A History of the Desire for Christian Unity, Volume II

The titles published in this series are listed at *brill.com/hdcu*

A History of the Desire for Christian Unity

Ecumenism in the Churches (19th–21st Century)

Directed by Alberto Melloni
Edited by Luca Ferracci

Volume II

Paths towards Communion

BRILL

LEIDEN | BOSTON

A project realized thanks to the contribution of Ministero dell'Università e della Ricerca (MUR), Ministero della Cultura (MiC) and Regione Emilia-Romagna.

Cover image: © Marc Chagall, c/o Pictoright Amsterdam 2021 Chagall ® Chagall is a registered trademark, owned by Comité Marc Chagall. Used with kind permission by Pictoright, Amsterdam.

The Library of Congress Cataloging-in-Publication Data is available online at
http://catalog.loc.gov /2021033875

Typeface for the Latin, Greek, and Cyrillic scripts: "Brill". See and download: brill.com/brill-typeface.

ISBN 978-90-04-44669-4 (hardback volume I)
ISBN 978-90-04-44851-3 (hardback volume II)
ISBN 978-90-04-44852-0 (hardback volume III)
ISBN 978-90-04-47241-9 (hardback volume IV)

This book is printed on acid-free paper and produced in a sustainable manner.

PRINTED BY DRUKKERIJ WILCO B.V. - AMERSFOORT, THE NETHERLANDS

Contents

Acronyms

AACC — All Africa Council of Churches
ACC — Anglican Consultative Council
ACCC — American Council of Christian Churches
ACER — Action Chrétienne des Étudiants Russes
ACK — Arbeitsgemeinschaft Christlicher Kirchen
ADL — Anti-Defamation League
AEA — Association of Evangelicals in Africa
AELC — Association of Evangelical Lutheran Churches
AELK — Allgemeine Evangelisch-lutherische Konferenz
AFSC — American Friends Service Committee
AGDE — Arbeitsgemeinschaft Diasporawerke in Europa
AICS — African Independent and Instituted Churches
AJC — American Jewish Committee
AJCF — Amitié Judéo-Chrétienne de France (Christian and Jewish Friendship in France)
ALC — American Lutheran Church
AMECEA — Association of Member Episcopal Conferences of Eastern Africa
ANC — African National Congress (South Africa)
APUC — Association for the Promotion of the Unity of Christendom
ARCIC — Anglican-Roman Catholic International Commission
ASEL — Acción Social Ecuménica Latinoamericana (Latin American Ecumenical Social Action)
BCC — British Council of Churches
BECS — Basic Ecclesial Communities
BEK — Bund der Evangelischen Kirchen in der DDR (League of Evangelical Churches in the German Democratic Republic)
BFSC — British Friends Service Council
BMS — Baptist Missionary Society
BWA — Baptist World Alliance
CALA — Consejo Anglicano Latinoamericano (Latin America Anglican Conference)
CALC — Clergy and Laymen Concerned
CALCAV — Clergy and Laymen Concerned About Vietnam
CAREE — Christians Associated for Relations with Eastern Europe
CBMS — Conference of British Missionary Societies
CCEE — Consilium Conferentiarum Episcoporum Europae (Council of the Bishops' Conferences of Europe)
CCEQ — Catholic Conference for Ecumenical Questions
CCG — Christian Council of Ghana
CCIA — Commission of the Churches on International Affairs
CCJ — Council of Christians and Jews
CCJP — Committee on the Church and the Jewish People
CCPD — Commission on the Churches' Participation in Development
CCR — Conference of Churches on the Rhine
CEAS — Comisión Episcopal de Acción Social (Episcopal Commission of Social Action)
CEC — Conference of European Churches
CELA — Conferencia Evangélica Latinoamericana (Latin American Evangelical Conference)
CELAM — Consejo Episcopal Latinoamericano (Latin American Episcopal Council)
CEPPLE — Conférence des Églises protestantes des pays latins d'Europe
CFC — Christian Frontier Council
CFR — Council on Foreign Relation
CICARWS — Commission on Inter-Church Aid, Refugees and World Services
CIEMAL — Council of Evangelical Methodist Churches of Latin America and the Caribbean

CIPAE	Committee of Churches for Emergency Aid
CJDP	Commission to Study the Bases of a Just and Durable Peace
CLADE	Congreso Latinoamericano de Evangelización (Latin American Congress of Evangelization)
CLAF	Comité Latinoamericano para la Preservación de la Fe (Latin American Committee for the Preservation of Faith)
CLAI	Consejo Latinoamericano de Iglesias (Latin American Council of Churches)
CMS	Church Missionary Society
CNBB	Conferência Nacional dos Bispos do Brasil (National Conference of Bishops of Brazil)
COCU	Consultation on Church Union
COINTELPRO	Counter Intelligence Program
Comintern	Communist International
COPEC	Conference on Christian Politics, Economics and Citizenship
CPA	Christian Partners in Africa
CPC	Christian Peace Conference
CPCE	Communion of Protestant Churches in Europe
CPLR	Conseil permanent luthéro-réformé
CPU	Church Peace Union
CRECES	Comunión Renovada de Evangélicos y Católicos en el Espíritu (Renewed Communion of Catholics and Evangelicals in the Holy Spirit)
CRRJ	Commission for Religious Relations with the Jews
CSCE	Conference on Security and Cooperation in Europe
CWC	Christian World Communions
CWME	Commission on World Mission and Evangelism
CWS	Church World Service
DFI	Dialogue with People of Living Faith and Ideologies
DÖSTA	Deutscher Ökumenischer Studienausschuss
EA	Evangelical Alliance
EACC	East Asia Christian Conference
EBF	European Baptist Federation
ECCB	Evangelical Church of Czech Brethren
ECUSA	Episcoapal Church in the United States of America
EIA	Entente Internationale Anticommuniste (International Anticommunist Entente)
EKD	Evangelische Kirche in Deutschland (Evangelical Church in Germany)
EKiR	Evangelische Kirche im Rheinland (Evangelical Church in the Rhineland)
ELCA	Evangelical Lutheran Church in America
ELCIC	Evangelical Lutheran Church in Canada
EMB	Evangelische Michaelsbruderschaft
ENCRISTUS	Encontro de Cristãos na Busca de Unidade e Santitade (Meeting of Christians in Search of Unity and Holiness)
EPHE	École pratique des hautes études
EPS	Ecumenical Press Service
ERF	Union nationale des Églises Réformées de France (National Union of Reformed Churches of France)
ESR	European Student Relief
FAO	Food and Agriculture Organization of the United Nations
FASIC	Fundación de Ayuda Social de las Iglesias Cristianas
FCC	Federal Council of Churches of Christ (in United States)
FCFC	Free Church Federal Council
FMEEC	Fellowship of Middle East Evangelical Churches
FPF	Fédération protestante de France (Protestant federation of France)
FPL	Foro Pentecostal Latinoamericano (Latin American Pentecostal Forum)
FRELIMO	Liberation Front of Mozambique
FSPC	Federation of Swiss Protestant Churches
FTL	Fraternidad Teológica Latinoamericana (Latin American Theological Fellowship)

FWCC	Friends World Committee for Consultation
GAW	Gustav-Adolf-Werk (Gustav Adolf Foundation)
GERT	Grupo Ecuménico de Reflexión Teológica (Ecumenical Group for Theological Reflection)
GRAE	The Revolutionary Government of Angola in Exile
HRROLA	Human Rights Resources Office for Latin American
HUAC	House Un-American Activities Committee
IBC	International Old Catholics Bishops' Conference
ICC	International Congregational Council
ICCC	International Council of Christian Churches
ICCJ	International Council of Christians and Jews
ICCLA	International Committee on Christian Literature for Africa
ICP	Institut Catholique de Paris (Catholic Institute of Paris)
IEF	International Ecumenical Fellowship
IFEB	Institut français d'études byzantines
IJCIC	International Jewish Committee on Interreligious Consultations
IKO	Interkerkelijk overleg
ILAFO	International League for Apostolic Faith and Order
ILC	International Catholic-Jewish Liaison Committee
IMBISA	Interregional Meeting of Bishops of Southern Africa
IMC	International Missionary Council
IMCCAJ	International Missionary Council's Committee on the Christian Approach to the Jews
IRC	International Red Cross
IRR	South African Institute of Race Relations
ISAL	Iglesia y Sociedad en América Latina (Church and Society in Latin America)
ISCE	International Society of Christian Endeavour
ITC	International Theological Commission
IWM	Interchurch World Movement
JDC	Joint Distribution Committee
JOC	Jeunesse ouvrière chrétienne (Young Christian Workers)
KEvK	Konferenz Evangelischer Kommunitäten (Conference of the Protestant Communities)
KRI	Katholieke Raad voor Israel (Catholic Council for Israel)
LCA	Lutheran Church in America
LCMS	Lutheran Church – Missouri Synod
LCUSA	Lutheran Council in the United States of America
LN	League of Nations
LRCS	League of Red Cross Societies
LWC	Lutheran World Convention
LWF	Lutheran World Federation
MAD	Mutually Assured Destruction
MPLA	The People's Movement for the Liberation of Angola
MWC	Mennonite World Conference
NAE	National Association of Evangelicals
NATO	North Atlantic Treaty Organization
NCC	National Council of Churches of Christ
NCCJ	National Conference of Christians and Jews (US)
NCWC	National Catholic Welfare Conference
NGOs	Non-Governmental Organizations
NHK	Nederlandse Hervormde Kerk (Dutch Reformed Church)
NIOD	Netherlands Institute for War Documentation
NLC	National Lutheran Council
NSCF	National Student Christian Federation
NSDAP	Nationalsozialistische Deutsche Arbeiterpartei (National Socialist German Workers' Party)
OAIC	Organization of African Instituted Churches
ÖAK	Ökumenischer Arbeitskreis evangelischer und katholischer Theologen (Ecumenical Study Group of Protestant and Catholic Theologians)
OAU	Organization of African Unity

OTSA	Orthodox Theological Society in America
PAC	Pan Africanist Congress (South Africa)
PCPCU	Pontifical Council for Promoting Christian Unity
PCR	Programme to Combat Racism
PHS	Presbyterian Historical Society
PIB	Pontificio Istituto Biblico (Pontifical Biblical Institute)
PIO	Pontificio Istituto Orientale (Pontifical Oriental Institute)
REC	Reformed Ecumenical Council
RELEP	Red Latinoamericana de Estudios Pentecostales (Latin American Network of Pentecostal Studies)
ROCOR	Russian Orthodox Church Outside of Russia
RSCM	Russian Student Christian Movement
SAE	Segretariato Attività Ecumeniche (Secretariat for Ecumenical Activities)
SALT	Strategic Arms Limitation Talks
SBC	Southern Baptist Convention
SCM	Student Christian Movement
SEA	Supreme Ecclesiastical Administration
SECAM	Symposium of Episcopal Conferences of Africa and Madagascar
SELK	Selbständige Evangelisch-Lutherische Kirche (Independent Evangelical-Lutheran Church)
SEPADE	Servicio Evangelico Para el Desarrollo (Evangelical Service for Development)
SIUC	South Indian United Church
SODEPAX	Society, Development, Peace (Ecumenical Commission on Society, Development and Peace)
SOTS	Society for Old Testament Studies
SPCU	Secretariat for Promoting Christian Unity
SWAPO	The South West Africa People's Organization
SWV	Sint-Willibrordvereniging (Society of Saint Willibrord)
UBS	United Bible Societies
UCKG	Universal Church of the Kingdom of God
UMC	United Methodist Church
UN	United Nations
UNCTAD	United Nations Conference on Trade and Development
UNELAM	Unidad Evangelica Latino Americana
UNEPREF	Union nationale des Églises protestantes réformées évangéliques de France (National Union of Protestant Reformed Evangelical Churches of France)
UNGA	UN General Assembly
UNITA	The National Union for the Total Independence of Angola
UNRRA	United Nations Relief and Rehabilitation Administration
UPCUSA	United Presbyterian Church in the United States of America
VELKD	Vereinigte Evangelisch-Lutherische Kirche Deutschland (United Evangelical Lutheran Church of Germany)
VRCS	Vsezagraničnoe russkoe cerkovnoe sobranie
WA	World Alliance for Promoting International Friendship through the Churches
WARC	World Alliance of Reformed Churches
WBF	World Baptist Fellowship
WCC	World Council of Churches
WCCE	World Council of Christian Education
WCCY	World Conference of Christian Youth
WCRC	World Communion of Reformed Churches
WJC	World Jewish Congress
WLM	West London Mission
WMC	World Missionary Conference
WPC	World Peace Council
WSCF	World Student Christian Federation
WSSA	World Sunday School Association
YMCA	Young Men's Christian Association
YWCA	Young Women's Christian Association
ZANU	Zimbabwe African National Union
ZAPU	The Zimbabwe African People's Union

Archives and Fonds

Archives

AAC	Archives d'Amay-Chevetogne
AACC	All Africa Conference of Churches archives
AAL	Archives de l'archevêché de Lyon
AAV	Archivio Apostolico Vaticano
ACI	Archives du Centre d'Étude Istina
ACO	Archives du Conseil Œcuménique des Églises, Geneva
ADDF	Archivio del Dicastero per la Dottrina della fede, Città del Vaticano
ADPJ	Archiv der deutschen Provinz der Jesuiten, Munich
AFscire	Archive of the Fondazione per le scienze religiose, Bologna
AG	Archives de la Communauté de Grandchamp, Areuse
AJOC	Archives d'Amay-Chevetogne, fund "Journées œcuméniques"
AKW	Kardinaal Willebrands Archief, Leuven
APDF	Archives de la Province dominicaine de France
ASRS	Archivio storico della Segreteria di Stato, Sezione per i rapporti con gli Stati e le organizzazioni internazionali, Città del Vaticano
BCC	Bishop's College Calcutta
BM	Basel Mission Archives
DT	Documentation de la Communauté de Taizé
EBAP	Erzbistumsarchiv Paderborn
GARF	Gosudarstvennyj Archiv Rossijskoj Federacii
GUA	Georgetown University Archives
IMC/CBMS	International Missionary Council/ Conference of British Missionary Society Archives
JFDP	John Foster Dulles Papers
KDC	Katholiek Documentatie Centrum, Universiteitsbibliotheek, Radboud Universiteit, Nijmegen
KU Leuven-CSVII	Katholieke Universiteit Leuven-Centrum voor Conciliestudie Vaticanum II (Center for the Study of the Second Vatican Council)
LACP	Lutheran Archives Center at Philadelphia
PUL	Princeton University Library
UCL-LG	Louvain-la-Neuve, Archives de l'Université Catholique de Louvain (UCL) – Centre Lumen Gentium
UUB	Uppsala universitetsbibliotek (Uppsala University Library)
WCCA	WCC Library and Archives, Ecumenical Center, Geneva

Fonds

AAEESS	Fondo Sacra Congregazione degli Affari Ecclesiastici Straordinari [in ASRS]
CFNA	Country Files North America [in WCCA]
DRBSC	Department of Rare Books and Special Collections [in PUL]
FD	Fonds Dumont [in APDF]
FDpy	Fondo Duprey [in AFscire]
FF	Fondo Johannes Feiner [in AFscire]
FJW	Fonds Johannes Willebrands [in KDC]
FWC	Fonds Willebrands Chevetogne [in AAC]
JLP	John Long Papers [in GUA]
PPP	Public Policy Papers [in PUL]

Journals, Lexicons, and Sources

Journals

AAS	*Acta Apostolicae Sedis*
ABTJ	*The Asbury Theological Journal*
ACM	*The American Church Monthly*
AHR	*The American Historical Review*
Am. Eccles. Rev.	*American Ecclesiastical Review*
APB	*Acta Patristica et Byzantina*
ASSR	*Archives de sciences sociales des religions*
BLE	*Bulletin de littérature ecclésiastique*
Cath(M)	*Catholica (Munster)*
Catholicité	*Catholicité: Revue d'information au service de l'Église universelle*
CBH	*Contemporary British History*
CC	*The Christian Century*
CEH	*Central European History*
Cenobio	*Cenobio: Rivista trimestrale di cultura*
CH	*Church History*
CHR	*The Catholic Historical Review*
Chrétiens et Sociétés	*Chrétiens et Sociétés XVIe–XXIe siècles*
CJT	*Canadian Journal of Theology*
Communio	*Communio: International Catholic Review*
Contacts	*Contacts: Revue Française de l'Orthodoxie*
CQ	*The Constructive Quarterly*
CQR	*The Church Quarterly Review*
CrSt	*Cristianesimo nella storia*
CTR	*Canadian Theological Review*
DBJ	*Dietrich Bonhoeffer-Jahrbuch*
DH	*Diplomatic History*
DR	*The Downside Review*
ECR	*Eastern Churches Review*
EcRev	*The Ecumenical Review*
EcTr	*Ecumenical Trends*
ELJ	*Ecclesiastical Law Journal*
epd-Dokumentation	*Evangelischer Pressedienst Dokumentation*
ERH	*European Review of History*
ETL	*Ephemerides Theologicae Lovanienses*
ETR	*Études théologiques et religieuses*
EvTh	*Evangelische Theologie*
Fronteiras	*Fronteiras – Revista de Teologia da Unicap*
GOTR	*The Greek Orthodox Theological Review*
GuL	*Geist und Leben*
HFJ	*Harvest Field Journal*
Hist. Jahr.	*Historisches Jahrbuch*
HRQ	*Human Rights Quarterly*
IBMR	*International Bulletin of Mission Research*
IDO-C	*Information documentation sur l'Église conciliaire*
IHR	*International History Review*
IJ	*International Journal*
IJMES	*International Journal of Middle East Studies*
IJSCC	*International Journal for the Study of the Christian Church*
IJST	*International Journal of Systematic Theology*
IKZ	*Internationale kirchliche Zeitschrift*
Irén	*Irénikon*
IRM	*International Review of Missions*
ITQ	*Irish Theological Quarterly*
JAAR	*Journal of the American Academy of Religion*
JCH	*Journal of Contemporary History*
JCS	*Journal of Church and State*
JECS	*Journal of Eastern Christian Studies*
JEPTA	*Journal of the European Pentecostal Theological Association*
JES	*Journal of Ecumenical Studies*

JGH	*Journal of Global History*
JMH	*The Journal of Modern History*
JoMaCC	*Journal of Modern and Contemporary Christianity*
JRAT	*Interdisciplinary Journal for Religion and Transformation in Contemporary Society*
JSAS	*Journal of Southern African Studies*
JTS	*The Journal of Transatlantic Studies*
KÅ	*Kyrkohistorisk Årsskrift*
KuD	*Kerygma und Dogma*
KZG	*Kirchliche Zeitgeschichte/ Contemporary Church History*
LOGOS	*LOGOS: A Journal of Eastern Christian Studies*
LS	*Louvain Studies*
LTP	*Laval Théologique et Philosophique*
MA	*Modern Age*
Medellín	*Medellín – theology and pastoral care for Latin America*
MEKGR	*Monatshefte für evangelische Kirchengeschichte des Rheinlandes*
MSR	*Melanges de science religieuse*
MT	*Modern Theology*
NBf	*New Blackfriars*
NCCR	*National Christian Council Review*
NRT	*Nouvelle Revue Théologique*
NZZ	*Neue Zürcher Nachrichten*
OCP	*Orientalia Christiana Periodica*
Œcumenica	*Œcumenica: revue de l'anglicanisme et des questions œcumeniques*
OPREE	*Occasional Papers on Religion in Eastern Europe*
ÖR	*Ökumenische Rundschau*
Pneuma	*Pneuma: The Journal of the Society of Pentecostal Studies*
PSV	*Parola, Spirito e Vita*
PT	*Political Theology*
R&RR	*Reformation & Renaissance Review*
REB	*Revue des études byzantines*
Recherches et débats	*Recherches et débats du Centre Catholique des intellectuels français*
Revue apologétique	*Revue apologétique: doctrine et faits religieux*
RHE	*Revue d'histoire ecclésiastique*
RHEF	*Revue d'histoire de l'Église en France*
RHPR	*Revue d'histoire et de philosophie religieuses*
RJKG	*Rottenburger Jahrbuch für Kirchengeschichte*
RM	*Rethinking Marxism: A Journal of Economics, Culture & Society*
ROC	*Revue de l'Orient Chrétien*
RSCI	*Rivista di Storia della Chiesa in Italia*
RSPT	*Revue des Sciences Philosophiques et Théologiques*
RSR	*Recherches de science religieuse*
RT	*Revue Thomiste*
RThPh	*Revue de théologie et de philosophie*
RTL	*Revue théologique de Louvain*
SBJT	*Southern Baptist Journal of Theology*
SHE	*Studia Historiae Ecclesiasticae*
SIDIC	*Service International de Documentation Judéo-Chrétienne*
SJT	*Scottish Journal of Theology*
SNTR	*St. Nersess Theological Review*
SocSci	*Social Sciences*
STK	*Svensk teologisk kvartalskrift*
StZ	*Stimmen der Zeit*
SVTQ	*St. Vladimir's Theological Quarterly*
TCBH	*Twentieth Century British History*
TCC	*Twentieth Century Communism*
Témoigner	*Témoigner: Entre histoire et mémoire*
ThB	*Theologische Blätter*
ThGl	*Theologie und Glaube*
ThLZ	*Theologische Literaturzeitung*
TNI	*The National Interest*

TP	*Textual Practice*
TS	*Theological Studies*
TThZ	*Trierer Theologische Zeitschrift*
UCCM	*The Union Christian College Magazine*
Vestnik RSChD	*Vestnik Russkogo Studenchenskogo Khristianskogo Dvizheniya*
VInt	*La Vie Intellectuelle*
VJHS	*Valahian Journal of Historical Studies*
VUCh	*Vers l'Unité chrétienne*
WEADM	*Western Equatorial Africa Diocesan Magazine*
WiWei	*Wissenschaft und Weisheit*
WuW	*Wort und Wahrheit*
ZDTh	*Zeitschrift für Dialektische Theologie*
ZKG	*Zeitschrift für Kirchengeschichte*
ZMP	*ZMP – Journal of the Moscow Patriarchate*
ZThK	*Zeitschrift für Theologie und Kirche*
ZwZ	*Zwischen den Zeiten*

Lexicons and Sources

ACO	*Acta conciliorum oecumenicorum*, ed. Eduard Schwartz, Johannes Straub & Rudolf Schieffer, Berlin, De Gruyter; series prima 1,1914–4,1948; series secunda 1,1948–3,2016.
ADA	*Acta et documenta Concilio oecumenico Vaticano II apparando: Series prima (antepreparatioria)*, Vatican City, Typis Polyglottis Vaticanis, 1960–1961.
ADP	*Acta et documenta Concilio oecumenico Vaticano II apparando: Series secunda (preparatioria)*, Vatican City, Typis Polyglottis Vaticanis, 1964–1995.
AS	*Acta Synodalia Sacrosancti Concilii oecumenici Vaticani II*, Vatican City, Typis Polyglottis Vaticanis, 1,1970–6,1978.
BBKL	*Biographisch-Bibliographisches Kirchenlexikon*, ed. Friedrich W. Bautz., Hamm, T. Bautz, 1,1975–34,2013.
Catholicisme	*Catholicisme: Hier Aujourd'hui Demain*, ed. G. Jacquemet, Paris, Letouzey et Ané, 1,1948–15,1998–2000.
CD	Karl Barth, *Church Dogmatics*, ed. Thomas F. Torrance & Geoffrey W. Bromley, London, T&T Clark, 2004.
CHC	*The Cambridge History of Christianity*, Cambridge, Cambridge University Press, 1,2005–9,2009.
COGD	*Corpus Christianorum Conciliorum Oecumenicorum Generaliumque Decreta*, ed. Alberto Melloni & Giuseppe Alberigo, 6 vols. to date, Turnhout, Brepols, 1,2006–.
DBW	*Dietrich Bonhoeffer Werke*, ed. Eberhard Bethge & others, Gütersloh, Gütersloher Verlagshaus, 1,1986–17,1999.
DBWE	*Dietrich Bonhoeffer Works in English*, Minneapolis, Fortress Press, 1,1996–17,2014.
DEM	*Dictionary of the Ecumenical Movement*, ed. Nicholas Lossky & others, Geneva, WCC Publications, 1991; ²2002.
Denz	*Enchiridion symbolorum definitionum et declarationum de rebus fidei et morum*, ed. Heinrich Denzinger & Peter Hünermann, Freiburg i.Br., Herder, 1991.
DHGE	*Dictionnaire d'Histoire et de Géographie ecclésiastiques*, dir. Alfred Baudrillart & others, Paris, Letouzey et Ané [Turnhout, Brepols], 1,1912ff.
DiKi	Dialog der Kirchen (series).
DMRFC	*Dictionnaire du monde religieux dans la France contemporaine*, dir. Jean-Marie Mayeur & Yves-Marie Hilaire, Paris, Beauchesne, 1,1985–12,2016.
DSAM	*Dictionnaire de spiritualité ascétique et mistique, doctrine et histoire*, ed. Marcel Viller, Paris, Beauchesne, 1,1937ff.

DThC — *Dictionnaire de théologie catholique*, ed. Alfred Vacant & others, Paris, Letouzey et Ané, 1,1903–15,1950; tables générales, ed. Bernard Loth & Albert Michel, 3 vols., 1951–1972.

HC — *Histoire du Christianisme des origines à nos jours*, ed. Jean-Marie Mayeur, Paris, Desclée, 1,1990–14,2000.

HThK Vat.II — *Herders Theologischer Kommentar zum Zweiten Vatikanischen Konzil*, ed. Bernd Jochen Hilberath & Peter Hünermann, Freiburg i.Br., Herder, 1,2004–5,2006.

KD — Karl Barth, *Kirchliche Dogmatik*, Munich, Kaiser, 1,1932–4,1967.

LA — "Agreement between Reformation Churches in Europe (The Leuenberg Agreement)," Mar 16, 1973.

LThK — *Lexikon für Theologie und Kirche*, ed. Michael Buchberger & others, Freiburg i.Br., Herder, 1st edition 1,1930–10,1938; 2nd edition 1,1957–14,1968; 3rd edition 1,1993–11,2001.

NPNF — *A Select Library of Nicene and Post-Nicene Fathers of the Christian Church*, ed. Philipp Schäff & Henry Wace, Edinburgh, T&T Clark, series prima 1,1886–14,1890; series secunda 1,1890–14, 1900.

ODNB — *Oxford Dictionary of National Biography: From the Earliest Times to the Year 2000*, ed. Henry Colin Gray Matthew & Brian Harrison, Oxford, Oxford University Press, 2004.

PL — *Patrologiae cursus completus: Series Latina*, ed. Jacques-Paul Migne, 217 vols., Paris, Migne, 1841–1855.

RGG — *Religion in Geschichte und Gegenwart*, ed. Hans Dieter Betz & others, Tübingen, Mohr Siebeck, 1998–2007.

TA — *Tomos Agapis: Vatican-Phanar (1958–1970)*, Rome/Istanbul, Imprimerie Polyglotte Vaticane, 1971.

THS — *Towards the Healing of Schism: The Sees of Rome and Constantinople: Public Statements and Correspondence between the Holy See and the Ecumenical Patriarchate (1958–1984)*, ed. Edward James Stormon, New York, Paulist Press, 1987.

TRE — *Theologische Realenzyklopädie*, Berlin, De Gruyter, 1,1976–36,2004.

WA — *D. Martin Luthers Werke: Kritische Gesamtausgabe (Weimarer Ausgabe)*, Weimar, 1,1883ff.

Conciliar Documents

AG — *Ad gentes*, in: COGD 3, 486–520.

DH — *Dignitatis humanae*, in: COGD 3, 475–485.

DV — *Dei Verbum*, in: COGD 3, 439–450.

LG — *Lumen gentium*, in: COGD 3, 296–350.

NA — *Nostra aetate*, in: COGD 3, 434–438.

OE — *Orientalium Ecclesiarum*, in: COGD 3, 351–359.

UR — *Unitatis redintegratio*, in: COGD 3, 360–375.

Notes on Contributors

Matteo Al Kalak, *University of Modena and Reggio Emilia*
Sandra Arenas, *Temuco Catholic University*
Nikolaos Asproulis, *Volos Academy for Theological Studies*
Gerhard Besier, *TU Dresden*
André Birmelé, *University of Strasbourg*
Nicla Buonasorte, *FSCIRE Bologna*
Christophe Chalamet, *University of Geneva*
Andrew Chandler, *University of Chichester*
Bruno Cherubini, *FSCIRE Bologna*
Keith Clements, *Conference of European Churches*
Catherine E. Clifford, *Saint-Paul University*
Will Cohen, *University of Scranton*
Viorel Coman, *Romanian Patriarchate*
Kisitu Davies, *University of KwaZulu-Natal*
Peter De Mey, *KU Leuven*
Joseph Famerée, *UCLouvain*
Luca Ferracci, *University of Modena and Reggio Emilia / FSCIRE Bologna*
Étienne Fouilloux, *Université Lumière Lyon II*
Leonhard Hell, *University of Mainz*
Dianne Kirby, *Trinity College Dublin*
Dino Knudsen, *Malmö University*
R. Simangaliso Kumalo, *University of KwaZulu-Natal*
Dietz Lange, *University of Göttingen*
Frieder Ludwig, *Kiel University*
Adalberto Mainardi, *Monastery of Cellole*
Saretta Marotta, *Ca' Foscari University of Venice*
Alberto Melloni, *University of Modena and Reggio Emilia / FSCIRE Bologna*
Friederike Nüssel, *University of Heidelberg*
Elisabeth Parmentier, *University of Geneva*
Rodrigo Polanco, *Pontifical Catholic University of Chile*
Michael Quisinsky, *University of Freiburg*
Silvia Scatena, *University of Modena and Reggio Emilia / FSCIRE Bologna*
Karim Schelkens, *Tilburg University*
Christoph Theobald, *Centre Sèvres – Paris*
Mauro Velati, *FSCIRE Bologna*
Matthias Wirz, *Radio Télévision Suisse*
Jurjen Zeilstra, *Utrecht University*
Peter Zimmerling, *University of Leipzig*

INTRODUCTION

Acceleration of the Impossible

Alberto Melloni

1 Premise

The second volume of the *History of the Desire for Christian Unity* focuses on years during which a transformation took place, and a greater success, though less fertile, was achieved than had been hoped for by the early 19th century interpreters of the ecumenical aspiration. In this volume the Fondazione per le Scienze Religiose has continued to benefit from the generous collaboration of scholars of various generational, denominational, and intellectual backgrounds. The time span examined here is not delineated by sharp lines, but by transitional periods. At its beginning lie the somnambulistic years preceding the Great War[1] and the four years of the bloody *katastrophé* that overwhelmed empires, turning them into nostalgia, myth, regret, retropias.[2] At its end is the prelude to the collapse of the Cold War and the USA/USSR polarization, a prelude that witnessed a series of entwined events (the oil crisis of 1973, the war against Israel in Kippur, the US defeat in Vietnam, the coup in Chile, the Portuguese revolution, Deng Xiaoping's return to power in China, Karol Wojtyła's election to the papacy[3]). Those who lived through this time and witnessed this epochal shift can be divided into two unequal groups. On the one hand, there were the many who saw what was not yet achieved ecumenically as delays in an objectively overwhelming journey that would either receive an extension (which instead never materialized) or that would demand much necessary and preventative reflection. On the other hand, there were the few who perceived the dangers of sterility and the demands of a difficult future[4] for one of the greatest movements in Christianity, which was about to measure itself against a world that was no longer ordered according to ancient "social" ideologies but by a new liberalism that went by the name of globalization.[5]

The object of this research is, as I have said, a metamorphosis. It is distributed over settings and initiatives that no one knows how to measure by any absolute parameters. It turns a hope of still unclear theological outlines, uncertain of its next institutional steps, standing at the alluring gates of a utopia, into a historical reality, as corporeal and visible as the unity of Christians and churches that

1 Christopher M. Clark, *The Sleepwalkers: How Europe Went to War in 1914*, London, Penguin Books, 2012. On the immediate debate it aroused, see Hanna Teichler, "Christopher Clark, *The Sleepwalkers: How Europe Went to War in 1914*," *Témoigner* 118, 2014, 197–199. A discussion of the positions can be found in Annika Mombauer, "Guilt or Responsibility?: The Hundred Year Debate on the Origins of World War I," *CEH* 48/4, 2015, 541–564. For the effects of the Great War on the path of ecumenism, see Frédéric Gugelot's chapter in the first volume of this work.

2 See Kryzstof Pomian, "Catastrofi," in: Ruggiero Romano, dir., *Enciclopedia Einaudi*, vol. 2, Turin, Einaudi, 1977, 789–803 and the analysis by Grégory Quenet, "La catastrophe, un objet historique?" *Hypothèses* 3/1, 2000, 11–20. The sociological hypothesis of "retropia" comes from Zygmunt Bauman, *Retrotopia*, Cambridge, Polity Press, 2017.

3 Here I am following Charles S. Maier, "Two Sorts of Crisis?: The 'Long' 1970s in the West and the East," in: Hans Günter Hockerts, ed., *Koordinaten deutscher Geschichte in der Epoche des Ost-West-Konflikts*, Berlin, Oldenbourg Wissenschaftsverlag, 2004, 49–62.

4 Giuseppe Ruggieri, "Il vicolo cieco dell'ecumenismo," *CrSt* 9/3, 1988, 563–615.

5 On Michel Foucault's well-known thesis that gave birth to neo-liberalism with the Walter Lippmann Colloquium of Aug 26–30, 1938, see Michel Foucault, *Naissance de la biopolitique: Cours au collège de France (1978–1979)*, Paris, EHSS/ Gallimard/Seuil, 2004.

it aspires to. It is a process that accelerates and is accelerated by institutions, periodicals, vocations, careers, books, monasteries, and cenacles, united by just two elements: first the conviction that there is nothing to be done except to put one's very existence on the line, whatever the cost, and second, the perception, in working through that process, of having reaped a harvest that makes the radicality of that choice make sense.

For the main figures of that existential experience, the results cannot be described in mere terms of strategies, merits, or politics (which must, however, play a part). Even the most sober sources and authors exuded the conviction of being caught up in the whirlwind that revitalizes bones as dry as those of Ez 37, of being set ablaze by the fire of a new Pentecost, as in Acts 2. They were drawing from mystical language and anchoring it to the raw flesh of historicity,[6] accounting for something unheard of on the level of the churches' self-understanding and doctrines.[7]

Study them today with historical-critical aims and awareness, we can recognize contours that are historically and physically palpable, rationally describable, and intellectually sound, even if they exceed the premises. We do this convinced that such knowledge does not come from an extrinsicist conflict of truths branded as "doctrinal" or from excising intentions as if they were some ideological veneer but that it derives from an effort devoid of fixed goals, focused on grasping, with the appropriate tools, epistemologically divergent meanings of religious conceptions and experiences.[8]

2 Progress and Threshold

If there were an angel of history for this "central" era of ecumenism *latu sensu* it would not resemble the celebrated *Angelus Novus* that Walter Benjamin describes in his theses on the concept of history, meditating on a 1920 work by Paul Klee. Benjamin's angel faces the past. Piling up at his feet he sees the wreckage of a world whose fragments cannot be reassembled. It is tragically wide-eyed, searching for what has shattered its wings, hopelessly battling the stormy wind we call "progress."[9] Mainstream ecumenism's angel of history (which has neither a Klee nor a Benjamin of its own …) certainly looks forward. It focuses on a threshold of which it cannot measure, against the sun, the distance. On the threshold's lintel, the angel can decipher two words taken from the creeds of the

6 Giancarlo Gaeta, "La mistica moderna sulla traccia di Michel de Certeau," in: Isabella Adinolfi, Giancarlo Gaeta & Andreina Lavagetto, eds., *L'anti-Babele: Sulla mistica degli antichi e dei moderni*, Genoa, Il melangolo, 2017, 3–20.

7 Yves Congar, in a lecture given at the Capranica College at the start of Vatican II in October 1962, stated this eloquently, see Giuseppe Alberigo, dir., Joseph A. Komonchak, ed., *History of Vatican II*, 5 vols., Orbis/Leuven, Maryknoll/Peeters, 1995. For an example, see the reconstruction by William K. Kay, "Pentecostal and Charismatic Convergence: A Divine Trajectory?," in: Peter Hocken, Tony L. Richie & Christopher A. Stephenson, eds., *Pentecostal Theology and Ecumenical Theology: Interpretations and Intersections*, Leiden, Brill, 2019, 65–84.

8 See my keynote lecture for EuARe 2024 "History and Its Religious Objects: Experiences, Discipline, Challenges."

9 The Italian translation of *Thesen über den Begriff der Geschichte* has a decisive introduction by Michele Ranchetti in Walter Benjamin, "Sul concetto di storia (1940)," in: Walter Benjamin, *Opere complete*, ed. Enrico Ganni & Hellmut Riediger, vol. 7, Rolf Tiedemann, ed., *Scritti 1938–1940*, Turin, Einaudi, 2006, 483–493. Predictably, the same can be said for the translation in Hannah Arendt, ed., *Illuminations*, trans. Harry Zohn, New York, Schocken Books, 1986, 253–264. The problem is deeply considered in Gershom Scholem, "Walter Benjamin and His Angel," now in Gershom Scholem, *On Jews and Judaism in Crisis: Selected Essays*, ed. Werner J. Dannhauser, New York, Schocken Books, 1976, 198–236. Although it uses literature in translation, an illuminating reference to Klee's *Schöpferische Konfession* (Paul Klee, *Creative Confession and Other Writings*, London, Tate Publishing, 2013) can be found in Riccardo Corcione, "*Angelus Novus*: Storia di un duplice alter ego, Walter Benjamin e Paul Klee (1920–1940)," *Cenobio* 65/2, 2016, 23–49. More recently, see Alexander Hope, "Figuring out Benjamin's 'Angel of History': 'Reading,' *Angelus Novus* and Sublime Metaphor," TP 34/6, 2020, 995–1020.

early church, "unity" and "visible," almost aspiring to distill the profound metric of the Nicene and Nicene-Constantinopolitan profession of faith.[10]

The rubble of the accompanying "hundred years' war" (the Great War, World War II, the Cold War, the post-Soviet wars), the blood of the struggles waged against colonialism with its various disguises and reincarnations, the realization that the deeper cultural paradigms of contempt (from anti-Semitism to antifeminism), all of which one had expected modernity to have eaten away, had only been dulled and camouflaged. They did not appear to the angel of ecumenical history as denials or even caveats. The most promising facts or the most disappointing events appeared to it as steps on a ladder to be climbed, ascending willingly – and voluntarily scaling it again, if necessary – strengthened by the irrevocable decision (or grace, if you will) to obey the command *Ut unum sint* that was delivered to all the churches. In this ascent, the angel and its ecumenical cohorts know that they will not necessarily see the finish line from any closer, but they can literally *sorprendere* (from Latin *super-prehendere*, to see over) it from a higher and more distant point.

Meanwhile, the angel of ecumenical history did not and could not see that, behind it, luminous and moving, a blameless superficiality had grown in which churches, theologies, and societies had realized that in the end the unbridled violence, the politeness of church hierarchies, dialogue as a profession, theological verbosity, and even the (*in se* laughable) contrast unleashed by the few but noisy ultra-confessional "right-wingers" of each tradition were enough to declare obsolete and useless the postulate that tearing apart churches is always the matrix of bloodier conflicts, present or to come.[11]

I allow myself this digression, certainly not to metaphorically skip over critical issues but to portray their far-from-common scholarly dimensions. Like it or not, there is no angel of history of the desire for Christian unity. There is, however, the desire and its history, which can be properly studied, that is, examined by taking into account that complex theological issues and entirely pragmatic material dynamics should be rigorously analyzed (and not merely by calling one's own superficiality "cultural history").[12] This demands intellectual struggle[13] and the radical rejection of simplifications that view the historical knowledge of great transcontinental processes as some lovely collection of arbitrary "core samples" locked in a nice, big tome that, in deference to the current trend, sports a nice "global" in the title.

The path traced here by an inner desire that has become a historically palpable event is marked by a contradiction running through the lives of institutions and persons: the "ecumenical" utopia has accelerated over the years and presents itself as a historical anticipation, but it also reveals the burden of the last mile. The fulfillment of processes long thought unrealizable arrives suddenly, disclosing a final hesitation, that makes what could have been epochal something local. The desire for unity would have been served by a

10 The rhyme coming at the beginning rather than the end (εἰς ἕνα, εἰς ἕνα, εἰς τὸ) and then, at 381 εἰς μίαν and the final ἕν. See Alberto Melloni, dir., Costanza Bianchi & Massimiliano Proietti, eds., *Storia e* traditio *del simbolo di Nicea e di Costantinopoli*, Bologna, EDB, forthcoming.

11 See Oliver McTernan, *Violence in God's Name: Religion in an Age of Conflict*, Maryknoll NY, Orbis Books, 2003. For more recent related developments, particularly in the African context, see Helen Nambalirwa Nkabala, "The Use of Violent Biblical Texts by the Lord's Resistance Army in Northern Uganda," *Transformation* 34/2, 2017, 91–100, part of the monograph *Special Issue on Religion, Hermeneutics, and Violence*.

12 See Alberto Melloni, "Sur le maniérisme dans l'histoire de l'expérience religieuse," *RHE* 117/3, 2024, 264–274.

13 That quality is found in analysis can be seen in the, in my opinion, exemplary work of Thomas William Ruston, *A Reparative Reading of the Eucharistic Ecclesiology of John Zizioulas and its Reception as Social Trinitarianism*, Ph.D. thesis, University of Birmingham, 2022.

multistage rocket theory (invented by mathematician Konstantin Ė. Tsiolkovsky decades before its application in the US space program), losing the initially necessary weight in order to climb. Ecumenism did not have any such theory to draw upon. It lived off the momentum of a generation that stayed on the scene and then, before unity became eucharistic, convinced itself that, after all, the unity achieved was the only unity that could be achieved, a historicist fallacy (even the early church was divided) that served to justify delaying. What was lacking in achieving the communion sought all along yet never achieved was not seen as a time given to be "redeemed,"[14] but as a *space* to be populated with dialogue.

And, as will be seen, the objective result of this proliferation, in itself blessed, will be two-edged. The dialogical quantity will enable the audience of the theologians involved to be enlarged (but also divided). It will make it possible to persuade (but also energize) the reluctant components to the path of unity within each denomination. It will enable the participation (but also indifference) of the mythical "public opinion," which no longer perceives division as a scandal or mixed marriages as a tragedy, but as an opportunity for "hospitality." If Vatican II had unnecessarily, prophetically, and clearly called a "truce" what all its contemporaries and posterity for decades would call "peace,"[15] then the time of confessional disarmament and ecumenical progress in the decades that are the subject of these studies could only be a *kairos* the historical sense of which can and must accurately take stock of the wastage.[16]

14 As in Jerome's translation of Ephesians 5. The 1985 document of South African theologians had taken the principle of propitious occasion for their reference, on which, see the essays in Robert McAfee Brown, ed., *Kairòs: Three Prophetic Challenges to the Church*, Grand Rapids, Eerdmans, 1990.

15 On GS 81, see Giovanni Turbanti, *Un concilio per il mondo moderno: La redazione della costituzione pastorale "Gaudium et spes" del Vaticano II*, Bologna, Il Mulino, 2000.

16 See Matteo Zuppi, *Nel nome della pace*, Bologna, EDB, 2024.

3 The Leading Figures up to 1948

Temporal distancing, hindsight, and the critical work behind many of the studies collected here show one reality, that what I will continue to call for the moment the "success" of ecumenism was fissured by frailties and delays because it was born fissured by both individual and ecclesial frailties and delays, which historical research shows to be greatly on the rise. The years from the Edinburgh conference to the theological awakening of the years between the two world wars – with the fascist *Machtergreifungen* passed by parliamentary consensus and the communist revolution born out of the ashes of the tsarist empire – did not entirely erase ambiguities, of which one was more relevant than the others. It stemmed from the unconfessed or unconscious idea that missionary competition among churches was to be fought not only and not so much because it constituted a scandal with respect to the command of Jesus, but because it weakened believers' response in the face of the spread of materialistic atheism. Unity (as well as poverty, a thirst for justice, and peace) was to be pursued, yes, out of obedience to the gospel, but even more so to improve an apostolic "performance," to make one's apologetics more "credible."[17]

This is documented, for example, by the Roman Catholic magisterium (not that it knew it better than Presbyterian theological reflection, but it said it more simply[18]). When, at the turn of the 1930s,

17 An interesting panorama (also for the date it was compiled) of the French-speaking Catholic context of the 1930s is given by André Charron, *Les Catholiques face à l'athéisme contemporain: Étude historique et perspectives théologiques sur l'attitude des catholiques en France de 1945 à 1965*, Montreal, Fides, 1973. A typical case is examined in Douglas Pratt, "Interreligious Dialogue: A Case Study Approach in Respect to the Vatican and the World Council of Churches," in: Martha Frederiks & Dorottya Nagy, eds., *World Christianity: Methodological Considerations*, Leiden, Brill, 2020, 179–203.

18 See John R. Fitzmier & Randall Balmer, "A Poultice for the Bite of the Cobra: The Hocking Report and Presbyterian Missions in the Middle Decades of the

the papacy thought it could and should overlook the ontological difference between communion with those who profess the Trinitarian faith and dialogue with those who "at least believe in God," which Pius XI posited as the discriminating factor between atheism and anti-theism, it provided evidence of this instrumental conception.[19] It was no accident that Rome had chosen the tarnished spectacles of the visions at Fatima ("Russia will be converted") to interpret the tragedy of a church like the Russian one, which, after missing the appointment with the reformatory foments of the early 20th century, had been swallowed up by the Leninist and then Stalinist system and, at least until the German attack on the Soviet Union,[20] had been oppressed by the Communist effort to unify the homeland by replacing the mediation of church with that of party and by replacing the body of St. Sergius, made incorruptible by his holiness, with the embalmed body of Lenin, raised to socialist worship by science.[21]

In this context, voices emerged that are no longer intellectually related singular entities, but true collective subjects: not solo voices, but "choirs" that came onto the scene and are given unequal attention in the following essays. Of these guiding forces I will mention three: theologians, historians, and authorities.

3.1 *The Theologians*

Theologians are complicated objects for the historian, whose own method should always (always) refrain from drying out their intentions by sucking out their "political" goals (or misunderstandings) or by constructing anachronistic tactics that ignore that these figures chose to belong to a church and to their particular church. History – and this is just a history book – must deeply understand the manner and the awareness with which theologians, committed to a confessional tradition, develop their search for "truer" data with the tools of exegesis, doctrinal history, and the meaning of liturgical stratifications. They are intellectuals seeking a new way, an older "Tradition," a forgotten originality, to dismantle the jumble of "traditions" that are often nothing more than antiquated nostalgia, obsessed with modernity.[22]

Theologians are often grappling with a dissatisfaction with the solutions available to the major spiritual families and willing to suffer the reaction of those who consider such arrangements immutable. The imposing intellectual architecture of liberal theology makes a (dogmatic?[23] fundamental?[24]) reaction more urgent, involving in the ecumenical debate the Bultmanns, the Barths, the Tillichs, and in their own way the Bonhoeffers – standard bearers of positions that imply and illuminate nodes of unity, but that certainly do not begin with that questioning. Greek-speaking Orthodox theology seeks a political revenge that instead will lead to mega-*katastrophé*, while Russian-speaking theology grows in the myth of the Slavophile

Twentieth Century," in: Milton J. Coalter, John M. Mulder & Louis B. Weeks, eds., *The Diversity of Discipleship: Presbyterians and Twentieth Century Christian Witness*, Louisville, Westminster Press, 1991, 105–125.

19 See Étienne Fouilloux, *Eugène, cardinal Tisserant (1884–1972): Une biographie*, Paris, Desclée de Brouwer, 2011, and Philippe Chenaux, *L'Église catholique et le communisme en Europe (1917–1989): De Lénine à Jean Paul II*, Paris, Cerf, 2009.

20 See Adriano Roccucci, *Stalin e il patriarca: La Chiesa ortodossa e il potere sovietico (1917–1958)*, Turin, Einaudi, 2011.

21 See Alexei Yurchak, "Bodies of Lenin: The Hidden Science of Communist Sovereignty," *Representations* 129/1, 2015, 116–157.

22 This was a summary made by Yves Congar, *La tradition et la vie de l'Église*, Paris, Cerf, 1984, on which, see Alberto Melloni, "Congar, Architect of the *Unam Sanctam*," *Louvain Studies* 29/3–4, 2004, 222–238.

23 Bruce L. McCormack, *Karl Barth's Critically Realistic Dialectical Theology: Its Genesis and Development (1910–1936)*, Oxford, Clarendon Press, 1997. See the essay by Christophe Chalamet in this volume.

24 Think of the US Presbyterian members of the FCC born in 1908 under Robert E. Speer, and also John Mott's IWM.

intelligentsia.[25] Roman Catholic theology, impoverished by the pervasive and obsessive Roman suspicion of "modernism,"[26] relegates the responsibility of thinking about possible theological participation in the unity movement[27] to religious orders, but exposes them to Roman repression that, when it comes, is fierce.[28] The difference between their confessional and ritual backgrounds does not erase the fact that, for them, disputes, hesitations, and aggressions are residual phenomena, to be handled with feigned caution, delay, even opportunism, a fake wait-and-see attitude and cunning detours, which have nothing to do with the rear projections of mediocrity that belong only to those who see them in others.

They are predominantly white, male, and European theologians, but not only. Since the late 1930s, a wider world has been in motion (if Tambaram had not been made unrepeatable,[29] or if Dietrich Bonhoeffer had remained in the United States ...[30]). A utopia that had Anglican and Scandinavian epicenters took on a broader agenda, with predominant *itinéraires européens d'expression française*.[31] The aforementioned Presbyterian (American), Dominican (especially French-speaking), and Jesuit (especially German-speaking) foyers, the sacred monsters of (Reformed) dogmatics, the great exegetical (evangelical) "schools" of the universities, the intellectual circles that, in the *entre-guerres* spirit, considered intellectual engagement seminal[32] – all of them expressed theologies that, as "militant," demand the appropriate research criteria.

Putting controversy about the true church (an expression of self-interested apologetics, on which there is little historical work to be done) aside, they see the equally rigorous study of both what unites and what divides the churches as a moral obligation. They are theologians who do not live to provide evidence of their own or a particular church's "role" or "ambitions," and they cannot be understood to be freeing themselves of complex issues by calling them "doctrinal" or signing up for the club of the *ignoratio elenchi*. They are persons

25 See the masterpiece by Andrzej Walicki, *W Kręgu Konserwatywnej utopii: Struktura i przemiany Rosyjkeigo Słowianofilstwa*, Warsaw, PWN, 1964; ET: Hilda Andrews-Rusiecka, *The Slavophile Controversy: History of a Conservative Utopia in Nineteenth Century Russian Thought*, Oxford, Clarendon Press, 1975. For a general and exhaustive overview of the Slavophile movement, see the essay by Jeremy Pilch in the first volume of this work.

26 See Claus Arnold & Giovanni Vian, eds., *The Reception and Application of the Encyclical* Pascendi: *The Reports of the Diocesan Bishops and the Superiors of the Religious Orders until 1914*, Venice, Edizioni Ca' Foscari, 2017.

27 The Dominicans of Le Saulchoir would do this with a Thomism different from the neo-Thomism of the Leonine era, developed as a firewall against modern philosophies and imbued with a historical sense and intellectual vivacity. It would also be done by the Jesuits in the rediscovery (think of Fourvière) of the Fathers of the Christian East, avoiding the mechanisms of Baroque theology, the expression of a regime of Christendom. On the issue, see the eminent studies of Étienne Fouilloux, *Yves Congar (1904–1995): Une vie*, Paris, Salvator, 2020; Étienne Fouilloux, *Marie Dominique Chenu (1895–1990)*, Paris, Salvator, 2022; as well as Étienne Fouilloux, *La Collection "Sources chrétiennes": Éditer les Pères de l'Église au XXe siècle*, Paris, Les Cerf, 2011; and Étienne Fouilloux, *Les éditions dominicaines du Cerf (1918–1965)*, Rennes, Presses Universitaires de Rennes, 2018. Finally, see the essay by Joseph Famerée in this volume.

28 Such as that suffered by the future Cardinal Congar, which he deemed similar to tactics by the Gestapo whose ways he had known as a member of the resistance, see Alberto Melloni, "Le système et la vérité dans le journaux d'Yves Congar," in: Gabriel Flynn, ed., *Yves Congar: Théologien de l'Église*, Paris, Cerf, 2007, 207–224.

29 See Jan van Lin, *Shaking the Fundamentals: Religious Plurality and Ecumenical Movement*, Leiden, Brill, 2002, and, in this volume, the essay by Frieder Ludwig on the IMC's first conference held in Tambaram.

30 See Karl Martin, ed., *Dietrich Bonhoeffer*, Darmstadt, WBG, 2015 and the essay by Peter Zimmerling in this volume.

31 This is the title of the monumental text by Étienne Fouilloux, *Les catholiques et l'unité chrétienne du XIXe au XXe siècle: Itinéraires européens d'expression française*, Paris, Le Centurion, 1982.

32 A bibliography can be found in Dominique Lejeune, *Les religions dans l'entre-deux-guerres en France*, Besançon, Doubs, 2019.

distributed along a generational continuum, with professions and intellectual interests, but are imbued with a unique passion, worthy of the oblation of self, of the risk of ending up in the nets of authority, or at the fringes of churches, blind and deaf to fascist and Nazi seductions. Having stern intelligences, they are possessed by a maddening industriousness, convinced that they can thus shape, with intelligence, severity, and industriousness, the limits of their own church and thus benefit the believing communities, with or without a certain amount of moralism about the faith of the simple.

3.2 *The Historians*

Alongside the theologians (or sometimes enjoying the intellectual flexibility of some of them) are the historians of a historiography that moves over vast terrains with post-positivist confidence. Old Testament exegetes, New Testament exegetes, antiquarians, patrologists, historians of the Middle Ages and the modern age, philologists of councils, Byzantinists, and historians of rituals take on problems that feed into an underlying ecumenical postulate: the historicity of division allows not only for a critical grounding of the Kantian principle of what unites but above all for the circumscription of the field of conflict. Not as its purpose but as its effect, their work documents that disagreements have cultural or transcultural implications. It shows that polychrome doctrine does not harm the unity of the faith and that a critical intelligence of the biblical given (once deconstructed with sharp tools) speaks, not less but more, to the believer and the soul of the churches. "Militant" historiography, then, as much as theology, but in a specific sense.

It is not therefore the militancy that postulates confessional treatises, explaining that the true church resists the ebb and flow of time because it is true and is true because it resists the ebb and flow of time, but a critical attitude. It is the keen awareness that the choice of object of one's work is never neutral and is fueled by a guarded intentionality in which every historian – apart from bigots and atheists who feel ideologically immunized by their membership in one cabal or another – knows that they are measured by the quantity and quality of their knowledge, working from primary sources with zero incidences of plagiarism.

3.3 *The Authorities*

A third force at work are the guardrails guiding the different churches. The institutional arrangements that express authority are quite different. There are heads who are not leaders, leaders who are not authorities, authorities who are not heads, and figures who encompass two or three of these variables. But each, in its own denominational sphere, expresses a somewhat "apex" instance. Leading figures of the globalization of the long century,[33] these authorities bring the multilateralist logic of the post-Great War era to the field of Christian faith in search of unity. It is a way of thinking that, in the 1920s, saw the League of Nations, at its core, as a replicable, adaptable, and even reassuring model. The collectors of consensus and money,[34] redistributors of ideas, producers of alarms and reassurances, all traverse a Europe where the myth of "Genevan" neutrality is crushed between Nazi-fascist totalitarianism (which maintains the promise of extermination) and Bolshevik totalitarianism (which betrays the promise of justice). They disembark in the land of Yalta, where Stalinist Russia had rebuilt a Soviet patriarchy that preserves the dream of a third Rome and the return of Constantine.[35]

33 Charles S. Maier, "Consigning the Twentieth Century to History: Alternative Narratives for the Modern Era," *AHR* 105/3, 2000, 807–831.

34 Also missing here is a "ledger" for ecumenism, which would also be important. The importance of such a text was already identified by Charles E. Harvey, "John D. Rockefeller, Jr., and the Interchurch World Movement of 1919–1920: A Different Angle on the Ecumenical Movement," *CH* 51/2, 1982, 198–209.

35 Peter Iver Kaufman, "Stepping Out of Constantine's Shadow," in: George E. Demacopoulos & Aristotle Papanikolaou, eds., *Christianity, Democracy, and the Shadow of Constantine*, New York, Fordham University Press, 2017, 202–218, and Alberto Melloni & others, dir.,

Within these authorities one recognizes a nucleus that could be called "spirituals," who, however, unlike the Franciscan "spirituals," are destined for apex roles. It is enough to recall Nathan Söderblom, Charles Brent, John XXIII, Athenagoras I, and Metropolitan Nikodim (Rotov). They were not an accident of history or a providential fluke, but proof that sowing credibility does not achieve results because it has "programed" them but produces them because it expects them.

4 Central Figures between Amsterdam and the Fall of the Berlin Wall

The reader will note that, during the time following the end of World War II, many things changed, but not the leading figures, not as "categories" or individuals, subject as they are to turnovers because of death. The stage that provided the initial impetus for overcoming confessional gravitational forces, therefore, was not left behind. This raises a crucial question from an interpretational point of view; namely, how to decipher a partial, slow, disordered shift.

What in academic and ecclesiastical worlds are called successions are actually processes of flanking, in which those trained in ministry in the 19th century (Nathan Söderblom was born in 1866, Angelo Giuseppe Roncalli and Paul Couturier in 1881, Athenagoras and Karl Barth in 1886, and Hamilcar Alivisatos in 1887) had readers and theological colleagues who experienced the Great War as children (Willem Visser 't Hooft was born in 1900, Oscar Cullmann in 1902, Edmund Schlink in 1903, Yves Congar in 1904, Dietrich Bonhoeffer and Eugene Carson Blake in 1906, Johannes Willebrands and Madeleine Barot in 1909, and Jean-Louis Leuba in 1912). The next generation came from the 1920s (Philip Potter was born in 1921, Emmanuel Lanne in 1923, José Míguez Bonino in 1924, Georg Kretschmar in 1925, Lukas Vischer and Giuseppe Alberigo in 1926, Jean-Marie Roger Tillard in 1927, and Martin Luther King and Nikodim [Rotov] in 1929) up to the World War II generation (John Zizioulas was born in 1931 and Konrad Raiser in 1938). The overlap between them mixed together readings and actions.

It also took some effort to expand the ecumenical maps. The ancient geography of ecumenism was marked by academic poles where Protestant schools were the strongest (Paderborn, Munich, Neuchâtel, Strasbourg), by active foyers where the engagement of different denominations was strongest (Bossey, Chevetogne, Dombes, Crestwood), and by places in Anglican and Lutheran Northern Europe where the hope for unity had arisen with those who personified it. Not on the ancient perimeter but within it, was the strengthening of the WCC's Geneva and Vatican II's Rome. The gravitational mass and events of these institutions drew questions and answers, but their constitutively planetary dimension opened new horizons. Indeed, the old "centers" of ecumenism carried with them from the crisis culture of the 1930s a naive and radical intellectual conviction: that understanding processes meant guiding processes, that interpreting problems solved problems, that gathering a limited number of thoughts, but those of pure intentions, generated enormous resources of pure thought for the great masses ...

It was a vision of self that prompted an overestimation of one's own importance, with a sincerity and pride that still influence historical work today, driven to read the ephemeral as proof of a merit that, if it were strong, would not be virtuous. The arrival of new dialogue partners did not erase these two-dimensional geometries but flanked them with questions and answers that added a third dimension, which transformed polygons into the sides of a polyhedron.

4.1 *The Price of Passion*

So, the identical glistens slowly. But not only that. There are two intertwined facts impacting the 40

Constantino I: Enciclopedia internazionale sulla figura, il mito, la critica e la funzione dell'imperatore dell'editto di Milano (313–2013), 3 vols., Rome, Istituto della Enciclopedia Italiana, 2013.

years of a bipolar world. The first is the success of ecumenism. Rather than measuring itself with utopias, dreams, delays, postponements, or small advances, it encountered great accomplishments, such as the aforementioned birth of the WCC (to which Soviet opportunism bestowed an Orthodox presence that was not taken for granted[36]) and the convocation of Vatican II (announced at the end of a week of prayer for Christian unity[37] where Pope John XXIII imposed a non-Catholic-Roman presence that made its ecumenicity the expression of an ecclesiology in the making).[38] These events were reflected in political gestures (the bi-confessional Christian party in Germany), public gestures (the Jerusalem embrace between pope and ecumenical patriarch), and the recognition of local experiences.

Those ecumenical successes were a prelude to and in part generated a second, no less relevant, fact: the collapse of the subjective and objective "cost" of ecumenical engagement. After a time when the aspiration for unity was exposed to challenges or condemnations and had forced in everyone a vigilance that was not meant to tone down but to preserve the desire for unity, ecumenical commitment no longer required mass heroism. Instead, it settled for a swath of virtuous skills, behind which were hidden very violent repressive actions (think of the Roman inquisition's doggedness against Tillard), which were isolated enough not to become either issues or cases.

A few examples – which certainly do not cover the Christian ecumene, but which seem to me to be expressive of the extent and significance of what I would describe as a reduction in the cost of ecumenical engagement and the quality of its product – include ecumenical monasticism, the federative process of Protestant alliances, and the role of public opinion.

The Christian radicalism that lives coenobium as a prophecy and/or pledge of an anticipated unity, future, and togetherness can be defined as "ecumenical." It had to carefully make its way past many pitfalls. The Schotenhof monastery (whose first spiritual director was Father Constantin Bosschaerts, a former colleague of John XXIII) never moved past bi-ritualism. The Amay monastery moved to its current location at Chevetogne in 1939, that is, nine years after the exile of its founder.[39]

Geneviève Micheli and the three other Reformed women who began the ecumenical adventure of Granchamp on Lake Neuchâtel in 1940 shared a desire for communal radicality with other French-speaking circles.[40] Antoinette Butte's intimate experience at Pomeyrol[41] took shape after 20 years of attempts, parallel to the "community" that received its rule from Roger Schutz on the hill of Taizé, until monastic vows were made in 1949.[42] These energetic experiences, taking place in parallel but all eloquent, did not have an easy life in the different churches of these creators of what Bonhoeffer had theologically interpreted as "communal life." On the Catholic side, Maria di

36 See Alberto Melloni, ed., *Vatican II in Moscow (1959–1965): Acts of the Colloquium on the History of Vatican II. Moscow, March 30–April 2, 1995*, Leuven, Bibliotheek van de Fac. Godgeleerdheid, 1997.

37 On the non-Catholic observers at Vatican II, see the essay by Mauro Velati in this volume, who also authored the monograph *Separati ma Fratelli: Gli osservatori non cattolici al Vaticano II*, Bologna, Il Mulino, 2014.

38 See Giuseppe Alberigo, "Ecclesiologia in divenire: A proposito di 'concilio pastorale' e di Osservatori a cattolici al Vaticano II," now in Giuseppe Alberigo, *Transizione epocale: Studi sul Concilio Vaticano II*, Bologna, Il Mulino, 2009.

39 On the Amay-Chevetogne Abbey and its founder Dom Lambert Beauduin see the essay by André Haquin in the first volume of this work.

40 See the essay by Silvia Scatena and Matthias Wirz in this volume on the rebirth of monasticism in the Protestant world and the personal testimonial by Minke de Vries, *Vers une gratuité féconde: L'expérience œcuménique de Grandchamp*, Paris, Parole et Silence, 2009.

41 Michel Clément, *Un monachisme protestant?: Spiritualités et règles de trois communautés protestantes en France: Reuilly, Pomeyrol, Villeméjane*, Paris, n. pub., 2012.

42 See Silvia Scatena, *Taizé, una parabola di unità: Storia della comunità dalle origini al concilio dei giovani*, Bologna, Il Mulino, 2018.

Campello initiated an ecumenical life of poverty in time to suffer all the Catholic condemnations of the 1920s.[43] And again, in 1967, the community of Bose, born around a cenacle of Bible reading devised by Enzo Bianchi, was struck down by the local bishop's interdict.

After that there were no condemnations, but there were also no significant new attempts. This is not a rebuke but a statement that it seems that, without a struggle, the ambition to anticipate tomorrow's unity in a way of life on par with all others lacks an inner urgency. If participating in the triumphal march toward visible unity becomes easy, free, or even fulfilling, then it is inevitable that this will not be the path taken by fiery souls or communities in distress in the early 21st century.

Another area where ecumenism emerged as a theological commodity is that involving the organization and reorganization of Protestant world federations (and, as a consequence, agreements of communion among churches). In 1947, at Söderblom's instigation, the LWC, which had originated in Eisenach in 1923, was transformed into the LWF, the main actor in important ecumenical agreements such as the 1984 Budapest agreement establishing the sharing of pulpit and altar among the churches of the federation, and the joint declaration with the Roman Catholic Church on justification signed in 1999. With regard to churches in the Congregationalist and Presbyterian traditions, the WARC was formed in 1970 (which is also this volume's chronological limit) from the convergence of the ICC, founded in 1891, and the Alliance of the Reformed Churches Holding the Presbyterian System, active since 1875, which brought together Reformed and Presbyterian churches of the United States and the British Isles.[44] At the 2010 synod held in Grand Rapids, Michigan, the alliance was transformed into a communion when the REC – which had originated in that same city in 1946 as the Reformed Ecumenical Synod – was added to form the WCRC (which in 2021 saw the separation from it of several North American Reformed churches that, in disagreement over sexual ethics, formed the ARC).[45]

It is an interweaving of histories that Catholic and Orthodox apologetics gladly gloss over, lamenting "Protestant" indecipherability or subsuming their dispositions into rough political categories. What is of interest here is quite different and does not presuppose any value judgment. The way that the authorities of the youngest Christian communities, arising out of the reforms of the 16th century, have sought internal cohesion and collective representation in the ecumenical context is based on a sophisticated and not overly onerous negotiating practice that celebrates a peace-making understanding, capable of including and accommodating fundamentally divergent doctrinal positions without a theological or intellectual toll.[46] Once again the expansion of "world" agreements, up to a certain point, was allowed, but at the beginning of the 21st century it would be shaken by the evangelical mood and an inability to address ethical issues (abortion, same-sex marriage) that, in many churches, had the same divisive capacity that war would bring to orthodoxy.

A third area in which the sources make it possible to touch upon the slow decline of the Christian desire for unity is that of "public opinion," understood as the place where opinions are formed and expressed, a place where their enunciation does

43 Mauro Velati, "L'ecumenismo di sorella Maria," in: Roberto Morozzo della Rocca, ed., *Maria di Campello: Un'amicizia francescana*, Brescia, Morcelliana, 2013, 119–146.

44 Marcel Pradervand & Fred Kaan, eds., *Proceedings of the Uniting General Council of the World Alliance of Reformed Churches (Presbyterian and Congregational) held at Nairobi, Kenya, August 20–30, 1970*, Geneva, WARC, 1970.

45 The history and ecumenical commitment of the major Protestant world communions are recounted in this volume by André Birmelé and others.

46 The bone of contention with tradition was recounted by one of the greatest historians of the 20th century, Roger Aubert, "Quatrième session du groupe de travail 'Alliance Réformée Mondiale/Église Catholique romaine', Woudschoten (18–23 février 1974)," *RTL* 5/3, 1974, 398–400.

not entail social exclusion.[47] This is not a matter of engaging in some trivial sociology of communication within the area of study that is theological, exegetical, and historical-religious.[48] However, it will be clear to the reader that there was a long period when the 20th century's "social" tools *par excellence* – journals – strove to connect and create an audience, to introduce – through rationing and daring – fundamental historical-theological questions, to create a language. They succeeded and saw their efforts crowned with success.

As in other spheres – Vatican II, for instance – an "influential spectator" was established, making its weight felt and determining editorial choices ranging from the Bible[49] to real literary cases such as the book on infallibility by Hans Küng, a Swiss theologian who, on the one hand, developed Brian Tierney's research on the Franciscan and medieval origins of the principle, while ignoring the historical interpretation that held until 1996 that Vatican I gave such a narrow definition that the papacy had objectively never been able to resort to it.[50] These are two extremes, but they point to the belief that knowledge can substitute for responsible action by those in charge who, downstream from the momentous lifting of excommunications between Rome and Constantinople in 1965, missed two major appointments with history.

4.2 *Selective Points*

Whether ecumenism's success heralds its decline is thus a historiographical question, and to confuse *post hoc* with *propter hoc* would be an unforgivable methodological blunder. The *post hoc*, indeed, is objective, but the *propter* is far more intricate. Chronologically, it harkens backwards and is affected by the systems of construction of doing theology. It also depends on the churches' own self-understanding and the instruments used in understanding their tradition and traditions. This stratification had to be analytically reconstructed in order to understand and judge the contradictions that made the time between 1968 and 1989 a canvas on which a different design took shape. While martyrdom (from Martin Luther King Jr.'s, to those of the Prague Spring, to the victims of the military regimes imposed throughout Latin America by Washington) returned to populate the horizon of the churches,[51] signs appeared of a "reaction" that seemed focused on the poor reception of what appeared to have been achieved.

Among the many moments studied here, it is worth mentioning the concelebration agreement devised by John Zizioulas and Pierre Duprey for Athenagoras I in 1970 but dropped due to the hesitations of Paul VI.[52] Or we might mention an epochal event such as the 1982 publication of the

---

47 This conceptual framework is the *Öffentliche Meinung* (public opinion) of Niklas Luhmann, *Die Politik der Gesellschaft*, ed. André Kieserling, Frankfurt a.M., Surhkamp, 2000, 274–318.

48 Worthwhile, not only for her keen observations on the life sciences, is Bernadette Beansaude-Vincent, *L'opinion publique et la science: A chacun son ignorance*, Paris, Institut d'Édition Sanofi-Synthèlabo, 2000.

49 The *Traduction Oecuménique de la Bible* grew out of an Orthodox proposal in November 1965 and was published under the editorship of François Refoulé, OSB – who had been deported to Austria for the *service du travail obligatoire* and who held a doctorate from Lund – and Rev. Georges Casalis – a militant anti-Nazi student of Barth and friend of Visser 't Hooft who was a witness at his wedding – see Gérard Billon & others, dir., *L'aventure de la TOB: Cinquante ans de traduction oecuménique de la Bible*, Paris, Cerf, 2010.

50 As often happened, this was all intuited by Yves Congar, "Après *Infaillible?* de Hans Küng: Bilans et discussions," *RSPT* 58/2, 1974, 243–252.

51 From this perspective, it is interesting to note the shared martyrology that was the fruit of the joint effort of the Bose monastic community and Faith and Order, started in 2004 and continued in 2008. The first proposal for an ecumenical martyrology dates back to the conference held by Faith and Order in Bangalore in 1978 as a result of the study "Witness Unto Death: Martyrdom as Ultimate Hope." See *Minutes and Supplementary Documents from the Meeting of the Commission on Faith and Order held at the Ecumenical Christian Centre Whitefield, Bangalore, India, 16–30 August 1978*, Geneva, WCC Publications, 1979, 42.

52 See Alberto Melloni, *Tempus visitationis: L'intercomunione inaccaduta fra Roma e Costantinopoli*, Bologna, Il Mulino, 2019.

report of the first ARCIC – epochal also because of its political implications, since it would have given NATO a unified confessional physiognomy – the rejection of which was imposed by then-Cardinal Joseph Ratzinger because of his idiosyncrasy regarding a use of the expression "traditions," which was not permitted by his ecclesiological essentialism.[53] Or again, we might note the thousandth anniversary of the baptism of Rus', which occurred in 1988 and was not accompanied by a convocation of the Holy and Great Council of the Orthodox Church which could have addressed the problems that, over the decades, have led to a schism between Moscow and Constantinople and to the Russian-Ukrainian fratricide.

We can also list the Lima agreement on BEM (Baptism, Eucharist, and Ministry) of 1982, which held the powerful instrument of a logic of consensus/convergence, but which failed to break out of the circuit of Faith and Order's theological atelier,[54] thus achieving far less than the agreements born out of the ecclesiologies of reconciled diversity such as the 1973 Leuenberg Agreement[55] – while the political welding of evangelical moods and the political right today experiments with a collaboration in which fundamentalist, ultra-liberalist, and supremacist ideologies seem like folklore.[56]

4.3 *The Crest and Counter-Evidence*

The research that converges in this history did not need to dwell on the events where a militant and triumphant ecumenism failed to prevent swelling pockets of contempt and murderous violence among Christians (for example, the civil war in Ireland from 1922 to 1998 or those that overflowed boundaries at the end of the USSR between 1991 and 2022). Rather, they are included and absorbed in the growing "practical" commitment, which emerged as early as the 1966 Geneva World Conference on Church and Society and then in 1968 at the Uppsala general assembly or again in 1975 at the Nairobi assembly. It is a different perspective, then, from the two lungs of the 1920s (Life and Work and Faith and Order, significantly transformed into a "commission" in 1948), which was illuminated by the construction of symbolic settings (from the embrace between Athenagoras I and Paul VI in Jerusalem in 1964 to the youth council in Taizé) and revisiting *vexatissimae* issues (the date of Easter, for example). It brings a fervor that reduces the amount of thought applied to unresolved problems, fills the void of communion with gestures of true fraternity, undercuts the instrumentalism of the political right seeking religious legitimacy that has anti-ecumenical periods (against Catholic-minded liberation theology, for example[57]) and then elaborates a combative ecumenism against the ghosts of modernity, resembling an international hate organization. What acceleration had made seem imminent thus turns out to be impossible at the moment that history turns the page, filing away that century that, short or long as it may have been, is certainly over.

Translated from Italian to English by Susan Dawson Vásquez and David Dawson Vásquez.

53 For the text of the *osservazioni* sent by Ratzinger to the heads of the Church of England, see *AAS* 74, 1982, 1062–1074. The text of ARCIC's first final report can be found in *Enchiridion Œcumenicum*, vol. 1, Sever J. Voicu & Giovanni Cereti, eds., *Dialoghi internazionali (1931–1984)*, Bologna, EDB, 1986, 3–159.

54 Luca Ferracci, *Battesimo Eucaristia Ministero: Genesi e destino di un documento ecumenico*, Bologna, Il Mulino, 2022.

55 Jan Gross, *Pluralität als Herausforderung: Die Leuenberger Konkordie als Vermittlungsmodell reformatorischer Kirchen in Europa*, Göttingen, Vandenhoeck & Ruprecht, 2018 and, in this volume, the essay by Elisabeth Parmentier.

56 Think of the apocalyptical theory presented in William Strauss & Neil Howe, *The Fourth Turning: An American Prophecy – What Cycles of History Tell Us About America's Next Rendezvous with Destiny*, New York, Crown, 1997 (Howe himself claimed to have given rise to the theology of Trump's presidency; see Neil Howe, "Where did Steve Bannon get his Worldview? From My Book," *The Washington Post*, Feb 24, 2017).

57 See Luca Ferracci, "The Vatican, Sandinista Priests, and Liberation Theology in the Papers of the Reagan Presidency," *CrSt* 44/3, 2023, 803–833.

Bibliography

Alberigo, Giuseppe, dir., Joseph A. Komonchak, ed., *History of Vatican II*, 5 vols., Orbis/Leuven, Maryknoll/Peeters, 1995.

Alberigo, Giuseppe, *Transizione epocale: Studi sul Concilio Vaticano II*, Bologna, Il Mulino, 2009.

Beansaude-Vincent, Bernadette, *L'opinion publique et la science: A chacun son ignorance*, Paris, Institut d'Édition Sanofi-Synthèlabo, 2000.

Chenaux, Philippe, *L'Église catholique et le communisme en Europe (1917–1989): De Lénine à Jean Paul II*, Paris, Cerf, 2009.

Congar, Yves, *La tradition et la vie de l'Église*, Paris, Cerf, 1984.

Ruston, Thomas William, *A Reparative Reading of the Eucharistic Ecclesiology of John Zizioulas and its Reception as Social Trinitarianism*, Ph.D. thesis, University of Birmingham, 2022.

Scholem, Gershom, *On Jews and Judaism in Crisis: Selected Essays*, ed. Werner J. Dannhauser, New York, Schocken Books, 1976.

PART 1

Contents: Preparation for the Unforeseen

∵

CHAPTER 1

Le Saulchoir and *Chrétiens désunis*

Joseph Famerée

1 Introduction

In the very day he joined the Dominican Order, on Dec 8, 1926, after having completed his novitiate in Amiens, Yves (religious name: Marie-Joseph) Congar entered the convent school of Le Saulchoir. This Dominican school of the province of France had previously been moved to Belgium, to Kain-la-Tombe near Tournai, just over the border, following the expulsion of the religious congregations in the early 20th century. Le Saulchoir is the name of the estate in Kain-la-Tombe where the convent school had been set up.

What was the prevailing intellectual climate at Le Saulchoir in 1926 when Congar arrived there, and how did it evolve until the second half of the 1930s, when the Dominican held his famous conferences of January 1936 in Montmartre, which would form the basis of his first book, *Chrétiens désunis*?[1]

Which theological development did Congar himself undergo during this period? What does this book contain? What significance does it have for the openness of Catholics, and of other Christians, to the desire for Christian unity?

These are the questions that will be addressed in the first three parts of this chapter, followed by a fourth part devoted to a few exemplary aspects of the reception of *Chrétiens désunis*.

1 Marie-Joseph Congar, *Chrétiens désunis: Principes d'un "œcuménisme" catholique*, Paris, Cerf, 1937; ET: *Divided Christendom: A Catholic Study of the Problem of Reunion*, trans. Muad A. Bousfield, London, Bles, 1939.

2 The Intellectual Climate at Le Saulchoir during the Years 1920–1930

Care must be taken not to present a mythological and oversimplified view of the history of Le Saulchoir, such as that which arose from a particular reception of the 1937 manifesto *Une école de théologie: Le Saulchoir*,[2] according to which there would have been a joyous Saulchoir (that of the regency of Marie-Dominique Chenu, focused entirely on its return to France), then a sorrowful Saulchoir (that of the Roman sanctions decreed against Chenu's manifesto in 1942 and against the crisis of the worker-priests in 1954), and finally a glorious Saulchoir (that of the contribution of certain of its members, above all Congar, to the conciliar project).[3] But what is it exactly about the years of Chenu's regency that concerns us here more directly?

Under the regency of Ambroise Gardeil, it became possible to attend two years of additional academic specialization after the institutional Dominican training in philosophy and theology. Although he himself was an advocate of the

2 Marie-Dominique Chenu, *Une école de théologie: Le Saulchoir*, Kain-lez-Tournai-Étiolles, Le Saulchoir, 1937; reissued in Marie-Dominique Chenu, *Une école de théologie: Le Saulchoir*, ed. Giuseppe Alberigo, Paris, Cerf, 1985, 91–173. For a more nuanced and sophisticated view of a certain theological diversity at the abbey in Kain, see Henry Donneaud, "Le Saulchoir: Une école, des théologies?," *Gregorianum* 83/3, 2002, 433–449.

3 According to the (not entirely humorless) characterization by Étienne Fouilloux, *Une Église en quête de liberté: La pensée catholique française entre modernisme et Vatican II (1914–1962)*, Paris, Desclée de Brouwer, 1998, 125; see pages 126–148 (which I sometimes follow closely) for a strictly historical reassessment of this "type of myth behind which it is not easy to discern the truth" (125).

speculative approach, Gardeil did not discourage more "positive" or "historical" orientations. Thus, Father Mannès Jacquin, who had been trained in the historical method in Louvain, launched the journal *Revue des sciences philosophiques et théologiques* in 1907 in cooperation with his fellow Dominican brothers Albert-Marie Blanche and Antoine Lemonnyer. In his book *Le donné révélé et la théologie*,[4] Gardeil argues in favor of a theological apologetics with claims to objectivity, even though he is well aware that theology remains a human construct, homogeneous with the "revealed given" but at the same time distinct from it: theological conclusions cannot be absolutized. World War I led to the dispersal of this first Le Saulchoir team around Gardeil.

Antoine Lemonnyer, regent of the school from 1911, endeavored to gather a second team together as soon as the war ended, with the moral support of Pierre Mandonnet, an emeritus professor from Fribourg who, however, did not join Le Saulchoir until 1927, one year after the arrival of the professed novice Yves Congar. Long before that, Chenu had joined the team as early as 1920. As noted by Étienne Fouilloux, "the Lemonnyer-Mandonnet phase in Le Saulchoir can be described as the incursion of historical criticism into the very heart of the work that was being conducted by the house," which thereby aligned itself with the method of biblical study applied by Father Marie-Joseph Lagrange in Jerusalem.[5] At the Kain *studium*, the objective was to resituate Thomas Aquinas within his own historical context and in relation to his sources.

In an initial effort to promote this scholarly endeavor, the Institut d'études thomistes was founded in 1920–1921, with Chenu as its secretary. This was followed by the creation of the Bibliothèque thomiste, which, in 1923, was taken over by the Société thomiste, itself established the previous year as a society that brought together members of the various Thomist currents of the day. However, the society's official organ, the *Bulletin thomiste*, proved so openly critical of the masters of the Dominican school that difficulties very soon began to arise between Le Saulchoir and Saint-Maximin, the Dominican *studium* of the province of Toulouse. As early as 1923, the Thomism of Le Saulchoir was accused "of sacrificing theology to philosophy, and above all to history."[6] The year 1925 witnessed the beginning of the publication of the *Somme théologique*, also known by the name *Revue des jeunes*, which was launched by Father Antonin-Dalmace Sertillanges in collaboration with the Kain convent school. At about the same time, Étienne Gilson became a regular visitor to Le Saulchoir and a friend of Chenu, whom he would assist, in 1931, in the creation of the Institute of Medieval Studies in Ottawa, similar to the one in Toronto.

Following the Saulchoir of Gardeil and the Saulchoir of Lemonnyer-Mandonnet, we now have Le Saulchoir of Chenu, who would succeed in combining the former's speculative orientation and the latter's medieval interests. Having arrived in Kain as early as 1920, he initially lectured on the patristic, Greek, and Latin sources of the Doctor Angelicus. The following year, he proceeded to teach a secondary course that enjoyed particular success among the students: that of the history of dogmas, renamed history of Christian doctrines. He not only demonstrated how orthodoxy had gradually emerged from deviations and heresies but also reconstructed the intellectual climate of the patristic and medieval discourses.[7] Passionate and nonconformist, Chenu was the central figure of the medieval project at Le Saulchoir and

4 Ambroise Gardeil, *Le donné révélé et la théologie*, Paris, J. Gabalda, 1910.

5 Fouilloux, *Une Église en quête de liberté*, 127.

6 Fouilloux, *Une Église en quête de liberté*, 129.

7 Congar would later write: "I still have the notes I took during his classes ... These pages hardly convey the wonderful feeling of reawakening, of being able to grasp the intelligence of what has been thought, of the dynamic development that I never ceased to experience while attending the classes of Father Chenu'"; see Yves Congar, *Journal d'un théologien (1946–1956)*, ed. Étienne Fouilloux, Paris, Cerf, 2000, 58.

worked tirelessly on the publications that related to it (bibliographical records, bulletins on the history of doctrines, lexicographical notes). However, he was "not a mere historian, and even less a philosopher," but "first and foremost a theologian ...; his primary goal was [to provide] a better scholarly justification for a theology that would be worthy of the name"[8] while seeking to prove that Aquinas was the first theologian to meet the requirements of Aristotelian science fully. This was Chenu, this was Le Saulchoir that Congar found upon his arrival in 1926.

In the early 1930s, Chenu's theology, and through him that of Le Saulchoir, underwent noticeable changes when he became "the real 'patron' of the house."[9] Successively promoted, in 1932, to master in theology and regent by the master general Martin-Stanislas Gillet, Chenu secured remarkable advancements for his *studium*: the status of a canonical faculty for philosophy and theology in 1937 and the return of the school to France on the eve of the declaration of war. Not only was he able to fill the gaps left behind, for instance, by the premature death of Marie-Dominique Roland-Gosselin, the philosophical mind, in 1934, but he also secured the collaboration of prominent seniors, notably Sertillanges for moral theology from 1928 and the biblical scholar Ernest-Bernard Allo on the eve of World War II. Most importantly, he was also able to find, among the graduates of the 1920s, "the young pillars of a team that was tied to him through bonds of friendship as much as by a substantial number of shared views: Marie-Joseph Congar, Henri-Marie Féret, and Thomas Deman, among others."[10] This team "set the tone at Le Saulchoir as early as the late 1930s,"[11] even though there was no lack of differing views around it, as would be revealed by the crisis of 1942 concerning Chenu. Le Saulchoir nevertheless acquired a certain reputation under Chenu's regency, to the point that the school became convinced that it had become "an educational model for the order" and "the template for the only Thomistic revival worthy of that name."[12] Then why not state this publicly? It was in this frame of mind that in 1937 Chenu wrote the booklet *Une école de théologie: Le Saulchoir*, which was initially intended for a limited distribution. However, it would ultimately unleash a storm of indignation, as it would come to be seen as "a sort of manifesto that presents the *studium*, and the theology developed by it, as exemplary models to the superiors and fellow brothers."[13]

Chenu did not forsake the Middle Ages after 1930. He succeeded to Father Mandonnet at the Société thomiste and at the library of the same name, and inherited the responsibility for the *Revue des sciences philosophiques et théologiques* from Roland-Gosselin, which he held until Congar took over in 1936, the year of the latter's conferences in Montmartre on the occasion of the Octave of Prayer for Christian Unity. By the late 1920s, however, the focus of Chenu's history classes shifted from the Middle Ages to the modern and contemporary periods (the problem of faith in the 19th century, the Modernist crisis). Becoming aware of the implications of centuries of Catholic intransigence, and having now also taken an interest in history as such (taking the economic, social, political, and cultural context into consideration), he launched "his great offensive against what he termed ... 'baroque theology,'" namely "the entire scholastic output, from the late Middle Ages to the dawn of the 20th century: five centuries ... in which the proliferation of commentaries only served to bury the thought of St. Thomas or of great contemporaries under thousands of formalistic and withered pages."[14] He would be joined by Congar

8 Fouilloux, *Une Église en quête de liberté*, 131.

9 Fouilloux, *Une Église en quête de liberté*, 132.

10 Fouilloux, *Une Église en quête de liberté*, 133. Elsewhere, Fouilloux would single out Chenu, Congar, and Féret as "the main trio of the school of theology"; see Congar, *Journal d'un théologien*, ed. Fouilloux, 54, note 186.

11 Fouilloux, *Une Église en quête de liberté*, 133.

12 Fouilloux, *Une Église en quête de liberté*, 133.

13 Fouilloux, *Une Église en quête de liberté*, 133.

14 Fouilloux, *Une Église en quête de liberté*, 135.

in this struggle.[15] For the regent of Le Saulchoir, "a theology worthy of that name is a spirituality that has found the rational instruments that suited its religious experience."[16]

It was above all during the 1930s, under Chenu, that history, in the sense of contemporary secular life, burst into Le Saulchoir with the arrival of the chaplains and leaders of the JOC: the economic and moral crisis, the rise of the fascist movement, the reaction of popular fronts, and so on. Looking at Christianity, at the world at work, the theologian discerns "'lieux' théologiques *en acte*"[17] which the church should take seriously if it wishes to reconnect with the major concerns of its contemporaries. The manifesto of Le Saulchoir lists six such loci: a missionary expansion that has been freed from "outdated colonialism"; the splendors of the Christian East; the birth of the ecumenical movement (with particular emphasis on this "theological loci" and the preceding one); the rise of the specialized Catholic action; the "pluralism of human civilizations"; and the "social restlessness triggered by the access of the popular masses to public and conscious life," in spite of the risk "of communist perversion."[18] For Chenu, these problems had become "far more important for the future of faith than many scholastic debates."[19]

The Copernican Revolution, which led to a shift from a deductive theology (one deduced from logical and doctrinal principles) to an inductive theology (one induced from facts), implies a new set of instruments. Chenu probably owed his awareness of church evolution to his erudition in the field of history, "but even more to a series of interpretations stemming either from his personal experience or from his intellectual insights."[20] On this last point, the Dominican acknowledged his debt to the Tübingen School, which criticized "the abstract intellectualism of the Aufklärung and its indifference towards history," and, by the same token, the modern scholasticism of textbooks and the growth of Catholic intransigence.[21] In a Catholic way of thinking, which the regent of Le Saulchoir interpreted as a dialectic between formalism and realism, it was essential that the living theology of the 20th century follow in the footsteps of the German school and rediscover realism, which had succumbed to a withering formalism, by combating the epigones of the so-called baroque theology and by seeking out, in the lives of human beings and of the church, those "'in act theological loci' that nowadays constitute an obligatory waypoint for the understanding of faith."[22] It should be noted here that it was precisely Chenu who introduced Congar to the works of a prominent representative of the Tübingen School, Johann Adam Möhler. Moreover, it is well known that the latter became a key point of reference in his ecclesiological (and thus ecumenical) reflection. We shall return to this topic later on.

After *Une école de théologie: Le Saulchoir* had been placed on the index in 1942, and following his banishment from the school,[23] the ex-regent no longer wielded any direct influence at Le Saulchoir. However, his two associates Yves Congar and Henri-Marie Féret, along with others, would continue to teach there in the spirit of "a school of theology" until their forced departure in 1954, in connection with the crisis of the worker-priests.[24] Regarding the heirs to the legacy of Chenu, in particular his friend Congar, Fouilloux even goes

15 Féret should also be included. All three of them conceived "the project of a joint work: a History of Theology," which failed to materialized due to their respective commitments; see Congar, *Journal d'un théologien*, ed. Fouilloux, 60–61.

16 Chenu, *Une école de théologie*, 75.

17 Chenu, *Une école de théologie*, 68 (italics original).

18 Chenu, *Une école de théologie*, 67–68.

19 Fouilloux, *Une Église en quête de liberté*, 137.

20 Fouilloux, *Une Église en quête de liberté*, 138–139.

21 Chenu, *Une école de théologie*, 66–67.

22 Fouilloux, *Une Église en quête de liberté*, 140.

23 See Robert Guelluy, "Les antécédents de l'encyclique 'Humani generis' dans les sanctions romaines de 1942: Chenu, Charlier, Draguet," *RHE* 81/3, 1986, 421–497.

24 See Jean-Pierre Jossua, "Le Saulchoir: Une formation théologique replacée dans son histoire," *CrSt* 14/1, 1993, 99–124.

so far as to ask the following question: "Might it not, in fact, seem reasonable to suggest that the latter incarnates Le Saulchoir better than Chenu himself?"[25] In other words: a successful transmission. On this point, the disciple is said to have equaled, if not even surpassed, the teacher: a Dominican vocation linked to the study of St. Thomas, amplified by history, then by apostolic experience.

Is this not how the intellectual climate of the years 1920–1930 at Le Saulchoir might be characterized, when Congar arrived there as a student and then assumed professorial and editorial duties? An understanding of history as a discipline and a method (applied, in particular, to the study of the Doctor Angelicus), a sense of history as the life of the contemporary world (notably through the apostolic experience of the JOC), an effort to bring clarity, the discernment of the formal aspect of a question, and the meticulous search for the truth which Congar would later associate with his study of Thomas Aquinas's thought (in conjunction with the ecumenical dialogue)[26] – this is the backdrop against which Yves Congar was to follow his own path.

3 Yves Congar at Le Saulchoir (1926–1939)

The person who arrived at Le Saulchoir of Kain on Dec 8, 1926, upon completion of his novitiate in Amiens, was born on Apr 13, 1904, in Sedan (French Ardennes), one of the main centers of French Protestantism in the 16th and 17th centuries. In this confessionally mixed area, Congar's parents had formed bonds of friendship with Reformed Protestants and Jews. As an adolescent, Yves would play with young Protestants and often had serious theological discussions with the pastor's son, especially as far as the issues of Mass and of the Eucharist were concerned. Moreover, the Protestant pastor had placed a small chapel at the priest's disposal after the Catholic church had been set on fire by the Germans in August 1914. The Dominican friar would later attribute his ecumenical vocation to these circumstances.[27] During these war years and those that immediately followed, he also acquired, according to his own testimony, the basic foundations of a solid and authentic awareness of the church: thanks to the devout life of the small parochial community of Sedan, and especially to the sermons of his priest, which, to use a typically Congarian expression, were "so full of Catholic doctrine and spirit";[28] thanks also to the influence of the Abbé Daniel Lallement, his mentor in Sedan, who introduced him to the reality of liturgy and religious life – by taking him, for the Vespers of the Transfiguration of Aug 5, 1919, to the French Benedictine monks of Saint-Wandrille, who had been living in exile in Conques (Belgian Ardennes), on the banks of the Semois, since 1904 –; and, finally, thanks to the inspiration he received from his mother, in whose library he had discovered *Le Mystère de l'Église* by Father Humbert Clérissac, a book that would greatly influence his thinking by introducing him to what he called "the poetry of Catholicism"[29] (it was also in his mother's library that he would later

25 Fouilloux, *Une Église en quête de liberté*, 141.

26 See *Jean Puyo interroge le Père Congar: Une vie pour la vérité*, Paris, Le Centurion, 1975, 38–40. The eloquent subtitle of this long interview is noteworthy.

27 See Yves Congar, *Une passion: L'unité: Réflexions et souvenirs (1929–1973)*, Paris, Cerf, 1974, 10. For the biographical details mentioned here, see 9–35; see also Jean-Pierre Jossua, *Le Père Congar: La théologie au service du Peuple de Dieu*, Paris, Cerf, 1967, 13–26, 43–51, 65–74, and 99–100; *Jean Puyo interroge le Père Congar*, 5–86; Étienne Fouilloux, *Les catholiques et l'unité chrétienne du XIXe au XXe siècle: Itinéraires européens d'expression française*, Paris, Le Centurion, 1982, 209–221; Étienne Fouilloux, "Frère Yves, cardinal Congar, dominicain: Itinéraire d'un théologien," *RSPT* 79/3, 1995, 379–388; Joseph Famerée, "Formation et ecclésiologie du 'premier' Congar," in: André Vauchez, ed., *Cardinal Yves Congar, 1904–1995: Actes du colloque réuni à Rome les 3–4 juin 1996*, Paris, Cerf, 1999, 51–70, which I largely follow.

28 Congar, *Une passion: L'unité*, 13.

29 *Jean Puyo interroge le Père Congar*, 74.

come upon the Assumptionist journal *L'Union des Églises*, which later became *L'Unité de l'Église*).

Such were the seeds of a calling that was not only ecumenical and ecclesiological but also, and simultaneously, priestly and religious, Dominican and Thomist. At least this is how Yves Congar would later look back on the consistency of his vocation.[30]

Prior to entering the Dominican novitiate in 1925, the young student had been admitted to the university Carmes Seminary in Paris and had attended philosophy classes for three years, notably those of a certain Jacques Maritain, at the Institut catholique. This is where he was initiated into scholastic Thomism before embracing a different approach to Aquinas at Le Saulchoir. As stated above, when Congar arrived at the Kain convent school in December 1926, he came upon a school characterized by its historical training, under the influence of the fathers Antoine Lemonnyer, Pierre Mandonnet, Marie-Dominique Roland-Gosselin, and especially Marie-Dominique Chenu, who was still very young. Le Saulchoir intensified the study of the biblical and patristic sources of the *Divus Thomas* and endeavored to read him more in the context of his own time by means of the then rapidly developing discipline of medieval studies.[31] This approach to Aquinas, replaced in his own time, could not but reinforce the down-to-earth realism and the love for a real, concrete life of our Ardennes-born student, not to mention the basis of his irresistible taste for history. A desire to return to the biblical and patristic sources and a feeling and concern for history. This already says everything about Congar.[32]

It is also necessary to note elements of a more directly defining, more personal, and more intentional nature that gradually shaped his theological project, in other words: his ecclesiological and ecumenical endeavor. The friar preacher thus prepared himself for the presbyteral ordination (Jul 25, 1930) by studying, on the one hand, the Gospel according to John along with the commentaries of Thomas Aquinas and Father Marie-Joseph Lagrange (as he would later confide, it was precisely while pondering chapter 17 of this gospel, in 1929, at the age of 25, that he definitely felt a calling to work towards the union of the disciples of Christ)[33] and, on the other hand, the theology of the "Eucharistic sacrifice," particularly in the book of the canon Eugène Masure, *Le sacrifice du chef*.[34] Prior to this, during his three years at the seminary and his four years of Dominican religious life, as he recalled, he had already, every day and to the best of his ability, offered himself to God to accomplish his will, under the very strong impression of a verse of the *Benedictus* at Lauds (it was "less said by me than said to me inwardly by Another"[35]): "Et tu, puer, propheta Altissimi vocaberis." Nothing here suggests a sense of exceptional vocation, but rather an effort to dedicate himself every day, in fidelity, to the will of God: a readiness to "prepare the ways of the Lord" according to the needs of the church and of the world. He would also relate this verse to his efforts – and I would add: to

30 Congar, *Une passion: L'unité*, 13–14.

31 André Duval, "Aux origines de l''Institut historique d'études thomistes' du Saulchoir (1920 et ss): Notes et documents," *RSPT* 75/3, 1991, 423–448; Fouilloux, "Frère Yves, cardinal Congar," 383–384.

32 Jossua, *Le Père Congar*, 13ff. and 166ff.

33 For the years 1929–1932, it is necessary to supplement, and sometimes correct, the recollections of *Une passion: L'unité* and the interview by Jean Puyo with "Mon témoignage," a handwritten fragment of memoirs written between 1946 and 1949: "From that moment, I have firmly held on to the idea of dedicating myself to unity, and especially to the reunion of the French Protestants, our closest separated brethren" (here already, the expression "separated brethren"!). Congar adds that Father Lemonnyer, his former regent, had "surprisingly understood, or even intuitively known and encouraged [this]"; Congar, *Journal d'un théologien*, ed. Fouilloux, 19–62, here 20–21. Must we understand this "surprisingly" as an indication that the orientation of our theologian was quite exceptional, and ultimately found little support in Le Saulchoir itself?

34 Eugène Masure, *Le sacrifice du chef*, Paris, Beauchesne, 1932; ET: *The Christian Sacrifice*, trans. Dom Illtyd Trethowan, London, Burns, Oates & Co., 1944.

35 Congar, *Une passion: L'unité*, 9.

his *pioneering* efforts – in ecumenical and ecclesiological matters.

As far as his more specifically intellectual formation is concerned, his lecturer's thesis (which concluded the cycle of Dominican studies) dealt with the unity of the church, a topic that he had chosen during the summer of 1928[36] and for which he had to "engage in intensive research and study," as "the topic was very vast," and also because he had never "been taught anything in this respect";[37] during the academic year 1928–1929, he also attended classes on the history of Christian doctrines, in which Father Chenu spoke to his students about the Faith and Order movement and its first ecumenical conference, which had convened in Lausanne in 1927 (as brother Congar noted, the professor hardly needed more than one hour a week to afford him new perspectives on a reality that had already existed in his mind).[38]

As already stated, it was at about the same time that Marie-Dominique Chenu brought Möhler to his attention: in the latter's works, the student in theology discovered the primary modern source that he needed; what the theologian from Tübingen had achieved in the 19th century would breathe life into his own work and become an ideal from which he would seek inspiration for his own reflection in the 20th century.[39]

Early in 1930, the future professor had also asked for a copy of a page by Father Marie-Benoît Schwalm in which the latter outlined what ecclesiology should be. The page was taken from the article "Les deux théologies: La scolastique et la positive";[40] it speaks of the necessity to apply the Thomistic analysis of society to the church-society, "a social subject of a special and supernatural kind."[41] The young theologian would be profoundly influenced by it for a time, although he soon realized that the Thomistic categories of society could not fully account for the ecclesial mystery; on the other hand, he drew lasting inspiration from other parts of Father Schwalm's text in which the latter expressed the desire that future ecclesiology might synthesize the scattered achievements of the centuries, finding inspiration in the thinking of the Fathers, popes, and theologians who elaborated this doctrine, and become "this treatise on the

36 "As early as 1930," according to "Mon témoignage"; see Congar, *Journal d'un théologien*, ed. Fouilloux, 21.

37 Congar, *Journal d'un théologien*, ed. Fouilloux, 21–22. Does not this lack of instruction on the unity of the church, which Congar deplores, corroborate the originality of his theological choice when compared to the prevailing interests of the study house of Kain? The title of his dissertation, "Amorces d'un traité de l'Unité de l'Église," is anticipatory and attests to the precociousness of his ecclesiological and ecumenical ventures. This lecturer's thesis (152 pages) can be consulted at APDF, V, 832 (Y. Congar), year 1931.

38 See *Jean Puyo interroge le Père Congar*, 75. In support of his ecumenical openness, Congar also mentions the apostolic endeavors of his Dominican province. A regular correspondence with the Norwegian mission was of particular interest to the future lecturer in theology and afforded him deep insights into the religious situation of that country. Likewise, the Russian seminary of St. Basil in Lille was located very close to Le Saulchoir, having been entrusted by Pius XI to the French Dominicans for the training of Russian Catholic priests of Eastern rite (established by the fathers Henri-Jean Omez and Christophe-Jean Dumont, this seminary, in conjunction with the affiliated study center Istina, was held in high esteem at Le Saulchoir from 1927 onward: exchanges between Lille and Kain, introduction to Eastern theology and liturgy etc.). Lutheran Protestantism and Orthodoxy thus existed for the students of Le Saulchoir, their existence having been communicated to them through fraternal testimonies; see Congar, *Une passion: L'unité*, 11; Jossua, *Le Père Congar*, 18; *Jean Puyo interroge le Père Congar*, 74; Congar, *Journal d'un théologien*, ed. Fouilloux, 21. Although he does not entirely deny it, Fouilloux is personally inclined to downplay the ecumenical influence exerted by Congar through these essentially missionary endeavors of the province of France; see Fouilloux, *Les catholiques et l'unité chrétienne*, 214ff.

39 *Jean Puyo interroge le Père Congar*, 48. "Over time," as he noted in "Mon témoignage," "increasingly viewed Möhler as a prophetic man who had astonishingly guessed what the century needed most"; Congar, *Journal d'un théologien*, ed. Fouilloux, 60.

40 Marie-Benoît Schwalm, "Les deux théologies: La scholastique et la positive," *RSPT* 2/4, 1908, 674–703; esp. the paragraph entitled "Traité de l'Église au point de vue scolastique," 686–691.

41 Schwalm, "Les deux théologies," 689.

church, a treatise on the socialized Son of God."[42] This idea would reappear, further elaborated, in the ecclesiological project that prompted Congar to launch the Unam Sanctam series in 1936–1937 with the publication of its first volume, *Chrétiens désunis*.

After passing his exams, in October 1931, the newly qualified lecturer had to begin teaching immediately in the first trimester of the academic year, acting as a substitute for Father Chenu, who had left for Canada in order to found the Institute of Medieval Studies in Ottawa. Hence, he had only six months of further studies, completed in Paris, from January to June 1932, by attending a few courses on rational sociology at the Institut Catholique (Abbé Lallement), those of Gabriel Le Bras and Étienne Gilson at the École Pratique des Hautes Études, and finally those of the pastors Auguste Lecerf (Reformed dogmatics) and André Jundt (Lutheran dogmatics) at the Faculty of Protestant Theology.[43] Convinced "that the mission of our generation was to press home, *within the church*, what was true about the demands and problems presented by Modernism," Congar also hoped to be able to "attend a few classes by Loisy, who was in his final year at the Collège de France and whose *Mémoires* [he] had just read." However, he was not permitted to do so by his provincial, Father Jourdain Padé, who, while he did authorize him to attend the courses of the Protestant faculty, did not see the point of doing so, estimating that "anything interesting which they might have to say could be found in their books." To which the young professor replied that his intention was "precisely to seek what cannot be found in the books," and understood, "ever better, that in all fields, nothing can replace direct, physical, living contact."[44]

Having returned to Le Saulchoir, Congar prepared himself to teach apologetics in a spirit that was quite different from that of his predecessors: even before reading Blaise Pascal in captivity, he had been deeply Pascalian in this field, never having believed in a rational argumentation; he would also emphasize the problems of interconfessional apologetics and, more generally, contribute to the rise of said discipline to the status of a truly fundamental theology. As early as 1933, he succeeded in transferring the *De Ecclesia*, which had hitherto been included in the apologetics program, to theology. His desire to draw up a broad treatise on the church also goes back to this time. The point of view and the plan adopted by his course in 1932 reveal that under the influence of Fr. Schwalm's article and of Abbé Lallement's sociology courses, he set about pondering the mystery of the church by applying the Thomistic categories of society to it, although he would gradually come to realize that these categories were unable to fully account for ecclesial reality.[45]

As already said, during his years of study and early professorship, the young Dominican had, as early as 1929, allegedly become keenly aware of his ecumenical vocation and had confided as much to his superiors, who did not voice any objections. Upon completion of his first ordination holidays,

42 Schwalm, "Les deux théologies," 689, see also Jossua, *Le Père Congar*, 20–24.

43 See Congar, *Une passion: L'unité*, 17f. For additional details on the Faculty of Theology at Boulevard Arago and on the crucial encounters that Congar had there (thus leading to the creation of ecumenical channels), see Fouilloux, *Les catholiques et l'unité chrétienne*, 218–220. The young Catholic theologian noted that: "No one at the faculty would tell me or ask me anything. I believe they viewed me with a certain sympathy, although they probably wondered what I was up to"; Congar, *Journal d'un théologien*, ed. Fouilloux, 27. Everything had yet to be done in the field of ecumenism…

44 Congar, *Journal d'un théologien*, ed. Fouilloux, 24, 26–27. Congar would often return to the legitimate demands of Modernism: "The goal was to give back theology its historical dimension and its dimension of a living religious knowledge"; Congar, *Journal d'un théologien*, ed. Fouilloux, 60; see also 59.

45 See *Cours d'ecclésiologie 1932–1933*, in: APDF, 832, 40, Congar explicitly distances himself from an apologetic approach (21). He wishes to draw up a theological treatise on the church (26) while remaining dependent on the Thomistic categories of causality (33ff.: final cause, material cause, efficient cause, formal cause); Jossua, *Le Père Congar*, 23f.

on Aug 14, 1930, he had the opportunity to visit the Dominican priory in Düsseldorf, where he discovered *Die Hochkirche*,[46] the journal that would soon be directed by Friedrich Heiler. At this time, the periodical placed greater emphasis on the Hochkirche movement, which sought to develop a "catholicizing" tendency within German Protestantism, than on ecumenism. Upon coming into contact with the Germanism, the French Dominican immediately realized that "even though he knew very little about it, there was something very profound to understand and discover in Luther."[47] The following summer, he visited the academic centers of Berlin[48] and "experienced the fascination of the historic sites of Lutheranism":[49] the Wartburg, Erfurt, Wittenberg. During the first semester of 1932, which he spent in Paris, he not only attended classes on Martin Luther and John Calvin but also frequented the Franco-Russian circle,[50] a meeting point for Orthodox Christians, Protestants, and Catholics where it was possible to mingle with Jacques Maritain, Nicholas Berdyaev, Sergius Bulgakov, Lev Gillet, and Emmanuel Mounier.[51] At the Institut Catholique, the Dominican ecclesiologist also made the acquaintance of the abbé Albert Gratieux, who held classes on Aleksey Stepanovich Khomyakov and the Slavophile movement. At about the same time,[52] he paid a visit to Dom Lambert Beauduin, then "exiled" in France, and confessed his aspirations and projects to him: nothing less than the desire to "embark on a renewal of ecclesiology in conjunction with a broad participation in unionist activities," as it was formulated in the language of the time.[53]

The theologian from Le Sauchoir then proceeded to put his idea into practice and acquainted himself with the terrain, so to speak, by visiting Amay-sur-Meuse (near Liège in Belgium) in late July and early August 1932. It is in this priory, which had been established by Dom Beauduin[54] in 1925 and relocated to Chevetogne in 1939, and at which the Latin and the Eastern (Slavonic) rites were celebrated simultaneously in two separate chapels, that Father Congar met abbé Paul Couturier. It was also at this very moment, during his stay at Amay, as the Dominican ecumenist would later learn, that the priest from Lyon received the inspiration to dedicate himself to the cause of unity and decided to promote his famous Week of Universal

46 He was able to borrow a few fascicles of this journal "from the library, even though some considered this strange or even dangerous, or expressed doubts about the seriousness of this movement." He later subscribed to the journal of this Lutheran "High Church," on which he wrote his first article concerning an ecumenical topic (in the Assumptionist journal *L'Unité de l'Église*, January–February 1931, 398–403). "I believe," as Congar also wrote, "that the articles read in late August and especially in early September 1930, in Düsseldorf, afforded me the first breath of ecumenical air"; Congar, *Journal d'un théologien*, ed. Fouilloux, 22–23.

47 Congar, *Une passion: L'unité*, 17.

48 He had some contacts with Protestants, notably when he paid a visit to Adolf Deißmann, professor of New Testament studies, then rector of the University of Berlin, who dedicated a book on Una Sancta to him; Congar, *Journal d'un théologien*, ed. Fouilloux, 23.

49 Citing the felicitous formulation of Fouilloux, *Les catholiques et l'unité chrétienne*, 217.

50 It is, in fact, the seat of the RSCM (placed at the latter's disposal by the YMCA) at 10 Boulevard Montparnasse.

51 See Congar, *Une passion: L'unité*, 18f.; *Jean Puyo interroge le Père Congar*, 76. Regarding these acquaintances, Congar makes enlightening comments about the "ecumenical" atmosphere of the time: "The father provincial [Jourdain Padé] told me that it was wrong of me to seek such contacts, that certain fathers of the monastery [of Faubourg-Saint-Honoré] (Father Chauvin) criticized me for this and had said to the father provincial: 'You are casting Father Congar into apostasy'"; Congar, *Journal d'un théologien*, ed. Fouilloux, 28.

52 If the first meeting with Dom Beauduin did indeed take place in Cormeilles-en-Parisis, Congar's dating of this meeting to April 1932 (Congar, *Une passion: L'unité*, 20–21) is problematical: following a brief stay in Strasbourg, the exiled monk of Amay left for En-Calcat on Apr 22, 1932, and did not arrive in Cormeilles until the spring of 1934, having left En-Calcat on Apr 4; see Fouilloux, *Les catholiques et l'unité chrétienne*, 221, note 74; Congar, *Journal d'un théologien*, ed. Fouilloux, 28, note 56.

53 Congar, *Une passion: L'unité*, 21.

54 On Beauduin and the monastery of Chevetogne, see the chapter by André Haquin in the first volume of this work.

Prayer for Christian Unity in order to infuse an entirely new spirit into the very Catholic Solemn Octave of Prayers for Unity of Christian World;[55] in the same spirit, in 1937, he would enter into a theological dialogue with a number of Protestant pastors, thus establishing the basis of what would come to be known as the Dombes Group.[56] In some way, and in anticipation of future developments, it was thus in the Benedictine priory of Amay that Catholic "doctrinal ecumenism" and "spiritual ecumenism" first crossed paths.

"With regard to the difficult 1930s, as the historian of contemporary French-speaking European ecumenism would write, there is absolutely no doubt that they bear the mark of Father Congar."[57] It is true, of course, that the latter was first and foremost professor at Le Saulchoir. "There, following the path laid out by his teacher, Father Chenu, he pursued his studies of medieval history and theology. However, the bulk of his 'external' activities and much of his already abundant output is, in one way or another, concerned with ecumenical issues."[58] The French Dominican became the main Catholic discussion partner in the ecumenical dialogue. From 1935, his initiatives, which he had to reconcile with his teaching obligations, succeeded each other "at a frightening pace," leading him "to the brink of physical and nervous exhaustion."[59]

The same year witnessed the birth of the *Cahiers pour le Protestantisme* (following a plan elaborated by Congar, the French publisher Éditions du Cerf, then at Juvisy, collected various pieces on Protestantism that had appeared in *La Vie intellectuelle* and published them in small pamphlets): the ecumenist, who bore the sole responsibility for this vast enterprise, and also frequently complained about it, wished to provide a much deeper understanding of contemporary "Protestant sensitiveness" and to present it through the actions of a number of "prominent personalities."[60] Fouilloux concludes:

> The *Cahiers* play a decisive role in the ecumenical career of Father Congar: it is they that accredit him – or make him appear suspicious – in different places; it is their publication that multiply the requests for collaboration. No less decisive is their role in the evolution of interconfessional relations in France: exactly contemporary with the first article of the Abbé Couturier, they raise the same topics – charity, objectivity – and attest, like him, to the rise of ecumenism in the Catholic context.[61]

Still in 1935, the Dominican was asked to participate in the "Franco-Russian retreats," gatherings that took place during the weekend of Pentecost and mainly brought together students of various confessions, Protestant, Orthodox, and, more recently, Catholic. The ecumenist from Le Saulchoir was thus not the inventor of these "retreats," although he did infuse them with a greater spirit of trust and frankness. He also endeavored to "provide a supporting framework" for the Catholic participants by launching a Parisian circle of theological studies that sketched the contours of "plenary Catholicism" (this circle would become the Fernand Portal group, named

55 Congar, *Une passion: L'unité*, 21–23.

56 See Étienne Fouilloux's contribution on Couturier and Catherine E. Clifford's contribution on the Dombes Group further bellow in this volume.

57 Fouilloux, *Les catholiques et l'unité chrétienne*, 207. For the following pages of this chapter, see Joseph Famerée, *L'ecclésiologie d'Yves Congar avant Vatican II: Histoire et Église: Analyse et reprise critique*, Leuven, Peeters, 1992, 33–35 and 401–402, on which I sometimes draw extensively.

58 Fouilloux, *Les catholiques et l'unité chrétienne*, 207.

59 Fouilloux, *Les catholiques et l'unité chrétienne*, 221; see *Jean Puyo interroge le Père Congar*, 78, 153. During the Week of Prayer for Christian Unity of January 1936 at Sacré-Cœur Basilica in Paris, "an incredible fatigue of the nervous system forced me to preach while holding on to the edge of the pulpit"; Congar, *Une passion: L'unité*, 35. It is well known that these conferences would furnish the basis of *Chrétiens désunis*.

60 See Congar, *Une passion: L'unité*, 27–29; Fouilloux, *Les catholiques et l'unité chrétienne*, 221–227.

61 Fouilloux, *Les catholiques et l'unité chrétienne*, 226–227.

after one of the main protagonists of the Malines Conversations between Catholics and Anglicans from 1921 onward).[62] Entirely produced in Belgium, *Au service de l'unité* was its liaison organ.[63] Father Congar sought to convene skills and good intentions. He tirelessly performed the "task of a reawakening and reunifying" in the service of unity.[64]

In late 1935, the chaplains of the Sacré-Cœur Basilica of Montmartre invited the Dominican to preach the Solemn Octave of Prayers for Unity of Christian World from Jan 18 to 25:[65] "There, on each day, following the very solemn celebration of vespers in the different rites of the Catholic Church, and usually under the presidency of a bishop, a sermon is delivered, which is followed by the Benediction of the Blessed Sacrament."[66]

Leaving spirituality aside and focusing on theological reflection, "in eight sessions that had more to do with lecturing than with homily," Congar outlined "a Catholic synthesis of the problem of unity that prefigured *Chrétiens désunis*," turning a traditional ceremony into "an event that provoked various reactions," while his name and his ideas attracted 800 to 2,000 people depending on the day. At the close of the conferences, the Orthodox and the Protestants would then drive him to exhaustion in the course of heated debates held at the Institute de théologie orthodoxe Saint-Serge or at the Federation of Protestant Students. Subsequently taken up in various cities, the repercussions of these conferences were at least as strong as those of the *Cahiers pour le protestantisme*.[67]

At about the same time, Congar became the theological advisor of L'Amitié. This association had arisen out of the comradeship of former students of the École Normale Supérieure and was, according to its statutes, restricted to members of the three orders of public or private education. It had recently opted for a confessional and ecumenical orientation. From 1936 to 1938, as Fouilloux was able to ascertain, the Dominican friar would go there to debate major doctrinal issues with the pastor Pierre Lestringant "in front of about fifty passionate listeners." Similar discussions took place in Douai. The Catholic participants asked him to organize special training. From then on, Congar was very much in demand, also by officials from the ecumenical movement, even if he was unable to respond to all requests.[68]

The experience of "the Englishman, of English culture, and of Anglican religion," which the French ecumenist still lacked, dates from the summer of 1936, when he decided to cross the Channel for the first time. He thus learned to appreciate the Anglican Church "for its admirable legacy, its worship, [and] its religious as well as humanistic ethos, which was both respectful and free."[69]

The previous year, Congar had agreed to provide a theological conclusion for the study which the journal *La Vie intellectuelle* had conducted on the current reasons for unbelief (Jul 31, 1935). The results of this study shocked him and convinced him of the necessity to restore "the true appearance

62 On this undertaking, see the chapter by Bernard Barlow and Martin Browne in the first volume of this work.

63 All issues of this liaison organ can be consulted in the Congar papers, see APDF, 832, 52, Groupe Portal.

64 See Congar, *Une passion: L'unité*, 29–32; Fouilloux, *Les catholiques et l'unité chrétienne*, 227–230.

65 The "initiative to dedicate the days that link the two feasts of the Chair of St. Peter in Rome and the conversion of St. Paul to the prayer for unity" was born in 1907 in the Anglican world, at the instigation of Father Paul James Francis Wattson, an Episcopalian minister, and of Rev. Spencer Jones, a "pro-papal" Anglican; it was approved as early as 1909 by Pope Pius X. Such is the explanation provided by Congar himself in the book that he wrote on the basis of his conferences of Montmartre, *Chrétiens désunis*, ix–x; Ruth Rouse, "Voluntary Movements and the Changing Ecumenical Climate," in: *A History of the Ecumenical Movement*, vol. 1, Ruth Rouse & Stephen C. Neill, eds., *1517–1948*, London, SPCK, 1954, 309–349, here 348–349.

66 As described by Congar, *Chrétiens désunis*, xi.

67 See Fouilloux, *Les catholiques et l'unité chrétienne*, 230–231.

68 See Congar, *Une passion: L'unité*, 32–33; Fouilloux, *Les catholiques et l'unité chrétienne*, 231–232.

69 See Congar, *Une passion: L'unité*, 33–35; Fouilloux, *Les catholiques et l'unité chrétienne*, 232–233.

of Catholicism."[70] In the wake of the "theological conclusion", the outlines of the French Dominican's original ecclesiological project gradually begin to emerge, in close connection, as we have already seen, with a strong ecumenical awareness.

It seemed to him that unbelief was, on the one hand, a consequence

> of the fact that the church showed people a face that betrayed, rather than expressed, its true nature, [which is] in conformity with the Gospel and with its own deep-rooted tradition. The proper answer, the positive conclusion, would consist in renewing our presentation [of ourselves] and, to this end, primarily our own vision of the church by moving beyond appearances and the juridical vision that were then, and have long been, predominant.[71]

With great lucidity, in the course of the 1930s, the ecclesiologist thus diagnosed a "deficit of incarnation and catholicity" on the part of the church: while the rest of the modern world, a humanistic and atheistic spiritual totality that is at odds with Christian totality, "pursues its own evolution and applies itself to resolving renewed problems, the church secludes itself and focuses inward on itself, forming a world apart, [one that is] strictly conservative [and] intent on guarding the deposit" of faith.[72]

> Hence, a huge portion of human activity, an entire growth of humanity, of human flesh – modern life with its science, its woes, its splendors – has not had in itself the incarnation of the Word; the church has not given its soul to this expanding body that was meant, like every human value, to receive the communication of the Spirit of Christ in order to become his body and give glory to God.[73]

Indeed, every expansion of the human in any one of the realms of creation must be met by a growth of the church, an incorporation of faith, a humanization of God. Such is the definition of ecclesial catholicity. The church is the universe as transfigured by grace into the image of God.[74]

Soon afterwards, as he launched the series Unam Sanctam, Congar specified his ecclesiological objective in the following manner: "To impart knowledge of the nature or, if you will, of the mystery of the church" by conveying "a notion of the large, rich, living church, full of biblical and traditional vigor."[75]

The fact that the series was launched with *Chrétiens désunis: Principes d'un "œcuménisme" catholique* was mainly due to the difficulties encountered in the translation of Möhler's *Die Einheit in der Kirche*,[76] which had been intended to symbolically inaugurate Unam Sanctam, but also a consequence of Congar's growing ecumenical commitment between 1935 and 1937.[77] By a happy

70 Fouilloux, *Les catholiques et l'unité chrétienne*, 238–239.

71 Congar, *Une passion: L'unité*, 44–45.

72 See Yves Congar, "Une conclusion théologique à l'Enquête sur les raisons actuelles de l'incroyance," *VInt* 37, 1935, 214–249, esp. 238ff., 3rd part.

73 Congar, "Une conclusion théologique," 241.

74 See Congar, "Une conclusion théologique," 242: this is already evocative of the qualitative conception of catholicity that would be further developed two years later in *Chrétiens désunis*.

75 According to the wording of the prospectus announcing the launching of Unam Sanctam (see APDF, V, 832, 43), quoted in Congar, *Une passion: L'unité*, 46–47. In this regard, it should be noted that from the very beginning, the French theologian had discerned the close bonds of solidarity that linked ecumenism, ecclesiological research, pastoral renewal, as well as the biblical and liturgical movements (see Congar, *Une passion: L'unité*, 41).

76 Johann Adam Möhler, *Die Einheit in der Kirche oder das Prinzip des Katholizismus: Dargestellt im Geiste der Kirchenväter der drei ersten Jahrhunderte*, Tübingen, Laupp, 1825; ET: *Unity in the Church, or, the Principle of Catholicism: Presented in the Spirit of the Church Fathers of the First Three Centuries*, trans. Peter C. Erb, Washington DC, Catholic University of America Press, 1996.

77 Fouilloux, *Les catholiques et l'unité chrétienne*, 239.

coincidence, the title of the series quite accurately describes the "ecumenical" aim of its first volume: to work towards the unity of the church, which is one (*unam*) and must become so once again in a wholly visible manner, and which is holy (*sanctam*).

What a work, indeed! *Chrétiens désunis*, the first comprehensive overview of the topic in French, was a standard reference book for over 15 years, as it "laid the theological groundwork for a status of ecumenism in a Catholic context," thus marking a crucial milestone in the field of doctrine, as Amay had been in the field of action and as the Abbé Couturier was in the process of becoming in the field of spirituality.[78] This doctrinal initiative would also generate a properly theologal – and no longer merely corporate or juridical – approach to church unity, as well as a qualitative – and no longer strictly quantitative, temporal, and geographical – perception of catholicity, to the point of expanding the notion of church to the very limits of the universe thanks to the original notion of ecumenicity. This undertaking represented a fundamental reform of the still dominant apologetic and juridical approach of the time.[79]

4 *Chrétiens désunis*

In his foreword, Congar states that the "speeches delivered by me on this occasion [the Octave of Prayer for Christian Unity at the Sacré-Cœur Basilica of Montmartre] in January 1936, having been re-elaborated and technically improved, form the basis of the present volume."[80] As specified by the subtitle of the work, the purpose of these speeches was to set forth the "principles of a Catholic 'ecumenism'" (note the quotation marks that enclose the word ecumenism, thereby signaling the particular meaning that is assigned to it). Precisely this topic is elaborated upon by Congar, again in the foreword: "This movement, which prompts the Christian churches to conceive the desire to restore the lost unity and, to this end, to understand themselves better and to understand one another, is the 'ecumenical' movement."[81] The goal of the latter is

> to prepare the reunion not only of the Christians but [also] of the various currently existing churches within a new unity. ... It is not the wish or the attempt to unite, into a single church, regarded as the only true one, Christian groups that are considered to be dissidents. It begins with the idea that no single Christian confession, in its present state, possesses the plenitude of Christianity; that even if one of them is true, it is nevertheless not, taken as a confession, in possession of the whole truth, but that other Christian values exist outside of it, not only among the Christians that are confessionally separated from it but in the other confessions or the other churches *as* confessions or *as* churches.[82]

The Dominican's open-minded approach and his effort to grasp, in a nuanced manner, the specific outlook of the ecumenism of his time are truly remarkable. As a Catholic, however, he could not accept that all existing Christian denominations had failed in some way or another and that each of them held only part of the truth, and that they thus needed to "unite in professing what is common to them in Christianity, in respect of their differences": if this is ecumenism, he maintains, then "there cannot be a Catholic 'ecumenism.'"[83] But, on the other hand,

78 Roger Aubert, ed., *Nouvelle Histoire de l'Église*, vol. 5, *L'Église dans le monde moderne: 1848 à nos jours*, Paris, Éditions du Seuil, 1975, 653; Fouilloux, *Les catholiques et l'unité chrétienne*, 207.

79 This did not fail to alarm the Roman authorities, who saw Congar as suspect from then on; see Congar, *Une passion: L'unité*, 54ff.; *Jean Puyo interroge le Père Congar*, 100ff.

80 Congar, *Chrétiens désunis*, xi.

81 Congar, *Chrétiens désunis*, xi–xii.

82 Congar, *Chrétiens désunis*, xii.

83 Congar, *Chrétiens désunis*, xii–xiii.

> if "ecumenism" – and this defines it as a specific movement of thought and action – is merely an awareness that there actually is a problem of church reunion, that this problem is not exhausted, or even fully addressed, by the exclusive pursuit of individual "conversions," but that there are good grounds to make a theological assessment of the dissident Christianities as Christianities, of the relationships of the dissident churches, as churches, to THE true church (the *Catholica*) and to its unity – then indeed can there be, and we even believe that there ought to be and that there is: a Catholic "ecumenism."[84]

This is precisely what *Chrétiens désunis* endeavored to do, namely to define the basis, the nature, and the conditions of a Catholic "ecumenism."

While he fully endorsed the doctrines of the Roman magisterium on ecclesial unity and dissidence, Congar nonetheless noted in a very astute manner, like Dom Thédore Belpaire (*Irénikon*, March 1930), that not all is said in these official documents: these define the ideal objective that must be reached, but "they say very little with regard to the concrete starting point and to the possibilities of moving towards this objective."[85] There is thus room for reflection on the "possible paths of a movement for the reintegration of dissident Christianities into the unity." It is the theologian's task "to define the limits, to establish the broad directions and the main reference points," and "to develop the notion of Christian reality as seen under the very conditions of its incarnation in humankind."[86] It is in this spirit that the French theologian's work must be understood, as a theology of the possible, moving along a fine line between the official stances of the Catholic hierarchy and the positive appraisal of the other Christians.[87]

Accordingly, the work was divided into four broad approaches.[88]

(1) An examination of the contemporary divisions: seeing and analyzing the facts in an objective manner; understanding the *theological* significance of these divisions beyond their mere description and documentation (chapter 1).
(2) An in-depth, positive, serene, and irenic theological (theologal) presentation on the *one* church, viewed under its two major aspects of unity (chapter 2) and catholicity (chapter 3).
(3) A presentation and critique of the main theories on the unity of the church that are found outside the Catholic Church: the liberal ideology of Stockholm (Life and Work) and the ideology of the "Ecumenical movement" (chapter 4); the Anglo-Catholic conception (chapter 5); an Orthodox ecclesiology inspired from Slavophile theology (chapter 6).
(4) A concluding examination of the concrete problem of a Catholic "ecumenism": what Christians dissidents and dissident Christianities are from the perspective of the one and only church (chapter 7); the broad lines of a concrete agenda of Catholic "ecumenism" (chapter 8).

From a strategic point of view, this first book by Congar may be said to have contributed to the loosening and, as far as possible, to the opening up of the Catholic ecclesiological exclusivism of the

84 Congar, *Chrétiens désunis*, xiii.
85 Congar, *Chrétiens désunis*, xiii.
86 Congar, *Chrétiens désunis*, xiv.

87 Following a remarkably well-documented analysis, Fouilloux is able to conclude that: "Father Congar did not tread a high road but a narrow, sinuous, and uneven path, in the middle of which he attempted to reconcile his desire to move forward and his concern that he might be cut off from the rear"; *Les catholiques et l'unité chrétienne*, 268.
88 See Congar, *Chrétiens désunis*, xiv–xv.

time, or, at the very least, to its breaching.[89] This is borne out both by the method employed and by the thereby elaborated, doctrinal content.

4.1 *Method*

The method, which is also "a concrete action program," pursues a threefold objective: a kind of psychological approach in the mutual relations with other Christians; a return to the roots and to the profound life of Christianity; the enablement of a reintegration into catholicity.[90]

(1) A psychological attitude that involves the abandoning of mutual prejudices and resentment; the carrying out of serious information work on one another; embracing charity for the purpose of procuring the maximum good for others; acting in a gentle and humble manner; being perfectly loyal and true; in short, being evangelical, fraternal, amicable.[91] This "irenic" method had also been elaborated, since 1925, at the abbey which Dom Beauduin had founded at Amay-sur-Meuse, where Congar had spent some time in 1932, at the same time as the Abbé Couturier; significantly, the journal of the union monks, launched in 1926, bore the Greek title *Irénikon*. This attitude, which would lead to great difficulties for the founder of this abbey, stood in stark contrast to that of the majority of Catholics. Ultimately, it also opened up the possibility of allowing oneself to be challenged by the elements of truth found among other Christians, precisely in view of a deeper and more comprehensive truth,[92] and thus of an enrichment, or even of a reform of the Catholic Church itself.

(2) A return to the roots and to the profound life of Christianity in which Christians are "truly less disunited," and "thereby rediscovering the external forms of unity."[93] This implies going beyond the letter and the system that are specific to each Christian confession, going back *together* to the deep roots, prior to the disunion, and, having arrived at this level of shared depth, rediscovering the expressions of unity. While Congar was not the only one to practice the *reditus ad fontes* at the time, it was to become his trademark, a truly methodological reflex that was meant to provide a basis for all ecclesiological and ecumenical reflection.

(3) The enablement of a reintegration into catholicity by means of a double effort of irenic and critical explication with regard to the separated brothers (this serene and peaceful explication being the best form of clarification in the eyes of Congar), but also by means of an intensified effort to increase the effectiveness of the catholicity of the Catholic Church itself, that is, its ability to assimilate any authentic spiritual query (this being the most crucial ecumenical work, the life of the church itself, more faithful to the grace of its catholicity). This points to an ecumenical methodology that includes ecclesial reform as an intrinsic element: not only should one strive to explain (and thus already to reformulate, up to a certain point) the Catholic doctrine to the separated brothers but also to reform the Catholic Church itself so that it might respond more faithfully and more fully "to the inner law and to the grace of its catholicity."[94]

(4) Concurrently with this "ecumenical" method, Congar is also convinced that the "reunion" of the churches is above all an "object of

89 According to the assessment of Fouilloux "Father Congar, less than ten years after *Mortalium animos*, achieved a major result that he generously ascribed to the Malines Conversations: 'showing that Rome was possible' [*Chrétiens désunis*, 212]"; *Les catholiques et l'unité chrétienne*, 268.

90 See Congar, *Chrétiens désunis*, 325–341, 402; Joseph Famerée, "Originalité de l'ecclésiologie du Père Congar," *BLE* 106/1, 2005, 89–112, esp. 99–101, on which I largely base myself.

91 "Irenicism," "loyalty," "comparativism," and "catholicity," these are the terms employed by Fouilloux, *Les catholiques et l'unité chrétienne*, 246–268 to describe this method.

92 "Obedience to truth was originally a law for us"; Congar, *Chrétiens désunis*, xvi.

93 Congar, *Chrétiens désunis*, 402.

94 Congar, *Chrétiens désunis*, 402; see also 339–340.

theologal hope and prayer":[95] a radically spiritual dimension underlies every ecumenical endeavor. In short, Congar lays down the principles of a method of "ecumenism" that is more specifically theological or doctrinal: an irenic and loyal attitude that banishes polemics; a serene, mutual discovery of the different Christian traditions, albeit without erasing doctrinal differences, in intellectual honesty; a comparison of the respective doctrines, but also the ability to criticize one another, in truth and fraternity.

4.2 *Doctrinal Content*

From a strictly theological point of view, what is new is the conception of catholicity that emerges here, which was to enable a first opening of the Catholic Church to "ecumenism": indeed, Congar endeavors to effect the transition from a strictly quantitative, temporal, and geographical notion of catholicity ("always widely present throughout the world"), which is also juridical and apologetic (only the Catholic Church is truly catholic, in the sense of this spatial-temporal universality), to a *qualitative* notion (catholicity is the church's ability to provide an incarnation of the Word for every human, cultural reality).[96] Every expansion of the human must be met by a growth of the church, a humanization of God. The church must even become the universe, transfigured by the grace of God. In this regard, Congar would speak of the ecumenicity of the church.

For Congar, the bedrock of catholicity thus lies in the plenitude of the grace of Christ: the principles of church unity have the capacity to extend the communication of divine life to all mankind and the ability to assimilate every human value. "The thus understood catholicity of the church is thus essentially Trinitarian and Christological":[97] it is in the Christ Jesus, the principle of salvation, and in his body, which is the church, that the relationship which exists between the unity of God and the multiplicity of the creature is founded. The church is a theandric reality in which all human reality redeemed by Christ is realized in him.[98] This catholicity of Christ is the principle of the church's catholicity. It is therefore "this capacity, which its principles of unity possess, to reach, transfigure, save, fulfill, and restore to unity all of humanity throughout the world, all that receives or can receive a human animation in the world."[99] This capacity is not only the constitutive law of the church, it is also a summons and an intrinsic requirement. One may thus speak of a dynamic universality of the divine truth of faith, of the baptismal incorporation into Christ, of sacramental graces, of the ecclesial life of mutual charity.[100]

Because its spiritual reality is incarnate, "all the principles of the unity of the church, whose catholicity is dynamic universality, have an external form, a face and an instrument of inner unity: catholicity is apostolic, corporate, and hierarchical, as is unity."[101] This external constitution was laid down either by the Lord or by the apostles and cannot be changed. There is no such thing as a "non-Roman catholicity": throughout history, the papacy has been the sole organ of unity and of the universal assumption of the many into one unity, and can indeed still be so.[102] Simultaneously, the church must adapt to the full diversity of the human substance that it must incorporate into the unity. Divine logic is the communication of life through assumption into the unity; human logic is the communication of life through division and dispersion, the burden of sin weighing down

95 Congar, *Chrétiens désunis*, 402.

96 See Congar, *Chrétiens désunis*, 115–148 (chapter 3, "La catholicité de l'Église une"); see also Joseph Famerée & Gilles Routhier, *Yves Congar*, Paris, Cerf, 2008, 57–71, which I often follow closely, and Famerée, *L'ecclésiologie d'Yves Congar avant Vatican II*, 42–53.

97 Congar, *Chrétiens désunis*, 117.

98 See Congar, *Chrétiens désunis*, 119, 121.

99 Congar, *Chrétiens désunis*, 121–122.

100 See Congar, *Chrétiens désunis*, 122–123.

101 Congar, *Chrétiens désunis*, 125.

102 See Congar, *Chrétiens désunis*, 126, note 1. In spite of the renewal of the notion of catholicity proposed by *Chrétiens désunis*, Congar's argumentation with regard to the papacy, in this particular case, remains dependent on standard post-Tridentine apologetics.

on and corrupting these natural accretions. Within the church, these two logics are articulated as the synergy of the "gift" of divine life (in Christ) and of the "activity" or active input of human beings.[103]

An extension of unity, ecclesial catholicity guarantees the respect and the fulfillment of human diversity while purifying it, not by way of denaturalization but through supra-naturalization. A great diversity of ways to lead a Christian life is legitimate and even necessary for the church.[104] At the same time, catholicity purifies the human diversities and lets them die in the face of their excessive particularism in order to let them enter the overarching unity of the whole. The Holy Spirit is the bond of both catholicity and unity.[105]

The Catholic Church is certain that it holds and represents the fullness of truth, in which the partial and antinomic conceptions – antinomic because they are partial – are reconciled in unity. The Catholic Church cannot accept "ecumenism" if it implies that the Church of Christ does not currently exist in the world. "The one church, Catholic and visible, exists in its unity, its catholicity, and its visibility," even if "its catholicity is imperfect," inasmuch as it "is initially only given as a dynamic potentiality."[106]

Indeed, "is there really no reason for us to admit that [the Church of Jesus Christ] is not yet fully Catholic"?[107] Under the aspect of its present realization, the catholicity of the church, though inalienable, "has its positive and negative sides, and it can be stated *a priori* that it is not currently perfect and probably never will be."[108] The Roman Church, fully Catholic from the point of view of the dynamic possibilities of its living substance, explicitly only realizes this catholicity in an imperfect manner, and in this imperfection, the division of Christianity plays a role.[109] There is some truth and a share of inalienable Christian values in all confessions, in spite of their separation, but this calls for a reintegration into catholicity. To this end, the church can only remain one if it proves Catholic with a more fully effective catholicity. It must engage "in a continuous reform of itself." Ecumenicity is the church itself, the church inasmuch as it develops its ecumenical worth.[110]

Catholic "ecumenism," according to Congar, thus begins and is able to develop when the Catholic Church recognizes that it currently only realizes its catholicity in an imperfect manner, that it must therefore continuously reform itself in order to be Catholic with a catholicity that is increasingly perfect, comprehensive, open, and receptive to the inalienable Christian values of the other confessions, precisely in order to reintegrate them into the catholicity. This was only a first expression of openness to other Christians (nonetheless crucial for the development of Catholicism and quite audacious for the period),[111] although this openness could intensify itself over time. Congar even offers a spur of the moment justification of his position in a letter to Father Maurice Villain: "What I have written and said may perhaps appear half-hearted in the near future. [But] at the time when I wrote and said it, this was not so."[112]

Having said this, let us examine how the "ecumenical" proposals of *Chrétiens désunis* were received at the time.

103 See Congar, *Chrétiens désunis*, 130.
104 See Congar, *Chrétiens désunis*, 137–142.
105 See Congar, *Chrétiens désunis*, 145.
106 Congar, *Chrétiens désunis*, 239.
107 Congar, *Chrétiens désunis*, 315.
108 Congar, *Chrétiens désunis*, 315–316.

109 A similar statement is found 27 years later in the decree on ecumenism issued by Vatican II, *Unitatis redintegratio* (§ 4).
110 See Congar, *Chrétiens désunis*, 339–341.
111 In the context of an acute tension between loyalty to the Catholic tradition and the inner urge to recognize the ecumenical movement: an "irresolvable contradiction," as stated by Fouilloux, *Les catholiques et l'unité chrétienne*, 246.
112 Y. Congar to M. Villain, May 13, 1939, copy, cited in: Fouilloux, *Les catholiques et l'unité chrétienne*, 247.

5 The Reception of *Chrétiens désunis*

This is the short description of *Chrétiens désunis* that can be found on the back cover of the Unam Sanctam prospectus announcing the fourth volume in the series, *Cathedra Petri* by Pierre Battifol, in 1938: "Bordin Prize of the Académie Française for 1938. Eight chapters outlining a positive theology of the church, of its unity, and of its catholicity, and confronting this theology with the doctrine of the Christian denominations that are separated from the Roman Church."[113] Even though this advertisement text is the work of those who conceived the series, it is nevertheless worth noting that *Chrétiens désunis* had already attracted the attention of the Académie Française, an institution whose primary interest is not theology. One should also mention that the prospectus announcing this volume was printed in 8,000 copies in French and 1,200 copies in English (to be sent to the ecumenical conferences of 1938).[114] An Italian version of the prospectus also exists.[115] All this conveys a certain idea of the effort to publicize the new series and its first volume.

Strictly by way of example, only two contemporary academic reviews of *Chrétiens désunis* will be discussed here: one published by Abbé Gustave Thils, doctor and *maître* in theology at Louvain, in *Ephemerides Theologicae Lovanienses*;[116] the other by a fellow Dominican brother of Congar, Vincent-Marie Pollet, in the journal *Angelicum* of the Dominican university of the same name in Rome.[117]

The review published by Thils singles out the main points in the Congarian argument: the divisions among Christians can only disappear if the spiritual intuition from which they arose is discerned; the divergences are maintained by the particular way in which each church conceives the unity of the universal church; the dissidents must be integrated into the *Una Catholica*, but a Catholic unity which, far from rejecting them, assumes all true values, as the catholicity of the church will thus be enriched by the visible expressions that it lacks. The conclusion is laudatory:

> This brief overview ... will at least give an idea of the scope of the overall conception. ... One could quote many passages that disclose the anguish of this apostle of union, his effort to highlight what the divergent ecclesiologies have in common, his loyalty to the defense of truth. In short, these "principles of a Catholic ecumenism" are a fine achievement, and one that will stand out in the context of unionist literature.[118]

A mirror of his time, Thils speaks of unionism and only uses the word ecumenism to cite the subtitle of Congar's book, not even mentioning the quotation marks in which the latter enclosed the word, thereby limiting the impact of his audacity.

Pollet, on the other hand, who was well-disposed towards his fellow Dominican brother and did not fail to mention "his usual brilliance," nevertheless expressed a far more restrictive view of Catholic "ecumenism" and of catholicity. In the opinion of the reviewer, who criticized Congar for having "perhaps" placed too much trust in the piety and the mysticism of the dissident Christians, the authentic values that persist among them are also found among the Catholics of the same cultural milieu. "A reunion would therefore only serve to manifest better, in Roman Catholicism, the values that are already inherent in it. The Catholicism of the Roman Church would only benefit from it insofar as it depends, in order to express itself, on numbers, divergences of temperament, of culture,

113 APDF, V, 832, 43.

114 An English translation of *Chrétiens désunis* was soon available in 1939: Congar, *Divided Christendom*.

115 See APDF, V, 832, 43: handwritten note by Congar in connection with the printed prospectus of Unam Sanctam and of *Chrétiens désunis*.

116 See Gustave Thils, review of Yves Congar's *Chrétiens désunis*, *ETL* 14, 1937, 684–686.

117 See Vincent-Marie Pollet, review of Yves Congar's *Chrétiens désunis*, *Angelicum* 15, 1938, 300–301.

118 Thils, review, 686.

etc."[119] Pollet falls short of embracing Congar's qualitative understanding of catholicity, according to which the reunion of the Christians will usher in a truly new reality compared to the current Roman Catholic Church, not to mention the fact that, in the eyes of the reviewer, the reunion is merely a "return to the church," even if it were an "achievement" and not a renunciation. And for the Thomist Pollet, even if this consideration is true with regard to individual souls, it is only so "per accidens" with regard to "their confessions themselves, which constitute communions, wholes that no longer communicate, or only in a distant or imperfect manner, with the Una Sancta." Noting that "it is even dangerous to insist too much on the unilateral character of the dogma and of Catholic theology from a defensive position" and pointing out various flaws (hasty generalizations, unhappy formulations, disputable judgments), the reviewer nevertheless recognizes that these "are merely the price to be paid for the author's unquestionable talent, which manifests itself (fully) in this brilliant essay." And concluding in a far less "ecumenical" manner than his fellow brother from Le Saulchoir: "Let us hope that the author will find emulators, and this time at least, let us rejoice that a Catholic has rekindled the flame on the altar upon which the dissidents, enamored of unity, will come to immolate their prejudices and make sacrifice of their divisions."[120]

Apart from this Catholic theological reception,[121] it is important to note how the work was perceived among the leading officeholders of the Catholic Church, here the master general of the Dominican order, Martin-Stanislas Gillet, echoes the misgivings of Rome. The following quotation represents the best part of a confidential letter which he addressed to Father Chenu, the regent of Le Saulchoir, on Jan 17, 1939:

> I must speak to you about the book by Father Congar, whose great merits no one disputes, but who has shown a talent to stir certain otherwise sympathetic minds. If I write to you about it, it is because I have been entrusted with the mission to do so and to forestall and mitigate certain warnings that might be issued in high places, if at all, under the pressure of certain theologians who, I repeat, recognize the exceptional merits of this book but deplore the *confusion* of certain pages that would gain from being corrected by the author (this concerns the pages 34, 35/50, *52*, 316, 319, 320, *330*). What Fr. Congar is mostly criticized for is that he relies more on *religious experience* for the control of the faith than on the definitions of the church and the dogmatic formulas. Here appended, you will find a synopsis of similar thoughts taken from recent works.
>
> In my opinion, this is what Fr. Congar should do. He should write me a letter in which he states that he has taken cognizance of the criticism that some have leveled at him in connection with certain pages of his book, especially those in which he talks about *religious experience*; that in his thinking, he has never desired to cast doubt on or contradict the magisterium of the church in any way; that, when addressing himself especially to our separated brothers, he placed the emphasis on what was most likely to convince them; that if he was wrong, he deeply regrets it and is ready, for a new edition, to make the corrections that he is asked to make. With this letter, which would be like a lightning rod for me, I would ward off the thunderbolt if ever it threatened this beautiful monument.

---

119 Pollet, review, 301.

120 Pollet, review, 301.

121 One might also cite the short, positive appraisal by the historian Léon Halkin from the University of Liège in Belgium: "I have not yet told you how highly I have thought of your book *Chrétiens désunis*, a truly remarkable work, utterly free of all compromise, and also of all vanity. I also admired the call for charity that you repeated in the most recent issue of *La Vie intellectuelle*. This will please Mounier, and do good to so many others!"; L. Halkin to Y. Congar, Dec 15, 1937, in: APDF, 832, 53, Groupe Portal.

> I believe that this should only be discussed *with Father Congar* and with no one else. It is safer for him, for us, for me, for the *convent school*, which is a faculty. I repeat that I have no knowledge of anything official or even unofficial; however, I thought I *sensed* some concerns; this is why I am taking the initiative.
>
> There is no cause for alarm, but there is reason to be cautious.
>
> This is why this letter is that of a *father*, a *friend*, and not that of a *judge*. On this note, I embrace Father Congar and you, and assure you once again of my fatherly affection in St. Dom.
>
> SMG[122]

It is the recourse of *Chrétiens désunis* to "religious experience" that gave cause for concern. Some suspected it of propagating what had been regarded as the subjectivism of Catholic Modernist theologians in the early 20th century: the religious feeling of the subject, which eludes the abstraction of the dogmatic formulas and the control of the magisterium. Far removed from any subjectivism and relativism, Congar's taking into account of religious experience was precisely what enabled him to recognize, respect, and appreciate the experience and the authentic Christian values of the "separated brothers." The request that Father Congar write a letter in which he would express his total submission to the magisterium of the church and his regret for eventual errors is somewhat surprising in the light of the fact that he had already clearly said all this in the foreword to *Chrétiens désunis*.[123] The letter would have no doubt given Congar an opportunity to clarify his intentions, but it would have mostly served as a tactical instrument in the hands of his superior general, as a "lightning rod" in case any threats materialized. Such prudence on the part of the master of the order says much about the diffuse atmosphere of distrust that reigned in Rome when it came to ecumenical issues.[124]

Ten years later, a letter which Congar had prepared but never sent, in this form, to the *socius* of the master of the order for the French-speaking realm testifies to the success and the resonance of *Chrétiens désunis* both among Catholics and in ecumenical circles.[125] However, the French Dominican would never obtain the authorization of the order's master, Father Manuel Suárez Fernández, to publish a second revised and expanded edition, which had been planned for 1949,[126] the first edition having been out of print since 1941. The word of caution that he personally wrote for this second edition at Le Saulchoir (in Étiolles)[127] on the feast of St. Dominic of 1948 is revealing with regard to how he viewed his own work ten years after its first publication, taking into account the criticism that had been leveled against him. In this text, he recalls that as a prisoner in Colditz in 1941, he had refused to approve a second edition. He had

> the feeling that many things, in this book, were no longer up to date; that even my ideas had evolved; that I viewed the issue partly in a new way: more imbued with history, psychology, and thus, I believe, in a more genuine way. Even with the excuse that the circumstances made it impossible for me to engage in this type of work, it seemed to me dishonest to reissue a text that predated the most recent developments of the ecumenical movement and the valuable intellectual

122 S.-M. Gillet to M.-D. Chenu, Jan 17, 1939 (copied, typewritten text), in: APDF, V, 832, 400.

123 Congar, *Chrétiens désunis*, xvi.

124 From his three-page "answer" to "Rme Père" Gillet, let me simply quote Congar's assessment of Luther, which was quite daring at the time: "In Brother Martin Luther, there was, *before he became a Lutheran*, a spiritual quest and an authentic spiritual feeling"; Y. Congar to S.-M. Gillet, Jan 26, 1939, in: APDF, V, 832, 400.

125 Y. Congar to A. Giraud, Mar 28, 1949, in: APDF, V, 832, 400, 3, document 4.

126 The manuscript of this hoped-for edition may be found at APDF, V, 832, 108.

127 In the vicinity of Paris, since 1939.

> strides that I have made. It was also my desire, in an eventual reedition, to take account of some of the critiques which, in the midst of an exceptionally favorable reception, had nevertheless been directed at me: either to respond to them or to benefit from them.

He then goes on to say that:

> Had I entirely followed the current flow of my thought, I would have had to write a book that would, in many ways, have been new, structured along different lines, with historical considerations that are only insufficiently sketched out here. Owing to a lack of time, I could not imagine writing such a book. Nor could I bring myself to reissue this text as it had been in 1937, with only a few corrections and additions. Between the ideal but impractical solution and the insufficient, and thus inacceptable, solution, I chose a middle course which, without satisfying me, could appease my strongest scruples. I made a certain number of additions, some of them considerable; everywhere I could, I did my best to mention, in the appropriate places, at least the most notable publications that had appeared since 1937; I corrected many flaws and clarified more than one point; finally, I rewrote all of chapter 4 and more than half of chapter 8 in an entirely new manner. … Due to these partial revisions, this already poorly written book, the result of a simple editing of speeches, is more unbalanced than ever. But why be surprised? It is the fruit of a compromise.[128]

And finally: "With regard to the ecumenical movement, I have the feeling that I have become, over the years, both more sympathetic and stricter; perhaps, in sum, more genuine."[129]

This retrospective view illustrates both the lucidity and the dynamism of the French theologian's ecumenical reflection, a manner of thinking that was constantly evolving and undergoing changes depending on the new facts that presented themselves to him: never contenting himself with the achievements of the past, always in search of a more complete and exact truth. It heralded Congar's increasingly pertinent and rigorous commitment to the desire and the quest for the unity of Christians, in spite of all the constraints and sanctions that he was to endure until his improbable rehabilitation soon after the announcement of an "ecumenical" council on Jan 25, 1959.

Translated from French to English by Robert Meyer.

Bibliography

Congar, Marie-Joseph, *Chrétiens désunis: Principes d'un "œcuménisme" catholique*, Unam Sanctam 1, Paris, 1937; ET: *Divided Christendom: A Catholic Study of the Problem of Reunion*, trans. Muad A. Bousfield, London, Bles, 1939.

Chenu, Marie-Dominique, *Une école de théologie: Le Saulchoir*, Kain-lez-Tournai, Le Saulchoir, 1937.

Famerée, Joseph, *L'ecclésiologie d'Yves Congar avant Vatican II: Histoire et Église. Analyse et reprise critique*, Leuven, Leuven University Press, 1992.

Famerée, Joseph & Gilles Routhier, *Yves Congar*, Paris, Cerf, 2008.

Fouilloux, Étienne, *Les catholiques et l'unité chrétienne du XIXe au XXe siècle: Itinéraires européens d'expression française*, Paris, Le Centurion, 1982.

Fouilloux, Étienne, *Une Église en quête de liberté: La pensée catholique française entre modernisme et Vatican II (1914–1962)*, Paris, Desclée de Brouwer, 1998.

128 See the manuscript of the hoped-for second edition of *Chrétiens désunis*, in: APDF, V, 832, 108, 1.

129 See the manuscript of the hoped-for second edition of *Chrétiens désunis*, in: APDF, V, 832, 108, 3.

CHAPTER 2

Ressourcement and the Rediscovery of the Fathers

Nikolaos Asproulis

1 *Ressourcement* Theologies: Prehistory, Figures, and Context

1.1 *Eastern Orthodoxy: From Philokalia to the Neo-Patristic Synthesis and Its Intermediate Loci*

To claim that the roots of the Orthodox *ressourcement* are immersed in the last decades of the 18th century might sound somewhat strange to the ears of someone little familiar with the history of theology. It is, however, commonplace nowadays to consider the publication of *Philokalia* as the starting point for the East's rediscovery of the Fathers. Although this affirmation tends, sometimes, to be underlined with all too much emphasis, one cannot at any rate underestimate the decisive role that the ascetic and monastic traditions played in the traditional orthodox consciousness.

The *Philokalia of the Holy Ascetics*, an imposing work published in Greek in 1782 in Venice by Saints Makarios of Corinth and Nicodeme of the Holy Mountain, is a collection of patristic and ascetic texts stretching from the 4th to the 14th century which sought to revive a certain spiritual tradition grounded in prayer and articulated in a three stage process: *purification* from the passions, *illumination* by the divine light, and *perfection*, that is, *theosis* (deification). The principal aim of the *Philokalia* was to bring to the fore a core aspect of the practice of theology, typical of the Fathers and at the time thought to be forgotten, in which both prayer and speculation about God were considered to be two complementary activities (one could even speak of a sort of proto-*ressourcement*). It was an aspect, in other words, far from the pitfalls of the post-Reformation Western spirituality that seemed to dominate the doctrine and the practice of the institutional church at the time.

After the fall of the Byzantine Empire (1453), most of the Orthodox lands found themselves under Ottoman authority, while theologians were wont in their speculations to adopt conceptual and methodological tools that were alien to the Orthodox tradition and typical of Catholics and Protestants. It was this group of factors, both political and cultural, that led to the so-called *pseudomorphosis* and Babylonian captivity of Orthodoxy.[1] In light of this, it becomes evident that the *Philokalia* is rightly seen "as a turning point in the history of Orthodox theology";[2] that is, it was part of a wider spiritual renewal stemming from Mount Athos,[3] which, departing from the modern style of practicing theology, promoted a thought and an ethos inspired by the Fathers and consisting of a direct vision of the divine glory bestowed on the practitioners of prayer and mystical ascesis. St. Gregory Palamas, a pioneer ascetic and theologian of the Hesychast tradition, known especially for his popularized and emblematic distinction between essence and energies in God, lies at the heart of this philokalic renaissance in Orthodox theology.

The *Philokalia* had a considerable impact on the Russian Orthodox world. Concurrently, and nevertheless well before the Greek version of the *Philokalia* was committed to print in Venice, St. Paisius Velichkovsky,[4] who was aware of the Hesychast spirituality practiced on Mount Athos,

1 See Georges Florovsky, "Western Influences in Russian Theology," in: George Florovsky, *The Collected Works*, vol. 4, *Aspects of Church History*, Belmont MA, Nordland Publishing, 1975, 157–182.

2 Andrew Louth, *Modern Orthodox Thinkers: From the Philokalia to the present*, London, SPCK, 2015, 3.

3 See Kallistos Ware, "Philocalie," *DSAM* 12, 1336–52.

4 See Louth, *Modern Orthodox Thinkers*, 4–6.

translated into Church Slavonic a selection of texts similar to those contained in Makarios's and Nicodeme's compilation. Velichkovsky's version appeared in 1793 as *Dobrotolubiye* and was destined to become far more popular in the Russian sphere than its Greek counterpart was. It appears then that the Hesychast tradition or vision, still alive on Mount Athos and rediscovered thanks to the printing of the two versions of the so-called *Philokalia*, should be considered the actual turning point of the patristic renaissance in the East. Thus, despite the Ottoman occupation and the dependence of post-Byzantine theology on Western influences,[5] a particular spirituality and style of theology had been preserved thanks to the holy men (*gerontes*) on the Holy Mountain, and, following a gradual development, was able to fuel a true patristic *ressourcement* in the East.

To a large extent, the rediscovery of the Fathers was mediated through the work of the Optina Monastery at the beginning of the 19th century, which was destined to be a great spiritual center for a considerable number of intellectuals – one need only think of Fyodor Dostoyevsky and his celebrated novel *The Brothers Karamazov* (1879); the news rapidly spread thanks to Slavophile thinkers closely linked to the Optina skete. Furthermore, the philokalic tradition would contribute in large part to the rise of the spiritual fatherhood of the institution, practiced by the so-called *startsy* (elders), who had the task of guiding younger monks towards a Christian life of rectitude and asceticism. The Optina Pustyn' would soon become the center "for a patristic revival"[6] with a considerable number of publications and translations of patristic-ascetic texts (around 200,000),[7] made thus available to a wider audience and to the libraries in the Russian theological academies. In this regard, it is necessary to mention the immense work of Philaret of Moscow. Inspired by this philokalic spirituality, he promoted and entrusted to the theological academies of Moscow, St. Petersburg, and Kiev the translation of a series of *Works of the Fathers* compiled between the 4th and the 7th centuries thanks to which "at the end of the nineteenth century, Russia had at its disposal, in its own language, the best patristic library in Europe."[8] The work would culminate in a considerable number of academic monographs on different patristic figures and themes.

Although a large swathe of Orthodox lands were experiencing a dark age under the yoke of the Ottomans, a limited encounter with the West, represented by its Enlightenment ideals, had already established a foothold in the modernization program of Peter I and Catherine II.[9] These developments, along with the glorious Russian victories in the Napoleonic wars, would subsequently contribute to the birth of an attitude that sought a particular Christian experience which it was thought only the Russian soul could offer to the West, which was considered rationalist and morally corrupt. Russian religious thought was divided in response to this preliminary encounter between the two worlds: on one side, there were the Slavophiles,[10] who distanced themselves from

5 For an overview of this period, see Georges Florovsky, *The Collected Works*, vol. 5, *Ways of Russian Theology: Part One*, ed. Richard S. Haugh, Belmont MA, Nordland Publishing, 1979, and vol. 6, *Ways of Russian Theology: Part Two*, ed. Richard S. Haugh, Vaduz, Buchervertiebsanstalt, 1987. See also Christos Yannaras, *Orthodoxy and the West: Hellenic Self-Identity in the Modern Age*, Brookline, Holy Cross Orthodox Press, 2006.

6 Andrew Louth, "French Ressourcement Theology and Orthodoxy: A Living Mutual Relationship?," in: Gabriel Flynn & Paul D. Murray, eds., *Ressourcement: A Movement for Renewal in Twentieth Century Catholic Theology*, Oxford, Oxford University Press, 2012, 495–507, here 498.

7 For further reading, see Sophie Deicha, "Patristics in Russia, the 19th Century," *GOTR* 44/1–4, 1999, 575–583.

8 Olivier Clément, "Les Pères de l'Église dans l'Église orthodoxe," *Connaissance des Pères de l'Église* 52, 1993, 25–26, as cited in: Louth, *Modern Orthodox Thinkers*, 10.

9 For instance, see Basil Dmytryshyn, ed., *Modernization of Russia Under Peter I and Catherine II*, New York, Wiley, 1974.

10 See the now classic Andrzej Walicki, *W kręgu konserwatywnej utopii: Struktura i przemiany rosyjskiego słowianofilstwa*, Warsaw, PWN, 1964; ET: *The Slavophile Controversy: History of a Conservative Utopia in Nineteenth Century Russian Thought*, trans. Hilda Andrews-Rusiecka, Notre Dame, University of Notre Dame Press, 1989.

Western ideological and intellectual currents, while on the other side there were the so-called westernizers, who embraced the ideas originating in the West.[11] Despite being much indebted to Wester philosophy (especially to German Idealism and Romanticism)[12] and despite their focus on the peculiarities of Russian culture in terms of its uniqueness, pride, and ability to comprehend the world (which would degenerating into a peculiar ethnophyletic ideology[13]), the bond that held the Slavophiles together was their constant appeal to the Orthodox patristic tradition for the inspiration required to confront political liberalism, capitalism and Western rationalism. This was clearly brought out by the relationship, direct or indirect, that the movement's main figures, Aleksey Stepanovich Khomyakov and Ivan Vasilyevich Kireyevsky, maintained with the Hesychast tradition of the Optina Monastery.

Kireyevsky, in particular, had not only been involved in the monumental publication of the patristic texts under the inspiration of Philaret, but had also supported the project financially.[14] For him "the Holy Fathers speak of a country they have been to" and they bear "testimony as eyewitnesses."[15] At the same time, Khomyakov, despite being deeply influenced by German Idealism (specifically, through the figure of the Catholic theologian Johann Adam Möhler),[16] would offer an original understanding of the "one" church in terms of the theological-cultural concept of *sobornost*, based on his investigations concerning unity (the church is *one*),[17] and on his being influenced by the spirit of the Russian *mir*. Despite certain shortcomings, Kireevsky and Khomyakov were both destined to become major catalysts of a patristic retrieval through which Russian religious thought would address modernity.[18]

To sum up, the "fundamental principles" of this growing interest in, or return to, the Fathers can be clearly traced in the monumental publication of the *Philokalia*, certainly as a weighty text but primarily as a vision, which was destined to have an enormous impact on subsequent generations. If one takes the "*Philokalia* project" on its own terms, it appears its intention was to give shape to a particular identity in a more or less polemical confrontation with certain instances of Western theology and culture. In other words, it tried to address the new challenges posed by modernity by drawing on the ancient patristic tradition, or at least on a specific current in this tradition – the ascetic writings – which, however, were often mixed with Idealist or other influences. Not having experienced the main historical milestones according to which modernity in the West took shape, beginning with the Reformation and the advance of secularization, most of Orthodoxy had long avoided any mutual and critical engagement with the Western world of the 19th century. This continued up until certain instances of *ressourcement* theology induced Slavophile thinkers to creatively address the challenges of modernity, and to

11 Parush Parushev, "The Slavophiles and Integral Knowledge," in: Ivana Noble & others, eds., *Wrestling with the Mind of the Fathers*, Yonkers, St. Vladimir's Seminary Press, 2015, 121–155. For more details on this movement see the chapter by Jeremy Pilch in the first volume of this work.

12 Brandon Gallaher, "'Waiting for the Barbarians': Identity and Polemicism in the Neo-Patristic Synthesis of Georges Florovsky," *MT* 27/4, 2011, 672–678. See also Parushev, "The Slavophiles," 131–132.

13 Parushev, "The Slavophiles," 149–155.

14 Parushev, "The Slavophiles," 139–40.

15 Ivan Kireevsky, "Fragments," in: Boris Jakim & Robert Bird, eds., *On Spiritual Unity: A Slavophile Reader: Aleksei Khomiakov, Ivan Kireevsky, with essays by Yury Samarin, Nikolai Berdiaev and Pavel Florensky*, Hudson, Lindisfarne Books, 1998, 276–291, here 288, 283, as cited in: Louth, *Modern Orthodox Thinkers*, 9.

16 See Paul Valliere, "The Modernity of Khomiakov," in: Vladimir Tsurikov, ed., *A.S. Khomiakov: Poet, Philosopher, Theologian*, Jordanville, Holy Trinity Seminary Press, 2004, 129–144.

17 See his major theological work "Tserkov odna" ["The Church is One"], in: Aleksey S. Khomyakov, *Polnoe sobranie sochinenij* [Complete collected works], vol. 2, Moscow, Universitetskaya tipografiya na Strastnom bulvare, [5]1907; ET: "The Church is One," in: Jakim & Bird, eds., *On Spiritual Unity*, 31–53.

18 See Valliere, "The Modernity."

do so, moreover, in a way that closely echoed their Western counterparts.

1.2 *Western Christianity: The Catholic "Proto-*Ressourcement*" of the 19th Century and Protestantism Looks to the Fathers*

The West's rediscovery of the Fathers, understood as a phenomenon that concerned Christianity in general and Catholicism more specifically, in conjunction with the renewal of interest in theology and patristics, cannot be understood without examining certain major figures of the 19th century. The Tübingen School, Maurice Blondel and John Henry Newman may be seen to be among the main architects of the patristic *ressourcement* in Western Europe.

In the case of the Slavophiles, Eastern Orthodoxy critically confronted the developments that had taken place in Western culture, that is, outside its own historical milieu, in particular, the spread of the Enlightenment ideas of political liberalism, economic capitalism, and individualism, Catholic theology instead strove to deal with modernity using its own means, reviving the medieval scholastic tradition as the most proper way of tackling the pursuits of modernity. The long hermeneutic tradition following the work of Doctor Angelicus was thus once again considered the necessary means by which the church could contain modern ideas and remain committed to a fully-fledged pre-modern *Zeitgeist*. Neoscholasticism, therefore, despite its variations (for example, "Baroque theology,"[19] the "Roman school," etc.) may be understood as a kind of *ressourcement* directed towards a return to a specific tradition that was considered at that time to be the sole foundation for Catholic theology.

Faced, therefore, with secularism and with the ideas of liberal modernity, along with science's subsequent break from the church as a source of authority,[20] and the progressive fervor of liberal Protestantism,[21] the Catholic Church "turned to the scholastics."[22] Pope Leo XIII's encyclical *Aeterni Patris* (Aug 4, 1879)[23] was decisive for the articulation of a system of theology which was based on Thomas Aquinas, but downplayed his particular historical context, transforming his thought into the exemplification of a "sacred metaphysics"[24] in a speculative and deductive way. Such close alignment with the scholastic interpretations of St. Thomas was not the only way, however, in which Aquinas's thought was understood during the 19th century, even though it was this understanding that was given utmost authority by the Church of Rome's struggle against modernity.

The so-called Roman school consisted of influential Jesuit-taught theologians at the Roman College. It was active from 1824 until 1879 or 1886,[25] and can be counted among the factors that

19 This is the term used by Marie-Dominique Chenu and Yves Congar to define the post-Reformation developments in Catholic theology. For instance, see: Elizabeth T. Groppe, "Yves Congar, French Priest," in: *Encyclopedia Britannica*, available at <https://www.britannica.com/biography/Yves-Congar> (accessed Mar 2, 2022).

20 Jürgen Mettepenningen, *Nouvelle Théologie – New Theology: Inheritor of Modernism, Precursor of Vatican II*, London, T&T Clark, 2010, 20.

21 Mettepenningen, *Nouvelle Théologie*, 25.

22 Jürgen Mettepenningen & Ward De Pril, "Thomism and the Renewal of Theology: Chenu, Charlier and their Ressourcement," *Horizons* 39/1, 2012, 50–68, here 53.

23 See Kevin L. Hughes, "Deep Reasonings: Sources Chrétiennes, Ressourcement, and the Logic of Scripture in the Years Before – and After – Vatican II," *Modern Theology* 29/4, 2013, 32–45, here 33–34; Jon Kirwan, *An Avant-Garde Theological Generation: The Nouvelle Théologie and the French Crisis of Modernity*, Oxford, Oxford University Press, 2018, 47.

24 Marie-Dominique Chenu & Jacques Duquesne, *Jacques Duquesne interroge le Père Chenu: "Un théologien en liberté"*, Paris, Le Centurion, 1975, 31: "But this list of theses had the effect of extrapolating a philosophical apparatus from St. Thomas, setting aside the very foundation of his thought and of his theology … It extracts the doctrine of St. Thomas from history; it de-temporalizes it; it makes it into a sacred metaphysics"; as cited in: Mettepenningen & De Pril, "Thomism and the Renewal of Theology," 53.

25 C. Michael Shea, "Ressourcement in the Age of Migne: The Jesuit Theologians of the Collegio Romano and the

indirectly contributed to patristic *ressourcement*. Drawing eclectically, not only on prominent scholastic commentators (such as Francisco Suárez[26] and Möhler) but also extensively on the Fathers of the church, this school aimed at "a creative retrieval ... of the patristic past," and an "expansion of the theology of tradition."[27] It is rather important to note in this regard that, in contrast to the Neoscholastic trend, the members of this tendency considered themselves to be "positive theologians," an expression that was used to emphasize the study of history, the Bible and the Fathers[28] and that echoed later developments, especially in *nouvelle théologie* and in the "internal pluralization" evident in the neo-Thomist philosophy of the first quarter of the 20th century.[29]

Just as Russian intellectuals had been divided over their approach to modernity into *pro* and *contra* camps, the same held for their Catholic counterparts. Even among Catholics there was no lack of theologians ready to take inspiration from various modern ideas and thus given to follow a different path in an attempt to bring the Catholic Church into a constant dialogue with modernity.

Figures such as Alfred Loisy, George Tyrrell, and Maurice Blondel stand out among the so-called Catholic Modernists.[30] Blondel describes the intellectual backdrop of his own generation as

> a milieu in which one vacillated from dilettantism to scientism, where Russian neo-christianism clashed with the rigorous virtuosity of radical German idealism; where ... in philosophy, not to say in religious pedagogy itself, the notional, the formal, even the unreal seemed to triumph; where the very efforts that one made to reopen the sources of a profound life ... ended only in symbolism, without succeeding in rehabilitating the concrete, the direct, the singular, the incarnate, the living letter ... a sacramental practice which introduces into our veins a spirit more spiritual ... a popular common sense and Catholic realism.[31]

In opposition to this, the Catholic Modernists attempted to go beyond the strict rationalist methodology and objectification of God typical of scholasticism by promoting an original understanding of the challenges posed by the historical-critical method and Kantian philosophy, especially in their experiential and historical dimensions. The Catholic Modernists sought, basically, to couple Christian faith with real world, highlighting the core importance of a historical methodology that seriously takes into account the concrete socio-cultural needs and demands of the world in its encounter with the church.

Hence we return to the name of Maurice Blondel, one of the most influential figures of Modernism.[32] Starting with a methodology strongly oriented along immanentist lines, with his trilogy (*L'Action, Lettre sur l'apologetique,*

Shape of Modern Catholic Thought," *Nota et Vetera*, 15/2, 2017, 579–613, here 581–582.

26 For the person and his work see Christopher Shields & Daniel Schwartz, "Francisco Suárez," in: Edward N. Zalta, *Stanford Encyclopedia of Philosophy*, available at <https://plato.stanford.edu/entries/suarez/> (accessed mar 2, 2022).

27 Shea, "Ressourcement," 584.

28 Shea, "Ressourcement," 585–586.

29 Mettepenningen, *Nouvelle Théologie*, 25ff.

30 It is interesting to note that in Nicholas Berdyaev's words "in a certain sense it is possible to call Khomyakov an Orthodox Modernist. There is in him a certain kinship with Roman Catholic modernism"; Nikolai Berdyaev, *The Russian Idea*, Hudson, Lindisfarne Press, 1992, 181, as cited in: Parushev, "The Slavophiles," 129, note 30. See also Gallaher, "'Waiting for the Barbarians'" and Valliere, "The Modernity.") This appreciation accounts for our own perspective according to which the real counterparts of Catholic *ressourcement* can be traced to the groups of the Russian Religious Renaissance and its precedents rather than in the majority of the neo-patristic theologians. See also below.

31 Frederic Lefèvre, *L'Itineraire philosophique de Maurice Blondel*, Paris, Aubier Montaigne, 1966, as cited in: Kirwan, *An Avant-Garde*, 44.

32 For an introduction to his life and work, see Oliva Blanchette, *Maurice Blondel: A Philosophical Life*, Grand Rapids, Eerdmans, 2010 and Oliva Blanchette "Why We Need Maurice Blondel," *Communio* 38/1, 2011, 138–167.

Histoire et dogme)[33] Blondel fought for a change in direction of Catholic philosophy and theology by insisting on the importance of the supernatural destiny of human action and the socio-historical character of its existence. By appealing to tradition, he desired to overcome the false dilemma of Neoscholasticism, which opposed dogma to history, providing an understanding of history rooted in action. Tradition is primarily preserved not in the moral actions of an individual or group of people, but in the collective *action* of the church itself. For Blondel, tradition acquires a clear historical and experiential character, becoming a sort of "living tradition." And even if Blondel does not appear to appeal to the Fathers to carry out the turn towards "immanence" in Catholic thought, his methodology was destined to carve out a path towards a patristic revival beyond the prevailing systems of Neoscholasticism.

Working backwards, the Tübingen School must certainly be included among the factors that gradually led, in the 19th century, to the patristic *ressourcement* in Catholic theology.[34] In contrast to the prevailing medieval model of the *summa*, which still guided the Catholic university theology of the era and considered all other disciplines ancillary to "theology as *one* science";[35] the first seeds of a gradual specialization of knowledge was gaining momentum and would eventually lead to the "robust call for disciplinarity"[36] that would be one of the distinctive traits of the Tübingen School. Such a call meant an important paradigm-shift in the way theology was practiced by scholastics in universities, since it went beyond a sterile, rationalistic and singular understanding of the reality of God in favor of a plurality of distinct perspectives (disciplines) that took the historical dimension of dogma seriously into account; albeit, the latter remained connected to an organic understanding of the living tradition.[37] Despite the influence of German Idealism (especially visible in the concept of "living tradition")[38] through its "two Johannes," Johann Sebastian von Drey and Johann Adam Möhler, the Tübingen School aimed at exploring the tradition, namely, the Bible and the Fathers,[39] by providing a methodological blueprint that would be recouped later in, among other places, the *nouvelle théologie*. Precisely with regards to Möhler, Yves Congar would argue that he "does not *use* the Fathers in order to *prove conclusions*" – in this sense, one can see the so-called theological conclusion of the scholastics – he instead tries to live them.[40]

In his now classic work, *Die Einheit in der Kirche*,[41] Möhler makes extensive use of the early Fathers in

33 Maurice Blondel, *L'Action: Essai d'une critique de la vie et d' une science de la pratique*, Paris, Alcan, 1893; ET: *Action (1893): Essay on a Critique of Life and a Science of Practice*, trans. Oliva Blanchette, Notre Dame IL, University of Notre Dame Press, 1984; Maurice Blondel, *Lettre sur les exigencies de la pensée contemporaine en matière d'apologétique et sur la méthode de la philosophie dans l'étude du probléme religieux*, Saint-Dizier, Thévenot, 1896; ET: *Histoire et Dogme: Les lacunes philosophiques de l'exégèse moderne*, La Chapelle, Imprimerie-librairie de Montligeon, 1904; ET: The Letter on Apologetics, and History and Dogma, trans. Alexander Dru & Illtyd Trethowan, London, Harvill Press, 1964.

34 For more details, see the contribution by Michel Fédou in the first volume of this work.

35 Grant Kaplan, "The Renewal of Ecclesiastical Studies: Chenu, Tübingen, and Theological Method in Optatam Totius," *TS* 77/3, 2016, 567–592, here 575 (italics original). For an overview of the main studies carried out in the second half of the 20th century on Möhler and the Catholic Tübingen School, see Luca Ferracci, "Johann Adam Möhler negli studi teologici del secondo Novecento: Principali linee di interpretazione," *CrSt* 42/1, 2021, 87–128.

36 Kaplan, "The Renewal of Ecclesiastical Studies," 574.

37 Kaplan, "The Renewal of Ecclesiastical Studies," 574.

38 Kirwan, *An Avant-Garde*, 163; Gallaher, "'Waiting for the Barbarians,'" 672–678.

39 Mettepenningen, *Nouvelle Théologie*, 16

40 See Yves Congar, "L'Esprit des Pères d'après Moehler," supplement of *La vie spirituelle* 55, 1983, 1–25, as cited in: Kaplan, "The Renewal of Ecclesiastical Studies," 568 (italics original).

41 Johann Adam Möhler, *Die Einheit in der Kirche oder das Prinzip des Katholizismus: Dargestellt im Geiste der Kirchenväter der drei ersten Jahrhunderte*, Tübingen, Laupp, 1825; new edition ed. Josef Rupert Geiselmann, Cologne, Hegner, 1957; ET: *Unity in the Church, or, the*

his attempt to argue against both an institutional scholastic understanding of the church and the Protestant axiom of *sola scriptura*. Reminiscent of similar ideas found in Khomyakov's thought,[42] by following the Fathers Möhler conceives the church in pneumatological and experiential terms, that is, as a community of the Spirit that goes beyond the clericalist and hierarchical conception that still prevailed in the magisterium of the time.[43] As has been rightly argued, this rediscovery of the patristic vision of the church was more "in tune with the Second Vatican Council than with the First"[44] a statement that points to the importance of this proto-*ressourcement* in Catholic theology.

Another emblematic intellectual and theologian of the 19th century is John Henry Newman.[45] His contribution to the patristic revival can be traced in his long scholarly career, during both his Anglican and Catholic phases. In his attempt to deal with the prevailing religious liberalism of his time, he turned to the Fathers, where he found authentic interpreters of the Bible and witnesses of the ecclesial experience. As scriptural interpreters, he wrote, the Fathers "acquaint us with the things Scripture speaks of";[46] while at the same time studying the Fathers offers a "vivid perception of the divine institution, the prerogatives, and the gifts of the Episcopate."[47] Newman's extensive study of the Fathers led to a monograph, important for its time, entitled *The Arians of the Fourth Century* (1833), in which his deep knowledge of the diverse traditions and schools of theology in the early church comes to the fore, and in which he attempted to address his own contemporary context with respect to the Anglican Church.[48] What was to become, however, his landmark contribution to the *ressourcement* spirit was his controversial *An Essay on the Development of Christian Doctrine*,[49] which appeared at about the time of his conversion to Catholicism.[50] Here, Newman appeals to the *history* of dogma, as it was defined during the patristic period, in order to overcome all static or closed conceptions of the church, which was better understood as a living reality than as a fixed institution.[51] Such a perspective was clearly directed against the (Neo)scholastic understanding of the church and theology, to the extent that Newman "found in the Fathers a theological method that was congenial to his own," and that permitted him to read the Fathers "as contemporaries, as participants in the theological conversations and controversies of his own day."[52]

To sum up this cursory overview of the prehistory of Catholic *ressourcement*, it has become clear that certain instances of Catholic theology embarked on a dialogue with their surrounding world by adopting modernizing ideas that could make the church's task of bearing witness more effective in the present. Against the abstract and speculative theological method of Neoscholasticism, which disembodied Christian faith of actual life, these theologians appealed to the Fathers as exemplars of how theology should be practiced in its encounter with a radically different world. This proto-*ressourcement*, despite its

---

Principle of Catholicism: Presented in the Spirit of the Church Fathers of the First Three Centuries, trans. Peter C. Erb, Washington DC, Catholic University of America Press, 1996.

42 Valliere, "The Modernity," 132.

43 Mettepenningen, *Nouvelle Théologie*, 16.

44 Mettepenningen, *Nouvelle Théologie*, 16.

45 See the contribution by Peter B. Nockles in the first volume of this work.

46 John Henry Newman, *Lectures on the Doctrine of Justification*, London, Longmans, Green and Co., 1908, as cited in: Michael Lang, "Newman and the Fathers of the Church," *NBf* 92/1038, 2011, 144–156, here 149.

47 John Henry Newman, *Lectures On Certain Difficulties Felt by Anglicans in Submitting to the Catholic Church*, vol. 2, *Lecture 12: Ecclesiastical History No Prejudice to the Apostolicity of the Church*, London, Longmans, Green, and Co., 1901, 371–372, as cited in: Lang, "Newman and the Fathers," 145.

48 Lang, "Newman and the Fathers," 147.

49 John Henry Newman, *An Essay on the Development of Christian Doctrine*, ed. James M. Cameron, Harmondsworth, Penguin, 1974.

50 Mettepenningen, *Nouvelle Théologie*, 16.

51 Mettepenningen, *Nouvelle Théologie*, 17.

52 Lang, "Newman and the Fathers," 156.

indebtedness to various philosophical trends, was not characterized by a polemical stance (least of all against the East); rather, it represented a dialogical and hermeneutical impulse characterized by a desire to bring the church into constant dialogue with the contemporary world.

From the early Reformation, Luther and the first Reformers sought to distance themselves from any dependence on Rome by appealing not only to the supremacy of the Bible but also to the (principally Greek) patristic tradition. This had a double aim: to reinforce the polemical battle in confrontation with the Roman Church[53] and to find an authority by which to establish their continuity with the ancient church.[54] For instance, during a disputation in Leipzig in 1519,[55] in reaction to the position of Johannes Eck, who accused the Orthodox Church of being schismatic or even heretical, Luther himself replied vehemently by pointing to the long history of the Eastern churches, especially the Church of Jerusalem and the Greek Church, as well as to their large number of great Fathers and theologians[56] not to mention the martyrs and saints who stepped out of the doors of the Orthodox Church over the previous 1,400 years, and who, at least in part, preceded the history of the Roman Church itself. Additionally, Philip Melanchthon, who took the initiative to organize the first *official* contact with the *primus* (*protos*) of Eastern Orthodoxy, the Ecumenical Patriarch of Constantinople,[57] was familiar with the patristic[58] and Greek philosophical background of Byzantine Orthodoxy; the first Reformers had made an appeal to them for allies. Calvin too would follow the same line on his own initiative, by drawing, although not without reservations, "a good deal on patristic support," as "defenders of our opinion" against the opponents of the early Reformation.[59] Calvin would look to the Fathers whenever they pointed ("by derivation")[60] to the supremacy and sufficiency of the Bible (*sola scriptura*).

An appeal to the Fathers as allies in the controversy of the Reformers against their opponents is also very evident among post-Reformation theologians, who, to such ends, gave life to a "Protestant patrology." From the moment that the patristic tradition was not considered "wholly corrupt," it constituted to their eyes an important "resource in controversy."[61] Figures such as John Owen were of this opinion – he saw his personal battles against divergent deviations from doctrinal orthodoxy reflected in the struggles of the early church against heresy[62] – or such as John Wesley – for whom the Fathers in general, and the ascetic tradition in particular, were decisive in "re-envisioning how the Church might be ... against the lack of spirituality" in his own age.[63]

By the early decades of the 19th century, however, the situation had changed profoundly. The rise of liberal Protestantism, which adopted the prevailing historical-critical methodology, led to a gradual devaluation of the Fathers as *testes*

53 John Webster, "Ressourcement Theology and Protestantism," in: Flynn & Murray, eds., *Ressourcement*, 482–494, here 484.

54 Carl Trueman, "Patristics and Reformed Orthodoxy: Some Brief Notes and Proposals," *SBJT* 12/2, 2008, 52–60, here 55.

55 See Ernst Benz, *Die Ostkirche im Lichte der Protestantischen Geschichtsschreibung von der Reformation bis zur Gegenwart*, Munich, Karl Alber, 1952, esp. 3–61.

56 "Cum in universa Ecclesia nulla pars dederit plures excellentiores scriptores quam Graeca"; Martin Luther, *WA* 2, 271ff., as cited in: Ioannis Karmiris, "Luther and Melancthon on the Orthodox Church," *Theologia* 34/1, 1963, 15.

57 For this encounter, see Benz, *Die Ostkirche*, 17ff.

58 Regarding the reception of patristic theology by Melanchthon see for instance: H. Ashley Hall, *Philip Melanchthon and the Cappadocians: A Reception of Greek Patristic Sources in the Sixteenth Century*, Göttingen, Vandenhoeck & Ruprecht, 2014.

59 Webster, "Ressourcement," 484–485.

60 Webster, "Ressourcement," 485.

61 Webster, "Ressourcement," 486.

62 Trueman, "Patristics," 53.

63 Ted A. Campbell, "Wesley's Use of the Church Fathers," *ABTJ* 51/1, 1996, 57–70, here 63.

veritatis, or "witnesses" of the Christian truth.[64] Unlike among the fathers of the Reformation, a new way of thinking arose with regards to the church's past. For instance, Adolf von Harnack and his students (among which Albrecht Ritschl) considered the history of the doctrine as an "acute Hellenization" of the evangelical faith,[65] and appealed to the need to reject the use of philosophy in theological discourse and to return to the authenticity of the gospel as distinct from its intermediate stages of development in the long process of church history.[66]

To sum up, while ambivalent from the outset, the attitude of the diverse Protestant traditions towards the Fathers pointed above all to their unique role in articulating and developing the Christian faith, especially as witnesses of the *magnalia Dei* in the history of the church and even more as interpreters of the revelation recorded in the Bible. Without downplaying the importance of the latter point, even in instances of polemical debate or of the radical rejection of the Roman tradition, the Fathers played a decisive role in the efforts of the Reformers to interpret and justify their faith and their continuity with the early church, while addressing their contemporary challenges.

64 See the contribution by Mark D. Chapman in the first volume of this work.

65 See Adolph von Harnack, *Das Wesen Des Christentums*, Leipzig, Hinrichs, 1900; ET: *What Is Christianity?*, trans. Thomas Bailey Saunders, New York, Harper & Row, 1957, 217–245. For a critical assessment of his view from an orthodox point of view, see Paul Gavrilyuk, "Harnack's Hellenized Christianity or Florovsky's 'Sacred Hellenism': Questioning Two Metanarratives of Early Christian Engagement with Late Antique Culture," *SVTQ* 54/3, 2010, 323–344.

66 On the contrary, see Jaroslav Pelikan, *Christianity and Classical Culture: The Metamorphosis of Natural Theology in the Christian Encounter with Hellenism*, New Haven, Yale University Press, 1993; Diogenes Allen & Eric O. Springsted, *Philosophy for Understanding Theology*, Louisville, Westminster John Knox Press, 22007.

2 *Ressourcement* Theology: Context, Trends and Figures

2.1 *20th Century Eastern Orthodox Theology: The Context*

Although a recovery of the patristic heritage through numerous scholarly publications and text editions had already taken place in Russia at the end of the 19th century and at the beginning of the 20th, the real explosion of the patristic *ressourcement* was triggered by the active presence of Russian émigrés in the West, especially in Paris, who had been expelled by the Bolshevik Revolution between 1922 and 1923.[67]

Despite having a significant impact on the political, social, and intellectual history of Europe, the footprint that the revolution left on the theology and spiritual life of Orthodoxy, while indirect, is something that normally goes almost unobserved. Yet, had the revolution never occurred, it might be argued that the map of contemporary Orthodox theology would have been very different. Although it might seem naive and exaggerated to argue that without the diaspora Russian theology would not have known a creative flourishing like the one it experienced in the first half of the 19th century, one may make just such an inference if one only bears in mind the general condition of the theological education provided in the universities of the Orthodox world. The Russian diaspora, in its *ressourcement* context, must in fact be recognized as the pivotal event of a true revival, if not resurrection, of Orthodox theology after a long period of historical and cultural slavery under the Ottoman regime and various Western influences. The encounter with the Catholic face of *ressourcement* that took place in Paris during the first decades of exile (1922–1947) – exemplary instances are the so-called Berdyaev colloquy and Vladimir Lossky's indirect encounter with Étienne

67 Ivana Noble & others, *The Ways of Orthodox Theology in the West*, Yonkers, St. Vladimir's Seminary Press, 2015. See also the contribution by Adalberto Mainardi in this volume.

Gilson[68] – and the birth of various ecumenical initiatives (for example, the case of the Fellowship of St. Alban and St. Sergius)[69] would contribute to a daring change for Orthodox theology in the direction of the church Fathers.

This shift of contemporary theological attention to its resources was manifested in the first congress of Orthodox theology, held in Athens in 1936,[70] in which eminent émigré figures such as Georges Florovsky and Sergius Bulgakov took part. The congress itself signaled an attempt on the part of the Orthodox theological elite of that time to liberate theology from its "Babylonian or scholastic captivity" (evident in particular from the 17th to the 18th century), to free its methodology from Western influences and to recover, thanks to the Fathers, the genuine Orthodox and ecclesial ethos. The legendary call to a "return to the Fathers," as it was explicitly proposed by Florovsky during the congress,[71] became the starting point for 20th century Orthodox theology and the determining outlook in its enterprise to articulate its own distinctive theological method and discourse after a long period of alienation.

The result, the establishment of the Institut de théologie orthodoxe Saint-Serge[72] in Paris in 1925, drove Orthodox theology towards a renewal, beginning with its own tradition. When reexamining the history of this esteemed and pioneering institute, one soon becomes well acquainted with its character and perspective. In the context of exile in Paris, where Orthodoxy's presence had been previously limited and where different intellectual trends within Catholic theology were already progressing, figures such as Sergius Bulgakov, Anton Kartashev, Georges Florovsky, Nicholas Afanasiev and others were to become the pioneering exponents of this creative and promising period for Orthodox theology and the first partners in a dialogue with different currents (not only theological, but also philosophical) of the Western intellectual tradition – a dialogue that did not disdain contact with the French existentialism of Gabriel Marcel and Jacques Maritain.[73]

Elsewhere throughout the 19th century, while the number of Orthodox Christians in America had steadily grown, the Orthodox Church had remained fundamentally an immigrant community served by bishops and priests sent from abroad, primarily from Russia. It was only in 1905 that Archbishop Tikhon (Bellavin), later to become patriarch of Moscow, recognized the need for a clergy born and raised in America and decided to establish a permanent seminary, leading finally, after many changes of course, to the inauguration in 1938 of St. Vladimir's Theological Seminary.[74] Despite a difficult first decade, the aftermath of World War II brought unexpected possibilities for the seminary's further growth and development under the deanship of Florovsky, Alexander Schmemann, John Meyendorff, and others. Since the 1950s, St. Vladimir's Theological Seminary and its journal would become the sole theological institute promoting and bearing witness to the Orthodox ethos in the English-speaking world.

Deeply inspired by these developments, a whole generation of Greek theologians representing the so-called theology of the 60s[75] would take

68 See Louth, "French Ressourcement," 500; Sarah Coakley, "Eastern 'Mystical Theology' or Western 'Nouvelle Théologie'?: On the Comparative Reception of Dionysius the Areopagite in Lossky and de Lubac," in: George E. Demacopoulos & Aristotle Papanikolaou, eds., *Orthodox Constructions of the West*, New York, Fordham University Press, 2013, 125–141.

69 For further details, see <http://www.sobornost.org> (accessed Mar 2, 2022).

70 Hamilcar S. Alivisatos, ed., *Procès-verbaux du premier congrès de théologie orthodoxe à Athènes: 29 Novembre–6 Décembre 1936*, Athens, Pyrsos, 1939.

71 See Georges Florovsky, "Western Influences in Russian Theology" and "Patristics and Modern Theology," in: Alivisatos, ed., *Procès-verbaux*, 212–231 and 238–242.

72 For further details, see <http://www.saint-serge.net> (accessed Mar 2, 2022).

73 Louth, "French Ressourcement," 501.

74 For further information, see <https://www.svots.edu> (accessed Mar 2, 2022).

75 For a critical overview of this movement, see *Le renouveau de la théologie grecque des années soixante à nos jours*, special issue of *Contacts* 69, 259–260, 2017.

the lead in this *ressourcement* and in the renewal of contemporary Orthodox theology. This multilateral current, including the metropolitan of Pergamon, John Zizioulas, Christos Yannaras, and John Romanides, by acquiring and reworking, in a peculiarly Eastern and Greek way, diverse aspects of the legacy of the émigrés theologians, produced rather important syntheses (for example, the "theology of personhood").[76]

Similar developments that may be traced through Romanian and Serbian Orthodox theology are often underestimated. Although the history of the reception of the patristic tradition in Serbian Orthodox theology began during the Middle Ages, one can only trace a certain patristic *ressourcement* during the first decades of the 20th century, especially through figures such as Nicholas Velimirović and Justin Popović. Their critical and rather often negative encounter with various progressive aspects of Western modernity (for instance, Popović speaks about a clear Arianism in European culture, to the extent that the "whole European philosophy … was contaminated by Arian yeast – to a certain extent religion too"),[77] was followed by an attempt to offer a different anthropological view (here one can even find the first seeds of a *relational* perspective). This view was based on a bold, patristic theology with a Christological stamp and various other sources of inspiration (ranging from Slavophiles to other Russian intellectuals, such as Pavel Alexandrovich Florensky) which would finally lead to a wider theological and liturgical renewal.[78]

Dumitru Stăniloae is widely considered to be the most important contributor to the patristic *ressourcement* in Romanian theology. Even before the true explosion of scholarly and spiritual interest in St. Gregory Palamas, Stăniloae published a monograph on his life and work[79] by making use of manuscripts of his unpublished works. Meanwhile, throughout his life's work, which included the translation and expansion of the *Philokalia* into the Romanian language,[80] he would appeal specifically to the Greek Fathers as his partners in order to initiate a dialogue with contemporary counterparts so as to tackle Western challenges in pursuit of the rediscovery of a common patristic tradition.[81]

2.2 *The Russian Religious Renaissance and Neo-Patristic Synthesis: The Dialogue Between Bulgakov and Florovsky*

It is commonplace in contemporary Orthodox scholarship to recall that there are two major, almost mutually exclusive trends in 20th century Orthodox theology: the so-called neo-patristic theology, represented mainly by figures such as Georges Florovsky and Vladimir Lossky; and the Russian religious renaissance, often labeled simply the "Russian school" or, the "Paris school,"[82] and represented primarily by Vladimir Sergeyevich Solovyov, Sergius Bulgakov and Pavel Florensky. These two important trajectories of Orthodox theology resulted from the Russian diaspora in the West, insofar as most of the so-called founders of both schools belonged to the first or second

76 See Pantelis Kalaitzidis, "New Trends in Greek Orthodox Theology: Challenges in the Movement Towards a Genuine Renewal and Christian Unity," *SJT* 67/2, 2014, 127–164.

77 Justin Popovic & Jovan Pejčić, *Zenica tragizma: Kratki spisi (1923–1940)*, Niš, Prosveta, 1998, 184, as cited in: Darko Djogo, "Serbian Neopatristic Theology (Some Aspects of History, Reception and Currents)," *Teologia* 4, 2012, 10–36, here 32.

78 For an overall, albeit somewhat uncritical, overview see Djogo, "Serbian Neopatristic."

79 Dumitru Stăniloae, *Viața și învățătura sfântului Grigorie Palama* [The life and teachings of St. Gregory Palamas], Bucharest, Editura Institutului Biblic și de Misiune al Bisericii Ortodoxe Romane, 2006 (1st ed. Sibiu, Tipografia Arhidiecezană, 1938).

80 See Louth, *Modern Orthodox Thinkers*, 127–142.

81 Viorel Coman, "Revisiting the Agenda of the Orthodox Neo-Patristic Movement," *DR*, 136/2, 2018, 99–117.

82 Hilarion (Alfeyev), "Orthodox Theology on the Threshold of the Twenty First Century," available at <http://orthodoxeurope.org/page/11/1/1.aspx> (accessed Mar 14, 2022).

generation of Russian emigrants.[83] Notwithstanding their somewhat common cultural and historical roots, the relationship between these eminent figures was marked by a deep and often hostile division, concerning above all their use and reception of the patristic heritage. This somewhat divisive split in the main body of modern Orthodox theology between the Russian and the neo-patristic schools was first pointed out by the late Alexander Schmemann,[84] and more recently by Paul Valliere.[85] At the same time, however, the supposed separation between the two currents of thought concerning the way in which they receive and appreciate the tradition of the Fathers has been boldly criticized as a naive oversimplification based primarily on ideological bias or ignorance of the particular context rather than on a careful reading of their work.[86] Thus it would appear that the time has come to question the predominant narrative by hypothesizing that if one is to appreciate the patristic retrieval in contemporary Orthodox theology, then a more inclusive conception that seeks to go beyond the prevailing division is required. Without enquiring into the details of the history, here we will refer to the major representatives of this debate, namely, Bulgakov and Florovsky.

Although they have often been deemed adversaries as a result of the Sophianism controversy,[87] Bulgakov and Florovsky both began their careers without any special training in theology (Bulgakov studied economics, Florovsky, history)[88] later, during the years they both spent in Paris, they developed a close and warm spiritual relationship of mutual appreciation. After all, they were destined to become the most creative minds in contemporary Orthodox theology. Although, while Bulgakov went almost unnoticed for much of the last century due to his frequently obscure thought and to his condemnation by the Moscow Patriarchate and the ROCOR for sophiology, Florovsky's theological program was to become the standard method for practicing Orthodox theology in subsequent years.[89]

But how do they understand the role of the Fathers in contemporary theology? As has been aptly put by Andrew Louth, although "*ressourcement* was claimed by those, such as Florovsky and Lossky, who saw the future of Orthodox theology as lying in the search for a 'neo-patristic synthesis,' in reality *ressourcement* was deeply embedded in the Russian enterprise of theology."[90] Indeed, in his article "Evcharističeskij dogmat" ("The Eucharist Dogma")[91] Bulgakov calls for a "return to the theology of the Fathers ... to the patristic doctrine ... [as] a true guide"[92] to theological discourse. A similar call can be found in Georges Florovsky. The latter would argue for "a reviving [of the] patristic style [as the] very premise of theological renaissance."[93] By this return to the Fathers, he sought to overcome a sterile "theology of repetition" ("'to *follow*' the Fathers does *not* mean just '*to quote*' them"),

83 They are the "fathers" and the "children" of the Renaissance, as is argued by Paul L. Gavrilyuk, *Georges Florovsky and the Russian Religious Renaissance*, Oxford, Oxford University Press, 2013, 42–59.

84 Alexander Schmemann, "Russian Theology: 1920–1972. An introductory survey," *SVTQ* 16/4, 1972, 172–194.

85 Paul Valliere, *Modern Russian Theology: Bucharev, Soloviev, Bulgakov: Orthodox Theology in a New Key*, Edinburgh, T&T Clark, 2000.

86 For instance, see Gavrilyuk, *Georges Florovsky*.

87 See Alexis Klimoff, "Georges Florovsky and the Sophiological Controversy," *SVTQ* 49/1–2, 2005, 67–100.

88 See Louth, *Modern Orthodox Thinkers*, 42–59, 77–93, respectively. See also Andrew Blane, ed., *Georges Florovsky: Russian Intellectual and Orthodox Churchman*, Crestwood NY, St. Vladirmir's Seminary Press, 1993; Robert Slesinski, *The Theology of Sergius Bulgakov*, Yonkers, St. Vladimir Seminary Press, 2017.

89 Louth, *Modern Orthodox Thinkers*, 42–45, 78–79 respectively.

90 Louth, "French Ressourcement," 499 (italics original).

91 Sergii Bulgakov, "Evkharisticheskiy dogmat," *Put* 20, 1930, 3–46, and 21, 1930, 3–33; ET: "The Eucharistic Dogma," in: Sergius Bulgakov, *The Holy Grail and the Eucharist*, ed. and trans. Boris Jakim, Hudson, Lindisfarne Books, 1997, 63–138.

92 Bulgakov, *The Holy Grail*, 82.

93 Florovsky, "Western Influences," 191–192.

by acquiring their "'mind,' their *phronema*."[94] The common quest of these two theologians towards a recovery of the patristic mind is clearly evident in the way in which they receive tradition (the Bible and the Fathers).

To begin with Florovsky, he argues for a certain *theological* use of the Scriptures: "The Bible is one indeed, and yet it is, in fact, a collection of various writings. ... The solution depends ultimately upon our conception of history."[95] Already in this reference to Scripture, Florovsky sees that the fundamental issue underlying the whole discussion of the interpretation of the Word of God is nothing less than its *historicity* as the fundamental axis upon which a theological appreciation of tradition rests. He counter-argues, therefore, against various tendencies in the history of the church and in contemporary biblical scholarship to undervalue the historical dimension of Revelation.[96] For him the "Bible is history,"[97] or rather *Heilsgeschichte*, in contrast to any tendency to understand the scriptural texts as *summae theologiae*. What then is the particular role of the Fathers in this respect?

According to the theologian, "the appeal to Tradition [here patristic] was actually an appeal to the mind of the Church, her *phronema*. It was a method"[98] of interpreting the *magnalia Dei* in the context of history. It was particularly in the context of delivering the apostolic faith that for the first time the authority of the Fathers came to the fore. For Florovsky, the Fathers "were witnesses of the permanence or identity of the *kerygma*."[99] What is really of value is not a mere "appeal to antiquity" or to a *consensus partum*,[100] on the contrary, it is an appeal to "the mind of the Fathers," – not in a literal sense, that is regarded as "an intrinsic term of reference in Orthodox theology."[101] As Florovsky himself describes the neo-patristic program, it "must be a *synthesis*, a creative reassessment of those insights ... granted to the Holy Men of old. It must be *Patristic* ... *ad mentem Patrum*. Yet it must be also *Neo*-Patristic, since it is addressed to the new age."[102]

In Florovsky's view, this patristic vision must not be seen as "an archaic manner or pose, and not just as a venerable relic, but as *an existential attitude*, as *a spiritual orientation*."[103] Tradition concerns then "a continuity of the abiding presence of the Holy Spirit in the Church,"[104] a definition shared by most of Florovsky's neo-patristic colleagues (such as Lossky)[105] or pupils (such as Metropolitan Kallistos Ware).[106] At the same time, it is not only historicity (that is, "ecumenism in time"),[107] but also Christ himself who is the

94 See Georges Florovsky, "St. Gregory Palamas and the Tradition of the Fathers," in: Florovsky, *The Collected Works*, vol. 1, *Bible, Church, Tradition: An Eastern Orthodox View*, Belmont MA, Nordland Publishing, 1972, 105–120, here 109 (italics original).

95 Georges Florovsky, "Revelation and Interpretation," in: Florovsky, *The Collected Works*, vol. 1, 17–36, here 28–29.

96 Here, Florovsky indirectly refers to Rudolf Bultmann's demythologizing project. See Rudolf Bultmann, *The New Testament and Mythology and Other Basic Writings*, ed. and trans. Schubert M. Ogden, Philadelphia, Fortress Press, 1984.

97 Florovsky, "Revelation and Interpretation," 29.

98 Georges Florovsky, "The Authority of the Ancient Councils and the Tradition of the Fathers," in: Florovsky, *The Collected Works*, vol. 1, 93–105, here 98.

99 Florovsky, "The Authority," 101.

100 Florovsky does not accept this term without serious reservations as is evidenced in the letter, G. Florovksy to D. Bateman, Dec 12, 1963, in: Anastassy Brandon Gallaher, "Georges Florovsky on reading the life of St. Seraphim," *Sobornost* 27/1, 2005, 61–63.

101 Florovsky, "St. Gregory Palamas," 105, 107.

102 Blane, "A Sketch of the Life of Georges Florovsky," in: Blane, ed., *Georges Florovsky*, 11–155, here 154 (italics original).

103 Florovsky, "St. Gregory Palamas," 113 (italics original).

104 Florovsky, "St. Gregory Palamas," 106.

105 Vladimir Lossky, *In the Image and Likeness of God*, ed. John H. Erickson, trans. Thomas E. Bird, Crestwood, St. Vladimir's Seminary Press, 1974, ch. 8, "Tradition and Traditions," 141–168, 152.

106 Timothy Ware, *The Orthodox Church: New Edition*, London, Penguin Books, ²1993.

107 See for an analysis, Matthew Baker, "Neopatristic Synthesis and Ecumenism: Towards the 'Reintegration' of Christian Tradition," in: Andrii Krawchuk & Thomas Bremer, eds., *Eastern Orthodox Encounters of Identity and Otherness*, New York, Palgrave MacMillan, 2014, 235–260.

ultimate *criterion* of truth,[108] to which the Fathers of the church bear witness as interpreters of the apostolic tradition.

Paradoxically, however, a very similar understanding of the role of the Fathers and the meaning of tradition can be also detected in Bulgakov, who was generally thought not to follow the Fathers as closely as Florovsky. In an early, yet still important, article entitled "Dogmat i dogmatika" ("Dogma and Dogmatic Theology"),[109] Bulgakov boldly contends that "the Word of God is the absolute criterion of theology," while "theology cannot include ideas that could not be directly or indirectly confirmed by the Word of God."[110] Eventually the Word of God, while not conceived as *summae theologiae*, "potentially includes a *summa* in itself," revealing its "divine-human character."[111] Furthermore, to the degree in which the Word of God also belongs to the church, it appears that it can be properly appreciated only in this context: "The Holy Scriptures must be understood in the light of Tradition."[112] Echoing, at this point, Florovsky's endeavor to value the authority of the Fathers, Bulgakov would raise a critical question with profound relevance to our topic. As he put it "dogmatic theology has to be 'according to the Fathers' and to agree with patristic tradition. But what does this mean?"[113]

By adopting the historical-critical methodology exemplified by the "contemporary resources and methodology" offered by modernity, Bulgakov wishes to approach the Fathers on their own terms[114] and to avoid projecting sterile anachronisms onto them. While he recognizes their authoritative status (as *testes veritatis*), the theologian nevertheless remained critical of any "rabbinic" reading that renders their texts "dogmatically infallible." According to Bulgakov, in essence, the patristic *texts* should be discussed within their particular context, taking into account all the available resources from church history, beginning with textual criticism.[115] After all, what really matters is not the texts in themselves (here lurks a kind of "patrological heresy"), already extensively analyzed in scholastic and Neoscholastic manuals and in theological conclusion in both East and West, but their *spirit*: "The real veneration of the Fathers must reverence not the letter but the spirit. The writings of the Fathers must have a guiding authority."[116] Opposed to "antiquity" as a criterion of truth, Bulgakov would also have asserted that the ultimate criterion of theology was the person of Christ ("the Christological question").[117] It is clear by now that for Bulgakov, as for Florovsky, historicity and the Christological axis constitute the foundations on which to build a patristic *ressourcement*.

Although the history of contemporary Orthodox theology still presents both theologians and their views as mutually exclusive, a closer reading of their texts reveals a far more common understanding of the character of the patristic tradition. This does not deny, however, that there are also differences between the two which are impossible to underestimate. For those familiar with their work, it is evident that, on the one hand, Florovsky appealed to the Fathers in order to find a common language and an ecumenical meeting ground in

108 Florovsky, "The Authority," 97ff.

109 Sergius Bulgakov, "Dogmat i dogmatic," in: *Zhivoie Priedanie: pravoslavie v sovremennosti* [Living tradition: Orthodoxy in modernity], Paris, YMCA, 1937, 9–24; ET: "Dogma and Dogmatic Theology," in: Michael Plekon, ed., *Tradition Alive: On the Church and the Christian Life in Our Time*, Oxford, Rowman & Littlefield, 2003, 67–80.

110 Bulgakov, "Dogma," 69.

111 Bulgakov, "Dogma," 70.

112 Bulgakov, "Dogma," 70.

113 Bulgakov, "Dogma," 70.

114 A similar call is suggested by modern patristic scholars, for example Nikolaos Loudovikos, "Dialogical Nature, Enousion Person, and Non-Ecstatic Will in St. Maximus the Confessor: The Conclusion of a Long Debate," *Analogia* 2/1, 2017, 81.

115 Bulgakov, "Dogma," 70.

116 Bulgakov, "Dogma," 71.

117 Bulgakov, *The Holy Grail*, 82.

his encounter with his Anglican counterparts,[118] even if his work ended up becoming a hermeneutical tool binding for contemporary theology. On the other hand, Bulgakov appealed to the authority of the Fathers using a contextual hermeneutic in order to bring the church into a dialogue with the challenges of modernity. He did so without fear of being critical of particular figures in the patristic tradition; or of adopting certain ambivalent and neglected views (as was the case with Apollinaris of Laodicea);[119] or even of calling for the need to reflect on the development of Christian doctrine (echoing perhaps Newman); or conceptualize in new terms the God-world relationship beyond, for instance, the Palamite distinction between essence and energies.[120] At the same time, one cannot underestimate both author's profound indebtedness to German Idealism, (a debt expressed in a more direct way by Bulgakov,[121] and in an indirect way by Florovsky, who makes ample use of Möhler's thought[122]) or the intellectual and cultural context in which they worked (Solovyov's work, pre-revolutionary Russia, emigration, Berdyaev colloquy and the birth of the Institut de théologie orthodoxe Saint-Serge). In addition, if one takes into account the variety of directions present within the so-called neo-patristic synthesis,[123] and if one compares them with the much more homogeneous character of the Russian school, there are clear signs of a need for a reconciliation of both perspectives.

2.3 *The* Ressourcement *in 20th Century Catholic Theology: The Context*

Following the radical challenges proposed by Modernism, the first decades of the 20th century represented, for Catholic theology, a struggle between two opposite tendencies. On the one hand, there was the institutional church, which combatted Modernism through the use of encyclicals (see the famous *Pascendi Dominici gregis*, 1907) and other methods, in the fear that what was considered to be a result of the Enlightenment and secularism, would swamp every form of knowledge. The outcome was the reintroduction of scholastic theology in the main seminaries and Catholic faculties and in particular of an interpretation of Thomism, which, by cutting theology off from its historical context, made it akin to a "sacred metaphysics."

On the other hand, the gradual success of communism in East Europe and the formation of the socialist regimes, united in the constant secularization of social life, as much in the East as in the West, contributed in a decisive way to the relaxing of the hold that the ecclesiastical authority had on society, whilst subjectivity and immanence seemed to become the cardinal points that guided the man of the 19th century in his understanding of existence and history.

It was this rather complex and fluid context, along with certain theological developments in biblical studies, ecclesiology, liturgics and ethics,[124] that paved the way to the *nouvelle théologie*.[125]

118 In Florovsky's view, "Patristics was one of the links" in Orthodox theology's enterprise to dialogue with other Christian traditions. See Andrew Blane & Thomas Bird, "Interview with G.V. Florovsky, Nov. 8, 1969," 76–77 (unpublished), as cited in: Baker, "Neopatristic Synthesis" in: Krawchuk & Bremer, eds., *Eastern Orthodox*, 238.

119 See for instance the extended use of Appolinaris in Sergius Bulgakov, *The Lamb of God*, trans. Boris Jakim, Grand Rapids, Eerdmans, 2008.

120 See Bulgakov, "Dogma"; Anastassy Brandon Gallaher & Irina Kukota, "Protopresbyter Sergii Bulgakov: Hypostasis and Hypostaticity: Scholia to the Unfading Light," *SVTQ* 49/1–2, 2005, 5–46.

121 See Brandon Gallaher, *Freedom and Necessity in Modern Trinitarian Theology*, Oxford, Oxford University Press, 2016, 48, *passim*.

122 See Gallaher, "'Waiting for the Barbarians.'"

123 See Coman, "Revisiting the Agenda," 102, where he distinguishes between different directions: "(a) a *historical-patristic-ecclesiological* direction ... (b) a *mystical-Palamite-philokalic* direction ... and (c) a *Eucharistic-liturgical- eschatological* direction" (italics original).

124 See Mettepenningen, *Nouvelle Théologie*, 27–29.

125 For a detailed exploration of the origin of the concept, see Mettepenningen, *Nouvelle Théologie*, 3–14.

Primarily located in Paris and francophone, the *nouveaux théologiens* attempted to rehabilitate history as the main ground of theological discourse, where the building blocks of theology (that is, the Bible, divine liturgy and patristics) are to be accessed; at the same time, they strongly criticized the rationalistic and speculative reflection of Neoscholasticism and Heinrich Denzinger's positive theology; finally, they attempted to bring the church into a constructive dialogue with modernity.[126] In this endeavor, *nouvelle théologie* was destined to play a decisive role in the renewal of Catholic theology, contributing, in spite of the mistrust and suspicion that initially encompassed it, to the important and necessary reforms adopted by Vatican II.[127]

The starting point of this Catholic *ressourcement* theology should be sought at Le Saulchoir,[128] a Dominican theological school near Tournai (now in Belgium, but at the time in France), whilst the Jesuit theology school of Lyon-Fourvière represented one of its principle centers of development.[129] A pioneer group of French Dominicans and Jesuits of both institutes, including prominent intellectuals such as the Dominicans Marie-Dominique Chenu, Yves Congar, Dominique Dubarle, and Henri-Marie Féret; and the Jesuits Jean Daniélou, Henri-Marie de Lubac, Henri Bouillard and others, would undertake the task to "refresh theology's bonds with history"[130] and the true life of the people by bringing the church and theology into a close dialogue with the quests of modernity.

2.4 *Chenu, de Lubac and Daniélou*

"Anyone who did not live through the years 1946 and 1947 in the history of French Catholicism has missed one of the finest moments in the life of the Church."[131] With these words Congar described the atmosphere within which the patristic revival slowly found a foothold in France, in the wake of the general renewal of theological disciplines previously touched on. However, one must be careful not to misunderstand the enthusiasm that lies behind Congar's words, insofar as the *ressourcement*[132] and the more general theological renewal contemporary to it provoked harsh reactions from the Church of Rome, reactions whose price the Dominican theologian paid in person. The term "nouvelle théologie" was coined and

---

Although originally intended to describe a positive development in the history of the Catholic theology, the concept itself never actually adopted a positive meaning or was used by the protagonists of the movement. Its negative connotations were due to the hesitancy on the part of the church to easily adopt any progressive developments, as well as due to the fact that the official exponents of the *magisterium* mainly linked it to the growing spirit of modernity. In this light, an authoritative voice of the church, Réginald Garrigou-Lagrange, "La nouvelle theologie ou va-t-elle?," *Angelicum* 23/3–4, 1946, 126–145, here 143, attempted to address the new trend by saying that the "nouvelle theologie will lead us back to Modernism." See also Mettepenningen, *Nouvelle Théologie*, 4–5.

126 Mettepenningen, *Nouvelle Théologie*, 9–11.

127 Kirwan, *An Avant-garde*, 252ff.; Gerald O'Collins, "*Ressourcement* and Vatican II"; Paul McPartlan, "*Ressourcement*, Vatican II, and Eucharistic Ecclesiology," both in: Flynn & Murray, eds., *Ressourcement*, 372–391, 392–404, respectively.

128 See Marie-Dominique Chenu, *Une école de théologie: Le Saulchoir*, ed. Giuseppe Alberigo, Paris, Cerf, 1985; Mettepenningen, *Nouvelle Théologie*, 41–82. See also the chapter by Joseph Famerée in this work.

129 Mettepenningen, *Nouvelle Théologie*, 83–114; Étienne Fouilloux, "A New 'Lyon School' (1919–1939)?," in: Flynn & Murray, eds., *Ressourcement*, 83–94.

130 Mettepenningen, *Nouvelle Théologie*, xiii.

131 Yves M.-J. Congar, *Chrétiens en dialogue: Contributions catholiques à l'Œcuménisme*, Paris, Cerf, 1964; ET: *Dialogue between Christians: Catholic Contributions to Ecumenism*, trans. Philip Loretz, London, G. Chapman, 1966, 32; Henri de Lubac, *At the Service of the Church: Henri de Lubac Reflects on the Circumstances that Occasioned His Writings*, trans. Anne Elizabeth Englund, San Francisco, Ignatius, 1993, 45, 48.

132 The concept itself was coined by the poet and social critic Charles Peguy, see Yves Congar, "Le prophète Péguy," *Témoignage Chrétien*, Aug 26, 1949, 1, as cited in: Gabriel Flynn, "A Renaissance in Twentieth-Century Catholic Theology," *ITQ*, 76/4, 2011, 323–338, here 327.

utilized, initially,[133] with polemical and demeaning intent on the part of those who accused the *noveaux théologiens* of Modernism; among them, the names Marie-Michel Labourdette[134] and Réginald Garrigou-Lagrange stood out.

The call for a renewal in theology, motivated by the inability of the church to effectively tackle the challenges of the times, would find its bold expression in the work *inter alia* of Chenu,[135] de Lubac,[136] and Daniélou.[137] Pioneers of *ressourcement* theology, these three theologians opposed the abstract and speculative approach of Neoscholasticism with all their energies; they appealed to history[138] as the ground of theological discourse, and on several occasions they emphasized the urgency that the church find new languages and tools to keep abreast of modernity. De Lubac, with his magisterial *Catholicisme*, sought in particular to overcome the traditional scholastic division between nature and grace by bringing to the fore a more inclusive notion belonging to Aquinas's account, one open to a perspective similar to the Greek patristic tradition.[139]

By frequently adopting the Modernist emphasis on the importance of the historical conditions for the development of human existence or of Christian doctrine itself,[140] the *nouveaux theologians* appealed to a return to the sources that was not a sterile "theology of repetition"[141] or an "escape into a dead past,"[142] but conversely helped the church to confront the "challenges of today."[143]

In the so-called manifesto of *nouvelle théologie*, *Les orientations présentes de la pensée religieuse* (1946), Jean Daniélou provides a detailed description of what he considered ought to be fundamental axes for the *ressourcement* movement, namely: (a) the return to the sources of Christian faith (for example, the Bible, the Fathers and the Divine Liturgy); (b) a fertile and open dialogue with the various currents in modern thought; and (c) a major greater involvement of the church in the new reality of things.[144]

In the light of these three axes, the "new theology," as perceived by the founders of the theological renewal, in this case by Daniélou, placed history at the center of theological reflection. And this was possible above all thanks to these theologians' encounter with various expressions of secular ideologies, such as Hegelianism and Marxism, which, each from a different perspective, made reference to history as the place of human action.[145]

This shift to history on the part of French-Catholic theology is also connected to its encounter both with Protestant theology and with the

133 The controversial term was used for the first time by Pietro Parente, secretary of the Holy Office, in his "Nuove tendenze teologiche," *L'Osservatore Romano*, Feb 9–10, 1942, 1.

134 Marie-Michel Labourdette, "La Théologie et ses sources," *RT* 46/2, 1946, 353–371.

135 See especially Chenu, *Une école de théologie: Le Saulchoir*; Marie-Dominique Chenu, "Classes and the Mystical Body," in: Marie-Dominique Chenu, *Faith and Theology*, trans. Denis Hickey, Dublin, Gills 1968, 185–201.

136 See Henri de Lubac, *Catholicisme: Les aspects sociaux du dogme*, Paris, Cerf, 1938; ET: *Catholicism*, trans. Lancelot C. Sheppard, London, Longman Green, 1950.

137 Jean Daniélou, "Les orientations présentes de la pensée religieuse," *Études* 249, 1946, 5–21.

138 See the emblematic essay by Jean Daniélou, *Essai sur le mystère de l'histoire*, Paris, Éditions du Seuil, 1953.

139 See Henri de Lubac, *Surnaturel: Études historiques*, Paris, Aubier-Montaigne, 1946. For such an interpretation that aims at reconciling the Greek patristic tradition with Aquinas in this respect, see Nikolaos Loudovikos, "Striving for Participation: Palamite Analogy as Dialogical Syn-energy and Thomist Analogy as Emanational Similitude," in: Constantinos Athanasopoulos & Christoph Schneider, eds., *Divine Essence and Divine Energies: Ecumenical Reflections on the Presence of God in Eastern Orthodoxy*, Cambridge, James Clarke & Co, 2013, 122–148.

140 See Henri de Lubac, "Le probléme du développement du dogme," *RSR* 35, 1948, 130–160.

141 As Henri de Lubac himself put it *Catholicisme*, 278: "To imitate primitive Christianity or the Middle Ages will not be enough"; as cited in: Kirwan, *An Avant-garde*, 167.

142 de Lubac, *Catholicisme*, 279–280, as cited in: Kirwan, *An Avant-garde*, 167.

143 Kirwan, *An Avant-garde*, 166.

144 Daniélou, "Les orientations," 7.

145 Daniélou, "Les orientations," 13–17.

Russian émigré theology of Florovsky.[146] In 1945, the Alsatian, Evangelical theologian Oscar Cullmann had already published what would become his classic work, *Christus und die Zeit*,[147] where he proclaimed the importance of history as the place of salvation from a biblical point of view and as a fundamental axis of Christian theology. Accordingly, in contrast to the Neoscholastic methodology, which had marginalized concern for history, Daniélou with a diligent effort, coupled the theological method with historical fact and grounded it in in patristic theology[148] (or on the "patristic system" as already noted in 1946).[149]

While Daniélou and other pioneering French theologians of the Lyon-Fourvière school were attempting in this way to reorient theology, the *Humani generis* Encyclical of Pope Pius XII (Aug 12, 1950) once again attempted to halt the coming theological ferment that was taking shape over the horizon. However, it was already obvious how the river of this renewal had triggered an irreversible process as was further confirmed by the aspirations generated by Vatican II and the following reforms.

The *nouveaux théologiens*, through all their efforts, attempted to revive Christian faith in a rapidly changing modern world. By their appeal to a return to the Fathers (aside from the Bible and the Divine Liturgy), these theologians emphasized the relevance of historical consciousness for the life of the church, and critically adopted those aspects of modernity that better aligned with their efforts to create an immanent methodology and a "communitarian spirituality."[150] Furthermore, the ecumenical dialogue that they were engaged in with their Orthodox and Protestant counterparts brought to the foreground the thought of the Fathers as a common ground of Christian unity. The evident polemical attitude with which they advanced their reevaluation of Neoscholasticism nevertheless accompanied a more inclusive understanding of *ressourcement* (not limited to the Fathers) and a true interest in social issues and in the concrete needs of the men of their time – one that demanded a response from the living church.

2.5 **Ressourcement** ***in Protestant Theologies***

Despite the fact that the appeal to the patristic tradition held in common by the early Reformers was principally directed against Rome, and despite the dominance of liberal Protestantism between the end of the 19th century and the beginning of the 20th, wherever theology had not been informed by the spirit of the Fathers,[151] in Catholicism, as in Protestantism, a revival of the interest in the common patristic tradition was evident, especially after Vatican II. Thanks to the growth of ecumenical dialogue, even Protestant theologians came to appreciate the patristic tradition in the context of exegetical and dogmatic study.

With his call "back to the sources" and by adopting a "*ressourcement* style," appealing not only to the Fathers of the early church but also to the 16th and 17th century writings of the Calvinist tradition, Karl Barth was the first to break with liberal Protestantism.[152] Although the *sola scriptura*

146 For the relationship between Daniélou and Florovsky see, Jean Daniélou, "Metempsychosis in Gregory of Nyssa," in: *The Heritage of the Early Church: Essays in Honor of the Very Reverend G.V. Florovsky*, Rome, Pontificum Institutum Orientalium Studiorum, 1973, 227–243; Daniélou *Essai*. One can find letters from their correspondence in Florovsky's archives in St. Vladimir Orthodox Seminary in New York.

147 Oscar Cullmann, *Christus und die Zeit: Die urchristliche Zeit und Geschichtsauffassung*, Zollikon, Evangelischer Verlag, 1946; ET: *Christ and Time: The Primitive Christian Conception of Time and History*, trans. Floyd V. Filson, Eugene, Wipf & Stock, 2018.

148 Jean Daniélou, "Christianisme et histoire," *Études* 254, 1947, 166–184.

149 Daniélou, "Les orientations," 10.

150 Kirwan, *An Avant-garde*, 174–192.

151 Jason R. Radcliff, *T.F. Torrance and the Consensus Patrum: A Reformed, Evangelical and Ecumenical Reconstruction of the Church Fathers*, Ph.D. thesis, University of Edinburgh, 2013, 1.

152 Karl Barth, *The Göttingen Dogmatics: Instruction in the Christian Religion*, vol. 1, trans. Geoffrey. W. Bromiley, Grand Rapids, Eerdmans, 1991, 40, as cited in: Webster, "Ressourcement," 487.

principle had guided the Reformers from the very outset, it should not be understood primarily in a negative sense; rather, it points to the church as the context within which the Bible must be read and heard.[153] It is widely recognized among the major Protestant traditions, in fact, that the Bible must not be treated "in isolation" from its context.[154] When the Fathers of the church were struggling against the heresies of their era, their work was primarily exegetical; in the sense that they tried to interpret the apostolic *kerygma* deposited in the Scriptures,[155] a process that gradually led them to the formulation of a Christian doctrine. That said, the Fathers never sought to build a conceptual system outside the ecclesial context. Their theological enterprise and interpretation firmly relied on the Scriptures, and their aim was to "come into the presence of the very Word of God."[156] Although a certain degree of discontinuity between the gospel and the church can be found in the various versions of Protestantism, what really matters in the end is that "*ressourcement* theology offers an invitation to Protestant theology to renew its vocation as an ecclesial science,"[157] in the sense that one cannot but take seriously into account the long history of theology and the church as a constant endeavor towards a reinterpretation of the various moments in the history of salvation.

The late Thomas F. Torrance was an exceptional exponent for the rejuvenation of the patristic heritage in Protestant theology. Against the failure of his Protestant counterparts to articulate a hermeneutic guide to patristic tradition,[158] Torrance constitutes a unique case where a clear commitment to the Greek Fathers played an effective role of authoritative support for a particular conception of Evangelical and Reformed theology. By grounding his view on the Christological account of the early Fathers of the church, such as Athanasius and Cyril of Alexandria, and the conception of *homoousion* (consubstantiability), Torrance endeavored to offer a particular "evangelical patristic dogmatics"[159] by which he sought to reconstruct the continuity of tradition not only with the Apostolic Church, but also with the church of the Fathers. Echoing with his "grand-narrative" the patristic retrieval, as it was developed by his close friend Georges Florovsky,[160] Torrance provided a *ressourcement* theology that pointed to the philosophical and ecumenical value of the Fathers, and aimed to reevaluate their importance for a dialogue between the church and the cultural setting in which it was immersed, especially that formed by scientific developments.

Analogous interest in a revival of the patristic tradition, above all the Greek one that arose from the encounter with dominant Hellenistic philosophy,[161] can be traced in figures such has Colin Gunton, who in formulating his own theology clearly appealed to the Cappadocian one,[162] or in the Anglo-Catholic theological movement of Radical Orthodoxy, which provided a positive, syncretic rereading of some aspects of Neoplatonic philosophy; of "pre-Scotist Christianity"; of the Greek patristic tradition (Dionysius the Areopagite, Gregory Palamas); of de Lubac; and of

153 Karl Barth, *Credo*, New York, Scribner, 1962, 180, as cited in: Webster, "Ressourcement," 488.

154 Hans Boersma, "Up to the Mountains with the Fathers: Evangelical Ressourcement of Early Christian Doctrine," CTR 1/1, 2012, 3–22, here 13.

155 Boersma, "Up to the Mountains," 8.

156 Boersma, "Up to the Mountains," 9.

157 Webster, "Ressourcement," 493.

158 Radcliff, *T.F. Torrance*, 3.

159 Especially with his *The Trinitarian Faith: The Evangelical Theology of the Ancient Catholic Church*, Cornerstones, London, T&T Clark, [2]2016. See Radcliff, *T.F. Torrance*, 92.

160 For their mutual relationship in terms of vision see, Matthew Baker & Todd Speidel, eds., *T.F. Torrance and Eastern Orthodoxy: Theology in Reconciliation*, Eugene, Wipf & Stock, 2015.

161 See towards this end, Allen & Springsted, *Philosophy*, xviii. See also Boersma, "Up to the Mountains," 14–15.

162 See Lincoln Harvey, ed., *The Theology of Colin Gunton*, London, T&T Clark, 2010.

Russian émigré theology, all in an attempt to propose a "re-enchantment of the world in Christ," by a creative rehabilitation of tradition and a honest dialogue with modernity.[163]

The search for a historical and critical hermeneutic approach to the past, but not necessarily negative, still constitutes today one of the principle challenges that contemporary Protestant theology finds itself confronted by. In appealing to the Fathers, diverse Protestant thinkers seek even today to find supporters for their interpretation of the Word of God in continuity with the life and experience of the early church in order to address, in a more or less authoritative way, the challenges posed by our current world. Without ignoring possible debts to contemporary philosophical influences (for example, Hegelianism, existentialism or phenomenology), and although a bold emphasis is rightly put on the priority of the Scriptures as the starting point of any Christian theological discourse, the Fathers are more or less now recognized as faithful interpreters and witnesses of the apostolic faith and experience of the early church. Witnesses who need to be heard again in our ever-changing context. As was once stated by an Anglican bishop, "we Anglicans do not always admire the hermeneutical methods of the Fathers, but we do recognize the conclusions to which the Fathers came."[164]

3 By Way of Conclusion: Back to the Fathers, "ad mentem Patrum" or beyond the Fathers?

Faced with the crisis of the modern age, sparked by the various political, cultural and intellectual developments in the West, pioneer theologians and intellectuals from the major Christian traditions intentionally addressed unforeseen problems by returning to the patristic tradition for inspiration. By appealing to history, the different *ressourcement* theologies attempted to question a particular speculative and rationalistic, Neoscholastic, and "baroque" theology that was still prevalent at that time; this theology separated tradition (Thomas Aquinas or the Fathers of the early church) from its context, either as a *summa* and "sacred metaphysics" or as *catenae* of texts and ideas (see the ambivalent concept of *consensus Patrum*) employed to support *a posteriori* the doctrine of the imperial or institutional church. Whether or not they were usually aware of the common influence exercised on them by German Idealism, in most cases the pioneers of *ressourcement* (in particular *nouveaux théologiens* and Russian religious renaissance thinkers)[165] adopted the core ideas of the spirit of modernity, such as the historical-critical hermeneutic method, in order to render the message of the gospel and Christian doctrine soteriologically effective for their age.

163 Adrian Pabst & Christoph Schneider, "Introduction: Transfiguring the World through the Word," in: Adrian Pabst & Christoph Schneider, eds., *Encounter between Eastern Orthodoxy and Radical Orthodoxy: Transfiguring the World through the Word*, Farnham, Ashgate, 2009, 1–25, here 2.

164 Kallistos Ware & Colin Davey, eds., *Anglican-Orthodox Dialogue: The Moscow Statement Agreed by the Anglican-Orthodox Joint Doctrinal Commission*, 1976, London, SPCK, 1977, 56.

165 It is interesting to note that the major figures in the Russian religious renaissance or even Slavophilism were more open to the quests of Modernism, as were their Catholic counterparts of *nouvelle théologie*, than certain protagonists of neo-patristic synthesis who seem in this respect closer to the various trends of Neoscholasticism. Despite being a paradox, in most cases, such as in Vladimir Lossky or John Romanides and others, the "return to the Fathers" of the Church led to a "patristic fundamentalism" that was not very different from Neoscholasticism.

Bibliography

Flynn, Gabriel & Paul D. Murray, eds., *Ressourcement: A Movement for Renewal in Twentieth-Century Catholic Theology*, Oxford, Oxford University Press, 2012.

Gavrilyuk, Paul L., *Georges Florovsky and the Russian Religious Renaissance*, Oxford, Oxford University Press, 2013.

Gonnet, Dominique & Michel Stavrou, eds., *Les Pères de l'Église au XXe siecle: Histoire, litterature, theologie: "L'aventure des Sources chrétiennes"*, Paris, Cerf, 1997.

Mettepenningen, Jürgen, *Nouvelle Théologie – New Theology: Inheritor of Modernism, Precursor of Vatican II*, London, T&T Clark, 2010.

Sarisky, Darren, ed., *Theologies of Retrieval: An Exploration and Appraisal*, London, T&T Clark, 2017.

CHAPTER 3

From Mission to Ecumenism: Istina

Étienne Fouilloux

1 Introduction

Who today would dispute the role played by the Parisian Istina center in the appearance and development of ecumenical concerns within the Catholic Church in 20th-century France? The contrast between this evidence and the near-total absence of Istina in the historiography of the ecumenical movement is therefore very surprising. The Benedictine abbey of Amay-Chevetogne, an exact contemporary of the Dominican center, celebrated the 50th anniversary of its foundation with a certain amount of pomp in 1976,[1] and celebrated its 75th anniversary in 2001;[2] moreover, a monumental biography has been devoted to its founder, Dom Lambert Beauduin.[3] Nothing of the sort exists for Istina: no anniversary celebrations, no history beyond a few short encyclopedic entries;[4] no biography, either, for Father Christophe-Jean Dumont, who was the heart and soul of Istina from 1932 to 1967: instead, there are just a few scattered or elliptic references and an Italian thesis from which a small book was extracted, albeit without any French translation.[5] As for the *Souvenirs d'un pionnier* collected by Dumont, they have yet to be published, and could hardly pass as true memoirs anyway; instead, they consist in a compilation of studies and reviews that had already been published by the Dominican friar and supplemented by a number of unpublished documents linked together by rather short commentaries.[6] Recollections and histories of Istina are thus entirely lacking, at least in the public domain.

Such an omission astonishes a historian who has spent much time working in the Dominican center and is therefore quite familiar with the wealth of its archives and with the broad spectrum of topics that they cover.[7] The following pages alone are not intended to fill this gap. They merely attempt to reconstruct the main stages of Istina's turbulent path, while at the same time advancing a few hypotheses regarding the silence that continues to linger over its history. Up to 1967, this path includes four quite distinct stages that will be examined in chronological order: that of the seminary of St. Basil in Lille, that of the intensification of relations

1 Jean-Jacques von Allmen & others, *Veilleur avant l'aurore: Colloque Lambert Beauduin*, Chevetogne, Éditions de Chevetogne, 1978.

2 Several articles on the abbey's history may be found in the monastery's journal, see *Irén* 75/4, 2002 and 76/2–3, 2003.

3 Raymond Loonbeek & Jacques Mortiau, *Un pionnier, dom Lambert Beauduin (1873–1960): Liturgie et unité des chrétiens*, 2 vols., Louvain-la-Neuve/Chevetogne, Collège Érasme/Éditions de Chevetogne, 2001. The work comprises over 1600 pages.

4 Christophe-Jean Dumont, "Istina (Centre d'Etudes)" and "Istina (Revue)," *Catholicisme* 6, cols. 220–221.

5 Ciro Bova, *Christophe-Jean Dumont: Una vita per l'ecumenismo*, Bari, Ecumenica Editrice, 1998; see furthermore my entry on Father Dumont in *Dictionnaire biographique des frères prêcheurs: Dominicains des provinces françaises (XIXe–XXe siècles)*, available at <journals.openedition.org/dominicains/1228> (accessed Mar 14, 2022).

6 Christophe Dumont, "L'Église romaine et le Mouvement œcuménique: Souvenirs d'un pionnier (1926–1967)," Archives de la province dominicaine de France (end of compilation dated Oct 11, 1981); for more information on this manuscript see Hyacinthe Destivelle, "*Souvenirs d'un pionnier*: Les Mémoires inédits du Père Christophe-Jean Dumont," *Istina* 54/3, 2009, 279–297.

7 See the passages dedicated to Istina in: Étienne Fouilloux, *Les catholiques et l'unité chrétienne du XIXe au XXe siècle: Itinéraires européens d'expression française*, Paris, Le Centurion, 1982; and, more recently, Michel Mallèvre's overview in his article, "Les Dominicains français et la promotion de l'unité des chrétiens au XXe siècle: Engagements personnels et institutions," in: Nicole Bériou, André Vauchez & Michel Zink, eds., *Les Dominicains en France (XIIIe–XXe siècle)*, Paris, Académie des inscriptions et belles-lettres/Cerf, 2017, 483–502.

between Russia and Christianity, that the opening to the ecumenical movement, and, finally, that of the ambiguous conciliar consecration.

2 A Russian Seminary in Lille

The downfall of the tsarist regime in 1917 gave rise to a veritable "Russian mirage" within Catholicism, the effects of which were felt right up to the highest circles of Rome. Prior to this, the osmosis between the Orthodox Church and the imperial state precluded any hope of missionary penetration into Russia, in spite of the religious freedom granted by Nicholas II in the aftermath of the revolutionary upheavals of 1905–1906. Failing to fully understand the implications of the restoration of the Moscow Patriarchate by the council of 1917–1918, the Vatican experts who advised the popes Benedict XV and Pius XI on Eastern matters estimated that the Russian Church was a tottering edifice that would not survive the downfall of its monarchical guardian and the early persecutions of the communist regime, and that its days were numbered. They thus concluded that the situation had never been more favorable to a conversion of Russia to Catholicism. But not to just any kind of Catholicism! Underestimating how wide the psychological gap between Eastern and Western Christians had become after centuries of separation, the papal advisers were tempted to reduce the schism to a small number of disagreements over dogma and, above all, to the issue of the liturgical ritual, which they erroneously believed was the main reason why the Russians remained attached to their church. Would it be enough to return to the strategy once relaunched by Pope Leo XIII? To develop a Catholicism of Byzantine-Slavic rite that would enable this still unspoiled people to detach itself from its bad shepherds and to return to the fold of Peter? The key requirement for the success of such a plan was to stop sending Latin missionaries to Russia and to replace them with a clergy of Eastern rite that was to be recruited from the emigrant community and trained in the West, as least initially, as long as the Soviet territory remained inaccessible.

Several projects to establish a Russian seminary were thus launched in the early 1920s. The Lille one was the first to be realized, somewhat fortuitously under Dominican patronage. L'Œuvre d'Orient took up the task on the initiative of Pope Pius XI himself, who provided vital financial support, locating itself in the ancient consulate of the Kingdom of Servia at 59 rue de la Barre, in the center of Lille. All that it lacked was a religious order or congregation that would be able to shoulder the responsibility for such an unusual foundation. When the Spiritans declined to do so,[8] the chapter of the Dominican province of France (that is, Paris) took up the challenge, more out of a sense of opportunity than out of true conviction:[9] placed under the patronage of St. Basil, the seminary opened its doors in autumn 1923, with two French friars and a handful of postulants. It was plagued by difficulties from the very beginning. The new foundation was sponsored by no less than four ecclesial institutions: L'Œuvre d'Orient provided part of the funding; Rome provided the rest and was intent on supervising the training through the Congregation for the Oriental Churches, then through the Pro Russia commission; the Order of Preachers agreed to furnish the supervisory personnel; and the diocese of Lille was to assist in the recruitment of the postulants. Only a miracle

8 Christian Sorrel, "Les congrégations religieuses masculines françaises en Orient (milieu XIXe–milieu XXe siècle)," in: Hervé Legrand & Giuseppe M. Croce, eds., *L'Œuvre d'Orient: Solidarités anciennes et nouveaux défis*, Paris, Cerf, 2010, 223–253, here 244.

9 The Dominican province of France already had a link to Russia in the person of Father Jean-Baptiste Amoudru, parish priest of Notre-Dame de France in St. Petersburg since 1907; see Nathalie Viet-Depaule's entry on Father Amoudru in the *Dictionnaire biographique des frères prêcheur*, available at <https://journals.openedition.org/dominicains/179> (accessed Mar 14, 2022). By accepting the responsibility for St. Basil's, the chapter hoped to improve the status of the province, with regard both to Rome and to France, where the order had no legal existence.

could prevent overlapping responsibilities and rivalries.[10]

The first two Dominican superiors of St. Basil's, François Foulon and Paul Duchaussoy, accepted the assignment out of pure obedience. Lacking any specific competence in Eastern matters, or even sympathy for the Russians and for Russia, they applied the rules that were then in force in Western seminaries. The boarding students were thus required to attain proficiency in French and to learn Latin before following the curriculum of theological studies at the Lille Catholic University. Their spiritual schooling took place through the practice of typically Western and Dominican devotions, for instance the Rosary. St. Basil's was thus very much like a normal seminary. The reactions to this Latinization program were not long in coming. The dispatching, in 1924, of a Bulgarian priest of Macedonian origin by the Congregation for the Oriental Churches did indeed allow for the celebration of religious services according to the Byzantine-Slavic rite; however, this was no more than a palliative that was unevenly appreciated by the Russian students. Meanwhile, the Roman authorities continued to deplore the insufficient Easternization of the institute.

But they were not the only reactions. In November 1923, Father Henri-Jean Omez was assigned to St. Basil's at his own request,[11] after having discovered Eastern Christianity through his dealings with tsarist soldiers, like himself prisoners of war in Germany between 1914 and 1918, from whom he had learned the rudiments of the Russian language and of Russian culture. Unlike the Fathers Foulon and Duchaussoy, he enthusiastically embraced the task that had been entrusted to him: immediately upon arriving at St. Basil's, he set about earnestly studying Russian and the Byzantine-Slavic liturgy, acquiring the right to celebrate it in November 1925. In July of the following year, he was joined at St. Basil's by his friend Father Christophe-Jean Dumont, five years his junior, who fully shared his desire for Easternization.[12] Several seminarians, recently converted Catholics or late vocations plagued with uncertainty, were in fact unwilling to accept the Latin mold into which they were being pressed, which led to a wave of dropouts. Following a series of internal frictions, the Fathers Foulon and Duchaussoy succeeded in being relieved of their duties, and the provincial chapter of summer 1927 entrusted St. Basil's to Father Omez.

The new superior was not in an enviable position. Overwhelmed by financial worries, he had no choice but to break with a suicidal policy. He also had to placate the prejudices of the Roman Pro-Russia commission, which only granted him a prolonged interim term and failed to draw up specific order. A clear "Eastern" shift and an active promotional campaign nevertheless succeeded in straightening the rudder. While his predecessors had ignored the diocese of Lille and the local Catholic community, Father Omez, developed a good relationship with Msgr. Achille Liénart, a young, dynamic bishop who had been appointed in 1928; he opened the seminary for the main liturgical celebrations and solicited invitations to introduce it to the outside world. Apart from their educational value, these events increased the prestige of St. Basil's and secured the financial support of members of the Catholic bourgeoisie in northern France, to which Omez and Dumont belonged.[13] While 28 candidates to the

10 For the history of St. Basil's, in her research Laura Pettinaroli has supplemented the archives of Istina with those of the Vatican, which we had not been able to consult; see Laura Pettinaroli, *La politique russe du Saint-Siège (1905–1939)*, Rome, École française de Rome, 2015, 430–434, 627–629.

11 For more on this pious man, see my entry in the *Dictionnaire biographique des frères prêcheurs*, available at <https://journals.openedition.org/dominicains/1931> (accessed Mar 14, 2022).

12 Omez was born in Tourcoing in 1892, Dumont in Valenciennes in 1897.

13 Supporters included Vladimir Dloussky, Viktor Richter, Paulin-Gérard Scolardi, and Alexandre Spassky, to whom we may add Lev Gedenov, who received part of his training in Lille; see Constantin Simon, *Pro Russia:*

priesthood attended the seminary, four ordinations were rewarded to the new leadership for their efforts, who were joined in 1927 by Father Antoine-Léon Hubatzek, born in Lille but of Czech origin.

The seminary's poor reputation nevertheless persisted, and the number of Russian emigrants with a suitable vocation was rapidly exhausted. It thus proved necessary to organize regular prospecting missions on the Baltic, Finnish, or Polish fringes of the Soviet Union, which had turned out to be inaccessible and tougher than expected, in order to allow the Dominicans of St. Basil's to approach Orthodox territories. The rare vocations awakened by these missions were frequently only Russian in name, and accordingly short-lived. Aware of the impasse, Father Omez and his associates began to cover their backs. In 1927, a study center thus discretely appeared in the shadow of St. Basil's; its name, Istina, Russian for religious truth, is merely a translation of the order's motto: *Veritas*.[14] Resolutely Dominican, it set out to document Russia's glorious Christian past as well as its fate since the Bolshevik Revolution. Its ultimate aim was to lay the groundwork for a change of course that would place the entire undertaking in a less explicitly missionary perspective than that of the seminary.

However, the team's primary agenda was still to keep it alive, a task that became even more difficult after the opening of the Collegium Russicum in Rome, entrusted to the Jesuits, in 1929. The blessing of the iconostasis and the formation of a choir completed the installation of the chapel, which held its first solemn service of Slavic rite before the public of Lille on Jul 3, 1928. Year after year, it then hosted liturgical celebrations that achieved a certain popularity thanks to the clarity of Father Hubatzek's translations and the goodwill of the local press. The limited amount of space in rue de la Barre soon proved insufficient. Having now gathered enough experience, the team of St. Basil's offered the monasteries, colleges, societies, and parishes of the region, and then also of Belgium and northern France, a program of liturgies and conferences accompanied by screenings that generated a real enthusiasm and contributed in a significant way to the Eastern awakening of the Latin congregations. The Congress of the 50th anniversary of the Eucharistic congresses inaugurated in Lille in 1881, held in Lille in 1931, is viewed as the culmination of this "Oriental circus":[15] it included a solemn service of Slavic rite and a synoptic speech by Father Omez on the Eastern churches and Christian unity.[16]

By appealing to the mystical riches of the Russian soul and the horrors of antireligious persecution, this first initiation sought to create an emotional bond on the basis of both the Eastern tradition and contemporary events. The veneration of the Feodorovskaya Icon of the Mother of God, a recent copy of which St. Basil's prided itself on possessing, provided the support of Marian devotion. Without leaving the path of unionism, which hoped that the promotion of the Slavic rite would lead to a wholesale conversion of Russia, the Dominicans of Lille proposed a soft variant that avoided offending Orthodox circles. The three-pronged approach "knowing, loving, praying," presented by Father Omez at the congress of Lille, did in fact involve a threefold examination of conscience: a better knowledge of Eastern Christianity to prevent the reduction of Catholicism to the sole Latin rite; the love of the separated Christians to preclude the denigration of their values and religious customs; and fervent prayer to transcend confessional interests in the one truth. The application of such principles would afford a nuanced view of the communities that were then qualified as dissident,

The Russicum and Catholic Work for Russia, Rome, PIO, 2009, 251–267.

14 First outlined in a project drawn up by Omez and dated May 5, 1927; first public mention in a printed invitation from June 1929; see Pettinaroli, *La politique*, 720–721.

15 An expression used by Father Hubatzek in a testimony offered to the present author in November 1969.

16 Henri-Jean Omez, *Les Églises d'Orient et l'unité chrétienne: Rapport présenté au Congrès Eucharistique de lille le 3 juillet 1931*, Paris/Boulogne-sur-Seine, Centre d'Études Istina, 1931.

whose defects could not obscure their rich spiritual heritage. An appreciation of Russian religious philosophy does not prevent one from deploring its "enlightenment," nor does it forbid one from praising the appropriateness of the encyclical *Mortalium animos* and the need for a magisterium in matters of faith.[17] From which followed the urgency of a "constructive apologetics" which, far from confronting the "dissidents" with their errors, was intended to persuade them to seek the fulfillment of their faith in the fold of Peter. In Lille, the frictions arising from a few conversions and mixed marriages did not tarnish the cordial relations with the Orthodox parish. However, the gap opened up between St. Basil's missionary vocation and the position taken externally by its representatives, a discrepancy that furthered the cause of its detractors, with a Jesuit from Lille named Michel d'Herbigny at their head, then all-powerful in Rome in matters of unionism as president of the Pro Russia commission.

A misstep on the part of Father Omez precipitated his fall. Curious to observe firsthand what was then happening in the Soviet Union, he took advantage of an opportunity to spend fifteen days there incognito in November 1931. Having left as one who viewed the "socialist paradise" with skepticism, he returned, if not convinced, as many other travelers had been at the time, then at least positively surprised by the Promethean efforts to develop the country and by the ardent zeal displayed by its young generation, with whom he was able to enter into contact thanks to his knowledge of Russian. In private conversations upon returning to France he thus conveyed balanced and by no means unsympathetic impressions that disconcerted the bourgeois audiences of the north and the French authorities, and even more so the Vatican leadership which, having not been consulted on the appropriateness of the journey, had prescribed discretion in this regard. This exhortation to caution had been reiterated by Msgr. Michel d'Herbigny and Pope Pius XI himself during the audience granted to Omez in January 1934. On Jun 24, 1932, the General Curia of the Order of Preachers called upon the provincial of France to remove the "culprit" from Lille. After a brief attempt to contest the decision, believing that he had been forbidden to write about his journey but not to talk about it, Father Omez finally complied, leaving the management of the moribund seminary to Father Dumont. Monsignor d'Herbigny made of Omez his last victim, getting rid of a man who had long tarnished his visibility, yet falling irrevocably into disgrace the following year in turn. In the very midst of the Roman reaction to the Stalinist purges, this discrepancy in the assessment of Soviet realities could not be tolerated: the imprudent actions of Father Omez precipitated his fall.[18]

A first, partial explanation for the paucity of historiography on the Istina center thus lies in its origins, which reveal a trauma that is all the more painful because it has not been healed. Unlike Dom Lambert Beauduin, who was brutally removed from Amay at the same time and under similar circumstances, Father Omez died in 1968 without ever having regained the smallest apostolate pertaining to Russia. Can it be that one of the key reasons for the silence on Istina lies in the impossibility, for the victims of the crisis of 1932, and especially for Father Dumont, to mourn this trauma and thus to objectify this early rift?

17 Pius XI, *Mortalium animos*, in: *AAS* 20, 1928, 5–16, which strongly condemns the nascent ecumenical movement. See in the first volume of this work the chapter by Marie Levant.

18 Léon Tretjakewisch was more severe in his judgement of the French Jesuit (see his *Bishop Michel d'Herbigny SJ and Russia: A Pre-Ecumenical Approach to Christian Unity*, Würzburg, Augustinus-Verlag, 1990, 222–228) than either Antoine Wenger in *Rome et Moscou (1900–1950)*, Paris, Desclée de Brouwer, 1987, 58–359 or Pettinaroli in *La politique*, 726–727, although the latter two do not exonerate Father Omez from all responsibility for his woes; an overview of the currently accessible evidence is provided in: Étienne Fouilloux, "Un dominicain français en Russie soviétique (1931)," *ASSR* 181, 2018, 265–283.

3 Russia and Christianity

Initially tempted to retreat to Le Saulchoir or Juvisy in order to further his Eastern specialization, Father Dumont was forced to clear up an entangled situation. His solidarity with Father Omez did not withstand the separation: realizing how slim the chances of collaboration within a Dominican team were, the deposed superior, who had books and information sent to him, urged his friend to leave St. Basil's and did not accept what he considered to be vain obstinacy, without fully understanding the constraints under which his former assistant had to work.[19] In fact, Rome's desire to maintain a welcoming center for Catholics of Byzantine-Slavic rite in northern France significantly reduced Dumont's room for maneuver, who nevertheless preserved St. Basil's from being transformed into a boarding school for Russian children. His counterproposal regarding the possibility of carrying on the work of the Istina study center outside of Lille having been rejected by Pius XI and by Msgr. d'Herbigny, he had no choice but to accept the solution prescribed by the Pro Russia commission on Mar 20, 1933: the seminary was to be closed, certainly, but the team in Lille was to be maintained for the pastoral care of the Russians of Eastern rite, under the responsibility of Cardinal Liénart, and for intellectual work in preparation for sending Dominicans to Russia, once this proved possible. A clause in the contract precipitated the end of the Omez-Dumont friendship: the Holy See considered itself the owner of the premises at 59 rue de la Barre, a claim that included the objects of daily or liturgical use and the library. Following a last-ditch struggle, the Dominican Order obtained the right to distinguish between donations to St. Basil's and donations to the Dominican Order's treasury, which were to be managed by Le Saulchoir. The motu proprio from December 1934, which put the house back under the supervision of the Congregation for the Oriental Churches, rather than the Pro Russia commission, confirmed this partition: the books and files remained Dominican property.[20]

Until 1947, the house retained this mixed status that kept it under a triple tutelage. That of the Roman authorities, which became less strict with the dismissal of Msgr. d'Herbigny, turned into open support when Father Dumont won the confidence of Cardinal Eugène Tisserant, who had been appointed secretary of the Congregation for the Oriental Churches in 1936.[21] That of the local ordinary, to whom Rome delegated its powers in matters concerning the Russian apostolate, was not particularly bothersome – Cardinal Liénart in Lille (until 1936), the auxiliary bishops of Paris who were responsible for foreigners, Msgr. Emmanuel-Anatole-Raphaël Chaptal and later Roger Beaussart, did not withhold support for Istina. And that of the order, finally, which continued to build up the team with a parsimony that was not entirely unjustified; none of the friars assigned to the team adapted easily to the specific tasks of the house, beginning with the learning of Russian; more importantly, none of them could long endure the austere and secretive leadership of Father Dumont, to whom the institute secretary Simone Dandois pledged his unfailing loyalty.

A second explanation for the lack of historical scholarship on Istina is that the trauma of 1932 left an indelible mark on Father Dumont, thereby further reinforcing his own reserved temperament. It would prompt him to surround his later work with jealous secrecy in order to better protect himself from publicity that was felt to be damaging. And as it turned out, Istina's further development

19 In his entry "Omez" for the encyclopedia *Catholicisme*, however, Dumont still thinks that he was "ousted without just cause" (fascicle published in 1983, col. 83).

20 Pettinaroli, *La politique*, 627–629.

21 "If the nomination of Msgr. Tisserand [sic] to the Oriental [Congregation] is confirmed, it would be very fortunate, since he is a great friend of the order and an enthusiastic reader of *La Vie intellectuelle*," wrote Dumont to Hubatzek on May 22, 1936; furthermore, he sent the cardinal a warm letter of congratulations on Jun 18, when the news was confirmed.

subsequently became closely interwoven with the biography of Father Dumont, for 35 years…

Neither the small number of St. Basil's parishioners from Lille nor the budgetary headaches – Father Omez's dismissal having led certain private donors to withdraw their support – were able to prevent the spectacular resurgence that occurred as early as spring 1933. After months of uncertainty, the "Oriental circus" resumed its tours, which had become ever more essential, under the direction of Father Hubatzek, although the latter was not able to celebrate liturgies in the Slavic rite until 1937. Articles describing St. Basil's work, new liturgical translations, and bulletins sent to the newspapers all perfected an already proven script, which also gained additional facets through the close relations that Hubatzerk developed with artistic, emigrant circles: on Oct 26, 1934, no longer content with accompanying religious services or enlivening certain liturgical feasts in northern France, the Dominican friar and his choir marked the 70th birthday of the Russian composer Alexander Gretchaninov by inaugurating a series of concerts that were praised by music lovers and local radio stations alike. Two months later, Istina lent its support to the Ikona society, which had organized an exhibition that had found great success, be it in Paris, Lille, or later in Strasbourg. After this, the move to Paris gave rise to a number of adaptation difficulties: the strong influence of the Russian-Catholic parish, the hardships of the times, and, occasionally, a certain degree of saturation were detrimental to the success of the tireless outreach efforts. The Eastern education of those who entertained close relations with Istina was assured through the establishment, in May 1933, of a prayer association for Russia. Each month, it submitted to its members a proposal to be developed at a venue or in a printed leaflet; although the latter was subject to periodic interruptions, Father Hubatzek's conferences for the society's members continued to be held in Paris until the spring of 1939.

Istina's activities were boosted by the arrival in Lille, in September 1934, of a prestigious collaborator: the converted historian and philosopher Julia Nikolaievna Danzas, a Dominican tertiary who had been rescued from the Soviet camps. The quality of her information and her passion for the task enabled Father Dumont to pursue the ambitious publishing program begun under the leadership of Father Omez. In 1934, the publishing house Éditions du Cerf accepted a monthly page on the USSR in the weekly newspaper *Sept*, as well as a bimonthly section entitled "Russia and Christianity" in *La Vie intellectuelle*, of which 14 appeared in the journal from Apr 10, 1934, to Nov 25, 1936. They simultaneously provided the material for its namesake journal *Russie et Chrétienté*, the first issue of which came out in April 1934; its title is said to have been conceived by Dominique Mesnard, who was briefly assigned to St. Basil's.[22] In 1935, 800 copies of the journal were printed for 500 subscriptions. It was soon supplemented by a book series entitled Istina, which was inaugurated with *Bagne rouge*,[23] the first woman's testimony on the Gulag, in which Julia Danzas gave a striking account of her experiences in various concentration camps, from Irkutsk to the Solovetsky Islands.[24] While the religious persecutions continued unabated in the USSR, shattering all hopes of missionary penetration, her competencies steered the work of the Istina center in the direction of a high-quality Sovietology, albeit one devoid of lenience, as it was not only based on the scrutiny of the official press and the monitoring of emigration but also on her own painful experiences at the hands of the new regime. Religious topics were nevertheless not neglected, far from it: in 1935, Julia Danzas published a

22 Yves-Dominique Mesnard, *Mes racines sont dans la mer*, Paris, France-Empire, 1982.

23 Julia N. Danzas, *Bagne rouge: Souvenirs d'une prisonnière au pays des Soviets*, Juvisy, Cerf, 1935.

24 Her name is not mentioned, but the short introduction signed "Istina" leaves no doubt as to her authorship. The scholar of Slavic studies Michel Niqueux has reconstructed her astonishing journey and unearthed numerous unpublished texts in the biography *Julia Danzas, de la cour impériale au bagne rouge*, Geneva, Éditions des Syrtes, 2020.

remarkable book entitled *L'itinéraire religieux de la conscience russe*,[25] which was followed, in 1938, by the seminal thesis of the Slavonic scholar Pierre Pascal on the schism of the old believers.[26] In the same year, the center took over the responsibility for its book series from the Éditions du Cerf, as well as for its journal *Russie et Chrétienté*, which was now independent of *La Vie intellectuelle* and published on a quarterly basis, though in a larger format.

Only the apostolate to the emigrants failed to make any progress in Lille. In countless reports, Father Dumont underscored how the modest number of Russians in northern France, and their mistrust of St. Basil's, reduced the success of its pastoral efforts to little more than nothing, with only about 15 people attending the regular services owing to the paucity of conversions. Moreover, the old idea of relocating to Paris, an influential center of Russian emigration, finally gained ground: the agreement of Aug 15, 1936, between the archdiocese of Paris and the Dominican province of France, placed the friars in charge of the Russian Catholic mission of rue François-Gérard, in the 16th Parisian arrondissement. The quality of their liturgy office, sermons, and spiritual assistance earned them a reputable success that was prolonged, in January 1938, by the monthly bulletin *Bessedy* (Interviews), and crowned soon thereafter by the Marian events – an exhibition, a triduum of prayer, and study days – that took place thanks to their initiative. "Our mission is rapidly expanding," affirmed Father Dumont, who was promoted to the rank of an archimandrite in the spring of 1938.

From a doctrinal point of view, Istina's output was in many ways characterized by a very conventional unionism. The center focused exclusively on the Christian East, which, for Father Dumont, found itself, *vis-à-vis* Catholicism, in a situation "totally different from the confessions that issued from the Reformation."[27] Protestantism was thus removed from the agenda, as was its extension, the emerging ecumenical movement. By virtue of its calling, Istina was primarily concerned with Russia, albeit without setting it apart from its religious environment: Father Dumont honored the invitation sent by the organizers of the first International Conference of Orthodox Theology, which convened in Athens in 1936. This unionism, which clearly subordinated spiritual harmony to the protection of religion, was more rigid than that of Father Omez. Deeply marked by the crisis that had led to the latter's departure, Dumont thought it necessary to increase the dose of anticommunism in order to rehabilitate Istina in Rome. For nearly two years, almost every leaflet published by the society and a significant number of issues of its journal described the flaws of Soviet society and denounced the atheism of the USSR. Little by little, however, the thoroughness of a first-hand documentation in contrast to easy polemics introduced indispensable nuances and led to the adoption of a detached view that caught the attention of the historian Aline Coutrot in the pages of *Sept*.[28] The treatment of "Holy Russia" and of its vicissitudes under the red star was somewhat adversely affected by such prioritizing of Soviet matters: *Russie et Chrétienté* waited until 1937 to launch a column on the life of the Orthodox communities in the USSR and another on those of the emigrants.

Few texts directly address the issue of divisions among Christians. Their perspective remains that of the return to the Roman fold, either individually or collectively, which is presented as an increasingly probable scenario since the revolutions of 1917. With their occasional conversions of Russians, and given the impossibility of penetrating Russia

25 Julia N. Danzas, *L'itinéraire religieux de la conscience russe*, Juvisy, Cerf, 1935.

26 Pierre Pascal, *Avvakum et les débuts du Raskol: La crise religieuse au XVIIe siècle en Russie*, Paris, Centre d'études russes Istina, 1938.

27 Christophe-Jean Dumont, *Pour l'Unité du monde chrétien: Le Centre d'Études Russes Istina* 19, 52, 1937, 90.

28 Aline Coutrot, *Un courant de pensée catholique, l'hebdomadaire "Sept" (mars 1934–août 1937)*, Paris, Cerf, 1961, 181–185.

itself, the Dominicans of Istina made the penetration of the emigrant community into one of their main objectives: the total circulation of *Bessedy*, of which 1,200 copies were printed, largely exceeded the number of people who regularly attended the services of the church in rue François-Gérard. However, its success cannot be explained without specifying that it was written in a peaceful tone and spirit. For Istina, the move to Paris was indeed an opportunity to return to the doctrine of Father Omez, a trend that had already set in towards the end of the Lille period. The weakness of the anticommunist front and the dissipation of the "Russian mirage" prompted the center to be wary of the risks of political contamination.[29] Moreover, the reactions of the emigrant intelligentsia led to the realization that an aggressive apologetics would be counterproductive. Dumont and Hubatzek accordingly began to reevaluate the Greco-Slavic dissents. Although they did not disrupt the Roman unity, they seriously undermined its catholicity. However, this did not prevent it from sharing a rich dogmatic and liturgical legacy with the mother church, in the face of which divergences that were viewed as minor, or at times even as the result of misunderstandings, appeared quite pale in comparison. The only thing that really separated Eastern and Western Christianity was an incompatibility of religious temperament, which had been exacerbated by history. All these positions were dear to the nascent Catholic ecumenism, notably to Father Yves Congar, who congratulated himself on a development that he himself had largely triggered with the publication of his main work, *Chrétiens désunis*, in 1937.[30] Father Dumont had actually been one of the censors who reviewed the book.

However, the method employed somewhat lagged behind these theological advances. A desire for loyalty did indeed imply the reconsideration of an approach to Orthodoxy that had often been blackened for the sake of the unionist cause; it entailed a symmetric struggle against the caricatures of Catholicism that circulated among emigrants, notably the assimilation of believers to the Latin rite: only the complete dismantling of mutual prejudices would be able to create a climate that was conducive to a rapprochement with the Russian diaspora. However, the concern for doctrinal integrity, along with the directives issued by the Vatican, made it very difficult to establish interconfessional relations: out of caution, Father Dumont contented himself with sporadic or discrete contacts, both with the youth movements and with the artistic circles of the emigrant community. "Irenic without lapsing into irenicism," this cautious approach was alarmed by the bold initiatives of Paul Couturier, a priest from Lyon, or of Dom Clément Lialine, a monk of Amay. Although Dumont was opposed to proselytism, he did not spurn defectors and held on to the hope of strengthening Russian catholicity. At the outbreak of World War II, the Istina center was balanced between its unionist mold, which it had divested of its domineering complacency, and a fledgling ecumenism that it hesitated to embrace.

Although Father Dumont escaped mobilization in 1940, this was not the case for Hubatzek, who was taken prisoner and did not rejoin Istina upon his return from captivity in 1941. As for Julia Danzas, she left Paris for Rome, where she died in 1942. Cardinal Tisserant then assigned the Russian priest Alexander Kulik to rue François-Gérard; while the Jesuits of the St. George Boarding School in Namur, who had taken refuge in Paris and were housed in the vicinity of rue François-Gérard, assisted father Dumont in his parish duties. Until the end of the war, however, the responsibility for Istina rested on his shoulders. In conditions marked by discretion and deprivation, he

29 Dumont nevertheless attended, in Switzerland, three sessions of the International Commission Pro Deo, an interdenominational organization dedicated to combatting the antireligious propaganda emanating from the Soviet Union (1934, 1935 and 1937).

30 Marie-Joseph Congar, *Chrétiens désunis: Principes d'un "œcuménisme" catholique*, Paris, Cerf, 1937; ET: *Divided Christendom: A Catholic Study of the Problem of Reunion*, trans. Muad A. Bousfield, London, Bles, 1939.

continued his patient work to promote an awareness of Eastern Christianity among the Parisian believers. Just when the USSR, owing to its decisive contribution to the fall of Nazism, made a strong comeback on the stage of international relations and in the consciousness of the Western world, the extensive information work carried out by Istina since 1927 finally bore fruit: armed with the accumulated firsthand documentation and to its informal contacts within the emigrant circles, the center was operational when Joseph Stalin's resurrection of the Moscow Patriarchate inaugurated a new phase in the relations between Western and Eastern Christians. All the collected intelligence, notably on the visits of Russian hierarchs to Paris, was passed on to the Roman Congregation for the Oriental Churches, of which Istina became one of the most reliable sources of information. At the same time, Father Dumont continued to expose the false or inaccurate ideas that circulated about the USSR.

Precisely that was the goal of the journal *Russie et Chrétienté*, which reappeared in 1946. Each of its issues provided translations of numerous original documents that were difficult to access, as well as authoritative reports on religious developments in Russia and in the emigrant community. Taken in charge again by the Éditions du Cerf, the journal struggled to regain its quarterly publication frequency of prewar years and soon began to feel the adverse effects of the Cold War: due to its structural deficits, it was discontinued by Cerf in 1947 and finally cancelled three years later. The book series Russie et chrétienté, published by the same editor, suffered a comparable fate in spite of a brief, prosperous phase illustrated by four hitherto unpublished works of high quality.[31] After the loss of his means of publication, Father Dumont could only make himself heard through the speeches and articles he was asked for, notably by his colleagues from Économie et Humanisme: the information provided on these occasions is still of the highest quality, but it is less abundant and more scattered.

The problems inherent to Istina were joined by the difficulties arising from its partnership with the Russian-Catholic parish in Paris: the latter mobilized too many forces for meager results and dissuaded eventual Orthodox discussion partners from entering into regular contact with "converters of Russians." Consequently, Father Dumont decided to ask the Congregation for the Oriental Churches to make these two poles of activity independent of each other. Cardinal Tisserant not only accepted the proposal but also supported it: the congregation itself purchased the large house chosen by Father Dumont in Boulogne-sur-Seine. The move was completed on May 16, 1947, and the responsibility for the congregation in rue François-Gérard was handed over to the successor appointed by Rome, Father Paul Gretchichkine. In February 1948, the cardinal archbishop of Paris, Emmanuel Suhard, inaugurated the chapel of Eastern rite at 25 boulevard d'Auteuil in Boulogne. In his dealings with the supervisory authorities, however, Father Dumont was very insistent that the Russian character of the institution be maintained. Moreover, he continued to attend the gatherings of Russian priests, as for instance that of Rome in November 1946. Notwithstanding this, the disassociation of the Istina center from the apostolate among the Russian emigrants marked a second, though now decisive step in its slow transition from unionism to ecumenism.

4 The Bridge to Ecumenism

This renewed change of direction took place in the midst of serious difficulties, notably with regard to funding: in its operational activities, the Istina center suffered from chronic deficits

31 Michel de Taube, *Rome et la Russie avant l'invasion des Tatars (IXe–XIIIe siècles)*, Paris, Cerf, 1947; Nicolas Arseniev, *La sainte Moscou: Tableau de la vie religieuse et intellectuelle russe au XIXe siècle*, Paris, Cerf, 1948; Archimandrite Spiridon, *Mes missions en Sibérie: Souvenirs d'un moine orthodoxe russe*, Paris, Cerf, 1950; Élisabeth Behr-Sigel, *Prière et sainteté dans l'Église russe*, Paris, Cerf, 1950.

and was only able to survive thanks to the regular and extraordinary subsidies that it received from the Congregation for the Oriental Churches. The gravest problems, however, concerned the staff: the carousel of short-lived appointments continued to play out around Father Dumont and his secretary, Simone Dandois. The two most humiliating failures involved the Dominican friar Irénée-Henri Dalmais (1946–1948) and the Marist Brother Maurice Villain, for whom the transition from the spiritual movement of Abbé Couturier to Father Dumont's leadership (1948–1949) proved impossible. It was not until the arrival of Father Marie-Joseph Le Guillou in 1952, and of the Romanian Friar Jean Goia in 1954, that Father Dumont was finally able to rely on permanent Dominican collaborators.

The influence that Istina acquired through its conversion to ecumenism is all the more remarkable. Having for a time believed that the collapse of the Soviet Union under the weight of the German assaults would lend renewed pertinence to the constitution of a branch of Byzantine rite within the Dominican Order,[32] Father Dumont rapidly became disenchanted. The passing of nearly the whole of Slavic Orthodoxy under the control of the Moscow Patriarchate, a major religious consequence of World War II, and the subsequent involvement of the patriarchate in the Cold War spelled the end of all hopes for an East-West rapprochement that had been raised in the final phase of the conflict and since the liberation. It was then that a preexisting idea was able to reappear in full light after having been overshadowed by the Eastern priority, namely, that of a lineage between the schisms of the 16th and 11th centuries. The Reformation that took place in the midst of Western Christianity had only occurred because the latter had been stripped, for almost 500 years, of that part of its original legacy that has been preserved in the East. Under these conditions, the focus on one or the other schism makes little sense: as a globally relevant issue, the unity of the separated Christians must be addressed at the global level. This was the line of argumentation adopted by Father Dumont on numerous occasions to justify Istina's involvement in ecumenism, which became evident from 1948 onwards, although traces of it had appeared at an earlier date. Indeed, the center had already developed an interest in the January Octave of Prayer for Christian Unity during the war years, although its perspective was quite different from that of Abbé Couturier. Father Dumont was one of the chief organizers of the Parisian celebrations from January 1942 to January 1948, whereupon he handed over his responsibilities to the diocesan service for foreign communities. He was also invited to speak at the Octave of Unity, both in France and abroad, even though he was not a particularly good orator. Most importantly, in 1942 he accepted the responsibility for a modest study circle in which he had his first opportunity to meet Protestants. In March 1948, the tradition of the "first Sundays" of Istina was begun in Boulogne: following the liturgy and Father Dumont's homily, monthly presentations prepared by the foremost specialists evoked the key points of current ecumenical affairs. Apart from Dumont himself, the speakers included Louis Bouyer, Yves Congar, Clément Lialine, Robert Rouquette and Maurice Villain. They were soon joined by two young Dominicans, Maurice René Beaupère and François Biot, who founded the Centre Saint-Irénée in 1953, Istina's little brother in Lyon, which would make a name for itself by organizing ecumenical trips, inaugurated in 1961 by a pilgrimage to the Holy Land, and by offering spiritual assistance to confessionally mixed couples. These activities were backed by the newsletters *Foyers mixtes* (1968) and *Chrétiens en marche* (1971), as well as by an impressive specialized library.[33] By late 1948, the mimeographed bulletin

32 "Rapport sur la constitution dans l'Ordre des Frères Prêcheurs d'une branche de rite byzantin," undated (1942?), 11 typewritten pages.

33 The library joined with the Henri de Lubac Library of the Catholic University of Lyon in 2017. On the birth of the Centre Saint-Irénée, see Étienne Fouilloux, "Une

Vers l'Unité chrétienne reiterated the substance of these meetings. The main voice of Istina's commitment to ecumenism, it provided high-quality information on the development of the ecumenical movement and on that of the Reformation confessions that could not appear in *Russie et Chrétienté*. From 1954 onwards, ecumenical training sessions for priests and laypeople rounded out the program. The comparison between the bulletin's prosperity and the journal's chronic deficit proved to Father Dumont that there was perhaps a public interest in ecumenism, whereas the desire to keep informed on Russian and Eastern affairs had greatly subsided. At the crossroads of this realization and of the now firmly anchored belief in the indivisibility of the issue of unity, the quarterly journal *Istina*, launched in 1954, marks the conclusion of the long journey that had led the center and its director from the "Russian mirage" to the reunification of Christianity conceived as a whole. The four sections that made up the new journal illustrate the successive stages of this evolution: "Russie et chrétiente," "Chrétientés orientales," "Orient et Occident," and "Problèmes de l'œcuménisme,".

The latter explains the discrete initiation, for the very first time, of regular talks with the Parisian representatives of the separated communities, which included: a circle of a rather pastoral nature in the case of the emigrants who had remained loyal to the Moscow Patriarchate; a circle of a more doctrinal character in the case of the instructors from the Institut de théologie orthodoxe Saint-Serge in Paris, the flagship of the exarchate of the Ecumenical Patriarchate, whose activities culminated in two colloquies, at the Abbey of Le Saulchoir, one on the *Filioque* of the Creed (1950) and one on the primacy of Peter (1953); and finally a circle of Lutheran pastors from the French capital. The close cooperation between Father Congar and Father Dumont soon extended Istina's influence beyond this local context. Unsettled by rumors of a condemnation of Catholic ecumenism that had come to his ears during a brief stay in Rome in the spring of 1946, the theologian from Le Saulchoir persuaded Dumont to address a "Note sur le movement catholique en faveur de l'unité chrétienne" to his most attentive dialogue partner, Msgr. Giovanni Battista Montini, pro-secretary of the Secretariat of State. Jointly drafted by the two Dominicans, but signed by Dumont alone and dated Dec 15, 1946, it pleaded in favor of a recognition of this movement by the Holy See, but failed to elicit a tangible response. The two friends then suffered a double setback: the meeting of the Catholics engaged in the work of unity, which had been scheduled to take place at their invitation in April 1947 at a seminary school in the vicinity of Le Saulchoir, was called off at the last minute due to an indiscretion; what is more, none of those whom they had chosen to observe the constitutive meeting of the WCC in Amsterdam, in the summer of 1948, obtained the necessary permission from Rome.

On the other hand, no obstacles were put in the way of the first unofficial meeting between the leadership team of the WCC and the group of Catholic theologians associated with Istina. The meeting was held in Boulogne in September 1949 and pastor Willem Visser 't Hooft, secretary general of the Genevan council, later noted that it had not been without consequences for the definition the council gave of itself at the meeting of its central committee in Toronto the following year.[34] Once again, Istina was chosen, this time by the Council on Foreign Relations of the Church of England for a meeting between these same theologians and some of the most prominent Anglican "scholars" on Apr 14–15, 1950. Father Dumont's caution with regard to the substance of the talks, and his discretion regarding the form in

affaire lyonnaise: La succession de l'abbé Couturier," *Chrétiens et Sociétés* 18, 2011, 105–135; see also the testimony of Maurice René Beaupère, *Nous avons cheminé ensemble: Un itinéraire œcuménique: Entretiens avec Béatrice Soltner*, Lyon, Olivétan, 2012.

34 Willem Adolf Visser 't Hooft, *Memoirs*, London, SCM Press, 1973.

which they were held, enabled Istina to assume an important function, namely that of a hosting venue for the first steps in a high-level ecumenical dialogue that was only just beginning to take shape in the early 1950s. The Dominican friar's balanced approach made his presence indispensable in numerous delicate situations. He thus lent a hand to the drafting of the conclusions reached at the conference of Catholic unionists and ecumenists at the Abbey of Grottaferrata, under Roman supervision and in a relatively tense atmosphere (Sep 19–22, 1950). Acting in a private capacity, he took part in the Orthodox boat trip on the occasion of the 19th centenary of St. Paul's preaching in Greece, which allowed him to establish contacts for the future (Jun 15–29, 1951). Istina organized a new meeting with the leaders of the WCC, at Presinge in Switzerland, on the topic of the *vestigia ecclesiae* (Nov 14–16, 1951). Dumont drew up the conclusions to the first CCEQ,[35] in which he played a key role alongside the Dutch organizers Johannes Willebrands and Frans Thijssen (Fribourg in Switzerland, Aug 11–13, 1952). He assisted in the capacity of a journalist at the third world conference of the Faith and Order commission, the doctrinal branch of the WCC (Lund, Aug 15–28, 1952). The role of Istina's director in interconfessional relations had probably never been as crucial as during these first, hesitant und entirely unpublicized approaches between 1949 and 1952.

From 1952 onward, and until the establishment of the Roman SPCU in June 1960, the CCEQ replaced Istina as the focal point of unofficial contacts with both the Genevan council and the churches and communities that belonged to it. Father Dumont paid close attention to its work, which Istina then took up, especially when it concerned the topics of the conferences and meetings of the developing ecumenical movement; however, he was no longer the key mediator in exchanges that were increasing in number and diversifying. This did not prevent him from continuing to play a role of his own, notably in the direction of the Greek East, since the relations with the Slavic East remained frozen. Invited to preach the Week of Prayer for Christian Unity in Istanbul in January 1953, he seized the opportunity to meet with Patriarch Athenagoras, with whom he began a promising dialogue.[36] In 1954, at the urging of Father Congar, Dumont collected various texts highlighting the coherence of a line of thinking that was both frank and unwavering even though it did not come from a professional theologian, publishing the results in the book series Unam Sanctam under the title *Les Voies de l'unité chrétienne*.[37] He also attended the second general assembly of the WCC, which convened in Evanston, near Chicago, during the summer of that same year, albeit as a journalist and not as an observer since the local ecclesiastical authority did not accept any observers. In May–June 1956, he undertook a long journey that took him first to Athens, where Father Marie-Joseph Le Guilloux would spend the 1956/1957 academic year, then to Istanbul, where he strengthened his ties with Patriarch Athenagoras, and finally to Geneva, the seat of the WCC.[38]

35 Mauro Velati, *Una difficile transizione: Il cattolicesimo tra unionismo ed ecumenismo (1952–1964)*, Bologna, Il Mulino, 1996; Peter De Mey, "Précurseur du Secrétariat pour l'Unité: Le travail œcuménique de la 'Conférence Catholique pour les questions œcuméniques (1952–1963),'" in: Gilles Routhier, Philippe Roy & Karim Schelkens, eds., *La théologie catholique entre intransigeance et renouveau: La réception des mouvements préconciliaires à Vatican II*, Louvain-la-Neuve/Leuven, Collège Érasme/Universiteitsbibliotheek, 2011, 271–308.

36 Valeria Martano, *Athenagoras, il patriarca (1886–1972): Un cristiano fra crisi della coabitazione e utopia ecumenica*, Bologna, Il Mulino, 1996.

37 Christophe-Jean Dumont, *Les voies de l'unité chrétienne: Doctrine et spiritualité*, Paris, Cerf, 1954.

38 "Relation d'un voyage accompli par le P. Dumont o. p., directeur du Centre d'Études 'Istina' à Athènes, Istanbul et Genève (mai–juin 1956)," Jun 29, 1956, 24 typewritten pages (with the handwritten annotation "confidential").

Istina and its director could thus not fail to rejoice at Pope John XXIII's announcement in January 1959 of the convocation of the 21st general council of the Catholic Church, one of the objectives of which was none other than the rapprochement of divided Christians. The years 1959–1960 were indeed prosperous ones for the center: even though the journal *Istina*, with its roughly 400 subscribers, was still plagued by deficits, the success of *Vers l'Unité chrétienne* was undeniable and justified the shift to a printed format in early 1959, with a print run of 1,500 copies. In 1960, Father Le Guillou published his monumental work *Mission et unité* in the series Unam Sanctam:[39] Father Dumont now had a theologian of international renown to assist him. In fact, it was in Istina and by the hand of Father Dumont that the greater part of the note of the CCEQ "Sur l'aménagement des relations entre l'Église catholique et les Églises séparées en vue de la restauration de l'unité" was drafted.[40] Dated June 1959 and encouraged by the papal initiative, it develops arguments in favor of Catholic participation in the ecumenical dialogue, which had been maturing for years, from the perspective of the council. Its limited but targeted diffusion, both in Rome and among the bishops, earned it a sizable readership.[41]

5 A Missed Consecration?

Father Dumont and his center thus seemed destined to play an important role in the preparation of the council. It was then that an unfortunate mishap occurred that came to be remembered as the "Rhodes incident." For the first time in its brief existence, the WCC convened its central committee on Orthodox territory, from Aug 19 to Aug 28, 1959. Father Dumont had been invited to attend as an observer, along with Johannes Willebrands and other Catholic specialists. For some time already, the French Dominican and a number of Greek, university theologians had been planning a bilateral meeting. As it had not been possible to hold this meeting before the Rhodes session, it had been postponed to Aug 21. Its Greek organizer, Professor Vasileios Ioannidis, not only failed to inform Geneva of this decision but even invited nearly the entire Greek delegation that was to attend the session of the central committee: some 50 prelates and prominent personalities. At the same time, some of the press referred to this evening as the beginning of talks between the Catholic Church and the Eastern churches; an official meeting was even announced for the following year in Venice. The leadership of the WCC, particularly its secretary general Visser 't Hooft, were furious. They accused the Catholic guests in general, and Father Dumont in particular, of having taken advantage of the Rhodes meeting to engage in factional activities that would bring back the days of unionism: the establishment of privileged ties between Rome and the East to the detriment of the predominantly Anglo-Protestant ecumenical movement – and this in the very context of the initial contacts that were to allow the Slavic churches under Soviet tutorship to join the Genevan council of churches, a membership that would become effective at its third assembly in New Delhi, in 1961. The criticism fell just short of accusing Father Dumont and his Greek dialogue partners of wanting to sabotage these preliminary negotiations, even though they had been discrete. This had, of course, not been the intention of Istina's director. Conciliatory statements were released that would ease the tension relatively quickly.[42]

39 Marie-Joseph Le Guillou, *Mission et unité: Les exigences de la communion*, 2 vols., Paris, Cerf, 1960.

40 But in cooperation with Rome's man of confidence in ecumenical matters, the Jesuit Charles Boyer of the Pontifical Gregorian University.

41 Giuseppe Alberigo, "Á l'aube de l'œcuménisme catholique," in: *Homo religiosus: Autour de Jean Delumeau*, Paris, Fayard, 1997, 714–720.

42 In addition to the recollections of the two main protagonists, Dumont and Visser't Hooft, see also Johannes G.M. Willebrands, "La rencontre de Rhodes," *VUCh*

The incident nevertheless put the finger on a real problem. Before New Delhi, the Eastern churches felt somewhat overwhelmed in the midst of the ecumenical council, in which a religious atmosphere of Protestant inspiration prevailed. Accordingly, some of their representatives may have been tempted not to stake everything on one card. Moreover, Father Dumont, whose commitment to ecumenism was undeniable, remained marked by a long history of unionism that he did not deny. He made no secret of his view that the Orthodox churches, with regard to the desired unity, were in a very different position from that of the Reformation churches and therefore deserved special treatment.

A further partial explanation for the paucity of historiography on Istina is thus that the aforementioned incident, in which the Dominican friar was not the sole active player but in which he was deeply involved, damaged his reputation by briefly calling his loyalty into question. While the convocation of the council appeared to be a good opportunity to hark back to the center's pioneering past on the subject of ecumenism, the Rhodes incident, which cast a shadow on its director, cut short any attempt at retrieving its memory.[43] Never again would Father Dumont regain the full confidence of the Genevan council, whose expanding relations with Rome would primarily take place via the Bea-Willebrands duo, who presided over the SPCU. Dumont undoubtedly became one of its influential members, and Istina played an active role at the origin of its French counterpart, but the incident increased his determination to assert the prominent rights of Eastern Christianity.

In July 1960, while the structures of the barely one-month-old secretariat were still ill-defined, he unsuccessfully pleaded with Cardinal Augustin Bea to create "two distinct organisms," one for the West, the other for the East, "which would demonstrate more clearly to the Orthodox that the Catholic Church very clearly distinguishes the nature of their separation from that of the Protestants: an almost total communion in faith and a structural identity in hierarchical and sacramental matters (validity of the priesthood, of the episcopacy, and of the Eucharist)";[44] he went on to give his support to the model of two departments within one and the same secretariat. He then expressed concern about the "conciliar agenda's overly exclusive orientation to an ecumenism polarized by the sole consideration of the churches stemming from the Protestant Reformation,"[45] and strove to set up a mixed working group between the Oriental Commission, a clone of the congregation of the same name, and the SPCU – but to no avail, as the former refused to even talk about it. It drew up its own decree on the basis of provisions and in terms whose insufficient ecumenical openness were publicly regretted by Dumont.[46]

The Istina center was well represented at the council: Father Le Guillou was a private expert in the service of Msgr. Matthieu Rougé, bishop of Nîmes. Father Dumont was an official expert of the SPCU. As such, he participated in the drafting of the decree on ecumenism, notably of paragraphs 14–18 of the third section, which are

13/1–2, 1960, 1–4; Jan Grootaers, *Rome et Genève à la croisée des chemins (1968–1972): Un ordre du jour inachevé*, Paris, Cerf, 2005, 49–51; and esp. Karim Schelkens, "L''affaire de Rhodes' au jour le jour: La correspondance inédite entre J.G.M. Willebrands et C.-J. Dumont," *Istina* 54/3, 2009, 253–277.

43 Yves Congar called for it in his ecumenical autobiography from 1964, but in vain: "Without seeking to be in the public eye, Father Dumont enjoyed the trust of all circles with whom he was called upon to work. ... He worked at the center of the tangle of relationships from which the web of Catholic ecumenism wove itself day after day, through bad and good periods. When history is written, it will be necessary to look in his direction, and I do not doubt that the records of Istina ... will then furnish an exceptionally rich documentation"; see Yves Congar, *Chrétiens en dialogue: Contributions catholiques à l'oecuménisme*, Paris, Cerf, 1964, xliv–xlv.

44 Note to Cardinal Bea from Jul 8, 1960, 2.

45 Dumont, "L'Église romaine," 199.

46 "Présentation du décret sur les Églises orientales," in *Documents conciliaires*, vol. 1, *L'Église, l'Œcuménisme, les Églises orientales*, Paris, Le Centurion, 1965, 225–232.

devoted to the Eastern churches that separated from Rome. However, he was still somewhat concerned about the direction taken by the council. There is no doubt that he was very pleased with the official endorsement of ecumenism by his church and with the gesture, crucial in his eyes, of the exchange of the kiss of peace between Paul VI and Athenagoras in Jerusalem in January 1964 and, even more importantly, the lifting of the mutual excommunications between Rome and Constantinople on Dec 7, 1965 – gestures that he witnessed with great emotion, and to which he had contributed significantly through his contacts with the Ecumenical Patriarchate in the early 1950s.[47] His legendary caution was nevertheless irked at the series of bold actions unleashed by the council, which seemed to him more harmful than beneficial to the cause of unity. Ever since the highly risky meeting of Grottaferrata in 1950, the Vatican authorities had learned to appreciate his careful judgment and the soundness of his doctrine. Accordingly, it came as no surprise that he was asked to go to Rome in 1967 in order to advise the Secretariat of State on matters relating to the rapprochement with the separated Christians. Father Dumont thus left the Istina center, to which he had dedicated 40 years of his life. His ecumenical situation underwent a dramatic change: having long been in an initiative position, he now assumed a supervisory function, as demonstrated in the late 1970s by his critical assessment of the Catholic Church's plan to join the ecumenical council.[48] Such a change of status did not fail to raise doubts among some of his former collaborators or associates. Thus began the final stage of the Dominican's career, which no longer had anything in common with the Istina center, with which he had identified himself for so many years. Moreover, his new function implied a duty of confidentiality that was hardly reconcilable with the drafting of memoirs. It was only after leaving office, in 1979, that he finally ventured to write his memoirs… though these cannot really be regarded as such, being rather a compilation of texts accumulated in the course of a long career that began in the service of unionism before shifting to ecumenism.

In the same year, 1967, Father Le Guillou founded the Institut supérieur d'études œcuméniques at the Institute catholique of Paris, thus reviving a stillborn project from 1950 under far more favorable circumstances. A new team under the leadership of Father Bernard-Dominique Dupuy secured the return of Istina to the Dominican fold in the new Parisian buildings of rue de la Glacière, in 1967–1968.[49] Unlike Father Dumont, Father Dupuy was a professional theologian and a disciple of Father Congar in ecclesiology. He boasted a philosophical culture that was superior to that of his teacher and had developed an interest in Judaism that would leave its mark on Istina's subsequent history. He thus assumed the leadership of a team that was much larger than any which Dumont had ever had. It is this team that would have to ride out the "Catholic crisis"[50] and the ecumenical turmoil of the 1970s, not, however, without internal friction. It was characterized by the coexistence of strong personalities whose later fortunes would contrast starkly with one another: some would abandon monastic life altogether (Xavier Charpe and Yves-Noël Lelouvier), while others would play an important role in the ecumenical movement (Albert-Marie de Monléon) or in the "restoration of order" that marked the papacy of John Paul II (Jean Miguel Garrigues).[51]

Translated from French to English by Robert Meyer.

47 Alberto Melloni, *Tempus Visitationis: L'intercomunione inaccaduta fra Roma e Costantinopoli*, Bologna, Il Mulino, 2019.

48 Grootaers, *Rome et Genève*, 51–56.

49 On this new phase of Istina's history, see the tribute to Bernard-Dominique Dupuy in the articles in *Istina* 55/3, 2010.

50 Denis Pelletier, *La crise catholique: Religion, société, politique en France (1965–1978)*, Paris, Payot, 2002.

51 See the latter's militant testimony, in Jean-Miguel Garrigues, *Par des sentiers resserrés: Itinéraire d'un religieux en des temps incertains*, Paris, Presses de la Renaissance, 2008.

Bibliography

Fouilloux, Étienne, *Les catholiques et l'unité chrétienne du XIXe au XXe siècle: Itinéraires européens d'expression française*, Paris, Le Centurion, 1982.

Fouilloux, Étienne, "Istina (1923–1967)," *Dictionnaire biographique des frères prêcheurs: Dominicains des provinces françaises (XIXe–XXe siècles)*, available at <https://journals.openedition.org/dominicains/1432>.

Grootaers, Jan, *Rome et Genève à la croisée des chemins (1968–1972): Un ordre du jour inachevé*, Paris, Cerf, 2005.

Mallèvre, Michel, "Les Dominicains français et la promotion de l'unité des chrétiens au XXe siècle: Engagements personnels et institutions," in: Nicole Bériou, André Vauchez & Michel Zink, eds., *Les Dominicains en France (XIIIe–XXe siècle)*, Paris, Académie des inscriptions et belles-lettres/Cerf, 2017, 483–502.

Pettinaroli, Laura, *La politique russe du Saint-Siège (1905–1939)*, Rome, École française de Rome, 2015.

Simon, Constantin, *Pro Russia: The Russicum and Catholic Work for Russia*, Rome, PIO, 2009.

Velati, Mauro, *Una difficile transizione: Il cattolicesimo tra unionismo ed ecumenismo (1952–1964)*, Bologna, Il Mulino, 1996

CHAPTER 4

The Debate on Ecumenism within Orthodoxy (1917–1948)

Adalberto Mainardi

1 Introduction: Church Unity and Orthodox Identity

In the first half of the 20th century, deepening relationships between Christians of various denominations provoked a turning point in Orthodox reflection on the church and Christian unity. The emergence of the ecumenical problem in Orthodoxy assumed the form of a workshop of ideas, methodologies, initiatives and interdenominational relations with specific characteristics. At the same time, the ecumenical question highlighted different ecclesiologies, bringing the definition of Orthodox identity back into play. During the 30-year period between 1917 and 1948 the Orthodox, and in particular Russian theologians in exile, were prominent players in the emerging ecumenical movement, which in turn stimulated Orthodox theological thought. The dates that I am conventionally taking as the *terminus a quo et ad quem* of this work correspond to watershed events at the historical and ecclesial levels. The first is the year of the Russian Revolution and of the founding of the Local Council of the Russian Orthodox Church. The second is the year of the founding of the WCC and the year when the council, convened in Moscow at the initiative of the Russian Orthodox Church, put the condemnation of the ecumenical movement on the agenda. Finally, both dates coincide with the radical political, social, and cultural rearrangements brought about by the two world wars.

The dissolution of the three great empires, Ottoman, Habsburg, and Russian, in which the majority of the Orthodox population had lived for centuries, drastically changed the Orthodox world's political and cultural references.[1] The genocide of the Armenian population; the pressure of the new Turkish government on the church of Constantinople, deprived of a majority of its faithful by the exchange of population between Greece and Turkey at the Lausanne conference in 1923; the Russian Civil War and the incipient religious persecution in the Soviet Union – all marked a highly dramatic moment for Christians in the East. The "only section of the Eastern community which was free from external pressures," as Nicolas Zernov observed, was that of the Russian exiles who, despite "having lost their right to speak officially in the name of their church, [had] recovered the inner freedom to decide on their policy in regard to the Christian West unaffected by state interference."[2]

The emigration of about one million Russians had transformed the abstract theological question of the relationship with other churches into a vital need to redefine the Orthodox ecclesial identity in a new context.[3] Daily mingling with Christians of other denominations obliged the exiles to face unprecedented problems, forcing them to set aside any feeling of self-sufficiency. "Our misfortune, emigration," recalled Metropolitan Eulogius (Georgievsky), "brought us into contact with a world that did not confess our faith ...

1 I mainly refer here to the Chalcedonian Orthodox churches. At the theological level, ecumenism in the Oriental Orthodox churches saw important developments in the second half of the 20th century.

2 Nicolas Zernov, "The Eastern Churches and the Ecumenical Movement in the Twentieth Century," in: *A History of the Ecumenical Movement 1517–1968*, vol. 1, Ruth Rouse & Stephen C. Neill, eds., *1517–1948*, Geneva, WCC Publications, ^{4}1993, 645–674, here 669.

3 See Antoine Arjakovsky, *La génération des penseurs religieux de l'émigration russe: La revue La Voie (Put') (1925–1940)*, Kiev/Paris, L'Esprit et la Lettre, 2002, 166. On the Russian emigration, see, Marc Raeff, *Russia Abroad: A Cultural History of the Russian Emigration (1919–1939)*, Oxford, Oxford University Press, 1990; and Nikita Struve, *Soixante-dix ans d'émigration russe (1919–1989)*, Paris, Fayard, 1996.

which obliged us to come out of our routine and isolation."[4]

The historiography on Orthodox ecumenism produced by the protagonists of the ecumenical movement has delivered two narratives. In the first, the Orthodox simply testify to the existence and truth of the one Church of Christ, which is the Orthodox Church. In the second, the manifestation of the desire for unity among Christians is seen as a spiritual event that requires dogmatic reflection in order to rethink the meaning of the church's unity. The two perspectives are reflected in the studies that Georges Florovsky and Nicolas Zernov prepared for the *History of the Ecumenical Movement* by Ruth Rouse and Stephen C. Neill that were devoted, respectively, to attempts at reunion from the 15th to the early 20th century and to the Eastern churches in the ecumenical movement between World War I and 1948.

Florovsky applied the interpretive framework he had tested in his reconstruction of Russian Orthodox theology in the modern age to the genealogy of ecumenism. To the extent that it assimilates philosophical, exegetical, and theological methods, as well as scientific conceptions and conceptual tools from the West, Orthodoxy loses itself in a "pseudomorphosis" (a term and concept borrowed from Oswald Spengler) that, while maintaining an exterior image of Orthodox piety, empties its soul.[5] Only a return to the spirit of the Greek Fathers would enable Orthodoxy to regain its identity and to clearly pose the central question of the ecumenical problem: "What is the universal church? And in what sense do schismatic bodies still belong to the church?"[6] It is a matter of understanding what church membership consists in, that is, of how to determine the boundaries of the church. The ecumenical task is to clarify "the + and the scope of those questions which the Orthodox were bound to ask, and will ask again and again."[7]

Zernov's essay, which replaced the contribution originally commissioned to the Bulgarian Stefan Tsankov, set the Russian diaspora's pioneers of ecumenism in the wake of the religious renaissance that had animated the Russian intelligentsia at the turn of the century and which had brought Orthodoxy and contemporary philosophy into dialogue.[8] In the ecumenical openness, they glimpsed an ecclesial event, a true *kairos* for Orthodox theology, and considered the "participation of Eastern Christians in the ecumenical event consonant with the true tradition of their church."[9]

The two visions of ecumenism corresponded to the two conceptions of the relationship between Orthodoxy and modernity. This was often characterized in terms of a "Modernist" current, which drew upon Vladimir Solovyov and was open to engaging with European philosophy and theology (in authors such as Sergius Bulgakov, Anton Kartashev, Boris Vysheslavtsev and Nicholas Berdyaev), or as a "neo-patristic" current (in Florovsky and Vladimir Lossky) aimed at revitalizing the perennial tradition of the church in opposition to what were seen as modern Western deviations.[10] This division, with its programmatic

4 Tatiana Manoukhina, ed., *Le chemin de ma vie. Mémoires du Métropolite Euloge*, Paris, Presses Saint Serge/Institut de théologie orthodoxe, 2005, 471.

5 Georges Florovsky, "The Orthodox Churches and the Ecumenical Movement prior to 1910," in: *A History of the Ecumenical Movement*, vol. 1, 171–215 (on "pseudomorphosis," see 182–187); see Georgi Florovsky, *Puti russkogo bogosloviya*, Paris, YMCA Press, [2]1981 ([1]1937); ET: Georges Florovsky, *The Collected Works*, vol. 5, ed. Richard S. Haugh, *Ways of Russian Theology: Part One*, Belmont MA, Nordland Publishing Company, 1979, and Florovsky, *The Collected Works*, vol. 6, *Ways of Russian Theology: Part Two*, ed. Richard S. Haugh, Vaduz, Büchervertriebsanstalt, 1987. For a criticism of the category of pseudomorphosis, see Dorothea Wendebourg, "'Pseudomorphosis': A Theological Judgement as an Axiom for Research in the History of Church and Theology," *GOTR* 42, 1997, 321–342.

6 Florovsky, "The Orthodox Churches," 214.

7 Florovsky, "The Orthodox Churches," 215.

8 See Nicolas Zernov, *The Russian Religious Renaissance of the Twentieth Century*, New York, Harper & Row, 1963.

9 Zernov, "The Eastern Churches," 673.

10 See, for example, Alexander Schmemann, "Russian Theology: 1920–1972, An Introductory Survey," *SVTQ* 16/4, 1972, 172–194, here 178; Peter A. Chamberas, "Georges Vasilievich Florovsky (1893–1979): Russian Intellectual Historian and Orthodox Theologian," *MA* 45/1, 2003, 49–66; Robert Bird, "The Tragedy of Russian Religious Philosophy: Sergei Bulgakov and the Future of Orthodox Theology," in: Jonathan Sutton & Wil van den Bercken, eds., *Orthodox Christianity and Contemporary Europe*, Leuven, Peeters, 2003, 211–228.

connotations, was not only projected onto an interpretation of the past but also had an effect on the present by polarizing intra-Orthodox debates on specific issues such as the limits of the church, dogmatic development and the possibility of intercommunion.

At the beginning of the 21st century, various aspects of research that might be grouped under the title of "deconstructing the myth of the Fathers" (among the émigrés) highlighted the limits of the above simplification.[11] Not only is there a constant study of the church Fathers in an author like Bulgakov, but the movement of a "return to the Fathers" is also indebted to Russian religious philosophy. The very idea of a neo-patristic "synthesis," notions such as those of the vision or spirit of the Fathers, of "a concrete experience of the divine," lead back through the philosophy of Pavel Florensky and Vladimir Solovyov to an idealist framework (Schelling) as mediated by the assimilation of Johann Adam Möhler's thought by the Slavophile school (Aleksey Khomyakov and Ivan Kireyevsky).[12]

Any exploration of the Orthodox contribution to the nascent ecumenical movement must take several factors into account, which will be covered in the following sections of this article. They include the experiences of dialogue and philosophical theological debate prior to the Russian Revolution, which was then woven into the Local Council of the Russian Orthodox Church in 1917–1918; the divisions and schisms that tore asunder the Russian Orthodox Church in the Soviet Union and in the diaspora after the Revolution; and the experience of Orthodox theologians, bishops and the laity in places of ecumenical exchange, in particular the Orthodox contribution to the world conferences on Faith and Order and Life and Work. It is in this complex tapestry that the ecumenical and ecclesiological visions of authors such as Sergius Bulgakov and Georges Florovsky, who played a leading role in the nascent ecumenical movement, are framed.

2 The Emergence of the Ecumenical Problem and the Moscow Council (1917–1918)

Between the 19th and 20th centuries, the Russian Orthodox Church underwent a significant period of theological confrontations and relations with Anglicans and Old Catholics.[13] In the dialogue with the former, the main obstacle was the

11 John Behr, "Passing Beyond the Neo-Patristic Synthesis," report to the international conference "Neo-Patristic Synthesis or Post-Patristic Theology: Can Orthodox Theology be Contextual?," Volos Academy of Theological Studies, Jun 3, 2010; Brandon Gallaher, "'Waiting for the Barbarians': Identity and Polemicism in the Neo-Patristic Synthesis of Georges Florovsky," *MT* 27/4, 2011, 659–691; Paul L. Gavrilyuk, *Georges Florovsky and the Russian Religious Renaissance: Changing Paradigms in Historical and Systematic Theology*, Oxford, Oxford University Press, 2013. On Florovsky, see also Andrew Blane, ed., *Georges Florovsky: Russian Intellectual, Orthodox Churchman*, Crestwood NY, St. Vladimir's Seminary Press, 1993; George Hunston Williams, "Father Georges Florovsky's Vision of Ecumenism," *GOTR* 41/2–3, 1996, 137–158. On Bulgakov, see in particular Catherine Evtuhov, *The Cross and the Sickle: Sergei Bulgakov and the Fate of Russian Religious Philosophy (1890–1920)*, Ithaca, Cornell University Press, 1997; Brandon Gallaher, "Bulgakov's Ecumenical Thought," *Sobornost* 24/1, 2002, 24–55; Antoine Arjakovsky, *Essai sur le père Serge Boulgakov (1871–1944): Philosophe et théologien chrétien*, Paris, Parole et Silence, 2006.

12 Yves Congar had already highlighted Khomyakov's debt to the Tübingen School: Yves Congar, "La pensée de Möhler et l'Ecclésiologie orthodoxe," *Irén* 12, 1935, 321–329.

13 See Florovsky, "The Orthodox Churches," 196–214; Bryn Geffert, *Eastern Orthodox and Anglicans: Diplomacy, Theology, and the Politics of Interwar Ecumenism*, Notre Dame, University of Notre Dame Press, 2010; Aidan Nichols, *Alban and Sergius: The Story of a Journal*, Leominster, Gracewing, 2018; Daniil A. Toporov, *Dialog Rossiyskoy Pravoslavnoy Tserkvi so Starokatolicheskim Dvizheniem vo vtoroy polovinye XIX–nachale XX veka* [Dialogue of the Russian Orthodox Church with the Old Catholic movement in the second half of the 19th to the early 20th century], Ph.D. thesis, Obshchetserkovnaya aspirantura i doktorantura imeni svyatykh ravnoapostolnykh Kirilla i Mefodiya, 2015.

question of the validity of Anglican ordinations. Paradoxically, the negative response of Leo XIII's *Apostolicae curae* in 1896 had reopened the debate. Professor Vasily Sokolov of the Moscow Theological Academy argued that, contrary to the pope's position, Anglican orders should be recognized by the Orthodox.[14] In short, two camps formed. In the first were those such as Chrestos Androutsos[15] and Metropolitan Antony (Khrapovitsky)[16] who considered it impossible to judge the validity of ordinations outside the church. In the second were those who considered it entirely possible to recognize a certain degree of "ecclesiality" in ecclesial communities separate from the Orthodox Church, a position that had an influential forerunner in Moscow Metropolitan Philaret (Drozdov).

In 1908, the fifth Lambeth conference decided to form a standing committee for relations with the Orthodox. In 1912, a society for the rapprochement of the Anglican Church and the Orthodox Church was formed in St. Petersburg; it would play a role at the council of 1917–1918.[17] The English societies for the study of the Christian East should not be overlooked either.[18] At an institutional level, it was in particular the Episcopalian Church in the United States that developed relations with the Russian Orthodox Church, which had existed in North America since the 18th century.[19]

As for the Old Catholics, contacts were initially established through the Society of the Friends of Spiritual Enlightenment, whose representatives participated in the Bonn conferences of 1874 and 1875.[20] A second, more doctrinally demanding phase of dialogue occurred in the 1890s when the Holy Council of the Russian Orthodox Church

14 See Vasily A. Sokolov, *Ierarkhiya anglikanskoy episkopalnoy tserkvi* [Hierarchy in the Anglican Episcopal Church], Sergiev Posad, Tipografya A.I. Snegirevoy, 1897; ET: *One Chapter from an Enquiry into the Hierarchy of the Anglican Episcopal Church*, London, The Church Printing Co., 1897. Similar conclusions were reached by Afanasii Bulgakov, whose work was translated into English as *The Question of Anglican Orders: In Respect to a "Vindication" of the Papal Decision*, trans. William J. Birkbeck, London, SPCK, 1899.

15 Chrestos Androutsos, *The Validity of English Ordinations from an Orthodox-Catholic Point of View*, trans. Frederick W. Groves Campbell, London, Grant Richards, 1909. The Greek original was published in 1903. See Geffert, *Eastern Orthodox and Anglicans*, 23–24.

16 Antony (Khrapovitsky), *Perepiska vysokopreosvyashchennogo Antoniya, arkhiepiskopa Kharkovskogo s predstavitelyami Episkopalnoy tserkvi v Amerike* [The most eminent Antony, archbishop of Kharkov, correspondence with representatives of the Episcopalian Church in America], Kharkov, Eparkhialnaya tipografiya, 1915, Hilarion (Troitsky) also intervened on the subject in defence of Antony's positions with a letter to Robert Gardiner in 1917 on the Faith and Order commission project: "Pismo g. Robertu Gardineru, sekretaryu komissii dlya ustroystva mirovoy konferentsii khristianstva" [Letter to Mr. Robert Gardiner, secretary of the commission organizing the world conference of Christianity], in: Hilarion (Troitsky), *Tvoreniya* [Works], vol. 3, *Tserkovno-publitsisticheskie trudy* [Ecclesiastical and publicistic works], Moscow, Sretensky monastyr, 2004, 495–540.

17 The purpose of the Russian Society for the Rapprochement of the Anglican Church with the Orthodox Church which was approved by the Holy Council according to its charter, was "to develop feelings of mutual esteem, understanding, and closeness between members of the Orthodox and Anglican Churches," and to "support and broaden the activity aimed at the reunification (*vossoedinenie*) of the Anglican Church with the Orthodox": *Ustav Russkago Obshchestva revniteley sblizheniya Anglikanskoy Tserkvi s Pravoslavnoyu* [Chart of the Russian Society for the Rapprochement of the Anglican Church with the Orthodox Church], St. Petersburg, Sinodalnaya, 1912, 1–2. As early as Apr 24, 1912, Ivan Pavlovich Sokolov gave the society a lecture on the validity of Anglican ordinations: "O deystvitelnosti anglikanskoy ierarkhii" [On the Validity of the Anglican Hierarchy], *Khristianskoe chtenie* 3, 1913, 374–400.

18 Nor should one overlook the Eastern Church Association, established in 1863–1864, and the Anglican and Eastern Orthodox Churches Union, established in 1906, which, on the eve of World War I, were later combined into the Anglican and Eastern Churches Association; see Nichols, *Alban and Sergius*, 6.

19 See Tim Noble, "Pravoslavná misie v Americe pred rokem 1920," in: Ivana Noble & others, eds., *Cesty pravoslavné teologie ve 20. století na Západ*, Brno, CDK, 2016, 109–156.

20 On this point, see the contribution by Franz Xaver Bischof in the first volume of this work.

established a specific commission for dialogue with Old Catholics, chaired by Archbishop Anthony (Vadkovsky) of Finland. It was at this stage that Vasily Bolotov presented his theses on the *Filioque*, "the most important contribution to the discussions"[21] on the position of Old Catholics and a milestone for Orthodox-Catholic dialogue.[22] Bolotov distinguished between dogmas and *theologoumena*, namely private theological opinions that enjoy a certain authority in the church because they are supported by the doctors of the church. The different arguments on the procession of the Holy Spirit in the East (as in Photius) or in the West (as in Augustine) had not disrupted communion among the churches, and therefore, as a *theologoumenon*, the *Filioque* could not, according to Bolotov, be considered an *impedimentum dirimens* to the reestablishment of communion with Old Catholics.[23]

The dialogue with Old Catholics outlined the ecclesiological problem: how is membership in the one church to be properly understood? The opinions of the Orthodox theologians who were engaged in dialogue diverged. There were those who considered the Old Catholics to belong to a true schism, which could only be healed by incorporation into the Orthodox Church (for example Patriarch Sergius (Stragorodsky) and Alexis Maltsev), and those who considered them a church whose Orthodoxy could be recognized and with whom communion could be reestablished without incorporating them in one of the historic Orthodox churches (for example Pavel Svetlov).[24]

The problem of unity with the Church of Rome was central to the concerns of literati and philosophers, from Dmitry Merezhkovsky to Vyacheslav Ivanov. Vladimir Solovyov's ecumenical thought is examined in another chapter.[25] Here it suffices to recall two aspects of his intellectual legacy that greatly conditioned – whether by affinity or opposition – Russian Orthodox thinkers in exile: the idea that all Christian doctrine depends on the "one fundamental dogma of divine revelation," the divine humanity of the incarnate word,[26] and the works on the development of dogma.[27] The contribution to reflection on Christian unity made by Russian religious philosophy, particularly Leo Mikhailovich Lopatin, Pavel Florensky, Nicholas Lossky and Nicholas Berdyaev, can be traced to Solovyov's theories.

Florensky expressed his most radical insights on ecumenism in a 1923 paper commenting on some of Lopatin's theses concerning a "World Union for the Rebirth of Christianity," over which much of the spirit of the Solovyov's *Three Conversations* hovers.[28] The ecumenical problem emerges here

---

21 Florovsky, "The Orthodox Churches," 208.

22 Irina G. Rusova, "Professor V.V. Bolotov and Roman Catholics," *Khristianskoe chtenie* 5, 2020, 5–53; Adalberto Mainardi, "Firenze vista da Mosca: Il Concilio di Ferrara-Firenze e la Chiesa ortodossa russa: Aspetti storiografici e implicazioni teologiche," in: Riccardo Burigana & Pierantonio Piatti, eds., *Un Concilio di oggi: La memoria, la recezione e il presente del Concilio di Firenze (1439–2019)*, Vatican City, Libreria Editrice Vaticana, 2022, 203–226.

23 Vasily V. Bolotov, *K voprosu o Filioque* [On the subject of *Filioque*], St. Petersburg, Merkusheva, 1914.

24 See Pavel Y. Svetlov, *Khristianskoe verouchenie v apologeticheskom izlozhenii* [Apologetic exposition of Christian doctrine], Kiev, Kul'zhenko, 1910.

25 See the contribution by Jeremy Pilch in the first volume of this work (esp. 212–219).

26 Vladimir S. Solovyov, *Istoriya i budushchnost teokratii (issledovanie vsemirno-istoricheskogo puti k istinnoy zhizni)* [History and future of theocracy: a study on the path of world history toward true life], in: Vladimir S. Solovyov, *Sobranie sochinenij* [Collected works], vol. 4, *1883–1887*, St. Petersburg, Obshchestvennaya polza, 1914, 295–296.

27 See Vladimir Soloviev, *Le développement dogmatique de l'église*, Paris, Desclée, 1991.

28 Pavel A. Florenskij, *Zapiska o khristianstve i kulture* [Note on Christianity and culture], in: Pavel A. Florensky, *Sochineniya* [Essays], vol. 2, Moscow, Mysl, 1996, 547–559. See Vladimir S. Solovyov, *Tri razgovora o voyne, progresse i kontse vsemirnoy istorii, so vkljucheniem kratkoy povesti ob antichriste i s prilozheniyam* [Three Conversations on War, Progress, and the End of World History, with a Brief Narrative of the Antichrist

as a problem of Christian culture threatened by Enlightenment ideology. Christian liturgy (the term "culture" deriving from *cultus*) as the union of the divine and the human in all its dimensions, he argued, is the key to unity.[29] The shared grounding in Christ is more important than the differences among Christians, which should not be eliminated but reconciled.[30] The patient work of conversion and spiritual regeneration is necessary, and every church must undertake it internally, for "no ecclesiastical chancery, no bureaucracy, and no diplomacy will inspire a unity of faith and love where there is none."[31] It is not ritual or even doctrinal differences that are "the real cause of the shattering of the Christian world, but a deep mutual disbelief at its core in faith in Christ, the Son of God who came in the flesh."[32] Unity is not achieved by neglecting the particularities and riches of each individual denomination. Indeed, for him, Christ's commandment of love would be broken if the concrete forms of a particular church's religious life were imposed on everyone.[33]

Florensky held that the narrow path between religious relativism and denominational identitarianism leads to the only possible solution to the problem of division: the conversion of each church to Christ's truth and the reality of liturgical life. It is essential that we recognize the work of the Spirit in other churches. "The Spirit is one, but the gifts are many; yet this awareness we have not made our own."[34] The exact meaning of the term "catholic" is not extensive or quantitative, for the Greek *katholikos*, first and foremost, indicates intensity and quality. Exclusivism with regard to other churches denies catholicity and leads to heresy. "Each church and confession, taken separately, reveals limitations, and in growing more rigid each one assumes the character of a cult. In contrast, the awareness of one's own limitedness and striving to complete one's gift with the gifts of others ... render each confession catholic."[35]

For Florensky, a catholic outlook coincides with the ability to penetrate the concrete forms of authentic religious life in each denomination.[36] The condition for unity in the Christian world is a change in thinking, a *metanoia* within each confession, which must abandon "the vain thought of its own riches and become firmly convinced that the immense treasure of the universal church" can be its own through Christ.[37] Florensky insisted on the problem of relations with the Church of Rome, particularly on "the primacy of honor and initiative at the Christian level that, by right, belongs to the bishop of Rome."[38] These elements would be found again in Sergius Bulgakov.

One of the most important events in the life of the Russian Orthodox Church, which affected the whole of Orthodoxy and drew the attention of the other Christian churches, was the Local Council (Pomestny Sobor) convened in 1917 after the abdication of the tsar and preparations spanning from 1905.[39] The council lay at the intersection

and with Appendices], St. Petersburg, Tipografiya Spb. T-va Trud, 1900; ET: *War and Christianity from the Russian Point of View: Three Conversations*, San Rafael, Semantron, 2007.

29 See Pavel A. Florenskij, *Filosofiya kul'ta* (*Opyt pravoslavnoy antropoditsei*) [Philosophy of cult (An essay in Orthodox anthropodicy)], Moscow, Akademichesky proekt, 2018. See also the contribution by Benedikt Kranemann & Adalberto Mainardi in the first volume of this work.

30 Florenskij, *Zapiska*, 552.

31 Florenskij, *Zapiska*, 552.

32 Florenskij, *Zapiska*, 552.

33 Florenskij, *Zapiska*, 553.

34 Florenskij, *Zapiska*, 555.

35 Florenskij, *Zapiska*, 555.

36 Florenskij, *Zapiska*, 556.

37 Florenskij, *Zapiska*, 558.

38 Florenskij, *Zapiska*, 558.

39 The decrees are published in Hilarion Alfeev, ed., "Concilium moscoviense 1917–1918," in: *COGD* 4/2, 2016, 734–881. See Günther Schulz, *Das Landeskonzil der Orthodoxen Kirche in Russland 1917/18 – ein unbekanntes Reformpotential*, Göttingen, Vandenhoeck & Ruprecht, 1995; Adalberto Mainardi, ed., *Il concilio di Mosca del 1917–1918: Atti dell'XI Convegno ecumenico internazionale di spiritualità ortodossa, sezione russa, Bose 18–20 settembre 2003*, Magnano, Qiqajon, 2004; Günther Schulz, Gisela-Afanasija Schröder & Timm C. Richter, eds., *Bolschewistische Herrschaft und orthodoxe Kirche*

of a complex reform movement in the Russian Church and civil society. One of the council's decisions that was most pregnant with consequences was the reestablishment of the patriarchate, two centuries after its suppression ordered by Peter the Great. In his remarks as a member of the council, Bulgakov foreshadowed the ecumenical significance of the patriarchate: at the end of the Constantinian era, the Russian Orthodox Church, along with the other churches, was called upon to face "the fundamental disease of the entire Christian world, the division between the Eastern and Western churches, which cannot fail to cause constant pain in the hearts of Christians."[40] Patriarch Tikhon (Bellavin), who had cultivated important relationships with the Episcopal Church during his tenure in North America (1898–1907), was elected. During the course of its work, the council decided on the establishment of a specific commission "on the union of the heterodox churches with the Orthodox church."[41] At the institutional level of ecumenical commitment, the council's decision to tackle the problem of Christian unity can be compared to the Patriarchate of Constantinople's encyclical of 1920.[42]

Among the reasons given for the commission's formation was the danger of atheism that "threatened not a single Christian denomination, but all Christianity."[43] Archbishop Evdokim (Meschersky) of the Aleutian Islands and North America,[44] the chairman of the commission, called less for work on ideal formulations about Christian unity and more concrete proposals taking into account the state of relations with Old Catholics, Anglicans, and Catholics.[45] The final report reflected this orientation, but the committee's discussions were broader. Positions ranged from the most open (including the president himself) to the most pessimistic.[46] Anton Kartashev, last ober-procurator of the Holy Council and first

in Russland: das Landeskonzil 1917–1918: Quellen und Analysen, Münster, LIT, 2005; Hyacinthe Destivelle, *The Moscow Council (1917–1918): The Creation of the Conciliar Institutions of the Russian Orthodox Church*, eds. Michael Plekon & Vitaly Permiakov, Notre Dame, University of Notre Dame Press, 2015.

40 Sergii N. Bulgakov, "Smysl patriarshestva v Rossi: Prilozheniye 1 k Deyaniyu 31" [The Significance of the patriarchate in Russia, Appendix 1 of the Proceedings no. 31], in: Aleksy Kolcherin & Aleksandr Mramornov, eds., *Dokumenty Svyashchennogo Sobora Pravoslavnoy Rossiyskoy Tserkvi 1917–1918* [Documents of the Holy Council of the Russian Orthodox Church from 1917–1918], vol. 5, *Deyaniya Sobora s 1-go po 36-e* [Proceedings of the council 1–36], Moscow, Izd. Novospasskogo monastyrya, 2015, 796–711, here 711.

41 See Günther Schulz, "Der Ausschuß für die Vereinigung der Kirchen des Landeskonzils der Orthodoxen Kirche in Rußland 3./16.8. bis 7./20.9.1918," *Kirche im Osten* 39, 1996, 70–100; Destivelle, *The Moscow Council*, 121–123; Aleksandr I. Mramornov, "Voprosy mezhdunarodnykh i mezhtserkovnykh otnosheniy na Svyashchennom Sobore Pravoslavnoy Rossiyskoy tserkvi 1917–1918 gg." [Issues of International and Inter-ecclesial Relations in the Holy Council of the Russian Orthodox Church of 1917–1918], *Vestnik MGIMO-Universiteta/Mgimo Review of International Relations* 66, 3, 2019, 176–201.

42 On this, see the contribution by Stylianos Tsompanidis in the first volume of this work.

43 "Zayavlenie ob obrazovaniem Otdela po voprosam mezhtsekovnykh kontaktov" [Petition for the Establishment of a Commission on Inter-church Contacts], Jul 19–Aug 1, 1918, in: GARF, F. 3431, op. 1, d. 494, f. 1, typescript. See also Günther Schulz, "Dokumente zu Ökumenischen Bezügen des Landeskonzils der Orthodoxen Kirche in Rußland 1917/18 und zu der Arbeit seines Ausschusses 'Vereinigung der Kirchen,'" *Kirche im Osten* 39, 1996, 189–191. (I thank Aleksandr Mramornov for providing me with the transcript of the committee minutes.)

44 He was born Vasily Ivanovich Meshchersky. In 1922, he joined the Renovationist schism and the following year was elected president of the Supreme Church Administration of the Renovated Church. He wrote a book on religious life in America: *Religioznaya zhizn v Amerike* [Religious Life in America], Sergiev Posad, Tipografiya Troitse-Sergievoy Lavry, 1915. For further reading, see Dmitry N. Nikitin, "Evdokim (Meshchersky)," in: *Pravoslavnaya Entsiklopediya* [Orthodox encyclopaedia], vol. 17, Moscow, Tsentr Pravoslavnaya Entsiklopediya, 2008, 115–117.

45 GARF, F. 3431, op. 1, d. 495, ff. 3–5v, typescript.

46 Bishop Simon (Shleev) pointed out how, in "The book of Patriarch Cyril" of 1644 (a controversial collection published under Tsar Michael I of Russia) the Latins were presented in the bleakest terms and that, in theology textbooks, they were "attributing doctrines to

minister of religion in the Russian Provisional Government, did not hide his pessimism concerning Christian unity, which he considered "practically and psychologically impossible and, even if not harmful, useless." However, the problem of Christian unity had to be brought before the Christian conscience because of the spread of nationalism: the renewal of European culture rooted in Christian fundamentals had to be close to the heart of the Russian Church.[47] Bishop Simon (Shleev) went further, calling for "a firm union, not backing away even from sharing prayer with the heterodox. Only by awakening friendship and love in their hearts can we hope to restore theological union (*edinenie*) with them."[48]

The society for the rapprochement of the Anglican Church with the Orthodox Church sent a letter to the patriarch, which was forwarded to the commission on Aug 31–Sep 13, 1918. "In these days of the most terrible world war," it reads, "the believer begins more and more to long painfully for Christian brotherhood, Christian love and the unity of the whole Christian world."[49] The letter, calling for the "long hoped-for time when Christians will indeed form one fraternal family under the leadership of our Lord Jesus Christ,"[50] proposed that the names of three hundred saints from England, Ireland, and Scotland be included in the new edition of the Russian Orthodox Church's *Synaxarium*, and that they be celebrated "on All Saints Sunday" according to the rite of one of the "ancient liturgies" of the Church of England (excluding "later Latin innovations").[51]

There was not enough time for the text of the resolution approved by the commission to be considered by the assembly of bishops before the council was interrupted, and it was thus not included in the collection of decrees. The resolution referred to the relations already established with Old Catholics and Anglicans ("The Holy Council ... joyfully considers the sincere efforts of Old Catholics and Anglicans for union [*k edineniyu*] with the Orthodox church") and called for the creation of a permanent commission within the Holy Council on the "future study of questions concerning the Old Catholics and Anglicans in the hope of overcoming the difficulties on the road to unity (*k edineniyu*)."[52] As Hyacinthe Destivelle points out, it is anachronistic to speak of "ecumenism" regarding the commission's work with respect to its motivation (a defense against militant atheism), its goal (jurisdictional reunification, *edinenie*, rather than unity in communion, *edinstvo*), or its means (bilateral dialogue with a doctrinally related church).[53] Nevertheless, the very fact that the Council had raised the issue of Christian unity and reached a decision shows how the problem of unity had attained full maturity in ecclesial consciousness. In their ecumenical efforts, the theologians of the diaspora would refer to the decisions of the council.

3 The Jurisdictional Fragmentation of the Russian Diaspora: The Places of Intellectual and Ecumenical Exchange

"When I left Russia," confessed Nicolas Zernov, "I was convinced that the only true church was the Orthodox Church and that all Christians in the West were victims of error. But after meeting the heterodox face to face I gradually changed

Catholics that they do not profess at all. We must correct and purify our books." GARF F. 3431, op. 1, d. 495, f. 5.

47 GARF F. 3431, op. 1, d. 495, f. 28–28v.

48 GARF F. 3431, op. 1, d. 495, f. 57.

49 GARF F. 3431, op. 1, d. 495, ff. 8–10. Among the letter's signatories was Metropolitan Benjamin (Kazansky) of Petrograd, who was sentenced to death by the Bolsheviks in 1922 and canonized in 1992.

50 GARF F. 3431, op. 1, d. 495, ff. 8–10.

51 GARF F. 3431, op. 1, d. 495, f. 10.

52 *Dokumenty Svyashchennogo Sobora* [Documents of the Holy Council], vol. 3, *Protokoly Svyashchennogo Sobora* [Protocols of the Holy Council], ed. Aleksy Kolcherin & Aleksandr Mramornov, Moscow, Izd. Novospasskogo monastyrya, 2014, 740 (Protocol of Sep 7–20, 1918). See Destivelle, *The Moscow Council*, 123.

53 Destivelle, *The Moscow Council*, 123.

my convictions."[54] The encounter with Western Christianity marked the transition from controversy to dialogue for an entire generation, for whom the church was no longer identified with a, now surpassed, historical model of Orthodoxy. In the years when leading figures of the Russian diaspora were taking part in the ecumenical initiatives of Life and Work (Stockholm 1925) and Faith and Order (Lausanne 1927), the Russian Orthodox Church in the diaspora was experiencing a series of internal divisions, shaped by the political situation.

During the Civil War, Patriarch Tikhon had already authorized the autonomy of the SEA of Southern Russia, which, after the rout of the White Army, reconstituted itself as the SEA abroad. Metropolitan Antony (Khrapovitsky) was elected primate at the ecclesiastical assembly of all Russian emigration (VRCS) that was held in Sremski Karlovci near Belgrade in November and December 1921. Metropolitan Antony, who had exchanged correspondence with Gardiner before the war and had maintained relations with the Anglicans,[55] viewed the recognition of Anglican orders by Patriarch of Constantinople Meletios IV (Metaxakis) in 1922 with concern. Only a council could settle such a question and the Russian Orthodox Church could not be excluded from it.[56]

The openly anti-Soviet stance of the Karlovci Synod led Patriarch Tikhon to appoint Metropolitan Eulogius (Georgievsky) head of the diaspora. The difference between the two souls of the Orthodox emigration – the Karlovci one, pro-monarchical, conservative, and distrustful of Western Christianity, and that headed by Eulogius, open to ecumenical contacts and engagement with contemporary culture – gradually grew until 1926 when the Karlovci Synod excommunicated Metropolitan Eulogius. The Moscow Patriarchate, struggling with internal schisms itself, was unable to intervene in the jurisdictional conflict that divided the Russian Orthodox diaspora.[57]

Upon the death of Patriarch Tikhon in 1925, the Bolshevik government would not allow the election of a successor, and the *locum tenens* of the patriarchal throne, Metropolitan Peter (Polyansky) of Krutitsy, was placed under arrest. In 1927, in an attempt to ensure the church's survival, the vicar of the *locum tenens* to the patriarchal throne, Sergius (Stragorodsky), signed a controversial declaration recognizing the Soviet state and declaring his loyalty to it.

This step by Metropolitan Sergius sealed a schism between Moscow and the ROCOR (Karlovci Synod). Metropolitan Eulogius, who had first defended Sergius's declaration as a choice for

54 Nicolas Zernov, *Sunset Years: A Russian Pilgrim in the West*, London, Fellowship of St. Alban and St. Sergius, 1983, 87, quoted in Nichols, *Alban and Sergius*, 17.

55 Antony (Khrapovitsky), *Perepiska*; Troitsky, *Pismo g. Robertu Gardineru.*

56 Patriarch Meletios' decision, followed only by the Church of Cyprus and Patriarch Damian of Jerusalem, aroused unease within Orthodoxy and was short lived. In 1923, Meletios was forced from the patriarchal throne by the Turkish government and, in order to preserve the patriarchate in Constantinople, British diplomacy did not defend him. On the political implications of the recognition of Anglican orders and the different reactions in the English Church, divided between Anglo-Catholics and Protestants, see Geffert, *Eastern Orthodox and Anglicans*, 86–99. On the relations between Constantinople and Moscow in interwar period, see: Mikhail Shkarovsky, *Konstantinopol'skaya i Russkaya Tserkov' v period velikikh potryaseniy (1910-e–1950-e gg.)* [The Church of Constantinople and the Russian Church during the great upheavals (1910s–1950s)], Moscow, Poznanie, 2019.

57 Struve, *Soixante-dix ans*, 71. On the schisms of the Russian Church during the soviet era, see Dimitry Pospielovsky, *The Russian Church under the Soviet Regime, 1917–1982*, vol. 1, Crestwood NY, St. Vladimir's Seminary Press, 1984; Ilya Solovyov, ed., *Obnovlencheskiy raskol: Materialy dlya tserkovno-istoricheskoy i kanonicheskoy kharakteristiki* [The Renovationist schism: documents for a historical-ecclesial and canonical overview], Moscow, Obshchestvo lyubiteley tserkovnoy istorii, 2002. On the Russian Orthodox Church outside Russia, see Andrey Kostryukov, *Russkaya Zarubezhnaya Tserkov' v 1925–1938 gg: Yurisdiktsionnye konflikty i otnosheniya s Moskovskoy tserkovnoy vlast'yu* [The Russian Church Abroad, 1925–1938: Jurisdictional conflicts and relations with Moscow church authorities], Moscow, Izd. PSTGU, 2011.

political neutrality, found himself at the center of opposing pressures as religious persecution in the Soviet Union grew. On Jun 10, 1930, he was relieved of his duties by Metropolitan Sergius for taking part in a prayer for "the suffering Russian Church," which had been organized in London on Mar 16 of that year at the initiative of the Archbishop of Canterbury Cosmo Gordon Lang. With the support of most of the clergy and faithful, Eulogius refused to resign; on Jan 17, 1931, Patriarch Photius received him into the jurisdiction of Constantinople with the erection of an autonomous archbishopric for the Russian Orthodox in Europe. Eulogius intended this as a temporary administrative break with Moscow, caused by the political emergency. Sergius, however, suspended him and his clergy *a divinis*. A minority of the emigres, including Nicholas Berdyaev and Vladimir Lossky, decided to remain under Moscow's jurisdiction in order not to betray the persecuted church.[58]

The schism made the opposition between the two attitudes toward the issue of Christian unity more rigid. The intransigent wing saw no problem: "Heretics and schismatics have from time to time fallen away from the one indivisible church, and, by so doing, they ceased to be members of the church, but the church itself can never lose its unity according to Christ's promise."[59] Where the intransigent position saw a dangerous misunderstanding, others discerned a painful provocation for theological thought and ecclesial consciousness: if the church is one, how should the fact that there are Christians outside the church (a fact demonstrated by the Orthodox recognition of the validity of some sacraments administered by other churches) be understood? The ecumenical challenge set Orthodox theology on two directions: inwards, to clarify the foundations of its own ecclesiology, and outwards towards the Christian West, surpassing the apologetic spirit of the past in order to restate the essential content of Orthodoxy.

To carry out the dual function of training clergy and establishing the foundations of a renewed Orthodox ecclesial self-awareness, Metropolitan Eulogius decided to establish the Institut de théologie orthodoxe Saint-Serge in Paris, which opened in 1925.[60] The project obtained financial support from numerous American and European donors, including the Appeal for the Russian Clergy and Church Aid Fund, chaired by Bishop Henry Russell Wakefield of Birmingham, and the YMCA, chaired by John Raleigh Mott.[61] Bulgakov served as dean of the institute and taught dogmatics, while the faculty included Anton Kartashev (church history), George Fedotov (hagiography), Bishop Cassian (Bezobrazov) (exegesis), Georges Florovsky (patristics), Maria Skobtsova, Nicholas Berdyaev and Basil Zenkovsky (philosophy).

Another fundamental moment of unification for the Orthodox diaspora was the RSCM, which emerged before the revolution as an interdenominational movement on the model of similar

58 Radovan Pilipovich, "Tserkovnye gruppirovki russkoy emigratsii (1920–1940) mezhdu Belgradom i Konstantinopolem" [Ecclesial Groupings of the Russian Emigration, 1920–1940: Between Belgrade and Constantinople], in: *Stoletie dvukh emigratsiy: 1919–2019, Sbornik statey* [A century of two emigrations: 1919–2019, collection of articles], Moscow-Belgrade, Institut slavyanovedeniya RAN-Informatika, 2019, 193–218, esp. 210–211.

59 Antony (Khrapovitsky), *Opyt Khristianskogo Pravoslavnogo Katikhizisa* [An Essay in Orthodox Christian catechism], Sremskie Karlovtsy, s.n., 1924, 58, quoted in Zernov, "The Eastern Churches," 672. Metropolitan Sergius (Stragorodsky) shares the same views, although he admits "a certain communion" with the schismatics, evidenced by the different discipline of admission into the church of the heterodox (baptism, chrismation, or repentance): Sergius (Stragorodsky), "Otnoshenie Tserkvi Khristovoy k otdelivshimsya ot nee obshchestvam" [The attitude of the Church of Christ towards separated communities], *Zhurnal Moskovskoi Patriarkhii* 1/2, 1931, 5–7; 1/3, 1931, 3–6; 1/4, 1931, 3–7.

60 Manoukhina, ed., *Le chemin de ma vie*, 366–372.

61 Arjakovsky, *La génération des penseurs religieux*, 212–213; Gavrilyuk, *Georges Florovsky*, 127–128. On the Institut de théologie orthodoxe Saint-Serge, see Donald A. Lowrie, *Saint Sergius in Paris: The Orthodox Theological Institute*, London, SPCK, 1954; *L'Institut de Théologie Orthodoxe Saint-Serge: 70 ans de théologie orthodoxe à Paris*, Paris, Hervas, 1997. On John Mott and the YMCA, see the contribution by Sarah Scholl in the first volume of this work.

associations in the Protestant world. Later, it was reassembled in the various centers of the Russian diaspora (Prague, Belgrade, Sofia, Paris). At the Pšerov congress, from Oct 1 to Oct 7, 1923, the two souls of the movement, the interdenominational and the Orthodox, managed to find some unity, partly due to the prominent personalities of the generation of "professors" such as Sergius Bulgakov, Pavel Novgorodtsev, Anton Kartashev, Nicholas Berdyaev, and Basil Zenkovsky. Under the French acronym ACER (Action Chrétienne des Étudiants Russes), the movement was reestablished. Zenkovsky was elected president and Lev Liperovsky secretary. Despite the Orthodox overtones, the movement collaborated closely with the YMCA representatives. In June 1926, the Karlovci Synod forbade the faithful to work with the YMCA and WSCF, declaring them organizations hostile to the Orthodox Church and controlled by Freemasonry. The condemnation bewildered the movement's leaders and marked another step toward estrangement between the two souls of Orthodox emigration.[62]

The movement's journal, the *Vestnik Russkogo Studencheskogo Khristianskogo Dvizheniya* (The Messenger of the RSCM) provides an important overview of ecumenical encounters in the new generation of emigration. The journal's ecumenical character was due, in particular, to the work of Lev Zander and Nicolas Zernov. An editorial in a supplement dedicated to the unity of the churches that came out on the eve of the war took stock of the "ecumenical problem." While the phrase was new, "the thought it encompasses is ancient" and speaks "of our terrible, great sin – the division of Christ's church – and calls us to reunification (*k soedinenyu*)."[63] The responsibility for the reunification of churches should not be left to theologians or the hierarchy alone because all are members of the body of Christ. The first step in ecumenism is "*to recognize the sin of the division of the churches as our personal sin.*"[64] The second is "*to perceive ourselves as members of one ecclesial Body*, even if fractured, and to feel pain for those who are not in communion with us, to have interest in them and feel love for them."[65] The task of the journal and the student movement was precisely to "awaken the consciousness of ecclesial unity, to learn about the lives of other Christians," in order to overcome the reciprocal insensitivity to, and ignorance of, one another.[66]

Along with Saint-Serge, we should remember the ecumenical initiatives of Nicholas Berdyaev, who had obtained the YMCA's support in organizing the Académie de philosophie religieuse in Paris and in publishing the journal *Put*, which was an essential forum for intra-Orthodox discussion and debate with Western thought from 1925 until the war.[67] The Russian philosopher organized seminars in his home on topics of theology and religious philosophy, including some of the most ecumenically controversial, in which Orthodox, Protestants, and Catholics participated. The opportunities of exchange with Western Christianity, both formal and informal, contributed to breaking down fences, relinquishing prejudices and misunderstandings, and fostering a greater comprehension of complexity, a participation from within each other's Christianity. "Every confession," Berdyaev would say, "discovered a

62 Arjakovsky, *La génération des penseurs religieux*, 135–138; Geffert, *Eastern Orthodox and Anglicans*, 110–120.

63 [Lev Zander & Nicolas Zernov], "Ot redaktsii," *Ekumenicheskiy listok*, supplement of *Vestnik*: *Organ tserkovno-obshchestvennoy zhizni* 14/2, 1939, 1–2, here 1.

64 [Zander & Zernov], "Ot redaktsii," 1 (italics original).

65 [Zander & Zernov], "Ot redaktsii," 2 (italics original).

66 [Zander & Zernov], "Ot redaktsii," 2.

67 The notice introducing the journal read, "*La voie* is an organ of Russian Orthodox thought. It seeks to continue the tradition associated with the names of Khomiakov, Dostoevsky and Solovyov, and believes in the possibility of creative development within Orthodoxy ... It will acquaint Russians with the spiritual currents in Europe and the life and thought of other Christian denominations"; Arjakovsky, *La génération des penseurs religieux*, 121.

different and little-known world, which was nevertheless, the same Christian world."[68]

4 Orthodoxy in the Ecumenical Movement: The Lausanne Conference (1927)

One of the reasons for the Orthodox distrust of ecumenism was the problem of proselytism. It had been raised as early as 1920 in Geneva with the preparatory meeting of Faith and Order[69] and was brought up again in a moving speech by Nicholas Glubokovsky at the conference on Life and Work in Stockholm in 1925.[70] It was thanks to persistent behind-the-scenes mediation and the conviction of some Orthodox exponents such as Archbishop Germanos (Strenopoulos) of Thyateira that the Orthodox finally participated in the first world conference on Faith and Order.[71] In 1927 at Lausanne, 13 Eastern churches were represented, of which 11 were Chalcedonian.[72]

Metropolitan Germanos (Strenopoulos) of Thyateira,[73] who had led the Orthodox delegation to the conference on Life and Work in Stockholm in 1925, was one of the cochairs in Lausanne. He distinguished between a "narrow sense" of unity, among members of the same church community, and a broad one, inviting the development of the idea of this larger unity, in which each church, while forming a body of its own members, is a member of a larger body, within which all these members form the one body of our Lord. It rejected the idea (with an implicit reference to the Catholic doctrine of "return") "according to which one Church, regarding itself as the one true Church, insists that those who seek reunion with it shall enter its own realm."[74]

68 Arjakovsky, *La génération des penseurs religieux*, 180. In attendance at the meetings were the Orthodox Boris Vysheslavtsev, Anton Kartashev, Lev Karsavin, Sergius Bulgakov, Basil Zenkovsky, Nicolas Zernov, Georges Florovsky, as well as the Protestants Philippe Boegner, Wilfred Monod, Pierre Maury, Suzanne de Dietrich; and the Catholics Jacques Maritain, Fr. Luis Gillet, Fr. Pierre Batiffol, Fr. Lucien Laberthonnière, Emmanuel Mounier, and Gabriel Marcel. Orthodox initiatives were matched by cautious openings on the Catholic side, amidst the persistence of the unionist model and the first ecumenical steps. Here I mention only: the Velehrad conferences initiated by Metropolitan Andrey Sheptytsky among Catholics, Greek Catholics, and Slavic Orthodox (in 1907, 1909, 1911, 1924, 1927, 1932, and 1936, the proceedings of which were published in *Slavorum literae theologicae*); the work of the "monks of unity" of the monastery of Amay-Chevetogne, the Dominican Istina Center. See the contributions by Laura Pettinaroli and André Haquin in the first volume of this work, and the essay by Étienne Fouilloux "From Missions to Ecumenism: Istina" in this volume.

69 Tissington Tatlow, "The World Conference on Faith and Order," in: *A History of the Ecumenical Movement*, vol. 1, 405–441, here 418. On accusations of proselytizing, see, for example, Valery Vilinsky, "Puti katolicheskoy propagandy" [Paths of Catholic propaganda], *Vestnik: Organ RSChD* 3, 4, 1928, 29–31.

70 Constantin Patelos, ed., *The Orthodox Church in the Ecumenical Movement: Documents and Statements (1902–1975)*, Geneva, WCC Publications, 1978, 127–131.

71 See Tatlow, "The World Conference" and the contribution by Luca Ferracci in the first volume of this work.

72 The Ecumenical Patriarchate of Constantinople, the Patriarchate of Alexandria, the Patriarchate of Jerusalem, the churches of Greece, Cyprus, Romania, Serbia, Bulgaria, Russia, Poland, Georgia, the Armenian Church, and the Syriac Patriarchate of Antioch: Herbert Newell Bate, ed., *Faith and Order: Proceedings of the World Conference, Lausanne, August 3–21, 1927*, New York, George H. Doran Company, 1927, 528. The Moscow Patriarchate could not send delegates, and the Karlovci Synod refused to participate in the conference. The two Russian delegates, Metropolitan Eulogius (Georgievsky) and Sergius Bulgakov, had been co-opted by the organizers despite the absence of an explicit mandate from Moscow. Two other Russian exiles, Nicholas Glubokovsky and Nicholas Arsenev, were delegates from the Bulgarian Orthodox Church and the Polish Orthodox Church, respectively. See the list of members with corrections and additions in WCCA, 231.001, and the Continuation Committee leaflet, "List of Commissions Already Appointed," May 1, 1926, in: WCCA, 231.001.

73 On whom, see Yannick Provost, "Le métropolite Germain de Thyatire (1872–1951): Un grand précurseur orthodoxe du mouvement œcuménique," *Contacts* 64, 2012, 404–429.

74 Bate, ed., *Faith and Order*, 20.

Metropolitan Stefan of Sofia stressed that faith implies unity and also the constant concern for it.[75] Serbian Bishop Nicholas Velimirović spoke on the Orthodox doctrine of the sacraments.[76] In the sessions on ministry and the confession of faith, Sergius Bulgakov caused a minor scandal when he began to speak on the veneration of the Mother of God (*Theotokos*). The president interrupted him, urging him to keep to the theme. Bulgakov insisted and was later allowed to resume his speech: the humanity of Our Lord is inseparable "from that of his Mother, the unspotted *Theotokos*. She is the head of mankind in the Church; Mother and Bride of the Lamb." The Orthodox Church hoped that Christian unity in worship would be achieved "not so much through the common acceptance of liturgical forms as through the energy drawn out by the irresistible attraction of spiritual beauty."[77]

Before the plenary sessions ended on Aug 18, the Orthodox delegates read a declaration. They explained that, in addition to the preamble and the call to unity, they would only vote on the first of the Lausanne conference's final reports ("The Message of the Church to the World: The Gospel") and would abstain from voting on those on the nature of the church, a common confession of faith, and ministry and sacraments, the basis of which they deemed "inconsistent with the principles of the Orthodox Church which we represent."[78] The abstention reflected a split within the Orthodox delegates, especially between the more conservative Greeks and more liberal Russians, fueled by the fear that the concluding reports would form the basis of a "unified church." In matters of faith, there could be no compromise. The points of disagreement concerned the apostolic tradition as the necessary complement of scripture and the divine institution of ministry in the three degrees of the episcopacy, presbyterate, and diaconate.[79] In the absence of a totality of the faith, agreement on a few points did not allow *communio in sacris*: no principle of economy was applicable in this case. Reunification could only occur on the basis of the common confession of faith of the undivided church of the seven ecumenical councils. On the other hand, the Orthodox hoped for cooperation with the other churches in the social and moral spheres and declared that they held a positive view of a partial reunification of the churches with shared dogmatic principles, as such a union would simplify the discussion for future union with the Orthodox Church.

In a brief response, Charles Brent recalled that the conference's purpose was not to offer a sufficient basis for union, but the opportunity to define points of agreement and disagreement clearly. The Orthodox declaration frankly and peacefully offered this clarity, but he called on everyone, however (including the Orthodox) to be responsible in studying the others' positions honestly and without prejudice.[80]

The Orthodox declaration made a great impression. Arthur Headlam, the bishop of Gloucester, who was very critical of the Orthodox position (calling it "historically untenable"[81]), believed

75 Bate, ed., *Faith and Order*, 48–53.

76 Bate, ed., *Faith and Order*, 286–290. On the ecumenical efforts of Nicholas Velimirović, see Juljia Vidović, "Saint Nicholas Velimirovitch (1880–1956)," in: Pantelis Kalaitzidis & others, eds., *Orthodox Handbook on Ecumenism: Resources for Theological Education*, Oxford, Regnum Books International, 2014, 269–272.

77 Bate, ed., *Faith and Order*, 209. Bulgakov dedicated a monograph to Marian veneration: *Kupina neopalimaya: Opyt dogmaticheskago istolkovaniya nekotorykh chert v pravoslavnom pochitanii Bogomateri* [The burning bush: an example of a dogmatic interpretation of certain features in Orthodox veneration of the Mother of God], Paris, YMCA Press, 1927; ET: *The Burning Bush: On the Orthodox Veneration of the Mother of God*, trans. Thomas Allan Smith, Grand Rapids, Eerdmans, 2009. On Bulgakov's Mariology and the autobiographical aspects related to it, see Andrew Louth, "Father Sergii Bulgakov on the Mother of God," *SVTQ* 49, 2005, 145–164.

78 Bate, ed., *Faith and Order*, 383.

79 Bate, ed., *Faith and Order*, 382–387.

80 Bate, ed., *Faith and Order*, 387.

81 Bishop of Gloucester [A. Headlam], "The Lausanne Conference and the Orthodox Eastern Church," *The Christian East* 8/4, 1927, 184–189, here 189. See "The Orthodox at Lausanne: The Bishop of Gloucester's

however that it was partly for show ("what is sometimes called a gesture") to assure their faithful at home that the delegates had not betrayed the Orthodox faith.[82] In fact, Orthodox participation in the discussions continued with the same commitment and conviction. In many ways, direct acquaintance and exchange, resolving misunderstandings and misinterpretations, were worth more than the final text of the reports.[83] Interestingly, in his reply to the Lausanne reports, the Patriarch of Alexandria Meletios II (Metaxakis) referred to the declaration as a clear and unanimous expression of "the opinion of the Orthodox Church"; any other reply would have been superfluous since "the Orthodox Church, including all the diverse autocephalous bodies, has but one mind and one desire upon questions of the faith." A definitive answer on the matter, however, could only come from the pan-Orthodox Council, whose convocation Meletios hoped was imminent.[84]

The experience at Lausanne signified Orthodox involvement in the ecumenical movement and was seen positively by the theologians who took part.[85] Arguing against the encyclical *Mortalium animos* of 1928, which had frozen hopes for the Catholic Church's participation in the ecumenical movement, Bulgakov considered the conference on Faith and Order to be the revelation of a *novum*, namely, a movement toward the unity of believers in Christ, an event sparked in history by the Spirit, which demanded to be recognized, considered theologically, and lived out concretely in its consequences.

It was, first and foremost, an event to be acknowledged: "Something *had happened* and those who took part hold the responsibility of the memory of this spiritual *event*."[86] Lausanne was a spiritual experience that infinitely exceeded the meeting's modest theological results, because "it was perceived in a new way and with a new force that the whole Christian world believes and loves Jesus the Lord ... is spiritually nourished by the holy Gospel and the Word of God, with the Holy Spirit who lives in it."[87] The ecumenical movement as a spiritual experience was born upon a Trinitarian foundation. This event had to be thought of theologically. The question of the very possibility of the enterprise attempted at Lausanne, to which Pius XI responded negatively, was the same question posed by the Orthodox. If no distinction can be made in the truths of faith between *fondamentalia* and *non-fondamentalia*, they still manifest (according to Bulgakov) in gradations. The distinction between *dogmata explicita* and *dogmata implicita* authorizes churches that do not yet recognize all the dogmas defined by the church to be welcomed on the same path towards unity. There is a seed "from which all of Christian dogmatics develops" (an idea that was dear to

Criticism," *Church Times*, Feb 3, 1928. To Headlam responded Germanos, Metropolitan of Thyateira, "The Orthodox Delegation at Lausanne and its Declaration," *The Christian East* 9/1, 1928, 9–15.

82 "Copy of the verbatim notes taken at the Session of the Church Assembly held on Friday 6th July 1928," in: WCCA, 231.001.

83 William Temple, then bishop of Manchester, reported how there was an early understanding between Lutherans and Greek Orthodox on the idea of the "invisible church," before realizing that, for the Greeks, the invisible church meant the faithful departed; "Copy of the verbatim notes."

84 "Communication to the Continuation Committee from His Holiness Meletios, Patriarch of Alexandria, April 29, 1930," in: WCCA, 231.002.2.

85 See Stefan Zankow, "Die Orthodoxe Kirche und die Bewegung für die Vereinigung der Kirchen," *Una Sancta* 3, 1927, 290–297; Nicolas Arseniew, "Gedanken über Lausanne," *Una Sancta* 3, 1927, 397–400; Nicolas Arseniev, "Lozanskaya konferentsiya" [The conference of Lausanne], *Vestnik RSChD* 3, 1928, 1–5; Sergii Bulgakov, "K voprosu o Lozannskoy konferentsii (Lozannskaya konferentsiya i entsiklika Piya XI *Mortalium animos*)" [The Lausanne question: the conference of Lausanne and Pius XI's encyclical *Mortalium animos*], *Put* 13, 1928, 71–82, now in Sergii Bulgakov, *Put Parizhskogo bogosloviya* [The way of Paris theology], Moscow, Izdatelstvo khrama svyatoy muchenitsy Tatiany, 2007, 140–154 (the following quotations refer to this edition); Sergius Bulgakov, "The Papal Encyclical and the Lausanne Conference," *The Christian East* 9/3, 1928, 116–127.

86 Bulgakov, "K voprosu o Lozannskoy konferentsii," 142.

87 Bulgakov, "K voprosu o Lozannskoy konferentsii," 141.

Vladimir Solovyov), a faith without which "there is no Christianity" that "in itself holds the possibility of accepting all dogma": the profession of Christ as "the Son of the living God" (Mt 16:16). Lausanne represented this moment of the dawn of primitive Christianity (as evidenced by the unanimous acceptance of the report on the gospel) that, while it should not stop at this initial stage, should by no means be downplayed. The Orthodox Church, which considers itself the *una sancta*, could not ignore it except by seriously sinning in negligence and insensitivity and, indeed, must "become all things to all people, so that by all means some may be saved," according to the Pauline example.[88]

Bulgakov cleared the ground of the misunderstanding, nourished by *Mortalium animos*, that ecumenism coincides with the elaboration of a *new* confession, one agreed to on the basis of an indistinct, dogmatic *amalgam* crafted to satisfy everyone. In fact, nothing is more alien to the Orthodox conception, which in this sense shares the Catholic ecclesiological maximalism: "Uniting all in the bosom of Orthodoxy."[89] It is on this point that Bulgakov presents the, perhaps, most original reflection for understanding the ecumenical event from the Orthodox perspective. The essence of the church lies in its being catholic (*soborna*), but this means two things at the same time. It is indeed "conciliar/catholic (*soborna*) not only in the sense of catholicity (*kafolichnost*), which is opposed to all spiritual provincialism, but also has the sense of being called to gather (*soborovanie*) hearts in love and unanimity." It is precisely this call to assembly worked by the Spirit in the name of Christ that constitutes the ecclesial element beyond the canonical boundaries of the (Orthodox) church.[90]

The Greek term that corresponds to this idea of gathering (*soborovanie*) is *ekklesia*, the assembly of those called. It is at this level, theological and spiritual at the same time and not merely spatial and temporal, that the universality of ecclesial being (*tserkovnost*) is located. Orthodoxy, remaining itself, "has the full possibility of *gathering in assembly* (*soborovat*) with non-orthodox Christians, aiding them in their search for the one and only true ecclesiality."[91] There is an objective working of the Holy Spirit toward unity that removes it from all calculations of worldly diplomacy, and it is founded in baptism, in faith in the Lord, in love for him, and in the gospel. It was "the true mystical soil for the union that is sprouting."[92] It was Bulgakov himself, moreover, who had introduced the term *sobornost* into the ecumenical debate with his speech on ministry in Lausanne:[93]

> Russian theology expresses the fundamental essence of Church unity in a word for which no other language has an equivalent. *Sobornost* connotes alike the catholicity of the church – the integral totality of its being – and its spiritual character as the oneness of its members in faith and love; its

88 Bulgakov, "K voprosu o Lozannskoy konferentsii," 148.

89 Bulgakov, "K voprosu o Lozannskoy konferentsii," 148.

90 Bulgakov, "K voprosu o Lozannskoy konferentsii," 149.

91 Bulgakov, "K voprosu o Lozannskoy konferentsii," 150 (italics original).

92 Bulgakov, "K voprosu o Lozannskoy konferentsii," 150.

93 The term *sobornost*, which Aleksey Khomyakov himself never used, was introduced by Yuri Samarin and Nikita Gilyarov-Platonov in the Russian translation of Khomyakov's French works and is derived from the ecclesiastical Slavic *sobornaya*, which translates the "catholic" (καθολική) of the Creed. See, Antonella Cavazza, *"La Chiesa è una" di A.S. Chomjakov: Edizione documentario-interpretativa*, Bologna, Il Mulino, 2006, 19 [f. 26v]; and Alexei S. Khomyakov, "Lettre au rédacteur de l'Union Chrétienne à l'occasion d'un discours du père Gagarine, jésuite (1860)," in: *L'Église latine et le Protestantisme au point de vue de l'Église d'Orient: Recueil d'articles sur des questions religieuses écrits à différentes époques et à diverses occasions par A.S. Khomyakov*, Vevey, Xenia, [2]2006, 273–280. Although Khomyakov did not use the term *sobornost*, neither Berdyaev nor Bulgakov hesitated in attributing its authorship to him. See Antonella Cavazza, "L'idea di sobornost' da A.S. Chomjakov al Concilio Vaticano II: Messa a fuoco del problema," in: Alberto Melloni, ed., *Vatican II in Moscow (1959–1965): Acts of the Colloquium on the History of Vatican II Moscow, March 30–April 2, 1995*, Leuven, Bibliotheek van de Faculteit Godgeleerdheid, 1997, 129–144. See also the contribution by Jeremy Pilch in the first volume of this work (esp. 203–210).

> outer aspect, as at all points resting on the freely-chosen unanimity of its members, and lastly its ecumenical character, which links it to all nations and subordinates to it all local churches. It is the conception of *sobornost*, summing up as it does the organic nature of the Church, which underlies the doctrine of the hierarchy in the Orthodox system.[94]

Recognized as an event of the Spirit and looking closely at its theological presuppositions, the desire for unity should have consequences in our lives. Bulgakov repeated the question raised by all of the Russian intelligentsia, "What is to be done?," and proposed creating a "symbolic" ecumenism, a comparative study of Christian confessions stripped of any apologetic spirit to circumscribe dissent and foster mutual understanding. In perfect harmony with Solovyov, Bulgakov suggested that heresies are one-sidedness of thought. It is necessary to step out of the logic of "abstract principles" in order to place different positions in the light of truth. Returning to an idea proposed by Friedrich Heiler,[95] Bulgakov proposed founding an institute for ecumenical studies with theologians of different orientations and denominations to openly address ecclesiological questions (the nature of church, priesthood, the sacraments, and justification), reiterating the need to address the consequences of the Nicene symbol. These included the veneration of the Mother of God, the issue "that most divides the Christian world."[96] However, Lausanne had been a turning point. The discussion could now take place between "friends seeking to understand one another … brothers and sisters in the Lord, even though they have been until now *fratres separati*."[97]

Florovsky, too, spoke on the nature of the ecumenical movement.[98] His starting point already measured the full distance from Bulgakov's conception of the ecumenical problem: the church "is not divided and is indivisible," but the "Christian world" is torn apart and on the "verge of collapsing."[99] Florovsky criticized attempts to restore the unity of the Christian world based on moral grounds since division "has, first and foremost, *dogmatic* significance. It is always a division in the faith, in the very experience of the faith."[100] Where Bulgakov had discerned an event of the Spirit, lovingly revealing a unity of faith grasped through a conversion of the theological *mens*, Florovsky sensed an attack on truth. Dogmatic minimalism threatened to steer the ecumenical movement into adogmatism. The moralism of fraternal love was but a call for "union in poverty, impoverishment, narrowness," where dogmas wind up being dissolved into "moralistic symbols and postulates."[101] True unity (*edinstvo*) can be realized "only in Truth, that is, in fullness and power, not in weakness and insufficiency."[102] The main point of departure from Bulgakov was a denial of gradualness in the revelation of dogma (inherited from Solovyov), because "the entirety of the fullness of knowledge is given from the beginning in the experience and consciousness of the church and must only be *recognized*."[103] The reestablishment of unity is properly *re*unification

94 Bate, ed., *Faith and Order*, 258.

95 Which he mentions in a footnote: Friedrich Heiler, "Ergebnisse und Forderung der Lausanner Weltkonferenz," *IKZ* 1, 1928.

96 Bulgakov, "K voprosu o Lozannskoy konferentsii," 154.

97 Bulgakov, "K voprosu o Lozannskoy konferentsii," 154.

98 Georgi Florovsky, "Problematika khristianskago vozsoedineniya" [The problem of Christian reunification], *Put* 37, 1933, appendix, 1–15. An editorial note (by Berdyaev) points out that, while "making room for the interesting article by Fr. Georges Florovsky," it did not "consider his view on Christian unification as the only possible one and admits other points of view."

99 Georgi Florovsky, "Problematika khristianskago vozsoedineniya" 2.

100 Georgi Florovsky, "Problematika khristianskago vozsoedineniya" 4.

101 Georgi Florovsky, "Problematika khristianskago vozsoedineniya" 5.

102 Georgi Florovsky, "Problematika khristianskago vozsoedineniya" 5.

103 Georgi Florovsky, "Problematika khristianskago vozsoedineniya" 5 (italics original).

(*pri-soedinenie*), which implies an adherence to the truth, and is a more precise concept than the idea of a generic process of Christian *unification* (*soedinenie*).[104]

Florovsky attributed to the Reformation an unsurpassable defect of anthropological minimalism, while Rome, which did not lack grace and sacraments, had separated itself through a lack of charity and dogmatic unanimity. Rome tended towards unity, but its haste to reestablish Christian unity under the Roman pontiff was the main obstacle to reunification. This was demonstrated by the error of Uniatism, because the division between East and West "is not in the rite or even merely in jurisdiction, but precisely in the faith and experience of life."[105]

Florovsky's ecclesiological maximalism led him to reevaluate Cyprian, who identified the canonical and charismatic boundaries of the church. Of course, Florovsky admitted the undeniable fact that the church recognizes the validity of the sacraments, even among schismatics. But while for Bulgakov the presence of the signs of the church beyond the visible church was a paradox that called for broadening the understanding of the mystery of church, for Florovsky it remained a historical antinomy that only eschatology could resolve definitively. Florovsky's article sparked a lively controversy in Berdyaev's journal, which involved the younger theologians Nicolas Zernov and Nicholas Afanasiev.[106] The latter, in particular, highlighted the emergence of a universalistic ecclesiology in Cyprian, which obscured an older ecclesiology outlined in Ignatius of Antioch that was centered on the Eucharist and in which communion among the churches did not presuppose a hierarchical, pyramid model.[107] This was the core of what would develop as Eucharistic ecclesiology, which Florovsky and Bulgakov both, for opposite reasons, looked upon with distrust.

5 From Lausanne to Edinburgh: Orthodoxy and Church Unity

Orthodox participation in the ecumenical movement required an answer to the question, "what are the dogmatic foundations of the 'ecumenical fact'?" Moreover, since ecumenism questioned the unity of the church, its clarification implied an ecclesiology. What is the church? How should the profession of its unity in the creed be understood? The Orthodox answer revolves around the concept of *sobornost*, that is, the "catholicity" of the church. For Bulgakov, *sobornost* entails the "very substance of Orthodox ecclesiology," without which charismatic foundation Orthodoxy appears to be an eclectic compromise between Catholicism and Protestantism.[108] The idea of "catholicity" can also be seen as Orthodoxy's main contribution to the interwar ecumenical movement. The understanding of this "catholicity," however, diverged depending on whether it was understood in continuity with, or in opposition to, its interpretation by Russian religious philosophy, which outlined two different conceptions of ecclesial tradition.

Intra-Orthodox theological debate in the 1930s was dominated by three events: the discussion of Bulgakov's proposal for partial intercommunion

104 Georgi Florovsky, "Problematika khristianskago vozsoedineniya" 14.

105 Georgi Florovsky, "Problematika khristianskago vozsoedineniya" 13.

106 Nikolay Zernov, "Sv. Kiprian Karfagenskiy i edinstvo vselenskoy tserkvi" [St. Cyprian of Carthage and the unity of the universal church], *Put*, 39, 1933, 18–40; Nikolay Afanasiev, "Kanony i kanonicheskoe soznanie" [Canons and canonical conscience], supplement of *Put* 39, 1933, appendix, 1–16; Nikolay Afanasiev, "Dve idei vselenskoy Tserkvi" [Two ideas of universal church], *Put* 45, 1934, 16–29. In the same journal, Florovsky responded with the article "O granitsakh Tserkvi" [On the boundaries of the church], *Put* 44, 1934, 15–26, which echoed his thoughts in Georges Florovsky, "The Limits of the Church," *CQR* 117, 1933, 117–131.

107 See the contribution by Benedikt Kranemann & Adalberto Mainardi in the first volume of this work (esp. 556–560).

108 Serge Boulgakov, *L'Orthodoxie: Essai sur la doctrine de l'Église*, Paris, Alcan, 1932; reprint: Lausanne, L'Age d'Homme, 1980, 71–72.

within the Anglo-Orthodox association of the Fellowship of St. Alban and St. Sergius, the condemnation of Bulgakov's Sophiology by the Moscow Patriarchate and the Karlovci Synod in 1935, and the first Orthodox theological conference in Athens in 1936.

In Lausanne, Bulgakov had identified the achievement of Christian unity with a "sharing of the same Cup at the Holy Table and by the ministry of a priesthood,"[109] but he thought then that this would happen only in the distant future.[110] The growing awareness that the unification of the Christian world was an urgency dictated by the Holy Spirit, which could not stop with the canonical solutions that had emerged in other historical contexts, convinced him of the need to take a concrete step. In 1933, he proposed that Orthodox and Anglican members of the Fellowship of St. Alban and St. Sergius participate in one another's Eucharist. The proposal sparked a lively debate that transcended the Fellowship's boundaries.[111] The first rift between the Orthodox engaged in ecumenical relations occurred over the sharing of the Eucharistic table.

In the same year, the YMCA Press published a collection of articles entitled *Khristianskoe vossoedinenie: Ekumenicheskaya problema v pravoslavnom soznanii* (Christian reunification: the ecumenical problem in Orthodox thought), with contributions from Sergius Bulgakov, Metropolitan Gennadios of Heliopolis, Metropolitan Nectarie of Bukovina, Nicholas Berdyaev, Anton Kartashev, Stefan Tsankov, Hamilcar Alivisatos, and Basil Zenkovsky.[112] Berdyaev noted that never before had there been "such a longing for unity," and that division within Christianity remained "the great scandal for the non-Christian and anti-Christian world."[113] Bulgakov's contribution to the volume was probably prepared to justify his proposal for intercommunion.[114] The essay, however, had a broader scope and was a systematic reflection on the foundations of ecumenism. He developed the arguments he had been mapping out since the mid-1920s in a series of essays on ecclesiology,[115] in particular in a talk in January 1927 at the St. Alban's Orthodox-Anglican conference on "The church and Non-Orthodoxy."[116]

109 Bate, ed., *Faith and Order*, 262.

110 Bulgakov, "K voprosu o Lozannskoy konferentsii," 148 (also in *Put* 13, 1928, 77).

111 The question has been studied widely, see: Dimitrios Filippos Salapatas, *The Fellowship of St. Alban and St. Sergius: Orthodox and Anglican Ecumenical Relations (1927–2012)*, Newcastle upon Tyne, Cambridge Scholars Publishing, 2018. See also: Brandon Gallaher, "Bulgakov and Intercommunion," *Sobornost* 24/2, 2002, 9–28; Bryn Geffert, "Sergii Bulgakov, the Fellowship of St. Alban and St. Sergius, Intercommunion, and Sofiology," *Revolutionary Russia* 17/1, 2004, 105–141; Bryn Geffert, *Eastern Orthodox and Anglicans*, 158–183; Sergei V. Nikolaev, "Spiritual Unity: The Role of Religious Authority in the Disputes between Sergii Bulgakov and Georges Florovsky concerning Intercommunion," SVTQ 49, 2005, 101–123; and Nichols, *Alban and Sergius*, 191–208.

112 *Khristianskoe vossoedinenie: Ekumenicheskaya problema v pravoslavnom soznanii*, Paris, YMCA Press, 1933. Regarding the volume, Zernov noted that the spectrum of positions on ecumenism ranged from the strict to the moderate to the bold, represented by the Russian diaspora at Saint-Serge: Nichols, *Alban and Sergius*, 194.

113 Nikolay Berdyaev, "Vselenskost i konfessionalizm" [Universality and Confessionalism], in: *Khristianskoe vossoedinenie*, 63–81, here 64.

114 Sergii Bulgakov, "U Kladezya Iakovlya (In. 4,23): O realnom edinstve razdelennoy Tserkvi v Vere Molitve i Tainstvakh," in: *Khristianskoe vossoedinenie*, 9–32; ET (abridged): "By Jacob's Well: On the Actual Unity of the Divided Church in Faith, Prayer, and Sacraments," *The Journal of the Fellowship of St. Alban and St. Sergius* 22, 1933, 7–17.

115 Sergii Bulgakov, "Ocherki ucheniya o Tserkvi" [Essays on the doctrine of the church], *Put* 1, 1925, 53–78; 2, 1926, 47–58; 15, 1929, 39–80; 16, 1929, 19–48; Sergii Bulgakov, "Does Orthodoxy Possess an Outward Authority of Dogmatic Infallibility," *The Christian East* 7/1, 1926, 12–24; Sergius Bulgakov, "The Problem of the Church in Modern Russian Theology," *Theology* 23, 1931, 9–14, 63–69; Sergius Bulgakov, "One Holy, Catholic, and Apostolic Church," *The Journal of the Fellowship of St. Alban and St. Sergius* 12, 1931, 17–31 (reprinted in *The Christian East* 12, 1931, 90–104); Sergius Bulgakov, "The Church – Holy – Soborny (Catholic)," *ACM* 32, 1932, 414–431. See Michael Plekon, "Still by Jacob's Well: Sergius Bulgakov's Vision of the Church Revisited," *SVTQ* 49/1–2, 2005, 125–143.

116 Sergius Bulgakov, "Outlines of the Teaching About the Church: Address given at the Orthodox & Anglo-

Analyzing the changing ecclesiastical discipline of the admission of the non-Orthodox into the church (baptism, chrismation, or a confession of faith) from Basil the Great to Theodore the Studite, Bulgakov noted the existence of an *ecclesia extra ecclesiam*. This did not mean an interconfessionalism based on indifference, but the recognition of the irresistible desire of the entire Christian world for the union of all. Alongside the centrifugal force of separation, a centripetal energy leading all Christians back to the (Orthodox) church was manifesting itself. In particular, the ancient canons governing the church's attitude toward heretics and schismatics could not be applied to the Anglican Church, which had never had any relationship with Orthodoxy. The only authentic attitude toward the non-Orthodox was one of ecclesial love.[117] Prayer, the Word of God, spiritual life, and baptism already constituted the content of an invisible communion between Orthodox and Protestants, hindered only by the absence of a rightly ordained priesthood (that is, an episcopal structure). Where this structure existed, however, as in the Anglican Church (and in the Roman Catholic Church), unity in the sacraments was preserved, even though these churches were separated from Orthodoxy "canonically in the sense of jurisdiction and dogmatically in a whole spectrum of differences, though these are powerless to invalidate the efficacy of the sacraments."[118] This is demonstrated precisely by the recognition of baptism. Dogmatic divergences, in fact, are superficial while "what constitutes ecclesial *unity* … lies deep within."[119] Unlike Berdyaev, for Bulgakov the foundation of Christian ecumenism lay not in mystical experience but in a fact, namely, unity "as the breath of the grace of the Holy Spirit, as the manifestation of Pentecost";[120] this was experienced in the sharing of prayer in the name of Jesus in the "direct efficacy of the Word of God (wrongly belittled in the face of the Tradition)" and especially in the sacraments. Bulgakov went so far as to question the "pseudo-axiom" (a contentious allusion to Antony Khrapovitsky and Florovsky), according to which sacramental communion must have prior dogmatic agreement as a condition, since a difference in some Christian dogmas cannot cancel "the unity of sacramental life." "Why is it considered essential to agree in advance on opinions and not vice versa, to seek in the unity of the sacrament the ways to overcome this difference? Why not seek the overcoming of the heresy in doctrines through overcoming the *heresy in life*, which is precisely division?"[121]

In the course of internal discussion at the Fellowship, Bulgakov went deeper into this line of argument. The Eucharist can be shared if it is not subordinated to a dogmatic maximalism that actually disavows the primacy of the Eucharistic dogma.[122] Recurrent in Bulgakov's reflection was the idea of dogmatic development dear to Solovyov that intercommunion requires a minimum of dogmatic agreement that nevertheless corresponds to the maximum of the church's shared dogmatic heritage. There are "Eucharistic" dogmas (such as belief in the incarnation) implied by the Eucharist itself, and "non-Eucharistic" dogmas specific to a time period in order to meet particular needs, and not all are on the same level for restoring unity. The intercommunion envisaged by Bulgakov was to be an initial seed, a "sacrament of reunion," which in this embryonic stage of

Catholic Conference," December 1926–January 1927 (typescript), in: Archives of the Fellowship of St. Alban and St. Sergius, available at <https://fsass.org/shop/archives/fr-sergius-bulgakovs-outlines-of-the-teaching-about-the-church/> (accessed Mar 20, 2023); then published in Sergius Bulgakov, "Outlines of the Teaching about the Church – The Church and Non-Orthodoxy," *ACM* 30, 1931, 411–423 and 31, 1932, 13–26; see Sergius Bulgakov, "Orthodoxy in its Relation to Non-Orthodoxy," *ACM* 40/4, 1936, 251–263.

117 Bulgakov, "Outlines," 27–29.

118 Bulgakov, "U Kladezya Iakovlya," 29.

119 Bulgakov, "U Kladezya Iakovlya," 13.

120 Bulgakov, "U Kladezya Iakovlya," 13.

121 Bulgakov, "U Kladezya Iakovlya," 30–31 (italics original).

122 Sergius Bulgakov, "Ways to Church Reunion," *Sobornost* 2, 1935, 7–15.

catholic unity needed an effort of canonical imagination capable of preserving diversity, eschewing any "sacramental cannibalism," any absorption of one church into any other.[123] The Anglican Church would become more and more "Anglican" as it approached Orthodoxy, and the Orthodox Church would better understand that the church is not identified with Byzantium. "Unity in orthodoxy is not obedience to the power of one church," but "one and the same life in love and in freedom and in holiness."[124]

Bulgakov's proposal drew sharp criticism on both sides of the fault line of denominational affiliations. Among the Orthodox, Nicolas Zernov, George Fedotov, Lev Zander and, after some initial confusion, Anton Kartashev were in favor (intercommunion was a creative act in response to a new situation where church diplomacy had failed).[125] The most intransigent critic was Florovsky: *communio in sacris* could never be a private action but was always a catholic action. To introduce intercommunion into an "arbitrary group" such as the Fellowship would have been an act that was "uncatholic, particularist, and even sectarian."[126] Objections also arose on the Anglican side.[127] After two years of discussion, Bulgakov's proposal was shelved, though not without leaving a trail of controversy and misunderstanding. He had put his finger on the sore spot of divisions between the churches. Only prophetic action could overcome the heresy in life (Eucharistic separation) without allowing itself to be entangled in the separation of theologies. On this point, he was misunderstood and accused of psychologism (by Florovsky) or sentimentalism (by Arthur Michael Ramsey). Metropolitan Eulogius himself dismissed the issue: Bulgakov's idea was "absolutely wrong" since only the totality of the ecclesial body could settle dogmatic differences.[128]

While Bulgakov's proposal on intercommunion foundered, his theology was the subject of several canonical condemnations, which raised some wariness even among the Anglicans about the degree to which his ideas conformed to Orthodox doctrine. On Sep 7, 1935, the vicar of the *locum tenens* of the Moscow Patriarchate, Metropolitan Sergius (Stragorodsky), issued a decree (*ukaz*) stating that Bulgakov had seriously deviated from Orthodoxy in Trinitarian doctrine (his interpretation of biblical *sophia* as divine *ousia*), soteriology (saying that the incarnation was independent of the fall), and eschatology (accusing Bulgakov of advocating a form of apocatastasis). The decree was based on a complaint by one Alexis Stravrovsky, an alumnus of the Saint-Serge, and a report by Vladimir Lossky to Metropolitan Elevtery, exarch for Western Europe of the Moscow Patriarchate. On Dec 27, 1935, Metropolitan Sergius issued a second decree, condemning Bulgakov's Christology. On Oct 30 of the same year, on the basis of a voluminous report by Archbishop Seraphim (Sobolev), the Karlovci Synod of the ROCOR condemned Bulgakov's Sophiology as heretical.[129]

123 Bulgakov, "One Holy, Catholic, and Apostolic Church," 95–96.

124 Bulgakov, "One Holy, Catholic, and Apostolic Church," 95–96. See Gallaher, "Bulgakov and Intercommunion," 22.

125 See Anton Kartashev, "The Paths Towards the Reunion of the Churches," *The Journal of the Fellowship of St. Alban and St. Sergius* 25, 1934, 7–13.

126 G. Florovsky to Members of the Executive, Oct 16, 1933, in: Archives of the Fellowship of St. Alban and St. Sergius, cited in Nichols, *Alban and Sergius*, 196.

127 Oliver Fielding Clarke, "The Healing of Schism," *The Journal of the Fellowship of St. Alban and St. Sergius* 25, 1934, 3–7. Arthur Michael Ramsey believed that rushing to intercommunion would compromise the understanding of the Eucharist as the "act of Christ in His one Body"; Nichols, *Alban and Sergius*, 204.

128 Manoukhina, ed., *Le chemin de ma vie*, 493.

129 On the matter, see Natalya Timyrovna Eneyeva, *Spor o sofiologii v russkom zarubezhe 1920–1930 godov* [The sophiological controversy in the Russian emigration of the 1920s and 1930s], Moscow, Institut vseobshchei istorii RAN, 2001; Bryn Geffert, "The Charges of Heresy against Sergii Bulgakov: The Majority and Minority Reports of Evlogii's Commission and the Final Report of the Bishops' Conference," *SVTQ* 49/1–2, 2005, 47–66; Aleksandr P. Kozyrev & Alexei E. Klimoff, "Materialy k 'sporu o Sofi,'" *Zapiski russkoy akademicheskoy gruppy v SShA/Transactions of the Association of Russian-American Scholars in the USA* 39, 2016;

As Bulgakov was not subject to the jurisdictions that had convicted him, there were no immediate canonical consequences. However, Metropolitan Eulogius, after asking him for a statement of defence,[130] was forced to appoint a special commission that included Jacob Ktitarev, Bishop Cassian (Bezobrazov), Georges Florovsky, Sergius Chetverikov, Anton Kartashev, Basil Zenkovsky, and Boris Sove.[131] Under attack was the theological orientation of Saint-Serge and, indirectly, the autonomous archbishopric itself. In 1937, the commission absolved Fr. Bulgakov of all charges of heresy, but a minority report by two members of the commission, Florovsky and Chetverikov, pointed out a number of weaknesses in his theology.[132] The affair generated an animated debate and had serious consequences, dividing the community of Russian émigrés.[133] It is not possible to go into the details of the theological controversy and its political implications here, but two aspects of Bulgakov's theology were directly connected to ecumenical issues: the relationship to tradition and the conception of church, which we will examine briefly in the next section.

In the year following the outbreak of the Sophia controversy, the first Orthodox theological conference was held in Athens; it was attended by representatives of the theological faculties of Bucharest, Chișinău, Belgrade, Warsaw, Paris, and Athens. Like the similar ecumenical conferences organized in the Balkans by Stefan Tsankov,[134] it may be said that the Athens congress was a fruit of the ecumenical movement, as Hamilcar Alivisatos, its indefatigable promoter, acknowledged.[135]

Robert F. Slesinski, "S.N. Bulgakov: Heresiarkh?," SVTQ 63/4, 2019, 423–446.

130 Sergii Bulgakov, "Dokladnaya zapiska predstavlennaya v oktyabre 1935 g. ego Vysokopreosvyashchenstvu mitropolitu Evlogiyu" [Memorandum from October 1935 to His Eminence Metropolitan Eulogius], in: *O Sofii premudrosti Bozhiey: Ukaz Moskovskoy Patriarchii i dokladnye zapiski prof. prot. Sergiya Bulgakova Mitropolitu Evlogiyu* [Sophia: the wisdom of God, decree of the patriarch of Moscow and the memorandum of Prof. Sergei Bulgakov to Metropolitan Eulogius], Paris, 1935, 20–53, some parts of which were published in Sergius Bulgakov, "Memorandum presented … to the Metropoliten Eulogius [Abstracts]," *The Christian East* 16, 1936, 48–49. Already in 1927, Bulgakov had had to produce a defensive memorandum following a letter from the synod of the ROCOR (dated Mar 18/31) accusing Metropolitan Eulogius of failing to monitor the Modernism of his associates, but in that case the metropolitan was satisfied with the theologian's response: "Dokladnaya zapiska, predstavlennaya professorom prot. Sergiem Bulgakovym mitropolitu Evlogiyu vesnoy 1927 g." [Memorandum presented by Archpriest Prof. Sergius Bulgakov to Metropolitan Eulogius in spring 1927], *The Christian East* 16, 1936, 54–64. Vladimir Lossky reacted argumentatively to Bulgakov's self-defence: Vladimir Lossky, *Spor o Sofii; 'Dokladnaya Zapiska' prot. S. Bulgakova i smysl Ukaza Moskovskoy Patriarkhii* [The controversy concerning Sophia: Fr. S. Bulgakov's "Memorandum" and the meaning of the decree of the Moscow Patriarchate], Paris, s.n., 1936.

131 Manoukhina, ed., *Le chemin de ma vie*, 533.

132 Florovsky's assertion that Bulgakov recanted (Blane, ed., *Georges Florovsky*, 67) has not been substantiated (Geffert, "The Charges," 54, note 30). On Florovsky's role in the commission, see Alexis Klimoff, "Georges Florovsky and the Sophiological Controversy," SVTQ 49/1–2, 2005, 67–100.

133 Berdyaev intervened in defence of Bulgakov in a particularly harsh tone: "Dukh Velikogo Inkvizitora (po povodu ukaza mitropolita Sergiya, osuzhdayushchego bogoslovskie vzglyady o. S. Bulgakova)" [The spirit of the grand inquisitor: concerning Metropolitan Sergius's *ukaz* condemning Fr. S. Bulgakov's theological conceptions], *Put* 49, 1935, 72–81. On the various voices in the debate, see Arjakovsky, *La génération*, 438–444. Bulgakov, referring to the Anglican idea of comprehensiveness, defended freedom of thought in areas that are not defined by dogma: Sergius Bulgakov, "Freedom of Thought in the Orthodox Church," *Sobornost* 6, 1936, 4–8.

134 In Bucharest (1933), Herceg Novi (1935) and Novi Sad (1936). On Tsankov, see Viktor Mutafov, *Stefan Cankov: odin iz osnovatelej ekumeničeskogo dviženija* [Stefan Tsankov: One of the founders of the ecumenical movement], Ph.D. thesis, PIO, 2013; Viktor Mutafov, "Padre Stefan Zankov: Un pioniere della riconciliazione tra i cristiani," in: Luigi d'Ayala Valva, Lisa Cremaschi & Adalberto Mainardi, eds., *Beati i pacifici: Atti del XXII Convegno ecumenico internazionale di Spiritualità ortodossa, Bose, 3–6 settembre 2014*, Magnano, Qiqajon, 2015, 263–271.

135 Hamilcar S. Alivisatos, ed., *Procès-Verbaux du premier congrès de théologie orthodoxe à Athènes, 29 Novembre–6 Décembre 1936*, Athens, Pyrsos, 1939, 58.

The project dated back to 1922 and had been developed in a series of meetings (Athens, 1930; Cambridge, 1932; Chamby, Switzerland, 1935), until the Theological Faculty of Athens assumed the organizational responsibilities. The congress' agenda included the definition of theological studies within Orthodoxy and specific topics such as the convocation of an ecumenical council, the internal and external mission of the church, relations with culture, state, and society, as well as several disciplinary and liturgical issues (the calendar, married clergy, fasting, etc.).

An underlying concern in the discussions was the unity of the Orthodox world. In his keynote address, Alivisatos – referring to autocephaly – warned against "nationalist tendencies arising from unilateral political directives," which erect "high walls between the different communities of Orthodoxy."[136] Estrangement between the different autocephalous churches had negatively impacted theological studies in a severe way. Only sincere cooperation and mutual respect and care for one another allow for a true progress of peoples and societies. Orthodox unity leads toward Christian unity. Before the Great War, it seemed impossible that representatives of different churches might come together; afterwards, it was only the Catholic Church that excluded itself.[137] For Alivisatos, the congress's goal was to become aware of "Orthodoxy's inner and external strength,"[138] in an effort to break down the walls erected between the churches by the "scholastic and fanatical" theology of the past, and thus to contribute to the work of promoting unity that the ecumenical movement was carrying out.

It was in Athens that Florovsky sounded his call for a new Hellenization of Orthodoxy in line with the spirit of the Fathers to respond adequately to the challenges of modernity.[139] His address should be considered alongside his argument, developed in his magnum opus the *Ways of Russian Theology*, of the "pseudomorphosis" of Russian theology due to Western influences: to the extent that it betrays the Fathers, Orthodox theology loses itself.[140] Arguing against Bulgakov's theological perspective, Florovsky proposed a "return to the Fathers" (which he identified entirely with the Greek Fathers) as a necessary prerequisite of any theological synthesis, beyond the modern deviations of Catholic scholasticism or Protestant confessionalism.

For his part, in Athens Bulgakov reiterated that ecclesiology was the problem of the age and, in his summary, formulated his ecclesiological theses; these were rooted – not explicitly – in his Sophiology. On the one hand, the church possesses an empirical being; on the other, it transcends time and space. It is supratemporal "and, *in this* sense, is the eternal foundation of the being and building of the world."[141] The world was made in view of the church, as expressed in the Shepherd of Hermas. For Bulgakov, the church was not simply a community of believers, but the principle of divine life in creatures. The fullness of the church will only be visible in the fullness of time, but the church's Trinitarian dimension – where each member is bound to the other, not as individuals but as part of the body of Christ "in the organic multi-unity (*Vieleinheit*)"[142] of the Father's love in the communion of the Holy Spirit – is already reflected in what Russian theology calls *sobornost*: the organic unity of the church in which each person's freedom is combined with the hierarchical principle that in turn exercises its ministry only in the unity of love.

The indebtedness of Bulgakov's ideas to German idealism was a constant source of criticism on the part of Florovsky, who, in his rebuttal of

136 Alivisatos, ed., *Procès-Verbaux*, 55.
137 Alivisatos, ed., *Procès-Verbaux*, 58.
138 Alivisatos, ed., *Procès-Verbaux*, 61.
139 Georges Florovsky, "Patristics and Modern Theology," in: Alivisatos, ed., *Procès-Verbaux*, 238–242.
140 Georges Florovsky, "Westliche Einflüsse in der russischen Theologie," in: Alivisatos, ed., *Procès-Verbaux*, 212–231.
141 Serge Bulgakoff, "Thesen über die Kirche," in: Alivisatos, ed., *Procès-Verbaux*, 127–135, here 128.
142 Serge Bulgakoff, "Thesen über die Kirche," 130.

Bulgakov's address, called the Russian term *sobornost* "new and dangerous."[143] It was less a matter of opposition of two ecclesiological models than of contention over the authentic interpretation of Orthodoxy and the debt one wishes to accord to Russian religious philosophy. The Sophiological dispute forms the backdrop to the argument over the idea of church.

6 The Debate over Church Unity: Bulgakov and Florovsky

The condemnation of Bulgakov's Sophiology had exposed two rival approaches to dogmatic theology. According to Florovsky, all revealed truths are always present in ecclesial tradition in their totality: historical development is merely the, sometimes difficult and contradictory, unveiling of this eternal content according to different historical situations. Changes are only formal, not substantial. As such, there is no dogmatic development and, in this sense, Solovyov was wrong. According to Bulgakov, however, theology is fundamentally historical because the very reality of the church, as divine humanity in history, is historical.[144] The problem of tradition became crucial for Orthodox theology, as evidenced by a collected work produced, largely, by professors of the Saint-Serge institute.[145] Only the incarnation and Trinitarian dogma, Bulgakov argued, are universally binding, while other theological doctrines (including ecclesiology, soteriology, and eschatology) do not possess the same dogmatic status.[146] The *consensus patrum* is a guide for thought, but is not normative, and a minor theological idea in the Fathers may prove theologically fruitful in a new context.[147] Each historical era has its own theological task and its own specific prophetic gift.[148]

Addressing the problem of the historicity of dogmas, Bulgakov recalled that "the tradition of the Fathers is by no means exhaustive," and for that reason it may prove "insufficient to give a satisfactory or exhaustive solution to those problems that recur in dogmatic reflection."[149] Therefore, if "in the divine foundation of the church is found all the fullness of revelation and all the fullness of life – *according to divinity* ... in the church's divine-human consciousness, insofar as temporality and relativity are interwoven into it, this fullness is realized only gradually and partially. This is why a *history* of dogmas is possible and indeed exists ... New dogmas arise and, in this sense, dogmatic development occurs."[150]

143 Bulgakoff, "Thesen über die Kirche," 135. The term had good fortune, and some applied it to intra-Trinitarian life: Vladimir Illyn, "The Nature and the Meaning of the Term 'Sobornost,'" *The Journal of the Fellowship of St. Alban and St. Sergius* 25, 1934, 5–7.

144 "In the empirical being of the Church, there is nothing that does not belong to history, that, in itself, is absolute and eternal"; Sergius Bulgakov, *The Bride of the Lamb*, trans. Boris Jakim, Grand Rapids, Eerdmans, 2002, 271 (ed. or.: Sergii Bulgakov, *Nevesta Agnctsa: O Bogochelovechestve*, vol. 3, Paris, YMCA Press, 1945). See Myroslaw Tataryn, "History Matters: Bulgakov's Sophianic Key," *SVTQ* 49/1–2, 2005, 203–218.

145 *Zhivoe predanie: Pravoslavie v sovremennosti* [The living tradition: Orthodoxy in the modern world], Paris, YMCA Press, 1937 (republished in Moscow, Svyato-Filaretovskaya Moskovskaya vysshaya Pravoslavno-khristianskaya shkola, 1997), with contributions by Sergius Bulgakov, Anton Kartashev, Ivan Lagovsky, Basil Zenkovsky, Nicholas Afanasiev, Vladimir Illyn, George Fedotov, Lev Zander, Cyprian Kern, Cassian (Bezobrazov), Boris Sove.

146 Sergii Bulgakov, "Dogmat i dogmatika" [Dogma and dogmatics], in: *Zhivoe predanie*, 8–25 (the Moscow 1997 reprint is cited here). The essay was included in *Bogoslovskaya Mysl*, Paris, Izdanie Pravoslavnogo Bogoslovskogo Instituta, 1942, 9–24. This is the position that Bulgakov defended in Edinburgh: Leonard Hodgson, ed., *The Second World Conference on Faith and Order: Held at Edinburgh, August 3–18, 1937*, New York, The Macmillan Company, 1938, 67.

147 See Gavrilyuk, *Georges Florovsky*, 141. See also Paul Valliere, *Modern Russian Theology: Bukharev, Soloviev, Bulgakov: Orthodox Theology in a New Key*, Grand Rapids, Eerdmans, 2000, 373–403.

148 See Sergius Bulgakov, "The Church Universal," *The Journal of the Fellowship of St. Alban and St. Sergius* 25, 1934, 10–15, here 14.

149 Bulgakov, "Dogmat i dogmatika," 15.

150 Bulgakov, "Dogmat i dogmatika," 20 (italics original).

One of the "dogmatic facts" that required further theological reflection was precisely the ecumenical movement. For Lev Zander (echoing Bulgakov) ecumenism, as a "great gathering (*soborovaniya*) of Christians of different denominations," is not just a place where the Orthodox can bear witness to the "one and only true church" (as for Florovsky), but an event inspired by the Spirit bearing witness to Christ, a "Christophany" that was to be an object of discernment, a calling and, at the same time, a task.[151]

Drawing out the consequences from the debate on intercommunion and Sophiology, Bulgakov outlined the foundations of Orthodox ecumenism. The starting point is not division, but the sacrament of unity: "The cup of Christ remains one, although those who approach him are divided. And it is the same Spirit who gives different charisms."[152] Deep within, in its sacramental life, the church remains one. Only from this irreducible fact of the one and holy church, of the *una sancta* "as the supreme and preeminent reality," is it possible to understand the "dogmatic paradox" of ecumenism, whereby there are different churches "each of which *is* church ... in the sense of belonging to the *una sancta*."[153]

Bulgakov distinguished between two dimensions of the church: the ontological, which refers to its essence, and the empirical, which is manifested in its historical existence. The church is the harmonious union in diversity, a "multi-unity" that, by grace, reflects the pluri-unity of the divine Trinity on the plane of creation. It is *one* in that it is "the body of Christ" (Rom 12:5; 1 Cor 6:15; 1 Cor 12:27) and, at the same time, it is plural in the diversity of charisms "the temple of the Holy Spirit" (1 Cor 3:16), an uninterrupted Pentecost manifesting the "manifold wisdom of God" (Eph 3:9–10). This plural unity of the *una sancta* is no longer visible in the historic churches, where diversity has been accentuated to the point of division. The ecumenical problem is all about overcoming the "hiatus between the mystical body of the church and the historical-hierarchical organization" in order to affirm "the *unity* of the church as the body of Christ, as life in Christ and in the Holy Spirit, with respect to which there are no confessional limits and no monopoly."[154]

Bulgakov's last work, *The Bride of the Lamb*, which was published posthumously, was dedicated to overcoming the antimony between the ontological and empirical dimensions of the church. The ecclesiological tome completes his great trilogy *O Bogochelovechestve* (On Divine-humanity). For Bulgakov, the gateway to the mystery of the church is Sophia. Sophia or the Wisdom of God (Prov 8:22–31) is divine *ousia*, the substance of intra-Trinitarian life that, in creation, manifests itself as created Sophia. This is not a fourth hypostasis, but the metaphysical foundation of the world that makes divine humanity possible, the incarnation of the Logos and the transfiguration of the cosmos in the Holy Spirit. It is precisely the church that is the "sophianic foundation of the world" (referring to *God's multifaceted* wisdom, Eph 3:9–11); it is "Sophia in both of her aspects, Divine and creaturely, in their interrelationship, which is expressed in their union."[155] In the Pauline ecclesiological texts (1 Cor 10:16–17; Eph 1:22–23, 2:10, 15–16, 18–22; Col 2:19), Bulgakov highlights the idea of gathering (*sobornost*): "The Church is an *organism* or a body, or generally a living multi-unity. In the Church, many members are united and diverse gifts are distributed, her living multi-unity being headed by Christ and quickened by the Holy Spirit."[156]

The antithesis between the church as, on the one hand, *pleroma*, fullness, and, on the other, as a

151 Lev Zander, "'I soglasno slavim vsesvyatago Dukha' (O sushchnosti ekumenicheskogo dvizheniya)" ['And together we will praise the Holy Spirit' (On the Essence of the Ecumenical Movement)], in: *Zhivoe predanie*, 136–158, here 136.

152 Sergii Bulgakov, "Una Sancta (Osnovaniya Ekumenizma)," *Put* 58, 1938–1939, 3–14, here 12.

153 Bulgakov, "Una Sancta," 3 (italics original).

154 Bulgakov, "Una Sancta," 7–8 (italics original).

155 Bulgakov, *The Bride of the Lamb*, 253.

156 Bulgakov, *The Bride of the Lamb*, 257 (italics original).

pilgrim community on earth (*ekklesia paroikousa*) is resolved by interpreting the church as "the unity of the supra-eternal Divine Sophia and the becoming creaturely Sophia":[157]

> The idea that the church as the body of Christ is the "fullness of him which filleth all in all" (Eph 1:23) refers precisely to this definition. What does this *plerōma* signify if not the eternal life of God, the Divine Sophia, who alone is worthy of being called "all in all"? … The Incarnation of Christ accomplishes … man's deification, which is precisely the power of the heavenly Church manifested in the earthly Church.[158]

The church as Sophia is the heavenly Jerusalem, descending from on high, but it is also the bride awaiting her bridegroom, "the created, earthly Church" that through the Spirit asks for this descent: "Heavenly and earthly, the Church is one in ground and limit, in entelechy, but she remains dual in the world process until the end of the world."[159] The mystical unity of humanity coincides with the mystery of the church, the body of Christ and, at the same time, temple of the Holy Spirit. This ecclesiology is "the doctrine of the sobornost of the Church, understood both ontologically and practically as the principle of gathering (Russ. *sobiranie*) and gatheredness (Russ. *sobrannost*) in love."[160] From this it follows, among other things, that the "organic and creative life of the Church ontologically *precedes* the hierarchical principle," even though later "hierarchy was advanced as the *prius* of the Church."[161] On the ecumenical level, this means that the hierarchical organization of the church is relative to history and not to its essence. The justification for the hierarchy lies in its connection with the Eucharist, not in dogma (as in the Roman Church) or in its denial (as in Protestantism), but in the principle of *sobornost*, that is, in the union of all in freedom and love. When Orthodoxy forgets this principle, it transforms (in a perfectly Roman spirit) "a hierarchy which rules over the Church in the capacity of an ecclesial oligarchy." The gift of Pentecost is the episcopate as an expression of the *sobornost* of the entire church, not the bishops as a historically verifiable succession.[162]

The church as an institution, "the 'visible' or empirical Church, does not wholly coincide with the church as Divine-humanity, with its noumenal depth, although the empirical is connected with, based on, and permeated by, the Church as Divine-humanity."[163] An *ecclesia extra ecclesia* is given beyond the institutional boundaries of the church; the church of Pentecost is not exhausted in the seven sacraments, nor do the divisions of the historical church touch the depths of the mystery of the church. The *una sancta*, as the incarnation of God renewed in Pentecost, moves the church to unity, overcoming in each "the spirit of confessionalism that supplants the universal unity with ecclesiastical provincialism."[164] The plurality of churches (*multae ecclesiolae*) is based on *ecclesia supra ecclesias*. The divisions between hierarchical systems that church history has handed down to the present must be considered in light of the meta-empirical and noumenal unity of the church, which subsists in the prophetic and kingly face of the historical church, while also calling it to sacramental and hierarchical unity. The face of the

157 Bulgakov, *The Bride of the Lamb*, 258.
158 Bulgakov, *The Bride of the Lamb*, 257.
159 Bulgakov, *The Bride of the Lamb*, 264.
160 Bulgakov, *The Bride of the Lamb*, 262.
161 Bulgakov, *The Bride of the Lamb*, 262–263 (italics original).
162 Sergius Bulgakov, "The Hierarchy and the Sacraments," in: Roderic Dunkerley, ed., *The Ministry and the Sacraments: Report of the Theological Commission Appointed by the Continuation Committee of the Faith and Order Movement under the Chairmanship of the Right Rev. Arthur Cayley Headlam*, London, SCM Press, 1937, 95–123, here 103 (Russian version: "Ierarkhiya i tainstva," *Put* 49, 1935, 23–47). See Sergius Bulgakov, "The Church Universal," 10–11.
163 Bulgakov, *The Bride of the Lamb*, 271.
164 Bulgakov, *The Bride of the Lamb*, 293.

church is turned simultaneously to heavenly contemplation as well as to earthly horizons.[165]

In Bulgakov, the emphasis falls on the pneumatic and eschatological moment of the church as a divine-human reality. Florovsky's perspective diverges precisely at this point: methodologically, because he finds it impossible to separate the historical from the noumenal aspect of the church, and theologically, because of the Christological orientation of his ecclesiology. Two studies from 1934 prepared for the meetings of the Fellowship of St. Alban and St. Sergius are illuminating on this matter.[166] Florovsky makes it immediately clear that "the Church is Christ's work on earth; it is the image and abode of His blessed Presence in the world."[167] A Christological foundation also permeates the charismatic dimension. On the day of the Pentecost, the Holy Spirit descended upon the church (the apostles and those who were with them, that is, the ecclesial *sobornost*), extending the dwelling of Christ among individuals in space and time, bringing his action in history to fullness. This action is the church, which represents the continuation of the divine-human union, humanity transfigured and regenerated. The mystery of the "final reunion in the image of the Unity of the Holy Trinity … is realized in the life and construction of the Church, it is the *mystery of sobornost, the mystery of catholicity*."[168]

Florovsky continued to work on his insights of the 1930s in his paper "The Church: Her Nature and Task" at the Amsterdam Assembly in 1948. A Christological anchorage of ecclesiology implies a personalistic conception of Christian life, which he did not see as guaranteed by the latent monism of Sophiology. The church is composed of persons, irreducible to mere elements of the whole, since "each is in direct and immediate union with Christ and His Father – the personal is not to be sacrificed or dissolved in the corporate, Christian 'togetherness' must not degenerate into impersonalism." The concept of "catholicity" (*sobornost*) is not exhausted in the idea of the organism, which "must be supplemented by the idea of a symphony of personalities, in which the mystery of the Holy Trinity is reflected (cf. John xvii, 21 and 23)." But the personal center of the church is in Christ, because "she is not an incarnation of the Holy Spirit, nor is she merely a Spirit-being community, but precisely the body of Christ, the Incarnate Lord."[169] This is the reason Florovsky prefers a Christological orientation in ecclesiology to a pneumatological one such as that of Aleksey Khomyakov and Johann Adam Möhler (and Bulgakov).

Unlike Bulgakov, who saw in *sobornost* an organic form of the succession of the gifts of the Holy Spirit in the church, Florovsky explained the notion of "catholicity" (*sobornost*) in terms of apostolic tradition and succession, that is, according to historical and not just charismatic categories. "The Church is an *apostolic Church* … created and sealed by the Spirit in the Twelve Apostles, and the Apostolic Succession is a living and mysterious thread binding the whole historical fullness of Church life into one catholic whole."[170] The objective aspect, which is the uninterrupted *sacramental* succession, and the subjective aspect, which is fidelity to

165 Bulgakov, *The Bride of the Lamb*, 293.

166 Georges Florovsky, "Sobornost: The Catholicity of the Church," in: Eric Mascall, ed., *The Church of God. An Anglo-Russian Symposium by Members of the Fellowship of St. Alban and St. Sergius*, London, SPCK, 1934, 51–74. When the article was reprinted in *The Collected Works*, the word *sobornost* was omitted, see Georges Florovsky, "The Catholicity of the Church," in: Georges Florovsky, *The Collected Works*, vol. 1, *Bible, Church, Tradition: An Eastern Orthodox View*, Belmont MA, Nordland, 1972, 37–55; Georges Florovsky, "The Sacrament of Pentecost: A Russian View on Apostolic Succession," *The Journal of the Fellowship of St. Alban and St. Sergius* 23, 1934, 29–34, as well as in Georges Florovsky, *The Collected Works*, vol. 3, *Creation and Redemption*, Belmont MA, Nordland, 1976, 189–200 (the following quote from *The Collected Works*).

167 Florovsky, "The Catholicity," 37.

168 Florovsky, "The Catholicity," 39 (italics original).

169 Georges Florovsky, "The Church: Her Nature and Task," in: Florovsky, *The Collected Works*, vol. 1, 57–72, here 67.

170 Florovsky, "The Catholicity," 45 (italics original).

the apostolic tradition, are inseparable. "Apostolic Succession must not be severed from Apostolic Tradition, and in fact never can be. Apostolic Tradition is not only a historical reminiscence … Tradition is not Church archeology but spiritual life. It is the memory of the Church."[171]

Florovsky reproached Khomyakov for pitting the charism of doctrinal infallibility (proper to the apostolic tradition) against sacramental power (established in apostolic succession), unduly separating them. The deposit of the true faith is indeed guarded by the whole church, but each local church finds its center and unity in its own bishop, "because through him it is included in the mysterious '*sobornost*' ['*catholicity*'] of the Church-body for all times."[172]

Sobornaya means simply "catholic," *katholike* from *kath'holou*, "according to the whole," indicating "the inner fullness and integrity of the life of the church." Florovsky noted that the expression *ekklesia katholike* did not primarily indicate the extension of the church over the whole earth, but of its orthodoxy, "the truth of the 'Great Church,' as contrasted with the spirit of sectarian separatism and particularism."[173] As support, Florovsky cited Ignatius of Antioch ("where there is a bishop, let there be the whole multitude; just as where Jesus Christ is, there too is the Catholic Church,") and Cyril of Jerusalem, for whom catholicity was an inner quality of the church, since "dogmas are taught *'fully, without any omission*, catholically, and completely' (*katholikôs kaì anelleipôs*)."[174]

Florovsky upended Bulgakov's appeal to history: the historical development of the church is not the progressive revelation of a noumenal reality but the unbroken witness of an event in history, the incarnation of Christ. The custodians of the veracity of this witness are the Fathers, "a constant and ultimate measure and criterion of right faith."[175] Only by acquiring this "mentality" (*phronema*) is it possible to rise to an authentic catholic consciousness, which coincides with a historical consciousness: "The Church recognizes and confirms dogmatic events as facts of history. God-manhood is a historical fact, not just a postulate of faith. Within the Church, history must provide the theologian with a genuine perspective. … for the life of the Church is tradition."[176]

The ecumenical problem was reconceived on historical grounds. Even for Florovsky, "*the very fact of division in the Church is a paradox and an antinomy*."[177] On the one hand, the force of Cyprian's principle *nulla salus extra ecclesiam* lies in its tautological character, "because *salvation is the Church*."[178] On the other hand, church history testifies that "the life in grace in schismatical bodies is not extinguished and exhausted."[179] There have been and are cases where the church even welcomes heretics without renewing their baptism and clerics in their ministerial rank. In the very form of its operation, the church testifies to the extension of its mystical territory beyond the canonical threshold. The ecumenical paradox lies entirely within the noncoincidence between the church's canonical and charismatic boundaries, which Cyprian had too hastily identified.[180]

Florovsky's perspective allowed for much less optimism about the future of the ecumenical movement than Bulgakov's vision. Both were certainly convinced that Orthodoxy was not one denomination among others but the church in its

171 Florovsky, "The Sacrament of Pentecost," 194.
172 Florovsky, "The Sacrament of Pentecost," 191.
173 Florovsky, "The Catholicity," 40.
174 Florovsky, "The Catholicity," 40–41, quoting Ignatius of Antioch, *Epistle to the Smyrnaeans* 8.2 and Cyril of Jerusalem, *Catechetical Lectures* 18.23.
175 Georges Florovsky, "St. Gregory Palamas and the Tradition of the Fathers," in: Florovsky, *The Collected Works*, vol. 1, 105–120, here 107.
176 Florovsky, *The Collected Works*, vol. 6, 296.
177 Florovsky, "The Sacrament of Pentecost," 200 (italics original).
178 Florovsky, "The Catholicity,'" 38 (italics original).
179 Florovsky, "The Sacrament of Pentecost," 197–198.
180 Georges Florovsky, "The Limits of the Church." Gallaher, "Bulgakov's ecumenical thought," 52, note 93, reveals the similarity of this article by Florovsky with Bulgakov's address "Outlines."

truth, not a church but the church.[181] Where Bulgakov saw the shoots of eschatological unity, however, Florovsky saw an abyss of separation from the church, an impossible compromise on the church's integrity. In both, the tension between a universalistic vision of church in a hierarchical sense and the perspective of Eucharistic ecclesiology that was beginning to take hold remained unresolved. From the late 1930s, Florovsky would avoid the term *sobornost*, which to him must have seemed hopelessly compromised by Bulgakov's Sophiology.[182]

7 Orthodoxy within the Ecumenical Movement: The Edinburgh Conference (1937)

The first two Faith and Order conferences are separated by a decade of intense theological (in the Continuation Committee) and organizational work. The organizing committee's rich and often complicated correspondence with the leaders of the autocephalous churches documents Orthodox interest in, and appreciation for, the ecumenical enterprise.[183] The Edinburgh conference in 1937 marked, in the words of Metropolitan Stefan of Sofia, "a notable advance in the whole spiritual atmosphere of the conference."[184] Metropolitan Germanos (Strenopoulos) of Thyateira led the delegation. Russians (including Bulgakov and Florovsky, Nicholas Afanasiev, Lev Zander, and Nicolas Zernov) made up about one third of the Orthodox delegates. Five sessions were scheduled: (1) "The Grace of Our Lord Jesus Christ"; (2) "The Church of Christ and the Word of God"; (3) "The Communion of Saints"; (4) "The Church of Christ: Ministry and Sacraments"; and (5) "The Unity of the Church in Life and Worship."

Among the Orthodox serving on the Continuation Committee elected in Lausanne were Hamilcar Alivisatos, Nicholas Arsenev, Stefan Tsankov, and Sergius Bulgakov. The section on the communion of saints was included at the insistence of the Orthodox. In the preparatory stage, Bulgakov had remarked that the point was so important that it could not be subsumed under others since it involved "the theology of the relationship between the militant church on earth ...

181 Boulgakov, *L'Orthodoxie*, 102, 211; Georges Florovsky, "The Ethos of the Orthodox Church," in: *Orthodoxy: A Faith and Order Dialogue*, Geneva, WCC Publications, 1960, 36–51, here 39.

182 In his "Father Georges Florovsky's Vision," Williams suggests that, because of Florovsky's influence, the term *sobornost* would not reappear on the WCC agenda until the 1970s.

183 For example, Patriarch Nicholas V of Alexandria, in his letter to Bishop William Temple dated Jun 22, 1937, with the appointment of Metropolitan Nikolaos of Aksum, patriarchal vicar in Cairo, as his delegate, stated that he, after his personal participation in the Lausanne conference, had always followed the work for church unity with great interest: "We have been given by God's grace the opportunity of assisting as metropolitan of Nubia at the time, at the Faith and Order conference at Geneva in 1920 and at Lausanne in 1927, and have followed since with great interest the meritorious efforts for the promotion of the relations among the Churches for the raising form the middle of the misunderstandings and for a better knowledge of the truth for an approachment and with the time and God's will, for the reunion in One Catholic and Apostolic Church, for the promotion of our Lord's will throughout the world and the restoration of its peace"; Nicholas V of Alexandria to the Most Rev. Archbishop of York William Temple, Jun 22, 1937, in: WCCA 232.004, Faith and Order, Edinburgh 1937, I, Greek original and English translation.

184 "I find a notable advance in the whole spiritual atmosphere of the Conference"; Hodgson, ed., *The Second World Conference*, 120. Among those represented in Edinburgh were the Ecumenical Patriarchate, Patriarchate of Alexandria, Patriarchate of Antioch, Patriarchate of Jerusalem, Patriarchate of Russia (Russian Church in exile), Church of Cyprus, Orthodox Church of Greece, Church of Bulgaria, Orthodox Church of Poland, Church of Albania, and the Orthodox Church of Latvia (which had been autonomous from the Patriarchate of Moscow since 1921). Other Eastern churches were the Assyrian Church, Orthodox Syrian Church of the East, Egyptian Orthodox (Coptic) Church, and the Apostolic Church of Armenia. See Hodgson, ed., *The Second World Conference*, 282–283.

and the triumphal church in heaven."[185] Bulgakov justified his insistence on the veneration of the Mother of God by the fact that "the correct understanding of this aspect of Orthodox liturgical life" would be helpful for the Protestant world, while its exclusion from the program would "make a painful impression on the whole Orthodox world, which is absolutely to be avoided."[186] The issue, moreover, was not merely pastoral but theological. At the heart of the church, "as its personification," Bulgakov identified the sanctifying reality of "the Most Holy and Most Pure Virgin Mother of God, who belongs to our world and to our humanity … and, at the same time, to the glorified humanity of Christ."[187] The final report simply mentioned the words of the *Magnificat* "all generations will call me blessed" (Luke 1:48) and the need for further study. One note specified that the Orthodox believe that the mother of the Lord, the *Theotokos*, should be venerated above all the saints and angels and all creation.[188]

The most controversial topics remained those of the session on "The Church of Christ: Ministry and Sacraments."[189] Bulgakov recalled the need for dogmatic reflection on the church. The main obstacle to reconciliation was the absence of a dogmatic definition of the church in the early centuries and the contentious nature of modern definitions after the Reformation. This problem opened up a more general one: the necessity of making a distinction "between dogmatic definitions which are obligatory and definitions concerning doctrinal differences."[190] This was not a matter of sacrificing the truth, but of seeking the possibility of reconciliation in all matters "not bound by obligatory definitions."[191]

Georges Florovsky, who chaired the session on ministry, contested the possibility of clearly separating dogma and doctrine, as proposed by Bulgakov, and warned against "the danger of substituting something new for the traditional and venerable doctrine of the past."[192] Lacking substantive agreement, they had to restrict themselves to exactly setting out the different conceptions. It would not be a step backward to acknowledge the real extent of the differences and the points at which the differences were irreconcilable, while it would have been heresy with regard to church history to regard them as mere misunderstandings or "to substitute for reunion of churches a confusion of churches."[193] Florovsky – who, after Edinburgh, on Bulgakov's own recommendation replaced him in his position in Faith and Order – proposed that the Continuation Committee work on a definition of church as a supernatural reality, centered on Christ's work and expressed by the metaphor of

185 S. Bulgakov to Canon L. Hodgson, Jul 10, 1935, in: WCCA 23.4.020/1, autograph.

186 Bulgakov to Canon L. Hodgson: "I have insisted almost in all conferences of the Cont[inuation] Com[mittee] and am continuing to insist that the question of the veneration of Our Lady and its importance for the Orthodox Church might be *explained not for a discussion, but for the information*, as a 'witness to what the worship and life of the Church mean' to the Orthodox people. I have a firm conviction that the right understanding of this side of worship of Orthodoxy would be helpful for the Protestant world. In contrary [sic] the exclusion of this point from the program may make a painful impression in the whole Orthodox world, which is in any case to be avoided" (italics original).

187 Bulgakoff, "Thesen über die Kirche," 133–134. See Sergius Bulgakov, "The Question of the Veneration of the Virgin Mary at the Edinburgh Conference and a Brief Statement of the Place of the Virgin Mary in the Thought and Worship of the Orthodox Church," *Sobornost* 12, 1937, 28–31 (reprinted in *The Eastern Church Quarterly Review* 3, 1938, 109–111); Sergius Bulgakov, "The Incarnation and the Virgin Birth," *Sobornost* 14, 1938, 32–37.

188 "The latter hold that the mother of our Lord, designated as *Theotokos* (God-bearer), the ever-Virgin, should be venerated as the highest of all saints and angels, and of all creation"; Hodgson, ed., *The Second World Conference*, 351 n. 1.

189 Rev. Donald M. Baillie, the president of the session, himself admitted this. Hodgson, ed., *The Second World Conference*, 135.

190 Hodgson, ed., *The Second World Conference*, 67.

191 Hodgson, ed., *The Second World Conference*, 67. See Bulgakov, "The Hierarchy and the Sacraments."

192 Hodgson, ed., *The Second World Conference*, 75.

193 Hodgson, ed., *The Second World Conference*, 74.

the body, "as the one people of God, as one glorious body, as the New Jerusalem."[194]

In the declaration accompanying the second revision of the final report, the Orthodox delegates acknowledged the progress made regarding the veneration of the Blessed Virgin and the saints. They found unexpected agreement on the topic of grace (lamenting only the failure to treat the notion of *synergia*, "cooperation"), and some convergence on the Word of God, while not fully agreeing on the relationship between Scripture and Tradition. ("We consider the church and not the 'Word' [that is, the written and preached Word] as primary in the work of our salvation.") With regard to the unity of the church in life and worship, they reiterated that "only one true church can be visible and exist on earth" and that intercommunion "must be considered the crowning act of a real and true reunion which has already been fully achieved by fundamental agreement in the realm of Faith and Order and is not to be regarded as an instrument for reunion."[195] The declaration read by Metropolitan Germanos, like that of Lausanne, sought to reunite the different souls of the Orthodox delegation in a unity of purpose: "Brethren! After having made this declaration in order to satisfy our consciences ... With you we bewail the rending asunder of the seamless robe of Christ. We desire, as you, that the members of the one Body of Christ may again be reunited, and we pray, as you, day by day in our congregations for the union of all mankind."[196]

In Edinburgh, the discussion of the proposal to unify the two branches of the ecumenical movement, which came from the ranks of Life and Work, tested the Orthodox on the degree of their ecumenical commitment.[197] On the Orthodox side, adhesion was conditioned by both theological issues (the doctrinal, constitutional, and liturgical differences in respect to the Reformed tradition) as well as organizational issues (the criteria for representation of the different autocephalous churches). In a memorandum drafted in the aftermath of the conference, Paul Anderson, an Ohio Presbyterian who had coordinated assistance to Russian exiles on behalf of the YMCA since World War I, identified three groups among the Orthodox delegates: those who were persuaded that the gap with other Christians was unbridgeable and for whom the non-Orthodox remained schismatics and heretics; those who saw signs of a return to the one, holy, catholic, and apostolic Church in the Protestant world; and, finally, those who were in favor of dialogue, convinced that Orthodoxy was flexible enough to allow for "an area of consensus" open to different interpretations of the tradition.[198]

The groupings did not reflect jurisdictional divisions, although in general the Romanians (absent in Edinburgh), along with some Greeks and Russians, supported the first position. Russians and

194 G. Florovsky to L. Hodgson, Sep 29, 1939, in: WCCA 23.4.020/2, WCC, Commission Faith and Order, Correspondence with Churches, departments, groups, 1934–1952/2, correspondence with Life & Work. "The one Church of God is not an earthly institution and not merely a human society, but a supernatural reality which is in the process of growth towards the world to come in which it will be consummated. It is the sphere of action of the Risen and Ascended Lord, all its members being in Christ and being knit together by a spiritual or charismatic kinship, all their gifts and activities continuing the work of Christ by the virtue of the Holy Spirit, originating from Christ and being co-ordinated by Him to the final goal. Then the church will appear in the age to come as the one people of God, as one glorious body, as the New Jerusalem ... This definition should be completed by some reference to the sacraments and the ministry, which are the Divinely intended and instituted means by which the actual growth of the Church is effectuated."

195 Hodgson, ed., *The Second World Conference*, 154–155. The English text of the declaration, with 16 signatures, is found in WCCA 23.4.020/1. Gennadios Limouris, ed., *Orthodox Visions of Ecumenism: Statements, Messages and Reports on the Ecumenical Movement (1902–1992)*, Geneva, WCC Publications, 1994, 15–17.

196 Hodgson, ed., *The Second World Conference*, 157.

197 Hodgson, ed., *The Second World Conference*, 192–204.

198 Paul Anderson, "Memorandum supplied to F.W.T." [Father William Temple], Edinburgh, Aug 11, 1937, in: WCCA, 232.003, Faith and Order Edinburgh 1937.1, ff. 1–2 (typescript).

Bulgarians were in the second camp, while the third position was ascribable only to "a few individuals." At the same time, Anderson warned that the Orthodox delegates were not always representative in all respects of the feeling of their churches and that it would take a long time for the Orthodox faithful to catch up with those who represented them. Indeed, it was often this awareness that held the Orthodox delegates back in the theological discussions.[199]

Anderson reflected the widespread feeling in Faith and Order that, in Edinburgh, many delegates perceived the Orthodox presence as "at best … an unfortunate necessity," and reported how the term "Pan-Protestantism" was "used by some Orthodox to describe what they believe to be the goal of a great many Protestants at Edinburgh."[200] Tied to this perception was the problem of Orthodox representation in a possible unified ecumenical movement, that would balance Protestant numerical dominance and take into account the proportions of the faithful (one hundred and fifty million Orthodox and two hundred million Anglicans and Protestants of various denominations). Moreover, the Orthodox churches were in a situation of material poverty and political precariousness in their home countries, while the Russian Orthodox Church, which accounted for two thirds of Orthodoxy, was prevented from taking part in the ecumenical movement for political reasons.[201] These problems were destined to be reopened when the WCC was established. Ecumenism was not only a problem of theological confrontation, but of a shared ecclesial journey.

8 Conclusions

We could place the contribution of Orthodox theology under the heading of a renewed relationship to tradition, calling for its return as an active principle in contemporary Christianity. Alivisatos likened this movement to the similar liturgical movement and the return to the sources in the Catholic sphere. If the encounter with tradition essentially responded to Orthodoxy's need to redefine itself, the new look at a shared heritage decisively lent greater depth to the ecumenical path. This extraordinary creative effort, in which the reflection of Russian theologians in exile played an almost maieutic role, took place on a two-fold level: on the one hand, it sought to understand Western Christianity beyond centuries-old prejudices, and, on the other, it attempted to grasp the meaning of Orthodox Christian witness in terms appropriate to the disenchantment with the modern world that was posing radical questions to the theology of all churches.

The ecumenism of Orthodoxy in the first half of the last century was not exclusively a theological movement, but an ecclesial, indeed also theological, response to historical provocations. The experience of the conciliar dimension of the church in the Moscow Council of 1917–1918, the precarious situation of the Orthodox in exile as well as those in Turkey and the Middle East, the redefinition of their identity and confrontation with the Christian West, the persecutions in the Soviet Union and divisions within Russian Orthodoxy – these were some of the traits that characterized Orthodoxy between the two World Wars and which conditioned its contribution to the ecumenical journey.

Having to account existentially and ecclesially for their faith, within the ecumenical movement the Orthodox posed essential questions about the nature of the church: what does the catholicity of the church mean? In what sense do separate communities belong to the *una sancta*? The ecumenical challenge prompted Orthodox theology to explore in greater depth its notion of church and the meaning of church unity, to discuss the relationship between dogma and history, between institution and charism, as well as to rediscover the theology of the Fathers and at the same time tradition as a pneumatological reality and not merely an unalterable heritage of

199 Anderson, "Memorandum supplied to F.W.T.," f. 2.
200 Anderson, "Memorandum supplied to F.W.T.," f. 2.
201 Anderson, "Memorandum supplied to F.W.T.," f. 3.

the past. In regard to each of these areas, Orthodox theology presented a wide spectrum of positions, and it would be reductive to delineate two opposing camps of modernists and traditionalists. The neo-patristic platform launched by Florovsky in opposition to Russian religious philosophy is actually indebted to the latter in many respects. At the same time, Bulgakov believed that Sophiology was a coherent development of insights present in the Fathers. Additionally, Orthodox theology saw other important developments germinate between the wars, such as the Eucharistic ecclesiology of Nicholas Afanasiev,[202] the mystical theology of Vladimir Lossky,[203] the work of Dumitru Stăniloae[204] and the liturgical theology of Alexander Schmemann.[205] Different orientations corresponded to different degrees of involvement with Western thought and the ecumenical movement, with outcomes more open to dialogue when the criterion of truth was posited as a common requirement and not used to define Orthodox identity.[206]

In 1948, after World War II, when the WCC was founded at the Amsterdam assembly, the Orthodox churches of communist bloc countries were not present.[207] The church conference of the heads and representatives of the autocephalous Orthodox churches, convened in Moscow in July 1948 with Joseph Stalin's support to celebrate the fifth centenary of the Russian Church's autocephaly, had branded the WCC as the organization of an "ecumenical church" with socioeconomic and political aims that contradicted the Christian ideal.[208] The conclusions of the Moscow confer-

202 See Nicolas Afanassieff, "L'Église qui préside dans l'amour," in: *La primauté de Pierre dans l'église orthodoxe*, Neuchatel, Delachaux et Niestlé, 1960, 9–64; Nicolas Afanassieff, *L'Église du Saint-Esprit*, Paris, Cerf, 1975. See also Aidan Nichols, *Theology in the Russian Diaspora: Church, Fathers, Eucharist in Nikolai Afanas'ev (1893–1966)*, Cambridge, Cambridge University Press, 1989.

203 Vladimir Lossky, *The Mystical Theology of the Eastern Church*, Crestwood NY, St. Vladimir's Seminary Press, 1997; Vladimir Lossky, *The Vision of God*, Crestwood NY, St. Vladimir's Seminary Press, 2013; Vladimir Lossky, *In the Image and Likeness of God*, Crestwood NY, St. Vladimir's Seminary Press, 2001. On the relationship between Lossky and the Russian diaspora, see Rowan Williams, *The Theology of Vladimir Nikolaevich Lossky: An Exposition and Critique*, thesis, University of Oxford, 1975, which has been translated into Russian: Rowan Williams, *Bogoslovie V.N. Losskogo: izlozhenie i kritika*, Kiev, Dukh i litera, 2009.

204 Dumitru Stăniloae, *Viaţa şi învăţaturile Sfântului Grigorie Palama* [The Life and Teaching of St. Gregory Palamas], Sibiu, Tipografia archidiecezană, 1938; Dumitru Stăniloae, *Ascetica şi Mistica Bisericii Ortodoxe* (1947), Bucharest, Ed. Inst. Biblic şi de Misiune al Bisericii Ortodoxe Române, 2002; FT: *Théologie ascétique et mystique de l'Église orthodoxe*, Paris, Cerf, 2011. See Viorel Coman, "Revisiting the Agenda of the Orthodox Neo-Patristic Movement," *DR* 136/2, 2018, 99–117.

205 Alexander Schmemann, *Introduction to Liturgical Theology*, Crestwood NY, St. Vladimir's Seminary Press, 1966; Alexander Schmemann, *Liturgy and Tradition*, ed. Thomas Fisch, Crestwood NY, St. Vladimir's Seminary Press, 1990.

206 See Gavrilyuk, *Georges Florovsky*, 190–191; Matthew Baker, "Neopatristic Synthesis and Ecumenism: Towards the 'Reintegration' of Christian Tradition," in: Andrii Krawchuk & Thomas Bremer, eds., *Eastern Orthodox Encounters of Identity and Otherness: Values, Self-Reflection, Dialogue*, New York, Palgrave-MacMillan, 2014, 235–260.

207 See Willem Adolf Visser't Hooft, "The Genesis of the World Council of Churches," in: *A History of the Ecumenical Movement*, vol. 1, 697–724, esp. 716–717.

208 Limouris, ed., *Orthodox Visions*, 18–19; Hilarion Alfeev, ed., *Conference of the Heads and Representatives of the Autocephalous Orthodox Churches: Moscow 1948*, in: *COGD* 4/2, 883–897, esp. 895–897. In attendance were the primates of the churches of Georgia, Serbia, Romania, and Bulgaria; Metropolitan Elias (Karam) of Lebanon represented the patriarchates of Alexandria and Antioch; and representatives of the Ecumenical Patriarchate and of the Church of Greece, who had joined the WCC and attended the celebrations but not the conference. Catholicos of All Armenians George VI attended as just a guest but signed the document on the Catholic Church and ecumenism. The assembly had been conceived and planned by the Soviet leadership since 1945 to foster the Moscow Patriarchate as the leader of world Orthodoxy: see Adriano Roccucci, *Stalin e il patriarca: Chiesa ortodossa e potere sovietico, 1917–1958*, Turin, Einaudi, 2011, 287–293; Daniela Kalkandjeva, *The Russian Orthodox Church, 1917–1948: From Decline to Resurrection*, London, Routledge, 2015, 307–344.

ence, however, were not followed by Orthodoxy as a whole. The debate over the "non-ecclesial" character of the WCC continued until the Toronto statement of 1950; Florovsky was among its most convinced inspirers.[209]

Some of the points address Orthodox concerns directly: "The World Council of Churches is not and must never become a superchurch" (III.1); "Membership in the World Council of Churches does not imply that a Church treats its own conception of the Church as merely relative" (III.4) nor does membership imply that "each Church must regard the other member Churches as Churches in the true and full sense of the word" (IV.4).[210] The WCC's role is that of an instrument that must diminish so that *una sancta* can grow. In 1961, the Moscow Patriarchate decided to join the WCC and, shortly thereafter, sent observers to Vatican II.[211]

Translated from Italian to English by Susan Dawson Vásquez and David Dawson Vásquez.

Bibliography

A History of the Ecumenical Movement 1517–1968, vol. 1, Ruth Rouse & Stephen C. Neill, eds., *1517–1948*, Geneva, WCC Publications, 41993.

Arjakovsky, Antoine, *La génération des penseurs religieux de l'émigration russe: La revue La Voie (Put') (1925–1940)*, Kiev/Paris, L'Esprit et la Lettre, 2002.

Arjakovsky, Antoine, *Essai sur le père Serge Boulgakov (1871–1944): Philosophe et théologien chrétien*, Paris, Parole et Silence, 2006.

Bulgakov, Sergius, *The Bride of the Lamb*, trans. Boris Jakim, Grand Rapids, Eerdmans, 2002.

Destivelle, Hyacinthe, *The Moscow Council (1917–1918): The Creation of the Conciliar Institutions of the Russian Orthodox Church*, Notre Dame, University of Notre Dame Press, 2015.

Florovsky, Georges, *The Collected Works*, vol. 5, *Ways of Russian Theology: Part One*, ed. Richard S. Haugh, Belmont MA, Nordland Publishing Company, 1979.

Florovsky, Georges, *The Collected Works*, vol. 6, *Ways of Russian Theology: Part Two*, ed. Richard S. Haugh, Vaduz, Büchervertriebsanstalt, 1987.

Gavrilyuk, Paul L., *Georges Florovsky and the Russian Religious Renaissance: Changing Paradigms in Historical and Systematic Theology*, Oxford, Oxford University Press, 2013.

Geffert, Bryn, *Eastern Orthodox and Anglicans: Diplomacy, Theology, and the Politics of Interwar Ecumenism*, Notre Dame, University of Notre Dame Press, 2010.

Khristianskoe vossoedinenie: Ekumenicheskaya problema v pravoslavnom soznanii [Christian reunification: the ecumenical problem in Orthodox thought], Paris, YMCA Press, 1933.

Nichols, Aidan, *Alban and Sergius: The Story of a Journal*, Leominster, Gracewing, 2018.

Patelos, Constantin, ed., *The Orthodox Church in the Ecumenical Movement: Documents and Statements (1902–1975)*, Geneva, WCC Publications, 1978.

Salapatas, Dimitrios Filippos, *The Fellowship of St. Alban and St. Sergius: Orthodox and Anglican Ecumenical Relations (1927–2012)*, Newcastle upon Tyne, Cambridge Scholars Publishing, 2018.

Zernov, Nicolas, *The Russian Religious Renaissance of the Twentieth Century*, New York, Harper & Row, 1963.

209 See Job (Getcha), "Georges Florovsky and the World Council of Churches," in: John Chryssavgis & Brandon Gallaher, eds., *The Living Christ: The Theological Legacy of Georges Florovsky*, London, T&T Clark, 2023, 393–407.

210 "The Church, the Churches and the World Council of Churches: The Ecclesiological Significance of the World Council of Churches" (1950), available at <www.oikoumene.org/resources/documents/toronto-statement> (accessed Mar 21, 2023).

211 On which, see Melloni, ed., *Vatican II in Moscow*.

CHAPTER 5

Abbé Paul Couturier and Spiritual Ecumenism

Étienne Fouilloux

1 Introduction

Abbé Paul Couturier, who composed the prayer for unity in which Christians from all continents and of all confessions join every January, is probably the 20th-century priest from Lyon who is best known across the world. A pioneer and an ardent promoter of a spiritual ecumenism approved by the highest ecclesial authorities in the Catholic, Orthodox, and Protestant churches, his life, work, and legacy should not pose any problems to historians, the more so as his archives can be accessed without too much difficulty.[1] However, this is not the case.

The conflicting reactions in the aftermath of his death gave rise to a first major question. On 27 Mar, 1953, Cardinal Pierre-Marie Gerlier contravened in his favor the rule in Lyon "that no word should be spoken in the church on the occasion of a priest's funeral." The cardinal's message is quite clear: "It is not only the friend, a devoted friend, who now speaks, but above all the archbishop of Lyon, who wishes to offer to the departed the sorrowful homage of his admiration, of his affection, and of his gratitude." But also: "Abbé Couturier has greatly honored this diocese. He has been a magnificent servant of the church. The church thanks him through my humble voice." He was "a precursor and a model" whose work for unity must be "continued in the same spirit."[2] In contrast, the obituary written by Abbé Montagnon, the superior of the society of the priests of St. Irenaeus or Carthusian priests, an institution in Lyon to which Couturier belonged, can barely conceal the thorns beneath the roses. Dated 1 Jun, 1953, it expresses some surprise over the "outpouring of affection and admiration" surrounding his mortal remains, while also pointing out that his "intensive activity" in the service of ecumenism "was carried out on the margins of the House's[3] 'works' and gradually drew him away from us to the point of monopolizing him." Most notably, it emphasizes "that teaching was not his vocation" and that he was not particularly successful at it due to the fact that he was not sufficiently grounded in the triviality of day-to-day life, which contradicted the "overflying" advocated by Couturier in his ecumenical course of action.[4] This rather harsh criticism provoked a reaction from Abbé Gabriel Matagrin, the future bishop of Grenoble, who resigned the following year from his position as spiritual director of the Institution des Chartreux (or simply: Les Chartreux), a prestigious private high school in Lyon at which Couturier had taught.[5] In the light of these testimonies, one may well ask whether

1 The papers of Abbé Couturier and of his disciple, the Marist Brother Maurice Villain, are preserved at the Abbey of Notre-Dame des Dombes, near Lyon, under the supervision of the Chemin Neuf community, which took over the abbey from the monks in 2001; the papers pertaining to the propagation of the January Week of Prayer for Christian Unity are stored in Lyon, at the center Unité Chrétienne.

2 "Never will we be able to forget what he has done for the unity of Christians, with regard to which our Holy Father recently told me how much he longed for its realization, and that it should therefore be the object of our ardent prayer to the sole One who is indeed able to grant its realization as He wills"; see *Paul Couturier, apôtre de l'unité chrétienne: Témoignages*, Lyon, Vitte, 1954, 45–47.

3 The so-called Maison (or Institution) des Chartreux on Croix Rousse Hill in the 4th arrondissement of Lyon.

4 Archives des Chartreux, double printed page with a black frame. The Sulpician priest Louis Richard appears to respond to its assessment in the note which he published in the *Semaine religieuse du diocèse de Lyon*, Sep 25, 1953, 511–514.

5 Gabriel Matagrin, *Le chêne et la futaie: Une Église avec les hommes de ce temps (entretiens avec Charles Ehlinger)*, Paris, Bayard, 2000, 42.

a mediocre high school teacher and a great ecumenist could actually coexist in one and the same priest – a first major question to investigate.

But did they really coexist or did one simply follow upon the other? A second key question, which Couturier's disciple and biographer, Maurice Villain, believed that he had settled. "The fact remained, however, that the willful destruction of personal papers – and especially of those that preceded the ecumenical career – carries with it an irreducible significance. This first Paul Couturier is abolished by decision of the second," as Villain wrote in the biography that remains the standard reference work to this day.[6] Hence the conclusion drawn a few years later that "Abbé Couturier was the disciple of no one in this world: he was instructed by the Holy Spirit alone."[7] Father Villain was enough of a historian to realize that he could not defend such a questionable point of view for long. His biography nevertheless devotes 9 pages to the first 40 years of the Carthusian priest's life, 36 to the years 1920–1937, and nearly 300 to the subsequent 15 years, the latter being those of his ecumenical activity, and also those in which Villain was his principal assistant. Unlike the Dominican Friar Yves Congar, who discovered his ecumenical vocation in 1929, at the young age of 25, and dedicated his life to the reconciliation of Christians, for Paul Couturier ecumenism was a late vocation: discovered at the age of 51, this vocation occupied only the last 20 years of his life. Was there thus a first Couturier, a modest science teacher at a large private high school, followed by a second Couturier, a pioneer of spiritual ecumenism? This second major question actually refers back to the first one: regardless of whether these two aspects of Couturier's personality can be shown to have existed simultaneously or successively, the duality remains – and confronts the biographer with the familiar questions regarding the consistency or inconsistency of a human life as well as its continuity or discontinuities.

In the case of Couturier, the duality seems so evident that it cannot fail to arouse suspicion, since the historian finds it difficult to accept that the ecumenist owes nothing to his long training and to the long-lasting activities that preceded it. At the risk of complicating the portrayal, we shall thus examine three instead of two Couturiers, or three phases of his life, with the aim of determining what the ecumenist owed to each of them: Couturier during his years of apprenticeship, be it in the context of his family or of his priestly, scientific, or even pedagogical training, prior to immersing himself in the rich Catholicism of Lyon; Couturier undergoing reeducation in this intellectual, spiritual, and apostolic milieu during the 1920s and early 1930s; Couturier the apostle of Christian unity, from the 1930s to the 1950s, the best known of all three. Finally, his legacy will also need to be addressed, along with those who embraced it. Such a course of action will perhaps add a certain depth to a process that has, so far, been far too determined by its outcome and focused too much on its final stage.

2 The Initial Phase of Education (1881–1920)

Nothing in this phase really portends the ecumenical blossoming of maturity and old age. But let us approach the problem from the other end: was the very particular ecumenism of Abbé Couturier in

6 Maurice Villain, *L'Abbé Paul Couturier: Apôtre de l'Unité Chrétienne*, Paris, Casterman, 1957, 18. The biography by the Anglican clergyman Geoffrey Curtis, a friend of the Carthusian priest, is very similar to that of Villain (*Paul Couturier and Unity in Christ*, London, SCM Press, 1964). For a more detached view of spiritual ecumenism, see my doctoral thesis: Étienne Fouilloux, *Les Catholiques et l'unité chrétienne du XIXe au XXe siècle: Itinéraires européens d'expression française*, Paris, Le Centurion, 1982, 269–345, 490–510, 625–648; and the study for the 50th anniversary of the Lyonnais priest's death: Étienne Fouilloux, "La vocation tardive de l'abbé Couturier," in: *L'œcuménisme spirituel de Paul Couturier aux défis actuels: Actes du colloque universitaire et interconfessionnel, Lyon et Francheville, Rhône, France, les 8, 9, 10 novembre 2002*, Lyon, Profac, 2003, 15–43.

7 Maurice Villain, "L'abbé Paul Couturier aujourd'hui," introduction to *Œcuménisme spirituel: Les écrits de l'abbé Paul Couturier*, Paris, Casterman, 1963, 15–38, here 30.

any way connected to the 40 years that one could call his hidden life?

2.1 *The Imprint of the Family*

At least three traits that determined the ecumenist's apostolate until his death can be linked to his family's situation. The first is of a purely economic nature. Born in Lyon in 1881 as the son of a small manufacturer, Couturier was, like his whole family, the victim of the poor business dealings of a father who died early. The consequence was a financial precariousness, bordering on poverty, that marked his youth and would continue to haunt him throughout his life. In spite of its reputation in Lyon, the Institution des Chartreux was not in a position to provide its members with a good income. And Paul Couturier was also in charge of his sister, Marie-Antoinette, who was three years older than him. Without this lifelong habit of parsimony, he would not have been so careful in his handling of the ecumenical budget, the meticulous keeping of which is attested by numerous accounting records found among his papers and in his correspondence. He is said to have relied on helpers, either voluntary or paid, for the laborious packaging of the brochures, posters, and other documents on unity and for the posting of these packages to various destinations in France or throughout Europe. The budgeting of the January week of prayer would obsess him until the eve of his death.[8] Like the day-to-day life of its inventor, spiritual ecumenism bears the mark of an austerity that is in many ways akin to poverty.

A second family-related constraint, this time, however, of a more ambivalent nature, was his sister Marie-Antoinette Couturier. After the death of their mother in 1918, Paul was somehow responsible for her, all the more so as she was afraid to live alone in the small, fourth floor apartment situated between the Saône and the Rhône, at 5 rue du Plat, and had asked her brother to move in with her. His superiors at Les Chartreux granted this request, but it isolated him from his fellow Carthusian brothers, who resided in a religious house where Couturier's room now only served him for receptions. Although he was sometimes compelled to silence her when someone came to visit him, this sister looked after Abbé Couturier in financial and spiritual matters, as shown by their correspondence. Very pious and quite assertive,[9] she was active on the sidelines of the initiatives launched by her brother, mobilizing the earthly and celestial networks that were familiar to her: she thus advised him to travel to England in September 1937 to attend the intercession for six recently deceased persons, among whom Marius Gonin, the key figure behind the publishing house Chronique sociale de France, the flagship of Catholicism in Lyon.[10] A usually discrete but all the more effective presence, Marie-Antoinette Couturier was both a responsibility and a vigilant guardian for the apostle of spiritual ecumenism.[11]

For the Couturiers, austerity was not only a material but also a moral issue. It can be assumed that Paul's upbringing was marked by a very strong rigorism that had lasting effects on his sensitive character, which was tormented by scruples. His first article, published anonymously in the Dominican journal *La vie spirituelle* (Mar 1, 1935), bears the title "D'une thérapeutique spirituelle du scrupule." "When a rigoristic, educational influence burdens one of these poor, hypersensitized temperaments with the heavy jurism of a falsely understood religion, [the result] is a distorted soul that is perhaps forever trapped in scruple."[12]

8 On Mar 10, 1953, he was still 315,000 francs short on a total of 830,000, in spite of the 50,000 donated by the industrialist Paul Gillet (see the latter's letter from Mar 3 and the letter of P. Couturier to Cardinal P.-M. Gerlier, Mar 10, 1953, in: AAL, 11, II, 205); the deficit was filled on the eve of his death.

9 According to the recollections of the Sisters of Reparative Adoration, in whose chapel in rue Henri IV (Lyon, 2nd arrondissement) the octaves of prayer were held between 1934 and 1938; see *Unité chrétienne*, 32, November 1973, 47–48.

10 See "Frère et soeur," *Unité chrétienne*, 32, November 1973, 43.

11 She died in 1960, surviving him by more than seven years.

12 "Que, sur un de ces pauvres tempéraments hypersensibilisés, une influence éducative rigoriste fasse peser le lourd jurisme [sic] d'une religion mal comprise,

Deliberately entrenched behind anonymity, this passage and a few others bear witness to his personal experience. The decisive encounters of the 1920s would doubtlessly help Couturier free himself of this handicap, as is also demonstrated by its objectivation in his writings. But are certain lingering effects of this handicap still detectable in the ecumenist's bearing? His rare, photographic portraits preserve the appearance of a face that has often been qualified as diaphanous, which draws attention through the depth of its gaze, the depth of a will and of a prayer directed towards its sole objective: the reconciliation of separated Christians. Yet what this face also expresses, along with a touch of sadness or fatigue, is a certain rigor that appears to exclude any pleasure that would distract from this goal, indeed even any kind of humor. Was Abbé Couturier someone who liked to laugh? One may doubt it.

Another distant legacy of the scruple was the meticulousness which he introduced into everything that pertained to the work for unity, notably into his celebrations of Mass, which grew exceedingly long due to the numerous remembrances of deceased people, which he felt were his duty. The same interpretation can be applied to the tone of the letters with which he besieged Cardinal Gerlier and other correspondents in order to obtain an authorization or collaboration. The certitude that he was the humble agent of a holy cause gave him a self-assurance that did not shrink from transgressing the hierarchical rules in order to demand support, and then to react to the slightest refusal as if it were a tragedy.[13] Can we not conclude that Couturier's obsession with personal fault, with the psychological suffering resulting from it, revealed a tendency to turn into an obsession with the collective faults that ran counter to unity, and into a quasi-physical suffering stemming from the harm that was being done to it?

2.2 *The Clerical Imprint*

A clerical imprint was already evident in his family, which included an aunt in the congregation of Nazareth and a great uncle as a priest, namely Louis Planus, who encouraged the young Paul to join the society of the priests of St. Irenaeus, to which he belonged, following the completion of his secondary education at the Lazarist institute in Lyon.

Ordained on Jun 9, 1906 – so between the two encyclicals of Pius X condemning the law of the separation of church and state, and shortly after Georges Clemenceau had put an end to the church inventories that were putting Catholic France to fire and sword – Couturier's clerical formation took place at the height of a sharp upsurge in anticlericalism. Even filtered by the walls of the seminary, this atmosphere of crisis cannot have given an already quite worried young man any reason to look forward to his future ministry with optimism.

Following his novitiate at Les Chartreux (1900–1901), he entered the diocesan major seminary, which was administered by the "gentlemen" of St. Sulpice. To be sure, the conflict between the two societies of priests over the formation of the clergy of Lyon was not what it had been a quarter of a century earlier.[14] The Carthusians had lost and their recruits had been forced to bow to the common law; however, a few traces of this conflict may still have lingered on at the beginning of the century.

c'est une âme faussée et pour toujours peut-être close dans le scrupule"; [Paul Couturier,] "D'une thérapeutique spirituelle du scrupule," *La vie spirituelle*, Mar 1, 1935, 141.

13 To cite just one example among many: "How could you not approve or at least not tolerate, turning a blind eye to everything while being informed of everything, these amicable yet rather infrequent encounters [of Protestant and Catholic personalities at Victor Carlhian's house]? What a terrible responsibility it would be to shrink back!!!"; letter of P. Couturier to Cardinal P.-M. Gerlier, Nov 25, 1943, in: AAL, 11, II, 205.

14 Georges Babolat, "Les Chartreux de Lyon," in: *Les Catholiques libéraux au XIXe siècle: Actes du Colloque internationnal d'histoire religieuse de Grenoble des 30 sept.–3 oct. 1971*, Grenoble, Presses universitaires, 1974, 453–462; Philippe Molac, *Les sulpiciens à Lyon au XIXe siècle*, Master's thesis, Université Lumière-Lyon 2, 1995.

Like his fellow students, the young Couturier's studies at the seminary provided him with a standard and sound academic background, that was more than brilliant, except perhaps in Holy Scripture with a professor such as Emmanuel Podechard. With the Modernist crisis looming on the horizon, audacity was hardly deemed appropriate in the formation of future priests. In the grand tradition of the French school of spirituality of the 17th century, the aim of the Sulpicians directors was to provide the diocese of Lyon with good, saintly priests, and not with intellectuals. More than a school of theology, the St. Irenaeus seminary was a school of piety, if not even of intense spiritual life, and one may well assume that this early instilling of the primacy of prayer over reflection, so characteristic of spiritual ecumenism, marked Abbé Couturier for life, like the majority of his fellow students. Moreover, the quasi-monastic regime of the house, with its close monitoring of conscience and very frequent confessions, was not made to allay his scruples. It even instilled a desire for cloistered life in him, which, if he had not had to take care of his sister, would have led him to the Trappist monastery of Notre-Dame des Dombes in the early 1920s, in spite of his poor singing skills.[15]

2.3 *The Imprint of Teaching*

After having completed his clerical formation at Les Chartreux, due to the dispersion of Sulpicians and the reorganization of the seminaries of Lyon following the separation law (1905–1906), Abbé Couturier, now the holder of a bachelor's degree in mathematics, was sent to the Catholic faculty of Lyon to earn the *licence de sciences* that would allow him to teach at the house. His diploma in his pocket, he began his high school teaching career in 1907 (it lasted until 1946).[16]

It is certainly in this area of his activity that the gap with spiritual ecumenism appears the greatest. Indeed, testimonies such as that of Jean Escoffier, who acknowledges the school teacher's role as an inspirational figure, are rare. In this case, the testimony refers to the vision of the world presented in a senior high school class in the late 1920s, during a natural science lesson.[17] In the same vein as Abbé Montagnon's, all the other witnesses describe Couturier's professional life more in terms of duty than of vocation, and mostly in terms of failure: at best, he was said to be boring, at worst he was jeered.

Without pretending to plead a cause that seems lost from the outset, the historian of ecumenism can nevertheless advance two arguments that point in opposite directions. The science teacher sometimes drew on his scientific knowledge, enhanced, it is true, by his dialogue with Victor Carlhian, in order to promote the reconciliation of Christians to which he dedicated himself at a late stage in his life. He thus compared the ambivalence of innovation in the field of religion to that of the geological cataclysm, which undoubtedly causes destruction but also leads to the emergence of new things.[18] There is therefore an analogy between the development of all living beings, which takes place "by way of an uninterrupted organic restructuring of the cells," and that which a Christianity in need of unity will hopefully undergo.[19]

A poor teacher of mathematics, physics, chemistry, and natural science, Abbé Couturier was nevertheless an excellent teacher of ecumenism. This

15 According to the repeated testimony of his cousin Louis Clément, who accompanied him to the monastery on a spring day of 1922, a testimony of which the oldest version appears in a letter to Maurice Villain dated Sept 8, 1957, in: Papiers Villain, Notre-Dame des Dombes (all the documents cited in the following stem from the same collection of Couturier-Papiers Villain, unless otherwise indicated).

16 According to Villain, Couturier spent three years at the Catholic faculty, from 1906 to 1909; however, the registry of personnel at Les Chartreux records that he had been licensed to teach natural sciences as early as 1907, which is more in keeping with the university curriculum of the time (teaching license being gained in one year).

17 Testimony of 11 handwritten pages for Villain's biography, dated 1928 by its author, in: Papiers Villain.

18 *Œcuménisme spirituel*, 193.

19 *Œcuménisme spirituel*, 199.

is consistently apparent from the way he propagated ideas through leaflets, brochures, and thin, assorted papers, which are easier to assimilate than thick volumes; from his recourse to images and music in order to popularize the cause, with some degree of success; and from his early use of the press and of radio to publicize converging opinions on a given topic, in the form of two- or three-sentence statements requested from personalities representing the various confessions.

These few clues show that the inventive ecumenist did not entirely eradicate the timid, private schoolteacher. However, the sum of these clues was evidently not enough to bring out the ecumenist.

3 A Second Formation (1920–1932)

Aged 33 in 1914, Abbé Couturier was eligible for the draft. He served as a nurse in the health services, but hardly anything is known about this episode of his life, though many of his companions assigned it pivotal importance. He does not appear to have served on or near the front line, but rather in the rear: in Lyon and its surroundings, where there was an influx of wounded and hospitals multiplied. In any event, the sight of so much suffering is bound to have reinforced his natural penchant for pessimism and dolorism.

His understanding of the world and of humankind did not undergo any decisive changes until the early 1920s, under the impact of two simultaneous encounters: one with the industrialist Victor Carlhian from Lyon, the other with the Jesuit Albert Valensin. While Couturier was probably introduced to Carlhian by one of the latter's nephews who went to school at Les Chartreux, the circumstances under which he met Albert Valensin remain unknown, as does the possible existence of a dialogue between the layman and the Jesuit.[20]

3.1 *The Layman*

Returning to better substantiated historical considerations, Father Villain spared no praise for the industrialist in his book *Portrait d'un précurseur*: "Let there be no doubt: Paul Couturier is Victor Carlhian's greatest conquest, and it was a layman who prepared the prophet of ecumenism for the church." Or even: "You were the John the Baptist of the herald of Christian unity, the precursor of this precursor."[21] But what can be said about him above and beyond hagiography? Born in 1875 into a family that originated from the Queyras massif in the Alps, Victor Carlhian dreamed of a university career on the fringes of mathematics, his specialty, and philosophy, his passion. However, a speech impediment and the obligation to ensure continuity in the family business, which specialized in the production of gilded fabrics, ruled otherwise. A militant of Marc Sangnier's politico-religious movement Sillon, which was suppressed in 1910, and heartbroken over the silencing of his teacher, the Oratorian Lucien Laberthonnière, he used his connections and his money to sponsor every significant expression of intellectual, spiritual, and apostolic openness in Lyon at the time of the anti-Modernist repression: the Chronique sociale; the parish of Notre-Dame Saint-Alban of Abbé Laurent Remillieux, ordained in the same year as Couturier; the Lyon group of medical, philosophical, and biological studies of Doctor René Biot; the philosophical society of Lyon. Similarly, his short

20 Perhaps such a meeting occurred through the spiritual group Eligi Principem Iesum (EPI) which had been founded by Colonel André Roullet in the immediate aftermath of the war with Albert Valensin as an adviser? But did Victor Carlhian actually belong to it? On this group, see Henri Hours, "L'E.P.I.," *Église à Lyon*, Feb 3, 1997, 63–64.

21 Maurice Villain, *Portrait d'un précurseur: Victor Carlhian (1875–1959)*, Paris, Desclée De Brouwer, 1965, 30 and 115. "Carlhian was for Couturier what Halifax had been for Portal: the layman who awakens the clergyman from a certain satisfied slumber"; apart from the latter term, which does not really suit Couturier, Maurice Villain's assessment is confirmed by Jean Guitton, "Portrait d'un laïc: Victor Carlhian," in: Jean Guitton, *Œuvres Complètes*, vol. 1, *Portraits*, Paris, Desclée de Brouwer, 1966, 727–775, here 764.

newsletter, *Le Van*, sorted through journals and books with great acumen.

In late May 1920, Carlhian purchased a property on the plateau of Vercors, at a locality named Saint-Ours in the commune of Veurey, where he planned to spend his summer vacations. He obtained the right to establish a household chapel on the property, which was inaugurated on Aug 18 and attended to by priests to whom he thus gave the opportunity to rest for a few days. Abbé Couturier served as its chaplain for the first time from Sep 12 to 19, 1920. He would return there every summer, for varying periods of time, until 1936 at the very least.[22] It was in this context that a lively dialogue between the layman and the priest developed, followed by frequent encounters during the school year, notably concerning the education of Carlhian's children.

According to the extant documents, this exchange meant more to Couturier than any other possible form of institutional mediation. He did not belong to the collaborative work group of the philosopher Jacques Chevalier, which Carlhian joined in 1921, soon after it had been founded.[23] He was rarely seen, save on exceptional occasions, at the sessions of the philosophical society of Lyon, where his intellectual background would have appeared too limited. However, the ideas and the works debated in these different circles reached him indirectly, through the intermediary of Carlhian, and entered into his thoughts, then into his work. This was the case in a field that interests us only marginally here: that of political ideas. As Saint-Ours's Golden Book explains: "One of them was a Sillonist. The other had strong sympathies for the Action française." The first exchanges must therefore have been quite tense. But the layman's power of persuasion eventually prevailed: unlike many of his fellow priests, Abbé Couturier had little sympathy for the Vichy regime, and even less for collaboration.[24]

This was even more true in the field of philosophy and of theology, where Carlhian's influence is clearly discernable in the beginnings of spiritual ecumenism. In January 1927, while reading *Le Van*, Couturier thus discovered a text by Jacques Chevalier entitled "Le progrès vers la Vérité", which he would distribute in mimeographed form and later use himself.[25] Truth is not given once and for all, immutable and complete; rather, it reveals itself progressively – a position with evident ecumenical implications. On Nov 7, 1930, Couturier thanked Carlhian for having given him a text written by the Lazarist Guillaume Pouget, the source of Jacques Chevalier's inspiration; indeed, the industrialist had taken it upon himself to edit Pouget's unpublished exegetical and theological texts for private use. In these writings, Couturier discovered the necessary dialectic between truth and charity that Jean Guitton would elaborate upon in his message for the octave of unity in January 1937.[26] On Sep 18, 1935, Couturier thanked Carlhian for having sent him Father Pierre Teilhard de Chardin's *Le Milieu Divin*, which the industrial disseminated in samizdat form, and which the Carthusian priest then passed on to some of his non-Catholic contacts so that they could read it.[27] The cosmic dimension that his desire for unity came to assume in the late 1930s and early 1940s would be incomprehensible without

22 These details are provided by Saint-Ours's Golden Book, a veritable treasure trove of information.

23 Unlike his friend Abbé Jules Monchanin, another priest of great renown from Lyon, who would settle in India.

24 Clearly sympathetic "to the MARÉCHAL and to his Government, who are working to help create a New Europe in which FRANCE will retain its dignity, its prestige, its territory, and sufficient independence, without which nothing would be achievable," the industrial Jacques Visseaux deplored that such a perspective did not interest the Carthusian priest, letter of Apr 1, 1943, in: Papiers Couturies.

25 *Œcuménisme spirituel*, 195–196.

26 *Revue apologétique*, March 1937, 340–345.

27 He notably sent it to Nicholas Arsenev and to pastor André-Numa Bertrand. See Pierre Teilhard de Chardin, *Le Milieu Divin: Essai de vie intérieure*, Paris, Éditions du Seuil, 1957; ET: *The Divine Milieu: An Essay on the Interior Life*, New York, Harper & Row, 1957.

this – at least partial – discovery of the Jesuit's grandiose vision.[28] The list could be extended even further: through the mediation of Victor Carlhian, Couturier glimpsed a universe of references that were entirely new to him, and thanks to which he would be able to structure some of his ecumenical institutions.

3.2 *The Jesuit*

However, the layman was not his only guide: alongside the latter – and perhaps in cooperation with him – stood the Jesuit Albert Valensin, a professor of theology at the Catholic faculty of Lyon whose intellectual and spiritual influence deserves to be taken out of the shadow of his younger brother, the philosopher Auguste Valensin, who was then lecturing at the philosophical department of the same institution.[29] In 1920, he initiated spiritual retreats for priests at the Villa Saint-Hughes of Saint-Égrève, close to Saint-Ours as the crow flies, which followed the model of the *Spiritual Exercises* of Ignatius of Loyola. Couturier immediately signed up for them. As the second retreat took place from Aug 31 to Sep 15, 1921,[30] after he had spent one month at Saint-Ours, it might be conjectured that he had already gone directly from Carlhian to Valensin in 1920. He also participated in the continuation of the experience during the school year, through regular meetings with Valensin: begun in the autumn of 1922, they dealt with various problems of spiritual life that affected the Jesuit's auditors, for instance: "On the guidance of scrupulous souls. On the nature of the scruple. The analysis of evil. Its causes. The spiritual therapy that it necessitates" (meeting of May 16, 1924).[31]

Albert Valensin and his brother Auguste are two of the main disciples of the philosopher Maurice Blondel in France. Although Carlhian entertained closer ties to Laberthonnière, it is nevertheless possible that he introduced Couturier to the master from Aix-en-Provence. Had he not associated with the Jesuit, however, it seems improbable that he would have written the following words to a reticent Maurice Villain on Aug 12, 1939: "In fact, Blondel had to wait for a less distrustful atmosphere, but it is not he who changed. ... He kept a low profile and let the storm pass. And this would bring us to the topic of the stern brothers who, among us, arrogate to themselves certain rights that have nothing irenic about them,"[32] for instance the right of denunciation. Thanks to Valensin and Carlhian, Abbé Couturier thus became acquainted with currents of thought that enabled him to emancipate himself from the textbook Thomism that he had absorbed at the seminary. Unlike the theological ecumenism of Father Congar, which is rooted in Thomism, the spiritual ecumenism of Abbé Couturier stands in another tradition: it is a distant product derived from the metaphysics of charity (Laberthonnière) and the philosophy of action (Blondel).[33]

However, Father Valensin's major contribution to spiritual ecumenism was not of an intellectual nature. In 1931, in Saint-Ours, on the occasion of the 25th anniversary of Couturier's ordination, Victor Carlhian presented him with a fictitious "retreat diary" written by an auditor of "Father Ignatius." In this document, the keys to which are not difficult to decipher, one may read the following:

28 See for example the meditation for the Protestant women's community of Grandchamp (Switzerland) in 1941, "Un aspect cosmique de la prière," in: *Œcuménisme spirituel*, 164–175.

29 Albert Valensin, *La vie intérieure d'un jésuite: Journal spirituel du P. Albert Valensin (1873–1944)*, Paris, Aubier-Montaigne, 1953.

30 *Semaine religieuse du diocèse de Lyon*, Apr 29, 1921, 365–366.

31 Invitation of May 13, in: Papiers Couturier.

32 V. Carlhian to M. Villain, Aug 12, 1939, in: Papiers Villain.

33 "The intellectual points of reference of Abbé Couturier undoubtedly played a decisive role in his discovery of spiritual ecumenism. These must be seen in Father Auguste Valensin, and thus in Blondel," wrote Father Yves Congar in *Chrétiens en dialogue: Contributions catholiques à l'oecuménisme*, Paris, Cerf, 1964, xxx. He mistook only the first name.

"I attained a better understanding, listening to Father Ignatius, of the Christian duty to live a faith that is always on the move, as it must always desire more light to think and work. Christianity is an obligation to [seek] progress."[34] The anonymous article on the "Thérapeutique spirituelle du scrupule" is more precise. Through a broad psychological and spiritual usage of the *Spiritual Exercises* of Ignatius of Loyola, "the obtained cures are often spectacular"; they enable one to cast off the "mummifying bandages of 'legalism.'"[35] Contrary to what was to be the rule, "the confession of the scrupulous person should therefore be rare, monthly, and preceded by a short examination." In this way, the royal road that had already been discerned at the seminary and encouraged by Pius X will be freed: "The Communion, having become a free aliment for this sick soul, will nourish him, warm him, and also enlighten him."[36] The power of persuasion of the great preacher that Albert Valensin was did not make an unrepentant optimist out of Couturier, but it did enable him to live his faith in a more pacified way, centered around Mass, which he considered to be the highlight of the day. The slowness with which he celebrated it quickly became proverbial, causing him to be replaced as chaplain of the Sisters of St. Charles, whom he had cared for since October 1936, before earning him a discrete chapel in the Basilica of Ainay, where he was able to officiate at his own pace.[37] As Carlhian aptly puts it, what Couturier discovered in Valensin was "a religion that welcomed every effort toward the good, the beautiful, and the true, a morality that was less concerned with avoiding evil than with proving, through personal dedication to others, the extent of his love for God."[38] Without this true deliverance, the Carthusian priest would have remained imprisoned in a religion dominated by the fear of sin and of its punishment, and would have never given birth to spiritual ecumenism.

This notwithstanding, Albert Valensin also had another, more direct impact on Couturier that proved decisive in another way. Together with several of his fellow Jesuit brothers, he had launched an initiative to help the Russian refugees who were flocking to Lyon after the war and the revolution. As early as 1923, he entrusted part of this task to Paul Couturier and his sister, who dedicated themselves to it wholeheartedly, initially on a purely material level, while gradually discovering a religious universe that was entirely alien to them. The Carthusian priest did not raise any objections when some of his protégés chose to join the Catholic Church, as shown by the speech which he delivered at a profession of faith on Pentecost Sunday 1927; however, his eagerness to proselytize was more irenic and more discrete than that of the majority of his contemporaries.[39]

For the sake of clarity, the description of the Catholic milieu of Lyon in the 1920s, which so deeply transformed Abbé Couturier, will be restricted to two of its emblematic figures. Many other names could be cited, such as those of Abbé Laurent Remillieux and of Abbé Jules Monchanin.[40] At the end of this development,

34 Cited in: Villain, *Portrait d'un précurseur*, 26.

35 [Couturier,] "D'une thérapeutique spirituelle," 144–145.

36 [Couturier,] "D'une thérapeutique spirituelle," 151–152.

37 According to the already cited testimony of Jean Escoffier.

38 Cited in: Villain, *L'Abbé Paul Couturier*, 23–24.

39 "Oh, of course! Far be it from my mind to ignore the fruits of holiness which the Spirit of God, by the ways of prayer and of the sacraments, has brought forth in the countless souls that have lived the rich treasure trove of Orthodox beliefs according to the rectitude of their sincere faith. I would feel honored to join all my Orthodox brothers in praying to Father John of Kronstadt and to St. Seraphim of Sarov, to name just a few of the illustrious saints that are better known among us Westerners. Of this treasure, as you know, there is indeed nothing that you should deny! Orthodox by formation, you remain so, but you add what is missing and thus become, as the Benedictine monks of the union say, a 'Catholic Orthodox.' It is, indeed, the joining of these two words that best represents your *de facto* rejoining of the Catholic Church"; text found on three handwritten and crossed out pages, in: Papiers Couturier.

40 For additional details, see Étienne Fouilloux, "Les racines de l'"oecuménisme spirituel,'" *Unité chrétienne*, 60, November 1980, 51–72; see also Étienne

the priest who had once been tormented by scruples, the educator who had felt uncomfortable in his teaching position could now reply to Simone Carlhian, the daughter of his friend, that his favorite quality was "prudent audacity" and his bedside book the Bible, that the concern that mattered most to him was to "reunite what was separated," and that his deepest aversion was "to shut oneself off."[41] His earlier handicaps had not vanished as if by magic, but his life as a priest had undergone a major transformation.

4 The Invention of Spiritual Ecumenism (1932–1953)

It is noteworthy that the crystallization of these early signs into a true ecumenical vocation took place at the priory of Amay-sur-Meuse, during the month that the Carthusian monk spent there in July–August 1932. It was in this house, which he already knew by reputation and from reading,[42] and although it had been hit very hard by the removal of its founder Lambert Beauduin and by Russification imposed from Rome, that he found the Benedictine peace that he had longed for so much, to the point of becoming an oblate of Amay in the following year, under the name of Benoît-Irénée, and of beginning all his letters with "Pax." Most importantly, it was also here that he perceived the mission that would occupy the last 20 years of his life: to work towards the union of the separated Christians. Even in its weakened state, the priory of Amay remained both a point of reference and a starting point, a place where Couturier learned of the existence of Mass for the extinction of schism, of the January octave of prayer, and perhaps of a formulation by Dom Lambert Beauduin that would inspire him: "The union will be rebuilt by the grace of God and when He wills it."[43]

However, nothing had prepared the Carthusian priest to put such a late vocation into practice. He had to learn nearly everything about the other confessions; but above all, he needed to define a method of work. Thus, his public life, as opposed to his previous hidden life, can be divided into three phases that are separated by the beginning and the end of World War II.

4.1 *From Unionism to Ecumenism*

The first phase was that of the tentative emergence of spiritual ecumenism from its unionist surroundings. Even as Abbé Couturier, in Amay, made the decision to devote his remaining energies to unity, he was already on the frontline of an initiative to establish a Russian chapel of Eastern rite in Lyon: inaugurated on Dec 18, 1932, it followed in the wake of a series of similar foundations that had begun in the West in the early 1920s.[44] From that very moment, he knew that the unionist path, which turned the uniate communities into bridges for the return of the Easterners to the Roman fold, was not the right one and that the Orthodox East feared these communities, often consisting of renegades, more than Latin Catholicism itself. The Carthusian priest would

Fouilloux, "Jules Monchanin dans les milieux intellectuels lyonnais de l'entre-deux-guerres," in: *Jules Monchanin (1895–1957): Regards croisés d'Occident et d'Orient: Actes des Colloques de Lyon-Fleurie et de Shantivanam-Thannirpalli, avril–juillet 1995*, Lyon, Profac-Credic, 1997, 53–71 and *DMRFC* 6.

41 Undated questionnaire appended to Villain, *L'Abbé Paul Couturier*, 353–354.

42 See the explicit reference to the positions of Amay in the abovementioned speech on the occasion of the profession of faith of a Russian.

43 See the monumental biography of the Benedictine monk: Raymond Loonbeek & Jacques Mortiau, *Un pionnier, dom Lambert Beauduin (1873–1960): Liturgie et unité des chrétiens*, 2 vols., Louvain-la-Neuve/Chevetogne, Collège Érasme/Éditions de Chevetogne, 2001, 1156–1158 on Couturier's visit there; and Thaddée Barnas, "L'abbé Paul Couturier et le monastère d'Amay-Chevetogne," *Irén* 75/4, 2002, 458–479. On Dom Beauduin and the Monastery of Amay-Chevetogne see the contribution by André Haquin in the first volume of this work.

44 Étienne Fouilloux, "Une fondation unioniste à Lyon en 1932," *Bulletin des Facultés catholiques de Lyon* n.s. 107, 1983, 39–46.

thus quickly distance himself from a chapel that he himself had helped establish. He was neither the first nor the last Catholic priest to make such a transition from unionism to ecumenism.

In January 1933, drawing on material from Amay, he decided to adapt the January union prayer for use in Lyon, intending to "cleanse [it] of petty-minded interpretations" (letter of Aug 27, 1935). However, this disassociation from the original Anglo-Saxon wording, notably in terms of the return to the Catholic Church, did not occur overnight. It was not until 1939 that Couturier clearly expressed the change of content that he had effected with regard to the latter.[45] It was also not until 1939 that his projects ceased to be couched in a vocabulary inspired by the triduum and the octave, which was too evocative of the "sacristy."[46] "One could just as well call it the Week of Christian Unity," he wrote in his first reference to this event in April 1938.[47] Both the brochure and the program for January 1939 thus introduced a definition that was entirely devoid of Catholic associations: "Universal prayer of Christians for Christian unity"; "for the unity of all Christians."

At the same time, Abbé Couturier, who had hitherto only met Russians in distress, went in search for official representatives of other confessions. On the side of Orthodoxy, he had been fortunate enough to have already met in Lyon in October 1934 the metropolitan Eulogius (Georgiyevsky), who presided over the main ecclesiastical jurisdiction of the Russian emigrant community in France under the aegis of the Patriarchate of Constantinople. But like many well-intentioned Catholics, he became somewhat lost in the quarrels between jurisdictions and gained the support of figures that were as much motivated by the struggle against communism as by the unity of Christians.[48] His only trustworthy intellectual and spiritual contacts at the time were two laymen: Nicholas Arsenev, whom he received in Lyon on Mar 30 and 31, 1938, and Lev Zander, a disciple of Father Sergius Bulgakov, the great theologian of the Institut de théologie orthodoxe Saint-Serge in Paris. This was still very little.

Another layman could be added to this duo: Serge Bolshakoff, an eminent representative, in England, of the ROCOR, an ecclesiastical jurisdiction that was antagonistically obedient to the pro-Soviet Patriarchate of Moscow. He founded the Confrérie Saint-Benoît, which entertained links to the Anglican Benedictines of Nashdom Abbey, of which he was an oblate. It was he who introduced Couturier to the Anglican circles that he frequented. All belonged to the small Anglo-Papalist fringe of the Church of England, which sometimes went even further than Roman Catholicism in its attachment to liturgical matters. The first Channel crossing, in September 1937, of a priest who could read English but had trouble understanding it and could not speak it[49] was essentially confined to these circles. A second trip, in July 1938, broadened the perspective by including major High Church communities such as Cowley, Kelham, or Mirfield. It also encompassed courtesy visits to the Archbishop of York, William Temple, and the Archbishop of Canterbury, Cosmo Gordon Lang.[50] A third trip, planned for the summer of 1939, did not take place on account of the world crisis, but also because of the veto imposed on Cardinal Gerlier by his counterpart from Westminster, Cardinal Arthur Hinsley: in spite of his discretion, the Carthusian priest had not requested any authorization, thereby incurring

45 See for example his letter to Gunnar Rosendal; P. Couturier to G. Rosendal, Nov 13, 1939, copy, in: Papier Couturier.

46 P. Courturier to S. Mourier, Dec 16, 1940, in: Suzanne Mourier's private papers.

47 In the journal *Œcumenica* 5/1, 1938, 65.

48 The scholar of Slavic studies Jules Patouillet warned him about these compromising offers of support; J. Patouillet to P. Couturier, Jun 7, 1937, in: Papiers Couturier.

49 His English-teaching colleague from Les Chartreux, the layman Joseph Guillermin, served as his interpreter.

50 On the specifics of his encounters, see the *"Curriculum vitae" unioniste* that he prepared in expectation of a third trip, seven typewritten pages, undated.

the wrath of the Catholic leadership in England.[51] Conversely, Lyon had welcomed several Anglicans, they too from the High Church. For that matter, Couturier made no secret of his lack of familiarity with Low Church circles.[52]

On the Protestant side, the results were equally disappointing. While the synod of Agen convened by the UNEPREF did, in June 1936, decide to participate in the January prayer, Couturier and his supporters had some illusions about his decision, which only concerned the "liberal" branch of French Calvinism, prior to its union with the "evangelicals" to form the Reformed Church of France, at the meeting of Lyon in 1938. Moreover, before the arrival of pastor Roland de Pury and with the exception of his predecessor Henri Hollard, the Protestants of Lyon were somewhat reserved towards what they perceived as a "courteous and clever offensive launched by our Catholic brothers," which must be met by "an … evangelization effort on the part of the Church," Reformed of course.[53]

On the eve of the war, Abbé Couturier's strongest ties to Protestants did not concern France, but the German-speaking area of Switzerland. His friend Laurent Remillieux put him in touch with the fraternity of St. John, composed of Reformed pastors from Bern who sought to restore the liturgy in their church: a prototype of a kind of Protestant High Church. From 1937 to 1942, a total of four meetings took place between this fraternity and a group of priests from Lyon: two in Erlenbach, in the canton of Bern (1937 and 1939), and two at the monastery of Notre-Dame des Dombes (1938 and 1942), hence the name first Dombes Group that they acquired in historiography. However, these meetings bore more resemblance to meditative, prayer retreats than to true theological exchanges, even if the invitation, by the Swiss, of a brother of Karl Barth, Peter, in 1938, and of the historian Otto Erich Strasser in 1939 did open the way for a true dialogue on the church (1939) or on spirituality (1942).[54] But apart from these discrete encounters, Couturier's attempts to reach out to Protestantism were limited to the pietist movement of the Third Order of Watchers, grouped around Wilfred Monod, and to the Swedish Lutheran pastor Gunnar Rosendal, who displayed strong Catholicizing tendencies. A solid relationship with the nascent WCC in Geneva had not yet been established.

It was nevertheless against this subdued background that Couturier laid the foundations of spiritual ecumenism. In January 1935, he interpreted a *nuancée* letter of the Metropolitan Eulogius as an authorization to invite Orthodox Christians to the events of the octave of prayer in Lyon. Triumphant reactions on the Catholic side and an Orthodox withdrawal on the other made it necessary to issue a clarifying statement, which Couturier wrote at Carlhian's house in Saint-Ours, in August, and sent to a number of theologians for comment. "It is not my impression that anything in these pages can offend the most delicate Catholic sensibilities," the Jesuit Henri-Marie de Lubac answered on Aug 24. "It is an outpouring of fanciful imagination without basis; it is neither serious nor sound. … This should not be published: it encourages all misunderstandings without being of help in bringing to light the true good intentions," retorted the Dominican Yves Congar in early October.[55] Following its rejection by a journal of the French publisher Éditions du Cerf, the seminal article entitled "Pour l'unité des chrétiens: Psychologie de l'Octave de prières du 18

51 Letters of the bishop of Nottingham (Sep 23, 1938) and of Cardinal Hinsley (May 15, 1939), in: AAL.

52 Letter to the Marist Brother Stanislas Cwiertniak from Feb 27, 1944, in: Papiers Villain.

53 V. R[ivet], "Chronique du mois," *Bulletin paroissial* (*de l'Église réformée de Lyon*), February 1936, 3.

54 The best record of these meetings – rather than the various writings of Father Villain, who joined them only in 1942 – is the testimony of pastor Lucien Marchand, the only French Protestant to have participated in them, in: Gaston Bordet, *Oecuménisme en Franche-Comté: Recherches sur les origines*, Besançon, Université de Franche-Comté, 1977, 81–98.

55 Letter to his fellow Dominican brother Pierre Boisselot, which the latter quotes in a letter to Christophe-Jean Dumont, Archives Istina, Paris.

au 25 janvier" thus appeared in the *Revue apologétique* in December 1935.[56]

In an awkward manner – one does not suddenly become a writer at the age of 54 – this article communicates the essence of the Carthusian priest's insights to the public. According to him, the faithful of the different Christian confessions are in a comparable psychological situation with regard to the separation: all are guilty and all must repent; all must therefore pray within their churches, in a spirit that will overcome the commitment to proselytism to make way for "a holy emulation without rivalry,"[57] addressing a convergent prayer to God for the restauration of unity. The difficulty evidently lies in the adopted perspective, which, at least temporarily, sets the dogmatic quarrels aside.

Two years later, again in the *Revue apologétique* which Couturier began to colonize,[58] the approach outlined was further specified in a long article published in two installments, under the more appropriate title: "L'universelle prière des chrétiens pour l'unité chrétienne."[59] The first draft had already provided the formulation that would ultimately impose itself: the unity for which one must pray is the "unforeseeable working of the Spirit," "as Our Lord Jesus Christ demanded and willed it."[60] In 1937, in a stroke of near genius, Abbé Couturier took up Jesus' great prayer for unity in the Gospel of John (ch. 17) and made it the centerpiece of what became the magical formula of spiritual ecumenism: the implored unity, "such as Christ wills it" (1939) and "by the means that he chooses" (1940), escapes confessional constraints. Whatever their church, all Christians can pray in this manner: it was enough to think it, but Couturier was to first one to say it aloud and practice it. Such a prayer in "spiritual emulation" allows for the "overflying" of "all demarcations and lets us rest in the Heart of our Christ";[61] and it is this "overflying," yet to be clarified, that will overcome historical and dogmatic quarrels. It is easy to see why the term is by no means exaggerated: Couturier's methodology represented a radical break with the preceding proselytism or with unionism, albeit one that was not without risk, as this "overflying" temporarily blurs the difficulties while unity has yet to be achieved, and because both the Catholic Church and the Orthodox Church consider that it exists within them.

From then on, Abbé Couturier continued to focus intently on this form of prayer. Year after year, he mobilized a growing number of both Catholic and Anglican religious communities for even the smallest ecumenical event. Moreover, he began to create a network of Christians who were determined to pray for unity on a regular basis. He also began to gather together lives that had pledged themselves to this cause, in the various confessions, at the moment of death. All of this shaped the contours of what would, somewhat later, become the "invisible monastery"[62] of Christian unity. However, this did not mean that the Carthusian priest had abandoned the field of ideas, of secondary importance to him but nevertheless necessary. At the various public or private January events that he organized in Lyon, he drew extensively on the rich intellectual breeding ground provided by the Catholic Faculties or the scholasticate of Fourvière, relying heavily on the Jesuits Pierre Chaillet, Henri de Lubac, Gaston Salet, and Albert Valensin, on Abbés Joseph Chaine, Jules Monchanin, Laurent Remillieux, and Louis Richard, but also on a layperson such as the philosopher Jean Guitton, who mediated the legacy of the Lazarist Fernand Portal, of Lord Halifax, and of Cardinal Désiré-Joseph Mercier. On the eve of the war, the think tank was expanded to include theologians from outside Lyon, such as the Belgian

56 Paul Couturier, "Pour l'unité des chrétiens: Psychologie de l'Octave de prières du 18 au 25 janvier," *Revue apologétique* 61/598, 1935, 684–703.

57 Couturier, "Pour l'unité des chrétiens," 693.

58 A total of 45 issues appeared from December 1935 to October/December 1939, of which 20 contained a text submitted by the Carthusian priest.

59 Paul Couturier, "L'universelle prière des chrétiens pour l'unité chrétienne," *Revue apologétique* 65/625, 1937, 411–427, and 65/626, 1937, 562–578.

60 Couturier, "Pour l'unité des chrétiens," 689, 693.

61 Couturier, "L'universelle prière," 421.

62 See Paul Couturier, "Le Monastère Invisible," in: *Œcuménisme spirituel*, 158–162.

Jesuit Émile Mersch (1938) or the Dominican Yves Congar (1939).[63] Spiritual ecumenism was born.

4.2 *The Time of Boldness and Danger*

This ecumenism went through unforeseen developments owing to the sad conditions that prevailed in France between 1940 and 1944. While Father Congar was being held as a prisoner of war, Lyon briefly became the undisputed capital of the movement, as well as, for a brief time, the intellectual and spiritual capital of a crippled French nation. At the same time, the atmosphere of semi-confinement that was so characteristic of the unoccupied zone until November 1942 also gave Couturier and his assistant, the Marist Brother Maurice Villain, ample opportunity for bold moves, which they did not refrain from making.

These bold moves pertained less to the diffusion of the formula of prayer than to its theological definition. In terms of diffusion, the weeks of prayer held in Lyon in the years 1940, 1941, and 1945 were reduced to their simplest expression. Couturier and Villain nevertheless continued to increase the number of easily distributable leaflets, for instance the proper of the Mass *ad tollendum schisma*, which had been discovered in Amay in 1932[64] and renamed Mass for Christian Unity (1940). The Carthusian priest even launched the tentative prototype of a journal, *Pages documentaires sur l'unité chrétienne*, which was discontinued after three issues; the Marist, for his part, launched a monograph series entitled Ad Unitatem, released by the publisher Arthaud in Grenoble.

Less visible from the outside, the imposed loosening of the ties with England was accompanied, in Lyon, by a distinct shift of priorities towards Protestantism. During the summer of 1939, Couturier met the Calvinist pastor Jean de Saussure, from Geneva. It was he who brought him into contact with the very recently established Protestant women's community of Grandchamp, whose spiritual care the Carthusian priest soon partly assumed through the meditations that he sent them. It was again Saussure who acted as an intermediary with the nascent WCC, which Maurice Villain visited for the first time in January 1941, and Saussure once more who brought together the team of Barthian or neo-Calvinist pastors who were present at Dombes in the autumn of 1942 for a first, very promising exchange on the conception of the church in the Pauline *Epistle to the Ephesians* a meeting that led to the formation of a second discussion group.

On the other hand, Jean de Saussure had nothing to do with the visit to Lyon, in December 1940, of the young Roger Schutz from Switzerland, who had only just arrived on the hill of Taizé. Couturier's and Villain's "ascent" to Taizé, on Jul 4 and 5, 1941, formed a bond that would play a significant role in the constitution of the nascent community and in its ecumenical mission, which was not initially clear. Roger Schutz and his friend Max Thurian also regarded the Carthusian priest as their "spiritual father."[65] While it is true that these overtures only involved groups that were well disposed towards Catholicism, which represented a rather small segment of francophone Protestantism, the change of preferred dialogue partner is nevertheless quite noteworthy.

With a great discretion that makes any historical reconstruction very difficult, the period of latency ushered in by the war also enabled the invisible

63 Revising his initial negative judgment, he wrote the following to Cardinal Gerlier: "Before leaving Lyon, I had a rather long meeting with Abbé Couturier. Even though everyone must remain responsible for his [own] deeds and words, I believe I should inform Your Eminence that I have found the positions of M. Couturier to be better founded and sounder than I had imagined. I found it important to offer this testimony in his favor"; Y. Congar to Cardinal P.-M. Gerlier, Sep 17, 1945, in: AAL.

64 "When can one say the mass for the return of the churches? *As with the masses in black*," question and answer on a loose leaf in the notebook "Amay 1932," in: Papiers Couturier.

65 "To our spiritual father, the Abbé Couturier, Roger Schutz and Max Thurian," dedication to Couturier in Roger Schutz, *Introduction à la vie communautaire*, Geneva, Labor et Fides, 1944. On these bonds, see Silvia Scatena, *Taizé, una parabola di unità: Storia della comunità dalle origini al concilio dei giovani*, Bologna, Il Mulino, 2018.

monastery of Christian unity to assume an active role, in the absence of a visible monastery whose activities had been cut short. Several of its groups began operating in the area of Lyon, in close collaboration with their non-Catholic counterparts, since the leadership did not permit mixed groups. In the various confessions, the circle of people dedicated to the prayer for unity thus grew to a certain size.

It was also during the war years that Couturier and Villain, professor of theology at the scholasticate of Oceanian missions in Sainte-Foy-les-Lyon, strove to lend greater weight to spiritual ecumenism by providing it with a theology of its own. Two significant brochures thus appeared under Couturier's name, albeit only *ad usum privatum* in order to circumvent ecclesiastical censorship.[66] The first entitled *À propos de la Bulle "Unam sanctam"*,[67] was written in response to an Anglican objection. It sought to prove that the theocratic leanings of Pope Boniface VIII belonged to an obsolete medieval context that had been recognized as such by some of his successors, notably by Leo XIII in the late 19th century. With regard to this borderline case, Couturier suggested that the outdated formulations of tradition should be put into perspective and that greater consideration should be given to the limits of papal infallibility. The second brochure entitled, *Dynamisme et loyauté*,[68] outlines a theory of "overflying," that is, of the overcoming of dogmatic differences in prayer. Without renouncing his loyalty to his own church, which he always respected, the Carthusian priest drew on the works of the philosophers Jacques Chevalier and Jean Guitton to illustrate the dynamic, not static, nature of truth, whose successive, always imperfect approaches could and should be improved through possible ulterior developments. In so doing, he unwittingly joined the debate on the value of theological conclusions and dogmatic formulations, a debate that caused a pamphlet by Father Marie-Dominique Chenu to be placed on the Index at that same time. A newcomer to theology, Couturier undoubtedly lacked the proficiency and the skills of the master from Le Saulchoir, but their intuitions had much in common.

However, these bold statements eventually led him into trouble. On May 14, 1941, the Holy Office asked Cardinal Gerlier for clarification regarding the preparatory leaflet for the week of 1941, which bore the local *imprimatur* that deferred to the "supreme" doctrinal authority. Why this document, which seems quite harmless in comparison to the aforementioned brochures? Probably because of its public dissemination. It states, for example, that: "The true Catholic, in the innermost depths of his soul, suffers great pain at the thought of everything that conceals the true face of the church from the eyes of his Christian brethren as well as from the eyes of the unbeliever." And also: "It is we, more than anyone else, who must rejoice with exultant joy at the news that our Christian brethren can experience, here or there, a great visitation from God."[69] Self-criticism and a call for a reform of Catholicism on the one hand, recognition of the blessings received by the non-Catholics on the other: this was a great deal for a traditional believer to digest, even more so for the Holy Office.

Accompanied by a personal letter from Gerlier, the report sent to Cardinal Francesco Marchetti Selvaggiani, the secretary of the Holy Office, attempted to save what could be saved. "Monsieur Abbé Couturier is a very highly esteemed priest, devoid of all ambition and driven only by an ardent desire for good. Unfortunately, his theological formation and his caution are not always

66 Three if one includes "Prière et unité chrétienne," the final reworking of the formula of prayer from 1935 to 1937. The first brochure probably dates from 1941 (it was sent to Madeleine Marcault on Sep 22), as does "Prière et unité chrétienne" (handwritten note by Couturier on Father Congar's copy, in: Archives de la Province dominicaine de France), while the second was probably written in late 1942 (criticism of Father Christophe-Jean Dumont in a letter from Mar 9, 1943).

67 Paul Couturier, *À propos de la Bulle "Unam sanctam"*, Lyon, G. Neveu, [1943].

68 See *Œcuménisme spirituel*, 195–213.

69 *Œcuménisme spirituel*, 120–121.

commensurate with his zeal."[70] "Living in a somewhat imaginary world," he "expounds the problem in a manner hitherto unknown to the average believer and employs formulations and expressions that cannot be endorsed."[71] In fact, they had already been censored several times by the diocesan authority: a simple warning without publicity would thus suffice. On Dec 16, the Holy Office accepted the conclusions of the archbishop of Lyon and entrusted him with the task of delivering a *monitum* of unspecified content to the person concerned.[72] This incident, which was kept secret, has been described in some detail, as this was the only time Abbé Couturier was sanctioned by Rome during his lifetime. In a manner that was to become a habit of his, Cardinal Gerlier warded off the blow by downplaying the matter before the Roman authorities, while striking a harsher tone in Lyon in order to prevent any relapse.[73]

Although not obviously connected to ecumenism, the next blow suffered by Abbé Couturier in the final months of the German occupation was more serious. Arrested by the Gestapo on Apr 11, 1944, and incarcerated in Lyon's Montluc prison where he was given up for dead by his friend and companion in misfortune, pastor Roland de Pury, he was released without charge on Jun 12. The reasons for his arrest remain unknown. His hostility to the anti-Semitism of the Vichy regime is well documented but was not expressed in public.[74] Moreover, not a single study on the Lyon Resistance mentions the name of the Carthusian priest. Did it appear in a notebook or a list of addresses discovered by the German police? This is conceivably the case. However, it is more likely that his previous correspondence with religious figures in Great Britain was deemed suspicious, along with his ties to Swiss Protestant circles. The ordeal nevertheless took a heavy toll on the 63-year-old man, possibly even marking a point of no return in the decline of his health.

4.3 *The Final Years*

Soon after the end of the war, he was released from his duties as a teacher and was thus able to devote all his remaining energy to ecumenism. But the years weighed more and more heavily on his shoulders, and soon illness also followed. Consequently, the end of his life is characterized by a rather sharp contrast between the growing success of his formula of prayer for unity and a feeling of weariness, or even of loneliness, in the face of the burdensome task of promoting and disseminating spiritual ecumenism.

Did he achieve any success? In a previous publication, I drew up a map showing the spread of the January week of prayer, in Couturier's formulation, throughout eastern France and beyond, along with its numerous local ties.[75] Accordingly, I shall merely quote the figures from the final report presented to Cardinal Gerlier on Mar 10, 1953, only a few days before Abbé Couturier's death:

70 Cardinal P.-M. Gerlier to Cardinal F. Marchetti-Selvaggiani, Oct 28, 1941, copy. The wording of the report is a little bit harsher: "He is a very virtuous priest, modest, pious, with an ardent zeal. ... The integrity of his intentions is beyond doubt. However, his zeal can sometimes push him beyond the limits of prudence, or even of orthodoxy"; Oct 18, 1941, copy, 1, in: AAL, 11, II, 205.

71 Cardinal P.-M. Gerlier to Cardinal F. Marchetti-Selvaggiani, Oct 28, 1941, copy, in: AAL, 11, II, 205.

72 See AAL, 11, II, 116/41. On this matter, see Olivier Georges, *Pierre-Marie Gerlier, le cardinal militant: 1880–1965*, Paris, Desclée de Brouwer, 2014, 310–313.

73 "I thus see no possibility, at the present time, of authorizing what I previously asked you to discontinue," the Cardinal wrote on Nov 26, 1943, in response to the letter from 25 November concerning the possibility of holding interconfessional meetings at Carlhian's house ("like Moses, you strike the rock with too much insistence"); Cardinal P.-M. Gerlier to P. Couturier, Nov 26, 1943, copy, in: AAL, 11, II, 205.

74 "I do not need to tell you why my sympathy for the Jews, which has always been great, is becoming even greater now that France is ... persecuting them ... Is it too strong a word? ... Is it a Nazi racial oppression filtered by France? Is it an autochthonous French product [stemming] from a nationalist reaction? ... May God have mercy on the persecuted"; he wrote on Oct 20, 1940, only days after the first statute on Jews, to a nun named Sister Albert le Grand Sanson (handwritten letter, with its original punctuation, preserved at the Fonds Couturier).

75 Fouilloux, *Les Catholiques et l'unité chrétienne*, 558.

73,000 forwarded tracts; 40,000 Masses for Christian unity; 5,500 posters and 7,000 brochures in response to 1,900 requests. While still contested, notably in Rome, the formula of prayer for Christian unity introduced by the Carthusian priest gained rapid popularity in Catholic circles and placed him at the head of a diffusion campaign that went beyond the strength of a single priest in poor health.

Did he suffer isolation and exhaustion? The departure of Father Villain for the Parisian region in 1948, after a brief stay at the Dominican Istina center, deprived Couturier of the disciple who had been his closest collaborator for ten years. No true replacement was found, other than in the form of material and occasional help: the Dominican Friar François Biot and the Jesuit Robert Clément, in the final days. From 1951, the Carthusian priest's distress was discretely alluded to in his correspondence, in the course of a series of angina pectoris attacks.

In spite of this, spiritual ecumenism continued to lay the groundwork for its undeniable expansion. Year after year, a growing number of priests and members of religious orders requested the ecumenical formation that they had not received during their ecclesiastical studies. In order to fulfill this desire, Couturier and Villain organized annual meetings known as the Journées du Châtelard, after the name of the Jesuit retirement home in the vicinity of Lyon where these events found a permanent venue in 1950, five years after their creation. Here, several hundred clerics of all kinds and of all areas were given a solid training by the best theologians. Many of them would become key players in the diffusion of ecumenism in their dioceses or congregations.

The second Dombes Group, for its part, began to meet on an annual basis following the resumption of its gatherings in 1946, one year in Switzerland (Presinge or Grandchamp), the next year at the Abbey of Dombes. With the additional support of a few renowned theologians (the Dominican Irénée-Henri Dalmais, the Marist Joseph de Baciocchi, or the Jesuit Gustave Martelet), it engaged in a systematic examination of the dogmatic differences between Catholicism and the legacy of the Reformation. During the first phase of its existence, until 1956, the group's activities were limited to this experiment in comparative theology, with two-way exchanges on the same topic, but without any attempt to formulate a joint approach to controversial issues. It was, at the time, merely a discrete forum, devoid of any influence and without any indication of the importance that it would later attain. Abbé Couturier continued to devote great care to the preparation of the meetings and to the recruitment of speakers, but he left the chairmanship to those whom he deemed more competent: initially Father Maurice Villain and his friend from Taizé, pastor Max Thurian. He rarely intervened, except to remind these intellectuals of the primacy of prayer when the *rabies theologica* took hold of them.[76]

For all that, the obligation to meet the growing demand for ecumenism with the limited means at hand did not diminish the inventiveness of the offer. Apart from its growing insistence on the necessity to take into account the living Christian values of separated Christian brothers and to subject the Roman Church to a reform that would make it more consistent with what it claimed to be, spiritual ecumenism joined the ranks of those who pioneered what was not yet known as the "repentance" promoted by Rome at the end of the 20th century. During the summer of 1946, Couturier announced an initiative that he had been brooding over since the war: he asked several hundred priests to celebrate Mass on Aug 24, St. Bartholomew's Day, in atonement for the massacres perpetrated against Protestants on that day, in 1572, by Catholics of Paris and Lyon.[77] In conjunction with pastor Jacques Delpech, the leader

76 Catherine E. Clifford, *The Groupe des Dombes: A Dialogue of Conversion*, New York, Peter Lang, 2005 and the essay in this volume by the same author.

77 See, the chapter on this topic published in a compilation owed to the Carthusian priest and authored by Paul Couturier, the historian André Latreille, and pastor Jean Cadier, "La Saint-Barthélemy, Jour de Réparation," in: *Unité Chrétienne et Tolérance Religieuse*, Paris, Éditions du Temps Présent, 1950, 104–123.

of an Evangelical mission in High Aragon, he drew attention to the precarious fate of the Protestant minority in the National-Catholic Spain of General Francisco Franco.[78] Not without a certain audacity, feared by Cardinal Gerlier, he did not shrink from addressing himself directly to the French Jesuit Charles Boyer, trusted confidant of the Roman circles in ecumenical matters, in an attempt to win him over to his point of view, albeit with little immediate success.[79] In terms of recognition, the Carthusian priest had to content himself with the title of an honorary archimandrite of the Melkite Church, bestowed by the patriarch Maximos IV on Apr 11, 1952.

5 A Varied Legacy

In spite of undeniable difficulties resulting from the growing exhaustion of its main architect, spiritual ecumenism was in full expansion when Couturier died on Mar 24, 1953, the victim of a final heart attack. Before his mortal remains, Cardinal Gerlier pledged to ensure the continuity of the deceased's ecumenical work, which was to prove difficult since the prelate insisted that the succession of the Carthusian priest remain within the diocesan orbit. Three of Couturier's disciples could legitimately lay claim to his legacy, although their emulation would not always be free of rivalry.[80]

5.1 *The Biographer*

Maurice Villain was the first and closest theological adviser to Abbé Couturier, whose insights he helped articulate and to whom he was very attached. However, he suffered from a threefold handicap. He belonged to a monastic order, whereas Cardinal Gerlier wanted a priest from his own diocese to succeed Couturier. He had left Lyon in 1948, when his superiors agreed to release him from his teaching responsibilities at the scholasticate of Sainte-Foy so that he could devote himself entirely to ecumenism, and settled in Paris. Finally, and most importantly, neither the ecclesiastical authorities nor some of his peers considered him theologically reliable: endowed with great sensitivity, he stretched some of his master's riskiest ideas to their limits instead of channeling them.[81]

He could also boast major assets: as the closest collaborator of the Carthusian priest for nearly ten years, he had prepared the École des Chartes before joining the Marist Brothers. He thus disposed of a historian's training, which he later cultivated as a professor of patrology and church history at the scholasticate of Sainte-Foy. In addition to the responsibility, in cooperation with Max Thurian, for the Dombes Group in its comparatist phase, there also fell to him the task of extracting from the papers of Abbé Couturier (as well as his own) a biography of his master. It appeared in 1957, with a foreword by the historian André Latreille from Lyon, and became a true success (the 4th edition was published in 1964). It was not perfect owing to a number of errors concerning certain details, but particularly on account of a questionable overall conception, of which the most evident flaws are the almost total silence on Couturier's life prior to ecumenism, the penchant for hagiography, and the tendency to credit Couturier with the theological conceptions of his biographer.[82]

Be that as it may, Father Villain's book, based as it is on the papers of which he was the custodian, and which he quotes abundantly, made the inventor of "spiritual ecumenism" known far beyond the small circle of those whom he had convinced, along with the further addition, in 1963, of his

78 On their dialogue, see Max Pribilla, "Intolérance Dogmatique et Tolérance Civile," in: *Unité Chrétienne et Tolérance Religieuse*, 124–146.

79 Correspondence of 1949–1951, published in *Unité chrétienne*, August 1974, 40–45.

80 Étienne Fouilloux, "Une affaire lyonnaise: La succession de l'abbé Couturier," *Chrétiens et sociétés* 18, 2011, 105–135.

81 Which would later cause him difficulties with the canonical censorship, on which he spoke at length in his own memoirs: Maurice Villain, *Vers l'unité: Itinéraire d'un pionnier: 1935–1975*, Dinard, Groupement pour le Service Œcuménique, 1986.

82 Villain, *L'Abbé Paul Couturier*, 380.

collected writings.[83] This twin accomplishment has yet to be matched. Moreover, it fulfilled its purpose: to reveal the ecumenical achievements of Abbé Couturier and his message to the Christian world.

5.2 *Father Michalon and* Unité Chrétienne

The task of ensuring the dissemination of the January week of prayer was immediately assigned to Pierre Michalon, a priest of Saint-Sulpice who was originally from Saint-Étienne (and thus belonged to the diocese of Lyon at the time). In his capacity as professor for Holy Scripture at the major seminary of Viviers, in the Ardèche, he had become aware of the drama of division. He had subsequently established contact with Abbé Couturier and organized meetings between priests and local pastors. At the time of Couturier's death, he was professor at the major seminary of Angers, and his superiors were unwilling to let him go immediately. It was not until the autumn of 1954 that he was finally assigned to the major seminary of Lyon, where he could devote himself entirely to ecumenism and assume the task of dissemination that had temporarily been entrusted to Abbé Jean-Paul Vincent, the chaplain of Lyon University Parish.

A man of great energy, Father Michalon gave the formula of prayer introduced by Couturier an increasingly broad geographical and confessional scope while successfully avoiding clashes with Roman circles, where the official doctrine remained focused on the prayer for the return of the separated Christians to the Catholic fold. A crucial threshold was crossed from 1957 onward, when the annual theme of the prayer week began to be formulated in collaboration with the Faith and Order commission of the WCC. It was this role in the promotion of the Carthusian priest's legacy that earned the Sulpician priest an appointment as consultant to the SPCU and allowed him to participate in the consecration of spiritual ecumenism by Vatican II, in its decree on ecumenism: "This change of heart and holiness of life, along with public and private prayer for the unity of Christians, should be regarded as the soul of the whole ecumenical movement, and merits the name 'spiritual ecumenism'" (*UR* § 8).

Father Michalon also founded the center Unité chrétienne in Lyon, which, in 1965, sponsored the creation of the first professorship for ecumenism in a Catholic theological faculty. In the following year, the center launched a small quarterly journal of the same name, *Unité chrétienne*, to support its activities and to provide a forum for feedback.[84]

6 The Dominican Branch

In the early 1950s, after Father Villain had left for Paris, a group of young monks stepped in to help Couturier prepare and expedite the textual material for the January week of prayer. Among them was the Dominican François Biot, the son of an important personality in the Catholic circles of Lyon, Doctor René Biot. His fellow Dominican Maurice René Beaupère had been a student of Abbé Couturier at Les Chartreux, from which experience he inherited an ecumenical vocation that he shared with his brother. However, Cardinal Gerlier's exclusion of the members of religious orders from the selection process prevented the two Dominican friars from applying for the succession.

In 1953, their superiors granted them permission to establish the Centre Saint-Irénée in Lyon, which had initially been conceived as a subsidiary of the Istina center in Paris but very soon became independent. In order to avoid a possible competition with Couturier's two other potential heirs, Fathers Biot and Beaupère – and later only Father Beaupère after Biot was appointed professor at the study house of L'Arbresle – launched three unprecedented initiatives that rested on a

83 *Œcuménisme spirituel*, 244.

84 Michalon's opinion on the history of ecumenism in Lyon was published in Pierre Michalon, "L'Abbé Couturier et l'Unité chrétienne," *Unité chrétienne* 32, 1973, 6–46. It provides a useful counterpoint to Father Villain's book.

strict parity between Catholics and non-Catholics, essentially Protestants: ecumenical pilgrimages, the first of which took place in the Holy Land in the spring of 1961, but which would later undergo considerable expansion; an interconfessional ecumenical formation by correspondence, or F.O.I. (Formation Œcuménique Interconfessionnelle), which came into existence in 1965; and last but not least, pastoral care for mixed households with spouses of different confessions, which involved the drafting of the Charter of Lyon in 1964 and the launching of the bulletin *Foyer mixtes* in 1968. In the context of these manifold activities, the library was not merely an ancillary service. From the very onset, Father Beaupère conceived of it as an indispensable tool of intellectual work in the service of unity taking the place of the pertinent reference library that was still lacking in Lyon. It is particularly noteworthy on account of its large collection of periodicals from all confessions and countries, built up through exchanges, at first with the Dominican journal *Lumière & Vie* when Father Beaupère was its director, in the 1960s, and then with the quarterly bulletin *Chrétiens en marche*, which has continued to be published against all odds until shortly before his death in December 2022.[85]

7 Conclusions

The coexistence of these three branches of the legacy bequeathed by Abbé Couturier has not always been easy. In their own respective way, however, each of them contributed to the spread of the strongly spiritual ecumenism introduced by the Carthusian priest. To conclude this cursory description of a life that seems astonishing in many respects, the historian must return to the stark contrast between the magnitude of the achievement and the modesty of its inspirer. Indeed, unlike Father Congar, Abbé Couturier was not exactly a prolific writer: the entirety of his scattered message constitutes a volume of merely 244 pages. And yet, this priest who had been destined to remain in the shadows due to his lack of fortune, intellectual formation, and connections, this teacher-priest who was also handicapped by severe psychological problems, nevertheless invented, under the name spiritual ecumenism, one of the most effective ways of bringing together separated Christians. Sometimes viewed with suspicion in his own church, in spite of the protection afforded by his discretion and by his archbishop, Abbé Couturier did not live long enough to witness the official recognition of his creation by Vatican II. Today, Abbé Couturier is known throughout the world as the one person who succeeded in imposing an unbiased prayer at the very heart of the movement for the reconciliation of separated Christians. Moreover, his numerous heirs brought his legacy to fruition, each in his own way. In 2010, he was even included in the list of saints venerated by the Church of England. Such a distinction would certainly have offended the modesty of the self-effacing priest from Lyon.

Translated from French to English by Robert Meyer.

Bibliography

Fouilloux, Étienne, *Les catholiques et l'unité chrétienne du XIXe au XXe siècle: Itinéraires européens d'expression française*, Paris, Le Centurion, 1982.

Fouilloux, Étienne, "La vocation tardive de l'abbé Couturier," in: *L'œcuménisme spirituel de Paul Couturier aux défis actuels: Actes du colloque universitaire et interconfessionel, Lyon et Francheville, Rhône, France, les 8,9, 10 novembre 2002*, Lyon, Profac, 2003, 15–43.

Fouilloux, Étienne, "Une affaire lyonnaise: La succession de l'abbé Couturier," *Chrétiens et sociétés* 18, 2011, 105–135.

85 In 2017, it became part of the Henri de Lubac Library of the Catholic University of Lyon. See the testimony of Maurice René Beaupère, *Nous avons cheminé ensemble: Un itinéraire œcuménique: Entretiens avec Béatrice Soltner*, Lyon, Éditions Olivétan, 2012 and Étienne Fouilloux, "Beaupère, Maurice," in: *Dictionnaire biographique des frères prêcheurs: Dominicains des provinces françaises (XIXe–XXe siècles)*, available at <https://journals.openedition.org/dominicains/1285> (accessed Apr 28, 2023).

CHAPTER 6

The Search for Christian Unity in Britain in the First Half of the 20th Century

Andrew Chandler

1 Introduction

Long before the 20th century, in 1734, Voltaire visited England and found himself delighted by the diversity which he encountered there. "This is the land of sects," he wrote amiably. "An Englishman, as a free man, goes to Heaven by whatever route he likes ... If there were only one religion in England there would be danger of despotism, if there were two they would cut each other's throats, but there are thirty and they live in peace and happiness."[1] The visitor to a foreign country can no doubt allow himself the luxury of enchantment but such a comment establishes the particular, and even peculiar, claims which the British example might still make within an international history of religion. How could a vision of a united Christian Church inspire, and persuade, in a society whose members had long cherished a freedom to make their own decisions – indeed, where religion thrived in so many states of conformity and criticism, assent and objection? How was one even to make a beginning, and by what methods should any attempt at union be made?

2 The Vision of the Church

Early in the 20th century, the Regius Professor of Divinity at Oxford, Henry Scott Holland, wrote a volume of essays and reminiscences, summoning up the characters whose lives had crossed his own and acknowledging their influence upon him. One of these sketches captured the figure of John Brown Paton, a Congregationalist minister:

> He had the fire of the prophet and the heart of a child. ... Always, he was breaking in upon our lethargies with some new and tremendous plan for saving all the world, or for uniting all the Churches. ... he had a special theory about the ideal Church, in its connexion with the Kingdom of Heaven, by which he denied to it the mingling of good and evil which is generally believed to be represented by the Parable of the Wheat and the Tares. But, whatever may be said of his exegesis here, he was profoundly loyal to his Vision of a pure and holy Church: and was ready to work with all good Christians for the Cause of the Master, and in the service of man.[2]

Henry Scott Holland was something more than a dry academic settled into the comforts of an established position in a historic university which an established church tended to regard as almost entirely its own.[3] His warmly admiring response to John Brown Paton reveals something significant to a historian of ecumenism: the stirring of a desire for the union of Christians at the beginning of the

1 Voltaire, *Letters on England*, London, Penguin, 1980, 37, 41. In writing of the English and their religion he devoted no less than four letters to the Quakers and placed them first. Thereafter, to the Church of England he dedicated only one letter; to the Presbyterians another. Then there followed a letter "On the Socinians, or Arians, or Anti-Trinitarians."

2 Henry Scott Holland, *A Bundle of Memories*, London, W. Gardner, Darton & Co., 1915, 286–287.

3 To read something of these qualities, see Stephen Paget, ed., *Henry Scott Holland: Memoir and Letters*, London, Murray, 1921.

20th century was not simply an argument which could be framed by a process. It had become an ideal and a growing cause, a part of the atmosphere of a hopeful age in which men and women might greet each other as collaborators and allies and share a belief in the accomplishment of great things. Without this impulse, and this atmosphere, the conventional things which ecumenists soon came to see as the definitions of their efforts would never have occurred: the arguments about faith and order, the intricacies of meetings and memoranda and the laborious drafting of official statements.

Indeed, the vision of the universal church had become something vividly alive in the minds of men and women across the Protestant churches. In 1905, Darwell Stone, the Anglo-Catholic priest and presiding authority at Pusey House in Oxford – and a figure very different from John Brown Paton or Henry Scott Holland – published a new book on *The Christian Church*. Here he wrote:

> One who has systematically pondered the ideas of unity which the New Testament and the writings of the Fathers suggest cannot acquiesce in the present state of the Church … Existing divisions among Christians are a scandal to the Christian name … spiritual energy is lessened and spiritual life marred because Christians are not outwardly at one. Necessary controversies use up time and strength which are all too sorely required for the progress of the Christian religion. Through exigencies of attack and defence, which cannot be avoided as things now are, the love of many is impaired … It ought to be the aim of each Christian to do what in him lies to promote outward union.[4]

Christians, insisted Stone, must realize the reality of their common ground. It was not something that lay beyond them. It existed now: "The inner unity of all the baptised as members of the body of Christ is momentous."[5]

3 The Acknowledgement of Pluralism

The 19th century had come to show the richness of Christian pluralism within a diverse United Kingdom. Popular enthusiasm for religion, too, reinforced this pluralism for there were so obviously different churches, chapels and communities alive and prospering in every city and town, and in most villages, too. Communities were not frozen in their own historical backgrounds but open to waves of internal migration and intricate patterns of change which altered attitudes and practices constantly. People had begun to understand their neighbors in terms of class, and religious adherence expressed it. In sum, one would almost certainly encounter people of a different Christian community in the course of daily affairs, even if one viewed them with reserve. People at large understood that membership of a particular congregation often owed far more to patterns of friendship, connection, locality and practical need, than they did to doctrine – though there was undoubtedly much doctrine in the air.

Familial patterns and shifts between generations showed that lives did not occur in narrow denominational boundaries. They were open to influences of all kinds. The Anglican theologian Frederick Denison Maurice was the son of a Unitarian minister and a Calvinist Baptist. It has been judged that a quest for a coherent, integrating theological vision lay at the heart of Maurice's mature contribution to his own church.[6] In the 20th century Archbishop Cosmo Gordon Lang was brought up in the Church of Scotland and had a

4 Darwell Stone, *The Christian Church*, London, Rivington, 1905, 451–453.

5 Stone, *The Christian Church*, 453.

6 For an attractive portrait, see Florence Higham, *Frederick Denison Maurice*, London, SCM Press, 1947, 11–28. For a later treatment of Maurice and his theological development, see Jeremy Morris, *F.D. Maurice and the Crisis of Christian Authority*, Oxford, Oxford University Press, 2005.

brother who was a minister in it.[7] The future archbishop, Arthur Michael Ramsey, grew up in a Congregationalist family in Cambridge.[8]

Popular anti-Catholicism had subsided in the last decades of the century, yet a gulf between Protestantism and Catholicism remained. In 1900, Roman Catholics were still viewed with suspicion and denied public space for worship and occasions. The building of an immense cathedral only a short walk from Westminster Abbey and Methodist Central Hall certainly showed that the Catholic Church had begun to claim public space with some purpose and growing confidence. In 1908, Archbishop Francis Alphonsus Bourne openly repudiated the prohibition of Eucharistic processions by pronouncing his blessing from the loggia of the cathedral.[9] A resentment of historical dispossession hung over Catholic life. Yet there was also a longing to be acknowledged and to take a place in the foreground. Indeed, the enduring power of Establishment religion could still be sensed in the degree to which those outside it, Protestant or Roman Catholic, still longed to be a part of its great services or occasions. At times they insisted that they all were a part of a shared history and in time would contribute gifts of genuine eloquence. The great lectern at Westminster Abbey was a benefaction of the BMS, donated in 1949 in memory of the great missionary and translator of the Bible, William Carey.

In truth, Anglicans and members of free churches still felt themselves to belong to distinct tribes and they could view each other with an intuitive suspicion. Anglo-Catholic Anglicans viewed Nonconformists with coldness and found that this was firmly reciprocated. Yet ecumenical encounters quietly prospered at the turn of the new century. In 1892, while still bishop of Rochester, the future archbishop of Canterbury, Randall Thomas Davidson, had attended the Reformed Baptist preacher Charles Spurgeon's funeral and accepted readily an invitation to pronounce the benediction. When another great Baptist name, John Clifford, marked the anniversary of a 50-year-long pastorate at Westbourne chapel, in 1908, he received a "fraternal greeting" from the archbishop: "Let me assure you of my respectful and sympathetic appreciation." To this Clifford replied, "we stand at different angles of Christian life; but there are large breadths of Christian thought and faith and work in which we are agreed."[10] Private patterns also showed connections of a happy kind. When a young member of the Faculty of Theology at Oxford (and future bishop of Oxford), Kenneth Kirk, went on holiday to Polperro in Cornwall, the local chapels shut down for the Sunday evening so that their congregations could go to hear him preach.[11]

In the affairs of the world, established and Nonconforming traditions alike increasingly found that they shared common ground in the new century. Public politics had once been divisive; now it seemed more likely to unite. Public platforms became a meeting place for Christians invited to address great issues. Bishop Hensley Henson, whose father had left the Church of England for the world of Nonconformity and whose stepmother was a German Lutheran, could write in the privacy of his journal about "the sects," but in 1902 he readily accepted invitations to speak to the Wesleyan WLM and the general assembly of the United Free Church of Scotland in Edinburgh and was cheered when he went there.[12] The bitter public debate about education which broke out at the turn of the century, and the friendship between Davidson and

7 See John G. Lockhart, *Cosmo Gordon Lang*, London, Hodder & Stoughton, 1949.

8 See Owen Chadwick, *Michael Ramsey: A Life*, Oxford, Clarendon Press, 1990.

9 See Ernest Oldmeadow, *Francis Cardinal Bourne*, London, Burnes, Oates & Washbourne, 1940, 369–398.

10 George K.A. Bell, *Randall Davidson, Archbishop of Canterbury*, vol. 1, London, Oxford University Press, ^{3}1952, 578–579.

11 Eric W. Kemp, *The Life and Letters of Kenneth Escott Kirk, Bishop of Oxford (1937–1954)*, London, Hodder & Stoughton, 1959, 105.

12 See Owen Chadwick, *Hensley Henson: A Study in the Friction between Church and State*, Oxford, Clarendon Press, 1983, 98–100.

the Methodist John Scott Lidgett might appear emblematic. The two met at an interdenominational conference on education in 1902; by the time of the 1906 education bill, Davidson and Lidgett were corresponding privately. They even bumped into each other on holiday in Sidmouth after the Sunday morning worship at the parish church. In 1906, a new campaign to promote Sunday observance united them without scruple: a public rally in May found Archbishop Davidson in the chair, Lidgett sitting on one side, and the duke of Norfolk, Henry Fitzalan-Howard, the outstanding Catholic layman, on the other. Davidson himself clearly found the arrangement revolutionary. Subsequently, a "Message to the nation" was jointly signed with the Roman Catholic archbishop of Westminster.[13] Perhaps the importance of such things should not be exaggerated, but they did show how often an ecumenical rapport could be observed at work within a confident, public-spirited, outward-looking denominationalism.

But what of questions of doctrine and of church order? There was much here to make the boldest idealist hesitate. The 20th century inherited much earnest activity in the sphere of Anglican–Roman Catholic meetings, and the name of Charles Lindley Wood, viscount of Halifax, still defined and symbolized much for those enthusiasts for the reunion of two episcopal churches.[14] However, a good deal of momentum had been dissipated by the papal bull of 1896, *Apostolicae curae*, which had stung Anglicans and affirmed what seemed to be an insuperable obstacle.[15] It seldom occurred to them that they, in turn, had presented Nonconformists with another such obstacle to reunion by insisting that almost everything in the life of the church derived from episcopal succession. These were now the questions which would come to define much – but not all – of the ecumenical activity of the 20th century.

4 The Ecumenical Age

The 1910 WMC in Edinburgh would hardly have mattered at all if Christians at large had not found that its ambitions rang true to their own experiences and hopes.[16] Ecumenism may be identified as a movement in Christian history, but it has often offered a useful term by which historians can assemble a variety of often quite different visions and initiatives. Some were formal, even official, while others were individualistic and even entrepreneurial.

Discussions about reunion for the most part lay in the hands of clergy. Accordingly, they emphasized doctrine, sacraments, rites and, almost above all, the recognition of orders. Yet the significant achievement of the wider movement of ecumenical Christianity in Britain was that it came to involve the hopes of a far greater number of people, and accordingly manifested a greater scale and ambition. The Christian laity in this age of popular voluntarism took much into its own hands. It provided the money to finance buildings and new activities; it fostered a growing commitment to the questions of society and themes of justice and politics; it set up evening classes and discussion groups and offered to young men and women not only a social home but an intellectual, cultural and political one. In particular, a good deal of the new basis and vigor of the ecumenism of the first half

13 See Alan Turberfield, *John Scott Lidgett: Archbishop of British Methodism?*, Peterborough, Epworth Press, 2003, 106–107.

14 John G. Lockhart, *Charles Lindley – Viscount Halifax*, 2 vol., London, Bles, 1935. But see, too, Sidney Dark, *Lord Halifax: A Tribute*, London, A.R. Mowbray & Co., 1934. Lord Halifax was, with Fr. Fernand Portal, a French Lazarist priest, the moving spirit of the Malines Conversations (1921–1925) between theologians of the Church of England and the Church of Rome. See on this topic the chapter by Bernard Barlow and Martin Browne in the first volume of this work.

15 See in this regard the contribution by Paul Avis in the first volume of this work.

16 See the contribution by Brian Stanley in the first volume of this work.

of the 20th century was to be found across the universities in the SCM.[17] Of all these things it was the commitment to reform society in an age of division and poverty which proved the most powerful basis for joint action. Already at the beginning of the new century, this was the ground on which Christians encountered one another, and they found that they often shared the same ideals. In reality, ecumenism already existed where the word itself was unknown; it could be observed in the midst of local communities and in the urban details of great cities and towns. It needed no language to describe it, no formal reports or agreements and no sanction from ecclesiastical authorities.

If the later 19th century had brought an age of denominations, it is important to acknowledge the extent to which the methods of denominationalism facilitated new ecumenical relations. These campaigns of institutional rationalization were at work across all traditions and they produced a great convening of committees, the building of central institutions, the patient and persevering labor of administration, the appointment of superintendents for district (Methodist) or area (Baptist), and the direction of denominational strategies. The General Presbyterian Alliance had been founded in 1875, the Ecumenical Methodist Conference in 1881, the ICC in 1891. The union of the Particular and General Baptists of the New Connexion in 1891 showed that theological identities were growing milder, more amenable to other strains. In 1892, an alliance between John Clifford and Hugh Price Hughes did much to yield a new National Free Church Council. By 1907, the many varieties of Methodism had coalesced in three main strains: Wesleyan, Primitive, and United. In 1932, all three would combine in one of the great acts of church union of the age.[18] However, even if the outward limits of denominationalism were defined firmly, at least some practitioners still looked beyond them even as they attended to their daily duties. By 1918, the secretary of the Baptist Union Council, John Howard Shakespeare, confessed that he was longing for reunion, even under episcopacy and even involving reordination. "The days of denominationalism are numbered," he wrote. "There is nothing more pathetic or useless, in this world, than clinging to dead issues, worn-out methods, and antiquated programmes."[19] Indeed, the burgeoning ecumenical movement attracted many of the leading lights in what was now being called the free church tradition. Increasingly it was wondered whether this emerging, coherent identity might present a firm basis for new conversations with the Church of England itself.

The Great War transformed British society from the top to the bottom and revolutionized, in particular, the relationship between the individual and the political state. In religion, much new thinking clung doggedly to denominational foundations. In October 1916, the two archbishops inaugurated a National Mission of Repentance and Hope in a service at Westminster Abbey. This proved to be a very Anglican affair indeed. The laity was to be organized in the parishes as a "bishop's company," something that was hardly likely to attract Nonconformists,[20] but what altered was to be found on the ground. Military chaplaincies now showed an opening to the place of the churches outside the established religion, yet in the strange worlds of the trenches denominational loyalties must have looked exceedingly remote.[21] An innovation such as the organization Talbot House (also

17 Tissington Tatlow, *The Story of the Student Christian Movement of Britain and Ireland*, London, SCM Press, 1933, 660–676.

18 See the celebratory Richard N. Wycherley, *The Pageantry of Methodist Union: Being a Pictorial Record of the Events Leading Up to and Consummating in the Historic Uniting Conference of 1932*, London, Epworth Press, 1936.

19 See Alfred C. Underwood, *A History of the English Baptists*, London, Kingsgate Press, 1947, 253.

20 For a general overview, see Bell, *Randall Davidson*, vol. 2, 767–774.

21 See Michael Snape, *God and the British Soldier: Religion and the British Army in the First and Second World Wars*, London, Routledge, 2005, 83–138; also Alan Wilkinson, *Dissent or Conform?: War, Peace and the English Churches (1900–1945)*, London, SCM Press, 1986, 38–42.

called Toc H) sought deliberately to ignore denominational divisions – as surely as it excluded social ones – or even the distinctions of rank.[22]

5 The 1920 Lambeth Conference and the "Appeal to All Christian People"

It was during these vital years of war that the first formal meetings of Anglicans and ensembles of free church leaders occurred. In 1914, leading lights of the Church of England and the free churches sat down together to discuss their differences and their hopes of unity. Two years later, they published a report, "Towards church unity"; a second followed in 1918. But what, if anything, would now follow, and who would take the initiative?

Arguably, the Church of England was increasingly coming to regard itself as the seat of a global denomination. This could be seen in the growing importance of the Lambeth conferences, which had begun in 1867. By the time of the sixth Lambeth conference in 1920, these decanal gatherings of the archbishops and bishops had grown in confidence and stature. They received reports, discussed their contents and issued statements, not setting down firm orthodoxies for dissemination across the church, but proposing new formulations and interpretations for the church itself and in the world at large.[23] These conferences had certainly gained in ecumenical ambition, at least partly thanks to the influence of Anglican missionaries who could not justify to themselves a refusal to work with those of other churches when there was so clearly need for unity. It was not always the case that missionary bishops, in particular, were "ecumenical progressives," or liberals. One of the most austerely watchful of the High Church colonial bishops was Frank Weston, bishop of Zanzibar. For Weston receiving communion and exchanging pulpits were things to be disavowed; he was not afraid to accuse other Protestants of heresy. In such a way, and only seven years before at a conference at Kikuyu, Weston seemed to stop the whole Anglican Church and every ecumenical ambition dead in its tracks for such reasons.[24]

At the beginning, the new Lambeth conference of 1920 gave little indication of new revelations to come. A committee on reunion, chaired by the archbishop of York, Cosmo Gordon Lang, showed barely a glimmer of life, let alone ambition. Yet suddenly, inexplicably, it began to gain an extraordinary momentum in the committee stage, and soon this had yielded not simply a set of safe and tidy resolutions but a new document, the "Appeal to All Christian People"[25] – a foundation for a new ecumenical ambition in this postwar world. The document's character was confident, even bold. The decision to address "people," not "churches" struck a chord. And in the very middle of this creative enterprise was none other than Bishop Weston himself, a man who was observed by Archbishop Davidson's energetic chaplain, George Bell, to be an "extraordinary mixture of generosity and menace."[26] If the appeal began with the authority of bishops it took a liberal view of their discretionary powers and encouraged them to innovate. Those powers were enlarged to accommodate local, and occasional revisions. Bishops could also approve an exchange of pulpits if necessary to furthering reunion. Even communion might be allowed to an unconfirmed Christian if a bishop at work in his own diocese saw fit.[27]

22 More widely, see Melville Harcourt, *Tubby Clayton: A Personal Saga*, London, Hodder & Stoughton, 1953; also Michael Snape, ed., *The Back Parts of War: The YMCA Memoirs and Letters of Barclay Baron (1915–1919)*, Woodbridge, Boydell & Brewer, 2009.

23 See Alan M.G. Stephenson, *Anglicanism and the Lambeth Conferences*, London, SPCK, 1978.

24 See Herbert M. Smith, *Frank Bishop of Zanzibar: The Life of Frank Weston D.D. (1871–1924)*, London, SPCK, 1926, 145–170.

25 "An Appeal to All Christian People," in: *Conference of Bishops of the Anglican Communion: Holden at Lambeth Palace July 5 to August 7, 1920: Encyclical Letter from the Bishops, with the Resolutions and Reports*, London, SPCK, 1920, 133–161.

26 See Bell, *Randall Davidson*, vol. 2, 1010.

27 The text may be found in George K.A. Bell, ed., *Documents on Christian Unity (1920–1924)*, first series, London, Oxford University Press, 1924, 1–14.

The appeal was promptly welcomed by the representative bodies of the Church of England. The reaction across the Protestant churches proved to be just as encouraging in the assemblies and annual conferences of the Baptist Union, the Presbyterian Church, the Congregational Union of England and Wales, the Primitive, United, and Wesleyan Methodists, the Society of Free Catholics and the Moravians. A joint committee of Baptists, Congregationalists, Presbyterians, Wesleyan, Primitive, and United Methodists, and one Moravian was duly convened. Their view was subsequently submitted to the two bodies which represented their combined interests, the Federal Council of the Evangelical Free Churches and the National Free Church Council, which published it. This response pronounced an "earnest and cordial" welcome.[28] The consequences of the "Appeal to All Christian People" would now define much of British ecumenism for most of the following decade and more than a little longer.

6 Anglicans and the Free Churches

The two councils which represented the various free churches[29] now collaborated in writing a response. Lambeth pronounced episcopacy itself a blessing and a vehicle to reunion. Yet, however invitingly it was robed, to Christians of the free churches the idea of bishops still represented a principal obstacle. They looked for episcopacy in the Scriptures and found no trace of it. Anglican bishops were appointed by the state, and freedom from the state was the very foundation on which Nonconformists stood. Many were suspicious of the powers of official institutions as things which might not express the spirit of the gospel. Nor did free church people accept that they were simply sects or minorities, splinters which had broken away from the main body of the church: "Our members are, it must be remembered, in a wider and larger Church fellowship than Anglicanism is … when a Congregationalist passes from his communion to Anglicanism he passes into a smaller Church fellowship." To enter the "Lambeth scheme of episcopacy" would cut them off from "all, or the greater part, of non-episcopal Christendom."[30] Indeed, it would be an act of schism – "and a treacherous kind of schism."

For Anglicans, the validity of orders proceeded uniquely from episcopal ordinations. Free church ministers did not look to have their ministry validated by a bishop or by the Church of England, but only by the mind of Christ. They were not sure that Christ set down "one form of polity for the Church," episcopal or any other. They now sought to view episcopacy with an "open mind"; but "we must add that we cannot be expected to consider any form of polity which claims to be an exclusive channel of grace or which fails to recognize the place and the rights of the Christian people in the affairs of the Church."[31] Moreover, it might be remembered that the Anglican view of episcopacy itself was not even shared by most Christians who professed episcopacy in other churches. In the matter of the spiritual freedom of Christians, the free churches were in no way averse to the making of some declaration of faith, although to set any such thing in stone left them uneasy. As for the authority of the state over the church, they could not accept something which must so plainly jeopardize or even "violate the rights of conscience."[32] However, the free churches wished still to respond productively. They insisted that they were hopeful, and would remain hopeful, because the Holy Spirit would guide them all and not least thanks to their own achievements in exchanging pulpits, intercommunion and working together in the world at large.

28 For a comprehensive gathering of responses, see Bell, ed., *Documents on Christian Unity*, 100–169.

29 See Edward Kenneth Henry Jordan, *Free Church Unity: History of the Free Church Council Movement (1896–1941)*, London, Lutterworth Press, 1956.

30 See Bell, *Documents on Christian Unity*, 130–131.

31 Bell, *Documents on Christian Unity*, 133.

32 Bell, *Documents on Christian Unity*, 137.

There was a joint conference at Lambeth Palace in November 1921. A new committee of 13 was appointed and it met in January, March, and April the following year. A report was then approved by the reconvened conference at Lambeth. It was clever, and often subtle. The nature of the church was something broad, and the reality of "representative and constitutional" episcopacy insofar as it was ancient, if not scriptural, might be accepted by "the greater part of Christendom, … as the means whereby this authority of the whole body is given." Councils of presbyters and congregational meetings should also be accepted by those who had looked to bishops. Altogether, the report insisted, "the acceptance of Episcopal Ordination for the future would not imply the acceptance of any particular theory as to its origin or character, or the disowning of past ministries of Word and Sacrament otherwise received, which have, together with those received by Episcopal Ordination, been used and blessed by the Spirit of God." The Nicene Creed should be accepted by all "as the sufficient statement of this corporate faith," with the Apostles' Creed used for services of baptism. However, diverse "use" of the creeds within a united church should be expected and accepted: "Assent should not be understood to imply the acceptance of them as a complete expression of the Christian Faith, or as excluding reasonable liberty of interpretation," for they affirmed essential things and were the inheritance of centuries.[33]

As subsequent resolutions passed by the annual assembly of the Federal Council of the Evangelical Free Churches showed, these formulations and definitions still left much hanging in the air. The defining principles of deliberation and activity, however, were now well established: public conferences commissioned private committees and those committees made their reports back to the commissioning conferences. Yet, although the members of the committees may have begun to convince themselves that they had gained vital ground, it could be seen that the wider constituencies still harbored doubts. The authority of a bishop was still something to be suspected. The validity of orders was still something unassured. When the annual assembly of the Federal Council took place in 1923, a new statement asked whether the very methods by which the hopes of church unity lived and worked were likely to realize the ambition itself: "The Union movement cannot – especially in the minds of the people – live entirely on private conferences and their reports." Not for the first time, they looked for "acts of unity," more genuine evidence of "fellowship and co-operation" in the life of what was already a universal church.[34] Some critics were offended that the validity of their own orders was still thrown into doubt. In an age of public democracy, they had gained still more confidence in the rightness of their own congregational principles of independence, and they were suspicious of ecclesiastical and clerical power. Nor could it be ignored that it was in the relationship between the Church of England and the state that a great difficulty remained, even though it may appear less and less offensive.

What followed from all this was duly deliberate. A single volume, *The Church of England and the Free Churches*, jointly edited by George Bell and William Lewis Robertson, was published in 1925.[35] It is difficult to discern consequences. Almost 100 years later, the book itself is very hard to find. The high moment of Lambeth was soon looking very like a figment of the past, and one that was soon gathering dust. Few things can be more obscure in the imagination than those which belong to a recent past.

33 Bell, *Documents on Christian Unity*, 143–151.

34 Bell, *Documents on Christian Unity*, 164–168.

35 George K.A. Bell & William L. Robertson, eds., *The Church of England and the Free Churches: Proceedings of Joint Conferences Held at Lambeth Palace (1921–25)*, London, Oxford University Press, 1925.

7 COPEC

In April 1924 an extraordinary gathering took place in Birmingham, a bastion of Quakerism, under the banner of the Conference on Christian Politics, Economics and Citizenship. COPEC was chaired by the young bishop of Manchester, William Temple, while the persevering, practical genius of the conference was to be found in the vision of a young Quaker, Lucy Gardner. It was explicitly an ecumenical rally of 2,500 men and women drawn from almost all denominations across the British Isles. Nor was this merely a domestic enterprise: guests came from many countries and returned afterwards with reports of a great achievement. An admiring Archbishop Nathan Söderblom remarked that COPEC was now a new word in the English language itself.[36]

The task of COPEC was firmly framed:

> The basis of this Conference is the conviction that the Christian faith, rightly interpreted and consistently followed, gives the vision and the power essential for solving the problems of today, that the social ethics of Christianity have been greatly neglected by Christians with disastrous consequences to the individual and to society, and that it is of the first importance that these should be given a clearer and more persistent emphasis ... Christianity has proved itself to possess also a motive power for the transformation of the individual, without which no change of policy or method can succeed. In the light of its principles the constitution of society, the conduct of industry, the upbringing of children, national and international politics, the personal relations of men and women, in fact all human relationships, must be tested. It is hoped that through this Conference the Church may win a fuller understanding of its Gospel, and hearing a clear call to practical action may find courage to obey.[37]

Accordingly, those who came to Birmingham received 12 preparatory reports written by groups commissioned by the main organizing body, seeking to inspire to study, to educate, and influence a wide readership. These included studies on international relations, war, crime, leisure, home, industry and property, education, family, and relations of the sexes.

To read the proceedings of COPEC is to glimpse a veritable who's who of British Protestantism at large in the first years of postwar ambition.[38] Moreover, they show the extent to which the movement drew from both the clergy and the laity, and how much it was defined by the participation of women. Temple was joined by a diverse representation of Anglican opinion, including Bishop Edward Stuart Talbot of Winchester, Charles Raven and Evelyn Underhill, Charles Cripps (Baron Parmoor), Bishop Hamilton Baynes, Constance Smith, Ruth Kenyon, and Ruth Rouse of the WSCF, while the Congregationalists Alfred Garvie and William Selbie, the Methodist William Frederick Lofthouse (also a Birmingham man, teaching at Handsworth College) and the Quaker Herbert Wood also spoke at various sessions.

Historians have wondered where all of this actually went, for there was no grand consequence, no further rally, no very obvious corollary in political, economic or social affairs. When the general strike took place in May 1926, it was hard to see the response of the churches as anything other than

36 For COPEC at large, see Edward R. Norman, *Church and Society in England (1770–1970): A Historical Study*, Oxford, Clarendon Press, 1976, 279–313; see also John Kent, *William Temple: Church, State and Society in Britain (1880–1950)*, Cambridge, Cambridge University Press, 1992, 115–134.

37 *The Proceedings of C.O.P.E.C.: Being a Report of the Meeting of the Conference on Christian Politics, Economics and Citizenship, Held in Birmingham, April 5–12 1924*, London, Longmans, Green, 1924, xi. The preliminary statement is produced at the beginning of each one of the 12 reports published for the conference.

38 *The Proceedings of C.O.P.E.C.*, iii–vi.

muddled (and unwanted).[39] However, there was a sinking of roots into the soil, including a Continuation Committee and further studies (*Rural Life*, a study published in 1927[40]). There was also an innovative housing project. The achievement of the COPEC venture was to crystallize, memorably, a new consensus before it dispersed into the private lives of clergy and laity at large in the world. Its fruits were to be found, if they could be found at all, in the details of personal, congregational, and communal experience.

8 The Hopes of Orthodoxy and the Silence of Roman Catholicism

In the later years of the 19th century something in the atmosphere of Anglicanism had, by degrees, altered. The identity of a Protestant, national church, once so solid, was breaking into a new curiosity about the Christian world at large and becoming more open to expressions which would once have been repudiated as effectively Roman Catholic or Orthodox. This yielded a place in worship to images and icons, the Virgin Mary and the veneration of saints. For a growing number of Anglicans, and not only Anglo-Catholics, the existence of the Orthodox world conjured up a marvelous vision of the ancient and universal Christian Church.[41]

Here, too, hopes of reunion thrived on high moments and dissolved into a good deal of quiet mutual study and the maneuvers of committees. If Anglicans and free church people remained absorbed in their difficulties, elsewhere, however, such study bore fruit. Relations between Anglicans and Orthodox now grew still warmer, and not only because both traditions had bishops. In July 1922, there came a breakthrough. The patriarch of Constantinople pronounced that Anglican orders were as valid in the eyes of his church as those of the Roman, Old Catholic, and Armenian churches, "inasmuch as all essentials are found in them which are held indispensable from the Orthodox point of view for the recognition of the 'Charisma' of the priesthood derived from Apostolic succession."[42] This statement encouraged a pattern of comparable acknowledgements from the patriarch of Jerusalem and the Church of Cyprus.

A great ecumenical service to celebrate the 1500th anniversary of the Council of Nicaea took place in Westminster Abbey, and the Orthodox world was richly represented. Such an occurrence presaged a new and more purposeful age of ecumenical diplomacy, in which the figure of the bishop of Gloucester, Arthur Cayley Headlam, became a dominant one. The excitements of this strain would come to matter to free church people, not because they shared them, but because they increasingly found that their own efforts were eclipsed by them. At the Lambeth conference of 1930 their resentment made itself felt.

As far as relations with the Roman Catholic Church were concerned, not all was extinguished by *Apostolicae curae*. In the Church of England, Protestant Evangelicals abjured any entangling compromises with a power they continued to suspect, while the broad body of the Church of England barely thought of Rome at all and, immune to curiosity, knew only the sufficiency of its own patterns and perimeters. Yet Anglo-Catholics were now enjoying a modest golden age, and their movement became increasingly visible across the parishes, not only by an increasingly common enthusiasm for vestments and the performance of ritual in worship, but also by the prolific creation of confraternities, sodalities and associations, and

39 See Norman, *Church and Society*, 338–341; also Kent, *William Temple*, 135–147; also Frederic A. Iremonger, *William Temple, Archbishop of Canterbury: His Life and Letters*, London, Oxford University Press, 1948, 328–344.

40 *Rural Life: A Report prepared by a Commission appointed by the Copec Continuation Committee*, London, Longmans, Green & Co., 1927.

41 These shifts are captured by Willem A. Visser 't Hooft, *Anglo-Catholicism and Orthodoxy: A Protestant View*, London, SCM Press, 1933.

42 See Stephenson, *Anglicanism and the Lambeth Conferences*, 155.

of pilgrimages to Walsingham (where a Catholic shrine coexisted with an Anglican shrine). Despite a ridiculed "popish" piety or contestation concerning matters of doctrine, many Anglo-Catholics in the Church of England leant heavily towards the Church of Rome. At large, Anglo-Catholics did what they could to thrive in a condition of irreducible ambiguity. A minority looked to the papacy itself for authority and made advances to their Roman neighbors. Mark Vickers has shown that a succession of quiet, private conferences between Anglican papalists and Roman Catholics took place at the outset of the 1930s. In 1932, these meetings were peremptorily extinguished by Cardinal Bourne.[43]

9 The Lambeth Conference of 1930 and the Joint Doctrinal Commission

The Lambeth conference of 1930, which took place under the presidency of Archbishop Lang, might have lacked the revelatory force of the "Appeal to All Christian People," but it showed the extent to which all these new ecumenical understandings had begun to refashion Anglicanism itself. The bishops now received reports on all that had passed since 1920 and examined various schemes and proposals. An Orthodox delegation, led by Patriarch Meletios II of Alexandria, was formally welcomed to Canterbury Cathedral; a later service at St. Paul's Cathedral was attended by the Orthodox but was avoided by the free churches who sensed that they had now been relegated to the margins by the patronage of new favorites. Indeed, it was the impressively present Orthodox who commanded the real interest of the 1930 conference, although many delegations, both national and international, were also there, and the vital ecumenical innovation of a joint doctrinal commission owed much to the Old Catholic archbishop of Utrecht, Franciscus Kenninck. Few at the conference of 1930 could have been unaware that the creation of a new, united Church of South India was beginning to gain ground and the cautious encouragement which was given for new work on this scheme did little more than delay an outbreak of controversy.[44]

Although their relations had now become brittle and defensive, the hope of union between episcopal Anglicans and nonepiscopal free churches had not been forgotten. They were reestablished in 1933. There duly appeared *A Sketch of a United Church*, a new report produced by a commission in membership carefully balanced between the Church of England and the various British free churches. Two years later there followed an *Outline of a Reunion Scheme for the Church of England and the Evangelical Free Churches of England*. Both these reports explored possible constructions of episcopacy that would satisfy in greater measure the principles held by all parties while also incorporating synodical and representative models that defined the governance of the free churches themselves. After all, a general practice might allow a variety of interpretations. The adoption of episcopal ordination, it allowed, "neither affirms nor excludes the view that Apostolic Succession determines the validity of the Ministry and Sacraments."[45] The effect of this was not widely or powerfully felt but a general disinclination was, even so, palpable. When the two free church councils merged, in 1941, they proceeded to produce a full, critical response to Anglican overtures.

43 See Mark Vickers, *Reunion Revisited: 1930s Ecumenism Exposed*, Leominster, Gracewing, 2017.

44 See Stephenson, *Anglicanism and the Lambeth Conferences*, 155–177; see, too, *The Lambeth Conference, 1930: Encyclical Letters from the Bishops with Resolutions and Reports*, London, SPCK, 1930, 110–151.

45 See *Outline of a Reunion Scheme for the Church of England and the Evangelical Free Churches of England*, London, SCM Press, 1938. The cautious preface is jointly the work of Archbishop Lang and Alfred E. Garvie.

10 Christian Thought across Denominational Borders

It was now widely held that Christians might, and should, freely work together for the salvation of the world. The cause of division was still doctrine and church order, not good works. What of the realm of Christian thought and scholarship? Here, too, for the most part, Protestants collaborated openly and with increasing confidence. When the Baptist Terrot Reaveley Glover had published his influential and popular study *The Jesus of History* in 1917,[46] the little book went out into the world fortified with a warm commendation by Archbishop Davidson: "I regard it as a high privilege to be associated with this volume." The academic world yielded some acknowledgement that the finest scholarship might emanate from any tradition. Naturally, Baptists took a tribal pride in a figure such as Glover, just as Congregationalists were proud of the achievements of William Boothby Selbie, the Methodists looked eagerly to William Frederick Lofthouse, and the Quakers smiled upon the publications of Herbert George Wood. A fine reputation often won an ecumenical acknowledgement and a wide readership across the churches.

It was true that the theological colleges, concerned as they were with the education of new priests and ministers, remained bastions of denominationalism. However, here, too, there were many conversations and intersections. Meanwhile, the journals represented the reflections of denominational constituencies: *Theology* was written by Anglicans and largely read by them, while *The Expository Times* was a regular feature of the reading life of free church ministers. Yet these journals published, and promoted, a wide variety of discussions on Christian unity. In academic scholarship alone, and in biblical studies above all, the denominations became largely irrelevant. Although the free churches produced a greater wealth in Old Testament scholarship (the president of the SOTS for a number of years was the Baptist Henry Wheeler Robinson), the Anglicans, in greater numbers fortified with the classical education of the public schools, dominated New Testament studies. Despite all this, there were only a few striking collaborations between individuals from different Protestant denominations. The Anglican William Oscar Emil Oesterley collaborated with the Baptist Theodore Henry Robinson on two books of fundamental significance to students of theology, *Hebrew Religion* (1930) and *An Introduction to the Books of the Old Testament* (1934).[47] The great, indeed heroic, achievement in biblical translation in these years proceeded from a prodigious, individualistic Scot, James Moffatt. Moffatt's New Testament achieved an immense readership, particularly across the free churches of Britain.[48]

11 The Place of British Christians within the International Ecumenical Movement

The leading lights of British Christianity throughout the first half of the 20th century remained, at least in some measure, idealists. They were vigorously active, and convinced ecumenists, who often divided their efforts among local, national, and international movements. William Temple, who became archbishop of York in 1928, and Bishop Headlam did much to define the Anglican investment in the Faith and Order movement, while George Bell achieved much the same effect in the parallel Life and Work movement. In 1933, Headlam also became the chairman of the new

46 Terrot R. Glover, *The Jesus of History*, London, SCM Press, 1917.

47 William O.E. Oesterley & Theodore H. Robinson, *Hebrew Religion: Its Origins and Development*, London, SPCK, 1930 and William O.E. Oesterley & Theodore H. Robinson, *An Introduction to the Books of the Old Testament*, London, SPCK, 1930.

48 James Moffatt, *A New Translation of the Bible containing the Old and New Testaments*, London, Hodder & Stoughton, 1926.

archbishop of Canterbury's CFR. The many connections which emerged in these contexts were animated by the new dramas of political life.

Needless to say, the crisis of totalitarianism on the European continent created a new context for Christian ecumenism, and although it complicated the efforts of its practitioners it also placed them squarely in the foreground of public life and affairs.[49] The persecution of Christians abroad provoked more and more people, both inside and outside the churches, to take a keen interest in ecumenical conferences which they would otherwise have barely noticed. Most conspicuous in these terms was the Oxford Conference on "Church, Community and State," a gathering of some 425 people from 120 countries which took place for two weeks in July 1937.[50] The effective genius of this memorable assembly was the prodigious Scottish layman, Joseph Houldsworth Oldham. Only weeks later there followed a great conference of the Faith and Order movement in Edinburgh. Ecumenical friendships grew more committed, and more productive, because they had come to matter in the world. Other relationships which might otherwise have remained sympathetic were heavily altered. The bishop of Chichester, George Bell, and the Congregationalist minister, Nathaniel Micklem, now met on new ground and became fast allies. By the same token, Bell became divided from his brother bishop, Headlam of Gloucester, for in German matters Headlam showed himself to be provocative and recalcitrant.[51]

The deepening crisis in world affairs in these years provoked a succession of ecumenical initiatives at Lambeth Palace, where Archbishop Lang convened conferences of church leaders to draft joint statements exhorting disarmament, supporting the League of Nations or pleading for the peaceful resolution of dangerous grievances. Lang himself was sharply aware that such ventures achieved very little indeed, if anything at all. Yet they showed that all participating churches acknowledged their place in the world of politics and sought to speak with a united voice. In 1938 and 1939, Lang's ecumenical diplomacy intensified and led him to attempt a vast intervention for peace on behalf of churches throughout the world. He was hurt by the predictable abstinence of the Roman Catholic Church and proved more successful in enticing the Orthodox. What came of all these efforts, heroic in their fashion, was rather little, but the archbishop of Canterbury could at least show the world that much of the Christian Church had not merely accepted the narratives of power and war as the world tumbled into catastrophe.[52]

12 World War II and the Sword of the Spirit

The coming of World War II was watched with growing dread by all Christians in Britain. For many it marked a tragic crystallization of what was by now a well-established confrontation with Nazism and the powers of totalitarianism at large. After the fall of France in the summer of 1940,

49 See, for example, Norman, *Church and Society*, 314–363; also Keith Robbins, *England, Ireland, Scotland, Wales: The Christian Church (1900–2000)*, Oxford, Oxford University Press, 2010, 241–261 and Adrian Hastings, *A History of English Christianity (1920–1985)*, London, Collins, 1986, 310–352. On how Christian responses to these international crises led to new pathways towards unity see the chapter by Keith Clements in this volume.

50 See *The Churches Survey their Task: The Report of the Conference at Oxford, July 1937, on Church, Community and State*, London, Allen & Unwin, 1937.

51 See Ronald Jasper, *Arthur Cayley Headlam Life and Letters of a Bishop*, London, Faith Press, 1960, 284–306; also Ronald C.D. Jasper, *George Bell, Bishop of Chichester*, London, Oxford University Press, 1967, 201–244; also Andrew Chandler, *George Bell, Bishop of Chichester: Church, State and Resistance in the Age of Dictatorship*, Grand Rapids, Eerdmans, 2016, 42–73.

52 See Andrew Chandler, "Munich and Morality: The Bishops of the Church of England and Appeasement," *TCBH* 5/1, 1994, 77–99; also, Andrew Chandler, "The Judgement of an Archbishop: Archbishop Lang and the morality of British Foreign Policy (1933–1939)," in: Keith Robbins & John Fisher, eds., *Religion and National Policy in the Twentieth Century*, Leiden, Brill, 2009, 183–224.

Cardinal Arthur Hinsley inspired the admiration of the new prime minister, Winston Churchill, when he remarked that it was better now that the hopes of freedom should rest with Britain and its empire alone. This may have seemed little more than patriotic bravado, but the desire amongst Christians to show a firm, expressive unity with the national state in the context of such an emergency was widely shared. It certainly brought Hinsley and his church into the foreground of national life.[53] Hinsley himself had now become increasingly at home with those who led the other churches, not least with Archbishop Lang, whom he met regularly at the Athenaeum club (it was Lang who proposed that he, too, become a member there). He also found that in his views of the war he had much in common with Bishop Bell.[54]

In October 1940, Hinsley took a bold step by writing a letter to *The Times* in the company of the archbishops of Canterbury and York and the moderator of the FCFC. Together they embraced the five peace points set down by Pius XII. Inspired by the Roman Catholic historian and writer, Christopher Henry Dawson, and without discussion with his own bishops, Hinsley summoned into life a new enterprise, the Sword of the Spirit, to unite Christian men and women who sought justice in war, in the conduct of international relations and in the pursuit of peace. Whatever the Roman Catholic bishops made of this, the laity set to work eagerly. Within weeks it could be seen that a movement of ecumenical study groups, lectures and meetings had almost unexpectedly sprung up. In a great public meeting at the Stoll Theatre in May 1942, Hinsley chaired a first session, on "A Christian International order," and Archbishop Lang chaired a second, on "A Christian Order for Britain." At the end of the meeting, Bishop Bell spontaneously proposed to Hinsley that he might lead them all in the Lord's Prayer. Hinsley did so. This was certainly a vivid moment in the history of Christian unity in Britain.[55]

On May 28, 1942, a new joint statement was published, largely drafted by Bishop Bell, announcing a commitment by the Church of England, the free churches and the movement itself to work through "parallel" action in religious affairs and "joint" action in the social and international realms. That year Temple and Hinsley also collaborated on a Christmas message to the people of occupied Europe. However, in these activities the limit of ecumenical cooperation between Protestants and Catholics had been reached. When Hinsley died in March 1943, there was a rather hasty redrawing of borders. Historians tend to view these events as striking moments which did not obviously build into enduring movements or achieve a recognizable change, but their symbolic presence touched much that moved, barely apprehended, beneath the surface of church life. The Sword of the Spirit remained alive in the minds of the Christian public, like a rumor which everyone wanted to be true and which turned out to be fact after all. Many Christians who looked to unity in the church remained hopeful because it had occurred at all.

The experience of war altered the very atmosphere of national life and naturally forged new loyalties across old borders, in religion as elsewhere. Old debates amongst Christians – about the nature and claims of the Christian Church, about the basis of the political state – had assumed new forms and acquired a new intensity. Indeed, it was widely heard that, in this war for civilization itself, the new visions of the dictators had found their essential refutation and their fundamental adversary in the Christian Church in all its branches. The ecumenical vision of Bishop Bell pressed that, in such a world as this, division was a luxury that Christians could barely afford. When

53 John C. Heenan, *Cardinal Hinsley*, London, Burns, Oates & Washbourne, 1944, 92, 98–99.

54 See George K.A. Bell, "Cardinal Hinsley," *Blackfriars* 24/278, 1943, 165–168.

55 See Michael J. Walsh, "Ecumenism in War-Time Britain: The Sword of the Spirit and Religion and Life (1940–1945)," *The Heythrop Journal* 23/3, 1982, 243–258 and 23/4, 1982, 377–394; also Jasper, *George Bell*, 245–255 and Hastings, *A History of English Christianity*, 393–398.

he wrote *Christianity and World Order* Bell turned to a succession of papal encyclicals in search of solid ground for a new, ecumenical Christian apologetic.[56] More in this vein came from the brilliant Presbyterian, William Paton, whose book *The Church and the New Order* even found its way into the hands of Dietrich Bonhoeffer in Germany.[57]

In this there was also a deepening of idealism and a growing hope for reform. It had become important to think about the condition of the world, and to think together. Groups of all kinds could be found busily at work, publishing articles, reports, and opinions. The Moot group of Oldham was one such meeting of minds; essentially an intellectual conclave it was naturally ecumenical in character.[58] In *The Christian News-Letter*, Oldham and his deputy Kathleen Bliss created an innovative, regular bulletin which could be easily pocketed and disseminated across a society busy with the prosecution of war. The *News-Letter* also produced a series of short books with authors hailing from a variety of denominational backgrounds or, in the case of the refugee Gerhard Leibholz, from Germany itself.[59]

13 Archbishop Temple

In the tumult of war British Christianity had found a new place in public discourse and also a new ecumenical breadth and ambition. Much of this settled on the figure of William Temple, who was enthroned as archbishop of Canterbury on St. George's Day in 1942. On that day, Temple contrasted a world beset by "more intense and fiercer competition, conflict and war between larger and ever larger concentrations of power" with a world fellowship of Christians, "the great new fact of our era," claimed by the labors of missionaries the world over and now marked out by the world conferences Stockholm, Lausanne, Jerusalem, Oxford, Edinburgh, Tambaram, and Amsterdam.[60] The significance of Temple was powerful. His readiness to speak on public platforms, his amiable charisma and obvious sympathy for the poorer and less privileged in society made him a "people's archbishop," while his intellectual generosity attracted admiration even from those who had their doubts. Those who sought the unity of Christians dared to hope for the future.

Temple's ecumenical credentials, not least as a presiding genius of many conferences of the Faith and Order movement, were formidable. Yet for all his idealistic force, his breadth and expansion, he remained very much a figure of an Anglican world, and the premises from which much of his own thought and experience proceeded declared this.[61] His commitment to episcopacy was adamant, although he allowed that it might be understood in different ways. He believed that hospitality might be offered to free church people at communion, but not reciprocity. He moved only by degrees towards a fuller, freer, exchanging (or "interchanging") of pulpits and also towards an idea of "supplementary" ordinations, whereby

56 George K.A. Bell, *Christianity and World Order*, Harmondsworth, Penguin, 1940.

57 William Paton, *The Church and the New Order*, London, SCM Press, 1941; see Eberhard Bethge, *Dietrich Bonhoeffer: A Biography*, London, William Collins, 1970, 643–646.

58 See Keith Clements, ed., *The Moot Papers: Faith Freedom and Society (1938–1944)*, London, Bloomsbury, 2015.

59 For a sense of the range of the series, see William Paton, *The Message of the World-Wide Church*, London, Sheldon Press, 1940; Oliver C. Quick, *Christianity and Justice*, London, Sheldon Press, 1940; Karl Barth, *A Letter to Great Britain from Switzerland*, London, Sheldon Press, 1941; Gerhard Leibholz, *Christianity, Politics and Power*, London, Sheldon Press, 1942. This world of debate is examined by John Carter Wood in *This is Your Hour: Christian Intellectuals in Britain and the Crisis of Europe (1937–49)*, Manchester, Manchester University Press, 2019.

60 William Temple, *The Church Looks Forward*, London, Macmillan, 1944, 1–7.

61 For a recent, critical analysis, see Edward Loane, *William Temple and Church Unity: The Politics and Practice of Ecumenical Theology*, Basingstoke, Palgrave Macmillan, 2016, 1–20, 205–226.

ministers might "receive" each other's rites of ordination. However, Temple did much to oversee the creation of a new BCC in 1942, the same year in which the CCJ was established. With the moderator of the FCFC, the Congregationalist, John Seldon Whale, he also produced *A Statement of Christian Belief*.[62] While this arguably did not mark a very splendid advance in Christian unity it certainly affirmed once again that Christians were often found to be united in questions of faith even though they were divided in those of order.

It would be hard to exaggerate the sense of shock which the death of Archbishop Temple provoked in 1944. It could hardly be denied that ventures in church unity had always thrived on a sense of idealistic expectation. This was exactly the quality which Temple had summoned. Now there was an acute sense of a void.

14 Archbishop Fisher and the Cambridge Sermon (1946)

Before he became archbishop of Canterbury in 1944, Geoffrey Francis Fisher had few credentials as an ecumenist, besides participating in the early work of the BCC. Fisher knew, however, that the primacy had now been redefined by the ecumenical efforts of his predecessors and he was determined to honor what he had inherited. In seeking to maintain the pursuit of Christian unity, he also enjoyed at least two conspicuous advantages: unencumbered by loyalty to a particular party of the church, he was strikingly open-minded; unbothered by eloquent illusions, he was purposefully, and resolutely, practical. In short, Fisher did not look for weighty conferences, studious committees and endless discussions. He sought results.[63]

As archbishop, Fisher now readily became president of the BCC. He commissioned theologians drawn from the Anglo-Catholic dimension of the Church of England to consider again the unity of the Christian Church and to publish a report. There followed another, by evangelicals, and then a third report, to some extent provoked by the first, by leading free church thinkers. The constructive effect of these endeavors was difficult to judge, though they undoubtedly inspired some debate and did something to establish a fruitful intellectual atmosphere.[64] Yet while this was going on the archbishop himself made a decisive move.

Fisher saw that in Britain itself the desire for Christian unity had languished. In characteristically brisk fashion, he decided to revive it in a single sermon, wholly the work of his own mind. He preached it at a service in Cambridge on Nov 3, 1946. Fisher observed how much had now been gained by ecumenical endeavor, which went on openly and without fuss among all churches, with the exception of Rome. He insisted, "on the theology of Redemption and Grace, of the Scriptures, the Creeds, the Sacraments, even of the Church itself, there are no barriers that reach up to heaven." What divided Christians lay instead in particular difficulties: in a disagreement about the ministry of the church, in the foundations and practice of procedure and government, in worlds of habit, the "idiom" of worship, and the manner of thought and speech. Much progress in discussions had been abruptly interrupted by the war. "How," he asked, "shall we begin again?" But he also added, significantly, "I sense a certain reluctance to begin at all."

Fisher had heard it said by "a distinguished theologian" that schemes of reunion should be set aside until more thought and prayer had occurred. Any wait for theological unanimity was bound to be a very long one indeed – and yet the churches continued to suffer from their disunity and there

62 William Temple & John S. Whale, *A Statement of Christian Belief*, London, SPCK, 1943.

63 See Edward Carpenter, *Archbishop Fisher: His Life and Times*, Norwich, Canterbury Press, 1991; also Andrew Chandler & David Hein, *Archbishop Fisher (1945–1961): Church, State and World*, Farnham, Ashgate, 2012.

64 See Andrew Chandler, "*Catholicity*: Anglicanism, History and the Universal Church in 1947," *IJSCC* 18/2–3, 2018, 236–251.

remained, for them all, one Christ. He acknowledged that the search for a constitutional unity faced severe obstacles. It might well be asked how much constitutions themselves really counted in the end? Surely it was now time to change the method. Suppose Christians chose instead a "process of assimilation, of growing alike," a "free and unfettered exchange of life in worship and sacrament between them as there is already of prayer and thought and Christian fellowship ... that they should grow towards that full communion with one another, which already in their separation they have with Christ"? "My longing," continued Fisher, "is not yet that we should be *united* with other churches in this country, but that we should grow to *full communion* with them." Their object should be to remove the barriers which blocked the "free circulation" of the whole Christian body.

Fisher admitted that episcopacy divided. However, episcopacy was something debated in itself; it had not, in practice, settled in one understanding and form, even in the churches which had it – not even in the Church of Rome. The nonepiscopal churches had accepted that episcopacy was an established fact, that it had a place in the universal church, and that it would continue to exist. Suppose Christians who repudiated bishops now took episcopacy "into their own system," thereby influencing and revising the idea of episcopacy itself in response to their own ideas, objections and understandings. "In such a giving and receiving of episcopacy," Fisher proposed, "there would be a mutual removal of a barrier between the folds." Christians might enter freely into each other's churches and into the full fellowship of worship that they found there. He concluded, invitingly, "cannot we grow to full communion with each other before we start to write a constitution? Have we the wisdom, the humility, the love and the spirit of Christ sufficient for such a venture as I have suggested?"[65]

This sermon inaugurated a new era of denominational conferences. In this Fisher himself took the lead, inviting a new ensemble of free church luminaries to Lambeth Palace. He now placed much responsibility in the hands of the bishop of Derby, Alfred Rawlinson. Once a Congregationalist, Rawlinson was a New Testament scholar who had also cowritten a book called *The Genius of the Church of England*.[66] To Lambeth also came the moderator of the FCFC, Howard Roberts. Fisher himself emphasized how important it was not to pursue a scheme of incorporation or absorption but simply to explore the importance of what they all might give and receive. Roberts took great heart from this meeting and wrote to Fisher, "I am persuaded that you have opened a way for an unprecedented advance in the cause of re-union."[67] This meeting inaugurated still further conferences. For all these efforts, the overall effect of five years of conversations and conferences was often impressive to those who attended but inconclusive in the minds of everyone else. As time slipped by, they also looked increasingly obscure. The same old binds appeared irreducible: without some agreement about episcopacy, there could be no agreement about orders; without an acceptance of orders, there remained the problem of giving and receiving communion.

The later 1940s certainly did witness a great deal of shared discussion and study. Some meetings brought surprises. In his memoirs, Nathaniel Micklem recalled an invitation to a small, private conference in Oxford of free churchmen and "strong Anglo-Catholics":

> For the most part we had long been friends, and we talked together with the utmost frankness. We met for no controversial purpose; our sole end was to define accurately and precisely where we differ. I remember a short discourse by Professor Gordon Rupp.

65 For the text itself, see Chandler & Hein, *Archbishop Fisher*, 163–168 (italics original).

66 Alfred E.J. Rawlinson, *Problems of Reunion*, London, Eyre & Spottiswoode, 1950, and Alfred E.J. Rawlinson & Charles Smyth, *The Genius of the Church of England*, London, SPCK, 1947.

67 Carpenter, *Archbishop Fisher*, 314.

> He had drawn up a careful list of Free Church criticisms of the Anglo-Catholic position and a parallel list of Anglo-Catholic criticisms of Free Churchmanship; each side recognised that his list was fair. The two lists were identical! We met for two or three days; we knew well that at some point there was profound difference between us, but at the end of our sessions we were utterly unable to define that point.[68]

At large, however, it could be seen that the suspicions of evangelicals and Anglo-Catholics had not disappeared: they were always somewhere about to agitate and warn of calamities. Systems of episcopacy, however elegantly designed and smoothly commended, remained objectionable to many free church people. For many, too, the preservation of Christian liberty was still hard to reconcile with a state church, however modest the connection might now be and however well that state behaved. Fisher continued to disavow a vision of incorporation and centralization, looking instead for full intercommunion, diversity and freedom.[69] Yet he also feared unlicensed innovations and the unraveling of church order. Perhaps, he mused, the churches could coordinate their administrative and organizational designs? But when Fisher launched ideas like these to his deputies or allies for development they tended to dwindle and then to disappear.

In 1950, the Rawlinson committee published *Church Relations in England*. This presented six points for the Church of England and the free church tradition to consider: that each was satisfied that the others maintained the apostolic gospel; that a free church would accept and indeed adopt a model of episcopacy and of future episcopal ordination; that communion might be given by priests of the Church of England to baptized Christians from the free churches, while Anglicans could still only receive communion from ministers of the free churches who had been episcopally ordained; that the Church of England would maintain its hope that episcopal confirmation be generally accepted throughout the free churches; that free churches would continue in freedom, relating as they saw fit to those churches which remained independent; and that this creation of "parallel" churches, united in intercommunion, should not be a point of conclusion but a stage on a continuing path towards the full achievement of union.[70] Fisher waited a year for the reaction to settle before placing this before the synods of the provinces of York and Canterbury. Yet neither at the time nor later did these proposals inspire a great stir, and a sense lingered that fundamental questions about church order had not really been answered. Looking back at this a decade later, the ecumenist Norman Goodall was left to observe, "it cannot be said that the result was a marked change in denominational attitudes."[71] However, he did perceive that a harbinger of a new relationship between Anglicans and Methodists lay in the report of 1950.

15 The State of Ecumenism in 1951

In Lent 1951, a series of sermons took place at Great St. Mary's in Cambridge on "The approach to Christian unity." The overall effect was, as the editor of the subsequent publication affirmed, a liberal one and it was not unhopeful: "There is at the present time a stronger and more genuine desire than ever before on the part of the Christian churches to understand each other and to emphasize the community of their origin and their purpose." Even so, it was perhaps the sermon of Bishop Bell, by now a veteran of many years and

68 Nathaniel Micklem, *The Box and the Puppets (1888–1953)*, London, Bles, 1957, 139.

69 Carpenter, *Archbishop Fisher*, 317.

70 See, for example, the assessment by James P. Hickinbotham, "Church Relations in England," *The Churchman* 65/2, 1951, 69–76.

71 Norman Goodall, *The Ecumenical Movement: What It Is and What It Does*, London, Oxford University Press, 1961, 110.

many conferences, which struck the most somber note. If only, he lamented, the churches at large had made the same progress in their search for unity that the governments of nations had made in manufacturing armaments and prosecuting wars. In such a world as theirs, could Christians continue to justify their divisions? Yet the churches appeared if anything increasingly defined by a "temper of isolation ... In all our churches, there is too little movement, and too much circumspection." The Roman Catholic Church looked farther off than ever before. As for the relations between Anglicans and free church people, despite some special permissions and some exchanging of pulpits, "we are no further forward in 1951 than we were in 1920." In the same 30 years in which so little had been achieved in Britain, Christians in India had achieved unity. Why was there this difference? It was because the church in South India knew, above all else, the utter importance of evangelism: "We have no overmastering passion to preach the Gospel to a non-Christian world." Unity, insisted Bell, demanded sacrifice – and too little had been sacrificed by their various traditions to achieve it. He went on, "because we cannot have perfection from our own point of view – and do we really think we have perfection in our own churches now? – are we to refuse to suffer irregularities and anomalies for a while? Dare we sit down and do nothing?"[72]

Bishop Bell argued that the more Christians in Britain knew of the work of the new WCC, and the more they invested in that work themselves, the more they would grow together and the greater their witness to the world would be. However, he was beginning to acknowledge how hard it was to make the international ecumenical movement meaningfully alive in the mind of the Church of England itself. Domestic ecumenism could only flourish within the sustaining context of a convincing, greater narrative. Denominationalism revealed only a retreat from the world. When the second great general assembly of the WCC took place at Evanston in 1954, Bell wrote a brief, popular study to bring the history of the ecumenical movement at large to the attention of British Christians.[73] Then he took off for the United States to see the general assembly for himself. Whatever Bell made of this, it was William Wand, the bishop of London, who revealed how uncomfortable an English Anglican might be in such company, grumbling at such an immense concentration of German theology, American money, and Dutch bureaucracy.[74] This remark reached the ears of Visser 't Hooft and must have confirmed an apprehension that in the great councils of international ecumenism the Anglicans must always look a little out of place.

16 Anglicans, Methodists, and Presbyterians

By the mid-1950s, it could be seen that what had for decades been the basic model of Anglican-free church discussions was in decline. Perhaps this was hard to resist: although ecumenical conferences tended to attract approachable leaders such as Micklem or Melbourn Evans Aubrey who, after all, had much in common, each of the various free churches still represented a distinct tradition, order and culture. Their views of the Church of England also proceeded from quite different premises. This was true of Methodism in particular. Many of the leading lights of Methodism, particularly if they hailed from its Wesleyan past, had no very profound objection to episcopacy, but the spirit of Primitive Methodism remained very much alive, too, and this was more firmly resistant to the adoption of bishops of any definition or description. At all events, Anglicans and Methodists now

72 *The Approach to Christian Unity: Sermons Preached before the University of Cambridge (1951)*, Cambridge, Heffer, 1951, 57–63.

73 George K.A. Bell, *The Kingship of Christ*, Harmondsworth, Penguin, 1954.

74 Willem A. Visser 't Hooft, *Memoirs*, London, SCM Press, 1973, 252.

began a sustained dialogue to explore a new union of two parts. These new conversations became an important labor of Bishop Bell's last years, and he certainly drove his Anglican colleagues hard. There was a glimmer of progress and a new, studious report for digestion by the two constituencies.[75] In this lay a foundation for later dramas.

When Archbishop Fisher sought to stir discussions between the Church of England and the Presbyterian Church of Scotland, he upset the bishops and the priests of the Episcopal Church of Scotland almost at once. Talks, once begun, ended abruptly in 1952. Yet Fisher charmed a suspicious general assembly of the Church of Scotland and persevered. In 1958, there appeared a new report proposing the exchanging of pulpits and the receiving of sacraments; there was also some creative examination of what Fisher called "assimilation," not least with reference to a reconciling of the principles of episcopacy and the presbytery. These ideas found favor in the convocations of York and Canterbury – but that was the easy part. It was the achievement of the Scots not to turn the report out altogether but accept the prospect of a year of committee-work and general deliberation. There could be no denying the power of the critics. An anniversary commemoration of the Reformation in Scotland simply made matters worse. A year later the whole venture crashed in the general assembly of the Church of Scotland.[76]

17 Deliberating in Secret: Anglicans and Roman Catholics

Under Cardinal Hinsley's successors a sense of separation was blandly reaffirmed. The happily ecumenical Bishop David Mathew now looked very like a fish out of water. Returning to Britain in 1953 after a long tour of duty as an apostolic visitor and delegate in Africa, he became a bishop-in-ordinary to the armed forces, a position which he did not want and for which he was barely suited. A sense of disappointment hangs over the later life of this remarkable priest who might have succeeded Hinsley.[77]

If Anglicans or free church people found themselves in a position to plead for the cause of unity, they were likely to earn the response that the Roman Catholic Church already possessed it.[78] Yet the rest was not quite silence. What occurred looked more like the silent diplomatic maneuvers which take place behind the scenes in the lives of nation states divided by an iron curtain. When Charles Boyer, a French Jesuit dispatched by the Vatican to observe the first general assembly of the WCC in Amsterdam in 1948, had met Bishop Bell, a private meeting followed in Rome itself. This revealed that the mind of Rome was not closed to new overtures. It also showed that the Cold War was fostering a need for Christian solidarity. These conversations continued and grew in size and intent. Increasingly, the Anglicans found an admiration for one of their hosts in particular: Msgr. Giovanni Battista Montini. Indeed, Montini was at home in Anglican company. During the war, he had befriended the British representative to the Holy See, Lord Francis D'Arcy Osborne, looking after the diplomat's valuable possessions in his own flat and allowing him to use his bath.[79]

Discretion was everything. When the European press got wind of these surreptitious exchanges and blew them up into something immense, the horrified participants scattered like the cast of a stage melodrama. However, the meetings continued. Two new conferences involved

75 See Robbins, *England, Ireland, Scotland, Wales*, 364–366; also Chadwick, *Michael Ramsey*, 333–346; also Hastings, *A History of English Christianity*, 548–550.

76 See Carpenter, *Archbishop Fisher*, 319–330.

77 See the biography of Bishop Mathew by Fergus Kerr in: *ODNB* 37.

78 A tone stoutly maintained by Christopher Butler, the abbot of Downside, in his introduction to John M. Todd, *Catholicism and the Ecumenical Movement*, London, Longmans, 1956, ix–xiv.

79 See Owen Chadwick, *Britain and the Vatican during the Second World War*, Cambridge, Cambridge University Press, 1988, 124–128.

larger numbers and a succession of safe houses. Between January 1952 and July 1962, a series of meetings took place in London, then in Rome, Cambridge, Assisi, and Oxford. In these a number of English Roman Catholics, carefully led by Archbishop John Carmel Heenan, played a growing part. Much of the substance of these meetings, however private they were, proved valuable. They also showed how much was changing within the Roman Catholic Church itself. Owen Chadwick, who observed much of this at close quarters, later noted how, by degrees, the Roman Catholics opened their minds to biblical criticism and in this found new common ground with their Anglican peers.[80]

18 Fisher at Large in the World of the Christian Church

It would be quite wrong to suggest that every ecumenical overture which had provoked new ventures in the search for unity in Britain in the first half of the 20th century had proceeded from the doorstep of Lambeth Palace. Equally, it would be mistaken to deny the centrality of the figure of the archbishop of Canterbury. In 1960, Archbishop Fisher clearly saw that retirement was upon him. He decided to make a tour of a wholly ecumenical character, first to Jerusalem, then to Istanbul and then to Rome. These were not merely valedictory visits, but ventures hopefully intent on Christian union. Fisher knew that the mind of the new pope, John XXIII, showed a new generosity, a new openness. There was proof of this in the establishment in 1960 of the SPCU. Fisher decided that he should meet the pope, regardless of obstacles or criticism. Even so, the Vatican appeared unsure as to how to receive him, and there was a certain amount of embarrassed scurrying about behind the scenes. Fisher still managed to be received at the Vatican: on December 2 the meeting took place. It lasted over an hour. A part of the tale, as Fisher told it, has become famous. John XXIII looked to the time when the separated churches might return to the mother church. Fisher gently repudiated this vision of returning. John XXIII, at first surprised by the objection, reflected briefly and then accepted the objection.[81]

Nothing of this was recounted at the time. No photograph was taken. The fact of the meeting was itself enough to do what Fisher intended – to make history. The meeting presented further evidence that ecumenism in Britain had never been merely a domestic affair but something which depended upon the reality of a great picture, a new sense of invitation, connection or illumination. Fisher, the practical man who looked for practical results, knew the power of symbolism. Now he was proud of his achievement, and rightly so. He had managed to outmaneuver and make awkward a reluctant curia and achieve, at a stroke, a new basis for an ecumenical future. “The period of the cold war between Churches is not altogether past,” he remarked cheerfully. “But it is passing.”[82]

19 Conclusions

The diversity that Voltaire had observed in 1734 was still well rooted 200 years later. It would be tempting to argue that the apparent failure of the cause of Christian unity in the first half of the 20th century revealed the continuing vitality of public and private religion and that unity would be a vision better served by declining numbers, waning beliefs and diminishing resources – and

80 See Owen Chadwick, “The Church of England and the Church of Rome, from the Beginning of the Nineteenth Century to the Present Day,” in: Edward G.W. Bill, ed., *Anglican Initiatives in Christian Unity: Lectures Delivered in Lambeth Palace Library (1966)*, London, SPCK, 1967, 73–107, here 94–101.

81 For three treatments of this meeting see Carpenter, *Archbishop Fisher*, 733–744; Chandler & Hein, *Archbishop Fisher*, 105–109, 235–238; also Chadwick, “The Church of England and the Church of Rome,” 100–104.

82 Chadwick, “The Church of England and the Church of Rome,” 104.

when society at large cared less about religion altogether.

An atmosphere of disappointment certainly hangs in the air and historians have not been slow to point to it. Yet it is too easy to judge that the ecumenical ventures which occurred throughout the first half of the 20th century failed to win what was so obviously sought. So much of the achievement was to be found in activity, not results. New lamps had been lit, and new tasks begun. It is better to see these things on their own terms, rather than as elements of a greater, failed ambition. It had been shown, clearly and insistently, that terms of unity had entered the basic vocabulary of British Christianity and displaced terms of division.

A state church had acknowledged the richness of independent confessions and met them respectfully and creatively. Indeed, at least some of the justifications by which Anglicanism existed had been extended and even redefined, at least for a time. Across the free churches there had been unions between kindred traditions, too, even if they often seemed more like practical acts of denominational revision than harbingers of a universal Christian Church. Sometimes it could be seen that ecumenical ventures had come to involve a renegotiation of relationships between clergy and laity, although the former usually came out very much on top in the end. Unity in church order must matter fundamentally to Christians themselves, particularly if they occupy positions of authority. It would be quite wrong to pretend that what was plainly a history of failure in this sense did not matter, but the accomplishment of a unity of witness and endeavor in a wide world of turmoil must surely have meant far more to a humanity which still sought the dawn of the kingdom of God. Christians in Britain had learnt that unity was something that could be understood, and realized, in many forms. It could exist in a single act, barely observed – or even in a single word. In all this, they at last had something of value to offer to the future of the whole Christian Church.

Bibliography

Bell, George K.A., *Documents on Christian Unity (1920–1924)*, first series, London, Oxford University Press, 1924.

Bell, George K.A., *Randall Davidson, Archbishop of Canterbury*, London, Oxford University Press, ^{3}1952.

Bill, Edward G.W., ed., *Anglican Initiatives in Christian Unity: Lectures delivered in Lambeth Palace Library (1966)*, London, SPCK, 1967.

Carpenter, Edward, *Archbishop Fisher: His Life and Times*, Norwich, Canterbury Press, 1991.

Hastings, Adrian, *A History of English Christianity (1920–1985)*, London, Collins, 1986.

Heenan, John C., *Cardinal Hinsley*, London, Burns Oates & Washbourne, 1944.

Jasper, Ronald C.D., *Arthur Cayley Headlam: Life and Letters of a Bishop*, London, Faith Press, 1960.

Jasper, Ronald C.D., *George Bell, Bishop of Chichester*, London, Oxford University Press, 1967.

Kent, John, *William Temple: Church, State and Society in Britain (1880–1950)*, Cambridge, Cambridge University Press, 1992.

Micklem, Nathaniel, *The Box and the Puppets (1888–1953)*, London, Bles, 1957.

Norman, Edward R., *Church and Society in England (1770–1970): A Historical Study*, Oxford, Clarendon Press, 1976.

Robbins, Keith, *England, Ireland, Scotland, Wales: The Christian Church (1900–2000)*, Oxford, Oxford University Press, 2010.

Stephenson, Alan M.G., *Anglicanism and the Lambeth Conferences*, London, SPCK, 1978.

Stone, Darwell, *The Christian Church*, London, Rivington, 1905.

Todd, John M., *Catholicism and the Ecumenical Movement*, London, Longmans, 1956.

CHAPTER 7

Kerygmatic Theology: Karl Barth and Rudolf Bultmann

Christophe Chalamet

1 Introduction

Kerygmatic theology, otherwise known as "dialectical theology," or the "theology of the Word," did not have as its primary purpose contributing to Christian unity. No particular desire for Christian unity animated its proponents in the early stages of its existence during World War I and during the decade or so that followed. Yet this theological school, with all its singular and distinctive voices (not only those of Karl Barth and Rudolf Bultmann, but also of Friedrich Gogarten, Emil Brunner, Eduard Thurneysen, and perhaps even of Paul Tillich for a while in the early 1920s), made a crucial contribution to the ecumenical movement in the 20th century. How did it do so? By focusing on the core of the Christian message and by seeking to interpret anew this core, with its various implications, for today. Despite the ever-recurring suggestion that "doctrine divides" whereas "action unites," it may well be that some of the most significant contributions to the quest for Christian unity have been (and are) certain theological constructs, whatever their confessional background, which most deeply enrich and renew our understanding of the Christian faith, the gospel, and the church as bearing witness to the gospel.

The present contribution centers on the two towering figures of "kerygmatic" or "dialectical" theology, namely, Karl Barth and Rudolf Bultmann. An obvious asymmetry soon becomes obvious when one considers Barth and Bultmann, and their respective commitment and contribution to the ecumenical movement. Barth was far more influential and significantly more committed to this movement than Bultmann ever was. Yet Bultmann, too, in his own, more indirect way, contributed to ecumenical dialogue and the quest for the unity of all Christians.

2 Karl Barth as "Ecumenicist"?

Ecumenism was hardly in Karl Barth's field of vision during his theological studies in Bern, Berlin, Tübingen, and Marburg (1904–1908).[1] "At the beginning of this century, as a I was studying theology, no mention was ever made that I could read a modern Catholic book. Protestants did not read such books."[2] Barth entered the practical world of the pastoral ministry, first in 1909 in Geneva as a vicar, and then in 1911 as the main pastor in the small town of Safenwil in the Swiss canton of Aargau. In Geneva, he was a young pastor-in-training, under the wings (at least for a short while) of Adolf Keller, who would

1 On Karl Barth and ecumenism, see esp. Thomas Herwig, "Barth und die Ökumene," in: Michael Beintker, ed., *Barth Handbuch*, Tübingen, Mohr Siebeck, 2016, 143–148. Michael Welker, "Karl Barth: From Fighter Against the 'Roman Heresy' to Leading Thinker for the Ecumenical Movement," *SJT* 57/4, 2004, 434–450; Willem Adolph Visser 't Hooft, "Karl Barth and the Ecumenical Movement," *EcRev* 32/2, 1980, 129–151; Klaus Alois Baier, *Unitas ex auditu: Die Einheit der Kirche im Rahmen der Theologie Karl Barths*, Bern, Lang, 1978; Thomas Herwig, *Karl Barth und die Ökumenische Bewegung: Das Gespräch zwischen Karl Barth und Willem Adolf Visser 't Hooft auf der Grundlage ihres Briefwechsels (1930–1968)*, Neukirchen-Vluyn, Neukirchener Verlag, 1998; Benjamin Dahlke, *Karl Barth, Catholic Renewal and Vatican II*, London, T&T Clark, 2012; and my article "Karl Barth on the Quest for the Church's Unity," *CrSt* 37/2, 2016, 343–359.

2 Karl Barth, "Über die Annäherung der Kirchen: Ein Gespräch zwischen Karl Barth und Tanneguy de Quénétain," *Junge Kirche* 24/6, 1963, 304–309, here 308.

eventually become a major figure in the ecumenical movement, and who would publish, as early as in 1931, the first monograph on the relationship between dialectical theology and the ecumenical movement.[3]

While in Geneva, Barth heard a conference delivered by John Mott, the well-known ecumenicist, who was holding a lecture tour in several Swiss universities. Barth attended Mott's lectures in Geneva (Feb 5–7, 1911); however, the speaker barely touched on ecumenism.

2.1 *Barth's Theological Breakthrough (1914–1918)*

In the fall of 1914, at the onset of the war, Barth began to question radically the theological training he had received, namely, a modern, liberal interpretation of Christianity. He was shocked to see that his revered teachers in Germany all supported their nation's belligerent attitude. Their way of legitimizing their country's decisions and initial attacks, such as the assault on Belgium, shook him to the core. He began to think that what he had been taught rested on problematic theological grounds. As Barth began reading the apostle Paul's Epistle to the Romans and taking copious notes, which would eventually become his commentary on Romans, or *Der Römerbrief*,[4] the question of the unity of the church remained very remote from him.

Barth's interest in theological dialogue with Roman Catholicism began in earnest in the 1920s. The Jesuit Erich Przywara wrote a long, profound review of the *Römerbrief*. This text was published in 1923, and despite some peculiar misinterpretations of his thought, it made an impression on Barth.[5] In it, Przywara, besides (mistakenly) viewing Barth's thought as, ultimately, monist and pantheist, singled out his Swiss colleague as a theologian who was genuinely Protestant.

In 1925, it was a Protestant colleague, Erik Peterson, whose Roman Catholic proclivities were well known to Barth (Peterson became a Roman Catholic in 1930), who wrote a pamphlet denouncing dialectical theology's errors.[6] Barth was called upon to clarify certain matters, particularly in respect to ecclesiology: the church, with its dogma, is *not* the prolongation of God's revelation in the incarnate Word.[7]

2.2 Analogia Entis *or* Analogia Fidei?

In 1925, Barth left the University of Göttingen, where he had been teaching since 1921, and where he was surrounded by (mostly) Lutheran scholars, to teach at the University of Münster. This move was significant, for Münster was a Catholic city at the time. During his five years there (1925–1930), Barth entered into a lively, fruitful dialogue with Roman Catholics. Leaving aside some of the marginal or superficial issues, which impeded true dialogue, Barth was beginning to allow Protestant theology to be questioned, quite radically, by Catholicism.[8]

3 Marianne Jehle-Wildberger, *Adolf Keller (1872–1963): Pionier der ökumenischen Bewegung*, Zürich, Theologischer Verlag, 2008; ET: *Adolf Keller (1872–1963): Ecumenist, World Citizen, Philanthropist*, trans. Mark Kyburz & John Peck, Eugene, Cascade, 2013.

4 Karl Barth, *Der Römerbrief*, Bern, G.A. Bäschlin, 1919 (second edition: 1922); ET: *The Epistle to the Romans*, trans. Edwyn C. Hoskyns, London, Oxford University Press, 1933.

5 Erich Przywara, "Gott in uns oder Gott über uns? Immanenz und Transzendenz im heutigen Geistesleben," in *StZ* 105, 1923, 343–362. Reprinted, in an abbreviated form, in Erich Przywara, *Ringen der Gegenwart: Gesammelte Aufsätze 1922–1927*, vol. 2, Augsburg, Benno Filser-Verlag, 1929, 543–578.

6 Erik Peterson, "What Is Theology?," in: Erik Peterson, *Theological Tractates*, ed. and trans. Michael J. Hollerich, Stanford, Stanford University Press, 2011, 1–14.

7 Karl Barth, *Die Theologie und die Kirche*, Munich, Kaiser, 1928; ET: "Church and Theology," in: *Theology and Church: Shorter Writings (1920–1928)*, trans. Louise Pettibone Smith, Eugene, Wipf & Stock, 2015, 286–306; Rudolf Bultmann, "The Question of 'Dialectic' Theology: A Discussion with Erik Peterson," in: James M. Robinson, ed., *The Beginnings of Dialectic Theology*, vol. 1, Richmond, John Knox Press, 1968, 257–274.

8 See especially Barth's article, "Der römische Katholizismus als Frage an die protestantische Kirche," *ZwZ* 6, 1928, 274–302; ET: "Roman Catholicism: A Question to the Protestant Church," in: *Theology and Church*, 307–333.

Conversely, Roman Catholic scholars were paying attention to the questions Karl Barth directly and forcefully addressed to them.

The theme of analogy became fairly important in these years, especially as a consequence of the conversations and debates with Pryzwara. Barth was critical of what he thought underpinned the notion of "analogy of being" (*analogia entis*), namely the postulate of a certain commonality between the Creator and the creature in light of the creation of human beings "in God's image" (*imago Dei*). If there is a commonality between the Creator and the creature, particularly in connection to the notion of "being" as a common category pertaining both to the Creator and the human creature, albeit in infinitely different way, then there might be a possibility for the creature, as creature, to be, at least potentially, open to God, just as there is a possibility for God to encounter his creature. To Barth, this notion of an intrinsic possibility, of an inherent quality present within the creature which enables it to be open "upwards," was literally an anathema. To him, it simply eliminated the person and work of Jesus Christ as the mediator, as the way which comes, unilaterally (at least at first), *from* God *to* the world, and not the reverse.[9]

Hence Barth came to consider the *analogia entis* as "the invention of Antichrist." The immediate context in which he made this pronouncement, in 1932, is important:

> I can see no third alternative between that play on the *analogia entis* which is legitimate only on the basis of Roman Catholicism, between the greatness and misery of a so-called natural knowledge of God in the sense of the *Vaticanum* [Vatican I], and a Protestant theology which draws from its own source, which stands on its own feet, and which is finally liberated from this secular misery. Hence I have had no option but to say No at this point. I regard the *analogia entis* as *the* invention of Antichrist, and I am of the opinion that *because of it* it is *impossible* to become Catholic. I add that all other reasons for not doing so are to my mind short-sighted and trivial (CD 1/1, xiii [rev., italics mine]).

Barth's claims in this passage continue to give pause to many. Przywara thought it was the kind of prank a school friend might typically make, and he took Barth's interpretation of his (Przywara's) teaching on *analogia entis* to be a "grotesque distortion."[10] Even today there is no agreement among specialists as to whether Barth misunderstood Przywara or not. What is clear is that Barth expressed a sharp, radical criticism of Roman Catholic theology as he launched what would become his massive project of a *Kirchliche Dogmatik*.

2.3 *The Turn to a More Positive Ecclesiology*

In those years of teaching in Münster and later in Bonn (1930–1935), Barth was reconsidering the topic of the church. He remained opposed to any form of ecclesial or ecclesiastical triumphalism, but he also moved beyond what can be seen as a certain negative one-sidedness, which came to the fore in his earlier ecclesiology (for example, in *Der Römerbrief*, 1922). In the first volume of his *Church Dogmatics*, Barth states that "God in Jesus Christ is the essence of the Church" (CD 1/1, 12), that "the being of the Church is identical with Jesus Christ" (CD 1/1, 41). Such pronouncements stand out when compared to the far more dialectical statements in the early 1920s, where the church was presented to a significant extent as contradicting the gospel: "The opposition between the Church and the Gospel is final and all-embracing: the Gospel

9 On the debate concerning *analogia entis*, see Keith L. Johnson's excellent study, *Karl Barth and the Analogia entis*, London, T&T Clark, 2008. For a different interpretation, according to which Barth did not accurately interpret Przywara's views, see John R. Betz, "Translator's Introduction" to Erich Przywara, *Analogia entis: Metaphysics: Original Structure and Universal Rhythm*, trans. John R. Betz & David Bentley Hart, Grand Rapids, Eerdmans, 2014, 1–115.

10 Erich Przywara, *In und Gegen: Stellungnahmen zur Zeit*, Nurnberg, Glock und Lutz, 1955, 278. See Betz, "Translator's Introduction," 112.

dissolves the Church, and the Church dissolves the Gospel," as Barth put it in *The Epistle to the Romans*.[11] The visible church is the church of Esau, the church "where no miracle occurs, and where, consequently, human beings are exposed as liars."[12] This church "may be seen at Jerusalem, or Rome, or Wittenberg, or Geneva."[13] The church of Jacob, on the other hand, the true church, remains invisible; it is "the unobservable, unknowable, and impossible Church," which has "neither place nor name nor history."[14] According to Barth in 1921, we can only speak of the church of Esau; yet we cannot forget that the true "theme" of the church of Esau is the church of Jacob.[15] The emphasis, in 1921, may have been on the "tribulation" of the church, but by then Barth already claimed that it is only when we recognize this tribulation or distress that we may discover hope.[16]

In the first volume of his *Church Dogmatics*, Barth underlines the profound connection between the being of the church and its Lord. Indeed, if Barth is able to identify the being of the church with Jesus Christ, it is because "the true Church" wholly depends, at all moments, on him: "It is because it lives by Jesus Christ ... that it is the true Church" (*CD* 1/2, 214).

Was Barth becoming a "crypto-Catholic"? Some thought so on the basis of the first volume of his *Church Dogmatics*, in which Barth defended the traditional Trinitarian and Christological doctrines, including the doctrine of the virgin birth. These were significant developments in Barth's theology, which opened the door to a fruitful dialogue with Roman Catholic and Orthodox theologians. This dialogue continued throughout the 1930s and became increasingly important after World War II, as the ecumenical movement entered a new phase with the creation of the WCC, and as the Roman Catholic Church was struggling against, and in favor of, major internal changes in the years leading up to Vatican II.

2.4 *Die Kirche und die Kirchen (1935)*

In 1930, Karl Barth entered into contact with Willem Adolph Visser 't Hooft, arguably the most significant ecumenicist in the 20th century. Visser 't Hooft was among the first to introduce Barth's theology to French- and English-speaking audiences. In 1931, Adolf Keller presented him as "a truly international apostle of the Barthian theology."[17]

The importance of this friendship, for both men, cannot be denied. It took a great deal of energy on Visser 't Hooft's part to convince Barth that (Barth) was the right person to contribute to the burgeoning ecumenical movement in the 1930s, as well as in 1948 at the founding of the WCC in Amsterdam. Visser 't Hooft worked tirelessly at involving Barth in ecumenism, and, given Barth's frequent reluctance, he was rather successful at it.

In February 1935, Barth agreed to give a series of four lectures in Geneva in July 1935 on "the Church and the Churches."[18] This was Barth's first major theological contribution to the topic of Christian unity – and a lasting one, since Barth integrated many insights from these lectures in *Church Dogmatics* 4/1, when he returned to the topic of Christian unity, as well as on other occasions (see *CD* 4/1, 668–685).

In the first lecture, entitled "The Unity of the Church," Barth stated that Christ is the unity of the church and, therefore, searching for the unity of all Christians means searching for, and returning to, Christ.[19] Consequently, the church must "submit

11 Barth, *The Epistle to the Romans*, 333.
12 Barth, *The Epistle to the Romans*, 341.
13 Barth, *The Epistle to the Romans*, 341.
14 Barth, *The Epistle to the Romans*, 342.
15 Barth, *The Epistle to the Romans*, 341.
16 Barth, *The Epistle to the Romans*, 345.

17 Adolf Keller, *Karl Barth and Christian Unity: The Influence of the Barthian Movement Upon the Churches of the World*, New York, Macmillan, 1933, 128; Willem Adolph Visser 't Hooft, *Memoirs*, London, SCM Press, 1973, 36–38.
18 Karl Barth, *Die Kirche und die Kirchen*, Munich, Kaiser, 1935; ET: *The Church and the Churches*, Grand Rapids, Eerdmans, 2005 (first published in English in 1936). The page numbers in what follows refer to this English translation.
19 In 1963, Barth stated that "converting" from Protestantism to Roman Catholicism, or vice-versa (or to yet

and subordinate itself on its human side, the side of its life, order, and teaching, to the standard which it derives from Christ, from God."[20] The church "must look back to its origin and essence, set its compass by that bearing, suffer itself to be purged and reformed by that standard."[21] Such statements may appear innocuous, but in fact they contain an immense program, upon which Vatican II, to give one particularly significant example, embarked. The church's being may be Jesus Christ, but there is still a certain gap, indicated above by the verbs "submit" and "subordinate," between the church and Jesus Christ. The identity of the church as Christ's body, does not mean an equality with Christ himself: as its head and as its "standard," Christ necessarily stands over the church in "its human side." There is a unity-in-distinction between Christ and the church, which is expressed in the fact that Jesus Christ is both the "being" of the church and its Lord, as the "head" of the ecclesial body.

Needless to say, Barth acknowledged the presence of both unity and multiplicity in the New Testament, with regard to the church, but he saw a predominance of unity over multiplicity. In the New Testament, "we find no relation of polarity or tension, or of mutual dependence, between the one church and the many gifts, persons, and the like; we find only a one-sided relation of dependence and derivation in which the multiplicities are subordinate to the unity."[22] This is a forceful theological statement, of which many modern historians of the primitive church, and others as well (including theologians), might disapprove.

Barth then makes another significant claim concerning the quest for the unity of the church: this quest can never become an end in itself. Such a quest would be "idle and empty," and "the forces of sin and the forces of grace" would both forcibly, and successfully, resist it.[23] In stating so pointedly that ecumenism can never become the goal, Barth is targeting the ecumenical movement and the "professional" ecumenicists, including his friends Visser 't Hooft and Adolf Keller.[24] In a letter he wrote to Keller on Dec 1, 1932, Barth already expressed his perplexity when "ecumenism itself literally becomes the goal."[25] Two and a half years later, after his lecture series in Geneva, Barth still remained ambivalent about the ecumenical movement precisely on this point.[26]

At the same time, he was convinced that the quest for the unity of the church is not optional for Christians: "If we listen to the voice of the Good Shepherd, then the question of the unity of the Church will most surely become for us a burning question."[27] The fact that there is "one Mediator" excludes "a multiplicity of Churches."[28] These statements are clear: in 1935, Barth stated that the question of Christian unity and the quest for this unity must be "for us a burning question."[29] In other words, here was a leading theologian endorsing the ecumenical movement's goal (if not its methods).

Barth was extremely forceful in his denunciation of disunity. In his second lecture, he stated that we need to deal with the multiplicity of the churches "as we deal with sin, our own and others," which therefore also means "as guilt": "We must not allow ourselves to acquiesce in its reality."[30] There are "signs of oneness" here and there, but

another Christian tradition), is a denial of the "invisible unity of the church"; Barth, "Über die Annäherung der Kirchen," 308.

20 Barth, *The Church and the Churches*, 7.

21 Barth, *The Church and the Churches*, 7.

22 Barth, "Über die Annäherung der Kirchen," 11–12 (rev.).

23 Barth, *The Church and the Churches*, 13 (rev.).

24 K. Barth to A. Keller, Dec 1, 1931, in: Karl Barth Archiv 9231.381, unpublished letter.

25 Quoted in Jehle-Wildberger, *Adolf Keller (1872–1963)*, 122.

26 Jehle-Wildberger, *Adolf Keller (1872–1963)*, 152, where Barth is quoted as saying: "All in all … for the moment this ecumenical business has not made much of an impression on me."

27 Barth, *The Church and the Churches*, 16.

28 Barth, *The Church and the Churches*, 14.

29 Barth, *The Church and the Churches*, 16.

30 Barth, *The Church and the Churches*, 22–23.

the multiplicity of the churches is a clear sign of our "real distress" and of our "failure."[31]

The third lecture centers on the "task of the uniting of the churches." Having said that this task is a "mandate" or a "command" (*Gebot*) from the Lord, Barth adds that the task at hand is "lofty" and "arduous" – it is a task "of super-human magnitude."[32] Only Christ's voice, his calling, can realize this uniting,[33] for it has nothing to do with the creation of "alliances" and "federations" among churches.[34] These may in fact lead to resurgences of "denominational self-consciousness,"[35] whereas true unity implies the common celebration of the Eucharist.

Barth then urges the ecumenical movement to be "cautious" and "modest" in its aims: no "hallelujahs"![36] This is another pique directed at the leaders of the movement. It is true that learning to know one another is important, even as it will lead the conversation partners to the realization of the depths that separate them, but should we imagine that a movement such as the ecumenical movement may lead the churches to their uniting? Caution is in order: "The uniting of the churches is too great a matter to be the result of a movement, however smart and comprehensive."[37] Such a movement can contribute to an "anticipation" of such uniting; not much more than that, but also no less than that.[38]

Barth had already suggested that this stance could have positive consequences in 1935, thirteen years before the controversy he sparked – notably along with Jean Daniélou – when he commented on the absence of an official Roman delegation – or even of individual Roman observers – at the 1948 Amsterdam general assembly and said that this absence was not to be deplored since it was coherent with the Roman Church's official stance.

> From this point of view, I am not distressed by the well-known and widely regretted reservation of the Roman See towards union movements of the past and present. It was and is needful that someone somewhere should make a stand against the excessive claims of all Church movements, and assert that the uniting of the churches cannot be produced. Rather, in obedience to the unity of the Church which is already accomplished in Jesus Christ, it can only be *found* and *recognized*. It is in this sense that I understand the papal refusal (which is certainly arrogant on their part) to take a hand in the efforts which have been made so far towards union.[39]

There is a tension which runs through these 1935 lectures: the ecumenical movement has full legitimacy, since the command to be one comes from Christ himself. However, the uniting of the churches cannot be achieved by a (human) movement – even a movement which is as well-intentioned and as encompassing as the ecumenical movement. Unity ultimately depends on God, who gives it. Yet this in no way excludes the call, addressed to all Christians, to listen to one another, to become closer to one another, at least as a kind of "anticipation" of the authentic unity, which only God grants.

"Unity" is much greater and deeper than "getting along," or even "understanding one another":

> Let us not deceive ourselves: the uniting of the churches into the unity of the Church would mean more than mutual tolerance, respect, and occasional cooperation; more than learning to know each other and to listen to one another; more than feeling one in some ineffable commonality. It would also

31 Barth, *The Church and the Churches*, 27 and 30 (rev.).
32 Barth, *The Church and the Churches*, 44.
33 Barth, *The Church and the Churches*, 45 (rev.).
34 Barth, *The Church and the Churches*, 36.
35 Barth, *The Church and the Churches*, 37.
36 Barth, *The Church and the Churches*, 37.
37 Barth, *The Church and the Churches*, 38 (rev.).
38 Barth, *The Church and the Churches*.
39 Barth, *The Church and the Churches*, 39 (rev., italics original).

> mean more than being really one in faith, hope, and love, and therefore able to worship together in one accord. Above all it would mean – and this would be the decisive test of the authenticity of all the rest – that together they confess, which means that together they also talk towards the outside, in the direction of the world, and in this way they could fulfill that commandment of Jesus on which the Church is based. … A uniting of the churches in the sense of that task which is so seriously laid upon the Church would undoubtedly mean a uniting of the confessions into one unanimous confession.[40]

Here a decisive aspect of Barth's understanding of the quest for the unity of all Christians becomes apparent: the importance of "confessing" the common faith. This is the heart of his vision of unity: Christians who are united and unanimous in their confessing the faith, not only in their assemblies of worship, but towards the world as well. Undoubtedly, the events in Germany, only 14 months before his lectures on church unity in Geneva with the Synod of Barmen (May 1934), made a deep and lasting impression on Barth (he mentions these events in the fourth lecture),[41] yet the important point is that the "uniting" of the church into a "unity" depends on a unanimous "confessing" of God and the gospel.

How can this be achieved? Barth lists four conditions: (1) it cannot happen out of confessional weakness, or (2) for secular motives (for instance, an aspiration to form an international union), or (3) as a result of a compromise in which the churches abandon (even by one iota) certain things which until then they deemed necessary to assert.[42] (4) "In the surrender of separation only one thing must be abandoned in this or that Church, namely a disobedience to Christ which may until now still be hidden to this Church."[43]

The fourth and final lecture, on "The Church and the Churches," opens with a call to engage in the practice "which all Church activity must presuppose": "The task of listening to Christ."[44] Barth continues with a call for honesty. The movement toward unity will take place only if the differences among the churches appear clearly, in a meeting "face to face" but also "over against each other, in sharp and surprising contrast."[45] We should not be afraid of true discussions and confrontations, even as we may be tempted to settle for a superficial peace.[46] "Theological dilettantes, amateurs, eclectics, and historians of all sorts"[47] hinder rather than foster the quest for unity. A "secret encounter and a secret community in the subject matter" will be present, despite all the differences, among those who articulate "a sound, consistently developed, and necessary 'yes and no'" in their dialogue.[48] A "true unity" was more present in the clash of 1529 in Marburg between Huldrych Zwingli and Martin Luther "than in certain contemporary situations, in which there is so much profession of supposed love that no one dared to ask with serious honesty about the truth, and thus to let a consistent claim and a consistent counter-claim to meet each other."[49]

The quest for unity cannot be separated from the quest for Christ's truth, and the quest for Christ's truth cannot happen without true hope and true love being present. Searching for Christ's truth is indispensable to the uniting of the churches, "even when its first result is that no one moves an inch from his position, and so the fact of division is at first accentuated."[50]

---

40 Barth, *The Church and the Churches*, 40–41 (rev.).

41 Barth, *The Church and the Churches*, 54.

42 Barth, *The Church and the Churches*, 41–43.

43 Barth, *The Church and the Churches*, 43 (rev.).

44 Barth, *The Church and the Churches*, 49.

45 Barth, *The Church and the Churches*, 57–58.

46 Barth, *The Church and the Churches*, 56–57.

47 Barth, *The Church and the Churches*, 57.

48 Barth, *The Church and the Churches*, 57 (rev.).

49 Barth, *The Church and the Churches*, 58 (rev.). Barth restates these insights in *CD* 4/1, 681.

50 Barth, *The Church and the Churches*, 58 (rev.).

Barth's lectures conclude with a call to engage in theology in all seriousness: "It is vital that once more in every Church, exactly with its own specificity and precisely because of this, with an ear attentive to Christ, sound, sober, rigorous, and real *theology* should be practiced again." But "in this sphere too, what is really authentic and decisive cannot be achieved by human hands."[51]

In 1931, Adolf Keller had published a monograph on "the way of dialectical theology through the Christian world" in which he asserted that "dialectical theology can no more evade the ecumenical movement than the latter can evade dialectical theology."[52] Both were needed *together*.[53] In a long letter to Keller from Dec 1, 1931, Barth expressed his impressions about Keller's book and the call it contained in the direction of both dialectical theologians and the ecumenical movement:

> But instead of making additional remarks on this or that particular point, you certainly will prefer to hear how I respond to chapter nine in your book, which from your standpoint certainly contains the most important thing you wished to say. I must begin by admitting that I feel personally challenged (in a positive way) when you regret, on page 188, that the dialectical theologians until now have lacked the necessary "immersion" in the ecumenical movement. But then tell me: how should one do this? I have read, and I do read from time to time, as a simple Christian, the messages which your conferences etc. address to society, but then I can only say that I read them with some alarm, for it is not clear to me whether I hear in them the Church calling for its own ecumenicity, or the Church testifying to it. It is so unclear that in this regard until now I do not feel myself called in the least (last year in Bern, I heard Söderblom and Deißmann at one of those occasions, and really I could not feel anything but a "refreshing irreverence").[54]

In December 1931, Barth was still deeply uneasy in relation to the ecumenical movement. He simply had little interest in what he heard from some of its leaders (especially the leaders of Life and Work). But Keller's book impressed something upon him – something Barth had not considered until then:

> It will amaze you, but it is true: while reading your book, for the first time I have actually tried to carry out the thought that the ecumenical movement and dialectical theology have something to do with one another, that the two can move side by side and even hand in hand.[55]

Yet Barth is not ready to simply accept Keller's injunction: dialectical theology and the ecumenical movement do not sit side by side as easily as Keller imagines. Rather, they stand on two very different levels, and they have very different aims. As a consequence, Keller's appeal is problematic.

Barth continues:

> I have tried, and I try, to speak to my readers and listeners, whoever and wherever they may be, occupying myself with the subject matter itself, and not in order to place them somewhere. I search for what is ecumenical so to speak on the spot, without caring for the geographical meaning of this term. And it seems, as the figure shows, that also on this geographical level things are not as bad as they should have been given my lack of interest for this aspect of the problem, and

51 Barth, *The Church and the Churches*, 59 (rev.).

52 Keller, *Karl Barth and Christian Unity*, 289 (rev.).

53 Keller writes: "It is exceedingly important that the Ecumenical Movement seriously consider the dialectical approach. It is, however, to be hoped that dialectical theology will also sense the seriousness of the ecumenical demand"; Keller, *Karl Barth and Christian Unity*, 291 (rev.).

54 K. Barth to A. Keller, Dec 1, 1931.

55 K. Barth to A. Keller, Dec 1, 1931.

> so I am in fact determined to continue in this manner.[56]

Barth's letter to Keller in December 1931 is a highly interesting document, which sheds light on his 1935 lectures in Geneva on "the Church and the Churches." It helps us understand what he meant by "ecumenism" and "ecumenical" and how he thought he himself, as a theologian, might be contributing to this endeavor: not by promulgating a word addressed across different countries, from one region of the world to another (as the leaders of the movement did, in his opinion, with their constant international travels and the survey of various regions of the world in Adolf Keller's book), but rather through a theological inquiry which goes to the heart of the matter, which is as it were the "seat" or the beating heart of ecumenism. This "seat," however, cannot be exchanged with ecumenism as such, it cannot be replaced by it. Ecumenism, he wrote to Keller in 1931, cannot formally become an end in itself, it cannot become the focus of human efforts as such:

> But what I do not quite understand, and what I find to be completely at odds with the meaning of my own work, is this, namely, that here ecumenism has been formally made into the goal, that you (differently from us) wish to speak from one country to another, from one Church to another, and to speak precisely of ecumenism in itself, as if this could be a theme of human work and human discourse.[57]

Barth's lectures on "the Church and the Churches" can be seen as part of his answer (for, as his letter to Keller shows, Barth was already committed to ecumenical dialogue, conceived as rigorous, robust theological dialogue, before 1935) to Keller's wish for a fruitful encounter between the new theological school and the ecumenical movement. These lectures can also be seen as a useful "blueprint" for the ecumenical movement. They both ground its necessity and urge this movement not to be naïve or too optimistic: serious work lies ahead, and even if that work is done, it will not magically produce "unity." "Unity" is a divine gift; what human beings may achieve is, at best, an approximation, already here and now, of this gift.

Barth's lectures remain important. In his own day, they were greeted as a kind of "conversion" on his part to the ecumenical movement: a conversion which did not entail the end of his critical position towards this movement, but a sort of public conversion nevertheless, since his lectures were soon published in his pamphlet series *Theologische Existenz heute*,[58] and shortly afterward translated into English (1936).[59]

Barth's contribution to ecumenical dialogue did not begin in 1935. As we have seen, his works were read with interest by Roman Catholics from the second edition of the *Römerbrief* on. However, these lectures delivered in Geneva in 1935 marked the first direct, public, and articulated word that Barth was expressing on the topic of Christian unity. His encounters, on the other hand, were becoming richer and broader. He was no longer simply a conversation partner for certain German-speaking Roman Catholic theologians, such as Erich Przywara and others. In April 1934, during a week of lectures and meetings in Paris, Barth met Jacques Maritain and Étienne Gilson, besides some younger theologians who were deeply interested in his theology and who would eventually contribute in highly significant ways to ecumenical dialogue and to Rome's commitment to ecumenism, first and foremost, Yves Congar. Here is how Karl Barth, in a text written shortly after his visit to Paris, reported on this encounter,

56 K. Barth to A. Keller, Dec 1, 1931.

57 K. Barth to A. Keller, Dec 1, 1931.

58 Karl Barth, *Theologische Existenz heute*, vol. 27, *Die Kirche und die Kirchen*, Munich, Kaiser, 1935.

59 Nils Ehrenström, "Movements for International Friendship and Life and Work, 1925–1948," in: *A History of the Ecumenical Movement*, vol. 1, Ruth Rouse & Stephen Charles Neill, eds., *1517–1948*, London, SPCK, ^{2}1967, 545–596, here 575.

which took place at the Dominican convent of Juvisy at the invitation of some Dominicans:

> Immediately following the first lecture, some young Dominicans approached me in a friendly manner to greet me, and they invited me to come share their table the next day. … Fifteen kilometers from Paris … we found a small convent built in a very original way, in a contemporary, rather revolutionary style. These "fathers" constitute an apparently very balanced and gifted group, they are involved under the guidance of a superior in the editing of journals and newspapers. … Among the guests, there were Étienne Gilson, the medieval scholar, and the convert Jacques Maritain, who are both sources of inspiration for the movement of scholarly renewal within French Catholicism. But during our conversation several of the monks showed as well that they are very deeply competent and clear-sighted; unsurprisingly, during the simple but physically invigorating meal to which we were invited, we came to talk about nature and grace, and other related topics, during a conversation which was not only loyal, but also almost fraternal, and which made it possible, on both sides, to bring to light all of the peaks and ridges.[60]

Such encounters were extremely important. They signaled the dawn of a new era in ecumenical dialogue, which would lead to new beginnings, in the 1960s and beyond. In his memoirs, Marc Boegner mentions how struck he had been, in April 1934, to see the intensity with which Yves Congar was listening to Barth's conferences in Paris.[61]

We see in Barth's report from the Spring of 1934 exactly the kind of attitude which he commends in his seminar lectures on "the Church and the Churches" (July 1935), namely, the call for rigorous, honest debate as the best way to make progress together; sharpness in theological thought and dialogue is not the enemy of a fraternal attitude – quite the contrary!

2.5 *Karl Barth and Ecumenism (1935–1947)*

Karl Barth's involvement in the ecumenical movement took a "back seat" in the ensuing years. Around 1937, with a few of his close friends, including Visser 't Hooft and Pierre Maury, for a while he envisioned a new journal, to be called "Doctrina."[62] However, Barth soon abandoned this project. Why did he do so? That same year was an eventful year for the ecumenical movement, first with the conference, on the (explosive!) theme of "Church, People, State," held in Oxford in July 1937. This conference turned out to be a great disillusion for Barth, who had expected the ecumenical movement to issue a very strong and clear critique of the German Christians (*Deutsche Christen*), but this simply did not occur.

On Jun 3, 1937, Adolf Hitler had prohibited any pastor from the German Evangelical Church to attend the Oxford conference. Only a few members of certain free churches, which refused to be involved in the German Church struggle, travelled to Oxford. The inaugural speech, by Archbishop of Canterbury Cosmo Gordon Lang, was rather weak: he said that it was not his duty to explain or address the obstacles the Evangelical German delegation had encountered with its own political authorities (Lang supported the appeasement approach of the British government at the time; he praised the Munich Agreement of September 1938 and called on that occasion for a day of thanksgiving

60 See Karl Barth & Pierre Maury, *Nous qui pouvons encore parler …: Correspondence (1928–1956)*, Lausanne, L'Âge d'Homme, 1985, 283–291, here 285–286. Visser 't Hooft mentions these encounters in his memoirs: Visser 't Hooft, *Memoirs*, 68.

61 See Marc Boegner, *L'exigence œcuménique: Souvenirs et perspectives*, Paris, Albin Michel, 1968, 99.

62 Karl Barth, *Gesamtausgabe*, sec. 5, vol. 43, *Karl Barth – Willem Adolph Visser 't Hooft: Briefwechsel*, ed. Thomas Herwig, Zürich, TVZ, 2006, 55.

to God).[63] The final "Declaration" only "regretted" the absence of the German delegation, without explaining the reasons for their absence.[64] Karl Barth kept abreast of events by means of various articles by Alphons Koechlin in the *Basler Nachrichten* and through discussions with Eduard Thurneysen. He was deeply disappointed and spoke of the "lemonade of the Oxford Declaration" regarding the German situation.[65] If his friends were unable to counter the cowardice which had prevailed in Oxford in July 1937 (and Barth was not sure whether he himself could have offered the kind of strong, sharp response he wished his friends had expressed during the conference), then it was a sign they were not ready to launch a new theological journal, entitled "Doctrina": "To me, it seems better to give up the project of confronting the world as bearing and representing a particular 'Doctrina.'"[66] "If we had a trumpet to blow into, then this horn should have been heard for the first time in Oxford … but this did not occur."[67]

Barth concludes his letter to Visser 't Hooft of Jul 27, 1937 on a personal note: "Dear friend, I know your heart hangs with the ecumenical movement and that you mean well with this. But I must tell you, something does not work for me in the particular logic and ethic and esthetic of this matter, and I would much prefer not to have to hear anything about it for a long while (*auf lange Zeit*)."[68] The young ecumenicist was hurt by these words and by the entire letter. His assessment of the Oxford conference was very different, and far more positive. He thought the conference inaugurated a new phase for the ecumenical movement; one in which the call for the church to be church was first voiced. This he took to be a sign that Barth's work, and the work of Barth's friends, was beginning to bear fruit.[69] Concerning the final declaration, which Barth had derided as "lemonade," he wrote that he himself and Barth's other close friend, Eduard Thurneysen, helped compose this document. In response to Barth, he described this "Declaration" as "good and right" (*gut und richtig*). Visser 't Hooft was shaken by his friend's letter and now wondered what Barth's position might be with regard to ecumenism as a whole, and also, more specifically, with regard to the deeper commitment Visser 't Hooft was about to make to this movement.[70] In an ensuing letter, Barth maintained his original assessment, providing a long, detailed exegesis of the final "Declaration" in order to show his friend what was so "bad" (*schlimm*) about it, and, worse even, what was so "bad" about the fact that his friends did not even realize how bad the document was.[71] To the Swiss theologian, the Oxford conference's final "message" (*Botschaft*) was vague and sentimental when mentioning the absence of the German delegation, instead of "naming" the problem, that is, Hitler's June decision, head-on and directly.

These letters of the summer of 1937 are typical of Barth's stance on ecumenism. He was ready to let himself become involved in it (as we saw with his lectures in Geneva in July 1935), but he also had little patience with the great international events of the ecumenical movement, especially when they led to compromise and a lack of clarity for, and therefore also against, the situation. In 1925, he had already been dissatisfied with the Stockholm conference, and the organizers were fully aware of his sentiments. Barth thought that the entire Life

63 *Karl Barth – Willem Adolph Visser 't Hooft: Briefwechsel*, 59, note 4.
64 *Karl Barth – Willem Adolph Visser 't Hooft: Briefwechsel*, 60, note 8.
65 See K. Barth to A.W. Visser 't Hooft, Jul 27, 1937, in: *Karl Barth – Willem Adolph Visser 't Hooft: Briefwechsel*, 60 ("die Limonade der Oxforder Erklärung"), and see the editor's notes (*Karl Barth – Willem Adolph Visser 't Hooft: Briefwechsel*, note 8).
66 *Karl Barth – Willem Adolph Visser 't Hooft: Briefwechsel*, 60.
67 K. Barth to A.W. Visser 't Hooft, Aug 18, 1937, in: *Karl Barth – Willem Adolph Visser 't Hooft: Briefwechsel*, 69.
68 K. Barth to A.W. Visser 't Hooft, Jul 27, 1937, 61.
69 A.W. Visser 't Hooft to K. Barth, Aug 15, 1937, in: *Karl Barth – Willem Adolph Visser 't Hooft: Briefwechsel*, 62–63.
70 A.W. Visser 't Hooft to K. Barth, Aug 15, 1937, 63.
71 K. Barth to A.W. Visser 't Hooft, Aug 18, 1937, 69–74.

and Work movement was like a "tower of Babel."[72] If Barth was led to contribute to the ecumenical movement, it was certainly not as a consequence of these gatherings, which many today see as the main stages in the ecumenical movement in the 20th century; it was, rather, his unrelenting interest in profound inquiry and reflection concerning the subject matter of Christian theology.[73]

This does not mean that Barth had no interest in the more institutional side of ecumenism. He repeatedly agreed, throughout the second half of his life, to take part in some of these international events. But he was well aware that his true contribution to ecumenism and to the quest for the church's unity was to be found in his groundwork, that is, his *Church Dogmatics*. "Each one in his place!" then, but each one abiding by the same demand, by the same "rules of play," namely: searching for clarity, so that others may be compelled to clarity as well. Barth simply deplored the fact that, in Oxford, these "rules of play" were not followed – "not even by [his] closest and most cherished friends."[74]

As we have seen, Barth was convinced that his major contribution to ecumenism was his long-term work on dogmatics. How did he view that work in relation to the "one Church"? Barth provides us with an answer in the second part of his *Prolegomena* (CD 1/2), a volume of 900 pages which was published in 1938, and in which he wrote that dogmatics must be "a dogmatics of the ecumenical Church"; it "should address the one universal Christian Church," and it should do so "in the spirit and name of the one universal Christian Church" (CD 1/2, 823).[75] However, this does not mean that dogmatics can "float" above the various churches and "the relative determinateness of faith" (CD 1/2, 823–824). The theologian is not called to imagine him/herself in a "watchtower" standing over the church's "distinctions and divisions"; this would be a "phantasy" (CD 1/2, 824). Hence, Christian dogmatics cannot have the ambition of providing a "combination" of the various Christian strands or traditions (CD 1/2, 824).

Here Barth shows once again that his vision of ecumenical dialogue does not entail any relativizing. He writes:

> We can only say that the compulsion of the Word of God leads to one, the one possible, confessional position – that of the Protestant Church. … Church dogmatics is Protestant dogmatics or it is not Church dogmatics. By "Protestant dogmatics" is here to be understood the dogmatics of the one holy, universal and apostolic Church, as it was purified and founded anew by the reformers of the 16th century and by the confession which adopted their testimony, and as it hears the Word of God in this as the only possible and normative determination. … when the Church is the true Church it is the Protestant Church (CD 1/2, 825).

These are very strong words. They reflect a central aspect of Barth's view of ecumenism, a view which is neatly summarized in this assertion: "It is only where adversaries are opposed with genuine dogmatic intolerance that there is the possibility of genuine and profitable discussion. For it is only there that one confession has something to say to the other" (CD 1/2, 827). We should not misunderstand these claims – and we should take note that Barth no longer expressed his views in this manner in later years. What Barth wished to say here is

72 See Jehle-Wildberger, *Adolf Keller (1872–1963)*, 94–96. See K. Barth to E. Thurneysen & G. Merz, Oct 4, 1925, in: Barth, *Gesamtausgabe*, sec. 5, vol. 4, *Karl Barth – Eduard Thurneysen: Briefwechsel (1921–1930)*, ed. Eduard Thurneysen, Zürich, TVZ, 1974, 371.

73 On these points see Keller, *Karl Barth and Christian Unity*, 15–16.

74 K. Barth to W.A. Visser 't Hooft, Aug 18, 1937, 75.

75 See also Barth, "Über die Annäherung der Kirchen," 304.

that one should really stand in one's tradition and be completely convinced of its legitimacy; this is the only way one may represent one's tradition. It is only when one is deeply and really convinced of the validity of one's tradition that one might make a convincing case, before others, concerning its validity. This does not mean one ought to ignore the positive elements present in other traditions, or the various shortcomings of one's own; it means, rather, that one must really be rooted somewhere – not just in the gospel, but in the gospel as it is interpreted in a given tradition – in order to really contribute to ecumenical dialogue. In 1924, that is, at the very beginning of his lifelong work on dogmatic theology, Barth was already convinced that Christian dogmatics is either ecumenical, or it is not Christian dogmatics at all.[76]

It thus appears that Barth remained a Protestant, indeed Reformed theologian throughout all these years – even as he seemed to embrace all the ancient dogmas, including the virgin birth, even as he aimed to articulate a dogmatics for the one universal church, and even as he stated that Protestants should celebrate the Lord's Supper at every Sunday worship.[77] His short statement about the *analogia entis* in the preface of *Church Dogmatics* 1/1 (1932), was by far not his only critical stance toward Rome in those years. In 1938, in *Church Dogmatics* 1/2, he made the accusation that Roman Catholicism "is rebellion against the authority of the Word of God, rebellion against canonical Scripture, rebellion against the fathers too and against every genuine confession" (*CD* 1/2, 667)! This incredibly forceful critique, buried as it was toward the end of a massive book, did not trigger the same reaction as his famous and brief pronouncement on *analogia entis* had six years earlier, as it was found in a much more visible section of his *Church Dogmatics* (namely, in the preface to the first volume). Yet it could – and perhaps should – have! Barth's indictment of Roman Catholicism, in 1938, just as in 1932, was not half-hearted. To those who thought that the Roman Church was too hierarchical and authoritarian, Barth was in effect replying that Roman Catholicism knows "too much" about authority, in obvious ways, but also, more surprisingly, "too little," namely, too little about true obedience to the true authority (of the gospel) (*CD* 1/2, 667).

Barth was not happy with the ecumenical movement in those years either. In a letter written in October 1942, Barth asked Samuel McCrea Cavert, an American clergyman, why the burgeoning WCC was not taking a concrete position on the current events:

> In recent years, I had many occasions to deplore the fact that, in Geneva, despite certain useful observations which were gathered, several reports which were produced, various preparatory studies which were made, various meetings and letter exchanges which took place, various technical assistance which was provided, but also on occasion (albeit at a more personal level) certain suggestions which were made to the churches which find themselves in the midst of the struggle and who suffer in it, despite all of this, "Geneva" and thus the ecumenical movement was never to be *heard* in the most decisive moments of what was unfolding in those years: not after 1933, at the time of the German Church struggle, not in the summer and fall of 1938, as the political storm was gathering, not in 1939 as it exploded, not at the time of the catastrophe of 1940, and not since then: it did not address any word of confession, of clarification, of encouragement and of consolation, to all Christians and all human beings, in the name of the churches which are concretely united there. Why did I, why do I, as an individual, have to send out such letters, when since 1925,

76 See Barth's circular letter, Feb 5, 1924, in: *Karl Barth – Eduard Thurneysen: Briefwechsel (1921–1930)*, 221.

77 On this point, see Keller, *Karl Barth and Christian Unity*, 15.

> always anew, so many beautiful words have been spoken and written on the unity, newly found in the ecumenical movement, of the Church of Jesus Christ? Why did "Geneva" leave it to me to speak out?[78]

Barth was rather annoyed by an ecumenical movement which was producing many reports and declarations without being able to say one clear, decisive word on the situation of the Protestant Church in Germany.

2.6 *Amsterdam (August 1948)*

The time came for the single most important ecumenical event that Barth would attend in his life – and attend it he did. Even more than that, he contributed to it and to its preparation the preceding year. The constitutive assembly of the WCC took place in Amsterdam in August 1948. Barth gave the keynote lecture, on the topic of "human disorder and God's design." In his talk, Barth overturned the title and argued it was more adequate to speak of "God's design and the world's disorder."[79] He expressed his concern that most of the preparatory work had focused on "the world's disorder" and paid only scant attention to "God's design," which is the one reality that sheds light on our world. If we presume to have solutions to solving the world's disorder and to reunite the Christian churches, do we not presume to be like "Atlas," who is "destined to bear the dome of heaven on his shoulders"?[80] In direct continuity with his 1935 lectures on "The Church and the Churches," Karl Barth called on all participants to "listen" to Christ, to avoid all sentimentalism with regard to the absence of Rome and Moscow at the conference, and to embark in a "movement away from every ecclesiasticism toward Jesus Christ."[81] Without this movement, it would be impossible for Christians from different origins to talk to one another, to listen to one another, and to become united with one another.[82]

In June 1949, Karl Barth was asked to comment retrospectively on the Amsterdam assembly. This unpublished lecture, entitled "Der Skandal der uneinigen Kirche," sheds light on his own involvement in, and assessment of, the working group known as section I at the Amsterdam conference.[83] One of the interesting claims he articulates in this lecture concerns the attempt, which was made in Amsterdam, to clarify the "disagreements within the agreement" and the "agreements within the disagreement." We need to search for convergences even in places where they do not seem to be present, and also to clarify where differences lie even in matters which seem to be shared. Then the question, of course, is to know whether the remaining "disagreements within the agreement" are truly divisive, or whether they can be accepted as non-divisive differences. But this process of clarification is indispensable if unity is not to be pursued at the cost of theological shallowness. The participants in section I were not charged with producing a confession of faith, but their final document begins with doxology and ends with a call for repentance, in hope, and with an eye toward a common confession of faith.[84] This is, needless to say, perfectly in keeping with Barth's view of ecumenical dialogue and its essential relationship with the act of "confessing" the faith.

2.7 *The Second General Assembly of the WCC in Evanston (1954)*

In 1950, Karl Barth was invited to take part in the general assembly of the WCC in Evanston, Illinois – another significant milestone in the ecumenical

78 Karl Barth, "Brief an einen amerikanischen Kirchenmann" (1942), in: Karl Barth, *Eine Schweizer Stimme (1938–1945)*, Zürich, Evangelischer Verlag, 1945, 272–302, here 299.

79 Karl Barth, "No Christian Marshall Plan," *CC*, Dec 8, 1948, 1330–1333.

80 Barth, "No Christian Marshall Plan," 1331.

81 Barth, "No Christian Marshall Plan," 1331.

82 Barth, "No Christian Marshall Plan," 1331.

83 Karl Barth, "Der Skandal der uneinigen Kirche," Jun 10, 1949, in: Karl Barth-Archiv 11210 (unpublished lecture).

84 Barth, "Der Skandal der uneinigen Kirche," 6.

movement, which had been decided for 1953 and which ultimately was held in August 1954.[85] On Oct 18, 1953, Barth wrote to Visser 't Hooft to inform him that he would not attend the general assembly: he had renounced his plan to embark on a North American lecture tour and had decided to give priority to the writing of his *Church Dogmatics*. Barth had participated in the preparation of the general assembly by actively contributing to three conferences: a ten-day conference in Rolle, Switzerland, on Jul 20–30, 1951; a second one, a year later, at the Ecumenical Institute in Bossey in September 1952 (Visser 't Hooft had to convince a reluctant Barth that his presence was needed there); and a third one, again in Bossey, in August 1953. These preparatory conferences were quite successful, despite some tensions, especially during the first one, between Barth, who refused to associate Communism with Nazism, and Reinhold Niebuhr who, as a North-American theologian, had a much more negative opinion of Communism. The Cold War was making itself felt within the ecumenical movement.

After this, Barth worked hard on his massive doctrine of reconciliation (part 4 of *Church Dogmatics*, volume 4/1 was published in 1953; the last volume of the doctrine of creation, 3/4, had been published only two years earlier, in 1951). Among the key topics which he began to consider anew in those years was that of "covenant" (*Bund*). This necessarily led him to reflect again on Israel, and it may have led him to realize that there was a large empty space, or a blind spot, in many quarters of the ecumenical movement, as was testified by the preparatory documents for the upcoming general assembly: where was Israel, in relation to the quest for Christian unity? Can the ecumenical movement simply bypass the question of Israel? By no means, if the aim of this movement is to reunite "the people of God," since Hebrews are the "original" people of God. Therefore, in those years and until the final year of his life, Barth repeatedly called on the ecumenical movement not to forget the reality of Israel. He went as far as to claim that "the separation from the Jews is *the* burning question in the ecumenical matter."[86] In *Church Dogmatics* 4/1, he presented "the existence of the Synagogue side by side with the Church" as "an ontological impossibility, a wound, a gaping hole in the body of Christ, something which is quite intolerable" (*CD* 4/1, 671). It must be said that Barth's desiderata with regard to the inclusion of Israel in the quest of Christian unity remain, to this day, unfulfilled.

2.8 *The Reception of Karl Barth's Theology by Roman Catholic Thinkers in the 1950s*

Some of the most significant studies on Karl Barth's theology were written by Roman Catholic scholars. The 1950s were a particularly important decade in this regard, with the publication of Hans Urs von Balthasar's masterful study, *Karl Barth: Darstellung und Deutung seiner Theologie*.[87] Barth had heard the lectures Balthasar had given in Basel, which were subsequently gathered in this book. The work remains a high point in the scholarship on Barth's thought and questioned some key theses, especially concerning how Barth supposedly moved from dialectical to analogical patterns in connection with his book on Anselm of Canterbury.[88]

85 On Barth and Evanston, see Herwig, *Karl Barth und die ökumenische Bewegung*, 195–225.

86 Herwig, *Karl Barth und die ökumenische Bewegung*, 221. See also Karl Barth, *Ad limina apostolorum*, Zürich, EVZ-Verlag, 1967; ET: *Ad limina apostolorum: An Appraisal of Vatican II*, trans. Keith R. Crim, Richmond, John Knox Press, 1968, 30 ("critical question" no. 5) and 36 ("critical question" no. 6).

87 Hans Urs von Balthasar, *Karl Barth: Darstellung und Deutung seiner Theologie*, Cologne, Jakob Hegner, 1951; ET: *The Theology of Karl Barth*, trans. Edward T. Oakes, San Francisco, Ignatius Press, 1992.

88 Karl Barth, *Fides quaerens intellectum: Anselms Beweis der Existenz Gottes im Zusammenhang seines theologischen Programms*, Munich, Kaiser, 1931. See also another very important milestone in Barth scholarship: Bruce L. McCormack, *Karl Barth's Critically Realistic Dialectical Theology: Its Genesis and Development (1909–1936)*, Oxford, Clarendon Press, 1995.

1957 then saw the publication of Henri Bouillard's three-volume work on Barth.[89] This was a very detailed study, which arguably did not attain the depth of Balthasar's insights. Barth had traveled to Paris with Balthasar in order to attend (among the public, not as a member of the jury) the oral defense of Bouillard's dissertation at the Sorbonne.

In that same year, Hans Küng published his book on the doctrine of justification.[90] Küng, who had befriended Barth, argued that Barth's doctrine of justification was remarkably compatible with the Council of Trent's teaching on this topic. Barth wrote a letter-preface to the book in which he approved of Küng's interpretation of his views on justification and marveled at this convergence.[91]

These were arguably the three most significant studies on Barth's theology by Roman Catholic scholars in the 1950s. Many others (with less a pronounced echo) would follow.

2.9 *Karl Barth and Vatican II*

Barth followed the development of the council with great interest, seeking firsthand accounts from some of its participants. He would undoubtedly have accepted the invitation he had received to be present in Rome as an "observer" if his health had permitted him to go to Rome for the final two sessions.[92] Despite his frail condition, subsequent to several extended stays in hospital, Barth eagerly travelled to Rome at the end of September 1966, invited by the SPCU.

His concern with the council did not primarily regard its consequences for the ecumenical movement, or for the relations between Rome and other churches. His interest rested on the fact that here was a church which was "centrally and actually" committed to "the renovation of its own house."[93] This was the key point, which might also become significant for Protestantism.[94] To consider the council primarily in relation to its ecumenical impact was insufficient, according to Barth.[95] It first had to be admitted that the council was a "landslide," a "*spiritual* movement."[96] Barth's admiration for Angelo Giuseppe Roncalli, Pope John XXIII, is obvious, when he describes him as a "very remarkable man," who urged the Roman Catholic Church to engage in "a reorganization – precisely around the gospel."[97] Furthermore, Barth sensed that some kind of "backlash" or "reversal" might take place in the lower orders, as some might wish to reject such a program.[98]

Barth wrote a detailed report of his visit to Rome and gave his overall impressions of what he had seen:

> As a result of the trip I gained a close acquaintance with a church and a theology which have begun a movement, the results of which are incalculable and slow but clearly genuine and irreversible. In looking at it we can only wish that we had something comparable, if it could avoid a repetition of at least the worst mistakes we have made since the sixteenth century. … Any optimism about the future is automatically excluded. But calm, brotherly hope is called for, together with a willingness in the meanwhile to conduct in both great and small affairs a thorough housecleaning of our own. … I returned from Rome just as stubbornly evangelical – I would really rather say, evangelical-catholic – as before.[99]

89 Henri Bouillard, *Karl Barth*, 3 vols., Paris, Éditions Montaigne, 1957.

90 Hans Küng, *Rechtfertigung: Die Lehre Karl Barths und eine katholische Besinnung*, Einsiedeln, Johannes-Verlag, 1957; ET: *Justification: The Doctrine of Karl Barth and a Catholic Reflection*, trans. Thomas Collins, Edmund E. Tolk & David Granskou, Louisville, Westminster John Knox Press, 2004.

91 For Barth's letter-preface, see Küng, *Justification*, lxvii–lxx.

92 Barth, *Ad limina apostolorum*, 9.

93 Barth, *Ad limina apostolorum*, 67. This text was first published in *EcRev* 15/4, 1963, 357–367.

94 Barth, *Ad limina apostolorum*, 68.

95 Barth, *Ad limina apostolorum*, 72.

96 Barth, *Ad limina apostolorum*, 68 (italics original).

97 Barth, *Ad limina apostolorum*, 69.

98 Barth, *Ad limina apostolorum*, 70.

99 Barth, *Ad limina apostolorum*, 17–18.

Barth was quite enthusiastic about the "house-cleaning" which was under way in Rome, but he still had pointed questions, such as these: Is the goal of this process a "reform," or is it something else?[100] (Barth was convinced this was a "reforming council"). What is the "measure" which is being used in this "aggiornamento"? What is the council "updating" the church toward?[101] Barth was concerned that "the modern world" might be the "measure" for some, even as the conciliar constitution on revelation, *Dei Verbum*, had placed the Word of God at the center of its understanding of divine revelation. Barth's question was related to his impression upon reading *Dei Verbum*: he was full of praise with regard to chapters 1, 3, and 6, but chapter 2 was somewhat problematic: it is "the great fit of weakness which befell the Council," there is a "painful weakness" in this chapter, its "darkness" is "considerable."[102] Why is this so? The reason is that it places tradition and the magisterial office of the church alongside and next to Scripture.[103] Mention of the tradition and the magisterium is not a problem in itself, since *sola scriptura* among Protestants should never be taken to mean "solitaria scriptura" and since Protestants also have certain normative (in a non-absolute, relative sense) documents (Barth mentions the 1934 Barmen Declaration). However, Tradition and the church's teaching office need to be clearly subordinated to Scripture, according to the Swiss theologian.[104] Scripture is not the "sole" authority, but it is the "supreme" one, as he sees it.[105] Here, the council should have "reformed" the teachings of the Council of Trent on Scripture and Tradition, according to Barth: it is not possible to venerate Scripture and the Tradition "pari affectu ac pietate."[106] In addition, Barth thought it was a mistake to see the church as a direct prolongation of God's revelation (see *LG* 52).[107]

Despite these criticisms, which may be expected from a Protestant theologian, Barth praised the dogmatic constitution on divine revelation; its shortcomings in the second chapter, he thought, were "more than compensated" by the strengths of the preceding and following chapters.[108] He was struck by the absence of natural theology, of anathemas, and of any apologetic tendency: there is only *one* source of revelation, namely the Word of God (not two, for example, the Word of God and Tradition, or the Word of God and human reason). The presence of the word "source" *in the singular* was momentous. This was a major step forward beyond Vatican I and "in contrast to it," something which is "new in content and method, something of which we must never lose sight in our evaluation of the council's teaching about God's revelation and which is also a criterion for judging its other pronouncements."[109] As Barth saw it, Vatican II meant that Jesus Christ had "inevitably stepped anew into the center of faith of the Roman Christians and the thought of the Roman theologians – just at the place where he seemed increasingly called into question by the discouraging development of the dogmas about Mary."[110]

Barth was focusing on what he took to be the best insights in the conciliar documents: those that point *forward*, to what lies ahead – not backwards, toward Trent and Vatican I – in order to critically assess less satisfactory aspects. Among these, there was the pastoral constitution on the church in the modern world (*Gaudium et spes*), which according to Barth did not presuppose a robust interpretation of the gospels and of Paul's Epistles; dialogue with the world is important, but needs to come second, after the necessary *proclamation* to the

100 Barth, *Ad limina apostolorum*, 55.
101 Barth, *Ad limina apostolorum*, 20.
102 Barth, *Ad limina apostolorum*, 51.
103 Barth, *Ad limina apostolorum*, 51.
104 Barth, *Ad limina apostolorum*, 49.
105 Barth, *Ad limina apostolorum*, 54.
106 Barth, *Ad limina apostolorum*, 50.

107 See Karl Barth, *Gesamtausgabe*, sec. 4, vol. 28, *Gespräche (1964–1968)*, ed. Eberhard Busch, Zürich, TVZ, 1997, 192; see also Barth, *Ad limina apostolorum*, 23.
108 Barth, *Ad limina apostolorum*, 52.
109 Barth, *Ad limina apostolorum*, 53–54.
110 Barth, *Ad limina apostolorum*, 69.

world.[111] Another weak point was the lack of any mention of the fact that the ecumenical movement, in the 20th century, had originated outside the Roman Catholic Church.[112]

These were some of the question Barth took with him when he traveled to Rome in September 1966. He was also commenting regularly, and mostly positively, about what was happening in Roman Catholicism in the many talks he gave in those years. For instance, in 1965, he spoke about the attempts to unite Rome and Protestantism as being "premature." Intra-Protestant dialogue must first begin to reunite the many different Protestant branches.[113] He might also have had in mind the "heretic elements," which he thought still existed in the Roman Church.[114] Mariology, especially, is so overgrown that it threatens "the vine by which it lived, that is, the work and word of God in Jesus Christ."[115]

A particularly interesting aspect of Barth's view of Roman Catholicism in those years concerns his preoccupation that, in reforming itself, it may repeat, in its own way, some of the Protestant errors in modernity.[116] Can it be the case that there may be "too much" movement, that things may be moving too fast? Yes, Barth seemed to be saying – yet at the same time he only wished Protestants would become more mobile too.[117]

2.10 *Karl Barth and Ecumenism: Concluding Remarks*

Karl Barth made a significant contribution to the ecumenical movement, primarily through his groundbreaking theological research, in the course of over five decades of theological scholarship of the highest order, and not only through the very broad echo his work found in many different regions of the world, but also through his personal, recurring involvement in this movement, beginning in the mid-1930s and the seminar he gave in Geneva in July 1935, then in Amsterdam in 1948, in the preparation of the Evanston assembly in 1954, and as an interested and critical observer of Roman Catholicism's renewal in the 1960s.

Not surprisingly for a Reformed thinker, Barth always propounded a "low" ecclesiology. He was convinced that the "order" of the church, while certainly not unimportant, could not be conferred any ultimate importance: "It certainly cannot be maintained that the existence of a synodal or episcopal organ to guarantee the unity of the communities is essential to the New Testament idea of the Church" (*CD* 4/1, 674). Such an order pertains to the *bene esse* of the church, namely, to its well-being, not to its *esse* (its very nature or essence). Jesus Christ is the Creator, "the basis and the guarantee" of the churches' unity (*CD* 4/1, 675).

Barth was not an optimist in regard to the prospects of reuniting all Christian churches. His vision of unity was in fact quasi-eschatological, although he acknowledged the progress which had taken place during his own life.[118] Even if a reuniting may not occur before the *eschaton*, this does not mean we simply have to wait for this unity! Christians are called to welcome this unity, and also to work towards it. What exactly is the goal? How should we think about this unity? Certainly not as a mix-up (*Durcheinander*) or fusion of the Protestant and the Catholic dimensions, but as a visible unity, and a Christianity "which can simply be called Protestant-Catholic," coming from Christ and moving towards Christ.[119] Barth had as little patience with any vision of unity which confuses the particular riches of different traditions and so falls into the trap of uniformity, as with any vision

111 Barth, *Ad limina apostolorum*, 27.

112 Barth, *Ad limina apostolorum*, 30.

113 Karl Barth, "Interview von George Puchinger" (April 1965), in: Barth, *Gespräche*, 185.

114 Barth, "Interview von George Puchinger," 189.

115 Barth, *Ad limina apostolorum*, 60.

116 Karl Barth, "Gespräch in der Basler Bruder Klaus-Gemeinde" (March 1967), in: Barth, *Gespräche*, 366.

117 Karl Barth, "Gespräch in der Basler Titusgemeinde" (June 1968), in: Barth, *Gespräche*, 467.

118 Barth, "Gespräch in der Basler Bruder Klaus-Gemeinde," 356.

119 Barth, "Gespräch in der Basler Bruder Klaus-Gemeinde," 356.

of plurality which promotes a mere juxtaposition of churches which ignore or, worse, despise one another. Disunity, that is, the fact that the various churches "are so different from one another and confront one another as such strangers that they cannot recognize and acknowledge one another, at any rate seriously, as the community of Jesus Christ" (*CD* 4/1, 675), is a scandal and a sin.

"Confessing" the faith together is a key marker of genuine unity, according to Karl Barth, whose view of ecumenism was shaped to a significant extent by the Barmen Declaration of May 1934. In one of the final volumes of his *Church Dogmatics*, Barth stated once again his vision of unity, in a passage in which he expressed high praises for the ecumenical movement, despite the fact that "what was said at Amsterdam or Evanston" made little impact on the world. He wrote:

> The outlook today [in the world] would be quite different if in some negotiations and conferences there were at least as honest and open and practical a concern for the union of the nations as there has been for the union of the churches at Edinburgh, Stockholm, Amsterdam, Evanston, etc., and as there is continually in Geneva, not in the Palace of Nations, but in *Route de Malagnou*, 17 [the seat of the WCC at the time] (*CD* 4/3.1, 38).

Visser 't Hooft was overjoyed to read these words.[120]

"We must learn to think more from the Bible," Barth said in 1965.[121] However, we also need to listen and talk to one another, "clearly and concretely," without sentimentality or any shallow irenicism; and such conversations require a very sound knowledge of ourselves too.[122]

"We will not see the one church; our children and grandchildren won't either," said Barth in June 1968; but even if a "being-together" is not yet possible, a "coming-together" is.[123] And Barth, who very much rejoiced at the sight of the movement Christians were making, in the last decades of his life, in the direction of unity, made a lasting contribution to this effort.

3 Rudolf Bultmann's Indirect Contribution

Rudolf Bultmann remains a towering figure in 20th-century biblical interpretation and systematic theology. He was not, however, a dogmatic theologian, and never dreamed of writing a "church dogmatics."[124] Neither did he directly contribute to the ecumenical movement through a personal involvement in conferences and other events of this type. His most significant direct engagement with the ecumenical movement is rather negative; it is his article, first published in 1951, in which he critically assesses the Christological confession (or "basis") of the WCC.[125]

Yet this relative lack of direct involvement in the ecumenical movement should not lead us to think that Bultmann's influence on ecumenism, in the 20th century, was insignificant or even marginal. Today, despite the efforts of a few scholars, his writings have lost much of the impact they had from 1940 to 1965, but in those years, which were

120 *Karl Barth – Willem Adolph Visser 't Hooft: Briefwechsel*, 302–303.

121 Barth, "Interview von George Puchinger," 194.

122 Barth, "Interview von George Puchinger," 195, as well as Barth, "Gespräch in der Basler Titusgemeinde," 465.

123 Barth, "Gespräch in der Basler Titusgemeinde," 465.

124 The index in Christof Landmesser, ed., *Bultmann Handbuch*, Tübingen, Mohr Siebeck, 2017 contains four entries on ecumenism; of these four, three concern other theologians (Ernst Käsemann and Nathan Söderblom). Konrad Hammann's biography contains only a few mentions of ecumenism. See Konrad Hammann, *Rudolf Bultmann: A Biography*, Salem OR, Polebridge, 2013, 168–169, 468–469, and 504.

125 Rudolf Bultmann, "Das christologische Bekenntnis des Ökumenischen Rates" (1951), in: Rudolf Bultmann, *Glauben und Verstehen: Gesammelte Aufsätze*, vol. 2, Tübingen, Mohr, 1952, 246–262; ET: "The Christological Confession of the World Council of Churches," in: Rudolf Bultmann, *Essays, Philosophical and Theological*, New York, Macmillan, 1955, 273–290.

crucial for the ecumenical movement, Bultmann was at the very center of the theological debates throughout the world. These debates included many Roman Catholic theologians (however, far fewer Orthodox scholars).

3.1 *Early Works as a "Dialectical" Theologian*

Soon after the end of World War I, Bultmann became known as an exegete of the New Testament and as an advocate of the *Formgeschichte*. However, he soon became known, in addition to this exegetical work, as a (critical) member of the dialectical school, alongside Karl Barth and Friedrich Gogarten – with a greater proximity, particularly (but not only) at first, to Gogarten than to Barth. By the mid-1920s, Bultmann was denouncing "liberal theology" – a move which pained and preoccupied his own teachers, including Wilhelm Heitmüller, his immediate predecessor at the University of Marburg.[126]

In 1925, Bultmann replied to Erik Peterson's sharp (and Catholicizing) criticism of dialectical theology (*Was ist Theologie?*).[127] At first, the plan was for Barth and Bultmann to write a joint response, but this project was soon abandoned and each wrote his own reply.[128] In his reply, Bultmann focuses on revelation as an "eternal event, yet as an *event*." He asserts that the difference between Peterson and the "dialectical" theologians lies precisely in this:

> If the *dialegesthai* of theology points in the direction of an *event* (and an event which occurs as it were from God) as its presupposition, then it follows that the object (*Gegenstand*) of theology, insofar as theology consists in talking about God, does not allow, strictly speaking, for any *dialegesthai* (we go that far, as dialecticians!), but rather that the only adequate manner of speaking of God is the message, or proclamation. ... [Peterson] does not derive his theological (dogmatic) concepts from the event-character of its object, and thus he loses theology's direct connection with proclamation. Instead, he finds his concepts in the "order of being," thanks to a supposed vision of essences.[129]

Bultmann has seen, with great acuity, the basic difference between Peterson and the dialectical approach. For Peterson, the Christ event finds its prolongation (*Verlängerung*) in dogma, and this prolongation is taken to be "a direct, unbroken prolongation, in no way as a real prolongation which is grounded in God's miracle through the Holy Spirit; it is a simple and undialectical continuity of revelation history with the history of the church. There lies our opposition."[130]

The debate between Barth and Przywara in the ensuing years, that is, in the late 1920s and early 1930s, is a clear confirmation of Bultmann's "diagnosis": it is possible to ground theology, namely the human discourse concerning God, on a notion of revelation as "event," but it is also possible to ground theology on a concept of "being," and on a notion of the continuity, despite all discontinuities, between divine and creaturely being. As Bultmann sees it, "God's own seriousness" remains *God*'s seriousness: it is not transmitted once and for all to any earthly reality, even if it is the church.[131] Dialectical theology is an attempt to "speak adequately," despite the impossibility of talking of God.[132] Yet Bultmann fully agrees with Peterson that "the actual meaning of the revelation is not the *paradox*," that in Christianity the point is not to state things through paradoxical assertions.

126 See, for further details, my book *Dialectical Theologians: Wilhelm Herrmann, Karl Barth and Rudolf Bultmann*, Zürich, TVZ, 2005, 157–160.

127 Peterson, *Theological Tractates*.

128 In what follows, I quote from Rudolf Bultmann, "Die Frage der 'dialektischen' Theologie," in: Jürgen Moltmann, ed., *Anfänge der dialektischen Theologie*, vol. 2, *Rudolf Bultmann – Friedrich Gogarten – Eduard Thurneysen*, Munich, Kaiser, 1963, 72–92.

129 Bultmann, "Die Frage," 78.

130 Bultmann, "Die Frage," 79–80.

131 Bultmann, "Die Frage," 80.

132 Bultmann, "Die Frage," 81.

Bultmann suggests that talking about paradoxes is not necessary, and that the term itself, just as the term "dialectic," as a "philosophically loaded term," could easily, and perhaps should, be omitted.[133] All things considered, by placing "the dogma" in direct, unbroken continuity with revelation itself, Erik Peterson has "suppressed the Holy Spirit."[134]

3.2 *Ecclesiological Insights (1929 and 1955)*

Rudolf Bultmann never reflected at length on the "unity" of the church. However, we can glean several pronouncements from his writings which may give us a sense of his thoughts on "unity." For instance, in 1955 Bultmann published an article titled "Die Wandlung des Selbstverständnisse der Kirche in der Geschichte des Urchristentums."[135] Here he dedicates a paragraph to the question of unity. We should note, however, that it is Bultmann the historian of early Christianity who is speaking here – not the systematic theologian (except for the very last sentence of the article, in which Bultmann claims that only a dialectical understanding of the church, in being linked to both the future and the present, to both transcendence and immanence, is faithful to the essence of the church).[136] He is writing in a descriptive, not prescriptive or normative, manner. Still, here are his comments on the "unity" of the early Christian community:

> The fact that the ecclesia understood itself to be the people of God meant also that it thought of itself as a *unity*. The gospel did not promise individual persons the salvation of their soul and immortality, as did the mystery cults; it called individuals together to the one congregation of God. In the mystery cults, to be sure, individual persons came together to form congregations, but the individual congregations, although they may have stood, viewed historically, in certain relationships to one another, neither constituted a unity nor were exclusive. As a matter of fact, of course, the Christian congregations also were formed by the convocation of individual persons. However, they did not think of themselves as a visible, empirical corporation, but as a manifestation of the invisible congregation of God to which they all had been called. All individual congregations belonged together in the one and the same ecclesia that here and there took visible form. This ecclesia is there before the individuals who were called into it. By his call the individual is summoned into a space or a sphere that extends invisibly, mysteriously, into the earthly space. And such a faith soon led to the speculation that the ecclesia is a preexistent heavenly entity.[137]

We should be careful not to extract too much from this text. It is interesting to see Bultmann comment on the "unity" of the community as preceding the inclusion of new members into it, and also on the plurality of Christian communities which, since the earliest stages of Christianity, had a sense of "belonging together in the one and the same ecclesia." In an article first published in 1929, on "church and teaching in the New Testament," Bultmann already distinguished between the "communities" and the "community" (*ekklesiai* and *ekklesia*), adding that the communities belong to the one community, "not as parts or limbs which, when joined together, constitute the whole; for the whole is present in each single community."[138]

133 Bultmann, "Die Frage," 84.

134 Bultmann, "Die Frage," 92.

135 Rudolf Bultmann, "Die Wandlung des Selbstverständnisse der Kirche in der Geschichte des Urchristentums," in: Rudolf Bultmann, *Glauben und Verstehen: Gesammelte Aufsätze*, vol. 3, Tübingen, Mohr, 1960, 131–141; ET: "The Transformation of the Idea of Church in the History of Early Christianity," *CJT* 1/2, 1955, 73–81.

136 For this "dialectical" understanding of the church, see Bultmann, "The Transformation of the Idea of Church," 81.

137 Bultmann, "The Transformation of the Idea of Church," 77 (italics original).

138 Rudolf Bultmann, "Kirche und Lehre im Neuen Testament," in: Rudolf Bultmann, *Glauben und Verstehen:*

Here we find an ecclesiological insight which has become fairly important for recent theologians and ecumenicists.

3.3 *Direct Comments on Church Unity*

Bultmann's direct comments on the unity of the church are very scarce. Even in his commentary on the Gospel of John, when commenting the famous verse of John 17:21, his analysis is somewhat laconic, stressing the eschatological dimension of the community (this unity is not the kind which "can be realized and organized in institutions and dogmas").[139]

On Jul 29, 1970, Bultmann sent a letter to Percy Ernst Schramm, the chancellor of the Orden pour le mérite für Wissenschaft und Künste, in which he makes it clear that he held the hope of a reunification of the Protestant and the Roman Catholic Church to be "an illusion."[140]

This rather negative stance was not new, in Bultmann's case. In 1925, the Theological Faculty of the University of Marburg had begun to think about how to commemorate, in 1929, the 400th anniversary of the famous Marburg dispute, during which Huldrych Zwingli and Martin Luther could not reconcile their views, especially on the interpretation of the Lord's Supper. Noticing the strong influence of British and North American clergymen in the ecumenical movement, Rudolf Otto, assisted by Martin Rade and Heinrich Hermelink, wanted the "original" country of the Reformation to assert itself as a leading ecumenical actor.[141] Hence, they eventually decided to invite Nathan Söderblom, with the primary aim of promoting intra-Protestant unity worldwide. Söderblom, however, declined the invitation.

On Nov 8, 1925, Bultmann wrote a long "declaration" (of nearly 10 pages), addressed to his colleagues at Marburg's Theological Faculty, in which he criticized this project. This text, which remained unpublished until 1980, is not well known and deserves our attention.[142] In these pages, Bultmann seeks to show how, as he sees it, his colleagues' project is erroneous and in point of fact intrinsically "dishonest" (the recurring German term Bultmann uses is "unwahrhaftig," which, needless to say, is a very strong criticism, since "Wahrhaftigkeit" was a key marker for modern, scientific or liberal theology). Why is it so? Because it rests on the false assumption that there is a communal Protestant spirit (*Gemeinschaftsgefühl*), including a German-Protestant spirit, which a conference might enhance or strengthen. Bultmann claims that such a spirit does not exist, that the theologians who are planning such projects are "an army of leaders without troops" ("eine Armee von Führern ohne Truppen").[143] In passing, Bultmann criticizes the 1925 Life and Work conference in Stockholm as an example of the triumph of Americanism, especially of its naiveté and optimism, which confuses its own political and economic morality with a Christian ethic.[144] As Bultmann sees it, Protestantism is not a given historical entity (*Grösse*) which must seek worldly standing or worldly power (*Weltgeltung*).[145] Such ambitions are best left to Roman Catholicism, according to Bultmann.

Gesammelte Aufsätze, vol. 1, Tübingen, Mohr, 1933, 153–187; ET: "Church and Teaching in the New Testament," in: Rudolf Bultmann, *Faith and Understanding*, trans. Louise Pettibone Smith, Philadelphia, Fortress Press, 1987, 184–219, here 195.

139 Rudolf Bultmann, *Das Evangelium des Johannes*, Göttingen, Vandenhoeck & Ruprecht, 1941; ET: *The Gospel of John: A Commentary*, trans. George R. Beasley-Murray, Oxford, Blackwell, 1971, 503 and 514–517, quote on 517 (the English version is translated from the 1964 edition).

140 R. Bultmann to P.E. Schramm, Jul 21, 1970, in: Orden pour le mérite für Wissenschaften und Künste, ed., *Reden und Gedenkworte: Zehnter Band, 1970/71*, Heidelberg, Lambert Schneider, 1973, 195.

141 See Günter Bezzenberger, ed., *Marburg im Kontext: Gedenkbuch an das Marburger Religionsgespräch*, Kassel, Verlag Evangelischer Presseverband Kurhessen-Waldeck, 1980, 50.

142 For Bultmann's declaration, see Bezzenberger, ed., *Marburg im Kontext*, 53–59.

143 Bezzenberger, ed., *Marburg im Kontext*, 55.

144 Bezzenberger, ed., *Marburg im Kontext*, 57.

145 Bezzenberger, ed., *Marburg im Kontext*, 57.

What Protestants should aim to achieve is not to "regain" or to achieve dominance on the world stage. Instead, their priority, also as they organize conferences, should be to strive for "a radical self-examination on whether it is right for us to speak of Protestantism, given the ... complete confusion of our theological concepts and the total disunity of Protestants, above all of the theologians."[146]

This document makes it clear that Bultmann was interested in genuine theological discussions, not in conferences which gloss over differences and difficulties or which circumvent the true theological issues. We see here the same call for *Sachlichkeit*, for radicalism and rigor in theological work, that we find in his colleagues and friends Friedrich Gogarten and Karl Barth. In 1925, the ecumenical movement still had to begin serious work on the very substance of the Christian faith.

3.4 *The Confessional "Basis" of the WCC*

On Feb 26, 1951, Rudolf Bultmann gave a lecture in Aarau at a conference of Swiss liberal (*freisinnig*) theologians. This lecture was subsequently published in two theological journals, as well as in the second volume of Bultmann's collected works, *Glauben und Verstehen*.[147] Bultmann had been asked by the organizers of the conference to evaluate the confessional basis of the WCC, namely, that "The World Council of Churches is composed of Churches which acknowledge Jesus Christ as God and Saviour (*Heiland*)." Bultmann usually liked to come straight to the point in his lectures, and thus within four pages the reader discovers that confessing Jesus Christ as "God" is very unusual in the New Testament; Bultmann sees only one passage, John 20:28, namely the confession of Thomas the apostle. Certainly, in many New Testament passages Christ "is looked upon and worshipped as a divine figure – as θεῖος, we might most conveniently say in Greek – and so as a god, but not simply as God."[148] When the New Testament brings the κύριος into close proximity to God, it should not be read as providing insight into his "nature" as such; it seeks, rather, to "give expression to his significance" as savior.[149] Hence the Amsterdam formula is completely one-sided, in Bultmann's opinion; it reproduces the old liberal one-sidedness, but in the other direction (thus forfeiting Christ's humanity).[150] It would have been far more adequate to talk about Christ as "the Word of God," or as "the Son of God," since it is "as such" that "he is God."[151]

Bultmann thus registered a deep disagreement with the "basis" of the WCC – even as he maintained that Christ can be said to be God if by "God" one means "the event of God's acting."[152]

3.5 *Rudolf Bultmann and the Quest for Unity*

Bultmann's contribution to the quest for Christian unity may have been indirect, but this does not signify that it was (and remains) insignificant. To the surprise of some of his colleagues who could not follow his approach, his works were received quite positively, albeit not uncritically, by several Roman Catholic theologians, in Germany, in France, and elsewhere.[153] Indeed, it can be said

146 Bezzenberger, ed., *Marburg im Kontext*, 58.
147 Bultmann, "The Christological Confession."
148 Bultmann, "The Christological Confession," 279.
149 Bultmann, "The Christological Confession," 280.
150 Bultmann, "The Christological Confession," 286.
151 Bultmann, "The Christological Confession," 287 and 290.
152 Bultmann, "The Christological Confession," 287.
153 See Barth, "Interview von George Puchinger," 196. Hermann Häring, "Ungeliebter Kronzeuge: Zur Bultmannrezeption in der katholischen Theologie," in: Bernd Jaspert, ed., *Rudolf Bultmanns Werk und Wirkung*, Darmstadt, Wissenschaftliche Buchgesellschaft, 1984, 379–395. See also Gotthold Hasenhüttl, *Der Glaubensvollzug: Eine Begegnung mit Rudolf Bultmann aus katholischen Glaubensverständnis*, Essen, Ludgerus, 1963; Heinrich Fries, *Bultmann, Barth und die katholische Theologie*, Stuttgart, Schwabenverlag, 1955; Maurice Boutin, *Relationalität als Verstehensprinzip bei Rudolf Bultmann*, Munich, Kaiser, 1974; André Malet, *Mythos et logos: La pensée de Rudolf Bultmann*, Geneva, Labor et Fides, 1962. More critically: Léopold Malevez SJ, *The Christian Message and Myth: The Theology of Rudolf Bultmann*, London, SCM Press, 1958.

that his theological work "had an astonishing resonance in the Catholic academic milieu," especially since biblical scholars within Roman Catholicism were becoming freer to rely on modern critical methods, but also as a consequence of Bultmann's openness to philosophy as a support for theology and his talk of a "point of contact" between the Creator and the creature.[154]

Nearly half a century after his death (in 1976), Bultmann's theology may appear rather remote to us. Yet his concern for the existential relevance of the Christian message still deserves to be taken seriously, even as we search for new ways of thinking about this relevance.

154 Hammann, *Rudolf Bultmann: A Biography*, 468.

Bibliography

Baier, Klaus Alois, *Unitas ex auditu: Die Einheit der Kirche im Rahmen der Theologie Karl Barths*, Bern, Lang, 1978.

Barth, Karl, "Der römische Katholizismus als Frage an die protestantische Kirche," *Zwischen den Zeiten* 6, 1928, 274–302; ET: "Roman Catholicism: A Question to the Protestant Church," in: K. Barth, *Theology and Church: Shorter Writings (1920–1928)*, trans. Louise Pettibone Smith, Eugene, Wipf & Stock, 2015, 307–333.

Barth, Karl, "Über die Annäherung der Kirchen: Ein Gespräch zwischen Karl Barth und Tanneguy de Quénétain," *Junge Kirche* 24/6, 1963, 304–309.

Barth, Karl, *The Church and the Churches, Grand Rapids*, Eerdmans, 2005.

Barth, Karl, *Gesamtausgabe*, sec. 5, vol. 43, *Karl Barth – Willem Adolph Visser 't Hooft: Briefwechsel*, ed. Thomas Herwig, Zürich, TVZ, 2006, 55.

Chalamet, Christophe, "Karl Barth on the Quest for the Church's Unity," *CrSt* 37/2, 2016, 343–359.

Dahlke, Benjamin, Karl Barth, *Catholic Renewal and Vatican II*, London, T&T Clark, 2012

Herwig, Thomas, *Karl Barth und die Ökumenische Bewegung: Das Gespräch zwischen Karl Barth und Willem Adolf Visser 't Hooft auf der Grundlage ihres Briefwechsels (1930–1968)*, Neukirchen-Vluyn, Neukirchener Verlag, 1998

Keller, Adolf, *Karl Barth and Christian Unity: The Influence of the Barthian Movement Upon the Churches of the World*, New York, Macmillan, 1933.

Visser 't Hooft, Willem Adolph, "Karl Barth and the Ecumenical Movement," *EcRev* 32/2, 1980, 129–151.

Welker, Michael, "Karl Barth: From Fighter Against the 'Roman Heresy' to Leading Thinker for the Ecumenical Movement," *SJT* 57/4, 2004, 434–450.

CHAPTER 8

The Rebirth of Religious Communities in Reformation Churches

Silvia Scatena and Matthias Wirz

1 Introduction

Since the second half of the 19th century and especially during the 20th, those churches that bear the marks of the Reformation witnessed, throughout Europe, an unexpected phenomenon: the emergence, at their cores as well as on their margins, of religious and monastic communities.[1] After four centuries of an apparently unanimous – or at least extensive – rejection of this *forma vitae* in general, and of religious vows in particular, Protestantism wound up welcoming and once again gradually accepting the various manifestations of a rule based community life. This recovery of the cenobitic form within the Protestant sphere is clearly of significant ecumenical worth and can be read as a "powerful factor of unity"[2] that preceded – and then accompanied – the commitment to the ecumenical movement of the churches to which these new communities were belonging.

In particular, these communities overcame a centuries-old, doctrinal opposition. Their founders had to open up to a tradition that the Protestant world as a whole had rejected and seek references outside their own theological and ecclesiastical contexts. If, for a few centuries, monastic life had been understood – and rejected – in the Protestant world as an exquisitely Catholic element, this return of forms of communal life embedded with the need for radical evangelical discipleship thus implied, constitutively, the acceptance of some qualifying elements of traditions belonging to the undivided church. Furthermore, these new community realities did not reject or deny the attainments of the Reformation. Rather they drew upon them in representing forms of commitment and spiritual expressions that could instead be a manifestation of it. To the extent that they sought to recover and reinterpret traditions and forms of life that were alien to their own confessional background, they thus demonstrated the existence in Protestant churches of an instance of openness to an authentic dimension of catholicity, to the universality of the "One Church."

This demonstration was realized both on a specifically doctrinal level and, above all, on the level of lived experience, since primarily it was in an existential sense – with the mere "eloquence" of the lives of their members – that these new community creations intended to constitute a "sign" of unity both for their own churches and for those sharing experiences similar to theirs. It was, above all, in this perspective, then, that the Protestant communities arising in the 19th and 20th centuries offered a unique and fundamental contribution to the emergence and development of an ecumenism that was actually experienced and which has increasingly nourished the entire ecclesial body.

---

1 While some Protestant communities express a certain mistrust of the adjective "monastic," preferring "cenobitic," in other Protestant contexts, the adjective is used indiscriminately to define every form of communal religious life without a clear distinction between the different forms of consecrated life (contemplative, diaconal, active etc.).

2 See Annie Perchenet, *Renouveau communautaire et unité chrétienne: Regards sur les communautés anglicanes et protestantes*, Tours, Mame, 1967, 9; François Biot, *Communautés protestantes: La renaissance de la vie régulière dans le protestantisme continental*, Paris, Fleurus, 1961, 17; Guglielmo Di Agresti, "Riforma e monachesimo ieri e oggi," *Studi Francescani* 68/1, 1971, 29–66, here 60; Michele Cassese, "Il monachesimo nel pensiero protestante," in: *Il monachesimo in Oriente e in Occidente*, Milan, Quaderni del centro interreligioso Henri le Saux, 1989, 73–110, here 103–104; André Birmelé, "Peut-on être moine et protestant?: Fondements d'une théologie monastique protestante," in: Sœur Évangéline, ed., *Protestantisme et vie monastique: Vers une nouvelle rencontre?*, Paris, Olivétan, 2015, 145–155, here 154.

2 The Survival of Coenobitic Experiences after the Reformation

It is common knowledge that the 16th century Reformation, initiated in a convent by the Augustinian monk Martin Luther, brought with it a very negative judgment of the religious *forma vitae*, to the point that the latter disappeared for several centuries in the churches marked by it. Borrowing partly from the judgments issued in previous centuries by authors such as John Wyclif,[3] the criticism of "monastic" life by the reformers of the 16th century – particularly as it appeared at the end of the Middle Ages (a decadent spiritual situation, intolerable material wealth, privileged canonical status, etc.) – focused essentially on the superior status accorded to the religious with respect to ordinary believers. The attack on the institution of monasticism was formulated first of all by Luther. The criticism assumed decidedly vehement tones, springing from his personal experience and in defense of his own actions, receiving a vigorous and detailed treatment in his *De votis monasticis judicium* (On Monastic Vows, 1521).[4] In this highly polemical treatise, the German Reformer targeted particularly the traditional vows of chastity, poverty, and obedience, which he accused of being a justification for acts contrary to the gospel. For Luther, a vocation (*Berufung*) no longer appeared as a call to enter a convent for salvation, but the call to live one's profession (*Beruf*) in the world in a Christian way. According to Bonhoeffer, "Luther invested his whole life in his call to the monastery. … God showed him through Scripture that discipleship is not the meritorious achievement of individuals, but a divine command to all Christians."[5] Taken up by Huldrych Zwingli,[6] John Calvin,[7] and the other principal Reformers, this criticism – received in the heat of the controversy – was also found in the various Lutheran and Reformed confessions of faith,[8] contributing to a hostility towards monastic vows and, more generally, towards monasticism as such, which became a profoundly defining element of Protestant identity. In the lands whose princes adhered to the Reformation, the goods of most of the convents were then, as is well known, secularized.

Even in this context, however, the Reformers themselves were already timidly open to a less negative evaluation of the phenomenon of religious life. With prudent allusions, in fact, a certain margin of freedom could exceptionally be recognized in the existence of this form of discipleship in which one could *secundum evangelium vivere*, without, however, any claim that such a life is better in the eyes of God.[9] The instances permitted

3 See Ian Christopher Levy, ed., *A Companion to John Wyclif, Late Medieval Theologian*, Leiden, Brill, 2006.

4 Martin Luther, *De votis monasticis judicium*, in: WA 8, 564–669. For a classic and still fundamental study, see René H. Esnault, *Luther et le monachisme aujourd'hui: Lecture actuelle de "De votis monasticis judicium"*, Geneva, Labor et Fides, 1964. See also Biot, *Communautés protestantes*, 21–50; Johannes Halkenhäuser, *Kirche und Kommunität: Ein Beitrag zur Geschichte und Auftrag der kommunitären Bewegung in den Kirchen der Reformation*, Paderborn, Bonifatius, 1978, 13–81; Marianne Carbonnier-Burkard, "La Réforme protestante et la critique du monachisme," in: Sœur Évangéline, ed., *Protestantisme et vie monastique*, 15–36.

5 Dietrich Bonhoeffer, *Nachfolge*, Munich, Kaiser, 1937; ET: *DBWE* 4, *Discipleship*, trans. Barbara Green & Reinhard Krauss, Minneapolis, Fortress Press, 2001, 47.

6 Huldrych Zwingli, *Kommentar über die wahre und falsche Religion*, in: Ulrich Zwingli, *Schriften*, vol. 3, Zurich, Theologischer Verlag, 1995, ch. 28, "Von den Gelübden."

7 John Calvin, *Institutes of the Christian Religion*, trans. Henry Beveridge, Grand Rapids, Eerdmans, 1989, book 4, ch. 13, 472–490. See Biot, *Communautés protestantes*, 51–77.

8 *Confessio Augustana* (1530), art. 27, available at <https://bookofconcord.org/augsburg-confession/> (accessed Sep 13, 2022); *The French Confession of Faith* (1559), art. 24, available at <https://www.ccel.org/ccel/schaff/creeds3.iv.vii.html> (accessed Sep 13, 2022).

9 See Halkenhäuser, *Kirche und Kommunität*, 60–81, which presents the texts of the Lutheran tradition, the clearest example of which is found in the Wittenberg Articles, the protocol that summarizes Luther's conversations with Henry VIII's English envoys in 1536 (70–71). Calvin also distinguished the "holy and legitimate monasticism" of the early church from that of the late Middle Ages (see Calvin, *Institutes*, 478–481, here 481).

in the wake of this recognition, however, were of short duration in the Protestant world of the 16th century. Where medieval monasteries survived the Reformation, mostly in Lower Saxony and Westphalia, this was mainly with a view to the formation of ministers of worship and mainly thanks to the efforts of (non-resident) pastors who ensured the monastery's management. In particular, we can think of the cases of Möllenbeck, Loccum, and Amelungsborn.[10]

With the Thirty Years' War and then, above all, with the Enlightenment, these residual monastic survivors in the Protestant sphere would be definitively dismantled. Because the ascetic rendering of the Christian message was by then no longer understood, and also because of the hardening of the controversy between Protestant Orthodoxy and Pietist currents – which affected even the social forms of Christian life – as well as the type of development that religious studies were undergoing, the cenobitic *forma vitae* would, in fact, wind up being emptied of meaning, substantially taken to be, as it was in Protestant theological circles, a "relapse from the pure doctrine of the Gospel into a pre-Christian state."[11] The exclusion of all forms of religious life from the ecclesial fabric of Protestantism then caused – as would be recognized in the 20th century – an "open wound."[12] There was no lack of attempts to heal this wound during the 18th century, seeking to overcome what was beginning to appear to be an ecclesial impoverishment. These were relatively brief experiences, linked to some non-monastic spiritual movements, but which – marked by a character of evangelical radicalism and a strong desire for community life – variously recovered a form of spirituality and *koinos bios* that was in some way similar to that of the religious life.

In particular, an essential crucible for this recovery was Pietism,[13] a powerful movement of spiritual awakening and an attempt to revive an ecclesial dynamism that significantly marked Protestant religiosity of the 17th and 18th centuries. Its programmatic creator, Philipp Jacob Spener, clearly foresaw the establishment of particular groups of more fervent and committed Christians (*collegia pietatis* or *ecclesiolæ*) gathering outside public worship for their own, individual edification and in the hope of conferring vitality and Christian authenticity to a gentrified institutional church. In the wake of these achievements – in addition to some more extreme, rigorous, and sectarian tendencies[14] – two precise achievements of community life stand out in particular, united by elements that would further distinguish the monastic communities that would arise in the Protestant sphere two centuries later: an insistence on the fraternal dimension of the ecclesial community, an openness to encounter and dialogue with Christians of other confessions, and a renewed consideration of the eschatological dimension of faith.

This is primarily a reference to Gerhard Tersteegen's *Pilgerhütte* in Otterbeck in the Rhineland. It was a resident community of men established in 1727 under the direction of this

10 See Halkenhäuser, *Kirche und Kommunität*, 82–105. On Möllenbeck, see Nicolaus Heutger, *Das Stift Möllenbeck an der Weser: Kanonissenstift, Windesheimer Chorherrenstift, Evangelisches Stift*, Hildesheim, August Lax, 1987. On Loccum, see Nicolaus Heutger, *Das Kloster Loccum im Rahmen der zisterziensischen Ordensgeschichte: Zum 100. Geburtstag von Johannes XI. Lilje, Abt zu Loccum, und zur Expo 2000*, Hannover, Theodor Oppermann, 1999, and Horst Hirschler & Ludolf Ulrich, eds., *Kloster Loccum*, Hannover, Lutherisches Verlagshaus, 2012. On Amelungsborn, see Nicolaus Heutger, *Das Kloster Amelungsborn: Werden, Wachsen, Wirken: Zum 100. Geburtstag von Christian Mahrenholz*, Hannover, Theodor Oppermann, 2000, and Hans-Jörg Dietsche, "Kloster Amelungsborn: Ein Sonderfall der Reformation," in: Anna-Maria aus der Wiesche & Frank Lilie, eds., *Kloster auf evangelisch: Berichte aus dem gemeinsamen Leben*, Münsterschwarzach, Vier-Türme, 2016, 49–52.

11 As expressed by the church historian Lorenz von Mosheim in his *Vollständige Kirchengeschichte*, quoted in Halkenhäuser, *Kirche und Kommunität*, 111.

12 See Walter Nigg, *Vom Geheimnis der Mönche*, Zurich, Artemis, 1953, 19.

13 See, among others, Johannes Wallmann, *Der Pietismus*, Göttingen, Vandenhoeck & Ruprecht, 2005.

14 See Halkenhäuser, *Kirche und Kommunität*, 135–143.

Reformed "saint in Protestantism,"[15] who was greatly influenced by Pietism but also an avid reader of the monastic literature of the undivided church and was particularly fascinated by the hermitic and mystical ideal. His cenobium – solid enough to survive until the beginning of the 19th century – gathered barely ten "Christians and pilgrims 'awakened' to the view of God's great eternity." These were Christians who withdrew from the world to lead a "hidden life with Christ in God," in prayer and manual labor, but who also engaged in visiting the sick, caring for souls, and in the missions.[16]

Another attempt at fraternal life that arose in the same years within Pietism, but certainly less explicitly monastic than the previous one, was that of the Herrnhuter Brüdergemeine in Saxony led by Count Nikolaus Ludwig von Zinzendorf modeled on the New Testament *koinonia*.[17] Animated by one who knew how to be a poet and a prophet, a traveler and an organizer, a mystic as well as an ecumenist *ante litteram* all in one, the experience was also an unprecedented achievement in Protestantism. In Herrnhut, some families – mainly from the church of the Moravian Brothers who had taken refuge on the count's lands in 1722 – started the novel practice of a shared life, the Brüder-Unität, forming a kind of vast community, whose days were divided into the celebration of various moments of daily prayer around which the various acts of daily life were integrated. In particular, the Herrnhut community was organized into small groups ("bands," then "choirs") that gathered at least once a week for a common meal, special prayer times, spiritual sharing or even a sacramental celebration of foot washing.[18] To "create" the community day, two biblical verses were chosen at random every morning to be distributed from house to house. Starting in 1731, these "watchwords" (*Losungen*) were collected and published annually in a single volume, whose editions soon began to spread in the Reformation churches where they nurtured the piety of many of the faithful and continue to do so today.[19] The Unitas Fratrum was a unique melting pot of shared interdenominational life. From its outset, in addition to the Moravian Brothers, Zinzendorf also welcomed Lutherans and Calvinists, faithful to the intuition of Christian reconciliation that had moved him from a very young age. Finally, a vigorous missionary program animated the community, leading the brothers and sisters, in less than 30 years, to settle in the most diverse geographical areas: from Greenland to the Caribbean, from Georgia to Suriname, from Persia to South Africa.

Although not properly cenobitic, the Herrnhuter Brüdergemeine therefore allowed a signifi-

15 See Walter Nigg, *Grosse Heilige*, Zurich, Artemis, 1946, 309–354, here 309. See also Cornelis Pieter van Andel, *Gerhard Tersteegen: Leben und Werk, Sein Platz in der Kirchengeschichte*, Vluyn-Neukirchen, Neukirchener Verlag, 1973, and Peter Zimmerling, "Gerhard Tersteegen (1697–1769): Pietist und Mystiker," in: Peter Zimmerling, *Evangelische Mystik*, Göttingen, Vandenhoeck & Ruprecht, 2015, 112–131.

16 See Halkenhäuser, *Kirche und Kommunität*, 119–126. See also Hansgünter Ludewig, "Herzensgebet und Pilgerhütte: Gerhard Tersteegen und die Anfänge evangelischer Kommunitäten," MEKGR 40, 1991, 103–126, and Horst Neeb, *Gerhard Tersteegen und die Pilgerhütte Otterbeck in Heiligenhaus (1709–1969)*, Düsseldorf, Archiv der Evangelischen Kirche im Rheinland, 1998.

17 See Erich Beyreuther, *Nikolaus Ludwig von Zinzendorf: Selbstzeugnisse und Bilddokumente, Eine Biographie*, Gießen-Basel, Brunnen, 2000. See also Peter Zimmerling, "Nikolaus Ludwig von Zinzendorf (1700–1760): Mystik in Alltag und Gemeinde," in: Zimmerling, *Evangelische Mystik*, 132–149.

18 See Hans Beat Motel, "Die Brüder-Unität: Ein ökumenisches Modell," *Una Sancta* 26, 1971, 60–67. See also Halkenhäuser, *Kirche und Kommunität*, 126–135; Peter Zimmerling, *Nachfolge lernen: Zinzendorf und das Leben der Brüdergemeinde*, Moers, 1990; and Dietrich Meyer, *Zinzendorf und die Herrnhuter Brüdergemeine (1700–2000)*, Göttingen, Vandenhoeck & Ruprecht, 2009.

19 The *Losungen* (*Paroles et textes pour chaque jour*) are published annually in German and French by Friedrich Reinhardt in Basel. In English, the *Moravian Daily Texts* are published in various formats by the Interprovincial Board of Communication of the Moravian Church in America. They are also available in some 20 other languages.

cant rediscovery of the unfulfilled call to communal life, influencing Protestant Christianity in the following centuries.

3 The Anglican Revival and Community *Diakonia*

3.1 *The Rebirth of Religious Communities in the Church of England*

Despite the aforementioned, karstic subterranean currents of brief experiences of community life, until the 20th century, examples of *koinos bios* remained the almost exclusive legacy of the Pietist heritage in the churches marked by the Reformation.

As early as the mid-19th century, a foreshadowing of the 20th century revival of consecrated community life in continental Protestantism was nonetheless noted in the Church of England, which – consistent with its insistence on continuity with the tradition of the great undivided church – had, in fact, always maintained a certain "nostalgia" for this form of Christian life.[20] It was a "nostalgia" with regard to which the role of the *Book of Common Prayer*, an essential source and reference of structured and objective *pietas*, certainly played a far from secondary role.[21] While the first official contribution to the theology of religious life from an Anglican point of view would have to wait until the 1970s,[22] the Church of England's recognition of this *forma vitae*, and concomitant legalization of religious vows by the English parliament, date back to the late 1880s, after the birth of the first two male religious communities, which emerged more than 20 years after the first sisterhoods.[23]

Already from the mid-1800s, there was in fact a blossoming of female communities in England. Consisting of slightly under 30 between 1850 and 1880, their number would continue to grow until and beyond the turn of the century.[24] These were communities that initially grew up around a parish and that remained small in size. They were mainly communities of "mixed life," in which the apostolic work and the outreach to "penitents" – the ill or destitute – earned them important recognition on the part of the various offices of the Anglican Church. In general, this did not undermine the structuring role of a common liturgy or the early affirmation of a contemplative dimension.

Seen until the mid-20th century as an expression of a specific component of Anglicanism, their origin can actually be traced back to the context of the particular religious vitality of the early Victorian age, set against the background of the profound changes brought about by the industrial and urban revolution. In particular, it also arose out of instances of ecclesial renewal proper to the Oxford Movement, starting from a peculiar reimagining of the Church of England as a historical concretization of the great undivided church of the first centuries of Christianity. The Anglican spiritual tradition undoubtedly offered a number of elements that were conducive to the rebirth of religious and monastic life. These included traces of conventual life dating back to before the Reformation that survived in the ancient universities of Oxford and, to a lesser extent, Cambridge,

20 See Mark D. Chapman, *The Fantasy of Reunion: Anglicans, Catholics and Ecumenism (1833–1882)*, Oxford, Oxford University Press, 2014, and Adalberto Mainardi & Matthias Wirz, "Expériences monastiques et mouvement œcuménique au XXe siècle," in: Luca Ferracci, ed., *Toward a History of the Desire for Christian Unity: Preliminary Research Papers*, Münster, LIT, 2015, 81–98.

21 See Thomas Seville, "La restaurazione della vita religiosa nella Chiesa d'Inghilterra nel secolo XIX," in: Nicola D'Acunto, ed., *Monachesimo e vita religiosa: Rinnovamento e storia tra i secoli XIX–XX*, San Pietro in Cariano, Gabrielli, 2002, 181–203.

22 See Donald Allchin, "Il monachesimo nella Communio anglicana," in: Donato Giordano, ed., *Il ruolo del monachesimo nell'ecumenismo: Atti del Simposio Ecumenico Internazionale*, Monte Oliveto Maggiore, Abbazia Monte Oliveto Maggiore, 2002, 161–173.

23 See Perchenet, *Renouveau communautaire et unité chrétienne*, 88–93.

24 See Owen Chadwick, *The Victorian Church*, vol. 1, London, Black, ²1970, 503–511, and Jacques Gadille, "Les îles britanniques," *HC* 11, 225–243.

besides the long list of devout Anglicans who in the 17th and 18th centuries endeavored to overcome traditional criticism of a rule-based form of community life, initiating or supporting in some cases actual experiences in this regard.[25] Nonetheless, the role of some Tractarians in the development of this movement of community rebirth is indeed hard to underestimate.[26] Among these, the name of Edward Pusey in particular should be recalled. Professor of Hebrew at Oxford and undisputed leader of Anglo-Catholicism, from the beginning of the 1840s – in 1841, he received the vows of Marion Hughes, the first woman to take this step in the Anglican Church – he convincingly encouraged the restoration of religious life in England by defending the nascent women's communities from the many criticisms soon to come from within and without different sectors of the Anglican clergy. These criticisms were not unrelated to the change in women's status that the new community phenomenon brought about, nor were they helped by several conversions to Catholicism.

It was Pusey in particular who encouraged the founding of the first Anglican women's community in a house in Park Village West, London, in 1845. About ten years later, that community joined with another founded in 1848 in the port slums of Davenport, thus giving birth to the Society of the Most Holy Trinity at whose mother house – Ascot Priory, Berkshire, from 1861 – Pusey spent the last years of his life. The Oxford professor, who became John Henry Newman's partner in ecumenical exchanges in the late 1860s, also inspired the Community of St. John the Baptist in Clewer as spiritual director of that new community's first superior. More than a few bishops entertained reservations about Pusey for his positions on the essential nature of religious vows and for his regard for certain Catholic practices (such as the preservation of the Eucharist and daily communion). The bishop of Oxford, Samuel Wilberforce, in the end, decided that, instead of Pusey, it would be the parish priest of Clewer, Thomas Carter, who would be responsible for organizing the life of the new community. Carter was rather more cautious on the matter of vows – like William Butler, founder of the Community of St. Mary the Virgin in Wantage. It was an issue that, predictably, was at the center of several debates among the various figures of the Church of England.[27]

Together with another early Tractarian, John Keble, Pusey was also one of the closest supporters of the Society of the Sisters of Bethany, founded in 1866 by Etheldreda Anna Bennett in Clerkenwell, at the time one of the poorest neighborhoods in London. She had been one of the first to experience the community at Park Village West where she had dedicated herself more intensely to her vocation, deciding to offer space and opportunities for retreat and silence to the men and women absorbed by the many commitments of social life. Among the few new communities that did not have a priest as its founder, the Society of the Sisters of Bethany adopted, like the other newly founded sisterhoods, the Augustinian rule in the form modified by Francis de Sales and Jane Frances de Chantal and, for prayer, the system of seven offices based on the breviary in the English Sarum rite, a variant of the Roman rite in use in Britain before the Reformation. Distinguishing themselves from other communities, the sisters of Clerkenwell did not fail to pay explicit attention, from the very beginning, to the theme of unity, introducing a

25 An example is the one promoted in the 17th century in Little Gidding by Deacon Nicholas Ferrar or the one initiated the following century by William Law who founded a non-monastic community in King's Cliffe with a simple and secluded life, observance of regular prayer hours, and the recitation of divine offices. On these and other attempts and experiences, see Seville, "La restaurazione della vita religiosa," and Olive Wyon, *Living Springs: New Religious Movements in Western Europe*, London, SCM Press, 1963, 39–61.

26 See Arthur M. Allchin, *The Silent Rebellion*, London, SCM Press, 1958, and Perchenet, *Renouveau communautaire et unité chrétienne*, 65ff.

27 See Seville, "La restaurazione della vita religiosa."

regular intercession for "the visible unity of the Catholic Church" in community prayer.[28]

One of Pusey's former pupils, on whom he probably exerted a great influence, was Richard Meux Benson. One of the priests closest to the Sisters of Bethany, he was a spiritual disciple of Butler and, from 1850, vicar of Cowley, a neighborhood on the outskirts of Oxford. He founded the first male religious community in the Church of England, the Cowley Fathers, formed at the end of December 1866 when Benson and two other priests made a vow in one another's presence to live a lifetime of celibacy, poverty, and obedience as priests of the Society of St. John the Evangelist. Officially recognized by the bishop of Oxford, who ratified its statutes and spiritual rule – including the vows – in 1884, the Society of St. John the Evangelist would lead a life that was, in some ways, monastic while soon becoming engaged in the intense labor of preaching, retreats, and parish missions.[29]

The first male communities emerged rather later than the women's communities, despite Pusey's early desire to establish a college of unmarried priests and the hopes in this regard ignited by Newman's retreat to Littlemore in 1842, before his passage to the Catholic Church. These new male communities had a somewhat different character from the new Anglican sisterhoods. While the latter generally found their main spark in a desire for consecrated life – which, in turn, was accentuated by a social context that favored their development in different ways – the male foundations were more marked by a missionary concern, both in parishes and on other continents. Contributing to the conviction concerning the importance of personal consecration and thorough education in the frame of a common life, was in effect, and not in an indifferent way, as much the awareness of a need for preaching that was better suited to the context of growing secularization, as likewise the demand for an adequate spiritual accompaniment, which came from the new women's communities.[30] The founding of the first explicitly monastic communities, and in particular the rebirth of a male Benedictine life, took place only in the 1920s with the founding of Nashdom Abbey. In this case it was once again the women that were the trailblazers, particularly the community founded in 1891 at St. Mary's Abbey in West Malling, which adopted the Rule of St. Benedict 15 years later.[31] In any case, the first male foundations established after the birth of the Cowley Fathers were, in general, more so than the latter, marked by a concern to modify the experience of common life with greater openness to the questions of their own time.

Seeking to offer a concrete response in this sense was the Community of Resurrection in Mirfield, the first of the new foundations established by Charles Gore, a member of that lively Oxford environment that combined the fervor of the first Tractarians with the reflection on a "social Christianity." Born of an idea for priestly community based on the Oratorian model, which was intended to take the form of shared life, prayer and study, without vows, it would, instead, progressively evolve towards a true religious community, both active and contemplative. This evolution culminated in 1892 with the lifelong vows professed by the first six brothers and the choice of a superior in the person of Walter Howard Frere, who was later recruited by Lord Halifax for the Malines Conversations.[32] Consecrated above all to a ministry for the formation of young priests – facilitating access to the priesthood even for children of modest families who were without a university education – and destined to become one of the most numerous and dynamic communities of the Anglican Church, the foundation

28 See Perchenet, *Renouveau communautaire et unité chrétienne*, 77.

29 See Perchenet, *Renouveau communautaire et unité chrétienne*, 80ff.

30 See Seville, "La restaurazione della vita religiosa," and Gadille, "Les îles britanniques."

31 See Perchenet, *Renouveau communautaire et unité chrétienne*, 109ff.

32 See Perchenet, *Renouveau communautaire et unité chrétienne*, 99–101.

of the Community of Resurrection would be followed, two years later, by that of the Society of the Sacred Mission of Kelham, which was also dedicated to priestly formation, not only in England, but also in South Africa and Australia. This last was founded on the initiative of Herbert Kelly, an heir – like Gore – to the liberal thought of Frederick Denison Maurice, professor of moral theology at Cambridge and often considered a precursor of the ecumenical movement but above all one of the initiators of so-called Christian socialism.[33] Like the Community of the Resurrection, the Society of the Sacred Mission soon developed a significant concern for the ecumenical dimension, which materialized especially after Kelly began to have contact with the WSCF in 1907, when Kelham's students started to regularly attend the WSCF conferences. Their attention to ecumenism also grew out of the contacts that were generally established by many of these early Anglican foundations with various Catholic religious communities.[34] The destination of a visit by Dietrich Bonhoeffer in March 1935 in search of impressions of other Christian traditions before he began his own attempt at *vita communis*,[35] the importance that knowledge of and relationships with many of these English communities would also have for the father of spiritual ecumenism in Lyon[36] is well known.

3.2 *Between the Awakening and Social Protestantism: The First Communities of Deaconesses*

While the Anglican communities – of which only the first ones have been mentioned here[37] – were recognized relatively early on by the bishops of the Anglican Church and while, in general, they essentially maintained the structure of Catholic religious orders,[38] the case of other contemporary experiences of reintroducing forms of community life in continental Protestantism was very different. Attempts were made, in different ways and with different outcomes, both in the unique and delicate context of French minority Protestantism and in German, Swiss, Dutch, and Scandinavian contexts. Their social and confessional milieu were very different from one another, but they were all variously affected by the profound transformations brought about by industrialization and the emergence of a "social question." It is no coincidence that all the new foundations that sprang up in the Protestant world between the middle and the end of the 19th century had both a religious and a social character assuming the features of "community diakonies," although the need for community did not always fully subscribe to the Diaconal option. this occurred above all in the contexts of a *Staatskirche*, where the dimension of outward service and a progressive tendency towards professionalism in carrying out significant social tasks often prevailed.

The vicissitudes of the many experiences in which the movement of Protestant diaconal communities was concretely expressed during

33 See Jeremy Morris, *F.D. Maurice and the Crisis of Christian Authority*, Oxford, Oxford University Press, 2005. For a brief profile of Maurice, see also the article by Paul Avis in the first volume of this work.

34 Again, see Perchenet, *Renouveau communautaire et unité chrétienne*, 101–106.

35 See Eberhard Bethge, *Dietrich Bonhoeffer: Eine Biographie*, Munich, Kaiser, 1970; ET: *Dietrich Bonhoeffer: A Biography*, Minneapolis, Fortress Press, 2000, 412–413. See also the contribution by Peter Zimmerling in this volume.

36 See the many pages Maurice Villain devotes to Paul Couturier's Anglican contacts and travels in England in his *L'Abbé Paul Couturier: Apôtre de l'unité chrétienne: Souvenirs et documents*, Paris, Casterman, [2]1957, 109–140, and the biography of the Chartreux priest by the priest of the Mirfield Community Geoffrey Curtis, *Paul Couturier and Unity in Christ*, London, SCM Press, 1964. On these Anglican networks established by Lyonese ecumenism, see Étienne Fouilloux, *Les catholiques et l'unité chrétienne du XIXe au XXe siècle: Itinéraires européens d'expression française*, Paris, Le Centurion, 1982, 322ff.

37 For an exhaustive but dated list, see again Perchenet, *Renouveau communautaire et unité chrétienne*, 469–473.

38 This is the reason why they have not been addressed in other contributions on the revival of Protestant communities. See, for example, Biot, *Communautés protestantes*, 14. See also Matthias Wirz, "'Risposta dell'uomo alla grazia': La rinascita del monachesimo in ambito protestante," *PSV* 75, 2017, 199–212.

the 19th century are difficult to summarize, the developments, conceptions, and organizational structures they assumed being so varied.[39] We shall thus concentrate here on only two main movements – that of the German *Mutterhausdiakonie*, to which the experiences of several other countries can also be traced, and that of the French deaconesses of Reuilly which, especially in its initial founding intentions, had a specifically communitarian religious vocation that was more accentuated than in other new foundations and which, more than in other cases, was directly influenced by the experience of the Awakening.

If deaconesses' houses sprung up here and there throughout Europe during the 19th century, it was Germany that was certainly this movement's chosen land, as evidenced by the establishment of an *ad hoc* study center, the Diakoniewissenschaftliches Institut, at the University of Heidelberg in 1854.[40] Especially at the beginning, the emergence of deaconesses was in particular an expression of the Protestantism of the Lower Rhine valley, of a Reformed inspiration, or of Bavarian Lutheranism of the Nuremberg region, which was free from ties to the state. Another important center of dissemination was also Bielefeld, in Westphalia. These were generally contexts in which the social awakening manifested itself in communities in predominantly Catholic contexts. Such communities were animated by a fervor and readiness to denounce the negative social and moral consequences of the upheavals wrought by large industries.[41]

Theodor Fliedner, a Lutheran from Nassau but influenced by the Reformed tradition of the Lower Rhine, established the first experience of a *diakonia* community in Germany. After visiting centers of the spiritual Awakening in the Netherlands, Scotland, and England on several occasions, in 1836 he founded the first mother house of deaconesses in Kaiserswerth, a small village on the right bank of the Rhine near Dusseldorf.[42] The outgrowth of a women's society for the poor and the care of the sick and a training school for evangelical healthcare workers set up in the Kaiserswerth's presbytery, the community founded by Fliedner was not only supposed to be a philanthropic work, aimed to address the absence of a nursing profession that had not existed in Germany until then. In establishing this first *Mutterhausdiakonie* to respond to the need to provide the institutions founded by the promoters of the German Social Gospel movement with a reliable and stable staff, Fliedner turned to the organization of the early church and carefully studied the rules of Catholic religious orders – particularly that of the Daughters of Charity of St. Vincent de Paul. It was from the latter that he took the idea of a particular habit, which would soon become the uniform of the German and Swiss deaconesses, and he also looked carefully at the seminary for missions in Barmen for the structuring of a Protestant community life. The *Gemeindeschwestern* did not take vows, but they renounced remuneration, submitted to the decisions made by the community's leadership, and understood celibacy to be a requirement of the vocation of service, committing themselves to remain unmarried for the entire time of their mission. They were primarily dedicated to the care of the sick and the destitute.

39 For an overview of the various formulations of communal *diakonia*, see again Perchenet, *Renouveau communautaire et unité chrétienne*, 268–329 and 474–475.

40 Without making any claim to completeness, see Herbert Krimm, *Das Diakonische Amt der Kirche*, Stuttgart, Evangelisches Verlagswerk, ²1965; Paul Philippi, *Die Vorstufen des modernen Diakonissenamtes (1789–1848) als Elemente für dessen Verständnis und Kritik: Eine motivgeschichtliche Untersuchung zum Wesen der Mutterhausdiakonie*, Neukirche, Neukirchener Verlag des Erziehungsvereins, 1966; Claude Bridel, *Aux seuils de l'espérance: Le diaconat en notre temps*, Neuchâtel, Delachaux et Niestlé, 1971, 39–47; and Ernst Schering, "Ordenserneuerung und Gestaltwerdung der Diakonie im Protestantismus des 19. Jahrhunderts," *RJKG* 6, 1987, 115–132.

41 In this sense, see Régis Ladous, "Le protestantisme: Du Vormärz à l'unité allemande," *HC* 11, 315–340.

42 See Dietmar Kruczek, *Theodor Fliedner: Mein Leben, für das Leben, Eine Biographie über den Gründer der Kaiserswerther Diakonie*, Neukirchen-Vluyn, Aussaat, 2002, and Perchenet, *Renouveau communautaire et unité chrétienne*, 294–299.

They immediately expanded rapidly, and in a short time new deaconess houses were opened in several other German cities.[43] Already at the beginning of the 1840s, the experience of Kaiserswerth's *Diakonissenhäuser* – reunited in 1861 at the Kaiserswerther Generalkonferenz – also spread from North Rhine-Westphalia to French-speaking Switzerland, between Lausanne and Vallorbe, in the restless canton of Vaud, which was shaken by the ferment of a religious dissidence of pietist connotation that had officially broke away from Vaud's *Landeskirche* in 1847.[44] It was in Echallens in particular that pastor Louis Germond, connected to the Awakening movement, founded the first Swiss house of deaconesses in 1842, following the example of Kaiserswerth. These *Mutterhausdiakonie* then moved to Saint-Loup in the aftermath of the break with the Église nationale made by an important fraction of the Vaud pastorate, to which Germond adhered, and which soon spread to several cantons of French-speaking Switzerland.[45] Even in German-speaking Switzerland, Kaisersweth did not fail to serve as a model for new communities. First and foremost was that of the deaconesses of Bern, born in 1844 on the initiative of Sophie von Wurstemberger, already a frequent visitor to the Pietist circles of the city and a founder of an association for the care of the ailing poor. Although the development of the Bernese *Mutterhausdiakonie* was initially slower, by the end of the 19th century the reputation of the deaconesses of Bern was such that, in 1908, the German empress Augusta Victoria called upon them to take over the management of the large Protestant hospital in Cologne and later that of Hamburg.[46]

The dimension of professionalization became more and more important in these early communal creations, which spread in parallel to the contemporaneous development of the Innere Mission, which was started in 1848 by Johann Hinrich Wichern, the great federator of a German social Christianity for the Christian reconquest of society as well as the founder of another *Mutterhaus* in Hamburg with deaconesses and lay "brothers."[47] A more communitarian and liturgical dimension, however, was to be found in another important *diakonia* community promoted in 1854 in the Bavarian presbytery of Neuendettelsau by the neo-Lutheran pastor Wilhelm Löhe who was very active in the liturgical and sacramental revival movement. A leading figure in 19th century German Protestantism, Löhe had not initially thought of founding a community, but after the experience of the first Neuendettelsau deaconesses, who gradually began to live together, he soon became convinced that a shared life was necessary to give support and continuity to the new *diakonia*. He started from the idea that a *diakonia* community represented first of all a "sign," a living example of what the church was intended to be. Without asking them to take vows, therefore, he recommended the practice of the evangelical counsels to the deaconesses.[48]

Due to the importance attached to the dimension of personal consecration and to the link between *diakonia* and *koinonia*, the Bavarian foundation promoted by Löhe was most similar to the Reuilly project of *diakonia* community. An experience that was begun in the Paris suburbs at the end of 1841 by Antoine Vermeil – a pastor who had served in Hamburg and Bordeaux before going to Paris in 1840, influenced by the Réveil movement since the years of his theological studies in Geneva – together with Caroline Malvesin, a governess from Bordeaux, already one of his parishioners, who was very touched by the preaching of

43 See Biot, *Communautés protestantes*, 119ff.

44 See Jean-Pierre Bastian, *La fracture religieuse vaudoise, 1847–1966: L'Église libre, la "Môme" et le canton de Vaud*, Geneva, Labor et Fides, 2016.

45 See Perchenet, *Renouveau communautaire et unité chrétienne*, 285–287.

46 Perchenet, *Renouveau communautaire et unité chrétienne*, 287–289 and 308–309.

47 See Halkenhäuser, *Kirche und Kommunität*, 145–156 and Ladous, "Le protestantisme."

48 See Halkenhäuser, *Kirche und Kommunität*, 156–172 and Judith Lena Böttcher, *Vowed to Community or Ordained to Mission?: Aspects of Separation and Integration in the Lutheran Deaconess Institute Neuendettelsau, Bavaria*, Göttingen, Vandenhoeck & Ruprecht, 2018.

Adolphe Monod, one of the most famous preachers and proponents of the spirituality of the Réveil in France in the first half of the 19th century.[49] Opened in November 1841 and officially inaugurated in April of the following year, the first house of deaconesses in Rue de Reuilly was thus born amid the eventful background of the France of the July Monarchy. This context was characterized by a renewed involvement of Protestants in national political life after the experience of the "Desert" and a clandestine existence, as well as by a social activism that was the expression of the theology of individual renewal typical of the Réveil, which reached Paris in the 1830s and continued until the rupture with the Reformed Church in 1848, and the concomitant constitution of the Union des Églises évangéliques libres; last but not least, it was a context also marked by a growing spirit of emulation and rivalry in the fields of charity and evangelization between a Catholicism that was also undergoing a process of renewal and new missionary zeal and a Protestantism that aimed to play catch-up on the national stage after a century-long delay.[50]

Against this background, the foundation of the first French-speaking *diakonia* community was born from the encounter between Vermeil's idea "to raise, under another name and without perpetual vows and the superstitions that spoil them, religious orders of women appointed to care for children, the ill, and the elderly" – the Catholic model of reference was mainly that of the Vincentian Daughters of Charity – and Malvesin's desire for a total consecration to God within the framework of community life.[51] This exigency, in the context of the difficult interconfessional relations of this juncture, was immediately combined in a meaningful way with that of intra-Christian unity. As Malvesin wrote to Vermeil in February 1841:

> For me, I feel that my work should be to act for the Lord to hasten the blessed moment when there will be only one flock guided by one Shepherd! ... Oh! When the time comes when we will no longer remember the words "Protestant" and "Catholic," except to give thanks to the Lord that they no longer exist and when the great Christian family will quench its thirst at the fountain of living water that will gush forth to eternal life.[52]

The founder of Reuilly's *diakonia* wanted the new community to be clearly oriented towards a communal form of religious life, which brought with it an intrinsic need for a lifelong commitment. Although at the time of their consecration by a laying on of hands, the deaconesses committed themselves to celibacy, obedience, and the sharing of goods for only a limited time – initially two years – these commitments, which were indefinitely renewable, were nevertheless understood as permanent by the nascent community, whose conception and *forma vitae*, more than others, appeared comparable to those of a "regular" Catholic community.[53] It was precisely

49 See Gustave Lagny, *Le réveil de 1830 à Paris et les origines des diaconesses de Reuilly: Une page d'histoire protestante*, Lyon, Olivétan, 2007, the reedition of a volume published in Paris in 1959 by the Librairie Protestante; Gérit Messie, *Les Diaconesses de Reuilly: Un germe fécond*, Paris, Cerf, 1992; Michel Paret, *Les diaconesses de Reuilly: Entre action médico-sociale et vocation religieuse communautaire, des sœurs protestantes et leurs œuvres, des origines à nos jours*, Ph.D. thesis, EPHE; Sœur Évangéline, "La fondation des Diaconesses de Reuilly, dans son contexte ecclésial et de société," in: Sœur Évangéline, ed., *Protestantisme et vie monastique*, 63–72; and Frédérick Casadesus & Karine S. Bouvatier, *Les Diaconesses de Reuilly à livre ouvert*, Lyon, Olivétan, 2017.

50 See Patrick Cabanel, *Histoire des protestants en France: XVIe–XXIe siècle*, Paris, Fayard, 2012, 954ff.

51 See A. Vermeil to C. Malvesin, Feb 6, 1841, quoted in: Perchenet, *Renouveau communautaire et unité chrétienne*, 275. For the full edition of the correspondence between the two founders of the Reuilly *diakonia*, see Caroline Malvesin & Antoine Vermeil, *Correspondance 1841: La fondation de la communauté des Diaconesses de Reuilly*, Lyon, Olivétan, 2007.

52 See C. Malvesin to A. Vermeil, Feb 10, 1841, quoted in: Perchenet, *Renouveau communautaire et unité chrétienne*, 277.

53 See Perchenet, *Renouveau communautaire et unité chrétienne*, 279, and Biot, *Communautés protestantes*, 125.

because of this resemblance to the "*corporations monastiques*" abolished by the Reformation that the new community's early years were far from easy, despite its initiation of numerous projects and rapid growth.[54]

In the context of the stark divisions between liberals and orthodox within the French Protestant minority, the new *diakonia* community immediately became the object of numerous attacks, both from the evangelical side and, above all, on the part of various exponents of liberal Protestantism who did not fail to reproach the "papist" deviations of the new community.[55] These attacks did not cease or slow down the development of the Reuilly community, but they nevertheless induced the two founders to reformulate the statutes of the new community, highlighting its social and welfare commitment, weakening its community spirit. Above all they contributed to spreading a current of strong distrust in Protestant circles towards this first form of consecrated community life reborn in French-speaking Protestantism. It was a distrust that would begin to ease up only in the mid-20th century, at the same time as progress in the ecumenical field, allowing the deaconesses to begin to redefine their project of community in the name of a return to their founders' most original inspiration.[56]

4 The Finkenwalde Experience and the New Search for a "Life in Common"

In the 1930s, an experience that was rather brief but theologically more significant for the further development of reflection on the question of community in the churches of the Reformation was undoubtedly that of the pastoral seminary of Finkenwalde in Pomerania directed by Dietrich Bonhoeffer from 1935 to 1937.[57]

Following the synods of Barmen and Dahlem in 1934, in order to ensure the formation of its ministers, the Confessing Church established five "preaching seminaries" together with the constitution of "fraternal councils" (*Predigerseminar*) for internal organization and the adoption of an ecclesiastical "emergency" law (*Notrecht*).[58] Starting in 1935, these seminaries allowed candidates for pastoral ministry to bypass the official training sites of the state church, which had become heavily polluted with the German Christians and the spirit of the regime. These "illegal" centers offered courses of a few months that candidates were required to follow after their academic training. The educational system of pastors in the German Protestant churches, in fact, after several years of university preparation in a theological faculty, provided a more practice-oriented training (preaching, liturgy, catechesis, pastoral care), after which candidates could present themselves for a "second exam," which permitted them access to ordination and the ecclesiastical ministry.

29-year-old Dietrich Bonhoeffer, qualified as a free lecturer, was assigned the supervision of the seminary in Pomerania by the fraternal council of the Union of Old Prussia, removing him from the pastoral ministry that he had undertaken 18 months earlier at a German parish in London. The operation of the seminary initially began in

54 See again Perchenet, *Renouveau communautaire et unité chrétienne*, 282, which specifically notes the two volumes by Catherine Valérie Boissier, wife of Count Agénor de Gasparin, *Des Corporations monastiques au sein du Protestantisme*, Paris, Meyrueis, 1854–1855.

55 See also the biographical entry by André Encrevé, "Vermeil Antoine," DMRFC 5, 486–487.

56 See Sœur Évangéline, "La fondation des Diaconesses de Reuilly."

57 See Wolf-Dieter Zimmermann & Ronald Gregor Smith, eds., *I Knew Dietrich Bonhoeffer*, London, Collins, 1966, 105–161; Paul-André Turcotte, *Réconciliation et libération: Théologie de la communauté chez Dietrich Bonhoeffer*, Montreal, Bellarmin, 1972; Bethge, *Dietrich Bonhoeffer*, 419–586; and Albrecht Schödl, *Unsere Augen sehen nach dir: Dietrich Bonhoeffer im Kontext einer aszetischen Theologie*, Leipzig, Evangelische Verlagsanstalt, 2006.

58 See Bernard Reymond, *Une Église à croix gammée?: Le protestantisme allemand au début du régime nazi (1932–1935)*, Lausanne, L'Âge d'Homme, 1980.

Zingst, near Stralsund, in a holiday home behind the dunes of the Baltic Sea in the spring of 1935. After a few months, a more stable accommodation was found in an isolated manor in Finkenwalde, in the Oder delta, not far from Szczecin.

The material conditions of the nascent institution were very uncertain, and seminarians were often forced – in order to have bread, furniture, and books – to beg from friendly Confessing parishes or even some well-to-do patrons who, at this stage of the *Kirchenkampf*, expressed their concern for the Confessing Church through their generosity. The director – whom the fraternal council had supplemented with a Reformed inspector of studies, Wilhelm Rott – immediately devoted himself to establishing a communal life, sharing his ecclesiastical salary, his well-stocked personal library, and his grand piano with the students. From its very first months, Finkenwalde's seminary, more than any other, effectively became a living community.

In his lectures, Bonhoeffer accorded particular preference to biblical theology with a focus on the Old Testament, which was in no way merely accidental at a time when many German Christians gave it just a cursory reading or even wanted to purge Christianity of it all together.[59] Significantly, in a time marked by the risk of compromising the faith and by the struggle to defend it, he also focused on a study of the confessional writings of the Reformation. Practical theology (homiletics, catechesis, and pastoral care) was clearly also part of the program of the formation of candidates for pastoral ministry.[60] This field was the area in which Bonhoeffer did not fail to emphasize the scandalous and provocative character of the Christian proclamation, strenuously defended in the context of a persecuted church, but not for that reason sealed up in a defensive or victimized attitude. Closely connected to this approach, therefore, was also an ongoing spirituality, which was to find particular expression in his lectures on "grace at a cost," which then became *Nachfolge* (*Discipleship*), published in 1937.[61] Above all, this teaching on the obedience demanded of a disciple of Jesus would radically differentiate Finkenwalde's *Predigerseminar* from the other German seminaries and was certainly the fundamental crucible from which the new institution's entire life emanated.[62] In these courses, Bonhoeffer fought against a slack interpretation of the faith, or "cheap grace," that did not bind the believer by any obligation and which was poisoning the Protestant churches. On the contrary, he argued, against the *koine* then in vogue in the gentrified church, that believing meant paying a price. For a disciple of Christ, grace is a "costly grace" that can only be experienced and transmitted through living it in an effective, and often even demanding, discipleship. "*Only the believers obey, and only the obedient believe* … He who does not obey cannot believe."[63] This message – as explosive as the tones that characterized all his lectures dedicated to the exegesis of the synoptic passages on discipleship and then to a profounder enquiry into some ecclesiological themes – deeply impressed his listeners. Many of them, in the face of what they perceived as an unhinging of their own theological system of reference, attempted to respond personally to the urgent questions posed to their church by that particular moment in history.

59 From the Finkenwalde period come his lectures on King David and on the reconstruction of Jerusalem in Ezra and Nehemiah, in: *DBWE* 14, 868–893, 917–930, and on prayer and the interpretation of the Psalms, in: Dietrich Bonhoeffer, *Gemeinsames Leben*, Munich, Kaiser, 1939; ET: *DBWE* 5, 155–181. See Fulvio Ferrario, *Bonhoeffer*, Rome, Carocci, 2006, 112–116.

60 His course lectures come to us through students' notes. See *DBWE* 15, 307–437. See Peter Zimmerling, *Bonhoeffer als praktischer Theologe*, Göttingen, Vandenhoek & Ruprecht, 2006.

61 See *DBWE* 4, and Bethge, *Dietrich Bonhoeffer*, 450–460.

62 See Bethge, *Dietrich Bonhoeffer*, 450. See also Martin Kuske & Ilse Tödt, "Vorwort der Herausgeber," *DBW* 4, 7–18.

63 *DBWE* 4, 63–64 (italics original). See Christiane Tietz, "'Nur der Glaubende ist gehorsam und nur der Gehorsame glaubt': Beobachtungen zu einem existentiellen Zirkel in Dietrich Bonhoeffers 'Nachfolge,'" *DBJ* 2, 2005, 170–181.

Consistent with that foundational course, the life of the seminary led by Bonhoeffer also had a very specific organization. If the, mainly theological but nevertheless spiritual, theme of *Discipleship* had to be developed in a real ecclesial context in order to be lived concretely, it had to be supported by a climate nourished by a truly shared *praxis pietatis*. That is why the director of Finkenwalde wanted to give the communal life of his candidate preachers the vigorous style of a true life community.[64] This approach responded to a thought that had fascinated Bonhoeffer for several years, the idea that the formation of a new generation of theologians should be the responsibility of "church-monastic schools, where the pure doctrine, the Sermon on the Mount, and worship are taken seriously – which for all three of these things is simply not the case," Bonhoeffer noted in a letter to his friend Erwin Sutz in 1934, "at the university and under the present circumstances is impossible."[65] The very future of the church depended on it, he wrote to his brother in January 1935, a few months before taking over the direction of the pastoral seminary; "the restoration of the Church must surely depend on a new kind of monasticism, which has nothing in common with the old but is a life of uncompromising discipleship, following Christ according to the Sermon on the Mount. I believe that the time has come to gather people together and do this."[66]

That framework gave Finkenwalde a densely packed schedule, a regular "rhythm" that in many ways was purposely patterned on a monastic day. In the morning, the Word of God broke the nocturnal silence (which had to be absolute), after which a morning service was celebrated in the chapel, beginning with the prayer of the psalms interspersed with refrains of songs and continuing with the reading of an entire chapter of the Old Testament and a passage from the New as a *lectio continua*. On Saturdays, the director held a brief meditation, on the other days he offered a spontaneous, quite clearly expounded prayer, which ended with the "Our Father," followed by a hymn and the final blessing. At that point, the candidates could have breakfast. Immediately afterwards, however, one of the practices that created the most difficulties was still waiting for them: individual biblical meditation, which lasted half an hour. For the pastor candidates, this time of recollection on scripture verses – which was not to be disturbed in any way – aroused several queries and reservations: uncertainty about the actual content of the meditation, difficulty in concentration, stray thoughts. Lectures followed this period of total silence and, before lunch, a half hour of singing. During meals in the refectory there was often a reading, which could also be taken from secular works. The afternoon was instead mainly dedicated to personal study. A time for conversation and music followed dinner; then, at 10 p.m., the entire community again gathered for night prayer, which lasted about three-quarters of an hour.

In order to maintain this rhythm and to help the students, who arrived at the seminary every six months, enter into the "style" of the house, at the conclusion to the first course (at the end of the summer of 1935) Bonhoeffer offered some candidates the opportunity of staying in Finkenwalde to establish a stable community with him. The council of the Confessing Church responded to the request by granting six brothers. This "practical, lived, and experienced fraternity," which represented something entirely unique in the context of Protestantism, was intended to support the ministry of preaching in the face of the isolation from which it suffered, aspiring to provide a concrete answer to the question of the essence of Christian life and obedience. Last but not least, it

64 Like his teaching on discipleship, the setting of shared communal life in the seminary – as well as the use of the auricular confession that Bonhoeffer asked to be practiced in Finkenwalde – gave rise to numerous criticisms and rumors. See G. Krause to D. Bonhoeffer, Feb 18, 1939 in: DBWE 15, 148–151, here 152. See also Bethge, *Dietrich Bonhoeffer*, 462–466.

65 D. Bonhoeffer to E. Sutz, Sep 11, 1934, in: DBWE 13, 216–218, here 217.

66 D. Bonhoeffer to K.-F. Bonhoeffer, Jan 14, 1935, in: DBWE 13, 284–285, here 285.

sought to offer a "spiritual refuge" in view of the worldly commitments that the new ministers were called to, especially during the storms of the *Kirchenkampf*.[67] The brothers of this *Bruderhaus* who gathered to endow the seminary life with an inner continuity were certainly not bound by "vows," however, they submitted to the discipline of prayer, assumed teaching assignments (within and outside the house), shared their financial resources, and committed themselves temporarily to celibacy.

This organization of communal life and the extensive time Finkenwalde devoted to prayer and personal meditation on Scripture were clearly not well accepted in all Protestant theological circles. Karl Barth, for example, after reading a text on the seminary's practices, wrote to Bonhoeffer that he could not "really say that [he] was pleased by what [he] read." In particular, he could not share "the kind of fundamental distinction between theological work, on the one hand, and edifying reflection, on the other."[68] Moreover, while he openly mistrusted the monastic tendencies that he saw in the *Bruderhaus*, the arrangement of the seminary's daily life aroused a suspicion of legalism in him. Bonhoeffer, for his part, defended the approach, referring even to Barth's own research (the latter had been expelled from Germany and was now a refugee in Basel). For *Bruder* Dietrich, theological work could, in fact, emerge

> only from within a life defined by morning and evening reflection on the word and by fixed times of prayer ... The reproach that it is somehow legal does not really concern me. What is legalistic if a Christian should learn what it means to pray and spend a good amount of his time learning to do so?[69]

The director of the seminary recognized the value of objectivity in his experiment. His indications were extremely practical and detailed, sometimes formulated in a very peremptory tone, in order, above all, to guard against prayer or meditation conditioned by moods or merely introspective needs. For Bonhoeffer, "the goal is not monastic isolation but rather the most intensive concentration for ministry to the world" in the light of inspiration offered by "a deaconesses' mother house."[70] To form the future pastors, he intended to offer them "not only theological working groups and occasional worship communities but also a more fixed, ordered, and regulated life in community."[71] In this way, as Christians, they would learn to unite prayer, doctrine, and discipleship in order to concretely live in obedience to the radical commandment of Christ. The preaching seminary thus constituted a "training ground" in preparation for work since "Christians, too, belong not in the seclusion of a cloistered life but in the midst of enemies"[72] even if, at the same time, Christian life is, in its essence, monastic, in that it is a response to the call of obedience to Christ in the cloister, which is "nothing else but world."[73]

It was out of Finkenwalde's fragmentary experience that the short work *Gemeinsames Leben* (*Life Together*) was born, written with the intention of putting into writing the contribution of the precarious foundation to the task – which Bonhoeffer considered truly ecclesial – of Christian community life.[74] The book – published in 1939, two years after the forced closure of the seminary and the interruption of Bonhoeffer's project of fraternity – was an immediate and lasting success even during the war years. Its author, on the basis of what he had learned, warned above all

67 See Dietrich Bonhoeffer, "To the Council of the Evangelical Church of the Old Prussian Union, Finkenwalde/Stettin, Sep 6, 1935 re: Establishment of a House of Brethren in the Finkenwalde Preacher's Seminary," *DBWE* 14, 95–99.

68 K. Barth to D. Bonhoeffer, Oct 14, 1936, *DBWE* 14, 268.

69 D. Bonhoeffer to K. Barth, Sep 19, 1936, *DBWE* 14, 254.

70 See Dietrich Bonhoeffer, "To the Council of the Evangelical Church," *DBWE* 14, 96–97.

71 *DBWE* 14, 95.

72 *DBWE* 5, 27.

73 *DBWE* 4, 48. On Bonhoeffer's relationship to monasticism, see Laurent Schlumberger, "Dietrich Bonhoeffer et le monachisme," *ETR* 57, 1983, 465–490.

74 See *DBWE* 5, 25–140.

theologically of the dangers of the communitarian ideal, distinguishing in particular a "psychic" love, of affinities between persons, and an authentically "spiritual" one, created and recreated daily by the Holy Spirit and mediated by Christ, the only one who allows a true distance between the brothers to be established. "Christ stands between me and others."[75] For Bonhoeffer, this affirmation should be the foundation of every Christian community life, making it a reality, not a mere flight of fancy; it is always given by God. This idea permeated all of Bonhoeffer's short text, even the more practical indications regarding times of solitude and sharing, service, the confession of sins, and the sacrament of the altar.

That the common life developed in Finkenwalde was not an escape from the world or one's responsibilities can be seen from the fact that, throughout the years when the seminary existed, Bonhoeffer never ceased to commit himself to the two fronts of ecumenical work and *Kirchenkampf* within the Confessing Church. At times, the radicality and audacity of his positions did not fail to frighten some of his students.[76] Various activities of preaching and teaching beyond the community also emanated from the seminary, which thus served as a spiritual center for the Confessing Church in Pomerania. Additionally, the director's desire to combine the realization of a Christian community based on the Sermon on the Mount with a strong ecumenical character and his opening the seminary's outreach in that direction was evident in his plans to visit the Church of Sweden with the candidates. Initially planned for the summer of 1935, the trip finally took place in March of the following year and earned Bonhoeffer a ban on his academic teaching by the Reich's national ministry of education.[77]

A considerable ecumenical influence was also fundamental in the seminary's "monastic" approach and the establishment of the fraternal house. Although some evangelical fraternities of pastors had begun to form after World War I in the spheres of the Berneuchen movement (Sydower Bruderschaft, Evangelische Michaelsbruderschaft),[78] as well as under the authority of the fraternal councils of the Confessing Church, Bonhoeffer did not draw much inspiration from them in establishing his community. While they showed that monastic attempts were admissible in the Lutheran Church, those experiences did not actually establish a true *vita communis* among their members. Instead, it was mainly all the visits Bonhoeffer made in March 1935 to the English communities that impassioned him to this *forma vitae* shaped by the practice of silence, the centrality of a rhythm to the day, and the regularity of common prayer, which convinced him of the fruitfulness of community life and its possible impact on the church as a whole. Significantly, it was during the same period that Bonhoeffer also contemplated going to India for a firsthand view of the community life and passive resistance practiced in the ashrams that had grown up around Gandhi.[79]

As a result, the experiment of Finkenwalde had a clear, significant ecumenical value in that it contributed, thanks to the rapid spread of *Life Together*, to the progressive recovery in Protestantism of a different understanding of monastic practices and community life. What emerged with it was therefore a new ecclesial conception. Following the struggles of the *Kirchenkampf*, in the wake of Finkenwalde's theologian and parallel to Barth's theology of revelation, it became possible to see "Christ existing as community" in the church.[80] The ecumenical scope of Bonhoeffer's community

75 DBWE 5, 43.
76 Eberhard Bethge, *Leggere Bonhoeffer*, Brescia, Queriniana, 2006, 73–84. On the Finkenwalde director's commitments to ecumenism and ecclesial politics, see 489–615.
77 See Bethge, *Dietrich Bonhoeffer*, 506–517.
78 See Halkenhäuser, *Kirche und Kommunität*, 182–209.
79 See Bethge, *Dietrich Bonhoeffer*, 406–409.
80 See DBWE 1. See also, Henry Mottu, *Dietrich Bonhoeffer*, Paris, Cerf, 2002, 63–86.

experiment thus acquired an ecclesiological dimension and a clear ecclesial relevance.

Through the testimonial presented in *Life Together*, Finkenwalde exerted a considerable influence on the formation of cenobitic communities that would soon emerge in different Protestant ecclesial circles.[81] Above all, it validated the choice of their founders for a radical, concrete obedience to Christ to be pursued in the sharing of a faith lived in common and in the search for a unified existence in and for Christ, without being shut off from the world. The German community of Imshausen, in particular, recognized "the importance of what Dietrich Bonhoeffer's service has given us in carrying out these reflections on the experience and life of Finkenwalde."[82]

5 The War as a Turning Point and the Cenobitic Renaissance in French-Speaking Protestantism

5.1 *Ferment of Renewal in French-Speaking Protestantism between the Two World Wars*

The theme and need of an entire generation, before the forced interruption of the experience at Finkenwalde and – in a completely independent way – the search to recover a communitarian perspective was also seen in the French-speaking context in reaction to the excessive individualism conveyed by the tendencies of hegemonic liberal Protestantism in the universities and Reformed churches of the 19th century. Even before the mid-1930s and the affirmation of a true *réseau barthien*, in Paris, Geneva, and Lausanne, the pillars of theological liberalism began to be increasingly questioned by a new generation of students and young pastors disappointed by the weakness of the message of their churches. Faced with a triumphant Nazi Germany, these churches appeared to them incomprehensibly timid and locked within the re-proposal of a theology of experience and moral conscience or of a social Christianity that did not pay enough attention to reflecting on the foundations of the faith.[83]

These departures from the optimism of the first postwar period and the urgency of a *redressement* towards a less atomistic conception of the church mainly took the form of a renewed concern for doctrinal firmness. It was primarily a neo-Calvinism that recognized and interpreted the spread need for theological renewal under the banner of a return to the Bible and the great traditional dogmas. In France and French-speaking Switzerland in the 1930s, this preceded and contributed to the reception of Barthian ideas by a young Protestant generation that sought, in the pastor from Basel, more of a prophet of the *Kirchenkampf* than a dialectical theologian. Promoted by Auguste Lecerf in Paris and by Jean de Saussure in Geneva, this movement of theological renewal, together with the Barthianism to which it was joined by the fundamental interest in a reaffirmation of the transcendence of the Word of God and Christian truths, was not without immediate repercussions in the ecclesiological realm – which saw a growing desire both for a more communal restructuring of the church and a new attention to sacramental themes – and for a spiritual and liturgical life.[84]

81 See Halkenhäuser, *Kirche und Kommunität*, 197, 203–204, and Minke de Vries, *Verso una gratuità feconda: L'avventura ecumenica di Grandchamp*, Milan, Paoline, 2008, 20–21.

82 See H. Eisenberg to A. Schönherr, Mar 9, 1986, cited in: "Postfazione dei curatori," in: Dietrich Bonhoeffer, *Vita comune: Il libro di preghiera della Bibbia*, ed. Gerhard Ludwig Müller & Albrecht Schönherr, trans. Maria Cristina Laurenzi, Brescia, Queriniana, 2001, 123–164, here 133.

83 In this sense, see in particular Bernard Reymond, *Théologien ou prophète, les francophones et Karl Barth avant 1945*, Lausanne, L'Âge d'Homme, 1985.

84 See Reymond, *Théologien ou prophète*, and Alain Probst, "Qu'est-ce que le néo-calvinisme?," *Revue Réformée* 134/2, 1983, 67–76. On the Genevan pastor Jean de Sassure, see Olivier Fatio, "Les sermons de guerre du pasteur de Saussure," in: Michel Porret, Jean-François Fayet & Carine Fluckinger, eds., *Guerres et paix: Mélanges offerts à Jean-Claude Favez*, Geneva, Georg, 2000, 591–613, and Silvia Scatena, *Taizé, una*

In this latter field, the reaction to the combined effects of religious Pietism and theological liberalism was mainly seen in French-speaking Switzerland, where a significant effort was made towards realizing a liturgical renewal that would respond to the concern for endowing spiritual life and preaching with a more solid biblical and dogmatic structure than that conveyed by an often misunderstood theology of experience or by the practical concerns of social Christianity.[85] This perspective guided the research of a group of pastors, Église et Liturgie, which gathered around Richard Paquier from the beginning of the 1930s. Paquier had begun to hypothesize the recovery of an overlooked social and communitarian dimension of worship and piety, a recovery with an ecumenical orientation, starting from a notion of "evangelical catholicity" that could be rediscovered through doctrinal and liturgical research into the first four centuries of the church, both Eastern and Western.[86] Concomitant with the development of a *Nouvelle liturgie* proposed to the church of Vaud in 1938, the commitment of this group of French-speaking Swiss pastors concentrated mainly on developing an *Office divin de l'Église universelle*, which was widely tested before being printed in 1943. For daily prayer, it drew from the Huguenot Psalter, the Roman breviary, the *Book of Common Prayer*, and the Eastern Church Office. Basically, it aimed at rediscovering, beyond reformed practice, the prayer of the ancient church while offering an answer to those who felt the need for a more objective and disciplined prayer.[87]

Moving within a completely different framework, the Parisian pastor Wilfred Monod, of Methodist origins, sought to concretize the widespread and unfulfilled aspirations for a more structured spiritual life that was attentive to the community dimension of the Christian faith. Active more or less during the same years and within the more general *mouvance œcuménique* that characterized the entire movement of renewal underway in Protestantism in the 1920s and 1930s, Monod was the original proponent of a social Christianity that was attentive to the new demands of spirituality and of personal and communal piety.[88] A professor of practical theology at the Protestant faculty in Paris, a brilliant preacher at the Oratory of the Louvre, and a prominent leader in the Life and Work ecumenical movement, Monod founded the Fraternité spirituelle des Veilleurs, a Protestant "third order," which he understood, in his own words, not in a "technical" sense, as in Catholic terminology, but as a reminder of an idea that had already been realized by St. Francis in the forms accessible to and permitted to him. In other words, it was a spiritual fraternity that truly represented the closest model of a recovery – on the part of French-speaking Protestantism – of the value of a "rule," a spiritual discipline within the framework of a community that was aimed at a "veritable catholicité," which was to be incessantly prayed for.[89]

parabola di unità: Storia della comunità dalle origini al concilio dei giovani, Bologna, Il Mulino, 2018, 15–16 and throughout. See also the article by Max Thurian, "Les grandes orientations actuelles de la spiritualité protestante," *Irén* 22, 1949, 368–394.

85 See André Bardet, *Un combat pour l'Église: Un siècle de mouvement liturgique en Pays de Vaud*, Lausanne, Bibliothèque Historique Vaudoise, 1988, 83ff. See also Irénée-H. Dalmais, "Le renouveau liturgique dans le protestantisme d'expression française," *La Maison Dieu* 19/3, 1949, 48–54.

86 The notion of "evangelical catholicity" was dear to Paquier, who, in turn, was influenced by Nathan Söderblom's ecumenical ideal drawn from the works of the Lutheran theologian Friedrich Heiler; see Friedrich Heiler, *Evangelische Katholizität, Gesammelte Aufsätze und Vorträge*, Munich, Reinhardt, 1926, on which, in particular, see Hans Hartog, *Evangelische Katholizität: Weg und Vision Friedrich Heilers*, Mainz, Matthias-Grünewald-Verlag, 1995, 219–236.

87 See "Église et Liturgie," in: Richard Paquier, *L'Office divin de l'Église universelle: Services du matin, de midi et du soir pour chaque jour de la semaine*, Geneva, Labor, 1943.

88 In particular, see Laurent Gagnebin, *Christianisme spirituel et christianisme social: La Prédication de Wilfred Monod (1894–1940)*, Geneva, Labor et Fides, 1987.

89 See Wilfred Monod, *Après la journée: Souvenirs et visions (1867–1937)*, Paris, Grasset, 1938, 323–342, and Wilfred Monod, *Dix années des Veilleurs ("Tiers-Ordre"*

The "third order" of the Veilleurs was established in 1923 in response to the need felt during World War I of "collaborating in the reconstruction of Europe" through a new community experience capable of sustaining a demanding spiritual life that fit the urgencies of the moment. Far from that often individualistic and disembodied piety that Monod so strongly reproached his own church for embracing, the order was comprised of Protestants of different denominations. They were Christians who did not live together but who were united by a fidelity to the shared commitment of a daily reading of the Beatitudes, by the desire to draw freely in prayer and liturgy from the "undivided treasure of Christianity," and by the preaching of a gospel that was both social and spiritual, "the only thing capable of avoiding the horrible specter of another world catastrophe."[90] The founder of the Veilleurs – which at the beginning of the 1930s already had more than 400 members in France and French-speaking Switzerland – did not limit himself to recovering the model of the "third order" by trying to adapt it to the gospel principles in a Reformed context. In an article in 1933 dedicated to the first years of the new spiritual fraternity, Monod also expressed hope for the creation, "in the future, of blessed houses in which young disciples of Christ could reside, unmarried men united in the holy struggles of the soul and the control of the body while pursuing their studies or business, and without a commitment to celibacy."[91] In his dream of establishing this sort of evangelical *phalanstère*, Monod also foresaw the possibility that, in the future, Christians might effectively find union through "intercessory prayer, study, and contemplation in a retreat house like the Port-Royal 'Solitaires' (Pascal remained a lay man)."[92]

5.2 *The Community of Pomeyrol*

Monod's concern for a renewal of piety and the recovery of a community perspective played an important role in the birth of the first "regular communities" in the Reformation area, all variously marked by the spirituality of the "third order" of the Veilleurs, to which belonged the initiators of the first two actual experiences of women's community life that arose in French-speaking Protestantism, in that melting pot of community vocations that was created during the war.

The first center in this search for community was born under the double inspiration of the Veilleurs and the Scout Movement; it was the resident women's group of Antoinette Butte established in Pomeyrol (Saint-Étienne-du-Grès), in Provence, during the first winter of the war. It was a small communal cell whose constitution was in line with the experience of retreats and hospitality that Butte had already started in Saint-Germain-en-Laye, in the region of Paris at the end of 1929.[93] It was a new experience, deeply linked to its foundress's personality and history. Born in Lorraine to a Catholic father and a Lutheran mother, baptized Lutheran and confirmed Calvinist, she soon became one of the main promoters of Protestantism's Scout Movement, the foundress and assistant national commissioner of the Éclaireuses unionistes. In 1923, at the age of 25, with her law studies, the start of a doctorate, and the beginning of the practice as a lawyer in Nancy already behind her, during a period of prolonged illness and forced inactivity, she had come to know

protestant) *20 Avril 1923–20 Avril 1933*, Alençon, Imprimerie Corbière et Jugain, 1933.

90 See Monod, *Dix années des Veilleurs* and Wilfred Monod, *Les Veilleurs* (*"Tiers-ordre" protestant*), in: DT, Jan 1, 1928, 15 pages of typed manuscript. This was a reprise of an article that appeared in the *Revue du christianisme social* 2/2, 1924, 124–154.

91 See Monod, *Dix années des Veilleurs*.

92 Monod, *Dix années des Veilleurs*.

93 On the community at Pomeyrol see, in particular, Biot, *Communautés protestantes*, 152–155; Perchenet, *Renouveau communautaire et unité chrétienne*, 352–362; Communauté de Pomeyrol, "Historique," *Foi et Vie* 76/6, 1977, 74–78; Michel Clément, *Un monachisme protestant? Spiritualités et règles de trois communautés protestantes en France: Reuilly, Pomeyrol, Villeméjane*, Paris, Ulmus Americana Editiones, 2012.

of the new spiritual fraternity of the Veilleurs and had entered the third order founded by Monod, whose influence was essential in her decision to undertake a venture of offering hospitality in a small retreat house in Saint-Germain-en-Laye on premises owned by the association of French pastors that were open to offering a place to those in search of solitude and silence.[94] Leaving her job in Nancy and her responsibilities in scouting, Butte immediately devoted herself full time to this new experience, to which she gave particular expression in her work *L'incarnation, la Sainte-Cène, l'Église*,[95] the outcome of her early spiritual and communitarian research that, from its outset, was spontaneously oriented towards ecumenism and which became increasingly characterized by a new approach to the sacraments.[96]

Despite its modest beginnings, the community that had begun in Saint-Germain-en-Laye in November 1929 gradually met with considerable interest, especially among students and the scouting ranks, so much so that, in 1937, the Nîmes committee of the Association des pasteurs de France, which had received the gift of a property in Pomeyrol, in the Bouches-du-Rhône department, asked to open there a second house of welcome and retreat. From the winter of 1939/1940, after the beginning of the war and the requisitioning of the Saint-Germain-en-Laye premises, it would, in fact, become the site of the first true attempt at a shared life for Butte and the two collaborators who joined her in Provence. In the context of the war and in a very precarious situation, this attempt immediately took on a twofold direction. On the one hand, it sought a rhythm and a form of common prayer that essentially drew upon the liturgy of the ERF, while also integrating prayers of other Christian traditions (Lutheran, Catholic, Orthodox, and Anglican), as well as elements from various contemporary experiences: the WCSF; the Veilleurs, from which a daily recitation of the "Beatitudes" at noon was taken; the Moravian Brothers; and the Quakers and the Moral Re-Armament, from which the practice of silent recollection followed by sharing was borrowed. On the other hand, it saw the deployment of an intense activity of extending hospitality to refugees and fugitives besides the many people and groups who chose Pomeyrol as a place of retreat, reunion, and meeting: students, catechumens, pastors. Before the property was requisitioned by German troops in February 1944 – the three residents, nevertheless, continuing their shared life in a nearby house – the small community cell in Pomeyrol hosted over 40 encounters.

After the Liberation, the Pomeyrol property was requisitioned again and used as a center to house Arabs awaiting repatriation before it was returned to the Association des pasteurs de France in 1947. Immediately after the war, therefore, the small nuclear community was temporarily installed in some barracks that had been abandoned by the Wehrmacht and continued both its intense labor of offering hospitality and its search for a form of fraternal and communal existence. It was a *forma vitae* that, while deliberately renouncing formalized rules, became, on the other hand, more and more structured and marked by the rhythm of common prayer – in 1950, Butte published a *Liturgie quotidienne*, the fruit of her almost 20 years of experience[97] – as well as consciously occupied with an intrinsic need for definitiveness. In November 1951, this led the first resident nucleus of Pomeyrol to the decision to take the first step of consecration, committing themselves to a lifelong poverty, celibacy, and mutual submission with a triple vow that Butte presented biblically as "a sacrifice inspired by grace … a voluntary religious commitment, a solemn promise received by God," which did not represent access to any state of perfection, but was rather a reactualization of

94 See Pierre Bolle's entry on "Butte, Antoinette," in: *Les protestants*, 110.

95 See Antoinette Butte, *L'incarnation, la Sainte-Cène, l'Église*, Lausanne, Payot & Cie, 1936.

96 See the 1981 letter from pastor Roger Chapal included in: Antoinette Butte, *Semences: méditations, lettres, témoignages*, Saint-Étienne-du-Grès, Oberlin, 1989, 36–39.

97 See Butte, *Semences*, 179.

baptismal consecration.[98] In September 1955, this same step from the consecration would therefore also be taken by a fourth sister, in the presence, and with the imposition of hands, of the regional president of the ERF, a sign that the new community was officially recognized by Southern French Protestantism, something by no means taken for granted.[99]

5.3 *The Grandchamp and Taizé Communities*

The decision to assume a lifelong commitment by the first three sisters of Pomeyrol preceded, by one year, a similar step by the first seven sisters of another new women's community formed in the small Swiss village of Grandchamp near Neuchâtel, also during the first year of the war.[100]

The two communities had very different formational contexts. Pomeyrol's location in the Cévenole region, close to the "sanctuary" of Huguenot memory that is the Cévennes, was very different from that of Grandchamp in the canton of Neuchâtel, whose church and theological faculty were more marked than others by Barth's theology, the ecumenical movement, and the various ferments of biblical, liturgical, and ecclesiological renewal that converged to offer a favorable framework for a communitarian rebirth.[101] The establishment of these two first regular women's communities in the Reformed territory was, nevertheless, characterized by a great spiritual affinity, both being born in the wake of the experience of the Veilleurs. In fact, Monod's Protestant third order included the unmarried nurse Marguerite de Beaumont, who was the first to settle in Grandchamp in 1936, in the house where a small group of women from French-speaking Switzerland had been holding retreats for five years. Beginning in April 1940, she inspired, in fact, a first attempt at community life with Marguerite Bossert and Irène Burnat, together with the spiritual animator of the group of women responsible for the retreats, the Parisian widow Geneviève Micheli, who in 1944 would be asked by the nascent community to become its "mother."[102]

Geneviève Micheli came from a French Protestant upper middle-class family and was a woman with a strong spiritual character. She was Monod's parishioner at the Oratory of the Louvre in the 1930s before leaving for Switzerland and starting a solitary life in a chalet in the Upper Engadine. Micheli was also familiar with the community of the Saint-Germain-en-Laye retreat house, where in 1939 she would have accompanied on a visit Marguerite de Beaumont, with

98 See the text "Les vœux" included in the special issue of *Foi et Vie* dedicated entirely to the Pomeyrol Community, 76/6, 1977, 27–30, and, in the same issue, "Quelques points de la vocation de Pomeyrol," 32–66, which, in many ways, has the weight of a "rule" for the community.

99 See Communauté de Pomeyrol, "Historique."

100 On the Grandchamp Community, see de Vries, *Verso una gratuità feconda*, and the introduction to the English edition of that work by its editor and translator Nancy S. Gower, "The Roots and Early History of the Community of Grandchamp," in: Minke de Vries, *The Fruits of Grace: The Ecumenical Experience of the Community of Grandchamp*, Eugene, Pickwick, 2017, 1–33. See also Fabien Gaulué, "Vers un 'monastère réel de l'unité chrétienne': Taizé et Grandchamp," in: *L'œcuménisme spirituel de Paul Couturier aux défis actuels: Actes du colloque universitaire et interconfessionnel, Lyon et Francheville, Rhône, France, les 8, 9, 10 novembre 2002*, Lyon, Profac, 2003, 130–156.

101 See Matthias Wirz, "Neuchâtel et le renouveau monastique au XXᵉ siècle (Grandchamp, Taizé, Bose)," in: *Cinq siècles d'histoire religieuse neuchâteloise: Approches d'une tradition protestante: Actes du colloque de Neuchâtel (22–24 avril 2004)*, Neuchâtel, Université de Neuchâtel, 2009, 387–402, and Gottfried Hamman & Roselyne Righetti, "La Faculté de Théologie," in: *Histoire de l'Université de Neuchâtel*, vol. 3, *L'Université, de sa fondation en 1909 au début des années soixante*, Neuchâtel, Gilles Attinger, 2002, 577–618.

102 On the birth of the community, see, in particular, the testimonial of Marguerite de Beaumont herself, *Du Grain à l'Épi: Recueil de souvenirs*, Le Mont sur Lausanne, Éditions Ouverture, 1995. For a general portrait of Geneviève Micheli, see "Témoignage de Jean-Louis Leuba," in: *Une vocation de femme: Geneviève Micheli*, Areuse-Le Mont-sur-Lausanne, Communauté de Grandchamp, 1996, 17–43.

whom she had had a great spiritual intimacy since the late 1920s. During that stay in Paris, as well as introducing Marguerite de Beaumont to Antoinette Butte – who was then about to leave for Pomeyrol where she would soon invite the first two residents of the nascent Swiss community to join her for a month-long formation in community life[103] – Geneviève Micheli also accompanied de Beaumont to Monod – who had already participated in a retreat at Grandchamp the year before[104] – as well as to the Benedictines of the Monastery of Sainte-Françoise-Romaine. The latter were a community that had, very early on, a remarkable ecumenical openness and whose prioress, Marie-Elisabeth de Wavrechin, had been in contact with Micheli.[105] Seeing more and more clearly that the establishment of a small community consecrated to biblically-centered prayer and spiritual accompaniment was an important contribution "in working toward the rebuilding of the world" and the anticipatory sign of a "dawn of a new era," Micheli clearly wanted to encourage the vocation of the "guardian" of Grandchamp to a life of silence and praise in a community setting.[106] In February 1940, this vocation was therefore enriched ecumenically by a decisive encounter in Lyon with Abbé Paul Couturier, to whom de Beaumont had been directed by pastor Jean de Saussure, the instructor of generations of young catechumens and a successful lecturer in Geneva, Lausanne, and Neuchâtel, as well as, as mentioned above, one of the leaders of the movement of theological and spiritual renewal in French-speaking Switzerland.[107] It was an encounter of stories and vocations that mutually confirmed each other: the father of Lyon's spiritual ecumenism saw in this mature woman with a contemplative spirit the cornerstone of the first, longed-for Protestant cell of his invisible monastery, and Marguerite de Beaumont, in turn, found in him a fundamental source of inspiration.[108]

Just a few months later, the meeting between Marguerite de Beaumont and the young Lausanne theology student Roger Schutz would have been equally decisive for the inauguration of the shared life of Grandchamp's first resident nucleus. Schutz, too, was in fact at the beginning of a complex search for community, motivated as much by an aspiration to a profound spiritual experience in a framework of lived fraternity as by the assumption of responsibility in the face of the challenges of contemporary humanity.

Schutz was the son of a pastor of the Église nationale of Vaud and a theology student at the faculty of the Free Church of Lausanne. After the difficult years of an adolescence weakened by pulmonary tuberculosis, for the young Schutz, the awareness of the potential for renewal and irradiance that a community could have was clearly combined, from the very outset, with the desire to concretely realize – with the "parable" of an evangelical community life – the yearning for peace and unity that flowed from the wounds of the 20th century. It was a yearning for unity that was therefore also articulated in an immediately ecumenical sense, also due to his family history, knowledge of the Veilleurs' experience, and his attendance of the WCSF environment, whose leadership would, in large part, be taken over by the WCC then in the process of formation. For the young man from Lausanne, the search for a *via communionis* that

103 See Perchenet, *Renouveau communautaire et unité chrétienne*, 354.

104 See the excerpts of a letter Monod wrote from Grandchamp to his wife in 1938, quoted in an address given by Sœur Linke, "Petite histoire croisée de Grandchamp, de Pomeyrol, des Abeillères et des Veilleurs," available at <www.protestants.org/page/924133-communautes> (accessed Sep 27, 2022).

105 See "Témoignage de Dom Philibert, Père Abbé du Bec Hellouin," in: *Une vocation de femme*, 75–83.

106 See G. Micheli to M. de Beaumont, Dec 25, 1939 and Apr 23, 1940, in: AG.

107 See G. Micheli to M. de Beaumont, Feb 28, 1940, in: AG.

108 See P. Couturier to J. de Saussure, Dec 26, 1939, in: Papers of Jean de Saussure, private documentation, Geneva; and P. Couturier to M. de Beaumont, Apr 3, 1940, in: AG; Minke de Vries, "L'accompagnement spirituel de l'abbé Couturier et la Communauté de Grandchamp," in: *L'œcuménisme spirituel*, 119–130.

was also visible among divided Christians would soon appear to be nothing more than an essential condition for the fulfillment of a gospel irreconcilable with any form of separation.[109]

For Schutz, too, as for Marguerite de Beaumont, the meeting with Abbé Couturier was in any case fundamental for pinning on ecumenism a community project that had not yet engaged in specific reflection on the issue of unity. The meeting between the Lyonese priest and the Swiss theology student took place shortly before Christmas 1940,[110] a few months after the latter arrived in the small Burgundian village of Taizé, a few kilometers from the remains of Cluny Abbey and just south of the demarcation line, which, until the complete occupation of France in November 1942, separated the area under direct German military occupation from the central-southern area under the control of the Vichy government. In search of a house for meetings and retreats for the small *confrérie* of Protestant students who had banded together, in April 1940, following his sharing of his first community projects with a few companions – it was a sort of third order whose members, although separated from one another, were committed to the model of the "Solitaires" of Port-Royal, namely, to a shared intellectual project and to following certain norms of spiritual discipline[111] – Schutz's choice of a place beyond the border of Swiss neutrality was clearly a response to a pressing need: to seek a center of gravity for his own spiritual search and his own commitment to community in a region that was clearly located within a set of non-random, geographical-spiritual coordinates and which, above all, was traversed by an enormous and constant flow of refugees.[112]

An inner concentration on, and close confrontation with, the reality and misery of war through frequently offering hospitality to refugees thus formed the fundamental forge in which some of the essential spiritual concerns of the young founder of the *clunisien* community project took shape. It was a project in which the student from Lausanne found precious collaborators in both de Beaumont and Couturier. He shared with de Beaumont his own spiritual resolutions as well as the prospects and difficulties of a community experiment that had to deal with the lack of a tradition in the Protestant world to draw on, a concern that weighed all the more heavily on those who wanted to "remain in favor of the Reformation."[113] It was with Couturier in particular that Schutz shared the first organic expression of his project: the *Notes explicatives* of the Communauté de Cluny, printed in Lyon in the autumn of 1941.[114] This was a foundational text in many ways, disseminated in Lyon by Couturier and in Geneva by Jean de Saussure and Suzanne de Dietrich, secretary of WCSF for ecumenical relations and a key figure in the biblical renewal of the last century. This first brochure undoubtedly helped to broaden the circle of those in Geneva who looked with attention and sympathy on the new Protestant community movement, but above all, it was the instrument of the meeting between Schutz and the first two young university students, the Genevans Max Thurian and Pierre Souvairan, who were willing to follow him to Taizé to form the resident nucleus around which the larger "Grande Communauté" would be formed.[115]

109 In particular, see the first chapter of Scatena, *Taizé*, 1–110 and 828–830.

110 See Roger Schutz, "Témoignage," in: Maurice Villain, ed., *Paul Couturier, apôtre de l'unité chrétienne: Témoignages*, Lyon, Vitte, 1954, 165–174.

111 See R.H., "Conférence de printemps pour les étudiants des universités romandes," *La Vie Protestante*, Apr 12, 1940, 7, and O. Delafontaine to R. Schutz, May 23, and Aug 8, 1940, in: DT. See also the project "Communauté des intellectuels chrétiens," undated, 4 pages of typed manuscript, Archives of WSCF, Yale Divinity Library.

112 Among Schutz's many testimonials, see, in particular, various fragments and diary pages published in Roger Schutz, *À la joie je t'invite: Fragments inédits, 1940–1963*, Taizé, Les Presses de Taizé, 2012.

113 See R. Schutz to M. de Beaumont, Jun 25, 1941, in: GA.

114 See *Communauté de Cluny: Notes explicatives*, Lyon, G. Neveu, 1941.

115 See Scatena, *Taizé*, in particular 82ff.

After plans changed due to the precipitation of the situation in France, which forced Schutz to return to Switzerland in November 1942, Geneva, not Taizé, became the setting of the search for a first communal *forma vitae*. It was in the city of Calvin that, between the end of 1942 and the fall of 1944, a small cell of communal life took shape, willing to commit annually to poverty and celibacy.[116] It was a cell – like the small resident group of Grandchamp that also moved to Geneva in the winter of 1942/1943 – which was soon structured around a daily recitation of the *Office divin de l'Église universelle*, a reformed and ecumenical adaptation of the Roman breviary that pastor de Saussure, the Genevan "godfather" of both these "regular" communities emerging in French-speaking Switzerland, hoped would create "a permanent religious bond."[117] It was a decisive period in which the first resident nucleus gathered around Schutz became aware of the uniqueness of its place within the broader *clunisien* spiritual grouping. The two years spent in Geneva also consolidated the bond of friendship and solidarity with the contemporary community research ongoing at Grandchamp, intensified relations with the leadership of the nascent ecumenical council, saw the first uneasy confrontation of this embryonic community experiment with the ecclesial environment of Geneva, agitated by the group's liturgical passion, and, last but not least, solidified Schutz's pleas for a Protestant form of community life that reinterpreted some of the founding elements of monastic life, with an attitude of both distance and sympathy towards it. Schutz raised these pleas in his licentiate thesis in theology, *L'idéal monacal jusqu'à Saint Benoît et sa conformité avec l'Évangile*, which he defended in Lausanne in April 1943, and in the dense short volume *Introduction à la vie communautaire*, the first detailed presentation of the Communauté de Cluny, which was published the following year by the prestigious Genevan publishing house Labor et Fides.[118] He finished this latter work just on the eve of his pastoral consecration in the Evangelical Reformed Church of Neuchâtel in July 1944.[119] The text essentially represented the expression of his ongoing research in which the fruit of a more personal and intimate experience – the discovery of the value of a structural spiritual discipline – became the center of gravity of a common life, which in turn was presented as both the protection of and stimulus to a unified inner life. Such an inner life was nourished by a daily prayer, which a communal life tended to make increasingly liturgical. There was also a brief but incisive reference to the *clunisien* community's earliest concerns regarding ecumenism and to its founder's hope that a sign of community in response to "a century of disintegration and disintegrated people" might also represent an effective stimulus of unity for churches that had become inured to the scandal "of the lacerated body of Christ."[120]

Although decisive, the period in which the Communauté de Cluny took concrete form in Geneva was a short one. In fact, in the aftermath of the liberation of Burgundy, the resident group – which a fourth member, Daniel de Montmollin, had joined in 1943 – immediately returned to Taizé, but not without passing first through Lyon to meet with Abbé Couturier. Slowed but not interrupted by Schutz's return to Switzerland, relations between the organizer of the Dombes Group meetings and the young *clunisiens* would become increasingly close after October 1944. This was a fundamental turning point for the effective shaping

116 See Scatena, *Taizé*, in particular ch. 2, 82ff.

117 See Jean de Saussure, "L'Office divin de l'Église universelle," *La Vie Protestante*, Jul 30, 1943, 4. The article hailed the first issue of the *Office* in July 1943 for the Geneva-based publisher Labor et Fides.

118 See Roger Schutz, *L'idéal monacal jusqu'à Saint Benoît*, License thesis no. 354, Theology Faculty of l'Église Évangélique Libre of the canton of Vaud, Lausanne, 1943, and Roger Schutz, *Introduction à la vie Communautaire*, Geneva, Labor et Fides, 1944.

119 On Schutz's pastoral consécration, see Scatena, *Taizé*, 143ff.

120 See Schutz, *Introduction à la vie communautaire*, 21, 13–17.

of a stable "communauté régulière évangelique."[121] The first postwar years in France will thus also be those of the entry of the small group *clunisien* into the composite scene of Francophone ecumenism and, if one dimension would therefore flourish in the most full in the small resident community, it will undoubtedly be the ecumenical one.[122] This dimension would unfold in both the search for frequent opportunities of contact with religious and priests of the region, and through Thurian's effort – in the context of his growing involvement in the postwar meetings of the second interconfessional Dombes "cell" – to develop the "principles of an ecumenical theology" with a view to a common reexamination of the essential truths confessed by Catholics and Protestants.[123] Protestant prophetism and movement of catholicity – also to be understood in the wake of the notion of an "evangelical catholicity" of the founder of the *Église et Liturgie* as the rediscovery of the "true (universal and ecumenical) Catholic Church, that of the Creed, in all its truth and primitive purity" – were, in particular, the early and main fixed point in the approach of the *clunisiens* to the ecumenical problem, whose key, in full tune with the Lyonnais father of spiritual ecumenism, was decisively identified in a parallel process of conversion and refocusing on Christ that inflexibly subordinated all theological work to a trust in the transformative power of shared prayer.[124]

In the decade following the first resident nucleus's return to France, the small village of Taizé would therefore progressively establish itself as a crucial center of French-speaking spiritual ecumenism, at the same time as an acceleration of the monastic evolution of the young Reformed community.[125] That acceleration, which between 1948 and 1949 materialized particularly in the resolution to cross the threshold that the resident group had hitherto been precluded from crossing, that is, the commitment to accept, through an explicit profession, the perpetual character of those exceptional life conditions – celibacy, community of goods and obedience to an authority – which were no longer presented as functional to the exercise of an ecclesial ministry or to the formation of a resident community but seen ever more clearly as a possible and evangelical state of life. This was the culmination of a process that grew out of the existential experience of the members of the first resident group, who had no doubts about the irrevocability of their choice of life, but who clearly felt the increasing need to ratify their inner determination to form a community existence that still presented a variety, and quite flexible degrees, of belonging. This "making commitments" – a term long preferred to that of "vows"[126] – was the conclusion which, as mentioned, the first communal nuclei of Pomeyrol as well as of Grandchamp would also soon reach.[127]

Although formally missing from the text of the commitments made at the time of profession, the concern with unity would increasingly appear, in a diverse variety of ways, at the center of the evolution of these first three regular communities, born in the context of French-speaking Protestantism, to which, before a growing differentiation of their respective paths, they would together pose the unavoidable "question of community." During the years of ecumenism's uncertain path and of the first "technical attempts" at dialogue between Rome and Geneva, the Communauté de Taizé-lès-Cluny – a name that was provisionally assumed before abandoning the

121 See the title of the third part of Schutz's licentiate thesis: "Une communauté régulière évangélique est-elle réalisable?."

122 See Scatena, *Taizé*, 202–233.

123 See M. Thurian to M. Villain, Apr 23, 1945, in: Papiers Villain, Notre-Dame des Dombes.

124 See, in particular, the article from 1946 by Roger Schutz & Max Thurian, "L'Eucharistie, sacrement de l'Unité," *Catholicité*, January 1946, special issue *VUCh* 30–32, and Max Thurian, "La communauté de Cluny," *Verbum Caro* 7/3, 1948, 108–124.

125 See Scatena, *Taizé*, in particular, 235–318.

126 See Roger Schutz, "Naissance de communautés dans les Églises de la Réforme," *Verbum Caro* 33/1, 1955, 14–28.

127 See de Beaumont, *Du Grain à l'Épi*, 136–137.

reference to the ancient Benedictine abbey altogether at the end of the 1940s – would be understood and presented more and more explicitly as a "foyer" of encounter between Christians of different traditions on their way to unity, affirming itself, in fact, as a very particular *haut-lieu* of French-speaking spiritual ecumenism. This affirmation would take place in the same years of an uneasy confrontation with the French Reformed sphere and, in particular, with the National Council of the ERF; in the years of the delicate structuring and exponential growth of the first group of residents; of the search for an empirical integration between a more contemplative and frankly monastic path and a more "centrifugal" one in view of a clearer "presence in the world" through penetration of the worker's milieu; and *last but not least* in the years of Schutz's drafting of the *Règle*.[128] Presented for the first time to the community on Easter Sunday 1952 and soon also adopted by the community of Grandchamp, it was a short and essential text, deliberately limited to "the minimum outside of which a community cannot be built in Christ" and, in a certain way, "open," and aware of being situated within a precise historical moment.[129] It was thus a text that would find in these very characteristics the main reason for its effective ability to shape the charism of the community as well as its enduring adaptability to the successive evolutions of the latter: a community always in search of delicate and evolving balances between changes and essential continuities, in the spirit of a rule for which "immobility" constituted a "disobedience" in following Christ. But it was also a text that contained, on the other hand, in its introduction, a fundamental reference to certain central, original, and inalienable needs: openness to all that is human, without religious or ideological discrimination, presence to one's own age, "the passion for the unity of the body of Christ."[130]

6 The New Protestant Communities in Germany

In the aftermath of World War II, even in the cradle of the Reformation – in a Germany where a theological dictionary could still apodictically affirm in 1941 that "Protestantism fundamentally rejects monasticism"[131] – there was a true blossoming of community life. In the first two decades of the postwar period, no less than ten communities were born within the panorama of the German Protestant churches.[132] From the middle of the century, despite the difficulties that diaconal houses encountered in the 19th century regarding being accepted as legitimate places of Christian community life, the view of the churches and of theology on "monastic" life began to change.

More than any other factor of a theological, ecclesial, or religious nature, in point of fact it was the reaction to the barbarity of Nazism and the horrors of war, along with the consequent spiritual upheaval, that had a catalytic effect on the birth of Protestant religious communities on German soil. Hence this context prompted – in diverse believers and independently of one another – the awakening of a strong need of community that materialized in the establishment of different experiences of shared life, all espousing, in different ways, a

128 See Scatena, *Taizé*, 318–446.

129 There have been several successive editions of the *règle*. For the latest, see *La Règle de Taizé*, Taizé, Les Presses de Taizé, 2010. Reference here, however, is made to the first manuscript version from the end of 1952, which is preserved in the community archives. On the "open" character of the *règle*, see, in particular, the text that would soon follow by Bruder Roger, *L'esprit de la Règle*, undated, 5 pages of typed manuscript, in: AG.

130 See *La Règle de Taizé*.

131 Winfried Zeller, "Mönchtum," in: *Calwer Kirchenlexikon*, vol. 2, Stuttgart, Calwer, 1941, 265–270, here 269. Still, three decades later, one could read in a German encyclopedia that "the Churches born of the Reformation rejected and reject monasticism." See the entry "Mönchtum" in *Brockhaus Enzyklopädie*, vol. 12, Wiesbaden, Brockhaus, 1971, 731.

132 For a list of the first postwar Lutheran communities, see Halkenhäuser, *Kirche und Kommunität*, 219–221.

desire for unity and reconciliation, often associated with no less strong a sense of repentance for the atrocities committed by Nazi Germany. These communities were not born outside history, but instead were fully aware of their place within it. "From the point of view of spiritual history, the contemporary movement of Protestant communities is absolutely incomprehensible without this experience of war, understood as a 'fatal' crisis of secularism,"[133] affirmed one of the agents of this rebirth. It therefore did not constitute – as a direct witness said – a "romantic effort to restore past forces, eager to return full speed to the Middle Ages, but, on the contrary, [it was] a revolutionary event."[134]

If the trauma of the war and the disintegration that it had generated produced, as a counter-reaction, the birth of places of community life in which to restore the interpersonal bonds that had been broken and to realize, concretely, the dimension of Christian fraternity, at the same time the simple appearance of these new communities shattered a real "Protestant taboo."[135] The monastic form of Christian life could thus find its place in the German Protestant churches as well. At various times in the first decades of their existence, however, these new community realities had to endeavor to justify this "place" on a scriptural and theological level.[136] In this effort they were clearly sustained by the vast current of renewal that had swept through German Protestantism in the first half of the 20th century – the "century of the Church" in the words of Otto Dibelius[137] – specifically permitting a reconsideration of the "charismatic" character of the church itself and a rediscovery of the collective and ecclesial dimension of Christian existence, which was decisive for the birth of the various new experiences of fraternity (*Bruderschaften*).[138] These were gatherings of Christians that were similar in many ways to Catholic third orders: arrangements that did not envisage a shared life or the abandonment of the family, but which asked their members to fulfill certain ecclesial commitments within the framework of sharing the same spirituality. It was not by chance that most of them emerged after World War I: some under the influence of the spheres of *diakonia* communities (in line with the idea that not only the bodies of the least among us required care, but also the "sick" body of Christ), others under that of renewal or moments of awakening within the church, arising particularly from youth groups to which such spheres – such as those of the Berneuchen Movement – endowed a Christian expression.[139]

These "fraternities,"[140] to which the new cenobitic communities born after World War II would refer, had developed against the backdrop of an overall transformation of the theological and spiritual climate under the banner of the emergence – in contrast to the dominant

133 See Olav Hanssen, "Gethsemane: Eine grundsätzliche Besinnung," *Evangelisches Gethsemanekloster: Brief für Freunde*, spring 2005, 15–25, here 19.

134 Erich Müller-Gangloff, "Gottes Volk als Bruderschaft," *Quatember* 17, 1953, 3–8 (here 7). In the same sense, see Biot, *Communautés protestantes*, 188–189.

135 See Siegfried von Kortzfleisch, *Mitten im Herzen der Massen*, Stuttgart, Kreuz, 1963, 15.

136 See Halkenhäuser, *Kirche und Kommunität*, 211–214, and Christoph Joest, "Die Entstehung von Kommunitäten in den Kirchen der Reformation," in: Athina Lexutt, Volker Mantey & Volkmar Ortmann, *Reformation und Mönchtum: Aspekte eines Verhältnisses über Luther hinaus*, Tübingen, Mohr Siebeck, 2008, 241–264, here 256–260.

137 See Otto Dibelius, *Das Jahrhundert der Kirche: Geschichte, Betrachtung, Umschau und Ziele*, Berlin, Furche, 1927.

138 See Halkenhäuser, *Kirche und Kommunität*, 180–205.

139 See Joest, "Die Entstehung von Kommunitäten," 245–249.

140 In German, these fraternal experiences are usually called *Bruderschaften* (or *Schwesternschaften*); unlike *Kommunitäten*, they do not involve the communally shared life of their members. The Bruderschaft des gemeinsamen Lebens (founded in 1905), the Hochkirchliche Vereinigung (1918), the Sydower Bruderschaft (1923), the Evangelisch-katholische eucharistische Gemeinschaft (1929), and the Evangelische Michaelsbruderschaft (1931) can be cited as examples of such experiences. For a detailed list, see Halkenhäuser, *Kirche und Kommunität*, 206–209.

Kulturprotestantismus – of a "theology of the Word" that replaced faith in the colorful progress of humanism with a strong theocentrism as well as the associated, radical questioning of the liberal synthesis between revelation and religion, nature and grace. With the affirmation of dialectical theology and Karl Barth's thought, it became clear that the kingdom of God, far from being reducible to the ethical and cultural progress of humanity, was instead the eruption of the eternal into history, an eruption that brought a judgment upon humanity and the world, thus opening the path to the possibility of "anomalous" Christian realizations, as the nascent communities would sometimes be, with their deeply eschatological existence.[141] At the same time, the contemporary movements of liturgical and sacramental renewal, which possessed a strong ecclesiological component, spontaneously oriented their reflection toward the fraternal structure of the church, also opening the door to new instances of community.[142] The contributions of the new historical research on the origins of Christianity and the related reevaluations of authentically Christian roots of monasticism[143] should not be overlooked in the flourishing of cenobitic communities in the German Protestant churches, as well as, above all, the awareness of the scandal of the division of Christians and the emerging ecumenical tension that contributed, in a fundamental way, to taking a new look at the dimension of the church's universality. It was a look in which confessional otherness would be considered to be the bearer of opportunities and gifts from which to learn, even within the framework of new forms of fraternal life.

The instances of community appearing in Germany after 1945 – mostly crystallizing the experiences of fraternity that had arisen in the first half of the century into diversified forms of coexistence – were clearly all permeated by this overall climate, which was essential for their, somewhat gradual, ecclesial recognition. Furthermore, against this more general background, the first German *Kommunitäten* began to crop up autonomously, starting from the sharing of common spiritual experiences and their founders' requests to live the *sequela Christi* more concretely and radically within the framework of small and dynamic fraternities of shared life. These communities, therefore, germinated "from below," so to speak, with a certain improvisation and, for the most part, in highly precarious states, often encountering a certain opposition from their own familial and ecclesial spheres.

While the members of these new Protestant communities very soon chose to adopt the "evangelical counsels," committing themselves to chastity, poverty, and obedience with a promise or even vows,[144] their *forma vitae* was rarely linked to any traditional type of religious life. The new *Kommunitäten*, therefore, could hardly be placed in the usual categories of "contemplative" or "active life." In fact, it was primarily the desire to follow Christ and for a shared life that inspired and justified their foundation, and it was only secondarily that the forms of gathering together – different in each instance – would take on concrete commitments in the ecclesial and social spheres. Rather than each community having a specific

141 See Barth's critical but kind evaluation of monasticism and appreciation of the original intentions of this phenomenon in a further piece: Karl Barth, *KD* 4/II, 10–18. In general on this point, see Fulvio Ferrario, *La teologia del Novecento*, Rome, Carocci, 2011. On the relationship of these renewals with the question of community, see Biot, *Communautés protestantes*, 169–179.

142 See Alfred Ehrensperger, "Liturgische Bewegungen in der evangelischen Kirche im 20. Jharhunderts," *Liturgisches Jahrbuch* 33, 1983, 236–250; and Hans-Christoph Schmidt-Lauber, "Liturgische Bewegungen," *TRE* 21, 401–406.

143 Already at the end of the 19th century, Adolf von Harnack was hoping for the return of monks to Protestantism. See Adolf von Harnack, "Was wir von der römischen Kirche lernen und nicht lernen sollen (1891)," in: Adolf von Harnack, *Ausgewählte Reden und Aufsätze*, Berlin, De Gruyter, 1951, 66–79, here 73–74.

144 See Christoph Joest, *Spiritualität evangelischer Kommunitäten: Altkirchlich-monastische Tradition in evangelischen Kommunitäten von heute*, Göttingen, Vandenhoeck & Ruprecht, 1995, 157–185.

forma vitae (more contemplative or more active), it was the ecclesial background of their founders – exercising a decisive influence on how the ecclesial and social presence of each *Kommunität* was understood – that allowed them to be categorized. Two groups can be roughly distinguished,[145] the first being the "Pietist" type communities, characterized in particular by the elements typical of the Protestant Christianity of the Awakening, with an emphasis on preferentially free prayer and more daring missionary activity (first among these were the communities of Darmstadt, Selbitz, and later Gnadenthal). The second were those of the "ecclesial" type, more marked by the movements of biblical, theological, and liturgical renewal and by a "high" sense of the church (among these, in particular, can be counted the communities of Casteller Ring and Imshausen in Germany and those that arose simultaneously in Sweden).[146]

The recognition of these communities as authentic realizations of Christian life by the churches of the Reformation was gradual.[147] One of their first joint public manifestations took place in February 1956 at the Evangelische Akademie in Tutzing, at a meeting where the members of the new *Kommunitäten* began to be (re)acquainted with one another and to reflect on their ecclesial role. That first meeting – an "event in the history of the Church," as it was later called by the then chaplain of Casteller Ring, Johannes Halkenhäuser[148] – permitted the German Evangelical churches to become aware of the existence of such realities together with their theological and ecclesiological significance. Three years after the meeting in Tutzing, a presentation of the new and varied fraternal experiences that had taken shape in the German Protestant churches after the war was, significantly, sent to press.[149] In reality, however, it was some Catholic authors who were the first to turn their attention to the strong theological value of the phenomenon of this flowering of community, pointing out in particular its important ecumenical value.[150] The effective and institutional reception of the communities by the German Evangelical church would only take place towards the end of the 1970s, the decade in which a KEvK was instituted. In particular, in May 1976, the Lutheran bishops of the VELKD issued a first official statement on regular communities[151] and, in 1979, the EKD then published an authoritative study on "evangelical spirituality" in which cenobitic communities were recognized as "legitimate expressions of Christian existence" and defined as "places of grace" (*Gnadenorte*).[152] This was clearly

145 See Halkenhäuser, *Kirche und Kommunität*, 214–217.

146 The birth of some regular Lutheran communities in Sweden was due in particular to the influence of the English monastic experiences of the previous century and the ecclesial renewal movement around the figure of Bishop Nathan Söderblom. See Ö. Eckman, "Iniziative monastiche nella chiesa di Svezia," in: *Monachesimo ed ecumenismo: Esperienze delle comunità protestanti*, Rome, Moniales Ordinis Servorum, 1967, 37–41; and Perchenet, *Renouveau communautaire et unité chrétienne*, 422–433.

147 See Johannes Halkenhäuser, "Die evangelischen Kommunitäten: Die ekklesiale und ökumenische Dimension ihres Lebens," *ÖR* 20, 1981, 121–132; and Christoph Joest, "Der Protestantismus und die evangelischen Kommunitäten," *Kerygma und Dogma* 42, 1996, 272–284.

148 See Halkenhäuser, *Kirche und Kommunität*, 213. For a contemporary and participatory account, see Erich Müller-Gangloff, "Die Evangelischen Kommunitäten," *Quatember* 20, 1956, 103–105.

149 See Lydia Präger, ed., *Frei für Gott und die Menschen: Evangelische Bruder- und Schwesternschaften der Gegenwart in Selbstdarstellungen*, Stuttgart, Quell-Verlag, 1959.

150 See, for example, Albert Görres, "Eine geistliche Lebensregel für Christen in der Welt," *GuL* 21, 1948, 237–238; and Friedrich Wulf, "Die Stellung des Protestantismus zu Aszese und Mönchtum in Geschichte und Gegenwart," *GuL* 27, 1954, 21–34.

151 See Lutz Mohaupt, ed., *Modelle gelebten Glaubens: Gespräche der Lutherischen Bischofskonferenz über Kommunitäten und charismatische Bewegungen*, Hamburg, Lutherisches Verlagshaus, 1976, 142–144.

152 EKD, *Evangelische Spiritualität*, Gütersloh, Gütersloher Verlagshaus, 1979, here 53–54. Other official position statements were further drafted: EKD, *Evangelische Kommunitäten* (1997); and EKD, *Verbindlich Leben: Kommunitäten und geistliche Gemeinschaften in der Evangelischen Kirche in Deutschland* (2007), which

a "paradigm shift"[153] in the German Protestant church which, abandoning its centuries-old opposition to the monastic *forma vitae*, now appointed a bishop to be responsible for these new ecclesial realities. From the middle of the following decade, a representative of the communities would also have a seat in the synod of the EKD.

It was, therefore, above all through their laborious insertion into the Protestant ecclesial panorama – an insertion that would remain legally delicate in the absence of a Protestant canon law[154] – that the first communities that sprang up in that land sought to express their ecumenical concerns.

The first was the community of the sisterhood of Mary in Darmstadt (Ökumenische Marienschwesternschaft),[155] which arose from the traumatic experience of the almost complete destruction of that city during the night of Sep 11–12, 1944, and which was led by the figures of Mother Basilea (Clara) Schlink and Mother Martyria (Erika) Madauss – formerly leaders of biblical study groups for girls within the Confessing Church; it was created as a place to live and pray, not without traces of a certain spiritual sorrow, as a sign of penance and with a view to reconciliation. From its early years, the sisters of the Marienschwesternschaft – the new community's name was intended to refer to the path of faith and obedience to God's will exemplified by the Lord's mother – in addition to three daily prayers, welcomed guests and engaged in biblical theatrical productions. They quickly experienced a rapid development that allowed them to diversify their activities, especially in the area of evangelization, opening various foundations in Germany and abroad. The adjective "ecumenical" that defined the community on its establishment (but which the sisters renounced in 1964, deciding to call their community Evangelische Marienschwesternschaft) irrefutably indicated the interdenominational scope of their unique concentration on the theme of reconciliation, for which the sisters engaged in daily communal prayer. From the outset, this commitment also included significant attention to dialogue with Israel.

Shortly after the establishment of the community in Darmstadt came that of the Communität Christusbruderschaft (Community of the Christ-Brotherhood)[156] in Selbitz, led by pastor Walter Hümmer and his wife Hanna (Frau Mutter), during the years of World War II, starting with the Pietist parish Awakening movement led by the couple. On Jan 1, 1949, seven sisters and four brothers took up a shared life in the rectory, around which other buildings were soon to be built. By the end of the following decade, the community already numbered just under 60 sisters and 10 brothers. From its earliest years, the life of the Christusbruderschaft was composed of prayer and service – while the brothers assisted the pastors

recognized a place for communities in the church's "constitution," see 25.

153 Peter Zimmerling, "Evangelische Kommunitäten: Monastische Spiritualität im Protestantismus," *Geist und Leben* 90, 2017, 360–368, here 363.

154 See Halkenhäuser, *Kirche und Kommunität*, 216–217, and Joest, *Die Entstehung von Kommunitäten*, 264.

155 See Mother Basilea (Clara) Schlink, "Die Œkumenische Marienschwesternschaft," in: *Frei für Gott und die Menschen*, 111–127; Mother Basilea (Clara) Schlink, *Immer ist Gott grösser: Sendung der Marienschwesternschaft*, Darmstadt, Œkumenische Marienschwesternschaft, 1963; Perchenet, *Renouveau communautaire et unité chrétienne*, 388–412; Marianne Jansson & Riitta Lemmetyinen, *Christliche Existenz zwischen Evangelium und Gesetzlichkeit: Darstellung und Beurteilung von Lehre und Leben der "Evangelischen Marienschwesternschaft" in Darmstadt*, Frankfurt a.M., Peter Lang, 1997; and Joela Krüger, "Die Revolution der Versöhner: Evangelische Marienschwesternschaft Darmstadt," in: *Kloster auf evangelisch*, 122–125.

156 See Walter Hümmer, "Die Christusbruderschaft in Selbitz," in: *Frei für Gott und die Menschen*, 184–194; Joest, *Spiritualität evangelischer Kommunitäten*, 309–342; Walter Hümmer, ed., *Denn er hatte seinem Gott vertraut: Zum Gedenken an Walter Hümmer*, Selbitz, Christusbruderschaft, 1999; and Schwester Beate Seibel, "Tritt ein in den Liebesraum Gottes: Communität Christusbruderschaft in Selbitz," in: *Kloster auf evangelisch*, 12–16.

in their ministry, some of the sisters worked in nursing while others were active in parishes (*Gemeindeschwestern*) – its mission was increasingly understood as a search for and the realization of a balance between the three dimensions of *leiturgia*, *martyria*, and *diakonia*.

Almost contemporaneously to that of the Christusbruderschaft was the founding of the Community of Casteller Ring,[157] born in 1950 as the result of the spiritual anxiety that the persecution by the Gestapo and the war aroused in many young people engaged in Christian scouting who were led by Christel Schmid, who became Mater Felizitas. From its very beginning, the focus of the sisters' life – who adopted the Rule of Benedict in order to reconnect with the monastic experience of the undivided church – was the monastic liturgy. "While everything was falling apart, we asked ourselves: Why is life still worth living? We experienced the power of shared prayer and the fact that we needed the sisters around us in order to live the Church of Christ," recalled one of the first nuns who would later succeed the foundress as prioress.[158] Relocated to Schwanberg Castle seven years after it started, the community – strongly influenced by the liturgical and sacramental reflections developed by Wilhelm Löhe – thus intended to establish itself and present itself essentially as a "prayer cell" for the world, expressing its original desire for the unity of the body of Christ primarily in this way.

The experience of *Kirchenkampf* and the resistance's political struggle against Nazism was at the origin of another new reality of shared life, that of the Community of Imshausen in Hesse.[159] During the war, its future foundress, Vera von Trott – sister of the resistance fighter Adam von Trott who was executed in 1944 – sheltered several Christians persecuted under Adolf Hitler's regime in an old mill. Towards the end of the war, an officer who was an ordained pastor and an objector to military obligations sought refuge with her. At the end of the hostilities, he decided to settle in Imshausen with von Trott and a few others who had joined them in the meantime. A small, stable community nucleus was thus formed, structured around the sharing of daily prayer – which soon became the monastic office – and an intense activity of offering hospitality and accompanying others, especially children, who were entrusted to them. A few years later, in 1955, this nucleus then formalized its commitment to community life and the observance of the evangelical counsels. Starting from full membership in the local church, an openness to the ecumenical dimension also soon became important, with the explicit concern for "the completeness of the one universal Church."[160]

Although a short time later than the experiences just mentioned, for their explicit intention to represent a living response to the fractures of history, we can also add – among the new German communities that arose in the early 1960s (Christusträger, Gethsemanekloster, Adelshofen) – the Jesus-Bruderschaft (Jesus Brotherhood) in Gnadenthal,[161] which arose out of the meetings

157 See Christel Schmid, "Der Casteller Ring," in: *Frei für Gott und die Menschen*, 145–150; Perchenet, *Renouveau communautaire et unité chrétienne*, 412–416; Maria Pfister, "Frei für Gott und das Kommen seines Reiches: Die (evangelische) Communität Casteller Ring Schloß Schwanberg," *Geist und Leben* 54, 1981, 385–390; Joest, *Spiritualität evangelischer Kommunitäten*, 235–269; and Halkenhäuser, *Kirche und Kommunität*, 231–237.

158 See the story of Schwester Maria Pfister quoted in Joest, *Spiritualität evangelischer Kommunitäten*, 238.

159 See Hans Eisenberg, "Die Communität Imshausen," in: *Frei für Gott und die Menschen*, 194–198; Perchenet, *Renouveau communautaire et unité chrétienne*, 417–419; Udo Waschelitz, "Die Kommunität Imshausen," in: Ingrid Reimer, ed., *Alternativ leben in verbindlicher Gemeinschaft: Evangelische Kommunitäten, Lebensgemeinschaften, Junge Bewegungen*, Stuttgart, Quell, 1979, 46–52; and Bruder Georg, "Unterwegs und ganz daheim: Kommunität Imshausen," in: *Kloster auf evangelisch*, 60–63.

160 Eisenberg, "Die Communität Imshausen," 197.

161 See "Die Jesusbruderschaft," in: *Frei für Gott und die Menschen*, 223–230; Halkenhäuser, *Kirche und Kommunität*, 227–231; Jesus-Bruderschaft, ed., *Orte der Hoffnung: Leben in Gnadenthal, Hennersdorf und*

of a group of young Evangelical Christians from West and East Germany. The genesis in 1961 of this new community experience was not accidental. The erection of the Berlin Wall in August of that year – and the separation between the two parts of Germany that it crystallized – was, in effect, interpreted as a stimulus to concretely and existentially unite their operational and prayerful forces in view of a reconciliation of, not only societies, but also and above all of the divided churches. Constitutionally ecumenical, in the following years the Jesus-Bruderschaft – dedicated to social work and hospitality, like the other new communities – would therefore accept among its members men, women, and families belonging to different Christian denominations, thus seeking to constitute an effective witness of communion in its "reconciled diversity."[162]

Translated from Italian to English by Susan Dawson Vásquez and David Dawson Vásquez.

Bibliography

Allchin, Donald, "Il monachesimo nella Communio anglicana," in: Donato Giordano, ed., *Il ruolo del monachesimo nell'ecumenismo: Atti del Simposio Ecumenico Internazionale*, Monte Oliveto Maggiore, Abbazia Monte Oliveto Maggiore, 2002, 161–173.

Biot, François, *Communautés protestantes: La renaissance de la vie régulière dans le protestantisme continental*, Paris, Fleurus, 1961.

Esnault, René H., *Luther et le monachisme aujourd'hui: Lecture actuelle de "De votis monasticis judicium"*, Geneva, Labor et Fides, 1964.

Halkenhäuser, Johannes, *Kirche und Kommunität: Ein Beitrag zur Geschichte und Auftrag der kommunitären Bewegung in den Kirchen der Reformation*, Paderborn, Bonifatius, 1978.

Joest, Christoph, "Die Entstehung von Kommunitäten in den Kirchen der Reformation," in: Athina Lexutt, Volker Mantey & Volkmar Ortmann, *Reformation und Mönchtum: Aspekte eines Verhältnisses über Luther hinaus*, Tübingen, Mohr Siebeck, 2008.

Lagny, Gustave, *Le réveil de 1830 à Paris et les origines des diaconesses de Reuilly: Une page d'histoire protestante*, Lyon, Olivétan, 2007.

Perchenet, Annie, *Renouveau communautaire et unité chrétienne: Regards sur les communautés anglicanes et protestantes*, Tours, Mame, 1967.

Präger, Lydia, ed., *Frei für Gott und die Menschen: Evangelische Bruder und Schwesternschaften der Gegenwart in Selbstdarstellungen*, Stuttgart, Quell-Verlag, 1959.

Scatena, Silvia, *Taizé, una parabola di unità: Storia della comunità dalle origini al concilio dei giovani*, Bologna, Il Mulino, 2018.

Schering, Ernst, "Ordenserneuerung und Gestaltwerdung der Diakonie im Protestantismus des 19. Jahrhunderts," RJKG 6, 1987, 115–132.

Schlumberger, Laurent, "Dietrich Bonhoeffer et le monachisme," *ETR* 57, 1983, 465–490.

Sœur Évangéline, ed., *Protestantisme et vie monastique: Vers une nouvelle rencontre?*, Paris, Olivétan, 2015.

Turcotte, Paul-André, *Réconciliation et libération: Théologie de la communauté chez Dietrich Bonhoeffer*, Montreal, Bellarmin, 1972.

Villain, Maurice, *L'Abbé Paul Couturier, apôtre de l'unité chrétienne: Souvenirs et documents*, Paris, Casterman, [2]1957.

Zimmerling, Peter, *Evangelische Mystik*, Göttingen, Vandenhoeck & Ruprecht, 2015.

Volkenroda, Hünfelden, Präsenz, 1995; Joest, "Die Entstehung von Kommunitäten," 252–255; and Bruder Franziskus Joest, ed., *Jesus-Bruderschaft Gnadenthal. Geschichte, Glaube, Gemeinschaft: Unser Leben auf den Punkt gebracht*, Holzgerlingen, SCM R. Brockhaus, 2019.

162 See Harding Meyer, *Versöhnte Verschiedenheit: Aufsätze zur ökumenischen Theologie I*, Frankfurt/Paderborn, Otto Lembeck/Bonifatius, 1998.

CHAPTER 9

The WMC in Tambaram in 1938 and Ecumenical Attempts in Africa and Asia

Frieder Ludwig

1 Introduction

"Unity may be theoretically a desirable ideal in Europe and America, but it is vital to the life of the church in the mission field. The divisions of Christianity may be a source of weakness in Christian countries, but in non-Christian countries, it is a sin."[1] These words pronounced by the Indian bishop Vedanayagam Samuel Azariah at the meeting of the Faith and Order movement in Lausanne in 1927 expressed the expectations of many participants at the WMC in Tambaram in 1938. This was the first meeting of the Protestant IMC at which non-Western Christians represented just over half of the 471 delegates.[2] The attempts at greater cooperation among the churches were characteristic not only of the situation in South India, where efforts towards church union had steadily progressed since the church ministers' conference at Tranquebar in May 1919, with the participation of Anglicans, Presbyterians, Congregationalists, and then Methodists as well, but also of the hopes of African participants. Christian Gonçalves Baëta from Ghana (then the Gold Coast) spoke in this spirit as one of the three speakers to address the assembly at the start of the meeting on the unity of the church and the concerns shared by all Christians.[3] The missionary conference was seen as a great necessity in his country, since by coming together the churches would be able to complement one another, enriching life in the process. In his address, Baëta highlighted the reciprocity of relations. He saw his own participation as a personal learning experience but also as an offer to others: "We come here to enrich others and we are prepared to place at their disposal the entire Christian experience of our country. ... We are hoping that we shall go away from this conference strengthened in the sense of unity in Christ."[4]

1 On Lausanne see Hermann Sasse, ed., *Die Weltkonferenz für Glauben und Kirchenverfassung: Deutscher amtlicher Bericht über die Weltkirchenkonferenz zu Lausanne, 3.–21. August 1927*, Berlin, Furche, 1929; a slightly different variation of the Azariah quotation (see Bengt Sundkler & Christopher Steed, *A History of the Church in Africa*, Cambridge, Cambridge University Press, 2000, 159) can already be found before Lausanne: see Vedanayagam Samuel Azariah, "Caste and Denomination," *HFJ* 41, 1921, 246–253, here 246: "The divisions of Christendom may be a source of weakness to the Church in Christian lands; but they are a scandal and a stumbling block in the mission field." However, a more widespread reception by the non-Western public (such as in Nigeria) did not commence until 1927/28.

2 Stephen Neill, *A History of Christian Missions*, London, Penguin Books, 1964, 518–519; on this, see also the list of participants arranged by country in: IMC, ed., *Addresses and Other Records*, Tambaram Series, vol. 7, London, Oxford University Press, 1939. Arthur Mitchell Chirgwin, *Under Fire: The Christian Church in a Hostile World*, London, SCM Press, 1941, 21–22., noted that this greater representation reflected the rapid growth of the "young churches": "When the Jerusalem Conference met in 1928 there were approximately 8,000,000 Protestant Christians in the mission field, when the Madras Conference met ten years later the number had reached approximately 13,000,000, an increase of 68%. During the decade there had been an increase of 40% in China, 50% in India and Japan, 100% in Africa, and 150% in Latin America. At no time in Christian history has such progress been made."

3 "In my country mission work was started more than 100 years ago. The people are themselves taking over the management of the churches; and they themselves support the churches"; "One World Christian Church. Significance of Missionary Conference at Tambaram. Christ's message: Delegates' Address," *The Madras Mail*, Dec 15, 1938.

4 "One World Christian Church,"

The desire to strengthen church unity was also expressed in the conference's closing recommendations. Spiritual fellowship was not enough:

> While we are profoundly thankful for the growth in brotherly love and understanding that has come with increased cooperation, and while we are convinced of the need for its yet further extension, there are certain parts of the Christian obligation which in our judgment demand more than a cooperative basis. In particular it has been found that in most cases cooperation in the great evangelistic task stops at the point where pastoral care is needed for the building up of the church. We can act together in the presentation of the Gospel to men and in winning of them to the Christian faith; but there is evidence that in the next necessary stage cooperation breaks down owing to divided church loyalty. From this standpoint therefore, as well as from the growing spirit of unity that has resulted from common working at a common task, has come in many fields a deep and growing conviction that the spirit of God is guiding the various branches of His church to seek for the realization of a visible and organic union.[5]

In this chapter, I shall first discuss West African approaches to the question of cooperation among the churches at the Tambaram conference before looking at Indian perspectives.[6] The talks about church union in South India, which began in 1919 and successfully culminated in 1947 with the foundation of the Church of South India, were followed throughout the world with great interest.

2 West African Approaches

Christian Baëta was the youngest of the 15 African participants at Tambaram, having just turned 30 (he was born on May 23, 1908), and represented his country's clear choice.[7] From 1930 to 1935, he had been a guest pupil of the North German Mission Society at their mission house in Basel, before going on to spend several months in Paris and in England.[8] He spoke fluent German, English, and French. His main aim in preparing for the conference was to discover the views of the people from the region he was representing. After receiving the documents from the IMC, he embarked on a nine-week journey throughout the Gold Coast,

5 IMC, ed., *The World Mission of the Church: Findings and Recommendations of the International Missionary Council, Tambaram, Madras, India, December 12th to 29th, 1938*, London, IMC, 1939, 154. T.V. Philip, *Edinburgh to Salvador: Twentieth Century Ecumenical Missiology*, Delhi, CSS & ISPCK, 1999, ch. 3, available at <https://www.religion-online.org/book-chapter/chapter-3-mission-and-unity/> (accessed Oct 5, 2022).

6 The account is mainly based on my postdoctoral thesis: Frieder Ludwig, *Zwischen Kolonialismuskritik und Kirchenkampf. Interaktionen afrikanischer, indischer und europäischer Christen während der Weltmissionskonferenz in Tambaram 1938*, Göttingen, Vandenhoeck & Ruprecht, 2000.

7 At the decisive meeting of the Christian Council of the Gold Coast, his name was at first not even mentioned among the possible candidates, but at the subsequent vote Baëta won a majority apparently without difficulty. The records do not provide any information about the exact course of the decision-making process: "Three names had been submitted to the Council, viz. Mr. J.C. de Graft Johnson, Rev. S.S. Odonkor, Rev. G.R. Acquash. It was decided that the candidate with the second highest number of votes should be regarded as 'second choice' candidate in case anything happened to prevent the first choice from going to the conference. Mr. Bardsley outlined the qualifications for the delegate which had been in the minds of the subcommittee. A vote was then taken, and Mr. Baëta was elected delegate, with Mr. Acquash as 'second choice'"; "The Christian Council of the Gold Coast, 10th session, Dec. 23rd, 1937," in: IMC/CBMS, West Africa, Gold Coast, box 267.

8 Extract from the "Brüderverzeichnis" (list of brothers) of the Basel Mission, in: BM, BV 2410. On Baëta, see Christian G. Baëta, "My Pilgrimage in Mission," *IBMR* 12/4, 1988, 165–168; John S. Pobee, *Religion in a Pluralistic Society*, Leiden, Brill, 1976; Theo Sundermeier, "Auf dem Weg zu einer afrikanischen Kirche: Christian G. Baëta, Ghana," in: Hans Waldenfels, ed., *Theologen der Dritten Welt: Elf biographische Skizzen aus Afrika, Asien und Lateinamerika*, Munich, C.H. Beck, 1982, 71–81.

starting on Jul 15, during which he visited numerous localities where he held meetings.[9]

In his report, he wrote that the idea of a gathering in Madras had made a great impression everywhere, and he had seen the willingness to work together everywhere he went. A number of points had been raised over and over again and were therefore particularly significant. The first of these was the enthusiasm with which the idea of a rapprochement among the different denominations had been welcomed. In some places, his visit had even been the initial impetus for an interfaith meeting, with moving speeches referring to Ps 133: "Gracious the sight, and full of comfort, when brethren dwell united." Everywhere people had seen a contradiction between the message's claim and the reality of fragmentation among the confessions, particularly in places where such differences could lead to violent clashes. Baëta therefore believed it made sense for the WMC to establish a liturgy for certain joint religious services. The clergy should also be instructed to refrain from polemical statements against other confessions.[10]

The second important point listed by Baëta was marriage: people all over the country were dissatisfied with the current state of affairs. Everywhere people gave the same answer when questioned about the reason for the church's preference for monogamy, namely that monogamy was a white man's custom and the church had come from the white man. Baëta hoped to get a definitive solution to this question at Tambaram: "Then if by any means possible, I wish to try to get a definite pronouncement either from the preliminary conference of African delegates only, or from the big conference itself, on the question whether or not there is anything in polygamy essentially alien to, and incompatible with profession of the Christian faith."[11]

These two points were also crucial for other West African delegates. All agreed that the different approaches to polygamy taken by the various churches were an obstacle to Christian Unity. One African delegate described precisely how this issue represented a major problem. One denomination would baptize a convert and his first wife, whereas another would not baptize the man at all but instead all of his wives (since each of them only had one husband). A third denomination would baptize everyone, while a fourth would make a selection. The South Indian union committee clearly had no inkling of such a state of affairs, which it saw as a previously unknown dimension of its own efforts: "Such a situation is obviously scandalous,"[12] was the verdict published in the *Church Union News and Views*.

Assistant Bishop Alexander Babatunde Akinyele of the Anglican Church firmly took a position of resolute adherence to the African Independent Churches. In a manuscript entitled *Relationship with Schismatic Bodies, and How to Cope with Them*, he pointed out the different European and

9 A statistical overview of the missions and churches in the Gold Coast is provided by Joseph I. Parker, ed., *Interpretative Statistical Survey of the World Mission of the Christian Church*, New York, IMC, 1938, 67: according to this, there were 984 organized churches and 626 other places where religious services were regularly held. A total of 251,773 were counted. The African staff consisted of 165 ordained ministers and 1,063 non-ordained catechists. The largest organizations in the country included the Methodist Missionary Society (129,091 members), Presbyterian Church of the Gold Coast founded by the Basel Mission and the Church of Scotland Foreign Mission (60,830 members), Ewe Church founded by the North German Mission Society, to which Baëta belonged (35,831 members), and the Anglican diocese of Accra (19,400). Independent African churches were not considered. Churches founded by African-Americans had a small membership (African Methodist Episcopal Zion Church with 5,000 members and African Methodist Episcopal Church with 812).

10 Report of Rev. Christian G. Baëta on his tour of the Gold Coast, July–September 1938, in: IMC/CBMS, West Africa, Gold Coast, box 267, 3–6.

11 Report of Rev. Christian G. Baëta on his tour of the Gold Coast, 7–8, here 7.

12 Dermott Monahan, "Church Union After Tambaram," *Church Union News and Views* 9/3, 1939, 52–54, here 53.

African perspectives: "When an Anglican churchman thinks or speaks of 'schismatic bodies' one great class of Christians from whom he is separated presents itself chiefly to his mind – the various non-conformist bodies, viz. Wesleyans, Methodists, Baptists, Presbyterians etc. We must be broader ... and think of the ... African Church who recently left the Church of England."[13] This drew attention to the independent African churches which had rapidly gained influence not only in Western but also in Southern Africa.

In this paper, Akinyele addressed the African Church as one of the organizations that had emerged from the first wave of the independent church movement, whereas in his response to the survey for the Tambaram conference he dealt at length with the Aladura (prayer) churches which had spread across Western Nigeria from the 1920s. Unlike the independent churches previously founded (such as the African Church in 1901), which had split off from the missionary churches in protest against European paternalism but which nonetheless still maintained similar structures and liturgies, the Aladura churches developed in a spontaneous and uncontrolled manner. At their heart were charismatic acts such as healing through prayer and visions.

A central figure in the late 1920s was Joseph Ayo Babalola, whose work was depicted as overwhelmingly positive by Akinyele. Babalola, a former member of the Anglican CMS, is reported as having had visions and hearing God's commandment to pray and preach. Akinyele states that his charisma and power quickly became apparent. Through Babalola's influence, thousands of people renounced their cult objects and expressed the desire to learn about God through Christ. Following the method of earlier Aladura preachers, and seizing upon an ancient traditional religious practice ("heathen custom"), he urged people to bring water, which he then blessed; people believed that the water could cure all ailments. Many cases of healing were indeed reported – although Babalola himself did not ascribe any significance to the water. The effect of his presence was generally extremely impressive:

> One can hardly help being impressed with Mr. Joseph Babalola; by his humanity, his simplicity, and his belief in his mission, and also by the awe and the reverence in which he was held by the vast crowds. The scenes along the roads leading to the town where he was then working, gave one a vivid picture of what must have happened along the roads of Palestine in the days of our Lord. – The blind, the lame, the sick, the leper, all were there, and occasionally there was the dead body being brought to him.[14]

On the other hand, there were also countless adherents or lesser prophets, men of a different caliber and less certain calling, people who, one might imagine, acted not entirely without financial interest. In many towns in Western Nigeria religious services, open-air and nocturnal vigils held by these "derivative Aladuras" were common practice and were often found near the Anglican churches. Besides prayers, choral music and proclamations, the ringing of a bell to drive away evil spirits was another important element. Many Anglican worshipers were drawn to these events, especially since the lay preachers were often former members of their congregation. These preachers were liable to misjudge the situation on occasion, leading to the deportation of one of them and the arrest of two others. Bishop Akinyele considered it important, therefore, to distinguish between the movement's original motivation and

13 Alexander Babatunde Akinyele, *Relationship with Schismatic Bodies, and How to Cope with Them*, in: Kenneth Onwuka Dike Library, University of Ibadan, Bishop A.B. Akinyele papers, box 13, undated manuscript, probably written in the 1920s or early 1930s (refers to a letter from 1922).

14 "The Madras Questionnaire," in: Kenneth Onwuka Dike Library, University of Ibadan, Bishop A.B. Akinyele papers, box 32, 1–2.

its repercussions in order to make the most of the revival for his own church:

> Whilst I had a good deal of sympathy with the work of Joseph Babalola, and felt that he had a living message, and that if our agents exerted themselves to get his converts into the church classes for instruction, much lasting good might be done, I fear that the presence and the preaching of his followers are a danger to the organized church life of the country, and quite possibly a greater danger still.[15]

The confrontation with the African Independent Churches was also linked to the question of the ecumenical acceptance of these groups, even though Tambaram was far from making this an explicit subject of the talks. The Aladura churches were generally open to the idea of working together. For example, pastors from the Anglican and Methodist churches, along with ministers from other African churches, such as the Cherubim and Seraphim Church, the first Aladura church founded in 1925, were invited to work in the committees and became actively involved in them.[16] However, this kind of ecumenism, which arose naturally in the congregations, represented a problem for European missionaries. The Anglican bishop of Lagos, Melville Jones, saw cause to issue an incisive warning in 1933: he was totally in favor of having things in common and even for organic union with the Wesleyans, but fraternizing with the African churches must be rejected. Taking part in the meeting of these churches would represent a betrayal of principles and therefore one should be on one's guard.[17]

However, it was not easy for African church leaders to satisfy this demand as these churches had often come into existence as the result of a revival, which in turn had an effect on the established churches. It was not uncommon for these divisions to run through families. For instance, Isaac Babalola Akinyele, the brother of Anglican Bishop Alexander Babatunde Akinyele, was a leading figure in the independent Christ Apostolic Church. Despite this, the two brothers had an excellent relationship, as shown when Alexander Akinyele wrote to his brother during his journey to Tambaram, thanking him for his support during the wedding of his daughter Ebun.[18]

At the conference, the African section turned to the question of the independent churches on Dec 22. Chief Albert John Luthuli gave the main talk, which was received with reservations by Alexander Akinyele. In his conference papers, the Nigerian bishop corrected Luthuli's introductory statement. Luthuli had written: "So far as I know the separatist movement and the growth of a multitude of religious sects is a phenomenon peculiar to South Africa among the younger churches." Akinyele amended this to "peculiar to the younger church in Africa." Luthuli then stated with reference to the *Christian Handbook of South Africa*[19] that there were now around 500 such groups; Akinyele scribbled in the margin: "The religious

15 "The Madras Questionnaire," 5.

16 Lamin Sanneh, *West African Christianity: The Religious Impact*, London, C. Hurst, 1983, 191.

17 *Western Equatorial Africa Diocesan Magazine*, 38/343, July 1933.

18 "I must take this chance to thank you for all you did during Ebun's marriage"; A.B. Akinyele to I.B. Akinyele, Allerton Vicarage, Liverpool, Nov 8, 1938, in: Kenneth Onwuka Dike Library, University of Ibadan, Bishop A.B. Akinyele papers, box 7. For further details, see: Frieder Ludwig, "United in Success: The biographies of the Akinyele brothers in contrast," in: Klaus Koschorke, ed., *"Christen und Gewürze": Konfrontation und Interaktion europäischer und indigener Christentumsvarianten*, Göttingen, Vandenhoek & Ruprecht, 1998, 246–258.

19 Christian Council of South Africa, ed., *Christian Handbook of South Africa*, Lovedale, Lovedale Press, 1938.

groups have also increased in Nigeria." These corrections can be found throughout the paper.[20]

Luthuli went on to call these African religious sects a cancer in the life of the church: by calling themselves Christian they prevented the growth of a spiritually healthy and strong African church. He saw the main reason for the appeal of these churches in the general dissatisfaction with the administration of the "European managed churches," in which Africans were granted very little executive power, as well as with the generally arrogant behavior of the European superintendents, whether overtly expressed or disguised. Another reason in his view were the personalities of church founders. They tended to be extremely ambitious, intent on earning a living or seeking to escape from the disciplinary measures of the missionary churches. The promise of freedom from taxes, or at least a reduction for the churches, and the prospect of representation on the church council exercised an enormous appeal in the congregations. Moreover, widespread illiteracy among the masses made them easily influenced "by every wind from Heaven or Hell." Further factors mentioned by Luthuli were national feeling and the denominational divisions among the European churches:

> NATIONAL FEELING: A genuine desire on the part of Africans to have something African and under African control. Religious liberty enjoyed in South Africa gives an African room to freely endeavour to do something alone and by himself and the increase in the number of groups who seem to express themselves along religious lines only is to my mind due mainly to the fact that in most spheres of life in South Africa, the African meets many restrictions, legal and otherwise.
>
> DENOMINATIONALISM: The unfortunate position of having disunity in the church as represented by denominations has no doubt been an object of emulation by Africans. He has perpetuated differences that are not of his own by conviction in most cases but by tradition.[21]

To combat these causes Luthuli recommended speeding up the general educational program, improving the training of ministers, who should be at least as highly qualified as their European counterparts, transferring positions of authority within the church hierarchy to Africans, and raising the awareness of white South Africans that they should be more liberal and Christian in their dealings with black Africans.

These debates brought the African Independent Churches to the attention of the Indian Christian media. As a commentary in *The Guardian* shows, the situation in South Africa received much attention: "It appears that schisms and sects are rampant in some countries, in Africa more than in any other. One reason adduced from Africa was with racial distinctions in the Church, the African did not feel at home there and preferred to attempt something of his own."[22]

At the same time, efforts towards church union in South India were equally of great interest to African participants. In 1935, Assistant Bishop Alexander Akinyele of Ibadan had already cited at length the article – with which I opened this chapter – by his Anglican Indian colleague Azariah, who had realized that although the attainment of ecclesiastical unity in Europe was a theoretical ideal, it was vital to life in the mission field.[23]

20 Albert John Luthuli, *The African Separatist Churches and Religious Sects*, in: Kenneth Onwuka Dike Library, University of Ibadan, Bishop A.B. Akinyele papers, box 32.

21 Luthuli, *The African Separatist Churches*, 2.

22 "World Missionary Conference, Tambaram," *The Guardian*, Dec 22, 1938, 820.

23 Akinyele in his presidential address at the start of the 6th Synod in Lagos, May 1935, *WEADM* 40/367, 1935.

3 Union Attempts in India

3.1 *Church Union Talks in South India*

The importance of the South Indian talks was undisputed at the ecumenical gatherings that took place throughout the 1930s. The second world conference on Faith and Order held in Edinburgh in 1937 stressed that the unification plan merited particular study since it represented an attempt to incorporate ecclesiastical bodies founded on completely different principles, namely the episcopal, Presbyterian, and congregational.[24]

In 1929, a first draft was published ("Scheme of Union"), which included recognition of the historic episcopate in constitutional form, albeit without the episcopate theory.[25] This draft became known in Europe through publications such as the pamphlet written by George Phillips, disseminated in the United Kingdom, and translated into German by the Basel Mission. The author pointed out "that the denomination in India was largely a matter of accident and geography rather than necessarily of conviction." If someone was talking about a Christian Indian from Nagapatam district, for example, the chances were that this person would be a Methodist since only the Wesleyan Methodist Missionary Society was active in that region. On the other hand, the majority of Christians in the Tinnevelly district were Anglicans from either the high church or low church tradition depending on the location. Phillips asked readers to imagine this situation transposed to England: it would be "as if all Christians in Essex were to grow up as Baptists, in Middlesex as Anglicans, and in Surrey as Presbyterians. This works perfectly well until people travel and settle in other counties. That is when the problems start." For this reason alone, the desire for unification was so characteristic of the Indian church. This was compounded by the increasing sense of nationalism, which leads to the "strong desire ... to be a true Indian as much as a true Christian."[26] In very similar terms, one of the best-known unification figures, the Anglican theologian Aiyadurai Jesudasen Appasamy, pointed out in his treatise *Church Union: An Indian View*, published in 1930, that the success of efforts towards union were closely bound up with the genius of India: "The measure of unity which has been attained thus has been possible because of the genius of the people for tolerance and broad-mindedness. This scheme is not being imposed upon us from outside." He also drew attention to the importance of the guru tradition.[27]

Appasamy was also the author of the "Manifesto on Church Union"[28] published the same year and cosigned by 171 Indian church leaders. Here it was affirmed that Indians had always stressed *bhakti* (loving devotion to God) and held the conviction that belief in God could be more effectively expressed through their most elevated feelings than through dogmas. According to this logic, a

24 Ernst Staehelin, *Das Glaubensgespräch der Kirchen: Die zweite Weltkonferenz für Glauben und Kirchenverfassung abgehalten in Edinburg vom 3.–18. August 1937*, Zollikon, Evangelischer Verlag, 1940, 337. The fact that international attention was on India can be seen for example in: Vedanayagam Samuel Azariah, "The Bishop's Letter," *The Dornakal Diocesan Magazine* 16/8, 1939, 1–8: "The World Conferences at Edinburgh and Tambaram in 1937 and 1938 both evinced great interest in the South India Scheme; and it is no exaggeration to say that the prevailing opinion among both Anglicans and non-Anglicans was that the proposals set out in the Scheme contain, in the main, practical considerations and wise provisions on which alone a visible union among the Reformed Churches would at any time become practicable. That being so, there would be a great disappointment throughout the world that we in South India let a scheme drop, a scheme which bears on it marks of God's guidance, respect for the past history of the negotiating churches and consideration for their age-long experiences."

25 Bengt Sundkler, *Church of South India: The Movement towards Union (1900–1947)*, Greenwich CT, Seabury Press, 1954, 167–168.

26 George Phillips, *Warum die Kirchen Indiens sich zu vereinigen wünschen*, undated (*c.*1930), in: BM, C-4-51, 6–7.

27 Aiyadurai Jesudasen Appasamy, *Church Union: An Indian View*, Madras, Christian Literature Society's Press, 1930; on this, see also the discussion on "Church Union," *Dornakal Diocesan Magazine* 7/7, 1930, 14–16.

29 Sundkler, *Church of South India*, 205–206.

unified church would reflect this spirit and create an atmosphere conducive to the Indian expression of Christianity.[29]

In the 1930s, deep-seated controversies among the different parties involved in unification endeavors came to the fore, such as over the understanding of the historic episcopate, the relationship between bishop and synod, the participation of the laity in Holy Communion, or the administering of the sacraments in the older Anglican congregations during a set interim period of 30 years. Despite this, Indian Christians consistently pushed ahead with unification efforts. In 1936, the Indian members of the joint committee wrote an open letter to Christians in Britain and the United States, stressing once again that the new church should be an organization that suited Indians, regardless of whether or not it was to the taste of the Fathers in the West.[30] In the following year, 116 Indian Christians, including Bihari Lal Rallia Ram, Vedanayagam Samuel Azariah, and Aiyadurai Jesudasen Appasamy, addressed the Indian public directly. In an appeal published in the *Madras Diocesan Magazine*, they described the attempts at union as mainly the result of an Indian initiative.[31]

3.2 *Rethinking Christianity in India*

However, not all Indian Christians were convinced by developments in the efforts towards church union. Objections came from unexpected quarters, namely, precisely from those forces that had accorded particularly strong support to links between Christianity and Indian culture. The criticism also found expression in the best-known publication of Indian Christians, which came to life in connection with the WMC of Tambaram: the anthology published by D.M. Devasahayam and A.N. Sudarisanam entitled *Rethinking Christianity in India*. Its authors later became known after the work's title as the Rethinking Group or Madras Rethinking Group. They included G.V. Job, S. Jesudasen, D.M. Devasahayam, E. Asirvatham, and A.N. Sudarisanam, who each contributed an article, while most of the articles were written by brothers-in-law Pandipeddi Chenchiah and Vengal Chakkarai, with five and three articles, respectively. Both of these lay theologians were already leading figures as part of the Madras Christo Samaj, an association of critical Indian Christians.

The Madras Christo Samaj emerged in 1913 out of the slightly older Young Liberals' League founded in 1904. The aim of the Young Liberals' League was to foster the unity of Indian Christians, while the Christo Samaj saw itself "as an expression of the new national spirit of the country on the one hand, and of the new spirit of communal and religious self-consciousness and self-realization that had taken hold of the Christian community on the other hand."[32] Conferences were held in Bangalore every year from 1917 at the initiative of the Samaj. Its publication forum was the *Christian Patriot*, where the church union model was called into question as too Western.[33] The Madras Rethinking Group developed its own understanding of Christian belief, which stressed

29 Sundkler, *Church of South India*, 205–206.

30 "A Union Problem (A Letter Addressed to the Editors of Church Papers in the West, Signed by the Indian Members of the Joint Committee of 1936 Apr 24, 1936)," *The South India United Church Herald* 28/4, 1936, 89–91.

31 "An Appeal to the Churches in India for Unity," *The Madras Diocesan Magazine*, 1937, 60–62.

32 *The Memorandum of the further Development and Expansion of Christianity in India*, presented by the Christo Samaj to Joseph H. Oldham Esq., 1921, Secretary of the IMC, on Dec 3, 1921, in: UTS Library, New York, "South Asia," 1. The memorandum was also printed in: *The Young Men of India* 33, 1922, 14–33.

33 On the *Christian Patriot*, see Klaus Koschorke & others, eds., *Discourses of Indigenous Christian Elites in Colonial Societies in Asia and Africa around 1900: A Documentary Sourcebook from Selected Journals*, Wiesbaden, Harrassowitz, 2016; Klaus Koschorke & others, eds., *"To give publicity to our thoughts": Journale asiatischer und afrikanischer Christen um 1900 und die Entstehung einer transregionalen indigen-christlichen Öffentlichkeit*, Wiesbaden, Harrassowitz, 2018. See also the monograph by Klaus Koschorke, *Owned and Conducted entirely by the Native Christian Community: Der "Christian Patriot" und die indigen-christliche Presse im kolonialen Indien um 1900*, Wiesbaden, Harrassowitz, 2019.

the immediacy of the encounter with Christ and for this reason at the same time sought a positive acceptance of "Hindu heritage" and dialogue through the "confluence of the spirits" in "India's spiritual laboratory." External forms, the vessels constructed around the message, represented an obstacle to both these aims. It is therefore hardly surprising that the Western concept of the church met with little enthusiasm among the group.

In the *Rethinking Christianity in India* anthology, criticism of (Western) missionary influence became the starting point for further reflections. In his introductory piece, G.V. Job argued that an Indian Christian had a better chance than a missionary of being heard by Hindus, as long as he was a good Indian. The Indian churches were currently no more than an imitation of their Western counterparts in terms of the structure of their religious services and their ecclesiastical hierarchy; India did not have its own theology and had not even created a decent heresy of its own.[34] The collective work was intended to show that the Indian church had developed the ability to think and act for itself and that Christianity had become an indigenous movement.[35]

Pandipeddi Chenchiah, in particular, explored the issue of ecclesiastical hierarchy and a possible Indian counter-model. He first of all made it clear that he had little sympathy for the Catholicism of the Roman variety. On the grounds of national interest alone there was no desire in India to encourage religions with trans-Indian loyalties. The spread of an Islam which regarded Turkey or Egypt as its spiritual mother was just as little in the national interest as a Catholic community oriented towards Rome gaining influence. But more important than the political grounds for rejecting "a church that wanted to put itself in the place of Jesus Christ," were the spiritual grounds. An Indian Christian gladly relinquished this Catholic church model – not because it was alien to him but because it resembled certain rituals which had also developed in Hinduism, such as veneration of the saints, relics, and belief in the sacraments. Modern and rational representatives of Hinduism themselves rejected these forms as pathological. Why should a Christian accept such foolishness in the name of Christ while rejecting it in Hinduism? Indian Christians did not want a new kind of religious slavery.[36]

In contrast to this, Protestantism undoubtedly had a stronger appeal through its sense of the individual, alertness to freedom of conscience, rejection of superstition, and opposition to the priesthood. However, one essential quality was also lacking here: the spirit. Doctrine was so dominant that it left no room for the growth of the spirit.[37] The church as it is known today (and here Chenchiah put the Catholic and Protestant churches in the same box) was not the plan of Jesus but had first come into being when the Holy Spirit had ceased to be a reality. Chenchiah developed these ideas through a short outline of the first centuries of missionary history:

> Twelve fishermen conquered the world. Thomas came to India. Philip planted the seed in Africa. Paul set ablaze Europe. Of the twelve, eight were too many for the world. Three were sufficient. Yet success seemed to have defeated its own end. When Rome was conquered – itself a miracle – the debacle came with unexpected suddenness. Conquered Rome, conquered Christianity. The weakness of life manifested itself in the hour of victory. The weakness was converted into strength. Hence the death of Christ and the birth of Christianity. When the disciple

34 G.V. Job, "The Christian Movement in India," in: D.M. Devasahayam & A.N. Sudarisanam, eds., *Rethinking Christianity in India*, Madras, Hogarth Press, 1939, 3–45, here 16–17.

35 D.M. Devasahayam & A.N. Sudarisanam, "Preface to First Edition," in: Devasahayam & Sudarisanam, *Rethinking Christianity*, V–VI, here V.

36 Pandipeddi Chenchiah, "The Church and the Indian Christian," in: Devasahayam & Sudarisanam, *Rethinking Christianity*, 83–102, here 94.

37 Chenchiah, "The Church and the Indian Christian," 95.

> felt that Jesus was taken away, he had the consolation that in exchange he had the Holy Spirit. But the Holy Spirit also left.[38]

Thus, India's Christians faced the alternative between continuing the path of evangelization through organization and conquest taken by the missionary churches, singing along to "Onward Christian Soldiers," on the one hand, or recapturing the Holy Spirit on the other.[39]

Chenchiah was hence bound to reject the South Indian model of church union as a continuation of Western ecclesiastical organization. In this respect, he was naturally able to invoke the long-standing criticism made by the group of Indian Christians involved in the negotiations of the early 1920s. A memorandum of the Madras Christo Samaj addressed to the secretary of the IMC, Joseph H. Oldham, in December 1921 summarized their criticisms of the unification plans: a major problem with the union undertaking was the leading role of missionaries. Indian support came from ministers and laymen dependent on missionaries and anxious to please them. However, this approach was like putting the cart before the horse or building a house before laying its foundations. Indian self-respect was injured not only by the manipulations of the missionaries but also by the fact that the union church perpetuated the Western churches' administrative, ecclesiastical, and evangelical machinery, which was alien to Indians. "Indian religion has laid far less emphasis on close organization and on costly institutions and has depended far more on the personal and voluntary service of unorganized religious workers of the type of the Sadhus."[40] Centralization of ecclesiastical authority and the far more complex machinery of a union church would represent the definitive triumph of a foreign system. This would cement the administrative and financial dependence on foreign missions. The document then criticized the mass conversions sought by the Western churches, mainly successful among the lower castes. Naturally one agreed that the gospel should be preached above all to the poor but the reasons for their conversion were sometimes questionable: "It is to the social and material aspirations of the lower classes that the method has largely appealed and the spiritual motive is not given the emphasis and preeminence that it always should claim."[41] The large number of newly converted Christians from the lower classes had not only led to further divisions in the Indian church but also given missionaries the legitimation to perpetuate their control function. The Samaj proposed a strict division between philanthropic social work and Christian mission as a potential solution.[42]

The shaping of the Samaj by converts from the upper castes is unmistakable in this memorandum. The portrayal of the model of church union as an initiative of Western missionaries must be seen in the context of internal Indian conflicts and power struggles, for in the efforts towards unification Indian Christians such as Bishop Azariah, but also Appasamy, had played a major role from the beginning.

Even more forthright than the Christo Samaj memorandum in their opposition to unification efforts were the Bangalore conferences, in which Chakkarai and Chenchiah also took part. At the seventh meeting held in 1923, D.M. Devasahayam affirmed that the union movement in India was not a popular movement but one imposed by foreigners who wanted to prove that the early apostolic church could be reproduced in the missionary field. He urged the conference to confirm the previous year's resolutions which had decided that (1) the existing churches were already equal members of a catholic church; (2) intercommunion and inter-celebration should have precedence on the organic union; and (3) union plans should be postponed until the Indian church had achieved economic, administrative, and

38 Chenchiah, "The Church and the Indian Christian," 99.

39 Chenchiah, "The Church and the Indian Christian," 101.

40 *The Memorandum of the further Development*, 16.

41 *The Memorandum of the further Development*, 17.

42 *The Memorandum of the further Development*, 18, 27.

intellectual independence. In a contribution following the discussion, the "secret diplomacy" of the negotiations was condemned and a demand made for an upfront and transparent approach. Another speaker who had clearly taken part in the union negotiations ("who was intimately connected with the movement") agreed that these talks were of little interest to the Indian people. He also told the conference that one of the leading negotiators had been unable to answer a question about who would pay the salaries of new bishops. He said that, in the event of church union the Church of England would provide funds to the SIUC, thus giving the impression that the union plan was nothing other than an Anglican takeover attempt. Finally, the chairman of the section, Rev. H.C. Balasundaram, summarized the discussions at the Bangalore conference about church union, concluding "that in the interests of Christian public the conference should put up a brave fight against the proposed union which, if it could accomplish anything at all, would accomplish our own spiritual ruin. In his short experience, he found that the leaders of this movement had a genius for non-essentials and that time and energy spent by them was worthy of a better cause."[43]

In *Rethinking Christianity*, Pandipeddi Chenchiah was able to draw on these earlier arguments. In his contribution on church union, he argued that every (new) convert thought the idea laughable that a union of the Church of England, of Scotland, and of the Lutheran Swedish and American churches, could result in an Indian church. The only reason this plan had survived was that religious people had no sense of humor. The entire notion was a joke. Union could only be achieved by replacing church consciousness with "Christ consciousness."[44]

The collected volume *Rethinking Christianity in India* was not met solely by voices of consensus, not even among Protestant Indian theologians. In a review, Paul Devanandan argued that the work was essentially limited to criticism and therefore repeated well-known positions, a point not without justification in the case of Chenchiah's church union article.[45] Nonetheless, the Chenchiah and Chakkarai circle did attempt at least to suggest their own alternative approach. In a memorandum from 1922, Christo Samaj pointed out two concrete examples serving to overcome denominational barriers which reflected an impulse similar to its own: "Concrete manifestations of our ideal are to be found in the Bangalore Residential High School – a purely Indian Christian effort – and the ashram of Tirupattur – a medical Home and Institutions where the ideals of brotherhood and service are being put to daily practice."[46]

The Christukula Ashram founded by doctors Savarirayan Jesudason (a member of Christo Samaj and later of the Rethinking Group) and Ernest Forrester Paton (brother of the IMC general secretary, William Paton) in Tirupattur in 1921 became particularly significant. It represented one of the first attempts to combine this form of religious life developed in classical Hinduism (the gathering in a hut or forest settlement under the direction of a guru) with Christianity. The ashram idea had long been forgotten, but since the late 19th and early 20th centuries, forces for Hindu reform had sought to revive it. Debendranath Tagore founded the Santiniketan Ashram in 1888, which was taken over by his son, the poet Rabindranath Tagore, in 1901.[47] In 1915, Mahatma Gandhi set

43 "The Seventh Bangalore Conference: Why do We Read the Bible? What Think Ye of Christ? Responsive Cooperation between Hindus and Christians. The Union Scheme Condemned and the Āshram Ideal to the Front," *The Christian Patriot*, Jun 2, 1923, 2–3.

44 Pandipeddi Chenchiah, "Church Union: A Study of Underlying Ideas," in: Devasahayam & Sudarisanam, *Rethinking Christianity*, 209–228, here 226.

45 Paul Devanandan, "Review: Rethinking Christianity in India," *NCCR* 59, 1939, 651–654, here 654.

46 Christo Samaj, "A Memorandum on Certain Problems of Missionary Effort and Christianity in India," *HFJ* 42, 1922, 7–14, 7.

47 Rabindranath Tagore summarized his ashram concept in a short essay "Is God to be Sought in Forests," in: Francis Acharya, ed., *Kurisumala: A Symposium on Ashram Life*, Kottayam, Kurisumala Ashram, 1974, 90–92. He put forward the view that the development of Indian religious thought was closely tied to withdrawal to the forest and contrasted this with the

up his Sabarmati Ashram near Ahmedabad in Gujarat, which he conceived as a training center for political and social reformers in a clear departure from the classical ideal of withdrawal for spiritual contemplation.[48] Other important new foundations were the yoga school at Kumbakonam (1909) and the Sri Aurobindo Ashram in Pondicherry (1910–1926). The Christian Ashram of Tirupattur was to a great extent inspired and influenced by these models. The church of Tirupattur's architecture resembled that of a South Indian temple, and devotion and services were designed with Indian symbolic acts, objects, and music. The hospital modeled its personal and individual relationship with patients on the guru-pupil relationship.[49]

The Bangalore conference also recognized the Christian ashram movement as a step in the right direction, and at its 1923 gathering one of the delegates drew up a vision of the Christian ashram in combining the attributes of a modern Hindu ashram with those of the famous Catechetical School in Alexandria. Although the prevailing feeling among the rest of the participants was that it would be more practical to start on a more modest project, it was clear to everyone that this form of uniting was far more preferable to merging in a union church. The *Christian Patriot* subsumed the discussions at the seventh Bangalore conference under the succinct subheading: "The Union Scheme Condemned and the Ashram Ideal to the Front."[50]

The ashram movement was also a topic dealt with in *Rethinking Christianity in India*. Chenchiah ended his church article with the conclusion that the immediate task to hand was to experiment. The idea of the ashram had been born at a time of great spiritual experimentation in India and had made an important contribution in both the past and the present. The political regeneration of modern India had been brought about by the Sabarmati Ashram, and in education and training at Santiniketan. Indian science had originated in the ashrams of Sri Aurobindo and Ramana Mahershi. Spiritual regeneration was also the result of an ashram. Ashrams were the precursors of the Christian Church in India.[51]

The anthology dedicated a contribution to ashrams. It was written by the cofounder of Tirupattur, Savarirayan Jesudason.[52] However, it was fairly general and the need for more far-reaching research was later emphasized at the Tambaram conference. Its participants included not only Jesudason as co-founder of the Christukula Ashram, but also Eli Stanley Jones from the ashram in Lal Bagh in

West's "city culture": "Thus in India it was in the forests that our civilization had its birth, and it took a distinct character from this origin and its environment. … In later days there came a time when these primeval forests gave way to cultivated fields, and wealthy cities sprang up on all sides. … But even in the heyday of its material prosperity the heart of India ever looked back with adoration, upon the early ideal of strenuous self-realization, and the dignity of the simple life of the forest hermitage … The West seems to take a pride in thinking that it is subduing nature; as if we are living in a hostile world where we have to wrestle everything we want from an unwilling and alien arrangement of things. This sentiment is the product of the city-wall habit and training of mind."

48 On this, see Mahatma Gandhi, *Mahatma Gandhis autobiographie: Die Geschichte meiner Experimente mit der Wahrheit*, Freiburg, Karl Alber, 1960, 347–349. This autobiography also contains a section on Shantiniketan (335–337).

49 On the Christian ashram movement: Ernst Pulsfort, *Christliche Ashrams in Indien: Zwischen dem religiösen Erbe Indiens und der christlichen Tradition des Abendlandes*, Altenberge, Telos, 1989; Helen Ralston, *Christian Ashrams: A New Religious Movement in Contemporary India*, Lewiston NY, Edwin Mellen Press, 1987; Friso Melzer, *Christliche Ashrams in Südindien*, Erlangen, Verlag der Ev.-Luth. Mission, 1976. A general description can be found in: Horst Rzepkowski, article on "Ashram," in: Horst Rzepkowski, *Lexikon der Mission: Geschichte, Theologie, Ethnologie*, Graz, Styria, 1992, 50–51, and Hans-Peter Müller, "Ashrams, christliche," *RGG* 4, 811. A good overview of the historical development of the guru concept is provided by Joel D. Mlecko, "The Guru in Hindu Tradition," *Numen* 29/1, 1982, 33–61.

50 "The Seventh Bangalore Conference," 2–3.

51 Chenchiah, "The Church and the Indian Christian," 102.

52 Savarirayan Jesudasen, "Ashrams," in: Devasahayam & Sudarisanam, *Rethinking Christianity*, 197–206.

Lucknow. Among the delegates there was also, besides Charles Freer Andrews, a prominent representative of a non-Christian ashram, since in the meantime the former missionary had become the vice president of the Santiniketan Ashram.

The Christian ashram movement was a topic discussed at the WMC, for example in connection with the training of missionaries. It was suggested that selected newcomers should first become acquainted with an indigenous form of religious life for a certain period of time: "It might be possible to arrange for a limited number of candidates to share, for a period of several months or possibly years, in the life of some indigenous institution such as the Christian ashrams in India."[53]

This idea was subsequently taken up at a seminar of British experts held at Woodbrooke College in Selly Oak in Birmingham. Eleonore Bowser from the BMS was rather skeptical. She held that Christian ashrams were not very suitable as an introduction since they did not represent India's ordinary church life, but were instead exceptional forms.

William Paton shared Bowser's skepticism, but at the same time pointed out another aspect that would have to be borne in mind and appreciated: "We must not forget the crucial fact of political subjection in relation to the feelings of Indian Christians. Psychological adjustments are still required of the missionary."[54] At this time, Christian ashrams were studied with interest as model attempts by quite an influential group within the international missionary movement. It was therefore only logical that in the period immediately following the Tambaram conference the Madras Rethinking Group sought to obtain a deeper understanding of this phenomenon, not turning their attention until later to other indigenization approaches, such as Christian yoga.

In 1941, Pandippedi Chenchiah, Vengal Chakkarai, and A.N. Sudarisanam published their *Asramas, Past & Present*. Chenchiah started by giving a brief etymological account of the term, which he derived from the root "śram" ("to strive"). He associated the origin of ashrams with the "Aryan immigration" (around 1500 BC, nomadic tribes who called themselves "Arya" invaded north-west India) and referred to the Brahmana literature (which evolved between 1000 and 700 BC) as evidence. After settling in the Punjab and Ganges valley, the heads of the families handed over the burden of responsibility to their sons while they and their wives withdrew to the forest for contemplation. They built huts, according to Chenchiah, and lived on fruit and vegetables. These hermitages were called *asramas*. When spiritual endeavors bore fruit, the ashram became a place of peace and harmony, a refuge. Chenchiah's description was extremely idyllic: travelers who had lost their way would be drawn by the smoke of the altar fire, animals escaping hunters found refuge here, and students in search of knowledge would journey there.[55] A central element was the founder personality, the *ṛṣi* or "seer." For every cultured Hindu an ashram conjured up the image of a forest with a flowing stream on whose banks there would be a hut; in front of the hut a tall tree under whose branched shade sat a *ṛṣi* with a distinguished beard in religious contemplation. His elderly wife could be found in the hut, one or two pupils nearby, and an altar with its sacred fire (*agni*) burning.

3.3 *Approaches in the Mar Thoma Church*

Another differently oriented Indian ecumenical vision was embodied by C.P. Mathew, one of the representatives of the Mar Thoma Church in Tambaram. He was not himself a priest but

53 "The Place, Function and Training of the Future Missionary," in: IMC, ed., *The Life of the Church*, Tambaram Series, vol. 4, London, Oxford University Press 1939, 251–293, 255.

54 "Conference on the Training of Missionaries," Woodbrooke College, Selly Oak, Apr 21–24, 1939, in: Rhodes House, Oxford, SPG-D Series 630/1.

55 Pandipeddi Chenchiah, "Asramas: Derivation and Meaning," in: Pandipeddi Chenchiah, V. Chakkarai & A.N. Sudarisanam, *Asramas, Past & Present*, Madras, Indian Christian Book Club, 1941, 1–8.

in fact a teacher at the Union Christian College in Alwaye (Kerala). Members of the Mar Thoma Church, the Anglican Church, and the Jacobite Syrian Orthodox Church worked together at this educational institution, which was founded in 1921. They were represented in Tambaram by the college's principal, A.M. Varki. As the first unified college in India resulting solely from an Indian initiative, Alwaye assumed a pioneering role. Its delegates at Tambaram acted confidently as representatives of a community that had its own political views, was economically independent, and whose roots predated the period of European colonialism and missionary initiatives. Mathew was clearly aware of the history of schisms within ancient Indian Christianity. He had already mentioned it in a short study, which was to serve the other delegates at the WMC as preparatory and background information. He described the tradition of the St. Thomas Christians, who traced their church's origins back to the activity of the Apostle Thomas, while also noting rather disapprovingly that historians disagreed about the authenticity of this tradition, but that it was reasonable to assume with certainty that there had been a Christian community in south-west India since the 3rd or 4th century.[56]

This appraisal by the Union Christian College professor was actually rather too circumspect. Reports of a very early Christian presence in South India appear quite plausible given the close trade relations between India and the Mediterranean in the 1st and 2nd centuries, as is proved by coin finds, among other things.[57] The doctrine of the Council of Chalcedon (451) on Christ's two natures was not accepted by the church in South India. From the 6th century onwards, there are increasing references to close links to the Nestorian Church of Mesopotamia and Persia. It is a disputed matter among scholars whether there were dependencies and how strong other influences were, particularly from the West Syrian (Monophysite) tradition, but also from the Western (Roman Catholic) one.[58] These issues became important later, after the arrival of the Portuguese in Kerala in 1498, because, as Mathew goes on to explain in his outline, this led to a series of missionizing attempts by the Roman Catholic Church and finally to a forced takeover at the Synod of Diamper (1599). Links to Mesopotamia were suppressed, and doctrine and liturgy adapted to the rules of Tridentine Catholicism. These measures were opposed by some, leading to a schism in 1653: "Then a considerable section rose in revolt against the supremacy of Rome and threw off the yoke which had been imposed on them by force." These congregations subsequently submitted to the authority of the Jacobite patriarch of Antioch.[59] The Jacobite or

56 C.P. Mathew, *The Witness of the Church: The Syrian Church of India with special reference to its Reaction through Centuries to Hindu Life and Thought*, Madras, Diocesan Press, 1937, 1.

57 Stephen Neill, *A History of Christianity in India*, vol. 1, *The Beginnings to AD 1707*, Cambridge, Cambridge University Press, 1984; see also Klaus Koschorke, "Der indische Subkontinent," in: Karl Müller & Werner Ustorf, eds., *Einleitung in die Missionsgeschichte: Tradition, Situation und Dynamik des Christentums*, Stuttgart, Kolhammer, 1995, 104–120, here 104–105. Mathias Mundadan in his *History of Christianity in India*, vol. 1, *From the Beginning up to the Middle of the Sixteenth Century*, Bangalore, Church History Association of India, 1989, opts for the 1st century, but bases this on his own ecclesiastical knowledge as a precondition. A compilation of important sources with references to India from early church authors (including Eusebius of Caesarea, Gregory of Nazianzus, and Ambrose of Milan) can be found in: M.K. Kuriakose, *History of Christianity in India: Source Materials*, Madras, Christian Literature Society, 1982, 1–8, although here the question that obviously arises is which geographical area is intended by "India" in each case.

58 A summary of the different points of view is given by: Paul Verghese, "Die dunklen Jahrhunderte," in: Paul Verghese, ed., *Die syrischen Kirchen in Indien*, Stuttgart, Evangelisches Verlagswerk, 1974, 21–32, esp. 21–22. For a survey of the contacts with the Western church before the 16th century, see Mundadan, *History of Christianity*, vol. 1, 116–144.

59 Mathew, *The Witness of the Church*, 2; see also Koschorke, "Der indische Subkontinent," 106. Teotonio R. de Souza, "The Indian Christians of St. Thomas and the Portuguese Padroado: Rape after a Century-Long

Syrian Orthodox community did indeed belong, like the Nestorian Church, to the "pre-Chalcedonian" churches (namely, those churches that did not recognize that council's canons), but their Monophysite orientation in fact represented the opposite extreme in the Christological controversy. The fact that this reorientation required explanation for the representatives of the oldest form of Indian Christianity is shown by Mathew's comments along with those of his colleague and superior, Varki, at the Tambaram conference. Mathew adopted a detached attitude and referred to the different positions:

> For long centuries from about the middle of the 6th century till the synod of Diamper the Malabar Church had been largely under Nestorian influences. A few of the historians who reject the Apostolic origin of the Malabar Church maintain that it was founded as the result of the missionary labours of the Nestorian Church. The Syrian Christians however generally not only deny the Nestorian origin of the Malabar Church but also maintain that it was never strictly and fully under the Patriarch of Babylon. They hold that though Nestorian Bishops were in this country and performed episcopal functions in the Syrian community for a long period, the community enjoyed always administrative autonomy. The long period of Nestorian influence does not seem to have left any permanent impress on the Syrian Church of the latter days.[60]

Varki, on the other hand, in his paper given at "The Growing Church" section and later published in the conference proceedings, showed a striking connection between historical analysis and Syrian Orthodox self-perception:

> Historians have tried to make out that the Orthodox Syrian Church in South India was at one time Nestorian and later Monophysite. The truth seems to be simply that these Christians, few in numbers, living among large non-Christian populations and without opportunities of frequent contact with Christian communities outside, welcomed with open arms whoever came from Asia Minor or Palestine or Persia without stopping to enquire into his precise doctrinal and ecclesiastical affiliations, and so quite probably the church at one time accepted Nestorian bishops and at another time Monophysite bishops without however accepting the doctrines which these bishops held. In one sense, therefore, the contentions of the historians may be true. In another and a truer sense this church has always kept its faith Orthodox and its succession apostolic.[61]

Therefore, there were already two distinct groups of St. Thomas Christians: one linked to Rome and the other a Jacobite Church under the authority of the Jacobite patriarch. The history of schisms continued in the Jacobite community with the arrival of missionaries from the Anglican CMS in the 19th century. Mathew underlines the fact that the aim of the CMS was not to recruit believers from the Syrian community, but that it was solely concerned to promote the education of St. Thomas Christians, to awaken them from their "spiritual sleep," and to purify the church of "what they considered to be corrupt practices and notions and thus to help the Church to become in its turn a missionary church in this vast non-Christian land." The CMS missionaries even worked with the Syrian metropolitan during a period, but serious disagreements arose later under a different metropolitan. The early CMS missionaries, as representatives of the Anglican Church's extreme evangelical wing, had

Courtship (1498–1599)," in: Koschorke, ed., *"Christen und Gewürze"*, 31–42 shows the extent to which contacts before 1599 were of mutual interest.

60 Mathew, *The Witness of the Church*, 7.

61 A.M. Varki, "The Orthodox Syrian Church in India," in: IMC, ed., *The Growing Church*, Tambaram Series, vol. 2, London, Oxford University Press, 1939, 220–233, 223.

not developed much appreciation of the rites, ceremonies, and teachings of the Oriental Church in Malabar. However, they alone could certainly not be held entirely responsible for the collapse in good relations.[62]

The Alwaye professor offered only a vague description of subsequent events in the preparatory document for Tambaram, but wrote at greater length in one of his later papers when recognized as an international expert on the history of his church, partly thanks to his contributions at the WMC in 1938. He explained in an article published in 1974 that the break between the CMS and the Syrian Church did not mean that the CMS's activity had not left any trace. Rather, it continued to have an effect in the field of religion in many different ways. Small Anglican congregations had been established in many places comprising mainly Syrian Christians and new converts from the lowest Hindu castes. Nonetheless, Mathew admitted that the missionaries took Syrians into their church only with great reluctance and after their entreaty. As can be seen clearly from their correspondence, the missionaries had no intention of setting up a Syrian branch of the Anglican Church in Travancore. However, the CMS's activity led to further divisions because a group was formed that wanted to remain within the Syrian Church while at the same time strongly influenced by the reform ideas of low church Anglicans. This resulted in a conflict since the majority of the Syrian Church was opposed to these reforms, which in turn culminated in a legal dispute in which the pro-reform group was defeated. This caused a split in the church between the two groups in 1888. The pro-reform group claimed that the Syrian Church of Malabar was independent, while the other faction remained under the authority of the patriarch of Antioch. Thus once again two churches were created where previously there had been just one – the Mar Thoma Church influenced by the CMS and the Syrian Orthodox Church.[63] However, this did not have the effect of consolidating the latter community. Another dispute came to the fore in 1909 when Patriarch Abdullah arrived from Syria, installed himself for two years, and excommunicated the Syrian Metropolitan Mar Dionysius in 1911. An endless series of disputes came before the courts.[64] At Tambaram, Varki gave an outline of the situation of Syrian Christianity based on the census of 1931. According to this, the Syrian community numbered approximately 1,180,000 people. Around 640,000 "Roman Syrians" were integrated into the Catholic Church, while the non-Roman section was divided between the Mar Thoma Church (150,000), the Anglican Church (23,000), the Syrian Orthodox Church, in turn split between the faction of the patriarch (170,000) and that of the catholicos (190,000), and others (7,000).[65]

Restoring unity to India's oldest church was the main concern of the IMC and the Anglican Church in India from 1929. The Anglicans felt bound to seek reconciliation between the patriarch and catholicos factions since the Roman Catholic Church could exploit the dispute to its own benefit and had already persuaded two bishops to come over from the Syrian Orthodox side.[66] In 1931, a provisional arrangement was reached: the church in India was granted certain rights of autonomy and the title of catholicos recognized.[67]

62 Mathew, *The Witness of the Church*, 3. Mathew does not even describe it merely as "spiritual sleep," but "spiritual stupor."

63 C.P. Mathew, "Die Ankunft der Kirchlichen Missionsgesellschaft und ihre 'Hilfsmission,'" in: Verghese, *Die syrischen Kirchen*, 85–114, here 104–105; on this, see also C.P. Mathew, "Ein neues Schisma und die Mar-Thoma-Kirche," in: Verghese, *Die syrischen Kirchen*, 115–128.

64 *A Note on the History of the Dissensions in the Jacobite Syrian Church in Travancore and Cochin*, in: K.C. Chacko to Metropolitan, Dec 8, 1930, in: BCC, Metropolitan box 2, file 2, Syrian Church Travancore 1929–1930, 1–3.

65 Varki, "The Orthodox Syrian Church," 222.

66 *A Note on the History of the Dissensions*, 4.

67 On this, see also Klaus Koschorke & Frieder Ludwig, *Anti-Denominationalismus und Nationalimus: Die Anfänge ökumenischer Kooperation in Asien und Afrika (unter besonderer Berücksichtigung Indiens und Nigerias) und ihr Einfluß auf die Ökumene-Bewegugn des*

Further attempts at agreement soon followed. Unlike the previous reconciliation talks, in which British and American representatives of the international mission movement had played an important role as mediators, the new discussions took their main impulse and direction from the initiative of Indian Christians in Kerala. From the mid-1930s, church union conferences among the Mar Thoma, Syrian Orthodox, and Anglican churches took place in which leading figures from the Union Christian College in Alwaye in particular played a decisive role.

As previously mentioned, this educational institution in Alwaye had been founded in 1921. It was the first non-Catholic Christian college in India founded by Indians themselves.[68] The driving force behind its foundation was primarily Chacko, who belonged to the Syrian Orthodox Church and had been first a student and then a teacher at Madras Christian College. His experience there convinced him that a similar institution would also be of great use in Kerala.[69] He succeeded in winning support for his idea from influential colleagues of his time in Madras, such as Mathew, V.M. Ittyerah of the Mar Thoma Church, and Varki of the Syrian Orthodox Church. He was also able to persuade the governing bodies of these churches and the heads of the Anglican diocese of Travancore and Cochin to support the project. The founders attributed special weight to the realization that the Union Christian College was in favor of Christianity's unity and wanted to counter the rivalry among the denominations in the field of education.[70] It was unique in south-west India in advocating such a program. "The Union College is the only enterprise of any kind in which the different sections of the Syrian Church are in any sense cooperating," observed the Protestant missionary *Harvest Field Journal*.[71] Moreover, the project was also welcomed by the non-Christian, Indian elite. Professor Sarvepalli Radakrishnan, then at University College in Calcutta, stated in his greeting:

> The institution appeals to me and ought to appeal to other non-Christians too for the following reasons: – It is likely to make those who come under its influence feel that religion is a living reality and not a dead routine. We hear it said often that India is a deeply religious country and perhaps also that too much religion has ruined her. In all such talk we seem to be confusing religion with rule and ritual, external ceremony and mechanical worship. It is good to say the prayers we have learnt at our mothers knees once or twice a day, but is it not much better to make religion a vital force of our lives determining every word, thought and deed? I hope at Alwaye you would try to kindle the spiritual sense, instill a larger vision and thus help people to respect each other's faith. Such mutual respect would be the necessary result of a true understanding of the spirit of religion that it is not a cult or a creed, a church or a ceremonial system, but an inner life which in the quiet depths of the soul seeks its way to God.[72]

Westens, Deutsche Forschungsgemeinschaft research project, ch. 10.1.3.

68 "This was the first non-Roman, Christian College in India owing its existence to Indian Christian initiative. All the non-Roman Christian Colleges in India had been managed by Western Missionary Societies"; V.M. Itteryah, "Union Christian College: A Survey of the first twenty-five years," in: *Union Christian College: A Survey of the First Twenty-Five Years (1921–1946)*, Alwaye, 1946, 2–3, archived in the Union Christian College Alwaye.

69 V.M. Ittyerah, *K.C. Chacko of Alwaye*, Kottayam, undated, archived in the Union Christian College Alwaye.

70 *The Union Christian College, Alwaye: Its Beginning and Growth*, undated, 1, archived in the Union Christian College Alwaye.

71 "Ut Omes Unum Sint: Notes on the Union Christian College, Alwaye," *HFJ* 42, 1922, 293–296, here 295.

72 *The Union Christian College Alwaye South India*, Madras, 1921, 4f., archived in the Union Christian College Alwaye.

One year later the poet Rabindranath Tagore inaugurated the first hall of residence. In his address, he highlighted that the college had the same ideals as the school he himself founded in the ashram in Santiniketan.[73]

The Alwaye model gave a strong impetus to ecumenical relations among Anglicans, Syrian Orthodox believers, and members of the Mar Thoma Church. These contacts and common points were intensified during the reconciliation attempts by the Anglicans to overcome the disagreements within the Syrian Orthodox Church. Talks had been taking place since the end of the 1920s in which the possibility of even closer collaboration was considered. However, at the first conference in Kerala in 1929 only representatives from the Mar Thoma Church and the Anglicans took part. They still discussed the idea of union, but the suggestion was rejected by the competent committee of the archbishop of Canterbury (the Eastern Churches Committee). The reason given was that the Mar Thoma Church was in a transition stage and one did not want to jeopardize relations with the larger Syrian churches.[74]

Therefore, representatives of the Syrian Orthodox Church were invited to the next round of talks. Two initial informal preparatory meetings were held in Thiruvella in February and June 1935. In May 1936, the Kerala Council of Church Union had its first official meeting. The fact that Chacko and Mathew were appointed joint secretaries there suggests that they wielded the most influence. Another participant from Union Christian College in Alwaye was Varki.[75] The aim of the talks was first to establish intercommunion among the three communities and work together on the common points of agreement.[76] However, at the second informal meeting a delegate of the Syrian Orthodox Church proposed that intercommunion should be linked to either an organic or a federal union.

Chacko supported this proposal, which was also welcomed by the representatives of the Mar Thoma Church. The Anglicans were somewhat taken aback by so much enthusiasm. They reminded the others that they were part of a worldwide community and therefore their diocese could not join an organic union with the Syrian churches without leaving the worldwide organization. They also made it clear "that their diocese along with the other Anglican dioceses in South India had gone too far with the South Indian church union scheme for them to withdraw at this stage." The following resolution was finally adopted:

> This conference heard with much sympathy an expression of the ideal of organic union put forward by Fr. Alexios and Mr. K.C. Chacko and agreed that not only the organic union of the three churches concerned, but also the Union of all the Churches of Christendom must be included in its vision as the ultimate goal of all Christians. The members of the Orthodox Syrian Church handed in a memorandum, to make clear their views on the matter and to show that to them the way of organic union seemed to be the only way of

73 "But cordial relations exist already between the Anglican Church and the Jacobite portion of the Syrian Church, and we are conscious of the fact that reunion with the Mar Thoma Church, which is viewed with the gravest suspicion by the other portions of the Syrian Christianity in India, would prejudice our friendly relationship with a much larger and more important body"; "Education in India: Speech by Poet Rabindranath Tagore when he declared open the first hostel of the Union Christian College in 1922," in: *Union Christian College Silver Jubilee Souvenir (1921–1946)*, Alwaye, 1946, 50–54, archived in the Union Christian College Alwaye.

74 M.G. Haig (secretary to the archbishop of Canterbury) to Lord Bishop of Travancore and Cochin, Lambeth Palace, Jul 13, 1929, Enclosure: Eastern Churches Committee, Jul 3, 1929, in: BCC, Metropolitan box 2, file 2, Syrian Church Travancore 1929–1930, 2.

75 *Proceedings of the Kerala Council of Church Union*, Kottayam, 1936, 2f., archived in the Union Christian College Alwaye.

76 Metropolitan, "Syrian Church Malabar," proceedings of church union conferences held at Tiruvala; Proceedings of the first conference held at the C.M.S. Bungalow, Tiruvala on Feb 15–16, 1935, 3, archived in Bishop's College Calcutta.

> intercommunion. The members of the Mar Thoma Syrian Church expressed their keen desire to realize this ideal of organic union and their readiness to explore its feasibility. Neither they nor the Anglicans were able to accept unanimously that organic union was the only way to intercommunion.[77]

This showed the limits to unification attempts between Christians from the St. Thomas and Anglican traditions respectively. Given that this approach represented a direct alternative to the Free Church-Anglican union model, when the latter finally culminated in the foundation of the unified Church of South India in 1947, the rival approach inevitably came to an abrupt end.

Mathew's ecumenical hopes were thus thwarted and his disappointment can be seen in his rather skeptical remarks about church union plans during and after Tambaram. At the WMC, he distanced himself from the large joint Holy Communion events held. He later wrote in an article published in the Indian *National Christian Council Review*:

> In this connection one is afraid that a little too much has been made of the great joint Communion that the Madras delegates had at Tambaram on Christmas morning. Its significance and impressiveness are not to be denied. It is a great thing that practically all the delegates knelt side by side to receive the Body and Blood of their Common Lord and that amongst those who assisted Bishop Azariah who was the chief celebrant, there were Chinese and Japanese and African and American and English bishops. So far it was catholic in a sense. But the celebrants were all of the Anglican communion. No Free Church Ministers would have been and could have allowed to assist in the celebration. A few days before this service, when there was a celebration by Free Church ministers, several of the delegates did not communicate, and I do not blame them for I myself was amongst them.[78]

In the same article, however, he also affirmed that greater unity in the Church of Christ was an urgent necessity and one which received much more recognition in countries like India than in the West.[79] But that should not mean that unpleasant realities could be simply swept aside by pleasant-sounding expressions such as "unity in diversity." There would be a lot more obstacles in the way on the path to intercommunion.

The representative of the Mar Thoma Church had no objection to the joint liturgies of the Word (without sacraments). When he traveled to England after the WMC as a member of the Madras follow-up team, he took part in the first church service in St. Paul's Cathedral jointly organized by Anglicans and Free Church members.[80] Mathew himself preached at various Anglican churches in the dioceses of Chichester (Eastbourne), Bangor, Liverpool, and Durham. This form of ecumenical exchange had been preceded by correspondence between the CBMS, which organized the follow-up event to Tambaram, and the head office of the Anglican Church in Lambeth Palace. The

77 Metropolitan, "Syrian Church Malabar," proceedings of the second conference, Jun 6 to Jun 8, 1935, 26f., archived in Bishop's College Calcutta.

78 C.P. Mathew, "The Madras Team to Great Britain," *NCCR* 59, 1939, 585–590, here 587–588.

79 Mathew, "The Madras Team," 587, 589. Following his stay in Britain after Tambaram, Mathew noted: "One was a little disappointed to learn that while in most places in Great Britain there was hardly any active hostility between the various Churches there was not much of positive cooperation either. That there is no active hostility or mutual recrimination is sofar good but certainly it is a poor ideal for the one body of Christ. … That the need for cooperation and union is felt more keenly in countries like India is not surprising. It is significant that it was mainly the delegates from the younger Churches at Tambaram who stated the case for union with clearness and vigour."

80 Mathew, "The Madras Team," 585. Mathew gave a similar account of his British stay in his college journal: C.P. Mathew, "After Madras, in Great Britain," *UCCM* 14/1, 1939, 10–13.

archbishop of Canterbury had left the decision about whether to invite a representative from the Mar Thoma Church to preach at Anglican churches to the bishops of each diocese.[81] During his stay in England, Mathew appears to have worked particularly closely with Rev. Ching-yi Cheng, the general secretary of the Church of Christ in China, whom he also described as a friend.[82]

His ecumenical horizons extended even further later in life. In the 1960s, Mathew not only wrote books explaining the differences and similarities between the beliefs of the Syrian Orthodox Church and the Mar Thoma Church,[83] but also took part in the full assembly of the WCC in New Delhi in 1961, where he was elected to the council's central committee. He was also an observer at Vatican II.[84] This path of engagement in the worldwide church was initiated in Tambaram. In a radio broadcast for the BBC Mathew explained the impact the conference had had on him:

> Of course, before I went to the Madras meeting, I knew that there were Christians in almost every country of the world. But this knowledge became much more real and vivid as I met the delegates from 69 countries, sat with them at meals and heard them talk about the conditions of their respective countries and churches. We discussed with them problems of common interest and prayed with them. I realized then how the Church of Christ is universal today in a greater degree than ever before in history.[85]

Translated from German to English by Fiona Robb.

Bibliography

Hallencreutz, Carl F., *Kraemer Towards Tambaram: A Study in Hendrik Kraemer's Missionary Approach*, Lund, Gleerup, 1966.

Jongeneel, Jan A.B., "Tambaram 1938: Hendrik Kraemer on Africa," *Missionalia* 37/1, 2009, 20–32.

Ludwig, Frieder, *Zwischen Kolonialismuskritik und Kirchenkampf: Interaktionen afrikanischer, indischer und europäischer Christen während der Weltmissionskonferenz in Tambaram 1938*, Göttingen, Vandenhoeck & Ruprecht, 2000.

81 S.H. Dixon (secretary of the CBMS) reminded the archbishop on Dec 7, 1938 of an earlier visit by A.M. Varki (although he clearly confuses his denomination): "You will remember that Professor Varki of Alwaye College, South India, as a member of the Indian Mission of Fellowship in 1932, was welcomed generally throughout the country in Anglican churches, and as far as I can understand, there was no difficulty about his preaching, provided the service was taken by the incumbent of the church. Prof. C.P. Mathew, M.A., is a colleague of Prof. Varki, and also a member of the Mar Thoma Syrian Church, and I presume there would be no objection to recommend him freely for preaching in Anglican churches. There will be in England only four weekends concerned, and if any difficulty were anticipated, I could write to the Bishops of the Dioceses, or I could say I had mentioned this to you and you had stated unofficially that you did not anticipate any difficulty." There was obviously no such quick conclusion at the archbishop's secretariat since the answer given two days later stated: "The Archbishop would be grateful if you could let him know something about Prof. C.P. Mathew. He notes that you state that he is a colleague of Professor Varki and also a member of the Mar Thoma Syrian Church. From this he presumes that he is an Indian and not an Englishman though his name might suggest the latter. As to these two having authority to preach in churches, His Grace asks me to make it clear that actual authorisation to preach in particular churches must be secured from the Bishop of the Diocese concerned"; Lambeth Palace Library, Lang papers 171.

82 Mathew, "The Madras Team," 385.

83 C.P. Mathew, "Agreement and Differences in Faith Concepts," in: *Orthodox – Mar-Thoma Dialogue*, Alwaye, n. pub., 1969 (original text in Malayalam).

84 C.P. Mathew & Madathilparampil Mammen Thomas, *The Indian Churches of Saint Thomas*, Delhi, Indian Society for Promoting Christian Knowledge, 1967, back cover.

85 C.P. Mathew, "Talk," in: CBMS, *World Christians and You: Broadcast Talks by Members of a World Christian Conference*, London, Edinburgh House Press, 1939, 25–28, here 26–27.

Mackman, Toshiko, *The Tambaram Conference 1938 and the Japanese Delegates' Response*, Ph.D. thesis, University of Birmingham, 2003.

Ranger, Terence, *Are We not also Men?: The Samkange Family & African Politics in Zimbabwe (1920–64)*, London, Baobab, 1995.

Conference Publications

IMC, ed., *The Authority of the Faith*, Tambaram Series, vol. 1, London, Oxford University Press, 1939.

IMC, ed., *The Growing Church*, Tambaram Series, vol. 2, London, Oxford University Press, 1939.

IMC, ed., *Evangelism*, Tambaram Series, vol. 3, London, Oxford University Press, 1939.

IMC, ed., *The Life of the Church*, Tambaram Series, vol. 4, London, Oxford University Press, 1939.

IMC, ed., *The Economic Basis of the Church*, Tambaram Series, vol. 5, London, Oxford University Press, 1939.

IMC, ed., *The Church and the State*, Tambaram Series, vol. 6, London, Oxford University Press, 1939.

IMC, ed., *Addresses and Records*, Tambaram Series, vol. 7, London, Oxford University Press, 1939.

IMC, ed., *The World Mission of the Church: Findings and Recommendations of the International Missionary Council, Tambaram, Madras, India, December 12th to 29th, 1938*, London, IMC, 1939.

IMC, *Questions for the IMC at Madras*, London, 1938.

IMC, *Who's Who of the Madras Meeting of the IMC*, 1938.

IMC, *World Christians and You*, London, 1939.

CHAPTER 10

Ecumenism between Communism and Nazism (1929–1948)

Étienne Fouilloux

1 Introduction

A cursory glance at how the international crisis of the 1930s and 1940s influenced the nascent ecumenical movement might only take note of its negative consequences. This crisis, of which World War II was merely the culminating point, also wrought havoc in the field of interconfessional relations and had a retarding effect on numerous developments. It is thus necessary, in a first step, to take stock of the losses sustained by ecumenism during the war, be it in terms of people, publications, or institutions. However, it would be wrong to dwell exclusively on the negative consequences of the crisis. Indeed, the war years were not only destructive ones for ecumenism, which in fact benefited from the war in at least two respects. The conflict led to a great intermingling of peoples of different religious affiliations who ignored each other when they were not fighting, since they had previously had little opportunity to meet. The shock of the mutual discovery was undoubtedly ambivalent: while it may have reinforced confessional identities, it also gave rise to new vocations for unity.[1]

However, the real ecumenical significance of the war lies elsewhere. As much a clash of totalitarian ideologies as a confrontation of armed forces, it threatened the Christian faith down to its very foundations. But the divided Christians, both under the totalitarian yoke and in the resistance movement, but not without hesitation or mistakes, were able to form a common front against the danger which they perceived to be the most threatening: Nazi paganism and its attempt to subvert Christianity by Aryanizing it. The movement for Christian unity, and especially its Genevan institutions, thus emerged stronger from a war that had led to the collapse of its main enemy. But aside from the Western allies, who were concerned about fundamental liberties and above all about religious freedom, the victorious side also included a Soviet Russia that paid little heed to such concerns. As a result, the movement for Christian unity, having only just been freed from Nazi hostility, soon found itself confronted with a resurgence of communist hostility. Rather than focusing on World War II in the strict sense, the ensuing developments can thus be subsumed under a broader and more appropriate periodization ranging from the ideological confrontations of the 1930s, which potentially triggered the war, to the settling of scores between the victors of the latter conflict at the onset of the Cold War. In such an approach, it is less a matter of scrutinizing the internal development, theological and spiritual, of the nascent ecumenical movement during the years of the global crisis than of determining to what extent the major "non-theological factor" which the crisis constituted weighed on such a development.

2 Losses and Delays

The final years of the war witnessed the disappearance of four personalities who, in different capacities, had played, or could have played, an important part in the efforts to bring about a rapprochement among separated Christians. Born in 1865, the Ukrainian uniate Metropolitan Andrey Sheptytsky was certainly very old, but it can nevertheless be assumed that the rapid succession

1 On this ambivalence, see Étienne Fouilloux, "Les catholiques francophones et l'œcuménisme (1939–1945)," in: *Miscellanea Historiae Ecclesiasticae*, vol. 6/4, *Les Églises chrétiennes dans l'Europe dominée par le IIIe Reich*, Brussels, Nauwelaerts, 1984, 529–546.

of regimes to which he was subjected in his latter years (Soviet in 1939, Nazi in 1941, and again Soviet in 1944) hastened his death, on Nov 1, 1944. Matters are clearer in the cases of Max Josef Metzger, Maria Skobtsova, and Dietrich Bonhoeffer, who were murdered because of their resistance to Nazism. A German priest born in 1887, Father Metzger closely associated pacifism with ecumenism. It was his pacifism that led to his arrest and to his death sentence, which was carried out on Apr 17, 1944. His disappearance made an orphan of the interconfessional brotherhood Una Sancta, which he had founded in 1938–1939 and which had enjoyed considerable success in Germany.[2] On Mar 31, 1945, the Orthodox nun Maria Skobtsova, apostle of the poor in the working-class neighborhoods of Paris, died in the Ravensbrück concentration camp for women to which she had been deported. Even more painful for the ecumenical movement was the death of the pastor and Lutheran theologian Dietrich Bonhoeffer, the hope of the WA and of the practical Christian movement Life and Work: a collateral victim of the failed assassination attempt against Hitler in July 1944, he was executed on Apr 9, 1945, at the Flossenbürg concentration camp.[3] His novel ideas on the embedment of Christianity in a world cut off from God would undoubtedly have featured prominently in the subsequent interconfessional dialogue.

Less painful owing to their temporary nature, certain war-related disruptions were no less damaging to the ecumenical movement. In spite of a few small-scale celebrations of the Week of Christian Unity in the various officers' prison camps (so-called oflags) in which he was held and of an attempt to learn Russian while in captivity, the French Dominican Yves Congar, who was regarded as the leader of a "Catholic ecumenism" since the publication of his pioneering book *Chrétiens désunis* in 1937,[4] rightly considered that the six years that lay between his mobilization in 1939 and his liberation from war captivity in 1945 were six lost years for both his ecumenical efforts and his theological work, just when these were about to come to fruition. Emblematic and well documented, his case is certainly not an isolated one. Numerous prisoners of war never recovered from their long confinement. Fortunately for the spiritual ecumenism, that of Abbé Paul Couturier and of pastor Roland de Pury, in the same prison of Lyon in the spring of 1944, did not last too long. They came out alive, if not unharmed.

On the publication side, the situation was hardly more encouraging. Synonymous with shortages, notably of paper, and with mass destruction, the war slowed down, when not brought to a complete halt, the editorial output. Ecumenical publications were in fact still rare, and mostly of recent date: they were the first to be affected by the restrictions. *Irénikon*, the pioneering journal of the community of Amay-Chevetogne in the field of ecumenism, was discontinued in 1940 and did not resume publication until 1945. *Russie et chrétienté*, the Parisian journal of the Dominican Istina center for Russian studies, suffered the same fate and had to wait until 1946 to resume a precarious existence. Similar interruptions also plagued the book series that were at least partly devoted to ecumenism, already few in number: the rare manuscripts published during the war in the series Unam Sanctam, which Father Congar had entrusted to his fellow Dominicans at the Éditions du Cerf, were those that had already been ready for publication before its dissolution, notably the Dominican theologian's own collection of studies entitled *Esquisses du mystère de l'Église* in 1942.[5]

2 On Metzger and, more generally, on the German Christian opposition to Nazism, see the contribution by Peter Zimmerling in this volume.

3 Ferdinand Schlingensiepen, *Dietrich Bonhoeffer, 1906–1945: Martyr, Thinker, Man of Resistance*, London, T&T Clark, 2010.

4 Marie-Joseph Congar, *Chrétiens désunis: Principes d'un "œcuménisme" catholique*, Paris, Cerf, 1937; ET: *Divided Christendom: A Catholic Study of the Problem of Reunion*, trans. Muad A. Bousfield, London, Bles, 1939.

5 Marie-Joseph Congar, *Esquisses du mystère de l'Église*, Paris, Cerf, 1942.

Apart from these notable human and material losses, the most damaging effects of the war on the ecumenical movement must be assessed in terms of delays. The founding of the Protestant Taizé Community, for example, was delayed by the war: the young theology student Roger Schutz had already discovered the hill of Taizé in Burgundy in 1940, but he was not able to settle there with his friends Pierre Souvairan and Max Thurian until 1944, after the liberation of the Cluny region.[6]

Above all, the war delayed the birth of the organization dedicated to promoting the rapprochement of Christians who were separated from Rome: Anglicans, Protestants, and Orthodox Christians. During the summer of 1937, the Oxford Conference, held under the auspices of the practical Christian movement Life and Work, and the Edinburgh conference, organized by the doctrinal movement Faith and Order, appointed a select committee to initiate the project. The conference convened by the same committee in Utrecht in May 1938 agreed on the name, structure, and doctrinal basis of the WCC: "The World Council of Churches is a fellowship of churches which accept our Lord Jesus Christ as God and Savior." The conference in Utrecht also appointed a Provisional Committee that established its seat in Geneva, from where it actively engaged in preparations for the constitutive assembly of the future council. The committee's leading figure, the Dutch Reformed pastor Willem Adolf Visser 't Hooft, would later remark that "no one expected that this provisional structure would have to last for ten years"[7] – the more so as the WCCY, held with great success in Amsterdam in July–August 1939, had demonstrated the impatience of the younger generations and their hope of witnessing the realization of unity with their own eyes. The Provisional Committee did actually stipulate that the constitutive assembly of the WCC should convene in August 1941.

The spread of the war, both in Europe and Asia, quickly rendered these plans obsolete. Moreover, its outbreak revealed strong differences of opinion within the member churches regarding the preferred stance which the emerging council should adopt *vis-à-vis* the belligerent nations. Divided, as early as 1939, between those who believed that it should restrict itself to a task of mediation, in view of restoring the peace without taking sides in the conflict, and those who estimated that it should condemn the dictatorial regimes, especially those of Germany and Japan, as aggressors and destroyers of liberties, it failed to agree on a common position before the spread of the conflict. Visser 't Hooft would later write that "from 1940 to 1945 the Council was unable to act normally through its responsible committees. It seemed at first that the war would not merely slow up the process of the formation of the Council, but might well lead to its complete disintegration."[8]

3 Building a Common Front

The history of ecumenism during World War II is nevertheless not reducible to a field of ruins – neither is the war itself at the climax of the military confrontation, which lasted from 1939 to 1945 in Europe, but from 1937 to 1945 in Asia. Unlike the preceding war of 1914–1918, this conflict was not only, and not primarily, a struggle of exacerbated nationalisms but a much more fundamental struggle between incompatible ideologies. On one side the Stalinist Communism that aspired to eradicate religion from the USSR, and on the other the Nazi ideology that aimed to replace the Judeo-Christian revelation with a new religion based on race, that used false scientific arguments to justify its

6 Silvia Scatena, *Taizé, una parabola di unità: Storia della comunità dalle origini al concilio dei giovani*, Bologna, Il Mulino, 2018; FT: *Taizé, une parabole d'unité: Histoire de la communauté des origines au concile des jeunes*, Tournhout, Brepols, 2020.

7 Willem Adolf Visser 't Hooft, "The Genesis of the World Council of Churches," in: *A History of the Ecumenical Movement*, vol. 1, Ruth Rouse & Stephen C. Neill, eds., *1517–1948*, London, SPCK, 21967, 697–724, here 704.

8 Visser 't Hooft, "The Genesis of the World Council of Churches," 709.

premises. In contrast to these totalitarian ideologies, liberal democracy endeavored more or less skillfully, and with varying success, to enlist the support of the Christians and their churches in its struggle against one or the other threat, or even against both.

In this life-and-death struggle, which began not in 1937–1939 but in 1929 (new legislation on religious associations in the USSR) and in 1933 (Adolf Hitler's accession to supreme power in Germany), each branch of disjointed Christianity used its own weapons, of which the year 1937 provided an impressive display: an intentionally rapid succession of encyclicals by Pius XI, directed against the racist Nazi ideology that "de-Judaized" Christianity (*Mit brennender Sorge*, Mar 14) and against the "intrinsic errors" of Communism (*Divini Redemptoris*, Mar 19);[9] the condemnation by Life and Work, at its second world conference in Oxford in July, of the dictatorial aspirations of the modern state, but also the movement's determination to support the "Churches under the Cross" and its defense of the church, in whatever form, as a pillar of fundamental liberties.[10]

Though distinct, these formulations of standpoints against the dangers of totalitarianism mutually reinforced each other. Moreover, they also encouraged the building of common fronts of predominantly spiritual orientation in an effort to counter the threats that weighed on the faithful and their churches. These common fronts created a situation in which Christians of different confessions who had until then hardly had the opportunity to interact now began to work together. It would certainly be misleading to say that their actions constituted ecumenism in the strict sense of the term, since their ultimate goal was not the unity of the separated Christians but "merely" the preservation of religious freedom in the countries where it was threatened and the defense of the Judeo-Christian tradition against the assaults of Soviet materialism or Nazi paganism.

3.1 *An Anti-Communist Ecumenism?*

The earliest plans to build such a common front were devised in 1930 in the wake of the protests against the resumption of persecution of Christians in the Soviet Union, following the restrictive decree on religious associations from Apr 8, 1929, and against the violent dechristianization campaigns that followed upon it. Pope Pius XI himself initiated the movement with his letter from Feb 2, 1930, to the vicar general of Rome, Cardinal Basilio Pompili, in which he called for a crusade of prayers against the persecution, not only in the Catholic Church but "in the entire Christian world."[11] Followed by a solemn reparation Mass in St. Peter's Basilica in Rome on Mar 19, the letter even elicited responses in the most remote catholic dioceses, be it in Mazara del Vallo in Sicily or in Phát Diệm in Indochina. It also found a strong echo in the churches that were separated from Rome. Even though the Patriarchate of Moscow, deprived of an incumbent since the death of Metropolitan Tikhon in 1925, was compelled by the Soviet authorities to deny the very existence of a persecution, other Orthodox churches thanked the pope, whose initiative sparked emulation in the Reformation churches, notably in the Anglo-Saxon world.[12]

9 Fabrice Bouthillon & Marie Levant, eds., *Pie XI, un pape contre le nazisme?: L'encyclique "Mit brennender Sorge" (14 mars 1937). Actes du colloque international de Brest, 4–6 juin 2015*, Brest, Éditions Dialogues, 2016; quoted according to Pius XI, *Divini Redemptoris*, in: AAS 19, 1937, 65–109.

10 Nils Ehrenström, "Movements for International Friendship and Life and Work, 1925–1948," in: *A History of the Ecumenical Movement*, vol. 1, 587–592.

11 *Chirografo al Cardinale Basilio Pompili, Vicario di Roma, sulle violenze compiute in Russia*, Feb 2, 1930, in: AAS 22, 1930, 80–93.

12 Laura Pettinaroli, "The Crusade of Prayers for Russia in 1930," in: Milla Bergström & Kirsi Salonen, eds., *The Holy See's Foreign Policies in Inter-War Europe*, Helsinki, Suomen Kirkkohistoriallinen Seura, 2016, 179–201; see also "La persécution religieuse en Russie," *La Documentation Catholique* 23, 1930, cols. 835–887 and 963–1015.

These outcries were convergent, not conjoined. Three year later, a new step was taken. The EIA, which had been combatting the Comintern since 1924 and had always sought support within the churches, created an interconfessional commission called Pro Deo in October 1933. The initiative was the brainchild of Dr. Yury Lodyzhensky, an influential member of the most conservative of the emigrant churches, the ROCOR, even though his office staff also included the Protestant attorney Jacques Le Fort or Abbé Henri Carlier, a Swiss journalist of considerable renown. Like the EIA, Pro Deo was based in Geneva but attempted to create national branches throughout the world, with varying success. It was at once a news agency that reported on the crimes of Communism, a center of propaganda that strove to prevent its spreading, and a lobby that tried, in vain, to prevent the USSR from entering the League of Nations in 1934. Although some of its initiatives were a definite success, particularly its traveling exhibition on the League of Militant Atheists, the influence of Pro Deo was far inferior to that of the antireligious propaganda emanating from Soviet sources.

Its organizers may not have represented their churches, but they were certainly not "irregular fighters" who lacked any sort of ecclesial backing. Long misunderstood by historiography, this Christian anti-Communism was in fact not entirely devoid of ecumenical aspirations. The names of ecumenists regularly appear in the guest lists of Pro Deo's annual assemblies and include Genevan officials of the emerging WCC (Henry-Louis Henriod, Alexandre de Weymarn) as well as Catholics such as Father Christophe-Jean Dumont, director of the Dominican Istina center, and Abbé Paul Couturier, the inventor of spiritual ecumenism. For Lodygensky, it was important that the struggle against Communism and the work towards Christian unity be closely intertwined, though more in the sense of a single front in the face of adversity than of a true doctrinal union. This was also the opinion of the Jesuits, whose superior general, Włodzimierz Ledóchowski, issued the slogan "advance separately, strike simultaneously" in May 1936. In 1934, they launched the bulletin *Unitas*, in which the propaganda for unity, in the sense of a return to Rome, stood alongside investigations into the progress of Communism in the Parisian banlieue.[13]

This type of activity did not fail to become the target of political exploitation, particularly by the Anti-Comintern, an agency created in the summer of 1933 by the propaganda services of the Third Reich for the purpose of mobilizing all forces that opposed Bolshevism, the nemesis of the Nazis. Only a few Western Christians succumbed to what could be termed an "ecumenism of collaboration," in the precise meaning that the expression would acquire in the course of World War II: Christians like Dr. Lodygensky and his family, prosecuted after the liberation of France, who agreed to help the Third Reich defeat Communism, be it on the front or in the rear. The situation in the Slavic territories conquered by the Wehrmacht was very different. Without going as far as to engage in explicit collaboration, certain Catholic dignitaries and the ROCOR did not look unfavorably upon the German victories, which led to a reopening of the churches, Orthodox or Uniate, although this development was soon adversely affected by the Soviet reconquest.[14] The antagonism between Soviet Communism and ecumenism would resurface during the Cold War.

13 This hitherto unexplored continent was happily discovered by Stéphanie Roulin, *Un credo anticommuniste: La Commission Pro Deo de l'Entente Internationale Anticommuniste ou la dimension religieuse d'un combat politique (1924–1945)*, Lausanne, Antipodes, 2010; see also Giuliana Chamedes, "The Vatican, Nazi-Fascism and the Making of Transnational Anti-communism in the 1930s," *JCH* 51/2, 2016, 261–290.

14 The French historian Xavier de Montclos was one of the first to emphasize the importance of this unanticipated "awakening": see Xavier de Montclos, *Les chrétiens face au nazisme et au stalinisme: L'épreuve totalitaire, 1939–1945*, Paris, Plon, 1983; for the Soviet point of view on this still sensitive issue, see Adriano Roccucci, *Stalin e il patriarca: La Chiesa ortodossa e il potere sovietico*, Turin, Einaudi, 2011.

3.2 *An Ecumenism of Resistance*

Far more important for the rise of the ecumenical movement was what could be called, by way of symmetry, the "ecumenism of resistance," meaning the joint spiritual struggle of Christians against Nazism, its paganism, or its distortion of the message of the gospel by a German Christianity cut off from its Jewish roots. Even before the war, this struggle had prompted the emerging ecumenical institutions to support the Confessing branch of the German Protestant churches, which faced persecution. Thus, the authorities in Berlin refused to issue passports to the members of the delegations which these churches wished to send to the conferences of Oxford and Edinburgh, as they included Confessing personalities. The German theologians, who had been very active in the preparation of these two conferences, were accordingly unable to attend. The only three German theologians present at Oxford belonged to small, rather unrepresentative Methodist or Baptist Churches, not to the large Lutheran or Reformed ones. When the conference expressed its support for the Confessing Church, they became indignant, insisted that Christians in Germany enjoyed full religious freedom, and expressed their gratitude that "God in his providence has sent a leader who was able to banish the danger of Bolshevism in Germany … and to give it a new faith in its mission and future."[15] The sharp reactions of the Nazi authorities to the conclusions of Edinburgh, and above all of Oxford, which warned the churches against the totalitarian threat, confirmed that the ecumenical movement as a whole was now considered an enemy by the regime, which instructed its policing services to keep a close eye on it: the archives of these services thus constitute a valuable source of information for the reconstruction of its history.

While numerous believers and pastors, Protestant or Catholic, supported Hitler until the end of the war, historiography has also showcased the spiritual struggle of a strong minority of them against Nazi dominance (*Kirchenkampf*), and especially the proven link between this struggle and the one for the union of the separated Christians, whether it be considered from the perspective of the Confessing part of the Protestant Church or rather from the perspective of the Catholic-based Una Sancta brotherhood.[16] The murder of two of the leading figures of this struggle, Metzger and Bonhoeffer, whom the Nazis sentenced to death in mock trials, is symbolic in this respect. This movement, which united *Kirchenkampf* and *Ökumene*, assumed such proportions in Catholic milieus that the Fulda Conference, the periodic gathering of the German bishops, decided to create a committee on ecumenical issues, which was entrusted to the bishop of Paderborn, Msgr. Lorenz Jaeger.

The boundary between spiritual resistance and resistance tout court, whether political or military, is porous. While that of Father Metzger was pacifist and non-violent, the resistance of the Munich student group known as the White Rose, in which an Orthodox engaged in militant activities alongside Protestants and Catholics, until its brutal suppression in 1943, also had political overtones. As for that of Dietrich Bonhoeffer, a member of Admiral Wilhelm Canaris' counterespionage service since 1940, it included links to the circles that prepared an attempt on Hitler's life.

Born in Germany, the ecumenism of resistance also took root in the only European country that successfully resisted the "brown tide": Great Britain. English Catholicism, a minoritarian but dynamic church, quickly responded to Pope Pius XII's call for a "spiritual crusade" for peace in his Christmas message of 1939.[17] Its

15 Text quoted by Ehrenström, "Movements for International Friendship and Life and Work," 588.

16 For the former, see Armin Boyens, *Kirchenkampf und Ökumene*, vol. 1, *1933–1939*, Munich, Kaiser, 1969, and Armin Boyens, *Kirchenkampf und Ökumene*, vol. 2, *1939–1945*, Munich, Kaiser, 1973; for the latter, see Jörg Ernesti, *Ökumene im Dritten Reich*, Paderborn, Bonifatius, 2007.

17 *Alla Curia Romana in occasione del Natale*, Dec 24, 1939; the Italian text can be found in: *Discorsi e Radiomessaggi di Sua Santità Pio XII*, vol. 1, *Primo anno*

head, Cardinal Arthur Hinsley, archbishop of Westminster, launched the movement Sword of the Spirit in August 1940,[18] with the collaboration of intellectuals such as Christopher Dawson and Barbara Ward. This movement sought to mobilize the British for a "crusade of prayer, study, and action" against the "pagan empires" and for a "new order of justice and peace."[19] Sword of the Spirit enjoyed great success in the British Isles and in the Commonwealth, as numerous Protestants and Anglicans became involved in it through a parallel movement, Religion and Life. On Dec 21, 1940, Cardinal Hinsley, along with the Anglican archbishops of Canterbury and York, Cosmo Gordon Lang and William Temple, and the moderator of the Free Church Federal Council, Walter H. Armstrong, signed a ten-point manifesto on the ongoing war and the desired peace: five of these points were taken from the pope's Christmas message and five from the conclusions of the Oxford conference.[20] Followed by a series of interconfessional meetings in the spring of 1941 and supplemented by several documents of the same type in the United States and the Commonwealth, this manifesto was one of the sources of the Atlantic Charter – signed on Aug 14, 1941, off the coast of Newfoundland, by the American president Franklin Delano Roosevelt and the English prime minister Winston Churchill – in which the Allies defined their war objectives. The two countries could thus rely on the Christian churches to provide a spiritual framework for their struggle against Nazism and its henchmen.

A spiritual resistance also arose in vanquished and occupied France, albeit under much more unfavorable conditions. In May 1941, the interconfessional refugee relief organization Amitié chrétienne was founded in Lyon on the initiative of two Protestants and under the auspices of both pastor Marc Boegner and Cardinal Pierre-Marie Gerlier. With the decisive support of the Jesuit Pierre Chaillet and Abbé Alexandre Glasberg, it essentially devoted itself to the rescue of persecuted Jews, especially during the wave of mass arrests that occurred during the summer of 1942.[21] At the same time, Father Chaillet and his colleagues from the Jesuit scholasticate of Lyon-Fourvière were making preparations for the publication of a clandestine organ of spiritual resistance. Originally called the *Témoignage catholique*, it became the *Témoignage chrétien* when Protestants such as pastor Roland de Pury became involved in its publication. Between November 1941 and August 1944, the notes and letters of the *Témoignage chrétien* engaged in a merciless struggle against Nazi paganism, against its phobia of Jews, and against the danger of contamination that it posed for the churches under its sway.[22]

This spiritual resistance naturally hoped for the defeat of the Third Reich and for an Allied victory. However, it waged its struggle in its own domain, that of helping the persecuted or rejecting Nazi ideology, and not on the political terrain *per se*. Is it nevertheless permissible to speak of "political ecumenism" in a situation that led Catholics, Protestants, Jews, and agnostics to work together in the Allied governments? Geoffrey Adams offered a positive answer to this question in a book that looked into the presence of firm

di Pontificato, 2 marzo 1939–1° marzo 1940, Vatican City, Tipografia Poliglotta Vaticana, 1955, 435–445.

18 See Eph 6:17.

19 Olivier Rota, *Les catholiques anglais et la "question juive" (1917-1967)*, Paris, Cerf, 2021, 392–393.

20 Thomas Moloney, *Westminster, Whitehall and the Vatican: The Role of Cardinal Hinsley, 1935–1943*, Tunbridge Wells, Burns & Oates, 1985, 186–204.

21 For a recent look into this little-known organization, see Madeleine Comte, "L'abbé Glasberg au secours des Juifs," in: Chrisrian Sorrel, ed., *Alexandre Glasberg, 1902–1981, prêtre, résistant, militant*, Lyon, LARHRA, 2013, 37–57.

22 See the standard study by Renée Bédarida, *Les Armes de l'Esprit: Témoignage chrétien (1941–1944)*, Paris, Les Éditions Ouvrières, 1977, and her biography of Pierre Chaillet entitled *Pierre Chaillet: Témoin de la résistance spirituelle*, Paris, Fayard, 1988; see also the more recent assessment by Patrick Cabanel, *De la paix aux Résistances: Les protestants en France (1930–1945)*, Paris, Fayard, 2015.

believers of the three confessions around General Charles de Gaulle in the France libre movement.[23] Such a broadening of the notion of ecumenism is open to debate, the more so as many of the personalities in question participated for reasons that had nothing to do with religious considerations. This blend of confessions was nevertheless a novelty for a country in which the notion of secular state had acquired a quasi-dogmatic status since the promulgation of the Law on the Separation of the Churches and State in 1905.

3.3 *A Suffering Ecumenism*

Sadly, the war created another situation in which Christians who had hardly ever had the chance to meet before then had the opportunity to do so: their captivity. The military victories of the Third Reich transformed the part of Europe under its control into a gigantic detention camp: a string of oflags for officers and stalags for enlisted men in which millions of prisoners of war of all nationalities and confessions were crowded together; and a network of deportation and extermination camps in which all those whom the Nazis viewed as their enemies suffered a slow or immediate death.

No form of organized religious life was tolerated in these camps, with the exception of Dachau, where the clerics were concentrated. This prohibition, and the harsh conditions of detention, did not stop inmates of different confessions from helping each other to survive. A prisoner for the entire duration of the conflict, pastor Martin Niemöller, leader of the German Confessing Church, thus developed cordial relations with the Catholic priests whom he met in various places of detention. In Ravensbrück, the French Reformed Protestant Hélène Roux and the Orthodox Maria Skobtsova endeavored to witness their faith in a manner consistent with that of their Catholic comrades in suffering, Geneviève de Gaulle or Germaine Tillion. The influx of Soviet prisoners of war, who were all considered communist agents, into the death camps caused many of the deported to recognize that persecution had not entirely extinguished faith in the USSR.

The religious situation of the prisoners of war was not as bad, since the Geneva conventions granted them the right to receive spiritual assistance from chaplains. More difficult to carry out among the scattered work *Kommandos*, the activities of the chaplains stimulated the spiritual life of the large camps, such as the stalags and especially the oflags. Since the officers were not compelled to work, idleness and a higher level of education fueled an intensive cultural and religious life in the oflags. Protestant and Orthodox Christians were usually in the minority, and thus subject to the more or less insistent proselytizing efforts of the Catholic majority, to which they responded with evangelization attempts. The intermingling and the encounters that resulted therefrom were thus not necessarily beneficial to the ecumenical cause, as the dialectic between the desire to conquer and the need to present a united Christian front was a delicate balance and varied in each local situation. Many prisoners of war nevertheless discovered ecumenism through a comparative reading of the Bible in occasion of the celebration of the January Week of Prayer for Christian Unity. A few ecumenical vocations even emerged in captivity, proving fruitful after the war in areas of historical confessional confrontation, as for instance the French regions of Tarn and Poitou.[24]

---

23 Geoffrey Adams, *Political Ecumenism: Catholics, Jews, and Protestants in de Gaulle's Free France (1940–1945)*, Montreal, McGill-Queen's University Press, 2006.

24 The partial study of this topic by Étienne Fouilloux, *Les catholiques et l'unité chrétienne du* XIX*e au* XX*e siècle: Itinéraires européens d'expression française*, Paris, Le Centurion, 1982, 454–467, has been taken up and completed by Delphine Debons, *L'assistance spirituelle aux prisonniers de guerre: Un aspect de l'action humanitaire durant la Seconde Guerre mondiale*, Paris, Cerf, 2012, 342–347.

4 Geneva's Hour

"But in the midst of the war years," as Willem Adolf Visser 't Hooft later wrote, "the tide turned. Instead of a period of stagnation the war proved to be a time of deepening and intensifying ecumenical fellowship."[25] This testimony carries weight, since it comes from someone who had also been one of the main architects of this turnaround, as a key player in the Provisional Committee of the emerging WCC. But he was more than that. Having decided not to seek exile in England or the United States, Visser 't Hooft made Geneva the hub of an important clandestine network known as the Swiss Route. Carefully compartmentalizing his activities, he was able to relay sensitive information back and forth between the Dutch resistance at home and the government of Queen Wilhelmina, which had taken refuge in London.[26] The Swiss Route was also used to fuel the spiritual resistance of the French newsletter *Témoignage chrétien* by providing it with theological ammunition. Moreover, Visser 't Hooft was one of several who vainly tried to convince the Allied governments to offer substantial help to the German resistance against Hitler.

Though Visser 't Hooft continually deplored that the emerging WCC could not speak with one voice during the raging war, his Genevan team nevertheless managed to stay in contact with the churches of the various Western belligerents. He himself was able to travel to France and even England by roundabout routes. The German citizen Hans Schönfeld and the Swede Nils Ehrenström were free to circulate in German-occupied Europe, and Alexandre de Weymarn turned the *Service œcuménique de presse et d'information* into an indispensable instrument of communication between the churches. In 1940, an Ecumenical Commission for the Chaplaincy Service to Prisoners of War was created in Geneva. Autonomous from the nascent WCC although it emanated from the latter, it was steered by the Swiss Protestants Alphons Koechlin, Jacques Courvoisier, and Olivier Béguin. It operated in the stalags and oflags, in collaboration with other Anglo-Protestant organizations, such as the YMCA, and in emulation of the Catholic chaplaincies or the Red Cross service, although this emulation sometimes turned into a competition.[27] As for the German pastor Adolf Freudenberg, who had been posted to Geneva in 1939, he set up an aid service for refugees that made it one of its principal tasks to provide relief to the Jews who were crowded together in the camps of southern France and to help their colleagues from the Cimade (founded in 1939) obtain their release, before finally convincing the Swiss authorities, with some difficulty, to grant them asylum in Switzerland. Here again, the borderline between ecumenical work and spiritual resistance was often blurred. The effectiveness of these two services was credited to the Genevan team: in occupied Europe, as Visser 't Hooft would later note, it was common to speak of "ecumenical meals" or "ecumenical shoes."[28]

Much like his teacher Karl Barth and his friend Dietrich Bonhoeffer, Visser 't Hooft had long been convinced that "the reality and vitality of the Ecumenical Movement will depend on the spiritual resistance against the evil forces which it can manifest in those many countries that are being submerged" by the Third Reich, as he wrote on Jun 14, 1940, to his colleagues from the provisional committees of London (William Paton) and New York (Henry Smith Leiper).[29] At the time, this conviction could not be heard by the main belligerents. The Allied victories lent it a relevance that it had previously lacked. Although the nascent WCC's inability to speak with one voice about the

25 Visser 't Hooft, "The Genesis of the World Council of Churches," 709.

26 Visser 't Hooft, "The Genesis of the World Council of Churches," *passim*. See also Willem Adolf Visser 't Hooft, *Memoirs*, London, SCM Press, 1973.

27 Debons, *L'assistance spirituelle aux prisonniers de guerre*, 134–136 and 143–152.

28 Visser 't Hooft, *Memoirs*, 132.

29 Visser 't Hooft, *Memoirs*, 126.

war could have led to its demise, it reaped the fruits of a stance that aimed to make it "spiritually indispensable for churches in time of need."[30] An impartial advocate of religious freedom, and of human rights in general, the WCC benefited greatly from the fact that it was perceived, in a Europe that was in the process of liberating itself, as one of the inspirers of the victory over Nazism.

In fact, it even prepared for the imminent victory by creating two new departments. The Department of Reconstruction and Inter-Church Aid, which was entrusted to the Scottish Presbytarian James Hutchinson Cockburn, was to assist in the material reconstruction of the European communities that had been ravaged by the war. In a first trip across the Atlantic, in the spring of 1945, Visser 't Hooft obtained $500,000 from John D. Rockefeller to accomplish this goal. The Commission of the Churches on International Affairs, created in partnership with the IMC, which preferred to retain its autonomy rather than blend in with WCC, prolonged the intercessory role that Geneva had sought to maintain during the war. It was explicitly conceived, in Anglo-Saxon manner, as a kind of Christian lobby with the ability to influence the new international institutions that were in the making. In this way, the WCC in formation took on a significance that it had not had at the beginning of the war – both materially, as the initially small team had grown steadily through the creation of new departments and could rely on increasingly large budgets, and above all morally, owing to its resolute commitment to struggle against the Nazi stranglehold on the Christians of Europe.[31]

5 From the War to the Cold War

But how representative was it? Some 50 churches had joined the WCC during the war, which increased the membership to over one hundred in its immediate aftermath. But Visser 't Hooft and his associates had hoped for much more, the more so as the conflict unexpectedly relaxed certain prior tensions. The WCC could not convene its constitutive assembly without settling the case of German Protestantism that had already poisoned interconfessional relations after World War I. The German Christian leadership had been swept away in the fall of the Third Reich and was replaced by leaders from the Confessing Church, several of whom had only just been released from prison. This change of direction in the higher echelons of the EKD opened the way for its admission of failure in the face of Nazism, the condition *sine qua non* for the normalization of its ecumenical situation. This admission was pronounced during a summit meeting with the envoys of the WCC, held on Oct 18–19, 1945, in the German city of Stuttgart, which lay in ruins. In the name of the entire EKD, its council declared: "We did fight for long years in the name of Jesus Christ against the mentality that found its awful expression in the National Socialist regime of violence" which is questionable "but we accuse ourselves for not standing to our beliefs more courageously, for not praying more faithfully, for not believing more joyously, and for not loving more ardently."[32] The Stuttgart Declaration of Guilt, which could have been more resolute but was considered nonetheless intolerable by numerous German believers and pastors, was deemed sufficient by the representatives from Geneva. It brought the German question to a successful and rapid conclusion by enabling the immediate integration of the EKD into the WCC.

The latter had not given up the hope of establishing ties with the two large churches that its representativeness lacked: the Roman Catholic Church and the Russian Orthodox Church. On the side of the Catholic Church, relations were at a standstill. As in World War I, Rome worried about the growing influence which the Anglo-Saxon Protestant world enjoyed as a result of the war, particularly

30 Visser 't Hooft, *Memoirs*, 133.

31 See the contribution by Jurjen Zeilstra in this volume.

32 English text available at <https://marcuse.faculty.history.ucsb.edu/projects/niem/StuttgartDeclaration.htm> (accessed Jan 10, 2023).

through the YMCA. Pope Pius XII held on to the unionist policy of his predecessors, which hoped for the "great return" of the Orthodox East, or at least of part of it, to the Roman fold, albeit with little success.

The Catholic ecumenism that had emerged during the 1930s in Germany, Belgium, or France was still too weak to be considered an alternative policy. In 1943, the pope nevertheless signed two key documents that might have heralded better days, as their ecumenical implications were not insignificant. The encyclical *Mystici corporis Christi* from Jun 29, 1943, certainly upheld the substantial identity of the Roman Church with the Church of Jesus Christ on earth, but it defined it in Pauline terms as a "Mystical Body" and no longer only as a hierarchical society. It also left a narrow opening through which the dissident Christians, who are said to "have a certain relationship with the Mystical Body,"[33] could slip through. As for the encyclical *Divino afflante Spiritu* from Sep 30, 1943, it freed the Catholic exegesis from the prohibitions that had hampered it since the Modernist crisis and thus opened the way for an eventual interconfessional collaboration around the biblical text. At the height of the conflict, these modest and delayed overtures found little echo and had almost no immediate consequences. The accumulating successes of the nascent WCC were perceived more as a threat than as an opportunity by the Roman authorities. Accordingly, they declined to send Catholic observers to the constitutive assembly of Amsterdam in 1948. It would take over ten years, a new pope, and the latter's announcement of a council, to unblock the situation on this side.

On the Allied side, with which the emerging council identified itself, Stalin's USSR figured prominently, even though no one could forget that he had attempted to eradicate Christianity throughout his territory in the 1930s. Would a common front against a persecuting Communism be rebuilt after the war? Nothing of the sort was to happen, as is demonstrated by the failure of the resumption of activities by the Pro Deo Commission in 1944–1945. At four meetings in Lausanne, Visser 't Hooft refused to assign a higher priority to the struggle against Communism than to the battle against Nazism, which he considered a priority. He thereby marginalized Dr. Lodygensky and his friends from the ROCOR, to the benefit of a burgeoning dialogue with the Catholic delegation from which Abbé François Charrière, the soon-to-be bishop of the Diocese of Lausanne, Geneva, and Fribourg, emerged as a key discussion partner.[34]

It should also be noted that the war had led to a major new development on the side of Moscow. In 1941, the Russian Church called for resistance against the German invader and mobilized what remained of its strength for the "great patriotic war": it even provided the funds to equip an armored division. Stalin was grateful for its participation in the national war effort and, in 1943, allowed it to fill the position of the patriarch, which had been vacant since Tikhon's death in 1925. Close to death in 1939, the Russian Church experienced a salutary respite, albeit under the close surveillance of the Council for the Affairs of the Russian Orthodox Church and of its chairman, the former chekist Georgy Karpov. Patriarch Alexy I, elected in 1945, and his operative in charge of international relations, Metropolitan Nicholas, expressed their desire to be informed about the emerging WCC. Geneva was delighted with this favorable disposition, and an initial meeting was arranged for 1946 in Prague. However, it was canceled by Moscow, so that Geneva remained without news of the patriarchate until the eve of the constitutive assembly in Amsterdam.

A few weeks earlier, the solemn celebration of the 5th centennial of its autocephaly, in July 1948, marked the resurgence of the Moscow Patriarchate and of its religious influence.[35] The

33 Pius XII, *Mystici corporis Christi*, Jun 29, 1943, §103, in: *AAS* 35, 1943, 193–248.

34 Roulin, *Un credo anticommuniste*, 411–418.

35 Laura Pettinaroli, "L'autocéphalie en Guerre froide: Tensions interconfessionnelles et réflexions sur

event combined a series of high-profile liturgical ceremonies and a conference of the leaders and representatives of the Eastern churches, who had traveled to Moscow for the occasion. Among the resolutions adopted by this conference, two were primarily concerned with interconfessional relations. A fierce denunciation of the papacy stigmatized its calls for a return of the Eastern Christians to the Roman fold as well as "its participation in the instigation of fratricidal wars, its struggle against democracy, and its defense of fascism."[36] This was nothing more than the ideological translation of an aggressive campaign against Roman uniatism that was taking place in the Soviet territories, notably through the brutal suppression of the Catholic churches of Eastern rite, first in the USSR, then in the people's democracies under Soviet domination, and through the forced reunification of their believers with Orthodoxy.

Less harsh in form, the resolution pertaining to the ecumenical movement was equally as negative in substance: falsely accused of preparing the creation of an "ecumenical church" through the "reduction of the prerequisites for the achievement of union," it was particularly criticized for subordinating its religious function to "the organization of social and political life" and to the constitution of a "force that wielded internal influence."[37] The allusion to Geneva's new fields of action in support of refugees, reconstruction, and lobbying was very clear, and behind it the accusation of subservience to the Western world under Anglo-American influence. Accordingly, the signatory churches refused to join the WCC and to be represented at its constitutive assembly.

This dealt a hard blow to the organization, which had been at pains not to appear too closely attached to the West, even though it depended on it for most of its material resources: at the Amsterdam assembly, the statements of the Czech theologian Josef Hromádka and of the American politician John Foster Dulles complemented each other in their assessment of the international situation and with regard to the role which Christians should play in the aftermath of the war. The archbishop Germanos (Strenopoulos), Metropolitan of Thyateria, who represented the Patriarchate of Constantinople in Moscow, did not attend the conference and thus did not sign its resolutions. Indeed, how could he have done so in the light of the fact that he himself was expected to become one of the WCC's five presidents and that Greek Orthodoxy viewed the renewed activity of the Moscow Patriarchate with great suspicion?[38] However, the resolutions did bear the signatures of the heads of churches under Soviet influence in Eastern Europe, as well as that of the envoy dispatched by the Orthodox Patriarchate of Antioch. This opposition seriously diminished the Eastern representativeness of the WCC. In what gave the impression of being a religious episode of the Cold War that now pitted the former Allies against each other, the revived Moscow Patriarchate gathered a front of ecumenical denial around itself, an ecclesial transposition of the communist bloc that would also persist until the détente of the early 1960s.[39] After having contributed to the spiritual defeat of Nazism, the ecumenical movement was, for more than a decade, confronted with the hostility of the world under communist influence.

From the 1930s to the 1950s, the fierce clash of ideologies that culminated in World War II was

l'unité à la conférence inter-orthodoxe de Moscou en 1948," in: Marie-Hélène Blanchet, Frédéric Gabriel & Laurent Tatarenko, dir., *Autocéphalies: L'exercice de l'indépendance dans les Églises slaves orientales (IXe–XXIe siècles)*, Rome, École française de Rome, 2021, 469–494.

36 "Résolution relative à la question 'Le Vatican et l'Église Orthodoxe,'" *Journal du patriarcat de Moscou*, 1948 (special issue), 23–25, here 24.

37 "Résolution relative à la question 'Le Mouvement œcuménique et l'Église orthodoxe,'" *Journal du patriarcat de Moscou*, 1948 (special issue), 29–30.

38 On this Greek distrust towards the "council" of Moscow, see Valeria Martano, *Athenagoras il patriarca (1886–1972): Un cristiano fra crisi della coabitazione e utopia ecumenica*, Bologna, Il Mulino, 1996, 140–144.

39 Roccucci, *Stalin e il patriarca*, 280–295.

evidently a crucial "non-theological factor" in the development of the ecumenical movement. Greatly benefiting from its spiritual resistance to Nazism and from the latter's collapse under the blows of the Allied attacks, it later suffered from the exclusion that had been forced upon it by Stalinist Communism, which viewed it as nothing more than the spiritual mask of Western imperialism under American leadership. It was not until the advent of a precarious peaceful coexistence of the blocs that this exclusion came to an end and that the churches under Soviet tutelage were able to join the WCC at its third plenary assembly, which convened in 1961 in New Delhi.

Translated from French to English by Robert Meyer.

Bibliography

Adams, Geoffrey, *Political Ecumenism: Catholics, Jews, and Protestants in de Gaulle's Free France (1940–1945)*, Montreal, McGill-Queen's University Press, 2006.

Bédarida, Renée, *Les Armes de l'Esprit: Témoignage chrétien (1941–1944)*, Paris, Les Éditions Ouvrières, 1977.

Bouthillon, Fabrice & Marie Levant, eds., *Pie XI, un pape contre le nazisme?: L'encyclique "Mit brennender Sorge" (14 mars 1937). Actes du colloque international de Brest, 4–6 juin 2015*, Brest, Éditions Dialogues, 2016.

Boyens, Armin, *Kirchenkampf und Ökumene*, vol. 1, *1933–1939*, Munich, Kaiser, 1969.

Boyens, Armin, *Kirchenkampf und Ökumene*, vol. 2, *1939–1945*, Munich, Kaiser, 1973.

Cabanel, Patrick, *De la paix aux Résistances: Les protestants en France (1930–1945)*, Paris, Fayard, 2015.

de Montclos, Xavier, *Les chrétiens face au nazisme et au stalinisme: L'épreuve totalitaire (1939–1945)*, Paris, Plon, 1983.

Ernesti, Jörg, *Ökumene im Dritten Reich*, Paderborn, Bonifatius, 2007.

Fouilloux, Étienne, *Les catholiques et l'unité chrétienne du XIXe au XXe siècle: Itinéraires européens d'expression française*, Paris, Le Centurion, 1982.

Moloney, Thomas, *Westminster, Whitehall and the Vatican: The Role of Cardinal Hinsley, 1935–1943*, Tunbridge Wells, Burns & Oates, 1985.

Roccucci, Adriano, *Stalin e il patriarca: La Chiesa ortodossa e il potere sovietico*, Turin, Einaudi, 2011.

Rota, Olivier, *Les catholiques anglais et la "question juive" (1917-1967)*, Paris, Cerf, 2021.

Roulin, Stéphanie, *Un credo anticommuniste: La Commission Pro Deo de l'Entente Internationale Anticommuniste ou la dimension religieuse d'un combat politique (1924–1945)*, Lausanne, Antipodes, 2010.

Schlingensiepen, Ferdinand, *Dietrich Bonhoeffer, 1906–1945: Martyr, Thinker, Man of Resistance*, London, T&T Clark, 2010.

Visser 't Hooft, Willem Adolf, *Memoirs*, London, SCM Press, 1973.

CHAPTER 11

Ecumenism in the Third Reich: The Pioneering Work of Dietrich Bonhoeffer and Max Josef Metzger

Peter Zimmerling

1 Introduction

It may be surprising to learn that the Third Reich turned out to be fertile ground for the process of ecumenical unity that emerged after World War II.[1] The shared experience of resistance to the National Socialist reign of terror and on the front line of World War II generated a previously unknown momentum for ecumenical efforts. In Germany, ecumenism gained even greater significance because the country's different confessions were more or less equivalent in size. Whereas in the early 20th century efforts to advance ecumenism were mainly due to the tensions arising from rivalry in the missionary work of the different faiths abroad, now the need for unity among the churches became a matter of urgency due to the developments in Europe itself.

As far as the Protestant side is concerned, my discussion will concentrate on Dietrich Bonhoeffer, who was one of the main representatives of the Confessing Church and one of the theologians most involved in ecumenical issues. He enjoyed excellent contacts with ecumenical groups and was one of the first to recognize the need for an ecumenical theology. Today he is probably best-known 20th century Protestant theologian. I shall also examine the ecumenical engagement of Max Josef Metzger, founder of the Una Sancta movement, who, presented astonishingly similar theological reflections at about the same time as Bonhoeffer. The similarities between the two are striking: Metzger's ideas were very close to those of Bonhoeffer, and his life also came to a violent end at the hands of the Nazis, although his insights in the ecumenical field, like those of his contemporary, did not have an effect until the decades after the war.[2] They were each prophetic thinkers whose ideas were regarded distrustfully by their own churches during their lifetimes.

2 Dietrich Bonhoeffer, a Pioneer of Ecumenism: Historical Background

Before he proceeded to make first the Protestant Church and then the Una Sancta movement the focal points of his life and work, it was anything but inevitable that Dietrich Bonhoeffer would study theology.[3] Although his family belonged to the Protestant Church, they neither attended services at the local congregation in the Berlin district of Grunewald nor were they active in any other capacity in the church. It was simply not part of their everyday life. Rather, Bonhoeffer's resolve to study theology was due to an inner calling: "Dietrich Bonhoeffer was one of those *homines religiosi* whose decision to dedicate his life to the service of God came early on, when still a child, and beyond the perception of any other human being. ... The election of a religious form of life for

1 On this subject, from the Catholic point of view, see the study by Jörg Ernesti, *Ökumene im Dritten Reich*, Paderborn, Bonifatius, 2007.

2 For more details on Metzger's ecumenical activity in Germany during the Third Reich and the war see in the first volume of this work the chapter by Paul Metzlaff.

3 I presented, for the first time, part of the following reflection in: Peter Zimmerling, *Bonhoeffer als Praktischer Theologe*, Göttingen, Vandenhoeck & Ruprecht, 2006.

the son of a bourgeois, scholarly Protestant household meant the study of theology."[4]

It was during a semester studying in Rome in 1924 that Bonhoeffer's interest in the empirical church began, prompted by his experience of the divine service in Catholic churches there. According to his extant diary entries, it was during Holy Week and Easter in Rome that the meaning of the concept of the church truly became clear to him: "The day [Palm Sunday] had been magnificent. It was the first day on which something of the reality of Catholicism began to dawn on me – nothing romantic, etc. – but I think I'm beginning to understand the concept of 'church.'"[5] Two other passages from the same diary entry reveal the cause of this new understanding. Of the morning Mass at St. Peter's, he wrote: "The universality of the church was illustrated in a marvelously effective manner. White, black, yellow members of religious orders – everyone was in clerical robes united under the church. It truly seems ideal."[6] Here for the first time *universality* as an essential attribute of the church became clear to Bonhoeffer. Concerning vespers in a convent of nuns on the same day, he observed: "The impression left by these novices was even greater than would have been left by real nuns, because every trace of routine was missing. Instead, it was worship in the true sense. The whole thing gave one an unparalleled impression of profound, guileless piety."[7] Here Bonhoeffer understood the meaning for the church of a *divine service* celebrated together.

In the question about the essence of the church, Dietrich Bonhoeffer had found, in Rome, the issue that would preoccupy him for the rest of his life. His engagement with the church was a natural consequence of the inner certainty that he had been called to theology. Soon the focus of his interest would not be so much his study of theology as a scientific discipline but rather the concretion of scientific-theological reflections about the church. Subsequently, both practical work for the church, which would soon include his ecumenical commitment, and theological reflection about it would go hand in hand.[8] Theory and practice would feed each other.

In his doctoral thesis entitled *Sanctorum Communio: Eine dogmatische Untersuchung zur Soziologie der Kirche*, on which he worked at the same time as his theology degree and first theology exam, Bonhoeffer conducted a scientific-theological investigation into what constitutes the essence of the church.[9] At about the same time, he was also gaining his first practical experience in the church. He became a helper at the Sunday school of his local congregation in Grunewald, where he held catechesis for children.[10] During this period, one of the fundamental themes of Bonhoeffer's subsequent involvement in the church can already be seen: not just proclaiming the Christian message, but working in the community. For him, the *vita communis* is part of being a Christian, at least in symbolic terms. Bonhoeffer invited the Sunday school children to his home and went on excursions with them. From the Sunday school group a youth group was created, which discussed difficult subjects in the spirit of a youth academy.[11] They held their meetings at Bonhoeffer's family home in Grunewald, and went to concerts and the opera together, often after an introduction to the work concerned by one of the group's members.

4 Carl Friedrich von Weizsäcker, "Gedanken eines Nichttheologen zur theologischen Entwicklung Dietrich Bonhoeffers," in: Hans Pfeifer, ed., *Genf '76: Ein Bonhoeffer-Symposion*, Munich, Kaiser, 1976, 29–50, here 30–31.

5 DBWE 9, 88.

6 DBWE 9, 88.

7 DBWE 9, 89.

8 To the same effect, see also Thomas Day, *Conviviality and Common Sense: The Meaning of Christian Community for Dietrich Bonhoeffer*, Ph.D. thesis, Union Theological Seminary, 1975.

9 On this point, see D. Bonhoeffer to his parents, Sep 21, 1925, in: DBWE 9, 148–149.

10 See Eberhard Bethge, *Dietrich Bonhoeffer: A Biography*, trans. Victoria J. Barnett, Minneapolis, Fortress Press, 2000, 91–94.

11 See Bethge, *Dietrich Bonhoeffer*, 94–95.

Once he had embarked upon it, Bonhoeffer never deviated from this path towards practical engagement in the church.[12] After receiving his doctorate and passing his first theology exam, instead of single-mindedly building his academic career, which his family and the rest of his acquaintances took for granted, he decided to enter the service of the church. He completed a year as a vicar in Barcelona in 1928. Again, in addition to the work of proclamation, Bonhoeffer wanted to share in the lives of community members. He learned of their lot in the course of his many visits to their homes and gained further insights by taking part in the German community's vibrant associations. After returning to Berlin, he completed his post-doctorate thesis entitled *Akt und Sein*,[13] a qualification that he needed in order to pursue a university career.[14]

After obtaining his doctoral habilitation he was still too young to be ordained as a minister in the Prussian Union of Churches and therefore spent the academic term of 1930–1931 on a scholarship at the Union Theological Seminary in New York.

This period is significant for Bonhoeffer's ecumenical engagement in two ways. It is at this time, before either the Third Reich or the *Kirchenkampf*, that he underwent a change of direction both towards a more personal devotion to Christ and towards ecumenism. The first of these, the shift towards a personal *faith in Christ*, was the result of his experience of worship and community in a black, Baptist congregation in Harlem.[15] Looking back on this time, he wrote to a friend:

> At that time, I was terribly alone and left to myself. It was quite bad. But then something different came, something that has changed and transformed my life to this very day. For the first time, I came to the Bible. That, too, is an awful thing to say. I had often preached, I had seen a great deal of the church, had spoken and written about it – and yet I was not yet a Christian but rather in an utterly wild and uncontrolled fashion my own master. I do know that at the time I turned the cause of Jesus Christ into an advantage for myself, for my crazy vanity. I pray to God that will never happen again. Nor had I ever prayed, or had done so only very rarely. Despite this isolation, I was quite happy with myself. The Bible, especially the Sermon on the Mount, freed me from all this. Since then everything has changed ... That was a great liberation. It became clear to me that the life of a servant of Jesus Christ must belong to the church.[16]

The passage shows that Bonhoeffer's experience of Christ concerned above all two aspects: first, a perception of the Bible as God's own speech, as "a love letter from God,"[17] and second, "a life of uncompromising discipleship, following Christ according to the Sermon on the Mount."[18] In his case, this took the form of working for "peace and social justice ... Christ himself."[19] From this moment onwards, Bonhoeffer is a "Sermon on the Mount Christian": his entire theology and biography from now until his work *Widerstand und Ergebung* must be understood as an attempt to fulfill the Sermon on the Mount. This biblical text had until then

12 See Bethge, *Dietrich Bonhoeffer*, 97–123.

13 The thesis is published in *DBWE* 2.

14 However, at the same time Bonhoeffer writes: "I feel in general that academic work will not hold me for long. On the other hand, I think it very important to have as thorough an academic grounding as possible"; Bethge, *Dietrich Bonhoeffer*, 128.

15 "Bonhoeffer acquired his most profound impression of a living congregation in the Abyssinian Baptist Church of his friend Frank Fisher in nearby Harlem, where he participated intensively for six months in both the Sunday school and worship," according to *DBWE* 10, 597.

16 D. Bonhoeffer to E. Zinn, Jan 27, 1936, in: *DBWE* 14, 134.

17 Bethge, *Dietrich Bonhoeffer*, 204. Carl Friedrich von Weizsäcker's interpretation is correct: "Thus his breakthrough to the Bible is not with the highly intellectual Letter to the Romans [as with Karl Barth], but the unbearably merciful simplicity of the Sermon on the Mount"; von Weizsäcker, "Gedanken," 41.

18 D. Bonhoeffer to K.-F. Bonhoeffer, Jan 14, 1935, in: *DBWE* 13, 285.

19 *DBWE* 13, 285.

been the domain of Catholic spiritualism, with the exception of Anabaptist and Radical Pietist traditions. It was an absolute novelty for mainstream European Protestantism at the time. It constitutes the basis of Bonhoeffer's pacifism, as well as his preference for ethical questions, including his insistence that the church should proclaim the concrete commandment in decisive ethical situations. "*Following* Christ – what that really is, I'd like to know – is not exhausted by our concept of faith."[20]

In New York Bonhoeffer also discovered the meaning of *ecumenism*. This was, perhaps, hardly surprising in a city with such a diversity of Christian denominations – unlike his native Berlin, where, apart from Catholicism, Christian groups outside the dominant Protestant Prussian Union of Churches were of little significance. Furthermore, many of the professors who taught at the Union Theological Seminary were founding members of the ecumenical organizations Life and Work and Faith and Order, which gave rise to the foundation of the WCC in Amsterdam after World War II.[21] Soon Bonhoeffer was not only working as a youth secretary in the incipient ecumenical movement, but was also addressing the question of the movement's existence as a church in lectures and essays. When he returned from New York, he was appointed honorary youth secretary at the WA meeting in Cambridge at the beginning of September 1931. He now spent much of his time and energy on ecumenical conferences, for whose preparation and organization he was partly responsible. Bonhoeffer's role as youth secretary of the WA was ultimately aimed at reaching an understanding between hostile nations based on their shared Christian faith. This also accounts for his commitment to pacifism, which included the rejection of any attempt to revise the Treaty of Versailles by violent means.

2.1 *Collaboration with the Confessing Church and on the Barmen Declaration*

Bonhoeffer was little known outside ecumenical organizations before Hitler came to power on Jan 30, 1933. This would now change. He became a public figure in the fight against the infiltration of German Christians into the Protestant Church. Together with Martin Niemöller, a pastor in the well-to-do Dahlem district of Berlin, and Gerhard Jacobi, pastor at the city's Kaiser Wilhelm Memorial Church, he was instrumental in building the Jungreformatorische movement, the precursor to the Pfarrernotbund and the Confessing Church. The German Christians won a huge majority at the ecclesiastical elections, which Adolf Hitler had called at short notice early in the summer of 1933. The Jungreformatorische movement responded by drawing up a confession aimed at highlighting the errors of this Protestant group sympathetic to Nazi ideology. Bonhoeffer was one of the two authors of the confession. However, the time was apparently not ripe for a broad, resounding ecclesiastical opposition and the attempt failed.[22]

Not until nine months later, at the end of May 1934, was the Barmen Declaration, largely attributable to Karl Barth, adopted and the Confessing Church founded at the first national German synod of the Confessing Church held in Wuppertal-Barmen. In October of that year, the church's emergency law was declared at the Confessing Synod in Berlin-Dahlem. In other words, the Confessing Church went on to create its own ecclesiastical structure, including its own examination boards and preachers' seminars.

The Confessing Synod of Barmen of 1934 set up the formulation of a systematic ecclesiology for the first time in Protestantism, including the doctrine on ecclesiastical order and office. The Barmen Declaration represented a necessary advancement upon the inadequate Reformation

20 *DBWE* 13, 136 (italics original).

21 See in the first volume of this work chapters by Dietz Lange, "The Life and Work of Nathan Söderblom," 585–614; and Luca Ferracci, "Charles Brent and the Faith and Order Project: From Its Origins to the Lausanne Conference of 1927," 615–639.

22 See Bethge, *Dietrich Bonhoeffer*, 300–304.

ecclesiology. The fact that today pastors in many German *Landeskirchen* are still ordained according to the Barmen Declaration is proof of its lasting importance.

After Hitler came to power, the German Christians endeavored to bring the Protestant Church into line with the Nazi regime and to secure the triumph of the *Führerprinzip* by creating the position of *Reichsbischof* to head the church. The Confessing Church reacted to this by drafting the new Barmen confession, one adopted by both Lutheran and Reformed members for the first time since the Reformation. "Only the state of persecution unprecedented in the history of the German Protestant churches gave the church a new ecclesiological awareness and confidence about its own identity."[23]

The significance of the Barmen Declaration, therefore, is certainly not restricted to being a fundamental document of the *Kirchenkampf* at the beginning of the National Socialist regime. Barmen also marked a break with the anti-institutional reservations of 19th-century Liberal Protestant theology. It became possible to overcome the institutional shortcomings of the Reformation understanding of the church as found in article 7 of the *Confessio Augustana*.

In the context of the Third Reich's Führer cult, the Barmen Declaration pointed out that there is no other source of revelation apart from the revelation of God in Jesus Christ (thesis 1) and that Jesus Christ is the only lord that man must obey (thesis 2).[24] The Declaration's Christocentric orientation became the theological foundation of the WCC after World War II. It also reminded everyone that the order of the church and its offices must reflect the content of its proclamation if it is to remain valid. For this reason, thesis 3 states:

> "Rather, speaking the truth in love, we are to grow up in every way into him who is the head, into Christ, from whom the whole body [is] joined and knit together" (Eph 4:15, 16).
>
> The Christian Church is the congregation of the brethren in which Jesus Christ acts presently as the Lord in Word and Sacrament through the Holy Spirit. As the church of pardoned sinners, it has to testify in the midst of a sinful world, with its faith as with its obedience, with its message as with its order, that it is solely his property, and that it lives and wants to live solely from his comfort and from his direction in the expectation of his appearance.
>
> We reject the false doctrine, as though the church were permitted to abandon the form of its message and order to its own pleasure or to changes in prevailing ideological and political convictions.[25]

Therefore, it is not enough to bear witness to Jesus Christ through the proclamation, as stated by Philip Melanchthon in article 7 of the *Confessio Augustana*. The church's mission goes beyond this, and consists in ensuring that in order to be credible a given form of ecclesiastical order must reflect the proclamation.[26] Just as with faith and obedience, message and order are interdependent and inextricably linked. Thesis 3 of the declaration establishes that not only the church's message and faith, but also its order and obedience, have proclamatory power.

Thesis 4 sets out in greater detail what this means in relation to the concrete form and duties of the ecclesiastical offices:

23 Eberhard Bethge, "Was heißt: Kirche für andere? Überlegungen zu Dietrich Bonhoeffers Kirchenverständnis," in: Eberhard Bethge, *Ohnmacht und Mündigkeit: Beiträge zur Zeitgeschichte und Theologie nach Dietrich Bonhoeffer*, Munich, Kaiser, 1969, 152–169, here 155.

24 See *The Theological Declaration of Barmen*, available at <https://cathedralofhope.org/wp-content/uploads/2019/03/The-Theological-Declaration-of-Barmen.pdf> (accessed Oct 17, 2022).

25 See *The Theological Declaration of Barmen*, 283.

26 See DBWE 6, 72–73.

"You know that the rulers of the Gentiles lord it over them, and their great men exercise authority over them. It shall not be so among you; but whoever would be great among you must be your servant" (Matt 20:25, 26).

The various offices in the church do not establish a dominion of some over the others; on the contrary, they are for the exercise of the ministry entrusted to and enjoined upon the whole congregation.

We reject the false doctrine, as though the church, apart from this ministry, could and were permitted to give to itself, or allow to be given to it, special leaders vested with ruling powers.[27]

Thesis 4 is not only opposed to the Third Reich's concept of office, with its apex in the cult of the Führer; it also represents a move away from the understanding of office prevalent until then in the Protestant Church, which saw it in terms of rulership. In contrast to this, in the light of the New Testament, ecclesiastical office must be understood as ministry for others, not rulership. During the *Kirchenkampf* period, office once again became what it had been in primitive Christianity and the time of the early church: not a privilege but rather a danger and a burden.[28]

The new understanding of office found in Barmen drew on the practical experience of the *Kirchenkampf*. The image of a participatory church became visible for the first time in Protestantism. The Reformation's demand for a universal priesthood was put into practice. When pastors were conscripted during the war, the laity, particularly women, increasingly assumed responsibility in the communities, which allowed for the emergence of the presence of all the talent necessary for community life.

Bonhoeffer did not attend either of the synods in Barmen or Berlin-Dahlem, because he had been working as a minister in London since October 1933. However, he became one of the few unwavering proponents of their decisions. He used his time in London to mobilize the German congregations in England and the various bodies of the ecumenical movement in favor of the Confessing Church, generally with successful results.[29] It was a major achievement when all the German congregations in England in the end joined together in the struggle against the *Reichskirche* government.

2.2 *Ecumenical Friendship with George Bell and Collaboration with the Military Resistance*

Bonhoeffer was only 27 when during his ministry in London in 1933 he became acquainted with George Bell, bishop of Chichester and member of the House of Lords, while Bell, who had been born in 1883, was, at 50, nearly twice his age.[30] The age difference alone made it anything other than a foregone conclusion that the two would become good friends. The radical difference in the political systems of their respective countries was another potentially complicating factor: on the one hand, Nazi Germany with its unlimited *Führerprinzip* becoming clearer by the day, and on the other, a democracy that had evolved in the course of many centuries. There was also a stark contrast between their theological traditions: a Reformation theologian modeled on Luther and Barth alongside a

27 *The Theological Declaration of Barmen*, 284.

28 See Kurt Scharf, *Brücken und Breschen: Biographische Skizzen*, Gütersloh, Gern Mohn, 1980, 71.

29 See Bethge, *Dietrich Bonhoeffer*, 392–406.

30 For more on this and on what follows, see: Peter Zimmerling, "Dietrich Bonhoeffer und George Bell – Ökumenische Freundschaft im Ernstfall," in: Christian Möller & others, eds., *Wegbereiter der Ökumene im 20. Jahrhundert*, Göttingen, Vandenhoeck & Ruprecht, 2005, 294–313. The correspondence between Bell and another major figure in the ecumenical movement, Willem Adolph Visser 't Hooft, is published by Gerhard Besier, *"Intimately Associated for Many Years": George K.A. Bell's and Willem A. Visser 't Hooft's Common Life-Work in the Service of the Church Universal: Mirrored in their Correspondence*, Cambridge, Cambridge Scholars Publishing, 2015. For a biography of the controversial bishop, see Andrew Chandler, *George Bell, Bishop of Chichester: Church, State, and Resistance in the Age of Dictatorship*, Grand Rapids, Eerdmans, 2016.

deeply Anglican churchman. Nonetheless, they discovered a surprisingly close agreement on fundamental beliefs at their very first meeting. Bell had succeeded Nathan Söderblom as the international president of Life and Work in 1932. Given that much of the work and members of this organization overlapped with those of the WA – Life and Work had actually originated from the WA in Stockholm in 1925 – ecumenical cooperation between Bell and Bonhoeffer almost inevitably arose.[31]

Their friendship revealed the urgency of their respective ecumenical commitments. Bell's intervention for friends in Germany cut across the ecclesiastical, individual and political spheres: first, he voiced his support for the Confessing Church in the ecumenical movement; second, he organized help for refugees from the Nazis in England; third, he backed the German resistance to Hitler in the British Parliament, government and otherwise in public. Bell paid for this engagement when he was rejected as a candidate for the archbishop of Canterbury in 1942. In its obituary of him, *The Manchester Guardian* wrote: "His chances declined at the same time as he made public his sympathy for Jews and Germans."[32]

There is unfortunately not enough room here to mention all the circular letters to ecumenical bodies, requests to ecumenical conferences, petitions to the German government and *Reichskirche* officials, and letters to *The Times*, by means of which Bell actively campaigned on behalf of the Confessing Church thanks to information received directly from Bonhoeffer. The main aim of this activity was to warn foreign churches against recognizing the *Reichskirche* government in Germany and to create ecumenical momentum for the emerging Confessing Church. His advocacy for the Confessing Church reached its high point when, as president of Life and Work, he sent a circular letter to all member churches on Ascension Day of 1934, two weeks before Barmen.[33] The letter, sent under pressure from Bonhoeffer and with his agreement, criticized the German *Reichskirche* in devastating terms: it represented the *Führerprinzip* and a violent regime, disciplinary measures and racial discrimination "without precedent in the history of the Church."[34]

Immediately following the pogrom of 1938, Bell founded the charity Christian Churches Committee for non-Aryan Christians.[35] This committee helped 31 persecuted German pastors and their families obtain a visa for Great Britain. To speed up the emigration process (also in favor of non-theologians, writers and artists), Bell was willing to act as personal guarantor for the refugees.

Bell's advocacy for "another Germany" opposed to the National Socialists became well known. As an active member of the House of Lords, he constantly raised awkward questions on the subject to Winston Churchill's government. He waged a war on two fronts: while he remained an outspoken opponent of the Nazis, he also fought against the increasingly prevalent view in Britain that there was no longer any need to distinguish between Nazis and Germans. On Apr 23, 1940, it was declared at London's Guild Hall in a speech approved by Churchill: "We are not trying to remove a cancerous growth from the German people, but Germany itself, which has become a cancerous growth on the European organism."[36] Bell believed that this perception made any friendship initiative and effort at reconciliation after the war far more difficult. His appeals for an end to the bombing of non-military targets also looked

31 On the origin of ecumenical organizations, see: Gerhard Linn, *Ökumene: Hoffnung für eine gespaltene Menschheit?*, Leipzig, Evangelische Verlagsanstalt, 1992, 50ff.

32 Cited in Eberhard Bethge, "George Bell und Forest Hill, Rede anlässlich der Namensgebung der George Bell Hall in London (Forest Hill) am 5. Februar 1994," *Bonhoeffer-Rundbrief* 64, 2001, 3–4.

33 See Bethge, *Dietrich Bonhoeffer*, 369–372.

34 Cited in Bethge, *Dietrich Bonhoeffer*, 370.

35 Ulrike Lange, "Bell, George Kennedy Allen," in: Markus Vinzent, ed., *Metzler Lexikon christlicher Denker*, Stuttgart/Weimar, J.B. Metzler, 2000, 83–85, here 84.

36 Cited in Edwin H. Robertson, "Solidarität mit dem Feind: Die Friedensinitiativen des englischen Bischofs Georg Bell," *Glaube und Lernen* 8/1, 1993, 46–58, here 53.

ahead to the period following the end of Hitler's Germany.[37] In a speech to the Upper House on Feb 9, 1944, Bell strongly rejected any indiscriminate bombing war on moral grounds: "The Allies stand for something greater than power. The chief name inscribed on our banner is 'Law.' It is of supreme importance that we who, with our Allies, are the liberators of Europe should so use power that it is always under the control of law."[38] Bell was mocked by the British public as "naive, 'a political bishop,' pro-German."[39]

Bonhoeffer was again personally involved in the *Kirchenkampf* after his appointment in 1935 by the *Bruderrat* (fraternal council) of the Confessing Church as director of one of its illegal preaching seminars. He held this position until 1940, and in a clandestine capacity from 1937.

Even after the education and training of pastors in eastern Pomerania was forced to come to an end by the war and the Gestapo in March 1940, Bonhoeffer continued to work from outside as a visitator for the Confessing Church. However, his main activity had long since been his direct participation in the conspiracy against Hitler. Throughout he never lost sight of the church, including as an institution, which is demonstrated in his work on *Ethik*[40] and his reflections from *Widerstand und Ergebung*[41] on the future form of church and Christianity after the war.[42]

Bonhoeffer, on behalf of the German resistance against Hitler, met Bell for the last time in May 1942 at the church's conference center in Sigtuna near Stockholm. Bell made notes of the discussions, which have been conserved, immediately afterwards.[43] Bonhoeffer even told Bell the names of the leading men in the conspiracy. He asked the bishop to inquire into the British government's conditions for peace for Germany after Hitler's fall. This was particularly urgent because a number of important officers in the military were hesitating to join the conspirators as long as Britain upheld its demand for Germany's "unconditional surrender." From June until August, Bell attempted to persuade the British government to give the German opposition a hearing and provide them with its support. Despite a personal meeting with the Foreign Minister Anthony Eden, however, the government was not willing to take any steps or provide any guarantees.[44] In the Foreign Office in London, people simply turned a deaf ear.[45]

Just how important ecumenism was to Dietrich Bonhoeffer is shown by the fact that his last words to come down to us concerned Bell, his most important counterpart in the ecumenical dialogue. This last surviving message indeed represents Bonhoeffer's ecumenical testament. It was delivered by Bonhoeffer's fellow prisoner, English Captain Sigismund Payne Best. Bonhoeffer had instructed him on Apr 8, 1945 to relay the message to Bell, just before he was transported to Flossenbürg concentration camp and on the day

37 Here, it suffices to point out that it has only been a few years since the taboo concerning the allied bombardments was broken and a controversial debate unleashed; see, for example, Jörg Friedrich, *The Fire: The Bombing of Germany (1940–1945)*, New York, Columbia University Press, 2008 (against), Richard Overy, *Die Wurzeln des Sieges: Warum die Alliierten den Zweiten Weltkrieg gewannen*, Stuttgart, DVA, 2001 (for). A lead article in *Der Spiegel* magazine referred to Bell's calls: Jochen Bölsche, "So muss die Hölle aussehen," *Der Spiegel*, Jan 5, 2003, 45.

38 Peter Raina, ed., *Bishop George Bell, House of Lords Speeches and Correspondance with Rudolf Hess*, Bern, Peter Lang, 2009, 61–62.

39 Edwin H. Robertson, *Unshakeable Friend: George Bell und die deutschen Kirchen*, London, CCBI, 1995.

40 *DBWE* 6.

41 *DBWE* 8.

42 On this, see Hans-Christoph von Hase, "Die Kirche muss gewagt werden: Zu Dietrich Bonhoeffers Gedanken über die Aufgabe der Kirche als Institution," *Die Innere Mission* 52, 1962, 37–47.

43 *DBWE* 16, 289–305.

44 See Patricia Meehan, *The Unnecessary War: Whitehall and the German Resistance to Hitler*, London, Sinclair-Stevenson, 1995.

45 See Ilse Tödt, "Ein Streiflicht: Das britische Außenministerium stellt sich 1942 taub," *Bonhoeffer-Rundbrief* 61, 2000, 4–6.

before his execution. Payne Best was an intelligence officer and, as such, professionally trained for such a task. After the war he remembered Bonhoeffer's words quite clearly, particularly since Bonhoeffer had repeated them to him twice so that he could learn them by heart.[46] Payne Best delivered Bonhoeffer's message to Bell by letter: "'Will you give this message from me to the Bishop of Chichester, tell him, that this is for me the end, but also the beginning – with him I believe in the principle of our Universal Christian brotherhood which rises above all national hatreds and that our victory is certain – tell him too, that I have never forgotten his words at our last meeting.' He gave me this message twice in the same words, holding my hand firmly in his and speaking with emotional earnestness."[47] Bonhoeffer's words are about so much more than his personal hope for resurrection, as suggested by the first part of his message, the only part to become known. Bonhoeffer dies trusting in the final victory of the kingdom of God, meaning a worldwide ecumenical brotherhood and sisterhood, beyond all strife and hate between nations. The scandalous effect such words would have in Britain at the very end of the war is shown by the fact that, for fear of being accused of treason, Captain Payne Best did not reveal them to Bell until Sep 17, 1946, nearly a year-and-a half after his return from Germany.

3 Towards an Ecumenical Theology: Prerequisites

The subject of Bonhoeffer's doctoral thesis is an investigation into the form and place of the church.[48] Working on a thesis having precisely this as its subject was a fundamental prerequisite in subsequently coming to terms with the idea of an ecumenical theology. Bonhoeffer explored the question of "whether and how the empirical and essential church could simultaneously be brought theologically under a *single* concept in both logical and sociological terms."[49] Expressed otherwise, his work dealt with where and how the church in which we believe reveals itself in the empirical church.[50] The believed reality of the church must not be allowed to remain merely believed but must assume a concrete form in the world, that is to say, it must become clear and tangible. This question preoccupied Bonhoeffer throughout his life, in ever changing approaches. It was a particularly topical subject in German Protestantism in view of contemporary events, first because of the end of the *Kirchenregiment* (church government) in 1918 and, second, even more so subsequently during the upheavals of the *Kirchenkampf*. Bonhoeffer reaches the conclusion that God's revealed will assumes a concrete, visible and intelligible form in the church, specifically in the visible form of the church. It seems clear that this conclusion brought him closer to the Catholic understanding of the church.

Insofar as Bonhoeffer refers to God's *revealed* will, it is implicit that he is speaking about the church as a *theologian*. He is concerned with the church of the third article of faith. In focusing his discussion of the church on the concept of revelation, Bonhoeffer reflects the ideas of Karl Barth's early dialectic theology. Yet he goes beyond this by discussing the church as a revealed reality set in Christ, which can also be empirically perceived and investigated, even by using sociological

46 See "Zwei Zeugnisse von der Ermordung Dietrich Bonhoeffers," in: Rainer Mayer & Peter Zimmerling, eds., *Dietrich Bonhoeffer aktuell: Biografie, Theologie, Spiritualität*, Gießen, Brunnen, ²2013, 90.

47 See DBWE 16, S.P. Best to G.K.A. Bell, Oct 13, 1953, 468–469.

48 DBWE 1. Among the studies of the text, see particularly: Day, *Conviviality*; Joachim von Soosten, *Die Sozialität der Kirche: Theologie und Theorie der Kirche in Dietrich Bonhoeffers "Sanctorum Communio,"* Munich, Kaiser, 1992; Rainer Ebeling, *Dietrich Bonhoeffers Ringen um die Kirche: Eine Ekklesiologie im Kontext freikirchlicher Theologie*, Gießen, Brunnen, 1996.

49 Ernst Wolf, "Vorwort" (Foreword) to the second edition of *Sanctorum Communio*, Munich, Kaiser, 1954, 5.

50 See the afterword by Joachim von Soosten, in: DBWE 1, 290–306.

methodology. The fundamentally Lutheran orientation of Bonhoeffer's theology is evident here, a legacy he inherited from his professors in Berlin, particularly the well-known Lutheran scholar Karl Holl. In addition to Karl Barth's revelation theology approach, two fundamental discoveries of Martin Luther determined Bonhoeffer's concept of the church foundation in Christ and the sociality of the church.

The Christological justification of the church is explained as follows: the church's foundation in Christ derives in terms of content from Christ's suffering and death for us; his death on the cross allowed humanity to share in the life of God without any prior work – when Luther elevated the doctrine of justification to the status of fundamental article of the church, Christ's representation on our behalf became a structural principle of the Christian community. "To become Christ to the other," says Luther. The principle of vicarious representation "gives Christian basic-relations their substantive uniqueness," writes Bonhoeffer.[51] Ecclesiology and Christology are brought together by the principle of representation. The close link between them is meant to be secured in both Luther and Bonhoeffer by the Christological focus of the concept of the church. The representative acts of individual members of the church take on a concrete form in their willingness to help through everyday tasks, in intercession and the forgiveness of sins granted to one another.

As regards the sociality of the church, that is to say its form of community, for Bonhoeffer the Reformation hallmarks of the church according to article 7 of the *Confessio Augustana* already show the fundamentally social dimension of the concept of the church. There can be no proclamation of the gospel or administration of the sacraments without an assembled congregation. Sociality is thus a constitutive element from the outset in the Reformation concept of the church as well; it does not in any sense rank second to faith. In this context, Bonhoeffer uses a phrase that for most people is the only text they know from the *Sanctorum Communio*: "Christ existing as church-community."[52] This saying has become truly independent and been released from its context in Bonhoeffer, taking on a meaning and role totally alien to Bonhoeffer's theology in the postwar Death of God theology.[53] How should this phrase be properly understand? The formula is first meant to express succinctly the church's Christological certainty. One should conduct oneself in the community in the same way as Christ lived. Second, it expresses the idea according to which members of the community being with and for one another is not only made possible by Christ's actions on our behalf, but has already become reality in him. In Christ, the church is unified as a person. "The unity of the church as a structure *is* established 'before' any knowing and willing of the members; it is not ideal, but real."[54] That is why there is also an irreversible inclination of Christ towards the community, also in terms of content. Linguistically, Bonhoeffer's formula alludes to the words of the Apostle Paul, who speaks of the community as the body of Jesus Christ and contrasts the collective person of the first man, Adam, with the collective person of the new man, Christ.

As a Protestant theologian, Bonhoeffer obviously realizes that the empirically existing church cannot simply be identified with the church of the third article of faith. The church which is capable of being empirically experienced is instead shaped by the interpenetration of the *sanctorum communio* and the *peccatorum communio*.[55] It can only be grasped through the dual characteristic of being simultaneously historical and religious, hence fallible, a community of men and women on the one hand, and the divinely ordained community of the

51 DBWE 1, 156–157.

52 DBWE 1, 189–192.

53 On this, see Dorothee Sölle, *Stellvertretung*, Stuttgart, Kreuz, ³1966, 121ff.

54 DBWE 1, 199 (italics original).

55 See DBWE 1, 214–216.

Holy Spirit on the other,[56] whereby for Bonhoeffer the confessing community is the source and goal of community reality.[57]

The aspect that was unique in Bonhoeffer's ecclesiological approach at the time was the attempt to initiate a dialogue between theology on the one side and social philosophy and sociology on the other. In this regard, it must be remembered that sociology was a completely new discipline at the time, founded by Max Weber in Heidelberg as recently as the turn of the century. In the prolegomena to his doctoral thesis, Bonhoeffer builds a bridge to social philosophy and sociology by developing a new concept of reality drawn from his study of German idealism. First, he relinquishes the central position of the cognitive subject. The modern idealist subject-object opposition is replaced by the "I-you" relationship. "I" as a person can originate in socially qualified terms only in opposition to an actual "you." In this regard, Bonhoeffer develops ideas taken from Max Scheler, Theodor Litt, and Eberhard Grisebach. He also draws on Emanuel Hirsch, who in his critique of idealism claimed to have superseded the epistemological question through the primacy of the ethical question. Hirsch's critique in turn leads to a concept similar to the "I-you" philosophy. Applied to the concept of the church, the "I-you" relationship allows the church to be understood in social-philosophical terms as the reality of the encounter between individuals. Bonhoeffer describes the church in this context as an *independent* sociological form. "*For Christian philosophy, the human person originates only in relation to the divine.*"[58] God's transcendence encounters the formation of personality in the ethical transcendence of the human encounter between "I" and "you."[59] Conversely, this means that the effect of the personal formation of the human "you" always occurs only indirectly; in other words, it is mediated: only when the Holy Spirit meets the concrete "you" "*does the other me become a You to me from whom my I arises.*"[60]

The introduction of the concept of person in Bonhoeffer's understanding of reality had a twofold effect: it is from the encounter between the divine "you" and the human "I" in the "you" of one's fellow human beings that the absolute significance of the one for the other arises. The fact that the human experience of being a person occurs merely indirectly through the "you," mediated through the divine "you," guarantees the personal freedom of the "I" against the arbitrariness of the "you."

Bonhoeffer adds to this ontic and ethical concept of person a general metaphysical concept of person. This allows him to explain why individuality and sociality originated simultaneously with regard to humanity's existence. The spiritual sociality of human existence according to the general metaphysical concept of person[61] leads to the realization that the sociality of the church is the aim of God's history with humanity: "God does not desire a history of individual human beings, but the history of the human *community*. However, God does not want a community that absorbs the individual into itself, but a community of *human beings*. In God's eyes, community and individual exist in the same moment and rest in one another."[62]

It is notable that Bonhoeffer's first academic work already contains many of the themes that would permanently shape his ecclesiological thinking. These include the realization that God encounters a human being in the "*you*." This is the basis of the line running through his theological thought that is steadfastly critical of individualism. Conversely, the idea that it is *God* who wants to encounter the individual guarantees

56 On this point and on and the following discussion, see Heinz Rüegger, *Kirche als seelsorgerliche Gemeinschaft: Dietrich Bonhoeffers Seelsorgeverständnis im Kontext seiner bruderschaftlichen Ekklesiologie*, Bern, Lang, 1992, 29.

57 See Ebeling, *Dietrich Bonhoeffers Ringen*, 46.

58 *DBWE* 1, 49 (italics original).

59 *DBWE* 1, 51.

60 *DBWE* 1, 55 (italics original).

61 *DBWE* 1, 73.

62 *DBWE* 1, 80 (italics original).

the individual's freedom. He will later write in *Nachfolge*, "there are no psychic immediacies."[63] Bonhoeffer continues to insist that the church must assume a concrete form, namely, become visible. The recognition of sociality as a fundamental category of faith inevitably leads to an opening and crossing of the church's frontiers, whereby Bonhoeffer does not justify the universality of the church on formal grounds, but on substantive ones. "Bonhoeffer strictly insists that the true church of Jesus Christ exists only where the vicarious representative witness of faith takes on a concrete form. On the other hand, however, this witness – precisely because as witness to Christ it has a universal content – points beyond any boundaries, rifts, and divisions imposed by human beings."[64]

4 Fundamentals of Bonhoeffer's Ecumenical Theology

Today it is taken for granted by German Protestant theologians that theology must be practiced in the ecumenical perspective. This could not be further from the case for the period between the two world wars. It is hard to imagine how little interest there was in ecumenism in the 1920s and 1930s in Germany, and no more than a tiny minority was involved in the emerging ecumenical movement. Of these, the New Testament theologian Adolf Deißmann stands out. Ecumenical theologians were complete outsiders at the time, like the young scholar Dietrich Bonhoeffer. His standard of living and his family connections permitted him to travel abroad, where he would live for lengthy periods, as early as the 1920s. This gave him a broader horizon than most other German theologians. His own theological reflections on ecumenism were stimulated by the ecumenical movement's ambivalent position on the *Kirchenkampf* in Germany, by the *Reichskirche* dominated by the German Christians, and by the Confessing Church. He was preoccupied with three main questions: the ecumenical movement's existence as a church; the proclamation of the concrete commandment by the ecumenical movement; and related to that, the tasks of an ecumenical peace council. All three questions run throughout his lectures and essays on ecumenism during his active involvement in the incipient ecumenical movement.

4.1 *The Need for an Ecumenical Theology*

His first major ecumenical speech was delivered at a conference of the WA in Čiernohorské Kúpele in Czechoslovakia in 1932 on the subject "Zur theological Begründung der Weltbundarbeit."[65] Bonhoeffer's train of thought starts with the premise that it is not enough at a time of increasingly stronger nationalist movements to retreat into the practice of ecumenical cooperation while ignoring the theological foundation of ecumenical action. The absence of theological reflection rendered ecumenical work defenseless against external accusations: "Whoever is involved in ecumenical work must allow himself to be chided as unpatriotic and untruthful, and every attempt to counter this is easily shouted down."[66] Bonhoeffer is convinced that the ecumenical movement originates from a new self-understanding on the part of the Church of Christ, is itself a church, and therefore must also develop a new theology.[67] He sets out ideas about what the fundamental lines of this new ecumenically shaped theology should resemble.

> What is this Christianity that we always hear so much about? Is it essentially the content of the Sermon on the Mount, or is it the message of reconciliation in the cross and resurrection of our Lord? What significance does the Sermon on the Mount have for our action? What meaning is there in the message from the cross? What relationship do

63 *DBWE* 4, 91.

64 Cited from von Soosten, "Afterword," in: *DBWE* 1, 304.

65 Bethge, *Dietrich Bonhoeffer*, 246–248; the lecture is published in: *DBWE* 11, 327–344.

66 *DBWE* 11, 352.

67 *DBWE* 11, 356–357.

> the forms of our modern lives have to the Christian proclamation? What do the state, the economy, and our social life have to do with being Christian?[68]

Bonhoeffer here touches on both of the questions which would later particularly absorb him: the significance of the Sermon on the Mount for being a Christian in the Protestant tradition (the subject of *Nachfolge*) and the orders of human life, which he later attempted to develop under the concept of mandate (in *Ethik*).

A year later, in 1935, Dietrich Bonhoeffer once again took up a theological position on the question of ecumenism, this time in his essay on "Die Bekennende Kirche und die Ökumene."[69] This was an attempt to move closer to answering the question of the continuing significance of each church's confession in the context of the growing ecumenical movement. This was the first time he raised the question of the church in the churches, one which would occupy the WCC in Geneva even more regularly after the war.

4.2 *Proclamation of the Concrete Commandment*

Bonhoeffer's starting premise that the ecumenical movement is the church leads him to take the view at Čiernohorské Kúpele that it is the movement's mission, given the difficulties and tensions of the age, to proclaim the concrete commandment (*konkretes Gebot*). What does he mean by this?

The proclamation of the concrete commandment will always encompass the political dimension.[70] However, proclamations by the church must not be confused with the ordinary everyday business of taking sides politically.[71] The proclamation of the concrete commandment can only occur by listening to the gospel of Jesus Christ and understanding a given situation. This goes beyond social and ethical statements and political resolutions, because it broaches the situation of humanity *coram deo* and, consequently, awakens in the world a spiritual moment not conditioned by humanity's actions, leading to a relativization of the political dimension. Christian Möller calls this, "grace's added eschatological value,"[72] which should not be relinquished through a false politicization of the church's proclamation. It is only in this sphere that the church can even dare to proclaim the concrete commandment.[73] The gospel promotes the proclaiming of the concrete commandment in a twofold sense. It keeps open the path of any "qualified silence" that might be necessary, while also opening the proclamation of the concrete commandment to the possibility of error. Bonhoeffer rightly points out that the church is first and foremost bound by its obligation to the truth, thus it would be a betrayal of truth if it were to hide behind vaguely held resolutions when it does not know the concrete commandment instead of admitting ignorance:

> Nothing good can come of pretending to act before the world and oneself as though one knew the truth, when in reality one did not know the truth … Qualified silence would perhaps be more appropriate for the church today than speech that is possibly very unqualified. That means a protest against every form of church [*Kirchentum*] that does

---

68 *DBWE* 11, 357.

69 See Bethge, *Dietrich Bonhoeffer*, 482–486.

70 Minds have long been divided on the question of the meaning of the political in the church. On this point, see Helmut Gollwitzer, *Wendung zum Leben: Predigten (1970–1980)*, Munich, Kaiser, 1980, foreword.

71 This distinction is hardly taken into account by Folker Albrecht and Ingo Baldermann (see their article "Propheten/Prophetie VI. Prophetie, praktisch-theologisch," *TRE* 27, 513–517).

72 Christian Möller, *Gottesdienst als Gemeindeaufbau: Ein Werkstattbericht*, Göttingen, Vandenhoeck & Ruprecht, ^{2}1990, 55f.

73 Rainer Mayer differentiates in this regard between the "basic confession of Jesus Christ" and the "daring to make a new situational confession," see Rainer Mayer, "Was wollte Dietrich Bonhoeffer in Fanø? Zur aktuellen Diskussion um ein Friedenskonzil ('Weltversammlung für Gerechtigkeit, Friede und Bewahrung der Schöpfung')," *Theologische Beiträge* 19, 1988, 73–89, here 89.

> not honor the question of the truth above all.[74]

Equally plausible, in my view, is Bonhoeffer's affirmation that the certainty that sins will be forgiven also remains the foundation of the concrete commandment: "The church may not command without itself believing in the forgiveness of sins and without pointing out its proclamation of the forgiveness of sins to everyone it commands."[75] The possibility of remaining silent and the reliance on forgiveness prevent the proclamation of the concrete commandment from becoming political in the sense of an ideology.[76]

This proclamation of the concrete commandment must be dared even when the churches are attacked by public opinion in the respective societies due to said proclamation. From our current perspective, it is hard to imagine the reaction triggered by the following sentences in Germany in the 1920s and 1930s, when it was still seething under the sense of humiliation caused by the Treaty of Versailles: "The churches bound together in the World Alliance believe that they recognize a very specific order as that commanded us by God today. The order of *international peace* is God's commandment for us today."[77] In retrospect, today we know what a blessing it would have been for the subsequent history of both Germany and Europe if Bonhoeffer had been able to influence public opinion with these words.

Bonhoeffer also criticizes the tendency in Anglo-Saxon countries, particularly the United States, to regard world peace as part of God's kingdom on earth. An almost disturbing biblical realism can be discerned in his own view: "International peace is not a reality of the gospel, not a piece of the kingdom of God, but rather a commandment of the wrathful God, an order of the preservation of the world towards Christ."[78]

4.3 *The Call for an Ecumenical Peace Council*

Bonhoeffer set out his views even more clearly at the ecumenical conference in Fanø in Denmark in 1934 than he had at Čiernohorské Kúpele.[79] National Socialism had come to power in Germany the year before. Bonhoeffer, together with his entire family, had no doubt that Hitler meant war for Europe and the world. This was behind his renewed call, inspired by his view of ecclesiology, for the ecumenical movement to proclaim the concrete peace commandment. He first argues that the loyalty of Christians to the church of Jesus Christ is far greater than to their own countries.

> Peace should exist because Christ is in the world, that is to say, peace should exist because there is a church of Christ for whose sake alone the entire world still lives. And this church of Christ lives in all nations and at the same time beyond any kind of national, political, social or racial frontier, and the brothers of this church are more inseparably joined through the commandment of the one Lord, Jesus Christ, whom they heed, than any ties of history, blood, class and language of men could bind.[80]

That this idea was far from self-evident at the time was demonstrated by the universal Catholic Church at the end of World War II a few years later. Hostility between Catholic Germans and Poles

74 Bonhoeffer in his lecture "Zur theologischen Begründung der Weltbundarbeit" (1932), DBWE 11, 358. German word clarification in the translation.

75 DBWE 11, 361.

76 Bethge states something similar when he writes: "*Prayer* prevents the actions of the justified from fanatical ideologies that transform innovators into poor representatives of their own cause"; Eberhard Bethge, "Beten und Tun des Gerechten: Dietrich Bonhoeffers umstrittenes Erbe," (1975) in: Eberhard Bethge, *Am gegebenen Ort: Aufsätze und Reden*, Munich, Kaiser, 1979, 39–47, here 47 (italics original).

77 DBWE 11, 364 (italics original).

78 DBWE 11, 365.

79 Bethge, *Dietrich Bonhoeffer*, 372–392.

80 DBW 13, 299 (German original); translated from the German – passage not included in the English translation.

was particularly intense in Upper Silesia, leading to horrendous acts of cruelty when the German population was expelled from this territory.

Needless to say, Bonhoeffer realized that his voice would not be heard on its own. He therefore called on the assembly at Fanø to assume its responsibility as an ecumenical peace council:

> How does peace come about? Who makes the call to peace so that the world may hear it, indeed is compelled to hear it, so that all nations must rejoice? A lone Christian cannot do this; he can indeed raise his voice and bear witness when others remain silent, but the world's powers can silently step over him. The different churches can also certainly bear witness and suffer – oh, if only they did so – but they too are crushed by the violence of hatred. Only the one great ecumenical council of the Holy Church of Christ of the entire world can say it in such a way that the world must grudgingly hear the word of peace and the nations rejoice, because this Church of Christ takes the weapons out of the hands of its sons in the name of Christ and forbids them to go to war and calls out the peace of Christ over a raging world.[81]

For much as Bonhoeffer's call may at first sound fanciful, looking back on history it actually seems quite realistic, certainly much more realistic than all the dreams of National Socialist or Communist world domination.

4.4 Nachfolge *as the Concretion of Faith: Reclaiming the Sermon on the Mount for the Protestant Church*

In 1934, Bonhoeffer wrote to his teacher and friend at the New York Union Theological Seminary, Reinhold Niebuhr: "It is high time to bring the focus back to the Sermon on the Mount, to some degree on the basis of a restoration of Reformation theology [see the *solus Christus* of the Barmen Theological Declaration], but in a way different from the Reformation understanding."[82] For Bonhoeffer, this is an attempt to link up directly with primitive Christianity, bypassing Reformation theology along the way, a theological intellectual path which would prove extremely fruitful for ecumenism after the war. By reclaiming discipleship for the Protestant understanding of faith, Bonhoeffer wants to overcome Protestantism's highly criticized lack of experience, its lack of concretion of faith. It is not without reason that in the New Testament the gospels, including the Acts of the Apostles, come before the Epistles of St. Paul. The message of justification and the Sermon on the Mount must be interpreted together. In his work *Nachfolge* of 1937, Bonhoeffer discovers what would later become the classic formulation for this: "*Only the believers obey, and only the obedient believe.*"[83]

The consequence of this approach in *Nachfolge* is a revision of the traditional Protestant proclamation of justification of the sinner from grace alone. Bonhoeffer accuses this position of largely proclaiming "cheap grace." It had overlooked the fact that faith and discipleship, namely, faith and obedience, are inextricably linked. The work begins with the famous passage: "Cheap grace is the mortal enemy of our church. Our struggle today is for costly grace. ... Cheap grace means grace as doctrine, as principle, as system. It means forgiveness of sins as a general truth; it means God's love as merely a Christian idea of God. Those who affirm it have already had their sins forgiven. ... Cheap grace means justification of sin but not of the sinner."[84]

In contrast, the Sermon on the Mount is for Bonhoeffer the paradigm of how costly grace must be proclaimed. He wants to learn from this text what this proclamation should resemble today.

81 *DBW* 13, 300–301 (German original); translated from the German – passage not included in the English translation.

82 *DBWE* 13, 183–184.

83 *DBWE* 4, 63 (italics original).

84 *DBWE* 4, 43.

"Costly grace is the gospel, which must be sought again and again, the gift which must be asked for, the door which must be knocked upon. Such grace is costly because it calls us to follow, and it is grace because it calls us to follow *Jesus Christ*. It is costly because it cost a man his life, and it is grace because it gave him life in the first place."[85] Bonhoeffer focuses all his efforts on making any flight into a premature spiritual interpretation of the Sermon on the Mount impossible, thus in non-binding religious interiority. This explains his insistence on "simple obedience," on a literal interpretation.

This is shown by a very vivid example:

> How is such a reversal possible? What has happened that the word of Jesus has to endure this game? That it is so vulnerable to the scorn of the world? Anywhere else in the world where commands are given, the situation is clear. A father says to his child: go to bed! The child knows exactly what to do. But a child drilled in pseudotheology would have to argue thus: Father says go to bed. He means you are tired; he does not want me to be tired. But I can also overcome my tiredness by going to play. So, although father says go to bed, what he really means is go play. With this kind of argumentation, a child with its father or a citizen with the authorities would run into an unmistakable response, namely, punishment. The situation is supposed to be different only with respect to Jesus's command. In that case simple obedience is supposed to be wrong, or even to constitute disobedience. How is this possible?[86]

One may perhaps be able to believe in God for oneself alone behind closed doors. However, discipleship can be lived only in the community with brothers and sisters. Through recognition of costly grace, which encompasses the discipleship of Christ, it becomes clear that the Christian community is absolutely essential for the life of individual Christians.

4.5 Gemeinsames Leben: *Overcoming Individualism, Subjectivism and Inwardness*

The premise that discipleship of Jesus Christ can only be lived in a community provides the subject for Bonhoeffer's next book, *Gemeinsames Leben*.[87] This work made a significant contribution to creating a right of abode for monastic spirituality in the Protestant Church. Bonhoeffer wrote down the roughly one hundred pages of this work in rapid succession in September and October 1938, a year after the Gestapo had sealed off the preachers' seminar and brethren house in Finkenwalde.[88] Of all Bonhoeffer's works, *Gemeinsames Leben* is the one that saw by far the greatest number of editions, as well as translations into all the major languages. It is divided into the following chapters: Community, The Day with Others, The Day Alone, Ministry, Confession and Communion. The work is the first attempt in Protestantism after a long time to reflect not only the organization of *individual* spiritual life, but also of the *common* spiritual life seen from the view of the entire church. Right from the preface, Bonhoeffer makes it clear that his reflections are intended to serve the church as a whole. "We are not dealing with a concern of some private circles but with a mission entrusted to the church. Because of this, we are not searching for more or less haphazard individual solutions to a problem. This is, rather, a responsibility to be undertaken by the church as a whole."[89] Bonhoeffer is nonetheless aware of the many objections to this task: "There is a hesitation evident in the way this task has been handled. Only recently has it been understood at all. But this hesitation must give way to the willingness

85 DBWE 4, 31 (italics original).
86 DBWE 4, 79–80.

87 DBWE 5, 25–140.
88 For details, see Bethge, *Dietrich Bonhoeffer*, 469–472.
89 DBWE 5, 25.

of the church to assist in the work."[90] In this short work, Bonhoeffer aimed to show that the lived existence of a Christian requires spiritual gathering if it is not to be dispersed into a mere attempt at improving the world.

4.6 Widerstand und Ergebung: *The Church for Others*

Bonhoeffer's last extended disquisition on the subject of the church can be found in his *Entwurf für eine Arbeit* contained in *Widerstand und Ergebung*.[91] He calls for a radical reorganization of the church, a structural revolution, including a deep-seated restructuring of the traditional office of pastor. Among the proposals were switching the church's financial administration to donations and abolishing the full-time office of pastor.[92] Ultimately, Bonhoeffer wants a "church without privileges."[93] These practical suggestions for restructuring the church might be dismissed as the ideas of an unworldly dreamer, except that they were the result of the rigorous evolution of Bonhoeffer's new Christological perspective developed in *Widerstand und Ergebung* and of the new definition of being a Christian that he formulated there. He justifies the church's reorganization by basing it on Jesus Christ's "being-for-others":[94] Jesus Christ is the human being who is there for others. The church behaves counter to this proclamation of Christ if it does not underline it through an appropriate form and exemplary conduct. In its discipleship of Jesus Christ, it must be the church for others.

Bonhoeffer criticizes the Confessing Church for "fighting during these years only for its self-preservation, as if that were an end in itself." Precisely in this regard it had proven *not* to be a church for others. That makes it at that time "incapable of bringing the word of reconciliation and redemption to humankind and to the world." Only when the church begins to behave according to the example of Jesus will the day come "when people will once more be called to speak the word of God in such a way that the world is changed and renewed."[95]

Bonhoeffer applies these ideas expressed in the *Entwurf für eine Arbeit* not only to the church in general but also to the office of pastor, which permits him to prepare the way for a new *understanding of office*. For him it had always been well established that Jesus Christ is the lord of the church and the world. However, his experience in prison made him realize even more clearly the implications of this for the form of the pastor's office, namely that this lord had always exercised his rule solely through powerlessness, ministry and the cross. The example of the suffering and impotent Jesus cast doubt on any type of clericalization and hierarchical tendencies in the church.

The *Entwurf für eine Arbeit* is informed by a vision of a new church which Bonhoeffer had in mind for the period after the fall of the Third Reich. He channeled his thoughts into the hope of being "of some service for the future of the church."[96] This desire was not realized in the immediate postwar period: not least thanks to the benevolence of the victorious powers, the church quickly acquired a new display of organizational power. Perhaps Bonhoeffer's wish will be fulfilled in our age, in which the definition of the church's foundations and of being Christian has been opened up again.

The internal coherence of Bonhoeffer's vision is certainly notable: he consistently makes his Christological ideas useful for ecclesiological action. If faith means participating in Jesus's existence

90 DBWE 5, 25.

91 DBWE 8, 499–504. On this point, see the different interpretation of Bonhoeffer's statement in Bethge, "Was heißt: Kirche für andere?," 152–169.

92 DBWE 8, 503.

93 This is the title of an article by Josef Smolik, who interpreted Bonhoeffer's ideas on this subject at the Bonhoeffer symposium in Geneva in 1976 from a Czech perspective; Josef Smolik, "Kirche ohne Privilegien," in: Pfeifer, ed., *Genf '76*, 129–145.

94 DBWE 8, 500–503.

95 DBWE 8, 389–390.

96 DBWE 8, 504.

and this takes concrete form in "being there for others" – namely with regard to the "neighbor within reach"[97] – the logical consequence is that "church is ... church only when it is there for others."[98]

The simplicity of Bonhoeffer's vision is impressive. The nature of Jesus Christ, the actions of the individual Christian and the church's mandate are all defined by love, "being for others." Ultimately these ideas represent a development of his fundamental belief adopted from Luther and discussed in the *Sanctorum Communio* that the church is justified in the vicarious actions of Jesus Christ on our behalf. The notion of vicarious representation leads the ethical thinker in Bonhoeffer to develop an ethics of love rooted in Jesus's twofold commandment: "And thou shalt love the Lord thy God with the love of thy whole heart, and thy whole soul, and thy whole mind, and thy whole strength. This is the first commandment, and the second, of the same ilk, is this, Thou shalt love thy neighbor as thyself" (Mark 12:30f). Bonhoeffer's vision of a renewed church will automatically remind readers of the words handed down to us concerning the external perception of the early church: "See how they love one another!" Bonhoeffer's vision aims at a renaissance of early Christianity, and indeed at a renewal of Christianity as defined by primitive Christianity.

The ecumenical dimension of Bonhoeffer's ecclesiology also comes to light here. Irrespective of the church concerned, ecclesiastical thinking leads to the church's being there first and foremost for the church or for its officeholders rather than for others.[99] In this way, the church satisfies itself and carries on complacently believing that it is needed. In other words, it remains static and takes it for granted that people will come to it of their own volition. Thus Bonhoeffer bases his notion of a church for others on his Christology: Jesus is the human being there for others. The church, therefore, has no need of itself. Like everyone, it needs Christ. Movement must therefore always be from Christ. Since Christ is there for the church, the church should, through him, also be there for people. If the church were to adopt Bonhoeffer's new understanding of office, it would have direct ecumenical consequences: a "church for others" can only exist in the form of a "church with others."

5 Striking Similarities between Dietrich Bonhoeffer and Max Josef Metzger and the Una Sancta Movement

In terms of their origins and career paths, the differences between Dietrich Bonhoeffer and Max Josef Metzger appear significant. However, upon closer inspection major similarities in their lives and ecumenical approaches become apparent. This "increasing convergence" is attributable to their shared background in a crisis-ridden Germany between the wars and their opposition to the Nazi regime.

5.1 *Biographical Parallels*

Metzger came from a family of Catholic teachers in southern Baden and grew up in the predominantly Protestant town of Schopfheim.[100] He graduated in Catholic theology from Freiburg im Breisgau and Fribourg in Switzerland, where he had a number of international contacts with fellow students, and completed his doctorate after his return to

97 *DBWE* 8, 501.

98 *DBWE* 8, 503.

99 I am grateful to my tutorial assistant, Nicolas Viziotis, for these insights.

100 On this point and on the subsequent discussion, see: Max Josef Metzger, *Christuszeuge in einer zerrissenen Welt: Briefe und Dokumente aus der Gefangenschaft (1934–1944)*, ed. Klaus Kienzler, Freiburg i.Br., Herder, 1991, 7–41; Walter Wilhelm Baumeister, *Max Josef Metzger: Ein Herold Christi, des Königs*, Meitingen, Kyrios, 1951; Christian Heß, *"Ohne Christus, ohne tiefstes Christentum ist Krieg": Die Christkönigsthematik als Leitidee im kirchlich-gesellschaftlichen Engagement Max Josef Metzgers*, Paderborn, Bonifatius, 2016.

Freiburg im Breisgau. He then intended to pursue a *habilitation*, but this possibility was rejected by the professor responsible. Metzger hence dedicated himself entirely to working for the church. One can observe a similar development with Bonhoeffer, in terms both of the early influence of international contacts and of a conscious shift from theological studies to church activity.

It is striking how strongly Metzger's work for peace among nations and the unity of the churches subsequently resembled Bonhoeffer's own. After being ordained as a priest in 1911 and working as a chaplain, Metzger became divisional chaplain on the French front in 1914. His experiences there would henceforth motivate him to advocate peace and understanding among Europe's nations. In 1917, he had already approached Pope Benedict XV with an "international peace program"[101] and in the same year founded the World Peace League of the White Cross. He gained an international reputation as a result of his participation or involvement in international peace congresses in the 1920s in The Hague (twice), Graz, Paris, and Luxembourg.

Metzger had already been appointed head of the secretariat general of the Austrian Kreuzbund in Graz in 1915, a welfare and social, diaconal organization. His work there made him realize that the laity's involvement in the church is crucial. In 1919, Metzger therefore founded the Mission Society of the White Cross, whose slogan was "Christ must be king" (1 Cor 15:25). This was renamed Society of Christ the King in 1927[102] and was run by the laity. When in that same year society members took over the running of a new clinic of the local Caritas association for the treatment of alcoholics, Metzger also moved to the town of Meitingen near Augsburg.

In 1938, Metzger founded the Una Sancta movement, which included non-Catholics, to foster ecumenical understanding between the two major Christian confessions in Germany. It was a new departure insofar as it signaled the Catholic Church's willingness to relinquish its claim to universal representation. Una Sancta groups soon began to form throughout Germany. At Pentecost in 1938, Metzger wrote to all the Protestant pastors in Germany inviting them to take part in ecumenical discussions. This led to the ecumenical congresses in Meitingen, in which theologians from different denominations took part. These first ecumenical meetings among the divided churches in Germany became the precursors to subsequent meetings after the war.

It is obvious that Metzger's activity in support of peace and the unity of the churches was a thorn in the side of the Nazis. Upon being incarcerated for the third time, after a few months in Plötzensee prison in Berlin, Metzger was condemned to death on Oct 14, 1943 by Roland Freisler, president of People's Court in Berlin. He was executed after a further six months of reclusion in Brandenburg-Görden prison on the Apr 17, 1944. The grounds given for his execution were a two-page peace memorandum that he intended to have taken to neutral Sweden. He was betrayed by a sympathizer of the Una Sancta circle in Berlin. Metzger was headstrong and determined, qualities which made him uncomfortable for the church hierarchy. He was well aware that people dismissed him as an "eccentric idealist."[103] and it was no coincidence that he was not employed as a parish priest. He himself admitted that his "spiritual outlook" was not that of a typical priest: "Religious officialdom, unworldliness, remoteness from reality, narrow-mindedness, legalism and traditionalism couldn't be more alien to me."[104]

101 Reprinted in Marianne Möhring, *Täter des Wortes: Max Josef Metzger, Leben und Wirken*, Meitingen, Kyrios, 1966, 215f.

102 After Pope Pius XI had proclaimed the Feast of Christ the King in 1925.

103 Metzger's own words in a text to the People's Court dated Sept 28, 1934, reproduced in: Metzger, *Christuszeuge*, 277.

104 Metzger, *Christuszeuge*, 276.

Rather, his perspective was shaped by primitive Christianity's view of the kingdom of God.[105] He therefore considered himself bound to the ethos of the Sermon on the Mount and remained a pacifist throughout his life.[106] This formed the spiritual foundation of his work on behalf of peace, social and ethical issues, and church unity.

It is truly remarkable how close Metzger's thinking in this sense resembles Bonhoeffer's own. For both, the Sermon on the Mount had assumed the role of the guiding principle of action. As a member of the Confessing Church, it was natural that Bonhoeffer would oppose the *Reichskirche*. Moreover, even within the Confessing Church he belonged to the decisive wing, known as the Dahlemites, who advocated that the resolutions of the synods of Barmen and Berlin-Dahlem should apply without any limitation. For Bonhoeffer, Dahlem's emergency church law established the binding framework for his ecclesiology. This explains his view that "whoever knowingly separates himself from the Confessing Church in Germany separates himself from salvation."[107]

Metzger had no doubt that he was fulfilling a prophetic mission for the church and the world in his work to foster peace among nations and church unity: "It [a strong and clear sense of mission] took hold early on, the knowledge becoming ever clearer, more vehement, that I had a great duty to fulfill in God's kingdom in the world which would manifest itself in the very orientation of my own way of life."[108]

Very much in the same vein as Metzger, Bonhoeffer also saw his work for the kingdom of God in the light of the Old Testament prophets. This can be seen particularly well in a sermon on Jer 20:7 delivered while working as a pastor with the German community in London.[109] It was held on Jan 21, 1934, four days before the leaders of the groups involved in the *Kirchenkampf* were received by Hitler in Berlin. In the run-up to this meeting, Bonhoeffer had tried to influence it directly by means of various interventions.[110] The sermon's immediate context was thus highly charged. This intellectual background throws into greater relief Bonhoeffer's prophetic self-perception, while also allowing him to reveal the deeper motivation behind his participation in the *Kirchenkampf*.[111]

In the case of Metzger, it is clear from a number of his writings that he was willing to suffer martyrdom for his cause.[112] His letters from prison, written shortly before his execution, show that he recognized the hopelessness of his efforts and

105 On this point and on the subsequent discussion, see Metzger, *Christuszeuge*, 276.

106 For more detail, see Metzger, *Christuszeuge*, 16–23.

107 *DBWE* 14, 656–678, here 675, essay entitled "On the Question of Church Communion" ("Zur Frage nach der Kirchengemeinschaft").

108 Metzger, *Christuszeuge*, 163 (letter from prison in Brandenburg on the first day of Advent in 1943).

109 *DBWE* 13, 349–353. The autobiographical themes in the sermon were already pointed out by Bethge (Bethge, *Dietrich Bonhoeffer*, 387–389). Jørgen Glenthøj in particular has attempted to discern the significance of the Jeremiah motif for Bonhoeffer's own understanding of discipleship; see Jørgen Glenthøj, "Dietrich Bonhoeffers Weg vom Pazifismus zum politischen Widerstand," in: Mayer & Zimmerling, *Dietrich Bonhoeffer aktuell*, 37–53. As Otto Dudzus before him in Dietrich Bonhoeffer, *Predigten, Auslegungen, Meditationen (1925–1945)*, ed. Otto Dudzus, vol. 1, Gütersloh, Kaiser, 1998, 42ff., Werner Kallen, *In der Gewissheit seiner Gegenwart: Dietrich Bonhoeffer und die Spur des vermissten Gottes*, Mainz, Matthias-Grünewald, 1997, 62ff. has recently read this sermon as Bonhoeffer's prophetic vocational story.

110 Bethge, *Dietrich Bonhoeffer*, 343–346; see also Klaus Scholder, *Die Kirchen und das Dritte Reich*, vol. 2, *Das Jahr der Ernüchterung 1934 Barmen und Rom*, Berlin, Siedler, 1985, 50ff.

111 Dudzus does not pay sufficient attention to the interconnection between both themes when he writes: "But this sermon's importance has absolutely nothing to do with the indicated circumstances and dangers but lies entirely in the inner story of this young prophet named by God to his ministry"; Dudzus, *Predigten*, vol. 1, 42.

112 Metzger, *Christuszeuge*, 37–41; on this, with respect to Metzger and Bonhoeffer see also Eberhard Schockenhoff, *Entschiedenheit und Widerstand: Das Lebenszeugnis der Märtyrer*, Freiburg i.Br., Herder, 2015, esp. 157–163.

offered his life to God as an atoning sacrifice for world peace and church unity: "I would be happy if, through offering my life, I could effectively serve the goal which my life strived for without apparent success."[113] Even before his imprisonment, he wrote to the members of the Society of Christ the King in his spiritual testament of Lent 1942: "Nothing could give my life a more meaningful end than being allowed to give my life for Christian peace in the kingdom of Christ."[114]

Again the similarity with Bonhoeffer is notable. Even in his early speeches and sermons Bonhoeffer's willingness to suffer martyrdom as the goal of being a disciple of Christ emerges again and again.[115] As early as 1932, he already expresses the belief that future Christians will have to pay with their lives to defend the truth of the gospel. They will have to prove that they protest even more obstinately and with purpose on this earth precisely because they are thinking of the above. The blood of new martyrs will be demanded from the church. "But this blood, if we really still have the courage and honor and faithfulness to shed it, will not be as innocent and untarnished as that of the first witnesses."[116] With these words Bonhoeffer actually anticipated his own fate after the war: many did not recognize his martyrdom as such for a long time, but regarded his execution merely as a consequence of his political resistance.

Bonhoeffer's willingness to suffer martyrdom also comes to the fore in his last conversation with George Bell in Sweden in May 1942. Just as Jeremiah saw for Israel, he sees the only chance for Germany's survival the acceptance of unconditional surrender, which meant renouncing any kind of negotiated peace. Defeat had to be accepted by the members of the resistance to Hitler as God's judgment of Germany. According to Bell's diary entries, Bonhoeffer said at the time:

> There must be punishment by God. ... We do not want to escape repentance. Our action to be such as well be understood as act of repentance and spoken out. Have been speaking to families whose anti-Nazi sons have been killed in Poland and ask why? He replied: our innocent ones suffer, as the innocent Poles suffer. Christians do not wish to escape repentance, or chaos if God wills to bring it on us. We must take this judgment as Christians. We take this act as fact of repentance; importance of *declaring* repentance (which I stressed).[117]

5.2 *Similar Ecumenical Aims*

It is notable that for both Metzger and Bonhoeffer their advocacy of world peace and the unity of the churches were inseparable. As we saw above, in his speech to the youth conference at Fanø in Denmark in 1934, held jointly by the WA and by Life and Work, Bonhoeffer, like Metzger before him at the peace conferences in the 1920s, spoke out clearly in favor of peace among nations. At the same time, Bonhoeffer called for an ecumenical peace council of the churches, since he believed that the message of peace would only have a

113 Metzger, *Christuszeuge*, 137 (letter dated Oct 10, 1943).

114 Cited in Metzger, *Christuszeuge*, 39.

115 For example, in his Sunday school address on the Sunday of the Dead in 1929: "You see, Christians much preferred to die than to deny their dear God; indeed, they were even glad that they might die, for they knew that soon all their cares and worries would be over, and that they would soon be in heaven, where there are no more tears, but rather nothing but joy"; *DBWE* 10, 557; or in a sermon for *Volkstrauertag* in 1932: "What does faithfulness of the community of Christ mean here other than calling [us] out into this furious raging again and again – unto exhaustion, unto humiliation, unto martyrdom – the words of Christ that there should be peace"; *DBWE* 11, 426.

116 *DBWE* 11, 459.

117 Diary entry by George K.A. Bell for May 31, 1942, *DBWE* 16, 300–301 (italics original). Bonhoeffer had indeed written such a confession of guilt already, long before the conversation with Bell, at the height of Hitler's military successes, *DBWE* 6, 138–143.

chance of being heard by the wider public if proclaimed by all the churches together.

In a memorandum written from prison during Advent 1939, Metzger for his part suggests to Pope Pius XII that he call a general ecumenical council.[118] This memorandum is Metzger's ecumenical testament. There, he writes that the council's task would be nothing less than "giving a new face to the reunited church."[119] In preparation, the pope should appoint a group of twelve experts to sound out the chances of a rapprochement. The meeting could take place in Assisi: "Assisi might be the appropriate location, as there the spirit of the *poverello*, revered by all Christians without distinction, would be conducive to an atmosphere of peace and reconciliation."[120] Even Metzger's very language shows similarities with Bonhoeffer's at Fanø: "The adversities of the age, which God uses to speak to us, require the last momentous efforts *in order to overcome the rupture in the Christian church* so that Christ's kingdom of peace can be made a reality in the whole world."[121] For Metzger, the contemporary political situation presented itself as the *kairos* to overcome the division of churches.

Even his diagnosis of this situation is strikingly similar to Bonhoeffer's. Metzger writes: "Whenever the law of divine order, which establishes the life of human beings living together in *truth, justice* and *love*, is abandoned, there is only *war and destruction*. Therefore, what we are living through is the dress rehearsal for the last judgment."[122] Like Bonhoeffer, Metzger has no doubt that the unity of the church can only be achieved by taking the spiritual path. A new start in unity is only possible by converting to Jesus Christ and his commandment. "The adversities of the age have fallen precisely on us and will humble us even further so that all together we will finally arrive at a great *metanoia*, a conversion from the ways of self-righteousness, blindness, pride, a complete turning to Christ, the prince of peace and the king of love."[123] The Christocentric orientation of Metzger's theology discernible in this passage links him to Bonhoeffer. The Barmen Declaration already bore this hallmark, as we have seen. After the war, the Christocentric approach would become the theological foundation of the WCC in Geneva and then, in the 1960s, of the proclamations of Vatican II.

Metzger is adamant that the main obstacles to church unity do not lie in dogmatic differences: "The real differences relate much more to *theological doctrines* and matters of *ecclesiastical discipline* than to questions of *revealed belief*."[124] In this context, he already anticipates the later ecumenical attempt at a solution: the aim of ecumenism is reconciled diversity rather than the leveling of differences. "The opposition between different intellectual *positions* is much stronger; but these cannot simply be identified with "truth" and "error" respectively. What are often involved are *ranges of tension* whereby under *una catholica*'s universality everyone is allowed to be right in some way."[125] This text anticipates the sociological view according to which a fundamental cause of the differences between the confessions, which can only be overcome with difficulty, lies in the relevant *habitus*.

It would appear that Pope Pius XII never received Metzger's ecumenical memorandum. He certainly did not react to it. Despite this, Metzger's views served to prepare the ground for an

118 Reprinted in: Metzger, *Christuszeuge*, 82–90.

119 Metzger, *Christuszeuge*, 89 (italics original).

120 Metzger, *Christuszeuge*, 89.

121 Metzger, *Christuszeuge*, 84 (italics original).

122 Metzger, *Christuszeuge*, 83(italics original). On this, see: Heß, *"Ohne Christus, ohne tiefstes Christentum ist Krieg."*

123 Metzger, *Christuszeuge*, 84 (italics original).

124 Metzger, *Christuszeuge*, 87 (italics original).

125 Metzger, *Christuszeuge*, 87 (italics original); similar ideas may be found in: Max Josef Metzger, "Theologische Abhandlung über das Königtum Christi: Vermächtnis aus der Todeszelle," in: *Maran Atha. Zum 25. Todestag von Dr. Max Josef Metzger*, Meitingen, Kyrios, 1969, 33–155, esp. 56f.

ecumenical rapprochement among the churches after World War II.

6 Conclusions

The ecumenical activity and commitment of Dietrich Bonhoeffer and Max Josef Metzger is shaped by three fundamental insights. First, the challenge to the Christian faith brought by the totalitarian regimes of the 20th century represented a significant external impetus for Christian churches to come closer together. Second, this situation in turn made the churches' ecumenically active members realize that assuming responsibility in society and working for the unity of the churches were inseparable aims. Finally, the mortal threat to Christian values and law forced Christians to become socially and ethically engaged and to stand up for peace and justice. Only on this basis was Christianity's permanent survival in Europe possible.

From a theological perspective, it was the common Christocentric basis shared by ecumenical advocates that enabled them after the war to emphasize what the confessions had in common rather than the differences among them. During the Third Reich, the critical-ideological potential peculiar to Christocentrism, showed itself to be fruitful. Against the background of the Nazi-imposed cult of the Führer, belief in Jesus Christ as the only lord in life and death brought an inner freedom beyond the reach of authoritarian demands.

Finally, the impact of the martyrdom of a series of ecumenical pioneers should not be underestimated.[126] The testament of the lives of Dietrich Bonhoeffer and Max Josef Metzger represented an ongoing ecumenical obligation for those who survived the war. Resistance to the reign of terror of totalitarian regimes turned them into "martyrs of undivided Christianity."[127] The experience of joint resistance has lost none of its force right up until today, as we were reminded a while ago when statues of the Lutheran martyr Dietrich Bonhoeffer and the Catholic martyr Maximilian Kolbe, together with those of eight others, were erected above the entrance door to Westminster Abbey. Eberhard Schockenhoff has defined four aspects that make the witness of the martyrs important for the future of Christianity and ecumenism.[128] First, the sacrifice of their lives serves as a reminder for "sober realism," which prevents us from suppressing the destructive potential of human beings in their dealings with one another. Furthermore, the martyrs remain a thorn in the side of a mainly conformist, Western Christianity. Third, they remind us that even the most extreme dedication to the realization of the kingdom of God is subject to eschatological reservation. Finally, they also force future generations to cherish the hope of the world's renewal through God.

Translated from German to English by Fiona Robb.

126 Schockenhoff, *Entschiedenheit*.

127 Schockenhoff, *Entschiedenheit*, 169.

128 For this and the subsequent text, see Schockenhoff, *Entschiedenheit*, 202–206.

Bibliography

Baumeister, Walter Wilhelm, *Max Josef Metzger: Ein Herold Christi, des Königs*, Meitingen, Kyrios, 1951.

Bethge, Eberhard, *Dietrich Bonhoeffer: A Biography*, trans. Victoria J. Barnett, Minneapolis, Fortress Press, 2000.

Bonhoeffer, Dietrich, "On the Question of Church Communion," DBWE 14, 656–678.

Ernesti, Jörg, *Ökumene im Dritten Reich*, Paderborn, Bonifatius, 2007.

Heß, Christian, *"Ohne Christus, ohne tiefstes Christentum ist Krieg": Die Christkönigsthematik als Leitidee*

im kirchlich-gesellschaftlichen Engagement Max Josef Metzgers, Paderborn, Bonifatius, 2016.
Metzger, Max Josef, *Christuszeuge in einer zerrissenen Welt: Briefe und Dokumente aus der Gefangenschaft (1934–1944)*, ed. Klaus Kienzler, Freiburg i.Br., Herder, 1991.
Möhring, Marianne, *Täter des Wortes: Max Josef Metzger, Leben und Wirken*, Meitingen, Kyrios, 1966.
Robertson, Edwin H., *Unshakeable Friend: George Bell und die deutschen Kirchen*, London, CCBI, 1995.
Zimmerling, Peter, *Bonhoeffer als Praktischer Theologe*, Göttingen, Vandenhoeck & Ruprecht, 2006.
Zimmerling, Peter, "Dietrich Bonhoeffer und George Bell – Ökumenische Freundschaft im Ernstfall," in: Christian Möller & others, eds., *Wegbereiter der Ökumene im 20. Jahrhundert*, Göttingen, Vandenhoeck & Ruprecht, 2005, 294–313.

CHAPTER 12

Transnational Movements and Pastoral Issues (1930–1950)

Keith Clements

1 Introduction

The period 1930–1950 saw world upheavals caused by totalitarianism and war on an unprecedented scale. In response, as never before, churches and Christians in general sought to engage in diaconal work for the relief of suffering, in joint efforts to strengthen the pastoral, educational, and evangelistic ministries of the churches, and in discerning the prophetic voice for peace, justice, and human rights. It was in responding to these crises in transnational ways that the desire for Christian unity led to new paths towards unity.

2 Transnational Movements and Their Organizations: The Scene in 1930

The start of the period under review saw well established transnational organizations and their associated movements, many of them chronicled earlier in these volumes, at work in a wide range of engagements for Christian unity, world missions and evangelization, peace and social justice, education and humanitarian relief. Prominent here were the long-established youth movements represented by the YMCA, the YWCA, and the WSCF. The IMC, fruit of the Edinburgh WMC of 1910, true to its name, was by its very nature transnational, and indeed during the period under review it was through its member mission organizations that much of the Western Churches's interest in the wider world found conscious expression.[1] In the aftermath of World War I, peace, reconciliation and the prevention of further conflicts had become of paramount concern, as seen in the activities of the WA, which had been formed at the outbreak of the conflict in 1914, and also such bodies as the Fellowship of Reconciliation, likewise formed on an international basis in 1914.[2] The issues of peace and social and economic justice were central to the Life and Work movement, launched at the Stockholm conference of 1925, and then given continuity and direction by the Universal Christian Council for Life and Work, and from 1928 its research office in Geneva. Concern for the visible unity of the churches which had begun before 1914 likewise was given new impetus by the experience of world conflict, finding focus and structure as a result of the first world conference on Faith and Order at Lausanne, in 1927, and its subsequent commission on Faith and Order.[3] Meanwhile practical, Christian humanitarian concern at international level was finding international expression, for example, in the initiative of the Swiss ecumenist Dr. Adolf Keller, who in 1920 founded the European Central Bureau for Relief (Inter-Church Aid), located initially in the Swiss Protestant Federation but with crucial moral and financial support from the FCC. Note should also be taken of other transnational movements and their organizations active at the time, such as the EA, the WCCE and, more controversially, the Oxford Movement.

Few could have anticipated the challenges that would face them in the next decade as the world plunged into a time of unforeseen turbulence,

---

1 On the IMC see the contribution by Kenneth R. Ross in the first volume of this work.

2 See the contribution by Gerhard Besier in the first volume of this work.

3 On the beginning of Life and Work and Faith and Order see the contribution by Dietz Lange in the first volume of this work, and the contribution by Luca Ferracci in the first volume of this work.

signaled first in 1929 with the Wall Street crash and the world financial crisis. This seriously affected the ability of such organizations to operate at an international level. Faith and Order, for example, had to relinquish its full-time secretariat. Paradoxically, the WA, though a less official body of the churches, managed to survive better than some thanks to the support, via the CPU, from the millionaire philanthropist Andrew Carnegie.

3 The International Scene (1930–1933): New Forebodings

In April 1929, Francis P. Miller, the editor at the time of *Student World*, the quarterly journal of the WSCF, called attention to a troubling paradox facing that organization. As its name implied, it was undoubtedly international in its nature and reach. Its head office was in Geneva and it also had offices in Australia, Canada, France, Germany, Great Britain, Holland, India, New Zealand, South Africa, and the United States. Its membership totaled 300,000 students including many in countries other than those mentioned, notably China and Japan. It would seem, therefore, to be well-placed for making a contribution to international peace. Yet, its discernible influence on world affairs seemed relatively weak – and those affairs were once again disquieting:

> The international situation makes it perfectly evident that the services of the Federation in the international field are as much needed now as they have ever been. The forces making for hatred and strife between nations may not be as obtrusive or vocal as they were before 1914, but their reticence does not mean that they are any less powerful or sinister. Worship of the National Being can become a more dangerous cult in industrialized modern democracies than it ever was in old fashioned monarchies and this cult is one of the great world religions at the present time. The East has yet to secure full justice from the West and the possibility of war will not cease until it does so.[4]

If the WSCF did not find its own role in the preparation of the world for a just and creative peace then, said Miller, "it may continue as a very useful international student telephone exchange, but it will not be the experimental model of the world community for which some of its members have hoped and dreamed."[5]

This mood of self-examination in the face of a changing world was a marked feature of the transnational Christian youth movements as they entered the 1930s, and it is notable how the WSCF, for example, attempted this taking stock of its work not by occupying a single, supposedly superior vantage point over the world as a whole, but by bringing together perspectives from the very different and changing contexts of students, for example in Germany, Japan, France, China, and South Africa, while at the same time launching a major review of "The Message of the Federation." The relative strength of the Christian student presence in India and the Far East was a vital factor in making the youth movements in their apprehension aware of the renewed dangers of war, since it was in the East that the most immediate danger was arising, most evidently in 1931 by the Japanese expansionism in China. Another factor promoting self-examination was the impact, in Europe at least, of Karl Barth's "theology of crisis" with its emphasis on the revealed Word of God in Jesus Christ and therewith its fierce criticism of all human pretentions to quasi-sacred greatness, not least that of the nations in their self-justifying pride. The Dutchman Willem A. Visser 't Hooft, who in 1932 became secretary of the WSCF (and

4 Francis P. Miller, "The International Task of the Federation", *Student World* 22/1, 1929, 1–3. Copies in WCCA. See the contribution by Sarah Scholl in the first volume of this work.

5 Miller, "The International Task of the Federation."

editor of *Student World*), was a devoted Barthian and under his leadership Bible study became a key feature of the movement, thanks especially to the French student leader Suzanne de Dietrich. It was remarkable that despite the drastic impact of the world financial crisis the WSCF was able to achieve so much in the time of mounting crisis in the 1930s. Visser 't Hooft himself comments:

> This was possible because the group of leaders of the Federation worked as a well-coordinated team with great unity of purpose. Francis Miller of the USA, Reinhold von Thadden and Hans Lilje of Germany, Pierre Maury and Suzanne de Dietrich of France, Robert Mackie and Eric Fenn of Great Britain, Augustine Ralla Ram of India and others gave as much time and thought to the Federation and trusted each other so fully that the General Secretary was part of a team the members of which were all active in one way or another.[6]

It was this shared vision and mutual trust that was to prove vital in maintaining the international ecumenical movement alive in the fateful days ahead. In 1932, the pioneering British ecumenist and secretary of the IMC Joseph H. Oldham, in thoroughly Barthian mode addressed an SCM conference in Bad Boll, Germany, on "The Dilemma of Western Civilization," and in that very same year the *Student World* promoted a major discussion of nationhood, nationalism, and war in the theological perspective, with articles by Hans Lilje, secretary of the German SCM, and several leading theologians. Indeed the WSCF was soon bringing virtually all the notable Protestant theologians of the time to the attention of its membership, and often of each other, too.

6 Willem Adolph Visser 't Hooft, *Memoirs*, London, SCM Press, 1973, 44.

4 Witness for Peace: Changing Agendas and Intergenerational Differences

The WSCF, YMCA, and YWCA had been founded primarily to promote Christian fellowship and pastoral support for and among students, and to encourage them to join the evangelical missionary enterprise. By 1930, however, the issues of international peace, justice, and reconciliation had moved to the top of their agendas. How, then, did they compare in intent and practice with those bodies specifically devoted to world peace, namely Life and Work and the WA? In September 1931, the WA held its eighth international conference in Cambridge, England. Dominating its agenda was disarmament, appropriately enough in view of the World Conference on Disarmament scheduled to begin in Geneva in the following year. The atmosphere in the WA was one of concern yet also of optimism. "World peace depends on world disarmament, and disarmament depends on you," ran a poster welcoming delegates to Cambridge, epitomizing the ethos of much of the WA: identify the issues that are wrong in the world and bring pressure on governments to address them. In Cambridge, however, there was a new development, namely, a special effort to engage youth in the enterprise. Not only was there a special preliminary conference for the 70 youth delegates, but a major structural innovation was also agreed upon with the setting up of a joint youth commission of the Alliance and Life and Work. This would have a joint secretariat in Geneva overseen by the Frenchman Henry-Louis Henriod and, moreover, three honorary travelling youth secretaries covering different areas of the world. The appointee for Germany and Central and Northern Europe was Dietrich Bonhoeffer. This concerted effort at youth recruitment generated a new challenge to the movement, for Bonhoeffer was not the only one in that age group to express strong dissatisfaction with the Alliance's production of bland declarations on peace and disarmament without any real *theological* analysis of what was happening in the world, and without any examination by the churches of what their own specific responsibility as members of the body of Christ in the world was. Optimistic religious pragmatism, too akin to that of secular liberalism, was not enough. In the WSCF and allied youth movements, and within the WA and Life and Work, a difference in emphasis and approach along generational lines was thus developing, with the younger elements looking for a much sharper-edged approach to international and social issues. When Adolf Hitler came to power in 1933, the threat to the ecumenical witness, and the need for it, became all the more real.

5 The Crisis in Europe: Responding to Totalitarianism (1933–1939)

The appointment of Adolf Hitler as chancellor of Germany on Jan 30, 1933 and thereby the advent of his National Socialist Party as the effective ruling force in the country, ushered in the most convulsive 20th-century phase in the life not only of Germany but in much of the rest of Europe, and indeed of the world, as well. By their very nature, the events in Germany demanded a transnational response from the ecumenical community. There had for several years been alarm outside Germany at the strident demands of the Nazi movement with its sinister neo-pagan ideology of "blood race and soil," its belligerent nationalism and, last but not least, its virulent anti-Semitism and other forms of racism. Now, however, much of this was being put into actual practice, as seen in the rapid suppression of all political opposition, the implementation of a police-state, and the first anti-Jewish measures including the enforced boycotts of Jewish-owned businesses and the removal from civic office and employment of so-called non-Aryans. For the churches both abroad and in Germany, however, there was the very immediate issue of how the German churches, Protestants and Catholic alike, would fare under the new regime and what their response to it would be. Notwithstanding the brutal methods of the Nazis, there were many in the German churches who welcomed Hitler's revolution with its perceived aims of national renewal. Sprinkling his speeches with references to "the Almighty" he promised a place for the churches in the new order, so long as they conformed to that order. Initially, the Catholic bishops in Germany had strongly attacked the Nazi ideology as incompatible with Christian teaching, but in 1933 the Vatican and the Nazi regime signed a concordat which essentially assured the church of the state's protection on condition that the church did not interfere with the state's policies.

5.1 *The German* Kirchenkampf *and Transnational Responses*

Soon after the Nazi takeover in 1933 there began the *Kirchenkampf*[7] prompted by the attempt of the so-called German Christians movement, a Protestant arm of the Nazi Party, to take over the German Evangelical Church. Their aim was for a "Reich church" under the leadership of a Führer-style Reich bishop, and purged of non-Aryan clergy. Opposition was initially mounted by the Pastors's Emergency League, led by the Berlin pastor Martin Niemöller, and it culminated in the Free Synod of Barmen in May 1934, which, in condemnation of the German Christians and under the leading inspiration of Karl Barth, drew up the famous Barmen Declaration, the founding charter of the Confessing Church. The Barmen Synod and its Declaration constituted, from the beginning, an ecumenical event. This was obviously so on the German level, bringing together as it did so many Protestants from the regional and confessional diversity of the German Evangelical Church. However, this intra-German and intra-Protestant ecumenism immediately exploded onto the wider ecumenical scene. Moreover, it soon became clear that such reportage and comment from abroad

7 For a comprehensive account of the *Kirchenkampf*, see especially Klaus Scholder, *The Churches and the Third Reich*, 2 vols., London, SCM Press, 1987–1988. More in particular see Peter Zimmerling's contribution on ecumenism in the Third Reich in this volume.

was not just *about* the *Kirchenkampf* but was a vital part of the conflict itself, as the Reich state and church authorities sought to counter not just pro-Confessing Church views but any reporting of "church turmoil" as malicious propaganda. Therefore, even on this immediate popular level, Barmen became a phenomenon in much of the *oikumene*.

Just days before the Barmen Synod, on Ascension Day 1934, George Bell, Anglican bishop of Chichester and president of the Universal Christian Council for Life and Work, issued a special message to the member churches of Life and Work regarding the German Evangelical Church.[8] This received wide international publicity. It voiced alarm at the autocratic methods being foisted on church government, the measures taken against oppositional pastors, many of whom were suffering harassment and imprisonment, and drew attention to other problems "which are the concern of the whole of Christendom" regarding the nature of the church, its witness, its freedom, and relationship to the secular power. A major factor in prompting Bell to issue this statement was the desperate appeal being made from within Germany by a number of pastors for a word of solidarity from the ecumenical fellowship, an appeal cogently conveyed to Bell by Dietrich Bonhoeffer, who at that time was in London as pastor of two German congregations there.[9] Those who met at Barmen knew, therefore, that the ecumenical world was watching, listening and praying with them – and waiting for the decisive word. Through its president, Life and Work had conveyed a message of pastoral concern and solidarity to a church bearing a costly and prophetic witness.

It has to be said that generally in the English-speaking world the German *Kirchenkampf* was persistently seen as one about "religious liberty" or "freedom of conscience" and Barmen as a stand for such freedoms. This was not how it was seen by those such as Barth and Bonhoeffer. Barth inveighed strongly against what he saw as the typically Anglo-Saxon misjudgment of the significance of Barmen, such as when visiting Britain in 1937 he declared the fight to be "not about the freedom, but about the necessary bondage, of the conscience; and not about the freedom, but the substance, of the Church."[10] Nevertheless, such sympathy and solidarity as was shown by churches outside Germany, and their admiration for Barmen – however incomplete their understanding of it may have been – as a symbol of opposition to the totalitarian regime, did matter to the Confessing Church. If there was at some points a misunderstanding from the outside world, at least it was a creative one.

All things considered, as far as the main ecumenical organizations and associated movements of the time are concerned, their consideration of the Barmen and the German *Kirchenkampf* reflected their particular self-understandings, interests, and relations with the German scene.

The IMC, given that its agenda was still largely that of the work of European and North American missionary societies in Africa, Asia, and Latin America, might have been expected to pay little attention to an intranational church dispute in Europe, but the case was quite the opposite. For one thing, the Nazi revolution had immediate and savage consequences for the German Protestant missions, and on two levels. First, parallel to the attempts to impose a *Gleichschaltung* (literally "unification") on the churches themselves, there was an attempt inspired by the German Christians to force all the mission bodies into one organization under a central control. Second, the regime's severe restrictions on the export of Reichsmarks meant that virtually overnight German work in the mission fields faced destitution and closure. Both these issues arrived on the London desk of the IMC secretary, the British ecumenical leader

8 For complete text, see George K.A. Bell, "A Message Regarding the German Evangelical Church to the Representatives of the Churches on the Universal Christian Council for Life and Work," *DBWE* 13, 144–146.

9 Bell, "A Message."

10 Karl Barth in *British Weekly*, Apr 22, 1937.

Joseph Oldham and his assistant William Paton, as the German mission leaders appealed for solidarity and help, and within their means the IMC leadership did respond.[11] This in itself impelled the IMC leaders to an innate sympathy with the church opposition in Germany. In its survey of developments in the "sending countries" for 1934, the year of Barmen, the IMC journal *International Review of Missions* reported on the difficulties being faced by the German missions but also that they were allied to the Confessing Synod and that the German Christian movement was "disintegrating."[12] Similarly, the following year it was reported that the growth of "neo-paganism" in Germany was being met by the uncompromising attitude of the Confessional Synod to "this new menace to Christ." Furthermore, from the early 1920s Oldham had been arguing that the mission agenda also had to embrace matters of international justice and peace along with traditional missionary aims. Perhaps there is no more telling clue concerning the pervasive effect of Barmen than the way in which Oldham himself was able to speak at an international SCM gathering in 1935 on "The Christian World Community," and with unmistakable echoes of the first Barmen thesis could ask what more momentous question there might be for a person than "whether there is a living Word which he may hear, which he may trust, which he can and must obey?"[13]

The responses of Life and Work and Faith and Order to Barmen and the *Kirchenkampf* clearly differed. Life and Work concerned itself with the responsibility of churches in the sociopolitical field, and Faith and Order with fundamental doctrines of the churches and the basis of the unity they sought. It is, therefore, obviously ironical that, while what was produced at Barmen was a Theological Declaration, while Barth and other framers of the declaration stressed its "theological" nature in order to distinguish it from any political or socioethical statement, it was not Faith and Order but Life and Work which engaged most closely with Barmen and with the following career of the Confessing Church. Certain reasons for this are quite clear. Given its agenda of ethical concern, Life and Work (together with the WA) could not avoid being already seriously tested by the overall German situation since the Nazi revolution of January 1933, as is seen in the resolutions on the persecution of Jewish and other minorities passed by the executive committee of Life and Work at its meeting in Novi Sad in September 1933, and the still more outspoken statements made by the WA in Sofia a few days later. As the *Kirchenkampf* unfolded during the winter of 1933–1934, the harassment and persecution of church opposition could hardly be ignored. Sympathy with the Pastors' Emergency League was a natural concomitant culminating, as has been noted, in the solidarity expressed in Bell's Ascension Day message to Life and Work members just days before Barmen.

Then, barely three months after Barmen, came the scheduled biennial meeting of the council of Life and Work on the Danish island of Fanø, Aug 22–28, 1934, in conjunction with the management committee of the WA and concurrently with a youth conference sponsored jointly by Life and Work and the WA. Fanø was the first major international ecumenical gathering since Barmen, and it was obvious that the German situation would dominate the agenda, bound up as this was with the final decisions to establish the theme of the 1937 Oxford conference: church, community, and state. The tensions and dramas of those six days are well documented.[14] They included Bonhoeffer's call for a universal church council to issue a declaration against war. Yet as far as the immediate future of the ecumenical movement was concerned, the crucial step was taken by Life and Work to identify with the Confessing Church

11 See Keith Clements, *Faith on the Frontier: A Life of J.H. Oldham*, Edinburgh, T&T Clark, 1999, 290.

12 William Paton, "Survey," *IRM* 24, 1935, 101.

13 Clements, *Faith on the Frontier*, 290.

14 See Scholder, *The Churches and the Third Reich*, vol. 2, 234–243.

as its German Protestant partner. A resolution was passed confirming Bell's Ascension Day message and condemning the autocratic methods of government with its attempts to ban free discussion in church. This was a blunt "no" both to the German Christians and to the Reich church led by Reich bishop Ludwig Müller and represented at Fanø by Theodor Heckel, director of the church foreign office who had made strenuous but counterproductive appeals to the gathering not to interfere in German affairs. The resolution declared unequivocally: "The Council desires to assure its brethren in the Confessional Synod of the German Evangelical Church of its prayers and heartfelt sympathy in their witness to the principles of the Gospel and of its resolve to maintain close fellowship with them."[15] Not that Fanø was a complete victory for the Confessing cause, for Theodor Heckel managed to have an additional clause inserted into the final resolution stating that the Council wished "to remain in friendly contact with all groups in the German Evangelical Church."[16] This sounded innocent enough at the time but it was to have troublesome consequences when attempting to respond to the Confessing Church's exclusive claim to be the Evangelical Church of Germany.

Faith and Order, on the other hand, never saw itself called to take sides in the *Kirchenkampf*, considering Barmen to be merely representative of one "party" within the German Church, and maintaining that Faith and Order had to be open to all churches that "accept the Lord Jesus Christ as God and Savior." Bonhoeffer and the Confessing Church leaders insisted that the "Reich church," which was open to the German Christian influence and had not subscribed to the Barmen Declaration, did *not* confess Christ as God and Savior but had subjected itself to worldly masters and powers and was the church of Antichrist. In the light of Barmen, the Reich church government could no longer claim to represent the Church of Christ in Germany and should not be invited to the ecumenical table.

In practice, Life and Work, thanks to that last-minute interjection by Theodor Heckel at Fanø, was never fully able to be as exclusive in its invitations to Germany as Bonhoeffer and his Confessing colleagues wished, but they had no doubt that Life and Work was essentially on their side. The 1937 Life and Work conference in Oxford delivered a substantial message of concern about the German situation and explicitly affirmed: "We are greatly moved by the afflictions of many pastors and laymen who have stood firm from the first in the Confessional Church for the sovereignty of Christ, and for the freedom of the Church of Christ to preach His Gospel."[17] The brief message to Germany from the Faith and Order conference in Edinburgh a few days later merely stated: "We are one in heart with all suffering Christians in your land."[18]

While there may have been some confusion among these ecumenical bodies, by contrast the WSCF was never in any doubt as to where its sympathies lay on the German scene. This was at least partly because so many of its present and former German leaders (such as Hans Lilje, general secretary of the German SCM 1924–1934) identified with the Confessing Church. Throughout the 1930s, Visser 't Hooft, secretary of the WSCF and a devotee of Karl Barth, was able to report first hand on his visits to Germany in *Student World*, and in 1935, for example, wrote: "The German Church stands at the crossroads, one road leading to new life, the other one leading to death" and commented that like St. Paul that church was learning that to suffer for Christ's sake was a gift. Moreover, crucially and prophetically he continued: "Whether it will prove

15 Universal Christian Council for Life and Work, ed., *Minutes of the Meeting of the Council: Fanø, August 24th–30th*, 1934, Geneva, Secretariat Universal Christian Council for Life and Work, 1934, 50–52.

16 Universal Christian Council for Life and Work, ed., *Minutes of the Meeting of the Council*, 51.

17 Joseph H. Oldham, ed., *The Churches Survey Their Task: Report of the Conference at Oxford, July 1937, on Church, Community and State*, London, George Allen & Unwin, 1937, 275.

18 Leonard Hodgson, ed., *The Second World Conference on Faith and Order Held at Edinburgh, August 3–18, 1937*, London, SCM Press, 1938, 39.

to be worthy of that gift is a matter which concerns the whole of ecumenical Christendom,"[19] a remark that Bonhoeffer himself could have made. It was in fact in the WSCF, which published articles, among others, by figures such as Karl Barth, Paul Maury and Visser 't Hooft himself, that the most intensive studies of the theological issues of the German *Kirchenkampf* and their implications for ecumenism occurred, not to mention also the *Evangelische Wochen* conferences organized by the SCM in Germany, which provided much-needed platforms for Confessing leaders like Martin Niemöller to encourage their communities.[20]

It is quite clear that during this tumultuous period the transnational movements IMC, Life and Work, WA, Faith and Order, WSCF, and other youth movements took on a new significance when internationalism itself came under threat. They were stretched to the limit in terms of material resources. Nor was there yet in place an overall body expressing fellowship across the *oikoumene*, although the 1937 Oxford and Edinburgh conferences, respectively of Life and Work and Faith and Order, were the preliminaries to the meeting very soon afterwards, which laid the groundwork of what would become the WCC. It was also true, however, that at this critical time the movements did not wait for organizational competence. Indeed, at times they were ahead of conventional considerations. The youth movements in particular had long enjoyed substantial Orthodox participation and were also providing a means of contact with ecumenically interested Roman Catholics, some of whom expressed a great appreciation of the preparatory material for the 1937 Oxford conference. It was, above all, a time of personal commitments, of vitally important friendships, exemplified, for instance, by those between George Bell and Dietrich Bonhoeffer, between Visser 't Hooft, Oldham, and William Temple, and also of the personal visits to Europe by Henry Smith Leiper, ecumenical secretary of the FCC, and other Americans. Leiper established many contacts in Germany, and during his visit of 1924 attended the Fanø conference, where he talked at length with Bonhoeffer and others. The links between North American and European ecumenical Christians were being consolidated at more than just organizational level.

5.2 *The Refugee Crisis from 1933 to 1939 and the Ecumenical Responses*

An immediate consequence of the Nazi revolution was the start of the exodus from Germany of people, overwhelmingly Jews, directly threatened by the regime. By 1939, approximately 282,000 Jews had left Germany and 117,000 annexed Austria. Of these, the largest number, 95,000, went to the United States, 60,000 to Palestine, 45,000 to Great Britain, and 75,000 to Central and South America. Some 18,000 also went to Shanghai in Japanese-occupied China. For their part, the churches outside Germany were challenged to make a transnational response on a scale beyond anything previously undertaken, and in so doing were discovering anew the dimension of unity which comes about through involvement in shared tasks of meeting human needs. Obtaining sound, accurate information about life on the ground in Germany was a main priority for concerned circles abroad. This task, however, was rendered more difficult by the conditions within Germany itself, which made any form of transnational partnership hazardous: those Germans overtly showing solidarity with Jews or helping them to escape abroad, and those with active international links, were judged by the regime to be engaged in un-German activities. Among the first to suffer was the eminent theologian, ecumenist, internationalist and social activist pastor Friedrich Siegmund-Schultze. In 1933, he was dismissed from his Berlin chair in social ethics and pedagogy and deported to Switzerland by the Gestapo on account of his aid to Jews. The WA in Germany was effectively shut down and the

19 Cited in: Keith Clements, *Ecumenical Dynamic: Living in More than One Place at Once*, Geneva, WCC Publications, 2013, 103.

20 See Visser 't Hooft, *Memoirs*, 84–99.

German SCM was banned in 1938. Transnational communication continued nevertheless. Visits from abroad were still possible right up until the outbreak of war (and for a time even afterwards if the visitor was from a neutral country). Leiper visited Germany every year from 1933 to 1939. Some visited specifically not only to assess dire situations, including conditions in the concentration camps, but to protest to government representatives about what they saw. One such visitor was the English Quaker Dorothy Buxton who, having been briefed by Oldham and Bonhoeffer beforehand, visited Germany in 1935, meeting both Protestant and Catholic leaders, and even had a (decidedly heated) exchange of opinion with *Reichsmarschall* Hermann Göring. In November 1938, following the notorious *Kristallnacht* attacks on Jews, a group of leading American Quakers visited Germany with the aim of meeting government figures. Previously, the AFSC had been providing direct relief in Germany (soup kitchens and kindergartens) but had intentionally not made any public protests about what was happening lest such work be jeopardized. The delegation was not able to meet any political figures, but was given an assurance by the Gestapo that their relief work would not be endangered.

A number of existing Christian humanitarian organizations mobilized their resources as best they could in order to meet the refugee crisis. In the first place, from 1920 there was the European Central Bureau for Relief (Inter-Church Aid), at the time closely associated with Life and Work. Specifically in response to the refugee crisis other organizations appeared, notably the International Christian Commission for Refugees, set up in 1933 by the European Central Bureau, Life and Work, and the WA, with Bishop George Bell, the president of Life and Work, as chairman. However, the most interesting phenomenon was the growth not of any single organization, but of several interlocking networks of bodies at the international level, working cooperatively and sharing information and expertise. Much of this cooperation took place at the personal level, involving trust, respect and friendship across national and denominational barriers. Indeed, it meant interfaith cooperation, too, for most significantly it involved Christian-Jewish collaboration at certain key points.[21] A key figure was Dr. Bernhard Kahn, a Swedish-born Jew, former secretary general of the *Hilfsverein der deutschen Juden* and from 1924 European director of the JDC. He himself fled Nazi Germany in 1933 and set up his office in Paris, from where he emigrated to the United States in 1939. "Throughout the 1930s, Kahn's office was the well-informed and well-connected hub for a network of representatives of all faiths who travelled to Europe on fact-finding missions and on refugee issues."[22] His primary Protestant partner in Berlin was Friedrich Siegmund-Schultze, and as early as 1932, the year before the Nazi takeover, he arranged a meeting with three key Protestant ecumenical figures visiting Berlin from the United States: Henry S. Leiper (mentioned above), Samuel McCrea Cavert, general secretary of the FCC, and Everett Clinchy, a Presbyterian pastor and a founder of the recently formed NCCJ. Kahn also arranged for Americans to meet Jewish leaders. Regular contact was maintained between Kahn and these visitors in the coming years. Kahn regularly visited the United States, as did Julius Richter, director of the German Protestant missions office in Berlin. In turn, the American ecumenists were in close touch, especially through Henry Leiper, with their European counterparts in Scandinavia, France, Great Britain and, in particular, Switzerland, where in addition to Adolf

21 On this and related topics grateful acknowledgment is made for the studies of Victoria J. Barnett, in particular: Victoria J. Barnett, "Communications between the German Resistance, the Vatican and Protestant Ecumenical Leaders," in: Christian Gremmels & Wolfgang Huber, eds., *Religion im Erbe: Dietrich Bonhoeffer und die Zukunftsfähigkeit des Christentums*, Gütersloh, Gütersloher Verlagshaus, 2002, 54–71; and Victoria J. Barnett, "Track Two Diplomacy (1933–1939): International Responses from Catholics, Jews and Ecumenical Protestants to Events in Nazi Germany," *KZG* 27/1, 2014, 76–86.

22 Barnett, "Track Two Diplomacy," 77.

Keller and the European Central Bureau, the ecumenical office in Geneva was increasingly engaged in the German scene. The American diplomat, James McDonald, the LN High Commissioner for Refugees from Germany from 1933 to 1935, also had extensive contacts with Jewish and Christian leaders in the United States, Britain and elsewhere in Europe and was instrumental in setting up meetings with Christian and Jewish leaders in New York and London, besides being active in raising funds for Jewish refugees.[23]

Thanks to Kahn, MacDonald and others a network thus emerged embracing key Jewish and Christian (both Protestant and Catholic) leaders at the international level. Victoria Barnett comments: "One immediate outcome of this network was the dissemination of detailed information about what was going on in the new Germany to religious leaders abroad, including harrowing reports of anti-Jewish violence."[24] She further states, as far as the US scene was concerned:

> It is … striking that there was not only activism from leaders of all three faiths [Protestant, Catholic, Jewish] but far more interreligious cooperation and communication than is commonly assumed in the literature. These US faith leaders were in contact with a European network that included members of the Confessing Church, the ecumenical movement, Catholic dissidents and clergy, and Jewish leaders.[25]

This transnational networking was to become even more crucial in wartime. It was already vital in generating a sense of solidarity with the oppressed.

23 McDonald resigned from the commission in 1935, frustrated by the lack of support from the US government.

24 Barnett, "Track Two Diplomacy," 81.

25 Barnett, "Track Two Diplomacy," 86.

6 The Transnational Movements and the Approaching War

World events outpaced the actual formation of the WCC, and the inaugural assembly would not take place until 1948, in Amsterdam. For the time being, the Council, with only an embryonic secretariat headed by Visser 't Hooft in Geneva, would be known as the "WCC in formation." This meant that even greater responsibility was placed upon the movements and their cooperation.

This was manifest above all in the WCCY, which under the banner "Christus Victor" took place in Amsterdam from July 24 to Aug 1, 1939, that is to say, barely five weeks before war broke out. It was a joint enterprise of the WSCF, the World YMCAs and YWCAs, the Ecumenical Youth Commission and the WA, with the additional collaboration of the IMC, the WSSA, the ISCE, and the Continuation Committee of the 1937 Edinburgh Faith and Order conference. Some 1,500 delegates from all continents attended concentrated days of encounter, bible study, worship, and discussion of youth's responsibility in that critical hour, and of what they expected of the churches. No official delegates were present from Germany, but that did not deter some 20 young Germans from bravely making their own way there. The closing message stated poignantly: "The nations and peoples of the world are drifting apart. The Churches are coming together … In war, conflict and persecution we must strengthen one another and preserve our Christian unity unbroken."[26] The conference may have appeared to be a once-only event, merely an idealistic gesture ineffective against the world set on war. Yet for many of the delegates it was a personally transformative experience of long-term significance, as in later life they ascribed their life-long commitment to the impact of that first experience at Amsterdam and the friendships which they had begun to make there. Furthermore, Visser 't Hooft maintained that the conference had

26 See Visser 't Hooft, *Memoirs*, 101.

a major influence on setting the style for future WCC assemblies, especially in its emphasis on bible study and shared worship; and it injected hope and direction into the movement itself just when outwardly everything was so discouraging.[27]

7 Being Transnational outside Europe and America

The movements and their organizations considered so far in this chapter had, or aspired to having, a global reach, but were largely founded, led and resourced by Christians and churches in Europe and North America. Therein lies a danger of assuming that the only significant ecumenical developments were either those in, or directed from, "the North." It is therefore important to note that even during the 1930s (if not earlier) there were transnational relationships and movements developing outside the North American-European axis that were intraregional rather than global. These were by no means essentially in competition with the more widely international bodies, and indeed the latter often acted as a vital means of communicating their concerns to the wider ecumenical community. This was very important since from a Northern perspective it might easily be assumed that throughout such movements there was a uniform understanding of what it meant to be "transnational" and what the value of such transnationality was. The very varied national contexts of the members, however, might well challenge such assumptions, especially where circumstances of tension or actual conflict arose.

One instance of where the notion of "transnationality" became particularly challenging was the Japanese expansionism in Manchuria in 1931–1932. The WSCF had active SCMs in both China and Japan. Western readers of the *Student World* in 1932 might well have been surprised by the strength of feeling that lay behind the article "Chinese Students in the Far Eastern Crisis" by Yao-tsung Wu of the YMCA Student Division in China, as he described the vehement (and occasionally violent) siege by thousands of students on the government in Nanking demanding united, patriotic action and a declaration of war against Japan.[28] As regards the attitude of Christian students, "on the whole not many of them take an attitude distinctly different from that of the non-Christian students. However, they are not so outspoken as the latter in advocating war." He concludes:

> Personally I rejoice to see the students act in the way they have acted ... [Last year] the students were quiescent because of Government suppression. They have now found a cause to put their efforts into for the time being, and they show us clearly that they are still full of vitality and vigour. Social change of a more fundamental character will be coming to this part of the world sooner or later and we have every reason to believe that in this, as in previous important changes, the students will once more be in the front line.[29]

As if to emphasize that Japanese Christians were no less concerned, the article is followed by three peace poems by Toyohiko Kagawa and a Mr. Takahashi. Such reports represented a plea that within the fellowship of the WSCF the particular conflicts and sufferings in Asia were as important as those in Europe, and indeed would require Asian solutions. The development of a regional Asian Christian consciousness owed much to the 1938 meeting of the IMC at Tambaram, India, "though Asian delegates to earlier world meetings had already expressed the need for their churches

---

27 See *Student World* 32/4, 1939, for students' impressions, including some critical questions on, for example, the absence of shared communion at the conference.

28 Yao-tsung Wu, "Chinese Students in the Far East Crisis," *Student World* 25/2, 1932, 156–162.

29 Wu, "Chinese Students," 162.

to work towards greater unity in life, partnership in mission and autonomy in administration."[30]

It was not only in Asia that a new transnational consciousness was germinating. Margaret Wrong, secretary of the ICCLA, reported in the *Student World* on her visit to Africa in 1939 under the title "What the Church Must Do in Africa."[31] Travelling from Kenya to the Gold Coast (present-day Ghana), she pointed to increasing evidence in all territories of a better contact with the rest of the world through trade and modern communications and education, and the changes that this would cause socially and culturally. Incumbent on the church was its calling to be truly a church that was both united and universal, and to address the racial and economic divides in Africa. "Increased contact is making the lack of unity increasingly evident in Africa." Significantly, she points to the Tambaram conference as a practical expression of belief in a universal church, and a recognition of the partnership of all people, nations and tongues in the work of the church. "At that meeting a group of African Christian leaders conferred with people of other races, and returned to Africa with a new vision of the universality of Christianity, as well as a more vivid understanding of the various tensions between Christianity and paganism, whether it be the paganism of the African tribe or of the western secular world." Compared to Asia, it took longer to establish an ecumenical body for Africa but it is evident that the seeds were being sown in the later 1930s. John S. Pobee comments that an all-Africa organization became possible only in the years after World War II, when African nationalism gathered momentum.[32]

8 Transnational Movements in Wartime (1939–1945)

The onset of war in Europe at the beginning of September 1939 inevitably disrupted the work of transnational organizations. For the next six years, much ecumenical work depended on personal contacts and informal networks which, despite the immense difficulties, persisted as movements.

The difficulties of obtaining a corporate action on the part of churches and ecumenical bodies was apparent in the period just before war itself. The churches, at and after the 1937 Oxford conference, had clearly affirmed that their fellowship could not and must not be sundered by war, and this represented a significant difference from their stance in 1914–1918. However, their capacity actually to prevent war, or to help bring the conflict to a just resolution once it had started, was quite another matter. Throughout 1939 there was a rush of initiatives taken by church leaders in the European democracies, with calls for prayer and joint public statements against nationalism and the use of force, together with proposals for conferences or procedures for arbitration. Bishop George Bell, for instance, suggested a meeting of theologians in Rome to "discuss fundamental principles in a true international order and in social justice." But the pope could not see the use of such a proposal when he had already, so it was argued, made the church's position on these matters perfectly clear. It was even more difficult to conceive how German theologians might be expected to participate in international talks in which they would have to discuss, if not issue public declarations about, concrete political questions that could not be raised at home. Visser 't Hooft was warned by German friends that in the present situation even those who personally felt sympathetic to such initiatives would feel the dice loaded against them if they so much as attended a conference held effectively under Western democratic auspices. The Scandinavian churches, for their part, were inherently disposed towards inclusive mediation,

30 Tosh Arai & T.K. Thomas, "Christian Conference of Asia," *DEM*, 169–170.

31 Margaret Wrong, "What the Church Must Do in Africa," *Student World* 33/1, 1940, 111–117.

32 John S. Pobee, "All Africa Conference of Churches," *DEM*, 17–19.

but even the Norwegian bishop Eivind Berggrav, a member of the WCC Provisional Committee and president of the WA, warned Bell of the danger of creating "a Maginot line" between churches in the democracies and those on the other side. But did this then mean that the churches in the democracies should stay silent? From Switzerland, Karl Barth had no inhibitions and in April urged that when war broke out a message be sent to the German people on behalf of all the churches, declaring that the war was not against them as such but against their criminal rulers, and that they as the people should ask themselves whether it was not their duty to do everything they could to end it and prevent a victory by their false leaders. From the United States came yet another proposal, this time for a small conference of experts in international affairs with theologians and church leaders. This did indeed meet in Geneva in July 1939 under the auspices of the WCC and the WA and even included two Germans, Wilhelm Menn and Otto Heinrich von der Gablenz, but no consensus was reached. Even among the Westerners there were strong disagreements about the attitude to be taken towards Nazi Germany. Nothing could be collectively addressed to the immediate situation. What did emerge was a document reflecting on the discussions, "The Churches and the International Crisis," which was sent out to churches and served as a useful discussion paper for the longer term.[33] The lack of ecumenical consensus before Sep 1, 1939, was to become even more apparent once war had begun.

8.1 *Divergent Witnesses (1939–1940)*

From the onset of hostilities, divergences grew still wider even among the churches of the allied and neutral countries. During the early months of the war, Visser 't Hooft was increasingly troubled by an apparent moral relativism in British, French, and Dutch circles: "There was such a fear of national self-righteousness and such a sense of the failure of all nations that very many refused to make up their minds about the basic issues of this war."[34] He laid some of the blame for this on the ecumenical movement itself and on the ambiguity of some of its achievements: "We had placed such an emphasis on the duty for the church to remain the truly ecumenical church that there was a danger that the church would be looked upon as a haven of refuge above the world and not give guidance to its members for their decisions in this world."[35] The basic divide lay between those who considered a negotiated peace with Nazi Germany to be still the best option, and those who believed the removal of the Nazi regime to be the prerequisite for a credible peace. The Scandinavian churches remained the most committed to mediation. To the meeting of the WCC administrative committee in Apeldoorn, Netherlands, in January 1940, Bishop Berggrav of Oslo brought a group from the Scandinavian churches who requested ecumenical consideration of the proposals he had already shared with church and political figures in London and Berlin. William Temple and the four British participants in Apeldoorn produced a statement on the conditions for peace. It stated the need for guaranteed sovereignty for the Czech, Slovak, and Polish peoples and for a definitive peace to be negotiated at a European congress including these peoples.[36] The statement had no effect whatsoever. The Administrative Committee itself tried to address the issues of the war, but the Scandinavian initiative had effectively stymied any further ecumenical action: the Scandinavians were reluctant to conceive any move without German involvement. Visser 't Hooft wanted a clear protest, at least, against such violations of humanity and freedom as were taking place. Marc Boegner of France and Alphons Koechlin of Switzerland supported him, but even such a word would be tantamount,

33 Visser 't Hooft, *Memoirs*, 111.

34 Visser 't Hooft, *Memoirs*, 114.

35 Visser 't Hooft, *Memoirs*, 111.

36 The French Protestant leader, Marc Boegner, refused to sign. See Visser 't Hooft, *Memoirs*, 118.

in the view of others, to aggravating the present conflict even further.[37]

Visser 't Hooft did not renounce his efforts to induce the ecumenical movement to utter a clear word of guidance, and in April wrote a long discussion paper on "The Ecumenical Church and the International Situation," which he circulated to a wide circle of colleagues. It received appreciation but also criticism, and of the latter none was more decisive than that by Archbishop William Temple, the most senior British figure involved. Evidently chastened by the experience at Apeldoorn in January, he now regarded any collective ecumenical voice as an impossibility. He noted a "plethora of counsels" among the churches but no consensus, and on a practical level the ecumenical movement itself did not at the time exist in a form that could speak as one voice. Instead, Temple wrote to Visser 't Hooft: "I want us all to prophesy individually, and to do this in contact with one another through your office, so the same message will be given ecumenically with a variety of emphasis."[38] While Temple was writing (May 20), his words were given added brutal weight as German forces, already occupying Denmark and Norway, stormed across Holland and Belgium and into France. North of the Alps, apart from Switzerland itself, little was left of "neutral" Europe. War had now torn through the very fabric of travel, communications and meetings within which ecumenical life had largely been woven since 1918. Even the WCC administrative committee could not meet again until January 1946. Visser 't Hooft later commented: "The provisional structure of the Council, which had not yet been authorized by the Churches, seemed altogether too shaky to stand the strain. It appeared for a time as though hardly any contacts could be maintained with the Churches."[39] Temple had in fact pointed to the way in which, remarkably, the ecumenical movement was to continue and in certain respects become profounder during the next six years. It did so largely through personal, and necessarily often surreptitious, contacts, for which the Geneva office was the vital nexus in this "diffused ecumenicity." There also now existed the Peace Aims Group, set up by the WCC and the WA as a means of permitting a constructive discussion among the churches, and with the intention of maintaining, via Geneva, contact with opposition groups in Germany. William Paton was secretary of this group in London, and William Temple chairman.

Besides Geneva, however, there were in neutral, or belligerent but unoccupied allied, territories centers of transnational communication and collaboration: London, where William Paton, secretary of the IMC, also served as an associate general secretary of the WCC as well as assisting the Peace Aims Group, and in places where Oldham was still active in fostering ecumenical study on public and international issues; New York, where Henry Smith Leiper, executive secretary of the FCC was, like Paton, an associate general secretary of the WCC, and who with the general secretary of the FCC, Samuel McCrea Cavert, formed a partnership deeply committed to engaging with Europe and the wider world; and, very significantly, the Vatican, which had its own diplomatic channels of communication with governments, embassies and international organizations besides with the worldwide Roman Catholic presence itself. Other religious bodies, including the Quakers, were of great international importance, especially in work on behalf of refugees and other victims of the war.

8.2 *War and the Widening Refugee Crisis*

A major challenge demanding the fullest possible services of movements and organizations was the

37 Visser 't Hooft, *Memoirs*, 119–120.

38 Visser 't Hooft, *Memoirs*, 123.

39 Willem Adolph Visser 't Hooft, "The Genesis of the World Council of Churches," in: *A History of the Ecumenical Movement*, vol. 1, Ruth Rouse & Stephen C. Neill, eds., *1517–1948*, London, SPCK, 1954, 697–724, here 709.

enormous refugee crisis and the needs of all the victims of the war. Among the first decisions of the Provisional Committee of the WCC in 1939 was the creation of an office in London to coordinate refugee work. Alfred Freudenburg, a Confessing Church pastor who had had to leave Germany on account of his non-Aryan wife, was appointed executive officer. Soon afterwards, the office relocated to Geneva, where it could work closely not only with other WCC staff but also the major international relief agencies associated with the LN and the IRC. Transnational coordination took place at several levels. The YMCAs and YWCAs throughout the war were highly active in relief work and in support in countries, wherever they were permitted to operate, among refugees and other war victims, prisoners of war and men and women in the armed services. Across the border in France, CIMADE, under its general secretary Madeleine Barot, from the early days of the war was heavily engaged in work within refugee and internment camps and, during the German occupation, in arranging clandestine shelters and escape routes out of France for Jewish people. As a student, Barot herself had been deeply influenced by the WSCF and the example of the Confessing Church. Other crucial figures in this enterprise were André Trocmé, Protestant pastor in the village of Le Chambon-sur-Lignon, where many Jewish children were hidden by the local population, and the mayor of the village, Charles Guillon, himself a pastor. But Guillon was also secretary general of the world YMCA and thus in constant touch with the WCC in Geneva, indeed a frequent visitor there, and so able to facilitate the secret transportation and reception of the young refugees in Switzerland. Major collaborating organizations in the network of which Geneva was the hub were the European Central Bureau for Relief (itself, of course, a transnational operation), the relief arm of the FCC, the AFSC and the BFSC. The role of the WCC (at the time in formation) was to be consolidated by setting up, in 1944, the Department for Inter-Church Aid and Refugee Service, into which the European Central Bureau was in due course incorporated.

8.3 *Networking for Communication and Information-Sharing*

A crucial task of the ecumenical networks in wartime was the communication of news and the sharing of information about conditions in war-affected countries, and the responses of the respective churches to these conditions. The EPS, which originated in early 1930s, was a ready means for this, at least for information which did not need to be kept confidential. The WSCF, for its part, was able to continue remarkably intact and active during the war, since besides Visser 't Hooft and Suzanne de Dietrich in the Geneva office its general secretary and editor, the Scotsman Robert Mackie, was based in Toronto, Canada. *Student World* maintained its quarterly appearance throughout the war. Evangelism in wartime China, the Universal Day of Prayer for Students, the church universal in time of war, Christian students in wartime, were among the topics that filled its pages during 1940 while, for example Liu Kwong Ching of the Chinese SCM, wrote a graphic and harrowing account of the repeated bombing of Kunming, and its effect on the life of students there. “You and we have grown up in a time of widespread suffering. The wholesale murdering of man and culture is confined to nowhere. Surely we are called to learn the deep lessons in it all, and they can only be won by those who are willing to pay the cost that it entails. May we be found worthy of our calling.”[40] Mackie pressed repeatedly in *Student World* for an honest examination by WSCF of its role now and in the aftermath of war. From Canada he was able to travel to South America and the Caribbean, and his travel diaries often appeared in *Student World*. One day in 1944 he “mysteriously” appeared in London, having travelled from Canada via Geneva, and gave a fascinating talk

40 Liu Kwong Ching, “Greetings from a Chinese Hillside,” *Student World* 34/1, 1941, 64.

"which enabled a group in London to share in what was happening to fellow Federation members in other countries especially in Germany and occupied Europe."[41] The travails in China, Japan and India no less than those of Europe continued to feature prominently in *Student World*.

Another instrument for collecting and disseminating information was provided in Britain by Oldham's *Christian News-Letter*, a fortnightly pamphlet, often accompanied by a lengthier supplement, which began publication soon after the outbreak of war, and which extended into the public domain the kind of concerns being discussed in Oldham's high-powered intellectual discussion group, "The Moot."[42] At times its readership totaled well over 10,000 in Britain alone. It was also taken up by the WCC in Geneva, and found its way to the United States and elsewhere in the English-speaking world. As well as stimulating debate on topics of war and war aims, social justice, education and the need for reconstruction following the war, the newsletter published a great deal of international news, particularly on the work of the churches even in distant corners of the world, from Russia to China, from Africa to occupied Europe. The supplements included articles written by eminent international figures, such as Karl Barth, John Foster Dulles, Reinhold Niebuhr, and Karl Jaspers. The newsletter was soon joined by a series of paperback books dealing at greater length with topics considered in the newsletter itself. It was in Geneva, in particular, that the newsletter was welcomed. Early in 1941, Visser 't Hooft expressed to Oldham his frustration that not enough copies were arriving there. The matter was crucially important in the early months of 1941, when the newsletter discussed almost exclusively Pope Pius XII's "five peace points," which were issued in December 1940, and the response of the British church leaders. Soon copies were arriving far more efficiently in Geneva, and in June 1941 Visser 't Hooft was able to tell Oldham that he had recently shown copies to a visitor to Geneva who, according to his carefully worded description, was clearly Adam von Trott, one of the leading figures in the so-called Kreisau Circle of the German resistance: "He was deeply impressed by it and said that this would help him a great deal with certain things on which he is working with his friends. The knowledge that there is a group such as the one of which you are the center who take this kind of attitude gives him and others real hope concerning the future."[43] By "this kind of attitude" he meant an alternative to the British demand for unconditional surrender by Germany.

There was thus in the making, however tenuous at times, some form of dialogue traversing the frontiers of the war, even including the opposition in Germany. This was also clear when Dietrich Bonhoeffer made his second wartime visit to Geneva on behalf of the Confessing Church and the Resistance, in September 1941. Bonhoeffer was presented by Visser 't Hooft with recent books of major importance by British Christians on the major issues of the war and on a just postwar settlement. The first was George Bell's *Christianity and World Order* (1940), in which Bonhoeffer's closest English friend reiterated his demand that a distinction be made between "German" and "National Socialist," and that efforts should be made via neutral channels to discover what terms of peace would be likely to create a lasting peace and not lead to a further poisoning of international relationships. Bonhoeffer read this gratefully and responded warmly to Bell in a letter from Switzerland: "The certainty of our ecumenical fellowship is growing and is a great comfort and encouragement. I have had the great pleasure and satisfaction to read your newest book and I am sharing your hope for a strong stand of the churches after the war."[44] The second book was

41 Robin Boyd, *The Witness of the Student Christian Movement: Church Ahead of the Church*, London, SPCK, 2007, 52.

42 See Clements, *Faith on the Frontier*, 363–405.

43 Clements, *Faith on the Frontier*, 397.

44 Dietrich Bonhoeffer, "Letter to George K.A. Bell," *DBWE* 16, 224.

William Paton's *The Church and the New Order* (1941). His book was but one manifestation of the intense interest in, and debate on, "peace aims" taking place in British church circles just then. Bonhoeffer in Geneva was immensely encouraged by reading all such material, which revealed a different British approach to the war and a postwar world from that provided by either Germany's propaganda machine or the British government's own public voice as heard on the BBC overseas service. Paton's book, however, demanded special attention because it suggested in some detail what an acceptable postwar Germany and Europe should look like, so Bonhoeffer set out his response in a paper which he wrote with Visser 't Hooft.[45] Immensely grateful for Paton's perception of the difficulties that would face a reconstruction of Germany in every sense, and also for Paton's appreciation of the value of the Confessing Church and its potential role in rebuilding relations after the war, he nevertheless warned that a non-Nazi government would need "to get such terms of peace that it has some chance to survive" and not be discredited in the eyes of its own people. This would need to be known in advance by the opposition. Furthermore, Bonhoeffer argued that Paton displayed too many Anglo-Saxon assumptions about the evident and immediate desirability of "human rights and liberties" in face of the omnipotent state, in a situation (like that in Nazi Germany) where *all* order had been destroyed. This was a striking example of an attempt at transnational ecumenical dialogue in the midst of conflict.

8.4 *Networking with the German Resistance*

At this point, explicit attention should be paid to the German resistance, which interacted and overlapped at times with the ecumenical movements. The German resistance was not a single organization or movement but comprised several distinct groups and circles. There was the opposition group within the *Abwehr* (German military intelligence), in which Dietrich Bonhoeffer's brother-in-law Hans von Dohnanyi, a senior civil servant, was a key figure, and into which Bonhoeffer himself from 1940 was coopted on account of his ecumenical contacts abroad. There was the group of academics, diplomats, civil servants, and some clergy grouped around Count Helmut James von Moltke, the Kreisau Circle. This included Adam von Trott and, on occasion, Hans Schönfeld of the Ecumenical Research Department in Geneva. Not dissimilar was the Freiburg Group of academics from the Albert-Ludwig University, which was formed after the *Kristallnacht* in 1938, and which had close ties with the Confessing Church, and the Stuttgart Circle, which formed around the industrialist Robert Bosch. Equally, it has to be said, much of the movement, whether in the *Abwehr*, the army itself, the Foreign Ministry, the Kreisau Circle or similar groups, was strongly imbued with Christian conviction and ethical values, both Protestant and Catholic. It might, therefore, be no exaggeration to describe the German resistance as itself an ecumenical movement since so many of its leading figures were marked by a common Christianity, although admittedly as resisters they were linked more immediately by the objective of overthrowing Hitler and the Nazi regime and replacing them with a non-Nazi government. Furthermore, not only was there a common basis of Christian values permitting the mutual trust that underlay the dangerous, underground discussions of those political objectives; there was one crucial dimension to the resistance whereby conscious Christian commitment, interchurch relations and actual ecumenical bodies played a vital role, namely, the international one. Their international links were a *sine qua non* of the main elements in the German resistance, for the fundamental reason that an overthrow of Hitler would not only need to be successful within Germany itself but would require recognition by the allied governments that a credible non-Nazi government had been brought into being, with which a negotiated peace would be possible. This meant

45 Dietrich Bonhoeffer & Willem Adolph Visser 't Hooft, "The Church and the New Order in Europe," *DBWE* 16, 528–539.

discussing a common cause with the allies on the basis of the fundamental human values of freedom, justice and dignity, in all of which the churches as represented in the ecumenical movement (and particularly, for example, at the Oxford conference of 1937) had a strong investment. Indeed, Klemens von Klemperer states, "transcending as it did, national interest in the realm of human rights, the foreign policy of the resistance may stand as a model for the human-rights policy which has evolved since World War II in a world still plagued by dictatorships."[46]

Before the war, some people in the German opposition had already been in contact with the British Foreign Office and with other European capitals. With the onset of war such contacts could only be very indirect, via neutral governments or consulates and other significant institutions in neutral countries. Of major significance here was the Vatican.[47] With the pope's approval, during the first six months of the war, the *Abwehr* circle, using the Bavarian Catholic lawyer Josef Müller as mediator, conducted clandestine discussions with British diplomatic representatives in the Vatican on a possible peace settlement. On both sides there were hopes of a positive outcome but in the end there was confusion about the exact terms of the agreement that had supposedly been reached, and the launch of Hitler's major Western offensive in April 1940 was the final blow to it. The Vatican nevertheless continued to be an important point of contact throughout the war. In the opposite direction lay neutral Sweden, the sole Nordic country to remain unoccupied during the war. Its state church had ready access to diplomatic channels, which added to its importance for the German resistance, although there was caution on the Swedish side lest its political neutrality be seen to have been violated.

For the Resistance, however, the most important neutral territory lay immediately next-door to Germany: Switzerland. In the first place, there was no lack of foreign consulates there, of both belligerent and neutral countries including, of course, Germany itself. There was, above all, Geneva, of equal importance in international terms to the capital of the Swiss Federation, Bern, on account of the major international organizations located there. The WCC office became a vital nerve center for the international dimension of the German resistance and its links with the outside world. Members of the Resistance who could travel to Switzerland on diplomatic passes had ready access to its staff. Adam von Trott visited several times. Hans Bernd Gisevius and Eugen Gerstenmaier also appeared there, as did Dietrich Bonhoeffer. In turn, Hans Schönfeld was able to travel into Germany, his travel facilities also being helped by his continuing (and in some eyes suspect) connection with the Reich church's foreign office. However, besides specific events, visits, plans, and discussions that took place in Geneva, a vital element in the whole picture of "resistance" was the reception and transmission of information about what was happening in Germany and the occupied lands, knowledge of which made the need for resistance and an overthrow of the Nazi regime, if not the actual military defeat of Hitler, a moral necessity. This included information about the most heinous of all crimes, the Jewish Holocaust. Victoria Barnett comments:

> It is clear from the archives in Geneva that ecumenical leaders were receiving detailed information from the onset of the war – including information that could only have come from German military and intelligence sources – and that the significance of this information was clear to them. Conclusive documentation of the [Jewish] genocide didn't come till 1942, but they interpreted the ominous early signs accurately.[48]

46 Klemens von Klemperer, *German Resistance against Hitler: The Search for Allies Abroad (1938–1945)*, Oxford, Clarendon Press, 1992, 171–180.

47 See Owen Chadwick, *Britain and the Vatican during the Second World War*, Cambridge, Cambridge University Press, 1986.

48 Barnett, "Communications," 61.

Such information was being transmitted to ecumenical partners abroad, including the FCC, and London. The ecumenical network was being used both to spread information about the crimes and to consult on which action (however hesitant) to take in the face of them. It was in May 1942 that transnational ecumenism and political resistance converged in the dramatic meeting between Dietrich Bonhoeffer and Bishop George Bell in Sweden, at which Bonhoeffer shared with Bell full details of the conspiracy to overthrow Hitler and replace the regime with a non-Nazi government, in the hope of obtaining encouragement from the Allied governments. Bell on his return to London relayed the information to the British government, however to no avail.

8.5 *The Refugees Again: Christian-Jewish Collaboration*

A concern for obtaining and sharing information on what was happening in Germany and occupied territories, political resistance to Hitler, attempts to set out the conditions for a "just peace," and the diaconal work for the victims of war and oppression were obviously frequently overlapping areas, and no more so than in responding to the huge numbers of refugees in Europe. Here, ecumenical networking necessarily extended into Christian-Jewish collaboration. One example was the joint visit to London in 1942 by Presbyterian Everett Clinchy of the US NCCJ, the Roman Catholic Father Vincent Donovan and Rabbi Morris Lazaron, who participated in London in the founding of the UK CCJ. As has been shown, such collaboration in response to the plight of the Jews had already been in operation since the first waves of Jewish emigration from Nazi Germany and the gathering of reports on the plight of Jews fleeing and of those trapped. As the war proceeded, information-sharing became both increasingly necessary yet also more hazardous if the identities of the sources living under Nazism were to be protected. There is strong evidence that much of the information on the Nazi crimes, whether planned or actually committed, was being collected and channeled through certain circles of the Resistance, notably that in which Hans von Dohnanyi was playing a key role.[49] It was on behalf of Dohnanyi that Bonhoeffer and the Bavarian Catholic Josef Müller were assigned to explore again which peace attempts the Vatican might support and which conditions for peace might be supported in the event of a successful coup. The knowledge of what was happening to the Jews in occupied Poland as well as in Germany gave added urgency to these explorations. In Geneva, the office of Visser 't Hooft (and, after 1939, of Adolf Freudenberg) was an active conduit for information on the German resistance (as, earlier, on the German *Kirchenkampf*). There was active cooperation between Christians and Jews, above all between Gerhard Riegner, head of the WJC, and Visser 't Hooft's office. During the war, Visser 't Hooft, Riegner, and Freudenburg met weekly, and one of the first mentions of the confirmation of the genocide of European Jews was issued jointly by the WJC and the WCC.

9 Reconstruction and Reconciliation (1945–1950)

It was evident that as the war entered its later stages in 1944–1945, thanks to transnational cooperation in all the fields mentioned, there was now a network where thinking on the future form of the world could be exchanged. The American churches' project on *A Just and Durable Peace*,[50] the work of the London Peace Aims Group, the efforts of the American Lutheran Fred Nolde and others, paving the way for a Universal Declaration of Human Rights to be built into the charter of the infant United Nations organization, all became material for joint transnational concern and discussion. Not everything could be publicized as yet. For example, papers of the Freiburg Group

49 Barnett, "Communications," 57.

50 FCC, *A Just and Durable Peace*, London, SCM Press, 1943.

on the responsibilities of the churches for society in a new Europe, were tantamount to treason in wartime Germany. Several of the group paid the ultimate price for their views when, in 1944, their memorandum was discovered by the Gestapo, yet their memorandum did eventually find its way to the WCC which was already considering its forthcoming priorities.

It could be said that the whole ecumenical enterprise at the end of World War II became a transnational movement for reconciliation following the most devastating conflict in human history. The tone was set by the meeting in October 1945, in Stuttgart, Germany, of representatives of the ecumenical movement from France, Great Britain, Holland, Switzerland, and the United States, with leaders of the German Evangelical Church. There was mutual, humble recognition, and the Germans on their own behalf prepared a statement of repentance, desire for reconciliation, and commitment to making a new beginning. Yet what was most urgent was the enormous task of providing relief for the victims of war and reconstructing living conditions and human communities, not only in Europe but in Asia and in parts of the Near East. The YMCA and YWCA at the local and regional level were brought fully into the program of the new WCC department of reconstruction and Inter-Church Aid which, in addition to its formal association with the UNRRA,[51] was working in close collaboration with the NCWC, the LWF, and the LRCS. Within months of being launched in 1946, as part of its refugee work in Europe the American-based CWS assisted the YMCA and YWCA in work with prisoners of war and in setting up summer camps where 41,000 undernourished children were fed.[52] These years also saw the start of work camps in which young people from different churches and nationalities spent time together physically working on reconstruction projects in war-damaged Europe, also sharing in local projects of lay witness and evangelism. First initiated by a consortium of churches and denominations in the United States, such ecumenical work camps were to develop into a regular program of the WCC's youth department in the 1950s and 1960s. The friendships formed through such experiences, often bridging the gaps between the belligerent nations in the recent war, proved to be vital ingredients in the postwar ecumenical movement.

9.1 *World Christian Youth Meets Again – and Raises Questions*

A most significant sign of the continued and renewed vitality of the youth movements was the second WCCY, which met in Oslo, Norway, from Jul 22 to 31, 1947, the first large-scale international ecumenical gathering after the end of the war. Like its predecessor which had met in the threatening circumstances of 1939, this was organized by the World YMCAs, the World YWCAs, the WSCF, and the WCC, now with its own youth department led by its secretary Francis House. Under the banner "Jesus is Lord," some 1,100 delegates came from nearly 80 countries and from all continents: more than 200 from Asia, Africa, and Latin America. The mood was optimistic but this was no postwar euphoria. Alex Johnson, the conference chairman, said in his opening remarks, "God has given the youth of His Church a unique opportunity to be here in our happy capital in the very same days when the world more and more is becoming terribly similar to the world of the first world conference of Christian Youth in Amsterdam, July 1939."[53] No Russians had been permitted to attend by their government, and the Japanese delegation had been refused permission by the Allied

51 UNRRA was succeeded by the IRO, another UN specialist agency, in 1947.

52 Geoffrey Murray, "Joint Service as an Instrument of Renewal," in: *A History of the Ecumenical Movement*, vol. 2, Harold E. Fey, ed., *The Ecumenical Advance (1948–1968)*, Geneva, WCC Publications, ^{2}1986, 199–231, here 212.

53 Cited in Paul Griswold Macy, ed., *The Report of the Second World Conference of Christian Youth: Oslo, Norway, July 22 to 31, 1947*, Geneva, WCC Publications, 1947, 7.

governments. Any euphoria was also tempered by the realization that coming together in Christ did not smooth away profound differences in outlook, and that there were no easy solutions to many of the problems the delegates had brought with them. Nevertheless, they departed with a note of true gratitude and a decisive commitment to facing the challenges ahead. Among them were some destined to play a major role in ecumenical life, including Philip Potter, general secretary of the WCC in the years 1972–1984.

The inauguration of the WCC in 1948 had been long awaited. Those whose ecumenical commitment had been bound up with the movements mainly agreed with it in principle, but with some reservations as to whether this represented a move towards centralization and a loss of their autonomy. The youth movements, in particular, but also the IMC could rightly claim that they themselves or their forerunners had been the prime stimulators and movers of the ecumenical movements from the early 1900s, and any diminution of their freedom would be a loss to the movement as a whole. On the other hand, the WCC could provide solid support and open up fresh channels for their work. Meanwhile the movements were themselves questioning certain of their inherited priorities. Within the WSCF, the British SCM was debating whether the time had come to discontinue the more traditional missionary outlook in which the SCM had been nurtured in the early 1900s, and for which the SCM had been a major recruiting agency right up until World War II. At the same time, questions were being asked in India and other countries now striving for independence about the relationship between any transnational movement working in a country and the nationalist movement of that country. This particularly applied to India in the 1940s, and also to China as it was released from the Japanese threat and was then faced with the advance of communist nationalism. Judging by articles in *Student World* and *International Review of Missions* during these years, these were delicate issues from both the international and the national perspectives.

9.2 *The Laity Movement*

There was also, however, one major transnational development in the later 1940s which can be said to be a child of the youth movements. This was the laity movement. In the preparatory volume for the 1937 Oxford Life and Work Conference on Church, Community and State, Oldham had written:

> Nothing could be plainer than that if the Christian faith is in the present and future to bring about changes ... in the thought, habits, and practices of society it can only do this through the living, working faith of multitude of lay men and women conducting the ordinary affairs of life. The only way in which it can affect business or politics is by shaping the convictions and determining the actions of those engaged in business and politics.[54]

It is not, said Oldham, the function of the clergy to tell the laity how to act in public affairs, but to confront them with the Christian demand and to encourage them to discover its application for themselves. These thoughts Oldham promoted further in his wartime *Christian News-Letter* and also the CFC, which he founded in 1942. After the end to the war, Oldham found in Visser 't Hooft a ready ally who was enthusiastically willing to develop the idea as an essential element in the new ecumenical phase. With the aid of a grant from the American millionaire philanthropist John D. Rockefeller, the Château de Bossey near Geneva was purchased and became the home of an Ecumenical Institute focusing on enabling young people from different countries to study together for the tasks of reconstruction in the world. Hendrik Kraemer, an eminent Dutch missiologist, himself a layman with a passion for the renewal of the church, and whose book *A Theology*

54 Willem Adolph Visser 't Hooft & Joseph H. Oldham, *The Church and Its Function in Society*, London, George Allen & Unwin, 1937, 117.

of the Laity[55] became a widely read bible for the laity movement, was appointed the institute's first director in 1947.

However, while the Ecumenical Institute and the WCC's department for the laity were important resources, neither Bossey nor Geneva was the true control center for the spiritual mobilization of the laity, for there was no single center as such. In Germany, the Evangelical lay academies were emerging as vital laboratories of learning what a Christian responsibility mission signified in modern secular and industrial society, and similar centers of lay education and renewal were appearing in Sweden, the Netherlands, Great Britain, the United States, and elsewhere. Linked by a common interest and the sharing of experience, the laity movement was a transnational phenomenon, extending much farther than the European-North American scene, and was discovering its own history. Jesudas M. Athyal states that virtually every ecumenical institution and missionary initiative in South Asia in the early 20th century was an initiative of the laity, particularly those nurtured by the YMCA, YWCA, and WSCF: "Throughout the century, as the region had an active presence in the ecumenical movement, it was widely acknowledged that a strong laity perspective was an integral component of unity and Christian witness, especially in the pluralistic context of Asia."[56] In that Asian development, Oldham had been a vital stimulus in the 1920s, along with John R. Mott. In India, the major ecumenical landmark in 1947 was the formation of the Church of South India, which represented not just interchurch restructuring but the assertion by Asians of the need for a genuinely Asian Christian presence and identity in the region, parallel to the movement for political independence and freed from the inherited Western denominationalism. This would not have occurred without powerful lay backing and leadership. Similarly in China, the desire for a united Christian Church free of Western domination and divisiveness, was powerfully fueled by the commitment of the laity.[57]

In conclusion, it can be seen that after the end of World War II the most distinctively national contribution to the laity movement, the German *Kirchentag*, significantly proved highly influential well beyond Germany. The *Kirchentag* movement was initiated by Reinhold von Thadden, an aristocratic lay member of the Confessing Church, who while suffering as a prisoner of war in Russia dreamt of a popular lay movement linking faith to daily life and social responsibility, and thereby overcoming the assumed dichotomy between Christian commitment and the public sphere, which had proved so fatal in allowing Nazism to reign over national life. He envisaged large-scale gatherings for Bible study, lectures, debates, recitals, drama, and celebratory worship. The first *Kirchentag* was held in the largely ruined city of Essen in August 1950, drawing more than 25,000 people to its program, while over 200,000 attended the closing assembly. The *Kirchentag* became a regular two-yearly event in the German calendar. While clearly German in its origins and ethos, it was always von Thadden's intention that the *Kirchentag* should be a truly ecumenical, transnational event. Visser 't Hooft was a main speaker at its early meetings. In due course, it did attract an ever-increasing international attendance, and highlighted issues of global concern, as it still does. While attempts to imitate the *Kirchentag* in other countries have never quite succeeded, except in more modest forms (although it should be noted that the Marama conventions of the Mar Thoma Church in South India were attracting and educating large numbers long before 1950),[58] the *Kirchentag* has proved to

55 Hendrik Kraemer, *A Theology of the Laity*, n.p., Regent College Publishing, 1958.

56 Jesudas M. Athyal, "The South Asian Presence in the Ecumenical Movement," *EcRev* 69/4, 2017, 557–569, here 567.

57 See Theresa Carino, "Chinese Churches and the Ecumenical Movement from an Asian Perspective," *EcRev* 69/4, 2017, 542–556, here 542.

58 David L. Edwards, "Signs of Radicalism in the Ecumenical Movement," in: *A History of the Ecumenical Movement*, vol. 2, 373–410, here 394.

be a continuing inspiration to the laity movement worldwide. It may justly be regarded, along with much else, as a gift from the 1940s to the transnational search for Christian unity and Christian engagement with the world.

Bibliography

A History of the Ecumenical Movement, vol. 1, Ruth Rouse & Stephen C. Neill, eds., *1517–1948*, London, SPCK, 1954.

A History of the Ecumenical Movement, vol. 2, Harold E. Fey, ed., *The Ecumenical Advance (1948–1968)*, Geneva, WCC Publications, ²1986.

Barnett, Victoria J., "Communications between the German Resistance, the Vatican and Protestant Ecumenical Leaders," in: Christian Gremmels & Wolfgang Huber, eds., *Religion im Erbe: Dietrich Bonhoeffer und die Zukunftsfähigkeit des Christentums*, Gütersloh, Gütersloher Verlagshaus, 2002, 54–71.

Barnett, Victoria J., "Track Two Diplomacy (1933–1939): International Responses from Catholics, Jews and Ecumenical Protestants to Events in Nazi Germany," *KZG* 27/1, 2014, 76–86.

Bonhoeffer, Dietrich, *Dietrich Bonhoeffer Works*, vol. 13, *London (1933–1935)*, ed. Keith Clements, Minneapolis, Fortress Press, 2007.

Bonhoeffer, Dietrich, "Letter to George K.A. Bell," in: Bonhoeffer, *Dietrich Bonhoeffer Works*, vol. 16, *Conspiracy and Imprisonment (1940–1945)*, ed. Mark S. Brocker, Minneapolis, Fortress Press, 2006.

Boyd, Robin, *The Witness of the Student Christian Movement: Church Ahead of the Church*, London, SPCK, 2007.

Clements, Keith, *Faith on the Frontier: A Life of J.H. Oldham*, Edinburgh, T&T Clark, 1999.

Jehle-Wildberger, Marianne, *Adolf Keller (1872–1963): Ecumenist, World Citizen, Philanthropist*, Eugene, Cascade Books, 2013.

Klemperer, Klemens von, *German Resistance against Hitler: The Search for Allies Abroad (1938–1945)*, Oxford, Clarendon Press, 1992.

Kraemer, Hendrik, *A Theology of the Laity*, London, Lutterworth, 1958.

Macy, Paul Griswold, ed., *The Report of the Second World Conference of Christian Youth: Oslo, Norway, July 22 to 31, 1947*, Geneva, WCC Publications, 1947.

Oldham, Joseph H., ed., *The Churches Survey Their Task: Report of the Conference at Oxford, July 1937, on Church, Community and State*, London, George Allen & Unwin, 1937.

Scholder, Klaus, *The Churches and the Third Reich*, 2 vols., London, SCM Press, 1987–1988.

Visser 't Hooft, Willem Adolph & Joseph H. Oldham, *The Church and Its Function in Society*, London, George Allen & Unwin, 1937.

Visser 't Hooft, Willem Adolph, *Memoirs*, London, SCM Press, 1973.

CHAPTER 13

The Una Sancta Movement and the Jaeger-Stählin Group in Germany

Friederike Nüssel

1 Origins of the Jaeger-Stählin Group

The so-called Jaeger-Stählin group refers to an ecumenical gathering of Protestant and Catholic theologians. The name, widely used in accounts of ecumenical history, derives from its two founders, Archbishop and Cardinal Lorenz Jaeger and Bishop Wilhelm Stählin. However, its official name[1] is in fact the Ökumenischer Arbeitskreis evangelischer und katholischer Theologen (Ecumenical Study Group of Protestant and Catholic Theologians).[2] It initially consisted of two different groups which held meetings in parallel from 1946. As Barbara Schwahn points out in her fundamental study on the group's origins and history, published in 1996, what is commonly referred to as the Jaeger-Stählin group is often associated with the Una Sancta movement.[3] However, such an assignation is completely misleading. Although some members of the Una Sancta movement also belonged to the ÖAK, because of the latter's "origins, links with the ecclesiastical hierarchy and, most importantly, its nature and aims," it must not only be clearly distinguished "from the Una Sancta movement in the strict sense,"[4] but must even, quite the opposite, "be classed as one of the Catholic Church's attempts to steer the Una Sancta movement ... on to the right path."[5] Many Roman Catholic bishops and theologians, as well as some Protestants observers too, suspected the Una Sancta movement of trying to achieve church unity "by simplifying theological problems and anticipating the fellowship of worship."[6]

1.1 *Foundation and Aims*

As already mentioned, the study group originally consisted of two separate groups, one Catholic and the other Protestant. They met for the first time on Apr 2 and 3, 1946, at the seminary in Werl

1 This name is commonly used when referring to the group's early history, but it does not appear in the sources that regard its foundation. Instead, *Arbeitskreis* (study group), *Arbeitsgemeinschaft* (study community) or *Theologenkomission* (commission of theologians) are used. On this, see Dominik Burkard, "Informanten, Türöffner, und Agenten: Erzbischof Lorenz Jaeger und seine (frühen) römischen Kontakte," in: Nicole Priesching & Gisela Fleckenstein, eds., *Lorenz Jaeger als Theologe*, Paderborn, Schöning, 2019, 33–80.

2 See Nicole Priesching, "Ein Konservativer Pragmatiker: Tagung über Kardinal Lorenz Jaeger als Ökumeniker," in: Katholische Nachrichten Agentur (KNA), Ökumenische Information (ÖKI), 39, September 2019, I.

3 Convinced that church unity could only be achieved by taking the spiritual path in converting to Christ, Max Josef Metzger founded the Una Sancta brotherhood in 1938. Private Una Sancta circles linked to the brotherhood were set up across Germany, playing an important role in the creation of ecumenical awareness and the dissemination of the ecumenical aim of church unity. An important instrument of the Una Sancta movement in this endeavor was its journal *Una-Sancta-Rundbriefe*, which served as a discussion platform for Protestants and Catholics. Its direction was taken over by Matthias Laros after the end of World War II, but he was relieved of this position in 1948 after the *Monitum*. The *Una Sancta* journal was then founded in 1953 under Thomas Sartory. On this, see Peter Lengsfeld, "Ökumenische Theologie als Theorie ökumenischer Prozesse: Die Kollusionstheorie," in: Peter Lengsfeld, ed., *Ökumenische Theologie: Ein Arbeitsbuch*, Stuttgart, Kohlhammer, 1980, 36–67, esp. 56. See also Gerhard Voss, "Una Sancta," *LThK* 10, 373f. For greater details concerning the roots of the Una Sancta movement, see the contribution by Paul Metzlaff in the first volume of this work, while for its developments during the period of the Nazi dictatorship and World War II, see in this volume Peter Zimmerling's contribution on ecumenism and the Third Reich.

4 Barbara Schwahn, *Der Ökumenische Arbeitskreis evangelischer und katholischer Theologen*, Göttingen, Vandenhoeck & Ruprecht, 1996, 22.

5 Schwahn, *Der Ökumenische Arbeitskreis*, 23.

6 Schwahn, *Der Ökumenische Arbeitskreis*, 23.

in the Soest district of Westphalia. The foundation of the Catholic group and the initiative to form a parallel Protestant group can be traced back to the archbishop of Paderborn, Lorenz Jaeger, and to that city's cathedral provost, Prof. Dr. Paul Simon. Jaeger had already appointed in 1944 "[Josef] Höfer together with Robert Grosche (1888–1967), Michael Schmaus (1897–1993), Karl Rahner (1904–1984), and Romano Guardini (1885–1968) to a study group under Paul Simon's direction charged with preparing an interconfessional study group."[7] Jaeger's guiding principle was his conviction that since the schism within the church had originally been caused by theologians it should "likewise be overcome through theological study."[8] Jaeger for his part was instructed by the Fulda Bishops' Conference, in consultation with the Protestant *Landesbischof* Stählin, "to monitor and influence the work of union."[9] To this end he was to set up a Catholic group, whose members were Joseph Lortz, Bernhard Rosenmöller, Gottlieb Söhngen, Gottfried Hasenkamp (editorial director), Robert Grosche, and Karl Schmitt.[10] At Dean Simon's initiative, the Protestant participants were the bishop of Oldenburg, Wilhelm Stählin, theology professors Heinrich Schlier, Peter Brunner, and Edmund Schlink, pastor Hans-Dietrich Mittorp from Paderborn, and Hermann Sasse. There was overall agreement that the aim was not to conduct "negotiations for union," but rather the initial intention was "to clarify shared terminology."[11] It is nonetheless worth noting that Joseph Lortz already foresaw talks on union in the dialogue arrangement. He considered it the shared belief of both parties "that the church of Jesus Christ could be found in the other confession."[12]

Apart from the debate about its aims, the newly created group also considered the question of its status and membership. On the Catholic side, the circle immediately enjoyed the recognition of ecclesiastical authority, in virtue of the instructions received by Archbishop Jaeger from the Episcopal Conference of Fulda. On the Protestant side, there were also attempts to have the group authorized by the EKD and secure the involvement of a member of the EKD's council. The EKD did indeed promise financial support but wanted the group to remain an independent working body rather than commission it officially. The reasons for this decision were undoubtedly multifaceted, but were probably connected to the fact that ecumenical activities were suspected of harboring catholicizing tendencies. Individual members such as Bishop Stählin in particular were accused of this. The EKD, which during its foundation phase had more than enough to contend with in the form of internal questions of confessionalization, kept its distance from this kind of conflict by renouncing an official mandate. To "reassure the Protestant positions,"[13] practical direction on the Protestant side was transferred to Edmund Schlink, who exercised this office for many years. In contrast, on the Catholic side there was less continuity in scientific supervision.[14]

1.2 *Cardinal Lorenz Jaeger*

Cardinal Lorenz Jaeger was born on Sep 23, 1892 in Halle an der Saale, the eldest of five children. His mother was a devout Catholic and his father a Protestant. This mixed confessional family situation had a profound effect on Jaeger in the context of the Saxon diaspora. After his father's premature

7 Burkard, "Informanten, Türöffner, und Agenten," 58.

8 See the quotation from Jaeger that Bishop Hermann Kunst and Cardinal Hermann Volk reproduced in their preface to the ÖAK's first publication in the Dialog der Kirchen series. See Karl Lehmann & Wolfhart Pannenberg, eds., *Glaubensbekenntnis und Kirchengemeinschaft: Das Modell des Konzils von Konstantinopel (381)*, DiKi 1, Freiburg i.Br./Göttingen, Herder/Vandenhoeck & Ruprecht, 1982, 5.

9 Cited from Schwahn, *Der Ökumenische Arbeitskreis*, 18.

10 See Schwahn, *Der Ökumenische Arbeitskreis*, 18.

11 See Stefan Höfer, "Una-Sancta-Bewegung," *LThK* 10, cols. 463–466, here 465.

12 This view is reproduced in Schwahn, *Der Ökumenische Arbeitskreis*, 22, n. 16 from the minutes of the 23rd meeting in 1962.

13 Wilhelm Stählin, *Via Vitae: Lebenserinnerungen*, Kassel, Johannes Stauda, 1968, 554.

14 See Schwahn, *Der Ökumenische Arbeitskreis*, 38.

death, the family moved to Olpe in Westphalia. In view of the family's financial hardship, Jaeger was offered a place in the orphanage of the Sisters of St. Francis of Perpetual Adoration so that he could complete his secondary school education at the church school. He went on to study Catholic theology in Paderborn and Munich, and philosophy in Münster. He was ordained as a priest in 1922. After a number of years working as a diaspora pastor and army priest, he was ordained bishop of Paderborn on Oct 19, 1941 in the midst of World War II. Even though ecumenical rapprochements between Catholics and Protestants had been rejected since 1928 as a result of the papal encyclical *Mortalium animos*, Jaeger was sympathetic to Protestant Christians and even when he was ordained as bishop he already spoke of "reunification in faith."[15] At his initiative, in 1943 a department for questions on reunification in faith was set up by the Fulda Bishops' Conference. While "mutual understanding, dialogue, and exchange"[16] were clearly important to him, he was not so much "a theoretician of ecumenism" as a "conservative pragmatist."[17]

In his study of Jaeger's role in the history of the foundation of the so-called Jaeger-Stählin group, Dominik Burkard concludes that Jaeger himself hardly ever appears in the documents relating to the group's practical discussions. The truly influential figure on the Catholic side was in fact provost Paul Simon. Burkard attributes Jaeger's low profile to his concern that "his views [might] be taken as authoritative."[18] Accordingly, "Jaeger's role in the creation of the 'study group' in 1946 ... should be described as the conclusion of a long and complex evolution."[19] This idea is confirmed by Volker Leppin,[20] who identifies a certain asymmetry at work in this formative period. There was hardly any contact between Stählin and Jaeger, while for Stählin his true counterpart in shaping the joint work was Paul Simon, who was the academic director of the Catholic side, and later his successor, Josef Höfer: "However, he [Höfer] lost the trust of his Protestant partners because of his failed attempt to deliver to the pope a Protestant response to the *assumptio* doctrine, with the result that Jaeger himself then came to the fore."[21]

Regarding the ensuing diplomatic dialogue between the EKD and the German Bishops' Conference, Jörg Seiler notes "that the ecumenist Jaeger wanted to exclude the progressive Una Sancta movement as far as possible, while at the same showing sympathy towards the Winfriedbund, for example."[22]

After the *Monitum* of the Holy Office *Cum compertum* in 1948 and the subsequent *Instructio De motione oecumenica*, "the archbishop of Paderborn became one of the most influential figures within the Bishops' Conference."[23] Jaeger's contacts with Rome had become institutionalized after "approval for ecumenical meetings and discussions [became] the Holy See's right of reserve, which was delegated to episcopal incumbents for

15 Wolfgang Thönissen, "Lorenz Kardinal Jaeger: Wiedervereinigung im Glauben als Gebot der Gegenwart," in: Christian Möller & others, eds., *Wegbereiter der Ökumene im 20. Jahrhundert*, Göttingen, Vandenhoeck & Ruprecht, 2005, 194–213, here 194.

16 Lorenz Kardinal Jaeger, *Einheit und Gemeinschaft: Stellungnahmen zu Fragen der christlichen Einheit*, ed. Johann-Adam-Möhler-Institut, Paderborn, Bonifatius, 1972, 12f.

17 See Nicole Priesching, "Ein konservativer Pragmatiker: Tagung über Kardinal Lorenz Jaeger als Ökumeniker," in: KNA, ÖKI 39, September 2019, IV.

18 Priesching, "Ein konservativer Pragmatiker," I.

19 Priesching, "Ein konservativer Pragmatiker," I.

20 Conference on Jaeger (see KNA 39, I); Katholische Akademie Schwerte conference Aug 29–30, 2019 with the leadership by Nicole Priesching, Paderborn.

21 Priesching, "Ein konservativer Pragmatiker," I.

22 On this point, see also Georg Korting, "Kleine Geschichte des Winfriedbundes: Eine katholische Initiative zur Wiedervereinigung der Christen im Wandel der Zeit," *Cath(M)* 67/4, 2013, 297–317, here 297: "The Winfriedbund can be classified as an early Catholic initiative, which worked to promote Christian reunification since the end of World War I, at first mainly focusing on the return of separated Christians to the Catholic Church, an aspect that was determinative in the Catholic Church until Vatican II."

23 Burkard, "Informanten, Türöffner, und Agenten," 36.

only three years."[24] As the delegate of the Fulda Bishops' Conference, Jaeger had to "direct in particular the activities of the different local groups as part of the coordination of so-called Una Sancta work. These groups had a coordination center at the Christkönigs-Institut in Meitingen, founded by Max Josef Metzger."[25]

Jaeger's influence became even stronger as a result of two other significant ecumenical initiatives. First, he founded the Johann-Adam-Möhler-Institut in Paderborn in 1956, where he assumed an important role in overcoming the division between the churches. Second, he was one of the cofounders of the SPCU based in Rome, and consequently played a decisive role in the preparation of the decree on ecumenism before and during Vatican II. "In December 1959, Archbishop Jaeger sent Cardinal Bea the plan to set up a commission on Christian unity, which was to deal with ecumenical issues during the council's preparation. Cardinal Bea gave his full approval in letters dated Jan 1 and 20."[26] On Mar 4, 1960, a letter was sent to Pope John XXIII requesting that such a commission be created.[27] Other than that of Augustin Bea, the advocate of ecumenism at the Holy Office, another name is inextricably linked to the foundation of the SPCU: that of Johannes Willebrands, secretary of the Catholic Conference for Ecumenical Questions. Jaeger was in touch with both of them. As a "member of an international committee of bishop guarantors for the Catholic Conference ... Jaeger persuaded Bea to take on the role of specialist and advisor for Una Sancta work."[28] In 1965, ten years before his death, Lorenz Jaeger was made a cardinal by Pope Paul VI.

According to Nicole Priesching, "Cardinal Lorenz Jaeger was not an ecumenical theologian but rather a controversial theologian in the traditional mold, who nonetheless was able to see the 'Protestant principle' as a corrective for the Catholic Church."[29] His ecumenical vision and hopes can be described in the context of an ecumenism of return, which clearly accounts for his involvement in ministering to converts. He vigorously rejected both intercommunion and the 1973 memorandum on ministries (*Ämtermemorandum*). This context must be borne in mind when reading his account of the first meetings of the two groups in Werl, offered as part of a speech delivered to mark his departure as an active member of the group in 1970:

> We said to ourselves then: now is the time, when our nation has collapsed spectacularly, to raise the banner of hope, to give some sign of common ground, and show our people the path into the future. The schism was originally caused by theologians, and must equally be overcome through theological study. Our aim then was nothing other than to clear away the debris, to investigate the substance of theological concepts circulating as common currency, so that we could once again understand one another in our dialogue. We honestly attempted to prepare the groundwork for one another from the perspective of theological controversy at the time and in this way create a renewed basis for dialogue.[30]

24 Burkard, "Informanten, Türöffner, und Agenten," 36.

25 Saretta Marotta, "Augustin Bea auf dem Weg zum Ökumeniker 1949–1960," *ZKG* 127/3, 2016, 373–393, here 379; The increasing number of marriages between members of different confessions promoted ecumenical efforts among the laity. An important center was the Christkönigs-Institut in Meitingen founded by Metzger in 1928. On this see also Saretta Marotta, "La genesi di un ecumenista: La corrispondenza fra Augustin Bea e il vescovo di Paderborn Lorenz Jaeger (1951–1960)," in: Luca Ferracci, ed., *Toward a History of the Desire for Christian Unity*, Münster, LIT, 2015, 159–191 and Saretta Marotta, *Gli anni della pazienza: Bea, l'ecumenismo e il Sant'Uffizio di Pio XII*, Bologna, Il Mulino, 2020.

26 Jaeger, *Einheit und Gemeinschaft*, 411.

27 See Jaeger, *Einheit und Gemeinschaft*, 411.

28 Priesching, "Ein konservativer Pragmatiker," 111.

29 Priesching, "Ein konservativer Pragmatiker," 111.

30 See the special edition of farewell speeches by Jaeger and Schlink and Stählin's reply at the 31st meeting in 1970, cited in: Schwahn, *Der Ökumenische Arbeitskreis*, 21f.

1.3 *Bishop Wilhelm Stählin*

Wilhelm Stählin was born on Sep 24, 1883 in Gunzenhausen, the youngest of eleven children, of whom only six survived. Son of a Lutheran pastor, after his father's early death he grew up in Augsburg, where he completed his secondary school education. His strict upbringing forbade any contact with Catholic pupils, so that inevitably he did not have any ecumenical aspirations in his youth. After studying theology in Berlin, Erlangen, and Rostock, he served as a pastor from 1917 to 1926. From 1926, he was professor of practical theology in Münster, where he served as the "antipode" to Karl Barth, who was teaching there at the same time. This contrast continued throughout World War II, when Stählin joined the Confessing Church for just a short time before distancing himself from it fairly quickly, but without joining the other side. He was bishop of the Evangelical Lutheran Church in Oldenburg from 1945 to 1952. As founder of the EMB, he led one of the most important liturgical movements.[31] He also took part in the first Protestant-Catholic theological conference in Hermsdorf just outside Berlin in Easter 1943.[32] He took over the leadership of the Protestant working group of the ÖAK from 1946, which he chaired until 1970, and died on Dec 16, 1975 aged 92 in Prien am Chiemsee. He published his memoires under the title *Via Vitae*, whose nearly 750 pages he had completed in October 1967, wherein he called his relationship to his confession "an unhappy love."[33] Bishop Hartmut Löwe, who for many years was the spiritual leader of the Protestant side, claims that Stählin's work for the ecumenical cause always sprang from a desire to remedy "the inadequate aspects of the reality of the church wherever he came across it."[34] Aware of the limitations of the confessional perspectives and their need to be complemented, "he pleaded for the recognition of 'legitimate differences,'"[35] and considered "any reunification program … unrealistic."[36]

1.4 *Edmund Schlink*

When the two study groups were officially united in 1968, after Vatican II, it was Edmund Schlink who proposed the name it still bears today: Ökumenischer Arbeitskreis evangelischer und katholischer Theologen.[37] Whereas the academic directors on the Catholic side changed with frequency, Schlink remained the Protestant group's director from the group's foundation and had a profound influence on it in this capacity until 1979.[38]

Schlink was born in Darmstadt on Mar 6, 1903, the son of a university professor in mechanics. He studied mathematics, natural sciences, and philosophy in Tübingen, Munich, Kiel, and Vienna from 1922 to 1925, but switched to theology early in 1926. However, his interest in the natural sciences continued despite this. Thus, Schlink wrote his doctoral thesis in Marburg on the subject of personality change, before studying theology with Karl Barth in Münster. After merely four semesters, he submitted his Master's thesis there in 1930. This empirical and psychological study on the emotional experiences of God was a contribution to the problem of natural religion. He had his first confrontations with the NSDAP while working in pastoral ministry. In 1934, Schlink completed his Habilitation thesis in Gießen with a work on the understanding of the proclamation. He taught at the Confessing Church's college in Bethel from 1935 until this was closed by the Gestapo in 1939. After a number of functions in different locations, he was appointed to the chair for dogmatics at the University of Heidelberg in 1946, setting up the first ecumenical university institute that very year. In 1950, together with Walter Freytag, he

31 See Hartmut Löwe, "Wilhelm Stählin: Nicht nur der Kopf, der ganze Mensch will glauben," in: Möller & others, eds., *Wegbereiter der Ökumene im 20. Jahrhundert*, 133–155.

32 See Stählin, *Via Vitae*, 247.

33 Stählin, *Via Vitae*, 731.

34 Löwe, "Wilhelm Stählin," 152.

35 Löwe, "Wilhelm Stählin," 152, quoting from Wilhelm Stählin's work on church unity.

36 Löwe, "Wilhelm Stählin," 152.

37 See Schwahn, *Der Ökumenische Arbeitskreis*, 21.

38 See Schwahn, *Der Ökumenische Arbeitskreis*, 37.

founded the DÖSTA. In the international ecumenical arena, he was a delegate at the general assemblies of the WCC in Amsterdam in 1948, Evanston in 1954, New Delhi in 1961, and Uppsala in 1968. He was the EKD's official observer at Vatican II from 1962 to 1965,[39] an experience which proved of great significance for his work in the *ÖAK*. He died on May 20, 1984, and he is considered one of the most important Protestant forerunners of ecumenism.[40] As Christoph Schwöbel notes, Schlink's understanding of ecumenism was nurtured by the "twofold approach of understanding ecumenism dogmatically and dogmatics ecumenically,"[41] and informed by his experiences during the German church struggle, the incipient ecumenical movement within the Protestant churches, and "the encounter with Roman Catholicism and the Eastern Orthodox churches."[42] Like Stählin, he saw the aim of ecumenical understanding not in the abolition of the different confessions but in "unity in diversity."[43] He associated this with the hope of "a multiplicity of churches open to one another, to which communion in the Lord's Supper and mutual recognition of ministries might increasingly bestow itself."[44]

1.5 *The ÖAK's Methods and Subjects*

During the foundation phase, the two groups were interested in discussing subjects of common concern and in becoming acquainted with one another through the exchange of theological ideas. Two gatherings a year were held to this end, one in the spring and one in autumn. In 1955, it was then agreed to meet only once a year during the week before Palm Sunday, a schedule which has been maintained to this very day. The jointly agreed subjects in the early years always included exegetical and doctrinal lectures from both sides. Lectures from other disciplines were accepted on a subject-by-subject basis. In 1949, however, the treatment of the doctrine on justification deviated from this rule. Hermann Volk and Wilhelm Maurer lectured from the Catholic perspective on the doctrine of justification in the confessional writings of the Evangelical Lutheran Church. Conversely, Peter Brunner[45] and Michael Schmaus gave presentations from the Protestant perspective on the Council of Trent's doctrine of justification.[46] This particularly fruitful meeting had been preceded in 1948 by one on the subject of faith, while the second meeting in 1949 was dedicated to conversion and repentance. In 1950 and 1951, the subjects of baptism and the power of

39 As Bishop Hermann Kunst and Cardinal Hermann Volk noted in 1982, besides Schlink there were many other members of the group as "fathers, advisors, and observers at the council" who were able to bring the fruits of the common knowledge to the world at large. See their preface in: Lehmann & Pannenberg, eds., *Glaubensbekenntnis und Kirchengemeinschaft*, 6.

40 See Christoph Schwöbel, "Edmund Schlink: Ökumenische Dogmatik," in: Möller & others, eds., *Wegbereiter der Ökumene im 20. Jahrhundert*, 232–254.

41 Schwöbel, "Edmund Schlink," 236.

42 Schwöbel, *Wegbereiter*, 237.

43 Edmund Schlink, "Die Kirche in Gottes Heilsplan: Die Ergebnisse der ersten Sektion der Weltkirchenkonferenz in Amsterdam," *ThLZ* 73/11, 1948, 641–652, here 651.

44 Schlink, "Die Kirche," 651.

45 Peter Brunner was, together with Edmund Schlink, a long-standing member of the ÖAK (1947–1981) and author of many works of scholarship. He should be ranked alongside Schlink in terms of his ecumenical position. Both worked closely together: "He was interned in Dachau concentration camp in 1935 because he had criticized the National Socialist regime. Brunner was one of the pastors released when the bishop of Chichester asked disapprovingly why pastors were being detained, although his release was on condition that he did not resume his previous activities, an order which he ignored. Schlink later brought him to Heidelberg as professor for dogmatics"; Schwöbel, "Edmund Schlink," 238). On some points, Brunner moved closer towards Catholic positions (see for example Schwahn, *Der Ökumenische Arbeitskreis*, 46). His interpretation of the Council of Trent is highly distinctive, which can be seen as the first "reassessment of the doctrinal condemnations in the ÖAK," even if at the time it was not "received positively" there; Schwahn, *Der Ökumenische Arbeitskreis*, 170.

46 See Schwahn, *Der Ökumenische Arbeitskreis*, 49. The examination of binding doctrinal statements of a tradition of interpreters from both confessions has been systematically applied recently by the dialogue group of theologians at Tübingen and Lateran University under the direction of Eilert Herms and Lubomir Zak.

the spirit were examined. It can be seen from this that soteriology and related issues formed the first major subject area of discussion. These themes were interrupted only in 1950, when, on the occasion of the declaration of the dogma of the bodily Assumption of Mary into heaven, it was decided to discuss the subject of the worship of Mary and the saints. The method practiced in the case of the doctrine of justification, of studying a particular tradition from the other confession's perspective, was repeated in a meeting on ecclesiology in 1962. Peter Brunner reflected on the ecclesiological status of the Roman Catholic Church from a Protestant perspective, while Heinrich Fries did the same for Protestantism from a Roman Catholic perspective. The planning of these lectures shows the great importance the group placed on reciprocity in its treatment of subjects based on the principle of *par cum pari*: they wanted to facilitate a dialogue among equals. Although minutes were taken of the proceedings, they were kept private. During the first ten years, the lectures and joint theses formulated at the sessions were not published in order to avoid giving any impression that union or consensus talks were at issue.

1.6 *The Challenges of Working Together*

Among the greatest challenges faced by the group in its early years were the 1948 *Monitum Cum compertum* and the 1949 *Instructio De motione oecumenica*. For the group, particularly its Protestant members, these pronouncements seemed to cast doubt as to whether dialogue was desired by the Catholic side and regarded as legitimate. There was much debate and intense consultation within the group. Finally, a declaratory interpretation of the proclamations by the group's Catholic side made it possible for Protestant members to agree to continue the group's meetings and for a joint group declaration to be sent to the EKD's council.[47] It is interesting to note in this context that the *Monitum* was understood by Catholics in Germany as a safeguard "against certain excesses and forms of enthusiasm (*Schwarmgeisterei*) of the Una Sancta movement in Germany"[48] and was explained to the group's Protestant members in this way. A letter from Jaeger to the Holy Office's assessor sent through Höfer confirms this assumption: "I have given this gentleman a twofold mission: to monitor Una Sancta's endeavors in Germany and to direct the study group of leading theologians. I have already been able to report in writing on a couple of occasions about this group's work."[49]

Similarly, Jaeger's initiative in the "creation of an office for ecumenical questions in Rome went in this direction: the subsequent SPCU was to observe not only ecumenical and confessional endeavors, but most importantly avert undesirable disruptions."[50]

Another challenge to the group's work came from the recognition of the Assumption of Mary as dogma in 1950. The Protestant side's criticism stemmed from the fact that this dogma was not only the first decision *ex cathedra* since Vatican I, but also the application *ex cathedra*, for the second time, of papal infallibility in doctrinal decisions, which had been proclaimed in the dogmatic constitution *Pastor aeternus* after the institution of the very same doctrine of infallibility. This was viewed as unsettling by the Protestant side, particularly since the dogma of *assumptio Mariae* lacked any biblical basis whatsoever. The ÖAK Heidelberg members, Edmund Schlink, Günther Bornkamm, Peter Brunner, Hans von Campenhausen, and Wilfried Joest, eventually drew up a statement in response. This became the first public document issued by ÖAK members, and was to be delivered to the pope via Josef Höfer. Unfortunately, due to difficulties in coordinating the timing attributable

47 On this, see Schwahn, *Der Ökumenische Arbeitskreis*, 68f., esp. n. 150.

48 This was how Schlink summarized the views of the Roman Catholic side in a letter to the president of *Katholikentag* (Catholics Day), Theophil Herder-Dorneich. The cited text can be found in Schwahn, *Der Ökumenische Arbeitskreis*, 64.

49 L. Jaeger to A. Ottaviani, Apr 8, 1949, in: EBAP, Nachlass Jaeger, 533. On this, see also Thomas Sartory, *Die ökumenische Bewegung und die Einheit der Kirche: Ein Beitrag im Dienste einer ökumenischen Ekklesiologie*, Meitingen, Kyrios, 1955, 91.

50 Burkard, "Informanten, Türöffner, und Agenten," 71.

to Höfer himself, and for which Bishop Hermann Volk apologized to the Protestant side, the document did not arrive at the arranged time. This caused much disappointment, particularly for Edmund Schlink, who argued against continuing the group's discussions, because of both the new dogma and the tardy delivery of the Protestant response. It was not without regret that he took this stand. However, the majority of the group's Protestant members were in favor of continuing. In solidarity Schlink decided to remain with them and the Catholic members, but found that the atmosphere and the kind of work had changed dramatically.[51] For its part the Catholic side immediately recognized the strain that the dogma put on ecumenical relations. They praised the Protestant response for its differentiated approach as well as its tone and style. In terms of substance, however, the Catholic theologians remained unconvinced by the Protestant criticisms and defended the new dogma, albeit proffering different reasons.

The papal curia's two pronouncements on ecumenism and the declaration of the doctrine of the Assumption as dogma caused the Protestant side to doubt the meaningfulness of continuing dialogue. In these early years, a third area of conflict arose on the Protestant side concerning the catholicizing position of Hans Asmussen. This led to Asmussen's expulsion from the EKD's council, while even the VELKD also assumed a critical attitude. Faced with the accusation of catholicizing interests, the ÖAK once again affirmed its position not to draw up any consensus formulas aimed at unification. The subjects chosen for the discussions were the theological controversies of the Reformation period and 17th century, together with "the transformation in modern thought since the Enlightenment and the rise of the natural sciences, with the resulting problems for relations among the different confessions."[52] Christianity's relationship to the world also had to be considered. The non-public nature of the talks was again confirmed, "although the possibility of a common public resolution was admitted. However, 'resolutions' in which one side had expressed its dissent to the other would not be published.'"[53] This reflected very much the VELKD's position. At its general synod of 1958 it defined the central ecumenical task as "acquiring a sense of the other church's self-conception, unburdened by prejudices and misjudgments."[54]

1.7 *Consolidation*

These challenges were experienced as serious crises for the group's ongoing collaboration.[55] Therefore, the opening up of the Roman Catholic Church towards ecumenism and the foundation of the papal SPCU represented a fundamental change to the conditions of the group's joint work. Meanwhile, the work of both ecumenical study groups in Germany was significant in preparing for Vatican II. Before the council, Cardinal Bea asked Jaeger and Schlink to inform him of the ÖAK experience. It can therefore hardly be a coincidence that chapter 1.4 of the ecumenical decree describes dialogue as the main form of implementing the ecumenical movement in a way highly consistent with the methods of the ÖAK. Vatican II contributed to the group's integrity and activity by allowing in 1968, on the basis of the Roman Catholic Church's new ecumenical openness, for the Catholic and Protestant groups to be merged officially into a single study group. The group would henceforth be an ecumenical body dedicated to the scholarly study of theological controversies. It could now publish its studies as the study group, in which the academic directors of both sides acted as editors.

51 See Edmund Schlink's retrospective remarks in his "Pneumatische Erschütterung," *KuD* 8, 1962, 221–237, esp. 231.

52 Schwahn, *Der Ökumenische Arbeitskreis*, 90.

53 Schwahn, *Der Ökumenische Arbeitskreis*, 90f.

54 Cited from Schwahn, *Der Ökumenische Arbeitskreis*, 91.

55 On this, see the preface in: Lehmann & Pannenberg, eds., *Glaubensbekenntnis und Kirchengemeinschaft*, 5.

2 The Development of Theological Study through Publications

The subsequent history of the so-called Jaeger-Stählin group after 1968 is largely tied to the scientific-theological treatment of controversial theological subjects, according to the group's own view of its role. Consequently, the resulting publications will be briefly outlined in the second part of this chapter. They can, in retrospect, be read as a scientific-theological response to the ecumenical concerns of the Una Sancta movement, with the difference that they sought to provide the theological foundation which Cardinal Jaeger and others found lacking.

2.1 *Creation of the Dialog der Kirchen Series and Its First Three Publications*

Even though for a long time the ÖAK did not make the lectures and theses from the study sessions available in publications of its own, many lectures were in fact published in other journals and collections, in particular the interim report in the volume commemorating Archbishop Jaeger and Bishop Stählin entitled *Pro Veritate: Ein theologischer Dialog*, edited by Edmund Schlink and Hermann Volk in 1963. Reports from individual meetings were published in book form thereafter. Not until 1982, however, did the ÖAK create the series Dialog der Kirchen. It would publish the results of its research there from then on and right through until today. The first volume is dedicated to the Niceno-Constantinopolitan Creed of 381 as a model for the connection between confession of faith and fellowship of churches. The external occasion for this was offered to the circle by the celebration of the 1600th anniversary of the Council of Constantinople in 1981. Regarding its subject matter, the internal reason within the group for jointly reconsidering this confession derived from the fact that the circle had previously been occupied with it on the occasion of the 450th anniversary of the *Confessio Augustana* of 1530, and had begun to debate the question of the role of confessional and church fellowship.

Two questions were central to grappling with the *Confessio Augustana*: first, the "question of which criteria in this document are overriding for the unity of the church";[56] second, to investigate the tension "that comes to light in such a confessional text, namely its status as both historical text *and* binding ecclesial reality."[57] A question to which little attention had been paid was central here, namely, to what extent "continuity and change in the concept and understanding of the church's confession" are to be understood as an autonomous "form of the manifestation of Christian belief."[58] It seemed logical in this respect to examine the Niceno-Constantinopolitan Creed as "the only truly ecumenical credo of the Christian churches"[59] in its significance for church and the fellowship of churches, and in this connection also to look at the link between pneumatology and ecclesiology and the question of the subsequent introduction of the *Filioque*, which was so fundamental to relations between the Eastern and Western churches. Therefore, the study first addressed the "origin and historical situation of the confession of faith of Constantinople,"[60] followed by the "*history of the influence* of symbol,"[61] giving special attention to the *Filioque* issue,[62] and finally the question of its "relevance for the state of

56 See Lehmann & Pannenberg, eds., *Glaubensbekenntnis und Kirchengemeinschaft*, 10, introduction.

57 Lehmann & Pannenberg, eds., *Glaubensbekenntnis und Kirchengemeinschaft*, 10, introduction (italics original).

58 Lehmann & Pannenberg, eds., *Glaubensbekenntnis und Kirchengemeinschaft*, 10, introduction.

59 Lehmann & Pannenberg, eds., *Glaubensbekenntnis und Kirchengemeinschaft*, 9, introduction.

60 See the paper by Wolf-Dieter Hauschild, "Das trinitarische Dogma von 381 als Ergebnis verbindlicher Konsensbildung," in: Lehmann & Pannenberg, eds., *Glaubensbekenntnis und Kirchengemeinschaft*, 13–48.

61 Lehmann & Pannenberg, eds., *Glaubensbekenntnis und Kirchengemeinschaft*, 10, introduction (italics original).

62 On this, see the paper by Reinhard Slenczka, "Das Filioque in der neueren ökumenischen Diskussion," in: Lehmann & Pannenberg, eds., *Glaubensbekenntnis und Kirchengemeinschaft*, 80–99.

contemporary ecumenical dialogue."[63] The study not only made advances in the sense of major substantive findings. In its consideration of the meaning of symbol for the fellowship of churches, the group was also able to reflect on methodological questions such as "the relationship between scripture and confession, scripture and councils (magisterium), doxology and dogma, the development of dogma in the early church and late antique metaphysics,"[64] and the reception of doctrinal decisions in new contexts.

Shortly after the publication of this work on the confession of faith, two further volumes in Dialog der Kirchen were published with the findings of previous symposia. The first was about the *Confessio Augustana*'s ecumenical scope, briefly mentioned above, under the title of *Evangelium, Sakramente, Amt und Einheit der Kirche*.[65] The second was a study on the sacrificial nature of the Lord's Supper, *Das Opfer Jesu Christi und seine Gegenwart in der Kirche*.[66] In the first of these, fundamental reflections on the understanding of church unity are set out at the end of the joint report. It is stressed that church unity is bestowed in the salvific event that constitutes the very basis of the church and is consequently first and foremost a gift (*Gabe*) and only then a duty (*Aufgabe*).[67] It can only be preserved in faith and restored in conversion and renewal. In line with article 7 of the *Confessio Augustana*, it is affirmed that the condition of unity can only "be binding on that which is necessary for the gospel's sake; there can and must be freedom in everything else."[68] Another joint affirmation is crucial, whereby it is held that unity as an "essential dimension" of the church encompasses diversity. Unity applies "horizontally in the contemporary church as well as vertically in its relationship to the church of previous centuries."[69] In the horizontal perspective, church unity is understood as the "fellowship (*communio, koinonia*) of churches ... which creates and represents churches in their respective locations and in this are able to develop diverse theologies, spiritualities, ways of life, liturgical and legal disciplines. In this respect, the church is always a conciliar fellowship."[70] As regards unity in the vertical sense, stress is placed on the church's historical continuity with the early church and the Trinitarian, Christological, anti-Pelagian, and anti-Donatist doctrinal decisions. The eschatological dimension is also clearly highlighted. The church has eschatological magnitude, is subject to judgment in that capacity, and is *semper reformanda*. The separation between the visible and invisible church is rejected, whereas the tension between visible form and spiritual dimension is highlighted: "It is the means of salvation (institution) and fruit of salvation (fellowship in the Holy Spirit). It is the holy church and the church of sinners."[71]

Evangelium, Sakramente, Amt und Einheit der Kirche is followed by the study on the sacrificial nature of the Lord's Supper. This sequence makes sense not only in terms of sacramental and theological, but particularly also on ecclesiological,

63 Lehmann & Pannenberg, eds., *Glaubensbekenntnis und Kirchengemeinschaft*, 11, introduction (italics original). See the paper by Theodor Schneider, "Der theologische Ort der Kirche in der Perspektive des dritten Glaubensartikels," in: Lehmann & Pannenberg, eds., *Glaubensbekenntnis und Kirchengemeinschaft*, 100–125.

64 Lehmann & Pannenberg, eds., *Glaubensbekenntnis und Kirchengemeinschaft*, 12, introduction.

65 Karl Lehmann & Edmund Schlink, eds., *Evangelium, Sakramente, Amt und Einheit der Kirche: Die ökumenische Tragweite der Confessio Augustana*, DiKi 2, Freiburg i.Br./Göttingen, Herder/Vandenhoeck & Ruprecht, 1982.

66 Karl Lehmann, ed., *Das Opfer Jesu Christi und seine Gegenwart in der Kirche. Klärungen zum Opfercharakter des Herrenmahles*, DiKi 3, Freiburg i.Br./Göttingen, Herder/Vandenhoeck & Ruprecht, 1986.

67 Lehmann & Schlink, eds., *Evangelium, Sakramente, Amt und Einheit der Kirche*, 184, thesis 1.

68 Lehmann & Schlink, eds., *Evangelium, Sakramente, Amt und Einheit der Kirche*, 184, thesis 2.

69 Lehmann & Schlink, eds., *Evangelium, Sakramente, Amt und Einheit der Kirche*, 184f.

70 Lehmann & Schlink, eds., *Evangelium, Sakramente, Amt und Einheit der Kirche*, 185, thesis 3.

71 Lehmann & Schlink, eds., *Evangelium, Sakramente, Amt und Einheit der Kirche*, 185, thesis 4.

grounds. The fundamental question for the sacrificial nature of the Lord's Supper, namely "whether the Lord's Supper/Eucharist can be called a sacrifice and even a 'sacrifice of the church,'" is essential to understanding the very nature of church. According to the editors Karl Lehmann and Edmund Schlink, this question is one of "the most difficult and disputed issues between Reformation and Roman Catholic theology."[72] In its exploration of the subject, the ÖAK goes beyond the state of the question reached in the *Das Herrenmahl* published by the Gemeinsame römisch-katholische/evangelisch-lutherische Kommission (Joint Roman Catholic-Lutheran Commission) in 1978.[73] No complete consensus had been reached here on the question of its sacrificial nature. In its final report, the ÖAK identifies "the Word from *self-surrender out of love*" as the center of the Christian understanding of sacrifice.[74] The "*singularity and unique nature of Christ's sacrifice* in his life and death" is highlighted. During the celebration, "the movement of surrender from God to human beings" is fundamental.[75] "Therefore, within this action of God for our salvation *a turning of human beings to God* is demanded and made possible, which is conveyed in the participation in God's turning to the world."[76] The Lord's Supper and the Eucharist are about making present Jesus Christ's voluntary self-surrender in the visible symbol of the meal, where the presence of Christ's sacrifice is transmitted through the power of the spirit. In remembering the death of their Lord and by praying, "*the congregation celebrating the Lord's Supper partakes of Jesus Christ's sacrifice*."[77] "Thus, the church's sacrifice does not mean the offering to God of a holy gift facing us on the altar through the hand of a human priest, but reception of the church in Christ's surrender, that is the *offering of ourselves* through, with and in Jesus Christ *as living sacrifice*."[78] In this treatment of the sacrificial nature, it can be seen that the ÖAK wants to express the church's active inclusion in the event of sacrifice, but not in such a way that the church itself is the subject of the event, but rather such that its involvement depends on Jesus's self-sacrifice, which occurred once for eternity and his promise of self-realization in the Words of Institution.

2.2 *Lehrverurteilungen, kirchentrennend?*

Undoubtedly the ÖAK's most influential work remains *Lehrverurteilungen, kirchentrennend?*,[79] which examined the subject of justification, the sacraments, and ministry. The study has its origin in Pope John Paul II's visit to Germany in November 1980. The pope met with the *Landesbischof*, Eduard Lohse, in Mainz. As a member of the ÖAK and chairperson of the EKD council, Lohse "urged an improvement in ecumenical cooperation regarding Sunday church services, Eucharistic communion and marriage between people of different confessions."[80] Afterwards a joint ecumenical commission was set up (1981–1985). This commission established that the ecumenical tasks first required a theological

72 Lehmann, ed., *Das Opfer Jesu Christi*, 9.

73 Gemeinsame römisch-katholische/evangelisch-lutherische Kommission, *Das Herrenmahl*, Padeborn/Frankfurt a.M., Bonifatius/Otto Lembeck, 1978.

74 Lehmann, ed., *Das Opfer Jesu Christi*, 231.

75 Lehmann, ed., *Das Opfer Jesu Christi*, 232.

76 Lehmann, ed., *Das Opfer Jesu Christi*, 232.

77 Lehmann, ed., *Das Opfer Jesu Christi*, 236. A joint statement reads: "We have nothing else to offer God that could please him other than Jesus Christ and his sacrifice. This can be the only sense when the congregation united in its Lord – and only through him, with him and in him itself – offers Jesus Christ to God by presenting his merit before the Father's eyes: his Son's obedient suffering consummated for once and eternity, by which the congregation believes its own life is surrounded." (236) However, this statement taken on its own would appear problematic from a Protestant point of view, at least insofar as the church comes to take on the role of the subject of the representation of the Son's self-sacrifice.

78 Lehmann, ed., *Das Opfer Jesu Christi*, 237.

79 *Lehrverurteilungen, kirchentrennend?*, vol. 1, Karl Lehmann & Wolfhart Pannenberg, eds., *Rechtfertigung, Sakramente und Amt im Zeitalter der Reformation und heute*, DiKi 4, Freiburg i.Br./Göttingen, Herder/Vandenhoeck & Ruprecht, 1986.

80 *Lehrverurteilungen, kirchentrennend?*, vol. 1, 9, introduction of the editors.

appraisal of controversial theological differences and how to handle the 16th century doctrinal condemnations at the Council of Trent and in Lutheran and Reformation confessional writings, since these called into doubt a common witness. The ÖAK was charged with the resulting task of a "cleanup of the past."[81] Specifically at issue were the interrelated questions of whether the accusations of the Reformation period "still apply to today's partner,"[82] and whether the joint statements achieved in convergence texts could be taken up by the churches. Chaired by Cardinal Volk and Bishop Hermann Kunst and under the academic directorship of Karl Lehmann and Wolfhart Pannenberg, the ÖAK worked between 1981 and 1985, subdivided into three separate groups on justification, sacraments, and ministry.

In order to fulfill its remit at the suggestion of Wolfhart Pannenberg, the ÖAK included Reformed theologians for the first time.[83] This was not least due to the fact that the fellowship of churches had become possible between many Lutheran, United, Reformed, and pre-Reformed churches through the Leuenberg Concord of 1973.[84] The doctrine of justification offered the basis for this fellowship among Protestants since it had not been the object of condemnation between the Reformed and Lutheran traditions. The doctrinal differences dividing the churches on Christology, the doctrine of predestination, and the Lord's Supper could be superseded in the Leuenberg Concord on this common basis. The Lutheran-Reformed consensus on the understanding of the Eucharist could therefore serve as a basis for the investigation of the ÖAK's questions regarding the Eucharist and the Lord's Supper in *Lehrverurteilungen, kirchentrennend?*. At the same time, the Leuenberg Concord, as Karl Lehmann and Wolfhart Pannenberg point out in the introduction to the book, had "acquired the function of an initial spark methodologically."[85] Unlike the Leuenberg Concord, however, in *Lehrverurteilungen, kirchentrennend?* "no 'concord' was sought which represents a binding agreement and seeks to restore the fellowship of churches directly."[86] Instead, the aim was solely a careful investigation and review of the condemnations. The lines of inquiry concerned who the precise target of the condemnations were, whether or not the "condemnation sentence (*Verwerfungssatz*) correctly identified the targeted position,"[87] whether or not "that statement of rejected doctrine still applies to the position taken by the partner in question today," and, if so, "what weight and importance ... the remaining difference" continues to have.[88]

In the redress to these fundamental questions, in the treatment of the doctrine on justification, the differences "as one understood them previously" are first analyzed, which relate to the understanding of original sin, the corruption of human nature, and concupiscence, the understanding of the human role and the effectiveness of justification, and of *sola fide*, assurance of salvation, and of good works and merits. In the next step, new insights are presented which open up the possibility of a reassessment. Finally, it is shown in respect to individual subjects of the rejected doctrines that the condemnations no longer apply to the partner nowadays, and to what extent. The joint conclusion states: "As far as the understanding of the justification of the sinner is concerned, the 16th-century condemnations discussed here by both sides no longer apply to the partner today in such a way as to have a divisive effect on the church."[89] This formulation immediately indicates that not all differences have been resolved or set

81 *Lehrverurteilungen, kirchentrennend?*, vol. 1, 10.

82 *Lehrverurteilungen, kirchentrennend?*, vol. 1, 11.

83 Schwahn, *Der Ökumenische Arbeitskreis*, 97.

84 See Michael Bünker & Martin Friedrich, eds., *Konkordie reformatorischer Kirchen in Europa (Leuenberger Konkordie)*, Leipzig, Evangelische Verlagsanstalt, 2013. On the drawing up process of this document, see the contribution by Elisabeth Parmentier in this volume.

85 *Lehrverurteilungen, kirchentrennend?*, vol. 1, 14.

86 *Lehrverurteilungen, kirchentrennend?*, vol. 1, 14.

87 *Lehrverurteilungen, kirchentrennend?*, vol. 1, 15.

88 *Lehrverurteilungen, kirchentrennend?*, vol. 1, 15.

89 *Lehrverurteilungen, kirchentrennend?*, vol. 1, 74.

aside, as established in the second point of the summary. However, in light of a review of the condemnations, the questions at issue are no longer "of the kind whose answer would mark the decision on the true and false church; in other words, that with them 'the church stands and falls.'"[90] They can now be regarded as "theological tasks to be taken seriously ... which must continue to be pursued, including in legitimate theological dispute, *within* the one church, which must not collapse because of them."[91] Finally, in a third point, the doctrine of justification is provided as a critical measure, namely in reference to the fact that the consensus reached on the condemnations again appears fragile where new doctrines are affected by the old doctrinal condemnations. The church's critical measure must serve to examine "whether the church's proclamation and practice corresponds to what is enjoined upon it by its Lord."[92] This examination of the condemnations of the theology of justification in *Lehrverurteilungen, kirchentrennend?* proved to be one of the fundamental prerequisites in drawing up the *Joint Declaration on the Doctrine of Justification.*[93] This declaration was signed on Reformation Day in 1999 by the President of the LWF and the President of the Pontifical Council for Promoting Christian Unity in Augsburg. The *Joint Declaration on the Doctrine of Justification* has since also been subscribed to by the World Methodist Council (2006), the Anglican Communion (2016), and the WCRC (2017).

Part 2 of *Lehrverurteilungen, kirchentrennend?* deals with the sacraments, looking first at the understanding and number of sacraments. This is followed by an examination of the doctrinal differences and condemnations in relation to the Eucharist/the Lord's Supper, confirmation, extreme unction, and marriage. Among the most important findings is that the difference in the number of sacraments need not be categorized as divisive between the churches, since, apart from the *sacramenta maiora* (baptism and the Lord's Supper), other church acts ordained by God are celebrated in Lutheran churches too. The examination of the condemnations concerning the doctrine of the Lord's Supper is particularly important. This includes problems in controversial theology, which were fundamental during the Reformation, namely the questions concerning the sacrificial nature of the Lord's Supper, the real presence of Christ, and the two forms of communion. In the discussion on the real presence, the redress succeeds, through a meticulous explanation of the origin and intention of the doctrine of transubstantiation, the reasons for its rejection in the Reformation, the Lutheran doctrine of ubiquity, and the Christological prerequisites, in describing the Catholic, Lutheran, and Reformed doctrine as three doctrinal forms, two of which agree on a given theological doctrine. Thus, Catholics and Lutherans agree on the doctrine of the real presence of the body, Catholics and Reformed share their rejection of the Lutheran doctrine of ubiquity and its Christological prerequisites, while Reformed and Lutherans for their part reject the doctrine of transubstantiation.[94] It also becomes clear that not only in the Catholic and Lutheran, but also in the Reformed doctrine following John Calvin, the true presence of Jesus Christ in the celebration of the Lord's Supper is known in relation to the elements and that the "clear and unequivocal confession of the true presence of Christ ... is not necessarily tied to the explanatory model ... proposed by the doctrine of transubstantiation or the doctrine of ubiquity."[95] As far as the sacrificial nature of the Mass is concerned, in *Lehrverurteilungen, kirchentrennend?* the ÖAK is

90 *Lehrverurteilungen, kirchentrennend?*, vol. 1, 74.

91 *Lehrverurteilungen, kirchentrennend?*, vol. 1, 75.

92 *Lehrverurteilungen, kirchentrennend?*, vol. 1, 75.

93 For the text of the declaration, see: Harding Meyer & others, eds., *Dokumente wachsender Übereinstimmung: Sämtliche Berichte und Konsenstexte interkonfessioneller Gespräche auf Weltebene*, vol. 3, *1990–2001*, Padeborn, Bonifatius, 2003, 419–441.

94 On this, see *Lehrverurteilungen, kirchentrennend?*, vol. 1, 104–108.

95 *Lehrverurteilungen, kirchentrennend?*, vol. 1, 107, thesis 2.

able to cite the study on the sacrificial nature of the Lord's Supper. It is agreed "that Christ's sacrifice on the cross can 'neither be continued or repeated, nor replaced or complemented,'"[96] and that the "liturgical and conceptual *division between sacrificium (sacrifice) on the one hand and sacramentum (sacrament) on the other*," which is decisive for understanding the sacrificial nature, "can be considered resolved in Eucharistic doctrine and practice."[97] A revision of the condemnations dividing the church is also achieved with regard to the prohibition of the lay chalice and thus to the question concerning which settlement talks fell apart after the Diet of Augsburg.

Part three of *Lehrverurteilungen, kirchentrennend?* looks at the subject of ministry, identifying the fundamental theological questions on the subject as well as major areas of agreement. These concern the concept and deployment of ministry, the sacramentality of ordination, the effect of ordination, the structure of ministry and succession of office, and finally the role of the papacy. Whereas with regard to the doctrine of justification and the Lord's Supper the condemnations could be reassessed in such a way that their power to divide the church could be deemed settled, this degree of clarification is not obtained for the question of ministry. In particular, the question of the historical apostolic succession in the episcopate and the jurisdictional power of the papacy are identified as fundamental questions requiring further study.

2.3 *Verbindliches Zeugnis*

It became clear to its members during the course of the ÖAK's work that the theme of the theological principles of the sources and of the criteria of theological knowledge are fundamental in exploring the question of truth in ecumenical rapprochement. This issue had already been dealt with in the early years. However, the work on *Lehrverurteilungen, kirchentrennend?* and the possibility of further agreement particularly on the question of ministry meant it made sense to address the methodological question thoroughly once again. This took place during the working sessions held from 1986 to 1998. The findings were published in three volumes under the heading *Verbindliches Zeugnis*. The first volume in 1992 is devoted to the subject *Kanon, Schrift, Tradition*,[98] the second volume (also 1992) contains contributions on *Schriftauslegung, Lehramt, Rezeption*[99] and an interim report. The third volume, which appeared in 1998, considers the relationship between *Schriftverständnis und Schriftgebrauch*,[100] and provides a wide-ranging concluding report. The studies clearly show that the traditional conflict over the Reformation principle of *sola scriptura* and the relationship between Scripture and Tradition has shifted in the light of contemporary standards because the origin of biblical texts and the collection of the biblical canon can themselves be seen as the result of the process of tradition. Although, in the Roman Catholic definition of the relationship, the critical role of Scripture with respect to tradition is not emphasized in the same way as it is by Protestants, the decisive question today is ultimately the magisterium's role and doctrinal authority, as the concluding report highlights.

2.4 *Gerecht und Sünder zugleich?*

In 2001, two years after the *Joint Declaration on the Doctrine of Justification* was signed, the ÖAK published *Gerecht und Sünder zugleich?*. This was part of the discussion on the *Joint Declaration*, in which

96 *Lehrverurteilungen, kirchentrennend?*, vol. 1, 90.

97 *Lehrverurteilungen, kirchentrennend?*, vol. 1, 92 (italics original).

98 Wolfhart Pannenberg & Theodor Schneider, eds., *Verbindliches Zeugnis*, vol. 1, *Kanon, Schrift, Tradition*, DiKi 7, Freiburg i.Br./Göttingen, Herder/Vandenhoeck & Ruprecht, 1992.

99 Pannenberg & Schneider, eds., *Verbindliches Zeugnis*, vol. 2, *Schriftauslegung, Lehramt, Rezeption*, DiKi 9, Freiburg i.Br./Göttingen, Herder/Vandenhoeck & Ruprecht, 1995.

100 Pannenberg & Schneider, eds., *Verbindliches Zeugnis*, vol. 3, *Schriftverständnis und Schriftgebrauch*, DiKi 10, Freiburgi.Br./Göttingen, Herder/Vandenhoeck & Ruprecht, 1998.

"the question of concupiscence and sin in the righteous [had proven to be] a particular obstacle."[101] As the ÖAK notes, it is disputable whether "the relevant formulations of the 'Official Common Statement,' which made signature possible in the first place, [had] explained this point of disagreement legitimately."[102] In a talk given to the full assembly of the German Bishops' Conference in autumn 1998, Cardinal Lehmann had admitted that the clarification of this formulation is "undoubtedly an acid test for the shared description of the reality of the justification of human beings."[103] The concluding report summarizes the results of the investigations from the perspectives of exegesis, of the history of dogma, of systematic-theological, of church law, and of liturgical science.[104] Its aim is not "to find a uniform theological formula which reduces the Protestant doctrine of 'righteous and sinner at the same time' and its traditional rejection by Catholics to a common denominator."[105] Rather, the ÖAK – taking as its point of departure that both sides "have their own confessional and ecumenical legitimacy based on a common fundamental belief"[106] – is concerned "to show that, in the question of 'righteous and sinner at the same time,' the divergent doctrines of the two confessions can be understood and interpreted under hermeneutical conditions accepted by both of them in such a way that they cease to represent mutually exclusive doctrinal statements but rather are able to serve as complementary corrections and additions in a shared interpretation of Holy Scripture and of ecclesiastical traditions."[107] First of all, the finding common to both confessions is crucial, whereby today most New Testament research interprets the relevant passage in "Romans 7:7–25 not as referring to righteous Christians but to people before their encounter with Christ."[108] It is true that "according to the current state of exegetical research the *simul iustus et peccator*, as Luther interpreted it in Paul following certain formulations of Augustine, does not have a solid basis in Romans 7."[109] Nonetheless, the formulation draws attention to the basic question in the Old Testament already touched upon of how it should "be explained and interpreted that members of a salvific community, even baptized Christians, also sin."[110] It is clear that for Paul carnal desire does not cease after baptism, but persists "in the thoughts and actions of Christians."[111] However, referring to sinner and righteous "is understood in the sense of radical asymmetry."[112] Tied to the Lutheran affirmation of the sinfulness of the righteous and the controlled sin is the task of explaining how the new constitution of humans can be appropriately expressed through baptism. On the other hand, the Catholic tradition teaches that "the lust (*concupiscentia*) latent in the Christian as the spark for sin (*fomes peccati*) is not 'sin' in the true sense of the word,"[113] because sin always implies an active, voluntary, and rational human involvement. This view raises "the question of the connection between sinful desire contrary to the ninth and

101 Theodor Schneider & Gunther Wenz, eds., *Gerecht und Sünder zugleich?: Ökumenische Klärungen*, DiKi 11, Freiburg i.Br./Göttingen, Herder/Vandenhoeck & Ruprecht, 2001, 7, foreword.

102 Schneider & Wenz, eds., *Gerecht und Sünder zugleich?*, 7, foreword.

103 Schneider & Wenz, eds., *Gerecht und Sünder zugleich?*, 7, foreword.

104 Schneider & Wenz, eds., *Gerecht und Sünder zugleich?*, 400–456.

105 Schneider & Wenz, eds., *Gerecht und Sünder zugleich?*, 406.

106 Schneider & Wenz, eds., *Gerecht und Sünder zugleich?*, 406.

107 Schneider & Wenz, eds., *Gerecht und Sünder zugleich?*, 406f.

108 Schneider & Wenz, eds., *Gerecht und Sünder zugleich?*, 408.

109 Schneider & Wenz, eds., *Gerecht und Sünder zugleich?*, 421.

110 Schneider & Wenz, eds., *Gerecht und Sünder zugleich?*, 421.

111 Schneider & Wenz, eds., *Gerecht und Sünder zugleich?*, 422.

112 Schneider & Wenz, eds., *Gerecht und Sünder zugleich?*, 422.

113 Schneider & Wenz, eds., *Gerecht und Sünder zugleich?*, 422.

tenth commandments (see Romans 13:9)"[114] and the problem of finding an appropriate "term for sin's devastating power," which comes alive again in the flesh of the Christian so "that he does not let himself be 'led by the spirit' (Galitians 5:16)."[115] In the report's exegetical section, the authors conclude that the undeniable differences specific to each confession cannot be played off against one another in the New Testament, but turn out to be "absolutely proper applications of the Pauline doctrine of justification."[116] After outlining historical developments, the fourth part provides a systematic reflection which, starting from preliminary hermeneutical considerations, analyzes the expression *simul iustus et peccator* in reference to a baptized person. Consideration is first given to what it means for the baptized person to be righteous, and then sin in the life of the Christian is examined. This anticipates the conclusion subsequently arrived at, namely, that the affirmation or rejection of "righteous and sinner at the same time" corresponds to different descriptions of the same reality. From a systematic-theological perspective, point 28 of the *Joint Declaration on the Doctrine of Justification* states that the justified "must all through life constantly look to God's unconditional justifying grace"[117] and that they do not escape from sin. In reflecting on the sinfulness of remaining concupiscence, the Roman Catholic side explores concupiscence as a determination contrary to God.[118] In conclusion, "despite the different approaches by the Catholic and Lutheran sides,"[119] a differentiated consensus and shared understanding can be established: "The baptized also sin according to their remaining desire contrary to God and must therefore judge themselves as *peccatores* for themselves and in relation to themselves. In Christ, on the other hand, who is the foundation of their faith, they are *iusti* and truly justified before God."[120]

2.5 *Church Ministry in the Apostolic Succession*

Gerecht und Sünder zugleich? concluded for the time being the ÖAK's exploration of justification theology. It then turned its attention once again to the subject of ministry. This had been discussed at a number of previous meetings: in 1969 in "Autorität in der Krise"; in 1971 in "Sacerdotium und Ministerium"; in 1974 in "Die Lehre von der Ordination unter Bezug auf die geltenden Ordinationsformulare"; in 1975 in "Presbyterat und Episkopat unter Bezug auf die apostolische Tradition"; and then as part of the study on the doctrinal condemnations. The first two meetings in 2002 and 2003 concentrated on keynote speeches, while the first two volumes appeared in 2004 with contributions on basic principles and questions, and on origins and transformations.[121] Two contributions deserve special mention: the in-depth exegetical study by Jörg Frey on "Apostelbegriff, Apostelamt und Apostolizität. Neutestamentliche Perspektiven zur Frage nach der 'Apostolizität' der Kirche"[122] on the Protestant side; and by Thomas

114 Schneider & Wenz, eds., *Gerecht und Sünder zugleich?*, 422.

115 Schneider & Wenz, eds., *Gerecht und Sünder zugleich?*, 422.

116 Schneider & Wenz, eds., *Gerecht und Sünder zugleich?*, 422.

117 Meyer & others, eds., *Dokumente wachsender Übereinstimmung*, vol. 3, 426.

118 See Schneider & Wenz, eds., *Gerecht und Sünder zugleich?*, 446f.

119 Schneider & Wenz, eds., *Gerecht und Sünder zugleich?*, 455.

120 Schneider & Wenz, eds., *Gerecht und Sünder zugleich?*, 422.

121 *Das kirchliche Amt in apostolischer Nachfolge*, vol. 1, Theodor Schneider & Gunther Wenz, eds., *Grundlagen und Grundfragen*, DiKi 12, Freiburg i.Br./Göttingen, Herder/Vandenhoeck & Ruprecht, 2004; *Das kirchliche Amt in apostolischer Nachfolge*, vol. 2, Dorothea Sattler & Gunther Wenz, eds., *Ursprünge und Wandlungen*, DiKi 13, Freiburg i.Br./Göttingen, Herder/Vandenhoeck & Ruprecht, 2004.

122 Jörg Frey on "Apostelbegriff, Apostelamt und Apostolizität. Neutestamentliche Perspektiven zur Frage nach der 'Apostolizität' der Kirche," in: *Das kirchliche Amt*, vol. 1, 91–188. This represents the most comprehensive exegetical study to date on the theology of ministry from a Protestant perspective.

Söding on "Geist und Amt. Übergänge von der Apostolischen zur nachapostolischen Zeit."[123] In the concluding report on points of agreement and differences in the third volume,[124] findings on the biblical witness, the course of church history, and confessional developments are brought together and supplemented by practical theological considerations. In the systematic-theological appraisal, there are reflections on the hermeneutics of "apostolic succession," the meaning of the church as a whole for the apostolic mission, and the differences between presbyterial and episcopal succession, forms of *episkopé*, and ecclesiological scope. The pneumatological perspective in terms of spiritual effectiveness is crucial here for the appraisal of apostolicity. This is proposed by the ÖAK following the study *Die Apostolizität der Kirche* by the Joint Roman Catholic-Lutheran Commission on Unity.[125] Whereas the findings on the relationship of the priesthood of all believers to the ordained ministry, the mission of the ministry, the necessity of *episkopé*, and the understanding of the apostolic succession are similar in content to those in *Die Apostolizität der Kirche* and *Communio Sanctorum*, the particular contribution of the ÖAK's works on ministry was in their historical depth.

2.6 *Other Studies*

In these studies on confession and church, on the doctrinal condemnations concerning justification, on the sacraments and ministry, on the understanding and relationship of scripture, tradition and magisterium, and finally on the theology of ministry, the ÖAK examined and made progress on the major theological controversies at the heart of Protestant-Catholic doctrinal ecumenism. The relevance of the study on church ministry in the apostolic succession was reinforced by the publication of the *Dominus Iesus* declaration in 2000. This pronouncement distinguished those churches that had not preserved the office of bishop in historical apostolic succession from their sister churches as ecclesial communities. Again this made it clear that recognition of the Reformation churches on the part of the Roman Catholic side and the possibility of a fellowship in the Lord's Supper and the Eucharist were contingent upon an agreement on the question of ministry and of apostolic succession. The study on church ministry in apostolic succession certainly brings clarity to the basic questions of the theology of ministry. Agreement on all the questions constitutive for the Roman Catholic side, such as the papacy's role and definition, could not be reached, however. The ÖAK members therefore decided to interrupt their investigation of questions of controversial theology and instead to take up a subject that was challenging for both churches. They began to examine the question of the theology of religions concerning whether there can be salvation outside the Christian faith. Christianity's relationship with non-Christian religions had been the main subject of the *Dominus Iesus* declaration. Their conclusions were published in 2012 in the work *Heil für alle? Ökumenische Reflexionen*.[126] While this volume undoubtedly included differences in religious and theological perspectives, there was general agreement on belief in the universality of the salvation given and revealed in Jesus Christ.

In anticipation of the Reformation's 500th anniversary in 2017, the ÖAK in its sessions from 2011 turned to the question of whether a common perspective and assessment of the Reformation were possible and, if so, how. This resulted in the study *Reformation 1517–2017: Ökumenische Perspektiven* (*Reformation 1517–2017: Ecumenical Perspectives*),[127]

123 Thomas Söding on "Geist und Amt. Übergänge von der Apostolischen zur nachapostolischen Zeit," in: *Das kirchliche Amt*, vol. 1, 189–263.

124 *Das kirchliche Amt in apostolischer Nachfolge*, vol. 3, Dorothea Sattler & Gunther Wenz, eds., *Verständigungen und Differenzen*, DiKi 14, Freiburg i.Br./Göttingen, Herder/Vandenhoeck & Ruprecht, 2008, 167–267.

125 *Das kirchliche Amt*, vol. 3, 261–263.

126 Volker Leppin & Dorothea Sattler, *Heil für alle. Ökumenische Reflexionen*, DiKi 15, Freiburg i.Br./Göttingen, Herder/Vandenhoeck & Ruprecht, 2012.

127 Volker Leppin & Dorothea Sattler, *Reformation 1517–2017: Ökumenische Perspektiven*, DiKi 16, Freiburg i.Br./Göttingen, Herder/Vandenhoeck & Ruprecht, 2014.

published in 2014. This was the first of the ÖAK's work to appear in a German-English bilingual edition. It provided a common view of the Reformation, taking into account the fact that this phenomenon was not confined to the Reformation churches alone, but that a thorough reform of the Roman Catholic Church also occurred in the same period. The Reformation's spiritual significance for church renewal was endorsed by both sides.

In addition to these projects, and after completion of the study on church ministry, the ÖAK also discussed the question of whether a joint declaration on the Lord's Supper was possible and even desirable, and, if so, in which form. These thoughts had been prompted by the fact that many of the group's members considered that the fundamental divisive differences in the church in the understanding of the Lord's Supper and the Eucharist had been resolved in *Lehrverurteilungen, kirchentrennend?*. The question of a joint declaration on the Lord's Supper gained in practical importance after the first two ecumenical *Kirchentage* in Berlin in 2003 and Munich in 2010. There was intense debate at both of these events about whether to hold a joint celebration of the Lord's Supper, which many of those attending fervently desired. The ÖAK initially considered an "*in via* declaration" on the Lord's Supper and the Eucharist. However, in the end it was decided at the meetings of 2016 and 2017 to draw up a joint declaration after all. This was completed in 2019 and announced at a press conference.[128] The document is called *Gemeinsam am Tisch des Herrn*.[129] Based on considerations in exegesis, ecclesiastical history, history of dogma, systematic theology, and liturgy, it states that mutual admission and participation of Protestant Christians in the Roman Catholic Eucharist and Roman Catholic Christians in the Lord's Supper is possible on theological grounds and can be recommended. However, it also states that a joint celebration or inter-celebration must still be ruled out because this would require a full fellowship of churches. The possibility of mutual participation in the Eucharist and the Lord's Supper is thus a step on the path towards greater fellowship but does not constitute the aim of the ecumenical endeavors pursued by the ÖAK since its foundation.

3 Retrospect and Prospect

From examining the history of the ÖAK, its work can be understood as a scholarly theological response to the Una Sancta movement and as a way of responding to that movement's concerns. The development from two parallel groups to a single one alone mirrors the profound changes in ecumenical relations between the Roman Catholic and Protestant churches. The ÖAK made a major contribution to both sides being able to acquire greater knowledge and understanding of their confessional differences, to recognize or rediscover their common beliefs, and pinpoint the historical circumstances and mutual misunderstandings in controversial theological points and resolve them in many aspects. Such a scholarly endeavor progresses more slowly and arduously than the ecumenical relations, which have long been nurtured in the parishes. It is nonetheless seen as essential by both church hierarchies in order to develop sustainable ecumenical ties. Precisely in terms of its contrast to the Una Sancta movement, the ÖAK has served the pursuit of church unity and continues to do so, just as many other bodies for dialogue at a regional, national, and international level do. Moreover, it clearly stated in 1982 that this unity does not exclude diversity but actually embraces it. Establishing what form of unity in diversity is possible and how the global ecumenical aim of visible unity in Catholic-Protestant ecumenism can be understood on a common basis are tasks of future ecumenical rapprochement.

128 See <https://bistumlimburg.de/beitrag/gemeinsam-am-tisch-des-herrn/> (accessed Oct 20, 2022).

129 The document is available at <https://www.uni-heidelberg.de/md/fakultaeten/theologie/oek/gemeinsam_am_tisch_des_herrn._ein_votum_des__kumenischen_arbeitskreises_evangelischer_und_katholischer_theologen.pdf> (accessed Oct 20, 2022).

A consideration of the group's history undoubtedly permits us to affirm that the understanding reached so far has transformed relations between the Roman Catholic Church and the Protestant churches in Germany and many other parts of the world. Rivalry and exclusion have been replaced by the desire to cooperate and friendly relations. A review of the history of religious conflicts, besides the contemporary experience of such conflicts throughout the world, shows how important it is to preserve and nurture this growing fellowship since we know precisely how fragile it is.

Translated from German to English by Fiona Robb.

Bibliography

Bünker, Michael & Martin Friedrich, eds., *Konkordie reformatorischer Kirchen in Europa* (*Leuenberger Konkordie*), Leipzig, Evangelische Verlagsanstalt, 2013.

Burkard, Dominik, "Informanten, Türöffner, und Agenten: Erzbischof Lorenz Jaeger und seine (frühen) römischen Kontakte," in: Nicole Priesching & Gisela Fleckenstein, eds., *Lorenz Jaeger als Theologe*, Paderborn, Schöning, 2019, 33–80.

Gemeinsame römisch-katholische/evangelischlutherische Kommission, *Das Herrenmahl*, Padeborn/Frankfurt a.M., Bonifatius/Otto Lembeck, 1978.

Harding Meyer & others, eds., *Dokumente wachsender Übereinstimmung: Sämtliche Berichte und Konsenstexte interkonfessioneller Gespräche auf Weltebene*, vol. 3, *1990–2001*, Padeborn, Bonifatius, 2003.

Jaeger, Lorenz Kardinal: *Einheit und Gemeinschaft: Stellungnahmen zu Fragen der christlichen Einheit*, ed. Johann-Adam-Möhler-Institut, Paderborn, Schöning, 2019.

Lehrverurteilungen, kirchentrennend?, vol. 1, Karl Lehmann & Wolfhart Pannenberg, eds., *Rechtfertigung, Sakramente und Amt im Zeitalter der Reformation und heute*, DiKi 4, Freiburg i.Br./Göttingen, Herder/Vandenhoeck & Ruprecht, 1986.

Marotta, Saretta, "La genesi di un ecumenista: La corrispondenza fra Augustin Bea e il vescovo di Paderborn Lorenz Jaeger (1951–1960)," in: Luca Ferracci, ed., *Toward a History of the Desire for Christian Unity: Preliminary Research Papers*, Münster, LIT, 2015, 159–191.

Pannenberg, Wolfhart & Theodor Schneider, eds, *Verbindliches Zeugnis*, vol. 1, *Kanon, Schrift, Tradition*, DiKi 7, Freiburg i.Br./Göttingen, Herder/Vandenhoeck & Ruprecht, 1992.

Pannenberg, Wolfhart & Theodor Schneider, eds., *Verbindliches Zeugnis*, vol. 2, *Schriftauslegung, Lehramt, Rezeption*, DiKi 9, Freiburg i.Br./Göttingen, Herder/Vandenhoeck & Ruprecht, 1995.

Pannenberg, Wolfhart & Theodor Schneider, eds., *Verbindliches Zeugnis*, vol. 3, *Schriftverständnis und Schriftgebrauch*, DiKi 10, Freiburgi.Br./Göttingen, Herder/Vandenhoeck & Ruprecht, 1998.

Priesching, Nicole, "Ein konservativer Pragmatiker: Tagung über Kardinal Lorenz Jaeger als Ökumeniker," in: KNA, ÖKI 39, September 2019.

Schwahn, Barbara, *Der Ökumenische Arbeitskreis evangelischer und katholischer Theologen*, Göttingen, Vandenhoeck & Ruprecht, 1996.

Stählin, Wilhelm, *Via Vitae: Lebenserinnerungen*, Kassel, Johannes Stauda, 1968.

Thönissen, Wolfgang, "Lorenz Kardinal Jaeger: Wiedervereinigung im Glauben als Gebot der Gegenwart," in: Christian Möller & others, eds., *Wegbereiter der Ökumene im 20. Jahrhundert*, Göttingen, Vandenhoeck & Ruprecht, 2005, 194–213.

CHAPTER 14

The Ecumenical Study Days of Chevetogne

Peter De Mey and Saretta Marotta

1 The Origins: The Longing for Ecclesiological *Ressourcement* of a New Generation of Louvain Theologians

On Jul 4, 1942,[1] a few months after Rome's condemnation of the work of the two Dominicans Marie-Dominique Chenu and Louis Charlier,[2] the Belgian Archbishop Jozef-Ernest Van Roey received a letter from the Holy Office urging him, without any further explanation, to prudently remove the theologian René Draguet from his teaching position at the Faculty of Theology in Louvain. On Jul 22 Draguet himself was informed of the measures taken by the Holy Office against him.[3] This decision struck very hard at the University of Louvain, where Draguet, a specialist in the field of doctrinal history and Eastern patristics, had held since 1927 one of the most important chairs, that of fundamental theology (*Dogmatica generalis*). The removal was the result of the thorough examination to which his course entitled "De notione, obiecto et methodo theologiae" had been subjected by the Holy Office in December 1941, the year when he published a general survey on the history of Catholic dogma.[4] It was common knowledge that the disputed book by Charlier was based on college notes taken during Draguet's courses,[5] whose studies focused on the notion of tradition, the role of the magisterium, the development of dogma and the methods of theology, which were all aspects of the "two sources of faith" question, that would finally be addressed by Vatican II.[6] When Draguet was removed from teaching, his students not only lost a mentor, but were severely affected in their theological research, in which they hoped to find a solution to the uncomfortable distance and frequent contradictions between speculative theology and Holy Scriptures. From March 1942, about 20 students and young researchers of the Faculty of Theology in Louvain had begun to meet monthly in a confidential "theological circle," to which some professors and Draguet himself had

1 Sections 1–3 of this contribution were written by Saretta Marotta, and sections 4–6 by Peter De Mey. All translations from French have been provided by the authors and by Susan Dawson Vàsquez and David Dawson Vàsquez (in the footnotes).

2 The censorship on their works (Marie-Dominique Chenu, *Une école de théologie: Le Saulchoir*, Etiolles, Le Saulchoir, 1937; Louis Charlier, *Essai sur le problème théologique*, Thuillies, Ramgal, 1938) intervened in February 1942 and the two Dominicans were removed from teaching, respectively from Paris and Louvain. See: *AAS* 34, 1942, 37 and 148; Robert Guelluy, "Les antécédents de l'encyclique 'Humani Generis' dans les sanctions romaines de 1942: Chenu, Charlier, Draguet," *RHE* 81, 1986, 420–497; Jürgen Mettepenningen, "L'Essai de Louis Charlier (1938): Une contribution à la nouvelle théologie," *RTL* 39, 2008, 211–232; Étienne Fouilloux, "L'affaire Chenu 1937–1943," *RSPT* 98, 2014, 261–352.

3 ADDF, *Censura librorum 1942*, 113/1942. The decision of the Holy Office against Draguet was taken on Jul 1. About the background to the removal, see Ward De Pril, *Theological Renewal and the Resurgence of Integrism: The René Draguet Case (1942) in Its Context*, Leuven, Peeters, 2016, 208–221.

4 René Draguet, *Histoire du dogme catholique*, Paris, Albin Michel, 1941.

5 Decision taken on Dec 17, 1941, in: ADDF, *Censura librorum 1942*, 113/1942. De Pril compares the work of Draguet and Charlier, claiming that, ever since the *Essai sur le problème théologique* had come out in 1938, rumors were circulating that Draguet was its real author. See De Pril, *Theological Renewal*, 16–17 and 85–119. Draguet himself, in a review of Charlier's book, pointed out that the Dominican – without his knowledge – had been heavily inspired by his course: see René Draguet, "Review of Essai sur le problème théologique by L. Charlier," *ETL* 16, 1939, 143–145.

6 On the debate, see Karim Schelkens, *Catholic Theology of Revelation on the Eve of Vatican II: A Redaction History of the Schema De fontibus revelationis (1960–1962)*, Leiden, Brill, 2010; Riccardo Burigana, *La Bibbia nel concilio: La redazione della costituzione "Dei verbum" del Vaticano II*, Bologna, Il Mulino, 1998.

been invited to speak, the latter during the circle's last meeting on Jul 19, three days before learning of the Holy Office's measure against him.[7] The discussions focused on the central place of the Bible in theology and the need for renewal in the Catholic Church, even if the term "adaptation" was preferred. After Draguet's removal, no further meetings took place in Louvain, and the 30-year-old Charles Moeller, one of the most active theologians in the circle, was looking for a more protected place than the university to continue these discussions.[8] Since 1941, he had re-established contact with the Benedictine monk and editor of the journal *Irénikon*, Clément Lialine, whom he had met ten years earlier as a fellow student in Louvain. Moeller probably thought that the Belgian monastery of Chevetogne might be the ideal place to continue this experience of joint research and discussion.[9]

Lialine, a Russian emigrant and convert from Orthodoxy to Catholicism who had entered the monastery of Amay-sur-Meuse in 1928 in order to devote himself to the work for Christian unity, was one of Lambert Beauduin's most remarkable disciples.[10] During the enforced absence of Dom Beauduin from Chevetogne (1931–1951),[11] he took care to keep his ideal alive and, deeply attached to the spiritual traditions of his country and his church of origin, he promoted a better knowledge of Eastern liturgy and theology in the West. Since he had maintained a correspondence with several friends from his theological studies in Louvain – among whom in particular Moeller – in that summer of 1942, on the eve of the feast of the Transfiguration,[12] he warmly welcomed his former fellow students into the monastery. They thus finally found a place to continue their discussions and also had the opportunity to familiarize themselves with Eastern spirituality. The meetings continued every year, always during the summer holidays. Lialine and these young theologians were obviously unaware that they had given birth to an institution that would exist until 1999.

From Aug 2 to 5, 1942, in the midst of World War II, Moeller, together with his 27-year-old colleague Roger Aubert,[13] converged on the monastery near Namur for the first of those "theological days"

7 The elected president for the session was the Benedictine Paul Denis. Lucien Cerfaux attended each session as professor. Also present at the meeting of Jul 19 was the Vice-Rector Léon-Joseph Suenens, the future archbishop of Malines (1961–1979) and one of the four cardinal moderators of the council. See the minutes of the sessions from Mar 23 to Jul 19, 1942, in: UCL-LG, Charles Moeller, papiers, 1942.

8 For more information on this theologian, see Fernand Colleye, *Charles Moeller et l'Arbre de la Croix: Crise de l'Église et désarrois du Monde. La vie d'un théologien du XXème siècle*, Paris, Publibook, 2007.

9 Étienne Fouilloux, *Les catholiques et l'unité chrétienne du XIXème au XXème siècle: Itinéraires européens d'expression française*, Paris, Le Centurion, 1982, 769, based on an interview with the author in July 1970. Moeller met Clément Lialine at the Benedictine abbey of Mont César in Louvain, where he received a significant part of his seminary studies.

10 Olivier Rousseau, "Dom Clément Lialine (1901–1958)," *Irén* 31, 1958, 165–182; Michel Van Parys, "Dom Clément Lialine: Théologien de l'unité chrétienne," *Irén* 76, 2003, 240–269.

11 Jacques Mortiau & Raymond Loonbeek, *Dom Lambert Beauduin visionnaire et précurseur (1873–1960): Un moine au cœur libre*, Paris, Cerf/Éditions de Chevetogne, 2005, 193–226.

12 Rousseau attributes the origin of the Ecumenical Study Days of Chevetogne to Lialine's initiative to bring together a small group of young theologians from Louvain on the occasion of some important Orthodox liturgical feasts, such as the Transfiguration on Aug 6 and the Feast of the Cross on Sep 14: "They [the ecumenical study days] had for their object the deepening, often prolonged in endless discussions, of the liturgical texts of these feasts which, in the Byzantine Rite, are of a very spiritual significance and of an incomparable doctrinal richness"; Olivier Rousseau, "Les journées œcuméniques de Chevetogne (1942–1967)," in: *Au service de la parole de Dieu: Mélanges offerts à Monseigneur André Charue, évêque de Namur*, Gembloux, Duculot, 1969, 451–485, here 452.

13 Moeller had introduced Aubert, who was at that time a doctoral student, to Lialine one year before. See the autobiographical memories written by Aubert to Moeller, Nov 25, 1952, in: UCL-LG, Charles Moeller, papiers, 1942. Aubert had become interested in ecumenism during his military service in Leopoldsburg, through the chaplain Guillaume Vander Elst, a disciple of Beauduin himself. See Colleye, *Charles Moeller*, 129–130.

which would be later officially called Ecumenical Study Days of Chevetogne (Journées œcuméniques de Chevetogne). The group involved in this first initiative was very small: no more than six people,[14] including four Benedictine monks and among them Théodore Strotmann, who would become a frequent speaker at the study days in the following years, and the New Testament scholar Jacques Dupont, from Saint-André-de-Clerlande, at that time a long-term guest of the monastery during his studies.[15] Despite the small number, the discussion, which was centered on the theme "Écriture et Magistère," was nonetheless of a high level, picking up the thread of the previous meeting in Louvain. The handwritten notes taken by Dupont and the report on the session written by Moeller, testify to the intensity of the discussion.[16] The Belgian theologians were dissatisfied about the extensive use of biblical expressions as a mere source of *auctoritates* for deductive theological affirmation (as if they were some "glosses to the Denzinger," according to a metaphor used by Draguet and taken up also in the Louvain circle). In Draguet's footsteps, the Chevetogne group advocated a double return to the two sources of revelation: on the one hand to the Holy Scripture and on the other to the authentic tradition of the church. Furthermore, they perceived the "fullness of Christian truth present above all and even only in the tradition of the living magisterium."[17] It was precisely the living magisterium that had to constitute the *regula proxima* for Christian faith and life. According to them, the tradition of the church consisted indeed not only of the extraordinary or explicit magisterium (the dogmatic definitions of councils and so on), but also of the ordinary magisterium, the living tradition of the church, which expresses itself in other ways, such as the liturgy in the first place. These reflections, which had previously given rise to a written consultation in Louvain on the subject,[18] were all issues with ecumenical implications, since also Protestant and Orthodox theologians had denounced the lack of vitality of Catholic theology. It is not by chance, therefore, that the starting point of the debates in Chevetogne, in addition to the results of the discussions of the Louvain theological circle, were the proceedings of the Orthodox Theological Conference that had taken place in Athens in 1936 and which Draguet had included in the program of his courses.[19] Thanks to two lectures delivered there by the theologian Georges Florovsky, Orthodox

14 "A half-dozen Catholics"; according to Albert Verdoodt, *Les colloques œcuméniques de Chevetogne (1942–1983) et la réception par l'église catholique de charismes d'autres communions chrétiennes*, Chevetogne, Éditions de Chevetogne, 1986, 7.

15 According to Jacques Dupont's notes (preserved in AAC, fund "Journées œcuméniques" – henceforth abbreviated as AJOC – and limited to the first three sessions, 1942–1945) and the memories of Aubert (letter to Moeller, Nov 25, 1952), the participants in this first meeting were: Clément Lialine; Charles Moeller; Roger Aubert; Jacques Dupont; Robert Van Cauwelaert; and Théodore Strotmann.

16 Moeller had probably hoped to publish this report in *Irénikon*, but from 1941 to 1944 the community was obliged to put its publication activities on hold. In 1953, Moeller collected the conference reports of the first ten years of the Ecumenical Study Days in a book that has remained unpublished: Charles Moeller, *Le mouvement pour l'unité à la croisée des Chemins: Dix années d'œcuménisme à Chevetogne, 1942–1951* (manuscript finished on Jan 19, 1953 and preserved in AJOC). Later this work was summarized in Verdoodt, *Les colloques œcuméniques*, which remained one of the few historical reconstructions of the Study Days, together with the essays of Rousseau, "Les journées œcuméniques" and Emmanuel Lanne, "Le rôle du monastère de Chevetogne au Deuxième Concile du Vatican," in: Doris Donnelly & others, eds., *The Belgian Contribution to the Second Vatican Council: International Research Conference at Mechelen, Leuven and Louvain-la-Neuve (September 12–16, 2005)*, Leuven, Peeters, 2008, 361–388.

17 Moeller, *Le mouvement pour l'unité*, part I, ch. 1–2.

18 The result of the consultation was a dossier of *vota* of each theologian about the "role of Holy Scripture today in systematic theology." The *vota* are collected in UCL-LG, Charles Moeller, papiers, 1942.

19 "[He] had the audacity, for the time, to put on the program the work of the Athens Conference of Orthodox Theology (1936) or that of S. Bulgakov"; Fouilloux, *Les catholiques et l'unité*, 769. The proceedings had been published in 1939: Hamilkar S. Alivisatos, ed., *Procès-verbaux du Premier Congrès de Théologie Orthodoxe à Athènes, 29 Novembre–6 Décembre 1936*, Athènes, Pyrsos, 1939.

theologians had identified the return to biblical and patristic sources as a way of reaching the heart of the church's true tradition. In the same year as the Jesuits of Lyons launched the collection of patristic texts entitled Sources Chrétiennes aiming to break with neoscholasticism,[20] the *ressourcement* thus constituted the original core and the starting point of the reflections of the study days of Chevetogne as well. In particular, the discussions of 1942 identified the confrontation with Orthodox spirituality and theology as a means of rediscovering the living tradition of the church, so that it was decided to devote the following meeting to a comparison of Eastern and Western ecclesiology.

"Les signes de l'Église dans le catholicisme et l'orthodoxie" was the theme chosen for the 1943 session, held just a few months after the publication of *Mystici corporis Christi*.[21] The theology of the sign applied to ecclesiology was an attempt to go beyond the ecclesiology of the encyclical and to interpret the hierarchical unity as a sign of the church and the church as a visible sign of Christ. This attempt to justify the importance of structures of authority in the divine economy functioned as a response to Orthodox ecclesiology, which considered charismatic holiness a prerequisite for the authority of bishops. The Chevetogne theologians claimed that obedience to a human and imperfect head, which does not necessarily presuppose sanctity, constitutes in itself a true act of faith, because it is an act of faith to see behind this authority a sometimes obscure sign of God. From the comparison between jurisdictional and charismatic authority, the discussions then moved on to the different concepts of holiness, for individuals and as a church. In contrast to the Orthodox ideal of a visible church that would find itself in a continuous state of saintliness and transfiguration, Catholics were aware that the holiness that became manifest at Pentecost is not typical for the daily life of the church but is only the necessary but momentary manifestation of a deeper sanctity, that is the humiliated and crucified holiness of the incarnate Christ. In short, while Eastern theology insists on the transfigured Christ of Mount Tabor, Western theology privileges the suffering, earthly Christ. Similarly, individual sanctity for Catholics was to be achieved by obeying God's will in inhabiting the world, while for the Orthodox the ideal of sanctity was a transfigured one, separated from the world, time, and space, an ideal of which hermit monks were an eloquent example. As a possible solution to the contrast between these different theological systems, Moeller suggested the maturation of a single "total ecclesial consciousness" ("une Église totale"), after the model of the Apostolic Church as another expression of *ressourcement*. Still, the participants in the Chevetogne

20 See Michel Fédou, "Sources Chrétiennes: Patristique et renaissance de la théologie," *Greg* 92, 2011, 781–796, here 797–788 (italics original): "The future collection Sources Chrétiennes did not only have the sole aim of making patristic texts known in French, but, by this very means, it was to contribute to a true renewal. The project implied, first of all, a distancing from a theology which, up until that time, was dominated above all by Thomist, or rather Neo-Thomist, scholasticism: it was a question of rediscovering, upstream, a direct and fruitful contact with the patristic sources, which was to have an impact on the very organization of theological disciplines." See the detailed reconstruction provided by Étienne Fouilloux, *La collection "Sources chrétiennes": Éditer les Pères de l'Église au XXe siècle*, Paris, Cerf, 1995.

21 The session was held from Aug 9 to 12, 1943 and was attended by: Lialine, Moeller, Aubert, Dupont, Luc Lialine (Clément Lialine's brother), Rousseau, the converted Lucien Morren with his wife Hélène ("Mr. and Mrs. Morren, converts from the University of Brussels, whose active presence gave to the exchange of views an overall particularity"; Jacques Dupont's notes in AJOC), Jean Leclercq, Ambroise Verkeulen and a not yet identified Abbé R. Felix. On Aug 10, further guests arrived: Van Cauwelaert, Gisbert Ghysens and some monks of Chevetogne's community, among whom also Strotmann and Stéphane De Vos. The list of participants is inferred from Jacques Dupont's notes in AJOC and Roger Aubert, "Conversations de Chevetogne. Août 1943. Confrontation des points de vue catholique et orthodoxe sur l'Église et en particulier sur la place de la Hiérarchie," in: UCL-LG, Charles Moeller, papiers, 1943.

conversations came to the conclusion that in the end the different ecclesiology (and Christology) of Orthodox and Catholics (differences which were also visible in their liturgies)[22] referred to two different anthropological perspectives and visions of the relationship of Christians with the secular world. Thus it was decided to devote the 1944 session to a reflection on the meaning of Christian humanism. However, this meeting had to be postponed due to the escalation of the war.[23]

2 Lialine's Leap Forward: From an International and Ecumenical Expansion to Clarifying the Meaning of Christian Humanism

After a temporary suspension, a third meeting was planned from Aug 20 to 25, 1945. This meeting bore numerous novelties, resulting from the personal imprint of Lialine, who worked more closely with Moeller in the organization of the ecumenical study days. First of all, the participation in the event increased considerably: 24 participants instead of 15 during the 1943 meeting, among whom were Gustave Thils, Jean Jérôme Hamer and Jean Giblet, and for the first time theologians from beyond the national borders of Belgium attended the conference.[24] The war being over, it was indeed possible for Lialine to invite some of his contacts abroad, especially from France, such as the Jesuit Jean Daniélou, founder of the Sources Chrétiennes series,[25] and the Dominican Yves Marie-Joseph Congar, who had just been released from German captivity:[26] both would become regular guests of the study days. From 1947 (the year before the *Monitum Cum compertum*),[27] this expansion would also become ecumenical, since the first non-Catholic speakers were invited, among whom were Max Thurian, from the Reformed Taizé Community, and Orthodox theologians from the Institut de théologie orthodoxe Saint-Serge in Paris. In this way, the Chevetogne conversations became a very valuable and exceptional experience of direct confrontation between theologians from the Catholic and other Christian confessions in the preconciliar era.

Secondly, from that moment on, the discussions were no longer left to free improvisation, but were stimulated by a precise program of keynote speeches. Even if the theme of Christian humanism was not completely removed from the agenda (and would be proposed again in 1947 and 1948), the new subject of the conference, "Les Églises au sortir de la deuxième guerre mondiale," was introduced by an opening speech by Roger Aubert, who

22 "The byzantine liturgy transports us mysteriously but truly into paradise ... The Latin liturgy, to the contrary, invites us to identify ourselves, in faith, with the humanity of Christ, which we know, also by faith, to be the mediator between God and us, and the bearer of divine life"; Charles Moeller, "Naissance de l'Église totale," in: UCL-LG, Charles Moeller, papiers, 1943, 4. It is a report of the 1943 session, substantially reproduced later in Moeller, *Le mouvement pour l'unité*. This report may have been sent to all the participants, including Jacques Dupont, who on Sep 8 replied to Moeller with a letter of observations (see Dupont to Moeller, Sep 8, 1943, in: AJOC, Jacques Dupont's notes).

23 "We agreed that it is a matter of anthropology that governs all differences between the two churches"; Olivier Rousseau, "Résumé des Conversations théologiques. Chevetogne, 6–12 août 1943," in: UCL-LG, Charles Moeller, papiers, 1943. "If there is one subject that stands out at the end of these discussions in 1943, it is that of supernatural anthropology"; Moeller, *Le mouvement pour l'unité*, part I, ch. 2, 39.

24 Moeller, Aubert, Felix, Giblet, Thils, Morren, Dupont, Rousseau, Clément Lialine, Luc Lialine, Edouard Beauduin (Dom Lambert's nephew), Strotmann, De Vos, Van Cauwelaert, Daniélou, Congar, Hamer, Jean Leclercq and the Benedictine monks from Chevetogne, Mont-César, and Clervaux, Georges Leclercq, Jean Hild, Hébert Roux, François Vandenbroucke, Jean van den Mensbrugghe and Marc Forêt (list taken from AJOC, Jacques Dupont's notes).

25 Daniélou also presented a contribution that was later published in Jean Daniélou, "Les orientations présentes de la pensée religieuse," *Études* 249, 1946, 5–21, and which is often cited as a "manifesto" of the *nouvelle théologie*.

26 Étienne Fouilloux, *Yves Congar (1904–1995): Biographie*, Paris, Salvator, 2020, 97ff.

27 See the contribution by Saretta Marotta in this volume.

gave a broad overview of recent developments in theological trends in Europe at the end of the war period.[28] Aubert illustrated the important changes in theological life between the two wars, such as the rise of the liturgical, biblical, and ecumenical movements, and the challenges associated with this transformation, both in the field of ecclesiology and in that of Christian humanism, which means the relationship between Christianity and the modern world, in light of the different anthropologies (pessimism and positivism) that had been established in the philosophical currents of the last 20 years. The speeches that followed clarified all these aspects one by one, and the return to the sources once again proved to be an essential method of analysis.[29] In particular, the intervention of the Benedictine Jean Leclercq opened up new perspectives,[30] leading to the awareness of the need to investigate theological and ecclesiological questions from a *historical* perspective, with an approach that was not obvious at that time and which was the same as that pursued by the incarnational theology of Le Saulchoir of Chenu and Congar (and condemned by Roman authorities).[31] Another concept that made its first appearance at the Chevetogne conversations precisely during the 1945 meeting was the ecclesiology of the "people of God," introduced by Lialine's intervention in opposition to the approach of the encyclical *Mystici corporis* and which would be further developed especially in the 1950s' sessions on ecclesiology.[32] However, although only three out of eight keynote speeches dealt explicitly with it, the main theme of the conference remained Christian humanism, which Moeller and Aubert, also thanks to the presence of Thils, saw as "the principal task of Christian theology."[33] As Aubert wrote later in his book of 1954:

> In its confrontation with modern thinking, theology has also been led to discover new objects of study, aspects of reality which the theologians in the past considered unnecessary to dwell on, in particular the place of lay people in the Church, the sense of human history in the eyes of the believer and the Christian understanding of temporal values, scientific progress, secular action.[34]

Moeller himself, concluding the report of the 1947 session, also stated:

> Is it not for this reason, among others, that the living magisterium is necessary, that is to say, in order to answer, in the course of the centuries, the new questions which arise for the Christian conscience? Does not our contemporary world ... present us with problems

28 This speech was published as Roger Aubert, "Les grandes tendances théologiques entre les deux-guerres," *ColMechl* 31, 1946, 17–36 and later its contents were developed in the book Roger Aubert, *La théologie catholique au milieu du XXe siècle*, Paris, Castermann, 1954.

29 Here is the complete list of interventions, taken from AJOC, Jacques Dupont's notes: Roger Aubert, "La vie théologique dans l'entre-deux guerres"; Charles Moeller, "Problématique générale de l'humanisme chrétien"; François Vandenbroucke, "Les bases ecclésiologiques du monachisme"; Jean Leclercq, "Médiévisme et unionisme"; Jean Daniélou, "Le mouvement de la pensée religieuse en France des dernières années"; Olivier Rousseau, "L'exégèse patristique"; Clément Lialine, "Deux essais récents de renouvellement théologique dans l'Orthodoxie (Boulgakov et Florovsky)"; Charles Moeller, "Réflexions sur le livre de Vladimir Lossky: La théologie mystique de l'Orient"; Charles Moeller, "Conclusions."

30 Dom Jean Leclercq, "Médiévisme et Unionisme," *Irén* 19, 1946, 6–23. Moeller commented that it was "a veritable revelation," having shown "the true face of the Middle Ages," exploring in particular the monastic context, strongly patristic and therefore closer to dialogue with the East than the usual historical prejudice suggests, seeing it as the starting point of the division among the Churches. See Moeller, *Le mouvement pour l'unité*, part II, ch. 1, 13–14.

31 Marie-Dominique Chenu, *Une école de théologie: Le Saulchoir*, ed. Giuseppe Alberigo, Paris, Cerf, 1985.

32 Rousseau, "Les journées œcuméniques," 456. The 1955 session in particular would reflect on the different "images" of the church, starting with that of the church as bride.

33 See Dries Bosschaert, *The Anthropological Turn, Christian Humanism, and Vatican II: Louvain Theologians preparing the Path for Gaudium et Spes (1942–1965)*, Leuven, Peeters, 2019.

34 Aubert, *La théologie catholique*, 52.

> unknown to the Fathers and which it is precisely the role of the teaching Church to resolve (of course in the light of fundamental Christian principles)? ... On the other hand, there are science and technologies. Will they remain outside? How can we bring them back to God?[35]

This new perspective, which had made its way into contemporary theology for some years, from Jacques Maritain to Karl Rahner,[36] explains why so many of the Chevetogne sessions were devoted to this topic, and particularly the 1947 session, dedicated to the theme of supernatural anthropology in light of the ancient tradition, both Western and Eastern, and which made an attempt to include non-Catholic theologians into the dialogue.

The 1947 session, "L'anthropologie chrétienne," had a rich program of 16 lectures, five of which presented by non-Catholics: the Orthodox Nicholas Arsenev, the Swedish Lutheran theologian Gunnar Rosendal, the Reformed Max Thurian and the two Anglicans Geoffrey Curtis and Patrick Thompson. Among the numerous speeches, which examined the different anthropological visions in past and present theological currents, ranging from patristics to contemporary theology,[37] for the first time the thinking of theologians of the Reformation was studied in Chevetogne, for example through the conference of Hamer on the theology of Karl Barth and that of Max Thurian on John Calvin.[38] The antinomy between the "incarnated" anthropological vision of the Western Church and the "eschatological" vision of the Eastern Church (but also the vision *soli Deo gloria* of the Reformation) was identified by Chevetogne theologians as one of the major obstacles to unity. Their proposal to work in the direction of a possible "earthly humanism" that is, of a human anthropology transfigured by the mystery of the incarnation, basically meant following the same line pursued by Life and Work. "It was therefore a question of *doing ecumenism* by studying what, in each tradition, is authentically Christian and not only what is opposed to a different confession. In this way, *the possibility of new dogmatic developments* had to be integrated into the research."[39] In Moeller's conclusion, it is already possible to note a desire to go beyond Lialine's "irenic methodology,"[40] which above all aimed to highlight fundamental

35 Moeller, *Le mouvement pour l'unité*, part II, ch. 2, 42–43. He had already published Charles Moeller, *Humanisme et sainteté: Témoignages de la littérature occidentale*, Paris, Casterman, 1946.

36 About the latter, see Anton Losinger, *The Anthropological Turn: The Human Orientation of the Theology of Karl Rahner*, New York, Fordham University Press, 2000.

37 See Moeller's long report, which summarizes each theological system in a chronological and historical overview and denounces the poverty of post-Tridentine theology in this respect compared to the past, in Moeller, *Le mouvement pour l'unité*, part II, ch. 2, 1–46.

38 Here is the complete program (taken from UCL-LG, Charles Moeller, papiers, 1947, where one can also find the text of each intervention): Charles Moeller, "Introduction"; Lucien Cerfaux, "L'anthropologie de saint Paul"; Geoffrey Curtis (monk of the Anglican community of Mirfield), "L'anthropologie de saint Irénée"; Olivier Rousseau, "L'anthropologie de la liturgie"; Charles Moeller, "L'anthropologie de l'école d'Antioche"; Gunnar Rosendal, "L'anthropologie du protestantisme"; Jean Chatillon, "L'anthropologie des Victorins"; Jean Jérôme Hamer, "L'anthropologie de Karl Barth"; Clément Lialine, "L'anthropologie des Pères ascétiques"; Yves-Marie-Jospeh Congar, "L'anthropologie chez S. Thomas"; Max Thurian, "L'anthropologie de Calvin"; Jean Giblet, "L'anthropologie de Philon d'Alexandrie"; Patrick Thompson (Anglican), "L'anthropologie chez les auteurs anglais de 1600 à 1830"; Roger Aubert, "L'anthropologie post-tridentine"; Nicolas Arseniev, "L'anthropologie russe contemporaine"; Charles Moeller, "Conclusions." The speeches of Chatillon and Thurian were published in *Irénikon* (respectively: Jean Chatillon, "Une ecclésiologie médiévale: L'idée de l'Église dans la théologie de l'école de Saint-Victor au XIIe siècle," *Irén* 22, 1946, 115–138 and 395–411, and Max Thurian, "L'anthropologie réformée", *Irén* 25, 1952, 20–52). The contribution of Giblet was later published as Jean Giblet, "L'homme, image de Dieu dans les Commentaires littéraux de Philon d'Alexandrie," *Studia Hellenistica* 5, 1948, 93–118, whereas Hamer's lecture was reworked in the book by Jérôme Hamer, *Karl Barth: L'occasionalisme théologique de Karl Barth. Étude sur sa méthode dogmatique*, Paris, Desclée, 1949.

39 Moeller, *Le mouvement pour l'unité*, part II, ch. 2, 4 (italics original).

40 Clément Lialine, "De la Méthode irénique," *Irén* 15, 1938, 3–28, 131–153, 236–255, 450–459.

differences among the confessions. This initial formulation of the goal of the study days, which moreover dealt with such general and broad themes, soon began to show its limitations. The theme of Christian humanism and supernatural anthropology was again proposed at the meeting in 1948, which was attended by such a small group that no traces or evidences of the conference are left; furthermore, Moeller reports that there were no planned interventions at that conference, as all the attention was focused on the founding assembly of the WCC in Amsterdam.[41] Be that as it may, this session, entitled "La théologie des réalités terrestres" (imitating the title of a book by Thils),[42] constituted the last act before the definitive abandonment of this theme, "too vast and complex for there not to be, sooner or later, a concern to return to the concrete."[43] From 1949 onwards, the discussion shifted towards more biblical and ecclesiological topics, each time followed in the title with the words "... and ecumenism." It was not merely by chance that this transition did coincide with the changing of the guard between Lialine and Olivier Rousseau in the organization of the ecumenical study days. The intellectual animation of which, however, also remained in Moeller's hands.

3 The "Rousseau Era": The Series "... and Ecumenism" to Discuss the Meaning of Tradition

Dom Olivier Rousseau was a close friend and collaborator of Dom Lambert Beauduin. Together they had conceived the project of the "monastery of the union" at Amay-sur-Meuse, although once it had been founded, Célestin Golenvaux, the abbot of Maredsous, the monastery to which Dom Olivier belonged, would not allow him to change community.[44] Finally allowed to join the Amay group in 1930, when the monastery was already experiencing a moment of strong conflict with Rome that would soon lead to Beauduin's exile, he became master of novices there and editor of *Irénikon* together with Lialine.[45] Strongly committed to the liturgical movement, Rousseau was also a scholar of patristics, taking furthermore an interest in Aramaic and Syriac sources, convinced that it was necessary to go beyond the Greek–Latin binomial in order to achieve a true ecumenical consciousness. It is probably due to him that the problem of the competition between the Ecumenical Study Days and the "Oriental days," both organized by the monastery of Chevetogne, was solved, by insisting that the former should not be limited only to dialogue with the Eastern churches. Rousseau himself would later write: "It was around Orthodoxy that our meetings began, and the dialogue should never be one-sided."[46] Another innovation introduced in the "Rousseau era" was the fact that from then on the journal *Irénikon* would publish the reports of the sessions written by Moeller, thus making the study days known to the public, even if the names of the individual speakers and participants were not always mentioned in the published reports.

The sessions of 1949, 1950, and 1951 constitute a single path of progressive awareness that developed in three consequential stages: from the initial

41 Moeller, *Le mouvement pour l'unité*, part III, introduction.

42 Gustave Thils, *Théologie des réalités terrestres*, Bruges, Desclée, 1946.

43 Fouilloux, *Les catholiques et l'unité*, 771.

44 Emmanuel Lanne also reports that Rousseau had been the true inspirer of the letter *Equidem verba* addressed by Pius XI to the Superior General of the Benedictines Fidelis von Stotzingen. Emmanuel Lanne, "Dom Olivier Rousseau: 1898–1984," *Irén* 67, 1994, 163–185.

45 On the events at Amay-sur-Meuse/Chevetogne and Dom Beauduin, see the contribution by André Haquin in the first volume of this work.

46 Rousseau, "Les journées œcuméniques," 462. Moreover, in his report on the 1949 session, he specified: "We would even say that a [four-way dialogue] is needed, given the important nuances that separate Greek Orthodoxy and Slavic Orthodoxy, nuances that are too often neglected in ecumenical meetings"; Charles Moeller, "Bible et Œcuménisme," *Irén* 23, 1950, 164–188, here 167, note 1.

reflection on the role of Holy Scripture in the church, to the centrality of the biblical theology in the ecumenical debate, and finally to the cruciality of the ecclesiological question. The choice of the theme for the 1949 meeting, "Bible et œcuménisme," was apparently based on an "almost banal" observation: the fact that common prayer resulting from the shared reading of a biblical page was a normal experience in ecumenical meetings.[47] In reality, this recognition of spiritual ecumenism as the primary source of practical and theological ecumenism was instead highly meaningful. In that summer of 1949, a year after the Holy See's *Monitum Cum compertum* that had reaffirmed the prohibition of any form of *communicatio in sacris*, the reference to the practice of common prayer during interdenominational meetings, mentioned even in the report of the session published in the pages of *Irénikon*,[48] was not a neutral statement. Moreover, in the aftermath of the bitter experience of Amsterdam, where the absence of representatives of the Catholic Church had been so polemically emphasized by theologians such as Karl Barth,[49] to reaffirm that the Bible was the common ground on which rapprochement among the confessions could take place, was a programmatic choice. It showed indeed that dialogue with Protestantism was intended as the starting point for the new Ecumenical study days led by Rousseau. As a matter of fact, since the beginning of the century, Catholic and Protestant exegetes had been confronted with the common challenge posed by historical criticism to the sacred texts, which risked reducing the Bible to a literary collection of historical myths. Scientific researches that had been carried out within each confession in parallel, starting from common questions but threading different paths, had been able to enter into dialogue with each other since the 1943 encyclical *Divino afflante spiritu*, which had sanctioned the legitimacy of the application of the historical-critical method in Catholic exegesis as well.[50] The 1949 session of the study days, however, was not a comparison of the results of various exegetical studies, but rather a confrontation of the relevance of the biblical movement in the different denominations. No traces of this conference remain in the Chevetogne archives, but a few pages of the Moeller diaries have survived, including the list of participants and scheduled speakers.[51] In addition to Paul Evdokimov from Saint-Serge representing Russian Orthodoxy and, for the Greeks, the deacon of Phanar, Chrysostomos (Costantinides), at that time a student at Louvain, three of the five non-Catholics present at the session were Reformed Christians.[52] Among

47 "In ecumenical meetings, a kind of 'de facto ecumenism' is manifested in the prayers said in common before the meetings ... The common reading of a page of Holy Scripture shows each time that the true 'place' where the 'Word' should be heard is in a praying community. Only then does it take on all its resonance. It may be said that this community experience is banal. We do not think so"; Moeller, "Bible et Œcuménisme," 164–165.

48 However, at the time when *Irénikon* printed the report of the session, the instruction *Ecclesia Catholica* had already appeared, correcting that monitum and specifying in particular that the common recitation of the Our Father during ecumenical meetings was licit. About this, see the contribution by Saretta Marotta in this volume.

49 Karl Barth, "Die Unordnung der Welt und Gottes Heilsplan," in: Focko Lüpsen, ed., *Amsterdamer Dokumente: Berichte und Reden auf der Weltkirchenkonferenz in Amsterdam 1948*, Bethel bei Bielefeld, Evangelischer Presseverband für Westfalen und Lippe, 1948, 136–146; See also Karl Barth, "No Christian Marshall Plan," *The Christian Century*, Dec 8, 1948, 1330–1333. Christophe Chalamet, "Karl Barth on the Quest for the Church's Unity," *CrSt* 37, 2016, 343–359.

50 See the recent synthesis of Michael Florian Pfister, *Ein Mann der Bibel: Augustin Bea SJ (1881–1968) als Exeget und Rektor des Päpstlichen Bibelinstituts in den 1930er und 1940er Jahren*, Regensburg, Schnell und Steiner, 2020 and François Laplanche, *La crise de l'origine: La science catholique des Évangiles et l'histoire au XXe siècle*, Paris, Albin Michel, 2006.

51 UCL-LG, Charles Moeller, cahiers: n. 44.

52 The other two were the Reformed pastor Émile Fabre from Lille and the art historian Louis Quiévreux. About 20 participants attended the conference. This is the complete program (taken from UCL-LG, Charles Moeller, papiers, 1949): Jean Daniélou, "Bible et Tradition"; Roger Aubert, "L'évolution de la science

their names, particularly noteworthy was that of the first female speaker of the ecumenical study days, Suzanne de Dietrich, one of the founders and directors, together with Hendrik Kraemer, of the Ecumenical Institute of Bossey, near Geneva,[53] where the reading and study of Scripture was the core of the formative course designed for lay people.[54] In this context, one of the main milestones gained during the 1949 meeting in Chevetogne was the consciousness that the Bible is not a private reading, but a word announced to a community: "The Word of God, before being a *written* word, is first of all a word *proclaimed* by God himself, transmitted in and by a community of believers, and whose meaning only does take on its *full meaning* when it is *heard*, religiously, by the community of redeemed."[55] That means that the imperatives of scientific exegesis remained secondary in the face of the need for an exegesis of faith, that is, a biblical theology. In addition to the demands of the scientific study of the Bible and its historical-critical exegesis, also the participants gathered in Chevetogne thus affirmed the need to safeguard a "spiritual reading" of the Scriptures,[56] in response to a demand that came from the very heart of the experience of believers but also from the liturgical experience: "How can we admit that the meditation of Christians, that is, their *spiritual life*, is based on uncontrollable and perhaps fanciful theological views? How can such a view be maintained, when this typological use of the Old Testament through the New is *the essential method of the Church in its Liturgy*?"[57] Here the influence of the liturgical movement[58] on the study days is

catholique autour de la Bible depuis le XIXe siècle"; Albert Denis, "Exposé des journées bibliques de Louvain"; Suzanne de Dietrich, "Le mouvement de la pensée religieuse protestante autour de la Bible au cours de ces vingt dernières années"; Paul Evdokimov, "La valeur religieuse de la Bible dans l'Orthodoxie"; Georges Chevrot, "La pastorale biblique auprès du peuple fidèle. Expériences d'un curé de grande ville"; Antonin-Marcel Henry, "Enquête sur les appétences et les répulsions des élites chrétiennes d'aujourd'hui concernant la Bible"; Louis Quiévreux, "La Bible et la piété populaire médiévale d'après les vitraux de la Cathédrale de Bourges"; Jean Giblet, "Exposé des journées biblique de Beauraing"; Roger Poelman, "Les expériences d'un professeur de religion dans une institution moderne concernant la lecture de la Bible." Evdokimov's contribution was later published as Paul Evdokimov, "La Bible dans la Piété orthodoxe," *Irén* 23, 1950, 377–386.

53 Hans Ruedi-Weber, *The Courage to live: A Biography of Suzanne de Diétrich*, Geneva, WCC Publications, 1995; Hans Ruedi-Weber, *A Laboratory for Ecumenical Life: The Story of Bossey (1946–1996)*, Geneva, WCC Publications, 1996. De Dietrich wrote a report of the session and sent it to the WCC headquarters: Suzanne de Dietrich, *Rapport sur la rencontre de Chevetogne, 29 septembre–2 octobre 1949*, 6 typewritten pages, in: WCCA, Study Department, D 97.

54 On the impact of the biblical movement on the ecumenical movement, see Matthias Haudel, *Die Bibel und die Einheit der Kirche: Eine Untersuchung der Studien von "Glauben und Kirchenverfassung,"* Göttingen, Vandenhoeck & Ruprecht, 2012.

55 Moeller, "Bible et Œcuménisme," 165 (italics original and ours).

56 The "spiritual" exegesis defended by the participants in the Chevetogne sessions was certainly not equivalent to the "pious" exegesis promoted by traditionalist Catholicism, as opposed to historical-critical exegesis (for example, the multi-volume commentary by Dolindo Ruotolo, which was so successful among the Italian bishops), but referred back to the reproaches that the *nouvelle théologie* and the *ressourcement* posed to scientific exegesis, contesting the absence of a biblical theology. See Anthony Dupont & Karim Schelkens, "Scopuli Vitandi: The Historical-Critical Exegesis Controversy between the Lateran and the Biblicum (1960–1961)," *Bijdragen* 69, 2008, 18–51; Saretta Marotta, "Augustin Bea e la disputa sulla storicità dei Vangeli," *Modernism* 6, 2022, 62–97, and Mauro Pesce, "Un bruit absurd? Henri de Lubac di fronte alla distinzione tra esegesi storica e esegesi spirituale," *Annali di Storia dell'Esegesi* 10, 1993, 301–353.

57 Moeller, "Bible et Œcuménisme," 175 (italics original).

58 In this regard, it is worth mentioning that the founder of Chevetogne Dom Lambert Beauduin, recently reintegrated into the community after his exile, was able to participate for the first time to the event. He had been one of the first animators of the Belgian liturgical movement. See Lucien Morren, "Preface," in: Verdoodt, *Les colloques œcuméniques*, 2: "And already, earlier, he [L. Beauduin] was given permission to participate in the 1949 session. He attended in the company of his good friend Msgr. Chevrot, the well-known Parisian

evident in the conviction that the liturgy, "existentially" loyal and conforming to the biblical tradition, constitutes the "first theological *locus* of the ordinary Magisterium,"[59] that is, a living tradition.

The 1950 session "Théologie de la Parole et œcuménisme"[60] (held this time in October, two weeks after the international congress of Catholic ecumenists organized in Grottaferrata by Charles Boyer and attended by Dom Rousseau and Dom Lialine)[61] focused on the problem of determining the identity of this much needed "biblical theology." Reflection on biblical theology implied reflection on the very content of preaching and catechesis, distinct moments of the same ministry of the Word, but with different objectives.[62] The point of departure was the observation that "all Christian denominations need to pronounce a *mea culpa* on the subject of the Ministry of the Word,"[63] since each denomination has lent more weight to one aspect while neglecting the others.[64] A large number of the reports at the 1950 session were devoted to the historical analysis of preaching and catechesis, looking for "the causes of this decadence" in the course of history.[65] As a result, these were identified with the end of the patristic era and the consequent dissolution of the intimate union among catechesis, liturgy, and the Word that had characterized it. Until the 13th century, theology was indeed identified with commentary on Scripture, while the theological *summae* did not go beyond the circles of specialists: for the faithful the reception of the Word was like the reception of the sacraments. However, between the 14th and

priest-preacher; how could those present not remember their tasty conversations!" Dom Beauduin also attended the following sessions until his death in 1960.

59 Moeller, "Bible et Œcuménisme," 184.

60 The conference took place from Oct 2 to 4, 1950 and was attended by 26 participants, almost a third of whom were non-Catholic. For this session as well, the archives only contain the list of scheduled talks and the list of participants.

61 See our contribution on the Catholic conference for ecumenical questions in this volume. Dumont and Congar were also present at Grottaferrata, but not at this meeting in Chevetogne.

62 "Preaching in the strict sense … is connected to the '*prophetic*' mission of the Church: … it must not seek to triumph over the person by presenting 'arguments of human persuasion,' we would say today, a secularized, 'humanist,' Christianity, in the non-religious sense of the term. Preaching brings 'the good news' not as a superior 'wisdom' (which it is in one sense), but as a 'paradox' that saves … Catechesis is no longer addressed to the person to convert him or her. Strictly speaking … it presupposes the Christian life. It seeks to instruct the Christian more deeply in the mysteries of revelation"; Charles Moeller, "Théologie de la Parole et Œcuménisme," *Irén* 24, 1951, 313–343, here 313–316 (italics original).

63 Moeller, "Théologie de la Parole," 324.

64 "In the area of *preaching*, our Protestant brothers and sisters are considerably ahead of us because they have developed a 'theology of the Word' … Our Orthodox brothers and sisters, on the other hand, suffer from an almost total absence of preaching. Their ecclesiology directs them more readily to liturgical catechesis … As for Catholic preaching, it seems that it is not sufficiently concerned to ground itself in a 'theology of the Word' … the teaching is too exclusively focused on morals, too inspired by a natural theodicy … In regard to *catechesis*, the situation is the opposite … The insistence of our Protestant siblings on the *kerygma* leads them to neglect catechesis"; Moeller, "Théologie de la Parole," 320–321 (italics original).

65 Moeller, "Théologie de la Parole," 324. Here is the complete program (taken from UCL-LG, Charles Moeller, papiers, 1950 and AJOC): Olivier Rousseau, "Introduction: Sens de ces réunions"; Jean-Louis Leuba (pastor in Basel), "L'efficacité de la Parole"; Chrysostome Baur, "Les grands prédicateurs de l'antiquité chrétienne: S. Jean Chrysostome"; Cyrille Lambot, "Les grands prédicateurs de l'antiquité chrétienne: S. Augustin"; Jean Leclercq, "Moyen-Age et prédication"; Aymon-Marie Roguet, "Expériences positives et négatives concernant la prédication: catholique"; Élie Mélia, "Expériences positives et négatives concernant la prédication: orthodoxe"; Jean-Louis Leuba, "Expériences positives et négatives concernant la prédication: protestant"; Olivier Rousseau, "Rapport sur le congrès unioniste de Grottaferrata"; Pierre Ranwez, "Notes sur l'histoire du Catéchisme"; Léon van der Elst (alias Jean de Vincennes), "Les affamés de la Parole"; Charles Moeller, "Conclusions." Ranwez's contribution was later published as Pierre Ranwez, "Réflexions sur le catéchisme et son histoire," *L'union*, April 1953, 39–46; May–June 1953, 37–47.

16th century the abandonment of the *lectio continua* of the Bible led to forgetting some texts; meanwhile, conferences on abstract theological topics multiplied, replacing images and biblical themes. Eventually, the Counter-Reformation would accentuate the polemical effort of catechesis and preaching by increasingly distancing them from the liturgy. Scripture thus became that florilegium, that "arsenal of evidence" which characterized the theology textbooks of the time. From this historical analysis, the participants in the Chevetogne meeting unanimously agreed on the urgent need to integrate the various aspects of evangelization along a single mystery, that of the Holy Scripture received by the ecclesial community.[66] These are Hamer's comments on the conference: "It seemed urgent ... to create without delay a great movement of enthusiasm for the 'Word of God.' ... Where does it draw its effectiveness from? Is it from the talent of the speaker, from his priestly character, or from the divine origin of his message? These various questions demand more profoundly doctrinal answers than have been given to them so far."[67] Since developing a theology of the Word is, after all, nothing other than restoring the importance of the "Church's prophetic role,"[68] the Chevetogne discussions came back to the role of the church in preserving and transmitting Word and tradition. From highlighting the need for a biblical theology, the session thus ended by returning to the dilemma of the relationship between Scripture and the magisterium, from which in 1942 the reflection of the group of theologians of Louvain and the first session of the study days had started. However, this time such reflection took place through a direct comparison with the other Christian confessions, and was, moreover, no longer limited to Orthodoxy alone, but also included the Reformed and Lutheran traditions.

"Tradition et œcuménisme" was the theme of the 1951 session, which tackled head-on the point on which ecumenical differences appeared most irreducible. And yet, on closer examination, even on this subject the greater mutual knowledge made it possible to dismantle age-old prejudices, such as the one that denied that the Protestant *sola scriptura* could ever accept the idea of tradition. The intervention of pastor Marc-Henry Rotschy (who had replaced Thurian at the last moment in presenting the paper "Tradition in Calvin's Theology") demonstrated instead the existence of a tradition in his church, in the same way as the Benedictine Paul De Vooght, an expert on early Reform movements, explained that even for John Wyclif the highest authority after the Bible was the tradition of the church Fathers (*consensus Patrum*).[69] However, it was mainly Edmond Ortigues' intervention that denounced how the doctrine of the "two sources of Revelation" was the result of a misinterpretation of the Council of

66 "This was one of the major conclusions of the October 1950 session – if not the most important ... The unanimity of all participants on its necessity was so impressive that it should be stressed"; Moeller, "Théologie de la parole," 330 (italics original).

67 Report by Hamer in: *Témoignage chrétien*, January 1951, cited in Rousseau, "Les journées œcuméniques," 465.

68 "To develop a theology of the Word is, after all, nothing other than to give a prophetic role to the Church, the same importance that one gives to its priestly role or its jurisdictional role"; Moeller, "Théologie de la parole," 331.

69 Here the complete program (taken from UCL-LG, Charles Moeller, cahiers: n. 45): Olivier Rousseau, "Exposé du programme de la semaine"; Lucien Cerfaux, "Analyse de la notion de Tradition chez S. Paul"; Paul De Vooght, "La Tradition chez les scolastiques et le préréformateurs (Wyclif)"; René Blanc, "La Tradition dans la théologie luthérienne"; Marc-Henry Rotschy," La tradition dans la théologie de Calvin"; Henry Renaud Turner Brandreth (Anglican parish of Paris), "La notion anglicane de la Tradition"; Pierre Kovalevsky, "Tradition et Sobornost dans la théologie Orthodoxe"; Edmond Ortigues, "La notion de Tradition d'après le Concile de Trente"; Jan-Hendrik Walgrave, "Newton et l'évolution du dogme"; Roger Aubert, "La théologie catholique contemporaine de la Tradition"; Charles Moeller, "Conclusions." The conference was attended by 39 participants among whom were many ecumenists like Christophe-Jean Dumont, Robert Grosche, and Frans Thijssen. Henri-Marie de Lubac was present for the first time.

Trent, which had initially preferred *regula* to the term *fons*:

> The serious and important fact to know is that the decree of the fourth session concerning the Scriptures and the Traditions was misunderstood and distorted by the polemic of the sixteenth century. … The thesis of two juxtaposed "sources" confused the humanist notion of historical source, a document from which earthly intelligence extracted its information, with the spiritual source of faith, which is Christ sanctifying his Church. … It is not a question of two sources/documents of Revelation, *de fontibus Revelationis*, as thousands of manuals have repeated, confusing the problem of the theological places, that is to say of the sources of theology, with the problem of Revelation, which has no source, because it is none other than Jesus Christ, the source of faith.[70]

If for Catholics tradition is not an autonomous source of revelation (the overcoming of the doctrine on the "two sources" would become one of the focal points at Vatican II),[71] on the other hand, *sola scriptura* does not really apply to other confessions either: "All Christians admit that Scripture is a norm only when it is read in *church-community*. It is not, therefore, the *littera scripta*, the written letter, that is authoritative, but the ecclesial proclamation of the message contained in the Book."[72] The reflection on the theology of the Word thus referred back to the ecclesiological question, highlighting the role of the community in the written fixation of revelation[73] and shifting the focus from the dialectic between Scripture and Tradition to that between revelation and church. It is the ecclesial community indeed that constitutes the theological place in which Scripture and Tradition are combined. However, reflecting on the relationship between the church and revelation meant once again reflecting on the magisterium, that is, the possibility for the church to transmit an active tradition as well as a passive one and the possibility of the evolution of dogma. On Nov 1, 1950, a month after the previous session of the study days of Chevetogne, Pope Pius XII had defined the dogma of the Assumption. As is well known, this was a veritable earthquake for ecumenical relations.[74] In fact, the papal bull *Munificentissimus Deus* said nothing about any scriptural argument, or about the alleged "traditions" about the death of the Virgin, but appealed only to the "faith of the Church," that is the faith of the faithful, offering a clear example of "active magisterium." The Catholics present at Chevetogne strongly defended how active tradition was already present in all the early councils, where notions such as *homoousios* or the Trinity did not belong to the biblical vocabulary but were concepts that already represented interpretations of the Scripture. They therefore defended the possibility of an active magisterium

70 Edmond Ortigues, "La tradition de l'Évangile dans l'Église d'après la doctrine catholique," *FoiVie* 49, 1951, 304–322, here 318–319. This contribution was also published in Edmond Ortigues, "Écriture et Traditions apostoliques au Concile du Trente," *RSR* 36, 1949, 271–299. The text of his speech in Chevetogne is in: UCL-LG, Charles Moeller, cahiers: n. 45, annexes. See also Moeller's comments in his report of the 1951 session: "There is only one source of faith and not two that are juxtaposed, without visible communion, and sometimes in opposition. This is undoubtedly the central discovery of the ecumenical meeting"; Charles Moeller, "Tradition et Œcuménisme," *Irén* 25, 1952, 337–370, here 346 (italics original).

71 See Schelkens, *Catholic Theology of Revelation*.

72 Moeller, "Tradition et Œcuménisme," 339 (italics original).

73 "The Bible, as a book, has been composed in the community and was meant primarily for its edification. The book and the Church cannot be separated"; Georges Florovsky, *The Collected Works*, vol. 1, *Bible, Church, Tradition: An Eastern Orthodox View*, Belmont MA, Nordland Publishing, 1972, 18, perhaps quoted in Pierre Kovalevsky's speech.

74 For an overview of the reactions, see *Irén* 23, 1950, 425–427; *VUCh* 28, 1950, 10–19 and *La Documentation catholique* 33, 1951, 235–250. Max Thurian's reaction is one of the most notorious: Max Thurian, "Le dogme de l'Assomption," *Verbum Caro* 5, 1951, 2–50.

by resorting to the notion of the church as the bride of Christ, spiritually united to him, assisted by the Holy Spirit, indissolubly and therefore also infallibly bound to her bridegroom.[75] The image of the *Ecclesia sponsa* would be the object of an entire session of the study days in 1955, but already in 1952 it had become clear that ecclesiology and, primarily, Christology, was what for Moeller constituted the hard core, the "crossroads" of all ecumenical confrontations. It was on the relationship between Christ and his church that the ecclesiologies of the different denominations diverged profoundly, especially among the Western churches. For Protestants, the church "exists only in act, in the very moment when God speaks to it, in the community. The church is entirely generated by Holy Scripture. When it no longer hears this divine Word, *it dies*. From then on, the church cannot judge Scripture but is always 'judged by it.'"[76] For Catholics, on the other hand, the church has a *permanent* charisma, which enables it to discover and promulgate the exact meaning of revelation. This is possible because of the church's condition as bride of Christ. Mariology, too, was ultimately reduced to an ecclesiological problem. By reflecting on the figure of Mary, Catholics defended their conception of the mediation of grace through the church. These different ecclesiological conceptions, "constitute two Christian universes that nothing, for the time being, will be able to bridge,"[77] as Moeller concluded in his 1953 manuscript reviewing the first ten years of activity of the Ecumenical Study Days of Chevetogne. However, the differences over Mariology and ecclesiology highlighted the fact that the core of the divergences was the interpretation of the figure of Christ, about which, in Moeller's view, nothing had changed since the debates that had animated the councils of the early centuries of Christianity, when the first schisms had occurred. Indeed, the *querelle* between Nestorians (a human Jesus) and Monophysites (a divine Jesus) never ended, but basically all the churches of today blame the others for not being faithful to the Council of Chalcedon, that is, either to humanize Christ or to deify him too much. The ecclesiological problem derives from this Christological problem, since the church is but an extension of the Incarnation. Especially because it is always Christology that constitutes the sole object of all controversies, Moeller concluded that it was necessary to go back and reflect on the origin of the schisms, starting with the schisms of the 4th century, which can also explain the prehistory of further divisions.

The 1952 session of the study days would indeed have as its theme "La théologie du schisme."[78] There were several reasons for this choice. The first was that on Sep 8, 1951 Pius XII's encyclical *Sempiternus rex Christus* had appeared, celebrating the 15th centenary of the Council of Chalcedon. Precisely in this encyclical, which recalled the terms of the debate among Nestorians, Monophysites, and Diaphysites, Pius XII extended the call for ecumenical unity also to the Miaphysite churches. Similarly, the organizers of the study days of Chevetogne were also convinced that it was necessary to involve the Eastern non-Chalcedonian churches in the ecumenical debate, starting from the study of their schism. The reflection of the 1952 session was not accidental for yet another reason: in August 1952 the third world conference of the

75 Moeller, "Tradition et Œcuménisme," 354–370.

76 Moeller, "Bible et Œcuménisme," 183 (italics original).

77 Moeller, *Le mouvement pour l'unité*, part III, ch. 1, 185.

78 The conference took place from Sep 30 to Oct 2, 1952 and was attended by 38 participants (among them there were also Nikos Nissiotis, from the WCC, and Johannes Willebrands, who a month earlier had just started the experience of the CCEQ). This is the program: Yves Congar, "La notion théologique du schisme"; Hilaire Duesberg, "Le schisme dans l'Ancien Testament"; Jacques Dupont, "Le schisme à partir du Nouveau Testament"; Charles Moeller, "Le schisme au temps des premiers conciles"; Maurice Pontet, "Notion du schisme chez S. Augustin"; Archimandrite Emilianos (Timiadis), "Séparation entre l'Orient et l'Occident"; Jean Leclercq, "Le grand schisme d'Occident"; Jacques Courvoisier, "Le schisme dans la tradition réformée"; Clément Lialine, "Brève communication sur une opinion orthodoxe récente concernant le schisme"; Jean Gribomont, "Schisme et appartenance à l'Église."

Faith and Order movement was held in Lund, and "Christ and his Church," along with the biblical roots of this relationship, was the theme of one of the three preparatory reports that had been sent in advance to the delegates, and in which the very notion of schism had been discussed, too.[79] The third reason was that in 1950 Dom Lambert Beauduin had returned from his exile and was reintegrated into Chevetogne. He would be 81 years old in 1954, precisely on the 900th anniversary of the Great Schism. Beauduin had always invited his monks to develop a scholarly interest in the first councils, particularly concerning the doctrine on the episcopate.[80] The decision to dedicate a miscellaneous volume collecting contributions on the first councils and the first schisms in the history of Christianity on the occasion of his birthday therefore seemed the most obvious choice.[81] Moeller's book on the first ten years of the Ecumenical Study Days was also probably intended to accompany these celebrations.

The meetings of 1952 and 1953 can therefore be seen as a single in-depth study of schisms: from those of the first centuries concerning the Christian East (1952) to that on the theology of grace at the origin of the Reformation (1953). Six of the eight lectures presented at the 1952 session were published in the two volumes offered to Dom Beauduin.[82] Of all the contributions, which mainly reported on the history of the various schisms over the centuries, the one by Congar was particularly noteworthy. It was perceived as "shocking" because of the interpretations that it offered and was therefore placed as an introduction to the first volume of the *Festschrift*:[83] for instance, when Congar blamed the schism of 1054 and the subsequent Council of Florence for the canonical separation of rites, which had become a clear sign of the separation of the churches, putting an end to the "healthy pluralism" that had characterized the Catholic Church in previous centuries.[84] Or, above

79 Faith and Order had also already used the notion of the church as the "people of God" for a long time. See Oliver S. Tomkins, *The Church in the Purpose of God: An Introduction to the Work of the Commission on Faith and Order of the World Council of Churches, in Preparation for the Third World Conference on Faith and Order to be Held at Lund, Sweden in 1952*, Chatham, Parrett & Neves, 1950; *Report of the Third World Conference on Faith and Order: Lund, Sweden: August 15–28, 1952*, London, John Roberts Press, 1952, esp. 7–11 and 16–17. See also Clément Lialine, "Le mouvement Foi et Constitution à l'étape 'Lund 1952,'" *Irén* 26, 1953, 146–161 and 256–282.

80 Emmanuel Lanne, "Il ruolo del monastero di Chevetogne al Concilio Vaticano II," *CrSt* 27, 2006, 513–545, here 514.

81 *1054–1954: L'Église et les Églises: Neuf siècles de douloureuse séparation entre l'Orient et l'Occident. Études et travaux offerts à Dom Lambert Beauduin*, 2 vols., Chevetogne, Éditions de Chevetogne, 1954–1955. The two volumes collected the contributions of 44 authors, two-thirds of whom Roman Catholics, the rest Greek and Russian Orthodox, Lutherans, Reformed, and one Anglican.

82 Yves M.-J Congar, "Neuf cents ans après: Notes sur le 'Schisme oriental,'" in: *L'Église et les Églises*, vol. 1, 3–98; Dom Jacques Dupont, "Le Schisme d'après Saint Paul," in: *L'Église et les Églises*, vol. 1, 111–127; Charles Moeller, "Réflexions sur les schismes à l'époque des premiers conciles," in: *L'Église et les Églises*, vol. 1, 241–260; Maurice Pontet, "La notion de schisme d'après saint Augustin," in: *L'Église et les Églises*, vol. 1, 163–182; Dom Jacques Leclercq, "Points de vue sur le Grand Schisme d'Occident," in: *L'Église et les Églises*, vol. 2, 223–240; Jacques Courvoisier, "Du Schisme dans la tradition et dans l'histoire des Églises réformées," *L'Église et les Églises*, vol. 2, 283–307.

83 "As for Fr. Congar, whose address caused a stir, he returned to the material he covered in his *Dictionnaire de théologie catholique* entry 'Schism,' bringing it up to date, insisting particularly on the importance of the local church in antiquity and the centralizing development in the West, which gave the notion of schism a different meaning from what it was in the past between particular churches"; Rousseau, "Les journées œcuméniques," 467. See Yves M.-J. Congar, "Théologie," in: *DThC* 15, 341–502.

84 "'In the sixth century in Rome … when a child was brought to the baptistery, the acolyte asked: In what language does he confess our Lord Jesus Christ? According to the answer, he recited the creed in Greek or in Latin.' Surely this state of things can be considered a wholesome pluralism … Before modern times, ritus meant concrete ritual, a manner of celebrating the liturgy, the concrete expression of one's faith … But since then – and who can say precisely when? – 'rite' became an abstract reality, a thing in itself; it became a separate entity and one begins to speak of *the* Oriental

all (this was the basic thesis of his contribution), when he stated that the process of "estrangement" between East and West had begun well before 1054 and the schism was nothing more than the final acceptance of this progressive distancing.[85]

As far as the 1953 session is concerned, although all the speakers were invited to participate in the second volume of the collective work *L'Église et les églises*,[86] there they dealt with other topics, so that none of the contributions presented at the session "La grâce et l'œcuménisme" was published in that volume or in the pages of *Irénikon*. Unfortunately, not even the texts of the speeches remain in the archives, but only brief summaries and notes, so that it is not easy to reconstruct the content of the session. However, it is clear from Moeller's account (although the names of the speakers were never mentioned in *Irénikon*) that one of the key contributions had been pronounced by Gérard Philips, from the University of Louvain, who had traced the origins of the concept of "created grace" in the history of Catholic theology from St. Augustine to the Council of Trent, showing that the doctrine against which Martin Luther railed was in fact a misinterpreted degeneration.[87] The Dominican Nikolaus Walty from Le Saulchoir then spoke about the Tridentine doctrine on grace, while two pairs of speakers, John Meyendorff from Saint-Serge and Endre von Ivánka from the University of Graz for the Orthodox churches, and Pierre-Yves Emery from Taizé and the pastor Henry Bruston from Lyons for the Reformed, illustrated respectively the concepts of "divinization" and "extrinsic grace" which were fundamental concepts for the theology of grace in the respective confessions.[88]

The 1953 session was attended by 38 participants, a number that had also been reached in the 1951 and 1952 editions. This progressive increase in the audience of the Ecumenical Study Days of Chevetogne was a characteristic mark of the "new Rousseau era." The new study days had a greater impact also through its representativity: Suzanne de Dietrich's participation in 1949 on behalf of the WCC was followed in 1950 by the participation of Jean-Louis Leuba, a member of the Faith and Order commission, and that of Nikos Nissiotis, associate director of Bossey, in 1952.[89] As the fame and importance of these study days increased, their echo reached even Rome, which was worried about them and tried to subject

rite … The question of rite has become identified with the very question of church"; Congar, "Neuf cents ans après," 39–40; ET: *After Nine Hundred Years: The Background of the Schism between the Eastern and Western Churches*, New York, Fordham University Press, 1959, 35–36 (italics original).

85 Congar, "Neuf cents ans après," 8, also 20–22, 52–63, 80–87, and 98.

86 Endre von Ivánka, "Palamismus und Vätertradition," in: *L'Église et les Églises*, vol. 2, 29–46; Jean Meyendorff, "Un mauvais théologien de l'unité au XIVe siècle: Barlaam le Calabrais," in: *L'Église et les Églises*, vol. 2, 47–66; Pierre-Yves Emery, "La Réforme du XVIe siècle et les conciles œcuméniques," in: *L'Église et les Églises*, vol. 2, 263–281. In the same volume, the contribution of Paul Evdokimov, who was not present at the 1953 session but was presumably initially invited as a speaker, is worth mentioning: Paul Evdokimov, "De la nature et de la grâce dans la théologie de l'Orient," in: *L'Église et les Églises*, vol. 2, 171–195.

87 Years later, Philips would return to this subject in greater detail: Gérard Philips, *L'union personnelle avec le Dieu vivant: Essai sur l'origine et le sens de la grâce créée*, Gembloux, Duculot, 1974. Moeller published the report of this session, as usual, in *Irénikon*. See Charles Moeller, "Théologie de la Grâce et Œcuménisme," *Irén* 28, 1955, 19–56. Because the issue quickly sold out, he invited Philips to provide some additions and publish the report as a small joint book. See Charles Moeller & Gérard Philips, *Grâce et œcuménisme*, Chevetogne, Éditions de Chevetogne, 1957.

88 Here is the complete program: Jean Meyendorff, "La théologie de la divinisation en Orient et dans le monde orthodoxe"; Endre von Ivánka, "Anthropologie de la grâce en Orient et en Occident"; Gérard Philips, "La théologie de la gratia creata"; Nikolaus Walty, "La doctrine de la grâce au Concile de Trente"; Pierre-Yves Emery, "Grâce externe et interne chez Calvin"; Henry Bruston, "La notion de la grâce dans la théologie réformée"; Charles Moeller, "Conclusions."

89 Verdoodt reported that in March 1952 a week of "ecumenical social days" was held in Chevetogne, organized in collaboration with the study department of the WCC of Geneva, on the Christian significance of economy and human work. See Verdoodt, *Les colloques œcuméniques*, 11–12. The meeting actually took place from Mar 28 to 31 and news of it also reached the Holy Office. See ADDF, Rerum variarum, 1948, n. 39, pos. 146.

them to its own authorization. The attempt was eventually thwarted thanks to the action of the prior of Chevetogne, Dom Thomas Becquet, and Bishop André-Marie Charue of Namur.[90] This way, the experience of the Ecumenical Study Days was able to continue its course, intensifying an ecclesiological reflection that would anticipate by several years the fundamental themes of Vatican II.

4 The Ecclesiological Conferences (1954–1958)

The organizers of the 1954 conference on "Baptême et Église," which was attended by 34 participants, may have been inspired by an article which the Dominican father Jean Jérôme Hamer had published a few years earlier in *Irénikon*.[91] On the basis of his analysis of the teaching of Western and Eastern church Fathers about the validity of the baptism when administered by heretics and schismatics, Hamer had come to the conclusion that, "even when administered outside the visible unity, baptism is by its proper nature a real element of the Church of Christ."[92] The recently nominated Louvain professor Albert Descamps was asked to give a lecture on the theology of baptism in the New Testament.[93] Due to his openness to the approach of the *formgeschichtliche Schule*, he was convinced that the New Testament reveals a "diversity of theologies of baptism."[94] Some accounts understand baptism as a rite of purification leading to the forgiveness of sins; others as the sign of accepting Christ and the Triune God; it was understood by another group as the "rite of initiation into the Church" or as a rite symbolizing "the mystical union to the Risen Lord." The theology of baptism today is invited to reflect this variety even more.[95] Bernard Botte, a Benedictine monk at the abbey of Mont César in Louvain, must have been invited because of his 1952 article on the interpretation of the baptismal rites.[96] The article contains a strong plea to the Sacred Congregation of Rites to restore the *Rituale Romanum*[97] and its rites for infant and adult baptism, as had been the case in 1951 with the Easter vigil. Since the lecture by Dom Botte is the only one of those comprising this conference to be published in full, it is a precious testimony to the intention of the organizers to ask a celebrated liturgist to reflect on the ecclesial significance of baptism.[98] For Botte, this requires attention to the three dimensions of the word ἐκκλησία in the New Testament: the liturgical assembly, the local church, and the universal church. For him, the significance of baptism as incorporation in the universal church is undisputed; in his time, the sense of belonging to the local church, and of being in regular contact with

90 Fouilloux, *Les catholiques et l'unité*, 772.

91 Jérôme Hamer, "Le baptême et l'Église: À propos des 'Vestigia Ecclesiae,'" in *Irén* 25, 1952, 142–164, 263–275.

92 Hamer, "Le baptême et l'Église," 275.

93 Albert Descamps, "Simples réflexions sur la théologie primitive du baptême chrétien," in: UCL-LG, Charles Moeller, carnets, n. 50, 1954, 1.

94 According to Jean Giblet, "Mgr Albert Descamps, exégète et théologien de Louvain," *RTL* 12, 1981, 40–58, Descamps combined the thematic approach of his teacher Cerfaux with Dibelian *Formgeschichte*. After the council, Descamps remained willing to reflect on baptism in relation to Christian unity, as appears from Albert Descamps, "Le baptême, fondement de l'unité chrétienne," in: Lorenzo de Lorenzi, ed., *Battesimo e giustizia in Rom 6 e 8*, Rome, Abbazia S. Paolo fuori le mura, 1974, 203–234.

95 "We must not synthesize these themes too quickly but rather study each separately for itself; rather than the artificial unity of a synthesis, we should prefer, in this case, the rich diversity of a tapestry to which a number of artists have contributed"; Descamps, *Simples réflexions*, 1.

96 Bernard Botte, "L'interprétation des textes baptismaux," *La Maison-Dieu* 32, 1952, 18–39.

97 "It seems obvious to me that it is, among our liturgical books, the one most in urgent need of a correction or even a reworking"; Botte, "L'interprétation des textes baptismaux," 36.

98 Bernard Botte, "Les rapports du baptisé avec la communauté chrétienne," *Les Questions Liturgiques et Paroissiale* 34, 1953, 115–126.

its bishop, besides a more regular attendance at its liturgy, needs to be emphasized.[99]

Three speakers from other ecclesial traditions also took the floor. The Protestant scholar who had originally been invited to the meeting, André Benoît, was a specialist in the theology of baptism in the 2nd century.[100] In an article written in the same period, he defended the "coexistence" of local parish and universal church in the early church. Unlike the Catholic tradition, however, for Protestants the notion of universal church is understood as the experience of the presence of Christ in the celebration of baptism and Holy Supper by the community.[101] Both the Anglican and Orthodox speaker point to the relationship between baptism and the resurrection of Christ and to the importance of the liturgy as *locus theologicus*. According to the Anglican priest Geoffrey Curtis, the Book of Common Prayer understands baptism as incorporation in the Risen Lord. Being united with Christ's resurrection becomes visible by the activity of the Spirit in us, not just for ourselves but for the whole of creation.[102] The Orthodox speaker, Élie Mélia, pointed to the importance of the rite of immersion, which signifies that the baptized person participates in Christ's sacrifice and in his resurrection. For him, baptism also means the inclusion in the local eucharistic community.[103]

In the following year, the community of Chevetogne organized a conference on "Ecclesia sponsa," the church as bride of Christ, with 41 participants. In the opinion of Henri Cazelles, the metaphor of the nuptial relation of Yahweh and Israel may have been developed in response to the presence of fertility cults and sacred prostitution in the religions of the ancient Near East.[104] The professor of New Testament studies at the Faculty of Protestant Theology in Geneva, Franz-Jehan Leenhardt, had probably been invited because he had paid attention to the church of the Acts of the Apostles in some of his previous writings.[105] The most important Pauline metaphor for the church is that of body of Christ, with its attention to both the mystical

99 See especially the conclusion to Botte, "Les rapports du baptisé avec la communauté," 124: "In requesting baptism, the catechumen asks to be incorporated into the universal church. They are perfectly aware of this. But this church is hierarchically organized ... Today, as in the first centuries, every Christian is incorporated into a local church, placed under the jurisdiction of a bishop. Of this, our Christians are not sufficiently aware." Botte's defense of the parish ended with a criticism of Catholic Action: "To dream of a *cura animarum* organized on the level of Catholic Action, according to social classes, would be, in my opinion, a dangerous utopia. In any case, at the present time, the parish remains the normal community of the Christian"; Botte, "Les rapports du baptisé avec la communauté," 126.

100 André Benoît, *Le baptême chrétien au second siècle: La théologie des Pères*, Paris, PUF, 1953. Benoît, a patrologist from the University of Strasbourg, was replaced by Pierre Regard, a Protestant pastor from Mons, Belgium.

101 See André Benoît, "La paroisse dans le christianisme primitif," *FoiVie* 50, 1952, 215–231, esp. 219–221.

102 See Geoffrey Curtis, "L'appartenance à l'Église par le baptême et l'incorporation au Christ et à sa Résurrection par ce sacrement," in: UCL-LG, Charles Moeller, carnets, n. 50, 1954. Curtis was a member of the Community of the Resurrection in Mirfield, a peculiar Anglican monastic experience.

103 See Élie Mélia, "L'insertion dans l'Église par le baptême dans la tradition de l'Église orthodoxe," in: UCL-LG, Charles Moeller, carnets, n. 50, 1954. Mélia, a former student of Sergius Bulgakov at the Institut de théologie orthodoxe Saint-Serge, was rector of the Georgian parish in Paris. His theological work was mainly a reflection on his pastoral experience. In the same period, Mélia had been invited to contribute to an important collective by Serge Verhovskoy, who had been professor at Saint-Serge from 1944 to 1952 and had accepted the invitation to teach dogmatics at St. Vladimir's Orthodox Theological Seminary. See Ilya Melia, "Malaja Cerkov': Prichod, kak christianskaja obščina" [The small church: The parish as Christian community], in: Sergey Verchovsky, ed., *Pravoslavie v žizni: Sbornik statej* [Orthodoxy in life: Collection of articles], New York, Chekhov Publishing House, 1953, 85–116. The article is about the relationship between the parish and the bishop. In the conclusions to this chapter, he warned against a twofold danger, minimizing the importance of the parish by not seeing her as the Church of Christ, and assuming that the parish is a self-sufficient entity.

104 Cazelles had only recently become professor at the ICP.

105 See especially Franz-Jehan Leenhardt, *Études sur l'Église dans le Nouveau Testament*, Geneva, Georg & Cie, 1940.

relationship between the faithful and Christ and to the sociological dimension of the church.[106] In another publication he discusses the conjugal relationship of Christ with the church in Eph 5 as a variation of the metaphor of the church as the body of Christ. We are united with Christ through the gift of the Holy Spirit, thanks to Christ's love for us culminating in the crucifixion.[107] This time, the typical attention to the patristic tradition focused exclusively on the Syriac East. *Irénikon* had already published a study in 1955 by the Syriac Catholic priest Gabriel Khouri-Sarkis on the feast of the consecration and the dedication of the church, which in the Syrian tradition opens the liturgical year.[108] The Jesuit François Graffin, who had been nominated professor of Oriental Christianity at the Catholic University of Paris in 1951, dealt with the same theme in the Ecumenical Study Days but on the basis of a richer collection of sources, namely the Syriac and Chaldean breviaries, and the homilies of the Syrian bishop Mar Jacob of Serugh. The main goal of his article, the only one from the 1955 conference to be published, was to make this rich liturgical tradition known in the West as well.[109] In his conference on the church as bride in the Orthodox tradition, theologian Boris Bobrinskoy highlights the doctrinal themes that resonate with this "nuptial symbolism." Among these are the relationship of God with Israel, the holiness of the church and the sinfulness of its members, its motherhood, the relationship between the Mother of God and the church, the one between church and wisdom in Sergius Bulgakov. After the conference, he sent a detailed overview of citations by church Fathers and Orthodox theologians on "L'action du Saint-Esprit dans l'Eglise-Epouse du Christ" to Moeller, partly in preparation for the next conference.[110]

Just a few months earlier, the CCEQ had organized its fourth meeting in Paris on a similar theme.[111] Its theologians sought to stimulate the Catholic reflection on the nature of the church by focusing on two important images, that of the church as bride and that of the church as body of Christ. Unlike in Chevetogne, the CCEQ gave the floor only to Catholic speakers who, as converts, were asked to explain the theology of their previous traditions. The conferences by Louis Bouyer, Joseph McGill, Willem Hendrik van de Pol and Johannes Peter Michael all expressed the need to emphasize the superiority of the Catholic view on this theme. Furthermore, the lecture by Swiss theologian Charles Journet offered a rich Catholic reflection on the image of the church as bride of Christ, which is able to express both the intimate relationship and the difference between the two.[112]

---

106 Leenhardt, *Études sur l'Église*, 42.

107 Franz-Jehan Leenhardt, "Réalité et caractères de l'Église," in: Georges Florovsky & others, *La Sainte Église Universelle: Confrontation œcuménique*, Neuchâtel, Delachaux et Niestlé, 1948, 59–91, here 74.

108 Gabriel Khouri-Sarkis, "La fête de l'Église dans l'année liturgique syrienne," *Irén* 28, 1955, 186–193. By means of quotations from the Syriac breviary the author praises the church as the bride of Christ, who receives and renders back Christ's love for her.

109 François Graffin, "Recherches sur le thème de l'Église-Épouse dans les liturgies et la littérature patristique de langue syriaque," *L'Orient Syrien* 3, 1958, 317–336. The journal was founded by Khouri-Sarkis two years earlier, and to the first issue contained the contribution by Olivier Rousseau "Actualité des Études syriennes," in *L'Orient Syrien* 1, 1956, 31–43.

110 Bobrinskoy, who had accepted the chair in dogmatic theology at the Saint-Serge only one year earlier, had been asked by the Georgian priest Melia to replace him. The theme of his lecture was to remain important in his mature ecclesiology. See Boris Bobrinskoy, *Le mystère de l'Église: Cours de théologie dogmatique*, Paris, Cerf, 2003. In the New Testament, the bridal imagery "is no longer an analogy; it is the reality of divine love, of Christ towards his church and towards every human soul that the Spirit entrusts to the Lord. It is the mystery of the eternal wedding of Christ and the church which becomes the foundation of human love"; Bobrinskoy, *Le mystère de l'Église*, 143. The section ends with a reflection on sinfulness and holiness in the church: Bobrinskoy, *Le mystère de l'Église*, 148–151.

111 See also our article on the significance of the CCEQ in this volume.

112 Charles Journet, "L'Église, Épouse du Christ," in: AAC, FWC, Dossier 3, 5. When treating the Chevetogne conference on "Ecclesia sponsa," Olivier Rousseau is attentive to the impact of this idea on the redaction of the

Journet was equally convinced that the Protestant reluctance to apply this image to the church can be countered by paying greater attention to the connection between pneumatology and ecclesiology. The Spirit is "the efficient personality of the Church."[113]

The Swiss Protestant exegete Pierre Bonnard, known for his welcoming reaction to *Divino afflante Spiritu*,[114] had been invited to the 1956 conference on "L'Esprit-Saint et l'Église" – attended by 34 speakers – in order to explain the New Testament background of this theme.[115] Describing the precise relationship between the Spirit and the church is a delicate issue. The Christian community *is* the temple of the Spirit (1 Cor 3:16) but individual Christians still are able to act against the Spirit. Bonnard follows Congar in speaking about a "covenant relationship" between church and Spirit, not that the infallibility of the ordained ministry could be derived from this image.[116] In the New Testament, ecclesiology is still characterized by "a spiritual monism" which is not in favor of making strict divisions between community members and their leaders.[117] The conference by Nicolas Koulomzine had also a strong focus on Scripture, especially on the Spirit as revealer of Christ in the New Testament and in the church.[118]

In his first contribution to the ecumenical study days, Emmanuel Lanne presented the contribution of patristic theology on this theme.[119] His attention goes first to the teaching of the African theologians, from Tertullian to Augustine, on the validity of the baptism administered by heretics. In his opinion, the famous conclusion to Book III of Irenaeus' *Adversus Haereses*, which Lanne quotes in Latin as "ubi enim Ecclesia, ibi et Spiritus Dei, et ubi Spiritus Dei, illic Ecclesia et omnis gratia,"[120] can be interpreted as a reflection on the boundaries of the church.[121] According to him, the Greek church Fathers Irenaeus of Lyons and especially Cyril of Alexandria remain very helpful for a contemporary theological reflection on the proper roles of Christ and the Spirit in the process of divinization.[122]

Since the topic of this session was thematically linked to that on grace, Moeller had asked Professor Philips once again to present the more recent Catholic teaching on the relationship between the Spirit and the church. He did not publish his lecture but integrated it into his course notes.[123]

Dogmatic constitution on the church *Lumen gentium*. See Rousseau, "Les journées œcuméniques," 472.

113 Journet, "L'Église, Épouse du Christ," 6.

114 Pierre Bonnard, "L'Encyclique *Divino Afflante Spiritu* et l'orientation de l'herméneutique biblique," *Revue de Théologie et de Philosophie* n.s. 38, 1950, 51–56. According to Bonnard, a professor of the New Testament at the Freie Fakultät Lausanne, with this encyclical "l'aube de l'herméneutique catholique romaine" had started, see Bonnard, "L'Encyclique Divino Afflante Spiritu," 51.

115 Pierre Bonnard, "L'Esprit saint et l'Église selon le Nouveau Testament," *RHPR* 37, 1957, 81–90.

116 Bonnard, "L'Esprit saint et l'Église," 85, in reference to Yves M.-J. Congar, *Esquisses du mystère de l'Église*, Paris, Cerf, ²1953, 160.

117 Bonnard, "L'Esprit saint et l'Église," 88.

118 Nicolas Koulomzine was already teaching at Saint-Serge but would become the successor to Cassian (Bezobrazov) on the chair of New Testament studies after the council. In Nicholas Koulomzine, "Images of the Church in Saint Paul's Epistles," *SVTQ* 14, 1970, 5–27, esp. 19, it becomes clear that he considers 1 Cor 12:3 – "no one can say Jesus is Lord except by the Holy Spirit" – as "*the* spiritual gift."

119 Emmanuel Lanne obtained his PhD from the École Pratique des Hautes Études in Paris and in the same year would be nominated dean of studies of the Pontifical Greek College of St. Athanasius in Rome. His lecture was only published in 1970 as "Lo spirito e la Chiesa nella teologia patristica," in: Emmanuel Lanne, ed., *Lo spirito Santo e la Chiesa: Una ricerca ecumenica*, Rome, Ave, 1970, 153–205.

120 Lanne, "Lo spirito e la Chiesa," 171.

121 "Those who do not have faith in the Church, are not of the Church and so they do not possess the Spirit, because the Spirit is Truth. They cannot quench their thirst with the draught of youth inside the Church, says Irenaeus, hence they reject the Spirit"; Lanne, "Lo spirito e la Chiesa," 173.

122 "In the Church we participate in the body and Spirit of Christ, which are two different aspects of the same reality"; Lanne, "Lo spirito e la Chiesa," 202.

123 See Gérard Philips, "De Spiritu Sancto et Ecclesia in theologia contemporanea," Louvain, 1957–1958. The centrality of this theme in his theological work also appears

Philips invited Catholic theologians to pay more attention to the Greek church Fathers when teaching Trinitarian theology. They would thus become more attentive to the union of the believer with each of the divine persons, "ad propria personarum" as Thomas Aquinas put it.[124] Philips insisted that the union between the church and the Holy Spirit is "a personal union, not a hypostatic one."[125]

The cycle of ecclesiological conferences ended in 1958 with one on "Présence réelle du Christ dans l'Eucharistie," once again attended by 34 participants. Moeller reports in his introduction how Professor Leenhardt, during their correspondence in preparation of the study day on "Ecclesia sponsa," had already made the suggestion to dedicate a part of that conference to a discussion of this theme. He had published *Le sacrament de la Sainte Cène* in 1948[126] and his 1955 study on the same topic had been well received by the Catholic theologian Joseph de Baciocchi.[127] Soon afterwards, *Istina* paid attention to this debate.[128] Moeller started to prepare a conference on unity and the Eucharist, but due to a meeting of the CCEQ in Chevetogne and the inauguration and consecration of the Byzantine Church in 1957, the study day took place only in 1958 and would bring together both Leenhardt and de Baciocchi. In his conclusions, indeed, Moeller warned that there is more than the scholastic debate on transubstantiation: there is "the role of the Holy Spirit, the divine presence in the other sacraments and in God's word, the relation of the Eucharist with the mystical body."[129]

The analysis of the institution narratives in the New Testament by Jacques Dupont, almost echoes Moeller's words.[130] The theological basis of the dogma of the real presence is the prophetic reference to Jesus' sacrifice on the cross in the institution narratives, which, however, have also become a "memorial."[131] The Orthodox theologian Nicolas Koulomzine, derived two theses from the same New Testament texts: "(1) The institution of the Eucharist cannot be understood differently from the institution of a sacrament, according to the will of our Savior; (2) The sacrament of the Eucharist cannot be understood other than

from the title of his *Festschrift*: *Ecclesia a Spiritu Sancto edocta (Lumen Gentium 53): Mélanges théologiques Hommage à Gérard Philips/Verzamelde Theologische Opstellen aangeboden aan Mgr. Gérard Philips*, Gembloux, Duculot, 1970.

124 See Gérard Philips, "Le Saint Esprit en nous: À propos d'un livre récent," *ETL* 24, 1948, 127–135.

125 See Gérard Philips, "L'Esprit-Saint et l'Église dans le développement de la Théologie Catholique," in: UCL-LG, Charles Moeller, carnets, n. 50, 1956. Unlike other Catholic theologians in his time, Philips showed great respect for the freedom of the believers and did not explain the personality of the church in such a way that the Holy Spirit would almost appear as the hypostasis of the church. See Claude Gérard, *Le Saint-Esprit et ses œuvres dans la pensée de Monseigneur Gérard Philips*, Rome, Pontificium Athenaeum Sanctae Crucis, 1995, 64–66.

126 Franz-Jehan Leenhardt, *Le sacrament de la Sainte Cène*, Neuchâtel, Delachaux et Niestlé, 1948.

127 Franz-Jehan Leenhardt, *Ceci est mon corps: explication de ces paroles de Jésus-Christ*, Neuchâtel, Delachaux et Niestlé, 1955. Joseph de Baciocchi, "Le Mystère eucharistique dans les perspectives de la Bible," *NRT* 87, 1955, 561–580, deplores the insufficient attention to Scripture and the exaggerated emphasis of Catholic theology on philosophical speculation: "First of all, it was necessary to see in what sense Eucharistic sacramentalism prolongs the structure of the Jewish Passover; and for this work, Franz Leenhardt's book was most valuable to me"; de Baciocchi, "Le Mystère eucharistique," 562.

128 Marie-Joseph Le Guillou, "Chronique bibliographique: Un débat sur l'eucharistie," *Istina* 3, 1956, 210–240.

129 Charles Moeller, "Conclusions," in: UCL-LG, Charles Moeller, carnets, n. 54, 1958, 4.

130 Jacques Dupont, "'Ceci est mon corps', 'Ceci est mon sang,'" *NRT* 90, 1958, 1023–1041, esp. 1026: "The real presence is, in fact, only one aspect of Eucharistic doctrine."

131 "The defenders of the dogma of the real presence sometimes tend to neglect or to blur the symbolic and figurative character of the Eucharistic rite ... Jesus announces by a prophetic action the sacrifice that he will accomplish on Calvary. It is an effective sign, however, because in eating this bread and drinking from this cup, the apostles truly enter into the covenant that the sacrifice of Calvary will seal ... It is from this perspective that one must ask the question of the real presence"; Dupont, "'Ceci est mon corps,'" 1035, 1037. Furthermore, Dupont approvingly refers to Leenhardt's work when saying that "from the prophetic, the rite has become a memorial."

ecclesial according to the intention of Christ."[132] Gisbert Ghysens, a Benedictine from Maredsous, made an attempt to reread the doctrine on the real presence and on transubstantiation from the Council of Trent in an ecumenical way. It is helpful to realize, as Henri de Lubac has shown in his *Corpus Mysticum: L'Eucharistie et l'Église au Moyen-Age*,[133] that the theologians of the late 12th and early 13th century used the term *substantia* in the broad sense of referring to the "reality" (*veritas*) of something.[134] It is advisable to explain the change in substance of the liturgical elements to be metaphysical and not physical.[135]

Franz-Jehan Leenhardt chose to make his mainly Catholic audience more familiar with the theology of Calvin on the presence of Christ in the Eucharist. The communion with the body of Christ is a mystery for Calvin, which is brought about "through the secret force of the Holy Spirit."[136] Joseph de Baciocchi reassured his Protestant readers that Catholic theologians have no difficulty in accepting the uniqueness of Christ's sacrifice and of God's reconciliation.[137] In the course of his careful exposition of the Catholic teaching on transubstantiation, including the "definitive" nature of the change of the elements,[138] insights were shared that after the council would lead to ecumenical rapprochement on this theme, such as the conviction that the term "transubstantiation" was not to be explained in reference to the Thomistic understanding of *substantia*.[139] Rousseau characterizes this session as "probably the most dense of all in view of the dialogue."[140]

5 Engaging in a More Intensive Preparation of Vatican II (1959–1962)

Immediately after the announcement of the council, the original plan to continue the theological reflection on the Eucharist was left aside.[141] Congar's suggestion to revisit the history of the previous councils up to Vatican I[142] and to invite more speakers than usual to this conference on "Les mouvements de l'Ecclésiologie à travers l'Histoire des Conciles"[143] was accepted. Less

132 See Nicolas Koulomzine, "Le caractère sacramental et ecclésial de l'Eucharistie d'après le Nouveau Testament et la tradition de l'Église orthodoxe," in: UCL-LG, Charles Moeller, carnets, n. 54, 1958.

133 Henri de Lubac, *Corpus Mysticum: L'Eucharistie et l'Église au Moyen-Age*, Paris, Aubier, 1944.

134 Gisbert Ghysens, "Présence réelle eucharistique et transsubstantiation dans les définitions de l'Église catholique," *Irén* 32, 1959, 420–435, esp. 431.

135 Ghysens, "Présence réelle eucharistique et transsubstantiation," 434, with a reference to Carlo Colombo, "Teologia, filosofia e fisica della transustanziazione," *La Scuola Cattolica* 83, 1955, 89–124.

136 Franz-Jehan Leenhardt, "La présence eucharistique," *Irén* 33, 1960, 146–172, here 149. "Calvin is concerned exclusively with the substance of the body of Christ, while the Catholics, beginning with substance, are interested in what in the bread undergoes a conversion"; Leenhardt, "La présence eucharistique," 155–156. Leenhardt does not hesitate to criticize the objections against Catholic theology found in John Calvin's *Traité de la Sainte Cène* harshly.

137 Joseph de Baciocchi, "Présence eucharistique et transsubstantiation," *Irén* 32, 1959, 139–161, esp. 140–141.

138 de Baciocchi, "Présence eucharistique et transsubstantiation," 152.

139 de Baciocchi, "Présence eucharistique et transsubstantiation," 154. Their dialogue also continued after the council, as appears from Joseph de Baciocchi, "Église et Trinité dans le mystère eucharistique: Méditation œcuménique," in: *L'Évangile, hier et aujourd'hui: Mélanges offerts au professeur Franz-J. Leenhardt*, Geneva, Labor et Fides, 1968, 241–249.

140 Rousseau, "Les journées œcuméniques," 474.

141 Olivier Rousseau, "Introduction," in: Bernard Botte & others, *Le Concile et les conciles: Contribution à l'histoire de la vie conciliaire de l'Église*, Chevetogne/Paris, Éditions de Chevetogne/Cerf, 1960, ix–xix.

142 See O. Rousseau to J. Willebrands, Feb 18, 1959, in: UCL-LG, Charles Moeller, carnets, n. 55, 1959. Since the CCEQ was thinking of discussing the upcoming council as well, Rousseau makes the suggestion that the CCEQ would in its conference focus on the theology of the council and the challenges to organizing one today. It would soon become clear, however, that the Paderborn conference on mission and unity would take place as scheduled and that the executive board of CCEQ would prepare a position paper on the council.

143 On Feb 17, 1959, Rousseau proposed eight names to Moeller: Hilaire Marot, Pierre-Thomas Camelot,

than a year after the conference, which took place in October 1959, all the papers, including an additional study by Congar, had been published in an edited volume.[144] Congar opened the encounter by raising four questions.[145] The opening question "whether collegiality is essential for the church and in which sense" indicates that the conference wanted to contribute to the renewal of the church, even when it focused on the history of previous councils. Other questions dealt with the canonical value of councils, which as collegial events are somehow in conflict with the monarchic and hierarchical constitution of the church, and with the question of who grants authority to the councils and what exactly this authority is. Finally, Congar hoped that their conference would also shed light on what makes a council "ecumenical."

Dom Botte was the only one to use the term collegiality in the title of his chapter, but he explained from the very outset that the title was imposed on him.[146] Still, he was convinced that the full establishment of the hierarchical church between the Councils of Nicaea and Chalcedon did not happen in complete discontinuity with the time of the New Testament, where both the collegial character of the group of the Twelve and the leadership of Peter are mentioned throughout.[147] The confirmation of the apostolic succession of the bishops in the first letter of Clement I was important to protect the unity of the church but it also enhanced communion relationships among bishops. Dom Hilaire Marot, the only monk from Chevetogne to take the floor, developed a similar reasoning in the second contribution, dealing with the period preceding the ecumenical councils. One should not consider them to be an absolute novelty. When in the pre-Nicene period regional councils were convened in reaction to certain difficulties, the underlying ecclesiology, according to Marot, was already that of an "ecclesiology of communion" based on "the local Church." Only a meeting of a substantial number of bishops, representing their local churches, is able to safeguard the unity and catholicity of the church through the unanimity of its teaching.[148] The professor of patristics and former rector of Le Saulchoir, Pierre-Thomas Camelot also repeats the point made by Marot: the institution of the council predates the ecumenical councils. The reunification of the Roman Empire made it possible to organize councils at a universal level that continued to express the unity and catholicity of the church.[149]

Hamilcar Alivisatos, Gérard Fransen, Jean Leclercq, Jean Meyendorff, Alphonse Dupront and Roger Aubert. He would thereby have two Orthodox speakers, and Meyendorff would have to comment on the unionist councils of Lyons and Florence as an Orthodox. In the program sent out to the participants on Aug 10, 1959, the decision was made to set off with a lecture on collegiality in the New Testament and in the apostolic Fathers, which was entrusted to Dom Botte. On the Council of Basel, Leclercq was replaced by Paul De Vooght, and on Lyons and Florence, Meyendorff by Joseph Gill. Congar was entrusted with providing a synthesis that would precede the concluding words by Moeller. The colloquium was able to attract 44 participants.

144 See Botte & others, *Le Concile et les conciles*. Two translations contributed to the wide reception of the book: *Das Konzil und die Konzile: ein Beitrag zur Geschichte des Konzilslebens der Kirche*, Stuttgart, Schwabenverlag, 1962 and *Il Concilio e i concili*, Rome, Edizioni Paoline, 1962.

145 Information derived from the notebooks of Willebrands and Jan Grootaers, Centre for the Study of the Second Vatican Council, KU Leuven.

146 Congar had coined the notion of collegiality in Yves M.-J. Congar, "Le peuple fidèle et la fonction prophétique de l'Église," *Irén* 24, 1951, 289–312, 440–466, esp. 446: "We must not hesitate to translate *sobornost'* as 'collegiality' or 'collegial principle.'" Rousseau had reviewed a number of publications that had picked up the term in Olivier Rousseau, "Propos sur la 'collégialité,'" *Irén* 29, 1956, 320–329.

147 Bernard Botte, "La Collégialité dans le Nouveau Testament et chez les Pères apostoliques," in: Botte & others, *Le Concile et les conciles*, 1–18.

148 Hilaire Marot, "Conciles anténicéens et conciles œcuméniques," in: Botte & others, *Le Concile et les conciles*, 19–43. The quotation comes from the conclusion on page 42. Thanks to his reflections on communion ecclesiology, his contribution was a key to this conference, in the opinion of Emmanuel Lanne. See Lanne, "Le rôle du monastère de Chevetogne," 366.

149 Pierre-Thomas Camelot, "Les Conciles œcuméniques des IVe et Ve siècles," in: Botte & others, *Le Concile et*

Few bishops from the West were present at the Councils of Nicaea, Ephesus, or Chalcedon, but the bishop of Rome was represented by his legates, and if the council had to approve canons in their absence, as was the case with canon 28 of Chalcedon, the approval of the pope was awaited. According to Camelot, it is not necessary to ask whether the council is above the pope or vice versa: "The Council takes place in union with the pope, just as the members are united to the head."[150] The idea of collegiality is present as the awareness to "collectively represent the unity of the body," particularly in the task of remaining faithful to the apostolic tradition, enlightened by Christ and inspired by the Spirit.[151] Congar enriched the volume with a historical study on the motif of the priority of the first four ecumenical councils. When in 519 Pope Hormisdas was finally able to recognize the Council of Constantinople, despite the complete absence of Latin bishops, this was accompanied by a statement which highlighted the value of the first four councils. The comparison of these councils with the four gospels by Pope Gregory the Great and with the four rivers of paradise (Gen 2, 9–10) by Isidore of Seville equally belongs to the *Wirkungsgeschichte* of this motif. With an appeal to the British medievalist Brian Tierney, Congar shows that in the 12th century canonists were convinced that popes were bound by the decisions of these councils and thus prepared the conciliar theories of later centuries.[152] He knows that the motif is important for the Anglican Church as well but is used by it in an exclusive way that is foreign to the Catholic tradition.[153] He especially hopes that a rediscovery of the value of the first four councils may serve the dialogue with the Orthodox, who commemorate the Councils of Nicaea and Chalcedon liturgically, as they also did with the seventh ecumenical council of 787.[154]

The Orthodox contribution to the colloquium and volume dealt with the fifth to eighth ecumenical councils, even if the Orthodox Church considers only the first seven to be ecumenical.[155] Hamilcar Alivisatos, who had been professor at the University of Athens for over four decades, had been promoting the Orthodox participation in the ecumenical movement since the 1920s. He welcomed the initiative of the Ecumenical Study Days as a way of filling the void that was caused "by the total absence of the Catholic Church in the ecumenical movement." Such initiatives allow "to prepare the necessary climate for future

les conciles, 45–73, here at 47–52. A few years later, Camelot published the monograph *Éphèse et Chalcédoine* as the second volume of Gervaise Dumeige, dir., *Histoire des conciles œcuméniques*, Paris, Éditions de l'Orante, 1962.

150 Camelot, "Les Conciles œcuméniques," 72.

151 Camelot, "Les Conciles œcuméniques," 66. As in the Council of Ephesus, the presence of Christ amidst the college of the apostles was symbolized by the enthronement of the Gospel.

152 Yves Congar, "La Primauté des quatre premiers conciles œcuméniques: Origine, destin, sens et portée d'un thème traditionnel," in: Botte & others, *Le Concile et les conciles*, 75–109, esp. 93–94. Reference is made to Tierney's 1951 dissertation that was published as Brian Tierney, *Foundations of the Conciliar Theory: The Contribution of the Medieval Canonists from Gratian to the Great Schism*, Cambridge, Cambridge University Press, 1955.

153 Congar, "La Primauté des quatre premiers conciles œcuméniques," 98.

154 "The dialogue between the Orthodox East and the Catholic West is being resumed today in new and favorable conditions. Sooner or later the question of ecumenical councils and their number will be addressed. It is not for us to say what the Orthodox position might be: open or rigid. It is up to us to prepare, on the Catholic side, the basis for proposals that could respond to an open Orthodox attitude"; Congar, "La Primauté des quatre premiers conciles œcuméniques," 109. See also Peter De Mey, "Preparing the Ground for Fruitful Dialogue with the Orthodox: An Important Motivation of the Ecumenical 'Avant-garde' during the Redaction History of *Lumen gentium*, *Unitatis redintegratio* and *Orientalium Ecclesiarum* (1959–1964)," in: Benoît Bourgine, ed., *Le souci de toutes les Églises: Hommage à Joseph Famerée*, Leuven, Peeters, 2020, 57–85.

155 Hamilcar S. Alivisatos, "Les conciles œcuméniques V^e^, VIe, VIIe et VIIIe," in: Botte & others, *Le Concile et les conciles*, 111–123.

official discussions."[156] The major historical point made in his article is the absence of the pope at the first seven ecumenical councils, which proves, in his opinion, that the supreme authority in the church lays with the council. He was convinced that Orthodox and Catholics need to return to the situation before the Schism. The East and the West have developed profoundly different structures of authority, but differences in local traditions at that moment were still deemed compatible with unity.[157]

The Louvain professor of canon law Gérard Fransen ended his contribution on the medieval councils with an impasse to be solved by later councils: how can the pope be the supreme legislator and judge in matters of faith and at the same time have to obey the canons of earlier councils?[158] The question was taken up by Paul De Vooght, who as a specialist of Jan Hus was asked to treat the topic of conciliarism at the Councils of Constance and Basel.[159] At the former, conciliarism appeared under two forms, pleas to convene councils more regularly or to entrust the ordinary governance of the church to the Roman curia.[160] The latter granted the council the highest authority in matters of faith and church reform, but once the pope had recognized the decisions taken there, the church was bound to his primacy. Even then, however, it maintained the right to question a pope's orthodoxy.[161]

The organizers had been able to invite some of the greatest historians of their time to summarize their insights on the last three councils of the Catholic Church. The British Jesuit Joseph Gill was working on the critical edition of the acts of the Council of Florence and could base his presentation on his recent monograph on the same event.[162] Even if the three Greek delegates that were present were in favor of the theological consensus that, despite the different theological explanation of the procession of the Holy Spirit, Greek and Latin saints had been inspired by the same Spirit, Gill was also attentive to the pressure they would have to face upon returning to Constantinople. The French historian Alphonse Dupront, who had been a professor at the Sorbonne since 1956, was a specialist on the crusades. As in other studies on the Council of Trent which he had published on the occasion of its fourth centenary, Dupront highlights in particular its sociological aspects: the provenance of the small number of council Fathers, the enormous impact of the absent pope on the council through his legates, the important role of the theologians both in defining the position of the absent Protestants and in presenting the Catholic tradition as a coherent whole.[163] The participants in Che-

156 Alivisatos, "Les conciles œcuméniques," 112. Alivisatos, "Les conciles œcuméniques," 112. Dom Rousseau honored him posthumously with a substantial in memoriam, see Olivier Rousseau, "Un grand œcuméniste: le Professeur H.S. Alivisatos," *Irén* 42, 1969, 523–531.

157 Alivisatos, "Les conciles œcuméniques," 122. See also Hamilcar S. Alivisatos, "Les deux régimes dans l'Église unie avant le schisme," in *L'Église et les Églises*, vol. 2, 105–116.

158 Gérard Fransen, "L'Ecclésiologie des Conciles médiévaux," in: Botte & others, *Le Concile et les conciles*, 125–141, esp. 141.

159 Dom Paul De Vooght, "Le Conciliarisme aux conciles de Constance et de Bâle," in: Botte & others, *Le Concile et les conciles*, 143–181. One year later he would publish his major monograph *L'Hérésie de Jean Huss*, Louvain, Publications universitaires de Louvain, 1960.

160 De Vooght, "Le Conciliarisme aux conciles de Constance et de Bâle," 147. As a result of the new constellation that, "it is for the pope to consecrate bishops, for the cardinals to create the pope. It was therefore impossible for the cardinals to be completely conciliarist in the manner of the bishops and the theologians"; De Vooght, "Le Conciliarisme," 148.

161 De Vooght, "Le Conciliarisme," 172–173 and 179.

162 Joseph Gill, "L'accord gréco-latin au Concile de Florence," in: Botte & others, *Le Concile et les conciles*, 183–194. Joseph Gill, *The Council of Florence*, Cambridge, Cambridge University Press, 1959. For a recent ecumenical study of this council, see Barbara Hallensleben & Antoine Arjakovsky, eds., *Le Concile de Florence (1438/39): Une relecture œcuménique/The Council of Florence (1438/39): An Ecumenical Rereading*, Münster, Aschendorff, 2021.

163 Alphonse Dupront, "Le Concile de Trente," in: Botte & others, *Le Concile et les conciles*, 195–243. See also Alphonse Dupront, "Du Concile de Trente: Réflexions autour d'un IVe centenaire," *Revue Historique* 206,

vetogne, as well as the many readers of the proceedings volume, will have greatly profited from the detailed presentation and evaluation of all the documents on ecclesiological issues of Vatican I by Louvain church historian Roger Aubert.[164] The author also indicates the limitations of this council to be remedied at the next: more attention needs to be paid to the role of the Holy Spirit in the church, to the theology of the episcopate and to the theology of the laity,[165] and ambiguous formulations (the characterization of the primacy of the pope as "vere episcopalis" and of his infallible teaching as valid "ex sese, non autem ex consensu Ecclesiae") need to be explained better in order to allow for a different reception from that of "papal centralization."[166]

In his conclusion, Congar makes use of the distinction between institution and life.[167] For the Catholic Church, the binding character of the canons of ecumenical councils is an institution of divine right. If other churches believe that decisions by a council need to be received by the church, then this creates a "serious divergence."[168] If in many contributions attention is paid to the collegiality of the bishops that is displayed during a council, then Congar deduced that this belongs to the life of the church.[169] He also expresses his sympathy for the notion of church as communion, because such an ecclesiology is both theological and anthropological,[170] while he also hopes that the next council will be open towards the "missionary, ecumenical and pastoral" questions that are addressed to it "by the world and by the others."[171]

1951, 262–280. The method of Dupront is welcomed as highly innovative by Marie-Dominique Chenu, "Vie conciliaire de l'Église et sociologie de la foi," *Esprit* 12, 1961, 678–689.

164 Roger Aubert, "L'ecclésiologie au concile du Vatican," in: Botte & others, *Le Concile et les conciles*, 245–284. The references to Louvain dissertations on aspects of Vatican I are a sign of the interest in this council in this university. Half of the speakers at a 1961 conference on fundamental theology also dealt with Vatican I. See Jean-Pierre Torrell, "Les grandes lignes de la théologie de l'épiscopat au Concile du Vatican: Le point de vue officiel," in: Georges Dejaifve & others, *Le Premier "symposium" internationale de théologie dogmatique fondamentale: Louvain, 31 août–2 sept. 1961*, Turin, Società editrice internazionale, 1962, 49–66; Georges Dejaifve, "'Ex sese, non autem ex consensu Ecclesiae,'" in Dejaifve & others, *Le Premier "symposium" internationale*, 67–81; and Gustave Thils, "L'infaillibilité de l'Église 'in credendo' et in 'docendo,'" in: Dejaifve & others, *Le Premier "symposium" internationale*, 83–122.

165 "Today, after half a century of progress in ecclesiology, accomplished in an atmosphere of scriptural and patristic renewal, a new council will be able to take up in much better conditions a formulation of the Catholic doctrine of the church that is both precise and harmonious"; Aubert, "L'ecclésiologie au concile du Vatican," 262.

166 "'The years following the council would bring a strengthening of the direct action of the pope over dioceses and, let us say it, of pontifical centralization. ... A well-balanced theology of the church nonetheless demands that this question be asked, just as practical life demands that its applications be regulated. Will this be the work of the second Vatican council? This is the secret to the future.'"; Aubert, "L'ecclésiologie au concile du Vatican," 284. An important document that can provide assistance in the process of reception is the 1875 declaration of the German episcopate, which had been translated and commented by the Chevetogne community. See Olivier Rousseau, "La vraie valeur de l'Épiscopat dans l'Église: D'après d'importants documents de 1875," *Irén* 29, 1956, 121–142.

167 Yves M.-J. Congar, "Conclusion," in: Botte & others, *Le Concile et les conciles*, 285–334.

168 Congar, "Conclusion," 300. This part of his conclusion even ends in a rather negative fashion: "In many ways, over the past fifteen years or so, our discussions have come back to this same point, which is that of an (irretrievable?) 'parting of the ways.'"

169 "Authority itself may not be collegial; its exercise must, to some degree and in some way, honor the demands of collegiality, of communion, and therefore, far from excluding them, encompassing and assuming, as co-responsible, all the other Christians who are part of the same body. On many occasions, in the course of our exchanges, we have found it interesting to distinguish between the constitution – legal form or structure – on the one hand and the concrete regime ... on the other"; Congar, "Conclusion," 302.

170 Congar, "Conclusion," 305–314.

171 "The next council must be a council in which the church, in examining itself in the light of the questions of the day, defines itself in a very open and generous way, not so much in itself and for itself than in its relationship to the world and in the relationship that the others have with it"; Congar, "Conclusion," 329.

Of the 1960 consultation on "L'Église locale et l'Église universelle," which was attended by 51 participants, only some contributions have been published. Half of the six speakers were non-Catholics, and the colloquium started with the Swedish Lutheran exegete Bo Reicke highlighting the notion of the local church in Paul[172] and the French Reformed pastor Hébert Roux treating the notion of the universal church in the letters of the same apostle.[173] Olivier Rousseau recalls that the rector of the Georgian parish in Paris, Élie Mélia, had impressed his audience with the then still innovative thesis that, within a sacramental ecclesiology, the Eucharistic community of the local church is the basis of the Orthodox understanding of catholicity.[174] The French patrologist Jean Colson discussed the articulation of the two notions in the 2nd century, from Clement I to Irenaeus of Lyons. In this period, the notion of church was applicable to both realities, even if the see and the bishop of Rome became very aware of their special role.[175] The title of the published version of Congar's lecture describes the historical evolution in church history from an ecclesiology of communion to an ecclesiology of the universal church.[176] Whereas in the former the church was understood as a communion of local churches, with bishops visiting one another and seeking to make unanimous decisions during synods and councils, especially since the Gregorian Reform, the papacy, with the help of the mendicant orders, imposed an ecclesiology of the universal church. In an attempt to learn from the Eucharistic ecclesiology of the Orthodox theologians of the emigration, Congar expressed the hope that this universal ecclesiology would be enriched by an ecclesiology of communion. *Mystici corporis* has shown the way, but the upcoming council needs to go further.[177] In broad strokes, Emmanuel Lanne discussed the evolution of the organization of the church at the provincial level

172 As a specialist on the first community of Jerusalem – see Bo Reicke, *Glaube und Leben der Urgemeinde: Bemerkungen zu Apg. 1–7*, Zürich, Zwingli, 1957 – the exegete explained that, even if Paul had encountered the Christian faith in the local church of Jerusalem, he understood each community as the local realization of the universal church. In Phil 2 Paul refers to Christ's proexistence to correct the imperfections of a local church which excels in diaconal service. See Bo Reicke, "Unité chrétienne et diaconie: Phil. ii I–II," in: Willem Corneli van Unnik, ed., *Neotestamentica et Patristica: Eine Freundesgabe Herrn Professor Dr. Oscar Cullmann Zu Seinem 60. Geburtstag Überreicht*, Leiden, Brill, 1962, 203–212.

173 See Hébert Roux, "La notion d'Église universelle dans les Épitres pauliniennes," in: UCL-LG, Charles Moeller, carnets, n. 56, 1960, 1. The entire intervention is preserved in: Archives de la Fédération Protestante de France, Hébert Roux, "Chevetogne," 1960. Roux argues that in the Pauline letters and especially in the Letter to the Ephesians Paul pays attention both to the catholicity – its being filled by Christ – and the universality – its universal mission – of the church.

174 Élie Mélia, "L'Église locale manifestation de l'Église catholique," in: UCL-LG, Charles Moeller, carnets, n. 56, 1960, 1. See Rousseau, "Les journées œcuméniques," 476. Similar ideas occur in Élie Mélia, "Point de vue orthodoxe sur le problème de l'autorité dans l'Église," in: John M. Todd, ed., *Problèmes de l'autorité: Un colloque anglo-française*, Paris, Cerf, 1962, 127–142, esp. 134: "The local church, in fact, in which the bishop exercises his primacy, has priority in the ontological order because it founds the Eucharistic community through sacramental communion with Christ, while the universal church, on the other hand, manifests the communion of Eucharistic communities with one another."

175 Jean Colson, "Église locale et Église universelle au IIe siècle," in: UCL-LG, Charles Moeller, carnets, n. 56, 1960, 1. Similar ideas can be found in chapters 3 and 4 of Jean Colson, *L'épiscopat catholique: Collégialité et primauté dans les trois premiers siècles de l'Église*, Paris, Cerf, 1963, 39–64.

176 Yves Congar, "De la communion des Églises à une ecclésiologie de l'Église universelle," in Yves Congar & Bernard-Dominique Dupuy, eds., *L'épiscopat et l'Église universelle*, Paris, Cerf, 1962, 227–260.

177 "This synthesis must be pushed today in the direction of a better consideration of the relationships between the particular church and the universal church, episcopacy and papacy"; Congar, "De la communion des Églises à une ecclésiologie de l'Église universelle," 256. "A theology of papal power, linked to an ecclesiology of the universal church, requires, in order to be fully in line with the tradition, to be harmonized with an ecclesiology of the church as communion, a theology of the power of bishops as power by divine right"; Congar, "De la communion des Églises à une ecclésiologie de l'Église universelle," 259.

and beyond, from the 1st to the 7th century.[178] His central argument is that, long before the Council of Nicaea, the church had already started to organize itself beyond the local level by accepting the preeminence of certain episcopal sees according to the twofold principle of their political significance in the empire and their apostolic origin.[179] This evolution would lead, in the 7th century, to the creation of the institution of the pentarchy.[180]

In his speech at the opening of the 1961 meeting on "L'Esprit-Saint, Esprit de verité et l'infaillibilité de l'Église," Dom Rousseau indicated that, in view of the upcoming council, the organizers had chosen to discuss an ecclesiological theme that would induce "a confrontation of positions useful for the advancement of the dialogue."[181] Rousseau knew that the infallibility of the church was "affirmed" by Catholics and Orthodox, but "denied" (or "discussed," as the introduction to the proceedings has it) by the Protestants. Even so, it had been entrusted to Jean-Jacques von Allmen, the Swiss Reformed pastor and professor at the University of Neuchâtel, who had also attended the previous conference, to highlight the first part of the title of the colloquium in his opening conference, which he did from a biblical perspective.[182] The indefectibility of the church is related to it being the result of the incarnation as God's work in Jesus Christ through the power of the Spirit. As a reality in time and space, the church is fallible and in need of repentance. Originally the organizers had not intended to focus on all the historical aspects connected to this theological topic but to study the vision of one theologian by way of example. According to Irenaeus of Lyons, as Bruno Reynders highlighted, the church disposed of a great instrument to counter heretic attacks, that is to say, the rule of faith. It was the task of bishops as successors to the apostles to summarize what the church had always taught. The words "infallibility" and "inerrancy" however, did not yet belong to Irenaeus' vocabulary.[183]

Since it was felt during the discussion that important historical information on the period preceding the one covered by the Louvain professor Gustave Thils was missing, two participants accepted to prepare a contribution to the volume. The French Dominican Bernard-Dominique Dupuy, who had started to attend the Ecumenical Study Days since his nomination as successor of Congar as professor of fundamental theology at Le Saulchoir in 1959, discussed the teaching authority of the church from the period of the

178 Emmanuel Lanne, "Églises locales et patriarcats à l'époque des grands conciles," *Irén* 34, 1961, 292–321.

179 He regularly comments on Francis Dvornik, *The Idea of Apostolicity in Byzantium and the Legend of the Apostle Andrew*, Cambridge MA, Harvard University Press, 1958.

180 In the introduction to this article, the reader already felt that during the council this monk would also combat Latinization and would defend the rights of the Eastern Catholic Churches: "The extremely centralized organization of the Western church, especially since the Middle Ages, the influence of the theology of Bellarmine on the church, and finally the immense prestige which the papacy has enjoyed since the Vatican council have been the principal factors which have contributed to the blurring in Catholic thought of the role and importance of the notion of the local church. We also know that a very clear tendency of a certain theology would like, in a more or less conscious way, to see in the patriarchate only a rather anachronistic honorific title and in the bishops only functionaries, temporary depositaries of the central authority for the section of the Catholic church whose charge is entrusted to them"; Lanne, "Églises locales et patriarcats," 292.

181 "Introduction aux journées œcuméniques de Chevetogne (25–29 septembre 1961)," in: UCL-LG, Charles Moeller, carnets, n. 56bis, 1961, 1.

182 Jean-Jacques von Allmen, "L'Esprit de vérité vous conduira dans toute la vérité," in: Olivier Rousseau & others, *L'infaillibilité de l'Église: Journées œcuméniques de Chevetogne 25–29 Septembre 1961*, Chevetogne, Éditions de Chevetogne, 1963, 13–26.

183 Bruno Reynders, "Premières réactions de l'Église devant les falsifications du dépôt apostolique: Saint Irénée," in: *L'infaillibilité de l'Église*, 27–52. Reynders, who was awaiting the permission to make a transfer to Chevetogne, had recently published *Vocabulaire de la "Démonstration" et des fragments de St. Irénée*, Chevetogne, Éditions de Chevetogne, 1958.

New Testament up to the 13th century.[184] Before the period of the ecumenical councils bishops and presbyters had already seen it as their duty to transmit the apostolic faith to new generations of Christians, but this could be carried out in a variety of creeds. Starting from the Council of Nicaea, the bishops exercised their teaching authority by expressing the *consensus patrum* in the form of binding creeds and canons.[185] In the medieval period, particular attention was paid to the promulgation of the symbols of faith by the pope. The pope continued to be held personally fallible, however, and it was insisted that the creeds needed to express the faith of the church.[186] Dom De Vooght, who had not missed a single conference since 1951, agreed to study the use of the term "infallibility" by Latin theologians from the 13th till the 15th century.[187] In the late 13th century Petrus Olivi coined the term *inerrabilitas* and applied it in first instance to the church and in a derived sense to the see of Rome and to the pope. For the 14th century, De Vooght focused on two theologians who started using the term *infallibilis*. The Catalan canonist Guido Terrena was the first to define as infallible the definitions of the pope that were the result of previous consultation with his cardinals and with the bishops that had convened in a council. This, however, does not apply to his teaching as a private person. The German Augustinian Hermann von Schildesche, on the other hand, was an early "papalist," and for the 15th century De Vooght followed the papalist line through a few other theologians from Prague, as well as through the Spanish Dominican Cardinal Juan de Torquemada. His most important conclusion, however, is a negative one, in that the great scholastic theologians, among whom Thomas Aquinas, remained reluctant to use the term.[188]

The Louvain professor Gustave Thils participated in the conference at the time when he was already an active member of the SPCU[189] and presented part of his ongoing research on Vatican I.[190] The first schema *De Ecclesia* in its chapter "De Ecclesiae infallibilitate" and the revised schema *De Ecclesia* in its chapter "De ecclesiastico magisterio" briefly affirm the *infallibilitas in credendo* of all the faithful as the foundation of the two forms

184 Bernard-Dominique Dupuy, "Le magistère de l'Église, service de la parole," in: Rousseau & others, *L'infaillibilité de l'Église*, 53–97. Because his paper was prepared after the conference, in the footnotes he could already refer to Yves Marie-Joseph Congar, *La tradition et les traditions*, Paris, Fayard, 1960.

185 "The formulations of the great councils are a determining moment in the exercise of the Magisterium and in the clarification of the infallibility of the church … Infallibility is only the translation on the level of the Magisterium of the doctrinal immutability affirmed at that time on the level of truth"; Dupuy, "Le magistère de l'Église," 81.

186 Dupuy, "Le magistère de l'Église," 94–96 contains an interesting discussion of Thomas Aquinas, *ST* II^{a}–II^{ae}, I, a. 9: "Utrum convenienter articuli fidei in symbolo *ponantur*" and a. 10: "Utrum ad Summum Pontificem pertineat symbolum fidei *ordinare*."

187 Paul De Vooght, "Esquisse d'une enquête sur le mot 'infaillibilité' durant la période scolastique," in: Rousseau & others, *L'infaillibilité de l'Église*, 99–146. His footnote references show the scholarly interest in this theme in those years. See Adolar Zumkeller, *Schrifttum und Lehre des Hermann von Schildesche O.E.S.A. († 1357)*, Würzburg, Augustinus-Verlag, 1959 and Pacifico Massi, *Magistero infallibile del papa nella teologia di Giovanni da Torquemada*, Turin, Marietti, 1957.

188 The conclusion is clear: "The most papalist of theologians, Juan de Torquemada, did not quite succeed in placing the pope fully above the council. It took another four centuries to develop this point of doctrine"; De Vooght, "Esquisse d'une enquête," 146.

189 Gustave Thils owed his nomination at the secretariat to his *Histoire doctrinale du mouvement œcuménique*, Louvain, Warny, 1955, and had already presented first drafts of proposals for the secretariat during its August 1961 plenary session in Bühl. See Peter De Mey, "Gustave Thils and Ecumenism at Vatican Council II," in: Donnelly & others, eds., *The Belgian Contribution to the Second Vatican Council*, 389–413.

190 Gustave Thils, "L'Infaillibilité de l'Église dans la constitution 'Pastor aeternus' du 1er Concile du Vatican," in: Rousseau & others, *L'infaillibilité de l'Église*, 147–182. See also Thils's works: *Primauté pontificale et prérogatives épiscopales: "Potestas ordinaria" au Concile du Vatican*, Louvain, Warny, 1961 and *L'infaillibilité du peuple chrétien "in credendo": Notes de théologie posttridentine*, Paris, Desclée de Brouwer, 1963.

of the *infallibilitas in docendo*, the one exercised by the college of bishops and the other exercised by the pope. The reason for the relative neglect of the *infallibilitas in credendo* in the documents of Vatican I was that this teaching was universally accepted and no difficulties remained to be solved by the council.[191]

This conference was also an ecumenical learning experience. The critical but constructive viewpoints expressed by non-Catholic theologians became important elements in Moeller's conclusion.[192] The ecclesiologist of Saint-Serge, Nicholas Afanasiev, proposed to reformulate the Catholic discussion on infallibility in terms of the notion of truth. The Orthodox Church is called to protect the truth which it had discovered with the assistance of the Spirit of truth. Hence decisions by an ecumenical council have to be verified by the church.[193] As he would repeat on other occasions, in his opinion the Orthodox Church and the Catholic Church shared a fascination for universal ecclesiology.[194] Within this framework, it was the ecumenical council's task to define the truth, but it was less clear for the Orthodox Church which body had to validate the decisions of a council, except that this could not be entrusted to the local churches. The two options were the emperor or the bishop of Rome; if one maintains this ecclesiology, then even an Orthodox theologian would nowadays ascribe this function to the pope.[195] Within the framework of a Eucharistic ecclesiology, which is more congenial to the Orthodox conscience in Afanasiev's opinion, the unity of God's church is safeguarded in the plurality of local churches establishing relations of communion with one another.[196] Thanks to the incomparable testimony delivered by the Church of Rome, one could eventually call infallible the decisions pronounced by the bishop of Rome in the name of his church.[197] According to the canon theologian of Exeter, Henry Balmforth, there is a strong awareness within Anglicanism that the church cannot err in its essential truths, while it insists that these truths can be discovered by means of a variety of ways: Scripture, the rule of faith, the liturgy, the *consensus fidelium* and theological reflection.[198] While continuing to believe that the definitions of Vatican I are not based on Scripture, the church Fathers, and the historical reality of the church in

191 Thils warns however: "Nothing is more contrary to the Vatican definition of 1870 itself than to imagine a pontifical Magisterium 'separated' from the church, without any organic 'connection' with it, and even 'distinct' from it in its normal and habitual exercise"; Thils, "L'Infaillibilité de l'Église dans la constitution 'Pastor aeternus,'" 180. His chapter also prepares the discussion on the active nature of the *infallibilitas in credendo* during Vatican II, see Thils, "L'Infaillibilité de l'Église dans la constitution 'Pastor aeternus,'" 173–174.

192 Charles Moeller, "Conclusion: Infaillibilité et Vérité," in: Rousseau & others, *L'infaillibilité de l'Église*, 223–255.

193 Nicolas Afanassieff, "L'Infaillibilité de l'Église du point de vue d'un théologien orthodoxe," in: Rousseau & others, *L'infaillibilité de l'Église*, 183–201. "Infallibility then belongs neither to a council nor to any person, whether the bishop of Rome or someone else; but it belongs to the truth held by the Church"; Afanassieff, "L'Infaillibilité de l'Église," 186. Rousseau explicitly mentions in his overview that "Afanasiev's presence was significant in this session"; see Rousseau, "Les journées œcuméniques," 478.

194 See the famous article he also allowed the Chevetogne community to publish: Nicolas Afanassieff, "Una Sancta," *Irén* 36, 1963, 436–475.

195 "Remaining on the terrain of universal ecclesiology, we can logically admit that it is indeed the pope who is the organ through which the reception by the church of the decisions of an ecumenical council is manifested"; Afanassieff, "L'Infaillibilité de l'Église," 192.

196 "Infallibility belongs to the union of the local churches in concord"; Afanassieff, "L'Infaillibilité de l'Église," 197.

197 "When the bishop of Rome speaks, his decisions can be infallible, if he thus manifests the church of Rome acting in agreement with all the other local churches"; Afanassieff, "L'Infaillibilité de l'Église," 200.

198 Henry Balmforth, "L'Infaillibilité de l'Église selon la doctrine de l'Église anglicane," in: Rousseau & others, *L'infaillibilité de l'Église*, 203–210. Balmforth was known for his book *The Royal Priesthood*, London, The Church Union, 1956. The Council on Inter-Church Relations of the Church of England had delegated five more Anglicans to the conference. A report by one of them, John de Satgé, was added in appendix to the volume. See John de Satgé, "Quelques réflexions sur la conference œcuménique de Chevetogne, septembre 1961," in: Rousseau & others, *L'infaillibilité de l'Église*, 257–263.

the first millennium, Anglicans might be willing to accept that the apostolic see of Rome enjoys "a primacy of honor, or of responsibility."[199] Finally, Jean Bosc, professor of dogmatic theology at the Faculty of Protestant Theology in Paris, explained the position of the Reformed churches in this debate.[200] His church denies the infallibility of the church (albeit not its indefectibility) because the authority of the Holy Scripture is guaranteed by God. In order to assist believers in interpretating God's Word, the church is free to convene councils or may decide on particular confessions of faith but these need to be received by the believers.

Moeller's conclusions show that the Catholic organizers had learnt a great deal from this ecumenical conversation. It was advised to substitute the biblical notion of truth for the technical term infallibility, to be more aware of the exceptional character of the extraordinary magisterium[201] and to appreciate the liturgical celebrations of the local church as instances in which both the infallibility *in credendo* and the infallibility *in docendo* can be practiced.[202]

The final colloquium in this series returned to the theme of collegiality. The meeting on "Les Douze" was attended by 49 participants. It took place two weeks before the start of the first session of the council but its conferences were not published in one volume. The first four conferences were dedicated to exegetical issues. Following his general interest in the link between the Old and the New Testament, the Swiss Reformed Old Testament scholar Wilhelm Vischer compared the use of the number twelve in both parts of the Holy Scripture. Vischer's main thesis is that Jesus is "the Israel of God" (Gal 6:16) who fulfilled God's promises to Israel in his life, death and resurrection.[203] The Louvain exegete Jean Giblet dealt with the Twelve in the synoptic gospels. Even if some scholars had started to question the well-known thesis of Karl Heinrich Rengstorff that the institution of the Twelve goes back to the historical Jesus and was inspired by the Jewish institution of the *Shaliah*, Giblet remains convinced that some biblical passages that refer to the Twelve belong to a very old tradition. Apart from the reference to the apostles in 1 Cor 15:5, there is the Semitic vocabulary in Mark 3:14, the acknowledgement of Judas as "one of the Twelve" in all three synoptic gospels, and the announcement that the Twelve will sit "on twelve thrones, judging the twelve tribes of Israel" in Matt 19:28 and Luke 22:28–30, which is in line with the eschatological character of Jesus' proclamation.[204] The conference by François-Paul Dreyfus, professor of New Testament studies at Le Saulchoir, aimed to put Paul in relation to the institutions of the Twelve and the

199 Balmforth, "L'Infaillibilité de l'Église selon la doctrine de l'Église anglicane," 210.

200 Jean Bosc, "L'attitude des Églises réformées concernant l'Infaillibilité de l'Église," in: Rousseau & others, *L'infaillibilité de l'Église*, 211–222. Bosc, who would become a member of the Joint Working Group between the WCC and the Catholic Church after the council, was already engaged in regular dialogues with Catholic theologians. See Jean Bosc, Jean Guitton & Jean Daniélou, *Le dialogue catholique-protestant*, Paris, La Palatine, 1960.

201 "On the other hand, in the acts of the extraordinary Magisterium, everything does not regard the faith, far from it. There is even the possibility of a council meeting without defining any point of faith … In other words, and if we may make the comparison, the definitions of the extraordinary Magisterium are similar to mountain paths, which make it possible to reach this or that point more quickly; but the path must not make us forget the mountain itself. The mountain, in this case, is the living tradition of the whole church assisted by the Spirit in proclaiming the truths of salvation"; Moeller, "Conclusion: Infaillibilité et Vérité," 251–252.

202 "The first organ of irrefutable proclamation of the truth of God is the liturgy of the local church"; Moeller, "Conclusion: Infaillibilité et Vérité," 237. This is a remarkable insight for a Catholic theologian in 1961.

203 "Précis de l'étude présentée par M. Wilhelm Vischer," in: UCL-LG, Charles Moeller, carnets, n. 57, 1962, 2 pages.

204 A comparison with the outline "Les Douze dans les évangiles synoptiques" in: UCL-LG, Charles Moeller, carnets, n. 57, 1962, 2 pages, shows that Giblet pronounced an identical lecture at the Colloquium Biblicum Lovanienses of August 1962 which he presided. See Jean Giblet, "Les Douze: Histoire et théologie," in: Jean Giblet & others, eds., *Aux origines de l'Église*, Bruges, Desclée de Brouwer, 1965, 51–64.

apostles. Even if at the level of the New Testament there is a difference in vocabulary between Paul, counting himself as one of the apostles, and Luke's never including Paul in the number of the Twelve, the occurrence of the words "from the beginning" in both Acts 1:22 and John 15:27 already anticipates the synthesis of the Twelve and the apostles in the post-apostolic church.[205] Finally, the rector and professor of New Testament studies from the Orthodox theological faculty of Saint-Serge in Paris, Msgr. Cassian (Bezobrazov), dealt with the Twelve in Johannine literature, which he considered a literary unity produced by the same apostle. He had a special interest in the symbolism of numbers. His most important conclusion was that nothing is said about apostolic succession in these writings.[206]

Two monks from the Chevetogne community had also prepared a contribution. Théodore Strotmann spoke about "The cult of the apostles in the Byzantine Liturgy"[207] and Hilaire Marot about "The notion of apostolicity and its titles in the tradition of the church."[208] The Byzantine liturgical tradition of the East praises the apostles Peter and Paul in an equal manner on Jun 29, a feast inherited from the Latin tradition. According to Strotmann, this praxis also has ecclesiological implications.[209] Honorific titles that had been applied exclusively to the pope since the Gregorian Reform (*Sedes apostolica*, *Summus Pontifex*, etc.) were, as Marot's detailed investigation shows, applied from the 5th to the 7th centuries to bishops as well.[210] In these years, the Belgian Jesuit Georges Dejaifve was mainly doing ecclesiological research on Vatican I,[211] but in the concluding lecture of this conference he dealt with "The succession of the Twelve in Roman Catholic tradition and theology."[212] By looking more closely at selected moments in the tradition, Dejaifve hopes to show that the relationship between the college of the Twelve and its head in the New Testament has in the Latin tradition become the relationship between the collegial authority of

205 François-Paul Dreyfus, "Paul, les Douze et les Apôtres," in: UCL-LG, Charles Moeller, carnets, n. 57, 1962, 2 pages.

206 Msgr. Cassian (Bezobrazov), "Les Douze dans les écrits johanniques," in: UCL-LG, Charles Moeller, carnets, n. 57, 1962, 1 page. In 1955, *Istina* had published – with much hesitation, as the foreword indicates, and accompanied by a lengthy response by Pierre Benoît – an article by the author dealing with a similar theme. See Cassian, "Saint Pierre et l'Église dans le Nouveau Testament (le problème de la primauté)," *Istina* 2, 1955, 261–304. In his opinion, Peter enjoyed the "hierarchical primacy" at no point in his apostolic ministry (267); his post-paschal appointment as pastor was qualitatively different from that of the other apostles but ended – thus he argued on the basis of John 21:23 – at the moment of his death (295–298). On the basis of the New Testament, one can only conclude that, "no church has inherited the primacy of the hierarchic center of Jerusalem in the Christian world" and that "Saint Peter died a martyr without leaving a successor." What he interestingly does not exclude is "the hierarchical primacy of one local church, like the primacy of the church of Jerusalem, presided over by Saint Peter and later by Saint James"; Cassian, "Saint Pierre et l'Église," 303–304.

207 Published as Théodore Strotmann, "Les coryphées Pierre et Paul et les autres apôtres," *Irén* 36, 1963, 164–176.

208 Published as Hilaire Marot, "La Collégialité et le Vocabulaire épiscopal du Ve au VIIe siècle," *Irén* 36, 1963, 41–60 and *Irén* 37, 1964, 198–226.

209 "Without diminishing the eminence of Peter's place among the apostles, the juxtaposition of the two coryphees expresses more a regime of government that is charismatic rather than directly juridical, a plenitude of governance that is polyarchic (the 'chorus' of the bishops of the universal church) rather than a monarchial shrinkage (the 'papal church')"; Strotmann, "Les coryphées Pierre et Paul," 175. The article had been published after the demise of Pope John XXIII and had been dedicated to his memory: "In memory of Pope John XXIII who called himself 'the humble successor of Peter and Paul.'"

210 For the implications for the discussion on collegiality, see Marot, "La collégialité et le vocabulaire épiscopal," 41: "This fact is not indifferent to a study of collegiality as it was then envisioned because it was, as we will see, to manifest the apostolic character of every episcopate ... that a series of expressions were created at that time."

211 See Georges Dejaifve, *Pape et évêques au premier Concile du Vatican*, Paris, Desclée de Brouwer, 1961.

212 Published as Georges Dejaifve, "Les douze apôtres et leur unité dans la tradition catholique," *ETL* 39, 1963, 760–778.

the college of bishops and the successor of Peter as their principle of unity.[213] At the time of the church Fathers, Cyprian sees the pope as the one in charge of the unity of the bishops, and according to Augustine Peter's successor is able to represent the college of bishops.[214] In the 12th century, the relationship between the pope and bishops is explained by making a distinction between the power of sacred order and the power of jurisdiction. The former is received from God and the latter from the one possessing the *plenitudo potestatis*, even if the canonists know that the pope needs the assistance of the college of cardinals and can eventually be deposed by a council.[215] In modern times, despite the crisis of Gallicanism, the Catholic Church has preferred to maintain the paradox that there are two subjects possessing the highest authority in the church.[216]

6 Conclusions

The sheer number of 18 Ecumenical Study Days which the Benedictine community of Chevetogne has organized between 1942 and 1962 makes it clear that this community has participated immensely in the ecumenical formation of Catholic theologians in the decades preceding Vatican II. The success of the study days is partly connected to the special setting and the outstanding personalities of some of the monks. Making the demanding journey to Chevetogne, participating in their bi-ritual life of prayer, and feeling warmly welcomed by the community made a profound ecumenical impact on the participants.[217] Religious communities often courageously defend their ideals and cherish a critical distance from Rome. This motivated the monks of Chevetogne to offer refuge to the young students from Louvain who had been confronted with the magisterium's distrust of *nouvelle théologie*. The role of the Chevetogne community, however, was not limited to being good hosts, but it also allowed many confreres – such as Clément Lialine, Olivier Rousseau, Théodore Strotmann, Hilaire Marot, and Emmanuel Lanne – to share their well-prepared scholarly work during these conferences.

In comparison to the ambition of the CCEQ to include all major ecumenical centers in Europe, the study days were narrower in scope and were oriented in particular towards francophone scholars. On the other hand, unlike the CCEQ, from 1947 the community started to invite Orthodox, Anglican, and Protestant theologians to present their views and participate in a truly ecumenical event. This opportunity for direct conversations between Catholic and non-Catholic theologians makes the Ecumenical Study Days of Chevetogne a distinctive and exceptional experience in the panorama of initiatives organized by Catholic ecumenism in the preconciliar period.

The high quality of the conferences was the result of the strategy to select well-known specialists on the topic assigned to them. Examples are Franz-Jehan Leenhardt and Joseph de Baciocchi on the real presence of Christ in the Eucharist, Gérard Philips on grace, Yves Congar on the Great Schism, Joseph Gill on the Council of Florence, Roger Aubert and Gustave Thils on Vatican I, and Nicholas Afanasiev on Eucharistic versus universal

213 Dejaifve, "Les douze apôtres et leur unité," 762.

214 Dejaifve, "Les douze apôtres et leur unité," 762–767.

215 Dejaifve, "Les douze apôtres et leur unité," 767–773.

216 Dejaifve, "Les douze apôtres et leur unité," 773–777. Hence Dejaifve is able to conclude: "The Western tradition, through the vicissitudes of its history, has tried to remain faithful to the precept of the Lord in keeping the ever-threatened balance between the one and the many within the church. Has it always succeeded in doing so in practice? This is a question that we leave open. Unfortunately, practice is not always up to the convictions of the faith, neither for individuals nor for the church"; Dejaifve, "Les douze apôtres et leur unité," 778.

217 "May the final reporter be allowed to say that the Amay-Chevetogne 'institution,' through the celebration of the liturgy, the attentive hospitality of the community and of its prior, also represents an 'event' which, each time, 'converts' the participants of these ecumenical meetings"; Moeller, "Conclusion: Infaillibilité et Vérité," 224.

ecclesiology. From the very beginning, the talent of fundamental theologian Charles Moeller to broaden the discussion in his concluding thoughts was appreciated. The scholarly ambition of the Chevetogne conferences also becomes clear when observing that many conferences were followed by valuable volumes edited by the Éditions de Chevetogne, whereas the CCEQ left it exclusively to the speakers to decide whether or not to publish their findings. As for the thematic focus, the Ecumenical Study Days were particularly interested in the renewal and reform of Catholic ecclesiology (openness to the world, collegiality, infallibility, and apostolicity), whereas those of the CCEQ were also interested in a systemic reflection on models of Christian unity and on the themes discussed in the WCC.

When studying the materials of the study days organized after the announcement of Vatican II, one feels that some of its innovative ideas were prepared there.[218] Lanne therefore calls these conferences "the far, then close preparation of Vatican II in Chevetogne."[219] Towards the end of the council the community reassumed this series of conferences and started to harvest its fruits to improve ecumenical relations between churches.[220]

218 In his overview, Lanne points to the connection between his own contribution to the 1960 conference on the local church and *Lumen gentium*, § 23, as well as Thils' intervention on infallibility and *Lumen gentium*, § 12. Lanne, "Le rôle du monastère de Chevetogne," 367.

219 Lanne, "Le rôle du monastère de Chevetogne," 370.

220 This took place especially in the 1964 conference on Vatican II and the ecumenical situation, and in the 1965, 1966, and 1968 sessions dealing with the three major documents *Lumen gentium*, *Dei Verbum*, and *Gaudium et spes*. See also Rousseau, "Les journées œcuméniques," 479–483.

Bibliography

1054–1954: L'Église et les Églises: Neuf siècles de douloureuse séparation entre l'Orient et l'Occident. Études et travaux offerts à Dom Lambert Beauduin, 2 vols., Chevetogne, Éditions de Chevetogne, 1954–1955.

Botte, Bernard & others, *Le Concile et les conciles: Contribution à l'histoire de la vie conciliaire de l'Église*, Chevetogne/Paris, Éditions de Chevetogne/Cerf, 1960.

Colleye, Fernand, *Charles Moeller et l'Arbre de la Croix: Crise de l'Eglise et désarrois du monde. La vie d'un théologien du XXème siècle*, Paris, Publibook, 2007.

Congar, Yves & Bernard-Dominique Dupuy, eds., *L'épiscopat et l'Église universelle*, Paris, Cerf, 1962.

De Pril, Ward, *Theological Renewal and the Resurgence of Integrism: The René Draguet Case (1942) in Its Context*, Leuven, Peeters, 2016.

Fouilloux, Étienne, *Les catholiques et l'unité chrétienne du XIXème au XXème siècle: Itinéraires européens d'expression française*, Paris, Cerf, 1982.

Lanne, Emmanuel, "Le rôle du monastère de Chevetogne au deuxième concile du Vatican," in: Doris Donnelly & others, eds., *The Belgian Contribution to the Second Vatican Council: International Research Conference at Mechelen, Leuven and Louvain-la-Neuve (September 12–16, 2005)*, Leuven, Peeters, 2008, 361–388.

Rousseau, Olivier & others, *L'infaillibilité de l'Église: Journées œcuméniques de Chevetogne 25–29 Septembre 1961*, Chevetogne, Éditions de Chevetogne, 1963.

Rousseau, Olivier, "Les journées œcuméniques de Chevetogne (1942–1967)," in: *Au service de la parole de Dieu: Mélanges offerts à Monseigneur André Charue, évêque de Namur*, Gembloux, Duculot, 1969, 451–485.

Verdoodt, Albert, *Les colloques œcuméniques de Chevetogne (1942–1983) et la réception par l'église catholique de charismes d'autres communions chrétiennes*, Chevetogne, Éditions de Chevetogne, 1986.

CHAPTER 15

Theological Foundations and Interpretations of the Ecumenical Movement during the First Half of the 20th Century: Orthodox Positions

Viorel Coman

1 Introduction

Unlike the Roman Catholic Church, which set out on an official ecumenical path only after Vatican II, the Orthodox Church showed interest in dialogue and conversation with other Christian denominations much earlier in the 20th century. Although the ecumenical spirit of the Orthodox Church has not gone uncontested by certain ultraconservative groups, it has nevertheless been a major protagonist in the ecumenical movement and has taken part in official gatherings from the beginning, contributing to the healing of divisions with the other Christian churches. That said, this chapter narrates the story of the Orthodox quest for an ecumenical path towards unity in the period between the 1930s and the 1960s, with a focus on (1) the unofficial encounters between the Orthodox Church and the Catholic Church due to the impressive ecumenical work of the Russian theologians of the Parisian diaspora, who sought theoretical and practical forms of rapprochement with the Catholics in France at a time when no dialogue was possible on an official level between the two churches; and (2) Georges Florovsky's contribution to the dialogue between the Orthodox Church and the Protestant churches within the WCC. In addition, there is a major insight that emerges from the narration of the story of the Orthodox quest for an ecumenical path towards unity from the 1930s to the 1960s: the most daring ecumenical models were proposed by Orthodox theologians who were seeking to bring their church closer to Roman Catholicism, and especially by Nicholas Afanasiev and André Scrima. Although the ecumenical reflections of Florovsky, who was involved in the development of the WCC, did not lack ecumenical courage in their willingness to interact with the Protestant world, his theological reflections were more cautious and did not go as far as the ecumenical models proposed by Afanasiev and Scrima in relation to Catholics.

2 Orthodox-Catholic Relations

With the promulgation of the encyclical *Mortalium animos* in 1928 by Pope Pius XI,[1] the Roman Catholic Church was prohibited from engaging in official ecumenical relations with other Christian churches, including the Orthodox Church. Nevertheless, despite the condemnation of the ecumenical activity at the time by the pope, the following decades saw the advent of a form of proto-ecumenism in relations between the Orthodox Church and the Catholic Church, albeit at the unofficial level of theologians and cross-denominational networks of like-minded ecumenists who sought to advance the cause of Christian unity in each tradition. From the 1930s to the 1950s, the Russian theologians of the Parisian diaspora formed "the ecumenical *avant-garde*"[2]

---

1 See the contribution by Marie Levant in the first volume of this work.

2 The expression "ecumenical *avant-gard*" is borrowed from the title of Peter De Mey's article "Preparing the Ground for Fruitful Dialogue with the Orthodox: An Important Motivation of the Ecumenical 'Avant-garde' during the Redaction History of *Lumen gentium*, *Orientalium Ecclesiarum* and *Unitatis Redintegratio*," in: Benoît Bourgine, ed., *Le souci de toutes les Églises: Hommage à Joseph*

within the context of the informal relationships between the Orthodox Church and the Catholic Church. However, in the 1960s it was Scrima who was foremost among those Orthodox theologians who served as bridge builders between the two traditions, and who made an important contribution to the warming of their relations, especially during Vatican II, which officially inaugurated the ecumenical turning point[3] in interactions between the Orthodox Church and the Catholic Church. The ecumenical turn in Orthodox-Catholic relationships constitutes a series of events in the early 1960s that took the Church of Constantinople and the Church of Rome from estrangement and animosity towards dialogue and cooperation, with the goal of recovering the lost unity between the Orthodox Church and the Catholic Church. The ecumenical turn launched the so-called dialogue of love between the two churches (from 1963 to 1975) and acted as a catalyst for the establishment of an official doctrinal dialogue between them, the so-called theological dialogue (from 1975 onwards).[4]

2.1 *Russian Orthodox Theologians in the Parisian Diaspora*

A major impetus in the rapprochement between the Orthodox Church and the Catholic Church in the decades prior to Vatican II was provided by the Russian Orthodox theologians and philosophers of the Parisian diaspora, who were forced to leave their native country and move West by the Bolsheviks at the beginning of the 1920s.[5] Most of them settled permanently in France, where they enriched the theological and cultural landscape of the country. Although their forced departure from Russia was a tragic and undesirable episode that should have never happened, it had positive implications for the growth of an Orthodox contingent in a predominantly Catholic and Protestant milieu, as well as for the ecumenical trajectory of Orthodox Christianity in the 20th century. The establishment of the Institut de théologie orthodoxe Saint-Serge in Paris in 1925 and the efforts of its professors – especially Sergius Bulgakov and Georges Florovsky – to make Orthodox Christianity better known in the West contributed to the rapprochement between Eastern and Western Christianity in a way that had not been possible before. Their informal interaction with the French Catholic world, which prepared for and anticipated the official ecumenical turn between the Orthodox Church and the Catholic Church in the 1960s, was facilitated via a series of encounters and mutually influencing theological projects that aimed at the renewal of both traditions.

First of all, these informal interactions between Orthodoxy and Catholicism surfaced from the 1930s onwards in meetings between several theological and philosophical associations and unofficial discussion groups. Even though most of these gatherings were not necessarily intended to provide platforms for ecumenical dialogue in the strict

Famerée, Leuven, Peeters, 2020, 57–86. The expression is used by Peter De Mey to define the group of Roman Catholic theologians who favored a new path for their church in the decade prior to Vatican II, namely that of ecumenical openness and dialogue. On the Parisian diaspora see the contribution by Adalberto Mainardi in the first volume of this work.

3 For a detailed description of the ecumenical turn in Orthodox-Catholic relationships, see Viorel Coman, *Bridge-Builder between East and West: André Scrima and the Ecumenical Turn in Orthodox-Catholic Relationships*, Leiden, Brill, 2024.

4 For the history of the official dialogue between Orthodoxy and Catholicism, see, especially, Patrice Mahieu, *Se préparer au don de l'unité: La commission internationale catholique-orthodoxe (1975–2000)*, Paris, Cerf, 2016; Patrice Mahieu, *Paul VI et les orthodoxes*, Paris, Cerf, 2012; and Giancarlo Bruni, *Quale ecclesiologia?: Cattolicesimo e Ortodossia a confronto. Il dialogo ufficiale*, Milan, Paoline, 1999.

5 The story of their departure from Russia is narrated by Lesley Chamberlain in her book *The Philosophy Steamer: Lenin and the Exile of the Intelligentsia*, London, Atlantic Books, 2006. See, also, Marc Raeff, *Russia Abroad: A Cultural History of the Russian Emigration (1919–1939)*, Oxford, Oxford University Press, 1990.

sense of the term, their relevance to the cause of inter-Christian unity should not be downplayed. These meetings brought together members of the Catholic, Protestant, and Orthodox intelligentsia in Paris where they shared common interests and subscribed to similar perspectives on the social, political, economic, cultural, and theological changes associated with their time. The participation of the Russian Orthodox theologians and philosophers of the Parisian diaspora in the meetings contributed to the development of greater understanding and rapprochement between their tradition and Catholicism. A few famous gatherings at private homes in Paris are illustrative in this regard and deserve to be mentioned: Nicholas Berdyaev's colloquia in Clamart (a suburb of Paris); the encounters at the house of Jacques and Raissa Maritain in Meudon; and Gabriel Marcel's Friday seminars (in rue de Touron).[6] Unfortunately, these meetings are poorly documented, with very few recorded sources which can be used to reconstruct them.

Among the exceptions to this paucity of documentation is the *Dieu Vivant* circle and its homonymous journal, which has recently received some attention from scholars.[7] The history of the *Dieu Vivant* circle can be divided into two stages: Marcel Moré's Sunday seminars (1941–1944) and the publication of the *Dieu Vivant* journal (1945–1955). A Parisian intellectual with a growing fascination with diverse nonconformist currents in vogue in the 1930s, such as personalism and surrealism, Moré's interest was captured by Christian spirituality and eschatology in the 1940s; this was due in particular to the violent context of World War II, which inspired in him and the participants in his seminars a sense of impending apocalypse. Moré's Sunday seminars started on Mar 29, 1941, lasted until 1945, and were attended by many Parisian theologians, philosophers, writers, historians, and anthropologists.[8] These encounters were frequently attended by Vladimir Lossky and other Orthodox figures such as Berdyaev. Even though the primary purpose of Moré's seminars was not an ecumenical one, the encounters gave Lossky and other Orthodox theologians the chance to diffuse the knowledge of Eastern Christianity and its rich patristic tradition among Catholics and Protestants. For example, at the seminar that took place on Oct 11, 1941, Lossky presented a paper on "La théologie de la Lumière chez Saint Grégoire de Thessalonique,"[9] which served his intention to familiarize Western theology and philosophy with the basic doctrinal and spiritual teachings of the Orthodox tradition. It has even been argued by Rowan Williams that Lossky's masterpiece, *Essai sur la théologie mystique de l'Église d'Orient*,[10] grew out of the Russian theologian's participation in

6 See, for example, the following publications, which focus on the informal ecumenical encounters between Orthodox and Catholic theologians and philosophers in the period before Vatican II in France: Bernard Hubert, ed., *Jacques Maritain et Nicolas Berdiaev: Un dialogue d'exception (1925–1948)*, Paris, YMCA Press, 2022; Ivana Noble & others, *The Ways of Orthodox Theology in the West*, Yonkers, St Vladimir's Seminary Press, 2015, 257–258; Donald A. Lowrie, *Rebellious Prophet: A Life of Nikolai Berdyaev*, Westport CT, Greenwood Press, ²1974, 198–201; Jacques Maritain, *Carnet de notes*, Paris, Desclée De Brouwer, 1965, 183–254; and Tim Noble, "Springtime in Paris: Orthodoxy Encountering Diverse Others Between Wars," in: Andrew Pierce & Oliver Schuegraf, eds., *Den Blick weiten: Wenn Ökumene den Religionen begegnet: Tagungsbericht der 17. Wissenschaftlichen Konsultation der Societas Oecumenica*, Leipzig, Evangelische, 2014, 295–310.

7 Étienne Fouilloux, *Christianisme et eschatologie: Dieu Vivant (1945–1955)*, Paris, CLD, 2015; and Viorel Coman, "Vladimir Lossky's Involvement in the *Dieu Vivant* Circle and its Ecumenical Journal," *ITQ* 85/1, 2020, 45–63.

8 Fortunately, the minutes of the first ten meetings have been preserved. See "Dix séances de vie spirituelle," *Digraphe* 86–87, 1998, 35–49.

9 Vladimir Lossky, "La théologie de la Lumière chez Saint Grégoire de Thessalonique," *Dieu Vivant* 1, 1945, 93–118. The article was republished in Lossky's book *À l'image et à la ressemblance de Dieu*, Paris, Aubier, 1967, 39–65.

10 Vladimir Lossky, *Essai sur la théologie mystique de l'Église d'Orient*, Paris, Aubier, 1944; ET: *The Mystical Theology of the Eastern Church*, London, James Clarke & Co., 1957; see also Rowan Williams, *The Theology of Vladimir Nikolaievich Lossky: An Exposition and Critique*, Ph.D. thesis, Oxford, University of Oxford, 1975, 21 (unpublished).

these seminars, and was written with the intention of introducing the mystically oriented tradition of Eastern Christianity to a non-Orthodox audience.

Moré's Sunday seminars ended in 1944, but their influence continued over the decade that followed, primarily due to the publication of the *Dieu Vivant* journal by the same group of intellectuals in attendance at the meetings, who decided to spread their ideas and agenda (the revival of the eschatological consciousness of the church and society) through published texts. The first issue of the journal came out in April 1945, and the last issue appeared in 1955. Moré served as the only permanent member of the journal's steering committee. The journal's peer-review committee had an ecumenical composition and consisted of four to five members. Apart from Jean Hyppolite, who held an atheistic worldview, all the other members of the peer-review committee were Christians of various traditions: Pierre Burgelin (Protestant), Vladimir Lossky (Orthodox), and Gabriel Marcel and Maurice de Gandillac (Catholics). Both Jean Daniélou and Henri-Marie de Lubac served as mentors of the journal. The journal's most famous contributors include names such as Jean Daniélou, Hans Urs von Balthasar, Oscar Cullmann, Gabriel Marcel, Martin Buber, Romano Guardini, Karl Barth, Yves Congar, and many others. In addition, many Orthodox found the *Dieu Vivant* journal to be a useful platform for disseminating Eastern Christian ideas in the West, especially the results of their engagement with patristic texts in the modern world. The journal benefitted from the contributions of Vladimir Lossky,[11] Georges Florovsky,[12] Alexander Schmemann,[13] Myrrha Lot-Borodine,[14] Elisabeth Behr-Sigel,[15] and John Meyendorff,[16] to name but a few. As well as the personal encounters and exchanges that the *Dieu Vivant* journal occasioned between Orthodox theologians and their Catholic friends, its articles also served as a bridge between the two separate Christian worlds, whose theologians, within the Parisian context, started to move gradually from polemical confrontations and animosities towards constructive dialogue and enriching conversations. Moreover, given the general failure of Orthodox journals published by the Russian diaspora in Paris to reach a wider audience, *Dieu Vivant* gave Russian theologians and philosophers the opportunity to make their voices heard in a non-Orthodox context.

Moreover, the rapprochement between Orthodoxy and Catholicism in the decades prior to Vatican II was mediated by the neo-patristic movement,[17] whose aim was to renew Eastern Christianity through a return to the principal sources of Christian faith, especially the Fathers of the church. The neo-patristic movement facilitated the rapprochement between the Orthodox Church and the Catholic Church in the sense that it followed a similar agenda to the French Catholic

11 Vladimir Lossky, "Du troisième Attribut de l'Église," *Dieu Vivant* 10, 1948, 77–89.

12 Georges Florovsky, "Les voies de la théologie russe," *Dieu Vivant* 13, 1949, 39–62; Georges Florovsky, "La Bible et l'Église," *Dieu Vivant* 21, 1952, 95–105.

13 Alexander Schmemann, "La Théocratie byzantine et l'Église orthodoxe," *Dieu Vivant* 25, 1953, 33–53.

14 Myrrha Lot-Borodine, "De l'absence des stigmates dans la chrétienté antique," *Dieu Vivant* 3, 1945, 81–89; Myrrha Lot-Borodine, "La Béatitude dans l'Orient chrétien: Mysterium spei," *Dieu Vivant* 15, 1950, 83–115; Myrrha Lot-Borodine, "Eucharistie chez Nicolas Cabasilas," *Dieu Vivant* 24, 1953, 123–134.

15 Elisabeth Behr-Sigel, "La prière à Jésus: Ou le mystère de la spiritualité monastique orthodoxe," *Dieu Vivant* 8, 1947, 67–94.

16 Jean Meyendorff, "Traditions et hiérarchie dans l'Église," *Dieu Vivant* 26, 1953, 79–91.

17 For a comprehensive introduction to the history and theology of the neo-patristic movement, see Viorel Coman, "The Orthodox Neo-Patristic Movement's Encounter with the Christian 'Other': An Ecumenical Hermeneutics of Receptivity," *TS* 81/3, 2020, 717–740; Viorel Coman, "Revisiting the Agenda of the Neo-Patristic Movement," *DR* 136/2, 2018, 99–117; Paul Ladouceur, "Treasures New and Old: Landmarks of Orthodox Neopatristic Theology," *SVTQ* 56/2, 2012, 191–228; Andrew Louth, "The Patristic Revival and its Protagonists," in: Mary B. Cunningham & Elizabeth Theokritoff, eds., *The Cambridge Companion to Orthodox Christian Theology*, Cambridge, Cambridge University Press, 2008, 188–202; and Sergey S. Horuzhy, "Neo-Patristic Synthesis and Russian Philosophy," *SVTQ* 44/3–4, 2000, 309–328.

ressourcement or *nouvelle théologie*,[18] which succeeded in overcoming the dominance of Neoscholasticism and in reviving modern Catholicism via a rediscovery of the patristic ethos of Christianity.

Considered to be the most influential movement in 20th-century Orthodoxy, the neo-patristic movement was initiated within the Russian diaspora in Paris by Georges Florovsky, whose call for a return *ad mentem patris* was embraced by the majority of Orthodox theologians in the second half of the last century: Vladimir Lossky, Dumitru Stăniloae, Justin Popović, and John Zizioulas, to name a few of them. The two papers presented by Florovsky at the first congress of Orthodox theology, held in Athens in 1936, are considered to be the manifesto of the neo-patristic movement and have provided a continuous point of reference for subsequent generations.[19] The movement initiated by Florovsky was not a homogeneous or uniform whole, but was defined by several characteristics of Greek patristic inspiration, such as a historical-patristic-ecclesiological direction; a mystical-Palamite-Philokalic direction; and a Eucharist-liturgical-eschatological direction.[20]

Like the French Catholic *ressourcement*, one of the guiding principles of the agenda of the neo-patristic movement was the departure from the influence of Western scholasticism, which had permeated the Orthodox way of thinking (ecclesiology, anthropology, ethics, etc.) for centuries, particularly from the 16th century onwards.[21] It is true that the emphasis on this quest to de-Westernize Orthodox theology could, at times, make it look as though it were the only axis of interaction between the neo-patristic movement and Catholicism, which in some very conservative circles led to the polarization between East and West. However, the neo-patristic movement cannot be reduced to this single dimension of the effort to purify modern Orthodox theology of the negative influences of scholasticism and its program certainly goes beyond this departure from Western theology. The members of the neo-patristic movement benefitted from the encounter with a similar movement within the context of French Catholicism and from the rediscovery of ancient texts by modern Western theologians. As John A. Jillions points out, "the very sources they use – biblical, patristic, canonical, conciliar and liturgical texts – come through editions and scholarly aids made possible by mainly Western scholars."[22] For example, from the moment of the publication of its first volumes at the beginning of the 1940s, the Sources Chrétiennes series, a bilingual collection of

18 Jon Kirwan, *An Avant-Garde Theological Generation: The* Nouvelle Théologie *and the French Crisis of Modernity*, Oxford, Oxford University Press, 2018; Gabriel Flynn & Paul D. Murray, eds., *Ressourcement: A Movement for Renewal in Twentieth-Century Catholic Theology*, Oxford, Oxford University Press, 2011; Jürgen Mettepenningen, *Nouvelle Théologie – New Theology: Inheritor of Modernism, Precursor of Vatican II*, London, T&T Clark, 2010; Hans Boersma, Nouvelle Théologie & *Sacramental Ontology: A Return to Mystery*, Oxford, Oxford University Press, 2009; and Brian E. Daley, "The *Nouvelle Théologie* and the Patristic Revival: Sources, Symbols, and the Science of Theology," *IJST* 7/4, 2005, 362–382.

19 These two papers presented by Florovsky in 1936 are: Georges Florovsky, "Westliche Einflüsse in der russischen Theologie," in: Hamilcar S. Alivisatos, ed., *Procès-verbaux du premier congrès de théologie orthodoxe à Athènes: 29 novembre–6 décembre 1936*, Athens, Pyrsos, 1939, 212–231; ET: "Western Influences in Russian Theology," in: George Florovsky, *The Collected Works*, vol. 4, *Aspects of Church History*, Belmont MA, Nordland Publishing, 1975; see also Florovsky's second paper presented at the congress in 1936: "Patristic and Modern Theology," in: Alivisatos, ed., *Procès-verbaux du premier congrès*, 238–242; the same text was republished by Florovsky in *Diakonia* 4/3, 1969, 227–232.

20 The identification of several directions within the neo-patristic movement pertains to Ioan I. Ică Jr. See Ioan I. Ică Jr., "Modern and Contemporary Orthodox Theology: Key Moments, Key Figures, Developments, and Assessments," in: Viorel Ioniță, ed., *Orthodox Theology in the 20th Century and Early 21st Century: A Romanian Orthodox Perspective*, Bucharest, Basilica, 2013, 21–94, esp. 76.

21 Viorel Coman, "Neo-Patristic Movement," *DHGE* 33, f. 192–193a, 347–353, esp. 347.

22 John A. Jillions, "Orthodox Christianity in the West: The Ecumenical Challenge," in: Cunningham & Theokritoff, eds., *The Cambridge Companion*, 276–291, here 277.

patristic texts commissioned under the leadership of certain *nouveaux théologiens* such as de Lubac and Daniélou, served both Catholic and Orthodox theologians in Paris and offered them a common tool for a genuine theological renewal that brought their traditions closer to each other. Even though it is difficult to trace the mutual theological influences between the French Catholic *ressourcement* and the neo-patristic movement, it suffices here to give the example of Afanasiev's Eucharistic ecclesiology, which not only provided Orthodox theology with an ecumenically relevant vision of the church pertaining to Orthodox-Catholic relationships, but also influenced the work of de Lubac, Congar, the ecclesiology of Vatican II, and other magisterial documents. It is no secret that the earliest drafts of Vatican II's dogmatic constitution on the church, *Lumen gentium*, referred Afanasiev's work.[23]

The rapprochement between Orthodoxy and Catholicism was brought about precisely by the Eucharistic ecclesiology as it was developed by Nicholas Afanasiev, a prominent Russian theologian from the Parisian diaspora who activated as a professor at Institut de théologie orthodoxe Saint-Serge in the French capital. Afanasiev's views on the church were elaborated in a series of articles and a fundamental monograph titled *L'Église du Saint Esprit*.[24] Among the most important articles published by Afanasiev on Eucharistic ecclesiology are: "La doctrine de la primauté à la lumière de l'ecclésiologie";[25] "L'Église qui préside dans l'amour";[26] and "Una Sancta: En mémoire de Jean XXIII, le pape de l'amour."[27] Unlike the ecclesiology of *sobornost*, developed in the 19th century by the Slavophiles in opposition to the Western Church doctrine, Afanasiev's Eucharistic ecclesiology was ecumenically oriented and sought to create bridges between Orthodoxy and Catholicism. As Kallistos Ware noted, any hint of a polemical approach is absent from the ecclesiological model proposed by Afanasiev.[28]

Afanasiev's reflections on the church[29] from an ecumenical perspective started from the premise that the various ecclesiological models that have emerged in the course of history can be reduced to two fundamental types: universal ecclesiology and Eucharistic ecclesiology. In his opinion, even though the universal type became predominant in Western Christianity and was equally adopted by Eastern Orthodoxy, it is not the earliest ecclesiological model of the church. As Afanasiev pointed out, "universal ecclesiology ... is not primitive ecclesiology, but quite the reverse: it has taken the place of a different ecclesiology which I call eucharistic."[30] That being so, what Afanasiev

23 See Peter De Mey, "An Investigation of the Willingness to Develop a Eucharistic Ecclesiology in Roman Catholic Magisterial Teaching on the Church and in the Orthodox-Roman Catholic Ecumenical Dialogue," in Mathai Kadavil, Jobin Puthuparampil, George Thomas Kallunkal, eds., *From Streams to Source: Essays on the Foundation of Malankara Theology. Festschrift in Honour of Dr. John Berchmans OIC*, Bethany Ashram, Bethany Vedavijnana Peeth, 2010, 111–132.

24 This monograph is the Ph.D. thesis of Afanasiev, defended in 1950. It has originally been written in Russian and published posthumously in 1971. The French translation came out five years later: *L'Église du Saint Esprit*, trans. Marianne Drobot, Paris, Cerf, 1975; ET: *The Church of the Holy Spirit*, ed. Michael Plekon, trans. Vitaly Permiakov, Notre Dame, Notre Dame University Press, 2007.

25 Nicolas Afanassieff, "La doctrine de la primauté à la lumière de l'ecclésiologie," *Istina* 4, 1957, 401–420.

26 Nicolas Afanassieff, "L'Église qui préside dans l'amour," in: Nicolas Afanassieff & others, eds., *La primauté de Pierre dans l'Église orthodoxe*, Neuchâtel, Delachaux et Niestlé, 1960, 7–64; ET: "The Church which Presides in Love," in: John Meyendorff, ed., *The Primacy of Peter*, Crestwood, St Vladimir's Seminary Press, 1992, 91–143.

27 Nicholas Afanasiev, "Una Sancta: En mémoire de Jean XXIII, le Pape de l'Amour," *Irén* 36/4, 1963, 436–475; ET: "Una sancta: To the Memory of John XXIII, the Pope of Love," in: Michael Plekon ed., *Tradition Alive: On the Church and the Christian Life in Our Time*, Lanham, Rowan & Littlefield, 2003, 3–30.

28 Kallistos Ware, "*Sobornost* and Eucharistic Ecclesiology: Aleksei Khomiakov and His Successors," *IJSCC* 11/2–3, 2011, 216–235, here 225.

29 The information on Afanasiev's ecclesiology relies on Viorel Coman, *Dumitru Stăniloae's Trinitarian Ecclesiology: Orthodoxy and the Filioque*, Lanham, Lexington Press/Fortress Academic, 2019, 231–236.

30 Afanasiev, "The Church which Presides in Love," 107.

attempted was a restoration of the prevailing self-understanding of the church during the first three Christian centuries after Christ.

According to Afanasiev, universal ecclesiology has its roots in the theology of the 3rd-century African bishop of Roman origins Cyprian of Carthage, whose main concern was to preserve the visible unity of the church which had been shaken by a series of schisms and internal problems. Cyprian's ecclesiological model, which addressed the question of church unity, drew inspiration from the organization of the Roman Empire, where the empirical unity of the provinces was guaranteed by the emperor. Of similar importance for Cyprian's theory of the unity of the church was the Pauline image of the body and its various organs or parts, which cannot exist and function properly without the whole.[31] The Russian theologian claimed that the bishop of Carthage constructed his theory of the universal church in light of the two aforementioned sources: a unique organism spread all over the world and divided into many parts (local churches). Each local church is only a part of the universal church and does not possess ecclesial value unless it is through its participation in the whole. Or, to put it differently, the ecclesial nature of each local church derives directly from its being rooted in the universal church:

> Fullness and unity are the possessions of this Church scattered *per totum mundum*, not of isolated local churches which, being merely *members* of the Church, can only possess part of the fullness. Any local church is not the "Catholic" Church ... the local churches taken all together form the universal, ecumenical Church. ... All the local churches together are the one and only Body of Christ, but the empirical Church is to some extent the sum of its separated parts.[32]

Afanasiev argued that, according to the basic tenets of such an ecclesiology, the episcopacy is regarded as the empirical requirement and proof of the church's unity. The principle of the unity of the church is the unity of the episcopacy, especially because just as God is one, Christ is one, and the faith is one, so the episcopate is one: "*Episcopatus unus est*, because the 'throne of Peter is one,' 'in which God has established and shown the source of all unity.'"[33] Each bishop, who is the head of a local church, is a successor of Peter and serves as a symbol of unity only as long as he stays in communion with all the bishops that form the one episcopate. As a matter of fact, what invests a bishop with the quality of being a sign of unity is his membership in the episcopal college, rather than his role of chief pastor of the diocesan community entrusted to him. The unity of the bishop with all the other members of the episcopal college is, in fact, a concrete sign that his local church pertains to the universal and Catholic Church. Cyprian defined the relation between a bishop and the church as follows: "The bishop is in the Church and the Church is in the bishop: any person who is not with the bishop is not in the Church [*episcopum in ecclesia esse et ecclesiam in episcopo et si qui cum episcopo non sit in ecclesia non esse*]."[34]

In Afanasiev's view, Cyprian's universal ecclesiology inevitably leads to the doctrine of primacy: just as there is one bishop at the head of every local church, so there should be one bishop at the head of the universal church. Afanasiev pointed out that, even though Cyprian did not state that the bishop of Rome should be considered the head of the universal church, his ecclesiology regrettably demands a doctrine of primacy. As Afanasiev said, "if we take the universal theory of the Church, we cannot refute the doctrine of universal primacy."[35] Furthermore, Afanasiev considered that the

31 Afanasiev, "The Church which Presides in Love," 93–95.
32 Afanasiev, "The Church which Presides in Love," 95 (italics original).
33 Afanasiev, "The Church which Presides in Love," 96; see also Afanasiev, "Una Sancta: To the Memory of John XXIII," 12.
34 Afanasiev, "The Church which Presides in Love," 97.
35 Afanasiev, "The Church which Presides in Love," 99.

teaching on the unity of the church as a universal reality renders almost impossible the reunion of the Orthodox Church and Roman Catholic Church after the schisms, because both believe that only one true church can exist and there cannot be two universal churches: "For the orthodox the only true Church is the orthodox church. For the catholics it is the catholic church."[36] In this case, reconciliation means the return of the separated part, which ceased to be the church, to the bosom of the true church (*una sancta*).

The problems raised by the concept of universal ecclesiology prompted Afanasiev to consider what he believed to be the ecclesiology of the apostolic age and of the following two centuries: the Eucharistic ecclesiology, whose theoretical expression is to be found in the letters of Ignatius of Antioch. That being so, Afanasiev claimed that, according to the basic principles of Ignatius' Eucharistic ecclesiology, from which the concept of a universal church was completely absent, "every local church was autonomous and independent – autonomous, for it contained in itself everything necessary to its life; and independent, because it did not depend on any other local church or any bishop whatever outside itself."[37] They were, therefore, independent and autonomous on the basis of the fact "that each local church was the Church of God in all its fullness,"[38] and not a mere part of a larger whole, as in the case of universal ecclesiology. This fullness of each local church did not derive from anything outside itself, but from the fullness of Christ in the Eucharist, for Christ is not partially but wholly present in the Eucharist:

> As the Body of Christ, the Church manifests herself in all her fullness in the Eucharistic assembly of the local church, because Christ is present in the Eucharist in the fullness of his body. This is why the local church possesses all the fullness of the Church ... the Church is where the Eucharistic assembly is. It is also possible to formulate this in another way. *Where the Eucharist is, there is the Church of God, and where the Church of God is, there is the Eucharist.*[39]

According to this ecclesiological model, the Eucharist rather than the bishop represents the distinctive empirical sign of the church, for all those who participate in the Eucharistic assembly belong to the church: "The limits of the Church are determined by the limits of the Eucharistic assembly."[40]

Afanasiev believed that when the Eucharist is understood as the principle of the unity of the church, the thesis that the bishop functions as a symbol of the local church is not excluded, because the bishop is included in the very concept of the Eucharist. The Eucharistic celebration could not exist without the bishop who presides over the assembly. However, unlike universal ecclesiology, which places the symbol of the church's unity in the bishop as detached from the local church, Eucharistic ecclesiology – Afanasiev pointed out – sees the true unity of the church in the unity of the body of Christ, that is, in the unity of Christ himself which finds concrete expression in the Eucharistic assembly.[41]

The Russian theologian was also perfectly aware that the Eucharistic ecclesiology might give the impression that, due to the fact that a large number of local churches exist, the one Church of God cannot exist, but only a plurality of churches. He stated, however, that Eucharistic ecclesiology does not function according to the rules of Euclidean arithmetic: one plus one is still one. In this regard, Afanasiev clarified that:

36 Afanasiev, "Una Sancta: To the Memory of John XXIII," 9.

37 Afanasiev, "The Church which Presides in Love," 107.

38 Afanasiev, "The Church which Presides in Love," 107.

39 Afanasiev, "Una Sancta: To the Memory of John XXIII," 14 (italics mine); see also Afanasiev, "The Church which Presides in Love," 109–110.

40 Afanasiev, "Una Sancta: To the Memory of John XXIII," 14.

41 Afanasiev, "Una Sancta: To the Memory of John XXIII," 14.

> The plurality of local churches does not destroy the unity of the Church of God, just as the plurality of eucharistic assemblies does not destroy the unity of the eucharist in time and space. In the Church, unity and plurality are not only overcome: the one also contains the other. The unity of the Church in its empirical life is manifested by a plurality of local churches, and the plurality of the local churches safeguards the unity of the Church of God in Christ.[42]

Even though each one of these local churches is of the same ecclesial value as the others, Afanasiev was not opposed to stating that "equality creates a hierarchy of churches grounded in the authority of witness." In other words, "the Church of God lives fully present in the eucharistic assembly of the local churches, but each of them has a different way and degree of making the presence actual in its own life. A local church will have higher authority of witness if it has a greater realization of the presence of the Church of God."[43] That being so, Afanasiev claimed that Eucharistic ecclesiology excludes the idea of primacy, which is but a legalistic expression and involves the power of a bishop over the whole universal church, but accepts that a local church sits at the head of the hierarchy and enjoys a certain priority. The notion of priority, however, does not imply that one local church and its bishop possess power over the other local churches, for no church can exercise any kind of power over the others: any power, of any kind, exercised by a local church over another local church would be exercised over Christ and his body; it simply means that "the church that had priority naturally possessed the highest degree of authority, together with the greatest love, and would always be ready to come to the help of churches in need."[44] For Afanasiev, when the authority of the church-in-priority is invoked, it is not an appeal to the judgement of a tribunal whose authority is absolute, but a local church appeals to the church-in-priority so as to find itself, by listening to the voice of the church which dwelt there.

As for the ecumenical question of the reunion between the Orthodox and the Roman Catholic Church, Afanasiev advanced the idea that according to the principles of the Eucharistic ecclesiology none of the two churches has ceased to be the true Church of God. According to the principle of universal ecclesiology, if one or another local church detaches itself from the church, that local church falls into an ecclesiological void; Eucharistic ecclesiology, however, Afanasiev highlighted, supports the idea that the break in fraternal communion does not render any of the local churches in doctrinal conflict devoid of ecclesiality. Afanasiev explained his claim by declaring the following: in the first three centuries after Christ, the many independent and autonomous churches were not scattered, but they lived in unity, mutual love, and concord with one another. The source of their unity, however, was guaranteed by the fact that each of them constituted diverse representations of the same Church of God which dwelt in them all. Because of this type of union, a local church "could not live in isolation from the others and could not remain a stranger to what happened in the other churches."[45] Everything that happened in one of them affected the other churches, for it happened in the Church of God. So each local church would accept or receive all that takes place in another church and vice versa. But when a local church steps out from this agreement of love, distancing itself from the fraternal communion, this exit indicates that the local church, deprived of communion, ceases to exist for all the other local churches, for there are no longer links through which this communion could be realized. However, according to Afanasiev, such a church "did not cease to remain itself the Church of God

42 Afanasiev, "The Church which Presides in Love," 109.
43 Afanasiev, "The Church which Presides in Love," 112.
44 Afanasiev, "The Church which Presides in Love," 113.
45 Afanasiev, "Una Sancta: To the Memory of John XXIII," 15.

despite its isolated situation."[46] The real manifestation of its existence as a church is the Eucharist. On the basis of these considerations, Afanasiev claimed that, in spite of all the doctrinal divergences between the Orthodox and Roman Catholic Church, their renewal of communion is still possible: none of them has ceased to incarnate the true Church of God and the Eucharist of both is valid. They both should share in Eucharistic communion to rediscover the unity that already exists between them.

Although Afanasiev's Eucharistic ecclesiology determined the trajectory of the Orthodox vision of the church in the 20th century, none of the modern Eastern theologians fully embraced its principles without stipulations and corrections. Nevertheless, his ecclesiology remains defined by the Orthodox ecclesiological model of the 20th century, which tried to go beyond the doctrinal polemics of the past and bring Eastern and Western Christianity closer to each other. In many ways, his quest for Orthodox-Catholic unity was continued with as much enthusiasm by another Orthodox theologian who played an essential role in the relationships between Constantinople and Rome in the 1960s: André Scrima.

2.2 *André Scrima*

Unlike Afanasiev, whose work in the field of Orthodox-Catholic relationships developed mostly at the theological and theoretical levels, Scrima's involvement in the work towards Orthodox-Catholic unity[47] had a more practical dimension. This is not to say that his theological vision lacked in substance. While his theology of Orthodox-Catholic unity is quite visionary and deserved serious attention, he remains better known for his role as a sort of a church diplomat who worked for the consolidation of the relationship between the Ecumenical Patriarchate of Constantinople and the Church of Rome during the 1960s, and especially during Vatican II, where Scrima was a "privileged channel"[48] of communication between Rome and Constantinople.

Scrima was born in 1925 in Transylvania, Romania.[49] After his academic training in philosophy (1944–1948), he decided to study theology (1949–1956) in Bucharest, at the Institute of Orthodox Theology.[50] The meetings of the Burning Bush Group,[51] an informal gathering of church and lay intellectuals that emerged in 1945 at the Antim Monastery in Bucharest, convinced him to embrace monastic life in the early 1950s. Working as an interpreter for Patriarch Justinian of Romania (patriarch from 1948 to 1977), in 1956 Scrima had the opportunity to meet two Indian politicians in Bucharest who offered him the chance to pursue doctoral studies at Banaras Hindu University in India. This providential encounter with the Indian politicians allowed him to leave Romania and move abroad, escaping the persecution suffered by the members of the Burning Bush Group at the hands of the communist regime. After his studies in India, Scrima decided to settle at the Deir El Harf Monastery in Lebanon, where he helped the spiritual and monastic revival of Christian life in the Orthodox Patriarchate of Antioch. Even though the Deir El Harf Monastery was the place where he resided most of the time, Scrima travelled quite often between Lebanon, Rome (the

46 Afanasiev, "Una Sancta: To the Memory of John XXIII," 18.

47 See, for example, Viorel Coman, "André Scrima's Contribution to the Ecumenical Turn in Orthodox-Catholic Relationships: A Historical Reconstruction (1957–1967)," *OCP* 86/2, 2020, 571–595. See, also, Coman, *Bridge-Builder*.

48 Mauro Velati, *Una difficile transizione: Il cattolicesimo tra unionismo ed ecumenismo (1952–1964)*, Bologna, Il Mulino, 1996, 415.

49 For a more detailed presentation of Scrima's biography, see Ioan Alexandru Tofan, *André Scrima, un "gentleman creștin"* [André Scrima, a "Christian gentleman"], Bucharest, Humanitas, 2021.

50 Now the Faculty of Orthodox Theology in Bucharest. From 1948 to 1989, its name was Institute of Orthodox Theology, because it was excluded from the University of Bucharest by the communists.

51 See Paul Ladouceur & Athanasios Giocas, "The Burning Bush Group and Father André Scrima in Romanian Spirituality," *GOTR* 52/1–4, 2007, 37–61.

Vatican), France (the Istina center in Paris), and Geneva (the WCC), especially after 1960 when he met Patriarch Athenagoras of Constantinople, who nominated Scrima a close collaborator for the improvement of Orthodox-Catholic relationships in the context of Vatican II.

Scrima's ecumenical activity in the service of Orthodox-Catholic unity can be divided into two major phases: the first one goes from the moment of his encounter with Athenagoras in 1960 until his nomination as a personal representative of the ecumenical patriarch of Constantinople at Vatican II in 1964; the second one goes from 1964 until the end of the council and the lifting of the anathemas between Constantinople and the Vatican.[52]

During the first phase, Scrima's ecclesial and diplomatic activity on behalf of the Ecumenical Patriarchate developed in three main directions. The first one is exemplified by Scrima's role as a privileged channel of communication for Constantinople with the members of the SPCU, both before the opening of the council and during its first sessions. Even though Constantinople did not send observers to the first session of the council, Scrima's close friendship with the members of the secretariat allowed him to keep the ecumenical patriarch abreast of the latest developments taking place at Vatican II. The second direction is defined by his efforts to keep the Ecumenical Patriarchate on the path of dialogue, especially after the 1962 incident concerning the Russian observers. The unexpected presence of the Russian observers at the first session of the council, without the prior information of Constantinople or any of the other Orthodox churches, upset the ecumenical patriarch to the point that many in the Phanar considered Rome responsible for undermining the role of the Church of Constantinople in the communion of Orthodox churches. Scrima's diplomatic skills and Athenagoras' unfailing support for the cause of Orthodox-Catholic unity avoided the escalation of a serious crisis between Constantinople and Rome. The third direction encapsulates his ecumenical work behind the scenes that led to the historic meeting between Patriarch Athenagoras and Pope Paul VI in Jerusalem in January 1964, which marked the ecumenical turn in the relationships between Constantinople and Rome.

During the second phase, Scrima's most important contribution to Orthodox-Catholic unity had to do with his participation in the third and fourth sessions of Vatican II as the personal representative of the ecumenical patriarch. Even though Scrima closely followed the work of the first two sessions of the council, it was only in 1964 that he was nominated a personal representative of Patriarch Athenagoras at Vatican II, contributing to the regular meetings of the SPCU with the non-Catholic observers and influencing the final version of some of the conciliar documents, especially *Lumen gentium*, *Unitatis redintegratio*, *Orientalium Ecclesiarum*, and *Dei Verbum*.[53] However, Scrima's outstanding accomplishment during this second phase remains his involvement in the preparations for the lifting of the 1054 anathemas between Constantinople and Rome, which is the event that crowns his activity as the personal representative of the ecumenical patriarch at Vatican II. The lifting of the anathemas at the end of Vatican II was the most important moment in the relationships between the Orthodox Church and the Catholic Church, and especially between Constantinople and Rome, after centuries of separation and mutual ignorance.[54] On

52 See, André Scrima, *Duhul Sfânt și unitatea Bisericii: "Jurnal" de Conciliu* [The Holy Spirit and the unity of the church: a "diary" of the council], ed. Bogdan Tătaru-Cazaban, Bucharest, Anastasia, 2004.

53 See, for example, Viorel Coman, "Mary as Mediatrix: André Scrima's Contribution to the Mariological Chapter of *Lumen Gentium*," *JECS*, 73/3–4, 2021, 291–316; Viorel Coman, "The Holy Spirit and Scripture: André Scrima's Contribution to Vatican II's Dogmatic Constitution on Divine Revelation *Dei Verbum*," *Religions* 14/12, 2023, 1454.

54 For Scrima's analysis of the event, see André Scrima, "The Lifting of the Anathemas: An Act of Reparation," *ECR* 1/1, 1966, 23–26.

the one hand, this epoch-defining event, which removed the mutual excommunications of 1054 from the memory of both traditions, was one of the many fruits of the historic meeting between Patriarch Athenagoras and Pope Paul VI, to which Scrima contributed significantly. On the other hand, the mutual nullification of the anathemas opened new paths and perspectives in the relations between Orthodoxy and Catholicism, paving the way for the 1967 exchange of visits between Patriarch Athenagoras and Pope Paul VI and precipitating the inauguration of the official theological dialogue between the Orthodox Church and the Catholic Church.

Scrima's diplomatic work for the rapprochement between the Orthodox Church and the Catholic Church was guided by a theological understanding of their existing unity that even today remains quite unique, due to its ecumenical openness. One fundamental idea shapes Scrima's entire theological vision of reconciliation between Orthodoxy and Catholicism: "There is a fundamental unity between the Orthodox Church and the Roman Catholic Church,"[55] despite the gradual separation between the two during the second millennium. Even though nowadays there is no Eucharistic communion between Orthodoxy and Catholicism, the Catholic Church ought to be "the main partner of dialogue for the Orthodox Church,"[56] especially because "everything that essentially constitutes the fullness of the Mystical Body of Christ pertains to both of them: the Sacraments, the Eucharist, the Tradition, *communio sanctorum*, the institutional structure of the church."[57] Scrima believed that the Orthodox Church and the Catholic Church must be understood as "two organic forms of expression of the one and the same apostolic heritage."[58] In his opinion, "both churches live separately the one and the same fundamental content of the apostolic faith, sacramental reality, and ecclesial structure. This means that both constitute two complementary ways of living the catholicity/sobornicity of the church."[59] The schism of 1054 alienated Orthodoxy from Catholicism and vice versa, but this process of estrangement did not mark "a fundamental rupture"[60] between the two.

In order to describe the progressive estrangement between Orthodoxy and Catholicism, Scrima made use of a three-stage schema of historical evolution. The first refers to the relationships between Eastern and Western Christianity during the first Christian millennium, when the unity between the two was preserved, despite tensions, conflicts, and different forms of church organization. The apostolic unity between them was not called into question by the existence of a theological pluralism, as Christian bishops shared the conviction that all of them pertained to the same church established by Christ and the apostles. As Scrima pointed out, "the East and the West communed (first millennium) with one another within the same church; they were complementary to each other, forming one single church in their legitimate diversity."[61] The second phase covers the period of the second millennium, which marked a gradual shift in the relations between the East and the West. The spirit of theological pluralism vanished and a mutual opposition between the two gradually started to govern their interactions, especially after the schism of 1054. Nevertheless, "the feeling that the church is still one was initially not lost. Nobody was speaking about two churches. The separation was rather a family quarrel, and the unity was not affected in any way."[62] But the

55 André Scrima, "Réflexions sur l'Église orthodoxe," *Écoute* 78, 1960, 21.

56 André Scrima, "Perspectives œcuméniques: Point de vue d'un orthodoxe," KU Leuven, 1965, 5, in: UCL-LG, Charles Moeller, papiers, 02040, 13 pages. The written version of this unpublished text has been established on the basis of the audio recording of a conference given by Scrima in Leuven.

57 Scrima, "Perspectives œcuméniques," 5.

58 André Scrima, "Orthodoxe und Katholiken: Ihre Besondere Situation in Geschpräch der christlichen Ökumene," *WuW* 2, 1967, 89–98, here 92.

59 Scrima, "Orthodoxe und Katholiken," 92.

60 Scrima, "Orthodoxe und Katholiken," 90.

61 Scrima, "Perspectives œcuméniques," 10.

62 André Scrima, "Vues orthodoxes sur Vatican II," 2. This four-page text is preserved in the Vatican II Archives of

fall of Constantinople in 1453 and the rise of the Reformation changed the situation in several ways: the sense of unity was almost completely lost as Eastern Christianity became a stranger to Western Christianity and vice versa; the Roman Catholic Church started approaching Eastern Christianity as it approached Protestantism; as a result, the language of reconciliation between the two was replaced by that of conversion;[63] and the peak of their estrangement was reached at Vatican I, which exclusively identified the *una sancta* with the Roman Catholic Church. Yet, a third stage in the relationships between the two churches was inaugurated at Vatican II, when Orthodoxy and Catholicism decided to take the road away from conflict and animosity towards communion and dialogue, an approach which continues to the present day.[64]

This understanding of the relationship between Orthodoxy and Catholicism led Scrima to say that any form of ecumenism between the two always takes place within the church (*una sancta*), and is aimed at finding the fullness of the church that is lived on both sides in a condition of separation. That being so, Scrima opined that the unity between Orthodoxy and Catholicism is not so much to be created or fabricated but actualized. Furthermore, for the Orthodox Church, any encounter or dialogue with the Catholic Church is an exercise of self-knowledge and self-introspection, especially because Catholicism is the complementary interlocutor of Eastern Christianity. To Scrima, the life of each church illuminates, enriches, and completes the other. A dialogue between the two is about becoming the other. This process of becoming the other does not mean an act of conversion. It means that both Orthodoxy and Catholicism must remain open to each other from within, in the sense that, for the Orthodox Church, the Catholic Church should not be seen as an external and distant partner in conversation. Catholicism should be part of Orthodoxy's identity and vice versa. That is to say that their mutual encounter from within is an act of reciprocal rediscovery of the other missing half without which neither is complete. For this reason, Orthodoxy must take an inclusivist stance towards Catholicism and vice versa.

Even though the ecclesiology developed by Scrima was not as elaborate as that of Afanasiev, his vision of the Orthodox-Catholic relationship shows the great ecumenical enthusiasm that nourished the minds and hearts of several Orthodox theologians in their attempts to establish bridges in the dialogue with the Catholics in order to pave the way towards reconciliation and reunion, especially in the decades prior to and during Vatican II. Nowadays, after the experience of the long process of building up an official dialogue between the Orthodox Church and the Catholic Church, much of the initial enthusiasm has cooled, with theologians of both traditions coming to realize that a millennium of separation cannot be easily healed. Nevertheless, the many attempts at providing a solid foundation for the Orthodox-Catholic dialogue between the 1930s and 1960s could serve as a source of inspiration for the revitalization of the culture of dialogue and conversation within both traditions, especially at moments when old tensions emerge and hopes seem to be slowly fading away.

3 The WCC: Georges Florovsky's Vision of the Limits of the Church

After the enriching experience of the dialogue between the Old Catholics and the Anglicans in the 19th century, the Orthodox churches' involvement in the WCC[65] in the mid-20th century marks their

Fr. Emmanuel Lanne at the Monastery of Chevetogne, Lanne Fund, no. 1465, 1–5. The text was written in 1964.

63 Scrima, "Vues orthodoxes sur Vatican II," 2.

64 Scrima, "Orthodoxe und Katholiken," 97.

65 See Athanasios Basdekis, ed., *Orthodox Kirche und Ökumenische Bewegung. Dokumente – Erklärungen – Berichte (1900–2006)*, Frankfurt a.M./Paderborn, Lembeck/Bonifatius, 2006; Gennadios Limouris, ed., *Orthodox Visions of Ecumenism: Statements, Messages and Reports on the Ecumenical Movement (1902–1992)*, Geneva, WCC Publications, 1994; Georges Lemopoulos,

most important gesture of ecumenical openness at the official level, even though not all Orthodox autocephalous churches joined the movement right from the beginning, owing to political reasons. In fact, the Orthodox churches were among the founding members of the WCC, as no less than five churches from the Eastern Christian world were present at its first assembly in Amsterdam in 1948: the Ecumenical Patriarchate, the archdiocese of the Greek Orthodox Patriarchate of Antioch in the United States, the Church of Cyprus, the Church of Greece, and the Ethiopian Orthodox Church. Most of the Orthodox churches from behind the Iron Curtain, including the Moscow Patriarchate, which initially criticized the ecumenical movement, joined the WCC in 1961 at its third assembly in New Delhi. The Orthodox churches were not only a founding member of the WCC, but the encyclical letter *Unto the Churches of Christ Everywhere*,[66] issued in 1920 by the Ecumenical Patriarchate to invite Christian churches to consider the formation of a sort of a League of Churches, inspired the formation of the WCC. Among the leading voices of early Orthodox ecumenism within the WCC, Georges Florovsky holds a place apart.

3.1 *Georges Florovsky*

There is no other Orthodox theologian who had a more important impact on the development of Eastern Christianity in the 20th century than Georges Florovsky. To many, he remains the most influential Orthodox theologian of the past century, especially owing to the fact that he is the architect of the neo-patristic direction of modern Eastern Christianity. Born in 1893 in Odessa, then part of the Russian Empire, Florovsky and his family were forced by the Bolsheviks to leave their country and move to Western Europe at the beginning of the 1920s. Florovsky spent his working life teaching in France (at the Institut de théologie orthodoxe Saint-Serge in Paris, from 1926 to 1948) and in the USA (at the St. Vladimir's Orthodox Theological Seminary in New York from 1949 to 1955; at the Holy Cross Greek Orthodox School of Theology in Brookline, Massachusetts, and at Harvard Divinity School, from 1956 to 1965; and at Princeton University in New Jersey, from 1964 onwards). Florovsky died in 1979 at 85 years of age.[67] His published work covers many theological topics, including patristics, church history, ecclesiology, and ecumenism.[68] Ecumenism was a central subject of reflection in Florovsky's writings, due to his participation in the formation and development of the WCC. As Job (Getcha), archbishop of Telmessos, pointed out, "in the WCC, Florovsky always represented the Ecumenical Patriarchate of Constantinople."[69]

"Historical Road Map of Orthodox Involvement in the Ecumenical Movement," in: Pantelis Kalaitzidis & others, eds., *Orthodox Handbook on Ecumenism: Resources for Theological Education*, Oxford, Regnum Books, 2014, 96–103; Georges Florovsky, "The Orthodox Church and the World Council of Churches," *St. Vladimir's Seminary Quarterly* 2/4, 1954, 111–118; and Nicolas Zernov, "The Eastern Churches and the Ecumenical Movement in the Twentieth Century," in: *A History of the Ecumenical Movement*, vol. 1, Ruth Rouse & Stephen C. Neill, eds., London, SPCK, 1954, 645–674.

66 "Encyclical of the Ecumenical Patriarchate, 1920: *Unto the Churches of Christ Everywhere*," in: Limouris, ed., *Orthodox Visions of Ecumenism*, 9–11; Natallia Vasilevich, "The 1920 Encyclical of the Ecumenical Patriarchate and the Proposal for a 'League of Churches': Translation or Interpretation?," *EcRev* 72/4, 2020, 673–682. See also the contribution by Stylianos Tsompanidis in the first volume of this work.

67 For a detailed presentation of Florovsky's biography, see Paul L. Gavrilyuk, *Georges Florovsky and the Russian Religious Renaissance: Changing Paradigms in Historical and Systematic Theology*, Oxford, Oxford University Press, 2013; Andrew Blane, ed., *Georges Florovsky: Russian Intellectual, Orthodox Churchman*, Crestwood, St Vladimir's Seminary Press, 1993.

68 Andrew Louth, *Modern Orthodox Thinkers: From the* Philokalia *to the Present*, London, SPCK, 2015, 77–93.

69 Archbishop Job (Getcha) of Telmessos, "Georges Florovsky and the World Council of Churches," in: John Chryssavgis & Brandon Gallaher, eds., *The Living Christ: The Theological Legacy of Georges Florovsky*, London, T&T Clark, 2021, 393–407, here 394.

Florovsky's engagement with the ecumenical movement began in 1937 at the Edinburgh conference, when Faith and Order on the one hand, and Life and Work on the other decided to merge to form the future WCC. After Edinburgh, Florovsky was elected as an Orthodox member of the Provisional Committee where he served from 1939 to 1948 and which was entrusted with the task of guiding the formation of the future WCC, as well as drafting its constitution. In 1948, at the first assembly of the WCC in Amsterdam, Florovsky was appointed a member of the central committee and was also invited to serve on the executive committee, a task he carried out until 1961. In 1952, at the Lund conference, Florovsky was elected a member of the Faith and Order commission, a position he honored until 1971.[70]

3.2 *Ecclesiology and Ecumenism*

In an article published in 2009, John Jillions rightly claimed that modern and contemporary Orthodox Christianity has no "unified approach to ecumenical engagement with other churches."[71] As Jillions pointed out, three different approaches coexist, each of them sharing a different view on the ecclesiological status of other Christian churches. The first approach – "the traditionalist model" – argues that the Orthodox Church is the only true Church of Christ whereas all other Christian churches cannot be properly called churches as they departed from the unity of the body of Christ and find themselves in a defective state of schism. The traditionalist model sees the goal of ecumenism as a return of all the other Christian churches to Orthodoxy.[72] The second approach – "the mainstream model" – which finds in Georges Florovsky a leading voice, equally argues that the Orthodox Church is the historical embodiment of the *una sancta* and the faithful continuation throughout the ages of the church established by Christ and the apostles. Nevertheless, unlike the traditionalist model, the mainstream model admits that other Christian churches possess degrees of ecclesiality, depending on how close they are to the Orthodox Church.[73] Florovsky's model is "the most widely accepted Orthodox model"[74] of ecumenical engagement. The third model – "the prophetic model" – which is promoted by Orthodox theologians such as Sergius Bulgakov and Nicholas Afanasiev, Anton Kartashev, and Nicholas Zernov, is the most ecumenically open, in the sense that these thinkers tried to find alternative ways of inter-Christian engagement that had the potential to open up the path towards a prophetic form of Christian unity.[75]

Although Florovsky subscribed to a model of ecumenical engagement that acknowledges degrees of ecclesiality outside the canonical borders of the Orthodox Church, his first explorations in the field of ecclesiology were rather exclusivist, which brought him closer to the traditionalist model at the time. According to Florovsky's early publications, especially "The House of the Father," "in the Church, a mosaic of different parts is impossible. There stand opposite each other not 'creeds' with equal rights, but the Church and the schism, united in spirit of opposition. It can be whole only through elimination, through a return to the Church."[76] No qualification is offered by Florovsky with respect to the ecclesial status of the Christian communities that are not in Eucharist

70 See Willem A. Visser 't Hooft, "Fr. Georges Florovsky's Role in the Formation of the WCC," *SVTQ* 23/3–4, 1979, 135–138; and Matthew Baker & Seraphim Danckaert, "Fr. Georges Florovsky," in: Kalaitizidis & others, eds., *Orthodox Handbook on Ecumenism*, 209–213.

71 John Jillions, "Three Orthodox Models of Christian Unity: Traditionalist, Mainstream, Prophetic," *IJSCC* 9/4, 2009, 295–311, here 295.

72 Jillions, "Three Orthodox Models of Christian Unity," 296–297.

73 Jillions, "Three Orthodox Models of Christian Unity," 297–301.

74 Jillions, "Three Orthodox Models of Christian Unity," 301.

75 Jillions, "Three Orthodox Models of Christian Unity," 301–308.

76 Georges Florovsky, "The House of the Father," in: Georges Florovsky, *The Collected Works*, vol. 13, *Ecumenism I: A Doctrinal Approach*, ed. Richard S. Haugh, Vaduz, Büchervertriebsanstalt, 1989, 58–80, here 79.

communion with the Orthodox Church. Every form of Christian organization that exists outside the canonical borders of the Orthodox Church is invited to return to Orthodoxy, which embodies the church universal or the *una sancta*. Florovsky's early ecclesiology was developed as a reaction to Sergius Bulgakov's ecumenical enthusiasm, which was open at the time to a form of intercommunion between the Orthodox Church and the Anglican Church.[77] However, with Florovsky's involvement in ecumenical activities from the 1930s onwards, his position departed from its strict traditionalist model and embraced a more nuanced tone. Florovsky's article "The Limits of the Church"[78] recounts his switch from one model to the other, without abandoning the idea that the Orthodox Church embodies most fully the Church of Christ.

Florovsky's ecumenical model, which was developed after the publication of "The Limits of the Church," promoted the idea that the canonical and sacramental borders of the church do not coincide entirely. That is to say that, outside the canonical walls of the *una sancta*, there is no complete absence of God's grace.[79] As Florovsky pointed out:

> The Church bears witness to the extension of her mystical territory even beyond her canonical threshold; the "outside world" does not begin immediately. ... As a mystical organism, as the sacramental Body of Christ, the Church cannot be adequately described in canonical terms or categories alone. It is impossible to state or discern the true limits of the Church simply by canonical signs or marks. Very often the canonical boundary determines also the charismatic boundary; what is bound on earth is bound by an indissoluble knot in heaven. But not always. And still more often, not immediately. In her sacramental, mysterious being the Church surpasses canonical measurements.[80]

What made Florovsky claim that "the wilderness without grace"[81] does not begin immediately outside the canonical walls of the *una sancta* was the ancient practice of the church, which did not baptize the schismatics and heretics returning to its bosom:

> The Church customarily receives adherents from sects and even from heresies not by *the way of baptism*, thereby obviously meaning or supposing that they have already been actually baptized in their sects and heresies. In many cases the Church receives adherents even *without chrism*, and sometimes also clerks [that is, clerics] *in their existing order*.[82]

To Florovsky, the fact that their sacraments were not reiterated at the moment when they joined the church showed that the Christians who departed from the *una sancta* still preserve a link with the church.[83] Since some non-Orthodox are received into the Orthodox Church via different means than baptism, it indicates that there are "different categories of 'the separated'" and, consequently, "degrees of Church membership."[84]

This distinction between the canonical and the sacramental borders of the church provided

77 See Anasstasy Gallaher, "Bulgakov's Ecumenical Thought," *Sobornost* 24/1, 2002, 24–55 and Anasstasy Gallaher, "Bulgakov and Intercommunion," *Sobornost* 24/2, 2002, 9–28.

78 Georges Florovsky, "The Limits of the Church," *CQR* 117/233, 1933, 117–131. Florovsky's article was republished in the volume by Brandon Gallaher & Paul Ladouceur, eds., *The Patristic Witness of Georges Florovsky: Essential Theological Writings*, London, T&T Clark, 2019, 247–256. I will be quoting from the volume edited by Gallaher and Ladouceur.

79 Florovsky, "The Limits of the Church," 247.

80 Florovsky, "The Limits of the Church," 248–249.

81 Florovsky, "The Limits of the Church," 250.

82 Florovsky, "The Limits of the Church," 248 (italics original).

83 Florovsky, "The Limits of the Church," 253.

84 Georges Florovsky, "The Doctrine of the Church and the Ecumenical Movement," *EcRev* 2/2, 1950, 152–161, here 158 and 160.

Florovsky with the necessary instrument to assist the Orthodox Church's ecumenical engagement. For Florovsky, the Orthodox Church's involvement in ecumenism is not an optional step but "a direct obligation emerging from the essence itself of the Orthodox consciousness and the obligation that lies for the true church to witness everywhere."[85] In other words, the presence of the Orthodox Church in the structures of the WCC is a missionary task as the Orthodox Church is called to give testimony to other Christians about "the apostolic faith and the Tradition in its integrity and fullness."[86] Florovsky's conviction that the task of the Orthodox Church in the ecumenical movement is to witness the fullness of the truth and grace it possesses has been so widely shared by such a wide majority of Orthodox Christians that it continues even today to be the main justification for the Orthodox Church's participation in bilateral and multilateral ecumenical dialogues. In this regard, Florovsky set the trajectory for the mainstream approach to the role of Orthodox Church in the ecumenical movement.

Although Florovsky drew a distinction between the canonical and sacramental borders of the church, which do not always coincide, he always emphasized that the WCC must be perceived neither as a supra-church nor as a reunion or fellowship of the churches.[87] This is to say that, for Florovsky, the membership of the Orthodox Church in the WCC should not be read as a recognition of the full ecclesiality of other churches by Eastern Orthodox Christianity, in line with a sort of "branch theory," which was seen by many as the ecclesiological vision behind the WCC. Florovsky's opposition to such a claim, which was also shared by other Orthodox theologians and ecumenists, was extremely strong, to the extent that it influenced the Toronto statement *The Church, the Churches and the World Council of Churches*[88] of 1950, which affirmed that the WCC is not the *una sancta* and is not "based on any one particular conception of the Church" (§ 3.3). Additionally, the Toronto statement clearly stated that membership in the WCC does not imply a relativization of one's own conception of the church.[89]

To many non-Orthodox, Florovsky's ecumenical vision remains quite traditional and makes the advancement of the inter-Christian dialogue difficult. Nonetheless, such a vision is not very different from that promoted by the Roman Catholic Church at Vatican II, which acknowledges that the Catholic Church is the *una sancta* and admits traces of ecclesiality outside the confines of Catholicism.[90] Even though Florovsky's ecumenical vision does not share the courage of other Orthodox thinkers such as Afanasiev or Scrima, its merit lies in its attempt to go beyond

85 Georges Florovsky, "Une vue sur l'Assemblée d'Amsterdam," *Irén* 22, 1949, 5–25, here 9.

86 Florovsky, "Une vue sur l'Assemblée d'Amsterdam," 9. Another model of ecumenical engagement was proposed in the 1970s by the Romanian Orthodox theologian Dumitru Stăniloae, who goes beyond Florovsky's claim that the Orthodox Church's role in the ecumenical movement proves the fullness it possesses. According to Stăniloae's concept of "open sobornicity," the Orthodox ecumenical engagement is also an opportunity for Eastern Christianity to enrich itself with the genuine theological and spiritual gifts of other Christian churches. See Dumitru Stăniloae, "Sobornicitatea deschisă" [Open Sobornicity], *Ortodoxia* 23/2, 1971, 165–180; Viorel Coman, "Open Sobornicity in Dumitru Stăniloae," in: Irina Paert, Alison Ruth Kolosova & Andreij Shishov, eds., *Companion to Conciliarity in Modern Orthodox Theology*, New York, Wiley-Blackwell, forthcoming.

87 Florovsky, "Une vue sur l'Assemblée d'Amsterdam," 6.

88 *The Church, the Churches and the World Council of Churches. The Ecclesiological Significance of the World Council of Churches. A Statement Commended to the Churches for Study and Comment by the Central Committee of the Council, Meeting at Toronto, Ontario, July, 1950*, Geneva, WCC Publications, 1950, English text available at <https://www.oikoumene.org/resources/documents/toronto-statement> (accessed Mar 26, 2024).

89 In addition to the Toronto statement, see Job (Getcha) of Telmessos, "Georges Florovsky and the World Council of Churches," 398–399.

90 Sandra Arenas, *Fading Frontiers?: A Historical-Theological Investigation into the Notion of the "Elementa Ecclesiae"*, Leuven, Peeters, 2021.

the traditionalist model and find a way to provide Eastern Christianity with the ecclesiological instruments to adhere to and support the work of the WCC.

4 Conclusions

From the 1930s until the 1960s, Orthodox Christianity developed different models of ecumenical engagement which showed its willingness to contribute to the emerging process of Christian reconciliation. Whereas, in their search for a rapprochement with the Catholic Church, Orthodox theologians such as Nicholas Afanasiev and André Scrima developed the most ecumenically open models of conversation and dialogue with Rome, a more moderate tone was adopted by Orthodox theologians involved in the work of the WCC, especially by Georges Florovsky. Afanasiev's and Scrima's approaches to Roman Catholicism have not been shared by the majority of Orthodox theologians, while Florovsky's explorations in the field of the Orthodox role in the ecumenical movement became normative for many Eastern theologians. However, what all these models of ecumenical engagement revealed was the motivation of Orthodox theologians to find ways of opening up a conversation with other Christian churches with a view to advancing together on the path towards unity at a time when the relationships between the different denominations had not yet been detached from the climate of hostility that had characterized their interactions for centuries.

Bibliography

Coman, Viorel, *Bridge-Builder between East and West: André Scrima and the Ecumenical Turn in Orthodox-Catholic Relationships*, Leiden, Brill, 2024.

Cunningham, Mary B. & Elizabeth Theokritoff, eds., *The Cambridge Companion to Orthodox Christian Theology*, Cambridge, Cambridge University Press, 2008.

Flynn, Gabriel & Paul Murray, eds., *Ressourcement: A Movement for Renewal in Twentieth-Century Catholic Theology*, Oxford, Oxford University Press, 2011.

Gavrilyuk, Paul L., *Georges Florovsky and the Russian Religious Renaissance*, Oxford, Oxford University Press, 2013.

Kalaitzidis, Pantelis & others, eds., *Orthodox Handbook on Ecumenism: Resources for Theological Education*, Oxford, Regnum Books, 2014.

CHAPTER 16

Theological Foundations and Interpretations of the Ecumenical Movement during the First Half of the 20th Century: Roman Catholic Positions

Leonhard Hell

1 Fundamental Ideas and Premises of Previous Representations of the Movement

> Oecumenism begins when it is admitted that others, not only individuals but ecclesiastical bodies as well, may also be right though they differ from us; that they too have truth holiness and gifts of God even though they do not profess our form of Christianity. There is oecumenism, says an active member of this movement, when it is believed that others are Christian not in spite of their particular confession but in it and by it.[1]

If these words of Yves Congar[2] that define ecumenism, not to mention those of his unnamed ecumenical witness, are still considered valid today, it follows that hardly anything that is driven by the desire for Christian unity is necessarily directly shaped "ecumenically." If one were to imagine a figure consisting of a series of concentric circles, ecumenism in the strict sense of the word would form the innermost circle, surrounded by ever-widening circles representing various Christian ideas of unity or attempts at church union. This model is in a clear state of tension with a second pattern, which had gained favor within Catholicism by the time of Vatican II at the latest. The same figure of circles is used to show belonging to the universal Catholic Church or orientation towards it.[3] Here the fulfilled unity of the church and the perfect integration into it can ultimately only be conceived of when the innermost circle's conditions and testimonies of unity are realized. The first concentric model, on the other hand, represents exactly the opposite idea: the true unity of Christians and the union of the churches in visible form are also (and indeed must be) attained precisely when the conditions and signs of this unity are defined differently (at least in part) according to each confession. The fact that the relevant texts of Vatican II, namely, *Lumen gentium* and especially *Unitatis redintegratio*, reflect this tension but were either unable or unwilling to resolve it accounts for the

1 Marie-Joseph Congar, *Chrétiens désunis: Principes d'un "oecuménisme" catholique*, Paris, Cerf, 1937, 173; ET: *Divided Christendom: A Catholic Study of the Problem of Reunion*, trans. Muad A. Bousfield, London, Bles, 1939, 135; also cited in: Yves Congar "Le développement de l'évaluation ecclésiologique des Églises non-catholiques – Un bilan," in: Gerard Békés & Vilmos Vajta, eds., *Unitatis Redintegratio 1964–1974: The Impact of the Decree on Ecumenism*, Rome, Pontificio Ateneo S. Anselmo, 1977, 63–97, here 65, where Congar claims a *ius primae noctis* for the introduction of this conception in Roman Catholic theology.

2 On Congar's life and work, see the contribution by Joseph Famerée in this volume. Since Congar has rightly been given his own chapter in this work, he will be mentioned only in passing in this contribution.

3 Whereas sections 14–16 of the *Lumen gentium* church constitution set these circles off from the center outwards, the first encyclical issued by Pope Paul VI, *Ecclesiam suam*, undertook the movement in the opposite direction through "discussion circles" (*colloquia*); see Paul VI, *Ecclesiam suam*, in: AAS 56, 1964, 609–659, here 654–659. As Congar, "Le développement," 70 already noted, in both cases there is the danger of ecclesiocentrism, which makes a specific church, namely, ones' own, the epitome of what a church is per se. In the case of the inner circle of ecumenism in the strict sense, there is naturally the risk of the opposite danger, namely, that what it truly means to be a church can be perceived at all only from outside all empirical ecclesial structures.

council's decisive yet incomplete step forward in Roman Catholic doctrine on the question. This step was necessary for the church to be able to open itself up to the ecumenical movement; and it was possible because many theologians and activists, while far from representing the majority view at the time, had previously paved the way through their words and deeds for this transformed doctrinal position.

In this context, it should be remembered that these individuals were not the first to take on this task since the 16th century.[4] In fact, in every period between the last formal so-called colloquies of the Reformation era and the first official bi- or multi-confessional dialogue of the postconciliar period there had been attempts or at least ideas about how to prevent the reality of schism from remaining a permanent state of affairs. A number of accounts by Catholic authors setting out to describe these endeavors had already been written in the 19th and early 20th centuries.[5] For the first half of the 20th century, which is the subject of this chapter, a comprehensive study is available only for the francophone regions,[6] while for many other languages and regions there are at least a number of general overviews.[7]

My aim here is not to remedy this deficiency for Catholicism as a whole. Rather, I must and can only confine myself to providing a survey of the Catholic theological reference points and views on the phenomenon, as well as the material and formal foundations of what is commonly referred to as the ecumenical movement.

If one shares Congar's definition of the heart of the ecumenical project, one must inevitably distinguish it from those approaches aimed at the return to the Catholic Church of Christians from other confessions, at corporate reunion, and at subordination to the primacy of the bishop of Rome, among other things. That is why in some languages a semantic distinction has been established between "ecumenism" and "unionism."[8] Even though this distinction may be able to claim a certain degree of validity on theological grounds, the question nevertheless arises as to whether it accurately represents the testimonies from the period in question, in this case the first half of the 20th century.[9] Some undoubted pioneers of ecumenism did indeed pursue a concept shaped by unionism in this sense, whether in their early

4 The judgment that recurs in the literature, or the self-perception of those involved, according to which they had worked together towards something or agreed about something for the first time since the schism, must be treated with absolute caution.

5 See Mathieu-Mathurin Tabaraud, *Histoire critique des projets formés depuis trois cent ans pour la réunion des Communions Chrétiennes*, Paris, Gauthier Frères & Cie, [2]1824; Gisbert Menge, *Versuche zur Wiedervereinigung Deutschlands im Glauben: Beiträge zur Kirchengeschichte*, Steyl, Verlag der Missionsdruckerei, 1920; see also the collection of texts in: Johannes Beumer, ed., *Auf dem Wege zur christlichen Einheit: Vorläufer der ökumenischen Bewegung von den Anfängen des Humanismus bis zum Ende des 19. Jahrhunderts*, Bremen, Carl Schünemann, 1966. From a Protestant theological perspective, see Friedrich Wilhelm Kantzenbach, *Einheitsbestrebungen im Wandel der Kirchengeschichte*, Gütersloh, Gütersloher Verlagshaus Gerd Mohn, 1979.

6 See Étienne Fouilloux, *Les catholiques et l'unité chrétienne du XIXe au XXe siècle: Itinéraires européens d'expression française*, Paris, Le Centurion, 1982.

7 For example, see José Desumbila, *El ecumenismo en España*, Barcelona, Editorial Estela, 1964; Jörg Ernesti & Wolfgang Thönissen, eds., *Die Entdeckung der Ökumene: Zur Beteiligung der katholischen Kirche an der Ökumenischen Bewegung*, Paderborn/Frankfurt a.M., Bonifatius/Otto Lembeck, 2008; Riccardo Burigana, *Una straordinaria avventura: Storia del Movimento ecumenico in Italia (1910–2010)*, Bologna, EDB, 2013.

8 This would appear to be the case mainly for Romance-speaking countries; see Desumbila, *El ecumenismo*, 89, 96 ("unionismo propiamente dicho" and "concepción unionista clásica" versus "ecumenismo"); Fouilloux, *Les catholiques et l'unite chretienne*; Mauro Velati, *Una difficile transizione: Il cattolicesimo tra unionismo ed ecumenismo (1952–1964)*, Bologna, Il Mulino, 1996.

9 Jean Guitton, *Œuvres complètes*, vol. 6, *Œcuménisme*, Paris, Desclée de Brouwer, 1986, 24, takes issue with Fouilloux's work and its underlying view: "The author of this book knew this history through documents; me, on my skin. Reading the book ... I did not recognize myself in it, although all the quotations he makes from my writings are correct. ... Mr. Fouilloux's implicit axioms are not my own."

days or throughout their lives, but a considerable number of them also believed in taking a twofold approach to achieving the aim of church unity: individual or corporate conversion on the one hand, and dialogue on the other. This is reinforced by the fact that language usage at the time in no way supports such a semantic opposition. This certainly applies to the individuals and groups working outside the Roman Catholic sphere. Neither Life and Work nor Faith and Order included the term "ecumenical" in their names. Anyone looking through the latter's fundamental texts will not find any quantitative or qualitative prominence for this semantic field, but instead frequently encounter expressions such as "unity/unité/Einheit" or "(re-)union/(Wieder-)Vereinigung."[10] This is also the case for the Catholic sphere, possibly even more so. To cite only one of the more noteworthy examples, in his review of Congar's *Chrétiens désunis*, which he warmly approved of it, the Louvain theologian Gustave Thils calls it "a beautiful work, which will leave its mark in the *Unionist* literature."[11]

Further questions arise regarding the now standard regional and historical division of developments within Catholicism. While the francophone and German-speaking areas have traditionally been identified as the most fertile ground of Catholic steps in the direction of opening up to ecumenism, studies dealing with other geographical areas have shown that further regions and languages should also be considered as playing a key foundational role. This discovery has shifted attention not only to the Anglo-American sphere, but also made scholars realize that the Romance-speaking areas, and not least Rome itself, should not be neglected. Similar questions would also have to be posed regarding the designation and demarcation of historical periods, which could be loosely paralleled with the publication years of the relevant Vatican documents, – such as *Apostolicae curae* (1896), *Mortalium animos* (1928), and *Cum compertum* (1948)/*De motione oecumenica* (1950)[12] – in order to occasionally identify these Roman doctrinal proclamations as none other than counter-responses to a Catholic ecumenism from below. Needless to say, the same question also applies to the periodization of the main phases of the non-Catholic ecumenical movement, whose dates are not that different, that is to the world conferences of Edinburgh (1910), Stockholm (1925), Lausanne (1927), Oxford

10 See Karl-Christoph Epting, *Ein Gespräch beginnt: Die Anfänge der Bewegung für Glauben und Kirchenverfassung in den Jahren 1910 bis 1920*, Zürich, Theologischer Verlag, 1972, esp. the appendix, 315–388. The same kind of language is used precisely in correspondence with Vatican recipients; the first letter (1914) of secretary Robert H. Gardiner to secretary of state Cardinal Pietro Gasparri also refers to "dissidia" and "dissidentes" – although here all Christians and churches are meant – as well as to the aim of "redintegranda" or "restituenda unitas Christiana," see Epting, *Ein Gespräch beginnt*, 360.

11 *ETL* 14, 1937, 684–686, here 686 (italics mine). The aim which the reviewer, whether rightly or wrongly, sees himself as sharing with the author is expressed on page 685 as follows: "The ultimate aim of the movement is the integration of dissidents into the *Una catholica*, but into a Catholic unity that, far from rejecting any real value, takes them all on and gives an answer to all, because it is the body of the One who possesses all fullness in Himself." On the author, see Joseph Famerée, "L'œuvre théologique de Mgr G. Thils (1909–2000)," *RTL* 31, 2000, 474–491.

12 An analogous approach would be a division according to pontificates, such as from Leo XIII until Pius XII. A mixed model combining these aspects is adopted by Roger Aubert, "Les étapes de l'œcuménisme catholique depuis le pontificat de Léon XIII jusqu'à Vatican II," in: Laurence K. Shook & Guy-M. Bertrand, dir., *La théologie du renouveau: Texte integral des travaux presentés au Congrès international de Toronto*, vol. 1, Paris/Montreal, Cerf/Fides, 1968, 291–307. In addition to this historical longitudinal study, the same author also wrote a cross-sectional study appearing in three editions at the end of the period under consideration here and more aimed at confessional families: Roger Aubert, *Problèmes de l'unité chrétienne: Initiation*, Paris, Éditions de Chevetogne, 1952 ([2]1961, [3]1965). On the other hand, a model divided in turn by chronology, subjects, and individuals is followed by Paul M. Minus, *The Catholic Rediscovery of Protestantism: A History of Roman Catholic Ecumenical Pioneering*, New York, Paulist Press, 1976.

and Edinburgh (both 1937), and Amsterdam (1948). Even if such a view of a development in phases can indeed still claim a certain justification, this must nonetheless be placed alongside the observation that a not insignificant number of the acknowledged participants in the debate have consistently held to one and the same concept, which tends to give rise to a picture of simultaneous asychronicities, rather than a clearly directed paradigm shift.

In order to avoid the pitfalls of these overarching organizing concepts, without being reduced to a mere juxtaposition of different points of view, while also offering a periodization – historically never entirely avoidable – I believe the most suitable approach is to structure the discussion around a series of what I shall call nodal points.[13]

2 Three Intersection Points

The first of these nodal points can be dated to around the mid-1920s. Leading up to it are traditions dating back to the late 19th and early 20th centuries, both in terms of ideas and the individuals involved in them. The main endeavors aiming at church unity from the Catholic point of view remained the ecclesiastical bodies of the Christian East and the Church of England, which were seen to be of a similar kind. At the same time, some individuals who had been engaged in this area over many years were still active. These included Cardinal Désiré-Joseph Mercier of Malines,[14] as well as the inspiration for his ideas, the Benedictine Lambert Beauduin, both in Belgium;[15] the French Lazarist Fernand Portal,[16] together with his manifold following in France;[17] the French Jesuit Michel d'Herbigny, who was mainly active in Rome and Eastern Europe; and the Greek Catholic Metropolitan Andrej Sheptytsky.[18] They had all grown up against the background of the attempts at church union pursued under Pope Leo XIII only to see them fail.[19] On the one hand, the situation changed as one pope succeeded another (from the strictly anti-Modernist Pius X, through Benedict XV, perceived by everyone as more open-minded, to the learned Pius XI, who was, moreover, close to Mercier). On the other, it was due to the course and outcome of World War I and the Russian Revolution. The latter brought cataclysmic change for Christian churches in Russia, also leading to the exile of Russian Orthodox believers in Central and Western Europe, and of Christians in the Near and Middle East. Finally, changes also occurred due to stronger links between France, Belgium, and Great Britain. In this context, a number of different initiatives came to the fore, forging ties with one another transcending confessional divisions; admittedly, most of these initiatives failed. A third determining factor was the creation of the ecumenical movement's emerging institutions. This context and the figures taking up positions within the movement gave rise to very different projects, in terms of both their aims and

13 If I am not mistaken, a similar structure appears to inform the collection of essays by Henry St. John, *Essays in Christian Unity: 1928–1954*, London, Blackfriars, 1955, although there it is mainly justified on autobiographical and bibliographical grounds (see page IX). On the latter, see Herbert Keldany, "Henry St. John O.P. (1891–1973)," *NBf* 61/761, 1980, 35–40.

14 See the contribution by Bernard Barlow and Martin Browne in the first volume of this work.

15 See the contribution by André Haquin in the first volume of this work.

16 See the contribution by Paul Avis in the first volume of this work.

17 Worth particular mention is Jean Calvet and his work: *Le Problème Catholique de l'Union des Églises*, Paris, J. de Gigord, 1921, 43f., which also contains – repeatedly – the formula "L'union n'est pas l'absorption," suggested then by Beauduin in the Malines conversations.

18 See Léon Tretjakewitsch, *Bishop Michel d'Herbigny SJ and Russia: A Pre-Ecumenical Approach to Christian Unity*, Würzburg, Augustinus-Verlag, 1990. Among the works of Michel d'Herbigny, see his *L'Unité dans le Christ*, Rome, PIO, 1923.

19 See the contribution by Laura Pettinaroli in the first volume of this work.

the personalities behind them, although they were by no means unconnected. These included such undertakings as the Malines Conversations,[20] the foundation of the Union Monastery at Amay (later Chevetogne),[21] the systematic creation of educational institutions such as the PIO in Rome[22] (founded in 1917 but which took some time to gain a footing), or the St. Basil seminar organized by the Dominicans, together with their Istina center in Lille (later mainly in the Paris area).[23] Just to take one example, that of Lambert Beauduin mentioned above. Besides being a lecturer in ecclesiology at the Benedictine college of Sant'Anselmo in Rome, Beauduin also studied at the PIO, was the "ghostwriter" of the memorandum read out by Mercier during the last of the Malines Conversations under his supervision, and was the driving force[24] and first superior of the monastery founded at Amay. He had previously established contacts with England and with the Dominican Christophe-Jean Dumont and his circle in Lille. Moreover, this entangled thread of activities, organizations, and figures also came to form a nodal point through its apparent dissolution. The latter, in fact, turned out to be simply a re-formation following the *Mortalium animos* encyclical of Pope Pius XI of 1928,[25] which delimits it both in time and subject-matter. There was also a generational shift in some of the main active figures: Mercier and Portal both died in 1926, and Beauduin lost at least institutional influence as a result of his forced exile.

The second nodal point can be located around the mid-1930s, with its epicenter in 1937. This was the year of the two ecumenical follow-up events to Stockholm and Lausanne – they were held in Oxford and Edinburgh respectively – but also the year of publication of the essential ecumenical theological work, *Chrétiens désunis*, by Yves Congar, cited at the start of this chapter. Two other decisive works for our context also appeared in 1937, one by the Louvain theologian Gustave Thils on *notae ecclesiae* and the other by the Bonn professor Arnold Rademacher, *Die Wiedervereinigung der christlichen Kirchen*.[26] Congar's work inaugurated his seminal Unam Sanctam series,[27] published in the Éditions du Cerf run by his fellow Dominicans. This series would henceforth set the parameters of the ecclesiological and ecumenical theological debate. The second work published in the series, originally intended to be the first one, was a new French translation of Johann Adam Möhler's *Die Einheit in der Kirche* of 1825.[28] This

20 See the contribution by Bernard Barlow and Martin Browne in the first volume of this work.

21 See the contribution by André Haquin in the first volume of this work.

22 See Gianpaolo Rigotti, ed., *Oriente Cattolico*, vol. 1, Rome, Valore Italiano, ^{5}2017, 17–27.

23 See Etienne Fouilloux's contribution to this volume: "From Missions to Ecumenism: Istina." Even older, founded in 1895, was the institution that subsequently became known as the IFEB of the Augustinians of the Assumption. The institute is also important for our subject, and had various branches in Istanbul, Athens, Bucharest, and Paris; it also published a journal, *Échos d'Orient* (later, *Revue des études byzantines*). Among its major writers are Martin Jugie, who also taught at the PIO, and especially Sévérien Salaville.

24 This refers not just to the Belgian foundation but also to the papal letter *Equidem verba* of 1924 addressed to the Benedictine abbot primate, written shortly before the monastery's foundation and actually making it possible; d'Herbigny and Mercier were again among those involved in this initiative; see Jacques Mortiau & Raymond Loonbeek, *Dom Lambert Beauduin, visionnaire et précurseur (1973–1960): Un moine au cœur libre*, Paris, Cerf, 2005, 86–92.

25 See the contribution by Marie Levant in the first volume of this work.

26 See Gustave Thils, *Les notes de l'Église dans l'apologétique catholique depuis la réforme*, Gembloux, J. Duculot, 1937; Arnold Rademacher, *Die Wiedervereinigung der christlichen Kirchen*, Bonn, Peter Hanstein, 1937.

27 See Étienne Fouilloux, *Les Éditions dominicaines du Cerf: 1918–1965*, Rennes, Presses Universitaires de Rennes, 2018, 168–171.

28 Johann Adam Möhler, *Die Einheit in der Kirche: oder, Das Princip des Katholicismus, dargestellt im Geiste der Kirchenväter der drei ersten Jahrhunderte*, Tübingen, Laupp, 1825; FT: *L'unité dans l'Église: ou, Le principe du catholicisme d'après l'esprit des Pères des trois premiers siècles de l'Église*, trans. André de Lilienfeld, Paris, Cerf, 1938.

work was an attempt to retrace a line of legitimacy from the previous century to the new theological departures of the 1930s.[29] At the same time, a bridge was being built by a French Jesuit from the *nouvelle théologie* circle, Pierre Chaillet, and the Tübingen dogmatician Josef Rupert Geiselmann, in order to connect the Tübingen of the first decades of the 19th century to the reshaping of Catholic theology in the mid-20th century. Building on this connection, two years later, in 1939, a volume to commemorate the anniversary of Möhler's death in 1838 was simultaneously published in French and German.[30] Once again, political and historical events played a formative role, this time not in a post- but a pre-war scenario. In this case, too, a number of threads intertwined at various points can be discerned. Hence, Pierre Chaillet was not merely the French initiator and editor of the bilingual work in memory of Möhler; he had already written the introduction to the translation of Möhler in Congar's series. The translator of Möhler's work was André de Lilienfeld, a convert from the Baltic region fluent in both French and German and a member of the first generation of novitiates at Amay.[31] Another figure with ties to Amay and Lyon, Chaillet's most important place of reference, and also to Congar, was Paul Couturier, who brought a new color to the intertwining threads.[32] Many of these figures had already floated down one of the many streams which over time would become the Week of Prayer for Christian Unity.[33] After Couturier joined them, these streams could gradually be channeled into the same garden. Couturier, that ceaseless shining light of what has ever since been known as "spiritual ecumenism," also drew his main influence from Amay, and, as an oblate, remained in contact with the monastery throughout his life. It was there that for the first time he met Congar, who became one of the most tireless preachers and speakers at the Week of Prayer.[34] Indeed, *Chrétiens désunis* arose from one of Amay's lecture series. Couturier, who was not himself a theologian, also promoted theologians from different schools of thought. Accordingly, he set up (again in 1937) the Dombes Group discussion circle,[35] among others with Chaillet from the Catholic side and the founders of Taizé[36] from the Protestants. Chaillet and Yves de Montcheuil, another Catholic member of this circle and co-author of the Möhler volume, shared with Lilienfeld the fate of many *résistance* activists in the coming years of war, which linked them, even if only in an ideal way, and not at a personal level, to some of their German brethren, in particular to the former leading light of spiritual ecumenism in the German-speaking countries, Max Josef Metzger.[37] Whereas Chaillet and Lilienfeld survived, Metzger and de Montcheuil fell victim

29 See the contribution by Franz Xaver Bischof in the first volume of this work.

30 Pierre Chaillet, ed., *L'Église est une: Hommage à Moehler*, Paris, Bloud & Gay, 1939; Hermann Tüchle, ed., *Die eine Kirche: Zum Gedenken J. A. Möhlers (1838–1938)*, Paderborn, Schöningh, 1939.

31 See Leonhard Hell, "Früher katholischer Ökumenismus im deutsch-französischen Wechselspiel," in: Ernesti & Thönissen, eds., *Die Entdeckung der Ökumene*, 53–80, here 67.

32 See the contribution by Étienne Fouilloux in this volume: "Abbé Paul Couturier and Spiritual Ecumenism."

33 A look at the entangled origins of this undertaking can be found in Fouilloux, *Les catholiques et l'unite chretienne*, 273–345.

34 This does not mean Couturier felt an affinity with Congar in every personal and theological respect. The same applies, *mutatis mutandis*, to the many other speakers and preachers taking part in Couturier's initiative: from the previously mentioned Dumont and Beauduin, through the Jesuit Jean Daniélou, and the convert Louis Bouyer, to the layman and philosopher from Portal's circle, Jean Guitton. Nonetheless, Couturier also enjoyed a closed theological milieu loyal to him, for example the Sulpician Louis Richard and especially the Marist Maurice Villain.

35 See the contribution by Étienne Fouilloux in this volume: "Abbé Paul Couturier and Spiritual Ecumenism."

36 See Silvia Scatena, *Taizé, una parabola di unità: Storia della comunità dalle origini al concilio dei giovani*, Bologna, Il Mulino, 2018, 76–81.

37 See Jörg Ernesti, "Metzger, Max-Josef s.v.," in: Ernesti & Thönissen, eds., *Personenlexikon Ökumene*, 147–149. For Metzger's own work, see Max Josef Metzger, "Aufbruch zur Una Sancta," *ThGl* 33, 1941, 16–22, reprinted in *ThGl* 99, 2009, 278–285. His theological contemporaries and successors include most importantly Matthias Laros; see Matthias Laros, *Schöpferischer Friede der*

to the National Socialist death-machinery. All this points towards the distinguishing feature and historical limits of this second nodal point; if on the one hand a theological basis and spiritual connotation that transcended confessional boundaries was added to the previously fostered aspiration for unity, it was actually – as in the case of the non-Catholic ecumenical movement, too – war and occupation that threatened to suspend the project at an institutional level, even though in religious terms these circumstances often made it seem more urgent than ever, even making it oftentimes possible.[38] Conversely, hindsight shows that *Mortalium animos* and similar measures from Rome, or even sometimes of local origin, by no means discouraged Catholic combatants or even cowed them into silence; nor were the Malines efforts of the personal circle around Mercier, Beauduin, and Portal invalidated as a result, nor do they even appear to have failed. However, the need to eliminate a certain level of naïveté became equally clear, as did certain undeniable strategic and tactical tendencies evident in previous endeavors. This gave greater prominence to Christianity as a whole and, within this, the Protestant world, particularly compared to its predecessors at the turn of the century and in the 1920s.

The third nodal point hovers around the late 1940s and early 1950s. Once again, a postwar decade saw the ecumenical movement of non-Catholic origin finally come together in the WCC (1948). This made it clear to the engaged contingent on the Catholic side that they would have to adopt a new approach, particularly in relations with their Protestant brothers and sisters. This moment was the result, first, of the experience of the recent past, which had shown that longstanding divisions could be overcome under the pressure of war and persecution. However, it was also an inherent part of the context of Christian democratic projects. They did not want to repeat the mistake of putting their trust in a political organization of a confessional character. Within Catholicism, this set of circumstances was determined by the contact, resumed as soon as possible at the end of the war and in the early postwar years, between people and organizations who had had pre-war ties. Meanwhile, new forces also entered the stage. The most enduring was the Dutch pair of Johannes Willebrands and Frans Thijssen, two priests who came from a movement aimed at helping converts, but who now, without renouncing their previous work, sought to join the European ecumenical scene. The tangible result was the CCEQ and the subsequent contact with the WCC in Geneva.[39] There had been plans for, and precursors to, both of these before the war. In 1938, in Le Saulchoir, Congar had assembled a similar, but still entirely informal discussion group.[40] One of his friends, Otto Iserland, a former worker at the IMC in Geneva before converting to Catholicism, suggested at the same time the "setting up of a Catholic central office for ecumenical and controversial theological questions."[41] It was only now that such plans could be implemented, just as the WCC also came to life. The multi-faceted outlook of worldwide Christianity towards all sides persisted throughout all this, even occasionally taking in its Jewish brothers and sisters.[42] The

Konfessionen: Die Una-Sancta-Bewegung, ihr Ziel und ihre Arbeit, Recklinghausen, Paulus, 1950.

38 Guitton, *Œuvres complètes*, vol. 6, 530–539.

39 See the contribution by Peter De Mey and Saretta Marotta in this volume: "The Catholic Conference for Ecumenical Questions." The organization's founders succeeded in integrating Rome's attempts to rally, but also to curb, Catholic theological ecumenism – for example, that of the French Jesuit theologian who taught in Rome, Charles Boyer, and his Unitas center, or of the conference in Grottaferrata in 1950 (see Fouilloux, *Les catholiques et l'unite chretienne*, 705–709, 833–845) – and at the same time managed to strip it of its leadership role.

40 See Fouilloux, *Les catholiques et l'unite chretienne*, 242–244; Hell, "Früher katholischer Ökumenismus," 72f.

41 Cited from Fouilloux, *Les catholiques et l'unite chretienne*, 241, n. 237.

42 Especially worth mentioning in this context is the Protestant convert to Catholicism, Karl Thieme; on him, see Leonhard Hell, "Unio Ecclesiae – Materia primaria: Bischof Albert Stohrs Einbindung in den entstehenden

focus on the different contingents of Protestant Christianity, which had already shaped pre-war debates, was further reinforced.

3 Forums and Organs

The situation around the time of these three nodal points was not only shaped by contacts transcending internal and external confessional boundaries, informal and official meetings and conversations, or fundamental monographs, and the like. Vital fertile ground for ideas was also provided by journals of the most diverse format, objectives, and readership. Not only did already existing, refounded, or new organs of more general theological or ecclesiastical content regularly make known the efforts beginning to emerge around church unity,[43] but new publications were also expressly set up for this purpose.[44] In some cases, individual articles or series of essays were collected in a single volume.[45] Besides the Catholic organs themselves, Catholic authors also wrote for journals and anthologies that did not have to account to the Catholic authorities and for publications with a bi- or multi-confessional orientation.[46] It is clear in many of these cases that the aim was to reach a wider audience than merely the circle of theologians or especially interested clergy. This is also shown by the fact that early ecumenical debates as a whole, regardless of whether on Christian democracy, questions of social ethics, or even liturgical renewal, by no means took place in a strictly insular theological and scholarly environment but increasingly in the wider environment of engaged Catholics. The principal theological works of the period and many lesser writings were often not written solely for the auditorium of colleagues or to be left on the writing desk. The context in which Congar's *Chrétiens désunis* originated has already been mentioned. Other notable works in this vein were those in German by Karl Adam;[47] the essays of Paul Simon on the subject of *Wiedervereinigung*;[48] the volume by Arnold Rademacher;[49] and those in French by

internationalen katholischen Ökumenismus und in die Vorbereitung des Zweiten Vatikanischen Konzils," in: Karl Lehmann, ed., *Dominus fortitudo: Bischof Albert Stohr (1890–1961)*, Mainz, Echter, 2012, 99–119, here 105f.

43 For example, *Ephemerides Theologicae Lovanienses, Revue des Sciences Philosophiques et Théologiques, Études, Blackfriars, The Month, Stimmen der Zeit, Hochland.*

44 For example, *Revue Anglo-Romaine, Revue de l'Orient Chrétien, Revue catholique des Églises, Revue (pratique) d' Apologétique, Roma e l'Oriente, Acta Academiae Velehradensis, L'Union des Églises* (later, *L'Unité de l'Église*), *Irénikon, Bulletin of the Confraternity of Unity* (later, *Reunion*), *Die Friedensstadt, West-östlicher Weg, Catholica, Russie et Chrétienté* (from 1954, *Istina*), *Orientalia Christiana Periodica, Der Christliche Orient, Eastern Churches Quarterly*, and *Unitas*. Of particular interest is *Oecumenica*, a journal that, despite its place of publication (London), appeared in French from 1934 to 1939 and published articles by Catholic authors despite the publisher (SPCK) being Anglican.

45 See Max Pribilla, *Um die Wiedervereinigung im Glauben*, Freiburg i.Br., Herder, 1926. This volume brought together a number of his contributions to the Jesuit organ *Stimmen der Zeit*; on Pribilla, see Jörg Ernesti, "Pribilla, Max, s.v.," in: Ernesti & Thönissen, *Personenlexikon Ökumene*, 182f.

46 In this regard, problems often, though not regularly, arose with the ecclesiastical supervision of these kinds of publications.

47 Karl Adam, *Das Wesen des Katholizismus*, Augsburg, Haas & Grabherr, 1924; Karl Adam, *Una Sancta in katholischer Sicht*, Düsseldorf, Patmos, 1948. See also Stephan Lüttich, "Karl Adams Weg zu seiner katholischen Sicht der 'Una Sancta': Ein Beitrag zum geistigen Kontext der frühen ökumenischen Theologie," in: Ernesti & Thönissen, eds., *Die Entdeckung der Ökumene*, 139–158.

48 See Jörg Ernesti, "Simon, Paul, s.v.," in: Ernesti & Thönissen, *Personenlexikon Ökumene*, 210f.; Simon's publications contain expressions such as "Wiedervereinigung der Christen," "Wiedervereinigung im Glauben," and "Wiedervereinigung der Kirchen."

49 Rademacher, *Die Wiedervereinigung*; Rademacher, therefore, also added a theological support to his work for a wider audience: Arnold Rademacher, *Die innere Einheit des Glaubens: Ein theologisches Prolegomenon zur Frage der Kirchenunion*, Bonn, Peter Hanstein, 1937, 8.

Charles Quénet,[50] Gabriel Brunhes,[51] or Charles Journet.[52] The most important forums for this new audience were associations of Catholic students, and academically trained people and seminars open to the public, which were intended to provide theological information and the exchange of ideas, as well as to serve religious empowerment. These included the Pentecost meetings of the Una Sancta brotherhood initiated by Metzger,[53] the various *semaines*[54] and *amitiés*[55] in France, and several sundry retreat days (*retraites, journées*) in various European countries. On these occasions, the range of participants increasingly went beyond members of one's own confession (or the own gender). It is noteworthy in this context that, despite the actual, although sometimes only apparent, existence of ecclesiastical prohibitions, encounters expressly among theologians of different confessions were regarded as not merely desirable but even absolutely essential.[56] Meeting this need in practice certainly did not come to a halt when the Malines Conversations ended, but instead continued in a series of different initiatives. English Catholics held meetings with papalist Anglican representatives;[57] French Catholic theologians – such as in the circle around Jacques Maritain,[58] in the Dombes Group,[59] or at a meeting in Bièvres (1937)[60] – found the dialogue with Orthodox or Reformed partners; German circles of theologians and laity prayed and debated together in Una Sancta groups. Furthermore, as early as in 1934, a high-ranking Catholic and Lutheran discussion forum started to meet, which would soon be revived after the war as the Jaeger-Stählin circle.[61] Going back even further in time are the congresses aimed particularly at Catholic and Orthodox dialogue which had been held since 1907 in Velehrad in Moravia. They continued into the late 1930s, and after the war there was an attempt to build on them in the United States.[62] This generally occurred with the benign knowledge of the local church hierarchy, sometimes also of Rome; Velehrad even received praise and support from Pope Pius XI in 1927.[63] In no way does this mean that ecumenically engaged Catholic theologians of this period were able to carry out their activities of publication and dialogue totally without

50 Charles Quénet, *L'Unité de l'Église: Les Églises séparées d'Orient et La Réunion des Églises*, Paris, J. de Gigord, 1923.

51 Gabriel Brunhes, *Christianisme et Catholicisme*, Paris, Beauchesne, 1924. This work by the then professor at the seminary in Dijon and subsequent bishop of Montpellier was provided with a foreword by Michel d'Herbigny and immediately reached three editions.

52 Charles Journet, *L'Union des Églises et le christianisme pratique*, Paris, Grasset, 1927. See also Fouilloux, *Les catholiques et l'unite chretienne*, 868–871.

53 See the contribution by Paul Metzlaff in the first volume of this work. See also the contribution by Peter Zimmerling in this volume.

54 First and foremost, of course, the prayer weeks started by Couturier in Lyon, from where they spread elsewhere, with their series of lectures and discussions; see Maurice Villain, *L'Abbé Paul Couturier: Apôtre de l'Unité Chrétienne*, Tournai, Casterman, 1957, 78–93.

55 See Fouilloux, *Les catholiques et l'unité chrétienne*, 108, 365, 750–755.

56 See St. John, *Essays*, 59f.: "The way to increasing unity of heart and mind lies in the growth of friendly contacts and in conferences, on the theological level, between representatives of the different parts of divided Christendom." This comes at the end of the 1940s, but deliberately looks back at the two decades following the Malines Conversations.

57 There, too, one felt on the traces of the Malines Conversations; see Mark Vickers, *Reunion Revisited: 1930s Ecumenism Exposed*, Leominster, Gracewing, 2017. One of the instigators of these meetings was the Dominican convert from Anglo-Catholic circles and friend of Congar, Henry St. John; see Vickers, *Reunion Revisited*, 226–229.

58 See Fouilloux, *Les catholiques et l'unité chrétienne*, 170; interlocutors from the Reformed tradition already took part here.

59 See Villain, *L'Abbé Paul Couturier*, 142–157; Hell, "Früher katholischer Ökumenismus," 60.

60 See Fouilloux, *Les catholiques et l'unité chrétienne*, 235f.; Hell, "Früher katholischer Ökumenismus," 72f.

61 See Jörg Ernesti, *Ökumene im Dritten Reich*, Paderborn, Bonifatius, 2007, 42–123. See also the contribution by Friederike Nüssel in this volume.

62 See Peter Esterka, "Toward Union: The Congresses at Velehrad," *JES* 8, 1971, 10–51.

63 The text of the papal letter can be found in: *AAS* 16, 1924, 326f.; see Esterka, "Toward Union," 25f., 31f.

impediment from ecclesiastical intervention or suspicion. However, the positions put forward in these forums were never subject to explicit anathema, nor were those defending them placed on the index solely for this reason, let alone excommunicated, nor were their teachings or publications banned.[64] On the contrary, these authors never openly criticized doctrinal pronouncements such as *Mortalium animos*, but rather, in the tried and tested manner, recognized their undoubted legitimacy while claiming that naturally their own position was not affected by this.

4 The *Una Sancta* between Reality, Loss, and Final Aim

As with all attempts aimed at the unity of the church(es), the people, groups, and organs active within the Roman Catholic Church had to reach a clear position on the unity of the church set out in the common creed – described with further criteria in the farther confessional stock and supported by teachings, acts, and institutions – in view of the obvious division, separation, and disunity of Christians and Christianities worldwide, and frequently locally too.[65] In the first place, there was the consensus anchored in doctrine and undisputed in theology according to which one's own church possessed the unity professed in the creed, as well as the doctrine and structure needed to preserve it, and the corresponding life needed to make this unity believed in a visible reality.[66] There was just as much clarity and consensus that this could not be derived from the perfection of earthly structures or the individual actions of its members, whether clergy or laity, but solely from the effective will of Christ to establish, equip, and consolidate his church so that, even in the face of all limitation and deficiency of institutional and moral means, it could comply on earth with this divinely willed and given unity, let alone with the singularity given to that faith and to the content given with this faith.[67] In this sense, the unity of the church is not an aim as yet to be achieved at some later time nor is it a datum that can never truly be reached on earth.[68]

However, it was equally clear that it would be objectively unreasonable and strategically pointless at this stage to ascribe to the Christians and their congregations not currently living in ecclesial unity with Rome this inherited division as if it were an actual transgression. This would still be the case even if one was firmly convinced that the schisms and heresies wherever identified in the past had been caused through culpable separation from the papal see of unity. A conceptual theological solution traditionally resorted to was that of a bona fide accepted and transmitted faith and church life, whose essence contained an intention (hidden to themselves and to the others) towards unity in the Catholic Church, but which so far lacked conscious and visible realization.[69]

However, many things were still open to discussion within this consensus. It seemed

64 Another subject that cannot be dealt with here is so-called Modernism and its representatives in the context of ecumenical questions.

65 For these and the subsequent questions discussed here, a guiding role is given to the Dominican Henry St. John. Most of his views could equally be illustrated through French (Richard or Villain) and German (Rademacher) voices. On the other hand, there were of course deviations from this consensus (such as in the cases of Jugie, Journet, Boyer, and others). The Jesuit Max Pribilla can be placed in the middle between these two groups.

66 See St. John, *Essays*, 3; Pribilla, *Um die Wiedervereinigung*, 15.

67 See St. John, *Essays*, 11: "We as Catholics hold the Church to be Christ's Mystical Body ... This doctrine is the fundamental basis of our belief in the Church ... From this doctrine flows that of the supremacy and infallibility of the Pope, which is the divinely constituted safeguard of life in Christ within the Church."

68 See St. John, *Essays*, 4, 81; Pribilla, *Um die Wiedervereinigung*, 15.

69 The distinction, long advocated in soteriology with regard to non-Christians, between belonging to the salvific community *corde* or *corpore*, as well as reference to a *votum* or *desiderium* is applied here more or less without qualification to non-Catholic Christians in their classification *vis-à-vis* the Catholic Church.

particularly problematic to determine the effective status resulting from this theory of the salvation, or indeed non-salvation of Christians in this situation, their membership or not in the body of Christ,[70] the fundamental difference between their being Christian and their membership in a given church,[71] and the consequences of all that for the pursuit of the aim of church unity. The target in this respect was generally individual conversion or corporate (re)unification. Very few theologians developed a position that discovered, a viable path out of separation to unity accessible from different directions.[72]

It proved even more difficult for most ecumenically inspired Catholic theologians of the time to define more precisely the deficit that must be ascribed to their own church in light of the manifold divisions and separations within Christianity. The simplest version that set out to define this inadequacy as merely quantitatively or only strategically, in terms of the outward efficacy of Christian faith was not adopted.[73] On the other hand, a qualitative definition was difficult to achieve on the basis of the fundamental consensus just described and led not seldom to rather vague formulas.[74]

5 The Catholic Church's Contribution to Overcoming the Division

One thing above all applies here, and evidently it applies not only to Catholics. Members of the church can bring about the unity of the church desired by God and longed for by Christ in one way only: through "a consuming desire for reunion."[75]

The first steps in overcoming the division are seen generally as the recognition and acknowledgement of the shared responsibility for the divisions of the past and the present,[76] together with, conversely and at the same time linked to it, understanding for the other side's sense of injustice,[77] and the appreciation of its positive aims and concerns.[78] All this would be capable of overcoming complacency, crusading mentalities, suspicions, and prejudice in order to establish a fundamental attitude of sympathetic friendship.[79] The realization that not only theoretical knowledge obtained from books would be required to achieve this but also, and above all, practical knowledge, particularly in the form of personal acquaintance

70 See St. John, *Essays*, esp. "Appendix III: Membership of the Church," 137–140.

71 "Admission to the visible structure of the Church is by the sacrament of baptism … Those who owe their baptism to the agency of a non-Catholic religious body … often adhere in good faith to the religious profession in which they have been brought up. By doing so they lose the actual status of membership in the Church. Since, however, their action is unculpable this status is still retained in desire, and the purpose of which it exists is not rendered ineffective. Persons in this condition therefore remain members of the visible structure of the Church *in desire* only, though in actuality, and in virtue of their desire, they are still in some measure participants in its inner life of grace. Their membership is therefore incomplete"; St. John, *Essays*, 137f. (italics original).

72 "Living unity of the church of God does not arise like a society through a deliberate merger … but comes about naturally among those moved by the divine spirit and through this spirit grow together into a holy family of God"; Rademacher, *Die Wiedervereinigung*, 86.

73 See the distinction between quantitative and qualitative catholicity made by Ambroise de Poulpiquet, Dominican theologian and victim of World War I, in: Ambroise de Poulpiquet, *La Notion de Catholicité*, Paris, Bloud, 1910, and its reception in Thils, *Les notes de l'Église*, 250–254.

74 See St. John, *Essays*, 4; the view of the Catholic preservation of what constitutes the essence of being a church *quoad substantiam*, develops along similar lines, for example, in Gustave Thils, *Histoire doctrinale du mouvement œcuménique*, Louvain, Warny, 1955, 172, 194.

75 St. John, *Essays*, 3; Pribilla, *Um die Wiedervereinigung*, 1.

76 See St. John, *Essays*, 21; Rademacher, *Die Wiedervereinigung*, 125.

77 See St. John, *Essays*, 20; Rademacher, *Die Wiedervereinigung*, 125.

78 See St. John, *Essays*, 20; Rademacher, *Die Wiedervereinigung*, 125.

79 See St. John, *Essays*, 12, 17–21; Pribilla, *Wiedervereinigung*, 50f., 76.

and encounter, was taken for granted by all these voices.

The Malines Conversations represented a lasting *lieu de mémoire* of emerging Catholic ecumenism, which proved to be a constant reference point for Catholic theologians and their positions. Beyond Congar's almost panegyrical dedication of *Chrétiens désunis*, there are a number of other positions that claimed legitimacy based on the Malines precedent. This was not because the event as such was seen as particularly successful, but because the "spirit" that had visibly manifested itself there left lasting traces.[80] Many were anxious to affirm that the anathema of *Mortalium animos* was in no way aimed at Malines, and therefore it was possible to proceed in the same spirit as this previous experiment in dialogue.[81]

6 The Significance of Non-Catholic Churches and Communities

At the start of this chapter, I cited the position that contends that all Christians outside the boundaries of the Catholic Church have received that which makes them Christians from their own ecclesiastical community, which must therefore be taken as an instrument of divine will, even if this might be to a very limited extent. As has been seen, Congar had indicated that this argument was formulated by him for the first time within Catholicism in 1937. This claim requires qualification at the very least. His English confrere, Henry St. John, put forward the view as early as 1934 – then with reference to his former church (Church of England) later on in the book version consistently extended to all ecclesiastical bodies and argued for syllogistically – that the sanctifying grace acquired through baptism, and the faith contained within it given by God, presupposed the action of the Holy Spirit; if this baptism and faith were acquired in a non-Catholic community, this would mean the divine spirit had undoubtedly employed that community for this purpose.[82] This equally holds true even when said non-Catholic church is not considered as such part of the *corpus Christi mysticum*.[83] This assumes that the true doctrine and true life considered as essentially forming the church and fostering unity in one's own community are alive in other communities too. It also assumes that this process did not occur through illegitimate alienation but divine preservation.[84] Finally, the conclusion follows that the treasures found outside the boundaries of the visible Catholic Church should also be appreciated and recognized by Catholics. This even goes so far as to recognize that aspects of the shared faith have often been preserved by the "others" in such a way as to reveal the practice of faith within Catholicism to be wanting.[85] This willingness to learn on the part of Catholics can, in turn, open

80 See St. John, *Essays*, 28. On the spectrum of such attitudes, see Hell, "Früher katholischer Ökumenismus," 57f.

81 "Time has shown that the words used in that encyclical were not directed against meetings of the kind held at Malines"; St. John, *Essays*, 28. See similar testimonies in: Hell, "Früher katholischer Ökumenismus," 63f. The Malines dialogue model continued to be seen as exemplary; see, for example, Ernesti, *Ökumene im Dritten Reich*, 58–63.

82 "Since the possession of sanctifying grace implies the presence of the virtues and gifts of the Holy Ghost, it follows that whatever truth a non-Catholic holds by divine faith has been taught him by the Holy Ghost, and if he has learned that truth through the religious body to which he gives his allegiance then the Holy Ghost has made use of that body for teaching it"; St. John, *Essays*, 18. The original piece goes back to a lecture held in 1934 and published as Henry St. John, "The Approach to Reunion," *Blackfriars* 16, 1935, 85–95, and formulated even more clearly in St. John, *Essays*, 89: "Then the Holy Ghost has made the Church of England His instrument for teaching it."

83 See St. John, *Essays*, 18; Max Pribilla, *Um kirchliche Einheit: Stockholm – Lausanne – Rom: Geschichtlich-theologische Darstellung der neueren Einigungsbestrebungen*, Freiburg i.Br., Herder, 1929, 217.

84 See St. John, *Essays*, 29; Rademacher, *Die Wiedervereinigung*, 23.

85 See St. John, *Essays*, 29; Rademacher, *Die Wiedervereinigung*, 88.

up the other communities to the fullness of teaching and practice of faith.[86] From here the doctrine of truly ecclesial elements flourishes in manifold ways far beyond the period under consideration. These elements could also to be found outside the boundaries of the church of Catholic confession, even if not in the same perfection or fullness.[87]

7 The Content and Significance of the Opposition between the Confessions

Overall it can be seen that at the center of the debate was one's concept of the church, not traditional doctrinal differences such as the doctrine of grace and sacraments or pneumatology.[88] The crucial factor for the majority of Catholic writers was the essential visibility of the church itself and of its unity, without witholding its invisible and supernatural dimension.[89] On this terrain, the perspectives of the different churches and their respective claims to truth were regarded as virtually incommunicable.[90]

The most important stumbling block within the field of ecclesiology, at least since the dogmatic definitions of 1870, was considered the question of doctrinal authority and the pope's universal primacy of jurisdiction.[91] The possibility of reaching an understanding was seen on two possible levels: first, the manner of "exercising" this authority should appear to be highly flexible;[92] second, the aim was to make clearer to one's partners in dialogue the place of the papal office and its prerogatives in the totality of the Catholic understanding of church and faith.[93]

With regard to the possible attempts at understanding with non-Catholic partners, what would subsequently be called the "hierarchy of truths" emerged gradually. The distinction, considered classically Protestant, between *articuli fidei fundamentales et non fundamentales* was indeed decidedly rejected, and the traditional doctrine of *fides implicita* was professed by many.[94] Nonetheless, this opposition was supplemented by the idea of an interconnected and entirely weighted fabric of individual doctrines.[95]

8 Bridging Roles Both Outside and Inside the Church

Bridges, or points of contact, among separated Christianities were seen essentially in those churches considered to be of a type akin to Catholicism,[96] such as the Eastern churches, with their structural, dogmatic, and spiritual closeness to the Roman Catholic Church,[97] as well as – with regard to Western Christianity – the churches of the Anglican tradition. Concerning the latter Catholics saw particular links to catholicizing,

86 See St. John, *Essays*, 29; Rademacher, *Die Wiedervereinigung*, 91.

87 Alternatively, one spoke of "elements," "values," or "principles" of being a church; see Hell, "Früher katholischer Ökumenismus," 76–78.

88 See St. John, *Essays*, 86; Rademacher, *Die Wiedervereinigung*, 56; Pribilla, *Um kirchliche Einheit*, 293.

89 "This visible organic unity, so we believe, was our Lord's plan for his Church because he knew it to be the only way by which his truth and grace could be preserved and the means of their propagation guaranteed"; St. John, *Essays*, 19.

90 See St. John, *Essays*, 36; Pribilla, *Um kirchliche Einheit*, 227.

91 See St. John, *Essays*, 62; Pribilla, *Um kirchliche Einheit*, 292.

92 See St. John, *Essays*, 61f.

93 "An integral part of the nature of the Church as it is conceived of by Catholics as a whole"; St. John, *Essays*, 61.

94 This even applies, for example, to Rademacher, *Die Wiedervereinigung*, 80.

95 See St. John, *Essays*, 71; Pribilla, *Um kirchliche Einheit*, 226.

96 Different "types" of non-Catholic Christianity and non-Catholic churches with varying degrees of proximity to Catholicism had already been discussed by Brunhes, *Christianisme et Catholicisme*, 74, 140, 395.

97 "The Eastern Orthodox Churches, which have retained that [Catholic] tradition almost complete"; St. John, *Essays*, 66.

sometimes even papalistic currents.[98] In the former case, there was also the sense that piers of the bridge had been built through the Uniate churches. Some were able to discern even in German Lutheranism, with its original "Hochkirche" current, such a possibility of cohesion.[99] On the other hand, more skeptical minds instead saw precisely these supposed links as disruptors. The Uniate churches must have appeared from an orthodox perspective precisely as a sign of Roman proselytism.[100] Concentration on the Anglo-Catholic movements tended to make the possibility of an understanding with the Church of England as a whole more difficult.[101] The same was true for the Hochkirche currents in German Protestantism. On the other hand, more traditionally inclined authors did not consider these kindred groups capable of community with the Catholic Church. Rather, their apparent proximity only served to conceal unsurpassable distances. There was also assumed to be a danger that the catholicizing tendencies in non-Catholic churches might join forces in a Catholicism without Rome.[102]

A similar phenomenon became apparent in tendencies internal to theology. On the one hand, after the liberal currents of the 19th century, a remarkable recovery of Orthodox doctrine faithful to the confession could be detected, particularly in the sphere of Karl Barth's theology.[103] On the other hand, it had to be admitted, precisely in relation to this example, that this offered absolutely no navigable course to church unity.[104]

Nevertheless, there was still agreement that Catholicism had much in common with many other Christianities, which could foster the unity of the church and which remained to be rediscovered and reassessed, particularly by Catholics. Catholic ecumenism thus emerged in the immediate context of other prominent contemporary currents, such as the liturgical movement,[105] the lay movement, and the *retour aux sources* to the Bible and patristics, on whose impact it drew.[106]

Another bridge consisted in the religious orders and their spirituality. This ranged from the previously mentioned real efforts in bi-ritual monasteries with a particular focus on the Christian East and the fostering of contact with the reawakened religious life in the Anglican, and even in the Lutheran and Reformed tradition (not least Taizé and its women's counterpart at Grandchamp). Of special significance for theologians was the idea of a virtual space of a supra-confessional order existing in Couturiers's "monastère invisible"[107] or the Una Sancta brotherhood of Metzger,[108] and, beyond the official Catholic sphere, in the ecumenical Franciscans of Friedrich Heiler.[109]

9 The Perception of the Ecumenical Movement in Catholic Theology

The ecumenical movement, in particular since it had assumed concrete form in the world conferences and continued to develop in institutional bodies and follow-up events, culminating in the official foundation of the WCC, was viewed with great interest by Catholic theologians from the very start. Nonetheless, their position was far from

98 See St. John, *Essays*, 39f.; Guitton, *Œuvres complètes*, vol. 6, 463–529; Pribilla, *Um kirchliche Einheit*, 21.

99 See Pierre Charles, *La Robe sans couture: Un essai de Luthéranisme catholique*, Bruges, Charles Beyaert, 1923; Pribilla, *Um die Wiedervereinigung*, 13f.; Rademacher, *Die Wiedervereinigung*, 117f.

100 See Thils, *Histoire doctrinale*, 219.

101 See Brunhes, *Christianisme et Catholicisme*, 416.

102 See St. John, *Essays*, 41; Pribilla, *Um die Wiedervereinigung*, 43.

103 See St. John, *Essays*, 42f.

104 See Pribilla, *Um kirchliche Einheit*, 35; Thils, *Histoire doctrinale*, 88.

105 See St. John, *Essays*, 71.

106 See St. John, *Essays*, 71; Pribilla, *Um die Wiedervereinigung*, 58f.

107 See Villain, *L'Abbé Paul Couturier*, 333f.

108 See Ernesti, "Metzger, Max-Josef s.v.," 147–149 and Metzger, "Aufbruch zur Una Sancta," 16–22.

109 See Jörg Ernesti, "Friedrich Heiler und das Franziskanertum – frühe ökumenische Brückenschläge," *WiWei* 68, 2005, 82–101.

unanimous, even if there was agreement on a basic set of fundamental criticisms. One of these was the vague demarcation of who could participate. This was indeed hardly surprising, bearing in mind that even within the movement itself this problem led to considerable readjustments. There was agreement on the Catholic side that necessary but certainly not sufficient standards had been set through these corrections. Moreover, it was common for individual sections of the movement to be appraised differently; Life and Work, in particular, was mainly seen more as a goodwill organization of liberal Protestantism than as a serious attempt to overcome the divisions among Christianity.[110] Some theologians contended that the political and social aims of this movement predominated over religious and ecclesial ones. The view of Faith and Order was different. The inescapable questions, also unavoidable from a Catholic point of view, regarding doctrine and the life of those churches involved were at the very least the clear subject of the talks in this forum.[111] However, there was still no acceptance of the methods and results of Lausanne and of the subsequent gatherings.[112] Nor could one support the dominant idea of Faith and Order, which held that the one church exists in the present merely in the various fragments or branches of the different individual confessional churches.[113]

However, most authors, despite their criticism, also sought to draw something positive from the ecumenical movement. This concerned less the fundamentals or objectives of Christian or even church unity, but more in a "psychological" realm as contemporaries themselves often described it. The intention, which derived from the recognition of the undeniable sinfulness of the divisions within Christianity, was appreciated in all quarters and the spirit to which it gave rise stressed the new mindset or atmosphere.[114] This spirit could also be seen as exemplary for Catholics, too, not least because the new general perspective would enable them to see first and foremost the major elements of faith held in common, instead of always scrutinizing limits and differences.[115] The resulting goal that came into view is described by many as a rapprochement.[116]

Before all criticism on the grounds of principle and detail, Catholic authors consistently maintained that the awakened longing for unity in the church and the reunification of Christians had to be interpreted as the effect of the divine spirit at work. This spirit would have to arouse among Catholics in particular repent, reform, and increased efforts towards the universal unity of all Christians in a single church.[117] This was not least because new enemies common to all Christians were visibly raising their heads, namely the totalitarianisms shaping the age. These were often lumped together as materialistic (including communist ones) and neo-pagan (including Fascist and National Socialist ones), and were at any rate perceived as a common danger.[118]

In this context, an opposing interpretation of the common view still prevalent today of the relationship between the Catholic Church and the ecumenical movement came to the fore: it was not the former that had rejected the latter, but vice versa.[119] This would be naïve if one were to see in this interpretation Rome's actual attitude to the repeated attempts to integrate the Catholic Church within the ecumenical institutions. What

110 See St. John, *Essays*, 74; Pribilla, *Um kirchliche Einheit*, 114.

111 See St. John, *Essays*, 75.

112 See Pribilla, *Um kirchliche Einheit*, 199; somewhat more optimistic with regard to Faith and Order is St. John, *Essays*, 75f.

113 See St. John, *Essays*, 4; Pribilla, *Um kirchliche Einheit*, 198.

114 See St. John, *Essays*, 10–13; Pribilla, *Um die Wiedervereinigung*, 47f.

115 See St. John, *Essays*, 11.

116 See St. John, *Essays*, 59; Pribilla, *Um die Wiedervereinigung*, 40.

117 See St. John, *Essays*, 15–24; Rademacher, *Die Wiedervereinigung*, 86–96.

118 See St. John, *Essays*, 7; Rademacher, *Die Wiedervereinigung*, 113.

119 See St. John, *Essays*, 73; Pribilla, *Um kirchliche Einheit*, 204.

it actually meant was that precisely the ecumenical movement's internal evolution had shown that unity without an understanding in the content and structure of belief,[120] and without taking into account the unavoidable sense of truth of the individual denominations and their members, was an illusion.[121]

10 Viable Aims

The distinction between different Christianities and types of church drawn from history and established in theology was common to many Catholic positions. Rarely was a concept assumed to be equally realizable for all churches or communities. Rather, in most cases a basic distinction was practiced between the Eastern churches, which were structurally similar, if not of identical constitution, and defined by a similar doctrine – especially with regard to the sacraments and ecclesiastical ministries, though a lightly pronounced distinction was made between the Byzantine and Eastern Orthodox churches in this context – and the non-Catholic churches and communities of the West, which differed by degrees in their structure and confession of faith. Where for many authors corporate union was and remained the preferred unifying means with regard to the Eastern churches,[122] for the Western churches the view was not so clear. It is true that here, too, there was a certain tendency towards the possibility of corporate union, particularly in relation to the Church of England or the Anglican community as a whole.[123] However, a similar idea was rarely considered feasible for the entire spectrum of Protestant churches, but here, too, any proselytism was increasingly rejected.[124] There was more of a preference for complementary routes to unity along parallel paths.[125] Only a few theologians, albeit admittedly very prominent ones, said at least implicitly goodbye to the aims of conversion to or corporate union with the Catholic Church. However, they saw in the intensive growth of the catholic element within their own church and in the extensive increase in encounter and dialogue with other Christians and churches the human element of that movement, which came from Christ and would lead to church unity by traveling along paths known only to him and which, therefore, could not be defined either structurally or doctrinally.[126]

On the other hand, there was a widespread consensus among Catholics on the definition of what would not be sufficient for true unity, namely, a mere church association that put aside dogmatic differences, something of which the ecumenical movement was often accused.[127]

On the whole, and this of course shows both the status and the attitude of Catholic theologians in this period, all these views, which were in some cases truly divergent, were accompanied without exception by the claim that they were in no way contrary to the official teaching of the church at the time.[128] In this sense, there was indeed a cer-

120 See St. John, *Essays*, 79; Pribilla, *Um die Wiedervereinigung*, 52.

121 See St. John, *Essays*, 78; Pribilla, *Um die Wiedervereinigung*, 31.

122 See St. John, *Essays*, 6; more skeptical in this respect is Pribilla, *Um kirchliche Einheit*, 306, but also Rademacher, *Die Wiedervereinigung*, 114.

123 See St. John, *Essays*, 6.

124 See St. John, *Essays*, 29; Pribilla, *Um die Wiedervereinigung*, 35.

125 See St. John, *Essays*, 29; Pribilla, *Um kirchliche Einheit*, 302.

126 This seems to me at least to be the, as mentioned, rather implicit concept which characterized the spiritual ecumenism of the Lyon kind and its theological supporters, but also the reunification theology of Arnold Rademacher.

127 See St. John, *Essays*, 9; Pribilla, *Um die Wiedervereinigung*, 7.

128 "The view of membership of the Church here set out is implicit in the Encyclical *Mystici corporis*"; St. John, *Essays*, 139. On the different – although all entirely open-minded – readings of *Mystici corporis Christi*, particularly in the German-speaking countries, see Thomas Sartory, *Die ökumenische Bewegung und die Einheit der Kirche: Ein Beitrag im Dienste einer*

tain fluctuation in the intensity of early ecumenical endeavors. These reacted not only to external political and historical circumstances but also to the restrictive measures and doctrinal pronouncements of their own church hierarchy, although they never completely came to a standstill in this period. Around the middle of the 20th century, a veritable flood of general accounts of ecumenism from a Catholic perspective were already able to take stock of the movement and spur on further engagement. These works continued to appear until immediately before Vatican II.[129] Among the latter's Fathers, theological preparatory bodies, and advisors all the aforementioned positions continued to exist,[130] and even most of them there would be able to identify a critical analysis of the texts the council issued.[131] The fact that in the aftermath of this historic church assembly there started a widespread willingness on the part of the Roman Catholic Church to initiate official discussions with non-Catholic churches, church associations, and confessional families, to participate in subdivisions of the WCC – in some cases even to work formally with them and ratify consensus by the ecclesiastical authorities, even by renouncing to urge the canonical authority of doctrinal teachings[132] – cannot be obviously inferred from the preparations of the first half of the century. Just as in other areas, the dynamic momentum of the event far transcended texts and subject matters.

Translated from German to English by Fiona Robb.

Bibliography

Ernesti, Jörg & Wolfgang Thönissen, eds., *Die Entdeckung der Ökumene: Zur Beteiligung der katholischen Kirche an der Ökumenischen Bewegung*, Paderborn/Frankfurt a.M., Bonifatius/Otto Lembeck, 2008.

ökumenischen Ekklesiologie, Meitingen, Kyrios-Verlag, 1955, 133–145. A very similar route had indeed already been followed for *Mortalium animos*, see St. John, *Essays*, 28 and Hell, *Früher katholischer Ökumenismus*, 57. The simultaneously elegant and ironic summing-up found in Bernard Leeming, *The Churches and the Church: A Study of Ecumenism*, London/Westminster MD, Darton, Longman & Todd/The Newman Press, 1960, 166f., still holds: "Individual Catholics, while accepting most loyally the instructions from Rome, lay different emphasis upon different aspects of the matter, and show a feeling varying from the distinctly warm to the distinctly cold."

129 See Carlo Boyer, *Unità cristiana e movimento ecumenico: Testi e documenti*, Rome, Studium, 1955; Thils, *Histoire doctrinale*; Johannes P. Michael, *Christen suchen Eine Kirche: Die Ökumenische Bewegung und Rom*, Freiburg i.Br, Herder, 1958; Sartory, *Die ökumenische Bewegung*; Maurice Villain, *Introduction à l'œcuménisme*, Tournai, Casterman, 1958; Gustave Weigel, *A Catholic Primer on the Ecumenical Movement*, Westminster MD, The Newman Press, 1959; Alberto Bellini, *Il movimento ecumenico*, Padua, Presbyterium, 1960; Marie-Joseph Le Guillou, *Mission et unité: Les exigences de la communion*, 2 vols., Paris, Cerf, 1960; Leeming, *The Churches and the Church*; Georges H. Tavard, *Petite histoire du mouvement œcuménique*, Paris, Fleurus, 1960; *Le Christ et les Églises*, Paris, Éditions Universitaires, 1961; Willem H. van de Pol, *De oecumene*, Roermond, Romen, 1961; Bernard Lambert, *Le problème œcuménique*, 2 vols., Paris, Le Centurion, 1962; Henri Daniel-Rops, *Ces chrétiens, nos frères*, Paris, Fayard, 1965, 601–703. A work by a Protestant author that appeared as the second volume in a Catholic series published by Thomas Sartory must be regarded as something of a curiosity, although nonetheless symbolic: Hans Weissgerber, *Die Frage nach der wahren Kirche: Eine Untersuchung zu den ekklesiologischen Problemen der ökumenischen Bewegung*, Essen, Ludgerus, 1963.

130 Even theologians such as Charles Boyer were members of the ecumenical vanguard of the conciliar institutions: the SPCU.

131 See, for example, Peter de Mey, "De Oecumenismo Catholico et de Opere Conversionum: The Relationship between Ecumenism and the Apostolate of Conversions before and during Vatican II," in: Stephan van Erp & Karim Schelkens, eds., *Conversion and Church: The Challenge of Ecclesial Renewal: Essays in Honour of H.P.J. Witte*, Leiden, Brill, 2016, 263–287.

132 This applies especially to the consensus declarations on Christology with Eastern Orthodox churches in their stance on the formulas of the Council of Chalcedon.

Fouilloux, Étienne, *Les catholiques et l'unité chrétienne du XIXe au XXe siècle: Itinéraires européens d'expression française*, Paris, Le Centurion, 1982.

Pribilla, Max, *Um die Wiedervereinigung im Glauben*, Freiburg i.Br., Herder, 1926.

Pribilla, Max, *Um kirchliche Einheit: Stockholm – Lausanne – Rom: Geschichtlich-theologische Darstellung der neueren Einigungsbestrebungen*, Freiburg i.Br., Herder, 1929.

Sartory, Thomas, *Die ökumenische Bewegung und die Einheit der Kirche: Ein Beitrag im Dienste einer ökumenischen Ekklesiologie*, Meitingen, Kyrios-Verlag, 1955.

St. John, Henry, *Essays in Christian Unity: 1928–1954*, London, Blackfriars, 1955.

Thils, Gustave, *Histoire doctrinale du mouvement œcuménique*, Louvain, Warny, 1955.

CHAPTER 17

Theological Foundations and Interpretations of the Ecumenical Movement during the First Half of the 20th Century: Protestant and Anglican Positions

Dietz Lange

1 General Context

20th century ecumenism belongs in the context of an ongoing process of a general internationalization, which characterizes much of 19th-century culture and politics. Cases in point are the Great Exhibition in 1851, the founding of both the Red Cross and the International Organization of Labor in 1864, the first modern Olympic Games in 1896, and the first Hague Convention in 1899.[1] Even more pertinent is the burgeoning interest in the history of religions, exemplified by much brilliant scholarship as well as the World's Parliament of Religions in Chicago in 1893.[2]

The main proponents of early ecumenical endeavors were Anglicans and some Protestant churches. The Anglican Communion became established internationally in the course of the rapid growth of the British Empire, particularly during the 18th and 19th centuries. Protestantism also went through a period of worldwide expansion, by means both of its missions and of emigration. Moreover, it generated a whole series of movements and institutions that overarched not only national boundaries but also denominational limits. This development had its roots both in the great revivals and in a more general unease with the predominant materialist mood of the age.[3] It resulted in institutions such as the EA (1846) and the APUC (1857), as well as in the YMCA (1844), the YWCA (1855), and the WSCF (1895); they all shared the so-called Paris basis, which included missionary endeavor, social justice, and peace. The international and interdenominational student conferences of the great revivalist preacher Dwight Lyman Moody in Northfield, Massachusetts, from 1888 onwards were to gain a special significance for ecumenism. Not only had Nathan Söderblom attended one of them, but so had one of the founders of the WSCF, the outstanding Methodist lay evangelist John R. Mott, whose clarion call "Evangelization of the world in this generation" became famous at the time. The most powerful impulse of all these activities was missionary in nature, but under the growing influence of the American Social Gospel and similar endeavors in Europe, issues of social ethics also played an increasing role. None of these movements was a product of theological reflection. Instead, they were concerned with practical problems in the mission fields, both foreign and domestic. However, even the theological reflections of the ecumenical movement remain incomprehensible in the absence of this lively scene.[4]

The trend towards internationalization was delayed in the established Protestant churches, however. The first Protestant denomination, the German Lutherans, had originally become institutionalized against its will. It had to organize itself in separate units along territorial lines and was dependent on the German princes for

1 See Reinhard Frieling, "Ökumene," *TRE* 25, 1995, 46–77.

2 See the contribution by Arie L. Molendijk in the first volume of this work.

3 See Kenneth S. Latourette, "Ecumenical Bearings of the Missionary Movement and the International Missionary Council," in: *A History of the Ecumenical Movement*, vol. 1, Ruth Rouse & Stephen C. Neill, eds., *1517–1948*, London, SPCK, 1954, 351–402.

4 See the contribution by Sarah Scholl in the first volume of this work and the contribution by Keith Clements in this volume.

protection. Others such as the Church of Sweden had joined the Reformation through royal decree. Regardless of the nature of their origins, many European Protestant churches continued to be state churches at the beginning of the 20th century. They adhered, though in various degrees, to the nationalism of their respective countries. It was not by accident that the new international tendencies had arisen outside the confines of the established churches, many of them in the United States. Only in the course of time did European churches become aware of the credibility problem their national character – let alone their nationalism – created.

Apart from this aspect, European Protestant churches had experienced internal divisions early on. Their efforts to overcome them by rigorous purges caused those dissidents that could afford it to leave their countries. In addition, many others also emigrated due to economic hardship, many of them to the United States. All these people founded dependencies of their home churches. Members of established churches like Anglicans, Presbyterians, and Lutherans often organized themselves in North America along the lines of their national origin, even though their different nationalities shared similar doctrines and forms of organization. The resulting multiplicity of denominations is another factor precipitating so many ecumenical initiatives in America.

Fierce polemics, attempts at proselytizing, needless duplication together with the challenge of a rapidly progressing secularization gradually led to a yearning for better relations among the various churches. Thus, the first half of the 20th century became the formative period of the ecumenical movement. In this space of time, a whole range of theologians, in particular Anglicans and Protestants, developed the basic ideas of church unity that still determine ecumenical debates today. They did this both in the intense discussions of ecumenical conferences and in individual statements, in books and in articles. In the following sections, the conferences will serve as a means of structuring this development, supplemented by typical and/or particular influential individual utterances.

2 The Anglican Initiative

One of the main roots of modern ecumenism as a movement for church unity dates back to an internal conflict within the Anglican Communion. This communion was originally the territorial church of the United Kingdom. Its affiliates in the colonies organized themselves analogously on the principle of regional autonomy. Their relative independence began to pose serious problems in 1863 when the Church of South Africa excommunicated a bishop on grounds of heresy. He refused to leave, and as a result the church split. This issue prompted the first Lambeth conference in 1867 to assert the authority of the mother church over the others in the British Empire.[5] The quest for a unified foundation of the Anglican faith soon spread out. The convention of the Protestant Episcopal Church in Chicago in 1886 took it up, determining the basic criteria in a short statement, which the Anglican Communion subsequently adopted and modified at its second Lambeth conference in 1888. In this form, as the Lambeth Quadrilateral, the statement became its basis for future ecumenical debates; it reads as follows:

a. The Holy Scriptures of the Old and New Testaments as containing all things necessary to salvation and as being the rule and ultimate standard of faith.
b. The Apostles' Creed as the Baptismal Symbol; and the Nicene Creed as the sufficient statement of the Christian faith.
c. The two Sacraments ordained by Christ himself – Baptism and the Supper of the Lord – ministered with unfailing use of

5 See Randall T. Davidson, dir., *The Five Lambeth Conferences*, London, SPCK, 1920, 3–12, 56, 72–75; Harold T. Lewis, *A Church for the Future: South Africa as the Crucible for Anglicanism in a New Century*, New York, Church Publishing, 2007, 11–22. See the contribution by Paul Avis in the first volume of this work.

Christ's words of Institution and of the elements ordained by Him.

d. The Historic Episcopate locally adapted, in the methods of its administration, to the varying needs of the nations and peoples called of God into the unity of His Church.[6]

The Lambeth conference considered these criteria to be not only the "inherent parts of the sacred deposit,"[7] as the Chicago convention had, but also the basis for the unification of all Christian churches. They were to provide the basis for a "brotherly conference … with representatives of other Christian Communions in the English-speaking races," for deliberations leading "either towards corporate Reunion, or towards such relations as may prepare the way for fuller organic unity hereafter."[8] These words definitely point beyond the confines of Anglicanism itself. However, the territorial and state-church view inherent in its concept of the church is still apparent, and the delegates' cautious optimism regarding the chances of convincing other Christian communions of the need for an episcopal organization actually reflects the relative isolation of Anglicanism from the rest of the Christian world at this time. This state of affairs requires a short explanation before we continue.

The doctrine of the indispensability of the historic episcopate dates back to the restoration period under Charles II; it was the essential element in the Act of Uniformity of 1662, which made it an "absolute condition" that the ministry be episcopally ordained.[9] The idea gained momentum after the Glorious Revolution of 1688. James II and William III were no longer the "godly princes" former kings had been. The civil authority of Parliament was now established. In such circumstances, uninterrupted apostolic succession of bishops by laying on of hands became an instrument for the church to assert its independence from secular institutions. The High Church wing gained in influence by claiming that the historic episcopate was a divine gift "that marks the sphere of covenanted grace." In other words, the church claimed authority based on *jus divinum*, which alone could validate its ministry.[10]

Subsequently, three different schools developed. They hold, in the terms of modern debate, either that apostolic succession belongs to the *esse* of the church, or to its *bene esse*, or its *plene esse*; in other words, in the last two cases, it merely bestows additional excellence to the church. The latter two positions imply, as Henry Chadwick put it, that it is not a dogma, not "a requisite sign and instrument of unity and continuity in the community," but merely refers to the authority of factual tradition. In other words, apostolic succession is a "historical" fact insofar as it is a guarantee of "decent order." Chadwick even calls the Act of Uniformity "un-Protestant."[11]

The High Church wing had its heyday in the Tractarianism of the 19th century, commonly known as the Oxford Movement. It produced the so-called branch theory, half a century before the

6 See Philip Schaff, *The Creeds of Christendom*, vol. 3, *The Creeds of the Evangelical Protestant Churches*, New York, Harper, ³1919, 947f.

7 See Davidson, dir., *The Five*, 158.

8 See Davidson, dir., *The Five*, 122. See also Günther Gaßmann, "100 Jahre Lambeth-Quadrilateral: Die anglikanische Einheitscharta und ihre ökumenische Wirkung," *ÖR* 37/3, 1988, 301–311.

9 See "Charles II, 1662: An Act for the Uniformity of Publique Prayers and Administrac[i]on of Sacraments & other Rites & Ceremonies and for establishing the Form of making ordaining and consecrating Bishops Priests and Deacons in the Church of England," in: *Statutes of the Realm*, vol. 5, John Raithby, ed., *1628–80*, 1819, 364–370. The text may be found at <http://www.british-history.ac.uk/statutes-realm/vol5/pp364-370> (accessed Jan 12, 2023).

10 See Richard A. Norris, "Episcopacy," in: Stephen Sykes & John E. Booty, eds., *The Study of Anglicanism*, London, SPCK, 1988, 296–309, here 305.

11 See Henry Chadwick, "The Quadrilateral in England," in: John R. Wright, ed., *Quadrilateral at One Hundred: Essays on the Centenary of the Chicago Lambeth Quadrilateral 1886/88–1986/88*, Cincinnati, Forward Movement Publication, 1988, 140–155, here 141–142; see also John R. Wright, "Heritage and Vision: The Chicago-Lambeth Quadrilateral," in: Wright, ed., *Quadrilateral at One Hundred*, 8–46.

second Lambeth conference.[12] The author of the branch theory is William Palmer,[13] whose basic thesis is that all churches retaining the creeds of the original undivided church and the apostolic succession of bishops – and these alone – are branches of the one true Church of Christ.

Some churchmen actually attempted to put this theory into practice early on. They formed the APUC in 1857, a small group of Anglican, Roman Catholic, and Orthodox churchmen. Their source of inspiration was Johann Adam Möhler's idea of unity in diversity.[14] However, the experiment turned out to be short-lived: a letter of the Holy Office to the English bishops in 1864 explicitly prohibited Roman Catholics from taking part in any such endeavor; the ruling was reaffirmed under Benedict XV in 1919.[15] However, the branch theory survived and exerted its influence right down to the Porvoo Common Statement of 1993.

12 See the contribution by Peter Nockles in the first volume of this work.

13 See William Palmer, *A Treatise on the Church of Christ: Designed Chiefly for the Use of Students in Theology*, 2 vols., London, J.G.F. & J. Rivington, 1838.

14 See Johann A. Möhler, *Die Einheit in der Kirche oder das Prinzip des Katholizismus: Dargestellt im Geiste der Kirchenväter der drei ersten Jahrhunderten*, Munich, Laupp, 1825; ET: *Unity in the Church, or, the Principle of Catholicism: Presented in the Spirit of the Church Fathers of the First Three Centuries*, ed. and trans. Peter C. Erb, Washington DC, Catholic University of America Press, 1996. See also the contribution by Michel Fédou in the first volume of this work.

15 An English translation of the letter can be found in Henry E. Manning, *The Reunion of Christendom*, London, Longmans, Green & Co., 1866, 79–84; see the decree *De participatione catholicorum societatis "Ad procurandam Christianitatis unitatem"*, in: *AAS*, 11, 1919. Add to this the apostolic letter by Leo XIII, *Apostolicae Curae*, in: *AAS*, 29, 1896–97, 193–203, which declares the Anglican orders null and void. On the dispute on the Anglican orders see the contribution by Paul Avis in the first volume of this work.

3 The First Protestant–Anglican Negotiations

One of the many subjects debated at the Lambeth conference of 1888 was the possibility of intercommunion with the Swedish Church. The crucial argument in favor of this was that the Swedes had an episcopal constitution and laid claim to apostolic succession. The church historian Herman Lundström had proved that all the Swedish bishops of the time of the Reformation were properly consecrated.[16] Moreover, the two churches had a similar origin in a royal initiative. On the other hand, the Church of England had adopted specifically Protestant tenets in its Thirty-Nine Articles, which also made them interesting partners for the Swedes.

These common features for a while concealed the persisting differences. To begin with, it was Calvinism, not Luther, which inspired the Thirty-Nine Articles. More importantly, the institutional element of the church played a much larger role for the self-understanding of Anglicans than for the Swedes, in that it explicitly postulated its state church character (Article XXXVI). The Church of Sweden, on the other hand, had its theological basis in Luther's approach of a revolt of the individual conscience against institutional overreach. All its earliest ministers had studied with Luther himself in Wittenberg, before Sweden was able to institute its own Protestant theological faculties. Thus faith for them was primarily a personal trust in God's mercy. They recalled that Luther had actually never intended to establish a new church. Moreover, they became acutely aware of the intrinsic problems of a state church when King Sigismund attempted to return the country to Catholicism. The synod of the church resisted him and subscribed to the *Confessio Augustana* in 1593. That move provided them with a certain measure

16 See Herman Lundström, "Ett officiellt uttlåtande om svenska kyrkans s. k. successio apostolica," *KÅ* 7, 1906, 266–268.

of independence from the king, even within the state-church system.

These are the concerns that one must bear in mind when considering the initiative Randall Davidson, the archbishop of Canterbury, took towards intercommunion with the Swedish Church in 1908. The Swedes had not reacted to the previous Anglican overtures of 1888 and 1897, because of their close ties to their US dependency, the Evangelical Lutheran Augustana Synod in North America, which was non-episcopal.[17] On this occasion, Davidson's efforts almost came to naught once again because the Swedish archbishop, Johan Ekman, was not interested in the question. Only by accident did events take a different turn. Nathan Söderblom, who was then still professor of the history of religions, visited Ekman one day. On that occasion, he saw Davidson's letter on the archbishop's desk and asked for permission to read it. In the end, Ekman entrusted him with contacting the Anglican side. For Söderblom, rapprochement with the Anglicans had been an "old dream,"[18] even though he was a Low Church man by heritage and conviction, and in no way a crypto-Anglican. Conversely, he considered Anglicans as essentially Protestant, in spite of the Anglo-Catholic minority's "shenanigans."[19] Be that as it may, he immediately set to work and arranged for Henry William Tottie, bishop of Kalmar, to take part in the Lambeth conference of 1908. This clergyman, of Scottish descent, belonged to the High Church wing of the Swedish Church. His diplomatic adroitness led to the invitation of an Anglican delegation to Uppsala for serious negotiations in 1909.

At this meeting, one of the most important subjects was the canonical compatibility of the two churches. Söderblom informed his Anglican counterparts that the Swedish Church did indeed cherish apostolic succession as a treasure, but did not consider it essential for the validity of the church's mission. Rather it adhered to the Lutheran view, "no particular organization of the church and of its ministry is instituted *jure divino*, not even the order and discipline and state of affairs recorded in the New Testament."[20] The Anglicans apparently did not raise any objections to this.

However, negotiations after this meeting were very slow. The war intervened and prolonged things even further. In the meantime, Söderblom made an effort both to make Anglicans better acquainted with the Swedish Church and to clarify further his conditions for intercommunion. He did this by means of two articles in *The Constructive Quarterly*, a short-lived (1913–1922) American interdenominational journal edited by the Episcopal layman Silas McBee.[21] The former article recounts the history of his church, emphasizing in particular the fact that it had retained its bishops in the Reformation, and that its episcopal constitution later served to bolster its independence from the king. The second article deals with the Protestant idea of freedom as its religious foundation, which has absolute priority over all issues of church constitution. This is the reason for limiting the significance of apostolic succession. On the other hand, Söderblom expressed his high esteem for the Thirty-Nine Articles of the Anglican Church as well as for its reverence for tradition.

Beyond the issue immediately at hand, Söderblom considered the talks with the Anglicans a first step towards a new *corpus evangelicorum*. In point of fact, he had already set his sights on an even wider perspective, a vision of some kind of unity for all of Christendom. Such an extension

17 See Davidson, dir., *The Five*, 122f., 252–257.

18 See Bengt Sundkler, *Nathan Söderblom: His Life and Work*, Lund, Gleerups, 1968, 88f.

19 The Swedish term is "högkyrkofasoner"; see Nathan Söderblom, *Religionsproblemet inom katolicism och protestantism*, Stockholm, Geber, 1910, 288.

20 See Nathan Söderblom's handwritten note *Statement as to the Doctrine of our Church about the Holy Ministry and the Ecclesiastical Constitution*, Sep 22, 1909, in: UUB, NSS C, kapsel 53, Intercommunion.

21 See Nathan Söderblom, "On the Character of the Swedish Church," CQ 3, 1915, 281–310; see also, Nathan Söderblom, "On the Soul of the Swedish Church," CQ 3, 1915, 506–545.

was to require further steps, however, which only the outbreak of the war in 1914 brought about; Söderblom had completed his articles before that. Nonetheless, they do contain the nucleus of his ecumenical conception. The *corpus evangelicorum* he envisaged was not a monolithic institution leveling out existing differences in doctrine, liturgy, and administration. Instead, its visible unity would be a dialectical process of cooperation and contest among separate church bodies.[22]

In reply to these articles, Arthur Cayley Headlam wrote his Bampton Lectures in 1920. He was at the time Regius Professor of Divinity in Oxford (and later would be Bishop of Gloucester, 1923–1945), a fairly liberal Anglican. His lectures begin by enumerating all the historical reasons for skepticism regarding apostolic succession in the sense of an uninterrupted laying on of hands: the earliest church was not hierarchically organized; the doctrine of succession itself did not exist before the Council of Trent, and so on. He maintains that true faith is alive even in nonconformist churches. Therefore, apostolic succession is not essential in the sense of being "necessary for valid Orders." Nonetheless, "it is necessary to secure Christian unity," for the practical reason that it can guarantee unified order. In Headlam's mind, this does not exclude the recognition of a differing kind of order in another church.[23]

Headlam's view on this issue considerably influenced the favorable opinion of the 1920 Lambeth conference on intercommunion. Yet Archbishop Davidson was still somewhat skeptical, especially with regard to the non-episcopal Swedish Lutherans in the United States. He suggested that succession might be deficient even in the Swedish Church, since its constitution lacked a diaconate. These misgivings notwithstanding, in the end he gave voice to cautious optimism. The conference finally conceded a green light,[24] and the Swedish bishops concurred in 1922. From then onwards, the bond forged between the two churches became one of the most important elements of the nascent ecumenical movement. In spite of a crisis at the Faith and Order conference in Lausanne, 1927, it persists until the present day, reinforced by the rising influence of the High Church wing in the Church of Sweden after World War II.

4 The WMC of Edinburgh 1910

The quest for church unity appeared to be particularly urgent in the missionary field. Native churches saw themselves confronted with European and North American controversies, which were foreign to them. Competition among missionary societies was widespread, even to the point of proselytizing. On the other hand, the mother churches clung to their respective heritages.[25] The internal divisions of the Christian Church thus increasingly appeared as a serious obstacle to any success in the field of missions. Apart from that, Islam was making rapid advances in Africa and other lands, becoming an

22 See Söderblom, "On the Soul," 544; in the Swedish version "cooperation" and "contest" are *samförstånd* and *tävlan* respectively, see Söderblom, *Svenska kyrkans*, 58f. Adolf von Harnack had uttered a similar idea earlier, using the image of a garden containing the castle of the Roman Church and the cottages of Protestant denominations: each denomination would keep its own lodging but share common responsibility for the garden's maintenance. See, Adolf von Harnack, *Aus Wissenschaft und Leben*, vol. 1, *Wissenschaft, Schule und Leben*, Gießen, Töpelmann, 1911, 225–250. However, the different quality of housing is missing in Söderblom's article, as is the idea of peaceful contest in von Harnack's deliberations.

23 See Arthur C. Headlam, *The Doctrine of the Church and Christian Reunion: Being the Bampton Lectures for the Year 1920*, London, J. Murray, 1923, 261–269, 307, 312, 314 (quotes on page 269).

24 See *Conference of Bishops of the Anglican Communion: Holden at Lambeth Palace, July 5 to August 7, 1920*, London, SPCK, [2]1922, 152f.

25 See WMC, ed., *World Missionary Conference, 1910: To Consider Missionary Problems in Relation to the Non-Christian World*, vol. 8, *Report of Commission VIII: Co-Operation and the Promotion of Unity*, Edinburgh, Oliphant, Anderson & Ferrier, 1910, 10, 34, 87. See also the contribution by Brian Stanley in the first volume of this work.

ever more serious competitor. The entanglement of foreign missions in colonial politics, economic interests, and Western culture further aggravated the situation. In addition, the mission churches themselves saw their home base being eroded by rapidly advancing secularization. All this provoked a quest for the very roots of Christianity: what is its essence, apart from denominational differences and the cultural heritages? Protestants such as Gustav Warneck and Nathan Söderblom pleaded for a careful acculturation of the Christian message, preserving Christianity from both syncretism and Western cultural idiosyncrasies. Missionaries should couple this with respect for other religions and carefully guide indigenous churches towards independence.[26] Hence, the Edinburgh conference was set up to deal with this situation. Its delegates eagerly responded to those modern ideas and recommended, above all, a thorough study of the history of religions as a prerequisite.[27]

Turning more specifically to the background of the conference itself, we find that the SCM played a decisive role in convening it. Founded in 1889, the movement became the autonomous British branch of the international WSCF. From the outset, it took a keen interest in evangelization and foreign missions. The general secretary of the SCM, Tissington Tatlow, was a member of the Church of England, and the general secretary of the WSCF was the Methodist John R. Mott. Their cooperation was instrumental in winning over the Anglicans for the concern of inter-church unity, upon which it had only touched in the Lambeth Quadrilateral. Mott and the Scottish SCM leader Joseph H. Oldham who had organized the conference came to chair its meetings. Their revivalist background was balanced by the numerous representations of all the Anglican factions. One member of the latter group who later became a prominent proponent of ecumenism was Charles Brent, at that time a missionary bishop on the Philippine Islands.[28] Delegates hailed from a wide variety of countries and missionary societies, although the vast majority were Anglo-American.[29]

In spite of their lively interest in the essence of the church, the delegates did not spend much time on lofty but abstract declarations but rather concentrated on the practical requirements of the situation abroad. Their recommendations include "comity" (that is, the assignment of one geographical region to one missionary society alone, in order to avoid competition), conferences, and the joint action of different missionary societies. Emphasis was to be placed not so much on doctrine but rather on fellowship and common worship. Nonetheless, the conference did raise the question of unity, which was to become the central concern of the ecumenical movement. It even coined the alternative of federative vs. organic, that is institutional, unity, which was to become one of the main contentions later on. A certain preference for organic union in the face of "heathenism" is obvious from the proceedings, on the assumption that missions require a church with one voice.[30] Such unity had already proved possible in the missionary field, even among churches with very different administrations such as Anglicans and Presbyterians. The examples cited are the then germinal Church of South India, several churches in East Africa, and one case in Australia. Anglican delegates may have seen their conviction that in

26 See Gustav Warneck, *Abris einer Geschichte der protestantischen Missionen von der Reformation bis auf die Gegenwart*, Berlin, M. Warneck, [9]1910, 511f.; Nathan Söderblom, "Missionens dårskap," in: *Tal och skrifter*, vol. 3, *Tal (1892–1927)*, Stockholm, Åhlén & Söners Förlag, 1933, 117–122.

27 See William H.T. Gairdner, *"Edinburgh 1910": An Account and Interpretation of the World Missionary Conference*, Edinburgh, Oliphant, Anderson & Ferrier, 1910, 137–149, 179.

28 On Charles Brent, see the contribution by Luca Ferracci in the first volume of this work.

29 See Latourette, "Ecumenical Bearings," 289; Tissington Tatlow, "The World Conference on Faith and Order," in: *A History of the Ecumenical Movement*, vol. 2, Harold E. Fey, ed., *The Ecumenical Advance (1948–1968)*, London, SPCK, 1970, 377–447, here 377f.

30 See Gairdner, *"Edinburgh 1910"*, 115–118, 187.

the end the Quadrilateral could somehow serve as a basis for unity vindicated.

Some representatives recommended cooperation on a federative basis as a first step toward more complete unity. Federative unity as an ultimate goal would have been the preferred position of Protestants. However, the roles of Anglicans and Protestants were sometimes interchangeable. Thus Julius Richter, a German Protestant professor of missions, insisted that some sort of central organization with "restricted powers"[31] was necessary; on the other hand, some very liberal Anglican delegates even considered full, "organic" unity as purely mechanical, unwieldy, even dangerous.[32] The conference did not reach a decision on this matter nor did it intend to do so. It had discussed neither the practical details nor the theological ramifications. Its primary concern was the broader question, that is to say whether a universal mission might lead the way to Christian unity.[33] Even so, the unsolved problem behind that question is the tacit assumption that home missions in secularized Western culture would have to overcome their differences in a way analogous to the experiments mentioned above. The complications involved in that expectation do not seem to have preoccupied the delegates.

5 The Impact of the Great War

The outbreak of World War I on Aug 1, 1914, abruptly pushed aside all doctrinal and organizational problems of church unity and brought its ethical aspects to the fore. The fact that nominally Christian nations were fighting a war against each other, a war that was to become one of the cruelest in history, was a shock widely felt. Worse still, scores of Christian ministers on either side preached hate sermons from their pulpits, worshipping the god-nation instead of the Father of Jesus Christ, as Nathan Söderblom succinctly put it in a famous sermon.[34] On the other hand, some remarkable peace initiatives protested against this militant nationalism. One example is the founding conference of the WA by Protestants (in part Quakers), at Constance, Germany, from Aug 2 to 3, 1914. The WA was to become a seedbed for the Life and Work movement. Protestant church representatives from the neutral countries launched a peace appeal on Nov 27, 1914. Shortly before, Pope Benedict XV had published his peace encyclical (on Nov 1).[35] Protest against nationalism and war dividing nations and churches was to become a major ecumenical issue. It determined the debates of the Stockholm and Amsterdam conferences and has remained on the agenda ever since. The impact of the war profoundly affected all the churches, adding to the confessional divisions a dangerous rift along the lines of nationality.[36]

6 The Lambeth Conference of 1920

Traces of this new emphasis also appear in the extensive debates of the conference of the Anglican bishops held at Lambeth Palace from Jul 5 to 7, 1920, although its primary purpose was to prepare for the preliminary Faith and Order conference, which was to convene in Geneva immediately afterwards, from Aug 9 to 12. Lambeth covered a whole range of subjects besides church reunion and missionary problems, such as marriage and family, industry and commerce, and international relations. All of these concerns center around one common idea, fellowship, the exemplary model

31 See Gairdner, *"Edinburgh 1910"*, 180–181, 189–190.

32 See Gairdner, *"Edinburgh 1910"*, 206.

33 See Gairdner, *"Edinburgh 1910"*, 91.

34 See Nathan Söderblom, "De två gudarne," in: Nathan Söderblom, *När stunderna växla och skrida*, vol. 2, *Teckningar, undersökningar och betraktelser*, Stockholm, Geber, ³1935, 103–112; GT: "Die beiden Götter," in: Nathan Söderblom, *Ausgewählte Werke*, vol. 2, *Christliche Frömmigkeit und Konfessionen*, Göttingen, Vandenhoeck & Ruprecht, 2012, 127–137.

35 See Benedict XV, *Ad beatissimi apostolorum*, in: *AAS* 6, 1914, 585–660.

36 See the chapter by Gerhard Besier and Frédéric Gugelot in the first volume of this work.

of which is the church. Reunion of the churches was the central theme of the conference, represented by the largest of its commissions. However, it maintained that such unity could not be an end in itself. For the "aim of mission is not only to make Christians, but to make Christian nations."[37] This is clearly a reaction to the war experience. The conference construed a direct link between church reunion and commitment for social and international justice. That allows for an analogy between the church and the League of Nations as "the most promising … attempt to advance towards the ideal of the family of nations." The background to this proposition is the Anglican idea of the church as the continuation of divine incarnation in Christ, which is to have its beneficent effects as a leaven in the social life of the world. The bishops call this a "miracle" wrought by the Holy Spirit.[38]

As for the reunion of the churches itself, the bishops in their "Appeal to All Christian People" referred to the Quadrilateral. However, they reformulated its fourth criterion in a characteristic fashion: "A ministry acknowledged by every part of the Church as possessing not only the inward call of the Spirit, but also the commission of Christ and the authority of the whole body." In the following sentence, they called the episcopate "the best instrument for maintaining the unity and continuity of the Church," not its *conditio sine qua non*.[39] They corroborated this view by the suggestion that ministers from non-episcopal churches may receive supplementary episcopal ordination. This would allegedly not imply a repudiation of their past ministry – a view that probably raised some eyebrows among non-Anglicans.

In spite of the modifications mentioned, this exposition demonstrates that the bishops were still finding it hard, if not impossible, to conceive of any kind of church union other than on an episcopal basis. They even stated in cheerful optimism: "We eagerly look forward to the day when through its acceptance in a united Church we may all share in that grace which is pledged to the members of the whole body in the apostolic rite of the laying-on of hands."[40]

Interestingly, in one instance church leaders actually took the bishops at their word. They assumed that the somewhat more lenient view on episcopal ordination expressed by the conference opened a venue for a real reunion, as it seemed to suggest the replacement of the "tactual line of succession" by a "principle." Under this assumption, it inspired the American Congregationalist Newman Smyth to initiate a negotiating process leading to a concordat with the Protestant Episcopal Church. The General Convention of the Episcopal Church after controversial debates adopted this document in 1922, although neither the National Council of Congregational Churches nor the House of Deputies of the Episcopal Church ever ratified it. Its provision of supplementary ordination for such Congregational ministers as desired it, while remaining members of their denomination, did become practical reality in a few cases, however. Yet the Concordat never had a living chance; it remained an episode and was officially terminated in 1961.[41] The point of contention was, needless to say, that this rite would in fact have made those Congregational ministers answerable to the bishop, as well as devalued their previous service. Negotiators on either side downplayed these implications. This is astonishing because for Congregationalists, any kind of episcopal oversight is contrary to their basic principle of the

37 See "Encyclical Letter from the Assembled Bishops," in: *Conference of Bishops*, 7–22, here 20.

38 "Encyclical Letter from the Assembled Bishops," 19–20.

39 "An Appeal to All Christian People," in: *Conference of Bishops*, 26–47, here 28.

40 "An Appeal to All Christian People," 28.

41 See Newman Smyth, *A Story of Church Unity: Including the Lambeth Conference of Anglican Bishops and the Congregational-Episcopal Approaches*, New Haven, Yale University Press, 1923, 43, 62–63, 80 (quote on p. 63); Newman Smyth, *Passing Protestantism and Coming Catholicism*, New York, C. Scribner's Sons, 1908; Schaff, *The Creeds of Christendom*, vol. 3, 953–956; Peter G. Gowing, "Newman Smyth and the Congregational-Episcopal Concordat," *CH* 33/2, 1964, 175–191.

autonomy of the congregation, derived from the Protestant idea of the priesthood of all believers. Newman did become aware of this problem but apparently did not consider it to be a major concern.[42]

7 The Role of Anglicanism in Faith and Order

The origin of the Faith and Order movement is closely connected to the name of the Episcopalian bishop Charles Brent, one of the delegates to the WMC in Edinburgh in 1910.[43] He was one of the truly great personalities of ecumenism.[44] A native of a small village in Canada, he was neither a scholar nor a systematic theologian by nature, but a deeply religious and inspiring person, a "prophet" with great personal authority.[45] At the time, he was a missionary bishop in the newly acquired American colony of the Philippines, an assignment that had greatly broadened his horizon. As for his view of the church, he followed Anglican inclusiveness, stating that the missionary task calls for both Protestant personal religion and Catholic discipline.[46] Moreover, he insisted that a pagan environment requires the cooperation of all Christians. This is what motivated his ideas on Christian unity. The Edinburgh conference of 1910 encouraged him to take the next step, soliciting for an interdenominational conference of all Christian communions on the problems of faith and order. He submitted a motion to that effect to the General Convention of the Protestant Episcopal Church in Cincinnati in October 1910 and obtained its acceptance.

It is no accident that this idea first took shape in the Episcopalian Church, the American branch of the Anglican Communion. Not only was it spared any political considerations as it was not a state church, but the mere presence of an extraordinarily large number of Christian communions in that country also lent a sense of urgency to such a move. It is therefore not surprising that Brent's proposal went through without any serious opposition. The foundation of the FCCC shortly before, in 1908, may have served as an additional stimulus.

Preparations for such a conference began in earnest after World War I. One person who was indispensable in this process was Robert Gardiner, a lawyer and secretary general of the Episcopal Church. A man of incredible knowledge and a masterful organizer, he carried the main workload. The visionary, however, was Brent. He sensed that the war had intensified the need for unity, since it had compounded confessional divisions with national antagonisms. His insight found its clearest expression in his speech at the World Conference of Life and Work in Stockholm in 1925, when he pleaded for the churches to become "a clearing-house for international forgiveness." In a passionate contribution to a debate at the same conference, he proclaimed his "belief that the Christian Church if it be so minded can, in the name of Christ, rule out war and rule in peace within a generation. I may be a fool, but if so I am God's fool."[47]

The Episcopalians/Anglicans remained dominant in the nascent movement at least until 1920, when the Geneva conference introduced joint leadership, and they have remained its eager proponents ever since. They had a clear vision, worked hardest to promote it and provided the lion's share of financial resources.[48]

42 See Smyth, *A Story*, 36f.

43 For the history of this movement, see Günther Gaßmann, *Konzeptionen der Einheit in der Bewegung für Glaube und Kirchenverfassung (1910–1937)*, Göttingen, Vandenhoeck & Ruprecht, 1979.

44 See his biography, Alexander C. Zabriskie, *Bishop Brent: Crusader for Christian Unity*, Philadelphia, The Westminster Press, 1948.

45 See Zabriskie, *Bishop Brent*, 187.

46 See Zabriskie, *Bishop Brent*, 145.

47 George K.A. Bell, ed., *The Stockholm Conference 1925: The Official Report on the Universal Christian Conference on Life and Work Held in Stockholm, 19–30 August, 1925*, London, Oxford University Press, 1926, 181.

48 See Tatlow, "The World Conference," 407–410.

Both the constitutive meeting of Faith and Order in Geneva in 1920 and its first actual conference in Lausanne in 1927 could boast a very large representation of Christian communions, even though the Roman Catholic Church had declined an invitation early on.[49] Exceptions were the Russians and the Germans who both had serious misgivings about what they conceived as Anglican imperialism. The German Protestants were not willing to subscribe to any organizational criterion for church unity such as the *successio apostolica*, which the Anglicans had stated in their Quadrilateral.

8 Cooperation beyond Doctrinal Differences (Stockholm 1925)

For the Life and Work movement, the central figure is Nathan Söderblom who had been installed as Sweden's Lutheran archbishop on Nov 8, 1914. He had been a professor of history of religion in Leipzig from 1912 until 1914. The outbreak of the war had shocked him to the same extent as so many others, and he was disappointed to see churchmen and theologians of all stripes uncritically parroting nationalist propaganda. He considered this a more serious threat to Christian unity than any previous one. Correspondingly, his ecumenical interests became more extensive in scope. Whereas his negotiations with the Anglicans had merely aimed at a new *corpus evangelicorum*, he now universalized his drive for unity to include all Christian communions. Simultaneously, his interests shifted from the doctrinal matters in his earlier talks with the Anglicans to focus more on the ethical implications of the antagonisms among Christians in the warring nations. Church unity was not to become an end in itself, but should serve the restoration of peace. This shift is one of emphasis, however, not an abandonment of the theological aspect. The emphasis on the practical issue of peace does not imply indifference to the truth. On the contrary, Söderblom thinks the churches should be engaged in a serious but peaceful "contest" or discourse, both learning from each other and upholding what conscience dictates. Such a contest must be coupled with "cooperation" concerning the ethical challenges of the age as its indispensable supplement. "Doctrine separates, but service unites," is the dominant slogan. However, separation by doctrine does not preclude unity in faith, which is the prerequisite for united service.[50]

The intimate connection between ecumenism and peace, promoted first by the WA and provided with a theological foundation by Söderblom, led to the foundation of the Life and Work movement in 1919. Söderblom would also become one of the vice presidents of Faith and Order, but Life and Work always took precedence for him because of the urgency of its task, whereas questions of doctrine and church jurisdiction were a project for a longer term.

As the war continued unabated, the question inevitably arose as to how to implement the work for peace beyond the mere appeals that had been drowned out by the ongoing noise of battle. This is where Söderblom's good working relationship with the Anglicans came into play. In August 1917, the British Council for Promoting an International

49 The reason for this refusal was expounded in the official decree by Pius X, *De participatione catholicorum societati "Ad procurandam Christianitatis unitatem,"* in: *AAS* 11, 1919, 309.

50 Willem A. Visser 't Hooft quotes that "slogan," which stems from Söderblom, out of context and seems to attribute to him both an indifference to the truth and the illusion that cooperation could function without some sort of agreement on the common basis of faith. Both assumptions are erroneous, see Nathan Söderblom, "Pater Max Pribilla und die ökumenische Erweckung. Einige Randbemerkungen," *KÅ* 31, 1931, 1–99, esp. 44–51. Visser 't Hooft goes on to say that what separates us are only "relative cultural or other human idiosyncrasies," which sounds like a rather casual dismissal of serious theological work, be it Catholic, Orthodox, or Protestant; see Willem A. Visser 't Hooft & Joseph H. Oldham, *The Church and Its Function in Society*, London, Allen & Unwin, 1937, 90–95 (quote on page 95).

Christian Meeting asked him to organize an ecumenical conference. Even before its missive arrived, an article by William Temple appeared, which also urged for such a conference to be held even before peace arrived. Söderblom immediately complied and suggested a date in November of that year, in connection with a conference of the WA. This proposal did not materialize, however, and nor did several other later ones, due to the war.

It was only on Aug 19, 1925 that the first Life and Work conference was finally able to assemble in Stockholm. Anglican-Protestant cooperation played a considerable role in its proceedings. Its agenda was so replete with urgent ethical issues arising from the aftermath of the war that participants were totally overwhelmed. Many delegations were but poorly prepared, but the most notable exception to that deplorable fact was the British delegation, consisting mainly of Anglicans. They had been preparing at the COPEC, inspired predominantly by the Low Church wing, in Birmingham the year before under the leadership of William Temple, at that time Bishop of Manchester (he was archbishop of Canterbury from 1942 to 1944). Their critical view of capitalist societies and their ideas of social reform played a major role in the Stockholm discussions.

For all the smoothness of cooperation on matters of practical ethics, this conference also revealed a major difference between Anglicans and Protestants, Lutherans in particular, regarding their theological backgrounds. It concerns the central subject of the conference, the kingdom of God. The choice of this subject makes perfectly good sense, since the kingdom of God is both the sole source and the purpose of the church and therefore the basis for its call to unity. Yet it was precisely this vital point that was interpreted in quite diverse ways. The Anglo-Saxons (including Anglicans) mostly adhered to the American Social Gospel line of thought, according to which the kingdom is an ideal society attained under God's guidance, but essentially achieved by human obedience to his will. The most vocal advocate of this view of the conference was the Anglican bishop of Winchester, Frank Theodore Woods. In his opening sermon, he proclaimed: "We believe in the Kingdom of Heaven. We are conspirators for its establishment. That is why we are here. That is the meaning of this conference."[51] Certainly, humans need divine assistance to succeed in that endeavor, and God is both the source of power and the Lord who disposes of the world's destiny. However, this does not detract in any way from the crucial importance of human activity. Thus Woods concludes that in Christ we can accomplish the impossible.[52]

Woods's most articulate opponent was the Lutheran bishop of Saxony, Ludwig Ihmels. He had been a professor of systematic theology in Leipzig prior to his installment in 1922 and thus knew Söderblom well. His theological starting point was the relationship between subjective experience of truth and objective divine revelation. The kingdom of God exclusively belongs to the latter sphere. It is nothing other than God's coming in Christ, eliciting faith in the human heart through the Holy Spirit. The church has to bear witness to this kingdom, a witness that is not limited to words but includes responsible social action within the so-called orders of creation (family, social relations, state). However, it is definitely not human activity, which brings about the kingdom of God.[53]

Söderblom took an intermediate position, maintaining that Anglo-Saxon and German views should supplement, not exclude each other. His approach was clearly Lutheran. The kingdom is divine in origin and nature, not human handiwork. However, he would not agree with conservative Lutherans that social order as such is God's creation. Rather, it is subject to transforming human activity, which is prone to distortion by sin.[54]

51 Bell, ed., *The Stockholm Conference*, 38.

52 See Bell, ed., *The Stockholm Conference*, 38–45, esp. 44–45.

53 See Bell, ed., *The Stockholm Conference*, 72–79.

54 See Nathan Söderblom, *Kristenhetens möte i Stockholm augusti nittonhundratjugofem: Historik, aktstycken, grundtankar, personligheter, eftermäle*, Stockholm,

The conference by no means succeeded in dissolving the controversy between the conflicting views on this issue. On the contrary, it has remained one of the most persistent ones in the history of the ecumenical movement. In the course of the following decades, the overall balance has been tilting towards the Anglo-Saxon position. Lutheranism, on the other hand, has made significant steps forward toward the position Söderblom promoted during that period of time.

9 Conflict in Lausanne 1927

The Stockholm conference received an overwhelming, predominantly positive, response worldwide. Yet continuing doctrinal division did not cease to preoccupy churchmen. Not only was there no chance of persuading the Roman Catholic Church to join the movement, but even those churches that had actively participated in the Stockholm meeting were as divided as ever on doctrinal matters. Obviously, any kind of rapprochement concerning the essentials of the Christian doctrine would be neither easy nor swift. Such is inevitably the case when the depth of conscience coincides with an entrenched tradition solidified by institutional rules and legal statutes. However, that conference had demonstrated that theological disagreement does not have to prevent active cooperation on the pressing problems in the social arena. On the other hand, the controversy on the notion of the kingdom of God had made it clear that the religious basis for such cooperation cannot be taken for granted but needs careful consideration. The newly awakened ecumenical enthusiasm rendered this desire all the more urgent.

Such was the background for the Lausanne conference. Its delegations represented nearly as broad a range of different churches as had the Stockholm meeting. However, this time they all carried their own non-negotiable basics in their baggage. This was especially true for the ecclesiological differences between Protestant and Anglican views, which had been concealed but not overcome by the agreement on intercommunion with the Swedish Church of 1922. They now began to come to the fore, consuming a considerable amount of the debates' time. Moreover, the tensions between the two contesting delegations were exacerbated by the fact that the High Church wing of the Anglican Communion was strongly represented. This gave rise to fears of a clash from the outset of the assembly;[55] an awful lot, therefore, depended on the wisdom of the leadership.

Fortunately, Bishop Brent had agreed to accept the presidency in spite of his severe heart problems. He combined uncompromising commitment with the necessary dose of pragmatism. In a preparatory pamphlet, he demanded that there be no "fixed conclusions" at the conference and suggested for its deliberations the "method of research" into questions such as: "What are the things which divide us? What are the things that unite?" At any event, the conference was not to become "a meeting for controversy … but an opportunity for eliciting from others the convictions which hold them, in order to establish sympathetic understanding among people of different minds." Hence a "bold and patient – above all, patient – experiment" was necessary.[56]

He essentially repeated these admonitions in his presidential address at the opening of the conference, warning delegates that the problem of church order posed a seemingly unsurmountable

Svenska Kyrkans Diakonistyrelses Bokförlag, 1926, 246, 252f., 257–259, 298.

55 See Reinhard Frieling, *Die Bewegung für Glaube und Kirchenverfassung (1910–1937): Unter besonderer Berücksichtigung des Beitrages der deutschen evangelischen Theologie und der evangelischen Kirchen in Deutschland*, Göttingen, Vandenhoeck & Ruprecht, 1970, 29, 65, 77; Friedrich Siegmund-Schultze, *Die Weltkirchenkonferenz in Lausanne (vom 3. bis 21. August 1927): Ein Schritt zur Einigung der Kirche Christi in Glaube und Verfassung. Erster Gesamtbericht*, Berlin, Evangelischer Pressverband für Deutschland, 1927, 12, 189f., 213–215.

56 See Charles H. Brent, *The Christian Way toward Unity*, Boston, The Secretariat, 1925.

obstacle for the time being. Personally, he would therefore "let this vexed subject lie for the present."[57] Though he was unwavering in his adherence to the conditions of the Quadrilateral as being of "permanent value," he stressed that the church must not consider the form of ministry as a matter of dogma. Episcopal constitution is not *conditio sine qua non* for unity.[58] In an effort to prevent antagonisms from flaring up, he thus tried to inspire a spirit of patience and hope: "May it not be that, all other things being settled, we will grow into it (that is, into unity) as did the early church?"[59]

Unfortunately, his prudent remarks did not quell the impatient desire of many delegates for tangible results. The level of controversy gradually mounted and came to a head in the debate on section VII "The Unity of Christendom and the Relation thereto of Existing Churches." Before presenting his report to the conference, Söderblom, its leader, carefully exposed the basic options available for the deliberations on unity.[60] He distinguished three possible approaches. First: "institutionalism," the way represented by Roman Catholicism, but also by conservative Lutheranism with its insistence on confessional unity. This approach obviously posed an obstacle to unity. Second: "spiritualism," which actually would be his personal preference but for its lack of coherence and duration. Third: his own suggestion, which he called "incarnationalism," a term alluding to the Anglican position, probably in order to provide a talking point that had the potential to bridge the gap between the parties. In point of fact, this term was somewhat misleading, inasmuch as it suggests the idea of the institutional church as a continuation of God's incarnation in Christ, something that contradicts his own Protestant way of thinking. In his report, Söderblom tacitly corrected himself, emphasizing that church organization is a provisional product of human making, indispensable though it is in practical terms. The essential unity of the church as the communion of believers is a unity in Christ, not one of organization. In practical terms, organic unity is therefore a "unity in multiplicity." It must not prevent common worship, in particular the common celebration of communion.[61] But it is essential, Söderblom continued, that there be room for "diverse types of doctrinal statement and of the administration of church ordinances." This sentence miraculously survived in the second draft of the report that the mainly Anglican protest against its first version had necessitated.[62]

This was the most unequivocal version of the Protestant position pronounced at the conference. In a more traditional way, the German Lutheran theologian Werner Elert stated, quoting article 7 of the *Confessio Augustana*: "For the true unity of the Church it is sufficient to agree on the doctrine of the Gospel and the administration of the sacraments."[63] This reference to 16th century confessional documents could, however, also be read as making their recognition a dogmatic requirement and thus an institutional criterion for church unity. More consistently Protestant was the Calvinist view of Eugène Choisy, a Reformed theologian from Geneva, whose allegiance to confessional writings was decidedly more liberal. He stressed that Christianity is not primarily an ecclesiastical organization; its unity consists in its reference to the person of Christ, whom the Bible witnesses and who is present in and through the

57 See Charles H. Brent, "The Call to Unity," *EcRev* 29, 1977, 162–166, here 166.

58 See Zabriskie, *Bishop Brent*, 191.

59 Brent, "The Call to Unity," 166.

60 For what follows, see Herbert Newell Bate, ed., *Faith and Order: Proceedings of the World Conference Lausanne, Aug. 3–21, 1927*, London, SCM Press, ²1928, 321–331.

61 Nathan Söderblom, "Randanmärkningar till Lausanne," *STK* 3/4, 1927, 336–381; Bengt Sundkler, *Nathan Söderblom: His Life and Work*, Lund, Gleerups, 1968, 408.

62 See Bate, ed., *Faith and Order*, 398 (for the first draft) and 436 (for the second draft). The second draft came to the floor only after Söderblom had left the conference.

63 For Elert's contribution to the conference, see Bate, ed., *Faith and Order*, 13–17, here 15; for the full text of the *Confessio Augustana*, see Philip Schaff, *The Creeds of Christendom*, vol. 3, *The Creeds of the Evangelical Protestant Churches*, New York, Harper, ³1919, 3–73, 11.

Holy Spirit. Outward unity could only be based on free consent, not on preconceived theological postulates. It should therefore be a unity in variety and love.[64]

On the other side of the aisle, there were the predominantly Anglican proponents of organic unity, which for them was tantamount to signifying episcopal governance. Most explicit among them at this conference was the highly influential Anglo-Catholic dean of the Theological Faculty of London University, Charles Gore, previously bishop of Birmingham and Oxford. He belonged to a group of Tractarians who in some ways were more liberal than their mentors had been, with an open mind for contemporary culture and for the challenges of historical-critical research on the Bible, if in a very conservative fashion. They were also sensitive to the social problems of their time. However, their stance was rigidly Anglo-Catholic when it came to church order.[65]

Gore left no doubt that Anglicanism would not cede an inch as far as episcopal ordination was concerned.[66] As he had written in an earlier book, he did not intend thereby to exclude common worship with members of other Christian communions, but to his mind that would fall short of unity "in definition."[67] Such true unity inexorably requires episcopal leadership; "a ministry not episcopally received is invalid." He thereby squarely contradicted the Protestant view that *rite vocatus* is nothing more than a matter of decent order. While it is true that God can sometimes work even through an invalid ministry, it is not for humans to discover when such is the case.[68] It is equally clear for Gore that the ministry must always be threefold (bishops, priests, and deacons), which would automatically render Protestantism deficient, since it has but one ministry and rejects any kind of hierarchy. Gore insisted that church organization had its origin in the appointment of the apostles by Jesus himself, "which must be regarded as true history." He alleged that scholars were increasingly accepting as a fact "that Christ instituted a visible society called the Church," bypassing the evidence to the contrary amassed by biblical criticism, especially after the discovery of the eschatological character of Jesus's preaching by Johannes Weiß and Albert Schweitzer. Thus, it is the visible church that is the body of Christ.[69]

This is the position that made him the most vehement opponent to Söderblom and to his "Report of Section VII," to the point of a barely veiled threat to terminate Anglican cooperation in Faith and Order.[70] He did not go to the length of following through with that threat, but the consequence of his uncompromising stance was crystal clear, as he had formulated it in another book published a few years previously, namely that there was no prospect for an organic union of the church "within the measurable future." He did add that "the union of Christians in their various sections for moral and social witness and service" was entirely possible, and they should vigorously pursue such a goal.[71] At first glance, this may remind the reader of Söderblom's principle of contest and cooperation. However, Söderblom as a Protestant did not envisage any ulterior goal for church unity

64 See Bate, ed., *Faith and Order*, 28–31.

65 See, Bate, ed., *Faith and Order*, 13, 16–24, 112–116.

66 For the following passage, see Gore's contributions to the conference, Bate, ed., *Faith and Order*, 161–165.

67 See Charles Gore, *The Church and the Ministry*, ed. Cuthbert H. Turner, London, Longmans, Green & Co., 1900, 92, 307.

68 See Gore, *The Church*, 305.

69 See Charles Gore, "Preface to the Fourth Edition," in: *The Church*, v–xvii, here vi, see also 53–68, 74. It should be noted, however, that according to Gore's later book: Charles Gore, *The Holy Spirit and the Church*, London, J. Murray, 1924, Jesus did not "found" the church, since it was already in existence in ancient Israel; he only "re-founded" it; Gore *The Holy Spirit*, 42, 51; see also Gore, *The Holy Spirit*, 61: the church is the same "theocratic society as in Israel, only refashioned and renewed."

70 See Bate, ed., *Faith and Order*, 402. See also Ramsey's characterization of Gore: "In temperament he was an autocrat," Arthur M. Ramsey, *From Gore to Temple: The Development of Anglican Theology between Lux Mundi and the Second World War (1889–1939)*, London, Longmans, Green & Co., 1960, 13.

71 See Gore, *The Holy Spirit*, 347.

beyond a federation of independent church bodies, organic only by means of love, better mutual understanding, and intercommunion between episcopal and non-episcopal churches. The contrast between the two protagonists can be epitomized in the more basic difference mentioned above: while Gore speaks of the visible church as divinely instituted and rejects the idea of an invisible church, for Söderblom, the visible church is a human institution. Common faith in Christ, which constitutes Christian unity, is an "invisible" or hidden unity, even though it does have visible consequences.[72]

Another, less rigid, Anglican voice was that of Arthur Cayley Headlam, bishop of Gloucester. As far as adherence to the conditions of the Quadrilateral is concerned, that is to the Bible, the ancient Creeds, and the "divinely appointed and divinely inspired ministry," he was equally as unequivocal as Gore. A united church must be an organic unity in the sense of a unified institution. A federation would not meet that requirement. However, Headlam emphasized that this did not mean attributing dogmatic infallibility to these criteria. They simply represented "the traditional expression of the faith in Christ." This in no way detracts from the essence of the church being the sacramental continuation of Christ's incarnation, but it does leave room for "great possibilities of diversity." One example Headlam explicitly mentions is the possibility of a union of different churches, each of them keeping their own bishops.[73] Though episcopal ordination is indispensable, a united episcopate remains a possibility in the distant future because there is no convincing way of denying any particular church the legitimacy of its claim to apostolic succession. Until that moment, one has to admit that, "because the Church is divided therefore all orders are irregular and no succession is perfect."[74] Headlam explicitly declined to propose a course from that state of affairs to final unity.

Even more conciliatory was the contribution of William Temple.[75] Although in many ways he agreed with Gore, from whom he had learned much,[76] his more philosophical background in Oxford Hegelian idealism constituted a very different approach. His basic view was that the whole world process exhibits an evolving union between God and man. The incarnation is both the apex of the evolution from matter to life, then onwards to mind and to spirit, and finally to incarnation and divine revelation. As he expressed it in a very condensed form in an earlier book, "the Incarnation … was a real enrichment of the Divine life."[77] This all-encompassing penchant to mediation includes his ecclesiology. On the one hand, an organism must have a structure, he said in Lausanne, and that structure should indisputably be the threefold ministry of deacons, priests, and bishops. The historic episcopacy with its apostolic succession is "a necessary part" of the evolution of the church and basis of its unity, because the church is "the continuation of … the Incarnation."[78] He was therefore adamant in pointing out that any kind of unity must be organic, that is a unified organization instead of a mere federation of separate bodies. Moreover, he argued – maybe with a twinkle in his eyes as he looked toward Protestant delegates – that the historic episcopate is an effective bulwark against Pelagianism. At the same time, he emphasized that church unity must be "elastic" – leaving open what exactly he meant by that.[79] In this way, he sought to mediate between strict adherence to

72 See Stephen Sykes, "Anglicanism and the Anglican Doctrine of the Church," in: Wright, ed., *Quadrilateral at One Hundred*, 156–177, here 163.

73 See Bate, ed., *Faith and Order*, 331–338 (quotes on pages 331–332).

74 See Bate, ed., *Faith and Order*, 333.

75 On Temple and, more in general, on the ecumenical ventures that occurred across the first half of the 20th century in Britain, see Andrew Chandler's contribution to this volume.

76 See Ramsey, *From Gore to Temple*, 146–161.

77 William Temple, *Christus Veritas: An Essay*, London, Macmillan, 1924, 280.

78 See Bate, ed., *Faith and Order*, 133–138 (quote on page 138).

79 See Bate, ed., *Faith and Order*, 138.

apostolic succession and the principle *ubi Christus ibi ecclesia*. As he succinctly put it in a personal letter to Arthur M. Ramsey: "If a Branch is partly severed, it still lives with the life of the tree. It suffers from the form of connection that is lost; it lives by what is left, and it is still a part of the tree."[80]

However, in the end even Temple's efforts to mitigate the basic disagreements between Protestants and Anglicans did not succeed. An indication of how deep their differences were is the fact that it was not possible to conduct a common celebration of the Lord's Supper in Lausanne. For those delegates who had participated in such an intercommunion at the Stockholm conference two years previously, this was a disappointment. The different composition and atmosphere of the Lausanne conference, and above all its more "dogmatic" mood, apparently made this outcome inevitable.

10 Protestant Theological Developments from 1925 to 1937

One phenomenon that strikes even the casual observer is a backlash to the ecumenical spirit of Stockholm, which was typical of nationalistic German Protestant theologians in these years. They would vigorously protest against any idea of the church as a vanguard for a reconciliation among nations. A vivid example is a declaration published by two leading Lutheran theologians, Paul Althaus and Emanuel Hirsch. The authors claim that international reconciliation was out of the question as long as "the others pursue a murderous policy against our nation," which referred to the Treaty of Versailles.[81]

Hirsch's view of the unity of the church was somewhat contradictory. On the one hand, he argued that divisions in the church have often had a purifying effect by preventing the dead weight of institutional power that suffocated the honest conscience and prevented free debate. On the other hand, he strongly pleaded for the unity of the church on the national level superseding the differences among the "dying" old confessional churches. This seems to indicate a rivalry between the Word of God as the religious basis of any church and the nation as a quasi-religious authority.[82]

Althaus's nationalism did not affect his ecclesiology in such a tangible way. His view of church unity was more traditionally Lutheran. For him, the authority of the church is expressed in its confession (in particular, the *Confessio Augustana*), which determines the correct interpretation of scripture, but does not claim infallibility.[83] This does not imply, however, that a confession is a matter of historical relativity, in a way that would facilitate plans to unite all Christian denominations in one single church body – something Althaus alleges Söderblom and Friedrich Heiler advocate. He apparently attributes some kind of timeless validity to the confessional refutations of Roman Catholicism, on the one hand, and of spiritualism, on the other.[84] He does maintain that no church is identical with the hidden essential church and that the word and the sacraments are sufficient criteria for defining a church body as Christian.

80 C. Gore to W. Temple, Apr 29, 1936, in: Ramsey, *From Gore to Temple*, 124.

81 See Paul Althaus & Emanuel Hirsch, "Evangelische Kirche und Völkerverständigung," *ThB* 10, 1931, 177–178, here 178.

82 See Emanuel Hirsch, *Leitfaden zur christlichen Lehre*, Tübingen, Mohr, 1938, 195–197.

83 See Paul Althaus, *Grundriß der Dogmatik*, vol. 1, Erlangen, Rudolf Merkel, ²1936, 75, 78.

84 As for the term spiritualism, Althaus may be alluding here to the encyclopedia entry by Ernst Troeltsch, "Kirche III: Dogmatisch," in: *Die Religion in Geschichte und Gegenwart: Handwörterbuch für Theologie und Religionswissenschaft*, vol. 3, Tübingen, Mohr Siebeck, ¹1912, cols. 1147–1155. Troeltsch contrasts what he deems the genuinely Protestant view of the church as a spiritual fellowship with the institutional view of the Roman Church. He does concede that some kind of institutional order is required for a large communion but vehemently criticizes its interpretation as institutionalized salvation, even in its Protestant version as an institution of the Word of God.

This does not prevent him from believing, however, that the Lutheran confession is a purer witness to the truth than any other.[85]

Over and against these voices, a new note was struck in the so-called rediscovery of the church by Otto Dibelius,[86] who was a student of Adolf von Harnack in Berlin. During a course of study abroad, the independence of the Church of Scotland made a deep impression on him. After a rapid career in the Evangelical State Church of Prussia's older Provinces, he became *Generalsuperintendent* of the church province of Kurmark in 1925. The best-known book of his long list of publications is *Das Jahrhundert der Kirche* of 1926.[87] The new century is assumed to have begun with the revolutionary end of the German Empire in 1918. A political conservative, Dibelius disagreed with the revolution's aim of a liberal state, even though he did uncompromisingly reject war (a position certain to provoke harsh criticism in the Germany of that time).[88] What is surprising, however, is the optimistic tone of his fanfare, a stark contrast with the somber mood of many of his contemporaries in view of a widespread estrangement from the church. It was to express his appreciation of the church's liberation from bondage to the state, which, he thought, offered a golden opportunity to open up to the needs of modern society. It finally had an administration of its own, and was answerable only to God. This was definitely a change for the better: "Ecclesiam habemus."[89] As a symbol of this independence, Dibelius pleads for the office of bishop to be introduced, analogous to the Swedish model. Reform of the bureaucratic administration would then have to follow.[90]

This new emphasis on the church does not amount to a High Church position, however. Dibelius insists that membership in the church is not necessary for salvation. However, even though Protestant religion is personal, it is not individualistic, because fellowship corresponds to the mind of Christ. This fellowship is not an end in itself, nor is it subservient to a hierarchy. It is nothing but an instrument of the will of Christ. To Dibelius's mind, that implies an "authoritative trait," because the authority alluded to is none other than that of divine revelation.[91] From these presuppositions, he derives a mandate for the church to provide the secular state and society in general with a sense of moral direction. The proper duty of the church is not ecclesiastical in a narrow sense of the word, but includes energetic activity in foreign and domestic missions, in shaping social relations in the image of the kingdom, and in pursuing an extensive cultural program.[92]

All this seems to suggest that such a church must be a unified organization. However, Dibelius is dealing here solely with the Evangelical Church of Germany, not with the church in an international or interdenominational perspective. The central concern of his book is the newfound chance for his own church to become true to its very essence. In its outward appearance, that church was a federation of several territorial churches, each with its own confessional basis as Lutheran, Reformed, or United. These differences do not seem essential to the author. Apparently, he agrees with the statement of the *Confessio Augustana*, article 7, that sharing word and sacrament is sufficient for

---

85 See Althaus, *Grundriß der Dogmatik*, vol. 1, 79–85; Paul Althaus, *Grundriß der Dogmatik*, vol. 2, Erlangen, Rudolf Merkel, [1]1932, 141; Paul Althaus, *Die christliche Wahrheit. Lehrbuch der Dogmatik*, vol. 1, Gütersloh, Bertelsmann, 1947, 275.

86 See Carsten Nicolaisen, "Dibelius, Otto s.v.," TRE 8, 729–731; Klaus Scholder, "Otto Dibelius (1880–1980)," *ZThK* 78/1, 1981, 90–104.

87 Otto Dibelius, *Das Jahrhundert der Kirche*, Berlin, Furche, 1926.

88 See Otto Dibelius, *Friede auf Erden?: Frage, Erwägungen, Antwort*, Berlin, Furche, [3]1933. See also the famous anti-war novel, which Dibelius frequently quotes, by Erich M. Remarque, *Im Westen nichts Neues*, Berlin, Propyläen, 1929; ET: *All Quiet on the Western Front*, trans. Brian Murdoch, New York, Alfred A. Knopf, 2018.

89 See Dibelius, *Das Jahrhundert*, 75.

90 See Dibelius, *Das Jahrhundert*, 93, 101, 181, 238, 255.

91 See Dibelius, *Das Jahrhundert*, 39, 89f., 113, 118–127, 130.

92 See Dibelius, *Das Jahrhundert*, 129, 223–231, 235f., 252–254.

defining the church. On the institutional level, he would add that the newly founded – in 1922 – federatively structured national church organization Deutscher Evangelischer Kirchenbund was a sufficient basis for unity.

Having said that, one must add that Dibelius does not content himself with the national level. His experience of being a delegate to the WMC in 1910, the Stockholm conference on Life and Work in 1925, and the Lausanne conference on Faith and Order in 1927 had not been lost on him. It made him emphatically recommend an "ecumenical atmosphere." By this "soft" formulation, he does not mean some kind of mirage, but essentially the unity in diversity which Söderblom had promoted. However, he differs from Söderblom in emphasizing the objectivity of the one truth, which he sees preserved in the Apostolic Creed as a summary of facts.[93]

It is not only in purely ecclesiastical terms that Dibelius looks beyond the borders of Germany, but also with regard to the political situation. He finds himself in agreement with the guidelines of the Life and Work movement, which conceived of ecumenical activity as a force of international reconciliation. The war experience had taught him how destructive nationalism is. His antidote is not an abstract internationalism but the idea of an international community thriving on the independent contributions of all nations.[94]

Dibelius's book met with sharp criticism, particularly from Karl Barth.[95] Barth wrote a passionate short article, reproving Johannes Schneider, editor of a church periodical, for an intolerable ecclesiastical triumphalism. He went on to include the "purple [that is, clerical] 'Century of the Church'"[96] in his polemic as an instance of ecclesiastical self-aggrandizement instead of honoring God alone. However, Klaus Scholder is probably correct in calling this argument unjust, because the two men were actually much closer to each other than Barth's invective suggests. Dibelius's courageous activity in the Confessing Church is proof of that.[97]

Barth's own position is exposed in the first volume of his *Kirchliche Dogmatik*. In its foreword, he explains why he has not continued his *Christliche Dogmatik* of 1927,[98] but set it out anew under a different heading in 1932. The new term "church" dogmatics means that its base is not religious experience, nor is it obliged to any existing theological school of thought; instead it is the self-examination of the church regarding its proclamation of the Word of God. The church owes its very existence to that revelation. For this reason, his *opus magnum* begins with two large volumes on the doctrine of the Word of God. Although God himself cannot be defined, his revelation is unequivocal. Therefore, it is the church, not the single scholar with his idiosyncrasies, which has to expound this revelation. Even though Barth does not claim infallibility for a church analogous to the Roman Catholic model, he does imply that the church is one, regardless of the many separate communions calling themselves churches. This diversity notwithstanding, unity must not remain "invisible" but find its expression in a common "confession," since all debates in the church ought to end up by explicitly asserting its authority, which in the final analysis belongs to the Word of God alone. The confession of unconditional allegiance to that word supposedly provides indubitable clarity. Barth would later

93 See Dibelius, *Das Jahrhundert*, 191f., 205, 213, 216, 254–256 (quote on page 245). As for the Creed, he disagrees with his teacher von Harnack who had vehemently criticized the Apostolic Creed and thereby triggered a passionate public dispute (*Apostolikumsstreit*) in 1892. However, he unmistakably craves respect for a free and unfettered theological science; see Dibelius, *Das Jahrhundert*, 219–223.

94 See Dibelius, *Das Jahrhundert*, 233, 241–248.

95 See Karl Barth, "Quousque tandem…?," in: Karl Barth, *"Der Götze wackelt": Zeitkritische Aufsätze, Reden und Briefe von 1930 bis 1960*, ed. Karl Kupisch, Berlin, Käthe Vogt, 1961, 27–32; Karl Barth, "Nachwort," in: Barth, *"Der Götze wackelt"*, 58–62; Otto Dibelius, *Antwort an Karl Barth*, Berlin, Kranzverlag, 1931.

96 See Barth, "Quousque tandem…?," 31.

97 See Scholder, "Otto Dibelius," 94f.

98 Karl Barth, *Die christliche Dogmatik im Entwurf*, Munich, Kaiser, 1927.

chide ecumenical conferences for not working on such a confession.[99]

Barth's assumption that those conferences should be able to permit all the vastly different Christian communities to agree on a single creedal, or confessional, formulation without resort to any kind of coercion seems astonishing. Did he believe that the grand design of his own theology would simply dwarf those differences to irrelevance? However, such an insinuation would not account for the historical context. Barth wrote these lines in 1940. His point of reference was the Barmen Declaration of 1934, by means of which the Confessing Church of Germany, uniting Lutheran and Reformed Christians, stood up to the attempt of the National Socialist government to subject the Protestant Church to its dictate. That group was under enormous pressure, and it had a clear-cut adversary, neither of which applies to ecumenical conferences. It is that context which makes comprehensible Barth's apparent demand that a meaningful church unity be expressed in a creedal formulation.

A text by the title *Die Kirche und die Kirchen* written a couple of years later seems to confirm this interpretation. The plurality of churches is, he declares, a consequence of sin. It is therefore not for humans to eliminate it. Efforts of the so-called ecumenical movement for a better mutual understanding are laudable, to be sure, but they will not by themselves obtain the goal of unity. His skepticism of the ecumenical movement is so strong that he can even commend the Roman Catholic Church for not taking part in it in the name of church authority, notwithstanding his criticism of its claim to infallibility.[100] His point is that church unity precedes all human efforts, consisting as it does in nothing other than Christ himself whose "Body" it is. If you earnestly search for the Christ of the Bible within your own particular church, not for some expedient of church politics, the church will "automatically be happening" in its midst.[101] It is his characteristic occasionalism, which for Barth relegates questions of church organization to virtual irrelevance.

To a certain extent, Dietrich Bonhoeffer echoes Barth's position. In an article of 1935, he describes the German Confessing Church as a reminder to the ecumenical movement of the need for a confession. He goes so far as to oppose vehemently the idea that different interpretations of the Christian faith could have equal rights: there is either truth or heresy! However, Bonhoeffer does not share Barth's criticism of the ecumenical movement. Rather, he suggests the creation of an "ecumenical council."[102]

Wilfred Monod, a close associate of Söderblom's, took a different approach. His was of a revivalist background. He had been a professor of practical theology at the Faculté de théologie protestante in Paris and president of the Union des Églises réformées of France in 1912. He was dismissed from his academic position because his practical church activities required too much of his time, but he did excel in the field of ecumenism. A silver-tongued orator and an energetic worker both for church reform in France and for the ecumenical movement, he contributed to both the Stockholm and

99 See Karl Barth, *Die Kirchliche Dogmatik*, vol. 1/2, Zürich, Evangelischer Verlag, 1940, 660.

100 See Karl Barth, *Die Kirche und die Kirchen*, Munich, Kaiser, 1935, 10ff., quote on page 15 (republished in Karl Barth, *Theologische Existenz Heute*, vol. 1, Munich, Kaiser, 1980); ET: *The Church and the Churches*, Grand Rapids, Eerdmans, ^{2}2005.

101 See Barth, *Die Kirche*, 20–24, here 22. See also Karl Barth, "Der Begriff der Kirche," in: Karl Barth, *Gesammelte Vorträge*, vol. 2, *Die Theologie und die Kirche*, Zürich, Evangelischer Verlag, 1928, 285–301.

102 See Dietrich Bonhoeffer, "Die Bekennende Kirche und die Ökumene," *EvTh* 2, 1935, 245–261, esp. 247, (quote on page 261). Bonhoeffer's better known monograph Dietrich Bonhoeffer, *Sanctorum Communio*, Berlin, Trowitzsch, 1930, representing his doctoral thesis that he finished at the age of 21, devotes only half a page to the problem of the "Church and the churches" (Bonhoeffer, *Sanctorum Communio*, 148). The unity of the single congregation takes absolute priority here; "Christ existing as community" is the somewhat extreme formula he expounds as his interpretation of the idea of the body of Christ. See also the contribution by Peter Zimmerling in this volume.

the Lausanne conferences. In a paper prepared for the Journeées sprirituelles of Valence in 1930, he castigated France's individualistic brand of Protestantism and passionately pleaded for a religious renewal. The church as the body of Christ has both an invisible and a visible aspect. The former is defined as the "perpetual presence of Christ on earth." This is what constitutes the essential unity of the church – not a doctrine, nor an organization. Church unity is to become visible, above all, in the common celebration of the Lord's Supper. Being a Methodist, Monod intended this in a strictly Protestant sense. Holy Communion was for him the superior external expression of the unity of faith in Christ, which is to bridge all differences in doctrine and church organization.[103] In a way, this concept is reminiscent of Söderblom's persevering negotiations with the Anglican Church on intercommunion, its actual performance at the Stockholm conference, and later his disappointment that the same did not happen in Lausanne in 1927. However, Monod makes no mention of the dialectic of contest and cooperation, so essential to Söderblom's ecumenical ideas, thereby restricting his concept to the purely religious realm.

We encounter an entirely different point of view in Helmut Richard Niebuhr's classic, *The Social Sources of Denominationalism*.[104] Niebuhr, an ordained minister of the E&R (an offspring of the Evangelic Church of the Old Prussian Union) and a professor of Christian ethics at Yale University, was one of the prominent American theologians of his time. He focuses, albeit not exclusively, on American Protestantism, which differs from its European counterparts by its complete independence from the state. His book carefully analyzes the multifarious social causes of church divisions: by class, sectarianism, nationality, settled citizens vs. new immigrants, and race. By means of this sociological approach, he proves that denominationalism is rooted in a complex combination of factors, over and above doctrinal matters. For this insight, he is indebted to Ernst Troeltsch's extensive work on church sociology.[105] However, Niebuhr does not consider denominationalism a natural consequence of the worldwide expansion of Christianity, having pertinent parallels in all other world religions, as Troeltsch did, but describes it as the "ethical failure" of ceding to the powers that be,[106] which reflects Karl Barth's characterization of it as an expression of sin.

The latter view seems reasonable enough when one looks at such "social sources" as nationalism and racism that Niebuhr so vividly described. Nonetheless, it appears to be rather one-sided when you look at the many factors involved in church divisions, and not all of said factors fall under the category of failure. Obvious cases in point are the cultural customs that immigrants brought with them from their native lands, not to mention the religious ones, such as the voice of conscience in matters of faith.

Not surprisingly, in his last chapter Niebuhr frames his solution to the problem of division in very general terms. He seems to think that some kind of "group action" by the churches and an ethics of love is all that is required.[107] This recommendation hardly does justice to the complexity of the problems that he himself had so thoroughly analyzed. The leading proponents of ecumenism had already offered some far more detailed practical proposals, none of which Niebuhr refers to. In view of his brilliant analysis, this is all the more regrettable.

103 Wilfred Monod, "Le mystère de l'Église," in: André-Numa Bertrand, Willfred Monod & Robert Will, eds., *L'Église: Rapports présentés*, Paris, Fischbacher, 1931, 1–42, esp. 38 (quote on page 19).

104 See H. Richard Niebuhr, *The Social Sources of Denominationalism*, New York, World Publishing Company, 1971.

105 See Ernst Troeltsch, *Gesammelte Schriften*, vol. 1, *Die Soziallehren der christlichen Kirchen und Gruppen*, Tübingen, Mohr, ^{3}1923.

106 See Niebuhr, *The Social Sources*, 3–25.

107 See Niebuhr, *The Social Sources*, 274, 278–284.

11 Anglicans and Protestants at Oxford and Edinburgh in 1937

The Oxford conference on Life and Work lasted for twelve days in July 1937. Its theme, church, community, and state, reflects the drastic changes in the world situation since 1927. Not only in Russia, since 1917, but now also in Germany, totalitarian regimes posed an existential threat to the Christian Church. In Russia, it suffered from outright persecution; in Germany, the regime tried to force the Protestant Church into submission to its ideology. The resistance of the Confessing Church to this pressure determined, at least implicitly, the agenda of the conference.

No German participants had been able to come. The Germans had already to a great extent been absent at the ecumenical youth conference on the island of Fanø, Denmark, in 1934, where just one official German delegate was present, sent by the *Reichsbischof*. (Nonetheless, the fact that Dietrich Bonhoeffer gave a speech there as well as a sermon on peace and international relations shows that the ecumenical ties, if under strain, were still functioning.[108]) In spite of its physical absence, however, the perilous situation of the German church was on everyone's mind, in Oxford as well as in Fanø. "Only slowly did Christians come to perceive that the rise of totalitarian systems had introduced a new era for the world and for the Church," a keen observer writes,[109] but this did occur at the Oxford conference, as is evident from its shift in emphasis compared to earlier ecumenical meetings. These had until this time been concerned with the problem of church unity. Now the confrontation with hostile pagan ideologies inexorably led to the more basic question: what makes the church the church? In tackling it, the conference unequivocally sided with the German Confessing Church.

The theological guidelines of this church were those of the "crisis theology" (the term for the Dialectical theology at the time), more precisely Karl Barth's version of it. The radicalism of his doctrine of divine revelation imposing itself with absolute sovereignty on the human mind and soul was foreign to both Anglican and most Lutheran delegates. However, Anglicans in particular appreciated Barth's clear-cut position in the political turmoil as a "prophetic teacher," and they linked this view to a recent rediscovery of the Bible in their own church.[110]

In spite of its unanimity on the political issues, the mood at the conference was ambiguous. On the one hand, the ecumenical movement had become an established institution by now. Among those present, Chairman Oldham, Gustaf Aulén, Anders Nygren, Emil Brunner, Leonard Hodgson, Willem Visser 't Hooft, and Henry P. Van Dusen were its best-known representatives at the time.[111] Against the external threat, the delegates experienced a closer communion with one another than had been the case at Lausanne ten years before. One aspect was clear, however: the isolation of Anglicans had patently diminished. On the other hand, the optimism that had characterized the Stockholm conference had vanished and given way to a sense of gloom.

Shortly after this conference, the other large ecumenical movement, Faith and Order, convened in Edinburgh from Aug 3 to 18, 1937. The encyclical *Mortalium animos* of 1928 had made it clear that any Roman Catholic participation in ecumenical endeavors continued to be out of the question.[112] Nor had any Germans arrived, like in Oxford a couple of weeks before. Yet again, the situation in

108 See Eberhard Bethge, *Dietrich Bonhoeffer: Theologe, Christ, Zeitgenosse*, München, Kaiser, 1967, 445–453; ET: *Dietrich Bonhoeffer: Theologian, Christian, Man for His Times: A Biography*, ed. Victoria J. Barnett, Minneapolis, Fortress Press, ^{2}2000, 385–391.

109 See Nils Ehrenström, "Movements for International Friendship and Life and Work, 1925–1948," in: *A History of the Ecumenical Movement*, vol. 1, 545–596, here 594.

110 Ramsey, *From Gore to Temple*, 129–144, here 141.

111 See Ehrenström, "Movements for International Friendship," 584.

112 See the contribution by Marie Levant in the first volume of this work.

Germany was tangibly present, and the conference just sided with the Confessing Church, in spite of the fact that most of its participants were strangers to its theological basis, Dialectical theology.

More remarkable is the fact that, as the minutes of the conference show, Anglicans had apparently become more self-critical of their approach to ecumenism. In his preface to the report on the conference, Leonard Hodgson recognized that the Anglican view of church order had proved to be a chief obstacle to church unity. Extensive negotiations took place on the several options of federation, organic unity, and corporate unity, besides intercommunion. No consensus was reached on this issue.[113] The conference did recognize, however, that each church body is a totality of doctrine, worship, and organization.[114]

That was not the only thorny subject the conference had to consider. The radical interpretation of the Word of God and divine grace by the crisis theology equally seemed to stand in the way of further progress in these deliberations, inasmuch as it tended to overestimate the unifying effect of a confessional formulation – and to underestimate the difficulties involved in achieving one. Thus in the end, there seemed to be more questions left open than solutions found. Hodgson concluded, "that the time was not yet ripe for a frontal attack on the problems presented by the doctrine of the church."[115]

Having said this, it is nonetheless worthwhile to observe the subtle changes in outlook since Lausanne. That is true especially for Bishop Temple, the principal exponent of the Anglican community at the Edinburgh conference. In his opening sermon, he exposed the typically Anglican *via media*: the Reformation was too one-sided, neglecting the truth of the other side. Had it been more conciliatory it might perhaps have avoided separation. In other words, what he thought was missing was a "balance of truth." For this reason, he deemed it all the more regrettable that once again "the great Church of Rome" was absent.[116] So far, none of this was new. However, later in the conference he fully acknowledged the radical questions posed by the new situation in the world. Nazi totalitarianism had promoted the idol of race in lieu of God. It had perfected the propensity to lying initiated by World War I propaganda, and it was preparing a new war. All this had led to a religious revival in Germany. Temple seems to imply that this development was a step beyond the rather provincial bickering of Christian churches amongst each other, finally redirecting attention to the two most prominent trends unfolding since the 19th century: the expansion of both secularism and Christianity. This was Temple's motivation when he spoke in his sermon about the widespread longing for fellowship and the unity of humanity as a challenge to the church.[117] The motto of the Oxford conference a couple of weeks previously, "let the church be the church," reverberated in it.

The shift in emphasis had consequences for Temple's views on the ministry of non-episcopal churches. Two addresses he delivered to high-level church bodies as archbishop of Canterbury several years later (May 25 and Jul 19, 1943) clearly show this. They were prompted by the seemingly remote situation of the Church of South India, which was preparing a union between Anglicans, Presbyterians, Congregationalists, and Methodists, to be finalized after Indian independence in 1947. He pointed out that, if the ministry of non-episcopal churches stood under the guidance of the Holy Spirit, they could legitimately join such a union. This was meant to be a statement of principle, reaching well beyond the immediate occasion. However, he hesitated: that concession would have to be preliminary, because non-episcopal ministry was still defective. One would therefore have

113 See Leonard Hodgson, ed., *The Second World Conference on Faith and Order Held at Edinburgh, August 3–18, 1937*, New York, Macmillan, 1938, 239–269.

114 See Tatlow, "The World Conference," 431–441.

115 See Hodgson, ed., *The Second World Conference*, 10.

116 See Hodgson, ed., *The Second World Conference*, 15, 17, 20 (quotes on page 17 and 20).

117 See Hodgson, ed., *The Second World Conference*, 44–49.

to assume that the "irregularity" would be terminated in due time, this means that episcopal rule would prevail in the end. The author's uneasiness shows that he was probing uncharted territory.

In spite of this insecurity, Temple did indicate the direction he was envisaging. The preeminent requirement for true unity, he insisted, should be "one of harmony, not of unison." This implies the all-inclusiveness of such a visible body of Christ. "The united Church should bring together all the elements of truth in all the several traditions, each sharpened as regards its definition and consequently as regards its cutting edge." He refrains from any suggestion as to how this vision could be implemented, however. In the final analysis, this "points to the action of God."[118]

The uncertainties were not restricted to the Anglican camp, as Protestants did not agree on the kind of church unity either. The Strasbourg Lutheran professor of theology Fernand Ménégoz repeated the slogan that federation does not suffice, without offering a viable alternative. The Basel Calvinist professor of church history Eberhard Vischer, a disciple of Adolf von Harnack, emphasized the fact that Jesus did not bring the church but the kingdom of God – which in itself is a non-answer to the practical question. The Swedish bishop of Lund, Anders Nygren, expressed the majority Lutheran view that we already possess a common message, which is far more important than outward unity.[119]

This unsatisfactory state of affairs may in part have been due, as many critics have pointed out, to inadequate preparation and to the brevity of the conference. That in turn could be attributed to the troubled times when the specter of a new war was already on the horizon. Be that as it may, the absence of progress in the discussions on ecclesiology in no way detracted from the strong sense of spiritual unity. This feeling did produce one solid achievement after all, which concerns the organizational level. The experience of fellowship reinforced the perception that had been developing for some time, that is to say, that the two branches of the ecumenical movement, Life and Work on the one hand, Faith and Order on the other, were increasingly covering the same ground. So, after lively discussions and obtaining the consent of Life and Work, the delegates decided to fuse the two movements.[120] There was one clear note of dissent, however. It came from Bishop Headlam, and he considered it important enough to include it in the minutes. His rationale was that a future world council of churches might consider it its official duty to speak out on public affairs, something he considered potentially detrimental.[121] In hindsight, this has proved to be a reservation worth considering. For although there can be no reasonable doubt that the responsibility of the church includes informed comment on the concerns of society, it can only too easily be tempted to furnish such comment with absolute religious authority, thus claiming potentially to overrule even the most knowledgeable specialists in the field.

12 Views on the Church at Amsterdam 1948

In order to understand the proceedings of the Amsterdam conference, one has to bear in mind two points. The first point is that ecumenical relationships had survived Nazi Germany. One outstanding example is George Bell, bishop of Chichester. He had always sharply distinguished between Germans and Nazis, while uncompromisingly condemning the latter. During the Third Reich, he had welcomed refugees from Europe

118 See William Temple, *The Church Looks Forward*, London, Macmillan, 1944, ch. 2, "Christian Unity and Christian Reunion," 8–25, and ch. 3, "The Background of the Reunion Problem," 26–30, here 26, 29.

119 See Hodgson, ed., *The Second World Conference*, 69, 72, 122.

120 See Hodgson, ed., *The Second World Conference*, 270–274; Tatlow, "The World Conference," 426.

121 See Hodgson, ed., *The Second World Conference*, 151, 184–188; Willem A. Visser 't Hooft, "The Genesis of the World Council of Churches," in: *A History of the Ecumenical Movement*, vol. 1, 697–724, here 703.

to the United Kingdom. He had even opposed the carpet-bombing of German cities by the Allies in 1943, which possibly cost him the See of Canterbury after William Temple's early death in 1944. Of particular interest here is his relation to Bonhoeffer. They met in Sigtuna, Sweden, in 1942.[122] Temple learned much from him about the German resistance. He thereupon strongly recommended supporting it to the British Premier Anthony Eden – unfortunately to no avail.

A helpful move on the German part was the Stuttgart Confession of Guilt, drafted by the highest representatives of the German Protestant churches in 1945. They acknowledged that they had not mustered sufficient courage to stand up to the criminal Nazi regime. Many of the authors had been members of the Confessing Church. Their resistance to the regime had earned them worldwide respect. Moreover, their main source of inspiration, dialectical theology, had gained increasing influence among Protestants throughout Europe.

The second point concerns the relationship of this conference to Stockholm 1925. On the one hand, there seems to be a striking analogy in that the Amsterdam meeting once again took place in the deep shadow of a barbaric war that had ended only a couple of years previously. Consequently, ethical issues, particularly the urgent need for peace, stood out prominently in the agenda. One might therefore be inclined to view it as just another Life and Work meeting. On the other hand, however, the impact of the dialectical theology made itself felt. The issues of church unity having been relegated to the background by the exigencies of the day, Barth and his disciples brought a more fundamental theological concern to the fore: the very essence of the church and its relation to the world of politics. That is what the conference's organizers had in mind when they coined its motto "Man's Disorder and God's Design."

In the wake of World War II, the specifically religious emphasis of the conference was on repentance. In the words of the American delegate Reinhold Niebuhr (elder brother of Helmut Richard Niebuhr): "The churches were more certainly in a process of renewal than in a process of reunion."[123] It is in this context that the unequivocally pacifist principle that war is contrary to the will of God is placed. That is a significant shift from the Stockholm conference in 1925, which had seen far more divided opinions on this issue. Even now, however, unanimity was not entirely without qualification. The camp of dialectical theology was unabashedly pacifist, but Niebuhr, who had been a vocal advocate for US entry into the war as the lesser evil, issued a timely warning, "peace as a political absolute is confusing. If we strive for political peace too desperately we deliver the world into the hands of those who have no scruples."[124] As a leading representative of Anglo-Saxon Christian realism, he questioned the self-assurance of the opposing Barthian camp with these words: "We seem always to be God rather than men in this theology, viewing the world not from the standpoint of the special perplexities and problems of given periods but *sub specie aeternitatis*."[125] This controversy presaged decades of divided opinions among Christians worldwide.

The Danish Lutheran Niels Hansen Søe voiced a different kind of criticism of Dialectic theology. He wondered why the proponents of the unifying power of confession were so preoccupied with the bygone situation of Nazi Germany and failed to address the ongoing breakdown in religious belief in the Western world. With regard to social ethics,

---

122 Bell locates the meeting in Stockholm (George K.A. Bell, *The Kingship of Christ: The Story of the World Council of Churches*, Harmondsworth, Penguin, 1954, 36f.); this is an error. Bonhoeffer's biographer Eberhard Bethge who carried out extensive research on the matter, leaves no doubt that it was Sigtuna: Bethge, *Dietrich Bonhoeffer: Theologian*, 760.

123 See Reinhold Niebuhr, "The World Council at Amsterdam," in: Reinhold Niebuhr, *Essays in applied Christianity*, ed. D.B. Robertson, New York, Meridian Books, 1959, 305–310, here 310.

124 See Reinhold Niebuhr, "The World Council and the Peace Issue," in: Niebuhr, *Essays*, 311–313, here 313.

125 See Reinhold Niebuhr, "We are Men and Not God," in: Niebuhr, *Essays*, 168–175, here 173.

he considered the discussions on war and peace, while necessary, to be one-sided and reminded his colleagues of the long-neglected, burning problem of racial minorities.[126] Both these issues, different though they are, point beyond the obvious limitations of the Amsterdam debates, defining future challenges of ecumenicity that later conferences would have to tackle.

Although the problem of church unity was not in the center of the stage at Amsterdam, the preparatory volume to the conference did include a few statements on the subject. Thus the archbishop of Armagh, John Gregg, repeated the traditional Anglican stance that there can be no church union without the Quadrilateral as its basis.[127] The Swede Gustaf Aulén expounded the equally familiar Lutheran position that the basis of church unity consists exclusively in the message of Christ in word and sacrament. This meant for him that the institutional church is not just of human making, because Christ is incarnate in his church. This betrays his High Church leanings. However, he did not blame the diversity of Christian churches on their sinfulness but called it a sign of the wealth of faith. Only when it turns into hostility and mutual condemnation would it become an expression of sin.[128] Finally, Karl Barth found church unity in the "event" of the divine gathering, which is the living congregation. This statement eschews the mundane problems posed by institutional reality, but it does reflect the more radical Calvinist version of the common Reformation idea of the priesthood of all believers, as opposed to episcopal forms of hierarchy.[129]

There is yet another reason, apart from the changed situation in the world, for the fact that the Lausanne controversy between Anglicans and Protestants did not erupt with renewed fervor in Amsterdam. This concerns an apparent attenuation of the Anglican position that was evident at the Lambeth conference of 1948, shortly before Amsterdam. The delegates introduced their official pronouncements on the unity of the church by referring to "the governing principles of any Anglican approach to reunion" as laid down in the Quadrilateral and in the "Appeal to All Christian People" of 1920. However, they asked for the diverse interpretations of the role of apostolic succession (as belonging to the *esse*, *bene esse* or *plene esse*, of the church) to be equally honored. This means that neither can "non-episcopal ministries [be regarded] as identical in status and authority with the episcopal ministry," nor can "the sacraments of non-episcopal bodies [be declared] to be null and void." It follows that the idea of a supplementary ordination for ministers of such bodies as recommended by the conference of 1920 is no longer an option, because it "has been found to involve theological difficulties."[130] These concessions helped the members of section I, which had been working on the question of unity, to be content with some brief, rather vague remarks. They considered it sufficient to praise the institution of the WCC as a step in the right direction.[131]

Indeed, the formal establishment of the World Council was the one important event at Amsterdam with regard to church unity. With it, Nathan Söderblom's dream of 1919 had finally come true. The chairman of the conference, Willem

126 See Niel Søe's contribution to the debate in Willem A. Visser 't Hooft, ed., *Man's Disorder and God's Design*, vol. 5, *The First Assembly of the World Council of Churches: Held at Amsterdam, August 22nd to September 4th, 1948*, London, SCM Press, 1949, 83.

127 See John A.F. Gregg, "One, Holy, Catholic, Apostolic Church," in: *Man's Disorder and God's Design: The Amsterdam Assembly Series*, vol. 1, *The Universal Church in God's Design*, London, SCM Press, 1948, 59–66, here 65f.

128 Gustaf Aulén, "The Church in the Light of the New Testament," in: *Man's Disorder*, vol. 1, 18–30, here 19, 29; Gustaf Aulén., *Kristen gudstro i förändringens värld: En studie*, Stockholm, Diakonistyrelsens Bokförlaget, 1967, 165–167.

129 Karl Barth, "The Church – The Living Congregation of the Living Lord Jesus Christ," in: *Man's Disorder*, vol. 1, 67–76, here 72.

130 See *The Lambeth Conference 1948: The Encyclical Letter from the Bishops; Together with the Resolutions and Reports*, London, SPCK, 1948, 50, 55.

131 *Man's Disorder*, vol. 5, 51, 53, 56.

Visser't Hooft, explicitly recalled the Stockholm conference of 1925 and referred to Söderblom's ecumenical ideas, calling the strategy of the new council one of "constructive and mutual challenge." However, the hope that he expressed in this paper that *Deo volente* the World Council might "suddenly take on the formidable authority of an organ of the holy Spirit," with its implied reference to Barth's idea of event, shows how much the ecumenical mood had changed.[132]

13 Outlook

The synthesis of Söderblom's dialectic of contest and cooperation, on the one hand, and the Barthian event metaphor, on the other, reflects an age of crisis when another long and devastating war had finally come to an end and a cautious hope that a new era of peace was about to begin. Over the years, that hope turned into a desire for continuity, for a reassessment of tradition, and for institutional security – a trend that was reinforced by the simultaneous rapid secularization in many parts of the Western world. This complex development turned out to be a boon for the Anglican position and to become a great challenge for the Protestant stance. The Anglican transformation of the Swedish Church and the accession of some Lutheran churches to the Porvoo Common Statement of 1993 are cases in point. Needless to say, the ecclesiological problems and differences so intensely debated by the two communions are still awaiting a solution.

Bibliography

Barth, Karl, *Die Kirche und die Kirchen*, Munich, Kaiser, 1935.

Bate, Herbert Newell, ed., *Faith and Order: Proceedings of the World Conference Lausanne, Aug. 3–21, 1927*, London, SCM Press, 21928.

Bell, George K.A., ed., *The Stockholm Conference 1925: The Official Report on the Universal Christian Conference on Life and Work Held in Stockholm, 19–30 August, 1925*, London, Oxford University Press, 1926.

Davidson, Randall T., dir., *The Five Lambeth Conferences*, London, SPCK, 1920.

Gairdner, William H.T., *"Edinburgh 1910": An Account and Interpretation of the World Missionary Conference*, Edinburgh, Oliphant, Anderson & Ferrier, 1910.

Gaßmann, Günther, *Konzeptionen der Einheit in der Bewegung für Glaube und Kirchenverfassung (1910–1937)*, Göttingen, Vandenhoeck & Ruprecht, 1979.

Headlam, Arthur C., *The Doctrine of the Church and Christian Reunion: Being the Bampton Lectures for the Year 1920*, London, J. Murray, 1923.

Söderblom, Nathan, "On the Character of the Swedish Church," CQ 3, 1915, 281–310.

Söderblom, Nathan, "On the Soul of the Swedish Church," CQ 3, 1915, 506–545.

Sykes, Stephen, "Anglicanism and the Anglican Doctrine of the Church," in: John R. Wright, ed., *Quadrilateral at One Hundred: Essays on the Centenary of the Chicago Lambeth Quadrilateral 1886/88–1986/88*, Cincinnati, Forward Movement Publication, 1988, 156–177.

WMC, ed., *World Missionary Conference, 1910: To Consider Missionary Problems in Relation to the Non-Christian World*, vol. 8, *Report of Commission VIII: Co-Operation and the Promotion of Unity*, Edinburgh, Oliphant, Anderson & Ferrier, 1910.

Wright, John R., "Heritage and Vision: The Chicago-Lambeth Quadrilateral,", in John R. Wright, ed., *Quadrilateral at One Hundred: Essays on the Centenary of the Chicago Lambeth Quadrilateral 1886/88–1986/88*, Cincinnati, Forward Movement Publication, 1988, 8–46.

Zabriskie, Alexander C., *Bishop Brent: Crusader for Christian Unity*, Philadelphia, The Westminster Press, 1948.

132 Willem A. Visser 't Hooft, "The Significance of the World Council of Churches," in: *Man's Disorder*, vol. 1, 177–195, here 188, 192. See also Jurien Zeilstra's contribution to this volume.

PART 2

Tempus Visitationis: *An Ecumenical Spring*

∴

CHAPTER 18

Willem A. Visser 't Hooft and the Early Years of the WCC: From Amsterdam 1948 to New Delhi 1961

Jurjen A. Zeilstra

1 Introduction

The first two intervals between the three assemblies of Amsterdam 1948, Evanston 1954, and New Delhi 1961 may be considered to have been times of expansion and efflorescence for the WCC. The concrete institutional design of the ecumenical movement contemplated from the late 1930s proved its relevance and had the effect of a renewal upon churches. The following chapter can in no way claim to offer an exhaustive picture, and many other stories could be told. The intention is to demonstrate that the whole project was more time-bound than those involved in it at the time realized. The life in which a strong illustration of this thesis can be found is that of the first secretary general of the WCC, the Dutchman Dr. Willem Adolph Visser 't Hooft.[1] In this chapter, his life is used as a lens through which to study the ecumenical development of the period.

In 1938, a rather young Visser 't Hooft was chosen as the first secretary general of the WCC which was in the process of being formed. He had earned his spurs as secretary from 1924, thanks to his European work among schoolboys of the YMCA and then, in the 1930s, as secretary of the WSCF. For Visser 't Hooft, the unity of the church in the 20th century did not represent an ideal to be pursued but a starting point, as he believed, a God given fact to be rediscovered. Faced with the disruptive forces unleashed by an uprooting modernity, totalitarian movements, and war at unprecedented scale, for him church unity was a beneficial starting point for action. Here he found not only his personal motivation, but also an assignment for society as a whole, considered by him to be a matter of obedience to God as well as duty. In his lectures and sermons, he frequently used the words "we must," and when summing up at the end: "Our marching orders are." The tension between reality and this alleged mission might be enormous. To be sure, the world was not eagerly awaiting the messages of Visser 't Hooft. Yet those who voted for him to become the secretary of the new organization were convinced he had a special contribution to make. They did not choose an easy-going character, but most of them were not to be disappointed. Visser 't Hooft put all the energy and creativity he had into the task. His postwar successes in this regard must have been surprising, even to him. Looking back in his memoirs, he gratefully realized that he had been fortunate to find himself in the right spot where his capacities had been appreciated at the most promising of times.[2]

During the early years of the war, for a short period, with the German armies sweeping across Europe, it seemed doubtful whether the ecumenical bureau in Geneva could be of any real use. Visser 't Hooft, posted to Geneva, had to be content with a very small staff in those difficult years.

1 Jurjen A. Zeilstra, *Visser 't Hooft (1900–1985): Living for the Unity of the Church*, Amsterdam, Amsterdam University Press, 2020. See also: Jurjen A. Zeilstra, "Une vie vouée à l'oecuménisme," *Positions Luthériennes* 67/1, 2019, 7–35.

2 Willem Adolf Visser 't Hooft, *Memoirs*, London, SCM Press, 1973, 342. See also Herman van Run interview with Visser 't Hooft, "Markant: Visser 't Hooft," NOS-televisie, Dec 8, 1977, Hilversum, Nederlands Instituut voor Beeld en Geluid.

However, a strong emphasis was soon placed on the practical work among refugees and prisoners of war, and an extensive international network thinking of postwar conditions for a true, durable peace followed. Towards the end of the war, funds quickly became available, and a growing number of paid employees could be put to work. Reconstruction and reconciliation now became very important. With church-supported work among refugees freshly integrated in the WCC organization, there was more work than Geneva could manage. Nevertheless, Visser 't Hooft and his colleagues in the immediate postwar years were gradually able to transform the WCC from an enterprise with a handful of employees into a medium-sized international nongovernmental organization.

Another urgent issue that Visser 't Hooft focused upon in 1945 was how to reconcile the German churches with churches in countries that had suffered from German aggression and how to enable them to help reintegrate their country into Europe. Visser 't Hooft consciously developed a profound view of this huge problem, which was closely connected to his approach to reconstruction and to his conviction that postwar Europe should ideally be a federal union built on Christian values.[3] His personal experiences as a young man during the aftermath of World War I, and during World War II, had taught Visser 't Hooft that churches paying attention to the questions concerning society should endeavor to go beyond moral indignation. Since 1918, for countless years the international atmosphere had been poisoned by nations blaming each other for causing the war. This game of blame should not be repeated after 1945, especially not in church circles. Visser 't Hooft now felt that he and his staff had a real chance to shape church interest in international affairs in a new ecumenical quality, and they did so expediently.

It was thanks to factors such as these that in 1948, only a few years after a devastating world conflict had rendered the nations apart, the founding assembly of the WCC in Amsterdam was a memorable highlight. Many participants in the founding meeting in the Amsterdam Concertgebouw, on Aug 23, 1948, were overcome with strong emotions, but not only those inside the building were impressed. This moment of church peace and dedication to "God's design" was a strong testimony to peace in a world full of disorder, at a time when the Cold War cast the frightening shadow of the atom bomb, and violent struggles for or against independence were occurring in many colonies. The Roman Catholic Church and the Russian Orthodox Church were not present in Amsterdam. Visser 't Hooft decided to consider it his personal challenge to overcome the objections of these two large churches and apply all energy of which he and his staff were capable to convincing them that they, too, had an important contribution to make in the ecumenical arena by becoming members of the WCC.

Although in order to present a comprehensible picture some small excursions beyond the years indicated will be necessary, this chapter focuses on the period from 1948 to 1961. This may be considered preeminently to have been the most fruitful era for both the ecumenical movement, in general, and the WCC, in particular. It must be evaluated as a time of strong ecumenical self-confidence. However, when one has to explain the reasons for this heyday, one has to account for the striking phenomenon that were its contextually bound reasons. Contemporaries thought of ecumenical growth and expected it to continue. However, many factors for the great successes of the institutional church-oriented approach to Christian unity were strongly time-bound, such as: (1) reconstruction; (2) reconciliation; (3) openness to church diplomacy; (4) true multilateral opportunities for developing a "responsible society"; (5) the opportunity to speak prophetically in a world eager for hopeful words; (6) the successful development of an international ecumenical study center; (7) a promising Eastern Orthodox membership; and last but not least (8) the beginnings of a Roman Catholic "aggiornamento." Those

3 Jurjen A. Zeilstra, *European Unity in Ecumenical Thinking (1937–1948)*, Zoetermeer, Uitgeverij Boekencentrum, 1995.

in charge, above all Visser 't Hooft, were convinced they were developing something that, despite alternating vicissitudes, could not but continue to grow, if not in quantity, undoubtedly in quality. However, at the end of the years considered here, signs were visible for those who did not close their eyes that, as in the story of Joseph in Genesis, after the years of ecumenical plenty, years of ecumenical hunger would almost certainly follow. Ecumenical pioneer Willem Visser 't Hooft, in his old age, was well aware of this.

2 Reconstruction: "Churches Worth Helping in Europe"

After the war, the staff of the WCC in Geneva expanded rapidly, supported in particular by American money from a number of sources. The WCC was an interesting recipient and distributor for the aid programs of American churches, as it was capable not only of distributing money, but also of setting up and guiding staff members on concrete projects. In the course of the 1950s in Geneva, a staff of 140 employees could be financed, a number which in the early 1960s grew up to 200. WCC refugee work cooperated closely with the United Nations in many countries. In the last year of war, Visser 't Hooft, together with the American Samuel McCrea Cavert, had worked hard on the reorganization of the ecumenical refugee work and its integration into the WCC. In October 1945, the new WCC Department of Reconstruction and Interchurch Aid was established. The Scot James Hutchinson Cockburn became its director. Successively, Adolf Freudenberg, Elfan Rees, Wolfgang Schweitzer, Richard Fagley, and Baldwin Sjollema directed this work. The Swiss pastor Alphons Koechlin became chairman of the Reconstruction Committee, but Visser 't Hooft was personally closely involved in many projects. Coordination was necessary particularly in connection with refugee work and the numerous activities established in order to support churches involved in postwar reconstruction. It became possible to acquire a picturesque villa in a park-like garden at 17 Route de Malagnou for use as an office building. During the following years other buildings in the vicinity were added. Visser 't Hooft left the day-to-day management of the finances of the WCC to his senior financial assistant, Frank Northam, who shared responsibility with the Swiss banker and anonymous donor to the organization, Gustave Hentsch.

Visser 't Hooft now saw golden opportunities to develop the WCC as a network for reconciliation and assistance in various places, not only in Europe. In the eyes of many people, the war had put the classic dogmatic contrasts among churches in a different perspective. Practical cooperation and church renewal had a new priority and, therefore, contacts were established and maintained from Geneva with Protestant churches in almost all European countries. In October 1945, for example, Visser 't Hooft himself went to the Netherlands to attend the first postwar synod of the largest Dutch protestant church, the NHK, in Amsterdam. Here he delivered a powerful speech on the new relevance of the church that had come to light amidst the ordeal of the war.[4] The church had learned anew to deliver a prophetic message to the world and to address itself to concrete problems in a way that appealed to both the masses and the elite. During the following years, the NHK, which for many decades had been institutionally paralyzed by its conflicting liberal and conservative wings, reorganized itself and in 1951 adopted a new church order with a strong missionary profile.

All over Europe many church buildings had been damaged or destroyed owing to the war, and there was often no money to make the necessary repairs or pay the pastors. However, as far as Visser 't Hooft was concerned, without neglecting financial needs, spiritual renewal was at the heart of the ecumenical message. He presented it in such a way that it became clear that the churches had come out of the war refined and now stood in the

4 *Wat er gebeurde in de Nieuwe Kerk op den Dam rond 31 October 1945*, The Hague, Boekencentrum, 1945.

world with open eyes. Churches had undergone a severe judgment and had learned an important self-searching lesson on justice and love for one's neighbor. Visser 't Hooft considered a postwar continuation and strengthening of this awareness essential, not only with regard to the reconstruction of Europe, but also to the conditions necessary for a sustainable European, indeed world, peace. In the 1947-draft of a four-year plan intended, in particular, for American contributors, he wrote:

> I have no doubt that there is more *real* Christianity to-day in Europe than 20 or 50 years ago. In Norway, Holland, France, Germany, Czechoslovakia, Hungary, Greece there are movements of *renewal* such as have not been seen for many generations. This is especially true among intellectuals. The Student Christian Movements are alive. The various types of professional lay associations show that large numbers of Christians mean business. And we have not had so much vitality in the *theological* realm for (perhaps) centuries. Do not give our American brethren the impression – which many have anyway – that Europe must be written off. It is important to show (and this is true) that there are churches *worth helping in Europe*.[5]

Visser 't Hooft urged his staff to stress the practical side of projects. He knew Americans' way of thinking and he wanted facts and concrete explanations, examples, and figures in order to impress them. Projects such as evangelization in Hungary, theological education in Berlin, and training for lay leaders, such as Kerk en Wereld in the Netherlands, had "to be sold," as it were, to American churches.

In general, Visser 't Hooft was a team worker when it concerned colleagues he estimated, but when it came to his position as secretary general directing his staff, *le patron* certainly wanted to maintain control. He wanted to inspire his employees but did not hesitate to throw them in at the deep end, and demanded initiative. He left them to work out the development of details on their own. With regard to refugee work in Rome, Vienna, and Athens, so-called field offices were set up. Emphasis was on indiscriminate practical assistance to refugees wherever possible. Immediately after the end of hostilities in 1945, the most attention was paid to Germany. With regard to churches in Poland and East Prussia, an important man in the field for Visser 't Hooft was Stewart W. Herman, an American Lutheran pastor who had worked for the Office of Strategic Services during the war but now offered his assistance to the WCC.

Germans living under Russian rule experienced difficult times after the collapse of the Third Reich. Those on the eastern side of the Oder–Neisse line were driven to the West, expelled and transported in livestock wagons to what was left of Germany. The estimate is that there were two million deaths among these *Heimatvertriebenen*. For a considerable period, effective help was nearly impossible. In the Russian zone of occupied Germany, pastor Heinrich Kloppenburg maintained contact with Protestant churches in the countryside and reported to Visser 't Hooft, who endeavored to support the workers in the field from Geneva but often felt powerless. Nonetheless, the ecumenical efforts made to help Germans in need during this breakdown of German society was not forgotten.

3 Reconciliation: "Help Us, So That We Can Help"

In the spring of 1945, Visser 't Hooft made a trip to the United States. For weeks on end, he had a tight schedule of meetings and speaking engagements and he preached in many churches. Despite the fact that the trip was a great success in terms of fundraising, Visser 't Hooft felt disappointed. People wanted to know about the ecumenical work among refugees, what was needed for the reconstruction of Europe, and what was the role

5 Willem Adolph Visser 't Hooft, Notes on the Draft Four Year Plan, Jul 15, 1947, in: WCCA, General correspondence, 797.

of the churches. Yet when he wanted to speak about the ill fate of the German resistance, which had struggled in vain not only against Hitler, but also for the future of a federal and unified Europe based on Christian values, few were interested. Americans were celebrating victory in Europe and were in a jubilant mood thanks to the defeat of the Nazis. It was expected that the surrender of Japan would soon follow. This festive mood, however, was accompanied by preoccupations about the growing influence of the Soviet Union in Eastern Europe. Visser 't Hooft realized that the European ideals, as fostered by resistance fighters such as Adam von Trott and Dietrich Bonhoeffer during the war, apparently did not now render the right paradigm for presenting the value of the ecumenical movement in America.

This did not mean that Visser 't Hooft himself abandoned the theme of European unity as an idea having Christian roots, and neither did his staff. The postwar reconstruction and the search for values that in the ecumenical movement were considered to be fundamental to Europe remained emphatically connected to their background in the resistance and the revival of the church:

> What then is the true *raison d'être* of European unity? What is the basis on which Europe can stand, be itself and accomplish its mission in the world? That question cannot be answered by historical or cultural analysis alone. For Europe has been visited by a great and terrible judgement of God. And the present mission of Europe can only be understood if we grasp the meaning of that judgement.[6]

It was Visser 't Hooft's strong belief that the church had come out of the war purified and with a God-given purpose of commitment. An exhausted Europe would undoubtedly rediscover this church as the place where the kingdom of God's promise of justice and peace had remained alive at times of barbarous repression. Churches aware of the newly risen opportunities would be able to counteract secularization and make a substantial contribution to the much-needed new spiritual foundations of society. Small pioneer groups of dedicated men and women were expected to break the international deadlock as ecumenical vanguards. The churches themselves were the building blocks upon which to build the new structures of salvation, but church leaders had to learn how to cooperate. According to Visser 't Hooft, it was an issue that concerned just as much socialists, who realized that the masses could not live by bread alone, as Christians from all denominations, who had come to be aware that moral advice and correct theology were insufficient for living churches.

Europe was, in the opinion of Visser 't Hooft, not a concept to defend, but an idea of unity in which to live. In the 2nd-century "Letter to Diognetus," he read what was said about Christians: "The soul is imprisoned in the body, but it sustains [*Or: constrains*] the body; Christians are detained in the prison of the world but they sustain [*Or: constrain*] the world."[7]

He believed in a special necessity of the time, which he thought of as an office of reconciliation.[8] People, in his opinion, urgently needed reconciliation with God, with themselves and with others. True reconciliation was only possible at the cross of Christ, that is, after people's readiness to confess their sins before God, in the faith that Christ had suffered for their forgiveness. Visser 't Hooft believed that no Christian had to be afraid of being

6 Willem Adolph Visser 't Hooft, "Europe," speech held in Gex at the reconstruction conference, March 1949. See Lucian N. Leustean, *The Ecumenical Movement & the Making of the European Community*, Oxford, Oxford University Press, 2014. Jan Schubert, *Willem Adolph Visser 't Hooft (1900–1985): Ökumene und Europa*, Göttingen, Vandenhoeck & Ruprecht, 2017.

7 "Epistle to Diognetus," in: Bart D. Ehrman, ed., *Apostolic Fathers*, vol. 2, Cambridge MA, Harvard University Press, 2003, 121–159, here 142, trans. 143 (italics original).

8 Zeilstra, *Visser 't Hooft (1900–1985)*, 259, 288.

considered, as such, an "outdated eccentric."[9] The great challenge he saw was to give credible expression to a religious conviction in a secularized world.

In 1945 Germany was in ruins: millions of people were displaced and the German churches were badly battered, torn inwardly, and morally damaged. The fear of nihilism, ongoing moral decay, and totalitarian communism was great. In particular, German youth raised concerns. The Nazi values with which they had grown up had now been annihilated. Visser 't Hooft must have had *déja vu* feelings when thinking back to the years following World War I when as an organizer and fundraiser he had been actively involved in ESR. Once again, all kinds of aid programs were being developed, but now he was in a far more influential position, and he was determined to maximize his options. The first great question was how to deal with the German churches. The majority of German believers had lived with the Lutheran notion of a special realm of the church, isolated from state affairs (two kingdoms doctrine). They had supported Hitler and, simultaneously, adhered to the experience of their faith as a spiritual cause. It was not until the government started to interfere directly in church affairs, for instance through the *Berufsverbot*, which denied the ministry to ethnically Jewish church pastors, that people became indignant. In 1934, the Barmen Declaration denounced state dominance over the church on biblical grounds.[10] An article against anti-Semitism, however, was lacking, and it was only a small minority within German Protestantism that resisted. The number of German church leaders that became convinced Nazis was limited. However, the reputation of the Confessing Church was not really impressive. The number of those who paid lip service to the regime for "tactical" reasons, such as the bishop of Hanover, August Marahrens, was large.

Nevertheless, even during the dark years of the conflict, Visser 't Hooft had always been convinced that after the war the German churches should, in an earnest way, be rehabilitated as soon as possible. In the interest of a durable peace, of the development of the ecumenical movement, and of a sound reconstruction of German institutions, feelings of hatred and rancor should not be allowed to take root as had occurred after World War I, which is why he deemed it necessary to recommence relationships as early as in autumn 1945. To anyone who wanted to hear, inside and outside the WCC, Visser 't Hooft made it clear that a genuine core of faith would enable a regenerated German Protestant Church to overcome the German crisis and would provide the necessary "good Germans" capable of leadership. He saw the Protestant Church as the only institution, in his words "the only coherent body" in Germany, suitable for social services and social work.[11] The church alone would be able to link the unavoidable political consequences to the Christian message. In this respect, his extensive network of contacts within the YMCA and the WSCF, built up during his career as secretary of those organizations, turned out to be useful. Thus, when after the collapse of the Third Reich reformist church leaders soon began to reorganize the predominantly Lutheran – and for a small part Reformed German Protestant – churches, he tried to be as well informed as possible. In the place of the DEK, the renewed EKD was now established.

In these circumstances Visser 't Hooft considered that a new and what he called a more "aggressive" form of evangelism was essential to fill the spiritual and moral void now threatening German society. He realized however that strengthening the ecumenical ties at this moment in time

9 Willem Adolf Visser 't Hooft, *Heel de kerk voor heel de wereld: Belang van de oecumene*, Utrecht, Ambo – Bosch & Keuning, 1968, 13.

10 See the contribution by Peter Zimmerling in this volume.

11 Willem Adolf Visser 't Hooft, "The Place of the German Church in Post-War Reconstruction," *Christianity and Crisis*, Jun 11, 1945, 4–7. Zeilstra, *Visser 't Hooft (1900–1985)*, 260–261.

would not be easy. A great distrust for anything German ran deep in the victorious nations, especially in countries that had suffered occupation. In Germany itself, church cooperation with the Allies now occupying the country was a delicate issue. The extensive bombings of German cities in the last years of the war had caused a great deal of anger. Christians in Germany were afraid to be seen as traitors when entertaining friendly relations with the Allied authorities or international organizations. Nevertheless, Visser 't Hooft was optimistic. Everywhere in Germany he saw people in desperate circumstances once again embracing real Christian beliefs and he trusted that the church could propose new, untainted politicians. He found a good example of one and saw a true ally in ecumenism in the later president of the Federal Republic, Gustav Heinemann. He realized that such Germans could not be expected to be accepted overnight internationally, but there was no time to lose. Disillusioned people could equally well be reached through evangelism as through dangerous propaganda.

Examples of the German church leaders that Visser 't Hooft appreciated were Otto Dibelius, Theophil Wurm, and the permanent representative in Geneva of the EKD, Reinhold von Thadden. They had turned their backs on nationalism, which they now openly denounced as a pagan power. The most important "good German" in the eyes of Visser 't Hooft was Martin Niemöller, who during World War I had been a conscript and submarine captain. Later as a civilian he became a theologian and pastor in Berlin. Niemöller joined the Nazi party, but when, after gaining power, Adolf Hitler started pursuing his Aryan campaign by banning Jews from jobs, Niemöller turned into one of the fiercest critics of the regime in the church. In 1938, this led to his seven-year imprisonment with the status of "personal prisoner of the Führer" and to great fame outside Germany.

As early as Oct 18 and 19, 1945, the first official contact of German church leaders with a delegation from the WCC in formation took place at a meeting in a badly bombed Stuttgart. Visser 't Hooft managed to reach the city together with Dutch missiologist Hendrik Kraemer, who had been interned in a concentration camp himself. Furthermore, the ecumenical delegation consisted of the French friend of Visser 't Hooft Pierre Maury, the American delegate for ecumenism Samuel McCrea Cavert, the American Lutheran Sylvester C. Michelfelder, the Swiss Alphons Koechlin, and the British Anglican Bishop George Bell. The whole enterprise was improvised. Obtaining visas had been very difficult even for this small group. The Norwegian delegation who had been expected in Stuttgart did not succeed in reaching the city in time.

Promising international ecumenical beginnings had been cut off in the 1930s by fascism, but personal contacts had survived through the war. This made Stuttgart possible. It was Visser 't Hooft's deliberate strategy to take the liberty to present the small ecumenical delegation at Stuttgart as representative of churches in the European countries that had suffered German aggression.[12] The most important outcome was that Visser 't Hooft invited the Evangelical Church to become a full member of the WCC in formation as soon as possible. In his personal notes to the meetings in Stuttgart, he jotted down: "Now want resume *full* relations for a) We need the witness of German Church in the ecumenical movement; b) We desire to help in the reconstruction of church life in Germany and to do our share in meeting the physical needs of the German people as churches and through the churches."[13]

The arrival of the foreigners surprised the Germans because Visser 't Hooft had not been able to give them notice in advance, but the Germans immediately adjusted their agenda. Without consulting leaders of member churches of the WCC,

12 They were delegates, able to speak on behalf of their churches. See minutes by Hans Asmussen, untitled, Stuttgart, Oct 25, 1945, in: WCCA, YDS-4, 31.

13 Willem Adolph Visser 't Hooft, personal notes, Stuttgart 1945, and "Main points to be made by World Council delegation in Stuttgart-discussions," draft, no date, in: WCCA, YDS-4, 29–30.

the secretary general proposed a process leading to a full recovery of ecumenical relations and discussed this with his delegation members. What was not clear at that moment was whether it would be possible to find enough common ground with the Germans, and not only with those present, to rebuild relations. Everything would depend on a German willingness to acknowledge their guilt in an honest and convincing way. Once in conversation with their hosts however, the foreign participants were impressed by the awareness of guilt on the part of these German church leaders and their willingness to express their regret. In a sermon by Martin Niemöller on Jer 14:7–11 at the eve of the conference on Oct 17, the Nazi period was interpreted as a judgment of God, to which only a full German confession of guilt could be an appropriate answer. In this service, Niemöller asked for God's forgiveness for the German people and for the church belonging to it.

This set the tone for the discussions the following day, when the German representatives heard Visser 't Hooft make an urgent appeal: "You have said: Help us. And this is what we want to do, but we return the word when we say: Help us to be able to help you. This is the meaning of our conversation."[14] What he wanted to hear were clear church statements about the guilt of the German people and a condemnation of Hitler's regime of terror and persecution over a large part of Europe, along with an explicit mention of the suffering that had ensued for the churches and the Jews. Only such a statement would allow Visser 't Hooft to call upon the churches in the countries that had suffered for forgiveness towards the German people and to organize substantial foreign aid to German churches. He was paid due attention. One of the most important forces behind the Stuttgart Declaration of Guilt was the pastor of Schöneberg, Hans Asmussen. As early as 1942, in the middle of the war, he had written a long letter to Visser 't Hooft expressing his confidence that under the surface of the war God was at work in the hearts of men and that questions of guilt had to be dealt with by the churches as soon as possible after an armistice, and not left to political propaganda. At the time, this letter made a deep impression on Visser 't Hooft, who himself had earlier spoken of a spiritual war behind the visible one, by which he meant a spiritual struggle in the heart of every person. This approach found its way into the final statement by the church leaders present at Stuttgart, which famous starting words are: "We are especially grateful for this visit, as our people are not just part of a larger society of suffering, but also part of a solidarity of guilt. With great pain in our hearts we declare: because of us, never-ending suffering was brought to many peoples and nations."[15]

The German delegates identified themselves with the German people, but their status was not clear. Could they really claim to represent German churches or even a German ecumenical council? Formally, they could not, and even less could they presume to speak on behalf of the German people as a whole. But neither could the delegation of foreigners claim to operate with proper mandate and consultation, when they stated:

> Our own churches and the World Council have not recognized sufficiently early and sufficiently clearly the evil force which had been let loose and have therefore not acted sufficiently courageously when there was still time to act. And we are too clearly aware of the witness and suffering of many in the German Church. We see clearly, in what happened to the German nation and church, "both the kindness [Güte] and severity of God [Ernst Gottes]."[16]

Although Stuttgart was controversial due to a lack of formal representation, in the German churches

14 Notes by Hans Asmussen, Stuttgart, Oct 25, 1945.

15 Notes by Hans Asmussen, Stuttgart, Oct 25, 1945.

16 Visser 't Hooft, personal notes, Stuttgart 1945 and "Main points to be made by World Council delegation in Stuttgart-discussions."

it made Visser 't Hooft the man with an extended hand. In the darkest hour of German history, he avoided accusations and showed the power of ecumenically-driven reconciliation.

Visser 't Hooft was very much aware that a meeting of a handful of ecclesiastical leaders did not mean that reconciliation had entered the hearts and minds of everyone. In those circumstances, however, he considered it reasonable to take the Barmen theses and the 1945 Treysa conference as having a binding effect in substance and as creating a new situation for the EKD. After all, by confessing their faith in front of a common enemy in Barmen in 1934, representatives of the Lutheran and Reformed churches had established the foundation of a confessing church that was developed anew after the war at Treysa. The next ecumenical challenge was a broad appropriation by all churches involved in the WCC in process of formation. In November 1945 Visser 't Hooft explained his view on the situation of the German church in a memorandum addressed to his ecumenical contacts.

During the years that followed, Martin Niemöller was the German *par excellence* able to provide the necessary continuation to this process. Visser 't Hooft wasted no opportunity to make Niemöller be seen internationally as a reliable representative of the other Germany, indeed even the contemporary prophet that Europe now needed. In March 1946, he asked Niemöller to commit himself to two months of ecumenical work involving isolated German congregations and the pastoral care for prisoners of war. The energetic and endearing Niemöller did not disappoint him. In the summer of 1946, Visser 't Hooft pulled many strings and used all his diplomatic skills with the Allies in order to make it possible for Niemöller to travel to the United States so he could make the case for the German Confessing Church and make the German resistance known on the other side of the Atlantic, which he promptly did, leading an enthusiastic Visser 't Hooft to write: "My question really amounts to this: are you quite sufficiently grateful for the quite wonderful work for which you are being used? There is almost no other man in the world whose word and work is so clearly and visibly blessed."[17]

The two had a frank way of communicating. Niemöller made no secret of his conviction that it would be crucial for a strong German delegation to be accepted without discussion and be taken seriously as co-founder of the WCC. Visser 't Hooft fully agreed, but in 1947 he was well aware that there was still much resentment in the European churches towards the German people, and he asked for patience.

> The great question is ... what will happen when the time comes for a frank discussion. At that time, two dangers will arise, namely, that the German Church should deny or minimize the particularly grave responsibility of the German nation for the suffering of these years and that the other churches should assume a Pharisaical attitude toward the German Church.[18]

In the end, he defied critics and was able to guarantee that the EKD would be permitted to send 20 official delegates to the first assembly at Amsterdam without fear of being accused, and allowed to participate without any reservation. Two additional places were reserved for the German Mennonites and Old Catholics.

Nonetheless, Visser 't Hooft took the great suffering that the German people had borne as a punishment from God. However, he saw no point in a human addition to that suffering. In order to ease the shortage of reliable church leaders and ministers, he advocated the early release of theologians who were in prisoner-of-war camps because they had served in the German army. It was not until 1947 that the WCC received permission from the Allied authorities ruling Germany to appoint a permanent ecumenical liaison representative for

17 W.A. Visser 't Hooft to M. Niemöller, Feb 17, 1947, in: WCCA 42.0059, general correspondence, 1026.

18 W.A. Visser 't Hooft to M. Niemöller, Feb 17, 1947.

the German churches. The Danish Lutheran minister Halfdan Høgsbro was prepared to accept this difficult position. He settled in Bad Homburg, near Frankfurt am Main in the American zone, and reported directly to Visser 't Hooft. The Germans had little confidence in the way the Americans and the British were treating them. To Høgsbro's suggestion that the WCC should be more involved in the trials against war criminals because, as he had observed, Germans had little confidence in the way the Americans and the British were treating them, Visser 't Hooft replied that Geneva lacked both the expertise and the competence to intervene. However, in particular cases the German church leaders themselves could always appeal to the CCIA in the person of its director Otto Frederick Nolde. The German churches were reinventing themselves. Finally, after much debate, and to the relief of Visser 't Hooft, the organization of an overarching EKD was accepted by the *Landeskirchen* as the representative church body of Protestant Germany that could apply for WCC membership.

4 Diplomacy: "Genuine Meeting of Minds"

In 1945, the victorious Allies decided to set up a new, more effective, United Nations Organization in place of the League of Nations, established in 1919, and 51 countries joined it. That human rights were to play an important part was welcomed in ecumenical circles, where it had often been argued that the League of Nations had lacked a spiritual root, or "a soul," according to some.[19] Nevertheless, no great expectations were held owing to the character of human nature, that was considered to be inherently sinful and incapable of living up to an optimistic concept such as human rights independently. In the first years of its attention to international relations, the WCC concentrated rather on religious freedom. As early as 1943, Visser 't Hooft pleaded for a permanent ecumenical body of expert theologians and lawyers specifically dedicated to international affairs. Not power, but ecumenical influence on the basis of a consensus among experts was sought. On the basis of his wartime experience, Visser 't Hooft became a great supporter of an active, ecumenical diplomacy, which mainly remained quietly behind the scenes but, if necessary, was to stand in the limelight of the media. Any suspicion that the churches were interfering in politics, however, had to be defused from the start. He was fortunate in that there was indeed a certain openness in this period towards church propelled diplomacy. That a considerable number of responsible politicians had been members of the YMCA, the WSCF or associated organizations, or had been educated in schools or churches with a background in the missions was also of great assistance.

An important start was made as early as on the eve of the war, in July 1939, in Geneva, when an ecumenical conference of lay experts in international relations took place in a vain attempt to prevent the war. Visser 't Hooft later saw this conference at the Hotel Beau-Séjour as the beginning of serious ecumenical thinking on international affairs, culminating in February 1946 in the founding of the CCIA as a joint organ of the WCC and the IMC. The experienced Leiden professor of international law and friend of Visser 't Hooft, Baron Frederik Mari van Asbeck, was chairman of the CCIA from 1948 to 1965. The daily management was in the hands of the Englishman Kenneth George Grubb and the American Frederick Nolde, realists when it was a matter of international politics. Good relationships with the United Nations were cherished, but care was taken to ensure that WCC staff members should not be involved in any decision-making of that organization. In 1948, Nolde wrote an important contribution on human rights for the Amsterdam assembly, in which with some hesitation he pleaded for the WCC to accept these as essential for a stable world order and as a basis for cooperation of the WCC with the United Nations and other organizations in the international sphere. However, in the early years of the WCC human rights were a concept

19 Zeilstra, *European Unity in Ecumenical Thinking*, 6.

associated with an autonomous view of man, and in general not wholeheartedly embraced in ecumenical circles. It was the policy of Visser 't Hooft, Nolde, and Grubb to put full emphasis on rights that guaranteed the Christian's freedom to exert one's personal religious conviction and to preach the gospel.

Visser 't Hooft and the American Walter W. Van Kirk managed as a duo the secretariat of the CCIA, but in effect it was predominantly Visser 't Hooft who, as a diplomat, presented its policy in public. His demand was that the members of the commission should always be careful to have precise information about the world of international relations and abstain from pious preaching. He was convinced that the politicians and diplomats whom they wanted to reach were not expecting moral indignation, but should be helped with an expert view and by Christian-charged ethics. With the unified authority of the churches, Visser 't Hooft hoped to be able to speak in public with a prophetic voice compatible with the 20th century, offering concrete proposals and recommendations. The core statements had to be values in order to be relevant, based on Christian convictions, and expressed in a way intelligible to all those truly interested.

Shortly afterwards, in June 1946, international tensions in the context of the Cold War rose considerably. Some people feared a third world war might break out and insisted on a prophetic word from the churches. However, Visser 't Hooft was cautious at the time and reacted in his typical fashion: "Now I do not believe in statements that are just drawn up in this office or by one or two offices and which have not grown out of a genuine meeting of minds."[20]

He wanted to wait until August 1946, when the CCIA would officially meet for the first time. Formulating a clear statement on the basis of consensus, however, proved to be far more difficult than he had initially thought. From the very start, there were great differences of opinion among the CCIA experts themselves. In the case of the Cold War, the question of how Christianity and totalitarian systems related to each other caused endless discussions. However, Visser 't Hooft successfully defended his *tertium datur* stand, carefully building up through the years an independent ecumenical profile as a surplus value in the church approach to the crises of the time. This ethically motivated refusal to be used, as WCC, by either West or East did not appeal to everybody, but during the 1950s proved to be respected by both people of the church and politicians.

5 Manifestation of Good Will: "Responsible Society"

In the meantime, the date of the official establishment of the WCC, Aug 23, 1948, was rapidly approaching, and the star of Visser 't Hooft as a leading actor on the stage of the ecumenical movement began to rise. In 1947 he was invited to deliver the so-called Stone Lectures at Princeton in the United States. The title of the main theme was "The Kingship of Christ," in which Visser 't Hooft presented an overview of the most important theological developments during the *interbellum* period and their consequences for the current situation. To his American audience he explained the clash between the totalitarian state and the church, particularly in Germany, but he also provided some examples based on the situation in Norway and the Netherlands. In regard to the problem outlined in his 1928 dissertation concerning the deplorable theological stalemate between European and American theology, he now expressed optimism.[21] An important lesson had in recent years been learned on both sides of the Atlantic: in Europe people had started to think more practically, while in the United States a

20 W.A. Visser 't Hooft to W.W. Van Kirk, Jun 4, 1946, in: WCCA, general correspondence 772.

21 Willem Adolph Visser 't Hooft, *The Kingship of Christ: An Interpretation of Recent European Theology*, New York, Harper & Brothers, 1948. Willem A. Visser 't Hooft, *The Background of the Social Gospel in America*, Haarlem, Tjeenk Willink & Zoon, 1928.

profounder theological exploration had occurred. Therefore, before too long, and with the right dedication, Visser 't Hooft expected a breakthrough in the European–American ecumenical dialogue. Concentration on the kingship of Christ could not but lead to a new transatlantic ecumenical rapprochement. With this view, for several years during the 1950s, Visser 't Hooft was able to influence the orientation of the WCC, not in a Christocentric sense alone, but by means of this Christocentrism he was building a mutual understanding between Europeans and Americans. One criticism that could be heard, and not only regularly in America at that time, was that "ecumenism" implied disregard for the truth and sheer relativism, which he decidedly rejected: "The ecumenical conversation must be a struggle for truth. Excessive politeness is sometimes a greater hindrance to ecumenical advance than frank facing of difference."[22] As far as Visser 't Hooft was concerned, in the ecumenical attitude the search for truth itself was at stake.

One of the wrinkles that had to be ironed out was the mistrust and suspicion between the two main precursory organizations of the WCC. Members of Faith and Order feared that the new council would be dominated by Life and Work. Even in 1937, during the Oxford Conference, Life and Work (with its focus on practical Christianity) seemed more eager to set up the WCC than Faith and Order (with its focus on the dogmatic aspect of faith and church order) at their meeting in Edinburgh that same year was. It seemed to them, not entirely without reason, that frequently practical work was higher on the agenda of the WCC than the substantive discussion of matters of faith. This anxiety was reinforced when the peace organization WA (established in 1914) was liquidated in 1948, with Life and Work resulting as its most important heir. In March 1948, Visser 't Hooft was attacked on this point by the secretary of Faith and Order, Canon Leonard Hodgson, professor at Oxford, who felt that the Life and Work study department was accorded too much room within the new council. The secretary general of the WCC, at this time still "in process of formation," stated that all organs of the WCC were in fact organs of the churches themselves and that there was no reason to fear that Faith and Order risked being submerged. During the 1950s, Visser 't Hooft did his utmost to develop the debate on questions of faith, in particular ecclesiology, through the department of Faith and Order. Nevertheless, Hodgson's worries were justified. In the second half of the 1960s interest in this type of consensus-seeking, faith-centered ecumenical debate quickly waned, while more themes related to social and racial issues, emancipation, environment, and peace activism gathered momentum. However, this development lies outside the scope of the present chapter.

A crucial aspect in regard to the Amsterdam conference was the invitation policy concerning keynote speakers. Visser 't Hooft wanted first-class experts, leaders in their field, not necessarily theologians, but men, and some women, capable of ecclesiological thinking. One of his victories was that he was able to persuade his favorite Reformed theologian, the Swiss Karl Barth, who had not exactly been a great admirer of the ecumenical movement so far, to deliver the opening speech. Barth's reputation was connected to the Barmen Declaration of 1934, when he and his fellow protesters took a firm stand against Hitler. He was a strong church-oriented thinker, who had founded his theology on an exegesis of biblical revelation. During the war, Barth had repeatedly urged Visser 't Hooft to raise his voice clearly against injustices as an ecumenical prophet. Somewhat reluctantly he went to Amsterdam in 1948, persuaded by Visser 't Hooft to overcome his dislike of what he considered to be ecumenical circuses. However, he impressed many with his passionate address, not sparing the idealists, when he warned against any unity constructed as a hubristic human project, a modern Tower of Babel.[23]

22 Willem Adolph Visser 't Hooft, "Ten Ecumenical Questions," Oct 21, 1947, in: WCCA, 994.2.11/19.

23 Clifford Jeapes, dir., *The First Assembly of the World Council of Churches, Amsterdam, 1948*, Geneva, Religious Films, 1948. Apart from his keynote address Barth did not have a very fortunate conference at Amsterdam:

The overture to the Amsterdam assembly on Aug 22, 1948 was a celebration in the Nieuwe Kerk, situated next to the palace in Dam Square. The actual establishment of the WCC took place the following day in the Concertgebouw, with the solemn pronouncement of the founding words by Geoffrey Fisher, archbishop of Canterbury, after the delegates had cast their votes. This was the milestone that had been awaited for over ten years. With a brutal war fresh in their memory, violent processes of decolonization in progress, and the Cold War threat of the atom bomb holding the world in its grip, members of very different churches felt connected and prepared to work together. The important element was that with churches renewed and united in a strong world organization, modernization did not necessarily have to result in materialism and secularization. Churches could face the challenge of a new era with inspired self-confidence thanks to their confidence in God. At least that is how their leaders, for the most part rather mature, white European and North American males, experienced it.

Amsterdam signified a consolidation and completion of the policy decided in Oxford and Edinburgh in 1937 and in Utrecht in 1938. Apart from lectures and working groups, there was a number of business meetings at which a whole series of decisions, having far-reaching consequences for the nature of the new council, had to be taken. Similarities to the United Nations were striking, and it was clear that the churches aimed to play a significant role in the postwar world. Theoretically and in canon law, Amsterdam had to invent itself. This was no synod or council, therefore there was no precedent. In principle, large assemblies of delegations from all the member churches would meet every six years. A central committee, elected by the assembly, would meet annually and choose a small executive committee. A secretary general was to manage the staff on a daily basis, and an *ex officio* secretary was nominated for both the central and the executive committees. He would be accountable to the assembly. At this stage, Visser 't Hooft was still convinced that the Bible principally offered one single true church model that could be rediscovered through Christian dialogue: "Our name [World Council of Churches, plural] indicates our weakness and our shame before God, for there can be and there *is* finally only one Church of Christ on earth. Our plurality is a deep anomaly."[24] When presenting the report of the Provisional Committee to the assembly, Visser 't Hooft warned: "Our common witness in word and deed has no substance and no convincing power unless that witness is rendered locally and nationally in all the [member] Churches."[25]

During the congress, he was later appointed as the secretary general for the coming period, *nemine contradicente*. WCC staff members were to be organized into departments under a director, personally responsible to the secretary general. Everything that occurred during the founding meeting would be interpreted politically by the outside world, even if it was intended in a spiritual sense. This was not the only reason why Visser 't Hooft was cautious: he did not want to raise too many expectations. Clear statements on current issues were expected from Amsterdam, but the secretary general was well aware that, with 147 member churches, reaching a consensus if only on the major themes would never be easy. Amsterdam was undoubtedly a milestone, but "World Council" still was a big word for an organization that had almost no representatives from Africa, South America, Eastern Orthodoxy, or the Roman Catholic Church. This could only be a start. The real work was yet to come.

In order to endow the discussions with real content, the Amsterdam theme "Man's Disorder and God's Design" was subdivided into four sections.

Jurjen A. Zeilstra, "What went wrong?: Karl Barth in Amsterdam 1948," *ZDTh*, 38/1–2, 2022, 133–156.

24 Visser 't Hooft, *Memoirs*, 210 (italics original). His opinion in this regard was to change during the 1960s.

25 Willem A. Wisser 't Hooft, *The Task of the World Council of Churches: Report Presented on Behalf of the Provisional Committee*, 1948, 4.

Visser 't Hooft was on his guard but, with such a large assembly and an overloaded program, moments of confusion and misunderstandings were unavoidable. The American John Foster Dulles, who had effected important ecumenical work during the war as president of the CJDP of the FCC, and who was soon to take office as the new secretary of state in the Dwight D. Eisenhower administration, came into conflict with the Czech theologian Josef Lukl Hromádka. Visser 't Hooft personally appreciated them both. Yet while Dulles became increasingly anti-communist during these years, Hromádka moved in the opposite direction and called for Christian cooperation with moderate communists. At Amsterdam, the final report of section III explicitly denounced both communism and capitalism, much to the satisfaction of the secretary general who was determined to maintain the independent stand of the WCC. He was convinced that "the Christian churches should reject the ideologies of both communism and laissez-faire capitalism, and should seek to draw men away from the false assumptions that these extremes are the only alternatives."[26]

It took some time before everybody understood that the WCC was taking its independence seriously. In the White House, in Washington, they certainly had not realized what the goals of the WCC were. On the eve of the Amsterdam conference, Visser 't Hooft was surprised to be visited by the American diplomat Myron Charles Taylor, who had been instructed by President Harry Truman to investigate how religious organizations such as the WCC could be mobilized in the fight against communism. After rejecting Taylor and receiving the Russian Orthodox Church refusal to participate to the conference, Visser 't Hooft felt confirmed in his opinion concerning the need for the WCC to sail on a strictly independent course.[27]

Visser 't Hooft considered the unity of the church to be a gift from God, which was what the churches, to his mind, were now rediscovering. The formula "Jesus Christ God and Savior" had its roots in the YMCA and in Faith and Order. As early as in 1938 it was adopted as the basis for the provisional WCC, and this was now formalized without any severe problems. Visser 't Hooft had always defended the phrase as the necessary pivot of faith and not as a confession, since the WCC had no pretentions about being a church, but with the potential of being extended, as was actually effected at the 1961 New Delhi assembly: "The World Council of Churches is a fellowship of Churches which confess the Lord Jesus Christ as God and Saviour according to the scriptures and therefore seek to fulfill together their common calling to the glory of the one God, Father, Son and Holy Spirit."[28] We shall return later to the reason for this addition.

This is not the place to offer a comprehensive analysis of the Amsterdam conference. For the moment it is sufficient to have exemplified the atmosphere of good-will in which there were real multilateral opportunities to develop what was called a "responsible society" further.[29] The phrase "responsible society" was coined for Amsterdam by Visser 't Hooft and Scottish ecumenical pioneer Joseph Houldsworth Oldham. They saw the churches as building blocks being lined up by the WCC to build the responsible society that corresponded to the 1950s search for stability and ethical order.

6 The Prophetic Voice from Geneva: "Das Wächteramt"

The words that stood out in the Amsterdam message were: "We intend to stay together."[30] The over-

26 *Man's Disorder and God's Design: An Ecumenical Study Prepared under the Auspices of the World Council of Churches*, vol. 3, *The Church and the Disorder of Society*, New York, Harper & Brothers, 1948, 195.

27 Visser 't Hooft, *Memoirs*, 225–227.

28 Willem Adolph Visser 't Hooft, "The Basis: Its History and Significance," *EcRev* 37, 1985, 170–174, here 173.

29 Joseph H. Oldham, "A Responsible Society," in: *Man's Disorder and God's Design*, vol. 3, 120–154.

30 *Man's Disorder and God's Design*, vol. 2, *The Church's Witness to God's Design*, London, SCM Press, 1948, 215.

arching and most complex theme of Amsterdam, however, was "Man's Disorder and God's Design." It had a sequel in the ambitious theme of the second assembly at Evanston in 1954, "Christ, the Hope of the World." The last assembly under the leadership of Visser 't Hooft was in 1961 in India, "Jesus Christ, The Light of the World." The striking aspect of all these catchphrases is their static formulation. They reflect a desire for stability, which is comprehensible after a violent war and with new, repeated threats of destruction on the horizon.

This was a fertile period in which the WCC was allowed to play the role of guardian angel of world peace. Within a decade it developed into a global religious nongovernmental organization with hundreds of employees. The world stage of the 1950s and the early 1960s represented the context in which the WCC now had to operate. It was characterized by a series of international crises occurring against the background of the Cold War, such as the war in Korea, the Soviet invasion of Hungary, the Cyprus and Cuba crises. Time and time again, events such as these were reason for the WCC staff either to issue a public statement or, in a number of cases, to opt for a diplomatic intervention.

The CCIA, predominantly consisting of well-informed lay experts, was almost continually on the alert. When effective action behind the scenes was sought, Visser 't Hooft and his staff preferred a silent diplomacy to the limelight of the media. Simultaneously, in a number of cases it was considered the task of the WCC to speak out with a prophetic voice and exercise consciously what Karl Barth had taught Visser 't Hooft to call the watchman's office: *das Wächteramt*. If sufficient support in the churches was lacking, Visser 't Hooft usually refrained from comment, as for instance in regard to the biblical legitimization and ecumenical and theological meaning of the modern state of Israel, founded just a few months before the WCC. In the case of South African apartheid, he was able to gain trust with a moderate diplomatic approach during his visit in 1952. The Cottesloe Consultation of 1960 brought the delegates of eight South African churches to an agreement, although some of the churches later rejected the outcome. However, during the Cyprus crisis in the late 1950s internal tension with the Anglicans within the ecumenical network arose. In regard to the Cuba crisis, Visser 't Hooft had to recognize that he had spoken out of turn. Nonetheless, in the end he managed to reinforce his mandate and was able to continue along the chosen path. In order to retain a flexible approach and the capacity to react quickly to developments, the secretary general considered that his mandate to speak out in public was renewed provided he did what he could to consult the ecumenical bodies concerned.

Visser 't Hooft did not fit into any previous profile of a secretary general. The task was unintentionally modeled after his personality. He was much more than an executor of plans designed by church leaders or approved by assemblies or synods. Visser 't Hooft was not only an erudite theologian but also an energetic character who led the office with a firm hand, revealing himself to be a skillful diplomat. He developed a vision and strategies, and gave alert responses to current developments in the world. His vast network and his extensive knowledge reinforced his growing authority within the ecumenical movement, in the churches, in the media, and among politicians. In the meantime, he held on to his Barthian convictions concerning a Christocentric ecclesiology. This was rather a rigid approach but was also straightforward. Somehow, and for a period, it helped to keep together the many varieties of Christendom that existed in the hundreds of member churches of the WCC.

The secretary general was not always successful in providing the concrete form that he envisaged to the connection between theology and the role that he saw for the WCC on the world stage. In order to involve more conservative churches in the work of the council, while also facing secularization and seeking to reinforce support within the member churches, in the 1950s he forcefully drew attention to the need for the renewal of the church. At times he overplayed his hand, or he bit off more than he could chew. This was the case during the second WCC assembly in Evanston in 1954, which had as its theme "Jesus Christ, Hope of the World." The choice of the theme "hope" at the time of the Cold War appeared too improbable to result in a clear stand and it created confusion of speech. While some maintained a more literal expectation of the second coming of Christ, others considered this a flight into transcendent thinking. In point of fact, what concerned Visser 't Hooft personally was really nothing less than saving the world. The unity of the church in this world could never be merely a marginal or purely internal church matter. His optimistic nature concealed a savior complex and a very pertinent idea of truth. This made him vulnerable when it became clear that the concrete renewal of the church that he so vehemently anticipated in the 1950s failed to carry the day and put a stop to a profound secularization in the long term, even threatening the very existence of traditionally organized churches.

7 Bossey Study Centre: Ecumenism as a New Theological Discipline?

In 1945 Visser 't Hooft gave a series of lectures on biblical social ethics at the theology faculty of the University of Geneva, in which he proposed a new methodological and ecumenically orientated approach to church history. According to him, a good reader understood that the Bible was not a book of ready-made rules and solutions, but that in its texts a person could gradually become aware of God's plan for the salvation of the world. As early as in the 1930s, Visser 't Hooft, as the secretary of the WSCF, had personally tried to establish something like an ecumenical study center in Geneva, but such plans faltered. After the war, he again explored the possibilities for it. In the postwar spirit of reconciliation and reconstruction, the idea of an international ecumenical study center was an appealing thought to many, and he was now successful.

In October 1946 the first courses started. Visser 't Hooft personally had the chance to show that he had not lost his skills as a fundraiser when he received a gift of one million dollars from the American businessman John D. Rockefeller Jr., half of which was intended for the Ecumenical Institute. In 1950, it became possible to purchase the small castle of Bossey, near Céligny, in order to house it. Bossey became an "energizing center" of encounter and study, a true ecumenical laboratory, where young people from all over the world could meet, discuss and learn about reconciliation, reconstruction, justice, and peace in an ecumenical atmosphere. Students were trained to profile themselves as open-minded Christians with ambitions in the public domain in their countries of origin. Missiologist Hendrik Kraemer, Suzanne de Dietrich, and Henry-Louis Henriod, all experienced WSCF staff members, took the lead, while numerous guest lecturers of fame and ecumenical experience were attracted there. There was a lay course, which on opening already had 30 entries, but the focus was on the theology course, which was aimed at older students of theology and young ministers.

Throughout the years, Visser 't Hooft himself gave many lectures, even in his old age. It was his ambition to develop what he called ecumenism as a new theological discipline. In February 1956, lecturing in Melbourne, he explained his ideas and argued in favor of a scientific, simultaneously value-driven study of the dynamic relations among churches.

> Ecumenism is the discipline which seeks to provide a comprehensive description of the faith and life of the Christian churches, as well as the ways in which they co-operate and manifest their unity and which also deals critically with the issues which have arisen as a result of the encounter between the churches for the churches themselves and the ecumenical movement.[31]

---

31 Willem Adolph Visser 't Hooft, "The Implications of the Ecumenical Movement for Theological Education," Melbourne and Bangkok, 1956, in: WCCA, 994.2.15/30.

According, explicitly, to Visser 't Hooft, this type of study should be more than "descriptive ecclesiology."[32] He thought of a dynamic and motivating curriculum that could be integrated well into missiology if only there were a good textbook. He expected the ecumenical movement to be very favorably promoted by means of the help of vibrant seminars in order to reflect better on the complicated challenges that the WCC now had to face in the modern world.

Visser 't Hooft considered most church historians to be far too influenced by secular historiography. What he urged was for a more personal approach and committed type of research and presentation. What was needed was what he called a "theological critique" of church history.[33] Even the handbook on the history of the ecumenical movement, for which Ruth Rouse acted as an editor and to which he himself contributed an article on the word "ecumenical," he found too factual.[34] He himself wanted to make a first contribution to his critique with his article "Our Ecumenical Task in the Light of History":[35] Visser 't Hooft considered making theological judgments about historical developments a necessary ecumenical endeavor. As an example, he thought of a critical ecumenical – theological analysis of the Reformation. He wondered to what extent this movement in the 16th century had been a true renewal of the church or to what extent the work of the devil, with the consequent division and violence.

32 Visser 't Hooft, "The Implications of the Ecumenical Movement for Theological Education."

33 Visser 't Hooft, "The Implications of the Ecumenical Movement for Theological Education."

34 Willem Adolf Visser 't Hooft, "The Word 'Ecumenical' – Its History and Use," in: *A History of the Ecumenical Movement*, vol. 1, Ruth Rouse & Stephen C. Neill, eds., *1517–1948*, London, SPCK, 1954, 735–740.

35 Willem Adolph Visser 't Hooft, "Our Ecumenical Task in the Light of History," *EcRev* 7, 1955, 309–320.

8 Cold War and Eastern Orthodoxy

The success of Amsterdam 1948 was interpreted by Visser 't Hooft as a victory of the Holy Spirit over the weaknesses of people and their divisions and an apex in the history of the church in a vulnerable phase of world history. However, he also saw its drawbacks, and two important rejections were examples of this. While relationships with the Greek Orthodox churches under Constantinople had always been good, the same could not be said about the contact with the Russian Orthodox Church. The invitation to this church and the churches in Eastern Europe that were related to it were rejected, since from Moscow it was reported that cooperation in the current form was impossible. Visser 't Hooft's reaction was that he might have accepted it if it had occurred for political reasons, but he considered the theological argumentation unacceptable. It was claimed by the Russians that the WCC was seeking to exercise power over member churches and thereby yield to the temptation that Christ had resisted, an allegation of course rejected by Visser 't Hooft. His view was that the Russian Church, which represented by far the largest part of Orthodoxy, was vital to the ecumenical movement. He was determined to do whatever he could to pave the way for Russian membership. First, he let the Russians know that they had not understood what the main concerns of the WCC were. Secondly, he developed a strategy to improve contact with them.

He considered it a vital matter for the ecumenical movement to regard these issues as urgent challenges. What was at stake was the significance of the church in the modern era, an urgent issue concerning all churches. According to Visser 't Hooft, both the Russian Orthodox Church and the Roman Catholic Church, in their rejections of the WCC in 1948 had not only misrepresented the identity of the council but also been inconsistent in their own self-understanding. Meeting in Toronto in 1950, the central committee adopted an important statement that explicitly rejected any suggestions that the WCC aimed to develop into a "superchurch." This constraint or disclaimer, already mentioned at Amsterdam, was now clearly expressed. For some, a huge world-church in one single organization was a feared nightmare, to others a vague ultimate ideal at the back of their minds. At Toronto it was now also stipulated that by joining the WCC a church did not recognize that all other members were fully-fledged churches. As far as Visser 't Hooft was concerned, the Toronto statement was only the beginning of a thorough ecclesiological reflection on the significance of the membership of the WCC.[36] The key question was what the ecumenical movement signified for the way in which each church thought about itself. Deriving from that, the next question was how people in every church thought about other churches.

Throughout the 1950s, Visser 't Hooft consciously relied on the independent course of the WCC as established at Amsterdam in 1948. Although he was well aware that this viewpoint was controversial, he implemented a consistent ecumenical policy involving both East and West. He was convinced that he was entrusted with a high calling to contribute to breaking the deadlock of the Cold War through the ecumenical idea of church. Theological insights in regard to Orthodoxy, which Visser 't Hooft explained in publications as early as 1933 and 1937, now repeatedly proved useful.[37] He successfully presented himself as an expert in the field of Orthodoxy. Systematically, he and his staff carefully avoided identification of the WCC with either West or East. Visser 't Hooft realized that those countries with churches under the Moscow Patriarchate were limited and restrained by Soviet regulations. With Josef Hromádka and Martin Niemöller venturing as pioneers to explore the possibilities of involving the Eastern Orthodox churches in the ecumenical movement, Visser 't Hooft was determined that the mandates derived from the Amsterdam and Evanston assemblies be used in order to do so, and for those churches to be nominated for membership in the WCC as soon as possible. What made him so resolute in this respect was a profound trust in the strength of the church proper. With its mystic core celebrated in a rich, heavenly oriented, mystic liturgy, the Eastern Orthodox Church cherished a valuable contemplative complement of being the church that, in his view, was much needed in the West with its strong emphasis on rational dogmatism, ethics, and an increasing focus on action in society, politically heavily influenced by strong secularizing tendencies. Vice versa, orthodoxy could be expected to be inspired by reflection on modern ethical issues. Apparently independent of historical circumstances, Eastern Orthodox membership could, Visser 't Hooft thought, intrinsically enrich the WCC. On several occasions, moments of Cold War crisis prevented the realization of his plan, for instance in 1956 during the Soviet invasion of Hungary, but Visser 't Hooft was not discouraged. In the end, he succeeded in convincing not only the Russian Church leadership, but also the Soviet authorities, that fruitful talks with the WCC were possible and would bear fruit for both sides. Serious meetings in Utrecht in 1959 ultimately resulted in the official nomination and full membership of the Russian, Rumanian, Bulgarian, and Polish Orthodox churches in New Delhi in 1961.

Visser 't Hooft himself made a notable impression on people and became a well-known speaker in Berlin at mass church meetings in the early 1950s, during periods of Cold War tension. One of the issues clearly revealing this, was his defense of Josef Hromádka. That this Czech theologian did not want to condemn Czech communists could be presented as a demonstration of an independent impartial course, but his refusal to condemn

36 "Statement on 'The Church, the Churches and the World Council of Churches': The Ecclesiological Significance of the World Council of Churches," in: Willem Adolph Visser 't Hooft, ed., *The Genesis and Formation of the World Council of Churches*, Geneva, WCC Publications, 1982, 112–120.

37 Willem Adolph Visser 't Hooft, *Le catholicisme non-romain*, Paris, A. Coueslant, 1933. Willem Adolph Visser 't Hooft & Joseph Houldsworth Oldham, *The Church and its Function in Society*, London, Allen & Unwin, 1937.

the Soviet invasion of Hungary in 1956 presented a new difficulty to Visser 't Hooft, and Hromádka lost a great deal of credit even with Visser 't Hooft on this occasion.

By consciously keeping the ecclesiological claims of the WCC modest, Visser 't Hooft and his staff took care to maintain the threshold of accession low. The Toronto statement of 1950 proved crucial. The fact that a member church did not automatically relativize its own identity was very important for churches that held the conviction that they were the true church, as the Russian Orthodox Church did. However, this entailed a cost, that is to say a certain vagueness concerning the ultimate goal of the movement, something that especially troubled those who appreciated higher levels of ecclesiological debate. If not a "superchurch," what was its ultimate aim? Was it really preparing the churches for full unity what was at stake?[38] It was a problem exorcised rather than solved. During the rapprochement with the Roman Catholic Church, slowly triggered from the early 1950s, this issue would become notably problematic and cause much confusion.

The secretary general's vision convinced many, but certainly not all. Objections arose, especially connected with suspicions that the Russian delegates, staff members, and employees would in the end abuse the WCC by exploiting it as a political podium. Visser 't Hooft was willing to listen to those who objected to Russian membership, but in his turn he was not convinced by them. To be sure, he was very much aware of the fact that the representatives of the Eastern Orthodox churches were not really free, most of the time, to express their opinions in public. But for this he wished to show patience and make allowances. He was confident, however, that all would end well thanks to the nature of the church itself, seeing very precisely the core light in the Russian Orthodox Church: the mystery of God's dwelling among human beings. The secretary general could not know that, precisely at the time when the Russian Orthodox Church became a member of the WCC, Nikita Khrushchev had started a new wave of religious persecutions in the USSR.

9 Roman Catholic Church: "Aggiornamento"

The second disappointing rejection in 1948 came from the Roman Catholic Church. Not that he had expected it to be a cofounder of the WCC, but Visser 't Hooft knew that there was a growing number of individual Roman Catholic members of the clergy who were very interested. However, the Roman Catholic *Monitum Cum compertum* of Jun 5, 1948 meant that no Roman Catholic was to attend an international meeting organized by the World Council (nor any other ecumenical gathering) without official permission. The Vatican now no longer condemned the (Protestant) ecumenical movement, as had been the case in 1928, but the request of the Dominican Yves Marie-Jospeh Congar to Cardinal Johannes de Jong, archbishop of Utrecht, to allow 14 Roman Catholic observers to attend the Amsterdam assembly was in vain. Nevertheless, there were interested Roman Catholics present in Amsterdam during the assembly. Without being literally present at the deliberations, they stayed at some distance from the meetings in a hotel and were carefully informed and provided with conference material by Visser 't Hooft. After the establishment of the WCC, in 1949, the Roman Catholic Church responded with the *Instructio De motione oecumenica* from the Holy Office which, among other things, recognized the ecumenical movement as worthy and inspired by the Holy Spirit.

Visser 't Hooft's strategic response to the Roman Catholic reluctant stand towards the predominantly Protestant ecumenical movement had always been to state that, just like the Russian Orthodox Patriarchate, the Roman Catholic Church leadership misunderstood the whole idea

38 Willem Adolph Visser 't Hooft, "The Substance of the Ecumenical Encounter," (unpublished text), Harvard, Dec 3–6, 1963, in: WCCA, 994.2.19/25.

of the WCC and that he was available to help clarify the issue. During a conference in the ecumenical center Istina in Paris, in September 1949, he discovered that many objections of the Roman Catholics to the ecumenical movement concerned, in their eyes, a defective understanding of the church on the part of the Protestants. His reaction was to put ecclesiology high on the agenda of the WCC. Furthermore, by developing knowledge of, and respect for, the Roman Catholic appreciation of tradition as a source of revelation along with the Bible, he hoped for a further rapprochement, needless to say, not intending in the slightest to diminish a single iota of the Protestant reverence for Scripture.

The secretary general found allies in the Dutch Roman Catholic priests Johannes Willebrands and Frans Thijssen of the SWV. After the lukewarm Vatican reaction to the establishment of the WCC in 1949, they endeavored to seek further contact with the Protestants. In 1952, Willebrands obtained permission from the Dutch bishops to set up a Catholic ecumenical association and became secretary of the CCEQ. Visser 't Hooft gladly responded and enjoyed the opportunity that a partly Dutch *entre nous* might then bring the churches closer together. In his opinion, this would not only help Rome to renew itself but also provide the Protestant churches with a deeper sense of unity. Visser 't Hooft never made a secret of the fact that it was his aim to make the Roman Catholic Church a member of the WCC. Willebrands had his own idea about the WCC, and Catholic ecclesiology was still rooted in the unionist idea of the return of non-Catholics back to the mother church. As long as this contrast in purposes did not become too concrete, everything went well. Neither Visser 't Hooft nor Willebrands apparently recognized that in due time their projects for each other were bound to fail. They both agreed to leave the most difficult questions to God.

Sometimes, things turned out for the worse due to clumsiness. This was the case in 1959 on the Greek island of Rhodes when Willebrands and the priest Christophe-Jean Dumont, present there in point of fact as observers for the WCC central committee, did not realize that they broke Visser 't Hooft's ecumenical rules by separately meeting the Orthodox representative attending the event. Once the media started to make things public, the story of an Orthodox–Roman Catholic rapprochement became viral. A very angry secretary general accused the Roman Catholics of amateurism, at best, or foul play, at worst, thereby spoiling the ecumenical atmosphere. A favorable consequence was that Rome realized that the ecumenical dossier required some coordination. Before long, in 1960, Visser 't Hooft gained a point of contact in the Vatican's SPCU. Rhodes was more than an incident, however. For a brief moment, it came to light how seriously different were not only the aims, but also the operating styles of the participants. A naïve but sincere Willebrands felt completely innocent when he unintentionally appeared to double-cross Visser 't Hooft's subtle strategies concerning the Eastern Orthodox.

In January 1959, Pope John XXIII took everybody, Protestants, Orthodox, and Roman Catholics alike by surprise by announcing a council. Initially, in Geneva, the impression was that delegates from all Christian denominations would be invited to go to Rome, but that proved not to be the case. What started with a Vatican initiative to bring up-to-date a corpus of canon law of 1917, quickly developed into a program of "aggiornamento" by means of which the church was to tackle questions of a new age.[39] For the new SPCU, presided over by Cardinal Augustin Bea with Willebrands as secretary, there was an important role to play in preparing Vatican II, which sessions started in 1962 and were brought to a close in 1965. There was a new openness, and those actively involved in the ecumenical dialogue, such as Willebrands and Visser 't Hooft, were able to utilize the council to have urgent issues discussed. Some of the

39 Karim Schelkens, John A. Dick & Jürgen Mettepenningen, *Aggiornamento?: Catholicism from Gregory XVI to Benedict XVI*, Leiden, Brill, 2014, 140 note 7, 146.

most important of these concerned freedom of religion, ecumenical relations, and mixed Protestant-Catholic marriages (the latter without success). To the outside world, Visser 't Hooft was careful not to exaggerate expectations, but he himself was impressed and cherished high expectations when, instead of the official Catholic monologue to which the WCC was accustomed, a new openness towards dialogue now emerged between the Roman Catholic Church and other churches.

In Geneva hopes for a Roman Catholic membership were still high, but in fact in the mid-1960s a period of considerable progress was drawing to a close. Vatican II consultations concerning ecumenism resulted, among other achievements, in the founding of the Joint Working Group with members of the WCC and of the Roman Catholic Church. This working group, of which much was expected, started its task in 1965 under the shared leadership of Visser 't Hooft and Willebrands, and is still active today.

After the retirement of Visser 't Hooft as secretary general the following year, it soon became obvious that this Joint Working Group was undoubtedly studying much and that cooperation on certain dossiers was encouraged, but that zest concerning renewal and concrete progress in ecumenical relations in Rome was virtually exhausted. Willebrands requested and received patience from the WCC, but when in 1969 Pope Paul VI, during his visit to the ecumenical center in Geneva, presented himself as the apostle Peter, Visser 't Hooft concluded that a brief, promising period of dynamism had come to an end. This was followed by a different, and once again more static, era in WCC relations with the Roman Catholic Church.

10 Changing Ecumenical Perspectives in a Changing World

Vatican II was still in progress when the WCC was itself unsuccessful in reaching the consensus in the ecumenical debate on ecclesiology for which Visser 't Hooft had asked at the Amsterdam conference in 1948. This became clear in 1963 at the Faith and Order conference in Montreal, where the German theologian Ernst Käsemann demonstrated that traces of at least seven ecclesiologies were recognizable within the New Testament. These were church models with ancient roots that could not easily be harmonized, not even by a fully comprehensive ecumenical dialogue, thus restricting the possibilities of consensus.[40] Ecumenical perspectives were now shifting rapidly in three other important ways: new member churches exerted their influence and changed priorities, the whole idea of classic Christian missionary work was now being challenged, and, perhaps most important, a new postwar generation had grown up. Most of these younger believers no longer aspired to listen patiently to expert religious leaders explaining God's plans for the world. The world of the fourth assembly in Uppsala in 1968 would definitely be a different place.

In New Delhi in 1961, this was still unknown territory, yet the signs of change to come were all there. A record number of 23 churches applied for membership: most of them were new churches that had developed out of missionary work in the former colonies in Africa, but noteworthy were also four Eastern Orthodox churches. The meetings were discernibly less dominated by older white men from Europe and North America. The IMC became an integral part of the WCC, at the very time when the juxtaposition of missionary work resulted in its identity crisis. Was it really the task of the Christian missionary to go to countries

40 See Ernst Käsemann, *Essays on New Testament Themes*, London, SCM Press, 1964. Interview with Hendrikus Berkhof, "Brood en Spelen," IKON-radio, Jul 6, 1985, Hilversum, Nederlands Instituut voor Beeld en Geluid. Only after a few years Visser 't Hooft was able to admit his acceptance of ecclesiological pluriformity in the New Testament. See the speech Visser 't Hooft gave at the synod of the Gereformeerde Kerken in Nederland, in: Kenmerk, IKOR-televisie, Sep 9, 1969, Hilversum, Nederlands Instituut voor Beeld en Geluid.

in Africa and Asia and convert people to the European way of believing in Christ?

Somehow the missions seemed to get stuck between secularization in the North and West and decolonization in the South and East. A fundamental insecurity had to face the new self-chosen paths of young churches. For Visser 't Hooft, missions were an irreplaceable pioneering part of the ecumenical movement, and he made it his aim to integrate the IMC into the WCC as soon as possible. He never denied local cultures their own interpretations of Jesus, provided they respected the exclusive role attributed to him in Western theology. This Christocentrism implied a strong aversion toward syncretism, meaning the uncritical mixing of elements from various religions. In his view, this was the wrong way to conduct interreligious dialogue.[41] When he encountered forms of syncretism, for instance when Buddha, Mahatma Gandhi, and Jesus were somehow placed on the same level, he strongly rejected it. He realized that missions were on the decline and would have to renew themselves in order to survive. However, he did not really have any clear ideas as to how this might be obtained. He had no intention of exchanging missionary work itself for equipollent interreligious dialogue and development aid, valuable as he thought the latter to be.

Visser 't Hooft, with his rich experience in youth organizations such as the YMCA and the WSCF, had always been a much appreciated speaker by young people, but after 1960 he increasingly felt a new tension with the young for whom everything took too long, and the achievements concerning church unity were not adequate. Ecumenical institutions that in the 1950s could be presented as symptoms of renewal, in the 1960s were rejected as old-fashioned elements protecting the *status quo* by representatives of a new, dynamic, and impatient generation. Extended negotiations on theologically and institutionally sustained church unity appeared to interest a new generation less and less. They did not really care for ecclesiology in a world that was rent by racism, proxy colonial wars defending capitalism, and a wealthy Western world fortifying itself. Visser 't Hooft wanted to demonstrate his understanding of these concerns, but his reaction was predominantly a call for patience and loyalty to Christian institutions. A more revolutionary social ethics replaced the responsible society, forms of liberation theology and the more activist call for justice and space for the rebellious freethinking young became key themes in the ecumenical movement. Visser 't Hooft understood that he needed to respond positively and he did so, for instance, in Uppsala in 1968. Yet time and again his urge to preach interfered, despite his desire to listen to the experiences of young people. He had always denounced forms of *œcuménisme sauvage*, or wild ecumenism, of groups celebrating intercommunion without church leadership approval. In the years before his death, a Visser 't Hooft by now impatient himself, thought the time was ripe to celebrate together, as Christians standing in different traditions, the Eucharist and the Lord's Supper as one community. As far as the authentic content of the experience was concerned, personally he considered consensus sufficient.[42] He was still self-confident in his faith, but also much less assured now as far as the vicissitudes of the times were concerned.

41 Willem Adolph Visser 't Hooft, *No other Name: The Choice between Syncretism and Christian Universalism*, London, SCM Press, 1963.

Bibliography

Leustean, Lucian N., *The Ecumenical Movement & the Making of the European Community*, Oxford, Oxford University Press, 2014.

Man's Disorder and God's Design: An Ecumenical Study Prepared under the Auspices of the World Council of Churches, 4 vols., New York, Harper & Brothers, 1948.

Schubert, Jan, *Willem Adolph Visser 't Hooft (1900–1985): Ökumene und Europa*, Göttingen, Vandenhoeck & Ruprecht, 2017.

42 Zeilstra, *Visser 't Hooft (1980–1985)*, 502.

Visser 't Hooft, Willem Adolf, *The Background of the Social Gospel in America*, Haarlem, Tjeenk Willink & Zoon, 1928.

Visser 't Hooft, Willem Adolf, *The Kingship of Christ: An Interpretation of Recent European Theology*, New York, Harper & Brothers, 1948.

Visser 't Hooft, Willem Adolf, *The Task of the World Council of Churches: Report Presented on Behalf of the Provisional Committee*, 1948.

Visser 't Hooft, Willem Adolf, *No Other Name: The Choice between Syncretism and Christian Universalism*, London, SCM Press, 1963.

Visser 't Hooft, Willem Adolf, *Heel de kerk voor heel de wereld: Belang van de oecumene*, Utrecht, Ambo – Bosch & Keuning, 1968, 13.

Visser 't Hooft, Willem Adolf, *Memoirs*, London, SCM Press, 1973.

Visser't Hooft, Willem Adolf, ed., *The Genesis and Formation of the World Council of Churches*, Geneva, WCC Publications, 1982.

Zeilstra, Jurjen A., *European Unity in Ecumenical Thinking (1937–1948)*, Zoetermeer, Uitgeverij Boekencentrum, 1995.

Zeilstra, Jurjen A., *Visser 't Hooft (1900–1985): Een leven voor de oecumene*, Middelburg, Skandalon, 2018.

Zeilstra, Jurjen A., "Une vie vouée à l'oecuménisme," *Positions Luthériennes* 67/1, 2019, 7–35.

Zeilstra, Jurjen A., *Visser 't Hooft (1900–1985): Living for the Unity of the Church*, Amsterdam, Amsterdam University Press, 2020.

CHAPTER 19

America and Ecumenism during the Cold War

Dianne Kirby

1 Introduction

The 21st century has seen a wealth of research and literature devoted to either the decline of religion in America or its growing grip on power.[1] There has been decline, largely in the mainstream liberal Protestant churches identified with the ecumenical movement[2] while the growth has been in the conservative churches, largely evangelical, fundamentalist, often anti-ecumenical. The power shift in terms of influence and access to power and funding has been from the ecumenical to the anti-ecumenical churches. The Cold War was the period in which the shift took place and was a significant contributor to, if not the main cause of it as the vehicle that facilitated America's assumption of a global role that irrevocably changed the nation and shaped the postwar world. The impact of the Cold War on the religiopolitical landscape of the United States is an immensely rich and complex story, riven by the diverse and conflicting sociopolitical and economic views of Christians, not to mention doctrinal differences.[3] For American ecumenists the emerging Cold War initially seemed an opportunity, but it proved instead a challenge to their place in American society with repercussions for their international colleagues. Early American ecumenists brought essential skills to the nascent ecumenical movement. John R. Mott was an institution builder, John Foster Dulles a political heavyweight, Reinhold and Helmut Richard Niebuhr intellectual activist theologians, not to mention others such as Henry P. Van Dusen, Francis P. Miller, Georgia Harkness, Samuel McCrea Cavert, and John Bennett who built the theological and organizational structures of Protestant international engagement. Heather A. Warren has rightly stressed the significance of American ecumenists owing to "their genius for organization that made them unique, a standing association of like-minded intellectuals with the managerial acumen and drive to develop the ecumenical idea into a reality."[4] At home, American ecumenists "unabashedly presumed leadership for determining America's moral code, defining its national ideals in terms of foreign policy."[5] Such presumptions

1 George Marsden, *The Twilight of the American Enlightenment: The 1950s and the Crisis of Liberal Belief*, New York, Basic Books, 2014; Ross Douthat, *Bad Religion: How We became a Nation of Heretics*, New York, Free Press, 2012; Joseph Bottum, *An Anxious Age: The Post-Protestant Ethic and the Spirit of America*, New York, Image Books, 2014; Susan George, *Hijacking America: How the Religious and Secular Right Changed what Americans Think*, Cambridge, Polity Press, 2008; Chris Hedges, *American Fascists: The Christian Right and the War on America*, New York, Free Press, 2007.

2 There is no regional ecumenical conference for North America. Both the Canadian Council of Churches and the NCC are independent. The Protestant churches – American Baptist churches, the Disciples of Christ, the Episcopal Church, the ELCA, the Presbyterian Church (USA), the United Church of Christ (earlier the Congregational Church), and the United Methodist Church – were a prevalent influence in American society from the colonial period until World War II. With political access and arbiters of the nation's moral values, they were part of the establishment.

3 Dianne Kirby, "The Cold War and American Religion," in: *Oxford Encyclopedia of Religion in America*, May 24, 2017, text available at <https://oxfordre.com/religion/display/10.1093/acrefore/9780199340378.001.0001/acrefore-9780199340378-e-398> (accessed Apr 12, 2024).

4 Heather A. Warren, *Theologians of a New World Order: Reinhold Niebuhr and the Christian Realists (1920–1948)*, Oxford, Oxford University Press, 1997, 5.

5 Warren, *Theologians of a New World Order*, 4.

did not change with the advent of the Cold War, but they most certainly had by the end of it.

Willem Adolph Visser 't Hooft, secretary general from the inception of the WCC, the institutional expression of the ecumenical movement, recalled in his *Memoirs* that "some of the gravest tensions in the life of the council were caused by the political and ideological divisions of the cold war period."[6] Visser 't Hooft's "turbulent post-war world"[7] saw the never static Cold War evolve through a number of stages, all of which entailed consequences for ecumenism in and beyond America. In the immediate aftermath of World War II there was hope that continued cooperation could engender a more peaceful and prosperous world order. Fear and mistrust prevailed, however, with each side blaming the other for the rising tensions, exacerbated by the Chinese communist revolution, the Soviet acquisition of nuclear weapons, and of course the Korean War, perhaps the coldest part of the Cold War. Albeit the peace potential offered by de-Stalinization failed to materialize, the encounter with MAD engendered by the Cuban Missile Crisis led eventually to a period of détente that offered the churches opportunities for peacemaking and engagement with their counterparts behind the Iron Curtain. This was followed, however, by a heightening of tensions over nuclear weapons and Ronald Reagan's Star Wars initiative. Reagan, who described himself as a born-again-Christian, mobilized the Christian Right as part of his electoral strategy of winning the White House and memorably referred to the Soviet Union as an "evil empire." Having revived the Cold War, he subsequently reversed stance and his presidency witnessed the final phase, the ending of the Cold War.

All stages of the Cold War, imbued throughout with the fear of nuclear warfare, were fraught with dangers for ecumenists. Their conviction, given urgent impetus by the two world wars, the Great Depression, and the rise of totalitarianism, was that Western civilization was in a crisis that required the churches to concern themselves intelligently and seriously with international affairs, as was reflected in new ecumenical structures, such as the CCIA, erected after the war.[8] Wartime disorganization, dislocation, and distress were perceived as creating a vacuum that presented opportunities for the renewal of Christian life, bringing hope out of chaos. Wartime rhetoric promised a new social and political order.[9] Combined with Christian insistence that the church could provide the common moral code a just and humane system required, there appeared a realistic prospect of reestablishing the church as an influential institution contributing to national and international reconstruction and revitalization.[10]

Theoretically, ecumenism is a strategy by which the church holds together as a distinct entity differentiated from political society. The intent is not to remain aloof from, but to engage with and influence the latter. The bold ecumenical claim for "the right of the church as an institution to occupy itself with the problems of this world," required access to and influence within society's corridors of power.[11] Given the extent to which the Allies drew on support from Christian leaders for their war effort, expectations were high.

6 Willem Adolph Visser 't Hooft, *Memoirs*, London, SCM Press, 1973, 219. It is worth noting that still today the Christian Right attributes culpability for the decline of the mainline Protestant churches to the ecumenical movement. See Joseph Bottum, "The Death of Protestant America: A Political Theory of the Protestant Mainline," *First Things*, August 2008.

7 Visser 't Hooft, *Memoirs*, 219.

8 Keith G. Robbins, "Britain, 1940 and 'Christian Civilization,'" in: Derek Beales & Geoffrey Best, eds., *History, Society and the Churches: Essays in Honour of Owen Chadwick*, Cambridge, Cambridge University Press, 1985, 279–300. See in this volume the chapter by Dino Knudsen.

9 Dianne Kirby, "From Bridge to Divide: East–West Relations and Christianity during the Second World War and Early Cold War," *IHR* 36/4, 2014, 721–744.

10 George Bell, "The Christian Church and World Peace," Jul 22, 1957, in: Lambeth Palace Library, Bishop George Bell Papers, vol. 349, 44–62.

11 Darril Hudson, *The Ecumenical Movement in World Affairs*, London, Weidenfeld & Nicolson, 1969, 3.

The churches had received notable government support for the postwar planning that they had undertaken during the war and contributed to the creation of the United Nations.[12] As the war drew to a close, political and ecumenical leaders looked to one another as a means to realize their respective postwar aims. Political hopes on the part of the government for a productive partnership with the churches in the postwar period were equally high. Christian missionaries had been forerunners for America's informal model of imperialism that unashamedly sought to remake the world in its own image. After World War I, missions were an "essential ingredient in the formation of American internationalism."[13] They were also an essential ingredient in the formation of the ecumenical movement, for which the financial and administrative responsibilities shifted to the United States when Europe was ravaged by World War II.[14] The Cold War would reveal how very different were ecumenical aims from those of the American government, and how unequal, in reality, was the church-state relationship. Secular maneuvering to secure Christian sanction for Cold War policies created a dilemma for ecumenical Christians: endorse America's Cold War project or adhere to ecumenical and prophetic aspirations. Adhering exclusively to the latter at a time when America's political establishment rather blatantly looked to weaponize Christianity, and indeed all moral and religious forces, carried huge risks, not least in terms of reducing their assumed political influence.[15] At the same time, certainly in the early years of the Cold War, anti-communist sentiments prevailed in all the churches. The inadequacies of their own nation seemed far less threatening than those of its Soviet and Chinese enemies. Many succumbed to the notion of "lesser evil" and endorsed the American mission.

2 Spiritual-Industrial Complex

It is important to recognize the huge impact on its own and other societies of America's promotion of the Cold War as a cosmic struggle between good and evil.[16] The early Cold War was an era when Christianity held an apparently meaningful societal role that embraced the political. It was a time when even the most secularized minds and institutions remained imbued with concepts that derived from a Christian ethos.[17] Its significance was reflected in the postwar construction of a "spiritual-industrial complex" to promote America's Cold War ambitions whilst containing those of the Soviet Union. A beneficiary of state sanction and commercial talent, the spiritual-industrial complex: "worked to foment a religious revival that was conceived in boardrooms rather than camp meetings, steered by Madison Avenue and Hollywood suits rather than traveling preachers, and measured with a statistical precision."[18] The nature of the revival was to advantage the most conservative anti-communist

12 John S. Nurser, *For All Peoples and All Nations: The Ecumenical Church and Human Rights*, Washington DC, Georgetown University Press, 2005.

13 Andrew Preston, *Sword of the Spirit, Shield of Faith: Religion in American War and Diplomacy*, New York, Alfred A. Knopf, 2012, 181. See also Andrew F. Walls, "World Christianity, the Missionary Movement and the Ugly American," in: Wade Clark Roof, ed., *World Order and Religion*, Albany, State University of New York Press, 1991, 147–172.

14 Dianne Kirby, "The Roots of the Religious Cold War: Pre-Cold War Factors," *SocSci* 7/56, 2018, available at <https://www.mdpi.com/2076-0760/7/4/56> (accessed Apr 12, 2024).

15 Dianne Kirby, "Truman's Holy Alliance: The President, the Pope and the Origins of the Cold War," *Borderlines: Studies in American Culture* 4/1, 1997, 1–17.

16 Ian Jones, "The Clergy, the Cold War and the Mission of the Local Church: England ca. 1945–60," in: Dianne Kirby, ed., *Religion and the Cold War*, Basingstoke, Palgrave Macmillan, 2003, 188–199.

17 Dianne Kirby, "Divinely Sanctioned: The Anglo-American Cold War Alliance and the Defence of Western Civilisation and Christianity (1945–48)," *JCH* 35/3, 2000, 385–412.

18 Jonathan P. Herzog, *The Spiritual-Industrial Complex: America's Religious Battle against Communism in the Early Cold War*, Oxford, Oxford University Press, 2011, 7.

churches, especially fundamentalist and evangelical. The Cold War climate perfectly suited American fundamentalist movements which were imbued with a Manichaean worldview with "a preference for dualities that tolerates no moderation or moderates, no compromise or compromisers."[19]

Initially, the postwar revival was welcomed by ecumenists. Churches belonging to the FCC were committed to spiritual recruitment and the department of evangelism was its largest branch by 1946. "The WCC's 'supreme call' in a 'global age,' Van Dusen had anticipated, was for 'united evangelism.'"[20] Billy Graham was invited to speak at the theological seminaries of Union and Princeton universities. Graham, criticized by Reinhold Niebuhr for disregarding social injustice, rallied to the latter's proposition that he deploy his prestige to buttress the burgeoning civil rights movement at a time when the shame of segregation marred America's moral position. A fragile partnership with opposition in both camps, the liberal-conservative rapprochement of the 1940s and 1950s was shattered by the Vietnam War.[21]

Today Cold War historians acknowledge that the Soviet threat was greatly exaggerated to facilitate "fear of the other" as the key mobilizing resource in transforming the Soviet Union from a wartime ally against fascism into a demonic threat committed to destroying all freedoms and religions.[22] Ecumenical leaders, as with most Christians of that era, were naturally, and for good reason, anti-communist and anti-Soviet. However, a defining tenet of ecumenism "is an understanding of human society that identifies fear of the 'other' as one of the greatest evils we face."[23] With a deliberately cultivated "fear of the other" at the heart of America's Cold War propaganda, some sort of collision between government and ecumenical forces was inevitable. Ecumenists initially succumbed, as did most of their fellow citizens, to America's ubiquitous Cold War propaganda. As Odd Arne Westad has asserted: "Contrary to the general perception at the time, it was the United States that was the propaganda master of the Cold War, in terms of both effort and resources spent."[24] In contrast, Soviet propaganda was clumsy and often counterproductive. Nonetheless, the ecumenical ideal demanded working toward the unity of all Christian churches, regardless of their location or political allegiances. This required engagement and dialogue with churches in communist regimes, a misunderstood and much maligned practice in America.

For ecumenists, the Cold War led to over four decades of testing church-state relations, exacerbated by the conflicting pressures from the domestic arena and those coming from the international ecumenical community. American ecumenists were subjected to competing demands. The transnational makeup of the ecumenical movement meant pressure not just from the Geneva headquarters of the WCC, but also from various national ecumenical bodies and international organizations. In the Cold War context of East and West mobilizing their respective religious resources, the pressure from the home front demanded loyalty in terms of adherence to the anti-communist consensus and support for the spiritual-industrial complex. America's deeply nationalist population subscribed to a view of their nation, assiduously cultivated in the early Cold War, as a benign force.

19 Martin E. Marty, "The Global Context of Ecumenism (1968–2000)," in: *A History of the Ecumenical Movement*, vol. 3, John Briggs, Mercy Oduyoye & Georges Tsetsis, eds., *1968–2000*, Geneva, WCC Publications, 2004, 3–22, here 7.

20 Mark Thomas Edwards, "Cold War Connections: The Vital Center of Liberal and Conservative Evangelicalism," in: Paul Mojzes, ed., *North American Churches and the Cold War*, Grand Rapids, Eerdmans, 2018, 449–463, here 460.

21 Edwards, "Cold War Connections."

22 Elaine Tyler May, *Fortress America: How We Embraced Fear and Abandoned Democracy*, New York, Basic Books, 2017.

23 Thomas Ryan, "What Does It Mean to Be Ecumenical?," available at <https://tomryancsp.org/WhatDoesItMeanTodayToBeEcumenical.html> (accessed Apr 12, 2024).

24 Odd Arne Westad, "The New International History of the Cold War: Three (Possible) Paradigms," *DH* 24/4, 2000, 551–565, here 558.

They were largely supportive of United States foreign policy.

From within the wider ecumenical movement, which included churches behind the Iron Curtain and across the developing world, came alternative views of the East-West conflict, and of America. The rise of fascism and communism in the 1920s and early 1930s originally brought church-state issues to the fore of ecumenical discussions.[25] These culminated at the 1937 Oxford conference, which offered strategic guidelines and practical suggestions for churches confronting a totalitarian state. The US was not a totalitarian state. Indeed, it provided all the essential conditions determined necessary for ecumenical churches to realize their primary duties.[26] This, of course, increased the imperative for American ecumenists to adhere to the movement's goals, elaborated during the 1937 Oxford conference on Church, Community, and State. These posited the state as the guarantor and servant of justice, but also insisted on the primacy of obedience to God over the state. It was the church's duty to criticize a state that departs from standards set out in God's word. Most important, the church had a "duty" of disobedience to a state that fails to uphold "the standards of justice set forth in the Word of God."[27] In contrast to most of their evangelical counterparts, ecumenical Christians aspired more to bringing Christianity into the world rather than people into the churches. Attempts to attain ecumenical goals and standards would bring ecumenical leaders into conflict with not only the Cold War state, but also non-ecumenical Christians and even many of their own clergy and parishioners.

In spite, or perhaps because of, the constitutional separation between church and state, America's manufactured postwar religious revival equated Americanism with Christianity and encouraged civil religion. According Christianity a leading role in the morality play drama intended to bolster America's ideological campaign, allowed the technically secular nation to target Marxist atheism, considered the Achilles' heel of Soviet communism. Ideologically America lacked a theoretical alternative that could match the universal appeal of communism with which the Soviets were armed. Instead, American propagandists elevated anti-communism to doctrinal status, a process facilitated by its religious roots, and combined it with the rhetoric of absolutist anti-communism to become a Western ideological counter to Marxism. Absolutist anti-communism claimed that communism was a supreme and unqualified evil bent on world domination. Christian anti-communism asserted communism was committed to the destruction of all religion.[28] From the blending of absolutist anti-communism with its Christian counterpart emerged the powerful propaganda construct of the godless Soviet bogey. It reinforced and added to America's portrayal of an irrational foe impervious to the normal modes of diplomacy, committed to the destruction not simply of the United States but also Christian inspired western civilisation. It provided the policy of containment with a moral framework crucial to consolidating support at home and abroad for America's assumption of the leadership of the free world.

The godless Soviet bogey became an immensely potent image to which most Christian leaders, and certainly their congregations, initially subscribed. However, it was subsequently questioned by a number of ecumenically-minded Christians as it came to inform the popular patriotism and civic

---

25 Dianne Kirby, "Christian Co-Operation and the Ecumenical Ideal in the 1930s and 1940s," *ERH* 8/1, 2001, 37–60.

26 These were identified as: (a) freedom to determine its faith and creed; (b) freedom of public and private worship, preaching, and teaching, (c) freedom from any imposition by the state of religious ceremonies and forms of worship; (d) freedom to determine the nature of its government and the qualifications of its ministers and members; (e) freedom to control the education of its ministers, to give religious instruction to its youths, and to provide adequate development of their religious life; (f) freedom of Christian service and missionary activity, both home and foreign.

27 Arne Hassing, *Church Resistance to Norway (1940–1945)*, Washington DC, University of Washington Press, 2014, 31.

28 Dianne Kirby, "Christian Anti-Communism," *TCC* 7/7, 2014, 126–152.

religion that marked America's postwar revival. Their concerns about the instrumentalization of Christianity and the way in which the American way of life was assigned the status of religion was not shared by the general population. For conservative Christians, particularly of the evangelical and fundamentalist varieties, the "godless Soviet bogy" became a determining component informing their worldview. They deemed as subversive ecumenical efforts to distinguish between Christian anti-communism and its Cold War religiopolitical counterpart.

3 John Foster Dulles

A key figure important to understanding American ecumenism and its relationship with government is John Foster Dulles. During World War II the ecumenical FCC had established the CJDP under his chairmanship. He was also a contributor to the United Nations project to which ecumenists were committed.[29] The commission's stated mission was to "clarify the mind of our churches regarding the moral, political and economic foundations of an enduring peace."[30] Dulles, with a wealth of political and Christian connections, subsequently attained one of the highest political offices in the land, becoming secretary of state under President Dwight D. Eisenhower. Notably, Eisenhower was himself involved with a variety of political groups concerned with shaping the postwar world, including a secret CFR project addressing postwar issues for the State Department.[31]

Together in the political realm, these two men would consolidate the religious cold war initiated under the Harry S. Truman administration. Of significance, therefore, is that none of the various politico-religious endeavors initiated during World War II sought to put the church at the core of the new world order. The political strategy was to instrumentalize the churches to help develop and secure the latter's acceptance. In cooperating with these initiatives, America's ecumenical leaders were working not for a new Christendom, but to persuade a churchgoing nation of the necessity of international cooperation, not isolation, once peace was secured. Such cooperation, at least in the short term, revitalized their relations with policymakers and their own position as players on the home front and in the international arena.

Dulles exemplified how easily some ecumenical churchmen in this period transited between state and church. Significantly, he came "to personify the Cold War as an unambiguous struggle between good and evil."[32] Whether speaking as a churchman or a statesman, Dulles was instrumental in cultivating "fear of the other." The end of World War II brought realization to Dulles that his nation was strong and united when confronted by danger. Peace, however, brought division over not simply what America's global role ought to be, but even whether it should have a global role, such being a radical departure from traditional US foreign policy.[33] Parochial, isolationist, anti-imperialist, suspicious of entangling alliances, the prospect of world leadership sat uneasily with the American people. Dulles became party to purposefully exaggerating the Soviet threat, considered necessary by the Truman administration, to persuade the American people to support the assumption of the global interventionism required to assure America's economic well-being.[34]

29 Nurser, *For All Peoples and All Nations*.

30 *Federal Council of the Churches of Christ in America, Biennial Report*, 1940, 182–184.

31 Ronald W. Pruessen, *John Foster Dulles: The Road to Power*, New York, Free Press, 1982, 186.

32 Leo Ribuffo, "Religion and American Foreign Policy," *TNI* 52, 1998, available at <https://nationalinterest.org/article/religion-and-american-foreign-policy-the-story-of-a-complex-relationship-760?page=0%2C3> (accessed Apr 12, 2024).

33 Walter Russell Mead, *Special Providence: American Foreign Policy and How It Changed the World*, London, Routledge, 2002.

34 Dianne Kirby, "John Foster Dulles: Moralism and Anti-Communism," *JTS* 6/3, 2009, 279–289.

When he became secretary of state responsible for upholding the Cold War consensus amongst America's allies, more than Soviet aggression, Dulles feared the lack of an international ethos in the West could cause disunity, undermining the sort of politically structured societies he envisioned: "Even if the Soviet threat were totally to disappear would we be blind to the danger that the West may destroy itself?"[35] Dulles was convinced that a universal values-based creed, namely Christianity, was essential for world order.

Dulles' accession to formal political power as secretary of state was in the family tradition, his grandfather and an uncle had also been secretaries of state. From 1919 when he was involved in economic and reparations negotiations at Versailles, through the 1930s when he became involved with the ecumenical movement's attempts to halt the tides of war, to World War II when he chaired the CJDP, the life of John Foster Dulles was marked by participation in crucial political and religious international developments. Following the war, he consolidated his reputation as a Christian statesman and strengthened his position in the Republican Party, especially as a bipartisan internationalist acting as a foreign policy advisor to the Democrat administration of President Truman.

Dulles' standing in the Christian community meant he was ideally placed to help first Truman and then Eisenhower construct a Cold War framework that arrogated Christianity as part of a religiopolitical campaign that fomented fear of the Soviet Union alongside an idealization of America that drew on the notion of divine choseness that has informed the nation's history, and indeed the very concept of America, from its colonial beginning.[36] With the waning of domestic Cold War repression, McCarthyism, Dulles was criticized by fellow ecumenists for his excessive self-righteous rhetoric and image as "a Presbyterian moralist ever ready – and eager – to do battle with the devil."[37] In the early Cold War, however, it was precisely these attributes "that had made Dulles so widely respected and his appointment as secretary of state such a foregone conclusion."[38]

4 Harry S. Truman and the WCC

The seeds of confrontation between ecumenical Christians and their respective states were sewn during the early Cold War when Truman, possessed of a seemingly sincere if simplistic faith, allowed himself to be persuaded by Franklin Delano Roosevelt's wartime representative to the Holy See, Myron C. Taylor, that: "The cause of Communism versus Christianity and Democracy transcends minor differences in Christian creeds."[39] Truman returned Taylor to the Vatican in 1946. In August 1947 the president affected a heavily publicized letter exchange with Pius XII, the locus of ideological opposition to and an avowed enemy of Soviet communism at a time when the Roman Catholic Church was deeply implicated in a range of anti-Soviet activities, as Eastern and Western policymakers well knew.[40] As each pledged their resources to a lasting peace built on Christian principles and an alliance based on shared moral and spiritual values, it was clear Truman sought to

35 John A. Bernbaum, Lisle A. Rose & Charles S. Sampson, eds., *Foreign Relations of the United States (1952–1954): Western European Security*, vol. 5, part 1, Washington DC, United States Government Printing Office, 1983, available at <https://history.state.gov/historicaldocuments/frus1952-54v05p1/d238> (accessed Apr 12, 2024).

36 This is a well-explored theme in American history books, see Conrad Cherry, ed., *God's New Israel: Religious Interpretations of American Destiny*, Chapel Hill, University of North Carolina Press, 1998.

37 Dianne Kirby, "John Foster Dulles: Moralism and anti-communism," *Journal of Transatlantic Studies* 6/3, 2009, 279–289, here 80.

38 Seth Jacobs, *America's Miracle Man in Vietnam: Ngo Dinh Diem, Religion, Race, and U.S. Intervention in Southeast Asia*, Durham, Duke University Press, 2005, 275.

39 M.C. Taylor to H.S. Truman, Jun 21, 1946, in: National Archives, Harry S. Truman Presidential Library and Museum, Taylor, Myron C. Papers, box 3.

40 Michael Phayer, *Pius XII, the Holocaust, and the Cold War*, Bloomington, Indiana University Press, 2008.

promote containment as a religio-moral obligation. Instead the alliance was widely interpreted as the launch of an anti-Red crusade.[41] Credited with the electoral defeat of the Italian Communist Party, it added a spiritual component to America's containment strategy, complementing the political and economic policies embedded in the Truman Doctrine and Marshall Plan.

Truman told his wife Bess, "if I can mobilize the people who believe in a moral world against the Bolshevik materialists ... we can win this fight."[42] Albeit the United States-Vatican alliance appeared to justify containment whilst blaming the Soviets for the breakdown in relations, some American ecumenical Protestant leaders expressed significant opposition to "any kind of diplomatic relationship that seems to unite Protestantism with Catholicism in a common war against Russia."[43] There was speculation in the American religious press that the pope was manipulating United States foreign policy to help him build up a Catholic western Europe.[44] As Robert Ellwood observed: "The working alliance between the world's two great anti-communist forces, the United States and the Vatican, ... made the spiritual children of Martin Luther uneasy."[45] Truman's plan, however, was but an extension into the international arena of America's spiritual-industrial complex.

As the diverse groups that made up the spiritual-industrial complex promoted patriotism and civic religion, Truman appealed in March 1946 for a moral and spiritual awakening, seeking support from America's key faith communities, Protestant, Catholic, and Jewish. All initially perceived a welcome enterprise.[46] The communist threat offered a culturally acceptable scapegoat against which clergy may have thought they could reforge the waning connection between religious duty, social participation, and national identity. However, the revival's superficiality and its preoccupation with capitalism and Americanism was cause for concern for numerous ecumenists.[47] Over time, the way in which Christianity was instrumentalized in service of the state, accompanied by apocalyptic rhetoric in a nuclear age, inevitably meant discord between America's ecumenical leaders and its political establishment.[48]

The way in which government interventions aimed at mobilizing religious resources would impact the ecumenical movement abroad as well as at home became apparent when Truman sought not simply to enroll it into his plans, but also wanted to secure the attendance of official papal delegates at the inaugural meeting of the WCC in Amsterdam in August 1948. Believing that the Soviet threat ought to unite all Christians, Truman disregarded, that is if he even knew about, the antipathy provoked between the ecumenical movement and the Vatican by the latter's 1928 encyclical *Mortalium animos*.[49] It indicted the former for theological indifferentism and woolly liberalism, part of the general failure of Protestantism,

41 See Alex Karmakovic, *The Myron C. Taylor Appointment: Background, Religious Reaction, Constitutionality*, Ph.D. thesis, University of Minnesota, 1967.

42 Robert H. Ferrell, ed., *Dear Bess: The Letters from Harry to Bess Truman (1910–1959)*, New York, W.W. Norton, 1983, 551.

43 Dianne Kirby, "Harry S. Truman's International Religious Anti-Communist Front, the Archbishop of Canterbury and the 1948 Inaugural Assembly of the World Council of Churches," *CBH* 15/4, 2001, 35–70, here 42.

44 See the editorial "Is the Cold War a Holy War?," *Christian Century*, Jan 11, 1950.

45 Robert S. Ellwood, *The Fifties Spiritual Marketplace: American Religion in a Decade of Conflict*, New Brunswick, Rutgers University Press, 1997, 52.

46 Harry S. Truman, *Address in Columbus at a Conference of the Federal Council of Churches*, Mar 6, 1946, available at <https://www.presidency.ucsb.edu/documents/address-columbus-conference-the-federal-council-churches> (accessed Apr 12, 2024).

47 Ellwood, *The Fifties Spiritual Marketplace*, 10–11.

48 For a meticulously researched account of this process for America's largest ecumenical body see Jill K. Gill, *Embattled Ecumenism: The National Council of Churches, the Vietnam War, and the Trials of the Protestant Left*, Dekalb, Northern Illinois University Press, 2011.

49 Pius XI, *Mortalium animos*, Jan 6, 1928. On *Mortalium animos* see the chapter by Marie Levant in the first volume of this work.

and forbade Catholic support for or countenance of a false Christianity quite alien to the one Church of Christ. Truman was aware of and had undoubtedly shared American Protestantism's inherent suspicion of the Catholic Church, viewed as propagandistic, opportunistic, power hungry, and "one of democracy's greatest enemies." During World War II American Protestants thought that Catholics were poised to pounce on democracy while it was weak and destroy it, believing that Catholicism was essentially totalitarian, the arch enemy of democracy and of its principle guardian, Protestantism.[50]

Protestant alarm over the president's partnership with the pope was compounded by the way in which McCarthyism reflected the hallmarks of Catholic anti-communism.[51] Ecumenical leaders feared that the Vatican was merging the Christian struggle against secularization, the *bête noir* of the church in the 19th century, with the secular crusade against Soviet communism as a means of influencing the Truman administration. The White House was inundated by Protestant protests organized against the presidential-papal alliance. Interestingly, Truman and Taylor were oblivious to the very existence of the ecumenical movement or the WCC in formation before Protestant leaders complained that America's alliance with the Vatican favored the Roman over the non-Roman churches and contravened the American principle of separation of church and state.[52]

Taylor met with significant Protestant leaders on Oct 20, 1947, in New York.[53] They impressed upon him that ecumenism and the WCC, were "of enormous significance for the religious freedom of the world" and had similar political potential to the Vatican. Confirming his lack of understanding of either, Taylor enquired of the WCC: "Would you call it the consolidated head of all Protestantism? Is it in constant session?." The Protestant leaders were keen to impress on the president's representative their global significance and to disabuse him of there being any political advantage in the alliance with the Vatican, which they feared might "involve us in war with Russia … The deadly antagonisms in Europe are between Catholicism and communism."[54] Expressing concern about the confusion between political goals and spiritual aspirations, they wanted a meeting with Truman in order that "the matter could be cast a little more realistically than it is being cast by the President." The desire for a meeting with the president reflected ecumenical aspirations to develop a Protestant theology for international engagement that would help shift the United States into accepting the moral responsibilities of a world power. Advising willingness "to cooperate so far as the spiritual condition of the world is concerned," they made it clear "some of us do not think that it can be done in the terms of a holy war."[55]

Rather than a "crusade," ecumenical Christians wanted meaningful engagement in politics and interchurch relations. They wanted to see a reduction in international conflict and a new international order. Misguided as they considered Truman's endeavors, he and Taylor seemingly offered the prospect of ecumenical access to power and influence. Hence, one month later, once in the presidential presence, the Protestant leaders

50 Gerald L. Sittser, *A Cautious Patriotism: The American Churches and the Second World War*, Chapel Hill, University of North Carolina Press, 1997, 107–109, here 107. There were Protestants who defended Catholics and accused their Protestant brethren of launching another anti-Catholic crusade. At the other extreme were Protestants who claimed that in addition to destroying democracy the Roman Church aspired to eventual world domination.

51 Robert L. Frank, "Prelude to Cold War: American Catholics and Communism," *JCS* 34/1, 1992, 39–56.

52 Meeting of Protestant clergymen with Myron C. Taylor, Oct 20, 1947, in: National Archives, Harry S. Truman Presidential Library and Museum, Taylor, Myron C. Papers, box 3.

53 Meeting of Protestant clergymen with Myron C. Taylor. Present were Samuel McCrea Cavert, FCC; Garfield Bromley Oxnam, Methodist; Edwin T. Dahlberg, Northern Baptist Convention; and William Pugh, Presbyterian Church.

54 Meeting of Protestant clergymen with Myron C. Taylor.

55 Meeting of Protestant clergymen with Myron C. Taylor.

proved notably receptive to the president's ideas about religious cooperation. Once, that is, they were reassured, falsely as it turned out, that Taylor's appointment was in no sense a first step towards diplomatic recognition of the Vatican. Following the meeting, correspondence between Truman and Bishop Garfield Bromley Oxnam revealed that he and his ecumenical colleagues endorsed Truman's plan and were: "Deeply impressed both by your spirit and by your approach to the world situation. A leader who seeks to 'implement the Sermon on the Mount' should have the full cooperation of the spiritual and moral forces throughout the world."[56]

Cooperation proved not to be forthcoming from the international leadership of the WCC, which Truman approached in 1948 through Taylor as the Protestant equivalent of the Holy See. Taylor referred to the WCC as the "Protestant Council in Geneva."[57] The Holy See represents the supreme authority and central government of the Roman Catholic Church, a hierarchical organization headed by the supreme pontiff, assisted by the Roman curia and its congregations, which act as the Vatican's state department. The WCC provides a voice for non-Roman Christendom, a collective voice that does not command but serves the churches. Its only authority consisted "in the weight which it carries with the churches by its own wisdom."[58] It lacked a titular head that carried supreme authority and was prohibited from acting in the name of its participating churches except so far as all or any of them commissioned it to do so.

1948 was a critical year in Cold War and ecumenical history, making it inevitable that the WCC inaugural assembly in Amsterdam became a forum for East-West disputation, most famously via Dulles and Czech theologian Josef Hromádka. Dulles' speech, significantly, argued the need for better organization of the churches against communism, effectively calling for what Truman wanted, a united international Christian anti-communist front.[59] He was opposed by Hromádka, who did not minimize the inherent dangers of communism, but who repudiated anti-communist solutions as futile, declaring: "The perils of communism cannot be overcome by equating it exclusively with totalitarianism and by marshalling all the possible and impossible groups against it."[60] At the end of the conference, the WCC, largely constituted of churches from North America and western Europe, opted for the responsible society in opposition to both totalitarian communism and laissez-faire capitalism. The repudiation of both ideologies was welcomed as ecumenism transcending the Cold War.[61] There was, however another critical factor, Truman's open and clumsy attempt to enroll the WCC into America's anti-communist crusade. Presidential intervention not only forced the WCC leadership to disavow the very side to which it was numerically and ideologically most inclined, but to do so in language that, in effect, suggested moral equivalence between it and the other side, despite the

56 G.B. Oxnam to H.S. Truman, Nov 15, 1947, in: National Archives, Harry S. Truman Presidential Library and Museum, G. Bromley Oxnam Papers, General Correspondence, Harry S. Truman, 1945–1951, Box 36.

57 Statement of Purpose: Mission of the Honourable Myron Taylor, Rome, 13 April 1948, in: National Archives, Harry S. Truman Presidential Library and Museum, White House Central Files: Confidential File No 2, Myron C. Taylor.

58 This was the formula used by William Temple in an explanatory memorandum of 1938. Willem Adolph Visser 't Hooft, *The Genesis and Formation of the World Council of Churches*, Geneva, WCC Publications, 1982, 93.

59 Willem Adolph Visser 't Hooft, ed., *Man's Disorder and God Design*, vol. 5, *The First Assembly of the World Council of Churches Held at Amsterdam, August 22nd to September 4th, 1948*, London, SCM Press, 1949.

60 "The Voice of Amsterdam," *Religion and the People* (November 1948). *Religion and the People* was a small circulation newsletter published by two left-wing Anglican priests. For more information about the journal and its constituency see: Dianne Kirby, "Ecclesiastical McCarthyism: Cold War Repression in the Church of England," *Contemporary British History*, 19, 2005, 185–201.

61 Kirby, "Harry S. Truman."

WCC's Western inclinations. Moreover, according to Visser 't Hooft, the WCC's stance against taking sides in the Cold War in 1948 meant that "the way was paved for the conversations with the Russian Orthodox Church which began at the time of the second assembly at Evanston (1954)."[62]

Ironically at the time, albeit Truman subsequently denounced the WCC for not supporting him, Taylor's interactions with ecumenical leaders exacerbated the Soviet's "deeply rooted suspicion that the World Council was controlled by Western political influences."[63] Consequently, the Orthodox churches in the Soviet bloc withdrew from participation, leaving a Western dominated council from which potential Soviet influence had been removed, an outcome that perfectly suited the Truman administration's agenda. Moreover and significantly, "Hromádka's speech at Amsterdam in 1948, calling for Christians to bridge the East/West divide, was generally forgotten in contrast to the warnings of John Foster Dulles about the threat of communism."[64] When the Korean War broke out in June 1950, the WCC "commended the United Nations, an instrument of world order, for its prompt decision to meet the aggression, and for authorizing police action."[65]

Unsurprisingly dissent came from the East. First from Bishop Albert Bereckzy of the Reformed Church in Hungary, followed by Dr. Tzu-ch'en Chao, the Chinese Amsterdam-elected WCC president. He resigned his office protesting that the WCC sounded "like the voice of Wall Street."[66] The statement served to encourage Truman to try yet again to bring the WCC into line with American propaganda. Taylor's efforts, as clumsy and transparent as ever, proved futile, causing a frustrated president to make a public announcement. Blatantly misrepresenting what he had been trying to do as a Christian rather than a political enterprise, Truman indicted the churches for not joining him. Shortly afterwards he proposed the appointment of an ambassador to the Vatican, which so outraged American Protestants it was withdrawn. Around the same time "a discreet inquiry" was made about accrediting an American ambassador to the WCC headquarters in Geneva.[67]

For all its advocacy of a rules-based system and a transnational order, the United States refused to be bound by either. The brutality inflicted on African-American citizens exposed the limited force of human rights within the United States. The overthrow of democratic governments by the CIA in Iran and Guatemala were modernized forms of imperial conquest that ignored America's own anti-colonial convictions as well as the ideals that supposedly informed the postwar world. The Truman-Taylor endeavors in the international arena impressed upon the WCC, and indeed the Vatican, the deeply political nature of America's religious cold war and the need to distinguish Christian concerns about communist ideology and Soviet bloc policies from what the archbishop of Canterbury, Geoffrey Francis Fisher, another Amsterdam-elected WCC president, privately called America's "will to dominate."[68]

Whilst the righteous nation narrative failed abroad, it was successful on the home front, including amongst ecumenical Protestants. The foremost scholar of the NCC, the American ecumenical movement's flagship body, Jill K. Gill, argues that: "The NCC led America's churches into

62 Willem Adolph Visser 't Hooft, *Has the Ecumenical Movement a Future?*, Belfast, Christian Journals Limited, 1974, 23.

63 Visser 't Hooft, *Memoirs*, 206.

64 Walter Sawatsky, "New Roles for CAREE since the Great Transformation," *OPREE* 20/3, 2020, available at <https://digitalcommons.georgefox.edu/cgi/viewcontent.cgi?article=1689&context=ree> (accessed Apr 12, 2024).

65 Visser 't Hooft, *Memoirs*, 220.

66 Visser 't Hooft, *Memoirs*, 224.

67 Visser 't Hooft, *Memoirs*, 227.

68 G.F. Fisher to C.F. Garbett, Nov 22–23, 1949, in: Lambeth Palace Library, Fisher, Geoffrey Francis (1887–1972), vol. 78, 3–5; Fisher was a key target of Taylor's overtures. See Dianne Kirby, "The Church of England in the Period of the Cold War," Ph.D. thesis, University of Hull, 1990; Dianne Kirby, "Anglo-American Relations and the Religious Cold War," *JTS* 10/2, 2012, 167–181.

battle against Cold War premises and policies."[69] However, Mark Thomas Edwards points out that ecumenical Protestants also led the Christian nationalist cause during the early years of the Cold War: "With the Christian libertarian banner, 'This Nation Under God,' literally hanging over their inaugural gathering, the NCC proudly asserted that the 'American way of life' was inseparable from Christian faith."[70]

Originally the NCC included 29 churches – 25 Protestant and 4 Eastern Orthodox with a combined membership of nearly 40 million – and 12 interdenominational agencies. Member churches were wide-ranging, including Presbyterian and Reformed, Disciples of Christ, Congregational (later United Church of Christ), Methodist (including African-American), Baptist, Lutheran, Episcopal, Moravian, Church of Brethren, Quakers, and Orthodox Russian, Syrian, Antiochian, Romanian, Ukrainian, and Greek. At its height it was one of the largest ecumenical organizations in the world with a budget in excess of 30 million dollars. Its leadership was vitally important to the success of ecumenism.[71]

The NCC was well aware of the red-baiting wreaked on its FCC predecessor for its Social Gospel roots, support for racial equality, labor rights, and business regulation. Born into McCarthyite America with the Korean War as a backdrop, the hostile environment to even the mildest challenges to the Cold War consensus demanded a self-conscious display of patriotism.[72] The NCC claim that it was founded in November 1950 to confront communism, materialism, and secularism reflected anti-communist as well as Christian concerns.[73] Visser 't Hooft, cognizant of the overwhelming pressure American policymakers were prepared to expend to bring Christian leaders globally into line, hoped to strengthen NCC adherence to ecumenical goals rather than those of the state by encouraging bonds with the wider ecumenical community.[74] He was countered at the founding assembly by Truman's secretary of state, Dean Acheson, whose address stressed the danger from "Red" China. Perhaps even more importantly, Truman thanked member churches for supporting freedom, indicating his anticipation that they would continue to do so.[75]

Assembly attempts to blend ecumenism and patriotism with internationalism and nationalism were reflected in the speeches of two key ecumenists, Hermann Morse, a strategic NCC creator, and its first president, Bishop Henry Knox Sherrill. Morse emphasized that a Protestant America could be the strongest world force against those seeking its conquest; Sherrill stressed the "building of a Christian America in a Christian world."[76] Both reflected NCC hopes to sustain their ecumenical convictions whilst retaining their influence within the administration and member churches and, at the same time, avoiding becoming a victim of McCarthyism and a fresh target for FCC detractors.

69 Jill K. Gill, "The National Council of Churches and the Cold War," in: Mojzes, ed., *North American Churches*, 99–132, here 131.

70 Edwards, "Cold War Connections," 453.

71 Paul A. Crow, Jr., "North America," in: *A History of the Ecumenical Movement*, vol. 3, 609–641.

72 The virulent distortions practiced against the ecumenical movement is illustrated by Alan Stang, *The Actor: The True Story of John Foster Dulles Secretary of State (1953 to 1959)*, Boston, Western Islands, 1968. Stang uses Dulles' statements made during World War II when the Soviet Union was an ally and government policy supported accommodation and cooperation in the interests of postwar peace to proclaim him part of a criminal conspiracy to capture the United States for communism.

73 Michele Rosenthal, *American Protestants and TV in the 1950s: Responses to a New Medium*, New York, Palgrave Macmillan, 2007, 39.

74 Gill, *Embattled Ecumenism*, 50.

75 Nathan H. VanderWerf, *The Times Were Very Full: A Perspective on the First Twenty-Five Years of the National Council of the Churches of Christ in the United States of America (1950–1975)*, New York, NCC, 1975, 19.

76 Henry Knox Sherril, "The Presidential Message," in: Robbins W. Barstow, ed., *Christian Faith in Action: The Founding of the National Council of the Churches of Christ in the United States of America*, New York, NCC, 1951, 143. See also Edwards, "Cold War Connections," 453.

Hopes for the latter proved futile. Despite sharing the same salvation-orientation and conservative concerns as their fellow American Protestants, the NCC found itself subject to similar attacks as those inflicted on the FCC for its identification with ecumenical principles of global justice and preference for a measured rather than an excessive anti-communism.[77] Foremost amongst its detractors was Carl McIntire's ACCC founded in 1941 that insisted that the NCC held the same pink people and perspectives as its "Marxian" forebear, the FCC, in a pamphlet asking: "How Red is the Federal/National Council of Churches?"[78]

The NAE, founded in 1942, joined the ACCC in condemning the NCC's involvement in secular politics, rather ironically given their future trajectory and that both organizations had their own Washington lobbyists. The NAE likened NCC worries about unregulated capitalism to communism and its support for the United Nations as putting the fate of the world into human hands rather than those of God.[79] Even more tellingly, however, were the assaults from the HUAC and Joe McCarthy, plus J. Edgar Hoover and the FBI. A striking Cold War characteristic was the way in which it was fought on two fronts and included domestic repression (McCarthyism in the USA, Titoism in the Soviet bloc) of those suspected of sympathies for the other side.[80] Ecumenists who reached through the Iron Curtain or simply supported progressive forces at home became suspect and could become subject to surveillance.

For Hoover ecumenists sympathetic to the Social Gospel were communist stooges, unwitting dupes of communism who, knowingly or unknowingly helped the communist cause.[81] The FBI and HUAC, the latter a recipient of the former's "intelligence," contributed to the conviction amongst churchgoers that there was a communist campaign to subvert America's churches. In 1948, HUAC issued a pamphlet, *100 Things You Should Know About Communism and Religion*. Joseph Brown Matthews, a self-declared former fellow traveler of the Communist Party USA and Methodist missionary, was appointed the research director for HUAC, after of course giving evidence to it.[82] In June 1953 Matthews published an article, "Reds in Our Churches," which claimed: "The largest single group supporting the Communist apparatus in the United States today is composed of Protestant clergymen."[83] Tellingly for the attitude of ecumenists at that time, support came from Reinhold Niebuhr who, wrongly, wrote that Matthews had made correct identifications.[84]

Determined that the American public remain vigilant against what he deemed Communist infiltration of their churches, Hoover encouraged Christians to spy on their brethren. FBI files show that the NCC came under particular scrutiny. They also show, specifically on Dec 3, 1953, important information, which the FBI chose not to disclose, that exonerated the NCC:

> Bufiles reflect certain derogatory information concerning Federal Council of Churches, later incorporated into National Council

77 Robert Wuthnow, *The Re-Structuring of American Religion: Society and Faith since World War II*, Princeton, Princeton University Press, 1988.

78 "How Red is the Federal/National Council of Churches?," New York, ACCC, n.d.

79 Allan J. Lichtman, *White Protestant Nation: The Rise of the American Conservative Movement*, New York, Grove Press, 2008.

80 Fred Halliday, *The Making of the Second Cold War*, London, Verso, 1983, 8.

81 Dianne Kirby, "J. Edgar Hoover, the FBI and the Religious Cold War," in: Steven P. Weitzman & Sylvester A. Johnson, eds., *The FBI and Religion: Faith and National Security before and after 9/11*, Berkeley, University of California Press, 2017, 67–84.

82 David Caute, *The Fellow-Travellers: A Postscript to the Enlightenment*, New York, Palgrave Macmillan, 1973, 312.

83 As cited in Robert Griffith, *The Politics of Fear: Joseph R. McCarthy and the Senate*, Amherst, University of Massachusetts Press, 1987, 230.

84 Reinhold Niebuhr, "Communism and the Protestant Clergy," *Look*, Nov 17, 1953, 37. Irony resides in Niebuhr himself being subjected to FBI investigation over his "radical" past.

> of Churches of Christ in America; however, much of this data has come from rival church groups. An investigation confined to contacts with informants of the New York Office in 1950, reflected that no data was indicating any Communist or subversive activities on the part of any persons affiliated with this organization.[85]

Telling for the attitude of Hoover toward ecumenical churchmen, Bishop Oxnam, one of the Methodist Church's most powerful bishops, a force in the FCC and the NCC, and the American WCC president, a massive presence in the liberal Protestant establishment, was targeted by the FBI despite being a patriotic anti-communist and an ardent opponent of the Soviet Union. Between 1922 and 1924, Special Agent A.A. Hopkins willfully and wrongly smeared Oxnam as a radical activist and advocate of the Soviet system. It was the foundation of a dossier that would grow to over 400 pages. Not only was Oxnam unaware of the file or the surveillance to which he was subjected, "to the day of his death he praised the Bureau and its leader, J. Edgar Hoover."[86]

Indeed, Oxnam even wrote an article published in June 1953, "How to Uncover Communists,"[87] in which he endorsed the FBI, "its thorough work, its loyalty to American traditions, and its spiritual leader, J. Edgar Hoover."[88] When, at his own request, he appeared before HUAC less than a month later, he in effect named names.[89] Oxnam thought himself vindicated, convinced he had cooperated to the full and refuted all charges against him at his hearing. HUAC, however, continued to see him as a supporter of liberal causes and hence a fellow traveler and did not cease to attack the bishop.[90] Oxnam exemplified the Cold War dilemma confronting liberal ecumenical Protestantism; they endorsed and supported a Cold War consensus that was used against them by conservatives unwilling to tolerate any criticism of or attempt to reform America's capitalist system or challenge its Cold War policies.

5 Eisenhower and the WCC

With the WCC, the NCC, and American policymakers resolute in their determination to influence each other, it was agreed that the second assembly of the WCC be held at Evanston in the United States in 1954. Naturally John Foster Dulles gave every assurance, unwarranted in some cases, that all bona fide delegates would receive entry visas. Eisenhower accepted the invitation to address the assembly. In his memoirs, Visser 't Hooft explained the importance of the WCC assisting the American churches as they were playing a decisive role in their nation's "great spiritual struggle"[91] and insisted that, given the uneasy climate in which the assembly was held, "it was most helpful that President Eisenhower came to address us."[92]

It was certainly helpful to Eisenhower, who had gleaned crucial lessons from Truman's ventures into the Christian realm. Truman had invoked the godless Soviet bogey to repudiate accommodation, negotiation, and compromise, and to move America into permanent military, political, and economic intervention on a world scale. It proved equally useful for Eisenhower as he confronted

85 Freedom of Information and Privacy Acts, National Council of Churches, HQ File 100-50869, section 7, available at: <https://archive.org/details/foia_National_Council_of_Churches-HQ-7/mode/2up> (accessed Apr 12, 2024).

86 Robert Moats Miller, *Bishop G. Bromley Oxnam: Paladin of Liberal Protestantism*, Nashville, Abingdon Press, 1990, 87.

87 Garfield Bromley Oxnam, "How to Uncover Communists," *Parade Magazine*, Jun 28, 1953.

88 As cited in Miller, *Bishop G. Bromley Oxnam*, 531.

89 *Testimony of Bishop G. Brompley Oxnam: Hearing before the Committee of Un-American Activities House of Representatives, Eighty-Third Congress, First Session, July 21, 1953*, Washington DC, United States Government Printing Office, 1954.

90 *Testimony of Bishop G. Brompley Oxnam.*

91 Visser 't Hooft, *Memoirs*, 250.

92 Visser 't Hooft, *Memoirs*, 251.

the Republican Party's potential isolationism and fiscal conservatism, allied electorates increasingly resistant to United States leadership, plus an unstable environment in which the United Nations was not yet effective and European unity remained elusive. However, rather than a state alliance with the leaders of organized religion, as pursued by Truman, Eisenhower used his office to move the nation toward a more direct identification with, if not embodiment of, religion itself.[93] Holding the second WCC assembly in America presented Eisenhower with a unique symbolic opportunity to demonstrate that a major world religious presence was being brought into alignment with the United States. It became an occasion to seemingly confirm America's position as the world's bulwark against the forces of anti-religious, totalitarian evil.

The attention given the assembly was confirmation of the high esteem then accorded Christian views, whether they derived from respected pastors, denominational leaders, theologians, or intellectuals. This was an era in which their opinions mattered and were sought, with some appearing on the covers of prestigious magazines such as *Time*.[94] The assembly drew more reporters than the Democratic convention, the establishment of the United Nations in San Francisco, the coronation of Queen Elizabeth, the funeral of Stalin, the peace conferences in Berlin and Geneva, all Roman Catholic events from the Holy Year to various Marian and Eucharistic congresses, the wars in Korea and Indochina, or the atomic tests in Nevada and the Pacific.[95] Opening the assembly, Eisenhower proclaimed faith "the mightiest force that man has at his command."[96] Communism was repeatedly condemned in speeches for its atheism and denial of human dignity and responsibility. Eisenhower's administration concluded with America's most celebrated theologian, Reinhold Niebuhr, proclaiming that the West had been successfully inoculated against communism "by the historical dynamism of the Judeo-Christian tradition."[97]

Interestingly, the Western emphasis on Judeo-Christianity was not replicated globally. In the developing world the emphasis was on "religion." In the Global South, Christianity was far too tainted with colonialism and imperialism to serve American ambitions. The Manichaean imagery of the Cold War and the distinction drawn between the godly United States and the godless Soviets, under both Truman and Eisenhower, affirmed the value of religion more than of any particular form.[98] Eisenhower, who regarded himself as the most intensely religious man he knew, was, according to historian William Lee Miller, "a fervent believer in a very vague religion."[99]

Notably in the 1950s, the most religious decade in American history, not only was a Christian amendment to the constitution rejected by Congress, but the Supreme Court, which had used the term "Christian" to describe the nation in 1931, in 1952 expressed itself as follows: "We are a religious people whose institutions presuppose

93 Kirby, "The Cold War and American Religion."

94 The change in the religiopolitical environment is encapsulated by two articles over 50 years apart: see *Religion and the Intellectuals*, New York, Partisan Review, 1951 and Alan Jacobs, "The Watchmen: What Became of the Christian Intellectuals," *Harper's Magazine*, Aug 14, 2016.

95 "Assembly in America," *The Christian Century*, Sep 1, 1954, 1031–1033.

96 As cited in Ellwood, *The Fifties Spiritual Marketplace*, 131.

97 Mark Silk, *Spiritual Politics: Religion and America Since World War II*, New York, Simon and Schuster, 1989, 107. Niebuhr's political positions changed according to Cold War events and his politics remain contested. He is lauded on the right for the "Christian realism," while on the left he is accused of apologetics that facilitated American militarism and expansion.

98 Michael S. Sherry, *In the Shadow of War: The United States since the 1930s*, New Haven, Yale University Press, 1995.

99 William Lee Miller, *Piety Along the Potomac: Notes on Politics and Morals in the Fifties*, Boston, Houghton Mifflin, 1964, 34, see also Jack M. Holl, "Dwight D. Eisenhower: Civil Religion and the Cold War," in: Mark J. Rozell & Glaves Whitney, *Religion and the American Presidency*, New York, Palgrave Macmillan, 2018, 133–152.

a Supreme Being."[100] It was further confirmation that political calculations not Christian convictions were the key factors in America's religious cold war. Ecumenical Christians increasingly realized that their only value to the state was if, and when, they supported it.

6 Consensus Breakdown

Heather Warren states: "By the late 1960s ecumenical Protestantism's consistent opposition to racism and war ironically made it a contributor to the dissolution of the national consensus that it had helped hold together for many years."[101] Certainly many ecumenists were active in opposing the Vietnam War and in promoting civil rights for African Americans in a context whereby the violence and injustice perpetrated against them and Vietnamese peasants rendered the depiction of the East-West confrontation as between good and evil untenable. Their role in breaking down the national consensus, if it was broken down, is complex. Certainly, ecumenical leaders considered they had played a vital role in the struggle for racial justice, securing success through church-state cooperation. This in turn persuaded them they retained the capacity to influence policymakers. They seemingly failed to appreciate that civil rights legislation was intricately bound up with repudiating Soviet propaganda that called attention to the deeply rooted racism that blighted American society. It was not a response to Christian concerns.[102] Just as Marxist atheism was the Soviet Achilles' heel at which American anti-communist propaganda aimed, America's deep-rooted racism was its Achilles' heel, targeted to tangible effect by Chinese and Soviet propaganda. The damage inflicted on America's moral standing by the treatment accorded its African American citizens demanded as a remedy precisely the sort of symbolic legislation enacted by the Lyndon B. Johnson administration in the 1960s. Nor can the ecumenical struggle against American racism be deemed entirely successful. Today: "The United States sometimes seems to be committed to amnesia, to forgetting its great national sin of chattel slavery and the violence, repression, endless injustices and humiliations that have sustained racial hierarchies since emancipation."[103] The contemporary Black Lives Matter movement destroyed the myth of a post-racial society ushered in by the electoral victory of President Barack Obama. Remarkably, given its negative impact in so many other areas, the Cold War struggle for hearts and minds globally had proffered a unique opportunity for church and state to work together in establishing racial justice and a better America. However, the Cold War proved a double-edged sword with regards to civil rights. Support could be and was portrayed as disloyal and pro-communist, as revealed by the treatment accorded Martin Luther King.[104]

The American ecumenical movement proved unable to overcome racist divisions even within the churches. The existence of African American churches – primarily Methodist, Baptist, and Pentecostal – reflected their exclusion or marginalization from full fellowship in America's churches. A major proponent of black theology, James Cone, who was also a leader in the Ecumenical Association of Third World Theologians, complained about the huge gap between theological doctrines about the church and the actual

100 The widely quoted statement is from the Supreme Court case *Zorach v. Clauson*, 343 U.S. 306, 1952, 313; see also Henry Patrick, "And I Don't Care What It Is: The Tradition of a Civil Religion Proof Text," *JAAR* 49/1, 1981, 35–47.

101 Warren, *Theologians of a New World Order*, 128.

102 See the special issue of *Diplomatic History* 20/4, 1996.

103 Thomas Laqueur, "Lynched for Drinking from a White Man's Well," *London Review of Books* 40/19, 2018, 11–15, available at <https://www.lrb.co.uk/the-paper/v40/n19/thomas-laqueur/lynched-for-drinking-from-a-white-man-s-well> (accessed Apr 12, 2024).

104 Sylvester A. Johnson, "Dreams and Shadows: Martin Luther King, Jr., the FBI, and the Southern Christian Leadership Conference," in: Weitzman & Johnson, eds., *The FBI and Religion*, 168–190.

practice of white church people.[105] Cone was also scathing about the failures of Black ecumenical churches "content with preaching sermons and singing songs about freedom," but which also failed to unite in Christ for "liberating suffering humanity."[106] Certainly the NCC provided a forum for and engaged with the new black theology, but their limited vision was exposed by their shocked response to James Forman's Black manifesto and demand for 500 million dollars reparations. At its core, black theology was a critique of the ethical failings and theological deficiencies of the white racist church, with the inherent implication that it could not be called Christian, that it was a heresy.[107]

Nonetheless, believing they had made a positive contribution to, and misconstruing White House cooperation in the realm of racial equality, ecumenical Christians mistakenly thought possible a church-state partnership in pursuit of peace and justice. They were to learn that whilst the status of their organizations and leadership, the size of their membership, and their global reach could get them into the corridors of power, the influence they could wield was negligible. How negligible would be rudely exposed by the Vietnam War.

7 Vietnam

The Vietnam War highlighted how the transnational nature of the ecumenical movement pushed American ecumenists toward a more critical stance of United States foreign policies and practices. The WCC New York office played an invaluable role in keeping American ecumenists abreast of global developments and ecumenical positions. Its links with the global ecumenical movement meant American ecumenists could access information beyond government position papers. In the mid-1960s material from the EACC and the Japan Christian Council for Peace in Vietnam confronted American ecumenists with harsh judgements of their nation and their own complicity. Even the NCC's Church World Service, a worldwide network for material and spiritual aid to the poor, the marginalized and the needy, stood indicted. It was central to NCC's work and consumed between 70 and 80% of its budget. It also brought the NCC into direct partnership with the WCC's program on interchurch aid, refugee service and development, and other ecumenical organizations. However, its collaboration with the American government to dispense relief helped support United States economic and military aims, detracting from the American ecumenical movement's standing as an independent entity.[108]

In addition to criticism from abroad, at home there was pressure on ecumenical leaders to address United States actions in Vietnam from young ecumenists in the NSCF, the editorial boards of *Christian Century* and *Christianity and Crisis*, pacifist and certain other denominational leaders. In December 1965 the NCC issued a cautious policy statement focused on America's unilateral military methods rather than more substantive issues such as goals, assumptions, and motives. But it was still amongst the first major mainstream organizations in the United States to criticize the government, as the White House noticed. Between 1965 and 1973 Vietnam was the dominant issue for American ecumenists. The ecumenical scrutiny to which Vietnam policies were subjected made it into a catalyst that led the movement to become more critical of Cold War policies generally, plus many other societal failings of which the war seemed symptomatic. Vietnam caused Niebuhr to voice

105 James Cone, *Speaking the Truth: Ecumenism, Liberation and Black Theology*, Grand Rapids, Eerdmans, 1986, 145–149.

106 Cone, *Speaking the Truth*, 149.

107 Steve De Gruchy, "Religion and Racism: Struggles around Segregation, 'Jim Crow' and Apartheid," in: *The Cambridge History of Christianity*, vol. 9, Hugh McLeod, ed., *World Christianities (c. 1914–c. 2000)*, Cambridge, Cambridge University Press, 2006, 385–400.

108 Gill, "The National Council of Churches."

shame for his nation[109] and question if the two superpowers were radically different and wondered had they not each revealed "similar imperialist impulses."[110]

Robert Bilheimer, head of the NCC Department of International Affairs and its Priority Program for Peace, recognized that Vietnam was a consequence of the worldview cultivated during the early Cold War, which fueled America's global interventionism. Bilheimer spent years as second-in-command to Visser 't Hooft at the WCC. He firmly believed the NCC should speak truth to power. He thought the Vietnam War could be used as a prism through which the nation could reflect on and realize the error of its ways. Certainly 1968, the year of the Tet Offensive, generally identified as a turning point in attitudes toward the war nationally, united NCC members in ecumenical witness. But for many the only goal was to end the war, not to transform American foreign policy. Moreover, if ecumenical denominational leaders held antiwar views, the same was not necessarily true of their laity which remained imbued with Cold War anti-communism and righteous patriotic fervor, unwilling to confront the darker side of the policies in the way desired by Bilheimer. Increasing tensions between leaders and laity meant the withdrawal of funds and support, creating rifts exacerbated by critics of American ecumenism keen to exploit the divisions.

As part of its antiwar activism, the NCC mobilized and supported grass roots activism, for example CALCAV. Formed in the autumn of 1965, CALCAV proclaimed dissent was a Christian tradition and declared: "To characterize every act of protest as communist-inspired or traitorous is to subvert the very democracy which loyal Americans seek to protect." CALCAV attracted FBI attention following the 1968 Spring Mobilization Committee to End the War in Vitanam.[111] It was subjected to the FBI's COINTELPRO program, which was linked to illegal CIA domestic surveillance programs that targeted the New Left and the neutralization of its leaders.[112] FBI surveillance revealed no evidence of communist affiliation or violent tendencies, yet CALCAV was still placed under Internal Security and Selective Service Act Investigations in the latter part of 1968. By the early 1970s as convictions grew that far from an aberration, Vietnam was symptomatic of numerous problems afflicting American society, including racism, poverty, and corporate power, CALCAV reflected ecumenism's broader analysis of America's social and political ills, changing its name to CALC.

Antiwar activism also included global collaboration with ecumenists and the interfaith community. Bilheimer forged ties over Vietnam with ecumenical organizations globally, even joining with the Canadian Council of Churches and Swedish congregations in 1969 to help draft resisters.[113] Critical was the changing makeup of the WCC, which was shifting from being a Western dominated organization to one wherein there was increasing representation from the developing and non-white worlds. These new elements brought with them their own experiences of colonial oppression and exploitation and the anger generated by United States foreign policy. This

109 Of his country's intervention in Vietnam, Niebuhr stated: "For the first time I fear I am ashamed of our beloved nation"; Richard Wightman Fox, *Reinhold Niebuhr: A Biography*, New York, Pantheon, 1985, 285.

110 Reinhold Niebuhr, "The Social Myths in the 'Cold War,'" *Journal of International Affairs* 21/1, 1967, 40–56, here 50. See also Ribuffo, "Religion."

111 Toward the end of 1966, the November eighth Mobilization Committee changed its name to the Spring Mobilization Committee to End the War in Vietnam, MOBE. It was a broad anti-war coalition made up of students, unionists, progressive religious leaders, civil rights and black power groups, women's organizations, Third World communities, and other members of oppressed constituencies. Tasked with organizing massive demonstrations in New York City and San Francisco in 1967, the protests attracted an estimated 500,000 participants.

112 Mitchell K. Hall, "CALCAV and Religious Opposition to the Vietnam War," in: Melvin Small & William D. Hoover, eds., *Give Peace a Chance: Exploring the Vietnam Antiwar Movement*, New York, Syracuse University Press, 1992, 35–52, here 39.

113 Mitchell K. Hall, *Because of Their Faith: CALCAV and Religious Opposition to the Vietnam War*, New York, Columbia University Press, 1990, 79–89.

meant additional pressure on American member churches to adhere to ecumenical ideals and to examine their own actions as well as those of their government. As with their Catholic brethren in Latin America, they had seriously to address taking a "preferential option for the poor" and oppressed.

It was an option that inherently challenged the traditional American ecumenical conviction and strategy that ecumenists could work with and influence the government. It took years of trying before Bilheimer realized that the government access accorded the NCC was owing to government assessments that the ecumenical movement could be politically useful. As the fortunes of the American ecumenical movement declined in terms of financial and lay support, the government felt less inclined to provide access and more inclined to disregard it. Ironically, this process occurred at the same time as young radicals within the ecumenical movement were becoming equally dismissive, albeit for very different reasons. They thought the NCC too close to the existing political order to be able to change it. The same view was held by other antiwar activists, particularly those on the secular left.

The full extent of the ecumenical dilemma was illustrated when the White House invited NCC input for fresh evaluations of the war. The report submitted was practical and moderate, reflecting the influence on ecumenists of the Niebuhr brothers and Christian realism.[114] However, tellingly, it provoked President Richard Nixon. He added the NCC to his list of enemies with all that implied – wire-tapping, IRS audits and slanderous castigation. Unable to mobilize ecumenists in support of his Vietnam policies, Nixon turned to evangelical leaders who were willing and able to provide moral endorsement and a voter base in return for access to political power. Not all, of course. Conservative and liberal Christians alike lacked a common foreign policy agenda. Heed must be paid to Axel R. Schäfer's reminder that: "Despite their often rabid anti-Communism, unapologetic patriotism, and emphasis on a strong military, conservative Protestants often remained Christians first and Americans second." As with their liberal counterparts, they could be "both accommodationist and adversarial, custodial and marginal."[115]

At the same time, as Gill emphasizes, anti-ecumenical evangelicals used the Cold War to their advantage to forge close relations with the Republican Party and supplant mainline Protestants as the go-to consultants of government officials by, in essence, providing automatic "God-cover" for American domestic and foreign policies. In addition, "evangelical Christianity proved willing to provide an aura of divine blessing to economic and political forces that propagated an uncritical exceptionalist view of American capitalism, while benefiting handsomely from the partnership." In contrast, when the NCC prove unwilling to unquestioningly promote free enterprise and other related "American" values, the Presbyterian oilman J. Howard Pew withdrew his financial support and indicted it as "the most subversive force in the United States," censuring churches that he claimed put sociopolitical and economic issues before evangelism.[116] Pew, along with the majority of Americans, was unwilling to relinquish Cold War convictions about the nation, its economic system, and its global role. Ecumenical attempts to make them do so would provoke the ire of powerful forces with consequential implications for the movement.

It is important to recognize that the major critics of the American ecumenical movement were very often funded by major right-wing groups, such as the Institute on Religion and Democracy, a Washington based neoconservative research institute that derived the bulk of its funding from right-wing foundations. The slander and

114 Mark Thomas Edwards, *The Right of the Protestant Left: God's Totalitarianism*, New York, Palgrave Macmillan, 2012.

115 Axel R. Schäfer, "Evangelicals and Empire: White Conservative Protestants in US Cold War Politics and Society," in: Mojzes, ed., *North American Churches*, 375–403, here 386.

116 Gill, "The National Council of Churches," 104.

gross distortions, which at the extreme spread fear that the ecumenical movement was creating a superchurch or leading the churches in the direction of Marxism, were refuted and disproved. However, the ubiquitous and unrelenting nature of the attacks had a deleterious impact effecting the sustainability and survival of many councils. The number of ecumenical organizations halved between 1967 and 1976.[117]

8 Peace and Nuclear Weapons

Hiroshima and Nagasaki, denounced as morally indefensible by the FCC in 1946, demonstrated the necessity of avoiding nuclear war.[118] However, what Niebuhr termed the "noxious demonry" of communism, an evil religion immune to moral or political suasion, justified America possessing the ultimate weapon: it was needed to deter the ultimate enemy.[119] The possession and use of nuclear weapons naturally preoccupied ecumenical churches and the Cold War context added further layers of contestation and controversy, not least over just war theory. For the historic peace churches – Mennonites, Quakers, and Brethren – nuclear weapons were always a major preoccupation. In a Cold War climate that equated peace and justice activism with support, intended or not, for the Soviet side, pacifist member churches' attempts to counter anti-communism, challenge the Cold War and reach out in reconciliation across the East-West divide, made them suspect institutions. In the West peace became a "dirty" word with what was derisively termed the Soviet-inspired peace movement castigated as a sinister ploy to weaken Western resolve.[120]

In the early Cold War amidst deteriorating East-West relations, the Soviet representative to the United Nations, Andrei Vyshinsky, made a simple proposal for disarmament. It alarmed Western leaders who feared that the Soviets had won a propaganda coup. Officially organized in 1949 and endorsed from the beginning by religious leaders in the Eastern bloc, the Soviet peace movement contrived to present a positive image of Soviet intentions, to cast the West as warmongering and provide a moral cause for collective religious action that would help protect rather than threaten the communist regimes. It appealed directly to Western Christians through a prism of religious and moral arguments that advocated coexistence, repudiated the Iron Curtain, and claimed ideological differences could reside peacefully in one world.[121] It struck a visceral chord that resonated with ecumenical Christians still scarred by the horror of war and apprehensive about nuclear weapons. After all, according to Ernst Lange, a minister of the EKD and WCC staff member: "The ecumenical movement *is* a movement for peace."[122] Referring to the "bogus division of mankind" as a "deadly menace," Lange insisted that the only way for the church to be one, holy, catholic, and apostolic was the ecumenical way: "And being ecumenical is at the same time the contemporary expression of peace, of *shalom*."[123]

Ecumenical Protestants, worried about a nuclear holocaust, were receptive to some sort of accommodation between the United States and the Soviet Union. Niebuhr, who defended America's right to a first strike in 1950, opposed

117 Crow, "North America."

118 Paul Boyer, *By the Bomb's Early Light: American Thought and Culture at the Dawn of the Atomic Age*, Chapel Hill, University of North Carolina Press, 1994, 202–228.

119 Reinhold Niebuhr, *Christian Realism and Political Problems*, New York, Scribner, 1953, 34.

120 Dianne Kirby, "Ecclesiastical McCarthyism: Cold War Repression in the Church of England," *CBH* 19/2, 2005, 187–203; Bruce Kent in conversation with Brian Wicker, *The Cold War Challenge to the Christian Churches*, Seminar 2, available at <http://www.explosionsolutions.org/coldwarkirby/> (accessed Jun 21, 2024).

121 Dianne Kirby, "The Cold War, the Hegemony of the United States and the Golden Age of Christian Democracy," in: *The Cambridge History of Christianity*, vol. 9, 285–303.

122 Ernst Lange, *And Yet It Moves: Dream and Reality of the Ecumenical Movement*, Geneva, WCC Publications, 1979, 147 (italics original).

123 Lange, *And Yet It Moves*, 147–148.

tactical first use in 1961 as "morally abhorrent."[124] The period of détente meant the government was also interested in rapprochement, albeit for different reasons. The steady deterioration of prospects for world peace and the escalation of the arms race in the period from 1976 to 1982 drew the attention of many churches to their responsibility to act before it was too late. Well before this period, however, a small number of ecumenical Americans had bravely opted to support the peace efforts of the Prague based CPC, founded in 1958 to highlight that peace and justice were valued by communist and Christian. The CPC was initially under the direction of Hromádka, respected for his courage and integrity.[125] In a gesture of ecumenical solidarity an American support group was established, CAREE. Following the suppression of the Prague Spring, the CPC became an overtly politicized agency under a new leadership that forced CAREE into a reevaluation of the relationship. A central consideration was that Westerners could be, and were, more critical of their government than their Soviet bloc counterparts. Nonetheless, in the words of CAREE president Charles West, it embraced an ecumenical policy "which tried to undergird all the churches in Eastern Europe spiritually, aware of the piety they embodied and the fears and temptations that beset them."[126]

The individuals involved were taking huge risks to demonstrate that dialogue was possible, that trust had to be built if the world was to avoid another global conflict and a possible nuclear Armageddon. Reflecting on the risks confronting American ecumenists working to build bridges across the East-West divide, Charles West jokingly told Paul Mojzes, both former CAREE presidents, "I think that you and I both have a file in the Stasi and the KGB and in the CIA."[127] The conversation, recorded in 2013 at Princeton Theological Seminary, confirmed Samuel P. Huntington's assertion that if religion is important, "governments will insist on controlling it, regulating it, suppressing or prohibiting it, or manipulating it to their own advantage."[128] However, understanding their importance to their governments also, to a degree, empowered the churches. Western ecumenists were concerned not to worsen the situation of Christians living in communist regimes, yet their Soviet bloc counterparts sometimes welcomed criticism because it directed attention to problems about which they could not freely speak. Moreover, as West explained from his own observations, CPC leaders such as Nikodim (Rotov) used ecumenical relations to their advantage with the aim of securing more freedom for the churches.[129]

"Part of a tradition of critical engagement in North America, CAREE represented scholars and churchpersons who were thinking together with those persons in Eastern Europe who finally decided that the World Council of Churches' effort at cooperation among churches globally had ended up, after all, as being too much a Western organization, politically speaking."[130] Concerns about the Western orientation of the WCC came to the forefront when delegates at the 1968 fourth WCC assembly in Uppsala were shown a film, *An Armed World*. The intent was to impress on the delegates the dangerous state of world affairs. Some delegates, however, considered the film Western Cold War propaganda as it "seemed not to be the dangers and destructiveness of war and injustice, but

124 John C. Bennett & others, "The Nuclear Dilemma – A Discussion," *Christianity and Crisis*, Nov 13, 1961, 200–204, here 202.

125 Church-state relations in Eastern Europe varied considerably and changed over time. See Paul Mojzes, *Religious Liberty in Eastern Europe and the USSR: Before and After the Great Transformation*, Boulder, Eastern European Monographs, 1992; Dianne Kirby, "The Churches and Christianity in Cold War Europe," in: Klaus Larres, ed., *A Companion to Europe Since 1945*, Oxford, Blackwell, 2009, 183–207.

126 Joseph Loya, "'For, Not of, the CPC': Christians Associated for Relations with Eastern Europe (CAREE) as a Study in Soft Power Peace Advocacy," in: Mojzes, ed., *North American Churches*, 492–507, here 496.

127 *The Cold War Challenge*, seminar 3.

128 Samuel P. Huntington, "Religious Persecution and Religious Relevance," in: Elliott Abrams, ed., *The Influence of Faith: Religious Groups and U.S. Foreign Policy*, Lanham, Rowman & Littlefield, 2001, 55–64, here 55.

129 *The Cold War Challenge*, seminar 3.

130 Sawatsky, "New Roles for CAREE."

the supposed necessity of maintaining the balance of nuclear terror – a balance always loaded in favor of the West."[131] CAREE certainly was not free from suspicion and tension with regard to its ecclesiastical counterparts from communist regimes, yet over time sufficient understanding developed to pioneer programs and projects bringing Christians together in a common struggle, albeit from a position of what has been termed "complex powerlessness," for peace and justice.[132]

In 1980, CAREE initiated the Institute for Peace and Understanding dedicated to Christian-Marxist dialogue, a dialogue that long predated the Cold War. Just as liberation theology was a Latin American phenomenon, Christian-Marxist dialogue was a European phenomenon that Americans observed, with limited participation, and Soviets suspected of ideological subversion intended to weaken the socialist world.[133] Although it is difficult to assess the impact of the peace churches, CAREE, Christian-Marxist dialogue, or the host of other bridge building exercises undertaken by the ecumenical movement, all were testimony to the courage and dogged determination of ecumenical Christians to challenge the Cold War narratives of both sides and keep Christian alternatives in the public realm.

It took till 1983 for the WCC to fully reject nuclear weapons, as part rather than leader of a wider movement within the churches responding to the massive arms buildup initiated by the Reagan administration. Reagan, adept at galvanizing the rhetoric of the religious cold war, resurrected the Truman-Eisenhower morality play presentation of the Cold War as a Manichaean conflict. He targeted conservative Christians for electoral support and secured office on a platform of tough talk with the "Russians." The escalation in words and weapons aroused consternation amongst American mainstream Christian leaders, ecumenical obviously and also Roman Catholic. Shortly after Reagan's election, Christian consternation was given voice at the Catholic bishops' conference where auxiliary bishop of Detroit Thomas Gumbleton warned: "It seems to me we are getting ever more close to the day when we will wage that nuclear war and it will be the war that will end the world as we know it."[134] Gumbleton's sentiments were equally those of his ecumenical counterparts.[135]

9 Conclusions

It was inevitable that the Cold War ideological conflict, even without state pressure, would cause ructions for the ecumenical movement. As Jan Rehman has pointed out, religions "are fields of social contradictions and struggles and, as critical and deconstructive biblical exegeses have demonstrated in abundance, their founding documents are not exempt from these struggles, but are traversed and riven by them."[136] United States Cold War interventions, given its farreaching power, worsened matters considerably. During the Cold War the United States and its communist opponents, all secular states, reverted to a traditional form of church-state relations in which those elements that supported the state were privileged over those that were critical. The FBI highlighted communist bloc attempts to mobilize religious forces whilst playing a critical role in the self-same procedure in America.

131 Norman Goodall, ed., *The Uppsala Report 1968: Official Report of the Fourth Assembly of the World Council of Churches (Uppsala, July 4–20, 1968)*, Geneva, WCC Publications, 1968, 57.

132 *The Cold War Challenge*, seminar 3.

133 *The Cold War Challenge*, seminar 3; Paul Mojzes, "An American Perspective on the Cold War's Impact on Christian Marxist Dialogue," in: Mojzes, ed., *North American Churches*, 508–532.

134 Kirby, "The Cold War and American Religion."

135 Protestant-Catholic relations changed immensely following Vatican II and the revolutionary papacy of John XXIII which reached out to the ecumenical movement and communist regimes. See Peter Hebblethwaite, *John XXIII: Pope of the Council*, London, Geoffrey Chapman, 1984; Dianne Kirby, "The Religious Cold War," in: Richard H. Immerman & Petra Goedde, eds., *The Oxford Handbook of the Cold War*, Oxford, Oxford University Press, 2013, 540–564.

136 Jan Rehman, "Can Marx's Critique of Religion Be Freed from Its Fetters?," *RM* 23/1, 2011, 144–153, here 151.

Ecumenism today suffers from negative connotations in America and the former communist regimes, particularly where nationalism has risen.[137] Post-Cold War America suffers still from messianic jingoism, remains susceptible to persecutory mania and large sectors of the population can still be mobilized for repression.[138] Yet Gill makes a positive assessment of American ecumenism's Cold War role, crediting it with moving the United States toward gender and racial equality and enlightenment values. She concedes its failure to shift the nation from its adherence to American exceptionalism, but argues that its many varied, and ultimately costly, actions

> produced a body of Christian thought that continue to challenge providential, nationalistic, American exceptionalism and policies that emanate from that. Over the years, its work helped to morally ground and legitimate the broader peace movement. And through its actions and partnerships, the NCC became a hub for building a counter-hegemonic network of progressive religious organizations that continues to articulate an ecumenical worldview. Though it paid a political and financial price for prophetic leadership during the Cold War, the council remains an unapologetic advocate of a human rights-based, justice-focused path to peace.[139]

As an assembly of churches placing emphasis on religious diversity, disagreement was inevitable within the American ecumenical movement. Cold War divisions exacerbated differences in areas where consensus ought to have prevailed and impinged decisively on church life. In many respects the churches' witness was determined by the way they viewed the conflict as well as by where they were situated geographically. Differing assessments of communism, capitalism, and the ideological struggle within the churches caused tensions that led to bitter disputes making common and authentic Christian witness difficult.[140] However, throughout, there were American ecumenists who persisted in promoting ongoing dialogue and reconciliation, who did speak truth to power in ways ecumenical leaders both sides of the Iron Curtain felt unable so to do. In assessing the way in which the Cold War came to a relatively peaceful ending, without resort to nuclear conflagration, the importance of ecumenical witness and ecumenical cooperation should not be discounted.

137 *The Cold War Challenge*, seminar 3.

138 Joel Kovel, *Red Hunting in the Promised Land: Anti-Communism and the Making of America*, London, Cassell, 1994, 237. Eight key attitudes and values have been determined to differentiate the white Donald Trump voter base from white non-Trump voters. Christian fundamentalism was one. David Norman Smith & Eric Allen Hanley, "The Anger Games: Who voted for Trump in the 2016 election and why," *Critical Sociology* 44/2, 2018, 195–212.

139 Gill, "The National Council of Churches," 131–132.

140 Lukas Vischer, "Major Trends in the Life of the Churches," in: *A History of the Ecumenical Movement*, vol. 3, 23–50.

Bibliography

Gill, Jill K., *Embattled Ecumenism: The National Council of Churches, the Vietnam War, and the Trials of the Protestant Left*, Dekalb, Northern Illinois University Press, 2011.

Herzog, Jonathan P., *The Spiritual-Industrial Complex: America's Religious Battle against Communism in the Early Cold War*, Oxford, Oxford University Press, 2011.

Hudson, Darril, *The Ecumenical Movement in World Affairs*, London, Weidenfeld & Nicolson, 1969.

Mojzes, Paul, ed., *North American Churches and the Cold War*, Grand Rapids, Eerdmans, 2018.

Preston, Andrew, *Sword of the Spirit, Shield of Faith: Religion in American War and Diplomacy*, New York, Alfred A. Knopf, 2012.

Rozell, Mark J. & Glaves Whitney, *Religion and the American Presidency*, New York, Palgrave Macmillan, 2018.

CHAPTER 20

Contemporary Church Diplomacy: The CCIA

Dino Knudsen

1 Introduction

When the Cold War replaced the Great Alliance of World War II, most transnational organizations inspired by this alliance – trade unions, women's organizations, and peace initiatives – either split, aligned themselves with one camp, or crumbled within a few years. However, one of the sole organizations able to resist the escalating East-West tensions and remain relatively independent during the conflict was a religious organization, the WCC.

Just as world religions predate modern states and the international system, religious organizations possess centuries of experience in withstanding forces that drive humans apart and in transcending the borders that divide them. They are masters of the noble art of diplomacy, whether to resist or accommodate the powers that be or in mediating among them, keeping the church intact and making its voice heard. Having faced the breakdown of international order in the 1930s and with Cold War tensions threatening to obstruct the formation of a new one after World War II, Christian churches reactivated and reinvented their diplomatic craft through the birth of the CCIA.[1]

This chapter investigates how the WCC churches, largely through the CCIA, developed a transnational diplomacy, including this diplomacy's internal and external effects. Two major historical processes characterized this period and fundamentally shaped the CCIA: (1) the East-West conflict, in which the absence of direct military confrontation made room for nonmilitary means, including the development of a cultural or spiritual cold war; (2) the conflict between the developed North and the developing South, including the process of decolonization in which hundreds of millions of people attained independence. In reality, these two processes were intertwined in a complex way, but for the sake of analysis, the initial focus of this chapter, after having introduced the CCIA, is on the East-West conflict. After this, and having documented the commission's diplomatic endeavors and impact on governance, the focus shifts, as does part of the development of the CCIA itself, to the North-South conflict. As we shall see, only by overcoming the challenges emanating from these two processes could the WCC emerge as a global council and fulfill an independent diplomatic role. However, this came with a loss of influence, especially in the corridors of power in Western capitals and the UN, as the commission in the 1970s substituted advocacy for action and placed the emphasis on empowering people instead of primarily engaging the powerful.

Diplomacy has traditionally been understood as the peaceful interactions among state actors, leaving nonstate actors out, or only in the margins, of the picture. However, the increased involvement of civil society in global governance in the second half of the 20th century has made it imperative to understand diplomacy as complex networks of relationships only partly controlled by traditional

1 Following Karsten Lehmann, *Religious NGOs in International relations: The Construction of "the Religious" and "the Secular,"* New York, Routledge, 2017, 8, current literature on the CCIA can be grouped into three categories: first, from a theological point of view, related to ecumenism, or from insiders; second, by historians or social scientists with a wider focus; third, an emphasis on the relationship between the CCIA and the UN. This contribution builds on, connects, and develops these different layers of scholarship, using sources from principally the WCCA, the Presbyterian Historical Society (Philadelphia) and the Princeton University Library (Princeton), as well as from the Lutheran Archives Center (Philadelphia) and the UN Archives (New York).

diplomats representing nation states. The concept of diplomacy has thus been diversified and broadened, including understanding the diplomat as not necessarily a foreign service official relying on hard power, but also a representative of a development agency, a human rights coalition, or a religious organization relying on soft power.[2]

There are many reasons why religious organizations are perfectly situated to perform key roles in diplomacy, including conflict prevention and resolution.[3] They are some of the largest and best organized civil society institutions, in some instances even more stable than local or national governments. Their networks stretch far and deep into society, even across borders, constituting potentially effective channels of communication. Social activism and experience in providing basic services, such as aid and health care, equip them with detailed local knowledge, even in the most remote places. Moreover, few can match their ability to formulate norms and values, including influencing public opinion, which provides them with a unique moral authority. These resources, together with access to top level decision makers, enable religious organizations to be unique diplomatic actors with the ability to frame and influence policy-making.[4] This was also the case of the CCIA.

2 Formation, Organization, and Methods

Many ecumenical councils in the early history of Christianity were rarely confined to church matters.[5] However, in more recent history, antecedents of the CCIA included the international peace efforts of Nathan Söderblom, archbishop of Uppsala and primate of Sweden, around the outbreak of World War I[6] and the WA in the interwar years.[7] The early Faith and Order conferences[8] and the Life and Work movement[9] should also be recorded, as well as the experience of the churches leading up to and during World War II, including the price the church paid for not engaging politically. In August 1947, in the Darmstadt Declaration the EKD confessed its guilt under the Third Reich. Heavily inspired by Karl Barth, one of the most influential Protestant theologians of the 20th century, the statement rejected the traditional Lutheran interpretation of the separation between the earthly and spiritual kingdoms. It was time for the church to play an active, independent,

2 Kathryn Hocstetler, "Civil Society," in: Andrew F. Cooper, Jorge Heine & Ramesh Thakur, eds., *The Oxford Handbook of Modern Diplomacy*, Oxford, Oxford University Press, 2013, 176–191; Jean-Robert Leguey-Feilleux, *The Dynamics of Diplomacy*, Boulder, Lynne Rienner Publishers, 2009, 3–4.

3 For a definition of religious NGOs, see Scott M. Thomas, *The Global Resurgence of Religion and the Transformation of International Relations: The Struggle for the Soul of the Twenty-first Century*, New York, Palgrave Macmillan, 2005, 101; Julia Berger, "Religious Nongovernmental Organizations: An Exploratory Analysis," *Voluntas* 14, 2003, 15–39, esp. 19, 29.

4 Kenneth Grubb, the CCIA's first chairman, eloquently and tellingly entitled his autobiography *Crypts of Power: An autobiography*, London, Hodder and Stoughton, 1971; Berger, "Religious Nongovernmental Organizations," 17, 20, 35; Peter Willets, *Non-Governmental Organizations in World Politics: The Construction of Global Governance*, London, Routledge, 2011, 5, 128, 161–162.

5 Donald W. Norwood, *Pilgrimage of Faith: Introducing the World Council of Churches*, Geneva, WCC Publications, 2018, xiv.

6 Antti Laine, Juha Meriläinen & Matti Peiponen, "Ecumenical Reconstruction, Advocacy and Action: The World Council of Churches in Times of Change, from the 1940s to the early 1970s," *KZG* 30, 2017, 327–341, esp. 333; Richard M. Fagley, "The First Twenty Years in Outline: A Brief Review of CCIA (1946–1966)," n.d. [1966], in: WCCA, CCIA 428.4.10, 2; also published in a shortened version in *The Churches in International Affairs: Reports 1970–1973*, Geneva, WCC Publications, 1974, 19–33. See also the chapter by Gerhard Besier in the first volume of this work.

7 Fagley, "The First Twenty Years," 2. See also the contribution by Keith Clements in this volume.

8 See *History and Structure*, available at <https://web.archive.org/web/20210211222027/http://www.wcc-coe.org/wcc/what/international/hist-e.html> (accessed Jun 28, 2023).

9 John S. Nurser, *For All Peoples and All Nations: The Ecumenical Church and Human Rights*, Washington DC, Georgetown University Press, 2005, 138, note 5.

and critical role in society, and not merely support the state.[10]

However, the immediate postwar impetus to form the CCIA came from the experience of the British Commission on Christian Social Responsibility and principally from the CJDP,[11] instituted in 1940 by the FCC. The CJDP developed into one of the most influential nonstate actors in postwar planning,[12] and brought together Christian leaders from various countries to Princeton University in July 1943 to form a consensus on postwar reconstruction.[13] Immediately after the war, the CJDP contributed extensively to building popular support for the United States joining the UN.[14]

The CJDP was directed by John Foster Dulles, to such an extent that it was known as the "Dulles Commission."[15] A devoted Presbyterian, lawyer, and diplomat, Dulles had served in the US delegation to the Paris Peace Conference in 1919, which produced the Treaty of Versailles. Dulles had been shocked by the total absence of any Christian impact, since churches could not expect to influence international affairs by the mere fact that leading Western statesmen happened to be Christians.[16] Moreover, the majority of the world's population was non-Christian. However, any minority, Dulles reflected after the war, if well organized and sufficiently animated, could make an impact on the majority.[17]

Such experiences and deliberations made Dulles play a leading role, in close collaboration with CJDP's Executive Director Walter Van Kirk, in organizing an international conference to create an ecumenical body for international affairs after World War II.[18] With this initiative, American ecumenists made two gains. First, they distanced themselves from the pacifism and isolationism that had characterized American churches prior to the war. Dulles himself had held isolationist views, but his participation in the Oxford Conference on Church, Community, and State in July 1937, had convinced him of the need for a thorough internationalist approach. Second, by speaking for the international church community, American ecumenists increased their global influence.[19]

Other reasons for establishing the CCIA included that a new, common Christian body was needed in order to access international political platforms, such as the UN, a move which simultaneously shielded individual churches from direct participation.[20] Individually, Protestant churches

10 Matthew D. Hockenos, "The German Protestant Debate on Politics and Theology after the Second World War," in: Dianne Kirby, ed., *Religion and the Cold War*, Basingstoke, Palgrave Macmillan, 2004, 37–49, esp. 40–41.

11 Nurser, *For All Peoples*, 129; *Reports 1970–1973*, 19; Fagley, "The First Twenty Years," 2.

12 Andrew Preston, *Sword of the Spirit, Shield of Faith: Religion in American War and Diplomacy*, New York, Anchor Books, 2012, 389, 394–396.

13 Otto Frederick Nolde, "Ecumenical Action in International Affairs," in: *A History of the Ecumenical Movement*, vol. 2, Harold E. Fey, ed., *The Ecumenical Advance (1948–1968)*, London, SPCK, 1970, 261–285, esp. 263; Ans J. van der Bent, *Christian Response in a World of Crisis: A Brief History of the WCC's Commission of the Churches on International Affairs*, Geneva, WCC Publications, 1986, 2.

14 *History and Structure*; Preston, *Sword of the Spirit*, 398–399.

15 Michael G. Thompson, *For God and Globe: Christian Internationalism in the United States Between the Great War and the Cold War*, Ithaca, Cornell University Press, 2015, 169.

16 Nurser, *For All Peoples*, 198–199.

17 *Transcript of a Recorded Interview with Dr. O. Frederick Nolde*, New York, Jun 2, 1965, The John Foster Dulles Oral History Project, PUL, in: WCCA, 428.10.10 JFDP, 428.10.10.2.

18 Willem Adolf Visser 't Hooft, *Memoirs*, London, SCM Press, 1973, 199; *John Foster Dulles and the CCIA, July 21, 1959*, in: WCCA, CCIA CFNA, USA General + Gov 1966–1978, U.S. Government, Secretary of State (John Foster Dulles), Consultations; *Draft, Memoirs of O. Frederick Nolde, June 17, 1972*, 6, in: LACP, box 1, O. Frederick Nolde Papers, folder "Memoirs, Draft, ca. 1971–1972."

19 Matti Peiponen, *Ecumenical Action in World Politics: The Creation of the Commission of the Churches on International Affairs (CCIA), 1945–1949*, Helsinki, Luther-Agricola-Society, 2012, 96–98, 115, 125; Lehmann, *Religious NGOs*, 83.

20 Laine, Meriläinen & Peiponen, "Ecumenical Reconstruction," 332–334.

wielded relatively little influence internationally and did not match Vatican diplomacy, which took place on both a state and a nonstate level, including through numerous Catholic agencies.[21] However, the churches stressed that their participation in politics was not for "political ends," since the CCIA did not "represent any particular interest or power."[22] Dulles himself warned that the churches should abstain from making "authoritative pronouncements in respect to detailed action."[23] The role of the churches was to provide spiritual leadership, including pointing out moral principles and broad strategies.[24] Nevertheless, this involvement in international affairs became a recurrent object of criticism in the following decades by conservative evangelicals, who thought this new creed was substituting for traditional mission and evangelism, and for those who thought it opened the doors to secularism.[25]

The founding conference of the CCIA was held at Cambridge, Aug 4–7, 1946. Half of the delegates present were Anglo-American, one third of the total number of delegates from the United States alone. Only two representatives of the Orthodox churches and one of the so-called younger churches from the developing world were present.[26] This composition reflected a situation and orientation which had a pervasive and persistent influence on the first two decades of the CCIA's existence.[27] English became the commission's *lingua franca*, and prior to 1966, only a limited number of CCIA documents was officially translated into other languages.[28] Over the years, the Anglo-American overrepresentation in the CCIA was attenuated by the inclusion of continental Europeans, but the southern hemisphere was not substantially represented before the 1970s.[29] Thus, the CCIA reflected the unequal distribution of power internationally, but ensured that the committee had access to the global power centers.

Ironically, the theological discussion proved divisive at the conference, therefore attention was paid exclusively to international affairs. However, except for the Americans, the themes were unfamiliar to many participants, some even questioned the UN. Furthermore, differences of methods emerged, as the Americans envisioned the CCIA to be a "high-powered" group, whereas the Europeans, including the British, were more cautious. Nevertheless, the participants decided to formally constitute the CCIA on Jan 1, 1947, which was later confirmed by the IMC and the provisional WCC, the CCIA's parent bodies.[30] The CCIA, it was decided, should serve "as a source of stimulus and knowledge" to both in their approach to international problems, "as a medium of common counsel and action, and as their organ in formulating the Christian mind on world issues and in bringing that mind effectively to bear upon such issues,"

21 Nurser, *For All Peoples*, 176–177.; Peiponen, *Ecumenical Action*, 160.

22 Willem Adolph Visser 't Hooft & Charles W. Ranson, "Introduction," *EcRev* 8, 1956, 361–363, here 362.

23 David P. Gaines, *The World Council of Churches: A Study of its Background and History*, Peterborough, R.R. Smith, 1966, 252.

24 *Address by John Foster Dulles on August 24, 1948 at the Assembly of the World Council of Churches at Amsterdam, Holland*, 2, in: PUL, DRBSC, PPP, box 39 "Reel 11 JFDP, WCC, 1948," folder "WCC, includes papers concerning the Amsterdam assembly, Aug 22–Sep 4, 1948."

25 Willem Adolf Visser 't Hooft, "The General Ecumenical Development Since 1948," in: *A History of the Ecumenical Movement*, vol. 2, 1–26, esp. 18–19.

26 Fagley, "The First Twenty Years," 2; to counter the imbalance, questionnaires had been sent to church leaders in 44 countries, but only 14 replied, perhaps due to chaotic postwar conditions, see Darril Hudson, *The World Council of Churches in International Affairs*, Leighton Buzzard, Faith Press for the Royal Institute of International Affairs, 1977, 30.

27 Fagley, "The First Twenty Years," 3; Kenneth G. Grubb, "Christian Approach to International Affairs – A Criticism," *EcRev* 8, 1956, 397–400, esp. 398–399.

28 Fagley, "The First Twenty Years," 2; *Reports 1970–1973*, 19–20; Nolde, "Ecumenical Action," 264.

29 Even then, quite a few representatives from the Global South, especially from Africa, were only employed for a short time, leaving for secular positions in their newly independent countries, see *Reports 1970–1973*, 34–35; Hudson, *The World Council of Churches*, 36.

30 Hudson, *The World Council of Churches*, 30; Peiponen, *Ecumenical Action*, 148–150, 196.

including representing them at the UN.[31] The CCIA thus sought to influence decision makers at both church and state level. Albeit a joint body, the commission was organizationally integrated into the WCC,[32] but had the flexibility to speak in its own name, although its high degree of autonomy was subject to consultation and review.[33]

The CCIA's budget was fairly modest. In 1948 it constituted $21,000, reaching $52,453 in 1954 (Evanston), $98,727 in 1961 (New Delhi), $120,746 in 1968 (Uppsala) and $257,405 in 1975 (Nairobi).[34] The commission was financed by the parent bodies. Funds came mostly, similarly to the WCC later, from US churches, but also from singular contributions, including the Rockefeller Foundation.[35]

Despite being one of its vice presidents, Dulles did not take active part in the CCIA's leadership, but contributed his authority, advice, and connections.[36] General oversight was assumed by Sir Kenneth Grubb (chairman), and Otto Frederick Nolde (director) led daily operations. A layman of the Church of England, Grubb had served as a missionary to South America, as chairman of the Institute for Strategic Studies, and in a number of church and state offices.[37] Nolde, handpicked by Dulles from the CJDP, was professor and later dean of the Lutheran Theological Seminary in Philadelphia.[38] Initially, they were employed part-time, but each had a small office staff to rely on and the assistance of international church departments, including the leadership of Willem Adolph Visser 't Hooft in Geneva, soon to be appointed secretary general of the WCC.[39] While Grubb worked out of an office in London, the CCIA headquarters was situated in New York, where Nolde acted as a representative to the UN.[40] In subsequent years, both were employed full time, and new officers were included. Richard Fagley, CCIA executive secretary, was added to the New York office in 1951, Elfan Rees served as representative in Europe from 1952, and André-Dominique Micheli became secretary in New York in 1955 and later in Geneva. Together with Alan R. Booth in London, they constituted the core officers in the CCIA's early decades.[41]

40 commissioners composed the CCIA (the number growing to 69 in 1970),[42] nominated (and later elected) by the parent bodies after deliberations with church leaders. These commissioners were not primarily selected on geographical or denominational grounds,[43] but as churchmen with experience in statecraft, especially those who could act as a door to the "corridors of power," facilitating direct representation at the highest levels. As few were qualified, the majority were laymen,

31 See *Outline of Proposal, an appendix*, 8, in: PUL, DRBSC, PPP, box 56 "Reel 20, JFDP, WCC, 1951," folder "WCC, Includes correspondence with Richard M. Fagley, Frederick Nolde, etc. 1951."

32 The CCIA was always more associated with the WCC than with the IMC, see Hudson, *The World Council of Churches*, 40.

33 Nolde, "Ecumenical Action," 268; Lehmann, *Religious NGOs*, 88; Peiponen, *Ecumenical Action*, 298.

34 Hudson, *The World Council of Churches*, 34–35.

35 For more on the US share of WCC budgets, see *Draft by Bill Murrah*, annex to *CCIA File: Draft on article about WCC by NACLA*, in: WCCA, CCIA CFNA, USA General + Gov, 1966–1978, Paper clips and publications 1966–1973; *Minutes of the First Meeting of the Commission Held at Woudschoten, Netherlands, on 17–18 August 1948*, in: PHS, box 27, FCC in America RG (Record Group) 18, FCC, 1894–1952, folder 18 "CCIA"; Peiponen, *Ecumenical Action*, 234–235.

36 Peiponen, *Ecumenical Action*, 234.

37 See *Draft by Bill Murrah*, 11; Lehmann, *Religious NGOs*, 86.

38 *Transcript of a Recorded Interview with Dr. O. Frederick Nolde*, 23–26; Lehmann, *Religious NGOs*, 84.

39 Nolde, "Ecumenical Action," 268; *Minutes of the First Meeting of the Commission*, 4.

40 Nolde, Nov 7, 1946, in: PHS, FCC in America RG 18, FCC, 1894–1952 , box 27, folder 17 "CCIA"; *The Commission of the Churches on International Affairs*, Grubb, Oct 23, 1946, 2, in: PHS, FCC in America RG 18, FCC, 1894–1952, box 27, folder 17 "CCIA."

41 Fagley, "The First Twenty Years," 6; *Reports 1970–1973*, 23; Nolde, "Ecumenical Action," 268; Lehmann, *Religious NGOs*, 88, 95.

42 Otto Frederick Nolde, *The Churches and the Nations*, Philadelphia, Fortress Press, 1970, 12.

43 Although recruitment seems to have taken place based on the traditional IMC division of territories, see Nurser, *For All Peoples*, 144.

and only three were women.[44] Only after the WCC assembly in Uppsala, 1968, did selection criteria start to include race, age, and culture.[45] Commissioners tended to stay for a long time in office, which later came at a cost to the commission's age composition. To some degree, this was counterbalanced by inviting global Christian youth organizations to nominate a representative each.[46]

Prominent names among commissioners included George Bell (bishop of Chichester and an ecumenical pioneer), Josef Hromádka (head of the Comenius Faculty of Theology and professor of theology of the Hussite Theological Faculty in Prague), Gustav Heinemann (later president of the Federal Republic of Germany), Reinhold Niebuhr, one of the most prominent American Protestant theologians, and Dulles himself, one of the most famous American Protestant laymen.[47] Only three members represented the younger churches.[48] The CCIA executive committee, usually consisting of 10–15 commissioners, convened meetings (at most once a year),[49] but due to a lack of resources, the CCIA only met in full at the WCC's septennial assemblies, meaning that in effect the officers led the commission. Decisions were taken by majority vote.[50]

The CCIA was aware of local developments around the world through soliciting information from special correspondents and about 400 churchmen globally, a network involving over 70 countries. In return, correspondents and churchmen received memoranda, bulletins, and so forth, from the commission.[51] The central nodes in this global network consisted of the international departments formed by churches nationally and/or regionally. Originally, the idea was to form these in each country and make them responsible for engaging with local governments. Only a few existed when the CCIA was founded, but 20 years later, the number had increased to 24. However, this organizational arrangement never became a truly global pattern: the flow of information to the CCIA from the local departments was not impressive, and contacts with governments were often left to the CCIA for a variety of reasons, including local inactivity.[52] To this came the CCIA's high-level contacts established through the UN, including to local governments, international organizations, NGOs, and others.[53]

The CCIA mixed two features ideally separated in state diplomacy. State diplomats do not formulate foreign policy, they execute it, but the commission combined being a sort of think-tank seeking to define foreign policy, and the instrument for implementing it. If the required expertise to take on this responsibility was not to be found in the churches, the CCIA would draw upon accessible institutions and foundations, including the

44 Nolde, "Ecumenical Action," 266–267; Fagley, "The First Twenty Years," 3–6; *Reports 1970–1973*, 20–22.

45 Hudson, *The World Council of Churches*, 43.

46 *Reports 1970–1973*, 20–22; Nolde, "Ecumenical Action," 266–267.

47 Grubb, *Crypts of Power*, 169; William Inboden, *Religion and American Foreign Policy (1945–1960): The Soul of Containment*, Cambridge MA, Cambridge University Press, 2008, 35; Peiponen, *Ecumenical Action*, 126–130.

48 Annex B, *Regulations for the Commission of the Churches on International Affairs, Woudschoten, Netherlands, August 17–18, 1948*, in: PHS, FCC in America RG 18, FCC, 1984–1952, box 27, folder 18 "CCIA."

49 *Regulations for the Commission of the Churches on International Affairs*, 3; see also Annex A to the same source; Hudson, *The World Council of Churches*, 44.

50 Fagley, "The First Twenty Years," 6; Annex A, *Regulations for the Commission of the Churches on International Affairs*, 26; Darril Hudson, "The World Council of Churches and Racism in Southern Africa," *IJ* 34, 1979, 475–500, esp. 476.

51 Fagley, "The First Twenty Years," 8; Nolde, "Ecumenical Action," 267; Annex E, *Commission of the Churches on International Affairs, June 30, 1948*; *Minutes of the Fifth Meeting of the Executive Committee at Emmanuel College, Toronto, Canada, 3–5 July 1950*, 17, in: PHS, FCC in America RG 18, FCC, 1984–1952, box 27, folder 18 "CCIA."

52 Fagley, "The First Twenty Years," 8; Hudson, *The World Council of Churches*, 45.

53 In Europe, Dulles connected the CCIA with German Bundeskanzler Konrad Adenauer, Jean Monnet and others, see Gerhard Besier, "80 Years of the World Council of Churches: Theological, Political and Societal Ambiguities," *KZG* 30, 2017, 294–311, 300.

secular arena.[54] However, due to limited resources, the focus of the commission was on specific international issues[55] rather than on overall long-term trends, which is why its work was often more *ad hoc* and pragmatic than systematic.[56]

Internally in the ecumenical movement, the CCIA would provide studies, analysis, and educate church- and laypeople in world affairs. Externally, the CCIA naturally yielded more authority on issues in which the churches were already experienced, such as aid and refugees. After the first ten years of the CCIA, in which Nolde focused on human rights, the following specialization in the commission crystallized: Nolde, disarmament; Rees, refugees; Micheli, human rights; Booth, African problems; Fagley, development (and population).[57]

At an early stage, the CCIA relied to a large degree on correspondence, but in time became alert to visiting the churches personally and to the importance of timing and trust in diplomacy. Thus, the CCIA began registering its points of view at the time and place of international political decision-making, including holding personal follow-up consultations and adjusting its advice along with evolving situations.[58]

Overall, the CCIA would take a range of different forms of actions, including: (a) monitoring, analyzing, interpreting; (b) delegations to churches and governments; (c) pastoral visits; (d) study teams; (e) confidential representation (to governments); (f) representations (to intergovernmental bodies); (g) support for action groups; (h) various efforts for peaceful solutions of conflicts.[59] It became standard procedure to count upon actions taken by the churches within the country or countries concerned when an international issue or crisis arose, yet the CCIA would also take independent action.[60]

While the ecumenical movement had primarily been headed by the British and French before World War II, the churches in the postwar world counted on an American lead, if not outright dominance. The CCIA did not constitute the ecumenical movement's first preoccupation with international affairs but represented a qualitative leap in this involvement. Previously, churches had often only risen to the occasion in times of crisis and rupture, meeting at conferences, issuing statements and praying. With the CCIA, the churches relied on a permanent instrument, although limited in size and budget, that developed the competencies, connections, and networks necessary for a continual advance of a Christian approach to international affairs, including the formulation of specific positions, policies, and programs, but also seeking for their acceptance and implementation in the secular arena.

3 Born into a Divided World

The WCC's founding assembly in Amsterdam in 1948 took place amidst increasing East-West tensions. The coup in Czechoslovakia earlier that year had shaken beliefs in collaboration with communist forces and many feared that the Berlin blockade was a prelude to war.

54 Nolde, "Ecumenical Action," 269; *The Church in International Affairs: Reports 1983–1986*, Geneva, WCC Publications, 1987, 8.

55 The CCIA's focus followed these criteria: (1) an inherently urgent problem; (2) of clear Christian concern; (3) about which there was substantial worldwide consensus; (4) which could be competently handled by a CCIA officer; (5) and for which there was a reasonable possibility that a contribution might be effective, or for which there was an overriding imperative for Christian witness, see Hudson, *The World Council of Churches*, 34.

56 *Reports 1970–1973*, 19–20; van der Bent, *Christian Response*, 6.

57 *Reports 1970–1973*, 23.

58 *Memorandum on Possible Future Program of the CCIA, Walter W. Van Kirk, July 30, 1948*, in: PHS, FCC in America RG 18, FCC, 1984–1952, box 27, folder 18 "CCIA"; Nolde, *The Churches and the Nations*, 15.

59 *The Church in International Affairs: Reports 1987–1990*, Geneva, WCC Publications, 1990, 31–32.

60 See *Notes on Actions in Connection with the Egyptian and Hungarian Crisis, O. Frederick Nolde, November 5, 1956*, 27, in: PHS, NCC RG4; General Secretary, 1950–1973, box 14, folder 25 "CCIA."

Political tensions spilled over into the churches. In the previous two years, serious efforts had been made to ensure the participation of the Russian Orthodox Church in the WCC,[61] but only a month before the assembly, a negative answer arrived from Moscow, where the Russian Orthodox Church and several Orthodox churches were celebrating the 500th anniversary of the autocephalous existence of the Russian Orthodox Church. By a majority vote, the Orthodox churches present in Moscow rejected joining the WCC.[62] The reasons advanced, apart from theological ones, were accusations varying from that the WCC represented "bourgeois" ecumenism to that the WCC was controlled by the Western powers, including that it sought to exert international influence.[63] However, some Orthodox churches, most importantly the Ecumenical Patriarchate of Constantinople, chose to join the WCC.[64]

At the assembly in Amsterdam, the CCIA had been entrusted with preparing section III, "The Church and the Disorder of Society." Eschewing moralistic denunciations of power politics, typical of earlier church gatherings, one of the draft documents described power as a basic reality in international relations, neither intrinsically good nor bad. Instead, the conclusion was that, although all great powers sought to expand, the cause of the present international tensions was "chiefly the Soviet Union."[65] Dulles offered another document that reached a similar conclusion. However, European Commissioners were generally less critical. Nolde, hardly a militant anticommunist himself, complained in a private memo that the Europeans refused "to specify the evils in the USSR without delineating in great detail the evils in the US."[66] Nevertheless, this approach of "share and share alike" ultimately formed the conclusion to the discussion of section III.

Before that, however, a famous verbal duel between Dulles and Hromádka, widely reported in the world press, took place on the podium. In his presentation, Dulles stated that the moral values essential for world peace were embodied, although imperfectly, in the Western democracies, and that communism was the greatest obstacle to realizing them. While acknowledging some similarities between the social and economic ends that "communists profess and Christians seek" and stating that the economy of a free society did not have to be *laissez-faire*, Dulles stated that the starting point of communists and Christians were antithetical. Christians believed in the dignity

61 See the strictly confidential source *Appendix to Minutes of Executive Committee, February 6–10, 1961, Minute of discussion in closed session on the Visit to Geneva of Bishop Nikodim*, 1–2, in: WCCA, 428.11.04.3 NY Office 1960–1962, folder "1961 January–June"; Visser 't Hooft, *Memoirs*, 198.

62 Vasil T. Istavridis, "The Orthodox Churches in the Ecumenical Movement (1948–1968)," in: *A History of the Ecumenical Movement*, vol. 2, 287–309, esp. 304; Elina Hellqvist, *The Church and its Boundaries: A Study of the Special Commission on Orthodox Participation in the World Council of Churches*, Helsinki, Luther-Agricola-Society, 2011, 27.

63 Hellqvist, *The Church and its Boundaries*, 27; Hamilcar S. Alivisatos, "Orthodoxy, Protestantism and the World Council of Churches," in: Constantin G. Patelos, ed., *The Orthodox Church in the Ecumenical Movement: Documents and Statements (1902–1975)*, Geneva, WCC Publications, 1978, 199–208, esp. 204. There is no consensus in the ecumenical historiography on what exactly caused the rejection. Hellqvist, *The Church and its Boundaries*, 26, states that it was caused partly by theological, partly by political differences. Georges Tsetsis, "The Meaning of the Orthodox Presence," *EcRev* 40, 1988, 440–445, esp. 441, writes that it was mainly due to Cold War tensions. Visser 't Hooft, *Memoirs*, 198, 205–206, 263, points to the same cause, but notes that inaccurate information and misinformation played a substantial role, apart from deeply rooted suspicions. However, Gaines, *The World Council of Churches*, 827, note 41, contends that many of the churches present in Moscow were well aware of the ecumenical movement.

64 There is no consensus in the research literature on how strong the Orthodox presence was at the WCC Amsterdam assembly. Tsetsis, "The Meaning of the Orthodox Presence," 441, states that it was weak. Alivisatos, "Orthodoxy," 201, states that it was strong. The estimate of Gaines, *The World Council of Churches*, 821–822, seems to be in between.

65 Inboden, *Religion and American Foreign Policy*, 43.

66 Inboden, *Religion and American Foreign Policy*, 45.

and worth of the individual, created in the image of God, whereas communists rejected moral law and God-given rights. This explained why communists ultimately relied on force and coercion, leading to totalitarianism. However, according to Dulles, communism was not a problem that could be solved by military means.[67]

Hromádka, however, contended that the West had mismanaged the problems facing humanity, reminding the audience of the failures in the Spanish Civil War and the Munich Agreement. Therefore, the East's reluctance to accept Western concepts of liberty, democracy, and justice was legitimate. For the first time in history, "the Eurasiatic East represented by the Soviet Union," was claiming an equal share in world leadership, Hromádka said, although he admitted that the USSR's actions were sometimes "ruthless and brutal." However, he distinguished communism from Nazism, because the former did not adhere to any "metaphysics that would elevate an earthly reality ... to the plane of an Absolute." Western supremacy in the world had ended, he declared, criticizing American capitalism for its emphasis on freedom rather than social security, whereas communism, "although under an atheistic form," contained "much of the social impetus" that the church had forgotten. However, the central problem was that in both the East and the West, man was no longer subordinate to God. "The whole of the civilized human race is sick," Hromádka stated, "and none is justified to claim a monopoly of means and medicines for the cure of the disintegrated international order." This did not equal indifference or neutralism in the face of injustice or oppression, Hromádka explained, but meant that the church should not "identify with a definite political cause" or be used by any power bloc. Rather, its mission was to "keep rival fronts in close touch with each other."[68]

Hromádka's position could not simply be explained away as appeasement to the new Czech regime, since he had demonstrated courage in the past, denouncing the Nazi regime at great personal risk. During the German occupation, Hromádka had fled and found refuge in the United States, where he lectured at Princeton Theological Seminary and the Union Theological Seminary in Philadelphia. Hromádka was not an ecumenical outsider but a Protestant professor of theology with firsthand knowledge of the movement and the United States that he was criticizing.[69]

If Hromádka's position did not convince everyone in Amsterdam, at least it was understandable and justifiable for many. His insistence on impartiality in power politics, in particular, found fertile ground, since, after all, the WCC's ambition was to become a *world* council, including the Orthodox churches under socialist rule. Here Dulles' approach seemed less fertile, openly advocating an alliance with the West, despite his admission of its imperfections and the references to a peaceful evolution of the international system. In the end it was decided, in line with what Barth advocated, to reject both capitalism and communism. Some Americans were truly frustrated by this, because they found it to be a simplistic comparison, although the rejection was directed against *laissez-faire* capitalism, not capitalism as such. Nonalignment had taken root in the WCC.[70] Two months later, Hromádka's was elected one of five presidents of the CCIA.[71]

---

67 *Address by John Foster Dulles*, 8.

68 *Assembly Commission IV on "The Churches and International Affairs," Our Responsibility in the Post-War World (First draft), by Professor Joseph L. Hromodka, Prague, February 1948*, 3–7, 17, in: PUL, DRBSC, PPP, box 39 "Reel 11 JFDP, WCC, 1948," folder "WCC, includes papers concerning the Amsterdam Assembly, Aug 22–Sep 4, 1948."

69 *Professor J.L. Hromadka*, in: WCCA, 450.004 Files from the WCC New York Office, Correspondence, Documents, "Joseph Hromadka."

70 The concept of "nonalignment" used in this chapter does not specifically refer to the Non-Aligned Movement, which included and still includes a wide range of nation states.

71 *Minutes of the Executive Committee of the Commission of Churches on International Affairs at Hotel Centraal,*

However, it was not enough for the WCC to reject power alliances: the new council also had to demonstrate a positive approach. Aside from contributing to competing economic systems coexisting peacefully, the assembly was unanimous in supporting the UN, including the adoption of an International Bill of Human Rights that involved freedom of religion.[72] Furthermore, the churchmen united around the concept of "responsible society," coined by Visser 't Hooft, emerging out of the discussion on how to balance the demands of freedom and justice within a democratic order, based on the recognition of essential human rights. It was not conceived as an alternative sociopolitical system, but as a guide and criterion for judging existing social orders.[73]

The nonaligned character of the WCC meant that national churches could not simply side with their respective governments when dealing with international affairs, but had to consider preserving ecumenical fellowship, including the formulation of an independent ecumenical voice. The first serious test of this stance had formed an important backdrop to the debates in Amsterdam.

Prior to the assembly, US President Harry S. Truman had attempted in vain to bring the nascent WCC in line with his foreign policy objectives. Truman, who was brought up in the Baptist Church, wanted an international religious alliance to form the moral and spiritual backbone of his containment strategy against international communism. He sought to keep the Orthodox churches out of the WCC, except for the Ecumenical Patriarchate of Constantinople, while involving, on the contrary, the staunchly anticommunist Roman Catholic Church. However, this plan found little support among the leading Protestants preparing for the WCC, both in the United States and worldwide. Visser 't Hooft politely, but firmly, refused to draw a WCC line at the so-called Iron Curtain. Instead, Truman turned to the archbishop of Canterbury, but failed to win him over. In the end, the centuries-old contradictions among the churches outweighed their common antipathy to communism. Many ecumenists still viewed the Roman Catholic Church as too authoritarian, hierarchical, and hegemonic to associate closely with it.[74]

In many ways, Pope Pius XII had pioneered the Cold War, and it was only during the 1950s that the Roman Catholic Church changed its stance. The American hydrogen bomb and the devastating effects of a possible third world war, but also Stalin's death in 1953, led the Roman Catholic Church to seek a way to ease tensions between East and West. In this way, and especially thanks to Vatican II in the 1960s, the Roman Catholic Church resumed a pioneering role, but contributed now to lay the basis for *Ostpolitik* and *détente* in the Cold War, including on human rights, social justice, and peace, and here it often operated in tandem with the WCC.[75]

A parallel change in the attitude of the Roman Catholic Church towards the WCC can be detected. Catholics were not allowed by the Vatican to participate in Amsterdam, and only after the Evanston assembly in 1954 did informal theological contacts intensify. The Vatican sent its observers to the third WCC assembly in 1961 in New Delhi, and a mere few weeks later, Pope John XXIII announced convening Vatican II the following year, changing

Amsterdam, 2nd September, 1948, 3, in: PHS, FCC in America RG 18, FCC, 1894–1952, box 27, folder 18 "CCIA."

72 Peiponen, *Ecumenical Action*, 290–294.

73 van der Bent, *Christian Response*, 7–8; Paul Abrecht, "The Development of Ecumenical Social Thought and Action," in: *A History of the Ecumenical Movement*, vol. 2, 233–259, esp. 241; Nolde did not believe in the designation of a particular economic or political system as Christians, see Nolde, *The Churches and the Nations*, 40.

74 Inboden, *Religion and American Foreign Policy*, 131–137; Peter C. Kent, "The Lonely Cold War of Pope Pius XII," in: Kirby, ed., *Religion and the Cold War*, 74; Preston, *Sword of the Spirit*, 413; Peiponen, *Ecumenical Action*, 162, 261.

75 Frank Coppa, "Pope Pius XII and the Cold War: The Post-War Confrontation Between Catholicism and Communism," in: Kirby, ed., *Religion and the Cold War*, 59–63; Nurser, *For All Peoples*, 179.

the ecumenical situation completely.[76] WCC observers were present at Vatican II, and in 1965, it was agreed to establish a Joint Working Group that would coordinate the relations between the WCC and the Roman Catholic Church annually.[77] In 1969, the pope visited the WCC headquarters in Geneva. Although this rapprochement did not lead to the Roman Catholic Church membership of the WCC, cooperation has since been strengthened, including on international affairs.[78]

The WCC was also courted by the East. This was potentially more dangerous because it touched a soft spot in the WCC, namely its central focus on world peace. Having stayed clear of Soviet power politics at the UN and being immensely successful in influencing the formulation of the UN's Universal Declaration on Human Rights (to which we shall return), the CCIA needed to demonstrate, in accordance with the impartial stand taken at Amsterdam, a sensitivity to the agenda of the churches in the Eastern Bloc, which the WCC still hoped to incorporate.

On Mar 15, 1950, the WPC called for a total ban on nuclear weapons in what became known as the Stockholm Appeal. In the following weeks, the appeal gained millions of signatories internationally, including those of prominent intellectuals, artists, and scientists. However, the WCC, acting with the CCIA, rejected the appeal as propaganda. "The Church must resist the danger of exploitation for political and propagandistic purposes by both sides," the CCIA noted, if it was to retain its credibility.[79] Indeed, the WCC rejected several attempts by the WPC to form an alliance due to the overlap between the WPC and Moscow's foreign policy aims. Meetings were held between the two organizations and contacts maintained informally, also in the 1970s, but were never translated into active cooperation.[80]

A similar situation developed with another prominent peace initiative, the CPC, founded in 1958 by Hromádka and based in Prague, which developed into a sustained platform for East-West dialogue. The CPC included many Protestant and Orthodox churches in the Eastern Bloc, including member churches of the WCC, and enjoyed the support of Barth, who saw it as an alternative form of ecumenism. The WCC was encouraged to become a member, as a way of seeking understanding and reconciliation between East and West. Nevertheless, the WCC never involved itself in the CPC, aside from unofficial representation, basically owing to the same concerns as it had with the WPC.[81]

The independent stand of the WCC meant that it did not form any alliance with Truman nor did it endorse the NATO, but it also resisted taking the bait from the East.[82] However, how to approach communism still constituted a burning question if the WCC were to succeed in its bold endeavor.

4 Friend or Foe?

From the outset, there was no consensus in the WCC on how to understand and deal with communism, neither as an ideology nor as a state power, which also reflected the highly diverse experiences of the churches. For example, exiled church leaders from the Baltic states, having seen their churches and countries recently annexed

76 See the contribution by Christoph Theobald on Vatican II and ecumenism in this volume.

77 Marlin VanElderen, *Introducing the World Council of Churches*, Geneva, WCC Publications, 1990, 27.

78 VanElderen, *Introducing the World Council of Churches*, 109–110; Visser 't Hooft, "The General Ecumenical Development," 16–17; for some joint WCC-Roman Catholic Church projects and collaboration in this area, see van der Bent, *Christian Response*, 10.

79 *The World Council of Churches and the Ideological Conflict of Our Time, Bossey, April, 1949*, 2, in: PHS, FCC in America RG 18, FCC, 1894–1952, box 27, folder 2 "General Secretary, Nolde."

80 Gaines, *The World Council of Churches*, 758–761; Visser 't Hooft, *Memoirs*, 227.

81 Besier, "80 Years"; Gaines, *The World Council of Churches*, 940, 1035; Paul Stefanik, "The Christian Peace Conference – Propaganda? ... or Prophecy?," *OPREE* 5/3, 1985, 45–56.

82 Peiponen, *Ecumenical Action*, 261–262, 344–345.

by the Soviet Union and the Russian Orthodox Church, appealed to reject communism as the anti-Christ.[83] Whereas in the Global South, especially in Asia and in the context of anticolonialism, many Christians believed in combining Christian theology and Marxism, including a united front with local communist parties.[84] However, the voices from the Global South were still marginal in the early decades of the WCC.

Seen from a Western and Central European perspective, communism did not constitute the same threat as Nazism had.[85] On the other side of the Atlantic, the American ecumenists were generally moderate anticommunists and centrists both theologically and politically. They considered themselves "realistic idealists" in international relations, and retained a strong commitment to internationalism, rejected American exceptionalism, and strove to reform the world permanently by abolishing war and eliminating poverty and inequality. Many believed in the ideals of democratic socialism, including the acceptance of an important role in central government.[86] They did not consider the Cold War, as Truman had, an essential contest between secularism and religion, but between people of the same faith.[87]

In a central study by the FCC, entitled *The Christian Approach to Communism*, communism was accepted as a domestic element in Western culture. "The strange paradox of our age," the study read, "is that Christendom, the matrix of Western civilization, has given birth to a monster that is taking steps to destroy her."[88] In a peculiar way, this FCC analysis mirrored Karl Marx's criticism of religion as both an expression of, and a protest against, real suffering.[89] According to the analysis, Christians only needed to look around them to discover the roots of the attraction of Marxism, "the evils prevalent in society."[90] In other words, communism was "the opium of the people" and its success highlighted the failure of the Christian Church itself.[91] Therefore, Christians needed to both learn from and combat against communism. Or as Nolde put it, the "primary answer of the Church to communism must be the renewal of the Church itself."[92]

The same basic message, but in a more radical form, echoed from the Global South. At Evanston, the Indian theologian Madathilparampil Mammen Thomas emphasized the "democratic social revolution" as the answer to communism and fascism. Dr. Gonzalo Báez-Camago, a Mexican

83 Gaines, *The World Council of Churches*, 777; Lucian N. Leustean, "Overview," in: Lucian N. Leustean, ed., *Eastern Christianity and the Cold War (1945–91)*, London, Routledge, 2011, 1–15, esp. 3.

84 Justin Reynolds, "From Christian Anti-Imperialism to Postcolonial Christianity: M.M. Thomas and the Ecumenical Theology of Communism in the 1940s and 1950," *JGH* 13, 2018, 230–251, esp. 234, 242.

85 This was a view shared by Karl Barth and Joseph Hromádka, see Norwood, *Pilgrimage of Faith*, 16.

86 David Little, "The Nolde Lecture, Lutheran Seminary of Philadelphia, Oct 1, 2013: The Legacy of Ecumenical Protestantism: Nolde Contribution," *Soundings* 98, 2015, 1–16, esp. 2–5; Preston, *Sword of the Spirit*, 354.

87 Gene Zubovich, "The Protestant Search for 'the Universal Christian Community' between Decolonization and Communism," *Religions* 8/2, 2017, 1–12, esp. 2.

88 *Resource Material – The Christian Approach to Communism*, 4, in: PHS, box 14, General Secretary, 1950–1973, NCC RG 4, folder 25 "CCIA."

89 Karl Marx, "A Contribution to the Critique of Hegel's Philosophy of Right," *Deutsch-Französische Jahrbüche*, February 1844, available at <https://www.marxists.org/archive/marx/works/1843/critique-hpr/intro.htm> (accessed Feb 27, 2023).

90 *Resource Material*, 7; in a similar vein, an earlier document of the IMC on the encounter with communism blamed the Christians for failing to live up to the teachings of Jesus and summarized the evils as: "The mounting pressure of population upon the land, with its resulting land hunger, undernourishment, and disease; the cry for a better life and opportunity; the increasing struggle for survival; the demand for self-determination; the revolt against the color bar and denial of equality of human rights; the disillusionment of the masses with the present order of society and their cravings for escaping the hopelessness of their lives." See *Missionary Policy in the Christian Approach to Communism, January 1949*, in: WCCA, 26.19.02/13, "WCC/IMC."

91 *Resource Material*, 4.

92 *The World Council of Churches and the Ideological Conflict of Our Time*.

Methodist, declared socially progressive governments the best bulwark against communism.[93] However, the Social Gospel that united ecumenists from both North and South was precisely what many conservative Christians in the United States, Evangelicals and Catholics alike, saw as a parallel to communism, especially in the heated atmosphere of McCarthyism.

Nevertheless, the prevailing consensus that gradually emerged in the WCC was that, while dialogue and collaboration – or even alliances, some would add in the Global South – with Marxists were acceptable, an adoption of their fundamental ideological premises was not.[94] This opened a *modus vivendi* with the churches in the Eastern Bloc, which to various degrees were controlled by the communist authorities.

5 Fragile Unity on Korea

Having spent the early years focusing on issues in which the churches shared a relatively high consensus, including aiding refugees and reconstruction, but also codifying human rights internationally, the CCIA found its unity seriously threatened by the Korean War. However, as divisive as the war potentially was for the WCC, it also provided an opportunity for the CCIA to demonstrate its worth.

Nine days after war broke out on Jun 25, 1950, the central committee of the WCC held a meeting. However, only one representative of the churches in China and none from Eastern Europe were present. At the meeting, the majority decided to support the so-called police action in Korea, under the auspices of the UN.[95] In the fall, the CCIA ceased this initiative within the UN, suggesting the formation of a UN corps of international peace observers. "I think you have hit on something that may be constructive for peace," Dulles replied to Nolde when consulted on the idea.[96] In November, the proposal was endorsed in a more extended form by the UNGA. Although the Peace Observation Commission subsequently had a checkered history, the underlying concepts for its creation constituted an early step in the history of UN peacekeeping.[97]

However, because the WCC decided to support the police action in Korea, and China intervened in the war on the North Korean side, Chinese churches effectively stopped their participation in the WCC.[98] Other churches also voiced criticism of what they saw as a pro-Western approach by the WCC and a dangerous spread of the conflict potentially leading to a world war.[99] Even the American-British axis in the WCC, so central to the CCIA, proved fragile as the war dragged on. In 1952, the British churches warned that it was "misleading and dangerous to oversimplify the situation in East Asia as a struggle of the democratic West against Communism," and recalled that "the struggle in Korea was not undertaken by the United Nations to fight Communism but to resist aggression." Moreover, they questioned whether the American "assumption that Communism has been imposed on China by force is adequate as a basis for policy," and suggested recognizing the Beijing government. "[W]e have long recognized the Moscow government: we have fought

93 Gaines, *The World Council of Churches*, 778.

94 For example, Charles Malik warned Christians not to compete with communism "on Communism's own ground," including rejecting its "dialectical-materialistic metaphysics"; see Charles Malik, "Positive Christianity and Communism," *EcRev* 8, 1956, 410–413, here 410–411.

95 Visser 't Hooft, *Memoirs*, 220.

96 Maureen R. Bergman & Joseph E. Johnson, eds., *Unofficial Diplomats*, New York, Columbia University Press, 1977, 126; Dulles recommended the CCIA proposal to the US government, see *Draft, Memoirs of O. Frederick Nolde*, 5.

97 Bergman & Johnson, *Unofficial Diplomats*, 124–126.

98 The Anglican priest Tzu-ch'en Chao stepped down as one of the WCC's five presidents because he found it irreconcilable to being a patriotic Chinese, see Gaines, *The World Council of Churches*, 761–762.

99 For an overview of positions on Korea in the WCC, see Visser 't Hooft, *Memoirs*, 222.

together with Communist armies for our respective national existences," they wrote.[100]

This criticism targeted *government* policies, but the British churches cautioned their American colleagues not to harmonize their stand with their government. Two years into the war, the clear message was that the British churches were not going to align with US government policies in East Asia, including the "rolling back" of communism in China implied by the US-led military incursions north of the 38th parallel.

6 Orthodox Ecumenism and Evanston as an Icebreaker

How to relate to communism assumed a particular meaning as far as Europe was concerned, and this was connected to Orthodoxy. The Orthodox Church is not one body in its organization, but a consociation of autocephalous churches, in which the Ecumenical Patriarchate of Constantinople is "first among equals." However, almost all the Orthodox churches were to be found behind the Iron Curtain.[101]

The Orthodox Church was not hostile to the modern ecumenical movement. Indeed, the WCC resembled a call first proposed by the Ecumenical Patriarchate of Constantinople in 1920 to form a "league of churches," parallel to the newly founded League of Nations.[102] And when possible, Orthodox churches participated in the ecumenical movement. In this movement, they themselves often met for the first time in centuries, due to the isolation and persecution they had undergone, including during the Ottoman Empire.[103]

Although the Orthodox churches had only been weakly represented at Amsterdam, this changed at the Evanston assembly in 1954, but it required some special connections. For the assembly to take place at Evanston, the WCC had imposed the condition that all duly named representatives were to be admitted to the United States. However, in preparation for the assembly, despite Nolde having warned Dulles (now US secretary of state) of "the serious repercussions, both at home and abroad" if visas were denied to participants, Dulles replied to Nolde that it would be very difficult to grant the necessary visas under the present law, not to mention the public opinion.[104] Dulles' references most likely concerned the so-called McCarran Act, which prevented persons promoting the establishment of a "totalitarian dictatorship" from entering the United States, and the atmosphere under McCarthyism.

To secure the visas, a WCC delegation met first with Dulles, then with President Dwight D. Eisenhower. Throughout 1953, Nolde followed up with Dulles,[105] and in November, the latter informed Nolde that he had personally spoken to the attorney general, who had indicated that he would be willing to grant the visas to accommodate Dulles. Dulles promised Nolde that he would "prepare the way."[106] Finally, 15 delegates from Czechoslovakia, Hungary, and East Germany were granted unconditional visas, and five with various

100 *Anglo-American Relations, Memo on Policies in East Asia, Prepared by a Group Representing the International Department, for the Consideration of Colleagues in the United States, May 1952*, 2–4, and K. Grubb to O.F. Nolde, Apr 23, 1952, both in: PUL, DRBSC, PPP, box 62 "Reel 22, JFD, 1952," folder "NCC, 1952."

101 Gaines, *The World Council of Churches*, 822; Alivisatos, "Orthodoxy," 202.

102 VanElderen, *Introducing the World Council of Churches*, 97. See also the chapter by Stylianos Tsompanidis in the first volume of this work.

103 Alivisatos, "Orthodoxy," 201; VanElderen, *Introducing the World Council of Churches*, 97–101.

104 *John Foster Dulles and the CCIA*, 4; J.F. Dulles to O.F. Nolde, Mar 21, 1953, in: PUL, DRBSC, PPP, box 73 "Reel 27, JFDP, 1953," folder "Frederick Nolde."

105 *Transcript of a Recorded Interview with Dr. O. Frederick Nolde*, 35; O.F. Nolde to J.F. Dulles, Mar 3, 1953; O.F. Nolde to J.F. Dulles, Mar 30, 1953; O.F. Nolde to J.F. Dulles, Apr 4, 1953, all letters to be found in: PUL, DRBSC, PPP, box 73 "Reel 27, JFDP," folder "Frederick Nolde."

106 O.F. Nolde to J.F. Dulles, Nov 9, 1953, in: PUL, DRBSC, PPP, box 73 "Reel 27, JFDP," folder "Frederick Nolde."

restrictions.[107] Their visit to the United States initiated church visits across the Iron Curtain and pioneered East-West cultural exchanges.

7 The Russian Orthodox Church Joins the WCC

The WCC-Russian Orthodox Church rapprochement after Amsterdam was initiated in 1952, when pastor Martin Niemöller, one of the world's best-known churchmen at the time owing to his previous imprisonment by the Nazi regime, paid a private visit to Patriarch Alexy I of Moscow, head of the Russian Orthodox Church. In his report to the WCC, Niemöller emphasized that the Russian Orthodox Church was truly Christian and that he had sensed regret on the part of Patriarch Alexy about the Russian Orthodox Church not belonging to the WCC.[108]

In 1954, Hooft received a verbal message from Metropolitan Nicholas (Yarushevich), in charge of the Russian Orthodox Church's foreign relations and peace campaigns, during a visit to Hungary. The latter would be glad to receive full information on the WCC and form closer contact. Subsequently, Hooft ensured that the Russian Orthodox Church received all the materials related to Evanston. A year later, contacts were kept alive through Bishop Otto Dibelius in Berlin, and Nicholas responded by urging the WCC to revise its attitude to the WCP. Prompted by the Eastern churchmen's visit to Evanston, an NCC delegation visited the USSR in 1956, and in return, Soviet churchmen visited the United States. Through these exchanges, the FCC proposed that the Russian Orthodox Church should meet with the WCC. However, due to the Hungarian uprising in the same year, the meeting was postponed and only realized in 1958, in Utrecht, Holland. It was of an initial and explorative character, but following this encounter, Russian Orthodox Church observers took part in WCC central committee meetings, and in 1961, Nikodim Rotov (who had succeeded Nicholas), privately stated that the time had come for the Russian Orthodox Church to apply for WCC membership.[109]

Negotiations took place in March 1961, when a Russian Orthodox Church delegation visited Geneva. One of the issues discussed was whether the Russian Orthodox Church might be represented at the CCIA's New York headquarters. However, because of the visa complications experienced earlier, the Russian Orthodox Church was encouraged to maintain relations with the CCIA and the UN through its Geneva office.[110] At the WCC assembly in New Delhi, 1961, the Russian Orthodox Church was finally integrated into the WCC. Only two churches voted against this, four abstained, and practically all the churches in the United States voted in favor.[111] Other Orthodox churches

107 O.F. Nolde to L. Thomas, Aug 19, 1954, in: PUL, DRBSC, PPP, box 85 "Reel 33, JFDP," folder "Frederick Nolde, 1954."

108 Visser 't Hooft, *Memoirs*, 263–265.

109 Most likely, this step by the Russian Orthodox Church also served to strengthen it *vis à vis* the Soviet state, which had begun new antireligious campaigns, see Adriano Roccucci, "The Experience of the Russian Orthodox Church during the Soviet Regime," in: Giuseppe Alberigo & Oscar Beozzo, eds., *The Holy Russian Church and Western Christianity*, London, SCM Press, 1996, 49–65, here 56–58; Tatiana A. Chumachenko, *Church and State in Soviet Russia: Russian Orthodoxy from World War II to the Khrushchev Years*, Armonk, M.E. Sharpe, 2002, 143–188; Dimitry Pospielovsky, *The Russian Church Under the Soviet Regime (1917–1982)*, Crestwood, St. Vladimir Seminary Press, 1984, 327–333; Visser 't Hooft, *Memoirs*, 263–266; Istavridis, "The Orthodox Churches in the Ecumenical Movement," 306; Gaines, *The World Council of Churches*, 795.

110 *Appendix to Minutes of Executive Committee*, 2.

111 Prior to Russian Orthodox Church membership of the WCC, the *New York Times* had printed accusations by the Orthodox Autocephalous Church and the Greek Catholic Church in Ukraine that the Russian Orthodox Church in tandem with the Soviet government had effectively destroyed them: see Gaines, *The World Council of Churches*, 803; more negative votes were

followed the Russian lead, so that between 1961 and 1965 all of them, except for the Albanian one, became members of the WCC. Together, they established a permanent office in Geneva.[112]

By including the Orthodox churches, the WCC not only changed the public's impression that it was essentially a Protestant club, but it also took real steps to abandon its exclusively Western character, structure, and orientation, thereby preventing the establishment of an Eastern equivalent to the WCC. Instead, Christians were united across the Iron Curtain, which gave the ecumenical movement an enormous boost. The Russian Orthodox Church did not obtain any concessions with respect to representation in New York or WCC participation in the WPC but noted the easing of East-West tensions and the idea of peaceful coexistence gaining a foothold as important ingredients in its decision to join the WCC. However, Protestant proselytism in the East continued to cause frictions in the WCC, as did the lack of experience in international affairs together with political and theological differences.[113]

Admitting the Orthodox churches to the WCC was not without challenges and risks. Theologically, these churches had affirmed their spiritual power by renouncing all secular power. However, their traditional subservience to the state meant that the churches had not been able to remain outside intrigues in both national and international politics.[114] Therefore, from a Western perspective, the risk was of a political nature: to what extent were the churches in the East under the control of their respective (communist) governments or used by them?

There were no doubts in the WCC that authorities in Eastern Europe kept a strict eye on the churches, including in international affairs, at times controlling appointments within the ecclesiastical hierarchy or denying visas for travel abroad.[115] In the USSR, the Russian Orthodox Church was expected to support the government's foreign policy, refrain from criticism, and report on useful contacts abroad. This obviously challenged the unity of the WCC, including the council's ambition to be critical towards both East and West.[116] However, Visser 't Hooft also noted how he envied the extent to which the Soviet government kept itself informed, in detail, about developments in the WCC, an interest he did not always find in the West.[117]

The change of guard in the leadership of the foreign relations of the Russian Orthodox Church, from Nicholas to Nikodim, initially nurtured hope. In Western media, Nicholas had resembled a propagandist for, and a collaborator with, the regime. Nikodim, who became one of the five WCC presidents in 1975, seemed more like an independent partner of the Soviet government.[118] Also, in time, the WCC's leaders learned to distinguish better between colleagues of the Russian Orthodox Church speaking for the record, meaning that it would be reported in Moscow, and speaking more independently for the church.[119]

cast against the inclusion of two Pentecostal churches, see *To the Member Churches in the U.S.A. of the World Council of Churches, December 1961, A Statement by Dr. Eugene Carson Blake*, in: WCCA, 428.11.04.3 NY Office 1960–1962, folder "1961 January–June."

112 Visser 't Hooft, "The General Ecumenical Development," 14–15; Tsetsis, "The Meaning of the Orthodox Presence," 441; Michael Bordeaux & Alexandru Popescu, "The Orthodox Church and Communism," *CHC* 5, 558–579, esp. 572.

113 For a list of early challenges with respect to orthodox involvement in the WCC, see Alivisatos, "Orthodoxy," 204–207.

114 Gaines, *The World Council of Churches*, 795, 822.

115 Gaines, *The World Council of Churches*, 804–805.

116 Hellqvist, *The Church and its Boundaries*, 31–32; Bordeaux & Popescu, "The Orthodox Church," 572.

117 Visser 't Hooft, *Memoirs*, 275.

118 Even in *tête-à-tête* conversations, Nikodim only admitted to individual cases of persecutions in the USSR and only when hard facts were laid before him, see Pospielovsky, *The Russian Church*, 359, 362; Gaines, *The World Council of Churches*, 1034–1035.

119 Eugene Carson Blake, "The World Council of Churches: East-West Church Relations (1966–1972)," in: Ans J. van der Bent, ed., *Voices of Unity: Essays in Honour of Willem Adolf Visser 't Hooft on the Occasion of his 80th Birthday*, Geneva, WCC Publications, 1983, 1–10, 6.

However serious the charges had been against the Russian Orthodox Church for subservience to the Soviet state or complacency in oppression of other churches in the USSR, the WCC leaders, assisted by the CCIA, saw it as their responsibility to bring the Russian Orthodox Church within the ecumenical fold, precisely because of the control the state extended over the Russian Orthodox Church. The paradoxical function of the Russian Orthodox Church during Soviet rule was that it potentially served both as a breeding ground for resistance to the regime and as its extended hand into civil society (including in the Soviet satellite states). However, the WCC leadership concluded that the true believers in the Soviet Union were not in the catacombs, but in the Russian Orthodox Church, including Christians both willing to compromise with the regime and those wishing to resist it. Ultimately, whether extending the Russian Orthodox Church a hand would benefit the latter or former had to be tested in practice.[120] Eugene Carson Blake, president of the NCC in the United States, and soon the successor of Visser 't Hooft as secretary general of the WCC, reminded his fellow American churchmen that the existence of Christian churches remained "the largest crack in the totalitarian structures of the USSR."[121]

8 Perforating the Iron and Bamboo Curtains

The pioneering visit of the Eastern churchmen to Evanston in 1954, and later the entry of the Russian Orthodox Church and other Orthodox churches into the WCC, led to church visits taking place between East and West. For example, Visser 't Hooft and Nolde visited the USSR as part of a WCC delegation in December 1959.[122] A Russian church delegation, including Protestants, visited the United States in 1963. Ten years later, the first visit by a Russian patriarch, Pimen, to the WCC headquarters in Geneva took place. A WCC delegation toured the USSR shortly after, and also held a preparatory discussion on the Nairobi assembly, to be held in 1975.[123]

Furthermore, there were visits by WCC delegations to other countries in the socialist camp. In 1956, Dr. Rajah B. Manikam, a Lutheran bishop in Tranquebar and the WCC's East Asia secretary, led the first visit to Mao Zedong's China. The visit was informal, and Manikam found the churches "self-supporting, self-administrating and self-propagating"[124] (in line with the Chinese so-called Three-Self Patriotic Movement at the time). As the state had taken them over, the churches no longer needed to provide funds for schools and hospitals and were tax-exempt. They enjoyed freedom of worship, he reported, including publishing books and periodicals, if they did not hold open-air meetings or speak out against the government.[125]

In a report "not to be published in any form," Manikam gave an account of the harsh criticism by Chinese church leaders of the alleged "political activities" of the WCC, its stance on Taiwan, and for having had a Western missionary representing the Chinese churches at Evanston. Moreover, the Chinese church leaders were skeptical about the WCC not supporting the WPC and made accusations that Dulles "controls your CCIA." However,

120 *On the Church Situation in the U.S.S.R., October 11, 1961*, in: WCCA, 428.11.04.3 NY Office, 1960–1962, folder "1961 January–June."

121 *To the Member Churches in the U.S.A. of the World Council of Churches.*

122 O.F. Nolde to G. Allen, Dec 20, 1959, annex to O.F. Nolde to P.D. Bernau, May 26, 1961, in: WCCA, CCIA CFNA, USA General + Gov, 1966–1978, US Government, Department of State (General); Gaines, *The World Council of Churches*, 799–801.

123 Pospielovsky, *The Russian Church*, 446.

124 Gaines, *The World Council of Churches*, 782.

125 These impressions were in the main confirmed by a report from the British Society of Friends that had visited China earlier, and by the former missionary of the Presbyterian Church in the United States to China, Rev. Charles C. West, see Gaines, *The World Council of Churches*, 182–187, 774–776.

the Chinese Christians wanted to renew the fellowship with the WCC (but not with the IMC).[126]

Manikam's encounter with Zhou Enlai, whom he described as the kindest prime minister he had met in East Asia, went more smoothly. Although Chou said that China had sent away "once and for all" those foreign missionaries who supported colonialism, he emphasized that the government had permitted others to stay and that churches enjoyed freedom if they did not "do wrong" or "upset the Government." He stressed that religious freedom was not being harmed by communists, but religious people themselves (mentioning specifically Catholics and Muslims, whom he accused of imposing their religious views on their children). Chou admitted that a majority of Chinese were religious and that communists only numbered nine million, but he expressed a hope that scientific advancements would make religion gradually fade away. In 1956, China still had to complete the so-called New Democratic stage of its revolution, which may explain the government's relatively soft stance on the churches, something that would change later, especially during the Cultural Revolution. However, Manikam also obtained information on imprisoned churchmen, considered counterrevolutionaries, and connected to Taiwan's Chiang Kai-shek, himself a Catholic.[127]

The efforts of the CCIA in this arena relied on the idea that building relations across Cold War frontiers, including developing mutual trust between individuals and groups, was the best way to ultimately prevent war.[128] The ability of the CCIA, and more generally of the WCC to overcome the rigidity of the US visa policy at the Evanston assembly, thereby realizing the first visit by a delegation of Eastern churchmen to the United States, contributed to breaking the ice between the two opposing camps. Starting from 1958, a more systematic travel and exchange program between the two superpowers took form, concerning science, technology, education, and culture, only to be limited in times of high tension, such as during the Soviet invasion of Afghanistan.[129] Whereas CCIA efforts in this arena did not lead to a continuous relationship with Chinese Christians, results were more positive when it came to Soviet Christians.

9 The Cold War Strikes Back

However, visits and exchanges between churches in the East and West were not without problems. For example, a WCC delegation to the Russian Orthodox Church in 1962 suspected that their host's exclusive focus on peace during discussions was the result of pressures exerted by the Soviet government. Independent conversations with church leaders were not possible and a case of state infiltration into the ranks of the Lutheran Church in Estonia was reported.[130]

An even more serious case was the first meeting of the WCC central committee behind the Iron Curtain, in Hungary, in the late summer of 1956. A few months later, in October–November, the Hungarian uprising took place and was subsequently

126 *Meeting of Bishop R.B. Manikam with Chinese Church Leaders at Peking on invitations from the I.M.C. and the W.C.C., March 17, 1956*, 1–6, in: WCCA, 450.004 Files from the WCC New York Office, correspondence, documents, Rajah B. Manikam; Gaines, *The World Council of Churches*, 782–787.

127 *Meeting of H.E. Chou-en-lai, Prime Minister of China with Bishop Manikam on March 27, 1956 at Peking*, 1–4, in: WCCA, 450.004 Files from the WCC New York Office, correspondence, documents, Rajah B. Manikam; see also the attached letter, R.B. Manikam to Dr. W.C. Merwin, May 15, 1956.

128 A letter to the editor, from Eric Schabacker, in: WCCA, 428.11.04.3 NY Office 1960–1962, folder "1961 January–June."

129 For more on cultural exchanges between the superpowers during the Cold War, see Yale Richmond, *Cultural Exchange and the Cold War: Raising the Iron Curtain*, University Park, Pennsylvania State University Press, 2003.

130 *Impressions of the visit of the delegation to the Russian Orthodox Church, June 1–2, 1962*, in: WCCA, 450.008 Files from the WCC New York Office, correspondence, Orthodox Catholic Church.

crushed by Soviet military intervention. In this situation, it was difficult for church leaders to take a stand. Metropolitan Nicholas offered material assistance to the suffering people of Hungary, but made no reference to the Soviet intervention.[131] The leaders of the three largest Hungarian churches (Roman Catholic, Reformed, and Lutheran) all committed themselves to the uprising, but after it had been suppressed, they were forced out of their ecclesiastical positions.[132] In the meantime, the WCC was attacked in the East for having contemplated the uprising at its meeting in Hungary.[133] Simultaneously, criticism from the West targeted the WCC for its relationship with proregime churchmen and administrators, prior to and after the failed revolution.[134] It was not easy to be a world council during periods of high tension and crisis.

Another test for the WCC was the Cuban Missile Crisis in 1962. The council warned against unilateral action on the part of the US government and called for the greatest possible restraint, but also stated that the Soviet missiles on the Caribbean Island constituted a great danger (later admitting that the United States had missiles on foreign soil closer to the USSR than the missiles in Cuba were to the United States). Any military action, the WCC emphasized, had to be in accordance with the UN Charter.[135]

Later still, in May 1968, when the Soviet Union crushed the so-called Prague Spring in Czechoslovakia by military intervention, the WCC wrote to the various Orthodox churches asking them to take a public stand. The Rumanians promptly replied that they protested the Soviet action, but no reply came from Bulgaria or East Germany, and Hungary was against taking any action. More importantly, no word came from the Russian Orthodox Church. The WCC decided to release a brief, but clear statement denouncing the intervention. A few weeks later, Nikodim sent a message through a friend: if the WCC absolutely "must do things like that, do them, but please don't ask us."[136]

After the defeat of the Hungarian uprising in 1956, Hromádka, who denounced the WCC's protest over Soviet intervention, had faced severe opposition when reelected to the WCC central committee.[137] Now Soviet military intervention had taken place on his own soil. However, the CPC, of which he was the chief architect, and whose members were highly outspoken against imperialism and colonialism, failed to take a clear stand. Consequently, Hromádka, who had backed the reforms to create "Socialism with a human face," resigned in protest. The events, he commented, constituted the "greatest tragedy" of his life.[138]

10 The CCIA between Diplomacy and Policy-Making

The CCIA nurtured a complex relationship with decision makers in both the East and the West, characterized by both conflict and consent, often walking on a knife's edge to preserve the churches' independent, critical stand, but also to maintain their influence and relevance.

The WCC made the UN paramount to its engagement in world affairs. Not only did it see the UN as the best option available for advancing human welfare, including world order and

131 Nolde, *The Churches and the Nations*, 64.

132 Gaines, *The World Council of Churches*, 787–789; Blake, "The World Council of Churches," 3–5.

133 VanElderen, *Introducing the World Council of Churches*, 27; Visser 't Hooft, *Memoirs*, 300–301.

134 Gaines, *The World Council of Churches*, 767, 790–791.

135 An early WCC statement on the crisis was issued before consulting the CCIA, which led to criticism of Visser 't Hooft, see Jurjen A. Zeilstra, *Visser 't Hooft (1900–1985): Living for the Unity of the Church*, Amsterdam, Amsterdam University Press, 2020, 327–329; Visser 't Hooft, *Memoirs*, 307; van der Bent, *Christian Response*, 47.

136 Blake, "The World Council of Churches," 7–8.

137 Gaines, *The World Council of Churches*, 755, note 10, 793.

138 Stefanik, "The Christian Peace Conference," 51; Ápád Welker, "The Christian Peace Conference and its Connections with the Communist State: The Case of Hungarian Churches in the Early 1960s," *VJHS* 20, 2013, 197–214.

intergovernmental cooperation,[139] but the establishment of the UN itself was also very much due to ecumenical efforts, in particular those of the FCC and the CJDP.[140] These two bodies were at the forefront in lobbying to have civil society represented in the UN, which paved the way for the CCIA to formalize its relationship to the UN as an NGO, representing both the WCC and the IMC.[141]

The CCIA maintained official contact with the UN, observed the General Assembly and Security Council meetings, kept in contact with the secretary general, received UN information and involved itself in a number of UN programs, specialized agencies, and so on.[142] The commission contributed to the UN in numerous ways in the fields of human rights, refugees, conflict resolution, disarmament, and development, among others, including being among the first to push the proposal that countries should allocate at least one percent of their national income to international development aid. This was unanimously adopted by the UNGA and later by the UNCTAD.[143] Moreover, the CCIA played a leading role in the UN's NGO community in the initial stages. Rees was elected chairman of the conference of NGOs, and Nolde was known as one of the most influential NGO representatives in the early UN system.[144]

One of the ways in which the CCIA continually contributed to the UN, was by providing information from its widespread networks, for example on human rights abuses around the world.[145] However, before that, the commission played a significant role in drafting the UN's Universal Declaration of Human Rights. Indeed, this declaration, adopted in 1948, might constitute the best example of how disproportionally a small but efficient committee impacted global governance.[146] Some even referred to article 18 of the declaration as "Nolde's article."[147]

At the center of the CCIA's attention in its early years was the safeguarding of religious freedom. This was not so much spurred on by the emergence of the so-called people's democracies in Eastern Europe, and the repression faced by Christians there, but by a more general concern for the impediments to global missionary activity. At the same time, these efforts were also directed against Catholic intolerance, especially in Southern Europe and Latin America.[148]

How the CCIA influenced the declaration has been documented in detail elsewhere.[149] Suffice it to say that by intervening in the diplomatic process at the UN, the CCIA ensured that the concept of "freedom of worship" was substituted in the declaration by the broader concept of the right to "freedom of thought, conscience, and religion," very

139 Gaines, *The World Council*, 553–555.

140 Inboden, *Religion and American Foreign Policy*, 30; Nurser, *For All Peoples*, 139, note 10; British churches also played a role, but were more hesitant than their American colleagues owing to their experience with the failures of the League of Nations, see K. Grubb to O.F. Nolde, Nov 13, 1946, 2.

141 O.F. Nolde, Nov 7, 1946.

142 *The Commission of the Churches on International Affairs, Joint Report on the Executive Chairman and the Director, August 17, 1948*, 14, in: PHS, FCC RG 18, FCC, 1894–1952, box 27, folder 18 "CCIA"; for an example of the CCIA and the UN secretary generals not following the same line, see R. Fagley to O. Dahlén, L.J. Niilus & E. Rees, Mar 20, 1972, in WCCA, 248.11.04.8, NY Office 1972–1974, 1972; Peiponen, *Ecumenical Action*, 232–234.

143 This idea was first developed at a meeting in Nyborg, Denmark, in 1958, but the churches originally thought that one percent might be too modest for the purpose, see Fagley, "The First Twenty Years," 22; Nolde, *The Churches and the Nations*, 13.

144 *Reports 1970–1973*.

145 *The Church in International Affairs: Reports 1974–1978*, Geneva, WCC Publications, 1979, 93.

146 Nurser, *For All Peoples*, ix, 176; Peiponen, *Ecumenical Action*, 223–230.

147 Lehmann, *Religious NGOs*, 95; in 1968, the CCIA was nominated for the Nobel Peace Prize for its human rights work, see O.F. Nolde to W. Kotschnig, Oct 3, 1968, in: WCCA, CCIA CFNA, USA General + Gov, 1966–1978, US Government, Department of State (General).

148 Nurser, *For All Peoples*, 174; Peiponen, *Ecumenical Action*, 101–102.; the question of religious freedom was instigated by the CCIA's concern to safeguard this right in the postwar Italian constitution, see *The Commission of the Churches on International Affairs, Joint Report on the Executive Chairman and the Director, August 17, 1948*, 22.

149 See especially Nurser, *For All Peoples*, and Peiponen, *Ecumenical Action*.

much to the wrath of the USSR.[150] In this difficult negotiating process, Nolde was aided by contacts in the US State Department, especially Dulles, who advised the Department, and was given access to high-level, sensitive information.[151] More generally, the CCIA relied on churches around the world to build a favorable public opinion of this article and exert pressures on their respective governments to accept and support it.[152] At this point, Nolde felt that the UN had finally acquired a soul.[153]

Having contributed to formulating the central human rights document of its time, the CCIA faced the far more challenging task of safeguarding its articles. To preserve this mission, the CCIA walked a narrow line between noncompliance with states abusing their power, and manifesting solidarity with the local churches suffering under it. This included not always publicly denouncing violations, because it might expose local churches, lead to greater oppression, and endanger WCC unity. The dilemma was that too harsh a criticism directed at authorities could simply force churches to retract from the WCC, blocking newly established channels of contact and dialogue, including those with the same authorities.[154]

This was a constant challenge in Eastern Europe where the Christian faith was deemed irreconcilable with Marxist doctrine, which led to church-state tensions, despite their official separation, formal constitutional rights, and declared policies of noninterference on the part of the authorities. The CCIA and the WCC would frequently express criticism to the embassies of the respective countries or work through Western governments, and they would refrain from asking the local churches to take part in these endeavors. Although silence did not equate inaction, this led to criticism of the WCC, which was not always unfounded, from both within and outside the churches, for accepting the abuse of human rights and not supporting dissidents strongly enough.[155]

The dilemma came to the fore at the WCC assembly in Nairobi, in 1975. Two Russian Orthodox priests urged the WCC to protest religious persecution in the Soviet Union, with specific reference to the Helsinki Final Act. By signing the accord, Soviet leaders had for the first time, in an international agreement, guaranteed to respect a wide range of human rights, including religious freedom. However, to the disappointment of many, the WCC protest was watered down following the advice of the Russian Orthodox Church leadership who feared a subsequent retaliation from Soviet authorities. Others in the WCC held that Christianity had emerged under totalitarianism – the Roman Empire – and would outlast it. Publicly criticizing the Soviet authorities was just as much an illusion to them as if the Christians had asked Nero to not burn Rome. However, in 1980, the WCC finally expressed a direct criticism of Soviet church policies.[156]

11 The Close Dance with Dulles' State Department

With its limited size and resources, the CCIA did not have the capacity to suggest a detailed foreign policy to be pursued by governments, but focused

150 Nurser, *For All Peoples*, 131, 147.

151 J.F. Dulles to O.F. Nolde, Apr 12, 1947, in: PHS, FCC RG 18, FCC, 1994–1952, folder 30 "General Secretary, Dulles"; *Minutes of the First Meeting of the Commission*, 4; *Transcript of a Recorded Interview with Dr. O. Frederick Nolde*, 29.

152 The CCIA received feedback to the draft declaration from churches in more than 37 countries, see *Minutes of the First Meeting of the Commission*, 6; Peiponen, *Ecumenical Action*, 111–114, 223–230.

153 Peiponen, *Ecumenical Action*, 335.

154 van der Bent, *Christian Response*, 40.

155 See a discussion of this delicate issue in the following reports: *Reports 1970–1973*, 133–135; *Reports 1983–1986*, 8, 24; *Reports 1987–1990*, 20, 132. *Draft, Memoirs of O. Frederick Nolde*, 28, explains how the churches sought to bring pressure on governments concerning these issues.

156 Gaines, *The World Council of Churches*, 1049, 1061–1063; Hellqvist, *The Church and its Boundaries*, 31–32; Hudson, *The World Council of Churches*, 287; Pospielovsky, *The Russian Church*, 450.

on issues of particular interest to the churches.[157] Bilateral relations with governments would ideally be pursued through local churches, but at times they were carried out directly by the CCIA or coordinated transnationally by the commission.[158]

Of particular importance is the CCIA's relationship with the US State Department. When preparing for the Cambridge conference, Nolde had consulted the department,[159] and this became standard procedure before important CCIA or WCC meetings. In this way, Nolde was able to take government thinking, input, and planning into account.[160] He also kept the State Department up to date on his travels abroad, for example when he was going to meet government representatives or the Moscow Patriarchate.[161] The State Department also kept itself informed on the commission's activities,[162] regularly receiving its materials[163] and making use of the information it offered. During World War II, churches had provided valuable information from enemy territories,[164] and as soon as the State Department became aware that an upcoming NCC delegation to Asia in 1952 (which included CCIA members) was concerned not only with "ecclesiastical matters," it made sure that it received a full report.[165] At the same time, the department included the CCIA in its efforts to build consensus around US foreign policy. Thus, the CCIA was invited to the Department's annual foreign policy conference for NGOs.[166]

Nolde worked with every US secretary of state since Cordell Hull, but at times he also contacted the US president directly, like he did with President Lyndon B. Johnson during the Vietnam War.[167] However, never was the relationship with government closer than during the Nolde-Dulles "partnership" in the 1950s. Dulles' background in the CCIA, shared interests, friendship, and trust[168] eased the commission's access to the department.[169] Apart from official contacts, the two men met informally two to four times a year, sometimes in Dulles' home, sometimes on trips abroad. For example, during the

157 *The Commission of the Churches on International Affairs, Joint Report on the Executive Chairman and the Director, August 17, 1948*, 19.

158 For example, this was the case when the Korean War began and later during the Suez Crisis, see *Draft, Memoirs of O. Frederick Nolde*, 25–26; *Outline of Proposal*, 13.

159 Nurser, *For All Peoples*, 130.

160 See O.F. Nolde to K. Grubb, Jan 27, 1959 and annexes to O.F. Nolde to J.F. Dulles, Apr 13, 1954, all in: WCCA, 428.10.10.3 JFDP, 428.10.10.

161 *Notes on Actions in Connection with the Egyptian and Hungarian Crisis*, 2, in: PHS, NCC RG 4, General Secretary, 1950–1973, box 14, folder 25 "CCIA"; O.F. Nolde to J.F. Dulles, Jun 11, 1958, in WCCA, 428.10.10 JFDP, 428.10.10.3 and US Department of State Consultations, Nolde, Mar 8 1955, in: WCCA, CCIA CFNA, USA General + Gov, 1966–1978, US Government, Department of State (General).

162 *State Department Consultations – 19 December 1956, Nolde to Grubb et al.*, annex to *State Department Consultation, Grubb to Nolde*, Dec 28, 1956, CFNA, USA General + Gov, 1966–1978, US Government, Department of State (General).

163 An arrangement renewed by Dean Rusk in 1961, see O.F. Nolde to P.D. Bernau, May 26, 1961.

164 Letter to J.R. Sharp, Jul 22, 1942, in: WCCA, 450.29 Files from the WCC New York Office, WCC + US Gov.

165 W.W. Van Kirk to J.F. Dulles, Oct 3, 1952, in: PUL, DRBSC, PPP, box 62 "Reel 22, JFDP, 1952," folder "NCC, 1952."

166 See R. Fagley to D. Rusk, Feb 28, 1967 and annexes, in: WCCA, CCIA CFNA, USA General + Gov, 1966–1978, National Foreign Policy Conference, Mar 16–17, 1965, Washington DC; this was also the case in 1958, see M.S. Rice to O.F. Nolde, May 6, 1958 and *Department of State, National Conference on U.S. Foreign Policy, October 30, 31, and November 1, 1951*, both in: WCCA, CCIA CFNA, USA General + Gov, 1966–1978, US Government, Department of State Meetings.

167 W. Shoemaker to O.F. Nolde, Jun 29, 1967 and W.J. Jorden to O.F. Nolde, Feb 6, 1968, both in: WCCA, CCIA CFNA, USA General + Gov, 1966–1978, US Government.

168 Dulles held Nolde in high esteem: at one point he told him that "any time you want a job as assistant secretary of state, it's yours," Nurser, *For All Peoples*, 28; in another instance, Dulles wrote to Nolde: "Fred, you are not talking like a churchman … I would be glad to have you down here helping me – as an Assistant Secretary of State … ." See *Consultation with the Secretary of State, 10th April 1958*, 2, 4, in: WCCA, CCIA CFNA, USA General + Gov, 1966–1978, US Government, Secretary of State (John Foster Dulles), Consultations.

169 *Transcript of a Recorded Interview with Dr. O. Frederick Nolde*, 27, 36.

Berlin foreign ministers' conference in 1954, Dulles informed Nolde during lunch about ongoing negotiations and that Molotov was being "impossible." Dulles considered walking out of the meeting, but instead, they discussed how to force Molotov to do so.[170] Consultations in larger groups took place once a year, but Nolde would also drop in occasionally to talk to Dulles.[171] He was "always available for advice, for suggestions, and for establishment of contacts," recounted Nolde, and there "was almost sufficient time" and "never a rebuff," even when the two men disagreed.[172]

According to leading US churchmen, Dulles never tried to misuse the church.[173] However, having returned from the NCC delegation to the USSR in 1956, Van Kirk and Roswell Barnes were asked by Dulles if they had anything "of a more intimate character to say" than the impressions reported to the press.[174] And after Evanston, the World Day of Prayer, which Eisenhower had called for when addressing the assembly, turned into a weapon in the Cold War, not the ecumenical initiative which had been the original intention of the WCC. Nevertheless, Nolde wanted the CCIA to link up with the follow-up initiative.[175]

Perhaps the best way to describe the relationship between the CCIA and the State Department is "mutually beneficial," as when Nolde, in connection to the Arab-Israeli conflict, kept Dulles informed about CCIA consultations with governments in the Middle East, or when Nolde asked Dulles to support suppressed Protestants in Spain and Columbia. And Nolde seems to have departed from the impartial stand of the WCC when he suggested that Dulles should include the following paragraph in a speech in San Francisco in June 1955: "Yet the Soviet Union must see that our action has been the necessary response to its own buildup of military strength and its threat for use of force to accomplish its own objectives of expansion."[176]

Nolde was thus often aligned with Dulles, but the CCIA was not the pawn of the government. When church-state interests failed to coincide, Nolde was ready to confront Dulles. Indeed, during the 1950s, ecumenists became increasingly disappointed with Dulles, as their perception of him as a Christian internationalist changed to that of a nationalist and Cold War hawk. Dulles' strategy of "massive retaliation" and "brinkmanship" openly disgusted them.[177] Thus, when the USSR announced a unilateral decision to cease its nuclear testing in the spring of 1958 Nolde put additional pressure on Dulles, who was reluctant to have the United States follow the initiative, threatening to publicly criticize the Eisenhower administration.[178] A heated meeting took place, in which

170 *Transcript of a Recorded Interview with Dr. O. Frederick Nolde*, 31–32.

171 *Transcript of a Recorded Interview with Dr. O. Frederick Nolde*, 31–32.

172 *Transcript of a Recorded Interview with Dr. O. Frederick Nolde*, 28, 34–38.

173 *Working for Peace as a Churchman, Roswell P. Barnes, May 22, 1961*, 5, in: WCCA, 450.002, Files from the WCC New York Office, John Foster Dulles.

174 J.F. Dulles to R. Barnes, Mar 24, 1956, in: PUL, DRBSC, PPP, box 100 "Reel 38, JFDP, 1956," folder "Roswell Barnes, 1956."

175 Letter to J.W. Hanes, Jul 8, 1955, in: PUL, DRBSC, PPP, box 96 "Reel 37, JFDP, 1956," folder "Frederick Nolde, 1955."

176 *Memo, Department of State, Office of the Secretary, May 31, 1955*, in: PUL, DRBSC, PPP, box 96 "Reel 37, JFDP, 1956," folder "Frederick Nolde, 1955," 2; Nolde and Dulles stayed in contact with regards to finalizing the speech, see Department of State to J.F. Dulles, Jun 8, 1955 and J.F. Dulles to O.F. Nolde, Jun 13, 1955, both in the same folder.

177 *Transcript of a Recorded Interview with Richard M. Fagley*, The John Foster Dulles Oral History Project, New York City, Dec 3, 1964, 10, 26–27, in: WCCA, 428.10.10 JFDP, 428.10.2; Preston, *Sword of the Spirit*, 460.

178 *Draft, Memoirs of O. Frederick Nolde*, 25, in: LACP, O.F. Nolde Papers, Box 1, Folder "Memoirs, Draft, ca. 1971–1972," O.F. Nolde to J.F. Dulles, Apr 8, 1958, and *Next Steps – Prevention of War and Promotion of Peace, Notes on an Address by Nolde, Director of the CCIA, at a Meeting of the U.S. Conference for the World Council of Churches, Buch Hill Falls, 18 April 1958*, 4, in: PUL, DRBSC, PPP, box 133 "Reel 52, JFDP, 1958," folder "Frederick Nolde, 1958"; *Consultation with the Secretary of State, 10th April 1958.*

Dulles lectured Nolde for over half an hour and urged him not to speak out in public. The meeting, according to Nolde, produced "more fireworks than any previous occasion."[179] However, the CCIA prevailed. After months of debate, in August the US and British governments declared their willingness to negotiate with the USSR about the cessation of tests. Dulles himself noted to Nolde how the administration's position "reflected as closely as possible the import and objectives" of the CCIA.[180] Afterwards, the churches were quick to pour oil on troubled waters. Barnes assured Dulles that whenever the churches had criticized his policies, it had "been an attempt to change public opinion so that you would have more elbow room to develop a politically possible foreign policy."[181]

Ultimately, an agreement to cease testing was not reached before 1963, in light of the Cuban Missile Crisis, and after considerable lobbying by the CCIA. The efforts of the latter were acknowledged even in Moscow. Having received a congratulatory cable from the pope, Khrushchev informed the Moscow Patriarchate that he thought that the WCC had contributed to such an extent to the agreement reached that he preferred not to publish news about the cable without a similar statement from the WCC.[182]

12 Peace Mediators: Korea, Sudan, and Eritrea

In certain instances, the CCIA was able to play a central mediating and peace-building role in civil wars. For example, in Korea in June 1953, progress towards an armistice had been brought to a standstill because of hostile actions by the South Korean government, which threatened to escalate the war. With negotiations broken off, Nolde offered Dulles to serve as an impartial intermediary to have them resumed. Dulles agreed and brought Nolde in, after clearance with the UN, for a consultation in Seoul between South Korean President Syngman Rhee, a Methodist, and the US assistant secretary of state for Far Eastern Affairs Walter Robertson.[183] Dulles placed all the necessary facilities, "both diplomatic and those which were under the jurisdiction of the armed forces," at Nolde's disposal, and Nolde conferred virtually on a day-to-day basis with both parties, including informing Dulles and President Eisenhower. Nolde's mediation ultimately contributed to the armistice between North and South Korea that effectively ended the war, although no peace agreement was ever signed. "Your mission," Dulles wrote, illustrates "the potential capacity of private

179 O.F. Nolde to J.F. Dulles, Apr 16, 1958 in: PUL, DRBSC, PPP, box 133 "Reel 52, JFDP, 1958," folder "Frederick Nolde, 1958."

180 *John Foster Dulles and the CCIA*, 6; however, an agreement on the cessation of tests of nuclear weapons was not reached before 1963.

181 R. Barnes to J.F. Dulles, Feb 23, 1959, in: WCCA, 450.002 Files from the WCC New York Office, Correspondence, John Foster Dulles; indeed, much points in the direction of Dulles not having completed a conversion from Christian internationalist to hawkish Cold War defender, as many ecumenists suspected he had. Privately, Dulles shared many of the concerns about nuclear weapons of his former church colleagues. Nolde acknowledged this, explaining it with the different responsibilities Dulles had to bear as an ecumenist and as a statesman. Furthermore, Nolde later correctly pointed out that, although Dulles received a great deal of criticism for his idea on "brinkmanship," it was actually John F. Kennedy who practiced it during the Cuban Missile Crisis, receiving widespread praise. For Nolde's observation, see *Transcript of a Recorded Interview with Dr. O. Frederick Nolde*, 10, 13; for a discussion of Dulles development in this period, see Preston, *Sword of the Spirit*, 460–462; John L. Gaddis, *The United States and the End of the Cold War: Implications, Reconsiderations, Provocations*, New York, Oxford University Press, 1992, 69–73; Inboden, *Religion and American Foreign Policy*, 226–256; the main positions in the debate on Dulles' development are summarized in Bevan Sewell, "Pragmatism, Religion, and John Foster Dulles's Embrace of Christian Internationalism in the 1930s," *Diplomatic History* 41, 2017, 799–823, esp. 800–801.

182 *Draft, Memoirs of O. Frederick Nolde*, 38.

183 *John Foster Dulles and the CCIA*, 3; for a detailed account of his involvement, see *Draft, Memoirs of O. Frederick Nolde*, 15.

organizations to exert an influence on public affairs," and he extended his gratitude to Nolde.[184] Nolde and Rees subsequently served as observers at the Geneva conference on Korea and Indochina from April to July 1954.[185]

Another WCC diplomatic success was reached in Sudan in 1971–1972, where the WCC played a mediating role between the Khartoum government and the South Sudan Liberation Movement. Most likely, it was the WCC's aid to refugees and financial assistance to liberation movements in Southern Africa that provided the necessary credibility for the WCC to assume this role. A peace agreement was signed in Addis Ababa in 1972. Emperor Haile Selassie, himself a member of one of the world's oldest Christian communities, hailed the influence of the WCC as of "lasting value." However, peace in Sudan proved to be temporary,[186] but the CCIA played a similar role in Eritrea and encouraged church contacts between Argentina and Great Britain during the Malvinas War.[187]

13 Decolonization and the Emergence of a Global Church

Protestants in Europe had once been devoted proponents and beneficiaries of colonial expansion, but following World War I ecumenical Protestants began calling for imperial disengagement. In doing so, they were not primarily moved by colonial rebellions or visions of the right to self-determination, but by the fear of a global export of European secularism.[188] At the same time, they felt compelled to develop a truly universal approach that could compete with socialist and communist internationalism.[189] The geographical and denominational limitations of the initial WCC might have been striking, as was the neglect of racial and colonial issues, but at Evanston Visser 't Hooft denounced colonialism.[190] However, it would take more than two decades for the WCC to develop a more consistent approach and begin a process of internal decolonization, spurred on by churches in the Global South.

Despite the principled stand taken at Evanston, in its early decades the CCIA took an overcautious attitude towards decolonization,[191] partly because the common ground between "older" and "younger" churches in this area was narrow. The pace of decolonization was an issue that divided those who favored a careful preparation of the colonized people's transmission to self-government from those, generally from the Global South, who had a more impatient approach.[192] Moreover, the CCIA had no precise guidelines on the far-reaching aspects of self-determination. Interdependence between North and South was viewed as instrumental to fellowship, but there was little awareness that interdependence between unequal partners easily leads to dominance and dependency. In other words, the issue of power was not critically addressed, and it was assumed that the interests of the developed and the less developed countries could be gradually reconciled.[193]

Therefore, instead of playing a pioneering role, the CCIA learned as it followed events from the

184 J.F. Dulles to O.F. Nolde, Jul 30, 1953, in: PUL, DRBSC, PPP, box 73 "Reel 27, JFDP, 1953," folder "Frederick Nolde"; Bergman & Johnson, *Unofficial Diplomats*, 121–122.

185 *Notes on a Report to the Central Committee of the World Council of Churches, by O. Frederick Nolde, August 4, 1955*, in: PUL, DRBSC, PPP, box 96 "Reel 37, JFDP, 1955," folder "Frederick Nolde, 1955"; Gaines, *The World Council of Churches*, 559.

186 *Reports 1970–1973*, 199–204.

187 van der Bent, *Christian Response*, 54, 58.

188 Udi Greenberg, "Protestants, Decolonization, and European Integration (1885–1961)," *JMH* 89, 2017, 314–354, esp. 314–318, 327.

189 Zubovich, "The Protestant Search," 5, 8.

190 Tahi Bonar Simatupang, "The East-West Tension, the North-South Imbalance – and JPIC?," *EcRev* 40, 1988, 399–404, esp. 401; Greenberg, "Protestants, Decolonization, and European Integration," 343.

191 Fagley, "The First Twenty Years," p. 19–20.

192 Fagley, "The First Twenty Years," 30.

193 Fagley, "The First Twenty Years," 19–20; van der Bent, *Christian Response*, 13–14.

sidelines and only gradually became involved. For example, when negotiations to transfer authority from the Netherlands to Indonesia were taking place in The Hague in 1949, the CCIA was represented in, or affiliated with, delegations on both sides, reflecting the Christian groups in both countries. This helped promote negotiations and became a model for how the commission would ideally contribute to problem-solving and reconciliation when Christians were represented on both sides of the fence.[194]

One of the bloodiest wars of independence in the 1950s took place in French Algeria. While many French Christians condemned the use of torture in the counterinsurgency warfare by the French state, they often did not question colonialism itself. French Christians had taken part in forming the WCC, and the latter found it difficult to distance itself from the former. This weakened the stand of the WCC on the issue. Initially, the WCC hoped for a reformed colonial presence in Algeria, but eventually realized that the greatest threat to a continued Christian presence in all of North Africa was the hardline stance of the supporters of French Algeria, including their claim to defend Christianity. Thus, Algeria became a wake-up call for the WCC: if Christians wanted to have any place in the postcolonial world, then they needed to take stock of their moral position.[195]

Another contemporary event also included the French churches. After the Suez Canal was nationalized, Israel, France, and Great Britain invaded Egypt in the fall of 1956. However, both the United States and the USSR were opposed to this action and applied pressure on the aggressors to withdraw. In this situation, the CCIA aimed to create a favorable to the withdrawal of French and British forces international public opinion. In the House of Lords, the archbishop of Canterbury had already stated that the action was a terrible mistake and in contravention of the letter of the UN Charter.[196] The statement was so remarkably strong that UN general secretary Dag Hammarskjöld asked Nolde to convey his personal greetings to the archbishop.[197] The commission asked the NCC to not make a unilateral statement, but to wait until the churches in Great Britain and France publicly denounced the action. While keeping Dulles informed, Nolde held consultations in Geneva, Paris, and London. Initially, most of the French church leaders consulted supported the action of their government, but after prolonged meetings they issued a critical statement, "born out of a real struggle," commented Nolde.[198]

14 Social Justice beyond the Cold War Divide: From Experts to Masses, from Advocacy to Action

The struggle against colonialism and domination thus influenced the WCC, but it would take the entrance of the so-called new and younger churches to make a truly sustained impact. This process was anticipated at the New Delhi assembly in 1961, to which churches from Asia and Eastern Europe were admitted, shifting the balance of influence from Western dominance in the WCC. At the assembly, the West came under fire for colonialism, paternalism, exploitation, domination, and white supremacy.[199] However, the

194 Bergman & Johnson, *Unofficial Diplomats*, 116; van der Bent, *Christian Response*, 44; for a more detailed account, see *Draft, Memoirs of O. Frederick Nolde*, 24.

195 Darcie Fontaine, *Decolonizing Christianity: Religion and the End of Empire in France and Algeria*, New York, Cambridge University Press, 2016, 117, 135, 210–211; after Leopoldo J. Niilus took charge of the CCIA in 1971, and with the backing of Nikodim, the CCIA reestablished relations with Algeria, see Lehmann, *Religious NGOs*, 9.

196 See Annex II to *Notes on Actions in Connection with the Egyptian and Hungarian Crisis*. Nolde, *The Churches and the Nations*, 65–66.

197 *Notes on Actions in Connection with the Egyptian and Hungarian Crisis*, 2.

198 *Notes on Actions in Connection with the Egyptian and Hungarian Crisis*, 3, 6.

199 Fontaine, *Decolonizing Christianity*, 211–212; Gaines, *The World Council of Churches*, 1039; contrary to Vatican II, the WCC took this opportunity to confess guilt for

paradigmatic shift from a primary focus on the East-West conflict to a focus on decolonization was expressed most clearly at the World Conference on Church and Society, held in Geneva in 1966.

For the first time, half of the 420 (mostly lay) delegates in Geneva came from developing countries. Their experiences and their yearnings for independence and development became central to the conference, which proved so radical that many from the so-called older churches, were disturbed by it.[200] The new voices heard in the WCC were not primarily concerned with passing moral judgements for or against capitalism and communism, which had dominated the debate at the Amsterdam assembly. Instead, they focused on their concrete experiences, as Christians, seeking independence, progress, and social justice. To them, postcolonial ecumenism provided a "third way," the realization of nonalignment. Visser 't Hooft's efforts to expand his concept of a "responsible society" to a "responsible world society" was met with criticism since participants did not believe in universalizing a Western concept, pointing to the failures of technical assistance, among other things. Instead, the theology of revolution was publicly advanced for the first time in a WCC context.[201]

These positions were further developed at the Uppsala assembly in July 1968, which took place amidst global student uprisings, protracted warfare in Vietnam, and civil unrest in the United States. A few months before the assembly, Dr. Martin Luther King, who had been chosen to preach the opening sermon, was assassinated. Since New Delhi, member churches in the WCC from the Global South had more than doubled, from 42 to 103 (out of a total number of 235), with African churches quadrupling, from 10 to 41. This context and the substantial change that the WCC was undergoing in these years altered its approach to international affairs. Quickly, the WCC's focus shifted in the following decade from a preoccupation with freedom and order to an emphasis on human dignity and justice. The approach similarly changed, from an orientation towards governments and international organizations to showing concrete solidarity and becoming involved in popular struggles.[202]

At the World Conference on Church and Society in Geneva, demonstrators had shouted "CCIA is CIA."[203] Generally, the CCIA was perceived as being too close to the US State Department and too Anglo-American, and for not being female, teetotal, or young enough.[204] At Uppsala, the commission met growing criticism, for example for its failure to represent the Global South[205] and for its quiet, diplomatic activities. It was demanded that focus be redirected from engaging the powerful to empowering people.[206] This loss of faith in the capacity of international political institutions to bring about substantial change also meant a

the churches' responsibility for anti-Semitism and the Holocaust, see Norwood, *Pilgrimage of Faith*, 24.

200 Katharina Kunter, "Not Only in the Shadows of the Cold War: Africa, Socialism and European Christianity," in: Katharina Kunter & Jens Holger Schjørring, eds., *Changing Relations between Churches in Europe and Africa: The Internationalization of Christianity and Politics in the 20th Century*, Wiesbaden, Harrassowitz, 2008, 109–188, esp. 117; VanElderen, *Introducing the World Council of Churches*, 28–29.

201 Kunter, "Not Only in the Shadows of the Cold War"; Bastiaan Bouwman, "From Religious Freedom to Social Justice: The Human Rights Engagement of the Ecumenical Movement from the 1940s to the 1970s," *JGH* 13, 2018, 252–273, esp. 269; Paul Abrecht, "The Development of Ecumenical Social Thought and Action," 254–256; Besier, "80 Years," 306; Reynolds, "From Christian Anti-Imperialism," 244.

202 Laine, Meriläinen & Peiponen, "Ecumenical Reconstruction," 336; Konrad Raiser, "International Affairs: Continuity and Discontinuity," *EcRev* 40, 1988, 372–381, esp. 377, 380; van der Bent, *Christian Response*, 8.

203 See Nurser, *For All Peoples*, 43, note 5.

204 Nurser, *For All Peoples*, 30.

205 Grubb, *Crypts of Power*, 168; other critics noted that the CCIA had not sufficiently developed a theological basis for its activities, leading to a lack in preaching the gospel and educating the churches in international affairs, see Nurser, *For All Peoples*, 107–108.

206 Raiser, "International Affairs," 380.

redefined relationship with the UN, which would no longer serve as the principal arena for the CCIA.[207]

These changes coincided with the CCIA undergoing a thorough reorganization. The commission had lost its principal guardian and privileged status in the WCC when Visser 't Hooft retired in 1966. Blake, his successor, closed the CCIA offices in New York and London and centralized the work of the WCC's international affairs in Geneva. In the following years, Grubb, Nolde, and Rees retired, Nolde having suffered a heart attack. Booth left for a position in a development organization and Micheli for the Red Cross.[208] Leopoldo J. Niilus became the new CCIA director. As a lawyer, not a theologian or missionary, and as an Argentinian, Niilus represented a changing of the guard taking place in the CCIA (except for Fagley who stayed on). However, the second-generation CCIA had less impact on, and enjoyed less autonomy from, the WCC, and it no longer served as its primary arm in world affairs.[209] Instead, the department of Church and Society, especially its PCR, made headway into former and unguarded CCIA territory, especially on the question of race.

15 The PCR

The question of race had not figured highly in the CCIA's first 20 years of existence. As WCC churches in South Africa were divided on the issue, including the Dutch Reformed churches that defended apartheid, it was difficult to find common ground, and the commission preferred to have the question dealt with at WCC level. At Evanston, racism within the church and society was criticized, but only after the Sharpville massacre in South Africa in March 1960 did a consensus emerge on strongly condemning apartheid, leading to the South-African Dutch Reformed churches withdrawing its membership of the WCC.[210] Another potential source of CCIA interest in race was the prevailing segregation in the US Southern states, but here the commission took no significant action, perhaps because all its American officers and staff were overwhelmingly WASP. However, things changed in the mid-1960s with the new agendas brought into the WCC from the Global South, and Blake – himself a US civil rights activist – assuming the leadership of the WCC.[211]

In 1969, the WCC established the PCR, which was intended to be a global program, but eventually focused on white racism. From 1970 to 1979, as part of the program, the WCC granted $2,634,000 to organizations involved in fighting racial oppression in southern Africa.[212] These special funds were destined for humanitarian purposes, such as education, health care, and aid to refugees, but as they were given to organizations that were also

207 Peter Lodberg, "Justice and Peace in a World of Chaos," in: *A History of the Ecumenical Movement*, vol. 3, John Briggs, Mercy Amba Oduyoye & Georges Tsetsis, eds., *1968–2000*, Geneva, WCC Publications, 2004, 323–343, esp. 331; Nurser, *For All Peoples*, 127; for an account of how the UN registered changing CCIA priorities, see *The Secretary-General's meeting with the newly appointed General Secretary of the World Council of Churches, Dr. Philip Potter, on 21 November at 12.30, Interoffice Memo Curtis Roosevelt to Georg Hennig, November 14, 1972*, in: UN Archives, S-0974-0013, series S-0974, box 13, file 1.

208 Fagley retired at the end of 1975; Blake, "The World Council of Churches," 8f.; Lehmann, *Religious NGOs*, 111; Nurser, *For All Peoples*, 52; however, Rees continued as a part-time consultant to the CCIA on UN and on Middle East affairs, see *History and Structure*; *Reports 1970–1973*, 34–37.

209 Lehmann, *Religious NGOs*, 109–111; the WCC Central Committee meeting in Addis Ababa in January 1971 made the CCIA less autonomous, and Philip Potter, who substituted Blake, saw the CCIA as merely one body of many conducting the WCC's foreign affairs, see Hudson, *The World Council of Churches*, 37.

210 VanElderen, *Introducing the World Council of Churches*, 25–26; Fagley, "The First Twenty Years," 12; Hudson, "The World Council of Churches and Racism," 478.

211 Hudson, *The World Council of Churches*, 110.

212 Hudson, *The World Council of Churches*, 138; *Reports 1974–1978*, 101.

involved in armed struggle,[213] and as grants were not subject to control, the program particularly shocked constituencies of essentially white people's churches and attracted worldwide attention, including allegations of supporting violence and terrorism.[214]

Earlier Christian discussions on violence had primarily related to the legitimate use of it by sovereign states, but now it concerned social justice. Whereas all churches could unite around the need for social justice, opinions differed on the means to reach it. The archbishop of Canterbury denounced the grants, urging them not to be limited to the struggle against white racism, whereas others in his church supported them.[215] Blake noted that "in the two hundred years in which force was practised by whites, no one interested himself in this theme." Philip Potter, his successor from the West Indies, said that the Third World was "compelled to take destiny into its own hands just as the Christians of Europe did when fighting Hitler." M.M. Thomas defended the program against "the *status quo* ideology of violence."[216]

In the end, the WCC neither endorsed nor condemned the use of violence, and ultimately a coalition of churches from the Global South, black churches in the United States, and churches in Eastern Europe ensured that the program was continued. In time, the program even received support from select Western governments and establishment figures, such as Queen Juliana of the Netherlands and the president of the Federal Republic of Germany, Dr. Heinemann, who both contributed to the program personally.[217] In 1972, the scope of the program was extended and economic boycotts and appeals for sanctions on South Africa were initiated.[218]

The program might not have made new friends in the power corridors in Washington, London, or Paris, but at the WCC's Harare assembly in 1998 Nelson Mandela was quick to acknowledge that it had constituted "a joint struggle for shared aspirations."[219] However, while enormously increasing the WCC's credibility in Africa, to the point that the CCIA became a mediator in the Sudanese civil war, the program also meant that agency shifted away from the CCIA and spread to other WCC bodies.[220]

16 From Individual Political to Collective Social Rights

The change in the WCC's approach to international relations, epitomized by its support for armed liberation movements in southern Africa, sprang from a desire to uproot the underlying causes of world misery, not merely deal with its effects, later summarized in the eloquent sentence "the tree of peace has justice for its roots."[221]

This also made it imperative for the WCC to redefine its relationship with human rights. As mentioned above, the CCIA was initially highly

213 Among the recipients were the MPLA, GRAE, and UNITA in Angola, FRELIMO in Mozambique, ZANU and ZAPU in Rhodesia, SWAPO in Namibia and ANC and the PAC in South Africa, see Hudson, "The World Council of Churches and Racism," 481.

214 *Reports 1974–1978*, 101; Hudson, "The World Council of Churches and Racism," 481.

215 However, in the WCC, the Salvation Army, the Presbyterian Church in Ireland, and the Evangelisch-Lutherische Landeskirche Schaumburg-Lippe suspended their membership in protest of the grants, see Tapiwa Mapuranga & Ezra Chitando, "The World Council of Churches and Politics in Zimbabwe: From the Programme to Combat Racism to Operation Murambatsvina (1969–2005)," in: Kunter & Schjørring, eds, *Changing Relations between Churches*, 119–133, esp. 124; and Hudson, "The World Council of Churches and Racism," 485.

216 Hudson, *The World Council of Churches*, 114, 118.

217 Hudson, *The World Council of Churches*, 118, 123; Hudson, "The World Council of Churches and Racism," 483–484.

218 Hudson, *The World Council of Churches*, 120–121; Laine, Meriläinen & Peiponen, "Ecumenical Reconstruction," 338.

219 Norwood, *Pilgrimage of Faith*, 83.

220 *Reports 1970–1973*, 135; Bouwman, "From Religious Freedom," 271.

221 Raiser, "International Affairs," 381.

successful in making human rights a common denominator in the WCC and influencing their formulation in the UN, but in time, this came at a cost at two levels. First, while the starting point for the churches was theological – man shaped in the image of God and freedom of religion as the fundamental right from which all others derived – Protestant principles had to be translated into a universal language to make any headway in international governance. By treading this path, Nolde eventually retreated to a language of secular liberalism, which paved the way for a secularized revival of the human rights concept in the 1970s. This would be dominated by nonreligious NGOs, such as Amnesty International and Human Rights Watch, sidelining the CCIA.[222]

Second, the CCIA faced a growing skepticism within the WCC towards the specific concept of human rights that was proposed. For example, M.M. Thomas objected to the lack of unity around the concept and the "kind of politics, which may be called Anglo-American," which emanated from it.[223] At the Nairobi assembly in 1975, it was concluded that "to work for human rights … also means to work at the most basic level towards a society without unjust structures."[224] This resulted in a movement away from the perception of human rights as predominantly civil and political, which had been at the center of CCIA's understanding, and an acceptance instead of social, economic, and cultural rights, including those of development and peace. This shift from individual to collective rights, with the emphasis on social justice, also accorded with the new theology of revolution, but it alienated the CCIA from more actively defending human rights and dissidents in Eastern Europe.[225]

The older generation of CCIA officers referred to this process as a "crisis" within the commission, framing it as a dichotomy between professionalism and dilettantism. Although this dichotomy obviously reflected a real change in methods, from primarily promoting advocacy in a UN setting to becoming directly involved with movements for social change and justice, the conflict was more fundamentally about how the new generation had taken over the older generation's favorite arsenal, human rights, but given it a somewhat new content.[226]

17 The Vietnam War and the Weakening of the Ecumenical Churches in the United States

Although Blake had supported Dulles' foreign policy, he developed into a strident critic of the Vietnam War at a time when the majority of American Christians still supported it.[227] The relationship with Richard Nixon administration deteriorated as the war dragged on. The NCC, the main financial backer of the WCC, had been one of the first major mainstream organizations in the United States to publicly criticize the government on Vietnam, leading President Nixon to later add the organization to his list of domestic enemies.[228] In March 1969, the ecumenical churches and the US government were still on speaking terms and the CCIA met with Nixon. He indicated that, while the government was still pursuing talks with the Vietnamese, "'action' would be sought

222 Lehmann, *Religious NGOs*, 84; Zubovich, "The Protestant Search," 7, 10.

223 Zubovitch, "The Protestant Search," 8; see also Reynolds, *From Christian Anti-Imperialism*, 241–242.

224 Raiser, "International Affairs," 378.

225 For example, the WCC did not support Charter 77 in Czechoslovakia or Solidarity in Poland actively enough, something that the WCC later apologized for, see Kunter, "Not Only in the Shadows of the Cold War," 113–114; *History and Structure*; Besier, "80 Years," 307; Bouwman, "From Religious Freedom," 269–271.

226 Lehmann, *Religious NGOs*, 112; for a summary of how historians have looked on the recasting of human rights within the WCC, see Bouwman, "From Religious Freedom," 271.

227 E.C. Blake to J.F. Dulles, Apr 3, 1957, PUL, DRBSC, PPP, box 114 "Reel 45, JFDP, 1957," folder "Rev. Eugene Carson Blake, 1957"; Besier, "80 Years," 306.

228 Besier, "80 Years," 306.

'underneath,'" possibly referring to the United States not ceasing military actions.[229]

At Uppsala, the WCC called upon the United States to cease the bombing of North Vietnam immediately and unconditionally. The CCIA followed the peace talks in Paris and Geneva and held numerous conversations with the four delegations present.[230] From 1972, the WCC called on the United States to withdraw its military presence in Indochina.[231] At this point, the State Department became inaccessible to the CCIA, now under the leadership of Niilus, blaming the commission in September 1973 for being one-sided and attacking the US government.[232] The CCIA, however, in the context of the emerging Watergate scandal, had already renounced any faith in Nixon, noting that the "Nixon gang" made "the pursuit of presidential power the chief business of the Administration."[233]

In the aftermath of World War II, the influence of the ecumenical, mainline churches in American society had reached its zenith, having contributed to formulating a foreign policy consensus, including incorporating the United States into binding international arrangements, notably the UN. Anyone in the US foreign policy establishment at that time, and for the next 20 years, had very likely grown up in a white, Protestant milieu, often associated with the ecumenical churches. However, the polarization that took place in American society in the late 1960s and 1970s, when the foreign policy consensus broke down and the foreign policy establishment was substituted by more fragmented and politicized elites, also undermined and marginalized the ecumenists. This gave way to a new alliance between the government and conservative evangelical churches in the United States, encapsulated in the Ronald Reagan administration in the 1980s, and had global ramifications.[234]

18 The End to *Détente* and the Cold War

While Nixon was not highly esteemed for his moral standards, the churches saw his administration's pursuit of *détente* in the Cold War in a more positive light, including the SALT I agreement, the opening to China, and the Helsinki process. The CCIA played an active role in the efforts leading up to the signing of the Helsinki Final Act in 1975, which included creating a human rights program to implement it. Moreover, *détente* also meant renewed dialogue with communist regimes and parties in Eastern and Western Europe.[235]

When East-West tensions reemerged in the late 1970s and early 1980s, the CCIA was concerned with the deteriorating power relations and played an active role in the new peace movements that developed internationally, including launching initiatives to prevent the proliferation of nuclear weapons and avoid nuclear war.[236] However, the CCIA no longer enjoyed a privileged relationship with the State Department, and the Reagan administration's policies in Central America in

229 *Aide Memoire on Conversation in Washington, D.C., 20 March, 1969, Fagley to Blake and Eugene Smith, March 24, 1969*, 1–3, and E. Smith to R. Fagley, Jul 2, 1969, both in: WCCA, CCIA, country files, USA 1972–1975, United States Government, Nixon administration, 1969–1974.

230 *Reports 1970–1973*, 36.

231 van der Bent, *Christian Response*, 48–49.

232 L.M. Rives to L.J. Niilus, Sep 4, 1973, in: WCCA, CCIA, country files, USA 1972–1975, United States Government, Nixon administration, 1969–1974.

233 R. Fagley to O. Dahlén and L.J. Niilus, May 23, 1973, in: WCCA, CCIA, country files, USA 1972–1975, United States Government, Nixon administration, 1972–1975; when President Gerald Ford pardoned Nixon, Fagley wrote Ford that this was "a very unwise exercise of your presidential prerogative," see R. Fagley to the president, Sep 13, 1974, same folder.

234 Dino Knudsen, *The Trilateral Commission and Global Governance: Informal Elite Diplomacy (1972–1982)*, New York, Routledge, 2016, 102f; Inboden, *Religion and American Foreign Policy*, 5–6, 29; Besier, "80 Years," 305–306.

235 *Statement of the National Council of Churches of Christ in the U.S.A. to the Democratic and Republican National Conventions 1972*, in: WCCA, CCIA CFNA, USA General + Gov 1966–1978, Paper clips and publications 1966–1973, 4–5; *CCIA Reports 1974–1978*, 173, 176–181.

236 *History and Structure*; *Reports 1983–1986*, 5.

particular led to conflict with the ecumenical churches, which demanded a stop to military aid to, and intervention in, El Salvador, Guatemala, and Honduras, and to covert operations in Nicaragua.[237] However, the CCIA supported the dialogue and easing of tensions between the two superpowers in the second half of the 1980s, and in the USSR church-state relations improved during *Glasnost*, during which time the Soviet president Mikhail Gorbachev met Patriarch Pimen twice.[238]

With the establishment of international order as its main concern when the CCIA was launched in 1946, the commission regretted the efforts to implement the so-called New World Order as the Cold War faded out. The UN authorized the Gulf War but exercised no effective control over it. The CCIA saw this as a failure, not the establishment, of world order.[239] However, positive steps toward overcoming the remnants of the Cold War era in the ecumenical churches themselves were taken in 1989, when the Christian community of North Korea was represented for the first time in an international ecumenical event at which the China Christian Council participated for the first time since 1956.[240] On the doorstep to a new dawn, the CCIA registered a process of continual secularization in the world, but also noted – in what one might call an almost prophetic vision – a resurgence of religion, concluding that "a new definitional struggle between religion and politics" was approaching.[241]

237 *Reports 1983–1986*, 126; in December 1989, the WCC protested the US invasion of Panama, see *Reports 1987–1990*, 167.

238 Leustean, "Overview," 6.

239 *Reports 1987–1990*, 20–21.

240 Lodberg, "Justice and Peace," 340; in September 1986, the CCIA was instrumental in organizing the first ever meeting between Christians from both North and South Korea in Switzerland, see *Reports 1983–1986*, 108–111.

241 *Reports 1983–1986*, 6.

19 Conclusions

In intervening in postwar international affairs and developing a transnational diplomacy, the ecumenical churches relied mainly on the successful experience of the US churches' in influencing their government's postwar planning and the establishment of international order. The composition of the CCIA, its orientation and methods essentially reflected the preponderant power of the United States in the postwar world. However, at the WCC Amsterdam assembly, it was resolved to walk the difficult path of nonalignment in the ongoing East-West conflict. Although the "vital space" for such an impartial stand was shrinking, the WCC managed in the main, contrary to most other transnational organizations at the time, to stay clear of power politics, including not taking the bait from neither the East nor the West. Thus, the WCC incarnated the hope of transcending the new barriers dividing humanity. A few churches, such as those of China, left the organization during times of tension and crises, but the overall tendency was the inclusion of an increasing number of churches from all over the world, including from behind the Iron Curtain. Thus, the WCC developed into a platform for East-West dialogue, including pioneering cultural exchange between the two power blocs, although this came at the price of not publicly raising a fierce, critical voice against the Eastern regimes. Moreover, by its influence on the formulation and execution of human rights globally, its efforts to rebuild war-torn societies, halt the arms race, mediate in local and international conflicts, and so on, the CCIA demonstrated the potential of Christian diplomacy, which included a wide range of specific techniques and procedures.

At the same time, the disagreements and contradictions among the Christian churches themselves, especially with the Roman Catholic Church, expressed the limitations of the WCC. The lack of unity in the ecumenical movement, among other things, meant that the CCIA never developed an international moral ethos, also open to other religions and secularists, as a basis for international institutions and relations. If people of the same religion could not unite, how could a divided humanity? Furthermore, the grand design of a global CCIA network in which the source of Christian diplomacy was local ecumenical knowledge and connections, commitment, and action, soon proved to be hollow. In many situations, the best the commission could hope for was a delayed local response to its visions, plans, and initiatives.

In its first decades, the CCIA failed to take the burning questions of the Global South into proper consideration, whether it was racism, colonialism, or the struggle for independence. Only with the entry of the so-called younger churches into the WCC and the demands they raised, did the focus of ecumenical Christians shift from the East-West conflict to the North-South divide. In the meantime, the CCIA became less influential within the WCC, where a loss of faith in international political institutions to bring about substantial change meant a redefined relationship with the UN. The CCIA, found itself no longer the primary arm of the WCC in world affairs. In the human rights arena, the earlier focus of the commission on individual, political rights was superseded by an emphasis on collective, social rights. Instead of primarily engaging the powerful in quiet diplomacy, as was the preferred method in the early decades of CCIA, the approach changed to empowering people and making a public display of this.

These developments led to a loss of CCIA influence in the corridors of Western capitals, where Nolde, in particular, had nurtured a close partnership with US secretary of state Dulles in the 1950s. Yet, the time when the ecumenical, mainline Christians had wielded influence in the US foreign policy establishment was long gone, as political polarization in the context of the Vietnam War gave way to the rise of new elites, favoring an alliance between the US government and conservative, evangelical Christians in the 1980s. However, in the Global South the status of the WCC peaked, especially due to its efforts starting from the 1970s onwards to assist liberation movements in Southern Africa who fought colonial and racial oppression. A criticism of this "utopian" approach – favoring direct contributions to popular movements instead of engaging experts and political decision-makers – developed in the WCC in the 1980s and the CCIA and its global network continued to be reduced in size and capacity. However, as the Cold War waned, the WCC emerged, not least in its efforts to decolonize itself, as a more truly global and independent council.

Bibliography

Bergman, Maureen R. & Joseph E. Johnson, *Unofficial Diplomats*, New York, Columbia University Press, 1977.

Hudson, Darril, *The World Council of Churches in International Affairs*, Leighton Buzzard, Faith Press for the Royal Institute of International Affairs, 1977.

Lehmann, Karsten, *Religious NGOs in International relations: The Construction of "the Religious" and "the Secular"*, New York, Routledge, 2017.

Nolde, Frederick, "Ecumenical Action in International Affairs," in: *A History of the Ecumenical Movement*, vol. 2, Harold E. Fey, ed., *1948–1968*, London, SPCK, 1970, 263–285.

Nurser, John, *For All Peoples and All Nations: The Ecumenical Church and Human Rights*, Washington DC, Georgetown University Press, 2005.

Peiponen, Matti, *Ecumenical Action in World Politics: The Creation of the Commission of the Churches on International Affairs (CCIA), 1945–1949*, Helsinki, Luther-Agricola-Society, 2012.

van der Bent, Ans J., *Christian Response in a World of Crisis: A Brief History of the WCC's Commission of the Churches on International Affairs*, Geneva, WCC Publications, 1986.

CHAPTER 21

Rome's Reluctant Ecumenical Progress: From *Mystici corporis Christi* (1943) to the Reception of *De motione oecumenica* (1949)

Karim Schelkens

1 Introduction

Early in the spring of 1944, amidst the turmoil of World War II, Pope Pius XII promulgated an encyclical entirely devoted to the memory of Cyril of Alexandria. In this document, the Roman pontiff reached out to "the Christian peoples of the East," underlining his joy at the fact that Christians in both the East and the West shared an equally deep veneration for this 5th-century church father. However, the pope regretfully added that his joy was "mingled with an equal regret that not all of them have come together into that desired unity of which he," St. Cyril, "was the ardent lover and promoter."[1] Such a statement on the part of a pope constitutes an interesting point of departure for this contribution: at a time of global armed conflict and on the eve of what would become the Cold War era, the Roman pontiff seemingly fostered an awareness of the need for Christians to "labor together in heart and endeavor for union in the one church of Jesus Christ, so that they may present a common, serried, united, and unyielding front to the daily growing attacks of the enemies of religion."[2] Further on, Pius XII underlined the need for Christians to discover what they had in common and stressed that a "variety of rites and customs, preserving inviolate what is most ancient and most valuable in each, presents no obstacle to a true and genuine unity."[3]

However promising and ecumenically sensitive these words may sound, the papal references to unity and legitimate diversity were only one side of the coin. Age-old divides proved difficult to bridge, and one is quickly compelled to ask: what is meant by unity here? And with whom? Just like many statements by Pius XII, the encyclical merely discussed Eastern Christianity and remained silent about Reformed Christianity. In 1944, the Catholic magisterium still followed the lineage of statements on "unity" made by predecessors ranging from Pius IX to Pius XI.[4] Having said that, one is hardly surprised when article four of *Orientalis Ecclesiae* proposes the traditional unionist approach, which had not only dominated 19th-century Catholicism, but was still vividly present in the 1928 encyclical *Mortalium animos*.[5] Pius XII did not distance himself from any of this, but instead asked that "those who ... are separated from the bosom and unity of the Church ... follow the example and custom of their ancestors in paying due respect to the Roman Primacy."[6] This brief, yet for non-Roman Christians unequivocal and rather arrogant clause sets the horizon for the story of Rome's position toward the ecumenical movement in the 1940s and the early 1950s.[7]

1 Pius XII, *Orientalis Ecclesiae*, in: *AAS* 36, 1944, 129–144, here 132.

2 Pius XII, *Orientalis Ecclesiae*, 132.

3 Pius XII, *Orientalis Ecclesiae*, 138.

4 See, in this regard, the contributions by Laura Pettinaroli and Marie Levant in the first volume of this work.

5 Pius XI, *Mortalium animos*, in: *AAS* 20, 1928, 5–16. See Manuela Barbolla, "La genesi della *Mortalium animos* attraverso lo spoglio degli Archivi Vaticani," *RSCI* 66, 2012, 495–538.

6 Pius XII, *Sempiternum Rex Christus*, in: *AAS* 43, 1951, 625–644, here 626.

7 This article owes a lot to earlier important studies, such as Jean-Marie R. Tillard, "The Roman Catholic Church and Ecumenism," in: Thomas F. Best & Theodore J. Nottingham,

As we will not discuss Rome and ecumenism under the era of John XXIII, the period examined here roughly spans the final 15 years of Pius XII's pontificate, a period marked by important political and societal shifts. A first aspect was the transition from the wartime era into the Cold War. These years witnessed the effects of Stalinism and its general suppression of religion, as well as the rise of secularism in the West. It was a period of stark contrasts, also characterized by the slow reconstruction of a devastated Europe and by the emerging political unification process that would eventually lead to the European Union.[8] In the year 1948, in particular, important turnabouts occurred, such as the approval of the Marshall Plan, or the proclamation of the Universal Declaration of Human Rights. All of these factors constitute the broad horizon necessary to frame the topic "Rome and ecumenism" after World War II.

On a more explicit and direct level, however, the first and perhaps most astute way of addressing the topic is this: in hindsight, and writing from a post-Vatican II perspective, one can safely claim that in the Vatican offices, in the official policies and in both the public and internal discourse of the Holy See, there was no ecumenism. On the other hand, this straightforward denial does not mean that writing about Rome and ecumenism before John XXIII boils down to describing a nonevent. Ecclesial Rome ought not to be understood solely through its public statements, and the above-cited sentences from the 1944 encyclical *Orientalis Ecclesiae* already indicated that the situation was ambiguous. That ambiguity only increased as the ecumenical movement succeeded in growing rapidly and in relative autonomy from Rome. The movement's momentum forced Rome to come to terms with it, all the more so since by its very nature it strove toward the unity of all Christians. The path toward the formal commitment of the Roman Church to the ecumenical movement witnessed in the conciliar era proved slow and complex, and was marked by several setbacks, the last of which occurred still in 1959, with a crisis that occurred during the central committee meeting of the WCC on the isle of Rhodes.

In the following, this evolution will be traced by looking at two subsequent phases, and the timeline runs fairly parallel to that of the major societal and political shifts of the era. First, a special focus will be set on the years between 1943 and 1948, marked by the transition from World War II to the early postwar period. This period was marked by the heritage of individual and shattered ecumenical initiatives of Catholics engaged before and during the war, as well as by an institutional effort to restore the closed type of Catholic ecclesiology that had prevailed in the interbellum. As indicated above, the year 1948 constituted an important marker for Western society. The same is true for the history of interchurch relationships: after the establishment of the WCC, the novelty of the postwar situation and the impossibility to return to the past were felt more deeply than ever. In the decade that followed, Rome's reluctant appreciation of the desire for Christian unity underwent many changes. The openness to reconsider Catholic ecclesiology entered some Roman milieus, helping to create a mixed attitude of rejection and openness. In the Holy Year of 1950 some setbacks were felt, but as of 1952 Rome's explicit "rejection" of ecumenism as a relativizing tendency and its traditional warnings against false irenicism and religious indifference, slowly disappeared from

---

eds., *The Vision of Christian Unity: Essays in Honor of Paul A. Crow, Jr.*, Indianapolis, Oikoumene Publications, 1997, 179–197, Lukas Vischer, "The Ecumenical Movement and the Roman Catholic Church," in: *A History of the Ecumenical Movement*, vol. 2, Harold E. Fey, ed., *The Ecumenical Advance (1948–1968)*, London, SPCK, 1970, 311–352, and the somewhat older yet well informed study by Gregory Baum, *That They May Be One: A Study of Papal Doctrine (Leo XIII–Pius XII)*, London, Bloomsbury, 1958.

8 This contribution will not focus on the alignment of political and religious endeavors to promote unity, however important they may be for a proper understanding of the era and of the ecumenical movement. For more background on this, see Lucian N. Leustean, *The Ecumenical Movement & the Making of the European Community*, Oxford, Oxford University Press, 2014, and Jurjen A. Zeilstra, *European Unity in Ecumenical Thinking (1937–1948)*, Zoetermeer, Uitgeverij Boekencentrum, 1995.

the public arena. In this regard, the French historian Étienne Fouilloux spoke of an "ecumenical thawing."[9]

2 Reframing Catholic Ecclesiology (1943–1948)

The frequently-heard conviction that at the end of World War II, the Catholic magisterium lacked any awareness of the importance of the ecumenical movement may bear some truth in it, but it requires a little historical nuance. As mentioned above, Rome is not to be identified too hastily with Catholicism as a whole. When, in 1944, Pius XII both praised the importance of Christian unity[10] and called upon non-Roman Christians to "return" to the true mother church, his awareness was contrasted. For one, the pope brought on and took for granted the condemnatory statements issued by his predecessors in recent decades, triggered by a rising ecumenical movement since the WMC in Edinburgh in 1910.[11] Not long after World War I, in May 1919, and heeding the advice of Cardinal Rafael Merry del Val, Pope Benedict XV had responded negatively to the invitation extended by Bishop Charles Brent to attend the conference at Lausanne.[12] Nine years later, after the completion of the ecumenical conferences at Stockholm and Lausanne, Pius XI defended the absence of Catholic representatives in these meetings by condemning all attempts at religious indifference in the aforementioned encyclical *Mortalium animos*.[13] That document cast a shadow on the ecumenical position of Rome in the interbellum and it would remain an inconvenient reference point until the eve of Vatican II.

On the other hand, the negative papal statements also resulted from an awareness that Catholics were increasingly involved in a variety of local initiatives and movements marked by a certain openness to dialogue with non-Roman Christianity. These efforts are elaborately discussed in other articles in this volume, yet their enduring presence before, during, and after World War II definitively had an impact on Rome's position regarding Christian unity. Therefore, such efforts will be only mentioned briefly here.

2.1 *The Contrasted War Heritage*

However devastating, the war itself functioned as a catalyst for the ecumenical movement in a broader sense, and Catholics were not alien to this evolution.[14] In his later career, the Dutch pastor Willem Adolph Visser 't Hooft,[15] often stated that the modern ecumenical movement was marked

9 Étienne Fouilloux, "Une longue marche vers l'œcuménisme: Istina (1923–1967)," *Istina* 55, 2010, 271–287.

10 It should be recalled that such hints had already also been made in the very first encyclical that Pius XII promulgated, on Oct 20, 1939. See Pius XII, *Summi Pontificatus*, in: *AAS* 31, 1939, 413–453.

11 For a survey, see John A. Radano, ed., *Celebrating a Century of Ecumenism: Exploring the Achievements of International Dialogue*, Grand Rapids, Eerdmans, 2012.

12 Jeffrey Gros, Eamon McManus & Ann Riggs, *Introduction to Ecumenism*, New York, Paulist Press, 1998, 28–29. For a detailed reconstruction of events, see Philippe Chenaux, "Le Saint-Siège et les débuts du Mouvement œcuménique: La Conférence de Lausanne (1927)," in: Andreas Gottsman, Pierantonio Piatti & Andreas E. Rehberg, eds., *Incorrupta monumenta Ecclesiam defendunt: Studi offerti a mons. Sergio Pagano, prefetto dell'Archivio Segreto Vaticano*, vol. 1/1, *La Chiesa nella storia: Religione, cultura, costume*, Vatican City, Archivio Segreto Vaticano, 2018, 213–226.

13 James F. Puglisi, ed. *Petrine Ministry and the Unity of the Church: "Toward a Patient and Fraternal Dialogue,"* Collegeville, Liturgical Press, 1999, On page 188, Puglisi claims that the papal rejection was inspired by the "intransigent" secretary of state Cardinal Rafael Merry del Val.

14 See Étienne Fouilloux's contribution "Ecumenism between Communism and Nazism (1929–1948)" in this volume.

15 For further information regarding his life and work, as well as bibliographical data, see the lemma by Karim Schelkens & Sandra Arenas, "Visser 't Hooft," in Michael Quisinsky & Peter Walter, eds., *Personenlexikon zum Zweiten Vatikanischen Konzil*, Freiburg i.Br., Herder, 2012, 280–282. Recently, a biography of Visser 't Hooft was published by Jurjen A. Zeilstra, *Visser 't Hooft (1980–1985): Living for the Unity of the Church*, Amsterdam, Amsterdam University Press, 2020. See also the contribution by Jurjen Zeilstra in this volume.

by the hand of Adolf Hitler, a belief he shared with one of his close confidents, the Swiss theologian Lukas Vischer. What both future Geneva officials hinted at was that the situation of armed conflict had spurred Christians not only to want to leave the military trenches, but also to abandon confessional entrenchment. The harsh life in prisons and concentration camps had produced an unexpected side effect of Christian solidarity and border-crossing friendships. Such personal encounters brought about the realization that the others were not working against "us," or against Christ, but in fact shared more than expected. Especially in Northern European countries, remarkable initiatives of cross-confessional cooperation, often in the context of underground resistance to the Nazi regime, occurred during the war years, not seldom building on preexisting initiatives.

In Belgium, for instance, the Malines Conversations, led by Lord Halifax and Cardinal Désiré-Joseph Mercier between 1921 and 1925 had demonstrated a willingness for dialogue between Catholics and members of the Church of England.[16] One of its key contributors, Dom Lambert Beauduin, would propel matters forward after the untimely closure of the conversations when he founded the monastery of Amay-sur-Meuse, which later moved to Chevetogne. This was a monastery that made use of Pius XI's call to the order of St. Benedict to engage in contact with Eastern Christianity. Instead of heeding the papal call to create cells of unionism within already existing Benedictine foundations, Beauduin established a new community in 1925, devoted to the prayer for Christian unity but without an interest to "absorb" other Christians into the Roman Church.[17] Chevetogne became a fertile ground and a place for exchange among Catholics interested in ecumenism, and as of 1942 its annual ecumenical study days constituted an important forum for exchange among ecumenically-minded Catholics.[18] Naturally, Chevetogne was not the only place, since the papal call in *Equidem verba* had triggered similar initiatives elsewhere. In 1925, the Benedictine convent at Niederaltaich led by Emmanuel Maria Heufelder also started its activities, and in the same year the French Dominicans – in particular Christophe-Jean Dumont – opened the Istina center, devoted to the aid for, and contact with, Orthodox Christians who had fled Russia in the aftermath of the 1917 revolution.[19] Often fluctuating between unionism and ecumenism, these local centers remained active after *Mortalium animos*.

In Southern France, the Taizé Community was founded in 1940,[20] while in Lyon Paul Couturier played a key role: he can be seen as the founder of "spiritual ecumenism," as a staunch promoter of the prayer for unity,[21] and also as an inspiring fig-

16 John A. Dick, *The Malines Conversations Revisited*, Leuven, Leuven University Press, 1989 and the contribution by Bernard Barlow and Martin Browne in the first volume of this work.

17 See Pius XI's 1924 apostolic letter *Equidem verba*. This document was not published in *AAS*, but a Latin and French version of it can be found in the Chevetogne booklet, Lambert Beauduin, ed., *L'Œuvre des moines bénédictins d'Amay-sur-Meuse*, Amay-sur-Meuse, Prieuré Bénédictin d'Amay-sur-Meuse, 1937, 7–11. For further information on the founding of Chevetogne, see Raymond Loonbeek & Jacques Mortiau, *Un pionnier: Dom Lambert Beauduin (1873–1960): Liturgie et Unité des chrétiens*, 2 vols., Louvain-la-Neuve/Chevetogne, Collège Érasme/Éditions de Chevetogne, 2001 and the contribution by André Haquin in the first volume of this work.

18 Olivier Rousseau, "Les journées œcuméniques de Chevetogne (1942–1967)," in: *Au service de la Parole de Dieu: Mélanges offerts à Monseigneur André-Marie Charrue, Évêque de Namur*, Gembloux, Duculot, 1969, 451–485.

19 For the history and the influences of the center see Étienne Fouilloux, *Les catholiques et l'unité chrétienne du XIXe au XXe siècle: Itinéraires européens d'expression française*, Paris, Le Centurion, 1982, 396–402 and 652–660, and more recently the aforementioned article by the same author "Une longue marche."

20 Silvia Scatena, *Taizé, una parabola di unità: Storia della comunità dalle origini al concilio dei giovani*, Bologna, Il Mulino, 2018, 47–59.

21 The prayer for Christian unity on the day that unites the feast of the chair of St. Peter and the conversion of St. Paul originates in a unionist fraction of the Anglican communion, under the impulse of the episcopalian

ure for the Dombes Group.[22] Couturier's initiative to unite Christians in prayer was already embraced by the ERF in 1936, and six years later the Faith and Order movement approved it. While my survey is anything but exhaustive, it suffices to indicate that recent studies underline the importance of such local experiences for the commitment to both political and ecumenical unification. For the francophone territory the landmark study remains that of Fouilloux, while more recently Jörg Ernesti has offered a valuable survey of Catholic commitment to interconfessional dialogue under the Third Reich.[23] Protagonists such as Lorenz Jaeger, who together with Ernst Wilhelm Stählin provided the basis for the ÖAK, and before them theologians such as Max Josef Metzger, the inspiring figure behind the Una Sancta movement, are now being studied in greater detail.[24] Even more recently, the NIOD has created a first survey, highlighting the importance of the IKO, which involved joint efforts of Reformed and Catholic churches in the Netherlands, active in resisting the Nazi regime.[25] While in the past the scholarly focus was set almost exclusively on the importance of such efforts for rescuing Jews from Nazi persecution during the war, attention is increasingly being paid to the postwar effects of such collaborations across confessional borders. It has become clear that wartime experiences had a strong effect,[26] not only on theology but also on the willingness of Christians to rethink their ecclesial self-perception. The foundations were laid to move beyond exclusivism into a willingness to acknowledge the value present in the religious other, whether Jewish or Christian.

None of the above features stands on its own. In order to understand Rome's position one needs to take a closer look at some key documents issued by Pius XII which, although not directly speaking out on ecumenical issues, did determine the evolution of Catholic self-understanding under his pontificate. When writing his renowned article on the ecumenical movement and the Roman Catholic Church under Eugenio Pacelli, Vischer noted "considerable tensions" between the theologians seeking ecclesial renewal on the one hand, and the magisterial discourse on the other.[27] That said, it is important to avoid focusing too much on *Mortalium animos*. In fact, the major reference point

Paul Wattson. In 1909 it gained the approval of Pope Pius X. For info, see Ruth Rouse, "Voluntary Movements and the Changing Ecumenical Climate," in: *A History of the Ecumenical Movement*, vol. 1, Ruth Rouse & Stephen C. Neill, eds., *1517–1948*, London, SPCK, 1954, 307–349, esp. 348–349. More details on Couturier can be found in Geoffrey Curtis, *Paul Couturier and Unity in Christ*, London, SCM Press, 1964, and see the edition of some of his writings by Maurice Villain, ed., *Œcuménisme spirituel: Les écrits de l'abbé Paul Couturier*, Tournai, Casterman, 1963. It should be observed here that already during the war, Couturier was criticized by theologians such as Louis Bouyer, who mockingly spoke of the good old Couturier and his "unionist sweetness." See Bertrand Lesoing, *Vers la plénitude du Christ: Louis Bouyer et l'œcuménisme*, Paris, Cerf, 2017, 192, note 1.

22 On Paul Couturier, see the contribution by Étienne Fouilloux "Abbé Paul Couturier and Spiritual Ecumenism," while on the continuation of the work of the Dombes Group see Catherine E. Clifford's contribution, both in this volume.

23 Jörg Ernesti, *Ökumene im Dritten Reich: Einheit und Erneuerung*, Paderborn, Bonifatius, 2007.

24 It is perhaps interesting to note that Metzger had written to Pius XII, in late 1939, asking for the convocation of a new and truly "ecumenical" council. On Metzger and the Una Sancta movement, see Leonard J. Swidler, *The Ecumenical Vanguard: The History of the Una Sancta Movement*, Pittsburgh, Duquesne University Press, 1966, and more recently Paul Metzlaff, "Der Una-Sancta-Kreis München: Seine Entstehung seit 1935 und seine Entwicklung bis 1945. Ein Rekonstruktionsversuch," in: Verein für Diözesangeschichte von München und Freising, ed., *Beiträge zur altbayerischen Kirchengeschichte*, vol. 57, Neustadt an der Aisch, Philipp Schmidt, 2017, 7–128.

25 See Bas von Benda-Beckmann, *De rooms-katholieke kerk en de grenzen van verzet in Nederland tijdens de Tweede Wereldoorlog*, Amsterdam, NIOD, 2015. This cooperative organization led to the well-known refutation of Jewish deportation by the churches in the Netherlands in 1942, in which Catholic Archbishop Johannes de Jong played an important role.

26 Also see the edition of the memoires of the Lutheran theologian Louis Bouyer, who, in 1939 converted to Catholicism. Louis Bouyer, *Mémoires*, Paris, Cerf, 2014.

27 Vischer, "The Ecumenical Movement," 314.

for Catholic ecclesiology was another, far more nuanced encyclical, which was published in 1943. Although *Mystici corporis Christi* has often been neglected by scholars investigating the ecumenical movement, it has recently regained some significance as a result of a renewed interest in the Catholic theological landscape of the 1930s and 1940s, characterized by a broad focus on revitalization, from the bottom up but not infrequently with the support of the magisterium.[28]

2.2 *Broadening Catholicism's Self-Understanding*

In this era, a multitude of *ressourcement* movements helped reshape the Catholic Church, ranging from the liturgical movement or Catholic Action to the biblical movement, and in several cases Pius XII's pontificate reluctantly permitted these movements to develop. A good example is the fact that Catholic biblical scholars experienced the pope's 1943 encyclical *Divino afflante Spiritu* as a "breath of fresh air after the storm."[29] All this had some effects on ecclesiological self-reflection. As early as in the 1930s, revival movements among others meant that biblical images of the church were rediscovered, and this evolution was picked up in magisterial discourse under the pontificate of Pius XII. The result was that, from the wartime years, Rome actively promoted an ecclesiology of the church as a mystical body, under the influence of the Dutch Jesuit Sebastiaan Tromp – who is known to be the "ghost writer" of Pius XII's encyclical *Mystici corporis*.[30]

Tromp, an expert in the study of Robert Bellarmine, placed Catholic Counter-Reformed ecclesiology of the 16th century and that of the early 20th century seamlessly in line.[31] What one found in the encyclical was mainly an institutional-hierarchical and legal interpretation of the ecclesiological image. This was in no way a coincidence, since, as the Chevetogne monk Nicolas Oehmen pointed out in some detail, Rome aimed at correcting theological misconceptions that offered a spiritualized perspective of the church.[32] This tendency was quite common among German theologians such as Karl Pelz, whose work *Der Christ als Christus* was relegated to the Index of Forbidden Books in 1940.[33] The encyclical contested this, and the ecclesiology was considered from the point of view of the church's visible structures (the sacraments, the ecclesiastical office structure – in which bishops were legally arranged under papal primacy), and that aspect remained *condicio sine qua non* for access to the invisible. Such ecclesiology elevated church structures to supra-historical entities that were not subject to change. The 1943 encyclical contained all this, and when later, in 1960, Tromp would draft the very first schema *De*

28 A survey of the importance of preconciliar movements is found in the volume of Gilles Routhier, Philippe J. Roy & Karim Schelkens, eds., *La théologie catholique entre intransigeance et renouveau: La réception des mouvements préconciliaires à Vatican II*, Louvain-la-Neuve, Collège Érasme, 2011.

29 Encyclicals such as *Divino afflante Spiritu* were welcomed as a relief among Catholic exegetes, who were aware that they had been accorded short shrift under the anti-Modernism of the early 20th century. In this regard, see in the first volume of this work the chapter by Mathijs Lamberigts, "The Catholic Biblical Movement between Fear and Hope." Characteristic is the reaction of the bishop of Namur. See Pie XII, *Encyclique sur les études bibliques*, Brussels, Éditions Universitaires, 1945, 7.

30 Pius XII, *Mystici corporis Christi*, in: *AAS* 35, 1943, 193–248. See Philippe Chenaux, *Pie XII: Diplomate et pasteur*, Paris, Cerf, 2003, 391–392. Tromp's affinity with this encyclical was mentioned early in comments, including that of Clément Lialine, "Une étape en ecclésiologie: Réflexions sur l'encyclique 'Mystici Corporis,'" *Irén* 19, 1946, 129–152, 283–317, and *Irén* 20, 1947, 34–54. Lialine already noted the affinity of the encyclical with Tromp's treatises.

31 Sebastianus Tromp, "Editor lectoribus," in: *Robertus Bellarminus, Opera oratoria postuma*, ed. Sebastianus Tromp, vol. 11, *Adiunctis*, Rome, Pontificia Universitas Gregoriana, 1969, 13.

32 Nicolas Oehmen, "L'ecclésiologie dans la crise: À propos de quelques livres récents parus en Allemagne," in: Nicolas Oehmen & others, *Questions sur l'Église et son unité*, Gembloux, Duculot, 1943, 1–11.

33 See on this tendency, the pages on "Corps mystique et magistère," in: *HC* 12, 156–158.

ecclesia for Vatican II, in a commission presided over by Marie-Rosaire Gagnebet, this perspective came to the fore again: the concept of the *ecclesia societas* and the *corpus mysticum* were considered to be *haud binae res*. To put matters in a nutshell, in 1943 the magisterium considered the mystical body of Christ, the Roman Catholic Church, and the Church of Christ as one single entity.[34]

The ecumenical implications seem unambiguous: the Catholic Church insisted on being the one true religion, and as far as the discourse on church membership was concerned, true Christians were those who really (*reapse*) and without any restriction belonged to the Church of Rome.[35] Membership and belonging were indiscriminate: only Roman Catholics really and fully belonged to the Church of Christ. For the other Christians there was at best a spiritual connection and the work of unity consisted in the work of conversion.

Why then pay attention to this encyclical? *Mystici corporis* did not contradict the traditional approaches, but it did open some doors: first of all, the tone of the document was less condemnatory and less drowned in apologetic jargon than previous Roman statements. Theologically speaking, the image of the mystical body extended Catholic reflection on the nature of the church beyond the mere juridical approach that had been dominant since Vatican I. In this way, the encyclical accepted the work of one of Tromp's confreres, Émile Mersch. In the 1930s, Mersch was influenced by the biblical movement, and had written elaborate studies in which he proposed the mystical body image as an open and inclusive concept, asking for a renewed attention to the mystical and pneumatological dimensions of the church.[36]

When the papal document was issued, the latter dimensions were not lost on Catholic theologians engaged in interconfessional contacts and in the aforementioned approaches, and for this reason they welcomed the encyclical as a step ahead. For instance, the Benedictine monk Jean Gribomont, a regular of the Ecumenical Study Days of Chevetogne, concluded that the encyclical's mention of a "perfect" belonging to the church allowed for a distinction, implying that other, "partial" realizations of that same belonging could exist.[37] Even if the encyclical coined church membership in terms of full belonging to the visible body, it did recognize the presence in other categories and faith groups of an inclination toward the mystical body, through their desire (*votum*) to satisfy God. Gribomont was not the only one to see this.

34 It sounded like this in the schema he wrote, under the section entitled *Ecclesia Catholica Romana est Mysticum Christi Corpus*. See the schema *De ecclesia*, in: *Schemata Constitutionum et Decretorum de quibus disceptabitur in Concilii sessionibus: Series secunda: De Ecclesia et de B. Maria Virgine*, Vatican City, Typis Polyglottis Vaticanis, 1962, 4–90, esp. 12.

35 In article 2 of an early draft of the schema *De ecclesia*, drawn up by Tromp and preserved in AAV, Conc. Vat. II, 739.117, this becomes clear: "Spiritual union with separated brethren: It is possible for those who wish to be members of the church to exist separately from it, yet the church knows that it is spiritually united with them, especially if baptized, though they lack the Catholic faith, yet nevertheless lovingly in Christ, they also participate in the communion of prayers, atonements and spiritual benefits."

36 The best introduction to the life and the ecclesiological work of Mersch remains that of Jean Levie, *Le P. Émile Mersch (1890–1940)*, which appeared as introduction to Émile Mersch, *La théologie du Corps mystique*, vol. 1, Paris, Desclée de Brouwer, 1949, vii–xxx. See also Jean Levie, "Le père Émile Mersch," NRT 67, 1945, 677–688. For Mersch's own work, see Émile Mersch, *Le Corps mystique du Christ: Études de théologie historique*, 2 vols., Louvain, Museum Lessianum, 1933. In 1944 followed the aforementioned study on the mystical body ecclesiology, Mersch, *La théologie du corps mystique*, posthumously published by his colleague Levie. This work was incidentally picked up and discussed by Yves Congar, "L'œuvre posthume du P. Mersch," *La vie spirituelle* 74, 1946, 117–124. Congar would later publish a similar historical and theological diptych on the notion of tradition, in which Mersch's oeuvre served as an example.

37 See Jean Gribomont, "Du sacrement de l'Eglise et de ses réalisations imparfaites: Essai de théologie du schisme," *Irén* 22, 1949, 345–367. In fact, Gribomont pointed out that the document stressed that "for even though by an unconscious desire and longing they have a certain relationship with the Mystical Body of the Redeemer"; Pius XII, *Mystici corporis*, § 103.

Already in 1937, around the time of the ecumenical conferences of Life and Work in Oxford and Faith and Order in Edinburgh, Yves Marie-Joseph Congar had explained the Catholic position in a way that abandoned the black and white rationale of *Mortalium animos*, pointing at the distinction between ecclesial incorporation *in voto*, on the one hand, and full and practical incorporation, on the other.[38] He, too, welcomed *Mystici corporis* as an opportunity to make room for a more refined ecclesiological discourse. Chevetogne monks such as Clément Lialine did the same. He seized the encyclical's openness to the mystical aspect of the church as an occasion to distinguish between the visible structures of the Roman Church, the mystical body, and the Church of Christ. Without abandoning the Roman claim to "fullness," the rediscovery of the mystical dimension of the church compels the creation of an open space, which would allow for the recognition of ecclesial life beyond Catholicism's visible and canonical confines.[39]

These "open" readings of *Mystici corporis* gained further ground when Pius XII published another encyclical in November 1947: *Mediator Dei*. This papal document dealt with liturgical matters, and once again it aimed at restoring theological misconceptions in the German areas.[40] Nevertheless, and perhaps somewhat against Rome's intentions, it was welcomed by Catholic ecumenists for offering a nuanced clause on the sacrament of baptism. Four years after *Mystici corporis*, the Vatican seemed to accept the ecumenically sensitive readings of the wartime encyclical when it indicated that through the sacrament the baptized belonged to the universal church. Strikingly, the latter was not defined as the Roman Catholic Church, but as the mystical body.[41]

2.3 *Rome versus Amsterdam: The* Monitum Cum compertum

While some saw the two aforementioned encyclicals as the beginning of a new period in

38 Marie Joseph Congar, *Chrétiens désunis: Principes d'un "œcuménisme" catholique*, Paris, Cerf, 1937, 209; ET: *Divided Christendom: A Catholic Study of the Problem of Reunion*, trans. Muad A. Bousfield, London, Bles, 1939. It is worth noting here that the experience of Istina and the study of the works of the Russian philosopher Nicholas Berdyaev – which he quoted in Nicolas Berdiaeff, *Esprit et liberté: Essai de Philosophie Chrétienne*, Paris, Editions "Je Sers," 1933, 345 – left their marks on Congar's ecclesiology. For an elaborate study of his thought, see Joseph Famerée, *L'ecclésiologie d'Yves Congar avant Vatican II: Histoire et Église. Analyse et reprise critique*, Leuven, Leuven University Press, 1992.

39 Lialine distinguished between members of the Church of Christ and members of the mystical body. See Lialine, "Une étape en ecclésiologie," 44; also see Pierre-André Liégé, "L'appartenance à l'église et l'encyclique Mystici Corporis Christi," *RSPT* 32, 1948, 351–357, who insisted on maintaining a difference between belonging to the mystical body and to the Catholic Church. Furthermore, Valentin Morel rejected *Mystici corporis*'s identification of the Roman Catholic Church with the mystical body of Christ. See Valentin Morel, "Le Corps mystique du Christ et l'église catholique romaine," *NRT* 70, 1948, 703–726. Some years later, Karl Rahner would also offer an interpretation of *Mystici corporis* that rejected a strict identification of the Roman Catholic Church with the mystical body of Christ. See Karl Rahner, "Die Gliedschaft in der Kirche nach der Lehre der Enzyklika Pius XII. 'Mystici Corporis Christi,'" in: Karl Rahner,*Schriften zur Theologie*, vol. 2, Einsiedeln, Benziger, 1955, 7–94, esp. 71–74.

40 For further background, see Theodor Maas-Ewerd, *Die Krise der Liturgische Bewegung in Deutschland und Österreich: Zu den Auseinandersetzungen um die "liturgische Frage" in den Jahren 1939 bis 1944*, Regensburg, Pustet, 1981.

41 Pius XII, *Mediator Dei*, in: *AAS* 39, 1947, 521–595, here 555. Two sources tend to identify Augustin Bea as the hand behind this "open" interpretation. See Jerome-Michael Vereb, *"Because he was a German!": Cardinal Bea and the Origins of Roman Catholic Engagement in the Ecumenical Movement*, Grand Rapids, Eerdmans, 2006, 134–143, and Josef Höfer, "Das geistliche Profil des Kardinal Bea," *Cath(M)* 26, 1972, 50–62, esp. 59–60. It is unclear whether this is correct, but in some studies it was underlined that *Mediator Dei* was a key reference point for Bea's ecumenical approach to the sacrament of baptism. See Emmanuel Lanne, "La contribution du Cardinal Bea à la question du baptême et l'Unité des chrétiens," in: Segretariato per l'Unione dei Cristiani, ed., *Atti del Simposio card. Agostino Bea (Roma 16–19 dicembre 1981)*, Rome, Pontificia Università Lateranense, 1983, 159–185.

ecclesiology, the litmus test came in the spring of 1948. At that moment, the announcement of the founding meeting of the WCC, which was to take place in the city of Amsterdam in August, with representatives of 147 churches, was widely advertised.[42] In the spring, the WCC staff had not sent an invitation to the Holy See as such, but preferred to invite individual Catholics. However, less than two months before the opening of the assembly, any hopes of having Catholic observers in Amsterdam were rapidly trampled on. On Jun 5, in the form of a *Monitum* entitled *Cum compertum*,[43] the congregation for the Holy Office, officially headed by the pope, issued a formal warning. The document was extremely brief and juridical, dryly listing existing regulations on *communicatio in sacris* and repeating the rules found in the 1917 Code of Canon Law. Yet its significance was greater. The document was interpreted as a return to the position of Pius XI and felt as a setback for both ecumenically minded Catholics, for the staff of the WCC, and for many others attending the assembly. In Amsterdam, the prominent voice of Karl Barth would go as far as to accuse Rome of "imperialism."[44]

The least one can say is that with *Cum compertum* the Vatican effectively distanced itself from the ecumenical movement. Commentators rapidly called to mind the old accusations of false irenicism and religious indifferentism,[45] but what also played a role in the period before the assembly was the presumption on the side of both the WCC and some Catholic theologians that the decision was in the hands of the local ordinary. In the case of Amsterdam, this was the archbishop of Utrecht, Johannes de Jong, who had been supportive of interconfessional collaboration during World War II; hence there was good hope that he would make his voice heard. In fact, in the spring of 1948 several requests arrived at the archdiocese. Archive correspondence shows that de Jong was initially in doubt, but not entirely against the idea of observers. However, he feared that unrealistic expectations might be raised, and in April 1948 he decided not to grant permission to theologians such as Johannes Willebrands[46] and Congar,[47] and

42 The story of the assembly is told, among others, by Willem Adolf Visser 't Hooft, "The Genesis of the World Council of Churches," in: *A History of the Ecumenical Movement*, vol. 1, 695–724.

43 Suprema Sacra Congregatio S. Officii, *Cum compertum*, in: *AAS* 40, 1948, 257.

44 On this, see Mauro Velati, *Separati ma fratelli: Gli osservatori non cattolici al Vaticano II (1962–1965)*, Bologna, Il Mulino, 2014. Barth's speech is found in Karl Barth, "Die Unordnung der Welt und Gottes Heilsplan," in: Focko Lüpsen, ed., *Amsterdamer Dokumente: Berichte und Reden auf der Weltkirchenkonferenz im Amsterdam 1948*, Bethel bei Bielefeld, Evangelischer Presseverband für Westfalen und Lippe, 1948, 136–146.

45 These "tendencies" had been condemned in the 1864 *Syllabus of Errors* by Pius IX, and moreover, what played a role was the painful memory of Catholics attending the World Parliament of Religions in 1893, after which they were censored by Leo XIII. On this remote background, see James F. Cleary, "Catholic Participation in the World's Parliament of Religions, Chicago, 1893," *CHR* 55, 1970, 585–609.

46 The story of Willebrands's alleged presence at the Amsterdam WCC assembly is told, among other places, in George Harinck & Lodewijk Winkeler, "The Twentieth Century," in: Herman J. Selderhuis, ed., *Handbook of Dutch Church History*, Göttingen, Vandenhoeck & Ruprecht, 2014, 521–644, esp. 594. For a reconstruction with ample proof of the fact that Willebrands and Visser 't Hooft encountered each other only in the mid-1950s, see Karim Schelkens, "Pioneers at the Crossroads: The Preconciliar Itineraries of W.A. Visser 't Hooft and J.G.M. Willebrands (1951–1961)," *Cath(M)* 70, 2016, 23–39.

47 J. de Jong to Y. Congar, Apr 6, 1948, in: ACI, de Jong touched upon the risky idea of sending Catholic observers, explaining that "we must be sure that the observers (in question) are not influenced by certain ecumenical theories that we do not agree with. This could lead to hopes that would never be realized. Therefore, we would like to reserve the right to designate the persons who may attend the conference." It is striking to note that throughout the 1950s the question of sending Catholic observers to non-Catholic assemblies, as well as the idea of inviting non-Catholics to Roman Catholic gatherings remained an item of discussion. See also the interesting article on this issue by Yves Congar, "La question des observateurs catholiques à la Conférence de Amsterdam, 1948," in: Lorenz Hein, ed., *Die Einheit der Kirche: Dimensionen ihrer Heiligkeit, Katholizität und Apostolizität: Festgabe Peter Meinhold*

informed Rome of the events, which helped trigger the publication of the *Monitum*.

This was one side of the story. Another issue was that the warning bore witness to Rome's suspicion of evolutions in the German ecumenical movement, and certainly of all too progressive Catholic tendencies in the German Una Sancta movement, which by now was under close surveillance by the Vatican.[48] The effect of the *Monitum*, in any case, was that it removed authority from the local church, since it applied canon 1325 – according to which Catholics, ordained or lay, could only participate or organize gatherings with direct Vatican permission – to the relatively new field of ecumenical gatherings. In conditions like these, bishops such as de Jong and Jaeger henceforth had to abide by the Roman *non possumus*. This unusual situation for the local bishops did not prevent the Dutch episcopate from publishing, four weeks after the *Monitum*, a pastoral letter on the ecumenical movement, asking their flock to pray for the successful outcome of the meeting.

The content of the letter mirrored the ambiguous situation: on the one hand, the bishops advocated Rome's call for a return of all non-Catholics to the mother church; on the other hand, they showed more diplomacy and awareness of what was happening, and did what the *Monitum* had omitted: they referred back to the wartime experience and expressed their admiration for the "great and authentic desire for unity in Christ" present in the ecumenical movement, as well as the fact that Catholics were also "guilty of the estrangement that has risen between us and non-Catholic Christians."[49]

One may conclude that until 1948, Rome was either not up to date with what happened on the local field or remained suspicious.[50] In its official discourse, the magisterium allowed for some rebalancing of Catholic ecclesiology, but Roman documents were in no way and at no time ecumenically inspired, and bluntly continued the old apologetic tradition to rank Protestants under the category of *dissidentes*. As Philippe Chenaux has pointed out, the pope's attitude toward the WCC, which he filed under the "Anglo-Protestant type ecumenism," was essentially hostile.[51]

Any signs of Roman outreach to other confessions were essentially in favor of encounter with Eastern Christianity, and even then such calls were inspired by unionism. The guiding principle that led to a more modest tone when discussing non-Roman Christians was rooted not in an ecumenical sensitivity, but in the awareness that the church needed to promote the peaceful coexistence of the peoples and to combat atheism. The unionist approach to the question of Christian unity dominated centers such as Unitas, led by the French Jesuit Charles Boyer from 1945, and the Vatican preferred this to Chevetogne, Istina, or Paderborn. It should come as no surprise that Boyer was among the few Catholics who effectively attended (albeit from a distance) the Amsterdam meeting,

zum 70. Geburtstag, Wiesbaden, Franz Steiner, 1977, 241–253.

48 Saretta Marotta, *Gli anni della pazienza: Bea, l'ecumenismo e il Sant'Uffizio di Pio XII*, Bologna, Il Mulino, 2019, 109, note 139, cites a reaction in *The Tablet*, which in turn published a report about a German speaker on the Vatican Radio, explaining the reasons behind the *Monitum* as follows: "We should like to point to the wild growth (*Wildwuchs*) which has made its appearance on the fringes of the Una Sancta movement, and which by now has penetrated deep into its center ... Joint services and joint prayers were by no means unusual."

49 The "Herderlijk Schrijven over de Oecumenische Beweging," *Katholiek Archief* 27, 1948, 543–547, dated Jul 31, 1948, was signed by Cardinal de Jong and Bishops Petrus Hopmans (Breda), Joseph Hubertus Gulielmus Lemmens (Roermond), Johannes Petrus Huibers (Haarlem), and Willem Pieters Adrian Musaerts ('s Hertogenbosch). John Pollard, *The Papacy in the Age of Totalitarianism (1914–1958)*, Oxford, Oxford University Press, 2014, 431, referred to this document in a very positive manner, somewhat neglecting the presence of the unionist perspective in it.

50 This was the case, for instance, regarding periodicals like the *Una Sancta Rundbriefe für interkonfessionelle Begegnung*, which adopted a very free and open manner when discussing ecumenical matters.

51 Chenaux, *Pie XII*, 365.

in the officious capacity of one of the journalists, many of whom were closely linked to the Roman milieu.[52] In all this, the Holy See's attitude served very little to avoid a landscape marked by the division between local ecumenical engagement in the transalpine countries, and unionist tendencies south of the Alps. A painstaking illustration of this divide is found in the severe words Congar wrote about Boyer in 1946: "As far as the ecumenical question is concerned, this man does not appear to have any true conviction, or any personal engagement."[53]

3 Leaving the Trenches (1949–1953)

Considering the above, one may ask why, in hindsight, several pioneers of ecumenism would insist that after 1948 Rome assumed a new approach to the ecumenical movement? The answer is complex: even among Catholics, the enthusiasm triggered by the Amsterdam assembly and the disillusion surrounding the Vatican attitude were hard to neglect. As a consequence, some local ordinaries, however limited their impact on the universal level may have been, rapidly endorsed new initiatives in their diocesan territories, which softened the perception of a Catholic anti-ecumenical stance.

At about the time when the *Monitum* appeared, the Dutch episcopal conference agreed to rename the traditional St. Peter Canisius Association for Apologetics, which investigated in depth into the apostolate of conversion and aimed at "guiding" Protestant pastors into the *Catholica ecclesia*. The new organization was no longer named after a Counter-Reform voice, but bore the name of St. Willibrord, whose apostolate occurred before the schisms of the 11th and 16th century. The SWV[54] was led by a new president, Willebrands. Although it continued its proselytic activities among Protestant pastors throughout the 1950s,[55] its general aims and agenda changed. The focus was extended and also included religious conversation with Dutch Protestants. This shift was not unique: in the same year and with the support of both the Congregation for the Oriental Churches and Cardinal Emmanuel Célestin Suhard, Istina also rearranged its activities. The impulse came from Dumont, who extended the center's attention beyond its traditional limitation to missionary work with the Russian Orthodox, henceforth adopting an integral perspective on the ecumenical movement.[56]

52 The Amsterdam experience gave rise to a new situation, in which Catholics, given the impossibility to attend as observers, attended ecumenical gatherings under the statute of "accredited journalists." In 1948, those doing so were Boyer, Maurice Villain, Jan Witte, and Frans Thijssen, all of whom were under the close watch of a member of the Holy Office, Tromp. On this, see Fouilloux, *Les catholiques et l'unité chrétienne*, 784–786. Also see the comments made by Yves Congar in his *Journal d'un théologien*, Paris, Cerf, 2000, 143–153.

53 Congar, *Journal d'un théologien*, 166–180, entry of Jun 17, 1946, 97. On Boyer and Unitas, see the memorial book published by members of the Ladies of Bethany Josefa Koet, Leideke Galema & Marion M. van Assendelft, *Hearth of Unity: Forty Years of Foyer Unitas (1952–1992)*, Rome, Fratelli Palombi, 1996.

54 Jan Jacobs, *Nieuwe visies op een oud visioen: Een portret van de Sint-Willibrord Vereniging (1948–1998)*, Nijmegen, Valkhof Pers, 1998.

55 Henk Witte, "Willebrands en de pastores convertiti," in: Adelbert Denaux, ed., *De Nederlandse jaren van Johannes Willebrands (1909–1960)*, Bergambacht, Uitgeverij 2VM, 2015, 83–114. It should also be said that in other places, such as Germany, this type of apostolate of conversion was common, one example being the story of the conversion of Rudolf Goethe, guided by the bishop of Mainz, an important case provided by Albert Stohr. See Leonhard Hell, "Unio ecclesiae – materia primaria: Bischof Albert Stohrs Einbindung in den entstehenden internationalen katholischen Ökumenismus und in die Vorbereitung des Zweiten Vatikanischen Konzils," in: Karl Lehmann, ed., *Dominus fortitudo: Bischof Albert Stohr (1890–1961)*, Mainz, Echter, 2012, 99–120.

56 The foundation of the new periodical, named *Vers l'Unité chrétienne*, testified to this redirection. See Fouilloux, "Une longue marche," 282.

3.1 *Spots of Ecumenical Unease in Rome*

As of 1948, changes occurred not only in northern Europe. In the Vatican, sporadic signs of a growing unease with the Roman attitude were to be seen. For instance, the Spanish Jesuit Angel Francisco Carrillo de Albornoz, a fervent promotor of the 1948 Human Rights Declaration, had been active in the curia but left Rome for want of freedom, to end up later by becoming a leading figure in the Secretariat on Religious Liberty of the WCC.[57] More important was that in the eyes of some Vatican officials it was clear that the *Monitum* was a *faux pas*, which called for some kind of correction. One of such amendments came from a substitute in the Vatican State Secretariat, Msgr. Giovanni Battista Montini. He had stood behind the 1945 appointment of Boyer at Unitas but he now granted an audience to Roger Schutz and Max Thurian in Rome. The Taizé brothers experienced the encounter as an act of "damage control," in which Montini confided to them that the *Monitum* in no way constituted an attack on the ecumenical efforts of non-Catholics, but was merely an internal disciplinary warning to "ecumenical groups lacking solidity and whose rather vague sense of charity risked compromising the Catholic truth as a clear and authorized witness."[58] Such events made it clear that, at least implicitly, ecumenism was on the Roman agenda.

Another proof of this change *en coulisse* occurred in the spring of 1949 when, in strict secrecy, Pius XII commissioned a small group of confidents to investigate the possibility of a new council. According to the pope, the council would discuss topics such as "God and his dominion," "the nature and end of man," and "the nature and role of the church." Regarding the last theme, the committee prepared statements on the growing popularity of the idea that every "sincere" person, even without baptism or without a visible dependence on the head of the church, is *vere et proprie* a member of the church. Apart from readdressing the question of ecclesial membership, they discussed the idea that, according to many, "dissidents" differed only in name from the Catholic faithful.[59]

The council's plans ended up in the archives, but again they disclose a growing concern. In that light it is interesting to notice that from 1948 Pius XII increasingly confided in one of the theologians involved in the council preparations: Augustin Bea.[60] The pope now appointed the German Jesuit as consulter to the Holy Office. At the time, Bea was still in charge as rector of the Pontifical Biblical Institute, but Pacelli had known him since his time as nuncio in Germany, and in Rome Bea had been the pope's private confessor since 1945. Bea's familiarity with the German ecumenical initiatives before and during the war were an asset, and after the death of Jaeger's Roman contact, Josef Grendel, Bea became the new liaison bridging the gap between the Roman environment and the German ecumenists.[61] Bea rapidly became Pacelli's eyes and ears in the Holy Office, and

57 On Albornoz, see John E. Witte Jr., "An Apologia for Religious Human Rights," in John Witte Jr. & Johan D. van der Vyver, eds., *Religious Human Rights in Global Perspective: Religious Perspectives*, The Hague, Martinus Nijhoff Publishers, 1996, 455–484, esp. 466.

58 Scatena, *Taizé*, 284–288, here 285. The original citation is in French and it did not remain without effect, since later that year Thurian published an article in which he relativized the importance of the *Monitum*. See Max Thurian, "À propos de l'Avertissement du Saint-Office du 5 juin 1948," *Verbum Caro* 2, 1948, 184–199.

59 See Giovanni Caprile, "Pio XI e la ripresa del Concilio Vaticano," *La Civiltà Cattolica* 117, 1966, 27–39; and Giovanni Caprile, "Pio XII e un nuovo progetto di Concilio Ecumenico," *La Civiltà Cattolica* 117, 1966, 209–227, both included as the first two chapters of Giovanni Caprile, ed., *Il Concilio Vaticano II: Annuncio e preparazione*, vol. 1/1, *1959–1960*, Rome, Edizioni "La Civiltà Cattolica," 1966, 3–35, esp. 23.

60 See Dominik Burkard, "Augustin Bea und Alfredo Ottaviani: Thesen zu einer entscheidenden personellen Konstellation im Vorfeld des Zweiten Vatikanischen Konzils," in: Franz Xaver Bischof, ed., *Das Zweite Vatikanische Konzil (1962–1965): Stand und Perspektiven der kirchenhistorischen Forschung im deutschsprachigen Raum*, Stuttgart, Kohlhammer, 2012, 45–66.

61 Saretta Marotta, "Ökumene von Unten: Augustin Bea di fronte alle attività del movimento tedesco Una Sancta,"

effects of his influence were soon visible, for example in the fact that the Vatican Radio suddenly granted an interview to the aforementioned Jaeger in the spring of 1948,[62] and in the papal address of Sep 5, 1948 to the Katholikentag in Mainz, in which Pius XII acknowledged "how urgent among many of your people, both Catholics and non-Catholics, the desire for unity is."[63]

3.2 *The Start of an Ecumenical Dawn: The Events of 1949*

In the second half of 1949, three events marked the fact that Rome took the desire for unity more seriously than before. These events were all the more significant since they helped remove internal divisions among Catholics, which in turn created a new position of the Roman Church as far as ecumenism was concerned. I shall briefly touch upon each of the events, then consider their consequences for the Catholic position *vis-à-vis* the ecumenical movement. The series started with a letter from the Holy Office, made public in August 1949. The letter did not explicitly deal with ecumenism, but it further elucidated Rome's understanding of the nature of the church.

Basically, the document was aimed at the anti-liberal-minded Boston theologian Leonard Feeney, who in turn refused to submit to the Vatican sanctions.[64] However, for various reasons, the "Feeney affair" turned out to be an important test-case for Catholicism's position on the possibility of salvation outside the church. The setting in itself helped considerably, since the controversy did not take place in a European setting, but in that of the United States, a country with a particular tradition of religious liberty. Moreover, since the war and certainly since the approval of the Marshall Plan, the United States rapidly grew into a dominant global political position, and many European nations were dependent on American support for the reconstruction of their economies after the war. Against this horizon, Feeney's interpretation of the patristic doctrine of *extra ecclesiam nulla salus* created both a politically and a theologically tense situation, up to the point that it forced the magisterium to take a public stance.

Catholics had often quarreled over the worth of the axiom – Congar would later refer to it as "this falsely clear axiom"[65] – which in its more evident and direct sense implied that outside the visible frontiers of the Roman Church no salvific value was to be found. Feeney, who felt that the 1948 *Monitum* justified his position, took this rigid stand and created some scandal with the claim that the baptism of desire was unavailing, which led him to declare publicly that all who were not members of the Catholic Church in the fullest sense were lost. He even went as far as to denounce Richard James Cushing, the Catholic archbishop of Boston, as a heretic for declaring that non-Catholics could be saved. In its letter the Holy Office not only defended the archbishop, it also rejected the rigid and exclusivist reading of the doctrine of salvation.[66] The affair lingered

CrSt 37, 2016, 541–611, and more recently her monograph, *Gli anni della pazienza*.

62 This was reported upon in the bulletin of the Istina center, *VUCh*, 1948, 6.

63 See the speech "Il radiomessaggio al 72o 'Katholikentag' in Magonza (5 settembre 1948)," in: *Discorsi e radiomessaggi di Sua Santità Pio XII*, vol. 10, *Decimo anno di Pontificato: 2 marzo 1948–1º marzo 1949*, Vatican City, Tipografia Poliglotta Vaticana, 1949, 179–185, here 183.

64 Leonard Feeney's name was closely connected to that of the St. Benedict Center, even though Feeney was not its founder. Located in Cambridge, Massachusetts, from March 1940, it was established by three lay persons: Catherine Clarke, Christopher Huntington, and Avery Dulles. After a part-time assignment, Feeney had become strongly committed to the center by the end of World War II. From 1945 his superiors granted Feeney permission to work full time. On the Feeney case, which was closely followed by theologians such as Congar, see among others Mario Carosio, "Extra ecclesiam nulla salus: Il caso Feeney," *CrSt* 25, 2004, 833–876.

65 Yves Congar, *Essais œcuméniques: Le mouvement, les hommes, les problèmes*, Paris, Le Centurion, 1984, 85.

66 For the letter *Suprema haec sacra* with criticism of Feeney's exclusivist position, see Fenton Feeney, "A Letter from the Holy Office," *Am. Eccles. Rev.* 127, 1952, 307–315. Subsequent studies on this controversy include those of George B. Pepper, *The Boston Heresy Case in View of the Secularization of Religion: A Case*

on for some years, until eventually, after Feeney's repeated refusal to comply with the order to go to Rome, the Jesuit was excommunicated in February 1953.[67]

The outcome of the Feeney case fueled the ecclesiological expectations of those who had already interpreted *Mystici corporis* in a broad sense. One month after the letter to the Boston archbishop and with approval of Cardinal Maurice Feltin, a group of theologians met in Paris at the Istina center: from the Roman Catholic side Congar, Dumont, Jean Daniélou, and Jean Jérôme Hamer attended, next to a group of theologians of various denominations, such as Visser 't Hooft and Oliver Tomkins, representing Geneva.[68] The WCC staff was preparing the 1950 central committee meeting in Toronto, and in that light they were in the midst of a discussion on the ecclesial nature of the WCC.

Congar and Visser 't Hooft played a key role in seeking a common ground: after a *tour d'horizon*, it was agreed upon that a common language was needed to discuss the nature of the true Church of Christ, and that it seemed crucial to reflect upon the possible subsistence of the elements of the true church in any particular Christian group.[69] What emerged was the centrality of the concept of the *vestigia ecclesiae*, and the idea that elements of the true church may be found to a larger or lesser degree in the various Christian communities. These notions had been explored by various theologians in the 1930s and 1940s, and in 1925 Beauduin had already written that Catholics engaged in the work of unity needed both to return "to the origins of Christianity and to the eras preceding the deplorable rupture of the 11th century, in order to rediscover the multiple vestiges of ecclesial resemblance," and they should "seek the numerous elements common to both West and East."[70]

The insights were not new, but in the postwar era their value became clearer. Visser 't Hooft appreciated the fact that Catholic theologians such as Daniélou insisted that those present should aim "to arrive at a dynamic conception of the *vestigia ecclesiae* for these traces of the church could be developed and lead to greater agreement."[71] The reception of the meeting would indeed be of major importance. In Chevetogne, Lialine was soon informed by Dumont and Daniélou,[72] and the idea circulated that Catholic ecumenists should invest in a type of permanent committee to coordinate their efforts on a larger scale. In July 1950, the WCC's third central committee meeting in Toronto, addressing the theme of "The church and the churches," picked up this thread. In its famous Toronto statement,[73] the WCC adopted the notion of *vestigia ecclesiae* as a guiding principle. On the side of Geneva, the reception was certified, but for Daniélou's wish to come true, a Roman intervention would be of assistance.[74]

Study in the Sociology of Religion, Lewiston, The Edwin Mellen Press, 1988. On the topic of the idea of salvation outside the church, see the book by one of Feeney's former students, Francis A. Sullivan, *Salvation Outside the Church?: Tracing the History of the Catholic Response*, New York, Paulist Press, 1992.

67 The decree of excommunication is found in *AAS* 45, 1953, 100.

68 On the meeting, see Willem Adolf Visser 't Hooft, *Memoirs*, London, SCM Press, 1973, 319–320, and Fouilloux, *Les catholiques et l'unité chrétienne*, 652–660. The most detailed reconstruction is found in the doctoral dissertation of Sandra Arenas, *Fading Frontiers?: A Historical-Theological Investigation into the Notion of the "Elementa Ecclesiae,"* Ph.D. Thesis, Leuven, KU Leuven, 2013, 66–67 (published in 2021 by Peeters).

69 Willem Adolf Visser 't Hooft, *The Genesis and Formation of the World Council of Churches*, Geneva, WCC Publications, 1982, 74.

70 Loonbeek & Mortiau, *Un pionnier*, 418–419, where the authors quote Beauduin commenting on Pius XI's 1924 apostolic letter *Equidem verba*. It should be added that Beauduin referred not only to the papal document but also to the Eucharistic congress in Amsterdam of 1924.

71 Visser 't Hooft, *Memoirs*, 320.

72 See the materials and C. Lialine to C.-J. Dumont, Oct 14, 1949, in: ACI, Correspondance Dom Clément Lialine (1948–1952).

73 Morris West, "Toronto Statement," in: *DEM*, 1008–1009.

74 It is striking to see that the Roman environment on the one hand created an openness for *ressourcement* on the level of ecumenical engagement, while in exactly the same period it curtailed the *nouvelle théologie*

Precisely between the aforementioned meetings in Paris and Toronto, the Holy Office spoke out on the ecumenical movement again. The new document was not a *Monitum*, but an *instructio*, bearing the title *De motione oecumenica*.[75] This magisterial document, signed by Cardinal Francesco Marchetti Selvaggiani and by assessor Alfredo Ottaviani, was not only different in tone, but also turned out to be the most comprehensive and authoritative Roman statement on ecumenism issued under Pius XII. Not surprisingly, the instruction started from a unionist perspective, and mindful of the pastoral letter of the Dutch bishops, Catholics were urged not to pay too much attention to the *défauts*[76] of their own church when studying the history of Christian divisions.

The instruction was almost sensational in that it echoed a sensitivity which had been previously lacking in the Vatican's rhetoric. Rome now recognized that the ecumenical movement stood "under the inspiration of the Holy Spirit." This pneumatological reference was embraced by ecumenists: since it implied that Rome acknowledged the activity of the Spirit outside its visible frontiers. Ecclesiologically speaking, this could be aligned with the doctrine of the ecclesial elements. Yet the instruction did more than this, it touched upon disciplinary matters, ensuring that the ecumenical movement would proceed "under effective supervision" and be given "prudent encouragement and direction," the authority partly returning to the hands of the bishops.[77] The local ordinary could approve of ecumenical encounters in his territory and check that the guidelines set down in the instruction were respected. In the case of international gatherings, the Holy Office remained responsible. Finally, the restrictive measures on the *communicatio in sacris* were softened, so that in the future Catholics attending ecumenical meetings could recite the Lord's Prayer or other approved prayers together with non-Catholics.

3.3 *From Grottaferrata to Fribourg: The Reception of* De motione oecumenica

On Dec 23, 1949, three days after the signing of an instruction that provided the correction Vatican officials such as Bea and Montini[78] had hoped for, Pius XII could be heard on the Vatican Radio. In his speech he looked ahead to 1950, announcing his hope that "the Holy Year might also welcome the great and centuries-long expected return to the one true Church of many believers in Jesus Christ, separated for various motives." The papal speech – crying out "why still separation, why still schisms?" – made it quite clear that Rome's recent recognition of the value of the ecumenical movement did not imply any questioning of its prerogatives.[79]

movement in which figures such as Congar and Daniélou played a central role. On the *nouvelle théologie*, see Étienne Fouilloux, *Une Église en quête de liberté: La pensée catholique française entre modernisme et Vatican II (1914–1962)*, Paris, Desclée de Brouwer, 1998.

75 Suprema Sacra Congregatio S. Officii, *Instructio ad locorum ordinarios "De motione oecumenica,"* in: AAS 42, 1950, 142–147. An English version was published in George K.A. Bell, ed., *Documents on Christian Unity: Fourth Series (1948–1957)*, London, Oxford University Press, 1958, 22–27.

76 For further background, see Peter De Mey, "L'évolution théologique et œcuménique de la 'Conférence catholique pour les Questions œcuméniques,'" in: Leo Declerck, *Mgr J. Willebrands et la conférence catholique pour les questions œcuméniques: Ses archives à Chevetogne*, Leuven, Peeters, 2015, 7–39. Henceforth we refer to this inventory as CCEQ archives.

77 Suprema Sacra Congregatio S. Officii, *De motione oecumenica*, 140–146.

78 For a survey of Bea's ecumenical path, see Saretta Marotta, "Augustin Bea auf dem Weg zum Ökumeniker 1949–1960," ZKG 127/3, 2016, 373–393 and Marotta, *Gli anni della pazienza*. For Montini, see the volume *Paolo VI e l'ecumenismo: Colloquio internazionale di studio (Brescia, 25–27 settembre 1998)*, Rome, Studium, 2001.

79 Radio message by Pius XII, on Dec 23, 1949; see "'Anno Santo, Anno di Dio': Il radiomessaggio natalizio al mondo," in: *Discorsi e radiomessaggi di Sua Santità Pio XII*, vol. 11, *Undecimo anno di pontificato: 2 marzo 1949–1º marzo 1950*, Vatican City, Tipografia Poliglotta Vaticana, 1950, 325–340, here 332.

In fact, Pius XII's radio appeal made it clear once again that the pope valued ecumenism first and foremost as a means to creating a united Christian front against militant atheism. This was the first thing the public heard, since the instruction only became public just over two months later, in early March 1950. Once it did appear, the document was enthusiastically received in Geneva, commented upon by Catholic ecumenists,[80] and regarded as a catalyst for action by Catholics adhering to the unionist perspective.

The reception of *De motione oecumenica* provides an interesting case at the end of this study, since it soon triggered the organization of two important, yet quite different, types of meetings, one in Grottaferrata, another in Présinge. Precisely the differences between these gatherings made it clear that in the early 1950s Catholicism still lacked a coordinated approach. As we shall clarify in our concluding reflections, the answer to that lacuna would eventually come from the country where the WCC was launched, the Netherlands. When it came to implementing the Vatican instruction, the first to jump on the wagon was Boyer.

From Sep 20 to 22, 1950, in the Greek Catholic abbey of Grottaferrata, just outside Rome, Unitas organized a gathering with some 18 experts, to discuss the work of unity.[81] The initiative to a certain extent reflected the isolated position of the organization amidst the Catholic ecumenical milieu of that time. Although representatives from several countries attended the meeting,[82] many of them were highly skeptical about its perspective and outcome. The concluding documents of the venue made it clear that the accent would fully remain on the apostolate of conversion of non-Roman Christians to Catholicism. This did not go unnoticed, and others such as Dutch Willebrands and Frans Thijssen, who were neither invited nor informed, would later stress that many Catholic ecumenists were still "wary of ecumenical initiatives originating in Rome," and even feared a clash between the Roman initiatives and those of others.[83]

These others consisted in the first place of Dumont and Congar, who had fostered plans to establish an overarching structure, analogous to the coordinating role Jaeger had played on behalf of the bishop conference of Fulda.[84] The French felt Boyer's Roman initiative had somewhat "hijacked" the occasion.[85] This was not entirely wrong, since the Grottaferrata meeting fell right in between two Roman initiatives that created serious obstacles for ecumenical advance: in August 1950, the encyclical *Humani generis* curtailed the *nouvelle théologie* movement, which, among other aspects, created a serious setback for *ressourcement* theology. In article 27, the magisterial document reaffirmed "that the Mystical Body and the Roman Catholic Church are one and the same thing," again creating confusion among ecumenists and

80 See the comment by Christophe Dumont, "L'Instruction du Saint-Office au sujet du mouvement œcuménique," *VUCh* 22/3, 1950, 2–8. Also see Dumont's later evaluation of the instruction, Christophe-Jean Dumont, "L'œcuménisme," *Recherches et débats* 27, 1959, 90–109.

81 On the meeting, see Fouilloux, *Les catholiques et l'unité chrétienne*, 705–711 and 835–845. See also "Chronique religieuse," *Irén* 23, 1950, 427.

82 The list of attendants was published in the Vatican newspaper, *L'Osservatore Romano*, on Sep 24, 1950, and mentions the presence of names such as Bouyer, Congar, Villain, Rousseau, Lialine, and others. It is clear from the list that Boyer had invited mostly people from the francophone milieus, leaving other centers underrepresented. For Germany, only Viktor Warnach was present and from the Netherlands Garcia van den Berck attended.

83 Willebrands recalled it as such in his introductory words to the volume of Koet, Galema & van Assendelft, *Hearth of Unity*, 10.

84 Wolfgang Thönissen, "Konsolidierung und Institutionalisierung der Ökumene: Die Aktivitäten des Paderborner Erzbischofs Lorenz Jaeger in den fünfziger Jahren des 20. Jahrhunderts," in: Jörg Ernesti & Wolfgang Thönissen, eds., *Die Entdeckung der Ökumene: Zur Beteiligung der katholischen Kirche an der ökumenischen Bewegung*, Paderborn, Bonifatius, 2008, 159–176.

85 Mauro Velati, *Una difficile transizione: Il cattolicesimo tra unionismo ed ecumenismo (1952–1964)*, Bologna, Il Mulino, 1996, 22.

strengthening the Roman unionist approach.[86] In the next to last article, the encyclical underlined that Catholics should not think, indulging in a "false 'irenicism,' that the dissident and the erring can happily be brought back to the bosom of the Church, if the whole truth found in the Church is not sincerely taught to all without corruption or diminution."[87] To cap this explicit return to past models and once again branding non-Catholic Christians as dissidents, in November of the same year, Pius XII formally promulgated the dogma of the assumption of the Virgin Mary,[88] which gave rise to considerable tensions between Protestants and Catholics, apart from the fact that several Catholic theologians questioned the need for this doctrinal definition.

Such odds did not prevent figures like Dumont from engaging in new initiatives. In November 1951, together with Tomkins, he organized a meeting at the Swiss abbey of Présinge, in the vicinity of Geneva. This encounter was quite different from the one of Unitas. Its scope extended well beyond the Roman milieu, the meeting was international, and it seriously aimed at bringing the Catholic world and the officials of the WCC into direct contact.[89] Those present helped prepare a conference of Faith and Order that would gather in Lund the following year. Also of interest is the fact that the Présinge meeting returned to the central theme of the ecclesial remnants[90] of talks from Congar[91] and from Tomkins.[92] In the end, the presence of two Dutchmen, Thijssen, a close friend of Willebrands, and the Dominican Piet Kreling, send by Willebrands to attend on behalf of his SWV, would turn out to be crucial. After Présinge, and in the conditions created by *De motione oecumenica*, the number of contacts and amount of correspondence between the leading voices in Geneva, the French Dominican, the ecumenical circles connected to Paderborn, and those connected to the SWV increased remarkably. The emergence of a broad international network of communications testified that a new phase was at hand although most of the contacts remained bilateral.

This was about to change, and already at the moment of the Présinge gathering informal preparations for establishing an overarching structure were underway. In the spring of 1951 Willebrands had been increasingly involved in discussions with Thijssen in order to prepare for what they initially called a "Conseil Œcuménique Catholique." In the summer of 1951, the two traveled around Europe in order to promote their initiative in Paderborn, Chevetogne, and Paris, but also in Rome. It was crucial, given the guidelines of *De motione oecumenica*, to gain support from within the Holy Office, and contacts were maintained with officials such as Tromp and Bea,[93] so that by September 1951 a first draft

86 Pius XII, *Humani Generis*, in: *AAS* 42, 1950, 561–578, here 571.

87 Pius XII, *Humani Generis*, 578.

88 Pius XII, *Munificentissimus Deus*, in: *AAS* 42, 1950, 753–771.

89 From the Catholic side, the people who attended were Dumont, Congar, and Hamer, along with Olivier Rousseau of Chevetogne, the Swiss theologian Charles Journet, the two Dutchmen Thijssen and Piet Kreling, and the British Benedictine monk Columba Cary-Elwes. Non-Catholic representatives were: Visser 't Hooft, Jean Bosc, Tomkins, Jean Courvoisier, Nils Ehrenström, Alexandre de Weymarn, Thurian, Hendrik van der Linde, Hendrik Kraemer, Suzanne de Dietrich, and Paul Evdokimov. See *Rapport rencontre de Présinge*, a report in French and Dutch, in: ACI (24 typed pages plus two introductory pages). The WCC secretary general's memoirs also refer to this meeting and to the importance of the ecclesiology of the "elements." See Visser 't Hooft, *Memoirs*, 320.

90 Theologians such as Vischer were well aware of the importance of the doctrine of the ecclesial elements, which was addressed during the central commission meeting of 1951 in Rolle, Switzerland. On this see Velati, *Separati ma fratelli*, 265.

91 Congar's talk built on the insights of his key work of 1937, where he had stressed the idea that Christian tradition had always recognized the existence of ecclesial value outside the "visible" church, thus challenging the ecclesiology that had emerged in Catholicism after the council of Trent. See various documents in CCEQ archives, "Dossier Présinge."

92 *Rapport rencontre de Présinge*, 6.

93 Bea was informed as early as in the spring of 1952. See "La 1ère réunion de la CCQŒ à Fribourg," in: CCEQ

for the "council" was ready.[94] The name alone – which would eventually be turned into Catholic conference – revealed the extent to which the Geneva WCC served as a model.[95] This period of informal preparations was closed a year later in Fribourg, when in August 1952 the CCEQ was officially launched. For the very same reason, several historians of ecumenism have signaled the year of 1952 as a turning point.[96]

4 Conclusions

The present survey on Rome and Ecumenism does not include a full reconstruction of the story of the CCEQ. This work has been carried out, and it will be addressed elsewhere in this volume.[97] Here it will suffice to point to the fact that, from its very first meeting in Fribourg until its last meeting in Gazzada in 1963, the CCEQ has assumed a pivotal role in reconnecting previously scattered and local initiatives. With this initiative, Catholic ecumenical engagement was able to further professionalize, even though it would take until 1960 before the question of observership was resolved,[98] and before Rome also had an official "address" for ecumenical contacts, which was felt by the painful experience of Willebrands and Dumont during the central committee meeting of the WCC in Rhodes.[99] The best way to illustrate the importance of the CCEQ is to provide the striking list of those engaged in it under the era of Pius XII, who were later appointed staff members (Jaeger, François Charrière, Thomas Holland, Josef Höfer, Charles Boyer, Gustave Thils, Pierre Michalon), and consultors (Hermann Volk, Francis Davis, Alberto Bellini, Joseph Feiner, Eduard Stakemeier, Thijssen, Janez Vodopivec, Dumont, Hamer, Maurice Bévenot, George Weigel, Georges Tavard) of the SPCU, headed by Bea and Willebrands.

In the following years, and given the fact that non-Catholics continued to find the Roman curia difficult to grasp, the CCEQ would serve as a central reference point. Invitations for observers at

archives. In a note of Apr 24, 1952, he was quite reluctant, judging that the situation in Rome was not ready for an "ecumenical council." He suggested starting by establishing a secretariat and a periodical, and making sure that the initiative came from the bishops and followed the principles of the Holy See.

94 J. Willebrands and F. Thijssen to L. Jaeger, Aug 21, 1951, in: CCEQ archives. "In general, the idea has already been discussed with Prof. Dr. S. Tromp S.J., member of the Holy Office in Rome. However, Father Tromp has not yet seen the concept as Your Excellency finds it here." In order to convince Tromp, Professor Jan Witte from the Gregorian University was contacted. In his response to the letter and the project for the "ecumenical council," dated Aug 28, 1951, Jaeger advised the two men to involve Bea, also in view of ensuring that their initiative would not outrule Boyer's Unitas.

95 Schelkens, "Pioneers at the Crossroads," illustrates the way in which the agendas of the WCC and the CCEQ ran parallel in the preconciliar era.

96 See for instance the volume by Velati, *Una difficile transizione*. The same goes for the aforementioned study of Fouilloux, "Une longue marche," 283, who affirms that "from 1952 until the creation of the Roman Secretariat for Christian Unity in June 1960, the Catholic Conference for Ecumenical Questions replaced Istina as the hub of unofficial relations both with the Geneva Council and with the member churches and communities."

97 Peter De Mey, "Précurseur du Secrétariat pour l'Unité: Le travail œcuménique de la 'Conférence catholique pour les questions œcuméniques' (1952–1963)," in: Roy, Routhier & Schelkens. eds., *La théologie catholique*, 271–308. See also Peter De Mey and Saretta Marotta contribution "The Catholic Conference on Ecumenical Questions" in this volume.

98 See for instance W.A. Visser 't Hooft to J. Willebrands, of Dec 16, 1953, in: CCEQ archives, in which the issue of sending Catholic observers to Evanston was raised but eventually, this time too, Rome would not permit official observers to go. Dumont, however, did go there on behalf of the CCEQ.

99 On the need for such an address, see Mauro Velati, "Un indirizzo a Roma: La nascita del Segretariato per l'unità dei cristiani (1959–1960)," in: Giuseppe Alberigo, ed., *Il Vaticano II fra attese e celebrazione*, Bologna, Il Mulino, 1995, 75–118, esp. 83–84. Regarding the Rhodes incident, see Karim Schelkens, "L''affaire de Rhodes' au jour le jour: La correspondance inédite entre J.G.M. Willebrands et C.-J. Dumont," *Istina* 54, 2009, 253–277.

meetings of the WCC would be discussed first with the board of directors of the CCEQ, and Catholic representation, still mainly under the statute of journalists, would henceforth be connected to this network. One of the organization's strongpoints was that it deliberately sought to include the various and often tense approaches within the Roman Catholic world, not casting aside the unionist tendencies, but integrating them. The consequence was that the CCEQ invited and brought together theologians from all sides within the Roman world, bridging the internal divide. Referring back to the above-cited words of Congar on Boyer, it was striking that both would be involved in the CCEQ. Besides this, it should be noted that this inclusive approach also implied that any initiative or meeting was discussed beforehand both with the local ordinaries and with members from the Roman curia.

This becomes clear when one glances through the archives of the CCEQ, which holds vast files of correspondence between Willebrands and the bishop of Fribourg, Charrière, preparing the first meeting. These two men made serious efforts to secure Roman confidence in their initiative. Several curial cardinals figured on the list of officials, besides those already mentioned above, such as Eugène Tisserant from the Congregation for the Oriental Churches,[100] Giuseppe Pizzardo, and Alfredo Ottaviani, who acted as the head of their respective congregations. Fribourg constituted a turning point for Rome and ecumenism, and from 1953, the year in which Couturier passed away, a new phase began.

100 Étienne Fouilloux, *Eugène cardinal Tisserant (1884–1972): Une biographie*, Paris, Desclée de Brouwer, 2011.

Bibliography

Declerck, Leo, *Mgr J. Willebrands et la Conférence catholique pour les questions œcuméniques: Ses archives à Chevetogne*, Leuven, Peeters, 2015.

Ernesti, Jörg & Wolfgang Thönissen, eds., *Die Entdeckung der Ökumene: Zur Beteiligung der katholischen Kirche an der ökumenischen Bewegung*, Paderborn, Bonifatius, 2008.

Famerée, Joseph, *L'ecclésiologie d'Yves Congar avant Vatican II: Histoire et Église. Analyse et reprise critique*, Leuven, Leuven University Press, 1992.

Fouilloux, Étienne, *Les catholiques et l'unité chrétienne du XIXe au XXe siècle: Itinéraires européens d'expression française*, Paris, Le Centurion, 1982.

Fouilloux, Étienne, *Une église en quête de liberté: La pensée catholique francaise entre modernisme et Vatican II (1914–1962)*, Paris, Desclée de Brouwer, 1998.

Routhier, Gilles, Philippe J. Roy & Karim Schelkens, eds., *Entre intransigeance et renouveau: La réception des mouvements préconciliaires à Vatican II*, Louvain-la-Neuve, Collège Érasme, 2011.

Velati, Mauro, *Una difficile transizione: Il cattolicesimo tra unionismo ed ecumenismo (1952–1964)*, Bologna, Il Mulino, 1996.

CHAPTER 22

The Catholic Conference for Ecumenical Questions

Peter De Mey and Saretta Marotta

1 Paving the Way: Grottaferrata, Presinge, Fribourg

In the Holy Year 1950,[1] after the promulgation of the *Instructio De motione oecumenica* on the Catholic commitment to Christian unity, an international conference of Catholic ecumenists was hosted near Rome, in Grottaferrata, promoted by the Unitas association, a semiofficial Roman center for ecumenical studies directed by the Jesuit Charles Boyer.[2] The meeting, held in Sep 19–22 and encouraged by the substitute of the Secretariat of State, Giovanni Battista Montini, and by the pope himself, was attended by 25 specialists, most of whom from the French-speaking area.[3] The participants perceived that the main purpose of the conference was to aggregate and control the activities of the actors of the nascent Catholic ecumenical movement, with the intention of associating and aligning them under the coordination of Unitas and Boyer. Yves Congar realized this very well: "Is there a plan, in the implacable logic of which we are going to be caught up without even being able to say 'ouf'? What is going to be asked of us, imposed on us? It seems undeniable that there was an intention, if not to absorb us, then at least to make us toe the line and to control us ... This impression is very vexing."[4]

Between 1945 and 1950, the Dominicans Yves Congar and Christophe-Jean Dumont had already tried to create a network of French Catholic ecumenists, also aiming to turn it into an interface for contacting the WCC in Geneva.[5] Their attempt failed because the local hierarchy was afraid of the reaction of the Roman authorities, in the climate of fear that followed the publication of the encyclical *Humani generis* on Aug 12, 1950.[6] The only way to achieve a coordination of Catholic ecumenism was to place it under the supervision of the episcopal hierarchy, as the Germans had done. The Fulda conference had indeed set up a commission for *Una-Sancta-Arbeit* in 1946, coordinated by the archbishop of Paderborn, Lorenz Jaeger.[7] Boyer was attempting to create a similar coordination, but on an international scale.

The Grottaferrata meeting culminated in the creation of a trio of coordinators who were supposed to provide the project with continuity: Dom Olivier Rousseau, from the Belgian monastery of Chevetogne, Christophe-Jean Dumont, from the French center Istina, and Boyer

1 Sections 1, 2, 3, and 6 were written by Saretta Marotta and sections 4, 5, and 7 were written by Peter De Mey.
For the inventory of the CCEQ archives in Chevetogne, see Leo Declerck, *Mgr J. Willebrands et la Conférence catholique pour les questions œcuméniques: Ses archives à Chevetogne*, Leuven, Peeters, 2015. All sources have been reported in English translated by the authors themselves.

2 Concerning *De motione oecumenica* see the contribution by Saretta Marotta in this volume. On Boyer see Fermina Alvarez Alonso, "Charles Boyer: Unitas in Italia per il mondo (1946–1956)," *Colloquia Mediterranea* 12, 2022, 203–223.

3 The list of the participants was published in *L'Osservatore Romano*, Sep 24, 1950, 1. On this meeting see Étienne Fouilloux, *Les catholiques et l'unité chrétienne du XIXème au XXème siècle: Itinéraires européens d'expression française*, Paris, Le Centurion, 1982, 705–709 and 835–845.

4 Yves Congar, *Journal d'un théologien (1946–1956)*, ed. Étienne Fouilloux, Paris, Cerf, 2001, 166–180, here 171 (Oct 19, 1950).

5 Fouilloux, *Les catholiques et l'unité*, 695–704.

6 For this encyclical, directed against the so-called *nouvelle théologie*, see Étienne Fouilloux, *Une Église en quête de liberté: La pensée catholique française entre modernisme et Vatican II (1914–1962)*, Paris, Desclée de Brouwer, 1998.

7 Jörg Ernesti, *Ökumene im Dritten Reich*, Paderborn, Bonifatius, 2007, 346–368.

himself. However, this continuity committee did not achieve its objective because of the divergences between the effervescent Catholic ecumenism of the French-speaking countries and the unionist approach of the Roman milieus and, in particular, of the Unitas association. The failure of the Grottaferrata meeting may explain why it was then possible to replace Boyer's project with another attempt, this time from the Netherlands.

At the Grottaferrata meeting only one priest, Garcia van den Berck, represented the Dutch ecumenists, in the absence of any members of the SWV, the main Catholic association in the Netherlands working for Christian unity and which in 1948 had come to replace its rather apologetic predecessor, the Apologetische Vereniging Petrus Canisius.[8] At the first World Congress of the Lay Apostolate in Rome in October 1951, the Dutch Jesuit Jan Witte had represented the SWV. Speaking in a plenary session on that occasion, Witte had launched the proposal for a "Conseil catholique œcuménique," anticipating a project under discussion in those months within the SWV.[9] During his trip to Rome in the autumn of 1951, Witte discussed the project with other Catholic ecumenists present at the congress to sound out their opinion on the proposal, receiving from Congar the following judgement: "if the thing comes to Rome, it's death!"[10] Despite the warning, Witte instead also discussed the proposal with some important men in Rome, such as the Jesuits Charles Boyer, Friedrich Kempf, Constant Van Gestel, Robert Leiber (Pius XII's private secretary), Sebastiaan Tromp, and Augustin Bea, the latter two consultors at the Holy Office.[11] In his report, Witte wrote that the purpose of the trip, apart from participating in the congress of the lay apostolate, was precisely that of "discovering in Rome the opinions of some members of the Holy Office (or other influential persons in our case) on a project to establish a 'Catholic ecumenical council.'"[12]

Witte's mission in Rome had been prepared by a round of consultations, in August 1951, by Johannes Willebrands, president of the SWV, and his friend and main collaborator Frans Thijssen with some French, Belgian, Swiss, and German personalities involved in Catholic ecumenical activities, in order to present the project of the "Conseil catholique œcuménique."[13] During their European trip, the two Dutch priests were welcomed, among others, by the Benedictine monks of Chevetogne and by Christophe-Jean Dumont, director of the Istina center in Paris.[14] The latter invited them to a meeting, scheduled for November 1951, between some Catholic theologians (including Congar)

8 Jan Jacobs, *Nieuwe visies op een oud visioen: Een portret van de Sint Willibrord Vereniging (1948–1998)*, Nijmegen, Valkhof Pers, 1998.

9 Fouilloux, *Les catholiques et l'unité*, 710. See also "Verslag Rome-reis van Pater J.L. Witte, S.J.," 3, in: AAC, FWC, dossier 5, 1: La préparation lointaine de la CCQŒ. Concerning the genesis of the project, Willebrands wrote in his diaries: "I vividly remember the moment when the thought entered my head. In 1950, in Hotel Noord-Brabant in Utrecht, during the break of meeting of the SWV. I always had the feeling that Divine Providence had given me the idea, yet, I had always felt powerless and worthless to be given such a responsibility"; Theo Salemink, ed., *You Will Be Called Repairer of the Breach: The diary of J.G.M. Willebrands (1958–1961)*, Leuven, Peeters, 2009, 151 (May 18, 1960).

10 "Verslag Rome-reis van Pater J.L. Witte, S.J.," 6. On Congar's first evaluations of the project of the CCEQ, see Mauro Velati, *Una difficile transizione: Il cattolicesimo tra unionismo ed ecumenismo (1952–1964)*, Bologna, Il Mulino, 1996, 33–34.

11 Alexandra von Teuffenbach, "Der Einfluss der Jesuiten der Päpstlichen Universität Gregoriana auf Papst Pius XII.," in: *Katholische Theologie im Nationalsozialismus*, vol. 1/2, Dominik Burkard & Wolfgang Weiss, eds., *Istitutionen und Strukturen*, Würzburg, Echter, 2011, 395–440.

12 "Verslag Rome-reis van Pater J.L. Witte, S.J.," 1.

13 See their report "Verslag van de Reis voor het Plan Katholieke Oecumenische Raad (2–18 august 1951)," in: AAC, FWC, dossier 5, 1: La préparation lointaine de la CCQŒ. The many versions of the "Plan voor een Katholieke Oecumenische Raad" and a number of translations are found in AAC, FWC, dossier 5, 2: Premiers projets d'un "Conseil œcuménique catholique."

14 Étienne Fouilloux, "Une Longue marche vers l'œcuménisme: Istina (1923–1967)," *Istina* 3, 2010, 271–287. For the activities of Chevetogne, see See the contribution on the Ecumenical Study Days of Chevetogne by Peter De Mey and Saretta Marotta in this volume.

and some members of the ecumenical commission Faith and Order on the subject of the *"vestigia ecclesiae."*[15] The meeting, which took place in Presinge, Switzerland, was also attended by some leading members of the WCC, such as the general secretary himself, Willem Adolf Visser 't Hooft.[16] Through this meeting, attended by Thijssen and another Dutch priest, the Dominican Piet Kreling, the leadership of the SWV made contact with the bishop of Geneva François Charrière, who had previously asked permission for their participation with the Holy Office, according to the *Instructio De motione oecumenica*.[17] It was indeed not easy to obtain the collaboration of the European bishops in the project. Despite the approval already granted by the Dutch episcopate, the attempt to meet that August with the archbishop of Lyon, Cardinal Pierre-Marie Gerlier, and the archbishop of Paris, Maurice Feltin, inexorably failed (the latter met Willebrands and Thijssen in December 1951 after the mediation of the archbishop of Utrecht, Johannes de Jong).[18] Among the ordinaries it was only possible to visit Jaeger, who was also the coordinator of the commission for ecumenical affairs on behalf of the German bishops. Jaeger was contacted in July 1951 and was the first to receive the two during their European "tour" in August.[19] Furthermore, it was he who suggested that they should contact certain personalities in Rome to receive the informal approval from the Roman authorities for the project. He recommended in particular that they first contact the Jesuit Augustin Bea, former rector of the PIB and at that time consultor of the Holy Office and confessor of the pope:

> You would do better, before making public your project and claiming the need "to create an international Catholic ecumenical movement, which should have its headquarters outside Rome, so as to clearly mark the difference with the Roman Congregations" to ask the competent authorities to ensure that in Rome there is agreement with your efforts. I suggest you address this question to Reverend Father Bea, former rector of the Biblical Institute and now consultor at the Holy Office, where he is particularly involved in these ecumenical matters. He will be able, in the most pertinent and secure way, to express an opinion on how far your project corresponds to the Roman intentions and whether the Holy Office will say an unconditional "yes" to what you have conceived.[20]

In addition to this, Jaeger invited Willebrands and Thijssen to participate in the next meeting of the German episcopal commission on ecumenism, scheduled to take place in Frankfurt in October. It was in Frankfurt that the two Dutch priests

15 On this theme, see what Congar wrote about the "elements of the Church" in Marie-Joseph Congar, *Chrétiens désunis: Principe d'un "œcuménisme" catholique*, Paris, Cerf, 1937, 302; ET: *Divided Christendom: A Catholic Study of the Problem of Reunion*, trans. Muad A. Bousfield, London, Bles, 1939. See also Sandra Arenas, *Fading Frontiers?: An Historical-Theological Investigation into the Notion of the "Elementa Ecclesiae,"* Leuven, Peeters, 2021.

16 About the meeting, see Fouilloux, *Les catholiques et l'unité*, 811–812; Velati, *Una difficile transizione*, 50–52; Karim Schelkens, "Pioneers at the crossroads: The preconciliar itineraries of W.A. Visser 't Hooft and J.G.M. Willebrands (1951–1961)," *Catholica* 70/1, 2016, 23–39, here 27–29. See also Thijssen's report in: AAC, FWC, dossier 16, 8: Presinge.

17 See F. Charrière to F. Thijssen, Oct 8, 1951 to ask him the names of the two Dutch delegates and the letters between Dumont and Thijssen, Oct 26, 1951 and Dec 8, 1951, in: AAC, FWC, dossier 19, 1: Correspondance.

18 "Bezoek aan Z. Hoogw. Excellentie Mgr. M. Feltin, aartsbisschop van Parijs, door dr. J. Willebrands en dr. F. Thijssen," Dec 12, 1951, in: AAC, FWC, dossier 5, 1: La préparation lointaine de la CCQŒ.

19 J. Willebrands and F. Thijssen to L. Jaeger, Jul 21, 1951, in: AAC, FWC, dossier 19, 1: Correspondance. See for a description of the visit in Paderborn "Verslag van de reis," 2–5.

20 L. Jaeger to J. Willebrands and F. Thijssen, Jul 28, 1951, in: AAC, FWC, dossier 19, 1: Correspondance. For the original German text, see Saretta Marotta, *Gli anni della pazienza: Bea, l'ecumenismo e il Sant'Uffizio di Pio XII*, Bologna, Il Mulino, 2019, 538–539.

came into contact (through the convert and journalist Johannes Peter Michael)[21] with Bishop Albert Stohr, who invited them to Mainz to attend the first ordination of a married Protestant minister, the former Lutheran pastor Rudolf Goethe, on Dec 23.[22] The meeting in Frankfurt was also the beginning of a closer collaboration with the Jesuits of the Sankt Georgen institute, in particular with rector Friedrich Buuck and Johannes Baptist Hirschmann, both of whom they had already visited during the August 1951 trip.[23]

Jaeger's suggestion to seek advice from Bea was taken up by Witte, as already mentioned, during his trip to Rome in October 1951. Among other Roman dignitaries contacted for the project of a "Conseil catholique œcuménique," the conversation with Bea was full of pertinent and useful suggestions. For example, he suggested rewriting the project using terminology strategically closer to that used in *De motione oecumenica* in order to place the initiative within the context of what was envisaged in the instruction. Furthermore, he recommended adopting Father Tromp's suggestion to place the new body under the protection of a trio of ecclesiastical supervisors, bishops de Jong, Jaeger, and Feltin: in this way, the Holy See would not be forced to give the initiative formal approval, which would inevitably undermine the new body in its relations with the ecumenical movement and for the same reason damage the Holy See.[24] These suggestions received by Witte were used in January 1952 by the SWV board in revising the draft of the "Conseil" so that a new version could be presented during the next trip to Rome undertaken by Willebrands and Herman Sondaal in April 1952. Following in Witte's footsteps, Willebrands and Sondaal visited many important individuals in Rome: first of all, the Dutch Jesuit Tromp, then Boyer, Van Gestel, Bea, and also Bernard Alfrink, coadjutor bishop of Utrecht, Petrus Canisius van Lierde, sacristan in the Apostolic Palace, and the Ladies of Bethany, a Dutch religious congregation of women who led the Unitas foyer.[25] Amidst the demotivating Tromp and the silent hostility of Boyer, who would prefer a Roman commission under the chairmanship of a cardinal,[26] Bea was one of the few in Rome who supported the proposal. The conversation with him once again was one of the most fruitful discussions of the whole visit and he would remain one of Willebrands' best contacts in Rome in the following years. The German Jesuit, who left them a typewritten page with observations on the project, made a suggestion which, once accepted, would mark the official start of the new organization's activities:

> Would it not be appropriate, first of all, to hold an international meeting of the bishops (or their representatives) primarily involved in ecumenical work and the best experts of the movement (but almost as a private meeting, without all the external apparatus)? This could for example take place during the summer holidays in a seminary.[27]

---

21 Michael was a journalist and editorial board member of the *Herder Korrespondenz*. By nature very polemical, he would later come into conflict with the leadership of the CCEQ, in particular for his opposition to Congar, being abruptly expelled in 1958 (he risked being dismissed from the *Herder Korrespondenz* as well).

22 See the correspondence between Thijssen and Stohr in: AAC, FWC, dossier 19, 1: Correspondance. For Stohr's involvement in the activities of the CCEQ, see Leonhard Hell, "Unio Ecclesiae – Materia primaria: Bischof Albert Stohrs Einbindung in den entstehenden internationalen katholischen Ökumenismus und in die Vorbereitung des Zweiten Vatikanischen Konzils," in: Karl Lehmann, ed., *Dominus fortitudo: Bischof Albert Stohr (1890–1961)*, Mainz, Echter, 2012, 99–119.

23 The conversations with Buuck and Hirschmann are reported in "Verslag van de Reis," 5.

24 Bea's meticulous corrections to the project are reported in "Verslag Rome-reis van Pater J.L. Witte, S.J.," 6–8.

25 See the handwritten report: "Romereis J. Willebrands – H. Sondaal (19 April–1 Mei 1952)," in: AAC, FWC, dossier 5, 1: La préparation lointaine de la CCQŒ.

26 C. Boyer to F. Charrière, Jun 23, 1952, in: Velati, *Una difficile transizione*, 42.

27 Bea's memorandum to Willebrands and Sondaal, Apr 24, 1952, in: AAC, FWC, dossier 5, 5: Correspondance avec d'autres personnalités. For the original German text see: Marotta, *Gli anni della pazienza*, 540.

Thus, in the following months, the SWV board decided to concentrate its efforts on organizing an international meeting, to be held in Fribourg and hosted by bishop Charrière. It was Charrière who, besides making the diocesan seminary available for the conference (as suggested by Bea), asked the Holy Office for permission for each participant, which proved particularly difficult in the case of Congar.[28] Congar was invited as speaker, along with the historian Hubert Jedin and the Benedictine of Chevetogne, Théodore Strotmann. With the sole exception of Jedin's historical contribution on Trent, all the speakers referred to topics on the current agenda of the ecumenical movement: Congar's intervention, based on his book *Chrétiens désunis*, recalled the theme of the Presinge meeting on the "elements of the church," while Strotmann's contribution was a survey of the work of the Faith and Order commission, to highlight the opportunities for collaboration.[29] The "private" meeting , which was the connotation given in the invitation letter, took place in Aug 11–13 and was attended by 24 theologians. Unlike the Grottaferrata conference, there was a better geographical distribution of participants, while the Italian presence was radically reduced, with only Boyer representing the Roman circles. The largest "delegation" came from Germany (whereas in Grottaferrata only the Benedictine monk of Maria Laach, Viktor Warnach, represented the German-speaking countries): in addition to Jedin and Warnach, the delegation also included Josef Höfer and Karl Schmitt, sent respectively by the bishops of Paderborn and Mainz, Karl Rahner, at that time resident in Innsbrück, Robert Grosche, editor of *Catholica*, and Karlheinz Schmidthüs, director of *Herder-Korrespondenz*. From Belgium, two monks from Chevetogne, Rousseau and Strotmann, the historian Roger Aubert and the Dominican Hamer attended the conference. From the Netherlands, Willebrands, Witte, Thijssen, and the Dominican Karel Pauwels were present. From France, in addition to Congar and Dumont, there were the Dominican Marie-Joseph Le Guillou from the Istina center, Henri Desmettre from Lille, and Eugène Fischer from Strasbourg, while from Switzerland there was the participation of Edmond Chavaz from Geneva, the Dominican Adolf Hoffmann from Fribourg, and Charrière himself. Some invitees were unable to attend the conference at the last moment. Among them was John Courtney Murray of Woodstock College in the United States, who had also previously attended the Grottaferrata meeting, as well as Chavaz, Congar, Dumont, Warnach, Hamer, and Rousseau.

Charrière's presence at the meeting was not the only expression of a bishop's approval of the project: in a circular letter sent to the invitees, Willebrands reported extracts from the enthusiastic reactions he had received from de Jong, Alfrink, Jaeger, Stohr, and even the apostolic vicar of Sweden, Johann Evangelist Müller, who was at that time dealing with the authorizations for Catholic observers at the Faith and Order conference in Lund at the end of August.[30] Archbishop Feltin of Paris wrote directly to Charrière, and his letter

28 See F. Charrière to A. Ottaviani, Jun 18, 1952 and Jun 28, 1952, in: AAC, FWC, dossier 5, 4: Correspondance avec cardinaux et évêques.

29 Here the titles of the scheduled interventions: "Kirchenspaltung und Ökumene historisch gesehen" (Jedin); "Les éléments d'Église parmi les chrétiens réformés et la réflexion ecclésiologique" (Congar); "Le Mouvement Foi et Constitution: Points de contact et possibilités pour un catholique d'aujourd'hui" (Strotmann). For a deeper look at the themes of the interventions, see Peter De Mey, "L'évolution théologique et œcuménique de la 'Conférence Catholique pour les questions œcuméniques' (1952–1963)," in: Declerck, *Mgr J. Willebrands et la Conférence*, 7–39, here 7–10. The texts of the contributions are in AAC, FWC, dossier 5, 6: Textes des conferences.

30 See Willebrands' circular letter of Jul 25, 1952, in: AAC, FWC, dossier 5, 3: Invitations. The original letters received from these bishops are in AAC, FWC, dossier 5, 4: Correspondance avec cardinaux et évêques. For the Catholic participation in Lund, see Fouilloux, *Les catholiques et l'unité*, 813–816.

was read out at the beginning of the conference.[31] These episcopal endorsements made it possible to satisfy the request of the Roman authorities to make the initiative the responsibility of the bishops and avoid the explicit authorization of the Holy Office. The new organization could thus have substantial freedom of action. Charrière became the third member of the bishops' board of guarantors in place of Feltin, and each conference would in future be chaired by the local bishop. Therefore, the coordinator of the "Conseil" would be named in the statutes as "secretary" and not "president," leaving this role to the bishops.

The main objective of the meeting in Fribourg was to lend a concrete form to the SWV's project for a "Conseil catholique œcuménique." The participants, who prior to the conference received the last draft of the project together with the texts of the planned talks, agreed to avoid the term "council" – which would have recalled the ecumenical council of Geneva, insinuating an erroneous parallelism – and preferred the provisional name of "Conférence catholique œcuménique," which would later become "Conférence catholique pour les questions œcuméniques."[32] The general secretariat of the new body, which should normally have continued to meet annually, was entrusted to Willebrands, while the final drafting of the statute was deferred to an executive board which initially consisted of almost the same members as the Grottaferrata Continuation Committee: Boyer somehow representing the Roman milieu, Dumont for France, Rousseau for Belgium, and Höfer for Germany.[33] Dumont himself, who had already drafted the conclusions of the 1950 meeting, wrote and read out a summary of the discussions at the end of the Fribourg conference.[34] The participants also established the main objectives of the CCEQ: to guarantee an effective contact between the different activities of Catholic ecumenism in the various countries; to promote scientific work on ecumenical questions, on the one hand, and ecumenical themes among the clergy and the faithful, on the other; to ensure mutual information among the members, especially on the evolution of the international ecumenical movement.[35]

As a matter of fact, the CCEQ in the following years represented an unprecedented opportunity to permit Catholic ecumenism in the various countries to be enriched through listening to similar experiences in other countries, as well as through the valuable contact and subsequent collaboration with the organizations of the international ecumenical movement. The CCEQ was above all a theological forge that prepared the renewal of Catholic ecclesiology at Vatican II.[36] However, for a long time, some fundamental differences on the very notion of "ecumenism" persisted among the members. These basic differences, which frequently caused difficulties and delays in the work of the CCEQ, would survive until the preparatory work of the Secretariat for Christian Unity.[37]

31 M. Feltin to F. Charrière, Jul 14, 1952, in: AAC, FWC, dossier 5, 4: Correspondance avec cardinaux et évêques.

32 The final decision was taken during a meeting in Paris: "Compte rendu de la réunion de la commission d'études," Nov 7, 1953, 3, in: AAC, FWC, dossier 3: Reunions du Comite directeur et de la commission d'etudes.

33 The hypothesis of an intentional continuity between Grottaferrata and the CCEQ is derived from Christophe-Jean Dumont, "L'œcuménisme," *Recherches et débats* 27, 1959, 90–109, here 106: "On the initiative of two Dutch priests, the project that had begun two years earlier in Grottaferrata was resumed."

34 Christophe-Jean Dumont, "Court résumé des échanges de vues," in: AAC, FWC, dossier 5, 7: Échanges de vues dans la réunion de Fribourg.

35 For the report of the results of the conference, see AAC, FWC, dossier 5, 8: Rapport et conclusions.

36 See Peter De Mey, "The Catholic Conference for Ecumenical Questions' Immediate Preparation of the Renewal of Catholic Ecclesiology at Vatican II," in: Luca Ferracci (ed.), *Toward a History of the Desire for Christian Unity: Preliminary Research Papers*, Münster, LIT, 2015, 141–157.

37 See Peter De Mey, "*De oecumenismo catholico et de opere conversionum*: The relationship between Ecumenism and the Apostolate of Conversions Before and During the Second Vatican Council," in: Stephan van

2 A Memorandum for the Evanston Assembly

After Fribourg, the work of the CCEQ was able to start properly. The second conference, already announced in Fribourg and planned for August 1953 in the seminary of Dijnselburg, near Utrecht, was in point of fact the first one to focus on the study of a particular theological or ecclesiological theme. It was the SWV, at Dumont's suggestion, that proposed as subject the topic of the next assembly of the WCC, scheduled for 1954 in Evanston, centered on the theme "Christ: the hope of the world."[38] Evanston was to be the second WCC assembly after Amsterdam in 1948 and it was expected that this time it would be possible for Catholics to be present as observers, as had been the case at the Faith and Order conference in Lund. The choice of the same theme as Evanston would ensure that those observers were prepared to represent the Catholic Church at that event, but it would also mark the beginning of the unofficial collaboration between the CCEQ and the WCC. The purpose of the Dijnselburg conference was in fact twofold: to prepare a memorandum on the theme of Christian hope to be offered to the assembly in Evanston, but also to plan a restricted meeting among some theologians of the CCEQ and some representatives of the WCC on the Evanston theme, as had already been done in Presinge for the theme of the elements of the church.[39]

However, some difficulties arose during the conference making the first goal unachievable. Two different approaches to the question emerged during the discussions and even the conference program took account of this diversity. On the one hand, there was an ecclesiological approach, close to the position of the German and Dutch members of the CCEQ, which subordinated the theme of the hope for the world to the question of the mediation of the church. On the other hand, there was a social and missionary perspective, close to the French sensibility and which gave priority to the possibility of collaboration among Christians for the renewal of humanity.[40] Understanding Christ or instead the church, as the hope of the world also implied a not insignificant diversity between the ecumenical visions of the members of the

---

Erp & Karim Schelkens, eds., *Conversion and Church: The Challenge of Ecclesial Renewal*, Leiden, Brill, 2016, 263–287.

38 See J. Willebrands to the executive board, Jan 25, 1953, in: AAC, FWC, dossier 7, 3: Correspondance et réactions concernant le 1er projet. See also the other topic proposals advanced by Willebrands to the SWV in the letter of Dec 4, 1952, in: AAC, FWC, dossier 7, 1: 1er et 2e projet.

39 See the invitation letter, Mar 23, 1953, in: AAC, FWC, dossier 7, 1: 1er et 2e projet. The meeting was attended by 30 participants. The largest group came from the Netherlands (11 people), whereas there were 7 Germans (Grosche, Schmidthüs, Schmitt, and also the historian Joseph Lortz, the journalist Johannes Peter Michael, the Benedictine of Niederaltaich Thomas Sartory, and the bishop of Mainz, Albert Stohr). The French and the Belgian delegations were almost identical to those who had attended the first meeting, with the addition of Maurice Villain and Jan-Hendrik Walgrave and with the absence of Aubert and Desmettre. No one came from Switzerland, but this time England, the United States and Sweden were represented, by, respectively, the Jesuit Maurice Bévenot, William Granger Ryan, and the Dominican Michel Bonnet de Paillerets. Boyer also attended the conference. For the complete list of the participants, see AAC, FWC, dossier 7, 8: Compte rendu.

40 This is also visible in the program, with two biblical-theological contributions on the subject of the alliance of God with his people in the Old and the New Testaments (Ansfried Hulsbosch, "L'attente du salut d'après l'Ancien Testament"; Robert Grosche, "Die Hoffnung im neuen Testament") and two contributions on the secular implications of Christian hope (Christophe-Jean Dumont, "L'espérance chrétienne d'après les travaux préliminaires à la seconde assemblée du Conseil œcuménique des Églises à Evanston U.S.A."; Johannes Peter Michael, "Erfüllt die katholische Kirche die Hoffnung der ökumenischer Christenheit?"). The meeting in Dijnselburg was the first conference of the CCEQ where some of the contributions were published, although in different periodicals: Ansfried Hulsbosch, "L'attente du salut d'après l'Ancien Testament," *Irén* 27, 1954, 1–20; Christophe-Jean Dumont, "L'espérance chrétienne d'après les travaux préliminaires à la seconde assemblée du Conseil œcuménique des Églises à Evanston (U.S.A.)," *Istina* 1, 1954, 80–106.

CCEQ. When the auxiliary bishop of Utrecht Bernard Alfrink gave his introductory speech as chair of the conference, the reactions to his ecumenical vision on the part of the French ecumenists were indeed strongly disappointed, as one can read in the memories of Maurice Villain, who attended the meeting representing the ecumenical circle of Lyon:

> What a surprise and what a shock! "We also do ecumenism," said the prelate at the beginning of his speech. But what kind of ecumenism was he talking about? The answer came in the second sentence: it was about converting Protestants, starting from the pastors, and the speaker explained in great detail the various conversion methods used in the archdiocese. I was sitting between Father Congar and Father Dumont. For each new sentence, we lowered our heads a little more. Finally, my head touched my knees.[41]

The final report of the Dijnselburg meeting also noted the difference between the line adopted by CCEQ members "from Catholic countries," who "wished to underline above all the temporal aspects of salvation and the importance of Christianity for the World," with an approach to the theme of Christian hope identical to that taken by the WCC, and the line defended by CCEQ members from "northern countries." Since Catholicism is a minority there, from a "long experience of cooperation with non-Catholics, in the field of social and political activity ... it has been learned that such cooperation does not bring people closer together as Christians ... . [T]herefore it is difficult to conceive that, when speaking of Christ, the hope of the World, this same Christ can be separated from his Church."[42] For these reasons the possibility of a meeting in common with some WCC theologians was put aside, whereas the task of drafting a Catholic memorandum for the Evanston assembly became the main objective of the third CCEQ meeting planned for April 1954 in Mainz. However, in the final discussion in Dijnselburg it was decided that the memorandum should be published as a private one by some Catholic theologians, not in the name of the CCEQ. This decision was taken, on the one hand, in reason of the many divergences between the members on how to deal with the subject but, on the other hand, also because this would keep "the status of the Conference as such still a private one."[43]

A restricted committee, consisting of Yves Congar, Louis Bouyer, and Hermann Volk, was to take charge of the drafting of the text, but at the meeting at the Istina center in Paris in November 1953 an enlarged commission, consisting almost exclusively of theologians coming mainly from the French (and Dominican) areas, already decided to entrust the drafting to father Congar alone.[44] This procedure was criticized by Charles Boyer,

41 Maurice Villain, *Vers l'unité: Itinéraire d'un pionnier (1935–1975)*, Dinard, G.S.O.E., 1986, 208. See also De Mey, "*De oecumenismo catholico*," 263–287.

42 "Report of the Second Meeting of the 'Catholic Ecumenical Conference' at the Seminary of Dijnselburg (6–9 August 1953)," 3, in: AAC, FWC, dossier 7, 8: Compte rendu. About the difficulties during and after the Dijnselburg conference, rendered evident especially in Michael's speech, see Velati, *Una difficile transizione*, 55–61 and Peter De Mey, "Précurseur du Secrétariat pour l'Unité: Le travail œcuménique de la 'Conférence catholique pour les questions œcuméniques' (1952–1963)," in: Gilles Routhier, Philippe J. Roy & Karim Schelkens, eds., *La théologie catholique entre intransigeance et renouveau: La réception des mouvements préconciliaires à Vatican II*, Louvain-la-Neuve/Leuven, Collège Érasme/Maurits Sabbebibliotheek, 2011, 271–308, here 277–280.

43 "Report of the Second Meeting," 13.

44 "Compte rendu de la réunion de la commission d'études," Nov 7, 1953, 1, in: AAC, FWC, dossier 3: Reunions du Comite directeur et de la commission d'etudes. This meeting was attended by the Dominicans Dumont, Congar, Le Guillou, Hamer, Bouyer, Marie-Joseph Bazille, in addition to Willebrands, Witte, and the prior of Chevetogne Clément Lialine. It was Congar who had asked to reformulate the composition of the commission in order to keep together "people who already know each other": Y. Congar to J. Willebrands, Oct 10, 1953, in: AAC, FWC, dossier 8, 1: Correspondance en préparation de la reunion.

who reacted to the first version of the text by saying that it was written in too "personal" a form.[45] Even at the meeting in Mainz, where Congar was absent, many objections were raised by other CCEQ members, and in the conclusions to the meeting Willebrands stated: "The discussions did not lead to any definite result, so it was decided to leave to the Central Committee the formulation of the final edition of these theses, which might then be published in some form or other."[46]

Owing to the non-unanimous approval of the document and because of the problems encountered by Congar in 1954 with the Roman authorities,[47] the revision of the draft finally changed hands and was entrusted to Dumont, while the memorandum itself was published anonymously in the journal *Istina*.[48] The document, however, arrived too late to be received by the WCC in preparation for the assembly, but an English translation was distributed among the participants in Evanston. Although it emerged at the end that it was not possible for a Catholic delegation to attend the WCC assembly as "observer,"[49] some Catholics were present as "journalists," including Dumont himself, who later published a detailed report for *Istina*.[50]

3 The Collaboration with the WCC on the Theme "the Lordship of Christ"

The preparation of the memorandum for the Evanston assembly brought the CCEQ closer to the work of the WCC, increasing the convergence of the agendas of the two organizations. The program of the Mainz conference, however, was not entirely dedicated to the theme of the memorandum: two speeches were scheduled, by Friedrick Buuck and Maurice Bévenot, on the ecclesiological issue of church membership, which was one of the most important topics studied at the time by the Faith and Order commission.[51] The fourth conference of the CCEQ,

45 C. Boyer to J. Willebrands, Mar 22, 1954, in: AAC, FWC, dossier 8, 1: Correspondance en préparation de la réunion.

46 "Report of the third Meeting of the CCEQ (21–24 April 1954)," 2, in: AAC, FWC, dossier 8, 2: Documents de la réunion de Mayence. It was not possible to find in the archives the final list of the participants at the conference, but the list of invitees amounts to 60 people, coming from Germany, Austria, France, Belgium, the Netherlands, Switzerland, United Kingdom, United States, Sweden (Bonnet de Paillerets), and Rome (Boyer).

47 Étienne Fouilloux, *Yves Congar (1904–1995): Une vie*, Paris, Salvator, 2020, 167–203; See also Alberto Melloni, "The System and the Truth in the Diaries of Yves Congar," in: Gabriel Flynn (ed.), *Yves Congar Theologian of the Church*, Leuven, Peeters, 2005, 277–302. This was the reason for Congar's absence in Mainz.

48 "Le Christ, L'Église et la grâce dans l'économie de l'espérance chrétienne (Vues catholiques sur le thème d'Evanston)," *Istina* 2, 1954, 132–158. "I believe that everything must be prepared for Mainz as if an agreement could be reached there. For this purpose, and even though the preparation of the next issue of our review *Istina* will be affected, I propose to rework Fr. Congar's first text, taking into account the criticisms that have already been made and his own reactions, which I hope to receive shortly ... I believe that if we want to have any chance of succeeding in this project of collective publication, we must start not from Fr. Congar's first text, but with a new text that takes into account the first criticisms"; C.-J. Dumont to J. Willebrands, Apr 5, 1954, in: AAC, FWC, dossier 8, 1: Correspondance en préparation de la réunion.

49 For the (failed) negotiations with the Holy Office for the sending of Catholic observers in Evanston, see Velati, *Una difficile transizione*, 61–72 and the documentation in AAC, FWC, dossier 17: Assemblée générale du COE à Evanston (1954).

50 Christophe-Jean Dumont, "Réflexions sur l'Assemblée œcuménique d'Evanston," *Istina* 3, 1954, 311–329.

51 There were scheduled also a speech by Clément Lialine about ecumenism and Orthodoxy and an intervention by Karl Thieme about the Jews: for both themes, it was the first time in the sessions of the CCEQ that these subjects were dealt with. Here is the complete program: "Dix thèses catholiques sur le thème d'Evanston, Jesus Christ, Ésperance du Monde" (Congar read by Dumont); "The Internal Plans of the Faith and Order Working Committee on the Theme of the Doctrine about the Church as Projected at Bossey, Aug. 11–19, 1953" (Bévenot); "Die Zugehörigkeit zur Kirche in katholischer und protestantischer Sicht" (Buuck), "La position spéciale de l'Orthodoxie dans le

held in Paris in 1955, also focused on an ecclesiological theme, namely the topic of "images of the church,"[52] which was also discussed a month later at the annual meeting of the Ecumenical Study Days of Chevetogne.[53] Furthermore, in January 1954, Johannes Willebrands and Willem Visser 't Hooft met for the first time. This visit by Willebrands to the WCC headquarters in Geneva marked the beginning of the collaboration and friendship between the two Dutchmen and also provided the basis for Dumont's presence as a "journalist" in Evanston.[54] Nine months later, in October 1954, Visser 't Hooft received Willebrands again, commenting on the results of the assembly and expressing the WCC's great appreciation for the memorandum received from the CCEQ: other regular meetings would follow in the following years, almost every six months.

After the Paris conference in August 1955, Willebrands proposed to Visser 't Hooft that the CCEQ study topics at the same time as the WCC and asked him for some suggestions. In his reply, sent in November 1955, the WCC general secretary welcomed the fact that "the ecumenical cause is best served by the fact that you and we are working separately on the same issues, but not apart from each other."[55] For this reason he proposed that the CCEQ should set aside the "classical" ecclesiological and theological topics typical of the work of the Faith and Order commission – such as tradition, the nature of the church, and so on, which were issues well investigated by both sides – and focus on the theme of "the lordship of Christ over the church and the world," which was a consequence of the Evanston theme and was the main issue of the then ongoing theological work of the WCC. Charged since 1955 with the deepening of this theme, the WCC division of studies, headed by Hans Heinrich Harms, would begin its task in July 1956 with a meeting in Arnoldshain, publishing in the same year a first dossier of studies as a result of its work.[56]

After Visser 't Hooft's letter, forwarded by Willebrands to the executive board of the CCEQ, a first meeting of a provisional study commission among the members of the conference was held in Paris in February 1956, with the participation of Dumont, Le Guillou, Hamer, Émile-Guillaume

problème œcuménique" (Lialine), "Katholische Thesen gegenüber jüdischen getrennten Brüdern zum Thema: Gottes Erlöserwirken in der Einheit mit seinem Gesalbten, die Hoffnung der ganzen Welt" (Thieme). Beyond the "Dix thèses," some of these contributions were later published: Maurice Bévenot, "La conception de l'Église dans le programme de travail de la Commission Foi et Constitution," *Istina* 2, 1954, 164–175; Clément Lialine, "La position spéciale de l'Orthodoxie dans le problème œcuménique," in: *1054–1954: L'Église et les Églises, neuf siècles de douloureuse séparation entre l'Orient et l'Occident: Études et travaux offerts à Dom Lambert Beauduin*, vol. 2, Chevetogne, Éditions de Chevetogne, 1954, 389–413; Karl Thieme, "L'espérance du monde: L'action rédemptrice de Dieu en union avec son Oint," *Istina* 2, 1954, 159–163.

52 The program consisted of three thematic blocks: (1) the church as "bride of Christ" (addressed by Heinrich Schlier to present it from the point of view of exegesis and Protestant theology, then by Charles Journet with regard to "classical Catholic theology"; (2) the church as "body of Christ" (Louis Bouyer for a Catholic and Pauline reading, Johannes Peter Michael and Willem Hendrik van de Pol for the Lutheran and Calvinist interpretation); (3) "La tâche de l'ecclésiologie devant les problèmes contemporains, tels qu'ils sont posées, non seulement par les Protestants, mais aussi par la situation catholique elle même" (Congar).

53 The meeting in Chevetogne, on the theme "Ecclesia sponsa," took place from Sep 27 to 30, 1955, whereas the conference of CCEQ in Paris, attended by 38 participants from 8 countries, was on Aug 1–4. The previous meeting in Chevetogne of 1954, like Mainz, also focused on the theme of the church membership, under the title "Le Baptême et l'Église." See the contribution on the Ecumenical Study Days of Chevetogne by Peter De Mey and Saretta Marotta in this volume.

54 Schelkens, *Pioneers at the crossroads*, 30. Later Willebrands also asked to publish the report on the Mainz conference in *The Ecumenical Review* (see Schelkens, *Pioneers at the crossroads*, 31).

55 W.A. Visser 't Hooft to J. Willebrands, Nov 14, 1955, dossier 10, 1.2: Correspondance.

56 Division of studies – WCC, *The Lordship of Christ over the World and the Church: A Report from the Consultation Held at Arnoldshain, Germany, July 5–8, 1956*, Geneva, WCC Publications, 1956.

Léonard, Thijssen, and Willebrands.[57] The issue was not easy because it also involved the question – already "the stone of scandal" at the conferences of Dijnselburg and Mainz – of the role of the church as mediator of the kingdom of Christ and in particular the question of the relationship between the church and secular power. It was decided, in consideration of the difficulty of dealing with a subject so distant from the usual themes of the CCEQ, to abandon the project of a meeting in 1956 for lack of time and to schedule the next conference a year later, in 1957 in Chevetogne. In Paris the many subthemes implied by the topic were also mapped out, listing them according to three different approaches: biblical, historical, and theological. This plan for a memorandum on the lordship of Christ was discussed by the executive board of the CCEQ at its session in Rome in May 1956, where Boyer, Dumont, Höfer, and Willebrands decided to assign the writing of the sections of the memorandum to three groups of scholars: Heinrich Schlier and Lucien Cerfaux for the biblical part, Roger Aubert, Joseph Lortz, and Ernst Walter Zeeden for the historical part, Joseph Gill, Hermann Volk, Jérôme Hamer, and Joseph Lecler for the theological part.[58] In the summer of 1956, Willebrands travelled to Germany and Belgium to discuss the historical aspect of the subject with Jedin, Zeeden, and Aubert. Due to time constraints it was suggested that he should contact the Jesuit Friedrich Kempf from the Gregoriana and Jean Leclercq, a Benedictine monk from the monastery of Clervaux in Luxembourg, who accepted the assignment.[59] Meanwhile, for the biblical part, both Cerfaux and Schlier agreed to write their part of the memorandum, with the collaboration of Jules-Marie Cambier and Rudolf Schnackenburg: this commission met in Bonn in April 1957. In the same days, the three scholars in charge of the theological part, Volk, Hamer, and Jan Groot, also met in Münster.[60]

The working method described above meant that when the fifth CCEQ conference took place in Chevetogne in August 1957, the drafting of the three parts of the memorandum on the lordship of Christ was still in progress. During the conference, therefore, only a first discussion of certain aspects of the question was possible. In his paper, Lucien Cerfaux summarized four contributions on the exegetical topic, prepared by each of the four members of his subcommittee (Schnackenburg, Schlier, Cambier, and Cerfaux himself). Only Groot presented a unified contribution as a result of the meeting in Münster, whereas for the historical part of the project there were even two speakers, Kempf and Leclercq, both speaking mostly about the Middle Ages.[61] This confusing situation was criticized by some conference participants, who disagreed on many points with the results of these preparatory studies.[62] Congar, above all, who had not been present at the meeting in Paris in February 1956, strongly called for a unified text, possibly written by a single person and properly by a theologian, who should necessarily maintain an approach based on Sacred Scripture and the

57 See Willebrands' handwritten notes "Bespreking Parijs (26–27 Februari 1956)," in: AAC, FWC, dossier 10, 1: La préparation et la correspondance.

58 See the report "Réunion du Comité directeur de la Conférence Catholique pour les Questions Œcuméniques (Rome, 29–30 Mai 1956)," in: AAC, FWC, dossier 10, 1.1: Comité directeur, voyages, rencontres.

59 See "Zusammenfassung Reise Deutschland, 28. Juli–11. August 1956 and Gespräch mit Prof. R. Aubert, Löwen 18. September 1956," in: AAC, FWC, dossier 10, 1.1: Comité directeur, voyages, rencontres.

60 "Réunion à Bonn du 30 avril 1957" and "Réunion consultative tenue à Münster du 25 au 27 avril 1957," in: AAC, FWC, dossier 10, 1.1: Comité directeur, voyages, rencontres.

61 Lucien Cerfaux, "Présentation des rapports sur: la Seigneurie du Christ sur le monde et l'Église d'après le Nouveau Testament"; Jan Groot, "Die Herrschaft Christi über die Kirche und die Welt"; Friedrich Kempf, "Die Katholische Lehre vom Vorrang der Kirche und ihrer Gewalt über das Zeitliche in ihrer Geschichtlichen Entwicklung seit dem Investiturstreit"; Jean Leclercq, "La royauté du Christ au bas moyen âge." The texts of the speeches are in AAC, FWC, dossier 10, 2.3.2: Les rapports de Chevetogne.

62 See Johannes Willebrands, "Rapport des discussions," in: AAC, FWC, dossier 10, 2.4: La discussion.

interpretation of history, without any excessive specialization in these branches:

> I felt a deep unease at Chevetogne because of the separation of the various chapters of theological work into areas of specialization, and at least one of them, the most fundamental, namely the biblical one, was stuck in the tightest circle of specialization. Now, in the project you have proposed to me, the separation between exegetes, historians and "theologians" still survives. A theological synthesis that does not emerge immediately and vitally from Scripture is a play of the mind that no longer satisfies anyone.[63]

A new restricted meeting in Paris in April 1958 with the participation of Willebrands, Dumont, Cambier, Groot, Hamer, and Congar himself decided again, as had already been the case with the Evanston document, to entrust the final drafting of the text entirely to Congar. This decision aroused the bitter opposition of Michael, who attended the Paris meeting as a representative of the *Herder-Korrespondenz*. In Chevetogne Michael harshly criticized the results of the study commissions, asking, on behalf of the journal's editorial staff, to introduce into the dossier, in the light of the German experience during the Nazi regime, a section on the need for the church's intervention in secular power.[64] In Paris, Michael's violent attack on Congar, whom he suspected of not being sufficiently loyal to Pope Pius XII and the traditional doctrine of the Catholic Church, soon led to his expulsion from the CCEQ (the journalist had in fact also dangerously directed his protest against the decisions taken in Paris at certain Roman personalities).[65]

Congar completed the task in November 1958, but in the following months he had to rewrite the text taking into account the comments of other CCEQ members. Finally, at the end of 1959, the memorandum was published in *Istina*, not in Congar's name, but officially as the result of the CCEQ's theological reflection on the lordship of Christ.[66] Four years after Visser 't Hooft's request of November 1955, the work was finally completed, but once again the CCEQ memorandum came too late, especially since the WCC division of studies had finished and published its work at the end of 1957.[67] However, the most important goal which CCEQ and WCC set themselves during their collaboration was to realize a meeting on the subject with theologians from both sides, as already envisaged at the time of the memorandum presented to the Evanston assembly. This project, along with parallel attempts to organize similar meetings with other ecumenical associations, such as the ILAFO, would dominate the efforts of the CCEQ in the later years of its existence.

During its November 1958 meeting, the executive board decided to dedicate their sixth conference, to be held in Paderborn in the fall of 1959, to a theme which was at the center of the attention within the WCC but of which Catholic observers were very afraid, that is the planned integration of the IMC and the WCC during the general assembly of 1961.[68] This "new orientation" of the WCC would

63 Y. Congar to J. Willebrands, Feb 5, 1958, in: AAC, FWC, dossier 10, 3.3: Correspondance.

64 "Stellungnahme der Herder-Korrespondenz zu der Dokumentation für die Konferenz von Chevetogne," in: AAC, FWC, dossier 10, 2.3.2: Les rapports de Chevetogne.

65 On the conflict Michael-Congar, see the detailed reconstruction in Marotta, *Gli anni della pazienza*, 299–317.

66 "La seigneurie du Christ sur l'Église et sur le monde, par un groupe des théologiens de la 'Conférence catholique pour les questions œcuméniques,'" *Istina* 2, 1959, 131–166. See also the explanations about the genesis of the text presented by Istina, "Le souverain domaine du Christ sur la création restaurée," *Istina* 2, 1959, 129–130.

67 Division of studies – WCC, *The Lordship of Christ over the World and the Church: Study Documents*, Geneva, WCC Publications, 1957.

68 The results of the conference would later be important for the preparation of the conciliar decree *Ad gentes*. Mauro Velati, "Œcuménisme et missions: La contribution des observateurs non catholiques à la rédaction du décret 'Ad gentes' du concile Vatican II," in: Paul Coulon & Alberto Melloni, dir., *Christianisme, mission et cultures: L'arc-en-ciel des défis et des réponses XVIe–XXIe siècles*, Paris, Karthala, 2008, 215–237.

lead either to better relations with the Catholic Church or to "an anti-Catholic movement."[69] After the announcement of the council, the executive board stuck to their original plan, since "the problems which the ecumenical movement poses to the Catholic Church" would then be fully revealed.[70] The usual introduction by the secretary would present "a historical and analytical overview of the development of the idea of missions in the ecumenical movement from Edinburgh 1910 till today."[71] The Belgian exegete Jules-Marie Cambier, who had just been nominated professor at the Université Lovanium in Léopoldville, explained on the basis of Scripture that the unity of the community was believed to be a practical necessity for the proclamation of Jesus.[72] Le Guillou was asked to give a presentation based on his recent dissertation on this theme.[73] Here he distinguishes a "Protestant" and a "Catholic" tendency in Protestant missiology. For the former, the church is mission in the sense that its sole task is to proclaim Christ to the world; for the latter it is the quality of its community life which makes the church missionary.[74] The Catholic approach to mission resembles the Catholic tendency in Protestantism. For Catholics, the required unity of communion is given "in the communion of the bishops around the bishop of Rome" but it is a communion characterized by a missionary dynamic.[75] Finally, Joseph Hofinger, an Austrian Jesuit, was invited because he was the promotor of the liturgical and catechetical renewal of the church in a missionary context. The seven international study weeks which he organized worldwide from 1956 to 1968

69 Johannes Willebrands, "Réunion du Comité Directeur: Collegio Bellarmino, Rome, 18–19 nov. 1958," Dec 27, 1958, 3, in: AAC, FWC, dossier 3: Reunions du Comite directeur et de la commission d'etudes. As one of the board members testified, "by integrating the International Missionary Council into the Ecumenical Council, the latter with its organization and resources will strengthen and multiply the Protestant missionaries where they are, and send them where they are not"; see Charles Boyer, "Malaise œcuménique," *Unitas* 11, 1958, 65–69, here 67.

70 Two-page report of the board meeting of Feb 26, 1959, sent by Willebrands to the members of the CCQE on May 16, 1959, 1, in: AAC, FWC, dossier 3: Reunions du Comite directeur et de la commission d'etudes.

71 Willebrands, "Réunion," 3. At the end of his speech he applied the conclusion of the second world conference on Faith and Order in Edinburgh 1937 to the upcoming council: "We humbly acknowledge that our divisions are contrary to the will of Christ, and we pray God in his mercy to shorten the days of our separation and to guide us by His Spirit into fullness of unity. … May this Council take place at a timely moment, more so than was the case with the Council of Trent in the time of the Reformation"; Johannes Willebrands, "Introduction au thème: Unité et mission," 6–7, in: AAC, FWC, dossier 11, 2: Documents.

72 Jules-Marie Cambier, "Quelques perspectives bibliques sur le thème Unité et mission," 4, in: AAC, FWC, dossier 11, 2: Documents.

73 See Marie-Joseph Le Guillou, *Mission et unité: Les exigences de la communion*, Paris, Cerf, 1960. See, for the text of his lecture, Marie-Joseph Le Guillou, "Mission et unité en perspectives protestante et catholique," in: AAC, FWC, dossier 11, 2: Documents; later published in *Istina* 4, 1959, 433–458.

74 Le Guillou, "Mission et unité en perspectives," 14: "Here? We are in the presence of two fundamental lines of thought, without which we would undoubtedly find the distinction between 'Catholics' and Protestants in the end, but without fully adhering to it: is it not the case that the purely Reformed tendency sees in the Church only a missionary event, whereas the 'Catholic' tendency insists more on the communion and cultural, let us say ontological, consistency of the Church, without, however, minimizing the mission in any way?" As an example of the first category he mentions the Dutch missiologist Johannes Christiaan Hoekendijk; Lesslie Newbigin is the prototype of the second category, and Le Guillou approvingly quotes his warning towards the planned integration of the IMC in the WCC: "The problem is not the coordination of missionary operations 'at the highest level.' 'It is the question of the integrity of the Church and its mission in all places'"; Le Guillou, "Mission et unité en perspectives," 15.

75 Le Guillou, "Mission et unité en perspectives," 20: "For us Catholics, too, the Church is defined as a missionary unity. It is a unity visibly given in the communion of the bishops around the Bishop of Rome, but this communional unity is essentially dynamic: it is entirely directed towards a double achievement, one of which is the image and prefiguration of the other: the missionary achievement, the eschatological achievement."

form the counterpart to Willebrands' initiative. In his lecture, he deplored the lack of ecumenical openness in Catholic missions.[76]

Ecumenism, meanwhile, after the announcement of the ecumenical council on Jan 25, 1959, had by then made its worldwide breakthrough in Catholic debate.

4 Ecumenical Formation for Future Council Fathers: The 1959 Memorandum

4.1 *Redaction History*

The idea of preparing a position paper on "the restoration of Christian unity"[77] on the occasion of the announcement of the council arose during an unexpected meeting of some members of the executive board of the CCEQ in Strasbourg on Feb 7–8, 1959. Willebrands had planned a meeting with Rousseau and Congar to discuss the theme of the next Ecumenical Study Days of Chevetogne. Dumont had made the journey from Paris to Strasbourg as well, so that the four of them found themselves discussing the future council. Dumont immediately asked questions about the potential contribution of the CCEQ: "What could our Conference be able to do? It seems that it has a responsibility and should take an initiative."[78] The CCEQ, being "the only international group" having "direct relations with the WCC" should educate the bishops of the Catholic Church and their theologians in view of the coming council. An urgent meeting of the executive board was scheduled for Feb 26. On Feb 21, Dumont informed Willebrands that he was almost ready with a first draft. Since in the meantime Willebrands had traveled to Geneva to collect the first reactions of the WCC to the announcement of the council, and since they also had to prepare the next CCEQ meeting in Paderborn, during the board meeting there was only time for a brief presentation of Dumont's draft. The members would study the document and send their remarks to the drafter. On Mar 1, Willebrands invited Dumont to the Dutch college in Rome for a discussion. Willebrands's diary expresses some preoccupations: "What will we do with this report? Will the executive board sign it? F. Boyer? Shall we send it to the bishops?"[79]

76 Joseph Hofinger, "Wie kann die kerygmatische und liturgische Bewegung im Bereich der katholischen Missionen die oekumenische Dimension aufnehmen?," in: AAC, FWC dossier 11, 2: Documents.

77 "Note du Comité Directeur de la 'Conférence Catholique pour les Questions œcuméniques' sur la restauration de l'Unité chrétienne à l'occasion du prochain Concile," Jun 15, 1959, 15 pages. Quotations in English are taken from the translation revised by Willebrands himself: "Memorandum from the Executive Committee of the 'Catholic Council for Ecumenical Questions' Concerning the Restoration of Christian Unity on the Occasion of the forthcoming Ecumenical Council," n.d., 33 pages. Unless otherwise indicated, all drafts and letters quoted in this section are found in AKW, dossier 34.

78 Salemink, ed., *You Will Be Called*, 76. See Istina, "Avec les yeux d'autrui," *Istina* 1, 1959, 3–6, here 5: "To those who, for many years or more recently, have taken to heart the great problem of the restoration of Christian unity falls the responsibility of sharing with the future Fathers of the Council the experience acquired in their contacts with their separated brethren and the fruits of the reflection which these contacts have suggested to them."

79 Salemink, ed., *You Will Be Called*, 82. The diary reports Boyer's "favorable response on the draft of the report" on Mar 3. See C. Boyer to C.-J. Dumont, Mar 2, 1959, in: APDF, FD. In his article on "Current Trends in Catholic Ecumenism" Boyer recognizes the existence of differences: "Since these differences exist it is better to consider them. It is perhaps the best way of attenuating them. It is also a way of making progress. An opinion which springs from sorrow for divisions and love of unity will always contain some valuable element of truth which the man who thinks otherwise is glad to assimilate. Truth is a fundamental good; it does not divide, it unites. It is the bread of the intelligence but one must often earn his bread by the sweat of his brow"; Charles Boyer, "Current Trends in Catholic Ecumenism," in: *Problems Before Unity*, Baltimore, Helicon Press, 1962, 58–70, here 69–70 (originally published as "Tendances actuelles de l'œcuménisme catholique," *Unitas* 14, 1961, 251–260, here 260).

On Mar 11 Dumont sent the next draft to Willebrands.[80] Nervous about the lack of any reaction, Dumont sent Willebrands a new letter on Mar 31, two days after Easter. In his opinion, the momentum had passed for a memorandum in the current form to be of any use. An early publication would have served the goal of preventing damage through ecumenically insensitive reactions from the Catholic side. But even during their board meeting of February he had warned that in his opinion the "Memorandum … Concerning the Restoration of Christian Unity on the Occasion of the forthcoming Ecumenical Council" seemed "too much for a rapid intervention, too little for a late intervention."[81] He hoped that Willebrands could help clarify whether a document in its current form still made sense. After discussing the memorandum with his fellow Dutch ecumenists Thijssen and Groot, on 2 April Willebrands sent his response to Dumont accompanied by two pages with suggestions for improving certain paragraphs. Willebrands was convinced that Dumont's initiative "maintains its entire relevance" and proposed to send it to the Holy Office as a somewhat broader understanding of their request to Willebrands to inform them about Protestant reactions to the announcement of the council.[82]

When Willebrands discussed the remarks made by the other board members with Dumont in Paris on May 13, special attention was paid to the authorship of the memorandum. Upon reading the first draft, Willebrands had noted: "The conference? Or: its executive board?"[83] The issue seemed to have been concluded during this meeting, since it was agreed that the executive board would have to approve the final version during its next meeting.[84] On Jun 2 Dumont sent a revised version[85] to his colleagues for feedback, but prior to the meeting of Jun 15–16 he received only Boyer's comments.[86] Even if the main drafter realized that each point of the memorandum would deserve a more elaborate treatment, the document was approved without difficulty.[87] It was agreed that the document would be sent to Cardinal Alfredo Ottaviani as secretary of the Holy Office, to Cardinal Eugène Tisserant as secretary of the Congregation for the Oriental Churches and to Cardinal Domenico Tardini as secretary of state and head of the Antepreparatory Commission. The Holy See was excluded as addressee in order to avoid having to inform them in detail about the intended receivers of the memorandum.[88]

80 C.-J. Dumont to J. Willebrands, Mar 11, 1959, 3 pages. This is the first draft of the memorandum which has been preserved in Willebrands' personal archives.

81 C.-J. Dumont to J. Willebrands, Mar 31, 1959, 1 page.

82 J. Willebrands to C.-J. Dumont, Apr 2, 1959, 1 page, accompanied by "Quelques remarques sur le Projet de 'Note' sur l'Unité chrétienne," 2 pages. In his letter Willebrands describes the significance of the memorandum as follows: "The main usefulness of this memorandum seems to me to consist in its informative character in the broadest sense of the word, that is giving a description of the current situation, warning the authorities by discovering the dangers it implies, presenting a line of thought and conduct by placing the milestones of a new development."

83 Anonymous notition in Willebrands' handwriting, kept in AKW, dossier 34.

84 The title of the memorandum would change from "Projet de 'Note' sur l'Unité chrétienne à l'occasion du prochain Concile" to "Note du Comité Directeur de la 'Conférence Catholique pour les Questions œcuméniques' sur la restauration de l'Unité chrétienne à l'occasion du prochain Concile."

85 C.-J. Dumont to J. Willebrands, Jun 2, 1959, including a self-critical message: "The more I reread my text, the more I find it inadequate. But I console myself with the thought that this will probably only be a first contact with the authorities."

86 C. Boyer to C.-J. Dumont, Jun 5, 1959, in: APDF, FD.

87 "Dumont's own criticism remains, that on the one hand the Note poses the whole problem of Christian Unity in its various aspects, while on the other hand the extreme conciseness of this exposition (inevitable, moreover, for a first explanation of the problem) makes one feel the need for a justification of each point mentioned"; "Réunion du Comité Directeur de la Conférence Catholique pour les Questions Œcuméniques, à Rome, les 15–16 juin 1959," Jun 20, 1959, 3 pages, 1, in: AAC, FWC, dossier 3: Reunions du Comite directeur et de la commission d'etudes.

88 "In the text the Holy See is indicated as the recipient. This fact seems to restrict the freedom to send it to others without having obtained the permission of the Holy

As a complement to previous research on the similarities of the memorandum with the final draft of *Unitatis redintegratio*,[89] the following analysis will show how the memorandum mainly reflects opinions which the main drafter Dumont had articulated in previous publications.[90] Relevant similarities and differences with the ecumenical views of other Catholic ecumenists will also be indicated.

4.2 *"Some Preliminary Psychological Difficulties"* (*§§ 3–9*)

At the start of the decade, Dumont had already paid attention to the "ecumenical experience" as a "psychological reality."[91] In preparation of the third world conference in Lund, the Faith and Order commission had prepared a report on "Non-Theological Factors that May Hinder or Accelerate the Church's Unity."[92] Among the "factors which are perpetuating divisions" a number of "psychological factors" had been mentioned, among others "emotional associations with certain words, especially as applied to others."[93] Of course the same awareness was widely spread among most Catholic ecumenists of that time.[94] Also the memorandum insists that the council Fathers should take "particular care in the choice of terms used to express our thought" (§ 6), and Dumont himself on other occasions asked for attention to such factors in order to improve the dialogue with the Orthodox.[95]

The first psychological difficulty which is discussed in the memorandum is the word "return." The many changes in § 5 illustrate that Dumont's opinion on this point was not easily accepted by the other members of the executive board. Boyer had mentioned twice that the Roman curia regularly uses the term in a sense which does not necessarily sound offensive to non-Catholic readers.[96]

See or at least without the Holy See being aware of it. One must be very careful not to embrace too much at the moment"; "Réunion du Comité Directeur," 1.

89 See Peter De Mey, "Johannes Willebrands and the Catholic Conference for Ecumenical Questions," in: Adelbert Denaux & Peter De Mey, eds., *The Ecumenical Legacy of Johannes Cardinal Willebrands (1909–2006)*, Leuven, Peeters, 2012, 49–77, esp. 56–68.

90 See for more information on his ecumenical significance Hyacinthe Destivelle, *Conduis-la vers l'unité parfaite: Œcuménisme et synodalité*, Paris, Cerf, 2018, 67–68. For a deeper comparison between Dumont's publications and the memorandum, see Peter De Mey, "La Note du Comité Directeur de la 'Conférence Catholique pour les Questions œcuméniques' sur la restauration de l'Unité chrétienne: Un votum anté-préparatoire non officiel à la veille du Vatican II," *Irén*, forthcoming, where it is also possible to find the original French texts of the document used here.

91 Christophe-Jean Dumont, "Le Mouvement Œcuménique et la doctrine de l'Église," *VUCh* 38, 1951, 3–9, here 6.

92 "Non-Theological Factors that May Hinder or Accelerate the Church's Unity," *EcRev* 4/2, 1952, 174–180. This discussion famously started with an article by Charles H. Dodd, "A Letter Concerning Unavowed Motives in Ecumenical Discussions," *EcRev* 2/1, 1949, 52–56.

93 "Non-Theological Factors," 177.

94 See Yves Congar, *After Nine Hundred Years: The Background of the Schism between the Eastern and Western Churches*, New York, Fordham University Press, 1959, 88; Jérôme Hamer, "Le concile œcuménique et l'Unité," in: *Qu'attendons-nous du concile?*, Bruxelles, La Pensée Catholique, 1960, 45–55, here 45.

95 "The gap is rather in a lack of knowledge of the psychological conditions of a rapprochement, a lack of knowledge which, unfortunately, gives rise to fears of a historical and even theological gap"; Christophe-Jean Dumont, "L'Église orientale catholique et le problème de l'Unité: Documents et Réflexions," *Istina* 4, 1960, 409–432, here 410. In June 1963, after the election of Pope Paul VI, in a private note to Augustin Bea, hoping that the cardinal would discuss its content with the pope, Dumont will insist: "The issue of schism and its cessation is 90% psychological"; see "Notes sur quelques points importants commandant les rapports entre Catholiques et Orthodoxes en vue de la restauration de l'unité canonique," in: Christophe-Jean Dumont, *L'Église romaine et le mouvement œcuménique: Souvenirs d'un pionnier (1926–1965)*, 239–244, here 239. This unpublished diary is being preserved in APDF. See also Destivelle, *Le Père Christophe-Jean Dumont*, 85.

96 "Paragraph 5 does not seem to me to be a happy one. It is likely to cause offence from the outset. The word 'return' is constantly used deliberately by the Roman Curia. It is found in the Instructio of the Holy Office: 'deque unica vera unione per reditum dissidentium ad unam veram Christi Ecclesiam.' It has a very good

While, according to the first draft, it would greatly help ecumenical relations if the term would be "avoided" by the bishops during the council, the final draft stops short of stating that the expression is "usually creating difficulties." It should not necessarily be avoided but carefully explained.[97] Willebrands had reacted in a different sense, and his request was attended to, as well. Dumont had made a second objection that the "dissident communities" could only with great difficulty return to a church which had substantially changed in form and content compared to previous centuries. For Willebrands, this was a matter of principle: the Catholic Church should not give the impression that it is opposed to change as such.[98] Dumont adds to this that we should also avoid giving the impression "that we attach an equal importance to that which is essential and to that which is accidental, to the unchangeable substance and to secondary determinations always subject to revision and transitory historic circumstances."[99] The last minute change of title of the memorandum from "Christian unity," to "the restoration of Christian unity" was perhaps connected to this ongoing reflection on "return" among the members of the executive board.[100]

With regard to the use of the word "church" the exigencies of Catholic doctrine do not seem to pose problems to the drafters of the text. "In strict theological parlance" the term does not apply to "dissident confessional groups,"[101] not even

meaning that the separated brothers are able to understand without taking offence"; C. Boyer to C.-J. Dumont, Mar 2, 1959, 1. See also C. Boyer to C.-J. Dumont, Jun 5, 1959, 1, in: APDF, FD: "The expression 'return' is used even in the latest documents of the Curia." Boyer would repeat the same point in "Les intentions de la Semaine de l'Unité," *Unitas* 13, 1960, 325–335, 332, and would even launch in a more substantial criticism against Catholic ecumenists in favor of a dialogue *par cum pari* and opposed to the language of "return" since it expresses the "superiority" of the Catholic Church in "Current Trends in Catholic Ecumenism," 61–65.

97 Perhaps for this reason the memorandum still refers at times to "the problem of reunion" (§ 3, § 20) and to "attempts at reunion" (§ 24).

98 "What makes the word 'return' odious does not seem to me first of all that it signifies a return to the Church of the sixteenth century, but rather that one senses with this word the idea of immobility on our side: we are in possession of the truth, of the unity, we do not move, while the others will have to move towards the place where we await them. It does not express the idea of dynamism, of growth from our side"; J. Willebrands to C.-J. Dumont, April 2, 1959, 1. See "Memorandum," § 5: "It is, moreover, important not to give our separated brethren the impression that we are determined to hold fast to our positions, leaving them the task of crossing the divide between us without our having to take the smallest step in their direction."

99 The similarity with certain ideas expressed by Pope John XXIII in his opening speech of the council *Gaudet Mater Ecclesia* is obvious. Boyer would, however, not have been opposed to this opinion. See Charles Boyer, "Comment concevoir l'œcuménisme catholique," *Unitas* 11, 1958, 97–104, here 102: "It is important to distinguish between what is essential and what is not ... In the domain of the accidental, the Church can change, as in fact she has changed. She abandons one use, perhaps long useful and beloved, to take up another which corresponds better to new conditions. Like humanity, the Church moves."

100 In one of the forewords collected in Christophe-Jean Dumont, "Unité donnée et Unité à faire," in: *Les voies de l'unité chrétienne: Doctrine et spiritualité*, Paris, Cerf, 1954, 208–213, here 211, he used the expression in a unionistic sense: "This is why we cannot conceive of the restoration of Christian unity in any other way than through the accession of all to the benefit of the three conditions which have never ceased to ensure, through the gift of God ever faithful in his promises, the indefectible unity of his Church." It is more likely, however, that the last minute change was inspired by the article which he had written immediately after the announcement of the council. See Christophe-Jean Dumont, "Le prochain concile et l'unité chrétienne," *VUCh* 109–110, 1959, 1–5, here 1: "The idea that non-Catholic confessions would be invited to participate in the Council was also suggested by the fact that the Council was related to the problem of the restoration of Christian unity."

101 The term "dissidents" was common theological parlance among Catholic theologians in those years. See Charles Boyer, "Le prochain Concile œcuménique," *Unitas* 13, 1959, 7–10, here 7: "A council where agreement would be sought with the dissident churches of the East" and Yves Congar, *Chrétiens en dialogue: Contributions catholiques à l'Œcuménisme*, Paris, Cerf, 1964, 31: "The integration into this Body would be, for the Dissidents, the healing of many wounds" (part of an article

"where it applies to a particular or local church as is the custom among the Orthodox"[102] (§ 8). The memorandum suggests alternative formulations to its readers. The preferred one is definitely the term "communion,"[103] and, "when the context is appropriate," one may also think of "confessions" or "denominations." In the final redaction Dumont exhorts Catholic bishops not to use "inverted commas" when speaking about the Orthodox.[104]

4.3 *"The Unprepared State of People's Minds" (§§ 10–19)*

In this section,[105] the memorandum wonders whether the bishops are sufficiently prepared to make objective statements concerning other Christian churches during the upcoming council. From this paragraph onwards, the document proceeds to deal separately with "the East" (§§ 11–15), then "the Anglican Communion" (§§ 16–18), and finally "the communions stemming from the Reformation" (§ 19).

The CCEQ is thankful about the growing interest in the Christian East under different popes since Leo XIII but wonders whether the bishops and theologians are ready to discuss the pending problems with it, let alone initiate a dialogue with the Orthodox.[106] The CCEQ is convinced that in order to improve relations with the Orthodox, the Catholic Church should renew its ecclesiology further, especially the reflection on the catholicity of the church.[107] Moreover, to create a greater awareness

on the ecumenical movement in the 1962 edition of the *Lexikon für Theologie und Kirche*). In "L'Église orientale catholique," 413, note 4, Dumont states that the substitution of the term "dissidents" for "Orthodox" in official magisterial texts is an "use, which can be regretted."

102 See, for a more nuanced position, Congar, *Chrétiens en dialogue*, 234–235: "For our purposes, it is sufficient to note that there can be Christian communities which have the quality of a local Church, but in an imperfect way, because of a lack of communion with the principles instituted by the Lord to structure the total Church. This seems to me to be the situation of the Orthodox Churches." This quotation is part of the revised edition of his famous article, "Note sur les mots 'Confession,' 'Église' et 'Communion,'" *Irén* 23, 1950, 3–36.

103 The preference for the term "communion" was broadly shared. See Marie-Joseph Le Guillou, "Église et 'Communion': Essai d'ecclésiologie comparée," *Istina* 1, 1959, 33–82, here 81 (italics original): "At the end of this long study of comparative ecclesiology, we wonder whether ecumenical dialogue should not be engaged around the notion and reality of *communion*." See also Congar, *Chrétiens en dialogue*, 241: "To adopt 'Communion' in preference to other words would respond well to the shift made in the last twenty years in the field of knowledge of other Christians from 'Symbolik' to 'Konfessionskunde' … 'Communion' encapsulates the values of 'Church' without prejudice to the questions that the use of this word does not fail to raise, at least for the Catholic theologian. The word 'communion' can be applied equally to the Catholic Church, the Orthodox Churches, Anglicanism (which officially calls itself, when referring to itself in its breadth, the 'Anglican Communion') and the various Protestant 'confessions.' Its use cannot offend anyone; it is a religious, indeed a properly Christian term.'" On the other hand, Congar was firmly opposed to the term 'confessions': "For my part, as a theologian, I am reluctant to refer to Christian communities, and in any case to the Catholic and Orthodox Churches, as 'denominations'" (Congar, *Chrétiens en dialogue*, 221) and "It is best to avoid 'confession' to refer to Christian communities or bodies" (Congar, *Chrétiens en dialogue*, 236).

104 In "L'Église orientale catholique," 413, note 4, Dumont even added the following comment: "To understand how the use of inverted commas can be felt by our Orthodox brothers as an affront, it is enough to ask ourselves how we Catholics would feel if they only called us 'so-called Catholics' or only wrote the title of our Roman 'Catholic' Church in inverted commas."

105 A comparison with two articles written in the same year, shows that this is definitely Dumont's own terminology. See his "Le prochain concile," 3, where he deals with the "unpreparedness of minds on both sides" and his "L'Église orientale catholique," 410: "Nothing would be more fatal than to have illusions in this area. As we have repeatedly stated, the preparation of minds, not only on the Orthodox side, but also on the Catholic side, is not sufficient to expect substantial results from the preparation of the Council in this way."

106 See Christophe-Jean Dumont, "Le Catholicisme romain et les Églises Orthodoxes," *VUCh* 99, 1958, 1–5, here 4. Boyer remained critical about this paragraph: "I don't like n. 12 at all, and I think it is at least useless"; C. Boyer to C.-J. Dumont, Jun 5, 1959.

107 The reflection on catholicity is found in two different paragraphs, which will be presented together: § 14

that catholicity means "unity in diversity,"[108] Catholic theologians and bishops still have to defend "the legitimacy of a triple pluralism, liturgical, canonical and theological" more strongly (§ 14).

Dumont had developed similar ideas in a 1954 article which contains a reflection on "the conditions of the unity in diversity within the Church." Once the church has accepted wholeheartedly "that unity should not be confused with uniformity" and that "true catholicity cannot exist where the unity of the Church would not be a unity in diversity," the same argumentation could be applied "to the unity that should be established between Christians who are separated in confessions or a variety of denominations. Uniformity is neither a condition of unity, nor a condition of reunion."[109] This needs to be realized in three fields. (1) Liturgical: because the Catholic Church mostly seems to respect the presence of Eastern-rite communities in its midst, the "legitimate plurality of rites" seems to be largely uncontested.[110] (2) Canonical: the efforts by Pius XII to promulgate initial portions of canon law on behalf of the Eastern Catholic Churches was for Dumont in 1954 "the clearest testimony" that this pluralism also had an impact on the "institutions" of the Catholic Church.[111] In light of the growing criticism of this codification among the Eastern Catholic Churches, the evaluation of the legitimate plurality in the field of canon law is less optimistic in the memorandum.[112] (3) Theological: in 1954, he justified theological pluralism by referring to "the diversity of schools in the bosom of the Catholic Church."[113] In view of the difficulties some of his own colleagues had experienced with Rome, the memorandum contains the courageous statement by Dumont that "the existence of the third (pluralism), the theological, seems scarcely acknowledged" (§ 14). The CCEQ

and § 49. Remarkably, even if growth in catholicity will also be beneficial for relations with the Anglicans and with the Protestants, it is treated in the document as part of a section dealing with ecumenical relations with the Orthodox.

108 In his contribution to the 1962 *Festschrift* of Boyer the secretary of CCEQ fully supports this reading. See Johannes Willebrands, "Catholic Ecumenism," in: *Problems Before Unity*, 1–14, here 6: "As a unity in a diversity, or in a plurality, she is the opposite of a monolith. She is world-embracing, or ecumenical."

109 Istina, "Justice distributive et Unité chrétienne," *VUCh* 68, 1954, 1–4.

110 Dumont, "Justice distributive," 1: "Of all the pluralisms entitled to exist in the Church, this liturgical pluralism is the most obvious and at the same time the most explicitly affirmed and the most effectively accepted." See "Memorandum," § 14: "If the first aspect (liturgical) has been largely outlined [ébauché]" and § 49: "A good step has been taken in this direction in terms of liturgical usage, but there is still some way to go."

111 Dumont, "Justice distributive," 3, under reference to the motu proprios *Crebrae allatae* (1949), *Sollicitudinem nostram* (1950) and *Postquam apostolicis* (1952); this effort concluded with the promulgation of *Cleri sanctitate* (1957). In the memorandum, and in another article published in the same year Dumont is aware that this codification also "had the unfortunate consequence of sheltering non-Catholics from Catholic influence by making contacts more difficult and less frequent" (§ 15). See Dumont, "L'Église orientale catholique," 410: "Surprising as it may seem, a number of measures have been taken recently which, far from favoring the role of unifier that is said to be expected from the united Oriental Churches, are rather likely to discourage the Orthodox from favorably considering the proposed union." See also Jose Maripurath Devassy, Astrid Kaptijn & Peter De Mey, "The Vota of the Eastern Catholic Churches and the Reform of Eastern Canon Law," in: Mathijs Lamberigts & Karim Schelkens, eds., *Vatican II after 60 years: Developments and Expectations Prior to the Council*, Turnhout, Brepols, 2023, 199–227.

112 See "Memorandum," § 14: "The second, the canonical, has only been tackled in part and the findings contested even by the oriental Uniate communities." The most profound criticism was pronounced during a 1958 synod by the auxiliary bishop of the Melkite Patriarch Maximos IV, Msgr. Pierre K. Médawar, and published in French as "De la sauvegarde des droits de l'Église orientale," *POC* 9, 1959, 224–242. Boyer would have preferred not to include such criticism. See C. Boyer to C.-J. Dumont, Mar 2, 1959, 1: "The end of this paragraph is not very respectful of the 'canonical measures' in question."

113 Dumont, "Justice distributive," 3: "The church has always been concerned to allow each person the greatest freedom in seeking the deepening of a formula or a systematization of the doctrine."

aligns itself indeed to the ongoing movement of theological *ressourcement* and indicates that the future Orthodox-Catholic dialogue will not benefit from scholastic theology, which is foreign to the Orthodox Church, but by the legitimate alternative of a more biblical and patristic one (§ 49). Of course, the memorandum is also aware that, "as far as the Orthodox themselves are concerned, people's minds are even more unprepared"[114] (§ 15).

The separate treatment of the Anglican Communion in the memorandum has ancient roots among Catholic ecumenists.[115] When returning to the leading question in this section, Dumont reminds his readers that the preparation already started with the Malines Conversations.[116] He mentions that, for Anglo-Catholics, "the question of the validity of their orders remains a grave difficulty to be overcome"[117] (§ 17). The establishment of the Church of South India has also revealed doctrinal tensions within the Anglican Communion on "the nature and the necessity of the episcopate" (§ 18) that would also have an impact on Anglican-Catholic dialogue.[118] The paragraph dealing with relations with the Protestant communions starts with a recognition of the seriousness and the amount of "dogmatic and canonical differences that any attempt at reunion would have to overcome" (§ 19). The mention of a number of promising High Church movements in the text (among which also the Taizé Community) and the invitation to Catholics to prepare themselves for the ecumenical work at the council by leaving behind "the attitude of Counter-Reformation" are the result of Willebrands' input.[119]

4.4 *"The Need to Distinguish without Dissociating" (§§ 20–23) and "Basic Difficulties" (§§ 24–26)*

The board of CCEQ also wanted to add some theoretical input to the later council Fathers, first by expanding on a key conviction in the ecumenical theology of the main drafter of the memorandum.[120] In his foreword to the December 1952 issue

114 Here, too, Dumont must have remembered his previous writings. See Istina, "Les arbres et la forêt," *Istina* 2, 1955, 129–133, here 132: "Has an equivalent progress been made on the part of both sides with regard to Roman Catholicism? … They sometimes become so obsessed with certain features of our Catholicism that they no longer see many other features in it which are no less important."

115 In 1937 Congar had already dedicated an independent chapter to the Anglican conception of unity. Similarly, Roger Aubert, who in *Problèmes de l'unité chrétienne: Initiation*, Chevetogne, Éditions de Chevetogne, 1953, 62 not only treats the Anglicans in a separate chapter, but even states that "the Church of England well deserves the name that a Swiss Calvinist theologian once gave it, and which it now boasts: the Bridge Church." For his part, Boyer treats the Anglicans in *Unus pastor: Pour la réunion à l'Église de Rome des Chrétiens séparés*, Toulouse, Apostolat de la Prière, 1950, under the heading "Protestantism." See Charles Boyer, *Christian Unity and the Ecumenical Movement*, London, Burns & Oates, 1962, 22.

116 Once again the memorandum prefers to be honest, however. See "Memorandum," § 16: "But it must to be admitted that the attitude of a considerable section [in the previous draft in French: 'de façon quasi unanime'] of the Catholic episcopate of the English-speaking countries until now would not appear to provide a favourable basis for any significant progress in this direction."

117 Here and in Christophe-Jean Dumont, *Comment les chrétiens se sont-ils séparés?*, Chevetogne, Éditions de Chevetogne, 1962, 28, he is aware of the existence of new historical research that deserves to be studied attentively, even if he is convinced that "the doctrinal basis and the historical considerations" of *Apostolicae curae* cannot be doubted. See also Boyer, *Christian Unity and the Ecumenical Movement*, 86: "Is that decision irrevocable? A few theologians think it not, but it is difficult not to see all the conditions for an infallible document in the Bull of 1896. However, it is understandable that Anglican ministers feel a repugnance when their orders are called in question. There are some who stay outside the Church for this reason alone."

118 Dumont provided further documentation on this in *Istina*. See "Remous dans l'Église d'Angleterre," *Istina* 4, 1955, 467–474.

119 J. Willebrands to C.-J. Dumont, Apr 2, 1959, 1.

120 The article "Le prochain concile et l'unité chrétienne" which he had published in the first issue of 1959 of *Vers l'Unité chrétienne*, contained a section title

of *Vers l'Unité chrétienne*, Dumont had already distinguished the Catholic and the Protestant understanding of the church and its visible unity while at the same time underlining the similarity between the Catholic and the Orthodox positions.[121] When assessing their attitude towards the episcopate, he knows it is possible to distinguish three groups: those for whom the episcopate is "a constitutive element of the sacramental structure of the ecclesial body," those who have not maintained the episcopate and those for whom the episcopate only contributes to the *bene esse* of the church.[122] The distinction that is found in the memorandum has only grown in complexity: "(a) Christian communions having preserved the form as well as the reality[123] of the sacramental structure of the episcopacy; (b) those communions having deliberately rejected this structure; (c) those having preserved the form although they have lost the reality"[124] (§ 20). The memorandum knows that the way to conceive the church also has implications for "the reality of the Eucharist"[125] (§ 20). On the basis of this distinction, Dumont expects "that reunion with the Orthodox may be more easily and more rapidly achieved than with the Protestants"[126] (§ 22) but he equally insists that it is important to orient our

"Distinguer les problèmes sans les dissocier": Dumont, "Le prochain concile et l'unité chrétienne," 4. See also Christophe-Jean Dumont, "Rome, Constantinople et Genève: L'œcuménisme au tournant," *Istina* 4, 1959, 415–432, here 422: "From the point of view of the Catholic faith a fundamental distinction must be made between the Orthodox Churches and the communions of the Protestant Reformation." Attention to "the link between the schisms" is the first characteristic of Dumont's ecumenical theology according to Destivelle, *Conduis-la vers l'unité parfaite*, 84.

121 See Christophe-Jean Dumont, "Unité de grâce et Unité visible," in: *Les voies de l'unité chrétienne*, 200–207 (this a reprint of a foreword of 1952 in *Vers l'Unité chrétienne*). Dumont, "Unité de grâce et Unité visible," 203: "Let us say straight away, to avoid any confusion, that our Orthodox brothers have the same demands on this point as we do, with the difference that they reject the doctrine of a primacy of divine right ensuring the cohesion of the ecclesial body," with § 21 of the memorandum: "It is of the utmost importance in matters concerning disunity not to give the Dissident Churches of the East *the impression that we put them on the same footing as the confessions resulting from the Reformation.*"

122 Dumont, "Unité de grâce et Unité visible," 203. He also mentions the confessions that defend these positions. See Dumont, "Unité de grâce et Unité visible," 204: "Between the two extreme conceptions we have sketched (the Catholic position and the most accused Reformed position) lies the whole range of intermediate confessions: Old Catholics, High Church Anglicans or Evangelicals, Lutherans of various tendencies, orthodox or liberal Reformed, etc."

123 In Dumont, "Le Catholicisme romain," 2 the formulation is slightly different: "The Reformed confessions have, of this structure, both the notion and the reality."

124 In "Le prochain concile," Dumont uses the terminology of "elements'" in this regard. See Dumont, "Le prochain concile," 2: "It should not be forgotten, moreover, that the problem of reunion is posed in a very different way in the eyes of the Roman Church, depending on whether one considers the Christian communions which have retained essential elements of the structure of the Church ... or the communions which have rejected them." The lack of attention to this theme in the memorandum is remarkable, because Dumont had even launched an invitation to other Catholic theologians to study this topic in Christophe-Jean Dumont, "Vestigia Ecclesiae," *VUCh* 32, 1951, 6–7. In *Le Mouvement Œcuménique*, 8, he even pleaded for "the elaboration of a Catholic theology of the *Vestigia Ecclesiae*." See Arenas, *Fading Frontiers*.

125 "Memorandum," § 20: "What is especially at stake is the reality of the Eucharist, the Lord's Sacramental Body, the significance of which is directly related to that of the Mystical Body, the Church, and the very existence of which depends on an ontological relationship with it." Willebrands gave already a nuanced assessment of the Protestant Lord's Supper in "Introduction à la conférence catholique œcuménique de Fribourg," 3, in: AAC, FWC, dossier 5: La première réunion de la CCQE à Fribourg (1952): "Protestants have retained the commemoration of the Lord's Supper, to which they no longer attribute the character of a sacrifice and in which many of them deny the *realis praesentia*. But they recognize in it an instrument of salvation and of the most intimate union with Christ."

126 See Dumont, "Le prochain concile," 2: "With such churches there is a problem of 'reunion' properly speaking by eliminating those few doctrinal differences which oppose them to us and which are generally few in number."

ecumenical efforts to both groups, since the history of their separation from the Catholic Church is interconnected.[127] The paragraph ends with the warning that an intensification of contacts with the Orthodox on the part of the Catholic Church should not hinder the ecumenical relations of the Orthodox churches with other churches, "whether or not within the framework of the World Council of Churches"[128] (§ 23). In light of these words, it is highly ironic that the main drafter of the memorandum, together with Willebrands, a few months later would fall precisely into this trap during the so-called Rhodes incident.[129]

When looking ahead to the difficulties that will need to be dealt with in future dialogues, Dumont explains that the doctrinal positions of the churches constitute "a fairly coherent whole" which is guided by a "first principle" to which "the members of a particular confession are the most deeply attached," up to the point of no longer seeing the value of the Catholic first principles (§ 24). The memorandum then mentions pairs of principles of which one is underemphasized by either the Oriental or the Protestant partner (§ 25). In an article in which he discusses the different articulation of "the sacramental and the juridical" with Catholics and Orthodox, Dumont places particular emphasis on reforms that are needed from the Catholic side, such as a stronger decentralization and better attention to the sacramentality of the church and its ministers, including the bishop of Rome.[130] The CCEQ finally asks for attention to some doctrinal formulations which cause problems to non-Catholics. Ecumenically it would be of great help if the magisterium were willing to provide "an authentic explanation of these formulas … by having recourse to a language more obviously biblical in its inspiration" (§ 26). Among the examples given are the "Ex sese, non ex consensu Ecclesiae" and the "Extra Ecclesiam nulla salus."[131]

127 This conviction was shared by other Catholic ecumenists, as well. See Yves Congar, *Aspects de l'œcuménisme*, Bruxelles, La Pensée Catholique, 1962, 18: "Certainly, Orthodoxy is different from Protestantism; in some respects it is even more different than Catholicism. Nevertheless, the Reformation might not have happened without the Eastern schism. There would have remained in Catholicism ferments of thought and a sense of transcendence which the development of devotions and even of theology in the Middle Ages have made us lose sight of."

128 In "Le Catholicisme romain," 5, Dumont refers to a Protestant weekly in which this fear had been expressed: "The decision to convene a council would be a clever maneuver to detach the Orthodox Churches from the Ecumenical Council in order to reduce it, in spite of itself, to an institution of purely Protestant inspiration and composition." See also J. Willebrands to C.-J. Dumont, Apr 2, 1959, 1: "Any attempt to break off relations between the Oriental Churches and the Ecumenical Council would demonstrate a lack of ecumenical attitude on our side and would risk ruling out the beginning of new contacts." Boyer's opinion of this paragraph was disregarded. See C. Boyer to C.-J. Dumont, Mar 2, 1959, 1: "I would delete this paragraph. The participation of the Orthodox in the Ecumenical Council may have some good effects. But the Oriental Churches would have the same reasons as the Catholic Church for staying out of the Council. To approve their way of acting seems to be a rebuke to the Catholic Church."

129 See Dumont, "Rome, Constantinople et Genève," 424: "Today in this field of ecumenism we are on shaky ground [un terrain mouvant], one could almost say explosive. A meeting that took place last August in Rhodes on the margin of the Central Committee of the Ecumenical Council between some Catholic personalities present as observers and the Orthodox delegates or guests of the Central Committee showed this clearly."

130 Christophe-Jean Dumont, "Catholiques et Orthodoxes à la veille du concile," *Istina* 2, 1961–1962, 189–208, esp. 196–201 ("Le sacramentel et le juridique").

131 See Congar, *Aspects de l'œcuménisme*, 72: "Although the Council cannot change any of the Catholic dogmas, it can explain them better, in such formulas and perspectives that some of the objections of our separated brethren would fall away. I am thinking, for example, of such points as the all-too-famous *Ex sese, non autem ex consensu Ecclesiae* of Vatican I." See for an interpretation of the "Extra Ecclesiam nulla salus" formula by Yves Congar, "'Hors de l'Église, pas de salut': destin et sens d'une formule," *VUCh* 58, 1953, 3–5.

4.5 *"The Present Situation" (§§ 27–41)*

According to the memorandum, in each of the three abovementioned groups of churches one encounters several "unfavorable factors," "favorable factors," and "factors with both favorable and unfavorable aspects" with regard to ecumenism. As regards the first category, there are sometimes decisions within the Catholic Church that are highly questionable for non-Catholics,[132] at other times developments within other churches or their ecumenical collaborations cause serious difficulties to Catholics[133] (§ 29). It is interesting to note that in his reaction Willebrands asked Dumont to add to the unfavorable factors the different method of establishing ecumenical relations between the personal contacts favored by the WCC and the rather impersonal "hasty audiences" granted by members of the Roman curia to non-Catholic ecumenical experts.[134]

The impressive list of favorable factors starts with those found in almost all communities: the awareness "of the harm caused by our divisions," the similarity of many pastoral problems Christian churches face and the need for common action in view of the societal problems of today[135] (§ 32). Boyer's request to remove a reference to Paul Couturier when referring to the commonly shared initiative of the Week of Prayer for Christian Unity was not complied with.[136] As far as the Orthodox are concerned, the CCEQ, among others, thankfully refers to the growing knowledge about Catholicism among circles of Orthodox

132 An example on the side of the Orthodox churches is "the opposition shown at the promulgation of each new dogma (the Immaculate Conception, Papal Infallibility) and even to that of the Assumption of the Blessed Virgin Mary, a doctrine nonetheless commonly received by these Churches" (§ 29). Charles Boyer would have fully supported this mention. See Boyer, *Christian Unity and the Ecumenical Movement*, 83: "In the East traditional doctrines were called in question as the Church of Rome recommended or defined them. Such was the case with the Immaculate Conception, and of the eucharistic Consecration effected by the words of Christ and not by the epiclesis." For Maurice Villain this attitude should lead to a self-critical reflection among Catholics. See Maurice Villain, *Introduction à l'œcuménisme*, Paris, Casterman, 1958, 121–122: "We understand why the Orthodox Church, which has always venerated the mystery of the Assumption, has refused to dogmatize it, that is, to stylize a definitive phrase around this belief, preferring to leave this truth in the penumbra of the mystery and in the sole manifestation of liturgical piety. … To our criticism, she would willingly reply that an imperative authority is not, to her liking, a sure sign of strength or interior maturity."

133 Among others the planned fusion of the IMC with the WCC (§ 31).

134 J. Willebrands to C.-J. Dumont, Apr 2, 1959, 2: "Contacts between the authorities, theologians of the Catholic Church and other Christian communions are almost completely lacking." Willebrands is implicitly pleading here for a new curial body that would be officially entrusted with such contacts.

135 Willebrands, "Catholic Ecumenism," 14: "A collaboration with our separated brethren in relief work and in reforming profane institutions in a Christian spirit. In this collaboration it is possible to give to the materialistic world, in a certain limited but real way, a common Christian witness, in which it will be manifest that a certain measure of common bonds always exists among Christians." This was one of the proposals which Willebrands had picked up during his visit with the leadership of the WCC during his visit in Geneva in Feb 23–26, 1959. See "Compte-rendu d'une conversation de Mgr. Willebrands, secrétaire de la Conférence Catholiques pour les Questions Œcuméniques, avec quelques dirigeants du Conseil Œcuménique des Églises à Genève… sur le sujet du Concile Œcuméniques, annoncé par le Pape Jean XXIII," Mar 7, 1959, 4, in: AAC, FWC, dossier 3: Reunions du Comite directeur et de la commission d'etudes: "In addition to the theological problem itself, there is the vast practical field of Christian life (on the international and social level, aid to refugees, to peoples undergoing social transformation, peace work, etc.). Could we increase the examples of collaboration that already exist, for example in refugee aid? It is hoped that a deeper collaboration will not be based only on the principles of natural law, but that there will be a collaboration between Christians, based on obedience to the commandments of the Gospel."

136 See J. Willebrands to C.-J. Dumont, Apr 2, 1959. For Boyer a reference to the formula of Couturier could imply "that unity can be achieved other than by the entry of other Christians into the Church of Rome"; see Boyer, "Les intentions," 334. He preferred the old formula of Paul Wattson: "For the return of all other sheep to the one fold of Peter."

emigrants[137] (§ 33). The memorandum is able to praise the growing number of contacts between Catholic ecumenists and their Anglican counterparts on the continent, but honestly mentions the difficulties of organizing such contacts in England and the United States (§ 34). The content of the paragraph dealing with favorable factors concerning "the communions stemming from the Reformation" (§ 35) was provided by Willebrands, who among others could refer to the opportunity that was given to specialists like himself to lecture about "the Catholic Church and its theology."[138]

In the final subsection, Dumont introduces specific groups to the council Fathers that provide both challenges and opportunities to Catholics. High Church movements have rediscovered values that are dear to Catholics and thus could favor "the establishment of more harmonious relations and reunion" (§ 37), even if Dumont is also aware that "these movements remain strongly attached to certain of the fundamental principles of the Reformation."[139] The Eastern rite communities in the Catholic Church are also discussed here. On the one hand, these communities make it clear to the Orthodox that the Catholic Church is "open to every legitimate diversity" (§ 38). The memorandum, however, also is very well aware that "their very existence and *a fortiori* their activity, even though they carefully abstain from all proselytism among the Orthodox, is looked upon by our separated Eastern brethren as a menace"[140] (§ 38). The hand of the former editor of *Russie et chrétienté* who continually included this item in each issue of *Istina*, is definitely recognizable in the paragraph dealing with the anti-communist attitude within the Catholic Church (§ 40). However, it also remains an ambivalent reality, especially in those cases when this attitude was inspired by Catholic apologetics.[141]

4.6 *"How Ought the Catholic Church to Give Expression to Her Goodwill?" (§§ 42–55)*

The final section, which was praised by several board members as the climax of the memorandum,[142] starts with a clear but prob-

137 See Lev Zander, *L'orthodoxie occidentale*, Paris, Centre d'études orthodoxes, 1958; ET: *Western Orthodoxy*, South Canaan PA, St. Tikhon Press, 1958 and the positive review by Olivier Rousseau in *Irén* 31, 1958, 308–335.

138 J. Willebrands to C.-J. Dumont, Apr 2, 1959, 2: "During the winter semester 1958–1959 the Catholic Church and its theology were studied at the Ecumenical Institute of Bossey under the direction of Catholic professors." See also the diary entries from Oct 27–Nov 11, 1958 in Salemink, ed., *You Will Be Called*, 49–56.

139 He is more outspoken on this in Dumont, "Remous dans l'Église d'Angleterre," 472: "It is because of these 'Protestant' principles, which are incompatible with certain 'Catholic' principles which we consider necessary, that in our view only the Church of England has to 'grow in catholicity' in order to become what it could and should be in a united Christendom. Hence our interest in certain elements of what is called Anglo-Catholicism."

140 See Congar, *After Nine Hundred Years*, 27: "The Orthodox reproach the Latins – and more precisely, Roman Catholics – for having ceaselessly exercised towards Orthodoxy a levelling and unchecked proselytism." See also Congar, *After Nine Hundred Years*, 38: "The existence of Uniate Churches and of a persevering effort of Rome to organize them, has been felt by the separated Eastern Christians as a veritable betrayal, as a lack of respect towards the East, as a refusal to take seriously … their reasons for not aligning themselves with a Latinized Catholicism. … However, it is a fact – and one would be wrong not to take it into serious consideration – that Uniatism appears to the Orthodox as being, by its profound presuppositions, the very caricature and contradiction of unity." Boyer would have difficulties considering these groups ambivalent. See Boyer, *Christian Unity and the Ecumenical Movement*, 18–19: "But not all Christians in the East are schismatic. … There are isolated groups of Catholics who keep their own language, liturgy and rite, and thus pave the way to unity for the dissident." In § 38 of the memorandum, Dumont presents a summary of his "Le Catholicisme romain," 1–5.

141 Apparently the memorandum preferred not to mention the persecution of Eastern Catholic Churches in communist countries. See Dumont, "Le Catholicisme romain," 3: "With the help of an atheistic civil power, the Uniate churches in the communist countries were forced to separate again from Rome and rejoin communion with the Orthodox churches."

142 J. Willebrands to C.-J. Dumont, Apr 2, 1959: "Numbers 42–57 of the memorandum seem to me to be the most important, they give the point. They seem to me

ably unexpected message to the future council Fathers: "It would be idle to imagine substantial results may be obtained in the efforts at restoring Christian unity if Catholics wait for non-Catholics to act alone" (§ 42). At the same time, the CCEQ is convinced that its recommendations have been made in great respect for "the dogmatic heritage of the Church or the sacramental and hierarchic structure she has received from the Apostles" (§ 43). The most important advice is to refrain from insisting on "the canonico-juridical aspect of the problem." The final goal of their ecumenical efforts remains for Catholics "the visible unity of the Church" as the "full communion of faith, discipline, and sacramental life."[143] On the way towards this goal Catholic ecumenists should develop a theology of "communion (koinonia)" (§ 44). This theological approach even has psychological advantages: "For if on the canonical level the question of the relationship of a local Church to the one, universal Church may be resolved only by an unequivocal 'yes' or 'no,' the reply to the question concerning communion within the objective content of the faith and sacramental life calls for an infinity of degrees and shades of meaning"[144] (§ 45). The second recommendation is "not to treat the dissident communions as though they were *objects* but rather to accept to speak with them as with *persons*" (§ 46) and hence enter into dialogue with them.

In the paragraphs discussing Orthodox-Catholic relations[145] the emphasis is also on what the Catholic Church ought to do, in view both of ecclesiological research and of drawing the practical consequences thereof. When the memorandum repeats its plea for liturgical, canonical, and theological diversity, it insists on the need for further research on "the nature and the form of the relations of communion between the different local churches." This includes reassuming the discussion on the powers of the bishop, which Vatican I had

very valuable"; C. Boyer to C.-J. Dumont, Mar 2, 1959, 1: "I have read your draft of a Memorandum carefully and, on the whole, I found it excellent. In particular, paragraphs 51 to 57 are really valuable. I hope that they will be noticed in high places as they deserve."

143 This was a traditional formulation of the ultimate goal of the ecumenical effort which Dumont defended on several occasions. See Dumont, *Unité de grâce et Unité visible*, 203: "For the Catholic theologian, visible unity is only real and complete if three conditions are met: unanimity in adherence to the same objective content of the faith, belonging to a unique hierarchically organized ecclesial body, participation in common in the same sacraments and, in particular, in the Sacrament of the Body and Blood of the Lord." More recently he had done so in the foreword Istina, "Traitement symptomatique et traitement spécifique," *Istina* 4, 1956, 369–373, here 371–372: "Unity in the Church's being necessarily involves a threefold element: unanimity in the profession of the same objective faith, belonging to the same hierarchically unified sacramental structure, and – as a consequence and as a sign – participation in common in the same equally sacramental worship. It is no longer merely a manifestation of unity, but the very constitution of the unity of the Church in its visible being. This is the organ – the threefold organ – to be restored in its integrity in all Christian confessions and among all Christian confessions."

144 One wonders whether Dumont may have been inspired by the partial communion that had been realized during the formation of the Church of South India. See Dumont, "Remous dans l'Église d'Angleterre," 470 (italics original): "There are various possible degrees of ecclesiastical communion: from communion properly so called or *full communion* (which presupposes total unanimity on the points considered to be binding on our faith and the identity of the fundamental elements of structure) a distinction is made for *restricted* or limited *communion*, which does not cover all areas of the sacramental life and which may not even be entirely reciprocal." Consequences for the Catholic Church are drawn by Louis Bouyer, "L'union des Églises du Sud de l'Inde," *Istina* 2, 1955, 215–237, here 234: "The Catholic Church itself does not teach an all-or-nothing theology where membership of its own body is concerned."

145 They are preceded by the only paragraph in the memorandum dealing with the "dissident Oriental Churches not in communion with the See of Constantinople" (§ 48). Here, too, the Catholic Church is asked to draw "the practical consequences from contemporary research emphasizing the fact that their opposition to the dogma of Chalcedon was verbal rather than real, the whole question being one of formulation; the true nature of the problem was scarcely understood at the time."

been unable to conclude,[146] as well as "the restoration, in law and in practice, of intermediate hierarchical levels (ecclesiastical provinces and national groups of provinces)."[147] Only on this basis might the Orthodox be able to reawaken "the conscience of the Roman primacy which they could recognize as that experienced before the Schism"[148] (§ 49). The executive board of CCEQ also proposes "the adoption of a progressive method": "An increasing collaboration in pastoral care and action, in theological and historical research; while ecclesiastical discipline concerning *communicatio in sacris* should prudently and gradually be adapted to present conditions" (§ 50).

The paragraphs dealing with the relationship with "the Protestant confessions" propose concrete reform measures within the Catholic Church that might be particularly appealing to "the so-called High Church movements" (§ 51). They include the promotion of a greater role of the vernacular in the liturgy, openness towards communion in both kinds and not imposing "the renunciation of the state of matrimony for those already married" (§ 55) in case of reordination.[149] The memorandum believes that such measures could "encourage their further development until they are ready to be received into the Catholic unity" (§ 51).

4.7 *Initial Reception of the Document*

During the following months, Willebrands and Dumont made great efforts to disseminate the memorandum, one of which was having it translated into Italian, German, and English. As for the curial addressees, Willebrands' diary mentions on Jun 22 that Tardini could not receive him because of a visit of General Charles de Gaulle. On the next day, he was cordially received by Cardinal Ottaviani. Ottaviani's secretary father Paul-Henri Philippe, commissioner of the Holy Office, promised that the memorandum would be transmitted to the Antepreparatory Commission and would "not be read through 'black glasses.'"[150] At a later stage, Cardinal Bea received the copy that had been sent

146 See the parallel formulation in Dumont, "Le Catholicisme romain," 4: "The growing interest in the theology of the local (or particular) Church fits in with a development that could provide the question of the Eastern schism with valuable elements for a solution; it is the beginning of a resumption, from below, of the preparatory work for the Vatican Council. Let us not forget that this Council is not finished; prematurely interrupted by political events, it still has to specify the responsibilities and the proper powers of the bishops, as a complement and counterweight to its declarations on the primatial role of the Bishop of Rome."

147 The following phrases in Dumont, "Catholiques et Orthodoxes," 199 reveal the authorship of this section of the memorandum: "A council could, however, go further along the road to reunion, and this by operating in the Latin Church the decentralization to which the episcopate unanimously aspires. ... The principle would be, in fact, the reinstatement of the intermediate levels of the ecclesiastical hierarchy, which have fallen into disuse even when they have not disappeared entirely from canon law: the ecclesiastical province grouping several dioceses under the responsibility of an archbishop, all the provinces of the same nation under that of a primate, perhaps also the Churches of the same continent or of the same fraction of a continent grouped under the leadership of a prelate who would be reminiscent of the patriarchs of the Church of the East."

148 Dumont's hope was surely based on articles such as Nicolas Afanassieff, "La doctrine de la primauté à la lumière de l'ecclésiologie," *Istina* 4, 1957, 401–420, and especially on its famous conclusion: "This refusal to recognize the present primacy must not be a rejection of that primacy which the Church of Rome has enjoyed since the end of the first century and which was the primacy of speaking for the Church of God to the whole Church" (Afanassieff, "La doctrine de la primauté," 419).

149 See Boyer, "Comment concevoir l'œcuménisme catholique," 102: "Quite recently, the reigning pope conceded to Lutheran ministers in Germany to receive priestly ordination, even though they were married. All of this makes it possible to ask Christians separated from the Roman Catholic Church to look at what in the Church is essential and irreformable." The reference is obviously to the ordination of Rudolf Goethe and others. About the affair of the converted and married former pastors see Marotta, *Gli anni della pazienza*, 149–166 and Henk Witte, "Willebrands en de pastores convertiti," in: Adelbert Denaux, ed., *De Nederlandse jaren van Johannes Willebrands (1909–1960)*, Bergambacht, 2VM, 2015, 85–113.

150 Salemink, ed., *You Will Be Called*, 106.

to Tardini and probably passed on to the pope himself. A private notice by Msgr. Pericle Felici, the secretary of the Antepreparatory Commission, well illustrates how the leadership of the Catholic Church was not only unprepared but even hostile towards the ideas on ecumenism carefully exposed by the CCEQ board:

> In my opinion, there is a lot of good will, but frankly, too much is demanded of the Church for the return of the separated brethren: to renounce terms, to bring theology into a purely biblical and patristic form, to have to find a way to satisfy all those who think in such a different and unstable way and follow a way of life so distant from the Catholic Church: it is a very hard task and above all risky for the Catholic Church, the only Church of Christ, the repository of truth. On the other hand, given the present situation of the separated brethren, it is absurd to think that the question of the return will be raised directly in the next ecumenical council: it is a slow task, to be done with much charity but also with much shrewdness, by prepared people. In any case, I would suggest passing the note on to some good theologian and jurist, who could indicate whether the points of agreement put forward in the note can be accepted with tranquility as a starting point. To me, some of the propositions and perspectives seem suspect.[151]

Dumont prepared letters to the members of the Catholic hierarchy and to the members of the CCEQ who would receive a copy of the note, as well as a one-page introduction on the history of CCEQ in case the memorandum were sent to bishops who were not yet familiar with their work. The letter to the members emphasized the confidentiality of this "first step." The memorandum should not be published or shared with non-Catholics, even if the members were welcome to use its ideas in their own conferences.[152] From the exchange of letters between Dumont and Willebrands, it can be deduced that the memorandum was definitely sent to the archbishops and cardinals of France as well as to bishops who supported the work of CCEQ, and to all the bishops in Belgium and the Netherlands.[153]

Even when it is difficult to measure the concrete impact of this initiative, the 1959 memorandum was definitely one of the most important initiatives taken by Roman Catholic ecumenical bodies in order to promote an ecumenical spirit within the Roman Catholic Church, or at least among its hierarchy, in the decade before Vatican II.[154]

---

151 "Nota di mons. Pericle Felici," n.d., in: ADPJ, Bea, Lc 1/4. See Vincenzo Carbone, *Il "Diario" conciliare di Monsignor Pericle Felici*, ed. Agostino Marchetto, Vatican City, Libreria Editrice Vaticana, 2015, 47 (Jul 16, 1959): "I report to His Eminence [Tardini] on a memorandum drafted by the Executive Board of the Catholic Ecumenical Commission. My judgement is unfavorable and I find it strange that the memorandum was also signed by Fr. Charles Boyer S.J. of the Gregoriana. His Eminence agrees to reprove it and still says he is amazed that the Secretariat of State gave him such a favorable report." See for a more detailed account Marotta, *Gli anni della pazienza*, 401–402.

152 C.-J. Dumont to J. Willebrands, Jun 29, 1959.

153 J. Willebrands to C.-J. Dumont, Jul 3, 1959; C.-J. Dumont to J. Willebrands, Jul 7, 1959; C.-J. Dumont to J. Willebrands, Jul 30, 1959; J. Willebrands to C.-J. Dumont, Aug 3, 1959.

154 Étienne Fouilloux, "'Mouvements' théologico-spirituels et concile (1959–1962)," in: Mathijs Lamberigts & Claude Soetens, eds., *À la veille du Concile Vatican II: Vota et réactions en Europe et dans le catholicisme oriental*, Leuven, Bibliotheek van de Faculteit der Godgeleerdheid, 1992, 185–199, here 197–198: "Its main interest is to precisely define the position of Catholic ecumenists even before the founding of the Secretariat for Unity and the drafting of the preparatory schemes for the Council: it can therefore be granted the status of *votum* of the Catholic ecumenical movement as a whole. … The *Note* is undeniably, among others, one of the distant sources not only of the decree on ecumenism, but also of other important decisions of the assembly. Its mixture of modesty, even prudence, and realistic hopes seems quite representative of the original and little-known phase from the Council's announcement to its autonomization from the Curia."

5 The CCEQ's Immediate Preparation of the Council

5.1 *Gazzada 1960: "Differences Compatible with Unity"*

The meetings of 1960 and 1961 had been conceived as twins. The meeting in Gazzada, dealing with "differences compatible with unity," discussed, according to Willebrands, "the horizontal pluralism," whereas the one in Strasbourg on renewal in the church would focus on "the vertical pluralism."[155] Dumont had already introduced this idea in 1954 in an article in *Vers l'Unité chrétienne*, in which he had reflected on the materials of the Evanston assembly. In his opinion, the WCC had asked the right questions – "What are the divergences compatible with unity and what are those that are not?" – but was unable to draw the right consequences from them.[156]

The consultation with the largest number of representatives of the hierarchy was the first one which took place on Italian soil, in Gazzada, near Milan, on Sep 19–23, 1960. The dogmatician from the archepiscopal seminary Carlo Colombo had invited the CCEQ on behalf of Cardinal Montini.[157] The invitation sent to the members on Mar 4, 1960, made it clear that they would have to discuss "the authentic and legitimate traditions" that have developed among the "separated communities," which the Catholic Church will have to "reunite and comprehend in its unity."[158] As Willebrands recalls in his opening address of the Strasbourg conference one year later: "The presence of three cardinals (Cardinal Alfrink, the archbishop of Utrecht, Cardinal Montini, the archbishop of Milano and Cardinal Bea, the president of the Secretariat for Christian Unity) created a new boost, which at the same time marked the importance of the ecumenical work and the interest which the hierarchy of the Church has in it."[159] That Cardinal Augustin Bea, the president of the recently created SPCU, was present and addressed the conference was particularly welcome. In his address, he recognized that "the Catholic Conference had been a kind of non-official preparation, together with other similar institutions, to the Secretariat for Christian Unity" and he explicitly referred to the fact that many of the members and consultors of the secretariat had been selected out of the active members of the conference.[160]

155 J. Willebrands to L. Bouyer, May 26, 1961, in: AAC, FWC, dossier 13, 3: Correspondance.

156 Istina, "Justice distributive et unité chrétienne," 4.

157 Willebrands visited Colombo for the first time in November 1958 for a discussion on how to enhance the interest in the Catholic Conference among Italian theologians. During a second visit, in June 1959, Willebrands received the invitation to contemplate a meeting of the Conference in Gazzada. He visited the place during a lecture tour in Northern Italy in February 1960 and informed the members of the board in his letter of Feb 16, 1960; see AAC, FWC, dossier 3: Reunions du Comite directeur et de la commission d'etudes.

158 Appendix to the announcement letter to the members of the Catholic Conference which Willebrands had sent out in four languages on Mar 4, 1960: "If the question of Unity is put in view of a reunion of the separated Christians in the *One* Church, as Our Lord desired and established her, the Church, in order to be really the gathering of the people of God, must clearly reunite and include in her unity all authentic and legitimate traditions which developed during the ages"; AAC, FWC, dossier 12, 1.2: Invitations, 1. This will be investigated in the fields of worship, institution, theology, and spirituality.

159 Johannes Willebrands, "Strasbourg," 1, in: AAC, FWC, dossier 13, 2: Conférences.

160 Augustin Bea, "Éminence, Excellence, Messeigneurs, Messieurs," 1, in: AAC, FWC, dossier 12, 4: Documents de la réunion de Gazzada. The speech by Bea had impressed Willebrands, as appears from his diary: "Early in the morning, Cardinal Bea arrives, and celebrates the Community Mass. The Cardinal speaks at the first session and responds to an hour and a half of questioning. This gathering is the high point of the Conference. We have never experienced anything like this before. The openness, the caring, the depth of Cardinal Bea makes a lasting impression. How many people are here, who have given their life to work for unity, to work for the separated brothers, without ever receiving any encouragement or gratitude from the hierarchical institutions? Now there is a special blessing from the Holy Father for their work. Later, Père Congar speaks about 'un miracle dans l'Église'"; Salemink, ed., *You Will Be Called*, 209 (Sep 21, 1960).

In his opening speech,[161] Willebrands made it clear that "the great task which we should accomplish in the encounter with separated Christians consists in revealing the catholicity of the Church more and more clearly." Willebrands exhorts Catholic believers to develop a "notional openness" (*ouverture notionelle*) towards the other churches, which thereafter has to be followed by an "existential openness."[162] If the executive board had chosen not to use the vocabulary of "elementa Ecclesiae" in the memorandum towards its own membership, the notion even helped to define ecumenism, which is the theological discipline "explaining how far and in what manner the theology and life of a Christian communion, separated from the Church, have preserved the '*elementa Ecclesiae*.'"[163]

Three theologians during the Gazzada conference proved to be advocates of legitimate diversity in the field of theology. According to the Dutch Augustinian Ansfried Hulsbosch, a long distance separates scholastic from biblical thinking,[164] but in his opinion Protestantism was even more infected by scholasticism than Catholic theology. The human person is entirely saved through divine grace and without any human cooperation.[165] The Benedictine Emmanuel Lanne explained that traditions, rites and disciplines could freely develop in the church during the first millennium, unless Holy Scripture or a general council had decided differently. It was St. Augustine in particular who stated that "the variety of local traditions adds to the beauty of the daughter of the king which the Church is."[166] In his presentation, the Jesuit Georges Dejaifve focused on the difference in "theological mentalities" in East and West and on the existence of an "Eastern" and a "Western ethos."[167] There exist, for example, two understandings of salvation:

> The East, in a more contemplative way, understands salvation as divinization, received by grace and stimulated by fleeing

161 Johannes Willebrands, "Gazzada 19.IX.'60," in: AAC, FWC, dossier 12, 4: Documents de la réunion de Gazzada.

162 Willebrands, "Gazzada," 2. This observation reflects the great impact of John Henry Newman on Willebrands. In his 1937 dissertation he even had upset the professors at the Angelicum with his uncommon appreciation of Newman. See Karim Schelkens & Henk Witte, eds., *Johannes Willebrands: De Denkleer van kardinaal Newman en haar toepassing op de kennis van God door het geweten*, Bergambacht, 2VM, 2013; Karim Schelkens, "J.H. Newman et l'œcuménisme catholique avant Vatican II," in: Mathijs Lamberigts & Ward De Pril, *Louvain, Belgium and Beyond: Studies in Religious History in Honour of Leo Kenis*, Leuven, Peeters, 2018, 275–288.

163 "Catholic Conference on Ecumenical Questions," in: AAC, FWC, dossier 12, 1: Liste des invités; invitations [a 2-page explanation on the conference theme added to the invitation of Mar 4, 1960], 1. At the same time, it is explained that, "only in the [Catholic] Church do these *elementa ecclesiae* have their source and true place."

164 Ansfried Hulsbosch, "Pensée biblique et pensée scolastique," 1, in: AAC, FWC, dossier 12, 4: Documents de la réunion de Gazzada. See Ansfried Hulsbosch, "Biblisches und scholastisches Denken," *TThZ* 70,1961, 129–155. In order to please the participants from various countries, Willebrands had asked Hulsbosch and Janez Vodopivec to prepare their lecture in German, following unsuccessful attempts to attract German theologians like Karl Rahner as speakers. More information on this Dutch Augustinian is found in Brian Heffernan, "Dutch Augustinian Theologians and the Second Vatican Council," *Analecta Augustiniana* 76, 2013, 415–445.

165 Hulsbosch, "Pensée biblique et pensée scolastique," 6–7.

166 Emmanuel Lanne, who was connected to the Pontifical Greek College of St. Athanasius in Rome, had been introduced to Willebrands through Höfer. In a letter of Apr 13, Willebrands had introduced Lanne's theme in Latin: "Licet salva unitate diverse sentire." After the conference, the contribution of the Benedictine from Chevetogne was published as: Emmanuel Lanne, "Les différences compatibles avec l'Unité dans la tradition de l'Église ancienne (jusqu'au XIIe siècle)," *Istina* 2, 1961–1962, 227–253.

167 Georges Dejaifve, "Orient et Occident – deux théologies – une seule foi," 2–3, in: AAC, FWC, dossier 12, 4: Documents de la réunion de Gazzada. The name of Dejaifve had already occurred among the first suggestions which Willebrands had sent to the executive board on Mar 7, 1960 because he had enjoyed reading his article "Orient et Occident Chrétien: deux theologies," *NRT* 82, 1960, 3–19.

> the world (according to the Plotinian ideas); the West as a work to accomplish, a deliverance of sins which one obtains through the moral effort of the Christian life on earth with the help of God.[168]

One also recognizes this double "ethos" in the field of mysticism and in the convictions about the knowledge of God that result from it. The East is in favor of "the way of negative or apophatic theology," the West of "affirmative or cataphatic theology," even if "both ways strongly affirm God's transcendence."[169]

Dejaifve knows that both traditions are much more opposed in the field of ecclesiology. Whereas Orthodoxy is "attentive to the eschatological aspect of the Church" and "looks at the Church on earth in the light of the final kingdom," in the West "one will never forget the historical character of the Church" with the danger that the outcome would be to "absorb the kingdom in the Church and to absolutize its institutional forms."[170] He is especially critical towards his own church:

> Our theologies have their limits. A revealed theology does not exist, even not our own one! ... Did we not too long pronounce monologues in the Catholic Church? Is it not the highest time to listen silently and humbly in order to observe how our separated brethren go their way towards God and to ask them to rejoin us, by following their own way? The Latin West and the Orthodox East are different, as different in their theologies and attitudes as a man and a woman. The divorce will only end when they have mutually felt the need to be in each other's presence, and when, being aware of their limits, they first seek to understand and to esteem one another in their differences, before loving one another and reunite.[171]

Concerning liturgical pluralism, in his speech in Gazzada the Dominican Irénée-Henri Dalmais hoped that the Catholic Church could come to a greater appreciation of the legitimate variety of the rites, especially in the East.[172] In the opinion of Dalmais, Dom Prosper Guéranger was wrong to assume that one had to impose the Roman rite everywhere as a guarantee of unity. He also warned about the return of similar convictions: "Some hope in a quite naïve way that one of the results of the following Council will be to get rid of this diversity which has been judged to be harmful for Catholic unity."[173] At the end of his article he discussed some "ecclesiological and ecumenical implications" and deplored, in the first instance, "the mutilation and adultering of traditional rites and institutions" in the Oriental Catholic rites, because of "a more or less elaborated form of Latinization." If such a tendency were maintained, it would be a disaster for our ecumenical relations with the Christians from the East, who are conscious of the fact that "juridical institutions, spirituality and theology are inseparable from liturgy."

It is a sign of the diversity of opinions within the CCEQ on this point that the Slovenian professor at the Urbaniana, Janez Vodopivec, in his contribution on "Unity in Diversity and the Missions,"

168 Dejaifve, "Orient et Occident – deux théologies," 4.

169 Dejaifve, "Orient et Occident – deux théologies," 7.

170 Dejaifve, "Orient et Occident – deux théologies," 13.

171 Dejaifve, "Orient et Occident – deux théologies," 14–16. In a letter to Dejaifve sent on May 6, Willebrands had also emphasized the need for a diversity of theological viewpoints: "In my opinion, it is precisely on the level of theology that pluralism should be recognised. The Orthodox reproach us (and on this point they are close to the Protestants) with a rationalized scholasticism marked by Wolfianism," in: AAC, FWC, dossier 12, 3: Correspondance.

172 Irénée-Henri Dalmais, "Signification de la diversité des rites au regard de l'unité chrétienne," in: AAC, FWC, dossier 12, 4: Documents de la réunion de Gazzada. This presentation was later published with the same title in *Istina* 3, 1960, 301–318. Dalmais probably was invited because of his book on *Les liturgies d'Orient*, Paris, Fayard, 1959.

173 Dalmais, "Signification," 5.

continued to defend the idea of the return to the Roman Catholic Church, while at the same time, when speaking about missions, considered a plurality of traditions as an added value:

> Only with the greatest spirit of sacrifice, which needs to be exercised from both sides, albeit not in an equal way, will our separated brethren rediscover the way to unity. Their quest should be facilitated or at least not be made more difficult. An organic reunion which will preserve the particularities of both parties by making them grow together, will be useful and necessary for both of them. The separated Christians will gain the entire living unity of the universal Church in its fullness and the Mother-Church for its part, while pushing for a renewal of plurality, will find in this Church a more complete expression of her internal richness, of the essential richness of the mystical body of Christ.[174]

In his lecture on "The Function of the Episcopacy in the Church and Its Relations with Papal Primacy," Carlo Colombo confronted his audience with the results of his "investigation of necessary and permanent elements as well as variable elements within the unique Church of Christ."[175] In Colombo's account on primacy, the reader is impressed by the primordial attention to the role of the pope as bishop of Rome.[176] He also seems ahead of his time when making a distinction between the essential elements of the primacy and the way in which they are exercised:

> It is unthinkable that the Church assumes forms of organization that would weaken the awareness of the primacy and its content or that diminish the constructive value of the full exercise of primacy for the life of the universal Church and of all its dioceses. One could however investigate whether it would not be possible to conceive of forms of collaboration between Pontiff and episcopate, forms that would allow to valorize the function of the bishop even more, not just towards the entire Church, as this was the case in the Ancient Church and as the separated brethren of the East would desire.[177]

Colombo ended his intervention with some remarkable *desiderata*: the nomination of bishops familiar with the traditions of their diocese,[178] and the development of juridical structures in favor of "collaboration between dioceses" analogous to the ancient patriarchates – he is thinking of episcopal

174 Janez Vodopivec, "L'unité dans la diversité et les Missions," in: AAC, FWC, dossier 12, 4: Documents de la réunion de Gazzada.

175 Carlo Colombo, "La funzione dell'episcopato nella Chiesa e le sue relazioni con il primato pontificio," 1, in: AAC, FWC, dossier 12, 4: Documents de la réunion de Gazzada. Colombo delivered his lecture in Italian, but a French translation of his speech was distributed to participants. See for the published version of his conference: Carlo Colombo, "La fonction de l'Épiscopat dans l'Église et ses relations avec la Primauté pontificale," *Istina* 1, 1961–1962, 7–32. When he gave this conference, Colombo already knew that he had been appointed as a member of the preparatory Theological Commission. During the council, he was the personal theologian and *peritus* of Cardinal Montini/Paul VI and became a titular bishop in 1964. See for more information on him: Luciano Vaccaro, ed., *Monsignor Carlo Colombo (1909–1991)*, Brescia, Morcelliana, 2003. A special issue of *La Scuola Cattolica* was dedicated to him in 2011, and one of the articles focuses on the same topic, treated by him during the 1960 meeting of the CCEQ. See Gabriele Cislaghi, "Episcopato e primato nella Chiese: Carlo Colombo e una questione ancora attuale," *La Scuola Cattolica* 139, 2011, 605–628.

176 Colombo, "La funzione dell'episcopato," 10: "The Roman Pontiff, the Bishop of Rome, has a twofold function of magisterium and a twofold jurisdiction: (a) episcopal jurisdiction, common with the other Bishops and pertaining to his own diocese ...; (b) primatial jurisdiction, exclusive to him and pertaining to the entire Church."

177 Colombo, "La funzione dell'episcopato," 12.

178 Colombo, "La funzione dell'episcopato," 17: "To facilitate this task of the bishop, it seems appropriate that the choice of bishops should also be determined in such a way as to ensure their task as interpreters and formators of the 'Christian spiritual tradition' of their Church."

conferences[179] and of what would later become the bishop's synod.[180]

A page of private notes by Willebrands is the only testimony of the concluding lecture by Congar on "The Obligation of Unity, Its Fields and the Means Necessary for Its Realization."[181] Some participants also collaborated in order to formulate practical *vota* after listening to the theoretical input of their colleagues.[182] Inspired by the typical way of collecting the concerns of the local churches during the ante-preparatory stage of the council, the executive board had called for this.[183] During its

179 Colombo, "La funzione dell'episcopato," 17: "A development in this direction is already the 'National Episcopal Conferences' whose competence could be deepened."

180 Colombo, "La funzione dell'episcopato," 18: "It is a question of seeing whether other forms of collaboration between the Episcopate and the Papacy are possible, different from those implemented so far and respectful of both dogmatic principles and venerable historical traditions. One such form could be the constitution in Rome of central bodies, perhaps of a periodic type, composed of members (Bishops) partly chosen by the Supreme Pontiff, partly elected by the national Episcopal Conferences, to which would be entrusted the task of examining and deciding all problems, of a doctrinal, disciplinary and spiritual nature, which might arise in order to reconcile the unity, universality and apostolicity of the one Church of Christ with respect and care for the spiritual traditions of the individual portions of the one Church and the proper pastoral competence of the bishops. Collegial decisions would, of course, only acquire value with the approval and promulgation by the Supreme Pontiff."

181 As appears from his May 4 letter to Congar, the title "L'obligation de l'Unité, ses domaines et les moyens par lesquels elle doit être réalisée" was imposed by Willebrands. For Willebrands's notes taken during the Gazzada conference, see AKW, dossier 34, 3: Reunion à Gazzada. Two case studies were introduced during the Gazzada conference as well, one by Professor Cyrille Vogel of the University of Strasbourg on a few points of discipline in the Greek Orthodox Church, and written documentation offered by the Jesuit Robert Clément, who discusses a tension he had observed in his pastoral ministry in Egypt between the juridical approach to sacraments of the Latin Church and the practice of Catholics rebaptizing Orthodox Copts.

182 Two of these texts formulate suggestions that will dominate the discussion on *De Ecclesiis orientalibus* and on *De oecumenismo* during the council. Rousseau, Duprey, and Clément presented recommendations for Eastern Catholics, Orthodox, and Latin Christians in the wake of the conference of Dalmais, who also signed the proposals. According to them, the rights of the patriarchs should be taken seriously, even in the College of Cardinals, and it is an anomaly that Rome has the right to regulate the application of Eastern rites; the teaching of the Catholic Church on *communicatio in sacris* and on mixed marriages should be revised in order to foster better relations with the Orthodox, and Latin Catholics should have more occasions to study the rich Eastern Catholic traditions. Dumont and Dejaifve made the suggestion that the Catholic Church should foster the creation of two bilateral commissions of Catholic and Orthodox theologians that would do work similar to Faith and Order and Life and Work. See "Projet de vœux consécutif à la conference du R.P. I. Dalmais OP sur la 'Signification de la diversité des rites au regard de l'unité chrétienne'" and "Suggestions concrètes présentées à la suite du rapport du R.P. Dejaifve, 'Orient et Occident: deux théologies, une seule foi' et de la discussion qui l'a suivi," both in: AAC, FWC, dossier 12, 5.3: Suggestions et voeux. During the council, Dumont would continue to write position papers in order to promote Orthodox-Catholic relations. See Peter De Mey, "Preparing the Ground for Fruitful Dialogue with the Orthodox: An Important Motivation of the Ecumenical 'Avant-garde' during the Redaction History of *Lumen gentium, Unitatis redintegratio* and *Orientalium Ecclesiarum* (1959–1964)," in Benoît Bourgine, ed, *Le souci de toutes les Églises: Hommage à Joseph Famerée*, Leuven, Peeters, 2020, 57–85, partim.

183 "Rapport de la session du Comité Directeur à Gazzada," Sep 19, 1960, 3, in: AAC, FWC, dossier 3: Reunions du Comite directeur et de la commission d'etudes: "Surely this is no longer the time to be satisfied with studies, reports, discussions, however good and profound they may be. Do we not have the obligation to help the Secretariat for Unity in its preparatory work for the Council, by communicating thoughts and concrete proposals? Certainly, the limited time at our disposal does not make this task easy. We will have to look for a method that will allow us to achieve maximum results. Perhaps we could ask small groups of people to draw some concrete conclusions from the work of this week, which will be read out at the end of the sessions and communicated to the Executive Board, which will present them to the Secretariat." During the following session of the executive board, another addressee was envisaged: "The Secretary will send them to the Secretariat for Christian Unity; and to the Oriental Commission, if Card. Bea deems it opportune for the conclusions that

conclusive meeting at the end of the conference, the board decided to contact the bishop of Strasbourg and his coadjutor in order to meet there in 1961 to discuss Pope John XXIII's favorite theme of "renewal in the Church" and to seek inspiration in Congar's "Vraie et fausse réforme dans l'Église and Hans Küng's "Konzil und Wiedervereinigung: Erneuerung als Ruf in die Einheit."[184]

5.2 *Strasbourg 1961: "Renewal in the Church"*

If the Gazzada meeting marked a significant shift in terms of the presence of three cardinals and the involvement of Italian theological circles, the Strasbourg meeting, which took place in Aug 21–25, 1961, registered another significant change in terms of participation. During the Gazzada meeting the executive board had expressed the need for "a greater participation of lay faithful and a presence of the female element."[185] They were of the opinion that one could no longer ignore the important ecumenical work of Catholic laity in the field of Life and Work, and one of the examples mentioned by Willebrands was The Grail, an ecumenically inspired international women's movement. They had their formation center in Willebrands' own diocese and offered administrative assistance to Willebrands for his ecumenical work both in the Netherlands and in Rome.[186] A preliminary program even includes the name of Marga Klompé, who was the first female minister ever in the Dutch government from 1956 and a committed Catholic. She shared Willebrands' interest in promoting Jewish-Christian relations in the Netherlands.[187] Due to his heavy workload as secretary of the SPCU, he only managed to write Klompé less than three months before the actual meeting with the request to speak about "The Place of the Lay Person in the Church."[188] In his letter, he indicates that "the place of the lay person in the apostolate of the church and in the Christianization of the world" can be derived from "the common priesthood of the faithful." When laity like Klompé are doing their best to change the structures of society, the church should appreciate this as an important dimension of church renewal, as well. Klompé had no time to prepare such a lecture but was still willing to attend the conference, even if she had observed on the final program that the topic of the laity was no longer on the agenda. In the end, however, she had to cancel her participation for medical reasons.[189] Three more women eventually participated in the Strasbourg conference: Maria Anna Johanna (Dé) Groothuizen, a former president of The Grail, who became in the same year observer for the Vatican with the FAO; Annie Perchenet, who coordinated L'Amitié, an association of Catholic and Protestant professors in France; and Lydia Simons, who was delegated by the general superior of the Ladies of Bethany.[190]

Soon after Gazzada, Willebrands received suggestions for the session on renewal from

directly concern the Eastern Churches"; "Session du Comité Directeur à Rome, le 15 Novembre 1960," 1, in: AAC, FWC, dossier 3: Reunions du Comite directeur et de la commission d'etudes.

184 "Réunion du Comité Directeur à Gazzada (Villa Cagnola) le 24 septembre," 2, in: AAC, FWC, dossier 3: Reunions du Comite directeur et de la commission d'etudes.

185 "Rapport de la session du Comité Directeur à Gazzada," Sep 19, 1960, 4, in: AAC, FWC, dossier 3: Reunions du Comite directeur et de la commission d'etudes.

186 See AKW, dossier 34, 344.

187 See especially chapter 8 of Karim Schelkens, *Johannes Willebrands: Een leven in gesprek*, Amsterdam, Boom, 2020, and Gerard Mostert, *Marga Klompé, 1912–1986: Een biografie*, Amsterdam, Boom, 2011.

188 J. Willebrands to M. Klompé, Jun 13, 1961, in: AAC, FWC, dossier 13, 3: Correspondance.

189 See also the subsequent exchange of letters on Jun 20, 1961; Jun 23, 1961; Jul 17, 1961; Jul 20, 1961; and Jul 31, 1961, in: AAC, FWC, dossier 13, 3: Correspondance.

190 Despite Rousseau's support, Willebrands did not respond positively to the request by the Belgian lay intellectual Jan Grootaers. See Willebrands' exchange of letters with Grootaers, Groothuizen, Simons, Perchenet, Rousseau, and Caroline van Voorst tot Voorst, in: AAC, FWC, dossier 13, 3: Correspondance. Among the relevant publications of Grootaers on this theme, see Jan Grootaers, "Tâches œcuméniques du laïcat," in: *Qu'attendons-nous du concile?*, 89–95.

Congar and Küng. According to Congar, since the CCQE wants to clear the way in particular for Catholic-Protestant dialogue, it should become clear what is good and what is bad reform for us and for them.[191] The holiness and the sacramental nature of the church should be explained clearly to the Protestants and someone should clarify how they apply the "simul iustus et peccator" to the church. In response to Congar's concrete suggestions, Willebrands would only contact Jedin in order to speak about ecclesial reform at Trent, but he had other priorities. Unlike Congar, Küng was of the opinion that the Catholic Church should also be willing to revise both its doctrine on the relation between the pope and bishops and the canonical elaboration thereof. For the conference, he suggested that Congar should treat the need for church reform, Jedin or others on selected themes from church history, Rahner on the renewal of church doctrine, Josef Andreas Jungmann on the renewal of the liturgy and, should no other specialist be found, he himself would be willing to give a presentation on the necessary renewal of canon law.[192] Küng made these suggestions in November, while shortly before Christmas, on his way home from Rome, the CCEQ secretary visited and approved the venue in Strasbourg.[193] Only on May 27, 1961, was Willebrands able to send a formal invitation to Küng to accept the lecture he had promised earlier, which Küng had to decline in view of other commitments.[194]

Congar's opening lecture on the fundamentals of renewal was a new version of his 1950 book *Vraie et fausse réforme dans l'Église*.[195] The first part of Congar's article presents the reasons for renewal in the church. A great deal of attention is paid to the expectations and criticisms of the separated brethren, and especially to the Protestant criticism of the Catholic Church, which is inspired by the intention to safeguard "the absolute primacy of God." Congar exhorts his fellow Catholic ecumenists: "It seems to me that the questions of the Reformation need to be taken into consideration."[196] Congar finds two important "principles for a solution" which are related to "the paradoxical condition of the Church" in Catholic ecclesiology. He elaborates them in two theses: "The Church is from top to bottom holy and made of sinners" and "The Church has been made by the sovereign act of God, and is to be made by human persons in history."[197] The opening conference by Congar was followed by two other substantial thematic contributions, one by the Oratorian Louis Bouyer, himself a former Lutheran pastor, and one by Professor Hermann Volk of Münster, who would become the bishop of Mainz less than one year later. According to Bouyer, the Roman Catholic

191 Y. Congar to J. Willebrands, Oct 7, 1960, 1, in: AAC, FWC, dossier 13, 3: Correspondance: "Since we are working in the perspective of dialogue with Protestants, we should ask ourselves what they – and what we – reject as the wrong kind of renewal. They don't accept just anything … and we don't either."

192 H. Küng to J. Willebrands, Nov 13, 1960, in: AAC, FWC, dossier 13, 3: Correspondance.

193 Salemink, ed., *You Will Be Called*, 248–249 (Dec 22–23, 1960).

194 Exchange of letters between Willebrands and Küng on May 27 and Jun 4, 1961 in: AAC, FWC, dossier 13, 3: Correspondance.

195 Yves Congar, "Les raisons et les exigences principales d'un renouveau. Péché et sainteté dans l'Église," in: AAC, FWC, dossier 13, 2: Conférences, and published as Yves Congar, *Comment l'Église Sainte doit se renouveler sans cesse*, Chevetogne, Éditions de Chevetogne, 1963. Congar's abovementioned letter of Oct 7, 1960 contained an aside on the future of his book: "Everywhere people say to me: 'But don't you want to republish this book, in view of the Council?' You know that a reprint was forbidden in 1952 or '53. I will not be the one to ask for anything. Everyone takes his own responsibility. I took the responsibility of writing this book; I did not take the responsibility of preventing it from pursuing a better career. It would eventually be up to those who made this decision to let me know, in one way or another, that times have changed"; AAC, FWC, dossier 13, 3: Correspondance. Still, his lecture for Strasbourg had been written anew and referred to new sources, such as Gerhart B. Ladner, *The Idea of Reform: Its Impact on Christian Thought and Action in the Age of the Fathers*, Cambridge MA, Harvard University Press, 1959.

196 Congar, "Les raisons," 3.

197 Congar, "Les raisons," 7–13.

magisterium can without difficulty subscribe to the principle of the "Ecclesia semper reformanda" (which was also the title of his conference), since it merely expresses the concept that the church, which is far from perfect, has to place itself under the judgement of the Word of God. There exists, however, neither in Protestantism nor in Catholicism, unanimity on how this principle has to be applied concretely. In very much the same way as Congar, he is able to say that the one church is characterized by two complementary aspects. On the one hand, it is safeguarded against error or sin through its infallibility. On the other hand, as *congregatio fidelium* the church is situated under God's saving judgment. Bouyer deplores the almost exclusive focus on papal infallibility in the Catholic Church, which is somehow understandable in his opinion, "as a reaction against the Protestant error."[198]

When accepting the late request from Willebrands to speak in Strasbourg, Volk hoped to be able to treat the theme differently from Congar by reflecting on "the relationship between the reality and the theological description of this reality, that is ecclesiology."[199] Volk is convinced that the renewal of ecclesiology that has taken place in *Mystici corporis Christi*, through the rediscovery "of the constitutive significance of the Holy Spirit for the Church," may contribute to renewal of the church itself. In the constructive part of his lecture, he therefore elaborates on three "fruits of the Spirit": the Spirit can help the church not to become exclusively juridical, to go further than simply tolerating diversity in its midst, and to promote a specific form of freedom, which in the Holy Scriptures is indicated as the freedom of God's children.[200]

The French Jesuit teaching at the Biblicum, Stanislas Lyonnet, believed that the biblical renewal which followed the publication of the encyclical *Divino afflante Spiritu* would bear several ecumenical fruits.[201] In the lecture of the Benedictine Olivier Rousseau, an overview of the history of the liturgical movement was followed by a discussion of contemporary challenges, such as the introduction of liturgical celebrations in the vernacular in the missions.[202] Among the ecumenical fruits of liturgical renewal, Dom Rousseau deemed it possible that churches would in the future commit themselves to achieve "a common edition of the Bible" or the common study of "the major treasures of Patristic thought." The conclusion to his article offers ample evidence that the CCEQ, especially with this conference on renewal in the church, was fully ready for the event which

198 Louis Bouyer, "Ecclesia semper reformanda," 7–88, in: AAC, FWC, dossier 13, 2: Conferences.

199 H. Volk to J. Willebrands, Jul 8, 1961, in: AAC, FWC, dossier 13, 3: Correspondance: "I think of the matter, at the moment, as being about the relationship between reality and the theological description of this reality, here ecclesiology; perhaps I could then present something of the thoughts of the essay, which has not yet appeared and which are probably somewhat different from Fr. Congar's remarks, and then discuss the ecumenical significance of these things." His lecture would be published as Hermann Volk, "Erneuerung der Ekklesiologie als erneuertes Selbstverständnis der Kirche und ihre ökumenische Bedeutung," *Catholica* 15, 1961, 241–270.

200 Hermann Volk, "Die Erneuerung der Ekklesiologie," esp. 14–21, in: AAC, FWC, dossier 13, 2: Conférences. "The Spirit of Christ as a superhumanly powerful principle gives the church a superhumanly grounded unity and gives it confidence to hold differences in unity in the power of this principle. The knowledge of the Spirit's power for unity gives the church the strength not only to bear possible differences within the church, but to regard them as a matter of course, because they are not an impairment of unity in the Spirit"; Volk, "Die Erneuerung," 20.

201 Stanislas Lyonnet, "Le renouveau biblique et l'œcuménisme," in: AAC, FWC, dossier 13, 2: Conférences. In a letter of Jul 10, 1961 Willebrands had reassured Lyonnet that Cardinal Bea had no objection at all with Lyonnet's participation. See Anthony Dupont & Karim Schelkens, "*Scopuli vitandi*: The Historical-Critical Exegesis Controversy between the Lateran and the Biblicum (1960–1961)," *Bijdragen* 69, 2008, 18–51.

202 Olivier Rousseau, "Le renouveau liturgique: Sa valeur pastorale de rechristianisation; valeur œcuménique du mouvement," 7, in: AAC, FWC, dossier 13, 2: Conférences.

would drastically change the outlook of the Roman Catholic Church:

> The result of the upcoming Council will for many be an important argument for or against what we have just said. It is legitimate to believe that the Holy Spirit will guide it and its results will be a precious and providential indication. We know very well, however, that all will not be done at once and one may presume that the result of the Council will only be a first step towards a larger evolution, of which the milestones have been put in place.[203]

6 The Efforts of the CCEQ to Organize Meetings for Catholic and Non-Catholic Theologians on the Eve of Vatican II

In November 1958, Willebrands obtained permission from Alfredo Ottaviani to hold the planned meeting among theologians of the WCC and the CCEQ on the subject of the lordship of Christ. On Dec 5, even a formal authorization from the Holy Office was granted.[204] By the end of the year, everything was ready for the meeting scheduled for October 1959 in Assisi, which was to be attended by 12 theologians from the CCEQ and an equal number of members of the WCC division of studies. In the midst of these efforts came the announcement of the council. The heated climate of expectations and fears in ecumenical circles made relations between Catholic and non-Catholics much more sensitive and vulnerable. This is the context that might explain how dramatic and disastrous the events of that summer, known as the Rhodes incident, were perceived to be.[205] In August 1959, Visser 't Hooft invited Willebrands and Dumont to Rhodes to attend the WCC central committee as "journalists." The main reason for that committee session was to prepare the integration of the Orthodox into the WCC, a process that would be completed at the third WCC assembly in New Delhi in 1961. Thanks to their presence on the island, Willebrands and Dumont were invited to a private, imprudent "dinner" with the Orthodox representatives aside from the official WCC talks, with the aim of organizing a shared workshop with Roman and Orthodox theologians in Venice for 1960. The Catholic-Orthodox "dinner," of which Visser 't Hooft was unaware, was picked up by the press and interpreted in the light of the future council as the dress rehearsal for a unification of the Roman and Eastern churches. The reaction of the WCC leaders, who accused the Catholics of applying *divide et impera* tactic, was fierce: "If you speak to the Press one more time, then, I must ask you to leave Rhodes immediately," Visser 't Hooft told Willebrands the day after the scandal. "I thought that I had invited the two most sensible Catholics, but I got the two dumbest ones."[206] Things escalated further in September, when Vatican Radio announced the Catholic-Orthodox meeting in Venice as "official," a mistake that revealed, among other things, the lack of a competent office in Rome responsible for ecumenical affairs. Despite Willebrands' efforts to carefully mend fences with the WCC, rebuilding

203 Rousseau, "Le renouveau liturgique," 7f. The remaining two lectures were case studies: Frédérick Manns, "Un exemple concret de renouveau dans l'Église: St. Bernard" and Théodore Strotmann, "La notion de renouveau chrétien dans la pensée de Berdjaev," in: AAC, FWC, dossier 13, 2: Conférences. The article of the latter was published on the occasion of the centenary of this birth in *Irén* 84, 2011, 33–52.

204 Willebrands' letter to Boyer, Dumont, Höfer, Cambier, Groot, Hamer, Volk, Schnackenburg, Kempf, Congar, Leclercq, Rousseau, Schmidthüs, Dec 27, 1958, in: AAC, FWC, dossier 10, 3.2: Préparation et projets pour la réunion d'Assise. See also J. Willebrands to A. Ottaviani, Nov 20, 1958, in: AAC, FWC, dossier 10, 3.3: Correspondance and Dec 1, 1959, in: AAC, FWC, dossier 4: L'Affaire de Rhodes.

205 For a detailed reconstruction, see Karim Schelkens, "L''affaire de Rhodes' au jour le jour: La correspondance inédite entre J.G.M. Willebrands et C.-J. Dumont," *Istina* 3, 2009, 253–277. See also the documentation in AAC, FWC, dossier 4: L'Affaire de Rhodes.

206 Salemink, ed., *You Will Be Called*, 128 (Aug 23, 1959).

the relations laboriously constructed over the previous years, the most dramatic and disastrous consequence of the "accident" was the cancellation of both meetings prepared by the CCEQ. Both the meeting in Venice with the Orthodox theologians and that planned for October in Assisi in collaboration with the WCC were canceled. The revocation was communicated to Willebrands in a letter from Hans Heinrich Harms a few weeks before the event:

> You will remember that after the unfortunate incident in Rhodes you asked me whether under those circumstances we could go on with our Assisi preparations. At that time, I was of the opinion that it would still be desirable to have this meeting, envisaged for such a long time ... Unfortunately, in the meantime the situation has changed. And this malaise has become all the greater because in these four weeks since the broadcast [of Vatican Radio], no effort has been made on the Roman Catholic side to clarify *publicly* the present confused situation.[207]

A further effort on the part of the CCEQ to enter into a lasting dialogue with the various expressions of the ecumenical movement deserves to be mentioned. From 1956 onwards, Willebrands established contacts with the ILAFO, an ecumenical association founded in 1951 with the aim of fostering understanding between Catholic-minded Christians of various communions within the WCC, promoting Catholic concerns such as the apostolic faith and apostolic succession (the "Apostolic Faith and Order").[208] Known today as IEF (since 1967), which also includes Orthodox and Roman Catholic members, at that time the ILAFO consisted mainly of Old Catholics, Lutherans, and especially Anglicans. Willebrands came into contact with Michael Bruce, secretary of the ILAFO, at the end of 1956 and shortly afterwards some members of the CCEQ were invited to attend the assembly organized by the ILAFO in Southwark in September 1957 on the themes, both very close to Catholic sensibility, of "the necessity of the episcopacy" and "the sacrifice of the Mass." Six members of the CCEQ were ready to participate, but the bishop of Southwark, Cyril Cowderoy, forbade Catholics from attending the conference.[209] Bruce and Willebrands decided to try again, this time arranging a private meeting between some CCEQ and ILAFO members at an *ad hoc* site under the hospitality of a sympathetic bishop. That is the reason why the meeting was fixed in Warmond for the end of April 1960. The themes were the same as those of Southwark ("the necessity of the episcopate" and "Eucharist as sacrifice") and the meeting was attended by 12 members of CCEQ and 12 of ILAFO.[210] Two years later, in June 1962, in Mirfield (England), a second joint conference was held between the two delegations, each composed of 15 members, on three themes: "the unity of the church and the unity of man"; "the twelve in the Bible"; "the apostolate of the twelve and the apostolate of the laity." The experience of collaboration between the two organizations, which led to another conference on conciliarity and primacy, held in Chevetogne in April 1964,[211] finally came to

207 H.H. Harms to J. Willebrands, Oct 1, 1959, in: AAC, FWC, dossier 4: L'Affaire de Rhodes.

208 Saretta Marotta, "The Dialogue and Collaboration between the International League for Apostolic Faith and Order and the Catholic Conference for Ecumenical Questions (1957–1964)," *JoMaCC*, forthcoming.

209 C. Cowderoy to J. Willebrands, Feb 23, 1957, in: AAC, FWC, dossier 15, 1.3: Correspondance. See also J. Willebrands to A. Ottaviani, Apr 15, 1957, in: AAC, FWC, dossier 15, 1.3: Correspondance.

210 For the CCEQ, the participants were: Rousseau, Dumont, Le Guillou, Bouyer, Moeller, Sartory, Küng, Francis Davis, Bévenot, Groot, Thijssen, Witte, Willem Hendrik van de Pol, and Willebrands. See the documentation in AAC, FWC, dossier 15, 1: La réunion à Warmond.

211 The meeting took place in Apr 6–10, 1963. The theme, collegiality and primacy, was declined in three aspects: scriptural, with the intervention only on the Catholic side prepared by Jacques Dupont; historical, with the speeches of Archimandrite Pierre Lhuillier together with Dom Hilaire Marot; theological, with Derek

an end after Vatican II, when the Roman Catholic members were included in the ILAFO (from 1966) and the CCEQ was dissolved.

With the creation of the SPCU, it seemed indeed as if the purpose of the CCEQ had been surpassed. Many members of the CCEQ were involved in the preparatory commissions of the council, most of whom in the new secretariat chaired by Cardinal Augustin Bea. Willebrands himself was appointed secretary of the new SPCU. For this reason, as exemplified by the organization of the Gazzada and Strasbourg meetings, it became very difficult for him and the other members to organize the annual conferences of the CCEQ. The last conference, which had been postponed for a year, took place again in Gazzada in Aug 26–30, 1963 and presented an overview of the ecumenical situation in different countries at the time of the council: it involved not only the countries traditionally in the vanguard of ecumenical dialogue, such as England (Bernard Leeming), Holland (Frans Thijssen), Germany (Heinrich Fries), the United States (Thomas Stransky), the Scandinavian countries (Hans Ludvig Martensen), and France (François Biot), but also Latin America (Jorge María Mejía), Africa (Joseph Blomjous), the Near East (Jean Corbon), and even Italy (Alberto Bellini) and Spain (José Maria Burgos). Willebrands's introductory report, on the other hand, was devoted to a general assessment of the participation of non-Catholic observers in the council up to that time. While the conference seemed to be intended to offer a *status quaestionis* to assess ecumenical urgencies in the various countries, it was in fact designed to raise awareness of the ecumenical issues among a wider audience than before, especially among bishops and council experts. More than 100 names were invited to the meeting, most of whom had not been involved in the work of the CCEQ until then, such as Bishop Blomjous of Tanganyika and theologians Fries, Otto Karrer, Giuseppe Dossetti, Roberto Tucci, etc.[212]

The Gazzada conference of 1963 thus differed greatly from the previous meetings, being more oriented towards a popularizing task "ad extra" rather than towards a theological reflection "ad intra" which was now taking place in the sessions and subcommissions of the secretariat. It is not surprising, therefore, that the Gazzada conference in 1963 constitutes one of the final acts in the history of the CCEQ. The other was the joint meeting in 1964 with the ILAFO in Chevetogne, and this was not by accident. The main reason why CCEQ members strove to continue the experience even in the challenging years of the council's preparation was precisely to help the secretariat to maintain contacts with ecumenical organizations. In this way, the final years of the CCEQ constituted a period of long transition, which lasted long enough for such a "transfer of power."

Above all, the long experience of collaboration with the WCC proved to be highly valuable for Bea's secretariat. In fact, after the Rhodes incident, the relationship between the CCEQ and Geneva went back to normal. In May 1961, it was even possible to carry out the project of a joint theological meeting among the members of the CCEQ and the WCC, a project which had been abandoned several times.[213] However, the theme originally intended for the Assisi meeting, the lordship of Christ, was finally abandoned, replaced by another theme, more urgent in view of the preparation of the council, which was "religious freedom." Even though there was in point of fact a subcommission within the secretariat charged with dealing with this theme,[214] the rules of the council did not fore-

Allen for the Anglicans and Georges Dejaifve for the Catholics.

212 The lists in AAC, FWC, dossier 14, 1: Invitations, participants, comptes.

213 See J. Willebrands to A. Bea, May 18, 1960, in: AKW, dossier 106: Correspondance avec le card. A. Bea. See also Velati, *Una difficile transizione*, 122–125.

214 See Silvia Scatena, *La fatica della libertà: L'elaborazione della dichiarazione "Dignitatis humanae" sulla libertà religiosa del Vaticano II*, Bologna, Il Mulino, 2004.

see the possibility of any direct contribution on the part of non-Catholics. In this sense, therefore, the semiofficial character that had always characterized the CCEQ proved to be very valuable for the secretariat, which took advantage of it in order to maintain the possibility of those informal meetings with Geneva.

7 Conclusions

The *Instructio De motione oecumenica* had made it possible for Catholic ecumenists to engage in international cooperation. The leading ecumenical centers were not eager to leave the initiative to the Roman center Unitas but accepted the proposal made by Dutch ecumenists to organize the CCEQ conferences in various dioceses throughout Europe with the approval of the local ordinary. Even if sometimes individual bishops did not allow the CCEQ to meet in their dioceses, the constant efforts of the CCEQ leadership to keep the Roman Curia informed about their plans and initiatives proved to be the right method. As the 1959 memorandum shows, by the end of the decade the CCEQ did not hesitate to honestly decry the unpreparedness of most Catholic hierarchs to accord central attention to the challenge of Christian unity during the council. After the Rhodes incident had shown the urgent need for a permanent ecumenical office in Rome, Pope John XXIII created the SPCU. In the wake of the nomination of the CCEQ secretary Johannes Willebrands as secretary of this new organism, many more members of the CCEQ were appointed members or consultors of the secretariat.

The most important Catholic association on ecumenism needed this first decade to overcome its own lack of preparation in the field of ecumenical theology as well. This became especially clear in the difficulty of presenting a common response to the Christological themes discussed by the WCC during this decade. The only solution was to entrust it to the most competent theologian, that is to say, Congar, to prepare his personal synthesis and reflection on the basis of the interventions during the CCEQ conferences in Dijnselburg, Mainz, and Chevetogne. Since Willebrands continued to hold the Dominican theologian in great esteem, he not only solicited his advice on the selection of speakers but regularly built conferences around major contributions published by the latter. The reconstruction of the genealogy of the theological ideas expressed in the 1959 memorandum on Christian unity also makes it clear that it was less the work of the entire CCEQ board than that of the main drafter, Christophe-Jean Dumont.

The memorandum has become a masterpiece of ecumenical formation for future council Fathers, asking them to be attentive to psychological sensitivities in the field of ecumenism, to treat the Christian East in a different way from the Protestant world while not neglecting the connections between the different schisms, and above all to become promoters of all legitimate forms of liturgical, canonical, and theological diversity both within and outside the church. The theological reflections of the CCEQ in the memorandum, but also the 1960 and 1961 conferences on "Differences Compatible with Unity" and "Renewal in the Church," would bear fruits in the work of the council, particularly in its Decree on Ecumenism.

Bibliography

Arenas, Sandra, *Fading Frontiers?: An Historical-Theological Investigation into the Notion of the Elementa Ecclesiae*, Leuven, Peeters, 2021.

Declerck, Leo, *Mgr J. Willebrands et la Conférence catholique pour les questions œcuméniques: Ses archives à Chevetogne*, Leuven, Peeters, 2015.

Denaux, Adelbert & Peter De Mey, eds., *The Ecumenical Legacy of Johannes Cardinal Willebrands (1909–2006)*, Leuven, Peeters, 2012.

Fouilloux, Étienne, *Les catholiques et l'unité chrétienne du XIXème au XXème siècle: Itinéraires européens d'expression française*, Paris, Cerf, 1982.

Fouilloux, Étienne, *Yves Congar (1904–1995): Une vie*, Paris, Salvator, 2020.

Jacobs, Jan, *"Naar één oecumenische beweging": De Katholieke Conferentie voor Oecumenische Vragen: Een leerschool en gids: 1951–1965*, Tilburg, Tilburg University Press, 1991.

Marotta, Saretta, *Gli anni della pazienza: Bea, l'ecumenismo e il Sant'Uffizio di Pio XII*, Bologna, Il Mulino, 2019.

Routhier, Gilles, Philippe J. Roy & Karim Schelkens, eds., *La théologie catholique entre intransigeance et renouveau: La réception des mouvements préconciliaires à Vatican II*, Louvain-la-Neuve/Leuven, Collège Érasme/Maurits Sabbebibliotheek, 2011.

Schelkens, Karim, *Johannes Willebrands: Een leven in gesprek*, Amsterdam, Boom, 2020.

Velati, Mauro, *Una difficile transizione: Il cattolicesimo tra unionismo ed ecumenismo (1952–1964)*, Bologna, Il Mulino, 1996.

CHAPTER 23

The "Controlled Growth" of Catholic Ecumenism under the Holy See of Pius XII: From Amsterdam 1948 to the *Instructio Ecclesia Catholica*

Saretta Marotta

1 Geneva 1946: the Revival of the International Ecumenical Movement

From Feb 20 to 23, 1946, the Provisional Committee of the WCC met in Geneva and, for the first time after the long interruption of the war, took up the threads of the process that would lead to the official constitution of the new international ecumenical body. The Holy See did not remain indifferent to this event, above all for very practical reasons because both the Swiss and the international press had given extensive coverage to two messages addressed by Catholic representatives to the members of the Provisional Committee. The first and more authoritative was from the new bishop of Lausanne, Geneva, and Fribourg, François Charrière, who had recently succeeded the late Marius Besson. Besson had been very concerned about religious pacification in Switzerland[1] and Charrière, who had written the letter in response to a visit he had received at his curia from one of the participants at the meeting in Geneva, the Swedish bishop of Växjö, Yngve Brilioth, also intended to continue along the same path of commitment as his predecessor, as he told the leaders of the WCC:

> We do not yet see how this union will come about, for we cannot eliminate our differences by a purely superficial common denominator. It would be a betrayal to give up one iota of the truths we have received. On the other hand, unity cannot be achieved by the triumph of one over the other, as happens on the temporal plane. Between the two extremes, which are the corrupting compound of what is true or the suppression of the adversary, there is room for the solution that is truly in the spirit of Jesus: reconciliation. How will this be achieved? It is too early to say. But for this miracle to happen, we all need to pray to the Father through our Lord, so that his kingdom may come in truth and love.[2]

Having learnt of this letter, the cardinals, members of the Holy Office, decided in their meeting on Mar 20, 1946, to call the new bishop to order, taking advantage of his forthcoming *ad limina* visit: "As soon as he arrives in Rome, have him interrogated by Msgr. Montini and, if it is true that he wrote it, give him a *miramur*."[3] The Roman authorities

1 Marianne Jehle-Wildberger, "Marius Besson und Adolf Keller: Ein frühes ökumenisches Gespräch," *Freiburger Zeitschrift für Philosophie und Theologie* 58/2, 2011, 505–530; Francis Python, "Prudence pastorale ou discours à l'usage des chrètiens modérés de Suisse romande?: L'oecuménisme patriotique de Mgr Besson (1920–1945)," in: Jacques Prévotat & Jean Vavasseur-Desperriers, dir., *Les "chrétiens modérés" en France et en Europe (1870–1960)*, Villeneuve d'Ascq, Presses universitaires du Septentrion, 2013, 133–140.

2 F. Charrière to Y. Brillioth, Feb 21, 1946, *La Liberté*, Mar 16, 1946, 4. Only two days later Charrière forwarded the text to the nuncio in Switzerland, Filippo Bernardini, "since this letter will probably be published"; F. Charrière to F. Bernardini, Feb 23, 1946, in: AAV, Arch. Nunz. Svizzera, b. 159, fasc. 438, f. 49. Here and elsewhere the original texts have been translated into English by the author.

3 Minutes of feria IV, Mar 20, 1946, in: ADDF, R.V. 1948, no. 39, b. 1, f. 5. This decision was taken only in reaction to the news of the message, which had come from an interview in *Le Monde* with Marc Boegner on Mar 2. A few days later, the Vatican received a detailed report from the nuncio in

clearly could not accept Charrière's statements. In their opinion, if it was true that not a "iota" could be dropped in the defense of Catholic doctrine, this certainly did not apply to non-Catholic interlocutors, who would necessarily have to renounce points of their own doctrine in order to return to the fold of the true church. As the encyclical *Mortalium animos*[4] had clearly explained, the solution to the problem of Christian unity, far from being nebulous, was one and one alone: the return of dissenters to the Catholic Church. To depart from this aim and method was nothing less than to embrace religious indifferentism. Even worse, therefore, was the second message that was sent on the part of a Catholic to the participants of the Geneva meeting, namely the "Message d'un prêtre catholique à ses frères orthodoxes et protestants réunis à Genève à l'occasion du conseil œcuménique des églises." It was the initiative of a priest from the diocese of Lille, Robert Prévost, who even had his text read out during the meeting by a delegate:

> Most Christians – if not to say all Christians – need to reform their thinking on this point. What is needed is a "conversion," a true change in mentality. … How many speak of the fullness of the church in a purely earthly sense, when this fullness of the church will only really be achieved on the great day of Christ? … You, my Orthodox and Protestant brothers, and we Catholics, all have an examination of conscience to make on this point. Let us not start by thinking that our neighbor needs it more than we do. If you want me to tell you what I think in the depths of my soul, I even believe that it is our Orthodox brethren who will have the least to do on this road to heavenly regeneration, in this reawakening of consciousness of our life as "risen in Christ."[5]

The message irritated the Roman authorities not only for its content, but also because it was an initiative taken without any official hierarchical mandate, neither from the bishop of the diocese of origin, Cardinal Achille Liénart,[6] nor from Charrière, who, when asked for an explanation by the apostolic nuncio in Switzerland, Filippo Bernardini, expressed his complete disappointment.[7] However, Prévost was convinced that he had been given a kind of unofficial mandate by none other than the Holy See, thanks to a lengthy negotiation that had taken place the previous year between Liénart and Giovanni Battista Montini, the substitute for the first section of the Secretariat of State, entrusted with general affairs. In point of fact, the cardinal Liénart had written to Pius XII in July 1945, asking him to instruct the priest from Lille, in the name of the Holy See, to continue at international level the work he was already doing in the diocese, namely the dialogue with

Switzerland, Filippo Bernardini, including the texts of the messages from Charrière and Robert Prévost, which will be discussed shortly. See F. Bernardini to D. Tardini, Mar 25, 1946, in: ASRS, AAEESS, periodo V, parte I, Svizzera, pos. 262, f. 11.

4 Pius XI, *Mortalium animos*, in: *AAS* 20, 1928, 5–16.

5 Robert Prévost, "Message d'un prêtre catholique à ses frères orthodoxes et protestants réunis à Genève à l'occasion du conseil œcuménique des églises," Feb 11, 1946, in: ADDF, R.V. 1948, n. 39, b. 1, ff. 66–68.

6 See Catherine Masson, *Le cardinal Liénart, évêque de Lille (1928–1968)*, Paris, Cerf, 2001. However, Cardinal Liénart, who, like the others, learned of the text of the message from the press, did not fail to congratulate him, confirming that he "fully approved the meaning" of the message and rejoicing "deeply in the echo it has met with our separated brethren"; A. Liénart to R. Prévost, Mar 9, 1946, in: ASRS, AAEESS, periodo V, parte I, Svizzera, pos. 262, f. 24. This letter was forwarded by Prévost to the Geneva leaders on Mar 11, 1946. They then passed it on to Charrière, who sent it to Bernardini.

7 "I made no secret to him that I had concerns and that I disapproved that he had not communicated this message to me before having it read in Geneva. Undoubtedly, Prévost depends on his bishop; but when an action of this importance takes place in a foreign diocese, it would be normal for a priest, before acting, to consult with the local bishop"; F. Charrière to F. Bernardini, Mar 19, 1946, in: AAV, Arch. Nunz. Svizzera, b. 159, fasc. 438, f. 56.

separated Christians.[8] Despite the rejection of the request, due to the strong reservations about the project and the person, of which Montini made no secret,[9] Liénart allowed Prévost to continue visiting various European countries to create contacts with Protestant and Orthodox ecumenists. His efforts were now about to culminate in the creation of a Catholic ecumenical secretariat in Geneva (with the help of the diocese of Lausanne, Geneva, and Fribourg, which provided him with premises) in order to establish a direct channel of dialogue between the leaders of the WCC and the Catholic Church. It was in this capacity that he intended to address his message to the Provisional Committee of the WCC. However, the Holy See did not become aware of the extent of Prévost's plans until months later, when, in June 1946, he explained them to nuncio Bernardini and asked for a meeting with him, as he had done with other nuncios and apostolic delegates, such as Angelo Giuseppe Roncalli in Paris and William Godfrey in London.[10] The nuncio in Bern was the first to alert Rome by writing to his superior, Domenico Tardini, substitute for the second section of the Secretariat of State, the section in charge of relations with states. The latter, after asking Montini for explanations (Montini had to justify himself and reiterate to Liénart that he had never given his consent to such an initiative),[11] directly appealed to the Holy Office asking to make a final decision on the Prévost case. This came in July 1947, after a lengthy examination by the Roman consultors, and resulted in a non-appealable refusal, to which the priest from Lille had no choice but submit.[12]

These public *démarches*, in which Rome was overwhelmed by the independent initiative of activists of Catholic ecumenism, and which coincided with the resumption of the activities of the provisional bodies of the WCC, imposed on the Holy See the urgency of a thoughtful reflection on the attitude with which it should approach the new body that was being created. Above all, the dilemma of the future world assembly, which was

8 A. Liénart to Pius XII, Jun 7, 1945 and R. Prévost to Pius XII, Jul 16, 1945, in: ADDF, R.V. 1948, n. 39, b. 1, ff. 141 and 142 respectively. Until that time, Prévost was chaplain of the spiritual movement Ad Lucem, which he had founded in 1931. See Florence Denis, "Entre mission et développement: Une expérience de laïcat missionnaire, l'association Ad Lucem (1945–1957)," *Le Mouvement sociale* 177, 1996, 29–47, esp. 30–31; Jean Pierre Ribaut, "Le Cardinal Liénart et 'Ad Lucem,'" *MSR* 54/3, 1997, 37–56.

9 "The careful and repeated study of his *Memoire* shows that reservations must be expressed, either about the doctrine and methods proposed, or even about the circumstances of a project whose inspiration does not seem to offer sufficient guarantees. Clearly, under these conditions, the approval requested could not be granted. Your Eminence will know better than anyone how to draw the wise conclusions from this examination"; G.B. Montini to A. Liénart, Oct 1, 1945, in: ADDF, R.V. 1948, n. 39, b. 1, f. 134. The examination of Prévost's project was entrusted to the Verbite Josef Grendel, consultor at the Holy Office, who did not fail to note the frequent recurrence of the word "conversion" in the exposition: "This expression is perhaps not accidental: it recurs so often that it obviously contains the essence of the purpose of this new movement"; Josef Grendel, *votum*, n.d., **ivi**, ff. 218–224.

10 R. Prévost to F. Bernardini, Jun 19, 1946, in: ASRS, AAEESS, periodo V, parte I, Svizzera, pos. 262, f. 4. Prévost himself speaks of these contacts with other nuncios in his letter.

11 G.B. Montini to F. Bernardini, Aug 27, 1946, in: AAV, Arch. Nunz. Svizzera, b. 159, fasc. 438, f. 39 and G.B. Montini to A. Liénart, Jul 27, 1946, AAV, Arch. Nunz. Svizzera, b. 159, fasc. 438, f. 40.

12 "It should be communicated to the Most Eminent Cardinal Liénart, bishop of Lille *iuxta mentem*: the Holy Office disapproves of the 'R.M.G.' [Rome-Moscow-Geneva] movement, which must be suppressed. The cardinal must forbid the priest Prévost to deal with such matters and invite him to devote himself to other ministries"; minutes of feria II, Jul 14, 1947, in: ADDF, R.V. 1948, n. 39, b. 1, f. 407. Moreover, the doubts about Prévost's project were also political, since he believed that the dialogue with Geneva should be balanced by a dialogue with the church in Moscow through the Ukrainian church. See Supreme Sacred Congregation of the Holy Office (hereinafter SO), "Svizzera. Consiglio ecumenico delle chiese. Circa il sac. Roberto Prévost. Relazione del giugno 1947," in: ADDF, R.V. 1948, n. 39, b. 1, f. 308. On Liénart's interest in dialogue with Ukrainian refugees, see Zénon Narozniak, "Le Cardinal Liénart et la communauté ukrainienne," *MSR* 54/3, 1997, 83–84.

soon to be convened, was already beginning to emerge and the Catholic Church would certainly be urged to participate in one way or another, not only by the leaders of the new movement, but above all by the impatient impulses of the ever-widening circle of Catholic theologians passionately concerned with the problem of Christian unity.

2 The Precedents

On Apr 23, 1946, Domenico Tardini received a visit at the Vatican from two members of the study department of the WCC, the pastors Howard V. Yergin and James Hutchison Cockburn. Their mission was to establish contacts with the Italian Protestant communities and with the Holy See in order to seek collaboration on the preparatory documents for the world conference planned for 1948, particularly on social issues and the relief of refugees.[13] Tardini dismissed the two guests rather rapidly, saying that while the Holy See "cannot but welcome with satisfaction any initiative that has charity as its goal and is inspired by feelings of rapprochement, etc.," "Catholics have their own organizations and act through them" and that "this is an action that does not hinder others, since the field of charity is so vast."[14] This was, after all, no different a response from that proffered by Pius XI and his secretary of state, Pietro Gasparri, to the leaders of Faith and Order in the audience of May 16, 1919,[15] and then ratified by the decree of Jul 4 of the same year.[16] The position of the Holy See, however, had not remained completely unchanged since that time. Indeed, the decree of 1919 had not prevented a Catholic journalist, the Jesuit Heinrich Sierp, editor of *Stimmen der Zeit*, from taking part informally in the preparatory meeting of Faith and Order in Geneva in August 1920, after the many requests that Robert Gardiner had made to Cardinal Désiré-Joseph Mercier over the previous few months.[17] Similarly, the fact that eight years later, on Jul 6, 1927, the Holy See reaffirmed this decree[18] did not prevent Msgr. Besson (who later justified himself by saying that he needed to obtain reliable information on the progress of the congress, as requested by the secretary of state Cardinal Gasparri) from allowing two Catholic observers, the Germans Max Josef Metzger and Hermann Hoffmann, to attend the Lausanne conference in August that year.[19] On both occasions it was probably a question of courageous, avant-garde actions on the part of the most ecumenically sensitive representatives of the episcopate, who more or less consciously disregarded the Holy See's instructions and were subsequently reproached for doing so. In more recent times, however, even after the encyclical *Mortalium animos*, the case at the Faith and Order conference in Edinburgh in 1937 was different. On that occasion it was indeed possible for some English Jesuits, among whom Maurice Bévenot, to obtain permission from their superior to be present as observers. Once again, this seems to have

13 Nils Ehrenström, "Notes for Dr. Cockburn: Study Department interests in Rome," Apr 16, 1946, in: ASRS, AAEESS, period V, parte I, Svizzera, pos. 262, f. 91.

14 Domenico Tardini, "Colloquio di mons. segretario con i pastori protestanti Hutchison Cockburn e Howard V. Yergin," handwritten account, Apr 30, 1946, in: ASRS, AAEESS, periodo V, parte I, Svizzera, pos. 262, f. 89.

15 See the contribution by Luca Ferracci in the first volume of this work.

16 SO, "Decretum de participatione catholicorum societati 'ad procurandam christianitatis unitatem,'" *AAS* 11, 1919, 309–316. See feria IV, Jul 2, 1919, in: ADDF, R.V. 1940, n. 2.

17 Étienne Fouilloux, *Les Catholiques et l'unité chrétienne du XIXe au XXe siècle: Itinéraires européens d'expression française*, Paris, Centurion, 1982, 178.

18 See SO, "Dubium: De conventibus (quos dicunt) ad procurandam omnium christianorum unitatem," *AAS* 19, 1927, 278. See feria IV, Jul 6, 1927, in: ADDF, R.V. 1940, n. 2.

19 See Philippe Chenaux, "Le Saint-Siège et les débuts du Mouvement œcuménique: La conférence de Lausanne (1927)," in: Andreas Gottsmann, Pierantonio Piatti & Andreas E. Rehberg, eds., *Incorrupta monumenta Ecclesiam defendant: Studi offerti a mons. Sergio Pagano, prefetto dell'Archivio Segreto Vaticano*, vol. 1/1, *La Chiesa nella storia: Religione, cultura, costume*, Vatican City, Archivio Segreto Vaticano, 213–226.

happened without the knowledge of the congregations of the Roman curia, but not of Pius XI, who had personally made arrangements with the general superior Włodzimierz Ledóchowski to ensure the secret presence of some Catholics at the event.[20] Not having been delegated by the Holy See, Bévenot did not present a report on the assembly to the Roman curia on his return, but had to do so three years later when, through the apostolic delegate Godfrey, he requested official authorization not only for his own participation in the constituent congress of the WCC, a congress that was assumed to be imminent but which the war postponed until 1948, but also for the meetings of the Preparatory Commission to be held shortly thereafter in Birmingham.[21] This time, given the clear will of the pope previously expressed, the Holy Office accepted the petition without difficulty and decided, on Jul 17, 1940, to "entrust the matter to the Most Reverend father general of the Society of Jesus, so that, without mentioning the Holy See, and after consulting the ordinaries, … he may select suitable persons":[22]

> This Supreme Congregation is not averse to your allowing – as by yourself, without ever mentioning the Holy See, and in agreement with H.E. the Most Rev. archbishop of Westminster and with H.E. the archbishop of Edinburgh – such participation to some fathers of the Society of Jesus within the limits and under the conditions indicated below, namely: 1 – to submit to the Preparatory Commission an exposition of Catholic doctrine on the subject to be dealt with at the congress, so that it may be published, together with the other writings, in the volume intended for the congress participants. The author must, however, include a declaration that he does not belong to the association; 2 – to attend the meetings of the Preparatory Commission as observers, and to speak only in the following cases: at the request of the commission, to clarify a point which has remained unclear in the written treatment; at the request of the commission, to illustrate a point of doctrine connected with the main argument; to correct the erroneous attribution to the Catholic Church of a doctrine which is not its own. … This Supreme Congregation has full confidence that Your Most Reverend Paternity will choose for such a grave and delicate task persons who are outstanding, especially in terms of theological competence and orthodoxy of thought.[23]

This authorization is not surprising when compared with the attitude of the Secretariat of State at the time: on Feb 14, 1939, the archbishop of York, William Temple, Anglican primate of England and chairman of the WCC Provisional Committee, had written to Secretary of State Luigi Maglione expressing a wish for cooperation, albeit in the knowledge that "the Church of Rome would not desire to be formally associated with the council":

20 The circumstances of the permission were reconstructed a few years later by Ledóchowski at the request of the general commissary of the Holy Office, the Dominican Giovanni Lottini: "We have not found any document from the Holy See granting Father Bévenot … the faculty to speak at the pan-Protestant congress on Faith and Order held in Edinburgh, England, in 1937. It seems, however, that the Holy Father Pius XI, who on several occasions condescended to speak to me about the tendencies of the Anglicans, wished for the presence of a father; and so I wrote to this father provincial. … The provincial, in accordance with my wishes, sent Bévenot there, not as a member, but as a simple observer"; W. Ledóchowski to G. Lottini, May 29, 1940, in: ADDF, R.V. 1940, n. 2.

21 See Bévenot's report on the Edinburgh conference, Apr 4, 1940, ADDF, R.V. 1940, n. 2.

22 Minutes of feria II, Jul 8, 1940, approved by feria IV on Jul 17, 1940 and ratified by the pope the following day, in: ADDF, R.V. 1940, n. 2. The decision of Jul 8, which accepted the *votum* drawn up by the Dominican Luigi Romoli, second companion of the commissary of the Holy Office was approved by a majority of 13 out of 15 consultors (the only dissenters being Alois Hudal and Franz Hürth).

23 F. Marchetti Selvaggiani to W. Ledóchowski, Jul 27, 1940, in: ADDF, R.V. 1948, n. 39, b. 1, f. 404.

> We hope that it may be permissible to exchange information with agencies of the Church of Rome on matters of common interest and that we should have the help from time to time of unofficial consultation with Roman Catholic theologians and scholars. Such sharing in our activities, as Roman Catholics may be ready to undertake, will be cordially welcomed by us as a manifestation of fellowship in Christ. At a time when all that Christians hold in common is menaced by forces of demonic power we venture to hope that we may have the benevolent sympathy of our Roman Catholic brethren as we attempt to recall men to the faith and obedience of the Lord Jesus Christ as the one hope for the salvation of the world.[24]

Maglione, through his apostolic delegate Godfrey, replied to this invitation with a substantially positive response:

> Your Most Reverend Excellency is requested to reply on my behalf to Mr. William Ebor [William Temple; Ebor is the Latin name of the see of York], explaining that there is nothing to prevent him from confidentially consulting the bishops and the apostolic delegate, just as there is nothing to prevent him from confidentially exchanging information and seeking the opinion of Catholic theologians, who will of course reply in their own name. Your Excellency will have the courtesy to add that the cardinal secretary of state did not reply to him directly, since, as is customary, he wished to inform the Holy See's representative in England of the matter and to give him the necessary instructions.[25]

Presumably, therefore, the WCC's request for Bévenot's cooperation was merely a follow-up to these agreements. In the light of this precedent, the visit of Yergin and Cockburn in April 1946 does not seem entirely out of the blue as it was based on a history of contacts and moderate cooperation, interrupted only by the world conflict. The 1939 correspondence between Maglione and Temple never came to the attention of the Holy Office, nor did the authorization given by Tardini to George Bell many years later, in November 1947, for the publication of this correspondence.[26] However, when in 1946 the question of Rome's participation in the efforts to found the WCC arose again, the congregation kept a record of the permission given to the English Jesuits to cooperate with the leaders of the international ecumenical movement: it was precisely from this precedent that a window of opportunity opened for the possibility of a positive response to the issue to be considered.

24 The letter had actually been prepared on Feb 10, 1939, but was not sent because of the simultaneous news of Pius XI's death. As Temple himself explained, the WCC delayed sending it until after the conclave had ended and the secretary of state had been appointed. W. Temple to L. Maglione, Mar 14, 1939, in: ASRS, AAEESS, periodo V, parte I, Stati Ecclesiastici, pos. 559, ff. 3–5.

25 L. Maglione to W. Godfrey, Jul 12, 1939, in: ASRS, AAEESS, periodo V, parte I, Stati Ecclesiastici, pos. 559, ff. 20–21. On 26 Jul, Temple replied to Godfrey that he was "most happy that the way is open for the measure of cooperation intimated in your letter"; W. Temple to W. Godfrey, Jul 26, 1939, in: ASRS, AAEESS, periodo V, parte I, Stati Ecclesiastici, pos. 559, f. 63.

26 In September 1947 Bell sent a request through Godfrey to the Secretariat of State to publish the correspondence between Temple and Maglione in his *Documents on Christian Unity* as evidence, albeit indirect, of the cooperation between the WCC and the Catholic Church (see Geroge Bell, ed., *Documents on Christian Unity*, Oxford, Oxford University Press, 1948, 298ff.). Surprisingly, Tardini replied that "all things considered, nothing stands in the way of such a publication" and even suggested that Maglione's dispatch to Godfrey of Jul 12, 1939 be published instead of Godfrey's consequent letter to Temple (D. Tardini to W. Godfrey, Nov 12, 1947, in: ASRS, AAEESS, periodo V, parte I, Stati Ecclesiastici, pos. 559, ff. 64–65).

3 Waiting for the World Assembly: the Holy Office Considers Sending Catholic Observers

Since March 1946, the day after the meeting of the Provisional Committee of the WCC in Geneva and the news of the two messages from Charrière and Prévost, the Holy Office had begun to compile a substantial dossier on the matter of Catholic participation in the future world assembly. On Apr 15, just before Tardini received the two WCC envoys at the Vatican, the dossier was entrusted to the Dutch Jesuit Sebastiaan Tromp to draft a *votum*.[27] In the weeks that followed, before Tromp submitted the result of his work to the Holy Office assessor Alfredo Ottaviani, by a mere coincidence, he was visited in his office and made the acquaintance of Yves Congar, the author of *Chrétiens désunis*.[28]

From May 10 to 30, the French Dominican was indeed in Rome for the first time, together with his confrere Henri-Marie Féret,[29] summoned by the master general of the order, Martin-Stanislas Gillet, to discuss the situation of the convent school Le Saulchoir after the Chenu case.[30] The two Dominicans took the opportunity to meet and talk to various prelates in the Roman curia. On the morning of May 17, they crossed the threshold of the Holy Office, but it was at the Pontifical Gregorian University in the afternoon that Congar, eager to meet the man to whom everyone referred as the ghostwriter of the encyclical *Mystici corporis*, conversed with consultor Tromp:

> We moved on to ecumenism. [Tromp] seems rather well up to date with regard to the externals and incidentals of the ecumenical movement. But he does not believe in it at all and does not see its relevance: they should come to agreement amongst themselves first, later one will see. ... He laughed at these things, for which I, for my part, have an entirely different regard. ... I told him that, in view of the next ecumenical congress in 1948, the plan for which he knows as well as I do, we will probably be asked to make some documentary contribution: to do some work setting out the Catholic viewpoint on this or that subject, perhaps, even, to give some talks at the Institute in Geneva. He replied that, in accordance with the categorical and repeated decisions of the Holy Office, one could not, in any manner, either from close at hand or at a distance, either directly or indirectly, participate in any activity of movements of this kind. He quoted these texts to me by heart, in Latin, and observed that the Holy Office had piled on the adverbial phrases in order to do away with any doubt whatsoever. One cannot collaborate with the dissenters in any way, he said, except in the political order, at the level of the Ten Commandments.[31]

Congar emerged from the meeting trembling with rage, convinced that Tromp was nothing more than a perfect specimen of the Roman system ("I hate the Gestapo wherever it is to be found," he had whispered to Féret that morning as he passed through the door to the Holy Office),[32] which saw "everything governed by an authoritative text, by a police regulation. Order reigns in Warsaw!"[33] Nevertheless, he would certainly have appreciated

27 A. Ottaviani to S. Tromp, Apr 15, 1946, in: ADDF, R.V. 1948, n. 39, b. 1, f. 74.

28 Marie-Joseph Congar, *Chrétiens désunis: Principes d'un "œcuménisme" catholique*, Paris, Cerf, 1937; ET: *Divided Christendom: A Catholic Study of the Problem of Reunion*, trans. Muad A. Bousfield, London, Bles, 1939.

29 Étienne Fouilloux, *Yves Congar (1904–1995): Une vie*, Paris, Salvator, 2020, 129–132. For the english translation of this book: Étienne Fouilloux, *Yves Congar: A life (1904–1935)*, Adelaide, ATf Press, 2023.

30 Michael Quisinsky, *Marie-Dominique Chenu: Weg, Werk, Wirkung*, Freiburg i.Br., Herder, 2021, 117–123; Étienne Fouilloux, "L'affaire Chenu (1937–1943)," *RSPT* 98/2, 2014, 261–352.

31 Yves Congar, *Journal of a Theologian (1946–1956)*, ed. Étienne Fouilloux, trans. Denis Minns, Adelaide, ATF Press, 2015, 130–133, here 131–132. Congar met Tromp alone, as Féret, tired, had returned to the convent of Santa Sabina in the early afternoon.

32 Congar, *Journal of a Theologian*, 119

33 Congar, *Journal of a Theologian*, 132.

the *votum* that Tromp delivered to Ottaviani nine days later, on May 26, 1946, containing his reflection on the question of how the Catholic Church should prepare for the founding assembly of WCC scheduled for 1948. It is not easy to establish whether the positions expressed by Tromp to Congar on that May 17 corresponded to his true thoughts at the time, or whether they were deliberately exaggerated, either by the memory of the latter, or by the intention of the former, due to a normal suspicion and reserve towards the Dominican whom Tromp was meeting for the first time. Even if these opinions were true, it is impossible to determine to what extent they were modified in the course of those weeks by the conversation with the French theologian. However, it is possible to find in Tromp's *votum* a direct consequence of the exchange of ideas with Congar, and in particular in the passage where he explicitly mentions the possibility of an invitation from Richard Kraemer to some Catholic theologians to hold lectures at the Ecumenical Institute in Bossey.[34] This was precisely one of the hypotheses put to him by the Dominican theologian, and certainly, given the strong skepticism that Tromp had shown towards what he called the "Rockefeller ecumenical foundation" and its director, Professor Kraemer of Leiden ("I have the impression that, for Tromp, 'nothing good can come out of' Leiden," Congar noted in his diary),[35] he could not have imagined that the Jesuit's opinion on the matter would be entirely favorable, inviting the cardinals of the Holy Office to "promptly decide whether such an invitation from non-Catholics can be accepted and, if so, under what conditions, in order to avoid scandal and unlawful forms of collaboration."[36] Generally speaking, the entire *votum* on relations to be established with the WCC was surprisingly positive. After tracing the history of the Holy See's pronouncements on the ecumenical movement, although recalling an abundance of negative precedents, ranging from the decrees of 1919 and 1927 to *Mortalium animos* and the failure of the Malines Conversations,[37] Tromp appealed in his report to that unique and remarkable precedent of the Catholic observers in Edinburgh in 1937, "qui dicunt votum catholicum non sine fructu bono fuisse," in order to formulate proposals which were certainly dialogical towards the new body:

> (3) The competent bishops (especially the Dutch bishops, if the 1948 congress is to be held in the Netherlands) should be instructed in good time as to how they should behave in view of the future ecumenical congress, so that there will be a single *modus agendi* approved by the Holy See.
> (4) It would be very useful to have Catholic observers present at the future congress, who would be allowed to explain the position of the Catholic Church in religious and mixed matters, for the better information of the members of the congress.[38]

Tromp also considered it appropriate for the pope "to send a short and very simple letter to the future ecumenical congress" in which he should praise "the desire of all to work together in defense of the order willed by God and Christ against the threats of the ungodly," explain "that the Roman Church, not out of pride or desire for domination,

34 "Quoad ad novum Centrum spectat pro studiis oecumenicis, erectum a munificentia Domini Rockfeller, in quo erunt duce professore reformato et missiologo Kraemer …: haud inverisimile est directores novi Athenaei etiam invitaturos docentes catholicos"; Sebastiaan Tromp, "De habitudine quorundam catholicorum ad consilium oecumenicum ecclesiarum habitum Genevae Februario 1946. Votum," May 26, 1946, 29, in: ADDF, R.V. 1948, n. 39, b. 1, f. 108.

35 Congar, *Journal of a Theologian*, 132.

36 Tromp, "De habitudine," 29–30.

37 See the contribution by Bernard Barlow and Martin Browne in the first volume of this work and Saretta Marotta, "Cardinal Mercier and the Malines Conversations: New Findings from the Vatican Archives," in: Leo Kenis & Jan De Maeyer, eds., *Joseph-Désiré Cardinal Mercier*, Turnhout, Brepols, forthcoming.

38 Tromp, "De habitudine," 29–30.

but out of love for the truth and obedience to Christ, cannot be present" and invite Protestants, Orthodox, and Anglicans to consider "whether the gospel, the seven ecumenical councils, and even the Roman Church's own consideration of its ecumenical unity and invincible stability, do not converge to the See of the One who, though unworthy, is the vicar of Christ on earth."[39] Partly because of the undisputed authority and prestige that Tromp enjoyed in the Roman theological consortium, the preliminary meeting of feria II of the Holy Office consultors, held on Jul 22, 1946, unanimously agreed with him. The consultors fully supported the *votum* submitted, emphasizing in particular two points in Tromp's conclusions which were, in their opinion, among those to be implemented most urgently, namely "the need for a papal intervention with a direct letter, not to the assembly, but to the ordinary of the place where the assembly is to be held and the need for competent persons attending the assembly as private observers, who, if necessary or requested, would be ready to clarify the thought and doctrine of the church."[40] They were convinced of this because they were aware that "this is required by the great importance of the matter itself" and that "until now the position of the Catholic Church has generally been negative, but it is opportune that even positive action be taken."

The sessions of feria II, that is, the Consulta on Tuesdays, concerned only the consultors of the congregation, who were the *periti* (theologians, canonists, moralists, biblical scholars, etc.) charged with studying the dossiers to be examined by the Holy Office and the *vota* on these dossiers, which were prepared in turn by one or two of them. For each dossier, the Consulta usually met ten days before the session of the cardinals members of the congregation, who instead met in feria IV, that is, each Thursday.[41] Because of the summer break, the consultors' decision of Jul 22 could not be ratified in feria IV until the autumn, on Oct 23. On that occasion, however, the cardinals opted for a *pro nunc dilata* (to postpone for the moment), preferring to wait for more information about the ecumenical congress (in particular the venue, program, and participants) before deciding what to do, but they agreed on the need for an intervention, "not, however, by the pope, but by the Holy Office, to reaffirm the principles and maxims so often proclaimed."[42]

From Tromp's idea of a message from the pope to the participants in the WCC assembly – an idea modified by the consultors into the more cautious hypothesis of a letter to be addressed to the bishop of the diocese or to the episcopate of the nation hosting the event – the project had thus been changed by the cardinals to the plan of an intervention by the Holy Office to reaffirm "the principles and maxims so often proclaimed." This was no small change, since it seemed to contradict the consultors' invitation to the pope to make "even positive" gestures towards the ecumenical question, after a hitherto generally negative practice. In any case, in that autumn of 1946, the question of sending observers still seemed to have been resolved in a positive sense: all that was awaited was the final choice of the assembly venue, so that the local church hierarchy could be contacted for the choice of theologians to be delegated.

The session of July 1947, which revisited the subject 12 months later, did not add much to what had been decided: "To hear the father general of the Jesuits on this matter and to instruct Father Tromp to hear the archbishop of Utrecht."[43] On the other hand, apart from the confirmation that the assembly would be held in Amsterdam in August 1948, there were still no new elements or information that might justify the drafting of a

39 Tromp, "De habitudine," 29–30.

40 Minutes of feria II, Jul 22, 1946.

41 Francesco Castelli, "La *Lex et Ordo S. Congregationis S. Officii* del 1911 e le edizioni del 1916 e del 1917," *RSCI* 66/1, 2012, 115–154, here 124–126.

42 Minutes of feria IV, Oct 23, 1946, in: ADDF, R.V. 1948, n. 39, b. 1, f. 124.

43 Feria IV, Jul 23, 1947, in: ADDF, R.V. 1948, n. 39, b. 1, f. 408.

new *votum*, even though the Holy See made considerable efforts to keep up to date on the matter, going so far as to subscribe to the bulletin "Service œcuménique de presse et d'information" through the nunciature in Berne.[44] Instead, what drew all the attention of the Supreme Congregation during the meetings of the consultors and cardinals of Jul 14 and 23, 1947 was the Prévost affair, on which Montini had asked the Holy Office in November 1946 to pronounce "a more precise word," since his repeated efforts to contain the free initiative of the priest of Lille and his Archbishop Liénart remained unsuccessful.[45] Even the printed position prepared by the Holy Office chancellery for these meetings devoted almost all its space to the examination of the movement planned by the priest of Lille,[46] the immediate suppression of which was decided, while, as far as the other point on the agenda was concerned (the WCC assembly), it repeated Tromp's previous *votum*, accompanied by a few new lines from the Jesuit summarizing the next operational steps.[47] It is noteworthy that the material distributed to the consultors and then to the cardinals in favor of participation included a concise pro memoria written by the Jesuit Camillo Crivelli – probably the result of the personal initiative of the scholar, professor of history of Protestantism at the Pontifical Gregorian University, and sent to the Holy Office by the Congregation for the Council on Dec 20, 1946[48] – and not another text that had come to the Holy Office's attention during the same period and was sent by Montini on Jan 15, 1947. This was the memorandum on Catholic ecumenism written by the French Dominican Christophe-Jean Dumont, director of the Istina center in Paris, and sent to the substitute of the Secretariat of State in December 1946.[49] Here, the French Dominican

44 It was Ottaviani himself who asked Bernardini "to receive continually, even after the Amsterdam assembly, the bulletin 'Service œcuménique de presse'"; A. Ottaviani to F. Bernardini, Feb 25, 1948, in: AAV, Arch. Nunz. Svizzera, b. 159, fasc. 438, f. 156.

45 G.B. Montini to A. Ottaviani, Nov 18, 1946, in: ADDF, R.V. 1948, n. 39, b. 1, f. 125. In June 1946, Prévost had gone to Rome to ask again for the mandate of the Holy See. Although since July 1946 Montini had made clear to both him and Liénart the opposition of the pope and the Secretariat of State to his project, which was, among other things, in open competition with Charles Boyer's Unitas association, founded almost at the same time, the ecumenist from Lille had, during the summer, taken his own initiatives to make contact with various European episcopates and non-Catholic interlocutors.

46 See SO, "Svizzera. Consiglio ecumenico delle chiese." It must be said, however, that the Prévost's initiatives had been monitored by the Holy Office since his message to the Provisional Committee of WCC in February 1946.

47 In particular, according to Tromp's proposals, these observers, who were to be chosen, as was later decided, by an appeal to the superiors of the religious orders, would be allowed to write opinions on the subjects of the Amsterdam congress and to speak orally, so that they could make their own contribution, albeit unofficially. See Sebastiaan Tromp, *votum*, Jul 6, 1947, in: ADDF, R.V. 1948, n. 39, b. 1, ff. 383–384.

48 Crivelli's text, which argued for the desirability of sending Catholic observers to the Amsterdam assembly, did not depart in principle from Tromp's argument and his reference to the Edinburgh precedent, and explicitly alluded to the contacts made in 1939 between the Provisional Committee of the WCC and the Holy See. See Camillo Crivelli, "Pro-memoria. Concilio ecumenico delle chiese. Nota informativa su origine, scopo e programma. Voto del consultore," n.d., in: ADDF, R.V. 1948, n. 39, b. 1, ff. 235–236.

49 On the memorandum, to which Congar also contributed and which was probably requested by the latter, see Fouilloux, *Les catholiques et l'unité chrétienne*, 898–903. Congar had met Montini on May 21, 1946 and had the impression "that perhaps a document is being prepared there on these questions; that a certain number of people would not be upset to see me condemned or disowned in it, that they are working for this"; Congar, *Journal of a theologian*, 134. The memorandum was thus an attempt to anticipate such a move, and indeed Dumont stressed in it, with reference to Catholic ecumenists: "It would be very detrimental to the cause ... if, in case one or the other position did not meet with the approval of the Holy See, it were to be disavowed in such a way or in such terms that it would lose all credibility with the dissidents whose trust it enjoys"; Christophe-Jean Dumont, "Note sur le mouvement catholique en faveur de l'unité chrétienne: Sa raison d'être, ses caractéristiques. Mesures à prendre pour assurer la rectitude de son développement et l'efficacité de son effort," 17 pages, in: ADDF, R.V. 1948, n. 39, b. 1, ff. 273–289, here f. 288 (14). The memorandum is also

asked the Holy See not to remain inactive in the face of the efforts of the international ecumenical movement and to create "within the Roman curia" a congregation or commission, analogous to the Congregation for the Oriental Churches, which would become "a center for information and coordination of all apostolic work undertaken with regard to the Protestant confessions."[50] He also called for the establishment of special chairs in Catholic universities dedicated to ecumenical dialogue, to encourage theological reflection on the problem, and for a study center in Rome analogous to the PIO.[51] Dumont's document does not seem to have aroused any reaction: in the archives of the Holy Office it is kept in a large folder, a kind of collection of news and informative notes on ecumenical movements and events in postwar Europe, but without any commentary or summary vote, that would prove that it had been sent to a consultor for study. Nor is there any mention of it in the various reports on the ecumenical movement prepared by the Holy Office chancellery for the consultors and cardinals. In short, it seems to have been ignored. One of the reasons for this could have been that Dumont was unknown to the Holy Office at that time: perhaps a different outcome would have been achieved if the text had been sent to the Congregation for the Oriental Churches, whose secretary, Cardinal Eugène Tisserant, could have presented it to the Supreme Congregation with more information and greater warmth.[52]

Dumont's proposal was not even mentioned in Tromp's new *votum* of Jan 25, 1948, now written in the run-up to the Amsterdam congress. In accordance with the mandate he had received the previous summer, in October Tromp had contacted Cardinal Johannes de Jong, archbishop of Utrecht, and asked for his opinion on the question of Catholic participation in the Amsterdam assembly. De Jong's reply, sent within a few weeks, provided a clear opinion:

> It does not seem appropriate to us that the Catholic Church should remain completely indifferent and ignore the congress. What is happening at this congress is also of great importance to us, at least in today's circumstances. ... If the committee preparing this congress were to offer Catholic observers the opportunity to explain in some way the thinking of the Catholic Church, I think it would be appropriate to seize this opportunity (I think this goes further than what has been allowed in the past: were not observers once nothing more than observers?). If there is a desire on the part of others to hear what the Catholic side thinks, it seems appropriate to us that the Catholic opinion should be expressed. This in itself implies that it is expedient for Catholic observers to be allowed to explain their positions further in a written vote.[53]

---

in the Dumont fonds in the archives of the Istina center, where Montini's reply of Jan 18, 1947 is found.

50 Dumont, "Note sur le mouvement catholique," 8. With regard to the approach to be adopted, the memorandum invited the Holy See to abandon the traditional method, which was aimed at individual conversions and which the French Dominican called "missionary" for this reason, pointing out that it had so far produced "extremely limited results" (3). To this approach, which had always seen the comparison among confessions in terms of confrontation and struggle, and which could therefore only be solved with the triumph of one side over the other, Dumont opposed the possibility of an alternative method, which, "creating a climate of mutual sympathy and trust, would be the only one capable of attracting souls to the truth" (4), and "exerting an impact on the influential circles of the same confessions, in order to awaken in them an evolution capable of leading them progressively to Catholic truth" (5). A new method, then, which Dumont did not hesitate to call "Catholic ecumenism" since, in his opinion, it could not be left to non-Catholics alone "a monopoly of a term which so well expresses the catholicity of the church" (6).

51 Dumont, "Note sur le mouvement catholique," 8.

52 Étienne Fouilloux, *Eugène cardinal Tisserant (1884–1972): Une biographie*, Paris, Desclée de Brouwer, 2011, 203–204, 399 and 417–418.

53 J. de Jong to S. Tromp, Oct 29, 1947, in: ADDF, R.V. 1948, n. 39, b. 1, f. 454. Tromp's letter to de Jong was on Oct, 12.

Encouraged by de Jong's positive opinion, Tromp therefore returned to reiterate that the sending of Catholic observers could not be postponed, but above all he did not renounce asking the cardinal inquisitors to reconsider the possibility of a message from the pope to the participants in the assembly: "Would it not be appropriate for the supreme pontiff ... to address a few words to the congress? ... Many will be grateful, many will perhaps laugh and accuse the pope of hypocrisy. But this also happened to Christ the Lord."[54] On Feb 23, the consultors unanimously approved ("affirmative cum debitis cautelis") Tromp's positions on the question of observers, considering the matter "in a certain sense already prejudged" on the occasion of the previous permission given to Bévenot in 1940 for the Birmingham meetings.[55] As for the action requested of the pontiff, they also considered it opportune, affirming that "the pope, as master of Christianity, should do something on this occasion," but they reiterated their preference for a letter with the same content, addressed rather to the cardinal primate of the Netherlands and accompanied by an appropriate information campaign, to be carried out not only through the local press, but also through "a series of articles to be prepared in the Holy Office and to be published in *L'Osservatore Romano* so that from now on a correct approach to the problem of the union can be given to the public." In order to complement the positions of Tromp with the decisions of the *consulta*, and thus to support them better before the plenary session of the cardinals (which had been rather hesitant the previous time), the consultors asked Josef Grendel at the last moment to add his own *votum* to the dossier to be voted on.[56]

Despite these efforts, however, the feria IV of Mar 10 turned out to be rather controversial: only three cardinals went along with the consultors' vote, while two pronounced a peremptory *non expedire*, both with regard to the observers and the papal letter ("non-Catholics already know Catholic doctrine"), and a sixth preferred to abstain.[57] The decision, therefore, remained in the hands of the pope, who, on the following day in the usual audience with the assessor of the Holy Office, announced:

> Concerning the papal letter: *non expedire* (the Holy Father does not wish, with a document of his own, to enhance the value of the conference, nor to confer on it the prestige that a papal act would give it, by giving it greater attention in the world). As for the observers: *mittantur* [let them be sent], with the precautions taken for the Birmingham meeting. ... But they should not be more than five or six (the Holy Father wants Father Congar to be excluded).[58]

54 Sebastiaan Tromp, "De Congressu oecumenico dissidentium Amstellodami 1948. Votum," Feb 1, 1948, 17, in: ADDF, R.V. 1948, n. 39, b. 1, f. 453.

55 Feria II, Feb 23, 1948, f. 481.

56 "Voto del Rev.mo p. Giuseppe Grendel, S.V.D. consultore," Feb 25, 1948, 12–16, in: ADDF, R.V. 1948, n. 39, b. 1, f. 484. Although he began with the clear statement that "the Catholic Church cannot just ignore the future meeting in Amsterdam," Grendel reiterated the preference for a letter from the pope ("opportune, not to say necessary from a pastoral point of view") to be addressed not to the assembly but to the archbishop of Utrecht, and the need to send observers authorized not by the Holy See but by the *ordinarius loci*, although chosen in agreement with the Holy Office, in order to "avoid anything official, and in general anything that could at least give the appearance of a *de facto* recognition of the congress"; "Voto del Rev.mo p. Giuseppe Grendel, S.V.D. consultore," f. 484.

57 Feria IV, Mar 10, 1948, in: ADDF, R.V. 1948, n. 39, b. 1, f. 483. The three cardinals who voted in favor of the consultors' decision were Marchetti Selvaggiani, Pietro Fumasoni Biondi, and Giuseppe Pizzardo. Nicola Canali abstained, while Raffaele Carlo Rossi and Domenico Jorio voted against it. The latter also drafted a written vote for the pope in which, in addition to requesting that Catholics be sent to Amsterdam as journalists and not as observers, he feared that a papal letter, "however vague and general, ... would be published and misunderstood by the sects and used to the exclusive advantage of the sects themselves, all of which are undoubtedly in bad faith and hostile to Rome, following the example of their leaders Luther, Calvin, etc."; "Voto di S.E. il Card. Jorio," in: ADDF, R.V. 1948, n. 39, b. 1, ff. 490–491.

58 Feria V, Mar 11, 1948, in: ADDF, R.V. 1948, n. 39, b. 1, f. 483. The pope also approved the plan to publish some articles in *L'Osservatore Romano*, as well as a pastoral letter from de Jong in which he recommended that "among

4 The Choice of the Observers and the Torpedoing of (and by) Congar

The decision about the observers to send to Amsterdam was expected to be one of the most challenging issues to be faced as far as Rome's relationship with the WCC was concerned. Tromp had already anticipated this *questio gravissima* in his January *votum* when, in submitting the three names (all Dutch) proposed by de Jong, he pointed out that Geneva already had its own preferences:

> It is clear that the observers must be people who are liked by both sides: the church and the ecumenical congress. Because if the dissidents do not like them, it does not work psychologically; if the church does not like them because they concede too much to their opponents, the dissidents will have false hopes, and the result will be great disillusionment and ultimately aversion to church authority. Certainly, many Catholics now serving the ecumenical cause will be acceptable to the dissidents, but can they be acceptable to the church? ... The observers must be people acceptable to both sides. However, we had the impression that both Congar and Villain had already been chosen by the other side.[59]

It was precisely Congar who, parallel to the examination of the Holy Office, made a move which, in spite of himself, would cause an upheaval in the matter, leading to a reexamination of the decision made on Mar 11. Indeed, on Feb 23, the same day as the consultors' meeting, the French Dominican wrote to Cardinal de Jong informing him that he had been "recently consulted, in a completely unofficial way, by the ecumenical organization of Geneva concerning the presence, desired by this organization, of a certain number of Catholic priests at the congress to be held next August in Amsterdam, that is, the World Council of Churches."[60] Geneva had received "more than 20 requests from Catholic priests" to attend the assembly, so, as Congar himself claimed, the French Dominican was asked to act as an intermediary for the WCC with the Dutch Catholic hierarchy in order to obtain "a list of about ten names" of those who could receive a direct invitation from Geneva.[61]

Real or misunderstood, the choice by the WCC leaders of the author of *Chrétiens désunis*, rather than a local bishop such as Charrière or de Jong, to assist in the negotiations was an unwise decision.[62] Receiving through de Jong Congar's letter in early March, the Holy Office chancellery began its own examination of the appeal. This could only begin with a summary of the precedents concerning the French Dominicans in the archives of the Holy Office, in particular the denunciation by Réginald Garrigou-Lagrange of *Chrétiens désunis* and the entire series Una Sanctam edited by Congar himself for the Éditions du Cerf.[63] At that time several

other things, he should say that no one can go and be an observer without his permission."

59 Tromp, "De Congressu oecumenico," 11 and 14.

60 Y. Congar to J. de Jong, Feb 23, 1948, in: ADDF, R.V. 1948, n. 39, b. 2, f. 956. A copy of the letter is reproduced in "Circa le idee diffuse dal p. Congar OP nella Collezione 'Unam Sanctam' da lui diretta e la Mozione 'Una Sancta': Breve relazione (marzo 1948)," in: ADDF, R.V. 1948, n. 39, b. 1, ff. 486–490, here ff. 487–488. Congar was referring to a conversation that he had with Georges Florovsky: see Congar, *Journal of a Theologian*, 145.

61 Congar to de Jong, Feb 23, 1948 in: ADDF, R.V. 1948, n. 39, b. 2, f. 956.

62 Later, Visser 't Hooft, in an internal WCC document written after the Amsterdam assembly and summarizing the course of the negotiations, denied that Congar had been given such a task of mediation, stating that the Dominican had misunderstood a simple request for suggestions. For details of the negotiations with WCC, see Saretta Marotta, "The Holy See and the Question of Sending Observers to the World Conferences of the International Ecumenical Movement," *JoMaCC* 3, 2024, 195–226.

63 These are the sentences denounced: "In this book we find an idea dear to Möhler, that religious doctrine is a systematization of *the religious experience*, which is itself defined as 'a way of feeling and living the Christian life or of constructing the religious object.' ... There is therefore a tendency to identify the Catholic faith with integral and common religious experience,

Jesuit theologians, including Henri-Marie de Lubac and Bévenot, came to the defense of the volume, and the matter ended with a simple warning and no practical consequences for Congar. However, it was the initial blemish on the Dominican's orthodox standing. The list of ten people drawn up by Congar "to the best of my ability" and submitted to de Jong for selection could therefore be tainted by such suspicions, and even be reason enough for the Holy Office to open a dossier on each of them. Maurice Villain, Bévenot, Willem Hendrik van de Pol, Alphonse Heitz, Vincent-Marie Pollet, Clément Lialine, Joseph Casper, Jean Daniélou, Max Pribilla, Jean Jérôme Hamer, with the addition of Henri Desmettre and Louis Kammerer as reserves, were all names that Congar presented as "Catholic priests who work for the reunion of our separated brothers and whose presence in Amsterdam seems desirable."[64]

De Jong entrusted to van de Pol the task of reviewing Congar's list. Interestingly, van de Pol was one of the three individuals, along with the Jesuit Jan Witte and the Franciscan Peter van Leeuwen, that the cardinal had suggested to Tromp as potential Dutch observers in October 1947. Van de Pol, a former Lutheran pastor who had converted, appreciated Geneva's goodwill in not forcing the Holy See into official contact on the issue, and was convinced that the WCC would then accept all the proposed names without making a selection. However, he did not tolerate the fact that "these observers belong exclusively to that faction known in the ecumenical world as irenic" and claimed that they "should be countered by the other side, less inclined to create illusions, so that the difference between the Catholic position and that of the dissidents be clearly presented."[65] His mistrust focused in particular on Villain, whose theological positions Tromp had already described in his *votum* as "dogmatic minimalism."[66]

Given these recent developments, the secretary of the Holy Office, Francesco Marchetti Selvaggiani, asked the pope to authorize Tromp to travel urgently to the Netherlands to discuss with de Jong and the other local ordinaries all the matters concerning the Amsterdam assembly personally.[67] After a marathon journey of more than 44 hours, an emergency meeting was held in Utrecht on Mar 30, attended by Tromp, Cardinal de Jong, the vicar general of Utrecht Jan Geerdinck, the bishop of Haarlem Johannes Petrus Huibers, and van de Pol. Of these, van de Pol was the most critical of the leaders in Geneva, and in particular of Willem Visser 't Hooft, whom he described as a "satis anti-Catholicum" figure:

> He is a very clever politician, who organizes things so that those who agree with him will be invited and those who disagree with him will be excluded. However, he is not omnipotent in this respect. He will certainly be indignant when he will hear that the request of Father Congar OP has not been accepted. Dr. van de Pol has no doubts that Father Congar's letter was written with the agreement of Dr. Visser 't Hooft, who would welcome Catholic observers, particularly those with an "irenic" approach.[68]

and to say that the conciliar definitions are a *one-sided and hardened* expression of this common, living and rich experience, to which we must always return in order to correct religious experiences that are too limited"; the dossier is in: ADDF, C.L. 1939, n. 15 (italics original). Remarks referring to: Congar, *Chrétiens désunis*, 149. On the effects, see Fouilloux, *Yves Congar*, 79–82.

64 Congar to de Jong, Feb 23, 1948, in: ADDF, R.V. 1948, b. 2, f. 957.

65 W.H. van De Pol to J. de Jong, Feb 25, 1948, letter reproduced in "Circa le idee diffuse," ff. 489–490.

66 "The principle of dogmatic *minimalism* dictates that theological sources must clearly distinguish between what pertains to faith and what does not. Where faith is not concerned, maximum freedom is allowed"; Tromp, "De congressu oecumenico," 12 (italics original).

67 A. Ottaviani to Pius XII, Mar 19, 1948, in: ADDF, R.V. 1948, n. 39, b. 1, f. 506. Having received approval from the pope the following day, Tromp departed on the evening of Mar 23.

68 Sebastiaan Tromp, "Colloquia cum Archiepiscopo Card. De Jong et Ep. Haarlemensi de Congressu

Van de Pol therefore persuaded the group to reject Congar's request and leave the choice of observers to de Jong alone. These could include three foreign names in addition to the three Dutch already chosen by the cardinal, and the group agreed to add Bévenot as an English speaker, Pribilla as a German speaker, and a Dominican, whose name could have been suggested by the father general Manuel Suárez Fernández himself, as a French speaker.[69] On Apr 6, the vicar of Utrecht then informed Congar of the negative outcome of his request, and asked him at the same time to inform Geneva that de Jong would use van de Pol's mediation instead of his own.

On his return to Rome, Tromp summarized the results of his journey in a report written on Apr 11 and submitted it to two other consultors, the Germans Josef Grendel and Franz Hürth. While the former had nothing to add, the latter, the moralist author of the encyclical *Casti connubi*,[70] raised serious doubts about Pribilla's name, which had nevertheless met with Grendel's warm approval.[71] Hürth also urged caution with regard to the plans for both a joint pastoral letter from the Dutch episcopate on the ecumenical theme and a response to the participants in the Amsterdam congress, should its leaders address a message to one of the local bishops: although de Jong and Huibers had discussed the two texts extensively and had agreed on a content grid, the German Jesuit recommended that they should not be sent unless a serious need arose in the course of time. Without passing through the consultors' meeting, the three reports by Tromp, Grendel, and Hürth went directly to the cardinals in feria IV, who, on Apr 21, 1948 and again on May 12 approved the first two without objection, except for indicating that they needed to hear the opinion of the first commissioner of the Holy Office, the Dominican Mariano Cordovani, about the identification of the French observer. However, it was the pope who, in both feria V which were to ratify these decisions, decided to adapt himself to the minority report, namely the one from Franz Hürth: on Apr 22, with regard to the two episcopal letters to be addressed to the faithful and to the congress, he specified that they should be sent "if and insofar as necessary. [It is better] to make as little noise as possible, in order not to contribute to highlighting the event (*iuxta votum Hurth*)"; on May 13, instead, he imposed the substitution of Pribilla's name for another observer of German nationality, to be identified for that purpose.[72] Shortly afterwards, becoming increasingly convinced by Hürth's theses, which called for the WCC assembly to be ignored as he foresaw a strong anti-Catholic outcome, the pope reversed this decision again, stating that he was "indeed of the opinion that the number of observers, instead of ***six*** as proposed in Fr. Tromp's report, should be reduced to *three*, if that is possible."[73]

Amstellodanensi," in: ADDF, R.V. 1948, n. 39, b. 1, ff. 570–576, here f. 571.

69 As for the French name, "it was decided not to consult the cardinal archbishop of Paris [Emmanuel Suchard] on the matter, as he was considered too close to irenic tendencies"; Tromp, "Colloquia cum Archiepiscopo," f. 572.

70 See Lucia Pozzi, "La Chiesa cattolica e la sessualità coniugale: L'enciclica *Casti connubii*," *Contemporanea. Rivista di storia dell'"800 e del '900* 3, 2014, 387–412 and Matthias Daufratshofer, *Das päpstliche Lehramt auf dem Prüfstand der Geschichte: Franz Hürth SJ als "Holy Ghostwriter" von Pius XI. und Pius XII.*, Freiburg i.Br., Herder, 2021.

71 Hürth accused Pribilla of being "too irenicus" and of a non-crystalline orthodoxy, probably because he was "born of a mixed marriage": "Est nimis 'irenicus'; est ortus ex matrimonio mixto, inde multa 'imponderabilia,' quae catholico non indigent ulteriore probatione, ipsum latent." The two vota of Grendel and Hürth, dated Apr 16 and 17 respectively, are found in: ADDF, R.V. 1948, n. 39, b. 1, ff. 587–589.

72 Feria V, Apr 22, 1948, in: ADDF, R.V. 1948, n. 39, b. 1, f. 590 and feria V, May 13, 1948, in: ADDF, R.V. 1948, n. 39, b. 1, f. 603. Feria VI and V, held in May, should have been limited to the simple approval of the letter for de Jong that Tromp had prepared in accordance with the decisions of Apr 21 and 22, in which he was to give the cardinal instructions for the assembly in Amsterdam, including the names of the six observers.

73 This is stated in the Holy Office's "Relazione" prepared on May 15, 1948, for feria IV on May 26, 1948, in: ADDF, R.V. 1948, n. 39, b. 1, ff. 615–619 (italics original).

These decisions had not yet been implemented when a memorandum sent by van de Pol to Tromp on May 10 changed the picture once again and definitively. As agreed, the Dutch convert had contacted Geneva (through his Protestant compatriot, Dr. Hendrik van der Linde, who was also close to conversion) to send the list of observers, whom it was Geneva's task to invite in a personal capacity, since the ecclesiastical authority could not send them officially on its own initiative. The response from Geneva was sharp:

> The list of observers given to archbishop [de Jong] by Father Congar is only one of the lists. The Ecumenical Council does not intend to invite all the people indicated by Father Congar, but to make a selection from all the lists, namely *ten people*. Since the Catholic Church does not officially indicate either representatives or observers, the choice of observers depends on Geneva. However, if it were officially communicated that a certain person would certainly not be accepted by the Catholic ecclesiastical authority, or, conversely, that such a person, who is very expert in ecumenical matters, would be welcomed by the Catholic Church, Geneva would take such a communication into account. The Ecumenical Council would not wish to invite as observers anyone other than those who have extensive experience in such matters, thanks either to studies of great importance or to ecumenical meetings.[74]

Geneva also made it clear, with reference to the Dutch candidates, that three observers of the same nationality could not be appointed and therefore only one could be accepted. At the same time, the WCC made it clear that it would be impossible for it to turn down requests for invitations from Catholics "with whom we have had a relationship of cooperation for many years," especially if such requests were made at the request of Catholic bishops or cardinals, "as has already happened in some cases."[75]

Such an answer from van der Linde was the death knell for the issue of sending observers, as Tromp well summed up:

> The opposition between Geneva and the Holy Office (by papal decree) is clear. The Holy Office wants no more than six observers, Geneva ten. The Holy Office wants three Dutch, Geneva only one. The pope does not want the observers to go as observers of the Catholic Church, but only as private persons, so he reserves the final decision on the appointment of observers by the other side for himself; Geneva claims the final decision for itself and wants to invite its own friends before the others, leaving it to the hatred of the Catholic Church to exclude almost publicly those friends who may have been recommended by a bishop or a cardinal.[76]

Van de Pol's proposal to inform Geneva that neither Congar nor Villain were *personas gratas* for Rome was impracticable for Tromp: "In fact, such a refusal would become public knowledge, and then not only would the note of exclusion be published, but also, if it were true that they had been approved by a bishop or a cardinal, a scandal would ensue." The impossibility for the Holy See to refer to a list defined *a priori* by extrinsic criteria, such as territorial origin, and thus to be forced

74 Willem Hendrik van de Pol, memorandum, May 13, 1948, in: ADDF, R.V. 1948, n. 39, b. 1, f. 605, summarizing what van der Linde had told him (italics original). The correspondence between van der Linde and Visser 't Hooft, which took place between April and May 1948, can be found in: WCCA, box 4201.1.2, dossier 3: Roman Catholic observers at the WCC assembly Amsterdam 1948, ff. 8–28. In particular, van de Pol's memorandum is based on the letter from Visser 't Hooft to van der Linde of Apr 30, 1948, in: WCCA, box 4201.1.2, dossier 3, ff. 10–11. On the correspondence between them, see Marotta, "The Holy See and the Question of Sending Observers," 208–209.

75 Van de Pol, memorandum.

76 Sebastiaan Tromp, "Nota," n.d., in: ADDF, R.V. 1948, n. 39, b. 1, f. 606.

into the embarrassment of expressing preferences and commenting on each candidate's theological qualities, quickly and ruinously led to the wreckage of the hypothesis of a Catholic presence in Amsterdam, as Tromp bitterly concluded, seeing no possibility of compromise: "There is nothing left to do but to choose: *either* to forbid the participation of Catholics altogether, ***or*** to send official observers, excluding all others."[77]

On May 24, 1948, the Holy Office consultors met again, for the first time since Congar's intervention and Tromp's subsequent trip, to pronounce a definitive word on the question of the Amsterdam assembly. Impressed by van der Linde's communications, through which it had become "self-evident that the organizers of the congress want to compromise the Holy See," they had become convinced of the need to "curb the exhibitionism of many Catholics," who included, as we shall see, not only Congar and Villain. Their resolutions, therefore, merely embodied a foreseen tragedy:

> To publish in *L'Osservatore Romano*, and then in the AAS, an official statement recalling the provision of canon 1325 which prohibits the intervention of Catholics in such congresses without the permission of the Holy See. This publication should be followed by an article or series of articles commenting on it. To write to Em. card. archbishop of Utrecht, so that in the meantime he may select some competent people who, without the title of observers, will follow the work of the congress as best as they can and who will be ready to answer and explain it in the Catholic press. The consultors also believe that it is appropriate to propose to the Holy Father that he write a document directly to clarify the Catholic position on the unity of the church.[78]

Due to time constraints, these resolutions were discussed by the cardinals at feria IV two days later, who, even more cautiously, rejected the third proposal, called for caution with regard to the second, and only confirmed the first point: "To propose a pontifical document which, starting from the fact of the Una Sancta, also deals with ecumenical congresses and also recalls the provision of canon 1325."[79] While a group of consultors led by Hürth drew up a draft declaration, the papal instructions arrived on Jun 3, approving the text.[80] The publication of what was to become the *Monitum Cum compertum* was thus finalized, and was communicated to de Jong in a letter of Jun 18 that left no room for any vestige of hope:

> First of all, we have thought it opportune to send you a copy of this supreme pontiff's *Monitum*, published in *L'Osservatore Romano* on Jun 6, 1948. … It is clear from the above *Monitum* that the question of sending Catholic observers to the Amsterdam congress has been resolved, and with a changed opinion: in order to participate in the congress, the express and prior authorization of the Holy See is indeed required.
>
> I inform you, however, that the Apostolic See will not grant this permission to anyone.[81]

77 Tromp, "Nota," f. 606 (italics original).

78 Feria II, May 24, 1948, in: ADDF, R.V. 1948, n. 39, b. 1, f. 614.

79 Feria IV, May 26, 1948, in: ADDF, R.V. 1948, n. 39, b. 1, f. 622.

80 Feria V, Jun 3, 1948, in: ADDF, R.V. 1948, n. 39, b. 1, f. 622. A first draft was prepared by Hürth on the morning of May 29, and corrected in the afternoon into a "schema reformatum'" with the help of Tromp and Joseph Creusen. On Jun 1, another version, the "schema denuo reformatum," was prepared with the help of Grendel. The schemas can be found in: ADDF, R.V. 1948, n. 39, b. 1, ff. 623 and 701–707.

81 F. Marchetti Selvaggiani to J. de Jong, Jun 18, 1948, in: ADDF, R.V. 1948, n. 39, b. 1, ff. 741–742. However, some representatives of the Catholic Church managed to attend the conference in the more discreet role of "journalists," under the supervision of Tromp, who had also been sent to the Dutch capital on the pretext of an academic conference. Among the Catholic journalists were Charles Boyer, Maurice Villain, and Jan Witte. See Fouilloux, *Les catholiques et l'unité*,

5 The *Monitum Cum compertum*: The Concurrent Guilt of German Catholic Ecumenism

For a long time it was felt that the *Monitum* of the Holy Office of Jun 5, 1948[82] constituted a clear and definitive response to the invitation of Catholic observers to Amsterdam and that it was drafted for that reason. Of these two statements, however, only the first is entirely true.

It is true that, from the *Monitum* onwards, all the negotiations then underway between bishops and theologians who wished to be sent to interconfessional initiatives (first and foremost the negotiations concerning Amsterdam) had to pass through Rome and were thus subject to the supervision of the Roman curia.[83] Hence, although canon 1325 recalled by *Cum Compertum*, provided for the possibility that in cases of urgency the special permission required by Catholics for such activities could be given by the local ordinary, in derogation of the pontifical one, a specific paragraph of the *Monitum*, added at the express wish of the pope, made it clear that in the case of "so-called ecumenical meetings" lay people and clerics "could not participate in any way without the prior consent of the Holy See."[84] However, the text of the *Monitum* also implied other norms that went beyond the dictates of the Code of Canon Law and constituted an overinterpretation of it. For example, the fact that if participation was forbidden, it was "much less licit for Catholics to summon and institute such kind of gatherings."[85] This clarification, together with the other two canons cited by the *Monitum*, canons 731 and 1258, which excluded common liturgies and forms of *communicatio in sacris*, seemed to have little to do with the WCC assembly. A report from the Holy Office chancellery in November 1948, summarizing the interpretative debate provoked by the *Monitum*, makes it clear that it was not written solely or even primarily with the Amsterdam appointment in mind: "However, the *Monitum* was also (or mainly) provoked by the custom that had become widespread, especially in Germany and France, of holding mixed conferences and sometimes even mixed liturgies. … Many of these conferences were promoted by those movements that have the name of Una Sancta."[86] Moreover, even the first version of the text preserved in the archives of the Holy Office had been conceived with a more explicit formulation:

> The Apostolic See is well aware of the care and skill of those, both ecclesiastics and lay faithful, who encouraged and exhorted by the letter of the encyclical *Mortalium animos*, have committed themselves, through prayer, study, and other appropriate means, to the task of recalling all non-Catholics to the integrity of the faith and to the unity of the church. This in no way conceals

793–796 and Congar, *Journal d'un théologien*, 143–153. On the assembly held from Aug 22 to Sep 4, 1948, which brought together 351 delegates from 147 churches, see Willem Adolf Visser 't Hooft, "The Genesis of the World Council of Churches," in: *A History of the Ecumenical Movement*, vol. 1, Ruth Rouse & Stephen C. Neill, eds., *1517–1948*, London, SPCK, 1954, 695–724.

82 Published in *L'Osservatore Romano*, Jun 6, 1948. Text also in SO, "Monitum Cum Compertum," *AAS* 40, 1948, 257.

83 As a result, while taking care to specify that it was a generally negative orientation and not dependent on the requirements of each candidate (As Bernardini explained to Charrière on the occasion of the rejection of Otto Iserland: "The rejection from Rome has nothing personal and is motivated by general reasons"; letter of 21.7.1948, in: AAV, Arch. Nunz. Switzerland, b. 159, fasc. 438, f. 180), the requests of the followings were handed over to Rome and systematically rejected Iserland, Villain, Desmettre, Pollet, Lialine, Congar, Witte, van de Pol and even Boyer, although he was recommended by Montini in July 1948; see ADDF, R.V. 1948, n. 39, b. 1, ff. 750ff.

84 SO, "Monitum Cum compertum." The pope had in fact asked that the text be amended by inserting a "reference to the permission which the Holy See must give to anyone who wishes to participate in both reserved and 'ecumenical' meetings"; feria V, Jun 3, 1948, in: ADDF, R.V. 1948, n. 39, b. 1, f. 622.

85 SO, "Monitum Cum compertum."

86 SO, "Circa un'interpretazione data al *Monitum* del Sant'Uffcio del 6 giugno 1948: Breve relazione (ottobre 1948)," Nov 24, 1948, in: ADDF, R.V. 1948, n. 39, b. 2, ff. 802–805.

> the merits of the "movement" called "Una Sancta." In recent times, however, some people in various places, driven by an excessive zeal (in their actions), have transgressed the limits properly established by the norms of the sacred canons and other prescriptions of the Apostolic See. Not infrequently they have participated, without legitimate authorization, in mixed meetings and gatherings of non-Catholics with Catholics. Sometimes this has gone so far as to violate the canonical prohibitions on *communio in sacris* with non-Catholics. Therefore, it seems appropriate to the most Eminent and Reverend Fathers to remind all the clergy and faithful of their duty to observe what is prescribed in this matter, especially in canons 1325 § 3 and 1258: matters that must certainly be observed also with regard to the assembly of non-Catholics to be held this year in Amsterdam, in which Catholics must not participate in any way.[87]

Thus, while the negotiations between the see of Utrecht and the WCC on the sending of observers were becoming increasingly intense and complicated, another issue had become entangled in the examination of the Holy Office, which, even more than the Prévost affair, contributed to the pessimism of the consultors and cardinals on ecumenical issues. This was perhaps the final reason why they felt the need to "curb the exhibitionism" of many Catholic ecumenists.

On Mar 15, indeed, the consultors had met to discuss a report presented by the German Jesuit Wilhelm Hentrich, who had studied and summarized a series of episodes and situations reported to the Holy Office in recent months concerning the activities of interconfessional dialogues promoted by Catholics.[88] In April 1947, the Benedictine Gregor Paletta had been denounced by a German layman (who had read the news in the newspapers) for having presided in Hannover, on the occasion of the Week of Prayer for Christian Unity in January, together with the Lutheran pastor Gerhard Kunze (who was also a liturgist), over a joint liturgical service of Catholics and Protestants, which had not been limited to the exchange of sermons, but had also included the recitation of Gregorian and Lutheran hymns and vespers.[89] Following this denunciation, Hentrich's investigations on behalf of the Holy Office had brought to light a whole series of similar occurrences,[90] some of which far more serious, such as the celebration of a Catholic Mass and a Protestant Lord's Supper at the same time in a Capuchin monastery in Stans, Switzerland, in July 1947, an event in the preparation of which the former Jesuit Otto Karrer, who had already been condemned by the Holy Office in 1942 for a book he had written,[91] had played a role. The reports collected by Hentrich covered the entire German territory and involved various priests and religious, but beyond the geographical distances they had as a common denominator a single matrix, namely the ecumenical movement Una Sancta, founded by the Catholic priest Max Josef Metzger, a martyr of the Nazis.[92] The size and pervasiveness of the Una Sancta movement had also been brought to the attention of the Holy Office by a detailed report submitted at the end of 1947 by the bishop of Mainz, Albert

87 "Primo progetto discusso e cambiato nella Consulta Patrum del 30.5.1948," in: ADDF, R.V. 1948, n. 39, b. 1, f. 623.

88 Wilhelm Hentrich, "Germania: De functionibus liturgicis a catholicis et acatholicis communiter peractis et de motione quae 'Una Sancta' appellatur. Votum," Feb 20, 1948, in: ADDF, R.V. 1948, n. 39, b. 1, f. 522.

89 The denunciation made by Heinrich Thönnissen on Apr 11, 1947 can be found in: ADDF, R.V. 1948, n. 30, f. 4. In this dossier other information from Germany was gradually collected, including reports from Albert Stohr.

90 The dossier collecting these cases is in: ADDF, R.V. 1948, n. 40.

91 Otto Karrer, *Gebet, Vorsehung, Wunder: Ein Gespräch*, Lucerne, Räber & Cie, 1941. See Liselotte Höfer & Victor Conzemius, *Otto Karrer: Kämpfen und Leiden für eine weltoffene Kirche*, Freiburg i.Br., Herder, 1985, 161–184.

92 Leonard Swidler, *Bloodwitness for Peace and Unity: The Life of Max Josef Metzger*, Philadelphia, Ecumenical Press, 1977; Jörg Ernesti, *Ökumene im Dritten Reich*, Paderborn, Bonifatius, 2007.

Stohr, who wished to make the Holy See aware of the question of the conversion of Lutheran pastors, opening up the future possibility of ordaining them to the Catholic priesthood despite being married, and of allowing those of them who were theologians to continue teaching in Catholic faculties.[93] Stohr had mentioned in his report the presence of hundreds of Una Sancta circles, whose activities he admitted were difficult to monitor. After Metzger's death, the movement was coordinated by his successor, Matthias Laros, who had also ended up on the Index Librorum Prohibitorum in 1942 for one of his works.[94] Laros himself was mentioned several times in Hentrich's report, particularly for his *Una Sancta Rundbriefe*, the bulletin addressed to the movement's sympathizers, in which he had, among other things, reserved words of praise for the numerous letters addressed to him by imprisoned soldiers, in which they levelled strong accusations against both Catholic and Protestant clergy concerning the prohibition of *communicatio in sacris*: "Is not this difference [between Protestant consubstantiation and Catholic transubstantiation] in reality nothing more than an opposition between human theories?,"[95] wrote one of them in a letter, to which Laros offered a considerable forum for debate by publishing it in the bulletin. In this regard, Laros had also cited as a virtuous example the case of a military chaplain who, in a concentration camp in the Urals, and owing to such a state of emergency, had celebrated a common Mass at Easter for 300 Catholic and 80 Protestant prisoners, also permitting the latter access to the sacrament of the Eucharist and receiving "approval post factum from the ecclesiastical authority."[96] Such publications by Laros, aimed at a large public (the bulletin was printed in tens of thousands of copies), could not but alarm the Roman authorities. On Mar 15, 1948, the Holy Office consultors therefore unanimously decided "to order, through the ordinaries, the priests Karrer and Laros to cease their activities with regard to the 'Una Sancta' movement since they were not suitable subjects for such a movement" and "to ask for detailed information and reports from the archbishop of Paderborn and from the three cardinals who will soon be coming to Rome."[97] In fact, the following months the first postwar *ad limina* visit of German bishops was to take place, and the first to go to Rome in April 1948 were the three German cardinals Josef Frings (Cologne), Michael von Faulhaber (Munich), and Konrad von Preysing (Berlin).[98] At the

93 I discuss this issue in more detail in Saretta Marotta, *Gli anni della pazienza: Bea, l'ecumenismo e il Sant'Uffizio di Pio XII*, Bologna, Il Mulino, 2019, 149–167.

94 Matthias Laros, *Das christliche Gewissen in der Entscheidung: Ein Werkbuch für religiöse Gemeinschaftsarbeit*, Cologne, Lahn, 1940. See Jörg Seiler, ed., *Matthias Laros (1882–1965): Kirchenreform im Geiste Newmans*, Regensburg, Pustet, 2009. On the Una Sancta movement under Laros' leadership see Saretta Marotta, "Ökumene von unten': Augustin Bea di fronte alle attività del movimento Una Sancta," *CrSt* 37/3, 2016, 541–611.

95 *Una Sancta Rundbriefe* 5, Nov 6, 1947.

96 *Una Sancta Rundbriefe* 5, Nov 6, 1947.

97 Feria II, Mar 15, 1948, in: ADDF, R.V. 1948, n. 39, b. 1, f. 521. The same more "precise information" was requested from the apostolic nunciature in Bern. The cardinals ratified the decision of feria IV on Apr 7, 1948 and decided, among other things, to "send Fr. Grendel to Germany to collect information"; minutes in: ADDF, R.V. 1948, n. 30, f. 73v. However, the removal of Karrer and Laros was postponed for the time being at the instigation of Grendel, who suggested that the respective bishops be recommended to implement practices of gradual marginalization: "It is imperative that both be removed from their positions as leaders of the organizations in question. But, as it seems to me, this must be done in the most discreet and unnoticed way, so that no harm is done. ... It seems to me that, before taking any action against him [Laros], it would be wise first to obtain information about everything, and especially of the best way to remove him, with the competent bishops"; J. Grendel to A. Ottaviani, Mar 15, 1948, in: ADDF, R.V. 1948, n. 39, b. 1, ff. 524–525. If it was not necessary to take other measures in the case of Karrer, this would not have been enough for Laros, for whom the Holy Office decided in January 1949 to remove him "ex auctoritate Sanctae Sedis," as Marchetti Selvaggiani informed the bishop of Trier, Franz Rudolf Bornewasser, on Jan 26, 1949 (ADDF, R.V. 1948, n. 39, b. 2, f. 1043).

98 On the contents of the *ad limina* reports of the German bishops in 1948, see Saretta Marotta, "Looking for Traces of the Ecumenical Question in the *relationes ad*

suggestion of the consultor Josef Grendel,[99] the archbishop of Paderborn, Lorenz Jaeger, who was responsible for the ecumenical commission within the Fulda bishops' conference, was added to the list, bringing forward his own trip by a few months.[100] Therefore, while a list of questions suggested by the pope was being prepared for the three cardinals to be interviewed,[101] and while Grendel himself was being sent to Germany with the same *interrogatorium* in hand to gather information,[102] Lorenz Jaeger was asked to prepare a detailed report on the ecumenical work in Germany over the past few years. Jaeger carried out his task and presented a comprehensive report on the state of the dialogue between Catholics and Protestants in Germany since 1945 at the pope's audience on Apr 16.[103] While the Holy Office consultors was ratifying the results of Tromp's trip to Holland on Apr 21 by deciding to send Bévenot, Pribilla, and a French Dominican as observers, Tromp was studying the Jaeger report. However, the Dutch Jesuit found the document lacking in information about the Una Sancta movement itself, but rather concentrated on giving an overall picture of the relations between the local and national hierarchies of the German Evangelical Church at the time, and thus on the reasons that drove some of its exponents, including some rather important ones (such as Hans Asmussen, president of the national council of the EKD and author, together with Martin Niemöller and Otto Dibelius, of the Stuttgart Declaration of Guilt),[104] to seek a dialogue with the Catholic Church. For Tromp, however, while considering theological discussions with such exponents useful if properly conducted, the hope nurtured by Jaeger and many other German bishops like Stohr that the internal divisions within Protestantism could lead to mass conversion was illusory. Indeed, even the archbishop of Paderborn concluded his report by calling for a decision by the Holy See on the question of the admission of married priests to the priesthood, who, in his view, could be the key to bringing the German Protestant Church closer to Rome, since they often brought whole communities with them to the Catholic Church at the time of their conversion. While Tromp was sympathetic to the problem of converted pastors and invited the Holy Office to open up the possibility of discussion and decision on a case-by-case basis, he remained very alarmed by what Jaeger's report revealed in the

---

limina of the German Bishops (1948–58)," *JoMaCC* 1/2, 2022, 343–368.

99 J. Grendel to A. Ottaviani, Mar 15, 1948, in: ADDF, R.V. 1948, n. 30, ff. 67–68.

100 See the minutes of the plenary session of Aug 17–19, 1943, in: Ludwig Volk, *Akten deutscher Bischöfe über die Lage der Kirche (1933–1945)*, vol. 6, *1943–1945*, Mainz, Matthias-Grünewald, 1985, 133–146, esp. 144. See also Aloys Klein, "Es begann mit der Una-Sancta-Bewegung: Die Fuldaer Bischofskonferenz in Verantwortung für die Einheit im Glauben," in: Josef Ernst & Stephan Leimgruber, eds., *Surrexit Dominus vere: Die Gegenwart des Auferstandenen in seiner Kirche. Festschrift für Erzbischof Dr. Johannes Joachim Degenhardt*, Paderborn, Bonifatius, 1995, 329–340; Wolfgang Thönissen, "Einheit und Erneuerung: Lorenz Kardinal Jaeger als Vorreiter der ökumenischen Idee in Deutschland," *ThGl* 94, 2004, 300–313.

101 "Interrogatorium ad obtinendas certas de rerum condicione informationes," Apr 22, 1948, in: ASRS, AAEESS, periodo V, parte I, Germania, pos. 899, ff. 3–4. The questionary was to better supplement the information already given with the *relationes ad limina*, which were based on an obsolete form from 1918.

102 Feria IV, Apr 7, 1948, in: ADDF, R.V. 1948, n. 30, f. 73: "Send Father Grendel to Germany to gather information."

103 Lorenz Jaeger, "Bericht über den Stand der Aussprache zwischen Katholiken und Protestanten in Deutschland seit 1945," in: ADDF, R.V. 1948, n. 39, b. 7, vol. 4, ff. 5–34. It is possible that the idea of Jaeger submitting a written report came from consultor Alois Hudal, who suggested taking advantage of the archbishop's presence in Rome to obtain information that would adequately supplement the *relationes ad limina*, complaining that "in their present form the five-year reports no longer correspond to the modern demands of life. Too much time elapses before the conclusions become reality and perhaps even exceed the scope of the consistorial congregation"; A. Hudal to A. Ottaviani, Mar 27, 1948, in: ADDF, R.V. 1948, n. 39, b. 7, f. 11.

104 Gerhard Besier & Gerhard Sauter, *Wie Christen ihre Schuld bekennen: Die Stuttgarter Erklärung 1945*, Göttingen, Vandenhoeck & Ruprecht, 1985; Wolfgang Lehmann, *Hans Asmussen: Ein Leben für die Kirche*, Göttingen, Vandenhoeck & Ruprecht, 1988.

background, namely the growth of experiences of interconfessional dialogue, mostly outside the control of the church. "The Una Sancta movement, which has spread all over Germany, shows that canon 1325 § 3 has apparently no longer been applied since Pius XII."[105] This had been denounced in an article by a Protestant journalist (Horst Michael, who would convert to Catholicism in 1950), which Jaeger had included among the appendices to his report, and from which Tromp concluded that: "Many conversations take place completely independently of the bishops. … There is therefore no doubt that many things are said in such conversations which cannot be approved: therefore, they are very dangerous"; that although "some conversations or meetings take place with the knowledge of the bishops," one could not be sure that even these were immune from "a certain tendency called 'the progressive assimilation of Catholic and Protestant dogmas.'"[106] Although Tromp's *votum* bears the date of Jun 2, when it was probably returned to Ottaviani, the reading of Jaeger's report had direct consequences on the final wording of the text of the *Monitum*. As Tromp himself admitted, "in the new version of the *Monitum*, the Una Sancta is not explicitly mentioned, since by this name is meant not only the apostate association of [Friedrich] Heiler and the even less commendable movement of Mr. Laros,"[107] but also a whole series of initiatives under the protection of bishops or religious orders such as the Benedictines, whose advantages Jaeger had well highlighted in his own report.[108] On the other hand, Jaeger's report had confirmed to the consultor that "there is no reason to remove from the *Monitum* the prohibition of discussions with Protestants on theological questions. On the contrary, there is a serious reason to maintain it."[109] However, the inclusion of the phrase "sine praevia Sanctae Sedis venia" (without the prior permission of the Holy See) in Tromp's explanations should have "made it clear that such talks can take place if they were properly conducted under ecclesiastical supervision."[110] Thus the same phrase that removed all hope for the would-be observers at the Amsterdam conference that the authorization of their local bishop would suffice, should in Germany have reassured the episcopal hierarchy that they could easily obtain the approval of the Holy See for the ecumenical initiatives they promoted, since it was precisely the ecclesiastical authorization that distinguished these activities from the uncontrolled Una Sancta movement. Or at least that was the interpretation Jaeger almost took for granted when, a few days after the appearance of the *Monitum*, he telegraphed Grendel in Rome to ask for confirmation of permission to hold not only the fifth conference of the specialist working group of Catholic and Protestant theologians, which he had sponsored and which was scheduled for that July, but also the annual congress of the Una Sancta movement which was to be held shortly afterwards, from Aug 26 to 29, in Seeshaupt near Munich.[111] Unexpectedly, and to the surprise of even the non-Catholics involved in these meetings,[112] the pope, in an audience with

105 "Eine Anknüpfung an 'Mortalium Animos' ist nicht geraten so wenig wie an Can. 1325 Par. 3., der Religionsgespräche mit Andersgläubigen untersagt. Die ausgebreitete Una-Sancta-Bewegung in Deutschland zeigt, dass dieser Canon seit Pius XII offensichtlich nicht mehr angewendet wird"; *Anlagen zum Bericht uber den stand der Aussprache zwischen Katholiken und Protestanten in Deutschland seit 1945*, in: ADDF, R.V. 1948, n. 39, b. 7, vol. IV, ff. 35 ss, annex no. 17.

106 Sebastiaan Tromp, "De Relatione Archiepiscopi paderbornensi de contactu mutuo inter protestantes et Catholicos Germaniae inde a 1945," Jun 2, 1948, in: ADDF, R.V. 1948, n. 39, b. 1, ff. 708–710, here 709.

107 Tromp, "De Relatione," f. 710.

108 About the work of Emmanuel Maria Heufelder and the Benedictine monastery of Niederaltaich see Marotta, "Ökumene von unten'."

109 Tromp, "De Relatione," f. 710.

110 Tromp, "De Relatione," f. 710.

111 J. Höfer to J. Grendel, telegram, Jun 15, 1948, in: ADDF, R.V. 1948, n. 39, b. 7, vol. 2, f. 14.

112 "Already on Jun 22, Prof. Dr. Höfer, rector of the archbishop's seminary in Bad Driburg, who is making the technical preparations for our conference on behalf of the archbishop of Paderborn, was able to inform all the participants in the previous meeting, together with the

the Holy Office assessor on Jun 17, approved both appointments, limiting himself to recommending "serious vigilance direction so that there are no doctrinal encroachments" and to make a detailed report later.[113] This only added to the already devastating disorientation caused by the *Monitum*, which Grendel himself had highlighted in his report after returning from the mission in Germany.[114]

authentic text of this decree [the *Monitum*], that our conference had already been expressly authorized by the Holy Office on Jun 18. … Prof. Höfer reported again how the German bishops themselves were greatly surprised by the issuing of this *Monitum* and with what remarkable speed, within three days, the request sent by telegram to Rome was answered by express permission to our conference"; W. Stählin to T. Wurm, Oct 2, 1948, in: Barbara Schwahn, *Der Ökumenische Arbeitskreis evangelischer und katholischer Theologen von 1946 bis 1975*, Göttingen, Vandenhoeck & Ruprecht, 1996, 64–65. Given the presence of Grendel in Germany at that time on behalf of the Holy Office (his departure from Rome, delayed by several months due to problems with travel permits, took place on Jul 5), the hypothesis I have put forward that he was the "man from Rome, who happened to be in Bad Driburg, and who has constant access to the same pope" whom Stählin, in the same letter, reports meeting during a conversation with Höfer in Bad Driburg on Jul 16, is therefore more than plausible: see Marotta, *Gli anni della pazienza*, 112–113.

113 Feria v, Jun 17, 1948, in: ADDF, R.V. 1948, n. 39, b. 7, vol. 2, f. 17. This decision was not without Grendel's intercession. In his letter to Ottaviani, Grendel warned: "If these two meetings were cancelled, not only would there be great embarrassment, but the impression would be created, unjustified in itself but certainly inevitable for non-Catholics, that the Holy See would forbid any such contact in the future"; J. Grendel to A. Ottaviani, Jun 16, 1948, in: ADDF, R.V. 1948, n. 39, b. 7, vol. 2, ff. 15–17. The report from November 1948, on the other hand, reveals that Hürth was completely against this: see SO, "Circa un'interpretazione."

114 Josef Grendel, "De motione Una Sancta in regionibus Europae centralis," Nov 30, 1948, 62 pages, esp. 24–26, in: ADDF, R.V. 1948, n. 39, b. 2, f. 991.

6 The *Instructio Ecclesia Catholica*: Directed Yet Again at Germans

In truth, the publication of the *Monitum* should have been accompanied by the appearance in *L'Osservatore Romano* of an explanatory article prepared within the Holy Office by one of the consultors, Msgr. Pietro Parente, and revised by his colleagues Hürth, Tromp, and Grendel. The article would have placed the *Monitum* in context, explaining how it was intended to call to account "some Catholics participating in unionist conferences" who, in the climate of enthusiasm generated by the revival of the international ecumenical movement, "have allowed themselves to go so far as to compromise dogma through doctrinal conciliations, [and] have participated in acts of mixed worship and administration of the sacraments to non-Catholics."[115] Despite the long work of drafting and then correcting the text, at the last moment the pope preferred to block its publication, "wishing to avoid reactions from Protestants"[116] and the text of the *Monitum* thus appeared in *L'Osservatore Romano* in its concise, dry form, which lent itself to multiple interpretations. However, an apparently well-informed German-speaking Vatican Radio announcer, the Jesuit Beat Ambord, had offered an illuminating interpretation of the *Monitum*, identifying German ecumenism as one of its main addressees, and his commentary, broadcast on the radio and then published in the *Neue Zürcher Nachrichten*, circulated quite extensively, being taken up and translated by other magazines,[117] to the point that Grendel (it is not excluded that he himself was the Vatican source quoted in Ambord's article) advised Ottaviani to forward it to the bishops who were asking for an explanation

115 Pietro Parente, "Ecumenismo e cattolicismo," draft, Jun 5, 1948, in: ADDF, R.V. 1948, n. 39, b. 2, ff. 725–729.

116 Feria v, Jun 17, 1948, in: ADDF, R.V. 1948, n. 39, b. 2, f. 735. "His Holiness does not see the point of publishing it, since the *Monitum* is very clear"; D. Tardini to A. Ottaviani, Jun 11, 1948, in: ADDF, R.V. 1948, n. 39, b. 2, f. 723.

117 For instance, *The Tablet*, Jun 12, 1948, 368.

of the *Monitum*:[118] "So it was stated in conclusion: not touched by this decree are the serious religious disputes, which take place in very small or quite small circles, and in which, for example, the differences between the various confessions are clearly studied and reported, and the Catholic point of view is emphasized with regard to the other confessions."[119]

This interpretation, which in essence seemed to limit the scope of the *Monitum* to private initiatives without ecclesiastical approval and to events similar to those in Amsterdam or, in any case, to "public conferences of a certain importance," was widely disseminated in the German-speaking countries and, more generally, in the countries into which the article had been translated, that is England and Holland, which led to the Holy See's indications being ignored once again.[120] This was illustrated by the case of the bishop of Basel, Franz von Streng, who, having obtained in a private audience with the pope the same permission given to Jaeger by telegram in mid-June, began to circulate this reply as an authentic interpretation of the *Monitum*, arousing the indignant reaction of Franz Hürth, who in October 1948 sent an alarmed memorandum to the pope and obtained a meeting of the Holy Office consultors to consider how an official correction could be made.[121]

Hürth's proposal, also supported by Tromp and Hentrich, who argued that a note should appear in *L'Osservatore Romano* stating that "a permission given or to be given by the Holy See in a particular case does not, as it is clear, constitute an interpretation of the decree,"[122] had to face the calm but tenacious opposition of Grendel, who, in the light of what he had observed during his recent trip to the German-speaking territories the previous July, called for more caution:

> A new public declaration would perhaps disturb the restored calm, and perhaps have harmful effects among the Protestants. … Therefore, in order to avoid any harm, in whatever form it might be feared, it would be good, before proceeding to a public declaration, to make contact with the ordinaries, and perhaps also to make use of them, in accordance with the directives of the Holy See, to bring about a just order in these matters, if this is necessary.[123]

Grendel therefore asked his colleagues in the Holy Office whether, instead of a new public prohibition, "an instruction to the bishops *for internal use*"[124] would not be preferable, which, by remaining confidential, would avoid the risk of deteriorating the already fragile Catholic-Evangelical relations, especially in Germany, where postwar necessities had forced the confessions to share various areas of cooperation, not least the mutual loan of places of worship, where the influx of refugees in 1947 had greatly altered the numerical relevance of religious minorities.[125]

118 "If I may be permitted to add my humble opinion at once, I would observe that, with regard to the clarification of the *Monitum* of Jun 5, one could perhaps privately refer His Excellency the archbishop to an article in the *Christliche Kultur* supplement of the *Neue Zürcher Nachrichten* of Jun 11 which contains a good explanation of the *Monitum* of Jun 5 with regard to its occasion, purpose and meaning"; Grendel to Ottaviani, Jun 16, 1948, ff. 15–16.

119 Beat Ambord, "Moderne Religionsgespräche. Das hl. Officium und die 'Una Sancta-Bewegung,'" NZZ, Jun 11, 1948.

120 SO, "Circa un'interpretazione," f. 803. On this attempt to relativize the scope of the Monitum's prescriptions and the subsequent battle of interpretation in the journals, see Marotta, *Gli anni della pazienza*, 125–126 and Fouilloux, *Les catholiques et l'unité*, 904.

121 Franz Hürth, memorandum, Oct 11, 1948, in: ADDF, R.V. 1948, n. 39, b. 2, ff. 812–814. Ten days later, in feria V, on Oct 21, 1948, the pope asked Ottaviani to deal with the subject in the *consulta*.

122 Wilhelm Hentrich, pro memoria, Oct 12, 1948, in: ADDF, R.V. 1948, n. 39, b. 2, f. 827.

123 Josef Grendel, "Parere: Circa un'interpretazione data al Monitum del Sant'Ufficio del 6 giugno 1948," n.d., in: ADDF, R.V. 1948, n. 39, b. 2, ff. 819–821, here f. 821.

124 Grendel, "Parere: Circa un'interpretazione," f. 821 (italics original).

125 "For example, after the *Monitum* it was feared that the Protestant priests would withdraw their agreement to

Meanwhile, the matter had become intertwined with the petition sent to the pope on Oct 18, 1948 by the bishops of Mainz and Speyer, Albert Stohr and Joseph Wendel respectively, who asked for a special dispensation *ad annum* (on an experimental basis for one year) to be able to continue ecumenical activities under their direct supervision, rather than applying to Rome for permission on a case-by-case basis.[126] At their meeting on Nov 24, the cardinal inquisitors therefore decided on a *pro nunc dilata*, postponing the two questions to a session at which the report on the results of Grendel's mission of the previous July would also be considered.[127] This decision shows how closely the Stohr-Wendel request and the question of the interpretation of the *Monitum* were linked, so much so that the latter seemed to be primarily a German question, though not exclusively so: "The *Instructio* should take into account not only the inconveniences caused [by Catholic ecumenism] in Germany, but also those in other countries where these conferences take place, for example in France, where they go further"; this is what the consultors recommended at their meeting after the Christmas break, on Jan 10, 1949, agreeing with Grendel that it was appropriate to "take the opportunity of the *Instructio* to clarify the scope of the *Monitum*."[128] On Jan 12, the meeting of the cardinals member of the Holy Office approved these decisions, with the significant exception of the last of the six proposals for action approved by the *consulta*, namely the recommendation, considered probably excessive and irrelevant, that "the *Instructio* should make it clear that Protestants who are convinced of the truth of the Catholic Church are obliged to make a formal transfer to it and not to remain in Protestantism on the pretext of better serving the unity of the churches."[129] At the same meeting it was also decided to grant the desired dispensation to Stohr and Wendel (as had already been the case for Jaeger and von Streng), on condition that the bishops would supervise the prohibition of *communicatio in sacris* and send an annual report to the Holy See, a task which Stohr faithfully fulfilled for years.[130] These were, after all, the conditions that would later be laid down in § 4 of the *Instructio Ecclesia Catholica*, the drafting of which was now underway and which, although it would not be published by the Holy Office until eleven months later, on Dec 20, 1949, had already been drafted in March 1949 in a version almost identical to the final one.[131] In the present state of the archival sources, it is not possible to determine with certainty the material authors of the text. However, Grendel certainly seems to be one of them, since he was responsible, among other things, for supervising the stylistic correction of the final text by the Latinists Antonio Bacci and Angelo Perugini of the Secretariat of Brief

use their churches for [Catholic] services. This would have been seriously detrimental to the already difficult task of caring for the souls of the refugees. In one diocese, because it is impossible to find other places that are in any way suitable, services are held in as many as seven hundred Protestant churches"; Grendel, "Parere: Circa un'interpretazione," f. 821. On the phenomenon of the viral spread of the practice of the *simultaneum* in postwar Germany, see Marotta, "Looking for Traces," esp. 354–357.

126 "Itaque petimus ad unum annum facultatem, talibus conventibus ex potestate delegata Sanctae Sedis licentiam praebere"; A. Stohr & J. Wendel to Pius XII, Oct 18, 1948, in: ADDF, R.V. 1948, n. 39, b. 7, f. 1.

127 Feria II, Nov 15, 1948, feria IV, Nov 24, 1948, and feria V, Nov 25, 1948, in: ADDF, R.V. 1948, n. 39, b. 7, f. 12. The voluminous report (over 60 pages) was completed by Grendel during the following week and submitted to the Holy Office chancellery on Nov 30 (see Grendel, "De motione Una Sancta").

128 Feria II, Jan 10, 1949, in: ADDF. R.V. 1948, n. 39, b. 2, f. 1038.

129 Feria IV, Jan 12, 1949, and Feria V, Jan 13, 1949, in: ADDF, R.V. 1948, n. 39, b. 2, f. 1038v. This was also the session that decided to proceed with the definitive removal, *ex auctoritate Sancta Sedis*, of Matthias Laros.

130 F. Marchetti Selvaggiani to A. Stohr, Jan 20, 1949, in: ADDF, R.V. 1948, n. 39, b. 7, f. 15.

131 "Schema instructionis Ordinariis locorum mittendae de Motione Oecumenica et de 'Una Sancta' (marzo 1949)," in: ADDF, R.V. 1948, n. 39, b. 2, ff. 1105–1112. This text already proposed the incipit "ecclesia catholica, etsi," which gave the *Instructio* its name, with an articulation and language very similar to the final text.

to Princes and the Secretariat of Latin Letters, respectively.[132] As mentioned above, it was indeed Grendel, then the clear spokesman for the German demands in the Holy Office, who had insisted, in both October and November 1948, on the idea of a general instruction to the bishops which would obviate the problem of dispensations granted on a case-by-case basis:

> It seems to me that the practice to be followed should at least be the same in all German dioceses. Otherwise there will be confusion. Now the German bishops, as several of them told me, wanted to discuss a uniform procedure together at their conference in Fulda in August this year and then present the result to the Holy See. In the event that it has not yet been presented, before answering the present question [of Stohr and Wendel] … we could perhaps address a request in this regard to the archbishop of Paderborn. This would provide a secure basis for such a uniform regulation in all dioceses.[133]

Furthermore, it was precisely the German bishops (along with the Swiss von Streng) who, in the months following the *Monitum*, had been the only ones to inundate the Holy See with constant and urgent requests for permission to hold interconfessional talks. Jaeger in particular, who was in constant contact with Grendel and probably received useful "encouragement" from him,[134] had proved tireless in this regard: in December he had sent a detailed report on the effects in Germany of the *Monitum* of the Holy Office of Jun 5, 1948, on conversations with Protestants,[135] and in February, despite the permission granted the previous month to Stohr and Wendel, he had continued to ask (often by telegram and also on behalf of other ordinaries) for urgent confirmation of conferences to be held in the months immediately following.[136] But it was in April that he took the most significant step, sending his own trusted theologian, Josef Höfer, to Rome, with the express mission of negotiating with the Holy Office special conditions for the German episcopate that would allow ecumenical activities to continue, delegating to the local ordinaries the faculties of dispensation and supervision in this regard.[137] Höfer, who remained in Rome for several weeks, during which period he met first Pius XII himself and then, on several occasions, the assessor Ottaviani and various

132 The exchange of material between the three, dated May 1949, is in: ADDF, R.V. 1948, n. 39, b. 2, ff. 1129–1138. On the role of Bacci and these secretariats in the drafting of encyclicals and papal texts during the pontificate of Pius XII, see Alejandro Mario Dieguez, "La 'fabbrica' delle encicliche: Il processo redazionale delle encicliche pacelliane e fonti per la sua ricostruzione," *JoMaCC* 3, 2024, 13–98.

133 Josef Grendel, "Parere in merito alla domanda degli Ecc.mi vescovi di Magonza e di Spira," Nov 17, 1948, in: ADDF, R.V. 1948, n. 39, b. 7, vol. 1, ff. 4–5.

134 On the collaboration between Grendel and Jaeger, see Marotta, *Gli anni della pazienza*, 111–141.

135 See Lorenz Jaeger, "Die Auswirkung des Monitums vom 5 Juni 1948," Dec 12, 1948, 12 pages, in: ADDF, R.V. 1948, n. 39, b. 2, f. 1093–1104. However, the text of the report was not sent by the Secretariat of State to the Holy Office until three months later, on Mar 30, 1949, that is when the first draft of the *Instructio* had already been completed (D. Tardini to F. Marchetti Selvaggiani, Mar 30, 1949, in: ASRS, AAEESS, periodo V, parte II, Affari generali, pos. 5, f. 329). Jaeger's report was immediately examined and summarized by Grendel for the congregation (Josef Grendel, note, Apr 10, 1949, in: ADDF, R.V. 1948, n. 39, b. 2, f. 1088–1092).

136 L. Jaeger to A. Ottaviani, Feb 21, 1949, in: ADDF, R.V. 1948, n. 39, b. 7, vol. 2, ff. 24–26, in which he asked for permission both for the next meeting of his *Kreis*, scheduled for Apr 4–7, in Bad Driburg, and for the Braunshardt talks under Stohr's patronage, which were to be held from Mar 24 to 26. The result of the request was positive in both cases (Feria V, Mar 24, 1949, in: ADDF, R.V. 1948, n. 39, b. 7, Vol. II, f. 33). On the Braunshardt circle see Hermann-Josef Braun, "Stohrs praktische Arbeit für die 'Una Sancta,' besonders in der 'Braunshardter Konferenz,'" in: Karl Lehmann, ed., *Dominus fortitudo: Bischof Albert Stohr (1890–1961)*, Würzburg, Echter, 2012, 121–137.

137 L. Jaeger to A. Ottaviani, Apr 9, 1949, in: ADDF, R.V. 1948, n. 39, b. 7, vol. 2, f. 35, published in Marotta, *Gli anni della pazienza*, 533.

consultors,[138] asked the Vatican authorities "not to destroy the efforts under way, but to allow them to develop according to the dispositions of the Holy See," and

> to grant to the Most Excellent ordinaries, in the form of the usual faculties of limited duration, the faculty to authorize, in the name of the Apostolic See, the organization of religious conversations in their own dioceses, while assuming responsibility, in accordance with the directives which they expect in this regard from the Holy See, both for the lecturers and for the other participants, and to report to the Holy See in the regular manner provided. This proposed and requested faculty does not apply to those religious conversations convened on a national or supranational basis.[139]

On May 5, 1949, the pope granted the requested permission, "since these are faculties similar to those contained in the forthcoming publication, *Instructio*."[140] Höfer thus succeeded in obtaining a list of dispensations, which Jaeger hastened to communicate to the plenary assembly of the Fulda conference a few months later, and which were granted by the Holy Office on a provisional basis for 12 months. By the end of the year they were to be confirmed by *Ecclesia Catholica*, which, however, was not published until the spring of the following year, when it appeared in the *Acta Apostolicae Sedis*.[141] Nevertheless, the list was passed to the ordinaries of the whole world well in advance, also in order to incorporate any latest changes, as established by the cardinals of the Holy Office in the session of Jul 27, 1949 and approved by Pius XII the following day: "Ask the Holy Father for permission to show the scheme to the most important bishops of Germany, France, England, and North America."[142]

7 Conclusions

Although dated Dec 20, 1949, the publication of *Ecclesia Catholica* was delayed as long as possible and did not appear in the pages of *L'Osservatore Romano* until Mar 1, 1950.[143] It was feared that it would provoke a reaction in the Catholic and non-Catholic world similar to that which followed the *Monitum Cum compertum*. However, the fact that the text of the new document was made known to the bishops several weeks before its publication gave them time to create quite a positive

138 The meeting with Pacelli took place on May 1, 1949, and that with Ottaviani on two occasions, on Apr 19 and May 6. When asked about the creation of a department or study commission for ecumenism in Rome, Ottaviani replied: "We cannot do it here yet. You have to do it from Germany"; see Josef Höfer, "Das geistliche Profil des Kardinal Bea," *Catholica* 26/1, 1972, 50–62, here 56. Höfer's account of the Roman meetings is in EBAP, Jaeger fond, dossier 18, U.S.-Arbeit.

139 Josef Höfer, "Relazione sul proseguimento dei conventi fra Cattolici e Protestanti in Germania controllati o diretti da Sua Ecc. l'arcivescovo di Paderborn. Proposte per il lavoro futuro," Apr 26, 1949, in: ADDF, R.V. 1948, n. 39, b. 7, vol. 2, ff. 36–44, here f. 44.

140 Feria V, May 5, 1949, in: ADDF, R.V. 1948, n. 39, b. 7, vol. 2, f. 44.

141 SO, "Instructio ad locorum ordinarios 'De motione oecumenica,'" *AAS* 42, 1950, 142–147.

142 Feria IV, Jul 27, 1949, and feria V, Jul 28, 1949, in: ADDF, R.V. 1948, n. 39, b. 2, f. 1196. In the summer indeed the pope authorized "a journey to Germany by Fr. Grendel, at the expense of the Holy Office, to speak about the *Instructio* to the three ordinaries already named (Cologne, Munich, Paderborn) and to others whom he thought it opportune to ask"; audience sheet, Aug 4, 1949, in: ADDF, R.V. 1948, n. 39, b. 2, f. 1158. The final text of the *Instructio* was approved, after the last changes had been made, at the session of feria IV, Nov 16, 1949, in: ADDF, R.V. 1948, n. 39, b. 2, f. 1235.

143 Publication was originally scheduled for Feb 25, 1950, and copies of the *Instructio* had already been sent to the nuncios. But the Secretariat of State had to wait for the go-ahead from the Holy Office: "A few days ago His Holiness told me that Your Excellency had made a remark about the document of the Holy Office which would delay its publication. Has this matter been resolved? Can we go ahead?"; G.B. Montini to D. Tardini, Feb 21, 1950, in: ADDF, R.V. 1948, n. 39, b. 2, f. 1443.

climate of expectation.[144] Even the WCC, while expressing concern that hierarchical oversight might place a heavy burden on contacts that had hitherto developed informally, recognized in the *Instructio* "certainly a document of considerable ecumenical significance ... [which] reveals to what extent the existence of the ecumenical movement has become a challenge in the Roman Catholic Church."[145] In particular, the preamble and the conclusion of the text, whose very title made it clear that the term "ecumenism" would be used even in the Catholic sphere, were surprising because of the undeniable change of tone in which Rome regarded the movement that had given rise to the Geneva institution, recognizing in it the "inspiration of the grace of the Holy Spirit."[146] If those in the Holy Office who considered it to be an authentic interpretation of the *Monitum* of 1948 – in particular to refute certain interpretations that denied its restrictive intention – rushed to offer this reading in commentaries published under their signatures in various journals,[147] it was undeniable that the *Instructio* provided Catholic ecumenists with a basis of rules and methods, a frame of reference on the terms of which they were allowed to continue their commitment. *Ecclesia Catholica* thus became almost a "Magna Charta" for preconciliar Catholic ecumenism, on the basis of whose parameters of tolerance it was able to adjust itself during the last decade of Pius XII's pontificate. It was, in point of fact, the reference to this *Instructio* that made it possible to draw up the plans for a "network" of Catholic ecumenists, as conceived by Charles Boyer at the Grottaferrata meeting in September 1950 and later effectuated by Johannes Willebrands with the CCEQ in 1952.[148] *Ecclesia Catholica* would thus provide these theological laboratories with the Cartesian axes on which to build the paths that would lead to the conciliar outcome at the end of the decade.

The decentralization of competences from Rome to the local ordinaries, and the consequent responsibility of the episcopate envisaged by the document, was to a large extent an echo of the German model: behind the call for the appropriateness and necessity of "collaboration of several bishops in the creation of organizations and offices for the supervision, control, and direction of all these activities,"[149] it is difficult indeed not to detect the suggestion of the exemplarity of the internal *referat* of the Fulda conference, which had already responded to these criteria. Moreover, even the admonition to watch over and, if necessary, to prevent the participation of the simple faithful in such meetings, which could bring them "little fruit and much danger" because they

144 In fact, in February 1950, the two *frères* of Taizé, Roger Schutz and Max Thurian, reported that they had heard of a "papal document which has recently been confidentially communicated to the bishops, which will soon appear in the *Acta Apostolicae Sedis* and which will explain the real meaning of the *Monitum* of Jun 6, 1948": Fouilloux, *Les Catholiques et l'unité*, 921. In fact, in January 1950, the bishop of Liege, Louis-Joseph Kerkhofs, had anticipated to Thurian the future publication of such a document, see Silvia Scatena, *Taizé, una parabola di unità: Storia della comunità dalle origini al concilio dei giovani*, Bologna, Il Mulino, 2018, 291.

145 "De Motione Ecumenica," *EcRev* 2/3, 1950, 296–298. Other reactions, including the personal one of Visser 't Hooft, can be found in WCCA, box 4201.1.1/6. Note, however, the efforts of Catholic ecumenists to promote an optimistic interpretation, for example Maurice Villain, "L'Église romaine devant le mouvement œcuménique," *Rythmes du monde* 24, 1950, 107ff. For an overview of non-Catholic reactions, see Fouilloux, *Les Catholiques et l'unité*, 918–923.

146 SO, "Instructio ad locorum ordinarios 'De motione oecumenica,'" 142.

147 Commentaries by Hürth (*Periodica de re morali canonica liturgica* 39, 1950, 204–209), Creusen (*NRT* 72/6, 1950, 647–649) and Parente (*Euntes docete* 3/1, 1950, 98–100) followed this line. At a meeting with Schutz and Thurian, Charles Boyer deplored this diversity of interpretation: "[The *Instructio*] was misunderstood in Rome, where it was interpreted in the opposite sense to that which we give it, and judged too generous"; Scatena, *Taizé, una parabola di unità*, 298.

148 On this subject, see the essay by Peter De Mey and Saretta Marotta "The Catholic Conference for Ecumenical Questions" in this volume.

149 SO, "Instructio ad locorum ordinarios 'De motione oecumenica,'" 146.

were not "well instructed and strong in the faith," seemed to be an implicit reference to the activities of the Una Sancta movement.[150]

Ecclesia Catholica's responsiveness to German needs is finally even more evident concerning the activities coordinated by Archbishop Lorenz Jaeger, especially in the case of the Catholic-Evangelical circle active in the diocese of Paderborn. In the wake of the 1948 *Monitum*, the Lutheran regional bishop, Wilhelm Stählin, had in fact asked Höfer how the document's references to *communicatio in sacris* were to be interpreted and whether the prohibition included the common prayer which the working group recited at the end of each meeting: convinced that this moment of sharing was "an indispensable condition of our theological dialogues," Stählin was in fact resolutely prepared to make the continuation of the experience dependent on this condition alone, declaring that "we could not and would not want to continue our promising work that has already begun if Rome were to express an explicit prohibition of such common prayers."[151] *Ecclesia Catholica* intervened to give a practically direct and almost textual response to this request, expressing a fundamental distinction regarding *communicatio in sacris*, which made it clear that no excommunication would be imposed if "the common recitation of the 'Our Father' or of a prayer approved by the Catholic Church, with which the same meetings are opened and closed, is introduced in interconfessional meetings."[152]

Precisely the clarification concerning the "Our Father," which opened up the possibility of prayer communion with the non-Catholic interlocutor by recognizing the spiritual value of the ecumenical effort, had an enormous innovative scope, which rightly did not escape the attention of non-Catholic ecumenists. A statement made in a personal capacity by WCC secretary general Willem Visser 't Hooft underlined, albeit cautiously, that "if I am not mistaken, this is the first document in which the Holy See explicitly allows Roman Catholics and Christians of other denominations to pray together, albeit with certain restrictions. This is a step forward."[153]

It was indeed a step forward which, although it could not remedy the Catholic absence at the 1948 Amsterdam assembly, certainly began a slow process of bringing even the Roman Catholic hierarchy closer to the burgeoning ecumenical movement that was changing Europe and the world.

Bibliography

Congar, Yves, *Journal of a Theologian (1946–1956)*, ed. Étienne Fouilloux, trans. Denis Minns, Adelaide, ATF Press, 2015.

Ernesti, Jörg, *Ökumene im Dritten Reich*, Paderborn, Bonifatius, 2007.

Fouilloux, Étienne, *Les Catholiques et l'unité chrétienne du XIXe au XXe siècle: Itinéraires européens d'expression française*, Paris, Centurion, 1982.

Fouilloux, Étienne, *Yves Congar (1904–1995): Une vie*, Paris, Salvator, 2020.

Marotta, Saretta, *Gli anni della pazienza: Bea, l'ecumenismo e il Sant'Uffizio di Pio XII*, Bologna, Il Mulino, 2019.

150 SO, "Instructio ad locorum ordinarios 'De motione oecumenica,'" 145.

151 W. Stählin to T. Wurm, Oct 2, 1948, in: Schwahn, *Der Ökumenische Arbeitskreis*, 64–65.

152 SO, "Instructio ad locorum ordinarios 'De motione oecumenica,'" 146.

153 The text of the statement, which has been picked up by much of the press, can be found in: WCCA box 4201.1.1/6. Charles Boyer told the Taizé brothers that the permission for the "Our Father" was "a stand against the opinion of certain English Catholic bishops who did not want it in their meetings with Anglicans"; Fouilloux, *Les catholiques et l'unité*, 920.

CHAPTER 24

The Christian World Communions

André Birmelé

1 Introduction

CWCs are leading actors on the contemporary ecumenical stage. These federations or alliances of churches with common denominational origins developed from the second half of the 19th century onward. Families of churches emerging from the 16th century Reformation, constituting the majority of the CWCs, spread to various countries through missionary activity and emigration. Hence there arose many local churches that, while claiming the same spiritual foundations, no longer had any special ties with the churches in their countries of origin holding the same values.

These church alliances were all characterized by their concern for universality. The creation of an international organization allowed many churches of the same family to discover the global aspect of their tradition. This contributed to the awareness of a bond of unity within the same confessional family, which gave the latter visibility in the global ecclesial reality. Even more important was the spiritual dimension. Many churches having the same tradition were becoming aware that, throughout the world, they were relying on the same doctrinal sources, the same confessions of faith, or the same creedal books that had once contributed to their emergence. This shared heritage transcended races, cultures, and countries. Formed from an identical historical background, the churches of the same family discovered that they had common traditions, shared forms of liturgy and worship, a similar piety, as well as convergent ethical and even sociopolitical approaches.

The references that internally characterize each of these alliances are not, however, shared equally by churches belonging to other confessional families, even if the concern for global visibility and having a shared spirituality is the same. These alliances differ greatly from one another. The number of faithful in the largest is unrelated to that of the others. Their structures are not comparable and reflect divergent self-understandings. Some see themselves as world churches while others only seek to be free associations of churches concerned with each local community's full autonomy.

These alliances, or federations, blazed the trail for ecumenism, contributing to the birth of the ecumenical movement that took place in the 20th century. From the outset, they saw themselves as a particular expression of the Church of Christ that transcends time and place, an expression often born in a particular context, yet an expression that wishes to make a unique contribution and to place its dogmatic and ecclesiological heritage at the service of the whole Church in its search for unity.[1]

Starting from 1957, the leaders of these global alliances have met annually to better understand their mission and interaction. In 1979, a careful theological reflection led to the name CWCs, which expresses a convergent understanding of the unity of the church and the commitment to the ecumenical movement on the part of each of the families of churches. This self-understanding needs to be clarified. It is connected to the overall vision of the WCC, since many of the major actors of the CWCs also have important responsibilities within it. However, this connection has also

1 These shared attitudes are mentioned in the definitions that the world confessional families formulated in 1962 and 1967. They can be found in the article by Harding Meyer, "Die Weltweiten Christlichen Gemeinschaften: Grundanliegen – Selbstverständnis – Ökumenische Verpflichtung," in: Harding Meyer, *Versöhnte Verschiedenheit: Aufsätze zur ökumenischen Theologie*, vol. 1, Frankfurt/Paderborn, Lembeck/Bonifatius, 1998, 183–196, here 186.

been contentious, a conflict essentially tied to the understanding of the confession and the model of unity desired and implemented by the CWCs. Nevertheless, the CWCs engage in contemporary ecumenical dialogue and play a role in declarations of communion between churches that were once opposed.

It is important to make one last introductory remark. These global alliances are free associations of churches, whose role is mainly consultative and federative. The particular churches that make up each alliance remain autonomous and are generally jealous of that autonomy, which they wish to preserve. Developments have certainly occurred or are in progress, and vary from one alliance to another. Additionally, the advice or choices advocated by the general assembly of a world communion is not binding on its member churches. This is a major difference from the Roman Catholic or Eastern Orthodox traditions, which recognize a more centralized power whose decisions are binding on all their members. This difference has generally led to great caution on the part of these two churches with regard to CWCs. However, they have always sent representatives to CWC gatherings, without seeing themselves as a CWC.

2 The Major CWCs

The churches of the Reformed tradition united in a world alliance as early as 1875; the Anglicans preceded them by organizing at an international level their first Lambeth conference in 1867. The Methodists held their first ecumenical world conference in 1881. The Lutherans did not organize at an international level until after their world conference in 1923. The Baptists did not take this step until 1968. The large confessional families (Anglicans, Lutherans, Reformed, Methodists, and Baptists) have more than 60 million faithful each. Smaller alliances (the MWC, Old Catholics, Quakers, the Salvation Army, the Disciples of Christ) often have fewer than a million members. The Seventh-day Adventists count more than 20 million faithful.

CWCs can certainly be defined by using the date of their emergence or their numerical size. However, it makes more sense to look at them from the perspective of their "ecclesial density": some – the largest – see themselves as a "church at the global level," while others understand themselves as non-binding federations of fully autonomous local churches.

2.1 *Communions with High "Ecclesial Density"*

2.1.1 The Anglican Communion

The Anglican Communion did not originally see itself as a global confessional family and did not establish a permanent international organization until after 1958, with central headquarters in London from 1963. By 1958, there were 19 autonomous Anglican churches, all of which were also members of the WCC. Today, their number has more than doubled. They are each in communion with the See of Canterbury and thus in communion with one another.[2]

Rejecting papal authority and strongly influenced by European reform movements (in particular, that of the Alsatian Martin Bucer), the Anglican Church sees itself as an autonomous church of the English nation and, in its cultural life and teaching, takes the *Book of Common Prayer* and the Thirty-nine Articles of Religion as its guiding texts. Similar churches quickly emerged in Ireland and Scotland. Without being subject to legislation by the Kingdom of England, they developed autonomously while taking into account the same liturgical and doctrinal norms. A major development took place in the 18th century following the 1776 United States' Declaration of Independence when, as a result of the declaration, the Anglican

2 See resolutions 13–17 in: *The Lambeth Conference 1958: The Encyclical Letter from the Bishops together with the Resolutions and Reports*, London, SPCK, 1958, 1.34–1.35. The *Wiley-Blackwell Companion to the Anglican Communion* is concerned mainly with the life of the communion today, and it contains a wealth of information on that topic. See Ian S. Markham & others, eds., *The Wiley-Blackwell Companion to the Anglican Communion*, Chichester, Wiley-Blackwell, 2013.

communities established on that continent no longer had political ties to England. Concerned with maintaining an ecclesial link with the Church of England, one of the new bishops, Samuel Seabury of Connecticut, asked in 1783 to be consecrated in London, but his request could not be granted, because the episcopal ordination included an oath of allegiance to the crown of England. The Anglican Church of Scotland, not bound to the English crown, agreed to consecrate him. In response to this fact, in 1789, the American Anglicans founded an autonomous convention, adopted a new prayer book, and constituted themselves as the Episcopal Church of the United States.[3] Other autonomous Anglican churches developed outside the British Empire. In the nations of the empire, however, the Church of England consecrated bishops and considered those dioceses as its own integral parts.[4]

One important development took place in 1867 and another in 1886. Various conflicts between and within autonomous Anglican churches had led the Anglican Church of Canada to ask the bishop of Canterbury to convene a worldwide consultative assembly. This was held in 1867 at Lambeth Palace, the seat of the primate of England. It decided to meet regularly, with consultations having no legislative or executive power. These Lambeth conferences have since been held every ten years, generally in the years ending in "8," except during the world wars.

For its part, the Episcopal Church of Chicago was concerned with the unity of all the autonomous Episcopalian churches in the United States. To this end, it drafted the Chicago-Lambeth Quadrilateral summarizing in four points the fundamentals of faith and the Christian Church: (1) Sacred Scripture, the revelation of the Word of God; (2) the Nicene-Constantinopolitan Creed; (3) two sacraments, baptism and the Lord's Supper; and (4) the historical episcopate. The Lambeth conference of 1888 adopted this quadrilateral with minor modifications: the addition of the Apostles Creed in point 2 and a greater emphasis on historical episcopacy. The Lambeth Quadrilateral became a standard reference for all the Anglican churches, and it would prove decisive in establishing the Anglican Communion at the Lambeth conference of 1958.[5]

Under the influence of the Oxford Movement, from the second half of the 19th century the emphasis was placed on the episcopal ministry and, in particular, the historical episcopate. In 1930, the Lambeth conference clarified that the Anglican Communion is understood as a communion within the one, holy, catholic, and apostolic church, in communion with the See of Canterbury. It added that this communion is made up of national churches that generally take the *Book of Common Prayer* as their point of reference for worship.[6] This reference is what is important, with no specification of a particular edition (1552 or 1662?) or mention of other prayer books in use by particular churches. The Thirty-nine Articles, instead, are mainly considered a historical reference. There is no common Anglican confession of faith, even though the different liturgical forms in use in the autonomous churches all refer to the Anglican liturgical tradition arising in the 16th century.

The question of reference being relativized, a crucial place was awarded to the communion of bishops, which ensured the continuity of the Anglican Communion in all matters of disputed interpretation, with the archbishop of Canterbury

3 Raymond W. Albright, *A History of the Protestant Episcopal Church*, New York, MacMillan, 1964.

4 See Rowan Strong, *Anglicanism and the British Empire (c.1700–1850)*, Oxford, Oxford University Press, 2007.

5 For more details on this major evolution, its antecedents, and its later significance, see John Robert Wright, ed., *Quadrilateral at One Hundred: Essays on the Centenary of the Chicago-Lambeth Quadrilateral (1886/88–1986/88)*, Cincinnati, Forward Movement, 1988, and the contribution by Paul Avis in the first volume of this work. On the father of the Chicago Quadrilateral, William Reed Huntington, see Huntington's own account, "The Anglican Communion: Our Ideals," in: *Pan-Anglican Papers: Being Problems for Consideration at the Pan-Anglican Congress, 1908*, London, SPCK, 1907.

6 See resolution 49, in: *The Lambeth Conference 1930: Encyclical Letter from the Bishops with Resolution and Reports*, London, SPCK, 1930, 55.

as the *primus inter pares*, an undisputed moral authority, but without direct power over the particular churches.

After the institutionalization of the worldwide Anglican Communion in 1958, the Lambeth conference of 1968 decided to establish the ACC, where each autonomous province is represented by a bishop, a priest, and a layperson. This smaller body (of about 100 members, while the number of bishops in the Lambeth conference exceeds 800) meets every 2–3 years and ensures unity and a strengthening of links between the autonomous Anglican churches.[7] This council faced many crises concerning the unity, identity, and mission of the Anglican Communion. The ordination of women to the ministry has been a central issue, first as priests and then, particularly, to the episcopal ministry. Long accepted in some provinces such as Australia, this became possible in England only in 2015. The controversy over homosexuality is even more serious. In 2008, the case of a homosexual American bishop made a normal meeting of the Lambeth conference impossible. A large number of bishops from the so-called Southern churches refused to travel to London, meeting in Jerusalem instead. This breakdown in the communion of bishops constituted a serious burden on the entire Anglican Communion and forced the archbishop of Canterbury not to convene the Lambeth conference in 2018.[8] The conference was then scheduled for 2020, but it was indeed held only in 2022.

2.1.2 The LWF

Along with the Anglican Communion, the LWF is the alliance that is most conscious of being a "global church." This development occurred in stages. Like the Anglican family, the Lutheran tradition had initially developed in Europe, with Germany and the Scandinavian countries becoming Lutheran as early as in the 16th century. Immigration had given rise to various Lutheran churches, mainly in North America, with some founded by German immigrants and others by Scandinavians. On the other continents, missionary work gave rise to Lutheran churches that were greatly dependent on the mission societies that had founded them.

The NLC of the United States and the AELK, founded in Germany in 1868, decided to convene a world conference in Eisenach, Germany in 1923. The purpose of the conference was to clarify the scope of the Lutheran confessions of faith and to organize mutual assistance among the 22 countries represented. The LWC – to which the large majority (over 80%) of German Lutheran churches belonged – met every six years, first in Copenhagen in 1929 and then in Paris in 1935, before being interrupted by World War II. The ideological proximity of some German churches to the national socialist regime dealt a severe blow to the organization's work that, after a preparatory meeting in Philadelphia in 1940, met for the last time in Uppsala in 1946.[9] The new political situation led Swedish bishop Nathan Söderblom, also a major player in the WCC, to promote the founding of the LWF in 1947 in Lund, Sweden. This international organization took over the missionary and social activities that German churches, now enjoying less credibility, had previously developed on a global level. These activities remain a major dimension of the LWF to this day, its Department for World Service being by far the largest item on its budget.

Fundamental theological reflection on the basis of the Lutheran confessions of faith, mutual assistance after the devastation of the war, missionary work in other continents, and responsibility within the ecumenical movement had been the cornerstones of the LWC's work, and they were

7 This mission was reaffirmed by the Lambeth Conference in 1988: *The Truth Shall Make You Free: The Lambeth Conference 1988. The Reports, Resolutions & Pastoral Letters from The Bishops*, London, Church House, 1988, 110ff.

8 See Paul Avis & Benjamin M. Guyer, eds., *The Lambeth Conference: Theology, History, Polity and Purpose*, London, Bloomsbury/T&T Clark, 2017.

9 For the history of the LWC, see Kurt Schmidt-Clausen, *Vom Lutherischen Weltkonvent zum Lutherischen Weltbund: Geschichte des Lutherischen Weltkonventes (1923–1947)*, Gütersloh, Gütersloher Verlagshaus Gerd Mohn, 1976.

taken up again as pillars of the LWF. The constitution adopted there provided for general assemblies every five years, the establishment of an executive committee with annual meetings and a secretariat in Geneva, and the creation of LWF national committees in all the countries where LWF churches are to be found. While its second article states that all LWF churches refer to the Lutheran biblical witness and confessions of faith, especially the *Confessio Augustana* and Luther's *Small Catechism*, as authentic expositions of God's Word, the third article adds that the LWF is a free alliance with no legislative binding power upon member churches, whose autonomy must always be preserved. The same article refers to the pillars of shared work mentioned above and adds that the global body may take up particular tasks at the request of one or more member churches.[10]

The nature of the LWF has changed over the years, gaining ecclesial density. Life within the federation has strengthened, and its links have evolved. The apartheid situation in South Africa was a major contributor to this development. Synods of white Lutheran churches in South Africa refused to allow black Lutheran Church members access to the Lord's Supper. Going beyond the non-interference stated in its constitution, the LWF decided at its general assembly – first in Dar es Salaam in 1977 and then in Budapest in 1984 – to exclude the white South African churches because of their refusal to extend communion to the black churches. Although this decision went beyond the prerogatives of its constitution, it was in line with its internal developments, as well as the result of intense theological work arising from the federation's engagement in international ecumenical dialogue. This work was largely carried out through the Lutheran Foundation for Interconfessional Research established by the general assembly in Helsinki in 1963, which later set up a research center in Strasbourg, France, in 1965, the Institute for Ecumenical Research.

A theological breakthrough had come from a new interpretation of article 7 of the *Confessio Augustana*, affirming that the unity of the church is communion in the celebration of the word and the sacraments. This is the necessary and sufficient condition for church unity. This vision of unity was first implemented in the Lutheran-Reformed and Lutheran-Anglican dialogues in Europe and, later on, in those on other continents. It resulted in declarations of communion with churches of other traditions, which also led to communion among the participating Lutheran churches. What was missing, however, was communion within the LWF itself. What was valid *ad extra* was not yet realized *ad intra*. In 1984, without yet declaring the LWF to be a communion of churches, the general assembly in Budapest took up the vision of unity based on article 7 of the *Confessio Augustana* and made it clear that the communion of pulpit and altar gives the Lutheran communion of churches its visible expression, an expression of the one, holy, Catholic, and apostolic church.[11] The final step was taken at the next assembly in Curitiba, Brazil, in 1990, which amended article 3 of the constitution: "The LWF is a communion of churches which confess the triune God, agree in the proclamation of the Word of God, and are united in pulpit and altar fellowship."[12]

Since then, the LWF has seen itself and acted as a "world church," like the Roman Catholic Church, while article 4 of its constitution emphasizes that its member churches remain autonomous. The decision of the general assemblies and its council do not replace the legislative and executive power of its member churches. An initial development occurred in 1999 when the *Joint Declaration*

10 "Constitution of the LWF," in: Jens Holger Schjørring, Prasanna Kumari & Norman A. Hjelm, eds., *From Federation to Communion: The History of the Lutheran World Federation*, Minneapolis, Fortress Press, 1997, 527–534.

11 A report of the Budapest assembly can be found in: Carl H. Mau, ed., *Budapest 1984: "In Christ Hope for the World": Official Proceedings of the Seventh Assembly of the Lutheran World Federation (Budapest, Hungary July 22–August 5, 1984)*, Geneva, LWF, 1985, 176.

12 "Constitution of the LWF," 530.

on the Doctrine of Justification was signed by both the Vatican and the LWF. The LWF had consulted with all the synods and member churches and obtained the mandate to do so, but it is still a singular example.

2.1.3 The Old Catholic Church

The origin of this CWC dates back to the 18th century. Dutch Catholics accused Rome of promoting Jansenism, and they established their own ecclesiastical jurisdiction in 1723. The rupture with the Holy See was consummated when the latter, which had already excommunicated these faithful, reestablished a Roman Catholic bishopric in Utrecht in 1851. The Old Catholic Church of Utrecht rejected the 1864 *Syllabus of Errors* as well as the dogma of the Immaculate Conception. Vatican I's proclamation of papal infallibility was a major event. It was rejected by a number of faithful and priests in the Netherlands, Germany, Austria, Switzerland, and in some Habsburg empire territories, including Czechoslovakia and Croatia.

In September 1871, a conference was held in Munich with more than 300 representatives of these groups, along with Anglican and Protestant observers. In 1874, the discipline of celibacy for priests was abandoned in some churches and, in the same year, a Catholic Christian faculty of theology was founded at the University of Bern. In 1877, the vernacular languages were adopted for the liturgy. In 1889, a union of these churches was established under the name of the Union of Utrecht, and it decided to send missions to England and North America.[13]

The Old Catholic Church remains anchored to the Catholic tradition and maintains a great majority of its teachings. Its practices, however, have moved away from those of the Roman church in several respects and to different degrees in different countries. Thus, in the Netherlands, Switzerland, Austria, Belgium, France, and Germany, this church admits married priests, the ordination of women, remarriage after divorce, contraception, and now, locally, the blessing of homosexual couples.

The Old Catholic Church emphasizes the autonomy of each diocese that constitutes it at the world level. The place of the laity is emphasized through the organization of both national and international congresses and the church's governance is assured by the IBC, which meets every two years under the presidency of the archbishop of Utrecht. This conference also includes laypersons elected by the local communities. Despite its small membership (less than half a million, two-thirds of whom are in North America), this church has played and continues to play an important role in the modern ecumenical movement. An active member of the WCC, it has been in full communion with the Anglican churches since the Bonn Agreement of 1931. Eucharistic hospitality is extended to many Lutheran and Reformed churches in Europe and the United States through various agreements. The church sees itself as a model of the one church, the ecclesial goal of the ecumenical movement.

2.1.4 The Seventh-Day Adventist Church

In the 19th century, following the preaching of the Baptist pastor William Miller, a revival movement developed in the United States. This movement, which expected Christ's imminent return, was called Adventism (from the Latin *adventus*, meaning "return"). When this return did not occur in 1844 as foreseen, the movement, originally composed of Christians of various denominations, split into various groups, the most important of which was the Seventh-day Adventist Church. The "Seventh Day" refers to the Sabbath (Saturday), the seventh day of the week, which the Adventists believe should be honored by the church today as the day of rest and worship, as it was in Old Testament times. Originally, the movement was intended to be supra-ecclesial, but the creation of a church was necessary to put a stop to various divergences. An initial conference was

13 On the history and life of this church, see Karl Prüter, *The Old Catholic Church: A History and Chronology*, San Bernardino, St. Willibrord's Press, ^{2}1996; Urs Küry, *Die Altkatholische Kirche: Ihre Geschichte, ihre Lehre, ihr Anliegen*, ed. Christian Oeyen, Frankfurt a.M., Evangelisches Verlagswerk, ^{3}1982.

founded in Michigan in 1860, before the establishment of a general conference in 1863, which has met every two years ever since. In 1864, the church began missionary work in Europe and then across the globe. The general conference was reorganized in 1901 and grants wide autonomy to the local churches (about 100 conferences and regional or national unions).

This worldwide church is characterized by a very important missionary and social outreach, which has led to its rapid growth, with more than 20 million baptized members today. From its beginning, special emphasis was placed on health and education. The internationalization of Adventism was accompanied by the creation of a large number of local institutions (schools, hospitals, printing houses, orphanages, and humanitarian organizations) directly serving the populations being evangelized. This work is supported by a vast communications network (the publication of printed materials, radio and television services, and the use of modern media).

As far as its doctrine is concerned, Adventism is characterized by a biblical fundamentalism. Having insisted on God's commandments and the faith of Jesus from its very beginnings, the Adventist church advocates a return to the primary truth of the biblical message, the indispensable condition for Christ's return, and since the message is clear, there is no need to write a common confession of faith for the entire church. This fundamentalist approach rejects historical-critical methods of exegesis as well as contemporary scientific approaches (evolutionary theory, for example).

Adventists are not much in favor of contemporary ecumenical approaches. They are not members of the WCC, although they have had some presence in the Faith and Order movement since 1927. In many countries, the Seventh-day Adventist Church has observer or associate status in national church organizations.[14]

2.2 *Communions of Independent Churches*

A second category of CWCs includes those with a lower ecclesial density. These CWCs are very concerned with upholding the independence of their member churches, and do not see themselves as "world churches." Some, however, are moving in that direction. Some do not want to go beyond the federation stage while others have a more continental character. They are mentioned here according to their decreasing ecclesial density.

2.2.1 The WCRC

The WCRC is the most recent CWC. It was formed in June 2010 in Grand Rapids, Michigan, in the United States, as a result of the merger of the WARC and the REC and is composed of 230 member churches from 108 countries, bringing together more than 80 million faithful, mainly from countries in the southern hemisphere. The two movements from which it sprang both have older roots.[15]

The WARC was founded in 1970 by the union of the Alliance of the Reformed Churches holding the Presbyterian System – born in 1875 and reuniting Reformed and Presbyterians in the United States and the British Isles – and the International Congregational Council, an independent confessional alliance counting over a million members.[16]

Unlike the LWF, the WARC did not focus on the theological achievements and confessions of faith of the 16th century and their significance for contemporary churches. A confession of faith, in its eyes, only makes sense when active and current in regard to the challenges of the contemporary world. Emphasis was placed on ethical

14 For a better understanding of the Adventist Church, see Raoul Dederen, ed., *Handbook of Seventh-day Adventist Theology*, Washington DC, Review & Herald, 2000, and the *Seventh-day Adventist Encyclopedia*, Washington DC, Review & Herald, 1996.

15 A complete list of the small continental or international alliances or federations is given in: Jean Jacques Bauswein & Lukas Vischer, eds., *The Reformed Family Worldwide: A Survey of Reformed Churches, Theological Schools, and International Organizations*, Grand Rapids, Eerdmans, 1999, 701–708.

16 On the process of the WARC's formation, see Marcel Pradervand, *A Century of Service: A History of the World Alliance of Reformed Churches (1875–1975)*, Edinburgh, St. Andrew Press, 1975.

and political issues, where the WARC engaged in pioneering work (defense of human rights, gender equality, commitment to justice, peace and the integrity of creation, economic injustice, and wealth distribution).[17] Opposition to apartheid in South Africa led to the exclusion of white Reformed churches in South Africa at the 1982 Ottawa general assembly. The Belhar (South Africa) confession of faith published in 1986 became a reference point for many WARC churches.

The REC was founded in 1946 as Reformed Ecumenical Synod and, before its merger into the WCRC, united about 40 churches of mainly Dutch origin from some 20 countries: 5 million faithful in the Netherlands, North America, and South Africa. Unlike the WARC, it was very concerned with the doctrinal heritage of the Reformation, especially the Calvinistic one. The REC was always interested in the unity of the whole Church of Christ, while convinced that such unity requires a better consideration of the Reformed heritage of the 16th century. It held general assemblies every four years on themes such as theological formation, catechesis, mission, and *diakonia*. Mutual assistance and contemporary issues (racism, wealth distribution etc.) were not overlooked, but those topics were not as central to its reflections as they were for the WARC.

In 2010, the merger of these two organizations into a single communion, the WCRC, took place in Grand Rapids, where the REC was headquartered. The WCRC's secretariat was established in Hanover, Germany. The process of achieving a genuine communion in which all Reformed and Presbyterian churches agree to be one world church has only just begun. Promising first steps have been made, however, such as the WCRC signing – after consultation with its synods – the *Joint Declaration on the Doctrine of Justification* between the LWF and the Catholic Church, in July 2017 in Wittenberg, at the WCRC's second general assembly. However, cultural, historical, and ethnic differences in many countries have resulted in a multiplicity of churches that are often in the minority, but still members of the WCRC, without churches being in true communion with one another.

17 For an overview of the WARC's position, see Odair Pedroso Mateus, *The World Alliance of Reformed Churches and the Modern Ecumenical Movement: A Selected, Chronological, Annotated Bibliography (1863–2004): Papers, Statements and Reports from Councils, Committees, Departments and Official Commissions*, Geneva, WARC, 2005. Two reference texts from 1951 and 1954 are included as appendices in this work. They indicate the basic orientation of the WARC.

2.2.2 The WMC

Methodism was originally a dissident branch of Anglicanism. It originated from an 18th century revival movement centered around John Wesley. Concerned with sanctification, students met for Bible reading, prayer, Eucharistic celebration, and social outreach toward the poor. Having stayed in the English colony of Georgia (today's United States), Wesley established some groups with the same practices there. After a moving personal experience that gave him the certainty of salvation, Wesley founded many groups within the Anglican Church, which he brought together in conferences, beginning in 1744. The American branch broke away from the Church of England in 1784, at the same time as the Episcopalian Church was born in the United States. Political differences, especially over slavery, caused American Methodism to break up into many fractions that did not reunite until 1968, with the founding of the UMC. In continental Europe, various small Methodist churches from different English missions first united in 1897 and again in 1905.

Even though Wesley himself did not want to break away from the Anglican Church, that is what happened to Methodists after his death. Methodism reproached Anglicanism for its tepid attitude. It argued that conversion must lead to authentic sanctification, which entails both a true personal spiritual life and a strong commitment to the love of one's neighbor. The foundation is the biblical message, which tradition, experience, and reason allow us to understand. Methodism has never developed a set of referential texts, and its final reference were always the preaching of John Wesley and the hymns written by his brother, Charles Wesley. Wesley had certainly insisted on the Thirty-nine Articles of the Church of England, which he had reduced to 25, but those versions differed from one Methodist church to another. At the ecclesial level, Methodism had various models, in some places episcopal and in others synodal presbyterian. Churches in a region or even a country met in these conferences which strictly respected the autonomy of each member church. Membership in a congregation was of various kinds, mainly distinguishing between converted and baptized members, on the one hand, and sympathizers, on the other.[18]

Large-scale missionary outreach spread Methodism to the whole world. Alongside those in England and the United States, large churches have sprung up in Africa (Nigeria and South Africa) and Asia (Korea and the Philippines). Today, the WMC has nearly 40 million baptized members and as many sympathizers. It met for the first time in London in 1881 (about 30 churches from about 20 countries). Today, it has about 40 national churches, all of which are members of the WCC, and some of them even its founders. Methodist churches in many countries are involved in ecumenical efforts and have become part of both national and continental ecumenical organizations. The WMC has participated in many interfaith dialogues and, in 2006, signed the *Joint Declaration on the Doctrine of Justification*. The signing came after consultation with each conference since the central organization cannot act directly on behalf of the churches.

2.2.3 The BWA

Like Methodism, which it preceded by over a century, the Baptist denomination also has its historical roots in England. In 1608, rejecting infant baptism, a group of Anglicans emigrated to the Netherlands, where religious freedom was guaranteed. There they met the Mennonites and other Anabaptists that had been established there since the 16th century, and they were influenced by the theological and spiritual choices of these communities. When they returned to England, they founded the first Baptist Church. In 1636, many Baptists emigrated to the British colony of Rhode Island in North America, which also guaranteed religious freedom. It was there that, through intense missionary work, Baptist communities developed, especially in the southern states, constituting the largest Christian family in the United States by 1800. Fewer Baptist communities were developed in England or, more generally, in continental Europe, as missionary outreach concentrated on the continents of Asia and Africa, instead.[19]

The majority of Baptists reject any formal categorization of faith, since no Baptist can speak for any other. This individualization of faith applies within each community and, logically, leads to a radical congregationalism. The church, which is always a local community, is a free association of autonomous believers who appoint their pastor. All community life is regulated at the level of the individual congregation and does not depend on supra-local organization. Nonetheless, certain characteristics common to all communities can be noted. The authority of the Bible is final and radical. The confessions of faith of the early church are certainly recognized, albeit without being normative. Emphasis is placed on individual conversion,

18 On the history of Methodism, see Randy L. Maddox, *Responsible Grace: John Wesley's Practical Theology*, Nashville, Kingswood Books, 1994, and Henry D. Rack, *Reasonable Enthusiast: John Wesley and the Rise of Methodism*, Philadelphia, Trinity Press International, 1989. For a more general overview, see James E. Kirby & William J. Abraham, eds., *The Oxford Handbook of Methodist Studies*, Oxford, Oxford University Press, 2009.

19 On the history of the Baptists, we refer to a collection of articles that is certainly old, but which remains invaluable: *Die Kirchen der Welt*, vol. 2, John David Hughey, ed., *Die Baptisten*, Stuttgart, Evangelisches Verlagswerk, 1964, and to Andrea Strübind & Martin Rothkegel, eds., *Baptismus: Geschichte und Gegenwart*, Göttingen, Vandenhoeck & Ruprecht, 2011.

which opens one to the grace of God given in Christ, the sole savior, and is marked by adult baptism by immersion, a ritual, non-sacramental act of confirmation. The Lord's Supper is also non-sacramental, the real presence of Christ residing in the renewal of the believer's confession of faith. Religious freedom and the separation of church and state are the best guarantees for every believer's freedom of conscience. Missionary work is fundamental and not only in non-Christian lands, being also aimed at Christians of other confessions, an old practice that still prevails in the most conservative circles.

These beliefs result in a very cautious attitude toward the contemporary ecumenical movement. Distrustful of any structural unity even in their own midst, a large number of Baptists see ecumenical efforts as the promotion of a world church, which they reject. However, a number of communities have moved beyond this position and are more open to national church organizations and even to the work of the WCC, and a few unions (about 15 out of more than 130 worldwide) are now members. On the other hand, some persevere in their reticence, a situation that does not fail to provoke numerous internal tensions. In 2004, for example, the United States' SBC, which was founded in 1845 in Augusta, Georgia, and has more than 15 million members, left the BWA, which they considered too liberal. The latter was founded in 1905 in London, meets at conventions held every five years, and numbers nearly 50 million believers.[20]

Because of its congregational system of governance, which leaves a great deal of autonomy to the local churches and within them to individual believers, specific points of doctrine may vary from place to place.

2.2.4 The MWC

The MWC unites about 100 churches from about 60 countries and has about 1.5 million members. It met in Basel in 1925 for the first time and has met every six or seven years since.

The year 1925 celebrated the fourth centenary of the Anabaptist movement. This movement, which originated in the Radical Reformation of the 16th century, was subject to numerous persecutions from its very beginning, not only on the part of states but also by other Christian families, including the historical Reformation currents (Reformed and Lutheran). Like Anabaptism in the 16th century, the Mennonite movement, which owes its name to the Dutch Anabaptist Menno Simons, has always been multifaceted. It was originally established in the Netherlands and more generally in the Rhine valley. Migration, following persecution, has always characterized this movement. Important communities settled in the Vistula valley (today's Poland) and then in North America. It is characterized by a strong missionary outreach, which has led to its expansion in Latin America and in some African countries. This missionary commitment is mainly the work of more liberal groups; the conservative ones (including the Amish current) set themselves apart from the modern world.[21]

The Mennonites are close to the Baptists, whose theology they have influenced. They reject infant baptism, advocate a return to the original biblical message, a radical separation of church and state, and congregationalism at the ecclesiastical level.

20 See Edward Glenn Hinson, "The Baptist World Alliance: Its Identity and Ecumenical Involvement," *EcRev* 46, 1994, 406–412.

21 For general studies on Anabaptism, see John D. Roth & James M. Stayer, eds., *A Companion to Anabaptism and Spiritualism (1521–1700)*, Leiden, Brill, 2007. More specifically, see Thomas A. Brady Jr., "The Cost of Contexts: Anabaptist/Mennonite History and the Early Modern European Past," in: Mark Jantzen, Mary S. Sprunger & John D. Thiesen, eds., *European Mennonites and the Challenge of Modernity over Five Centuries: Contributors, Detractors, and Adapters*, North Newton, Bethel College, 2016, 1–23. Finally, see also the Global Mennonite History Series (with translations into French, Spanish, Dutch, and German), which has five volumes, one for each continent where Mennonite communities live and operate. For the English edition, see John A. Lapp & C. Arnold Snyder, eds., *Global Mennonite History Series*, 5 vols., Intercourse, Good Books/Pandora Press, 2003–2012.

Their particular characteristics are pacifism (many refuse to serve in the military) and non-resistance (the refusal to use force against another person).

The founding of the MWC has led to a certain openness to other churches and the contemporary ecumenical movement. Various dialogues have taken place which, in 2011, led to a reconciliation with the Lutheran family.[22] The aim of these rapprochements, however, is not ecclesial communion with other confessions.

2.2.5 The Disciples of Christ

The Disciples of Christ is a movement that broke away from the Presbyterian (Reformed) Church in the early 19th century. There were, in fact, two movements, one, called the Christians, led by Barton Stone, and the other, the Disciples of Christ, led by Thomas Campbell. Without uniting, the two movements pursued the same goal, restoration of the unity of the Church of Christ, primarily the unity of the various Presbyterian denominations founded by Scottish and Irish immigrants in the United States. Both movements were convinced that unity would only be restored by a radical return to the biblical witness and life of the first Christians, and the rejection of all magisterial teaching after that. Such an approach could only come from individual believers. Both groups developed an intense missionary outreach, which gave rise to many small communities in several countries around the world. Like the Baptists, they shared a congregational vision of the church and professed the doctrinal independence both of the local communities and of individual believers. However, they did not share the Baptist understanding of the sacraments, and they embraced the Reformed tradition. While close, the two movements also came into conflict, as with question of the use of musical instruments in worship, for example.

The two movements were not united until 1960 with the founding of the church of the Disciples of Christ, which was joined by the Churches of Christ, dissident congregations that had emerged within the same movement. This federation of churches (half a million members) holds conventions every five years. The vast majority of its congregations are in the United States. The Disciples of Christ branch agreed to approach ecumenism in the 20th century and was a founding member of the WCC in 1948. After the merger in 1960, this concern was shared by all the federation's member churches.

2.2.6 The Salvation Army

William Booth, originally an Anglican and later a Methodist preacher, worked in the slums of East London.[23] In response to the overwhelming social misery he witnessed there, he founded the East London Christian Mission in 1865, and in 1878 he reorganized it according to a military model and called it Salvation Army. He was its first general, sending his troops all over the world, and hence the movement was present on all the continents by 1890. The foundation of missionary outposts was always accompanied by the establishment of free clinics and social institutions to improve the inhabitants' living conditions. This way, the Salvation Army has brought about changes in the social legislation of many countries.

Theologically, the Salvation Army stands in the tradition of the 16th century Reformation. However, it does not espouse particular doctrines. The sacraments are not celebrated in a traditional way; its hymns and liturgy are not subject to any specific pattern. Worship is a constant call to conversion.

---

22 *Healing Memories: Reconciling in Christ*, Geneva/Strasbourg, The Lutheran World Federation/The Mennonite World Conference, 2010. The second part of this report includes a historical presentation of the Mennonite family.

23 See David W. Taylor, *Like a Mighty Army?: The Salvation Army, the Church, and the Churches*, Eugene, Pickwick, 2014, and Henry Gariepy, *Christianity in Action: The International History of the International Salvation Army*, Grand Rapids, Eerdmans, 2009.

The Salvation Army sees itself as a church and is indeed one of the CWCs. It is not a member of the WCC but maintains friendly relations with other Christian denominations everywhere.

2.2.7 The Religious Society of Friends, the Quakers

This movement was founded in England in the 17th century by Anglican dissidents under the leadership of George Fox. Fox reported that he felt a "quaking in the name of the Lord," hence the name Quaker that was later adopted by his followers. This movement, influenced by Puritanism, is convinced that the divine dwells in every human being. They discover this by listening to the Word of God and by conforming to it. Every person is free in their own convictions, they see no need for a creed, for sacramental piety, or for any ecclesial mediation, and even less need for a hierarchical ecclesial structure. Life is modeled after the primitive church and its fraternal life. From there it is a matter of committing oneself to the dignity and equality of all human beings, the same rights for women and men, and the promotion of peace. It holds that true transformation of the world cannot be the fruit of an ideology, but can only result from an exemplary life of discipleship.[24]

The movement, which originated in England, spread to North America in the 17th century, and then to some Latin American and African countries in the 20th century. Some branches of the Quakers are close to the evangelical movements. In 1927, the world conference of the Friends gathered the American and European sections. Ten years later, the African and Latin-American section gave life to the FWCC; it meets every four years and has about 350,000 members (a third in Africa and a third in North America).

3 The Theological Focus of CWCs

The presentation made above of the different confessional alliances highlights the diversity of these federations. As already mentioned in the introduction, what they have in common is the overcoming of borders, races, cultures, and countries, as well as a concern for endowing this overcoming with a structural visibility and an awareness of their universality and continuity, not only geographical but also historical. This dimension of universality was not originally inherent in the ecclesial families emerging from the Reformation, which constitute the majority of these alliances. Rather, the churches of the Reformation insisted on universality in the sense of the ultimate and spiritual dimension of the church, without seeking to give it visibility at that time. Today, these various alliances are not only aware that each one is a spiritual reality transcending time and place, but they have also understood that this reality requires visibility and structure, even if the latter are not comparable from one family to another.

3.1 *Confessionalism and Confessional Identity*

The leaders of the world alliances have met regularly since 1957, and one of their first concerns was overcoming confessionalism. The existence of these confessional families was contested from the very beginning of the modern ecumenical movement. Indeed, they were reproached for their confessionalism, meaning a familial claim to be the sole bearer of truth, and to see its adherence to its confession of faith as the only way to express and live the Christian faith. Such an attitude, which leads to contention, even the exclusion of any other approach, was a phenomenon characterizing many alliances in their early days. Some questioned the legitimacy of other denominational alliances by challenging, at least partly,

24 A classic and comprehensive introduction to Quakerism still remains the one by Barry Reay, *The Quakers and the English Revolution*, New York, St. Martin's Press, 1985. More specifically on the development of Quakerism, see Leonard S. Kenworthy, *Quakerism: A Study Guide on the Religious Society of Friends*, Dublin IN, Prinit Press, 1981. For its spirituality, see instead Douglas V. Steere, ed., *Quaker Spirituality: Selected Writings*, Mahwah, Paulist Press, 1984.

others' ecclesial and doctrinal authenticity. Such an attitude has existed for centuries and has often characterized Christian families, which was the case even before the birth of global alliances.

However, any similar reproach was no longer valid in the second half of the 20th century, when the alliances learned to see themselves as an authentic and universal expression of the one Church of Christ without claiming exclusivity. This observation applies at least to the largest of these alliances and quickly became evident in their regular meetings. It is further confirmed by the fact that the birth of many alliances gave rise to the foundation of parallel movements of the same tradition, which were and remain confessionalist. One example is the LCMS, which criticized and still criticize the LWF for being too liberal, convinced that only a fundamentalist reading of the Lutheran symbolic texts permits an authentic approach to gospel truth. The same phenomenon has characterized the Methodist and Reformed families.[25] The fact that the majority of today's CWCs no longer hold to specific confessional texts is in itself a sign of this evolution.

The overcoming of confessionalism does not mean abandoning confessionality, that is each alliance's conviction that its historical, spiritual, and theological heritage is of great value and needs to be preserved, without claiming exclusivity. Further, this heritage needs to be reformulated in light of progress in biblical research and of theological pluralism, as well as in light of the societal and political challenges that every ecclesial family is now facing.

Furthermore, all these alliances have insisted and continue to insist on their ecumenical engagement, as they are convinced that they have a particular uniqueness that could benefit the whole ecumenical movement. The initial problematic has changed into that of the compatibility of denominational identity with ecumenical engagement.

The confessional alliances' first meetings were faced with the questioning of the very notion of "confession" in various ecumenical circles. Does the search for unity in the church not require the end of denominations, a complete rethinking so that a church that is truly one may emerge? Is not the confession of faith a specific fact that depends on the precise moment that gives rise to it, without being linked to the transmission of a family's particular heritage? In the ecumenical movement, not least at the level of the WCC, many voices were calling for the end of all confessional alliances.

Between 1957 and 1977, confessional alliance meetings addressed these issues.[26] A vision of the unity of the whole church rooted in confessional alliances without absolutizing them was gradually developed and, over the years, its relevance was confirmed. In particular, it was agreed that church unity should not be confused with uniformity, and that the one church is open to diverse expressions of the faith. Separation and diversity are not synonymous, diversity is an integral part of unity. It is not a matter of overcoming differences as such, but of transforming the character of difference itself. Any separating difference must become a legitimate difference expressing the wealth of the Church of Christ.

Global confessional alliances, therefore, are in no way opposed to the search for unity. On the contrary, they can and should be a pivotal point in the search for unity, with each alliance contributing its own distinctive spiritual and theological insights to the global ecumenical choir. The creation of alliances primarily enables each confessional family to achieve a common witness, mission, and service within itself. Each confessional family experiences

25 On this subject, see Harding Meyer, "Konfessionelle Weltbünde zwischen Konfessionalismus und Entkonfessionalisierung," *Una Sancta* 26, 1971, 51–59, esp. 53.

26 The history of these encounters has been authored by the then secretary general of the WARC, Edmond Perret, "The Conference of Secretaries of World Confessional Families 1957–1977," in: Yoshiro Ishida, Harding Meyer & Edmond Perret, eds., *The History and Theological Concerns of World Confessional Families*, Stuttgart, Kreuz Verlag Erich Breitsohl GmbH & Co., 1979, 43–72.

fellowship in worship and even the exchange of ministers among that family's churches. Each alliance has established an organization that goes beyond the particular church and preserves the communion within that family, even if the authority of these supra-local structures is relative. Such organizations cannot impose upon the particular churches, which remain autonomous. Thus, a vision of the unity that can be achieved through a true rapprochement of these alliances is laid out. In 1957, the tools for this to come about had not yet been developed. From the beginning, the search was considered the common task of the confessional alliances that wished to be part of the tradition of the church common to all Christian families while bringing their own specific touch. They saw themselves as specific expressions of the *una sancta catholica ecclesia*, even if they did not (yet) recognize one another as legitimate expressions of the Church of Christ. This was the concern and the approach of the first meetings after 1957.

3.2 *The Model of Unity*

An important development in the world confessional alliances coming together occurred with the participation of the Orthodox churches from 1961, and then of the Roman Catholic Church after Vatican II. These two churches do not see themselves as confessional families, a reality that they consider to be unique to Protestantism. Nevertheless, they decided to participate in these regular meetings. Vatican II's affirmation that the Church of Christ "subsists in" the Catholic Church has led to many being more open towards the latter. It means that the Church of Christ can also exist outside the Roman structure.[27] After Vatican II, the Roman Church's approach was comparable to those of the world confessional alliances: they saw themselves as an expression of the one Church of Christ, as being fully church without being the entire church.

The Lutheran theologian Harding Meyer was invited to present a paper on the major theological convictions of the world confessional families at the 1978 meeting of the world confessional alliances. His text was unanimously praised, and the secretaries of the families present adopted it as a charter defining their self-understanding and ecumenical purpose.[28] This charter emphasizes the historical continuity of the Christian faith and life in the specificity of each Christian confessional alliance as well as the legitimate diversity that is expressed in each of them (§ 11). The central affirmation, however, is that of the common confession of the one, apostolic faith within the catholic church, of which the confessional alliances are "specific" manifestations (§ 18). It is recalled that this understanding has been repeatedly affirmed by Anglicans and Lutherans (§§ 16 and 17) and is now being affirmed by Roman Catholics and even Orthodox (§§ 19–21). The "subsistit in" of Vatican II can be accepted by the vast majority of the world's confessional alliances because it also expresses their self-understanding (§ 19). In order to overcome all the ambiguities attached to the term "confession," the charter proposed to speak no longer of a "world confessional alliance" but of a "Christian World Communion" (§ 35), a name that would be officially adopted in 1979.[29]

The CWC model of unity was now clearly defined. Specificity does not mean separation or division. The fact that the Christian faith and the one Church of Christ have different expressions is legitimate and does not contradict either the unity in faith or the unity of the catholic church (in the original sense of that term). Thus, the

27 See the dogmatic constitution *LG* 8 and the decree on ecumenism *UR* 4.

28 Text published in Harding Meyer, "Basic Theological Concerns of World Confessional Families," in: Ishida, Meyer & Perret, eds., *The History and Theological Concerns*, 15–42.

29 In a commentary on the charter, Meyer casts the name of the particular CWC as the last name or family name, with the denominational designation as the first name. See Harding Meyer, "Die Weltweiten Christlichen Gemeinschaften: Ökumenischer Auftrag und Identität," *ÖR* 41, 1992, 419–434, esp. 428.

starting point of the dialogue between the CWCs is made clear. The primary task is bilateral dialogues between the different CWCs so that they may come to fully recognize each other (§§ 23–25). The logical outcome is a vision of unity, that of "unity in reconciled diversity." This expression, which is now commonplace and marks all subsequent efforts within the ecumenical movement, was used for the first time in this charter (§ 27).

This model of unity is also concerned with the historical continuity of the Christian faith, which must be stripped of all the seeds of division that, for too long, have often accompanied it. It is not a question of cementing any status quo, but of doing everything possible to ensure that, in dialogue, the preservation of continuity is accompanied by a true evolution of each CWC, which, while remaining identical to itself, increasingly understands itself as an ecclesial expression alongside others whose legitimacy it no longer disputes (§ 36ff). The preservation of Christian identity does not mean maintaining rigidities. A church that is identical to itself evolves according to time and place. Identity presupposes and includes transformation and evolution.

4 The Contribution of the CWCs to the Wider Ecumenical Movement

The WCC was founded in 1948 by a majority of churches that were also members of world confessional alliances, the future CWCs. Leaders of the four major alliances (Anglican, Lutheran, Methodist, and Reformed) played a leading role in its establishment. They were convinced that the model lived out in each of their alliances could and should be extended to a broader ecumenical identity, the stated purpose of their alliance being, as shown above, each church surpassing itself together with its commitment to the unity of the entire Church of Christ. The confessional alliances were the precursors of the WCC and should not be understood as movements opposed to it.

4.1 *Two Divergent Models of Unity*

The question of the distinction between confessional and ecumenical identity within the WCC was raised at the outset and was repeatedly addressed in the WCC's early assemblies. The question that arose was that of unity. Is what is sought a unity without particular denominations or is there room for different denominational identities?[30] Tensions were frequent and grew stronger over the years, especially after 1960, when the first polarizations occurred. Some saw confessional identity and ecumenical commitment as opposed realities, two notions that were mutually exclusive in their eyes. Maintaining denominational identities would only lead to a "problematic puzzle"[31] that would keep the churches divided. The young African, Asian, and Latin American churches were the first to challenge the existence of the world alliances, which they saw as transferring to the WCC the problems of the European and, later, North American churches, which they had inherited from the 16th century but were unable able to solve.[32]

The tensions between the WCC and the CWCs, most of which members were and continue to be major players within the WCC, should not be exaggerated. The people involved did not see the CWCs as a competitor to the WCC, especially since many of the WCC's activities were carried out in full cooperation with the confessional alliances, avoiding duplication from the beginning; such duplication would not have made sense. The dispute concerns a very specific point: the model of unity and the way to achieve it.

30 Regarding this issue, see Harold E. Fey, "Confessional Families and the Ecumenical Movement," in: *A History of the Ecumenical Movement*, vol. 2, Harold E. Fey, ed., *The Ecumenical Advance (1948–1968)*, London, SPCK, 1970, 115–142, which cites numerous interventions at WCC general assemblies.

31 Quoted by Lewis S. Mudge, "'Weltkonfessionalismus' und Ökumene," *Lutherische Rundschau* 13, 1963, 50–60, here 58. Mudge reports on conferences held at a meeting between the WCC and the CWCs in 1962.

32 Various examples in Fey "Confessional Families and the Ecumenical Movement," 120–126.

In order to understand this issue, it is important to recall the model of unity implemented by the WCC. At its general assembly in New Delhi in 1961, the WCC was the first to propose a vision of unity:

> We believe that the unity which is both God's will and his gift to his Church is being made visible as all in each place who are baptized into Jesus Christ and confess him as Lord and Saviour are brought by the Holy Spirit into one fully committed fellowship [*koinonia*], holding the one apostolic faith, preaching the one Gospel, breaking the one bread, joining in common prayer, and having a corporate life reaching out in witness and service to all.[33]

The assembly was not able to specify in detail what this "fully committed fellowship" entailed, but the general orientation was clear: the WCC wanted to move from a federation of churches existing side by side towards a different ecclesial quality.

The next step was the WCC assembly in Uppsala in 1968, which, not without referencing the recently concluded Vatican II, introduced the idea of a universal council: "The members of the World Council of Churches, committed to each other, should work for the time when a genuinely universal council may once more speak for all Christians, and lead the way into the future."[34] The more pneumatological vision of *koinonia* proposed at New Delhi was thus complemented by a more structural reality to be used for its realization. The following general assembly held in Nairobi in 1975 added:

> The one Church is to be envisioned as a conciliar fellowship of local churches which are themselves truly united. In this conciliar fellowship, each local church possesses, in communion with the others, the fullness of catholicity, witnesses to the same apostolic faith, and therefore recognizes the others as belonging to the same Church of Christ and guided by the same Spirit.[35]

The theological insistence on the pneumatological dimension of catholicity and conciliarity, which was also emphasized in Nairobi, was thus accorded secondary importance. Above all, the debate was structural and focused on "a conciliar fellowship of local churches which are themselves truly united." Is this an organic union, or even a merger of local churches called to form a "fully committed fellowship" in a place, nation, or region? The assembly seemed to be moving in this direction by calling for the "surrender of the denominational identities"[36] and adding that the "organic union of separate denominations to form one body does mean a kind of death which threatens the denominational identity of its members, but it is dying in order to receive a fuller life."[37]

The opposition between the two models of unity was obvious. The WCC proposed that the local churches unify or even merge, leaving behind their ancient (confessional) affiliations. These churches could then meet again in a universal council, the ultimate expression of unity. The path proposed was that of a geographical criterion, with any place (region or country) seeking to achieve a truly united church, an organic type of unity. The CWC model used another criterion, that of confessional families, which now extended beyond particular places. "Unity in reconciled diversity" is based on a rapprochement between existing world families and admits a legitimate diversity within the local churches. This vision included the hoped-for

33 *The New Delhi Report: The Third Assembly of The World Council of Churches 1961*, New York, Association Press, 1962, 116.

34 See Norman Goodall, ed., *The Uppsala Report 1968: Official Report of the Fourth Assembly of the World Council of Churches (Uppsala July 4–20, 1968)*, Geneva, WCC Publications, 1968, 17.

35 David M. Paton, ed., *Breaking Barriers, Nairobi 1975: The Official Report of the Fifth Assembly of the WCC (Nairobi, 23 November–10 December 10, 1975)*, London, SPCK, 1976, 57–69, here 60.

36 Paton, ed., *Breaking Barriers*, 65.

37 Paton, ed., *Breaking Barriers*, 63.

council, but the latter was called to be the place of unity that would bring the confessional families together at the global level.

The WCC's general assembly in Vancouver in 1983 also focused on society's major ethical issues, in particular the concern for peace, justice, and the care for creation. It emphasized the indispensable link between faith, sacraments, ministry, and conciliar structures on the one hand, and ethical commitment in this world on the other. This openness to more ethical and political questions was accompanied by the realization that unity and diversity, even denominational unity and identities, are not necessarily antagonistic. The unity sought is that of the church as a conciliar community "in its full richness of diversity."[38]

The vision advanced in Vancouver was taken up and systematized by the Canberra assembly in 1991, which approved the text "The Unity of the Church as Koinonia: Gift and Calling."[39] This text explicitly recognizes the validity of diversities – including theological traditions, that is, confessional identities – that "are integral to the nature of communion" provided that they do not render "impossible the common confession of Jesus Christ as God and Savior." Diversity is a positive component of unity, not a flaw that remains and must be accommodated. This change marked a significant step forward because it ended the heated debates about models of unity of the previous years.[40] The final stage in the discussion of the vision of unity came in the preparations for the Harare assembly in 1998. The new political situation – mainly the collapse of the Soviet Union and its consequences for world order – the significant progress in some bilateral dialogues, the reservations of the wider Orthodox family, and the emergence of Third World churches had led to a rearrangement of the ecumenical landscape. The WCC was therefore compelled to redefine its idea and common vision. Its very existence and ability to offer a conciliar structure at the global level that would unite all churches was being questioned. The orientation proposed and adopted in Harare saw the WCC as a general framework within which churches and groups of churches strived to achieve visible communion, not in a general way, but through privileged relationships that are established in a more *ad hoc* way between the various partners. The approach of the CWCs could find a place here.

4.2 *Multilateral and Bilateral Dialogues*

On the basis of the Uppsala decisions, the WCC had initiated a subsequent multilateral dialogue that would provide all churches with a common reference. It entrusted this task to its theological commission, Faith and Order, whose preparatory work in Accra in 1974 had had significant influence on the Nairobi assembly. The first draft was reformulated and, in 1981, led to the famous text *Baptism, Eucharist, and Ministry* (BEM).[41] This text was widely accepted by the churches; it proposed convergences that would allow the local churches to reach consensus as a basis for their local unity. It should be added that this text was the work of many theologians who were also involved in the CWCs. They did not consider it necessarily in opposition to the CWCs, but rather an indispensable general framework within which bilateral

38 David Gill, ed., *Gathered for Life: Official Report VI Assembly World Council of Churches (Vancouver, Canada 24 July–10 August 1983)*, Geneva/Grand Rapids, WCC Publications/Eerdmans, 1983, 45.

39 Michael Kinnamon, ed., *Signs of the Spirit: Official Report Seventh Assembly (Canberra, Australia, 7–20 February 1991)*, Geneva/Grand Rapids, WCC Publications/Eerdmans, 1991, 172–174. John Paul II referred to this text in his 1995 encyclical *Ut unum sint*.

40 This is the point that was most strongly criticized, especially by the authors of the previous declarations, in particular that of Nairobi. See Lukas Vischer, "Is this really 'the Unity We Seek'?: Comments on the Statement on 'The Unity of the Church as Koinonia: Gift and Calling,' Adopted by the WCC Assembly in Canberra," *EcRev* 44, 1992, 467–478.

41 *Baptism, Eucharist and Ministry*, Geneva, WCC Publications, 1982. On BEM, see Luca Ferracci, *Battesimo Eucaristia Ministero: Genesi e destino di un documento ecumenico*, Bologna, Il Mulino, 2021.

exchanges could also develop between confessional families.[42] This was not the option chosen by the WCC leadership and in particular by those in Faith and Order, who understood BEM as the foundation of the "conciliar community" for the purpose of "organic union."

In spite of being broadly accepted by the churches, the BEM undertaking did not produce the desired results and did not lead to any "unity" of local churches, those that existed in, for example, the Indies, being prior to BEM. After 1990, this text was even somewhat forgotten. The decisions taken in Harare in fact note the difficulty of a multilateral dialogue that, while providing a necessary framework, does not allow the necessary progress in the quality of relations between local churches. A federal framework open to regional ecumenical movements, confessional families, and, where appropriate, the Catholic Church, on the other hand, makes it possible to envisage differentiated developments between the various partners within the WCC itself, which is a forum that makes encounter and dialogue possible.

Bilateral dialogues generally undertaken between two confessional families existed throughout the 20th century. After 1960, they increased and were reinforced by the entry of the Roman Catholic Church into this process after Vatican II. Dialogues were initiated between local, regional, and national churches, but above all between the CWCs as such. It is not possible to mention all of these dialogues since the conclusions to those between the CWCs today are over 4,000 pages long.[43] It is mainly the four major CWCs (Anglicans, Lutherans, Methodists, and Reformed), besides the Roman Catholic Church and the Orthodox churches, that have conducted these dialogues. The results are remarkable and have made it possible to overcome many of the controversies inherited from history. They have also made it possible to move beyond the time when CWCs were seen as rigid and uncompromising defenders of their identities and a hindrance to ecumenical progress.

The common conviction of these dialogues, that of a "unity in reconciled diversity," is very different from that proposed by the WCC. Full ecclesial communion demands communion in the preaching of the word and the celebration of the sacraments (baptism and the Lord's Supper) as well as the full recognition of, and thus full communion in, each other's ministry. However, the path towards this communion is different from that imagined by the WCC.[44] It is a matter of seeking in bilateral dialogue a consensus that puts an end to the reciprocal condemnations declared in years past. Multilateral dialogue does not allow a consensus to emerge because it brings together in a single process a large number of representatives from a wide array of families. At most, it allows for convergences, which often resemble compromises. Bilateral dialogue, on the other hand, allows two families to directly tackle the themes that set them apart and to propose to the churches ways in which they can achieve a new quality of relationship. There is no need to mention here the great

42 Wolfhart Pannenberg, "Die Arbeit von Faith and Order im Kontext der ökumenischen Bewegung," *ÖR* 31, 1982, 47–59, esp. 59.

43 The most complete collection of the conclusions from the international dialogues is that published in German and in English. See Harding Meyer & Lukas Vischer, eds., *Growth in Agreement: Reports and Agreed Statements of Ecumenical Conversations on a World Level*, New York/Geneva, Paulist Press/WCC Publications, 1984; Jeffrey Gros, Harding Meyer & William G. Rusch, eds., *Growth in Agreement II: Reports and Agreed Statements of Ecumenical Conversations at the World Level (1982–1998)*, Geneva/Grand Rapids, WCC Publications/Eerdmans, 2000; Jeffrey Gros, Thomas F. Best & Lorelei F. Fuchs, eds., *Growth in Agreement III: International Dialogue Texts and Agreed Statements (1998–2005)*, Geneva/Grand Rapids, WCC Publications/Eerdmans, 2007; Thomas F. Best & others, eds., *Growth in Agreement IV: International Dialogue Texts and Agreed Statements (2004–2014)*, 2 vols., Geneva, WCC Publications, 2017.

44 This is very rapidly recognized by the representatives of the WCC who note the breakthroughs made by the bilateral dialogues. See Nils Ehrenström, "The World Confessional Families in the Service of Unity," *EcRev* 26, 1974, 265–277, esp. 267–268 and 272–273.

advances that have taken place, as it is beyond the scope of this presentation. Two examples may serve to illustrate this approach and show how the CWCs are major actors in the contemporary ecumenical movement, a fact that I noted in the introduction to this chapter.

The first example is that of the dialogues between the families that emerged from the Reformation: Lutherans, Reformed, Anglicans, and Methodists. These dialogues have been primarily carried out at the local level and then verified internationally. However, dialogue is not an end in itself, it can only propose to the churches some theological conclusions on the basis of which they can, through their synods, issue and approve a statement that effectively transforms the ecclesial quality of the bonds with other families. The reception and approval of these conclusions can only occur at the local level, in keeping with the self-understanding of the CWCs, where each church remains autonomous. These processes have given rise to many declarations of communion between churches that continue to refer to their own traditions but recognize in the other family an authentic and legitimate expression of the one Church of Christ. They have opened the way for the communal celebration of the Word and sacraments, to the passage not only of believers but also of ministers from one family to another, as well as to the constant search for a common witness and service. In this process, unity is no longer a dream but a reality. Numerous examples attest to this.[45]

The second example is that of the dialogue of the Lutheran, Reformed, Methodist, and Anglican families with Rome. On the basis of the results of 30 years of dialogue, Lutherans and Roman Catholics signed the *Joint Declaration on the Doctrine of Justification* in 1999. This agreement expresses the ecumenical understanding of the CWCs: the same confession of faith can be expressed by different formulations expressing a fidelity to different heritages. It states that unity does not mean uniformity; legitimate difference is not only tolerated but is part of the consensus. The gospel is the same. This agreement lifts the old condemnations inherited from history, holding that they no longer apply to the other church in the current state of its teaching. It is certainly not a matter yet of full communion, but a first, decisive step has been taken. This declaration was signed by the Roman Church on one hand, and the LWF on the other, with the latter having consulted all the synods of its member churches and obtained their mandate to sign the declaration. As noted above, the WMC signed the declaration in 2006, and the WCRC did the same in 2017. Just as with the Lutherans, the Methodists and the Reformed consulted all the synods of their member churches, since the global

45 Ten declarations of communion have been proclaimed on different continents between churches of the Reformation. The oldest is the Leuenberg Agreement of 1973, which established communion between Lutheran, Reformed, United, Waldensian, and Moravian churches in Europe. On this, see the contribution by Elisabeth Parmentier in this volume. The Lutheran and Reformed churches of the United States followed in 1997, signing *A Formula of Agreement*, while those of the Near East signed the Amman Declaration in 2006. In that same year, the signatory churches of the Leuenberg Agreement proclaimed their communion with the Methodist churches with the so-called Vienna Declaration. Dialogue between Lutheran and Reformed churches and the Anglican Communion ended in Germany with the Meissen Declaration (1988), and in France with the Reuilly Declaration (2001), which, unlike the former, did not include only the Church of England, but also all the British Anglican churches. The Lutheran churches of Scandinavia and the Baltic countries declared their communion in 1992 with the Porvoo Common Statement. In the US, the Lutheran church entered into communion with the Episcopal (Anglican) Church with the adoption of the agreement *Called to Common Mission* in 2001; their Canadian counterparts reached a similar agreement that year with the Waterloo Declaration. Finally, in Australia, the Lutheran and Anglican traditions reached an agreement called *Common Ground – Covenanting for Mutual Recognition and Reconciliation*, in preparation for a declaration of communion, that some churches have not yet ratified (on these dialogues, see my contribution in this volume, "The Lutheran-Anglican Dialogue and the Declaration of Communion").

organization did not have any authority without their direct mandate. The archbishop of Canterbury also approved the declaration on Oct 31, 2017, following a decision of the ACC, without ratification by the particular Anglican churches.

These two examples illustrate the ecumenical process implemented by the CWCs. The progress is real, and although there is still a long road ahead, the CWCs are today a major feature of the ecumenical landscape.

Translated from French to English by Susan Dawson Vásquez and David Dawson Vásquez.

Bibliography

Avis, Paul & Benjamin M. Guyer, eds., *The Lambeth Conference: Theology, History, Polity and Purpose*, London, Bloomsbury/T&T Clark, 2017.

Bauswein, Jean Jacques & Lukas Vischer, eds., *The Reformed Family Worldwide: A Survey of Reformed Churches, Theological Schools, and International Organizations*, Grand Rapids, Eerdmans, 1999.

Fey, Harold E., "Confessional Families and the Ecumenical Movement," in: *A History of the Ecumenical Movement*, vol. 2, Harold E. Fey, ed., *The Ecumenical Advance (1948–1968)*, London, SPCK, 1970.

Gariepy, Henry, *Christianity in Action: The International History of the International Salvation Army*, Grand Rapids, Eerdmans, 2009.

Healing Memories: Reconciling in Christ, Geneva/Strasbourg, The Lutheran World Federation/The Mennonite World Conference, 2010.

Hinson, Edward Glenn, "The Baptist World Alliance: Its Identity and Ecumenical Involvement," *EcRev* 46, 1994, 406–412.

Ishida, Yoshiro, Harding Meyer & Edmond Perret, eds., *The History and Theological Concerns of World Confessional Families*, Stuttgart, Kreuz Verlag Erich Breitsohl GmbH & Co., 1979.

Kenworthy, Leonard S., *Quakerism: A Study Guide on the Religious Society of Friends*, Dublin IN, Prinit Press, 1981.

Kirby, James E. & William J. Abraham, eds., *The Oxford Handbook of Methodist Studies*, Oxford, Oxford University Press, 2009.

Meyer, Harding, "Konfessionelle Weltbünde zwischen Konfessionalismus und Entkonfessionalisierung," *Una Sancta* 26, 1971, 51–59.

Meyer, Harding, "Basic Theological Concerns of World Confessional Families," in: Yoshiro Ishida, Harding Meyer & Edmond Perret, eds., *The History and Theological Concerns of World Confessional Families*, Stuttgart, Kreuz Verlag Erich Breitsohl GmbH & Co., 1979, 15–42.

Meyer, Harding, "Die Weltweiten Christlichen Gemeinschaften: Grundanliegen – Selbstverständnis – Ökumenische Verpflichtung," in: Harding Meyer, *Versöhnte Verschiedenheit: Aufsätze zur ökumenischen Theologie*, vol. 1, Frankfurt/Paderborn, Lembeck/Bonifatius, 1998.

Perret, Edmond "The Conference of Secretaries of World Confessional Families 1957–1977," in: Yoshiro Ishida, Harding Meyer & Edmond Perret, eds., *The History and Theological Concerns of World Confessional Families*, Stuttgart, Kreuz Verlag Erich Breitsohl GmbH & Co., 1979, 43–72.

Prüter, Karl, *The Old Catholic Church: A History and Chronology*, San Bernardino, St. Willibrord's Press, [2]1996.

Schjørring, Jens Holger, Prasanna Kumari & Norman A. Hjelm, eds., *From Federation to Communion: The History of the Lutheran World Federation*, Minneapolis, Fortress Press, 1997.

CHAPTER 25

Christian Partnership in Africa at the End of Colonization

R. Simangaliso Kumalo and Kisitu Davies

1 Historical and Cultural Setting of Ecumenism in Africa

The historical development of ecumenism in the African continent dates as far back as the beginning of the missionary era in the 19th century, through the work of the missionaries and their supporting agencies.[1] Arriving from either Europe or North America, the early white missionaries in Africa found a generally hostile environment in the predominantly black continent, where the culture and language were different from their own, and they thus adopted an ecumenical approach to their activities by crossing denominational lines to support one another. Linked to this collaborative approach was the fact that the missionary bodies had received the official support of their nations during the so-called "scramble for Africa,"[2] particularly following the Berlin conference of 1884–1885 which had legalized the right of European states to occupy African countries and to expand their work without any consultation of the African peoples themselves.[3] Despite coming from various denominations and being sponsored by different missionary societies, circumstance dictated that they collaborated once they were in the mission field,[4] and as a result, in most parts of Africa, missionaries intermingled with one another and even shared their ideas on how to convert the Africans, who were ofttimes resistant to the Christian message.[5] Nevertheless, they kept their denominational identities and their missionary gains apart. Importantly, however, we can assert that the ecumenical collaboration among the missionary groups accounts for both the success of the missionary project as a whole and the successful colonization of the continent by their home governments.[6] Through a combination of practical challenges and a passion for the mission of the church, together, the missionaries laid the foundation for ecumenism in Africa. On the one hand, they "used the principle of divide-and-rule to keep the African people divided, through Christian denominationalism,"[7] and on the other, they depended on some form of ecumenism for the continued success of their work.

1 See James Amanze, *A History of the Ecumenical Movement in Africa*, Gaborone, Pula Press, 1999. Gabriel Setiloane posits that ecumenism in Africa started at the bedrock of the missionaries, see Gabriel Setiloane, "The Ecumenical Movement in Africa: From Mission Church to Moratorium," in: Charles Villa-Vicencio & John W. de Gruchy, eds., *Resistance and Hope: South African Essays in Honour of Beyers Naudé*, Grand Rapids, Eerdmans, 1985, 137–147.

2 See Thomas Pakenham, *The Scramble for Africa: The White Man's Conquest of the Dark Continent from 1876 to 1912*, London, Abacus, 2014.

3 Jesse Mugambi, *From Liberation to Reconstruction: African Christian Theology after the Cold War*, Nairobi, East African Educational Publishers, 1995, 197.

4 Among the missionary societies that sent missionaries were the following: the Methodist Missionary Society; the Society for Christian Missions; the London Missionary Society (1795); the Edinburgh Missionary Society and the Glasgow Missionary Society (both 1796); the Netherlands Missionary Society (1797); the Church Missionary Society (1799); the Wesleyan Methodist Society (1813); the German Missionary Society (1815); the North German Missionary Society (1836); and the Board of Foreign Missions.

5 Nosipho Majeke, *The Role of the Missionaries in Conquest*, Cumberwood, APDUSA, 1987; see also Richard Elphick & Rodney Davenport, eds., *Christianity in South Africa: A Political, Social and Cultural History*, Cape Town, David Philip Publishers, 1997, 52.

6 Majeke, *The Role of the Missionaries in Conquest*, 53.

7 Mugambi, *From Liberation to Reconstruction*, 198.

2 The Development of Ecumenism in Africa

The development of ecumenism in Africa can be classified within four stages. The first of these can be clearly identified with the arrival of Western missionaries from different ecumenical bodies in the 19th century, which came with the aim of evangelizing Africa and expanding the colonial project on behalf of their home governments.[8] This was the moment in which missionaries first began to help one another across denominational lines in order to secure a foothold in African communities and firmly establish their mission work.[9] They also collaborated with merchants and magistrates who worked with them.

The second stage of ecumenical development is characterized by the growing sense of rivalry among the missionaries themselves as they saw their endeavors flourishing.[10] At this time, each agency was concerned with expanding their own work, resources, and influence among the African people.

The third stage of development took place in the second half of the 20th century, with the emergence of African elites who had been educated in mission schools and who now began to represent the interests of the African people.

The fourth stage concerns the institutionalization of ecumenism in Africa, which harkens back to the WMC held in New York in 1900, held with the aim of bringing together "various mission organisations working in Africa to find ways of co-ordinating their work in the continent."[11] This gathering was followed by the WMC of 1910 convened in Edinburgh, where the decision was taken "not to separate mission and ecumenism" in Africa.[12] The 1926 WMC in Le Zoute, Belgium, accordingly adopted the same theme of "The Christian Mission in Africa." It is significant to note that while these WMCs were taking place, churches across different African countries were already forming their own Christian councils, an early example being the CCG, established in 1929.[13] The firm establishment of ecumenism in Africa is therefore indelibly marked by the development of ecumenical consciousness. The movement gained particular impetus at the meeting of African church leaders in Uganda in 1958, where the resolution was taken to form the AACC, a body which was to be inaugurated in 1963. From this important initiative, a number of regional Christian councils sprung up across the continent. The quest for ecumenism, therefore, finally received its continental support and drive, leading to the formation of various ecumenical bodies with different foci and emphases on ecumenism and the mission of the global church.

3 Christian Partnership in Africa

The desire for unity and fellowship led to the founding of numerous ecumenical bodies around Africa. Among these, it is imperative to highlight some of the most important operating at continental level.

Founded in 1963, the AACC is the largest ecumenical fellowship on the African continent, representing about 140 million Christians and

8 See James R. Cochrane, *Servants of Power: The Role of English-Speaking Churches in South Africa (1903–1930)*, Johannesburg, Raven Press, 1987.

9 Colin Bundy, *The Rise and Fall of the South African Peasantry*, Cape Town, David Philip, ²1988, 29–64; see also Jean Comaroff & John L. Comaroff, *Of Revelation and Revolution*, vol. 1, *Christianity, Colonialism, and Consciousness in South Africa*, Chicago, University of Chicago Press, 1991; John L. Comaroff & Jean Comaroff, *Of Revelation and Revolution*, vol. 2, *The Dialectics of Modernity on a South African Frontier*, Chicago, University of Chicago Press, 1997.

10 Setiloane, "The Ecumenical Movement in Africa," 137.

11 David N.A. Kpobi, "Evangelicals and African Ecumenism," in: Isabel Apawo Phiri & others, eds., *Anthology of African Christianity*, Minneapolis, Fortress Press, 2016, 834–840, here 834.

12 Kpobi, "Evangelicals and African Ecumenism," 834. On the 1910 Edinburgh WMC see the contribution by Kenneth Ross in the first volume of this work.

13 Kpobi, "Evangelicals and African Ecumenism," 835.

173 national churches and regional Christian councils in 42 countries. Drawing on the theme of "Freedom and Unity in Christ" of its maiden assembly in Kampala, Uganda, the AACC has been identified with struggles for the decolonization of Africa, African nationalism, development, human dignity, and Christian unity. The association has long believed in the participation of all churches in the development of the African continent, and in line with this mission, it has accompanied churches across Africa in their involvement in the struggle for independence from colonial powers. At the present time, the AACC continues its vigilance on issues confronting the broader continent, but also on those faced by particular churches in local contexts. In this way, it offers a platform for collective voices and collective actions, basing intervention on the values of social and economic justice, health and wholeness, international relations (governance, ethics, and morality), and on its foundational programs which include theology, mission and evangelism, ecumenical growth, and interfaith relations.

The AEA, on the other hand, represents national evangelical fellowships in the whole continent, though its membership also extends to include international non-governmental Christian organizations, in addition to development and missionary agencies based within the continent. Since its foundation in 1966, the association has grown to comprise 40 evangelical fellowships as full members, which are called upon to "join in common concern to live and proclaim the Good News of Jesus amongst all nations and peoples, seeking holiness, justice, and transformation at every level: individual, family, community and culture."[14]

With a particular focus on empowering youth, women, and children, the AEA has contributed to the transformation of African societies, especially in the area of social justice. Over the years it has conducted various programs on theology and Christian education, evangelism and mission, ethics, peace and justice, relief and development, communication, youth and sports, as well as leadership development and church mobilization for advancing the kingdom of God and societal transformation on the African continent.

Another ecumenical body in Africa, the OAIC,[15] was established in 1978 with an aim to provide the continent's fast-growing churches with "a forum for sharing their concerns and hopes, and … to enable them to minister effectively to the needs of their members and their communities."[16] The association was founded following an invitation that Pope Shenouda III of the Coptic Orthodox Church of Alexandria based in Cairo had extended to the leaders of independent churches from seven African countries. Among the major concerns or objectives of the association was the desire for fellowship, as well as the promotion of theological and biblical teaching, and the theological training of its members. The OAIC has worked greatly towards ecumenical partnership and has established chapters in a number of countries, such as Kenya, Uganda, Tanzania, Botswana, Zimbabwe, Ghana, Madagascar, Nigeria, and the Democratic Republic of Congo, as well as the South African provinces of Eastern Cape and Western Cape.

The SECAM is a Catholic association founded in 1969 and headquartered in Accra, Ghana. Within each country, national episcopal conferences are held, assembled in regional groupings like the AMECEA and the IMBISA.

The CPA is one of the most significant forums through which African churches unite for consultation and cooperation, and through which they aspire for a common vision and mission that lead to mutual Christian witness. The CPA's influence on Christian partnership in Africa has largely been shaped by their response to a number

14 See the mission of the AEA available at <https://aeafrica.org/what-we-do/> (accessed Mar 27, 2024).

15 See <https://www.oikoumene.org/en/church-families/african-instituted-churches/oaic> (accessed Mar 27, 2024).

16 Masilo Molobi, "The Ecumenical Vision of the Organization of African Independent Churches from an Educational Perspective," *SHE* 37/1, 2011, 87–102, here 93.

of issues affecting the continent, including those of social justice, liberation, and Christian unity, as well as those pertaining to the experience of underdevelopment which had impacted many African societies since the early postcolonial era. While development was beginning to emerge as a medium for social justice, underdevelopment continued to promote injustices and confrontations within society. It was necessary, therefore, that churches initiated cross-denominational dialogue regarding important questions pertaining to the church as a whole: how would it identify itself with the poor? How could it speak of development without mentioning concepts such as liberation of the poor? How could development promote peace and justice while the churches' poor continued to be marginalized?[17] At the WCC 1975 conference in Nairobi, therefore, the idea of development was a central point of discussion, perceived by bodies such as the CCPD as "a liberating process aimed at social justice, self-reliance and economic growth."[18]

Ecumenism in Africa has developed through close relations with the WCC, though this is not to suggest that the African churches' struggles regarding humanitarian social issues such as political liberation, development, and peace and justice were only triggered through the influence of WCC initiatives. Indeed, ecumenical bodies in Africa such as the AACC have a long history of "deep awareness of the theoretical reorientations of the aims of development from the narrow focus on economic growth,"[19] though their mission has expanded over the years to address broader "concerns for human well-being and environmental sustainability – and more recently to a focus on sustainable development – with its triple emphasis on the social, economic, and environmental dimensions of development."[20]

4 The Achievements of Ecumenism in Africa

The ecumenical movements in Africa have made a number of accomplishments since their inception, which range from increasing ecumenical cooperation across denominational lines to supporting the collaborative struggle for independence and encouraging the development of African leadership, to name but a few. Their first achievement involved the development of the ecumenical identity of the African churches, which were constructed with the aim of engaging the churches with the critical issues concerning the African people during the postcolonial era. Underpinning the new African ecumenical identity was a theology that guaranteed advocacy for development without discrimination, as well as the theological conviction that all humans were created equal and that together, man and woman had been entrusted with the care of creation. In line with these fundamental principles, at the 1969 Abidjan conference, the AACC reiterated their belief that humans were "each entitled to a share of the world's wealth according to their needs, and are stewards of the same."[21]

The second achievement of ecumenism in Africa was the reconception of Christian churches as spaces of liberation and not suppression. What is more, from the churches' point of view, liberation was not only perceived in terms of political liberation from colonialist powers, but also in terms of liberation from widespread internal corruption, from oppressive African-led regimes,

17 *In Search of a Theology of Development: Papers from a Consultation on Theology and Development Held by Sodepax in Cartigny, Switzerland, November, 1969*, Geneva, SODEPAX, 1969, 152.

18 Teddy Chalwe Sakupapa, "The Ecumenical Movement and Development: The Case of the All Africa Conference of Churches (AACC), 1963–2000 (Part 1)," *SHE* 44/3, 2018, 1–15, here 5.

19 Sakupapa, "The Ecumenical Movement and Development," 5.

20 Sakupapa, "The Ecumenical Movement and Development," 5.

21 All Africa Conference of Churches, *Engagement: The Second AACC Assembly, "Abidjan 1969"*, Nairobi, All Africa Conference of Churches, 1970, 108.

from human rights violations, and from oppressive policies such as the apartheid in South Africa.[22]

Attempts to frame churches as spaces of liberation are evident from the proceedings of various ecumenical conferences organized in Africa, including the Lusaka assembly of November 1976 held in Kitwe, Zambia, which explored the concept of liberation in the spiritual, political, educational, social, and ecclesiastical spheres. A milestone in this process was the 1964 Mindolo consultation in former Northern Rhodesia, on "Christian Practice and Desirable Action in Social Change and Race Relations." The consultation, organized by the WCC, the AACC, the liberal South African Institute of Race Relations, and the Mindolo Ecumenical Foundation in Northern Rhodesia, brought together more than 50 Christian leaders, all critics of apartheid, and proposed the WCC PCR.[23]

The concept of liberation as an identity framework for church partnership encouraged churches to commit themselves to addressing issues of social transformation, especially as far as economic liberation was concerned. Churches such as those under the umbrella of the AACC were preoccupied by the need to address various socio-economic issues, particularly those affecting the marginalized groups of society including women, youth, childless women, sex workers, and refugees,[24] as well the need to confront the threats posed by increasing militarization and contemporary ideological battles such as that between capitalism and socialism. For economic liberation to take place churches had to work together and, at the same time, discern ways of increasing access to education. It was under this impulse that the churches became aware of the need to carry out research and to critically listen to the voices of society's most underrepresented and vulnerable. The Research and Development Consultancy Service, created by the AACC in 1982, emphasized the need for the communities to participate in the production of knowledge, especially in cases directly affecting them. This insistence was rooted in the conviction that "people, regardless of educational levels and occupation, possess important practical and empirical knowledge that allows them to operate in their current environments."[25]

The third achievement of ecumenism in Africa was its role in the endeavor of African Christians to end the continent's reliance on foreign intervention in the effort to eradicate social challenges such as poverty, hunger, and food insecurity. The postcolonial churches saw foreign dependence as pernicious with regards to addressing these concerns, with official Research and Development Consultancy Service documents arguing that African churches' dependence on foreign aid had been partly responsible for "the root causes of hunger and food insufficiency in Africa,"[26] and ecumenical bodies such as the AACC observing that African Christian communities had to involve themselves in calls for Christian witness as opposed to calls for foreign assistance because the "international link alone produced structural relationships internally that reproduce poverty and underdevelopment."[27] Ecumenism thus required the cross-denominational collaboration of African churches to tackle key issues affecting African

22 As Sakupapa goes on to observe, these cases of oppression had permeated African societies in "most postcolonial African states from the late 1970s to early 1980s"; Sakupapa, "The Ecumenical Movement and Development," 6.

23 Thembeka Doris Mufamadi, *The World Council of Churches and Its Programme to Combat Racism: The Evolution and Development of Their Fight against Apartheid (1969–1994)*, Ph.D. thesis, University of South Africa, 2011.

24 Sakupapa, "The Ecumenical Movement and Development," 7; Efiong Utuk, *Visions of Authenticity: The Assemblies of the All Africa Conference of Churches (1963–1992)*, Nairobi, All Africa Conference of Churches, 1997, 150.

25 Research and Development Consultancy Service, Quality of Rural Life: Programme Proposed for Intensified Rural Development Action by the African Churches, 1986, in: AACC archives, box 03-05-06, file no. 41, 13.

26 *Lomé 87, You Shall Be My Witnesses: Official Report of the Fifth AACC General Assembly*, Nairobi, All Africa Conference of Churches, 1988, 40.

27 *Lomé 87, You Shall Be My Witnesses*, 40.

societies, though independently of foreign assistance. Many interpreted this approach as a form of Christian witness; the 1987 AACC Lomé assembly, for example, discouraged African churches continued dependence on foreign aid while firmly insisting that "Christians should see it as their responsibility to fully participate in the social, political and economic life of their country."[28]

The postcolonial ecumenical movements' fourth accomplishment was the development of their own theologies – understood as "theologies cooked in an African pot"[29] – which responded to the social-economic challenges facing the African continent and which mandated the church to take a leading role given the numerical growth of Christianity in Africa. Theologians and church leaders of the continent were motivated by emerging theological reflections from African natives, such as the Kenyan theologian Jesse Mugambi and his theology of reconstruction, which argued that the church should play a significant role in facilitating social transformation. The theology of reconstruction became a focus of ecumenical movements such as the AACC.[30] For Mugambi, it was delusional to speak of the numerical growth of Christianity in Africa while social challenges such as poverty, corruption, civil wars, and hunger persisted throughout the continent. In fact, the theologian even posed the penetrating question: "How can the most religious continent in the world be abandoned by God to perish in poverty, in debt and under the yoke of the great powers of the world?"[31]

In Mugambi's view, there is an inevitable need for a new world order in which all individuals, from professionals to the unskilled, from religious leaders to lay Christian communities, and in fact all members of society were to participate in the reconstruction process which, according to the Kenyan theologian, was a common good for wider African society.[32] However, he adds that this would not simply come automatically; on the contrary, it would require the church to renew itself in order to reflect the present state of affairs. In redefining its identity, the church ought to see that theological engagements, debates, and dialogues "should be reconstructive rather than destructive … inclusive rather than competitive."[33]

The fifth achievement of ecumenism in Africa was the adaptation of the gospel to African cultures and philosophies. Ecumenical ambitions and current Christian partnership in Africa have advanced social integration by promoting a form of Christianity based on the African concepts of *ubuntu* (humanity) and neighborhood. These two concepts are related and are considerate of the humanity of the other, encouraging mutual relationships while strongly discouraging confrontation. For example, in East Africa, ecumenism is taught and propagated along the concept of neighborhood in an effort to reclaim the Christian unity that pertained before the radical separation produced by Western Christianity over the centuries.[34]

We can define neighborhood as "the quality of or state of an African Christian being a brother or sister to the other person,"[35] standing against

28 *Lomé 87, You Shall Be My Witnesses*, 114.

29 See Klaus Fiedler, Paul Gundani & Hilary Mijoga, eds., *Theology Cooked in an African Pot*, Zomba, Association of Theological Institutions in Southern and Central Africa, 1998.

30 As Sakupapa notes, "by the time of the AACC Addis Ababa Assembly in 1997, the paradigm of reconstruction [strongly advocated for by Kenyan theologian Jesse Mugambi] had become a central theological theme within the AACC"; Sakupapa, "The Ecumenical Movement and Development," 10.

31 Mugambi, *From Liberation to Reconstruction*, 163.

32 Jean-Claude Loba-Mkole, "Bible Translation and Reconstruction Hermeneutics," *APB* 20/1, 2009, 28–44.

33 Mugambi, *From Liberation to Reconstruction*, 13.

34 As Christopher Byaruhanga can admit: "It is in the neighbourhood setting that people in East Africa: i. come to know one another … ii. identify the new signs of the times and creatively respond to them"; Christopher Byaruhanga, *The History and Theology of the Ecumenical Movement in East Africa*, Kampala, Fountain Publishers, 2015, 3.

35 Byaruhanga, *The History and Theology of the Ecumenical Movement in East Africa*, 3.

a divided Christianity which carries ahead the confrontations that existed between various missionary groups as Christianity was being introduced to Africa for the first time. Through the lens of neighborhood, it would be impossible to contemplate a divided Christianity, as this would be a source of confusion from an African point of view. Instead, the growth of ecumenical thought and practice in Africa can be seen through the plethora of denominational diversity and tolerance that is gradually developing in the continent.[36]

The sixth accomplishment of ecumenism in Africa concerns the translation of the Bible and its use and fellowship, which is by no means an achievement realized within recent decades, but rather a prolonged development whose origins can be traced back to the arrival of Christianity in Africa in the 3rd century, when the Bible was translated into the Bohairic and Sahidic Coptic dialects of Egypt.[37] The Bible's translation into many indigenous African languages is arguably one of the major milestones for the ecumenical project in Africa, having helped to bring together protestant missions and guarantee that, despite differences between denominations, they can still work together for a common good. It is imperative to note that prior to Africa's political independence from colonial powers, Bible translation was chiefly the prerogative of colonial missionaries, and it served as an important mandate for Christian mission in Africa. Due in part to a lack of competence in indigenous languages, many Bible translations were difficult to understand in local contexts as they contained a number of grammatical mistakes. In recent decades however, Bible translation seems to have been taken over by ecumenical agencies such as the AACC, which has worked since its establishment to ensure that African societies have "access to the Word of God in clear and readable translations … done under the direction of the AACC by competent first language speakers of the particular language themselves."[38] Additionally, not only has the AACC called for and facilitated Bible translation in Africa, but it has also initiated calls for joint translations and for the publication of the Bible in the vernacular. Today, it is therefore extremely common to witness Sunday readings based on the standardized versions of the Bible approved by the Roman Catholic, Anglican, and Protestant church authorities in Africa.

5 Challenges Faced by Ecumenical Efforts and Ambitions in Africa

The experience of the CPA from the end of the colonial project and thereon has been complex, its work having been characterized by waves of pro-ecumenical and anti-ecumenical processes. Furthermore, even within the pro-ecumenical camp, partnership has been influenced by varying attitudes towards institutional ecumenical directives, with some advocating for a top-to-bottom approach while others insisting upon the need for grassroots ecumenical initiatives. Grassroots ecumenism, as Richard Werbner puts it, brings "people together in local settings, despite and

36 As Philip Jenkins states: "Often, relations between expanding denominations are cordial or at least non-confrontational, on the grounds that each church has plenty of room to grow, with ample likely converts. In much of Africa, different denominations have evolved good working relationships in form of conferences, or federations of Christian churches"; Philip Jenkins, *The Next Christendom: The Coming of Global Christianity*, Oxford, Oxford University Press, 2011, 155.

37 Byaruhanga, *The History and Theology of the Ecumenical Movement in East Africa*, 3. Byaruhanga thus contends: "Beginning in the late nineteenth-century missionary societies actively promoted Bible translation on the continent as a first step towards evangelization. In 1816, the Gospel of Mark was translated and published into one of the languages of Sierra Leone. In 1835, Madagascar produced the first complete Bible. In 1857, a complete Bible was translated in one of the languages of Botswana and South Africa. Ghana had a complete Bible translated in 1866; and in Eastern Africa, Krapt translated the Bible in 1844"; Byaruhanga, *The History and Theology of the Ecumenical Movement in East Africa*, 111.

38 Byaruhanga, *The History and Theology of the Ecumenical Movement in East Africa*, 111.

without effacing their religious differences; [it] is often a yearning, an ideal and a hope of highly valued religious unity and spiritual fellowship."[39] From a broader perspective, irrespective of diverse approaches to ecumenism, the CPA has been faced with the need to tackle theological problems and their contribution to humanitarian crises. Issues such as racism, social justice, social welfare, public service, international peace, and church and state relationships have been critical for African Christianity partnership. Addressing these challenges is of critical importance if the ecumenical journey is to remain meaningful to Christian witness in present-day Africa.

It cannot be said that the period of the 20th century during which most African states gained political independence from their colonial oppressors was a bed of roses for the CPA. Indeed, the CPA had to deal with the continued challenges of apartheid and post-apartheid struggles in South Africa the genocide, post-genocide, and reconciliation challenges in Rwanda, and the civil conflicts affecting countries such as Angola, the Democratic Republic of Congo, and Northern Uganda, to mention only a few.

With regards to the anti-apartheid struggle, ecumenism played a significant role by serving as a fulcrum of motivation for society in the fight against racial segregation. In this case, it can be argued that a grassroots approach to ecumenism had been adopted as opposed to an institutional one.[40] The apartheid in South Africa became a target for ecumenical struggles and a testing ground for the possibility of Christian partnership. It is paradoxical to note that while the Christian religion had been key in providing theological justification for the apartheid system through the NHK, it was slow in condemning the system in others. At the same time, it was essential in supporting defiance against apartheid in addition to promoting reconciliation in the post-apartheid era.[41]

However, ecumenical gains in this African region continue to be undermined by divisive anti-ecumenical theology such as that proposed by the UCKG, whose teachings have accused ecumenism of being anti-Christ and which have warned that "its supposed emphasis on 'love and peace' masked a dark ambition to establish a world order in which 'one government led by the anti-Christ and assisted by his beast (the false prophet) held sway."[42]

6 The Future of Ecumenism in Africa

While ecumenism has been applauded for supporting social movements and the development of new theologies "cooked in an African pot" such as African theology, the theology of reconstruction, and others, the work of the ecumenical project is not yet complete. Its newly developed theologies have been condemned by some for failing to guard society against oppressive forces akin to colonialism and excessive political control, moreover its theories and teachings have not yet succeeded in ridding the continent of ethnic conciseness, patriarchy, and other ills such as xenophobia. What is more, glaring questions surrounding Africa's troubled past remain unanswered; how, for example, could a genocide in which Africans slaughtered

39 Richard Werbner, "Grassroots Ecumenism in Conflict – Introduction," *JSAS* 44/2, 2018, 201–219, here 206.

40 "At the base of the Church – in local communities, in youth, students and working-class organisations – the type of struggle waged was more radical and more ecumenical than at the level of church hierarchies"; Graham A. Duncan & Anthony Egan, "The Ecumenical Struggle in South Africa: The Role of Ecumenical Movements and Organisations in Liberation Movements to 1965," *ELJ* 17/3, 2015, 269–282, here 271.

41 Charles P. Ryan, "Church and State in the 'New' South Africa," *PT* 11/6, 2010, 894–908; Kairos Theologians, *The Kairos Document: Challenge to the Church: A Theological Comment on the Political Crisis in South Africa*, Braamfontein, Skotaville Publishers, 1986; Stuart C. Bate, "The Church under Apartheid," in: Joy Brain & Philippe Denis, eds., *The Catholic Church in Contemporary Southern Africa*, Pietermaritzburg, Cluster Publications, 1999, 151–186.

42 Werbner, "Grassroots Ecumenism in Conflict – Introduction," 214.

one another based on their ethnic and religious backgrounds have possibly taken place in a nation as religious as Rwanda? Likewise, how can a country such as South Africa, with its rich Christian heritage and commitment, experience xenophobia responsible for the killing of hundreds of African immigrants? The main challenge for the ecumenical movement in Africa today, then, is to understand how Christian denominations can cooperate to promote reconciliation and unity in postcolonial, postindependence Africa, since at the root of many of the ills of African society – from the widespread poverty afflicting much of the continent to the more localized instances, like xenophobia in South Africa and genocide in Rwanda – is the churches' alleged complicity.[43] Nevertheless, the once-collaborative nature of church-state relations in most African countries has given way to an institutional form of ecumenism in which the state offers its overarching direction to churches regarding their partnership. This has been a bone of contention within the less dominant churches, such as the new Pentecostal groups, AICs, and other Christian ministries, who have perceived this as a form of overt control. For scholars such as Richard Werbner, this opposition comes as no surprise, especially as it involves calls for a top-down unity: "Such top-down unity is contested and arouses suspicion that the institutional ecumenism is a mere trap: it is seen to be a political move for dominance by one church over others, perhaps to return to rejected colonial control."[44]

As a consequence, the ecumenical movement has to continue strengthening its collaboration among its member churches while simultaneously developing new models of church-state relations. These will enable the church to make a demonstrable contribution to the development of the African continent, whether socially, economically or politically.

43 See Christine Schliesser, "From 'a Theology of Genocide' to a 'Theology of Reconciliation'?: On the Role of Christian Churches in the Nexus of Religion and Genocide in Rwanda," *Religions* 9/2, 2018, 1–14.

44 Werbner, "Grassroots Ecumenism in Conflict – Introduction," 213.

Bibliography

Amanze, James, *A History of the Ecumenical Movement in Africa*, Gaborone, Pula Press, 1999.

Byaruhanga, Christopher, *The History and Theology of the Ecumenical Movement in East Africa*, Kampala, Fountain Publishers, 2015.

Molobi, Masilo, "The Ecumenical Vision of the Organization of African Independent Churches from an Educational Perspective," *SHE* 37/1, 2011, 87–102.

Mugambi, Jesse, *From Liberation to Reconstruction: African Christian Theology after the Cold War*, Nairobi, East African Educational Publishers, 1995.

Sakupapa, Teddy Chalwe, "The Ecumenical Movement and Development: The Case of the All Africa Conference of Churches (AACC), 1963–2000 (Part 1)," *SHE* 44/3, 2018, 1–15.

Schliesser, Christine, "From 'a Theology of Genocide' to a 'Theology of Reconciliation'?: On the Role of Christian Churches in the Nexus of Religion and Genocide in Rwanda," *Religions* 9/2, 2018, 1–14.

Setiloane, Gabriel, "The Ecumenical Movement in Africa: From Mission Church to Moratorium," in: Charles Villa-Vicencio & John de Gruchy, eds., *Resistance and Hope: South African Essays in Honour of Beyers Naudé*, Grand Rapids, Eerdmans, 1985, 137–147.

Werbner, Richard, "Grassroots Ecumenism in Conflict – Introduction," *JSAS* 44/2, 2018, 201–219.

CHAPTER 26

A Foundational Ecumenical Event: The Non-Catholic Observers at Vatican II

Mauro Velati

1 The Background

In many ways, the experience of the non-Catholic observers at Vatican II left its mark on the events of the council, and also on the course of relations among churches in the decades that followed.[1] The observers' presence saved the conciliar magisterium from the temptation of self-referentiality, physically representing the various Christian worlds capable of challenging the church on the faithfulness to its founder's message. It opened up horizons of encounter which, until then, were difficult to imagine. Finally, it constituted a significant precedent for subsequent experiences of collaboration which, under the current pontificate, are increasingly represented in terms of a humble and patient sharing of gifts and perspectives.

The roots of the experience of the observers at Vatican II date back to the years after World War II, when a movement of mutual rapprochement between the churches and ecumenical organizations on the one hand, and episcopal structures such as those of Catholicism and the Eastern patriarchates on the other, took place. As is well known, the birth of the WCC in 1948 was received negatively by the authorities of the Roman Church. In many Catholic circles, however, it raised considerable interest and, especially in the French- and German-speaking areas, various initiatives to start a dialogue with the Protestant world in general, and with the WCC in particular, were developed. Among such initiatives, the CCEQ played an increasingly important role. It had been founded in 1952 by the Dutch priest Johannes Willebrands, and bore the indirect blessing of the Holy Office. It aimed at coordinating the efforts of various centers that sought to develop an ecumenical theology of a genuinely Catholic nature in Europe and elsewhere.[2] Among the aims of the CCEQ was also the establishment of direct dialogue with the WCC, which was seen as a sign of the unitive tension that characterized mainly the world of the Reformed and Anglican churches. Willebrands's first contacts with the secretary general of the WCC, Willem Adolph Visser 't Hooft, were facilitated by their common Dutch background. The first attempt at a collaboration, the project of sending Catholic observers to the WCC's general assembly in Evanston in 1954, was blocked by the opposition of the local Catholic hierarchy. It was precisely from this failure, however, that wider collaboration began on a joint theological study on the theme of "The Lordship of Christ over

1 This essay is based on the work carried out for the editing of the extensive research then included in Mauro Velati, *Separati ma fratelli: Gli osservatori non cattolici al Vaticano II (1962–1965)*, Bologna, Il Mulino, 2014, to which I also refer the reader for a detailed list of the archival collections consulted (15–18). Among the most important of those are, of course, the Vatican Apostolic Archives (the Vatican II Collection), the archives of the WCC in Geneva, the archives of the Centre d'Études Œcumenique of the LWF in Strasbourg, the archives of the French Protestant Federation in Paris, and other important private archival collections of the observers themselves and of the Catholic bishops and theologians present at the council.

2 Mauro Velati, *Una difficile transizione: Il cattolicesimo tra unionismo ed ecumenismo (1952–1964)*, Bologna, Il Mulino, 1996. See also Peter De Mey and Saretta Marotta contribution "The Catholic Conference for Ecumenical Questions," in this volume.

the World and over the Church."[3] Thanks to the contribution of some of Europe's most important theologians, the CCEQ prepared a comprehensive study that was then put in relation with the perspectives that emerged from the encounter among the churches of the WCC.

The first mixed meeting between representatives of the CCEQ and the WCC was scheduled to take place in 1960 in the mystical setting of Assisi. That project, however, was also a total failure. Repercussions of the so-called Rhodes incident caused the meeting to be cancelled. Some CCEQ proponents, in particular the French Dominican Christophe-Jean Dumont, had attended the WCC's central committee meeting in Rhodes in August 1959. It had been the occasion of an initial contact between Catholic representatives and those of Greek Orthodox churches. When the Roman authorities suddenly publicized the project for a Catholic-Orthodox meeting in Venice, however, the WCC leadership suspected an opportunistic move on the part of the Catholics. The relations with Geneva were being used for a very different goal, that of a rapprochement among the churches of episcopal structure, which was certainly in competition with, if not against, the initiatives of the Protestant world. The Rhodes crisis turned out to be a kind of growth that actually paved the way for subsequent developments. In 1961, Visser 't Hooft's strategy of "widening the field" of the WCC's membership obtained its first successes. At the general assembly in New Delhi, some of the Orthodox churches, including the Russian one, entered the WCC fraternity and finally a Catholic delegation, albeit not directly connected to the CCEQ, was able to participate in the proceedings. This was a necessary, although insufficient, background for the beginning of a strategy of collaboration in view of the celebration of Vatican II, which, in the meantime, had been announced by Pope John XXIII with his well-known address of January 1959 and whose preparations had begun in autumn 1960.

In this more general trend of rapprochement, each of the interlocutors obviously maintained his own specific sensitivities and options. For the WCC, in Visser 't Hooft's project, it was a matter of creating an authentic fellowship of churches, without any exclusions, made on the basis of a mutual recognition of the ecclesial nature and the genuine Christian roots of the interlocutors.[4] For the Orthodox churches it was, in good measure, a matter of finding support in the West given the harsh existence they were facing. The Patriarchate of Constantinople had seen its numbers greatly reduced and was still feeling the effects of the secularist politics of Kemalism. The Russian Church had been hit hard by the Soviet power and was fighting for survival, seeking a difficult collaboration with the regime. The novelty of Nikita Khrushchev's years could be seen not so much in an easing of the persecution, which instead became even harsher in the early 1960s, as in the regime's willingness to seek dialogue on an international level, accrediting itself externally through ecclesiastical channels as well.[5] On the Catholic side, theological and canonical assumptions of a so-called unionism, that is, the idea of a union between the churches understood as "incorporation" into the Catholic Church, remained largely unchanged. John XXIII's pontificate, however, had introduced significant novelties, at least in terms of perspectives. In the first months, the announcement of the council had generated exaggerated expectations as to the ecumenical scope of the assembly, even evoking the idea of a council of

3 "The Lordship of Christ over the World and over the Church," *EcRev* 11, 1958–1959, 437–449.

4 See Willem Adolf Visser 't Hooft, *Memoirs*, London, SCM Press, 1973. See also the contribution by Jurjen A. Zeilstra in this volume.

5 Adriano Roccucci, "Russian Observers at Vatican II: The 'Council for Russian Orthodox Church Affairs' and the Moscow Patriarchate Between Anti-Religious Policy and International Strategies," in: Alberto Melloni, ed., *Vatican II in Moscow (1959–1965): Acts of the Colloquium on the History of Vatican II (Moscow, March 30–April 2, 1995)*, Leuven, Bibliotheek van de Faculteit Godgeleerdheid, 1997, 45–69.

union following the model of the Council of Florence of 1439. The strategic novelty introduced by Pope John XXIII was the birth of the SPCU, brought about through the proposal of German Bishop Lorenz Jaeger and endorsed and supported by newly appointed Cardinal Augustin Bea, who was the early interlocutor of Willebrands and of the CCEQ's works.[6] In fact, the SPCU became a continuation of the CCEQ, although it had very different goals and prestige, and brought about a decisive change in Catholicism's position toward the ecumenical movement, actually representing that "place in Rome"[7] that had long been called for by non-Catholics.[8]

Headquartered in Rome, the SPCU stood alongside the bodies of the curia but established itself as a new agency in its conception, procedures, and above all in its entirely international composition. In fact, it represented the first piece of the curial reform that had already been called for during Pius XII's pontificate. Willebrands and Bea were in charge of its structure, following the guiding principles drawn up with the CCEQ in the previous years. Some of the European bishops directly involved in matters concerning relations with non-Catholics were therefore part of it: Jaeger, archbishop of Paderborn, the true inspiration of Bea's proposal to John XXIII; François Charrière, bishop of Lausanne, Geneva, and Fribourg; Joseph-Marie-Eugène Martin, archbishop of Rouen; Emiel-Jozef De Smedt, bishop of Bruges; John Carmel Heenan, archbishop of Liverpool, and others. Some of the best European theologians, and not only those working in the area of ecumenism, were appointed as members or consultors. Among these were Gustave Thils of Leuven, who was to be a protagonist of the drafting of the council's declaration on ecumenism, Hermann Volk of Münster, the Swiss Johannes Feiner, the Italian Alberto Bellini, and the Dominican Christophe-Jean Dumont, an expert on issues of Orthodox Christianity. Hence the number of men linked in various ways to the curia was very limited: Michele Maccarrone, professor of ecclesiastical history at the Pontifical Lateran University, and the French Jesuit Charles Boyer, professor at the Pontifical Gregorian University.

From the very beginning, the SPCU sought to act as a privileged interlocutor with the non-Catholic authorities through a broad interpretation of its powers as defined in its statute, even going beyond the indications from Pope John XXIII. The story of Visser 't Hooft asking to meet Bea as president of the new body is well known. Mentioning the request to the pope, the Jesuit cardinal received a provisional response on the need to proceed with caution. In fact, he decided to let the times ripen, and the meeting was held in Milan in 1960; it took place, however, in great secrecy.[9] The SPCU's activity became immediately the focus of public interest, and it soon had to deal with the hostility of other sections of the Roman curia. On the one hand was Alfredo Ottaviani's Holy Office that had, until then, managed relations with non-Catholic churches and controlled the theological and pastoral activities of Catholic ecumenists. On the other was the Congregation for the Eastern Churches, which was interested in keeping alive the unionist concern and the role of the Eastern Catholic Churches, whose existence had proved to be an obstacle in the dialogue with Orthodoxy. It was not, therefore, easy for the SPCU, which staff members found themselves working amid many difficulties, including logistical and organizational ones, to pursue a unified line of renewal and dialogue that represented the entire Catholic world.

6 Saretta Marotta, "La genesi di un ecumenista: La corrispondenza fra Augustin Bea e il vescovo di Paderborn Lorenz Jaeger (1951–1960)," in: Luca Ferracci, ed., *Toward a History of the Desire for Christian Unity*, Münster, LIT, 2015, 159–192.

7 See Mauro Velati, "'Un indirizzo a Roma': La nascita del Segretariato per l'unità dei cristiani (1959–1960)," in: Giuseppe Alberigo, ed. *Il Vaticano II fra attese e celebrazione*, Bologna, Il Mulino, 1996, 75–118.

8 On the subsequent developments of the SPCU, see the contribution by Bruno Cherubini in this volume.

9 Agostino Bea, *Ecumenismo nel Concilio: Tappe pubbliche di un sorprendente cammino*, Milan, Bompiani, 1968, 36.

2 Enactment

On a historical level, the process of rapprochement described above was intertwined with more general aspirations and demands for dialogue and international détente. The council, like a good part of John XXIII's magisterium, rooted as it was in church renewal, seemed to represent these trends well, hence it could be, even at an ecumenical level, a decisive occasion. The expectation that the non-Catholic churches would be involved in the council was strong and was manifested in the early months of 1959 in an intense debate on the nature of the council itself. Once it was made clear, however, that it would not be a council of union – and even less an "ecumenical" one in the modern sense – the question of what possible forms this involvement would take remained unanswered. Visser 't Hooft's proposal, then taken up in several quarters, was to involve non-Catholics in the preparations for the council through the establishment of consultatory commissions. In December 1960, however, in initiating the preparatory commissions' works, the pope clarified there would be no consultation, but that the results of the preparation would be gradually made known through the media.

The topic was put on the agenda of the SPCU since its first meeting of December 1960. It was not merely a question of organization or representation. The idea of non-Catholics participating directly at certain moments during the council was, in fact, part of a much broader framework of theological, canonical, and liturgical reflection that took shape in the months of preparation, outlining an organic project of renewal and dialogue with them.[10] Thanks to the commitment of the SPCU, the principle of an invitation to non-Catholics was accepted, not without resistance from those who feared that it might undermine the monolithic image of Catholicism. Unlike accredited journalists, in fact, observers were to attend the sessions in person, directly experiencing the dynamics and exchanges between the various personalities of the world episcopate. Active participation of the observers, however, was not allowed, and was only partially brought about through Willebrands's invention of Tuesday meetings with the SPCU.

The experience of the non-Catholic observers at the council, therefore, is an important, albeit brief, chapter in a longer history – that of the relations among Christian churches during the decisive transition between the 1950s and 1960s.[11] It is the story of (exclusively male) people of various origin and ecclesiastical status who, in many cases, played a leading role in their respective churches. Should the role played by Oscar Cullmann in the debate on ecumenism in the 1970s and 1980s be remembered here?[12] For his part, Edmund Schlink published a powerful "ecumenical dogma" in the 1980s, which still represents today one of the most articulate and coherent proposals in the field of the theology of unity.[13] Nor can we forget the fact that two of the Orthodox delegates became in subsequent years the main leaders of their churches: the Armenian Neshan Sarkissian – who became catholicos of Cilicia with the name Karekin II and then of the whole Armenian Apostolic Church as Karekin I – and the Syrian Ignatius Zakka I Iwas, patriarch of the Universal Syriac Orthodox Church. In its own way, Lukas Vischer's existential trajectory is also significant, even though he did not hold any high-level hierarchical position. He was undoubtedly one of the leading figures in the panorama of ecumenical theology, especially from

10 Mauro Velati, *Dialogo e rinnovamento: Verbali e testi del segretariato per l'unità dei cristiani nella preparazione del concilio Vaticano II (1960–1962)*, Bologna, Il Mulino, 2011.

11 For an overall history of the ecumenical movement after the council, see, *A History of the Ecumenical Movement*, vol. 3, John Briggs, Mercy Amba Oduyoye & Georges Tsetsis, eds., *1968–2000*, Geneva, WCC Publications, 2004.

12 Oscar Cullmann, *L'unité par la diversité: Son fondement et le problème de sa réalisation*, Paris, Cerf, 1986.

13 Edmund Schlink, *Schriften zu Ökumene und Bekenntnis*, vol. 2, *Ökumenische Dogmatik*, Göttingen, Vandenhoeck & Ruprecht, 1983.

the time of his work with the commission on Faith and Order, of which he was the director for many years (1966–1979).[14]

No women appear in this group, even though there are indications of an attempt to have them enter this male-dominated arena. In the spring of 1964, the leadership of International Congregational Council evaluated the possibility of sending a woman to Rome. The proposal came from Caroline Middleton DeCamp Benn, an English writer, educator, and proponent of a moderate Christian feminism who was involved in the English governing bodies of congregationalism. Douglas Horton, the head of the Presbyterian delegation had expressed doubt about the choice, not so much for theological reasons, but for reasons of opportuneness, as the appointment could have created tensions with their Catholic counterparts.[15] Anyway, the request was duly sent to Rome in May 1964 and received a negative response. Willebrands was forced to recall the continuity of Catholic tradition that precluded women from access to ministries and therefore from the right to participate in councils.[16] The paradoxical fact is that this all happened shortly before Paul VI decided to admit lay auditors – among whom there were women – to participate in the council.

Based on the official list drawn up by the SPCU, the total number of observers who participated in the council at different times reached 168.[17] However – particularly in the final sessions – there was the constant phenomenon of "conciliar tourism." Prominent people from the various churches asked the SPCU for permission to participate in the council's work for a few days, or even for a single meeting. This brought the Czech pastor Josef Hromàdka and the Orthodox theologians Hamilcar Alivizatos and Georges Florovsky, the Baptist William Barry Garrett, and the executive secretary of the MWC, Cornelius J. Dyck, to Rome. When Visser 't Hooft himself was in Rome, he received permission to attend the council sessions. It is also well-known that the SPCU sought Karl Barth's presence, which was impossible to obtain due to the Swiss theologian's precarious health condition. The number of non-Catholics who participated in the council was therefore certainly greater than that recorded in the official lists. The observers were then divided into two basic groups – delegate observers (148) and guests of the SPCU (20). In the first group were observers entrusted with a full mandate by their churches; in the second were individuals already linked in various ways to Catholicism and thus invited at the initiative of the SPCU, or members of churches that did not wish to be officially represented. In this second category were included Roger Schutz and Max Thurian, members of the

14 There is currently no biography of Vischer. See Michael Quisinsky, "The Ecumenical Dynamic of Vatican II – Lukas Vischer Between Geneva and Rome," *CrSt* 34, 2013, 273–314.

15 Horton wrote: "The appearance of a woman [among the observers] ... would mean the guests were taking an initiative that the hosts were not permitting themselves"; D. Horton to R. Calder, Apr 10, 1964, quoted in: Theodore Louis Trost, *Douglas Horton and the Ecumenical Impulse in American Religion*, Cambridge MA, Harvard Divinity School, 2002, 224. In that same letter, Horton advised Ralph Calder, the International Congregational Council executive in London, not to even raise the question with the SPCU. Afterward, he wrote to Willebrands to apologize for what had happened; see Trost, *Douglas Horton*, 225.

16 Trost cites the letter from Willebrands to Calder in which the secretary of the SPCU indicated the impossibility of giving non-Catholic Christians a permission that was not even accorded to Catholics; J. Willebrands to R. Calder, Jul 1, 1964, quoted in: Trost, *Douglas Horton*, 225. In fact, permission to attend the council was then opened to female auditors at the behest of Paul VI beginning with the third session. There were eight religious and seven lay women auditors.

17 See *Observateurs-délégués et hôtes du Secrétariat pour l'unité des chrétiens au deuxième concile œcuménique du Vatican*, Vatican City, Typis Poliglottis Vaticanis, 1965. The summary table actually shows the names of 152 observers and 22 guests (for a total of 174). Some of them, however, appear as representatives of different churches or organizations and are thus listed twice. To give just one example, Vitaly Borovoj was a delegate observer not only of the Moscow Patriarchate but also of the Church of Georgia. For all of this data, see Velati, *Separati ma fratelli*.

Taizé Community,[18] – which had already been in contact with the Holy Office in the preparation of unofficial talks between bishops and Protestant pastors – but also individual theological figures such as the abovementioned Cullmann and the Dutchman Gerrit Cornelis Berkouwer. The distinction between delegates and guests, however, proved more functional to the delicate balance of inter-ecclesial relations than substantial, given that participation in observer activities was the same for both groups.

From a quantitative point of view, the observers' activity in Rome was not uniform. Some of them, 48 in all, were listed as substitutes, standing in for the official observers, thus sometimes their stay in Rome lasted only a few days. Only a small group of observers (24) participated in all the council sessions, and in two cases – the representative of the EKD Edmund Schlink and the Anglican Bernard Pawley – their stay in Rome had already begun during the preparations for the council, for the former in the spring of 1962 and, for the latter, as early as March 1961.[19] There was a greater number of observers (45) who were present for at least two of the four sessions; and it is clear that it is in this narrower group that the core of the observers' experience should be identified.

From a representational point of view, the observers were the expression of a substantial portion of the world's Christianity. In fact, they came from as many as 32 churches or ecclesial organizations of various types (34 if we take into consideration the presence of two members of Pentecostal and American Baptist churches, albeit at an informal level, among the SPCU's guests).[20] There is a clear prevalence of figures from the Protestant or Anglican worlds (109 observers, including two Old Catholics, compared to 59 from the various Eastern churches), which can be easily explained on the one hand by the extreme variety and fragmentation of Western Christianity and, on the other, by a certain mistrust of the Orthodox world towards the Roman Catholic initiative.

The two best represented continents were undoubtedly Europe (68 observers) and North America (56), illustrating the prevalence of the Euro-Atlantic area, which could also be seen in the provenance of the Catholic episcopate participating in the council. The presence of representatives of Third World churches was of little relevance, although the 22 observers of Asian origin and the 18 Africans should be mentioned. The presence of only one Latin American (the Methodist José Miguez Bonino) certainly reflected the scanty non-Catholic presence on that continent, but also probably the persistence of confessional tensions in that geographical area. Finally, the presence of Frank L. Cuttriss, an Anglican priest who was the delegate of the Australian Council of Churches, completes the panorama of this significant assembly of world Christianity.

3 The End of Isolation

What is usually defined as the moment of the Catholic Church's entrance into the ecumenical movement appears, in historical analysis, to be a far more intricate and complex phenomenon than the picture that emerges from superficial readings. Longer term phenomena were intertwined in the concrete experience of the observers' presence in Rome. The complexity of the Eastern ecclesial political scene was at the origin of a delay in the

18 On Taizé, see Silvia Scatena, *Taizé, una parabola di unità: Storia della comunità dalle origini al concilio dei giovani*, Bologna, Il Mulino, 2018, 493–581.

19 See the reports by Bernard Pawley in Andrew Chandler & Charlotte Hansen, eds., *Observing Vatican II: The Confidential Reports of the Archbishop of Canterbury's Representative, Bernard Pawley (1961–1964)*, Cambridge, Cambridge University Press, 2013, 31–404.

20 There were many ecclesial organizations that, for different reasons, were not part of the group of observers. On the Orthodox side, the Greek, Romanian, Albanian, Bulgarian, Polish, Finnish, Czechoslovakian, and Cypriot churches, as well as the Patriarchate of Jerusalem, were not represented. On the Protestant side, the BWA, Pentecostal and Evangelical groups, and, in general, the many groups hostile to the ecumenical movement's development were absent.

arrival of Orthodox delegates. Conversely, the progressive rapprochement between Catholicism and the WCC, prepared by the work of Willebrands and the CCEQ, was a positive influence on the attitudes of most non-Catholic churches, leading in a few years (1968) to a lively debate on the Catholic Church's participation in the Genevan council.[21] On the Catholic side, the need to make up for a certain delay with respect to the ecumenical debate intersected with a tendency to broaden the ecumenical partnership that peaked at the aforementioned New Delhi assembly. In a certain sense, the observers' experience was the result of this climate and these demands, as proved by its typical mode of international assembly. The role played by the relationship between some Catholic protagonists and the secretary general of the WCC Visser 't Hooft can hardly be underestimated, in both its negative and positive aspects.

As unpredictable as it was unforeseen, the unfolding of the council was the background against which these new relationships took shape, and this was not without rejections, conflicts, and resistance. It is difficult to give the events an organic or orderly profile. The process was as quick as it was complicated. Many of the main events that marked the development of relations among the churches had random aspects. At the start of 1964, it was only the promptness of Patriarch Athenagoras I that enabled a project of spiritual pilgrimage, such as Paul VI's trip to the Holy Land, to be transformed into a starting point for dialogue between the Catholic and Orthodox churches. Even the modality of inviting observers, opting to privilege contact with individual confessional organizations, had unpredictable consequences, even before the end of the council, in the immediate development of a tapestry of bilateral relations destined to change the face of the ecumenical movement. It was, in fact, an outcome unforeseen by the WCC leaders, since that council was born in 1948 as a fellowship of churches that favored a multilateral approach by gathering the various interlocutors on equal footing, and detaching their representation from a quantitative criterion based on the size of each ecclesial body. This walking together of the churches exceeded – and in a way excluded – a path of bilateral relations, able to adjust their speeds depending on the dialogue partners.

Additionally, the WCC underwent a moment of real transition during the years of the council. The end of Visser 't Hooft's secretariat, which was handled and experienced in a very confused and problematic manner, overshadowed the debate on future developments, that had highly critical aspects but which remained mainly in the background of the WCC's development dynamism. It was precisely the observers' experience that showed how Visser 't Hooft's efforts to develop the WCC's project – in the sense of a real centralized governance, a non-church at the service of the other churches – had its limits, surpassed on the one hand by the awakening of the Catholic Church (which was also a potential international competitor) and, on the other, by developments in relations among the churches and by the different attitude of the Orthodox world. The voices that had been raised calling for a restructuring of the WCC in the direction of an inter-ecclesial agency for dialogue had been rejected in the name of fidelity to the original project and to the legacy of its founding fathers, of whom Visser 't Hooft himself was the guardian. But things were not the same in 1965. The Catholic Church, with its doubts and resistance, and the advances and slowdowns that always accompany its conduct in the area of ecumenism, had become – to all effects – a partner in the dialogue among churches. Owing to its prestige and size, it was automatically placed at the center of a network of relationships that inevitably intertwined with one another, often clashing with the one woven by the WCC in the previous decades.

The Orthodox churches in turn played an important role in redefining the positions that

21 See Jan Grootaers, *Rome et Genève à la croisée des chemins (1968–1972): Un ordre du jour inachevé*, Paris, Cerf, 2005.

had been initiated after the council. Under the presidency of Athenagoras, Constantinople had made its own field choice, strengthening its uncertain position with regard to Turkish power and its alliance with the West.[22] The Russian Orthodox Church, spurred by the Soviet powers for reasons of political expediency, had returned to dialogue with the Christian world, with its entry into the WCC being approved at the end of the 1950s. From certain points of view, the Orthodox world seemed to want to recover that dynamic role that had marked its actions at the very beginning of the ecumenical movement with the patriarchal and synodal encyclical of Patriarch Joachim III of 1902.[23] But behind this dynamism lurked internal conflicts and weaknesses that had been highlighted by the very invitation of observers to the council. Moscow pushed to obtain some goodwill, along the lines of a policy of cooperation between the churches of the WCC. The Phanar, under the pressure of a direct relationship with the visceral moods of the Greek people and hierarchy, stood by and watched, initially rejecting an alignment of participation in the council to then embrace the initiative from the beginning of 1964, establishing a direct contact with the papacy. At the end of Vatican II, the positions seem to have been reversed. Moscow's role had been overshadowed within the equalized horizon of multilateral relations in the WCC, while Athenagoras had become the symbol of a "dialogue of charity,"[24] recovering, at least symbolically, his representative role in the Orthodox world. The lifting of anathemas that had concluded the last session of the council, despite its scarce efficacy, confirmed for many the sense of the beginning of a new era. This new season of relations between Catholics and Orthodox could be read, as indeed some on both sides did, as a qualitative leap, the definitive detachment from a condition of dialogue somehow protected by others within the institutions of the ecumenical movement.

4 The New Catholicism

It was without doubt Catholicism that experienced the rapid development of conciliar events in an even more confused and traumatic manner. It had witnessed the overturning of an official position towards the ecumenical movement that dated back to the 1920s. As was emphatically stressed in all the observers' reports, the approval of the decree *Unitatis redintegratio* in 1964 – beyond the skirmishes and eventual regrets as to how it came about – represented a point of no return.[25] Catholicism found itself in need of adopting a policy and making precise and engaging choices with regard to the movement for unity. At first, the prevailing attitude was unquestionably that of reception and listening. Over the years, the experience of the WCC had created a vocabulary, an agenda of the most urgent problems, and a style of relationships and rules shared by the various dialogue partners. The SPCU arose in 1960 from precisely those Catholics who had been a part of this fertile soil in previous years. Vatican II, as it had been imagined by John XXIII, constituted the ideal

22 See Valeria Martano, "L'ortodossia e gli altri," in: Andrea Riccardi, ed., *Le Chiese e gli altri: Culture, religioni, ideologie e Chiese cristiane nel Novecento*, Milan, Guerini e Associati, 2008, 175–195.

23 The English text of the encyclical can be found in Constantin G. Patelos, ed., *The Orthodox Church in the Ecumenical Movement: Documents and Statements (1902–1975)*, Geneva, WCC Publications, 1978, 27–33.

24 See the contribution by Nicla Buonasorte in this volume.

25 There is still no overall reconstruction of Catholicism's journey in its relations with the ecumenical movement. The opening of the Vatican archives for the pontificate of Pius XI has afforded a clear view of the positions taken in the 1920s and 1930s, including the encyclical *Mortalium animos*. See Alberto Guasco & Raffaella Perin, eds., *Pius XI: Keywords: International Conference (Milan 2009)*, Münster, LIT, 2010. Further studies are awaited on the more recent period following the opening of the papers of Pius XII's pontificate.

framework for this effort: a "new Pentecost" that would lead to the renewal of Catholicism, making it capable of presenting a different face to other Christians as well. In the preparatory phase of the council, the SPCU's first acts highlighted precisely this effort to listen and self-review. The doctrine of the council was to touch on some of the hottest points of contention with the Protestant world, offering a renewal, if not in substance, then at least in tone and nuance, in the sense of a rapprochement with the world of the Reformation. On the other hand, the attitude of ecumenical circles did not forgo explicitly providing the essential points against which the reformational project had to be measured (recognition of the ecumenical movement, religious freedom, and mixed marriages being some of the main ones).

From the very outset, the desire to listen and an empathetic attitude were also at the base of the relationship established with the observers in Rome. A clear sign of this was the continual request for opinions and judgements on the events of the council and on the issues under discussion by the bishops, as well as the weekly Tuesday meetings, which the Old Catholic representative Werner Küppers dubbed "the observers' para-council."[26] The observers participated in all of the assembly's activities with the council Fathers, including liturgical moments. Several times, however, the role of the cafés and the network of conferences and meetings that took place outside the proper council were highlighted precisely because they permitted a less formal and more genuine interaction. Observers and bishops experienced the occasion for meeting new people and make new discoveries along lines that were, reasonably, primarily of nation and language. It thus happened that the Hungarian Lutheran theologian Vilmos Vajta had contact, for the first time, with the Hungarian bishops, the only Catholic delegation present from behind the Iron Curtain.[27] At the same time, the French and German Protestant observers established relations with the Spanish episcopate, which at the time represented a very un-ecumenical Catholic sector, at odds with the local Protestants on the burning issue of religious freedom.[28]

The Tuesday meetings were part of this dense network of gatherings and relationships, and the most official aspect of the ecumenical dialogue on conciliar matters could be seen against this background. The exchange within these meetings was initially aimed at gathering the observers' opinions and impressions concerning the life of the council and the documents presented during the proceedings. Soon, however, it became a fertile labor of comparison and encounter among the different perspectives, constituting a rough outline for future theological dialogues. In the first session, it was unclear what the observers' role was, and some of them were concerned about asking the leaders of their respective churches to be able to intervene during the meetings, and which authority to attribute to the content reported. By the second session, a level of familiarity had been acquired and, if anything, it is possible to note an opposite trend. That is to say, there was a request by the observers that the texts of the drafts presented at the council be rewritten in "ecumenical" terms, going beyond the nature of the council itself, which was not aimed at union but at renewal in the Catholic Church in the face of the challenges of the modern world. On the other hand, this second period put precisely the most current issues of ecumenical dialogue on the table (ecclesiology, Mariology, ecumenism). It was, therefore, a mature phase of the non-Catholic observers' presence who, in this

26 "Réunion des Observateurs," Nov 19, 1963, in: UCL-LG, Charles Moeller, papiers, 1944, 3. For an overview of the presence of Old Catholic observers, see Peter-Ben Smit, "Silence is Golden: Freedom of Speech and the Old Catholic Observers at the Second Vatican Council (1962–1965)," in: Peter-Ben Smit & Eva van Hurk, eds., *Parrhesia: Ancient and Modern Perspectives on Freedom of Speech*, Leiden, Brill, 2018, 177–198.

27 Velati, *Separati ma fratelli*, 178.

28 Velati, *Separati ma fratelli*, 399–403.

period, felt as if they were fully part of the conciliar adventure.

The third session, instead, allowed them to deal with issues of a more "external" nature: from religious freedom to the topic of religions, from the church's relationship with the world to its missions. Concerning these matters, it was harder to find an internal unity among the observers. The various churches were affected by the same divisions that emerged among the council Fathers, and they often experienced the same difficulties in determining their historical and theological significance. Certainly, the topic that seemed decisive for the observers was that of religious freedom. Among the Reformed and Lutheran delegations there was a shared awareness that the council's fate would be determined precisely by whether Catholicism would accept religious freedom. This was the reason behind the last week of the third session's dramatic evolution, which needless to say constituted one of the moments of crisis in the relationship between the observers and the council precisely because the vote on the draft of religious freedom was postponed, and because of the corresponding occurrence of last-minute changes inserted into the document on ecumenism at the behest of Paul VI.

In the fourth session, the non-Catholic observers' participation undoubtedly reached its highest level, even if the pope's scruples had risked calling its continuation into question in the previous spring.[29] Not only did the number of meetings with the observers increase (11 during this session as compared to 9 in 1963) but the level and quality of their contribution became significant. There was the case – unique but very meaningful – of the conciliar commission for the missions collecting the observers' amendments and proposals along with those of the Catholic bishops and addressing them directly to the revision of the text.[30] It is no coincidence, therefore, that, according to many, the height of ecumenicity in the conciliar texts should not be considered mostly or solely in the decree *Unitatis redintegratio*, but rather precisely in the decree on missions *Ad gentes*. Additionally, the fourth period saw the unfolding of a wider dimension of the encounter and dialogue between churches that went well beyond the discussion on the council's schemas and, hence, the Tuesday meetings. These meetings had become part of a wider context that saw – to give just a few examples – the start of the activity of the Joint Working Group between the Catholic Church and the WCC, the preparation of the joint declaration between Rome and Constantinople on the purification of memory, and, finally, the prayer shared by the observers with the pope and council Fathers that was held on Dec 4, 1965. That undoubtedly represented the culmination of the non-Catholic observers' active participation in the council.[31]

The Tuesday meetings were also the womb wherein the observers' most important contributions on particular conciliar schemas took shape. It was precisely on the issue of ecumenism that the observers' contribution was significant. This began during the second session: when the conciliar text was taking shape with the overcoming of the unionist perspective still present in the preparatory texts, the observers offered decisive ideas for its revision. A proposal from the delegate of the WCC, Lukas Vischer, for example, was at the origin of the drafting of a preface aimed at the official recognition by the Catholic Church of the history of the 20th-century ecumenical movement. It was

29 Antoine Wenger was the first to reveal how, under pressure from Pericle Felici, Pope Paul VI had considered the possibility, in April of 1965, of cancelling the presence of the observers at the council. See Antoine Wenger, *Le Cardinal Villot (1905–1979)*, Paris, Desclée de Brouwer, 1989, 52.

30 Mauro Velati, "Œcuménisme et mission: La contribution des observateurs non Catholiques à la rédaction du décret 'Ad gentes' du Concile Vatican II," in: Paul Coulon & Alberto Melloni, dir., *Christianisme, mission et cultures: L'arc-en-ciel des défis et des réponses XVIe–XXIe siècles*, Paris, Karthala, 2008, 215–237.

31 Giuseppe Alberigo, *Ecclesiologia in divenire: A proposito di "concilio pastorale" e di Osservatori a-cattolici al Vaticano II*, Bologna, Istituto per le Scienze Religiose di Bologna, 1990, 35–38.

an overcoming of the negative position that had emerged in 1948 when the WCC was established.[32]

The third chapter of the schema *De oecumenismo*, a kind of overview of the Christian world from the Catholic point of view, garnered the most severe criticism from the observers. A document drawn up by Vischer proposed the deletion of the entire chapter, perhaps to be replaced with the proposal of some topics for possible dialogue among the churches. For the Anglicans, it could only be maintained if the character of its discussion was clearly specified. Only as a discussion internal to the Catholic Church could it have meaning. For others, it was a matter of significantly amending it. There was the widespread observation regarding a certain forced irenicism which, in undermining the true points of division among the confessions, completely distorted the vision of the work of ecumenism. In the version presented in 1964, the text had been amended with the inclusion of a better-balanced viewpoint increasingly aligned with the request of many observers to render the chapter as a simple picture of the ecumenical situation, as honest and faithful as possible to the various actors' intentions.

Many problems, however, remained. For the Protestant observers, the question of terminology was decisive, and they requested an act of generosity on the Catholic side in granting the label of "church" for all denominational groups, overcoming doctrinal prejudices in the use of the term. There was a lively debate and, in the end, at least some of the observers accepted a dual designation – "churches" for the Oriental ones and "ecclesial communities" for the Reformed – that was introduced into the drafts thanks to the amendments of sympathetic bishops. Vischer himself supported the idea of a "hierarchy" in doctrinal truths affirmed by the magisterium that was proposed as an amendment by the Italian Bishop Andrea Pangrazio, which was then added to the final draft. The French Calvinist Hébert Roux endorsed the inclusion of an explicit request for forgiveness on the part of Catholicism for past behavior contrary to true ecumenism. Paul VI's address on Sep 29, 1963 at the opening of the second session of Vatican II, containing a first draft of this request for forgiveness, paved the way. Finally, a decidedly important point was that concerning the relationship between ecumenism and the seeking of conversions, the latter being widespread in Catholicism in the years before the council. Furthermore, on this point, the address by the delegate of the EKD, Edmund Schlink, led to a fine-tuning of the text, which better expressed the novelty of the ecumenical choice and the Catholic Church's commitment to that path.

The observers' frankness in expressing their criticism of the schema clearly highlighted radical differences in the vision of Christian unity. That is why, at the meeting of Nov 19, 1963, the SPCU theologian Frans Thijssen emphasized some fundamental points to be borne in mind when approaching the schema, in a precise attempt to correct the concordist approach of some of the observers' comments. Starting from a series of quotations of WCC documents, Thijssen proposed looking at the schema as the expression of a church reflecting on itself.[33] In this sense, it was not possible – except at the cost of breaking the rules of the game of true ecumenism – to expect a church to strip itself of that vision of itself that belongs to faith:

> It seems clear to me that it is not against the idea of ecumenism if a Church meditating upon itself establishes its attitude out of its own vision of what the Church is. This is why I believe that various remarks made last week on the schema infringe upon the rules of play for a true ecumenism. If, for example,

32 For an overview, see Velati, *Una difficile transizione*, 319–487.

33 Claude Soetens, "The Ecumenical Commitment of the Catholic Church," in: Giuseppe Alberigo & Joseph Komonchak, eds., *History of Vatican II*, vol. 3, Leuven/Maryknoll, Peeters/Orbis Book, 2000, 257–345, esp. 291.

> a Church is asked to drop or not express a point – one perhaps not in conformity with the faith of other Churches but precisely for them a point of its lived faith – then the rules are broken. For that Church then, it would be an infidelity to itself and thus a disservice to ecumenism. This would be true for the Roman Catholic Church if one questions the position of the See of Rome or the idea of the fullness of catholicity as such.[34]

Thijssen's clarifications were intended to set some limits to the criticism in the observers' comments in an honest and frank spirit, in the concrete situation of a Catholic council where, for the first time in history, the issue of the separated communities was being discussed, moreover in the presence of their representatives. The novelty of the meeting clearly could not erase the fact of the existence of radical differences in the very concept of Christian unity. This fact also emerged in the observers' reflections, which noted the existence of two different conceptions of ecumenism, and thus doubts about the use of the term in council documents. From this point of view, Vischer's document mentioned above was clear:

> The critical remarks which have been made above show that the schema *De oecumenismo* is based upon an understanding of the ecumenical task which differs at decisive points from that of the member churches of the World Council. It develops an ecumenism in which the Roman Catholic Church stands at the center. The claim to be the one and only church, and above all the claim to universal jurisdiction (which, however, is barely mentioned in the schema) has the effect of making it necessary that the Roman Catholic Church constitute the center of the dialogue. Theological convictions regarding the nature of the church determine the ecumenical method in such a way that non-Roman churches are urged, even in the present stage of dialogue, to recognize the Roman Catholic Church as the ecumenical center. Consequently, the declaration that the Roman Catholic Church is the one and only church is immediately followed by a consideration of the relation of the separated brethren to the Roman Catholic Church, and consequently also the non-Roman churches are immediately evaluated by reference to the Roman Church. In contrast, the churches gathered together in the World Council proceed from the premise that Christ is present in the member churches, and it is therefore their concern to manifest in their meeting together the unity which is given in Him. The individual churches differ widely in their understanding of this unity. Some are convinced that unity in historical continuity has been preserved in their churches, while others take the view that no single church can advance the claim to have preserved unity. Such differences can lead to acute tensions within the World Council. Yet in the confession of the Triune God, all the members find themselves drawn together into the fellowship of dialogue, and in this fellowship they can pray to God for the manifestation of the unity given in Christ. We must be clear about this. This schema does not present an ecumenicism which allows the whole of Christendom to come together in order to speak to one another. It rather presents a view which is determined by Roman Catholic ecclesiology. Strictly speaking, its title should read not *De oecumenismo*, but *De oecumenismo catholico* ... . In emphasizing the difference between these views, we have no intention of characterizing *De oecumenismo* as un-ecumenical. We would simply like to call attention to the fact that this text has not yet achieved an understanding of a dialogue in which all the churches can participate. In order to achieve that, it will be necessary first to conduct intensive conversations on the

34 "Réunion des Observateurs," 1.

> nature of true ecumenism. The schema *De oecumenismo* does provide a valuable basis for this conversation.[35]

The case of the document on ecumenism was, without a doubt, the most significant one, but it was not isolated. On various other topics related to the remaining conciliar documents, the observers' particular participation was important in guiding the work of the experts in the commissions. During the first session, the schemas being examined were those formulated by the preparatory commissions which, in many ways, did not meet the expectations of either the bishops or the observers. The only one that received some praise and active interest was the liturgical schema that, more than the others, had benefitted from the results of the preconciliar renewal movement. It was in the second session that the issues dearest to the non-Catholic observers appeared, in a form that was, among other things, renewed by the intervention of what has been called the "second preparation" for the council. For the delegates from the Protestant world, there was great interest in the schema on ecumenism and, naturally, for the schema on the church. According to Vischer, ecclesiology represented a sort of receptacle of all the divisions. This is why a group of observers gathered around the representative of the WCC began to work on a joint proposal on the topic of the church. It was also a crucial issue for the Orthodox delegates, who were anxiously awaiting for a revision of the doctrine of primacy, in the sense of greater collegiality, while they considered the position on ecumenism much less important. In this early phase, however, their presence was still of little significance due to the absence of delegates from Constantinople and from most of the churches in the Greek area. In the third and fourth sessions, other decisive documents of conciliar renewal appeared, concerning the Word of God, religious freedom, ecumenism and the Oriental Churches, mixed marriages, dialogue with other religions, relations with the modern world, and missions. Here, the observers' interest was strong, and their contribution, reaching its culminating point in the aforementioned *Ad gentes*, was substantial. The less important documents were those of a nature more internal to Catholicism (the priesthood and its formation, Christian education, religious life, the laity, and means of social communications) which did not garner particular attention.

It was also an opportunity for many bishops and theologians who had never dealt with ecumenism to discover a different dimension of their own Catholicity and, at the same time, to grasp the plurality of expressions of Christianity in the modern world. The wave of sympathy towards Protestantism that was shown at various levels within the body of Catholicism was probably linked to the analogous trend towards a certain type of modernization characteristic of advanced societies in the 1960s. In the presence of the observers in Rome, it found a new face of a Protestantism open to dialogue, one that was less tied to anti-Roman diatribes than in the past. In the same way, the encounter with Orthodox Christianity gave rise to a movement of rediscovery of the Eastern tradition, well summed up by the spread of a culture of Eastern icons and ascetic texts within a Catholicism thirsting for spirituality in an increasingly secularized society. In short, the council, along with the wider experience of the ecumenical movement, provided a series of keys of shared interpretations of the Christian reality that were able to interrupt the common tendency to monologue that was typical of the previous phase. For non-Catholics as well, this helped give Catholicism a new image, far from the conflicting images of the past. It should not be forgotten that, for the most part, the world of non-Catholic churches approached the council with an attitude that was often poisoned by prejudicial and distorted opinions that, in some way, were echoed even in the attitudes of the observers. A certain superficial and contentious view

35 Lukas Vischer, "Remarks on the Schema De Oecumenismo" (translated from the German), Nov 18, 1963, in: UCL-LG, Charles Moeller, papiers, 1946, 9.

of the Catholic tradition also appeared in their reports, especially in the context of discussions on Marian piety and the hierarchical constitution of the church.

However, the very way the meeting was conducted played a fundamental role. It was the rediscovery of the conciliar instrument that also opened new perspectives in the style of ecumenical relations. Vatican II brought about, at least in part, a dream of the forerunners who, in the years of conflict and totalitarianism, had imagined the idea of a council of unity. For example, Max Josef Metzger had written about it to Pius XII at the end of 1939, asking to start preparations for a true "ecumenical council" by gathering the representatives of the various Christian churches in the evocative setting of Assisi.[36] Furthermore, the debate following Vatican II often returned to that issue. In 1968, at the general assembly of the WCC in Uppsala, the project of a universal council of the churches was launched. In Nairobi in 1975, the watchword was that of building a "conciliar community" of churches.[37] Beyond any actual possibility of implementing these projects – most of which remained unfinished – the insistent reference to the issue of conciliarity remained both a methodological need and an essential component of the churches' ecumenical journey in the closing decades of the 20th century.

For Vischer, the very model of conciliar practice among the churches would lay the foundations for a rethinking of the role of the pope himself within the ecumenical totality. In the framework of a global reflection on its role, the ecumenical movement itself could also be considered "a shared introductory exercise to conciliar practice."[38] On the Catholic side too, the need to repeat the experience of welcoming and communion that the council had achieved continued to crop up. At the Second Episcopal Conference of Latin America, in Medellin, the local episcopate granted the observers of the other churches access to Eucharistic Communion, setting a precedent that was destined to provoke many discussions.[39] On a minor scale, and considering due differences, both the meeting in Assisi in 1968 and the ecumenical celebration of May 7, 2000 commemorating the martyrs of the 20th century, manifested the same need for encounter and communion experienced during Vatican II.[40] These and other events have shown the need for Catholicism to also update the observers' experience, in short making it a normal practice of ecclesial life.

5 Members of the Council?

Vatican II and the observers' experience constituted a model for encounters in the following years. The observers' experience at the council marked a point of no return even in the history of the councils of the Catholic Church, inaugurating a new model of "ecumenical" assemblies, not only in the original sense of the term (universal), but in a new

36 See Max Josef Metzger, *Christuszeuge in einer zerrissenen Welt: Briefe und Dokumente aus der Gefangenschaft (1934–1944)*, Freiburg i.Br., Herder, 1991, 89.

37 For a brief summary of the topic, see Emmanuel Lanne, "Conciliarity," *DEM*, 212. See also the WCC document *Councils and the Ecumenical Movement*, Geneva, WCC Publications, 1968.

38 Lukas Vischer, "Petrus und der Bischof von Rom: Ihre Dienste in der Kirche," in: Heinrich Stirnimann & Lukas Vischer, eds., *Papsttum und Petrusdienst*, Frankfurt a.M, Lembeck, 1975, 35–50, here 50. See also Lukas Vischer, *Ökumenische Skizzen*, Frankfurt a.M, Lembeck, 1972, as well as the WCC document "Councils, Conciliarity, and a Genuinely Universal Council," *Study Encounter* 10/2, 1974, 1–24.

39 Silvia Scatena, *In populo pauperum: La chiesa latinoamericana dal concilio a Medellin (1962–1968)*, Bologna, Il Mulino, 2008, 504–510.

40 See Mauro Velati, "Gli altri: Ecumenismo e religioni," Concilium 4, 2005, 49–63. On the meeting in Assisi, see Alberto Melloni, "La rencontre d'Assise et ses développements dans la dynamique du Concile Vatican II," in: Joseph Doré, ed., *Le christianisme vis-à-vis des religions*, Namur, Artel, 1997, 99–130. On the meeting developments, see Jean-Dominique Durand, *Lo "spirito di Assisi": Discorsi e messaggi di Giovanni Paolo II alla Comunità di Sant'Egidio: Un contributo alla storia della pace*, Milan, Leonardo International, 2004.

sense of openness to non-Catholic churches. From that moment on, there has not been a synodal moment within the church, at a local or universal level, that has not raised the issue of the participation of representatives of the various non-Catholic churches. To tell the truth, there were even those who considered the experience of Vatican II to be a logical development of the efforts, in view of a reunion of Christians, that had already been made following the schisms. In this sense, the experience of the observers at the council was linked with the presence of theologians and representatives of the non-Catholic churches during the Council of Florence in 1439 or during the many imperial diets convened after the schism of 1517 by Charles V to repair the religious rupture and to restore peace in Europe. This continuist interpretation captures the formal aspect of participation but probably underestimates the new context within which Vatican II was situated (during the century of the ecumenical movement), overshadowing the decisive fact of the new approach that Catholicism developed with regard to unity in the passage from unionism to ecumenism.[41]

Given the changing variety of councils from antiquity to modern times, the question of the possibility of considering the observers to be full "members" of the council was asked.[42] The observers' contribution to the conciliar discussion was not minimal. The secretary general of the WCC reported a Catholic theologian's affirmation that, if every passage of the conciliar documents that were in some way influenced by the observers were to be marked in red, the effect would be that of a body of very colorful texts.[43] In a more properly historical perspective, the emphasis might perhaps be reduced. Some concrete examples of these interventions had already been seen in the field of ecumenism. However, they took place in such varied forms and channels that it is very hard to quantify them. It is also difficult to separate the intention of the observers from similar trends already occurring in Catholicism. Among the theologians of the commissions themselves, who were working on the texts, there was, in some cases, a vigilant attention to the possible elements of concordance among the confessions. Frequently, the final effect on the texts was precisely the result of these parallel tendencies, which did not fail to include even the bishops. It should not be forgotten that, since the preparatory phase, the very program of the SPCU's work was focused on inclusion of the non-Catholic point of view in the discussion of the texts.

Beyond the question of the members' status there were those who saw in the observers' work a true enrichment of the ecclesiastical magisterium, which was capable, in this case, of going beyond a narrow understanding of its role at the service of the church:

> In a way analogous to that of the Catholic faithful and theologians, the Magisterium has already listened to members of other Christian Churches and Ecclesial Communities in their capacity as observers, guests, and fraternal delegates when carrying out its specific role. As a result, they have helped the teaching office to present the substance of the deposit of the faith in new ways which are relevant for the times as well as providing insights that have led to a deeper understanding of that deposit. Such assistance should not be seen as a surrender but the logical and positive consequence of the Catholic Church's recognition of the actual status of non-Catholic Christians.[44]

Beyond specific influences on the texts, the observers' presence had a considerable impact

41 Christopher Thomas Washington, *The Participation of Non-Catholic Christian Observers, Guests and Fraternal Delegates at the Second Vatican Council and the Synods of Bishops: A Theological Analysis*, Rome, Pontificia Università Gregoriana, 2015, 18–73.

42 Alberigo, *Ecclesiologia in divenire*, 14–16.

43 Visser 't Hooft, *Memoirs*, 330.

44 Washington, *The Participation of Non-Catholic Christian Observers*, 319.

from other points of view to the extent that it would justify the use of the term "members." The possibility of a "silent memory" of the divisions, witnessed by their presence at the sessions, the spiritual communion experienced during the liturgies, culminating in the prayer of Dec 4, 1965, the exchange achieved in the informal meetings during the proceedings (not only at the council's cafés but also in the many surrounding initiatives, often at an elevated theological level), were just some of the aspects of an "effective" and "affective" participation in the council, even though it was not sanctioned by a direct and official inclusion as official council members. Compared to the past, Vatican II introduced a significant precedent for the future celebration of councils, since it was no longer just an internal affair within a single church, but a moment of grace and openness to the other. Yves Marie-Joseph Congar spoke of a "circumincession" of churches within a community gathered in Jesus's name which true meaning, however, awaited eschatological realization.[45]

All in all, the experience of the observers at Vatican II cannot be understood without a comprehensive view of the conciliar experience that the most recent debate on its historiographical interpretation has brought to light. Beyond general discussions on the aspects of continuity or rupture with respect to the past, the research in recent years has highlighted the scope of the "event" of the council, going further than a simple consideration of the texts,[46] and it is precisely to this peculiar dimension of the council that the experience of the non-Catholics present in Rome seems to belong in its own right. It represents the most immediate and certain response to John O'Malley's question as to whether something actually happened at Vatican II.[47] Even the aspect of the intersection between the observers' requests and the process of drafting the text of the conciliar documents must thus be located within the global context of the relations and rapport established progressively as the four sessions unfolded, which constitutes the very meaning of the event.

The progress of the historiographical inquiry into this specific aspect of the conciliar event has been rather contradictory. On the one hand, it was able to benefit from the immediate publication of direct sources. The diaries of Douglas Horton and the memoirs of Robert McAfee Brown and Hébert Roux,[48] to mention only a few examples from the years following the council, constituted valuable primary material in reconstructing the history of the observers. In point of fact, this initial phase was not followed by adequate historiographical interest in the subject. It should be recognized – as Lukas Vischer noted at the time – that the *History of Vatican II*, directed by Giuseppe Alberigo, also kept track of the observers'

45 "In these conditions, the observers' participation was something other than just an ornament that enhanced the show. It specified and granted 'others' entry into our consciousness and our presence into theirs. It is the sign of a type of 'circumincession' of the Churches, each of which has its own personality within a fundamental community of faith and baptism in the name of the Lord Jesus"; Yves Congar, *Le Concile de Vatican II: Son église, peuple de Dieu et corps du Christ*, Paris, Beauchesne, 1984, 96.

46 This is the key to the historiographic interpretation that is also at the base of Giuseppe Alberigo & Joseph Komonchak, eds., *History of Vatican II*, 5 vols., Leuven/Maryknoll, Peeters/Orbis Books, 1995–2006. For a recent comparison between different theories on this text/event dialectic, see Peter Hünermann, "Der 'Text': Eine Ergänzung zur Hermeneutik des II. Vatikanischen Konzils," *CrSt* 28, 2007, 339–358, and Christoph Theobald, "Enjeux herméneutiques des débats sur l'histoire du Concile Vatican II," *CrSt* 28, 2007, 359–380. For a different type of interpretation, close to a traditionalist point of view, see Roberto De Mattei, *Il Concilio Vaticano II: Una storia mai scritta*, Turin, Lindau, 2010.

47 John W. O'Malley, *What Happened at Vatican II*, Cambridge MA, Harvard University Press, 2008.

48 See Douglas Horton, *Vatican Diary 1965: A Protestant Observes the Fourth Session of Vatican Council II*, Philadelphia, United Church Press, 1966; Robert McAfee Brown, *Observer in Rome: A Protestant Report on the Vatican Council*, Garden City, Doubleday, 1964; Hébert Roux, *Le concile et le dialogue œcuménique*, Paris, Seuil, 1964.

contribution.[49] In subsequent years, however, a large amount of unpublished documentation has permitted a general picture of the impact that individual observers presence had on the council, and of the variety of approaches that they brought forth with regards to Catholicism, to emerge, even if this is not well highlighted by their particular perspectives.

It makes sense that points of view should remain personal, just as the different confessional visions must remain decisive for an overall judgement on the council. Despite this, all the work, the internal dynamics, and the concrete impact of the observers' presence emerge in the documentation. The theological view of their reactions, logically, is influenced to a greater extent by the origin and mentality of the various delegates. From this point of view, André Birmelé has already written much that is important and, perhaps, only a specific analysis of the actions and relationships of the observers characterized by a greater theological competence might provide an exhaustive picture.[50] It should be borne in mind, among other things, that shortly after Vatican II many of them published very important articles on their view of the council's results. A view of individual paths, though, does not suffice. Only a comprehensive reconstruction can bring out the events, the dynamics, and the reciprocal relationships among the observers and with the council. The goal is to grasp the phenomenology of an encounter rather than to develop a complete theological view.

It is clear that this choice runs up against a question that Étienne Fouilloux had already posed in an initial article on the matter.[51] Can the observers be considered a group? Is it not rather a matter of considering individual personalities or confessional subgroups? An investigation in this direction is needed, and the studies already initiated by Margarethe Hopf (on Edmund Schlink), by Michael Quisinsky (on Lukas Vischer), and by Michael Attridge (with the publication of Eugene Fairweather's conciliar diary)[52] bode well for the future. All this will help reveal the opposing poles and the dynamics in which the presence of the observers to the council was played out. On the one hand, we have the constant attempt to make the group of observers assume a fictitious identity not only for strategic reasons (as some observers close to the WCC thought) but also because of the practical need to give substance to a significant group of personalities present in Rome who became partners in the dialogue with Catholicism. On the other, there is also the demonstration of the practical non-existence of a common strategy or even just a possible collective judgement on the events of the council. The observers' reactions – documented in their reports – paint a greatly varied and often contradictory picture. Personal initiatives were often decisive, presenting many difficulties not only for those who, like Vischer, tried to organize common strategies, but also for the Catholics themselves.

It is well known that, for the entire duration of the council, there was a steering committee of observers working on coordinating initiatives. The results of that group were rather modest. Many of the initiatives in the pipeline did not find unanimous support from the delegations, and

49 Lukas Vischer, "*Storia del Concilio Vaticano II*: Reactions and Comments by an Observer at the Council," *EcRev* 49, 1997, 348–353.

50 André Birmelé, "Le Concile Vatican II vu par les observateurs des autres traditions chrétiennes," in: Joseph Doré & Alberto Melloni, eds., *Volti di fine Concilio: Studi di storia e teologia sulla conclusione del Vaticano II*, Bologna, Il Mulino, 2000, 225–264.

51 Étienne Fouilloux, "Des observateurs non catholiques," in: Étienne Fouilloux, ed., *Vatican II commence … Approches francophones*, Leuven, Bibliotheek van de Faculteit der Godgeleerdheid, 1993, 235–261.

52 Margarethe Hopf, *Ein Osservatore Romano für die Evangelische Kirche in Deutschland: Der Konzilsbeobachter Edmund Schlink im Spannungsfeld der Interessen*, Göttingen, Vandenhoeck & Ruprecht, 2022; Quisinsky, "The Ecumenical Dynamic of Vatican II"; Michael Attridge, "A Canadian Anglican at Vatican II: The Activity of Eugene R. Fairweather," in: Michael Attridge, Catherine E. Clifford & Gilles Routhier, eds., *Vatican II: Expériences canadiennes – Canadian Experiences*, Ottawa, University of Ottawa Press, 2011, 341–359.

therefore ultimately it was resorted to the strategy of gathering support at a personal level. One of the moments when the division and hostility toward a common strategy became acute was the consultation held in the summer of 1964 at Rummelsberg with the goal of establishing some coordination among the delegations. The initiative came from the WCC which, even in the first session, had already proposed a common timing and attitude towards the council to the confessional delegations. It was precisely in that context that difficulties, especially from some Anglican observers, emerged, and it was clear that a united front was impossible.[53] It should be borne in mind that the see of Constantinople had, until that moment, played a very personal game and that Athenagoras had set himself objectives that went far beyond the observers' participation in the council, anticipating a direct link with Pope Paul VI in what has been called the "dialogue of charity."

6 The Postconciliar Period

The difficulties and embarrassment witnessed here are the clearest sign of the first stages of dialogue; such was the observers' experience in Rome. Far from demonizing or minimizing it, perhaps believing it to lead to an alleged slide toward the Protestantization of Catholicism or the deleterious effects of a reduction of the council's freedom, 50 years later this experience remains one of the richest and most profound moments of unity experienced by Christians and, as such, it became the start of a process of rapprochement characteristic of the postconciliar period. The observers' experience extended beyond the conclusion of the council into various initiatives of bilateral dialogue in which the Catholic Church participated. Bea and Willebrands's SPCU, once its function at the council had been completed, became the driving force behind a multifaceted activity of contact and theological dialogue. It is true that its statute was still provisional, given its lack of a clear institutional foundation and the particularity of its role, which was essentially linked to the work of the council. From December 1965, the SPCU was among the commissions charged with the application of the council while it awaited a redefinition of its goals to arrive from the work of the commission established by Paul VI in 1967 for the reform of the Roman curia.

This did not mean a divestment of its every activity. The council's program and the necessities of the dialogue initiated with the other churches required various completions both in regard to the relations themselves and as far as the church's own pastoral oversight was concerned. For those reasons, the SPCU continued the process of preparing the Ecumenical Directory that had already been envisioned from its first meetings in 1962, and which had been made increasingly necessary by the fact that the council had revealed the diversity of approaches and mentalities present in the Catholic Church with regard to ecumenical question. The conciliar declaration *Unitatis redintegratio* had established the general principles of the Catholic ecumenical position, but it was then necessary to translate those principles into concrete norms. The work was slowed down by the complexity of the factors in play and by the SPCU's choice to launch a triple consultation of regional episcopates from around the world, of selected representatives of the non-Christian churches, and of curial offices, including the new Congregation for the Doctrine of the Faith and the Secretariat of State. It was precisely from the former Holy Office that came the greatest resistance, and it was handled with a certain embarrassment by the heads of the SPCU. Only in May 1967 was the first part of the Ecumenical Directory published, that concerning the creation of ecumenical commissions at a local level, the question of baptism by non-Catholic churches, and the issue of *communicatio in sacris* among Christians of different confessions.

The imprint of the SPCU's work was innovative in the context of the departments of the

53 Velati, *Separati ma fratelli*, 335–339.

Roman curia; this was also true because it aimed at a progressive decentralization, with the direct and continuous involvement of episcopates from all over the world. The experience of the consultation, in fact, was repeated in that same period (between mid-1966 and April 1967) on the issue of collaboration between the SPCU and the UBS for the purpose of a joint work of translation of the original texts and greater dissemination of the Bible in various local contexts. In different ways and to different degrees, the consultation was also carried out for an issue considered essential by non-Catholics, but which remained unresolved by the council, that of mixed marriages. In this area, despite claiming a role of no secondary importance, the SPCU had to submit to the decisions of the Congregation for the Doctrine of the Faith and other organs of the curia, being thus inevitably marginalized by the definition of the Catholic position. In March 1966, the *Instructio de matrimoniis mixtis* was published, expressing a position far removed from the inroads made by the SPCU during the council in the dialogue with members of the non-Catholic churches. On the other hand, decentralization had not played a positive role in this area, given the restrictive positions expressed by influential resident bishops.

The SPCU's most detailed and massive work in the postconciliar period, however, remains that tied to developing relations between Catholicism and the other churches, viewed as the natural continuation of the season of conciliar dialogue.[54] It is clear that there was a very close link between the activity of the observers at the council and the subsequent implementation of structures for theological dialogue between the various churches. Relations with the churches were finally freed from the common dominating pattern of the preconciliar period. On the one hand, the Catholic Church had used diplomatic channels, surreptitiously identifying non-Catholic churches with their nations of provenance. It is well known that relations between Catholics and Anglicans were often handled through the British embassy in Rome and the Holy See's apostolic delegation in London. This created a confusion in plans – certainly owing to the need to compensate for the lack of a direct tie between the churches – which, in the long run, highlighted a political rather than purely religious aspect. On the other hand, Catholicism in the 1950s, animated by a mysticism of "return" that imagined a future passage of large sectors of the non-Catholic churches into the Roman one, tended to establish organic relationships with the pro-Catholic groups present in the other churches (Eastern unionists, High Church Anglicans, Lutheran associations such as Hans Asmussen's Die Sammlung) with the intent of assisting that transition. Far from producing good results in terms of conversions, such a policy only further deteriorated relations among the churches.

From this point of view, the SPCU's novel approach and the observers' positive experience constituted a radical break, inaugurating a new manner of church-to-church relations, free from political interference or unionist assumptions. The only case where it was rather difficult to separate the two aspects (ecumenism and diplomacy) was that of the Russian Orthodox Church, which sent a delegation to the council that included spies for the Soviet regime. The story of the liberation of Metropolitan Josyf Slipyj in 1963 involved an unprecedented diplomatic intervention on the part of the SPCU, assisted in the endeavor by diplomats of Western countries such as Italy. However, it was a wholly unique situation that cannot be taken as an example of the entirety of relations among the churches.

In this sense, the experience of the council paved the way for a completely new and properly ecumenical network of relationships. The original relationship was that among the men of the SPCU and the WCC; as early as 1964, the latter and the Catholic Church had initiated a structured relationship with the creation of the so-called Joint

54 André Birmelé, "Nos dialogues œcuméniques et les défis contemporains," in: Ferracci, ed., *Toward a History of the Desire for Christian Unity*, 257–270.

Working Group, which first met in November 1965 alongside the council. In that multilateral manner, Visser 't Hooft had also aspired to resolve the issue of the encounter between the various churches and the Catholic Church, but quite quickly had to resign himself to seeing the contemporary and parallel blossoming of a wider network of bilateral relations. Along this path, the LWF was the trailblazer. A beginning to the dialogue had already been decided in Rome during Vatican II, thanks to the mediation of the observer delegates, including two such great theologians as Kristen Ejner Skydsgaard and George Arthur Lindbeck. In a specific study, Skydsgaard had also laid the foundations for the first meeting of the joint Catholic-Lutheran commission in April 1966. In his opinion, it was a matter of seizing the *kairos* of the council and, on the Lutheran side, of adopting a self-critical attitude in order to learn from the lesson of internal renewal proposed by Catholicism with Vatican II. The WMC took the same path a short time later and, thanks to the work of its president, Fred Pierce Corson, who had attended the council as a delegate and who was able to overcome the entity's significant resistance, in 1966, decided to launch a commission of dialogue with Catholicism. In contrast was the attitude of the WARC which, in keeping with the WCC line, had decided at the Strasbourg meeting in 1966 to restrict contact with Catholicism in the activities of the Joint Working Group. Soon, however, their position changed and, in 1969, work on a joint Reformed-Catholic commission began. The same path was taken by other minority churches, such as the Quakers and the Disciples of Christ, which within a few years took similar steps toward dialogue with Catholicism.

The case of the Anglican Church did not escape these trends either, although perhaps it had its own peculiarities. The Anglican delegate Bernard Pawley had established a rather close bond with Paul VI, who considered the Anglicans to be the closest to Catholic sensibilities among the Western churches. Archbishop Arthur Michael Ramsey had followed the council's work less enthusiastically but had accepted the pope's proposal for a visit to Rome in 1966. Even in the midst of the controversy and difficulties caused by the publication of Paul VI's aforementioned instruction on mixed marriages, which was far removed from the requests of non-Catholics, the visit took place in November of that year and formalized the decision to set up a joint group for theological dialogue. As far as the Orthodox Church was concerned, the situations were also varied. The personal bond between Paul VI and Athenagoras was strengthened by the delegation sent from the Phanar to the last two sessions of the council. It included the Romanian-born monk André Scrima, who played an important role in the delicate relations between the SPCU – mainly in the person of Pierre Duprey – and the patriarch of Constantinople. After the council, the exchange of visits made by the two ecclesiastical leaders to Istanbul and Rome set the seal on a reborn understanding between the two Romes. However, the beginning of a stable form of collaboration through a structure of theological dialogue was postponed for several years because the path chosen by Athenagoras was that of the "dialogue of charity." The collaboration established by the SPCU with the Orthodox Russians also followed its own peculiar path, focused indeed on theological confrontation but specifically on the issues of the relationship between churches and society. These were the dominant themes of the Leningrad conference in December 1967, which brought together the delegations of the Roman Catholic Church and the Orthodox Russian Church in a fruitful exchange. It represented the summit of an understanding destined to suffer in the following years from the fickleness of the Soviet regime's politics, which maintained close control over the Orthodox Church.

This and other events show the extraordinary fruitfulness of the experience of the encounter born in Rome in 1961 with the arrival of the first delegates and observers from the different churches, which would have been inconceivable without the setting of an epochal event such as Vatican II but was certainly prepared for by a development of men and ideas that had been present in Catholicism since the years following the Modernist crisis, culminating in the creation of that key body that was the SPCU of Bea and Willebrands.

Translated from Italian to English by Susan Dawson Vásquez and David Dawson Vásquez.

Bibliography

Alberigo, Giuseppe, *Ecclesiologia in divenire: A proposito di "concilio pastorale" e di Osservatori a-cattolici al Vaticano II*, Bologna, Istituto per le Scienze Religiose di Bologna, 1990.

Attridge, Michael, "A Canadian Anglican at Vatican II: The Activity of Eugene R. Fairweather," in: Michael Attridge, Catherine E. Clifford & Gilles Routhier, eds., *Vatican II: Expériences canadiennes – Canadian Experiences*, Ottawa, University of Ottawa Press, 2011, 341–359.

Birmelé, André, "Le Concile Vatican II vu par les observateurs des autres traditions chrétiennes," in: Joseph Doré & Alberto Melloni, eds., *Volti di fine Concilio: Studi di storia e teologia sulla conclusione del Vaticano II*, Bologna, Il Mulino, 2000, 225–264.

Chandler, Andrew & Charlotte Hansen, eds., *Observing Vatican II: The Confidential Reports of the Archbishop of Canterbury's Representative, Bernard Pawley (1961–1964)*, Cambridge, Cambridge University Press, 2013.

Fouilloux, Étienne, "Des observateurs non catholiques," in: Étienne Fouilloux, ed., *Vatican II commence … Approches francophones*, Leuven, Bibliotheek van de Faculteit der Godgeleerdheid, 1993, 235–261.

Hopf, Margarethe, *Ein Osservatore Romano für die Evangelische Kirche in Deutschland: Der Konzilsbeobachter Edmund Schlink im Spannungsfeld der Interessen*, Göttingen, Vandenhoeck & Ruprecht, 2022.

Roccucci, Adriano, "Russian Observers at Vatican II: The 'Council for Russian Orthodox Church Affairs' and the Moscow Patriarchate Between Anti-Religious Policy and International Strategies," in: Alberto Melloni, ed., *Vatican II in Moscow (1959–1965): Acts of the Colloquium on the History of Vatican II (Moscow, March 30–April 2, 1995)*, Leuven, Bibliotheek van de Faculteit Godgeleerdheid, 1997, 45–69.

Scatena, Silvia, *Taizé, una parabola di unità: Storia della comunità dalle origini al concilio dei giovani*, Bologna, Il Mulino, 2018, 493–581.

Velati, Mauro, *Una difficile transizione: Il cattolicesimo tra unionismo ed ecumenismo (1952–1964)*, Bologna, Il Mulino, 1996.

Velati, Mauro, *Separati ma fratelli: Gli osservatori non cattolici al Vaticano II (1962–1965)*, Bologna, Il Mulino, 2014.

Vischer, Lukas, "*Storia del Concilio Vaticano II*: Reactions and Comments by an Observer at the Council," *EcRev* 49, 1997, 348–353.

Washington, Christopher Thomas, *The Participation of Non-Catholic Christian Observers, Guests and Fraternal Delegates at the Second Vatican Council and the Synods of Bishops: A Theological Analysis*, Rome, Pontificia Università Gregoriana, 2015.

CHAPTER 27

Fraternal Rivalry and Convergences: The "Leap Forward" of Vatican II

Christoph Theobald

1 Introduction

In the history of Christian ecumenism, Vatican II represents a decisive moment of "passage", the dimensions and stakes of which we have not yet finished measuring. During this assembly, Catholicism left behind an "ecumenism of return" and embarked upon the unpredictable paths of a shared search for unity. It was a turning point that could not occur without repercussions on the entire ecumenical movement.[1] Thanks to the many observers from other churches and their active presence, a symmetrical exchange began between them and the Roman Catholic Church. It left its mark on the conciliar texts and on the ways of proceeding thereafter. At the same time, it influenced, even modulated, the trajectory of the WCC and bilateral relations between churches, which then began to multiply. In a short time, a true "leap forward" was thus achieved, to use a spirited metaphor of Pope John XXIII who, in his opening address to the council on Oct 11, 1962, echoed precisely this expectation of "the Christian, Catholic, and apostolic spirit of the whole world."[2]

One must, therefore, analyze what happened during these seven years from the perspective of the non-Catholic observers and through the lens of the supporters of the ecumenical movement.[3] However, it is also necessary to consider the ecumenical event that was Vatican II from the perspective of the conciliar actors themselves. Their insight, supported by institutional transformations within the assembly, and above all the results of their work, must be understood: not only the documents, but also what was said – in *UR* 11 – of the dialogue and fraternal rivalry that, entering gradually into the conciliar customs, was experienced first by the conciliar assembly and observers, and then thought about and formulated as an ecumenical maxim and method.

More than half a century after the end of the council, this double result appears in a new light today. Not only has research on Vatican II and its reception entered a new, intercontinental phase that can now take advantage of a much broader documentary foundation, but the ecumenical movement has also undergone important

1 See especially Étienne Fouilloux, *Les catholiques et l'unité chrétienne du XIXe au XXe siècle: Itinéraires européens d'expression française*, Paris, Le Centurion, 1982; Mauro Velati, *Una difficile transizione: Il cattolicismo tra unionismo ed ecumenismo (1952–1964)*, Bologna, Il Mulino, 1996 and Mauro Velati, *Separati ma fratelli: Gli osservatori non cattolici al Vaticano II (1962–1965)*, Bologna, Il Mulino, 2014.

2 See the main passage of the Italian version of Pope John XXIII's opening address *Gaudet Mater Ecclesia*, which was greatly transformed and "doctrinalized" in its Latin translation: "But from a renewed, serene, and tranquil adherence to the whole teaching of the Church, in its entirety and precision, as it still shines forth in the acts of the Councils of Trent and Vatican I, the Christian, Catholic, and apostolic spirit of the whole world expects a leap forward toward a doctrinal penetration and a formation of consciences in more perfect conformity with fidelity to authentic doctrine, with this doctrine being studied and presented through the forms of inquiry and literary formulation of modern thought. The substance of the ancient doctrine of the deposit of faith is one thing, and the formulation in which it is clothed another. And it is the latter that must be taken into great account, with patience if necessary, measuring everything by the forms and proportions of a teaching authority primarily pastoral in character," in: Alberto Melloni, *Papa Giovanni: Un cristiano e il suo concilio*, Turin, Einaudi, 2009, 324–325. English translation available at <https://jakomonchak.files.wordpress.com/2012/10/john-xxiii-opening-speech.pdf> (accessed Jun 26, 2021).

3 See the contribution by Mauro Velati in this volume.

developments, ebbs and flows,[4] which reexamine its decisions, made during the *tempus visitationis* and thus also reconsider the work of the council. Thanks to ecumenical dialogue, the partners have discovered that their differences are not so much about a particular point of doctrine as about the "perspectives" (or *Denkformen*)[5] from which they consider the whole of the Christian mystery. Thinking of the dispute between East and West, Yves Marie-Joseph Congar affirmed that "it is the identical that is different"[6] and, since the *Joint Declaration on the Doctrine of Justification* in Augsburg in 1999, people have taken to speaking of a "differentiated consensus" or even more recently of a "differentiating consensus."[7] This "systemic" aspect of the question of Christian unity, which requires a reinterpretation of the entire tradition,[8] hardly appears in the historical works of the past century, nor in the different generations of commentaries.[9] It was, however, present at Vatican II, and was thought out by several actors, translated into institutional reality, and subjected to conflicts and negotiations among council Fathers, theologians, and observers before being found in the corpus of the 16 documents and becoming the object of postconciliar reception. This intertextual, systemic aspect should certainly be given more attention today, if not just for the simple fact, to which little thought is given, that the SPCU did not stop its conciliar work with the promulgation of the decree on ecumenism *Unitatis redintegratio* but brought other texts to completion. Our journey, which will follow the historical trajectory of the council, will attempt to show this.

2 From the Announcement of the Council to the Holy See's Full Recognition of the SPCU

As soon as John XXIII announced a forthcoming council on Jan 25, 1959 at St. Paul's Outside the Walls, the chessboard of future actors was laid out.

In his address in Italian to the consistory, the pope spoke of a "*general Council* for the universal Church" from which he expected "a light for the edification and joy of the whole Christian people." At the same time, he addressed "a friendly and renewed invitation to the faithful of the *Churches separated from us* to take part in this banquet of

4 See Christoph Theobald, "Le renouveau œcuménique au XXe siècle: Flux et reflux," in: Nagi Edelby & Souraya Bechealany, eds., *Le défi de l'Église Une: Mission de la revue œcuménique francophone* (*Actes de colloque de Beyrouth – 12–14 novembre 2015*), Beirut, CERPOC, 2018, 15–31.

5 Joseph Famerée, *Ecclésiologie et œcuménisme: Recueil d'études*, Leuven, Peeters, 2017, 352–359.

6 Yves Congar, *Une passion: L'unité. Réflexions et souvenirs* (*1929–1973*), Paris, Cerf, 1974, 108.

7 See Frédéric Chavel, "Luther et la théologie luthérienne dans le mouvement œcuménique: Bilan des avancées réalisées et évaluation des obstacles à surmonter," *RSR* 105, 2017, 403–423, here 409, note 11.

8 See Christoph Theobald, "Que nous est-il permis d'espérer? L'œcuménisme: Un seuil à franchir. À propos de deux ouvrages qui font date," *CrSt* 40, 2019, 411–452.

9 Without a doubt, the very genre of commentary makes an intertextual approach difficult. Compared to the commentary edited by Herder (*²LThK*) and the volumes of commentary of the *Unam sanctam* collection (vols. 51–77, 1966–1968), *HThK Vat.II*, has the advantage of entrusting several texts to one commentator. Thus, the decrees *Orientalium Ecclesiarum* and *Unitatis redintegratio* are commented on by Bernd Jochen Hilberath. The fifth volume (*Die Dokumente des Zweiten Vatikanischen Konzils: Theologische Zusammenschau und Perspektiven*, Freiburg i.Br., Herder, 2006) attempts a cross-sectional analysis, which the authors call a "calligraphic sketch" of the council. They note the "learning process" that took place in and through the conciliar assembly, without making a connection between this conciliar "experience" and the corpus as a whole, or even with the desire for a pastoral and ecumenical reinterpretation of the entire Christian tradition, as announced in Pope John XXIII's opening address. As for Giuseppe Alberigo & Joseph A. Komonchak, eds., *History of Vatican II*, 5 vols., Leuven/Maryknoll, Peeters/Orbis Books, 1995–2006, it places the drafting of the texts managed by the SPCU within the interplay of tensions between the assembly in its conflicting configuration, the papacy, the curia, and popular opinion – in this case, its representatives in the persons of the observers – leaving the theological orientation of the entirety of Vatican II in the background, except for Giuseppe Alberigo's concluding question in which he rightly defines Vatican II as an "epochal change."

grace and fraternity to which so many souls aspire from every corner of the earth."[10] The text that the curia sent to the cardinals, however, no longer spoke of a "general council" but of an "ecumenical council." It avoided mention of the churches but expressed an intention to the faithful of the communities separated from us, not to participate in a banquet of grace, but to "*follow us* in this search for unity and grace."[11] This very first indication of the Roman curia distancing itself from the newly elected pope's more open and more modest project[12] already announced two different approaches in preparing for the council.[13] As for the representatives of the other churches and ecumenical organizations, the Ecumenical Patriarch Athenagoras I, Willem Adolph Visser 't Hooft for the WCC, and many other personalities of the ecumenical movement took the signal of the Roman announcement very seriously, while tempering the enthusiasm that was expressed during the months that followed. Apprehension regarding the Roman Church remained strong, with a certain fear that it might monopolize a new stage of ecumenism (as could be seen from the text of the announcement in its curial version or from other "omissions" in *L'Osservatore Romano*)[14] or might even take steps that would undermine interconfessional understanding within the ecumenical council – the Rhodes incident in August of 1959 being one example among others.[15]

This shifting terrain began to stabilize somewhat from the moment that Pope John XXIII specified his intentions, set up a pre-preparatory commission on Pentecost of 1959, announced the name of the future council on Jul 14, 1959, and initiated preparations proper with the motu proprio entitled *Superno Dei nutu* on Pentecost, Jul 5, 1960.[16] While, from the outset, he insisted on the pastoral goal of a renewal of the church, formulating the ecumenical aim in terms of "cooperation" (not of "return"),[17] the stripping away of the pre-preparatory consultation and its transformation into a series of *quaestiones*, as well as the institution of ten preparatory commissions modeled on the organization of the curia, resembled a readjustment in the rule of a powerful administration that was imperturbably pursuing the doctrinal and disciplinary logic of the "ecumenical" councils of Trent and Vatican I.[18] The only two

10 See the critical edition of the Italian text by Melloni, *Papa Giovanni*, 296 (lines 245–249) and 297 (lines 310–324) (italics mine).

11 *ADA* 1, 5–6 (italics mine).

12 On this distancing, which became more and more systematic, see Giuseppe Alberigo, "The Announcement of the Council: From the Security of the Fortress to the Lure of the Quest," in: Giuseppe Alberigo & Joseph A. Komonchak, eds., *History of Vatican II*, vol. 1, *Announcing and Preparing Vatican Council II: Toward a New Era in Catholicism*, Leuven/Maryknoll, Peeters/Orbis Books, 1995, 1–54.

13 See Giuseppe Alberigo, "Preparing for What Kind of Council?," in: Alberigo & Komonchak, eds., *History of Vatican II*, vol. 1, 501–508.

14 Alberigo, "The Announcement of the Council," 15–20.

15 For this phase, see Velati, *Una difficile transizione*, 101–135; see also Alberigo, "The Announcement of the Council," 26–30.

16 *ADA* 1, 93–96.

17 Here is the conclusion to which Giuseppe Alberigo came after a detailed analysis of the set of interventions of Pope John XXIII during this stage: "Pope John wanted a Council that would mark a transition between two eras, that is, that would bring the Church out of the post-Tridentine period and, to a degree, out of the centuries-long Constantinian era, into a new phase of witness and proclamation, and would also recover substantial and abiding elements of the tradition considered able to nourish and ensure fidelity to the gospel during so difficult a transition," Alberigo, "The Announcement of the Council," 33–44, here 42. See also my analysis of the address of Pope John XXIII from the perspective of the "conscience herméneutique de Jean XXIII," in: Christoph Theobald, *La réception du concile Vatican II*, vol. 1, *Accéder à la source*, Paris, Cerf, 2009, 233–257, esp. 234–235, note 3 where is presented an analysis of 14 speeches.

18 See the analysis of Étienne Fouilloux, "The Antepreparatory Phase: The Slow Emergence from Inertia (January, 1959–October, 1962)," in: Alberigo & Komonchak, eds., *History of Vatican II*, vol. 1, 55–166.

new features were the Commission for the Apostolate of the Laity and, above all, the SPCU.

Confined at the time to functioning as a link with "those who, bearing the name of Christians, are separated from this Apostolic See,"[19] the SPCU, its formation, and its increasing influence on the work of the assembly will serve as a guideline in this first part.

2.1 *The Difficult Birth of an Ecumenical Logic*

Mauro Velati has traced the emergence of the SPCU, its roots in the CCEQ, Pope John XXIII's rapid decision on Mar 13, 1960 to entrust it to Cardinal Augustin Bea, and its vague description in *Superno Dei nutu*, where it was not given the status of a preparatory commission but of a secretariat.[20] This apparent limitation reveals the conflict of interpretation of which it was henceforward to be the object. While the secretary of the pre-preparatory commission, Cardinal Domenico Tardini, understood this designation as an act of prudence in the face of the novelty of ecumenical questioning, John XXIII – in a communication to Bea on May 17, 1960 – saw it as leaving room for greater freedom.[21]

The progressive enlargement of the SPCU's competencies was to be based on two vectors: the expansion of the circle of relations outside Roman Catholicism as well as the growing possibility of intervening during the preparations and, eventually, during the council itself. It was a fragile process that would only stabilize during the first intersessional period, in March 1963. As for the first vector, the SPCU's natural interlocutors were the churches that emerged from the Reformation and the WCC,[22] Cardinal Bea having declared himself unqualified on issues concerning the Orthodox churches.[23] However, on Sep 18, 1960, the SPCU's circle of relations was extended when Pope John asked it to prepare a text on the church and the Jewish people.[24] The desired cooperation with the Commission for the Oriental Churches, which for the moment held a monopoly on rapprochement with Orthodoxy, was reduced to a single meeting in March 1961. But that commission's inaction and the Orthodox desire to work with the SPCU instead finally led, at the end of the year, to the full responsibility for "ecumenical diplomacy" being entrusted to the secretariat,[25] not without leaving a potential for conflict that would contaminate future relations between the commission and the SPCU. The latter's first plenary session in November 1960, and its establishment of subcommissions, allows us to grasp the extent of the network of relations covered and especially the level of reflection it rapidly reached. It was subcommission IV, "De laicatu et tolerantia," which reported on the new conditions of communication in modern societies in a world that was becoming increasingly unified and marked by the pluralism of religious conceptions and attitudes. It was also this subcommission that

19 *ADA* 1, 95.

20 Velati, *Una difficile transizione*, 175–204; see also Mauro Velati, *Dialogo e rinnovamento: Verbali e testi del segretariato per l'unità dei cristiani nella preparazione del concilio Vaticano II (1960–1962)*, Bologna, Il Mulino, 2011, 15–94. This introduction to the collection of the principal documents of the SPCU gives a precise and detailed picture of its gestation, its formation, and its itinerary.

21 Velati, *Una difficile transizione*, 198.

22 Velati, *Una difficile transizione*, 205–210, reporting the first meeting between Cardinal Bea and the secretary general of the WCC, Visser 't Hooft, in Milan in September 1960. See also Velati, *Una difficile transizione*, 36–37.

23 Velati, *Una difficile transizione*, 192–193; see also Velati, *Dialogo e rinnovamento*, 115, 156; see also Joseph A. Komonchak, "The Struggle for the Council During the Preparation of Vatican II (1960–1962)," in: Alberigo & Komonchak, eds., *History of Vatican II*, vol. 1, 167–350, esp. 263.

24 See Velati, *Dialogo e rinnovamento*, 46–55; see also the introduction to the commentary on *Nostra aetate* by Johannes Oesterreicher, in *LThK*, supplement H.S. Brechter & others, eds., *Das zweite Vatikanische Konzil*, vol. 2, Freiburg I.Br., Herder, 1967, 406–414.

25 See Velati, *Una difficile transizione*, 210–218; see also Komonchak, "The Struggle for the Council," 323–324.

drew up an initial outline of *De libertate religiosa*[26] in 1961, a topic that Visser 't Hooft had indicated as an ecumenical prerequisite as soon as the council was announced.[27] All the conditions were met for a final opening of the circle of relations to the religions of the world, which did not take place until November 1964.[28]

As for the possibility of intervening in the preparations for and, ultimately, during the council itself – the second vector of the SPCU's expanded competence – it was contested from the start, especially by the Theological Commission. In his opening address to the first plenary session held on Nov 14–15, 1960, Cardinal Bea affirmed that the secretariat "is not merely an 'information-office,' but can also prepare materials regarding Christian unity and which therefore might be proposed to the Council."[29] Established for this purpose, the subcommissions – initially 10 and eventually 14 – had the task of preparing *vota* to be sent to the various preparatory commissions. This was effected for a certain number of them, such as the *vota* on the members of the church (subcommission I) and on its hierarchical structure (subcommission II) addressed to the Theological Commission, or those sent to the Liturgical Commission (subcommission VI) and to the Commission for the Discipline of the Sacraments (subcommission VII) etc.[30] The tacit presupposition of this approach was that ecumenicity must be a dimension of all the issues to be dealt with by the council. On a practical level, this implied the formation of mixed commissions with the SPCU's participation.[31]

However, the indifference of certain commissions, and even the Theological Commission's categorical refusal to collaborate with the men of the SPCU,[32] led, from the third plenary session of Apr 16–21, 1961, to a fundamental change in strategy. The SPCU began to draw up preparatory schemas, the very first being that concerning religious freedom,[33] followed at the fifth plenary session of Nov 27–Dec 2, 1962 by that on Judaism,[34] both

26 It is now possible to follow this development in detail, thanks to the collection of the texts and minutes of the secretariat's debates, in Velati, *Dialogo e rinnovamento*, 247–283 (second plenary session of Feb 6–9, 1961), 379–394 (third plenary session of Apr 16–21, 1961), 589–611 (fourth plenary session of Aug 26–31, 1961); see also Komonchak, "The Struggle for the Council," 296–300.

27 See Velati, *Dialogo e rinnovamento*, 42.

28 Beginning with the second plenary session (Feb 6–9, 1960), the question of the relationship with non-Christians was posed in the *votum*, prepared by Bishop Emiel-Jozef De Smedt, *De caritate Ecclesiae erga fratres absentes et erga non christianos*, see Velati, *Dialogo e rinnovamento*, 262–272.

29 See Velati, *Dialogo e rinnovamento*, 155.

30 For a global vision, see Komonchak, "The Struggle for the Council," 266–271 and 285–293. For a detailed presentation, accompanied by documents and the minutes of the debates, see Velati, *Dialogo e rinnovamento*, 187–210 and 315–335 (for subcommission I); 210–229 and 335–350 (for subcommission II); 409–437 (for subcommission VI); 438–478, 611–632, and 691–716 (for subcommission VII).

31 At the fifth plenary session (Nov 27–Dec 2, 1961), Cardinal Bea recalled the desire of the pope "that pastoral questions [be] considered by all commissions" (Velati, *Dialogo e rinnovamento*, 690); this should apply analogically to "ecumenical questions." However, at this moment in the conciliar preparation, the secretary of the Central Preparatory Commission had already envisioned the creation of a committee to gather texts on "the principal problems of pastoral technique" (see Komonchak, "The Struggle for the Council," 174–175, here 174). For its part, the SPCU was moving in a different direction.

32 It was first on the subject of ecclesiological questions (dealt with by subcommission II and then by subcommission I) that, beginning in February 1961, relations between the SPCU and the Theological Commission deteriorated, with the latter refusing to establish a mixed commission; see Komonchak, "The Struggle for the Council," 173–174 and 291–292.

33 Velati, *Dialogo e rinnovamento*, 391; see also Komonchak, "The Struggle for the Council," 298–299. The text of the Theological Commission on church and state and the text of the SPCU on religious freedom, as well as the debate of the Central Preparatory Commission on the two texts, can be found in *ADP* 2/4, 657–672 and 676–746.

34 Velati, *Dialogo e rinnovamento*, 729–745, esp. 738–745, where the minutes on the discussion that led to a decision to draft a decree can be found. The text, submitted to the Central Preparatory Commission in June 1962,

sent in February 1962 at the pope's express request directly to the Central Preparatory Commission.[35] It was a few days before this fifth plenary, at a time when the contradictions between the Theological Commission and the SPCU had become evident,[36] that Bea asked that the *vota* already drawn up on the Word of God be transformed into an outline for a pastoral decree.[37] At the fourth plenary session in Bühl of Aug 26–31, 1961, it was decided to form a new subcommission (XIII) on the relationship between Scripture and Tradition to counter the Theological Commission's *De fontibus revelationis*.[38] This text arrived too late at the Central Preparatory Commission, which had already revised its "competitor," but the decree on the Word of God was examined in June 1962.[39] It can be seen here that the "Latin" epicenter of the ecumenical question was becoming clearer and a common principle was emerging from the series of questions dealt with by the SPCU.[40] A final pastoral schema on Catholic ecumenism was drafted during the August 1961 session and amended during the fifth and sixth plenaries before being completed in Rome and discussed by the Central Preparatory Commission in June 1962.[41] Approved on several occasions by John XXIII, this strategic change naturally led – at the beginning of the council's first period (Oct 22, 1962) – to the SPCU's full recognition as the eleventh conciliar commission, but without the council being able to elect its members.[42]

What was the effect of this two-fold expansion on the reception of an ecumenical perspective, a multifaceted one, within the entities preparing for the council? It should be noted that, for various reasons, it remained very limited until the beginning of the first period. The SPCU was, first of all, confronted with the Theological Commission's systemic and juridical perspective which, like the *Suprema Congregatio* of the Holy Office, continued to be oriented in line with the conciliar doctrine of Vatican I. Several indicators of

was withdrawn for diplomatic reasons, see *ADP* 2/4, 22–23; see also Komonchak, "The Struggle for the Council," 296–300.

35 See Komonchak, "The Struggle for the Council," 266.

36 The many references by Cardinal Bea in the minutes of the discussions of the fifth plenary session can be found in Velati, *Dialogo e rinnovamento*, 675–676, 687, 738, and 743.

37 See Velati, *Dialogo e rinnovamento*, 675, note 488; see also Komonchak, "The Struggle for the Council," 272–274.

38 See Komonchak, "The Struggle for the Council," 267–271; Velati, *Dialogo e rinnovamento*, 762–789 and 914–921.

39 *ADP* 2/4, 816–834; see Komonchak, "The Struggle for the Council," 272–274.

40 In effect, the question of the Word of God had been on the agenda since the third plenary in April. In introducing the debate on the text of Prof. Hermann Volk, Bea spoke for the first time of its status as the "foundation of our doctrine" and added: "From the ecumenical point of view, it is of great importance because the Protestants often reproach us for not giving Sacred Scripture enough consideration," Velati, *Dialogo e rinnovamento*, 404; in the same text, see the remark of the cardinal at the beginning of the debate on *De Verbo Dei* during the fifth plenary, see Velati, *Dialogo e rinnovamenteo*, 688.

41 The prehistory of this schema begins with the work of subcommission IX on "The Central Ecumenical Problem According to The Current Orientation of the World Council of Churches in Geneva, and Especially its Conception of Unity"; see Velati, *Dialogo e rinnovamento*, 283–298 (second plenary) and 478–488 (third plenary). It was in July 1961 that the objective of subcommission III was established, and it engaged in the gradual drafting of the new text *De oecumnismo catholico*; see Velati, *Dialogo e rinnovamento*, 511–588 (fourth plenary), 654–656, and 663–673 (fifth plenary, during which a discussion was held on the text of Gustave Thils, *Pro decreto doctrinali elaborando "De oecumenismo," Suggestiones*), 823–870 (sixth plenary). The text sent to the Central Preparatory Commission as well as the corresponding chapter of the Theological Commission, chapter 11 of *De Ecclesia*, and the discussion of the Central Preparatory Commission on these two texts can be found in *ADP* 2/4, 785–812.

42 *AS* 1/1, 78 and 261. See also Andrea Riccardi, "The Tumultuous Opening Days of the Council," in: Giuseppe Alberigo & Joseph A. Komonchak, eds., *History of Vatican II*, vol. 2, *The Formation of the Council's Identity: First Period and Intersession (October 1962–September 1963)*, Leuven/Maryknoll, Peeters/Orbis Books, 1997, 1–67, esp. 44–46.

this perspective should be recalled here.[43] The main part was the clear and sharp demarcation of a hierarchical order, between doctrine, on the one hand, and the "principal problems of pastoral technique"[44] on the other. As for the doctrinal aspect, it was necessary to distinguish between its form and content. According to those in charge of the Theological Commission (Cardinal Alfredo Ottaviani and Sebastiaan Tromp), the form had to remain determined by contemporary needs "defined [as in Vatican I] almost exclusively in terms of defending the deposit against errors."[45] One should be content to formulate theses (in response to the pre-preparatory *quaestiones*), with only the principal actors in the Theological Commission expected to have a global view of the deposit of faith and its interpretation. This interpretation was still determined by the system of Roman Neoscholasticism, a kind of "normal science" (in the language of Thomas S. Kuhn) that would be imposed on the whole of Catholicity.[46] The order of doctrinal content was established in December 1960: a new profession of faith would precede an outline on the church (*De Ecclesia*), followed by another on the sources of revelation (*De fontibus revelationis*), and three more dealing with dogmatics and morals (*De deposito fidei pure custodiendo, De ordine morali individuali*, and *De ordine morali sociali*).

Ecclesiology, therefore, came first and provided the focus of the doctrinal preparations, with the question of the "members of the church" (discussed in chapter 2 of *De Ecclesia*)[47] being of particular ecumenical importance. An explanatory *votum* on this subject, written by Tromp in May 1961, revealed a keen awareness of the systemic character of post-Tridentine Catholic ecclesiology. As an aside, it also helps explain why Pope John's announcement of a "general council" on Jan 25, 1959 was immediately transformed into an "ecumenical council": "To admit that heretics and schismatics, forty-five per cent of all Christians, are really members of the Church would make it difficult to defend the ecumenical character of Trent and Vatican I, would require that heretical and schismatical bishops be invited to Vatican II, would deny the unity of the Church, and would ruin its claims to infallibility."[48]

The systemic form of the doctrinal content of ecclesiology, therefore, determined not only – on a horizontal level – the heretical and schismatic status of non-Catholic Christians, but also – on a vertical level – the function of authority and magisterium within the church (as is also evident from chapter 7 of *De Ecclesia*),[49] another crucial issue in the ecumenical debate on the regulating bodies of the faith. From this point of view, the subcommission's report on the amendments to *De Ecclesia* from session XII of Jul 17, 1962 is a masterpiece of systemic argumentation, taken to its limits in its general observations.[50] Here the subcommission took up all the disputes with the SPCU and, in perfect accord with the status it attributed to itself in chapter 7 of *De Ecclesia*,[51] went so far as to affirm that "the disagreements on the above points

43 See Bernard Sesboüé & Christoph Theobald, eds., *Histoire des dogmes*, vol. 4, *La Parole du salut*, Paris, Desclée, 1996, 227–344, and Theobald, *La réception du concile Vatican II*, vol. 1, 208–217.

44 See Komonchak, "The Struggle for the Council," 174.

45 Komonchak, "The Struggle for the Council," 235.

46 Sesboüé & Theobald, *Histoire des dogmes*, vol. 4, 468–470.

47 For the text of and the debate on this chapter, see *ADP* 2/3, 990–1037.

48 Komonchak, "The Struggle for the Council," 292.

49 For the text of and the debate on this chapter, see *ADP* 2/4, 621–656.

50 *ADP* 4/3.2, 187–194.

51 *ADP* 2/4, 624. See especially the following formula: "Romanus enim Pontifex non per se solum magisterium suum exercet, verum id ex parte committere potest etiam Sacris Congregationibus aliisque peritorum Consiliis, quae ad hoc ab ipso instituuntur, ut, non sine Spiritus Sancti adiutorio, doctrinam salutis in Ecclesia tueantur intemerateque ut ab omnibus servetur invigilent. Decisionibus ideo ac declarationibus istorum quoque coetuum, quamvis infallibili atque irreformabili sententia non muniantur, non externum dumtaxat obsequium, sed religiosa debetur et de se interior mentis adhaesio."

cannot be resolved by the Central Commission, which lacks both the legal and the practical jurisdiction. Indeed, it does not have any doctrinal authority and, while there is a very great freedom of criticism, it is however impossible to seriously respond to the objections."[52]

Therefore, the SPCU came up against the "unionism" or "ecumenism of return" doctrinally founded by the Theological Commission without having the immediate means to propose an alternative perspective so firmly argued, even sharing, in part, their "opponent's" presuppositions. This was a second reason for the limited effect of its interventions.

First of all, we can see the SPCU's difficulty – at a time when its offer to collaborate with the Theological Commission was systematically rejected – to free itself from the institutional demarcation between doctrine and discipline or "pastoral" care. The question emerged in the debates on *De Verbo Dei* that took place during the fifth plenary in November–December of 1961, when Cardinal Bea recognized that "the dogmatic aspect belongs to the question of '*De fontibus revelationis*,'" which fell under the Theological Commission's authority but did not exclude a pastoral, spiritual, or liturgical treatment based on a "theological exposition of the question."[53] During the same plenary, a similar debate took place on the status of *De Iudaeis*, which led to the elaboration of a "theoretical-practical decree" (the cardinal's expression) to be submitted to the Central Preparatory Commission and to the preparation of some "suggestions": theological ones for *De Ecclesia* and practical ones for the subcommission that dealt with *De libertate religiosa*.[54] It is then natural to ask if the former were sent to the Theological Commission. It seems they were not and that, at the time, Cardinal Bea relied only on the Central Preparatory Commission to advance the perspective of the SPCU.[55]

As for the themes, it is clear that, from the outset, the secretariat endorsed the presupposition, undoubtedly widely shared by all the preparatory commissions, that ecclesiology should become the axis of the council. This point of departure was even solemnly stated in the *proemium* to the *votum* of subcommission II "De structura hierarchica Ecclesiae."[56] The architecture of the series of subcommissions reflects this, in particular the entry on the question of the "members" of the church (subcommission I) and the question of its structure (subcommission II), highly controversial ecumenical points. The evolution of these two subcommissions can be seen in the *vota* and the minutes of the debate. In an effort to clarify the particular status of non-Catholic Christians between non-Christians and the Catholic Church on the basis of the famous implicit *votum* on membership in the church, subcommission I shifted from a conception that considered "separated brethren" to be members of the mystical body (and absolutized the image of the body) to one that relied on a hierarchy of "means of grace" and "constitutive elements of the Church" (which necessitated recourse to a wider range of biblical images).[57] At the same time, subcommission II moved from a conception that took papal "primacy," as defined

52 *ADP* 4/3.2, 192.

53 See the minutes of the debate in: Velati, *Dialogo e rinnovamento*, 687–690, here 688.

54 Velati, *Dialogo e rinnovamento*, 738–745, esp. 744.

55 Velati, *Dialogo e rinnovamento*, 743.

56 Velati, *Dialogo e rinnovamento*, 214–216.

57 The passage from one schema to another is perfectly explained in the "methodological remarks" that precede the new edition of the *vota* by Jean Jérôme Hamer, "De christianorum acatholicorum ordine ad Eccclesiam" (with the amendment that added a *votum* on the biblical images), in: Velati, *Dialogo e rinnovamento*, 318–319 and 328–329. The first explanation of this passage was given by Prof. Volk in an intervention in the discussion during the second plenary (Velati, *Dialogo e rinnovamento*, 206). This intervention and the "methodological remarks" are the first draft of the future *LG* 14, 15, and 16. In a brief intervention by Hamer, the concept of *conjunction cum Ecclesia* can already be found, taken up in *LG* 15.

by Vatican I,[58] as its starting point to another vision of the church based on Christ the incarnate Word, and started from what is shared by all Christians, namely their status as the "people of God."[59] These two documents, sent to the Theological Commission, were, therefore, on the same ground as the commission and attempted, by traditional means, to introduce ecumenical "breaches" into its "doctrinal edifice."

It was only with three other texts that the SPCU began to change its perspective, focusing more on what is common to all Christians while still the object of controversy and thus undoubtedly of misunderstandings that needed to be clarified: the question of religious freedom and the conception of the Word of God, tied to the relationship between Scripture and Tradition. These two questions (intimately linked to one another) lie close to the very principle of Christian tradition and its divisions. The debates on the first question, *De libertate religiosa*, which emerged from subcommission IV's ecclesiological work on the priesthood of the faithful and the condition of the laity in the church, revealed the difficulty of departing from the Catholic distinction between thesis and hypothesis – which was considered by other confessions and by common sense as opportunistic – in order to maintain the theologality of the faith, sustained by grace, and to trust, as far as propagation was concerned, supernatural means and not a State whose only end is the common good.[60] The challenge of this ecumenical transformation was seen even more clearly in the debates on the Word of God and on the relationship between Scripture and Tradition, since the council had to take the Protestant reproach of not according Scripture sufficient consideration seriously.[61] The formula by which "the Church cannot exist or be thought of without the Word of God" and its definition as "minister of the Word of God [*verbi Dei ministra*], subject to the supreme authority of the God who speaks" (*De Verbo Dei* 7, at the center of the schema)[62] is Lutheran in flavor, a liberation from the ecclesiocentrism underlying the entire conciliar preparations. More than any other schema, *De Verbo Dei* reveals an awareness that the ecumenical debate and the difficulties of faith in the modern world do not concern any particular point of doctrine but the totality of the mystery (*De Verbo Dei* 1 and 2).[63] It was precisely in this way that it reached the level of a principle and manifested for the first time the unity of ecumenical and pastoral perspectives. At the same time, the schema, at least implicitly, recognized that the post-Tridentine church unilaterally emphasized the sacramental aspect of the mystery and took into account what Catholics could learn from the Protestant insistence on the Word as the "power of God" and as "nourishment" (*De Verbo Dei* 10).[64]

There were some hesitations, however, partly due to differences within the SPCU, the most obvious of which concerned the problem of the material sufficiency of the scriptures, which in the end was left unresolved.[65] The question was not without ecumenical importance, as the council would show. It is true that the SPCU's subcommission XIII on Tradition and Holy Scripture affirmed that particular dogmas are included in the apostolic deposit (*De Traditione et Sacra Scriptura* 1). This general formulation, however, did not settle the question of the status of the dogmatic in relation to the kerygma, nor that of the legitimacy of any

58 Velati, *Dialogo e rinnovamento*, 213–224; see also the summary of the contradictory discussion by Cardinal Bea, who already set forth a different orientation, Velati, *Dialogo e rinnovamento*, 228–229.

59 Velati, *Dialogo e rinnovamento*, 342–346.

60 The final discussion during the fourth plenary brought together the arguments in the best light; see Velati, *Dialogo e rinnovamento*, 600–611.

61 This remark was repeated several times by Cardinal Bea (Velati, *Dialogo e rinnovamento*, 404, 688, and 891) and was presented in a more general way at the beginning of the report by Prof. Volk, see Velati, *Dialogo e rinnovamento*, 395–396.

62 *ADP* 2/4, 818.

63 See *ADP* 2/4, 816–819; see also the speeches by Prof. Volk, in: Velati, *Dialogo e rinnovamento*, 677 and 873.

64 See *ADP* 2/4, 818; see also Velati, *Dialogo e rinnovamento*, 399–401, 406, 408, and 680–681.

65 See Velati, *Dialogo e rinnovamento*, 915–921.

particular doctrinal development (of the Marian dogmas, for example). As for the relationship to history, everything suggests that the hermeneutical problems raised by modern exegesis (literary genres etc.), which were the focus of bitter discussion in 1961, remained outside the concerns of the two subcommissions.

A global vision of the SPCU's ecumenical logic certainly appeared in the last text, the pastoral decree *De oecumenismo catholico*,[66] but certain aporias were also revealed. No doubt, owing to the demarcation already mentioned, the SPCU's debates finally led to a renunciation of the idea of preparing a dogmatic study for the Theological Commission, although this was initially foreseen,[67] Gustave Thils having prepared a text *De oecumenicitate*[68] in view of "providing a framework for a work on ecumenism."[69] In retrospect, this renunciation was regrettable, because the different versions of the text and the discussions to which they gave rise addressed the main issues of contention, such as the distinction between conversion and ecumenical dialogue, equality (*aequalitas*) in the exchange – restricted by some and defended by others – as well as the aim of ecumenism: living together (*conviventia*),[70] the recognition by Catholics that "they also bear part of the responsibility of the past,"[71] and that they can learn from others.[72] In light of this initial awareness, the pastoral decree remains relatively weak, essentially reiterating the theme of the "means of grace" and the "constitutive elements of Church," which are directed towards their fullness in the Catholic Church, understood as a "general means of salvation."[73] At the beginning of the council's first intersessional period, however, it played a decisive catalytic role.

On the eve of Vatican II, the emergence of a genuine ecumenical logic that might replace that of the heads of the Theological Commission remained unclear. Certainly, the magnitude of the change at stake, attributed to the Holy Spirit,[74] was perceived. In addition to the president and the secretary of the SPCU, men capable of thinking and promoting this change, such as Hermann Volk, who became a bishop in 1962, Bishop Emiel-Jozef De Smedt, Thils, and others emerged. But what was affirmed of the principle of Christian tradition, namely the Word of God and the faith, and of the overall unity of the Christian mystery, approached differently by the various confessions or churches,[75] remained relatively marginal in relation to the ecclesiocentric logic that determined all the preparations.

2.2 *Debates on the Pastorality and Ecumenicity of the Council's Teaching: The First Session*

The opening address of the council, already mentioned at the beginning of this chapter, did however produce a certain reorientation that the Latin translation of John XXIII's Italian manuscript risked weakening.[76] Following the lines of the work by Alberto Melloni, if the order of the

66 This vision was introduced by the *relatio* of Cardinal Bea to the Central Preparatory Commission, which retraced the history of the *motio oecumenica*, shared by all the churches; see ADP 2/4, 801–804.

67 Velati, *Dialogo e rinnovamento*, 863.

68 The different versions of the text are found in Velati, *Dialogo e rinnovamento*, 542–549, 663–666, and 833–847.

69 Velati, *Dialogo e rinnovamento*, 666.

70 Velati, *Dialogo e rinnovamento*, 670.

71 Velati, *Dialogo e rinnovamento*, 547.

72 Velati, *Dialogo e rinnovamento*, 553 and 555. See also a formula in the first version of the report that tries to relativize the Catholic Church's perfect condition: "Even supposing that the conditions of the Catholic Church's existence is perfect, one can legitimately ask whether, to be faithful to the spirit of the apostles, one should not avoid imposing on the separated Christians what is not indispensable, and to let them enter into the dwelling place of the Lord, with all their own assumable traditions, even if they are less perfect and less well developed," Velati, *Dialogo e rinnovamento*, 546–547.

73 ADP 2/4, 786.

74 See for example Velati, *Dialogo e rinnovamento*, 547–548.

75 See Theobald, *La réception du concile Vatican II*, vol. 1, 222–223.

76 See the summary of the different versions and the analysis of the composition of the text in: Melloni, *Papa Giovanni*, 258–271 and 299–335.

manuscript (which was translated into Latin on the eve of Oct 11, 1962)[77] is restored, then the doctrinal part of the text (which follows the historical part on the councils)[78] begins with what the pope called the salient point of the council. This reverses the Theological Commission's preparatory perspective and introduces the principle of pastorality, considering the Christian mystery as a totality destined to shape consciences,[79] this programmatic passage being followed by its biblical foundation.[80] In the Italian manuscript, the development on Christian unity comes immediately after the doctrinal part, suggesting a link between the pastorality of the doctrine and its ecumenicity. It has a completely different tone from the Latin version. While the official text, delivered on Oct 11, 1962, focused on the Catholic Church – which knows that it is intimately united to Christ's prayer and prays that "Christians separated from this Apostolic See desire to be united with us" – the manuscript certainly affirmed that "the Catholic Church has remained faithful to Christ's testament ... and to the successor of Peter, *Vicarius Christi*," at the same time recognizing that "it continues to suffer from the division of the very first flock," referring to Jesus' prayer "with loud cries and tears" (Heb 5:7). Common to both versions, the threefold "radiation of the great mystery of unity" – the manuscript speaks of the *Sacramentum unitatis* – is manifested among three categories of people who, however, – contrary to the Latin text – are not characterized by their relationship to Catholics but in relation to Christ and to themselves: Christians "belonging to the various confessions of the innumerable believers in Christ, Orthodox and Protestants etc. and those belonging to the various non-Christian religious families ... also redeemed by Christ's Blood."[81]

Two days after the opening of the council, Cardinal Bea made the proposal, discussed on Oct 19 by the Secretariat for Extraordinary Affairs, to begin a debate during the council session on the pastoral character of the magisterium in order to then make a choice from among the texts and to begin their revision or a redrafting.[82] The initiative of Bea and other cardinals, such as Giovanni Battista Montini, was rejected. Beginning on Oct 22 the council began to work on the texts, with the principle of pastorality – and the ecumenicality it implies, we must add here – only able to intervene in the debate on this or that planned text, without ever influencing their planning; a parallelism between the principle and the planning of conciliar work being now established.[83]

Discussions thus began on the outline on the liturgy and continued with *De fontibus revelationis* and a brief outline on the means of communication before lingering, at the end of the first period, on *De Ecclesiae unitate "Ut omnes unum sint"* prepared by the Commission for the Oriental Churches, and on the Doctrinal Commission's *De Ecclesia*. Two ecumenical milestones can be identified along this winding path: the provisional solution of the controversy on *De fontibus revelationis* reached on Nov 21 by John XXIII instituting the first mixed commission, composed of members of the Doctrinal Commission and the SPCU,[84] and the assembly's positive vote on Dec 1

77 Melloni, *Papa Giovanni*, 262.

78 This first part, influenced by a theology of history, finishes with a thanksgiving (see Melloni, *Papa Giovanni*, 315–316).

79 See Melloni, *Papa Giovanni*, 324–325.

80 See Melloni, *Papa Giovanni*, 325–326.

81 Melloni, *Papa Giovanni*, 329–331; this passage follows a brief paragraph on the history of the divisions, which were preceded by the earliest Christianity under "the seal of unity, sanctified by the blood of the martyrs" (Melloni, *Papa Giovanni*, 329).

82 The text has been published by Giuseppe Alberigo, "Concilio acefalo?: L'evoluzione degli organi direttivi del Vaticano II," in: Giuseppe Alberigo, ed., *Il Vaticano II fra attese e celebrazione*, Bologna, Il Mulino, 1995, 193–238, esp. 219–224.

83 See the summary of Bea's text and the elaboration of the thesis of "parallelism" in: Theobald, *La réception du concile Vatican II*, vol. 1, 281–283.

84 *AS* 1/3, 260.

requesting that a single document be composed by amending the Commission for the Oriental Churches's *Ut omnes unum sint* and integrating it with the SPCU's *De oecumenismo* and chapter 11, "De oecumenismo," of the Doctrinal Commission's schema *De ecclesia*.[85] After the recognition of the SPCU as the 11th commission at the beginning of the first period, these two events marked a veritable turning point. From then on, its "central role" was recognized by the majority of the assembly as that of being "a force for balance in the most sensitive doctrinal questions."[86]

At the same time, the leading figures of the SPCU intervened in an increasingly concerted manner during the debates in the council sessions,[87] being able to rely on other bishops and other conciliar experts among whom a "majority" in favor of John XXIII's orientation began to take shape with difficulty. As for the liturgy, they insisted on introducing the vernacular, which was standard in the liturgy of the Protestant separated brethren,[88] as well as on communion under both species and on concelebration, which should no longer have presented a factor of division.[89] It was in the debates on the schema *De fontibus revelationis*, *Ut omnes unum sint*, and *De Ecclesia* that they succeeded in clarifying the ecumenical spirit or style of future conciliar texts, in close connection with their pastoral style. Karl Rahner, in fact, in the *generalia* of his *Disquisitio brevis de Schemate "De fontibus revelationis"* (distributed to the council Fathers at the beginning of November) and his *Animadversiones de schemate "De Ecclesia"* (distributed to the Fathers at the end of November in 1,300 copies), was the first to point out and articulate the lack of pastoral style and ecumenical spirit of these texts,[90] points that were later taken up by most of the Fathers of the majority. Rahner connected not only the proposal of truth and its possible reception (*indoles pastoralis*) but also more specifically the Catholic proposal of truth and the possibility of separated brethren to "feel that we are not obscuring what they legitimately defend as true and as their own possession."[91]

In the council session, Cardinal Bea and Bishop De Smedt took the floor several times, the first to criticize the lack of pastoral or ecumenical form in the two dogmatic schemas[92] and to anticipate the solution of a fusion of the three schemas on unity,[93] and the second to make ecumenicity more explicit.[94] De Smedt's first speech was the very first sign of the emergence of an ecumenical metadiscourse, that is, a discourse on method. Approached in terms of doctrine and style (*in aliqua doctrina et in stylo alicuius schematis*), this method presupposed first of all a principal distinction between "*admitting* Christ" and "the *way in which* to access

85 AS 1/4, 9 and 141.

86 This is according to the assessment of Giuseppe Ruggieri in his two chapters on the doctrinal debates of the first period, see Giuseppe Ruggieri, "The First Doctrinal Clash," and "Beyond an Ecclesiology of Polemics: The Debate on the Church," in: Alberigo & Komonchak, eds., *History of Vatican II*, vol. 2, 233–266 and 281–357, here 316.

87 In his very first intervention on the subject of the schema on the liturgy, Bea again recalled the need for collaboration between commissions and noted the "admirable progress of the ecumenical desire," in: AS 1/1, 407–408, here 408.

88 See for example AS 1/1, 356 and AS 1/2, 664.

89 AS 1/2, 23–24, 58 and 77.

90 See Karl Rahner, "Disquisitio brevis de Schemate 'De fontibus revelationis'/Kurze Untersuchung des Schemas 'De fontibus revelationis,'" in: Karl Rahner, *Sämtliche Werke*, vol. 21/1, *Das zweite Vatikanum: Beiträge zum Konzil und seiner Interpretation*, Freiburg i.Br., Herder, 2013, 237–261, esp. 237–247; and Karl Rahner & Otto Semmelroth, "Animadversiones de Schemate 'De Ecclesia'/Bemerkungen zum Schema 'De Ecclesia,'" in: Rahner, *Sämtliche Werke*, vol. 21/1, 298–339, esp. 298–300; see also the correspondence between Karl Rahner and Herbert Vorgrimler, in: Herbert Vorgrimler, *Karl Rahner verstehen: Eine Einführung in sein Leben und Denken*, Freiburg i.Br., Herder, 1985, 191–193.

91 Rahner, "Disquisitio brevis," 243.

92 AS 1/3, 48–51 (Nov 14) and AS 1/4, 227–230, esp. 229 (Dec 4).

93 AS 1/3, 709–712, esp. 710 (Nov 29). The day before, the patriarchal vicar of the Melkites of Damascus, Archbishop Joseph Tawil, had already made this proposal, see AS 1/3, 660–661.

94 AS 1/3, 184–187 (Nov 19) and AS 1/4, 142–144 (Dec 1).

Christ," a distinction that functions as a condition of possibility for an ecumenical dialogue whose goal is not reconciliation but first and foremost the dissipation of prejudices and misunderstandings.

> In recent decades, a new method has been introduced ... What characterizes it is that it is not only concerned with truth but also with the *way in which* the doctrine is presented so that it can be accurately understood by others. In this way, Christians of different denominations help each other so that they can understand more clearly and accurately a doctrine to which they do not adhere.[95]

This was what should happen during the council, he added, if the presence of non-Catholic observers was taken seriously. The presentation of this method was followed by four conditions of application: (1) to know the Orthodox and Protestant faith, liturgical life, and theology well; (2) to know their opinions on our doctrine and which points were understood accurately or not; (3) to know what, according to non-Catholics, was lacking or not sufficiently elucidated in Catholic doctrine; and (4) to examine if there were, in our way of speaking, forms or formulations that are difficult for non-Catholics to understand.[96]

To complete this ensemble of a great coherence, we must add the addresses of Bishop Volk who, given his place on the list of bishops, could only intervene on *De Ecclesia*[97] on Dec 7, 1962, at the end of the first period, having already delivered his written remarks on *De fontibus revelationis* and *Ut omnes unum sint*.[98] He was the one who gave the most precise and unified indications on the pastoral and ecumenical form of doctrine in itself. The last of his three addresses deserves to be cited for its great conciseness. While recognizing certain positive qualities of the schema on the church, he criticized it by saying that it

> does not have enough of a *sense of the Gospel for the Catholic faithful, for those who are separated from us, or for the world as a whole*. The council can and must propose the dogmatic doctrine on the church itself as gospel, which means *evanggelion*, and thus that dogmatic doctrine is, in itself, truly pastoral. If doctrine has no salutary force in itself, neither can pastoral work add it. Therefore, the two must not be separated. Such evangelical doctrine serves *ecumenical* needs at the same time. These needs cannot be met, ever, by concessions, but only by proposing the faith that the church professes of itself as richly as it appears in Holy Scripture, which considers the church an essential part of God's salvific work. It is not enough, therefore, to oppose heresy, which holds only a part of the revealed truth, with the other part. Only the *whole* can show that the part is a part. The most noble and not always easy task of Catholic theology, therefore, is to always propose, in the doctrine itself, the totality of the thing, *at least in its principles*.[99]

With these two speeches by Bishop De Smedt and Bishop Volk, the alternative between an ecumenism of return and another "logic" that was at least as coherent – that of "ecumenical dialogue" or even of a "dialogical" conception of the Christian tradition – was clearly posed for the first time.

2.3 *Institutional Stabilization of Competencies and Reference Texts: The First Intersession*

However, far from being won in December 1962, the ecumenical cause was left to the institutional reorganization of the council and to what became

95 AS 1/3, 184 (italics original).

96 See AS 1/3, 185. Bishop De Smedt also informed the assembly for the first time that the Theological Commission had refused any collaboration in the preparatory phase of the council.

97 AS 1/4, 386–388.

98 AS 1/3, 364–366 and 831.

99 AS 1/4, 388 (italics mine).

known as the "second preparation."[100] At the penultimate general congregation of the first period, on Dec 5, 1962, John XXIII had announced the establishment of a Coordinating Commission, which began its work at the end of January 1963. In addition to the architectural plan of all the conciliar texts, selected according to the aims of the council,[101] this commission had to rule on two major ecumenical problems that had remained unresolved: the work of the mixed commission on the former *De fontibus revelationis*, now called *De divina revelatione*, and the future of the three preparatory texts on ecumenism.

As for the mixed commission, supervised by Cardinal Achille Liénart of the Coordinating Commission, it met five times at the end of the first period. During the intersessional period, it met four more times, finally having to acknowledge, after "emotional confrontations similar to the violent discussions within the same mixed commission at the beginning of December 1962,"[102] that it could not reach a consensus on the essential, ecumenically central point, namely the relationship between Scripture and Tradition. This increase in contention, accompanied at times by the transgression of the rules of the game on the part of the minority of the commission, clearly shows that this is the epicenter of the paradigmatic conflict that was being played out between the two "logics," and it is understandable that the text disappeared from the agenda after the last meeting until the intersession between the second and third periods, with important consequences for the entire council.

The other problem was not solved until the second session of the Coordinating Commission between Mar 25 and 29, 1963. It was a question of applying the assembly's vote of Dec 1, 1962 to elaborate a single text from the SPCU's schema, that of the Commission for the Oriental Churches, and chapter 11 of the Doctrinal Commission's *De Ecclesia*.[103] After bitter conflicts with Cardinal Amleto Giovanni Cicognani, president of both the Coordinating Commission and the Commission for the Oriental Churches, and his surprising about-face, the SPCU finally obtained, on the last day of the Coordinating Commission's session, full responsibility for ecumenical relations (to be dealt with in chapter 3 of the future decree) while the Commission for the Oriental Churches had to limit its field of action to the Eastern Catholic Churches.[104] Thus ended the jurisdictional conflict that had appeared as early as March 1961 between the SPCU and the commission, sacrificing, however, the small Melkite minority present in the latter and their allies who, as we shall see, were in no way committed to the unionism of the majority of the Eastern Catholics.

A rereading of the three preparatory texts on ecumenism allows us to understand the positions under debate, especially the evolutions that took place during the first intersession. Chapter 11 of the schema *De Ecclesia* claims, according to its relator, to deal only with the strictly dogmatic principles that should govern Catholic ecumenism, leaving the SPCU to deal with the practical norms for ecumenical action.[105] Coming at the end of *De Ecclesia*, the text[106] asserts from the outset – in the form of a thesis – that because of its foundation by Christ as "unum et unicum signum

100 See the contribution of Jan Grootaers, "The Drama Continues Between the Acts: The 'Second Preparation' and Its Opponents," in: Alberigo & Komonchak, eds., *History of Vatican II*, vol. 2, 359–515.

101 See Theobald, *La réception du concile Vatican II*, vol. 1, 376–381.

102 See Grootaers, "The Drama Continues Between the Acts," 385; the texts of the debates are presented on pages 385–391.

103 *AS* 1/4, 9 and 141.

104 *AS* 5/1, 480–481 and 512. See also Grootaers, "The Drama Continues Between the Acts," 380–381 and 463–468. He concludes his account: "The step thus taken was very important for the future of the ecumenical dialogue. The 'unionist' school of interconfessional relations ... lost the privileged position ... while the truly ecumenical view of dialogue won a new authority in keeping with the prevailing wishes of the Council"; see Grootaers, "The Drama Continues Between the Acts," 468, and note 282.

105 *AS* 1/4, 125.

106 *AS* 1/4, 81–91.

levatum in nationes,"[107] "nothing can ever intrinsically violate its unity,"[108] hence the conclusion that the historical separations were from the Catholic Church (*De Ecclesia* 48) and that they can only be resolved by inviting the separated Christians and communities to rejoin it (50 and 51). What sounds to contemporary ears like a strategy of immunization is based here on the Eucharist, "*sign and source* of [the church's] unity before the whole world." Because of this, the church, "when schisms and heresies arose," has never ceased to affirm "that it would only admit to eucharistic worship those who, in communion with a bishop linked to the Roman See, professed the one, true and entire faith" (49).[109] Certainly, the text also concedes – in the classic form of a "hypothesis" – that the Catholic Church recognizes the "bonds" between it and the separated brethren, even salvific elements, but it immediately adds that the council "firmly teaches that the fullness of revelation was entrusted by Christ solely to the Catholic Church, that it cannot be divided, and that, therefore, it is there that it must be acknowledged by all Christians" (49 and 51). It is indeed towards this fullness that the "elements" and "bonds" tend, the recognition of fullness in Catholicism being the condition for possessing the inheritance of Christ.[110] This being maintained, the Catholic Church has no difficulty in rejoicing in the "ecumenical movement" (*motio oecumenica*) outside itself and, with a certain prudence, within it, a movement in any case directed by the Spirit of Christ towards her (52 and 53). *Communicatio in sacris* is authorized in certain strictly limited cases, without ever being considered a means of promoting unity (54). On the other hand, collaboration between Catholics and separated Christians in society is considered an excellent means of overcoming mutual suspicions and prejudices (55).[111]

In the face of the systemic conciseness of this chapter, drafted by Fr. Jan Witte, the proposal of the long schema of the Commission for the Oriental Churches,[112] especially oriented towards the Orthodox churches, seems diluted, even though it was based on the same presupposition: "Because of our fidelity to the will of Christ, we profess and declare that there is only one church, even in its earthly condition, and this true church is the one governed by the successor of Peter. Consequently, there is no other church that could profess itself true and unique" (7).[113] As the writer of this schema and its relator in the council sessions, Fr. Athanasiy Velyki, shows, its contents are distributed in three parts, a first one (1–12) dealing with the theological unity of the church, founded on the unity of government or, visibly, in Peter; a second (13–47) consecrated to the means of reconciliation in the broad sense of the term, be they supernatural means like prayer or theological, liturgical, canonical, psychological, and practical means; and a third (48–52) on the mode and conditions of reconciliation in a strict sense, intended to be more particularly adjusted to those from the East. While in the first two parts non-Catholics are called *dissidentes*, in the part on reconciliation they are called *redeuntes*.[114]

As for the third text that, after the vicissitudes already mentioned and many others,[115] it was finally adopted by the SPCU during its May 1962 plenary and sent directly to the council Fathers.[116] This text was based on the work of Fr. Witte and

107 *AS* 1/4, 81. This was already the understanding of Vatican I (see *Denz*, 3014).

108 *AS* 1/4, 81.

109 *AS* 1/4, 82 (italics mine).

110 *AS* 1/4, 81–83.

111 *AS* 1/4, 83–87.

112 *AS* 1/3, 528–545.

113 *AS* 1/3, 530.

114 *AS* 1/3, 531–543.

115 See Grootaers, "The Drama Continues Between the Acts," 429–435, and Bernd Jochen Hilberath, "Theologischer Kommentar zum Dekret über den Ökumenismus Unitatis redintegratio," *HThK Vat.II* 3, 69–223, esp. 95–96, which report how *De oecumenismo*, discussed in February 1962 first by three and then by two subcommissions, was gradually able to be released from the controlling authority of the Doctrinal Commission.

116 See Grootaers, "The Drama Continues Between the Acts," 434.

Fr. Velyki, drafters of the first two texts, who were joined by Bishop Johannes Willebrands on the SPCU's pastoral decree *De oecumenismo catholico*. The "synthesis" was composed, beginning in February 1962, in three mixed subcommissions, resulting from the three commissions concerned, thus fixing the outline of the future decree: I, "De oecumenismi catholici principiis," II, "De oecumenismi exercitio," III, "De Ecclesiarum Orientalium peculari consideratione." It was only during the second session of the Coordinating Commission, in March 1962, that chapter 3 acquired a division in two parts. Entitled from that point forward "De christianis ab ecclesia catholica seiunctis," this chapter included a first section bearing the old title, announcing the development in regard to the Eastern churches, and a second, "De communitatibus inde a saeculo XVI exortis," followed, at that time, by a fourth chapter "De catholicorum habitudine ad non christianos et maxime ad iudaeos," and a fifth, "De libertate Religiosa."

One might think that this work of "synthesis" would make it impossible to arrive at a dialogical conception of the Christian tradition. However, a comparison of the texts shows that the strategy of the Bea/Willebrands team, without doubt actively supported by John XXIII, succeeded not only in allowing the council to decide in November 1962, on the basis of a text that was ecumenically indefensible, in favor of a mixed commission, but moreover for the SPCU to obtain the leadership in this commission, without completely excluding the two other partners. The result was the conciliar schema *De oecumenismo*.[117] It was more evolved than the one proposed in June 1962 to the Central Preparatory Commission[118] and effectively sounded the death knell for any ecumenism of return. Several theological mutations guaranteed this. I present them here according to their "logic," proposing to return later to the third chapter of the schema, which was dedicated to the Orthodox and the Protestants.

117 AS 2/5, 412–441.

118 ADP 2/4, 801–804.

From the beginning (*De oecumenismo* 1), the unity, indeed the uniqueness, of the Church of God is presented without any reference to the Catholic Church and its own hierarchical structure,[119] so that the other churches and confessions could recognize themselves in it. The language is thus purely historical-scriptural,[120] including the necessary references to baptism, ministries, and the apostolic college with the blessed Peter. The approach is inductive and leads to a formulation that, in a single movement, unites the diversity of charisms of the one people of God, which thus becomes the "signum levatum in nationes," its proclamation of peace to the whole human race, and its pilgrimage of hope to the final homeland, this "holy mystery of the unity of the Church" that finds its model and its principle in the unity of the Father, Son, and Holy Spirit.[121]

The separations referred to in what follows are not mentioned in reference to the Catholic Church as we find in the documents of the other two commissions,[122] but occur within the Church of God. This is the second transformation, decisive because it opens the door to true communication. The relationship of the brethren separated from the Catholic Church (*De oecumenismo* 2) is consequently thought of in a wholly positive way, on the grounds, however, of a distinction between a "*perfect* communion" and a "*certain* communion with us," based on "goods" or interior and visible "elements" through which unity is manifested, or even on a set of "holy actions."[123] The only reservation that limits the symmetry between the partners, already present in the preceding text by the

119 The schema *Ut omnes unum sint* already abandoned, in its first three paragraphs, references to the Catholic Church and adopted scriptural language, introducing however, from paragraph 4, the societal reference of Catholic theology and, finally, in paragraph 5, "Catholic doctrine" (see AS 1/3, 528–529).

120 This was already the case in the first two paragraphs of the *Ut omnes unum sint* schema, which also introduced baptism, see AS 1/3, 528.

121 AS 2/5, 412–413, here 413.

122 AS 1/3, 530 (7) and AS 1/4, 81 (48).

123 AS 2/5, 413–414 (italics mine).

SPCU,[124] is in fact the affirmation, taken from the famous letter of the Holy Office to the archbishop of Boston Richard James Cushing (Aug 8, 1949),[125] according to which the church – the SPCU's text adds "the *Catholic Church of Christ*" – is "the general aid to salvation" and "in which alone, therefore, can be obtained," according to the schema, "the fullness of the means of salvation."[126]

In the wake of what was written before, the term "ecumenism" received for the first time a broad definition (*De oecumenismo* 3) which included, without covering them, the desires and efforts of non-Catholic Christians: "This term designates the movement and action ordered towards *that* unity of Christians that Jesus Christ asked of his father in an intense prayer,"[127] with the goal that "*this* fullness of the Christian legacy enjoyed by the one, holy, catholic, and apostolic church, may manifest itself in the world, in these times, in a more perfect way, and that it may be made more accessible." This presupposes the recognition that, because of the divisions and notwithstanding the renewed affirmation of the status of the Catholic Church, "it is becoming more difficult [for the church] to express, in the very reality of its life, the fullness of catholicity in all its aspects" and that it can learn something from the separated brethren, "allowing itself to be edified by all that the Holy Spirit accomplishes in their hearts."[128]

The practice of ecumenism builds on this historical and dynamic conception of "Catholic fullness" and combines suggestions outlined in the three preparatory texts, the central point being that dialogue can lead each one to a greater fidelity to one's own vocation.[129] Chapter 2 of the schema puts the means in a certain order: interior renewal, with a reminder of the movements of biblical renewal, conversion of heart, the call to an evangelical life, and common prayer for unity are at the top, followed by mutual knowledge among separated brethren, ecumenical formation, a new way of expressing and expounding the doctrine of the faith that is comprehensible for all, and cooperation in all areas.[130]

If we take as a reference Bishop De Smedt's address, delivered on Nov 19, 1962,[131] we must recognize that the schema (*De oecumenismo* 10) summarized his instructions on the style of expression (*modus*) of doctrine, perhaps too succinctly, but at the same time integrated them into a global process, referred to as the "renewal" of the church, whose contours and possible limits were not yet established. This would be done, at least partly, during the second and third periods of the council.[132]

3 Towards a Catholic Ecclesiology "Acceptable" to the "Ecumenical Movement" (Second and Third Periods)?

In the meantime, the Catholic Church had changed pontificates and it was Paul VI who, on Sep 29, 1963, inaugurated the second period with a long address that, in setting out the aims of the council, also made explicit its ecumenical purpose.[133] While affirming from the outset that only the Catholic Church could offer "the other Christians ... the unity in which they themselves should participate," the pope promoted an ecumenism that respected the *varietates* in the *unitas* and asked, for the first time, forgiveness from God and from the separated brethren for the

124 *ADP* 2/4, 786.

125 See *Denz*, 3870.

126 *AS* 2/5, 414.

127 *AS* 2/5, 416. Chapter 11 of *De ecclesia* (52 and 53) used the concept of the "ecumenical movement" but oriented it towards communion with the Vicar of Christ (*AS* 1/4, 83–84). The decree *Ut omnes unum sint* (39 and 41) used "ecumenical action" (*AS* 1/3, 540–541) and tied "true ecumenism" to the need to "correctly distinguish Catholic truth from the different systems" (21), in *AS* 1/3, 535.

128 *AS* 2/5, 414–416.

129 *AS* 2/5, 420.

130 *AS* 2/5, 420–423.

131 *AS* 1/3, 184–187.

132 *AS* 2/3, 422–423.

133 *AS* 2/1, 193–195.

mistakes made by the Catholic Church. During his reception of the observers on Oct 17, he returned to these points and relied on forgiveness – "reciprocal if possible" – to turn his gaze to the future – "a newness to be generated, a dream to be realized" – following St. Paul who, "forgetting what is behind," said he was running "towards the goal" (Phil 3:13–14). It was on this path, he said, that "the great dialogue takes place, the duration of which no one can determine today, given the still unresolved doctrinal differences."[134]

Compared to the previous year, the number of churches represented by the observers had increased. However, the Patriarchate of Constantinople was still not represented. On Sep 20, Paul VI wrote directly to Athenagoras I a handwritten letter containing the same idea of forgetting the past and the same quotation from the letter to the Philippians. This was the first since the letter Gregory XIII sent to Jeremias II on Mar 7, 1584, and remained unanswered until Nov 22, 1963. It was only when the pope's trip to the Holy Land began to take shape, a trip announced in his address at the closing of the second period on Dec 4,[135] that relations with the Phanar were established and a meeting between the pope and Patriarch Athenagoras I was planned. This decisive meeting on Jan 5 and 6, 1964, at the beginning of the second intersession, led to a considerable intensification of the relations between the two sees. This made it possible, in September 1964, for the Holy Synod to accept the Vatican's invitation to send observers from the patriarchate to the third session of the council.

The events then began to gather speed. The third pan-Orthodox conference in Rhodes (Nov 1–15, 1964) opened the possibility of engaging with the Catholic Church in a "dialogue of charity," a concept employed there for the first time. And the following year the idea emerged of the reciprocal lifting of the anathemas of 1054. Hyacinthe Destivelle has traced in detail the birth and achievement of this idea that led, on Sep 7, 1965, to a common, solemn celebration held during the last session of the council and at the same time in the patriarchal cathedral of St. George in Istanbul, each in the presence of a delegation from the other church.[136] Written in French, the common declaration, read out during the celebrations, perfectly summarized the point of arrival of the ecumenical relations between these two sister churches:

> Since they are certain that they express the common desire for justice and the unanimous sentiment of charity which moves the faithful, and since they recall the command of the Lord: "If you are offering your gift at the altar, and there remember that your brethren has something against you, leave your gift before the altar and go first be reconciled to your brother" [Matt 5:23–24], Pope Paul VI and Patriarch Athenagoras I with his synod, in common agreement, declare that:
>
> a) They regret the offensive words, the reproaches without foundation, and the reprehensible gestures which, on both sides, have marked or accompanied the sad events of this period.
>
> b) They likewise regret and remove both from memory and from the midst of the Church the sentences of excommunication which followed these events, the memory of which has influenced actions up to our day and has hindered closer relations in charity; and they commit these excommunications to oblivion.

134 "Allocution du pape Paul VI," *Istina* 10, 1964, monographic number *Le décret conciliaire sur l'œcuménisme: "Unitatis redintegratio"*, 519–522, here 520–521. For the relationship of Paul VI to ecumenism, see Velati, *Una difficile transizione*, 373–378.

135 AS 2/6, 569–570.

136 Hyacinthe Destivelle, *Conduis-la vers l'unité parfaite: Œcuménisme et synodalité*, Paris, Cerf, 2018, 35–65. On the consequences, see Alberto Melloni, *Tempus visitations: L'intercomunione inaccaduta fra Roma e Costantinopoli*, Bologna, Il Mulino, 2019.

> c) Finally, they deplore the preceding and later vexing events which, under the influence of various factors – among which, lack of understanding and mutual trust – eventually led to the effective rupture of ecclesiastical communion.
>
> Pope Paul VI and Patriarch Athenagoras I with his synod realize that this gesture of justice and mutual pardon is not sufficient to end both old and more recent differences between the Roman Catholic Church and the Orthodox Church. Through the action of the Holy Spirit those differences will be overcome.[137]

Accompanied by numerous symbolic gestures, in particular the return of the relic of the head of St. Andrew to the church of Patras,[138] the meeting of January 1964, and the communications that followed it, generated a new point of departure. I note this result in advance here, but in fact it represents a finishing line of the "leap forward" desired by John XXIII, because it determined to a large extent the ecclesiological dynamics of the second and third periods of the council, but it also explains some of the tensions between Catholicism and the non-Catholic churches and communities.[139] The WCC reacted with irritation to what it saw as a bilateral Catholic-Orthodox dialogue taking shape in Paul's opening address of the second period announcing the "great dialogue," as well as his reception of the observers and invited guests on Oct 17, 1963. This fear was only heightened by the meeting between Paul VI and Athenagoras. Added to this was a Catholic opinion that saw the council as a true beginning of ecumenism, not to mention many Roman blunders, such as the celebration, in the midst of the conciliar debate on ecumenism, of the transfer of the relics of a Ukrainian and Uniate saint, considered by the Russian Church responsible for the martyrdom of Orthodox saints, or the prohibition of welcoming Oscar Cullmann, a guest of the SPCU, to hold a lecture at a pontifical university. This more dramatic side of the "step forward" should not be forgotten, because, as we shall see, it also determined what happened next.

Certainly, during the second and third periods, the assembly also completed the drafting of the constitution *Sacrosantum concilium* on the sacred liturgy and the decree on the media of social communications *Inter mirifica* (promulgated on Dec 4, 1963), and made progress in its work on other schemas, especially the one on revelation. But it was the three ecclesiological texts, promulgated on Nov 21, 1964, and their ecumenical implications, that were at the center of the concerns of the council Fathers and observers. For reasons that will become apparent in what follows, I shall discuss them in the reverse order of their promulgation, beginning with the decree *Unitatis redintegratio* and finishing with the constitution *Lumen gentium*.

3.1 *Raising the Question of "Christ's Will for the Church"*

The history of the drafting of the decree on ecumenism is well known.[140] Let us simply recall that the text arrived at the council session on Nov 18, 1963 accompanied by a booklet of 191 amendments (for the first three chapters), added by the SPCU on the basis of observations received

137 *AS* 4/7, 651–654, here 652–653.

138 During the 86th general congregation on Sep 23, 1964, Paul VI exposed this relic in front of the altar where it was venerated by all the bishops and Orthodox observers; see *AS* 3/2, 285–288.

139 See especially Velati, *Una difficile transizione*, 393–400, and Claude Soetens, "The Ecumenical commitment of the Catholic Church," in: Giuseppe Alberigo & Joseph A. Komonchak, eds., *History of Vatican II*, vol. 3, *The Mature Council: Second Period and Intersession (September 1963–September 1964)*, Leuven/Maryknoll, Peeters/Orbis Books, 2000, 257–344, esp. 289–295.

140 See Werner Becker, "Einführung," ²*LThK* 13, 11–39, esp. 20–39; Hilberath, "Theologischer Kommentar," 95–103; Velati, *Una difficile transizione*, 378–412.

after the schema was submitted.[141] On Nov 21, it was adopted as the basis for the future decree. In February 1964, the SPCU studied all of the observations sent by the Fathers before the beginning of, during, and after the second period, and it drafted a new version of the text[142] that was proposed for the assembly's vote between Oct 5 and 8, 1964.[143] The *expensio modorum*, that is the vote on the amendments accepted by the plenary of the SPCU, took place on Nov 10, 11, and 14.[144] It seemed that everything was now ready for a conciliar promulgation on Saturday, Nov 21, which was announced after the last vote.

On the following day, the so-called Black Week of the council began. Paul VI cancelled the vote on *De libertate religiosa*[145] and intervened in two of the three texts that had already been voted on and were therefore ready to be promulgated: *Lumen gentium* and *Unitatis redintegratio*. At the "request of the higher authority,"[146] the SPCU distributed, on "black Thursday," 19 *modi* to be introduced into *Unitatis redintegratio*,[147] without the possibility of debate. Certainly, the text was voted on the next day and received almost unanimous support, and the experts recognized that on "the substance [of the three chapters], the content itself remained unchanged";[148] however, the effect on the council Fathers and the observers and guests was catastrophic.[149] Throughout the third period, "the minority pursued its agenda relentlessly" using "every possible procedural loophole to rein in the progress of the Council," and capitalizing "on the temperament of Paul VI to win little victories," not without revealing the "ambiguities" and "compromises" of the texts and the fragility of the majority.[150]

But what about these texts, primarily *De oecumenismo*? As shown in the *relatio* delivered on Oct 4, 1964 at the time of the presentation of the new version of the text,[151] the principal modification consisted in the change of the title of the first chapter, which no longer spoke of a Catholic ecumenism but of the one ecumenism, approached according to "Catholic principles."[152]

This paradigmatic conversion required, on the part of Christians and their churches, the unprecedented ability to combine at least three different points of view. First of all, the questioning of each of the Christian partners on "Christ's

141 The text of the schema (except for chapters 4 and 5 on the "relationship of Catholics to non-Christians and in particular with the Jews" and on "religious freedom," which later found their autonomy), can be found in: *AS* 2/5, 412–431; the summary of the observations received by the SPCU in: *AS* 2/5, 442–445; the proposed amendments in: *AS* 2/5, 446–467; and the speeches in: *AS* 2/5, 468–481.

142 *AS* 3/2, 296–317; the lengthy written *relatio* can be found in *AS* 3/2, 330–344.

143 Oral *relatio* of the first chapter and the outcome of the votes in: *AS* 3/3, 280–282, 316–317, and 366; oral *relatio* of the second chapter and the outcome of the votes, in: *AS* 3/3, 328–329 and 367, and *AS* 3/4, 48; *Relationes* of the third chapter and the outcome of the votes in: *AS* 3/4, 10–15, 48 and 75.

144 *Relatio* and the outcome of the votes on the amendments to the preamble and first chapter in: *AS* 3/7, 11–48 and 59; *relatio* and outcome of the votes on the amendments to chapter 2 in: *AS* 3/7, 412–421, and 451; *relatio* and outcome of the votes on the amendments to chapter 3 in: *AS* 3/7, 669–702 and 711.

145 See the highly detailed analysis of Louis Antonio Tagle, "The 'Black Week' of Vatican II (November 14–21, 1964)," in: Giuseppe Alberigo & Joseph A. Komonchak, eds., *History of Vatican II*, vol. 4, *Church as Communion: Third Period and Intersession (September 1964–September 1965)*, Leuven/Maryknoll, Peeters/Orbis Books, 2004, 338–452. The author's balanced assessment also shows that some obscurities remain, especially regarding the origins of the *modi* proposed by the pope after the Nov 21 vote.

146 Yves Congar, "Décret sur l'œcuménisme 'Unitatis redintegratio,'" in: *Documents conciliaires*, vol. 1, *L'Église, l'œcuménisme, les Églises Orientales*, Paris, Éditions du Centurion, 1965, 163–192, here 168.

147 *AS* 3/7, 422–423.

148 Congar, "Décret sur l'œcuménisme 'Unitatis redintegratio,'" 169.

149 The statement is from Yves Congar, *My Journal of the Council*, Collegeville MN, Liturgical Press, 2012, 690.

150 According to the evaluation in Tagle, "The 'Black Week' of Vatican II," 450.

151 *AS* 3/2, 296–317.

152 *AS* 3/3, 281.

will for the church [*circa Ecclesiam*]" (4 § 2);[153] a questioning to which an answer was sketched out in *De oecumenismo* 2, which is a kind of Catholic replica of article 1 of the constitution of the WCC. This WCC article was perfectly summarized in the newly added preamble of *UR* (1 § 2).

Second, the recognition by the Catholic Church of its own point of view, both on what it perceives of Christ's will *circa Ecclesiam* – there are indeed affirmations, for example on the role of Peter and on apostolic succession, that the others did not share – and on its way of perceiving the position of the "separated brethren," which was sketched out in *De oecumenismo* 3. It went as far as possible in describing what was "common," while introducing at the end of number 4 the distinctions already developed in previous versions between "*the whole plenitude* of the means of salvation, entrusted to the Catholic Church," and "the *means* of salvation used by the Spirit of Christ," which are the separate churches, between "the *general* means [*generale auxilium*] of salvation" and the "*particular* means [*auxilia*]" (a term implied in 5).

Finally, the entry into a common movement – the "ecumenical movement" – carried along by the self-questioning of all and the dialogue among all in regard to the common goal: "That by this path ... all Christians may find themselves gathered together in a common celebration of the Eucharist, in the unity of the one and only church," as stipulated in 4 § 3. The articulation of these three points of view implies, if taken seriously and driven to their logical conclusion, a "decentering" of Catholicism that no longer compares the others to itself but situates itself along with the others in relation to the will of Christ.

This "ecclesiological perspectivism" was rooted in a true historical pneumatology prompted by the ecumenical movement that *Unitatis redintegratio* interpreted as a "sign of the times" (*UR* 4 § 1, see also 1 § 2). It suddenly brought to light two aspects of the Christian tradition that had not been perceived before: the "unfathomable" depth of its Christian vision of grace, quoting the letter to the Ephesians (Eph 3:8),[154] and at the same time the plurality of "views" on it, which requires a theology of communication.

This "internal differentiation" of the mystery is not easy to perceive – it was a real novelty after the history of Christian heresies – and is even less easy to live, because it requires new skills on the part of the communities and their pastors and theologians. Therefore, it necessarily has a "principled" side, developed in the first chapter, and a "process" side, set out in the second chapter on the practice of ecumenism. Unlike previous versions of the text, these two sides are perfectly unified, each referring to the other, so that the "way" or the "manner of proceeding" (see *UR* 1 § 3) reflect the principles and vice versa. The same coherence characterizes the "process" of the second chapter which, while being substantially enriched, remains structurally the same as in the preparatory texts.

The enrichment is, however, significant and concerns the two sides of the dialogue inspired by the Holy Spirit – the self-questioning and the relationship to the other – as well as the relationship to the truth. The self-questioning must be integral, as is suggested by the introduction of the term *reformatio* (*UR* 4 § 2, and 6 § 1), previously missing from the conciliar language,[155] and, as far as doctrine is concerned, the recalling of the Roncallian principle (in the Italian version)[156] with its distinction between the deposit of faith and its formulation.

153 *AS* 3/2, 300. This formula is completely open, if one compares it with *De oecumenismo* 3 § 1 proposed in Nov 1963.

154 This development is due to Cardinal Paul-Émile Léger who, criticizing the expression "the Catholic Church possesses the whole truth," relied on Eph 3:8, whose citation can be found in n. 11 of the definitive text of *De oecumenismo*; see his address in: *AS* 2/6, 10–12. On the other addresses by the cardinal and his "petition" to John XXIII, see Theobald, *La réception du concile Vatican II*, vol. 1, 302, note 4.

155 It was also Bishop Volk who introduced the vocabulary of "reformatio" in his address on Nov 21, 1963, in: *AS* 2/5, 687–689. See also Theobald, *La réception du concile Vatican II*, vol. 1, 297–306.

156 See Melloni, *Papa Giovanni*, 324–325.

As for the relationship with the other, 9 speaks of "meetings of the two sides" where "each can deal with the other on an equal footing [*pari cum pari*]." This is valuable "especially for discussion of theological problems." The importance of this *pari cum pari* is also clear from the SPCU's response to those who wanted to delete this phrase: "The expression must be retained, because it indicates *the essential condition of all dialogue*."[157]

The fruit of this type of communication, free from any false irenicism (*UR* 11 § 1) but capable of self-criticism, is a new relationship to truth. It was already present earlier,[158] thanks to the Lutheran rule, known as the Meldenius rule: "In necessariis unitas, in dubiis libertas, in omnibus caritas"[159] (*UR* 4 § 7). It is expressed in chapter 2 with the help of what is called the "hierarchy of truths" in Catholic doctrine that "vary in their relation to the fundamental Christian faith" (*UR* 11 § 3).[160] The difference between these two approaches, both accepted by the council, resides in the space accorded to freedom (between unity and charity), which is perhaps broader in Lutheranism which locates the *adiaphora* therein, although the Catholic reception (*UR* 4 § 7) opens it up very widely, covering everything from the spiritual life to theological education. However, they have in common the "change of order" (*metabasis eis allo genos*), constitutive of the "hierarchy of truths" (*in omnis*), namely the passage, never acquired once and for all, to "charity" (*UR* 4 § 7) or to "love of truth, charity, and humility," or even to "fraternal rivalry" (*UR* 11 § 3), in relation to the "unfathomable riches of Christ" (Eph 3:8).

The last chapter of *Unitatis redintegratio* has a special status,[161] for while the first two chapters introduce a real ecumenical "logic" into the history of the Christian tradition, the third proposes a more precise historical-theological discernment of the "divisions" that took place in the East and those that were produced in the West. We shall return to the first part of this chapter, which deals with the Eastern churches, when we look at the document on the Eastern Catholic Churches. As for the second part on "Separated Churches and Ecclesial Communities in the West," we have already seen a certain irritation and fear on the part of the Protestant observers that a bilateral Catholic-Orthodox dialogue would take place without the other partners. The written *relatio* of October 1964 is well aware of this and defends, for this reason, the treatment of the two divisions and their effects in the same chapter while distinguishing between different types of "ecumenism."[162] Without defining these "churches and ecclesial communities," *Unitatis redintegratio* indicates, in four points, what connects the separated brethren and what are the "important differences ... especially in the interpretation of revealed truth," points that serve at the same time as "a basis and encouragement for [ecumenical] dialogue" (*UR* 19 § 4). These are the confession of Christ (*UR* 20), the love for and veneration of the Holy Scriptures (*UR* 21), sacramental life, with a new paragraph on the Eucharist (*UR* 22), and life with Christ (*UR* 23).

Mauro Velati reports on the frankness of the observers in general and the delegates of the WCC in particular, their impact on the texts, and the more institutional exchanges during the meetings of the SPCU on Nov 12 and 19, 1963. He also reports on the reaction of Frans Thijssen who, in the name of the SPCU, responded to the observers in introducing the principle that a church, which "meditating upon itself establishes its attitude out

157 *AS* 3/7, 418 (italics mine).

158 In the first schema, presented on Nov 18, 1963; the rule can be found in 3 § 4, see *AS* 2/5, 415.

159 See Joseph Lecler, "À propos d'une maxime citée par le Pape Jean XXIII: In necessariis unitas, in dubiis libertas, in omnibus caritas," *RSR* 49, 1961, 549–560; Joseph Lecler, "Note complémentaire sur la maxime: In necessariis unitas, in non necessariis libertas, in omnibus caritas," *RSR* 52, 1964, 432–438.

160 The expression was proposed by Bishop Andrea Pangrazio, in: *AS* 2/6, 32–34. See also Theobald, *La réception du concile Vatican II*, vol. 1, 302.

161 See the abovementioned written *relatio* and oral *relationes*.

162 See *AS* 3/2, 340–341.

of its own vision of what the Church is," cannot be called anti-ecumenical.[163]

As relevant as this reply is, it does not erase certain difficulties in the text, as summarized, for example, by the observer-delegate of the Alliance of Reformed Churches holding the Presbyterian System, pastor Hébert Roux. He questioned a certain asymmetry in the two parts of chapter 3 of *Unitatis redintegratio*, which remains silent about the doctrinal divergences between East and West (in pneumatology and ecclesiology) while affirming them in the relations between Catholics and Protestants and referring, in regard to the separated churches and ecclesial communities in the West, to the New Delhi Statement, without mentioning it, in speaking of the Orthodox churches, which were also signatories.[164] As for the substance, he questioned the relationship between the pneumatology of *Unitatis redintegratio* and its ecclesiology, asking "whether, in posing the problem of unity in terms of communion,[165] the decree ... grants its full meaning and real scope to the person and work of the Holy Spirit as the *one who realizes* full communion, and whether in a certain way the visible institution, the place and instrument of this communion, did not in the end become its *cause*."[166] On the basis of this questioning, the observer criticized the juridical and quantitative aspect of the terminology of "elements" (*UR* 3 § 2) and "means of salvation" (*UR* 3 §§ 4–5) and noted the questionable application of the Christological and eschatological category of "pleroma" to the church,[167] notwithstanding the fact that the entire argument is based on the (undoubtedly more fundamental) attestation to the Holy Scriptures and the ancient Tradition of the church (*UR* 3 §§ 5, and 21).

3.2 *How to Emerge from a Gregorian Ecclesiology or the First Steps towards a Restoration of the "Patriarchal Institution"*

As far as the first part of chapter 3 of *Unitatis redintegratio* on the Eastern churches is concerned, it is impossible to understand it without connecting it to the decree *Orientalium Ecclesiarum*, drawn up under the responsibility of the Commission for the Oriental Churches. Let us recall that, during the first intersession, in March 1963, a division of competencies took place between this commission and the SPCU in which the former had to restrict itself to dealing with the churches in union with Rome. The commission was dominated by a majority of Eastern patriarchs and bishops of a Uniate sensitivity, and by Latin experts of the same style. Only the Melkites, and their head Patriarch Maximos IV, defended an ecclesiology acceptable to the Orthodox. They had as their ally a Latin, Abbot Johannes Maria Hoeck, president of the Benedictine congregation of Bavaria. Their cohesion and their theological strength were evident for the first time during the debate on the schema *Ut omnes unum sint* on Nov 27, 1962, during the celebrated "Melkites' day,"[168] when the differences, and above all the symmetries, between the Latin church and the Eastern churches were suddenly made clear during the council session.

163 See Velati's contribution "A Foundational Ecumenical Event: The Non-Catholic Observers at Vatican II" in this volume, as well as Soetens, "The Ecumenical commitment of the Catholic Church," 290–293.

164 Hébert Roux, "Le Décret sur l'œcuménisme 'Unitatis redintegratio,'" in: Jean Bosc & others, *Points de vue de théologiens protestants: Études sur les décrets du concile Vatican II*, Paris, Cerf, 1967, 89–107, esp. 95.

165 See *UR* 2 § 2: "It is the Holy Spirit, dwelling in those who believe and pervading and ruling over the Church as a whole, who brings about that wonderful communion of the faithful. He brings them into intimate union with Christ, so that He is the principle of the Church's unity."

166 Roux, "Le Décret sur l'œcuménisme," 99 (italics original).

167 Roux, "Le Décret sur l'œcuménisme," 99–101.

168 The expression "Melkites' day" is from Bishop Néophytos Edelby, the most influential theologian of the Melkites. See Neophytos Edelby, *Souvenirs du concile Vatican II (11 October 1962–8 décembre 1965)*, Rabieh, Greek Melkite Research Center, 2003, 142; see also Ruggieri, "Beyond an Ecclesiology of Polemics."

The main issue at stake in this difference is the conception of the relationship between the "particular churches" and the "universal church." The term "particular churches" was used in *Lumen gentium* almost as a synonym for dioceses with barely a connection to its local roots. These inconsistencies were clearly shown in the sole debate on *Orientalium Ecclesiarum* in the council sessions,[169] which took place between Oct 15 and 20, 1964, when chapters 2 and 3 of *Lumen gentium* had already been voted on. Hoeck was one of the most critical and most visionary: "The constitution *De Ecclesia* [23] certainly alludes to the patriarchal structure," he acknowledged in his speech on Oct 19, 1964, "but in such an obscure way and without even naming it, that experts in the field have difficulty recognizing it."[170] He concluded his presentation:

> One may wonder, and in fact many do wonder, if it belongs to our council, *which is practically a Latin council*, to decide these kinds of questions that affect the Eastern churches, since in our decree [5], as well as in the decree *De oecumenismo* [16], it is solemnly declared that the Eastern churches have the right[171] and the duty to govern themselves according to their own disciplines. Are we not contradicting ourselves by dealing with their discipline? Should we not at least, before proceeding to a general vote, ask the Easterners whether they want the council to pronounce on these questions by a universal vote? The only question, or almost the only question, which certainly has come up throughout the whole council is that of the patriarchal structure of the whole church, but this question, as we have said, was only very inadequately touched upon.[172]

In Hoeck's mind, this question of the "patriarchal structure" obviously had very important constitutional consequences. In particular, it raised

> the question of knowing whether it was opportune to establish new patriarchates ... One could also ask whether it would not be appropriate to divide the Latin church into several patriarchates (not only honorary ones), because it is much too large in comparison with the other churches, and it is always tempted as a result to treat the other particular churches as minorities and to oppress them. In this way, too, it is easy to remedy the excessive centralization that everyone complains about.[173]

It must be recognized today that what is suggested, in this proposition that is both about principles and practical, is a most audacious "reframing" of the ecclesiology of *Lumen gentium*. Other interventions from the small Melkite minority went in the same direction.[174] Hoeck's proposal to confide "the whole of this question," that is, that of the patriarchates, "which is the pivot of the whole problem of the union with the Orthodox churches" to a new mixed commission, formed of members of the commissions on faith, on bishops, on ecumenism, and the Commission for the Oriental Churches, was unsuccessful. Perhaps it was too ambitious, especially at this stage of the council, because, according to Hoeck's wish, this "new study" should have been undertaken "not only for our decree [*Orientalium Ecclesiarum*] but also and above all for the constitution *De Ecclesia* and the decree *De episcopis*."[175]

In regard to the two texts of the SPCU and the Commission for the Oriental Churches, it should be noted that, thanks to the tenacity and competence of the Melkites and their allies, it

169 The text of the schema can be found in: *AS* 3/4, 485–493; the written *relatio* in: *AS* 3/4, 494–516.

170 *AS* 3/5, 72–75, here 73.

171 Paul VI's amendment changed the terms *ius* and *officium* to *facultas*.

172 *AS* 3/5, 74 (italics mine).

173 *AS* 3/5, 74.

174 See, for example, the intervention of Bishop Elias Zoghby on Oct 16, 1964, in: *AS* 3/5, 32–34.

175 *AS* 3/5, 73–74.

is *Orientalium Ecclesiarum* that offers the most historical-canonical and theological precision concerning the positioning of the particular churches and patriarchates within the whole of ecumenical ecclesiology. While adopting historical language in the first part of chapter 3 (UR 14), the decree *Unitatis redintegratio* superimposes on it the language of Latin-Roman ecclesiology that distinguishes the "[separated] Churches of the East" and "the Catholic Church" (UR 14 § 4).[176] It does so, of course, in coherence with the principles of the first chapter. *Orientalium Ecclesiarum* is certainly based on the same presuppositions (OE 1 and 3), but it succeeds in introducing some decisive perspectives for the future of ecumenical dialogue with the East.

In tension with the pontifical correction (UR 14 § 4), *Orientalium Ecclesiarum* maintains first of all the insistence on the rights of the Eastern churches: "The Sacred Council ... solemnly declares that the Churches of the East, as much as those of the West, have a full right and are in duty bound to rule themselves [*iure pollere et officio teneri regendi*], each in accordance with its own established disciplines" (OE 5).

It then manages to incorporate a definition of the term "particular church" that avoids the Latin reduction to the entity of the "diocese" and emphasizes that the church is a communion of churches, each with its own autonomous hierarchy. The equivalence between the terminology of "particular church" and the more classic "rite" is introduced at the last moment, giving the term a much broader meaning than just liturgical:[177] "The Holy Catholic Church, which is the Mystical Body of Christ,[178] is made up of the faithful who are organically united in the Holy Spirit by the same faith, the same sacraments and the same government and who, combining together into various groups which are held together by a hierarchy, form separate Churches or Rites" (OE 2). This definition, which in some way distinguishes between the two levels of a "community of *fideles*" and an "organic" grouping of "communities" under the same autonomous or "autocephalous" hierarchy, is valid for the churches of the East and the West (OE 3 and 5). This is a considerable achievement, complemented by the affirmation that, in an ecclesiology of communion of churches, diversity enhances their unity. The diversity of "ways of life" (patrimony, discipline, liturgy etc.) is linked to "different needs of time and place" (OE 2).

The section on "Eastern Rite Patriarchs" (OE 7–11) tells of "the patriarchate, as an institution," which "was recognized by the first ecumenical councils" (OE 7), a section that specifies the definition of a particular church or rite, is of extreme ecumenical importance.[179] Three points in particular are worth noting. First, there is the determination "that their [the Oriental patriarchs'] rights and privileges should be reestablished in accordance with the ancient tradition of each of the Churches and the decrees of the ecumenical councils" and that these are "those that obtained in the time of union between East and West," although they should be adapted somewhat to modern conditions (OE 9 §§ 1–3). Second, there is the affirmation of the internal canonical autonomy of the patriarchs, specified by reference to "patriarchs *with their synods*" (OE 9 § 4). Finally, there is number 11, which opens onto the future: "Seeing that the patriarchal office in the Eastern Church is a traditional form of government,

176 It should be noted in particular that *Orientalium Ecclesiarum* is peppered with references to the conciliar and Roman tradition, whereas the first part of the third chapter of *Unitatis redintegratio* is content with a detailed description, both positive and admiring, of the Eastern tradition, making only a final allusion to the Council of Florence.

177 OE 3 and AS 3/8, 558.

178 This phrase corresponds more to the Western tradition.

179 Let us note that the request to rule, in UR 14, on the "question discussed between Catholic theologians, to know whether, yes or no, the Eastern Churches, variously instituted by the apostles, are by divine right in a different condition from that of the (local) churches of the West (that of the Roman primate always excepted, which is of divine right)," the SPCU proposed "keeping silent" (AS 3/7, 675); this decisive point thus remained open and was left to subsequent ecumenical debate.

the Sacred Ecumenical Council ardently desires that new patriarchates should be erected where there is need, to be established either by an ecumenical council or by the Roman Pontiff." Bishop Néophytos Edelby is right in affirming that these "paragraphs are undoubtedly the keystone of the whole patriarchal edifice that the council wished to restore." He also adds, "The Catholic Church, if it decides sincerely to carry out this restoration, will remove one of the greatest obstacles to the union of the churches."[180]

Therefore those two decrees, the one on ecumenism and the one on the Eastern Catholic Churches, each in different ways, make an appointment with the future. This applies above all to the way of proceeding or communicating (*modus* and *via*), developed in the second chapter of *De oecumenismo*. Consistent with the principles of the first part, this *modus procedendi* places each "church and ecclesial community" under the obligation to seek the will of Christ *circa Ecclesiam* and to expound, in ecumenical dialogue, "the authentic and unquestionable meaning" of their own doctrine. But intertextuality and the debates also reveal, within the same Christian tradition now in the process of becoming "ecumenical," lines of demarcation carefully guarded by the conciliar minority but kept mobile by the presence of the SPCU, the observers, and the Melkite minority with its allies. On the Protestant side, this demarcation gave rise to the fear of the Latin risk of juridicism, based on an analytic or cumulative conception of the ecclesial elements and means of salvation, and, on the Eastern side, there was the tendency, subsequent to the Great Schism, to confuse Latin universality with that of the universal church and to impose Roman centralism. In the background to these battles on the front lines was the dogmatic constitution on the church *Lumen gentium*, a kind of shadow that hung over the debates just mentioned and under which the ecumenical forces of the council endeavored to move forward, leaving the difficult question of the relationship between these three texts to later generations.

3.3 *The Decrees on Ecumenism and on the Eastern Catholic Churches: A Critical Rereading of the Dogmatic Constitution on the Church?*

Apparently, this question did not arise, because the first of the two decrees is clearly situated in the wake of the constitution *Lumen gentium*, where "the doctrine concerning the church was already set forth," as indicated in *De oecumenismo* 1 § 3, and in the clarifications given, on two occasions, by the *relationes* that accompany that text.[181] These indications, however, leave untouched the question of the precise relationship between *Lumen gentium* and *Unitatis redintegratio*, all the more so since the *relatio* of 1964 reiterated a distinction between a "doctrinal constitution" and a "pastoral decree" that the SPCU itself had criticized,[182] as if the doctrine of *Lumen gentium* were not already

180 Néophytos Edelby & Ignace Dick, *Les Églises orientales catholiques: Décret "Orientalium Ecclesiarum"*, Paris, Cerf, 1970, 349 and 354.

181 See the *relatio* of Bishop Joseph-Marie-Eugène Martin on Nov 18, 1963, during the first reading of *De oecumenismo*: "Insuper nostrum decretum omnino et evidenter praesupponit doctrinam expositam in Constitutione dogmatica 'De Ecclesia'"; AS 2/5, 473; see also the *relatio* on Sep 23, 1964, during the second reading: "Rogat Secretariatus, ut prae oculis habeatur decretum *De oecumenismo* non esse constitutionem dogmaticam, sed decretum pastorale, quod niti potest et debet doctrina in Constitutione dogmatica '*De Ecclesia*' fuse exposita et in decreto *De oecumenismo* non repetenda. Secretariatui neque necessarium neque utile videtur iterum proponere totum tractatum dogmaticum de Ecclesia. *Sufficiens ei videtur efferre principia aliqua theologica, quibus in lucem ponatur unitas illa quam Christus pro Ecclesia sua voluit. Ne fiat integer tractatus theologicus, in capite primo elementa doctrinalia praecipua unitatem Ecclesiae spectantia modo tantum compendiario, nihilominus, ut nobis videtur, sufficienter claro proponuntur.* Evidens est tam Catholicis quam fratribus separatis haec elementa accipienda et interpretanda esse iuxta doctrinam integram Ecclesiae catholicae multoties iam et variis modis declaratam"; AS 3/2, 336–337 (italics mine).

182 See Theobald, *La réception du concile Vatican II*, vol. 1, 292–294.

pastoral! How, then, can we understand the exposition of the first chapter of *Unitatis redintegratio* "Catholic principles of ecumenism" if, according to the authors, they "highlight the unity that Christ willed for his church"?[183] Is it enough to understand *Unitatis redintegratio* as focusing on one aspect of *Lumen gentium*, clarifying it and concretizing it with pastoral details, without touching other elements of the text? Or does it bring something new, to the point of shedding new light (perhaps even a critical one) on the constitution promulgated at the same time? One can understand the reaction of many interpreters when they wondered whether the authors' careful reference to *Lumen gentium* might not be a strategy to protect what is actually new.[184]

In order to respond to these questions, it would be necessary to analyze the evolutions of conciliar ecclesiology, starting from the constitution on the sacred liturgy *Sacrosantum concilium*, then deal with *Lumen gentium* as well as *Unitatis redintegratio* and *Orientalium Ecclesiarum*, and finally examine the decree on missionary activity *Ad gentes*, promulgated on the last day of the council; there is not enough room for that here. However, we can adopt this intertextual approach for the three texts promulgated in 1964 and record, from an ecumenical point of view, how the difference in their perspectives shifts Catholic ecclesiology.

It is undeniable that *Unitatis redintegratio* introduced a new perspective on *Lumen gentium*, starting from a theology of ecumenical communication which is not to be understood primarily as the ecclesial replica of a philosophy of communication (which it is as well), but as a true rerooting of ecclesial understanding in the *modus conversationis Christi* (see DV 7 § 1), in its *via* (UR 4, 6, 9, and 11) and those of the apostles or in their *modus agendi* set forth in *Dignitatis humanae* (DH 12). This is what emerges from an intertextual analysis of all the documents developed by the SPCU. This led the council to effect a real change of perspective on itself and on the church, and to enter into ecclesiology no longer solely from the Catholic point of view, as was still the case with *Lumen gentium*, but on a basis common to all, formulated in relationship to what, according to their traditions, the one and the others perceive of the will of Christ.

This other perspective then, which is situated in a way obliquely to the overall course of *Lumen gentium*, invites a new evaluation of its stages. When the ultimate referent is no longer the current image of the Catholic Church but – moved "by the Holy Spirit" (see UR 1 and 4) – the ecumenical movement within itself and in the other "churches and ecclesial communities," the second part of chapter 2 of *Lumen gentium* (LG 13–15, which tell about the note of "catholicity," the Catholic faithful, and the separated brethren) is in a way reorganized and reintegrated into a single movement that begins in the first chapter, especially at its end (LG 8), precisely at the point where, for the first time, the effective historicity of the church is touched upon. In *Unitatis redintegratio*, the journey effectively begins immediately with the separated brethren, and then integrates them into the perspective proper to Catholicism (treated in LG 8 and 14). Above all, it no longer treats the relationship between non-Catholic churches or communities and the Catholic Church in terms of "elements" to be integrated into a Catholic "whole" which is certainly that of Christ (LG 8 and 15), but it at least suggests that these elements cannot be understood without the ecclesial or communal subjects that, in each historical case, are constituted in a particular way according to all (*simul sumptis*) the elements available and effectively realized (see UR 3 § 2).

Conversely, what in LG 14 is affirmed of the "full incorporation" into the Catholic Church in regard to salvation – that is, that a person can be in the church "in a 'bodily' manner and not 'in his heart'" – must be said of all the churches and ecclesial communities and hence represents a decisive factor of relativization of the elements in

183 *AS* 3/2, 336.
184 See the analysis of the reactions in Hilberath "Theologischer Kommentar," 104–108.

relation to the essential and necessary "incorporation into Christ" (*UR* 3 § 1). From these ecclesial groups referred by *Unitatis redintegratio* to the one Church of Christ, the text moves somewhat to the unity of the people of God, discussed in *LG* 13 and in *UR* 2 § 5, and especially in *UR* 4 § 6. This universalist perspective, like the eschatological utopia of the gospel of peace that underlies and supports it, is in some way "brought closer" to the historical reality of the churches and the church as it is traced in *Lumen gentium*, especially in chapter 7, although it is not missing from its first two chapters. It thus exercises a double function that does not appear as such in *Lumen gentium*: it relativizes the differences between churches and ecclesial communities in relation to the one goal, and it also makes clear the particularly Catholic insistence on the unity already given from the beginning and subsisting in the Catholic Church (*UR* 4 § 3).

Let us add (going back even further) what the decree on ecumenism says of the testament given by Christ Jesus (*UR* 2 § 1) and of the pneumatological principle of ecclesiology, which considerably expands what *Lumen gentium* affirms concerning the foundation of the church (*LG* 5, 3, and 4), even though *Unitatis redintegratio* ignores the distinction between the historical Jesus and the birth of the church, a distinction which necessarily affects the question of the will of Christ *circa Ecclesiam*.

In regard to *Orientalium Ecclesiarum*, its own perspective succeeded, at least on one point, in displacing the ecclesiology of *Lumen gentium*. The absence of the "patriarchal institution" in *Lumen gentium*, as it was called in *OE* 7 and 11, and sharply criticized by Hoeck on Oct 19, 1964, was corrected *in extremis*. In the final version of *Lumen gentium*, put to the vote on Nov 17, there were two amendments. Added as a kind of annex to number 23 on the relations within the episcopal college, its last paragraph speaks of "various churches … organically united," according to the plan of divine providence. It is in this context that they are now called "the ancient *patriarchal churches*," which "enjoy their own discipline, their own liturgical usage, and their own theological and spiritual heritage," not failing to add the reservation "preserving the unity of faith and the *unique divine constitution of the universal Church*."[185] The repercussions of this final amendment on the rest of chapter 3 and on a historical-theological rereading of the whole of *Lumen gentium* in an ecumenical perspective remain open by definition.

The three texts, promulgated at the end of the council's third period, are certainly ranked by the distinction between constitutions and decrees, but the simple fact of appearing in the same conciliar corpus exposes them to an intertextual reading and thus to tensions, even contradictions,[186] or simply openings, left to their postconciliar reception. The principal ecumenical issue, that is, that "all are led to examine their own faithfulness to Christ's will for the Church" (*UR* 4 § 2) was now established. From this, there emerges a distinction between two levels of language, a meta-discourse of ecumenical communication (*de exercitio*) that in a way allows one to pass through the door of the ecumenical movement and a discourse proper to Catholicism that submits its own tradition to a critical rereading, taking its point of departure from the criterion of the relationship of all to the will of Christ and to the unfathomable riches of his grace. It is on this level that the lines of demarcation that we have been examining are manifest, lines defended by some, and kept mobile, even porous, by others.

To conclude this section, let us return to Bishop Volk's repeated insistence on the fact that Christian "doctrine" forms a "whole" that only exists under "different forms of Christian life." They retain all their legitimacy "as long as the one [*una*] and integral [*tota*] doctrine and grace of Christ appears in them." This is true "at least in principle."[187] It does not seem that, in November 1964, the council had yet defined what these principles were.

---

185 *AS* 3/8, 85–86 (italics original).

186 For example, between *UR* 16 and *OE* 5 on the "faculty" or "right" and "duty" of the churches of the East and West "to govern themselves according to the disciplines proper to them."

187 See *AS* 1/4, 388, quote in *AS* 2/5, 688–689.

4 Ecumenical Access to the Source and the Preaching of the Gospel to All Creatures (Fourth Period)

One might think, however, that, with the promulgation of *Unitatis redintegratio*, the ecumenical journey of Vatican II had come to an end. Nonetheless, the Black Week and the violence that broke out at the heart of the council clearly showed that the council was in the midst of a true "paradigm crisis," in which a minority challenged the rules of the game because it felt, legitimately or not, that it was not being heard. Paul VI's management of this major conflict in Vatican II must be evaluated in this context.[188] The time following this crisis, the third intersession and the last period of the council, was of decisive importance because it was the time when the texts were delivered that reflected, according to the preparation by the SPCU, the epicenter of the ecumenical problematic. These texts were the constitution *Dei Verbum*, the decree on religious liberty *Dignitatis humanae*, the one on the relationship of the church to non-Christian religions – in particular Judaism – *Nostra aetate*, and, to a lesser extent, the pastoral constitution *Gaudium et spes*. The purpose of this last part is not to go through these documents but to show how they give access to the very principles of a Christian tradition that was becoming ecumenical.

One of the last texts of the council, the decree on missionary activity *Ad gentes*, which also rereads and "reframes" *Lumen gentium*, returning to the purpose of the council, can orient us:

> Missionary activity among the nations differs from *pastoral activity exercised among the faithful* as well as from *undertakings aimed at restoring unity among Christians*. And yet these two ends are most closely connected with *the missionary zeal* because the division among Christians damages the most holy cause of preaching the Gospel to every creature and blocks the way to the faith for many (*AG* 6 § 6).

4.1 *Accessing the Source*

The strength of the last mention of the ecumenical cause comes from the fact that it is related to pastorality, as envisioned by John XXIII in his opening address of the first period, and with pastoral activity, and was oriented towards "the holy cause of preaching the Gospel to every creature" (*UR* 1 § 1).[189] By focusing on this purpose, the council left behind the ecclesiology that was its main concern until the end of the third period.

The SPCU was involved in this return to the principles of the Christian tradition since the preparatory phase when, as will be recalled, it drew up several texts, in particular the two schemas on the Word of God and on the relationship between Scripture and Tradition and two others on Judaism and religious freedom. The conflicts between the SPCU and the Theological Commission on these questions were discussed above. During the first period of the council, these conflicts spread to the entire conciliar assembly. This led, after a vote on the schema *De fontibus revelationis* on Nov 20, 1962, which obliged the council to continue its discussion of a text that it had overwhelmingly rejected, to an intervention by John XXIII, who referred it to a mixed commission, composed of members of the Doctrinal Commission and the SPCU.[190]

The nine sessions of the mixed commission between Nov 25, 1962 and Mar 4, 1963 ended in failure.[191] It is true that the text as a whole was considerably improved, but the active minority and the majority were unable to reach an agreement on the question of the wider scope of the content of Tradition in relation to Scripture, an

188 See Sesboüé & Theobald, *Histoire des dogmes*, vol. 4, 468–470, and Theobald, *La réception du concile Vatican II*, vol. 1, 338–359.

189 This reference to Mark 16:15–16 is the expression par excellence of the missionary trajectory of the tradition, which is found in many conciliar texts in a structuring position (*LG* 1, 17 and 19; *UR* 1; *AG*, 1 and 6; etc.).

190 See Ruggieri, "The First Doctrinal Clash," 249–266.

191 See the two reports of Cardinal Liénart who, in the name of the Coordinating Commission, followed *De divina revelatione*: *AS* 5/1, 60–62 and 445.

anti-ecumenical position, also called theory of the two sources, defended tooth and nail by the minority as the keystone of the Catholic edifice.[192] It is understandable that the text sent to the Fathers on Apr 22, 1963 was not discussed during the second period. It was thanks to a brief remark by Paul VI in his closing speech of the second period[193] that the text surfaced during the second intersession and was discussed, in a new version (elaborated by a new subcommission), between Sep 30 and Oct 6.[194] After the amendment by the commissions concerned, the text of *De divina revelatione*[195] was sent back to the council Fathers, at the end of the Black Week, on Nov 20, 1964, with the announcement that the vote would take place only during the final period. The vote was held on Sep 20 and 21, 1965, while the assembly continued its debate on religious freedom. The result showed that the text had succeeded in gathering a very large majority.

However, on three crucial points, the number of *non placet* votes was clearly higher: the relationship between Tradition, Scripture, and the magisterium (DV 8–10); the effect of inspiration on the truth of the Scriptures (DV 11); and the historical-critical question of the historicity of the gospels (DV 10). These three points of contention are clearly situated within the anti-Modernist doctrinal system, mentioned several times, and more precisely concern the field of the mediations of revelation. While the minority continued to defend a verbal and doctrinal conception of revelation and faith, the majority insisted on a kerygmatic and economic conception, emphasizing the "intrinsic link between events and words" in revelation[196] and its sacramental structure. It cannot be denied, however, that great ambiguities remain. For, on several occasions, the text simply superimposes the biblical and patristic or "personalist" approach and the scholastic and doctrinal perspective.[197] The work of going through the 1,498 *modi* and their examination by the Theological Commission between Sep 29 and Oct 11, besides the appeal of the minority to Paul VI and his request to discuss again, *in fine*, the three amendments in the presence of the president of the SPCU, Cardinal Bea (on Oct 19, 1965), manifestly demonstrate that the doctrinal conflict remained at its epicenter[198] and, dare we say it, still remains there.

The reactions of some of the conciliar Fathers, of the *periti*, and of the observers, confirm that the constitution *Dei Verbum* represents a compromise. Congar's prudent judgment, given on the same day as its promulgation, Nov 18, 1965, could be found coming from the pen of other figures: "A great text which provides theology with THE MEANS of

192 See Johannes Feiner, "La contribution du Secrétariat pour l'unité des chrétiens à la Constitution dogmatique sur la Révélation divine," in: Bernard-Dominique Dupuy & others, *La Révélation divine: Constitution dogmatique "Dei verbum"*, vol. 1, Paris, Cerf, 1968, 119–153, esp. 136–153; Riccardo Burigana, *La Bibbia nel concilio: La redazione della costituzione "Dei verbum" del Vaticano II*, Bologna, Il Mulino, 1998, 171–253; see also Ruggieri, "Beyond an Ecclesiology of Polemics," 347–357 and Grootaers, "The Drama Continues Between the Acts," 385–391. The judgments on this stage are diverse: while the expert from the SPCU Johannes Feiner emphasizes the achievement of refusing to decide the question of the greater material extension of the tradition (Feiner, "La contribution du Secrétariat," 152), others stress, rather, the "distressingly impoverished," very provisional compromise obtained, and the ambiguity of the positive report of Cardinal Liénart (see Grootaers, "The Drama Continues Between the Acts," 390).

193 See *AS* 2/6, 566–567.

194 See the detailed analysis of the debate by Hanjo Sauer, "The Doctrinal and the Pastoral: The Text on Divine Revelation," in: Alberigo & Komonchak, eds., *History of Vatican II*, vol. 4, 194–231.

195 *AS* 4/1, 336–381.

196 AS 4/1, 337.

197 See, for example, number 5 on faith; see also the *relatio* which justifies this overlap, in: *AS* 4/1, 345, *relatio* of n. 5 (B).

198 See the detailed analysis of the course of *Dei Verbum* during the fourth period, Christoph Theobald, "The Church Under the Word of God," in: Giuseppe Alberigo & Joseph A. Komonchak, eds., *History of Vatican II*, vol. 5, *The Council and the Transition: The Fourth Period and the End of the Council (September 1965–December 1965)*, Leuven/Maryknoll, Peeters/Orbis Books, 2006, 275–362.

becoming fully evangelical."[199] Let us set out the main achievements and the most important ecumenical difficulties.

The drafter of the preparatory schema, Bishop Volk, to whom we owe the preamble of *Dei Verbum*, cannot have failed to see his different interventions confirmed, in particular that of Oct 6, 1964. Formulated then as a wish but eventually successful, it expressed his insistence on the intertextual link between the first chapter, "Revelation Itself," chapter 6, "Sacred Scripture in the Life of the Church," and *Sacrosantum concilium* (33, 35, 51, and 56).[200] This link was to be founded on a conception of the Word of God and its hearing as event and as quasi-sacramental.[201] As he said in 1964, "in this sense, it is clear that the Holy Scripture has a special importance: for in it is the Word of God and this Word is not only contained in it, for in the liturgy Holy Scripture is incensed, but not Tradition, and in that space, one proceeds to enthrone Holy Scripture but not Tradition."[202] In his commentary on *Dei Verbum*, Henri-Marie de Lubac also emphasized this point,[203] and Archimandrite André Scrima, the Phanar delegate, took the same approach, questioning the relationship between revelation and liturgy in the text: "One might have desired a stronger doctrinal emphasis on the interweaving of the economy and the liturgy. Indeed, the constitution does speak of this in its final chapter ... We are thinking, however, of a deeper aspect: its basis in mystery, if we may so put it."[204] From an intertextual perspective, we can turn here to the first part of chapter 3 of *Unitatis redintegratio*, which, in response to the hesitation expressed, proposes one of the few "intertextual" formulations that links (1) the heart of Christian revelation and its economic form, as it is formulated in DV 2; (2) liturgy and Eucharist, at least implicitly presented in *Dei Verbum* under the form of "sacramentum voluntatis suae" (DV 2) and in chapter 4 (DV 21); (3) and the building up of the church through the celebration of the Eucharist in the particular churches, as it is presented in LG 26.

> The sacred liturgy ... in which the faithful, united with their bishop, have access to God the Father through the Son, the Word made flesh, Who suffered and has been glorified, and so, in the outpouring of the Holy Spirit, they enter into communion with the most holy Trinity, being made "sharers of the divine nature" [2 Pt 1:4]. Hence, through the celebration of the Holy Eucharist in each of these churches, the Church of God is built up and grows in stature and through concelebration, their communion with one another is made manifest [UR 15 § 1].

As for the distinction between Scripture, Tradition, and the magisterium, the theory of the two sources is certainly given less emphasis but remains – especially after the intervention of Paul VI – in the background of the text (DV 9), and the magisterium is clearly established as being at the service of the Word of God (DV 10). The official observer of the LWF, Kristen Ejner Buhl Skydsgaard, acknowledged the openness of *Dei Verbum* on this issue, which is controversial in Catholicism, but also noted that "it is clear enough to say that it remains

199 Congar, *My Journal of the Council*, 845 (capitals in the text).

200 *Sacrosantum concilium*, in: COGD 3, 260–287.

201 The day before, the Melkite Bishop Edelby had spoken in a similar vein: "Sacra Scriptura est realitas liturgica et prophetica. Est proclamatio potiusquam liber scriptus. Est testimonium Spiritus Sancti circa Christum, cuius tempus praecipuum atque privilegiatum est celebratio Liturgiae eucharisticae"; AS 3/3, 306–309, here 306–307. See also Edelby, *Souvenirs du concile Vatican II*, 276–278 (Oct 5–6, 1964).

202 AS 3/3, 344.

203 See Henri de Lubac, "Commentaire du préambule et du chapitre I," in: Dupuy & others., *La Révélation divine*, vol. 1, 157–302, esp. 301–302.

204 See André Scrima, "Révélation et tradition dans la constitution dogmatique 'Dei verbum,'" in: Bernard-Dominique Dupuy & others, *La Révélation divine: Constitution dogmatique "Dei verbum"*, vol. 2, Paris, Cerf, 1968, 523–539, here 527. Quoted translation in Theobald, "The Church Under the Word of God," 356.

a clear line of demarcation between the Roman Catholic Church and the churches that emerged from the Reformation."[205] Edmund Schlink, also an official observer for the Lutherans, emphasized the possibilities the text offers for ecumenical dialogue, noting in particular the concomitance and proximity between the conciliar debate on tradition and the report of section two of the fourth world conference on Faith and Order held in Montreal in July 1963. He thus expressed his conviction that *Dei Verbum* would give Roman theology a biblical structure (Congar also said this), but immediately added: "It would be going too far, in my opinion, if one hoped that the constitution would produce essential transformations of certain central contents of the faith consciousness of Roman Catholicism."[206]

This reservation can be expressed in different ways. Someone like Cardinal Paul-Émile Léger insisted to the end on the difference between the apostolic tradition and the post-apostolic tradition in order to safeguard the transcendence of the Word of God in relation to the church and its post-apostolic tradition.[207] The same demand was formulated, in a critical manner, by Schlink.[208] Another way of formulating these reservations is found in the intervention of Cardinal Albert Gregory Meyer, who drew the attention of the council to "the limits and defects of the pilgrim church"[209] and asked that the critical function of the Scriptures be introduced into the text.[210] This was done at the beginning of the fourth period, but in a very attenuated fashion.[211]

As for the place of critical exegesis, which is decisive in the ecumenical questioning of the will of Christ *circa Ecclesiam*, the debates did not end with the preparatory phase. They crystalized in number 19 of chapter 4 of *Dei Verbum*, which discusses the historicity of the gospels. They continued until the reception of the last three *modi* of Paul VI on Oct 19, 1965.[212] While Skydsgaard

205 Kristen E.B. Skydsgaard, "Report No 5 of the Fourth Session of the Second Vatican Council" (Nov 19, 1965), ACO 7.24, 3–4.

206 Report of Edmund Schlink (summary by Micksey of reports 30 and 31), in: Konfessionskundliches Institut Bensheim, Evangelischer Bund Archive, E. Schlink. See also its further development, which was very nuanced, Edmund Schlink, "Écriture, tradition et magistère selon la constitution Dei verbum," in: Dupuy & others, *La Révélation divine*, vol. 2, 499–511, esp. 510–511.

207 See especially the intervention of Cardinal Léger on Oct 1, 1964, in: *AS* 3/3, 182–185; it came from the Montreal group (see Gilles Routhier, "L'itinéraire d'un Père conciliaire: Le Cardinal Léger," *CrSt* 19, 1998, 89–147, esp. 128–141), but its sentiment was equally shared by others who intervened, like, for example, Bishop Joannes van Dodewaard who reported on chapters 3–6 (*AS* 3/3, 229).

208 Schlink, "Écriture, tradition et magistère," 511: "The historical witness of the apostles and the early community is not clearly emphasized as constituting the pre-established normative 'vis-à-vis,' and because of this is critical of the contemporary Roman Church and the pope." The distinctions in *DV* 7 between the "inspiration," "prompting," and "help" of the Holy Spirit show a difference between the apostolic tradition and the Scriptures on the one hand, and "the tradition that continues in the church" on the other. No doubt it was difficult at that time to hold both the transcendence of the Word of God and the constant dialogue between God and the bride of his Son, defended by Bishop Volk and others.

209 *AS* 3/3, 150.

210 Here is the alternative formula proposed by Cardinal Meyer, in: *AS* 3/3, 151: "However, this living tradition does not always progress or grow in all of its elements. For when on her earthly journey the church contemplates what is divine, she can fail [*deficere*] and has indeed failed [*deficit*]. For this reason, she carries Sacred Scripture as a perpetual norm and, as it brings life to her, she corrects herself unceasingly and makes herself more perfect."

211 The version sent to the Fathers on Nov 20, 1964 still contained the following formula; see *AS* 3/3, 102 and *AS* 4/1, 371 and 375: "It is necessary, therefore, that all ecclesial preaching, as well as the Christian religion itself, should always refer to Sacred Scripture as their norm and the authority by which they are regulated and judged." The final version simply says, "all the preaching of the Church must be nourished and regulated by Sacred Scripture" (*DV* 21). See the same criticism, expressed by Joseph Ratzinger in his commentary on *Dei Verbum*, ²*LThK* 13, 515–528, esp. 524–525.

212 See Theobald, "The Church Under the Word of God," 350–353, and Peter Hünermann, "The Final Weeks of the Council," in: Alberigo & Komonchak, eds., *History of Vatican II*, vol. 5, 363–483, esp. 369–379.

remarks in his report that most bishops had a rather fundamentalist conception of the Bible, Schlink was rather admiring of the fact that the Catholic Church was the first among the churches to have said, in the field of critical hermeneutics, that the plurality of genres and forms of expression in the Scriptures has a properly dogmatic function. Without denying Skydsgaard's observation, one can add that the reception of the biblical chapters of *Dei Verbum* (chapters 3–6) in postconciliar Catholicism shows that, in the end, Schlink was right.

The critical remarks regarding the ambivalent conception of the faith in *Dei Verbum* have already been mentioned.[213] From an intertextual perspective, it should not be forgotten that the SPCU also bore full responsibility for the declaration on religious freedom *Dignitatis humanae*, which found its independence from *Unitatis redintegratio* at the Coordinating Commission's meeting of Apr 16, 1964.[214] It should also be remembered here that Visser 't Hooft had made it a prerequisite for ecumenical dialogue with the Catholic Church and that the SPCU's very first preparatory schema was precisely the one on religious freedom. The same ecumenical reasons for dealing with this issue were clearly indicated in the *relatio* presented by Bishop De Smedt on Nov 18, 1963.[215] It was necessary to take the other confessions' aversion to the Catholic Church's stance on this, even criticism of it as Machiavellian, into account. To a large extent, that state of mind resulted from the contradictory fact that, where the church was in the minority, it claimed freedom for itself, but denied it to other ecclesial communities in situations where it was the state religion.

It is not possible here to go into all the problems that this text posed with regard to the search for truth – "it leaves untouched traditional Catholic doctrine on the moral duty of men and societies toward the true religion and toward the one Church of Christ" (*DH* 1 § 4) – or the relationship between church and state. Any problems here are ecumenical problems because they are solved differently by the Orthodox churches and the Latin churches (Roman and Protestant). But it is the return to the principle of faith that must be addressed here.[216] The second part of *Dignitatis humanae* not only "reframes" the theology of faith of *Dei Verbum* (*DV* 5) but also creates a link with the relational perspective of point 7 of this constitution, which roots the tradition in the encounter (*modus conversationis*) between Jesus and the apostles. Certainly, the substance of these two texts is the same. But the focus of *Dignitatis humanae* (*DH* 10) on the freedom of the "act of faith" and the omission of the assent to doctrine reinforces the central axis of the relationship between God and person, and even integrates the idea of God's self-revelation in the act of faith, something that *DV* 5 does not do. This self-revelation, recalled at the beginning of point 11, is realized in the relational interplay between Jesus and his listeners, completing "on the cross the work of redemption whereby He achieved salvation and true freedom for men" (*DH* 11 § 2). The text adds: Christ "bore witness to the truth, but He refused to impose the truth by force on those who spoke against it." Here we have the most complete formulation of the *modus* of communication, based on a conformity between the evangelical truth and the manner of proposing it (*DH* 12 § 1 and 14 § 3), the *modus* or *via*, as Bishop De Smedt had defended it from the first period of the council.

The reactions, especially on the Protestant side, were mixed, as was the case during the bitter debates that almost brought the decree to an end.[217] The SPCU was accused of having been too

213 See *AS* 4/1, 345, *relatio* of n. 5 (B) and the address of Bishop Volk in: *AS* 3/3, 344–345.

214 See *AS* 5/2, 293 and 479–480.

215 See *AS* 2/5, 485–495, esp. 486 and Velati, *Dialogo e rinnovamento*, 600–611.

216 See the analysis in Theobald, *La réception du concile Vatican II*, vol. 1, 802–811.

217 See Gilles Routhier, "Finishing the Work Begun: The Trying Experience of the Fourth Period," in: Alberigo & Komonchak, eds., *History of Vatican II*, vol. 5, 49–184.

lenient in regard to the amendments of those opposing the schema.[218] This was undoubtedly the price to be paid for the passage of the text, which is marked by a series of ecumenical inconsistencies, such as the insistence on the doctrine of the Catholic magisterium of the time, not subject to the work of reinterpretation, as Bishop De Smedt demonstrated.[219] In order to introduce the missionary mandate given by Christ in Matt 28:19–20, therefore, the text affirmed from the outset, and without nuance, that – we believe – the "one true religion subsists in the Catholic and Apostolic Church, to which the Lord Jesus committed the duty of spreading *it* abroad among all men" (*DH* 1 § 2). The same affirmation is made towards the end of the declaration: "For the Church is, by the will of Christ, the teacher of the truth" (*DH* 14). This leads the text to redefine, once again, the function of the magisterium (see already *LG* 25 and *DV* 10), reintroducing here the distinction between "the truth which is Christ" and "those principles of the moral order which have their origins in human nature itself" (*DH* 14 § 3). It is, therefore, not surprising that – in the two parts of the declaration, entitled respectively "General Doctrine [*ratio*] on Religious Freedom" and "Religious Freedom in the Light of Revelation" – Protestant readers will find the classic Catholic distinction between natural theology and revealed theology.[220] Perhaps this judgment is unfair if one takes into account the theological-political aim of the text and its inductive approach toward the "roots … of the doctrine of freedom" (*DH* 9). On the other hand, we can understand their regret that the declaration remains so timid in recognizing the "way of acting that was hardly in accord with the spirit of the Gospel or even opposed to it" – an admission that is immediately counterbalanced by the affirmation of the continuity of the church's teaching (*DH* 12 § 1) – and that it does not speak of the freedom of Christians within the church. These points of view were shared by certain conciliar Fathers and *periti*.

4.2 *The Church's Relationship with the Jews*

One might ask why the text on the church's relationship to the Jews should be treated in the context of ecumenism. The significant history of the drafting of this text answers this question and also sheds light on the continuation of these sad relations. One must recall that, on Sep 18, 1961, Pope John XXIII asked Cardinal Bea and the SPCU to prepare a *Decretum de Iudaeis*.[221] From the preparatory phase, which began that way, to the promulgation of the declaration on the relation of the church to non-Christian religions *Nostra aetate*, on Oct 28, 1965, the council had traversed a "dramatic" path of conversion and discernment.[222]

At least four versions of the text can be distinguished. Conceived in 1961 by the SPCU, the *Decretum de Iudaeis* was proposed to the council assembly on November 1963 as chapter 4 of *Unitatis redintegratio* (with chapter 5 being on religious freedom).[223] Before this initial text (I) could be discussed and voted on,[224] a new, more restricted version (II) – this time in the form of an appendix to *Unitatis redintegratio* (*Declaratio altera*) – was sent to the council Fathers and discussed at the

218 See John Moorman, *Vatican Observed: An Anglican Impression of Vatican II*, London, Dartmon, Longman & Todd, 1967, 162.

219 *AS* 2/5, 485–495.

220 These section titles are not given in the English translation, but appear in the Latin text, as well as other translations. See Louis Joubert, "La Déclaration sur la liberté religieuse" and Albert Finet, "La Déclaration sur la liberté religieuse: Plaidoyer pour la 'liberté chrétienne,'" in: Bosc & others, *Points de vue de théologiens protestants*, 129–138, esp. 135 and 139–148, esp. 146.

221 See Velati, *Dialogo e rinnovamento*, 46–55, and ²*LThK* 13, 406–414.

222 Roman A. Siebenrock justly notes, in his commentary, that "the drama of the origins of the text has disappeared in the text itself," see Roman A. Siebenrock, "Theologischer Kommentar zur Erklärung über die Haltung der Kirche zu den nichtchristlichen Religionen," *HThK Vat.II* 3, 591–693, here 675.

223 Text I is found in: *AS* 2/5, 431–432 and the *relatio* of Cardinal Bea in: *AS* 2/5, 481–485 (69th general congregation).

224 See *AS* 2/5, 682.

beginning of the third period, in September 1964.[225] As no vote was taken, the text was once again endangered: the Coordinating Commission, which had already intervened in the drafting of version II,[226] tried to move it, this time to *Lumen gentium*, where it would appear as an appendix. Expanded to include other religions (according to the wishes of many of the Fathers), a third text (III)[227] was finally proposed on Nov 18, 1964 under this new conception[228] and submitted at the very end of the third period – surprisingly without discussion – to a vote. After difficult debates within the SPCU, a certain number of amendments were still introduced between the third and fourth sessions and proposed in October 1965 with the definitive text (IV),[229] now independent of any other attachment, for the assembly's assent.

Each time, Cardinal Bea justified the changes. On the first occasion, he insisted on the balance between, on the one hand, "an ecumenism in the strict sense that concerns only Christians" (which was dealt with in only three chapters of the decree) and, on the other hand, "the special bond between the church, the chosen people of the New Covenant, and the chosen people of the Old Covenant, a *bond* that is common to all Christians" (and this was therefore dealt with separately in the form of an appendix).[230] The second time, the ecumenical framework disappeared in favor of ecclesiology, *Lumen gentium* already being the "dogmatic" place where Judaism and other religions were dealt with and where a pastoral appendix could be better placed.[231] In 1965, when the declaration found its "independence" from an ecumenical ecclesiology, it was more within the sphere of *Dei Verbum* and its universalist conception of grace and revelation (see, in particular, *DV* 3).

Now, beneath the peaceful appearance of this consideration lies an extreme tension, because the two parts of *Nostra aetate*, numbers 1–3 dealing with non-Christian religions and number 4 dealing with Jewish-Christian relations, are not articulated at all. On this decisive point, the declaration that was finally adopted was a compromise that did not succeed in reconciling quite violent opposition within the council itself or in its societal resonance, especially in the West and Near East. On the one hand, there were those in Europe who remembered the Shoah and the responsibility of Christians. In his first *relatio* in 1963, Cardinal Bea did not hesitate to name anti-Semitism and the extermination of Jews in Germany under the Nazi regime, as well as the collusion of certain Christians with Nazi propaganda, as reasons for the council to deal with the question of the relationship with Jews.[232] On the other hand, there were those who, arguing from a strict conception of ecumenism, were opposed to this treatment within a decree on Christian unity or who even feared – as did the Eastern patriarchs, and not without reason – the negative effects of *De Iudaeis* on the Christians of the Near East.[233] The political pressures, from both the state of Israel and the Arab regimes, were very real indeed. That might explain, at least in part, the diplomatic hesitations and postponements imposed by the Coordinating Commission and its president, Cardinal Cicognani, who at the same time exercised the function of secretary of state. Despite Paul VI's courageous and promising

225 Text II is found in: *AS* 3/2, 327–329, and the *relatio* in: *AS* 3/2, 558–564.

226 See the *relatio* of Cardinal Bea in: *AS* 3/2, 561–562; see also the intervention of Bishop John Carmel Heenan, member of the SPCU, on the "inferences" without ecumenical sensitivity in the drafting of the text: *AS* 3/3, 37–39, esp. 39.

227 *AS* 3/8, 637–643.

228 The *relatio* of Cardinal Bea (*AS* 3/8, 649–651) justifies this move at length and relates it to the new title of the text: "On the Attitude *of the Church* in regard to Non-Christian," *AS* 3/8, 649 (italics original).

229 The definitive text is found in: *AS* 4/4, 690–696, the *relatio* in: *AS* 4/4, 697–722, and the fourth *relatio* of Cardinal Bea in: *AS* 4/4, 722–725.

230 *AS* 3/2, 562 (italics mine).

231 *AS* 3/8, 649.

232 *AS* 2/5, 483–484.

233 See the addresses of the five patriarchs during the general discussion: AS 2/5, 527–528; 541–542; 542–545; 557–558; 558–560.

trip to the Holy Land in January 1964, these oppositions became ever stronger.

This was seen in the surprising reaction of the Melkites at the time of the closure of the great debate on text II on Sep 29, 1964.[234] Their reaction, which was by no means isolated, was all the more astonishing since the 1964 debate on the *De Iudaeis* took place at the same time as that on the particular churches and the patriarchates, when the Melkites took the visionary position mentioned above. Compared to the Latins, they showed, in both cases, the same feeling of abandonment and combative self-defense, undoubtedly heightened by a long experience of suffering. This must be remembered over 50 years later, at a time during which the distressing fate of the churches of the Near East has rather worsened. Without realizing the terrible connection between anti-Semitism, the extermination of the Jews by the Nazi regime, and the founding of the State of Israel, the Melkites put their finger on a real problem, another line of demarcation or conflict: as if one could so simply separate theological questions from political ones!

This is not the place to analyze the declaration, whose limitations, and even ambiguities, were due in large part to the history just mentioned, and are sufficiently well known.[235] We shall content ourselves with simply noting the importance of the historical and exegetical work that made it possible for it to arrive at this result and to inscribe it in this very first sketch of a Christian theology of Judaism that, for its time, was quite remarkable. It can be found in Cardinal Bea's four *relationes*[236] and, above all, in the *Expensio modorum* of number 4.[237] In *modus* 82, we read that "the Secretariat for Promoting Christian Unity in no way intends to decide in what sense [*quonam sensu*] the Jewish people," according to the words of the dogmatic constitution *De Ecclesia* 16, remains "most dear to God" by election, "on account of their fathers."[238] This is a decisive "opening" that, in the history of the reception of the declaration, gave rise to great debates on what could be said, in a Christian theology of the Jewish people, about its positive position in the economy of salvation *post mortem Christi*.

From an ecumenical point of view,[239] it is particularly significant that number 4 of the declaration on the mystery of Israel refers exclusively to the Scriptures. The Reformed historian Fadiey Lovsky wrote:

> The reasons for the 1965 changes to the 1964 text on the Jews are contingent, however regrettable ... The starting point and the method are beyond criticism. This is a considerable event: that is why the Council's text has reformational value. That is why Protestants can recognize in it a message that is addressed to them as well and can thank the council for it.[240]

234 Edelby, *Souvenirs du concile Vatican II*, 269 (italics mine): "We take up and finish the declaration on Jews and non-Christians. This is, in general, a long plea in favor of the Jews. *The council has demonstrated, in its majority, to have more understanding for the Jews than for the non-Catholics*! One hardly hears two Latin bishops, one from Cameroon and one from Smyrna, praising Islam. Bishop Sfeir takes up this theme. Archbishop Tawil courageously asks the council fathers this question: why this special declaration for the Jews ... We are disgusted"; see also the notices on the 149th and 150th general congregations where the final amendments and the definitive text were voted on: "Not being able to bring down this draft declaration, we succeeded at least in rendering it inoffensive," Edelby, *Souvenirs du concile Vatican II*, 349–351, here 350.

235 See especially the historical works that relate both the attempts to bring down the text and the adjustments to allow it to pass, without succeeding in overcoming the resistance: Johannes Oesterreicher, "Kommentierende Einleitung," ²*LThK* 13, 406–478, esp. 458–474; Siebenrock, "Theologischer Kommentar zurErklärung," 633–643.

236 See AS 2/5, 481–485; AS 3/2, 558–564; AS 3/8, 649–651; AS 4/4, 722–725.

237 AS 4/4, 705–717.

238 AS 4/4, 715.

239 This is not the place to discuss the Jewish reaction.

240 Fadiey Lovsky, "La Déclaration sur les relations de l'Église avec les religions non chrétiennes," in: Bosc &

The reaction of Visser 't Hooft no doubt reflects that of many observers: "Anti-Semitism thus represents a denial of the Christian faith itself. The WCC tried to say this at its assembly in New Delhi in 1961. We are glad that all the churches are now seeking to inaugurate a new attitude towards the Jewish people and thus to begin to repair their many past mistakes."[241]

4.3 *Proclaiming the Gospel to All Creation*

If we remember that the first ecumenical conference in Edinburgh in 1910 dealt with mission and gave the delegates of the churches of other continents the opportunity to stigmatize the divisions among Christians as a major obstacle to the spread of the gospel, and if we remember that the prehistory of the decree *Unitatis redintegratio* goes back to a detailed analysis, by the newly instituted SPCU, of the link between unity and mission as conceived by the WCC,[242] we must be attentive to the ecumenical scope of the decree *Ad gentes*, promulgated in the last days of the council. This text, like *Unitatis redintegratio*, refers from the outset to "the holy cause of preaching the Gospel to every creature" (*UR* 1), referring simply to the leitmotif of the council, namely Mark 16:15. It is also a summary and a final rereading of the whole range of conciliar themes and insistences. *Unitatis redintegratio* is thus amply cited.

I have already provided the central, in a way programmatic, passage of the chapter on doctrinal principles (*AG* 6), which links the pastoral and ecumenical causes of the council to that of mission. Let us note four other occurrences. Chapter 2, which deals with the missionary beginnings of the church, addresses in its third article "Forming a Christian Community," and here recalls the "charity … between Catholics of different rites" and "the ecumenical spirit" which "should be nurtured in the neophytes":

> Insofar as religious conditions allow, ecumenical activity should be furthered in such a way that, excluding any appearance of indifference or confusion on the one hand, or of unhealthy rivalry on the other, Catholics should cooperate in a brotherly spirit with their separated brethren, according to the norms of the Decree on Ecumenism, making before the nations a common profession of faith, insofar as their beliefs are common, in God and in Jesus Christ, and cooperating in social and in technical projects as well as in cultural and religious ones. *Let them cooperate especially for the sake of Christ, their common Lord: let His Name be the bond that unites them!* This cooperation should be undertaken not only among private persons, but also, subject to approval by the local Ordinary, among churches or ecclesial communities and their works (*AG* 15 § 4).

The next number of the same article deals with the formation of seminarians in the spirit of ecumenism (*AG* 16 § 5). The last two passages are found in chapter 5 on "Planning Missionary Activity" (*AG* 29 § 4) and in chapter 6 on "Cooperation" (*AG* 36 § 2). They advocate "fraternal cooperation as well as harmonious living with the missionary undertaking of other Christian communities, that as far as possible the scandal of division may be removed."

With this final ecumenical word, the council thus united with the beginning of the movement of the same name. Having for the first time traversed the whole range of disputes starting from the church, in the fourth period it continued its

---

others, *Points de vue de théologiens protestants*, 149–169, here 168.

241 Olivier Rousseau, "Chronique de la IVe session du concile," *Irén* 38, 1965, 473–501, here 494, note 1.

242 See votum 2 drafted by Hamer, in: Velati, *Dialogo e rinnovamento*, 285: "b. To emphasize the intimate relationship that exists between unity and evangelization, according to the words of Christ (John 17:21) … c. To declare that the renewal efforts in the church are in no way intended to make the church stronger and more imposing in the eyes of the world but simply to make it more capable of carrying out, in the strength of the Holy Spirit, it humbler service of witness 'to the ends of the earth' (Acts 1:8)."

decentering movement and returned, on the one hand, to the principle of the Christian tradition, the Word of God, and, on the other hand, oriented itself towards its recipients. In this way, it introduced into its own Latin form the future potential for an ecumenical conversation.

5 Conclusions

Undoubtedly, the "leap forward" desired by John XXIII in his opening address of Oct 11, 1962 was achieved by Vatican II. This becomes even more apparent when we combine – according to an epistemological perspective possible today – a historical or genetic reading of the conciliar event, sensitive to the forces in play and in conflict, with an intertextual reading of the documents that is attentive to the progressive reframing of the texts, at work up until the last days of the council.

We can thus see the first formulation of what can be called an ecumenical "logic" or "grammar." A real paradigm shift was achieved through an unprecedented implementation of a collective intelligence within Roman Catholicism. The new paradigm consists in the displacement of the prevailing doctrinal system via the Catholic principles of ecumenism towards an evangelical *modus communicationis*. This *modus* inaugurated an open and permanent process of self-questioning and dialogue about the will of Christ *circa Ecclesiam*; it was a *modus* now borne, within Catholicism, by a new institution, that of the SPCU, whose permanence was already envisaged during the council's preparatory period.[243]

Certainly, at the end of the council, demarcations – both confessional and of a different nature – still existed and were even more visible. They were present throughout the entire work of Vatican II, and gradually became clearer and, in a way, exposed their principles: the initial demarcation between commissions or between what is doctrine and what is a matter for pastoral reflection; the boundary between the Orthodox churches and the Latin church, on the one hand, and between churches of the Latin tradition, Rome and the Protestant churches, on the other; the tension between attention to the "spiritual" relationship of the church to the Old Testament and to the Jewish people, as well as the condemnation of anti-Semitism, and the focus on the political stakes of this relationship; and, finally, the tension between the different ways of conceiving tradition.

These tensions, demarcations, or fissures within the conciliar corpus and the vision which it conveys in 1965 appeared in a more pronounced light. Would they or would they not be introduced into the new mode of self-questioning and dialogue proposed by the council to the churches, and would they be simultaneously placed before "the unfathomable riches of Christ" (Eph 3:8)? The future of ecumenism would depend on this. The tensions could then be able to be transformed into convergences within a differentiated and differentiating ecumenism grounded – according to *UR* 11 – on the imitation of the gospel (see Rom 12:10).

Translated from French to English by Susan Dawson Vásquez and David Dawson Vásquez.

243 The votes of subcommission XI "De permanentia secretariatus" were discussed during the fifth and sixth plenaries; see Velati, *Dialogo e rinnovamento*, 745–762 and 898–914.

Bibliography

Alberigo, Giuseppe & Joseph A. Komonchak, eds., *History of Vatican II*, 5 vols., Leuven/Maryknoll, Peeters/Orbis Books, 1995–2006.

Bosc, Jean & others, *Points de vue de théologiens protestants: Études sur les décrets du concile Vatican II*, Paris, Cerf, 1967.

Congar, Yves, *My Journal of the Council*, Collegeville MN, Liturgical Press, 2012.

Destivelle, Hyacinthe, *Conduis-la vers l'unité parfaite: Œcuménisme et synodalité*, Paris, Cerf, 2018.

Famerée, Joseph, *Ecclésiologie et oecuménisme: Recueil d'études*, Leuven, Peeters, 2017.

Fouilloux, Étienne, *Les catholiques et l'unité chrétienne du* XIXe *au* XXe *siècle: Itinéraires européens d'expression française*, Paris, Le Centurion, 1982.

Melloni, Alberto, *Papa Giovanni: Un cristiano e il suo concilio*, Turin, Einaudi, 2009.

Rahner, Karl, *Sämtliche Werke*, vol. 21/1, *Das zweite Vatikanum: Beiträge zum Konzil und seiner Interpretation*, Freiburg i.Br., Herder, 2013.

Theobald, Christoph, *La réception du concile Vatican* II, vol. 1, *Accéder à la source*, Paris, Cerf, 2009.

Theobald, Christoph, *La réception du concile Vatican* II, vol. 2/A, *L'Eglise dans l'histoire et la société: L'Évangile et l'Église*, Paris, Cerf, 2023.

Velati, Mauro, *Una difficile transizione: Il cattolicismo tra unionismo ed ecumenismo (1952–1964)*, Bologna, Il Mulino, 1996.

Velati, Mauro, *Separati ma fratelli: Gli osservatori non cattolici al Vaticano* II *(1962–1965)*, Bologna, Il Mulino, 2014.

CHAPTER 28

Bringing Ecumenism into the Postconciliar Period: The SPCU and the Ecumenical Directory (1965–1970)

Bruno Cherubini

1 Introduction

In December 1964, the council Fathers began leaving Rome to return to their home dioceses after the end of the general sessions of Vatican II. For many of them, it was a bittersweet departure. The previous weeks had witnessed the crowning of the dreams and efforts of a lifetime with the promulgation of historic documents such as *Lumen gentium* and *Unitatis redintegratio*, but several shadows had fallen over their achievements. The events of the so-called Black Week had challenged the relationship between pope and council and dampened some of the more courageous statements made by the latter. Above all, however, those events dramatically raised the question of the council's reception.[1] In fact, Paul VI's doubts about the results of Vatican II, and the growing influence on him by conservative and curial voices were brought to light. Once the council was over, the latter would be the only ones remaining in Rome, with an ability to influence the process of reception and thus, possibly, to gradually and silently dismantle the achievements of the council.

As far as *Unitatis redintegratio* was concerned, Paul VI's changes to the decree were more formal than substantial, but they confirmed the doubts, already present in ecumenical circles, that despite the obvious goodwill, the pope would not, or could not, fully understand the work carried out in recent years by the SPCU under Augustin Bea and Johannes Willebrands .[2] Before he was elected to St. Peter's throne, Giovanni Battista Montini had a traditionally unionist formation, tempered only by an attitude to dialogue that had led him, both during his years in Rome and his time in Milan, to initiate contact with the non-Catholic world, in particular with the Anglicans.[3] The new pope's attitude towards other Christian denominations, however, was traditional rather than that of an ecumenist. It should come as no surprise, therefore, that there was a substantial gap between his

1 The term Black Week designates that of Nov 14–21, 1964, during which Paul VI directly intervened in the drafting of certain conciliar schemas of great importance (*De Ecclesia, De libertate religiosa, De oecumenismo*), reintroducing into the text by authoritative *fiat* certain propositions held by the minority and rejected by the assembly in the previous years. See Louis Antonio Tagle, "The 'Black Week' of Vatican II (November 14–21, 1964)," in: Giuseppe Alberigo & Joseph A. Komonchak, eds., *History of Vatican II*, vol. 4, *Church as Communion: Third Period and Intersession (September 1964–September 1965)*, Leuven/Maryknoll, Peeters/Orbis Books, 2004, 338–452, esp. 406–417. See also Jan Grootaers, "Le crayon rouge de Paul VI: Les interventions du pape dans le travail des commissions conciliaires," in: Mathijs Lamberigts, Claude Soetens & Jan Grootaers, eds., *Les commissions conciliaires à Vatican II*, Leuven, Bibliotheek van de Faculteit Godgeleerdheid, 1996, 317–351; Pierre Duprey, "Paul VI et le décret sur l'œcuménisme," in: *Paolo VI e i problemi ecclesiologici al concilio: Colloquio internazionale di studio (Brescia 19–20–21 settembre 1986)*, Brescia, Istituto Paolo VI, 225–258, and Mauro Velati, "L'ecumenismo al concilio: Paolo VI e l'approvazione di *Unitatis redintegratio*," *CrSt* 27/2, 2005, 427–476, esp. 427–456.

2 Vischer commented in a similar way on the historic encounter with Paul VI in 1964, addressing Willebrands, who could only share his doubts. See Mauro Velati, *Separati ma fratelli: Gli osservatori non cattolici al Vaticano II (1962–1965)*, Bologna, Il Mulino, 436–439, esp. 438. Regarding the SPCU and its activity during the council, see the contributions by Mauro Velati; Christoph Theobald; and Peter De Mey and Saretta Marotta in this volume.

3 See Howard Root, "Montini and Anglicans: 1955–1966," in: *Paolo VI e i problemi ecclesiologici al concilio*, 268–272.

perspective and the experiences and programs of an organization whose members, starting with Willebrands, had dedicated their entire lives to Christian unity. For Montini, the years of the council had signified a profound experience of opening himself up to an awareness of the ecumenical question. Yet this very gap, together with the unprecedented (and perhaps unexpected) authoritarianism demonstrated during the Black Week, represented a major concern for the SPCU.

The work of the commission, therefore, could not come to an end with that of Vatican II. The idea of postconciliar existence of the commission was by no means new, as it had been present since the very first discussions in the SPCU, but there had never been any illusion thatthis would be simple. Its work had been constantly hindered by the very circles that were now awaiting the end of the council in order to take hold of the reins of the church again. Paul VI's haste to close the council as soon as possible had become almost proverbial by the beginning of 1965. The SPCU had therefore only a few months in which to ensure a survival suitable for its mission, and Bea and Willebrands found themselves fighting a battle on several fronts during this intersessional period. On the one hand, they had to complete their conciliar tasks, now represented by the drafting of the two controversial schemas *De Iudaeis* and *De libertate religiosa*. On the other, they had to succeed in carving out an institutional role for themselves in the curia that would allow adequate autonomy and responsibility for the SPCU. Finally, they had to use this autonomy and responsibility in order to ensure that the process of reception would remain faithful to the council.

2 Postconciliar Projects: The Ecumenical Directory

In early 1965, it should be noted, it was less a question of whether the SPCU would survive than of how it would do so. In describing church dialogue as tripartite – towards non-Catholics, non-Christians, and non-believers – in his first programmatic acts, the pontiff had, in fact, established ecumenism as the first of the founding pillars of his pontificate.[4] The SPCU, in the few years of its existence, had already demonstrated its extreme effectiveness, and not just that. It had established a dense network of official and unofficial relationships with the other Christian churches and with the ecumenical movement. This had afforded Bea, Willebrands, and the other members of the commission an experience that was completely unheard of in the Roman curia, and had also allowed them to gain the trust of their dialogue partners, which essentially made them irreplaceable. For this reason, long before the council's end began to loom heavily on the horizon, the SPCU was already involved in projects that went well beyond the Vatican assembly: I need only mention, by way of an example, the formation of the ecumenical and interconfessional dialogues, already in their first stages as early as April 1964.[5]

There remained, however, the problem of the SPCU's responsibilities *ad intra*, that is, the problem concerning the reception of *Unitatis redintegratio*. While a clash with the Holy Office of prosecretary Alfredo Ottaviani began to emerge immediately, the commission embarked on a plan that would have naturally brought the issue under its responsibility. Hence, during the plenary meetings of March 1965, the members of the SPCU approved the idea of drafting an Ecumenical Directory for the application of the ecumenical decree.[6]

4 See Paul VI, *Ecclesiam suam*, in: AAS 56, 1964, 609–659.

5 This refers to the Milan meeting of April 1964. See Mauro Velati, *Una difficile transizione: Il cattolicesimo tra unionismo ed ecumenismo (1952–1964)*, Bologna, Il Mulino, 1996, 439–445.

6 This was not the only extra and postconciliar project of the SPCU with similar characteristics: think, for example, of the question of the ecumenical translation of the Bible or of mixed marriages. However, this was certainly the one that best encapsulated all the problems represented by this phase of Vatican II. See Mauro Velati, "Il Segretariato per l'unità dei cristiani tra centro e periferia (1960–1975),"

Where did the idea come from? Already in the summer of 1961, the SPCU had prepared a general outline for a document, called a "Directory," which was very similar in tone and purpose to a curial instruction. The inspiration probably came from some liturgical *directoires* that had circulated in France in the 1950s.[7] The project had been abandoned but, by the second session, some of the Fathers had begun to ask that the ecumenical decree's promulgation be accompanied by a Directory defining those disciplinary questions that *Unitatis redintegratio*, by its nature, could not address. The idea was much appreciated, and similar requests were made for almost all the schemas under discussion. One cannot help noticing, however, that the first requests in this sense came from members of the conservative minority who spoke of a Directory that was "approved by the Holy See" as the only way to stem the risk of indifferentism.[8]

On Nov 25, 1963, the SPCU also officially expressed itself on the matter in an address by Cardinal Bea. The Jesuit gave assurances that the future Directory would serve as a protection against the dangers of a false ecumenism but, at the same time, would provide the bishops with the necessary tools to apply *Unitatis redintegratio* in their dioceses. Only the local ordinaries, not Rome, had the necessary familiarity with the situation at the local level.[9] The difference between the minority's request and Bea's promises could not have been clearer: in spite of the initial, diplomatic mention of the dangers of a false ecumenism, it is clear that the SPCU's project reflected a completely different idea of the postconciliar period. While the minority, as early as the second session, was thinking of a way to contain unwelcome results of the council through curial channels, the SPCU, as an expression of the majority, was instead trying to find a way to make the council flow into the ordinary practices of church governance. The insistence on the role of the local churches bishops, which was only superficially similar to the indications in the *Instructio De motione oecumenica* of 1949, clearly put the ecclesiological recovery of the *communio ecclesiarum* that was simultaneously taking place in the discussion on *De Ecclesia* on the table.

3 First Steps, First Obstacles

During 1963 and 1964, the Directory almost completely disappeared from the council's agenda. On the other hand, once the general outlines of what it should be were established, it was necessary to wait for the promulgation of *Unitatis redintegratio* to even begin imagining its actual content. The first opportunity to do so was on Mar 4, 1965, during the meeting of a subcommittee of the SPCU's plenary session.[10] In his opening address on Mar 1, Bea had mentioned the fact that the drafting of

in: *Paolo VI e l'ecumenismo: Colloquio internazionale di studio (Brescia, 25–26–27 settembre 1998)*, Brescia, Istituto Paolo VI, 167–196; Mauro Velati, "Bibbia ed ecumenismo: L'azione del Segretariato per l'unità (1963–1970)," in: Luca Ferracci, ed., *Toward a History of the Desire for Christian Unity: Preliminary Research Papers*, Münster, LIT, 2015, 201–220.

7 See Mauro Velati, *Dialogo e rinnovamento: Verbali e testi del Segretariato per l'unità dei cristiani nella preparazione del concilio Vaticano II (1960–1962)*, Bologna, Il Mulino, 2011, 790–815, esp. 811.

8 See *AS* 2/6, 340.

9 About a month later, Bea returned to the subject, reiterating that the Directory would address those questions that were too specific to be included in a conciliar document and that the bishops would have a central role in its application. See *AS* 2/6, 15 and 365. In the same period, Joseph-Marie-Eugène Martin also addressed the issue, reiterating the same concepts, see *AS* 2/5, 476.

10 Based on the surviving documentation, it seems that the Directory had not even been discussed at the preparatory meeting of the periti, called a "consulta." In reality, Willebrands, in a reconstruction a few years later, spoke of the Directory as resulting from "some surveys" carried out among the Fathers of the SPCU in March 1965. It is not clear whether with this expression he intended the discussion during the plenary session or other forms of less formalized consultations. We can, however, affirm with some certainty that this was the first official meeting devoted to the project. See Johannes Willebrands, "Introduction à la discussion du Project de Directorium de re Oecumenica," Jun 7, 1966, in: UCL-LG, Gustave Thils, papiers, 1022.

an Ecumenical Directory, "aut directorii," would be discussed.[11] The president's mention of multiple directories suggests that the idea of radically entrusting the matter to the *communio ecclesiarum* was still circulating: not a single, universal Roman Directory, but various directories under the responsibility of local authorities. The local dimension, after all, informed most of the ecumenical experiences of the Fathers present at the discussion, precisely because of the way Catholic ecumenism had developed during the preconciliar period.

It is not possible to reconstruct the discussion completely from the sparse accounts that remain of the meeting, but, from its results, it can be gathered that, at least for the moment, the idea of several local directories was set aside, or at least it was decided to concentrate the SPCU's energies primarily on a universal Directory. The following day, the Fathers approved a questionnaire that would be sent to the SPCU members, posing nine questions that were to guide the selection of themes to be included in the future Directory. Having approved the resolutions and concluded the meeting, all that was missing was the pope's official approval for the project, which was granted during an audience with Cardinal Bea on Apr 24.[12]

3.1 *The* Animadversiones circa directorium de motu oecumenico

The instrument of episcopal consultation was, and still is, a classic tool of governance in the Roman curia. While traditionally it had been above all a way in which the congregations shaped and instrumentalized consensus among the bishops, Vatican II allowed a more genuine use of the instrument to develop. The SPCU had adopted the practice, but the questionnaire on the Directory was different. In fact, it had been designed for a project that did not strictly concern a conciliar schema. This opened the possibility, for the first time, to address the episcopate *extra concilio*. Mentioning the Directory, Yves Marie-Joseph Congar recorded in his journal entry of May 3: "Willebrands would like to be able to proceed to a rather wide consultation. To have the authority to do this he had sought the authorisation of the Pope, because the Secretariat is at present only an organisation linked to the Council: one would need to be assured that some other organism would not consider itself more suitable."[13]

Entrusted with the task of drafting an extraconciliar document, the SPCU thus found itself without the sufficient authority – at least formally – to do so, and several "competitors" claimed the same role for themselves. Willebrands's desire for a "broad consultation" reflected the need to project it beyond the council as soon as possible, in order to legitimize its position even further than the increasingly narrow framework of Vatican II at the time. Paul VI momentarily denied authorization, but then requested that the questionnaire also be sent to "competent entities and people."[14] In addition to its own members, therefore, the SPCU also sent the questionnaire to various "friends" and collaborators (such as Congar himself) and to the existing ecumenical commissions. While the pontiff's decision clearly served to avoid exacerbating conflicts between the SPCU and the other commissions and related congregations, the pope also seemed to share Willebrands' concerns about the need for as broad a base as possible on which to found the Directory. This was not just a matter of form or legitimacy, however. Involving the church in its entirety meant that it also had to be part of the drafting phase of the Directory, which otherwise would be little more than just another Roman instruction, despite its focus on the local churches. For the time being, however, the project remained in Willebrands' purview.

11 "Sessiones Secretariatus: 1 März 1965: Prolusio," Mar 1, 1965, in: AAV, Carte Bea, box 10, folder "1965. Sessiones Secret," 2.

12 Willebrands, "Introduction à la discussion," 1.

13 Yves Congar, *My Journal of the Council*, Collegeville MN, Liturgical Press, 2012, 754.

14 Willebrands, "Introduction à la discussion," 1.

During the first days of May, the SPCU gathered the responses that had arrived in Rome and organized them in a voluminous dossier entitled *Animadversiones circa directorio de motu oecumenico*.[15] It was divided into nine sections: the first two concerning the state of ecumenism at the local level and the ecumenical commissions, the third conditional Baptism, the fourth the formula of abjuration, the fifth and sixth prayers for unity and *communicatio in sacris* and *in spiritualibus*, the seventh relations with the Orthodox. Finally, the last two permitted the Fathers to make their own proposals, particularly on the subject of ecumenical dialogues.

The *Animadversiones* showed a very fragmented and incomplete panorama of Catholic ecumenism in the twilight of the council, partly because of the very diverse backgrounds of those questioned. While some sections – especially the first four – are extremely rich in perspectives and suggestions, evidently due to the interest in them on the part of the ecumenical movement in the preceding years,[16] others betray a certain embarrassment. Consider, for example, the questions on *communicatio in sacris* and *in spiritualibus* in which the tension between ecumenical desires, Roman directives, and more or less local practices had created a situation that was still blocked but which, as would soon become clear, was ready to explode.

3.2 *The First Draft of the Ecumenical Directory*

As planned between March and April, the *Animadversiones* were to serve as the basis for drafting a first version of the Directory, which took place during the May plenary. As for the plenary discussion, the accounts that remain of it testify that the main concern continued to be the question of the role of the local churches in the reception of the decree.[17] Emiel-Jozef De Smedt,

15 The document to which this refers is *Animadversiones circa directorium de motu oecumenico*, in: UCL-LG, Charles Moeller, papiers, 2124–2133.

16 Take, for example, the question of conditional baptism. Already recognized as a major problem in the context of interconfessional relations for some time, it was one of the recurring themes in the local interconfessional agreements (the *Animadversiones* cite, for example, the directives of Bishop Marius Besson of Lausanne-Geneva-Fribourg, dating back to the 1930s). Between the end of the 1950s and the beginning of the 1960s, it was the object of debate in the pages of *Una Sancta*, with the contributions of various Lutheran and Catholic theologians, including Frans Thijssen. The responses of the *Animadversiones* reveal the great success the articles published in the journal *Parole et Mission* had had, especially in the French-speaking world. These articles were taken up first by the French episcopate to draw up some provisional directives on the recognition of non-Catholic baptism and then by the *Animadversiones* themselves as a possible source for the Directory. See Hans Asmussen, "Fünf Fragen an die Katholische Kirche," *Una Sancta* 11/2, 1956, 127–130; Frans Thijssen, "Sakrament und Amt bei den Nichtkatholischen Christen: Versuch einer Antwort auf die fünf Fragen von D. Hans Asmussen DD," *Una Sancta* 14/1–2, 1959, 82–108; Hans Asmussen, "Das 'Offenbare' und das 'Verbogene' (Antwort an den Bruder Franz Thijssen)," *Una Sancta* 14/3, 1959, 187–197 esp. 184–194; Frans Haarsma, "Die Gültigkeit der Taufe in nicht-katholischen Kirchen," *Una Sancta* 17/3–4, 1962, 181–187; Bernard-Dominique Dupuy & Robert Clément, "Qui est baptisé et qui ne l'est pas?," *Parole et Mission* 11, 1960, 569–591, esp. 570–571; Joseph Hoffmann, "L'Église veut-elle le rebaptême des non-catholiques?," *Parole et Mission* 22, 1963, 419–441, esp. 426–427.

17 For the documentation on this plenary session, see "Monday, morning 09:00," May 10, 1965, in: AAV, Conc. Vat. II, box 1431, folder 1 "Plenarie: Corrispondenza – Appunti," s.f. 4 "Plenaria: 9–14 maggio 1965 – Appunti"; "Lundi 10 mai 1965," May 10, 1965, in: AAV, Conc. Vat. II, box 1431, folder 1 "Plenarie: Corrispondenza – Appunti," s.f. 4 "Plenaria: 9–14 maggio 1965 – Appunti." The Moeller fond contains a handwritten note on the May 10 meeting, in: UCL-LG, Charles Moeller, papiers, 3552, but it breaks off before the discussion of the Directory; "Reunion – Directorium," [n.d.], in: UCL-LG, Charles Moeller, papiers, 2116, contains a handwritten transcription by Moeller of the May 11 discussion, and the beginning of the transcription of the May 12 meeting. For Willebrands's notes on the proceedings of the entire plenary, see also "Appunti," [multiple dates], in: AAV, Conc. Vat. II, box 1431, folder 1 "Plenarie: Corrispondenza – Appunti," s.f. 4 "Plenaria: 9–14 maggio 1965 – Appunti," and for the May 11 discussion, see esp. 7–8. Willebrands's agendas help

for example, called for the document to consist of rigid and precise directives so that the bishops could operate without error in such a difficult environment. John Carmel Heenan returned to the proposal of different directories for the different local contexts, but Cardinal Bea was adamant in affirming that the SPCU should be the final point of reference for local authorities: "Praeses conf[erentiae] Episcopalis ad nos referat."[18]

In reference to this meeting, Congar wrote in his diary, "Extremely serious work. No verbosity. When I consider what Catholic ecumenism is today, at the summit, I am astounded. It is fantastic! THE STEP HAS BEEN TAKEN!"[19] After the frustrations of 1964, the steps forward permitted by *Unitatis redintegratio* began to become concrete facts, which a pioneer of ecumenism such as Congar could finally see realized. Not only did the mission of a lifetime for him and others like him seem to be destined for a happy conclusion, but it had all occurred in the space of very few months.

On May 14, the first draft of the Ecumenical Directory was ready. It consisted of six chapters: "De commissionibus oecumenicis instituendis"; "De baptismi validitate a ministris ecclesiarum et ecclesialum communitatum a nobis seiunctarum collati"; "De professione fidei," "Precationes pro unitate christianorum"; "De communicatione in sacris"; and "De conversatione ecclesiastica cum fratribus orthodoxis." One of the most remarkable aspects of this first draft was undoubtedly the first chapter, which worked on planning a network of diocesan and "territorial" commissions having the function of coordinating and supervising local ecumenical activities, at the center of which was the SPCU. The commissions, therefore, acted as intermediaries between the ecumenical impulses "from below" and the SPCU in Rome. The following chapters were structured in a similar way. Each chapter tried to implement some points from *Unitatis redintegratio* (recognition of the baptism of separated brethren, the possibility of *communicatio in sacris*, the "special relationship" with the Orthodox), contextualizing it in contemporary doctrine and canon law but, above all, attempting to encourage the local churches as much as possible to find the most suitable forms and ways of application. This was especially clear, for example, in the chapter "Precationes pro unitate christianorum," which consisted of only a few concrete indications as to how occasions of prayer shared with non-Catholics could (and should) be conducted, concerning for example, the location, the vestments, the type of prayers etc. Needless to say, because of the very nature of the document, disciplinary indications could not be overlooked, and it is not surprising that they were mainly found in the chapter on *communicatio in sacris*. Hence, at this point, the spirit of openness to the local churches' contribution was far less developed than elsewhere, giving way instead to a much more traditional approach. However, the drafting was entirely provisional, particularly with regard to this subject.[20] Approval in the plenary session did not mean that the document was ready, but rather that it was sufficiently developed to be discussed again at the next plenary session scheduled for the autumn.

establish the chronological succession of the meetings of the SPCU, see Leo Declerck, ed., *Les agendas conciliaires de Mgr J. Willebrands, secrétaire du Secrétariat pour l'unité des chrétiens*, Leuven, Peeters, 2009, 179–182. *Directorium Oecumenicum*, May 14, 1965, in: UCL-LG, Gustave Thils, papiers, 940. UCL-LG, Gustave Thils, papiers, 953 contains the final draft of May 1965; UCL-LG, Charles Moeller, papiers, 2111–2122 instead contains the different drafts of the same month.

18 "Appunti," 7.

19 Congar, *My Journal of the Council*, 766 (capitals in the text).

20 According to Willebrands, a meeting on the theme of *oratio communis* and ecumenical dialogue, or on *communicatio in sacris*, as reported by Maxim Hermaniuk, was held on May 15. The fact that a meeting took place the day after the official draft of the text clearly indicates how it was immediately conceived as provisional. See Declerck, ed., *Les agendas conciliaires de Mgr J. Willebrands*, 182; see also *The Second Vatican Council Diaries of Met. Maxim Hermaniuk C.SS.R. (1960–1965)*, Leuven, Peeters, 2012, 238.

3.3 *Surviving the Summer*

As the end of the council drew near, the SPCU was not alone in moving toward the postconciliar period. With the creation of the Consilium ad exsequendam Constitutionem de Sacra Liturgia for the liturgical reform and the secretariats for non-Christians and non-believers, Paul VI had already begun to design an institutional structure dedicated to implementing the reception of Vatican II. Its contours, however, remained poorly defined. During the summer of 1965, the pro-secretary of the Holy Office Ottaviani, through a letter to the council secretary Pericle Felici, sought to test the waters in regard to the drafting of a Directory for the application of *Unitatis redintegratio*. Both cardinals, prominent members of the minority, had distinguished themselves during the years of Vatican II for their opposition to the SPCU and its projects. Ottaviani was thus trying to obtain support from within the central offices of the council in order to take control of the reception of the ecumenical decree. Felici replied that there were no other similar projects at the time and that, generally, the reception of conciliar documents was the business of the corresponding curial congregation, implying, therefore, that in the case of the ecumenical decree this was the Holy Office.[21]

It is very difficult to believe that Felici could truly have been unaware of the fact that an Ecumenical Directory had already been in the works since at least March. Instead, it seems rather likely that this forgetfulness was intentional. During that period, relations between Bea, Felici, and Ottaviani were particularly tense.[22] Two months later, on Aug 27, Bea's office received a letter from the Secretariat of State, signed by Angelo Dell'Acqua.[23] With it, the SPCU was officially instructed to draw up a "directory for the ecumenical apostolate,"[24] which would be submitted for approval to the council's Theological Commission and to the Secretariat of State. The SPCU was also urged to provide for its drafting as soon as possible. The two indications had rather important implications. In fact, after the unofficial green light given in April, Paul VI had formally entrusted the task of drafting the Directory to the SPCU, which kept it within conciliar procedures. In asking that it be done quickly, the pope also seemed to hope that, by being approved before the council closed, it would remain a Vatican II document, as far removed as possible from curial influences. This was hardly a remote danger, as Ottaviani's interests a few weeks earlier had demonstrated, but it became even more concrete at the beginning of September, when the cardinal requested in writing that Bea submit the Directory to the Holy Office for its final approval.[25] As Velati

21 P. Felici to A. Ottaviani, Jul 20, 1965, in: *AS* 6/4, 361. Ottaviani's request can be found in A. Ottaviani to P. Felici, Jul 9, 1965, in: *AS* 6/4, 346–347.

22 In addition to the issues related to the Directory and those linked to the schemas on non-Christians and religious freedom, the clash on mixed marriages was also looming on the horizon. The council had entrusted the issue to Paul VI, who was to prepare a motu proprio based on the discussions held in the assembly. Work had begun without the direct involvement of the SPCU; for this reason Bea asked Felici in June that the commission be informed of the work, but he received a negative response. See A. Bea to P. Felici, Jun 25, 1965, in: *AS* 6/4, 332; the response of Jul 2, 1965, in: *AS* 6/4, 342. However, the SPCU still counted on pontifical protection. In that period, Congar wrote in his diary: "The Holy Office had said to Willebrands: tell Cardinal Bea that he can no longer speak as Fr Bea. He cannot go on speaking, as he does, about brothers and a common home. – Willebrands replied: Tell that to the Pope! He's the one who speaks like that"; Congar, *My Journal of the Council*, 772.

23 No trace of the letter remains in the consulted archives. The evidence of its existence and content is to be found in different sources: from Willebrands's reconstruction of the stages of the Directory in 1966, from the citations made during the September plenary, and from the registry of the correspondence of the SPCU. See "Prot. 1667," in: *Protocollo – Corrispondenza in arrivo, Dicembre 1964 – gennaio/giugno 1966*, 3, in: AAV, Conc. Vat. II, box 1423; Willebrands, "Introduction à la discussion," 1; "Sessiones Secretariatus. Mense Sept. Prolusio," Sep 15, 1965, in: AAV, Carte Bea, box 10, folder "1965. Sessiones Secret."

24 Willebrands, "Introduction à la discussion," 1.

25 Willebrands, "Introduction à la discussion."

notes,[26] this request implied a deviation from the ordinary editing practice for conciliar documents. Ottaviani was attempting to distance the Directory from the control of the council and the SPCU. In this sense, Dell'Acqua's letter was providential (probably not by accident) because it provided Bea with the necessary authority to reject Ottaviani's request: by Paul VI's own will, the Directory would remain the business of the SPCU.

3.4 *The Second Draft:* Communicatio in Sacris

Having ensured its competence over the drafting, the SPCU could return to working on the Directory. In the following two months, it drew up the Directory's second draft, finishing its work on Nov 20.[27] The knot that needed untangling was the *communicatio in sacris* with Protestants. The Fathers undertook a revision of the paragraphs of the May version in order to bring them more in line with the ecclesiology of *Unitatis redintegratio*. The earlier version had stated that, where communion did not exist, *participatio sacramentalis* with separated brethren was not possible; therefore, since there was no communion with Protestants, sharing in the sacraments with them was, in fact, impossible. While the May text affirmed this principle in a fairly clear-cut manner, in the second draft, the Fathers emphasized the existence of different degrees of communion with Rome and attempted to define with greater precision the exceptional cases when *communicatio* was permissible.

This was developed in two paragraphs, which can be found in two different versions of the text, one of which was even presented to the non-Catholic observers and the Joint Working Group in November.[28] However, they had disappeared from the text that was delivered to the Theological Commission and the Secretariat of State. Since we do not have sources that might reveal the SPCU's internal discussions, it is not possible to say with certainty what prompted the members to remove these two paragraphs. The persistence of meetings on this subject in the SPCU's working calendar suggests that it had also been difficult to reach an internal agreement. Attempting to define more clearly what these exceptional cases might be may have seemed too challenging or too controversial. Perhaps it was feared that going into too much detail about particular circumstances might ultimately inhibit the local churches' ability to interpret the Directory's norms with the necessary autonomy.[29] The SPCU was content to settle for listing some very general principles which, moreover, were not very problematic. Certainly, the SPCU found itself having to maneuver within very narrow margins given the gravity of the topic, especially with the prospect of an examination by a hostile Theological Commission just over the horizon.

26 Velati, "Il Segretariato per l'unità dei cristiani tra centro e periferia," 172.

27 Declerck, ed., *Les agendas conciliaires de Mgr J. Willebrands*, 261, and Willebrands, "Introduction à la discussion," 2, give slightly different dates.

28 The meetings with the separated brethren bore no particular fruit, other than some criticisms of the regressive character of a few of the propositions (especially regarding conditional baptism). The general impression one gets is that there was a certain frustration on the part of the SPCU's non-Catholic collaborators, due no doubt to their being tired at the end of the council and to the perceived timidity of Bea's commission. See Velati, *Separati ma fratelli*, 609–611. Regarding the Joint Working Group, see the contribution by Michael Quisinsky in this volume.

29 A brief, handwritten note by Gustave Thils on the minutes of the Theological Commission's meeting that was to discuss the Directory seems to suggest that even the indication to abandon the discussion on *communicatio* with Protestants had come to Bea from Felici (or from the secretary of state Angelo Dell'Acqua). However, the note is decidedly difficult to interpret and there is no similar reference either in the notes of Charles Moeller or in the "diaries" of Sebastiaan Tromp or Felici. A letter dated Oct 13, 1965 from Dell'Acqua "regarding directory" is reported in the SPCU's correspondence register, but is not cited in any other source. See, Gustave Thils, "Examen des Directoire œcuménique par la Comm. Theol. les 29/11, 30/11, 1/12 1965," [n.d.], in: UCL-LG, Gustave Thils, papiers, 980, 1; "Prot. 1989," inside *Protocollo – Corrispondenza in arrivo*.

3.5 *Supervising the Council's Reception*

Between Nov 29 and Dec 1, the Theological Commission met to discuss the Directory.[30] It is immediately evident that an attempt was made to propose, once again, some of the topics and watchwords that the council had largely rejected in previous years but which the minority continued to try to impose behind the assembly's back. For the most part, in these cases, modifications were suggested that sought to restrict the ecumenical openness of the Directory, without however intervening deeply in its structure.[31] Some, such as Carlo Colombo[32] or the canonist Sebastiaan Tromp, showed instead that they had a more general vision. It was precisely Tromp who compiled the report to be sent to the SPCU in which the individual observations made by the Fathers of the commission assumed broad, at times even exaggerated, proportions.[33] The observations on local directives, for example, became a criticism of the Directory's eurocentrism. Discussing *communicatio in sacris*, the Theological Commission had much to say about the chapter's general structure. It criticized the very idea that *communicatio* was practicable or, in the case of Protestants, even possible. Notwithstanding the elimination of the two paragraphs on exceptional cases, it was precisely the ambiguity of the one on Protestants that aroused perplexities in the commission.

These two points among the otherwise varying criticisms made by the Theological Commission bring out two main aspects. Beyond certain polemical exaggerations in discussing the local dimensions of the Directory, the most interesting point was the desire to identify the bishops' conferences as the local churches' natural point of reference concerning ecumenical issues. This was not a surprising approach and must have seemed the inevitable collegial evolution of the principles of the 1949 instruction. In fact, it was no coincidence that similar comments had initially come from Bea as well. Albert Prignon, however, testifies to how the news that the Theological Commission was discussing entrusting the drafting of local directories to the bishops' conferences had caused a very concerned reaction from the SPCU.[34] In the two years that had passed since the president's

30 Thils, "Examen des Directoire œcumenique."

31 An example of the criticism of one of the paragraphs of the Directory in the chapter on *communicatio in sacris* concerns the mention of the "common faith." The Fathers of the commission suggested that the expression be replaced by "Catholic faith" or "true (Catholic) faith." There were also other cases, as in the proposal to replace the expression "iusta (de) causa" with "gravi (de) causa" (Thils, "Examen des Directoire œcuménique," 15–16). While Congar, commenting on the discussion concerning the Directory during the SPCU's plenary wrote "a step has been taken!" Albert Prignon, in his diary, noted: "We found ourselves as in the worst days of 1963, when we began to discuss the outline on ecumenism"; Albert Prignon, *Journal conciliaire de la 4e Session*, eds. Leo Declerck & André Haquin, Louvain-la-Neuve, Publication de la Faculté de Théologie, 2003, 253.

32 The presence at the meeting of Carlo Colombo, the pope's "personal theologian," should be noted. He had taken, especially in that period, to participating directly in the Theological Commission's work. If his mere presence is not enough to demonstrate the pope's direct and personal interest in the drafting of the Directory, due to the commission's simultaneous work on *Dignitatis humanae*, it can be said with certainty that the pontiff would at least have been informed *a posteriori*. See Jan Grootaers, *Actes et acteurs à Vatican II*, Leuven, Leuven University Press, 1998, 287–300; Franco G. Brambilla, "Carlo Colombo e G.B. Montini alle sorgenti del concilio," in: Luciano Vaccaro, ed., *Monsignor Carlo Colombo (1909–1991)*, Brescia, Morcelliana, 2003, 93–136.

33 See Sebastiaan Tromp, "Relatio actorum in Commissione Doctrinali (29–30 Nov. et 1 Dec. 1965) circa Directorium de re oecumenica," Dec 18, 1965, in: UCL-LG, Charles Moeller, papiers, 2136; See also M.-L. Ferrari, *I diari del padre Tromp, Segretario della Commissione Dottrinale al Concilio Ecumenico Vaticano II*, Master's thesis, Università degli Studi di Modena e Reggio Emilia, 2004/2005, 373ff.

34 "The Theological Commission met again to discuss the ecumenical directory. I was not there and I have not heard any news yet. In any case, practically speaking, the directory will not come out as it is now. If I understand correctly, it will be published in two stages: a more general one that holds for all and another which will be left variable according to regions and countries, at the discretion of the bishops' conferences. The Secretariat held a very lively meeting on the subject this

first statements much had changed, and the SPCU found itself with a much more complicated task than might perhaps have been imagined in 1963. The unraveling of events related to reception had made it clear that recourse to *communio ecclesiarum* now had to find a delicate balance, with the affirmation of the SPCU itself as the central and final authority on Catholic ecumenism. The Theological Commission, in suggesting that the authority of reception be distributed between Rome and the episcopal conferences was, in fact, turning the SPCU's own weapons against it, weakening its authority. As the reception of *Sancrosanctum concilium* was demonstrating, the local churches were proving to be suitable terrain for creating veritable strongholds of traditional doctrine against conciliar innovations.[35]

On the other hand, the comments on *communicatio* revealed the second aspect of the commission's criticism: the demand that the document specify the terms of its directives with utmost precision. As a doctrinal matter, vagueness on the issue could not, of course, be allowed, but also, perhaps, the comments were expressed in order to oblige the SPCU to admit the impossibility of ecumenical practice, highlighting its insurmountable limitations. The superficial contradiction between this aspect of the Holy Office's tactic and its recourse to the authority of the bishops' conferences was actually resolved in the idea that the latter should not so much *receive* the council as *limit* it in its local application.

3.6 *Curializing the Council, Conciliarizing the Curia*

The pontiff's interest in the SPCU's fate did not end with the August letter. In November he asked Felici for a proposal for an institutional organization of the postconciliar bodies. Despite the cardinal's initial hesitations,[36] when his proposal became the motu proprio *Finis concilio oecumenico Vaticano II*, the SPCU was mentioned in a paragraph explicitly dedicated to it, which formalized its transformation from a conciliar commission to a curial dicastery. As already mentioned, Paul VI's interest in the SPCU was not dictated by a personal sympathy but was part of a project that involved various forces within and external to the Roman curia. Quoting a conversation he had had with Charles Moeller, Jan Grootaers noted how his colleague indirectly linked the success of the Directory's editorial process with a kind of "protection" that the second section of the Secretariat of State accorded to Bea and his team.[37] For all intents and purposes, the SPCU was a key piece in Paul VI's pontifical project.

Shortly after the promulgation of *Finis concilio*, however, news arrived that the Directory would have to be subjected to further examination by the Secretariat of State and the Holy Office, recently renamed the Congregation for the Doctrine of the Faith.[38] The implications were enormous: why, a few months after removing it from

afternoon. Bishop De Smedt returned from it very fatigued again"; Prignon, *Journal conciliaire*, 246.

35 The most famous example, of course, is that of Cardinal Giuseppe Siri and his diocese in Genoa: see Nicla Buonasorte, *Siri: Tradizione e Novecento*, Bologna, Il Mulino, 2006, 325–427, esp. 381ff. Other examples are those of the bishop of Regensburg Rudolf Graber and the archbishop of Diamantina Geraldo de Proença Sigaud. See Daniele Menozzi, "L'anticoncilio (1966–1984)," in: Giuseppe Alberigo & Jean-Pierre Jossua, eds., *Il Vaticano II e la Chiesa*, Brescia, Paideia, 1985, 433–465.

36 See the notes by Felici, Nov 20, 1965, in: *AS* 6/4, 635–636; Dec 13, 1965, in: *AS* 6/4, 694–695; "Nota circa la costituzione degli Organismi postconciliari," Dec 20, 1965, in: *AS* 6/4, 710–713; Dec 22, 1965, in: *AS* 6/4, 719; Jan 8, 1966, in: *AS* 6/4, 738, and "Emendationes Schematis Motu proprio 'Finis Concilio,'" *AS* 6/4, 741.

37 See Jan Grootaers, "Moeller," in: *Agenda 33 "Beatenberg,"* Jul 19, 1965, KU Leuven-CSVII, Jan Grootaers, 4507; Jan Grootaers, "Père Chr. Dumont O.P.," in: *Agenda 34 "Basile Krivoc,"* Sep 4, 1965, KU Leuven-CSVII, Jan Grootaers, 4732; Jan Grootaers, "Conversation Lukas Vischer," in: *Agenda 40 "Prignon Philips,"* Oct 12, 1965, KU Leuven-CSVII, Jan Grootaers, 5521.

38 Motu proprio of Dec 7, 1965 by Paul VI, *Integrae servandae*, in: *AAS* 57, 1965, 952–955. The congregation's observations can be found in "Osservazioni della commissione ristretta della congregazione per la Dottrina della Fede e di alcuni reverendissimi consultori

Ottaviani's domain, had the pontiff brought the Directory back under his final authority? The decision could even be read as a denial of what Dell'Acqua had communicated in August. Had the protection granted to the SPCU by the second section of the Secretariat of State already come to an end? Or, as had already happened and would happen again and again in the future, had Paul VI succumbed to pressure from the conservatives in the curia? The pope's growing sympathy with the positions of the minority dictated by a concern for avoiding a schism at the council increasingly evolved during the phase of transition toward the postconciliar period into a greater preoccupation with the effects of a "disorderly" reception and incorrect interpretations of the council documents. This was also evident in *Finis concilio* itself, which provided that the postconciliar commissions would be presided over by the presidents of the corresponding congregations, thus repeating the "original sin" of the preparations for Vatican II, that is, curial control over the commissions.[39] Perhaps Paul VI hoped to be able to neutralize the negative influence of the curia through the upcoming reform, which effectively was supposed to "conciliarize" it.

This did not mean that the pontiff had abandoned the project of a faithful reception of the premises of Vatican II but rather that he was trying to find a subtle balance that might meet the needs of its various components. In confirmation of this, at the end of February it was decided to proceed to a consultation of the episcopate before definitively approving the Directory: with the "curialization" of the SPCU, the possibility of truly acting on a universal scale had arrived.[40]

4 Towards the Final Draft

At the beginning of March, a restricted commission of the SPCU, chaired by Willebrands, held a meeting with the task of integrating the suggestions into a single text to be sent to the bishops' conferences.[41] Many of the suggestions made by the Theological Commission to the Congregation for the Doctrine of the Faith were ignored. Confirming the importance that the SPCU attached to it, the first chapter remained practically intact, with the exception of a small addition aimed at defending the rights of the universal church with respect to local customs. The only notable addition was paragraph 29, in the chapter on *communicatio in spiritualibus* and *in sacris*, which perfectly represents the delicate balance the SPCU sought to strike between local and Roman needs. It brought together many of the key words in the Theological Commission's requests, granting the bishops' conferences the faculty to draw up specific directives to avoid the danger of indifferentism and proselytism. The new paragraph also gave them the right to modify the Directory's norms, just as the commission had requested. In order to defuse the risk of an excessive proliferation of these exceptions, which would have emptied the document of any efficacy, they were to have a merely transitional character.

(A.C. 12.I.66)," [n.d.], in: UCL-LG, Charles Moeller, papiers, 2138.

39 Pierre C. Noël, "Le travail post-conciliaire: Les attentes du groupe de la Domus Mariae et l'organisation de l'après-concile," in: Joseph Doré & Alberto Melloni, eds., *Volti di fine concilio: Studi di storia e teologia sulla conclusione del Vaticano II*, Bologna, Il Mulino, 2000, 267–308, esp. 273.

40 Willebrands, "Introduction à la discussion," 3.

41 The other members of the commission were Janez Vodopivec, Heinrich Ewers, Jean Jérôme Hamer, Emmanuel Lanne, and John Long. See Johannes Willebrands, "Agenda de bureau," Mar 1, 1966, in: KU Leuven-CSVII, Joahnnes Willebrands, folder 774. The completed text was "Directorium de re oecumenica," [n.d.], in: UCL-LG, Charles Moeller, papiers, 2146.

The events of 1965 and the beginning of 1966 show how, with respect to its initial intentions, the SPCU's focus began to shift in the direction of its "Roman" role: "Praeses conf[erentiae] Episcopalis ad nos referat."[42]

4.1 *The Bishops*

A few days later, then, the March text was sent to the episcopal conferences, the nuncios, and the apostolic delegates. These observations were also gathered in a thick dossier entitled *Animadversiones et suggestiones super Schema mense Martii 1966*.[43] Comparing the recurring themes of the new *Animadversiones* with those of the curial objections to the Directory, one notices both different priorities and interesting parallels. In the *Animadversiones* of the bishops, particularly those from Africa and Latin America, the accusation of eurocentrism returned.[44] The missionary origins of many of the bishops who were questioned – in particular those from Africa and Asia – and their distance from the European ecumenical world of the SPCU were reflected in the various, impassioned defenses of the term "proselytism," which for them represented not an abuse of power against separated brethren but legitimate apostolic outreach in territories where the church had yet to establish a strong presence. The bishops did not seem as eager as the Theological Commission to entrust the bishops' conferences with the responsibility of coordinating local ecumenism. On the contrary, most of them asked the SPCU not only for the utmost precision in the directives, but also for a good number of them, so that all possible problems would have a ready solution. In the case of the episcopate, it is likely that the focus of the question weighed primarily on concerns about discipline and orthodoxy, unlike the Theological Commission which made the same request but with broader objectives. The majority of those concerns were of a decidedly practical nature but, in some cases, even though they were in the minority, the bishops expressed exclusively doctrinal perplexities, needless to say mainly focused on the paragraphs concerning communion with Protestants.

The *Animadversiones* of March definitely made things difficult for the SPCU, which saw the same local churches asking Rome to restrict, as far as possible, their own margins of intervention in the reception of *Unitatis redintegratio*. Relying on the *communio ecclesiarum* increasingly proved to be a double-edged sword for the SPCU, which was forced to take into consideration positions that were decidedly more regressive than its own – positions that, in some cases, were even more or less consciously anticonciliar. It is difficult to say to what extent the episcopate's action of curtailment came as a surprise for the dicastery. The years of Vatican II had been ones of constant engagement with the most diverse realities of the church, often positively, but it could hardly be expected that the conciliar operations might faithfully replicate the diocesan contexts.

---

42 "Appunti," 7.

43 *Animadversiones et suggestiones super Schema mense Martii 1966*, [n.d.], in: UCL-LG, Charles Moeller, papiers, 2139, 2140, 2142, 205pp. The text referred to is the copy conserved in the Moeller fond, which has a different marking for each section of the dossier. The three sections are entitled "Conferentiis Episcoporum," in: UCL-LG, Charles Moeller, papiers, 2139; "Singuliis Episcopis," in: UCL-LG, Charles Moeller, papiers, 2140; "Supplementum," in: UCL-LG, Charles Moeller, papiers, 2142. Note that UCL-LG, Charles Moeller, papiers, 2141 consists of 20 typed pages containing the "Recommendation for Diocesan Commissions for Ecumenical Affairs" transmitted by the Bishops' Commission for Ecumenical Affairs – USA. In the absence of other information, it is legitimate to suppose that it was sent as a sort of collective *animadversio* of the US bishops, in a manner not unlike the way in which, during the previous year, some North American bishops had sent their local directories in response to the questionnaire on the opening of the work.

44 "Of necessity, the compiler of this provisional directory had to keep in mind the conditions generally existent for example in Europe. They did not, perhaps could not, envisage the conditions in mission territories where the Roman Catholic Church is in a minority, struggling to stabilize herself"; see the words by Paul Finbar Ryan in "Singuliis Episcopis," 15.

4.2 *The Pope: Defending the Rights of the Apostolic See*

Paul VI's interventions in the Directory were not yet over. His *modi* arrived in the SPCU signed by the Secretariat of State "following the indications of the Holy Father."[45]

The changes to the first chapter are highly significant. In his *modi*, with almost surgical precision, the pope took care to note that the ultimate reference point for ecumenical activities "from below" should always be the Apostolic See. In some cases, the SPCU had been eliminated as the final reference of the ecumenical commissions, replaced by the Apostolic See. Undoubtedly, this operation could not have sounded very pleasant to Bea or Willebrands. At least in theory, however, the Apostolic See did in fact include the SPCU itself, which was now part of it. Pierre Michalon, in a commentary on the final text of the Directory published shortly after its promulgation, explicitly supported this thesis, thus rendering it in a certain sense the official interpretation.[46] The pontifical edits fit perfectly into the more general design of curial reform that the pope was planning for the postconciliar period. Beneath the literal surface of the pontiff's *modi*, Paul VI wanted to make sure that the SPCU and its activities were part of the overall operations of the curia, in order to blunt its exceptionalism and integrate it into the routine mechanisms of government. At least in the immediate moment, as Michelon seems to show, this choice did not seem to be interpreted as a depletion of its prerogatives, or at least there was no reason to complain about it publicly.

4.3 *The Final Draft*

At the beginning of June, the plenary session of the SPCU finally met. The Fathers were called upon to compile a new text, the definitive one, taking into consideration the *modi* received since December. The Directory would have to be submitted to the Holy Father and the Congregation for the Doctrine of the Faith for further approval, which it was hoped, at this point, would be a mere formality.

All of Paul VI's *modi* were accepted with the exception of one. On a single occasion, the plenary felt it could ignore the pontiff and retained the indication of the SPCU as the final reference in Rome for the diocesan commissions. The Fathers were evidently rather cautious about placing their trust in the curial reform, which by mid-1966 was only characterized by papal promises and certain measures that were little more than symbolic.[47]

The issue of *communicatio in sacris*, along with the first chapter on the commissions, had proven to be the major difficulty of the Ecumenical Directory. In spite of the requests for clear and precise indications, the SPCU tried to leave as much room as possible for interpretation, both to allow the local churches to develop the concrete application

---

45 The pope asked for a copy of the Directory at the end of February. For this reason, his modifications were made on the then obsolete text of November. During the following month's plenary meeting, two documents were presented to the Fathers of the SPCU: a text of the Directory modified according to all of Paul VI's indications and a document in which only the most relevant modifications were underlined. The latter were decidedly limited in number. See "Alcuni ritocchi nel testo di novembre 1965 fatti dalla Segreteria di Stato in seguito alle indicazioni del Santo Padre," Jun 1, 1966, in: UCL-LG, Charles Moeller, papiers, 2135; "Testo di novembre 1965, ritoccato dalla Segreteria di Stato in seguito alle indicazioni del Santo Padre," Jun 13, 1966, in: AAV, Carte Bea, box 30, folder "Sessio Secr. 7–14 Jun. 1966."

46 Pierre Michalon, "Commento al Direttorio ecumenico," *IDO-C*, 1967, Dossier 18–19, 17.

47 The final point in the list of tasks of the diocesan ecumenical commissions should have read, as suggested by Paul VI: "Relationes cum commissione ecumenica territoriali … Insuper, si rerum adiuncta id suadeant, nuntis utilis ad Apostolicae Sedis mittantur, quibus haec in obeundis muneribus ad rem pertinentibus possit adiuvari." The text of the plenary was closer to the original text: "Curare rationes cum commissione oecumenica territoriali intercedentes … Insuper, si rerum adiuncta id suadeant, nuntis utilis ad Secretariatum ad Christianorum Unitatem fovendam mittantur, quibus hic in obeundis muneribus ad rem pertinentibus possit adiuvari"; see "Alcuni ritocchi nel testo di novembre 1965," 1.

of the norm, and also evidently because of the impossibility of taking a clear stand on topics where theological debate, even at the ecumenical level, had yet to sufficiently mature. Also included in the text was a brief treatment of exceptional cases that would allow *communicatio* with Protestants, based largely on the paragraphs eliminated in November.

The Directory's "external" reworking had brought out more clearly its spirit of compromise. It was now evident that the document was such by nature. It was precisely with its programmatic opening to the episcopate that the contradiction inherent in its dual focus of discipline and decentralization emerged rather violently, much more so than in the Theological Commission's objections. The ample room for maneuvering that the first drafts left to the local churches had gradually narrowed, at least in those contexts where the bishops' delay on the *status quaestionis* risked compromising the goals achieved by Vatican II. It is not clear to what extent the SPCU was aware of this limitation. Certainly, there was an awareness that a change of pace had occurred in its activity, both in having to relate to the whole church on an entirely new level, and in having to follow a pontiff whose timidities and doubts were causing increasingly evident delays. However, the discussion in the June plenary session does not seem to bear witness to any concrete consequence of this awareness. The SPCU was unaware, unwilling, or unable to find the necessary instruments to transform the Directory, whether this was an explicit choice of the new ecumenical dicastery or a simple consequence of the document's "literary genre." The document's promulgation, which was hoped to be imminent, would provide a fundamental test of the effectiveness of the approach adopted.

5 *Ad Totam Ecclesiam*

At the conclusion to the June plenary meeting, the SPCU delivered the Directory to the Congregation for the Doctrine of the Faith for its final examination prior to promulgation. In the following months, with only a couple of exceptions, the Directory disappeared from the ecumenical dicastery's agenda.[48] In December, Bea contacted the secretary of the congregation, Pietro Parente, to ask him for an explanation. The cardinal responded that he had no information and that Bea would have to wait until after the holidays to receive any news.[49] This was creating a certain discontent in the dicastery. The delay was already a problem in itself. Not only did it create a state of paralyzing waiting in the local churches,[50] but the longer it went on, the greater was the risk that the Directory would be born already outdated, given the continual evolution of the ecumenical movement in the period of fervent enthusiasm of the mid-1960s.

While the SPCU was preparing the Directory, in fact, awareness of the problem of intercommunion was growing in the ecumenical movement. In the eyes of its leaders, the openness toward *communicatio* in *Unitatis redintegratio* had suddenly made it possible, almost within reach. If, on the one hand, the churches themselves were beginning

48 The journal of the SPCU of 1966 recorded three meetings on the Directory: one with Dell'Acqua in July, one with the cardinal prefect of Propaganda Fide Gregorio Pietro Agagianian in October, and one with Charles Moeller of the Congregation for the Doctrine of the Faith in August. It is more than likely, however, that these refer to the second part of the Directory, work on which had begun precisely during that June plenary. See "Journal SCUF 1966," Jul 1, 1966; Jul 4, 1966; Jul 13, 1966; Aug 3, 1966; Oct 28, 1966, in: KU Leuven-CSVII, Joahnnes Willebrands, folder 830.

49 "Journal SCUF 1966," Dec 16, 1966, in: KU Leuven-CSVII, Joahnnes Willebrands, folder 830.

50 "The main obstacle has been the delay in publishing the long-awaited *Directorium*. For instance, meeting in plenary session, the bishops of Rhodesia decided that they could not freely and without prejudice to the ecumenical movement elsewhere in the world, accept the invitation of the Anglican bishops to enter into formal dialogue, until the *Directorium* had clearly defined the status of such a confrontation"; see Donal Lamont, "Report on Ecumenical Movement in Rhodesia," [n.d.], in: AFscire, FF, 1185, 1.

to move in this direction,[51] on the other the drive from below that struck the Christian communities was far more visible. In the case of the Catholic Church this was accompanied, however, by profound concerns of a disciplinary nature. Already in June, Cardinal Ottaviani's famous letter *Cum oecumenicum concilium* listed the dangerous developments of ecumenism among the risks of the council's reception.[52] At the local level, the hierarchy was beginning to engage in the first countermeasures, such as the censure of the activities of the Dutch ecumenical association Sjaloom at the beginning of 1967. Willebrands himself supported the resolutions of the local bishops during a series of meetings in his native country.[53] The SPCU recognized that the climate was changing and, during the April 1967 plenary session, it approved the formation of a commission dedicated to the study of the problem of intercommunion.[54] The feeling of being at the head of a potentially explosive phenomenon was well summarized by Thijssen: "We find ourselves in a difficult situation. Is the direction announced here a true development of ecumenism ... or is it a liberal tendency that undermines true ecumenism?"[55]

Between February and April, the stalemate in which the Directory had found itself was finally cleared. Within a few weeks, the ex-Holy Office convened a joint meeting with the SPCU, the Congregation for the Oriental Churches, and Propaganda Fide, during which the final text of the document was established.[56] The Congregation for the Doctrine of the Faith had probably achieved its goal: unable to intervene in the text in any significant way, it had attempted a last-ditch effort to sabotage the document by making it as obsolete as possible. Considering that the SPCU had delivered the text in June, only a few weeks before the letter *Cum oecumenicum* was sent to the bishops, it is also possible that Ottaviani was waiting for the results of his operation, perhaps hoping that the bishops would furnish him with the legitimacy to modify or even reject the Directory.

The text prepared by the commission only slightly modified the June text. However, it reintroduced some of the observations made by the Theological Commission over a year earlier, which had been deleted by the SPCU in 1966. The nature of these modifications seems to confirm, in any

51 Other than the first steps within the framework of bilateral and multilateral theological dialogues one thinks, for example, of the failed intercommunion between Paul VI and Athenagoras I, which engaged the energies of Rome and Constantinople for about a decade; see Alberto Melloni, *Tempus Visitationis: L'intercomunione inaccaduta fra Roma e Costantinopoli*, Bologna, Il Mulino, 2019; See also the introduction by Alberto Melloni in this volume.

52 Ottaviani's letter was part of the abovementioned strategy of anticonciliar circles to influence the reception of Vatican II through the manipulation of the bishops. The letter, which was supposed to remain secret, was published by the French press and caused strong reactions from the entire Catholic world, including the pope. Despite this, it is still rather doubtful what Paul VI's actual role was in the drafting of the letter. In any case, most of the episcopal conferences more or less explicitly rejected Ottaviani's theses. See Christian Sorrel, ed., *Renouveau conciliaire et crise doctrinale: Rome et les Églises nationales (1966–1968)*, Lyon, LARHRA, 2017.

53 See Wim Boelens, "Esperimenti ecumenici in Olanda e in Belgio," *Concilium* 5/4, 1969, 207–217; "Olanda – L'episcopato prende posizione contro le intemperanze ecumeniche," *Il Regno – Attualità* 22, 1967, 127.

54 It is not possible to reconstruct on which occasion the project was formulated, but it was probably during one of the meetings of the staff in the period between the two plenaries. See "Programme pour la réunion du Secrétariat pour l'unité des chrétiens du 7 au 15 juin 1966, à Rome," Jun 16, 1966, in: AAV, Carte Bea, box 30, folder "Sessio Secr. 7–14 iun. 1966," and "Plenary session of the Secretariat," [n.d.], in: AFscire, FF, 1180.

55 Frans Thijssen, "Sur la question de 'l'intercommunion' et 'communion ouverte' entre l'Église catholique et les Églises issues de la Réforme," [n.d.], in: AFscire, FF, 668, 3; See also Bernard-Dominique Dupuy, "'Communicatio in sacris' et Inter-communion: Réflexions doctrinales et pastorales (résumé)," [n.d.], in: AFscire, FF, 667; "Zur Communicatio in Sacris zwischen Katholiken und Angehörigen der getrennten Ostkirche," [n.d.], in: AFscire, FF, 669.

56 See "Presentazione del direttorio ecumenico fatta alla stampa da S.E.R. Mons. Giovanni Willebrands il 26 maggio 1967," *Service d'information* 2/2, 1967, 13–15, here 14.

case, that the cause of the long stalemate on the Directory was more of a "political" nature than one motivated by real doctrinal concerns: the tensions between the two dicasteries remained very high. Among other things, in that very same period, Bea and Ottaviani were at loggerheads on the mixed commission for the synod of bishops.[57]

The 1967 plenary session took place from Apr 19 to 28. It was not considered necessary to discuss the text approved by the mixed commission. The work on the Directory had moved on by then to the second part, and work on that had begun the previous June with two schemas on formation and ecumenical dialogue. Instead, the last days of the plenary session were completely taken up with the discussion on intercommunion. At the end of the plenary, the SPCU was received in audience by Paul VI, the first time that the whole office met with him. It was on that occasion that the publication of the first part of the ecumenical Directory was officially announced. The text was promulgated on May 14, 1967, Pentecost Sunday, entitled *At totam Ecclesiam*. After almost a year of suspension, the construction site was officially closed, but another essential chapter had begun: would the Directory work?

5.1 The Integration of the SPCU into the Roman Curia

I have already noted how curial reform represented the central point of Paul VI's project for the reception of the council. He had been a fervent supporter of the need for this reform since the years of his experience in the Secretariat of State, and his ascent to the papal throne finally gave him the opportunity to act in complete freedom.[58] The issue was entwined with Paul VI's – also already noted – increasingly solitary exercise of his governing faculties. A very clear example of this process can be found in the history of the commission for the reform of the curia, nominated by the pope during the council but whose activity would always remain secondary to papal decisions. The pope understood that his entire pontificate – at least as far as it was possible to foresee – would be dedicated to the reception of Vatican II; every long-term project would necessarily be informed by it, and every initiative of his would have to be characterized by fidelity to its results. Progressively, it seemed that Paul VI could, or more likely wanted to, assure such fidelity only by means of his personal intervention, due to the divisions that Vatican II created. This, of course, created a short circuit, especially in regard to questions of episcopal collegiality. In fact, many of the decisions that most influenced the role of the bishops and the curia in the postconciliar period came unilaterally from Paul VI, creating more than a few problems, as in the case of the establishment of the synod of bishops.

After the announcements made during the council, the year and a half that passed between its conclusion and the summer of 1967 had been rather quiet. The only measure of any importance had been the reorganization of the Holy Office with the motu proprio *Integrae servandae*.

---

57 At that time, the two dicasteries were competing for control over the commission that was to prepare the work of the synod on mixed marriages. During the preparations, the work was monopolized by the Congregation for the Doctrine of the Faith, which also managed, at the last moment, to reject the contribution of the SPCU. On the other hand, the events of the synod permitted the ecumenical dicastery to establish control over the matter. For a general overview of the synod, see Antonino Indelicato, *Il sinodo dei vescovi: La collegialità sospesa (1965–1985)*, Bologna, Il Mulino, 2008.

58 For the curial experience of Paul VI, see, among others, Robert A. Graham, "G.B. Montini Substitute Secretary of State (in tandem with Domenico Tardini)," in: *Paul VI et la modernité dans l'Église: Actes du colloques de Rome (2–4 juin 1983)*, Rome, École Française de Rome, 1984, 67–84; Andrea Riccardi, *Il "partito romano": Politica italiana, Chiesa cattolica e Curia romana da Pio XII a Paolo VI*, Brescia, Morcelliana, 2007, 247–306; See also Angelo Maffeis, "Giovanni Battista Montini e il problema ecumenico: Dagli anni giovanili all'episcopato milanese," in: *Paolo VI e l'ecumenismo*, 39–96. For a wider panorama of Montini's role, see Andrea Riccardi, *Il potere del papa da Pio XII a Giovanni Paolo II*, Rome/Bari, Laterza, 1993, esp. 223–341.

Anticipation had generated many expectations and a certain nervousness. In his diary, Grootaers reported the rumors that the pope "willingly" and repeatedly told "certain bishops" not to worry since the future reform would remain faithful to the decisions of Vatican II.[59] The pontifical acts that finally constituted the backbone of the reform were the apostolic constitution *Regimini ecclesiae universae*,[60] the true reform of the curia, and the motu proprio *Pro comperto sane*,[61] which incorporated the diocesan bishops into the curia, both promulgated in July 1967. The inclusion of the episcopate in the central governance of the curia was one of the central points of the governing program of Paul VI, a natural consequence of the new conciliar ecclesiology. The SPCU had played an important role in establishing its modalities, so much so that Charles Moeller could point to it as one of the entities that inspired the reform.[62] It is not possible here to go into the details of the changes; it is sufficient to recall the prominent role it gave to the Secretariat of State and to say that, as a result of it, the SPCU had not only been inserted organically within the curia but that it also constituted one of the foundation stones of the new Pauline era.[63] The "victory" brought about by the promulgation of the Directory and the events of the synod of bishops regarding mixed marriages had minimized the threat of the Congregation for the Doctrine of the Faith. However, some dark clouds were gathering on the horizon, revealing just how fragile the affirmation of the postconciliar church over the preconciliar one actually was. The "new men" of the Pauline curia, such as the prefect of the Congregation for the Doctrine of the Faith Franjo Šeper or the secretary of state Jean-Marie Villot, both "diocesans," did not really shine in terms of initiative or incisiveness in their governing actions. Some of the leading figures of the conciliar era, for example Charles Moeller or Léon-Joseph Suenens, gradually lost favor with Rome and were marginalized. The opponents of the council, including Ottaviani himself, although weakened, remained in the curia,[64] maintaining direct contact with the pontiff. It was precisely the role of the pontiff that was the fundamental weak point of the reform: in concentrating everything on the Secretariat of State, the pope was in fact placing all the work of the curia under its direct control.

As for the SPCU, the fact that it was invested with the responsibility for embodying the Pauline reform rendered it particularly susceptible to the phenomena mentioned here. The contact between the pope and Bea was direct, but this meant that so was the control. Even before the

59 Jan Grootaers, "Mgr. Prignon," Apr 29, 1967, in: *Agenda 56: "3/4/67-29/4,"* KU Leuven-CSVII, Jan Grootaers, 7764.

60 Paul VI, *Regimini ecclesiae universae*, in: *AAS* 59, 1967, 885–928.

61 Paul VI, *Pro comperto sane*, in: *AAS* 59, 1967, 881–884.

62 See Jan Grootaers, "Lorsque conversation avec Monsegnieur C. Moeller," in: *Agenda 57: "Alberigo 19/04/67-15/05/67,"* KU Leuven-CSVII, Jan Grootaers, 7791.

63 For some references, see the chapter on the reform of the curia in Giles Routhier, *Vatican II: Herméneutique et réception*, Anjou, Fides, 2006, 171–211; Joseph Famerée, "'Responsabilisation' des conférences épiscopales et concessions de 'facultés' aux évêques: Signes de décentralisation?" in: Doré & Melloni, eds., *Volti di fine concilio*, 27–52; Joseph Famerée, "Le décret Christus Dominus: Une reconfiguration du ministère épiscopal?," *RTL* 46, 2015, 490–514; Karim Schelkens, "From Superno Dei Nutu to Regimini Ecclesiae: The Secretariat for Christian Unity and the 1968 Reform of the Curia," in: Paul van Geest & Roberto Regoli, eds., *Suavis Laborum Memoria: Chiesa, Papato e Curia Romana tra storia e teologia: Scritti in Onore di Marcel Chappin SJ per il suo 70° compleanno/Church, Papacy, Roman Curia between History and Theology: Essays in honour of Marcel Chappin SJ on His 70th Birthday*, Vatican City, Archivio Segreto Vaticano, 2013, 167–181. For a historical perspective, see also Enrico Galavotti, "Sulle riforme della curia romana nel Novecento," *CrSt* 35/3, 2014, 849–890.

64 When, after *Regimini ecclesiae universae*, Bea and Ottaviani placed their mandate in the hands of Paul VI, the pontiff rejected the resignation of the former and accepted that of the latter. However, his trusted man Paul-Pierre Philippe became secretary of the Congregation for the Doctrine of the Faith, and Ottaviani, as "prefect emeritus," maintained his right to participate in meetings.

death of the German Jesuit in 1968, Jean Jérôme Hamer, a long-time collaborator of the SPCU but whose positions on doctrine were becoming progressively more cautious, began to take on a more important role in the dicastery. *Regimini Ecclesiae Universae* had forced several prominent members of the dicastery to be "downgraded" to simple consultors because they lacked episcopal dignity, and some of the most radical increasingly ended up being removed in the following years.[65] Integration into the Roman curia signified not only an increase in the SPCU's ability to act, but also the beginning of its true curialization that, if at the moment was only *in nuce*, would become particularly evident in the following years.

6 The Failure of the Directory: The Eucharistic Crisis

In April 1968, Hamer gave a lecture at Berkeley during which he argued that, while intercommunion should be considered both the means and the realization of Christian unity, given the present state of affairs, it was absolutely impossible to engage in it.[66] Indeed, it was even an obstacle on a path that was otherwise characterized by a perhaps slow but certain movement forward. Paul Minus Jr., a Methodist theologian, later commented in Gregory Baum's journal *The Ecumenist* that Hamer's lecture had revealed the existence at the time of "a mood of disfavor in some key hierarchical circles."[67] The lecture had a certain resonance, so much so that it was often cited in the following months by those who wanted to show that the only orthodox position on *communicatio* was that of a clear rejection.

The end of the council had released various tensions in the Catholic Church, mostly preexisting, which were finally reaching their breaking point on several fronts, not only in regard to ecumenism.[68] From the end of 1967, Paul VI began to speak of a "crisis of obedience" that in his opinion risked to deeply undermine the very structure of the church.[69] The idea of the centrality of hierarchy in ecclesiology had characterized his thought from an early age, but after the end of the council it was becoming more rigid. This was not the sole feature of the crisis: the pope increasingly seemed to assign the council at least partial responsibility for the crisis. Was the pope losing confidence

65 A very clear example of the tensions between the world of the theologians and Rome can be found in the story of the ITC. See Emanuele Avallone, *La Commissione Teologica Internazionale: Storia e prospettive*, Venice, Marcianum Press, 2016.

66 Jérôme Hamer, "Stages on the Road to Unity: The Problem of Intercommunion," *One in Christ* 4/3, 1968, 235–249. For news of the conference, see "Les étapes sur le chemin de l'unité: Le problème de l'intercommunion. Conférence du Jérôme Hamer, O.P., secrétaire adjoint du Secrétariat pour l'Unité des chrétiens," *La Documentation Catholique* 50/65, 1968, coll. 829–842.

67 Paul Minus, "Intercommunion Now?," *The Ecumenist* 6/6, 1968, 186–189, here 186. The book by Jérôme Hamer, *L'Église est une communion*, Paris, Cerf, 1962, was very influential in defining the ecclesiological doctrine of Vatican II. Godfrey Diekmann summarized Hamer's position on intercommunion as a perfect representative of the official "Roman" position, contrasting it, instead, with the more open position of Gregory Baum: see Godfrey Diekmann, "Dimensioni ecumeniche e problemi dell'intercomunione," *IDO-C* 1968, Dossier 38, 9.

68 For some references, see Denis Pelletier, *La crise catholique: Religion, société, politique*, Paris, Payot, 2002; Leo Declerck, "La réaction du cardinal Suenens et de l'épiscopat belge à l'encyclique Humanae Vitae: Chronique d'une déclaration (juillet–décembre 1968)," *ETL* 84, 2008, 1–68; as well as Jörg Ernesti, ed., *Paolo VI e la crisi postconciliare/Paul VI. und die Nachkonziliare Krise: Giornate di studio/Studientage* (*Bressanone 25–26 febbraio/Februar 2012*), Brescia, Istituto Paolo VI, 2013.

69 The occasions, between the end of 1967 and 1968, were different, the most relevant being the letter sent to the European congress of national directors for priestly vocations (*L'Osservatore Romano*, Dec 7, 1967), the address for the feast of the Presentation of Jesus in the Temple (*L'Osservatore Romano*, Feb 2, 1968), or the general audience of Oct 17. The latter was an occasion in which he directly connected the issue of the crisis of obedience with that of the normativity of the conciliar documents (*L'Osservatore Romano*, Oct 17, 1968).

in the capacity of the council to manage its own reception? His reliance on the curia, however reformed, seemed to suggest this. Certainly, in public as much as in private, Paul VI expressed his confidence in and his fidelity to Vatican II. The enthusiasm for ecumenical activity, however, had already begun to be a concern of the pontiff for some time. As early as Sep 7, 1966, during a general audience, Paul VI had spoken of "dissonances ... perhaps suggested by the desire for openness to the non-Catholic world, often credited by references to the recently concluded council, almost as if the council authorized calling the truth of the faith into question."[70]

The need expressed "from below" to engage in intercommunion had made episodes such as that of the aforementioned Sjaloom association grow in number and magnitude, with corresponding Roman interventions. During the summer of 1968, as many as three episodes of "Eucharistic disobedience" took place. Their political, theological, and ecumenical relevance was so great that Rome was obliged to react in a far more vigorous manner than with simple reminders from the local bishops.

The first episode was the famous "Pentecost intercommunion" in Paris.[71] The second episode was the intercommunion occurred during the meeting of the WCC in Uppsala.[72] Finally, there was the admission of non-Catholic observers to the Eucharistic table during the closing ceremony of the Medellín conference.[73] If the first two episodes provoked strong censorship reactions, the third convinced Rome that a real change was required. While on the two previous occasions intercommunion took place either in open rebellion to the authorities or in a clandestine manner, at Medellín the permission to go ahead with it was given by the local ordinary as well as by the prefect of the Congregation for the Discipline of the Sacraments. To justify their admission to communion, the observers had invoked the very paragraph of the Directory on *communicatio* with Protestants, thus emphasizing their full adherence to Roman directives. A few weeks after the event, a "Nota circa l'applicazione del Direttorio ecumenico" was published, dated Oct 5, and printed the following day in *L'Osservatore Romano*. The note made it very clear from its first paragraph that the cause of its publication was the events of the preceding months in which, "here and there," Protestant and Anglican Christians had been allowed to participate in Eucharistic communion. The note reasserted the text, giving a rather restrictive reading to the categories used by the Directory, particularly in the case of the passage referred to by the Medellín observers. The hostility identified by Minus was becoming a reality: in November 1968, during the annual plenary, Paul VI addressed the SPCU, reminding it that the Directory was not "a collection of advice" but "a true Instruction, an exposition of the discipline to which those who truly wish to serve ecumenism must submit."[74]

Since at least the fall of 1968, the Directory had assumed a function as a disciplinary instrument that was much more explicit than the initial intentions of its drafters. Together with the new curial role of the SPCU, there was a progressive diminishing of the dialogical relationship with the local churches, that had characterized, even in a conflictual sense, the drafting of the document, both in intention and in practice. In addition to the abovementioned question of the process of its drafting,

70 Philippe Chenaux, *Paul VI: Le souverain éclairé*, Paris, Cerf, 2015, 223.

71 See Pelletier, *La crise catholique*, as well as Denis Pelletier & Jean-Louis Schlegel, eds., *À la gauche du Christ: Les chrétiens de gauche en France de 1945 à nos jours*, Paris, Seuil, 2012, esp. Yann Raison du Cleuziou, "À la fois prêts et surpris: Les chrétiens en Mai 1968," 297–322. See also Étienne Fouilloux, *Les Chrétiens français entre guerre en Algerie et Mai 1968*, Paris, Parole et Silence, 2008, and the introduction by Alberto Melloni in this volume.

72 See the contribution by Gerhard Besier in this volume.

73 For a more in-depth treatment of the path of the Latin-American church that led to the Medellín conference, see the contribution by Sandra Arenas and Rodrigo Polanco in this volume.

74 *L'Osservatore Romano*, Nov 14, 1968.

which had repeatedly and in different forms sought to resort to the *communio ecclesiarum*, the role of the local churches was well represented in the paragraphs of the Directory, albeit in a constant dialectic with the responsibilities of the SPCU as the central authority of Roman ecumenism. Paul VI, in this and other comments of the period, seemed to be unaware of the proactive role of the local churches in the reception of the Directory's norms.[75] This is not what the SPCU had in mind, as we have already seen. Consider also, for example, the statements of Cardinal Lorenz Jaeger, who in the same period asserted that the Directory simply provided an "overall framework" that the bishops' conferences would have to use in order to fashion their own norms, more suited to the individual local realities. Analogously, in the presentation of the document to the press, Willebrands stated that "it should be completed by Directives of a local character in the various territories."[76] Shortly after the promulgation of the document, in June 1967, a meeting of the ecumenical commissions was held, which was intended precisely to foster its diffusion and reception at the local level and, at least in its intentions, was to be the first in a series of regular appointments to promote dialogue between the center and the peripheries. Significantly, these regular appointments would not be reconvened for a long time. It can be no coincidence that the suspension of these meetings corresponds with the emergence of the crisis of the late 1960s. It is not possible to say whether this was a conscious choice or whether other matters simply took center stage, relegating the meetings of the ecumenical commissions to the background. However, even if the latter were the case, it could be symptomatic of a loss of confidence in the local churches' ability to play an active role in dialogue with Rome, at least for the time being.

This evolution necessarily brought with it a reflection on the instrument of the Directory itself, beginning precisely with its normative rigidity. The SPCU, despite its own role in the curialization of postconciliar ecumenism, continued to imagine new kinds of dialectics between Rome and the local churches. During his report to the plenary meeting of 1969, Secretary Hamer, in dealing with the problem, even went so far as to establish a curious contrast between the Directory, "a normative text sealed with the highest approval," and "other types of documents," which would be more flexible, and which the SPCU would have to prepare for the episcopal conferences.[77] These other documents were nothing more than two texts on ecumenical dialogue and proselytism whose drafting was, by that time, practically completed. In the initial projects, drawn up between 1966 and 1967, these were to become the third and fourth parts of the Directory, but they had become mired in various editorial vicissitudes.[78] While the previously cited text on formation had already seen the light of day in May 1969 as the "second part" of the Ecumenical Directory, between the plenaries of 1968 and 1969 various doubts on the other two had emerged. In part, these were due to their overlapping with themes dealt with by the Joint Working Group, but in light of what has been said about the ineffectiveness of the first part, one cannot help but suppose that the SPCU was engaged in course-correcting efforts. The Directory had proven to be too rigid an instrument. Its normative

75 One thinks, for example, of the almost simultaneous address he gave in St. Peter's to Czechoslovakian pilgrims during the Week of Prayer for Christian Unity in January 1969, reported in *L'Osservatore Romano*, Jan 23, 1969.

76 These statements by Jaeger and Willebrands should not be taken too literally: we have seen how, by the time they were made, the hypothesis of local directories had already been dropped for some time. Rather, they indicated the possibility of the churches playing an active role in the reception of the document, as was foreseen by the text itself. "Presentazione del direttorio ecumenico," 15; "Dichiarazioni del card. Jaeger sul 'Direttorio Ecumenico,'" *Unitas* 22/4, 1967, 232.

77 See Jérôme Hamer, *Assemblée plénière du Secrétariat pour l'unité des chrétiens, 18–28 novembre 1969*, n.d., in AFscire, FF, 1118, p. 14.

78 For more details, see Bruno Cherubini, *Presagi di un inverno ecumenico: Il Direttorio di Paolo VI*, Bologna, Marietti, 2023.

character, however tempered, could easily be directed against the very intentions of the dicastery and thus actually stifle, rather than bring out, the ecumenical vitality of the local communities. Paul VI approved the downgrading of the latter two documents once he had given "the matter serious consideration."[79] This expression might allude to a certain perplexity on the pope's part. As already seen, he had become much more inclined to entrust this type of task to "true and proper instructions" rather than to such vague and flexible documents. In spite of this, the "minor" character of the topics discussed here (at least in respect to those in the first part) must have convinced the pontiff to give his approval to the SPCU's project. The document on dialogue would be published almost a year later in *Service d'information*, with the title "Réflexions et suggestions concernant le dialogue œcuménique,"[80] with the status of "a working instrument at the disposal of ecclesiastical authorities for concrete application of the Decree on ecumenism." With the emergence of these two documents, the Directory was officially completed with the publication of the second part, in May. The document on proselytism, after some additional treatment by the SPCU's commissions, was eventually cancelled due to "a tendency in the text to see things from a Latin perspective."[81]

7 New Directions

For the following year's plenary session, the plan was to proceed with a more profound survey of the problem of intercommunion at the local level.[82] According to the resulting *Rapport synthétique*, most of the responses indicted that cases of intercommunion were sometimes decided in an "emotional climate, or based on sentimental or psychological motives, or at events publicized by the mass media" so that the precise instructions of the ecclesiastical hierarchy often went unnoticed. According to the report, the pressure from Protestant churches in favor of intercommunion contributed, together with the repetition of cases such as those of Uppsala or Medellín, to weakening the confidence of Catholics in the soundness of the position of their own church. "The masses of the faithful" did not understand the directives coming from Rome and misunderstood their theological character, interpreting them as simple, odious obligations of a juridical nature.[83] It was therefore necessary to address the problem with a different approach that was more pastoral and less one-sided, one that would allow the faithful to understand the close link between the Eucharist and the unity of the church, taking into account the ever-changing and vital landscape of the ecumenical movement. In this, the episcopal conferences were to assume an important role in acting as intermediaries between Roman requirements and the local realities. Above all, they were not to "formulate directives that appeared to be a justification of the status quo."[84] The central problems in the relationship between Rome and the local churches – between the SPCU and the bishops, ecumenical commissions, and episcopal conferences – in the end, continued to recur substantially unchanged despite all the reforms, decisions, and directories promulgated in the previous years. Something, however, had happened in the meantime. In the period after the end of Vatican II,

---

79 Jean Willebrands, "Nota Explicativa: Introduction to the Document on Ecumenical Dialogue," *Service d'information* 12/4, 1970, 3–4, here 3.

80 Jean Willebrands, "Réflexions et suggestions concernant le dialogue œcuménique: Document de travail à la disposition des autorités ecclésiastique pour l'application concrète du Décret sur l'œcuménisme," *Service d'information* 12/4, 1970, 5–11.

81 "La session plénière: 18–28 novembre 1969," *Service d'information* 9/1, 1970, 3–14, here 3.

82 See "Convocazione plenaria 1969," Jul 8, 1969, in: AFscire, FF, 1107; "Questionnaire sur l'Intercommunion Eucharistique," Jul 3, 1969, in: AFscire, FF, 1110, 4 pp.

83 Pierre Michalon, "Questionnaire sur l'Intercommunion Eucharistique: Rapport synthétique," [n.d.], in: AFscire, FF, 758.

84 Michalon, "Questionnaire sur l'Intercommunion Eucharistique," 4.

a paradoxical reversal of positions had occurred: the SPCU came to be accused (or accused itself) of the same matters for which it had blamed the curia, and especially the hated Holy Office, during the council. This admission of the problem, frank as it was, sounds like a true awareness on the SPCU's part of the seriousness of the problem and the inadequacy of its own means.

In part, what had been hoped for in the report of the plenary session was already happening. It should not be underestimated that, in parallel to the disciplinary measures, the Roman offices were actually beginning to look for a different perspective from which to address the Eucharistic problem. Even though the process of its curialization was already underway, the SPCU did not renounce remaining as faithful as possible to its original mission. For example, in June 1969 a mixed commission with the Congregation for the Doctrine of the Faith produced a report on the question of intercommunion. The majority report introduced the theme of open communion, very timidly linking the steps forward of the section on *communicatio* with Protestants to "limited forms" of open communion. In other words, the report seemed to want to resolve the problem by recasting the issue posed by *Unitatis redintegratio* with respect to the possibility of *communicatio in sacris* within a different doctrinal framework than that of intercommunion, which had characterized the Roman interventions up to that point. It is also worth mentioning the minority report that, while in principle sharing the conclusions of the majority, called for a stronger emphasis on the theme of the mutual recognition of ministers by the churches. Both reports reflected a significant advance, and both themes – open communion and the mutual recognition of ministers – would then, as is well known, become central to the ecumenical debate in the 1970s (and not only then, particularly as far as the ministry was concerned).[85] Here, therefore, the post-Paris (and Uppsala, and Medellín) discussion had evolved and borne fruit. The mixed commission had succeeded in untangling the controversy into two separate arguments, differentiating the issue and opening new possibilities for application. If, in fact, the window of opportunity for a stable intercommunion with Protestants was gradually closing through the issuing of notes and instructions, that of Eucharistic hospitality remained open.

Despite these openings, or perhaps because of them, after 1969 the attitude of the SPCU towards intercommunion proper did not change radically, at least in the short term. The early years of the 1970s, in spite of the evolution in the tone of the discussion and the absence of episodes of great import like those of 1968, saw in fact a veritable stream of Roman calls for obedience and respect for the norms of the Directory, testifying to the permanence of a disciplinary approach, one of doubtful efficacy. The results of the reflections made between the summer and autumn of 1969 were condensed in the declaration on a common Eucharist of January 1970.[86]

8 Conclusions

The story of the Directory is emblematic of how the reception of ecumenism in the Catholic Church after Vatican II was a difficult and contradictory process from the outset. It represented one of the greatest successes of the council, as well as one of its characteristic features, and for this reason it was also one of the main targets of its opponents. The

85 "Relazione di maggioranza circa la communicatio in sacris e l'intercomunione," Jun 20, 1969, in: AFscire, FF, 748; "Relazione di minoranza circa la communicatio in sacris e l'intercomunione," Jun 24, 1969, in: AFscire, FF, 749; "Commissione mista tra la S. congregazione per la dottrina della fede e il Segretariato per l'unione dei cristiani," [s.d.], in: AFscire, FF, 678.

86 "La position de l'Église catholique en matière d'eucharistie commune entre chrétiens de diverses confessions: Déclaration du Secrétariat pour l'Unité des chrétiens," *La Documentation Catholique* 52/68, 1970, coll. 113–116; See also *L'Osservatore Romano*, Jan 12–13, 1970.

pressure point on which the council's opponents were able to concentrate their forces was Paul VI, with his understandable concerns for the unity of church and doctrine and his consequent timidity and insecurities.

Ecumenical practice, the energies of which had been released by *Unitatis redintegratio*, had proven to be a disruptive force within the Catholic Church, potentially capable of upsetting it from head to toe. Both its proponents and its opponents were aware of this, and it was particularly evident in the question of *communicatio in sacris*. From the pope's point of view, obedience to Roman directives was necessary to temper that natural "impatience" that was also positive insofar as it was bearer of prophetic elements but dangerous because it risked damaging the slow, difficult path that passed through theological reflection, dialogue, and agreements with other churches. The "crisis of obedience" had made it more important than ever to emphasize submission to the Holy See, especially in ecumenical matters, and the Directory, by its very nature, seemed the perfect instrument for doing so. On the other hand, however, the intention on which its drafters insisted was exactly the opposite: it was not to force the aforementioned energies into doctrinal and canonical enclosures, as the "prudent" voices demanded in order to stifle them, but rather to provide them with a framework within which they might break free as clearly, organically, and satisfactorily as possible.

One cannot help but emphasize how never, until 1968, had the Directory been considered an *Instructio*, the most classical and curial of Roman instruments. On the contrary, if in public discourse its novel character had often been diplomatically toned down (it is enough to recall the various, classical references to indifferentism), we can see how the SPCU had made a great effort to ensure that, both in its contents and in its drafting, it reflected as much as possible the new postconciliar climate despite its clear disciplinary objective, in a certain sense adapting it to the new context. The forcing of the issue that took place during the turning point of 1968 had indeed been prepared in previous years by the internal discussion of the drafting process, but the point of no return was certainly Medellín when, for the first time, ecumenical practice – not by chance in the area of *communicatio in sacris* – was imposed in forms outside the direct control of Rome but with the approval of the hierarchy. This made the danger of disobedience – even within that element that he still considered, despite Vatican II, the foundation stone of Catholic ecclesiology – far more concrete in the eyes of the pope. Paul VI's idea of being able to personally accompany the reception of Vatican II at a prudent and judicious pace, clashed with a reality that was proceeding much faster than the pope was willing to tolerate.

This rethinking of the Directory *ex post* could only further damage its profound meaning. The SPCU was well aware of this. It was precisely from within its ranks that the initiative arose to abandon the project and replace it with other, more flexible instruments that would remain more faithful to its original mission. Needless to say, the failure of the Directory does not signify a failure of the reception of ecumenism in the Catholic Church in general but rather an awareness that this was not the right way to go about it. There were in fact several directions taken by the SPCU, primarily that of theological dialogue or even intercommunion with Constantinople. Within the Catholic Church, as already mentioned, energies were shifted to the study of the question of the ministry, as if to admit that before engaging in *communicatio*, especially with Protestants, it was necessary to solve previous problems.[87] This approach, however, signified two things. On the one hand, that it was already decided to give preference to an ecumenism "from above," renouncing the desire to stimulate the local churches that had been the principal objective of the SPCU at the time of the council. On the other hand, it meant that intercommunion, the

87 This, not coincidentally, dragged on from the beginning of the ecumenical movement: see the contribution by Paul Avis in the first volume of this work.

crowning achievement of the ecumenical movement, the enacting of the unity of the church, which in 1965 had seemed within reach, was postponed to an indefinite future, postponed until agreements and doctrinal elaborations could be achieved, which, in retrospect, can be said to have been proven to be rather ineffective.

The role of the SPCU in this process is clear. With its own institutionalization, it sought the means to be able to have a concrete effect on the church. However, precisely this institutionalization carried within it the germs of its own loss of incisiveness, as Christophe-Jean Dumont had already lucidly noted in 1965.[88] Its insertion into the Roman curia gave it an authority that its founders could only dream of but, at the same time, inserted it into a mechanism that, especially in the long run, weakened its ability to interpret and effectively apply the impulses of the ecumenical movement to the Catholic Church.

88 Christophe-Jean Dumont, "Pour faire le point," *VUCh* 18/6, 1965, 53–56.

Translated from Italian to English by Susan Dawson Vásquez and David Dawson Vásquez.

Bibliography

Chenaux, Philippe, *Paul VI: Le souverain éclairé*, Paris, Cerf, 2015.

Cherubini, Bruno, *Presagi di un inverno ecumenico: Il Direttorio di Paolo VI*, Bologna, Marietti, 2023.

Doré, Joseph & Alberto Melloni, eds., *Volti di fine concilio: Studi di storia e teologia sulla conclusione del Vaticano II*, Bologna, Il Mulino, 2000.

Paolo VI e l'ecumenismo: Colloquio internazionale di studio (Brescia, 25–26–27 settembre 1998), Brescia, Istituto Paolo VI, 2001.

Sorrel, Christian, ed., *Renouveau conciliaire et crise doctrinale: Rome et les Églises nationales (1966–1968)*, Lyon, LARHRA, 2017.

CHAPTER 29

Ecumenism in Latin America after Vatican II: Evangelical Demands and Institutional Compromise

Sandra Arenas and Rodrigo Polanco

1 From Vatican II to the Medellín Conference (1968): Towards a New Concept of the Church

During the 19th and 20th centuries independence, republican and secular concepts, and the steady establishment and growth of the Reformed churches were gradually remapping the socio-religious scene for Catholicism. The public presence and social influence that Protestantism had begun to demonstrate led, for over a century and a half, to rejection by the Catholics, religious polarization, and public proselytism, which had been creeping into the culture.[1] Only through Vatican II and its early reception by the continental Catholic Church was this direct Catholic opposition mitigated; together with the acknowledgment of a theology of its own in a new sociopolitical context, a way of being a church was modeled in hegemonic Catholicism that would usher in ecumenism.

1.1 *The Socio-Religious Environment Prior to the 1960s Changes*

The 19th century was marked by hostility towards the Catholic Church in many liberal republics; seeking to remedy this issue, concordats would be signed from 1852 (Guatemala). These accorded increasing freedom to certain religious groups, although Catholicism would continue to be officially recognized as the state religion in countries such as Peru, Argentina, and Paraguay. In other cases, such as in Chile, Uruguay, and Brazil, the separation of church and state would be introduced gradually, enabling freedom of religion to be achieved far more quickly.[2]

Robert Bellarmine's model of the church, deeply rooted in Latin American Catholic self-understanding as a result of the direct influence of the Counter-Reformation in Spain during the 16th and 17th centuries, refrained from acknowledging any other foreign expression of Christianity. It tried to protect Catholic hegemony, both in religious matters and in terms of the privileges it granted in the public arena. However, at the beginning of the 20th century, Catholicism began to experience a kind of Protestant ambush and felt besieged by the groundbreaking revolutions, ideological liberalism, and seminal exodus of Catholics from popular backgrounds to the Protestant world, particularly to the Pentecostal Church. The image of an ambush is powerful; this feeling of harassment allowed for the development of studies and nascent theological thought, as well as an almost critical reflection on the possibilities for a new Catholicism. As a result, in the 1930s, the Catholic Church started to carry out a kind of reconquest of what was considered lost ground, assumed to belong to the church by right. Social Catholicism, for its part, rejected the marginal and subordinate role that the liberal state had granted to the church with no prospect of developing a Christian social

1 Proof of this was the use of pejorative expressions such as "cults" to refer to these institutions, as well as the express prohibition of religious freedom. See Walter Hanisch, "Protestantismo en Chile," *Mensaje* 26, 1954, 25: "There are 25 Protestant cults with 470 churches or services in the whole country ... Each cult carries out its own particular work."

2 See Sol Serrano, *¿Qué hacer con Dios en la República?: Política y secularización en Chile (1845–1885)*, Santiago, Fondo de Cultura Económica, 2008.

order. This rejection later became a Catholic social movement by means of Catholic trade unions, Catholic schools, Catholic universities, Catholic press etc., which sway and impact drew attention, in particular in the 1930s and 1940s. Against this militant backdrop in the public arena, the spread of Protestantism was physically impossible.

This anti-Protestant surge continued, practically unabated, until Vatican II. By then, however, the institutional geopolitics of the Roman Catholic Church had moved from its European center, and now Brazil, Colombia, and Mexico (along with the Philippines and the United States) were counted among the epicenters of Catholicism of the time. The population of Latin America had also grown substantially, implying greater Catholic hegemony. The processes of urbanization and industrialization that had been underway since the 1930s saw a sharp increase in the 1950s and 1960s; however, besides bringing populations closer together,[3] this also led to urban marginalization and underdevelopment in rural areas, where Pentecostal Protestantism was gradually consolidating its hold. In fact, as we shall see further below, this gradual movement from rural to urban, with its uprooting and need for cultural reconfiguration, had to offer believers an experience of faith adapted to the new situation they were suffering, which a certain Protestant religiosity could well manage. As a result, the ecclesial fringes began to shift and blur. This "other" started building local communities, although until Vatican II it was widely marginalized as irrelevant and discriminated against by the hegemonic church as non-Christian. No other institutional expression of Christianity was acknowledged except Roman Catholicism; in addition to constituting 92% of the population in the 1960s, there was an increased awareness that half of all the Catholics in the world were found on this continent.

1.2 *A Latin American Pentecost*

A common metaphor in Latin American theology and historiography that refers to the period after Vatican II is the "Latin American Pentecost."[4] This phrase shows the pneumatological shift, expressed through the powerful event of the Holy Spirit, that led to the reprogramming of the Christian agenda in the region. Thus, the local community had slowly been acquiring a theological density that would then be reflected in the interim between the council and the conference held in Medellín (1968), expanding in that assembly. CELAM II tried, on the one hand, to receive inspiration from the council and, on the other, to develop it at a local/regional level.[5] The self-awareness of being a regional and collegiate church had to be supported by doctrine and pastoral practice.

Vatican II had brought about a decisive change in Catholic self-awareness and, particularly in the years immediately after the council, there were moments of enthusiasm and creativity in ecumenical matters. Religious pluralism already existed, and now the theological and doctrinal framework was also favorable. Nevertheless, the experiences of shared knowledge had mainly occurred in the hands-on missionary and liturgical domains, far less in the theological field, and practically not at all in terms of doctrine. Furthermore, the WCC assembly held in Uppsala one month prior to the Medellín conference also provided its member churches with the rationale behind true Catholicity and the use of the action of the Holy Spirit in matters of missionary and ecclesial renewal; it was the responsibility of the churches to ensure social wellbeing and active participation in all social change.[6]

3 See José Míguez Bonino, "Unidad cristiana y reconciliación social: Coincidencia y tensión," *Cuadernos de Teología* 2/2, 1972, 109–123, esp. 110.

4 See for example, Eduardo F. Pironio, "Latinoamérica: 'Iglesia de la Pascua,'" *Criterio* 1652, 1972, 520–526.

5 See Alberto Ramírez, "La Conferencia de Medellín y la Teología de la Esperanza," *Cuestiones teológicas* 35/84, 2008, 235–254, esp. 239.

6 A good analysis carried out from a different angle – from the "South" – can be found in Gerald H. Anderson, "Uppsala 1968: The World Council's Fourth Assembly," *Philippine Studies* 16/2, 1968, 391–398.

At that time, cultures were questioning churches in regard to the gospel, and the churches were aware of their mission as a whole, in both a religious and human sense. As an event, the Latin American Pentecost was experienced as a missionary boost in a baptized but not sufficiently evangelized continent, in a context where an awakening awareness of discrimination was increasingly being viewed as a manifestation of God and a criticism of evangelization. Protestantism was also becoming more united in the continent. Between 1949 and 1969, the CELA brought together between 18 and 40 different churches, addressing issues on the Christian agenda relating in particular to public commitment.[7] The increase in the number of Evangelical Pentecostals, which began in the 1950s, continued with a vengeance in the following decade.[8] Thus, ecclesial self-awareness was redrawn around apostolic activity but within the framework of an inculturation of the Christian message and the development of a theology that would respond to sociopolitical needs. With the tension typical of a process of change on this scale, the "figure" of the church that emerged, both in praxis and in theology, could be described as that of a socially engaged Christian population, expressed in various ways (for example, through BECs). This would come to shape a certain model of ecumenical relations.

1.3 *Transformation and a New Climate of Conflict*

The Protestant-based ecclesial and ecumenical model had somewhat different characteristics in the churches and ecclesial communities that arrived in the continent through immigration in the 19th and 20th centuries (such as the Lutherans from Germany, the Anglicans from England, and the Orthodox Christians from the Middle East), compared to those that appeared as a result of the missionary upsurge brought about by international missionary organizations from the United States in particular, which demonstrated strongly apolitical Evangelical Protestantism.[9] This resulted in internal divisions and tensions with the nascent regional ecumenical movement. The criollo Pentecostal movement, which arose partly as a result of internal divisions within Methodism and partly thanks to strong support from missionaries, had introduced a "religious hybrid" that expanded in line with the emergence of Evangelical Pentecostalism. In fact, the mixing of official Catholic, indigenous, and traditional Evangelical elements formed, at its roots, an ecclesiality that placed a heavy emphasis on all things local, focused on worship and preaching the Word of God, and included the presence of traditional Latin American caudillismo.[10]

Thus, in the late 1960s, Latin American leadership began to emerge in the Evangelical Protestant world on the basis of an evangelizing model that swung between two core ideas. On the one hand, there was the central idea held by the fifth assembly of the CWME in Willingen (Germany) in 1952, namely that mission is an attribute of God and the Holy Trinity is its model; therefore, the sending of missionaries to preach the Word is unavoidable, essential to community life, and inherent to divine nature. On the other hand, there was the core idea held by the CWME in Mexico in 1963,[11]

7 See Orlando Costas, *Oaxtepec 1978: Unidad y misión en América Latina*, San José, CLAI, 1980, 87. The Roman Catholic Church was present neither at the Geneva conference on church and society in 1966, which had around 50 representatives from Latin America, nor at the UNELAM consultation in São Paulo in 1967.

8 Public commitment went hand in hand with this increase in numbers, although partisan political involvement only began in the 1980s and continues to this day. See José Luis Pérez Guadalupe & Sebastián Grundberger, eds., *Evangélicos y Poder en América Latina*, Lima, KAS/IESC, 2019, 19, 22.

9 This subsequently became more nuanced and also diversified, leading to internal divisions.

10 See Jean-Pierre Bastian, "De los protestantismos históricos a los pentecostalismos latinoamericanos: Análisis de una mutación religiosa," *Revista de Ciencias Sociales* 16, 2006, 38–54, esp. 49–50.

11 The CWME was born when the IMC joined the WCC in New Delhi in November 1961. Mexico represented an area of key missionary expansion for the region; for this reason, the WCC decided that the CWME would meet in Mexico City from Dec 8 to 19, 1963. See WCC, *Minutes of*

which was part of the WCC, that was considered radically in Uppsala in 1968, which moved away from the God-church-world circle and placed the world as the *locus* where God continues to meet humanity. Today, the dialectical relationship of God-world-church would best represent being a church to others.

From a Catholic standpoint, although ecumenism as a pastoral-theological matter did not play an important role in CELAM II,[12] the ecclesiological dynamism that developed there did, and this brought about lasting change in future ecumenical relations. From then on, churches became increasingly sensitive when it came to establishing channels of permanent cooperation in response to social needs, which conflicted with the internal polarization in Protestantism and Catholicism caused by diametrically opposed pastoral-theological emphases and spiritual beliefs: individual conversion versus social transformation,[13] and confessional Christianity versus testimonial Christianity.[14] In general, they resorted to transformation without defining its content and, therefore, prevented it from receiving a more significant renewal.[15]

2 The First Institutional Steps

Although ecumenism had existed for half a century in the Evangelical churches of Latin America, it was only after the changes brought about by Vatican II that the Latin American Catholic Church joined the ecumenical movement for fundamentally Evangelical reasons. In the period after the council this ecumenism, which, in its broadest sense, had theological roots, would be developed in three directions: on an ecclesial basis, with institutional initiatives, and in socio-theological reflection.

2.1 *The Initial, Isolated Steps*

During Vatican II, in the different Catholic ecclesial communities, Catholic priests and Evangelical pastors, besides ecclesial groups and communities, began organizing private initiatives, contacting one another in order to pray together and share their life of faith. There were, for example, joint panels to deal with mutual relationships, fraternal gatherings to become acquainted with each other, and new joint associations for social work.[16] It can be assumed, therefore, that a kind of grassroots ecumenism was the first thing to emerge in the field of Catholic-Evangelical ecumenical relations, and this occurred within the context of the council changes, opening up an ecclesial world that had hitherto been unknown, scorned, or feared. This Catholic opening-up – the product of a new way of conceiving the church – was warmly welcomed by the Evangelical churches that had already experienced their own ecumenical development over 50 years before, including in Latin America.[17]

the Second Meeting of the Commission on World Mission and Evangelism, Mexico City, December 8th–19th, 1963, London, Commission on World Mission and Evangelism, 1963. Nevertheless, the inculturation of the gospel in a pluricultural and religious context would only be established at the WCC assembly held in Salvador de Bahía, Brazil, in 1996.

12 See José Oscar Beozzo, "Medellin: Inspiration et racines," in: Joseph Doré & Alberto Melloni, eds., *Volti di fine concilio: Studi di storia e teologia sulla conclusione del Vaticano II*, Bologna, Il Mulino, 2001, 361–393; Silvia Scatena, *In populo pauperum: La chiesa latinoamericana dal concilio a Medellín (1962–1968)*, Bologna, Il Mulino, 2008; and Hans-Jürgen Prien, *Christianity in Latin America (Revised and Expanded Edition)*, Leiden, Brill, 2013, 554.

13 See Gottfried Brakemeier, *Preservando la unidad del Espíritu en el vínculo de la paz: Un curso de ecumenismo*, Quito, CLAI, 2008, 53–54.

14 This varied understanding of ecclesiality also brought about parallel initiatives in 1969: CELA III and CLADE I.

15 See Luis Alberto Gómez de Souza, "El postconcilio o el riesgo del ghetto narcisista," *Vispera* 1/1, 1967, 40–42.

16 See Sandra Arenas & Rodrigo Polanco, "Aproximación histórico-teológica a la cuestión ecuménica en Chile," in: Sandra Arenas & Rodrigo Polanco, eds., *Ecumenismo: Un panorama latinoamericano*, Santiago de Chile, Ediciones Universidad Alberto Hurtado, 2021, 143–186.

17 See the contribution by Juan Sepúlveda in the first volume of this work.

2.2 *Institutional Ecumenism*

One of the products of Vatican II in Latin America was the strengthening of CELAM, which was founded in 1955 "as a pastoral and theological organization authorized in the continent"[18] and which gradually fell in step with global changes and the ecumenical awakening. In 1955, CELAM I in Rio de Janeiro established the undersecretariat for the preservation and propagation of the catholic faith, a subsection of which was the defense of the faith;[19] in 1959, this became the CLAF, whose aim was to "preserve the Catholic faith in the face of non-Catholic movements, especially communism, Protestantism, spiritism, Freemasonry, and superstition."[20] In 1966, during its tenth annual meeting, the CELAM established the department of ecumenism, which was formalized the following year in Lima, in order to put the guidelines of *Unitatis redintegratio* into practice.[21] Its first president was His Eminence Antonio Quarracino (bishop of Nueve de Julio, Argentina), his executive secretary was the Argentinian priest Jorge María Mejía, and its headquarters were located in Buenos Aires.

During the first few years, work was carried out with those who previously, in their own countries, had already been interested in ecumenism. At the start, there was enthusiasm but, at the same time, there was a lack of mutual awareness between Catholics and Protestants, and obvious confusion regarding the different churches. In addition, as a general rule, "the nascent ecumenism was limited to the higher ranks and pastors, and it did not involve the Christian people."[22] Thus, the first steps consisted in carrying out studies that analyzed the state of ecumenism in Latin America, studying the documents issued by the SPCU, and achieving a rapport and holding meetings with other Christian traditions and ecumenical entities, such as the CALA and the LWF. Other movements were also approached that had previously been considered sectarian (for example Pentecostal churches, Assemblies of God, Adventists, Baptists). Reaching out to the UBS and being impressed by the world of the Reformation in the biblical sphere had possibly the greatest impact. In 1965, the CELAM approved the Latin American ecumenical edition of the New Testament (with the specialist participation of Hispanic Americans, both Catholic and Protestant), produced in collaboration with the monks of Taizé.[23] In 1968, the secretary of the department of ecumenism participated as an observer in the regional conference of the Americas, held by the UBS in Oaxtepec, Mexico. And in 1974, the first Latin American meeting of Bible scholars was held and attended by 30 specialists, both Catholic and Protestant. This was accompanied by the Catholic Church's strong Bible dissemination strategy.

The new spirit was crowned by the invitation of 11 Protestant observers to CELAM II in Medellín,[24] to which was responded in kind with the presence of Catholic observers invited to CELA III in Buenos Aires in 1969.[25] It is interesting to note that

18 Rodrigo Polanco, "Cambios en la conciencia eclesial en América Latina, previo a la Conferencia de Medellín (1968): Estudio a partir de la literatura clasificada en la base de datos 'Seladoc,'" presented at the international congress "Medellín 50 años después: Memoria y perspectivas de future," Pontificia Universidad Católica de Chile, Santiago, Nov 5–8, 2018. Now published in *CrSt* 41, 2020, 171–224, here 214.

19 See I Conferencia General del Episcopado Latinoamericano (1955), "Conclusiones," chapter 11, in: Consejo Episcopal Latinoamericano, *Las Cinco Conferencias Generales del Episcopado Latinoamericano*, Bogotá, San Pablo, 2014, 54–57.

20 "Conclusiones de la 3ª Asamblea ordinaria del Celam," 1958, quoted in Patricio Merino-Beas, "El diálogo ecuménico animado desde el Celam," *Theologica Xaveriana* 184, 2017, 387–410, here 392.

21 Merino-Beas, "El diálogo ecuménico," 388–397, esp. 394.

22 Merino-Beas, "El diálogo ecuménico," 396.

23 See Silvia Scatena, *Taizé, una parabola di unità: Storia della comunità dalle origini al concilio dei giovani*, Bologna, Il Mulino, 2018, 566–568.

24 See Hernán Parada, *Crónica de Medellin: Segunda Conferencia General del Episcopado Latinoamericano*, Bogotá, Indo-American Press Service, 1975, 259. See therefore Silvia Scatena, "'Um só Senhor, uma só fé': a esperança ecumênica de Medellín," *Fronteiras* 1/2, 2018, 397–414.

25 See Dafne Sabanes Plou, "Latin America," in: *A History of the Ecumenical Movement*, vol. 3, John Briggs,

the participation of the observers in the Medellín conference was far more active than at Vatican II, since the working groups and writing committees for the concluding documents had been combined. Furthermore, in particular, the request made by five of the observers to remain behind at the end of the conference and receive communion during the Eucharist at the close of the assembly must be remembered as a symbolic and performative gesture. The request was granted and the gesture was later continued by other communities in different parts of the continent.[26]

These institutional steps at a central level were replicated by the various national episcopates, always on the basis of a clear evangelical belief. For instance, in the Southern Cone, varying structural and existential initiatives were carried out in order to increase the desire for unity which was catalyzed by the optimism that was spreading throughout the continent in the 1960s. In Buenos Aires, an archdiocesan committee for ecumenism was formed in 1967, and the episcopal conference created the national secretariat for ecumenism in 1971.[27] In Paraguay, on Aug 5, 1967, the ecumenical movement of Paraguay was launched with a declaration signed by priests, pastors, and laypeople of the Catholic, Lutheran, and Methodist churches, the Disciples of Christ, and the Salvation Army; and, in 1969, the Acción Ecuménica de Asunción was formed.[28] In Brazil, the first ecumenical body in which Catholics were represented had already been created in 1957, the GERT (Lutherans, Methodists, Anglicans, and Catholics), and after Vatican II, the CNBB added ecumenism to its general guidelines for pastoral action. This led to the creation of several important ecumenical organizations, such as the Servicio de Consejería Interconfesional (1969) and the Consejo de Iglesias para el estudio y reflexión (1970).[29] In Peru, the Week of Prayer for Christian Unity was already being celebrated at the start of the 1960s, but since 1965 it has officially been an initiative of the Peruvian episcopal conference.[30] And in Chile, also in 1965, in light of *Unitatis redintegratio*, the episcopal conference requested the creation of diocesan secretariats for ecumenism and formed the national department of ecumenism. In 1966, the Week of Prayer for Christian Unity was celebrated and the national ecumenical days were held. All of the above helped to raise awareness on the ecclesiological importance of ecumenism.[31]

2.3 *Political Ecumenism*

In the 1960s, at the same time as these institutional initiatives, another form of ecumenism emerged in the continent from the Evangelical and, later, Catholic populace, that Julio Barreiro defined as "political ecumenism."[32] This was born from "the sociopolitical climate faced by Christians needing to find solutions to burning issues in Latin American society."[33] The strong feeling of social optimism that went hand in hand with the people's fight for structural change with regard to justice and peace in the continent raised an urgent question in the Christian consciousness as to the role of the gospel at this historic juncture. Different groups across the length and breadth

Mercy Amba Oduyoye & Georges Tsetsis, eds., *1968–2000*, Geneva, WCC Publications, 2004, 565–589, esp. 565–567.

26 See Scatena, *In populo pauperum*, 504–507, and, with further documentation, Scatena, *Taizé, una parabola di unità*, 675–680.

27 See Norberto Padilla, "El camino del ecumenismo en la Argentina," in: Arenas & Polanco, eds., *Ecumenismo: Un panorama latinoamericano*, 53–70.

28 See Diana Durán, "Apuntes para una historia del ecumenismo en el Paraguay," in: Arenas & Polanco, eds., *Ecumenismo: Un panorama latinoamericano*, 71–92.

29 See Elías Wolff, "Elementos para una historia del ecumenismo en Brasil," in: Arenas & Polanco, eds., *Ecumenismo: Un panorama latinoamericano*, 93–108.

30 See Juan Miguel Espinoza, "El episcopado peruano posconciliar y el ecumenismo: un desafío pastoral pendiente (1960–2010)," in: Arenas & Polanco, eds., *Ecumenismo: Un panorama latinoamericano*, 109–142.

31 See Arenas & Polanco, "Aproximación histórico-teológica."

32 See Zwinglio Dias, "Evaluación crítica de la práctica ecuménica latinoamericana," *Cristianismo y sociedad* 60, 1979, 3–30, here 7.

33 Dias, "Evaluación crítica," 5.

of the continent concluded that, in the light of the pressing needs of such an unfairly oppressed population, theological and institutional differences did not matter; rather, it was an imperative requirement of the gospel to join the liberation movements, with all Christians united as one. There were never any official church movements; these movements were constituted by laypeople and were gradually distancing and removing themselves from ecclesial structures. Although these movements would enter a crisis at the end of the decade, owing to their loss of Christian identity, they were the seed that would grow over the next two decades into liberation theology and the Christian fight for human rights.[34]

3 Ecumenism Assumes Different Forms: From Medellín to the New Millennium

On the Catholic side institutional ecumenism, from the Medellín conference until the new millennium, following its decisive arrival in the continent as a result of Vatican II's renewal, had its ups and downs.

3.1 *Strengthening Ecumenical Praxis: Structure*

In 1972, CELAM's department of ecumenism became the section on ecumenism, an offshoot of the general secretariat, with a view to influencing and being more closely involved in all the episcopal body's activities. This permitted the creation of committees and meetings such as the CELAM-CALA joint committee and the joint Methodist-Catholic group meeting in Buenos Aires in 1977. It also facilitated the presence of CELAM observers at the assembly held by the CIEMAL, the organization of courses in ecumenism in different countries across the subcontinent, the organization of Bible study groups, and regular meetings between Latin American delegates for ecumenism, among others.[35]

Furthermore, the CELAM provided both evidence of the spirit of ecumenism and guidance for the continent's Catholic churches. The Medellín conference and, in a different manner, the Puebla conference (1979) demonstrated the importance of the subject and were attended by observers (who were active in the committees) from other churches. The Medellín conference did so through the actions mentioned above, although there was no particularly conclusive reflection, while the Puebla conference did so with the fourth chapter of its final document, dedicated to the subject: "Dialogue for communion and participation" (nn. 1096–1127). This text, having briefly outlined the council doctrine on ecumenism, frames it within the evangelizing perspective guiding the document (n. 1096) and highlights the importance of ecumenism in the search for "human advancement" and the "defense of human rights and the building of justice and peace" (n. 1107). In this text, Latin American ecumenism is emphasized and encouraged. However, the document does not include a more complete reflection in relation to the challenges faced as a result of Christian ecclesial diversity throughout the continent.[36]

Conversely, there was a major change with CELAM IV in Santo Domingo (1992). The meeting was preceded by a backlash against liberation theology and the popular church, along with the ever-increasing involvement of the Vatican to ensure that the conference did not reinforce these new, notable expressions of Latin American Christianity. This meant that ecumenism ceased to be an important topic. This time, incomprehensibly, observers from other Christian churches were

34 See Dias, "Evaluación crítica," 6–8.

35 See Merino-Beas, "El diálogo ecuménico," 397–399.

36 *Documento de Puebla: III Conferencia General del Episcopado Latinoamericano* available at <https://www.celam.org/documentos/Documento_Conclusivo_Puebla.pdf> (accessed Aug 2, 2023). See also Juan Carlos Urrea Viera, "La reflexión episcopal acerca del ecumenismo en América Latina y el Caribe," *Medellín* 23/91, 1997, 375–391, esp. 384–386.

not invited (later, in response, Catholic observers would not be invited to the third general assembly of the CLAI in Concepción, Chile, in 1995).[37] Although the final document of Santo Domingo mentions ecumenism and encourages continuation of the dialogue (n. 132), its focus is "fundamentalist cults" and the "new religious movements or free religious movements" (nn. 139–152).[38] In spite of the fact that these were important distinctions, both conceptually and in pastoral terms, handling of the subject was no longer directly geared towards ecumenism and, moreover, treating the new independent Evangelical churches as "cults" restricted and affected the ecumenical movement enormously.

From then on, institutional ecumenism faced difficulties that slowed its progress. In 1995, in its analysis of the ecclesial situation across the continent during its ordinary general assembly, the CELAM recognized how little interest the local Catholic churches had in ecumenical matters. Thus, in light of the 1995 encyclical *Ut unum sint* by John Paul II, the CELAM devised a global plan to boost ecumenism. It suggested, among other things, encouraging and supporting the national secretariats for ecumenism in Latin America and the Caribbean; analyzing the phenomenon of Pentecostalism after carrying out a joint Latin American seminar with the CLAI; ecumenical training of pastoral workers; issuing publications about ecumenical dialogue; and promoting dialogue with historical churches and their associations.[39] In the diocesan churches, this was accompanied by activities under the same banner: the creation of secretariats for ecumenism, the annual celebration of the Week of Prayer for Christian Unity, numerous events promoting mutual understanding and dialogue, regular publications containing ecumenical news, the widespread dissemination of ecumenical versions of the Bible, the joint celebration of ecumenical liturgies on national holidays, the creation of several types of ecumenical groups with different social purposes, the creation of theological fellowships for the joint study of relevant topics, reciprocal invitations between representatives of other churches to meeting opportunities, and, in addition to all of the above, social ecumenism, theological ecumenism, and ecumenism relating to human rights. Nonetheless, two points must be stated: despite the efforts made to integrate all these initiatives into the lives and theology of the Catholic people of God, in general, they remained the concerns of the elite or of people who had a special interest in the subject. Secondly, over the last two decades, interest has markedly declined (also at the leadership level) in terms of resources invested, dedicated staff, and activities carried out.[40]

Furthermore, in the context of the Great Jubilee of 2000, the declaration by the Congregation for the Doctrine of the Faith, *Dominus Iesus* on the unicity and salvific universality of Jesus Christ and the church (2000), was also a considerable blow to Latin American ecumenism. It led to unease in non-Catholic churches as well as in Catholic groups

37 See Sabanes Plou, "Latin America," 584.

38 Available at <https://www.celam.org/documentos/Documento_Conclusivo_Santo_Domingo.pdf> (accessed Aug 7, 2023).

39 See José Luis Lacunza, *El ecumenismo en América Latina y el Caribe: Una visión histórica y proyectiva*, presented at the Seminar on Ecumenism, Mexico City, Aug 4–6, 1998. For the history of institutional ecumenism in Latin America after Vatican II, in addition to the texts cited in this paper, see María Teresa Porcile Santiso, "Ecumenismo en América Latina," *Medellín* 6/22, 1980, 186–199 (summarized in *Mensaje Iberoamericano* 198, 1982, 5–8); Edin Sued Abumanssur, "Ecumenism in Latin America: Between the Marketplace and the Desert," in: Virginia Garrard-Burnett, Paul Freston & Stephen Dove, eds., *The Cambridge History of Religions in Latin America*, New York, Cambridge University Press, 2016, 729–738; and Edward L. Cleary, "The transformation of Latin American Christianity, c.1950–2000," in: *The Cambridge History of Christianity*, vol. 9, Hugh McLeod, ed., *World Christianities (c.1914–c.2000)*, Cambridge, Cambridge University Press, 2006, 366–384.

40 See Padilla, "El camino del ecumenismo"; Durán, "Apuntes para una historia"; Wolff, "Elementos para una historia"; Espinoza, "El episcopado peruano"; Arenas & Polanco, "Aproximación histórico-teológica."

that were more inclined towards ecumenism.[41] In addition, since 2000, "the decrease in CELAM's resources, its restructuring and awareness-raising about the growth of the Pentecostal movement, and the drop in historic churches meant that the number of different ecumenical activities fell"[42] not only at the central level but also in local churches, as was painfully expressed at the latest meeting of bishops responsible for ecumenism and interreligious dialogue at the episcopal conference of Latin America and the Caribbean, held in Buenos Aires in November 2016.[43] CELAM V, held in Aparecida (2007), despite its support for ecumenism (including, once again, invitations to observers from other Christian churches), did not manage to reverse this trend.

3.2 *The Spirituality of Liberation*

Nevertheless, there was another vibrant and effective kind of ecumenism that had come to be characteristic of Latin American Christianity, which we can call "liberationist grassroots ecumenism," The ecumenical experiences of liberation, defense of human rights, and social commitment arose from a theological and ecclesiological "grassroots ecumenism." Since the end of the 1960s, a new awareness of the church was surfacing among many Latin American Christians who felt challenged by the history of suffering and injustice among their people. These believers began to gather in various parts of the continent to reflect upon their faith from a historical praxis of liberation. Theologists such as Gustavo Gutiérrez from Peru (Catholic), Rubem Azevedo Alves from Brazil (Presbyterian), and José Miguez Bonino from Argentina (Methodist) were developing what would come to be known as liberation theology.[44] Gutiérrez provides a good description of this new type of ecumenism:

> Meetings between Christians from different creeds but with the same political approach are becoming more frequent. This gives rise to ecumenical groups, often marginal to their respective ecclesiastical authorities, in which Christians share their faith and their efforts to create a more just society. The common struggle makes the *traditional* ecumenical programs seem obsolete (a "marriage between senior citizens," as someone has said) and impels them to look for new paths towards unity.[45]

Here, "unity is not an end unto itself" but "can and must occur, in accordance with the building of the Kingdom of God among men and for men."[46] With this solid social and theological foundation, "the ecumenical issue [was] reconsidered in terms of the practice of popular pastoral care and [required] new strategic positioning by ecumenical movements."[47] In some countries, especially in Brazil, this new type of ecumenism was based on a wide network of BECs which met frequently to discuss the Bible and discover the signs of God in Latin America, connecting the Word of God to the oppressed population's desires for liberation. These communities received considerable support in the 1980s from the Catholic Church (particularly after the Medellín and Puebla conferences), which led to a new way of thinking about the church known as popular church. At the time, the BECs had key political influence in some countries in the continent, particularly in Central America. This way of thinking about the church was also articulated in Protestant areas, albeit in a more limited manner.

However, in light of the difficulties that pastoral work bearing the stamp of liberation entailed, coupled with the strong reaction of the dictatorships

41 See Sabanes Plou, "Latin America," 584.
42 Merino-Beas, "El diálogo ecuménico," 402–403.
43 The authors of the text attended this meeting.
44 See Sabanes Plou, "Latin America," 568.
45 Gustavo Gutiérrez, *Teología de la liberación: Perspectivas*, Salamanca, Sígueme, 1990, 149; ET: *A Theology of Liberation: History, Politics, and Salvation*, Maryknoll, Orbis Books, 1988.
46 Dias, "Evaluación crítica," 27.
47 Dias, "Evaluación crítica," 11.

of the time, and given that the support of ecclesial leadership could not always be counted on, the communities had to become stronger through an institutional framework of mutual cooperation. As a result, at that time, the FTL (1970), the ASEL, founded in 1975 as a continuation of the ISAL, which had ended its activities in that year, and what then became the CLAI (1978), among others, were created as forms of support for better social, political, and theological work.[48] During this decade, the ecumenical dialogue of liberation greatly increased through meetings and centers for theological dialogue, as we shall explain in greater detail below.

Nevertheless, it is important to remember that this process has not been without conflict. For instance, the different interpretations of the human rights violations of the political and military regimes in the region led to divisions within the churches, precisely because of the church theology underpinning their praxis. On the one hand, there was the two kingdoms doctrine, which was apolitical by definition; on the other, there was a more social and democratic theology, which considered the involvement of Christian communities in the public and political arena as an internal requirement of their mission. Yet some traditionally apolitical Pentecostal churches also explicitly supported certain dictatorial regimes, such as Pinochet's in Chile. Later, with the end of the dictatorships in Latin America, the installation of the neoliberal model, and the *ad intra* revival experienced by the churches, all such instances of social-liberation commitment were reduced or permanently ceased, although contextual theology saw diversification and renewal.

4 The Political Dimension of Faith, Human Rights, and Ecumenical Praxis

In 1972, the then Bishop of Mar del Plata (Argentina), Eduardo Francisco Pironio, wrote that "the Latin American church's time has come."[49] He referred to the process of shaping one's identity, which required, in his opinion, "the spiritual richness of partner churches."[50] Since the 1960s, the social, economic, and political situation in the continent had been suffering a crisis: in addition to exacerbating political polarization, a series of military dictatorships had brought about greater social inequality, together with its correlative forms of oppression, corruption, and social injustice. In the 1980s, these regimes gradually began to withdraw, with countries returning to democratic political systems that would be fully established by the early 1990s. During this 30-year period, a local ecclesiological-ecumenical model had been created that responded to fragmentation, social inequality, and the violation of basic human rights. Nevertheless, this process was thrown into a critical state in the 1990s as a result of multiple factors, both political and religious, including the fear of the communities themselves that they would lose their identity and their members. Although this subject will be discussed in detail at a later stage, a summary look at its theoretical foundations is provided here.

4.1 *The Political Dimension of Faith*

During that time, on their program agendas, institutionalized ecumenical organizations had managed to emphasize the strong connection between the social, political, and economic context described above and awareness of the inescapable political dimension of faith, something that only came to the surface once the model of Christianity was detached from the state.[51] Having said that, these agendas were designed according to the view held by believers that local communities had seen what was known as a "massive breakthrough

48 See Sabanes Plou, "Latin America," 571–572.

49 Pironio, "Latinoamérica," 520.

50 Pironio, "Latinoamérica," 520.

51 See Prien, *Christianity*, 453.

of the poor,"[52] had "evangelizing potential,"[53] and had an ecclesial identity that had been revealed by said breakthrough and potential. Ecclesial faith, and the ecumenism that this necessarily implied, faced the unavoidable challenge of developing within this contextual outlook, since a grassroots social movement had arisen that included workers' organizations, trade unions, and neighborhood organizations in which Christians were the main players, although this was not without its setbacks.[54] Indeed, an appropriate interaction between churches and the world was at stake here, as well as the relationship between the religious sector, politics, and the spiritual, within earthly realities. The whole movement was fed by the communal and ecumenical reading of the Bible, in which the political-liberation dimension was not a marginal detail but part of the deeper, inescapable core of a person's faith in Jesus Christ. Since it was at the heart of the biblical message, liberation had to become a shared prayer and underpin the social commitment of Christians without hesitation.

To the same extent that the grassroots social and ecclesial movement was developing, a landmark project that criticized capitalism and imperialist domination, particularly in North America, was being devised, where the prospect of democratizing social spaces was guiding relationships characterized by equity. Through the instrumental use of political and sociological interventions, the Christian theology that emerged in the early 1970s became more prominent and aware of the fact that Latin America (and the so-called Third World in general, with its own nuances) was suffering the consequences of powerful international structures of domination and dependence on the capitalist system which, when combined with local structures of domination, had sparked a discriminatory process of development, a dependent political and economic system, high inflation, exploitation of the most vulnerable individuals, concentration of power, gender inequality, ethnic discrimination, and so on. It was clear that economic development had not resulted in the wished-for human welfare, and that this was an undeniable sign that there was oppression taking place that was not desired by God. As a result, the oppression-liberation antinomy was established as the theological-praxis paradigm for churches and ecclesial communities, providing extra-ecclesial common ground upon which to unite social forces promoting liberation. Ecclesiology was then reconsidered from this shared ground, articulating the notions of discipleship and the kingdom of God as the structuring concepts of the local basic community. Likewise, the spiritual experience of following Jesus had to be inseparable from the fight for freedom, because in this agonist process relationships of kinship and fraternity among all members of the public were at stake on both an intrahistorical and an eschatological level. Consequently, the common ground of ecumenical life now consisted of questioning ecclesial faith and its relationship to historical development, since "the demands of justice in the Kingdom of God in an obedient and radical discipleship"[55] jeopardized the public arena.

As a result of the foregoing changes, together with the decision of the churches and ecclesial communities to focus on the poor and fight against poverty, ecumenical relations in the continent started to thrive in a profound and effective

52 As shown at the Fourth International Ecumenical Congress of Theology, held in São Paulo from Feb 20 to Mar 3, 1980. See "Eclesiología de las Comunidades Cristianas Populares: Documento del IV Congreso Internacional ecumeénico de Teologia," *Medellín* 6/22, 1980, 282–296, here 283.

53 *Documento de Puebla*, n. 1147.

54 The churches still did not have the theological or doctrinal support necessary to sustain these social-revolutionary processes, since they were only then being created. In this respect, Prien's interpretation is vague, simply putting forward a "lack of preparation" by the Catholic and Protestant reformist middle class. See Prien, *Christianity*, 452.

55 *Carta a las Iglesias cristianas y organismos ecuménicos de América Latina*, Oaxtepec, Mexico, Sep 26, 1978, available at <https://www.yumpu.com/es/document/read/31027855/oaxtepec-consejo-latinoamericano-de-iglesias-clai> (accessed Aug 8, 2023).

way; although this had not been their main or even conscious intention, it was nonetheless a sign of the kingdom of God. There were opportunities for liturgical celebrations, missionary outreach, and theology to be deployed with the increasing introjection of the political awareness of ecclesial faith. The process was framed globally in the making of history: "The poor in the Third World are fighting tooth and nail to achieve unity in their mutual struggle against all forms of colonialism, neocolonialism, and imperialism. Churches must be involved in these efforts,"[56] precisely because of the public nature of the faith that they professed. This would be ecumenism in the service of, and dependent on, unity and justice for the Latin American people.

4.2 *Human Rights*

It is worth pointing out that this subject can be found at three points in time. The joint work to safeguard fundamental human rights was an immediate ecumenical response to the military regimes across the continent. Indeed, since the sociopolitical contexts were similar, the suffering and responses thereto tended to be comparable: strict authoritarian regimes, political corruption, state-sponsored violence, murder, torture, social destabilization, and increased poverty. In addition, in relation to the Sandinista revolution, the climate of civil violence was aggravated not only in Nicaragua and Guatemala, but also throughout Central America; the Southern Cone saw an influx of both refugees from this region and refugees fleeing the internal conflict in Mexico. The state-sponsored violence inflicted by military dictatorships was experienced across practically the whole continent and also had dire consequences for the communities of the faithful, whose members suffered martyrdom. This all quickly mobilized the ecclesial communities, in which an ecumenical response arose without being planned as such.

In this context, several ecumenical schemes were implemented more permanently, such as the Vicariate of Solidarity in Chile,[57] the joint endeavors of CEAS and Peace and Hope International in Peru,[58] and the CIPAE in Asunción, Paraguay. These were then reinforced by larger bodies, such as the HRROLA, created by the WCC in 1975 in Nairobi, which gave rise to, and left its mark on, local forums in the Southern Cone, Mexico, Brazil,[59] and Central America, even before the CLAI was founded.[60] It should be added that the WCC office played a crucial role in the Protestant movement in relation to the defense of fundamental rights.

56 See "Eclesiología de las Comunidades Cristianas Populares," 295.

57 For an analysis of the Vicariate of Solidarity as an ecumenical agency, see Roberto Garretón, "Derechos humanos: La fuerza de la verdad: El Comité Pro Paz y la Vicaría de la Solidaridad," *Persona y Sociedad* 17/3, 2003, 77–86; and Juan Sepúlveda, "La defensa de los derechos humanos como experiencia ecuménica," *Persona y Sociedad* 17/3, 2003, 21–28. See also the works by Alexander Wilde, ed., *Las Iglesias ante la violencia en América Latina: Los derechos humanos en el pasado y el presente*, Mexico City, FLACSO, 2015; Alison J. Bruey, *Bread, Justice, and Liberty: Grassroots Activism and Human Rights in Pinochet's Chile*, Madison, University of Wisconsin Press, 2018; and Patrick William Kelly, *Sovereign Emergencies: Latin America and the making of global human rights politics*, Cambridge, Cambridge University Press, 2018.

58 Rolando Iberico, "El ecumenismo de los derechos humanos en el Perú: Colaboración entre la Comisión Episcopal de Acción Social y Paz y Esperanza," in: Arenas & Polanco, eds., *Ecumenismo: Un panorama latinoamericano*, 291–321, esp. 295–301.

59 Brazil was a forefather of ecumenical work in this regard. One of the most significant meetings of the time was the second ecumenical meeting on human rights, held in São Paulo in January 1983, in which 15 Catholic and Protestant organizations committed to this endeavor took part. See SEDOC, *II Encontro Ecumênico de Direitos Humanos*, 15/162, June 1983, 1155–1279.

60 A WCC delegation visited CELAM on Feb 8, 2018. Dr. Fernando Enns, a German Mennonite theologian and member of the WCC central committee, said that, internationally, the churches of Latin America had been important agents of peace and justice. For a brief review, see Sabanes Plou, "Latin America," 572–573 and 577–578.

Catholicism on the continent, however, did not always react in a unified way. Some national churches, such as the Chilean Catholic Church, were active and diligent when it came to forming ties with other churches and ecclesial communities involved in the initiative promoted by the WCC and subsequently endorsed by the CLAI. Conversely, the Argentinian Catholic Church, for instance, was much more reluctant to become involved, at that stage, with a movement that would mean publicly taking a stance against the dictatorial military regime. Awareness of the ethical and social significance of the gospel, of the requirement to act with partiality towards victims, and of the ecumenical implications of this partiality was neither linear, immediate, or uniform. The same could be said for the Protestant churches. Furthermore, the different relationship that each church in each country had with the government also exerted its own influence.

While the political setting was changing and democracies were being restored, these same ecumenical bodies were also involved in the processes relating to truth, justice, and reparation. For example, in 1988 certain Protestant institutions organized an interregional meeting on human rights in Asia and Latin America, in which three Asian countries, Argentina, and Chile took part. It would be those two Latin American countries, together with Uruguay, Paraguay, and Brazil, which, in their transition to democracy, would be assisted by the prohuman rights ecumenical movement in investigating the crimes committed by the regimes. This resulted in conclusive reports that helped *a posteriori* to ensure greater justice for both victims and aggressors.[61]

The gradual journey of this ecumenical movement has illustrated a "path to spirituality," a concrete way of living a Christian life in situations where life, peace, and social justice are not being protected. This has led to permanent benefits in relation to the awareness of what it is to be a Latin American church.

5 Developing an Ecumenical Theology/Ecclesiology in Latin America

In Latin America, *praxis* guides and precedes theory. The ecumenical experiences that we have described facilitated the development of ecclesiological thinking of an ecumenical nature, which increasingly fell in line with the ecclesial experiences outlined. Three theological experiences/paths can be observed.

5.1 *University Research*

Immediately after Vatican II, the Catholic Church managed to (re)train its pastoral workers along council lines, which also served to encourage ecumenism. Against this backdrop, many faculties and centers for theological studies introduced one or more courses on ecumenism as part of their core programs for theological studies and preparation for priestly ministry. In some of those centers, such as the Universidad Católica de la Santísima Concepción in Chile, departments for ecumenical studies and scientific publications on the characteristics of ecumenism in various contexts were created. All of the above have involved socio-theological studies and reflections in relation to the culture and social reality of the various Christian churches. This has resulted in a better understanding of the cultural context in which the ecclesial communities have been developing. For Catholicism, this has been an opportunity to better understand the considerable progress made by the Pentecostal churches as well as by other new ecclesial experiences.[62]

61 The WCC office for human rights provided support for the Mothers of the Plaza de Mayo in Argentina; FASIC assisted the National Commission for Truth and Reconciliation in Chile; in Brazil, aid was coordinated by a Presbyterian minister and the archbishop of São Paulo. See Sabanes Plou, "Latin America," 577–578.

62 See Arenas & Polanco, "Aproximación histórico-teológica."

5.2 *Liberation Theologies*

A richer and more widely disseminated form of theological reflection emerged from grassroots communities committed to liberation (and the presence of theologians in said communities) and their associations of theologians. In the light of their new understanding of ecumenism, this serious reflection was rooted in the Latin American context and mindful of "the profound political changes that were taking place in the continent."[63] For example, the aforementioned ASEL was particularly relevant in the development of Latin American political-theological thought through the promotion of numerous activities and the publication of the journal *Cristianismo y sociedad*, which it had inherited from the earlier ISAL experience. Similarly, the FTL has promoted both reflection and publications concerning social issues as well as participation in conferences and meetings, but always maintaining, of course, an institutional independence with respect to its leaders. The frequent meetings of these theologians encouraged the creation of different centers for study, ecumenical reflection, and social sciences, such as in Costa Rica, Managua, Lima, Santiago de Chile, Caracas, Mexico, and Brazil. Furthermore, the theologians also attended and contributed to the Puebla, Santo Domingo, and Aparecida conferences, and they were involved in peace processes, for example, in Central America and Argentina. Their aim was threefold: to train Catholic and Protestant leaders from the communities in order to encourage processes of liberation, to help raise awareness of the new historical ecumenical process that was emerging from the grassroots, and to support the various processes of change which were underway in the region.[64]

This new model of unity for the church has been explained by Miguez Bonino.[65] For this renowned theologian, the main issue consists in posing the question of unity properly. His theological assumptions are as follows: "An ecumenism that is aware of its intrinsic contextuality is necessary" and it must distance itself from any illusion of universality; "the problem of unity of God's people must be presented during the times of suffering and hope in which the Latin American people were living;" and "more important than asking what the church *is*" is "the question about what it is *for*." Therefore, the true "scandal in Latin America is not the existence of different denominations" but "the polarization within each church … concerning the meaning of the Christian faith and its place and value in the historical situation."[66] On the basis of these premises, the ecumenical question has changed in order to now ask *where* the true church is and no longer *what* it is. He concludes that:

> The ecumenical movement must give up the attempt to erect one of the existing ecclesial entities as "the full measure" of ecclesial reality against which one could measure the "ecclesial density" of the rest. The search for unity is the struggle for the church as it strives to take shape in the quest for a new kind of human life in a new society.[67]

"Unity, therefore, is *based on the separation* of the practices and values of the kingdom itself."[68] Unity is not the aim. The aim is the kingdom. And often the kingdom involves division and struggle. Ecumenism must focus on the kingdom and not on the churches.

63 See Sabanes Plou, "Latin America," 571.

64 Sabanes Plou, "Latin America," 572–581.

65 See José Míguez Bonino, "A Latin American Attempt to Locate the Question of Unity," in: *What Kind of Unity?*, Geneva, WCC Publications, 1974, 51–62.

66 Jorge Scampini, "La participación latinoamericana en Fe y Constitución (1927–1991): Un espacio de verificación del diálogo teológico en y desde América Latina," in: Arenas & Polanco, eds., *Ecumenismo: Un panorama latinoamericano*, 189–224, here 206, in which Scampini summarizes the thoughts of José Míguez Bonino set forth in the abovementioned text.

67 In accordance with the summary provided in Scampini, "La participación latinoamericana," 207.

68 Dias, "Evaluación crítica," 27.

5.3 *Theological Dialogues*

In most Latin American countries there has been, in general, a lack of interest on the part of the churches and ecclesial communities to create and maintain forums for theological dialogue, which explains the nonexistence, to this day, of large scale, multilateral, regional dialogue.[69] Despite this, on an institutional, national, and sometimes regional level, the theological commissions formed, and the bi- and multilateral dialogues conducted, have made some progress through reflection combined with ecumenical documents issued by higher ecclesial bodies. Efforts have been made to receive them from a Latin American perspective. Among them, the text *Baptism, Eucharist and Ministry*, from the commission on Faith and Order convened in Lima, Peru, in 1982, was very important, as it provided the opportunity for many "mutual recognition agreements" to be drafted between the different churches throughout the continent, with a subsequent theological reflection on their rationale.[70] There are also the multilateral declarations on the mutual recognition of baptism in Chile (1999) and Brazil (2007). Likewise, the *Joint Declaration on the Doctrine of Justification* (1999) permitted many theological meetings and pastoral reflections concerning the 1517 schism, while the publication of the Catholic Church's *Code of Canon Law* (1983) enabled steps to be taken towards reconciliation in terms of pastoral practice, and led to ecclesiological reflection upon the institutionality of each of the churches. In addition, many study seminars have been organized, for example in Brazil, to reflect upon the practical implications of the documents originating from the higher bodies.[71] This has allowed for a nascent contextual reflection that has contributed to the universal development of ecumenical theology. Finally, to mark 500 years since the Catholic-Lutheran split, an international conference was held, among other commemorative events, in Santiago de Chile to provide an overview of ecumenism in Latin America and the Caribbean.[72]

6 The Rise of New Divisions

The third millennium has brought new challenges for ecumenism. The new social and ecclesial reconfiguration, together with the dwindling interest in the subject and the as yet unattained expansion of ecumenism at the grassroots ecclesial level, has led to new divisive factors that pose a challenge to this important ecclesial dimension in a new way.

6.1 *Fear of the Loss of Identity*

In the 1990s, the ecclesiastical authorities began the slow process of returning to the more structural and institutional aspects of church life and mission, since they were concerned by the exodus of believers and the alleged blurring of the church's identity owing to the substantial involvement of many communities in the sociopolitical processes of the continent. This process was apparent and widely known in the Catholic Church, and it was reflected, for instance, in the Catholic bishops appointed during that time (secure in their doctrine, more than prophetic in their actions), but this was also the case in many Protestant and Evangelical churches. For example, as stated by Jean-Pierre Bastian:

69 Bonino maintained, in the mid-1990s, that "unity as a mission – evangelizing and social – makes sense in the self-understanding of Latin American Protestantism; unity as a predominantly doctrinal or ecclesiastical project does not evoke interest or response," in: José Mìguez Bonino, *Faces of Latin American Protestantism*, Grand Rapids, Eerdmans, 1997, 131.

70 See Luca Ferracci, *Battesimo Eucaristia Ministero: Genesi e destino di un documento ecumenico*, Bologna, Il Mulino, 2020.

71 See examples in Wolff, "Elementos para una historia."

72 See Sandra Arenas & Rodrigo Polanco, "Congreso Internacional 'Recuperando la historia del ecumenismo en América Latina y el Caribe,'" *Teología y Vida* 58/2, 2017, 251–254.

> The Evangelical churches that were not taking part in the ecumenical movement associated with the World Council of Churches formed a group in 1969, at [CLADE I], and joined the international Evangelical movement led by the Billy Graham organization[73] ... From then on, the conferences organized by conservative Evangelicals involved a strategy to fight against the international ecumenical movement and the Latin American movement in particular ... These Evangelical leaders, regrouped into national Evangelical alliances, adopted positions strongly in support of the military regimes, such as in Chile and Guatemala.[74]

As a result, not only were rifts formed between leaders and their communities, but also the institutional churches distanced and separated themselves from the ecumenical centers and groups that, to this day, support and encourage these social movements, but have been gradually marginalized.

6.2 *Hegemonizing Tendencies*

The traditional cultural, social, and political hegemony maintained by the Catholic Church in the continent has been challenged by the Protestant churches since the beginning of the 20th century. By way of an example, in the presidential elections in Peru (1990), Guatemala (1990), and Brazil (2018), the so-called Evangelical vote was a deciding factor in the final result (with the election of Alberto Fujimori, Jorge Serrano Elías, and Jair Bolsonaro respectively), in contrast to the traditional influence exerted by the Catholic Church in previous years. Conversely, although its involvement with ecumenism as a result of Vatican II made it seem as if this would be the end of the Catholic Church's hegemonizing behavior, the legal struggle that many small grassroots churches face in order to be recognized as having the same rights as the traditional churches, particularly the Catholic Church, has, in places such as Peru[75] and Chile, provoked a renewed hegemonizing reaction on the part of the Catholics, who have slowed down all ecumenical progress and dismissed the other churches.

6.3 *New Ethical and Cultural Challenges*

The continued search for a theology more open to cultural pluralism has meant that communities and groups, ecumenical groups in particular, have been looking deep into the new topics on the cultural agenda, like gender issues, environmental concerns, relationships with indigenous religions and cultures, and so on. The challenges that these issues present to traditional ecclesiastical culture and ethics have led to tensions within the churches and, consequently, to a statement of their traditional identity, with the ensuing mistrust of groups, study centers, and any ecumenical publications not subject to hierarchical mentorship or monitoring. In short, added to the widespread lack of interest in ecumenism is the fact that certain groups which, in practice, are ecumenically important, are being marginalized by traditional ecclesial institutionalism owing to their way of thinking and of perceiving themselves as a church.

7 New Ecumenical Configurations in the Light of Cultural Changes

7.1 *The Meteoric Ecumenical Rise of Pentecostalism*

In today's Latin America, the Pentecostal movement is "one of the most dynamic expressions of Christianity, both for its rapid growth and for the highly militant nature of its followers."[76] Currently,

73 Jean-Pierre Bastian, *Breve historia del protestantismo en América Latina*, Mexico City, Casa Unida de Publicaciones, 1986, 162.

74 Bastian, *Breve historia del protestantismo*, 155–156.

75 See Espinoza, "El episcopado peruano."

76 Juan Sepúlveda, "El crecimiento del movimiento pentecostal en América Latina," in: Carmelo Álvarez, ed., *Pentecostalismo y liberación: Una experiencia latinoamericana*, San José, DEI, 1992, 77–88, here 77.

these churches account for between 10% and 15% of the Latin American population, but in some countries, such as Brazil, Guatemala, and Chile, the number is even higher (and may be up to 30% of all Christians). This has resulted in profound changes to religion in Latin America and, therefore, has also influenced ecumenism in different ways.[77] Nevertheless, it must be borne in mind that "Latin American Pentecostalism is extraordinarily diverse." "There is a kind of Pentecostalism that has arisen independently from, and practically simultaneously to, that of North America." This is the case in Brazil and Chile, where the said independent origin has resulted in a more indigenous church with deep cultural roots. There is also another kind of Pentecostalism that has "a missionary background, is generally North American in origin, [and] is financially dependent on an organization." This type of Pentecostalism emerged in the majority of Latin American countries, particularly in Central America. However, in spite of their more dependent origins, today these churches have achieved considerable autonomy and are similar to the other aforementioned churches. It should also be added that, as a third distinguishing feature, institutional fragility and private leadership has furnished Pentecostalism with a tendency towards fragmentation, thus further deepening its diversification.[78]

There is no simple explanation for this tremendous growth. Traditionally, it has been understood "as an efficient religious response to a crisis ... among the working classes" consisting in "a particularly intense experience of God, capable of offering" a new meaning to life, inconceivable within the limits normally provided by society.[79] In any case, it is clear that it is "a transformation of folk religion"[80] along the lines of acculturation that combines Protestant doctrinal principles, some aspects of popular Catholicism,[81] a little like Catholicism without a priest (this is the theory held by Pierre Channu, 1965), and a little of the indigenous religions of the continent (especially among the indigenous communities), together with the reorganization of traditional caudillismo.[82] "This coordination with folk religion ... has also taken

77 See Bastian, "De los protestantismos históricos," 47. For the history of Protestantism in Latin America, see Jean-Pierre Bastian, *La mutación religiosa de América Latina: Para una sociología del cambio social en la modernidad periférica*, Mexico City, Fondo de Cultura Económica, 1997; David Martin, *Tongues of Fire: The Explosion of Protestantism in Latin America*, Oxford, Blackwell, 1990; Bonino, *Faces of Latin American Protestantism*; Arturo Piedra, *Evangelización protestante en América Latina: Análisis de las razones que justificaron y promovieron la expansión protestante (1830–1960)*, 2 vols., Quito, Consejo Latinoamericano de Iglesias, [2]2005; David Stoll, *Is Latin America Turning Protestant?: The Politics of Evangelical Growth*, Berkeley, University of California Press, 1990; Calvin L. Smith, ed., *Pentecostal Power: Expressions, Impact and Faith of Latin American Pentecostalism*, Leiden, Brill, 2011; Stephen Dove, "Historical and Ideological Lineages of Dissenting Protestantism in Latin America," in: *The Oxford History of Protestant Dissenting Traditions*, vol. 4, Jehu J. Hanciles, ed., *The Twentieth Century: Traditions in a Global Context*, Oxford, Oxford University Press, 2019, 315–337; Virginia Garrard, "Dissenting Religion: Protestantism in Latin America," in: *The Oxford History of Protestant Dissenting Traditions*, vol. 4, 359–383; David Martin, "Otro tipo de revolución cultural: El protestantismo en Latinoamérica," *Estudios Públicos*, 44, 1991, 39–62; Ramón Castillo, "Iglesia y Sociedad en América Latina: Protestantismo y revolución en cambio de época," *Presencia Ecuménica*, 78, 2013, 24–29; Juan Carlos Urrea Viera, "Ecumenismo en América Latina y el Caribe: Mirada histórica y proyectiva," *Servicio* 243, 2000, 35–41.

78 Juan Sepúlveda, "Die Pfingsbewegung und ihre Identität als Kirche," *Jahrbuch Mission* 26, 1992, 145–153, here 146–147.

79 Sepúlveda, "El crecimiento," 87.

80 Bastian, "De los protestantismos históricos," 49.

81 It should not be forgotten that a significant number of Pentecostals were nominally Catholics beforehand, and that upon their conversion, they brought their own subconscious Catholic baggage to their Pentecostal setting. There is greater continuity between Pentecostalism and Catholicism than either church would believe (see Miguel Álvarez, "A Century of Pentecostalism in Latin America," in: *Global Renewal Christianity: Spirit-Empowered Movements Past, Present, and Future*, vol. 2, Vinson Synan, Amos Yong & Miguel Álvarez, eds., *Latin America*, Lake Mary, Charisma House, 2016, xxix–xlviii).

82 See Bastian, "De los protestantismos históricos," 49–51.

place in some historical Protestant churches, whose religious practices have become more Pentecostal in nature and who have achieved a certain increase in numbers, especially in indigenous and rural settings" (Mexico, Brazil, Puerto Rico).[83] This has, furthermore, raised questions about whether all these movements can be considered Protestantism in the traditional sense of the word, or whether they would be better understood as new religious movements. Nevertheless, regardless of whether or not one agrees with these theories, it must be noted that this demonstrates the huge challenges to ecumenism that Latin American Pentecostalism presents.

7.2 *Different Ecumenical Experiences*

Catholic-Pentecostal ecumenism has reshaped ecumenism in Latin America. The example of the dialogue pursued for more than 40 years between some classical Pentecostal churches and the SPCU has shown that "the participation of classical Pentecostals in ecumenical dialogue has not only led to new challenges, it has also brought about new opportunities"[84] by involving noninstitutional movements. Indeed, the need to explicitly describe "the models of unity emerging out of this dialogue"[85] and, when faced with "the absence of the typical channels for ecumenical reception in the classical Pentecostal constituency," the need to find alternative ways to communicate the results of the dialogue, such as using the dialogue participants and witnesses as ecumenical agents,[86] are clear examples of new challenges that are, at the same time, valuable opportunities to advance the kind of ecumenism that has tended to be halted by more official bodies.

"On the other hand, the official engagement of Pentecostal churches in the ecumenical movement is still virtually unknown" but has been considerably more extensive than commonly thought. For instance, "in 1961, the *Iglesia Pentecostal de Chile* and the *Misión Iglesia Pentecostal* joined the WCC as the first Pentecostal members."[87] These were "followed by several other Pentecostal churches in Latin America, Africa, and the USA, although the majority of Pentecostals do not seem to favor official membership status."[88] In this respect, "Latin American Pentecostalism has been a particular stronghold of ecumenical commitment since the 1960s … Pentecostal churches contributed significantly to the formation of the [CLAI] in 1982"[89] and have been active participants in the UNELAM and SEPADE, among other ecumenical organizations. Furthermore, the creation of the RELEP in Mexico in 1998 should be highlighted, as it "contributed enormously to the formation and awareness-raising of the theological, social, and historical identity of Pentecostalism in Latin America" through both numerous articles issued to date and the FPL, which was established in 2011 in Lima as "a venue for meeting and sharing."[90]

The multidimensional nature of the Pentecostal movement allows us to see that there is no single typology that can be used to describe ecumenism as practiced by Pentecostals and, in general, by charismatic Christians. In the continent, first of all, these churches have been practicing interdenominational ecumenism, in other words, ecumenism "between Pentecostals and other Evangelical denominations and historical

83 Bastian, "De los protestantismos históricos," 50.

84 Jelle Creemers, "Dance to the Beat of Your Own Drum: Classical Pentecostals in Ecumenical Dialogue," *JEPTA* 35, 2015, 58–68, here 64.

85 Jelle Creemers, *Theological Dialogue with Classical Pentecostals: Challenges and Opportunities*, London, T&T Clark, 2015, 5, quoted from Veli-Matti Kärkkäinen, *Spiritus ubi vult spirat: Pneumatology in Roman Catholic-Pentecostal Dialogue* (1972–1989), Helsinki, Luther-Agricola-Society, 1998, 34.

86 Kärkkäinen, *Spiritus ubi vult spirat*, 281.

87 Harold D. Hunter, "Global Pentecostalism and Ecumenism: Two Movements of the Holy Spirit?," in: Wolfgang Vondey, ed., *Pentecostalism and Christian Unity*, vol. 1, *Ecumenical Documents and Critical A ssessments*, Eugene, Pickwick, 2010, 20–33, here 26 (italics original).

88 Wolfgang Vondey, "Pentecostals and ecumenism: becoming the church as a pursuit of Christian unity," *IJSCC* 11, 2011, 318–330, here 324.

89 Vondey, "Pentecostals and ecumenism," 325.

90 Patricio Merino-Beas, "Pentecostalismo en América Latina: Panorámica," in: Arenas & Polanco, eds., *Ecumenismo: Un panorama latinoamericano*, 377–402, here 395.

non-Catholic churches."[91] There, Pentecostal participants have had the opportunity to meet up and share with Catholic observers and guests. Moreover, the aforementioned RELEP and the FPL have consistently shared their reflections with Catholic theologians guests. It must be said that, in all these ecumenical initiatives, the majority of committed Pentecostals generally have an academic background.[92] However, there are also other, nonacademic events that have recently been providing a rich and inspiring ecumenical experience. Several meetings between Pentecostals and charismatic Catholics across the continent, which are primarily for prayer and praising the Holy Spirit, take place. They are neither committees nor councils representing the churches; they are simply open prayer meetings which hope and trust that reconciliation among Christians will lead to a "new Pentecost." An example of this is the platform ENCRISTUS, which was set up in Brazil in 2007 and also has replicas in other countries, such as the CRECES.[93] As part of the Catholic Charismatic Renewal in Argentina, Pope Francis himself, while he was Archbishop of Buenos Aires, held three "meetings at Luna Park, which can hold 7,000 people. Three meetings of Evangelicals and Catholics" and two "three day spiritual retreats for pastors and priests together, preached also by pastors and a priest or bishop."[94]

7.3 *Rethinking Ecumenism*

From these experiences of mutual gathering and sharing, the concept of "ecumenism of the Spirit" has been born as an "experiential, dynamic, celebratory, and devotional" ecumenism, one that "does not specify institutional forms, structural commitments, or formal decisions."[95] Connected to this concept is that of the "pentecostality of the church," which seeks to overcome "an exclusionary and reductionist understanding of individual Pentecostalism, since each ecclesial singularity would not exhaust the pneumatological/Pentecostal dimension of the whole church." The Pentecost, which is what enabled the breaking down of "cultural and linguistic barriers," is what could eliminate social segregation, gender segregation, and every other kind of discrimination today; therefore, it is what will make internal communion among the different churches possible.[96] In this regard, all Christian churches are, or must be, Pentecostal, the Catholic Church included.[97]

Consequently, this interdenominationalism has its own resources and follows unique ecumenical paths. It is not surprising that many Evangelicals seek to rethink ecumenism in Latin America as something that has to be further removed from the current, more visible ecumenical structures; they petition these structures for a reorganization that would allow them to understand and more fully accept their own way of being Protestants. This is what has been named a "neo-ecumenical movement" that has led, as we have shown, to "numerous reconciliation processes between different Evangelical sectors and with other sectors of Christianity."[98] However, these very same churches are facing the growth of so-called prosperity theology, which, through the religion of consumerism and megachurches welcomed by neoliberal economies and far right regimes and based on charismatic leaders, the vast sums of money they receive, and the strength of their communication skills, offer a religious experience of

91 Merino-Beas, "Pentecostalismo en América Latina," 389.

92 See Hunter, "Global Pentecostalism," 31.

93 See Marcial Maçaneiro, "Católicos y pentecostales en reconciliación: Diez años del Encristus-Brasil," in: Arenas & Polanco, eds., *Ecumenismo: Un panorama latinoamericano*, 335–376.

94 Pope Francis, *In-Flight Press Conference of His Holiness Pope Francis from Sweden to Rome*, Nov 1, 2016, available at <https://www.vatican.va/content/francesco/en/speeches/2016/november/documents/papa-francesco_20161101_svezia-conferenza-stampa.html> (accessed Jul 27, 2023).

95 Merino-Beas, "Pentecostalismo en América Latina," 390 (quoting Carmelo Álvarez).

96 Merino-Beas, "Pentecostalismo en América Latina," 392, the concept of pentecostality of the church has been taken from Bernardo Campos.

97 See Álvarez, "A Century of Pentecostalism," xlvi–xlvii.

98 Hugo Córdova Quero, *El desafío del diálogo: Historia, definiciones y problemáticas del ecumenismo y la pluralidad religiosa*, Buenos Aires, GEMRIP, 2014, 38.

such an individual nature that any ecumenical practice is rendered unsuitable. We could talk here about postdenominationalism. These debatable ecclesial forms have already been criticized by the FTL. In addition, the expansion of fundamentalist trends within Pentecostalism and Catholicism has been another obstacle to ecumenism, in this case because ecumenism is considered unorthodox.

8 In the Light of New Cultural and Ethical Configurations

8.1 *The Ethics of* Buen Vivir

On the whole, visible unity is considered to consist of unity in apostolic faith, sacramental life, ministry, and mission. However, it has become increasingly clear that common responses to ethical and moral problems are another essential characteristic of visible unity, given that the way in which Christians and the communities respond to moral challenges affects the understanding and practice of unity. Milton Mejía has recently supported the insurmountable work of the churches and ecclesial communities in this respect:

> As churches and ecumenical movements, we have the challenge of dialoguing with and accompanying communities that are promoting ways to re-create the economy, taking from our ancestor's worldviews and the thinking of our critical tradition. Based on these experiences and the biblical-theological perspective of an abundant life for humans and the clamor of creation awaiting its redemption, we can contribute to a new way of thinking that allows us to recreate our way of life as humans and with nature.[99]

As a new and fresh paradigm, a network of rural and urban communities has appeared, gradually building an epistemic independence from the Eurocentric models of modernity that have tended to perpetuate cultural colonization in spite of geographical decolonization. This points directly towards the deconstruction of the idea of development and this growing network has emerged as an alternative by means of which to collectively build a new model for relations between human beings and nature. The concept of *buen vivir* (good living) surfaced in Ecuador, although it would be a mistake to consider it a purely Andean project. In fact, *buen vivir* has been expanding as it has been broadening its horizons, and it deals with creating new socio-natural relationships as a community: a collective creation of a new corporate organization with independent spaces for structuring and management which are recreated spaces of power, with gender and generational balances, and which produces local alternatives connected on a global scale in a varied manner. Some churches and ecclesial communities have played an active and vital role in this process of shared learning, and there is even a kind of ecumenical theology associated with them. Proposals such as that of *buen vivir* play a pivotal role in the emergence of new worldviews.[100]

8.2 *Sexual Diversity*

In Latin America, the situation that the LGBT+ communities face every day is hard, unfair, and violent as a result of the age-old homophobia entrenched in the continent's culture. In Christian

99 Milton Mejía, "The Economy of Life, Buen Vivir, and the Search for Alternatives in Latin America and the Caribbean," *EcRev* 67,2015, 208–213, here 213.

100 This is the case for Fernando Vega, who documented that ancient Andean cultures have been crucial in the shifts and rebuilding experienced by liberation theologies, and the exchange between the two can be seen as having initiated great possibilities for deployment. See Fernando Vega, "Teologia de la liberación y buen vivir," in: Alejandro Guillén García & Mauricio Phélan Casanova, eds., *Construyendo el Buen Vivir: I encuentro internacional del programa de cooperación universitaria e investigación científica*, Cuenca, PYDLOS, 2012, 115–134.

sectors, coexisting with normalized violence is religious discourse that attempts to justify, by using anthropological and biblical arguments, prejudice towards, and the marginalization of, these groups. As is normal in the Latin American context, there are also many Christian believers among the members of this community who have seen their faith in God profoundly questioned, if they have not already been entirely ostracized by the churches and communities. Faced with this reality, groups have sprung up that reflect upon the relationship between sexual diversity and faith, and which offer a place where both can be felt freely and peacefully without contradiction. An example of this is the El Camino inclusive ecumenical Christian community, founded in Peru in 2009.[101]

Ecumenism is an essential part of the identity of these communities and collectives. Indeed, because their reflection stems from a sincere search for God, usually at odds with certain ecclesial positions but seeking to create an opportunity from the marginalization they have suffered, the ecumenical character of their new community structure becomes part of their true definition. Many members of these communities left their own denominations and churches because they were unable to reconcile the condemnatory ethical discussions heard there with their own experience of a welcoming and inclusive God, especially after they found a true, inclusive fellowship in their new community, that breaks with many of the previous denominational divisions. As a result, ecumenism here takes the form of a shared rereading and critique of the teachings of the Bible, which deconstructs the traditional and discriminatory forms of reading in order "to do justice to God,"[102] maintaining "Christianity as a community of love, decrying all images that have made God into a discriminatory being and the church into an institution that perpetuates this."[103]

Here, we have encountered a specific kind of ecumenism, one born from an experience of segregation, contrasted with a new experience of integration, that provides new and valuable elements with which to understand ecumenism as devotion to an inclusive God, and which calls into question the kind of ecumenism that perpetuates a framework of differentiation.

9 A New Understanding of Ecumenism?

José de Jésus Legorreta asks: "How can we understand unity as proclaimed in the practices and reflections about ecumenism in a context in which being fragmented and different are of value?" How can we understand it, particularly when frequently "the preference for unity is usually a matter of power"? As a result, questions concerning the kind of unity being sought, whether there is a need for it, and even the actual possibility of it, are now unavoidable in ecumenical discussions. In Latin America, these questions are gaining new momentum as a result of their context.[104]

As we have outlined, this tension towards unity, faced by every ecumenical movement, has been shaped in the Latin American continent more within the framework of Evangelical praxis, in response to the social and political setting, than from a critical reflection on the *oikouménē* and its ecclesiological implications. The now-established diversification of religious faces in general – and

101 See Enrique Vega-Dávila, "Ecumenismo desde la diversidad sexual: La experiencia de 'El Camino,'" in: Arenas & Polanco, eds., *Ecumenismo: Un panorama latinoamericano*, 341–354.

102 Juan Fonseca, "El Camino: Experiencias de una comunidad inclusiva en Lima," in: Genilma Boehler, Lars Bedurke & Silvia Regina de Lima Silva, eds., *Teorías queer y teologías: estar… en otro lugar*, San José, Departamento Ecuménico de Investigaciones, 2013, 261–267.

103 See Vega-Dávila, "Ecumenismo desde la diversidad sexual," 349.

104 José de Jesús Legorreta, "Hacia un nuevo paradigma de unidad para el ecumenismo en un contexto pluralista," in: Arenas & Polanco, eds., *Ecumenismo: Un panorama latinoamericano*, 405–418, here 406.

Christian faces in particular – within a social environment with a growing appreciation of the diverse, has meant that new ecumenical practices have emerged, such as those hitherto described. It is clear, however, that the theological systematization of these experiences to allow for bi- or multilateral dialogue is still in its infancy. Moreover, with very few exceptions, there are no good precedents at this level, since, throughout our history, we have failed to think theologically about intra-Christian relationships.

From this perspective, in ever-increasing socially tumultuous contexts, Christian unity was not discussed theoretically; it was merely demanded in practice, which, during the decades of transition to democracy, undermined even the communication of that particular way of understanding and existing in unity. Not even the official institutional intraecclesial ecumenical events were accompanied by any mildly satisfactory reflection. It seemed, moreover, that neither institutional unity nor a kind of functional unity fitted into the agenda on the continent at the time, which expected a reassertion of difference. Identity is shaped by, and based upon, difference, with the potential that this unlocks to respond evangelically to the questions of today. All this invites us to move away from the ecclesiological paradigm in which unity is fictional and move towards one in which ecumenical relations are marked by meaningful mutual learning about different community styles, theological accents, and pastoral forms. Nevertheless, questions today require creative Christian responses, which also imply quality theological reflection.

Translated from Spanish to English by Kelly Harrison.

Bibliography

Abumanssur, Edin Sued, "Ecumenism in Latin America: Between the Marketplace and the Desert," in: Virginia Garrard-Burnett, Paul Freston & Stephen Dove, eds., *The Cambridge History of Religions in Latin America*, New York, Cambridge University Press, 2016, 729–738.

Arenas, Sandra & Rodrigo Polanco, eds., *Ecumenismo: Un panorama latinoamericano*, Santiago de Chile, Ediciones Universidad Alberto Hurtado, 2021.

Bastian, Jean-Pierre, *Breve historia del protestantismo en América Latina*, Mexico City, Casa Unida de Publicaciones, 1986.

Bastian, Jean-Pierre, "De los protestantismos históricos a los pentecostalismos latinoamericanos: Análisis de una mutación religiosa," *Revista de Ciencias Sociales* 16, 2006, 38–54.

Dias, Zwinglio, "Evaluación crítica de la práctica ecuménica latinoamericana," *Cristianismo y sociedad* 60, 1979, 3–30.

Hunter, Harold D., "Global Pentecostalism and Ecumenism: Two Movements of the Holy Spirit?," in: Wolfgang Vondey, ed., *Pentecostalism and Christian Unity*, vol. 1, *Ecumenical Documents and Critical Assessments*, Eugene, Pickwick, 2010, 20–33.

Merino-Beas, Patricio, "El diálogo ecuménico animado desde el Celam," *Theologica Xaveriana* 184, 2017, 387–410.

Míguez Bonino, José, "A Latin American Attempt to Locate the Question of Unity," in: *What Kind of Unity*?, Geneva, WCC Publications, 1974, 51–62.

Prien, Hans-Jürgen, *Christianity in Latin America* (*Revised and Expanded Edition*), Leiden, Brill, 2013.

Sabanes Plou, Dafne, "Latin America," in: *A History of the Ecumenical Movement*, vol. 3, John Briggs, Mercy Amba Oduyoye & Georges Tsetsis, eds., *1968–2000*, Geneva, WCC Publications, 2004, 565–589.

Sepúlveda, Juan, "La defensa de los derechos humanos como experiencia ecuménica," *Persona y Sociedad* 17/3, 2003, 21–28.

Vondey, Wolfgang, "Pentecostals and ecumenism: becoming the church as a pursuit of Christian unity," *IJSCC* 11, 2011, 318–330.

CHAPTER 30

Tomos Agapis: Origins and Consequences

Nicla Buonasorte

1 Introduction

On the morning of Dec 7, 1971, Cardinal Johannes Willebrands, president of the SPCU, accompanied by White Father Pierre Duprey, was received at the headquarters of the Ecumenical Patriarchate of Constantinople in Istanbul by Patriarch Athenagoras and 13 metropolitans. He had brought with him the first edition of a ponderous volume entitled *Tomos Agapis: Vatican-Phanar (1958–1970)*.[1] The copy presented to the patriarch bore Pope Paul VI's signed dedication. Copies were also given to the other metropolitans present.

On the following day, the two Catholic representatives participated in a meeting with the synodal commission for pan-Christian affairs, presided over by Metropolitan Meliton (Hatzis) of Chalchedon,[2] who stressed the importance of the *Tomos Agapis* as a testimonial to the progress made between the Catholic and Orthodox churches. Willebrands responded in the same vein, pointing to the *Tomos* as a sign of a true communion that already existed between the two churches, and proposed holding a symposium of Catholic and Orthodox theologians for a shared study of the theology that had inspired the documents of the *Tomos* and its implications.[3] These few lines are enough to show the importance that both parties attributed to this volume's publication.

2 The *Tomos Agapis*: What It Is, What It Is Not

The 735 pages of the *Tomos Agapis* are a compilation of 284 documents: a meticulous diary of the correspondence, visits, speeches, and meetings at various levels that took place between the heads of the church of old Rome and those of the New Rome, between the Vatican and the Phanar, the sees of the successors of the apostles Peter and Andrew, from 1958 to 1970. The idea for the publication, which received Athenagoras's immediate support, can be traced back to the Holy Synod's dean, Metropolitan Meliton, who discussed it with the secretary of the SPCU in Istanbul in December 1968.[4]

The characteristic practice of exchanging correspondence between the various churches in the first centuries of Christianity was a way of achieving *koinonia* that was widespread in the Christian community, and which was nourished by the reciprocal welcome of letters and letter bearers. The *Tomos Agapis*, therefore, was part of this traditional typology, which often also had a canonical significance.

1 *Tomos Agapis. Vatican-Phanar (1958–1970)*, Rome/Istanbul, Imprimérie polyglotte vaticane, 1971; ET: Edward James Stormon, ed., *Towards the Healing of Schism: The Sees of Rome and Constantinople*, Mahwah NJ, Paulist, 1987.

2 Meliton (Hatzis) was a member of the central committee of the WCC and representative of the patriarch to the general assembly. After his studies at the school of Halki, in 1943 he moved to the United Kingdom, where he was responsible for the Greek Orthodox in Manchester and Liverpool. He became one of the main collaborators of Athenagoras and his successor Dimitrios, in particular for relations with the Catholic Church. See *DEM*, 665–666.

3 The account of the meeting in the notes of Pierre Duprey, in: AFscire, FDpy, 3.31. This document is the basis of the "Rapport sur le voyage du card. Willebrands à Istanbul du 6 au 10 décembre 1971," in: Alberto Melloni, *Tempus visitationis: L'intercomunione inaccaduta fra Roma e Costantinopoli*, Bologna, Il Mulino, 2019, 307–314.

4 *THS*, "Preface," 24.

The title's meaning, explained by Metropolitan Damaskinos (Papandreou) and Fr. Duprey during a press conference held in January 1972, emphasizes love – *caritas* – as the inspiration for resuming contact between the Church of Rome and the Ecumenical Patriarchate.[5]

In Greek, *tomos* indicates a patriarchal or synodal decree, a letter, and therefore, by synecdoche, the entire corpus of correspondence exchanged between the two patriarchal sees. It is a love letter, then, of the rediscovered fraternal *agape* between the Orthodox and Catholic churches. The title, however, also refers to the meaning of "tome," a part of a more complex and larger work.[6] This meaning can be well understood in a chronological sense because other exchanges of letters, visits, gestures, and goals may well have followed, as in fact happened. But the *Tomos Agapis* is also (and perhaps above all) the documentary fallout of a substantially greater work: the path of the conversion of Christians in time called to unity, to the one chalice to be shared "so that the world may believe" (John 17:21). It is a journey in which Peter and Andrew will recognize that they are brothers, and the Orthodox and Catholic churches are sisters, reproposing a vocabulary that stretches back to the time of the undivided church and that will have its own story, which is still to be written.

One can leaf through the pages of the *Tomos* as through the agenda of a very busy time that brought the two churches very close to the reconstitution of that unity that the protagonists – repeatedly and with an insistence that only an evangelical parrhesia could inspire – had indicated as the goal, one that would be achieved when they could receive communion from the same chalice, an event that has not happened, but the expectation of which is no less compelling for that.

In this succession of letters, telegrams, invitations, visits, thanks, exchanges of gifts and well wishes, reflections, accelerations, slowdowns, perspectives, desires, hopes, and sometimes silences, the two undisputed key players emerge. The two men were of different ages, born, raised, and educated far from each other, in two different ecclesiological cultures. From time to time, they were supported or opposed by the churches they represented. They were aware of the greater responsibility emerging in their life stories, a responsibility from which they did not shirk. In this sense, some moments along the path undertaken – after a distance of over half a century – still preserve their extraordinary symbolic import: the first of all of these moments, the meeting between pope and patriarch held in Jerusalem in 1964, was a sign that the path toward encounter runs not only along the guiderails of documents, commissions, and theological study, but also and mainly along those of the personal and prophetic choices of individuals and communities. These choices would not always and not necessarily be followed by a corresponding advance along the path toward the unity of the churches. The pilgrimage to Jerusalem was the first icon of the dialogue of charity, the basis for a true theological dialogue (which was only officially opened in 1980 by Dimitrios I and John Paul II) that – in the hopes of the leaders of that time – would lead to the restoration of full sacramental unity.[7]

The volume, therefore, does not focus on any specific event but represents the establishment of individual and generational itineraries that took shape at institutional, theological, and spiritual turning points to which the documents bear witness. In the pages of the *Tomos Agapis*, one will not find behind-the-scenes accounts of what happened outside the spotlight of the official

5 See Jacques E. Desseaux, "Introduction: Le chemin des retrouvailles," in: Jean XXIII & others, *Le livre de la charité (1958–1978)*, Paris, Cerf, 1984, 9–42, esp. 10.

6 See "Tomos s.v.," in: Geoffrey W.H. Lampe, ed., *A Patristic Greek Lexicon*, Oxford, Clarendon Press, 1961, 1396.

7 There is an overview of the contents in Traian Valdman, "'Tomos Agapis': Testimonianza della ripresa delle relazioni fra la Chiesa Cattolica Romana e la Chiesa Ortodossa," *Vita Monastica* 149, 1982, 9–29.

meetings, in that patient work that often ran into obstacles and misunderstandings on both sides, and which are collected in the personal archives of the key players. One will only find hints of what the world and Christians were experiencing in those fast moving and often confusing decades. One will not find theological speculations, new canonical formulations, or the reflections of the internal debates that preceded and followed every official event and that had the power to influence every subsequent step. Above all, what is written is what happened, obviously not what did not take place. It is quite natural, therefore, that it always has a positive point of view, which, in the end, can be vaguely self-congratulatory. With this caveat, historians can take inventory of the topics dealt with in the book in order to identify the lines along which they have grown or, on the contrary, have run aground. Additionally, Christians can draw points for spiritual reflection from them, sounding out events from the perspective of salvation history.

The documents are presented in chronological order without contextualization, critical apparatus, or notes. A very brief preface, signed by Cardinal Willebrands and Metropolitan Meliton explains that publication came about because those texts, testimonials of a shared life that was gradually being reestablished, of a new experience of unity and communion, needed to be better known by all the faithful so that they could be made the object of reflection and become a shared heritage. An equally dry introduction, drafted by the members of the joint commission that had been tasked with the book's publication, explained the purely chronological choice of the documents' arrangement because of its greater objectivity and adherence to the unfolding of concrete reality and historical events.[8] Given the importance of the reciprocal visits in the tapestry of new relations, the communications concerning them were also included, in a smaller font. On the other hand, documents of a personal nature or that did not have any direct ecclesial import were excluded. As an accompanying tool, there are indexes by subject and for each event of particular importance. As for language, the original texts – in Greek, French, or Latin – are found on the left-hand page while their translation appears on the right.

3 Walking Together

While such an achievement had been unthinkable only a few years earlier, the *Tomos Agapis* was born at a time when the path of rapprochement undertaken by the two churches was going through a phase of enduring expectation that, however, would never (not yet?) be fully satisfied. The historical context onto which this expectation was grafted was complex, and the need for the greater involvement of the lay faithful was also felt. Previously excluded from decision-making processes, the laity were now increasingly ready, especially in the Catholic Church, to personally assume the responsibilities arising from their baptism, officially marking on many occasions and in many ways the end to their passive subordination.

In the 1960s, the worldwide political, social, and economic landscape was experiencing a series of upheavals and accelerations, tensions, protests, and changes played out among nations, social groups, men and women, and the elderly and the young, with an unexpected role also interpreted by believers. At every level, what was possible seemed to approach what was real in every aspect of society. Decolonization had brought new players to the forefront of history, the Cold War had reached its climax with the Cuban missile crisis, the horizon of peaceful coexistence seemed to open up new scenarios, while the protest of the youth, with its disruptive charge, was on the rise,

8 The members of the joint commission in charge of its publication were Damaskinos (Papandreou) and Bartholomew (Archontonis), for the Orthodox, and Pierre Duprey and Christophe-Jean Dumont for the Catholics.

calling even war into question, first and foremost that of Vietnam.[9]

In the short period of time encompassed by the documents of the *Tomos*, covering about 12 years, the definition of the religious "other" changed in a radical way for both churches. At the end of the 1960s, the lexicon revealed the path taken under the banner of a renunciation of a strategy of polemics, thanks to which the lost sheep, the heterodox, and the excommunicated people again became persons and, in this perspective, brothers and sisters. Beyond the resistance and rejection on the part of certain individuals and groups, the theologies of the two churches, in the diversity of their previous paths, had accepted the reestablishment of unity as a common horizon, taking the first millennium as a reference for the situation of the undivided church, admittedly a rather symbolic choice. In particular, Catholicism's delicate and never definitive passage from unionist positions to the shores of an ecumenism that had been condemned until a short time before and, on the Eastern side, the pacification of the memory of the Crusades and the Council of Florence, represented the condition *in fieri* that promised to clear the obstacles of centuries-old divisions and open new paths for the churches.

Historically the Orthodox Church had lived and experienced the complexity of plurality at the doctrinal and practical levels, a reality that Rome did not know or recognize in its own sphere. From the doctrinal point of view, this facilitated a participation in international organizations and meetings with other churches that had already assumed a stable and organized character in the first decades of the 20th century, and which led to the Orthodox Church entry into the WCC in 1961. "The ecumenical dimension" can be defined as "an integral part of the Orthodox ecclesial self-consciousness."[10]

While the Orthodox had enjoyed an experience of gradual entry into the ecumenical project, Catholics had not. John XXIII and his call for the council brought needed recognition to the contribution of theologians and intellectual milieus who had lived through decades of ostracism, mistrust, hostility, and even real canonical sanctions for their pioneering positions and research.[11] In this way, a heritage of contributions to the foundation and growth of an ecumenical theology was rediscovered, one that finally overcame polemics, particularisms, and proselytism, inaugurating a path shared among the great historical churches which it accompanied with a critical eye.[12]

9 See the account of its impact on the ecumenical movement, especially after the fourth assembly of the WCC in Uppsala in that fateful year of 1968, in Eugene Carson Blake, "Uppsala and Afterwards," in: *A History of the Ecumenical Movement*, vol. 2, Harold E. Fey, ed., *The Ecumenical Advance (1948–1968)*, London, SPCK, 1970, 410–445. The role of the Christian student movements in the protest years is instead analyzed by Risto Lehtonen, *Story of a Storm: The Ecumenical Student Movement in the Turmoil of Revolution (1968 to 1973)*, Grand Rapids, Eerdmans, 1998.

10 See Adalberto Mainardi, "I prodromi dell'ecumenismo in ambito ortodosso: Intuizioni, eventi, testimoni," in: Andrea Pacini, ed., *Oltre la divisione: L'intuizione ecumenica e il dialogo interreligioso*, Milan, Edizioni Paoline, 2011, 75–103, here 78. There is a detailed history of Orthodox participation in the ecumenical movement in Gennadios Zervos, *Il contributo del Patriarcato ecumenico per l'unità dei cristiani*, Rome, Città Nuova, 1974, updated, in German, in: Reinhard Flogaus & Jennifer Wasmuth, eds., *Orthodoxie im Dialog: Historische und aktuelle Perspektiven*, Berlin, De Gruyter, 2015. On the limits and stumbling blocks of this participation, see instead Razvan Porumb, *Orthodoxy and Ecumenism: Towards an Active "Metanoia,"* Oxford, Peter Lang, 2019.

11 See Étienne Fouilloux, *Les catholiques et l'unité chrétienne du XIXe au XXe siècle: Itinéraires européens d'expression française*, Paris, Le Centurion, 1982. A suggestive glimpse is offered by Roger Aubert, "Les étapes de l'œcuménisme catholique depuis le pontificat de Léon XIII jusqu'à Vatican II," in: Laurence K. Shook & Guy-M. Bertrand, eds., *La théologie du renouveau: Texte intégral des travaux présentés au Congrès international de Toronto*, vol. 1, Paris, Cerf, 1968, 291–307. On the paradigm shift, see the synthesis in Joseph Famerée, "Pour l'œcuménisme: Evolution de L'Église catholique depuis Vatican II," *RTL* 27, 1996, 47–77, and Christoph Theobald's contribution on Vatican II and *Unitatis redintegratio* in this volume.

12 For a synthesis of the history and the horizons of this path, see Giovanni Cereti, "Le teologie ecumeniche,"

From this perspective, the *Tomos Agapis* also becomes a resource for reconstructing the first steps of a shared ecumenical theology, revealing a process in its concrete unfolding.

For Aristocles Matthaiou Spyrou – the future Athenagoras, elected patriarch of Constantinople in 1948 after a long experience in the United States as archbishop of America's large Greek Orthodox community – promoting church unity began within Orthodoxy itself and its national variations, continued within ecumenical organizations, and then, naturally, turned to the Catholic Church.[13]

The first document of the *Tomos Agapis* is dated Oct 7, 1958. It is a message from Patriarch Athenagoras expressing compassion and care for the seriously ill Pope Pius XII. The first contact with Pope John XXIII took place immediately after the conclave, with a press release published by the Associated Press on Oct 30, 1958, in which the patriarch expressed his pleasure at the election of the former apostolic delegate to Istanbul.[14] Although that important biographical item was not explicitly mentioned, it is clear that the new pope was well known in the circles of the patriarchate and the Orthodox Church.[15] Angelo Giuseppe Roncalli had spent the period from 1935 to 1944 in Istanbul, living in the newly established Turkey of Kemal Atatürk, who had chosen the path of a strict separation between state and religion, opting for absolute secularism. The dissolution of the Ottoman Empire had led to a substantial upheaval of the *millet* system, depriving the patriarch of Istanbul's see of important aspects of his role, and causing a drastic decline in the Christian population.[16] Orthodoxy, therefore, was not unaware of the biography of the new pope (who, even in his private diaries from his time in Turkey, uses the terms "Orthodox brothers" and "Greeks," never "schismatics") who would graft onto the theme of peace the promising foundation of a dialogue at the highest levels. In fact, in his Christmas message of 1958, John XXIII took up and, in a way, responded to the patriarchal encyclical of 1920 *Unto the Churches of Christ Everywhere*, which proposed a world alliance of all religions modeled on the League of Nations.[17] It was a call that Rome had not responded to at the time, but which John XXIII had not forgotten. Athenagoras responded to this move in January 1959, making himself available for every concrete step necessary to respond to the world's expectations of peace and to achieve the unity of the church, based "to be sure ... not in the state of division and disagreement in which it has been for centuries past, and still is."[18]

in: Giuseppe Alberigo, Giuseppe Ruggieri & Roberto Rusconi, eds., *Il Cristianesimo: Grande Atlante*, vol. 3, *Le dottrine*, Turin, Utet, 2006, 1265–1283, and Gustave Thils, *Histoire doctrinale du mouvement œcuménique*, Paris, Desclée de Brower, [2]1963.

13 See Olivier Clément, *Dialogues with Patriarch Athenagoras*, Brookline, Holy Cross Orthodox Press, 2022; Aristide Panotis, *Les pacificateurs: Jean XXIII, Athénagoras, Paul VI, Dimitrios*, Athens, Edition de la Fondation européenne Dragan, 1974; Valeria Martano, *Athenagoras il patriarca (1886–1972): Un cristiano fra crisi della coabitazione e utopia ecumenica*, Bologna, Il Mulino, 1996.

14 *THS* 3, Oct 30, 1958, 27–28. The patriarch praised the words of John XXIII on peace, identifying it as the most urgent horizon for the salvation of humanity.

15 On Roncalli in Istanbul, see *Edizione nazionale dei diari di Angelo Giuseppe Roncalli-Giovanni XXIII*, vol. 4/1, Valeria Martano, ed., *La mia vita in Oriente: Agende del delegato apostolico, 1935–1939*, Bologna, Istituto per le Scienze religiose, 2006, and *Edizione nazionale dei diari di Angelo Giuseppe Roncalli-Giovanni XXIII*, vol. 4/2, Valeria Martano, ed., *La mia vita in Oriente: Agende del delegato apostolico, 1940–1944*, Bologna, Istituto per le Scienze religiose, 2008; a historical framework is given in Alberto Melloni, *Fra Istanbul, Atene e la guerra: La missione di A.G. Roncalli (1935–1944)*, Genoa, Marietti, 1992.

16 Sia Anagnostopoulou, *The Passage from the Ottoman Empire to the Nations-States*, Istanbul, Isis, 2004 and Dimitris Stamatopoulos, "From Millets to Minorities in the 19th-Century Ottoman Empire: An Ambiguous Modernization," in: Steven G. Ellis, Gudmundur Hálfadanarson & Ann K. Isaacs, eds., *Citizenship in Historical Perspective*, Pisa, Plus, 2006, 253–273.

17 *THS* 4, Christmas 1958, 28–29. See Mainardi, "I prodromi dell'ecumenismo," 81, and the contributions by Stylianos Tsompanidis and Vaslios N. Makrides in the first volume of this work.

18 *THS* 5, Jan 1, 1959, 30–31.

3.1 *Orthodox in Rome, Catholics in Constantinople*

Between 1959 and 1962, there were numerous contacts between the patriarch and various Catholic figures, including the mayor of Florence, Giorgio La Pira, who visited the Phanar in January 1960. But it was certainly the announcement of the council that would become Vatican II that accelerated the building of a solid relationship with New Rome. This is testified by the increase in official communications between the two places and then the correspondence concerning the possibility for the separated churches to send observers to the council sessions, conducted in particular by the newly founded SPCU, with its president, the elderly and very active German biblical scholar, Cardinal Augustin Bea,[19] and its secretary, the Dutch bishop, Johannes Willebrands.[20]

Meanwhile, in the pages of the *Tomos Agapis*, a dense network of exchanges unfolded, and other leading voices began to appear: the Romanian Archimandrite André Scrima, Cardinal Bea, Bishop Willebrands, and Metropolitan Maximos of Sardis, the president of the commission for pan-Christian affairs. Mutual visits began as well. In February 1962, Willebrands went to Istanbul, meeting the patriarch, the metropolitans of the Holy Synod, and the members of the commission for pan-Christian affairs.[21] The outcome of the meeting was positive for both sides, so much so that he was invited to return after Easter.

It was in a letter from Athenagoras to Bea on Apr 12, 1962 that the expression "sister churches" in reference to the Orthodox and Catholic ones was used for the first time. The patriarch, responding to the president of the SPCU, expressed the "desire for the rapprochement of the sister churches and the restoration of unity in the church" and confirmed his willingness to contribute as much as he could to reestablishing this unity.[22]

As is well known, the request to send two trusted clergymen or theologians for the first session of Vatican II was not accepted by the Ecumenical Patriarchate, which found itself in a particularly delicate situation with respect to the internal balance within Orthodoxy, while instead representatives of the Russian Church were present.[23] On the eve of the council's opening, Cardinal Bea wrote to the patriarch in response to the communication received personally from Metropolitan Emilianos (Timiadis), the patriarchate's envoy, on the impossibility of sending observers. Understanding the internal difficulties that such a request might cause, Bea gave assurances that everything possible would be done to continue the fraternal relations between the two churches, and expressed the hope that the council itself could effectively contribute to the creation of ever-closer ties.[24] Emilianos had long been the representative of the Patriarchate of Constantinople to the WCC in Geneva and was Willebrands's valuable contact for his first visits to Istanbul. They had also participated together in the informal meeting held in May 1961 at the WCC on the issue of religious

19 For a precise reconstruction of the SPCU's path, see Mauro Velati, "'Un indirizzo a Roma': La nascita del Segretariato per l'unità dei cristiani (1959–1960)," in: Giuseppe Alberigo, ed., *Il Vaticano II tra attese e celebrazione*, Bologna, Il Mulino, 1995, 75–117, and Mauro Velati, *Dialogo e rinnovamento: Verbali e testi del segretariato per l'unità dei cristiani nella preparazione del concilio Vaticano II (1960–1962)*, Bologna, Il Mulino, 2011. On Bea, see Stjepan Schmidt, *Agostino Bea: Il cardinale dell'unità*, Rome, Città Nuova, 1987 and now Saretta Marotta, *Gli anni della pazienza: Bea, l'ecumenismo e il Sant'Uffizio di Pio XII*, Bologna, Il Mulino, 2019.

20 See Adelbert Denaux & Peter De Mey, eds., *The Ecumenical Legacy of Johannes Cardinal Willebrands (1909–2006)*, Leuven, Peeters, 2012. The contacts with Constantinople are documented directly in his diaries: see Theo Salemink, ed., *"You Will Be Called Repairer of the Breach": The Diary of J.G.M. Willebrands (1958–1961)*, Leuven, Peeters, 2009, and Leo Declerck, ed., *Les Agendas conciliaires de Mgr. J. Willebrands, secrétaire du Secrétariat pour l'Unité des Chrétiens*, Leuven, Peeters, 2009.

21 *THS* 8, Feb 27, 1962, 33–34.

22 *THS* 10, Apr 12, 1962, 35.

23 On the matter of the observers, see Mauro Velati, *Separati ma fratelli: Gli osservatori non cattolici al Vaticano II (1962–1965)*, Bologna, Il Mulino, 2014, and also his contribution on the same matter in this volume.

24 *THS* 21, Oct 10, 1962, 42.

freedom. He had been proposed as an observer of the WCC to Vatican II, but his appointment had been blocked by a Russian veto. To inform Rome of the impossibility of sending observers to the council, Athenagoras decided to send Emilianos in person, in order to better explain the reasons for the refusal, so as to safeguard the friendly relations being established between the two churches.

The end of the council's first session was also the occasion of Fr. Duprey's first official trip to Constantinople as undersecretary of the SPCU. Bea sent him in December 1962 to offer an account of the work carried out in Rome.[25]

In June 1963, it was Bea who announced Paul VI's election to the throne of Peter to Constantinople and the other Eastern patriarchal sees, returning to the ancient but obsolete custom of irenic letters that presented the newly elected bishop of Rome to the patriarchs of the Eastern churches.[26] The patriarchate's response, the ancient *grámma timês*, a letter of congratulations for the election, would arrive in September, preceded by the letters of many other Orthodox churches.[27] In the letter from Metropolitan Maximos of Sardis, who signed as chairman of the commission for pan-Christian affairs, the appellation of "holy sister church" reappeared in the way he addressed Rome.[28]

The new Roman pontiff wrote directly to Athenagoras on Sep 20, 1963, calling himself simply the successor to the leader of the apostles and listing the elements preserved by both churches: the gospel, baptism, the priesthood, and the Eucharist. He then said that he was "solicitous for all that concerns the unity of Christians, and all that can help to restore perfect harmony among them."[29] This was the first letter sent from a pope in Rome to Constantinople since that of Gregory XIII to Jeremias II in 1584 to inform him of the adoption of the new calendar. Two months after Paul VI's letter, on Nov 22, Athenagoras' reply was sent from the Phanar, but it only arrived in Rome in December.[30] It also took up the theme of carrying out the Lord's will in unity and fraternity.

In the meantime, despite the kind of "affectionate rapprochement by the representatives of the various Christian confessions,"[31] the patriarchate decided to again decline the request to send its representatives to Rome for the second session of Vatican II. It was only in the following year, for the third session, and in a very different climate, that a delegation from the Phanar

25 *THS* 23, Dec 8, 1962, 43–44. Pierre Duprey, born in 1922 in Croix, in northern France, entered the society of the Missionaries of Africa, and pursued his studies in Tunis, Rome, Athens, and Beirut. He met Athenagoras in 1954 in Istanbul and established a personal relationship with the patriarch that would prove to be invaluable over the following years. In Beirut, he studied Arabic at St. Joseph University and formed a network of friendships with those who would become pioneers of ecumenism in the Middle East, some of whom he met later as observers during Vatican II and as leaders of various Eastern churches. In Jerusalem, between 1956 and 1963, he taught at St. Anne's seminary, dedicated to the formation of Greek Catholic priests. It was Athenagoras himself who invited him and four other Catholics, as journalists and thus without official representation, to the first pan-Orthodox conference in Rhodes in 1961. The following year he was called to Rome as an interpreter for the non-Catholic observers. In January 1963, John XXIII named him undersecretary of the SPCU. Over 20 years later, he became secretary of the new PCPCU. He was ordained titular bishop of Thibaris by John Paul II in 1990, and died in 2007. See also the Orthodox tribute to him in Jean-Marie R. Tillard, ed., *Agapè: Études en l'honneur de Mgr Pierre Duprey M.Afr., Évêque titulaire de Thibar*, Geneva, Centre Orthodoxe du Patriarcat œcuménique, 2000.

26 *THS* 29, Jun 25, 1963, 49.

27 Velati, *Una difficile transizione*, 419.

28 *THS* 32, Sep 9, 1963, 51–52.

29 *THS* 33, Sep 20, 1963, 52–53, here 52. On Giovanni Battista Montini's ecumenical background and its development, see Yves Congar, "L'œcuménisme de Paul VI," in: *Paul VI et la modernité dans l'Eglise: Actes du colloque de Rome (2–4-juin 1983)*, Rome, École Française de Rome, 1984, 807–820; Angelo Maffeis, "Paolo VI e l'ecumenismo," in: Pacini, ed., *Oltre la divisione*, 107–135; Patrice Mahieu, *Paul VI et les orthodoxes*, Paris, Cerf, 2012, and finally Philippe Chenaux, "Paul VI, un cheminement œcuménique," in: Benoît Bourgine, *Le souci de toutes les Églises: Hommage à Joseph Famerée*, Leuven, Peeters, 2020, 15–28.

30 *THS* 35, Nov 22, 1963, 53–54. On the delays, see Martano, *Athenagoras il patriarca*, 465–466.

31 See Velati, *Separati ma fratelli*, 234.

composed of Archimandrite Panteleimon (Rodopoulos), Archpriest John Romanides – both from the American diaspora – and the rector of the Greek Orthodox Church of Rome, Archimandrite Maximos (Aghiorgoussis), arrived in Rome. They were joined by Fr. Scrima, the personal representative of Patriarch Athenagoras, who had a close relationship with Duprey.[32] It was Scrima who had met Willebrands in October 1960, informing him of Athenagoras's desire to meet John XXIII in Corfu. Since then, he had been the main mediator between Rome and Constantinople.

3.2 *The Meeting in Jerusalem*

The period of difficulty that the two churches experienced in their relations between 1962 and 1963, when the resistance of the synod emerged along with the bitterness that followed the promulgation of the encyclical *Aeterna Dei sapientia* for the 15th centenary of the death of Leo the Great, which sounded like a challenge to the primacy of Constantinople, was interrupted – or rather, bypassed – by Paul VI's decision to go on pilgrimage to the Holy Land in January 1964. Arising from concerns other than ecumenical ones,[33] Pope Paul VI's idea, however, was immediately echoed by Athenagoras and became something more, something different, undergoing what Giuseppe Alberigo called "a happy and fruitful 'heterogenesis of ends,'" with important repercussions for the work of Vatican II.[34] On Dec 6, 1963, the patriarch, with his prophetic enthusiasm, well aware of the situation within Orthodoxy, which was anything but cohesive, repeated his desire that

> all the heads of the holy churches of Christ, of the East and West ... were to meet one another in the holy city of Sion, so that in a common contribution of spirit and heart, and with warm prayers ... that they might open up, in the spirit of unity, a new and blessed road ... which would lead further to the restoration of all things, according to his will.[35]

Duprey immediately left for the Phanar to offer news of the conciliar session that had just ended and to exchange ideas and requests concerning the upcoming journey, which had taken on a value that had not been foreseen just a short time before. In addition to political and diplomatic implications, there were ecclesiological questions linked to the history of those territories and churches, which the parties solved with skillful diplomacy. The representative of Rome expressed Paul VI's wishes to the patriarch clearly: "I tell him that it is a pilgrimage: the most religious, most simple, most in the spirit of penance possible ... The pope does not want anything theatrical, nothing that makes waves. He does not want us to speak about

32 André Scrima, a Romanian archimandrite, kept up informal relations between the Phanar and the Vatican without an official mandate. His biographical and spiritual path took him from being a monk in Romania, then a hermit in India, to being a disciple and collaborator of Athenagoras. See Anca Manolescu, "La pace cristiana come dialogo: Padre Andrei Scrima," in: John Behr & others, eds., *Beati i pacifici: Atti del XXII Convegno ecumenico internazionale di spiritualità ortodossa* (*Bose 3–6 settembre 2014*), Magnano, Qiqajon, 2015, 287–296, and Viorel Coman, "André Scrima's Ecumenical Vision and Its Relevance for the Post-Conciliar Orthodox Church," *SVTQ* 64/3–4, 2021, 181–210.

33 Paul VI was thinking of a pilgrimage characterized by simplicity, prayer, and penance, possibly meeting the different Christian denominations in the process. See Mahieu, *Paul VI et les orthodoxes*, 72–83.

34 Giuseppe Alberigo, "The New Shape of the Council," in: Giuseppe Alberigo & Joseph Komonchak, eds., *History of Vatican II*, vol. III, *The Mature Council: Second Period and Intersession* (*September 1963–September 1964*), Leuven/Maryknoll, Peeters/Orbis Books, 2000, 493–514. The expression has not been translated in the English edition and is therefore taken from the Italian: "La nuova fisionomia del concilio," in: Giuseppe Alberigo & Alberto Melloni, eds., *Storia del concilio Vaticano II*, vol. 3, *Il concilio adulto: Il secondo periodo e la seconda intersessione* (*settembre 1963–settembre 1964*), Leuven/Bologna, Peeters/Il Mulino, 1998, 513–534, here 528.

35 *THS* 36, Dec 6, 1963, 54–55, here 55.

a meeting at the ecclesiastical summit, but of a pilgrimage."[36]

At the end of December, Metropolitan Athenagoras (Kokkinakis) of Thyateira went to Rome to discuss the program for the trip and the meeting.[37] The almost total silence on the part of the heads of the other churches and Christian denominations quickly made the patriarch realize that the Jerusalem meeting would only be a meeting of two. The metropolitan evoked the image of two pilgrims, called to climb the same mountain from two different sides in order to meet at the top.[38]

Shortly afterwards, another image, that of the two successors of the apostles embracing, quickly made its way around the world, becoming the icon of an expectation, a hope, but also the testimonial of an "already" that had overcome not only theological reticence, centuries of distance, and doubts and coldness, but which was in itself a sign to be interpreted.[39] It would be naïve to overestimate the results of that meeting, but it is clear that the relations between the churches, in that moment, found a strong connection for the continuation of their journey, and that the impression conveyed beyond words and communiqués was equally as profound. Christian life overcame theology, as Athenagoras affirmed, "hierarchs do, theologians explain."[40]

Among the documents gathered in the *Tomos Agapis*, those related to the meeting in Jerusalem are particularly dense in content and portentous for the future. On Jan 5, 1964, on the Mount of Olives, the patriarch, in the apostolic delegation of Jerusalem, delivered a speech in Greek that was read in French translation by Archimandrite Symeon. After emphasizing that an event of exceptional scope and importance in the history and life of the church was taking place, Patriarch Athenagoras expressed his hope that the meeting might "be the first glimmer of dawn of a shining and holy day in which the Christian generations of the future will receive communion in the holy Body and Blood of the Lord from the same chalice, in love, peace, and unity, and will praise and glorify the one Lord and Savior of all."[41]

Here the issue of intercommunion, destined to accompany the entire subsequent ecumenical journey, came strikingly into play, underlined by the gifts exchanged between the two: Athenagoras placed an *encolpion*, a sign of episcopal dignity, around the pope's neck while Paul VI offered the patriarch a chalice, which Athenagoras would use in Bethlehem two days later, during the celebration of the Orthodox Christmas. Shortly after his return to Rome, the pope received some bottles of Patmos wine from Constantinople, brought by Athenagoras of Thyateira, for celebrating the Eucharist. The pope immediately appreciated the meaning, a gesture "which symbolizes, in spite of our differences, the abiding efficacy of the one sacrifice of Christ, and our sharing in the same priesthood and the same sacraments."[42]

The following day, Paul VI returned the visit, going to the patriarchate of Jerusalem's summer residence where, in alternation, the patriarch and the pope read the prayer of Jesus in chapter 17 of John's Gospel, in a *communicatio in sacris* that was

36 Notes of Duprey on the trip to Istanbul, Dec 9, 1963, in: AFscire, FDpy, 3.10. On Rome's attention to the Orthodox world during Vatican II, see Lukas Vischer, "The Council as an Event in the Ecumenical Movement," in: Giuseppe Alberigo & Joseph A. Komonchak, eds., *History of Vatican II*, vol. 5, *The Council and the Transition: The Fourth Period and the End of the Council (September 1965–December 1965)*, Leuven/Maryknoll, Peeters/Orbis Books, 485–539.

37 The protocol of the visit was signed by Angelo Dell'Acqua and by Athenagoras of Thyateira: see the appendices to *Tomos Agapis*, "Protocole de réception," "Ordre des cérémonies religieuses en la cathédrale patriarcale," "Cérémonie de prière dans la cathédrale du Saint-Esprit en présence du pape Paul VI et du patriarche Athénagoras Ier," 626–643; partly given in English in *THS*, Appendix I, 477–480.

38 *THS* 44, Dec 28, 1963, 58–60.

39 The event had continual coverage by the Italian national television, RAI. See Federico Ruozzi, *Il Concilio in diretta: Il Vaticano II e la televisione tra informazione e partecipazione*, Bologna, Il Mulino, 2012, 396–400.

40 See Melloni, *Tempus visitationis*, 43.

41 *THS* 48, Jan 5, 1964, 61–62, here 62.

42 *THS* 55, Jan 16, 1964, 66.

no less real than a sharing of the chalice that the excommunications still in effect seemed to prohibit, but which the meeting substantially overcame. Here too, words and emotions did not mask the difficulties of the path undertaken but, once again, as Duprey's words emphasized, "the gesture becomes theology."[43]

At the end of two days of unexpected emotional, theological, and spiritual intensity, the pope and the patriarch, with the agreement of the Holy Synod, issued a communiqué that, eschewing diplomatic language, fixed the event in memory as a point of no return, broadcasting it to all the faithful as "a brotherly gesture, inspired by the charity of Christ, who left his disciples the supreme commandment to love one another, to pardon offences seventy times seven, and to be united among themselves."[44] Forgiveness, therefore, a sign and prelude of things to come, offered traces of the path that would soon experience new accelerations. The reflection carried out by the SPCU immediately afterwards, starting from the ecumenical significance that the pilgrimage had assumed, enumerated the possible practical effects of the meeting, including the exchange of apostolic legates between the sees, the initiation of epistolary exchanges on the occasion of major Christian feasts, the creation of a committee for cultural collaboration, meetings of a theological and pastoral nature, as well as the cessation of the attribution of sees located in the Eastern territories to titular bishops, possibilities that would soon be made real. On the basic theme of the reestablishment of full communion, it was clear to all that "it would be useless and fruitless to tackle them head on today. It is necessary to recover the habit of thinking together on all the levels where it is possible before being able to approach this question meaningfully in a spirit of understanding."[45]

After 525 years, a pope and a patriarch met in Jerusalem. It had been at the Council of Ferrara-Florence in 1438 that Pope Eugene IV had initially demanded that Patriarch Joseph II kiss his foot.[46] It was there that the deepest fracture had occurred, which led to backdating to 1054 a split which had not been felt by contemporaries in that sense.[47]

Returning to Rome, Paul VI, awaited by a crowd of faithful Romans, reflected on what he had just experienced and stressed how it could be transformed into a fact of great historical importance, speaking of the seeds from which good fruit could sprout. Gestures and signs took on magisterial, not merely symbolic, significance. From the time in Jerusalem there was an acceleration of relations and a deepening of its contents with more personal and engaged tones, which often referred in some way to the experience that had been shared and that would soon blossom in the lifting of the excommunications.[48]

3.3 *Abolishing the Excommunications*

An occasion to put the question of the separation between the churches on the agenda arrived promptly when the prospect of a visit to Rome by

43 Pierre Duprey, "I gesti ecumenici di Paolo VI," in: Giuseppe Camadini, ed., *Paolo VI e l'ecumenismo: Colloquio internazionale di studio (Brescia, 25–27 settembre 1998)*, Brescia/Rome, Istituto Paolo VI/Studium, 2001, 198–214.

44 *THS* 50, Jan 6, 1964, 64.

45 "Rapport sur les implications œcuméniques du voyage du Saint Père en Terre Sainte," in: AFscire, FDpy, 7.1.

46 On this episode, see Joseph Gill, *The Council of Florence*, Cambridge, Cambridge University Press, 1959, 105.

47 On this, see the essay by Yves Congar, "Neuf cents ans après: Notes sur le 'Schisme oriental,'" which opens volume one of Lambert Beauduin, ed., *1054–1954: L'Église et les Églises, neuf siècles de douloureuse séparation entre l'Orient et l'Occident*, 2 vols., Chevetogne, Éditions de Chevetogne, 1954, 3–95, but also Francis Dvornik, "The Schism Between East and West," *ECR* 1, 1966, 6–11, and Giuseppe Alberigo, ed., *Christian Unity: The Council of Ferrara-Florence (1439/39–1989)*, Leuven, Peeters, 1991.

48 On the event and its scope, see the synthesis of Valeria Martano, *L'abbraccio di Gerusalemme: Cinquant'anni fa lo storico incontro tra Paolo VI e Athenagoras*, Milan, Paoline, 2014.

Athenagoras led to the discussion of the need to avoid creating confusion by continuing the reciprocal excommunications, considered by some to have expired with the Council of Ferrara-Florence of 1438–1439.[49] Even during the Vatican II sessions, the Ukrainian Bishop Maxim Hermaniuk posed the question broadly to probe sentiment on the topic. It was Hermaniuk who had previously proposed the simultaneous abolishing of the condemnations at a meeting of the SPCU in September 1964.

Between the different sensibilities of the documents on the matter approved by the council, *Unitatis redintegratio* and *Orientalium Ecclesiarum*, and the resistance present in both churches, however, a clear will to proceed along the path taken in Jerusalem was inserted. Many perceived the historical and symbolic weight of the excommunications of 1054 as an anachronistic and spiritually unacceptable obstacle. In fact, under Latin canon law, the penalty had expired on the death of the person who received it. For the Orthodox, beyond its canonical force, the anathema extended to the entire community of believers. On the ground, however, there were rather serious issues to be addressed: in particular, proselytism, uniatism, second baptism, and the *Filioque* in the text of the Creed.[50] It was a question of attributing substantial meaning, through a symbolic gesture, to the change in the situation existing between the two churches. Although lifting the excommunications would not suddenly erase the existing problems, an element destined to ferment in the churches in the following decades was introduced: reflection on the past in order to achieve forgiveness and purification of the heart – a different level from the canonical and juridical ones but which would open the way to successive dialogue.[51]

In November 1964, the pan-Orthodox conference of Rhodes established that dialogue with Catholics could be opened "on an equal footing."[52] Paul VI had sent a message to the conference noting Vatican II in progress and the simultaneous meeting in Rhodes of their brothers in Christ.[53] The first hints at the possibility of a gesture of reparation came in the early months of 1965 when, during his visit to Rome, Metropolitan Meliton emphasized the favorable circumstances that allowed for the establishment of theological dialogue as soon as possible. In April 1965, Bea, visiting Athenagoras, highlighted how the dialogue of charity was not limited to the mere exchange of visits but was concretized in the path of each church in preparation "for all that unity involves, and by so doing to work strenuously together to bring about that complete unity which the Lord intended."[54] Many steps had already been taken: the encounter in Jerusalem, the increasing number of meetings, and the restitution of relics kept in Rome to the various Orthodox churches testified to this. The eloquent gesture that Paul VI had desired to make to the church of Patras – the return of the head of St. Andrew, which Rome held since 1462 – recognized the apostolic foundation of the church in Greece, one of those least in favor of dialogue with Catholics.[55] A few months later, in October, the relics of St. Sabas were returned to the Patriarchate of Jerusalem. These practices, initiated by Paul VI and continued again in May 1996 with the return of the relics of St. Titus to the church of Crete, would be kept up by his successors to the papal throne.

Reconciliation, here as in other cases, is undoubtedly a process and not an isolated act. Cancelling the excommunications would be the final, public seal of a profound journey, which would not end with the closure of Vatican II. In 1965, when Bea

49 Among these was also Paul VI. See Velati, *Separati ma fratelli*, 630–634.

50 Velati, *Separati ma fratelli*, 629–639.

51 From this paradigm, Mahieu also draws all the acts of purification of memory carried out by John Paul II during his pontificate. See Mahieu, *Paul VI et les orthodoxes*, 92.

52 Zervos, *Il contributo del Patriarcato ecumenico*, 44.

53 THS 76, Oct 29, 1964, 80.

54 THS 93, Apr 3, 1965, 92–94, here 93.

55 Cardinal Bea announced Paul VI's decision, in: THS 66, Jun 20, 1964, 75–76. Athenagoras's response in: THS 67, Jun 27, 1964, 76.

and Willebrands listened in Istanbul to Athenagoras recalling the expectation of the whole world for a liberating word that would finally abolish the wall of schism and reestablish the unity of all, the possibility of a public act began to take on a more defined shape on both sides.[56]

Meliton and Chrysostomos of Myra brought to Rome the gift of an icon of Peter and Andrew, the coryphaeus and the protocletus of the apostles. In the course of their visit they suggested, according to Bea's reconstruction in his letter to Athenagoras of Oct 18, 1965, to "make a new and combined study, going right to the heart of the matter, of a canonical question which for nine centuries has helped to complicate and poison the relations between the Roman Catholic Church and the Patriarchate of Constantinople."[57] A joint commission was then established to work out a formula that could be published simultaneously in Rome and Istanbul.[58]

The commission's work – which minutes of a meeting are reported in the *Tomos Agapis*[59] – led to a joint statement – recorded by the Dominican Christophe-Jean Dumont for the SPCU – and the procedural arrangements for a public ceremony to be held on Dec 7 simultaneously in Constantinople and Rome.[60] In the French text, the joint declaration began with the words "pénétrés de reconnaissance envers Dieu."[61] The Orthodox Church would endorse the document with a patriarchal tome and the Catholic Church with a papal brief, read during the solemn liturgical ceremonies.[62] Noting that among the obstacles in the path of fraternal relations between the two churches "there looms the memory of the decisions, actions, and painful incidents which came to a head in 1054 in the sentence of excommunication passed on the Patriarch Michael Cerularios and two other persons by the legates of the Roman See, led by Cardinal Humbert" and that the authors of those actions did not intend to sever the ecclesial communion between the sees of Rome and Constantinople, Pope Paul VI and Patriarch Athenagoras I in his synod declared that they "remove from memory and from the midst of the church the sentences of excommunication" which followed the reprehensible words and gestures expressed by both sides.[63]

A Catholic delegation consisting of Cardinal Lawrence Joseph Shehan, archbishop of Baltimore, Enrico Nicodemo, archbishop of Bari, Msgr. Michele Maccarrone, and fathers Dumont and John Long from the SPCU arrived in Constantinople, while in Rome the Orthodox delegation was led by Metropolitan Meliton.

On Dec 7, 1965, the feast of St. Ambrose, a saint venerated by both churches, in St. George's Cathedral at the Phanar, Cardinal Shehan sat beside Patriarch Athenagoras. After singing the gospel of the Good Shepherd, a deacon solemnly proclaimed the joint declaration. The patriarch then read his tome and, together with the Catholic

56 THS 94, Apr 3, 1965, 94–97.

57 THS 119, Oct 18, 1965, 115–116, here 116.

58 THS 121, Nov 16, 1965, 117–118. The commission was composed, on the Catholic side, of Willebrands as president, Michele Maccarrone, president of the Pontifical Committee for Historical Sciences, the prefect of the Vatican Library, the Jesuit Alphonse Raes, Dumont, director of the Istina center, the Salesian canonist Alfons Stickler, and Duprey as secretary. On the Orthodox side, it was made up of Metropolitan Meliton (Hatzis) as president, Chrysostomos of Myra, Gabriel (Premetidis), secretary of the Holy Synod, Athenagoras (Anastasiades), and Fr. Evanghelos Galanis, while André Scrima and Pavlos (Menevisoglou), undersecretary of the Holy Synod, were the secretaries.

59 THS 124, Nov 23, 1965, 123–125.

60 On Christophe-Jean Dumont, consultor of the SPCU, see the entry by Étienne Fouilloux, in: *Dictionnaire biographique des frères prêcheurs: Dominicains des provinces françaises* (*XIXe–XXe siècle*), <https://journals.openedition.org/dominicains/1228> (accessed Aug 10, 2023).

61 THS 127, Dec 7, 1965, 126–128, 126: "Full of gratitude towards God."

62 Patriarchal tome of Athenagoras, THS 129, Dec 7, 1965, 130–131 and brief of Paul VI *Ambulate in dilectione*, THS 128, Dec 7, 1965, 128–129, respectively.

63 THS 127.

cardinal, gave the blessing to the faithful present. The Our Father was prayed in Greek and Latin.[64]

Meanwhile, in St. Peter's Basilica in Rome, the joint declaration was recited during Mass and Cardinal Bea read the apostolic letter *Ambulate in dilectione*. The council's applause signaled the assembly's unanimous consent, and Paul VI and Meliton exchanged an embrace of peace before descending into the Vatican grottoes, where the metropolitan went to pray at the tomb of John XXIII and to leave nine red roses on that of Leo IX, the pope who reigned in 1054.

The joint declaration of Athenagoras and Paul VI, approved and acclaimed by the Fathers, was included in the official collections of the council documents and then approved together with the apostolic letter *In Spiritu Sancto* with which Paul VI closed Vatican II on Dec 8, 1965.[65]

Interpretations of the meaning, limits, and potential of that event were not unanimous; nevertheless, its importance must be stressed. In fact, it was not only a kind of preparatory act for the theological dialogue that would follow the dialogue of charity then in progress, but also the manifestation of a new theological and ecclesiastical paradigm in the mutual relations between the two churches. The reestablishment of ecclesial charity, the purification of memory, the ecclesiology of the sister churches, and the model of unity in diversity can be considered as points of no return in the subsequent reflection, arising from the theological sense inherent in those acts and gestures.[66] Professor Joseph Ratzinger, in a later reflection on the *Tomos Agapis*, referred to the situation after the lifting of the excommunications and the renewal of memory as a process that not only concerned canon law but that had a properly theological nature, characterized by the immediate goal of full communion and by the kingdom of God as its supreme objective.[67]

4 Towards a Shared Chalice

What had been prophesized by the embrace in Jerusalem and legally sanctioned in December 1965, with its intrinsic liturgical quality, opened the doors to the next step, the fulfilment of a desire shared by the pope and the patriarch: communion with the same chalice. The dialogue of charity, theological dialogue, and sharing at the table were the stages of a single path. This was already clearly set forth in the words of Meliton in Rome in February 1965, when he spoke of "that bright day of the Lord, in which those of the West and those of the East, after the ancient fashion of our common martyrs, confessors, and fathers, will eat the same bread and drink from the same chalice and confess the one faith."[68]

As intended by the leading figures at the time, what is technically defined as intercommunion was meant to be a full recognition of the common belonging to the one Church of Christ, rediscovering the gestures of the first millennium.[69] It could

64 The tome was also signed by Thomas of Chalcedon, Chrysostomos of Neocaesarea, Jerome of Rodopolis, Symeon of Irinopolis, Dorotheos of the Prince's Isles, Maximos of Laodicea, Chrysostomos of Myra, Cyril of Chaldia, Meliton (Hatzis), and Emilianos of Miletus.

65 "Pauli Papae VI et Athenagorae Patriarchae Constantinopolitani declaratio communis," *COGD* 3, 550–552.

66 On the entwining of the different theological and ecclesial dimensions, the observations of Destivelle are fundamental: Hyacinthe Destivelle, "La signification ecclésiologique de la levée des anathèmes de 1054: Pour une théologie du dialogue de la charité," *CrSt* 38, 2017, 51–84.

67 "Rapport sur le colloque ecclésiologique entre théologiens orthodoxes et catholiques: 'Koinonìa,' Vienne 1–7-avril 1974," in: AFscire, FDpy, 109.1, 8.

68 *THS* 87, Feb 16, 1965, 85–87, here 87.

69 Authoritative exponents of Orthodox theology spoke of sharing at the Eucharistic table as a step that was by now ready to be taken, made concretely possible by the 1964 meeting between Athenagoras and Paul VI in Jerusalem and then by the solemn lifting of the excommunications in December 1965. See: Nicholas Afanasiev, "L'Eucharistie, principal lien entre les Catholiques et les Orthodoxes," *Irén* 38, 1965, 336–339; André Scrima, "The Lifting of the Anathemas: An Act of Reparation," *ECR* 1, 1, 1966, 23–26 and John D. Zizioulas, "La communauté eucharistique et la catholicité de

be said that this objective summarized the entire path documented by the *Tomos* and, even more, that of the ecumenical movement. The lifting of the excommunications did not, however, have the automatic effect of reestablishing intercommunion, despite the full recognition of the two churches' shared sacramental reality. As Metropolitan Meliton emphasized at the inception of the work of the joint commission in November 1965: "This act does not mean the restoration of full communion between the Roman Catholic and Orthodox churches ... Nor does it imply the restoration of a common sacramental life."[70]

The situation was that of a separation without excommunication, of a division without juridical attributes, what the theologian Vlassios Phidas, ten years later, would call *akoinonisìa*.[71] There was a need for a shared outlook, especially according to the Orthodox point of view. Paradoxically, however, it was mainly Patriarch Athenagoras who repeatedly raised the issue of concelebration with Pope Paul VI. While, from a canonical standpoint, intercommunion was not possible, the patriarch's insistence on sharing the chalice with the pope appeared as a means to reaching unity, not the crowning of a finished journey. In light of these overtures, the initiatives of unauthorized intercommunion that were spreading in both churches in different environments certainly factored into the call for prudence.[72]

Faced with the difficulties that emerged among the clergy and among the people, and even among the bishops, the project of concelebration and the sharing of the chalice seemed to stall for a long time. In December 1969, Athenagoras affirmed that "this is the hour for Christian courage,"[73] while Paul VI shortly afterwards referred, with a curious formulation, to the "prudent boldness"[74] to which both were called in advancing towards the common altar of the Lord. On the strength of the conclusions of the work of a small secret commission operating in Switzerland in the spring of 1970,[75] which outlined a possible canvas for concelebration, it was Paul VI who returned to this theme in 1971, affirming the presence of the Spirit in the desire to quickly arrive to the day "when at the conclusion of a liturgy celebrated together we shall be able to drink together from the same chalice of the Lord."[76] For Athenagoras, the gesture – a sign of a renewed experience of life – could have been accomplished without the theological agreement of the different churches, placing itself in the realm of prophecy and shared sign: visible unity "is not a work to be left for human considerations and deliberations, given that the designs of men are unsure (Wis 9:14), but something to be experienced in the life of Christ, which finds continued existence in his Body, the church."[77]

It was an idea of unity that recalled that of the college of the apostles; therefore, "it is not a question of a uniformity which would reduce all to itself, but of the unity of a body where harmony consists in the complementarity of the members,"

l'Église," *Istina* 14, 1969, 67–88 (translated as "Eucharist and Catholicity" and included in *Being as Communion: Studies in Personhood and the Church*, Crestwood, St. Vladimir's Seminary Press, 1993, 143–169).

70 *THS* 122, Nov 22, 1965, 118–121, here 120.

71 "Rapport sur le colloque ecclésiologique," 7.

72 See Mahieu, *Paul VI et les orthodoxes*, 189–191. On the unauthorized intercommunion of 1968 in the episodes of Paris, Uppsala, and Medellín, see the first-hand analysis by Alfredo Marranzini, "Il problema dell'intercomunione oggi" and "La chiesa cattolica e l'intercomunione," *La Civiltà cattolica* 120/4, 1969, 228–240 and 430–442; Francesco Coccopalmerio, *La partecipazione degli acattolici al culto della chiesa cattolica nella pratica e nella dottrina della Santa Sede dall'inizio del secolo XVII ai nostri giorni: Uno studio teologico sull'essenza del diritto di prendere parte al culto cattolico*, Brescia, Morcelliana, 1969, which looks at the issue from the point of view of canon law, and Luigi Santini, "Il problema dell'intercomunione," *Testimonianze* 12, 1969, 133–153.

73 *THS* 277, Dec 7, 1969, 228.

74 *THS* 279, Dec 22, 1969, 229.

75 See "Rapport de la commission mixte Église catholique-patriarcat œcuménique sur la possibilité d'une concélébration entre le pape et le patriarche œcuménique," in: Melloni, *Tempus visitationis*, 276–285.

76 *THS* 283, Feb 8, 1971, 231–232, here 232.

77 *THS* 284, Mar 21, 1971, 232–234, here 234.

according to Willebrands.[78] Once again, however, the exchange of letters and intentions was not followed by the concrete achievement of intercommunion; the path still seemed hindered by a weighty historical heritage, as Cardinal Willebrands explained.[79] One of the most difficult problems to manage was certainly that of the fate of the Eastern Catholic Churches.[80] But several factors made the achievement of that gesture – which would have meant so much in the history of the church – inappropriate in the judgment of the possible agents, including the resistance within the two churches, in particular on the Catholic side, from the Congregation for the Doctrine of the Faith, and the danger of a split within the Orthodox world.[81]

The *Tomos* does not go beyond a chronological account of these events, limiting itself to what was written in the official exchange. Nevertheless, rereading the correspondence from those years sheds light on the leaders' evangelical audacity and reflects the climate of expectation for an event that, for a long time, seemed imminent. For this, as for many other issues, it is necessary to know what was happening behind the scenes with the other major figures and artisans of the dialogue, to use the term that Meliton and Chrysostomos of Myra applied to Fr. Duprey as an "inspired and sincere artisan of the sacred cause."[82]

What emerges in the letters and documents published in the *Tomos* is the official and public part of the patient work constructed by the collaborators of Athenagoras and Paul VI, made up of the meetings and studies, relationships and common perspectives, in which men representing the two churches, but also their own lived experience, encountered one other.

This is why we can say that the authors of the *Tomos* are not only those who signed the documents, but all those, whose names often do not appear even once, who were the indispensable weavers of the threads and tapestries that became the fabric of the churches' journey. These include, first and foremost, the members of the SPCU (alongside Willebrands and Bea: Jean Jérôme Hamer, Dumont, Duprey, Emmanuel Lanne) and Damaskinos (Papandreou), John Zizioulas, Meliton (Hatzis), Maximos of Sardis, Chrysostomos of Myra, Chrysostomos of Neocaesarea, Bartholomew (Archontonis), Scrima, and Athenagoras of Thyateira.

5 Publishing the History

It soon became clear that it was necessary not to lose track of such a great patrimony of correspondence and meetings, which was becoming more and more valuable, and to make it an object of a *paradosis* addressed to all Christians.

In January 1969, a letter from Willebrands to Athenagoras announced that Paul VI had accepted the suggestion of the synodal commission that he and Duprey had met in Istanbul in December 1968 "to make preparations for publishing the various speeches and letters exchanged between the Church of Rome and the Orthodox churches in these recent years."[83] To achieve that goal, a joint commission of four members was created. Willebrands communicated that the representatives appointed by the Catholics were Duprey and Dumont. The same letter proposed an initial working session in Istanbul and a second in Rome. The reply from Istanbul, in early July, gave notification that the Orthodox members would be the Very Reverend Archimandrite Damaskinos

78 *THS* 275, Nov 30, 1969, 223–227, here 226–227.

79 See Mahieu, *Paul VI et les orthodoxes*, 194.

80 See André de Halleux, "Uniatisme et communion: Le texte catholique-orthodoxe de Freising," *RTL* 22, 1991, 3–29; Robert F. Taft, "The Problem of 'Uniatism' and the 'Healing of Memories': Anamnesis, Not Amnesia," *LOGOS* 41–42, 2000–2001, 155–196; and Hervé Legrand, "Les enjeux ecclésiologiques de l'uniatisme vus du proche-orient chrétien," *Science et Esprit* 65/1–2, 2013, 117–132, esp. 121.

81 Melloni, *Tempus visitationis*, 97–99.

82 Notes on the Orthodox delegation's trip to Rome, Mar 27, 1965, in: AFscire, FDpy, 2.28.

83 *THS* 245, Jan 19, 1969, 206–208, here 207.

Papandreou, director of the Orthodox Centre at Chambésy near Geneva, and the Reverend Deacon Bartholomew (Archontonis) from the staff of the Sacred Theological College of Halki.[84] From Willebrands we know that by July 1969 a first inventory of the texts had already been drawn up.[85]

A meeting of the joint commission took place in the autumn of 1969 in Istanbul, followed by others, reaching the decision to close the volume with Paul VI's January 1970 letter to Athenagoras, and adding as an appendix the two letters exchanged between the patriarch and the pope between February and March 1971, just before the printing of the *Tomos*. In all, there were 284 documents.

The title chosen had only one other attested precedent. Curiously enough, it was an anti-Latin work dating back to 1698 by Dositheus II, patriarch of Jerusalem, a staunch defender of the Greek theological tradition. Profoundly anti-Catholic and anti-Protestant, it too was entitled *Tomos Agapis*.

The official presentation, as we have seen, took place at the patriarchate in December 1971. During a private meeting with the Catholic delegation, Athenagoras reiterated his position, referring to the pope, as he often did, as "my brother, Paul II," linking his magisterium to that of the apostle Paul:

> We are the same church. I believe in tradition. I have nothing that separates me from my brother. Nothing that I disagree with him on. The filioque, infallibility, primacy, do I accept them? Of course I do! It would be crazy to ask a church to renounce its treasures, its dogmas, in order to create union. It is necessary to respect mutual traditions, to understand them reciprocally. These differences of conception existed during the centuries when we had sacramental communion. We must reject any negative attitude towards one another. We must not wait any longer. We have to put things in motion. Here in 1965, in two days, a commission ... repaired nine centuries of division in two days of work. Why did this happen? Because on both sides we wanted to reach a fair conclusion. It is necessary to continue. This is a matter that transcends all diplomacy.[86]

In January 1972, during the Week of Prayer for Christian Unity, a delegation from Constantinople, led by Metropolitan Meliton of Chalcedon, presented the volume – with a dedication from Athenagoras – to Pope Paul VI. The patriarch had signed the book with the words:

> To Pope Paul VI, beloved and venerated older brother, Athenagoras of Constantinople dedicates this volume that contains the relationship of the origin and growth of charity between the churches of Rome and Constantinople, with hope in the Lord and with the wish that He will grant that we may write its epilogue on the shared holy altar with His precious blood.[87]

From a quantitative point of view, the trend of documents published for each year graphically reflects the course of relations and the concentration of events and appointments. While from 1958 to 1961 there were but a few, that number rose to 16 in 1962, growing to 48 during 1965 and to 60 in 1967, a sign of the great work that was

84 *THS* 259, Jul 8, 1969, 215. On Damaskinos see Maria Brun, "Damaskinos Papandreou: Eine Biographie," in: Maria Brun & Wilhelm Schneemelcher, eds., *Eucharisteria: Festschrift für Damaskinos Papandreou, Metropolit der Schweiz, zum 60. Geburtstag am 23. Februar 1996*, Athens, Ekdotike Athenon, 1996, 229–253. Bartholomew (Archontonis) became ecumenical patriarch in 1991 as Bartholomew I.

85 *THS* 261, Jul 19, 1969, 216.

86 AFscire, FDpy, 3.31.

87 "Relations interconfessionnelles," *Irén* 45, 1972, 92–102, here 93, note 2. *Irénikon* devoted part of its first issue of 1972 to chronicling the visits to Constantinople in December 1971 and to Rome in January 1972 for the exchange of volumes with the respective dedications of the pope and patriarch, and to commenting on the importance of the publication.

unfolding between the two churches in those years. Subsequently, exchanges diminished, while remaining significant, until the closure of the *Tomos* in 1970.

The 1971 edition in Greek and French was not the only one. Precisely due to its character as a collection in progress and a documental accumulation and because of its objective, namely the transmission of the churches' path to the Orthodox and Catholic faithful, it soon became necessary to publish translations and updates.

Chronologically, the first edition was the Spanish one, without texts in the original languages, published in Madrid in 1973 by the Biblioteca de Autores Cristianos.[88] 22 documents were added to those of the original edition, encompassing statements through Jan 6, 1973. We know from a letter from Duprey that 2,000 copies were sold in the first year.[89] In Vienna in 1978, the Pro Oriente foundation printed the German translation of the *Tomos*, updated to 1976.[90] This edition had ten more documents than the original, including texts issued up until Jan 25, 1976. In 1984, a French volume was published in Paris, including documents through 1979.[91] Only 59 documents of the original 284 were republished, to which were added 34 for the following years with the new protagonists: Patriarch Dimitrios I and Pope John Paul II. The first new text included was Paul VI's speech on Jan 24, 1972, during the prayer at the Lateran Basilica with the Orthodox delegation led by Metropolitan Meliton, whom the pope called "the bearer of a book which history will make its own,"[92] referring to the gift of the copy of the *Tomos Agapis* signed by Athenagoras. He expressed the wish that they be able to add a new, definitive, and magnificent page to that book: the page of unity. The last document published, at n. 93, is the joint declaration of John Paul II and Dimitrios I of Nov 30, 1979, in which they announce the opening of theological dialogue and extend the horizon of dialogue and collaboration to all believers of other religions and to all persons of good will.

In 1987, the English edition quoted here was published in the United States, including documents through 1984, the result of translation work done by the Australian Jesuit Edward James Stormon and introduced by Paulist Father Thomas Stransky, who had played an important role during the council years in drafting the document *Nostra aetate*. The first copy of the work was given to John Paul II by Patriarch Dimitrios in December 1987 during a visit to the Vatican. The included texts number 481, the last one dated Jun 28, 1984: it is a letter from John Paul II to Stylianos (Harkianakis), primate of the Greek Orthodox Archdiocese of Australia, who had participated in the meeting with the pope in Rome as a member of the Orthodox delegation during the visit for the feasts of Saints Peter and Paul. Stylianos himself also signed a presentation as did the Catholic archbishop of Melbourne, Frank Little.

For the Slavic languages, the Russian translation did not appear until 1996, and the Ukranian one was published in 2001. The work in Russian was published by the Catholic publishing house Zhizn's Bogom, established in Brussels in 1945 and an important cultural center for the Russian diaspora in Europe.[93] The Ukrainian edition was

88 *Al encuentro de la unidad: Documentación de las relaciones entre la Santa Sede y el Patriarcado de Constantinopla 1958–1972*, Madrid, Biblioteca de Autores Cristianos, 1973.

89 Duprey mentions this in a letter to the superior general of the Missionaries of St. Paul in Lebanon, Habib Bacha, asking him to keep some copies of the volume in their bookstore and possibly to publish a review of it in their journal, noting that "this book is practically unknown in Lebanon and the Middle East"; P. Duprey to H. Bacha, Jul 25, 1975, in: AFscire, FDpy, 5.

90 *Tomos Agapis: Dokumentation zum Dialog der Liebe zwischen dem Hl. Stuhl und dem Ökumenischen Patriarchat (1958–1976)*, Innsbruck, Tyrolia, 1978.

91 Jean XXIII & others, *Le livre de la charité*.

92 Jean XXIII & others, *Le livre de la charité*, n. 60, Jan 24, 1972, 157–159, in English in: *THS* 241–244, here 242.

93 *Tomos Agapis: Vatikan-Fanar (1958–1970)*, Brussels, Zhizn's Bogom, 1996.

published by Dukh i Litera, which was established in Kiev in 1992.[94]

6 Things and Words

The substance of the *Tomos* is formed by the maturation of themes and horizons that are not taken for granted at the outset, which were constructed month after month, visit after visit, and meeting after meeting. The very fact of the actualization of the encounter itself became a theological act.[95] Reflection was carried out on the weight of the past and on the necessity of forgiveness, on the meaning of memory from a theological point of view and the need, on both sides, to purify it so that it could be the secure basis for subsequent steps of rapprochement.

The language reflects the reworking of ancient categories and, at the same time, highlights the search for a new vocabulary comparable to that in use in previous centuries. The permanence and novelty of the words are the mirror of the (re)discovery of the value of what is indicated, a creative act that illuminates with new meaning what was often not new, indeed what was often very ancient, belonging to the discourse of the first Christian centuries.

Among the expressions found in the *Tomos*, of particular interest is the representation of the two churches as "sisters." The expression "sister churches" belongs to the lexicon of the undivided church,[96] and its history before and after the recurrences found in the *Tomos* makes it particularly suitable to be considered a sort of thermometer of the quality of ecumenical relations.

In a certain sense, the expression acquires new theological meaning in the aftermath of the lifting of the anathemas,[97] but it was used for the first time in the correspondence between Athenagoras and Cardinal Bea in April 1962. In the same way, after the death of John XXIII, he referred to the late pope at a meeting of the Holy Synod as the "venerable leader of our sister Church of Rome."[98] Rome was also called sister church in the Easter greetings of 1964.[99] If the Orthodox made use of this expression frequently (see for example the address of Metropolitan Meliton to Pope Paul VI on the occasion of the Constantinopolitan delegation's visit to the pope),[100] on the Catholic side it appeared for the first time in an official document by Paul VI, the brief *Anno ineunte* of Jul 25, 1967, an important turning point for the ecumenical discourse.[101] In it, the pope refers to the conciliar decree *Unitatis redintegratio*, recalling the expression "sister churches" in use among the Eastern churches.[102] In the same way, Paul VI continued, "our churches for centuries lived like sisters [*sororio more*]" and, in the present time, the Lord calls them to again "recognize themselves as sisters." The Orthodox Church was, therefore, confirmed in its full ecclesiality, and the debate was opened on what the nature of the Petrine primacy in a newly united church might be.[103]

94 Natalya Ivanivna Kocchan, ed., *Tomos Agapis. Dokumenty pro vidnosyny Ryms'kogo i Konstantynopol's'kogo Prestoliv u 1958–1984 rr.*, Kiev, Dukh i Litera, 2001.

95 See Destivelle, "La signification ecclésiologique," 78–80.

96 See the thorough inventory of the indications found in the Christian literature of the first centuries in Emmanuel Lanne, "Eglises-sœurs: Implications ecclésiologiques du Tomos Agapis," *Istina* 20, 1975, 47–74. On the relations between the churches in the first three centuries, see Michael A. Fahey, "Ecclesiae sorores ac fratres: Sibling Communion in the Pre-Nicene Christian Era," *Proceedings of the Catholic Theological Society of America* 36, 1981, 15–38.

97 See Hyacinthe Destivelle, *Conduis-la vers l'unité parfaite: Œcuménisme et synodalité*, Paris, Cerf, 2018, 59–61. See also the study by the Orthodox theologian Will T. Cohen, *The Concept of "Sister Churches" in Catholic-Orthodox Relations since Vatican II*, Münster, Aschendorff, 2016.

98 *THS* 26, Jun 4, 1963, 44–45, here 45.

99 *THS* 58, Mar 27, 1964, 71.

100 *THS* 87.

101 *THS* 176, Jul 25, 1967, 161–163.

102 On the importance of the conciliar document in the process of rapprochement, see Jean XXIII & others, *Le livre de la charité*, 38–41.

103 See Maximos Vghenopoulos, "Il perdono tra le chiese: Il 'Tomos Agapis,'" in: Luigi d'Ayala Valva, Lisa Cremaschi

At the end of Athenagoras's visit to Paul VI in Rome in October 1967, the joint declaration, albeit in the usual prudent and measured language of official communications, resumed this trend of mutual recognition by stressing that the meeting of the pope and the patriarch had contributed to their churches rediscovering themselves as sister churches once again.[104]

Beginning with these years, new theological perspectives developed on both sides and the practice of referring to each other as sister churches became part of the standard vocabulary of the exchanges, thanks also to the reflection of and on Vatican II, especially on the theme of local churches in Catholic ecclesiology.[105] Congar spoke of a new epoch inaugurated by the two great leaders.[106]

This new era, strengthened by the bilateral meetings that punctuated the theological dialogue that began after the dialogue of charity (such as the declaration of the joint commission that met in Balamand in 1993) would not, however, be free of attempts at revisionism.[107] If the term "sister churches" constitutes the bricks with which this dialogue was patiently being built, it would also be the unacceptable horizon for those groups that obtained, in 2000, the *Note on the Expression "Sister Churches"* from the Congregation for the Doctrine of the Faith, led by then-prefect Joseph Ratzinger, whose doctrinal scope has long been debated, as well as the same congregation declaration *Dominus Iesus* on the unicity and salvific universality of Jesus Christ.

6.1 *The Liturgy in the* Tomos Agapis

For Christians, the liturgy constitutes the space and time in which communion among the baptized is made present and visible. In the *Tomos*, the horizon of the reestablishment of full sacramental communion is evident, becoming clearer and more explicit as the years go by. And this horizon is clearly liturgical, so much so that it is difficult to separate ecumenism and liturgy. There are numerous references to the desire to celebrate a common liturgy, a Eucharist in which both sides share in the same chalice.

The Eucharist, as the unifying center of Christianity, develops its potential when the celebration becomes the revelation of the church to itself and to the world.[108] In this, Orthodox theology undoubtedly has a historically constituted sensitivity built in the sign of the *koinonia* developed among the different churches. Catholicism can draw upon this, rediscovering the nucleus of a *status ecclesiae* that is a shared and permanent element, separated from the *statuta ecclesiae* where

& Adalberto Mainardi, eds., *Misericordia e perdono: Atti del XXIII Convegno ecumenico internazionale di spiritualità ortodossa (Bose, 9–12 settembre 2015)*, Magnano, Qiqajon, 2016, 307–319.

104 *THS* 195, Oct 28, 1967, 181–182.

105 See Mahieu, *Paul VI et les orthodoxes*, 166–167, and Joseph Famerée, *Ecclésiologie et œcuménisme: Recueil d'études*, Leuven, Peeters, 2017.

106 This is Congar's phrase in Congar, "L'œcuménisme de Paul VI."

107 See Hervé Legrand, "La théologie des églises sœurs: Réflexions ecclésiologiques autour de la Déclaration de Balamand," *RSPT* 88/3, 2004, 461–496. On its controversial reception in Catholicism and Orthodoxy, see Ronald G. Roberson, "Catholic Reactions to the Balamand Document," *ECJ* 4, 1997, 54–73; Michel Stavrou, "Les 'Ambigua' du document de Balamand pour sa réception du coté Orthodoxe," in: Comité Mixte Catholiques-Orthodoxes en France, ed., *Catholiques et orthodoxes: Les enjeux de l'uniatisme, Dans le sillage de Balamand*, Paris, Cerf, 2004, 323–342, esp. 327–328; and John S. Romanides, "Orthodox and Vatican Agreement: Balamand, Lebanon, June 1993," *Teologia* 64/4, 1993, 570–580. This last is an example of a severe Orthodox criticism of the Balamand document. More generally, on the anti-ecumenical retreat of Orthodoxy in the last quarter century, see Paul Ladouceur, "On Ecumenoclasm: Anti-Ecumenical Theology in Orthodoxy," *SVTQ* 61, 2017, 323–355; Paul Ladouceur, "Neo-Traditionalist Ecclesiology in Orthodoxy," *SJT* 72, 2019, 398–413; and Vasilios N. Makrides, "Orthodox Christian Rigorism: Attempting to Delineate a Multifaceted Phenomenon," *JRAT* 2, 2016, 216–252.

108 On this aspect, see the reflections of John D. Zizioulas, *Eucharist, Bishop, Church: The Unity of the Church in the Divine Eucharist and the Bishop during the First Three Centuries*, Brookline, Holy Cross Orthodox Press, 2001.

the different forms do not erode the substantial content.[109]

In a certain sense, the entire journey recounted in the volume can be read as a liturgy in which mutual welcoming moves on to the request for forgiveness as a preliminary penitential moment prior to listening to the Word of God and to the *communicatio in sacris*, which becomes the icon of rediscovered unity that will finally conclude the book in becoming what, to this day, is the *Tomos Agapis*.

It is precisely the importance of the liturgical moment that seems to me to be emphasized in the intensified relations between the Orthodox and the Catholic churches. First, the ceremony of the lifting of the excommunications, held simultaneously in Rome and Istanbul in 1965, constituted a true and proper liturgical form, all the more solemn because, on the Catholic side, it was celebrated during an ecumenical council. Moreover, the *Tomos Agapis* gives, as an appendix, the *ordo* followed for the liturgy of the Word celebrated in St. Peter's Basilica by the pope and the patriarch in October 1967, in which the absence of the eucharistic liturgy echoes as a warning not to let human tardiness delay the arrival of that day in which we "reach the hour of that perfect communion."[110] The words of the prayer of Paul VI resound with the painful breach in unity based on "the same proclamation of the Gospel and the same baptism, and are sharers in the same sacraments and gifts of the Spirit and together enjoy the protection of Mary" and the impossibility of "that full fellowship which would be a witness to the world." For this division, for the sins against unity that have accumulated in the past centuries, he expresses a request for forgiveness.[111]

A liturgy was also celebrated in Istanbul by Cardinal Willebrands during the trip in which he presented the *Tomos* to Athenagoras. In the Catholic Church of St. Anthony, a liturgy was celebrated for the feast of the Immaculate Conception, with the representative of the patriarch, Metropolitan Kallinikos of Lystra, Metropolitan Chrysostomos of Myra, and Metropolitan Gabriel of Koloneia, as well as the secretary of the Holy Synod, Archimandrite Pavlos (Menevisoglou), present. The Grand Rabbi of Istanbul David Asseo was also present among them.[112]

The value of liturgy in the ecumenical journey, therefore, is difficult to underestimate, and it is important to emphasize its connection with the dialogue between the two churches. It is precisely the liturgy that nourishes the ferment of the ecumenical journey, just as the Eucharist is the ferment of Christian life. At the end of the joint theological meeting held in Vienna in April 1974, for example, during the closing liturgy held in the Orthodox Cathedral of the Holy Trinity, the homily was given by Fr. Duprey, while during the Mass celebrated in the Cathedral of St. Stephen, Metropolitan Damaskinos (Papandreou) preached.[113]

7 What Authority for the Future?

Precisely because of its unique genesis and the declared intent that distinguishes it, the *Tomos* can be classified under different profiles. From a material point of view, it is a collection of documents that punctuate the path of the second half of the 20th century, a historical source for years to come. From a canonical point of view, it could be placed in line with canonical collections, comparable to the ancient "canons of the Fathers" of the

109 Alberigo's reflections on synodality provide a parallel resource: Giuseppe Alberigo, "Sinodo come liturgia?," *CrSt* 28, 2007, 1–40, esp. 10. An important place in the theological reflection on the *koinonia* of the churches is rightfully assigned to Jean-Marie R. Tillard, *Church of Churches: The Ecclesiology of Communion*, Collegeville MN, Liturgical Press, 1992. Also important is the later Jean-Marie R. Tillard, *Flesh of the Church, Flesh of Christ: At the Source of the Ecclesiology of Communion*, Collegeville MN, Liturgical Press, 2001.

110 *THS*, Appendix 4, 495–508, here 503–504.

111 *THS*, Appendix 4, 495–508, here 503–504.

112 See Melloni, *Tempus visitationis*, 308.

113 Alfred Stirnemann, "La Fondation 'Pro Oriente,'" *Istina* 20, 1975, 3–5.

Eastern Church and to the papal decrees of the Western Church, without forgetting the numerous references to the conciliar decisions it contains, decisions that are normative sources for the church. Theologians stress its value as a testimony to the path of conversion and rapprochement between the two churches, even without drawing the implicit conclusions that one would expect. In this regard, there has been talk of a sort of lack of correspondence between the gestures made by the churches and the full recognition of the new reality that has been created: "The impression remains that the churches are now making gestures that belong to a context, both theoretical and practical, which they nevertheless refuse to recognize. In other words, it is a matter of a 'future' that is already present and yet not recognized."[114] Some refer to the ecclesiological experience summarized in the *Tomos Agapis* to enucleate the method and principles to be esteemed in the future ecumenical journey, with other Christian churches as well.[115]

From the beginning, the welcome received by the volume has not hidden the existing stalemate on substantial aspects. An editorial in *Irénikon* underlines that joy at its publication must avoid superficial enthusiasm as well as a disenchanted reaction. The *Tomos Agapis* is only a preamble, and it is necessary to transform the principles that it enunciates and the goal to which it tends – that of the mutual recognition of the legitimacy of the respective traditions – into a concrete reality.[116]

The chronicle published by Giovanni Caprile in *La Civiltà Cattolica* on the occasion of the presentation of the volume to Paul VI by the Orthodox delegation during the Week of Prayer for Christian Unity has a celebratory tone. The *Tomos Agapis* is defined as a prototype, hinting at other volumes in preparation, bearing witness to the ecumenical journey made by the Holy See with the other Orthodox patriarchates.[117] In reality, to date, the *Tomos* remains an *unicum* in the written panorama dedicated to Catholic Church's bilateral relations with other Christian churches.

The acknowledged value of the *Tomos* as "one of the milestones in relations between the two churches"[118] does not, however, obscure the wound that exists when the churches refer to unity and communion as "imperfect," however real. It is probably this unresolved knot that casts a shadow on the overall importance of all the material collected, whose "result" was not what its crafters expected. An initial assessment was offered by the theological Koinonia conference held in Vienna in 1974, a realization of what had been hoped for at the time of the presentation of the *Tomos Agapis* to the patriarch in 1971, and which had come about even earlier as a proposal among the members of the commission charged with preparing the publication.[119] Organized and hosted by the Pro Oriente foundation of Vienna, together with the Centre Orthodoxe du Patriarcat Œcuménique of Chambésy and the SPCU, it remains a point of reference for later studies.[120]

114 See Giuseppe Ruggieri, *Cristianesimo, chiese e Vangelo*, Bologna, Il Mulino, 2002, 100.

115 See Valdman, "'Tomos Agapis,'" which identifies eleven ecumenical principles to follow in ecumenical work. On the theological dialogue that followed, see Dimitri Salachas, *Il dialogo teologico ufficiale tra la Chiesa cattolico-romana e la Chiesa ortodossa: Iter e documentazione*, Bari, Centro ecumenico "S. Nicola" padri domenicani, 1994 and Patrice Mahieu, *Se préparer au don de l'unité: La commission internationale catholique-orthodoxe (1975–2000)*, Paris, Cerf, 2016.

116 "Editorial," *Irén* 45, 1972, 3–6.

117 Giovanni Caprile, "Roma e Costantinopoli," *La Civiltà Cattolica* 123/1, 1972, 382–389.

118 See Vghenopoulos, "Il perdono tra le chiese," 308.

119 "The idea of such a colloquium had originated in the commission tasked with preparing the publication of the *Tomos Agapis*. It soon became clear that it would be useful to have a meeting of Catholic and Orthodox theologians to clarify the presuppositions and theological implications of the documents contained in this volume and also to draw practical consequences for the pastoral care and the life of the Catholic and Orthodox churches"; "Rapport sur le colloque ecclésiologique," 1.

120 The acts of the colloquium were published in *Istina* 20/1, 1975.

Half a century later, it is fitting to question what happened or did not happen among the churches. Are there consequences still to come or have we stopped at the level of desire and vision without any effects in the daily life of the churches? The path taken in these decades has also been described as a myth, as if to underline its limits and a supposed asymmetry in the evaluation of the gestures of reconciliation that have actually been implemented.[121] If the *Tomos* is a "gesture" that can be equated with the gestures that it gathers together, then Duprey's reflection on a sort of almost physiological delay of theology with respect to reality is probably still valid,[122] a reflection that, in different terms, was also posed by Athenagoras himself.[123]

References to the *Tomos* are, by now, customary on the part of the magisterium of both churches, a sign that it has entered into the common cultural and spiritual patrimony, even if there is not yet a shared theological elaboration of the conceptual difficulty underlying the still unsolved problems, that is, concerning the relationship between unity and pluralism and its reflections.[124] The path developed has become a model for the relations between the Catholic Church and the other churches, both in the context of the Reformation and the Orthodox churches. Even with the differences that shape considerations in the Catholic and Orthodox spheres, the reflection on time in the church that unfolded in the 20th century has been fundamental. If the time of the church and the time of history are no longer parallel and incommunicable universes, it is legitimate to reconsider remote events from new perspectives, eliminating any political superfetations and misunderstandings that can now be overcome.

Certainly, this is a solid basis upon which to build, which well underscores the value of the "human factor" that, at a precise historical moment, decided to respond with a surprising personal commitment to the Holy Spirit's call for unity, or, in less spiritual terms, to the scandal of division among Christians.[125] The canonical and theological implications of the dialogue undertaken between the churches has now reached a point of no return, even if it has not been able to avoid more or less long moments of slowdown or a lack of energy on both sides.[126] In any case, the perspective from which to judge an ecclesiastical journey must take the long view into account and not an event-driven history, a spiritual perspective and not only a canonical one.

One may wonder, however, whether the *Tomos* also has a further significance. Considering the repeatedly renewed consensus of the highest leaders of the two churches regarding the path to unity, it seems to me that it is possible to identify in this act of consensus a source that surpasses, in the hierarchy of canonical sources, particular rights and which indicates a clear horizon toward which their successors are called to move. It says that the ecumenical path cannot be regulated or weighed down by particular laws or by future, eventually different, choices made by leaders of the Christian churches. Referring once again to the church of

121 See Andrea Strübind, "Myths of Religious Reconciliation," *KZG* 27/2, 2014, 244–256.

122 Yves Congar's diary records a meeting with Fr. Duprey on Sep 14, 1965, during which the White Father said that he was convinced that "if one were to FORMULATE today the implications of these gestures and messages it is likely that Rome would retreat from such a formulation of ideas. The gestures will create a familiarity and when that has been done, one day, the formulas will be able to be accepted. And that goes not only for Rome. Among the Orthodox, the theologians are behindhand about the real ecumenical situation"; Yves Congar, *My Journal of the Council*, Dublin, Dominican Publications, 2012, 774 (capitals in the text).

123 See Clément, *Dialogues with Patriarch Athenagoras*, where the patriarch emphasized the freedom of pastors in regard to theologians.

124 On this, see the synthesis by Giuseppe Alberigo, "Unità, divisione, ecumenismo," in: Giuseppe Alberigo, Giuseppe Ruggieri & Roberto Rusconi, eds., *Il Cristianesimo: Grande Atlante*, vol. 2, *Ordinamenti, gerarchie, pratiche*, Turin, Utet, 2006, 612–626.

125 "The *Tomos Agapis* is the historical record of the acts brought about by the Holy Spirit," according to Vghenopoulos, "Il perdono tra le chiese," 318.

126 See Mahieu, *Paul VI et les orthodoxes*, 124.

the first millennium, it is important to recall that the most important canonists were bishops and that, therefore, canon law and pastoral care were aspects of the same responsibility.[127]

If unity is to be the sacrament of tomorrow's church, the *Tomos* certainly represents an inescapable reference point, showing the path that has been covered despite difficulties, a path that is not afraid of diversity and plurality. As elsewhere in church history, it is then the reception of an act that decides its value. Once again, the fact that the volume was written to submit the texts to the reflection of the Christian people, as its editors assert, underlines that it is they who are the true actors, capable of directing the church (or not) towards a time that has not yet come.

Translated from Italian to English by Susan Dawson Vásquez and David Dawson Vásquez.

Bibliography

Alberigo, Giuseppe, ed., *Christian Unity: The Council of Ferrara-Florence (1439/39–1989)*, Leuven, Peeters, 1991.

Clément, Olivier, *Dialogues with Patriarch Athenagoras*, Brookline, Holy Cross Orthodox Press, 2022.

Cohen, Will T., *The Concept of "Sister Churches" in Catholic-Orthodox Relations since Vatican II*, Münster, Aschendorff, 2016.

Denaux, Adelbert & Peter De Mey, eds., *The Ecumenical Legacy of Johannes Cardinal Willebrands (1909-2006)*, Leuven, Peeters, 2012.

Destivelle, Hyacinthe, *Conduis-la vers l'unité parfaite: Œcuménisme et synodalité*, Paris, Cerf, 2018.

Famerée, Joseph, *Ecclésiologie et œcuménisme: Recueil d'études*, Leuven, Peeters, 2017.

Flogaus, Reinhard & Jennifer Wasmuth, eds., *Orthodoxie im Dialog: Historische und aktuelle Perspektiven*, Berlin, De Gruyter, 2015.

Fouilloux, Étienne, *Les catholiques et l'unité chrétienne du XIXe au XXe siècle: Itinéraires européens d'expression française*, Paris, Le Centurion, 1982.

Mahieu, Patrice, *Paul VI et les orthodoxes*, Paris, Cerf, 2012.

Mahieu, Patrice, *Se préparer au don de l'unité: La commission internationale catholique-orthodoxe, (1975-2000)*, Paris, Cerf, 2016.

Martano, Valeria, *Athenagoras il patriarca (1886–1972): Un cristiano fra crisi della coabitazione e utopia ecumenica*, Bologna, Il Mulino, 1996.

Salachas, Dimitri, *Il dialogo teologico ufficiale tra la Chiesa cattolico-romana e la Chiesa ortodossa: Iter e documentazione*, Bari, Centro ecumenico "S. Nicola" padri domenicani, 1994.

Thils, Gustave, *Histoire doctrinale du mouvement œcuménique*, Paris, Desclée de Brouwer, 21963.

Tillard, Jean-Marie R., *Church of Churches: The Ecclesiology of Communion*, Collegeville MN, Liturgical Press, 1992.

127 For a synthesis, see Ken Pennington, "La legge nelle tradizioni cristiane," in: Alberigo, Ruggieri & Rusconi, eds., *Il Cristianesimo: Grande Atlante*, vol. 2, 647–663.

CHAPTER 31

Aarhus 1964 and the Dialogue between Eastern and Oriental Orthodox Churches

Will Cohen

1 Historical and Thematic Overview

The modern encounter between representatives of the Oriental Orthodox and Eastern Orthodox churches was an occasion of mutual surprise. Each side perceived in the understandings and articulations of the other a reflection of its own faith, to a degree that the centuries of separation between them would not have led either to expect. It was in August 1964, in Aarhus, Denmark, in the context of a meeting of the Faith and Order commission of the WCC, that renowned theologians from the two families of churches that had been formally separated since the Council of Chalcedon (451) were brought together for informal dialogue. In the commission's official minutes from Aarhus, which run to more than 100 pages, the item "Conversations between Ancient Oriental and Orthodox Churches" is summarized in a single paragraph:

> Dr. Vischer[1] reported that, in response to a suggestion made to the Working Committee two years previously, it had at last been possible to arrange an informal consultation between representatives of Chalcedonian and non-Chalcedonian churches; and this had been held in Århus during the previous few days. This meeting was not under the formal auspices of Faith and Order, but was arranged by a small preparatory group consisting of Dr. N.A. Nissiotis,[2] Fr. Paul Verghese,[3] and Dr. Lukas Vischer. The members of the group had expressed appreciation of the opportunity provided by Faith and Order. The meeting had proved very successful and held much promise for the future. All participants had been grateful for this opportunity for contact, and in their discussions had found far more agreement than had originally been thought possible. Many of their differences were seen to be mainly concerned with terminology.[4]

1 For Lukas Vischer's work in Faith and Order see the contribution by Michael Quisinsky in this volume.

2 Nikos Nissiotis was a theologian of the Church of Greece and an official observer at Vatican II. See Thomas Stransky, Marios Begzos & Alain Blancy, "Nikos Nissiotis: Three Sketches," *EcRev* 48/4, 1996, 466–475.

3 Fr. Paul Verghese of the Syrian Orthodox Church of Malabar (India) was the WCC's associate general secretary.

4 *Minutes of the Meeting of the Commission and Working Committee, 1964 Aarhus, Denmark, Commission on Faith and Order*, Geneva, WCC Publications, 1965, 79. Besides Verghese and Nissiotis, the theologians who participated in the discussions were, on the Chalcedonian, or Eastern Orthodox, side: Bishop Emilianos (Timiadis) of Meloa, Fr. Georges Florovsky, Fr. John Romanides, Fr. Vitaly Borovoy, Fr. John Meyendorff, Johannes Karmiris, and Gerasimos Konidaris; the latter two participants were from the Church of Greece, Borovoy from the Russian Orthodox Church, Meyendorff from what was to become the Orthodox Church in America, Florovsky and Romanides from the Greek Orthodox Archdioceses of North and South America (under the Ecumenical Patriarchate), and Timiadis of the Ecumenical Patriarchate. And on the non-Chalcedonian, or Oriental Orthodox, side: Archbishop Tiran Nersoyan, Bishop Neshan Sarkissian, Bishop Mar Severios Zakka Iwas, Metropolitan Mar Thoma Dionysius, Fr. Like Siltanat Habte Mariam Worquineh, Fr. V.C. Samuel, Karam Nazir Khella, and Getatchew Haile; Worquineh and Haile were of the Ethiopian Orthodox Church, Nersoyan and Sarkissian of the Armenian Apostolic Church (in Sarkissian's

In the joint statement produced at the conclusion of the Aarhus meeting, the consultation of theologians observed: "Our inherited misunderstandings have begun to clear up. We recognize in each other the one orthodox faith of the Church. Fifteen centuries of alienation have not led us astray from the faith of our Fathers."[5] More specifically, after noting the centrality of the teaching of St. Cyril of Alexandria in the consultation's deliberations, the joint statement said:

> On the essence of the Christological dogma we found ourselves in full agreement. Through the different terminologies used by each side, we saw the same truth expressed. Since we agree in rejecting without reservation the teaching of Eutyches as well as of Nestorius, the acceptance or non-acceptance of the Council of Chalcedon does not entail the acceptance of either heresy. Both sides found themselves fundamentally following the Christological teaching of the one undivided Church as expressed by St. Cyril.[6]

Three further unofficial consultations, or "study meetings," between the Eastern and Oriental Orthodox took place over the next two decades – in Bristol (1967), Geneva (1970), and Addis Ababa (1971). The joint statement issued at the Bristol meeting elaborated on what the two traditions had always maintained about the divinity and humanity of Christ:

> Ever since the fifth century, we have used different formulae to confess our common faith in the One Lord Jesus Christ, perfect God and perfect Man. Some of us affirm two natures, wills and energies hypostatically united in the One Lord Jesus Christ. Some of us affirm one united divine-human nature, will and energy in the same Christ. But both sides speak of a union without confusion, without change, without divisions, without separation. The four adverbs belong to our common tradition. Both affirm the dynamic permanence of the Godhead and the Manhood, with all their natural properties and faculties, in the one Christ. Those who speak in terms of "two" do not thereby divide or separate. Those who speak in terms of "one" do not thereby commingle or confuse. The "without division, without separation" of those who say "two," and the "without change, without confusion" of those who say "one" need to be specially underlined, in order that we may understand each other.[7]

As Nissiotis notes in his introduction to the report on the second study meeting in Bristol, the dissemination of the report on the first study meeting in Aarhus had been "met with a positive reaction in many parts of the world."[8] Interest and support from a number of leading hierarchs in both Eastern and Oriental churches, as well as from across the Orthodox world more broadly, was such as to give good reason already to see the informal meetings at Aarhus and Bristol as a preparation for a more official stage in the dialogue between the two Eastern traditions which, Nissiotis was confident in saying, would be forthcoming. The purpose of the official dialogue would be nothing less than to "discuss the possibility of re-establishing full church communion with one another."[9]

case, the Catholicosate of Cilicia), Zakka of the Syrian Orthodox Church, Dionysius and Samuel of the Orthodox Syrian Church of the East, and Khella of the Coptic Orthodox Church.

5 "August 14th, 1964, Evening Session: An Agreed Statement," *GOTR* 10/2, 1964–1965, 14–15, here 14.

6 "An Agreed Statement," 14.

7 "Study Group of Eastern and Oriental Orthodox Theologians, Bristol, 29th July 1967: Agreed Statement," *GOTR* 13/2, 1968, 133–135, here 133–134. The actual adverbs alluded to in the quotation, *adiairetos* (without division), *achoristos* (without separation), *atreptos* (without change), and *asyngchytos* (without confusion), were used in the Chalcedonian Definition of the Faith. They were also used prior to Chalcedon by St. Cyril.

8 Nikos A. Nissiotis, "Introduction," *GOTR* 13/2, 1968, 125–130, here 125.

9 Nissiotis, "Introduction," 125.

The reason hopes for this prospect ran as high as they did in 1968 was definitely because of how the first two informal theological consultations had been able to make such robust mutual affirmations of each other's Christological understandings. Christology, after all, had been the overt point of contention in the schism that had broken out between the two traditions in the 5th century, with the Oriental Orthodox opposed to the Christological formula of Chalcedon endorsed by the Eastern Orthodox. It is true that other areas of possible difficulty in achieving a full restoration of unity were occasionally mentioned at Aarhus and Bristol along with the Christological issue. When they were, however, at that stage of the informal dialogue it was almost in passing and as though they bore little significance compared to the fundamental disagreement over Christology. "The differences in liturgical forms, canon law, customs and practical issues, as well as in the names of certain Fathers of the Church venerated by different churches, need not be a problem," said the Greek Orthodox theologian Johannes Karmiris in the discussion following his presentation at Aarhus of a paper concerned with unification around the Christology of Cyril of Alexandria. "These [issues] do not separate; the precise formulation of the Christological dogma is the only thing that needs to be done."[10]

However, by late summer 1970 and the early days of 1971, when the Geneva and Addis Ababa consultations took place respectively, the perception of what constituted the most serious challenge in the dialogue had shifted. By then, many of the participating theologians[11] had come to take much more seriously, as potential stumbling blocks in the dialogue, the kinds of ecclesiological questions that Karmiris had merely touched upon back in 1964, including especially the question of what to do about the anathemas issued by one tradition against those deemed saints by the other. In fact, the consultation at Addis Ababa focused exclusively on this question and on matters specifically related thereto, such as how saints come to be authoritatively identified as such.

The Russian Archpriest Vitaly Borovoy, himself an advocate for the lifting of the anathemas, nevertheless spoke strongly in his paper at Addis Ababa about how thorny the issues surrounding their lifting were proving to be:

> The question of discontinuing the efficacy of the anathemas and mutual condemnations, and the recognition of saints, appears extremely complicated, very delicate and indeed the most difficult problem in the whole complex of "rapprochement" between the Orthodox churches which accept the Council of Chalcedon and those Eastern churches which do not accept the council.[12]

Fr. Borovoy goes on to say that this question is "far more difficult than the reaching of agreement about the foundations of a unified understanding by both sides of Christological formulae and about the correct interpretation of the dogmatic definition of the Council of Chalcedon."[13]

Fr. John Meyendorff, a proponent of reunification who had participated in the dialogues from their inception, shared Fr. Borovoy's perception that ecclesiological issues were emerging as a greater challenge than the doctrinal ones. "Our real problem is how we should deal with Tradition. I am optimistic about real agreement on Christology. The problem is not just the acceptance of certain councils, but how we should deal with the whole range of problems connected with

10 "Discussion: Concerning the Paper of Professor Karmiris," *GOTR* 10/2, 1964–1965, 75–81, here 78.

11 The number of participants had by this point increased, at Geneva, to 10 on the Oriental Orthodox side and 18 on the Eastern Orthodox side, and at Addis Ababa, to 16 on the Oriental Orthodox side and 13 on the Eastern Orthodox side.

12 Vitaly Borovoy, "Recognition of Saints and Problems of Anathemas: A Summary of the Views of N. Berdyaev, S. Bulgakov and A.V. Kartashev," *GOTR* 16/1–2, 1971, 245–259, here 245.

13 Borovoy, "Recognition of Saints and Problems of Anathemas," 245.

Tradition."[14] More specifically, elsewhere Fr. Meyendorff mentioned the mutual anathemas:

> The schism has led to opposing views and anathemas concerning people like Leo of Rome and Flavian of Constantinople, on the one side, and Dioscorus of Alexandria, Philoxenus of Mabbugh, and Severus of Antioch on the other. In some ways, since our churches are churches holding strongly to tradition and continuity, this problem might be seen as more agonizing and difficult than the doctrinal agreement itself.[15]

In spite of these concerns and their increasing prominence in the third and fourth consultations, and the fact that no clear solution to them was yet envisioned, the members of the study group expressed the view that, in any case, it was time for the encounter between their traditions to move from the level of an informal consultation of theologians to that of an official dialogue of the churches themselves. In lieu of a joint statement, the meeting at Addis Ababa concluded with the issuance of a "summary of conclusions." 11 of the 12 conclusions itemized there concerned the ongoing question of the lifting of the anathemas and the need for further reflection and education to shed light on the rationale for doing so. The summary's 11th point recommended that a study be undertaken by historians and theologians of the church to consider "distinctions between universal, national and local saints, as well as of the processes by which they came to be acknowledged as such," but it also went on to state that "the lifting of anathemas need not await the results of such a study."[16] The consultation seemed to be coming up against the intractability of certain apparently secondary problems that it did not think warranted allowing its progress to be stalled, given that what originally had been considered the much more formidable hurdle, the Christological disagreement, had been cleared with such surprising ease. The final point in the summary states:

> Perhaps we should conclude this statement with the observation that this is now the fourth of these unofficial conversations in a period of seven years. It is our hope that the work done at an informal level can soon be taken up officially by the churches, so that the work of the Spirit in bringing us together can now find full ecclesiastical response. In that hope we submit this fourth report to the churches.[17]

More than a decade would pass in which no further meetings of the informal consultation were held. But the hope of entering a new phase marked by official ecclesial dialogue between the two traditions did come to be realized in 1985, with the first meeting of the Joint Commission for Theological Dialogue between the Orthodox Church and the Oriental Orthodox Churches, in Chambésy, Switzerland.[18] The main purpose of the official dialogue's initial meeting was to agree upon and implement "a concrete form

14 "Minutes," Geneva, Aug 16–21, 1970, *GOTR* 16/1–2, 1971, 9–43, here 33.

15 John Meyendorff, "Chalcedonians and Non-Chalcedonians: The Last Steps to Unity," *SVTQ* 33/4, 1989, 319–329, here 325 (ed. or.: "The Last Steps to Unity," in: M.K. Kuriakose, ed., *Orthodox Identity in India: Essays in Honor of V.C. Samuel*, Bangalore, Rev. Dr. V.C. Samuel 75th Birthday Celebration Committee, 1988, 105–117, here 112–113).

16 "Addis Ababa Consultation, January 22 and 23, 1971," *GOTR* 16/1–2, 1971, 210–259, here 213.

17 "Addis Ababa Consultation," 213.

18 The question of precisely how to name the two sides of the dialogue was actually the opening subject of discussion at the official dialogue's initial meeting in 1985. "The first part of our discussions centered on the appellation of the two families in our dialogue." See "Communiqué of the Joint Commission, Chambésy, Switzerland, 10–15 December 1985," in Christine Chaillot, ed., *The Dialogue Between the Eastern Orthodox and Oriental Orthodox Churches*, Volos, Volos Academy Publications, 2016, 435.

of methodology to be followed,"[19] and a simple description of this methodology was offered in the communiqué issued at the conclusion of the meeting: "A joint subcommittee of six theologians was set up, three from each side, with the mandate to prepare common texts for our future work."[20] It was agreed that Christology would be the theme addressed first and that the subthemes would be "a) Problems of terminology b) Conciliar formulations c) Historical factors d) Interpretation of Christological dogmas today."[21] The communiqué also made note of the dialogue commission's preliminary judgment that the papers and agreed statements from the informal consultations at Arhus, Bristol, Geneva, and Addis Ababa would serve as a basis for its own work.[22]

The next plenary meeting of the Joint Commission took place three and a half years later, in June 1989, at the St. Bishoy Monastery in Wadi El Natrun, Egypt,[23] and produced the first of what would be two agreed statements by the Joint Commission in the space of a little more than a year. The Joint Commission's communiqué says of the first agreed statement that it was "adopted by the Joint Commission for transmission to our churches, for their approval and as an expression for our common faith, on the way to restoration of full communion between the two families of churches."[24]

Several points from the agreed statement bear highlighting. First, the Christology of St. Cyril is presented as the foundation of the dogmatic agreement between the two traditions, and particular mention is made of Cyril's formula "one incarnate nature [*physis*] (substance [*hypostasis*]) of God the Word." The agreed statement's inclusion of the word hypostasis in parentheses after *physis* when it quotes Cyril's famous phrase is notable. At first, it may appear that this is included in order to indicate how the word *physis* is to be understood, as signifying the unique person of Christ rather than the nature understood as "substance." However, the agreed statement goes on to say, "it is not the case that our Fathers used *physis* and *hypostasis* always interchangeably and confused the one with the other. The term *hypostasis* can be used to denote both the person as distinct from nature and also the person with the nature, for a *hypostasis* never in fact exists without a nature."[25] One of the central dilemmas surrounding the mystery of the incarnation the two traditions have wrestled with has been how, on the one hand, the divine hypostasis takes on human nature while, on the other hand, the assumed human nature, if it remains distinct, is then not correlated with any second, that is strictly human, hypostasis ("of its own," as it were). In other words, if it is true that "a *hypostasis* never in fact exists without a nature," for Chalcedon it is not reciprocally true in the incarnation that a nature never exists without a hypostasis (precisely corresponding to it). Part of the non-Chalcedonian difficulty in seeing how Chalcedon could not have been Nestorian lay in their difficulty in seeing how a second, distinct (human) nature could entail anything less than a second, distinct (human) hypostasis.

The agreed statement of 1989 takes almost verbatim the language of the Bristol consultation when it states:

19 "Communiqué of the Joint Commission," 435.

20 "Communiqué of the Joint Commission," 435.

21 "Communiqué of the Joint Commission," 435.

22 Of the participants in one or more of the informal consultations of 1964, 1967, 1970, and 1971, the following individuals were also among the members of the official dialogue commission that began in 1985: John Romanides, Damaskinos (Papandreou), and Mesrob Krikorian.

23 The Coptic Pope Shenouda III of Alexandria addressed the commission in its opening session and asked the participants to find a path forward to the restoration of unity between the two families of churches. See "Communiqué of the Joint Commission, St. Bishoy Monastery, Egypt, 20–24 June 1989," in: Chaillot, ed., *The Dialogue*, 436.

24 "Communiqué of the Joint Commission, St. Bishoy Monastery," 436.

25 "Agreed Statement of the Joint Commission, St. Bishoy Monastery, Egypt, 20–24 June 1989," in: Chaillot, ed., *The Dialogue*, 437–438, here 437 (italics original).

> The four adverbs used to qualify the mystery of the hypostatic union belong to our common tradition – without commingling (or confusion) (*asyngchytos*), without change (*atreptos*), without separation (*achoristos*), and without division (*adiairetos*). Those among us who speak of two natures in Christ, do not thereby deny their inseparable, indivisible union; those among us who speak of one united divine-human nature in Christ, do not thereby deny the continuing dynamic presence in Christ of the divine and the human, without change, without confusion.[26]

The second agreed statement, issued at the conclusion of the Joint Commission's third plenary meeting in Chambésy, in September 1990, highlighted that the Eutychian and Nestorian heresies alike are condemned by both families of churches. It emphasized that the unity (without commingling, change, separation, or division) of the divine and human natures in the one Christ entails specifically the unity (without commingling, change, separation, or division) of divine and human wills and energies. And it specified that "the natures with their proper energies and wills," once these are united hypostatically at the incarnation of the Logos, are distinguished "'in thought alone' (*'te theoria mone'*)".[27] This last point that the divine and human natures in Christ can be distinguished only in contemplation has been viewed by Orthodox critics of the second agreed statement as a retreat from the Christological teaching of Chalcedon.

After seven numbered paragraphs focused on Christological issues, paragraph eight of the second agreed statement turns to the matter of reception of ecumenical councils. It states, incontrovertibly, that both families accept the first three, but then goes on to say that the teachings on Christology that have just been explicated in paragraphs one through seven of the second agreed statement are, in the view of the Orthodox, "the teachings also of the four later councils of the Orthodox Church," that is, of Chalcedon and the subsequent councils the Orthodox regard as ecumenical. The Oriental Orthodox, meanwhile, are said to "consider this statement of the Orthodox as their interpretation. With this understanding," the paragraph continues, "the Oriental Orthodox respond to it positively."[28] It is significant that the second agreed statement leaves room for the Oriental Orthodox to refrain from affirming directly the Christology articulated in the councils of Chalcedon and Constantinople II (553) and III (680–681), and considers it sufficient that they "respond positively" to how their Orthodox dialogue partners now interpret those councils as having been in line with the Christological articulations presently put forward.

The second agreed statement calls on both families to lift "all the anathemas and condemnations of the past which now divide us" so that "the last obstacle to the full unity and communion of our two families can be removed by the grace and power of God." The question of just how the lifting of anathemas is to be undertaken is left open, as something that "should be decided by the churches individually."[29] Implicit in the brief latter statement is a recognition that neither family of churches is going to be likely to lift the anathemas against the other through one authoritative decision of that family as a single body. Here questions raised by Fr. Georges Florovsky at Aarhus appear: "Who can coordinate the various local or national churches? Who will prepare this confessional formula on behalf of the churches? We have to have a full meeting of the bishops on both sides. Who will convene this?"[30]

26 "Agreed Statement of the Joint Commission," 437–438.

27 "Second Agreed Statement and Recommendations to Churches, Chambésy, Switzerland, 23–28 September, 1990," in: Chaillot, ed., *The Dialogue*, 440–441, here 440.

28 "Second Agreed Statement and Recommendations to Churches," 440.

29 "Second Agreed Statement and Recommendations to Churches," 441.

30 "Discussion: Concerning the Paper of Professor Karmiris," 80.

Along with the second agreed statement, the 1990 meeting in Chambésy produced "Recommendations on Pastoral Issues" that suggested a variety of steps to be taken in preparation for the unity of the two families of churches. These suggestions ranged from exchanges of visits by "heads of churches and prelates, priests and lay people," along with students and faculty of theological schools, to publications of the documents of the Joint Commission and supporting materials, and to commitments to no longer "rebaptize members of each other ['s church]."[31] Additionally, the pastoral recommendations included brief sections on ecumenical relations, service to the world, and mission. A paragraph in the section on ecumenical relations proposed organizing joint Orthodox/Oriental Orthodox consultations on "crucial issues in which our two families agree fundamentally and have disagreements with the Roman Catholic and Protestant churches."[32] This particular proposal calls to mind another of the concerns Fr. Florovsky expressed at the very beginning of the modern dialogue between Eastern and Oriental Orthodox, in Aarhus, when he responded to comments that had seemed to characterize Chalcedon as an essentially Eastern council and the Tome of Leo as being of relatively little importance to it.[33]

> I should like to be an *advocatus diabolus* [sic.] because I feel the need. First I am wholeheartedly in favour of a reconciliation between Eastern churches, but I am not for over-emphasis on the East. Eastern ecumenism is a contradiction in terms. The West also belongs to the *oikoumene*. We cannot afford to forget the West – and the Tome of Leo. The Christian tradition is universal. The Byzantine Church was afraid of precipitating a schism by rejecting Leo. We must also be careful.[34]

The fourth and, as of this writing, last plenary meeting of the Joint Commission took place in November 1993, again in Chambésy. The communiqué issued at the conclusion of the session, which spanned six days and included 15 participants from each side, stated that the meeting's purpose was "to consider the procedure for the restoration of full communion."[35] The lifting of the anathemas was the main focus of the text. The communiqué proposed that "the lifting of the anathemas should be made unanimously and simultaneously by the heads of all the churches of both sides, through the signing of an appropriate ecclesiastical act, the content of which will include acknowledgement from each side that the other one is Orthodox in all respects."[36] Here, somewhat in contrast to its 1990 pastoral recommendations, the commission seems to envision, now, one sweeping pronouncement to which all the individual churches of both families will be signatories. Yet the precise mechanism for coordinating the decision is still not indicated. The text concludes by saying that the lifting of the anathemas should imply "that restoration of full communion for both sides is to be immediately implemented" and by urging that a number of practical steps be consequently taken, including a series of visits by the cochairs of the Joint Commission to the heads of all the local churches

31 "Recommendations on Pastoral Issues of the Joint Commission, Chambésy, Switzerland, 23–28 September 1990," in: Chaillot, ed., *The Dialogue*, 442–444, here 442.

32 "Recommendations on Pastoral Issues of the Joint Commission," 443.

33 "Chalcedon adopted above all the teaching of St. Cyril," said Professor Karmiris. "The synod did not base itself on the Tome of Leo. The Tome of Leo is a piece of paper among many materials in the Council. Papal delegates asked for its adoption as definition, but the Eastern fathers refused. Egyptians, Palestinians, Illyrians, all refused, including the bishops of Illyricum who were under the jurisdiction of Leo. We have our own fathers who are the true teachers of the faith," in: "Discussion: Concerning the Paper of Professor Karmiris," 78.

34 "Discussion: Concerning the Paper of Professor Karmiris," 80.

35 "Communiqué of the Joint Commission, Chambésy, Switzerland, 1–6 November 1993," in: Chaillot, ed., *The Dialogue*, 445–446, here 445.

36 "Communiqué of the Joint Commission, Chambésy, Switzerland, 1–6 November 1993," 446.

and the appointment of a liturgical subcommittee to look at "the liturgical implications arising from the restoration of communion." By its invocation of such expressions as "the outcome of the dialogue" or "our common understanding of the Orthodox faith which has led us to overcome the divisions of the past," the communiqué repeatedly gives the impression that the dialogue has been completed.[37]

However, on an official level, no pan-Orthodox or pan-Oriental Orthodox acceptance of the conclusions of the dialogue commission followed in the months and years after its last meeting in 1993. The reasons for the hesitation of many of the local Orthodox and Oriental Orthodox churches to ratify the commission's conclusions (among the Eastern Orthodox, only the churches of Antioch, Alexandria, and Romania[38] have declared their acceptance of the Joint Commission's conclusions, and among the Oriental Orthodox only the churches of Antioch, Alexandria, and Malankara-India)[39] may vary from one to the other. The Holy Synod of the Russian Orthodox Church, for its part, in a preliminary statement in 1994 expressed the view that the 1990 second agreed statement "cannot be considered as a definitive text" and that the Joint Commission's work ought to continue,[40] quite contrary to the impression conveyed by the commission itself in 1993 that its work had successfully come to an end. The same Holy Synod asserted further, in a subsequent 1997 text, that the second agreed statement "contains ambiguities in some Christological formulations," yet still without specifying the precise nature of its concern.[41] It is to be noted, whatever the views expressed were, that matters had come full circle in terms of what was initially considered the paramount obstacle by those engaged in the theological consultations in the 1960s: it is again on the dogmatic, Christological level, rather than on the (apparently less foundational) ecclesiological level, that an objection was being raised here by the Holy Synod of the Russian Orthodox Church in its 1997 decision. By this time, however, objections to the Joint Commission's conclusions had also been raised by monastic communities on Mount Athos as well as Old Calendarist groups in Greece, and, in these cases, the critical focus tended to be more ecclesiological than strictly Christological.[42]

A dozen years passed in which the work of the Joint Commission appeared finished, yet its findings were not adopted by the two families of churches, except in the cases of the few local

37 "Communiqué of the Joint Commission, Chambésy, Switzerland, 1–6 Novembre 1993," 446.

38 See "Statement of the Romanian Orthodox Church on the Official Theological Dialogue, Decisions of the Holy Synod, Bucharest, Romania, 8–9 December 1994," in: Chaillot, ed., *The Dialogue*, 456: "The Holy Synod of our church ... has decided ... 1. To take note of and to approve the conclusions of the dialogue between the Orthodox Church and the Oriental Orthodox churches." See also in the same volume "Statement of the Orthodox Church of Antioch, Damascus, 12 November 1991: On the Relation between the Eastern and Syrian Orthodox Churches," 454–455.

39 See the "Statement of the Coptic Orthodox Synod on the Theological Dialogue: Letter of Metropolitan Bishoy of Damiette to Metropolitan Damaskinos of Switzerland, Egypt, November 1990," in: Chaillot, ed., *The Dialogue*, 453.

40 "Statement of the Russian Orthodox Church on the Official Theological Dialogue, December 1994," in: Chaillot, ed., *The Dialogue*, 457.

41 "Statement of the Russian Orthodox Church on the Official Theological Dialogue: Decisions of the Holy Synod, Moscow, Russia, February 1997," in: Chaillot, ed., *The Dialogue*, 458. In the same text, we read that "the Russian Orthodox Church has special historical and ecclesiastical grounds to promote the success of the dialogue with the Oriental Orthodox churches. Our church throughout her history has protected and defended the Orthodox East."

42 With reference to the reactions from Mount Athos, John Erickson has written, "This opposition to the work of the Joint Commission does not appear to be based on Christological concerns." John H. Erickson, *Beyond Dialogue: The Quest for Eastern and Oriental Orthodox Unity Today*, paper given at the Symposium on the 1700th Anniversary of Christian Armenia, Oct 27–28, 2000, St. Vladimir's Seminary, Crestwood, NY, available at <http://www.svots.edu/content/beyond-dialogue-quest-eastern-and-oriental-orthodox-unity-today> (accessed Sep 4, 2023). On this issue see also Paul Ladouceur, "Orthodox Critiques of the Agreed Statements Between the Orthodox and the Oriental Orthodox Churches," *SVTQ* 60/3, 2016, 333–368.

churches mentioned above. Then in 2005, an Inter-Orthodox Theological Committee for Dialogue between the Orthodox Church and the Oriental Orthodox Churches was convened by Ecumenical Patriarch Bartholomew. Comprising Eastern (Chalcedonian) Orthodox theologians and hierarchs alone, it was charged with considering the remaining obstacles in the dialogue between the Chalcedonian Orthodox and the non-Chalcedonian Oriental Orthodox. Needless to say, the very existence of this committee constituted an admission from the Orthodox side that the official dialogue that had last met in 1993 had not succeeded after all in resolving all the outstanding issues between the two families of churches. In its communiqué, the inter-Orthodox committee indeed spoke of the need to look further at what were now retrospectively deemed "the obscurities of paragraph 8 of the 2nd Agreed Theological Statement,"[43] concerning the Oriental Orthodox view of the councils regarded by the Orthodox as ecumenical from Chalcedon forward. Underscoring a fresh sense of the unavoidability of addressing the difficult question of the status of those councils, and in what appeared to be a call for more effective Orthodox efforts at persuading the Oriental Orthodox of said councils' dogmatical legitimacy, the inter-Orthodox committee noted further that "the ecclesiological importance of recognizing and including the doctrinal definitions of the IV, V, VI, and VII ecumenical synods must be promoted more fully through special studies on their Cyrillian basis."[44] Also necessarily on the agenda were "the reservations of the Russian Orthodox Church with respect to the text of the Agreed Statements,"[45] as these had been flagged in the Russian Orthodox Church Holy Synod's 1997 decision voicing concerns over Christology.

In November 2014, the prospect of an actual resumption of the official dialogue between Orthodox and Oriental Orthodox was signaled by a two-day meeting of a Joint Commission's working group in Athens. Of the two cochairmen of this commission, which had never been formally disbanded although it had held no plenary meetings in over 20 years, the chair on the Oriental Orthodox side remained Bishop (then Metropolitan) Bishoy of Damietta,[46] while on the Orthodox side, Metropolitan Emmanuel (Adamakis) of France had been appointed to succeed the late Metropolitan Damaskinos (Papandreou) of Switzerland, both of the Ecumenical Patriarchate. In his opening speech at the meeting, Metropolitan Emmanuel called for a robust theological response to the various objections to the agreed statements that had been raised in the intervening years, often, he suggested, for reasons of prejudice and polemics.[47] At the same time, the working group recognized that in spite of the excellent efforts of the commission's subcommittees throughout the years of the official dialogue, it was nevertheless the case that, since 1993, "some churches [had] raised some serious issues that require further clarification such as lifting of anathemas, common enumeration of the Seven Ecumenical Councils, mutual recognition of saints and some questions on Christology."[48] The working group alluded to "solutions to these issues" already envisioned and proposed by participants in the Joint Commission, but acknowledged a need for such solutions to be "communicated effectively to the clergy, monks, schools of theology and people on both sides to arrive at a consensus,"[49] here being recognized as

43 "Communiqué Issued by the Inter-Orthodox Theological Committee for Dialogue between the Orthodox Church and the Oriental Orthodox Churches: Orthodox Centre of the Ecumenical Patriarchate, Chambésy, Switzerland, 13 March 2005," in: Chaillot, ed., *The Dialogue*, 447–448, here 447.

44 "Communiqué Issued by the Inter-Orthodox Theological Committee for Dialogue," 447.

45 "Communiqué Issued by the Inter-Orthodox Theological Committee for Dialogue," 447.

46 Bishop Bishoy passed away in 2018 and he has been replaced by Boulos, the Coptic bishop of Greece.

47 "Communiqué Issued by the Working Group of the Joint Commission, Athens, Greece, November 24–25, 2014," in: Chaillot, ed., *The Dialogue*, 449–450.

48 "Communiqué Issued by the Working Group of the Joint Commission," 450.

49 "Communiqué Issued by the Working Group of the Joint Commission," 450.

not yet achieved. While the working group concluded its statement on a more positive note by observing that three local Orthodox churches and three churches from the Oriental Orthodox side had indeed "already declared their acceptance of the agreed statements and proposals from the Joint Commission,"[50] a sense of uncertainty about whether and how a broader level of acceptance would ever be realized was, unmistakably, a key factor in the working group's very existence, its focus, and outlook.

In the weeks leading up to the June 2016 Holy and Great Council of the Orthodox Church on the island of Crete, an essay cowritten by Orthodox and Oriental Orthodox scholars that was sponsored by the OTSA, and published online and in a volume of essays distributed at the council, expressed the hope that the latter would include discussion of the dialogue and prospects for unity between Orthodox and Oriental Orthodox in its deliberations. Although the authors themselves seemed to recognize that in Crete there would be no decisive steps taken in regard to the issue, given the lack of consensus among local churches, they expressed concern that in the most recent preconciliar draft of the document on ecumenical relations there was no direct mention of the dialogue with the Oriental Orthodox, whereas in an earlier, 1986 version of the document a section specifically about bilateral discussions with the Oriental Orthodox had been included.[51]

> Lest the possibility of restored communion between Eastern and Oriental brothers and sisters in Christ flounder, we wish for this issue to remain in the atmosphere of the 2016 council under the agenda item "Relations of the Orthodox Church," in hope that a future such council will take dramatic action for the rightful restoration of communion between the Orthodox Church and the Oriental Orthodox churches.[52]

However, the Council of Crete did not reincorporate mention of the dialogue with the Oriental Orthodox in its text on ecumenical relations.[53]

In April 2018, the working group of the Joint Commission met again, in Antelias, near Beirut, Lebanon, but apparently did not issue a statement. A notice about the meeting that appeared on the website of the Ecumenical Patriarchate's permanent delegation to the WCC mentions that a plenary meeting of the Joint Commission was planned for late October 2018. But as of this writing, no plenary meeting has actually taken place, and the reason for this is likely to be found in the internal crisis within the Orthodox Church concerning the *Tomos* of autocephaly granted by the Ecumenical Patriarchate to Orthodox communities in Ukraine who have continued to be regarded by the Moscow Patriarchate as schismatic.[54] As a result of the steps taken by the Ecumenical Patriarchate in this process of granting autocephaly, the Moscow Patriarchate has severed communion with the Ecumenical Patriarchate and withdrawn from participation in any commission chaired or

50 "Communiqué Issued by the Working Group of the Joint Commission," 450.

51 Carrie Frederick Frost & others, "In the Hope of Restoration of Communion between the Orthodox and Oriental Orthodox Churches," in: Nathanael Symeonides, ed., *Toward the Holy and Great Council: Theological Reflections*, New York, Department of Inter-Orthodox, Ecumenical & Interfaith Relations, 2016, 42–44; reprinted in: Chaillot, ed., *The Dialogue*, 509–510.

52 Frost & others, "In the Hope of Restoration of Communion," 44.

53 Energy on the ecumenical question was taken up instead, at Crete, with a heated dispute over what may be considered the prior ecclesiological question of whether the name of "church" could properly be applied to any ecclesial body outside the canonical boundaries of the Orthodox Church at all. For overview and analysis of this issue, offered by a Lutheran scholar, see Dagmar Heller, "The (Holy and Great) Council of the Orthodox Churches: An Ecumenical Perspective," *EcRev* 69/2, 2017, 288–300.

54 On this issue see Nicholas E. Denysenko, *The Orthodox Church in Ukraine: A Century of Separation*, DeKalb, Northern Illinois University Press, 2018, and Andrii Krawchuk & Thomas Bremer, *Churches in the Ukrainian Crisis*, London, Palgrave Macmillan, 2016.

cochaired by a representative of the latter, which includes the Joint Commission.

2 Analysis of Key Issues: Christological Issues

Neither in the 5th century controversy nor in the modern dialogue has the dispute between Chalcedonian and non-Chalcedonian Christians ever been simply a matter of each side's rejecting the stance of the other in any kind of symmetrical manner. Divisions are often assumed to arise this way (because one side says X and not Y while the other says Y and not X, each side as certain as the other that it alone is correct), but closer examination of most divisions in Christian history, and certainly of the division over Christology at Chalcedon, shows that the respective views of each toward the other are by no means so neatly commensurate. Those who adhered to Chalcedon's two-natures Christology did not view the one-nature Christology of Chalcedon's opponents in the same way that the latter viewed the former. In fact, the possibility of interpreting the one-nature Christology in an orthodox manner was never a matter of dispute. The dispute centered very much instead on whether the two-natures Christology could be considered orthodox. On the dogmatic level, both at the time and in the modern encounter between the two traditions, it has thus always been Chalcedonian Christology that has had to justify itself to its critics.

This point can sometimes be obscured by the fact that on a superficial level, non-Chalcedonians may be as easily associated with the heresy of Eutyches (in whose theology Christ's humanity is compromised) as Chalcedonians may be associated with the heresy of Nestorius (in whose theology the human Jesus is separated from the divine Logos). The fact that both two-natures and one-nature Christology, taken to an extreme, result in heretical positions can make the dispute look symmetrical. However, there is this disproportion: then and now, insofar as non-Chalcedonians have always explicitly rejected Eutyches, Chalcedonians have accepted the differentiation, that is the possibility of a one-nature Christological formulation that is not Eutychian (Dioscorus I of Alexandria, it is often pointed out, was condemned by Chalcedon not for dogmatic reasons but for disciplinary ones); but not so in the reverse: non-Chalcedonians have tended not to differentiate between an acceptable and an unacceptable form of two-natures Christology. For them, there is no two-natures Christology that is not Nestorian, and hence a departure from the Christology of St. Cyril whom both sides hold up as orthodox. At least this has been the non-Chalcedonian position historically.

The burden of proof in the modern dialogue has thus, on the dogmatic level of Christology, fallen on the Eastern Orthodox to clarify that their tradition's two-natures Chalcedonian formula is no descent into Nestorianism, but conforms rather to the Christology of St. Cyril. As Karmiris pleaded at the conclusion of his paper delivered at the 1964 Aarhus consultation:

> May, therefore, the eastern [that is, oriental, non-Chalcedonian] brethren re-examine the subject touched upon here in the spirit of Christian brotherliness and love, and *may they then revise their attitude to the fourth ecumenical council and the Orthodox Catholic Church*, especially since they claim that they reject the extreme Monophysitism of Eutyches, whom they personally condemn as did the great Council of Chalcedon, a council which they falsely consider to be Nestorian in tendency.[55]

The point is that it was not the Chalcedonian members of the consultation who were being asked to revise their attitude to the Oriental Orthodox, not, that is to say, on the dogmatic question of their dialogue partner's Christological orthodoxy, because

55 "Discussion: Concerning the Paper of Professor Karmiris," 74 (italics mine).

on that question they were not in the same need of being persuaded of it.[56]

In light of what is being said here, it must have been a remarkable moment in the consultation in Aarhus when, in the discussion that followed Karmiris' paper, Fr. V.C. Samuel led off the responses of the non-Chalcedonian theologians by saying, "if this is the position of the Eastern Chalcedonians, then we are in complete agreement."[57] Archbishop Severios Zakka Iwas added in the same vein: "From our discussion so far I come to feel that there are no insoluble problems of doctrine between us concerning the Incarnation of our Lord Jesus Christ."[58] From this comment and similar ones that followed in Aarhus and in subsequent meetings, it is possible to see why there was so much hope for reconciliation between the two traditions.

In later phases of the dialogue, there were admittedly questions of Christology posed by the Chalcedonian side that demanded a response from the non-Chalcedonians. One was the question of non-Chalcedonian regard for the teachings of what the Orthodox deem the sixth ecumenical council (Constantinople III, 680–681) on the two energies and two wills of Christ. The earliest phase in the modern dialogue, focused as it was on Chalcedon itself, did not accord much consideration to this question, but it entered into discussions within the official dialogue, as evidenced by the appearance of the words "energy" and "will" already in the 1989 agreed statement and again in two places in the 1990 second agreed statement. In the latter text, the first of the two places is in paragraph 3: "Both families agree that the hypostasis of the Logos became composite (*synthetos*) by uniting to His divine uncreated nature with its natural will and energy, which He has in common with the Father and the Holy Spirit, created human nature, which He assumed at the Incarnation and made His own, with its natural will and energy."[59] While this sentence makes reference both to a divine nature and a human nature, and to a divine will and energy and a human will and energy united in Christ, it does not clarify whether one must say that, after the union, there is one (one nature, one energy, one will) or two. Cyril Hovorun has observed that, whereas Chalcedon allows both one-nature and two-nature expressions, Constantinople III in point of fact allowed "only the language of two *energeiai* and wills. This difference," he notes, "makes an agreement on the issue of activities and wills in Christ even harder to achieve than the agreement on Christ's natures."[60]

In paragraph 4 of the second agreed statement, we find the words "natures," "energies," and "wills" all invoked in the plural, suggesting that the non-Chalcedonians appear to have come to be able to affirm not only that "the Orthodox are justified in their use of the two-*natures* formula"[61] but that they are also able to affirm a proper use of the two-energies and two-wills formulas of Constantinople III. However, a qualification, included in the same sentence in paragraph 4, as to how the divine and human natures, energies, and wills may be distinguished from one another – "'in thought alone' ('*te theoria mone*')" – was a source of subsequent Orthodox criticism of the second agreed statement's way of framing the Christological resolution. The French Orthodox theologian Jean-Claude Larchet has expressed concern that with the phrase "in thought alone,"

56 As we shall see below, if the Chalcedonians have long been held in suspicion by the non-Chalcedonians on dogmatic grounds, the non-Chalcedonians have been held in perhaps just as much suspicion by the Chalcedonians on nondogmatic grounds, beginning with the condemnation of Dioscorus, and persisting up to the present day as the question of the acceptance of Chalcedon's ecumenicity continues to be put before the non-Chalcedonians.

57 "Discussion: Concerning the Paper of Professor Karmiris," 75.

58 "Discussion: Concerning the Paper of Professor Karmiris," 75.

59 "Second Agreed Statement," 440.

60 Cyril Hovorun, "The Issue of Wills and Energies in the Perspective of the Dialogue between the Eastern Orthodox and Oriental Orthodox," in: Chaillot, ed., *The Dialogue*, 134–146, here 134.

61 "Second Agreed Statement," 440 (italics mine).

the distinction between Christ's divine and human natures after the union becomes "a pure distinction of reason which does not correspond with a real distinction."[62] Larchet sees this as a "retreat from the dogmatic declaration of Chalcedon"[63] and a recrudescence of the particular Christology of Severus of Antioch for whom, according to Larchet,

> reality is attributed only to the composite nature or hypostasis of Christ … the human nature of Christ having no longer any real subsistence and only being distinguished in thought (in theory, such that a distinction in reason does not correspond with a real distinction) from the moment that the Word becomes the Word incarnate.[64]

Yet it should be noted that the phrase of greatest concern for Larchet, "in thought alone," is one invoked not only by the non-Chalcedonians throughout the centuries but by Constantinople II itself, which Orthodox recognize as the fifth ecumenical council, in its seventh anathema, condemning anyone who "does not consider the difference of those natures … be only in the onlooker's mind."[65] What is proscribed by this anathema is an understanding of the incarnate Logos' human nature that would imagine the possibility of its being isolated from the Logos' divine nature, which it cannot be, except in thought, now that everything done humanly must be predicated also of Christ as God, and everything done divinely must be predicated of Christ as man, according to the *communicatio idiomatum*.

As to whether professing that after the union there continue to be two natures able to be distinguished "in thought alone" means denial of their continuation in reality, it certainly would not necessarily have to be so. If we ask why the non-Chalcedonians hesitate to make that affirmation more explicit, here we return to the dilemma mentioned earlier about the nonreciprocal relationship between hypostasis and nature. However, before picking up that thread, a brief terminological clarification is in order. It is often, and rightly, recalled that Cyril was capable of using the term *physis*, which normally we translate as "nature," in more than one way. In the famous phrase "one incarnate nature of God the Word" what Cyril meant by "one nature" was what Chalcedon would mean by "one hypostasis" – that is, one being, one subject. Cyril at other times used *physis* to mean nature as either divine or human – what cannot be both without ceasing to be what it is (namely one or the other). In the first usage, "nature" is the site of the divine and/or human natures and in that sense can be composite. In the second usage, "nature" is purely uncreated (and thus consubstantial with God) or purely created (consubstantial with us).

With this twofold interpretive possibility for "nature" in mind, we may now move on to the larger or deeper issue, and see perhaps more clearly how it goes beyond just a confusion of language alone. If we understand "nature," for purposes of the present discussion, in the second of the two meanings adumbrated above, namely to mean that which is always only either divine or human and never both, then the following difference between Chalcedonian and non-Chalcedonian understandings may be suggested: for Chalcedonians, there can be no hypostasis (individuated being) without a nature in the sense meant here, but there can be such a nature without a corresponding hypostasis. The human nature is assumed by the hypostasis of the Logos (is *enhypostasized*, in the concept of Leontius of Jerusalem) and remains distinctly human nature *sans* human hypostasis. By contrast, in the thinking of Severus and non-Chalcedonians

62 Jean-Claude Larchet, *Personne et nature: La Trinité – Le Christ – L'homme: Contributions aux dialogues interorthodoxe et interchrétien contemporains*, Paris, Cerf, 2011, 77.

63 Ladouceur, "Orthodox Critiques," 340.

64 Larchet, *Personne et nature*, 81.

65 "Constantinople II: 553," in: Norman Tanner, ed., *Decrees of the Ecumenical Councils*, vol. 1, *Nicaea I to Lateran V*, London/Washington DC, Sheed & Ward/Georgetown University Press, 1990, 105–122, here 117.

following him, there could not remain a distinctly human nature after the union without also implying or entailing a distinct human hypostasis corresponding with it. So it is that for non-Chalcedonians the distinction of natures after the union can be no more than a distinction "in thought alone." To say anything stronger than that of the two natures after the union would be to imply a second hypostasis corresponding to the second, assumed nature, and thus would be Nestorianism. In short, Chalcedonian Christology could speak of a single hypostasis in two natures, while non-Chalcedonian could not speak of two natures (unless "in thought alone") except in two hypostases. As Norman Russell has put it, "for Severus and his followers it was axiomatic that there could be no 'nature' without its corresponding *prosopon* – 'person' in the sense of 'external representation' (*ouk esti physis aprosopos*). 'Two natures' in Christ for the *Severans* entailed two *prosopa* – which was the Nestorian position."[66]

This helps to shed light on the liturgical language in the Coptic tradition, critically highlighted by Larchet, that seems to flatly deny any duality of natures or wills in Christ after the union. The Word that became man is described in the Coptic liturgy as "*consubstantial with the Father in divinity and consubstantial with us in humanity*; not two persons nor two forms, *and also not known in two natures*, but one God, one Lord, one hypostasis, one will, one nature of the Word God incarnate."[67] If Russell is correct in stating that for non-Chalcedonians it is "axiomatic that there could be no 'nature' without ... 'person' in the sense of 'external representation,'" then it makes perfect sense that from an insistence on "not two persons nor two forms" (on which Chalcedonians would also insist) it must follow "also not known in two natures" (which Chalcedonians would not want to say). Further discussion between the two partners in the dialogue would seem to benefit, then, from a heightened attention to the particular question of the possibility of a nature without a corresponding hypostasis. The dogmatic commitment, so evidently shared by both traditions, to the consubstantiality "with the Father in divinity" and "with us in humanity," not just before but after the union, to which the Coptic liturgical language here bears witness, offers the solid point of departure for this further discussion.

In the language of "one will" and "one nature," also attested in the Coptic liturgy just quoted, it is obviously one divine-human will and one divine-human nature according to the non-Chalcedonian understanding. Paul Ladouceur has noted that the willingness of the Oriental Orthodox to accept the second agreed statement's language of natures and wills in the plural in their dialogue with the Orthodox stands uneasily with something asserted in a later 2014 agreed statement, to which the Oriental Orthodox were also signatories, in their dialogue with the Anglican Communion. There it is stated, in section 8 of the common text: "He who wills and acts is always the one hypostasis of the Logos incarnate with one personal will."[68] However, the question may be raised as to whether the adjective "personal" coming between the two words "one will" might not open space for further discussion on this point as well, by which it may be discovered that the two traditions are not really locked in intransigent and mutually incompatible positions, as Larchet worries. Every act of Christ is after all the single act of one person, every movement of the will also the single movement of one person. On this, both traditions agree. Both also agree that, as Hovorun puts it, "the humanity of Christ was moved by his divinity," but this fact "does not

66 Norman Russell, "Cyril of Alexandria's Mia-physis Formula in the Christological Debates of the Fifth and Sixth Centuries," in: Chaillot, ed., *The Dialogue*, 94–112, here 102–103 (italics original).

67 As quoted by Larchet, *Personne et nature*, 84–85 (italics original).

68 *Christology: Agreed Statement by the Anglican-Oriental Orthodox International Commission, Holy Etchmiadzin, Armenia, 5–10 November 2002, Revised Cairo, Egypt, 13–17 October 2014*, London, Anglican Consultative Council, 2015, cited in Ladouceur, "Orthodox Critiques," 348.

deprive the former of its own will"[69] in the view of the Orthodox, whereas in the view of the Oriental Orthodox it does seem to call into question whether after the union there is a human will that can be spoken of as other than the "one personal will."

As Hovorun concludes in speaking of the Orthodox view, the idea of Christ's humanity being moved by his divinity does not imply that there was a single will but that "the human will was completely subservient to the divine one."[70] In a relevant passage from Gregory of Nazianzus that was subject to rival interpretations between the two traditions, a passage that references the moment in Gethsemane when Jesus asked the cup to pass from him and then added "nevertheless not my will but thine be done" Gregory observes about the Son of God that it was not that "he would oppose will to will."[71] It seems clear that it is this opposition of wills that the non-Chalcedonians are insistent on ruling out with their invoking of the "one personal will" of Christ. Gregory states in the same passage that "His willing cannot be opposed to God, seeing it has altogether become divine."[72] However, what the dyothelite position makes clear is that the impossibility of opposing will to will in Christ is not a matter of necessity but of freedom, not a mechanical or merely chemical union but a lived one. Insofar as there are two wills, "one divine and another human, which was deified,"[73] this was a deification that actually happened continuously, was always happening at every moment in time, within the life of Christ, so that it could not merely have been complacently predicted as though nothing were at stake in it after that initial moment of divine-human union at Christ's conception. Viewed from this perspective, one may hope that the "one personal will" which the non-Chalcedonians have reason to affirm, since in Christ will cannot be opposed to will, can be shown to be compatible, from their perspective too, with the two wills in Christ whose perfect alignment in history is always a dramatic realization rather than a merely formulaic fact.

The foregoing analysis of certain Christological issues which still need to be further discussed in the dialogue may appear to be at odds with the opening assertion of this section that the burden has been on the Chalcedonians to persuade the non-Chalcedonians of their, the Chalcedonians', orthodoxy. Has it not rather come to seem that the onus is on the non-Chalcedonians to justify their positions on the dogmatic level, after all? It is indeed the case that the later phases of the dialogue did raise several issues that would require some response from the non-Chalcedonians. We have noted especially two. (1) Whether they might grant that "in thought alone" does still leave room for understanding the two natures in Christ after the union to be actually two in reality, even though how we can distinguish them is only in thought and not otherwise. And (2) whether in regard to the acting and willing of Christ, the fact that will is never opposed to will in him – that is, that the human will is so perfectly subservient to the divine that there is never a moment in Christ's entire existence when it is otherwise than a single personal act of willing that he does – may be seen as compatible with the real difference and duality of wills in him, a human one and a divine one throughout his earthly life (even though, again, for us distinguishable only in thought, as united with one another as they are), thereby preserving the actual, temporally dramatic significance of his obedience again and again, at every moment and in real human freedom.

Yet even though these probing questions are put to the non-Chalcedonians by the very content of Chalcedonian and neo-Chalcedonian Christology and do demand of them a yes or a no, the disequilibrium, on the level of the dogmatic positions

69 Hovorun, "The Issue of Wills and Energies," 146.

70 Hovorun, "The Issue of Wills and Energies," 146.

71 "Über den Sohn," in: Gregor von Nazianz, *Die fünf theologischen Reden: Text und Übersetzung mit Einleitung und Kommentar*, ed. Joseph Barbel, Düsseldorf, Patmos, 1963, 12^{1-18} (or. 30), 170–217, esp. 194–197, quoted by Hovorun, "The Issue of Wills and Energies," 145.

72 Hovorun, "The Issue of Wills and Energies," 146.

73 Hovorun, "The Issue of Wills and Energies," 146.

of the respective families of churches, described at the beginning of this section, is not thereby removed or reversed, for it remains the case that the larger question that both of these particular ones are asking is still whether the non-Chalcedonians can agree that Chalcedon's Christology is orthodox. Should the non-Chalcedonians be able to affirm openly and with confidence the orthodoxy of Chalcedonian (and neo-Chalcedonian, as further developed at Constantinople II and especially Constantinople III) two-natures Christology, this would be more than sufficient to dispel any remaining questions the Chalcedonian side may have about the orthodoxy of the one-nature Christology of the non-Chalcedonians.

Yet what are the prospects of such an unequivocal affirmation of Chalcedon on the dogmatic level on the part of the Oriental Orthodox, and is it really fair or wise to expect this of them? In spite of the willingness of the Oriental Orthodox to affirm current Orthodox interpretations of Chalcedon, they have not indicated that they are close to affirming that such interpretations render Chalcedon itself, for them, orthodox. On the contrary: "By all means, you continue to believe in Chalcedon; but do not expect us to accept Chalcedon." So stated Fr. Liqe Siltanat Habte Mariam of the Orthodox Church of Ethiopia. Likewise Bishop Severios Zakka Iwas (who would later become Syrian Orthodox patriarch of Antioch as Ignatius Zakka I Iwas): "When we say we accept the faith, we mean the faith that the church had before Chalcedon, formulated by the three ecumenical councils accepted by all. Let us be quite clear; Chalcedon is not acceptable to us." Further, Fr. Paul Verghese (later Metropolitan Paulos Mar Gregorios) of the Malankara Orthodox Syrian Church: "There should be no misunderstanding of the position of the non-Chalcedonian churches; there will be no formal acceptance of Chalcedon." Also Metropolitan Philipose Mar Theophilos of the Malankara Orthodox Syrian Church: "It will be helpful if Chalcedonians would realize the strong feeling against Chalcedon in non-Chalcedonian churches. That is a historical reality which arguments may not be able to overcome. Prof. Karmiris wants that a new formula should be developed; but let us be quite clear that that should not be an attempt to get the non-Chalcedonians to accept Chalcedon."[74] These were all statements made at the Geneva consultation in 1970. Roughly ten years later, before an inter-Orthodox commission meeting in Chambésy, Pope Shenouda III of Alexandria of the Coptic Orthodox Church stated: "As for the ecumenical councils, we accept the first three ... We reject the Council of Chalcedon ... I can say very frankly that all the Orientals cannot accept the Council of Chalcedon."[75]

Although it was a step forward in many ways, the 1990 second agreed statement was not able to achieve in equal proportion an utter clarity of affirmation of both Chalcedonian and non-Chalcedonian formulations, due to the Oriental Orthodox attitude toward Chalcedon reflected in the comments above. Describing the 1990 agreed statement's treatment of the two communions' differing Christological expressions, Lutheran theologian Dorothea Wendebourg observed that "an unequivocal preference is expressed for one of the disputed formulations – and decidedly not for that of Chalcedon, but for the language of 'one nature.'"[76] Two decades earlier, Fr. John Romanides had expressed the view

74 "Minutes," 29–31.

75 As reported in Metropolitan Chrysostomos (Costantinides) of Myra, "Dialogue of the Orthodox Church with the Ancient Oriental Churches," *Theologia* 51/1, 1980, 222–232, here 229–230; quoted in "Concerning the Dialogue between the Orthodox and Non-Chalcedonian Churches: A Memorandum of the Sacred Community of Mount Athos," May 14–27, 1995, available at <http://orthodoxinfo.com/ecumenism/mono_athos.aspx> (accessed Sep 5, 2023).

76 Dorothea Wendebourg, "Chalcedon in Ecumenical Discourse," *Pro Ecclesia* 7/3, 1998, 307–332, here 318. Wendebourg adds: "The declaration on which final agreement was reached in actual fact represents the victory of the Oriental view, in that it lifts up the formula of Cyril as the common solution, at the expense of the Chalcedonian discourse of the two natures in

that either Chalcedon is dogmatically acceptable or not, and "the Chalcedonians must reject Chalcedon" or "the non-Chalcedonians must accept the dogmatic teaching of Chalcedon as Orthodox."[77] Notably, here he does not say that if Chalcedon is indeed orthodox, as the Chalcedonians obviously have contended, then the Oriental Orthodox must abandon or renounce the truth of their own, differing articulation. His insistence is simply that the orthodoxy of Chalcedon be affirmed as well if there is to be true unity of faith.

If we are to gain a fuller appreciation of why no unequivocal and robust affirmation of Chalcedon on the dogmatic level has been forthcoming from the Oriental Orthodox or has even appeared to them as something they could ever conceivably offer, in spite of their willingness to accept the faith of the Orthodox today, and if we are to be able to find a way through the seemingly immovable obstacle posed by this stated unwillingness of the Oriental Orthodox to accept Chalcedon, we must consider another aspect of the dialogue, also involving a crucial disproportion in the ways that each tradition regards the other. This is the aspect that concerns not the tensions around dogma but those around discipline, at Chalcedon and thereafter. On this level, the disproportion runs in the other direction from what we have seen with respect to the dogmatic: here, it is decidedly the non-Chalcedonians who have been in the defensive position of having their side questioned by the Chalcedonians (much as on the dogmatic level it has been the Chalcedonians in the defensive position of having their side questioned). It is to an analysis of this aspect of the dialogue that we now turn.

Christ"; Wendebourg, "Chalcedon in Ecumenical Discourse," 321.

77 "Minutes," 23.

3 Analysis of Key Issues: Ecclesiological Issues

The ecclesiological issue that has garnered by far the most attention within the dialogue between Orthodox and Oriental Orthodox has been that of the historical anathemas issued by each side against saints of the other.[78] As noted earlier, the 1971 informal consultation at Addis Ababa was devoted almost entirely to this matter. Space does not permit a consideration of all the various angles and complexities presented in the consultation's papers and discussions on the question, but the following analysis will attempt to bring certain perhaps underappreciated points into focus, and shed greater light on their significance. Three things stand out as particularly worthy of consideration in regard to the specific terms of the anathemas issued within each tradition against the other, and how they have functioned within the respective traditions. (1) No anathema issued from the side of the Oriental Orthodox tradition (for example against Pope Leo I) was ever leveled on a disciplinary basis, that is, having to do with disobedience *vis-à-vis* ecclesiastical authority, as was the case with the condemnation of Dioscorus at Chalcedon; (2) if each side admits fallibility in its historic anathemas by now lifting them, this would mean quite different things for the respective sides, precisely insofar as the Oriental Orthodox tradition's anathemas of key figures at Chalcedon (such as Leo) was, and is, far more closely bound up with dogma and therefore more deeply woven into its identity, and also because an undoing of the dogmatic condemnations (which were directed only from the Oriental Orthodox side against the Orthodox and not vice versa) would put the spotlight more glaringly on the disciplinary charge of disobedience against the Oriental Orthodox side;

78 See John Zizioulas, "Ecclesiological Issues Inherent in the Relations between Eastern Chalcedonian and Oriental Non-Chalcedonian Churches," *GOTR* 16/1–2, 1971, 144–162.

and (3) this would demand either of the Orthodox a much greater recognition of the non-definitive status of Chalcedon in the latter 5th century (up to the mid-6th century), or would demand of the Oriental Orthodox a sense of remorse over the intransigence of Dioscorus and Severus of Antioch in their refusal to consider Chalcedonian theologians of their day to be orthodox, or some of both.

Proceeding then to the first of these three points, it is a well-known fact often averred during the dialogues that Dioscorus was not condemned by Chalcedon for doctrinal reasons, but for reasons of discipline. The acts of the council addressed Dioscorus directly, stating the following:

> On account of your contempt for the divine canons and your disobedience to this holy and ecumenical council, because, in addition to the other crimes for which you have been convicted, you did not present yourself even when summoned a third time by this holy and great council according to the divine canons to answer the charges brought against you, know that on the present thirteenth day of the month of October you are deposed from the episcopate by the holy and ecumenical council and deprived of all ecclesiastical rank.[79]

Among the alleged crimes of Dioscorus mentioned by the bishops was that of receiving Eutyches back into communion against the decision of 448 of the Home Synod (ἐνδημούσα) of Constantinople (and doing so even before the 449 "Robber Council," as Pope Leo called it, had convened), not permitting Pope Leo's Tome to be read at the 449 council, and the excommunication of Leo just prior to Chalcedon.[80] Another offense mentioned repeatedly was Dioscorus' having ignored a threefold summons to appear at the Council of Chalcedon. At the fifth session, when the wording of the Chalcedonian Definition was being discussed, the question arose as to whether Dioscorus was being condemned also on grounds of heresy. The acts record the clear response of Archbishop Anatolius of Constantinople, who stated: "It was not because of the faith that Dioscorus was deposed. He was deposed because he broke off communion with the lord Archbishop Leo and was summoned a third time and did not come."[81] Clear as it was at Chalcedon that Dioscorus' deposition was disciplinary and not dogmatic, and in spite of his later writings clearly rejecting the Christology of Eutyches,[82] Dioscorus would later come to be associated in Orthodox tradition with the Eutychian heresy, for example at Constantinople III where together with Eutyches he was named "hated of God,"[83] and in the letters of Justinian, who labeled Dioscorus heretical on the basis of a single spurious excerpt, at odds with abundant evidence from Dioscorus' otherwise long-known writings affirming the double consubstantiality of Christ.[84] On the basis of the latter and of the acts of Chalcedon itself, Orthodox participants in the dialogue with the Oriental Orthodox since Aarhus have had little trouble integrating a careful scholarly

79 ACO, II, 1,2,41; see the English translation of the minutes of Chalcedon, in Richard Price & Michael Gaddis, eds., *The acts of the Council of Chalcedon*, vol. 2, *Sessions II–X – Session on Carosus and Dorotheus – Session on Photius and Eustathius – Session on Domnus*, Liverpool, Liverpool University Press, 2005, 112–113.

80 Ilias Kesmiris, "Controversial Aspects in the Christology of Dioscorus of Alexandria," in: Chaillot, ed., *The Dialogue*, 113–133, esp. 126.

81 Session 5, quoted by Kesmiris, "Controversial Aspects in the Christology of Dioscorus," 127.

82 See Kesmiris, "Controversial Aspects in the Christology of Dioscorus," 127, on Dioscorus' condemnation of Eutyches and of the latter's Christology.

83 See "The Definition of Faith," NPNF, second series, 14, 344–346, here 344. For further discussion of the misleading "theological shorthand" by which Dioscorus' name was included with Eutyches' at Constantinople III, see John H. Erickson, "Anathema: An Obstacle to Reunion?," SNTR 3, 1998, 67–75.

84 Kesmiris, "Controversial Aspects in the Christology of Dioscorus," 128.

rehabilitation of Dioscorus in what concerns his doctrinal position.

It is important at this point to underscore the incommensurability thus obtained between the Orthodox view of Dioscorus, which has room for this sort of rehabilitation, and the Oriental Orthodox view of figures like Flavian, Leo, and the Fathers of Chalcedon in general. An Oriental Orthodox rehabilitation of the latter figures necessarily entails a much deeper procedure of what we may call surgical hermeneutics, to be carried out by Oriental Orthodox theologians today, because of how these representatives of the Chalcedonian tradition were condemned not on disciplinary but on dogmatic grounds.

Although in this sense perhaps the demand placed on the Oriental Orthodox is disproportionate, encouragement may be drawn from precedents and models of permitting careful historical scholarship to prune away excesses and distortions that may have accrued to a given figure in the context of polemics, even where dogmatic questions are concerned. A remarkable openness to reassessment in light of further information, should it emerge, was demonstrated in fact by a group of 12th-century Armenian theologians who entered into discussion with Byzantine officials in order to consider the conditions the latter had laid down for restoring communion between them.[85] Interestingly, the subject of discussion in the passage below was none other than Dioscorus, whom the Byzantines were apparently asking the Armenians to anathematize as one of the conditions for restoring unity. What is remarkable is that the Armenian dialogue partners were not utterly closed to taking such a step if they were given persuasive new grounds for doing so. They were not attached to the view of Dioscorus they had always had to such a degree that they would not revise it in accordance with a more accurate perspective of him, if they were provided with it.

> In 1179 when the … catholicos convened a council in Hromklay to consider the nine demands of the Byzantines for union, the Armenian fathers were cautious about Dioscorus. They stated that until now they had never heard of his being in agreement with Eutyches, and cited the letter of the eighth century Byzantine patriarch Germanus who had asked the Armenians to anathematize only Eutyches and no one else. They stated that their predecessors had already anathematized Eutyches but insisted that the Greeks provide the texts of Dioscorus' and Eutyches' writings for examination, and added that if there were any doctrinal similarities, then they would be willing to anathematize Dioscorus with those in agreement with Eutyches.[86]

Needless to say, in this particular instance, the Oriental Orthodox, represented by these Armenian Fathers, were considering moving from an affirmation to a condemnation of a figure long venerated in their tradition. However, if that was something to which they were open through further study, then one can also imagine they would have been open in principle to moving from a condemnation to an affirmation of figures long reviled by their tradition, such as Pope Leo. Rather than saying that on no account could they ever change their minds about something long held in their tradition, they were willing to hear more and think again.

85 See Isabelle Augé, *Églises en dialogue: Arméniens et Byzantins dans la seconde moitié du XIIe siècle*, Leuven, Peeters, 2011; Boghos Lévon Zekiyan, "St. Nersēs Šnorhali en dialogue avec les grecs: Un prophète de l'œcuménisme au XIIe siècle," in: Dickran Kouymjian, *Armenian Studies/Études arméniennes: In memoriam Haig Berbérian*, Lisbon, Calouste Gulbenkian Foundation, 1986, 861–883; Peter Halfter, "L'Église arménienne entre la papauté et les Byzantins aux XIIe et XIIIe siècles," in: Isabelle Augé & Gérard Dédéyan, eds., *L'Église arménienne entre Grecs et Latins: Fin XIe–milieu XVe siècle*, Paris, Geuthner, 2009, 63–78.

86 Krikor Maksoudian, "Reconciliation of Memories: The Maligned Dioscorus," *SNTR* 3/1–2, 1998, 37–44, here 42.

One of the things it would mean to move from here to point (2) then, if Oriental Orthodox were to be genuinely persuaded of Chalcedon's orthodoxy in light of further study and discussion, and on that basis lift their anathemas against its leading figures, would be that the very identity of the Oriental Orthodox tradition might be thrown open to a possibly destabilizing degree, that is to say to the extent that its identity rests on a self-definition in opposition to Byzantine Orthodoxy. While both traditions have defined themselves in contrast to each other in significant ways, the dynamic is not equally strong in both directions. For numerous historical and cultural reasons, not least the comparative sizes of the two families of churches, besides the much closer identification of the Orthodox Church with imperial power throughout the Byzantine period, which often meant that Oriental Orthodoxy suffered political marginalization, the consciousness of the Orthodox Church would be affected far less dramatically by an unqualified embrace of the Oriental Orthodox churches than the Oriental Orthodox would be by an unqualified embrace of the Orthodox. Although a vocal contingent of rigorists within the Orthodox Church have strenuously objected to the prospect of union with the non-Chalcedonians, the greater portion of Orthodoxy appears quite comfortable with such a prospect, far more so than with the prospect of restored unity with, say, the Roman Catholic Church, a scenario which presents for the Orthodox some of the very kinds of psychological and cultural-historical anxieties that appear to weigh upon the Oriental Orthodox when turned toward the possibility of being united with the Orthodox. It is the anxiety of being engulfed in a larger and historically overbearing other.

What else, one may ask, could account for the intensity of some of the hostile reactions alluded to by Oriental Orthodox dialogue participants that have been directed against those in their tradition who have wandered too close to a place of positive appraisal of Chalcedon? In one illustration of the "strong feelings against Chalcedon" that Theophilos had spoken of, Mesrob Krikorian noted at the consultation in Geneva that "in the 13th century an Armenian catholicos agreed to accept Chalcedon, but he was killed by the people."[87] Although the prounionist metropolitan of Moscow, Isidore of Kiev, on his return from the Council of Florence did not meet quite so severe a fate as this at the hands of his outraged Orthodox coreligionists of the 15th century, the anecdote recounted by Krikorian brings to mind this and other examples of Orthodox resistance to Latin "papism," reflected in the mantra invoked by anti-Western sectarians of more recent years, "Orthodoxy or death!" One may speculate that the symbolic power of opposition to Chalcedon may function within Oriental Orthodoxy similarly to how opposition to Rome has come increasingly to function within Orthodoxy over the past handful of centuries. As a means of identifying an area where something has gone wrong and requires careful attention, this kind of symbolic function is not necessarily wrong, but when it prevents the very possibility of looking further and thinking more deeply about how and why one's own tradition recoiled from another's, then it can stifle receptivity to a fuller picture of the truth of what transpired, and impede any possibility of genuine encounter, not only with the other's tradition but with the real depth and range of the resources of one's own.

If the Oriental Orthodox were to concede the orthodoxy of Chalcedon, this would then seem to put all the burden squarely on them to account for the resistance their forefathers raised against it and passed on to them. Here again the Orthodox might begin to appreciate the difficulty of being placed in such a position by considering what it would be like to remove from their dialogue with the Catholic Church the substance of their various doctrinal objections, so that what would be left would be only the question of why communion had been broken to begin with. In the one case as in the other, dogma and discipline seem to be in a certain tension within the dynamics of

87 "Minutes," 29.

the dialogue, with charges concerning the former holding charges concerning the latter in check.

If that is the case, then one aspect of the way forward, turning now to point (3), might be for the Orthodox to do as much as possible in the context of their dialogue with the Oriental Orthodox to highlight that the canonical "disobedience" of Dioscorus can only be understood as having taken place in the context of a highly fluid and ambiguous ecclesiastical environment. Dioscorus would have had good reason to suppose that the Council of Chalcedon would have no more standing in the life of the church's progress than any number of other supposedly ecumenical councils had had. This is by no means a matter of suggesting that he was right about Chalcedon: from the Orthodox point of view, which it may be hoped that the Oriental Orthodox might also be able to share, Dioscorus was not right about it, not right about the heterodoxy of the Tome of Leo nor of dyophysitism per se. Yet his disobedience may also be recognized as a mistake made in very confusing and trying circumstances, in which it was hardly clear to the majority of Christians in Byzantium whether Chalcedon was or was not to be viewed as authoritative. As the church historian Evagrius Scholasticus wrote of the council's reception, or lack thereof, in the latter part of the 5th century:

> In those days the Council of Chalcedon was neither proclaimed in the holy churches nor openly rejected. Each church leader acted in the way that he thought was legal. One camp supported all of its acts and formulas, did not correct its definitions and could not imagine how it was possible to change even a letter [Chalcedonians]. A second party not only rejected the Council of Chalcedon and all its acts but also anathematized it together with the Tome of Leo [extreme anti-Chalcedonians]. A third group, basing themselves on Zeno's "Henoticon," disputed among themselves the issue of one or two natures. Some of them stuck to the letter, others [moderate anti-Chalcedonians], inclined to peace, called each church to be responsible for its own fate and urged the church leaders not to have communion with each other.[88]

However, such acts of imagination on the part of the Orthodox in thinking about the anathema leveled against Dioscorus for disciplinary reasons might also be accompanied, on the Oriental Orthodox side, by a creative and humble readiness to undo, through their own present charity, whatever excessive suspicion there was in Dioscorus of the orthodoxy of the Chalcedonian Fathers. If it is true that "Dioscorus' Christology lacked flexibility" and was therefore "not able to adopt the Chalcedonian interpretation of Cyril's Christology,"[89] this has not been the case with respect to the Oriental Orthodox dialogue partners of today who, in spite of their abovementioned hesitancy in directly affirming Chalcedon as ecumenical, have responded positively to Orthodox interpretations of that council. It may also be readily acknowledged, on the Orthodox side, that non-Chalcedonian suspicion of leading figures at Chalcedon because of their surface resemblance and sometimes close association with Nestorian-leaning theologians, like Theodore of Mopsuestia or Theodoret of Cyrrhus (condemned fully or in part by the Orthodox themselves at Constantinople II, but not yet at Chalcedon where they were accepted), is little different and hardly less reasonable than the Orthodox's condemnations (for example, at Constantinople III) of Dioscorus for the latter's close association with Eutyches (even though Dioscorus himself had later condemned that figure's more extreme Christology). Furthermore, it should not be forgotten that even Pope Leo had written at one point in praise of Eutyches for his zeal in opposing

88 Evagrius, *Ecclesiastical History* 3, 30, cited in Hilarion (Alfeyev) of Podolsk, "The Reception of the Ecumenical Councils in the Early Church," *SVTQ* 47/3–4, 2003, 413–430, here 421.

89 Kesmiris, "Controversial Aspects in the Christology of Dioscorus," 133.

Nestorianism, a fact that might complicate a facile Orthodox judgment of Dioscorus that he should never for a moment have entertained a positive regard for Eutyches. In short, the possibility of seeing everything clearly at a given moment in time was highly remote for most Christians, even for saints of one tradition or the other, indeed even for ecumenical councils themselves when one is compared with the next.

4 Conclusions

We have seen the profound hopes engendered by the encounter between Orthodox and Oriental Orthodox beginning at Aarhus in 1964, and the immense progress made in the official dialogue between them that culminated in the 1990 second agreed statement and the 1993 communiqué recommending the mutual lifting of anathemas. Of the various outstanding issues of Christology and ecclesiology that a close examination of these texts and some of the critical responses to them has brought to the fore, none appears to be of such scale or obduracy as to impede further progress in the dialogue toward that eventual unity of the two families of churches that the Aarhus meeting inspired its participants to think possible. Yet the dialogue today has not fully resumed since its last plenary meeting in 1993. An initial explanation for the lack of further plenary meetings was certainly that the dialogue commission had considered its work essentially completed at the point when it left off: a perspective that by 2005 came to be recognized as having been too sanguine, as the inter-Orthodox committee of that year, convened by Patriarch Bartholomew, was charged precisely with looking again at what needed further attention in both the Christological and ecclesiological spheres of the dialogue. However, another and more concerning reason why the dialogue has not been picked up again has subsequently emerged, and this can be seen from the cancellation of the plenary meeting scheduled, finally, for late October 2018, a full 25 years since the last. No public announcement about the meeting's cancellation appears to have been made, but inquiries with officials in the Ecumenical Patriarchate yielded the information that the Church of Cyprus, which was hosting the meeting, had decided to cancel it due to two factors: the death on Oct 2, 2018 of Metropolitan Bishoy, cochair of the Joint Commission on the Oriental Orthodox side, and the decision of the Holy Synod of the Russian Orthodox Church on Oct 15, 2018 to sever Eucharistic communion with the Ecumenical Patriarchate.[90]

This decision of the Moscow Patriarchate – made in response to interventions by Ecumenical Patriarch Bartholomew in Ukraine, intended to prepare the way for the granting of a *tomos* of autocephaly, as requested by the Ukrainian parliament after decades of schism and the recent Russian military incursions in Crimea – had as one of its repercussions the withdrawal of Russian Orthodox participation from any commission headed by a representative of the Church of Constantinople. Hence, members of the Moscow Patriarchate have ceased their participation on all pan-Orthodox ecumenical dialogue commissions, including that between the Orthodox and the Oriental Orthodox. It may be hoped that this cessation is temporary, and indeed according to information I received from the Ecumenical Patriarchate, the Church of Cyprus in 2020 had intentions of rescheduling the plenary meeting, which were unrealized due perhaps to the pandemic, and the Phanar continues to consider reviving the formal dialogue. Whether it will indeed go forward and, if it does, what status it will have for the Orthodox family of churches should Russian Orthodox participation be lacking, remain serious questions. Since the *tomos* was formally granted in January 2019 by the Ecumenical Patriarchate to those now constituted as the Orthodox Church of Ukraine, the chances of an imminent return of the Russian Orthodox

90 I am grateful to Archdeacon John Chryssavgis of the Ecumenical Patriarchate for providing me with this information in an email exchange of March 2019.

participants to the Joint Commission have diminished significantly. Should the dialogue go forward, its status for the Orthodox churches, particularly if it were to attain further clarity about Orthodox restoration of unity with the Oriental Orthodox, would be surrounded by the same kind of ambiguity that has characterized the decisions of the Council of Crete, from which the Moscow Patriarchate and three other local Orthodox churches were absent in June 2016.

These issues of internal disunity in the Orthodox Church pose the largest impediment today to the ongoing progress of the dialogue with the Oriental Orthodox. We may recall that these issues were raised, at least implicitly or as a potential problem, at the very beginning of the informal stage of the dialogue at Aarhus itself, in the question posed by Fr. Florovsky: "Who can coordinate the various local or national churches?"[91] It is the question of the relationship between conciliarity and primacy at the level of the Orthodox Church as a whole, a question that has bedeviled relations between Moscow and Constantinople and appears to be no closer to a solution now than it was over 50 years ago when Fr. Florovsky raised it.

Many Orthodox who lament the ecclesiastical battles and dysfunctions on the institutional level, where the autocephalous churches do not manage to find a way to embody the unity to which the church is called, take solace in what they often perceive to be a greater spirit of unity at the grassroots level, both interjurisdictionally among Orthodox themselves and ecumenically *vis-à-vis* the Oriental Orthodox. With respect to Orthodoxy's dialogue with the latter, while the official positions of the local Orthodox churches remain at odds with each other, with only a few local churches willing thus far to endorse the conclusions of the Joint Commission, and the rest either non-committal or opposed, the fact is that the situation on the ground in many contexts, from the Middle East to North America, has vastly improved in terms of the readiness of people from the two traditions to embrace one another. While official dialogue has been at a standstill, mutual contacts and cooperation have multiplied and deepened, through everything from intermarriage and concelebration of services to exchanges of seminarians and faculty. At St. Vladimir's Orthodox Theological Seminary in New York, a full 25% of the incoming class of 2018 was composed of students from Oriental Orthodox churches.[92] In many Orthodox parishes in the United States, Oriental Orthodox Christians are welcomed to communion as a matter of course.[93]

These developments are real and have the potential to make a meaningful impact on future relations between the respective families of churches. Yet they also contain the seed of potential danger when considered together with the paralysis on the institutional level that has put the official dialogue with the Oriental Orthodox indefinitely on hold. The danger is that of a bifurcation between the practice and the teaching of the church, in this case of the Orthodox Church in its understanding of its relation to the Oriental Orthodox.

It is often thought that once mindsets change on the ground, the leadership of the church will inevitably follow, that is to say that teaching will sooner or later follow practice. This may happen sometimes, but not always. For at other times, when people on the grassroots level "get out ahead of" the hierarchy and do what they feel in their conscience is right before God, the result is not a change of teaching but only an increase in cynicism, even in despair, concerning the possibility of anything but paralysis from the official

91 See "Discussion: Concerning the Paper of Professor Karmiris," 80.

92 See <https://www.svots.edu/headlines/svots-welcomes-31-new-students-academic-year-begins> (accessed Sep 4, 2023).

93 See Emmanuel Lanne, "Quelques questions posées à l'Église orthodoxe concernant la 'communicatio in sacris' dans l'eucharistie," *Irén* 72/3–4, 1999, 435–452; and Radu Bordeianu, "Eucharistic hospitality: An Experiential Approach to Recent Orthodox Theology," *JES* 54/1, 2019, 5–24.

organs of the church. In other words, the chasm only widens between what people in fact do and what the church teaches they are to do, with the consequence that teachings of all kinds, on a great range of matters, come to be taken less and less seriously by the faithful. Soon it is seen as being of only relative importance whether what the church officially teaches comes to align with what people in their hearts feel they ought to do, or not; for people will go ahead and do it anyway, and this is sometimes celebrated as a kind of power of the people of which no hierarchical authority can deprive them.

Such an approach, while very understandable in a particular circumstance, such as that of the quest for Orthodox/Oriental Orthodox unity, where it may be felt that official talks have already dragged on too long and that it is time for action, may have unforeseen consequences that might be undesirable to Orthodox and Oriental Orthodox alike, who share an ecclesiology that emphasizes the importance of arriving together at a common mind through a conciliar process. If one renounces any attempt to make teaching and practice consistent with each other, the potential is there to "get out ahead of" the official church on all kinds of issues and make it seem less and less imperative to live, act, and speak as a united body, but only as so many individuals or ideological factions each going their own way. For this reason, rekindled efforts to advance the international dialogue between Orthodox and Oriental Orthodox Christianity remains vitally important.

Bibliography

Augé, Isabelle, *Églises en dialogue: Arméniens et Byzantins dans la seconde moitié du XIIe siècle*, Leuven, Peeters. 2011.

Chaillot, Christine, ed., *The Dialogue between the Eastern Orthodox and Oriental Orthodox Churches*, Volos, Volos Academy Publications, 2016.

Commission on Faith and Order, *Minutes of the Meeting of the Commission and Working Committee: 1964 Aarhus, Denmark*, Geneva, WCC Publications, 1965.

Constantinides, Chrysostomos (Metropolitan of Myra), "Dialogue of the Orthodox Church with the Ancient Oriental Orthodox Churches," *Theologia* 51/1, 1980, 222–232.

Holy Monastery of Gregoriou, *Ὁ θεολογικός διάλογος Ὀρθοδόξων καὶ Ἀντιχαλκηδονίω*, Mount Athos, Holy Monastery of Gregoriou, 2018.

Ladouceur, Paul, "Orthodox Critiques of the Agreed Statements between the Orthodox and the Oriental Orthodox Churches," *SVTQ* 60/3, 2016, 333–368.

Larchet, Jean-Claude, *Personne et nature: La Trinité – Le Christ – L'homme: Contributions aux dialogues interorthodoxe et interchrétien contemporains*, Paris, Cerf, 2011.

Maksoudian, Krikor, "Reconciliation of Memories: the Maligned Dioscorus," *SNTR* 3/1–2 ,1998, 37–44.

"Papers and Discussions between Eastern Orthodox and Oriental Orthodox Theologians: The Bristol Consultation, July 25–29, 1967," *GOTR* 13/2, 1968, 131–320.

Russell, Norman, "The Eastern Orthodox-Oriental Orthodox Dialogue Hits Stormy Waters: Two Recent Publications on the Debate," *IJSCC* 21/1, 2021, 32–41.

"Third Unofficial Consultation between Oriental Orthodox and Eastern Orthodox Theologians, Geneva, August 16–21, 1970," *GOTR* 16/1–2, 1971, 1–209.

Torrance, Iain, *Christology after Chalcedon: Severus of Antioch and Sergius the Monophysite*, Norwich, Canterbury Press, 1988.

"Unofficial Consultation between Theologians of Eastern Orthodox and Oriental Orthodox Churches, August 11–15, 1964: Papers and Minutes," *GOTR* 10/2, 1964–1965, 7–160.

Wendebourg, Dorothea, "Chalcedon in Ecumenical Discourse," *Pro Ecclesia* 7/3, 1998, 307–332.

CHAPTER 32

Lukas Vischer and the Faith and Order Commission in the 1960s

Michael Quisinsky

1 Introduction: Faith and Order between "Tremendous Extension" and "Promising Chaos"

The 1960s were a challenging decade for ecumenism. The first ecumenical achievements obtained in the prewar period entered a phase of institutional consolidation; at the same time, the WCC as the central ecumenical institution changed its outlook in order to expand and become profounder so that new members, in particular the Orthodox, might join it; Vatican II permitted the Roman Catholic Church to become an ecumenical partner, linked to the need to find new institutional arrangements and to rethink the entire theological framework of the unity sought.[1] Incidentally, the newly-built ecumenical center in Geneva opened its doors in the same year as Vatican II came to an end.[2] Last but not least, it was the time when a new generation of ecumenists entered the stage. Their best representative was Lukas Vischer.[3] Needless to say, he who was called "Mr Faith and Order,"[4] did not work alone. Moreover, as far as the succession of generations within the ecumenical movement is concerned, one can speak of a kind of congenial sense of unity between the young Reformed pastor Vischer and Willem Adolf Visser 't Hooft,[5] first secretary general of the WCC.

During Vischer's time as study secretary of the Faith and Order commission from 1961 to 1966, and as its director from 1966 to 1979, Faith and Order was at the very heart of the abovementioned ecumenical challenges. In 1957 a committee chaired by Oliver Tomkins was asked to take charge of a study on the future of Faith and Order. In 1960, the executive committee of the WCC met in St. Andrews and accepted the report of the Faith and Order commission concerning its future.[6] The world assembly in New Delhi in 1961 also accepted this report with its challenging diagnosis: "The achievement of unity will involve nothing less than a death and rebirth for many forms of church life as we have known them."[7] The analysis of its tasks showed that the Faith and Order commission looked for a new dynamic, dealing in a constructive way with the rapidly changing situation in the world and within Christianity. In the report, reference is made to forthcoming challenges, such as a broadening and deepening of the study program, theological assistance for member churches on the way to a church union, closer relationship to regional groups, and the establishment of contacts with the Roman Catholic Church. New Delhi not only accepted the contents of the future work of Faith and Order, but also decided to reinforce its institutional possibilities. When Lukas Vischer

1 A good introduction is offered by Konrad Raiser, "Fifty Years after the Second Vatican Council: Assessing Ecumenical Relations from the Perspective of the World Council of Churches," *EcRev* 67/2, 2015, 285–294.

2 Willem A. Visser 't Hooft, "Dedication of the Ecumenical Centre, 11 July, 1965," *EcRev* 17/4, 1965, 382–384.

3 Michael Quisinsky, "Vischer, Lukas," in: Michael Quisinsky & Peter Walter, eds., *Personenlexikon zum Zweiten Vatikanischen Konzil*, Freiburg i.Br., Herder, ²2012, 279–280. In the present chapter, Vischer's writings are quoted according to their accessibility for the author.

4 Geiko Müller-Fahrenholz, "Address given at the Memorial Service Held for Lukas Vischer," *EcRev* 60/3, 2008, 305–313, here 305.

5 Karim Schelkens & Sandra Arenas, "Visser 't Hooft, Willem Adolf," in: Quisinsky & Walter, eds., *Personenlexikon*, 280–282. See the contribution by Jurjen A. Zeilstra in this volume.

6 See "Report of the Commission on Faith and Order on the Future of Faith and Order," *EcRev* 13/1, 1960, 61–68.

7 "Report of the Commission on Faith and Order," 113.

joined the Faith and Order commission in 1961 as its study secretary, he thus had a kind of working program, an institutional embedment and a clear expectation that Faith and Order had to reinforce the theological reflection of the ecumenical cause. Having said this, he also became the driving force in the implementation of the multifold tasks attributed to Faith and Order. Moreover, this working program was part of a profounder reflection of the self-understanding of the WCC, for in 1959 Bishop Lesslie Newbigin had presented a paper dealing with "churchly unity." This paper then constituted the beginning of the report on the future of Faith and Order presented at the central committee of the WCC meeting 1960 in Rhodes[8] and constituted the basis for the "New Delhi Statement on Unity" of 1961.[9]

In his report on the activities of the Faith and Order commission and secretariat from New Delhi 1961 to Uppsala 1968, Vischer describes first the "tremendous extension" of Faith and Order's work in the early 1960s and then the "promising chaos"[10] of Montreal 1963, which was extremely important for its coincidences with Vatican II. If Vischer changed the impression of many delegates that Montreal was a "chaos," it is a proof of his spiritual and organizational skills that he could inverse the negative dynamic expressed by this word, insisting rather on the new possibilities offered by it. In fact, Faith and Order had to deal not only with a rapidly changing and increasingly complicated situation in the world, but also with fundamental changes within the Christian churches, often resulting from Vatican II and its impact on both the Roman Catholic Church and the other churches and communities. As a result, different bilateral and multilateral working methods had to be developed.[11] In dealing with ecclesiastical and ecclesiological topics, Faith and Order became more and more aware of its own nature as an ecclesial movement.[12]

With regard to the multifold topics discussed within the Faith and Order commission, the present chapter tries to elucidate the similarities to, and parallelism with, Vatican II.[13] This having been said, the special focus on Lukas Vischer, who pleaded as early as in 1961 for the importance of working "on parallel lines"[14] between Vatican II and the world assembly of the WCC in New Delhi, makes it possible to identify some of the most profound implications of this parallelism for the evolution of ecumenism in the long run. As a non-Catholic observer (and, as we shall see, active

8 On the impact for the relationship to the Roman Catholic Church see Karim Schelkens, "L'affaire de Rhodes' au jour le jour: La correspondance inédite entre J.G.M. Willebrands and Ch.-J. Dumont," *Istina* 54/3, 2009, 253–277.

9 See "New Delhi Statement on Unity" in *New Delhi Speaks: The Message of the Third Assembly (New Delhi (18 November–5 December 1961): With the reports of the Assembly's Sections on Christian Witness, Service and Unity and an Appeal to all Governments and Peoples,* London, SCM Press, 1962, 116-135, available at https://www.oikoumene.org/resources/documents/new-delhi-statement-on-unity (accessed Feb 26, 2024). For a comparison between the Faith and Order's proposal inspired by Newbigin and the final text see Ernest A. Payne, "Working out the New Delhi Statement on Unity," *EcRev* 14/3, 1962, 296–304, esp. 298–300.

10 *New Delhi to Uppsala, 1961–1968: Report of the Central Committee to the Fourth Assembly of the World Council of Churches,* Geneva, WCC Publications, 1968, 51–59, here 51 and 54.

11 *New Delhi to Uppsala, 1961–1968,* 58–59.

12 Nikos A. Nissiotis, "The Importance of the Faith and Order Commission for Restoring Ecclesial Fellowship," in: *Sharing in One Hope: Reports and Documents from the Meeting of the Faith and Order Commission,* Geneva, WCC Publications, 1978, 13–19. See also Nikos A. Nissiotis, "Le texte de la Commission 'Foi et Constitution' du C.O.E. Baptême, Eucharistie, Ministère, en tant qu'exemple du dialogue œcuménique multilatéral et Communautaire," in: *Les dialogues œcuméniques hier et aujourd'hui,* Chambésy, Centre Orthodoxe du patriarcat œcuménique, 1985, 233–247, esp. 236–238.

13 In this sense, the present chapter both presupposes and completes the very dense and source-rooted presentation of Faith and Order by Meredith B. Handspicker, "Faith and Order 1948–1968," in: *A History of the Ecumenical Movement*, vol. 2, Harold E. Fey, ed., *The Ecumenical Advance (1948–1968)*, Geneva, WCC Publications, 1986, 143–170.

14 Lukas Vischer, "The World Council of Churches and the Vatican Council," *EcRev* 14/3, 1962, 281–295, here 288.

participant) at Vatican II, Vischer's theological and spiritual, organizational and relational skills marked the greatest achievement of the Faith and Order commission and made of it the center of a far-reaching and influential ecumenical network. After being unified with Life and Work, Faith and Order played an outstanding role within the WCC and beyond it, densely concentrated in the commission sessions in Aarhus 1964, Bristol 1967, and Leuven 1971. Even if it was far from being the only topic, the event and process of Vatican II, its reception and hermeneutics played a very important role on Faith and Order's agenda in the 1960s. Following the observations, reflections, and insights of Vischer concerning Vatican II thus means following a central part of ecumenical history and, in particular, the ecumenical work in progress in that period.[15] This is particularly true of the coincidences between the topics discussed at Vatican II and within the Faith and Order commission, especially at the fourth world conference on Faith and Order in Montreal in 1963. Perhaps the most notable of these convergences is the notion of catholicity, widely debated in Montreal, which within a few years led to a better understanding of conciliarity and thus to the wish, expressed in Uppsala in 1968, for a universal council in which the churches could regain their lost unity.[16] Therefore, in the following, a first point will deal with Vischer's analysis of Vatican II, a second point will deal with Montreal and, finally, a third section will deal with the notion of catholicity. As an epilogue, one of the newborn forms of church life predicted in the report on the future of Faith and Order will be mentioned.

2 Vatican II: An Ecumenical Council?

When Pope John XXIII announced the Vatican II "ecumenical council" in 1959 in Rome, the WCC, the "Protestant Rome", was faced with several challenges. Needless to say, it was clear that the terms "ecumenical" and "council" did not mean the same with respect to the future event in Rome and the institution in Geneva. However, it was also quite naturally clear that the different meanings of the terms can only be considered to be linked together. The same is true of the assemblies in New Delhi in 1961 and in Rome from 1962 onwards.[17] On the one hand, it was clear that the council involved the multifaceted work of the WCC since "something new has happened,"[18] commented secretary general Visser 't Hooft in reference to the council itself,[19] and again on the council he said on another occasion: "Nostra res agitur."[20] On the other hand,

15 Parts of this chapter are based on several publications presenting my research in the archives of the WCC: Michael Quisinsky, "The Ecumenical Dynamic of Vatican II: Lukas Vischer between Geneva and Rome," in: Michael Quisinsky, *Katholizität der Inkarnation: Christliches Leben und Denken zwischen Universalität und Konkretion "nach" dem II. Vaticanum / Catholicité de l'Incarnation: Vie et pensée chrétiennes entre universalité et concrétion (d') après Vatican II*, Münster, Aschendorff, 2016, 80–121; Michael Quisinsky, "Lukas Vischer als 'nichtkatholischer Beobachter' von Konzilsereignis, Konzilsrezeption und Konzilshistoriographie," in: Quisinsky, *Katholizität der Inkarnation*, 124–149; Michael Quisinsky, "Ökumenische Perspektiven auf Konzil und Konziliarität: Lukas Vischer und die Vision eines 'universalen Konzils,'" in: Quisinsky, *Katholizität der Inkarnation*, 436–451; Michael Quisinsky, "L'héritage de Lukas Vischer sur Vatican II à l'heure de l'encyclique 'Laudato si,'" in: Philippe Chenaux & Kiril Plamen Kartaloff, eds., *Il Concilio Vaticano II e i suoi protagonisti alla luce degli archivi*, Vatican City, Libreria Editrice Vaticana, 2017, 41–58. Once again, I have to express my gratitude to the archivist of the WCC Hans von Rutte.

16 Quisinsky, "Ökumenische Perspektiven auf Konzil und Konziliarität," 439–442.

17 Vischer, "The World Council of Churches."

18 "Report of the General Secretary to the Central Committee, at Paris, 1962," *EcRev* 15/1, 1963, 74–81, here 78.

19 See also his "Report of the General Secretary to the Central Committee, Rochester, 1963," *EcRev* 16/1, 1964, 92–100, here 98, where he warns against any "competition" between two centers of ecumenical activity.

20 "Report of the General Secretary to the Central Committee, at Paris," 77. Vischer often refers to this sentence: see Lukas Vischer, "The Ecumenical Movement and the Roman Catholic Church," in: *A History of the Ecumenical Movement*, vol. 2, 311–352, here 329; see also Lukas Vischer, "The Council as an Event in the

the very fact that the activities of the WCC were multifaceted raised the question as to how to react to the papal announcement and, what was even more important, to the invitation by the newly founded SPCU,[21] presided over by the Jesuit biblical scholar, Cardinal Augustin Bea.[22] The different members of the WCC had different approaches to the forthcoming council and to this invitation, connected among other aspects both to their internal constitution and to their involvement in the WCC.[23] While it seems that the Vatican would have preferred to nominate the ecumenically experienced German theologian Hans Heinrich Harms[24] observer of the WCC,[25] within the WCC there was no unanimity about whether they should send any observer or none at all.[26]

Ecumenical Movement," in: Giuseppe Alberigo & Joseph A. Komonchak, eds., *History of Vatican II*, vol. 5, *The Council and the Transition: The Fourth Period and the End of the Council (September 1965–December 1965)*, Leuven/Maryknoll, Peeters/Orbis Books, 2006, 485–539.

21 Its very foundation had important repercussions on the ecumenical movement: Willem A. Visser 't Hooft, "The Calling of the World Council of Churches," *EcRev* 14/2, 1962, 216–226. See also *The New Delhi Report: The Third Assembly of the World Council of Churches 1961*, New York, Association Press, 1962, 171–175, esp. 175.

22 Philippe J. Roy, "Bea, Augustin," in: Quisinsky & Walter, eds., *Personenlexikon*, 48–50. See also Saretta Marotta, *Gli anni della pazienza: Bea, l'ecumenismo e il Sant'Uffizio di Pio XII*, Bologna, Il Mulino, 2019.

23 Mauro Velati, *Separati ma Fratelli: Gli osservatori non cattolici al Vaticano II (1962–1965)*, Bologna, Il Mulino, 2014, 28–81 and 112–123.

24 Hans Heinrich Harms, "Wie es war im Anfang. Persönliche Erinnerungen an den Anfang der Beziehungen zwischen dem Vatikan und dem Ökumenischen Rat der Kirchen," in: Hans Vorster, ed., *Ökumene lohnt sich: Dankesgabe an den Ökumenischen Rat der Kirchen zum 50jährigen Bestehen*, Frankfurt a.M., Lembeck, 1998, 62–74.

25 Mauro Velati, *Una difficile transizione: Il cattolicesimo tra unionismo ed ecumenismo (1952–1964)*, Bologna, Il Mulino, 1996, 294.

26 Lukas Vischer, "Storia del Concilio Vaticano II: Reactions and Comments by an Observer at the Council," *EcRev* 49/3, 1997, 348–353, esp. 351.

2.1 *Vatican II between Rome and Geneva*

The decision was made to send the young secretary of the Faith and Order commission's study group, Lukas Vischer, to Rome. During the first period, Vischer was the WCC's sole observer, and it was only in the second session that the Greek Orthodox theologian Nikos Nissiotis[27] was sent to Rome as the WCC's second observer.[28] The choice of Vischer, a theologian of only 35 years of age, aroused various comments. The eminent Protestant scholar, Oscar Cullmann,[29] professor in Paris and Basel and no less than Vischer's *Doktorvater*, deplored that the WCC did not send a "front row" theologian.[30] Later, Cullmann became himself an important Protestant, ecumenical voice at Vatican II.[31] In this role, he worked together with Vischer, whose theological habitus was nevertheless in no way restricted to being his teacher's pupil. On the contrary, as early as in his doctoral thesis, Vischer showed an interest in topics far beyond a narrow conception of the

27 Michael Quisinsky, "Nissiotis, Nikos," in: Quisinsky & Walter, eds., *Personenlexikon*, 199–200.

28 See also Lukas Vischer, "Grenzgänger zwischen Ost und West," in: *Nikolaos Ang. Nesiōtes: Thrēskeia, philosophia, kai athlētismos se dialogo: Anamnēstikos tomos* [Nikos A. Nissiotis: religion, philosophy, and sport in dialogue: in memoriam], Athens, M.P. Grigoris, 1994, 349–353.

29 Michael Quisinsky, "Cullmann, Oscar," in: Quisinsky & Walter, eds., *Personenlexikon*, 84–85.

30 This is reported by Yves Congar in his council diary. See Yves Congar, *My Journal of the Council*, Collegeville MN, Liturgical Press, 2012 (Jan 30, 1964).

31 Thomas K. Kuhn, "Oscar Cullmann und das Zweite Vatikanische Konzil," in: Guy Bedouelle & Mariano Delgado, eds., *La réception du Concile Vatican II par les théologiens suisses / Die Rezeption des II. Vaticanums durch Schweizer Theologen*, Fribourg, Academic Press, 2011, 113–140. See also Armin Mettler, "Die Materialien zum Zweiten Vatikanischen Konzil im Cullmann-Archiv," in: Martin Sallmann & Karlfried Froehlich, eds., *Zehn Jahre nach Oscar Cullmanns Tod: Rückblick und Ausblick*, Zürich, Theologischer Verlag, 2012, 149–160, and Margarethe Hopf, "Oscar Cullmann als Gast auf dem Zweiten Vatikanischen Konzil," in Sallmann & Froehlich, eds., *Zehn Jahre nach Oscar Cullmanns Tod*, 161–178.

Reformation and Protestantism,[32] rooted in a biblical hermeneutics.[33] Be that as it may, Cullmann's contemporary judgement is historiographically echoed by Étienne Fouilloux, who asked whether the nomination of Vischer was not "an elegant way to participate without getting too involved."[34] It goes without saying that Fouilloux continued by remarking that the choice revealed itself to be an excellent one, and this judgement is underlined by further research[35] as Vischer, who modestly attributed his nomination to his apparent "relatively unimportant position"[36] within the WCC, became rapidly not only an observer but also an actor in Vatican II. And this happened for several reason. First, Vischer in some way acted with two mandates, an official one and an unofficial one. As to the official mandate, it was defined by the role of the observers, and as far as the unofficial one was concerned, it resulted from Visser 't Hooft's encouragement to take every useful initiative.[37] Second, he increasingly became the coordinator of the observers. Besides numerous activities, the most prominent aspect of this role was the redaction by Vischer of a letter in the name of the observers to the council Fathers, read *in aula* on Dec 4, 1965 and welcomed with warm, voiced approval.[38] Needless to say, this led to some raised eyebrows within the group of observers and ecumenists.[39] Third, Vischer's outstanding organizational and theological skills were combined with pastoral sensibility,[40] influencing not only the work of Faith and Order, but also some conciliar documents, such as *Gaudium et spes*. Moreover, Vischer was one of the main architects of an ecumenically unprecedented convergence between Vatican II and the work of the Faith and Order commission, as is shown by the parallelism of the council and the fourth world conference on Faith and Order. Finally, the apparent disadvantage of his age turned into an advantage because Vischer became an actor not only in Vatican II but also in its reception and historiography.[41] This kind of personal continuity constituted a rather exceptional course, and it directly influenced the work of the Faith and Order commission, whose director Vischer became in 1966, and of the entire WCC until 1979, when the rule of mandates restricted by a time limit had to be applied to the Swiss theologian. It is no exaggeration to say that it is thanks to Vischer, among other things, that Vatican II became an ecumenical council in both meanings of the term. As to his own work within, and for, Faith and Order, the conciliar experience enriched him profoundly and transformed his theological thinking, which nevertheless remained faithful to its theological and spiritual roots within the Reformed Church of Switzerland as part of the ecumenical movement. It is therefore worthwhile following closely some of Vischer's most

32 Lukas Vischer, *Basilius der Große: Untersuchungen zu einem Kirchenvater des vierten Jahrhunderts*, Basel, Friedrich Reinhardt, 1953.

33 See his habilitation thesis: Lukas Vischer, *Die Auslegungsgeschichte von 1 Kor 6, 1–11: Rechtsverzicht und Schlichtung*, Tübingen, Mohr Siebeck, 1955. Shortly before his death, Vischer, deploring a very difficult period for the ecumenical movement caused among others by the non-reception of Vatican II, insisted again on the importance of the biblical witness – in a certain way, this text took stock of Vischer's activities and became a kind of "spiritual testament": Lukas Vischer, "Schwierigkeiten bei der Befragung des Neuen Testaments," in: Lukas Vischer, Ulrich Luz & Christian Link, eds., *Ökumene im Neuen Testament und heute*, Göttingen, Vandenhoeck & Ruprecht, 2009, 21–49.

34 Étienne Fouilloux, "Des observateurs non catholiques," in: Étienne Fouilloux, ed., *Vatican II commence …: Approches francophones*, Leuven, Peeters, 1993, 235–261, here 242.

35 See especially Velati, *Separati ma Fratelli* and Velati, *Una difficile transizione*.

36 Vischer, "Storia del Concilio Vaticano II," 351.

37 Vischer, "Storia del Concilio Vaticano II," 351.

38 See *AS* 4/1, 56. For the reactions see among others Congar, *My Journal of the Council* (Dec 4, 1965).

39 Congar, *My Journal of the Council* (Feb 3, 1964).

40 During his vicariate in Feuerthalen, the theologian Gottfried Locher was his superior. From 1953 to 1961, Vischer served as parish pastor in Schaffhausen-Herblingen, a lively town at the Swiss-German border.

41 Quisinsky, "Lukas Vischer als 'nichtkatholischer Beobachter.'"

important insights during the process and events of Vatican II.

2.2 *Vischer's Reports on Vatican II*

At the outset of Vatican II, the council had to discover itself, as did Vischer. He began to write reports to Visser 't Hooft regularly, communicating his observations, one might say to a certain extent, "to whom it may concern" in Geneva. The very first of these reports seemed rather confidential, as Vischer, like any other council protagonist, had to enter into a conciliar dynamic that was only just beginning. The more the council discovered itself, the more the very role of the different protagonists became explicit. As far as Vischer's reports are concerned, their confidential tone diminished with his growing sense of becoming an actor in Vatican II. The conciliar dynamic made it less necessary to send confidential notes to Geneva, since "[e]verything that happened, and even a little more (*omnia et quaedam alia*) has been fully reported in the newspapers."[42] Thus, the scope of Vischer's messages was to develop better communication networks in order to make the voice of the ecumenical movement heard in Rome. One of Vischer's main goals in this process was to identify "basic ideas." After the first session, Vischer named five of them: (1) a new view on the relationship between the church and the contemporary world; (2) a renewed ecclesiological thinking; (3) a reinforcement of the authority of the bishops; (4) a profounder and more extensive dialogue with non-Roman Christians; and, as one reads in the opening speech of John XXIII, (5) a recognition that a distinction must be drawn between the substance of faith and its formulation in a particular time or place.[43] Vischer was, incidentally, one of those who understood immediately that the ground-breaking dimension of the latter point had implications for the many theological issues at stake in the ecumenical movement and for the very methodology of dialogue.[44] He also understood the unity of these five basic ideas. In this sense, he drew a parallel between the growing importance of the word "oecumenicus" and that of the word "pastoralis," one of the most programmatical terms in the conciliar language.[45] Combining idealistic visions and sober realism, Vischer was aware of the different meanings in the use of the word "oecumenicus," as he illustrated while dealing with the question as to how to take part in a dialogue concerning truth. Yet these differences were merely another reason for him to participate in this dialogue from the theological point of view.[46] He also identifies one of the main institutional challenges of the question of the nature of dialogue:

> The Roman Catholic Church – despite its openness – cannot regard itself as a member of a fellowship of divided churches. It may take part in a dialogue which creates a relation between itself and the non-Roman churches. But it can hardly speak of a dialogue which unites all the separated churches with one another. The churches belonging to the World Council of Churches have a different concept. They have formed an alliance. They are bound by a fellowship of dialogue and of *diakonia* – a fellowship which does not prevent them from being completely themselves but which at the same time means that they have deep obligations to one another.[47]

After the first session, it was quite clear as to how these different concepts would evolve. The Catholic Church had to deal with what Vischer

42 Lukas Vischer, "Report on Second Vatican Council," *EcRev* 16/1, 1963, 43–59, here 44.

43 Vischer, "Report on Second Vatican Council," 45.

44 See Quisinsky, "The Eumenical Dynamic of Vatican II," 85–89.

45 Vischer, "Report on Second Vatican Council," 49. See now Gilles Routhier, "A l'origine de la pastoralité de Vatican II," *LTP* 67/3, 2011, 443–459, invoking the roles of John XXIII as well as that of ecumenists Yves Congar and Augustin Bea.

46 Vischer, "Report on Second Vatican Council," 50.

47 Vischer, "Report on Second Vatican Council," 53–54.

identifies as a somewhat paradoxical situation, that is that it wanted to be ecumenically active without belonging to the WCC. As for the WCC, it had to face the question concerning how to deal with this new and unusual ecumenical partner, but also with "what importance it [the WCC] attaches to membership."[48] The question is even more complex, for Vatican II was just at the outset, and the first session was "like the opening of a floodgate."[49]

While it was anything but clear what exactly the dynamic inaugurated by the first session's opening speeches would be, it was clear that there was one. This can be seen as a major insight of the second session that "witnessed for the first time a full discussion on the problems of the ecumenical movement" and had "to spell out in detail what 'ecumenism' was as Roman Catholics understood it."[50] This dynamic was groundbreaking, for the Roman Catholic Church had to abandon a concept of other Christians, and therefore of itself, that was bound to the Counter-Reformation, without knowing in advance "what other foundations could be used."[51] Being confronted with this kind of "open question"[52] was a new situation for the Roman Catholic Church. This dimension of uncertainty and challenge accumulated at the council between the Catholic Church and the ecumenical movement, which was experiencing a particularly delicate passage in its existence. In this sense, Vischer saw the importance of the future conciliar decree on ecumenism, but he also considered its limits:

> Although the schema on ecumenism is extremely important for the relationship between the Roman Catholic and the non-Roman churches, its significance must not be over-estimated. The future of ecumenical relations will not be determined only by this text. Admittedly, it will shape the ecumenical convictions of countless Roman Catholic Christians. Nevertheless the future course of mutual relations will be determined just as much by the way in which the Roman Catholic Church puts the ecumenical idea into practice. Since it has not yet taken part in the ecumenical movement, it must now find its own style.[53]

In agreeing to deal in one way or another with the ecumenical dynamic, the Roman Catholic Church could no longer conceive of its own ecclesiology and theology in a static way: "We must not forget that the ecumenical movement is dynamic in character and relations cannot be permanently regulated by a declaration of principles,"[54] and, one might add, not even by principles confined to the conciliar documents[55] of the Roman Catholic Church, which therefore could not constitute "a final word."[56] In order to enter into a permanent relationship with the ecumenical movement, it would be clear that the very principles of the

48 Vischer, "Report on Second Vatican Council," 54.

49 Vischer, "Report on Second Vatican Council," 54.

50 Lukas Vischer, "Roman Catholic Ecumenism and the World Council of Churches," *EcRev* 16/4, 1964, 378–394, here 378. It is noteworthy that Vischer's article deals with the "Roman Catholic ecumenism," formulation also used by Marie-Joseph Congar, *Chrétiens désunis: Principes d'un "œcuménisme" catholique*, Paris, Cerf, 1937; ET: *Divided Christendom: A Catholic Study of the Problem of Reunion*, trans. Muad A. Bousfield, London, Bles, 1939. Later, the preparatory scheme *De Ecclesiae unitate* became entitled "Decree on ecumenism," marking a shift in the very understanding of ecumenism by the Roman Catholic Church.

51 Vischer, "Roman Catholic Ecumenism," 378.

52 Vischer, "Roman Catholic Ecumenism," 378.

53 Vischer, "Roman Catholic Ecumenism," 379. As to the category of "style," it is noteworthy that it became later on a major category of the conciliar hermeneutic, see Joseph Famerée, ed., *Vatican II comme style: L'herméneutique théologique du Concile*, Paris, Cerf, 2012.

54 Vischer, "Roman Catholic Ecumenism," 379.

55 As early as during the second session, Vischer refers to the hermeneutical impact of the interdependence of the different future documents, see for example Vischer, "Roman Catholic Ecumenism," 383–385.

56 Vischer, "Roman Catholic Ecumenism," 380.

Roman Catholic Church "will be infringed."[57] In this sense, the Roman Catholic Church had to go through the same experience as the other ecumenical partners previously had. Incidentally, Vischer clearly saw that this was a great challenge for the Roman Catholic Church and that it was anything but an easy task.[58]

Needless to say, the same is true for the WCC. Therefore, the executive committee of the world council held in 1964 in Odessa,[59] based on both the programmatic text "New Delhi Statement on Unity"[60] and on the new situation emerging with Vatican II, discussed the new era of ecumenism and the future challenges relating to the fact that in the eyes of the ecumenical partners of the WCC the Roman Catholic Church had joined the ecumenical movement. In this new situation, several points were particularly important for the divided churches seeking unity, such as (1) the mutual confession of Jesus Christ, superseding differences in the understanding of ecclesiology and unity; (2) the principle of equality of rights within the WCC although no church was obliged to consider ecclesiologically the other churches in the same way as it conceived itself; (3) solidarity among the divided churches; (4) the understanding of universality accentuating the ever concrete realization of the church in individual places. Insofar as the Roman Catholic Church considered the WCC to be a useful instrument, but did not want to become a member, Vischer believed it to be even more crucial that the "churches joined together in the World Council must conversely ask themselves to what extent the ecclesiology of a church which has not hitherto been one of their number would alter the existing fellowship."[61] Thus the ecclesiological horizon of the Toronto statement *The Church, the Churches and the World Council of Churches*,[62] even if it still remained an important guideline, could no longer be considered sufficient either by the Roman Catholic Church or by the member churches of the WCC. In the search for new expressions,

> [t]he Roman Catholic Church and the World Council must therefore remain in close contact. The Roman Catholic Church needs the World Council if it is not to leave out of account in its ecumenical work the diverse and multilateral reality of Christendom. It needs the World Council if it is to share in the problems which concern, not individual churches as such, but the churches collectively. The World Council, on the other hand, needs contact with the Roman Catholic Church if it is not to slip into holding a view of the ecumenical task which is truncated from the outset. It must take up the questions addressed to it by the Roman Catholic Church. Close contact is also necessary because its member churches also stand in a relationship ... attended by particular problems.[63]

To express this in other words, even if in 1964 Vatican II was far from being completed, it was already clear that a new spiritual, theological, and institutional expression of the relationship between the Roman Catholic Church and the WCC was needed. Vischer considered three points to be particularly important for the shared responsibility resulting from this situation: (1) the Roman

57 Vischer, "Roman Catholic Ecumenism," 379.

58 Vischer, "Roman Catholic Ecumenism," 382. See also the meeting in Rummelsberg on "Relations between the World Council of Churches and the Roman Catholic Church" with discussions on Vatican II introduced by Lukas Vischer, Nikos Nissiotis and Edmund Schlink (Ans J. van der Bent, *Six Hundred Ecumenical Consultations (1948–1982)*, Geneva, WCC Publications, 1983, 18–19).

59 The Odessa statement is published in *EcRev* 16/3, 1964, 323–328.

60 *The New Delhi Report*, 316–322.

61 Vischer, "Roman Catholic Ecumenism," 390.

62 *The Church, the Churches and the World Council of Churches: The Ecclesiological Significance of the World Council of Churches: A Statement Commended to the Churches for Study and Comment by the Central Committee of the Council, Meeting at Toronto, Ontario, July, 1950*, Geneva, WCC Publications, 1950.

63 Vischer, "Roman Catholic Ecumenism," 392–393.

Catholic Church had to acknowledge explicitly its responsibility for ecumenism; (2) the ecclesiological differences should not justify the absence of relationship but become the object of relationship; (3) notwithstanding theoretical differences and practical difficulties, there were already common tasks urging the churches to work together. In this sense, the first two sessions of Vatican II clearly indicated a decisive evolution, but also the fragility of the situation:

> The Vatican Council can do much to help make such a cooperation a reality. Much will depend upon the way, and above all the spirit, in which the decree on ecumenism is revised. The discussions in connection with the decree which will take place within and outside the Council can help a long way towards bringing about an awareness of the problems … and towards bringing them at least a few steps nearer a solution.[64]

Of course, all now depended on whether "the bishops go this far."[65]

After the third session, leading to a "confusing picture,"[66] Vischer saw an ambiguous situation. On the one hand, new perspectives were opened by the conciliar texts and drafts – especially *De oecumenismo* and *De Ecclesia* – and they went far beyond what could be hoped before Vatican II. On the other hand, "the results have two faces, just as on ancient coins Janus, the god of gateways, has two faces."[67] While on one side there was a change of pace in relations with non-Roman Catholic churches, on the other side there was the transformation of classical theological positions and the traditional Roman organization. Thus, the "deepening of fellowship" and the "renewal of differences"[68] went hand in hand. More concretely, the decree *De oecumenismo* raised the question about which relationship and cooperation should be established between the Roman Catholic Church and the WCC. In mentioning the ecumenical movement and quoting the basis of the WCC, "the decree acknowledges that the ecumenical problem lies in the relationship of *all* the churches to one another."[69] Beyond rather technical questions on ecumenical structures and methods, the third session clearly revealed that the difficult and ambiguous situation of the Roman Catholic Church with the combination of rapid changes and a need to understand what had happened at the council "also concerns the non-Roman churches. Even in their separation, the separated churches are still so close to one another that any development in one church affects them all."[70] Therefore, no church could be merely an observer. One might say that the non-Roman churches, therefore, had a coresponsibility for Vatican II, just as the Roman Catholic Church had a coresponsibility for the ecumenical movement and the WCC. The third session somehow revealed the true question without offering an answer to it, that is "how a fellowship of dialogue and cooperation can come about between the churches."[71] Vischer proposed attaining a common understanding of words such as "dialogue," "ecumenical relations," and "cooperation," along with the implications and consequences of what was meant by those words. Now that the Roman Catholic Church wanted to be involved in one way or another in the ecumenical conversation, the non-Roman churches had to be able to bear a common witness. This implied a reflection on the role of the WCC both in its internal function and in its

64 Vischer, "Roman Catholic Ecumenism," 394.

65 Vischer, "Roman Catholic Ecumenism," 394.

66 Lukas Vischer, "Report on the Third Session of Second Vatican Council," in: *Central Committee of the World Council of Churches: Minutes and Reports of the Eighteenth Meeting, Enugu, Eastern Nigeria, Africa January 12th to 21st, 1965*, Geneva, WCC Publications, 1965, 91–102, here 100.

67 Vischer, "Report on the Third Session," 92.

68 Vischer, "Report on the Third Session," 92.

69 Vischer, "Report on the Third Session," 94 (italics original).

70 Vischer, "Report on the Third Session," 100.

71 Vischer, "Report on the Third Session," 101.

cooperation with the Roman Catholic Church. He insisted that the difficulties of the Roman Catholic Church after its ecumenical reversal of stance corresponded to the difficulties encountered by the non-Roman churches. Therefore, Vischer pleaded that all the churches should tackle this question together.

The situation changed once again with the fourth session. The texts had to be completed and the reception of Vatican II had to be prepared. Globally impressed by the different results of Vatican II, without ignoring the ambiguous aspects and the unresolved questions, Vischer admitted that there was a problem to "maintain an over-all view."[72] As for the ecumenical question, there "existed the danger that after the promulgation of this Decree [*Unitatis redintegratio*] the Council would regard the dialogue with the ecumenical movement as closed and that the spirit of the Decree on Ecumenism would not penetrate the remaining texts."[73] This would have led to a kind of isolation of the ecumenical question within the conciliar text corpus, and finally would have limited the future fellowship of the Roman Catholic Church in the ecumenical movement. On the one hand, Vischer summarized, "[a]s a whole, the fourth session withstood this danger."[74] On the other hand, only the "prerequisites"[75] for the integration of the ecumenical thinking had been created. These prerequisites were founded in several conciliar documents. Thus for the concrete reception of Vatican II, other texts beyond the conciliar documents were also important. The most important text was the "so-called Directorium"[76] that imparted directives for the future ecumenical work. The existence of this text, along with its content, had a major hermeneutical impact, for the SPCU wanted to handle a small number of themes "in order not to hinder the spontaneous development of the ecumenical movement."[77] To express it in other words, in Rome, at least the SPCU conceived the council as a beginning and the reception as an ongoing dynamic. This dynamic was both theological and institutional, and both dimensions were grounded in spirituality. In this sense, Vischer considered "[o]ne of the most significant events ... the service which the Pope and the bishops celebrated with the observers in *S. Paulo fuori le mura*"[78] for it not only honored the work of the observers but encouraged the participation of Catholics in ecumenical prayers. While the existence of the directorium clearly implies that Rome, or at least the SPCU, acknowledged an ongoing dynamic after Vatican II which could not but go beyond the council, this very document tried to "limit the spontaneous character of the ecumenical movement."[79]

The situation after the fourth session was thus more ambiguous than ever and challenged both the WCC and the Roman Catholic Church. Having said this, one can conclude that Vischer's reports were the expression of his ever-increasing role as a bridgebuilder between the WCC and Vatican II, for his networking constituted a very effective dimension of his conciliar participation.

2.3 *Vischer's Ecumenical Networking and Bridgebuilding*

Invited by the SPCU as an official observer, Vischer used the opportunity of the first session to extend his contacts. He complemented his ecumenical network with numerous contacts with Catholic bishops and theologians. A central role in this process was played by the Dutch theologian, ecumenist and later archbishop Johannes Willebrands,

72 Lukas Vischer, "After the Fourth Session of the Second Vatican Council," *EcRev* 18/2, 1966, 150–189, here 153.
73 Vischer, "After the Fourth Session," 186.
74 Vischer, "After the Fourth Session," 187.
75 Vischer, "After the Fourth Session," 187.
76 Vischer, "After the Fourth Session," 187. Vischer refers to SPCU's *Ad totam Ecclesiam* in: *AAS* 59, 1967, 574–592. See the contribution by Bruno Cherubini in this volume and Bruno Cherubini, *Presagi di un inverno ecumenico: Il direttorio di Paolo VI*, Bologna, Marietti 1820, 2023.

77 Vischer, "After the Fourth Session," 187.
78 Vischer, "After the Fourth Session," 187 (italics original).
79 Vischer, "After the Fourth Session," 189.

secretary of the SPCU.[80] As secretary of the CCEQ from 1952 to 1960,[81] Willebrands was involved in the ecumenical dialogue even before Vatican II and was able to take advantage of this rather discrete activity of the preconciliar years once he was called upon to build, together with Cardinal Bea, an ecumenical structure within the Vatican. During Vatican II, the relationship between Willebrands and Vischer became decisive.[82] After the first session, Willebrands invited Vischer to communicate to him some of the ecumenical observers' impressions and thoughts concerning the schemata.[83] In order to answer this demand, Vischer discussed matters with other theologians at the WCC and prepared an extensive evaluation from a WCC perspective, which he sent to Willebrands in an extensive letter on Jan 18, 1963.[84] In this letter, with his typical diction, he mentioned the difficulties of the task. Moreover, he added that several intentions of the WCC could already be introduced into the conciliar debates and discussions within the commissions. As for the institutional dimension of the difficulties, Vischer identified what would be one of the main topics of his entire ecumenical engagement: the foundation and organization of the WCC and the ecclesiological consequences resulting from it.[85] It would become increasingly clear that this topic challenged both the WCC and the Roman Catholic Church. As for the latter, and more concretely the council, Vischer stated the need for a new hermeneutic of controversial theological questions, for if the council merely repeated the traditional way of describing differences it would repeat the traditional hostile reactions. For Vischer, there existed a specific way of overcoming this danger: theological reflection, even on classical topics, had to be done in light of the problems and challenges of the contemporary world, thereby surpassing the old controversial-theological impasses. By considering new questions together, old questions could appear in a new light. After this hermeneutical introduction, Vischer mentioned several theological insights resulting from the ecumenical process during the recent years and decades. First, he proposed that the metaphor of the body of Christ,[86] which was particularly important for the Roman Catholic Church, could be extended, as was the case in the ecumenical movement, and be completed by other metaphors, such as the People of God. Second, he

80 Karim Schelkens, "Willebrands, Johannes Gerardus Maria," in: Quisinsky & Walter, eds., *Personenlexikon*, 288–289.

81 See Peter De Mey, "Précurseur du Secrétariat pour l'Unité: Le travail œcuménique de la 'Conférence Catholique pour les questions œcuméniques' (1952–1963)," in: Gilles Routhier, Philippe Roy & Karim Schelkens, dir., *La théologie catholique entre intransigeance et renouveau: La reception des mouvements préconciliaires à Vatican II*, Louvain-la-Neuve/Leuven, Collège Érasme/Universiteitsbibliotheek, 2011, 271–308; Peter De Mey, "Willebrands' contributions to the Catholic Conference for Ecumenical Questions (1952–1963)," in: Adelbert Denaux & Peter de Mey, eds., *The Ecumenical Legacy of Johannes Cardinal Willebrands (1909–2006)*, Leuven, Peeters, 2012, 49–77; and the contribution by Peter De Mey & Saretta Marotta, "The Catholic Conference for Ecumenical Questions" in this volume. It is also still interesting to consult the chapter "Œcuménistes catholiques et Conseil œcuménique des Églises," in: Étienne Fouilloux, *Les catholiques & l'unité chrétienne du XIXe au XXe siècle: Itinéraires européens d'expression française*, Paris, Le Centurion, 1982, 777–817.

82 See Leo Declerck, *Les agendas conciliaires de Mgr. J. Willebrands, secrétaire du Secrétariat pour l'unité des Chrétiens*, Leuven, Peeters, 2009.

83 Later, the SPCU organized, almost every Tuesday, a meeting with the observers in order to discuss the schemata (see Declerck, *Les agendas conciliaires*, 3, note 17, and Velati, *Separati ma fratelli*).

84 L. Vischer to J. Willebrands, Jan 18, 1963, in: WCCA, Personal papers Lukas Vischer, 994.3.50.21/1. Of course, not all the observers were in line with Vischer's increasingly leading role, see for example Declerck, *Les agendas conciliaires*, 64, note 420 or Congar, *My Journal of the Council* (Feb 3, 1965).

85 "In the Ecumenical Council we are not in a position to comment on the schemata on the basis of a confession. It is a community of churches of different confessions, and it goes without saying that its individual member churches would express themselves in a much more specific, comprehensive and probably also more critical way on a text drafted by Roman Catholics"; Vischer to Willebrands, 2.

86 Vischer to Willebrands, 3.

referred to the "New Delhi Statement on Unity," which dealt with the missionary dimension of the church as a central issue of the WCC. More exactly, he would prefer the Roman Catholic Church not to consider any longer the mission as one *munus* along with others, but as a characteristic dimension of its being. Third, he referred to the WCC's dealing with sin and sinners in the church as a possible model for a better articulation of this problem within the schema *De Ecclesia*. Fourth, he pleaded for a better articulation of the gifts of the Spirit in the conciliar documents, referring to the important Orthodox contributions to this question within the WCC. Fifth, he insisted on the frequently used formulation within the ecumenical movement and the WCC that the church had to be a servant and a serving church. Finally, sixth, he mentioned the possibility of increasing the depth and extension of the eschatological aspect of the conciliar texts, which could be attained by integrating the experiences in this domain that had occurred within the ecumenical movement. Needless to say, there are no linear evolutions which might prove that Vischer's letter directly influenced the further discussions of Vatican II, but the comparison between some final conciliar texts and Vischer's proposals is worthy of note. First, *Lumen gentium*, indeed, not only completes the metaphor of the body of Christ with the metaphor of the People of God, but also accords a central position to the latter. Second, the decree on the missionary activity of the church *Ad gentes* clearly considers that the mission is an overriding aspect of the church, not just one activity among others. Insofar as Catholic ecumenists such as Yves Congar contributed to this shift, one could argue that they were able to do so because their ecumenical learning included a growing sensitivity towards such insights. Third, Vatican II did indeed acknowledge the reality of sin within the church (*LG* 8). Fourth, *LG* 12 deals with charismata.[87] Fifth, Vatican II speaks indeed of the *ministratio* of the church in *LG* 4, and, sixth, one can consider the eschatological ecclesiology of *LG* 48 to be one of the most far-reaching openings of Vatican II.[88] Even if there is no single causal link between Vischer's letter and the final documents of the council, there is a striking parallelism which helps to measure the ecumenical achievements of Vatican II. It goes without saying that if it were true that the role of recommended ecumenists such as Yves Congar played a major role in these parallelisms, one could theorize from a hermeneutical and ecclesiological perspective the fact that contingencies and hazards resulting from individual biographies may be as important as formal decisions of institutions such as the WCC. There can be no doubt, however, that both dimensions are intrinsically linked together. The very contact between Vischer and Willebrands is an example of this correlation, as are the encouraging signs that Vischer saw in Augustin Bea; the Swiss theologian would often refer to the cardinal's proposal that the scheme *De Ecclesiae unitate* began by speaking of the need for internal reform within the Roman Church, rather than with the traditional unionist discourse.[89]

Having said this, beyond personal ties and institutional connections, major theological issues had their own dynamic, namely the need for clarification regarding what was meant by the term "church." Indeed, in the same letter to Willebrands, Vischer considered that the question as

87 It is noteworthy that the intervention of Cardinal Léon-Joseph Suenens was prepared by Hans Küng (see Hans Küng, *Erkämpfte Freiheit: Erinnerungen*, Munich, Piper, 2002, 473–475), Vischer's fellow countryman, whose dissertation on Karl Barth's understanding of justification (Hans Küng, *Rechtfertigung: Die Lehre Karl Barths und eine Katholische Besinnung*, Einsiedeln, Johannes Verlag, 1957) constituted a major step in Roman Catholic theology. Notwithstanding the fact that Küng's conciliar strategy of not participating in the commission is the complete contrary of Congar's habitus, it was once again an ecumenist who participated in the realization of one of Vischer's desiderata.

88 See Michael Quisinsky, *Geschichtlicher Glaube in einer geschichtlichen Welt: Der Beitrag von M.-D. Chenu, Y. Congar und H.-M. Féret zum II. Vaticanum*, Münster, LIT, 2007, 367–376.

89 Vischer to Willebrands, 7.

to whether non-Roman Catholic Christians were members of the body of Christ had a deep impact. According to Vischer, the answer to this question depended on which kind of dialogue could be practiced. If for Vischer the ecclesial reality of the non-Catholic churches was taken for granted, he knew the inherent difficulties that both Catholics and non-Catholics found in defining what exactly this ecclesial reality might mean. Therefore, he pleaded for a conciliar text that would recognize *a priori* the ecclesial reality of the other churches in order to open a dialogue.[90] As for Vischer, neither the discussion among Roman-Catholics nor the theological positions among the ecumenical partners were already sufficiently clear for any precise definition, with its subsequent implications. Thus, opening the dialogue by recognizing ecclesial reality beyond the Roman Catholic Church would in the long run be the most important and the most profound achievement of the council. Incidentally, it was this processual view of the council that needed to look continually beyond its texts that Vischer would increasingly apply as his specific conciliar hermeneutics.

3 Montreal and Vatican II: Perspectives of a Convergence

The process of Vatican II involved both the Roman Catholic Church and the ecumenical movement. Naturally, this is true generally speaking, ignoring institutional and structural dimensions. While it is almost impossible to measure the impact of the general atmosphere, it is all the more important to consider institutional ties, such as the participation of non-Roman Catholic observers and structural parallelisms, for example the similarities between Vatican II and the fourth world conference on Faith and Order in Montreal (Jul 12–26, 1963). Two months after his letter to Willebrands, "at a point midway between the end of the first session of the Vatican Council and the opening of our Fourth World Conference on Faith and Order,"[91] Vischer met him during a discussion in Bossey near Geneva between Roman Catholic and Faith and Order theologians.[92]

We therefore have to take a closer look at the fourth world conference in Montreal. After the first three conferences held in Lausanne in 1927, Edinburgh in 1937, and Lund in 1952, this one took place at a crucial moment. The ecumenical partners gathered in Montreal were aware of the changing situation in the world which demanded a new and renewed commitment to unity and mission, and they also were aware that the WCC and the Roman Catholic Church had to work together in this enterprise. This is illustrated, incidentally, by two best-sellers of the "well-provided conference bookstall,"[93] that is John A.T. Robinson's *Honest to God*[94] and Xavier Rynne's *Letters from Vatican City*.[95] As far as Vatican II was concerned, it goes without saying that there was no single strategy accepted by all the theologians present in Montreal. Roger Mehl stated in the opening address of the world conference "that the churches belonging to the World Council do not regard the Vatican Council as an event which does not concern them, but as an event which affects them all because it really concerns the history of the true universal church."[96] Inversely, Catholic ecumenists, such as Gustave Thils, were aware that Montreal affected

90 Vischer to Willebrands, 7.

91 Patrick C. Rodger, "Report of the Faith and Order Secretariat to the Central Committee on Current Developments in the Field of Christian Unity," *EcRev* 15/1, 1963, 81–88, here 83.

92 Declerck, *Les agendas conciliaires*, 3.

93 Patrick C. Rodger & Lukas Vischer, eds., *The Fourth World Conference on Faith and Order: The Report from Montreal 1963*, London, SCM Press, 1964, 20, note 1.

94 John A.T. Robinson, *Honest to God*, London, SCM Press, 1963.

95 Xavier Rynne, *Letters from Vatican City: Vatican Council II (First Session): Background and Debates*, New York, Farrar, Strauss and Company, 1963.

96 Cited in Rodger & Vischer, eds., *The Fourth World Conference on Faith and Order*, 10–11.

them, too.[97] As was to be expected, in his opening address Mehl also referred to the remaining difficulties, as did Hans Heinrich Harms, who asked whether there was any chance of a real dialogue between equals, questioning, by the way, the Roman Catholic understanding of the Holy Spirit.[98] As for Karl Barth, he warned that the ecumenical partners "shall do best to concentrate not on the new relations now possible with Rome but on what is happening in and to Rome herself, and to ask whether we are similarly open to the word of the Spirit."[99]

In his letter sent to Willebrands, who was also present in Montreal,[100] after the first session of Vatican II Vischer stated that the convergence of issues dealt with in Rome and Montreal was quite astonishing. Expressed in concrete terms, as parallel issues he named first ecclesiology, second the question of the Tradition and the traditions, and third the ministry and the divine service. For Vischer, this convergence was anything but accidental. It resulted rather from the fact that the question of unity unavoidably led to these issues and questions.[101] Once again, the convergence of issues resulting from an inherent theological dynamic was seconded by personal ties and constellations. In fact, Montreal "marked a new stage of the participation of Orthodox delegates and Roman Catholic observers."[102]

Going far beyond the different issues while finding the connections among them, Montreal started with a first general session on "Catholicity" on Jul 15, 1963. It is impossible, indeed, to overestimate the importance of this general dimension that tied together the five sections in which the membership conference was divided: "The Church in the Purpose of God"; "Scripture, Tradition and Traditions"; "The Redemptive Work of Christ and the Ministry of the Church"; "Worship and Openness of Christ's Church"; "'All in Each Place': The Process of Growing Together." The work in the different sections, leading to five section reports, dealt with issues concerning both the churches' self-understanding and the external perception of the WCC and ecumenical notions in a more general way. For example, the first section's report is divided into four chapters: "Christ, New Creation, Creation"; "The Church: Act and Institution"; "Christ, the Church and the Churches"; "The Church and the World Council of Churches." While the latter point in particular had to deal with a highly conflictual difference of positions within and outside the WCC, a parallel can be seen in the first chapter, considering the church from creation to fulfilment, with the salvation-historical approach of Vatican II, even though it must be clear that the notion of salvation history played a different role in Montreal (where Ernst Käsemann warned against any salvation-historical romanticism and perhaps even triumphalism) and in Rome (where the notion of salvation history might be a means of limiting a certain neo-scholastic tendency towards abstraction and triumphalism).[103]

In the third section, to take just one other example of these parallelisms, the awareness grew that the question of ministry led to a "recovery of a doctrine of the whole Church as the people of God, and of a positive and indeed creative understanding of the laity in consequence."[104] This may be considered parallel to what was experienced during the redaction of *Lumen gentium*, where the notion of People of God was finally considered to

97 See for a contemporary testimony Gustave Thils, *Histoire doctrinale du movement œcuménique*, Paris, Desclée de Brouwer, 1962, 83.

98 Rodger & Vischer, eds., *The Fourth World Conference*, 17.

99 Rodger & Vischer, eds., *The Fourth World Conference*, 20.

100 Declerck, *Les agendas conciliaires*, 42–44.

101 Vischer to Willebrands, 2.

102 Rodger & Vischer, eds., *The Fourth World Conference*, 19–20.

103 On the notion of salvation history in the ecumenical debates, see Geiko Müller-Fahrenholz, *Heilsgeschichte zwischen Ideologie und Prophetie: Profile und Kritik heilsgeschichtlicher Theorien in der ökumenischen Bewegung zwischen 1948 und 1968*, Freiburg i.Br., Herder, 1974. For a contextualization of Montreal's dealing with the notion, see Müller-Fahrenholz, *Heilsgeschichte zwischen Ideologie und Prophetie*, 38–39.

104 Rodger & Vischer, eds., *The Fourth World Conference*, 26.

be central, relegating the chapter of the hierarchy to a secondary role; moreover, and in line with what was already stated in *Lumen gentium*, but also in *Gaudium et spes*, the decree *Apostolicam actuositatem*, notwithstanding its eventual limits, can be seen as a groundbreaking achievement for any understanding of laity. As for the works of section four, there seems to be, on the one hand, a rather different approach on the part of Rome and Montreal, the world conference considering the contemporary state of worship far more explicitly. On the other hand, even if the starting point, the implications, and the proposed solutions are quite different, general questions concerning the Communion and the *communicatio in sacris* could not be eluded either in Rome or in Montreal. Finally, the fifth section dealt with some of the topics that were also contained in *Gaudium et spes*, *Ad gentes*, and *Unitatis redintegratio*. Notwithstanding the different approaches and arguments, implications and consequences, one can see that there was – *cum grano salis* – a certain parallelism between the issues.

In this sense, the similarity between the title of the second section's report, "Scripture, Tradition and Traditions"[105] and the title of the two-volume publication *La Tradition et les traditions*[106] by Yves Congar is particularly striking. Needless to say, Congar's book is not a conciliar text, but it had a certain influence on the conciliar conception of Tradition and Revelation, and this surpassed Congar's own influence as a peritus. Furthermore, references to Congar can be found in the history of the redaction of the section report.[107] Both Montreal and Congar distinguished between Tradition with a capital T and a variety of traditions, even if the distinctions are not exactly the same: while Montreal (§ 39)[108] considers the gospel itself to be Tradition and introduces a third term, "tradition" with a small t, designating the process of tradition, Congar's Tradition (with capital T) corresponds rather to this secondary term. The question of the relationship between Scripture and Tradition/tradition and continuity/discontinuity appears behind these differences.[109] However, notwithstanding these differences, the very parallelism shows "that in Roman Catholic theology the concept of tradition is undergoing serious reconsideration" (§ 44).[110] This is all the more true since there are also parallelisms between Montreal and *Dei Verbum*,[111] this reconsideration itself, in fact, can be considered revolutionary; in this sense, *Dei Verbum* was a milestone for the ecumenical movement. Jean-Louis Leuba showed that while *Dei Verbum*, establishing the predominant role of the Scripture, superseded post-Tridentine approaches considering Scripture and Tradition on the same level, Montreal surpassed the simplest interpretation of the *sola scriptura* principle. The common horizon of both transgressions saves the historical understanding of Revelation with its implications for the understanding of Man and World.[112] One can conclude that after Montreal, it was even clearer that the main challenge for the relationship between the Roman Catholic Church and the WCC and its member churches was ecclesiology, in particular the role of the magisterium.[113] One might also add, with Vischer:

105 Rodger & Vischer, ed., *The Fourth World Conference*, 50–61.

106 Yves Congar, *La Tradition et les traditions*, 2 vols., Paris, Fayard, 1960–1963. See especially "La pensée protestante contemporaine devant le problème de la tradition," in: Congar, *La Tradition et les traditions*, vol. 2, *Essai théologique*, Paris, Fayard, 1963, 215–243 (for Congar's dialogue with leading ecumenical theologians).

107 Rodger & Vischer, ed., *Fourth World Conference*, 23.

108 Rodger & Vischer, eds., *The Fourth World Conference*, 50.

109 See also Quisinsky, "The Ecumenical Dynamic of Vatican II," 100–112.

110 Rodger & Vischer, eds., *The Fourth World Conference*, 51.

111 See for example among Rodger & Vischer, eds., *The Fourth World Conference*, 50–51 (§ 45) and *Dei Verbum* 9 and 10.

112 Jean-Louis Leuba, "La Tradition à Montréal et à Vatican II: Convergences et questions," in: Bernard-Dominique Dupuy, ed., *La Révélation divine: Constitution dogmatique "Dei verbum"*, vol. 2, Paris, Cerf, 1968, 475–497.

113 Achim Buckenmaier, *"Schrift und Tradition" seit dem Vatikanum II: Vorgeschichte und Rezeption*, Paderborn,

> that the Constitution (*Dei Verbum*) nevertheless further the ecumenical dialogue. While not invalidating the hitherto existing doctrine, by emphasizing the importance of the Scriptures it asserts that the Church must always and in every case be responsible to Scripture in its statements, and even if it does not draw "its certainty solely from Scripture," it has nevertheless – especially in ecumenical dialogue – become significantly more difficult to verify any statement in any other way than by Scripture. With this, a promising development has been initiated.[114]

As far as Faith and Order was concerned, the work on the topics of Scripture and Tradition continued, notably in the sessions of Aarhus 1964 and Bristol 1967, when the different interpretations of their relationship revealed itself to be an imminent challenge.[115] This included a general reflection on hermeneutics,[116] going beyond technical questions concerning the combination of Scripture and Tradition. It also included a new awareness of the common history of the undivided Christian churches in the patristic period.[117] It should be noticed that the Bristol session also dealt with the topic "God in Nature and History," which indicates the general challenges of contemporary world views surrounding any theological and *a fortiori* ecumenical question.[118]

For the Faith and Order movement, Montreal was anything but a triumphal event. It goes without saying that it marked the end of one period and the beginning of a new one. Yet as the Faith and Order members came to realize a year later in their meeting in Aarhus, the new situation was rather confusing.[119] Having said this, what Vischer describes here seems to be the unavoidable challenge posed by a change in ecumenical generations, and a context in which such a change was marked by a kind of globalization of ecumenism. The new ecumenical situation occurred with Vatican II and the parallelism between the council and Montreal made it clear that the comfortable ecumenical routine had become outdated: "We know one another; indeed we know one another only too well; when we meet for ecumenical conferences, the first impression is not the discovery of new faces but the comforting feeling of being together again among old friends."[120] In order to avoid this routine, Vischer pleaded, to a certain extent on an organizational level, for a recognition of the new situation, marked by the presence in Montreal of the Catholics and the Orthodox as well as by the increasing discussions among the WCC member churches attempting to institutionalize unity. He also sought a greater commitment and stability of purpose of Faith and Order's work. This included, among other points, a focus on the life of the churches and the pastoral situation rather than on theological specializations, even if they existed in their own right and were more necessary than ever; an ecumenical work whose timing was not only dictated by the world conferences; a better evaluation of the achievements and the remaining difficulties; the need for both bilateral theological conversations and regional Faith and Order conferences. On the theological level, Vischer sought the identification of the general

Bonifatius, 1996, 239. In the same sense Vischer, *After the Fourth Session*, 156.

114 Vischer, "After the Fourth Session," 156.

115 *New Directions in Faith and Order: Bristol 1967: Reports – Minutes – Documents*, Geneva, WCC Publications, 1968, 32–49.

116 See the meeting of Basel 1964 and Heidelberg 1967 on the topic "The Significance of the Hermeneutical Problem for the Ecumenical Movement," in: van der Bent, *Six Hundred Ecumenical Consultations*, 18.

117 Meetings were held in Aarhus 1964, Hamburg 1965, and Saloniki 1966, see van der Bent, *Six Hundred Ecumenical Consultations*, 19.

118 The section report is published in *New Directions in Faith and Order*, 7–31. For a contextualization, see also Lukas Vischer, "Report of the Secretariat to the Commission on Faith and Order," in: *Faith and Order Louvain 1971: Study Reports and Documents*, Geneva, WCC Publications, 1971, 200–211, here 200–201.

119 Lukas Vischer, "The Faith and Order Movement at the Beginning of a New Period," *Mid-Stream* 4/2, 1964, 6–17, esp. 6.

120 Vischer, "The Faith and Order Movement," 6.

issues, admitting that not all the questions could be dealt with simultaneously: "We must clarify first the deepest questions, we must examine the presuppositions upon which the whole of the life and doctrine of the church is built; and only then can we apply ourselves to the specific questions, which we have not yet been able to set aside. If we deal first with the specific problems, we end up inevitably in culs-de-sac."[121] Vischer proposed nothing less than a new ecumenical method, dealing with fundamental issues, on the one hand, and combining theory and practice, doctrine and Christian life, on the other. The latter point was nothing other than the method proposed by Vatican II, especially by *Gaudium et spes*, which, according to Pope Francis, "revolutioned" theology by the reciprocal relationship between dogma and pastoral care.[122] Furthermore, even though he criticized a "Christological method" that was taken too superficially,[123] Vischer described some of the fundamental theological challenges as Christology-rooted, thus establishing (without saying so and referring rather to Lund) another parallelism between Vatican II and Montreal:

> We must first raise the fundamental questions which broke out in Montreal. So the program which we have set before you contains the proposal to set up studies on "Creation and Redemption," "Spirit, Order and Organization," and on the hermeneutical question. In the course of their work, almost all the sections of Montreal decided that the greatest difficulties are to be found in these places. In what way is God, the Father of Jesus Christ, also at work in the whole creation? What do we say of the work of the Holy Spirit in the church? By what criteria do we expound the scriptures? None of these themes has so far been dealt with in our movement.[124]

Indeed, these were also questions implicated in the discussions and documents of Vatican II. Most prominently, this is shown by Vischer's activities and reflections on *Gaudium et spes*.[125] Just as the documents of Vatican II required reception and hermeneutics, the "New Delhi Statement on Unity," also needed further depth and extension. For Vischer, it was clear that this was the next task of Faith and Order.

Simultaneously with the parallelisms to Vatican II, Faith and Order thus "has entered upon a new phase."[126] Vischer described both the challenges of this new phase and the necessary theological horizon in order to deal with them. As for the challenges themselves, their description sounds like a working program that Vischer had developed:

> The search for unity has become, much more than it formerly was, a common search for the very center of our faith. But does that entirely describe the change? Have we simply received a sharper and more comprehensive view of the problem of unity? Does the change not also have another and much deeper basis? The separated churches have been living together for years. They face together the great test to which the whole of Christendom is being subjected. They are together faced with questions to which they do not have the answers. Thus their fellowship does not only depend on their overcoming the inherited basic principles

121 Vischer, "The Faith and Order Movement," 12–13.

122 See Michael Quisinsky, "Prolegomena einer Theologie 'auf der Grenze': Papst Franziskus und die theologische Erkenntnislehre," *Theologie und Glaube* 107/2, 2017, 137–156.

123 Vischer, "The Faith and Order Movement," 14.

124 Vischer, "The Faith and Order Movement," 14.

125 See Quisinsky, "The Ecumenical Dynamic of Vatican II," 113–119. See still Carmen Aparicio Valls, "Contributo di Lukas Vischer alla *Gaudium et spes*," in: Carmen Aparicio Valls, Carmelo Dotolo & Gianluigi Pasquale, eds., *Sapere teologico e unità della fede: Studi in onore del Prof. Jared Wicks*, Rome, Editrice Pontificia Università Gregoriana, 2004, 3–19.

126 Vischer, "The Faith and Order Movement," 15.

> which separate them; it depends primarily on their standing the test together. This circumstance must have its proper effect on the Faith and Order movement. If the churches wish to grow into unity, then they must apply themselves increasingly to the central questions, before which they all stand in the same perplexity. They must try to break through to new affirmations. In this way they will become more closely bound together than through the treatment of the clerical confessional antitheses, which in comparison seem almost like para-theological problems; and many of the old differences will lose their force, to the extent that the churches succeed in saying together something new.[127]

This plea for a new departure, incidentally, was echoed by the Catholic ecumenist and future cardinal Roberto Tucci, quoting his fellow Jesuit brother Karl Rahner's *dictum* of Vatican II as a "beginning of a beginning."[128] If this implied a new hermeneutic which could be parallelized with that of Vatican II, especially with that of *Gaudium et spes*, it also implied the germ of what would become decades later the "differentiated consensus," for in both cases the encounter of confessional expressions of the faith led not only to a new understanding of the past, but also to a new insight that went beyond any simple juxtaposition, addition, or accumulation of the traditional positions of the different ecumenical partners. As for the horizon on which this challenge could be seen, Vischer identified it as the task of expressing the catholicity of the church in a new way. In the perspective of what would later be called globalization, Christianity had to find new forms of universal unity, which included taking into account that different churches had different conceptions of catholicity, but that all churches had to grow in their catholicity.[129] As far as the ecumenical dialogue with the Roman Catholic Church was concerned, a discussion on the understanding of catholicity seemed to be of the utmost importance, particularly in the light of Paul VI's Encyclical *Ecclesiam suam*.[130] "Should it therefore not be one of our next tasks to consider together the true essence of Catholicity? Must we not ask one another, in what way the one people of God can be manifested in all the world?"[131] Vischer pointed out that the WCC, in general, and Montreal, in particular, dealt with the church above all in its local manifestations and rather left open the question as to how to conceive of the universality of the church. "Must we then not ask ourselves, as a next step, what is the relationship between the universal and the local church?"[132] One could answer this question formulated by Vischer by referring to the complementarity between Montreal and Vatican II, for at first sight Vatican II tended to accentuate the universal dimension of the church, which was also to a certain degree in continuity of approach with Vatican I. Yet Vatican II also insisted on the local church, particularly when dealing with the ecclesiogenetic function of the Eucharist and hence the importance of local eucharistic communities (*LG* 23). Be that as it may, as Vischer concluded, "this question as to the proper way of expressing catholicity naturally goes far beyond the confines of the Faith and Order movement. It must be approached in various ways. But it does concern us also."[133] Anticipating what he would propose two decades

127 Vischer, "The Faith and Order Movement," 15–16.

128 Roberto Tucci, "The Ecumenical Movement, the World Council of Churches and the Roman Catholic Church," in: Norman Goodall, ed., *The Uppsala Report 1968: Official Report of the Fourth Assembly of the World Council of Churches, Uppsala July 4–20 1968*, Geneva, WCC Publications, 323–333, here 327.

129 In this sense, it is interesting to read the interpretation of the shift from "est" to "subsistit in" in paragraph 8 of *Lumen gentium* by Roberto Tucci, "The Ecumenical Movement," 326.

130 See Istituto Paolo VI, ed., *"Ecclesiam Suam": Première lettre encyclique de Paul VI. Colloque international, Rome 24–26 octobre 1980*, Brescia, Studium, 1982.

131 Vischer, "The Faith and Order Movement," 16.

132 Vischer, "The Faith and Order Movement," 16.

133 Vischer, "The Faith and Order Movement," 17.

later in support of an ecumenical church history,[134] Vischer justified in what followed that Faith and Order would reexamine the councils of the early church in order to see more clearly the universal dimension of the church then and in the future. This having been said, the strength of Vischer's vision for Faith and Order was perhaps that he not only had a clear view of the theological implications and necessities of the current situation, but that he was also able to place the theological work within manifold ecumenical activities: "It is just when we recognize the limitations of all theological thought that it becomes all the more important really to understand the Faith and Order movement as movement."[135] Vischer described here the need for, and the impact of, a spiritual ecumenism, once again anticipating what would later be theorized.[136]

4 Catholicity: a New Perspective of Reciprocal Acknowledgement on the Horizon

In Montreal, the notion of catholicity, which is more precise and dynamic a term than New Delhi's "unity,"[137] came into Faith and Order's spotlight. As early as in New Delhi in 1961, the notion of catholicity "was indicated …, but its 'marks' were not given."[138] Moreover, it was obvious that "[f]urther impetus was given to consider catholicity by the calling of the Second Vatican Council in 1962" since "[a] number of Faith and Order Commission members were observers at the Council" and this "increase in communication was furthered by the presence of Roman Catholic observers"[139] in Montreal. In fact, during the general session on Catholicity (Jul 15), it was Vischer who "drew attention to the way in which the ecumenical movement had avoided the use of the term 'catholicity' because of its past polemical associations with the self-assertion of separated churches; but he insisted that we had now to listen to the word and the idea and to explore it together."[140]

At Montreal, lectures were held by the Orthodox Vitaly Borovoy,[141] also a non-Catholic observer at Vatican II, who spoke of catholicity as both "possession" and "basic task," and by the Methodist Claude Welch,[142] who pleaded for a profounder exploration of this notion on the part of the Protestants. Needless to say, as early as in the next general session of Jul 16, 1963, which dealt with "The Church in the New Testament," statements such as the plea of the Protestant theologian Ernst Käsemann to consider rather the eschatological dimension of unity than a constructed *Heilsgeschichte* revealed the inherent difficulties of any reconsideration of catholicity.

Resuming and introducing the Montreal debates, Vischer developed a far-reaching definition of catholicity, "a dynamic term," and pleaded that the task of the ecumenical movement should contribute to the "growth of true catholicity." This also implied focusing once more on Jesus Christ, linking catholicity to Incarnation: "When we speak of catholicity, we confess the one Lord, who is the Lord of the whole world, who embraces all things, but who is also at all times the corner-stone on which the Church is built."[143] In reality, then, the notion of catholicity rapidly became one of

134 Quisinsky, "Lukas Vischer als 'nichtkatholischer Beobachter,'" 142–144.
135 Vischer, "The Faith and Order Movement," 17.
136 Bernd Jochen Hilberath & others, eds., *Ökumene des Lebens als Herausforderung der wissenschaftlichen Theologie: Tagungsbericht der 14. Wissenschaftlichen Konsultation der Societas Oecumenica / Ecumenism of Life as a Challenge for Academic Theology: Proceedings of the 14th Academic Consultation of the Societas Oecumenica*, Frankfurt a.M., Lembeck, 2008.
137 *New Delhi to Uppsala, 1961–1968*, 52–53.
138 Handspicker, "Faith and Order," 149.
139 Handspicker, "Faith and Order," 149.
140 Rodger & Vischer, ed., *The Fourth World Conference*, 16.
141 Karim Schelkens, "Borovoj, Vitali," in: Quisinsky & Walter, eds., *Personenlexikon*, 59–60. For his statement, see Vitaly Borovoy, "The Meaning of Catholicity," *EcRev* 16/1, 1963, 26–32.
142 Claude Welch, "Catholicity," *EcRev* 16/1, 1963, 33–42.
143 Lukas Vischer, "Preface," *EcRev* 16/1, 1963, 24–25, here 25.

the most influential ecumenical topics, integrating both concrete questions and a unifying leitmotif. In a certain way, Vischer also formulated here what increasingly became one of his favorite personal hermeneutical instruments. In so doing, he stood on the ground of two general insights articulated in Montreal, that is, first, that one needed to discuss "catholicity in terms of its 'qualitative' character" and, second, that a special accentuation of catholicity was in the spotlight: "The whole Catholic Church is present in every local congregation gathered for the hearing of the Word and the celebration of the Lord's Supper. Granted that this is the heart of catholicity, what does it mean for the organized life of the Churches?"[144]

As Vischer pointed out in Montreal and later, the main challenge of the post-Vatican II era was to deal with ecumenical questions in light of catholicity, and with catholicity in light of ecumenism. One year after Montreal, the Faith and Order commission met in Aarhus and insisted on the importance of a dynamic process of analyzing the understanding of catholicity and enquiring into it at greater depth.[145] It goes without saying that this was not an easy process, owing to the very dynamic inherent to the notion of catholicity and to the various changes occurring in the different churches and communities,[146] since the notion of catholicity implies in a very direct form the question of the relationship with the Roman Catholic Church, even if it is clear that catholicity surpasses the latter's boundaries. In fact, as early as 1937, the Roman Catholic ecumenist Yves Congar, called the "father of Roman Catholic ecumenism"[147] by Willem Adolf Visser 't Hooft,[148] pointed out, in his groundbreaking study *Chrétiens désunis*, the challenge of this notion for both the Roman Catholic Church and the ecumenical partners.[149] 30 years later, Vatican II was able to describe the universality of the church with the notion of catholicity, which not only implies an internal dynamic within the Catholic Church and its parts, but goes beyond them by referring to other Christians and finally all mankind (*LG* 13). Thus, the Roman Catholic Church not only improved its own understanding of the relationship between the local churches and the universal church (see the famous "in quibus et ex quibus" in *LG* 23) but could recognize outside itself "elementa plura sanctificationis et veritatis ... quae ut dona Ecclesiae Christi propria, ad unitatem catholicam impellunt" (*LG* 8). As far as ecumenical work was concerned, Vatican II acknowledged that the divisions among Christians rendered the realization of the "plenitudinem catholicitatis" impossible (*UR* 4), immediately adding that this was one of the major reasons why Catholics should contribute to the ecumenical activities around the world.

In this sense, there were concrete results of the atmospheric progress and theological insights of

144 Handspicker, "Faith and Order," 150.

145 *New Delhi to Uppsala, 1961–1968*, 53.

146 John St-Helier Gibaut, "La Catholicité, Foi et Constitution et l'unité de l'Église," in: François-Xavier Amherdt & others, eds., *Vers une catholicité œcuménique?: Actes du colloque "Ensemble et divers. Vers une catholicité œcuménique?" à l'Institut œcuménique de Bossey, les 6 et 7 septembre 2010*, Fribourg, Academic Press, 2013, 209–230, esp. 214, note 4, remarks that the Montreal documents on catholicity do not appear in the conference's report. This said, by studying the "longue durée," he can show that notwithstanding this fact, the dynamic of the notion of catholicity highly impacted the work of Faith and Order. If this dynamic clearly was at work, it leads to a way of conceiving of theology as an expression of the orthopraxis, the catholicity being a gift and a challenge rather than a quantifiable criterium for truth and orthodoxy.

147 Willem Adolf Visser 't Hooft, *Memoirs*, London, SCM Press, 1973, 319.

148 On Visser 't Hooft, who in 1949 met Catholic ecumenists in the Dominican study centre Istina in Paris, and Congar, see *Istina* 48/1, 2003 (monographic number entitled *Deux pionniers de l'unité: Yves Congar et Willem Adolf Visser 't Hooft*).

149 Congar, *Chrétiens désunis*, 115–148. For the importance of the notion in Congar's work and Congar's role in its exploration, see Joseph Famerée & Gilles Routhier, *Yves Congar*, Paris, Cerf, 2008, 57–79. See the contribution by Joseph Famerée in this volume. One year before Congar, the notion was thematized by Gustave Thils, "La notion de catholicité de l'Église dans la théologie modern," *ETL* 13, 1936, 5–73.

Vatican II and Montreal. At the Aarhus meeting in 1964, the working committee of Faith and Order appointed a study group which presented, in Bristol in 1967, the basis of the text discussed during the world assembly of the WCC in Uppsala in 1968, and was entitled "The Holy Spirit and the Catholicity of the Church."[150] The Christological definition of catholicity of Montreal was extended to a trinitarian one. As a possible expression of this catholicity, the idea of a universal council was articulated.[151] In line with Montreal, the notion of catholicity was somehow completed by the notion of conciliarity, and several studies in this direction were initiated.[152] Notably, in Aarhus and Bristol, the importance of the conciliar process in the ancient church was dealt with.[153] After the prospect of a universal council on the part of the world assembly in Uppsala 1968, the world assembly in Nairobi 1975 pleaded for a conciliar fellowship. This preeminence of conciliarity was somehow prefigured in Vischer's analysis of 1961, when he compared New Delhi and the future Vatican II in light of the history of church councils.[154] Moreover, he spoke there of the importance of reception, indeed a major issue for the post-Vatican II situation.[155] In line with Lukas Vischer's vision of 1961, the Uppsala document "The Holy Spirit and the Catholicity of the Church" also invoked the fact that true catholicity was a gift and a challenge, and also insisted that human failure could not destroy catholicity as a gift. Inversely, it was stated that it is the humans' task to make catholicity manifest in history. As for these manifestations, they were manifold and diverse, but they also, and in the first place, demanded a common search for theological expressions. In this sense, at the end of the 1960s, there were many old and new problems, but there was also a new sense of unity in theological research. More than ever, Faith and Order thus stood spiritually and institutionally at the core of a complex theological dialogue.

5 Epilogue: Faith and Order and the Joint Working Group

The promising results of ecumenical reflections within the Roman Catholic Church and within the WCC, along with the results of ecumenical networking between the former and the latter, contributed to a psychological and institutional change in the relationship between these new ecumenical partners. In considering this shift, Visser 't Hooft even articulated "a certain 'nervousness' in Geneva that Rome was becoming the new centre for ecumenical initiative."[156] If one can say that Faith and Order was a kind of theological think-tank within the WCC, the recently founded Joint Working Group[157] constituted a new quality of theological partnership between the WCC and the Roman Catholic Church in which Vischer

150 "The Holy Spirit and the Catholicity of the Church", in: Goodall, ed., *The Uppsala Report 1968*, 11–19.

151 See Michael Quisinsky, "Ökumenische Perspektiven auf Konzil und Konziliarität: Lukas Vischer und die Vision eines 'universalen Konzils,'" in: Quisinsky, *Katholizität der Inkarnation*, 436–451.

152 *New Delhi to Uppsala, 1961–1968*, 58–59.

153 *New Directions in Faith and Order*, 49–58. For the study meetings in Oxford (August 1965) and Bad Gastein (July 1966) see van der Bent, *Six Hundred Ecumenical Consultations*, 20.

154 Vischer, *The World Council of Churches and the Vatican Council*, 289–294.

155 Vischer, *The World Council of Churches and the Vatican Council*, 292. See the later Alois Grillmeier, "Konzil und Rezeption: Methodische Bemerkungen zu einem Thema der ökumenischen Diskussion der Gegenwart," *Theologie und Philosophie* 45/3, 1970, 321–352.

156 Gabriel Flynn, "Vatican II and the World Council of Churches: A Vision for Receptive Ecumenism or a Clash of Paradigms?," *LS* 33/1–2, 2008, 6–29, here 24.

157 Roberto Tucci, "The Ecumenical Movement," 341–350; Lukas Vischer, "The Activities of the Joint Working Group between the Roman Catholic Church and the World Council of Churches 1965–1969," *EcRev* 22/1, 1970, 36–69; Jared Wicks, "Collaboration and Dialogue: The Roman Catholic Presence in the Ecumenical Movement during the Pontificate of Paul VI," in: Istituto Paolo VI, ed., *Paolo VI e l'ecumenismo: Colloquio internazionale di studio (Brescia, 25–27 settembre 1998)*, Brescia, Studium, 2001, 215–267.

played a central role.[158] With its first research topic, "Catholicity and Apostolicity,"[159] the Joint Working Group, consisting in theologians from the WCC and the Roman Catholic Church, directly took up the discussions within Faith and Order, endowing it with an even more ecumenical dimension. In point of fact, since 1964, the idea of a joint commission of theologians from the WCC and the Roman Catholic Church had obtained increasing support, and it was accepted in January 1965 in Enugu by the meeting of the central committee;[160] in February 1965, when cardinal Bea visited the WCC headquarters in Geneva, he confirmed its approval by the SPCU.[161] Needless to say, the Joint Working Group had a merely deliberating function and tried to work in a flexible way without generating new structures. Furthermore, for Vischer, the foundation of the Joint Working Group "cannot be regarded as a final solution" but "must rather be the preparation of more satisfactory solutions."[162] To a certain extent, this Joint Working Group responded to Vischer's judgement after the fourth session of Vatican II: "The question of our reciprocal relationships will probably have to accompany us for a while without being solved, and we can, therefore, only make progress by paying attention to the doors God may open."[163] Notwithstanding its limitations, but believing that the doors opened by God would not be closed by humans, the Faith and Order commission was a natural partner for theological ecumenical collaboration, and when it was about to "study the fundamental issues that continually arise in the dialogue between the Roman Catholic Church and the other Churches,"[164] the theologians of Faith and Order on the one hand and the Roman Catholic Church on the other hand rapidly extended its field, working among other topics such as "Non-Christian Religions"; "Laity and Unity"; "Service to Humanity"; "The Study of Proselitism"; "Mixed Marriages"; "National and Local Councils"; and "Bible Translation."[165] In June 1967, 15 theologians of both the WCC and the Roman Catholic Church dealt with questions in the field of church and society, among others.[166] This shows the complexity of the task of conceiving of catholicity, a notion that nevertheless can more than any other clarify some of the hermeneutical and institutional challenges, concentrated in the "essential question"[167] of the concrete form of the relations between the WCC and the Roman Catholic Church.

158 For Vischer's active role in the conceiving of the future Joint Working Group, see the statement adopted in Rochester 1963: "Relations with the Roman Catholic Church. Statement adopted by the Central Committee," *EcRev* 16/1, 1963, 107–108.

159 "Joint Working Group between the Roman Catholic Church and the World Council of Churches: First Official Report," *EcRev* 18/2, 1966, 243–255, esp. 247. For the meetings in Nemi (May 1967), Oud Poelgeest (December 1967), and Rome (May 1968) see van der Bent, *Six Hundred Ecumenical Consultations*, 21; see also *New Delhi to Uppsala, 1961–1968*, 59 and *Joint Working Group between the Roman Catholic Church and the World Council of Churches: Seventh Report*, Geneva, WCC Publications, 1998.

160 "Relationships between the World Council of Churches and the Roman Catholic Church: Statement adopted by the Central Committee at Enugu," *EcRev* 17/2, 1965, 171–173.

161 *Joint Working Group between the Roman Catholic Church and the World Council of Churches.*

162 Vischer, "After the Fourth Session," 189.

163 Vischer, "After the Fourth Session," 189.

164 *First Report of the Joint Working Group between The Roman Catholic Church and the World Council of Churches*, Geneva, n. pub., 1966, 4.

165 "Joint Working Group between the Roman Catholic Church and the World Council of Churches: Second Official Report," *EcRev* 19/4, 1967, 461–467.

166 Max Kohnstamm, "Report to the General Secretary of the World Council of Churches Concerning the Exploratory Committee on Society, Development and Peace of the World Council of Churches and the Roman Catholic Church, June 1967–June 1968," in: *The Uppsala Report 1968*, 348–354. Participants in the first meeting were Joseph Grémillion, Pio Laghi, Jean Jérôme Hamer, Henri de Riedmatten, Vittorino Veronese, Auguste Vanistendael, Max Kohnstamm, Philip Potter, Paul Albrecht, John C. Bennett, Vitaly Borovoj, Axel von dem Bussche, Richard Fagley, André-Dominique Micheli, Samuel Parmar and Lukas Vischer (Kohnstamm, "Report to the General Secretary," 349–350).

167 "Joint Working Group between the Roman Catholic Church and the World Council of Churches: Second Official Report," 462.

While the Roman Catholic Church's membership in the WCC did not seem to be possible,[168] its membership in Faith and Order became even more important. If it is clear that a theological commission is only as good as its members are, one understands the significance of the presence of Vischer, the bridgebuilder between Vatican II and Faith and Order, between Rome and Geneva, in this Joint Working Group. Like few others, Vischer stands for the unity of the notions of catholicity and conciliarity for

> it may well be of immense importance for relations between the Churches if the Roman Catholic Church should, following the experience of the Second Vatican Council, succeed in giving conciliar form to the structures of the common life of the Church as a whole. The ecumenical movement could thereby receive a new impetus. Therefore, it is not good enough to view this assembly from a distance or to take cognizance only of possible sensational secondary features. The theme itself [the relationship between Rome and the Episcopal Conferences] demands our passionate participation.[169]

If this link was expressed in Uppsala in 1968, it was so as a result of both the conciliar experience of Vatican II and the ecumenical experience within the WCC and beyond it. That both conciliarity and ecumenism entered a crisis from the 1970s constituted a new challenge for the characteristic combination of realism and optimism that distinguished Lukas Vischer, who continued to leave a profound mark on Faith and Order in a new chapter of its history.[170]

168 See also Thomas F. Stransky, "Roman Catholic Membership in the World Council of Churches?," *EcRev* 20/3, 1968, 205–224; Lukas Vischer, "The World Council of Churches, Fellowship of all Churches," *EcRev* 20/3, 1968, 225–244. See now Jan Grootaers, *Rome et Genève à la croisée des chemins (1968–1972): Un ordre de jour inachevé*, Paris, Cerf, 2005.

169 Lukas Vischer, "Some Considerations Regarding the Joint Working Group between the Roman Catholic Church and the WCC: Report to the Central Committee," *EcRev* 21/4, 1969, 354–359, here 358.

170 Quisinsky, "Ökumenische Perspektiven auf Konzil und Konziliarität," 439–449.

Bibliography

Handspicker, Meredith B., "Faith and Order 1948–1968," in: *A History of the Ecumenical Movement*, vol. 2, Harold E. Fey, ed., *The Ecumenical Advance (1948–1968)*, Geneva, WCC Publications, 1986, 143–170.

New Delhi to Uppsala, 1961–1968: Report of the Central Committee to the Fourth Assembly of the World Council of Churches, Geneva, WCC Publications, 1968

Quisinsky, Michael, "Lukas Vischer als 'nichtkatholischer Beobachter' von Konzilsereignis, Konzilsrezeption und Konzilshistoriographie," in: Michael Quisinsky, *Katholizität der Inkarntion: Christliches Leben und Denken zwischen Universalität und Konkretion "nach" dem II. Vatcanum/Catholicité de l'Incarnation: Vie et pensée chrétiennes entre universalité et concrétion après Vatican II*, Münster, Aschendorff, 2016, 124–149.

Quisinsky, Michael, "Ökumenische Perspektiven auf Konzil und Konziliarität: Lukas Vischer und die Vision eines 'universalen Konzils,'" in: Michael Quisinsky, *Katholizität der Inkarnation: Christliches Leben und Denken zwischen Universalität und Konkretion "nach" dem II. Vaticanum/Catholicité de l'Incarnation: Vie et pensée chrétiennes entre universalité et concrétion après Vatican II*, Münster, Aschendorff, 2016, 436–451.

Quisinsky, Michael, "The Ecumenical Dynamic of Vatican II: Lukas Vischer between Geneva and Rome," in: Michael Quisinsky, *Katholizität der Inkarnation: Christliches Leben und Denken zwischen Universalität und Konkretion "nach" dem II. Vaticanum/Catholicité de l'Incarnation: Vie et pensée chrétiennes entre universalité et concrétion après Vatican II*, Münster, Aschendorff, 2016, 80–121.

Quisinsky, Michael, "L'héritage de Lukas Vischer sur Vatican II à l'heure de l'encyclique 'Laudato si,'" in: Philippe Chenaux & Kiril Plamen Kartaloff, eds., *Il Concilio Vaticano II e i suoi protagonisti alla luce degli archivi*, Vatican City, Libreria Editrice Vaticana, 2017, 41–58.

Rodger, Patrick C. & Lukas Vischer, eds., *The Fourth World Conference on Faith and Order: The Report from Montreal 1963*, London, SCM Press, 1964.

Velati, Mauro, *Separati ma Fratelli: Gli osservatori non cattolici al Vaticano II (1962–1965)*, Bologna, Il Mulino, 2014.

Vischer, Lukas , "The World Council of Churches and the Vatican Council," *EcRev* 14/3, 1962, 281–295.

Vischer, Lukas, "Report on Second Vatican Council," *EcRev* 16/1, 1963, 43–59.

Vischer, Lukas, "Roman Catholic Ecumenism and the World Council of Churches," *EcRev* 16/4, 1964, 378–394.

Vischer, Lukas, "The Faith and Order Movement at the Beginning of a New Period," *Mid-Stream* 4/2, 1964, 6-17.

Vischer, Lukas, "Report on the Third Session of Second Vatican Council," in: *Central Commitee of the World Council of Churches: Minutes and Reports of the Eighteenth Meeting, Enugu, Eastern Nigeria, Africa (January 12th to 21st, 1965)*, Geneva, WCC Publications, 1965, 91–102.

Vischer, Lukas, "After the Fourth Session of the Second Vatican Council," *EcRev* 18/2, 1966, 150–189.

Vischer, Lukas, "The Activities of the Joint Working Group between the Roman Catholic Church and the World Council of Churches 1965–1969," *EcRev* 22/1, 1970, 36–69.

Vischer, Lukas, "The Council as an event in the Ecumenical Movement," in: Giuseppe Alberigo & Joseph A. Komonchak, eds., *History of Vatican II*, vol. 5, *The Council and the Transition: The Fourth Period at the End of the Council (September 1965–December 1965)*, Leuven/Maryknoll, Peeters/Orbis Books, 2006, 485–539.

CHAPTER 33

Through a Maelstrom of Events: The WCC from Uppsala to Nairobi (1968–1975)

Gerhard Besier

1 The 1966 Geneva World Conference on Church and Society

In 1966, Willem Adolph Visser 't Hooft's departure as the first secretary general of the WCC marked the end of an era,[1] a deep divide separating him from his successor, Eugene Carson Blake. In the former's autobiography, the Dutch polyglot contently observed how when he addressed people in their native language, they "seemed to forget that I was a visitor and made me feel at home among them," adding how he "always felt rather miserable when I had to speak through an interpreter."[2] In contrast, Blake, from the United States, spoke only English and was almost 60 years old by the time he took office. Ultimately, it was more of a changing of the guard than a generational shift.

Unlike that of his predecessor, Blake's appointment was not without major turmoil. Initially, the executive committee had appointed 45-year-old pastor Patrick C. Rodger of the Scottish Episcopal Church, in doing so bypassing the WCC's central committee which only learned of the appointment later, through the press. In retaliation, the central committee assembled its own nominations committee which almost unanimously elected Blake, a former stated clerk of the UPCUSA, as the WCC's new secretary general in Geneva in February 1966. As a member of the central committee since 1954 and of the executive committee since 1955, Blake was considered for his reputation as both an experienced ecumenist and an excellent leader.

Though at that moment in history tensions between the global North and South were growing, those felt between East and West had by no means died out. This can be seen in the fact that, when it was necessary to find a replacement for Visser 't Hooft, the churches of the Eastern bloc countries – whose influence in the WCC had grown significantly since the Russian Orthodox Church had joined the movement in 1961 – sought to impede the appointment of someone from the United Kingdom or North America as secretary general, albeit ultimately in vain.

Meanwhile, even before the question of electing a new secretary general had appeared on the horizon, the theme for the WCC's upcoming 1966 world conference in Geneva had already been determined. At the central committee's 1962 meeting in Paris, the WCC's department of church and society had expressed its strong interest in choosing a theme in the area of social ethics, a possible title being "God, Man, and Contemporary Society." The following year, at the central committee's meeting in Rochester, delegates approved the proposed topics of discussion and commissioned a considerable number of theologians (mostly experts in Christian ethics and social issues), but also jurists and political scientists, to prepare four preliminary studies on the following themes: Christian social ethics in a changing world; responsible government in a revolutionary age; economic growth in a world perspective; and person and community.

While such a wealth of material could not possibly be discussed to its full extent across the 14 days of the 1966 Geneva world conference, its content

1 On Visser 't Hooft and the first decade of the WCC, see the contribution by Jurjen A. Zeilstra in this volume.

2 Willem Adolph Visser 't Hooft, *Memoirs*, London, SCM Press, 1973, 340–341.

was nonetheless summarized effectively within the final message that the conference addressed to the member churches of the WCC. It declared that it was the task of Christians to strive for "basic changes in society without too much delay," and maintained that those who called themselves brothers in Christ were to take "a more radical and revolutionary position"[3] on the problems in the world. Speaking in Geneva and referring to his own personal experience with the struggle against racism and the defense of civil rights in the United States, Blake asserted that the church had to "identify clearly with the cause of the poor, the discriminated against, the prisoner, the disadvantaged, and the marginalized." The church, continued the newly appointed WCC secretary general, was to "act as a church, taking a stand and joining with those in society who cannot win the struggle for justice, freedom, or equality on their own."[4] It was with Blake's impassioned words that the so-called theology of revolution, as it had come to be known, would thus be incorporated into the WCC's language and agenda.[5]

Blake wanted nothing less than for all of Christendom to rally behind him in his fight against poverty and racism. The Roman Catholic Church would be the first to miss the roll call. While Rome's admittance to the WCC had not been included among the council's short-term goals, closer cooperation between the Church of Rome and the Genevan council on areas of human development and peace seemed to be within reach, especially after the exploratory talks that took place during the 1966 world conference. Indeed, there was no shortage of encouraging signs from the Holy See. In January 1967, the Roman Catholic Church established the Iustitia et pax pontifical commission and, in March of the same year, Pope Paul VI promulgated the encyclical *Populorum progressio*, on the development of peoples. At its first meeting in April 1967, Iustitia et pax expressed its "desire to work as closely as possible with the World Council of Churches,"[6] a wish that would be fulfilled the following year with the founding of SODEPAX, an institute dedicated to research on matters of development and peace, the secretariat of which was held jointly by Catholics and Protestants of the WCC. Its first milestone was an international conference on the subject of world development, held in Beirut at the end of April 1968. In the years to come, SODEPAX would receive considerable financial support from many Western foundations, which also raised high hopes regarding the possibility of ecumenical cooperation between Rome and Geneva on ethical and social issues. However, the WCC left it to the general assembly of July 1968 in Uppsala to decide on the future of continued cooperation with the Catholic Church.[7]

Meanwhile, the global situation of apparent détente characterizing relations between the East and West in 1966 and 1967, alongside internal equilibrium within the WCC, appeared to encourage greater cooperation between the Genevan ecumenical movement and the Catholic Church, albeit only to counterbalance the growing influence of the socialist countries' churches within the council and to dampen the tensions that their ascendency entailed. For example, at the central committee meeting held in Candia, Crete, in August 1967, the Eastern Orthodox delegates declared by minority vote that "the origin of the Vietnam tragedy is the entirely unjustified military

3 *World Conference on Church and Society: Official Report*, Geneva, WCC Publications, 1967, 49.

4 The quotations are translated from the German text Hanfried Krüger, ed., *Appell an die Kirchen der Welt: Dokumente der Weltkonferenz für Kirche und Gesellschaft, Berlin*, Kreuz Verlag, 1968, 104–106.

5 A selection of the papers given at the Geneva conference is offered by Harvey G. Cox, ed., *The Church Amid Revolution: A Selection of the Essays Prepared for the World Council of Churches Geneva Conference on Church and Society*, New York, Association Press, 1967.

6 *Central Committee: Minutes and Reports of the Twentieth Meeting: Heraklion, Crete, Greece, (Aug 15th–26th, 1967)*, Geneva, WCC Publications, 1967, 145.

7 See Joseph J. Spae, "SODEPAX: An Ecumenical and Experimental Approach to World Needs," *EcRev* 26, 1974, 88–99, and Leopoldo J. Niilus, "Efforts for Human Rights of the World Council of Churches and of SODEPAX," *Concilium* 124, 1979, 86–91.

intervention of the USA in the internal life of the Vietnamese people," and that the "withdrawal of the American troops from the territory of Vietnam, without any condition, is absolutely necessary."[8] The socialist delegates also tried, unsuccessfully, to persuade the rest of the central committee to unanimously condemn the Israeli aggression in the Middle East, referencing the conflict that would go down in history as the Six-Day War of June 1967.

2 Uppsala 1968: The Fourth WCC General Assembly

The tensions listed above were not the only ones to color the fourth general assembly of the WCC, held in Uppsala from Jul 4 to 20, 1968. Delegates from the West and what was then known as the Third World also showed that the rifts running through the universal church were very deep. Differing perspectives between traditional theologians and those oriented toward the social sciences, clashing views between conservatives and liberals, between high church members and Presbyterians, between established Christianity of Northern Europe and that of the new churches of the global South emerging alongside the decolonization process, and tensions between youth movement delegates and church dignitaries at the Uppsala convention: all of these rendered the assembly of over 1,000 representatives and participants a seething cauldron. Norman Goodall, who edited the assembly report, commented:

> The whole tone and temper of Uppsala made it clear that a new age is upon us. The winds of change have become hurricanes ... The issues discussed in the following pages [of the report] and the forces which thrust them, often violently, upon the attention of the assembly illustrate the startling newness of the Christian task and the largely uncharted territory into which the ecumenical movement moves. Within the domestic life and leadership of the WCC change is no less in evidence. [These changes] become symbolic of what may well prove to be a radical change of direction with consequences which cannot yet be measured.[9]

A series of tragic world events unfolding in the prelude to the assembly and the general climate of tension at Uppsala acted as a trigger for the upheaval witnessed at the conference: Apr 4 of that year saw the assassination of Martin Luther King Jr., who had agreed to give an official address at Uppsala, while in May the European unrest of 1968 was ignited in Paris. In the meantime, the war in Vietnam had come to a head with the United States government's increasingly harsh response against those demonstrating in the streets in favor of peace, while southern Africa was ravaged by wars of liberation, Mao Zedong's government brought on the Cultural Revolution in China, and the global South continued its descent into an unending spiral of poverty, violence, and agony.[10]

It was particularly the student uprisings, which peaked in Europe during the so-called May 68 in France, that caused turmoil among the Uppsala delegates, especially among the younger participants. Appointed by the WCC executive committee at the behest of the WSCF, the YMCA, and the YWCA, young representatives brought the struggles and aspirations of the student movement with them to the assembly. First and foremost, the youth representatives desired "to make [their] contribution to the total engagement of the

8 *Minutes and Reports of the Twentieth Meeting*, 269.

9 Norman Goodall, "Editorial," in: Norman Goodall, ed., *The Uppsala Report 1968: Official Report of the Fourth Assembly of the World Council of Churches (Uppsala, July 4–20, 1968)*, Geneva, WCC Publications, 1968, xii–xx, here xx.

10 See Risto Lehtonen, *Story of a Storm: The Ecumenical Student Movement in the Turmoil of Revolution*, Grand Rapids, Eerdmans, 1998, 2. More generally, see, Gerd-Rainer Horn, *The Spirit of '68: Rebellion in Western Europe and North America (1956–1976)*, Oxford, Oxford University Press, 2007.

church and the individual believer in the work for peace, social justice, and the equal right of all men to food, education, and work." Additionally, they criticized the advanced age of the vast majority of delegates present in Uppsala which, in the young participants' own words, testified to how forms of "imperialism and paternalism are perpetuated by the structure and theology of the WCC."[11]

In front of the cathedral of Uppsala, where all the participants had convened for the assembly's opening ceremony, signs were displayed protesting an arrogant church in a hungry world and reminding those present of the biblical theme which they themselves had chosen for the conference: "Behold, I make all things new" (Rev 21:5). Swedish police were even called in to protect the general assembly, and in an impassioned speech former WCC youth leader Albert Hendrik van den Heuvel called for young people to finally have a voice in the assembly's decision-making processes. Despite the complexity of the situation, however, the assembly succeeded in carrying out its assigned task of providing reflections on what had been accomplished since the last assembly in 1961 and outlining the WCC's guidelines for the next seven years.

On Jul 7, the fourth day of the proceedings, the Uppsala cathedral again found itself the stage of an unprecedented event, destined to have significant repercussions on the process that the churches had recently undertaken in their return to sharing the Eucharistic table. While a lengthy and complicated debate on intercommunion was being held in the assembly, the Church of Sweden decided to invite all the baptized present at the assembly to join in its own Eucharistic celebration. Having taken place away from cameras and journalists, the Uppsala intercommunion would not have caused the stir that it did if not for the revelation made in the Jul 26 issue of *Time*, divulging that some Catholic observers had also been in attendance.[12] The result was a harsh reprimand from the Catholic bishop of Stockholm, John Edward Taylor, and the personal intervention of Cardinal Johannes Willebrands, president of the SPCU, who was also present at Uppsala as a guest and who was quick to specify on the pages of *La Civiltà Cattolica* that no Catholic present at the assembly as an observer had received communion during that celebration.[13]

Again, in this instance, the Uppsala assembly's impatience in rushing to resolve a problem for which theologians and churches seemed to have no answer found its justification in a series of similar experiments, played out in different contexts but on dates very close to that of the conference. Just over a month earlier, on Jun 2, the day of Pentecost, 70 Christians in Paris – including Catholic priests, pastors, and lay persons – had celebrated the Eucharist together in an apartment on Rue de Vaugirard, explaining their reasons in a letter given to the press and addressed to both the archbishop of Paris, Cardinal François Marty, and to the president of the FPF, pastor Charles Westphal.[14] The year of intercommunion, as 1968 has come to be known, then drew to a close with the Medellín

11 Goodall, "Editorial," xv.

12 "The World Council: From the Sacred to the Secular," *Time*, Jul 26, 1968, 66–67.

13 An account was given of Willebrands's clarification that "none of the observer-delegates" had participated in the Eucharist, while "a few Catholics present in Uppsala in a non-official capacity did, in fact, receive communion in Eucharistic celebrations presided over by non-Catholics," in an interesting way of describing the rite. See "Attività della Santa Sede," *La Civiltà Cattolica* 3, 1968, 395–400, here 396.

14 The related dates and facts are reconstructed in Yann Raison du Cleuziou, "À la fois prêts et surpris: Les chrétiens en Mai 68," in: Denis Pellettier & Jean-Louis Schlegel, eds., *À la gauche du Christ: Les chrétiens de gauche en France de 1945 à nos jours*, Paris, Éditions du Seuil, 2012, 297–322, esp. 317–319. Cardinal Marty responded with a very critical and firm note, see "L'Église catholique et l'intercommunion: Note de Mgr Marty," *La documentation catholique* 65, 1968, 1212–1214. Equally assertive was the response of the FPF that came shortly thereafter, in June: "Résolution du Conseil de la Fédération protestante de France," *Christianisme social* 176, 1968, 385–592.

incident, in which some non-Catholic observers present at CELAM II received communion during the assembly's closing concelebrations.[15]

Having concluded just three years earlier, Vatican II loomed large over the events of 1968. For many of the delegates – especially those who had participated in the council's work as observers – it had instilled hope in the possibility that a new chapter in ecumenical relations with the Catholic Church be inaugurated. Indeed, it was thought that insisting on the contextuality of Christian action – the world setting the agenda for the church – was the most efficient way of bridging the gap between the ecumenical movement and Roman Catholicism. Such an authoritative voice as that of the editor of *La Civiltà Cattolica* (and future cardinal) Roberto Tucci asserted that, despite ecclesiological differences, Rome and Geneva should work to prepare for the day when the Roman Catholic Church joined the WCC. The Uppsala general assembly welcomed this suggestion and declared in its statement on the relations with the Roman Catholic Church that the Joint Working Group should continue to consider the question of Rome's incorporation into the WCC. In affirmation and support of this stance, nine Catholic theologians, officially selected by the Vatican, were appointed as full members of the Faith and Order commission.[16] In the wake of these decisions, the delegates also decided to reappoint the joint secretariat which would head SODEPAX for a further three years.

In his closing report to the assembly, Visser 't Hooft stressed that theological and social-ethical issues were not to be handled separately.[17] Unanimously elected honorary president for life by delegates representing the now 241 churches of the WCC, Visser 't Hooft would continue to make his presence felt in the affairs of the ecumenical body which he had helped found in 1948, while his successor Blake announced from the outset that he would only remain in office until the next general assembly.

3 Soviet Tanks in Prague and the WCC's Reactions

Four weeks after the conclusion of the WCC's fourth general assembly, Warsaw Pact countries initiated a military intervention against the reformist socialist government in Prague. Evangelical Bishop Kurt Scharf of Berlin, who happened to be in the city on Aug 21, 1968, managed to bring an appeal from the synodal council of the ECCB to the West before the borders were closed. The document, which was accompanied by a letter asking the "Christian churches around the world" to intercede with international organizations on behalf of the Czech people and local churches, stated that the country's sovereignty and freedom had been "violated by an external attack," and that the Czechoslovakian churches had supported "our people's efforts for regeneration up to that point." Its authors continued:

> In these efforts, we see the continuation of our best national and spiritual traditions. In the name of our entire church, we protest the direct threats to this process of regeneration, the violation of our state sovereignty, and the occupation of our country by foreign armies, and we demand their withdrawal.[18]

15 See Silvia Scatena, *In populo pauperum: La chiesa latinoamericana dal Concilio a Medellín (1962–1968)*, Bologna, Il Mulino, 2008, 504–507.

16 See Jan Grootaers, "An Unfinished Agenda: The Question of Roman Catholic Membership of the World Council of Churches (1968–1975)" *EcRev* 3, 1997, 305–347.

17 See Willem Adolph Visser 't Hooft, "The Mandate of the Ecumenical Movement," in: Goodall, ed., *The Uppsala Report*, 313–323.

18 *Evangelischer Pressedienst ZR für Informationsabteilung*, Aug 23, 1968, in: WCCA, General Secretariat, Confidential Correspondence on Czechoslovakia 1968, quoted in Armin Boyens, "Ökumenischer Rat der Kirchen und Evangelische Kirche in Deutschland zwischen West und Ost," in: Gerhard Besier, Armin Boyens & Gerhard Lindemann, *Nationaler Protestantismus*

On Aug 28, 1968, senior WCC officials expressed their views on the matter in the following terms:

> We deplore the military intervention into the internal affairs of Czechoslovakia … We note that the new leadership of the Communist Party of Czechoslovakia was attempting reform of the party and of the state by legal means, in no way unfriendly to its eastern neighbors, and that these reforms aimed at enlargement of spiritual and intellectual freedom were and are overwhelmingly supported by the people of Czechoslovakia … We fear the effect of this ill-considered action by the USSR and its allies, because of its damage to the confidence of peace-loving people everywhere … We appeal to the government of the USSR to reconsider the policy which dictated the military intervention, to remove all its troops from Czechoslovakia at the earliest possible moment, and to renounce the use of force or its threat upon its allies.[19]

On Sep 14, 1968, Patriarch Alexy I of Moscow issued a statement whose tone could not have contrasted more wildly with that taken by the WCC, criticizing the language used by the central committee's chairman, the Indian M.M. Thomas, condemning in particular his description of the Soviet army's entry into Prague as a "military intervention":

> The armies of the allied countries, which temporarily have entered into Czechoslovakia – will not interfere in the internal affairs of the Czechoslovak Socialist Republic … The temporary entry of the five allied armies into Czechoslovakia … was necessary for the protection of the socialist structure in Czechoslovakia, to which the Czechoslovakian people is devoted and the very existence of which was threatened by the destructive activities of anti-socialistic forces.[20]

According to the Russian Orthodox Church's version of events, the Warsaw Pact's intervention in Prague was a relief measure intended to protect the Czechoslovakian people threatened by plots orchestrated by the enemies of socialism.

At the WCC's central committee meeting held in Canterbury in August 1969, secretary general Blake revisited the WCC's statement on the events in Czechoslovakia issued the previous year, recalling how the churches of some Eastern European countries had criticized its form and content. In addition to supporting a national church in obvious distress, the statement had served to demonstrate the WCC's impartiality toward the powers involved in the Cold War. Blake commented:

> While the situation in which our member churches find themselves varies widely, it should be understood by this committee that it will always be the attempt of the WCC to be just to all sides of every international conflict even when it is not easy for the churches always to accept the intention or approve the action taken.[21]

---

und Ökumenische Bewegung: Kirchliches Handeln im Kalten Krieg (1945–1990), Berlin, Duncker & Humblot, 1999, 27–321, here 145.

19 *Statement on Czechoslovakia issued by the Officers of the Central Committee of the World Council of Churches*, Aug 27, 1968, in: WCCA, General Secretariat, Confidential Correspondence on Czechoslovakia 1968, quoted in Boyens, "Ökumenischer Rat der Kirchen," 146.

20 *From the Patriarch of Moscow and All Russia. To: The Chairman of the Central Committee of the World Council of Churches, Mr. M.M. Thomas*, Sep 14, 1968, 1, in: WCCA, General Secretariat, Confidential Correspondence on Czechoslovakia 1968, quoted in Boyens, "Ökumenischer Rat der Kirchen," 148.

21 *Central Committee: Minutes and Reports of the Twenty-Third Meeting: University of Kent at Canterbury, Canterbury, Great Britain (Aug 12th–22nd, 1969)*, Geneva, WCC Publications, 1969, 138.

With this appeasing rhetoric, the WCC essentially aligned itself with the policy of détente pursued by the two superpowers and their allies.[22]

4 The PCR

The idea behind WCC's PCR – which was formally launched in 1969 – has a long history, dating back to the 1937 world conference held by Life and Work in Oxford.[23] On that occasion, participants had decisively rejected the racist ideology of National Socialism and its glorification of Aryanism, judging such ideas to be, "in fact, totally unfounded and completely foreign to the innermost nature of the Gospel."[24] In 1948, at the WCC's inaugural general assembly in Amsterdam, delegates reiterated their condemnation of racism, while six years later at the second general assembly held in Evanston, Illinois, they called on member churches to "renounce racial segregation and degradation in all forms and to work for its elimination in their own lives and in society."[25] They were words that as many as five Boer churches in South Africa – all of which members of the WCC – would categorically reject.

On the political level, the OAU formed in Addis Ababa in 1963 was boycotting South Africa and working to keep the issues of apartheid and racism on the United Nations' agenda. That same year, 100 African churches gathered in Kampala, Uganda, where they established the AACC. With their help and thanks to the support of the IRR, which was critical of the Pretoria government's apartheid policy, in 1964 the WCC organized a consultation on "The Christian and Race Relations in Southern Africa" in Mindolo, Zambia, with its primary discussion centered around the legitimacy of the use of violence in struggles for liberation.[26] While the tendency to favor peaceful forms of resistance was still predominant, after the Geneva conference of 1966 and the concomitant spread of the so-called theology of revolution through Geneva's ecumenical circles, the WCC's attitude toward armed struggle appeared to radically change.

First, they sought to gain a foothold in the Catholic Church, especially after the March 1967

22 See Klaus Hildebrand, *Geschichte der Bundesrepublik Deutschland*, vol. 4, *Von Erhard zur Großen Koalition (1963–1969)*, Stuttgart, Deutsche Verlags-Anstalt, 1986, 337; and Carole Fink & Bernd Schaefer, eds., *Ostpolitik, 1969–1974: European and Global Responses*, New York, Cambridge University Press, 2009.

23 See Claude E. Welch Jr., "Mobilizing Morality: The World Council of Churches and Its Program to Combat Racism (1969–1994)," *HRQ* 23, 2001, 863–910, esp. 872–882.

24 See Armin Boyens, "Die Südafrika-Problematik und der Ökumenische Rat der Kirchen in Genf," *KZG* 9, 1996, 232–250, here 233, and, more recently, Philippe Denis, "Reunion of Christendom or Ecumenism?: Relations Between Catholics and Protestants Before Vatican II in the South African Magazine The Southern Cross," *RHE* 106, 2011, 546–570. For articles and documents on the issue from the years 1937 to 1967, see Klaus-Martin Beckmann, ed., *Die Kirche und die Rassenfrage*, Berlin, Kreuz-Verlag, 1967; and Klaus-Martin Beckmann, ed., *Rasse, Kirche und Humanum: Ein Beitrag zur Friedensforschung*, Gütersloh, Gütersloher Verlagshaus Gerd Mohn, 1969.

25 Boyens, "Die Südafrika-Problematik," 236.

26 In his report on the role of Christians in a rapidly changing social climate, Visser 't Hooft also addressed the issue of violent resistance: "Christians have always been and still are deeply divided on this point. Calvin warned against the use of violence ... It is safe to say that the difference between violent and non-violent resistance is not as absolute as radical pacifists claim. Both are forms of pressure, or rather counterpressure. Both are ethically compromised because they use power and the use of power is never pure. It should be added that violence has its own dynamic because it generates new violence. Moreover, violence between national social and racial groups in general creates a deep rift that makes any form of peaceful coexistence almost impossible to achieve. The deepest division between peoples is a river of blood. ... It seems to me that most situations offer many more opportunities for nonviolent resistance than most people realize"; Willem Adolph Visser 't Hooft, "Die Rolle der Christen im rapiden Wendel der Gesellschaft," in: Willem Adolph Visser 't Hooft, *Hauptschriften*, vol. 1, *Die Ganze Kirche für die ganze Welt*, Stuttgart, Kreuz-Verlag, 1967, 82–95, here 91–92.

encyclical *Populorum progressio*'s scathing condemnation of racism, poverty, injustice, and exploitation, as well as its statements almost justifying revolutionary insurrection against tyrannies. In August, at the first central committee meeting chaired by Blake, delegates adopted a statement on racism in which they affirmed their willingness to seek the support and cooperation of the Roman Catholic Church. The issue was then referred to the Joint Working Group between Rome and Geneva, while Blake, alongside a number of Catholic representatives from the United States, hoped that the WCC, the pope, and the patriarch of Constantinople would draft a joint document against all forms of racism to be presented before the United Nations on Mar 21, 1968, the International Day for the Elimination of Racial Discrimination.[27] However, since the initiative would prove ineffective and the Joint Working Group between Rome and Geneva made no progress, Blake instead decided to present his own "Program of Study and Action for the Elimination of Racism" at the Uppsala world assembly.

His proposal, however, did not find unanimous support among the delegates, the majority of whom leaned toward methods and forms of resistance that would exclude the use of armed struggle. As a result, the motion was sent back to the central committee with the request to present an improved version of it.[28] Once revised in Uppsala, the amended version instructed the department on church and society to conduct preparatory consultations that would serve to prepare a "crash programme ... on the urgent matter of racism."[29] The first of these, held in 1969 in Notting Hill, London, from May 19 to 24, focused on white racism and the use of violence in combatting racial discrimination.[30] The hope expressed in the concluding report was that the WCC churches, working under a "principle of reparation," would recognize that they had "benefitted from racially exploitative economic systems" and would agree to "immediately allocate a significant portion of their total resources ... to organizations of the racially oppressed."[31] A similar demand for redress – in this case from white US churches toward black churches – had already been made a month earlier on Apr 26 by black preacher James Forman in his "Black Manifesto."[32] The report of the Notting Hill consultation culminated in the ardent declaration that "if all other attempts fail, the WCC and its churches will support resistance movements, including revolution, aimed at overthrowing the

27 See T.P. Melady to Paul VI, Vatican City, Aug 31, 1967 (copy), in: WCCA, General Secretariat, Race, Frequent Race-Post Uppsala 1968–70, folder "Race general 1967–70." In late September, not having received a reply, Thomas Patrick Melady, the representative of Pax Romana at the United Nations, then wrote to a monsignor in the Secretariat of State announcing his visit to Rome on Oct 9. Additionally, he proposed a meeting in Geneva where the pope, the ecumenical patriarch, and the secretary general could sign the joint declaration. There was no response from Rome. See T.P. Melady to Msgr. P. Laghi, Sep 25, 1967, transcript for Blake, in: WCCA, General Secretariat, Race. Frequent Race-Post Uppsala, 1968–70, folder "Race general 1967–70," both letters quoted in Boyens, "Ökumenischer Rat der Kirchen," 158.

28 Goodall, ed., *The Uppsala Report*, 192.

29 *Central Committee: Minutes and Reports of the Twenty-Second Meeting: Uppsala, Sweden (2nd and 3rd July, 18th and 20th July, 1968)*, Geneva, WCC Publications, 1968, 8.

30 The WCC staff point persons were: Eugene Carson Blake (speaker); Rena Karefa-Smart (research secretary of the department for cooperation between men and women in the church, family, and society); Baldwin Sjollema (director of the PCR from 1969); and David Gill (theologian and pastor of the Congregational Union of Australia and, from 1970–1982, a member of the WCC's directive staff).

31 *Minutes and Reports of the Twenty-Third Meeting*, 274.

32 See the complete text of the "Black Manifesto," in: Gayraud S. Wilmore & James H. Cone, eds., *Black Theology: A Documentary History*, Maryknoll, Orbis Books, 1979, 80–89. For further literature on the topic see: Jill K. Gill, *Embattled Ecumenism: The National Council of Churches, the Vietnam War, and the Trials of the Protestant Left*, DeKalb, Northern Illinois University Press, 2011; and Leilah Danielson, Marian Mollin & Doug Rossinow, eds., *The Religious Left in Modern America: Doorkeepers of a Radical Faith*, New York, Palgrave Macmillan, 2018.

political and economic tyranny that makes racism possible."[33]

Though the proposal for redress espoused in the document was met with no open opposition during the meeting, in an exchange of internal notes some observers warned the central committee against adopting the program as it had been outlined at the Notting Hill meeting. In a letter addressed to the director of Faith and Order Lukas Vischer, the Russian Orthodox Church's representative to the WCC, Fr. Vitaly Borovoy, expressed his concerns that such demands could be used as a pretext for making political accusations against the United States, South Africa, Rhodesia, and the West in general, leading the churches of those countries to reduce their economic contributions to the WCC and causing serious repercussions for the body's already precarious financial situation.[34]

The PCR that the central committee finally launched in Canterbury, in August 1969, consisted of two components: the actual text of the program, accompanied by a statement condemning racism, especially that perpetrated by white people, and the establishment of a special fund – initially to cover a period of five years – to finance specific operations. On a theological level, discrimination on the basis of race would be treated as a sin, while racism, the document continued, did not constitute an immutable human characteristic and could therefore be effectively fought and defeated, as was the case with slavery and other manifestations of human sin: "In the light of the Gospel and in accordance with its principles and methods," it was proclaimed, "Christians must be involved in this struggle and, wherever possible, in association with all people of goodwill."[35]

The WCC thus appealed to its churches "to move beyond charity ... and sacrificial action leading to new relationships of dignity and justice among all men and to become agents for the radical reconstruction of society."[36] The financial resources needed to put the project into practice came from the above-mentioned special fund. The WCC led by example, pouring a hefty 1,470,104.99 USD from its already meager funds into the new program's coffers: an endowment that was not without controversy, as the central committee's finance commission reported in the records.[37]

The concrete implementation of the project was entrusted to a special secretariat coordinated by the Dutch sociologist Baldwin Sjollema and placed under Blake's direct responsibility. Requesting that their example be followed, the central committee called on member churches to raise at least 300,000 USD to be distributed amongst "organizations of oppressed racial groups [and] organizations supporting victims of racial injustice whose purposes are not inconsonant with the general purposes of the World Council."[38] Initially, the reaction of members was rather lukewarm, especially in response to the request for increased donations and fundraising for the project. In fact, the executive committee's resolution to offer financial support to liberation movements in southern Africa in their humanitarian tasks, sparked heated debates when it was announced in early September 1970, attracting criticism from not only within, but also from outside the association of partner churches.[39] For example, Anglican Bishop Alphaeus Hamilton Zulu, a black South African and one of the WCC's presidents, refused to support the special fund and spoke against the anti-racism program not only in his own country

33 Hanfried Krüger, ed., *Ökumenische Bewegung (1969–1972)*, Korntal, Evangelischer Missionsverlag, 1975, pp. 68–69. See also Klaus-Martin Beckmann, *Rasse, Entwicklung und Revolution: Der Notting-Hill-Report und zugehörige Dokumente*, Stuttgart, Evangelischer Missionsverlag, 1970.

34 V. Borovoy to L. Vischer, no date, probably early August 1969, in: WCCA, 994.3.50.2, Relations with Eastern Europe (files of Lukas Vischer), folder "Documents on Russian Orthodox Church 1969–1970–1971," quoted in Boyens, "Ökumenischer Rat der Kirchen," 160.

35 *Minutes and Reports of the Twenty-Third Meeting*, 271.

36 *Minutes and Reports of the Twenty-Third Meeting*, 273.

37 *Minutes and Reports of the Twenty-Third Meeting*, 277.

38 *Minutes and Reports of the Twenty-Third Meeting*, 277.

39 See "Texte zum Rassismusbeschluß des Ökumenischen Rates," *epd-Dokumentation* 51, 1970.

but also in a series of lectures delivered across the United States.[40] He was joined in his reproval by Ben Marais, a professor at the University of Pretoria who had written to Blake accusing him of being a "subsidizer of violence"[41] and calling for the program's withdrawal.

On Sep 15, 1970, the council chairman of the EKD, Bishop Hermann Dietzfelbinger, wrote to Blake to express his disquietude over the executive committee's resolution to finance African liberation movements, as well as to request "appropriate clarifications" in view of the upcoming EKD council meeting.[42] In a message addressed to his congregations, Dietzfelbinger declared that "even in such cases, Christianity cannot renounce its fundamental principle of rejecting the use of violence in political and social conflicts,"[43] and a meeting held between 19 senior representatives of the EKD and a delegation of nine WCC members would prove incapable of assuaging the formers' doubts and apprehension. At times, even the line espoused by Blake on the issue of violence appeared undecided; while on the one hand he declared himself faithful to the idea of a "redistribution of power from the powerful to the powerless," on the other he asserted that the WCC would never abandon its "traditional support for nonviolent action and reconciliation efforts."[44] Additional exchanges between German bishops and the WCC secretary general further reinforced the EKD's reservations about the PCR. Ultimately, most of the regional churches, as well as the EKD, agreed to support the PCR in principle as long as only voluntary donations and not church tax revenues were used. In contrast, the BEK had taken a vastly different tack, deciding to hold a "special fundraiser as part of their Bread for the World campaign" to financially aid the WCC initiative.[45]

The dispute over the WCC's PCR had ended up raising questions about the nature of the church itself. As the minutes of the 1971 central committee meeting in Addis Ababa demonstrate, not only the EKD, but also other WCC churches were calling for discussion on ecclesiological issues of principle. In fact, the 1971 delegates demanded "a study be undertaken under WCC auspices on violent and non-violent methods of social change in view of the growing concern about this issue among Christians in every part of the world."[46]

In August 1973, the WCC's church and society department submitted a new survey for approval to the central committee meeting in Geneva, which reported the existence of at least three different perspectives on the use of force among the WCC member churches:

(a) Some believe that nonviolent action is the only possibility consistent with obedience to Jesus Christ. ... Nonviolent action is for them a witness to the transcendent power of God

40 During a lecture tour of the United States, Bishop Zulu clarified his reservations about the special fund. He was concerned that "no government could accept the situation where all the churches were allied with those who were supporting enemies who sought to overthrow the government"; J. Smith to E.C. Blake, Sep 22, 1971, in: WCCA, General Secretariat Central Committee 1968–1975 (Uppsala-Nairobi), Correspondence with presidents and officers, folder "Smith, Rev. Dr. John USA 1968–75," quoted in Boyens, "Ökumenischer Rat der Kirchen," 163.

41 "Letter to Dr Carson Blake," *Pro Veritate* 9, 1970, 12.

42 H.W. Dietzfelbinger to E.C. Blake, Sep 15, 1970, in: WCCA, General Secretariat, Race, folder "PCR 1970–71," quoted in Boyens, "Ökumenischer Rat der Kirchen," 164.

43 "Erklärung des Rates der EKD an die Gemeinden," *epd-Dokumentation* 45, 1970, 22–23.

44 E.C. Blake to H.W. Dietzfelbinger, Oct 6, 1970, attached: Position statement of the secretary general of the WCC on the EKD's declaration to the congregations, Sep 24, 1970, 3, section 6, in: WCCA, General Secretariat, Race, folder "PCR 1970–71," quoted in Boyens, "Ökumenischer Rat der Kirchen," 165.

45 A. Schönherr to E.C. Blake, Jan 9, 1971, in: WCCA, General Secretariat, country files, Eastern Europe – DDR (incl. CC), vol. 1, 1971–81, quoted in Boyens, "Ökumenischer Rat der Kirchen," 167. Bishop Albrecht Schönherr was then president of the BEK.

46 *Central Committee: Minutes and Reports of the Twenty-Fourth Meeting: Addis Ababa, Ethiopia (Jan 10th–21st, 1971)*, Geneva, WCC Publications, 1971, 55.

in Jesus Christ, a way of faith which will be justified by him and his power alone.

(b) Some are prepared to accept the necessity of violent resistance as a Christian duty in extreme circumstances. Not only must the cause be just and all other possibilities exhausted, but also there must be reasonable expectation that violent resistance will attain the ends desired, the methods must be just and there must be a positive understanding of the order which will be established after the violence succeeds. Violence will then be understood as the *ultima ratio*. …

(c) Some find themselves already in situations of violence in which they cannot help but participate. Nonviolence does not represent itself as an option unless they would withdraw totally from the struggle for justice. In this situation the problem becomes to reduce the sum total of violence in the situation and to liberate human beings for just and peaceful relations with each other … The problem of Christian responsibility, then, is to humanize the means of conflict and to build structures of peace wherever possible within it.[47]

The central committee further declared that there were "forms of violence in which Christians may not participate," including "the conquest of one people by another or the deliberate oppression of one class or race by another." Christians would not be permitted to employ "torture in all forms," nor could they engage in "the holding of innocent hostages, or the deliberate or indiscriminate killing of innocent non-combatants." The central committee also noted that "methods and techniques of non-violence, in the struggle for a just society" were far from exhausted and that a more thorough exploration of these deserved "the strongest possible support from the WCC and the churches."[48]

The PCR had not only caused heated controversy among WCC member churches, but it also contributed to the undermining of relations between Geneva and Rome. In the authoritative opinion of Fr. Christophe-Jean Dumont, there were as many as eight reasons as to why the Roman Catholic Church should not join the WCC, one of which was the excessive frequency with which the latter took sides in major international issues or sided with factions and liberation movements despite not enjoying the same diplomatic status as the Catholic Church.[49] Negotiations initiated by both sides under the best auspices in 1970 had thus already stalled. In July 1972, a report on Rome's possible membership of the WCC concluded that the Catholic Church's entry into the body was not an option for the foreseeable future, citing a long list of reasons for the decision which adjudged the incompatibility of their respective ecclesiologies (that is, the notion of a single church against the aspiration for a communion of churches) as the primary issue.[50]

The optimism and ecumenical enthusiasm that had characterized the years from 1966 to 1968 had, in short, given way to a cautious distancing whose effects were soon felt. When the first secretary of SODEPAX, Jesuit George Harold Dunne,

47 See the study "Violence, Nonviolence, and the Struggle for Social Justice," in: Michael Kinnamon & Brian E. Cope, eds., *The Ecumenical Movement: An Anthology of Key Texts and Voices*, Geneva, WCC Publications, 1997, 216–218, here 217.

48 "Violence, Nonviolence, and the Struggle," 217.

49 In a study from 1997, Catholic historian Jan Grootaers reported Dumont's concerns as follows: "The juridical status of the Holy See remains a considerable obstacle to membership of the WCC, especially because of the readiness of the WCC to speak out on international affairs, an area in which the two bodies did not at all have the same status in terms of international diplomacy. On this point – a sensitive one for both Geneva and Rome – Dumont referred specifically to difficulties which could be posed by the WCC's commitment to action to combat racism, including financial support to organizations, notably in southern Africa, which used violent means in the liberation struggle"; Grootaers, "An Unfinished Agenda," 315.

50 See "Patterns of Relationships between the Roman Catholic Church and the World Council of Churches," *EcRev* 24, 1972, 247–288.

left Geneva at the expiration of his term, Rome hesitated to appoint a successor, waiting for clarification from WCC leadership on what the joint commission's life expectancy was to be. For the Holy See, the problem lay in ensuring that SODEPAX would not become an independent entity with its own program and structure, but remain only a direct link between Rome and Geneva.[51] Against the background of SODEPAX's partial failure and Rome's disinclination to joining the WCC, it was unsurprising that Blake, in his last report as secretary general read to the central committee meeting in Utrecht in 1972, expressed his pessimism regarding the future of ecumenical relations between Geneva and Rome.[52]

5 The End of Blake's Term in Office: Taking Stock

At Addis Ababa in January 1971, the central committee regretfully noted Blake's letter of resignation, dated Jul 8, 1970, and appointed an 18-member committee to find his successor.[53] Blake's merits certainly included his efforts to make the WCC's work more effective and to relieve the secretary general of some of their administrative work; moreover, it was Blake who presented the central committee in Addis Ababa with the first results of the administrative reform that the WCC had begun ten years earlier in New Delhi, when the IMC had merged with the Genevan council.[54] The staff had been divided into three planning sections: unit 1 included Faith and Order, CWME, the working group on church and society, and the working group for dialogue with men of living faiths and ideologies; unit 2 consisted of the CCPD, the CCIA, the PCR, and CICARWS; and unit 3 was in charge of education (general and Christian education), communication, publications, and the handling of relations with regional and national Christian councils.

This structural reform, however, failed to solve the WCC's constant problem of funding. Under Blake's presidency, staff had significantly increased in number and the salaries of its employees had also been considerably augmented. To compensate for its financial difficulties the WCC had, up to that time, relied mainly on assistance from the EKD, whose membership dues had almost quintupled between 1960 and 1966, growing from 125,000 DM to 600,000 DM.[55] In November 1967, at the request of the director of the WCC's finance and administration branch, Frank Northam, the EKD agreed to further increase its contribution by 33%, from 600,000 to 800,000 DM.[56] Two years later, Blake again approached the West Germans with a request for a special grant. Initially, he had estimated the financial deficit to be covered at 1 million DM,[57] but due to declining contributions from US member churches, the deficit to be repaired had risen by 1.3 million DM. By the end of the following year, contributions to the WCC's general budget from the EKD would total 2.8 million DM.[58] In 1972 alone, a total of 4,703,718 DM

51 *Central Committee: Minutes and Reports of the Twenty-Fifth Meeting: Utrecht, The Netherlands (12–23 August, 1972)*, Geneva, WCC Publications, 1972, 215–219.

52 *Minutes and Reports of the Twenty-Fifth Meeting*, 133–137.

53 *Minutes and Reports of the Twenty-Fourth Meeting*, 99–100.

54 *Minutes and Reports of the Twenty-Fourth Meeting*, 161–171.

55 See the annotations of Frank Northam from 1971, no date, in: WCCA, Germany, Federal Republic, EKD Finance 1966–74, cited in Boyens, "Ökumenischer Rat der Kirchen," 173.

56 See Northam's report of Nov 8, 1967, in: WCCA, General Secretariat, Confidential Correspondence Visits to Germany, folder "West Germany 1967–69," cited in Boyens, "Ökumenischer Rat der Kirchen," 174.

57 The PCR, with its special fund, had contributed to this deficit, as seen in a letter to the German members of the central committee, Aug 17, 1969, in: WCCA, General Secretariat, Frequent Correspondence Cu-Ge up to December 1970, folder "Dietzfelbinger," cited in Boyens, "Ökumenischer Rat der Kirchen," 174.

58 See Frank Northam, *Summarized presentation to the Council of the EKD, February 1970 of urgent financial needs*, Feb 9, 1970, in: WCCA, General Secretariat, Confidential Correspondence Visits to Germany, folder

entered the WCC coffers from the churches in Federal Germany, establishing the EKD as the primary funder of the WCC. By way of comparison, one need only consider that the contributions of all United States' churches to the WCC's general budget in 1969 was only 2.8 million DM.[59]

In fact, unlike the German ones, other churches reacted by reducing payments and donations during instances in which Geneva adopted resolutions that were contrary to their convictions, such as the implementation of the PCR and its special fund. Blake was also far less successful than Visser 't Hooft in avoiding polarization within the body he headed. In Utrecht, in August 1972, the central committee finally addressed the problem in a letter to the churches entitled "Committed to Fellowship," which stated:

> To some people in some countries, it has seemed as if the WCC has turned from being a fellowship of the churches concerned to serve the unity of the church, into a group bringing pressure on the churches for certain social or political activities. This is not so ... Many of us in our churches experience the agonizing discomfort of the polarization of opinion into two or more warring camps. Here in Utrecht we have realized that we shall not be spared the same experience in the WCC. The Programme to Combat Racism has sparked off vivid controversies. ... Most difficult of all, we are becoming aware just how all-pervasive are the structures of racism and of economic oppression and thus how the struggle for justice inevitably divides us. ... The church does not have to seek out where she can enter the battles of our time; they are raging through our own community. ... In witnessing, we can but press on to make full use of that fellowship for greater justice. ... The church's unity must allow ample space for diversity and for the kind of open, mutual confrontation and correction that we have glimpsed this week.[60]

6 The New Secretary General: Philip Potter, a Representative of the Third World

On Aug 16, 1972, assistant secretary general and director of the CWME Philip Potter was unanimously elected by the central committee to serve as the new WCC secretary general for a five-year term. In the media, the Jamaican Methodist was portrayed as a representative of the Third World – not least because he was black, despite having lived in Europe, where he had held various positions within the ecumenical movement since 1948. Potter spoke German and French fairly well, but like Blake relied on an interpreter during official meetings. In his inaugural address, he invoked a fellowship of churches that was to be made "alive and real," and added, "I stand with you in the knowledge that we will not only stay together, but grow together and go forward together, and suffer together under the sign of the Cross and in the power of the risen Lord."[61]

At the central committee meeting in Utrecht in 1972, the head of the working group in charge of implementing the PCR, Sjollema, reported that a fifth priority had been added to the four already featured on the group's agenda, which concerned "the global economic structures that reinforce racism, emanating principally from Western powers." Sjollema's proposed solution was "the implementation of an investment policy in southern Africa."[62] Considering that foreign outlay in the

"West Germany 1970–71," cited in Boyens, "Ökumenischer Rat der Kirchen," 174.

59 See the petition to the German members of the central committee, in: WCCA, General Secretariat, Frequent Correspondence Cu-Ge up to December 1970, folder "Dietzfelbinger," cited in Boyens, "Ökumenischer Rat der Kirchen," 175.

60 *Minutes and Reports of the Twenty-Fifth Meeting*, 142–143.

61 *Minutes and Reports of the Twenty-Fifth Meeting*, 64.

62 *Minutes and Reports of the Twenty-Fifth Meeting*, 24.

region had the effect of reinforcing the white minority regimes, the report recommended that the WCC sell all existing holdings and cease to invest in companies involved in business activities in southern African countries. What is more, the capital resources available to the WCC were no longer to be deposited in banks that cultivated business dealings with these countries, and all member churches and Christians in general were expected to follow Geneva's example. Also attached was a list with the names of businesses and banks to boycott, particularly those conducting business in southern African countries.

Caught in a frenzy over his mission, by mid-December 1971 Sjollema had already called for the entire WCC staff to focus on combatting racism perpetrated by white people and to align all its resolutions and programs with the principles and the agenda of the PCR. At the second WMC in Bangkok, held between late December 1972 and early January 1973 on the theme "salvation today," delegates drafted a letter to the churches in which Sjollema's thoughts were closely echoed:

> The scandals of racism, of social injustices, of economic and political oppression, the tragic shame of the Indochina war or the bloody suppression of liberation movements, the dehumanization of technological civilization and the threat that it poses for the future of humanity, all these challenge Christians urgently to express in action the salvation of Jesus Christ.[63]

In response to the proposal for a form of moratorium on payments by missionary societies to beneficiary churches in the global South, the delegates offered the following statement:

> We have also examined more radical solutions, such as the recent proposal for a moratorium in the sending of funds and personnel for a set period of time. The whole debate on the moratorium springs from our failure to relate to one another in a way which does not dehumanize. The moratorium would enable the receiving church to find its identity, set its own priorities and discover within its own fellowship the resources to carry out its authentic mission. It would also enable the sending church to rediscover its identity in the context of the contemporary situation.[64]

The WMC's resolutions sparked fierce criticism, especially within conservative evangelical circles. On Feb 26, 1973, Horst Bürkle, director of the Institute of Missiology and Studies of Religion at the University of Munich's Faculty of Protestant Theology, posed the question as to whether "our sister churches be deprived henceforth, of our personal and financial contributions and instead be offered as new partners to groups fighting against existing political systems?"[65]

Those among the conservative evangelicals who had always harbored reservations about the WCC now had the excuse to bring within their ranks even those who had refrained from openly criticizing the Geneva-based ecumenical organization. As the rift between conservative evangelicals and the WCC deepened, it became apparent that it was not only Western evangelicals who strongly criticized the WMC, but also the Russian Orthodox Church. On Aug 7, 1973, a week before the central committee's Geneva meeting, Patriarch Pimen of Moscow had written to central committee chairman M.M. Thomas to express his dismay over the letter to the churches sent in January by the delegates of the Bangkok conference:

63 *Bangkok Assembly 1973: Minutes and Report of the Assembly of the Commission on World Mission and Evangelism of the World Council of Churches (December 31, 1972, and January 9–12, 1973)*, Geneva, WCC Publications, 1973, 2.

64 *Bangkok Assembly 1973*, 106.

65 *Epd-Dokumentation* 17, 1973, 60ff.

> Nothing is said about the ultimate goal of salvation, in other words, about eternal life in God; nor does anything point to the moral improvement and perfection as an indispensable condition for the achievement of this goal. … In the documents there are statements that have no clear and direct confirmation by the Scriptures.[66]

Essentially, Pimen refused to share in the view that "where there are no conditions of life worthy of man, one cannot even speak of salvation today." According to the patriarch, "salvation is not an adjunct to human existence or an 'excess' available only for those who are already in favorable conditions, but it is a bringing of man to a fulness of being from the state he is in now."[67]

To remedy the situation, already in early 1973 Potter, having taken office on Nov 1, 1972, sought to contact as many member churches as possible, beginning with those that had most heavily criticized him. For example, in May 1973, the FSPC had produced an internal document on the antiracism program of the WCC which was intended to serve as a basis for discussion. It began with a series of very specific questions: "Was it the task of the church to interfere in economic and political life? Was the WCC not one-sided in its choice of African voices? How did the WCC arrive at decisions? What authority did WCC statements have?"[68]

In his first report as the new secretary general submitted in August 1973, Potter could not avoid the need to address the grievances of the churches regarding the social programs that the WCC had promoted since Uppsala, seeming to show more sympathy toward the theological criticisms raised by the Orthodox Church than toward those put forward by the Western churches. He acknowledged that the former had the honesty and the courage to squarely face what they "regard as unfortunate trends in the World Council" while in response to the Western churches' accusation that there was an "apparent absence of rigorous theological work," he countered that "the theologians of the older churches in Europe can no longer speak for others and in certain historical and scholastic forms."[69] With this decisive affirmation, Potter betrayed his lack of regard for the theological traditions from which the WCC had emerged.

At the 1973 meeting, however, what most captured the central committee's attention was the document on "Violence, Non-Violence, and the Struggle for Social Justice."[70] Its first draft had been criticized for failing to mention the situation in Eastern Europe, though when the issue was later included in a new preface to the document, it was the leaders of the Eastern churches who protested.[71] The solution, it was decided, was to remove from the text any reference to the state of Christianity on the other side of the Iron Curtain.

Originally, the subsequent 1975 assembly was programmed to be held in the Indonesian capital, Jakarta. The central committee had already accepted an invitation to that effect at the 1972 Utrecht meeting, and communicated the choice of venue to its member churches.[72] While hosting a WCC general assembly constituted a prestigious occasion for Indonesia, the anticommunist regime of general Haji Mohammed Suharto – who had seized power in 1965 by way of a military

66 The text of the letter from Patriarch Pimen to the WCC's central committee is quoted in: Constantin G. Patelos, ed., *The Orthodox Church in the Ecumenical Movement: Documents and Statements (1902–1975)*, Geneva, WCC Publications, 1978, 47–52, here 49, 51.

67 Patelos, ed., *The Orthodox Church*, 50.

68 Elisabeth Adler, *A Small Beginning: An Assessment of the First Five Years of the Programme to Combat Racism*, Geneva, WCC Publications, 1974, 49.

69 *Central Committee: Minutes and Reports of the Twenty-Sixth Meeting: Geneva, Switzerland (22–29 August 1973)*, Geneva, WCC Publication, 1973, 141–142.

70 *Minutes and Reports of the Twenty-Sixth Meeting*, 19–23.

71 Walter Müller-Römheld, "Kontinuität und Wandel: Die 26. Zentralausschußitzung des Ökumenischen Rates der Kirchen in Genf 1973," *ÖR* 22, 1973, 513–524, esp. 520.

72 *Minutes and Reports of the Twenty-Fifth Meeting*, 74.

coup – was considered a political enemy by the USSR. Suharto was very open to economic investment from NATO countries and had cooperated closely with both the United States, which appreciated his liberal economic policies, and the Federal Republic of Germany. On the domestic front, however, Suharto acted brutally against his political opposition, ordering the assassination of communists and students critical of his government during the years marking his rise to power, culminating in a death toll estimated between 400,000 and 1 million between 1965 and 1966, in addition to annihilating Indonesia's Chinese population.

In mid-February 1974, the Russian Orthodox metropolitan and member of the WCC's executive committee Nikodim (Rotov) expressed his church's desire that the location of the fifth general assembly scheduled for the following year be changed, stating that the political situation in Indonesia was an impediment to delegates from socialist countries, that the climate was unhealthy, and that the city of Jakarta was too far from Russia and too expensive for the Moscow Patriarchate. Metropolitan Juvenal (Poyarkov), supporting his colleague, let it be known in advance that none of the delegates from the USSR would attend the assembly were it to be held in the Indonesian capital. In light of the protests received, the central committee reconsidered the question at the West Berlin meeting of August 1974 and, upon the recommendation of the executive committee which had met in mid-February of that year in Bad Saarow, it was decided that the assembly be moved from Jakarta to Nairobi.[73]

7 The WCC's Discussion on Human Rights from 1971 to 1975

In response to the supplication of the American, Swedish, and German churches, in Addis Ababa in 1971 the central committee addressed the issue of human rights for the first time. After intense discussion, it was decided that the CCIA be charged with the task of organizing a consultation "to focus member churches' concern on human rights."[74] Reflecting the urgency of the issue, in the spring of 1972 the general synod of the NHK penned an open letter to Blake expressing "their concern about the disregard for human rights in Eastern Europe."[75]

The issue thus returned to the top of the central committee's agenda at its 1972 meeting in Utrecht and then again in Geneva in August 1973, on which occasion the delegates received a 10-page report from the CCIA on the subject and the program of the human rights consultation they had begun to organize the year prior. It was an extremely realistic report in which the commission acknowledged the possibility that "it might not be possible to carry out in full the plans outlined because of the absence of adequate financial support."[76] Instead, at the central committee's meeting of August 1974 in West Berlin, delegates learned that the conference would be held in Austria in October of that year.[77]

The WCC seemed to have reverted to the position it had taken during the third assembly meeting of 1961 in New Delhi, when it recognized "the Universal Declaration of Human Rights, proclaimed by the United Nations in December 1948, as an important instrument in promoting respect for and observance of human rights and fundamental freedom," adding that as religious liberty had "a distinctive Christian basis, we regard this right as fundamental"[78]

In fact, ever since the Russian Orthodox Church's admission to the WCC in 1961, the council had no longer publicly addressed the issue of

73 *Central Committee: Minutes of the Twenty-Seventh Meeting: Berlin (West) (11–18 August 1974)*, Geneva, WCC Publications, 12–15.

74 *Minutes and Reports of the Twenty-Fourth Meeting*, 69.

75 *Epd-Dokumentation* 24, 1972, 2ff.

76 *Minutes and Reports of the Twenty-Sixth Meeting*, 59.

77 *Minutes of the Twenty-Seventh Meeting*, 38.

78 Willem Adolph Visser 't Hooft, ed., *The New Delhi Report: The Third Assembly of The World Council of Churches (1961)*, New York, Association Press, 1962, 160.

human rights violations, and instead it sought to resolve problems reported by member churches through back-channel diplomacy. For example, in April 1972, Visser 't Hooft, who had by then already retired, personally intervened with the church and state authorities in Moscow after the writer Aleksandr Isayevich Solzhenitsyn[79] – who would soon be exiled from Russia – wrote a public letter to the patriarch of all Russia the previous month, denouncing ongoing violations of religious freedom in the territories of the USSR.[80]

The following year, Potter made his first visit to Moscow to speak on the criticisms he was receiving from certain member churches and address the international pressure that was weakening his image as secretary general. CCIA director Leopoldo Juan Niilus was perfectly in line with the secretary general's defensive and discreet strategy, convinced as he was that open protests by the WCC regarding the lack of religious freedom in the USSR would only upset the new climate of European détente and cooperation.[81] He believed that the issue of human rights in the socialist countries would be resolved through negotiations conducted by the CSCE. As proof of this, on Easter 1973, when the general synod of the NHK addressed a letter of protest to the Soviet ambassador in The Hague over the treatment of the families of 45 evangelical Christians in the USSR who had been "sentenced to heavy penalties even though, according to our conception of justice, they have committed no crime other than that of holding religious services without explicit authorization,"[82] the WCC, which had received a copy of the letter, refrained from involving itself in the matter, although an internal note stated that the issue would require preliminary consultations with the Moscow Patriarchate. In any case, the letter was never given publicity in the ecumenical press that gravitated around the WCC.

The human rights consultation that took place from Oct 21 to 26, 1974 in St. Pölten, Austria[83] brought about a radical change in the way ecumenical circles in Geneva perceived the issue of human rights. The 1948 Declaration of Human Rights was based on the tradition of the Enlightenment, which emphasized individual human rights and exalted the freedom and autonomy of the person and as such engendered a disregard for "the social conditions of securing human existence."[84] Communism, in contrast, understood human rights as "the collective demands of … groups that remain unfulfilled in the social order of the non-socialist world,"[85] which included the right to work, to an education, to housing, to adequate remuneration, and to protection from exploitation.

In St. Pölten, the delegates reached an agreement on the following six points:

(a) There is a basic human right to life – including the whole question of

79 Born in 1918, Aleksandr Solzhenitsyn, the Russian writer, mathematics lecturer, and dissident, was sentenced to the internment in a gulag from 1945 to 1953. In 1962, with Nikita Khrushchev's permission, he published the novel *One Day in the Life of Ivan Denisovich*. In 1970, he was awarded the Nobel Prize for Literature. In 1974 he was stripped of citizenship and expelled from the USSR, and in 1976 he emigrated to the United States. He returned to Russia in the early 1990s, where he died in 2008.

80 Alexander Solzhenitsyn, *A Lenten Letter to Pimen, Patriarch of All Russia*, Minneapolis, Burgess, 1972.

81 See the memo from L.J. Niilus to P. Potter, *First part, Mar 1, 1973, Confidential*; supplement to the report by William C. Fletcher, "Religion and Soviet Foreign Policy 1945–1970," Mar 2, 1973; *Second part of my confidential memo of Mar 1, 1973*, Mar 5, 1973, in: WCCA, General Secretariat, country files, Eastern Europe, folder "USSR 1973–83," cited in Boyens, "Ökumenischer Rat der Kirchen," 201.

82 Letter from the General Synod of the NHK to the ambassador of the USSR in The Hague, German translation, no date, in: WCCA, 994.3.50.2, Relations with Eastern Europe (files of Lukas Vischer), folder "Documents on the Russian Orthodox Church 1969–1970," quoted in Boyens, "Ökumenischer Rat der Kirchen," 201.

83 *Human Rights and Christian Responsibility: Report of the Consultation, St. Pölten, Austria, (21–26 October 1974)*, Geneva, WCC Publications, 1975.

84 Ulrich Scheuner, "Die Menschenrechte in der ökumenischen Diskussion," *ÖR* 24, 1975, 152–164, here 157.

85 Scheuner, "Die Menschenrechte," 157.

survival, of the dangers and violations consequent on unjust economic, social and political systems and of the quality of life.

(b) There is a right to enjoy and maintain a cultural identity – which involves questions such as nations self-determination, rights of minorities, etc.

(c) There is a right to participate in decision-making within the community – which involves the whole question of effective democracy.

(d) There is a right to dissent – which preserves a community or system from hardening into authoritarian rigidity.

(e) There is a right to personal dignity – which involves condemnation, for example, of torture or of protracted imprisonment without trial.

(f) There is a right to chose [*sic.*] freely a religion or belief which includes freedom, either alone or in community with others and in public or private, to manifest his religion or belief in teaching, practice, worship and observance.[86]

Most of the participants had thus come out in favor of a collective understanding of human rights,[87] an aspect that was hotly debated within the WCC. In fact, several observed how the St. Pölten consultation's focus on human rights and the possibility of realizing them had failed to consider provisions for concrete interventions in favor of Christian individuals and groups in the USSR who suffered harassment and were denied religious liberty.[88]

It was only with the signing of the CSCE's final act, which took place in Helsinki on Aug 1, 1975, that the claims of Eastern bloc dissidents and activists were finally provided with a basis in international law. A wave of outcry over human rights violations in the USSR thus reached the West, but this time the WCC – probably out of fear of diplomatic backlash and interfaith friction – did not find itself at the forefront.

8 Nairobi 1975: The Fifth General Assembly and the Issue of Religious Freedom in the USSR

The WCC's fifth assembly, held in Nairobi from Nov 23 to Dec 10, 1975, had chosen the theme "Jesus Christ Frees and Unites." During the preparatory phase and without prior authorization from the Geneva leadership, Tibor Bartha, bishop of the Reformed Church in Hungary and president of the WCC in Hungary, invited churches from the USSR, Czechoslovakia, Poland, East Germany, Romania, Bulgaria, Yugoslavia, Cuba, and Hungary – all members of the WCC – to a consultation to be held in Budapest in mid-October of 1975.[89] Bartha only informed Potter after the invitations had already been sent, inviting him to attend the meeting and offering to send one of his delegates to Geneva to explain the initiative in detail.[90] Though Potter declined the invitation, he promised that someone from his staff would represent him in Budapest, and also suggested that Károly Tóth, president of the CPC, carefully examine the WCC's assembly workbook and other preparatory materials for

86 *Human Rights and Christian Responsibility*, 3.

87 See Lukas Vischer, *Relations with the Churches in the USSR in 1975*, 2, in: WCCA, 994.3.50.2, Relations with Eastern Europe (files of Lukas Vischer), vol. 2, folder "Four reports on visits to the USSR 1962; 1966; 1968; 1975," cited in Boyens, "Ökumenischer Rat der Kirchen," 203.

88 *SEG appointed staff group to follow up St. Pölten Human Rights consultation, Thursday, November 14, 1974*, three typewritten pages and 12 handwritten pages, in: WCCA, CCIA, St. Pölten Staff meeting on Human Rights, cited in Boyens, "Ökumenischer Rat der Kirchen," 203.

89 See *Protokoll-Programm und Teilnehmerliste*, in: Bundesarchiv, D O-4, 496; Bundesarchiv, D O-4, 1157, cited in Boyens, "Ökumenischer Rat der Kirchen," 210.

90 T. Bartha to P. Potter, Jul 9, 1975, in: WCCA, General Secretariat, country files, Eastern Europe, DDR (incl. CC), Eastern Europe general 1979–1985, cited in Boyens, "Ökumenischer Rat der Kirchen," 213.

the Nairobi assembly.[91] From the archives, there appear to have been no reservations on Geneva's part toward initiatives such as Bartha's which strove for the formation of church factions in line with particular political interests or specific confessional strategies. On his return from Budapest, Konrad Raiser – who in 1992 would be elected secretary general himself, and was at the time a member of Faith and Order – reassured Potter that the conference convened by the churches east of the Iron Curtain could not boast of any tangible success, nor had they succeeded in agreeing on a common line, and that, on the contrary, differences between the various countries and their respective churches had emerged even stronger than before.[92]

The substantial failure of that meeting, however, did not shield the Nairobi assembly from further tensions. On the third day of the conference, an English translation of the "Message to the Delegates of the Fifth WCC Assembly,"[93] was featured in the Kenyan newspaper *Target*. The posting, which had been written by Russian Orthodox priest Gleb Yakunin and layman Lev Regelson, and addressed to Potter and the rest of the delegates on Oct 16, 1975, denounced the plight of the many persecuted Christians around the world, especially those suffering oppression by the Soviet regime. They reported on the closure of 10,000 Orthodox churches between 1959 and 1965, the destruction of an Orthodox church in Zhytomyr in August 1975, the forced psychiatric treatment of dissidents, the arrest of lawyers who had defended worshippers unjustly oppressed by the political authorities, the sentencing to hard labor of those who wished to leave the country, and the confiscation of presses that printed the Bible. Delegates representing the Russian Orthodox Church expressed their utmost displeasure, especially since during previous visits to the USSR the CCIA staff members had explicitly reassured them that they had no intention of putting the issue of religious freedom in the USSR on the agenda in Nairobi.[94] Their additional complaint about having not been consulted prior to the letter's publication was met with the response that *Target* did not constitute an official organ of the WCC and thus no one, not even the secretary general, could intervene with censorship or bans. However, the publication's editorial board itself offered the Russian Orthodox delegates a chance to counter the accusations, allowing Metropolitan Juvenal to thus admit that events similar to those listed had "occurred in the life of the church and are still occurring,"[95] but add that they had clearly been exaggerated by the authors of the letter, who had violated the laws of the USSR with their missive. In late December 1975, the Russian Orthodox Church removed Yakunin from his ecclesiastical office without notice.

During the assembly, Potter and other staff members attempted to prevent any discussion of the issue of religious freedom in the USSR from taking place. During a press conference, the secretary general mentioned the letter that the two Russian dissidents had addressed to the assembly, though when asked if and when the letter would be discussed by the delegates, Potter replied that

91 P. Potter to T. Bartha, Aug 9, 1975, in: WCCA, General Secretariat, country files, Eastern Europe, DDR (incl. CC), Eastern Europe general 1979–1985, cited in Boyens, "Ökumenischer Rat der Kirchen," 213.

92 K. Raiser memo to P. Potter, Oct 24, 1975, *Re: Consultation in Budapest*, in: WCCA, General Secretariat, country files, Eastern Europe, DDR (incl. CC), Eastern Europe general 1979–85, quoted in Boyens, "Ökumenischer Rat der Kirchen," 214.

93 "The Suffering Church Appeals for Prayers and Help – Message to the Delegates to the Fifth Assembly of the World Council of Churches by the Rev. Gleb Yakunin and Lev Regelson, Members of the Russian Orthodox Church," in: Michael Bordeaux, Hans Hebly & Eugen Voss, eds., *Religious Liberty in the Soviet Union: WCC and USSR – A Post-Nairobi Documentation*, Kenston College, Centre for the Study of Religion and Communism, 1976, 40–53.

94 See Lukas Vischer, *Relations with the Churches in the USSR in 1975*, February 1976, 8, in: WCCA, 994.3.50.2, Relations with Eastern Europe (files of Lukas Vischer), vol. 2, folder "Four reports on visits to the USSR 1962; 1966; 1968; 1975," cited in Boyens, "Ökumenischer Rat der Kirchen," 215.

95 "The Suffering Church Appeals," 162.

for technical and legal reasons only WCC-affiliated churches and their official delegates could submit motions to the assembly or propose items for the agenda. In truth, the official record of the Nairobi conference reports discussion of the problem of religious freedom in the USSR, but does not explicitly mention the message of the two Muscovite dissidents.[96] The Swiss delegate Jacques Rossel suggested that the USSR be reminded that it had signed point seven of the Helsinki Accords but, faced with the protests from Russian Orthodox metropolitans Nikodim and Juvenal, this proposal and another of similar tenor were ignored. The final draft of the Nairobi report stated only that "the assembly has devoted a substantial period to the discussion of the alleged denials of religious liberty in the USSR," a summary considered insufficient by certain delegates, who successfully insisted that the final text be amended to read: "The assembly requests the general secretary to see to it that the question of religious liberty be the subject of intensive consultations with the member churches of the signatory states of the Helsinki Agreement and that a first report be presented at the next central committee meeting in August 1976."[97] Although the USSR was not explicitly mentioned anywhere in the text, the Russian Orthodox delegates resorted to abstention to express their disapproval of an atmosphere which they said was the result of a mixture of "haste, nerves, emotion, and divisiveness," as well as to accuse the other delegates of allowing themselves to be influenced by "sinful passions and divisions."[98]

The nomination committee's vote on the prospective presidents further reinforced the impression that the WCC was at the mercy of internal tensions in Nairobi. Well before the meeting in the Kenyan capital, the Russian Orthodox Church had proposed Nikodim for the shortlist of six names from which the WCC steering committee would be elected, despite it being common knowledge that he was also chairman of the CPC, a rival organization in Geneva. However, no one on the WCC staff raised the issue of his dual roles and the conflicts of interest that this might have entailed, and the decision was left to the discretion of the assembly. There, it was the secretary general of the NHK, van den Heuvel – who had been offered the post of secretary of the CPC 11 years earlier and had turned it down because Visser 't Hooft had reminded him of the gospel dictate against serving two masters (Matt 6,24) – who worked particularly hard to convince many of the delegates to vote against Nikodim.[99] In response to van den Heuvel's maneuvers, the Russian delegates resorted first to protests and then, in light of their impotence, to threats, even announcing that the Russian Orthodox Church would seriously consider its withdrawal from the WCC.[100] In the end, Nikodim, who had always shown absolute loyalty to the party apparatus in the past, was elected *en bloc* with the other five presidents in a capacity that permitted him to attend all meetings of the

96 David M. Paton, ed., *Breaking Barriers: Nairobi 1975: The Official Report of the Fifth Assembly of the World Council of Churches*, London/Grand Rapids, SPCK/Eerdmans, 1976, 169–170.

97 Paton, ed., *Breaking Barriers*, 174.

98 Paton, ed., *Breaking Barriers*, 172.

99 In October 1964, when van den Heuvel was invited to assume the position of secretary of the CPC's committee on ecumenical affairs by Professor Josef Hromádka, he first approached Visser 't Hooft to ask his opinion. Visser 't Hooft answered him the same day: "I do not think that you should accept ... And that for the simple reason that you would be in the unenviable position of having to serve two masters." Albert van den Heuvel followed the secretary general's advice and rejected Hromádka's offer. See the private and confidential memo from Van den Heuvel to Visser 't Hooft, Oct 29, 1964, and the memo from W.A. Visser 't Hooft to A.H. van den Heuvel, *Private and Confidential*, Oct 29, 1964, in: WCCA, General Secretariat, Prague Peace Conference, Confidential 1958, folder "Christian Peace Conference 1960–1968," both cited in Boyens, "Ökumenischer Rat der Kirchen," 218.

100 See *Personal Account of L. Vischer, Interesting details on a nominations-process in the WCC*, 3, in: WCCA, 994.3.50.4, Relations with Eastern Europe (files of Lukas Vischer), vol. 4, folder "Fünfte Vollversammlungen des WCC in Nairobi (Nov./Dez. 1975)," cited in Boyens, "Ökumenischer Rat der Kirchen," 218.

23-member executive committee and have a say in the appointments and dismissals of staff members. Additionally, all of the confidential documents of the WCC's innermost management group became accessible to him. It is today an established historiographical fact that Nikodim was also working as a KGB agent.[101]

In spite of some criticism of Potter's performance, the churches from socialist countries did not oppose his reelection when it was proposed at the 1976 central committee meeting in Geneva. The minutes of that meeting read: "In a closed session, Archbishop Scott presented the unanimous recommendation of the executive committee that Dr Philip Potter be appointed for a second term as general secretary for five years from Nov 1, 1977. The central committee unanimously agreed."[102]

Translated from Italian to English by Susan Dawson Vàsquez and David Dawson Vàsquez.

101 See Boyens, "Ökumenischer Rat der Kirchen," 91–99.

102 *Central Committee: Minutes and Reports of the Twenty-Ninth Meeting: Geneva, Switzerland (10–18 August 1976)*, Geneva, WCC Publications, 1976, p. 55.

Bibliography

Adler, Elisabeth, *A Small Beginning: An Assessment of the First Five Years of the Programme to Combat Racism*, Geneva, WCC Publications, 1974.

Besier, Gerhard, Armin Boyens & Gerhard Lindemann, *Nationaler Protestantismus und Ökumenische Bewegung: Kirchliches Handeln im Kalten Krieg (1945–1990)*, Berlin, Duncker & Humblot, 1999.

Cox, Harvey G., ed., *The Church Amid Revolution: A Selection of the Essays Prepared for the World Council of Churches Geneva Conference on Church and Society*, New York, Association Press, 1967

A History of the Ecumenical Movement, vol. 3, John Brix, Mercy Amba Oduyoye & Georges Tsetsis, *1968–2000*, Geneva, WCC Publications, 2004.

Kinnamon, Michael & Brian E. Cope, *The Ecumenical Movement: An Anthology of Key Texts and Voices*, Geneva, WCC Publications, 1997.

Krüger, Hanfried, ed., *Appell an die Kirchen der Welt: Dokumente der Weltkonferenz für Kirche und Gesellschaft*, Berlin, Kreuz Verlag, 1968.

Schjørring, Jens Holger & Norman Hjelm, eds., *History of Global Christianity*, 3 vols., Leiden, Brill, 2018.

Visser 't Hooft, Willem A., *Die Welt war meine Gemeinde: Autobiographie*, Munich, Piper, 1972.

Zeilstra, Jurjen A., *Visser 't Hooft, 1900–1985: Living for the Unity of the Church*, Amsterdam, Amsterdam University Press, 2020.

CHAPTER 34

Historians and Ecumenism: Western Christianity between Catholic Revisions and Inter-Denominational Efforts

Matteo Al Kalak

1 Introduction

There are many avenues to be explored regarding the ways in which the ecumenical movement and its needs have been presented in historical studies, though none would be able to exhaust the full complexity of the topic. Here I have chosen to adopt a specific perspective that allows the field to be narrowed down without diminishing the complexity of the debate.

The following pages intend to trace the historiographical repercussions of a primarily theological debate that took place during a particularly eventful period for the ecumenical movement, the era between the 1930s and 1970s. More specifically, as a guiding thread I have chosen the historical reconstructions regarding the split in Western Christendom, which allow to focus on the change of attitude in Catholic historiography and its attempts to arrive at shared reconstructions with its Protestant counterparts. It goes without saying that this choice means excluding debates concerning different but no less crucial areas, such as the recovery of a deeper understanding of the ancient church (think of the work of figures such as Henry Chadwick or Henri-Irénée Marrou) or, in another vein, of the fraught question of the Eastern tradition and of the values that – as seen by the ecumenical movement – were fundamental (among the many of these, one should at least mention Joseph Hajjar's writings on collegiality or the reflections put forward by Francis Dvornik on the relationship between East and West).

Therefore, without wishing to underestimate the weight that engagement with the early church or with the Eastern tradition had in the work of many historians of Christianity across the same years investigated here, I have chosen to focus on a narrower sphere, so as to better grasp the elements of both change and persistence within the interpretive paradigms. To this end, I will consider four historians who, in different ways, pioneered the approaches to reading the Catholic-Protestant divide that are considered here. For efficiency's sake, my analysis will focus on a few works to be taken as paradigmatic references through which to probe the wider production of the scholars considered and to better discern the defining points of their thought. Finally, I will attempt to understand the extent to which the interpretive revisions introduced were able to produce an ecumenical history of the church and, reversing the initial perspective, I will pose questions about history's ability to exert a significant influence on doctrinal and ecclesiological reflections.

2 Reversing the Perspective: Joseph Lortz

No individual marked as significant a turning point in the approach to reading and interpreting the figure of Martin Luther as Joseph Lortz, whose work offers a useful starting point from which to embark on the path outlined above. Up until the threshold of the contemporary era, intransigent readings of Luther were well-known, and characterized the three centuries of the modern age. According to the established narrative in Catholic circles, he had been the architect of a revolt against the power of the church, engendering a long chain of errors. Somewhat anticipated by humanism's claim to authority, via gradual mutations Luther's rebellion would later give rise to rationalism, to the Enlightenment, and to modern deviations of positivism, socialism, and to the "plague" of laicism.[1]

A priest and professor of history at the prestigious universities of Braunsberg, Münster, and Mainz, Lortz had been one of the first to break this pattern of interpretation, proposing a radically different reading of Luther.[2] In reality, attitudes toward the theologian-reformer had already begun to change within the Protestant camp as well, where biographies of Luther, such as those of Otto Scheel[3] and Heinrich Böhmer,[4] had already called for the need to consider new documents and perspectives, even to the extent of proposing the inauguration of platforms explicitly intended for interdenominational collaboration, as Alfred von Martin had done in his *Luther in ökumenischer Sicht*.[5]

In line with what was happening in the Protestant circles, on the Catholic front Lortz found himself committed to overcoming the reconstruction offered by the Jesuit Hartmann Grisar[6] and the more refined – but still nonconciliatory – reconstruction put forward by the Dominican Heinrich Johann Denifle.[7] Recasting the stereotypes established by Johann Cochlaeus in the 16th century,[8] the two historians presented Luther (and everything stemming from him) as a man afflicted with pathologies, psychoses, and profligacy of various kinds. The Reformer's monstruous and deformed traits were accentuated, and he was painted as an immoral character whose rebellion against Rome primarily derived from psychological compensations for a failed and delusional life. These psychopathological characterizations of Luther were destined for long-lived popularity, enduring until Erik Homburger Erikson's famous study.[9]

With a reconsideration that was in some ways anticipated by Sebastian Merkle[10] and spurred

1 There are numerous studies on the intransigent reaction and the relationship between church and modernity. I will limit myself to mentioning the overview given in Daniele Menozzi, *La Chiesa cattolica e la secolarizzazione*, Turin, Einaudi, 1993.

2 On Lortz's historiographic career and the interpretive revision he promoted, the comments made by Massimo Marcocchi, "Prefazione all'edizione italiana," in: Joseph Lortz, *La Riforma in Germania*, vol. 1, Boris Ulianich, ed., *Premesse, inizio, primi risultati*, Milan, Jaca Book, 1971, vii–xxx, remain valid (original German: Joseph Lorzt, *Die Reformation in Deutschland*, 2 vols., Freiburg i.Br., Herder, 1939–1940; ET: Joseph Lortz, *The Reformation in Germany*, 2 vols., London, Darton, Longman & Todd, 1968). For the precedents by which Lortz measured himself, see the analysis by Patrizio Foresta, "The Catholic Damnation and Redemption of Luther," in: Alberto Melloni, ed., *Luther: A Christian between Reforms and Modernity (1517–2017)*, vol. 2, Berlin, De Gruyter, 2017, 735–751, with detailed bibliographical references. In addition to these contributions, for more information on Lortz, see Boris Ulianich, "In memoriam Joseph Lortz (1887–1975)," *Rivista di storia e letteratura religiosa* 11, 1975, 781–801 and Gabriele Lautenschläger, "Lortz, Joseph Adam," *BBKL* 5, 241–244.

3 Otto Scheel, *Martin Luther: Vom Katholizismus zur Reformation. Auf der Schule und Universität*, 2 vols., Tübingen, J.C.B. Mohr, 1917.

4 Heinrich Böhmer, *Der junge Luther: Martin Luther und die Reformation: Mit 39 Abbildungen nach Holzschnitten und Kupferstichen des 16. Jahrhunderts*, Gotha, Flamberg, 1925.

5 Alfred von Martin, ed., *Luther in ökumenischer Sicht: Von evangelischen und katholischen Mitarbeitern*, Stuttgart, Frommans, 1929.

6 Hartmann Grisar, *Martin Luther: His Life and Work*, St. Louis, B. Herder Book Company, 1930.

7 Heinrich Denifle, *Luther und Luthertum in der ersten Entwicklung. Quellenmäßig dargestellt*, Mainz, Kirchheim, 1904–1909.

8 Johannes Cochlaeus, *Commentaria Ioannis Cochlaei, de actis et scriptis Martini Lutheri Saxonis ...*, Mainz, Behem, 1549.

9 Erik H. Erikson, *Young Man Luther: A Study in Psychoanalysis and History*, New York, Norton, 1958.

10 I am referring, for example, to the essay by Sebastian Merkle, "Gutes an Luther und Übles an seinen Tadlern," in: von Martin, ed., *Luther in ökumenischer Sicht*, 9–19, which calls for a study of Luther that is free from the animosities of confessional controversy. Merkle had already expressed a similar sentiment in his 1904 review of Denifle's work in *Deutsche Literaturzeitung* 25, 1904, 1226–1240.

on by a growing ecumenical sensibility,[11] Lortz examined Luther in a new light. In his analysis, dating back to the 1930s, the historian pointed to the Reformer's genuine intentions, which were not to promote a rift within Christendom. Rather, it was the Roman curia's inability to fully grasp the significance of the issues raised by Luther, which were by no means foreign to Catholic reformism, that was responsible for causing the denominational fracture: a difference in language and a basic misunderstanding was what ultimately led to the split between churches. As has been noted elsewhere, Lortz's theses would be revisited in the documents of Vatican II, particularly in *Unitatis redintegratio*,[12] and his interpretive paradigm would garner a wide following within Catholic historiography.

However, in order to fully understand Lortz's intellectual and historiographical journey, it is worth reflecting, at least in passing, on a few passages featured in the two works that brought about this reversal. I am referring in particular to *Geschichte der Kirche in ideengeschichtlicher Betrachtung*,[13] which first appeared in 1932 and which was the subject of numerous reissues and translations, and *Die Reformation in Deutschland*, which surfaced around 1939–1940 before enjoying similar success. Setting aside a discussion – which is by no means of secondary importance – regarding the editorial history of the two works and their respective revisions, what is most important here is to call attention to their contents concerning the Protestant Reformation.

In his *Geschichte der Kirche*, Lortz did not mince words when identifying Luther's schism as "the greatest catastrophe which has ever befallen the church from its beginning until the present day."[14] After downplaying the rift with the Eastern Church, since it had not been motivated by radical divergences (Rome and the East shared the same type of sacramental and hierarchically structured church), Lortz introduced two fundamental concepts: that the Reformation had also – directly and indirectly – had a "multifaceted and far-reaching influence"[15] on the Catholic Church, and secondly, that the emergence of the ecumenical movement had brought the schism's true motives to light: "The full significance of the impact of the Reformation on the Catholic Church was not revealed until today, precisely in the awakening of ecumenical thought, which embraces the entire church. Now it is becoming clear how the Reformation arose from the deepest interior of the church and how its ideas were originally directed toward a positive reform of the church from within its own bosom."[16]

This presents us with a "Catholic" Luther to rediscover, that is, a reformer whose roots were set in the thought of the church of his time, with its demands for reform and renewal. Lortz reappropriates the Augustinian of Wittenberg, opting not to pursue the doctrinal differences that arose from the Reformation (differences that, he admits, underpin "a form of Christianity diverging

---

11 In later years, revisiting his own experience, Lortz tried to present the ecumenical achievement of his research as an objective result: "When I set out on my work *Die Reformation in Deutschland*, it was by no means my aim to address the positive aspect of the Reformation in a very spirited or heartfelt way, especially in the gigantic – but also disruptive – person of Luther that was under discussion. ... This was a result that I seized, as it were, according to the means I had available, from the facts"; Joseph Lortz, *Mein Umweg zur Geschichte: Ein besinnlicher Rückblick auf der Journee des Anciens d'Echternach, 10. Oktober, 1959*, Wiesbaden, Steiner, 1960, 33, quoted in Marcocchi, "Prefazione," xiv.

12 See *UR* 3–4 and Marcocchi, "Prefazione," xxviii.

13 Joseph Lortz, *Geschichte der Kirche in ideengeschichtlicher Betrachtung: Eine Sinndeutung der christlichen Vergangenheit in Grundzügen dargestellt*, Münster, Aschendorff, 1936.

14 As this and other citations are not present in the English edition, the translator referred to the Italian: Joseph Lortz, *Storia della Chiesa nello sviluppo delle sue idee*, vol. 2, *Evo moderno*, Alba, Edizioni Paoline, 1967, 92.

15 Lortz, *Storia della Chiesa*, vol. 2, 93.

16 Lortz, *Storia della Chiesa*, vol. 2, 93.

substantially from the Catholic attitude"[17]), and instead investigates the genesis of the schism, with the evident desire to reassimilate it through a deeper understanding of its causes.

The central subject of his analysis, therefore, is not the instigator of the Reformation, but rather the factors that brought it into existence. Treating the Reformation movement as "a *contest* concerning the true form of Christianity,"[18] Luther is no longer regarded as the unruly and lustful monster he was characterized as in Denifle and Grisar's works, but as an interpreter of far-reaching sentiments that the church had failed to confront. His starting point was "a dreadful struggle of conscience carried on with great earnestness for the salvation of his soul,"[19] and it was the convergence of his doubts – both spiritual and existential – with those of the climate in which he was immersed that made him a reformer: an innovator not so much in the criticisms he made of Rome,[20] but in the impact that these criticisms had by virtue of his charisma and energy.

Lortz thus moves in two directions. On the one hand, he dampens Luther's prominence by framing it within the cultural context of his time. On the other, he rereads Luther's actions in positive terms, trying to pick out what the Reformer said that could be considered "right" and "legitimate" (that is, Catholic). Indeed, in one passage, Lortz – not a little boldly – attributes to Luther an almost providential function: "It must, of course, be conceded that the Protestant attack is another source of inner Catholic reform activity in the sixteenth century. Through it, many dormant Catholic forces were awakened, and the Catholic reform was hastened, permanently kept alert, and in many ways shown the direction which it was to take."[21]

It was a provocative statement that overturned the traditional framework through which to interpret the Reformation and, to some extent, echoed the judgments already made by some of Luther's contemporaries. The Saxon monk's protest was an event through which God spoke to the church, so that "any responsible attempt to study the Reformation as anything other than the judgment of God must be ruled out."[22] If we exclude emotionally-charged or apologetic readings, then it cannot fail to be seen "how the leaders [of the Reformation] who stand against the church by no means proclaim only heresy."[23]

What stems from this is a complex and articulate assessment of Luther's character, a man rich in positive insights (his marked Christocentrism, the importance of faith, his exaltation of Bible reading, and his theology of the cross), though also responsible for work that engendered "sad results for the church," the worst being that "Christendom was rent asunder and its forces were seriously hampered in the missions and in the growing struggle in the civilized world."[24] Explicitly referencing the developments of the ecumenical movement, Lortz thus reinterprets the historical events of the most serious schism suffered by Christendom in new terms, calling attention to the factors that allowed the Reformation to take place: socio-cultural conditions, ecclesiological motives, and, as is well known, a pluralism of positions and doctrinal options that created a *theologische Unklarheit* proving decisive in the rift between Wittenberg and Rome.

The interpretative framework that Lortz laid out in the *Geschichte der Kirche* can be found again, with some variations, in his monumental *Die Reformation in Deutschland*, which appeared just a few years later. The topic of *theologische Unklarheit* is repeatedly returned to in this later work and proposed as "one of the keys which to some extent unlocks the riddle of the colossal

17 Lortz, *Storia della Chiesa*, vol. 2, 92 (italics original).
18 Lortz, *Storia della Chiesa*, vol. 2, 95 (italics original).
19 Lortz, *Storia della Chiesa*, vol. 2, 97.
20 Lortz writes: "It is indeed true that Luther enunciates scarcely a single thought which cannot be traced back to a number of theologians, critics, and preachers before his time"; Lortz, *Storia della Chiesa*, vol. 2, 97.
21 Lortz, *Storia della Chiesa*, vol. 2, 98.
22 Lortz, *Storia della Chiesa*, vol. 2, 98.
23 Lortz, *Storia della Chiesa*, vol. 2, 98.
24 Lortz, *Storia della Chiesa*, vol. 2, 163.

apostasy."[25] According to Lortz, without recognizing this cultural precondition it would be impossible to understand how Luther's initiative took on the characteristics of a "revolution in the church."[26] The work, therefore, insists on the "historical necessity" of the Reformation, a theory aimed at explaining "how any church revolution such as the one accomplished in the sixteenth century could have been possible at all, and how it was, in a deeper sense, necessary."[27] This necessity can only be grasped if historical causes are taken into account, moving beyond the Reformation's "actual and immediate causation" and seeking to understand its "foundation, precondition, and preparation."[28]

In *Die Reformation in Deutschland*, Lortz returns to the idea that the responsibility for the schism cannot be attributed solely to Luther, but that it also fell on a Catholic hierarchy that was unable to grasp the depth of the questions posed by the Reformation, and which was itself trapped in the grips of doctrinal confusion, abuses, corruption, excessive taxation, clericalization, commodification of sacred things etc.[29]

According to Lortz, then, it was Catholicism's shortcomings and instability that made Luther a revolutionary heretic, producing a paradoxical situation based on a misunderstanding (*Missverständnis*): wracked by inner doubts about justification and grace, the young Luther – the same one described in Lucien Febvre's famous biography a few years earlier[30] – had set himself against a putative form of Catholicism, one which did not correspond to the actual repository of the faith:

> We are now able to recognize the basic error of the view which made Luther's struggle so hopeless for him. He wanted to be assured experientially of his being in a state of grace. He had to know it, better, to *feel* it. In his pre-Reformation period, not to know if one were in a state of was the same as not to be in that state. No one could affirm that this is the Catholic view. Within himself, Luther wrestled and overthrew a Catholicism that was not Catholic.[31]

In Lortz's view, the supposition that Luther was opposed to a non-Catholic Catholicism implied a need to reconsider the *Hercules Germanicus* as an expression of a Catholic world in search of purification and reform.

These comments should be sufficient in providing us with an understanding of how, despite the many aversions that Lortz's assessment of Luther aroused, such a revision was in line with attempts to encourage a rapprochement between Christian denominations, in an explicit relationship with instances of reconciliation that Lortz himself did not hesitate to promote.[32]

3 Insurmountable Limits: Hubert Jedin and Ecumenism

Within the new historiographical climate, Hubert Jedin established himself as one of the most influential scholars of the Council of Trent and of church history in the modern era.[33] A Catholic

25 Lortz, *The Reformation in Germany*, vol. 1, 156.
26 Lortz, *The Reformation*, vol. 1, 157.
27 Lortz, *The Reformation*, vol. 1, 3–4.
28 Lortz, *The Reformation*, vol. 1, 5.
29 See, for example, Lortz, *The Reformation*, vol. 1, 84–126.
30 Lucien Febvre, *Martin Luther: A Destiny*, New York, E.P. Dutton & Co., 1929. It should be remembered how Febvre already insisted on the cultural framework of Luther upbringing, and how he concentrated on the Reformer experience before the confessional fracture.

31 Lortz, *The Reformation*, vol. 1, 200 (italics original).
32 Joseph Lortz, *Die Reformation: Thesen als Handreichung bei ökumenischen Gesprächen*, Meitingen, Kyrios Verlag, 1940; and, in an already preconciliar climate, Joseph Lortz, *Einheit der Christenheit: Unfehlbarkeit und lebendige Aussage*, Trier, Paulinus Verlag, 1959.
33 Among the extensive bibliography on Jedin's work and historiographical output, I would merely point to the special issue of *CrSt* 22/2, 2001, which is devoted to Jedin, and to Heribert Smolinsky, ed., *Die Erforschung der Kirchengeschichte: Leben, Werk und Bedeutung von Hubert Jedin (1900–1980)*, Münster, Aschendorff, 2001.

priest and lecturer at the University of Breslau and later at Bonn, Jedin admittedly held more moderate positions than Lortz, and it would not be excessive to consider him on a very different position confronted with his distinguished colleague.

Evidence that Jedin only partially accepted Lortz's revision can be found in the first volume of his *Geschichte des Konzils von Trient*, a lengthy 1949 study on the "prehistory" of the council published a decade after *Die Reformation in Deutschland* and translated into English soon after.[34] Following an outline of the long and turbulent path of successive attempts at reform made by the late medieval councils, from those of Constance and Basel to Lateran V, Jedin set the stage with a chapter entitled "Luther's 'Reform' and Council."[35]

Certain traits of Lortz's "Catholic Reformer" appeared to survive in Jedin's analysis, though they were juxtaposed with considerations that also pointed to the serious errors of a theologian monk who had set off on a dangerous path away from the church.

In keeping with well-established rhetoric, Jedin's depiction of the Augustinian of Wittenberg opens with a portrait the Christian Luther's inner torment in which the usual ingredients can be found: fear of God's impending justice with regard to sin, the impossibility of achieving divine purity through personal works and sacrifice, and the inner abyss of a sinful humanity. As Jedin reminds us, confession was no longer able to assuage the future Reformer's anxiety, whose condition of suffering and deep distress is emphasized without, however, making any pathologizing claims. He then addresses the *Missverständnis* that Lortz had insisted upon. Luther's case was undoubtedly that of a *de facto* Catholic who went against a pseudo-Catholicism, yet there was also the issue of Luther's own misunderstanding, deluding himself that he had found the solution to his theological disquietude: "Then there came a day when *he fancied he had found a solution* [to his torment]: his notion of God had been all wrong! The study of the epistle to the Romans *convinced him* that the justice of God before which he trembled is not exacting, does not condemn, but is wholly beneficent."[36]

As can be seen, the tone is cautious. In Jedin's description, the Augustinian's insights are nuanced and ascribed to a subjective and delusory condition. The Silesian historian does not refute Lortz's assertion that Luther's target was an inauthentic Catholicism, arguing that the remedy Luther prescribed was in fact "a prerequisite, as well as the very heart, of a lived Christianity, and therefore, cannot be at variance with Catholic dogma."[37] The Reformer railed against a doctrine of grace which was erroneous even from a Catholic point of view, and challenged a degenerate scholasticism: "Just as he imagined that his 'tower experience' had taught him to shake off a theory of grace which he wrongly thought to be that of the Catholic Church – for it was not – so now he fought a scholasticism which had forsaken its best traditions."[38] Nevertheless, Jedin emphasizes how Luther quickly went astray and departed from the truth, describing his principle of *sola fide* as a "fateful formula" that envisions salvation as resulting from "faith alone, without works."[39] Faced with something falsely Catholic, then, Luther counters with an equally non-Catholic formulation: "To the erroneous teaching of the nominalist school, that unaided nature is able to love God above all things, Luther opposes the thesis of its utter corruption, so that justification is exclusively God's work."[40] Thus, as much as Jedin strives to acknowledge Luther's traits of catholicity, he neither considers them as the means through which to reconcile the Reformer with the church nor as the key

34 Hubert Jedin, *Geschichte des Konzils von Trient*, 4 vols., Freiburg i.Br., Herder, 1951–1975; ET: *A History of the Council of Trent*, 4 vols., St. Louis, B. Herder Book Co., 1957–1976.

35 Jedin, *A History*, vol. 1, 166–196.

36 Jedin, *A History*, vol. 1, 167 (italics mine).

37 Jedin, *A History*, vol. 1, 167.

38 Jedin, *A History*, vol. 1, 167

39 Jedin, *A History*, vol. 1, 168.

40 Jedin, *A History*, vol. 1, 168.

with which to engineer a subsequent ecumenical rapprochement.

The analyses that surface from the pages of the *History of the Council of Trent* maintain margins of ambiguity on these aspects, though on the whole they end up falling back on the view of Luther as a rebellious outsider of the church. For this reason, while the Reformer was yet to draw the ecclesiological conclusions that would result from his doctrinal and spiritual reflections, by 1517 he already found himself "no longer within the church, though he knew it not. He only realized the bearing of his theological opinions and drew the conclusions which led to his conception of the church when the controversy over indulgences suddenly made him the center of public interest and the leader of a powerful movement."[41]

Furthermore, Lortz's investigation into the underlying causes of the Reformation – the combination of factors that, as he explained, had formed the basis upon which Luther's protest could effectively be launched – was also met with relatively lukewarm reception in Jedin's analysis. While he agreed that Luther was part of a much broader framework and that his success was partially owed to a concurrence of proximate and remote causes (from the abuses perpetrated around indulgences, to the deep-rooted decadence of the church, and to the *natio germanica*'s desire for revenge against Rome), Jedin staunchly maintained that this state of affairs had added error to error, claiming "these were the reasons why so many of Luther's adherents fell into the fatal error that they were not following a heretic and were, therefore, not cut off from the church."[42]

In short, Jedin's estimation sees the heretical Luther prevail over the Catholic Luther, and while the historian had no difficulty in recognizing the limitations within the ecclesiastical hierarchy of the time, and the obvious distortions of the Catholic doctrine and its interpretations, he strongly circumscribes and relativizes Luther's catholicity.

41 Jedin, *A History*, vol. 1, 169.

42 Jedin, *A History*, vol. 1, 177.

Shifting our focus from Luther to the other protagonists mentioned in the "prehistory" of the Council of Trent, it becomes clear as to whom Jedin proposes to the reader as a positive – and alternative – model to Luther: the young Gasparo Contarini who, around the same time as Luther's tower-experience (*Turmerlebnis*) underwent a similar experience of enlightenment in Venice.[43] The future cardinal – who would become a leading figure in religious dialogue with Protestants in the 1540s – did not take a path away from the church, but lived through reform requests without breaking ecclesial unity. Jedin's was thus a reproposal of the primacy of the Catholic Reformation (that is, of the efforts of "self-reform among the 'members' of the church" occurring well before Luther and progressively endorsed by the papacy) over the Protestant Reformation.[44]

It was precisely regarding this point that Jedin distanced himself from Lortz. In spite of the Catholic ideas and principles that might be identified within Lutheran thought – even those most valuable and closely tied to the fundamental tenets of his theology – the Augustinian of Wittenberg's beliefs could not be reconciled with Catholic doctrine tout court, particularly in light of that which was defined at Trent. It was a conviction that Jedin would also make explicit later in his career. In 1969, in the midst of the postconciliar climate, he devoted an article to what he judged to be overly "inclusive" interpretations of Luther.[45]

43 See Jedin, *A History*, vol. 1, 377. Even more so, see Hubert Jedin, "Ein 'Turmerlebnis' des jungen Contarini," *Hist. Jahr.* 70, 1951, 115–130. For a critical analysis of Jedin's interpretation of Contarini, I refer the reader to Gigliola Fragnito, *Gasparo Contarini: Un magistrato veneziano al servizio della cristianità*, Florence, Olschki, 1988.

44 This definition of Catholic Reformation is taken from Hubert Jedin, "Catholic Reformation or Counter-Reformation?," in: David M. Luebke, ed., *The Counter-Reformation: The Essential Readings*, Malden MA, Blackwell, 1999, 19–45, here 34.

45 Hubert Jedin, "Mutamenti della interpretazione cattolica della figura di Lutero e loro limiti," RSCI 23, 1969, 361–377.

After welcoming the fact that Catholic historiography had now distanced itself from the likes of Cochlaeus's biography of Luther, he listed the dangers posed by those who wanted to go beyond the realm of simple historical analysis to "wholly embrace" Luther's religious ideal and, in the final analysis, those who stubbornly "wanted to consider him Catholic":[46]

> While I appreciate the commitment surrounding Luther's theology, I must also point out a danger in the most recent efforts to present a transformed image of him: I am convinced that it is impossible to integrate all of Luther, all of his personality, all of his theology, into the Catholic Church, to make him – if you will permit me the simplification – a Catholic.[47]

Although he accepted the findings of the most recent historiography on Luther and acknowledged, in no uncertain terms, that the Reformer was not "the sole culprit of the schism" or even "the deciding or deliberate party responsible for it,"[48] Jedin could not refrain from raising the pertinent question: "Where do you think that the concept of church lies in Luther? Where the unequivocal denial of the magisterial and pastoral office binding in conscience, the denial of the hierarchical structure of divine right?"[49]

In simple terms, a Catholic Luther inexorably collapses when examined in relation to the doctrinal foundations of the Catholic hierarchy. Despite all efforts, in Jedin's analysis the historical Luther constitutes the main obstacle to a theological Luther, assimilated to Catholicism only by virtue of phenomenological or existential readings. Jedin concludes:

> I must confess that, with the best of good will, I cannot integrate Luther into Catholicism. Can one gloss over these facts [Luther calling the pope Antichrist] to take refuge in an existentialist view of his theology? Can Luther be abstracted from history? To ask the question is, in my opinion, tantamount to answering it in the negative.[50]

4 The Issue of the Origins as a Path to Reconciliation: Erwin Iserloh

While Jedin, as has been mentioned, identified the insurmountable limits of rehabilitating Luther from a Catholic perspective, one of the students he shared with Lortz – Erwin Iserloh[51] – supported the idea of a rapprochement between Catholics and Protestants on historical grounds. Marked by his aversion to the Nazi regime, and having received the priestly ordination in 1940 from the hands of Clemens August von Galen, the young Iserloh made his debut with a dissertation, supervised by Lortz himself, on the eucharistic theology of Johannes Eck.[52] His work, which built upon "Lortz's synthesis of the Reformation and Jedin's work on pre-Tridentine theology," expounded the "inadequacy of Catholic theology's response" to many of Luther's objections.[53]

Iserloh got his habilitation with Jedin in 1951, and over the following years turned his attention toward the origins of the Catholic-Protestant schism, aided by the Institute of Ecumenical

46 Jedin, "Mutamenti della interpretazione," 368.
47 Jedin, "Mutamenti della interpretazione," 370.
48 Jedin, "Mutamenti della interpretazione," 372.
49 Jedin, "Mutamenti della interpretazione," 371.

50 Jedin, "Mutamenti della interpretazione," 373.
51 An updated directory of studies and biographical entries devoted to Iserloh can be found on the Historische Kommission für Westfalen website.
52 Iserloh's dissertation, defended in 1941–1942, was published eight years later: Erwin Iserloh, *Die Eucharistie in der Darstellung des Johannes Eck: Ein Beitrag zur vortridentinischen Kontroverstheologie über das Messopfer*, Münster, Aschendorff, 1950.
53 "Nota biobliografica," in: Erwin Iserloh, *Lutero tra Riforma cattolica e protestante*, Brescia, Queriniana, 1970, 7.

Theology in Münster, whose direction had been entrusted to him between 1965 and 1967. His most famous work on the posting of Luther's 95 theses dates back to the years of his tenure there (generally dated between 1962 and 1968), and was the subject of fierce debate. Within it, Lortz's student questioned the basis of what had taken place in Wittenberg, concluding that, in reality, the posting never happened in the way it had been relayed from generation to generation.[54] It was Iserloh's intention to

> conquer Luther, although with all due caution, in the renewed conciliar and post-conciliar ecumenical mood: if the posting never happened, then Luther was not the main factor responsible for the rift in Latin Christianity and the emergence of the different European confessional families.[55]

His analysis was aimed at corroborating Lortz's findings and explaining the rift between Catholics and Protestants as the result of a misunderstanding, subsequently exacerbated by the promulgation of inconsistent origin myths (the provocative posting of the theses).

Like his teacher, Iserloh wasted no time in associating the revision of the figure and the work of Luther with the watchwords of the ecumenical movement, which was enjoying a boom at the time. On this point, it may be helpful to retrace the structure and the arguments of a collection of essays printed in 1974, entitled *Luther und die Reformation*.[56] It emphasized the need to reread and reinterpret the figure of the Reformer in light of ecumenical demands. The preface to the work, dated Jun 24, 1974, was a manifesto of ecumenical militancy, and made explicit the function assigned to historical research in the context of Christian dialogue:

> Notwithstanding a lamented "oblivion of Luther," books on the Reformer and his work are stacking up. If, however, I have decided to present a few essays and articles here, taken from already published collected works, it is because I hope to place some emphasis that attempts to complete the image of Luther, which has ossified in a unilaterally confessional sense. This is especially true of some essays [that] explain why, in the doctrine of justification, *articulus stantis et cadentis ecclesiae*, distinctions that divide the churches should no longer be permitted. May this collection show how historical research on the church, directed toward ecumenism, is not only worthwhile in clearing ruins and rubble but also in providing an important contribution to reworking the problems posed to us.[57]

Lortz's legacy is so palpable in this passage that it requires no special comment. It would not be superfluous, however, to spend some time exploring the conception of history that these premises reveal. First of all, the idea of history here is closely tied to the problems of the day, and in overt service to the questions and urgencies of the present. Iserloh proposes a framework that entrusted the

54 Erwin Iserloh, *Luthers Thesenanschlag: Tatsache oder Legende?*, Wiesbaden, Steiner, 1962. On this and further editions of Iserloh's text, see Uwe Wolff, *Iserloh: Der Thesenanschlag fand nicht statt*, Fribourg, Institut für Ökumenische Studien der Universität Freiburg Schweiz, 2013. On the debate provoked by Iserloh, see, most recently, the reconstruction by Patrizio Foresta, "The Posting of the Theses: The History of a Mith," in: Melloni, ed., *Luther*, 185–202 (with an updated bibliography).

55 Foresta, "The Posting of the Theses," 185.

56 Erwin Iserloh, *Luther und die Reformation: Beiträge zu einem ökumenischen Lutherverständnis*, Aschaffenburg, Pattloch Verlag, 1974; the following quotations are adapted by the translator from the Italian edition, *Lutero e la Riforma: Contributi a una comprensione ecumenica*, Brescia, Morcelliana, 1977.

57 Erwin Iserloh, "Premessa," in: Iserloh, *Lutero e la Riforma*, 7.

task of healing and cancelling present-day divisions to historical-philological argumentation.

Let us look, for example, at the emphasis on the doctrine of justification. An analysis of Luther's theology, Iserloh argued, shows that the Reformer had no schismatic intentions but meant, if anything, to appeal "to an older Catholic tradition: Augustinianism."[58] Therefore, on this basis, it was appropriate to more carefully review and reconsider the significance of his doctrinal revision of the issue of justification.

In a detailed analysis, in which the fruits of his youthful studies on Occamism emerged, Iserloh went on to explain the concepts of *iustitia*, *gratia*, *donum*, and *iustificatio* in Luther's thought during the early years of the protest.[59] Beyond the complex argumentation, what is interesting to note is the conclusion that the scholar reaches. If the contemporary reader, detaching oneself "from the theological formulation, look[s] at the intended *res*, the differences in controvertist theology become, on many sides, irrelevant," and certainly weaker than what the contentious language used by Luther himself suggests.[60]

According to Iserloh, this redressed understanding of the young Luther, this resolution of the misunderstanding and the subsequent historically-based "correction" of Luther's image, was to crash like a tidal wave over confessional divisions, revealing their groundlessness and accelerating their reabsorption. However, when Iserloh himself shifts from history of theology to an analysis of the Catholic context, his tone changes, becoming discernibly less optimistic:

> Certainly, the Catholic still has several questions to address to Luther. Questions of such weight that ecclesial communion is not yet possible … In the theological evaluation of Luther's work, the concepts cannot be brought to agreement so quickly. But as far as his biography and the understanding of what motivated and preoccupied him, against the background of the 16th century, there are hardly any divergences today that deeply separate Catholic and Protestant studies.[61]

Iserloh's proposal, therefore, seems to lapse into a kind of "culturally" based ecumenism: if there cannot be communion in ecclesial praxis due to divisions having become too deeply entrenched, there could still be – or already is – unity in sharing an interpretation of Luther's message.

Recognizing the discrepancy between the conceptual level and ecclesiological level in Iserloh's analysis reveals its weakness. The division between Catholic and Protestant does not depend only – nor even primarily – on the spark that was genuinely or allegedly ignited by Luther, but rather on the many centuries of sedimentation of the churches that were born after 1517, and on the doctrines and practices they codified respectively. To paint a picture, even having established that it was not Luther who lit the spark, but a distorted reception of his claims or the short-sighted rigidity of the Catholic hierarchy, the fire that nonetheless broke out 500 years ago is not thereby extinguished, nor its effects diminished.

Reconsidering the causes of the Reformation, therefore, is only part of the problem. Rehabilitating the young Luther does not, in itself, also mean embracing the mature Luther or his legacy. Iserloh does not always seem to be aware of this limit. His emphasis on the Reformer's early activity, at many points, occupies the stage entirely. Moreover, his examination of the young Luther encompasses that of the Catholic Luther, and the two of them constitute "much more than just a few unresolved problems in Luther's biography." Indeed, as Iserloh

58 Erwin Iserloh, "La posizione di Lutero nella tradizione teologica," in: Iserloh, *Lutero e la Riforma*, 39–61, here 61.

59 Erwin Iserloh, "Gratia e donum: Giustificazione e santificazione secondo lo scritto di Lutero Contro il teologo lovaniense Latomus (1521)," in: Iserloh, *Lutero e la Riforma*, 129–153, esp. 138ff.

60 Iserloh, "Gratia e donum," 153.

61 Erwin Iserloh, "Lutero nella visione cattolica ieri e oggi," in: Iserloh, *Lutero e la Riforma*, 155–176, here 176.

himself points out, "ultimately, here we decide whether Luther's new theological position ... was – and is – in itself such as to produce a schism in the church."[62]

Though it was important and of clear symbolic significance, Iserloh's interpretation failed to generate the doctrinal revision that he had hoped for. The weight of a nearly five-centuries-long rift could not be alleviated by new frontiers of research, and the churches needed to find other means through which reach out toward one another.

5 Historical Exegesis as an Instrument of Ecumenism: Giuseppe Alberigo

A parallel and, in many ways, convergent path to Iserloh's acquisitions was that of Giuseppe Alberigo, who, starting from the study of the Protestant Reformation and reactions to it, widened his sights to encompass the entire history of the church. Another point uniting the two authors was their apprenticeship with, and subsequent distancing from, Jedin and some of his main positions.

Alberigo was born in 1926 to a Lombard family.[63] In 1953, he became involved with the Centro di documentazione which Giuseppe Dossetti had founded in Bologna to encourage projects in religious research that required long-term analysis. Dossetti promptly guided his disciple-friend toward history, placing him under the guidance of two of the most influential personalities in the fields of church history and Christian studies at the time: Delio Cantimori and the aforementioned Jedin. He immediately identified the Council of Trent and the rift between Catholics and Protestants as decisive turning points to focus on, and in 1959 he published his monograph *I vescovi italiani al concilio di Trento*, which was imbued with the already-profound influence that developments in Catholic historiography on the subject had had on the scholar.[64]

Although unlike for Lortz and Iserloh the urgencies of ecumenism were not mentioned among the motivations for his work, it would be Alberigo himself who would reveal, 30 years later, how the text had arisen from the sidelines of the deliberations of the CCEQ, a group formed with the intention of "raising theological and historical awareness of Catholicism"[65] with respect to the problems of division and the possible reunification of Christians. The Benedictine Jean Leclercq, who would consistently distinguish himself within the ecumenical movement, was the one to have extended an invitation to the Lombard scholar.

A careful reading of *I vescovi italiani* allows us to discern Alberigo's effort to understand and rehabilitate many of the reasons adopted by Protestants. If, for example, we consider a topic such as

62 Erwin Iserloh, "Il giovane Lutero e l'inizio della Riforma," in: Iserloh, *Lutero e la Riforma*, 63–89, here 63.

63 For a biographical profile of Alberigo, see Giovanni Miccoli, "Alberigo, Giuseppe," *DBI* 2014, available at: <www.treccani.it/enciclopedia/giuseppe-alberigo_%28Dizionario-Biografico%29> (accessed Oct 31, 2023); Alberto Melloni, "Giuseppe Alberigo, 1926–2007: Appunti per un profilo biografico," *CrSt* 29, 2008, 665–702. On the Centro di documentazione, I will limit myself to mentioning Daniele Menozzi, "Alle origini del Centro di documentazione (1952–1956)," in: Angelina Alberigo & Giuseppe Alberigo, eds., *"Con tutte le tue forze": I nodi della fede cristiana oggi: Omaggio a Giuseppe Dossetti*, Genoa, Marietti, 1993, 333–369; and Paolo Prodi, *Giuseppe Dossetti e le officine bolognesi*, Bologna, Il Mulino, 2016; Giuseppe Alberigo, ed., *L'"officina Bolognese" (1953–2003)*, Bologna, EDB, 2004.

64 Giuseppe Alberigo, *I vescovi italiani al concilio di Trento (1545–1547)*, Florence, Sansoni, 1959.

65 Alberigo recalled the genesis of his work on the Italian bishops at the Council of Trent in Giuseppe Alberigo, *Nostalgie di unità: Saggi di storia dell'ecumenismo*, Genoa, Marietti, 1989, 8. On the CCEQ, see Peter De Mey, "Johannes Willebrands and the Catholic Conference for Ecumenical Questions (1952–1963)," in: Adelbert Denaux & Peter De Mey, eds., *The Ecumenical Legacy of Johannes Cardinal Willebrands (1909–2006)*, Leuven, Peeters, 2012, 49–77, and the contribution by Peter De Mey and Saretta Marotta "The Catholic Conference for Ecumenical Questions" in this volume. A broader contextualization can be found in Mauro Velati, *Una difficile transizione: Il cattolicesimo tra unionismo ed ecumenismo (1952–1964)*, Bologna, il Mulino, 1996.

the translation of Scripture, which – a few years after the publication of Alberigo's work – would animate Catholic debate in the wake of Vatican II, we see a willingness to refute the traditional apologetic arguments in order to recover the legitimate demands that had inspired the Protestant community. According to Alberigo, although it had become commonplace "that Bible translation might even have been the forerunner of the Lutheran Reformation," it could not be ignored that "every movement of renewal or reform in the church has rooted its foundational attitude in a recovery of sensitivity and awareness regarding Scripture, understood as the essential cornerstone of the whole life of the church."[66] The conclusions that were drawn from this observation were interesting:

> It was improper to blame the Lutheran crisis on the revival of interest in and dissemination of the Bible. Arguably, it would not be difficult to reverse the position and twist the accusation, maintaining that one of the factors of the success of the Protestant Reformation was precisely the relatively limited dissemination of the Bible in the vernacular. More than anything, the abandonment of Holy Scripture had deleterious consequences in pastoral practice.[67]

Alberigo's words echoed the need to place the Protestant Reformation and the primacy of Scripture upon which Luther insisted within a broader context, free from the conditioning of the Catholic-Lutheran controversy. The Lutherans were not wrong in returning to the Bible to reform the church, and in no way could reading the Bible be blamed for the Protestant schism. On the contrary, familiarity with Scripture was a value that Catholics also needed to recover. Posing the question in Lortz's terms, it would have to be asked whether Lutheran claims against a devaluation of Scripture were directed toward an effectively Catholic stance or whether, conversely, the Protestant case aimed at bringing down a "non-Catholic Catholicism" (and as such could be considered Catholic itself).

In Alberigo's analysis, then, the discussion on the causes of the Reformation, which has been repeatedly evoked in the preceding paragraphs, would resurface under a different guise. The exploration of the issue, in this case, began with reflections on the non-residency of bishops and clergy invested with the duty of the care of souls. Alberigo explained that "to the extent that the council presented itself as the historical result of the needs for ecclesiastical renewal over the previous hundred years, it was easy to foresee that residency would be one of the most debated topics at Trent."[68] From Pius II's projects of reform to the *Consilium de emendanda ecclesia*, "the problem of residence was an issue of increasing importance, tending to transform from one of the main instances of reform into the 'problem' of the entire reform of the church upon which all other aspects were conditioned and, in the end, depended."[69] Therefore, if the reform – for it to be considered as such – had to resolve the scourge of an absent clergy that was distracted from its duties, Alberigo also wondered about the origins of evil, unearthing among the structural causes what he described as "a serious distortion of the very ideal of the ecclesiastical function whereby the priestly mission and pastoral commitment had come to be clouded in favor of the more conspicuous and humanly satisfying aspects of social and temporal importance [connected with the episcopal office]."[70] He identified

66 Alberigo, *I vescovi italiani*, 271–272. In the first footnote there, Alberigo railed against the anti-Lutheran attitudes adopted in the apologetics of his day (particularly those fomented by the Jesuits of *La Civiltà Cattolica*) who, in order to challenge the Reformer's attacks on the church's ignorance of the Scriptures, extolled their wide dissemination with arguments that were difficult to support.

67 Alberigo, *I vescovi italiani*, 272.

68 Alberigo, *I vescovi italiani*, 395.

69 Alberigo, *I vescovi italiani*, 404.

70 Alberigo, *I vescovi italiani*, 400–401.

the root of that deviation with a "dissociation … between legal system and moral norm,"[71] a dissociation that received an interesting comment:

> This point is paramount for locating this and other aspects of ecclesiastical decadence within a historical setting. One of the constants throughout the conciliar discussion would be precisely the conviction that many prelates had of the legitimacy of the existing system, except in regard to some of the most scandalous abuses. In the history of the church, this blurring of abuse with normal ecclesiastical practice, indeed, this transformation of abuse into a practical norm, has always constituted one of the most insidious dangers. It resulted in the most tenacious resistance to reform, which for many even came from a sincere conviction. Also stemming from this attitude was the need, felt by the Reformers, to harken back to the early church, bypassing the systems then in force.[72]

It is difficult not to hear in these words a statement of principle that, examining the causes of the Protestant schism and the consequent response drafted at Trent, entrusted to a scrupulous historical reflection, free of confessional partiality, the task of understanding the origins of the divisions, in view of their possible solution.

In the interpretation proposed by Alberigo, the schism of 16th-century Christendom was the result of both the centuries-long decline of the church, to which the Catholic hierarchy had failed to respond adequately, and a juridical confusion (a kind of *Rechtsunklarheit* that mirrored Lortz's *theologische Unklarheit*) resulting from insufficient historical analysis. For some, who had correctly distinguished abuse from the norm (that is, the Catholic and Protestant "reformers"), it was necessary to restore the church by means of a return to its origins and to the gospel. Others (that is, many Catholic bishops), however, were incapable of grasping the abuse as such, equating it with the very norm itself. In both cases – and this is perhaps the most relevant point – the actors had operated in good faith, with sincere motives and a genuine interest in church reform. It was the recuperation of this common concern that could provide the foundation for ecumenical dialogue or, at least, a mutual understanding that would soften the discord. Within this framework, the historian becomes an essential player in service of church reform, with the task of bringing back lost clarity, allowing for the correct interpretation of contested elements, thus falling upon historical investigation, applied with its scholarly methods.

But what most distinguishes Alberigo from the authors examined thus far are the developments of his research trajectory. Driven by the impetus of the ecumenical movement and the changing backdrop brought about by Vatican II, he would cease to assign a pivotal role to the Catholic-Protestant divide and would instead, on the one hand, introduce a broader chronology, and on the other, ascribe greater prominence to reflection on the early church and the Eastern tradition. The church historian becomes a historian of Christianity, moving from a dimension in which institutions dominate to one in which considerations related to a common spiritual source and to the lacerations caused over time prevail instead. Luther and the schism between Catholics and Protestants thus tend to be diluted within a broader history,[73] whose future unity – as Alberigo theorized in a collection devoted to the topic – could come to pass through a Christian ecumenical council. In it, the rigid structures of the churches would give way to methods that recalled the early church, and the action of the Holy Spirit would make it possible to dismantle the traditional juridical structures

71 Alberigo, *I vescovi italiani*, 401.

72 Alberigo, *I vescovi italiani*, 401–402, note 1.

73 See Giuseppe Alberigo, "Dinamiche religiose del Cinquecento italiano tra Riforma, Riforma cattolica, Controriforma," *CrSt* 6, 1985, 543–560.

and forms of representation that are harmful to reunification.[74]

6 An Ecumenical History of the Church?: Limits and Failures of an Experiment

Alberigo's development – sensitive, as we have seen, to the turn that Catholic historiography underwent with regard to Luther, but soon directed toward broader horizons – questioned a limitation that, in many aspects, church historians repeatedly noted when considering an ecumenical perspective. The reasons that inspired Lortz, Iserloh, or Jedin – to cite the cases reported here – to focus on Lutheran "trauma" are obvious. However, it is equally evident, as was mentioned at the outset, that their argumentations relegated the distancing from the Eastern tradition to the background, albeit while nobly acknowledging the latter's greater doctrinal proximity to Rome.

This is an example of how rarely historians, faced with an ecumenical perspective and the challenges of dialogue among churches, were able to fully embrace the complexity of the issue, focusing on only some of the divisions that occurred within Christendom at the expense of others. It is thus useful to ask whether, somehow, this limitation was being overcome when the historians mentioned herein, and the academic communities that they belonged to, set out to write an ecumenical history of the church.

We can find an interesting example in *Ökumenische Kirchengeschichte*, a work compiled between 1970 and 1974 by a sizeable group of scholars – including Alberigo and Iserloh – and headed by both the Catholic Raymund Kottje, professor of historical studies in Bonn, and the Protestant Bernd Moeller, former chair of church history in Göttingen.[75] In the preface to the Italian edition published in 1980–1981, it was precisely Alberigo who pointed out the work's shortcomings:

> The reader may wish for a better integration of the history of the Eastern Christian tradition, now concentrated exclusively in the fourth part of the first volume, risking that it remains somewhat extraneous and peripheral with respect to the history of the Western tradition. It is all the more reason to hope that adequate attention be given to the non-Chalcedonian churches in the future.[76]

Alberigo's observations were more than fair: the first volume, devoted to antiquity, after having explored early Christianity, dealt with the delicate transition from the pre- to post-Constantinian era. After that, the study came to the beginnings of monasticism, to then dwell on the entire history of the Eastern Church from its origins to the 20th century. The second volume focused on the Christian West – from the disintegration of the Roman Empire to the Gregorian age – on papal theocracy, scholasticism, the turbulent era of the Great Schism, and the movements founded by Peter Waldo, John Wyclif, and Jan Hus, before concluding with a segment on the Peace of Westphalia in 1648 and a long section dedicated to the Protestant Reformation, the Catholic Reformation, and the Counter-Reformation.

74 See Giuseppe Alberigo, "Per un concilio ecumenico cristiano," in: Alberigo, *Nostalgie di unità*, 148–156. *Nostalgie di unità* is a collection of various articles that Alberigo had published in the late 1970s and 1980s. For a contextualization of his output, see also Giuseppe Alberigo, "Istanze di comunione per una ecclesiologia cristiana," *CrSt* 16, 1995, 407–430, and Giuseppe Ruggieri, "Lo storico Giuseppe Alberigo (1926–2007)," in: Daniele Menozzi & Marina Montacutelli, eds., *Storici e religione nel Novecento italiano*, Brescia, Morcelliana, 2011, 33–52, esp. 44–45.

75 Raymund Kottje & Bernd Moeller, eds., *Ökumenische Kirchengeschichte*, 3 vols., Mainz, Matthias-Grünewald, 1970–1974. The work has had numerous reeditions, revised and corrected, which continue to this day.

76 Giuseppe Alberigo, "Prefazione all'edizione italiana," in: Raymund Kottje & Bernd Moeller, eds., *Storia ecumenica della Chiesa*, vol. 1, *Chiesa antica e Chiesa orientale*, Brescia, Queriniana, 1980, 5–7, here 6. This translates the third German edition of *Ökumenische Kirchengeschichte*, published that same year. All quotes from this text are adapted into English by the translator.

Lastly, the third and final volume reviewed the European churches (Catholic and Lutheran), the upheavals of the French Revolution, the developments of 19th-century European Christianity, and the challenges that the modernity of the 20th century posed to churches. A special section served as an epilogue, tracing the history of the ecumenical movement in Protestant, Catholic, and Orthodox spheres.

As can be deduced from this brief description, the analysis focused mainly on Europe and particularly on the dialogue between Rome, as the heart of Catholic universalism, and the Germanic world associated with Luther's legacy. The historiographical categories, the periodization of eras, and the problems considered were taken almost exclusively from the European experience, and very few questions were raised on the forms of Christianity in other regions of the world, from Africa to the Americas, or on issues relating to Christian encounters with other religions and cultures in the Far East. The choice of denominations represented was similarly limited and limiting, restricted to Protestant, Catholic, and to a lesser extent Orthodox, while neglecting to consider the churches that split from them. Neither should the fact that only two Orthodox authors – the theologian Anastasios Kallis and Metropolitan Stylianos (Harkianakis) – feature throughout the entire work be overlooked.

In summary, *Ökumenische Kirchengeschichte* appears to be the result of a disproportionately Eurocentric dialogue that was predominantly shaped by the demands of the Catholic-Protestant confrontation, with all its consequences.

For the purposes of this piece, the work's preface and epilogue are equally significant in revealing – through the dilemmas treated by the historical analysis – the anxieties and difficulties that the ecumenical movement was anticipating and, to a large extent, already encountering. From its outset, the project bore its contradictions and structural limitations, beginning with the definition of the relationship between historiography and ecumenical dialogue. The project's innovative method aimed at "bringing historians and theologians of the major Christian confessions together so as to arrive at a common account of church history," with the intention to foster mutual understanding and to create "an overview seeking to discover and communicate the extent to which church history possesses, within the different Christian branches, a coherent image of its object."[77]

It constituted an effort to establish a common denominator, a sort of shared description of the past. The method involved one Protestant and one Catholic assuming joint responsibility for overseeing the various sections of the volume, and in the few spaces reserved for the Orthodox traditions, a Catholic and a Protestant served as editors. If the authors disagreed on a single point, "the particular opinion of the co-author [would be] indicated in a note given in italics and bearing the initials of their name."[78]

Despite these premises and the clearly professed desire to offer the broadest synthesis possible, certain aspects still emerged that pointed to unresolved conflicts. Iserloh, although participating, expressed his strong misgivings about the first two chapters of the *Kirchengeschichte* (dedicated to Jesus of Nazareth and the early Christian community), and alongside protests in favor of a non-confrontational and shared historical vision, he expressed skepticism regarding the project's ability to actually affect ecumenical dialogue: "The editors and contributors hope that they have managed to remain immune to the ecumenical 'illusionism' prevalent today. ... It is not permissible to expect a solution to the conflicts of Christendom from our work. Historical research can only allow a better understanding, not the elimination of aporias."[79] It was an affirmation, not too thinly veiled, that extinguished easy optimism: however closely Catholics and Protestants might have

77 Raymund Kottje & Bernd Moeller, "Prefazione degli editori dell'opera," in: Kottje & Moeller, eds., *Storia ecumenica della Chiesa*, vol. 1, 8–10, here 8.

78 Kottje & Moeller, "Prefazione," 9.

79 Kottje & Moeller, "Prefazione," 8.

worked on together in the attempt to arrive at a common conception of church history, historical reconstruction could not induce an effective rapprochement between Christians.

The same contradictions reappeared in the epilogue of the third volume. The two editors compiled, in retrospect, a balance sheet on the work conducted, describing their "experiment" as a "contribution to the discussion" on "whether an ecumenical history of the church can be achieved."[80] Kottje and Moeller's remarks give the impression that the answer is once again uncertain. Indeed, they distanced themselves from the model proposed by Ernst Benz in his *Kirchengeschichte in ökumenischer Sicht*,[81] arguing for the impossibility of reducing or diminishing the role of individual Christian denominations, as Benz had done. According to Kottje and Moeller, the different churches that the various historians hailed from in fact served as indispensable sources of cultural and spiritual inspiration, and not merely a point of origin in which ecclesiastical conceptions and conditionings were rooted:

> The church historian also belongs to a Christian denomination; and this is precisely our situation, or, to put it in solemn words, our destiny, and we would be doing something unnatural, something artificial, if we wanted to disregard or go beyond this fact. ... Despite all efforts to maintain objectivity, in reality [the historian] cannot abstract from this even in historiographical work, especially as it is usually about the history of these same ecclesial communities. ... We cannot proceed as [Ernst Benz and his inspirer Kenneth Scott Latourette] did and begin by affirming in principle the pluralism of the Christian churches.[82]

The historian seems to surrender to theology, declaring the impossibility and inappropriateness of detaching oneself from their denomination of origin. The writing of an ecumenical history therefore becomes the compilation of "a common inventory,"[83] a shared description of events that marked Christianity's evolution from a common matrix. Even if the last words of the volume reported the hope for "a rapprochement between the confessions"[84] as a result of the work undertaken, the two editors circumscribed their ecumenical commitment within the bounds of scholarly exchange and collaboration. What is lacking is the effective will to impact the process of doctrinal and ecclesial reconciliation and to make history an element capable of propelling the ecumenical movement forward.

Fueling the contradictions listed above were the tense conditions in which the historical discipline found itself during its never-peaceful confrontation with theology and doctrinal issues. The historians examined in the present study – as well as the authors of *Ökumenische Kirchengeschichte* – sought to break free from the subjugation imposed on history by apologetics and controversistic theology, and move away from controversy by placing documentary data, the reconstruction of the protagonists' socio-cultural contexts, and a rethinking of doctrinal formulations as historically determined artifacts back at the center of attention. The expectation was that history's rediscovered and reassigned prominence could affect theology and, above all, influence the structures of the churches by bringing them closer together and enabling them to heal the wounds that had arisen out of misunderstandings and mutually misguided interpretations. Based on the evidence

80 Raymund Kottje & Bernd Moeller, "Epilogo: Il senso e i limiti di una storia ecumenica della chiesa," in: Raymund Kottje & Bernd Moeller, eds., *Storia ecumenica della Chiesa*, vol. 3, *Età moderna*, Brescia, Queriniana, 1981, 369–371, here 369.

81 Ernst Benz, *Kirchengeschichte in ökumenischer Sicht*, Leiden, Brill, 1961.

82 Kottje & Moeller, "Epilogo," 371.

83 Kottje & Moeller, "Epilogo," 371.

84 Kottje & Moeller, "Epilogo," 371.

provided by the facts, however, that expectation was ultimately left unfulfilled: theology seems neither willing to lose nor to share its primacy, whichever direction it takes. To cite two opposing cases among those reflected upon in the present study, on the one hand, Jedin was forced to defend the inadmissibility of a distortion of the documentary evidence (Luther calling the pope the Antichrist) in the name of an inclusive "recatholicization" of his doctrine and on the other hand, Lortz and Iserloh's arguments for a "Catholic" Luther were not conducive to a quick restoration of ecclesial communion.

History – including that concerned with ecumenism – retracts when faced with the resilience of theology, and even more so when faced with the juridical and hierarchical apparatuses of the churches. A space of legitimacy is carved out which, while refraining to prescind from religious and doctrinal demands, is distinct from the latter. Studying is a terrain offering a meeting point built upon a shared reconstruction of facts and, to a large extent, their interpretation. One does not, however, go further by attempting to draw conclusions or suggest consequences that, from a given historical reconstruction, could in some way be considered binding. Those who do so are, in most cases, looked upon suspiciously by the churches, and, not infrequently, expelled or ostracized from them.

Historiographical reflection thus seems to anticipate the crisis and the deadlocks of the ecumenical movement as a whole, shedding light on the entanglements produced by the various religious denominations with their many structures and traditions and, on another level, those produced by the conditioning of a Christianity that is often too Eurocentric, legalistic, and Westernized.

Translated from Italian to English by Susan Dawson Vásquez and David Dawson Vásquez.

Bibliography

Alberigo, Giuseppe, *I vescovi italiani al concilio di Trento (1545–1547)*, Florence, Sansoni, 1959.

Iserloh, Erwin, *Lutero tra Riforma cattolica e protestante*, Brescia, Queriniana, 1970.

Iserloh, Erwin, *Luther und die Reformation: Beiträge zu einem ökumenischen Lutherverständnis*, Aschaffenburg, Pattloch Verlag, 1974.

Jedin, Hubert, *Geschichte des Konzils von Trient*, 4 vols., Freiburg i.Br., Herder, 1951–1975; ET: *A History of the Council of Trent*, 4 vols., St. Louis, B. Herder Book Co., 1957–1976.

Jedin, Hubert, "Mutamenti della interpretazione cattolica della figura di Lutero e loro limiti," *RSCI* 23, 1969, 361–377.

Jedin, Hubert, "Catholic Reformation or Counter-Reformation?," in: David M. Luebke, ed., *The Counter-Reformation: The Essential Readings*, Malden MA, Blackwell, 1999, 19–45.

Kottje, Raymund & Bernd Moeller, eds., *Ökumenische Kirchengeschichte*, 3 vols., Mainz, Matthias-Grünewald, 1970–1974

Lortz, Joseph, *Geschichte der Kirche in ideengeschichtlicher Betrachtung: Eine Sinndeutung der christlichen Vergangenheit in Grundzügen dargestellt*, Münster, Aschendorff, 1936.

Lortz, Joseph, *Mein Umweg zur Geschichte: Ein besinnlicher Rückblick auf der Journee des Anciens d'Echternach, 10. Oktober, 1959*, Wiesbaden, Steiner, 1960.

Lortz, Joseph, *La Riforma in Germania*, ed. Boris Ulianich, ed., Milan, Jaca Book, 1971.

Prodi, Paolo, *Giuseppe Dossetti e le officine bolognesi*, Bologna, Il Mulino, 2016.

Ruggieri, Giuseppe, "Lo storico Giuseppe Alberigo (1926–2007)," in: Daniele Menozzi & Marina Montacutelli, eds., *Storici e religione nel Novecento italiano*, Brescia, Morcelliana, 2011, 33–52.

Ulianich, Boris, "In memoriam Joseph Lortz (1887–1975)," *Rivista di storia e letteratura religiosa* 11, 1975, 781–801.

CHAPTER 35

Christians and Jews: A Dialogue *Sui Generis*

Mauro Velati

1 Introduction

Judaism and Ecumenism are two terms that seem quite distant from one another. On the one hand, we have a civilization and religion that is thousands of years old; on the other, a historical, Christian phenomenon of the 20th century. Nevertheless, they are intertwined in the more general events of recent history. The Christian churches' revision of their attitude toward the Jewish people has matured over the last century within a climate of much broader phenomena, such as the spread of anti-Semitism in Europe, the rise of totalitarianism, and the extermination of Jews during World War II.[1] However, it has never been simply a question of social justice or of defending the rights of minorities. Even in the darkest moments of anti-Semitism, underground currents within the various churches conveyed an awareness of the unique relationship between Jews and Christians, and that awareness also nourished the desire for unity.

Vatican II was the culmination of this complex interweaving of the demands of ecumenism and interreligious dialogue. *Nostra aetate* undoubtedly represents a Catholic manifesto of openness to dialogue with different religions, but its deep genesis can be traced back to the meeting between John XXIII and Jules Isaac, a Jewish professor who had seen his family destroyed in the maelstrom of the Shoah. For reasons that were certainly extrinsic, the original text was presented to the council Fathers as an additional chapter of *De oecumenismo* and, by their will, was expanded into a special declaration. Neither a commonly defined religion, nor properly an ancient Christian confession, Judaism found no place within the narrow theological categories of the time. In addition, there was the enduring Jewish mistrust of Christian appropriation of their historical and religious heritage. In any case, Karl Barth's well-known statement in 1966 – "the ecumenical movement is driven by the Spirit of the Lord. But we should not forget that there is finally only one genuinely ecumenical question: our relations with the Jewish people" – still represents a significant challenge

1 On the development of relations between Catholics and Jews, see John Connelly, *From Enemy to Brother: The Revolution in Catholic Teaching on the Jews (1933–1965)*, Cambridge MA, Harvard University Press, 2012. On the more recent period, see Philip A. Cunningham, Norbert J. Hofman & Jospeh Sievers, eds., *The Catholic Church and Jewish People: Recent Reflections from Rome*, New York, Fordham University Press, 2007. On the dialogue between Jews and Christians in general, Marianne Moyaert & Didier Pollefeyt, eds., *Never Revoked:* Nostra aetate *as Ongoing Challenge for Jewish-Christian Dialogue*, Leuven/Grand Rapids, Peeters/Eerdmans, 2010, and Piero Stefani, "Le chiese cristiane e il popolo ebraico 'dopo Auschwitz,'" in: Giuseppe Ruggieri, ed., *Le chiese nel Novecento*, Bologna, EDB, 2002, 165–193. On the relations between the ecumenical movement and the Jews, the material in the archives of the WCC in Geneva is essential. For the Catholic Church, there are only documents related to Vatican II (in the Vatican II collection of the Archivio Apostolico Vaticano) that, unfortunately, have not yet been studied systematically. For the earlier period, the section of the archives related to the pontificate of Pius XII has recently been opened, and interesting new developments are expected, not just for the period of World War II. There are also many private collections of the main figures, such as those of John Maria Oesterreicher and Karl Thieme, which Connelly has already studied. For the period after the council, the papers of the CRRJ are currently not available, and private collections are scarce. Historians need to work on this in the future. Gerhart Moritz Riegner gives an important account from the Jewish perspective, see Gerhart M. Riegner, *Never Despair: Sixty Years in the Service of the Jewish People and of Human Rights*, Chicago, Ivan R. Dee, 2006.

to the historical understanding of the relations between ecumenism and Judaism.[2] It was not just a wish but an acknowledgement of relations that were already in place within the diverse body of Christianity. At its core, it was an attempt to understand – and thus to not trivialize or instrumentalize – the mystery of Israel, even going beyond the usual categories of Christian theology.

Barth's voice, moreover, was not an isolated one. In 1964, during the years of the council, the Canadian Dominican Bernard Lambert, taking his cue from Paul VI's trip to the Holy Land in January 1964, already characterized the course of Vatican II as a passage from Rome to Jerusalem and saw reconciliation between Jews and Christians as the foundation of all ecumenism.[3] A few years later, the Protestant scholar Fadiey Lovsky would speak of the people of Israel as the "pivot" of ecumenism.[4]

These are a few examples out of many, which reflect a very precise historical moment, that is, the passage to a new ecumenical awareness in the Christian churches. Before the council, when the relationship with the Jewish world was still mediated by the categories of mission and supersession, the situation was quite different. Taking different paths, both Catholics and Protestants started down a road of openness to the Jews that is still developing and can serve as an object for study, starting at least with World War II. The Orthodox churches should be treated differently, but that is a complex issue because of the intertwining of two factors that characterized the Eastern context in the 20th century: on the one hand, the persecution of the Eastern European churches, which brought about their isolation from the rest of Christendom; on the other hand, the birth of the state of Israel, which radically changed the perspective of Christians of Arab origin and occasioned the rebirth of very virulent forms of anti-Semitism.

The complexity of the relationship between ecumenism and dialogue with the Jews shows the specific and completely "asymmetrical" nature of the relationship between Jews and Christians. On the one hand is Christianity, a religious creed that is confronted with its own origin and traces its filiation along a different religious lineage. On the other hand is an ancient religion, Judaism, that looks at Christianity as one of the many products of its own history without, however, acknowledging its epochal character. One, a religion characterized by its universalism and the other a faith that coincides with a people.[5]

2 The Ecumenical Movement and the Jews

In the history of the modern ecumenical movement, the issue of the relationship with Israel has not held a central position. Ecumenism began as a specifically Christian movement, marked by the ideal of a visible unity among the churches and closely tied to the development of the missionary movement, continuing a long trend coming from the mid-19th century. As a religion that does not share a faith in Jesus Christ, Judaism remained extraneous to this area of encounter. Throughout the 20th century, however, there were numerous contacts and relationships between the two different trajectories: that of ecumenical dialogue and a focus on Judaism. All Christian churches have

2 The phrase is cited in Paul van Buren, *A Christian Theology of the People of Israel*, San Francisco, Harper, 1984, 351. See also Cornelius Adriaan Rijk, "L'œcuménisme et le dialogue," *SIDIC* 1/3, 1968, 14–17, here 17.

3 Bernard Lambert, *De Rome à Jérusalem: Itinéraire spirituel de Vatican II*, Paris, Éditions du Centurion, 1964, 257–259.

4 Fadiey Lovsky, *La déchirure de l'absence: Essai sur les rapports de l'église du Christ et du peuple d'Israël*, Paris, Calmann-Lévy, 1971, 232 and 256.

5 In the documents of dialogue between Christians and Jews, it is common to affirm the asymmetrical character of the relationship. For example, see the WCC document "Ecumenical Considerations on Jewish-Christian Dialogue," Jul 16, 1982, published in *The Theology of the Churches and the Jewish People: Statements by the World Council of Churches and Its Member Churches*, Geneva, WCC Publications, 1988, 34–42, esp. 36.

long thought of their relationship with the Jews in terms of proselytism and mission – the "accursed people" could only find salvation in denying the faith of their fathers and in recognizing Christian revelation.

Among Protestants, this type of activity took place within the missionary societies that, starting from the beginning of the 1700s, had developed a formation program for those specializing in missions to the Jews. The progressive coordination of these societies' efforts at the international level led, in 1921, to the foundation of the IMC.[6] During both the Edinburgh conference of 1910 (the first meeting of the WMC as well as the origin of the ecumenical movement's efforts) and the time of the actual foundation of the IMC, attention to the Jews was non-existent. In the panorama of world-level missions, which was opening to the prospect of encounters with the great Asian religions and the world of Islam, the small Jewish presence – scattered over so many countries of the world – appeared rather insignificant. It was the insistence of the English missionary societies that put the question of missions to the Jews on the agenda, starting down a path that, a few years later, would lead to the foundation of the IMCCAJ. In 1927, this organization's history began in two places symbolic of the Jewish presence in Europe – Budapest and Warsaw – and its evolution reflected the changes and transitions in the Protestant world's awareness of the Jews during that century.[7]

For several decades, the history of the missionary efforts of the IMCCAJ ran parallel to the history of the beginnings of the WCC in Geneva, which speaks to the struggles in Protestant consciousness during the decades before and after World War II. In the 1930s, the rise of Nazism with its anti-Semitic agenda was destined to change – at least in Europe – the context of the missionary societies. Many institutions associated with them, including the Institutum Judaicum Delitzschianum in Leipzig, had been suppressed by the Nazi regime. The missionary societies played an active role in assisting "non-Aryans" and in helping those affected by the persecution. Establishing a condemnation – albeit weak – of anti-Semitism was the beginning of a critical reflection that, however, did not in the least question the fundamental unionist character of the missions' activity. Already in the 1920s, the condemnation of various forms of anti-Semitism (whose religious character was generally denied) was often motivated by the simple observation that it constituted an obstacle to the work of religious propaganda in the Jewish world. Only in 1937, at the Vienna conference of the IMCCAJ, did general secretary Conrad Hoffmann Jr. clearly express awareness that Nazi anti-Semitism constituted a radically new experience compared to the past, and thus also required a new attitude from the churches. In that context, the assembly approved a declaration intended for the Oxford conference of the Life and Work movement, one of the two branches of the nascent ecumenical movement, which contained a vigorous stance against anti-Semitism:

> We desire to record our conviction that in contemporary anti-Semitism we face an extraordinary menace against which all Christians must be warned. All forms of hatred and persecution must be deplored by Christians, and their victims must be succored; but there exists today a type of racial anti-Semitism and anti-Semitic propaganda inspired by hatred of everything springing from Jewish sources; and this creates more crucial issues for Christianity than ordinary outbursts of race feeling. Christian churches must be warned that they cannot be silent

6 For the history of this organization up until its merger with the WCC, see the contribution by Kenneth R. Ross in the first volume of this work.

7 The history of the IMCCAJ has been exhaustively reconstructed by Allan R. Brockway, *For Love of the Jews: A Theological History of the International Missionary Council's Committee on the Christian Approach to the Jews (1927–1961)*, Ph.D. thesis, University of Birmingham, 1992.

> in the presence of this propaganda, still less connive at or participate in the extension of its errors and falsehoods, without betraying Christ, undermining the basis of the church, and incurring the most severe judgment of God.[8]

The declaration was not actually adopted by the Oxford assembly and ended up being watered down within a more general condemnation of all forms of racism. Nevertheless, it remains significant of what the experience of the missionary societies – although far from recognizing the religious specificity of Judaism – had developed and that, in various ways, would flow into the history of the ecumenical movement.

The years following World War II were fundamental, both for the history of the ecumenical movement and for the unfolding of relations with the Jewish world. A real perception of the dimensions of the tragedy of the Shoah slowly began to emerge. Within the Christian churches, the self-critical reflection on complicity with anti-Semitism and the lack of reaction to Nazism reached increasingly radical conclusions capable of overturning the very foundations of the religious perspective on Judaism. The Jewish world itself – through figures such as Jules Isaac – encouraged this process of revision in theological and catechetical terms. The various churches' attitudes differed according to their internal workings and logic. Among Catholics, the many voices calling for Pope Pius XII to explicitly intervene went unanswered.[9]

The Protestant world had not taken a unitary line, but the unifying sign of a reparatory attitude, aware of the negative potential of the traditional view of Judaism that had developed within the churches, existed in its various expressions. From this point of view, the 1947 Darmstadt declaration, by the EKD *Bruderrat*, was one of the most significant documents, given the role played by sectors of German Protestantism in supporting Adolf Hitler's anti-Semitic campaign.

> There was bound to be a bitter retribution for the fact that anti-Semitism rose and flourished not only among the people (who still seemed to be a Christian nation), not only among the intelligentsia and in governmental and military circles, but also among Christian leaders. And when finally this radical anti-Semitism, based on racial hatred, destroyed our nation and our churches from within, and released all its brutal force from without, there existed no power to resist it – because the churches had forgotten what Israel really is, and no longer loved the Jews. Christian circles washed their hands of all responsibility, justifying themselves by saying that there was a curse on the Jewish people. Christians had ceased to believe that the promise concerning the Jews still held good, they no longer preached it, nor showed it in their attitude to the Jews. In this way we Christians helped to bring about all the injustice and suffering inflicted upon the Jews in our country.[10]

Jews and Christians had often found themselves united in the suffering of the war, and the years after the liberation of Europe were a time when the desire for collaboration between people and institutions on the two sides found concrete expressions. The first CCJ was born in 1942 in Great Britain, but it was followed by similar experiences in the postwar years. The Oxford international conference on "Freedom, Justice, and Responsibility" in 1946 and the subsequent meeting in Seelisberg in 1947 were intended to provide a theoretical basis for a revision of the theological approach to Jews, and coincided with the founding of the ICCJ. These conferences did not appear out of nowhere but were the expression of a movement that had involved representatives of Judaism and the Catholic and Protestant churches since the

8 Brockway, *For the Love of the Jews*.

9 Connelly, *From Enemy to Brother*, 211–236.

10 Cited in Mauro Velati, "The Debate on *De Judaeis* and Ecumenical Dialogue," in: Neville Lamdan & Alberto Melloni, eds., *Nostra Aetate: Origins, Promulgation, Impact on Jewish-Catholic Relations*, Berlin, LIT, 2007, 145–162, here 147.

1920s, especially in the Anglo-Saxon context. It is the story of Jewish-Christian cooperation that its main historian – the English Methodist William Wynn Simpson – traces back to the contacts between Martin Buber and some Christian friends in the climate of a "presentiment of catastrophe" in the early months of 1914.[11] A few years later, in the United States, in response to the racist initiatives of the Ku Klux Klan, the Committee on Good Will between Jews and Christians was born, the seed of the future NCCJ that was established in 1928. In England, in these same years, the Society of Jews and Christians was founded to promote common initiatives in education and welfare. It would play an important role in the 1930s, aiding Jewish refugees fleeing Hitler's Germany. Viewed with suspicion by many sectors of both Judaism and the Christian churches, these initiatives of cooperation played an important role in the two sides' acquiring knowledge about each other and overcoming prejudices. Certainly, important problems remained in the very setting of their work, which would give rise to long debates: the risk of indifferentism, the question of common prayer, or the need to balance collaboration with an exclusivist conception of religious freedom that many of the participants did not want to relinquish.

The two conferences mentioned above, as well as a third in Fribourg in 1948, arose from the desire for international coordination among the groups working in this area. The main nucleus remained that of the American and English councils, but local groups had also formed in Germany, South Africa, Australia, Switzerland, Italy, France, and other countries. The Ten Points of Seelisberg were the manifesto of the Christian churches' commitment against discrimination and racism, without neglecting considerations of some theological aspects of Jewish-Christian dialogue. Catholic representatives had also participated in the document's drafting. In the unfavorable context of Pope Pius XII's church, they acted as pioneers and, in most cases, were converts. This is one of the paradoxes of this affair. It was precisely the targets of conversion efforts who became the best advocates of Judaism in the Catholic world.

When the first assembly of the WCC met in Amsterdam in 1948, these different paths in the Protestant world – missionary societies, councils of Christians and Jews, and the ecumenical movement – intersected. Some of the most important members of the IMCCAJ participated in the assembly. Hoffmann – then the association's secretary – was in charge of committee IV, section B, whose theme was the study of the Christian approach to the Jews. Along with others, he had worked on much of the preparatory material. In this committee, the report "The Christian Approach to the Jews" was born. While not among the acts that the assembly officially approved, this was commended to the churches for their serious considerations. It was a transitional document that, while innovative with respect to the common feeling of many of the WCC member churches, remained firmly anchored in considering the Christian approach in a missionary mode, without a theological deepening of the theme of the relationship between Christianity and Judaism. Even in the final section, recommending that the WCC sponsor more detailed studies, the proposed agenda was limited to listing three avenues of research: the basis of modern anti-Semitism, opportunities for cooperation between Jews and Christians in civil and social fields, and the issue of the state of Israel. Regarding the condemnation of anti-Semitism and the recognition of the sins of Christians, while the text was unequivocal (often repeating that "anti-Semitism is sin against God and man"), the general perspective was still that of Christian evangelism, with the significant affirmation of the "parish approach": "The fulfillment of this commission requires that we include the Jewish people in our evangelistic task" and again

11 William W. Simpson, "Co-Operation between Christians and Jews: Its Possibilities and Limitations," in: Göte Hedenquist, ed., *The Church and the Jewish People*, London, Edinburgh House Press, 1954, 117–142, here 117. See also William W. Simpson, *Jews and Christians Today: A Study in Jewish and Christian Relationships*, London, Epworth, 1940.

"our churches must consider the responsibility for missions to the Jews as a normal part of parish work, especially in those countries where Jews are members of the general community."[12]

After Amsterdam, the vision deriving from the history of the missionary societies was destined to be compared more and more closely with the approach of the Goodwill Movement, which dampened missionaries' evangelistic zeal in the name of tolerance and interreligious cooperation. The leaders of the IMCCAJ, whose influence persisted within the WCC – even in the absence of a special section – showed themselves willing to reconsider some assumptions of the entire Christian approach to the Jews. This was demonstrated by the work *The Church and the Jewish People*, published in 1954, as an expression of the commitment to in-depth study undertaken by the assembly in Amsterdam. The volume was edited by the secretary of the IMCCAJ, Göte Hedenquist, and collected the contributions of scholars who were linked, in various ways, to the committee's work, along with two Jewish voices, Rabbi Leo Baeck and the professor of history of religions Hans-Joachim Schoepfs, of the University of Erlangen.[13] The transitory nature of this work was expressed in Allan R. Brockway's assessment "everything had changed and nothing had changed."[14] Viewed within the long history of the IMCCAJ, it showed the growth in the Christian approach to Jews with the recognition of some essential information, such as the real meaning and permanent validity of the Old Covenant. On the other hand – while according space to the Goodwill Movement's approach in Simpson's article on Jewish-Christian cooperation – the core of the missionary approach was reaffirmed, which was well expressed by the words of Robert Smith: "The fundamental basis of this concern is the belief that the Gospel must be extended to the Jews on the same terms as to other peoples."[15]

Hedenquist's book represented the contribution of the IMCCAJ to the preparations for the general assembly of the WCC scheduled for August 1954 in Evanston. Unlike in Amsterdam, the committee leaders did not play a significant role in the assembly. That is why the Evanston debate – an occasion of great conflict and polarization on the topic of Israel – more accurately shows the mood and opinions of the wider ecumenical movement. The assembly's theme was "Christ, the Hope of the World," and the official report actually made no mention of Israel. In the provisional texts distributed to the assembly, however, after Hans Lilje's introductory report, there were two references to Israel, the first of which became an object of discussion. It called for "a statement of the New Testament concept of the ultimate fulfilment of God's promise to the people of ancient Israel, and the consequent special responsibility of the church of Christ for the proclamation of the hope in Christ to the Jews."[16] During the debate, three different positions were compared. The delegate of the Coptic Church, Makary El Souriany, asked for the phrase to be deleted for political reasons, because of possible repercussions in the Middle East. Charles Phelps Taft II, a layman of the ECUSA, objected to the mention of the missionary perspective towards the Jews, which was bound to jeopardize relations with the Jewish world. Hendrikus Berkhof, of the NHK, instead defended the purely religious meaning of the mention of Israel, citing Rom 9:11. The final vote on the reference resulted in 195 votes for its deletion and 150 for its retention. The proposal had received a not insignificant amount of support and, for that reason, at the end of the debate a statement on the hope of Israel was proposed and signed by some of the delegates – including Philippe Maury, Thomas F. Torrance,

12 *The Theology of the Churches*, 5–9, here 5–7.

13 See Hedenquist, ed., *The Church and the Jewish People*.

14 Brockway, *For Love of The Jews*.

15 Robert Smith, "The Christian Message to Israel," in: Hedenquist, ed., *The Church and the Jewish People*, 189–200, here 189.

16 Brockway, *For Love of The Jews*.

Joseph Sittler, Josef Hromádka, Edmund Schlink, and Martin Niemöller – and attached to the official report.[17]

The Evanston debate cannot be reduced to dissention between pro-Semites and anti-Semites or Zionists and anti-Zionists but appears as a more complex issue reflecting the tension between a missionary approach and the need to dialogue with the Jewish world. In the background there was certainly also the contrast between a European approach that was more attentive to the theological aspect (due to the reflection on the experience of the Shoah) and a North American one that was more pragmatic and tied to the missionary imperative.

In 1961, when the general assembly of the WCC was held in New Delhi, some hoped that a step forward could be made, with respect to Evanston, by adopting a motion on the relationship with Israel that was more theologically compromised. In reality, the divisions and differences remained intact, and the secretary general himself, Willem Adolph Visser 't Hooft, intervened to block any attempt to reopen the controversial issue, speaking with authority on rejecting the presentation of an amendment by the delegate of the FSPC: "On the contrary, the Jews remain God's chosen people (cf. Rom 9–11), for even their rejection for a time must contribute to the world's salvation."[18] The assembly approved a declaration on anti-Semitism that developed a position similar to that of Amsterdam. The only new element was the insertion of a brief phrase on the rejection of the accusation of deicide that anticipated the developments in the theological debate of the years to come ("in Christian teaching, the historic events which led to the Crucifixion should not be so presented as to fasten upon the Jewish people of today responsibilities which belong to our corporate humanity and not to one race or community").[19]

3 The Trajectory of the Catholic World

For a long time, the Catholic world and the ecumenical movement found themselves on opposing sides, with an attitude of ill-concealed hostility due to the refusal by the papal magisterium to recognize the goodness of the efforts of Protestant and Orthodox ecumenism. Although separated in their initiatives, Catholics and non-Catholics found themselves side by side in the storm of World War II and in the tragic discovery of the destructive potential that anti-Semitism had accumulated over the years since the beginning of the century.[20] All the different Christian denominations, before and during World War II, had – in different ways and to different extents – experienced the surrender to anti-Semitic political or religious ideologies. After the conflict ended, pioneering initiatives took root in the Catholic world as well, destined to prepare the ground for the council's turning point.

The trailblazers of ecumenism and those of dialogue with Judaism were clearly in the minority in Pius XII's church, vaguely tolerated but always surrounded by an attitude of mistrust due to fear of indifferentism and false irenicism, to use the terminology consecrated by the encyclical *Humani generis*. In 1950, the Holy Office issued a *Monitum* to Catholics warning against efforts to collaborate with those of other faiths. It was aimed at initiatives of Jewish-Christian dialogue and, in particular, at the activities of the ICCJ. As a result, a Roman inspection of Gertrud Luckner's Freiburg

17 *The Theology of the Churches*, 10–11.

18 Willem Adolph Visser 't Hooft, ed., *The New Delhi Report: The Third Assembly of the World Council of Churches (1961)*, New York, Association Press, 1962, 149.

19 *The Theology of the Churches*, 12.

20 On the impact of the World War II on the ecumenical movement, see Étienne Fouilloux's contribution "Ecumenism between Communism and Nazism (1929–1948)" in this volume.

circle was carried out by Jesuit fathers Robert Leiber, Augustin Bea, and Charles Boyer.[21]

In this situation, attempts to develop a reflection on the relationship between Christian unity and Judaism were understandably rare. The pioneers long insisted on the need to consider Jews from the same perspective that Catholic ecumenism regarded the so-called separated brethren, that is, from a perspective of a rediscovery of the other, of a reevaluation of a common heritage. For Christians, it was a question of the common faith in Jesus Christ; for Jews, of a more generic universal brotherhood based on the Old Covenant. It was not yet dialogue but rather a change in attitude: from conquest to fraternity. In the 1930s, Jesuit Joseph Bonsirven moved in a similar direction, rejecting the path of collective conversion and instead insisting on treating one another as brothers and sisters, overcoming ignorance and widespread misunderstandings.[22]

With the postwar period, the initiatives for dialogue and mutual understanding that had begun in the 1930s received a boost. The Austrian-born priest John Maria Oesterreicher, trained in the world of Christian unionism, played an important role. Born into a Jewish family, he had converted to Catholicism in the 1920s and had chosen the path of priesthood, finding himself beginning his ministry during the years of the Nazi rise to power. Founder of the *Erfüllung* newspaper, he was one of the first to promote forms of cultural resistance to the rampant anti-Semitism, even before the annexation of the Austrian territory to the Third Reich. In Europe, the situation of relations between Catholics and Jews was complicated by the effects of the Nazi extermination and by a cancellation process that seemed the only way to erase the memory of the many complicities and tolerances on the Christian side. After World War II, Germany was a destroyed and dismembered country, where the Jewish presence had been considerably reduced. At the same time, however, it was precisely in Germany that, according to John Connelly, the true driving force behind the change – that is, the sense of the shared suffering endured by Jews and Christians during the war – took root.[23] It became the basis of an attitude of reciprocal openness, which was completely new at a time when, it is as well to recall, the memory of the extermination of Jews as a historical event was not yet part of the common heritage of European consciousness.

In 1955, the theologian Karl Otto Thieme, connected to the Freiburg circle, published his six theses on the ecumenical aspect of Jewish-Christian dialogue.[24] It was a reflection born within the specific context of ecumenical dialogue.[25] In fact, Thieme had worked on the drafting of a Catholic contribution to the Evanston assembly, prepared

21 Thomas Brechenmacher, *Der Vatikan und die Juden: Geschichte einer unheiligen Beziehung vom 16. Jahrhundert bis zur Gegenwart*, Munich, Beck, 2005, 229–230. The *Monitum*, probably dated to Oct 28, 1950, was not published in *AAS* but was sent with a communication from the secretary of state to the German bishops (see Elias H. Füllenbach, "Das katholisch-jüdische Verhältnis im 20. Jahrhundert: Katholische Initiativen gegen den Antisemitismus und die Anfänge des christlich-jüdischen Dialogs in Deutschland," in: Reinhold Boschki & Albert Gerhards, eds., *Erinnerungskultur in der pluralen Gesellschaft: Neue Perspektiven für den christlich-jüdischen Dialog*, Paderborn, Schöningh, 2010, 143–163, esp. 154–157).

22 On Bonsirven see Laurence Deffayet-Loupiac, "Le rôle du Pére Bonsirven dans le renouveau du dialogue Judéo-chrétien dans l'entre-deux guerres," *RHEF* 89, 2003, 81–103. On a figure who was the opposite of Bonsirven and his history of anti-Semitism, see the recent work of Nina Valbousquet, *Catholique et antisémite: Le réseau de Mgr Benigni (1918–1934)*, Paris, CNRS Éditions, 2020. For the evolution that took place in the Catholic world, see the essays by Renato Moro, Gabriele Rigano & Alberto Melloni in: Andrea Riccardi, ed., *Le Chiese e gli altri: Culture, religioni, ideologie e Chiese cristiane nel Novecento*, Milan, Guerini, 2008, respectively 29–56, 57–95, and 97–122; see also Connelly, *From Enemy to Brother*, 174–236.

23 Connelly, *From Enemy to Brother*, 175.

24 Karl Thieme, "Der ökumenischen Aspekt der christlich-jüdischen Begegnung: Sechs Thesen zur innerchristlichen Diskussion," *Freiburger Rundbrief* 29–32, 1955–1956, 9–14.

25 On the German issues, see Füllenbach, "Das katholisch-jüdische Verhältnis," 143–163.

by the theologians of the CCEQ. Thieme, defined by Connelly as a "forgotten pioneer," was very significant in the development of Jewish-Christian relations. He, too, was a convert, born into a Protestant family and embracing Catholicism in the early 1920s. After having contributed, along with Oesterreicher and others, to the Catholic resistance in the fight against Nazi anti-Semitism in the years before the war, he participated in the first meetings between Jews and Christians and, in 1950, experienced what he called a conversion to dialogue, inspired by the reading and study of St. Paul's Letter to the Romans.[26]

Other examples can be found in the literature of that group of trailblazers who, within the space of a decade – from Seelisberg to the Apeldoorn conference of 1960 – had become spokesmen for a significant revision of Catholic teaching on the Jews. In France, Paul Démann, a Hungarian Jew who had converted to Catholicism and become a priest in the Congregation of the Our Lady of Notre-Dame de Sion, did not hesitate to recognize the mutual interdependence between the development of ecumenical efforts and Catholicism's opening to the Jews.[27] In the two areas, the goals were different, but the means and methods of action to overcome prejudices and rediscover a positive relationship of fraternity were identical. In Holland, the Dominican theologian Karel Pauwels, secretary of the KRI, posed the question concisely: "Is the mystery of Israel an ecumenical matter?"[28] He acknowledged the scant attention that the topic of the mystery of Israel had received in the history of the ecumenical movement and observed that, strictly speaking, ecumenism had a starting point (faith in Jesus Christ) that was incompatible with the Jewish religion. According to Pauwels, however, it was evident that Christians and Jews shared a common heritage. Israel possesses the gift of God in the Bible (even if considered differently and limited to the part of the Old Covenant). Ecumenical dialogue remained the model for a renewed approach to the Jewish world, in the search for common points of those *vestigia ecclesiae* that had played an important role in the nascent phase of the ecumenical movement.

It is clear from this brief indications how the discovery of a link between ecumenism and dialogue with Judaism could provide the pathway for Catholic reflection to think the relationship with Judaism in a different way, looking for common elements and, above all, to exit the wastelands of the missionary attitude that, from a historical point of view, had not achieved the desired results and which, by then, had shown its limitations from a theological point of view, at least to the most thoughtful minds. Similar reflections are also found in a text by pastor Jacques Martin, a founder of AJCF. Reflecting on the tasks and purposes of AJCF in 1958, Martin pointed precisely to the ecumenical movement's model. In his view, there was a need for "an attitude comparable to that which drives the ecumenical movement: the spirit of every encounter is that of a disinterested friendship; but at the same time, we have to fundamentally rediscover the sense of a common vocation and the meaning of our differences."[29] Martin also went into detail about a possible agenda for dialogue by inviting Christians to reflect on Judaism's ecclesiological significance.

4 The Turning Point of Vatican II

Chance and will were interwoven in the origins of *Nostra aetate*, which stemmed from Jules Isaac's proposal to John XXIII to make the council an occasion for overcoming the so-called teaching of contempt. The pontiff's choice to entrust the study

26 On Thieme's conversion, see Connelly, *From Enemy to Brother*, 190–209.

27 Paul Démann, "Juifs et chrétiens à travers les siècles," *Lumière et vie* 37, 1958, 91–110, esp. 108–109.

28 Carolus Franciscus Pauwels, "Ist das Mysterium Israel eine ökumenische Frage?," *Freiburger Rundbrief* 45–48, 1959–1960, 8–10.

29 Jacques Martin, "L'Amitié Judéo-chrétienne," *Sens* 293, 2004, 621–628, here 626.

of the subject to Cardinal Bea and the SPCU was not automatically seen as a sign of awareness of the intimate bond between the Jewish question and ecumenism. After all, Bea was an established biblical scholar and specialist in the Old Testament. He was also a Jesuit, and it was precisely in Ignatian circles that awareness of the church's magisterium on Israel and anti-Semitism was most alive, as evidenced by proposals made in the preparatory phase.[30] In the SPCU's work the two issues – ecumenism and Judaism – travelled on parallel but carefully distinct tracks. Bea and his collaborators were well aware of the fact that the issue of Judaism would never find a place on the agenda of either a dicastery or the newly created Theological Commission. That is why the SPCU found itself playing a valuable substitute role. Near the end of the preparatory phase – in June 1962 – two different documents were drafted, the first draft of *De Iudaeis* and the schema *De oecumenismo catholico*.

After a few months – a gap determined by the Secretariat of State's decision to remove the document on the Jews from the council's agenda – it was again John XXIII who allowed Bea to resubmit a draft on the issue in a reedited version. In the summer of 1963, then, the bishops received *De Iudaeis* in the form of a chapter of the schema on ecumenism. Was it a tactical move to protect the schema? Such an impression is confirmed by the insertion in the same draft of the schema of another chapter, one dedicated to religious freedom, which had already aroused considerable opposition.

The debate in the council session began with an examination of the draft in its entirety. In their addresses, many bishops also touched upon the placement of that fourth chapter on the Jews, naturally expressing different positions and wishes. Already at this early stage, the Eastern bishops' opposition – convinced that the chapter's discussion would aggravate relations with the Arab world – was evident. This attitude was reflected, for example, in the addresses of patriarchs Stéphanos I Sidarouss, Ignatius Gabriel I Tappouni, and Maximos IV Sayegh, who demanded the chapter be set aside.[31] Other bishops thought the chapter should be removed because it was not well-integrated into the ecumenical schema. The Canadian Paul-Émile Léger – like many others – feared the non-Catholics' reactions to the juxtaposition of ecumenical dialogue with that with Judaism. The very meaning of ecumenism as an effort of unity among those who share faith in Jesus Christ was, it seemed, obscured by the schema's structure.[32] Opinions on the chapter's fate were not unanimous. For Ermenegildo Florit and Casimiro Morcillo González, the right place for it would have been in one of the other schemas then being prepared (*De Ecclesia*, *De missionibus*, or else *De praesentia Ecclesiae in mundo*),[33] given the relevance of the issue of the relationship between the Old and New Covenants. For the Spaniard Josep Pont i Gol, on the other hand, what was needed was a specific schema on dialogue with religions that would also include Judaism, Islam, and the Eastern religions.[34] That was the perspective that was subsequently embraced in the development of *Nostra aetate*.

A few of the Fathers, however, were willing to accept the chapter's insertion in the ecumenical schema, but their acceptance was generally only

30 See the opinion of the PIB, "De antisemitismo vitando," which was sent out during the preparatory consultations, now available in *ADA* 4, 1, 131–132.

31 The texts of the addresses are in *AS* 2, 5, 527–528 (Tappouni), 541 (Sidarouss), and 542–545 (Maximos IV).

32 *AS* 2, 5, 550–552.

33 *AS* 2, 5, 606–608, here 608 (Morcillo: "Methodus oecumenica diversimode procedere debet pro christianis et pro non christianis, etiamsi filii sint Abrahe"), *AS* 2, 5, 665–667, here 666 (Florit: "Rationes prorsus singulares inter Ecclesiam et filios Israel legitimam reddunt tractationem etsi breviorem huius quaestionem"). See also the speech delivered by Fr. Paul-Pierre-Yves Dalmais, which was signed by six other African bishops ("Il ne faut pas mettre tout le monde dans le même sac"; *AS* 2, 5, 782–783, here 783) and that of Gregorio Modrego y Casaus (who asked that the chapter be included in *De Ecclesia*), *AS* 2, 5, 807–808.

34 *AS* 2, 5, 746–749, esp. 746. See also the address written by Jan Van Cauwelaert (825–826).

on certain conditions. It would be necessary, they said, to modify the very setting of the schema in line with a perspective that tended to broaden the concept of ecumenism well beyond the historical meaning it had assumed. Ecumenism, then, would indicate the church's constant concern for the salvation of all persons, whether Jewish or pagan (León Bonaventura de Uriarte Bengoa),[35] and would be transformed into an irenic attitude of openness towards all expressions of thought and human religiosity. The address by the Swiss Angelo Giuseppe Jelmini also ran along these lines.[36] In the speeches, however, the issue of chapter's acceptance was always linked to these conditions; it was given no justification of its own. The only bishop to clearly provide a reason for accepting the ecumenical schema's structure was the Mexican Sergio Méndez Arceo, who emphasized the existence of a shared heritage between Jews and Christians.[37]

The matter was also discussed by the non-Catholic observers, and it is interesting to note that – during the sort of parallel council of meetings with the SPCU – it was precisely the representatives of liberal Protestantism who advocated for the prospect of maintaining the chapter in the ecumenical schema. The American Unitarian George Huntston Williams proposed that the issue be divided into two large chapters, ecumenism proper and religious freedom (which would include the relationship with the Jews and anti-Semitism). The International Association for Liberal Christianity and Religious Freedom delegate, Lambertus Jacobus van Holk, appreciated the chapter on the Jews for its prophetic weight in the context of the fight against racism. Finally, the Quaker Douglas V. Steere reflected on the impossibility of a profound renewal in the church without consideration of those outside it (non-believers, Jews, followers of the great religions). The position of the Protestant and Anglican representatives was far more nuanced and careful to safeguard the uniqueness of ecumenism as an intra-Christian reality. The WCC's representative, Lukas Vischer, to give just one example, advised the secretary of the SPCU Johannes Willebrands from the beginning to separate the fourth chapter entirely from the ecumenical schema, and on several occasions expressed his preference for the solution of including *De Iudaeis* in the schema on the church.[38]

The matter of the ecumenical schema was resolved in the agreement between the SPCU and the council's governing bodies. In April 1964, the Coordinating Commission decided to transform chapter 4 into a *Declaratio altera de Iudaeis et non christianis*, thus partway meeting the concerns that had emerged in the SPCU. However, in order to quell the controversy, a condition was set to include mentions of Islam and the church's attitude towards other religions. On this basis, Willebrands commissioned the two theologians Yves Marie-Joseph Congar and Charles Moeller to draft a new version of the text on the Jews along with two other sections on universal brotherhood (with an explicit mention of Islam) and the condemnation of all forms of discrimination.[39]

The appointed commission's decision – constrained by different needs and pressures – opened the way to the drafting of a true and proper schema that incorporated the chapter on the Jews within a global discourse on the Catholic Church's attitude towards other religions. This was

35 *AS* 2, 5, 629–631, esp. 631.

36 *AS* 2, 5, 600–602, here 601–602: "Neque dicatur quaestio de Iudaeis schemati nostro aliena esse. Haec quaestio maxime attinte ad elaborandam unionem interomnes christifideles quia, 1. schisma inter Synagogam et Ecclesiam est fons omnium aliorum schismatum, et, 2. ut S. Paulus ait, totius conversio et adsumptio erit vita ex mortuis [Rom 11:15]."

37 *AS* 2, 5, 615–618, esp. 617.

38 Mauro Velati, *Separati ma fratelli: Gli osservatori non cattolici al Vaticano II (1962–1965)*, Bologna, Il Mulino, 2014, 318–319.

39 Giovanni Miccoli, "Two Sensitive Issues: Religious Freedom and the Jews," in: Giuseppe Alberigo & Joseph A. Komonchak, eds., *History of Vatican II*, vol. 4, *Church as Communion: Third Period and Intersession (September 1964–September 1965)*, Leuven/Maryknoll, Peeters/Orbis Books, 2003, 95–193, esp. 142–144.

the perspective of *Nostra aetate*. The time was not yet ripe for an in-depth reflection on the unique relationship between Judaism and Christianity or on this new approach's potential in reference to the ecumenical ideal. This new schema also did not articulate the historical implications of the events of the Shoah for Catholicism. The council document, however, initiated a process of revision of the theology of supersession and went far beyond past positions that had been formulated within the ecumenical movement.

The path of the new text encountered some difficulties between the third and fourth council sessions due to the tensions between the SPCU – custodian of the original version of the discourse on the Jews that hinged on abandoning the accusation of deicide – and the Theological Commission – behind which Pope Paul VI was also at work and which intended to downplay the epochal significance of this turning point. These tensions reflected the polarization that had also sprung up among the bishops and among the public at large. On the one hand, the American and Central European bishops (those most affected by the tragedy of the Shoah) pressed for an opening towards the Jews while, on the other hand, the Middle Eastern episcopate and traditionalist groups saw the accusation of deicide as an untouchable element in Catholic tradition. Bea presented an initial text to the conciliar assembly in September 1964, which was discussed in the general congregation.[40] Among the bishops' addresses, Cardinal Giacomo Lercaro's, which adopted a decidedly original perspective, was extremely important. Recognizing the specific religious vocation of Israel did not derive from motivations of a historical or political nature but from the "rediscovery of the theology of the mystery of the church," which was why it should be closely linked to the treatment of the document on the church and the liturgical constitution.[41] After an initial approval of the text with 1,651 *placet* (out of 1,996 voters) and the gathering of amendments, it began to take its definitive shape. The part on the Jews occupied chapter 4 and remained one of the most controversial points until the end. Following Lercaro's proposal, behind which Giuseppe Dossetti's pen was to be found, the opening sentence of *NA* 4 reads: "As the sacred synod searches into the mystery of the church, it remembers the bond that spiritually ties the people of the New Covenant to Abraham's stock."

The final version, in a much softer form, was released in the summer of 1965. The explicit mention of dropping the accusation of deicide was deleted and anti-Semitism was simply decried. In October of the same year, the text returned to the council Fathers and, despite a last attempt to block it by the traditional bishops of the Coetus Internationalis Patrum, it was approved and promulgated. At the final vote on Oct 28, 1965, 88 Fathers voted *non placet* out of a total of 2,309.[42] Much resistance had been overcome, but through a compromise that sacrificed some of the pioneers' demands.

The council period was an important turning point for the ecumenical movement[43] because in 1961 the IMC merged with the WCC, with the consequent integration of the IMCCAJ into the WCC's structures. It was a very important step for the ecumenical movement that extended its base but, above all, returned in some way to its origin, with

40 There is not yet a comprehensive reconstruction of the path of *Nostra aetate*. For this period, see Miccoli, "Two Sensitive Issues," 95–96, and John M. Oesterreicher, "The Genesis of *Nostra aetate*," in: John M. Oesterreicher, ed., *The New Encounter between Christians and Jews*, New York, Philosophical Library, 1986, 103–295.

41 Giuseppe Alberigo, "L'esperienza conciliare di un vescovo," in: Giacomo Lercaro, ed., *Per la forza dello spirito: Discorsi conciliari del card. Giacomo Lercaro*, Bologna, EDB, 1984, 7–62, here 40. The text of Lercaro's address is on pages 103–109 of the book.

42 See Mauro Velati, "Completing the Council's Agenda," in: Giuseppe Alberigo & Joseph Komonchak, eds., *History of Vatican II*, vol. 5, *The Council and the Transition: The Fourth Period and the End of the Council (September 1965–December 1965)*, Leuven/Maryknoll, Peeters/Orbis Books, 2006, 185–273, esp. 211–221 and 226–227.

43 See Velati, "The Debate on De Judaeis and Ecumenical Dialogue."

the acceptance of the missionary component. The integration of the two structures took place through the establishment of a new division within the WCC called CWME. The fate of the IMCCAJ had already been discussed in the previous two years. Having discarded the hypothesis of its dissolution, two possibilities remained: it either entered the new division on mission or was to be placed in the division on study. Those who supported the latter option insisted on the need to take into account the sensitivities of the Jewish world, which did not like any mention of evangelism. Inclusion in the division on study, however, would require a radical transformation of the committee's activities and interests, which arose from pastoral concerns. For that reason, at the moment of the final decision during an extraordinary meeting of the committee in March 1960, the first option prevailed.

Its inclusion in the WCC inevitably required a reformulation of the committee's aims and working methods. This is what Allan R. Brockway called the "identity crisis" of the IMCCAJ. The new committee's name became Committee on the Church and the Jewish People, adopting the formula conceived by Hedenquist for his 1954 book. Beyond names, however, it was the very spirit of the work that faced new challenges. During the committee's meeting that took place in Holland on the eve of the New Delhi assembly, the theme "Dialogue or Proclamation?" was chosen, and it was not a rhetorical question.[44] In his report, the Dutchman Johan Hendrik Grolle was not afraid to question the very concept of mission: "The concept of 'mission' does not correspond to the scriptural relation of church and Israel to one another." He argued that the fundamental unity between the Old and New Covenants, between Israel and the church of Jews and Gentiles, made the inclusion of Jews among the recipients of missions impossible. Grolle thus noted that the time had come for a new attitude, summed up by the word "dialogue."[45] However, debate showed the existence of differing opinions. Hedenquist himself disagreed with the use of the word "dialogue" and preferred to speak of "witness."[46]

Positioning the committee within the division on mission proved to cause even greater difficulties in relations with the Jews. When Gerhart Moritz Riegner, European representative of the WJC, received the first official communication from the committee's secretary, Anker Gjerding, he was surprised by the official heading "World Mission and Evangelism" and did not fail to complain to the WCC secretary general. Visser 't Hooft's response was frank, "but even with all the sympathy that I have for you, I cannot change Christian theology. Missionary effort is part of that theology."[47] He betrayed an intrinsic difficulty that was typical of the situation of ecumenical circles in those years. The incident was soon closed and collaboration between Riegner and the WCC continued over the years through the personal connection with the general secretary, not with the office of the CCJP.

The new committee's secretary was elected in September 1960 and had experience in the mission to the Jews. Of Danish descent, Gjerding had served as a teacher at the Tabeetha School of the Church of Scotland in Jaffa as a representative of the Danish Israel Mission, and had previous experience with the YMCA and in pastoral parish ministry. He had no doubt about the ultimate purpose of Jewish contact, which needed to hold fast to the gospel's missionary mandate. In his travel notebooks there recurs a concerned consideration of the radical tendencies prevalent in those involved in Christian-Jewish dialogue that called for the explicit renunciation of efforts towards individual conversions. In spite of this, he carried

44 *Minutes of the 28th Meeting of the International Council Committee on the Christian Approach to the Jews at Hillerod (Holland)*, in: WCCA, Dec 26, 2006, WCC/IMC Committee on Church and the Jewish People: ICCAJ annual meetings, 2.

45 *Minutes of the 28th Meeting*, 8.

46 *Minutes of the 28th Meeting*, 4.

47 Riegner, *Never Despair*, 475.

out important work in resuming the committee's endeavor, which was faced with a panorama of great changes.

In those early years, the efforts of the CCJP also incorporated theological study, stimulated by the broader context of the work of the WCC. In fact, the position of Visser 't Hooft and some components of the Faith and Order commission appeared much closer to ecumenical concerns in the search for dialogue – on an equal footing – between Jews and Christians. This orientation was undoubtedly influenced by the debate taking place simultaneously in Catholicism. From the general secretariat came the proposal for a consultation between Christians and Jews to be held in Bossey in the fall of 1963, which was to involve the CCJP. The idea did not immediately come to fruition because, during the first contacts with its Jewish counterpart, a fundamental divergence of views emerged on the topic of the possible consultation. While the WCC asked to deal with theological issues, Rabbi Marcus Miller, of the Synagogue Council of America, insisted on practical cooperation on ethical and social issues.

Halfway through 1964, a three-year Faith and Order project for a comparison between the various churches on the theological topic of the church-Israel relationship also began. The project was directed, and not by chance, by Vischer who, as an observer in Rome, had followed the first part of the debate on *De Iudaeis* and had grasped its importance for the churches' self-awareness. In reality, there was strong resistance to approving this project.[48] Just ten years after the Evanston assembly, the fear of disagreements and ruptures was still very strong. In September 1964, the first consultation opened in Geneva, with the participation of 12 theologians of different denominational backgrounds. Most of the member churches of the WCC were represented, with the exception of the Orthodox ones. The document resulting from this first meeting was then submitted to a wider consultation (with the involvement of the Catholic theologian Wolfdieter Theurer) and constituted the framework of what would be the first theological document from the ecumenical movement on the theme of the church-Israel relationship, the Bristol statement *The Church and the Jewish People* of 1967.

The 1964 document with the same title established some firm points on which there was broad agreement: the relationship with Israel has its own uniqueness since it concerned the people "formed" by God, who were the instrument of God's action in history and, as such, also have something to say to Christians today. God has not forsaken his people and their age-old suffering is not the result of infidelity but rather of a distorted vision that transformed Christians into persecutors. The document highlighted the disparities in vision on the issues of the relationship between the first and second Covenants and especially on the church's mission to the Jewish people. Once again, the missionary perspective and what we might broadly call the ecumenical perspective conflicted. For some, the need for an attitude of humility and listening to the Jews did not eliminate the possibility of a more explicit missionary proclamation – even if not in the form of proselytism. For others, its attitude could not be the same as that towards others since the church and the people of Israel together form "the one people of God." In this way, the relationship was seen "more in terms of an ecumenical engagement than of a missionary task" and resulted in the possibility of dialogue described in the following terms:

Both partners have to start from what they have in common; that is, from God's revelation as attested in the Old Testament, not trying to convert one another, but rather searching together and questioning one another, trusting that together they will grow into a fuller understanding. Whatever form this fuller understanding may

48 Gjerding reports this in a note to the CCJP's president, Bekker (A. Gjerding to R. Bekker, Jul 3, 1964, in: WCCA, 26.12.17/28, Committee on the Church and the Jewish People, 1.)

take, Christians should be willing to leave this in the hands of God, confident that the true knowledge of God will always include recognizing him in his revelation in Christ.[49]

The document's fourth paragraph also dwelt on the topic's ecumenical relevance. There was no assumption of such a perspective as I outlined at the beginning, that is, the incorporation of the relationship with Israel as the ecumenical problem par excellence. Rather, it affirmed a perspective that recognized the contribution of the relationship with Israel to the ongoing discussion among the churches. In this sense, some aspects were mentioned, such as the return to a common consideration of the Old Testament, the need for a clarification of Christology and the Trinitarian doctrine, the engagement with the eschatological perspective, and the dimension of particularity. From this perspective, the influence of Jewish-Christian dialogue was not direct, but stood as a kind of reinforcement of the ecumenical dynamic:

> We believe that the church's re-thinking of her theology with regard to the problem of Israel and her conversation with the Jewish people can be of real importance to the ecumenical movement. For in this way questions are posed which touch the very foundation and centre of Christian faith.[50]

The document was then discussed by the member churches of the WCC and would be published in its final version in 1967, at the end of the three-year working period.[51] The emphasis on the ecumenical relevance of the theme of dialogue with the Jews remained, but the issue was destined to find less and less space in the work of ecumenism, as shown by the evolution of the work of the WCC, crowned with the 1982 publication of the document "Ecumenical Considerations on Jewish-Christian Dialogue."

5 Finding Space for Dialogue

As can be seen during the 1960s, a turning point in the Christian world toward the rejection of anti-Semitism and a renewal in the approach toward the Jews took place mainly from an ecclesiological rethinking that went back to the origins of Christianity and was nourished by the rediscovery of patristic theology. The most important Jewish organizations followed this process with interest, not without direct lobbying to support the cause of change. Although not officially credited, the presence of representatives of Judaism at the council was undoubtedly a significant phenomenon, also because of the indirect impact they had in the debate on *De Iudaeis* through the SPCU's mediation.[52] Their positions on the matter, however, clearly had a very different nature from those arising from the intra-Christian discussion, and that is why the subsequent developments of Jewish-Christian dialogue – which became increasingly organized and structured – could not fail to highlight these profound differences, going far beyond the perspectives of the theological debate on Israel and the church. One could point to some specific issues that acquired importance, besides the theological question, in the development of relations between Jews and Christian churches in the period between the end of the 1960s and the beginning of the new millennium: the historical perspective (memory of the Shoah), the educational challenge of overcoming reciprocal prejudices, the political question

49 *Report on the Consultation on the Church and the Jewish People held in Geneva, 21–26 September 1964*, March 1965, 9 pages, in: WCCA, 26.12.10/1, 7.

50 *Report on the Consultation on the Church.* A collection of the reactions that were elicited among the churches by the document can be found in *Comments on the Report of the Consultation on the Church and the Jewish People held in Geneva, 21–26 September 1964*, May 1966, in: WCCA, 26.12.10/1, 1–70.

51 *The Theology of the Churches*, 13–28.

52 Claire Maligot, "Les enjeux internes des démarches juives auprès du concile Vatican II," *Tsafon* 8, 2015, 123–152.

triggered by the birth of the state of Israel and rekindled by subsequent conflicts, and, finally, the question of the relationship between dialogue and mission.

These perspectives were set out within a network of relations that had been built starting from the late 1960s between Christian churches and Jewish groups, according also to a specific asymmetry between, on the one hand, institutions with undisputed authority (such as most Christian churches, but not the WCC) and, on the other, Jewish organizations that were often fragmentary, lacking any particular doctrinal authority, and involving a complex intertwining between laity, rabbinate, and Israeli politics. It is impossible to summarize the countless relationships between individual churches and Jews on a national or local level, but it may be useful to spend some time on the story of the Catholic Church and the main ecumenical body, the WCC, to which many of the international federations of Protestantism referred. The relations of Judaism with these two elements of Christianity have been described as parallel paths that assumed different dynamics at different times: "Relations with Catholics and Protestants often followed parallel paths, but progress did not proceed simultaneously, and at any given time one would have moved beyond the other."[53] This was the case in the occasions already mentioned, such as the firm position taken in Amsterdam in 1948 or the publication of *Nostra aetate* by the Catholics. However, it would continue to be the same in the following decades, given the difference in the two bodies' natures, styles, and working mechanisms.

After the council, the Catholic Church was faced with the challenge of applying the measures and requests set forth in the approved documents. In the liturgical field, this need had already led to the creation of the Consilium ad exsequendam constitutionem de sacra liturgia before the council concluded its work. In the ecumenical field, the first part of the Ecumenical Directory had already been published in 1967, which touched on some of the most urgent questions in the relations among the churches.[54] The application of *Nostra aetate* was certainly more complex precisely because the dialogue with other religions did not have that background of relations and contacts typical of the ecumenical movement. It should be added that the specific Vatican Secretariat for Non-Christians, created in 1964 by Paul VI, had not shown many signs of vitality, often leaving the task of relating with non-Christian religious groups to the local Catholic authorities. In the case of the Jews, however, the SPCU maintained responsibility, with the specific internal commission that had worked on drafting *Nostra aetate*, led by the Dutch priest Cornelius Rijk.

The problems of applying chapter four of *Nostra aetate* were not unlike those of applying *Unitatis redintegratio*. It was a question of a different vision of the other penetrating the consciousness of the Catholic faithful, dispelling prejudices and overcoming unmotivated fears. There was, however, a certain degree of greater complexity in the case of the Jews, due to the lack of a common religious background. In 1969, in one of the SPCU's internal documents, four different attitudes of Catholics towards the Jews were noted: those who understood *Nostra aetate*'s message (the essential nature of Judaism for Christian self-consciousness), those who remained indifferent (also because, at times, they were not interested in a direct relationship with the Jews), those who maintained a variety of anti-Semitic prejudices, and, finally, those who considered Judaism to be a secularized religion and therefore devoid of any religious significance.[55] The possibility of understanding and living *Nostra aetate*'s message was therefore played out along the spectrum of these different gradations.

In the years following 1965, Catholicism enthusiastically embraced dialogue on a national and

53 Riegner, *Never despair*, 319.

54 On the Directory, see the contribution by Bruno Cherubini in this volume.

55 "The Relations between the Church and Judaism," *Information Service* 9, 1970, 19–20. The text offers no indication of its author, but it was one of the experts of the SPCU.

local level. Especially in countries where the Jewish presence was significant, spontaneous initiatives for dialogue were started. The most active churches were those in the United States, in Latin America, and in some European countries such as France, Belgium, the Netherlands, and Germany. In these countries, which had a historical presence of Judaism, the bishops' conferences set up a special secretariat on the model of the Roman one and appointed specific contacts for dialogue with Jews. In some cases, they went so far as to issue practical directives to the faithful, preceding an instruction by the Roman curia. This was the case, for example, for the CELAM and the bishops' conferences of the United States, Belgium, England, and the Netherlands.[56] Even larger was the number of countries where, in a less official way, spontaneous associations had sprung up to act in this field, such as the SAE, founded in Italy in the early 1960s by a lay scholar, Maria Vingiani, who combined her interest in ecumenism with that of dialogue with the Jews.

An initial synthesis of their experiences took place in Rome during a meeting organized by Rijk and Willebrands in April 1969, with 21 experts from 14 different countries present. In the preparatory texts, a theological perspective and a vision of the Jewish question that was indebted to *Nostra aetate*'s ecclesiological approach still prevailed. Dialogue with the Jewish world, it was stated, could lead to a deepening of the church's self-reflection and, in particular, two points were noted from which the most fruitful developments were to be expected: the concept of "salvation history" and the concept of the world as "God's permanent creation." The document also reiterated the importance of the link between ecumenism and Jewish-Christian dialogue, along the lines indicated by Karl Barth, mentioned above:

> Since the problem of relations with Jews is tied to the very mystery of the church ("Nostra aetate"), all Christian churches are *de facto* involved in the problem. It has therefore an *ecumenical* aspect, which it is important to emphasize in the context with which we are dealing. The Christian churches are divided, and we are seeking the unity willed by the Lord. This unity cannot be built except by a return to the common sources, to the origins of faith.[57]

In this phase, many of the initiatives of dialogue with Judaism undertaken by dioceses or episcopal conferences had precisely this ecumenical character, that is, of collaboration with the other Christian churches present in the territory. The extension of the concept of ecumenism implied in these developments was formulated as follows in the document cited: "This spirit can be called ecumenical insofar as the term expresses concern to know the other as he is and as he defines himself; concern to love and respect him in his convictions and in the conceptions which rule his life."[58]

The meeting also gave birth to an official document that was discussed in the plenary of the SPCU but was never published. Among other things, it aimed at laying the foundations for relaunching activities by the section of the SPCU for dialogue with the Jews in the context of *Nostra aetate*'s upcoming fifth anniversary, which proved to be very favorable. The need for a step forward, from the institutional point of view as well, was already presented to Paul VI at the beginning of 1970 by Robert Aron, a French writer of Jewish origin and author of foundational studies on Jesus's childhood and relationship with Judaism. Aron asked the pontiff to establish a special commission to

56 A partial overview of these stances is found in Jorge María Mejía, "Teaching on Jews and Judaism: Requirements of Official Bodies in the Roman Catholic Church," in: International Catholic-Jewish Liaison Committee, *Fifteen Years of Catholic-Jewish Dialogue (1970–1985)*, Vatican City, Libreria Editrice Vaticana, 1988, 75–86.

57 "The Relations between the Church and Judaism," 20 (italics original).

58 "The Relations between the Church and Judaism," 20.

deal with relations with the Jews, enclosing a dossier of the most important issues to be addressed. Even before that, however, it was Riegner, by then secretary general of the WJC, who raised the question of which body to approach in relations with Catholicism. This may seem to be a minor problem, but for the Jews it was a fundamental point, as demonstrated by the analogous case of relations with the WCC, which Riegner conducted not through the office of the CCJP, but directly with the secretary general, Visser 't Hooft.

In regard to Catholics, the issue stood in different terms but was no less problematic. Riegner and others had already pointed out the paradox of an office for relations with the Jews set within a larger office dedicated to relations between Christians to the heads of the SPCU. In spite of these insistences, in 1967, the curial reform introduced by Paul VI with the motu proprio *Regimini Ecclesiae universae* had not brought about any changes, pushing dialogue with the Jews back into an undefined limbo. On the Catholic side, there was a concern not to put the Jews on the same level as other non-Christian religions, by entrusting them to Cardinal Paolo Marella's dedicated secretariat, and keeping them in the orbit of Bea's SPCU, who had "invented" dialogue with the Jews. The lack of a breakthrough in this direction, that is to say, towards a truly autonomous commission associated with the SPCU, however, worried the leaders of Jewish organizations and became the greatest obstacle to the decision to open direct dialogue between the two parties.

On the other hand, it was precisely in this phase that relations with the WCC accelerated. Riegner, in liaison with Visser 't Hooft, had organized an initial joint meeting between the leaders in Geneva and those of the WJC in June 1968, encouraged by the publication of the Bristol statement the previous year. 33 representatives of the various Christian churches (including a few Catholics) and ten Jews of various geographical and theological backgrounds were present. A few weeks later, the general assembly of the WCC at Uppsala blessed the agreement, even though there was no specific document dealing with the subject. Indeed, at Visser 't Hooft's behest, secrecy was maintained during this first phase, which also covered the second meeting in May 1969. The caution led to not publicizing the meetings, not so much because of doubt about their success, but because of the presence of different sensibilities within the WCC. The fact that they were serious, however, was demonstrated by the establishment of a liaison committee for the coordination and preparation of the joint sessions. It was the Christian side that asked that the third meeting, scheduled for February 1970, receive the minimum publicity needed to render the agreement manifest.

It was a somewhat uncertain beginning, but it would inaugurate a period of significant changes. Even the Jewish side had to adjust in order to provide a credible interface to the dialogue with Christianity, and it was from these experiences that the idea of the constitution of a new organism that would gather its different components was born. Until then, the first referent had been the WJC, an entirely secular association and essentially the representative of the diaspora. On the one hand, it was necessary to include some representative segment of the religious sectors of Judaism (and therefore the Synagogue Council of America became a partner) and, on the other, there was a will to connect in some way to Israeli society, precisely because, for Jews, religion and people were closely linked. A strong impulse also came from the AJC and, at the end of the 1960s, the IJCIC was born as a liaison body between these different organizations, destined to become the main actor in Jewish-Christian dialogue.

Internal developments in the dialogue with the WCC also became a stimulus for acceleration within Catholicism. In 1968, the SPCU had gone through the uncertain stage of the transition between the management of Bea, who had by then fallen ill, and the new presidency of Willebrands. At the end of 1967, Riegner had attempted a new approach to solving the question of the statute of the commission for the Jews. Rijk's response came only eight months after his request, highlighting

Rome's hesitancy. The opportunity to stimulate action came at the beginning of 1969. The WJC was to hold a conference in Rome in the early days of January, and its leaders were contacted by Vittorino Veronese with a proposal for an audience with the pope. Israeli diplomacy imposed a stop to the initiative, to Riegner's great disappointment. A few days after the conference, a second attempt by the Catholics, mediated by Rijk this time, was more successful. A few days earlier, a communiqué from the Holy See had harshly condemned the bombing of the Beirut airport by the Israeli army, provoking a public outcry in Israel. To make amends for the gesture, Paul VI himself wanted to proceed with the plans for an audience, which was held on Epiphany of 1969 and during which the pope read a communiqué with positive overtones on the relations between the Holy See and the Jewish people. The Jewish delegation was struck by the warmth of the pope's words and especially by the fact that he used the expression "Jewish people" rather than "Jewish religion" several times.[59]

Out of a potential diplomatic incident, a new situation arose that was intended to prepare for official dialogue between the two sides. In the summer of 1969, Riegner, Rijk and Henry Siegman, then secretary of the Synagogue Council of America, met in London to prepare the project. In November, during another meeting, Siegman and Rijk agreed on the text of a Memorandum of Understanding that would be the basis for wider discussion between the parties. Finally, in December 1970, representatives of the IJCIC were guests of the SPCU in Rome, and, in that context, the decision evolved into establishing a stable connection between the two parties in the form of the ILC, which met for the first time a year later, in December 1971. This was not the first meeting between representatives of the Catholic Church and Jewish leaders, but it was the beginning of a permanent, high-level contact within the framework of a multi-year program. It was also a direct exchange between the two partners, outside the broad ecumenical context already mentioned several times. The foundations were probably laid here for development in Catholic-Jewish dialogue that, out of an originally ecumenical-ecclesiological context, extended its horizons to broader issues, imposed partly by current events (the progressive deterioration in the Middle East crisis after the 1967 war) and partly by the specific needs of the dialogue partners.

59 Riegner, *Never Despair*, 272–274.

6 Speaking to One Another in Order to Understand One Another: Building an Agenda

During the December 1970 meeting, an agenda was established on two levels: mutual relations and shared interests. On the first level, the questions relating to the history of anti-Semitism and to possible remedies in favor of cultural change were included, intentionally leaving the issue of shared heritage for a later stage in the dialogue.[60] In the second meeting, the topics of religious freedom and the protection of human rights were given priority. This meeting of the ILC brought out the asymmetrical nature of the relationship, at a time when the Catholic partners continued to see in the dialogue an interreligious dynamic (leaving the political aspect of the question to Vatican diplomacy, in particular, to the Secretariat of State), while the Jewish partners made no distinction between religion and politics. This situation had also forced Catholics to reconsider the choices made during the council to approach the dialogue with Jews in the same way as an ecumenical one. At the meeting in Rome in December 1970, not only the officials of the SPCU but also representatives of other curial offices (the

60 "At a later stage, studies might be undertaken of the common heritage of Jews and Christians in order to further the understanding both of each other and of their common responsibility to humanity and the world." The text of the memorandum is in: International Catholic-Jewish Liaison Committee, *Fifteen Years*, xv–xvi.

Congregations for the Doctrine of the Faith, for Catholic Education, for the Eastern Churches, and the Iustitia et Pax commission) were already present. Among the members of the ILC, in addition to experts from the Jewish section of the SPCU, was then included in 1971 the archbishop of Marseilles Roger Etchegaray, who was then president of the council of Euriopean bishops' conference. During the common discussion, the first two topics that emerged for a future work program went well beyond the field of theology, concerning the relationship between community, people, and land in the two religious traditions, and the theme of religious freedom and human rights. These were the themes of the 1971 Paris meeting.

The importance of this opening to direct dialogue can also be measured by the fact that it affected the structural aspect on the Catholic side. As we have seen, for some time the Jewish side had been asking for the creation of a true and proper entity dedicated to the question, albeit linked to the SPCU. The process was rather lengthy, but, in October 1974, the CRRJ was created, chaired by the president of the SPCU but directed by an independent secretary and consisting of representatives from various backgrounds. With a perfect symmetry, it came into being at the same time as an analogous body for dialogue with Muslims, based at the secretariat for non-Christian, showing once again the preponderance of diplomatic concerns at the heart of the Holy See's policy.

Paul VI's choice put the Jewish world in a position to accept dialogue more easily, after the institutional issue had also been resolved in Geneva. In fact, in 1973, as part of a general restructuring of the offices of the WCC, the responsibility for relations with the Jews was transferred to the newly created subunit DFI. This decision was the result of the central committee's meeting in Addis Ababa in 1971, when the first important WCC's document on interreligious dialogue – "Christians in Dialogue with Other Faiths," drawn up in Zurich the previous year by a group of theologians from various churches – was discussed. On that basis, the DFI was born, inserted within the unit on Faith and Witness and entrusted in its direction to an Indian theologian, Stanley Jedidiah Samartha. The WCC solution did not follow the same path as that of the Catholics, placing relations with Jews within a very broad framework such as that of dialogue with religions and contemporary ideologies. It was the sign of a different way of understanding those same relations and each group's own relationship with the Jewish world, going beyond that ecclesiological-ecumenical basis that was affirmed so clearly in the 1960s. Only at the beginning of the 1990s did internal debate begin in Geneva on the possibility of moving the issues related to the dialogue with Jews to the Faith and Order section. However, that debate had no practical consequences, leaving the institutional framework unchanged.

The CRRJ created by Paul VI and entrusted to a new secretary, the Dominican Pierre-Marie de Contenson, did not take long to enter into the heart of the problems of dialogue with an approach that was now broader and more dynamic than in the past. One of the new secretary's first acts was a trip to Palestine, in November 1974, during which he met important representatives of the Jewish world, such as the two chief rabbis of Jerusalem, and of the local Christian community.[61] The need for a line that would somehow be direct with the Jews of Israel was clear. Acceleration also occurred in doctrinal and pastoral workings with the publication of the document "Guidelines and Suggestions for Implementing the Conciliar Declaration 'Nostra aetate' (n. 4)."[62]

Mention has already been made of the document prepared in April 1969 by a group of experts of the section of the SPCU dedicated to Judaism. Before its publication, a provisional version of the text was circulated by Cardinal Lawrence Joseph Shehan, which elicited a great deal of interest but,

61 A short report on the trip is found in "Relations with the Jews," *Information Service* 27, 1975, 32–37.

62 Commission for Religious Relations with the Jews, "Guidelines and Suggestions for Implementing the Conciliar Declaration 'Nostra aetate' (n. 4)," *Information Service* 26, 1975, 1–7.

in fact, impeded its progress. It was only a few years later that the project was resumed and brought to completion, with a very different approach, due to the fruits of the experience of dialogue within the ILC. It presented itself as a text of an "almost exclusively practical" nature, characterized by a note of "sobriety." The intention to propose a "Christian theology of Judaism"[63] was excluded from the outset because the time was not ripe, but the ecclesiological perspective was not abandoned nor was the ecumenical significance of *Nostra aetate* forgotten. In fact, the conclusion of the document stated:

> The problem of Jewish-Christian relations concerns the church as such, since it is when "pondering her own mystery" that she encounters the mystery of Israel. Therefore, even in areas where no Jewish communities exist, this remains an important problem. There is also an ecumenical aspect to the question: the very return of Christians to the sources and origins of their faith, grafted on the earlier Covenant, helps the search for unity in Christ, the cornerstone.[64]

The text, intentionally presented within the framework of the 1975 Holy Year, dedicated to renewal and reconciliation, was meant to be the first step in the dialogue between Jews and Christians that was the purpose of the new commission's establishment. In this sense, it went beyond the affirmations of *Nostra aetate* by trying to flesh out the new spirit of mutual relations. In itself, however, it was a completely unilateral step in the presentation of a program that Catholicism as an institution was delivering. For this reason, it did not fail to provoke negative reactions among the dialogue partners. Compared to *Nostra aetate*'s scanty formulation, the Jewish reactions recognized the text of the guidelines as fully appreciating Judaism as a living religion, endowed with its own self-understanding of faith, going beyond the sometimes caricatured vision of a religious patrimony clinging to the conditions of the Pharisaic age. The document praised the experiences of collaboration already taking place at the local level and advocated a renewed commitment to collaboration in the social area and in efforts for peace. The condemnation of anti-Semitism and repudiation of persecutions were also explicitly reiterated, returning to *Nostra aetate*'s formulations.

There were, however, several reasons for dissatisfaction that emerged in Jewish circles. For the document's Catholic authors, the most vehement reactions were largely tactically and politically motivated, deriving from the extreme variety and division of the global Jewish community.[65] Nevertheless, they constituted a real obstacle to the development of dialogue. For some Jewish members, the clear affirmation of the duty of Christian proclamation, even though the text emphasized that this was to be effected with respect for religious freedom that explicitly referred to *Dignitatis humanae*, demonstrated the persistence of an attitude of proselytism.[66] Orthodox Judaism was scandalized by the mention of the possibility of common prayer, which was proposed on very basic grounds ("a common meeting in the presence of God, in prayer and silent meditation")[67] and with specific aims, such as supporting activities for peace and justice.

A fundamental aspect of Jewish self-understanding, however, remained unrecognized in the commission's document: the relationship

63 Commission for Religious Relations with the Jews, "Guidelines and Suggestions," 1.

64 Commission for Religious Relations with the Jews, "Guidelines and Suggestions," 6–7.

65 "These criticisms must always be interpreted either in reference to problems of Israeli internal politics or in the framework of the constant tensions and rivalry that may exist between the different Jewish organizations"; "Relations with the Jews," 33. This refers to de Contenson's report for the SPCU plenary of Feb 17–24, 1975.

66 An overview of Jewish reactions is found in "Relations with the Jews."

67 Commission for Religious Relations with the Jews, "Guidelines and Suggestions," 4.

between faith, people, and land. It was no coincidence that this was the issue that was most forcefully imposed by the Jewish side during the definition of the ILC's agenda.[68] The crucial point in the debate that followed the publication of the guidelines soon became the lack of any mention of the State of Israel. The Catholic side had chosen not to introduce political considerations into the document, but this was a manner of reasoning that was alien to their dialogue partners. It was even more so since a reference of this kind to the political dimension, with an explicit appreciation of the presence of the state of Israel had already been proposed in a previous document of the French episcopate, dated March 1973, on the attitude of Christians towards Judaism.[69]

The first step in the dialogue between Catholics and Jews already revealed all its possible weaknesses, forcing the Vatican commission's leaders to admit the "pre-dialogical" character of the guidelines, designed to lay the foundations for dialogue among Catholics, but not themselves the fruit of dialogue. Catholicism seemed to be moving on its own, outside a dialogical process, and this was, after all, the reproach underlying many Jewish reactions. On the other hand, Catholicism's rigidity was well known and, even in the ecumenical field, similar attitudes had been assumed. One thinks, for example, of the intercommunion affair, prompted a few years earlier by Athenagoras I's desire to concelebrate with the pope in order to show the basic unity binding Catholics and Orthodox, which was scuttled by widespread slowness and resistance.[70] In the case of dialogue with Judaism, the difficulties of the Holy See's international projection, the powerful return of anti-Semitism as an essential element of Archbishop Marcel François Lefebvre's schismatic fundamentalist program, and the extremely varied panorama of global Catholicism, which perceived the Jewish question in very different ways, all added to the problem.

The document produced in Geneva was another story. The CCJP had merged into the DFI in 1973, beginning work – perhaps in imitation of the Catholic guidelines – on a new document on the specific theme of relations with the Jews and beginning a vast consultation among the churches belonging to the WCC. The project that the DFI launched at the time was actually broader, taking into consideration the theme of dialogue with non-Christian religions and ideologies. The general assembly of Nairobi in December of 1975 had dedicated a special session to the subject, becoming the basis of a document called "Dialogue and Community," and the debate revealed an extreme polarization of positions. The antithetical views of those supporting Christian unity and those in favor of religious pluralism clashed. The final document inaugurated the churches' commitment to interreligious dialogue, but in its preamble there was a clear reaffirmation of the duty of proclamation to non-Christians. On the specific issue of Judaism, the conflict was in some ways even stronger, because it was imbued with political rather than religious content. The assembly in Nairobi was the first time that observers of various religions, including a Jew, were present. There was no explicit position taken on the theme of Jewish-Christian dialogue, but during the debate there were several references to the situation in the Middle East, with the emergence of radical positions ranging from the exaltation of the birth of the State of Israel, based on theological motivations, to the absolute rejection of Zionist imperialism. In fact, in the conclusions to the conference, the topic of a religious dialogue was completely obscured in favor of a clear political position for Israel's withdrawal from the 1967 borders and for

68 The issue had been addressed at the meeting in Antwerp in 1973, see Walter Würzburger & Raphael Judah Zwi Werblowsky, "Land, People and Nation in Jewish Perspective," in: International Catholic-Jewish Liaison Committee, *Fifteen Years*, 3–7.

69 "L'attitude des chrétiens à l'égard du Judaïsme: Orientations pastorales du Comité épiscopal français pour les relationes avec le judaïsme," *La documentation catholique* 55, 1973, 419–422.

70 Alberto Melloni, *Tempus visitationis: L'intercomunione inaccaduta fra Roma e Costantinopoli*, Bologna, Il Mulino, 2019.

the self-determination of the Palestinian people.[71] It was the beginning of a process that would lead the WCC to look at the issues of the Middle East from an increasingly political, anti-imperialist point of view.

However, this did not prevent its internal bodies from continuing to develop interreligious dialogue. The specific subunit decided to take up the theme discussed in Nairobi with the convocation of the Chiang Mai conference in April 1977. Through the work of 86 delegates of the various churches, coming from 36 different countries, a new document took shape that represented a framework of rules and principles of the churches of the WCC in regard to the challenge of interreligious dialogue, *Faith in the Midst of Faiths: Reflections on Dialogue in Community*.[72] It constituted the context in which the specific directives for dialogue with individual religious expressions would be published in subsequent years. In fact, however, the only area that produced a specific document was that of relations with the Jews. After the WCC's central committee had definitively adopted the Chiang Mai document in 1979, making a recommendation to the member churches, the CCJP was able to again take up the discussion carried out in 1975 and begin the drafting of a document of specific directives. Here the intervention of the Jewish representatives themselves, Riegner in particular, was decisive, both for encouragement in the enterprise (proposing the "Guidelines" published by Rome as a model) and for its concrete realization. From the very start, in fact, the project was sent to its Jewish counterpart, which was able to contribute with written comments and documents during the entire period of its drafting. In mid-1981 the text was approved by the CCJP and was submitted to a new consultation of the churches, until it met with a final approval by the central committee in July 1982. It was then sent to the churches as the official WCC document entitled "Ecumenical Considerations on Jewish-Christian Dialogue."[73]

Significantly, the text opened with an introductory section that was entirely dedicated to an interpretation of the dialogue between faiths and the meaning of a Christian position on Judaism. It was necessary, it said, to avoid the risks of an external classification of the other, seeking rather a "mutual questioning" and clearly separating what one faith could affirm about the other from what the other affirms about itself: "The WCC guidelines do not predict what partners in dialogue may come to learn about themselves, their history, and their problems. Rather they speak within the churches about faith, attitudes, actions, and problems of Christians."[74] While this was true in general for any kind of dialogue, in the case of relations with the Jews it was necessary to bear in mind the particular asymmetry mentioned above, that is, the fact that "while an understanding of Judaism in New Testament times becomes an integral and indispensable part of any Christian theology, for Jews, a 'theological' understanding of Christianity is of a less than essential or integral significance."[75]

These considerations and the revision of the text by the Jewish representatives produced a document that, in some ways, was less assertive, where the uncertainties and divisions between the positions of the WCC churches emerged clearly but, as Riegner himself was able to affirm, was more explicit on many of the crucial points of dialogue. In this way, the historical genesis of the theology of supersession that Christianity intended to overcome was clearly highlighted. The link between people and land was clearly affirmed, thus recognizing the right of a Jewish state to exist, even if balanced by an analogous recognition of the legitimate aspirations of the Palestinian people. The responsibility of Christianity in the persecutions was expressly stated, linking the Shoah directly to the teaching of contempt cultivated within strands of European Christianity ("Teachings of

71 See the two declarations "The Middle East" and "Jerusalem," in: *The Theology of the Churches*, 31–33.

72 See Stanley Jedidiah Samartha, ed., *Faith in the midst of faiths: Reflections on dialogue in community*, Geneva, WCC Publications, 1977.

73 See *The Theology of the Churches*, 34–42.

74 *The Theology of the Churches*, 35–36.

75 *The Theology of the Churches*, 36.

contempt for Jews and Judaism in certain Christian traditions proved a spawning ground for the evil of the Nazi Holocaust").[76] At the same time, however, it highlighted the existence of large sectors of world Christianity (in non-European continents) that did not have a first-hand experience of Jewish persecution and, for this reason, held a different position on Jewish-Christian dialogue.

The document was far less explicit about the theological and ecclesiological aspects of dialogue between Jews and Christians, emphasizing instead the still undefined character of the subject, which required further reflection on the part of Christian theologians. Any consideration of the ecumenical nature of this dialogue was also dropped. On the point of greatest sensitivity for Protestants, that is, the question of a missionary duty towards the Jews, room was left for the recognition of the plurality of views found within the WCC. The necessity of mission was explicitly affirmed as a Christian duty, but equally explicit was the rejection of proselytism, expressed with a quote from the 1971 document of the Joint Working Group between the Catholic Church and the WCC (in some ways with the authority of a truly ecumenical stance). There followed, however, an honest and detailed picture of the divergences among Protestants in conceiving the idea of mission to the Jews:

> There are Christians who view a mission to the Jews as having a very special salvific significance, and those who believe the conversion of the Jews to be the eschatological event that will climax the history of the world. There are those who would place no special emphasis on a mission to the Jews, but would include them in the one mission to all those who have not accepted Christ as their Saviour. There are those who believe that a mission to the Jews is not part of an authentic Christian witness, since the Jewish people finds its fulfilment in faithfulness to God's Covenant of old.[77]

The document's unfinished and non-definitive character received its final confirmation in the conclusion, where it hoped for the churches' maximum freedom to express "their understanding of Judaism in other languages, styles, and ways than has been done in these Ecumenical Considerations."[78]

7 A Form of Dialogue *Sui Generis*

At the beginning of the 1980s, the dialogue between Christians and Jews had found its first formulation in the attempts, as we have seen, to place a framework of lines of conduct maintaining a general value alongside the specific institutional structures (the Vatican commission and the CCJP, at the global level). Finding something similar within Judaism would be pointless since, although the number and quality of the dialogue partners had progressed significantly in this field as well, with the gradual addition of other Jewish organizations, there was no central authority capable of playing that role. The decisive role of singular, important personalities and of the IJCIC certainly remained, but this was always within a context that could not aspire to a global representation of Jews around the world. Even the turning point that occurred in 2003, with the launch of direct dialogue between the Vatican and the Rabbinate of Israel did not, from this point of view, introduce any significant novelty.

The first ten years of the ILC's work produced a model of dialogue that had no precedent and, for this reason perhaps, proceeded at times with difficulty. While in ecumenical dialogue Catholicism experimented with a form of mediation rooted in the common elements of Christian heritage, with the aim of extending their perimeter

76 *The Theology of the Churches*, 40.

77 *The Theology of the Churches*, 42.

78 *The Theology of the Churches*, 42.

through a theological reworking, here the question was rather the contrary. The study of the shared heritage that linked Jews and Christians was postponed. Rather, it brought to light what had, until then, constituted the decisive point in a relationship that had always been conflictual, namely anti-Semitism and the weight of elements that it had absorbed from the Christian tradition, together with what was defined as the primary issue, that is, the relationship between people, religion, and land. Alongside these were questions of common interest, specifically, those related to collaboration in the area of human rights, religious freedom, dialogue with other religions, and tackling the phenomenon of the secularization of contemporary society. Confirming the asymmetrical nature of this dialogue was the agenda, drawn mainly from the concerns of one of the two partners, the Jewish one. From a material point of view, in fact, the 1970 memorandum returned to most of the points of the dossier presented to Paul VI by Robert Aron a few months earlier.

From 1971 to today, the ILC has developed along these lines in a series of 24 meetings at intervals that were not always fixed, which is also due to the emergence of new difficulties in the relations between the two parties. It has drawn a geography of dialogue that is quite interesting in order to understand the issues at stake. The first three meetings took place in France and Belgium (Paris, Marseilles, and Antwerp) and, on the occasion of the first ten years of *Nostra aetate*, meetings were held in Rome (January 1975) and in Jerusalem (March 1976). The latter represented an important step for a discreet first contact with the Chief Rabbinate and especially for the visit of the two delegations to the Yad Vashem museum, in commemoration of the Shoah. In some cases, the symbolic value of the place chosen stood out, as with the meetings in Venice (March 1977) and Toledo-Madrid (April 1978). It was Riegner who proposed holding the meeting in Spain, with the presence of the primate-archbishop of the Catholic Church as a sort of reparation for the expulsion of the Jews in 1492. In 1979, the meeting was held in Germany for the first time, in Regensburg, a choice that certainly demanded a psychological effort on the Jewish side but which became a powerful element of reconciliation. For the occasion, the ILC received a message from the German Chancelor Helmut Schmidt, in which he expressed thanks for the Jewish delegation's courageous choice. During the meeting, the two delegations also visited the former concentration camp of Flossenbürg, where the Lutheran theologian Dietrich Bonhoeffer had spent his last days.

At times, the place and the issues addressed were closely intertwined, recalling each other, as in the case of the 1981 meeting in London, dedicated to secularism's challenge to religions, or that of September 1982 in Milan, in an Italy that was still affected by the threat of terrorism, when the sanctity of human life in a situation of violence was discussed. In 1984, the focus of attention was the theme of the youth. After the reports of the experts – the Italian Salesian Riccardo Tonelli and Rabbi Gordon Tucker of New York – time was allocated for the testimonials of four young people, two from each religion.[79] The main horizon was that of the challenge of youth who appeared distant not only from the religious sphere but also from the structure of a society that was increasingly dominated by materialism and consumerism, in a phase during which even the era of commitment that arose in the 1960s was experiencing its own crisis (as Marloes Andersen, a young Dutch Catholic, pointed out).[80] Faced with this challenge, Avraham Burg and David Kessler, from the Jewish point of view, emphasized the responsibility of educators and the need for a synthesis between Zionism and Judaism. The

79 See Gordon Tucker, "Youth and Faith," in: International Catholic-Jewish Liaison Committee, *Fifteen Years*, 228–238.

80 See <http://www.christianunity.va/content/unitacristiani/it/commissione-per-i-rapporti-religiosi-con-l-ebraismo/ilc---international-catholic-jewish-liaison-committee-/incontri/11----1984-27-29-marzo-amsterdam--comunicato-stampa-sul-tema---g/en.html> (accessed Feb 22, 2024).

other Catholic representative was Claudio Betti from the Community of Sant'Egidio in Rome who, while insisting on the needs of young people in a complex moment, testified to the experience of faith possessing a strong communal character. It is also worth noting the ILC's timing of the decision to meet in September 1990 in Prague, in the heart of Eastern Europe, which was experiencing a phase of great upheaval after the fall of communism and the tearing down of the Berlin Wall. In fact, anti-Semitic sentiment was growing in the post-communist countries.

As far as procedures were concerned, the ILC meetings had their own particularity. Unlike the ecumenical dialogue meetings, they were not aimed at drawing up common documents. The experts' reports provided the basis for a somewhat extemporaneous discussion that made no claim to completeness and – as far as we know – was not even documented in minutes of the meetings. The Catholic side usually drew up a summary in rather general terms, which was then sent to the presidents of the bishops' conferences for purely informative purposes.[81] Internally, the two sides then continued working on exploring the issues addressed in greater depth. Between one session and another there were then one or more meetings of a restricted committee intended to prepare for the next meeting. Due to the committee's archives being closed, however, it is not certain that minutes of those meetings exist. In the absence of a specific purpose for the work, the plenary session, in many cases, became the occasion for a free exchange of opinions on current issues.

In the first phase of the ILC's work, the dominant themes were essentially those tied to the nature of the relationship between religion, people, and land, and to those related to human rights (particularly religious freedom).[82] With regard to the former, dialogue was in no way easy since it brought into play a radical polarity between Christian-Catholic universalism and Jewish particularism, with its strong link between people and religion. On the Jewish side, making this connection understood was a fundamental step towards achieving the goal of full recognition of the reality of the state of Israel on the part of Christians. The issue, however, remained problematic, and this was demonstrated by the outbreak of new controversy in 1985 when, on the occasion of the 20th anniversary of *Nostra aetate*, a new document was published by the Roman commission: "Notes on the Correct Way to Present the Jews and Judaism in Preaching and Catechesis in the Roman Catholic Church." The theme was catechesis, but the document included mention of the existence of the state of Israel that provoked a negative reaction in the Jewish world. For many, the text's recognition of the existence of Israel ("the existence of the state of Israel and its political options should be envisaged not in a perspective which is in itself religious, but in their reference to the common principles of international laws"[83]) seemed to reject the very perspective that had often been affirmed within the ILC. It

81 Thus was the case, at least in the late 1970s, as is shown by the documentation preserved in Louvain-la-Neuve and dating back to Charles Moeller, vice president of the Roman commission between 1975 and 1980. See the document related to the Madrid session: Secretariat for Promoting Christian Unity Commission for Religious Relations with Judaism, *Seventh Meeting of the Joint Liaison Committee between the Catholic Church and Judaism: Information for Episcopal Conferences and Oriental Synods*, n.d., 3 pages, attached to the SPCU's letter of May 19, 1978, to the presidents of the episcopal conferences, now in UCL-LG, Charles Moeller, papiers, 3342. It is not known, however, whether sending such reports to the presidents was already customary earlier.

82 Some of the texts have been published in International Catholic-Jewish Liaison Committee, *Fifteen years*, for example, Walter Würzburger & R.J. Zwi Werblowsky, "Land, People and Nation in Jewish Perspective"; Ignace de la Potterie & Bernard-Dominique Dupuy, "People, Nation, Land: The Christian View," 8–14; and Louis Henkin, "Judaism and Human Rights," 15–25.

83 "Notes on the Correct Way to Present the Jews and Judaism in Preaching and Catechesis in the Roman Catholic Church," available at <http://www.christianunity.va/content/unitacristiani/en/commissione-per-i-rapporti-religiosi-con-l-ebraismo/commissione-per-i-rapporti-religiosi-con-l-ebraismo-crre/documenti

is true that these criticisms probably did not grasp the limited scope of the document's affirmation, intended simply to circumscribe the area in which to find a future agreement between Israel and the Holy See. However, it was accompanied by other statements that seemed to go in a similar direction. Riegner emphasized another, more general point: "Christians are invited to understand this religious attachment [to the Holy Land] which finds its roots in biblical tradition, without however making their own any particular religious interpretation of this relationship."[84] But was not respecting Jewish sentiment without adopting it a way of denying what the document affirmed in another point, namely the permanence of the value of the Old Covenant? Immediately after the document's release, at the ILC meeting in Rome, Geoffrey Wigoder did not hesitate to speak of an inability on the part of Catholicism to understand Judaism's profound self-awareness.[85]

This episode shows how there were persistent difficulties in understanding, precisely regarding the fundamental question posed by the Jews at the beginning of dialogue. In other ways, the 1985 document made an important contribution to the development of relations. Wigoder himself acknowledged this by stressing other important points, including a reevaluation of the figure of the Pharisees, aimed at dispelling clichés accumulated over the course of two millennia, and the full acceptance of Christianity's Jewish roots. This was dealt with at length in the document's third paragraph, the incipit of which read: "Jesus was and always remained, a Jew."[86] The document's publication was part of a phase of great development of sensitivity towards Jews, initiated by the election of the new pope, John Paul II, who came from a context of strong Jewish presence and had personally developed ties with many Jews (such as his old friend and fellow student Jerzy Kluger).[87] His election elicited positive reactions in the Jewish world, with a multitude of messages and requests for contacts. In addition to the two audiences granted respectively to a delegation of the AJC in February 1982 and to members of the ADL in March 1984, there was the entirely new practice of holding numerous meetings at the local level with Jewish communities during his first apostolic journeys. Among these it is sufficient to mention the one in November 1980, when he met the representatives of the German Jewish community, during which the pope gave a speech that Riegner considered a fundamental contribution to developing a Christian theology of Judaism.[88] In this first phase of his pontificate, which culminated with the historic visit to Rome's synagogue in April 1986, Pope John Paul II's contribution to dialogue with the Jews was direct and abundant, as was also seen – within a Catholic context – by his significant speech at the congress of delegates of the bishops' conferences in March 1982.[89]

The controversies that arose after the publication of the "Notes on the Correct Way to Present the Jews" were thus woven into the context of a great development in mutual relations, and seemed to confirm the providential reading that Charles Moeller had made, ten years earlier, on the occasion of the first difficulties that arose after the publication of the "Guidelines." For Moeller, dialogue demanded certain essential requisites of the partners, among which were profound humility, prudence, and patience. The succession of

-della-commissione/en2.html> (accessed Nov 27, 2023).

84 "Notes on the Correct Way."

85 Geoffrey Wigoder, "A Jewish Reaction to the 'Notes'," in: International Catholic-Jewish Liaison Committee, *Fifteen Years*, 255–269. Wigoder also expressed regret that the document's text had not been the subject of consultation with the Jewish counterpart prior to its publication.

86 "Notes on the Correct Way."

87 For a biographical profile, see Andrea Riccardi, *Giovanni Paolo II: La biografia*, Cinisello Balsamo, Edizioni San Paolo, 2011, esp. 38–43.

88 The text of the pope's discourse, held in Mainz on Nov 17, 1980, can be found in International Catholic-Jewish Liaison Committee, *Fifteen Years*, 301–302.

89 Now in International Catholic-Jewish Liaison Committee, *Fifteen Years*, 304–305.

events and statements, starting with *Nostra aetate*, had shown the unfolding of a sort of "divine pedagogy, which knows how to use even our stupidity and weakness for good and for peace." Recalling Jacques-Bénigne Bossuet's well-known axiom that "God writes straight with crooked lines," Moeller saw this unfolding precisely in the area of Jewish-Christian relations since, there more than in other areas, "the most concrete and practical reflections are paralleled by the highest reflections and those mysteries which remain the most difficult."[90] Ten years after Moeller's words, the new difficulties that arose from the publication of the "Notes on the Correct Way to Present the Jews" began to be overcome, opening the way to one of the most climactic moments of the dialogue, John Paul II's visit to the synagogue of Rome – during which he uttered the well-known phrase "you are our dearly beloved brothers, and in a certain way, it could be said that you are our elder brothers" – and Rabbi Elio Toaff's subsequent participation in the prayer for peace in Assisi in October of 1986.[91]

8 The Cold Shower of Reality

By the mid-1980s, the ILC's progress underwent a period of relative crisis, with meetings suspended for a period of five years. The agenda's implementation, decided more than 20 years earlier, had encountered numerous difficulties. On one point there was undeniable progress, namely the overcoming of stereotyped images of the other that had circulated in both Christian and Jewish circles. On the matter of the relationship between dialogue and mission, the Catholic attitude was less intransigent than that of some Protestant churches and, at the ILC's meeting in Venice in March 1977, a report by Tommaso Federici opened the way for clarification in regard to Judaism.[92] The theological dialogue on the shared patrimony between Christians and Jews had been postponed for some time, leaving room only for sporadic specific initiatives, and it was mainly the Catholic side that regretted this. During a meeting of the CRRJ at the end of the 1970s, one of the experts, the Holy Ghost Father Roger Le Déaut, noted: "We have moved – perhaps too hastily – from theoretical to practical questions."[93] On the issue of the recognition of the State of Israel, a solution was still far from being found, especially after the deterioration in the Israeli-Palestinian conflict and the proclamation of Jerusalem as the capital of the State of Israel.[94] Finally, the matter of the memory of the Shoah and the responsibilities of the Christian world in the spread of the virus of anti-Semitism in Europe in the 1930s – which, not by chance, was at the origin of the crisis in the mid-1980s with the eruption of the affair over the Carmelite convent at Auschwitz – was still unsolved. The issue became the center of public discussion, with the Jewish side expecting a stronger stance from John Paul II.

The scenario had changed a great deal since December 1965, when Vatican II came to an end. The approval of *Nostra aetate* had introduced a break in the continuity of a magisterium that had looked at the Jews through a series of traditional interpretations but, unlike what had happened in the ecumenical field with the active presence of non-Catholic observers, the Jewish

90 "Conference of Msgr. Moeller in USA," *Information Service* 30, 1976, 27–30, here 29.

91 For a valuable testimony on these two events, see Elio Toaff, *Perfidi giudei, fratelli maggiori*, Milan, Mondadori, 1987, 233–245. The pope's discourse held in the synagogue of Rome, can be found in: International Catholic-Jewish Liaison Committee, *Fifteen Years*, 321–325. See also, Eugene J. Fisher & Leon Klenicki, eds., *Pope John Paul II on Jews and Judaism (1979–1986)*, New York, US Catholic Conference, 1987.

92 Tommaso Federici, "Mission and Witness of the Church," in: International Catholic-Jewish Liaison Committee, *Fifteen Years*, 46–62.

93 *Riunione dei consultori della Commissione per i rapporti religiosi con l'ebraismo (4 maggio 1978, Casa Internaz. del clero)*, May 8, 1978, 1, in: UCL-LG, Charles Moeller, papiers, 3343.

94 Silvio Ferrari, *Vaticano e Israele: Dal secondo conflitto mondiale alla guerra del Golfo*, Florence, Sansoni, 1991, 184–189.

world had remained practically absent from the council Fathers' horizon. Archbishop Hélder Pessoa Câmara proposed concluding the council with a ceremony in St. Peter's Square, at the center of which would be a recitation by the pope, flanked by the heads of other Christian churches, of a request for forgiveness in the form of a prayer spoken before the chief rabbi. The idea was not even considered. Câmara himself saw it as "a dream."[95] After the council, however, the time had come for a true and actual encounter with the Jews. The original ecumenical and ecclesiological approach of the Christian theology of the 1960s had to give way to a different agenda, one more embedded in the problems and realities of history. It will be interesting to investigate the contours of this second and decisive phase – which has been treated summarily here – once the availability of documents permits a more accurate and informed investigation.

Translated from Italian to English by Susan Dawson Vásquez and David Dawson Vásquez.

Bibliography

Brechenmacher, Thomas, *Der Vatikan und die Juden: Geschichte einer unheiligen Beziehung vom 16. Jahrhundert bis zur Gegenwart*, Munich, Beck, 2005.

Connelly, John, *From Enemy to Brother: The Revolution in Catholic Teaching on the Jews (1933–1965)*, Cambridge MA, Harvard University Press, 2012.

Cunningham, Philip A., Norbert J. Hofman & Jospeh Sievers, eds., *The Catholic Church and Jewish People: Recent Reflections from Rome*, New York, Fordham University Press, 2007.

Cunningham, Philip A., *Seeking Shalom: The Journey to Right Relationship Between Catholics and Jews*, Grand Rapids, Eerdmans, 2015.

Eugene J. Fisher & Leon Klenicki, eds., *Pope John Paul II on Jews and Judaism (1979–1986)*, New York, US Catholic Conference, 1987.

Füllenbach, Elias H., "Das katholisch-jüdische Verhältnis im 20. Jahrhundert: Katholische Initiativen gegen den Antisemitismus und die Anfänge des christlich-jüdischen Dialogs in Deutschland," in: Reinhold Boschki & Albert Gerhards, eds., *Erinnerungskultur in der pluralen Gesellschaft: Neue Perspektiven für den christlich-jüdischen Dialog*, Paderborn, Schöningh, 2010, 143–163.

International Catholic-Jewish Liaison Committee, *Fifteen Years of Catholic-Jewish Dialogue (1970–1985)*, Vatican City, Libreria Editrice Vaticana, 1988.

Kessler, Edward, *An Introduction to Jewish-Christian Relations*, Cambridge, Cambridge University Press, 2010.

Lovsky, Fadiey, *La déchirure de l'absence: Essai sur les rapports de l'église du Christ et du peuple d'Israël*, Paris, Calmann-Lévy, 1971.

Miccoli, Giovanni, "Two Sensitive Issues: Religious Freedom and the Jews," in: Giuseppe Alberigo & Joseph A. Komonchak, eds., *History of Vatican II*, vol. 4, *Church as Communion: Third Period and Intersession (September 1964–September 1965)*, Leuven/Maryknoll, Peeters/Orbis Books, 2003, 95–193.

Moyaert, Marianne & Didier Pollefeyt, eds., *Never Revoked*: Nostra aetate *as Ongoing Challenge for Jewish-Christian Dialogue*, Leuven/Grand Rapids, Peeters/Eerdmans, 2010.

Oesterreicher, John M., "The Genesis of *Nostra aetate*," in: John M. Oesterreicher, ed., *The New Encounter between Christians and Jews*, New York, Philosophical Library, 1986, 103–295.

Riegner, Gerhart M., *Never Despair: Sixty Years in the Service of the Jewish People and of Human Rights*, Chicago, Ivan R. Dee, 2006.

The Theology of the Churches and the Jewish People: Statements by the World Council of Churches and Its Member Churches, Geneva, WCC Publications, 1988.

Velati, Mauro, "The Debate on *De Judaeis* and Ecumenical Dialogue," in: Neville Lamdan & Alberto Melloni, eds., *Nostra Aetate: Origins, Promulgation, Impact on Jewish-Catholic Relations*, Berlin, LIT, 2007, 145–162.

95 See Velati, *Separati ma fratelli*, 644.

CHAPTER 36

Protestant America and Ecumenism in the 1960s and 1970s

Luca Ferracci

1 A New Beginning for Ecumenical Dialogue in Mainstream Protestantism

On May 26, 1961, Eugene Carson Blake, a prominent figure in the UPCUSA, former president of the NCC and an influential voice in the civil rights movement, appeared on the cover of *Time*. It was not the first time the prestigious magazine had dedicated its frontispiece to a clergyman or, as in this case, to a leading representative of the ecumenical movement. In 1927, it was the pencil portrait profile of Charles Brent that was framed (actually more to celebrate his ecclesial leadership than the ecumenical achievements of Faith and Order) and, in December 1961, it would be Willem Visser 't Hooft's turn, behind whose shoulders gleamed a cross. It brightened the background that was as gloomy as the postwar Europe that the "world churchman"[1] – as the caption called him – had restored light and hope to from the pews of the Amsterdam assembly of 1948.[2]

It would be another five years before Visser 't Hooft left the leadership of the WCC in Blake's hands, but *Time* already seemed to have clear ideas about who was the most suitable candidate to take up his impressive legacy.

The reason for that early investiture was a speech that Blake gave on Dec 4, 1960 at the Episcopalian cathedral in San Francisco, where he had urged Presbyterians, Episcopalians, Methodists, and the faithful of the United Church of Christ to rediscover unity in one "truly catholic and truly reformed" church that would pave the way for the ultimate reunification of the whole of Christ's church.[3] It had been decades since mainstream Protestantism in the United States had learned to coexist and come together at a national level in order to meet the common challenges of secularization, social problems, and evangelization in urban suburbs as well as distant territories where America cast its protective shadow, or simply to witness within the Christian life to the same cohesion that had bound the nation together in the face of the threat of an atomic war. There were also no shortages of attempts at union that had failed because of a stubborn unwillingness to give way on points deemed at odds with one's ecclesial tradition.[4]

1 See the front cover of *Time*, Dec 8, 1961.

2 See the contribution by Jurjen Zeilstra in this volume.

3 Eugene C. Blake, "A Proposal Toward the Reunion of Christ's Church (Grace Cathedral, San Francisco, December 4, 1960)," in: Keith Watkins, *The American Church that Might Have Been: A History of the Consultation on Church Union*, Eugene, Pickwick, 2014, 205–215.

4 During World War I, the continuing need for military chaplains accompanying US soldiers deployed on the fronts of Europe prompted the idea of indiscriminately employing Episcopalian and Congregationalist pastors ordained according to a shared rite recognized as valid by both churches. The request for a "supplementary" ordination made by the Episcopalian Church provoked a rejection by the Congregationalist Church. By 1937, dialogue between the Episcopalian and Presbyterian churches had instead taken off. In 1946, after the war's end, a proposal for union was drawn up. It was the Episcopalians to upset the table this time, dragged away by a conservative minority reluctant to see the bishop's authority diminished in favor of a collegial type of community government. Things did not go better in 1949, when it was the Methodist Church's turn. Six years later, the immaturity of ecumenical relations between the two churches that emerged on the issue of intercommunion convinced both sides to suspend talks. On the proposal for a joint military ordinariate of Episcopalians and Congregationalists, see Peter G. Gowing, "Newman Smyth and the Congregational-Episcopal Concordat,"

The time had come, Blake said, to take ecumenical relations to another level, where basic interdenominational cooperation would give way to full communion within an ecclesial space dominated not by the need for doctrinal uniformity and governance, but by the urgency of realizing at a local level the universal unity that churches around the world had long been committed to seeking in large ecumenical bodies such as the WCC. Exactly 50 years from when Brent had nominated the ECUSA to head the initiative for a world conference on issues of doctrine and constitution – which would later become Faith and Order – at the Cincinnati general assembly, it now fell to America's oldest Christian denominations to translate the achievements of half a century of theological dialogues into a mature form of church fellowship. And the achievements were not few, according to Blake.

The first thing the united church of tomorrow could put to good use was the realization that mutual acceptance of ministerial structures would require renouncing past controversies about the precedence of episcopal order over presbyteral or congregational order and repudiating any right of preemption over the ordination of ministers and pastors. In essence, Blake proposed starting from the episcopal, or oversight, function concretely existing in all churches in order to find a compromise that would harmoniously merge the vertical and horizontal components of ecclesiology. This would mean cutting off the extremes. These were, on the one hand, the episcopalian temptation to an authoritarian and top-down conception of ecclesial life and, on the other hand, any "democratic" interpretation of the presbyterian-synodal system. In fact, this was the path that the ecumenical movement had long taken in its theological dialogues on the ministry dating back to the first world conferences of the interwar era.

His two other points were an attempt to explain, in practical terms, how the Presbyterian and Episcopalian traditions could agree, on the basis of a common tradition inherited from the Apostolic Church, on the confession of faith crystallized in the Nicene-Constantinopolitan symbol, and the sacraments of baptism and the Eucharist. While in the latter case it would be sufficient to recognize the sacraments as authentic vehicles of grace instead of symbolic acts to avoid entering into laborious theological negotiations, in the case of the creed it would be a matter of mitigating what Blake called the "over-traditional" position of Episcopalians and the hostility of the free churches to binding themselves to any formula of faith expressed over time.

Blake held that the latter was an attitude that, in the midst of a century of rapid social and cultural change, had opened a door in multi-faceted US Christianity to currents of religious relativism and personalism that threatened to turn the entire church established by Christ upside down. Moreover, at that precise historical juncture, it was the urgency of fortifying against the rampant secularization of North American society as well as of spiritually arming the nation against the Marxist atheism threatening the very existence of the West that, according to Blake, required the American churches, Protestant and non-Protestant, to achieve the unity that was no longer deferrable in time and no longer concealable behind administrative federations or simple denominational unions.

Blake's address marked the foundational act of the COCU, one of the most important (and ill-fated) attempts at union enacted by the historical denominations of North American Protestantism, but certainly not the first. The so-called Philadelphia Plan (1920) and Greenwich Plan (1949) – both arising in historic contexts, the end of World War I

CH 33/2, 1964, 175–191. On the dialogue between Episcopalians and Presbyterians, see Charles Duell Kean, *The Road to Reunion: The Role of the Episcopal Church in the Movement for Christian Reunion*, Greenwich CT, Seabury Press, 1958. On the failure of the project of intercommunion between Episcopalians and Methodists, see Thomas Ferguson, "Caught in the Parent Trap: Anglicans and Methodists in the USA," in: C. Franklin Brookhart & Gregory V. Palmer, eds., *That They May Be One?: The Episcopal-United Methodist Dialogue*, New York, Seabury Books, 2014.

and the beginning of the Cold War, that were far from easy – were also projects that could be traced back to the large denominational families of US Protestantism (Presbyterians, Episcopalians, Disciples of Christ, and Congregationalists, in this case). Those attempts, however, declared themselves programmatically disinterested in the theological issues at stake in ecumenical dialogue and were instead concerned with the preservation of a North American *pax christiana* that would safeguard the nation's social order and economic well-being, which were threatened by Marxist atheism.[5]

None of these plans, however, not even the boldest one that was presented by Blake in 1960, started from assumptions or insights that were original for the time. Christian unity as a universal antidote to secularization and atheism had already been a powerful trigger in the early 20th century for those churches, Protestant and Orthodox, that were convinced that only together could they defeat a modernity that seemed to relegate them to a role subordinate to states, ideologies, and socialist internationalism. This thinking was obviously shared by the church in Rome, but it remained imprisoned in a self-referentiality that seemed impossible to shake. Even identifying a *quod requiritur et sufficit*, condensed in the apostolic faith and the sacraments, was by no means new, dating back to a 19th century elaboration of the first common basis of Christian unity entirely thought out in the Anglican context.[6] These were centuries-old solutions to problems that had remained essentially unchanged over time, to which was added the obvious concern for the prominence of a fully emancipated Catholicism at the national level and the ongoing change in the religious fabric of Anglo-Saxon America that was making the liberal and ecumenical voice of the historical churches increasingly out of tune with the great choruses rising from the evangelical and conservative world.

2 The NCC: Between Social Commitment and Theological Negotiations

The FCC, born in 1908 in the aftermath of the Second Great Awakening and out of the growing evangelical alliance of the late 19th century, was the precursor to the NCC, which was christened in the heat of the Cold War and McCarthyism. On Nov 28, 1950, in Cleveland, Ohio, 25 Protestant and four Orthodox denominations sealed their union before the Bible and under a banner bearing the words "This Nation Under God." There seemed to be no trace left of that Christian labourism that had given birth to the Social Gospel movement at the turn of the century. The ecumenical and pan-Christian call to arms that

5 On the Philadelphia Plan, see "A Plan of Union for Evangelical Churches in the U.S.A.," in *Minutes of the General Assembly of the Presbyterian Church in the United States of America*, vol. 20, Philadelphia, Office of the General Assembly, 1920, 118–122. The fate of this, as well as the subsequent Greenwich Plan, is discussed in Samuel McCrea Cavert, *Church Cooperation and Unity in America: A Historical Review (1900–1970)*, New York, Association Press, 1970. For a comprehensive overview of all the ecumenical dialogues that took place in the United States from the mid-20th century to the beginning of the 21st century as well as the history of the COCU and its substantial failure, see Michael Root's chapter in the third volume of this work, some of the content of which this essay anticipates.

6 Such projects were not new in the North American religious scene. Others, remaining only on paper, were advanced by William Augustus Muhlenberg at the 1853 General Convention of the Episcopalian Church (the so-called Muhlenberg Memorial) and by William Reed Huntington in his book *The Church Idea: An Essay towards Unity*, New York, Dutton, 1870, which, in effect, was the manifesto of the Chicago-Lambeth Quadrilateral, the compass for a century and a half of ecumenism in the Anglican Communion. The most comprehensive overview on the matter remains Donald Herbert Yoder, "Christian Unity in Nineteenth-Century America," in: *A History of the Ecumenical Movement*, vol. 1, Ruth Rouse & Stephen Charles Neill, eds., *1517–1948*, London, SPCK, 1954, 221–259. In the first volume of this current work, see the essay presenting Paul Avis's understanding of 19th-century Anglican theology and its contribution to the birth of the ecumenical movement.

President Harry S. Truman desired now required churches to support their country in its weighty global burdens. There was a demand that the puritanical and theocratic matrix of the American "holy experiment" be recovered to encapsulate it in an aggressive and muscular Christian nationalism reduced to the rhetoric of the "chosen nation" and the "redeemer of the world."[7]

The gritty spirit displayed in Cleveland, however, did not take long to crumble under multiple external stresses, which allowed liberal currents to assert themselves within the NCC. Freed from the binary pincers of the Cold War, those forces sought an escape through a message that closely interwove pacifism, ecumenism, and, in some isolated cases, non-alignment. The impatience with the excesses reached by the wartime rhetoric in the early 1950s was joined by attacks from those in the Christian right – then on the crest of a wave and seeking political accreditation – who were pointing their finger at the liberal genome inscribed within the genetic code of the NCC churches, which not even the purification of nationalism had been able to cleanse completely. This was happening while Reinhold Niebuhr, the most influential and polished theologian on the US Protestant scene at the time, was recommending against confusing a global defense of religious freedom – one of the cornerstones of the liberal universalism that the United States embodied and professed – with a new form of imperialism that would risk isolating the world's leading nation.[8]

Visser 't Hooft was well aware that there was a way and the space for those cracks to turn into a breach. He insisted that the WCC's second world assembly, scheduled for 1954, be held in the United States. The Evanston, Illinois, conference thus became an opportunity to draw the NCC into the ecumenical movement's orbit, since North America was considered too important to leave it to the ideological battles of the Cold War or withering "Westernist" discourse that was only useful in justifying the fractured world order launched at the Yalta Conference in 1945. Having reactivated traditional social receptors and rejected the call to become the purveyors of an exceptionalist nationalism bent to the binary patterns of the Cold War, the NCC churches thus opened up to the transformations of the 1960s, to the student and pacifist protests during the harshest stages of the Vietnam War, and to the movements of 1968, developing a youthful and idealist subculture that, not infrequently, found its fulfillment precisely in ecumenism.

Especially from the 1970s onward, a marked and at times preponderant interest in the hottest geopolitical contexts emerged within the WCC. From the struggle against apartheid in South Africa to the defense of human rights trampled by dictatorships in Latin America, the NCC churches would unhesitatingly support the efforts of an ecumenical multilateralism that was trying to regain its footing thanks to the thrust of anti-imperialist pacifism. At the same time, they endured the criticisms that a certain fundamentalist evangelicalism, often attached to Western conservative circles, directed toward them for indirect complicity with Marxist subversion and the ethical laxity that Christianity as a whole was suffering.[9]

But the NCC's ecumenical potential was not entirely exhausted in the tense advocacy campaign. It fell to Blake, in the final foreshortening of his brief presidency (1954–1957), to import the

7 This topic is covered extensively in Diane Kirby's chapter in this volume. See also Paul Mojzes, ed., *North American Churches and the Cold War*, Grand Rapids, Eerdmans, 2018. On the ecumenical implications of the Social Gospel, see Gary Dorrien's chapter in the first volume of this work.

8 See Mark Edwards, "'God Has Chosen Us': Re-Membering Christian Realism, Rescuing Christendom, and the Contest of Responsibilities during the Cold War," *Diplomatic History* 33/1, 2009, 67–94, and William C. Inboden, "The Prophetic Conflict: Reinhold Niebuhr, Christian Realism, and World War II," *Diplomatic History* 38/1, 2014, 49–82.

9 Jill K. Gill, *Embattled Ecumenism: The National Council of Churches, the Vietnam War, and the Trials of the Protestant Left*, DeKalb, Northern Illinois University Press, 2011. On religious pacifist activism during the Cold War in general, see Andrew Preston, *Sword of the Spirit, Shield of Faith: Religion in American War and Diplomacy*, New York, Alfred A. Knopf, 2012.

model of multilateral dialogue adopted in Geneva by Faith and Order onto Yankee soil. Indeed, in Evanston, the WCC had encouraged church representatives to undertake concrete regional initiatives of dialogue. Thus, the idea of scheduling the first North American conference on ecumenism, entitled "The Nature of the Unity We Seek," for 1957 in Oberlin, Ohio, arose from a joint effort by the NCC, the US branch of the WCC, and the Canadian Council of Churches. The conference was open to Baptist, Orthodox, and Quaker delegations, as well as to the symbolic but significant presence of two Catholic observers.[10]

Not unlike the general conferences that the Genevan-based Faith and Order had held in Europe from 1927 onward, the Oberlin meeting was also limited to recording a very basic consensus and, in a message to its churches, repeated the urgency of seeking a degree of unity that was sufficient to end the divisions in North American Christianity.[11] As for the rest, each played their part according to script: the Baptists raised questions about infant baptism, the Lutherans about the presence of Christ in the Eucharist, and the Orthodox left the table convinced they already possessed all the elements of the unity that was being so laboriously sought.

The results may not have been astounding but, at the very least, the Oberlin conference had succeeded in bringing North American ecumenism – which, traditionally, had been more interested in federal rather than organically-based unions – into tune with the Genevan chessboard where the committee at 150 Route de Ferney had long been focusing its attention on the sacraments and the nature of church. Two years later, in 1959, the NCC also tasked its Faith and Order study department with initiating a series of multilateral dialogues that could solidly include American Orthodox, Catholics, and Pentecostals.[12] Their agenda followed, to the letter, that given by the newly appointed study secretary of the Faith and Order commission of the WCC, Lukas Vischer. In 1963, with Vatican II in full swing, it was time to delve into the ecclesiological significance of the councils (the topic was among those proposed by Vischer following his inauguration as secretary)[13], while after 1968 – in the aftermath of the ecumenical assembly in Uppsala and the experiences in Medellín and Paris – the focus turned to working on the problem of intercommunion.[14]

In 1970, it seemed to be the time to convene a second general council for North America that would replicate the one in Oberlin, but a year later the NCC's financial situation caused those plans to be cancelled.[15] This did not, however, prevent the commission from continuing to closely follow the work of its Genevan namesake (and counterpart) over the next decade. Indeed, from the WCC's Nairobi general conference in 1975 onward, the watchword became conciliar fellowship, and the NCC's Faith and Order commission was at the forefront of North American churches making their contribution to the theological definition of this

10 Fathers John Sheerin and Gustave Weigel were part of a group of 40 observers sent to Oberlin from churches and denominations that had not yet officially joined the project. See the list of delegates in the conference's report: Paul Sevier Minear, ed., *The Nature of the Unity We Seek: Official Report of the North American Conference on Faith and Order, 3–10 September 1957, Oberlin, Ohio*, St. Louis, Bethany Press, 1958, 289–301.

11 The reports of the 12 sections (four for each of the three divisions) are given in: Minear, ed., *The Nature of the Unity We Seek*, 167–269.

12 On the history of the Faith and Order studies of the NCC, see William A. Norgren, *Faith and Order in the USA: A Brief History of Studies and Relationships*, Grand Rapids, Eerdmans, 2011.

13 See the chapter by Michael Quisinsky in this volume.

14 See Faith and Order Commission of the NCC in the USA, "The Ecclesiological Significance of Councils of Churches (1963)," in: Joseph A. Burgess & Jeffrey Gros, eds., *Growing Consensus: Church Dialogues in the United States, 1962–1991*, Mahwah, Paulist Press, 1995, 585–613. Regarding the Eucharist and early experiments in intercommunion, see the study by Lewis S. Mudge, *The Crumbling Walls*, Philadelphia, Westminster Press, 1970, and the document by the Faith and Order Commission of the NCC in the USA, "The Eucharist in the Life of the Church: An Ecumenical Consensus," *The Ecumenist* 8/6, 1970, 90–93.

15 See Norgren, *Faith and Order*, 48–50.

model of unity and playing their part in building a full and visible "conciliar community."[16]

In the United States there were three conferences devoted to BEM (*Baptism, Eucharist, and Ministry*) by the time Geneva was ready to issue the document and then to consider its reception in the churches. One meeting took place just before the 1982 Lima assembly, the second immediately after BEM was published, and a third was held in 1986 to review the first responses to the document that had arrived at the Faith and Order headquarters in Geneva.[17]

It was a small number, however, compared to the 14 consultations that the North American Faith and Order organized between 1982 and 1989 on the second major study project completed in Geneva, "A Common Expression of the Apostolic Faith Today."[18] For the occasion, Black, Pentecostal, Orthodox, and numerous free churches in America (for the most part, Mennonites and Quakers) were called in turn to give an ecumenical interpretation of the apostolic faith for modern times and to take the Nicene-Constantinopolitan Creed of 381 as the early church's first model of unity.[19] But direct confrontation with denominations that did not perceive themselves to be strictly dependent on a particular confession or symbol of the faith ended up highlighting an internal contradiction in North American Protestantism: that between an ecumenism that was more sensitive to doctrinal differences – of which the large, established churches of the North Atlantic were the main expression – and another that was more attentive to non-theological factors – a label that covered a spectrum of subjects that ranged from gender issues to social hardships and that, instead, united the radical wing of the Reformation with the disjointed world of the Black churches, a legacy of slavery and social segregation.[20]

It could not, however, be said that this internal dynamic within the North American commission was at odds with what was happening globally in the multilateral theological dialogue of those

16 See the document reporting the study's findings, "Conciliar Fellowship: A Study of the Commission on Faith and Order of the National Council of the Churches of Christ in the U.S.A.," in: Joseph A. Burgess & Jeffrey Gros, eds., *Building Unity: Ecumenical Dialogues with Roman Catholic Participation in the United States*, Mahwah, Paulist Press, 1989, 458–483. The text also presented a straightforward analysis of the main obstacles slowing the North American churches' path to conciliar fellowship, including those of a social nature such as American culture's insistence on the concept of competition (477) and the absence of a true theology of the church in the doctrinal equipment of many US denominations (481).

17 The texts produced by the second BEM conference were published in Jeffrey Gros, ed., *The Search for Visible Unity: Baptism, Eucharist, Ministry*, New York, Pilgrim Press, 1984, while the report of the third meeting can be found in Lydia Veliko & Jeffrey Gros, eds., *Growing Consensus II: Church Dialogues in the United States (1992–2004)*, Washington DC, United States Conference of Catholic Bishops, 2005, 487–495.

18 For the text of the study, see *Confessing the One Faith: An Ecumenical Explication of the Apostolic Faith as it is Confessed in the Nicene-Constantinopolitan Creed (381)*, Geneva, WCC Publications, 1991. In 1988, the NCC's Faith and Order commission had already produced a booklet on the subject intended for internal circulation: *Confessing the One Faith: The Origins, Meaning and Use of the Nicene Creed: Grounds for Common Witness*, Cincinnati, Forward Movement Publications, 1988.

19 S. Mark Heim, ed., *Faith to Creed: Ecumenical Perspectives on the Affirmation of the Apostolic Faith in the Fourth Century*, Grand Rapids, Eerdmans, 1991, ix–xxi, here xvii. A list of these consultations can be found in S. Mark Heim, "The Holy Spirit Consultation: An Introduction," in: Theodore Stylianopoulos & S. Mark Heim, eds., *Spirit of Truth: Ecumenical Perspectives on the Holy Spirit*, Brookline, Holy Cross Orthodox Press, 1986, 1–4, esp. 2. Speeches from the conference with Pentecostals, held in October 1986 at the Fuller Theological Seminary in Pasadena, California, were collected in Jeffrey Gros, "Confessing the Apostolic Faith from the Perspectives of the Pentecostal Churches," *Pneuma* 9/1, 1987, and in the section *"Confessing the Apostolic Faith from the Perspectives of the Pentecostal Churches": Pasadena, California Consultation, 22–24 October, 1986*, in: *One in Christ* 23/1–2, 1987. The results of the colloquium with African American and Afro-Caribbean churches that took place in December 1984 were published in David T. Shannon & Gayrud S. Wilmore, eds., *Black Witness to the Apostolic Faith*, Grand Rapids, Eerdmans, 1988.

20 See the summary document of the 1989 Faith to Creed conference in Heim, ed., *Faith to Creed*, 198–204.

years. In a 1988 article, Letty Mandeville Russell, cochair of the North American group collaborating on The Unity of the Church and the Renewal of Human Community project promoted by the WCC in collaboration with the NCC, listed all the reasons that had led to "old style ecumenism" becoming a historical relic. The list began with a denunciation of the lack of attunement shown with contemporary topics and languages (from the feminist question to that of hierarchical relations in Western society and the church and including a theology that was increasingly losing its ethnocentric connotations). It concluded with the request that away from a unity hounded by doctrinal convergences – which, moreover, were not proving particularly effective in terms of ecclesial reception – there should be an unhesitating move toward a unity based on a shared discernment of how various social contexts influenced and determined the way the church felt.[21]

The call, far from being an isolated one, did not fall on deaf ears. Since the 1990s, the NCC theological commission had never turned its attention away from the most controversial topical issues. The change of pace, however, was not enough, even in North America, to halt the slow shutdown of theological dialogue that still holds the world's ecumenical efforts in check.

3 The Challenge of Evangelical Fundamentalism and Neo-Evangelicalism

So far, we have looked at the ecumenical efforts of the historical denominations of US Protestantism – and its representative body, the NCC, based in New York City, a cradle of progressive culture. On issues such as the fight against racism, support for international peace and cooperation policies, as well as the reaffirmation of the principle of separation of church and state, those denominations are still capable of expressing themselves with a degree of clarity that is often lacking in the more liberal component of the national political landscape. As early as the beginning of the 20th century, however, the denominational identity of those churches, so deeply woven into the social fabric of white, Anglo-Saxon America, began to fade against the steady pull from an evangelicalism that can be described as "fundamentalist" in its basic historical-theological connotation. Emerging in the late 19th and early 20th centuries as a reaction to "modernizing" exegesis based on the historical-critical method and certain excesses of liberal theology, this effervescent US evangelical world has since broken down into such different tendencies that, today, it is difficult to identify a singular interpretive perspective.[22] In its history, however, there are figures and steps that have marked some obvious discontinuities or emphasized accelerations in processes already underway, or else that have established balances that have remained unchanged over time.

The war against liberal theology and its modern instances in the economic and social spheres certainly did not earn fundamentalism the conquest of the grand university bastions of historic Protestantism. While it remained firm in its northern strongholds, in the segregationist society of the South, fundamentalists were reaping support among the Disciples of Christ: early Pentecostals, Mennonites, Anabaptists, and the member churches of the SBC, which in time would become the movement's main denominational base. They even went so far as to proselytize among numerous historical churches that had sprung up with the

21 Letty M. Russell, "Unity and Renewal in Feminist Perspective," *Mid-Stream* 27, 1988, 55–66.

22 The term "fundamentalism" arose, beginning in 1910, from the large-scale dissemination of a series of pamphlets, "The Fundamentals," which were intended to recall the fundamental principles of Christianity, the cornerstone of which was the Bible's infallibility. In 1920, conservative Baptist publicist Curtis Lee Laws called for a general conference on the fundamentals that would curb liberal theology and recover the authentic spirit of the faith of the Fathers. Frances FitzGerald, *The Evangelicals: The Struggle to Shape America*, New York, Simon & Schuster, 2017, 71–72.

settlements of Swedish Baptists, Dutch Reformed, and German Lutherans. It was during this period that, ousted from the universities and power centers of the large mainstream churches because it was seen as obscurantist and internally divided into a pulp of churches and congregations, fundamentalist evangelicalism developed a sectarian mentality and an attitude of self-representation as a minority of "saints" in perpetual struggle against the enemies of the Christian religion.[23]

The landscape changed dramatically after World War II, and not just as a result of the staggering growth in participants at Sunday worship, which, for a variety of reasons, almost all of which can be attributed to the apocalyptic climate generated by the first nuclear tests, occurred in the immediate postwar period. In his elaborate study of the history of the evangelical movement in the United States,[24] Matthew Avery Sutton describes the masses of workers, largely from the Sun Belt, who were baptized in the waters of American patriotism during the war and were thus fully integrated into the national fabric. Pouring into the suburbs of the large industrial cities of the North (following a trend that was, admittedly, already underway since the years of the New Deal), they created veritable fundamentalist enclaves in what were traditionally impregnable bastions of the main historical churches of Protestantism.[25]

It was in this climate that the figure of Billy Graham emerged. Born into a Presbyterian family in North Carolina but ordained a ministry by the SBC, Graham is the first real transitional figure in this story.[26] It was thanks to this preacher of extraordinary oratorical skills that the so-called neo-evangelicalism was born. It was a current that soon became the majority in US evangelicalism. It knew no denominational boundaries and, in obedience to the perceived mission assigned by God to the US people, aspired to address North American Christianity as a whole, Catholics and Orthodox included.[27] Leaving old anti-liberal prejudices, with all their coterie of polemics, to the more conservative fringe – which gladly kept the definition of "fundamentalist" for itself – Graham was, in fact, the one who redeemed the churches of the South from the political apathy in which ideological millenarianism, disinterested in world affairs, had kept them confined. He brought them fully into the country's political life where they could benefit from proximity to power, both Democratic and Republican, for which they would pay the price in the long run.[28]

Moreover, these were years when the concurrence of different elements following one after the other – the shock of 1968, the spread of feminism and student protests, the explosion of the racial question, and the ultimate urbanization of

23 On this issue, see Nancy T. Ammerman, *Bible Believers: Fundamentalists in the Modern World*, New Brunswick NJ, Rutgers University Press, 1987, and Barry Hankins, *Uneasy in Babylon: Southern Baptist Conservatives and American Culture*, Tuscaloosa, The University of Alabama Press, 2002.

24 Matthew Avery Sutton, *American Apocalypse: A History of Modern Evangelicalism*, Cambridge MA, Harvard University Press, 2014, 266, 310.

25 An example is the story of J. Frank Norris, a Texas preacher trained at the Southern Baptist Theological Seminary in Louisville. In the 1930s, he founded the First Baptis Church of Fort Worth and then the WBF in Detroit, under whose tent he gathered a populous Baptist community composed mostly of Southern workers employed in the city's large automobile factories. Norris's goal was to separate the First Baptist Church of Detroit from the Northern Baptist Convention, which he considered infested with Modernist tendencies. Norris was an anti-Semite (publicly referring to the *Protocols of the Elders of Zion*), anti-Catholic, and a life-long, bitter opponent of Franklin D. Roosevelt's economic policies. Barry Hankins, *God's Rascal: J. Frank Norris & the Beginnings of Southern Fundamentalism*, Lexington KY, The University Press of Kentucky, 1996.

26 Among the most recent studies on the issue, see Steven P. Miller, *The Age of the Evangelicalism: America's Born-Again Years*, Oxford, Oxford University Press, 2014.

27 See Richard V. Pierard, "From Evangelical Exclusivism to Ecumenical Openness: Billy Graham and Sociopolitical Issues," *JES* 20/3, 1983, 425–446.

28 Of course, the bibliography on Graham is vast and so, in addition to Steven P. Miller, *Billy Graham and the Rise of the Republican South*, Philadelphia, University of Pennsylvania Press, 2009, I prefer to refer the reader directly to FitzGerald, *The Evangelicals*, 143 ff.

rural masses from the South – was pushing up the growth curve of a Christian right that had made it its mission to arrest the decline in morals that threatened to destroy the "objective" norms of private morality and public ethics.[29]

As is well known, Ronald Reagan's ascension to the presidency in 1981 aligned the political affairs of the Republican Party with those of a certain Christian fundamentalism that shared with the president a passion for mass communication and a Manichean worldview of the spiritual competition with the USSR. Supported by an unparalleled media network whose leading men were the televangelists Jerry Falwell, Pat Robertson, Jimmy Swaggart, Jimmy Bakker, and Oral Roberts, the New Religious Right attempted, not always successfully, to steer the country's political agenda for more than a decade by constantly beating the drum of the four cornerstones of its program: the reintroduction of prayer into public schools, the fight against abortion, the preservation of US Christian traditions, and the introduction of policies to support the family and its traditional values.[30]

The golden moment of the Reagan era was followed by the Christian Coalition's "crossing into the wilderness" during Bill Clinton's two Democratic presidencies, then a rekindling of the flame with the election of George W. Bush, then a polarization around Barack Obama's health care choices, up to a forced support for Donald Trump. Evangelicalism, even though with mixed political fortunes, has remained a steadily growing component in North American society.

At the level of interdenominational relations, these churches have never excelled in ecumenical sensitivity. In fact, while acknowledging their rootedness in the fundamentals of classical Protestant theology and sharing the principles of *sola fide*, *sola gratia*, *sola scriptura* with the historical Reformation churches, these Christians have always been protective of their ecclesial autonomy – more often than not obtained after severing ties with the denominational family they belonged to – as well as entrenched in theological positions and readings of history that they considered non-negotiable. Having now set aside the anti-Modernist polemic of the early 20th century, but not the battles against evolution or critical exegesis of the Bible, it is now, more than ever, ethical positions that divide historic Protestantism from radical evangelicalism, especially in its political and ideological variant. Conflicting views on issues such as bioethics or homosexuality, in fact, constitute recent points of disagreement that merely widen a theological divide that dates back to the very birth of the evangelical movement.

The corpuscolar form of this Christian galaxy did not, however, prevent successes in experiments with interdenominational coordination or institutional structures that were new and in some respects revolutionary for a movement that, in its decentralized, horizontal, and anti-hierarchical nature, had historically grounded itself on an ideal identity and an indispensable theological foundation. In 1941, Presbyterian pastor Carl McIntire, a pioneer of an evangelicalism that did not disdain political engagement and did not accept compromise on the foundations of the movement, took the personal initiative to establish the ACCC, which brought disparate and minority sectors of Christian conservatism together. The main

29 Regarding this, see Angela M. Lahr, *Millennial Dreams and Apocalyptic Nightmares: The Cold War Origins of Political Evangelicalism*, Oxford, Oxford University Press, 2007.

30 There is a wide range of studies devoted to the subject of the intersections between foreign policy and the evangelical galaxy in the US in the 1970s and 1980s. On interaction between executive bodies and religious lobbies and the role of a president's faith, see Sara Diamond, *Roads to Dominion: Right-Wing Movements and Political Power in the United States*, New York, The Guilford Press, 1995, and William Steding, *Presidential Faith and Foreign Policy: Jimmy Carter the Disciple and Ronald Reagan the Alchemist*, New York, Palgrave Macmillan, 2014. For a closer look at the advocacy activities in defense of human rights and religious freedom carried out by churches globally, see the thorough study by Lauren Frances Turek, *To Bring the Good News to All Nations: Evangelical Influence on Human Rights and U.S. Foreign Relations*, Ithaca, Cornell University Press, 2020.

element of their cohesion was their aversion to what was then still called the FCC, that they saw as a hotbed of Modernist tendencies, a den of undercover Marxists, and, as such, the ideal target of a smear campaign aimed at flushing out enemies of the faith in the darkest hour of American history.[31] In 1947, McIntire aimed even higher, founding the ICCC, whose aim was to thwart the emergence of the WCC, which was then in the final stages of its complicated gestation.

It was two of his students, however, who get the credit of starting the most successful evangelical covenant. In 1942, two New England pastors, Harold Ockenga and J. Elwin Wright, established the NAE in Chicago, which gladly refrained from including the adjective "fundamentalist" in its name in order to open itself to all those components of America's Protestantism that no longer reflected the liberal dogmatism of the historical churches, beginning with Pentecostal groups, especially the Assemblies of God which were then in a phase of whirlwind growth. It was a choice that, in the span of little more than a decade, enabled the NAE – which had begun from a base of about 700,000 members belonging mostly to small Pentecostal denominations, the SBC, and the Missouri Synod Lutherans – to triple its membership and come to closely challenge, in terms of numbers and political clout, the denominational monopoly of the historical churches.

While, internally, relations between the NAE and the NCC were always marked by competition, relations with the WCC were certainly no better. Especially since the 1970s, intense grassroots propaganda campaigns deployed by the NAE media network described the Genevan ecumenical council as the coordinating center of a plan for the destruction of Christianity devised by international Freemasonry with the help of an elite of liberal theologians and financed with donations from unsuspecting US taxpayers.[32] The long list of accusations levelled against the WCC and its many ecumenical relief efforts included that of harboring Guevarist theological troublemakers – who were nothing but exiles hunted down by the military juntas of their respective countries[33] – and of being complicit in worldwide Marxist subversion, cultivating, under cover of humanitarian actions, groups of self-styled Christians in the service of communist dictatorships that oppressed churches and challenged the United States' continental supremacy.[34]

31 Immediately after the founding of the NCC, the ACCC published and circulated a pamphlet entitled "How Red Is the National Council of Churches?," in which it openly accused the rival organization of aiding communists and obstructing "clean-up" operations conducted by Washington intelligence. Gill, *Embattled Ecumenism*, 47–48.

32 Melani McAlister, *The Kingdom of God Has No Borders: A Global History of American Evangelicals*, Oxford, Oxford University Press, 2018.

33 Finding asylum in Geneva, in addition to Brazilian pedagogist Paulo Freire – who had been forced into exile after a military coup that ended João Goulart's government – were Methodists Julio de Santa Ana and Emilio Castro, fleeing Juan María Bordaberry's repression (Castro would go on to serve as WCC secretary general from 1985 to 1992), and Argentine jurist Leopoldo Juan Niilus, a Lutheran who was banned in 1969 by the Buenos Aires government for criticizing the ruling military junta's poor respect for human rights. It was thanks to their contributions, coordinated by Argentine Methodist José Míguez Bonino, that the ISAL study commission, set up by the WCC as early as 1961, and the SODEPAX, a mixed Catholic-Protestant research group established in 1968, became arenas of ecumenical reflection on the issues of emerging liberation theology for nearly 15 years. Additionally, they forged international networks that were decisive in launching ecumenical campaigns in defense of civil rights. On the history of ISAL and the contribution of the Protestant and South American "cell" exiled in Geneva, see Annegreth Schilling, *Revolution, Exil und Befreiung: Der Boom des lateinamerikanischen Protestantismus in der internationalen Ökumene in den 1960er und 1970er Jahren*, Göttingen, Vandenhoeck & Ruprecht, 2016.

34 On Nicaragua in the Sandinista decade (1979–1990) and how decisive the church mobilization strategy promoted by the Reagan administration proved to be, see Lauren Frances Turek, "Ambassadors for the Kingdom of God or for America?: Christian Nationalism, the Christian Right, and the Contra War," *Religions* 7/12, 2016, 151. The NAE was not lacking in initiative either:

Missionary activity, from the very beginning of the evangelical movement, has been the most powerful catalyst of its growth process, but it was also an ideal space from which to challenge the liberal internationalism of the WCC and its princely North American branch. It should not be forgotten that what transported generations of missionaries to the southern latitudes of the globe was not only the urgency of regaining for the gospel the masses dispossessed by Catholic obscurantism or the welfarist zeal of Protestant missionary work dating back to the late 19th century, but above all the conviction that only a large-scale evangelical mobilization would hasten the fulfilment of millenarian predictions about America's destiny to realize the last earthly kingdom of peace and fruitfulness. This accounts for the early coalescence between US imperialism in its various phases and forms, from late 19th century puritanical and ethnically based imperialism to its contention with the USSR for global supremacy, and an evangelicalism eager to compete at even the international level with a liberal Protestantism that was no longer capable of conquering the world with its modern, scientific rationalism.

A rather recent current of studies, however, has pointed out that, already since the 1970s, within this "imperialist" missionary outreach that came from a Christian co-responsibility for US plans of hegemony, there has been a slowly growing feeling of a need to break out of the binary pattern of the Cold War in order to let a cosmopolitan and pluralistic ethos rid evangelical missions of the arrogant paternalism of the colonial phase.[35]

The First International Congress on World Evangelization that took place in Lausanne, Switzerland, from Jul 16 to 25, 1974, attended by 2,700 participants from more than 150 countries, was not only the first clear demonstration of the global dimension achieved by evangelicalism but also an opportunity to again discuss the theoretical foundations of a missionary practice untethered from Western ethnocentrism and to challenge liberation theologies with a faith entrenched in the world's problems that claimed to be free of any political or ideological contamination.[36] The churches' representatives convened in Lausanne at the Palais de Beaulieu, a year after the Bangkok conference where the WCC had called for a "missionary moratorium" in order to breathe new life into an ecumenism that could no longer keep pace with the changing world. They came at the invitation of Billy Graham, who had been a tireless promoter of that conference, and they signed a pact to finish the work begun a generation earlier by the forebears of that missionary revivalism that had set the churches on a path toward reconciling their divisions.[37]

---

on a regular basis it promoted campaigns against the NCC and WCC, blaming them for their liberationist sympathies and their complicity with communist subversion in Latin America.

35 For example, see David A. Hollinger, *Protestants Abroad: How Missionaries Tried to Change the World and Changed America*, Princeton, Princeton University Press, 2017. On the value and limits of this tendency in the literature, see Mario Del Pero, "Religione, politica estera e attività missionaria: Importanza e limiti del *global turn*," *Il mestiere di storico* 12/1, 2020, 22–36.

36 Dominating the scene was Ecuadorian theologian René Padilla, who indicted the cultural imperialism of the West conveyed by US missionary action and forcefully posed the question of a missionary practice still bound to ethnocentric views and colonial styles. Padilla was also the most influential representative of an authentically "Evangelical" liberation theology that, unlike liberal-Protestant or Catholic theology, claimed to be immune from Marxist contamination and ideological drift. In this regard, see Al Tizon, *Transformation after Lausanne: Radical Evangelical Mission in Global-Local Perspective*, Oxford, Regnum Books, 2008, in particular 17–52.

37 On the generation of John Raleigh Mott and the other pioneers of the ecumenical movement, see Sarah Scholl's scholarly insight in the first volume of this work. On the Bangkok missionary conference sponsored by the WCC at a moment when its center of gravity was shifting from the North Atlantic axis to southern latitudes, see Katharina Kunter & Annegreth Schilling, "'Der Christ fürchtet den Umbruch nicht': Der Ökumenische Rat der Kirchen im Spannungsfeld von Dekolonisierung, Entwestlichung und Politisierung," in: Katharina Kunter & Annegreth Schilling, eds.,

4 Pacifist Sympathies

Identifying evangelical fundamentalism with the religious right or calling it anti-ecumenical in its entirety would be incorrect. Before the pious born-again Baptist Jimmy Carter was elected to the White House and even before Reagan seduced the conservative Christian vote with imagery steeped in nostalgia for the good old days, American evangelicalism exhibited a certain apathy toward politics and a blatant disorganization from an electoral standpoint. In the agricultural and depressed South, many fundamentalist Christians supported the welfare policies of the New Deal, and Pentecostals joined farm unions. On the conservative front, the vague anti-prohibitionist movement of the 1930s and 1940s became a political option for the Republican Party only in 1964 when Barry Goldwater, winning but suffering a boycott at the ballot box by the liberal wing of his party, challenged outgoing President Lyndon B. Johnson on a programmatic platform that was genuinely conservative in economic and social issues. To the far right, religious leaders such as the aforementioned Carl McIntire were stoking the embers of "red danger" and questioning the NCC's patriotic loyalties with the intent of undermining its credibility in the eyes of the institutions and their respective congregations. In the middle of the pack was Billy Graham, a phenomenal preacher of Christian patriotism – equally distant from both political extremes, apart from a costly infatuation with Richard Nixon – who, had he not embraced the cause of fighting apartheid, would have remained confined to his quarrelsome Southern enclave.[38]

Beneath the surface of a diverse Christian conservatism, that blessed America and marched with Martin Luther King Jr. and that refrained from rubbing salt in the wounds of denominationalism but did not work too hard to heal them, flowed a river of liberal and progressive culture. It emerged in the restless and troubled 1960s, marked by the escalation of the Vietnam War, the mounting of student protests, and the shattering of King's dream of racial harmony one night on the balcony of a Memphis motel, and became an evangelical presence that was less noisy and visible than the one propagated by the major television networks of the Christian right, but no less incisive in American public life.[39]

Radiating centers included Wheaton College, the forge of more than a generation of neo-evangelical leaders starting with Graham himself, and Fuller Theological Seminary in Pasadena, California, founded after World War II to counterbalance the anti-intellectualism and poor social commitment of early fundamentalism.[40] It was at Fuller that Carl Ferdinand Howard Henry – the author of a witty booklet against the movement's theological rigidity[41] and, beginning in the 1960s, a leading columnist for *Christianity Today*, the magazine founded by Graham to bring the evangelical voice to the heart of national life – had risen to prominence among the faculty. In 1966, Wheaton on its part hired John Alexander, a young

Globalisierung der Kirchen: Der Ökumenische Rat der Kirchen und die Entdeckung der Dritten Welt in den 1960er und 1970er Jahren, Göttingen, Vandenhoeck & Ruprecht, 2014, 19–74.

38 See Lyman A. Kellstedt & Mark A. Noll, "Religion, Voting for President, and Party Identification, 1948–1984," in: Mark A. Noll, ed., *Religion and American Politics: From the Colonial Period to the 1980s*, Oxford, Oxford University Press, 1990, 355–379, and Daniel K. Williams, *God's Own Party: The Making of the Christian Right*, Oxford, Oxford University Press, 2010.

39 See David R. Swartz, *Moral Minority: The Evangelical Left in an Age of Conservatism*, Philadelphia, University of Pennsylvania Press, 2012.

40 On the history of Wheaton College, see Michael S. Hamilton, *The Fundamentalist Harvard: Wheaton College and the Continuing Vitality of American Evangelicalism (1919–1965)*, Ph.D. thesis, University of Notre Dame, 1995, and Paul M. Bechtel, *Wheaton College: A Heritage Remembered (1860–1984)*, Wheaton, Harold Shaw Publishers, 1984. On Fuller Theological Seminary, see George Marsden, *Reforming Fundamentalism: Fuller Seminary and the New Evangelicalism*, Grand Rapids, Eerdmans, 1987.

41 This is referring to his *The Uneasy Conscience of Modern Fundamentalism*, Grand Rapids, Eerdmans, 1947.

white professor with a long history as an activist for Black civil rights in the Chicago suburbs.

Pastor Jim Wallis, who was not affiliated with either insotitution, had been raised in a strictly observant evangelical community, the Plymouth Brethren; he founded a resident community of Christian witness, prayer, and service to the marginalized in Washington, DC, in 1975. This was the result of an earlier experiment attempted in 1971 at Trinity Evangelical Divinity School in Deerfield, Illinois, when the excesses of some preachers' bellicose rhetoric during the most intense phase of the Vietnam offensive convinced Wallis and a few other students to establish the grassroots community, which would also be open to mainstream Protestants and Catholics. It aimed to preserve a remnant of pacifist and anti-militarist culture in the country. The called themselves Sojourners and founded a magazine, *The Post-American*, that, after the move to the nation's capital, would assume the same name as the community, which is the one it retains still today. In the 1980s, during the long tug-of-war between the Reagan administration and Sandinista Nicaragua, which was accused of harassing churches that did not align themselves with the directives of the revolutionary government in Managua, *Sojourners* would be one of the few voices out of tune in the media chorus of the big TV stations of the Christian right.[42]

Politically, the turning point seemed to come with the 1972 presidential election. While the vast majority of conservative evangelicals succumbed to the lure of Nixon and his promise to dismantle the Johnsonian Great Society, progressive sectors supported the Democratic challenger, George McGovern. That choice opened the way, the following year, for the creation of a progressive platform that, in Chicago, adopted such a peremptory and bold statement on the issues of war, racism, and social inequality that the NCC leadership could not help but state that it strongly agreed with the document's drafters.[43]

In a way, Carter's victory represented the swan song of this evangelical progressivism and any beneficial effect it might have had on interdenominational relations. The comeback of the Christian right in the Reagan era branded any experience of faith steeped in passion for social justice and peace as unpatriotic, while politics learned to twist themes and refrains dear to the churches into the bait of an ecumenism that redefined the country's religious physiognomy with a conservative bent.

Translated from Italian to English by Susan Dawson Vásquez and David Dawson Vásquez.

Bibliography

Gill, Jill K., *Embattled Ecumenism: The National Council of Churches, the Vietnam War, and the Trials of the Protestant Left*, DeKalb, Northern Illinois University Press, 2011.

McAlister, Melani, *The Kingdom of God Has No Borders: A Global History of American Evangelicals*, Oxford, Oxford University Press, 2018.

Norgren, William A., *Faith and Order in the USA: A Brief History of Studies and Relationships*, Grand Rapids, Eerdmans, 2011.

Sutton, Matthew Avery, *American Apocalypse: A History of Modern Evangelicalism*, Cambridge MA, Harvard University Press, 2014.

Swartz, David R., *Moral Minority: The Evangelical Left in an Age of Conservatism*, Philadelphia, University of Pennsylvania Press, 2012.

Tizon, Al, *Transformation after Lausanne: Radical Evangelical Mission in Global-Local Perspective*, Oxford, Regnum Books, 2008.

42 Christian Smith, *Resisting Reagan: The U.S. Central America Peace Movement*, Chicago, University of Chicago Press, 1996, esp. 3–58, and Swartz, *Moral Minority*, 233–254.

43 Swartz, *Moral Minority*, 183 and, above all, Mark A. Lempke, *My Brother's Keeper: George McGovern and Progressive Christianity*, Amherst, University of Massachusetts Press, 2017.

CHAPTER 37

The Intercommunion That Never Happened

Alberto Melloni

1 The Background to a Missed Opportunity

1.1 *Expectations in the Phanar and the Vatican (1959–1963)*

The possibility of restoring Eucharistic communion between Old and New Rome has its roots in the history of Vatican II, accompanying its stages.[1] For Pope John XXIII, already in his personally handwritten announcement of the council, the council was an "invitation" to other churches "to take part in this banquet of grace."[2] The language was softened in the official version; however, that horizon of unity was intuited and pursued by Rome, particularly through the birth of an office dedicated to dialogue with the other churches that was given an equal standing (it is a "secretariat") with the other curial offices.

Entrusted to Cardinal Augustin Bea, who had been very prudent in the preceding years, the secretariat was staffed – on the one hand by Johannes Willebrands and Pierre Duprey, and on the other by Christophe-Jean Dumont and Emmanuel Lanne – with people capable of providing the context to overcome the unionism and gatekeeping in the face of a "spiritual" ecumenism that would become in the 21st century the mark of a suffocating minimalism. In preparing for the council, the SPCU's role[3] involved producing its own documents[4] and drafting observations on the documents of other preparatory bodies,[5] as well as, on the level of symbolic gesture, securing in 1962 the presence of other Christians at the council's opening. It was delicate work, as can be seen in two incidents occurred during the preparatory phase. One – the so-called Rhodes incident[6] – was the direct contact between two Catholics, accredited as journalists, and some metropolitans, which made the ecumenical movement think that Rome was undermining the WCC for a dialogue with the neighboring tradition, in a logic that was actually outdated.[7] The other arose from a passage in the encyclical *Aeterna Dei sapientia*, which was promulgated by Pope John XXIII on Nov 11, 1961,

1 This essay is an excerpt of my *Tempus visitationis: L'intercomunione inaccaduta fra Roma e Costantinopoli*, Bologna, Il Mulino, 2019, which I also mention for its references to Karim Schelkens, "Seeking Full Communion: Some Notes on the Dialogue Between the Vatican and the Phanar," *Notes and Documents* 22/23, 2012, 65–83. In preparing that work, he researched the papers of Fr. John Long, SJ, which I find irreparably mutilated by the loss of a page of the final document. I will also refer to *Tempus visitationis* for the many documents I cite here, which are gathered there in the *Dossier delle fonti, 1964–1975*, 123–366.

2 See the contribution by Christoph Theobald in this volume.

3 See Mauro Velati, *Una difficile transizione: Il cattolicesimo tra unionismo ed ecumenismo (1952–1964)*, Bologna, Il Mulino, 1996, 175–319.

4 For the process preparing the *Decretum de Judaeis*, which was rejected in the main preparatory commission and certainly did not end its journey in the nets of the Holy Office, see Neville Lamdan & Alberto Melloni, eds., *Nostra Aetate: Origins, Promulgation, Impact on Jewish-Christian Relations. Proceedings of the International Conference, Jerusalem, 30 October–1 November 2005*, Berlin, LIT, 2007.

5 See Giuseppe Ruggieri, "The First Doctrinal Clash," in: Giuseppe Alberigo & Joseph A. Komonchak, eds., *History of Vatican II*, vol. 2: *The Formation of the Council's Identity, First Period and Intersession (October 1962–September 1963)*, Leuven/Maryknoll, Peeters/Orbis Books, 1997, 233–266.

6 See Karim Schelkens, "'L'Affaire de Rhodes' au jour le jour: La correspondance inédite entre J.G.M. Willebrands et Ch. J. Dumont," *Istina* 54/3, 2009, 253–277, and Hyacinthe Destivelle, "Souvenirs d'un pionnier: Les Mémoires inédits du Père Christophe Jean Dumont," *Istina* 54/3, 2009, 279–297.

7 This is why the CCEQ was established, which Willebrands founded and provided the driving force for, on which see the chapter by Peter De Mey and Saretta Marotta in this volume.

marking the 1500th anniversary of Pope Leo I's death. On the issue of canon 28 of the Council of Chalcedon of 451, the encyclical reiterated – as Pope Pius XII had in 1951 – Leo the Great's legitimate opposition to the *intentatam iniuriam*[8] that the canon established. It was a provocation that soured relations with the Phanar at the time, precisely on the eve of Patriarch Athenagoras I's great ecumenical endeavor in 1962. That effort extended a welcome to Andreas Rinkel, the Old Catholic archbishop of Utrecht, and then also to Arthur Michael Ramsey, archbishop of Canterbury,[9] as well as to Willebrands, the secretariat's number two, who, in February 1962, was looking for a way to bring Orthodox observers to Vatican II[10] and who perceived an extraordinary ecumenical intensity in the two conversations he had with the patriarch on Feb 14 and 19 of that year.[11]

Returning to the Phanar on Jun 1 with a letter of invitation to the council, Willebrands had to deal with Constantinople's refusal to send observers to Vatican II. The refusal was due to intransigence in Athens,[12] which the patriarch would circumvent thanks to Emilianos (Timiadis), a Constantinopolitan Orthodox prelate, who attended the council as an observer for the WCC instead of the Orthodox.

Unaware of the surprising, disruptive move by the Moscow patriarch – who, on orders from the Kremlin, had sent two observers to Vatican II – Constantinople's policy of *non recevoir* became a *felix culpa*.[13] It forced a continuation of direct dialogue with the patriarch and, 14 months later, allowed dialogue between Old and New Rome to be revived on a basis of fraternal gestures. The council acted as a foundation and a framework for the gestures, beginning with the letter *Mirabilis ille*[14] on Epiphany of 1963, which reimagined a new preparation for Vatican II, indicating those three areas – ecumenism, religious freedom, Judaism – regarding which the secretariat was still unsure whether they were to be the appendices of a very capacious *De Ecclesia* or addressed in another format and incorporated in varying forms.[15]

8 John XXIII, *Aeterna Dei sapientia*, Nov 11, 1961, in: AAS 53, 1961, 785–803.

9 See Karim Schelkens, "Envisager la concélébration entre catholiques et orthodoxes?: Johannes Willebrands et Athenagoras de Costantinople," *Istina* 57/2, 2012, 127–157, esp. 132.

10 For Willebrands's report on the meeting at Ariccia on Feb 9, 1961 where the question regarding invitations to fraternal delegates was proposed, see Mauro Velati, *Dialogo e rinnovamento: Verbali e testi del Segretariato per l'unità dei cristiani nella preparazione del Concilio (1960–1962)*, Bologna, Il Mulino, 2011, 301.

11 The text of the "Compte rendu du voyage à Costantinople, 14–21 février 1962," in: KDC, FJW, 284, should be the original while an Italian version is found in the same archive, and a copy is also found in ASV, ACVII SU, 321.2.

12 See Alberto Melloni, *L'altra Roma: Politica e S. Sede durante il concilio Vaticano II (1959–1965)*, Bologna, Il Mulino, 2000, 126–128.

13 Willebrands's letter to Athenagoras requesting that observers be sent is dated Jul 14, 1962 (Schelkens, "Envisager la concélébration," 136), while between Sep 27 and Oct 2 Willebrands went to Moscow to invite Russian observers. Indeed, the hasty arrival of delegates from the Russian Church, Vitaly Borovoy and Vladimir Kotlyarov, put the New Rome in a difficult situation as it found itself bypassed by Moscow because of an acceleration due to the political interests of the Soviet Union, which did not want to miss the opportunity. This had significant ecclesiological consequences. It was as if the ideology of the Third Rome, which took over from the Second Rome occupied by Turkish concerns, had found a way to validate itself on the international stage thanks to the papal invitation and – an irony of history – thanks to the diplomatic skills of Archbishop Francesco Lardone, the nuncio in Turkey handling the relationship between Rome and Moscow. On this, see Adriano Roccucci, "Russian Observers at Vatican II: The 'Council for Russian Orthodox Church Affairs' and the Moscow Patriarchate between Anti-Religious Policy and International Strategies," in: Alberto Melloni, ed., *Vatican II in Moscow (1959–1965): Acts of the Colloquium on the History of Vatican II, Moscow, 30 March–2 April 1995*, Leuven, Bibliotheek van de Faculteit Godgeleerdheid, 1996, 45–69. See also Andrea Riccardi, *Il Vaticano e Mosca (1940–1990)*, Rome-Bari, Laterza, 1992, 253–259, and Melloni, *L'altra Roma*, 122–125.

14 John XXIII, *Mirabilis ille*, Jan 6, 1963, in: AAS 55, 1963, 149–159.

15 See Enrico Galavotti, "Il concilio continua: Giovanni XXIII e la lettera *Mirabilis Ille* del 6 gennaio 1963:

In the second conciliar period, the Romanian monk André Scrima provided better information. He was accredited not as an observer, but as the *apocrisiarius* of the patriarch himself. Athenagoras followed the proceedings and welcomed Rome's first grand gesture. On Sep 20, 1963, he received a letter signed by Pope Paul VI. It was the first correspondence from a pope since the letter with a far different tone that Pope Gregory XIII had sent to Patriarch Jeremias II Tranos in 1584, informing him of the new calendar, and it was the only one in 909 years not to demand submission. Carefully drafted by Willebrands, Duprey, and Dumont,[16] the text of the papal letter, obviously, included the Eucharist among the goods safeguarded by both churches.[17]

1.2 Osculum pacis: *Jerusalem and Rome (1964–1965)*

The letter was sent when the trip to Jerusalem had not yet been decided and prior to the overwhelming events of the second period that led to the approval of liturgical reform, the clarification introduced by the votes of October 1963, the ballot on the placement of *De beata*, Josef Frings's *j'accuse* against the Holy Office, the postponement of the programmatic encyclical, and, not least, the presentation of the secretariat's first document to the council.[18] The first formulation of a draft of *De oecumenismo* in the council session proved that the secretariat not only had the protection of the late pope and enjoyed the confidence of the reigning one but that it also intended to engage the will of an assembly steeped in the issue of ecumenism but which was still unsure about the issues of religious freedom and the church's relationship with Jews. It seemed wise to extract those issues and address them in statements of their own, bringing only the three chapters on ecumenism to a vote and postponing discussion to the third council period.

This was the setting of Paul VI's idea for a pilgrimage to Jerusalem that, however, had more internal objectives, or rather, ones dear to the newly elected pope.[19] Announced on Dec 4, 1963, the trip brought about an intense exchange with the Phanar[20] because, surprisingly, Athenagoras declared that all church leaders should go to Jerusalem to pray together for Christian unity.

Introduzione e sinossi critica," in: Alberto Melloni, ed., *Tutto è grazia: In omaggio a Giuseppe Ruggieri*, Milan, Jaca Book, 2010, 115–169.

16 Schelkens, "Envisager la concélébration," 139, refers to minutes of Sep 20, 1963, found in GUA, JLP (the minutes are not numbered but identified by the date sent).

17 "The task which the Lord has confided to us as successor in this see to the leader of the Apostles makes us solicitous for all that concerns the unity of Christians, and all that can help to restore perfect harmony among them. Let us entrust the past to the mercy of God, and listen to the advice of the Apostle: 'forgetting what is behind us, I am stretched forth towards that which is ahead, that I may seek to seize it even as I am seized by him.' We have been seized by him through the gift of the good news of salvation, by the gift of the same Baptism, and of the same priesthood, in which the same Eucharist is celebrated – the one sacrifice of the one Lord of the Church"; *Tomos Agapis. Vatican-Phanar (1958–1970)*, Rome/Istanbul, Imprimérie polyglotte vaticane, 1971, 33, Sep 20, 1963, 82; ET: Edward James Stormon, ed., *Towards the Healing of Schism: The Sees of Rome and Constantinople*, Mahwah, Paulist Press, 1987, 33, Sep 20, 1963, 52. It formally acknowledged the greeting that was extended by Maximos of Sardis on Sep 9 congratulating Giovanni Battista Montini on his election to the papacy (the previous June), see Giancarlo Bruni, *Quale ecclesiologia? Cattolicesimo e Ortodossia a confronto: Il dialogo ufficiale*, Milan, Edizioni Paoline, 1999, 14–15.

18 See Joseph Famerée, "Bishops and Dioceses and the Communications Media (Nov 5–25, 1963)," in: Giuseppe Alberigo & Joseph A. Komonchak, eds., *History of Vatican II*, vol. 3, *The Mature Council, Second Period and Intersession, September 1963–September 1964*, Leuven/Maryknoll, Peeters/Orbis Books, 2000, 117–188; and Alberto Melloni, *Il concilio e la grazia: Saggi di storia sul Vaticano II*, Milan, Jaca Book, 2015, 237–302.

19 See Philippe Chenaux, *Paolo VI: Una biografia politica*, Rome, Carocci, 2016.

20 See the exchange between Gustavo Testa and Willebrands of Dec 10 in: Leo Declerck, ed., *Les Agendas conciliaires de Mgr J. Willebrands, secrétaire du Secrétariat pour l'Unité des Chrétiens*, Leuven, Peeters, 2009, 83–84.

Lukas Vischer, from the WCC, dismissed the proposal as "unrealistic."[21] Indeed, no one welcomed the suggestion that would minimize a visit of complex implications, both political[22] as well as ecclesiological. Given that Orthodoxy claimed the greater dignity of the oldest and most uninterrupted presence in Jerusalem,[23] an impeccable solution[24] was found between Duprey, Willebrands, and Angelo Dell'Acqua on the one hand and the patriarch's representatives on the other in the days between Dec 10 and 30. It was decided that it would be Athenagoras to welcome the pope of Rome,[25] whose intentions, far from ecumenical, were described in an article on Jan 1, 1964, which was signed by Willebrands.[26]

Instead, the meeting "on equal footing" desired by Athenagoras became a true leap forward. On Jan 5, at the tail end of the visit, Athenagoras and Paul VI met at the nunciature, on Jordanian territory.[27] They talked and embraced, a first in 525 years. The next day, Epiphany in the Latin calendar, the pope went to Bethlehem and, returning to the old city, visited the Orthodox patriarch to return the patriarch's visit and pray with him, each reading one verse at a time of the passage from John 17.[28]

These two moments of contact, on Sunday and Epiphany, exceeded all expectations, not only for their emotional intensity, but also for the level of theological depth and spiritual authenticity. The two embraces and exchange of gifts – the pope gave Athenagoras a chalice and the patriarch gave Paul VI a pectoral cross, which he immediately donned[29] – shattered all half measures.

Athenagoras had his own explanation for the event. He offered it preventatively to Greek journalists who, on the ramp of the airplane recounted the alarm with which monastic circles viewed the theological question underlying the meeting between the champion of Orthodoxy and the pope of Rome. For the patriarch, "hierarchs do, theologians explain."[30]

1.3 *Dealing with the Consequences: Rome (1964–1965)*

In order to capitalize on the embrace of peace, a delegation from the secretariat visited Istanbul between Apr 10 and 20, 1964, where explosive actions – to say the least, as reported to the secretariat of state[31] – were discussed: a visit by Athenagoras to Rome; the return of St. Andrew's

21 See the phone call between Willebrands and Vischer of Dec 10 in: Declerck, ed., *Les Agendas conciliaires de Mgr J. Willebrands*, 83–84.

22 An overview is given in Marlen Eordegian, "British and Israeli Maintenance of the Status Quo in the Holy Places of Christendom," *IJMES* 35/2, 2003, 307–328 and Silvio Ferrari & Andrea Benzo, eds., *Between Cultural Diversity and Common Heritage: Legal and Religious Perspectives on the Sacred Places of the Mediterranean*, Abingdon, Routledge, 2014.

23 For an idea of the background of the discussion, see the controversial Siméon Vailhé, "L'érection du patriarcat de Jérusalem, 451," *ROC* 4, 1899, 44–57. On Vailhé, an Assumptionist, see Vitalien Laurent, "Le P. Siméon Vailhé (1873–1960)," *REB* 18/1, 1960, 5–18.

24 On Duprey's audience at the Phanar, see *THS* 38, Dec 11, 1963, 56. See also Schelkens, "Envisager la concélébration," 140.

25 On Dell'Acqua's signature on the Dec 30, 1963, meeting's protocols, see GUA, JLP.

26 Johannes Willebrands, "Aspetti ecumenici del pellegrinaggio di Paolo VI," *Rocca*, Jan 1, 1964, 15–16.

27 Valeria Martano, *Athenagoras, il Patriarca (1886–1972): Un cristiano fra crisi della coabitazione e utopia ecumenica*, Bologna, Il Mulino, 1996, 466–471.

28 The reading, which was not planned in advance, took place by passing back and forth the Biblicum edition of the New Testament in Greek and Latin edited by Augustine Merk that Willebrands had with him, which was its third edition from 1948 that had been published posthumously. Willebrands's annotated copy is in KDC, FJW, 367. The eighth edition of Merk's work, edited by Carlo Maria Martini, had come out the year of the Jerusalem meeting.

29 See Yves Congar, "L'œcuménisme de Paul VI," in: *Paul VI et la modernité dans l'Église: Actes du colloques organisé par l'École française de Rome (Rome 2–4 juin 1983)*, Rome, École Française de Rome, 1984, 807–820.

30 The quoted phrase spoken to the journalists is referred to in a diplomatic dispatch; see Melloni, *L'altra Roma*. See also Hyacinthe Destivelle, "La signification ecclésiologique de la levée des anathèmes de 1054: Pour une théologie due dialogue de la charité," *CrSt* 38/1, 2017, 51–84. Previously see Martano, *Athenagoras, il Patriarca*, 472.

31 See the typed pages "Venuta a Roma del Patriarca Ecumenico Athenagoras," in: GUA, JLP, 3 fols.

head, a spoil of Latin plunder,[32] to the church in Patras (this was to be a priority[33]); and even a formal lifting of the 11th century excommunications.[34] Although the memorandum to the secretariat of state made it clear that a meeting between the pope and the patriarch in the Vatican should not give rise to "confusion,"[35] it was evident that the cessation of the condemnations – which some considered already annulled[36] – would make the issues of concelebration and intercommunion inescapable. That was precisely what was alluded to in October during the debate in the council session after the presentation of the schema *De oecumenismo*.[37] Studies by Yves Congar,[38] and later an article from 1966 by André Scrima, who was very close to Athenagoras, corroborated the expectation that the excommunications would be nullified.[39]

Intercommunion, however, remained a hazy and allusive background issue even during the fall of 1964, when the decree on ecumenism was being prepared. It faced discussion affected by the gloomy climate of that moment of Vatican II when the minority was attempting to blackmail Paul VI with the alarm of a rupture with tradition,[40] the significance of which neither the observers nor the majority understood.[41]

It was not insignificant that the episode of the corrections to *De oecumenismo* held special meaning in the series of authoritative addresses that the pope gave in what came to be called the Black Week of the council.[42] Taking up the papal pen to correct 18 points of a text that the assembly had first voted on paragraph by paragraph, then in its entirety, could have convinced observers and the churches that Catholic adherence to the principle of ecumenical dialogue was superficial or baseless.[43] Instead, the tremendous work by Willebrands and the secretariat transformed the most dramatic episode of the Black Week into an occasion to demonstrate their credibility and to guarantee the text of *Unitatis redintegratio* to the churches.[44] It was in paragraph 15 of that text that a decisive statement on the Orthodox churches was made, decreeing that:

32 See Schelkens, "Envisager la concélébration," 142, note 54.

33 On this, see "Rapport sur le voyage à Patras de Mgr Willebrands et du père Duprey (18–22 mai 1964)," in: *Dossier delle fonti*, doc. 1, May 23, 1964, 129–132.

34 See Declerck, ed., *Les Agendas conciliaires de Mgr J. Willebrands*, 109–112.

35 See "Venuta a Roma del Patriarca Ecumenico Athenagoras," 2.

36 Pope Paul VI was among many who considered these to have been annulled by the decisions of the Council of Ferrara-Florence of 1438–1439; see Mauro Velati, *Separati ma Fratelli: Gli osservatori non cattolici al Vaticano II (1962–1965)*, Bologna, Il Mulino, 2014, 630–634.

37 It was the Ukrainian Catholic Archbishop of Winnipeg, Maxim Hermaniuk, who spoke on Oct 7, 1964, with a few lines (penned by Lanne and/or Dumont) explaining that, after the death of Pope Leo IX, Cardinal Humbert of Silva Candida had been the one to condemn the Orthodox as heretics, whereas "as historical studies now show, no dogmatic truth had, in fact, been questioned," see *AS 3/4*, 10–13. The Canadian metropolitan's choice was also explained in his address at the secretariat plenary, in which he indeed proposed the simultaneous annulment of the condemnations of 1054, see Jaroslav Skira & Karim Schelkens, *The Second Vatican Council Diaries of Met. Maxim Hermaniuk, C.Ss.R. (1960–1965)*, Leuven, Peeters, 2012, 188–190.

38 Yves M.-J. Congar, "Neuf cents ans après: Notes sur le 'Schisme oriental,'" in: *1054–1954: L'Église et les Églises: Neuf siècles de douloureuse séparation entre l'Orient et l'Occident. Études et travaux sur l'unité chrétienne offerts à dom Lambert Beauduin*, vol. 1, Chevetogne, Éditions de Chevetogne, 1954, 3–98.

39 André Scrima, "Rom und Kostantinopel nach der Nichtigkeitserklärung der Banbullen," in: Franz Hummer, ed., *Orthodoxie und Zweites Vatikanum*, Freiburg i.Br., Herder, 1966, 185–191.

40 Claude Soetens, "The Ecumenical Commitment of the Catholic Church," in: Alberigo & Komonchak, eds., *History of Vatican II*, vol. 3, 257–345.

41 See John W. O'Malley, *What Happened at Vatican II*, Cambridge MA, Harvard University Press, 2010, 165–185.

42 On the Black Week, see Luis Antonio Gokim Tagle, "The 'Black Week' of Vatican II (Nov 14–21 1964)," in: Giuseppe Alberigo & Joseph A. Komonchak, eds., *History of Vatican II*, vol. 4, *Church as Communion, Third Period and Intersession, September 1964–September 1965*, Leuven/Maryknoll, Peeters/Orbis Books, 2003, 387–452.

43 Velati, *Separati ma fratelli*, 420–430.

44 Velati, *Separati ma fratelli*, 481–502.

> These Churches, although separated from us, possess true sacraments, above all by apostolic succession, the priesthood and the Eucharist, whereby they are linked with us in closest intimacy. Therefore some worship in common (*communicatio in sacris*), given suitable circumstances and the approval of Church authority, is not only possible but to be encouraged.[45]

"Quaedam communicatio in sacris," the formula drafted by the secretariat, received some comments,[46] but respected the incipient character typical of the conciliar reforms,[47] above all having for its subject not individuals or emergency circumstances but the churches in their function as custodians of the faith.

In those same days, however, *Orientalium Ecclesiarum*, the decree on the Eastern churches in union with Rome, received the council's final approval and – reflecting a logic drawn from the history of individual conversions, Latinization, and proselytism – used a very different argument in paragraphs 27 and 28:

> Without prejudice to the principles noted earlier, Eastern Christians who are in fact separated in good faith from the Catholic Church, if they ask of their own accord and have the right dispositions, may be admitted to the sacraments of Penance, the Eucharist and the Anointing of the Sick. Further, Catholics may ask for these same sacraments from those non-Catholic ministers whose churches possess valid sacraments, as often as necessity or a genuine spiritual benefit recommends such a course and access to a Catholic priest is physically or morally impossible.
>
> Further, given the same principles, common participation by Catholics with their Eastern separated brethren in sacred functions, things and places is allowed for a just cause.

Here, intercommunion was being used as a tool for proselytism to expand the Catholic Church's boundaries through the Eastern rite churches already in communion with it, posing a dramatic problem to Vatican II's *sui generis* ecumenicity.[48]

For some, John Meyendorff, for example,[49] it was proof that there was a theological disjunction that made intercommunion inadmissible because – as the Orthodox metropolitans of America (the Standing Conference of Canonical Orthodox Bishops in the Americas) had written in their Jan 22, 1965 statement[50] – the Eucharist can only be the goal of unity, not the means to achieve it.[51] For others, however, there was some leeway: Nicholas Afanasiev writing in *Irénikon* in 1965,[52] Scrima in the *Eastern Churches Review* in 1966,[53] and John Zizioulas at the meeting of Faith

45 *UR* 15, Jun 18.

46 See Tagle, "The 'Black Week' of Vatican II," 406–416. On the pope's position, see *Paolo VI e l'ecumenismo: Colloquio internazionale di studio (Brescia, 25–27 settembre 1998)*, Brescia/Rome, Istituto Paolo VI/ Studium, 2001.

47 On the incipient nature of the conciliar reforms, which did not prescribe a manual for renewal but rather initiated a process, see Alberto Melloni, *Papa Giovanni: Un cristiano e il suo concilio*, Turin, Einaudi, 2009, 235.

48 See Giuseppe Alberigo, *Transizione epocale: Studi sul Concilio Vaticano II*, Bologna, Il Mulino, 2009, 325–326 and Melloni, *Il concilio e la grazia*.

49 On Meyendorff's position, see Emmanuel Lanne, "Quelques questions posées à l'Église orthodoxe concernant la *communicatio in sacris* dans l'eucharistie," *Irénikon* 72/3–4, 1999, 435–451.

50 "Vatican II: A Preliminary Reaction," *St. Vladimir's Seminar Quarterly* 9, 1965, 26–37, see also the declaration in *St. Vladimir's Seminar Quarterly* 9, 1965, 38.

51 A stern conference against intercommunion was held in May, on which see George A. Galitis, *The Problem of Intercommunion from an Orthodox Point of View: A Biblical and Ecclesiological Study*, Athens, Ekdotiki Athinon, 1968.

52 Nicolas Afanasieff, "L'Eucharistie, principal lien entre les Catholiques et les Orthodoxes," *Irénikon* 38, 1965, 336–339.

53 André Scrima, "The Lifting of the Anathemas: An Act of Reparation," *ECR* 1/1, 1966, 23–26.

and Order in Leida in 1967, all spoke of sharing the Eucharistic table as an already developed step, in fact made more urgent by the 1964 meeting between the patriarch and the pope in Jerusalem and then by the acceleration of events in 1965.[54]

Actually, in 1965, it was the other issue – the nullification of the excommunications – that returned to the forefront. The reports of the trips of Willebrands and Duprey in April and then May of 1964 hinted that that goal was within reach and, that summer, the pan-Orthodox conference in Rhodes decided on opening a dialogue with the church in Rome "on an equal footing," although without stating how or where. This indicated an openness that Metropolitan Meliton (Hatzis) communicated to Rome in January 1965, presenting it to the pope as a first step in a "general preparation through creating favorable circumstances and studying the various issues of dialogue."[55]

1.4 *How to Lift the Excommunications*

That lifting the excommunications would offer favorable circumstances was a circumlocution that hid the substance of a proposal that, in April 1965, Bea and Willebrands believed to have heard from Athenagoras during their, by that time, customary spring visit, when the patriarch spoke of undoing the schism. Actually, Athenagoras's choice of words implied something more than the mere juridical annulment of a penalty that, at least in Latin law, had ended with the recipient's death. However, during the summer, when Meliton again returned to Rome, bringing the striking icon of Peter and Andrew embracing as a gift, the proposal was formulated with precision and rather narrowly.[56] To the reconciliation recorded in the *Tomos Agapis*, Paul VI then added a letter of thanks to the patriarch for the openness approved at Rhodes. In mid-July, Willebrands and Duprey returned to the Phanar to deliver it, along with a Greek translation of Pope John XXIII's *Giornale dell'anima*.[57] Meanwhile, the situation in Rome was not entirely tranquil and this came to light in the following weeks.

On the one hand, Michele Maccarrone, a medieval church historian, proposed to Amleto Giovanni Cicognani the convening of a "safe" commission to prove that the Council of Ferrara-Florence of 1438–1439 had not lifted the excommunications and that everything therefore had to be done from scratch. Maccarrone also used medieval precedents to argue that the meeting in Jerusalem had not altered the distance between the churches by one iota.[58]

On the other hand, the secretariat – insisting instead on the properly theological and ecumenical dimensions of the gesture – reaped its first success on Oct 9, 1965, when Paul VI and Metropolitan Emilianos (Timiadis) of Silyvria, observer from the Patriarchate of Constantinople, agreed to a joint Catholic-Orthodox commission to study a suitable formula. Jeopardized by the metropolitan's off-the-cuff loquacity, the news was brought back

54 See Jean D. Zizioulas, "La communauté eucharistique et la catholicité de l'Église," *Istina* 14, 1969, 67–88; published as "Eucharist and Catholicity," chapter 4 of John D. Zizioulas, *Being as Communion: Studies in Personhood and the Church*, Crestwood, St. Vladimir's Seminary Press, 1993, 143–169.

55 See Patrice Mahieu, *Paul VI et les orthodoxes*, Paris, Cerf, 2012, 84–85 also for the message from Paul VI signed "bishop of Rome," and Athanasios Papas, *Rome & Constantinople: Pope Paul VI & Metropolitan Meliton of Chalcedon*, trans. George Dion Dragas, Rollinsford, Orthodox Research Institute, 2006.

56 See Velati, *Separati ma fratelli*, 634–635.

57 On the importance of this text as restoring the papacy to the ranks of spiritual masters, see Alberto Melloni, "La semplicità del bene: Indagine sui primi lettori del *Giornale dell'Anima* di A.G. Roncalli-Giovanni XXIII," in: *Un cristiano sul trono di Pietro: Studi storici su Giovanni XXIII*, Gorle, Servitum, 2003, 326–349.

58 In Michele Maccarrone, *Studi su Innoncenzo III*, Padova, Antenore, 1972, Maccarrone had dealt with the principle laid down by Thomas of Capua that "Si Papa suis litteris excommunicatum salutat, non propter hoc eum absolvit" (taken from Thomas von Capua, *Die* Ars Dictandi, ed. Emmy Heller, Heidelberg, Winters, 1929). However, Innocent III himself specified (Feb 21, 1205) that such nullity only applied if the salutation was given "per ignorantiam vel neglegentiam aut occupationem nimiam vel etiam per subreptionem" (*PL* 215, 542B).

covertly[59] and entrusted to a commission that included, besides himself, none of Maccarrone's suggested candidates. However, there was the noted scholar Alfons Maria Stickler along with the specialist in Byzantine liturgical history, Alphonse Raes of the PIO, the ever-essential Father Dumont, and the Jesuit John Long who, judging from his papers, acted as the commission's secretary.

Dumont drafted an initial outline in French, which was discussed by Willebrands's small group in Rome.[60] After that step, it was shown to Scrima, the patriarch's personal representative to the council. That move reveals the level of trust that existed between the secretariat and Athenagoras's men.[61] The most (but not overly) relevant points of discussion were few: the Orthodox asked and were allowed to refer to the faithful, not only to the leaders of the church; there was discussion on whether to regret or condemn the offenses that had been exchanged (they chose to regret, *regretter*, both the gestures and the acts);[62] reparations for, in addition to forgiveness of,[63] historical wrongs was another issue, a formula that was cut after Bea consulted the Holy Office. On Dec 4,[64] a formula that passed every Vatican screening and that reflected the secretariat's expectations was accepted by Athenagoras without any objection.

This was not because the patriarch shared Rome's prudent sentiments but because he wanted to show his trust in the pope of Rome's credibility in achieving his dream of a shared chalice. On Dec 4, therefore, the permanent synod of the church of Constantinople approved the same formula that Rome endorsed in the declaration "Pénétrés de reconnaisance." In its opening, that declaration expressed its commitment to accept the call of grace for fraternity, advancing the idea that dialogue for *communio plena* leads back to the "sacramental life, which obtained among them throughout the first thousand years of the life of the Church."[65]

59 Schelkens, "Envisager la concélébration," 144, note 62, quotes Eugene Fairweather's diary entry of Oct 11, 1965, where the Anglican theologian says that he learned from Metropolitan Emilianos that the pope intended to "lift the excommunications," but that he was reassured by Willebrands that it was the metropolitan himself who had proposed it and that the pope was merely "responding" to him tactfully. Once again, therefore, we see the secretariat's technique of using strategies of misdirection to conceal highly delicate negotiations in order to avoid leaks. On the still unpublished source, see Michael Attridge, "A Canadian Anglican at Vatican II: The Activity of Eugene R. Fairweather," in: Michael Attridge, Catherine E. Clifford & Gilles Routhier, eds., *Vatican II: Experiences Canadiennes / Canadian Experiences*, Ottawa, University of Ottawa Press, 2011, 341–359.

60 Long conserved the papers, see "Projet de déclaration commune," Nov 15, 1965, in: GUA, JLP, 3 fols.

61 See Declerck, ed., *Les Agendas conciliaires de Mgr J. Willebrands*, 261. On the neutralizing of Maccarrone and Stickler's trip to Istanbul, see Velati, *Separati ma fratelli*, 634–635.

62 See "Projet de déclaration commune."

63 On the underlying philosophical problem, see Paul Ricœur, *Memory, History, Forgetting*, Chicago, University of Chicago Press, 2006. At the time, the two closest references were Hannah Arendt, *The Human Condition*, Chicago, University of Chicago Press, 1958, and Vladimir Jankélévitch, *Forgiveness*, Chicago, University of Chicago Press, 1967.

64 The day on which the permanent synod approved the text in Constantinople and the pope prayed for the first time at St. Paul's Outside the Walls in Rome with Protestant, Anglican, and Orthodox representatives.

65 *THS*, 128, Dec 7, 1965, 128–129, here 128. "It is for this reason that Pope Paul VI and Patriarch Athenagoras I in his Synod, being certain that they are expressing the common desire for justice and the unanimous feeling of charity of their faithful people, and remembering the Lord's command: 'If you bring your gift to the altar and there recall that your brother has anything against you, leave your gift at the altar, and go first to be reconciled with your brother (Matt 5:23–24), declare in mutual agreement: (a) that they regret the offending words, the baseless reproaches, and the blameworthy symbolic acts which on both sides marked or accompanied the sad events of this time; (b) that in the same way they regret and remove from memory and from the midst of the Church the sentences of excommunication which followed, the remembrance of which acts right up to our own times as an obstacle to our mutual approach in charity, and they condemn these to oblivion; (c) that they deplore, finally, the troublesome precedents and the further happenings which, under the influence of various factors, including misunderstanding and distrust on both sides, eventually led to a real rupture of ecclesial communion"; *THS* 127, Dec 7, 1965, 126–128, here 127.

On Dec 7, the "nullifications" were ceremonially instated in the form of a revocation. Reversing the gesture of the 1054 rupture, Meliton placed, not a bull, but a bouquet of roses on the tomb of Pope John XXIII. At the Phanar, the declaration was read and a common blessing given. A deluge of commentary followed and there was a feeling that the division of the eucharistic table had its hours numbered.

The two sides of the cancelled schism held different lines of thought. Rome followed the insights of the 1964 "Rapport sur les implications œcuméniques du voyage du Saint-Père in Terre sainte,"[66] the real working guide for the following five years. It envisaged a return to the *status quo ante* that had been instrumental to the reformatory movements,[67] like the liturgical movement: "All rapprochement is based on a mutual recovery of the fundamental unity that exists between the Catholic Church and the Orthodox Church."[68]

In Constantinople, a different group was forming around the monumental figure of the patriarch, including Meliton, Metropolitan Chrysostomos (Costantinides) of Myra, Metropolitan Emilianos (Timiadis) of Silyvria, the Archdeacon Bartholomew (Archontonis), as well as the noted Damaskinos (Papandreou), and the theological stature of John Zizioulas.

Those were the two trends in thought that framed the historical problem of "what to do?" regarding the communion that had been rediscovered and accepted without any meaningful opposition. Almost clandestinely, Duprey spoke about it to Meliton in Nea Smyrni at the house of the latter's cousin. On Mar 19, 1966, the two ecumenists noted that there had been no raising of shields.[69] They discussed a possible papal act against proselytism, of the patriarch having a representative in Rome, and how to excise the irritating language that still existed – at Vatican Radio, for example. A report from Duprey to Bea summarized some demands and produced small fruit. The proposal to resurrect the ancient tradition of Easter letters (the *litterae communionis*) marked an acknowledgement of the need to extend a gesture of peace toward all the Orthodox churches that was understandable to the mind and spirituality of the Christian East. And an important signal was given from the Orthodox side in April, with the publication of a new liturgical office in *Ekklesia*, the official journal of the Greek Church. Approved by the synod, it was released on the feast of the apostle Peter, composed by the patriarchate's hymnographer, Gerasimos Mikrayannanitis. This hymn to the apostle saw the return of expressions that had been removed from the printed tradition of the hymnal: *coryphaeus*, *protothron*, summit, and first cathedra.[70]

1.5 *The Turning Point of Sep 10, 1966*

But it was Athenagoras who again changed the pace. Duprey met with him face to face on Sep 10. The White Father quickly jotted down some notes[71] about what the elderly man was saying on an increasingly thick series of slips of paper – later transformed into a complete typewritten record.[72] He wanted to reciprocate the visit of all the patriarchs, discussing with them about going to Rome to achieve the results that would take them "where God wills," which had a minimum threshold: "A pastoral agreement of intercommunion."[73] It

66 *Dossier delle fonti*, doc. 2, Mar 21, 1966, 133–137, esp. 136.

67 Routhier did not understand this, see Gilles Routhier, "La réception dans le premier *De Ecclesia* des mouvements de renouveau préconciliaire," in: Gilles Routhier, Philippe J. Roy & Karim Schelkens, eds., *La théologie catholique entre intransigeance et renouveau: La réception des mouvements préconciliaires à Vatican II*, Louvain-la-Neuve/Leuven, Collège Èrasme/Maurits Sabbebibliotheek, 2011, 199–211.

68 *Dossier delle fonti*, doc. 2, 136.

69 See *Dossier delle fonti*, doc. 2, 133–135.

70 Even Cardinal Jean-Baptiste Pitra's Greek hymnal, printed in Rome by Propaganda Fide in 1899, had failed to notice the dropping of several Petrine titles from the ancient manuscripts.

71 See "Appunti manoscritti della conversazione tra Pierre Duprey e il patriarca Athenagoras," in: *Dossier delle fonti*, doc. 5, Sep 8 and 10, 1966, 144–147.

72 "Rapport sur la conversation du père Duprey avec le patriarche Athénagoras (10 septembre 1966)," in: *Dossier delle fonti*, doc. 6, Sep 20, 1966, 148–153.

73 "Appunti manoscritti," 145 and "Rapport sur la conversation," 149.

was an act that recognized the pope's leadership – an expression that Athenagoras later replaced with the liturgical one *coryphaeus* – and that transformed the oblivion of hatreds into the premise of communion in Christ. The experience of the lifting of excommunications became an example of the role of theology. "How long did it take theologians to resolve the issue of the anathemas?" Two days, because there was "charity on both sides."[74] The conversation covered many issues, with other persons joining in. Duprey reported everything, and the expression "pastoral agreement of intercommunion" – which could simply refer to measures to regulate Eucharistic hospitality or to accompany mixed couples – did not seem to impress him at all. He would come to understand later.

On Nov 30, for the feast of St. Andrew, Duprey again accompanied Willebrands to Istanbul for a new conversation with the patriarch.[75] Athenagoras confirmed that he had the whole synod on his side, sharing a view that he directly stated: "We are ready to drink from the same chalice … The differences that exist now existed in the ten centuries when we were in communion."[76]

The patriarch saw Paul VI in the role of a "great prophet" – a title of John the Baptist – that is, as one who "not only foresees the future, but prepares for it."[77] Willebrands reacted very cautiously. He mentioned the talks in place with the LWF and the Anglican Communion, almost as if to hold back the acceleration that Athenagoras was proposing. He did so unsuccessfully, however. The patriarch wanted to celebrate the first anniversary of the lifting of the excommunications and demanded that this "new atmosphere take a more concrete form."[78]

Other topics were also mentioned this time, leaving the issue of intercommunion in the background. But it was clear that Athenagoras understood the importance: preventing the lifting of the excommunications from remaining an isolated monument, without the hierarchs and churches being able to draw the appropriate consequences of that act at the level of participation at the eucharistic table. It was in this context that the visits that Paul VI and Athenagoras exchanged in the late summer of 1967 appeared to onlookers as bearing promises and meanings that once again exceeded individual wills.

On Jul 26, 1967, Paul VI's visit to Istanbul flirted with an ambiguity. It was not the reciprocation of Athenagoras's visit to Jerusalem, since Paul VI was the guest in that holy city and the patriarch was the host. But it was perceived that way, as a reciprocal extension of trust, evoking an impression that Meyendorff gave voice to. In the second edition of his book *L'Église orthodoxe hier et aujourd'hui*, he identified the trip as overcoming an "image"[79] of the pope that was an obstacle to dialogue. Duprey would mention it in the conclusions of his note on the concelebration in February 1970.[80]

Athenagoras's visit to Rome came on Oct 26, this one returning the pope's visit to the Phanar. It would not be an occasion to celebrate together though, of course. Actually, in some ways, it resembled the unfruitful visit that the patriarch had stated that he did not want to make. In the fraternal atmosphere during the shared prayer in St. Peter's, nuances between the two "preparations," which the pope and the patriarch alluded to, surfaced.

Publicly, Athenagoras said that the proximity of the altar was a sign of preparing with "heart and spirit for the future advance to a common Eucharist."[81] That meant an interior preparation, which did not presuppose intermediate steps.

74 "Rapport sur la conversation," 150.

75 See "Rapport du voyage à Istanbul de S. Ém. Mgr Willebrands (30 nov.–3 déc.)," in: *Dossier delle fonti*, doc. 7, Dec 10, 1966, 154–159, esp. 154.

76 "Rapport du voyage," 154–155.

77 "Rapport du voyage," 155.

78 "Rapport du voyage," 155.

79 Jean Meyendorff, *L'Église orthodoxe hier et aujourd'hui*, Paris, Éditions du Seuil, ^{2}1969 (^{1}1960), 173–174.

80 See [Pierre Duprey,] "Nouvelle note sure l'éventuelle concelebration eucharistique du pape et du patriarche Athénagoras," in: *Dossier delle fonti*, doc. 27, Feb 12, 1970, 271–275.

81 *THS* 189, Oct 26, 1967, 171–174, here 172.

Paul VI, on the other hand, after recalling the failures of previous attempts at unity, emphasized the freedom "from every political consideration"[82] that the churches were enjoying (which, thinking of the conditions in Turkey, was not the most exact diagnosis) and saw in those external circumstances the possibility "to take active steps on their own part so as to make possible the restoration of full communion."[83] That is, he posed the problem of preparation as an act of doctrinal will and dialogue clearly not fulfilled by the lifting of excommunications.

Mediated or immediate then, the question of a shared celebration of the Eucharist was not resolved with a dramatic turn, but neither was it entrusted to theological engineering or ecumenical diplomacy. If Rome hoped to get away with a *dilata* of ecumenical proportions, 1968 would have been a disillusion for everyone, Paul VI first of all.

1.6 *The Overflow of Practice*

The prospect of the two hierarchs and the two churches sharing communion from the same chalice as a prophetic omen of the possible anticipation – without a change in norms – of the full reception of one another in the Eucharist experienced a sudden cooling. The decades-long history of unsuccessful discussions on intercommunion, the dramatically circumscribed or ephemeral affair of one-sided agreements, all had a temporary but sharp reversal. The issue of intercommunion bifurcated and resumed flowing along divaricated and familiar riverbeds.

On the one hand, it again became a matter to be worked out theologically in ecumenical circles, with all the typical theological rigor and impotence when moving from doctrinal or doctrinal-historical questions into those of the lived liturgy of the people of God. That would be the case with the document from Faith and Order, the WCC think tank in 1968.[84]

On the other hand, in practice, the issue of intercommunion overflowed with a series of gestures and acts that enjoyed, or suffered from, very diverse degrees of notoriety. In 1967, the Dombes Group approved a document that permitted an established practice of "Eucharistic hospitality" from 1972 onward.[85] In the Anglican Communion, the committee chaired by Oliver Tomkins decided, by a majority vote, to supersede the mentality of individual exceptions, extending the idea of an agreement among churches, which would fail at the Lambeth conference.[86] In the Russian Church,

82 *THS* 190, Oct 26, 1967, 174–178, here 174.

83 *THS* 190, 176.

84 In 1968, Catholic theologians also joined Faith and Order, and the document "Accord œuménique sur l'Eucharistie" of that year marked one of the steps in the drafting process of the BEM (*Baptism, Eucharist, and Ministry*) document, on which see Luca Ferracci, *Battesimo Eucaristia Ministero: Genesi e destino di un documento ecumenico*, Bologna, Il Mulino, 2021.

85 See the contribution by Catherine E. Clifford in this volume.

86 Appointed by the Bishop of York in 1965, a commission chaired by Oliver Tomkins began discussing "admission to the Holy Eucharist" and published the report *Intercommunion Today: Being the Report of the Archbishops' Commission on Intercommunion*, London, Church Information Office, 1968. That document from the Anglican Communion analyzes the three existing approaches in the denominational landscape: (1) that inspired by the church Fathers which, because of doctrinal disagreements, denies access; this pertains to the churches of Orthodoxy and Catholicism; (2) that of the churches of the Reformation, which admits to intercommunion on the basis of the real unity given by baptism and the freedom of the spirit that breathes in everyone beyond denominational barriers; and (3) that which considers ecumenical dialogue to be unprecedented and requires the adoption of intercommunion practices among neighboring communities or churches (esp. 45). The Tomkins commission unanimously adopted the principle of the admission of individuals to the Eucharist as a sign of the communion sought. By ten votes to four, it approved the principle that intercommunion is to be encouraged among churches engaged in ecumenical dialogue. In 1972, on the basis of the Tomkins report, Lambeth adopted canon B 15a, which admitted baptized persons from other churches to the Eucharist in Anglican churches,

a synodal *ukaz* in 1969 established that the sacraments requested by Catholics and Old Believers could not be denied.[87] The decision was inconsistent with the thinking out of Constantinople,[88] shortly preceding the recognition granted by Moscow (without Constantinople's prior consent) to the autocephaly of the Russian American Church,[89] which developed its own practice and dialogue on the issue.[90]

As if that were not enough, there were also those who, like Chiara Lubich, reported Athenagoras's words as if they were shared confidences, revealing things to the pope that he was unaware of. But Paul VI was informed on everything, and the secretariat was irritated with the Focolare Movement founder's naivete in sending the Secretariat of State an agenda that it had not been involved in. Duprey had to make up for it with a note downplaying the matter, but he knew that Athenagoras was not seeking the pastoral agreement of intercommunion – based on a shared faith and geared toward regulating practice – that he had asked for in September 1966. Duprey understood that the patriarch no longer thought of intercommunion as a gesture that would strike out and cleanse the centuries of conflict, as he had said to Willebrands. He was thinking of a "concelebration," which was called for by the blood of the martyrs and that, therefore, demanded obedience, not permission or support. In May 1969, he condensed that vision into a call for the churches who had adopted the Julian and Gregorian calendars to celebrate a single Easter.[91]

Public opinion among Catholics, however, had to realize that, in 1968, the possibility of regulating the permits and prohibitions that had upheld the schism was fading. Effectively, at that moment in time, intercommunion was a problem that still seemed unsolvable only for the authorities, who rightly set themselves to figuring out how not to turn a blind eye to the question of "visible" unity. For the Christian people, however – including the Catholic camp, which was buffeted by the winds of Vatican II reforms – sharing the Eucharistic table was a non-issue.[92] Even when demonized as "wild

while the intercommunion agreement between the Church of England, Methodists, Moravian Brethren, and the Reformed Church failed to reach a quorum of the synod.

87 On Dec 16, 1969, as reported in *ZMP* 42, 1970, the holy synod, "examined the cherished cases in which Old Believers and Catholics present themselves in Orthodox churches to receive the holy sacraments. Having deliberated to clarify the prescriptions that, in cases in which Old Believers and Catholics present themselves in Orthodox churches to receive the sacraments, these should not be denied them." It included a communiqué signed by the (future patriarch) then-Metropolitan Alexy (Ridiger) of Tallin. On Sep 28, 1971, a *ukaz* of the bishops of the ROCOR decided instead that non-Orthodox could only be accepted into the church through baptism, a position accounted for in Andrei Psarev's essay, "The 19th Canonical Answer of Timothy of Alexandria: On the History of Sacramental Oikonomia," *SVTQ* 51/2–3, 2007, 297–320.

88 An analysis of the ten-year discussion can be found in Kallistos Ware, "Communion and Intercommunion," *Sobornost* 7/7, 1978, 550–567. Ware had taken stock of the issue of non-intercommunion in the diaspora in his article "Intercommunion: Where Does the Orthodox Church Stand Today?," *Eastern Churches Newsletter* 59–60, 1971, 14.

89 See Michael A. Fahey, "Orthodox Ecumenism and Theology: 1970–78," *TS* 39/3, 1978, 446–585.

90 For the first statement of the dialogue, exactly on the Eucharist, see John Borelli & John H. Erickson, *The Quest for Unity: Orthodox and Catholics in Dialogue. Documents of the Joint International Commission and Official Dialogues in the United States (1965–1995)*, Crestwood, St. Vladimir's Seminary Press, 1996, 45–46.

91 See "Pour une commune celebration de la fête de Pâques," in: *Dossier delle fonti*, doc. 13, May 1969, 179–184.

92 On the fact that the practice was experienced as a dutiful manifestation of the coming unity, see, for example, the editorial by John Coventry, "Ecclesial and Individual Intercommunion," *One in Christ* 1, 1971, 1–6. Personally engaged to apply brakes on the subject, Augustin Bea penned "L'eucaristia e l'unione dei cristiani," *La Civiltà Cattolica* 116/3, 1965, 401–413; two essays by Alfredo Marranzini also appeared in the same journal: "Il problema dell'intercomunione oggi," and "La chiesa cattolica e l'intercomunione," *La Civiltà cattolica* 120/4, 1969, 228–240 and 430–442. The issue was studied from the perspective of canon law by Francesco Coccopalmerio, *La partecipazione degli acattolici al culto della chiesa cattolica nella pratica e nella dottrina della Santa Sede*

intercommunion," Christians of different confessions were steadfastly convinced that they could break bread together and share the same chalice. This conviction burst into the public consciousness during three moments of intercommunion that took place in 1968 in different ways – by consensus or by inspiration – and that marked a point of no return.

In Paris on Jun 2, 1968, 61 people – two-thirds of whom were Catholic and one-third Protestant – celebrated Pentecost with a domestic liturgy in the home of Anne and Jacques Retel on Rue Vaugirard.[93] The celebration had diverse elements: eight priests, seven pastors, and a few notable names; the anaphora of St. Basil; communion under the two species in a rite that structurally followed the postconciliar Roman missal; and finally a letter to the archbishop of Paris, Cardinal François Marty, and to the president of the FPF, pastor Charles Westphal, informing them of what had transpired and explaining the reasons for such a provocative gesture. They were convinced, from the core of the "political struggles of our time," of the need to give voice to the "revolutionary significance of the Gospel," to assert the fact that "real Christian unity today transcends denominational boundaries," and proclaiming to all Christians "on the streets," of the task of giving substance to ecumenical embodiment.[94] In the name of practicing what was said to have been established, the gesture rejected any comparison to a publicity stunt. However, its echoes in the media, on the heels of that May in France, gave their public provocation an immense reverberation.[95]

One month later, the WCC's fourth assembly was held in Uppsala, where the topic of intercommunion was discussed in an *ad hoc* session between Jul 4 and 9, 1968. There was an unprecedented Catholic presence at the – as Luigi Sandri's report called it – "exasperating and entangled" debate.[96] In a certain way, the knot was cut through by the Church of Sweden's decision to invite all the baptized present at the assembly to its table. Consummated on Jul 7, this intercommunion only became a public fact on Jul 26, 1968, when *Time* published an article that revealed the participation of Catholic observers.[97] Rome imposed a kind of denial from Willebrands,[98] which was repeated from Stockholm by Catholic bishop John Edward Taylor.[99] However, it was a fact that the Catholics present, with or without the endorsement of "delegate" Catholics, responded to the liturgical call

dall'inizio del secolo XVII ai nostri giorni: Uno studio teologico sull'essenza del diritto di prendere parte al culto cattolico, Brescia, Morcelliana, 1969. A different position was taken by Luigi Santini, "Il problema dell'intercomunione," *Testimonianze* 12, 1969, 133–153. Of quite different biblical and theological depth was the work of Jean-Marie Tillard, "L'eucharistie et la fraternité," *NRT* 91/2, 1969, 113–135.

93 See Dominique Damamme & others, dir., *Mai-juin 68*, Paris, Les Éditions de l'Atelier, 2008, 56–59.

94 See the caution of Catherine Berry Stidsen, "Danish Bishop on Ecumenism," *Journal of Ecumenical Studies* 1, 1970, 196–198.

95 On the presence of Robert Davezies and André Laurentin for the Catholic side and Jacques Beaumont, George Casalis, and Jacques Lochard for the other side, see Olivier Landron, *Le cardinal Marty: 1904–1994: La force tranquille*, Paris, Cerf, 2017. The stance at the time was published as an article: François Marty, "L'Église catholique et l'intercommunion," *La Documentation catholique* 1520, 1968, 1212.

96 See the account by Antonio Matabosch, *Upsala 1968: IV Asamblea del Consejo Mundial de las Iglesias*, Barcelona, Facultad de Teologia de Barcelona, 1969. In Italy it was recounted by Luigi Sandri, "Le 'cose nuove' di Uppsala: Rassegna e bilancio conclusivo della IV assemblea generale del CEC," *Il Regno – Documentazione cattolica* 165/16, 1968, 317–332, here 324.

97 "The World Council: From the Sacred to the Secular," *Time*, Jul 26, 1968, 66–67.

98 Willebrands made a distinction in the section "Attività della Santa Sede," *La Civiltà cattolica* 119/3, 1968, 395–400. With an interesting formula of qualifying the worship, he stated that "none of the observer-delegates" had participated in the Eucharist, while "a few Catholics present in Uppsala in an unofficial capacity did in fact receive communion in eucharistic celebrations presided over by non-Catholics"; "Attività della Santa Sede," 396.

99 Marranzini, "Il problema dell'intercomunione oggi," 231.

to eat/drink with a spontaneity that showed the power of practice over all else.[100]

Finally, at the beginning of September, there was the intercommunion that occurred during the assembly of the continental episcopate in Medellín, convened following the Eucharistic congress in Bogotá, whose devotional evocations aimed to dampen rather than flame the desire for a shared table among the baptized from divided churches.[101] The first major event of Catholic synodality since the 1967 Ecumenical Directory, the Medellín assembly enjoyed the presence of "observers" (the Vatican II term also used by the WCC in Uppsala[102]) from other churches who had been invited by the ecumenical department of the CELAM. Their meaningful presence was felt at qualitative and quantitative levels, taking part in discussions and especially at liturgical moments when the spiritual import made the sacramental distance between the Christians of different denominations seem senseless.

This led some to think of how to spontaneously force the status quo, and they planned to show up to share in the Catholic Eucharist without making distinctions. Taking another route, five observers preferred to send a letter asking to share communion "at least once," appealing to Catholic discipline. In fact, point no. 55 of the Ecumenical Directory admitted non-Catholics to the sacrament of the altar celebrated by a Catholic minister when faced with urgent reasons, which the letter strikingly recognized as the Pauline dictate (2 Cor 5:4) of Christ's charity that compels believers. The Directory referred decisions regarding intercommunion to the sensitivity and responsibility of the bishops' conferences, and the observers thus put the question to the continental conference, evidently endowed with synodal authority.[103]

The request of the five observers was approved by the conference presidents, including Cardinal Antonio Samorè, then-president of the Pontifical Commission for Latin America, for the close of the conference. Their participation in the liturgical celebration on the evening of Sep 5[104] was authorized in a "personal" capacity.[105] Unlike Paris and Uppsala, this was a decision that might have hinted at a change in course from the rhetoric of exceptionalism that some churches, primarily the Catholic Church, had employed. As has been well documented, the Holy See outdid itself with a vehement disavowal,[106] which did not erase the fact that, at Medellín, it had been proven that the petition for full communion could not be reduced to some spontaneous insurgency, over which all control was lost.[107]

Indeed, those three "cases" in 1968 showed that unprovocative practices had fermented within the

100 According to Wilhelm Köster, "La Cuarta Asamblea General del Consejo Ecumenico de las Iglesias," *Razón y fe* 178/848–849, 1968, 245–251, here 249, only "a small circle, which included some young Catholics, showed a deplorable lack of group discipline." See also Vilmos Vajta, *"Intercommunion" avec Rome?*, Paris, Cerf, 1970. The consultation promoted by the WCC in late March of 1969 produced the document "Beyond Intercommunion: On the Way to Communion in Eucharist," in: *Faith and Order. Louvain 1971. Study Reports and Documents*, Geneva, WCC Publications, 1971, 54–77.

101 Silvia Scatena, *In populo pauperum: La Chiesa latinoamericana dal Concilio a Medellín (1962–1968)*, Bologna, Il Mulino, 2008, 505–509.

102 On the problem, see Mauro Velati, *Separati ma fratelli.*

103 The text of the Ecumenical Directory is in *AAS* 59, 1967, 574–592. See also the contribution by Bruno Cherubini in this volume.

104 According to Boaventura Kloppenburg, "A Segunda Conferência Geral do Episcopado latino-americano," *Revista Eclesiástica Brasileira* 28/3, 1968, 623–626, the observers received "holy communion under the two species," a specification found only in that journal, which seems plausible, since Vatican II itself recommended communion under the two species, body and blood, for "solemn" services (626).

105 In Vajta's work, it is stated that participation was allowed "in a private capacity … so the churches thus represented cannot be considered directly involved"; Vajta, *"Intercommunion" avec Rome?*, 13.

106 See "Rome met l'accent sur le danger des initiatives 'inoportunes' en matière d'intercommunion," *Informations catholiques internationales* 325, 1968, 15, which references the *Note* that Bea published on Oct 6, 1968.

107 Scatena, *In populo pauperum*, 505–508.

fabric of the churches, starting in the ecumenical monasteries and Taizé – with a certain theological attention vouchsafed for by prior Brother Roger – which had the practice of distributing daily the Eucharist consecrated in a Catholic liturgy and holding Sunday Masses in the Roman rite attended by young persons of different denominational affiliations who were convinced that they were at the forefront of an inescapable reconciliation of Christians who had been separated by time.[108] But they also said that the authorities lacked the ability to question and discern between what may have been mere improvisation and what instead was the *de coelo sonus* whose authority was felt by so many.

2 Tempus Visitationis

The one not giving in to the reduction of the matter of discipline and prudence remained Athenagoras. When he again received Duprey, on Mar 17, 1969, his vision was the same as in 1966: "This communion will be done," the White Father noted, trying to capture the words of the patriarch, who was well aware of the right/duty of theologians to discuss as well as the duty/right of the hierarchs to act.[109] It was a position that – in light of Paul VI's visit to Geneva and other important acts of dialogue – was to determine the secretariat's plenary in the second half of November, at the end of which they all had to surrender to what appeared as a higher will.[110]

2.1 *The Force of Destiny*

This force revealed itself anew at the Phanar, where Athenagoras received Willebrands, now cardinal president of the secretariat, accompanied by Duprey, Jean Jérôme Hamer, and Eleuterio Fortino, on Dec 1, 1969. The delegation had intended to give news of the extraordinary synod celebrated in Rome and the secretariat's plenary, but the patriarch had another agenda. Taking Willebrands by the hand, he explained that he was a man who could not "escape his destiny" – complete with the quote of Giuseppe Verdi – and that "this destiny is God's will."[111] It was a communion that the archbishop of the New Rome felt he was involved in without having planned for it:

> When I went to Jerusalem [in 1964], the pope offered me a chalice. I had not asked for or expected it, but he knew I wanted it, and he offered it to me. What divides us? Nothing, absolutely nothing. The pope will not have to change anything, the infallibility of the Church has always existed. I am always with the pope. He is the true head, and we all follow him, and I want to celebrate the Eucharist with him. Take courage and prepare for it.

108 The question was debated by Max Thurian, *Le pain unique. Simple réflexion sur l'eucharistie et le ministère*, Taizé, Les Presses de Taizé, 1967; ET: *The One Bread*, trans. Theodore DuBois, New York, Sheed and Ward, 1969.

109 "Note manoscritte di Pierre Duprey a colloquio con il patriarca Athenagoras," in: *Dossier delle fonti*, doc. 12, Mar 17, 1969, 172–178, here 172; Athenagoras said it to the *To Vima* correspondent as he left for Jerusalem.

110 See "Prolusio de Son Éminence le cardinal Jean Willebrands," in: *Dossier delle fonti*, doc. 17, November 1969, 202–208. See also "Plenary Session 1969," in: *Pontifical Council for Promoting Christian Unity: Information Service* 9/1, 1970, 3–11, which describes the genesis of the secretariat's document on intercommunion, included in the file (21–23), which was supposed to give an apologia for the Directory and reiterate cautions that turned out to be inapplicable (it would be interesting to make an analytical comparison with the instruction from 1972, on which see Francesco Coccopalmerio, "Comunione ecclesiale e *communicatio in sacris*: Un commento all'Istruzione del Segretariato per l'Unione dei Cristiani in data 1° giugno 1972," *La Scuola Cattolica* 100, 1972, 458–471, and Francesco Coccopalmerio, "L'intercomunione, problema ecclesiologico," *La Rivista del Clero Italiano* 53, 1972, 857–860).

111 "Rencontre du cardinal Willebrands avec Sa Sainteté le patriarche Athénagoras Ier à Istanbul, 1–2 décembre 1969," *Dossier delle fonti*, doc. 21, Dec 9, 1969, 230–233, here 231.

> Courage alone will not be enough: be bold, then, but you must do it.[112]

The report of the meeting recounted the emotions of those present and the objections raised, all of which concerned Orthodoxy. The decision of the Patriarch of Jerusalem, Benediktos I, who had banned intercommunion, was quoted, as was Archbishop Iakovos (Koukouzis) of North and South America, who took a "strict stand against all forms of intercommunion,"[113] and finally an, also negative, article by the auxiliary of Belgrade that had been published in the *Frankfurter Allgemeine Zeitung* was noted. "What will the reaction be in the Greek Church?"[114] asked the astute guests, as if to provoke a response that would allow for delay.

Athenagoras knocked them all down, saying "the [Greek] bishops are good" and would follow the patriarch if the pope would take the initiative: "The pope has to make the decision and I can and want to follow him. The initiative cannot begin from me. It is the pope who must decide it, and when the pope has decided it, the people and the Orthodox churches will accept it, and the governments as well."[115]

Athenagoras offered an analogy to the Jerusalem trip, where he had not asked anyone's opinion and that, in the end, had resulted in a success whereby, together, Willebrands and Meliton "had repaired a nine-century long mistake in two days." The concelebration had to be done in a similar fashion, "I will come to Rome. Prepare this step and be quick about it. You have one, two, even six months, but no more than six."[116]

2.2 *"Up to the North Pole"*

On his way out, Duprey confided to Athenagoras that Paul VI had told him he was willing to go to the North Pole to "concelebrate"[117] with the patriarch, proposing Malta for the concelebration. It was a curious choice of destination because, at the end of the 19th century, Malta was seen as a refuge for a conclave threatened by revolutionaries. It was as if the British island could be neutral territory, resurfacing not to escape an enemy, but to celebrate a fraternal bond. Athenagoras did not let the opportunity drop, responding that "it is not necessary to do it at the North Pole, we can do it at St. Peter's Basilica in Rome."[118]

It was in this tone of acceptance that the subsequent conversation with Meliton also unfolded. Duprey admitted that, faced with such clarity, he could not fail to communicate it to the pope, adding that he would give Paul VI a "theological note summarizing all the positive elements of such an act."[119] Reaching such a "decisive" point in relations required an "act of communion" between the two churches, not just between the two persons, and what would be celebrated "must be given as a sign."[120]

Once again, Meliton allowed himself to be caught up in some concerns, possibly only as a way of pandering to Duprey's earlier resistance. In any case, he acknowledged, in no uncertain terms, that the patriarch's desire had "the breath of the Spirit" and that "God will help overcome the difficulties"[121] of the gesture, preparing for which he announced that he would soon travel to Rome. Duprey revisited the thought that, in order not to trigger the Orthodox fringes, who might paint the concelebration as a capitulation, it could be

112 "Rencontre du cardinal Willebrands," 230. A summary of the visit can be found in "Official Visit of the Cardinal President to the Ecumenical Patriarchate," *Information Service* 9, 1970, 14–16.

113 In reality, it was the consequence of the agreement of Dec 12–13, 1960, signed at Worcester by Catholics and Orthodox, which said that "serious differences exist in our understanding of the Church, eucharistic discipline, and pastoral practice, which now prevent us from communicating in one another's Churches"; see "Orthodox-Catholic Agreement on the Eucharist," *ECR* 3/1, 1970, 74.

114 "Rencontre du cardinal Willebrands," 231.

115 "Rencontre du cardinal Willebrands," 231.

116 "Rencontre du cardinal Willebrands," 231.

117 "Rencontre du cardinal Willebrands," 231.

118 "Rencontre du cardinal Willebrands," 231.

119 "Rencontre du cardinal Willebrands," 232.

120 "Rencontre du cardinal Willebrands," 231.

121 "Rencontre du cardinal Willebrands," 231.

celebrated outside of Rome the first time, in Crete, for example, which Meliton accepted.

2.3 *If Two Days Were Few ...*

On dismissing his guests on Dec 2, Athenagoras repeated his case to Willebrands, jesting that, while two days' work had been enough to lift the excommunications, two extra work days might be necessary to prepare the concelebration... Willebrands understood and, on Dec 22, he had an audience with Paul VI to present him with the conditions, implications, and the steps to overcoming the state of separation without excommunication that the two churches were locked within. He brought with him the closing document on the subject of intercommunion that would be published on Jan 7, 1970.

Covered by that public ban that had been imposed on Catholics without great conviction, the patriarch's proposal for concelebration arrived on Paul VI's desk as a kind of "application" of the agreement on the lifting of the excommunications. In the secretariat, it found space for discussion, as happened with other issues as well, in relative secrecy, if not complete isolation.[122] It was the strategy adopted so many times during the council. Problems, especially difficult or very difficult ones, were left to develop in a supportive environment, then a broad explanation of the solution adopted could be divulged to the outside world. And so, work on the issue progressed in the secretariat's Roman offices without consulting the episcopate or other curial bodies until receiving the (papal?) endorsement to explore the problem with their Orthodox contacts. But the council was no more, and its rumblings, which gave both fright and comfort, which gave insight and stirred tensions, turned out to be a sorely missed resource.

2.4 *Implications*

Everything, therefore, had to be decided rationally. The lengthy "Notes sur le implications d'une éventuelle concelebration eucharistique entre le pape et le patriarche Athénagoras," which Willebrands personally assumed responsibility for, was outlined in December 1969.[123] It was divided into two parts.

The first dealt with the ecclesiological implications, of which there were five: the act to be performed would be an "act of church" celebrated by Paul VI and Athenagoras as "heads of the churches"; the concelebration mentioned by the Vatican II decree on ecumenism (*UR* 5) manifested "visibly the communion that exists"[124] in sacramental identity; with the concelebration, from the Orthodox side, the pope's primacy would be accepted by a church that did not reject it *de jure* and that had complained that its exercise "has often, in fact, been confused with the pope's ministry as patriarch of the West" and, from the Catholic side, would imply a church that recognizes the bishop of Rome's ministry of communion without calling the "canonical autonomy" of the churches into question; the Western councils after the 11th century would be considered as "responding to the historical needs of the Western Church"[125] and their ecumenicity would have to be reshaped, as the Latin church had done throughout the premodern age, according to the studies by Vittorio Peri;[126] and the initiation of the end of the dual jurisdiction between churches united with Rome and the Orthodox churches presupposed a direct dialogue with the few authority figures (Maximos V Hakim, Josyf Slipyi, Antonios Varthalitis, and the various Romanian voices) as well as the assurance

---

122 Congar rebuked him.

123 See "Notes sur les implications d'une éventuelle concelebration eucharistique enre le pape e le patriarche Athénagoras [signed by J. Willebrands]," in: *Dossier delle fonti*, doc. 20, Dec [22], 1969, 225–229.

124 "Notes sur les implications," 225.

125 "Notes sur les implications," 226.

126 See Vittorio Peri, *I concili e le chiese: Ricerca storica sulla tradizione d'universalità dei sinodi ecumenici*, Rome, Studium, 1965; see also Alberto Melloni, "Concili, ecumenicità e storia: Note di discussione," *CrSt* 28/3, 2007, 509–547, later published in Melloni, *Il concilio e la grazia*, 633–664.

that the Orthodox churches would offer them an "honorable solution."[127]

The second part concerned the practical implications, which dealt with three aspects: the risk of a schism in Orthodoxy, which Athenagoras ruled out (but no one could predict Moscow's position), had to be evaluated with an initial concelebration in a patriarchal church in order to avoid the sense of a capitulation to Rome, which could provoke a divisive uprising within Orthodoxy by the other churches; relations with the churches entering into communion with Rome could not be the same as those underway with the united churches; and the idea that theological debate would clarify any problems – it being understood that the *Filioque* was not a problem, if interpreted, according to the Florentine dictate, as equivalent to the *per Filium*.

The conclusion to the document was multifaceted: "There are certainly risks, but we are faced with circumstances that are quite unique in the history of the church and in which it is difficult not to see an invitation from the Holy Spirit." The effects that this would produce were explained as the beginning of a journey into a new situation. At the moment, "political factors do not poison this endeavor"[128] as they did in the 13th and 15th centuries or from the 16th to the 18th century, which allowed responsibility for the new situation to be taken, which even Meyendorff had seen represented in the symbolic act ("symbolic" in the Eastern sense) of going as a brother to visit Athenagoras in 1967. The act was "bold, but, if it is enacted, would not be isolated,"[129] and it would show how the church today does not want to solve theological problems by political means, but to deal theologically with non-theological problems as well. A canonical act by the pope would thus have to give a sense of the decision and also prove that Rome did not consider Athenagoras as "representative of all Orthodoxy,"[130] which a canonical act by the patriarch himself could mean.

Willebrands's note was given to a group of three scholars – Wilhelm de Vries,[131] Dumont,[132] and Duprey – for their opinion. Two divergent responses were given, one from de Vries and another from Dumont, while Duprey kept for himself a final consideration noting the distance between the two views.

De Vries explained in 34 points that the act would give a sign that the Catholic Church was not asking for anything and that it accepted what he called Athenagoras's "theological liberalism."[133] In his view, the patriarch wanted to take "theological discussion off the table on the path to reunion,"[134] suggesting, with some malice, that the project of the *lex Ecclesiae fundamentalis* entrusted by Paul VI to a commission to revise the code of canon law be the bench trial for this intention.

For his part, Dumont distinguished the "question of principle" from the "question of expediency" regarding an act that could be understood as merely the patriarch's access to the pope's Mass. The question of principle was dismissed with a few words ("in itself and from a theological perspective alone, nothing absolute stands in the way of a Eucharistic concelebration between the Holy

127 "Notes sur les implications," 227.

128 "Notes sur les implications," 228.

129 "Notes sur les implications," 229.

130 "Notes sur les implications," 229.

131 The Jesuit historian was the author of *Orthodoxie und Katholizimus: Gegensatz oder Ergänzung?*, Freiburg i.Br., Herder, 1965; "Das ökumenische Ereignis des 7. Dezember 1965," *StZ* 177/1, 1966, 65–69; and "Rom, Konstantinopel, Moskau heute," *Stimmen der Zeit* 183/1, 1969, 45–62.

132 Christophe-Jean Dumont was the director of the Istina center in Paris and an important figure in French ecumenism. He did his studies at Le Saulchoir and researched the conditions of the church in the Soviet Union. See Hyacinthe Destivelle, "*Souvenir d'un pionnier*: Les Mémoires inédits du Père Christophe-Jean Dumont," *Istina* 54/3, 2009, 279–297.

133 "Quelques réflexions au sujet d'une éventuelle concélébration eucharistique du pape Paul VI et du patriarche Athénagoras Ier," in: *Dossier delle fonti*, doc. 22b, Jan 1, 1970, 241.

134 "Quelques réflexions," 240.

Father and Patriarch Athenagoras"[135]), but the question of expediency, already raised by Meliton (does Athenagoras have the consensus that allows him to take this step?), remained. Dumont set out six points beginning with the recommendation to "acquire sufficient prior assurance" [*sic*!] that the other churches would not have an unfavorable position, even if they did not take the same position. In this regard – his second point – Dumont believed that the ecclesial act should be framed in a solemn way by the idea of the restoration of a preexisting unity and justified by the fact that the rediscovered fraternity no longer explains mutual exclusion from the Eucharist. This would establish a path that the other Orthodox churches could follow.

Given "the profound and general aspiration of the Christian people for the reestablishment of full unity and their impatience,"[136] Dumont said that one must ask whether the overall effect of this solemn gesture in the communities and among the faithful is "to be feared or hoped for." His response to the dilemma was twofold: it was to be hoped for if it were an "undisputed fact" for all of the Orthodox churches, circumventing any quibbles with a fundamental agreement. However, it was to be feared if it were chosen by Constantinople alone, because it would produce effects like those following the Council of Florence, "above all if the patriarchate passes to Athenagoras's successor," opening a schism of opposing churches. "This would increase the animosity of these churches towards the Catholic church, which would be accused of having consciously or unconsciously divided Orthodoxy."[137]

On Feb 2, Louis Bouyer drafted another "Note sur les implications d'une éventuelle concelebration eucharistique entre le pape et le patriarche Athénagoras,"[138] attempting to respond to de Vries' and Dumont's objections[139] by identifying two types of consequences of a gesture that had to make it clear "that unity must not be reestablished on a minimum but on a recovered fullness."[140]

The canonical consequences derived from the observation that it would be "illusory" to think that concelebration has a private dimension. It had to be a gesture that engaged "the fullness of the authority proper to each, considering the complete union between the churches directly involved as currently possible."[141] Regarding the question of the authority of the councils following the separation and of the dogmas defined by them, along with the Marian dogmas that de Vries had covered, this could be resolved on the assumption that, whatever "philosophical-theological forms"[142] the definitions were inspired by, the intention of the councils was always and only to remain faithful to the doctrine taught by the Fathers. The exercise of papal power over the Latin church and its patriarchal nature precluded that the forms used for its exercise in the Western Church could or should be extended to the other churches. Regarding Pius IX and Pius XII's Marian definitions, Bouyer thought it was possible to maintain them "as definitive, but still susceptible to, first of all, being clarified and even of being completed, given that the authentic churches of Christ – which have never erred in the faith although accidentally separated from their

135 "Sur une éventuelle concélébration eucharistique du pape et du patriarche œcuménique," in: *Dossier delle fonti*, doc. 22c, Jan 1, 1970, 245–249, here 246.

136 "Sur une éventuelle concélébration," 247.

137 "Sur une éventuelle concélébration," 247.

138 [Louis Bouyer,] "Note sur les implications d'une éventuelle concelebration eucharistique entre le pape e le patriarche Athénagoras," in: *Dossier delle fonti*, doc. 25, Feb 2, 1970, 262–266.

139 [Wilhelm de Vries,] "Nota sulle implicazioni di una eventuale concelebrazione eucaristica tra il papa ed il patriarca ecumenico," in: *Dossier delle fonti* doc. 24, Feb 2, 1970, 255–261. This note, from Feb 1 or 2, I attribute to him from the copy in GUA, JLP. It asks a question ("is it possible to be Catholic without positively recognizing the truth of the faith defined by Vatican I on the primacy and personal infallibility of the pope?," 255) repeating the general definitions of Trent and Vatican I.

140 [Bouyer,] "Note sur les implications," 262.

141 [Bouyer,] "Note sur les implications," 263.

142 [Bouyer,] "Note sur les implications," 263.

center of unity throughout the centuries – return to communion."[143]

On both the Orthodox and Catholic sides, the psychological consequences had to avoid false interpretations. This could be done by making it clear that the same condition of full communion could be reached with the autocephalous churches without presuming any automatic application, explaining that, after this communion, neither the pope nor the patriarch should "feel free to make a similar gesture toward other non-Orthodox churches (particularly Anglicans and Old Catholics)." At the same time, it would need a "very precise and energetic statement from the sovereign pontiff so that a generalized intercommunion in the West between Catholics and Protestants not be thought to have been authorized."[144]

A shorter "Note sur un projet de concelebration Paul VI-patriarche Athénagoras,"[145] dated Feb 10, indicated only the "reasons for an affirmative response," taken from the documents of the previous five weeks, that is, the "'how' from the procedural point of view" and the "'how' from the 'theological' point of view of 'canon law.'"[146] The arguments were then developed, and it concluded with a reference to Dom Lambert Beauduin's well-known paper "L'Église anglicane unie non absorbée" (1925),[147] which had marked the beginning of a Catholic ecumenism by sensing, even in the lexical fragility of the time, that it was necessary to move past a mentality of return and annexation.

On that date, the opinion that Willebrands had asked from Duprey also arrived.[148] It took into account a reworked document by the secretariat: "Nouvelle note sur l'éventuelle concélébration eucharistique du pape et du patriarche Athénagoras."[149] It encouraged referring not to "a," but "the" concelebration, showing a prudence in labelling the eventuality, which still however had an air of possibility. This new note took stock of a discussion arising from the unexpected occurrence of both the aforementioned decision of the Russian Church's Holy Synod to not deny to Catholic and Old Believers the communion and the Orthodox sacraments,[150] as well as Paul VI's words of Jan 21, 1970.[151] The thawing of reservations also explains the sequence of opinions: Duprey argued that de Vries' memorandum was clearly against the possibility because it adopted an "insufficiently historical and dynamic point of view" and, therefore, held that intercommunion could only take place after the resolution of all dogmatic disputes. He also included an entire section of the Bouyer document that dismantled those objections. In his report, Duprey showed how the Dominican was "favorable on the principle of concelebration but was very reserved in his

143 [Bouyer,] "Note sur les implications," 265.

144 [Bouyer,] "Note sur les implications," 265–266.

145 [Charles Moeller,] "Note sure une projet de concelebration Paul VI-patrarche Athénagoras," in: *Dossier delle fonti*, doc. 26, Feb 10, 1970, 267–270.

146 [Moeller,] "Note sure une projet," 268–269.

147 [Moeller,] "Note sure une projet," 270.

148 Willebrands, on Jan 14, had given him the summary of the meeting in Constantinople, the *nota* by Paul VI and the two memorandums of de Vries and Dumont. Duprey was scheduled to bring the Bouyer memorandum to Geneva on Feb 5, something which was not possible and which explains the arrival of his note in Rome only on Feb 10. Bouyer would later write the previously mentioned essay on *koinonia* for the Pro Oriente 1974 meeting, which later was published as "Gedanken zu möglichen Widerherstellung der Kommunionsgemeinschaft zwischen der orothdoxen in der Katholischen Kirchen, Aktuelle Perspecktiven," in: Pro Oriente, ed., *Auf dem Weg zur Einheit des Glaubens*, Vienna, Tyrolia, 1976, 127–136.

149 [Duprey,] "Nouvelle note."

150 The meeting in October 1969 between Willebrands and Nikodim (Rotov) in Leningrad could have influenced this decision, see [Duprey,] "Nouvelle note," 271.

151 In his general audience on Wednesday, Jan 21, 1970, during the Week of Prayer for Christian Unity, Paul VI said, "Where is the unity of faith, of charity, of ecclesial communion? The difficulties seem insurmountable! Ecumenism seems to be consumed in an illusory effort! ... But could not Peter, then, some say, renounce so many of his duties, and could not Catholics and dissidents celebrate together the highest and most definitive act of the Christian religion, the Eucharist, and proclaim the longed-for unity finally achieved? Unfortunately, not like this."

prudential evaluation of the circumstances that would make it concretely possible."[152] Finally, it pointed out how very felicitous formulas on unity in diversity appeared in the Bouyer report, such to make it the decisive synthesis, from the secretariat's point of view.

With these nuances, the scales tipped to the pro side and suggested an extension of the part of Willebrands's note on ecclesiological implications to be discussed later with Metropolitan Meliton so that, for example, "a small joint commission could be formed to study the possibility and the how of the proposed concelebration."[153] It had not taken two days or even two months, but two months and ten days for a fundamentally positive decision to be reached within the secretariat for unity and Paul VI's ecumenical entourage.

2.5 *A Quartet at Work*

As Duprey had imagined,[154] a joint *ad hoc* committee had to deal with the proposed concelebration in detail. It was a very small group of four: Fr. Duprey of the secretariat, Fr. Lanne of Chevetogne Abbey, a longtime advocate of Catholic ecumenism before and during the council, Fr. Zizioulas, already a prominent theologian, and Archimandrite Damaskinos (Papandreou), who was to be consecrated metropolitan that year and stationed in Geneva in order to work with the WCC and oversee the Centre Orthodoxe du Patriarcat Œcuménique that were located there.

The quartet's first two meetings were held in Chambesy, at the very modern premises of the Centre Orthodoxe. It was a long session, first from Apr 27 to 29, 1970, and a second time around May 15, which shortly thereafter reached an agreement on a report of the joint committee established at a short meeting held in Zurich between Jun 5 and 7 of that year. The report was strictly confidential, reserved for the two supreme authorities, recommending it not be released until after a final agreement had been reached.[155]

The report was presented as the fruit of a final meeting, following those of the previous April and May, and opened with a "fundamental" consideration[156] regarding the "requisites necessary for unity"[157] between the two churches, in the sense of the cogency discussed at the council of Jerusalem in Acts 15:28. A list of the commonalities of the faith was accompanied by a specific ecclesiological consideration, evoking the Vatican II formula *in quibus et ex quibus*:

> In each of the local churches, in the bosom of which and from which the mystery of God's love that saves us by making us children in the Son is realized, each bishop established by God as the shepherd of his people safeguards, in agreement with all the others, that the faith received from the Fathers be kept intact and inspire the faithful to imitate Christ, who is the way, the truth, and the life.[158]

Following that, however, was an evocation of the call of the saints and martyrs so dear to Athenagoras: "Through the communion of saints may [the faithful] enter into the innumerable cloud of witnesses who from the beginnings down to us have been and will be faithful to He ... who comes."[159] Faith, sacraments, and the episcopacy were thus presented as foundational to that "unity experienced by the undivided church of the first millennium,"[160] which constituted the idea of reference. The question, then, had to be posed starting from that analysis.

152 [Duprey,] "Nouvelle note," 272.
153 [Duprey,] "Nouvelle note," 275.
154 Moeller imagines a practical arrangement on Feb 10, see [Moeller], "Note sur un projet de concélébration."

155 See "Rapport de la commission mixte Église catholique-patriarcat œcuménique sur la possibilité d'un concelebration entre le pape et le patriarche œcuménique," in: *Dossier delle fonti*, doc. 28, Jun 6, 1970, 276–285.
156 "Rapport de la commission mixte," 276.
157 "Rapport de la commission mixte," 277.
158 "Rapport de la commission mixte," 277.
159 "Rapport de la commission mixte," 277.
160 "Rapport de la commission mixte," 277.

"Does this unity, a presupposition of concelebration, exist between the Catholic and Orthodox Churches?" The answer is historical: over the centuries, an "atmosphere of controversy and non-theological factors" have exacerbated the conflict and let mutual accusations of heresy fly. Today, marked by "greater serenity, ... serious historical works," and an awareness of "cultural conditioning," the question is posed differently. "We then ask why we could not concelebrate between Catholics and Orthodox, given that we have, on one side and the other, the sacraments, and notably the same priesthood that celebrates Christ's unique sacrifice, and hierarchies that mutually recognize one another and the same fundamental faith."[161]

The report observed that this faith could see new divergences emerge,[162] which only served as a reminder that, even in ancient times, communion did not presuppose entirely identical views, but that was never experienced as a cause that "compelled a rupture of communion."[163] Divergences that were "compatible within the same faith"[164] were actually useful in distinguishing the faith that comes from the apostolic tradition from expressions of each theological "culture," and they gave historical context to the anathemas subsequent to the levying of excommunications, which made it possible to take the missing step, that is, "rediscovering themselves as sister churches and progressively resolving a dispute inherited from a reinterpreted past."[165]

The answer to the initial question, therefore, presented itself as a positive one: there was a unity sanctioned by mutually recognized sacraments and hierarchies and a "fundamental faith,"[166] with misunderstandings regarding the formulations of that faith that prevented the sacramental communion between the two churches today. It thus had to be asked whether a unity of faith existed between the two churches.

Regarding the doctrine of the faith, the report noted that, despite the dogmatizing unique to the Latin tradition, "the shared faith of the undivided church and participation in the realities of the mystery of the church have been maintained without interruption in both one and the other church."[167] There was, therefore, a common profession of faith despite Catholic dogmas. The dogmas concerning ultimate ends, the sacraments, justification, and the free, rational, and gratuitous character of the act of faith are all issues that the West had defined in relation to its own affairs and that the East was asked not to reject as illegitimate, without requiring recognition of their formulation. Regarding pneumatology and the epiclesis, the *Filioque* was explained as a necessary defense for the Latin church, never questioned before the rupture. The proposal was, therefore, to renounce rejecting one another's formulas as illegitimate and to let a convergence find a way to reexpress itself through fraternal relations. Regarding the powers and function of the pope, discussion began from the fact that the Eastern tradition recognizes the bishop of Rome's "special authority *in the* Church"[168] that – in the form used by Leo the Great and Gelasius I – was never challenged in the East, although it had a "different conception"[169] of that reality. This allowed for the possibility of a shared agreement in the interpretation of Vatican I formulas and Eastern theology, following which it would be possible "to begin to live and to think together again."[170] The Marian definitions of the Immaculate Conception and the Assumption

161 "Rapport de la commission mixte," 277–278.

162 The reflection on Vatican I is very interesting because it observes that already between the 4th and 6th centuries the self-understanding of the Petrine ministry developed in Rome did not match the idea of the Orthodox.

163 "Rapport de la commission mixte," 278.

164 "Rapport de la commission mixte," 278.

165 "Rapport de la commission mixte," 279.

166 "Rapport de la commission mixte," 279.

167 "Rapport de la commission mixte," 280.

168 "Rapport de la commission mixte," 280 (italics mine).

169 "Rapport de la commission mixte," 281.

170 "Rapport de la commission mixte," 281.

were not shocking to the East and thus could also be taken up.

"At the end of this examination, therefore, we can respond to the preliminary question posed above in the affirmative. The dogmas defined by Catholics after the separation did not break the unity of faith existing from their origins between the Catholic Church and the Orthodox Church."[171]

The conclusion was thus conditioned on a pure inner will:

> A concelebration between the pope and the patriarch, therefore, is possible, provided that, from both sides, there is an expression of the will to resume a shared life and that, in the recommencement of this new life together, guided by the Holy Spirit, we will strive to deepen this shared faith in a mutual respect for the particular traditions of East and West.[172]

"Conditions and doctrinal consequences" could be drawn from this, the first of which would be a communication from each of the two leaders explaining the meaning and consequences of the step to be taken to their faithful. It is interesting that – *argumentum ad hominem* – care was taken to point out that, on the Catholic side, this was only the implementation of paragraph 17 of the conciliar decree *Unitatis redintegratio*. In this explanation, which called for "joint consultation," the intentions expressed in the joint declaration of Oct 28, 1967, on "mutual respect for one another's traditions," would be carried out for both sides. For the Orthodox side, only a consultation of the different Orthodox churches was recommended, to "prepare the faithful"[173] and to show the practical consequences.

Listed among the "canonical conditions and consequences,"[174] was instead the principle of the reestablishment of "normal canonical communion" [*sic*] among the churches, which dispensed with all obstacles to a shared life. "This consequence shall be announced in a general way, according to a formula that shall be finalized jointly before the concelebration takes place."[175]

Effects ranged from mixed marriages (and issues concerning the indissolubility of marriage, on which "the shared conviction of the two churches has been expressed, for centuries, with different pastoral attitudes"[176]) to what Paul VI had called "the rearticulation" of the two hierarchies. A number of comments were made on the subject concerning: the Byzantine rite churches in communion with Rome, for whom a "progressive reintegration" was envisaged; the condition of Latin Catholics living in the East, for whom an "articulation"[177] in the context of the synodal life of the Orthodox churches was envisaged; the Orthodox and Catholics of the Byzantine tradition in the West, based on compliance with canons on "unity of a place's hierarchical authority";[178] participation in an extended universal collegiality. The status of non-Byzantine Eastern Catholics (Maronites, Syrian Catholics, Coptic Catholics, Armenian Catholics, Chaldeans, and Syro-Malankara Catholics) remained an open question.

Finally, there were "pastoral conditions and consequences" that were examined and touched upon: "Psychological preparedness," the "moral certainty" of the lack of irreducible opposition on the part of one or the other church; the value of Eastern Catholics' "dual loyalty"; and the pope's clear statement that this step did not imply or authorize a "generalized intercommunion"[179] between Catholics, Anglicans, or Protestants in the West.

171 "Rapport de la commission mixte," 281.
172 "Rapport de la commission mixte," 282.
173 "Rapport de la commission mixte," 282.
174 "Rapport de la commission mixte," 283.
175 "Rapport de la commission mixte," 283.
176 "Rapport de la commission mixte," 283.
177 "Rapport de la commission mixte," 284.
178 "Rapport de la commission mixte," 284.
179 "Rapport de la commission mixte," 285.

The last step was to implement the concelebration.

> It seems premature at the present stage to specify the forms to carry out the act envisaged. For the moment, it seems sufficient to say that two concelebrations are desirable. For psychological reasons and to emphasize that it was his initiative, as the patriarch has repeatedly stressed, if the Holy Father accepts, the first concelebration may take place in an Orthodox church and according to the Orthodox liturgy (in Istanbul or Crete, for example). The second, preferably held in the days following the first, may take place in Rome according to the Roman liturgy. If it is agreed to concelebrate, then the other arrangements can be worked out jointly.[180]

Thus ends the monumentally important document, repeating its key expressions: the concelebration was the beginning of a reestablished "shared life"[181] that would allow legitimately distinct traditions to be understood as variants that were respected in the past and will be respectable in the future. "In common," describes how life would be lived after the concelebration and how doctrinal, canonical, and pastoral problems that were anything but simple could be unraveled, refusing to see – as during the era of "misunderstandings" – the presence of a Byzantine-rite Catholicism or the existence of post-division dogmas as insuperable obstacles. Was this the dawn of an ecumenical Pentecost?

2.6 *Devil's Advocates*

Just the opposite. The conclusion of the work must have exacerbated tempers, for on Oct 14, 1970, Duprey wrote, at Hamer's behest, a personal note rebutting the accusation that he "wanted to direct"[182] Secretary Hamer and Cardinal Willebrands in matters concerning the secretariat's policy on the East. He stated that he was willing to step down, as Thomas Francis Stransky had, after ten years of service. The positive conclusion must have brought up old doubts, which were capable of wrecking the project.

Reading the documentation, which became increasingly rarefied, one gets a sense of Fr. Lanne's resistance. He was not convinced that Athenagoras had his finger on the pulse of his church and thought that a step that could divide Orthodoxy should not be taken.

Resistance must also have surfaced within Paul VI, who asked for the opinion of Fr. Paul-Pierre Philippe, the most influential and reactionary Dominican in the Holy Office. If a braking mechanism was what was sought, Philippe was the ideal candidate to provide a powerful one. As expected, or perhaps desired, the Dominican warned Paul VI against adopting an ordinary and not exceptional form of intercommunion. The exact tenor of the reply is not known, but we do know that the argument that most affected Paul VI (as in other instances) was the one that warned of a disruption in regard to the ordinary magisterium of his predecessors. It was not a postponement, it was the decision to not take advantage of an opportune time, one which would never reappear.

2.7 *The Delusion of the People of God*

In December 1971, Willebrands went to Constantinople to celebrate the fifth anniversary of the lifting of the anathemas and to bring a copy of the *Tomos Agapis*, the collection of the acts that, over 12 years, had changed the tone of relations between Rome and Constantinople.[183] A detailed account of the Dec 7 conversation between the

180 "Rapport de la commission mixte," 285.
181 "Rapport de la commission mixte," 282.

182 [Pierre Duprey], "Note personnelle pour le père Hamer," in: *Dossier delle fonti*, doc. 29, Oct 14, 1970, 286–288, here 286.
183 See the contribution by Nicla Buonasorte in this volume.

Dutch cardinal and Athenagoras shows the old man's indomitable energy, remaining vigilant for unity, as well as his lucidity at registering that it was not his own expectations that were disappointed, but those of the people of God. The indomitable prophet did not give up, but he knew that "the Day will come, for we believe."[184] That profession of faith has been waiting for almost half a century for those who have the courage to take up the prophets' scroll and, with messianic meekness, to say once again that that day is a today, God's today.

Translated from Italian to English by Susan Dawson Vásquez and David Dawson Vásquez.

Bibliography

Congar, Yves M.-J., "Neuf cents ans après: Notes sur le 'Schisme oriental,'" in: *1054–1954: L'Église et les Églises: Neuf siècles de douloureuse séparation entre l'Orient et l'Occident. Études et travaux sur l'unité chrétienne offerts à dom Lambert Beauduin*, vol. 1, Chevetogne, Éditions de Chevetogne, 1954, 3–98.

Martano, Valeria, *Athenagoras, il Patriarca (1886–1972): Un cristiano fra crisi della coabitazione e utopia ecumenica*, Bologna, Il Mulino, 1996.

Meyendorff, Jean, *L'Église orthodoxe hier et aujourd'hui*, Paris, Éditions du Seuil, ^{2}1969 (^{1}1960), 173–174.

Schelkens, Karim, "Envisager la concélébration entre catholiques et orthodoxes?: Johannes Willebrands et Athenagoras de Costantinople," *Istina* 57/2, 2012, 127–157.

Tomos Agapis. Vatican-Phanar (1958–1970), Rome/Istanbul, Imprimérie polyglotte vaticane, 1971; ET: Edward James Stormon, ed., *Towards the Healing of Schism: The Sees of Rome and Constantinople*, Mahwah, Paulist Press, 1987.

Velati, Mauro, *Una difficile transizione: Il cattolicesimo tra unionismo ed ecumenismo (1952–1964)*, Bologna, Il Mulino, 1996.

184 "Rapport sur le voyage du card. Willebrands à Istanbul du 6 au 10 décembre 1971," in: *Dossier delle fonti*, doc. 33, Dec 6–10, 1971, 307–314, here 310.

CHAPTER 38

The Groupe des Dombes (1954–2011)

Catherine E. Clifford

1 Introduction

Initially founded in 1937 by Abbé Paul Couturier, a devout Catholic priest in Lyon, the Groupe des Dombes gathers pastors and theologians from the Catholic, Lutheran, and Reformed traditions in French-speaking Europe for the purpose of dialogue. The group takes its name from the abbey of Notre Dame des Dombes, the main setting for their meetings until the departure of the Trappist community in 1998. Since then, the members participating in this discussion have continued to meet annually at the Benedictine abbey of Pradines in the Loire region of France. Couturier, perhaps better known for his influence on the Week of Prayer for Christian Unity and as the originator of the approach of spiritual ecumenism, which Vatican II upholds as the "soul of the whole ecumenical movement" (*UR* 8) considered common prayer, theological dialogue, and institutional conversion or reform to be inseparable aspects of the comprehensive activity required for the reestablishment of Christian unity. These three elements are consistently held together in the ethos of the Groupe des Dombes.

The first phase in the life of the Groupe des Dombes (1937–1953) is explored in greater detail elsewhere in this work.[1] The early years of the dialogue might be characterized as a period of reestablishing the bonds of trust after centuries of estrangement. Those initial conversations took place in a context in which Catholics and Protestants continued to regard each anotherith suspicion. Pope Pius XI had condemned the emerging ecumenical movement in his 1928 letter, *Mortalium animos*,[2] and Catholic canon law generally outlawed participation in non-Catholic worship except when required by civic duty. Nonetheless, the cardinal archbishop of Lyons and primate of Gaul, Pierre-Marie Gerlier, gave his support and protection to Couturier's project. Meeting discretely and in houses of prayer – alternating between Protestant centers and the abbey of Notre Dame des Dombes, this experimental phase became a laboratory for new forms of common prayer that would frame the context for an exchange of views on a host of theological issues.

From 1942 to 1953, meetings were cochaired by Paul Couturier and Jean de Saussure, the Protestant pastor of the St. Pierre cathedral in Geneva and a leader of the Faith and Order movement. New relationships were forged in the crucible of World War II, when a number of participants found themselves together in prisoner of war camps, in resistance movements, or in efforts to protect Jews from deportation. By 1949, following the foundation of the WCC, the Vatican issued an instruction recognizing the Spirit's initiative in the wider ecumenical movement and authorizing the participation of Catholics in ecumenical meetings.[3] A climate of confidence and mutual trust was slowly established.

Following the death of the founder in 1953, members of the Groupe des Dombes developed a more intentional methodology of theological ecumenism, thus identifying unanticipated areas

1 See the contribution by Étienne Fouilloux in this volume, "Abbé Paul Couturier and Spiritual Ecumenism."

2 Pius XI, *Mortalium animos*, AAS 20, 1928, 5–16. See also the contribution by Marie Levant in the first volume of this work.

3 Suprema Sacra Congregatio S. Officii, *Instructio ad locorum ordinarios: De motione oecumenica*, AAS 42, 1950, 142–147.

of theological convergence between Protestant and Catholic traditions. Their initial discoveries were recorded in a series of short theses that went unpublished until the period of Vatican II, when the Catholic embrace of ecumenism and commitment to dialogue emboldened them to bring their project into the light of day.[4] More than any other ecumenical dialogue, the Groupe des Dombes has sought consistently and intentionally to hold together growth in theological agreement and the need for the reform of church structures and practices. From the outset, it has understood that the path to full ecclesial unity consists in a "conversion of the churches." This insight is reflected in the group's published statements of theological convergence on issues as diverse as the Eucharist (1971), ministry (1972), episcopal ministry (1976), sacramental theology (1979), the ministry of the bishop of Rome (1985),[5] Marian doctrine and piety (1997–1998),[6] the exercise of authority in the church (2005),[7] and the Lord's Prayer (2011).[8] The Groupe des Dombes' fundamental insight concerning the conversion of the churches, deeply rooted in Couturier's vision of spiritual ecumenism and the driving force of its theological method, is clarified and developed in the ground-breaking ecclesiological study, *For the Conversion of the Churches* (originally published in French in 1991).[9]

The remainder of this contribution will explore the theological contributions of the Groupe des Dombes from 1954 to the present day, with particular attention to this call for the conversion of the churches. It will examine both the emergence of new theological insights and the development of a finely-honed methodological approach to the work of theological ecumenism.

2 Theological Discovery and Ecclesial Responsibility

From 1954 to 1960, membership of the Groupe des Dombes increased from about two dozen to 40 participants. This required a period of transition to enable new members to familiarize themselves with the culture and practice of the dialogue. Among the key contributors in this period were Roland de Pury, Pierre-Yves Emery, Max Thurian, Jean de Saussure, Jean Bosc, Joseph de Baciocchi, René Girault, and Gustave Martelet. Throughout the 1960s, Maurice Villain, heir to Couturier, and Henry Bruston, pastor of the Lutheran Church in Lyon, would serve as Catholic and Protestant copresidents. Having established an approach to dialogue within a context of shared prayer and mutual respect, they applied a largely comparative methodology to the study of church-dividing doctrines. Their aim was to arrive at a correct understanding of each other's positions. At each meeting, representatives presented papers on Protestant and Catholic understandings respectively, including traditional or confessional teaching and contemporary studies. In the process, they began to clarify areas of misunderstanding, revealing how many commonly held ideas were actually a mischaracterization of the other's position. At the same time, they began to uncover significant

4 See *Ecumenical Dialogue in Europe: The Ecumenical Conversations at Les Dombes (1937–1955) Inspired by the Abbé Coutourier*, London, Lutterworth Press, 1966, 52–59. The original French versions are in "Les Thèses," *Verbum Caro* 70, 1964, 45–53, and "Thèses des 'Dombes,'" *Unité chrétienne* 23, 1971, 41–52.

5 The aforementioned contributions can be found in Catherine E. Clifford, ed., *For the Communion of the Churches: The Contribution of the Group des Dombes*, Grand Rapids, Eerdmans, 2010.

6 Alain Blancy, Maurice Jourjon & the Dombes Group, *Mary in the Plan of God and in the Communion of the Saints: Towards a Common Christian Understanding*, New York, Paulist Press, 2002.

7 Le Groupe des Dombes, *"One Teacher": Doctrinal Authority in the Church*, Grand Rapids, Eerdmans, 2010.

8 Groupe des Dombes, *"Vous donc, priez ainsi": Le Nôtre Père, itinéraire pour la communion des Églises*, Paris, Bayard, 2011. To date, no English translation of this document has been published. This chapter was completed prior to the publication of Group des Dombes, *"De toutes les nations…": Pour la catholicite des Églises*, Paris, Cerf, 2023.

9 *For the Conversion of the Churches* (1991), in: Clifford, ed., *For the Communion of the Churches*, 149–223.

areas of theological consensus behind differences of theological language or emphasis.

As they moved forward, the group was guided by a set of principles that, however inchoate, would come to be widely accepted in theological ecumenism. It was Maurice Villain that listed those hermeneutical principles that, according to the Groupe des Dombes, were preconditions for ecumenical dialogue.[10] The first of them is a recognition that there is an ordering of revealed truths; the second, that there exists a legitimate plurality or diversity of theological expressions; and the third that doctrine, far from being a static reality, is subject to development as the church grows in its understanding of revelation. The understanding of an order in Christian doctrine, foreshadowing what Vatican II would later call the "hierarchy of truths" (*UR* 11), was sometimes referred to by protagonists of the group as a "Christological concentration,"[11] that is, seeing various theological questions in their relation to the central confession of faith in Christ, truly God and truly human, the second person of the divine Trinity. An intentional application of these principles permitted the Dombes theologians to address theological differences with a proper sense of proportion and to identify significant areas of theological convergence.

2.1 *The Theses of 1956–1970*

Beginning in 1956, Max Thurian began to take note of those areas of agreement in a series of brief theses intended to serve as an aide-mémoire for members of the group. They became a point of reference designed to ensure continuity and to avoid unnecessarily going over points that had already been treated. At the time, no one envisioned their publication. If there was a greater openness on the part of Catholic authorities to ecumenical meetings, the members nonetheless felt their work was best conducted with considerable discretion. The theses and the progression of questions treated in this period laid the groundwork for the emergence of more extensive affirmations of theological agreement inside the ecumenical movement, especially in the wake of Vatican II. Beginning from a consideration of theological anthropology and progressing to a consideration of the mediating role of the church and its ministry, we see how the group sounded out some of the most significant areas of Protestant-Catholic disagreement rooted in the conflict of the 16th century Reformation, and centering largely on the doctrine of grace and human agency.

The theses of 1956 were the fruit of three years of meetings, in which the dialogue examined the topics of Christology, pneumatology, and original sin, respectively. In its 1954 meeting the members of the group verified that in the creeds and in the Chalcedonian doctrine of incarnation the Lutheran, Reformed, and Catholic traditions could affirm a sound basis of their common faith. By 1956, they chose to approach the question of theological anthropology by way of the doctrine of original sin. This conversation took place against the background of sometimes acrimonious debate within Catholicism, concerning the relationship of grace and human nature. Surprisingly, they concluded that the Council of Trent's doctrine of justifying grace did not differ essentially from that of the Reform.[12] Both maintained that there

10 Maurice Villain, *Introduction à l'œcuménisme*, Paris, Casterman, 1959, 236–275.

11 Jean Bosc, "Qu'est-ce que pour nous l'œcuménisme?," *Verbum Caro* 18, 1964, 18–26, here 19. This concentration on the Christological confession of faith corresponds to the priority or centrality that the decree on ecumenism gives to the foundation of the Christian faith. For a fuller exploration of Vatican II's notion of the hierarchy of truths, see: Catherine E. Clifford, "L'herméneutique d'un principe herméneutique: La hiérarchie des vérités," in: Gilles Routhier & Guy Jobin, eds., *L'autorité et les autorités: L'herméneutique théologique de Vatican II*, Paris, Cerf, 2010, 69–91. The Dombes theologians applied this principle in an exemplary manner in their study, see Blancy Jourjon & the Dombes Group, *Mary in the Plan of God*, as we shall see below.

12 In this same period, the young Hans Küng would complete a doctoral thesis showing the convergence of

is no salvation apart from God's free and unmerited gift of grace. Together they could affirm that if human people are created with an aspiration for God, they remain wounded by sin and reliant upon God. Through the work of the Spirit, they are enabled to respond to the free gift of grace, offered "through the initiative of God who justifies in Jesus Christ."[13] God is at work in both the desiring and in the active response of those who are justified and do good works.

The theses of 1957 and 1958 considered the mediating role of the church in the economy of grace. The teaching of 1 Tim 2:5 provides the guiding principle: "There is one God and one mediator between God and mankind, the man Christ Jesus." All other mediations are subordinated to the primacy of Christ's and must refer back to him. Thus, in the celebrations of Word and sacrament, the mediation of Christ himself is rendered real. The text of the theses affirms that the efficacious nature of the sacraments derives neither from the holiness of the minister nor from the rites of the church, but from the action of Christ himself through the Holy Spirit. This same principle grounds the sacramental nature of the church itself.

Turning their attention to the church as body of Christ, the Dombes theologians sought to address Protestant concerns regarding the church identifying itself with the incarnate Christ, as Pius XII had done in his 1943 encyclical *Mystici corporis Christi*.[14] According to its critics the language used exalted the institutional form of Catholicism to provide an uncritical, self-justifying narrative, one that was resistant to self-examination and reform. Protestant theology rightly cautioned against an uncritical or direct identification between Christ and the historical church, a human community marked by sin. At the same time, it was acknowledged that Protestant ecclesiologies centered in the notion of the *communio sanctorum* had at times fallen into a regrettable tendency to dissociate the visible church and the ecclesial body of Christ. Affirming the appropriate use of Paul's language to refer to the community of those baptized into Christ, the Dombes theologians insisted that the church can never be considered apart from its living bond with Christ and the Spirit.[15] They acknowledged the need to maintain a necessary distinction: "Jesus Christ is the head of this body, so that the organic unity which he has with his church does not affect his lordship over her. This lordship establishes a distinction which does not compromise the reality of the relationship of the Bridegroom and Bride which exists between Christ and his church."[16]

The theses of 1959 to 1962 centered on the ministries of the church, including the exercise of pastoral authority, apostolicity, and the priesthood of the ordained within the context of Christ's priestly ministry and that of the whole church.[17] Building on the consensus concerning the primacy of Christ and his sovereign authority over the life of the church, the group was able to affirm, in 1959,

Trent's teaching on the doctrine of justification with the thought of the Reformed theologian Karl Barth: Hans Küng, *Justification: The Doctrine of Karl Barth and a Catholic Reflection*, London, Thomas Nelson & Sons, 1964.

13 *Ecumenical Dialogue in Europe*, 53.

14 Pius XII, *Mystici corporis Christi*, AAS 35, 1943, 193–249.

15 Bonnard finds a corrective for both Catholic and Protestant positions in the Pauline corpus: "While Roman Catholic doctrine and pastoral practice tend inexorably towards *confusion* between the head and his body, and current pseudo-Protestant interpretation unduly *separates* Christ from his church, the New Testament describes a *living relationship* between this head and this body."; Pierre Bonnard, "L'Église corps du Christ dans le paulinisme," *RThPh* 8, 1958, 268–282, here 269 (italics original).

16 *Ecumenical Dialogue in Europe*, 55.

17 Recognizing the especially difficult nature of the question posed by the sacerdotal character of ministry in the Protestant-Catholic dialogue, a small subcommittee of the Groupe des Dombes was established, that met several times to carry out preliminary work in Lyon during the interval between the 1960 and the 1961 meetings. Several papers from this meeting were published, see Paul-André Harlé, "Sacerdoce et ministère dans le nouveau testament: Une approche du sujet," *Verbum Caro* 15, 1961, 357–371; Jean Bosc, "Ministère et sacerdoce universel en doctrine réformée," *Verbum Caro* 15, 1961, 372–377; Joseph de Baciocchi, "Ministère et médiation sacerdotale," *Verbum Caro* 15, 1961, 378–389.

the need for genuine pastoral authority in the church. This authority, however, was understood as derived from Christ himself. It had to be conformed to his model of service for the building-up of the church and be exercised in a manner that respected the dignity and freedom of all the baptized. In 1960, the Dombists undertook a study on the apostolicity of the church, continuing to establish a framework within which they might later approach the differing ways of structuring the church and its ministries. They began by affirming that the whole church is apostolic – sent by Christ, the one sent by the Father, to continue his mission in the world.

Against this broad ecclesiological background, the Groupe des Dombes explored the understanding of priesthood and ordained ministry at its 1961 meeting. Protestant doctrine sought to maintain the priority of Christ, the one high priest, and to affirm the spiritual priesthood of the baptized faithful (1Pt 2:9). At the same time, it was suspected that Catholic claims concerning the priesthood of the ordained served to create a priestly caste, an order of mediators between Christ and the baptized, in ways that diminished the priestly character of all the faithful. Catholic theology, on the other hand, explicitly viewed the ordained priesthood as a special case of instrumental mediation within the priestly people of God.

Further progress on this question was made in 1962, when the dialogue extended its discussion to consider "the sacerdotal action of Christ in the sacerdotal activity of the church."[18] The theses reflected a broad level of agreement on the unique nature of Christ's salvific self-gift, made present and active through the ministry of the church:

> Christ is present now in his church ... It is by participating in his living presence that we share, through the Holy Spirit, in the action by which he saves us. The redemptive act of Christ on the cross, accomplished once for all, cannot be repeated; but its power is eternally active in the perpetual intercession of the Son, the eternal high priest, with the Father.[19]

It is striking to note the effort to avoid the charged language of the 16th century controversies – terms such as sacrifice, expiation, offering. In the language of the Scriptures, the Dombists found a mutually agreeable vocabulary to articulate a common understanding of the faith.

No theses were recorded in the meetings of 1963 or 1964 as the work of the Groupe des Dombes embarked upon a much broader and more complex study of the role of the Holy Spirit in the church. The years from 1963 to 1970 marked a transition as a new generation joined the ranks of the dialogue. New participants included Hébert Roux, Bernard Sesboüé, Michel Leplay, and Étienne Goutagny. It also marked the beginning of a transition in methodology. Where the period from 1954 to 1964 had been characterized by a largely comparative approach to Protestant and Catholic positions, it became increasingly clear that a more historically critical approach to the respective doctrinal traditions was warranted, one that paid closer attention to the various factors (historical, social, and cultural) influencing developments on each side, if they were to identify the roots of what seemed to be intractable conflict. The areas identified in the theses of 1965 to 1970 as requiring further study by the churches would be the core of the work of the group for years to come.

The Orthodox theologian Paul Evdokimov was invited to the conversation of 1965, which centered on the doctrine of the Holy Spirit. The group readily acknowledged the need for Western theology to examine the role of the Spirit and recover a more robustly Trinitarian perspective. No theses were produced in the 1966 meeting, which was held at Taizé and coincided with an early gathering of young people on the Burgundy hill. In a passionate exchange with the Dombes theologians, these youths issued an appeal asking the group to address the urgent matter of Eucharistic sharing. In response to the fast-changing ecumenical climate

18 *Ecumenical Dialogue in Europe*, 59.

19 *Ecumenical Dialogue in Europe*, 59.

in the wake of Vatican II, the Groupe des Dombes would spend several of the following years focusing on the study of the Eucharist and the related question of the recognition of ministries.

Vatican II had set the door ajar on this question by its recognition of the ecclesial character of Protestant churches (*LG* 15; *UR* 19, 22 and its positive evaluation of the many elements of the church, expressions of their corporate life of faith that the Spirit does not hesitate to use as means of salvation (*LG* 8; *UR* 3). Among these is the celebration of the Eucharist, although the decree on ecumenism expresses the reserve that, "we believe [the churches separated from Rome] have not retained the proper reality of the Eucharistic mystery in its fullness, especially because of the absence of the sacrament of Orders" (*UR* 22). This reservation is connected to the Catholic understanding of the ministerial structure of the church the role of the bishops, who are charged with ensuring that the church remains in the faith of the apostles. Nonetheless, the decree also foresaw the possibility of limited sacramental hospitality when it set out a twofold principle intended to guide the pastoral practice of the church. First, "witness to the unity of the church" (*UR* 8): as long as the churches are not in full communion with one another, sharing in the Eucharist, the highest expression of communion in faith and ecclesial life, is generally excluded. Even so, because the sacraments are a means of grace and other Christians may find themselves in need and freely request it, the Catholic Church "sometimes commends this practice" (*UR* 8). This provision invites an active discernment of those circumstances in which Catholic ministers mightuitably respond with generosity to those in situations of genuine pastoral need. Catholics, on the other hand, are not authorized to receive the sacraments from Protestant ministers due to the reservation expressed above, which amounts to a non-recognition of the orders of Anglican priests and Protestant pastors.[20]

The theses of 1967 to 1970 lay the foundations for several substantial agreements that would emerge throughout the 1970s. Those of 1967 acknowledge the important influence of theological and liturgical renewal in Catholic sacramental theology and in the renewal of sacramental life within the churches of the Reformation. They note the growing convergence in the understanding of Eucharistic doctrine, in particular in the understanding of Christ's sacramental presence and his unique sacrifice. In light of this growing agreement, they ask whether Catholics might take more seriously the presence of God's Spirit in the life and ministry of Protestant communities and whether they might envision the occasional practice of intercommunion, that is, reciprocal Eucharistic sharing.

The theses of 1968 turn to the root of the impasse on sacramental sharing in the doctrine of apostolic succession, understood as the persistence of the faith of the apostles within the whole church. They affirm that continuity in the handing down of the apostolic mission is inseparable from a faithful preaching of the Word and conformity of life to the demands of the gospel. Furthermore, they suggest that any recognition of ministries must entail a confession of each church's failure to maintain one or another of these three aspects of apostolicity (ministry, proclamation, witness) in the course of time.

2.2 *Initial Insights into the Necessary Conversion of the Churches*

In the theses of 1969 and 1970 we find the Groupe des Dombes' first explicit references to the necessity of a conversion or *metanoia* of the churches. The members of the dialogue, profoundly aware of both growing theological consensus and the urgent need for common witness, rightly identified reconciliation and the establishment of communion as works of the Holy Spirit. The reconciliation of the churches, they noted, necessarily required a mutual recognition of ministries, which they suggested might be concretized in a reciprocal imposition of hands in a gesture of reconciliation and epiclesis. The liturgical action envisaged was

20 These provisions would be codified in canon 844 of 1983. See *Code of Canon Law: Latin-English Edition*, Washington DC, Canon Law Society of America, 2012.

neither a reordination nor a mere canonical validation of one another's ministries; it was understood rather as an act of recognition of the work of the Spirit in the life of the church. It would be carried out in a context of conversion and repentance where each church would frankly admit its shortcomings and failure to maintain the faith of the apostles in its integrity. While the Groupe des Dombes did not consider such a reconciliation to be imminent, its hope was that a period of more generous interim sacramental sharing might create the conditions for such a possibility.

Girault described the 1970 meeting of the Groupe des Dombes as a real turning point. The methods employed to this point seemed to have exhausted their usefulness. By the end of that meeting, which centered on the ecclesiology of the communion of saints, the members experienced an "immense fatigue" that came from going around in circles. When asked how they could possibly move forward, a Catholic member averred:

> "We are not sufficiently committed to the goal of ecclesial conversion!" A Protestant continued, "Unity is worth the pain of sacrifice. We must reflect on our *metanoia*." The [co]president formalized the state of the question: "We must pass from platonic considerations to the point of view of life changes. We must leave these theses to [formulate wishes for] an ecclesial *metanoia*." No one contested this. From then on, all became clear.[21]

From that point on, the method of the Groupe des Dombes would not limit itself to the clarification of theological ideas or the elaboration of consensus on the points of faith. Increasing attention would be paid to necessary reforms in the concrete life and practice of the church.

The Dombes theologians undoubtedly found a warrant for such an approach in *Unitatis redintegratio*, which explicitly links the work of ecumenical dialogue between competent experts to the ongoing reform of the church. The decree stipulates that the "primary duty" of Catholic theologians "is to make a careful and honest appraisal of whatever needs to be done or renewed in the Catholic household itself, in order that its life may bear witness more clearly and faithfully to the teachings and institutions which have come to it from Christ" and the apostles. That self-examination must lead them "to undertake with vigor the task of renewal and reform" (*UR* 4).

The members of the Groupe des Dombes had already begun to ask what practical consequences must follow upon the growing convergence on Eucharistic doctrine or the emergence of a common understanding of the ordained ministry. Engagement in a common search for a fuller understanding of the gospel brought to light shortcomings in certain aspects of each church's teaching and pastoral practice which stood in need of self-correction or rebalancing. The Dombists became more acutely aware of their responsibility to bring these discoveries to the attention of the churches. This feature would become the hallmark of the Groupe des Dombes' published work as they consciously carried out their mission of calling the churches to fuller unity.

2.3 *The Authority of an Independent Dialogue*

One of the principal goals of Vatican II was the reestablishment of church unity (*UR* 1). To enable the council to attend to this concern, Pope John XXIII established a new office, the SPCU.[22] Among its many tasks during the conciliar period was to facilitate the participation of official non-Catholic observers, among whom were members of the Groupe des Dombes. Pastor Hébert Roux represented the ERF and the WARC, and brothers Max

21 René Girault, "Fifty Years of Ecumenical Dialogue: The Groupe des Dombes," *Ecumenical Trends* 24, 1989, 73–78, here 77.

22 For a comprehensive study, see Mauro Velati, *Una difficile transizione: Il cattolicesimo tra unionismo ed ecumenismo (1952–1964)*, Bologna, Il Mulino, 1996; and Mauro Velati, *Separati ma fratelli: Gli osservatori non cattolici al Vaticano II (1962–1965)*, Bologna, Il Mulino, 2014.

Thurian and Roger Schutz the Taizé Community. Pierre Michalon, director of the Unité Chrétienne center in Lyon, and heir to Couturier's project of promoting spiritual ecumenism,[23] served as a consultor to the SPCU. Within the context of the council itself, delegates from the various churches indicated a desire to continue their exchange with Catholic representatives. This led to the establishment of a series of official bilateral dialogues between official delegates of the Catholic Church and the other confessional communities, including the LWF (1967), the WMC (1967), the Anglican Communion (1970), the WARC (1970), Pentecostal leaders (1972), and later the Eastern Orthodox (1980) and Oriental Orthodox (2004) churches.

In the face of this new development, members of the Groupe des Dombes were compelled to reflect on the unique nature of their own dialogue. Indeed, they would be asked what authority, if any, accrued to their work, given that they did not possess an official mandate from their churches. What effect could they expect to have on the life of the churches as a private, independent group? This became a more pressing question as they began to issue explicit calls for the reform of the churches. The members of the group were placed in the creative tension of striving to maintain uncompromising loyalty to their respective ecclesial traditions while at the same time seeking to show the churches which areas of their doctrines and pastoral practices were most in need of what the Dombists called a process of ecclesial *metanoia*.

Reflecting on the authority of the texts produced by the Groupe des Dombes, Sesboüé, writing in 1974, observed: "*Private* authority does not mean to say *no* authority."[24] As the dialogue began to produce a new kind of agreed statement, it sought to attain the highest possible degree of consensus and adherence to the text by all participants. These documents, now addressed to the members and authorities of their churches (Catholic, Lutheran, Reformed, and others), were intended to provoke further reflection and action. While the texts from Dombes were in no way binding to the churches and possessed only limited moral authority, the rigor of the Dombists' theological work was recognized as exemplary by other ecumenical scholars who welcomed their contributions to the broader conversation initiated by Vatican II. Having pioneered the work of ecumenical dialogue in the generation preceding the council, they served as a model for those who now embarked upon the work of more formal, officially mandated dialogues. At the same time, the Groupe des Dombes would continue to play a prophetic role. Its independence from ecclesiastical authorities gave it greater freedom to face difficult questions and to speak frankly of the challenges facing the churches.

3 Theological Breakthroughs: Doctrinal and Institutional Conversions (1970–1985)

The 1970s were marked by a series of significant theological breakthroughs on questions long considered to be church-dividing. Much of the theological ground had been prepared for this convergence in the explorations of the 1950s and 1960s. This maturation of biblical, liturgical, and theological renewal started in the mid-20th century, and was now supported by the significant developments contained in the teaching of Vatican II. In rapid succession, the group published a series of consensus statements on Eucharistic doctrine (1971), ministry (1972), episcopal ministry (1976), and on the Holy Spirit and the sacraments (1979). In the same period, statements of ecumenical consensus on the Eucharist and ministry emerged from official Lutheran-Catholic and Anglican-Catholic dialogues, as well as from

23 On the issue of Couturier's heirs, see the abovementioned contribution by Étienne Fouilloux in this volume, "Abbé Paul Couturier and Spiritual Ecumenism."

24 Bernard Sesboüé, "Quelle est l'autorité des accords œcuméniques?," *Unité des chrétiens* 14, 1974, 27–28 (italics original).

the Faith and Order commission of the WCC, often identifying similar areas of agreement.[25]

It was if a logjam had burst, and pent-up new energies were now released, allowing the grace of shared faith to flow freely. What set the work of the Group des Dombes apart from other dialogues were its calls for conversion and renewal in church teaching and pastoral practice. While it is not possible to present the full extent of the material covered in the extensive corpus of publications from this period on, we shall endeavor to identify key features, drawing particular attention to the conclusions that the Groupe des Dombes attempts to draw in each case for the conversion of the churches.

3.1 *Towards a Common Eucharistic Faith*

The 1971 agreed statement, "Towards a Common Eucharistic Faith,"[26] is presented by the Groupe des Dombes as an effort to articulate a shared profession of Eucharistic faith. It was written in a context of crisis marked by movements that contested traditional ecclesial authorities and expressed impatience with previously accepted social and ecclesial roles and boundaries. The Dombists addressed the Catholic conference of bishops, the national councils of the Lutheran and Reformed churches, and the whole Christian people as they sought to discern the appropriate conditions for a responsible and informed pastoral practice of Eucharistic sharing that would respect their differing sacramental disciplines. In an effort to present both theological consensus and its concrete application, the text was written in two parts – one theological and the other pastoral.

The document does not hesitate to affirm that the members of the group found themselves in "substantial agreement" on Eucharistic doctrine.[27] Disputed questions of the 16th century conflict pertaining to the sacramental presence of Christ and the sacrificial character of the liturgy are entirely reframed thanks to a renewed understanding of the Eucharist as both thanksgiving and memorial. The Eucharist is presented as both the action of Christ and the church's "great act of thanksgiving" for all that God has accomplished "in the creation and redemption of the world" and continues to accomplish "through the coming of his kingdom."[28] A recovery of the biblical notion of Eucharist as a memorial (*anamnesis*) (see 1 Cor 11:23–26) helps to clarify the nature of Christ's presence in the signs of bread and wine. Those Reformers (Martin Luther, John Calvin) who defended a doctrine of sacramental realism and the Council of Trent had referred to the Eucharist as a memorial, even though the understanding of this term was soon attenuated by polemicizing debate. The Dombes document reads:

> Christ, with everything he has accomplished for us and for all creation, is present himself in this memorial, which is also a foretaste of the kingdom. The memorial, in which Christ acts through the joyful celebration of his church, implies this representation and anticipation. Therefore it is not only a matter of calling to mind a past event or even its significance. The memorial is the effective proclamation by the church of the great work of God.[29]

Furthermore, the document sustained that it is through the invocation of the Holy Spirit by

25 Henry Robert McAdoo, ed., *Modern Eucharistic Agreement*, London, SPCK, 1973. The Faith and Order text contained in this collection is an early draft of the consensus statement on the Eucharist that would appear in *Baptism, Eucharist, and Ministry*, Geneva, WCC Publications, 1982.

26 "Towards a Common Eucharistic Faith (1971): Doctrinal Agreement on the Eucharist," in: Clifford, ed., *For the Communion of the Churches*, 13–24.

27 "Towards a Common Eucharistic Faith," 13. The group indicates their debt to the work of the Faith and Order commission's study, "The Holy Eucharist" in: *New Directions in Faith and Order: Bristol 1967*, Geneva, WCC Publications, 1968, 60–68.

28 "Towards a Common Eucharistic Faith," 14.

29 "Towards a Common Eucharistic Faith," 14.

the gathered community together with Christ's "heavenly intercession" that the sacramental signs derive their efficacy.[30] The sacramental signs thus become for us "the gift of Christ's person ... the real, living, and effective presence of Christ."[31] The text affirms that by sharing in this sacramental communion with Christ, Christians are reconciled to him and to one another and "become the servants of reconciliation among [people] and witnesses to the joy of the resurrection."[32]

An area of persistent disagreement which the text identified as requiring further study was that of differing customs in relation to the Eucharistic elements following the liturgical celebration. Catholics, who retain some of the consecrated bread or hosts, were reminded that "the primary purpose of reserving the Eucharist is for its distribution to the sick and the absent," rather than for adoration, as many had come to believe. For their part, Protestants were encouraged to be more consistent in their practice by showing greater "respect due to the elements" by consuming them "without precluding their use for the communion of the sick."[33] Even while acknowledging the need for fuller agreement on the mutual recognition of ministries, the Dombes theologians asked, given this high degree of consensus on Eucharistic doctrine, that "access to communion should not be refused for reasons of Eucharistic belief to Christians of another denomination."[34] In so doing, they were effectively inviting the churches to set aside the negative supposition that other Christians do not share a common Eucharistic faith. The remaining obstacle to full sacramental sharing was to be found in the questions of ministry and apostolic succession, questions which they now pursued with a new sense of urgency.

3.2 *Towards a Reconciliation of Ministries*

The Groupe des Dombes' document on the theology of ministry, "Towards a Reconciliation of Ministries,"[35] bears the subtitle "Points of Agreement between Roman Catholics and Protestants," an indication of both the complexity of the question and the limited nature of the consensus achieved. The document followed a progression established in some of the Dombes' earlier studies relating to the questions of apostolicity, priesthood, and ordained ministry. Beginning with a reflection on Christ's own ministry, it moved on to consider the ministry of the whole church, locating its reflections on the nature of ordination and pastoral ministry within the one established by God to serve the whole church. It concluded by returning to the proposal first made in the theses of 1969 for a liturgical act that might express the mutual recognition and reconciliation between Protestant and Catholic ministries.

Among the most significant elements of agreement identified in the document were the dependence of all ministries upon Christ, the model of ministry as service; the apostolic character of the whole church sent in mission and service to the world; and, carrying forward an insight uncovered earlier and rooted in Irenaeus' reflections on the succession of ministers in the church, that apostolic succession entails three essential features, namely, "continuity in the transmission of the ministerial function, fidelity in preaching to the teaching of the apostles, and a life in keeping

30 "Towards a Common Eucharistic Faith," 15.
31 "Towards a Common Eucharistic Faith," 16.
32 "Towards a Common Eucharistic Faith," 18.
33 "Towards a Common Eucharistic Faith," 16–17. For an understanding of the Catholic practice of reserving the sacramental species, see: Council for the Implementation of the Constitution on the Liturgy, *Instruction on Worship of the Eucharistic Mystery*, Boston, St. Paul, 1967, 31–32: "It would be well to recall the primary and original purpose of reserving the sacred species in church outside Mass is the administration of Viaticum. Secondary ends are the distribution of communion outside Mass and the adoration of our Lord Jesus."
34 "Towards a Common Eucharistic Faith," 20.

35 "Towards a Reconciliation of Ministries (1972): Points of Agreement between Roman Catholics and Protestants," in: Clifford, ed., *For the Communion of the Churches*, 25–36.

with the gospel and the demands of mission."[36] In a highly original manner, the document reflects on the sacramental nature of ordination through a consideration of the representative role of the minister, which is to "signify the church's dependence on Christ."[37]

A pastoral commentary that accompanies the agreed statement spoke of the ordained minister as one who is at the same time a member and representative of the community and a representative of Christ. The ministry becomes an "efficacious sign" in the church when, through the ministry of Word and sacrament, it leads the Christian community to the source of its life, mission, and unity.[38] The same commentary affirmed the priestly character of pastoral ministry, especially in the intercessory prayer of the Eucharistic liturgy in which the presider shares with the people Christ's intercession for the church.[39] The invocation of the Holy Spirit signified in the imposition of hands in the rite of ordination had to be understood in the ecclesial context of the call, election, and giving of a mission by God.

While recognizing the need for further reflection on the concrete historical form of the differing ministerial structures in the Protestant and Catholic traditions, including the concrete form of ministerial succession, the document concluded with a more fully developed proposal for the mutual recognition and reconciliation of ministries. However tentative, this study rested upon the conviction that any future *metanoia* or reconciliation would require a concrete symbolic expression, one that speaks of a new reality:

> We do not feel that a purely theological agreement can suffice to carry the churches the rest of the way towards unity. Our doctrinal agreement on the pastoral ministry already constitutes a reconciliation in faith; if it is accepted, the reconciliation will still need to be intimated by acts on the part of the churches.[40]

The document echoed the Groupe des Dombes' earlier proposal for a sacramental act of recognition expressed through the mutual imposition of hands, to signify both an act of repentance and of recognizing the apostolic character of one another's ministries, a mutual act of invoking the Holy Spirit and commissioning for service to the world.[41]

At the same time, the Dombists acknowledged that, in examining the life of their respective churches, they discovered that each "is in conflict with our mutual beliefs about the ministry,"[42] that is to say, they recognized a gap between their common understanding of ministry and the actual reality of each one's ministerial structure and practice. From this awareness and drawing upon the "complementary virtues"[43] they had begun to discover in one another's practice, they formulated a call for the conversion of the churches. They called upon Catholics to recognize that even in spite of "the defects and deviations" from traditional forms of ministry apparent in Protestant communities, and "despite the shared sin of separation," God has remained faithful and given them "that continued living in an apostolic succession of faith a ministry of the word and sacraments, whose value is manifested by its fruits."[44] Essentially, they were invited to recognize that even without a historical succession of bishops (episcopal succession), these ministries had effectively served the faithful transmission of the apostolic faith, whose effects are evident in the corporate ecclesial life of Protestant communities. Furthermore, they were invited to

36 "Towards a Reconciliation of Ministries," 27.

37 "Towards a Reconciliation of Ministries," 28.

38 "Commentaire," in: Groupe des Dombes, *Pour une réconciliation des ministères: Éléments d'accord entre catholiques et protestants*, Taizé, Les Presses de Taizé, 1973, 33–57, esp. 44–45.

39 "Commentaire," 47–48.

40 "Towards a Reconciliation of Ministries," 32–33.

41 "Towards a Reconciliation of Ministries," 35.

42 "Towards a Reconciliation of Ministries," 33.

43 "Towards a Reconciliation of Ministries," 33.

44 "Towards a Reconciliation of Ministries," 33.

consider that such a ministry has been faithfully handed down through a structure of "presbyteral succession."[45] As part of the conversion required for the mutual recognition of ministries, Catholics were urged to further develop "a more collegial pattern"[46] in the exercise of ministry at every level of their own ecclesial life. For their part, Protestant communities were called to acknowledge "by reason of the situation created by the rupture in the sixteenth century … that we are deprived, not of the apostolic succession, but of the fullness of the sign of this succession," understood as a personal exercise of episcopal ministry, which they were now invited to revive.[47] They were further exhorted to reconsider the practice, extant in a number of communities, of permitting non-ordained persons to preside at celebrations of the Lord's Supper.[48]

These far-reaching suggestions certainly met with resistance and skepticism, particularly among Reformed churches, where they were perceived as a betrayal of a long-established doctrine and practice.[49] Nevertheless, in hindsight, they retain their relevance even today.

3.3 *The Episcopal Ministry: Oversight in the Local Church*

Seeking to deepen and broaden the convergence achieved on the question of ministerial recognition, the Groupe des Dombes was one of the first dialogues to explore directly the matter of episcopal ministry in its 1976 statement "The Episcopal Ministry."[50] Where the previous statements on the Eucharist and ministry took the form of brief affirmations of common faith, this document contained a more fully developed exposition of the biblical and historical bases of the church's theology and practice. Its use of the term *episcopos* was drawn from the Greek New Testament and early Christian writings in reference to an incipient ministry of oversight, leadership, and a service of unity in the local church, one whose form was not fixed until the late 2nd or 3rd century.[51] The term was employed here to preclude any judgment or inference of opposition between so-called episcopal or nonepiscopal churches, that is to say, those churches that have bishops and those that do not. The document reflected a general consensus on the necessity of *episkopé*, a ministry of oversight in one form or another, as a constitutive element of the church. It respected the conviction of the Reformation churches that their ministries were genuinely apostolic and invited readers to consider that beyond a diversity of church polities, both Catholic and Protestant traditions sought to remain faithful to the essential structuring of the church, including a practice of *episkopé* that is at once collegial and presidential.[52] The Dombists further specified their use of the word *metanoia* in this document, stating that they understood it to designate "a change that affects not only inner dispositions and customs, but also ecclesial

45 "Towards a Reconciliation of Ministries," 33; For more on the question of presbyteral succession, see Harry J. McSorley, "The Roman Catholic Doctrine of the Competent Minister of the Eucharist in Ecumenical Perspective," in: Paul Empie & T. Austin Murphy, eds, *Lutheran and Catholics in Dialogue*, vol. 4, *Eucharist and Ministry*, Washington DC, USCC Publications, 1970, 120–137; and Harry McSorley, "Recognition of a Presbyteral Succession?," in: Hans Küng & Walter Kasper, eds., *The Plurality of Ministries*, New York, Herder and Herder, 1972, 23–32.

46 "Towards a Reconciliation of Ministries," 34.

47 "Towards a Reconciliation of Ministries," 34.

48 "Towards a Reconciliation of Ministries," 34–35.

49 See, for example, Roger Mehl, "La réconciliation des ministères est-elle déjà possible?," *RHPR* 53, 1973, 223–227; and Christophe-Jean Dumont, "Eucharistie et ministères: À propos des 'Accords des Dombes': Essai de critique constructive," *Istina* 18, 1973, 155–207.

50 "The Episcopal Ministry (1976): Reflections and Proposals Concerning the Ministry of Vigilance and Unity in the Particular Church," in: Clifford, ed., *For the Communion of the Churches*, 37–58.

51 The earliest suggestion of a monepiscopal structuring of the local church is commonly attributed to Ignatius of Antioch. See Franciscus Xaverius Funk, ed., *Patres Apostolici*, vol. 1, Tubingen, Libraria Henrici Laupp, 1901, 236, 266, 281. For a comprehensive study of the question, see: Francis A. Sullivan, *From Apostles to Bishops: The Development of the Episcopacy in the Early Church*, New York, The Newman Press, 2001.

52 "The Episcopal Ministry," 46 and 52.

institutions in their functioning and, if necessary, in their structures."[53]

Among the important insights drawn from their examination of the historical evolution of ministerial structures, the Dombes theologians draw our attention to the decline of the late medieval episcopate as a key factor contributing to the 16th-century fracturing of the Western Church, and conditioning the ministerial life of the Reformation communities: "The way in which this ministry functioned in fifteenth- and sixteenth-century Catholicism led most Reformation churches to try to find other types of institutions in which the ministry of *episkopé* could nonetheless operate." This, and the fact that they found no clear warrant for the ministry of bishops in the New Testament, led them to establish presbyteral forms of ministerial succession and church governance.[54] Elsewhere, they noted that in this period the ministry of bishops had taken on a form rooted in the structures and priorities of the existing social order, and no longer reflected its essential character of service to the gospel:

> In her official documents the church acknowledged this, but perhaps saw it too much as a matter of a series of personal failings on the part of individual bishops. We think much more needs to be admitted. The real situation was that as a result of the social models it adopted, the episcopal institution itself appeared to be contrary to the gospel.[55]

Finally, this study revealed that, in practice, the ministry of *episkopé* is at once personal, collegial, and rooted in a particular church, that is to say, in a community of the people of God gathered in a given place. The renewal of the exercise of *episkopé* in both Catholic and Protestant traditions required the restoration of a proper balance among these dimensions. In order to arrive at a "more evangelical exercise of the bishop's ministry," Catholics were urged to carry forward the fundamental orientations of Vatican II by preaching the gospel "in a language that is accessible to people today," by forming bishops who embrace "an increasingly genuine pastoral closeness to the Christian people," by developing a more "collegial and synodical life" in each diocese, and by paying "attention to the emergence of new church forms."[56] In practice, this would have meant rethinking the processes for the election of bishops, structures of decision-making within the diocese and for collaborating with other particular churches in each region.

Reformation churches were invited to recognize that a genuine episcopal ministry continued to be exercised in their communities in the form of synodal gatherings, regional councils, or by individuals, frequently inspectors or moderators who oversaw the unity of the church in a given region. Deeper theological and doctrinal reflection was called for in order that these communities might recover the value of a personal ministry of *episkopé*, learning from those churches that have "preserved or rediscovered the episcopate." The recovery of such a ministry was envisioned as a diversification of functions that need not preclude "the historical equality of pastors."[57]

3.4 *A Neglected Insight: A Sacramental Pneumatology*

In its 1972 statement on ministry, which spoke of ordination as a "sacramental sign,"[58] the Groupe des Dombes already acknowledged the need for a fuller reflection on the meaning of sacramentality in order to strengthen the ecclesiological bases of its consensus on ministry. The Dombes theologians recognized that, despite the considerable progress made toward agreement on the meaning of baptism, Eucharist, and ministry, "the churches still in fact remain divided in the way

53 Group des Dombes, *Le ministère épiscopal: Réflexions et propositions sur le ministère de vigilance et d'unité dans l'Église particulière*, Taizé, Les Presses de Taizé, 1976, 12 (translations are mine).

54 "The Episcopal Ministry," 38.

55 "The Episcopal Ministry," 53, note 13.

56 "The Episcopal Ministry," 53.

57 "The Episcopal Ministry," 56–57.

58 "Towards a Reconciliation of Ministries," 31.

they understand the sacraments and do not even give them the same importance in their lives."[59] The root of this difference resides in the differing approach to the mediation of grace and salvation through the agency of the church and the instrumentality of its ministry. As the Lutheran theologian André Birmelé has noted, the Groupe des Dombes is one of the first dialogues to attend to this persistent and fundamental difference.[60] It is sometimes expressed in the reticence of Protestant ecclesiology to consider the visible structures and ministries of the church as having any immediate link, participation, or instrumentality in relation to Christ's unique mediating role in the economy of grace and salvation. Catholic and Orthodox theologies, on the other hand, speak more readily of the divinely willed structure of the church and its ministries as participations in the mystery of Christ, or as spaces for an encounter with the living Christ.

The first part of the text "The Holy Spirit, the Church, and the Sacraments" explored the biblical roots for a sacramental theology in an exploration of the New Testament's reference to the mystery (*mysterion*) of Christ (Col 2:2; 3:4; Eph 3:4; 5:32; 6:19; 1 Tim 3:9; Mark 4:11), in whom we encounter the self-communication of God. The term was extended to the sacramental actions of the church where, through the Spirit, that same reality is made present and active.[61] In a brief historical sketch, the Dombes theologians argued that a decline in medieval theology led to an unbalanced emphasis on the efficacious nature of the sacramental signs, minimizing the responsibility of faith on the part of the receiver. Reacting to an overly mechanistic and external understanding of the sacraments, many Reformers focused on interior realities, resulting at times in an impoverished appreciation of the effective role of the sacramental signs. The modern renewal of sacramental theology was presented as an opportunity for the recovery of a more balanced sacramentality in both traditions.[62]

That renewed vision was rooted in a fresh appreciation of the role of symbols in human experience, of the active character of the Word of God, and of the power of the Holy Spirit in the epicletic prayer of the church. Beyond the development of a richly grounded understanding of sacramentality, the text suggested that although Catholics and Orthodox Christians differ from the Reformation churches in regard to the number of sacraments, all can agree to a certain priority to be attributed to those of baptism and Eucharist. The Reformers consider the latter as sacraments "in the strict sense," given the unambiguous biblical evidence linking them directly to Christ. Other liturgical actions of the church – confirmation, reconciliation, anointing, ordination, and marriage – remain a part of Protestant pastoral practice and are considered to have a sacramental character or to be sacraments in an analogous sense. Contemporary Catholic theology recognizes a certain "hierarchy of sacraments."[63]

Compared to any of the other documents published in that decade, this study by the Dombes theologians was less concerned with concrete pastoral practice, and remained on a somewhat abstract or theoretical level. Rather than inviting the churches to reexamine their pastoral life, it concluded with a series of brief theses reminiscent of their earlier work, expressing a shared theological understanding.[64] René Girault remarks that despite the importance of this agreement for deepening consensus on the understanding of the sacraments and the mediation of the church and its ministries, it remained one of the least read of all their contributions.[65]

59 "The Holy Spirit, the Church, and the Sacraments (1979)," in: Clifford, ed., *For the Communion of the Churches*, 59–94, here 59.

60 André Birmelé, "Un travail de pionnier," *Unité des Chrétiens* 67, 1987, 28.

61 "The Holy Spirit, the Church, and the Sacraments," 61.

62 "The Holy Spirit, the Church, and the Sacraments," 62–66.

63 "The Holy Spirit, the Church, and the Sacraments," 67.

64 "The Holy Spirit, the Church, and the Sacraments," 92–94.

65 Girault, "Fifty Years of Ecumenical Dialogue," 76.

3.5 *The Ministry of Communion in the Universal Church: A Methodological Turn*

Continuing its pioneering efforts, the Groupe des Dombes published one of the earliest ecumenical studies on the vexing matter of the papacy in its 1985 study, "The Ministry of Communion in the Universal Church."[66] While it did not claim the same degree of doctrinal agreement reflected in previous agreed statements, this text acknowledged that the reconciliation among churches must entail an ecumenical reception of the Petrine ministry. The document laid out a number of challenges that had to be tackled by Protestants and Catholics, pointing to the bases for a shared understanding of the nature of the bishop of Rome's unique ministry and calling for a renewed exercise of its mission.

This statement reflected another important transition in the methodology adopted by the Groupe des Dombes. The affirmation of theological consensus was now somewhat displaced by a new attention to the sustained study of history and of the biblical witness. Significantly, the examination of history, in particular the history of doctrines, preceded an exploration of the biblical witness. While such an approach may seem counter intuitive, this procedure served the ecumenical project of critical self-examination. The practice of "critical history"[67] enabled the group to illuminate those moments when the various decisions or efforts to appropriate the faith in the past may have been tainted by bias due to "historical and cultural contingencies and … human weakness," leading at times to a "selective reading and a skewed interpretation" of the Scriptures.[68] This critical study of history seeks to uncover the deep, sometimes unconscious roots of division. Only by clarifying the operative biases in their respective traditions will the churches be freed to engage together in a converted rereading[69] and reappropriation of the Scriptures, to arrive at a fuller understanding of their message.

The historical development of the papacy in the first millennium reveals the important witness of the Church of Rome and the gradual recognition of its bishop as a successor or vicar of Peter, acknowledged by others as possessing a primacy of honor and presiding in charity over the unity of the churches. The development of a monarchical style of church governance in the Middle Ages, within a context of separation from the churches of the East, contributes to the elaboration of a highly centralized form of church governance where the Patriarch of the West functioned in isolation from other patriarchal leaders. In the Reformation period, despite their skepticism regarding the features of the late medieval papacy that prevented

66 "The Ministry of Communion in the Universal Church (1985)," in: Clifford, ed., *For the Communion of the Churches*, 95–147. Other early studies include the work of the ARCIC, "Authority in the Church I," and "Authority in the Church II," in: Anglican-Roman Catholic International Commission, *The Final Report*, London, SPCK, 1982, 49–67 and 81–98; see also *Differing Attitudes Toward Papal Primacy*, available at <http://www.usccb.org/beliefs-and-teachings/ecumenical-and-interreligious/ecumenical/lutheran/attitudes-papal-primacy.cfm> (accessed Jan 3, 2024).

67 This term is taken from the work of Bernard Lonergan, where he describes the functional specialty of dialectics, a task of particular concern to those engaged in ecumenism. See Bernard Lonergan, *Method in Theology*, New York, Herder and Herder, 1972. Elsewhere I have applied Lonergan's discussion of method to interpret the approach of the Groupe des Dombes, in particular their engagement in the promotion of intellectual, moral, and religious conversion in the life of the churches. See: Catherine E. Clifford, *The Groupe des Dombes: A Dialogue of Conversion*, New York, Peter Lang, 2005; Catherine E. Clifford, "Lonergan's Contribution to Ecumenism," *Theological Studies* 63, 2002, 521–538; and Catherine E. Clifford, "Dialogue and Method: Learning from the Groupe des Dombes," *One in Christ* 38, 2003, 42–57. For an extended reflection on this methodological turn by a member of the group from this period, see Gottfried Hamman, "Aspects herméneutiques du travail du Groupe des Dombes," *Variations herméneutiques* 9, 1998, 47–59.

68 *For the Conversion of the Churches*, 98.

69 This term is drawn from *For the Conversion of the Churches*, 165. The French expression "relecture convertie" is rendered in the English as "'converted' reinterpretation."

it from serving the unity of faith, Protestant reformers did not endorse a complete rejection of the papal office. At Vatican I (1869–1870), the focus on papal authority gave rise to a centralized, ultramontane vision of the church, eclipsing the early church's vision of its service to a diversity of churches in communion. Vatican II, with its insight into the coresponsibility of all the bishops, incorporated into the episcopal college together with the bishop of Rome and participating with him in the governance of the universal church (*LG* 22–23), marks the beginning of a recovery of that communal ecclesiology and a shift away from an overemphasis on the personal ministry of the pope.

The respective biases of the churches were reflected in their varied interpretations of Matt 16:17–19.[70] Catholics, seeking a warrant for the unique ministry of the bishop of Rome, view Peter "in a privileged manner" as the rock upon which Christ built the church. Orthodox churches, who conceive church unity as a communion of diverse churches founded by the apostles, see Peter as representing "all the apostles and thus all of the apostolic sees."[71] In contrast, Reformation churches tend to read this text without reference to the institutional structure of the church, seeing Peter as "the first among those who confess their faith in Christ."[72] In these diverse interpretations of a key biblical passage, the Dombes theologians saw a reflection of each tradition's preference for emphasizing the personal, the collegial, and the communal dimensions of the papal office.[73] They envisioned the conversion of the papacy as the recovery of the correct balance of its diverse functions as bishop of the local Church of Rome, patriarch of the West, and servant of communion within the universal church. Where the Catholic Church was invited to consider how the exercise of the papacy might be enhanced by a greater devolution to the bishops, who share a common ministry of oversight with the bishop of Rome, Reformation churches were urged to discover how the reception of a renewed papal ministry might give a visible and concrete expression to their participation in the catholicity of the wider church.

4 Methodological Clarifications and New Applications (1986–2005)

Following this series of internationally recognized contributions to the wider ecumenical conversation on sacramental theology and the structuring of ecclesial ministries, the members of the Groupe des Dombes took a step back. In view of the 50th anniversary of their founding in 1987, copresidents Alain Blancy, French Reformed pastor and assistant director of the Bossey Ecumenical Institute from 1971 to 1981, and Maurice Jourjon, professor of patristics and dean of the Faculty of Theology, Catholic University of Lyon, invited the members to reflect on their vocation, to clarify their methods, their accomplishments, and their presuppositions in conversation with a small number of church leaders.

In this period, the members of the Groupe des Dombes were concerned by the emergence of new movements of fundamentalism within the churches. These groups often expressed suspicion or misunderstanding of the ecumenical project and sought to reassert closed confessional identities. The result was the production of the 1991 document, *For the Conversion of the Churches*, an extended reflection on the ecclesiological presuppositions of the dialogue's persistent concern for the renewal of theology, church structures, and practice. In this phase of its work the group also embarked upon two lengthy studies that entailed a rigorous application of its finely tuned methodology to study the complex of questions relating to Marian doctrine and the interconnected loci of

70 "The Ministry of Communion in the Universal Church," 126–130.

71 "The Ministry of Communion in the Universal Church," 129.

72 "The Ministry of Communion in the Universal Church," 129.

73 "The Ministry of Communion in the Universal Church," 129–130 and 137–146.

authority in the life of the church. It is impossible to do justice to these ground-breaking studies in this space. Once again, our focus will be on their central insights.

4.1 *The Ecclesiological Insight of For the Conversion of the Churches*

For the Conversion of the Churches was at the same time both a clarification of the Groupe des Dombes' self-understanding and an extended reflection on the nature of theological ecumenism. Following the model adopted in the previous studies, this text explored the theme of conversion in the history of the church and in the biblical witness. Its central thesis is summed up in the following assertion: "Far from excluding each other, identity and conversion call for each other: there is no Christian identity without conversion; conversion is constitutive of the church; our confessions do not merit the name of Christian unless they open up to the demand for conversion."[74] Human identity is a living reality that evolves and develops through a constant interaction with others in a dialectic of integration and differentiation, identification and self-affirmation, communion and autonomy. So too, the collective reality of the church is constructed through an unending process of self-constitution. The text warned against fundamentalist movements that seem to have in common "a rejection of the ecumenical movement." It observed:

> The typical feature of all forms of fundamentalism is their clinging to the values and customs of the past, without distinguishing the essential from the secondary. Everything is equally sacralized and absolute; and sometimes the most exterior aspects, which are inherently also the most transient (dress, details of ritual, etc.), become the symbol of affirming an intransigent and even secondary identity.[75]

In contrast, the Groupe des Dombes insisted that "*conversion is an essential constituent of an identity that seeks to remain alive and, quite frankly, faithful to itself.*"[76]

The document helpfully distinguished three levels of identity at play in the life of the church, namely, the Christian, the ecclesial, and the confessional. Briefly, Christian identity is deeply personal, yet anchored in the corporate and "existential confession of faith in relation to Christ, which is enshrined in the trinitarian confession and professed in the church."[77] Its touchstone is the creed of the universal church. Ecclesial identity is closely related to this first level since belonging to the church is closely bound up with Christian identity. It is lived out in concrete local communities, each of them oriented toward an eschatological horizon. "No confessional church can be identified as it stands with the church of Jesus Christ. In this sense ecclesial identity is the very goal of the ecumenical movement: 'May the church be fully the church!'"[78] The separation of the churches stands as a wound in their catholicity. Because they are marked by division and remain gatherings of sinful human people, the churches, even at this fundamental level, remain *semper reformanda*, always in need of renewal and reform.

Finally, the level of confessional identity refers to the various denominations of Christianity, many of which are identified by the specific confessional affirmations of faith developed in the defining moments of their history. Catholic and Orthodox churches are reticent about applying this framework, given that they understand themselves to identify closely with the one Church of Christ. Even so, their own theological traditions do not consider such an identification as exclusive of other ecclesial bodies, all of which participate to varying degrees in the identity of the one church. While all belong to the Church of Christ, this

74 *For the Conversion of the Churches*, 151.
75 *For the Conversion of the Churches*, 153–154.
76 *For the Conversion of the Churches*, 154 (italics original).
77 *For the Conversion of the Churches*, 154.
78 *For the Conversion of the Churches*, 156.

participation can only be lived out within the context of a particular church with its unique theological, spiritual, liturgical, and canonical traditions.

The central insight in this exploration related to the ambiguity of confessional identity, which is susceptible to absolutizing or classicism where the culture of a single church is taken as the only acceptable expression of ecclesial identity. This amounts to the effective inversion of the priority of Christian and ecclesial identities, replacing them with an inordinate attachment to the particularities of the confessional form. Confessional conversion is required to bring the separated churches into full ecclesial communion. Such conversion will require a sustained engagement in "a discernment based on the gospel in order to gather together all the positive values in support of the rich diversity of forms in the church and abandon their sinful dimension."[79]

The ecumenical movement is itself understood as a movement of conversion, one that incites the churches to assume their evangelical responsibility to become church in the fullest sense. This document was widely received and greatly influenced the reflections of other theologians and church leaders during a period of ecumenical soul-searching. It helped to make the expression "the conversion of the churches" a commonplace one in contemporary ecclesiology and ecumenical conversation.

4.2 *Applying the Hierarchy of Truths: Marian Doctrine versus the Horizon of a Common Profession of Faith*

In yet another complex study, the Groupe des Dombes devoted the next decade to Marian piety and theology, working with renewed clarity and confidence to produce *Mary in the Plan of God and in the Communion of the Saints*, which initially appeared in two parts, published in 1997 and 1998. While Marian doctrine was not the cause of division in 16th-century Reformation, the document's careful rereading of history revealed how Mary became, in later centuries, the focal point for the hardening of Protestant and Catholic sensibilities in matters relating to "soteriology, anthropology, ecclesiology, and hermeneutics."[80] She thus became a kind of test case for ecumenical consensus on a host of issues. The Dombes theologians felt an urgent need to address the matter "due to a disordered revival of ill-informed Marian piety that is only aggravating the tensions already existing between the churches in regard to the place of Mary, or even tensions arising within one and the same church."[81] Among the features of the phenomenon within Catholicism during this period was an organized campaign to request a new dogmatic definition of Mary as coredeemer and Mediatrix of all graces.

A rigorous examination of early developments of Marian doctrine, including the creedal affirmation that the only begotten Son of God was born of the Virgin Mary and her recognition as *Theotókos* or "Mother of God" at the council of Ephesus, reveals that these are primarily biblical and Christological expressions of faith. The priority of the common faith expressed in the creed serves as a hermeneutic for evaluating later doctrinal developments in both Marian devotion and in the Catholic definition of the dogmas of the Immaculate Conception (1854) and of the Assumption (1950). Within the Reformation churches, Mary remains a model of Christian obedience and faith. While these communities confess the virgin birth of Christ in the creeds, they find no warrant in the Scriptures to justify any assertion of Mary's Immaculate Conception or "miraculous

79 *For the Conversion of the Churches*, 163.

80 Blancy, Jourjon & the Dombes Group, *Mary in the Plan of God*, 51. This study was built on work previously accomplished by the American Lutheran-Catholic Dialogue in: Hugh George Anderson, James Francis Stafford & Joseph A. Burgess, eds., *The One Mediator, the Saints, and Mary: Lutherans and Catholics in Dialogue*, Minneapolis, Augsburg Fortress, 1992.

81 Alain Blancy & Maurice Jourjon, "Preface for Part I," in: Blancy, Jourjon & the Dombes Group, *Mary in the Plan of God*, 9–13, here 10.

birth," nor her Assumption or any "participation in the work of salvation."[82]

Following a survey of both historical developments and of the biblical witness concerning Mary, the text provided a series of important clarifications and invited both Catholics and Protestants to revisit their divergent traditions in light of the elements of convergence they had identified. First, following the exemplary approach of Vatican II's teaching, which presented Mary in the context of Christ and the church, it recalled that the Catholic proclamation of the dogmatic teaching on the Assumption took place on the feast of All Saints. Mary's Assumption is not to be understood as an exclusive privilege, but as a foreshadowing and a participation in the resurrection of the body promised to the entire communion of saints. It serves as a sign "of a salvation which is not reserved for her alone but which God wishes to bestow on all believers."[83] Responding to Protestant concerns that the dogma of the Immaculate Conception removes Mary from the basic human need for God, the text was careful to insist that this extraordinary protection from the effect of original sin had to be understood as a work of God's justifying grace in view of the Incarnation. It was a free gift of God's grace and not due to the personal merits of Mary. Consequently, "to the extent that Catholics admit that Mary's fiat at the Annunciation was possible only by the grace of God, they can rightly present the Immaculate Conception as a radical expression of the grace through which it pleased God, from the very beginning, to make it possible for Mary to agree to God's plan." By the same token, Protestants could better understand that the Catholic teaching "did not remove Mary from the human condition" but prepared her to respond freely to God's offer "just as every other redeemed creature does."[84]

Finally, the Dombes theologians invited both traditions to place these teachings properly within the hierarchy of truths (*UR* 11) and acknowledge that, if differences remained on these questions, they did not weaken the communion of faith in Christ. Because the Marian dogmas developed following the separation of the churches, the Groupe urged that these teachings should not be imposed as a condition for reestablishment of ecclesial communion. Protestants were asked not to "judge them contrary to the gospel or to the faith," but to see them rather as "legitimate conclusions" that flow from Catholic reflections within the coherence of faith in Christ.[85] Given that a diversity of opinion existed on this matter for centuries within the Western Church, a divergence of views needed not preclude communion in the heart of faith. Protestants were further challenged to correct their relative silence concerning Mary and to rediscover the important place accorded to her in the Scriptures, in the traditional prayer of the church, and in the writings of the Reformers.

4.3 *The Multifaceted Exercise of Authority: "One Teacher"*

Another decade of careful study gave birth to the highly original and ambitious study, *"One Teacher": Doctrinal Authority in the Church*, published in 2005. Following a similar methodology, the Groupe des Dombes explored here the divergent attitudes of Protestants and Catholics toward the complex interplay and the normative role of the Word of God in the Scriptures; toward other authoritative texts, including the creeds, the teachings of the ecumenical councils, and later confessions; toward the discernment and conscience of persons and of the whole people of God; and finally toward the authoritative role of persons in ministry, from individual pastors to the episcopal college and the primacy of the bishop of Rome.

A key insight emerging from the group's exploration of history was the recognition that the

82 Blancy, Jourjon & the Dombes Group, *Mary in the Plan of God*, 50.

83 Blancy, Jourjon & the Dombes Group, *Mary in the Plan of God*, 104.

84 Blancy, Jourjon & the Dombes Group, *Mary in the Plan of God*, 106–107.

85 Blancy, Jourjon & the Dombes Group, *Mary in the Plan of God*, 117.

Protestant tradition emerged from a crisis of authority in the Western Church. The effect of this was an enduring resistance to any identification between "a normative truth (the reflective image) with the instance of its proclamation (the reflective mirror)." The Lutheran and Reformed traditions have tended to locate doctrinal authority in the complex configuration of Scripture, the individual conscience, the public witness of the believing community, and in the "witness [of] normative texts, understood as symbolic – *confessions of faith*, *ecclesiastical disciplines*, or *catechisms*."[86] In practice, this gave rise to "an unstable dynamic" and a "principle of ambivalence" that has left a tension between Scripture, personal conscience, the confession of faith, and the church largely unresolved.[87] Conflicting interpretations of Scripture and claims to the absolute freedom of conscience have at times given rise to new divisions.[88] This stood in marked contrast to the Catholic experience of a highly centralized magisterium operating in the modern councils of Trent, Vatican I, and Vatican II – often at a remove from the discernment of the *sensus fidelium*, the discernment of faith operative in the gathered people of God. This theme, while present at Vatican II (*LG* 12), became increasingly important in the postconciliar period with its recognition of the necessity for an active reception of church teaching.

To overcome these important divergences, the Groupe des Dombes invited both traditions to a renewed exercise of authority, taking again the normativity of a structure that balances the personal, collegial, and communal dimensions of the church.[89] It further invited both traditions "to develop principles for a common doctrinal interpretation of texts that we recognize together as authoritative, including first, the Scriptures, then confessions of faith and the documents of the councils of the early church."[90] Another area that is identified as needing further clarification is the "link between the individual conscience and the collective conscience of the established community."[91] Although the group did not envision the goal in terms of an identical structuring of church polities, it judged that important reforms were needed to permit a mutual recognition of the value of these differentiations in the functioning of structures and processes of discernment and decision-making in one another's traditions. These questions are still of great importance today, as the churches struggle to respond to new moral and ethical issues.

5 Returning to the Roots of Spiritual Ecumenism

The most recent publication of the Groupe des Dombes, "*Vous donc, priez ainsi*" (Pray then in this way, Matt 6:9), appearing in 2011, represents another soul-searching moment in the life of the dialogue and a return to the roots of its vocation in Couturier's vision of spiritual ecumenism. In a context where the wider ecumenical movement was faced with an accumulation of theological advances that remained largely unreceived by church authorities,[92] this work urged the churches to return to the very sources of the call to Christian unity in their practice of common prayer with and for one another. While the work of the Dombes theologians had since then largely been directed toward the reconciliation of divisions in the Western Church dating from the 16th-century

86 Groupe des Dombes, *"One Teacher"*, 40 (italics original).
87 Groupe des Dombes, *"One Teacher"*, 49.
88 Groupe des Dombes, *"One Teacher"*, 52–53.
89 Groupe des Dombes, *"One Teacher"*, 125.
90 Groupe des Dombes, *"One Teacher"*, 125.
91 Groupe des Dombes, *"One Teacher"*, 127.
92 In this context, Walter Kasper, then president of the PCPCU, published a significant survey "in order not to forget the constructive outcome of the last decades"; Walter Kasper, *Harvesting the Fruits: Basic Aspects of Christian Faith in Ecumenical Dialogue*, London, Bloomsbury, 2009, 2. On the new challenges facing the ecumenical movement, see: Michael Kinnamon, *Can a Renewal Movement be Renewed?: Questions for the Future of Ecumenism*, Grand Rapids, Eerdmans, 2014.

Reformation, now they acknowledged that the global ecumenical context had shifted in the last half century due to the growing prevalence of new Pentecostal and Evangelical movements. The presence of the majority of Christians in the global south and the increasing contextualization of theology were changing "the very nature of ecumenism."[93] Within this new context the Groupe des Dombes proposed an extended meditation on the Lord's Prayer, inviting Christians everywhere to hear anew the urgent call for the reconciliation of all those who are sons and daughters of the same Father, brothers and sisters in Christ.

An overview of the role of the Lord's Prayer through the trajectory of history revealed that this basic confession of faith in the mercy of God and in the power of forgiveness became, in the context of division, tainted by confessional bias. The presentation of the Our Father in the catechisms of the Lutheran and Reformed churches linked it to the mark of church unity, suggesting that its recitation in common would contribute to the edification of the churches as they asked for daily bread, forgiveness, and liberation from evil.[94] Catholic catechisms of the Counter-Reformation period presented it as a form of prayer "for the return of dissidents to the one Catholic Church (in the confessional sense of the word)" and not as a form of prayer in communion with other Christians.[95]

In this new document the Groupe des Dombes urged the churches not to take for granted the experience of the last century, in which Christians rediscovered the practice of praying with and for one another. Indeed, they called Christians once again to draw from it the practical consequences of their fellowship in Christ: to pray with and for one another as often as able, to study the Scriptures together, to give a common witness in society, to renounce the condemnations and negative judgements of the past, to respect those differences which are not church-dividing, and to recognize more fully the fidelity of the ecumenical partner to the message of the apostles.[96] Saying the Lord's Prayer is an invitation to mutual forgiveness and to continue working for the day when it will be possible to share together the bread of his table. At the same time, if the present juncture of the ecumenical movement brings with it new and unanticipated trials, or the temptation to abandon ship, the Lord's Prayer serves as an intercession for the help of God to sustain us as we continue along the path to full ecclesial communion.

6 Conclusions

For more than 80 years, the Groupe des Dombes has provided an exemplary witness of faithful service to the search for Christian unity. Its character as an independent voluntary association, combined with the longevity of its members' participation, have enabled it to carry out its task with an unequalled clarity of purpose and theological rigor, the fruits of which are evident in its many contributions to the ecumenical life of the churches. The Dombists' insights into the necessity of going beyond theological agreement to consider the practical dimensions of ecclesial renewal in the conversion and reform of church structures and practice are now widely accepted by other interchurch dialogues as they turn their attention to the need for ecumenical learning on the path toward ecclesial communion. Faithful to the vision of Paul Couturier, the Groupe des Dombes continues to remind us that the way to Christian unity entails a deep commitment to common prayer, to unity in the theological and doctrinal expression of the faith, and to renewing the living witness of the churches: three inseparable dimensions of ecumenical life.

93 Group des Dombes, *"Vous donc, priez ainsi"*, 18–21, here 19.

94 Group des Dombes, *"Vous donc, priez ainsi"*, 71.

95 Group des Dombes, *"Vous donc, priez ainsi"*, 90.

96 Group des Dombes, *"Vous donc, priez ainsi"*, 148.

Bibliography

Clifford, Catherine E., *The Groupe des Dombes: A Dialogue of Conversion*, New York, Peter Lang, 2005.

Clifford, Catherine E., ed., *For the Communion of the Churches: The Contribution of the Group des Dombes*, Grand Rapids, Eerdmans, 2010.

Dumont, Christophe-Jean, "Eucharistie et ministères: À propos des 'Accords des Dombes': Essai de critique constructive," *Istina* 18, 1973, 155–207.

Ecumenical Dialogue in Europe: The Ecumenical Conversations at Les Dombes (1937–1955) Inspired by the Abbé Coutourier, London, Lutterworth Press, 1966.

Hamman, Gottfried, "Aspects herméneutiques du travail du Groupe des Dombes," *Variations herméneutiques* 9, 1998, 47–59.

Sesboüé, Bernard, "Quelle est l'autorité des accords œcuméniques?," *Unité des chrétiens* 14, 1974.

CHAPTER 39

The Leuenberg Agreement: A Pioneering Model of Church Communion between Reformation Churches in Europe

Elisabeth Parmentier

1 Origins and Goals of the Leuenberg Agreement

The Leuenberg Agreement, signed in 1973 between Lutheran, Reformed, and United churches in Europe and in the Rio de la Plata in Latin America, is an innovative ecumenical model that made it possible to lift the mutual condemnations that had separated the Lutheran and Reformed churches in the 16th century and to establish a church communion of 105 churches linked to the Reformation.[1] The Leuenberg Agreement itself called upon its signatories to not only "declare" but also to "realize" this communion of churches,[2] which, however, remain anchored to their respective traditions and confessions of faith. They retain their doctrinal texts and their confessions of faith but act in concert in all possible domains as a church communion. The family formed as a result of the signing of the Leuenberg Agreement, which today goes by the name of CPCE was also expanded to include other Reformed churches, such as the Methodist churches that joined the church communion by issuing a separate declaration in 1993.[3]

Following the historical developments the Agreement documented by Elisabeth Schieffer and the two fathers of the document, Marc Lienhard and Wilhelm Heinrich Neuser,[4] the results of the benefits of this model will be expounded here: bonds of communion among Lutheran and Reformed churches; forms of recognition between the CPCE and the Anglican churches; new dialogues in Europe (for example with the Baptist churches); twin declarations on other continents.

After four centuries of separation, the Lutheran and Reformed churches began to move closer together in the 20th century. In the opinion of historians, the tragedy of the two world wars led to the realization that the reconciliation of peoples could only take place through the reconciliation of the churches. The Lutheran and Reformed churches had already found themselves on common ground, notably in the pietist movements and in missionary undertakings, in the joint drafting of the Barmen Declaration, or in shared minority situations.

---

1 The number of member churches is lower (95 churches) today since several of these churches have gone through the processes of church unification (in the Netherlands, in France, between East and West Berlin, Berlin and Upper Lusatia, in Belgium, Scotland, and in the United Kingdom).

2 "Agreement between Reformation Churches in Europe (The Leuenberg Agreement)," Mar 16, 1973, English text available at <https://www.leuenberg.eu/download/leuenberg-agreement/?wpdmdl=943&ind=1590131974637> (accessed Jan 16, 2024).

3 See "Leuenberger Kirchengemeinschaft – Methodistische Kirchen: Gemeinsame Erklärung zur Kirchengemeinschaft (1993)", available at <https://www.leuenberg.eu/documents/archive/> (last accessed Jul 8, 2024). These churches were the United Methodist Church Central Conference of Central and Southern Europe; United Methodist Church Central Conference of Germany; United Methodist Church of Italy; United Methodist Church, Nordic and Baltic Area; the Methodist Church in the United Kingdom (the Methodist Church in Ireland plus the Methodist Church in Great Britain); Evangelical Methodist Church of Portugal; Evangelical Methodist Church of Argentina.

4 See Elisabeth Schieffer, *Von Schauenburg nach Leuenberg: Entstehung und Bedeutung der Konkordie reformatorischer Kirchen in Europa*, Paderborn, Bonifatius, 1983; Marc Lienhard, *Lutherisch-Reformierte Kirchengemeinschaft heute: Der Leuenberger Konkordienentwurf im Kontext der bisherigen lutherisch-reformierten Dialoge*, Frankfurt a.M., Lembeck, 1972; and Wilhelm Neuser, *Die Entstehung und theologische Formung der Leuenberger Konkordie 1971 bis 1973*, Münster, LIT, 2003.

The Leuenberg Agreement lists four factors that led to this rapprochement: the "grappling with the questions of modernity, the development of biblical research, the church renewal movements, and the rediscovery of an ecumenical perspective" (LA § 5). It also acknowledges that the churches have changed and that their confessional disputes have accordingly evolved. A common life already existed in some countries, as for instance in Germany, the Netherlands, and France. In France, where the Lutheran and Reformed churches all have minority status, the close proximity of their historical destinies had enabled them to conclude an agreement as early as 1968 with the drafting of the three Theses of Lyon focused on the Word of God and Holy Scripture; baptism; and the Lord's Supper.

From 1956 to 1960, experts' discussions were organized by the WCC, through the intermediary of the Faith and Order commission. The Arnoldshain conversations studied "The authority of the Holy Scriptures for the proclamation of the Church" (1957), "The presence of Christ" (1958), "The presence of Christ in baptism" (1959), "The presence of Christ and the Lord's Supper" (1960).[5]

Since these results needed to be harmonized in view of concluding church agreements, they were taken up by the Schauenburg conversations – held in Bad Schauenburg from 1964 to 1967 –, which allowed for the elaboration of several theses: "The word of God and the presence of God" (1964), "Theses on the Law" (1965), "Theses on the confession of faith" (1966).[6] They ascertained the existence of common foundations that opened up the possibility of a church communion. From 1969 to 1973, the dialogue conducted at Leuenberg (near Basel) focused on church communion and the separation of churches. Marc Lienhard notes that the aim of these meetings was a church communion based on the common foundations that had already emerged. A report from 1970 recommended that a church communion be established by means of an agreement oriented around three defining moments: a statement in which the churches agreed on a common understanding of the gospel (which the report of 1970 formulates as the "unique mediation of Jesus Christ" for our salvation, the "heart of scripture" – as taken up in paragraph 12 of the Leuenberg Agreement – expressed in the doctrine of justification by faith); a statement affirming that the doctrinal condemnations no longer applied to the present-day church and that the differences were no longer divisive; a statement of communion in the field of preaching and in the Lord's Supper.[7]

Two major changes characterized the Leuenberg conversations: the participation of the LWF and of the WARC and the inclusion of church leaders and pastors in the group of experts. The issue became an ecclesial one: the participants asked themselves how this fellowship might be realized and opted in favor of a church communion. The work on a preliminary agreement began in 1971[8] but was not based on the "organic union," a model that had been around since 1925 (for example in the United Church of Canada) and which involved the relinquishing of confessional names and identities, which was out of the question for these churches. The LWF was already familiar with the concept of *Kirchengemeinschaft*, or church communion.[9] Harding Meyer notes that the understanding of

5 Division of studies – WCC, *The Lordship of Christ over the World and the Church: A Report from the Consultation Held at Arnoldshain, Germany, July 5–8, 1956*, Geneva, WCC Publications, 1956.

6 See the report of Schauenburg in: *Auf dem Weg*, vol. 1, *Lutherisch-reformierte Kirchengemeinschaft: Berichte und Texte*, Zürich, TVZ, 1967, 31–43; also in: Schieffer, *Von Schauenburg nach Leuenberg*, appendix A, 39–54.

7 The report from 1970 is printed in: *Auf dem Weg*, vol. 2, *Gemeinschaft der reformatorischen Kirchen: Berichte und Dokumente des lutherisch-reformierten Gespräches in Europa*, Zürich, TVZ, 1971, 8–21. Also in: Schieffer, *Von Schauenburg nach Leuenberg*, appendix A, 55–67.

8 For a historical account of these negotiations in French, see Marc Lienhard, "La Concorde de Leuenberg: Origines et visée," *Positions luthériennes* 37/3, 1989, 170–189.

9 André Birmelé, *La communion ecclésiale: Progrès œcuméniques et enjeux méthodologiques*, Paris, Cerf, 2000.

this concept was guided by three principles:[10] the communion (*koinonia*) is not realized by way of agreements but as a gift of Christ. It is the communion with Christ that establishes Christian communion; this communion must be made visible and lived in faith, the sacraments, the ministry and a common ecclesial life, witness and service; communion must be lived in a legitimate diversity.

Harding Meyer also summarizes the notion of church communion as applied to the Leuenberg Agreement in the following manner:

> "Church communion" is the full realization of the unity of the Church in faith, sacramental communion, communion in the ministry, and communion in the life and activities of the churches of different confessional traditions. It is borne by a basic consensus in the understanding of the gospel and of its transmission in word and sacrament. In the light of this basic consensus, the doctrinal condemnations pronounced in the past are no longer applicable to the partner in his present situation.[11]

2 The Text of the Leuenberg Agreement

2.1 *Why an Agreement* (Konkordie)*?*

The very term "agreement" – in German "Konkordie," an echo of the Wittenberg Concord of 1536 that was intended to bring peace following the theological quarrels at the Colloquy of Marburg (1529) – suggests that this document aimed at effecting a reconciliation. It is named after the place where it was drafted, Leuenberg, near Basel, although the full title specifies the parties involved: "Agreement between Reformation Churches in Europe" (in addition to the churches of the Rio de la Plata). The family arising from the Leuenberg Agreemnt initially referred to itself as the Leuenberg Church Fellowship (Leuenberger Kirchengemeinschaft; Communion ecclésiale de Leuenberg). In 2003, the executive committee opted in favor of Community of Protestant Churches in Europe (Gemeinschaft evangelischer Kirchen in Europa; Communion d'Églises protestantes en Europe). Three major problems remained unsolved in this choice: firstly, the designation left out the churches of the Rio de la Plata; moreover, while the German term *evangelisch* (meaning "originating in the gospel") cannot be translated as "evangelical," even the adjective Protestant certainly does not have the same connotation; finally *Kirchengemeinschaft*, understood in the maximalist sense of mutual commitment and not merely as a federation or mere council of churches, is poorly rendered as community in the English translation, making it difficult for the English-speaking churches to grasp the exact nature of the commitment implied by the communion of these churches.

2.2 *The Gospel and the Understanding Thereof in the Doctrine of Justification*

The 49 paragraphs of the Leuenberg Agreement lay out a path divided into four sections: "The Road to Fellowship"; "The Common Understanding of the Gospel"; "Agreement Regarding the Doctrinal Condemnations of the Reformation Period"; "The Declaration and Realization of Church Fellowship."

This itinerary identifies the criteria of interpretation and the realities of history, then considers whether a "common understanding of the gospel" can be mutually recognized and whether the sermons and sacraments reflect this understanding. The assertion that the condemnations are obsolete opens up the possibility of a church communion that should be lived.

Therefore, the Leuenberg Agreement is based on a common understanding of the gospel that had been confirmed in previous doctrinal talks. The gospel ("the living Word of God in Jesus Christ," LA § 6), the event of salvation in Christ proclaimed to humanity, is termed "the message

10 Harding Meyer, "La communion ecclésiale selon la Concorde de Leuenberg," *Positions luthériennes* 37/3, 1989, 208–222, here 212.

11 Meyer, "La communion ecclésiale," 218.

of justification as the message of the free grace of God" (LA § 6.1). According to various confessions of faith, it is formulated in the doctrine of justification: "The Reformers expressed the true understanding of the Gospel in the doctrine of justification" (LA § 8a).

The churches acknowledge that they exist by reason of the same message of justification in Christ, but that they interpret it differently in their doctrinal developments, their sermons, and their liturgical and catechetical forms of expression. The doctrine elaborates on the message that is inherent to it and which guides it in relation to different times and contexts. This fundamental distinction between message and doctrine is also applied to the confessions of faith: "They [the churches] have learned to distinguish between the fundamental witness of the Reformation confessions of faith and their historically conditioned thought forms" (LA § 5).[12]

The second part of the Leuenberg Agreement, pertaining to the actual realization of the church communion, implicitly applies the same method: the body of Christ is unique but manifests itself in different expressions of piety, forms of worship (*Gestaltungen des Gottesdienstes*), and church disciplines, but these differences do not divide the church: "In fidelity to the New Testament and the Reformation criteria for church fellowship, we cannot discern in these differences any factors which should divide the church" (LA § 28), although it is stated that these doctrinal differences should continue to be examined. Not only does this difference have a right to exist, the communion actually draws nourishment from it: "Any union detrimental to the lively diversity of styles of preaching, ways of worship, church order, and diaconal and social action would contradict the very nature of the church communion" (LA § 45). The commitment to ensure this difference for the communion also protects the minority churches (LA § 45).

2.3 *The Reference to History and the Developments in Theology (LA §§ 3–16)*

The participating churches (not only the Reformation churches but also those that predate it) were long divided, but their perceptions of each other have now changed (LA § 3). The historical retrospective emphasizes two novel aspects: an already real rapprochement, and repentance: "Thankful that they have been led closer together, they confess at the same time that the struggle for truth and unity in the Church has also been, and remains, marked by guilt and suffering" (LA § 1).

Yet, it was precisely the foundation in Christ that had been a source of polemics. This is why the churches, after agreeing on the meaning of justification, applied themselves to the task of clarifying the issues of preaching, baptism, the Lord's Supper, Christology, and predestination (LA §§ 17–26). It was no longer a matter of detailing the preceding dialogues but of putting the common understanding of the gospel into practice (LA §§ 6–16):

> With this understanding of the Gospel we take our stand on the basis of the creeds of the early church and reaffirm the conviction, common to the Reformation confessions of faith, that the unique mediation of Jesus Christ in salvation is the heart of scripture and that the message of justification as the message of God's free grace is the measure of all the Church's preaching (LA § 12e).

Justification is not the only way to express the message of grace, but for such churches this doctrine has a normative function, which will be tested by intra-Reformation controversies.

2.4 *The Agreement with Regard to the Conflicts of the 16th Century (LA §§ 17–28)*

A certain amount of confusion may arise from the reading of the three controversial issues (the Lord's

12 Here, the expression "fundamental witness" translates the original German "das grundlegende Zeugnis," which constitutes the foundational proclamation, expressed in "geschichtlichen Denkformen" – distinguishing between *Grund* and *Formen*.

Supper, Christology, and predestination), as the explanation is short. The analysis of preaching and baptism (LA § 13–14a) is limited to two paragraphs, without evoking the dilemma between a believer's baptism and baptism as a gift of grace, since the addressees are the Lutheran and Reformed churches, not the heirs of the Anabaptists. The text expounds the entry into the community of salvation and the new creation, the call to conversion, the entry into the church, and the daily conversion to faith, through the "power of the Holy Spirit" (LA § 14a). Justification is followed by sanctification, thereby combining the respective emphases of the Lutheran and Reformed traditions.

A joint statement connects the *loci* of Christ's presence: "In preaching, baptism, and the Lord's Supper, Jesus Christ is present through the Holy Spirit" (LA § 13). In what way is quickly said: as far as the Lord Supper is concerned, "in the Lord's Supper, the risen Jesus Christ imparts himself in his body and blood, given up for all, through his word of promise with bread and wine. He thus gives himself unreservedly to all those who receive the bread and wine; faith receives the Lord's Supper for salvation, unfaith for judgement" (LA § 18).

The manner of Christ's presence, a contentious issue that opposed Huldrych Zwingli and Martin Luther in Marburg in 1529, does not stand at the center of the formulation. Action verbs dominate, along with the linking of the acting word of promise with the elements, which is completed in the following paragraph by the gift realized "in the act of eating and drinking" (LA § 19). It is thus the sharing that is decisive and not the medium of this presence. The statement that Christ gives himself "to all those who receive" is to be understood more in the Lutheran sense of the *manducatio impiorum.*

With regard to Christology, the text states: "In the word of promise and in sacrament the Holy Spirit, and so God's self, makes the crucified and risen Jesus present to us" (LA § 21).

Could the Risen One mingle with the limits of human flesh when he is glorified? This contentious Reformed issue is given a pneumatological answer: it is through the Spirit that this presence is imparted, but it is the glorious body of the Crucified One that is meant (with Lutheran emphasis on the reality of incarnation). The joint assertion that Christ is "truly present" shifts the focus from the insistence on the elements to relational considerations.

On predestination the document reads that "in the Gospel we have the promise of the unconditional acceptance of the sinners by God. All who trust this promise can know that they are saved and praise God for their election. For this reason we can speak of election only with respect to the call to salvation in Christ" (LA § 24).

The predestination to damnation is therefore rejected (LA § 25), which is in line with the position of the contemporary Reformed churches that no longer accept this aspect of the Calvinist doctrine.

2.5 *Overcoming Doctrinal Condemnations and Sharing the Sacraments*

At every point in the Leuenberg Agreement, it is unequivocally stated that the condemnations no longer apply to the current doctrinal position (LA §§ 20, 23, 26, 27, 32): "The condemnations … are inapplicable to the doctrinal position. This does not mean that the condemnations pronounced by the Reformers are irrelevant; but they are no longer an obstacle to church fellowship" (LA § 27). Moreover, the remaining differences no longer separate the participating churches (LA § 28).

Consequently, these churches declare that "they accord each other table and pulpit fellowship; this includes the mutual recognition of ordination and the freedom to provide for intercelebration" (LA § 33).

It is thus not only a matter of engaging in Eucharistic hospitality but of allowing for the possibility of sharing a Lord's Supper according to another liturgy in one's own church, since the fullness of the proclaimed and celebrated gospel is recognized in it. This sharing, which necessitated a mutual familiarization, truly planted the seeds of a shared future between the churches of Leuenberg.

2.6 *Ministry*

Paragraph 33 associates the ministry, in the service of preaching and of the administration of the sacraments, with a lapidary formula stating that the participating churches mutually recognize the ordination to the ministry and are willing to welcome each other's pastors and parishioners. Not only is there no new ordination or consecration but a church may even employ a pastor from another member church of the CPCE. In the paragraph relating to the concrete realization of the communion, the text makes it quite clear that the Leuenberg Agreement does not modify "the rules in force in the churches with regard to the induction to a pastoral charge, the exercise of this ministry, and the organization of congregational life" (LA § 43). Certain churches may also ordain deacons, lay preachers, and biblical scholars in addition to pastors, without requiring the others to do so. However, in spite of the mutual recognition of the ordination in principle, it cannot be ruled out that the educational requirements may not be compatible. Accordingly, these topics are to be addressed in future theological debates.

Another difficulty has to do with the term "intercommunion," which is rarely used today, namely in the difference between intercelebration and intercommunion. Intercelebration (which is recommended in LA §33) is explained above with the word "concelebration": a pastor can celebrate in another church of the Leuenberg communion; it is not the same as intercommunion which is only reciprocal hospitality. It differs from the concelebration by two pastors, since a Reformed pastor may celebrate a liturgy in a Lutheran or Methodist worship service, or vice versa.

3 The Characteristics of Consensus

3.1 *A Sufficient Consensus that Includes Everything*

The Leuenberg Agreement defines a foundation that is solid and sufficient (*satis est*) to carry different positions with regard to doctrine and church praxis. It is not to be seen as a lowest common denominator or as a vague compromise. This consensus may be considered holistic because it touches on the entire spectrum of faith.

The text however does not specify that this focus on the gospel as recognized in preaching and in the sacraments is based on article 7 of the *Confessio Augustana*: "And to the true unity of the Church it is enough [*satis* est] to agree concerning the doctrine of the Gospel and the administration of the Sacraments."[13] While the formulation "it is enough" suggests that one is content with the minimum (and thus with a minimum consensus), the Latin *satis est* expresses the fullness: everything contained in it.

3.2 *A Differentiated/Differentiating Consensus*

In the second ecumenical generation since Vatican II, after having engaged in a comparative quest for convergences in doctrine, the bilateral ecumenical dialogues sought to ascertain the extent to which each church is able to recognize the basic truths that underlie the faith of other churches. The consensus supports the differences that remain in the expressions of this doctrine – hence the name given to this model, which was long referred to as a differentiated consensus but now tends to be known as a differentiating consensus.[14] André Birmelé defines it in the following manner: "Each statement, in its first chapter, reiterates the common understanding of the

13 The English text of the *Confessio Augustana* is available at <https://bookofconcord.org/augsburg-confession/> (accessed Jan 16, 2024).

14 Theodor Dieter advocates this second qualifier because it clearly indicates that the consensus embraces the differentiation of distinct doctrinal orientations, this diversity being considered an inherent aspect of the fundamental agreement, as long as nothing contradicts it. See Theodor Dieter, "Vom Projekt 'Lehrverurteilungen – kirchentrennend?' zur 'Gemeinsamen Erklärung zur Rechtfertigungslehre,'" in: André Birmelé & Wolfgang Thönissen, eds., *Auf dem Weg zur Gemeinschaft: 50 Jahre internationaler evangelisch–lutherisch/römisch-katholischer Dialog*, Leipzig/Paderborn, Evangelische Verlagsanstalt/Bonifatius, 2018, 119–141. The explanation is on page 132.

gospel. The differences that now remain are part of the unity. They are not only legitimate but an expression of the incarnation of the Church of Jesus Christ in situations that are different and thus require differentiated answers."[15]

The differentiations are encountered at various levels: between the message of the gospel and its culturally and historically determined expressions, which constitute the doctrine. On a second level, one might also add the differentiation between fundamental articles of faith and secondary statements. If the signatory churches of the Leuenberg Agreement consider that what binds them together is sufficient for the church union, it is not because they content themselves with it but because the gospel itself provides the incentive to establish and build their communion.

4 From Doctrinal Consensus to the Church Communion (*LA* §§ 29–49)

In the sense intended in this Agreement, church fellowship means that, on the basis of the consensus they have reached in their understanding of the gospel, churches with different confessional positions accord each other fellowship in word and sacrament and strive for the fullest possible cooperation in witness and service to the world (LA § 29).

As the document shows, the aim of the Leuenberg Agreement was to transform the relations among the churches, not only with respect to the conflicts of the past but also for the future. Accordingly, these paragraphs contain specific provisions for the concretization of the second stage of the Leuenberg Agreement: after having declared the church communion, it is now time to realize the communion of Protestant churches in Europe.

The challenge lies not only in the assertion that the churches concerned are "of different confessional positions" but in the fact that they remain so, since they are not united in an undifferentiated denomination and organization but together nonetheless they form one and the same ecclesial family: "The participating churches are convinced that together they participate in the one Church of Jesus Christ and that the Lord frees them for and calls them to common service." (LA § 34). They celebrate their faith together, bring each other their gifts, and commit themselves to the most credible common witness.

5 The Realization of the Communion: Worship and Life in the Regions

The fully committed communion is founded on preaching and the shared sacraments. According to the *Confessio Augustana*, what is sufficient (*satis est*) for the unity declared therein, and for the definition of the church, refers to the communion received in Christ, the gospel. It is received and manifests itself visibly and perceptibly in preaching (in the broad sense: witness) and in the shared sacraments delivered by the ministry.

5.1 *The Centrality of Worship*

Paragraphs from 30 to 34 recapitulate the commitment assumed by signing the Leuenberg Agreement.

The communion arising from worship was the first priority in order to overcome the separation of the churches, this communion being fostered by the sharing of the Lord's Supper, made possible by the lifting of the doctrinal condemnations. Contrary to the belief of the Catholic and Orthodox churches, for whom Eucharistic sharing only becomes possible upon finalization of the unity, these churches benefited from the sharing of the Lord's Supper, allowing them to experience the communion at the local and regional level.

As the *Confessio Augustana* had specified that the unity of the church did not require identical rites and ceremonies, liturgy had not been a source of contention in the 16th century, and the Leuenberg Agreement does not address it. Since the general assembly of the CPCE in Belfast in 2001, a collection of common hymns, "Colours of

15 Birmelé, *La communion ecclésiale*, 284.

Grace," has also been available, and the churches have taken to sharing their liturgical resources on their website.[16] The general assembly in Florence (2012) adopted a study of the current challenges facing worship in various contexts.[17] These joint liturgical developments represent much more than a mutual exchange of information, namely a new and henceforth shared theological tradition.

5.2 *A Realization Begun in the Regions*

Building on already existing partnerships and connections, the Leuenberg Agreement developed a vision that underlined the importance of the regions: "It is in the life of the churches and congregations that church communion becomes a reality" (LA § 35).

As early as the first general assembly in Sigtuna (1976), the leaderships of the participating churches encouraged the strengthening of the bonds of Lutheran/Reformed solidarity among minority churches, which often enjoyed closer ties due to the political realities of shared regional identities. With the progressive construction of Europe after the 1960s, the communion benefited from existing networks. In France, for example, the two Lutheran (Reformed Church of France and Evangelical Lutheran Church of France) and the two Reformed churches (Protestant Reformed Church of Alsace-Lorraine and the Protestant Church of the Augsburg Confession of Alsace-Lorraine) already engaged in close cooperation prior to the Leuenberg Agreement and had formed the CPLR, the cornerstone of their joint endeavors and of their broader ecumenical dialogues. In 2007, this council adopted the name Communion protestante luthéro-réformée, an outward sign and an instrument of the developments encouraged by the CPCE, whereas the FPF brings together a very large proportion of the French Protestant churches of all denominations without these being able to declare that they are in mutual communion. In Germany, where the regional churches are either Lutheran, Reformed, or United depending on the respective federal state, worshippers have had the possibility, since 1970, to join another territorial church without difficulty, while the Leuenberg Agreement allowed the EKD to define itself as a church encompassing a diversity of ecclesial expressions that are in communion with one another. In the countries of Eastern Europe, on the other hand, where historical and social conflicts have often separated the Lutheran and Reformed churches, new initiatives were necessary to bring about a rapprochement.

Regional groups were activated or created in order to provide for common guidelines and mutual adjustments in ecclesial resolutions.

The CCR, created in 1961 to forge bonds of peace between the peoples on both sides of the Rhine,[18] participated actively in the CPCE before officially becoming a regional group in 2008.

The CEPPLE, established in 1950 by the pastor Marc Boegner (then copresident of the WCC) in order to assist the very small Protestant churches of Southern Europe, became the fourth regional group of the CPCE in 2014.

The South East Europe Group was created in 1975 by Johannes Hanselmann, Lutheran bishop of Bavaria, in order to enable exchanges with the churches of the Eastern European countries. This group brings together 28 churches at regular gatherings attended by church leaders and theologians who prepare theological studies commissioned by the CPCE's executive committee.

The Leuenberg North West Group was founded in 1990 by Peter Beier, the president of the EKiR, shortly before he became president of the CPCE; it comprises delegates from Belgium, Alsace, Luxemburg, and the Rhineland.

The churches of the Rio de la Plata provide for their own coordination, as do the five Scandinavian

16 See <https://www.leuenberg.eu/topics/liturgy/> (last accessed Jul 1, 2024).

17 "Anchor in Time – Protestant Worship in Southern, Central and Eastern Europe between Continuity and Change," a German version of the text is available at <https://www.yumpu.com/de/document/view/21242709/bleibe-in-der-zeit-community-of-protestant-churches-in-europe> (last accessed Jul 8, 2024).

18 Marc Lienhard also served as president of the Lutheran Church in Alsace-Moselle and as president of the CCR.

churches, which have not all signed the Leuenberg Agreement.[19]

6 The Four Major Tasks

The Leuenberg Agreement specified four tasks to which the member churches were to apply themselves: witness and service (LA §§ 36); the continuing theological task (LA §§ 37–41); organizational consequences (LA §§ 42–45); ecumenical aspects (LA §§ 46–48).

We shall address them in a different order from that of the Leuerberg Agreement in order to avoid repetitions.[20] The ecumenical developments will be discussed in detail in the seventh section of this chapter, which is devoted to the reception of the Leuenberg Agreement.

6.1 *The Communion: a Loose Framework and the Need to Ensure the Sustainability of Decisions*

"This declaration of church communion does not predetermine provisions of church law on particular matters of inter-church relations or within individual churches. The churches will, however, take the Agreement into account in considering any such provisions" (LA § 42c).

The Leuenberg Agreement thus specifies that the respective law of the signatory churches takes precedence and that it does not strive for an "organic union" (LA § 44), as it wishes to avoid uniformization and the loss of the minority churches' freedom to make decisions (LA § 45).

An executive council chaired by three presidents and organized by a secretary general coordinates the guidelines agreed upon by the church delegates during the general assembly that convenes every five–six years. Eight assemblies have been held to date: Sigtuna (1976), Driebergen (1981), Strasbourg (1987), Vienna (1994), Belfast (2001), Budapest (2006), Florence (2012), and Basel (2018). The secretariat relocated from Strasbourg (from the Institute for Ecumenical Research, where it was directed by Martin Weyerstall) to Berlin (under the guidance of Dr. Wilhelm Hüffmeier, then president of the EKU) in 1987, then to Vienna in 2006, where Bishop Michael Bünker has handed over the directorship to pastor Mario Fischer.

Since the guidelines issued by the assemblies do not have the binding authority of the Leuenberg Agreement,[21] they rely on the synods and the church leadership. The possibility of a joint decision-making body (a European synod) was evoked at the general assembly of Belfast (2001) but met with resistance. Church leaders still struggle to overcome this difficulty, notably through joint meetings and mutual participations in church synods at the regional level. In 2006, the general assembly of Budapest approved statutes that granted the CPCE an independent legal status and improved its ability to issue common guidelines. Having become a council, the body that coordinated the work between the assemblies was reinforced through the addition of expert groups (now called advisory boards) on ethics (2007), ecumenism (2009), and, since the assembly of Florence, ecclesiology (2012).

6.2 *Joint Witness and Service*

"The preaching of the churches gains credibility in the world when they give a united witness to the Gospel. The Gospel liberates and links together the churches for common service. … The struggle for justice and peace in the world increasingly requires that the churches assume a common responsibility" (LA § 36a).

19 The Lutheran churches of Finland and Sweden are not among the signatories but participate in the theological and ecumenical work.

20 These points were summarized in 2014 in an interim report drafted for the general assembly of Basel, which convened in September 2018. The report, modified and approved in Basel, and entitled "Kirchengemeinschaft – Church Communion – Communion ecclésiale," is available in English at <https://www.leuenberg.eu/download/general-assembly-basel-2018/?wpdmdl=322&ind=1590132661734> (accessed Jan 16, 2024).

21 Translated from the German "verbindlich," which André Birmelé translates in French as "qui oblige" ("which obligates").

The formation of the CPCE was propitiously associated with comparable developments on Europe's path to reconciliation, where the same questions were being asked. The churches, which had a head start over the political institutions in this field, were already experienced in the work of reconciliation.[22]

It was starting from the general assembly of Belfast of 2001 that the churches demonstrated a greater awareness of political and social issues in order to bring forward "a Protestant voice in Europe."[23] A pastoral position is dedicated to the work with the European authorities in Brussels, in cooperation with the CEC. In addition to the regular interviewing of personalities linked to the CPCE, the secretariat published the trilingual journal *Focus* from 2007 to 2016. The presidium and the council draw up communiqués on current issues.

Since 2009, the CPCE has been linked to the AGDE, a working committee that coordinates the activities of the institutions that offer assistance to the diaspora of Protestant churches in Europe. The GAW funds support programs for scattered Protestant communities, even beyond Europe, in partnership with the CPCE.[24]

6.3 *The Continuing Theological Task*

> The common understanding of the gospel on which the church fellowship is based must be further deepened, examined in the light of the witness of Holy Scripture, and continually made relevant to a contemporary context.
>
> The churches are tasked with studying further the remaining doctrinal differences that persist within the participating churches and between them without being grounds for division. These include: hermeneutical questions concerning the understanding of scripture, the confession of faith, and Church; the relation between law and gospel; baptismal practice; ministry and ordination; the "two kingdoms" doctrine and the doctrine of the sovereignty of Christ; Church and society. Consideration also has to be given to newly emerging problems relating to witness and service, order and practice (LA §§ 38–39).

As the quote here highlights, the hallmark of the CPCE within the ecumenical movement is the quality of its theological studies.

The general assembly of Sigtuna decided to bring church theologians together for doctrinal conversations. The studies commissioned by the assemblies are developed in such groups and sent to all the churches, then reviewed on the basis of the latter's responses and submitted to the next general assembly for adoption. Although these doctrinal studies do not carry as much authority as the Leuenberg Agreement, they develop a common tradition and shared doctrinal positions in the face of the challenges of contemporary society and in dialogue with the other churches.[25]

---

22 Elisabeth Parmentier, "Grenzüberschreitungen für ein versöhntes Europa: Baustellen für die evangelischen Kirchen und ihre Theologie," in: Martin Friedrich, Hans Jürgen Luibl & Christine-Ruth Müller, eds., *Theologie für Europa: Perspektiven evangelischer Kirchen/Theology for Europe: Perspectives of Protestant Churches*, Frankfurt a.M., Lembeck, 2006, 69–80.

23 A notable achievement was the joint declaration of the CPCE and the CCR on the challenges of migration and asylum, which formulated what the churches had already expected from the European Union as early as 2004. This so-called Liebfrauenberg Declaration is available at <https://www.leuenberg.eu/download/miscellany/?wpdmdl=876&ind=1590133444192> (accessed Jan 16, 2024).

24 In its annual publication, GAW has published various articles relating to the CPCE, for instance, in 2016, on the Protestant diaspora and the implementation of the Leuenberg Agreement in the Protestant minority churches, see Wilhelm Hüffmeier & others, eds., *Die evangelische Diaspora: Die Verwirklichung der Leuenberger Konkordie in evangelischen Minderheitskirchen*, Leipzig, Gustav-Adolf-Werk, 2016. This volume contains the most up-to-date articles on the current situations in the various regions.

25 The studies can be consulted on www.leuenberg.net, where most of them can be downloaded; others were first published in the series Ökumenische Perspektiven, then in a German version (Leuenberger Texte).

6.3.1 The Articulation of the Two Kingdoms Doctrine and the Doctrine of the Lordship of Christ (1976–1981)

In 1976, the general assembly of Sigtuna commissioned a study on the articulation of the doctrine of the two kingdoms and of the lordship of Christ, which was adopted at Driebergen in 1981.[26] The aim of this study was to ascertain whether the Lutheran doctrine affirming the Christian freedom to belong to the kingdom of God while respecting the temporal authorities might potentially lead to a divisive conflict with the Reformed churches that proclaim the lordship of Christ in all areas of day-to-day life. As in the case of the Leuenberg Agreement, the study assessed whether the two doctrines could be mutually recognized as faithful expressions of the understanding of the gospel in the field of social and political commitments. The assembly adopted this study, which concluded that the difference did not run counter to the fundamental agreement that gave rise to the communion.[27]

6.3.2 "The Church of Jesus Christ" (1987–1994)

Adopted at the general assembly of Vienna in 1994, the text entitled "The Church of Jesus Christ: The Contribution of the Reformation towards Ecumenical Dialogue on Church Unity"[28] was the most important to date. This jointly adopted ecclesiological study, even if it carries less authority than the confessions of faith and catechisms of the churches themselves, reiterates their meaning and furnishes more explicit hermeneutical keys to the distinctions of the Leuenberg Agreement, both with regard to the shared declaration of communion and to its realization. The study develops a first in-depth reflection on the ministries that is equally as valuable for the member churches of the CPCE as for their partners in ecumenism.

Consisting of three chapters – "The Nature of the Church as the Community of Saints," "The Community of Saints in Today's Society," "The Unity of the Church and the Unification of the Church" –, the text draws distinctions that are typical of Reformation theology. It distinguishes between the "foundation," the "shape," and the "mission" of the church:

> The foundation of the church is God's action to save humankind … in Jesus Christ. In this fundamental action God himself is the subject, and consequently the church is an object of faith. Since the church is a community of believers the shape of the church has taken various historical forms. The one church of faith (singular) is present in a hidden manner in churches (plural) shaped in different ways. The mission of the church is its task to witness before all humankind to the gospel of the coming of the Kingdom of God in word and action.[29]

The issue at stake here is the distinction between God's work, this being the "event" of salvation from which the church lives, and its own task. Its origin and its foundation are beyond its reach.[30] The church celebrates this work of God by offering that from which it lives: the preaching and the sacraments that constitute it – hence the insistence on a definition of the church that does not

26 The report of the general assembly of Sigtuna in German is published in: Marc Lienhard, ed., *Zeugnis und Dienst reformatorischer Kirchen im Europa der Gegenwart*, Ökumenische Perspektiven 8, Frankfurt a.M., Lembeck, 1977. The report of Driebergen in German is published in: André Birmelé, ed., *Konkordie und Kirchengemeinschaft reformatorischer Kirchen im Europa der Gegenwart: Texte der Konferenz von Driebergen/Niederlande (18. bis 24. Februar 1981)*, Ökumenische Perspektiven 10, Frankfurt a.M., Lembeck, 1982, 108–114.

27 Wilhelm Hüffmeier, ed., *Evangelische Texte zur ethischen Urteilsfindung/Protestant texts on ethical decision-making*, Leuenberger Texte 3, Frankfurt a.M., Lembeck, 1997.

28 "The Church of Jesus Christ: The Contribution of the Reformation towards Ecumenical Dialogue on Church Unity," May 9, 1994, English text available at <http://www.reformiert-online.net/agora2/docs/309.pdf> (accessed Jan 16, 2024).

29 "The Church of Jesus Christ," 7.

30 "The Church of Jesus Christ," 7.

expound what it does but what it benefits from.[31] Its mission is to witness, not to maintain itself. Its shape is in the service of this witnessing: "The visible church, in fact, has the task of witnessing in its shapes and forms to its original nature."[32] The visible church is not fully identified with the invisible church, but the latter expresses itself through the visible reality. In the same vein, the text does not wish to separate witness and service (or worship and *diakonia*), which derive from the same mission. Moreover, this mission requires ministries,[33] to which numerous pages were devoted, but they will be examined later. The text then proceeds to develop the dimensions of the Christian mission: worship, witness, service, and communion. A second part analyzes the challenges in today's pluralistic society, then expounds the model of unity, the meaning of consensus, and the status of difference. Unity is understood in the same way as the church: as the gift of the communion in Christ.

Certain churches, such as those of Norway and Denmark, were able to sign the Leuenberg Agreement only after their questions had been answered by this text. This document was also of great value in the agreements with the Anglican churches.

6.3.3 "Church and Israel" (1994–2001)

After adopting the study on the church, the general assembly of Vienna took yet another step, albeit toward its origins: how can the church consider itself the people of God without giving further thought to the chosen people? A study on the church and the people of Israel was an indispensable necessity in order to promote mutual trust. "Church and Israel: A Contribution from the Reformation Churches in Europe to the Relationship between Christians and Jews"[34] was the first study shared by Reformation churches of different European countries, which did not have the same relationship with Judaism, due in particular to the modern State of Israel. The new approaches formulated in the text represent groundbreaking achievements: the churches will refrain from asserting that Christianity is the completion and fulfillment of Judaism and that the aim is to convert people of Jewish faith. The term "people of God" can be mutually recognized, as the election of the Jewish people and of the church calls on both to convert to God. The ways of salvation are not viewed as two parallel ways, or as an exclusively Christian way, but as a common salvation that does not imply a unity of the two peoples.[35] The text offers practical possibilities to move beyond stereotypes and distorted portrayals of each other.[36] The conclusion apologizes for 20 centuries of Christian animosity and for the coresponsibility in the rejection and false interpretation of biblical texts.[37]

6.3.4 The Missional Challenges (2001–2006)

Between Belfast and Budapest, the churches of the CPCE, being well aware of the declining membership of the historical churches in Europe and of their weakness in the transmission of faith, developed a set of non-proselytizing missional guidelines – hence the title of the corresponding study, "Evangelising – Protestant Perspectives for the Churches in Europe,"[38] which was prepared by the Leuenberg North West Group as a forward-looking position paper and not as a doctrinal study. Its

---

31 "The Church of Jesus Christ," 8.

32 "The Church of Jesus Christ," 10.

33 "The Church of Jesus Christ," 13.

34 "Church and Israel: A Contribution from the Reformation Churches in Europe to the Relationship between Christians and Jews," Jun 24, 2001, English text available at <https://www.jcrelations.net/fr/article/church-and-israel-a-contribution-from-the-reformation-churches-in-europe-to-the-relationship-between-christians-and-jews.pdf> (accessed Jan 16, 2024). In this context, Israel does not refer to the political reality of the country but to Judaism.

35 "Church and Israel," 22.

36 "Church and Israel," 33.

37 "Church and Israel," 37.

38 "Evangelising – Protestant Perspectives for the Churches in Europe," September 2006, English text available at <https://www.leuenberg.eu/download/general-assemblies-up-to-2012/?wpdmdl=2045&ind=1602669442195> (accessed Jan 16, 2024).

diffusion was hampered by too much confidentiality, in spite of the fact that it announced social and ecclesial changes as early as 2006.

Belfast also commissioned an agenda for the life of the church communion, "The Shape and Shaping of Protestant Churches in a Changing Europe,"[39] which seeks to promote exchanges and to strengthen the communion through guidelines of mutual responsibility and the acceptance of mutual inquiries and corrections. At the same time, the South East Europe Group submitted the agenda "Shaping the Church, Gaining the Future,"[40] which supplemented the preceding one by offering guidelines for strengthening the bonds of communion without adding to the complexity of its structure.

6.3.5 Baptism and the Lord's Supper (1981–1987)

With regard to baptism, the Leuenberg Agreement appears to contradict itself, since paragraph 14 presents its characteristics as an integral part of the fundamental agreement, in a formulation that does not distinguish between confessing baptism and baptism as a gift of grace. Yet in paragraph 39, "baptismal practice" is listed among the theological topics that are in need of further study. Sacramental communion requires a deeper understanding of the praxis. A regional study was thus projected in 1981 at Driebergen and presented at the general assembly of Strasbourg in 1987, but not adopted. It was not until the assembly of Vienna in 1994 that the study on baptism and the Lord's Supper was finally adopted.[41]

This text employs the term "sacrament" as visible word, parallel to the audible word of preaching, but also "sign" or "sacramental sign." Baptism and the Lord's supper are events of the justification, of the reconciliation and communion in Christ. Concerning baptism, the text highlights the gift of the Holy Spirit and articulates promise and faith ("is simultaneously a gift of God and a human response").[42] Particular importance is attached to the link between baptism, the Lord's Supper, and the church (which is also found in LA § 14): "Thus baptism results in being incorporated into the community of believers. ... Baptism establishes and seals alliance to the universal and apostolic Church. ... This is made concrete by membership in one single congregation and church,"[43] while the person who has received the baptism is also called upon to bear witness to her/his faith, as s/he forms the basis of the universal priesthood.

With regard to the Lord's Supper, the text pays particular attention to the meal of joy and to eschatological hope, while not obscuring the importance of the forgiveness of sins and of repentance. The perspective is not individualistic but concerns the church communion: "In the Lord's Supper the Church becomes visible as communion. At the same time each eucharistic celebration is the sign, remembrance and challenge of the fact that the received gift stands in the communion of all believers and in the solidarity with the world to which God's redemptive will is addressed."[44] Eucharistic hospitality is recommended but the presidency must be linked to an explicit mandate from the church and the celebration must emphasize the bond with all churches.[45]

39 "The Shape and Shaping of Protestant Churches in a Changing Europe," Apr 7, 2006, English text available at <https://www.leuenberg.eu/download/general-assemblies-up-to-2012/?wpdmdl=2045&ind=1602669450744> (accessed Jan 16, 2024).

40 "Shaping the Church, Gaining the Future," Oct 5, 2005, English text available at <https://www.leuenberg.eu/download/general-assemblies-up-to-2012/?wpdmdl=2045&ind=1602669452387> (accessed Jan 16, 2024).

41 "On the Doctrine and Practice of Baptism" and "On the Doctrine and Practice of the Lord's Supper," in: Wilhelm Hüffmeier, ed., *Sakramente, Amt, Ordination / Sacraments, Ministry, Ordination*, Leuenberger Texte 2, Frankfurt a.M., Lembeck, 1995, 7–14 and 15–24; the English text is available at <https://www.leuenberg.eu/download/leuenberg-texts/?wpdmdl=911&ind=1590132396292> (accessed Jan 16, 2024).

42 "On the Doctrine and Practice of Baptism," 8.

43 "On the Doctrine and Practice of Baptism," 10.

44 "On the Doctrine and Practice of the Lord's Supper," 18.

45 "On the Doctrine and Practice of the Lord's Supper," 18.

The text also raises the question of praxis: welcoming children is possible and left to the discretion of the churches. Allowing non-baptized persons to partake of the Lord's Supper, on the other hand, is not normally possible; the prerequisite of baptism should be pointed out, but without coercion. The same question is also raised with regard to those who have formally left the church: the event of baptism itself is not repealed, and the church has an ongoing pastoral responsibility for those who have left the community.[46]

The debate on baptism and its relevance for the entire process of baptismal life was taken up again at a later date in the CPCE, this time in the context of a dialogue with the churches of the EBF.[47]

6.3.6 Scripture, Confession, Church

A document of major importance concerns Scripture and the confessions of faith. While not in itself a divisive issue, the Leuenberg Agreement includes it in its list of theological topics that require further study. The presence of evangelical-type churches among the Protestant minorities made it necessary to address the question of interpretation methods, particularly the rejection of the historical-critical method. The relinquishing of confessions of faith by certain Reformed churches made theological clarification a perilous undertaking, since culture imposes its criteria more easily than the Bible. What is the meaning of *sola scriptura* in this case? And what authority can ancient texts still have in the face of current reality? In an age marked by the fear of religious fanaticism or fundamentalistic readings, the general assembly of Budapest (2006) mandated a doctrinal conversation group to prepare a study on the topic "scripture, confession, church." This text expounds the current issues: fundamentalistic tendencies, radicalizations, or the relativization of biblical statements, problems related to preaching and the confessions of faith. Adopted in Florence in 2012, it is intended to allow for further discussions within each member church.[48]

6.3.7 Ministry or Ministries? (1987–2012)

Ministry and ordination had already been mentioned among the topics that required further study. The general assembly of Driebergen had cast aside all divisive aspects of the ministry of the proclamation of the gospel and the administration of the sacraments, which form the basis of the communion. All churches agreed to recognize that its institution is fundamental, but that the forms through which it is expressed may differ depending on the context. The general assembly of Sigtuna commissioned a study to determine how far the diversity endorsed by the fundamental agreement could go.

The general assembly of Strasbourg adopted the Neuendettelsau Theses (1982–1986).[49] These define the consensus on ministry and ordination, the understanding and the structure of the ministries, the meaning and the practice of ordination, and the "service of *episkopé*." They were supplemented by the Tampere Theses (1986),[50] which were integrated into the "Church of Jesus Christ."

---

46 "On the Doctrine and Practice of Baptism," 10.

47 See Wilhelm Hüffmeier & Tony Peck, eds., *Dialog mit der Europäischen Baptischischen Föderation (EBF) und der Gemeinschaft Evangelischer Kirchen in Europa (GEKE) zur Lehre und Praxis der Taufe/Dialogue between the Community of Protestant Churches in Europe (CPCE) and the European Baptist Federation (EBF) on the Doctrine and Practice of Baptism*, Leuenberger Texte 9, Frankfurt a.M., Lembeck, 2005.

48 Michael Bünker, ed., *Schrift – Bekenntnis – Kirche/ Scripture – Confession – Church*, Leipzig, Evangelische Verlagsanstalt, 2013.

49 "Amt-Ämter-Dienste-Ordination (Neuendettelsau-Thesen)/Ministry-Ministries-Services-Ordination (Neuendettelsau Theses)," in Hüffmeier, ed., *Sakramente, Amt, Ordination*, 25–27. The report of Strasbourg in German is published in: André Birmelé, ed., *Konkordie und Ökumene: Die Leuenberger Kirchengemeinschaft in der gegenwärtigen ökumenischen Situation*, Frankfurt a.M., Lembeck, 1988, 64–66.

50 "Thesen zur Amtsdiskussion heute (Tampere-Thesen)/ Theses on the Current Discussion about Ministry (Tampere Theses)," in: Hüffmeier, ed., *Sakramente, Amt, Ordination*, 117–120.

The first thesis, "Word-Church-Ministry," specifies that the churches from both traditions "concur that 'the ordained ministry' belongs to the being of the church." However, "the ordained ministry in itself alone does not guarantee the true being of the church but remains subordinate to the word of God." Moreover, the responsibility for preaching and for the sacraments lies with "the whole congregation."[51]

The second thesis, "General Priesthood-Ordained Ministry," describes the priesthood (witness) of the believers and the ministry as mutually dependent. The ministry "rests upon a particular commission of Christ," but stands together with the congregation "under the word of God."[52]

The third thesis, "The Service of Leadership (episkopé)-Ecumenical Perspectives," emphasizes that the Lutheran, Reformed, and United churches do indeed have a ministry of *episkopé* both in the individual congregation and at the supra-regional level, but that this responsibility "does not only fall to the ordained ministry" but is assumed hand in hand with the other services (notably the synod, which consists largely of laypeople). This service of *episkopé* is to be understood "as a service of the word for the unity of the church"; furthermore, "no single historically-derived form of church leadership and ministerial structure should or can be laid down as a prior condition for fellowship and mutual recognition."[53]

The theses arrive at a "fundamental consensus" that emphasizes the priesthood of all believers in witness and service while stressing the need for a "structured ministry" in which the ministry conferred through ordination would partake.[54] The ministries assume various forms that are determined by the respective mission (which, in these churches, includes Bible scholars, evangelists, preachers). The (historical) episcopal ministry is conceived as a sign of the visible unity, although the ministry and the *episkopé* cannot in themselves alone guarantee the true being of the church.

The different ways of organizing the life and action of the churches (of which the *episkopé* is a part) "do not refer to the foundation but to the shape of the church."[55] Thus, different structures of ecclesial authority and different manners of organizing the ministries do not stand in the way of communion because they do not concern the being of the church. However, diversity is also clearly limited by the sovereignty of the gospel.

In 2006, the general assembly of Budapest mandated a group to follow up on the topic "Ministry, Ordination and Episkopé," in a study adopted by the general assembly of Florence in 2012.[56]

Paragraph 76 directly takes up the thread of the Tampere theses: "In a broader sense, and corresponding with former documents of the CPCE, the understanding of episkopé emphasises the tasks of pastoral oversight as well as spiritual leadership and governance within the church."[57] Regardless of whether this *episkopé* is exercised by personal or collegial ministries, all the churches of the CPCE link it to synods: "This reflects the fact that the 'order of ministries' (cf. nos. 38seqq.), instituted to serve the ministry of all Christians, is broader than the ministry of word and sacraments."[58] The final recommendations include a strong statement in favor of opening the pastoral ministry to women.[59]

51 "Thesen zur Amtsdiskussion heute (Tampere-Thesen)," 118.

52 "Thesen zur Amtsdiskussion heute (Tampere-Thesen)," 118.

53 "Thesen zur Amtsdiskussion heute (Tampere-Thesen)," 119.

54 "The Church of Jesus Christ," 117.

55 "The Church of Jesus Christ," 117.

56 Michael Bünker & Martin Friedrich, eds., *Amt, Ordination, Episkopé und theologische Ausbildung/Ministry, Ordination, Episkopé and Theological Education*, Leipzig, Evangelische Verlagsanstalt, 2013.

57 Bünker & Friedrich, eds., *Amt, Ordination, Episkopé*, 61.

58 Bünker & Friedrich, eds., *Amt, Ordination, Episkopé*, 61.

59 Only the Lutheran Church of Latvia and the Sub-Carpathian Reformed Church no longer ordain women after having previously done so. The Lutheran Church of Poland has so far never authorized the ordination of women. But as signatories of the Leuenberg Agreement, they cannot refuse to recognize the ordination and the pastoral ministry of female theologians from the other churches of the CPCE.

A novelty is the encouragement to find a common policy for the requests of homosexual persons wishing to receive ordination. The reiterated goal is "unity in reconciled diversity."[60]

In parallel to study of doctrine, the interchangeability of pastors between the member churches also necessitated international consultations in order to harmonize the training requirements for the ordained ministry.[61]

6.3.8 Ethics: Christian Faith and Freedom (1987–1994) and Law and Gospel (1994–2001)

Taking the message of justification as its starting point, the first ethical study asks what Christian freedom means in the life of the world. A more delicate question is the relationship between law and gospel: if the Reformation insists on the centrality of the gospel that liberates, how can this be reconciled with the affirmation of the law that demands? Luther, in a Pauline manner, accords preference to the gospel, whereas John Calvin (and later John Wesley), with his insistence on election and sanctification, expounds the importance of the law.[62] The CPCE sought to ascertain whether these categories allowed for ethical decision-making. In 2001, well before the current ethical debates, the general assembly of Belfast instructed the churches to pursue the difficult quest in search of criteria for ethical decision-making from a Protestant point of view, based on the study of the law and the gospel. The study proved a long and arduous task, and was unable to furnish real answers.[63] Contemporary events showed that this priority had been justified, even though all faith-based organizations are confronted with these challenges and have published comparable studies of their own, albeit without really being able to solve the conflicts.

Today, the debates on bioethics, sexual ethics, and migrations divide societies and churches alike. Several studies on issues of ethical relevance have been adopted and shared by the general assemblies, notably on questions pertaining to end-of-life decisions and the care for the dying, but also on the ethics of reproductive medicine.[64] These discussions reveal the importance of the link to cultures.

6.4 *Socio-Historical Identities and Their Implications for the Communion*

The fourth aspect of the results of the Leuenberg Agreement, the "responsibility to promote the ecumenical communion of all Christian churches" (LA § 46), will be addressed in the next section. Here, we shall only consider the implications of socio-historical identities. The CPCE had placed the focus on doctrinal debates, with almost no consideration of historical and cultural identities. After the fall of the Berlin Wall in 1989, the South East Europe Group conducted a study on socio-political changes in Central and Eastern Europe as well as on nationalist conflicts. The study on church, people, state, and nation, was adopted in 2001 at Belfast.[65]

---

60 Bünker & Friedrich, eds., *Amt, Ordination, Episkopé*, 65.

61 Documented by Michael Beintker, "Perspektiven für die Aus- und Fortbildung von evangelischen Pfarrerinnen und Pfarrern in Europa. Zum Stand der Diskussion in der GEKE," in: Hüffmeier & others, eds., *Die evangelische Diaspora*, 66–72.

62 Wilhelm Hüffmeier, ed., *Das christliche Zeugnis von der Freiheit/The Christian Witness on Freedom*, Leuenberg Texts 5, Frankfurt a.M., Lembeck, 1999, 125–126.

63 Michael Bünker & Martin Friedrich, eds., *Law and Gospel – A Study, also with Reference to Decision-Making in ethical Questions*, Leuenberger Texte 10, Frankfurt a.M., Lembeck, 2007.

64 See the report of the CPCE "A Time to Live, and a Time to Die: An Aid to Orientation of the CPCE Council on Death-hastening Decisions and Caring for the Dying," available at <https://www.leuenberg.eu/download/ethics/?wpdmdl=860&ind=1590133164855> (accessed Jan 16, 2024) and CPCE, ed., *"Before I formed you in the Womb …": A Guide to the Ethics of the Reproductive Medicine from the Council of the Community of Protestant Churches in Europe*, Munich, Evangelischer Presseverband, 2017.

65 Wilhelm Hüffmeier, ed., *Kirche-Volk-Staat-Nation: Ein Beitrag zu einem schwierigen Verhältnis/Church, People, State, Nation: A Contribution to a Difficult Relationship*, Leuenberg Texts 7, Frankfurt a.M., Lembeck 2002.

The text shows to what extent the confessional identities were forged by territorial conflicts and proposes criteria for avoiding such constellations, notably by distinguishing between "possibilities of identification" (language, culture, religion) and "identity,"[66] which is not limited to one's belonging to a people or one's nationality. Two publications captured the experiences of the CPCE churches with respect to their identities in historical contexts: *Evangelisch in Europa* and *Theologie für Europa*.[67] Confessional identities are both a source of pride in diaspora situations and a hindrance to European and ecumenical work.

This led the CPCE to reflect on methods of reconciliation that would be more sensitive to identity-related obstacles. A narrative method was tested from the 2000s: "Healing of Memories," a joint program of the CPCE, the CEC, and the GAW from 2005 onward,[68] in Romania. The churches, supported by the expertise of the universities, revisited the stereotypes of "the other," the foundational narratives, and the readings of history. The same method was applied by the CCR, in collaboration with the ACK, on both sides of the Franco-German border and documented in a joint publication in 2013.[69]

These methods permit a better assessment of the historical, social, and economic realities without renouncing the doctrinal consensus.

7 The Reception and the Responsibility to Promote the Ecumenical "Communion of all Christian Churches"

The term "reception" refers to the manner in which the signatory churches appropriated the Leuenberg Agreement, how they assign it authority in the realization of church communion, and how they mediate its benefits in their own contexts: "Reception is a process in which a church or a church tradition appropriates a truth that does not derive from itself, but which it recognizes and receives as a formulation of faith."[70] The main aspects have already been described in the preceding section, with the exception of the ecumenical reception, the fourth task mentioned in the Leuenberg Agreement: "In establishing and realizing church fellowship among themselves, the participating churches do so as part of their responsibility to promote the ecumenical fellowship of all Christian churches" (LA § 46d).

These churches strive to establish relations with several different types of partners.

According to paragraph 47, "they hope that the overcoming of their previous separation will influence churches in Europe and elsewhere who are related to them confessionally. They are ready to examine with them the possibilities of wider church fellowship."

Paragraph 48 evokes the relations between the LWF and the WARC, which have in the meantime become global communions.

Paragraph 49 addresses the relationship with other confessions: "They also hope that the church fellowship will provide a fresh stimulus to encounter and collaboration with churches of other confessions. They affirm their readiness to set their doctrinal conversations within this wider context."

66 Hüffmeier, ed., *Kirche-Volk-Staat-Nation*, 144.

67 Wilhelm Hüffmeier & Udo Hahn, eds., *Evangelisch in Europa: 30 Jahre Leuenberger Kirchengemeinschaft/Being Protestant in Europe: 30 Years of the Leuenberg Church Fellowship/Être Protestant en Europe: 30 ans de la Communion ecclésiale de Leuenberg*, Frankfurt a.M., Lembeck, 2003; Friedrich, Luibl & Müller, eds., *Theologie für Europa*.

68 Dieter Brandes, "Versöhnung der Konfessionen in Europa," in: Hüffmeier & Friedrich, eds., *Gemeinschaft gestalten*, 250–254.

69 Klaus Blümlein & others, eds., *Kirchengeschichte am Oberrhein: Ökumenisch und grenzüberschreitend*, Ubstadt-Weiher, Verlag regionalkultur, 2013.

70 "Kirchengemeinschaft – Church Communion – Communion ecclésiale," 20.

7.1 *The Reception in the Confessionally Related Churches*

The reception of the Leuenberg Agreement could not impose itself in the churches because synods retained autonomy in their decisions. Only the quality and the pertinence of the agreement, as well as its implementation in the regions, would prove fruitful and enduring.

7.1.1 The Controversy over the Authority of the Leuenberg Agreement

A major debate focused on the authority of the Leuenberg Agreement, which states that it cannot be regarded as a new confession of faith (LA § 37) since it unites churches that maintain the authority of their respective texts. Nonetheless, these identities find themselves modified through mutual recognition, bonds of communion, and joint witness. These bonds were viewed favorably in countries where preexisting partnerships were only too eager to receive official confirmation (Germany, France, Switzerland, Italy). However, the great diversity of local situations led to different types of criticism.

7.1.2 The Ambiguities of the Method Employed by the Text

A major criticism of this method came from the ranks of the Protestants themselves: the Finnish theologian Tuomo Mannermaa saw it as a minimalist consensus[71] that only affirms the agreement over the common understanding of the gospel and allows for the lifting of the doctrinal condemnations, without going more deeply into questions pertaining to Christology, predestination, and the Lord's Supper.

In fact, the Leuenberg Agreement had no intention of initiating a unification process; its hermeneutical method was based on article 7 of the *Confessio Augustana*, even if the latter is only implicitly alluded to in the text. Moreover, it only touched upon the contentious issues, albeit without pretending to be exhaustive. It thus proved necessary to expand on the topic of ecclesiology, notably in "The Church of Jesus Christ."

The Finnish theologian Simo Peura deplores the lack of clarity in the method, as the Leuenberg Agreement lays out a dual hermeneutical framework: the distinction between the message and its doctrinal expressions, and the distinction between the core agreement and what it can bear.[72] In the author's opinion, this ambivalence means that it is perilous to seek the consensus in the analysis of the contents, which explains why the discussion about the interpretation of the Lord's Supper remains ambiguous.[73]

7.1.3 A Protestant Bloc?

The signing of the Leuenberg Agreement by a first sizable group of churches did not dispel the fears of other related churches. The Scandinavian churches, which exist in closer proximity to Orthodox and Anglican churches, did not see any point in doing so. Minority churches feared assimilation and the loss of their identity, despite the assurances of the Leuenberg Agreement that the communion would under no circumstances lead to uniformization and to the loss of the minority churches' freedom of decision (LA § 45). In addition, the German churches were suspected of dominating the CPCE because of their logistical and financial involvement.

A point of criticism raised after 2003 pertained to the characterization of churches as Protestant, which, as we have already seen, had been chosen

71 Tuomo Mannermaa, *Von Preussen nach Leuenberg: Hintergrund und Entwicklung der theologischen Methode der Leuenberger Konkordie*, Hamburg, Lutherisches Verlagshaus, 1981.

72 Simo Peura, "Leuenberg und die ökumenische Methode der Gemeinsamen Erklärung zur Rechtfertigungslehre," in: Jari Jolkkonen, ed., *Unitas Visibilis: Studia Oecumenica in Honorem Eero Huovinen Episcopi Helsingiensis*, Helsinki, Luther-Agricola Gesellschaft, 2004, 174–194, esp. 178.

73 Another family of churches rejected the Leuenberg Agreement by considering it a "minimal consensus": the European branch of the SELK (issued from the Missouri Synod), which regards the Book of Concord of 1580 as the sole doctrinal interpretation.

to translate the German adjective *evangelisch*, and which the churches that were more oriented to ecumenical fellowship with the other Christian churches viewed as inappropriate due to its connotations of competition. It was also feared that the Leuenberg Agreement would lead to the creation of a Protestant bloc that was more concerned with the number of member churches than with their theological consensus, and that minority churches or those that had survived persecution would look to it as a counterforce to the Catholic Church.[74]

7.1.4 Eurocentrism

As we have seen, the earliest signatories of the Leuenberg Agreement also included the Evangelical Church of the River Plate (Argentina, Uruguay, Paraguay) and the Waldensian Church of the River Plate Reformed Church in Argentina, which subsequently enlisted the participation of the local Evangelical Methodist Church of Argentina and of the United Evangelical Lutheran Church of Argentina. A representative regularly took part in the general assemblies. After 2003, however, they felt disavowed by the change of name, which placed Europe at the center. The CPCE encouraged them to form a regional group, but their ecclesial context is strongly influenced by the Missouri Synod, which excludes any church communion with Reformed churches. The CPCE nevertheless continues to cultivate this bond, with the result that the Evangelical Lutheran Church in Ecuador joined the CPCE at the general assembly of Florence in 2012.[75]

7.1.5 The Deficiencies of the Model of Communion

The Scandinavian churches of Iceland, Denmark, Sweden, and Finland, which were involved in the theological work, wished to delve deeper into the issue of the ministry. In 1992, while still unwilling to sign the Leuenberg Agreement, they concluded the Porvoo Common Statement with the Anglican churches in the concerned regions. As we shall see below, this statement emphasizes the ministry of unity of the *episkopé* that attests and lends visibility to the altar and pulpit fellowship. While the Leuenberg Agreement seeks to establish the communion by means of structures, the Porvoo Common Statement insists on the sign of the *episkopé* as the visible bond of unity. Was this declaration compatible with the Leuenberg Agreement? A broad consultation held in 1995 led to the conclusion that the agreements were indeed compatible, as each had been drafted in a specific context.[76] The Porvoo Common Statement, which brings together Reformation churches that have all maintained an episcopal system in their historic sees, does not seek to extend this requirement to other contexts and thus does not relativize the structural liberty conceded to the local churches under the terms of the Leuenberg Agreement. Conversely, the churches linked by the Leuenberg Agreement became increasingly preoccupied with the necessity of formulating binding ties for the communion.

On Nov 19, 1999, the Church of Norway signed the Leuenberg Agreement – while also emphasizing the importance of the ministry of *episkopé* for

74 This criticism of the Protestant bloc is evoked in the 1984 memorandum "Reformation Churches and the Ecumenical Movement," in: Erich Geldbach, ed., *Ökumene in Gegensätzen*, Göttingen, Vandenhoeck & Ruprecht, 1987, 184–230.

75 See Wilhelm Hüffmeier, "Genug und doch zu wenig? Die Leuenberger Konkordie in der Kritik," in Wilhelm Hüffmeier & others, eds., *Die evangelische Diaspora*, 40–42.

76 Wilhelm Hüffmeier & Colin Podmore, eds., *Leuenberg, Meissen and Porvoo: Consultation between the Churches of the Leuenberg Church Fellowship and the Churches involved in the Meissen Agreement and the Porvoo Agreement/Leuenberg, Meissen und Porvoo Konsultation zwischen den Kirchen der Leuenberger Kirchengemeinschaft und den an der Meissener Erklärung und der Porvoo-Erklärung beteiligten Kirchen*, Leuenberger Texte 4, Frankfurt a.M., Lembeck, 1996 document a consultation between the churches involved in the agreements of Leuenberg, Meissen, and Porvoo (held at Liebfrauenberg, Sep 6–10, 1995).

the visibility of the communion in the protocol of agreement. The Lutheran Church of Denmark, which was also a signatory of the Porvoo Common Statement, signed the Leuenberg Agreement on May 13, 2001. The Lutheran Church of Iceland, also signatory of Porvoo, signed the Leuenberg Agreement on July 2, 2020. The "Church of Jesus Christ" served as the basis for this commitment.

7.2 *The Joining of the Confessional Churches: the Methodist Churches*

The entry of the Methodist churches into the CPCE modified the distinction between historic churches and confessing churches. The method was innovative: these churches did not become participants in the church communion through the Leuenberg Agreement but on the basis of a declaration that stated their concerns regarding the issue of sanctification, along with the common understanding of baptism as a confessing response of the believers and as a gift of grace.[77] This declaration was adopted at the general assembly of Vienna in 1994 and sent to the different Methodist churches of Europe for signing.[78] Seven Methodist churches and church unions have become members of the CPCE since 1998.

7.3 *The Dialogues with Protestant Churches That Do Not Subscribe to the Agreement on the Sacraments: the Baptist Churches*

Since the general assembly of Vienna, the CPCE has been engaging in cooperative work with the Baptist churches in Europe. A local mutual recognition already existed among the Waldensian, Baptist, and Methodist churches in Italy (1990).[79] The text specified that owing to what they already held in common, "in spite of the gravity and importance of this problem (baptism), it does not constitute an obstacle to full communion between our churches" (§ 3.8). Indeed, the theological foundation is common to them all, in particular the relationship to the confession of faith (§ 3.9). Moreover, the New Testament assigns greater importance to the fruits of baptism than to its form (§ 3.10).

After 1999, the CPCE, in collaboration with the EBF, explored the possibility of a mutual recognition of baptism, as well as of a statute linking these churches to the CPCE, and succeeded in establishing the text of a corresponding agreement.[80] This agreement endorses the statements of the Leuenberg Agreement up to paragraph 12. It does not polarize between confessing baptism and baptism as a gift of grace, but considers the whole path of initiation to Christian life, the baptismal dynamism, rather than a single act. The Baptists assure that instead of rebaptism, a personal declaration of faith can confirm the previously received baptism (IV, § 11), while the churches of the CPCE pledge not to celebrate baptism without insisting on faith (IV, § 12). These churches mutually recognize that they participate in the one Church of Jesus Christ, joined together by the Holy Spirit, the unity of which is given as the body of Christ and not through baptism itself (III, § 3).[81]

77 This path had already been opened by the globally conducted dialogues with the Lutheran churches (1984) and the Reformed churches (1987), which had come to conclusion that nothing stood in the way of certain forms of communion whenever the churches were ready.

78 See "Leuenberger Kirchengemeinschaft."

79 "Documento sul reciproco riconoscimento fra chiese battiste metodiste valdesi in Italia," italian text available at <https://chiesavaldese.org/wp-content/uploads/2023/01/doc_recipr_riconoscim.pdf> (last accessed Jul 8, 2024).

80 "The Beginning of the Christian Life and the Nature of the Church/Der Anfang des christlichen Lebens und das Wesen der Kirche Ergebnisse des Dialoges zwischen EBF und GEKE," in: Wilhelm Hüffmeier & Tony Peck, eds., *Dialog zwischen der Europäischen Baptistischen Föderation (EBF) und der Gemeinschaft Evangelischer Kirchen in Europa (GEKE) zur Lehre und Praxis der Taufe/Dialogue between the Community of Protestant Churches in Europe (CPCE) and the European Baptist Federation (EBF) on the Doctrine and Practice of Baptism*, Leuenberger Texte 9, Frankfurt a.M., 2005, 9–51.

81 The text of this mutual commitment with the Baptist Federation is published in Michael Bünker & Bernd Jaeger, eds., *Frei für die Zukunft. Evangelische Kirchen*

As far as their response is concerned, however, at a broader European level the Baptist churches cannot agree on a joint decision, so that their approval remains uncertain. A cooperation between the churches of the EBF and the CPCE was ratified at the general assembly of Florence in 2012.

7.4 *Twin Declarations on Other Continents: A Formula of Agreement and the Amman Declaration*

The Leuenberg Agreement inspired two agreements in other continents.

First of all, in 1997, following a series of dialogues that had begun as early as 1962, the declaration known as "A Formula of Agreement" established full communion between the ELCA, the American Presbyterian Church (USA), the Reformed Church in America and the United Church of Christ.[82] Concurrently with the future churches of Leuenberg, they realized that the conflict between Luther and Zwingli at the Marburg Colloquy could be overcome, although the corresponding report entitled "Marburg Revisited" had no practical consequences. The Leuenberg Agreement was not deemed adequate for these churches, which did not have the same history of mutual proximity as their European counterparts. A second attempt, "An Invitation to Action" in 1983, enjoined these churches to issue a declaration to the effect that the condemnations of the 16th century were obsolete.[83] The next report, "A Common Calling" (1992), proposed a declaration in which the differences would be integrated into the full communion. It was on this basis that "A Formula of Agreement" was signed in 1997,[84] in which full communion was declared along with the recognition of the sacraments and ministries that are interchangeable. The remaining differences are not divisive. Mutual affirmation and admonition constitute a particular emphasis of this text, which also insists on the necessary links between the executive organs of the churches and the pursuit of joint theological work.

The Amman Declaration in 2006 also established full communion between 15 Reformed and United churches and one Lutheran church in the Middle-East.[85] The Amman Declaration follows the rationale of the Leuenberg Agreement by developing the common understanding of the gospel as the foundation of the communion (§ 2). A historical timeline provides an overview of the efforts to achieve unity since 1911, which were brought to a successful conclusion with the FMEEC. The Episcopalian churches and the Methodist Church did not participate in the Amman Declaration, but the latter invites them to sign as soon as they are ready to do so (§ 13). The model of unity is described in precise terms, following a procedure that is very close to that of the Leuenberg Agreement, also including the stage of declaration and realization. The churches mutually recognize the Christian faith, liturgical life, the sacraments, the celebration of the Lord's Supper to which the other churches are invited,

in Europa/Free for the Future. Protestant Churches in Europe. Documents of the 7th General Assembly of the Community of Protestant Churches in Europe, Florence, Italy, September 20–26, 2012, Leipzig, Evangelische Verlagsanstalt, 2013, 208–214.

82 "A Formula of Agreement," English text available at <http://d3n8a8pro7vhmx.cloudfront.net/unitedchurchofchrist/legacy_url/5362/foa-text.pdf?1418429584> (accessed Jan 16, 2024).

83 The texts and conclusions of "Marburg Revisited" may be found in: James E. Andrews & Joseph A. Burgess, *An Invitation to Action: The Lutheran-Reformed Dialogue, Series III, 1981–1983*, Philadelphia, Fortress Press, 1984.

84 The "Formula of Agreement" is the final step in this path, and has included the theological part of "A Common Calling". See the text available at <https://download.elca.org/ELCA%20Resource%20Repository/A_Formula_Of_Agreement.pdf> (last accessed Jul 1, 2024).

85 "The Amman Declaration. Agreement of full mutual recognition of Lutheran and Reformed Churches in the Middle East and North Africa," *Reformed World* 56, 2006, 204–208. It involves the Lutheran Church in Jordan and the Holy Land, the Synod of the Nile and the Presbyterian Church in Egypt, the Evangelical Church Union of Lebanon, the Evangelical Church of Kuwait, and the Synod of the Evangelical Church in Iran.

the ministries, and the *episkopé* (§§ 19–20). They accept the mutual participation in worship, concelebration, the participation of pastors and bishops in the ordinations, the interchangeability of pastors, and even the reciprocal participation in synods. Moreover, the text of the declaration also insists on a joint formation of pastors and on commitment to the ecumenical movement. The emphasis linked to context-specific issues is visible in the attention paid to interreligious dialogue (§ 21), the commitment to being a prophetic voice for social justice (§ 21d), human rights and struggle (§ 21j).

7.5 *The Dialogues with Other Christian Churches: Declaration of Communion with the Anglican Churches*

The Leuenberg Agreement was an important source of inspiration for three agreements signed with the Anglican churches in Europe: the Meissen Agreement, the Porvoo Common Statement, and the Reuilly Declaration.

As early as the international dialogue of Niagara (1987), the Anglican Church recognized the true faith, baptism, confession, and liturgy, and thus the apostolicity of the Christian Church preserved in the Lutheran and Reformed churches.[86] However, the churches of the Anglican Communion requested that these churches accept that, for them, the episcopal ministry is a sign (according to Niagara a "valuable symbol"[87]) of apostolic fidelity, and that an Anglican bishop be present at episcopal ordinations in order to manifest the link to the universal church. This was accepted in the declaration "Called to Common Mission," which established full communion between Episcopalians and Lutherans in America.[88] In the agreement "Called to Full Communion," concluded between Canadian Episcopalians and Lutherans and signed in Waterloo, Canada, in 2000, the respective bishops are invited to the episcopal ordinations (§ 2).[89] In Europe, on the other hand, the churches of the CPCE chose to follow different paths, with the agreements of Meissen, Porvoo, and Reuilly.

7.5.1 The Meissen Agreement

In 1988, by virtue of the Leuenberg Agreement, the Lutheran, Reformed, and United churches in Germany acted jointly as a church communion by signing the Meissen Agreement with the Church of England, which recognized their ecclesiality and their ordination.[90] However, full and visible communion (unity) was not achieved in it, because only a recognition – but not a reconciliation – of the Protestant ministry had been possible. The German churches did not comply with the Niagara Report request regarding the transmission of the sign of apostolicity by the Anglican bishops at ordinations. This permitted a mutual Eucharistic hospitality but not an interchangeability of ministers.

7.5.2 The Porvoo Common Statement

Concluded in 1992 between the Lutheran churches of the Scandinavian and Baltic countries and the Anglican churches of the British Isles, the Porvoo Common Statement brought together churches that had all maintained an episcopate in their historical sees, and thus shared the sign of the historical transmission of apostolicity.[91] It proclaimed a mutual recognition of these churches in faith, in the sacraments, which may be celebrated in common, in the mutual welcoming of parishioners, and in the recognition of duly ordained

86 "The Niagara Report: Report of the Anglican Lutheran Consultation on Episcope," September 1987, in: Sven Oppegaard & Gregory Cameron, eds., *Anglican–Lutheran Agreements: Regional and International Agreements (1972–2002)*, Geneva, Lutheran World Federation, 2004, 87–128.

87 "The Niagara Report," 19.

88 "Called to Common Mission: A Lutheran Proposal for a Revision of the Concordat Agreement," in: Oppegaard & Cameron, eds., *Anglican–Lutheran Agreements*, 231–242.

89 "Called to Full Communion (The Waterloo Declaration)," in: Oppegaard & Cameron, eds., *Anglican–Lutheran Agreements* 243–248.

90 "On the Way to Visible Unity – A Common Statement," in: Oppegaard & Cameron, eds., *Anglican–Lutheran Agreements*, 129–144.

91 "The Porvoo Common Statement," in: Oppegaard & Cameron, eds., *Anglican–Lutheran Agreements*, 144–176.

ministers. It also requested that the sign of ordination in the historical episcopal succession of the whole church be manifested by the presence of an Anglican bishop.

7.5.3 The Reuilly Declaration

Signed in 2001 by the Lutheran and Reformed churches of France and the Anglican churches of the British Isles, the Reuilly Declaration affirmed the mutual recognition of these churches, with the same problem of the historical episcopal succession.[92] It nevertheless goes beyond Eucharistic hospitality thanks to its mutual recognition of the *episkopé*, albeit in different forms. The churches can mutually welcome each other's ministers. In this declaration, the Anglican churches recognize the existence of true *episkopé* in the Lutheran and Reformed churches. The text encourages the churches to continue to work towards communion, something which the CPCE had desired, but not realized, for the whole of Europe.

7.6 *The Dialogue with the Catholic Church*

The Catholic reactions to the Leuenberg Agreement were characterized, even among the ecumenists involved in this dialogue, by a strong criticism of the model of unity. The criticism is consistent with Catholic ecclesiology: the Leuenberg Agreement is considered too lightweight ("minimalistic") for the problem of the ministry.[93] The ministry is central to the Catholic Church, since it is the college of bishops, in communion with the successor of Peter, bishop of Rome, that establishes and expresses Roman-Catholic unity.

Another problem lies in the method of differentiated consensus: what is the status accorded to difference? Is it really recognized, or is it only a transitional stage pending a future harmonization of the differences in view of a full consensus?[94] The Catholic approach would be that the other truths of faith, especially the issue of the church and its episcopal constitution, necessitate further declarations. In addition, the church communion must be based on clear authority structures and binding ties among the signatory churches.[95]

This criticism confirms that the ministry remains a divisive issue in the dialogue with the Catholic Church. The Reformation churches are asked whether they can consider the apostolic structure of the church itself, in particular the threefold ministry, in its ancient historical reality:

> Could the Protestant churches thus accept that the signs and methods of institutional continuity that emerged during history (episcopal succession, threefold ordained ministry) be recognized (once more) as "obligatory" and indispensable to the church, certainly insofar as they serve "the gospel of the radical gratuity of salvation and of its unconditional reception"?[96]

---

92 "The Reuilly Declaration," English text available at <https://www.churchofengland.org/sites/default/files/2017-11/reuilly_english.pdf> (accessed Jan 16, 2024).

93 "If the ministry is of divine institution, it belongs to the foundation of the Church and thus does not fall solely within the scope of the visible ecclesial institution"; Wolfgang Thönissen, "Sur le chemin de la communion des Eglises?: Au sujet de la Concorde de Leuenberg depuis une perspective catholique," in: Michel Deneken & Elisabeth Parmentier, eds., *La passion de la grâce: Mélanges offerts à André Birmelé*, Geneva, Labor et Fides, 2014, 205–226, here 221.

94 Bernard Sesboüé, *Sauvés par la grâce: Les débats sur la justification du XVIe siècle à nos jours*, Paris, Éditions des Facultés jésuites de Paris, 2009, 236–237.

95 In this respect, Hervé Legrand recognizes an ecclesiological dissymmetry or even a "serious ecclesiological deficit" in the lack of a joint, regularly convening synodal authority. See Hervé Legrand, "Comment progresser vers la communion quand les ecclésiologies sont dissymétriques et même séparatrices?," in: Deneken & Parmentier, eds., *La passion de la grâce*, 189–204, esp. 195.

96 Joseph Famerée, "Ministère – Ordination – Episkope: Un point de vue catholique sur le document de la CEPE," *Positions Luthériennes* 63/1, 2015, 3–18, here 15–16. This issue also includes an article by Martin Hirzel, "Ministère – Ordination – Episkope: Genèse, rédaction et enjeux d'un texte doctrinal," *Positions luthériennes* 63/1, 2015, 19–31, who sheds light on the genesis and the drafting of the study *Amt, Ordination, Episkopé und theologische Ausbildung/Ministry, Ordination, Episkopé and Theological Education*.

The problem also lies in the "obligatory"[97] nature of the teaching and of a pastoral decision taken with the authority of the ministry "after the latter has been in serious interaction and dialogue with the whole people of God."[98]

There will be occasion to discuss these questions, since regular discussions between the CPCE and the Catholic Church on the topic of ecclesiology have been held since 2013. A first document was adopted at the general assembly of Basel in 2018.[99]

7.7 *Consultations with Orthodox Churches in Europe*

It was not the intention to establish an official dialogue with the Orthodox Church in addition to the global bilateral dialogues. Nevertheless, in order to overcome mutual prejudices, the churches of the CPCE took advantage of the participation in the CEC, a platform shared by the European Orthodox churches, in order to strengthen the bonds. This attempt at rapprochement benefited from the dynamics generated by the Charta Oecumenica in 2001.[100] Three consultations (2002, 2004, 2006) were held to discuss "The Church of Jesus Christ" and the ecclesiological models. If the model of unity that does not value the bond of the bishops remains unacceptable for the churches of Orthodox tradition, a communion of churches that maintain a certain autonomy and share mutual commitments is familiar to them, as are the issues of authority and the difficulties that arise therefrom when attempting to agree on a joint policy.

The CPCE is currently striving to share its thoughts and reflections more widely with representatives of other churches and religions, notably by organizing the forum "Europe's Churches Turn to the Future" during two days of the general assembly (Sep 24–25, 2012), in order to reflect about changes in the 21st century and the necessity to offer ways of spiritual renewal.

8 Current Issues and Future Challenges

Finally, the issues that continue to preoccupy the member churches or have recently arisen should also be addressed.

Firstly, it is necessary to consider that although the CPCE has constantly sought to improve the quality of the bonds of communion, it has so far not been possible to establish a joint synod with the authority to make decisions. However, these bonds are not merely structural; they also imply that the churches make the theological studies known in their parishes and in their training programs. The communion demands a willingness to che churches to allow themselves to be corrected and questioned, and to refrain from making decisions without taking the sister churches into account. Since the general assembly of Florence in 2012, a group appointed by the CPCE has been entrusted with the development of the communion. Following an assessment of the ecclesiological model, the part of the document drafted by the group on current challenges mentions *Verbindlichkeit*, reception, and catholicity.[101] In relation to these bonds of fellowship, the binding character is first and foremost the ecclesiological quality, that is, the factor that constitutes authority for these churches. They "are church together,"[102] in accordance with the model of

97 In the sense of German *verbindlich* (binding), a recurrent problem for the CPCE.

98 Famerée, "Ministère – Ordination – Episkope," 16.

99 "Joint CPCE-PCPCU Report on Church and Church Communion," adopted by the general assembly of Basel in September 2008, available in English at <https://kjt.ee/wp-content/uploads/2018/09/CPCE-PCPCU-Report-E.pdf> (accessed Jan 16, 2024).

100 CEC & CCEE, "Charta Oecumenica: Guidelines for the Growing Cooperation among the Churches in Europe," April 2001, English text available at <https://www.ceceurope.org/wp-content/uploads/2015/07/ChartaOecumenica.pdf> (accessed Jan 16, 2024).

101 See "Kirchengemeinschaft – Church Communion – Communion ecclésiale," 17.

102 "Kirchengemeinschaft – Church Communion – Communion ecclésiale," 24.

"unity in reconciled diversity."[103] The CPCE's theological work is its true mark of quality and has so far been the mainstay of its authority. However, this may not be sufficient. In fact, as stated above, the Leuenberg Agreement wished to clearly mark the place of difference. But to what extent can it be tolerated when the rise of conservative currents manifests itself within these very churches? The conservative wing of American Lutheranism, represented by the Missouri Synod and the Wisconsin Evangelical Lutheran Synod, wields some influence over certain member churches of the CPCE. Thus, in the Lutheran Church of Latvia, which ordained women as pastors from 1975 to 1993, the synod has rescinded this decision. This signatory church of the CPCE did not hold any consultations with the sister churches. In spite of the lack of pastors, which compels some of them to continue working beyond the age of retirement or makes it necessary to ordain 18-year-old men, Archbishop Jānis Vanags denies women access to a ministry that remains possible in the Church of Latvia abroad. Since the fundamental agreement on gospel and sacraments is not called into question, the objections voiced by the other churches have no authority.[104] However, this is not an ethical but rather an ecclesiological issue that touches upon the question of the function and meaning of the ministry.

Another challenge concerns the so-called socio-ethical issues, which do not pertain to conflicts over the truths of faith but to decisions of social or ecclesial relevance that can give rise to potentially divisive discussions.

The CPCE has so far never been in danger of breaking apart, and its signatory churches continue to pursue their catholicity in the conviction that unity in reconciled diversity is a promising model for the future.

As this article was first written in 2018, it is not possible to add a development for these last years. The CPCE followed the guidelines decided at the Basel assembly and developed important reflections on a "Theology of Diaspora"; on church communion; and the work is beginning on Interreligious dialogue. Many diaconal projects were organized in these years of new-coming wars, for instance projects for "Euro-Orphans". Europe seemed to become again an important family of mutual solidarity, but after more than two years of war, increasing migratory movements, poverty and environmental disasters, worry and anxiety take over from sharing. The ninth general assembly of CPCE will take place on Aug 27–Sep 2, 2024 in Sibiu, Romania, and its tone was one of hope: "In the Light of Christ – Called to Hope."

Translated from French to English by Robert Meyer.

103 "Kirchengemeinschaft – Church Communion – Communion ecclésiale," 21.

104 In another situation, the intervention of CPCE officials had a positive effect. In the Lutheran Church of Poland, which belongs to the CPCE but has not so far approved the ordination of women, the episcopal conference, in 2006, added the request that the congregations refuse to accept that pastors from other churches celebrate the sacraments. The CPCE officials were able to argue that this request contradicted the recognition of the ordinations of the other churches that had signed the Leuenberg Agreement. This church is not compelled to ordain women, but it must recognize the female ministry of the other churches in the CPCE, which it agreed to do.

Bibliography

Birmelé, André, *La communion ecclésiale: Progrès œcuméniques et enjeux méthodologiques*, Paris, Cerf, 2000.

Hüffmeier, Wilhelm & others, eds., *Die evangelische Diaspora: Die Verwirklichung der Leuenberger Konkordie in evangelischen Minderheitskirchen*, Leipzig, Gustav-Adolf-Werk, 2016.

Lienhard, Marc, *Lutherisch-Reformierte Kirchengemeinschaft heute: Der Leuenberger Konkordienentwurf im Kontext der bisherigen lutherisch-reformierten Dialoge*, Frankfurt a.M., Lembeck, 1972.

Neuser, Wilhelm, *Die Entstehung und theologische Formung der Leuenberger Konkordie 1971 bis 1973*, Münster, LIT, 2003.

Oppegaard, Sven & Gregory Cameron, eds., *Anglican–Lutheran Agreements: Regional and International Agreements (1972–2002)*, Geneva, Lutheran World Federation, 2004.

Schieffer, Elisabeth, *Von Schauenburg nach Leuenberg: Entstehung und Bedeutung der Konkordie reformatorischer Kirchen in Europa*, Paderborn, Bonifatius, 1983.

Sesboüé, Bernard, *Sauvés par la grâce: Les débats sur la justification du XVI*[e] *siècle à nos jours*, Paris, Éditions des Facultés jésuites de Paris, 2009.

CHAPTER 40

The Lutheran-Anglican Dialogue and the Declarations of Communion

André Birmelé

1 Introduction

The dialogue between the Lutheran and Anglican churches has led to developments that present some of the most significant fruits of the contemporary ecumenical movement. The conclusions of worldwide dialogues have been received by the local churches and have led to declarations of communion in various countries and continents which put an end to past oppositions and express the unity that has been achieved today. If they so wish, the faithful of one tradition can become part of a community of the other family and, in many cases, there is even the possibility that ministers can move from one church to the other. The process that led to this major ecumenical breakthrough is the subject of the present contribution.

2 The Two Partners and Their Conception of Unity

2.1 *Historical Landmarks*

In the 16th century, the two families broke off their relationship with the Roman Catholic Church, but initially contact was frequent. The Alsatian reformer Martin Bucer was decisive in laying the theological foundations of Anglicism, and the Wittenberg Concord, drafted in 1536, was aimed at sealing the union. However, this text was partly motivated by political intentions, in particular by a concern for England and the German Lutheran states' common opposition to the pope and to the German Holy Roman emperor.[1] Due to separate political developments, contact became more sporadic, and it was not until the colonial era that closer connections were made.[2] Relations between the two families became more frequent thanks to the fact that from the 19th century Anglican and Lutheran communities lived side by side in different countries around the world.

It was not until the 20th century that more significant rapprochements also took place in Europe. Contact between the Anglicans in the British Isles and the Lutherans in Scandinavia intensified. As early as 1909, Eucharistic communion was proposed, along with a possible mutual recognition of the episcopal ministry. There were also attempts at union on the Indian subcontinent, but in other countries (such as the United States), such attempts were doomed to fail.[3]

1 See Amy Nelson Burnett, "From Concord to Confession: The Wittenberg Concord and the *Consensus Tigurinus* in Historical Perspective," *R&RR* 18/1, 2016, 47–58 and Charles P. Arand, James A. Nestingen & Robert Kolb, *The Lutheran Confessions: History and Theology of The Book of Concord*, Minneapolis, Fortress Press, 2012.

2 For example, already at the dawn of the 18th century a mission founded by Bartholomäus Ziegenbalgm, member of the Lutheran clergy, in Tranquebar (India) under the patronage of the Lutheran Church of Denmark, was transferred through Lutheran initiative to the Anglican city of Madras, thus beginning a cooperation between Anglicans and Lutherans that would last more than a century. See Peter Vethanayagamony, *It Began in Madras: The Eighteenth Century Lutheran-Anglican Ecumenical Ventures in Mission and Benjamin Schulze*, Delhi, ISPCK, 2010.

3 For the history of these relations through the centuries, see "Anglican-Lutheran Agreements. A Brief Orientation by Bishop David Tustin (UK) and Professor Michael Root (USA)," in: Sven Oppegaard & Gregory Cameron, eds., *Anglican-Lutheran Agreements: Regional and International Agreements* (1972–2002), Geneva, Lutheran World Federation, 2004, 11–21.

It was only after World War II, from 1945 onwards, that the two families formed global structures and gradually became CWCs. There is no need to go into detail about this evolution here, which is the subject of a separate chapter of this work.[4] Let us simply recall the major facts.

The LWF was established in 1947 and continued the work already begun by the Lutheran World Convention in 1919, four years before the latter official foundation, in August 1923.[5] In the beginning, the structure remained a federation, with each participating church retaining its full autonomy. The member churches achieved greater unity only gradually. The decisive step was taken at the seventh general assembly in Budapest in 1984[6] where the unity of the church was understood as communion in the Word and sacraments. Such communion was necessary and sufficient for unity *ad intra* and *ad extra*. As a consequence, there would be no need to harmonize either the theological assertions proper to each church or their structures as long as they allowed for communion in the Word and sacraments, and thus for a mutual recognition of the other community as an authentic expression of the one Church of Christ, the one, holy, catholic, and apostolic church. It was now a matter of working towards the manifestation of the unity of the church that is given in Jesus Christ.

The next step was a modification of the initial constitution. During its eighth assembly in Curitiba in 1990, the LWF became a communion of churches that established *koinonia* among all the Lutheran churches belonging to the federation.[7] From then on, the LWF understood itself as a world church and equipped itself to work as such. The LWF's governing bodies are its general assembly, which normally meets every six years, and its council, which meets annually. These two bodies have the authority to make decisions that are binding for the communion that the LWF represents. The LWF has now been able to confirm the conclusions of formal ecumenical dialogues with other Christian families, dialogues that had begun well before the LWF understood itself as a communion.

In the Anglican family, the breakthrough came in 1867 when the first Lambeth conference was held at Lambeth Palace, the seat of the archbishop of Canterbury.[8] The conference was called to deal with issues that threatened to divide the communion. The 76 bishops gathered at the time probably did not realize that these episcopal meetings would become a regular institution in Anglican life. The present Lambeth meetings bring together all the diocesan bishops of the communion and are held every ten years, in years that end in an eight. A representative number of auxiliary and assistant bishops have also participated in recent meetings. Thus, about 800 bishops gathered at the 1998 conference that was held at the University of Kent in Canterbury. While not a legislative body, the Lambeth conference adopts resolutions that

4 See my chapter on the CWCs in this volume.

5 For the history of the Lutheran World Convention, see Kurt Schmidt-Clausen, *Vom Lutherischen Weltkonvent zum lutherischen Weltbund: Geschichte des Lutherischen Weltkonventes (1923–1947)*, Gütersloh, Mohn, 1976. The constitution of the LWF of 1947 can be found in: Jens Holger Schjørring, Prasanna Kumari & Norman Hjelm, eds., *Vom Weltbund zur Gemeinschaft: Geschichte des Lutherischen Weltbundes (1947–1997)*, Hannover, Lutherisches Verlagshaus, 1997, 465–466; ET: Jens Holger Schjørring, Prasanna Kumari & Norman Hjelm, eds., *From Federation to Communion: The History of the Lutheran World Federation*, Minneapolis, Fortress Press, 1997, 527–528.

6 A report of the Budapest assembly can be found in: Carl H. Mau, ed., *Budapest 1984, "In Christ – Hope for the World": Official Proceedings of the Seventh Assembly of the Lutheran World Federation, Hungary, July 22–August 5, 1984*, Geneva, Lutheran World Federation, 1985, 176–177.

7 The assembly amended article 3 of the constitution as follows: "The LWF is a communion of churches which confess the triune God, agree in the proclamation of the Word of God, and are united in pulpit and altar fellowship"; Schjørring, Kumari & Hjelm, eds., *From Federation to Communion*, 530.

8 See the contribution by Paul Avis in the first volume of this work; Paul Avis, ed., *Anglicanism and the Christian Church: Theological Resources in Historical Perspective*, London, T&T Clark, ^{2}2002; and Paul Avis, *The Identity of Anglicanism: Essentials of Anglican Ecclesiology*, London, T&T Clark, 2008.

provide an interesting and representative photograph, taken every ten years, of the communion's opinion on current issues.[9] It attempts to be a body that strengthens the unity of the communion by drawing on the experience of the whole college of bishops and deliberating, in a spirit of prayer and dialogue, on the good of the whole church. Provinces have often submitted Lambeth conference resolutions to their own synods, but this process is not automatic.

At present, the Anglican Communion does not have a legislative body whose decisions are binding on all. Although each province promulgates its own ecclesiastical constitution, in practice there is an implicit awareness of membership and mutual dependence within the worldwide communion.[10] Anglicans currently recognize four global Instruments of Communion or structures of unity within the communion: the Lambeth conference, the Primates' meeting, the ACC, and the archbishop of Canterbury. The first three instruments are recently established conferences or councils. The ministry of the archbishop of Canterbury is the only one of these institutions that dates back more than 150 years. A special place is attributed to the ACC, founded by a corresponding resolution of the Lambeth conference of 1968.[11] It was established to share information, to study inter-Anglican relations (the division into and creation of provinces), to set guidelines for world missionary activity, and to maintain and promote cooperation, dialogue, and relations with other Christian churches. As with the Lambeth conference, the decisions of the ACC are not binding on the provinces, unless the latter take the initiative to transform its decisions at their level into positions relevant to their ecclesiastical law.

These few historical landmarks explain why official international ecumenical dialogues between these two Christian traditions are conducted by the LWF council on the Lutheran side and the ACC on the Anglican side.

2.2 *The Vision of Unity*

For the Lutheran churches, the necessary and sufficient condition for true unity of the church was already affirmed in 1530 by the *Confessio Augustana*. Article 7 of this confession of faith states: "And to the true unity of the Church it is enough to agree concerning the doctrine of the Gospel and the administration of the Sacraments."[12]

The church is defined there in reference to the means God uses to communicate his grace, preaching, and the sacraments. Thus, and only thus, does God create, recreate, maintain, and complete the church. As marks of the church, the Word and sacraments do not replace the traditionally affirmed *notae*, which are unity, holiness, catholicity, and apostolicity. Quite the contrary. The Word and the sacraments celebrated in conformity to the gospel permit the discovery of where the one, holy, catholic, and apostolic *ecclesia* exists. The continued existence of the church is not assured by an ecclesiastical structure but by the authentic celebration of the Word and sacraments.

It is important to clarify that this approach does not exclude the church's ministry. Ministry is essential for the preaching of the gospel and the celebration of the sacraments, and is at their service. Moreover, it is entrusted to the whole church. The forms and structures that have arisen in history have their meaning, but in no way do they have an absolute character. Diversity in them is possible and legitimate. The forms taken by this unique ministry of the whole church are

9 See Paul Avis & Benjamin M. Guyer, eds., *The Lambeth Conference: Theology, History, Polity and Purpose*, London, T&T Clark, 2017.

10 Henry Robert McAdoo, "Authority in the Church; Spiritual Freedom and the Corporate Nature of Faith," in: Stephen W. Sykes, ed., *Authority in the Anglican Communion: Essays Presented to Bishop John Howe*, Toronto, Anglican Book Centre, 1987, 69–93.

11 The texts of the resolutions (the last one of which, number 69, instituted the ACC) can be found in Roger Coleman, ed., *Resolutions of the Twelve Lambeth Conferences (1867–1988)*, Toronto, Anglican Book Centre, 1992.

12 Article 7 of the *Confessio Augustana* is available at <https://bookofconcord.org/augsburg-confession/> (accessed Jan 22, 2024).

legitimate insofar as and because the Word and sacraments are offered in accordance with the gospel. The Lutherans, therefore, have not "forgotten" the ministry, but unity in it is a consequence, not a prerequisite. When there is consensus in the understanding of the Word and sacraments and the authenticity of their celebration in the sister church, then unity is given, and this unity includes the mutual recognition of ministries.

At first glance, the Anglican approach seems different. While it, too, emphasizes the authentic celebration of the Word and sacraments in defining the church and its unity, the Lambeth Quadrilateral of 1888 adds the historical episcopate as a necessary sign of unity.[13] This definition of unity initially applied to unity within the Anglican Communion, but it is understood that the elements that establish the unity of a particular church are the same as those that found the unity of the church in a much wider sense.

There is a certain asymmetry between the Lutheran conception and this Anglican approach. The Anglicans insist on a historical succession in the episcopal ministry. The question of the common exercise of ministry, secured by the insistence on the historic episcopate, will be and is hotly debated in the dialogue between all the families stemming from the Reformation.

One thing must be emphasized, however: in the Anglican tradition, the ministry, even that of the bishop in historical succession, is not placed on the same level as the celebration of Word and sacraments. Therefore, while desiring a visible unity in the exercise of the *episkopé* as well, the Anglican Communion recognizes the churches that have not preserved this tradition as authentic expressions of the one Church of Christ. Even more than that, it recognizes the ministries and ordained ministers of these churches, while desiring to achieve a common exercise of ministry that goes beyond the mutual recognition of ministries and is expressed in a visible and common structure. This will be made clear in the declarations of ecclesial communion that will be presented later. A certain communion is already given, but its full visibility still requires, according to the Anglican understanding, this common exercise of *episkopé*.

This asymmetry is important, but this difference will be worked on so that it loses its separating character and no longer remains an obstacle to full communion. On this point there is a notable difference between the Anglican approach and that of the Roman Catholic or Orthodox churches.[14]

Thus, Anglicans and Lutherans agree that full communion requires communion in the preaching of the gospel, communion in the celebration of the sacraments, and communion in the ministry, that is, the mutual recognition of the ordained ministry that proclaims the word and celebrates the sacraments. Full communion means unity, not uniformity. It is not a matter of eliminating all the differences, therefore, but of transforming them so that the churches can recognize each other as full and authentic expressions of the one Church of Jesus Christ. An important step on this path to communion is theological dialogue. Churches have conducted these dialogues, and global organizations have commissioned experts for this

13 The Lambeth Quadrilateral cites the following four essential points: (1) the Holy Scriptures; (2) the Apostles' Creed; (3) the two sacraments of baptism and the Supper of the Lord; (4) the historic episcopate. The first step was to define the four elements that form the basis for the worldwide Anglican Communion, which was born from a first meeting in Lambeth in 1867; such a meeting has been held every 10 years since 1878. The text of the Lambeth Quadrilateral can be found in Coleman, ed., *Resolutions of the Twelve Lambeth Conferences*, 13. See also Alan M.G. Stephenson, *Anglicanism and the Lambeth Conferences*, London, SPCK, 1978, 64–67. On the centenary of the quadrilateral, see John Robert Wright, ed., *Quadrilateral at One Hundred: Essays on the Centenary of the Chicago-Lambeth Quadrilateral (1886/88–1986/88)*, Cincinnati, Forward Movement Publications, 1988.

14 See my "Episkopos, episkopé, cattolicità e costituzione della Chiesa: Grosse sfide per le Chiese riformate," in: *La relazione fra il Vescovo e la Chiesa locale: Antiche e nuove questioni in prospettiva ecumenica*, Venice/Rome, Istituto di Studi Ecumenici S. Bernardino/Centro Pro Unione, 2007, 189–216.

purpose who have been able to reach a significant theological consensus.

3 The International Anglican-Lutheran Dialogue

In 1968, the Lambeth conference and the executive committee of the LWF decided to set up an international Lutheran-Anglican dialogue. This led to a first text in 1972, the Pullach Report.

3.1 *The 1970–1972 Dialogue: the Pullach Report*

In analyzing the 1972 Pullach Report,[15] it is useful to do a quick review of the numerous points that create consensus between the two families. There is full agreement on the sources of authority: this point concerns the reference to Holy Scripture and the confession of faith of the first centuries, the importance of the Reformation confessions of faith, as well as the relationship between Scripture and Tradition (§§ 17–50). The church is understood to be the community (communion) of believers where the Word is faithfully preached and the sacraments administered in conformity to the gospel (§ 61). The agreement extends to the understanding of baptism (§§ 64–66) and the Lord's Supper (§§ 67–69), and the necessity of an ordained ministry for the preaching of the Word and the celebration of the sacraments (§§ 73–78).

The remaining disagreement concerns the necessity in the church of a historical apostolic succession in the episcopate. The debate was lively and the question of historical succession in the episcopal ministry was not really settled. It even gave rise to reservations on the part of some of the Anglican members, which are mentioned in the final text. It was agreed, in any case, that this succession is a particular gift from God to the church, a visible sign of unity through the centuries. Despite the absence of this succession in the majority of Lutheran churches, the Anglicans nevertheless noted that these churches know "true proclamation of the Word and celebration of the sacraments." They stated that they "gladly recognize in the Lutheran churches a true communion of Christ's body, possessing a truly apostolic ministry" (§ 85). The Lutherans stated that "those Lutheran churches which have not retained the historic episcopate are free to accept it where it serves the growing unity of the church in obedience to the gospel." They affirmed that they "recognize the churches of the Anglican Communion as true apostolic churches and their ministry as an apostolic ministry in unbroken succession, because they see in them the true proclamation of the gospel and right administration of the sacraments" (§§ 89–90).

The report proposed an extension of the intercommunion already experienced between Anglicans and Lutherans in certain Scandinavian countries to Lutheran churches in other countries, joint worship where possible, social action, and certain common structures. This development was to be accompanied by a continuation of joint theological reflection (§§ 96–108).

The report was approved by the executive committee of the LWF and by the Lambeth conference of 1978.

3.2 *Decentralized Dialogues and the 1983 Cold Ash Report*

In the implementation of these conclusions, it was decided to verify their relevance by establishing decentralized groups in various regions (United States, Europe, Tanzania).

In the USA, after two series of dialogues, an official agreement was reached in 1982[16] and approved

15 "Report of the Anglican-Lutheran International Conversation 1970–1972," in: Oppegaard & Cameron, eds., *Anglican–Lutheran Agreements*, 23–46. Here and elsewhere in the text the relevant paragraphs of reports and documents are given in parentheses.

16 "The Agreement: Common Resolution," in: William. A. Norgren. ed., *What Can We Share? A Lutheran-Episcopal Resource and Study Guide*, Cincinnati, Forward Movement Publications, 1985, 6–8.

by the Lutheran churches (the Lutheran Church of America and the American Lutheran Church) and the Episcopal churches (Anglicans). This agreement included all the theological conclusions in the Pullach Report. It noted the consensus on the understanding of the Word of God and the sacraments and the difficulty that remained for the full mutual recognition of ministries (the historical succession of the episcopate). On this basis, it proposed a broad collaboration in a number of areas (worship, spirituality, social action, education) and established an "interim sharing of the Eucharist."[17]

Theologically, there are three important elements that stand out: (1) this agreement led to ecclesial decisions. The churches are engaged at the level of their synods and here is a mutual recognition of churches that do not refer to identical confessions of faith (symbolic books). (2) It is specified that there is no question of full communion given the difference in the understanding of episcopal ministry. The progress made in the dialogue and the journey together is, in the eyes of the Lutherans, sufficient for full communion, but not for the Anglicans. What is visualized and concretized in the interim sharing of the Eucharist is only a step on the road to full ecclesial communion (even if this interim aspect is theologically debatable). (3) The churches committed themselves to continuing their theological dialogue with the aim of achieving full recognition of the ministries.

In Europe, the dialogue led to a publication in 1983 of what is called the Helsinki Report.[18] This is characterized by a remarkable deepening of the issues where the Pullach Report had already recognized a consensus: justification by faith, baptism, Eucharist, worship. It also detailed the question of ministry and, in particular, the close relationship and mutual dependence (but not confusion) between the universal priesthood of all believers and the ministry charged with the celebration of the Word and sacraments, since the latter was not seen as a simple emanation of the universal priesthood. There was also agreement on the understanding of ordination.

The most interesting breakthrough in this report is the consensus on apostolicity: historical succession in the episcopal ministry is essential but does not guarantee the apostolicity of the church. It is an expression of this apostolicity. The church is apostolic insofar as the preaching of the gospel and the celebration of the sacraments are in conformity with the gospel. This apostolicity finds its expression in the historical succession of the episcopal ministry, but it is not this succession that guarantees the church's apostolicity.

The consensus in the understanding of the Word and sacraments permitted, as a consequence and up to the present day, joint celebrations while waiting for a full communion that would also include the full recognition of ministers, including the episcopal ministry. The Helsinki Report made recommendations in this sense (such as mutual invitation to the Eucharist). It further proposed concelebrations and mutual participation in the ordination of pastors and bishops in order to achieve an integration of ministers and the possible passage of a minister from one church to another (§ 64).

Unlike the American report, the European one was not submitted directly to the synods of the churches. The conclusions of the European and American reports were taken up in the 1983 international so-called Cold Ash Report.[19] This report is a summary of the achievements of the regional dialogues and calls for detailed theological work on the question of episcopal ministry in order to achieve full communion.

17 "The Agreement: Common Resolution," 8.

18 "The Report of the Anglican-Lutheran European Regional Commission," Helsinki, August–September 1982, in: Oppegaard & Cameron, eds., *Anglican-Lutheran Agreements*, 47–68.

19 "Report of the Anglican-Lutheran Joint Working Group," Cold Ash, Berkshire, England 1983, in: Oppegaard & Cameron, eds., *Anglican-Lutheran Agreements*, 69–86.

3.3 *The Dialogue on Episcopal Ministry: The 1987 Niagara Report*

The text is introduced by a chapter on the being of the church and its mission. It emphasizes that "linear" succession cannot be understood as the sole criteria for the fidelity and apostolicity of the church (§ 20).[20] Even though the mission of the church calls for the apostolic ministry and the ministry of unity, apostolic succession is a sign (*nota*) of the whole church (§ 21). Because the church is founded on God's fidelity, it can rejoice in the symbols of continuity given to it, including continuity in episcopal and presbyterial ministry. These symbols must always be newly reinterpreted (§§ 29–30).

The text then speaks of the necessity for ecclesial structures. These structures cannot be absolutized but must be the object of a critical oversight in the name of the gospel. They also include a ministry of unity (or leadership), an important function of which is to ensure the link between the local church and the universal church. "The mere presence of a bishop ... will not *guarantee* the preservation of *koinonia* ... nor will the absence of such a bishop entail its destruction" (§ 53).

In the third part, the Niagara Report discusses the "truths we share" in ten points presented over 20 paragraphs (§§ 60–80). These are brief (two pages in all) and evoke the fundamentals that all subsequent declarations of communion will repeat without modification, even if the order of these points will not always be the same. These points set out the consensus on the authority of Scripture and the confessions of faith, liturgy, baptism, Eucharist, salvation in Christ, the church and its mission, ministries, as well as eschatological expectation. On the subject of ministry, these ten points emphasize the universal priesthood and the necessity of the particular ministry given by God to his church. It includes the conviction "that a ministry of pastoral oversight (*episcope*), exercised in personal, collegial and communal ways, is necessary to witness to and safeguard the unity and apostolicity of the Church" (§ 69).[21]

These convictions show that there is no longer any serious obstacle to full communion between the two churches (§ 71) and, therefore, a mutual recognition of "each other's ministries of *episcope*" is desirable and possible (§ 75).

On the basis of this theological consensus, the report proposes a four-step path.

(1) The approval by the synods of the local churches of the consensus on the fundamental aspects of the faith and the mutual recognition of the other church as "a true Church of the Gospel" (§ 112).

(2) The establishment of "provisional structures to express the degree of unity so far achieved": Eucharistic communion and concelebration, regular meetings of church leaders, mutual invitations, common work, joint theological formation, shared missionary projects, an exchange of pastors, and so on. (§ 113).

(3) In order to achieve a joint episcopal ministry, requests were made to both sides. First of all Lutherans were asked: to adopt the term "bishop" everywhere to designate the pastor of pastors; to not limit bishops' ministry in time, to make it clear that it is not a mere administrative responsibility; to make it clear that only a bishop has the authority to ordain pastors; and to invite an Anglican bishop to participate in the laying on of hands at the installation of a Lutheran bishop. On the other hand, Anglicans were asked: to insert the affirmation of the full authenticity of Lutheran ministries into their canonical books; to develop structures for a periodic collegial review of the bishop's ministry; and to invite a Lutheran bishop to participate in the laying on of hands at the installation of an Anglican bishop.

---

20 "The Niagara Report: Report of the Anglican–Lutheran Consultation on Episcope," September 1987, in: Oppegaard & Cameron, eds., *Anglican–Lutheran Agreements*, 87–128.

21 See also paragraph 79 of the Pullach Report.

(4) Once these conditions are met, the two traditions could enter into full ecclesial communion, which goes beyond the common celebration of the Word and sacraments and includes a common ministry. The document proposes the mutual recognition of ministries of *episkopé* and envisages a concrete path to achieve this: the approval by the synods of the churches of a consensus on the fundamental elements of the faith; the establishment of provisional structures expressing the degree of consensus reached; the establishment of a common episcopate that will come about through the mutual invitation and reciprocal laying on of hands by bishops from the different traditions at episcopal ordinations; the declaration of full ecclesial communion that includes communion in the Word and the sacraments, a common ministry, and a common commitment to mission and witness. This full communion will be fully visible and will correspond to the unity of the church (§§ 81–110).

The Niagara Report's conclusions were endorsed by the world organizations of both traditions. The Lambeth conference in 1988 recognized the substantial convergence and called on the Anglican churches to take steps in this direction by approving the conclusions of the Niagara Report at the synodal level, by deciding to recognize the other church, and by instituting an interim sharing of the Eucharist. The LWF responded in similar terms at its global assembly in Curitiba in February 1990. It did not endorse the idea of an interim sharing of the Eucharist since, for them, Eucharistic communion, by definition, cannot be interim.

3.4 *Other International Dialogues*

To complete the summary, two other international dialogues between the Lutheran and Anglican families must be added. The first was concluded in 1996 and focused on the "diaconate as an ecumenical opportunity."[22] It emphasized the importance of this ministry for the church and insisted on the need to ordain deacons who serve both the church's worship and the church's social commitments. Its significance for the dialogue aimed at establishing ecclesial communion is, however, secondary. The second dialogue was an assessment made in 2002, 15 years after the Niagara Report.[23] The assessment is positive and looks back at the declarations of communion made by the churches at the natural and continental levels, declarations to which we shall return below.

Another dialogue, that of the Anglicans with the WARC (now the WCRC), must be mentioned.[24] It resulted in the 1984 report "God's Reign and our Unity."[25] This document takes its starting point more from local situations but arrives at the same theological conclusions as the dialogues between Lutherans and Anglicans: an agreement on the understanding of the Word and sacraments and the difficulties regarding the understanding of the episcopal ministry with a continuity of historical succession. There has been no further international dialogue between these two families. A new stage was only introduced **in 2014**, without yet being able to present a final report. It is important to mention the Anglican-Reformed dialogue given that some declarations of communion at the national and continental level also include Reformed churches in some European countries.

22 "The Diaconate as Ecumenical Opportunity," in: *Anglican Lutheran Agreements*, 177–199.

23 "Growth in Communion," in: *Anglican Lutheran Agreements*, 275–337.

24 On the process of the WARC's formation, see Marcel Pradervand, *A Century of Service: A History of the World Alliance of Reformed Churches (1875–1975)*, Grand Rapids, Eerdmans, 1975. The WCRC was formed in June 2010 in Grand Rapids, Michigan, in the United States, by the merger of the WARC and the REC and is composed of 230 member churches from 108 countries, bringing together more than 80 million faithful, mainly from countries in the southern hemisphere. See my article on CWCs in this volume.

25 "God's Reign and our Unity: The report of the Anglican-Reformed international commission, 1981–1984," English text available at <https://www.anglicancommunion.org/media/104250/1984_aco_warc_gods_reign_our_unity.pdf> (accessed Jan 22, 2024).

4 Declarations of Communion

One of the major difficulties of the contemporary ecumenical movement is the passage from the conclusions of the dialogues to an effective transformation of the life of the local churches and the relationships among them. How do we move from a consensus among theologians to ecclesial communion?

The churches influenced by the Reformation have been confronted with this problem since the first decades of contemporary ecumenical developments and have developed a new methodology for receiving these conclusions at all levels of their ecclesial life. They have chosen to start from the theological agreement achieved in the dialogues, which, however, are not asked to be approved or rejected as such. These conclusions, in fact, are only the result of the work of theologians-who are certainly acting at the behest of the churches-and ultimately bind only the participants in the dialogues. It is therefore necessary to reach a short declaration that could be approved by the synods and thus create a new ecclesial situation. The churches appropriate the conclusions of the dialogues and draw up a text that declares a new quality to their relationship and, in the case of the churches marked by the Reformation of the 16th century, the full mutual recognition on the basis of communion in the celebration of the Word and sacraments. This text is submitted to the synodal bodies and comes into force after their approval.

This methodology is not new. The history of the churches in the 20th century has various examples where, at the national level, the churches of the Reformation tradition have come together, regrouped, and have, in certain cases, even decided to merge. This is particularly true of the European Lutheran and Reformed churches, which in various countries have reached declarations of communion. These declarations, which were the basis for and accompanied these relationships, were made by independent national churches but did not go beyond the "local" setting of a particular country. It was only in the context of the contemporary ecumenical movement that the traditions that emerged from the Reformation became aware, theologically, of the catholicity of the church and, at the organizational level, of the global dimension that now characterized each confessional family. In this new context, the European Lutheran and Reformed churches tried to transcend national frameworks in order to reach interconfessional agreements that would apply on a worldwide, or at least continental, level. This led to the Leuenberg Agreement, which resulted in a Lutheran-Reformed communion at the European level in 1974, a communion soon joined by the Methodist churches.[26]

The Lutheran-Anglican dialogue also had to meet this challenge. The approach was different, although the results were the same. Since the two ecclesial families concerned are structured in world communions, it was decided to start from the conclusions of the international dialogues and then to ask the national or continental churches to implement them at their level by drawing up declarations of communion that would be submitted to the synods and effectively transform the local situation. This approach was the only possible one, given that there was hardly any situation where national dialogues had preceded the global dialogue. It is this approach that was approved by the world organizations of both traditions. It was therefore the one implemented by the Lutheran and Anglican churches in various countries throughout the world. The four steps proposed by the Niagara Report were followed everywhere.

This way of carrying things out is ecumenically interesting because this path is familiar and aims to serve the whole ecumenical movement. It is a major step in the process of reception, which is the urgent task of current ecumenical efforts.[27]

26 For these declarations, especially the Leuenberg Agreement, see the contribution by Elisabeth Parmentier in this volume.

27 On this point, see Yves Congar, "La 'réception' comme réalité ecclésiologique," *RSPT* 56/3, 1972, 369–403; Jean-Marie Tillard, "'Reception': A Time to Beware of False Steps," *EcTr* 14/10, 1985, 145–148; and above all Jean-Marie Tillard, *Église d'Églises: L'ecclésiologie de communion*, Paris, Cerf 1987; Günther Gaßmann,

Theological consensus is not in itself synonymous with communion. It is only the prerequisite that then needs to be translated into the life of our churches. Reception does not simply mean information or acceptance. It is a complex process of appropriation and translation of consensus to the level of all ecclesial life. It must be concluded by a synodal decision. Theologically, it is necessary, in the phase of reception, to verify whether the theological agreements proposed at the international level truly conform to the theological identity of the particular local churches. The theological dimension is, however, only one aspect alongside other elements (lived reality in place and time, visible rapprochement of local communities, reconciliation of particular histories, and so on). Many non-doctrinal factors thus come into play in this phase that cannot be resolved through international theological dialogues.

For the sake of clarity, it is advisable to start with the declarations of communion in Europe and then move on to the North American continent and to developments in Australia.

4.1 *The European Declarations*

The European steps towards communion between Lutherans and Anglicans have given rise to three declarations: the Meissen Agreement (1988), the Porvoo Common Statement (1992), and the Reuilly Common Statement (2001). These three declarations follow each other in time, and it is easy to see that there has been a theological evolution due not only to the passage of time but also to geographical contexts. The first text concerns relations between the Church of England and the German Protestant churches, the second relations between the Anglican churches and the Scandinavian and Baltic Lutheran churches, and the third those between these same British churches and the French Lutheran and Reformed churches.

4.1.1 The Meissen Agreement

The first declaration of communion in Europe that linked the German Protestant churches and the Anglican Church of England is the Meissen Agreement.[28] The text was completed in 1988 and submitted to the synods, but there was no final acceptance on the part of the Church of England until January 1991.

The starting point of the dialogue that led to this declaration has an amusing side. The archbishop of Canterbury, Robert Runcie, had participated in the celebrations commemorating Luther's 500th birthday in 1983. He was probably unaware that the city where these celebrations took place, Erfurt, was under the jurisdiction of a German United church, a church that includes both Lutheran and Reformed traditions. Noting the close proximity of the celebration to the Anglican tradition, he invited the host church to enter into dialogue for true church fellowship. As a result, all German churches – including the United churches and not only the Lutherans – entered into dialogue. On the Anglican side, the dialogue partner was limited to the Church of England, without including the other Anglican churches of the British Isles. It was thus a "tri-alogue" which, for the German churches, was logical since they were in full communion with each other through the Leuenberg Agreement.

Theologically, this dialogue merely reiterated the common convictions set out in the first world dialogues; the drafting of the Niagara Report had not yet been completed at that time and occurred concomitantly with the work of the Meissen commission.

In its first paragraphs, the text recalled the ecclesiological convictions held in common: the church as a sign and instrument of the kingdom of God, and the church as communion. It added that full visible unity must include a common confession of faith in words and action, the sharing of

"Rezeption im oekumenischen Kontext," *ÖR* 26/3, 1977, 314–327 and John Zizioulas, "The Theological Problem of 'Reception,'" *Centro Pro Unione* 26, 1984, 3–6.

28 "On the Way to Visible Unity: A Common Statement," in: Oppegaard & Cameron, eds., *Anglican–Lutheran Agreements*, 129–144.

one baptism, the celebration of one Eucharist, and the common service of a reconciled ministry (§ 8).

In paragraphs from 9 to 15, the document spoke of the communion already achieved and the broad doctrinal agreement on Scripture; the early and 16th century confessions of faith; salvation in Christ; the sacraments of baptism and the Eucharist; the church; ministries, and in particular the ordained ministry as God's gift to the church and constitutive of the church; the apostolicity of the church; the need for personal, collegial, and communal leadership; and eschatological expectation. These points of consensus are also those stated in the Niagara Report, a simultaneity that arose due to the fact that members of the Meissen commission were also members of the international Lutheran-Anglican dialogue.

While insisting on the ministry's need for leadership (*episkopé*) exercised in a personal, collegial, and communal way (§ 15), the report specified that there was as yet no identity of views on the historical succession in the episcopal ministry and that this question required further dialogue (§ 16). This was not, however, to prevent decisive steps being taken on the path towards communion. Paragraph 17, therefore, which is the Meissen declaration itself, declared mutual recognition as the true church of Jesus Christ, mutual recognition of the authentic celebration of the Word and sacraments, and mutual recognition of the ordained ministry as a gift of God and an instrument of grace. This mutual recognition of the ministry remained incomplete, however, pending full ministerial recognition, which would be possible once a common understanding of the episcopal ministry had been reached.

The interchangeability of ministers was thus not yet possible. This restriction did not mean that a German pastor could not work in the Church of England or vice versa an Anglican priest in a German Protestant parish. Cooperation was possible, but each minister acted under the responsibility of the bishop of their church of origin. This situation would only change when a common episcopate was granted. At such a point, the interchangeability of ministers would be achieved, the minister concerned then passing to the responsibility of the bishop of the diocese where s/he worked.

Establishing a common episcopate still came up against the English requirement of accepting the episcopate in its historical succession, which the German churches could not consider as a necessary condition for full, visible unity.

This disagreement also meant that there could be no question of a concelebration of the Eucharist by ministers of both traditions, a common practice in Anglicanism where several ministers celebrate the Lord's Supper together. It would always be either an Anglican or a Protestant Eucharist, the characterization of the celebration depending on the minister saying the Eucharistic prayer (§ 17 B vi). Furthermore, it was necessary to avoid any imposition of hands by a bishop of the other tradition during an ordination. The absence of a common episcopate was seen to forbid such a sign. The signatory churches committed themselves to continuing their search for full communion in this ministry.

The Meissen Agreement was a decisive first step since it gave concrete expression to the visible unity possible between Anglicans, Lutherans, and Reformed. The agreement logically concluded with a number of very practical recommendations concerning the participation of Anglicans in the church life of German Protestant congregations and vice versa.

Concrete steps were planned to achieve the decisive rapprochement on the matter of the episcopate. A follow-up commission was set up and began work in 1988. It has not yet been able to solve the problems that remained open at the time of the signing and implementation of the agreement.

It should be added here that dialogue with the German Lutheran churches alone would perhaps have been easier. The presence of the United churches (often of the Reformed tradition) did not simplify the process, since those churches are rather reluctant to accept a supra-local church leadership of the episcopal type. Nevertheless, the Meissen Agreement was, and is, a major step forward, even if it still required further theological dialogue.

4.1.2 The Porvoo Common Statement

The Porvoo Common Statement[29] established communion between 13 Lutheran and Anglican churches in northern Europe. The agreement was finalized in the Finnish town of Järvenpää on Oct 13, 1992, and is named after the nearby town of Porvoo where a Eucharistic service was held on the preceding Sunday for all participating churches. The agreement came into effect definitively after its approval by the synods of all the churches involved.[30] This declaration went beyond the simple recognition of one another as true expressions of the one Church of Christ and communion in the preaching of the Word and the celebration of the sacraments. It achieved a common exercise of the episcopal ministry that gave greater visibility to unity and allowed for the full interchangeability of all ministers. In this it differs from other European declarations.

Before turning to the Porvoo text itself, we must mention an important change in the Anglican understanding of the unity of the church, at least at the European level. Generally speaking, the unity of the church is understood as full communion. According to the paragraph 53 of the 1972 Pullach Report, full communion is synonymous with communion in the Word and sacraments: "Altar and pulpit fellowship." In the dialogue leading up to the 1983 Cold Ash Report, full communion also was seen to necessarily include a common episcopate.[31]

The Anglican insistence on full communion was intended, on the one hand, to avoid the proclamation of communion in the Word and sacraments without consequences for the concrete life of the churches. On the other hand, it was a matter of achieving a common exercise of the ministry of leadership without excluding the need for the constant reform of every form of church life.

Lutherans have always been quite reticent regarding the Anglican insistence on full communion. In their eyes, it is given as soon as there is communion in the Word and sacraments. The idea that full communion could be surpassed by a fuller communion has always been foreign to them. This does not mean, however, that the unity of the church can do without the concrete bonds that make this communion more visible.

Ten years later, Anglicans became more cautious in their use of the notion of full communion or full unity as they became aware that full communion has an eschatological dimension. The goal of the ecumenical process was not abandoned, but its ultimate realization was seen to depend on God alone. In the early 1990s, the Anglican churches entered into dialogue with the Moravian churches. The notion of full communion was set aside in favor of the need for communion in the Word and sacraments and for the bonds of communion that must necessarily accompany any declaration of communion.[32] This approach was also taken in paragraph 8 of the Meissen Agreement, which spoke more generally of the need for "bonds of communion which enable the church at every level to guard and interpret the apostolic faith, to

29 "The Porvoo Common Statement," in: Oppegaard & Cameron, eds., *Anglican–Lutheran Agreements*, 145–176.

30 See the report of the cochair of the Porvoo conversations, David Tustin, "The Background and Genesis of the Porvoo Common Statement," in: Ola Tjørhom, ed., *Apostolicity and Unity: Essays on the Porvoo Common Statement*, Geneva/Grand Rapids, WCC Publications/Eerdmans, 2002, 3–14. See also Günther Gaßmann, "Das Porvoo-Dokument als Grundlage anglikanisch-lutherischer Kirchengemeinschaft im nördlichen Europa," *ÖR* 44/2, 1995, 172–183.

31 See paragraphs 25 and 26 of the Cold Ash Report. See also Michael Root, "The Phrase 'Full Communion' as a Statement of the Ecumenical Goal: A Dossier," in: William G. Rusch, ed., *A Commentary on "Ecumenism: The Vision of the ELCA"*, Minneapolis, Augsburg Fortress, 1990, 142–153.

32 *Anglican-Moravian Conversations: The Fetter Lane Common Statement with Essays in Moravian and Anglican History*, London, Church House Publishing, 1996.

take decisions, to teach authoritatively, to share goods, and to bear effective witness in the world." In the title of paragraph 8 Meissen nevertheless speaks of a "full, visible unity," and here we point out the comma between full and visible. It is therefore not simply a question of the full visibility of unity, but of full unity on the one hand and visible unity on the other.

As will be seen, this comma would disappear not only in Porvoo text, but also in the Reuilly Common Statement.

The notion of full communion did not reappear in the Porvoo Common Statement, and yet it was the agreement that led to the establishment of a common episcopate. Porvoo only speaks of the need for a fuller visible embodiment and fullness of communion to be given at the end of time (§§ 22 and 28), concepts that are also present in the agreement with the Moravian churches.

Referring to the international Lutheran-Anglican dialogues and their proposals, the Anglican churches in the British Isles and the Lutheran churches in Scandinavia and the Baltic states have been able to take more concrete steps towards visible church unity. In this dialogue, given the absence of a Reformed presence, the partners were able to accept all the conclusions of the international Lutheran-Anglican dialogue, including the proposals of the Niagara Report. The Porvoo Common Statement is the translation of these conclusions in northern Europe.

It should be added that some of these churches had long-standing privileged relationships. In addition, the Lutheran churches in Sweden and Finland had not experienced a break in the historical succession of the episcopate in the 16th century. For this reason, Eucharistic hospitality with the Church of England was also common. In the decades prior to the agreement, these relations were extended to other Lutheran churches in the Scandinavian and Baltic countries and to other Anglican churches in the British Isles.[33] But Porvoo does much more than confirm this state of affairs. The agreement establishes ministerial communion between these churches through the establishment of a common episcopal ministry.

The first four parts should be distinguished from the much shorter fifth part (§§ 58–61), which is the statement of communion itself. The first two parts are, first of all, a description of the context and situation and a more general reflection on the church and its mission. The emphasis is on a common understanding of the church as communion with particular emphasis placed on the common mission of the church in society (§§ 10–13). It makes clear that this common understanding of visible unity does not seek uniformity. The third part takes up the ten fundamental theological affirmations formulated in Niagara (§ 32) without modification, but in a different order.

The central point is to be found in the fourth chapter on the episcopacy, the partly controversial issue of earlier local relations. It is in this chapter that Porvoo embraces Niagara and goes further than Meissen. The apostolicity of the church does not depend on historical succession in the episcopal office, rather "apostolic succession in the episcopal office is a visible and personal way of focusing the apostolicity of the whole Church" (§ 46). Porvoo thus makes it clear that uninterrupted historical succession in the episcopal ministry is only a sign, which does not in itself guarantee the apostolicity of the church. "The use of the sign of the historic episcopal succession does not by itself guarantee the fidelity of a church … Nonetheless, the retention of the sign remains a permanent challenge to fidelity and to unity, a summons to witness to, and a commission

33 See Sydney Lynton, "Anglo-Swedish Church Relations 1638–1831," *Theology* 66/519, 1963, 372–374. For the history of relations between the Swedish and Anglican churches up to 1922 see Carl Henrik Lyttkens & Neil Tomkinson, *The Growth of Swedish-Anglican Intercommunion between 1833 and 1922*, Lund, Gleerups, 1970. See also Suzanne B. Geisler, "Step on the Swedish Lutheran Road to Anglicanism," *Historical Magazine of the Protestant Episcopal Church* 54/1, 1985, 39–49. More generally see John Toy, "Unplanned Excursions: Anglican Relations with the Scandinavian Churches," *Theology* 73/602, 1970, 359–363 and Lars Österlin, *Churches of Northern Europe in Profile: A Thousand Years of Anglo-Nordic Relations*, Norwich, The Canterbury Press, 1995.

to realize more fully, the permanent characteristics of the Church of the apostles" (§ 51). The importance of the sign of the laying on of hands by a bishop at the ordination of a new bishop is thus emphasized, and it established that this practice would be common procedure in the future.

There was, however, a problem to be solved. Some Lutheran churches participating in this agreement had not preserved historical succession in the episcopate (Norway and Denmark, for example). As churches, the document states, they have maintained an authentic apostolic succession and are now "free to recognize the value of the sign [of historical succession] and should embrace it without denying their own apostolic continuity" (§ 57). Since succession in an episcopal see is more important than personal succession (§ 49), these churches have the fullness of authentic apostolic succession. Conversely, the churches that have kept the sign can recognize the full apostolicity of churches where the episcopal chain has been interrupted at some point in history (§§ 52–53). This approach allows for the full mutual recognition of present-day ministries, including ministries of oversight and leadership. It was agreed that the sign of historical succession in the episcopate, where it existed, would be maintained and also that it would be introduced in the future where the chain had been momentarily interrupted. To this end, bishops from other churches would participate in future episcopal ordinations.

The Porvoo statement itself, which was submitted to and approved by the synods, constitutes the brief concluding part. It is composed of a declaration of the mutual recognition of one another as legitimate expression of the one Church of Christ, of communion in the celebration of the Word and the sacraments based on a common confession of faith, and of the mutual recognition of the existing episcopates, which now allowed for a common exercise of this ministry.

The agreement concludes by proposing a full visible unity that included, in addition to the mutual recognition and invitation already mentioned in the Meissen Agreement, the full interchangeability of ministers ordained by a bishop in the historical succession and the laying on of hands by bishops of other traditions at an episcopal ordination. This meant, in fact, an integration of all bishops into the historical episcopal succession.[34] The whole is framed by a common missionary commitment and practical arrangements for effective cooperation at all levels.

4.1.3 The Reuilly Common Statement

French Lutherans and Reformed have been in dialogue with British Anglicans since 1993. The dialogue began in Reuilly where it was hosted by a community of deaconesses and it led to a declaration of communion in 1999, which was celebrated at services in 2000 and 2001 in both England and France. Like the Meissen dialogue, it is in fact a tri-alogue, the French Reformed having joined the Lutherans in this process.

There is no need to go into detail about the basic theological consensus set forth in the Reuilly Common Statement.[35] The whole report "Called to Witness and Serve," presents in its first part the understanding of unity; chapter 5 focuses on the agreement of faith, the consensus on Scripture, salvation, baptism, the Lord's Supper, the church and its mission in this world, and the expectation of the kingdom of God. It is a restatement of the points of consensus stated at Niagara in the order adopted by the Porvoo declaration. Although they do not call for special comment, these points are obviously essential.

The dialogue shows the awareness that the understanding of ministry – and especially that of apostolic succession – requires further study. This is, as we have repeatedly said, the classic area of

34 See Ingolf Dalferth, "Ministry and the Office of Bishop According to Meissen and Porvoo: Protestant Remarks about Several Unclarified Questions," in: *Visible Unity and the Ministry of Oversight: The Second Theological Conference held under the Meissen Agreement between the Church of England and the Evangelical Church in Germany*, London, Church House Publishing, 1997, 9–48.

35 The text of the statement is published in *Called to Witness and Service: The Reuilly Common Statement with Essays on Church, Eucharist and Ministry*, London, Church House Publishing, 1999, 1–46.

dispute between Lutherans and Reformed on the one hand, and Anglicans on the other. That apostolic succession is limited to transmission from bishop to bishop and from bishop to priests by the laying on of hands at ordination is a misunderstanding that was quickly cleared up. Anglicans emphasize that the indispensable apostolic succession is the succession of the whole church in the apostles' teaching. The Reuilly statement is unequivocal: "The apostolicity of the Church, as fidelity to the apostolic teaching and mission, is manifested in a *successio fidelium* through the ages" (§ 36). It cannot, therefore, be reduced to the historical apostolic succession of ministers, even if the latter is a particular expression of the apostolicity of the whole church. Anglicans thus confirm that the apostolicity of the whole church affirmed by all traditions is primary; the historical succession by the imposition of hands by the bishop is only a particular sign expressing the apostolicity of the whole church. This being so, Anglicans recommend the use of this sign in the church as a whole, but its absence does not prevent them from recognizing "that a continuity in apostolic faith, worship, and mission has been preserved in churches which have not retained the historic episcopal succession" (§ 39). Anglicans, Lutherans, and Reformed thus recognize "one another's ordained ministries as possessing not only the inward call of the Spirit but also Christ's commission through the Church … [and that] personal, collegial, and communal oversight (*episkope*) is embodied and exercised in all our churches in a variety of forms" (§ 46).

Anxious to preserve their sign of historical succession in the episcopate, in the Reuilly statement, Anglicans introduced a distinction between communion in the Word and sacraments on the one hand, and full visibility of unity on the other. For Anglicans, the full mutual recognition expressed by communion in the Word and sacraments must be accompanied by concrete elements that structure the unity and give it real visibility. They wanted to arrive at a single leadership of the church through a ministry of oversight (the episcopacy) exercised in common. This new stage would not mean more communion, but it would give communion greater visibility.

It is here that we must note the evolution that had occurred since the Meissen Agreement. The famous comma, mentioned above, between full and visible unity has disappeared (§§ 21–29). There is communion, but it is not yet fully visible. It is this full visibility that is the goal. Lutherans and Reformed "can recognize in the historic episcopal succession a sign of the apostolicity of the Church. They do not, however, consider it a necessary condition for full visible unity" (§ 38). In this statement, furthermore, and this is another difference with respect to the Meissen Agreement, they did not claim that Anglicans should abandon their practice of historical succession in the episcopal ministry which, in their view, gives the necessary visibility to unity. The consequence of this development is clearly seen in the statement itself (§ 46). In it, Anglicans recognized that the ministry of leadership and oversight (the episcopacy) was present in the Lutheran and Reformed churches, even if expressed in a different form. It is also a visible sign in these traditions that expresses the unity and continuity of the church (§ 46a vi). This mutual recognition of the *episkopé*, which Meissen had not been able to achieve, was the breakthrough achieved at Reuilly. It preceded a later stage of "the reconciliation of churches and ministries" (§ 27).

Nevertheless, in the absence of the adoption of the sign of historical succession in the episcopal ministry, a common exercise of the *episkopé*, granted in the Porvoo statement, was not yet possible. In spite of this reservation, church communion was declared: every parishioner could move from one community to another. This was also true for ministers, even if, for the time being, a Lutheran or Reformed minister serving in an Anglican church remained under the authority of his or her church of origin and vice versa.

Like Meissen and Porvoo, Reuilly set up a follow-up commission to foster relationships at the local level and to seek a "wider unity." This included "deepening relationships within and between our three world communions and supporting efforts towards closer communion between Anglican, Lutheran, and Reformed churches in Europe and in those parts of the world where good relations between our church families already exist" (§ 48).

4.2 *Dialogue in North America and Australia*

4.2.1 Agreements in the USA

In the United States ECUSA and ELCA[36] exist in the same communities. ECUSA also has a province outside the United States that includes Central America, Ecuador, Colombia, Venezuela, Haiti, and the Dominican Republic and the Republic of Honduras, while ELCA includes the Bahamas.[37]

Official dialogue between ECUSA and the churches of the LCUSA (the former organization of ELCA that included the Lutheran Churches-Missouri Synod) began in 1969. This dialogue concluded its work in 1972 with a positive report to the churches, but it was not pursued because the churches were facing major internal problems (for example, the ordination of women, liturgical renewal, and so on).

A second dialogue was initiated in 1977, and its work was submitted to the national church bodies in 1982 as "The Agreement: Common Resolution." I have already mentioned this dialogue, which proposed the interim sharing of the Eucharist. With the exception of the Lutheran churches of the Missouri Synod, the participating churches recognized each other's baptisms (without exception), recognized each other as churches, and as churches in which the gospel is preached purely and the sacraments administered correctly. A third round of dialogues began in 1983. Its purpose was to clarify open questions that needed to be resolved before full communion could be established between these traditions. Two official publications were produced.[38]

After a six-year reception process, under the aegis of a joint coordinating committee, the concordat of agreement was put to a vote in 1997 by the two governing bodies of the ELCA and ECUSA, which met within two weeks of each other. The text was adopted by an overwhelming majority at ECUSA's general convention while the ELCA general assembly was six votes short of the required two-thirds majority. At the initiative of the ELCA, a small team was appointed by the two presiding bishops of the two churches to propose a revised version of the concordat, to be named "Called to Common Mission."[39] After a reception process in both churches, this document, containing a revised proposal for full communion between the two churches, was submitted to the ELCA in the summer of 1999 and to ECUSA in 2000. Approved by the final governing bodies of both churches, the relationship of full communion was celebrated in Washington on the feast of the Epiphany 2001 and at various regional events in the following weeks and months.

36 ELCA was formed as a church in 1988 through the merger of the ALC, the LCA, and the AELC. This development, which has been welcomed, has created particular problems for joint ecumenical engagement, given the more reserved attitude of the former ALC toward ecumenical developments. See W. Kent Gilbert, *Commitment to Unity: A History of the Lutheran Church in America*, Philadelphia, Fortress Press, 1988.

37 Raymond W. Albright, *A History of the Protestant Episcopal Church*, New York, Macmillan, 1964.

38 William A. Norgren & William G. Rusch, ed., *Implications of the Gospel*, Cincinnati, Forward Movement Publications, 1988 and William A. Norgren & William G. Rusch, ed., *"Toward Full Communion" and "Concordat of Agreement"*, Cincinnati, Forward Movement Publications, 1991. In its second part, the second document contained the proposal for full communion and the specific steps the two churches needed to take toward that end. Briefly summarized: ECUSA agreed to suspend its "Preface to the Ordinal" in the *Book of Common Prayer* in order to make the interchangeability of presbyters possible between ECUSA and the ELCA, while the ELCA declared its readiness to accept ministers from ECUSA without requiring their prior acceptance of the *Confessio Augustana*. Reciprocal participation in the consecration/installation of new bishops was intended to bring about a reconciliation of the two churches' episcopal ministries.

39 "Called to common mission: A Lutheran Proposal for a Revision of the Concordat of Agreement," In: Oppegaard & Cameron, eds., *Anglican–Lutheran Agreements*, 231–242.

In the first place, "Called to Common Mission" is directly comparable to the conclusions of the dialogues that led to the European agreements presented above. Since the report of the Niagara international dialogue had been issued in the meantime, the "Concordat of Agreement" and its successor, "Called to Common Mission," included the ten points of consensus on the major themes of the Christian faith (§ 5).

Divergence arose over the episcopal ministry. Unlike in the Porvoo statement, to which "Called to Common Mission" is related, the Episcopalians did not agree to recognize the preservation of true apostolic succession in the Lutheran churches or, therefore, the immediate establishment of a common episcopate, as Porvoo did. The Episcopal proposal, in agreement with the Lutherans preparing the statement, was that since American Lutherans had not preserved the sign of historical succession in the episcopate, a gradual integration of ministries should occur. By inviting Episcopalian bishops, from the time of the signing, to participate in the episcopal ordination of future Lutheran bishops, full integration could be achieved after about two generations. The significance of the sign of the historical episcopate was thus increased and became a condition for the recognition of the Lutheran episcopate, which was not the case with Porvoo.[40] This proposal did not receive the required two-thirds majority at the ELCA synod in the summer of 1997 in Philadelphia. Despite further discussions, this point was not changed in the version of "Called to Common Mission" adopted in the summer of 1999 by the Lutherans and in 2000 by the Episcopalians.

"Called to Common Mission" makes it clear that, for Lutherans, full communion was now given, while for Episcopalians, the adoption of "Called to Common Mission" merely opens a path that will not be completed until all Lutheran bishops have been integrated into the new common episcopate in historical succession (§ 14).

The statement of communion proposed by "Called to Common Mission" was implemented, but opposition within ELCA remained real. In order to appease the minority of Lutherans who continued to oppose "Called to Common Mission," the 2001 ELCA general assembly responded to a unanimous request of the ELCA bishops' conference by unilaterally providing a mechanism for synodical bishops in unusual situations to make an exception to the rule that a bishop should preside at all ordinations. The presiding bishop of the Episcopal Church reacted immediately, noting that, because of its unilateral nature, the decision was unfortunate and damaging to "Called to Common Mission." Such events hindered the declaration's reception, the fruits of which have been slow to materialize.

It should be noted that "Called to Common Mission" concludes with an emphasis on common mission and the constant search for the unity of the church across the traditions involved in "Called to Common Mission":

> Entering full communion ... will bring new opportunities and levels of shared evangelism, witness, and service. It is the gift of Christ that we are sent as he has been sent (John 17:17–26), that our unity will be received and perceived as we participate together in the mission of the Son in obedience to the Father through the power and presence of the Holy Spirit (§ 29).

Moreover, a joint commission, "fully accountable to the decision-making bodies of the two churches" (§ 23), was established. This joint commission was intended to be not only advisory but to "work with the appropriate boards, committees, commissions, and staff of the two churches concerning such ecumenical, doctrinal, pastoral, and liturgical matters as may arise" (§ 23). The establishment

40 See Michael Root, "A Striking Convergence in American Ecumenism," *Origins* 26/4, 1996, 60–64, as well as his previous article "Anglican-Lutheran Relations: Their Broader Ecumenical Significance," *One in Christ* 30/1, 1994, 22–33, esp. 26. See also his "Gemeinsame Mission: Anglikanisch-lutherische Kirchengemeinschaft in den USA," *Evangelische Kommentare* 33, 2000, 41–42.

of this commission was a logical consequence of the full communion proclaimed in the introduction to "Called to Common Mission," according to which, "full communion includes the establishment locally and nationally of recognized organs of regular consultation and communication" (§ 2).

4.2.2 The Waterloo Declaration

The ELCIC was founded in 1986 and has a membership of approximately 200,000 people from immigrant communities in various European countries.[41] It was born of the regrouping of various smaller Lutheran communities of different ecclesiologies according to the tradition of their countries of origin and the influence of pietistic movements. At the time of its foundation, the ELCIC entrusted the ministry of governance to persons who would be called bishops. Additionally, there is a more conservative Lutheran Church in Canada, the Missouri Synod, which does not participate in ecumenical efforts. The Anglican Church of Canada has approximately 3 million members.

The declaration of communion, the Waterloo Declaration,[42] is a short text of a few pages that states, from its introductory paragraphs, that the churches concerned do not see the need to redo, at new cost, all the theological work that had made it possible to arrive at the declarations of communion in Europe and the United States. It refers to the Niagara Report and its ten fundamental consensuses, without repeating them.

Full communion is described as:

> A relationship between two distinct churches or communions in which each maintains its own autonomy while recognizing the catholicity and apostolicity of the other, and believing the other to hold the essentials of the Christian faith. In such a relationship communicant members of each church would be able freely to communicate at the altar of the other and there would be freedom of ordained ministers to officiate sacramentally in either church. Specifically in our context we understand this to include transferability of members; mutual recognition and interchangeability of ministries; freedom to use each other's liturgies; freedom to participate in each other's ordinations and installations of clergy, including bishops; and structures for consultation to express, strengthen and enable our common life, witness, and service, to the glory of God and the salvation of the world. ("Introduction," § 7)

It is thus a relationship between two distinct churches or communions in which each maintains its autonomy while recognizing the catholicity and apostolicity of the other and believing that the other holds the essential elements of the Christian faith. In such a relationship, communicant members of each church would be able to communicate freely at the altar of the other, and ordained ministers would be free to officiate sacramentally in both churches. Specifically, in this context we intend this to include transferability of membership, mutual recognition and interchangeability of ministries, freedom to use each other's liturgies, freedom to participate in the other's ordination and installation of clergy, including those of bishops, and consultation structures to express, strengthen and enable our common life, witness and service, for the glory of God and the salvation of the world.

The most interesting point concerns the problem of the episcopal ministry in historical succession. The question is not treated in detail. It is merely affirmed that there is full and immediate recognition of the respective episcopates ("Affirmations," § 1–3), which is to be reflected in the participation and laying on of hands in any new ordination of bishops by bishops of both

---

41 On the process that led to the birth of ELCIC, see Norman J. Threinen, *Fifty Years of Lutheran Convergence: The Canadian Case-Study*, St. Louis MO, W.C. Brown Co., 1983.

42 "Called to Full Communion: The Waterloo Declaration," in: Oppegaard & Cameron, eds., *Anglican–Lutheran Agreements*, 243–248.

traditions ("Commitments," § 1–3). The fact that not all Lutherans have preserved the sign of historical succession in the episcopal ministry was not a problem in this decision. Thus, the interchangeability of ministers from different traditions was assured.

The part called "Declaration of Full Communion" consists of a single sentence: "We declare the Evangelical Lutheran Church in Canada and the Anglican Church of Canada to be in full communion."

The Waterloo Declaration is much closer to the Porvoo Common Statement, where full communion was achieved immediately upon the signing of the agreement, than to "Called to Common Mission," which envisages full communion only after the ordination of all ministers with the participation of an Anglican bishop who shares in the historical succession.

In the Waterloo Declaration the churches resolved "to establish appropriate forms of collegial and conciliar consultation on significant matters of faith and order, mission and service" and "to encourage regular consultation and collaboration among members of our churches at all levels, to promote the formulation and adoption of covenants for common work in mission and ministry, and to facilitate learning and exchange of ideas and information on theological, pastoral, and mission matters" ("Commitments," §§ 5–6).

4.3 *The "Common Ground" Convention in Australia*

There are approximately 100,000 Lutherans and 4 million Anglicans in Australia.[43] Dialogue between the Anglican Church of Australia and the Lutheran Church of Australia began in 1972 and has resulted in joint statements on the Eucharist, ministry, and baptism, as well as on *episkopé* and unity.

The document called "Common Ground"[44] is a convention and not yet a declaration of communion. It concludes with the statement: "We recognise each other as churches that, despite our failings, stand in the continuity of apostolic faith and ministry" (§ 4.1). These conclusions include the invitation for Anglican bishops to participate in Lutheran ordinations in order to establish historic apostolic succession throughout the episcopate (§§ 24.2–3).

"Common Ground" is a solemn commitment to walk together toward full communion. No formal decision has yet been made by the churches involved in this process.

5 Theological Assessment

5.1 *A Fundamental Consensus*

The fundamental consensus affirmed by all these statements has two aspects.

First, it concerns a common vision of unity. Ecclesial communion is communion in celebrating the Word and sacraments of baptism and the Eucharist. Such communion necessarily includes an agreement on ministries and entails the mutual recognition of those ministries.

The second fundamental consensus concerns Sacred Scripture, confessions of faith, an understanding of baptism and the Eucharist, of ministry, and Christian hope. Such consensus is complementary to the first and makes a declaration of communion possible. It was explicitly formulated in the Niagara Report of 1987. It is summarized in ten points that have been taken up in all declarations on communion both in Europe and in

43 On the history of these two faith communities in Australia, see: Alfred Brauer, *Under the Southern Cross: History of the Evangelical Lutheran Church of Australia*, Adelaide, Lutheran Publishing House, 1985 and Bruce Kaye, ed., *Anglicanism in Australia: A History*, Carlton VIC, Melbourne University Press, 2002.

44 "Common Ground: Covenanting for Mutual Recognition and Reconciliation between The Anglican Church of Australia and the Lutheran Church of Australia," 2000, in: Oppegaard & Cameron, eds., *Anglican–Lutheran Agreements*, 249–268.

North America, even if they have not always been arranged in the same way.

The issue of ministry, and in particular the episcopal ministry, has been central to all the regional dialogues that have led to statements of communion. First of all, there is consensus on the necessity of the ordained ministry, which is seen as constitutive of the church. It extends to the need for the ministry of supervision and oversight, the episcopal ministry (*episkopé*).

It is important to note that, in all the statements, Anglicans recognize the presence of an ordained ministry in other churches. The mutual recognition of ministries does not depend on the particular form that, for historical reasons, this ministry has taken in the different traditions. Anglicans go even further and recognize the presence of an authentic episcopal ministry in churches that have not preserved the historical succession of bishops. In Europe, this is particularly true of Reuilly. Anglicans, however, distinguish between a recognition of ministries and the full recognition of ministries. In their view, the latter requires communion in the episcopal ministry, an episcopate exercised in common.

Porvoo takes this additional step and considers succession in the episcopal see to be sufficient, which allows for immediate integration into the communion of bishops from churches that have not preserved the historical succession of bishops that Porvoo establishes. Dialogues in the United States has not taken this step. On the other hand, dialogue in Waterloo has.

It should be added at this point that Anglicans do not assert in any dialogue that the common exercise of the episcopal ministry is the guarantee of a church's apostolicity. It is only an expression of it, which Anglicans nevertheless consider necessary. A common episcopate, therefore, is not a prerequisite for the communion in the Word and sacraments declared in all the agreements, but rather is the necessary consequence of it. It is on this very point that there is a fundamental difference between the approach of Lutherans and Anglicans on the one hand, and Roman Catholics and Orthodox on the other. For the latter, communion in the Word and sacraments remains impossible as long as a common exercise of the episcopacy is not present.

5.2 *Compatibility of Statements of Communion*

Does this difference in the importance given to the historical succession in the episcopal ministry not express an incompatibility between the different declarations of communion? Would the communion declared in Porvoo be fuller than that declared by Reuilly? That there are different degrees of communion in the dialogue with other traditions, for example, with the Church of Rome, is obvious. Communion in that case does not reach a mutual recognition of ecclesiality, ministries, or the common celebration of the Word and the sacraments. But when communion is present and declared, as is the case in all Lutheran-Anglican agreements, can we still speak of a communion that lacks fullness?

The question has been asked many times and has even given rise to encounters devoted to the problem.[45] Some argued that Porvoo was more complete than the communion of Meissen or Reuilly. The majority, however, were of the opinion that such a comparison made little sense. If, as in the above-mentioned statements of communion, it is affirmed together that everything necessary for salvation is present in the other church and thus that the other family is church in the full sense of the word, than there is no reason to speak of a more or less full communion. Just as in any marriage, there is no more or less. There are, however,

45 For example, the symposium at Liegfrauenberg, Alsace, in September of 1995: Wilhelm Hüffmeier & Colin Podmore, eds., *Leuenberg, Meissen and Porvoo: Consultation between the Churches of the Leuenberg Church Fellowship and the Churches involved in the Meissen Agreement and the Porvoo Agreement/Leuenberg, Meissen und Porvoo Konsultation zwischen den Kirchen der Leuenberger Kirchengemeinschaft und den an der Meissener Erklärung und der Porvoo-Erklärung beteiligten Kirchen*, Leuenberger Texte 4, Frankfurt a.M., Lembeck, 1996.

different ways in which this union is expressed. This is also true within each CWC. Thus, within the LWF, which is a communion of churches, the expression of communion for French Lutherans with German Lutherans is different from that which connects French Lutherans to those of South East Asia. The diversity of expressions is not a sign of a lesser communion but only a translation of a different geographical proximity. The same reflection applies to declarations of communion between two sister churches. Depending on the time and place, the expression of communion is different. These different expressions can be explained, in part, by non-doctrinal factors.

Dialogue and progress, therefore, are easier when it is a matter of large national churches that are also in the majority in their geographical country. The Church of England and the Scandinavian Lutheran churches are the best examples of this. Their ecclesial conception is still strongly influenced by the idea of a national church, which undoubtedly has contributed to their coming together. These churches are certainly marked by the Reformation of the 16th century, but the Reformation took place in a certain continuity, without the clashes, violence, ruptures, and even religious wars that marked the continental churches. The result is a different understanding of the relationship between the church, culture, and the majority society. Opposition to other Christian traditions, and to the Roman Church in particular, does not bear the memory of fratricidal struggles. Such an identification between church and nation is absent in the majority of other Protestant churches in Europe, where churches belonging to different traditions exist in the same geographical location, communities that, despite their proximity, have known a long tradition of separation. In these situations the data are quite different from those of some large "multitudinist" churches.

The question of compatibility arises, however, because declarations of communion between Lutherans and Anglicans have also given rise to asymmetrical situations. Sweden is one example. Through its membership in the LWF, it is in communion with all Lutheran churches. This fact leads to the interchangeability of ministers. Because of the Porvoo Common Statement, this church has joined in a common episcopate with the Anglicans. Does the Church of Sweden have two types of ministerial recognition that are not identical?

This situation becomes even more complex for the Lutheran churches in the Baltic countries that are signatories of Porvoo. The Baltic Lutheran churches are also signatories of the Leuenberg Agreement so, logically, a Reformed pastor can exercise his ministry in those churches. What is his status in the eyes of Porvoo? A further complication arises from the communion with the Methodists declared by the signatory churches of the Leuenberg Agreement (especially in Germany), which also includes the interchangeability of ministers. The Church of England has not declared itself to be in ecclesial communion with the Methodist tradition as regards the Word and sacraments.

There is no need for multiple examples of such asymmetry, which may be theoretical but are nevertheless real. The situation is complex and the displacement of the various processes of reception needs to be accompanied with care and oversight. The current situation cannot continue but it would be wrong to consider it as inconsistent or disordered. The only abnormal situation is that of the division of the churches, which has been historically inherited. It is, therefore, inevitable that the reestablishment of visible unity will give rise to surprising moments where the total loyalty of all to the whole is required in order to overcome a complex but temporary situation.

5.3 *The Problem of the Visibility of Communion*

The theological question that remains unresolved in the various statements of communion does not concern the understanding of the ministry of oversight and leadership as such, the reality of which exists for Anglicans even in churches that have not preserved historical succession. The issue is different. Common episcopal ministry is also fundamental for Anglicans because it makes the communion that exists visible. The final ecumenical challenge is the full visibility of unity.

The difference between Meissen and Reuilly, on the one hand, and Porvoo and Waterloo, on the other, concerns the visibility or perceptibility of unity. This difference is not a matter of a few principles of application but a theological difference that has to do with the structures of unity that have to accompany the new quality of communion.

While committing themselves to a common life and mission, Meissen and Reuilly – unlike Porvoo – do not give themselves the means for a common leadership of the church. The declaration set up working groups to coordinate the measures to be taken in order to deepen the achievement of communion. But even the enumeration of very concrete measures[46] cannot hide the fact that there are still no structures of unity in which the new communion is embedded or that can carry it forward.

For Anglicans, the structure of unity hinges upon the ministry of church unity, the episcopal ministry. This approach is shared by Scandinavian and Baltic Lutherans and this convergence made Porvoo possible. The Lutherans and Reformed in continental Europe are not ready to enter into such a structure of unity which corresponds neither to their theological conviction, which rather emphasizes the synodal element, nor to their history, nor to their spiritual tradition. One cannot blame them for this. Nevertheless, they should be challenged and asked which structures of unity they would be willing to consider.

It is not a question of appropriating the British or Nordic model, but of seeking a framework that contributes to giving full authority to the declarations of communion, a framework that allows the one church to live effectively as one church, beyond the classical boundaries of nations or confessions, a framework that avoids being locked within a spiritualist ecumenism that is not lived out in the daily life of the churches. More generally speaking, the question arises as to the appropriate way to live unity in mutual loyalty and with the advantages and constraints that any engagement between churches also represents.

To avoid any misunderstandings: creating an additional ecclesiastical institution would not solve anything. It is only a matter of providing the means to make joint decisions that are valid for the churches involved in the declaration. This is the obstacle to efforts towards unity between Lutherans and Reformed in all countries.

The European example is telling. Bound by the Leuenberg Agreement, the churches have formed the CPCE, which regularly holds general assemblies to take stock of the progress made and to define its next steps. Every effort to achieve, for example, a common synod has been systematically rejected by the general assemblies. This was the case in Belfast in 2001 and again in Basel in 2018. The mere mention of such a possibility provokes outcry and passionate reactions in the continental European Lutheran and Reformed churches. This simple fact also reveals that these families' relationship to the problem of the exercise of authority in the church is often insufficiently clarified, and even ambivalent. Contemporary ecumenical exchanges, however, are leading these churches to a growing awareness of the need for an ecclesial structure to accompany the declarations of communion. A constitution that governs the life, unity, and exercise of authority in church life is indispensable. It is not a matter of the *esse*, but of the *bene esse* of the church. It is, therefore, not necessary in the same way as the Word and the sacraments celebrated in accordance with the gospel. However, no church and no communion of churches can do without it.

The challenges of the Anglicans are thus not only justified but necessary for the other churches marked by the 16th century Reformation. Porvoo as well as CCM believed that they could meet this challenge by establishing a common episcopate. The approach is attractive and could be

46 See, for example, paragraph 44 of the Reuilly Common Statement.

a real step forward on the road to unity, but one wonders if it is really possible. Recent developments in the Anglican communion raise doubts. The open homosexuality of an Episcopal bishop in the United States has led to a breakdown in the Episcopal communion within the Anglican family.[47] The Lambeth conference of Anglican bishops from around the world was to be held in 2008. It turned out to be unusual because it gathered in Lambeth only those Anglican bishops who did not reject homosexuality. Those opposed to such an understanding of humanity met in Jerusalem. The following conference planned for 2018 could not be held. It was then scheduled for 2022, but many bishops indicated that it would not be possible for them to celebrate the same Eucharist with bishops who are not opposed to the sexual practice that they reject. The Lambeth conference of 2022 failed to resolve the problem, that remains a separating difference within the Anglican communion.

Making a common episcopal ministry the linchpin that would give visibility to the communion declared is a move that seems fruitful. Recent developments in the Anglican communion, however, do not encourage the Lutheran and Reformed families in thinking that establishing a single episcopate would be an effective sign on the way to visibility of unity.

Statements of communion, along with the decisive ecumenical breakthroughs they have achieved, demonstrate that the question of visible structures of unity remains a task for the future, not only in dialogues but also within each church family involved in communion statements between the Lutheran and Anglican traditions.

Translated from French to English by Susan Dawson Vásquez and David Dawson Vásquez.

47 For a more detailed survey of the tensions and breakdowns in the last decades in the Anglican Communion see Christopher Craig Brittain & Andrew McKinnon, eds., *The Anglican Communion at a Crossroads: The Crises of a Global Church*, University Park PA, Penn State University Press, 2018.

Bibliography

Arand, Charles P., James A. Nestingen & Robert Kolb, *The Lutheran Confessions: History and Theology of The Book of Concord*, Minneapolis, Fortress Press, 2012.

Avis, Paul, *The Identity of Anglicanism: Essentials of Anglican Ecclesiology*, London, T&T Clark, 2008.

Brittain, Christopher Craig & Andrew McKinnon, eds., *The Anglican Communion at a Crossroads: The Crises of a Global Church*, University Park PA, Penn State University Press, 2018.

Hüffmeier, Wilhelm & Colin Podmore, eds., *Leuenberg, Meissen and Porvoo: Consultation between the Churches of the Leuenberg Church Fellowship and the Churches involved in the Meissen Agreement and the Porvoo Agreement/Leuenberg, Meissen und Porvoo Konsultation zwischen den Kirchen der Leuenberger Kirchengemeinschaft und den an der Meissener Erklärung und der Porvoo-Erklärung beteiligten Kirchen*, Leuenberger Texte 4, Frankfurt a.M., Lembeck, 1996.

Oppegaard, Sven & Gregory Cameron, eds., *Anglican–Lutheran Agreements: Regional and International Agreements (1972–2002)*, Geneva, Lutheran World Federation, 2004.

Österlin, Lars, *Churches of Northern Europe in Profile: A Thousand Years of Anglo-Nordic Relations*, Norwich, The Canterbury Press, 1995.

Schjørring, Jens Holger, Prasanna Kumari & Norman Hjelm, eds., *From Federation to Communion: The History of the Lutheran World Federation*, Minneapolis, Fortress Press, 1997.

Index of Names